THE BALLPLAYERS

BASEBALL'S ULTIMATE BIOGRAPHICAL REFERENCE

THE BALLPLAYERS

BASEBALL'S ULTIMATE BIOGRAPHICAL REFERENCE

EDITED BY MIKE SHATZKIN

MANAGING EDITOR: STEPHEN HOLTJE

PICTURE EDITORS: MARK RUCKER & JOHN THORN

Created and Developed by
Mike Shatzkin & Jim Charlton

ARBOR HOUSE
WILLIAM MORROW
New York

Copyright © 1990 by Mike Shatzkin & Jim Charlton

Editor: Mike Shatzkin
Managing Editor: Stephen Holtje
Picture Editors: Mark Rucker & John Thorn
Associate Editors: Bob Carroll, Jane Charnin-Aker, Shepard C. Long
Copy Editor: Frederic Schwarz

Created and developed by Mike Shatzkin & Jim Charlton
Design & layout by Robert Bull Design

Recognizing the importance of preserving what has been written, it is the policy of William Morrow and Company, Inc., and its imprints and affiliates to have the books it publishes printed on acid-free paper, and we exert our best efforts to that end.

Library of Congress Cataloging-in-Publication Data

The Ballplayers: baseball's ultimate biographical reference/edited
  by Mike Shatzkin; managing editor, Stephen Holtje; picture
  editors, Mark Rucker & John Thorn; created and developed by Mike
  Shatzkin & Jim Charlton.
    p.   cm.
  ISBN 0-87795-984-6
    1. Baseball players—United States—Biography—Dictionaries,
  2. Baseball players—Biography—Dictionaries.   I. Shatzkin, Mike.
  II. Holtje, Stephen.   III. Charlton, James, 1939–   .   IV. Title:
  Ballplayers.
  GV665.A1B323   1990
  796.357′092′2—dc20   89-77086
                                                                CIP

Printed in the United States of America

First Edition

1 2 3 4 5 6 7 8 9 10

ACKNOWLEDGMENTS

A project this big doesn't get done without a lot of help from a lot of people.

Stephen Holtje handled the enormous job of trafficking about 6,000 entries to and from contributors and editors and in and out of computer files, wrote many entries, and edited many others.

Shep Long contributed to every aspect of this book's creation during over two years on the project.

Jim Charlton helped nurture the idea for *The Ballplayers* into a real concept, assembled much of the SABR research team, and gave us the benefit of his special knowledge of the Chicago Cubs.

Lee Simmons was the original acquiring editor of this book and provided cogent early criticism to assure the book's consistency and authority.

Alan Williams added his special touch to sharpen our style.

Bob Carroll and Jane Charnin-Aker drafted a large portion of the book from the contributions of our researchers and provided a great number of entries themselves.

Many of our researchers made special contributions in particular areas of baseball history: Merritt Clifton on Japanese, Mexican, and minor leaguers; Fred Ivor-Campbell on the 19th century figures; A.D. Suehsdorf on the early 20th century; Frank Phelps on scouts and in drawing up lists of other non-player categories. Norman Macht, Jack Kavanagh, and Morris Eckhouse deserve special thanks for the sheer number of entries they researched. Stewart Wolpin and Chris Renino handled many of the most important subjects. Dick Clark not only double-checked statistics in Negro League articles against the latest research, he also coordinated the survey used to decide which players should be included and assembled the researchers for the bios.

Richard Topp, former chairman of SABR's Biographical Committee and currently SABR's president, gave us special expertise on birth and death dates and managerial records. Fred Schwarz meticulously checked every word and semi-colon, and John Metcalf gave us valuable criticism on our content.

Thelma Morris and Mike Sparrow of the Cleveland Public Library assisted in the use of their wonderful baseball collection, and Rick Minch and Sue Gharrity of the Indians' public relations office provided help far beyond their normal duties.

Special thanks to Mark Rucker and John Thorn for the pictures, to Bob Bull for an inviting and readable design, to Vance Weaver for his patient typesetting expertise, to Stephen Dydo and Cory Lynn for computer help, and to Andy Dutter for fostering, orchestrating, and coordinating more help from our publisher than any author has the right to expect.

My personal thanks go to my parents, Leonard and Eleanor Shatzkin, for a lifetime of indulging my interest in baseball and fostering my interest in books; to my wife, Martha Moran, the special person who makes many things possible; and to Mary Foster, who in 1955 introduced me to this wonderful game.

Mike Shatzkin
December 6, 1989

THE METHODOLOGY OF THE BALLPLAYERS

The nature of *The Ballplayers* required that we the select the subjects for entries. Clearly the concept of "complete," which is a useful guideline for *The Baseball Encyclopedia*, would be impossible even to define for a book including so many subjects other than ballplayers and managers–club and league histories, awards, publications, scouts, Japan Leaguers, Negro Leaguers, Mexican Leaguers, executives, umpires, journalists, and broadcasters.

We set an objective standard for inclusion of 20th-century ballplayers, progressively tougher as we went further back in time:

> 1950-present: 500 at-bats or 100 innings pitched through the 1989 season
> 1920-1950: 750 at-bats or 250 innings pitched
> 1900-1920: 1,000 at-bats or 500 innings pitched

The objective standard required the inclusion of nearly 5,700 ballplayers and managers. We added ballplayers who did not play enough to meet the numerical criteria, but whom we thought people would want to look up. So Choo-Choo Coleman, Jim Thorpe, Herb Washington, and Eddie Gaedel, among others, got in the book.

It was also necessary to assign each entry an appropriate length. The "text value" of a particular subject is often based on facts not contained in statistics. So Mickey Rivers, Moe Berg, and Germany Schaefer got more space than their statistical records would have indicated.

We made subjective decisions as to which 19th-century ballplayers, Negro Leaguers, etc. to include. *The Ballplayers* includes entries for over 1,000 names and topics other than 20th-century ballplayers and managers.

There is a statistical summary for the ballplayers and managers which we call the top line. With the understanding that comprehensive individual statistics are published elsewhere, our objective for the top lines was to create a factual snapshot of the player or manager's career. A unique element of the top lines in *The Ballplayers* is the assembled All-Star selection information, which is not part of the player records in *The Baseball Encyclopedia* or *Total Baseball*, but which we felt was an important component of the quick summary we wanted to present.

We also present the player's major awards (MVP, Cy Young, Rookie of the Year, and Gold Glove), usually available only in year-by-year lists.

The statistics (games, batting average, home runs, and RBI for hitters; innings pitched, won-lost record, and earned-run average for pitchers), seasonal accomplishments (league leaderships, awards, 20-win seasons, and All-Star selections), post-season play information, and Hall of Fame induction dates in the top lines provide a quick locator of an entry's place in baseball history. Even the basic information for these rudimentary top lines came from a variety of sources and required some interpretation.

The 1988 edition of *The Baseball Encyclopedia* was our principal source for major league stats, but Neft & Cohen's *Sports Encyclopedia: Baseball* (St. Martins, 1988 edition) and *Total Baseball* were used to check facts. All statistics are up to date through the 1989 season.

We were fortunate to have the services of Richard Topp, the former chairman of SABR's Biographical Committee. He reviewed entries for birth and death dates, kept us current with new research in career statistics and managerial records, and let us know whenever he noticed a major omission from the body of an article.

Dick Clark made SABR's monumental, ongoing compilation of statistics from the Negro Leagues available to us, keeping us up to date with new research.

Top line information for stadiums was taken from the landmark SABR publication *Green Cathedrals,* by Philip Lowry.

In the course of creating *The Ballplayers*, we also used every book on baseball history we could get our hands on, team media guides going back over many years, and the personal recollections of trustworthy observers. We checked every fact we could and tried to label uncheckable speculation for what it is. The "editorial office" for *The Ballplayers* remains open to improve future editions with new information and leads on information that we get from any source, as well as to add the continuing developments about the people involved with our national pastime. Contributions of additional information from our readers are greatly appreciated and will be carefully reviewed for inclusion in subsequent editions. Unfortunately, the sheer paperwork demands prevent us from acknowledging each contribution. Please write to us at:

The Ballplayers
c/o William Morrow & Company
105 Madison Avenue
New York, NY 10016

AN EXPLANATION OF

1. Name most known by during career.
2. Given first and middle names, if significantly different from name known by during career.
3. Nickname(s).
4. Years of birth and death.
5. Positions played for significant amounts of time. These may not include all positions; included are the player's primary position for each year of his career, positions played for more than 50 games over the course of his career, and positions played for 5% of his career.
6. Years in the major leagues, but not including years in which the player was on the roster but did not play.
7. Teams played for in the majors, not including teams of which the player was the property but for whom he did not appear in a major league game. The current team name is used for all teams still in existence; well-known defunct teams of the 20th century are also identified by name.

   Teams are listed in the order in which the player appeared with them, but are listed only once even if the player returned to them later.
8. The boldfaced team is that for which the player played the most, determined by games (offensive players) or innings pitched (pitchers).
9. If a team name changed because of a franchise move, the continuity of the franchise is shown by a backslash.
10. Career batting average , home runs, runs batted in.
11. Career innings pitched (rounded off to the nearest full inning), wins-losses, earned-run average.
12. "—" stands for "no average" (no official at-bats).
13. In a player's career statistics, a lack of home runs or RBI is significant, so topline data would show "0 hr" or "0 rbi." However, many players have no home runs or RBI in either LCS or World Series play; in such cases, the statistic is simply omitted.
14. Managerial statistics are won-lost record and winning percentage.
15. Years of awards and achievements are shown by the last two numbers, since the century is

Stretch Rickenbach - [Johann Sebastian] (Spandex) - 1931 - . 1B-OF-LHP 1949, 53-65, 69 Yankees, **Browns/Orioles**, Angels, Braves 1745 g, .289, 357 hr, 1157 rbi; 365 ip, 27-30, 3.68. 20 wins: 49 *1 LCS, 1 g, —. 3 WS, 16 g, .326, 3 hr, 7 rbi*
Manager 1972-75 **Braves** 285-237, .549. First place: 73 1 LCS, 3-4, .429
☞ Rookie of the Year - 49; MVP - 49, 57-58; Cy Young - 49; Led League - ba 56-58, 60, rbi 56, w 49, All-Star - 49, 57-62; Gold Glove - 62; Hall of Fame - 1987
The rookie sensation of 1949 etc. etc. (QED)

easily deduced from context. Awards are complete through 1988; 1989 awards available when we went to press are included. MVP awards include the Chalmers Award and league awards given prior to the inauguration of the BBWAA MVP Award.
16. "Led League" includes ties for the lead and follows *The Baseball Encyclopedia* by generally using the qualifying standards of the time.
17. All-Star selections include years in which a player was selected by the All-Star manager or elected by the fans but was unable to play in the game due to injury, military service, or retirement. Sources were *The Sporting News Dope Book* and *Official Baseball Register* and *USA Today*.
18. The initials of the primary researcher(s) of the article. A key to researchers' identities is at the back of the book, followed by short biographical sketches.
19. If a player was born with a different name than he used during his career, that name is given.
20. Despite our best efforts, some birth and death dates could not be tracked down. This is shown by "Unk." If a possible but not definitely established date exists, it is shown with a question mark.
21. Defunct teams are identified by the city name followed by the initials of the league.

THE TOP-LINE FORMAT

(13) (19) (20)

Crotchety Ghiezer - [Albert Colin, born Shtablinow Zbnivfstieck] (Old Steak 'n Brains, The Russian Wrassler) - Unk.-1936. SS-2B-C 1875-96, 1903 Hartford (NA), Indianapolis (NL), Reds, Chicago-Pittsburgh (UA), Louisville (AA), **Dodgers**, Braves, Yankees NA: 29 g, .253; ML: 2149 g, .301, 0 hr, 1006 rbi (inc.)

(21) (22) (23) (24)

Manager 1914 *Pittsburgh (FL)* 22|44, .333.
Umpire NL 1899-1902, AL 1904-09, 29-35 *3 WS, 1 ASU*

The yclept Russian from Chicago . . . . (GS)

(25)

22. A few 19th-century teams switched cities midseason; they are shown with a hyphen.
23. National Association statistics are shown separately, because fewer categories are available.
24. Some statistical categories are not complete, especially RBI, which were not kept track of by the American Association or by the National League in some years. SABR is currently reconstructing these statistical gaps.
25. Umpires' records include years umpiring (broken down by league) and numbers of World Series, LCS, and All-Star Games worked (for many years the umpires for these contests were chosen by their respective leagues on merit).

ADDITIONAL NOTES

There is often insufficient information regarding Negro, Japan, and Mexican leaguers; the toplines of players in these categories often contain frustrating gaps. Japanese statistics are available–in Japanese. We will have them in the next edition. SABR's Negro Leagues committee is currently attempting to reconstruct complete career statistics, but their efforts are proceeding year-by-year; thus, we have some yearly statistics for most players, but career statistics for very few. Mexican statistics are interrupted in 1984, when they were lost in a devastating earthquake.

Negro Leaguers who also played in the white major leagues have their statistics listed separately. Their All-Star selections in both leagues are listed on the same line, but are separated; the same applies to league leads in major categories.

No headings in categories such as "Executive," "Scout," or "Broadcaster" are given in the toplines of men who had major league playing careers.

THE BALLPLAYERS

BASEBALL'S ULTIMATE BIOGRAPHICAL REFERENCE

Hank Aaron [Henry Louis] (Hammerin' Hank) — 1934– . OF-1B 1954–1976 **Braves**, Brewers 3298 g, .305, 755 hr, 2297 rbi. *1 LCS, 3 g, .357, 3 hrs, 7 rbi. 2 WS, 14 g, .364, 3 hr, 9 rbi*
☛ *Most Valuable Player—57. Led League—ba 56, 59. Led League—hr 57, 63, 66–67. Led League—rbi 57, 60, 63, 66. All-Star—54–76. Gold Glove—58–60. Hall of Fame—1982.*

Aaron was normally not an excitable sort. One observer remarked that Aaron seemed to be looking for a place to sit down when he approached the batter's box. Robin Roberts, who gave up Aaron's first home run, remarked that Aaron was the only batter he knew that "could fall asleep between pitches and still wake up in time to hit the next one."

On a muggy April night in Atlanta in 1974, relief pitcher Tom House carried a baseball in from the left-field bullpen. When he handed the ball that had eclipsed the most important record in baseball to the unemotional record breaker, House reported that there were tears in Aaron's eyes. Perhaps the emotion was in response to his 715th home run, breaking Babe Ruth's career record, but more likely it was in thanks that the ordeal was finally over. It was an ordeal similar to the one undergone by Roger Maris 23 summers earlier, one difference being that Aaron's pursuit of Ruth had racial implications to many. Aaron received hate mail and death threats and, when he failed to get number 714 at the end of the 1973 season, he left an entire off-season for speculation and building expectations. The tears may have been the reaction to a giant weight being lifted off his shoulders.

Aaron was able to become the all-time home run champ by sustaining a relatively unspectacular but remarkably consistent career. He was never hurt badly enough to be out of the lineup for an extended period of time. He was not a particularly aggressive baserunner, so his legs suffered little wear and tear. He controlled his weight throughout his career. His remarkable physical condition allowed him to average 33 HR a year, hitting between 24 and 45 HR for 19 straight years. He drove in more than 100 runs 15 times, including a record 13 seasons in a row. He

was an All-Star in each of the 23 seasons he played. Sometimes lost among the home run hullaballoo are Aaron's two batting titles and four Gold Gloves for his play in right field. He was consistent and dangerous, and he quickly gained the respect he was to enjoy through his entire career. Early in his career, the Braves played the Dodgers with Jackie Robinson at third. Aaron twice faked bunts, but Robinson didn't budge. After the game, Aaron asked him why he didn't move in. Robinson told him, "We'll give you first base anytime you want it."

Aaron had an understated style that could make him look lazy. He wasn't. He didn't play high school ball in Mobile, Alabama, which somehow hatched the strange story that he batted crosshanded early in his career. He played semi-pro ball when he was 15, and was the shortstop for two seasons with the Indianapolis Clowns in the Negro leagues. In May 1952, the Braves paid $7,500 for Aaron, who spent the next season and a half tearing up three different minor and winter leagues. He desegregated the Braves in 1954 after Bobby Thomson broke a leg in spring training to open a spot. Aaron joined a powerful lineup featuring Eddie Mathews and Del Crandall that needed a final link.

Aaron won his first batting title in 1956, his third ML season. He came close to the Triple Crown the following year with league bests of 44 homers and and 132 RBI, but he finished third in the batting race behind Stan Musial and Willie Mays. Aaron blamed an ankle injury (he twisted it when he stepped on a bottle thrown onto the field) for slowing him up at bat. One of those 1957 homers is reputedly Aaron's own favorite: the homer that clinched the 1957 NL pennant. For his efforts that season, he won his only MVP award. In the Braves' World Series win over the Yankees, he batted .393 with three more homers and seven RBI.

In 1959, Aaron won his second batting title with a .355 average and led the league in slugging with a .636 average. In that year's All-Star Game, he singled in the tying run in the eighth inning, then scored the eventual winner on Mays's triple. In 1963, he again threatened to win the Triple Crown. He led the league with 44 HR and 130 RBI, but

Hank Aaron

again finished third in the batting race with a .319 average, beaten by Tommy Davis (.326) and Roberto Clemente (.320). He won HR titles in 1966, when he also won his final RBI crown, and in 1967, the Braves' first two seasons in Atlanta. The Braves won a wild NL Western Division race in 1969, but lost in the LCS in three games to the Mets, despite an Aaron homer in each game, seven RBI, and a .357 average.

It was around this time that Aaron was acknowledged to be a serious threat to Ruth's lifetime record. Heretofore soft-spoken and reserved, Aaron became more vociferous on the treatment of blacks in baseball's upper echelon. In 1970, soon after collecting his 3,000th hit, he stated frankly: "I have to tell the truth, and when people ask me what progress Negroes have made in baseball, I tell them the Negro hasn't made any progress on the field. We haven't made any progress in the commissioner's office. Even with Monte Irvin in there, I still think it's tokenism. I think we have a lot of Negroes capable of handling front-office jobs. We don't have Negro secretaries in some of the big league offices, and I think it's time that the major leagues and

baseball in general just took hold of themselves and started hiring some of these capable people." His quest for racial equality did not interrupt his chase of Ruth. In 1971, he had a career-high .669 slugging average and slammed 47 HR to climb to third place on the all-time list with 639, behind Ruth and Willie Mays. With 34 more in 1972, he passed Mays to go into second place. At the age of 39 in 1973, he cracked 40, the most HR ever for a player his age, ending the season one homer off the record. When the 1974 season opened, the Braves preferred he sit out the first series in Cincinnati so he'd hit the record shots in Atlanta. Aaron and Commissioner Bowie Kuhn thought not. And Aaron didn't leave people in suspense long, hitting a 3–1 pitch off Jack Billingham in his second at-bat on Opening Day, the first homer to be struck at the new Riverfront Stadium. He sat out the next game before the scene shifted back to Atlanta. On April 8, a Monday night game on national TV, he leaned into a 1–0 fastball from Dodger lefty Al Downing. He hit the ball with his weight on his front foot, as was his custom, on a slow arc into the left-field bullpen, where reliever House made a nice catch. As he jogged around the bases, easily and emotionlessly with his head down, he was congratulated by the Dodger infielders. He was met at home plate by a small mob, including his mother.

Aaron finished the year with 20 homers. Soon after the season was over, the Braves sent him to Milwaukee, where he hit 22 HR in two seasons for the Brewers. He finished his career tops all-time in HR, RBI, total bases, and extra-base hits, second in at-bats and runs (tied with Ruth), and third in games played and hits (3,771). He currently works in the Braves' front office. /(SEW)

Tommie Aaron — 1939–1984. 1B-OF 1962–63, 65, 68–71 **Braves** 437 g, .229, 13 hr, 94 rbi. *1 LCS, 1 g, .000*

Half the answer to the trivia question, "What brother combination hit the most homers?" the younger Aaron played regularly only as a rookie, batting .231. He managed in the minors and coached for the Braves until dying of leukemia at age 45. /(BC)

Don Aase — 1954– . RHP 1977–82, 84– Red Sox, **Angels**, Orioles, Mets 1071 ip, 63–59, 3.76 ☛ *All-Star—86.*

Aase was an erratic starter his first four seasons with Boston and California, and was permanently switched to relief in August 1980. Undergoing elbow surgery, he didn't pitch in the majors from late 1982 until June 1984. He signed with the Orioles as a free agent in 1985, went 10–6 with 14 saves, and became a All-Star in 1986, earning a club-record 34 saves. An arm injury held him to only eight innings in 1987. /(BC)

Ed Abbaticchio — 1877–1957. 2B-SS 1897–98, 1903–05, 07–10 Phillies, **Braves**, Pirates 855 g, .254, 11 hr, 324 rbi. *1 WS, 1 g, .000*

Abbaticchio was the first prominent player of obvious Italian ancestry. He led the National League with 610 at-bats for Boston in 1905. When the 1908 season ended with a playoff between the Cubs and Giants, Abbaticchio's Pirates were a half-game out. They had lost the pennant when Abbaticchio's apparent grand slam against the Cubs was called foul. Later, a woman who was struck by the ball sued for damages and swore in court that the ball had been fair. /(JK)

Abbott & Costello — *Comedians*

The Baseball Hall of Fame has a gold-plated recording of Abbott & Costello performing their best-known routine, "Who's on First?" in which a befuddled Costello asks Abbott about the peculiarly-named players of a baseball team. Who is the first baseman, What plays second, I Don't Know is the third baseman, and the shortstop is named I Don't Give a Darn.

Straight man William "Bud" Abbott came from a circus family. In 1936 he teamed up with Lou Costello (nee Cristillo), a fellow burlesque performer who had been a Hollywood stunt man. Their early radio success on the "Kate Smith Show" led to a program of their own and (beginning in 1940) a film career of 38 Grade-B movies. By the time they had a TV series in the early 1950s, their act had gone stale and the two comedians had developed a strong mutual antipathy. /(TF)

Glenn Abbott — 1951– . RHP 1973–81, 83–84 A's, **Mariners**, Tigers 1285 ip, 62–83, 4.39. *1 LCS, 1 ip, 0.00*

On the final day of the 1975 season, the 6'6" Abbott combined with three other A's pitchers (Vida Blue, Paul Lindblad, and Rollie Fingers) to no-hit the Angels. Claimed by Seattle in the expansion draft in 1977, he played for the Mariners longer than any other player on their original Opening Day roster, twice winning 12 games. He missed the entire 1982 season due to illness. /(NLM)

Jim Abbott — 1967– . LHP 1989– **Angels** 181 ip, 12–12, 3.92

Abbott is the most successful pitcher ever to go directly from college to the majors. Angels manager Doug Rader raised eyebrows when he put Abbott, who was born without a right hand, into his rotation out of spring training. Many thought it was done for the publicity, but after struggling early, Abbott proved the doubters wrong. /(WOR)

Spencer Abbott — 1877–1951. *Minor League* Star.

A troublesome nature kept Abbott moving from club to club, mostly in the lower reaches of the Giants' system. His 34 years of managing (1903–06, 1910–11, 1913–14, 1919–34, 1936–43, 1946–47) set a since-broken minor league record; he spent that time with 24 teams, winning five pennants. He was a coach with the Senators in 1935. /(MC)

Ferdinand A. Abell — 1833–1913. *Executive.*

One of the founders of the Brooklyn club in 1883, Abell put up the money to build Washington Park, Brooklyn's home grounds until Ebbets Field was built. Brooklyn joined the National League in 1890; their players were paid so well none went over to the Players' League and the Superbas won the pennant. In 1898 Abell consolidated the team with Baltimore and won two pennants, but the Brooklyn club was heavily raided by the American League in 1901 and Abell refused to raise salaries to meet the competition. /(NLM)

Al Aber (Lefty) — 1927– . LHP 1950, 53–57 Indians, **Tigers**, A's 389 ip, 24–25, 4.18

The Cleveland native won 24 games for Spartanburg in 1949 and threw a five-hitter for the Indians in his only ML appearance before serving overseas in 1951–52. Despite the long layoff, the sinkerballer returned to become a competent Tiger reliever. /(JCA)

Ted Abernathy — 1933– . RHP 1955–57, 60, 63–72 Senators, Indians, Cubs, Braves, **Reds**, Cardinals, Royals 1148 ip, 63–69, 3.46

Ironman submariner Abernathy struggled with control and injuries before finally enjoying his first good year in the majors at age 29 with Cleveland in 1963 (7–2, with 12 saves). With the Cubs in 1965, he was named NL Fireman of the Year when he led the league with 31 saves. Two years later with the Reds he again was Fireman of the Year and again led in saves (28). He had 148 career saves. /(MC)

Al Abrams — 1904–1977. *Writer*
Abrams joined the Pittsburgh *Post-Gazette* in 1926 and was its sports editor from 1947 to 1974. He continued his column, "Sidelights on Sports," after he retired. /(NLM)

Cal Abrams — 1924– . OF 1949–56 Dodgers, Reds, Pirates, **Orioles**, White Sox 567 g, .269, 32 hr, 138 rbi
Abrams, who was pegged out at home by Richie Ashburn to preserve the Phillies' 1950 pennant, was a weak-armed singles hitter. After three bench-warming years with Brooklyn, his best season came with the 1953 Pirates (.286, 15 HR). /(BC)

Jim Acker — 1958– . RHP 1983– **Blue Jays**, Braves 694 ip, 26–40, 3.78. *2 LCS, 12 ip, 0–0, 0.73*
Originally a Braves farmhand, Acker slipped badly after his 7–2, 10-save season with Toronto in 1985, and was traded back to Atlanta in mid-1986. In 1987 Acker led the Braves with 14 saves. His brother Bill was an NFL lineman. /(BC)

Tom Acker (Shoulders) — 1930– . RHP 1956–59 **Reds** 380 ip, 19–13, 4.12
Acker was a hard-throwing reliever who was 10–5 with four saves for the Reds in 1957, but his ERA was 4.97 and stayed over 4.00 in his remaining two ML seasons. /(FK)

Cy Acosta [Cecilio] — 1946– . RHP 1972–75 **White Sox**, Phillies 187 ip, 13–9, 2.65
The Mexican-born reliever was the ace of the Chicago bullpen in 1973, winning 10 and saving 18. After shoulder, elbow, and eye injuries disabled him for much of 1974, he never won another game. /(JCA)

Jose Acosta — 1891– . RHP 1920–22 **Senators**, White Sox 213 ip, 10–10, 4.51
Jose Acosta was one of a host of Cubans (which included his younger brother Merito, an outfielder) signed by Washington during the 1920s. The 5′6″ 134-lb hurler had back-to-back 5–4 seasons in 1920–21. /(NLM)

Jerry Adair — 1936–1987. 2B-SS 1958–70 **Orioles**, White Sox, Red Sox, Royals 1165 g, .254, 57 hr, 366 rbi
The often dour Adair brought a light bat, steady hands, and a tough attitude to the game. Hit in the mouth by a wild throw during the first game of a doubleheader in 1964, he took 11 stitches and returned to play the entire second game. He holds the ML record (with Bobby Grich and Joe Morgan)

for fewest errors in a season by a second baseman (five, in 1964). He also set ML records with 89 consecutive games and 458 chances without an error from July 22, 1964 to May 6, 1965 with the Orioles.
After hitting .300 for Hankyu in Japan in 1971, he returned to the States and was a coach for the A's and the Angels. /(BC)

Ace Adams — 1912– . RHP 1941–46 **Giants** 553 ip, 41–33, 3.47
☛ *All-Star—43.*
Ace (his given name) was the relief star of Mel Ott's wartime Giants. Beginning in 1942, he led the NL in games pitched three straight years and in games finished four straight. His 70 appearances and 67 in relief in 1943 set ML records. He topped the league in saves in 1944 and 1945 (13 and 15), but the next year he jumped to the then-outlaw Mexican League. /(JD)

Babe Adams [Charles Benjamin] — 1882–1968. RHP 1906–07, 09–16, 18–26 Cardinals, **Pirates** 2995 ip, 194–140, 2.76. 20 wins: 11, 13 *2 WS, 28 ip, 3–0, 1.29*
Except for a single game he lost for St. Louis in 1906, Adams pitched his entire major league career with Pittsburgh. After a brief stay with the Pirates in 1907, the quiet Hoosier rejoined the team as a 27-year-old rookie in 1909 and helped them win the pennant with a 12–3 mark. The Pirates went into the World Series against Ty Cobb and the Detroit Tigers with staff ace Howie Camnitz laid up with tonsillitis. Even though Adams ranked fifth on the club in wins, manager Fred Clarke chose him as the opening game pitcher on a tip that the righthander's style resembled that of Dolly Gray, an AL pitcher who'd handled the Tigers well during the season. Adams won Game One 4–1, Game Five 8–4, and, on two day's rest, clinched the series 8–0 to become the first pitcher to win three games in a seven-game series.
Over the next half-dozen years, Adams was the Pirates' ace, winning 22 games in 1911 and 21 in 1913. A sore arm threatened his career in 1916, and he returned to the minors. He was 34–16 in less than two minor league seasons before the Pirates brought him back. In both 1919 and 1920 he posted 17-win totals. He led the NL with eight shutouts in 1920. In 1925, when he was a 43-year-old reliever, he made another World Series appearance, pitching one scoreless inning against the Senators.
Adams was never a hard thrower and his sore arm cost him what speed he had, but he could put the

Babe Adams with the Pirates

ball exactly where he wanted to. In 1920, he walked only 18 men in 263 innings. He allowed a mere 430 bases on balls for his career. /(BC)

Bobby Adams — 1921– . 3B-2B 1946–59 **Reds**, White Sox, Orioles, Cubs 1281 g, .269, 37 hr, 303 rbi

Adams fashioned a 14-year career after spending 3 years in the military, but was a regular only in 1952–53. He was a handy infielder and a dependable pinch hitter who rapped six consecutive pinch hits in 1958. On April 19, 1952, Adams and Grady Hatton led off a game with back-to-back home runs against Pittsburgh's Mel Queen. Adams's brother Dick was with the A's briefly and his son Mike lasted parts of five seasons with three different teams. /(JK)

Buster Adams [Elvin] — 1915– . OF 1939, 43–47 Cardinals, **Phillies** 576 g, .266, 50 hr, 249 rbi

A wartime slugger, Adams's top year was 1945, when he hit .287 with 22 homers and 109 RBI splitting time between the Phillies and Cardinals. His nickname stemmed from his resemblance to the Buster Brown shoe company logo. /(MC)

Franklin P. Adams — 1881–1960. *Writer.*

Franklin P. Adams was a columnist for the New York *Globe*. On July 10, 1908, the composition room called to tell him that his column was eight lines short. Adams, on his way to a Giant-Cub matchup at the Polo Grounds, quickly scrawled out eight lines entitled "Baseball's Sad Lexicon": "These are the saddest of possible words, Tinker-to-Evers-to-Chance. Trio of bear cubs and fleeter than birds, Tinker-to-Evers-to-Chance. Ruthlessly pricking our gonfalon bubble, Making a Giant hit into a double, Words that are weighty with nothing but trouble. Tinker-to-Evers-to-Chance." Adams was later an ace panelist on the radio show "Information Please." /(WOR)

Glenn Adams (Addie) — 1947– . DH-OF 1975–82 Giants, **Twins**, Blue Jays 661 g, .280, 34 hr, 225 rbi

The DH in 326 ML games, Adams pinch-hit in more than half of his other appearances. With the help of his only ML grand slam, he drove in eight runs in one game, June 26, 1977, setting a Twins record. /(AB)

Sparky Adams [Earl John] — 1894–1989. 2B-3B-SS 1922–34 **Cubs**, Pirates, Cardinals, Reds 1424 g, .286, 9 hr, 394 rbi

The versatile Adams spent 1923 and 1924 as the Cubs' semi-regular shortstop, but came into his own when he was switched to second base for 1925 after second baseman George Grantham was traded to Pittsburgh for shortstop Rabbit Maranville. Adams led NL 2B in putouts, assists, total chances per game, and fielding average at his new position. Playing regularly, he led the league in at-bats for the first of three straight seasons and finished third in steals with 26, scoring 95 runs while batting .287. The leadoff batter improved to .309 in 1926, again scoring 95 runs, and finished second in steals (27) and third in hits. In 1927 he was moved around the infield more, playing 60 games at second base, 53 at third base, and 40 at shortstop. He scored a career-high 100 runs, finished fourth in the league in steals with 26, and hit .292. NL champion Pittsburgh sent Kiki Cuyler, who had fallen into disfavor with management, to the Cubs for Adams and Pete Scott in 1927. Adams once again replaced Grantham at second base as Grantham moved to first.

Adams's average fell off over the next two seasons, and in 1929 he was used in a utility role. After the season he was sold to the Cardinals. Used at third base, he helped St. Louis to two straight pennants, leading NL third basemen in fielding both seasons and in double plays in 1931. In the notorious rabbit-ball season of 1930, when the league batting average was .303, all eight Cardinal regulars (300-plus at-bats) hit .300, the only time in history that has happened. Adams contributed a career-high .314. In St. Louis's 1931 World Championship year, he led the league with 46 doubles and tied with teammate Pepper Martin for third in steals with 16. Another member of the Gas House Gang, Frankie Frisch, finished first with 28 and the Cardinals led the league in stolen bases.

In 1932 a knee injury kept Adams out for most of the year. In early May 1933 he went to the Reds along with Paul Derringer and Allyn Stout for Leo Durocher, Dutch Henry, and Jack Ogden in the deal that completed the cast of characters in the classic Gas House Gang. In Cincinnati Adams joined George Grantham again. But Adams's knee injury had deprived him of his speed, and although he was a regular for a year and a half, his average dropped off and his major league career ended. /(SFS)

Joe Adcock — 1927– . 1B-OF 1950–66 Reds, **Braves**, Indians, Angels 1959 g, .277, 336 hr, 1122 rbi. *2 WS, 9 g, .250, 2 rbi.*
   Manager 67 **Indians** *75–87, .463*
☛ *All-Star—60..*

Although he was played out of position, platooned, and frequently injured, Adcock retired as the twentieth most prolific home run hitter of all time and seventh among righthanded hitters. A natural first baseman, the 6'4" 220-lb slugger platooned with Ted Kluszewski when he joined the Reds in 1950, then switched to left field to keep both bats in the lineup. Traded to the Braves in 1953, he returned to first base and appeared in a career-high 157 games. On July 31, 1954, he hit four home runs and a double in a game against the Dodgers at Ebbets Field. His 18 total bases still stand as the one-game record. A broken arm in 1955 and broken leg in '57 held him to half-seasons, but in his healthy 1956 he hit .291, with 38 homers and 103 RBI. He was often platooned in later years, but in 1961, when he played in 152 games, he had 35 home runs and a career-high 108 RBI. Traded to the Indians in 1963 and sent on to the Angels the next year, Adcock

played through the '66 season as a platoon player and pinch-hitter. In 1967 he became manager of the Indians, but when the team finished eighth he was fired. Ironically, the main criticism of his managing was that he insisted on platooning the team's top sluggers, Leon Wagner and Rocky Colavito. /(MC)

Bob Addie — 1911–1982. *Writer*

Addie covered the Senators for 37 years with the Washington *Times-Herald* and the Washington *Post*. His column, "Addie's Atoms," appeared in *The Sporting News*. In 1981 Addie received the J.G. Taylor Spink Award. He was married to Pauline Betz, four-time U.S. women's tennis champion. /(NLM)

L.H. Addington (Leroy) — 1894–1956. *Writer*

For many years a member of the editorial staff of *The Sporting News* and publicity director for the National Association, Addington wrote a column, "In the Bullpen," that appeared regularly in *TSN* in the 1920s and 30s. /(NLM)

Bob Addis — 1925– . OF 1950–53 Braves, **Cubs**, Pirates 534 g, .281, 2 hr, 47 rbi

Addis was speedy but lacked power. After hitting .295 with 13 doubles in 93 games for the 1952 Cubs, he was given just 15 at-bats in 1953, and left the majors. /(BC)

Grady Adkins — 1897–1966. RHP 1928–29 **White Sox** 363 ip, 12–27, 4.34

Adkins showed promise as a 31-year-old rookie, going 10–16 with the fifth-place 1928 White Sox. But the next year he couldn't get anyone out, finishing 2–11 with a 5.33 ERA. /(BC)

Tommie Agee — 1942– . OF 1962–73 Indians, White Sox, **Mets**, Astros, Cardinals 1129 g, .255, 130 hr, 433 rbi. *1 LCS, 3 g, .357, 2 hr, 4 rbi. 1 WS, 5 g, .167, 1 hr, 1 rbi*
☛ *Rookie of the Year—66. All-Star—66–67. Gold Glove—66, 70.*

The speedy outfielder originally signed with the Indians for a $60,000 bonus. He was later sent to the White Sox along with Tommy John in a three-team trade. In 1966, his first full season, he hit 22 homers and led AL outfielders in putouts to earn Rookie of the Year honors. Traded to the Mets two years later, Agee helped them win the 1969 pennant with his leadoff hitting, including a career-high 26 homers. In the WS, he starred in the Mets' Game Three victory with a home run and two outstanding catches. /(AB)

Harry Agganis (The Golden Greek) — 1930–1955. 1B 1954–55 **Red Sox** 157 g, .261, 11 hr, 67 rbi

A brilliant athlete and a New England favorite, Agganis was a baseball and football star at Lynn Classical H.S. and Boston University, making All-American as a quarterback. He signed for a reported $35,000 with the Red Sox and after only one minor league season jumped to the majors. His death of leukemia during the 1955 season set Boston hopes for the future back for several seasons. A good fielder who led AL first basemen in assists in 1954, he had 11 HR in 434 at-bats in his rookie season and was hitting .313 at the time of his death. /(EW)

Sam Agnew — 1887–1951. C 1913–19 **Browns**, Red Sox, Senators 560 g, .204, 2 hr, 98 rbi. *1 WS, 4 g, .000*

Agnew was a Browns regular for three seasons (1913 through 1915) and led American League catchers in errors in two of them because of a scattergun arm. In 1915 he committed 39 errors. /(WAB)

Juan Agosto — 1958– . LHP 1981– **White Sox**, Twins, Astros 392 ip, 24–18, 3.46. *1 LCS, 0.1 ip, 0–0, 0.00*

The Puerto Rican born Agosto was signed at age 16 by the Red Sox in 1974, but spent his first full ML season with the 1984 White Sox. Chicago fans unkindly labelled the reliever "Juan Disgusto: the Master of Disaster" when he failed too often with the game on the line. He matured with the Astros; in 1988, he went 10–2. /(RL)

Luis Aguayo — 1959– . SS-2B-3B 1980– **Phillies**, Yankees, Indians 568 g, .236, 37 hr, 109 rbi

A utility infielder and pinch-hit specialist for the Phillies, Aguayo made his ML debut in 1980, but did not have 100 plate appearances in a season until 1985. In 1987 he hit 12 HR in only 209 at-bats, and his final home run eliminated the Mets from the pennant race in the last week of the season. /(SG)

Rick Aguilera (Aggie) — 1961– . RHP 1985– **Mets**, Twins 549 ip, 40–32, 3.53. *2 LCS, 12 ip, 0–0. 0.75. 1 WS, 3 ip, 1–0, 12.00*

As the Mets' fifth starter, Aguilera went 10–7 each of his first two years. He pitched three innings of scoreless relief in the Mets' dramatic 16-inning LCS clincher over the Astros in 1986. He was hit hard in Game Two of the World Series in relief of loser Dwight Gooden. Aguilera also surrendered two tenth-inning runs in Game Six, but was the winning pitcher after the Mets' spectacular three-run come-back in the bottom of the inning.

His best season, an 11–3 mark in 1987, was interrupted by three months on the DL in the middle of the year. An elbow operation kept Aguilera out for most of 1988, and David Cone took his place in the rotation. Aguilera was used in relief in 1989 and, throwing harder than previously, he soon won the righthanded closer role from Roger McDowell. Dealt to the Twins in mid-season in the five-man package that brought Frank Viola to the Mets, Aguilera returned to a starting role.

Aguilera hit .278 in his first major league season and has been used as a pinch-hitter. He was a third baseman at Brigham Young University and played on the same team with Cory Snyder, Wally Joyner, and Scott Nielsen. /(SH)

Hank Aguirre — 1932– . LHP 1955–70 Indians, **Tigers**, Dodgers, Cubs 1375 ip, 75–72, 3.25
☛ *Led League—era 62. All-Star—62.*

Equally adept at delivering screwballs and one-liners, Aguirre was switched from the bullpen to the starting rotation by the Tigers in 1962 and responded by leading the AL in ERA (2.21) while posting a 16–8 mark. A notoriously poor hitter, he hit below .040 in seven seasons and had a career BA of .085. /(AB)

Willie Aikens — 1954– . 1B-DH 1977, 79–85 Angels, **Royals**, Blue Jays 774 g, .271, 110 hr, 415 rbi. *1 LCS, 3 g, .364. 1 WS, 6 g, .400, 4 hr, 8 rbi*

In 1980 Aikens became the first player ever to have two multiple home run games in the same World Series when he blasted a pair in Game One for the Royals and repeated in Game Four. Named Willie Mays Aikens for the Hall of Famer, the 220-pound slugger topped 20 homers three times. Aikens's lack of fielding skills was legendary, and he should have been a DH, but Hal McRae already filled that role for the Royals. Aikens's involvement with drugs led to his suspension by the Royals and a 1984 trade to Toronto, where he DHed with little success. /(FJO)

Danny Ainge — 1959– . 2B-3B-OF 1979–81 **Blue Jays** 211 g, .220, 2 hr, 37 rbi

A basketball star at Brigham Young, the fiery Ainge was a 6'4" infielder-outfielder with the Blue Jays. After three years of failing to hit major league pitching, he quit baseball to join the NBA Boston Celtics. /(BC)

Eddie Ainsmith — 1892–1981. C 1910–24 **Senators**, Tigers, Cardinals, Dodgers, Giants 1068 g, .232, 22 hr, 317 rbi

A steady catcher for 15 seasons despite little offensive production, Ainsmith was a smooth handler of pitchers and an aggressive player. In a one-sided game on June 26, 1913, the Senators' catcher stole second, third, and home in the ninth inning, courtesy of the casual attitude taken by Athletics' pitcher Chief Bender. All of Ainsmith's excursions went unchallenged, but were scored as stolen bases. /(JK)

Jack Aker (Chief) — 1940– . RHP 1964–74 **A's**, Pilots, Yankees, Cubs, Braves, Mets 747 ip, 47–45, 3.28

A rugged, sidearming sinkerballer, Aker relieved in all 495 of his ML games, saving 123. The nickname "Chief" refers to his Potowatomie Indian ancestry, fierce presence, and effectiveness. He was AL Fireman of the Year with the 1966 A's, going 8–4 with a 1.99 ERA and 32 saves—a ML record until 1970. In August 1967, the Kansas City players, with Aker as their representative, became embroiled in a feud with owner Charley Finley. Having enraged Finley, Aker found himself pitching less and less. He was chosen by the Pilots in the 1968 expansion draft and was soon traded to New York. As a Yankee, he led the staff in saves in 1969 and recorded a 2.06 ERA in both 1969 and 1970, despite undergoing career-

threatening spinal surgery over the intervening winter. He pitched with pain the rest of his career. When the Yankees acquired Sparky Lyle in 1972, Aker was dealt to the Cubs, and led their bullpen in saves and wins. He later became a successful minor league manager and Cleveland's pitching coach. /(JCA)

Vic Albury — 1947– . LHP 1973–76 **Twins** 372 ip, 18–17, 4.11

Vietnam veteran Albury was sometimes impressive with the Twins but erratic, a victim of wildness and a chronic sore arm. He sometimes played in the field in the minors, but his hitting ability was of no use in the DH-employing AL. /(MC)

Santo Alcala — 1952– . RHP 1976–77 **Reds**, Expos 68 g, 249 ip, 14–11, 4.76

The 6'5" Dominican had a flashy 11–4 mark in 1976 with the "Big Red Machine," but his 4.70 ERA revealed his reliance on the Cincinnati bats. Traded to Montreal, he fell to 3–7. /(BC)

Mike Aldrete — 1961– . OF-1B 1986– **Giants**, Expos 425 g, .277, 15 hr, 138 rbi. *1 LCS, 5 g, .100, 1 rbi*

A lefthanded reserve who can play anywhere in the outfield, Aldrete enjoyed his best season in 1987, hitting .325 with 9 HR and 51 RBI when Giants regulars Candy Maldonado and Jeffrey Leonard were injured much of the season. He was traded to the Expos for Tracy Jones before the 1989 season. /(SCL)

Vic Aldridge — 1893–1973. RHP 1917–18, 22–28 **Cubs**, Pirates, Giants 1601 ip, 97–80, 3.76. *2 WS, 26 ip, 2–1, 4.91*

Aldridge was a steady hurler for the Cubs, going 47–36 from 1922 through 1924, and the Pirates, for whom he won 15 games in each of their 1925 and 1927 pennant-winning seasons. He had complete game wins over Coveleski and the Senators in Games Two and Five of the 1925 World Series, winning 3–2 and 6–3. In the seventh and deciding game, he couldn't get out of the first inning, but though the score was 4–0 after one, the Pirates came back to win 9–7.

In February 1928, the disgruntled Aldridge was traded to the Giants for 34-year-old Burleigh Grimes, who had clashed with New York manager John McGraw. Aldridge held out, joined the Giants late, and was waived after a dismal showing. Grimes, meanwhile, led the NL with 25 wins. /(JK)

Jack Aker

Dale Alexander (Moose) — 1903–1979. 1B 1929–33 **Tigers**, Red Sox 662 g, .331, 61 hr, 459 rbi
☛ *Led League—ba 32.*

In his first two years with the Tigers, the right-handed-hitting Alexander showed a powerful bat but an iron glove. Then in 1931, as his fielding began to improve, he lost his home run swing, hitting only 3 after two 20-plus seasons. When his BA dipped to .250 in June of the next year, the Tigers traded him to the Red Sox for aging outfielder Earl Webb. "Moose" suddenly went on a batting tear, hitting .372 for the rest of the season to end with an AL-high .367 BA. But his fielding was still a liability and his power was gone. When he hit a weak .281 as a part-timer in 1933, his ML career was over. /(EC)

Doyle Alexander — 1950– . RHP 1971– Dodgers, **Orioles**, Yankees, Rangers, Braves, Giants, Blue Jays, Tigers 3367 ip, 194–174, 3.76. *3 LCS, 23 ip, 0–4, 8.61. 1 WS, 6 ip, 0–1, 7.50*
☛ *All-Star—88.*

Dour Doyle Alexander moved around enough to become the fourth pitcher to record wins over all 26 teams. He became increasingly effective late in his career, by developing an assortment of pitches, speeds, and deliveries, and relying more on guile and control than overpowering stuff. In 1983 Alexander seemed like a journeyman pitcher at the end of his career when he put himself on the disabled list (and in Yankee owner Steinbrenner's doghouse) by injuring his hand punching a concrete wall in frustration. He was picked up by the Blue Jays and, though he started out by losing his first six games, he turned it around with a club record 8-game winning streak. He went on to win a club record 17 games the following season. In 1985 he won 17 games again, including the game that clinched the AL East pennant on the penultimate day of the season. He accused Toronto management of not wanting to win badly enough to pay him what he felt he was worth, and after badmouthing local fans, was traded to Atlanta, where his pitching was uninspiring. Traded to Detroit midway through the 1987 season, Alexander had a 1.53 ERA and a 9–0 record in an exciting pennant race for the Tigers, including two dramatic victories over the Blue Jays in the final days of the season. Often a slow starter, he had a surprisingly good first half in 1988, earning his first All-Star selection. However, he pitched less well for the remainder of the season as the weak Tigers were beset by injuries and fell out of first place. /(TF)

Gary Alexander — 1953– . C-DH 1975–81 Giants, A's, **Indians**, Pirates 432 g, .230, 55 hr, 202 rbi

Strikeouts and throwing errors short-circuited Alexander's ML career. Splitting the 1978 season between Oakland and Cleveland, he led all ML catchers with 27 homers but also led the ML with 166 strikeouts while batting only .225. The next year, his 18 errors led all ML catchers. /(ME)

Grover Cleveland Alexander
(Pete) — 1887–1950. RHP 1911–30 **Phillies**, Cubs, Cardinals 5189 ip, 373–208, 2.56. 20 wins: 11, 13–17, 20, 23, 27 *3 WS, 43 ip, 3–2, 3.35*
☛ *Led League—w 11, 14–17, 20. Led League—era 15–17, 19–20. Led League—k 12, 14–17, 20. Hall of Fame—1938.*

Pete had difficulty with everything in life except pitching. He was a solitary man and said little, and that in a small, whispery voice. His teammates respected him, and his longtime catcher, Reindeer Bill Killefer, was his friend.

Alexander's alcoholism was well known even before Ronald Reagan portrayed it in the movie "The Winning Team." But in spite of rumors of his pitching drunk or badly hung over, alcohol had no discernible effect on Alexander's performance until late in his career. He also suffered from epilepsy, which was sometimes mistaken for drunken behavior. The disease first appeared in 1918 during his service in France with the artillery, which partially deafened him. Despite his problems, Alexander was one of the most successful pitchers in ML history.

Many of his minor league experiences were inauspicious. Playing for Galesburg, IL, of the Central Association in 1909, he tried to break up a double play and took the shortstop's relay directly in the head. Unconscious for two days, he awoke with double vision. Galesburg sent him to Indianapolis (American Association), but, still disoriented, he broke three of the manager's ribs with his first pitch. Indianapolis sent him home and sold his contract to the Syracuse Chiefs of the International League over the winter. By spring, his vision had cleared and he won 29 for the Chiefs, including 15 shutouts.

The Phillies acquired Alexander for $750 in 1911. As a rookie, he led the NL in wins (28), complete games (31), innings pitched (367), and shutouts (7). Four of the shutouts were consecutive; one was a 1–0 win over Cy Young, then in his final season.

Alexander's greatest years were in Philadelphia (1911–17), despite a right-field wall in the Baker Bowl that was only 272 feet from home plate. He won 190 games (one-third of the team's total for the period), won 30 or more three straight years, 1915–17, and led the NL in every important pitching statistic at least once. His 16 shutouts in 1916 is still the ML record.

Traded with catcher Bill Killefer to the Cubs in 1917 for a battery of considerably lower caliber and $55,000, Pete won another 128 games for Chicago. But when Joe McCarthy took over as manager in 1926, he sent his drinking pitcher to the Cardinals for the $6,000 waiver price.

Alexander was ungainly, with a shambling walk; his uniform never seemed to fit properly, and his cap looked a size too small. Yet his pitching motion was economical, apparently effortless, and marvelously graceful. His windup was minimal, his stride short, his delivery three-quarters overhand. His right arm swung across his chest and the ball seemed to emerge from his shirtfront. He warmed up quickly. On the mound he was deliberate but without wasted time or motion.

He had a live fastball that moved in on right-handed hitters and a sharp-breaking curve. He had no changeup as such, but could change speeds on both the fastball and the curve to achieve the same effect. He kept the ball low and on the outside of the

Grover Cleveland Alexander

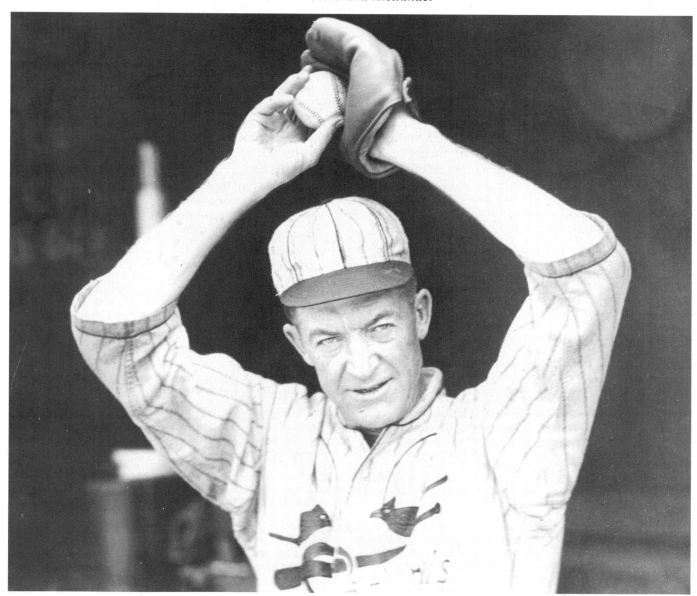

plate. His control was extraordinary (career: 1.65 walks per 9 innings), and batters who tried to wait him out usually fanned.

His most famous victim was Tony Lazzeri of the Yankees. In the seventh inning of the final game of the 1926 WS, with the Cardinals ahead 3–2, the Yankees had two out and the bases loaded. Alexander, who'd won two games, including a complete game the day before, relieved for St. Louis. On four knee-high pitches, he struck out Lazzeri, then pitched two more hitless innings to wrap up the World Championship.

After his 1926 heroics, Alexander got his best contract ever: $17,500. He responded with 21 wins in 1927, but he was 40 years old. The whiskey and age were taking their toll. After leaving the majors, he pitched in demeaning circumstances with touring teams until he was 51. He retired believing his 373 wins placed him one ahead of Christy Mathewson for the most career NL victories, but later statistical research added another win to Matty's total. /(ADS)

Hughie Alexander — 1917– . OF 1937 **Indians** 7 g, .091, 0 hr, 0 rbi

A fast, strong centerfielder, Alexander was an All-Star in both his minor league seasons, hitting .348 with 28 HR and 102 RBI for Fargo-Moorehead (Northern League) in 1936 and .344 with 29 HR in only 79 games for Springfield (Mid-Atlantic League) in 1937. He played in seven games with the Indians that year, but in December 1937 he mangled his left hand in an oil-drill accident and it was amputated.

Alexander became a scout for Cleveland in 1938 and signed Allie Reynolds and Dale Mitchell for the Indians. He joined the White Sox in 1952 and the Dodgers in 1956. Before he left the Dodgers for Philadelphia in 1970, he signed three-quarters of their 1970s infield: Steve Garvey, Ron Cey, and Bill Russell. He was made chief scout of the Phillies in 1979, and in 1987 followed Dallas Green to the Cubs as special player consultant. /(FVP)

Andy Allanson — 1961– . C 1986– **Indians** 395 g, .246, 12 hr, 112 rbi

A lithe, take-charge catcher, Allanson's handling of the 1986 Cleveland pitching staff was in part responsible for the Indians' resurgent, 84–78 mark. He was named the Topps All-Rookie catcher. Despite his size (6'5", 220-lb), he didn't homer until his 1,025th pro at-bat, in the Kingdome that June 23. The Indians, feeling they were perhaps a better-hitting, veteran catcher away from contention, signed Rick Dempsey for 1987, demoting Allanson. Cleveland

finished dead last (61–101). Allanson was again the starting catcher in 1988. /(JCA)

Bernie Allen — 1939– . 2B 1962–73 **Twins**, Senators, Yankees, Expos 1139 g, .239, 73 hr, 351 rbi

Allen, a T-quarterback from Purdue, had his best major league season his rookie year, with career highs in homers (12), RBI (64), and BA (.269). After that, his bat faded, and he was mostly a part-time defensive specialist. In five seasons with the Twins, he hit .318 as a visitor in Washington, but batted just .193 in 1967 after his trade to the Senators. /(BC)

Bob Allen — 1937– . LHP 1961–63, 66–67 **Indians** 274 ip, 7–12, 4.11

Allen posted a 2.98 ERA with five saves in his final season as an Indians reliever, but his 0–5 mark earned him a one-way ticket to the Pacific Coast League. /(MC)

Dick Allen — 1942– . 1B-3B-OF 1963–77 **Phillies**, Cardinals, Dodgers, White Sox, A's 1749 g, .292, 351 hr, 1119 rbi. *1 LCS, 3 g, .222*
☛ *Rookie of the Year—64. Most Valuable Player—72. Led League—hr 72, 74. Led League—rbi 72.*

Talented, controversial, charming, and abusive, Allen put in 15 major league seasons, hitting prodigious homers and paying prodigious fines. Called "Richie" at first, in mid-career he became, adamantly, "Dick." He was praised as a money player and condemned as a loafer.

He made 41 errors at third base (which he had not played in the minors) for the Phillies in 1964, but his 29 home runs, 91 RBI, 201 hits, and .318 BA earned him Rookie of the Year honors. A deep cut on his right hand, which he reported having suffered while pushing a stalled car, affected his throwing and the Phillies made him a first baseman/outfielder in 1967. He hit 40 home runs in 1966 and 177 through 1969, but off-the-field behavior brought him a 28-day suspension, a $500-a-day fine, and a trade to the Cardinals at the end of '69. The swap proved doubly controversial when Curt Flood refused to report to the Phillies and challenged the reserve clause in court, forcing St. Louis to substitute Willie Montanez. The Cardinals passed Allen on to the Dodgers after one year, and they traded him to the White Sox a year later. Each trade added to Allen's reputation as an unmanageable loner.

In 1972, with easygoing Chuck Tanner as his White Sox manager, he led the AL in homers (37),

Dick Allen

RBI (113), walks (99), and slugging percentage (.603) and was named MVP. In 1974, he was on his way to a similar year when he "retired" with a month left to play, giving no reason. Despite his vacation, he led the AL with 32 home runs.

The Sox traded him to Atlanta for cash and a player to be named later in December 1974, but before he could play for the Braves they sent him to the Phillies in May 1975 for Barry Bonnell, Jim Essian, and cash. When Essian was turned over to Chicago as Atlanta's player to be named later, he'd been swapped for Allen twice in less than half a year. After two sub-par years in Philadelphia and one in Oakland, Allen retired for good, still an enigma. His brothers Ron and Hank played in the majors. /(BC)

Ethan Allen — 1904– . OF 1926–38 **Reds**, Giants, Cardinals, Phillies, Cubs, Browns 1281 g, .300, 47 hr, 501 rbi

Allen, who never played in the minors, was a trim, lefthanded-hitting outfielder, who hit consistently well over a 13-year ML career. A bright, articulate man, he later served as the motion picture director of the NL, became a successful college baseball coach, and authored several books on baseball playing techniques. /(FS)

Frank Allen (Thin Man) — 1889–1933. LHP 1912–17 **Dodgers**, Pittsburgh (FL), Braves 970 ip, 50–66, 2.93

Allen suffered through three losing seasons with the Dodgers (in the best of them, 1913, he went 4–18—the worst record in the majors—despite a better-than-average 2.83 ERA). He was making $2,000 a year in 1914 when he jumped to the Federal League at the end of the season. It proved fortunate for the 6'1" 158-lb Allen, who finished second in the league with 23 wins and six shutouts in 1915. The highlight of his season came early, when, on April 24, he no-hit St. Louis, walking four and striking out two to defeat Bob Groom 2–0.

After the demise of the Federal League, he became a Brave and continued to pitch well (8–2, 2.07), but dropped off to 3–11, 3.94 in 1917. /(NLM)

Hank Allen — 1940– . OF 1966–70, 1972–73 **Senators**, Brewers, White Sox 389 g, .241, 6 hr, 57 rbi

The older brother of Dick and Ron Allen shuttled between Triple-A and Washington from 1966 through 1970. Tabbed "indifferent" by several managers, he had good speed, a fair arm, and trouble hitting righthanders. /(JCA)

Johnny Allen — 1905–1959. RHP 1932–44 Yankees, **Indians**, Browns, Dodgers, Giants 1950 ip, 142–75, 3.75. 20 wins: 36 *2 WS, 4 ip, 6.23*
☛ *All-Star—38.*

The tempestuous, hard-throwing Allen had shouting matches with team officials and umpires. He had a spectacular 17–4 rookie record with the Yankees in 1932, but a sore arm two years later and his habitual angry holdouts provoked his trade to the Indians in 1936. He was 20–10 that year, and won his first 15 decisions in 1937 before dropping a final 1–0 heartbreaker to Detroit. In 1938, he put together a string of 12 wins in a row before hurting his arm, and from then on was used as a spot starter and reliever. Pitching for Brooklyn in the 1941 WS, he held the Yankees scoreless in three relief appearances. /(JD)

Lee Allen — 1915–1969. *Writer.*

For ten years the historian at the Baseball Hall of Fame, Allen was formerly a feature writer for the

Cincinnati *Enquirer*, served as public relations director for the Reds, and also conducted radio and TV programs in Cincinnati and Philadelphia. Known as "Baseball's Walking Encyclopedia," he brought 55 cartons of books and record files with him to Cooperstown. Allen often spent time in small towns ferreting out information about old players. Among his books: *The Official History of the Cincinnati Reds, The History of the World Series, The National League Story,* and *The American League Story.* He played a major role in the compilation of the original *Baseball Encyclopedia.* /(NLM)

Lloyd Allen — 1950- . RHP 1969-75 **Angels**, Rangers, White Sox 297 ip, 8-25, 4.70

Allen was an Angels' bullpen hopeful in the early 1970s, and had his best year in 1971 (15 saves, 2.49). Although he pitched a seven-inning no-hitter for San Jose (California League) in 1968, he had a 1-12 record in the majors as a starting pitcher. /(SFS)

Maury Allen — 1932- . *Writer.*

Allen, a writer for the New York *Post* and *Sports Illustrated*, wrote *Where Have You Gone, Joe DiMaggio?* in 1975. His other books include *Baseball's 100* and *Now Wait a Minute, Casey.* /(NLM)

Mel Allen [Melvin Allen Israel] — 1913- . *Broadcaster.* ☛ *Hall of Fame—1978.*

The voice of Mel Allen is as resonantly warm and friendly as it is deep and authoritative. First heard on the radio in 1935, when he did football games for the University of Alabama, Allen continued on the air through the 1980s narrating television's "This Week In Baseball."

He became famous as the "Voice of the Yankees" (1939-64), a job and a team he loved. His home-run call, "That ball is going, going, gone!" became a trademark, as did his frequent exclamation, "How about that!" In 1978 he and Red Barber were the first broadcasters voted into the Hall of Fame (in the so-called Writers' Wing). /(MG)

Neil Allen — 1948- . RHP 1979-88 **Mets**, Cardinals, Yankees, White Sox 985 ip, 58-69, 3.85

Allen's emergence as a bullpen stopper in 1980 was one of the Mets' few bright spots in the first part of the decade. The clubhouse cut-up had seasons of 22, 18, and 19 saves (1980-82). After a poor start in 1983, at which point Allen confessed an alcohol problem, the Mets traded him to the Cardinals, who were unloading Keith Hernandez for suspected drug use. Hernandez became a team leader on the Mets;

Allen bounced around and hit bottom in 1987, when he was 0-8 for the White Sox and the Yankees. It was his second stint with the Yankees; in 1988 he pitched an unusual shutout for them. Relieving in the first inning with none out and a runner on first base, he picked off the runner; a special scorer's decision gave him a shutout, but not a complete game. /(SH)

Newt Allen [Newton Henry] (Colt) — 1901-1988. 2B-SS-OF-MGR Negro Leagues 1920-48 Kansas City Tigers, All-Nations, Kansas City Monarchs, St. Louis Stars, Detroit Stars, Homestead Grays, Cincinnati Clowns 640 g, .293, 16 hr

For 23 years, Newt Allen was the foundation of the powerhouse Kansas City Monarch teams that won 10 league championships. He was just 5'7" and 169 lbs, but displayed amazing strength and endurance in his baseball travels. Considered the premier second baseman during the formative years of the Negro National League, he made fielding his position an art. Former teammate Chet Brewer said, "Newt was a real slick second baseman, he could catch the ball and throw it without looking. Newt used to catch the ball, throw it up under his left arm; it was just a strike to first base. He was something! Get that ball out of his glove quicker than anybody you ever saw."

Allen attended Lincoln High School in Kansas City, MO with future Monarch teammates Frank Duncan and Rube Currie. The three organized a local team called the Kansas City Tigers, named after the school mascot. After a brief amateur career, in 1921 Allen joined the semi-pro Omaha Federals, for whom he was playing second base when discovered by Monarch owner J.L. Wilkinson. He signed with the All-Nations, toured with them for most of 1922, and was promoted to the Monarchs in October.

The switch-hitting Allen was a line-drive hitter and a skilled bunter. Aggressive on the basepaths, he was not afraid to break up a double play. He twice led the Monarchs in hits, doubles, and stolen bases. He paired with shortstops Willie Wells, Jesse Williams, and Dobie Moore to form extraordinary DP combinations. As Monarch captain, he led his club to the Black World Series in 1924, 1925, and 1945. In the first BWS, against Hilldale in '24, he had seven doubles and batted .281. His best year was 1929, when he hit .330 and led the team with 24 doubles and 23 stolen bases. In 1930 he batted .356.

Allen spent parts of the 1931 and 1932 seasons with the St. Louis Stars, Detroit Stars, and Homestead Grays, as well as with the Monarchs. In 1937 the Monarchs joined the newly-formed Negro American League; with Allen as their manager, they won five pennants (1937, 1939–42). In 1942, at the age of 41, Allen made his final BWS appearance; he batted .267 in the Monarchs' four-game sweep of the Homestead Grays.

Playing in Cuba for two winters, he batted .313 for the Almendares club in 1924–25 and .269 for the Habana team in 1937–38. He toured Japan, the Philippines, and the Hawaiian Islands with other Negro Leaguers. In 24 recorded games against major league competition, he batted .301. /(LL)

Gary Allenson (Hardrock) — 1955– . C 1979–85 **Red Sox**, Blue Jays 416 g, .221, 19 hr, 131 rbi

Allenson was International League MVP with Pawtucket in 1978. He shared catching duties in Boston with Carlton Fisk, and later Rich Gedman. He might have lasted longer had he been better able to hit major league breaking pitches. /(JCA)

Gene Alley — 1940– . SS-2B 1963–73 **Pirates** 1195 g, .254, 55 hr, 342 rbi. *3 LCS, 8 g, .040. 1 WS, 2 g, .000*
☛ *All-Star—67–68. Gold Glove—66–67.*

In 1966, the slight, soft-spoken Virginian teamed with second baseman Bill Mazeroski for a ML-record 215 double plays. A mediocre hitter, Alley was a good bunter, and an excellent hit-and-run man. He won Gold Gloves in 1966 and '67. A 1967 shoulder injury reduced his effectiveness and along with knee problems caused him to consider early retirement several times. He persevered through 1973. /(JCA)

Bob Allison — 1934– . OF 1958–70 **Senators/Twins** 1541 g, .255, 256 hr, 796 rbi. *2 LCS, 5 g, .000, 1 rbi. 1 WS, 5 g, .125, 1 hr, 2 rbi*
☛ *Rookie of the Year—59. All-Star—59, 63–64.*

A college fullback and all-around athlete, Allison admitted, "Hitting is the hardest thing I have ever tried to learn in my life." Learn he did. The Missourian ranks third among Twins home run hitters. His 30 in 1959 helped him become AL Rookie of the Year, and five times he hit 29 or more. He and roommate Harmon Killebrew were the first ML players to combine for two grand slams in one inning (7/18/62). In 1963 he led the AL in runs scored (99) and he hit homers in three consecutive at-bats on May 17. Burly #4 was a hustling fielder—his backhand diving catch in Game Two of the 1965 World Series was a typical effort—and an aggressive, hard-sliding baserunner. Killebrew once said of him: "He wants to win at everything—cards, ping pong, handball, or baseball. He wants to be first on the airplane and first on the bus." /(JCA)

All-Star Game — 1933–

Arch Ward, the sports editor of the Chicago *Tribune*, put together the first All-Star Game in 1933 as a part of Chicago's Exposition that year. The contest has retained its basic form ever since: teams of NL and AL stars, usually chosen by the fans and the year's All-Star managers, compete against each other in a mid-summer exhibition game.

For the first game, played in Comiskey Park, the managers were the senior pilots of their respective leagues: the recently retired John McGraw for the National League and Connie Mack, still going strong in his thirty-third straight year as manager of the Philadelphia Athletics. In subsequent years the pennant-winning managers of the previous season guided the teams, and in the years 1935–46 they selected the entire lineup. From 1947 to 1957 the vote for the starting lineup was returned to the fans, but Cincinnati fans stuffed the ballot box in 1957, producing a starting lineup with only one non-Reds player. The Cardinals' Stan Musial joined Reds Ed Bailey, Johnny Temple, Roy McMillan, Don Hoak, Wally Post, Frank Robinson, and Gus Bell. Commissioner Ford Frick kicked Post and Bell off the team to make room for Hank Aaron and Willie Mays, and took the vote away from the fans, giving it to the players, coaches, and managers. It was returned to the fans in 1970. Each year, various sportswriters and broadcasters decry the injustices of the latest vote, as reputations, rather than current performances, govern voter preferences. Ballot stuffing in Oakland and a weak crop of AL catchers made the A's Terry Steinbach a starter in 1987 (he was batting .218 at the time), but Steinbach became the hero of the game, winning the MVP award with a solo homer and two RBI. In 1989, Mike Schmidt was elected to start at third base for the NL despite having retired in May, and Jose Canseco was named to the AL starting lineup after missing the entire first half of the season with an injured wrist (neither one played).

There have been many memorable moments in the All-Star Games. The aging Babe Ruth won the first Game with a three-run homer, setting an early pattern of AL dominance by the younger league's abundance of superstar sluggers. The 1934 game featured Carl Hubbell striking out Ruth, Gehrig, Foxx, Simmons, and Cronin consecutively, the first three on twelve pitches with two runners on in the first inning. He then struck out Lefty Gomez, the

AL pitcher; Hubbell's six strikeouts in an All-Star Game have since been tied but not bettered. However, the AL won the game and took the 1935 contest too, before the NL finally won in 1936.

An unfortunate incident occurred in the 1937 game when Earl Averill's line drive hit Dizzy Dean on the toe. When told by the doctor that the toe was fractured, Dean said, "Fractured, hell! The damn thing's broke!" He hurt his arm by favoring his foot when he came back, shortening his Hall of Fame career.

The first shutout was recorded by the NL in a 4–0 victory in 1940, Paul Derringer getting the victory with support from Bucky Walters, Whit Wyatt, Larry French, and Hubbell. The AL was 12–4 in the first sixteen years of the mid-summer contest, including a thrilling 1941 victory on Ted Williams's three-run homer with two out in the bottom of the ninth inning and the AL down 5–4. The 1942 contest was followed a day later by a game won by the AL All-Stars 5–0 over Mickey Cochrane's Service All-Stars (mostly major leaguers in the military). In a losing cause in 1943, the NL's Johnny Vander Meer was the first pitcher to equal Hubbell's six strikeouts. The 1944 Game featured Phil Cavaretta setting an All-Star mark by reaching base five times (triple, single, three walks). In 1946 Ted Williams returned from military service to hit two HR (including the famous clout off Rip Sewell's blooper pitch) with four hits and five RBI as the AL won 12–0.

The 1949 game saw the first black All-Stars: Jackie Robinson, Don Newcombe, and Roy Campanella for the NL, and Larry Doby for the AL. In the 1950s the NL began to even the overall record, winning seven of the eleven contests (there were two All-Star Games each season starting in 1959). The most exciting All-Star Game of the decade was the 14-inning contest of 1950, tied on a Ralph Kiner HR in the ninth and won by a Red Schoendienst homer. Larry Jansen pitched one-hit ball for five innings and struck out six. Ted Williams broke his elbow while robbing Kiner with a catch against the wall in the first inning, but Williams stayed in the game and had an RBI single in the fifth inning. Williams had also saved the 1949 contest with a running catch of a Don Newcombe liner that was slicing away from him with the bases loaded in the second inning.

In the 1960s the NL went 11–1, with one tie. Some have attributed this to senior circuit teams' earlier willingness to sign black players who became superstars, such as Willie Mays, Ernie Banks, Willie

Stargell, and Bob Gibson. Stan Musial, helped by the two-contest-a-year format that continued through 1962, set an All-Star record by playing in 24 games. Denny McLain pitched three perfect innings in the 1966 contest, but the NL won yet again on a game-winning 10th-inning single by Maury Wills that drove in Tim McCarver. In 1967 Tony Perez homered in the 15th inning off Catfish Hunter to give the NL a 2–1 victory in the longest All-Star Game ever. Pitching dominated the game to such an extent that there were 30 strikeouts, including 6 by Ferguson Jenkins. Rico Carty became the first player elected as a write-in candidate as his comeback season caught the ballot makers by surprise in 1970. The NL won that year on 12th-inning singles by Pete Rose, Billy Grabarkewitz, and Jim Hickman. Rose scored the winning run in a famous home-plate collision with catcher Ray Fosse that broke Fosse's collarbone. He was never the same afterwards. The win was the NL's eighth in a row, and they started a new streak of 11 straight in 1972. Lee Mazzilli was the surprise hero in 1979, tying the game with an eighth-inning HR in his first All-Star at-bat and then walking in the ninth with the bases loaded for the win. The only AL win in the 1970s came in 1971, when Reggie Jackson crushed a mammoth home run that caromed off a light standard atop the right-field roof at Tiger Stadium.

The AL finally reached parity in the mid-1980s starting with their 1983 victory, which featured the first-ever All-Star grand slam, by Fred Lynn. Dwight Gooden was the youngest All-Star ever in 1984 at the age of 19, and he and Fernando Valenzuela struck out six consecutive batters between them, breaking Hubbell's mark. Valenzuela equaled Hubbell's individual feat in 1986, striking out Don Mattingly, Cal Ripken, Jesse Barfield, Lou Whitaker, and pitcher Ted Higuera consecutively. The NL won another extra-inning game in 1987 on a two-out 13th-inning triple by Tim Raines; they have won all eight extra-inning affairs and lead the series, 37–22./(SH)

Mel Almada — 1913–1988. OF 1933–39 **Red Sox**, Senators, Browns, Dodgers 646 g, .284, 15 hr, 197 rbi

The Browns traded their longtime star, Sammy West, to Washington for this Mexican-born leadoff hitter in June 1938, and Almada batted .342 the rest of the way. His skills disappeared during the off-season, and a poor start in 1939 resulted in his sale to Brooklyn. /(JK)

Bill Almon — 1952– . SS-3B-OF-2B-1B 1974–88 **Padres**, Expos, Mets, White Sox, A's, Pirates, Phillies 1236 g, .254, 36 hr, 296 rbi

Almon attended Brown University in his native Providence, Rhode Island, was named *TSN* College Player of the Year, and was the first player chosen in the June 1974 draft, signing with the Padres for $100,000. Tall and rangy, Almon became starting shortstop for San Diego in 1977, but Ozzie Smith came along in 1978 and Almon was relegated to utility duty. Released by the Mets in 1980, in 1981 Almon was second in AL Comeback Player of the Year voting, batting .301 for Chicago, the best batting average for a starting AL shortstop in 11 years. He returned to a utility role with Oakland and Pittsburgh. /(ME)

Roberto Alomar — 1968– . 2B 1988- **Padres** 301 g, .282, 16 hr, 97 rbi

The younger son of Sandy Alomar, Sr., who is now a Padre coach, Roberto became the regular Padres second baseman in 1988, hitting .266 with 24 stolen bases. /(JFC)

Sandy Alomar [Santos Conde] — 1943– . 2B-SS-3B 1964–78 Braves, Mets, White Sox, **Angels**, Yankees, Rangers 1481 g, .245, 13 hr, 282 rbi. *1 LCS, 2 g, .000* ☛ *All-Star—70.*

Alomar played every position but pitcher and catcher in the majors. A light hitter, he became a regular with the 1968 White Sox after he learned to switch hit. Though he led AL second basemen in errors in 1968 and 1969, most observers considered the errors a by-product of his exceptional range. He was California's everyday second baseman for five years, played 648 consecutive games from 1969 to 1973, and in 1971 led the league with 689 at-bats—a since-broken AL record for a switch hitter. Sold to the Yankees in 1974, he led the AL in fielding at 2B in 1975. He stole 20 or more bases in seven seasons, and 227 lifetime. He became a manager in his native Puerto Rico, and a coach for the Padres, the team that signed his sons Roberto, an infielder, and Sandy, Jr., a catcher. /(MC)

Felipe Alou — 1935– . OF-1B 1958–74 Giants, **Braves**, A's, Yankees, Expos, Brewers 2082 g, .286, 206 hr, 852 rbi. *1 LCS, 1 g, .000. 1 WS, 7 g, .269, 1 rbi* ☛ *All-Star—62, 66, 68.*

The oldest and the only power hitter of the Alous, Felipe spoke out loudly and often for Latin Ameri-can players, arguing that they were underpaid and overly criticized for being "hot dogs." A tall, solemn man, Felipe was among the first born-again Christians to come to the big leagues. His finest year was 1966 with the Braves when he hit 31 homers and batted .327, his 218 hits and 122 runs leading the league. Felipe seldom struck out. Later he became a batting coach and minor league manager with the Montreal Expos. San Francisco fans still recall he scored the winning run in the Giants' come-from-behind victory over the Dodgers in the final game of the 1962 playoff. /(JD)

Jesus Alou (Jay) — 1942– . OF 1963–79 **Giants**, Astros, A's, Mets 1380 g, .280, 32 hr, 377 rbi. *2 LCS, 5 g, .429, 1 rbi. 2 WS, 8 g, .150, 3 rbi*

Jesus, the biggest but slowest of the three Alou brothers, was usually called "Jay" by broadcasters, who feared a report "Jesus strikes out!" might be construed as blasphemy. When he joined Felipe and Matty on the Giants late in 1963, they appeared as the only ML all-brother outfield. The next season, when Felipe was traded, Jesus replaced him as the Giants' rightfielder. A competent contact hitter, he lacked Felipe's home run power and Matty's speed. He later played on Oakland's 1973-'74 World Champions, mostly as a DH or pinch hitter. /(JD)

Matty Alou — 1938– . OF-1B 1960–74 Giants, **Pirates**, Cardinals, A's, Yankees, Padres 1667 g, .307, 31 hr, 427 rbi. *2 LCS, 8 g, .333, 2 rbi. 2 WS, 13 g, .139, 1 rbi* ☛ *Led League—ba 66. All-Star—68–69.*

The 5'9" 160-lb Matty was the best hitter for average and the fastest of the three Alou brothers as well as the smallest. The feisty Dominican had his finest year when he came from the Giants to the Pirates in 1966, leading the league in batting at .342. In 1969 he topped the NL in hits and doubles. The only lefty of the Alous, he lined hits to all fields and batted .300 seven times. As a late-season pick-up in 1972, he hit .381 in the LCS and helped Oakland to their first World Championship. He and Felipe played together in the 1962 Series against the Yankees, and played together near the ends of their careers on the 1973 Yankees. The three brothers were together on the same team only briefly when Jesus came up in 1963 to join the Giants, but did all start one game together in the outfield. /(JD)

Whitey Alperman [Charles Augustus] — 1879–1942. 2B 1906–09 **Dodgers** 450 g, .237, 7 hr, 141 rbi

Alperman was the Dodgers' starting second baseman in 1906, '07, and '09. He hit a career-high .252

in 1906 and tied for the NL lead in triples in 1907 with 16. He also led NL second basemen with 6.2 chances per game in 1907 and 42 errors in 1909. /(JM)

Walt Alston (Smokey) — 1911–1984. 1B 1936 **Cardinals** 1 g, .000, 0 hr, 0 rbi.
    Manager 1954–76 **Dodgers** 2040–1613, .558. First place: 55–56, 59, 63, 65–66, 74 *1 LCS, 3–1, .750. 7 WS, 20–20, .500*

Alston carved out a Hall of Fame career as a manager of the Brooklyn and Los Angeles Dodgers. A product of the "Cradle of Coaches," Miami (Ohio) University, Alston tried almost every position during a 13-year minor league playing career (1935–47). Initially a third baseman, he moved to first base in 1936 and led the Mid-Atlantic League with 35 homers. Promoted to St. Louis, Alston struck out in his only major league at-bat. His first managerial assignment came while he was still a player, with Portsmouth (Mid-Atlantic League) in 1940. He led the circuit in homers (28), but the club finished sixth. The following two years, Alston led the Mid-Atlantic League in homers and RBI. He moved up, as player only, to Rochester (International League), but was released in 1944. Branch Rickey, who knew Alston from his days as the Cardinal's GM, hired him as player-manager at Trenton (Interstate League) on July 28, 1944, beginning Alston's 33-year run as a skipper in the Dodgers' organization. He spent two seasons at Trenton, one at Nashua, one at Pueblo, and two at St. Paul. After leading St. Paul to the Junior World Series in 1949, Alston was promoted to Brooklyn's top minor league club, Montreal. During four seasons in Canada, guiding many of Brooklyn's future stars, Alston's Royals never finished below second place. Finally, on November 24, 1953, Walter O'Malley named Alston to replace Charlie Dressen, who wanted a multi-year contract, a Dodger taboo. Alston served under 23 consecutive one-year contracts. Following charismatic helmsmen like Leo Durocher, Bert Shotton, and Dressen, Alston kept a low profile in the dugout. A quiet, dignified leader, Walt refused to panic following a disappointing second-place finish in 1954. He proved he was boss in 1955, quelling clubhouse turmoil just before the start of the season. With a lineup of stars, Alston led Brooklyn to its only World Series victory in 1955 and a pennant in 1956. Alston adapted to his talent: the power-laden Brooklyn clubs, the pitching-rich Los Angeles Dodgers of the 1960s, and the young team of the 1970s. Sandy Koufax, Don Drysdale,

Walter Alston

and Maury Wills led the group that earned four pennants in eight seasons from 1959 to 1966. Steve Garvey, Dave Lopes, and Ron Cey headed Alston's last great team. At age 62, Alston guided his 1974 Dodgers to a seventh and final World Series. He was honored as Manager of the Year six times by Associated Press and five times by United Press International. In eight All-Star Game assignments, he was the winning manager a record seven times. Alston was the first 1970s manager inducted into the Hall of Fame. /(ME)

Dave Altizer (Filipino) — 1876–1964. SS-OF-1B-2B-3B 1906–11 **Senators**, Indians, White Sox, Reds 514 g, .250, 3 hr, 116 rbi

After serving with the Army in China and the Philippines during the Boxer Rebellion and the Spanish-American War, Altizer played every position but pitcher and catcher. He was known for shouting "No, no, no" whenever he was tagged out. In 1908 he invented a postcard with a photo of William Jennings Bryan which, when held up to the light, also showed a photo of the White House. Altizer later umpired in the minors. /(NLM)

George Altman — 1933- . OF 1959–67 **Cubs,**
Cardinals, Mets 991 g, .269, 101 hr, 403 rbi
☛ *All-Star—61–62.*

The lefthanded hitter improved his average each of
his four years as a Cub regular, reaching a career-
high .318 in 1962. In 1961 he had 27 home runs,
led the NL in triples (12), and hit an All-Star Game
pinch homer. Traded to the Cardinals in 1963, his
home run production and BA plummeted. After
another poor year with the Mets, he returned to the
Cubs for three years as a pinch hitter.

Playing in Japan for Lotte and Hanshin,
1968–75, he hit .309 with 205 HR, and credited
martial arts training for his improvement. /(JCA)

Joe Altobelli — 1932- . 1B-OF 1955, 57, 61 **Indians,**
Twins 166 g, .210, 5 hr, 28 rbi.
Manager 1977–79, 83–85 **Giants,** Orioles 439–406,
.520. First place: 83 *1 LCS, 3–1, .750. 1 WS, 4–1, .800*

Although only a weak-hitting utility man in three
ML seasons, Altobelli was successful as a manager.
He was Manager of the Year three times in 11 minor
league seasons, and earned the same honor in 1978
when he brought the San Francisco Giants in third.
In 1983, his first year as manager of the Orioles, he
won the AL pennant and defeated the Phillies in the
WS./(FK)

Nick Altrock — 1876–1965. LHP 1898, 1902–09,
12–15, 18–19, 24, 29, 31, 33 Louisville (NL), Red Sox,
White Sox, Senators 1515 ip, 82–75, 2.67. 20 wins:
05–06 *1 WS, 18 ip, 1–1, 1.00*

Altrock was a standout for the early White Sox,
winning 20 games plus one in the WS for the 1906
"Hitless Wonders." A sore arm ended his active
career, but in his many years as a ML coach he
made token playing appearances through 1933.
Florid-faced, with a shock of unruly hair that
whitened with age, Altrock was famous for his
clowning in the coaching box and before games,
teaming first with Germany Schaefer and later with
Al Schacht./(JK)

George Alusik (Turk, Glider) — 1935- . OF 1958,
61–64 Tigers, **A's** 298 g, .256, 23 hr, 93 rbi

The 6'4" 175-lb Alusik had fair home run power in
his lanky frame but no chance of breaking into the
Tigers' Colavito-Bruton-Kaline outfield. Sold to the
A's, he platooned with lefthanded hitter Manny
Jimenez and became a useful pinch-hitter./(FJO)

Luis Alvarado (Pimba) — 1949- . SS-2B-3B
1968–74, 76–77 Red Sox, **White Sox,** Indians, Cardinals,
Tigers, Mets 463 g, .214, 5 hr, 84 rbi

Named International League MVP in 1969, Alvarado failed to hit in three trials with Boston. Traded
to the White Sox on December 1, 1970 with Mike
Andrews for Luis Aparicio, he was expected to
replace Aparicio at shortstop. But the slick-fielding
Puerto Rican with the quick release never hit above
.232./(RL)

Jose Alvarez — 1956- . RHP 1981–82, 88 **Braves**
162 ip, 8–9, 2.99

This relief pitcher finally stuck in the majors at the
age of 32. He began his career in the Braves' system,
was let go by them and by three other organizations,
and was picked up again by the Braves in
1986./(SFS)

Max Alvis — 1938- . 3B 1962–70 **Indians,** Brewers
1013 g, .247, 111 hr, 373 rbi
☛ *All-Star—65, 67.*

The consistent and popular Texan had lifetime highs
of .274 and 22 homers as a rookie in 1963. A
career-threatening bout with spinal meningitis disabled him for six weeks in 1964, but he made a
remarkable comeback and was an All-Star in 1965.
In both 1963 and 1967, he was voted the Indians'
Man of the Year./(JCA)

Brant Alyea [Garrabrant Ryerson] — 1940- . OF
1965, 68–72 Senators, **Twins,** A's, Cardinals 371 g, .247,
38 hr, 148 rbi. *1 LCS, 3 g, .000*

Slow afoot and a frequent strikeout victim, Alyea
had one outstanding season. In 1970, in only 94
games, he hit .291, with 16 homers and 61 RBI, to
help push the Twins to the AL West title./(MC)

Joey Amalfitano — 1934- . 2B-3B 1954–55, 60–67
Giants, Astros, Cubs 643 g, .244, 9 hr, 123 rbi.
Manager 1979–81 **Cubs** 66–116, .363

Amalfitano signed with the Giants as an 18-year-old
bonus baby in 1954, and under the rule of the time
had to be kept on the ML roster, hindering both the
Giants' pennant chances and his own development.
After finally receiving some minor league training
(1956–59), he returned to the Giants as a utility
infielder, never hitting enough to hold a regular
position. He coached for several ML teams, and in
1979–82 he was one of the Cubs' "rotating"
managers./(JD)

Ruben Amaro — 1936– . SS-1B 1958, 1960–69
Cardinals, **Phillies**, Yankees, Angels 940 g, .234, 8 hr,
156 rbi
☛ *Gold Glove—64.*

Although his weak bat and some hard luck limited
him to reserve roles most of the time, the personable
Mexican's glove, range, and versatility kept him in
the majors for 11 years. When Yankee shortstop
Tony Kubek was forced to retire after the 1965
season, New York traded infielder Phil Linz to the
Phillies for Amaro. His three years in New York
were plagued by injuries, which started with a
collision with leftfielder Tom Tresh in his first week
in a Yankee uniform. /(AB)

Wayne Ambler — 1915– . SS-2B 1937–39 **Athletics**
271 g, .224, 0 hr, 73 rbi

Although he was offered a $5,000 bonus by a NL
club just before his graduation from Duke University, Ambler signed with Connie Mack's Athletics,
explaining: "Mr. Mack paid for my entire college
education without ever asking for an accounting or
my signature on a contract." /(NLM)

American Association — 1882–1892. League.

The American Association was formed by midwestern clubs who resented the National League's
ban on beer and Sunday baseball. Dominated by the
St. Louis Browns of brewing magnate Chris von der
Ahe, the league thrived, quickly making peace with
the NL. However, the Players' League revolt undid
the AA, which (on the advice of the NL) expanded
to 12 teams in 1890 to directly compete with the
PL, a disastrous move that exacerbated the ills of
that strife-torn year and led to the AA's being
absorbed by the NL after the 1891 season. /(SH)

American League — 1901–

The American League was the brainchild of Ban
Johnson, the president of the Western League,
which was the strongest minor league in the 1890s.
It was upgraded by Johnson and former major
leaguer Charles Comiskey, the owner of the St. Paul
franchise. By 1900 it was renamed the American
League, and in 1901 it went into open competition
with the National League, the only other major
league at the time. Comiskey moved the St. Paul
club to Chicago, and the new league also competed
with the NL head-on in Boston and Philadelphia;
the other franchises were in Detroit, Milwaukee,
Cleveland, Baltimore, and Washington.
  Johnson stocked his new league with major league

players by starting a bidding war for their services,
ignoring the reserve clause in the NL contracts. The
low salaries paid by NL clubs, enforced with a
$2,400 salary maximum, made it easy to lure stars
such as Cy Young, John McGraw, Willie Keeler,
Napoleon Lajoie, Ed Delahanty, Jesse Burkett, and
others. Connie Mack signed Lajoie for the Philadelphia Athletics by offering him a $6,000 contract,
and Lajoie won the Triple Crown with 14 HR, 125
RBI, and a tremendous .422 average (still the AL
record). When a Pennsylvania court ruled that
Lajoie had to return to the Phillies, Johnson convinced Mack to transfer the highly desirable star to
the Cleveland franchise to keep him in the AL. For a
while, Lajoie did not accompany the team on trips
to Philadelphia, a small consolation to Mack. This
kind of owner solidarity helped the young league
survive the war with the senior circuit, although it
certainly helped that the AL outdrew the NL in all
three cities in which they both competed in 1901.
The Milwaukee franchise moved to St. Louis for
1902 and, now competing in four cities, the AL
once again outdrew the NL in head-to-head competition; overall attendance for the eight-team league
was 2,228,000 in a 136-game schedule compared to
the NL's 1,684,000.
  After the 1902 season, there was a peace settlement between the two leagues; the NL sought a
merger, but Johnson knew he had the upper hand,
and held out for full acceptance by the NL. The only
concession the AL had to make was to promise not
to place a franchise in Pittsburgh; they did move the
Baltimore club to New York, they were allowed to
keep all the players they had taken from the NL, and
the AL reserve clauses were to be respected. The
American League based its popularity on its contrast
to the rowdyism of the National League, with
Johnson especially noted for his strong support of
the league's umpires. In the NL an arbiter's authority depended largely on his own presence (which is
how Bill Klem became famous), but Johnson stood
behind all of his umpires and tolerated very little
abuse of them by players or managers. This was a
major element in John McGraw's decision to move
to the NL's New York franchise, and McGraw tried
to block the AL's move of the Baltimore club to
New York. The bad feelings between McGraw and
Johnson led to another conflict the next year. The
revival of the two-league concept allowed the resumption of postseason play in 1903 with the
inaugural World Series, won by the Boston Pilgrims
over the Pirates, but when McGraw's Giants won in
1904, he refused to play the Pilgrims. He did deign

to meet Mack's Athletics in 1905, and the Series has continued uninterrupted ever since, as has the peace between the two leagues.

The profitable American League expanded its schedule to 154 games in 1904. It had good luck in attracting young talent that turned out to be of superstar caliber. Ty Cobb, Shoeless Joe Jackson, Ed Walsh, Addie Joss, Tris Speaker, Walter Johnson, and most of all Babe Ruth brought the AL more publicity, and helped the junior circuit win twice as many World Series as the NL through 1918.

In 1919 the Black Sox scandal rocked the game as key members of the seemingly invincible White Sox threw the WS to the Reds for payoffs from gamblers. The AL's antidote was the legendary Babe Ruth. He had set what many considered to be an unbreakable record in 1919 by hitting 29 HR for Boston (19 ahead of the runners-up). After being sold to the Yankees for the 1920 season, Ruth benefited from several changes regarding the ball: it was livelier, it was cleaner (the spitball was outlawed), and it wasn't kept in play until it was falling apart. Ruth hit an unprecedented 54 HR in 1920 with his then unorthodox (and later much-copied) uppercut swing, and he proved to be quite a gate attraction. League attendance was over five million, more than a million and a half above the previous high and a million better than the NL total. Ruth's 54 HR was 35 ahead of runner-up George Sisler, but Ken Williams adopted the new strategy and soon he, Bob Meusel, Al Simmons, Lou Gehrig, and Joe Hauser were breaking the 20-HR barrier as Ruth set a new standard with 60 HR in 1927. When the next generation came along in the 1930s with the new style as a normal part of their repertoire, stars like Jimmie Foxx, Earl Averill, Hank Greenberg, Indian Bob Johnson, Joe DiMaggio, Hal Trosky, and Rudy York hit 30 HR regularly, occasionally challenged Ruth's record, and enabled the AL to dominate in the early years of the All-Star Game.

Ban Johnson continued as the autocrat of the American League until 1927, but his control over all of baseball slipped after the Black Sox scandal led to the appointment of Judge Landis to the new office of Commissioner. The peace settlement back in 1903 had included the founding of the National Commission, a triumvirate composed of the AL and NL presidents and Cincinnati owner Garry Herrmann that decided disputes between clubs and between clubs and players. Johnson had been able to dominate this board, but met his match in Landis. It didn't help that the scandal also precipitated a break between Johnson and Comiskey. Johnson resigned

when it became apparent to him that he was never going to remedy the situation. Ernest S. Barnard became AL president, but he died in 1931 and was succeeded by Will Harridge, who lasted a record 28 years.

Meanwhile, the Yankee dynasty that Ruth had started shared power with such mini-dynasties as the Senators (1924–25, '33), the Athletics (1929–31), and the Tigers (1934–35); New York won 14 AL pennants between 1921 and 1943. The Yankees also won the World Series ten times in that period; four additional AL victories added to American League domination of the postseason. In the tradition of Ruth, the AL was a hitters' league, and offense drew in the fans in numbers the NL couldn't match. In Boston, owner Tom Yawkey and general manager Eddie Collins paid dearly for West Coast stars Ted Williams and Bobby Doerr, and the Red Sox became respectable for the first time since Harry Frazee had sold off Ruth and others to pay the debts on his Broadway shows. But the two Hall of Famers brought Boston only one pennant (1946).

Yankee hegemony reached its peak after the war: from 1947 to 1964 they won fifteen AL pennants and ten World Series, including a record five straight under manager Casey Stengel (1949–53). This new Yankee dynasty was built around Mickey Mantle, Yogi Berra, and Whitey Ford and featured strength at every position and the solid pitching of the "Big Three": Allie Reynolds, Vic Raschi, and Ed Lopat. GM Ed Barrow and farm director George Weiss had put together the AL's best minor league system, and the dynasty seemed self-perpetuating. Al Lopez was elected to the Hall of Fame as a manager largely on the strength of being the only manager to take the flag away from New York in the 1950s, winning in 1954 and 1959. Managing Cleveland from 1951 to 1956 and Chicago starting in 1957, he finished second every other year in the decade.

The first AL franchise move in 50 years came when the St. Louis Browns moved to Baltimore for the 1954 season. Harridge's reign ended in 1959, and former All-Star Joe Cronin succeeded him as AL president. The 1960s brought more change, and (eventually) the end of the Yankee dynasty. The AL jumped the gun on expansion to get a California franchise (the Los Angeles Angels) and to let Calvin Griffith get out of Washington. Griffith's original Senators became the Minnesota Twins and a new franchise took their place in Washington. The ten-team structure required a 162-game schedule, which instantly led to controversy. Roger Maris, having adapted his swing to the short right-field porch at

Yankee Stadium, hit 61 HR in 1961 to break Ruth's season record. But Ruth had hit 60 in only 154 games. Commissioner Ford Frick, a former ghostwriter and drinking buddy of Ruth's, ruled that Maris had to match or set the record in the same 154 games; after that span of time, Maris had 59 HR. The infamous asterisk that Frick placed next to Maris's record was later overturned by the rules committee.

The biggest change in baseball was not the length of the schedule or the location of the franchises. In 1962 the Player Development Plan was adopted to deal with the troubled minor leagues, which had been losing money and teams for years. A plan to distribute the talent to stock the minors (and eventually, of course, the majors too) followed in 1965 with the introduction of the annual free-agent draft. The Yankee franchise had already developed the problems that would bring it crashing down to last place in 1966 after a sixth-place finish in 1965, but their inability to buy up all the young talent in the future doomed them to a lengthy stretch of mediocrity. The Yankee collapse ended the last vestiges of AL dominance. New York had lost the last two World Series, and the NL was winning the All-Star Game almost every year; AL teams had been slower than their NL counterparts to sign up minority talent, and the imbalance was great. AL attendance dropped off radically in 1965. As the Yankees lost their attraction, the NL drew five million more fans than the AL.

Baltimore became the new league dynasty thanks to their fine farm system and to the wise acquisition of Frank Robinson from the NL's Reds. Robinson won the Triple Crown in his first AL season (1966) and led the Orioles to their first-ever World Championship, something their precursors, the Browns, had never won. Baltimore became truly dominant after the second expansion in 1969, when the 12-team league was split into two divisions. They won three straight AL flags (1969–71), with division titles in 1973–74, and added another AL pennant in 1979.

The move to divisional play was an effort to get around the problem of too many losers each season. With two divisions in each league, more teams could contend, and do so later in the season. The newly minted Pilots lasted just one season in Seattle, moving to Milwaukee in 1970. The Kansas City Royals, better judges of young talent, became a Western Division dynasty later in the decade. Kansas City was available for an expansion franchise because Charlie Finley, the maverick owner of the Athletics (whom he rechristened the A's), had

moved his team to Oakland in 1968 in an effort to duplicate the attendance success of the Dodgers, Giants, and Angels on the West Coast. He failed at that, but he succeeded in building one of the most exciting teams in the league. Based on the superstar talents of Catfish Hunter, Vida Blue, Reggie Jackson, and Rollie Fingers, the team won five consecutive division titles (1971–75) and three straight World Championships (1972–74) and led the league each year in clubhouse vendettas and player-owner squabbles. Just to make sure they got attention, Finley literally changed the face of baseball by offering them rewards for growing mustaches, and also outfitted them in a variety of green, gold, and white uniforms.

Meanwhile, the league dealt with continuing attendance problems by approving a radical rule change, the designated hitter (DH). Allowing another player to bat for the pitcher perked up offense and attendance. This step was taken in the last year of Joe Cronin's administration. In 1974 Lee McPhail (the son of former owner Larry McPhail) took over the AL presidency.

What broke up the A's, and revived the fortunes of the Yankees, was the advent of free agency. Hunter showed the shape of things to come when he became a free agent after Finley reneged on part of his contract. George Steinbrenner, the New York owner, acquired Hunter's services with an unheard-of $3.5– million-dollar, five-year contract in 1975. Pitchers Andy Messersmith and Dave McNally challenged the reserve clause that year and won. Thereafter, players could, with varying restrictions, sell their services to the highest bidder after fulfilling certain requirements as to length of service. Finley's players hated him and seized the chance to escape. Finley saw trouble coming and traded or sold his best players when he could. Jackson and Ken Holtzman were traded to Baltimore for Don Baylor and Mike Torrez (although Finley was unable to hang onto Baylor and traded Torrez to the Yankees after less than two seasons). The sales of Joe Rudi and Rollie Fingers to the Red Sox and Vida Blue to the Yankees, for a million dollars each, were voided by Commissioner Bowie Kuhn "in the best interests of baseball."

The Yankees, besides signing many former A's—in addition to Hunter in 1975, they got Jackson and Ken Holtzman for 1977—assumed the characteristics of those Oakland teams: internecine feuding ameliorated by common opposition to the owner. They also had the success typical of the A's, winning three straight league titles (1976–78) and two World Series (1977–78). At the end of the

1980s, they were still the last team to repeat as World Champions.

Free agency is seen as a major factor in the new era of parity, with almost every team winning at least one division title, the exceptions in the AL being Cleveland and Texas. The Texas franchise has largely continued the losing tradition of its ancestors, the Senators. The team moved to Arlington, Texas after the 1971 season, bringing about a league realignment, with Milwaukee and Texas switching divisions. But the biggest change came in 1977, when the AL expanded again (this time without corresponding expansion by the NL). The addition of the Toronto Blue Jays and Seattle Mariners gave the AL 14 teams, and it adopted a much-criticized balanced schedule that resulted in each team playing more games outside its division than within it. At the time, the Western Division was considerably weaker than the East, and the Western clubs wanted more home dates against the East's more established and better-drawing teams.

Red Ames with the Giants

Interest in baseball boomed after the 1977 expansion, linked by many observers to the fact that almost every team had a turn at winning (the Mariners joined Texas and Seattle as the have-nots, but Toronto won its division in 1985). Dr. Bobby Brown, a former Yankee star and former part-owner of the Texas club, succeeded McPhail as AL president in 1984. /(SH)

Red Ames [Leon Kessling] — 1882–1936. RHP 1903–19 **Giants**, Reds, Cardinals, Phillies 3192 ip, 183–167, 2.63. 20 wins: 05 *3 WS, 11 ip, 0–1, 2.45*

In his major league debut, Ames threw a five-inning no-hitter against the Cardinals (9/14/03). He went on to pitch on four Giants pennant-winners; for the 1905 World Champions, Ames went 22–8, Christy Mathewson 31–8, and Joe McGinnity 21–15. Though Ames never again won more than 15, he remained a dependable New York starter through 1912. In the season opener on April 15, 1909, he no-hit Brooklyn into the 10th inning and went the route, losing 3–0 in the 13th.

Ames lost a league-high 23 games for Cincinnati in 1914 but, oddly, tied for the NL lead with six saves. With the Cardinals, his seven saves in 1916 and eight relief wins in 1917 were also NL highs. /(JK)

Sandy Amoros — 1930– . OF 1952, 1954–57, 1959–60 **Dodgers**, Tigers 517 g, .255, 43 hr, 180 rbi. *3 WS, 12 g, .161, 1 hr, 4 rbi*

The Cuban native, who spoke almost no English, was never more than a semi-regular in the Dodger outfield, but he's remembered for one great play, generally listed among the most outstanding in World Series history. In Game Seven of the 1955 WS, his sprinting catch of Yogi Berra's drive down the leftfield line was the key to Brooklyn's victory. According to winning pitcher Johnny Podres: "As great a catch as Amoros made, his relay to Pee Wee [Reese] (to double up Gil McDougald) was even better." When a reporter asked Amoros if he thought he would make the catch, he said, "I dunno. I just run like hell." /(TG)

Anaheim Stadium (The Big A) California Angels 1966– . LF-333, CF-404, RF-333

A modern, three-level stadium 36 miles from Los Angeles, Anaheim Stadium was designed for baseball, opening in 1966 with almost all of its 43,250 seats along the foul lines, and unenclosed in the outfield. It took its nickname, The Big A, from the massive left-field scoreboard, which was supported by a 230-foot-high Angels logo, a letter A with a halo. That scoreboard was forced into the parking lot in 1980 when double-decked outfield seating was added to accommodate the NFL's Rams, making Anaheim a fully enclosed ballpark and raising the baseball capacity to its present 64,593. The playing field remains natural grass. /(SCL)

Larry Andersen — 1953– . RHP 1975, 77, 79, 81–89 Indians, Mariners, Phillies, **Astros** 724 ip, 27–28, 3.33. *1 LCS, 5 ip, 0–0, 0.00. 1 WS, 4 ip, 0–0, 2.25*

A well-known clubhouse prankster and cutup, Andersen spent 10 years in the minors with brief stints in the ML every other year from 1975 to 1981, when he arrived to stay with Seattle. His 2.65 ERA as a middle reliever that year led the Mariners' staff. His offbeat questions, such as "why do we drive on the parkway and park in the driveway," gained him national attention with the Astros. /(SG)

Allan Anderson — 1964– . LHP 1986–88 **Twins** 496 ip, 37–25, 3.72
☛ *Led League—era 88.*

A second-round draft pick in 1982, Anderson finally lived up to his potential in 1988, going 16–9 and leading the AL with a 2.45 ERA despite pitching in the batter-friendly Metrodome. /(WOR)

Bob Anderson — 1935– . RHP 1957–63 **Cubs**, Tigers 841 ip, 36–46, 4.26

Anderson was the number-two man in the Cubs' rotation in 1959 (12–13, 4.13) and 1960 (9–11, 4.11). Moved to the bullpen by Chicago's "College of Coaches" in 1961, he was less effective. Traded to Detroit for Steve Boros after the 1962 season, he had his only winning record in 1963, his final year, going 3–1 in limited relief use. Traded to Kansas City in the Rocky Colavito deal that winter, he never made it back to the majors. /(JFC)

Brady Anderson — 1964– . OF 1988– Red Sox, **Orioles** 188 g, .210, 5 hr, 37 rbi

This Maryland native came to the Orioles in the deal that sent Mike Boddicker to Boston. The speedy centerfielder proved to be a high-percentage basestealer with the ability to draw walks. /(JFC)

Bud Anderson — 1956– . RHP 1982–83 **Indians** 149 ip, 4–10, 3.68

A minor league starter, Anderson was twice called up in mid-season as a reliever for the Indians. He had 7 saves in 1983 but only a 1–6 record. /(ME)

Craig Anderson — 1938– . RHP 1961–64 Cardinals, **Mets** 192 ip, 7–23, 5.10

The name Craig was unlucky with the early Mets. Anderson lost 16 straight with the original 1962 team and 19 in a row over three years. In NL history, the latter streak was rivaled only by teammate Roger Craig's 18 straight defeats in 1963. /(JCA)

Dave Anderson — 1960– . SS-3B-2B 1983– **Dodgers** 662 g, .232, 13 hr, 116 rbi. *1 LCS, 4 g, .000. 1 WS, 1 g, .000*

A bad back hindered Anderson's quest for the Dodgers' starting shortstop job after he was voted the Pacific Coast League's top prospect at Albuquerque. While he didn't continue the Pee Wee Reese, Maury Wills, and Bill Russell legacy as an everyday player, he became a valuable utility man. He contributed significantly in the Dodgers' 1988 World Championship season by filling in for injured regular Alfredo Griffin. /(TG)

Fred Anderson (Spitball) — 1885–1957. RHP 1909, 13–18 Red Sox, Buffalo (FL), **Giants** 986 ip, 53–58, 2.86

The 6'2" 180-lb Anderson spent his most productive years with Buffalo of the Federal League, going 13–16 in 1914 and 19–13 in 1915. He had an 8–8 mark for the NL champion 1917 Giants, with a 1.44 ERA. He had three saves in 1918 to tie for the NL lead. /(JM)

George Anderson — 1889–1962. OF 1914–15, 18 **Brooklyn FL**, Cardinals 269 g, .287, 5 hr, 69 rbi

A lefthanded-hitting leadoff man with reported 3.2-second speed to first, Anderson was a solid Federal League player unable to earn a job in the ML after the Feds folded. /(NLM)

Harry Anderson — 1931– . OF-1B 1957–61 **Phillies**, Reds 484 g, .264, 60 hr, 242 rbi

An outstanding spring training in 1957 won the lefthanded slugger promotion from Class A to the majors. In his sophomore year, he batted .301 with 23 HR and finished third in the NL with 97 RBI. But he led the league in strikeouts, and a chronic problem making contact hastened his ML exit. /(AL)

Jim Anderson — 1957– . SS-3B 1978–81, 83–84 Angels, **Mariners**, Rangers 419 g, .218, 13 hr, 86 rbi. *1 LCS, 4 g, .091*

A high school All-American at Granada Hills, CA in 1975, Anderson played six ML positions, including catcher, but failed to hit in any of them. /(NLM)

John Anderson (Honest John) — 1873–1949. OF-1B 1894–99, 1901–08 **Dodgers**, Washington (NL), Milwaukee (AL)/Browns, Yankees, Senators, White Sox 1627 g, .290, 48 hr, 976 rbi

Anderson was born in Norway. He broke in as an outfielder, and while the switch-hitter batted well, his fielding was terrible; he was moved back and forth between the OF and first base several times. For Brooklyn and Washington in 1898, he led the NL with 22 triples and a .494 slugging average. He hit .330 for the 1901 Milwaukee AL franchise in its only year of existence; the team became the St. Louis Browns in 1902. As a 1906 Senator, Anderson led the AL with 39 stolen bases. /(AJA)

Mike Anderson — 1951– . OF 1971–79 **Phillies**, Cardinals, Orioles 721 g, .246, 28 hr, 134 rbi

Before injuries and illness spoiled his career, Anderson excelled as a defensive rightfielder and showed promise as a hitter. /(AB)

Ollie Anderson — Unk.–1945. *Umpire* FL 1914

Anderson, who umpired for 40 years in 14 different minor leagues, including Texas, Pacific Coast, and American Association, worked 5,000 consecutive games before an auto accident hospitalized him in 1936. When players objected to his calls, his standard reply was, "I wish I were Santa Claus so I could give you everything you want." /(RTM)

Rick Anderson — 1956– . RHP 1986–88 **Mets**, Royals 97 ip, 4–4, 4.75

Anderson finally got the call at the age of 29 and contributed a 2–1, 2.72 record to the 1986 World Champion Mets. He was traded to the Royals in the deal that brought David Cone to New York.

Anderson pitched an 8–0 no-hitter against Shreveport on May 12, 1979 while with Jackson (Texas League). /(SFS)

Sparky Anderson [George Lee] (Captain Hook) — 1934– . 2B 1959 **Phillies** 152 g, .218, 0 hr, 34 rbi.
   Manager 1970– Reds, **Tigers** 1758–1362, .563. First place: 70, 72–73, 75–76, 84, 87 *7 LCS, 18–9, .667. 5 WS, 16–12, .571*

Named Manager of the Year twice in the NL and once in the AL, Anderson is the first manager to win more than 600 in both the NL and the AL and the first to win World Championships in both leagues. His 18 LCS wins lead all managers. He won the NL pennant in his first season, and in nine years at Cincinnati, he won five division titles, four pennants, and two world championships, only once

finishing below second place. He became known as Captain Hook for his frequent early removal of his starting pitchers in an era when that strategy was still unusual. It was a policy dictated by necessity. The "Big Red Machine" was based on offense, and often Anderson lacked a quality rotation. Also, many of the Reds' best starters—Gary Nolan, Don Gullett, and Wayne Simpson—were injury-prone and could not be overworked. But the Reds developed some of the best relief corps in the majors, including Clay Carroll, Wayne Granger, Tom Hall, and Pedro Borbon.

Moving to Detroit in June 1979, Anderson won the World Championship in 1984 and a division title in 1987. He became known for his unbounded optimism and a tendency to overstate his case to reporters. He called Kirk Gibson "the next Mickey Mantle" and handed less-talented players such as Chris Pittaro and Torey Lovullo regular jobs, praising their talents to the maximum, only to see them play themselves back to the minors within months. White-haired since his playing days, the avuncular

Sparky Anderson

Anderson missed time due to nervous exhaustion in 1989, when the Tigers finished a distant last. That season was only his second losing record in his first 20 years of managing.

Starting out with six seasons in the minor league farm system of the Dodgers, Anderson was traded to the Phillies and became their regular second baseman in 1959, his only big league season. After returning to the minors, he became a manager in 1964 at Toronto. Following four more seasons as minor league manager, he returned to the NL in 1969 as a coach for San Diego. He accepted a coaching post with California for 1970 but then was hired to manage Cincinnati. /(AL)

Ivy Andrews (Poison) — 1907-1970. RHP 1931-38 Yankees, Red Sox, **Browns**, Indians 1041 ip, 50-59, 4.14. *1 WS, 6 ip, 3.18*

Periodic arm miseries led Andrews to develop an assortment of pitches to replace his lost fastball. His best year was 13-7 in 1935 with the seventh-place Browns. /(JL)

Mike Andrews — 1943- . 2B 1966-73 **Red Sox**, White Sox, A's 893 g, .258, 66 hr, 316 rbi. *1 LCS, 2 g, .000. 2 WS, 7 g, .250, 1 rbi* ☛ *All-Star—69.*

Erratic in the field, Andrews had some sting at bat. Oakland picked him up in mid-1973 as a backup second baseman for the pennant drive, but when he made two key WS errors, owner Charlie Finley maneuvered him onto the disabled list, enraging teammates, fans, press, and Commissioner Bowie Kuhn. Andrews was reinstated and received a standing ovation at Shea Stadium. Angry at Finley for provoking the embarrassing incident, A's manager Dick Williams resigned during the off-season. Mike's brother Rob later played in the NL. /(AB)

Nate Andrews — 1913- . RHP 1937, 39-41, 43-46 Cardinals, Indians, **Braves** 773 ip, 41-54, 3.46 ☛ *All-Star—44.*

After four failed trials lasting less than 40 innings, Andrews escaped the minors during WWII to lead the NL with 20 losses in 1943 and was 16-15 in 1944. His career fizzled when the regulars returned from the war. /(JK)

Rob Andrews — 1952- . 2B 1975-79 Astros, **Giants** 493 g, .251, 3 hr, 91 rbi

The younger brother of Mike Andrews had no power, but his fielding consistency made him a useful backup second baseman. /(EW)

Joaquin Andujar — 1952- . RHP 1976-88 **Astros**, Cardinals, A's 2153 ip, 127-118, 3.58. 20 wins: 84-85 *3 LCS, 18 ip, 1-1, 5.00. 2 WS, 17 ip, 2-1, 3.12* ☛ *Led League—w 84. All-Star—77, 79, 84.*

Referring to himself as "one tough Dominican," the colorful Andujar reached his peak in the mid-1980s as a Cardinal workhorse who worked well on three days' rest. Coming from the Astros, who hadn't been able to handle his unique personality and had misused him in the bullpen, Andujar's 15-10, 2.47 record in 1982 helped St. Louis to a World Championship. He won the LCS clincher 6-2 as the Braves were swept in three games, and had a 1.35 ERA in the World Series, winning Games Three and Seven.

After dropping off to 6-16 in 1983, Andujar led the NL in wins, shutouts, and IP in 1984, going 20-14 with a 3.34 ERA and four shutouts in 261.1 IP. His 21-12 record in 1985 led the Cardinals as they captured the NL pennant, although he pitched poorly in the last two months after four great months and was 1-5 with a 5.76 ERA after August. He continued to struggle in the postseason, getting hit hard in two LCS starts and losing Game Two to the Dodgers. In the World Series, the Royals knocked him out in the fifth inning of Game Three as he lost 6-1, and he had a disastrous relief appearance in Game Seven. Called in in the fifth inning when the Cardinals were already losing by a wide margin, he gave up a hit and a walk and was then ejected, along with manager Whitey Herzog, for complaining vociferously about the umpiring.

Andujar was traded to Oakland that winter and his career wound down amidst injuries and accusations by him that his downfall was caused by a conspiracy against him (he never offered any specifics). One of his injuries with the A's came while taking batting practice despite being in the AL, where the DH rule prevented him from hitting. Although he batted just .127 lifetime, he considered himself quite a hitter, and switch-hit by an unusual system: if he didn't trust the control of the pitcher he was facing, he would go against the usual lefty-righty percentages and bat so that his pitching arm was the more protected back arm. /(SH)

Roger Angell — 1921- . *Writer*

A 1942 graduate of Harvard, Angell joined *The New Yorker* in 1962. His regular reports about baseball for that magazine have been collected into successful and respected books, including *The Summer Game* (1972), *Five Seasons* (1977), *Late Innings* (1982) and *Season Ticket* (1988). /(NLM)

Cap Anson [Adrian Constantine] (Pop)1851–1897. 1B-
3B-C 1871–97 Rockford NA, Philadelphia NA, **Cubs** NA
245 g, .352; NL 2276 g, .334, 96 hr, 1715 rbi (inc.)
  Manager 1879–98 **Cubs**, Giants 1297–957 .575
☛ *Led League—ba 79, 81, 88. Led League—rbi 81, 86,
88, 91 . Hall of Fame—1939.*

A premier batsman and leader, Anson is widely
regarded as the foremost on-field baseball figure of
the 19th century. He led the NL in hitting three
times and was the first man to get 3,000 hits. As a
manager, he took his Chicago team to five pennants.
Counting five years in the National Association, he
played 27 seasons at the highest level of baseball
competition and was a regular each year. He was
stern, iron-willed, and incorruptible, and his influence went far beyond the field as baseball became
the national game.

After a year at Notre Dame, the 19-year-old
Iowan turned pro in 1871 with the Rockford Forest

Cap Anson

Citys of the National Association, the forerunner of
the NL. The following season, he joined the Philadelphia Athletics as a third baseman and first
baseman. In five NA seasons, he hit over .350 four
times. One of the first players signed by William
Hulbert when he launched the NL in 1876, Anson
helped the Chicago team (then called White Stockings) to the first NL pennant, hitting .356.

Although he'd played mostly as a third baseman
and catcher in his early years, when he became
playing manager in 1879, he put himself permanently at first base. The stocky six-footer was no
artist in the field. He holds the all-time record for
most errors committed by a first baseman, but he
played at a time when gloves were not used and
errors were common. Longevity also helped account
for his error record.

He made up for his fielding shortcomings with his
bat. In all but two of his 22 NL seasons, he topped
.300. He led the league in 1879, 1881, and 1888,
with his .399 in '81 his personal high. He led the
league in RBI four times and five times drove in
more than 100 even though teams played fewer than
100 games each season until 1884. Line-drive singles were his hallmark, although he twice led in
doubles and totaled 532 two-base hits over his long
career. He hit 96 home runs, but 21 came in 1884,
when the White Stockings played at Lake Front
Park, with a 180-foot left-field foul line. He had five
homerless seasons.

Anson managed the White Stockings to three
straight pennants from 1880 to 1882 and two more
flags in 1885 and 1886. An innovator, he encouraged basestealing, devised hit-and-run plays,
and was one of the first to rotate pitchers. The first
manager to institutionalize preseason training, he
laid down strict training rules for his players and
sometimes enforced them with his fists. He had an
explosive temper and could be a cruel bench jockey
and umpire baiter. Many of the greatest stars of the
19th century played for him, but none outshone
him.

Anson participated in baseball tours of England
in 1874 and of the world in 1888–89. He improved
the quality of play in his time and spread the game's
popularity. He raised the caliber of players with his
own integrity and principles. Yet, at the same time,
he was a bigot who once pulled his team off the field
rather than play against a team with a black player.
He is often cited as a force in the banning of black
players from ML baseball, an unwritten rule that
persisted until 1947. That Anson was a racist is
beyond question. The extent of his influence in

keeping blacks out of the majors in the 19th century is debatable.

Anson became part-owner of the White Stockings in 1888, but he won no more pennants in the 1890s. The team was so linked with his image that when he finally left after the 1897 season, they were known for a while as the "Orphans." He managed the Giants for 22 games in 1898, then left baseball. When he later had financial problems, the NL attempted to establish a pension for him, but he rejected it. In 1939, he was named to baseball's Hall of Fame. /(AJA)

Johnny Antonelli — 1930– . LHP 1948–50, 1953–61 Braves, **Giants**, Indians 1992 ip, 126–110, 3.34. 20 wins: 54, 56 *1 WS, 11 ip, 1–0, 0.84*
☛ *Led League—era 54. All-Star—54, 56–59.*

One of the first "bonus babies," the tall, dark-eyed Antonelli signed with the Boston Braves for $65,000 in 1948 and pitched only in spots, mostly in relief, before leaving for military service in 1951–52. His 1954 trade to the Giants for Polo Grounds hero Bobby Thomson temporarily infuriated New Yorkers, but Antonelli silenced the critics with a 21–7 mark for Durocher's world champions. He led the NL in winning percentage (.750), ERA (2.30), and shutouts (6), and had a win and a save in the WS. He won 20 again in 1956 and 19 for the San Francisco transplants of 1959, leading the NL in shutouts again in both seasons. His 26 career shutouts constitute 21% of his ML wins. /(JD)

Luis Aparacio (Little Looie) — 1934– . SS 1956–73 **White Sox**, Red Sox 2599 g, .262, 83 hr, 791 rbi. *2 WS, 10 g, .286, 2 rbi*
☛ *Rookie of the Year—56. All-Star—58–64, 70–72. Gold Glove—58–62, 64, 66, 68, 70. Hall of Fame—1984.*

Playing side by side with Nellie Fox during the late 1950s and early 1960s, Aparicio helped form the nucleus of one of the slickest-fielding infield combinations in baseball. His 506 stolen bases ranked him seventh all-time when he retired, and he holds the lifetime shortstop records for games, double plays, and assists and the AL records for putouts and total chances. He dominated on a season-to-season basis too; in the first thirteen years of his career, he led AL shortstops eight consecutive years in fielding, seven times in assists, four times in putouts, twice each in total chances per game and double plays, and only once in errors.

Aparicio succeeded Chico Carrasquel, continuing the Venezuelan connection that gave the White Sox amazing depth at shortstop for years. Chicago was so confident in him as a rookie that they traded Carrasquel, a perennial fan favorite, to Cleveland for Larry Doby. Named Rookie of the Year in 1956, Aparicio led the league in stolen bases for the first of nine straight years. White Sox manager Marty Marion advised Aparicio to shorten his stance and stride into the pitch. Then he was told to play deeper to gain more range. His cannonlike arm took care of the rest. Bill Veeck arrived on the scene in 1959 and was amazed. "He's the best I've ever seen. He makes plays which I know can't possibly be made, yet he makes them almost every day."

Always a steady hitter, but never one of the great ones, Aparicio relied on his speed to make things happen in an era known for lead-footed sluggers. With Aparicio leading off followed by Fox in the lineup, Chicago had a deadly hit-and-run duo that helped catapult them to their first pennant in 40 years. Fittingly, it was Aparicio who fielded the ground ball off of Vic Power's bat that clinched it on September 22, 1959. In 1963, a new general man-

Luis Aparicio

ager decided a house-cleaning was in order, so Aparicio was sent to the Orioles. He established a since-broken AL shortstop record for fielding percentage that year (.983) and remained long enough to get into another World Series in 1966. He had lost some speed, but compensated by becoming a better hitter. Returning to Chicago in 1968, he enjoyed some of his finest years. He topped the .300 mark for the only time in his career in 1970, a year in which his team finished dead last in the standings with 106 losses. Aparicio played his 2,219th game on September 25, 1970 in front of a mere 2,000 fans to break Luke Appling's record of games played at shortstop. Rumors abounded that he was to be the Sox manager at the start of the 1971 season, but instead the club traded him to Boston for Mike Andrews. Aparicio finished his career in 1973, and in 1984 he took his place in the Hall of Fame. Now residing in Venezuela, his son's name is Nelson, after Luis's long-time sidekick Nellie Fox./(RL)

Bob Apodaca — 1950- . RHP 1973-77 **Mets** 362 ip, 16-25, 2.86

The righthanded reliever was 3-4 with 13 saves and a 1.48 ERA for the Mets in 1975, despite suffering a broken nose during the season. He retired after spending all 1978 and '79 on the disabled list with an elbow injury./(KT)

Luis Aponte — 1953- . RHP 1980-84 **Red Sox**, Indians 220 ip, 9-6, 3.27

This successful Venezuelan reliever retired for three years after four years in the Red Sox system. Playing in the Inter-American League in 1979, he developed an amazing fork ball and was resigned by the Red Sox./(EW)

Pete Appleton [born Peter William Jablonski] — 1904-1974. RHP 1927-28, 1930-33, 36-42, 1945 Reds, Indians, Red Sox, Yankees, **Senators**, White Sox, Browns 1141 ip, 57-66, 4.30

An accomplished pianist and college bandleader at the University of Michigan, Pete opted for a baseball career at graduation. He played under his real name until 1933, then had it legally changed to Appleton. Used mainly in relief for most of his ML career, his best year was 1936, when he started 20 games for the Senators and finished 14-9./(LRD)

Luke Appling (Old Aches and Pains) — 1909- . SS-3B 1930-43, 45-50 **White Sox** 2422 g, .310, 45 hr, 1116 rbi ☛ All-Star—36, 39-43, 46-47. Hall of Fame—1964.

Voted the greatest living White Sox player in a 1969 fan poll, Appling was almost a member of the Chicago Cubs. After two years at Oglethorpe University, Appling signed with the Atlanta Crackers (Southern Association). He was sold to the Cubs late in the 1930 season, but thanks to the intervention of Milt Stock (Eddie Stanky's father-in-law), Appling joined the White Sox in a cash transaction that also involved little-known outfielder Doug Taitt. There was nothing remarkable about Appling's first two seasons. His arm was powerful, but his throws were inaccurate, and sometimes wound up in the stands. Worse yet was his penchant for muffing the most routine ground ball.

The arrival of Jimmy Dykes as manager in 1934 had a positive effect on the young shortstop. Dykes cajoled, pleaded, and instilled confidence. When Appling finally realized that he wasn't going to drive the ball out of spacious Comiskey Park, he adjusted his stance and became one of the most productive hitters of the decade. With a keen batting eye, the leadoff hitter would foul off pitch after pitch before selecting just the right one, or drawing one of his many bases on balls. Legend has it that on one occasion, Appling fouled off seventeen straight pitches before hitting a triple, and his 1,302 lifetime walks (with a high of 122 in 1935) ranks 23rd all-time.

In his greatest year, 1936, Appling led the AL with a .388 average. It was the first batting title won by a White Sox player. He also had a club-record 27-game hitting streak and a seven-for-seven performance over three games. In 1943, at age 35, he won his second batting title. He hit .300 15 times.

Appling held down the shortstop position for nearly twenty years. In that time, he established ML shortstop records for games played and double plays and AL records for putouts and assists; all were later broken by Luis Aparicio. In spite of his everyday play, he acquired the epithet "Old Aches & Pains" through 20 years of complaining about his various physical ailments, the condition of the infield ("I swear, that park must have been built on a junkyard!" As it turned out, he was right), and salary disputes with General Manager Harry Grabiner. A $5,000 bonus promised him for winning the batting title in 1936 was later rescinded. In disgust he tore

Luke Appling

up his 1937 contract. Owner J. Lou Comiskey weathered the storm, and when Appling was ready to play, he was given a new contract. This time he signed on for another year, even though it was $2,500 less than what he wanted. Elected to the Hall of Fame in 1964, Appling worked as a batting instructor for the Atlanta Braves in the 1980s and rekindled memories with a home run off Warren Spahn in the first Cracker Jack Old-Timers' Game. /(RL)

Luis Aquino — 1965– . RHP 1986, 88– Blue Jays, **Royals** 182 ip, 8–9, 3.57

Aquino was converted to starting in 1989 and thrived in the new role. The Puerto Rican native pitched a 2–0 no-hitter against Columbus (International League) on June 20, 1988 while with Omaha (American Association). /(WOR)

Ramon Arano — 1939– . Mexican League.

The 5'8" 160-lb Arano didn't impress big league scouts but nonetheless became the only pitcher ever to win over 300 games in a single minor league, setting Mexican career marks for games, innings, wins, losses, hits, runs, earned runs, and strikeouts. His totals are complete only through 1984, as 1985 records were lost in the Mexico City earthquake. Except for three games with Oklahoma City at the end of '62, Arano never pitched outside of Mexico. Breaking in with Aguascaliente, he spent 11 years with the Mexico City Reds and eight with Cordoba, where he twice won 19 games. Arano also pitched for Poza Rica, Veracruz, Saltillo, Reynosa, and Coatzcoalcos. /(MC)

Jimmy Archer — 1883–1958. C-1B 1904, 07, 09–18 Pirates, Tigers, **Cubs**, Dodgers, Reds 846 g., .250, 16 hr, 296 rbi, *2 WS, 4 g, .143*

Dublin-born Archer took over as the Cubs' catcher in 1909 when star Johnny Kling was a season-long holdout. Archer, perhaps the best-throwing catcher of his time, made Kling expendable in 1911. Archer's right arm had been terribly burned by hot tar in an industrial accident. In healing, the muscles shortened but were left with a unique strength, enabling him to throw from the squat. This became his trademark. He led NL catchers in assists in 1912. /(JK)

Jose Arcia (Flaco) — 1943– . SS-2B-OF 1968–70 Cubs, **Padres** 293 g, .215, 1 hr, 35 rbi

This native Cuban's nickname, Flaco, means "thin," an apt description for the 6'3" 170-lb utility man. He hung on with the expansion Padres for two years, but didn't hit enough to last. /(WOR)

Frank Arellanes — 1882–1918. RHP 1908–10 **Red Sox** 410 ip, 24–22, 2.28

In 1909, as the replacement for Cy Young in the Red Sox pitching rotation, the swarthy Arellanes had his one decent year, (16–12, 2.18 ERA), giving up only 1.68 walks per nine innings. He relieved between starts and led the AL with 8 saves. /(EC)

Hank Arft (Bow-Wow) — 1922– . 1B 1948–52 **Browns** 300 g, .253, 13 hr, 118 rbi

A long-ball hitter, Arft hit a triple and a homer in his first game. He led the league in fielding in 1948 and 1950. He lives in St. Louis and runs a successful mortuary business. /(WB)

George Argyros — 1937– . Owner.

Argyros was described by then-NL president A. Bartlett Giamatti as "the James Watt of baseball" (after Reagan's Secretary of the Interior). The deforestation of the Mariners under Argyros has included the trades of such stars as Bill Caudill, Shane Rawley, Ivan Calderon, Danny Tartabull, Phil Bradley, and Mark Langston for a few overage catchers and minor leaguers unlikely to become major league stars. When Argyros bought the Mariners in 1981, he made himself the focus of an advertising campaign called "Playing Hardball" and promised to stamp the team with his own personality. When he sold the franchise in 1989, the Mariners had yet to have their first winning season. A friend of former Commissioner Peter Ueberroth, Argyros has led the major leagues in fiscal restraint, with the lowest salaries to go with the lowest winning percentage. Having the parsimony of a Calvin Griffith without the baseball acumen, Argyros has hired executives from his real estate and airline investments rather than baseball people. His managerial genius was best demonstrated in the 1986–87 off-season when the Mariners gave all their players salary cuts (including the few who played well), and then suggested they attend seminars on positive thinking. /(TF)

Buzz Arlett [Russell Loris] — 1899–1964. OF-1B 1931 **Phillies** 121 g, .313, 18 hr, 72 rbi

The handsome switch-hitter did not reach the majors until he was 32, despite an awesome minor league record. In his one ML year with the Phillies, he hit well but was a lackadaisical fielder. The 6′3″ 225-lb Californian began as a pitcher with Oakland of the Pacific Coast League in 1918 and won 108 before becoming a full-time outfielder in 1923. When he retired after 1937, his minor league career marks included a .341 BA and 432 HR. He hit four home runs in a game on two occasions with Baltimore (International League) in 1932. In 1984, the Society for American Baseball Research voted him the outstanding player in minor league history. /(LRD)

Harold Arlin — Unk.–Unk. *Broadcaster.*

On August 5, 1921, Arlin called the first baseball game ever to be broadcast on radio, describing the Pirates' 8–5 victory over the Phillies from a Forbes Field box seat for Pittsburgh's station KDKA. That fall, Arlin worked the first-ever football broadcast as well, a college game between Pitt and West Virginia. /(SL)

Steve Arlin — 1945– . RHP 1969–74 **Padres**, Indians 790 ip, 34–67, 4.32

Arlin threw an Eastern League no-hitter as a Phillies farmhand on July 25, 1967. With the struggling young Padres, he led the NL with 19 losses in 1971 and 21 in 1972. On July 18, 1972, he had a no-hitter with two outs in the ninth when Philadelphia's Denny Doyle singled. That season, he also had a one-hit 1–0 victory, went 10 innings allowing one hit before being relieved in another game, and had two other two-hitters. Of his 34 career wins, 11 were shutouts. Arlin practiced dentistry while still an active player. Arlin's grandfather, Harold Arlin, was the first announcer to broadcast a baseball game. /(MC)

Arlington Stadium Texas Rangers 1972– . LF-330, CF-400, RF-300

Arlington Stadium opened in 1965 as Turnpike Stadium for the local Texas League club, before joining the ML when the expansion Senators moved in as the Rangers. It is a single-level bowl-shaped stadium with no roof at all over the grandstand. Because of its openness it appears larger than its 35,698 capacity, second smallest in the ML. The field is natural grass with little foul territory, and is sunk below ground, so fans enter the stadium in the upper levels of the grandstand. A large Texas-shaped scoreboard stands behind the left-center field seats, and eight tall light towers ring the stadium. Almost all the Rangers' home games (including Sundays) are played at night due to the oppressive summer afternoon heat. Arlington Stadium is adjacent to the Six Flags Over Texas amusement park and is halfway between Dallas and Fort Worth. /(SCL)

Tony Armas — 1953– . OF-DH 1976– Pirates, **A's**, Red Sox, Angels 1432 g, .252, 251 hr, 815 rbi
☛ *Led League—hr 81, 84. Led League—rbi 84. All-Star—81, 84.*

A popular power hitter, Tony Armas was one of baseball's top sluggers until injuries took their toll. Developed in the Pittsburgh organization, he went to Oakland in a blockbuster, nine-player deal on March 15, 1977. Various injuries held him back until 1980, when he hit .279 with 35 HR and 109 RBI. He was *TSN* AL Player of the Year in 1981, tying for the league lead in homers and games played, but leading the league in strikeouts. The free swinger was traded to Boston for the more consistent Carney Lansford in a five-player deal. Armas peaked in 1984 (.268, 43 HR, 123 RBI). He was named to *TSN* and *UPI* postseason AL all-star teams and was Boston's co-MVP. From 1980 to 1985, Armas hit more homers than any AL player. The Venezuelan's next two seasons were ruined by leg injuries. He was replaced by Dave Henderson in the Boston outfield and released after batting just once in the 1986 World Series. He became a valuable role player for the Angels. /(ME)

Bill Armour — 1869–1922. Manager 1902–06 **Indians**, Tigers 382–347, .524

Armour was credited with finding and buying Ty Cobb for $500 while he was Tigers manager. In 1907 he bought a one-third interest in the Toledo club of the American Association. He later scouted for the Cardinals and was business manager for the minor league Milwaukee Brewers and Kansas City Blues in 1914–15. /(NLM)

Jack Armstrong — 1965– . RHP 1988- **Reds** 108 ip, 6–10, 5.33

The Reds made Armstrong their first-round draft pick in June 1987. He pitched a 4–0 no-hitter against Indianapolis on August 7, 1988 while with Nashville (American Association). /(JFC)

Mike Armstrong — 1954– . RHP 1980–87 Padres, **Royals**, Yankees, Indians 338 ip, 19–17, 4.10

Armstrong was a reliable set-up man for Dan Quisenberry in the Royals' bullpen in 1982 and 1983. He relied on a sinking fastball, hard slider, and forkball, and a submarine motion that was difficult to follow. /(FJO)

Morrie Arnovich (Snooker) — 1910–1959. OF 1936–41, 46 **Phillies**, Reds, Giants 590 g, .287, 22 hr, 261 rbi. *1 WS, 1 g, .000*
☛ *All-Star—39.*

A stocky, line drive hitter with little home run power, Arnovich hit a career-high .324 in 1939. /(JD)

Jerry Arrigo — 1941– . LHP 1961–70 Twins, **Reds**, Mets, Cubs 620 ip, 35–40, 4.14

After four years working mostly in relief, Arrigo started 31 games for the 1968 Reds. He responded with his best season, 12–10 and a 3.33 ERA. /(MC)

Fernando Arroyo — 1952– . RHP 1975, 77–82 **Tigers**, Twins, A's 535 ip, 24–37, 4.44

Never a hard thrower, Arroyo finessed his way into the Detroit rotation after Mark Fidrych's injury in 1977, but lost 18 games. In the 1981 strike-shortened season, he went 7–10 with his only sub-4 ERA (3.94). /(CC)

Luis Arroyo (Yo-Yo) — 1927– . LHP 1955–57, 59–63 Cardinals, Pirates, Reds, **Yankees** 531 ip, 40–32, 3.93. *2 WS, 5 ip, 1–0, 3.86*
☛ *All-Star—55, 61.*

On July 22, 1960, the pudgy Arroyo's acquisition by the Yankees was little noticed; he'd had mixed results in previous trials with three NL clubs, but he mystified AL batters with his screwball. In 1961, he was recognized as the league's top reliever, having taken a direct hand in 44 of the Yankees' 109 victories with 15 relief wins and 29 saves, both AL highs. His reliability contributed to Yankee ace Whitey Ford's first 20-win season. Arroyo then added a WS win, but a sore arm the following spring ended his dominance. /(GDW)

Richie Ashburn — 1927– . OF 1948–1962 **Phillies**, Cubs, Mets 2189 g, .308, 29 hr, 586 rbi. *1 WS, 4 g, .176, 1 rbi*
 Led League—ba 55, 58. All-Star—48, 51, 53, 58, 62.

The ultimate singles hitter, Ashburn hit leadoff for 15 years, batting over .300 nine times, winning two batting titles and finishing second three times. He is

Richie Ashburn

also the most recent player to hit .300 in his last season; he batted .306 for the expansion Mets and was their only All-Star. He became a Phillies broadcaster in 1963 and is a familiar short and smiling figure who wears an Irish hunting cap.

An All-Star in his first season, Ashburn knew how to get on base, leading the NL in walks four times. He was a model of consistency. He batted 6-for-10 and scored four runs in five All-Star games, and only once did he fail to score at least 84 runs in a season for the Phillies. A spray hitter with little power, 86 percent of his hits were singles. He reached his season high for homers (seven) with the Mets in his last year, playing in the Polo Grounds with its short distances down the lines.

Together with Robin Roberts, Jim Konstanty, Del Ennis, Curt Simmons, and Granny Hammer, he was a core player on the 1950 Philadelphia Whiz Kids, who won the NL pennant on the last day of the season over the Dodgers. On May 20, 1951, he singled eight times in a doubleheader. /(SEW)

Alan Ashby — 1951- . C 1973- Indians, Blue Jays, **Astros** 1370 g, .245, 90 hr, 513 rbi. *2 LCS, 8 g, .129, 1 hr, 3 rbi*

Ashby provided the Astros with 10 seasons of fine catching, quality game calling, and respectable hitting. Houston often tried to displace him with prospects like George Bjorkman, Luis Pujols, John Mizerock, and Mark Bailey, but Ashby beat off successive challenges to keep the regular job year after year. It finally took a bad back and Craig Biggio in 1989 to send Ashby packing; he was released after refusing a trade to Pittsburgh. From 1979 into 1985, he was battered by Joe Niekro's knuckleballs. "All the broken fingers and broken toes I can remember were caused by the knuckler," Ashby said. He was disabled five times with Houston. He tied a NL record for most no-hitters caught: Ken Forsch's (4/7/79); Nolan Ryan's (9/26/81); and Mike Scott's division title clincher (9/25/86). A switch-hitter who was much stronger lefthanded, he became the first Astro to homer from both sides of the plate in the same game on September 27, 1982. /(JCA)

Emmett Ashford (Ash) — 1914-1980. *Umpire* AL 1966-70 *1 WS, 1 ASU*

The first black umpire in the majors, Ashford was hired at age 51 to get five years to qualify for a pension. A loner off the field, Ash was a showboat on the diamond who dressed impeccably for the job wearing jewelry that included flashy cufflinks. In 1982 a Little League field in Los Angeles was named in Ashford's honor. /(RTM)

Tucker Ashford (Thomas) — 1954- . 3B 1976-78, 80-81, 83-84 **Padres**, Rangers, Yankees, Mets, Royals 222 g, .218, 6 hr, 55 rbi

The second player in the 1974 draft, Ashford's weak bat kept him from sticking as the Padres' regular third baseman in 1977. After 18 ML and minor league stops as a player, he became a manager in the Mets' farm system. /(FJO)

Bob Aspromonte — 1938- . 3B 1956, 1960-71 Dodgers, **Astros**, Braves, Mets 1324 g, .252, 60 hr, 457 rbi. *1 LCS, 3 g, .000*

One of many major leaguers produced by Brooklyn's Lafayette High School (including his brother Ken and Sandy Koufax), Aspromonte debuted at age 18 and struck out in his one at-bat with Brooklyn. At the time of his retirement, he was the last active ex-Brooklyn Dodger. He was a regular with the original Houston expansion team in 1962 and stayed through 1968. The celebrated bachelor set a NL record for third basemen with 57 consecutive errorless games in 1962 and added a since-broken NL record for fewest errors at 3B (11) in 1964. He was strictly pull hitter until 1967, when he batted a career-high .294 by hitting to all fields. Supplanted by Doug Rader the following season, he was the last original Colt .45 to leave the franchise. /(JCA)

Ken Aspromonte — 1931- . 2B-3B 1957-63 Red Sox, Senators, **Indians**, Angels, Braves, Cubs 475 g, .249, 19 hr, 124 rbi.
Manager 1972-74 **Indians** 220-260, .458

The elder of the Brooklyn-born brothers, this flashy-fielding second baseman led the Pacific Coast League in hitting in 1957 (.337) but was inconsistent in the majors. During the 1959 season Ken collected three hits in a game on five different occasions for the Senators. He came closest to being an everyday player in 1960 after being traded to the Indians, for whom he played 117 games, finishing with a career-high .288 average. /(RTM)

Brian Asselstine — 1953- . OF 1976-81 **Braves** 284 g, .254, 12 hr, 68 rbi

A speedy outfielder who showed flashes of power, Asselstine spent much of his career shuttling between the Braves and their Richmond farm club. He had finally won a regular ML job in 1978 when he broke his ankle after 39 games and missed the rest of the season. /(JCA)

Paul Assenmacher — 1960– . LHP 1986– **Braves**, Cubs 279 ip, 19–15, 3.58. *1 LCS, 0.2 ip, 0–0, 13.50*

Assenmacher was signed by the Braves out of a 1983 tryout camp. As a rookie in 1986, he went 7–3 (2.50) with seven saves in 61 appearances, mostly as a lefthanded setup man for Gene Garber. He spent the first month of 1987 on the DL and in 1988, he was tied for the NL lead in appearances, with 54, when he was disabled with recurring shoulder problems. He was 8–7 with five saves in 1988, posting a 1.16 ERA away from Atlanta-Fulton County Stadium but a 4.87 ERA at home. In mid-1989 he was acquired by the Cubs for their successful stretch drive. /(JCA/SCL)

National Association — 1871–1875. League.

The National Association of Professional Base Ball Players, formed in March 1871, was the game's first professional league. Any professional or semi-pro club could enter the NA pennant race simply by paying a $10 fee, and each club was responsible for scheduling its own games with the other contenders. Eight to thirteen clubs began each of the association's five seasons, but each year one to six clubs failed to finish. Only three of the twenty-three clubs that competed in the NA played all five years: Mutual of New York, Athletic of Philadelphia (which won the first NA pennant), and Boston's Red Stockings (who won the other four). /(FIC)

Astrodome Houston Astros 1965– . LF-330, CF-400, RF-330

Called the Eighth Wonder of the World when it opened in 1965, Houston's cavernous Astrodome was the world's first domed stadium. It was erected adjacent to Colt Stadium, home of the Astros in their three seasons as the Colt .45s, and was intended to protect players and fans from the sweltering Texas heat more than to prevent rainouts. In its first season, the Astrodome had a natural grass playing field, and the 4,796 panes of glass in the roof were clear, allowing light through to help the grass grow. Unfortunately, during day games the intense glare made it difficult to see fly balls, and the indoor grass was dying anyway. The roof was painted for the 1966 season, and an artificial playing surface—AstroTurf—was developed. On April 8, 1966 the Astros and Dodgers played baseball's first game on artificial turf.

Inside, the Astrodome is indeed a marvel. Circu-lar, with five seating levels and air conditioning to keep the temperature at 72 degrees for every game, it has a roof 208' above the playing field at its highest point, the equivalent of an 18-story building. A huge American flag is suspended in dead center field, and baseball's largest scoreboard runs 474' across the back wall. Still, the stadium proved to be not quite large enough when Mike Schmidt hit a speaker hanging from the roof in center on June 10, 1974 (the ball fell for a single). And on June 15, 1976, the Astrodome suffered its only rainout when torrential storms flooded the Houston streets and made it impossible to get to the stadium.

The Astrodome has always favored pitchers, and although the dimensions have been shortened from their original 360–420–360, the ball still does not carry well here, reducing the number of home runs. Only three home runs have ever been hit into the stadium's highest level, by Jimmy Wynn, Doug Rader, and Andre Dawson.

Today the Astrodome is hardly as unique as when it opened. The Twins and Mariners both play in larger domed stadiums, and the Astrodome's 45,000 capacity makes it the NL's second-smallest facility. /(SCL)

Joe Astroth — 1922– . C 1945–46, 49–56 **A's** 554 g, .254, 13 hr, 156 rbi

On September 23, 1950, Astroth had six RBIs in an inning, a feat accomplished by only nine others in modern baseball. A fine handler of pitchers, Astroth was Bobby Shantz's personal catcher in 1952, when Shantz won 24 games and the MVP award. /(RTM)

Keith Atherton (Country) — 1959– . RHP 1983–88 A's, **Twins** 527 ip, 33–38, 3.98. *1 LCS, 0.1 ip, 0–0, 0.00 1 WS, 1 ip, 0–0, 6.75*

It took a switch from starting to relief in his sixth year as an A's farmhand to get Atherton to Oakland. With the fastball his only good pitch, he was often touched for home runs. Traded to Minnesota in May 1986, he went 0–7 in August but saved 10 on the season, then was a set-up man for Jeff Reardon and the 1987 World Champions. /(JCA)

Atlanta Braves — 1966– . Team. 1773–2040, .465. *NL West Champions 69, 82*

The first major league team to move to the rich baseball territory of the Southeast, the Braves have struggled despite being located in a booming city and establishing a strong regional (later national) broadcasting network. Ten years after their arrival, attendance had sunk to 534,672 and only the club's purchase by Ted Turner kept the franchise in Georgia. Divisional championships in 1969 and 1982 and Henry Aaron's successful quest for Babe Ruth's career HR record have been the team's high points. In 1973 the Braves became the only team in history with three 40-HR sluggers, as Aaron, Darrell Evans, and Davey Johnson all topped that mark. /(PB)

Atlanta-Fulton County Stadium (The Launching Pad) Atlanta Braves 1966– . LF-330, CF-402, RF-330

One of baseball's earliest circular multi-decked stadiums, Atlanta-Fulton County Stadium was completed in 1965 and by the mid-70s had become known as The Launching Pad for the frequency with which home runs were hit there. Despite reasonable distances to all the fences, local atmospheric and weather conditions make the stadium a slugger's heaven, regularly the scene of more home runs than any other NL park. From 1967 until the early 1980s, Chief Noc-A-Homa, the Braves mascot, who resided in a teepee behind the outfield fence, would celebrate each Braves homer with victorious whooping and dancing, and on April 8, 1974, Hank Aaron hit his 715th career HR to pass Babe Ruth for the all-time ML lead. The stadium features a natural grass surface and distinctive vertical supports on the exterior and is located near three major interstate highways, providing easy access to fans from around the Southeast. It has a capacity of 52,003 and is also home to football's Atlanta Falcons. /(SCL)

Toby Atwell [Maurice Franklin] — 1924– . C 1952–56 Cubs, **Pirates**, Braves 378 g, .260, 9 hr, 110 rbi
☛ All-Star—52.

This Army Air Corps veteran almost saw his career come to an end when he hurt his knee sliding while playing for Montreal in 1949. Atwell's 1952 rookie season was his most productive offensively; he hit .290 for the Cubs. /(RTM)

Bill Atwood (Dad Gum) — 1911– . C 1936–40 **Phillies** 342 g, .229, 7 hr, 112 rbi

Nicknamed "Dad Gum" because it was his strongest expletive, the mild-mannered Atwood hit .302 as a rookie for the Phillies, but was never more than a part-time player. /(JK)

Rick Auerbach — 1950– . SS-2B-3B 1971–81 **Brewers**, Dodgers, Reds, Mariners 624 g, .220, 9 hr, 86 rbi

Handed the Brewers shortstop job at age 21, Auerbach kept it for part of 1971 and all of 1972. His weak bat cost him the starting job, but he lasted

seven seasons as a utility man and pinch hitter elsewhere. /(MC)

Don August — 1963– . RHP 1988– **Brewers** 291 ip, 25–19, 4.18

A member of the 1984 Olympic baseball team, August was the Astros' first-round pick in the June '84 draft. Acquired by Milwaukee in the Danny Darwin deal in 1986, he moved into the Brewer rotation in 1988 and had his best season, going 13–7 with a 3.09 ERA. /(SFS)

Jerry Augustine — 1952– . LHP 1975–84 **Brewers** 944 ip, 55–59, 4.23

Named to the 1976 AL All-Rookie Team (9–12, 3.30) as a starter, most of Augustine's career was spent in the bullpen. He retired in the Brewer's top ten in eight major pitching categories. /(JCA)

Eldon Auker (Big Six) — 1910– . RHP 1933–42 **Tigers**, Red Sox, Browns 1963 ip, 130–101, 4.42. *2 WS, 17 ip, 1–1, 4.67*

A submarine pitcher, Auker lost Game Seven of the 1934 World Series to Dizzy Dean after winning Game Four 10–4. In 1935 his 18–7 (.720) mark led the league in winning percentage. He pitched the first night game in St. Louis on May 24, 1940, losing to Bob Feller and Cleveland 3–2. He was a good-hitting pitcher, compiling a .308 mark in 1936. His lifetime average was a capable .187 with six homers. He developed his underhanded style of pitching because of a shoulder injury he had suffered while playing football for Kansas State University, where he starred in basketball as well as baseball. /(WB)

Doug Ault — 1950– . 1B-DH 1976–78, 80 Rangers, **Blue Jays** 256 g, .236, 17 hr, 86 rbi

Chosen by the Blue Jays in the November 1976 expansion draft, Ault helped them win their first-ever game and tied an Opening Day record with two homers. He had career highs of 11 HR and 64 RBI in 1977, his only season as a regular. /(WOR)

Jimmy Austin (Pepper) — 1879–1965. 3B-SS-C 1909–23, 25–26, 29 Yankees, **Browns** 1580 g, .246, 13 hr, 390 rbi.
Manager 1913, 18, 23 **Browns** 31–43, .419

Born in Wales, Austin was one of the best third basemen of his day. In his twelve seasons as a regular, he led the AL five times in total chances per game, four times in double plays, twice each in putouts and assists, and once in fielding average. An inconsistent hitter, he compensated by drawing walks and stealing bases, pilfering 244 lifetime with a high of 37. The switch-hitting chatterbox is most famous for a photo of him at third base, attempting to avoid the flying spikes of Ty Cobb. He signed with Pittsburgh of the Federal League but never reported, as the Browns matched the contract.

Austin was the first of Branch Rickey's "Sunday Managers" with the Browns (Rickey would not enter a ballpark on a Sunday due to an early promise to his mother). Austin had three short stints as the Browns' interim manager. The last four years of his playing career each consisted of just one game, including his sole appearance behind the plate. He coached with the Browns until 1932, when he joined the White Sox for seven years. /(WB)

Rick Austin — 1946– . LHP 1970–71, 75–76 **Indians**, Brewers 136 ip, 4–8, 4.62

Up and down for two years with the Indians, Austin earned a second chance with the Brewers with a strong season (2.33 ERA) in 1974 with the Hankyu Braves of the Japan Pacific League. /(MC)

Sam Austin — Unk.–Unk. *Writer.*

One of the earliest and best New York baseball writers, Austin covered the game for the New York *Herald* for more than 30 years beginning in the 1880s. /(NLM)

Earl Averill [Howard Earl] — 1902–1983. OF 1929–41 **Indians**, Tigers, Red Sox 1669 g, .318, 238 hr, 1165 rbi. *1 WS, 3 g, .000*
☛ *All-Star—33–38. Hall of Fame—1975.*

The Veterans Committee named outfielder Averill to the Hall of Fame 34 years after his final season. He is still the Indians' all-time home run leader with 226 (thanks in part to the short fence in old League Park) and holds Cleveland career records in six offensive categories. His number 3 is one of only three retired by the Indians.

"The Earl of Snohomish" (his hometown) grew up in the state of Washington and played semi-pro ball before signing with San Francisco of the Pacific Coast League in 1926. After three .300 seasons in the PCL, including .354 with 36 home runs and 173 RBI in 1928, the 5'9" 172-lb lefthanded hitter was purchased for a reported $50,000 by Cleveland. On Opening Day, 1929, he became the first AL player to homer in his initial big league at-bat. His 18 HRs (then a team record) and .331 BA in his rookie season helped establish him as one of the Indian's most popular players. A graceful but unspectacular

Earl Averill, Sr. with the Indians

centerfielder, he led all AL outfielders that year with 388 putouts, but his arm, injured in high school, was not strong.

In 1930, Averill hit .339, and on September 17 walloped three home runs in the first game of a doubleheader and another in the second game to become the first ML player to hit four homers in a twin bill. His 11 RBI that day set an AL record. A dead pull hitter, he slammed 32 homers in both 1931 and '32. He became one of the most feared hitters in the league; on August 29, 1932, Red Sox pitchers walked him five consecutive times. He had an off-year (.288) in 1935, largely because he burned his hand testing Fourth of July fireworks, but he bounced back in 1936 to lead the AL with 232 hits, and hit .378, second only to Luke Appling's .388.

His line drive in the 1937 All-Star Game broke Dizzy Dean's toe, an injury that indirectly ended Dean's career. That same year, just before a June game, Averill suffered temporary paralysis in his legs. X-rays revealed a congenital spinal malformation which forced him to change his batting style. His BA and home run output slipped.

He was showered with gifts, including a new Cadillac, on "Earl Averill Day" in Cleveland in 1938. Cleveland fans were outraged the following June when he was traded to Detroit for marginal pitcher Harry Eisenstat and cash. Averill hit .280 in a part-time role for the 1940 pennant-winning Tigers. His son, Earl Douglas, played seven years in the majors. /(JCA)

Earl Averill [Earl Douglas] — 1931- . C-OF-3B 1956, 58-63 Indians, Cubs, White Sox, **Angels**, Phillies 449 g, .242, 44 hr, 159 rbi

Averill came up as a catcher with the Indians, the team with which his father, Howard Earl Averill, fashioned a Hall of Fame career. In 1961, his only solid season, the righthanded hitter batted .266 with 21 home runs for the Angels in their first year. /(JM)

Bobby Avila (Beto) — 1924- . 2B 1949-59 **Indians**, Orioles, Red Sox, Braves 1300 g, .281, 80 hr, 465 rbi. *1 WS, 4 g, .133*
☛ *Led League—ba 54. All-Star—52, 54-55.*

The Indians signed Avila for only $17,500 out of the Mexican League, where he was already a star. The first Mexican to have real ML success, he was the Indian second baseman for eight years and became a national hero in his own country. In a 1951 game at Boston, he hit three homers, a single, and a double. In 1952 he led the AL in triples (11). He won the AL batting title in the Indians' 1954 pennant-winning year when he hit .341 despite playing half the season with a broken thumb.

An adept bunter and daring baserunner, his soccer training paid off several times when he intentionally kicked the ball out of defenders' mitts while sliding. Cleveland manager Al Lopez said Avila had "a fine swing, a sharp eye, a good spirit of competition . . . and a world of confidence in himself."

Dealt three times between December 1958 and July 1959, the dapper, well-educated Avila returned to Mexico in 1960, becoming a politician and, later, president of the Mexican League. /(JCA)

Benny Ayala [Benigno] — 1951- . OF-DH 1974, 76-77, 79-85 Mets, Cardinals, **Orioles**, Indians 425 g, .251, 38 hr, 145 rbi. *1 LCS, 1 g, --, 1 rbi. 2 WS, 5 g, .429, 1 hr, 3 rbi*

Puerto Rico-born Ayala homered in his first ML at-bat (8/27/74) but didn't stick on a ML roster until the Orioles acquired him in 1979. One of the Orioles' role players, he hit 33 homers and had 120 RBI in only 692 Oriole at-bats. /(MC)

Doc Ayers [Yancy Wyatt] — 1890-1968. RHP 1913-21 **Senators**, Tigers 1429 ip, 66-79, 2.84

Ayers earned his nickname by studying medicine. As a ballplayer, he spread germs through the AL as a spitball pitcher. His best year was 14-9 with the 1915 Senators. He was one of the pitchers given special dispensation to continue throwing the spitter after it was banned following the 1919 season. /(JK)

Joe Azcue [Jose Joaquin] (The Immortal Azcue) — 1939- . C 1960, 62-70, 72 Reds, A's, **Indians**, Red Sox, Angels, Brewers 909 g, .252, 50 hr, 304 rbi
☛ *All-Star—68.*

"The Immortal Azcue" was traded to Cleveland in 1963, just hours before their starting catcher broke his hand. The Cuban was less fortunate when he hit into the ML's first unassisted triple play in 41 years (July 29, 1968), turned by Washington's Ron Hansen. He caught no-hitters by Sonny Siebert of the Indians (6/10/66) and Clyde Wright of the Angels (7/3/70) and hit .280 in 1968, his All-Star year. He was a season-long holdout in 1971. /(JCA)

Charlie Babb — 1873–1954. SS 1903–05 Giants, **Dodgers** 347 g, .243, 0 hr, 116 rbi

After his rookie year with the Giants, Babb was traded to Brooklyn along with pitcher John Cronin for veteran shortstop Bill Dahlen. Babb hit .265 in 1904 for the Dodgers but was only fair in the field. /(BC)

Johnny Babich — 1913– . RHP 1934–36, 40–41 Dodgers, Braves, **A's** 592 ip, 30–45, 4.93

After pitching without much success in the NL during the mid-1930s, Babich went 14–13 with the Athletics in 1940. Five of his wins helped deny a fifth straight pennant to the Yankees, who finished two games behind the league-leading Tigers. /(JK)

Wally Backman — 1959– . 2B 1980– **Mets**, Twins 852 g, .277, 15 hr, 191 rbi. *2 LCS, 13 g, .256, 4 rbi. 1 WS, 6 g, .333, 1 rbi*

Backman was a Mets platoon regular whose speed and high on-base percentage made him a valuable number-two hitter. The switch-hitter teamed with leadoff hitter Len Dykstra (both used against right-handers) to become known as the "Partners in Grime" for their hustling, dirty-uniform style of play for the 1986 World Champions. Backman hit .320 that season and led the Mets with five runs in the LCS against the Astros. In Game Three he led off the ninth inning with a bunt single and scored on Dykstra's HR as the Mets won 6–5, and in Game Five he led off the 12th with an infield hit, advanced to second on a wild pickoff throw, and scored the winning run on Gary Carter's single. In the climactic Game Six, his 14th-inning single drove in a go-ahead run in the seesaw finale, and he scored the Mets' third and final run in the game-winning 16th-inning rally.

Backman was the Mets' first-round pick in the June 1977 draft, but although he hit .323, .278, and .272 in his first three trials with the Mets (1980–82), his mediocre fielding kept him from winning the second-base job. He impressed Tidewater (International League) manager Davey Johnson in 1983, and when Johnson became the Mets' manager in 1984 he brought Backman with him and was rewarded with 68 runs and 32 stolen bases. In Backman's only year as a regular, 1985, he led NL second basemen in fielding.

The Mets traded Backman to Minnesota after Gregg Jefferies hit .321 in the final months of 1988, and in 1989 he played every day for the Twins when not injured. /(SH)

Mike Bacsik — 1952– . RHP 1975–77, 79–80 **Rangers**, Twins 173 ip, 8–6, 4.43

Ranger pitching coach Sid Hudson called Bacsik "one of those kids who didn't quite have enough to make it." Bacsik was 4–2 in relief for the Twins in 1979. /(KT)

Fred Baczewski (Lefty) — 1926–1976. LHP 1953–55 Cubs, **Reds** 279 ip, 17–10, 4.45

The highlights of Baczewski's brief career were an 11–4 record for the sixth-place 1953 Reds and an 11-hit shutout of Pittsburgh in 1954. /(FK)

Red Badgro [Morris Hiram] (Bad Girl) — 1902– . OF 1929–30 **Browns** 143 g, .257, 2 hr, 45 rbi

Like Jim Thorpe, Ernie Nevers, and George Halas, Badgro made more of a name for himself as a football player than a baseball player. An end who had starred at the University of Southern California, he played with all three New York football teams, the Yankees, Giants, and Dodgers, from 1927 to 1936. In 1981 he was the oldest man ever elected to the Professional Football Hall of Fame.

In baseball, he hit a powerless .284 in 1929 and dropped to .239 in 1930. /(WB)

Bugs Baer (Arthur) — 1876–1969. *Writer.*

Baer was a columnist and cartoonist for King Features Syndicate. His column, "One Word Led to Another," ended with the closing of the New York *World-Journal-Tribune.* His quips were widely admired. Among the more famous: "Bodie was out trying to steal second. His head was full of larceny, but his feet were honest," and "DiMaggio, who popped out in his first four at-bats, could have done all his hitting in a chimney." /(NLM)

Jim Bagby, Sr. (Sarge) — 1887–1954. RHP 1912, 16–23 Reds, **Indians**, Pirates 1828 ip, 127–87, 3.10. 20 wins: 17, 20 *1 WS, 15 ip, 1–1, 1.80*
☛ *Led League—w 20.*

The slender, strong-armed Bagby won 23 games in 1917 and 17 in each of the next two seasons. In 1920, when Cleveland won its first pennant, he led the AL in wins (31), winning percentage (.721), innings (339–2/3), hits allowed (338), and relief wins (6). In the WS against Brooklyn he lost Game Two but came back to win the Game Five. Bagby went the distance, giving up 13 hits but only one run, and became the first pitcher to hit a WS home run. Two other WS firsts by teammates helped him: Elmer Smith's grand slam homer and Bill Wambsganss's unassisted triple play. Bagby's son Jim, Jr., also became a major league pitcher. /(ME)

Jim Bagby, Jr. — 1916–1988. RHP 1938–47 Red Sox, **Indians**, Pirates 1668 ip, 97–96, 3.96. *1 WS, 3 ip, 0–0, 3.00*
☛ *All-Star—42–43.*

The son of Jim Bagby, Sr., this 6′2″ 170-lb right-hander reached his career high of 17 wins in each of his All-Star years (1942–43). He led the AL in starts both years, but he missed much of 1944 in the Merchant Marine and thereafter never won more than eight games. /(SFS)

Stan Bahnsen — 1944– . RHP 1966, 68–82 Yankees, White Sox, A's, **Expos**, Angels, Phillies 2528 ip, 146–149, 3.61. 20 wins: 72
☛ *Rookie of the Year—68.*

Bahnsen was 1968 AL Rookie of the Year, going 17–12 (2.05) for the Yankees. He had thrown a seven-inning no-hitter with Toledo in 1966 and a seven-inning perfect game with Syracuse in 1967. In his 1966 major league debut, he struck out the side at Boston.

Bahnsen faltered in 1969 and then had two 14-win seasons. Desperate for third-base help, the Yankees dealt him to the White Sox straight up for Rich McKinney in December 1971. Bahnsen went 21–16 in 1972 but set a since-broken ML record by being removed in 36 of his 41 starts. On August 21, 1973, against Cleveland, he had a no-hitter with two outs in the ninth when Walt Williams bounced a single over a drawn-in Bill Melton at third. Bahnsen won 18 in 1973 but lost a league-high 21. On May 15, 1974, Bahnsen defeated Minnesota 1–0, retiring the first 23 batters before allowing a Bobby Darwin single.

In a second career as a reliever, Bahnsen appeared in 55 and 57 games for the 1979 and 1980 Expos, and 25 games for the 1981 Eastern Division Champions. /(RL)

Ed Bahr — 1919– . RHP 1946–47 **Pirates** 219 ip, 11–11, 3.37.

The Canadian was a rookie success in 1946 (8–6, 2.63), leading the Pirate staff in ERA. The next year his control problems made him a victim of the "sophomore jinx." /(ME)

Scott Bailes — 1961– . LHP 1986– **Indians** 492 ip, 31–41, 4.70

When the Indians were owed a player from Pittsburgh in mid-1985, they chose Bailes, a Double-A reliever with sharp breaking stuff. He jumped to the majors the next spring and went 10–10 with seven saves, setting a Cleveland rookie record for most relief wins (eight). Though unable to throw too often, making him better suited to starting, he continued to be shuttled between the rotation and the bullpen. /(JCA)

Bill Bailey — 1889–1926. LHP 1907–12, 14–15, 18, 21–22 **Browns**, Baltimore (FL), Chicago (FL), Tigers, Cardinals 1084 ip, 36–76, 3.57

After an impressive 4–1 debut in 1907 with the Browns, Bailey's career consisted entirely of losing records, including a 3–18 mark in 1910 and an 8–20 record in 1915 in his second year in the Federal League. /(WB)

Bob Bailey — 1942– . 3B-OF 1962–78 Pirates, Dodgers, **Expos**, Reds, Red Sox 1931 g, .257, 189 hr, 773 rbi

Bailey signed with the Pirates for what was believed to be a record bonus of $175,000 in 1961. He was *TSN* Minor League Player of the Year in 1962 and the regular Pirate third baseman for the next four years. The Dodgers traded Maury Wills for Bailey and Gene Michael in December 1966, but Bailey hit only .227 for two consecutive years, and Los Angeles sold him to the expansion Expos.

Bailey hit well for the Expos. Manager Gene Mauch often said: "Bailey means wood. Bailey doesn't mean leather." An opponent added: "They called him Beetle, after the comic strip character. He fielded like a comic strip character." As the starting third baseman in 1972–73, he made 39 errors. Mauch also tried him at 1B and OF.

The Montreal fans developed a love-hate relationship with the slow-footed streak hitter who grounded into 216 lifetime double plays. In 1970 Bailey hit .287 with 28 homers, including one of the longest shots in Astrodome history on August 16. When he was traded in December 1975, he was the leader in nine of ten Expo career batting categories. /(JCA)

Ed Bailey — 1931– . C 1953–66 **Reds**, Giants, Braves, Cubs, Angels 1212 g, .256, 155 hr, 540 rbi. *1 WS, 6 g, .071, 1 hr, 2 rbi*
☛ *All-Star—56–57, 60–61, 63.*

Sharing catching duties with Smokey Burgess on the 1956 Reds, the 6'2" 205-lb Bailey hit 28 home runs as the team tied a National League record by hitting 221. Bailey hit 20 homers in 1957 and 21 in 1963, and was in double figures five other years, but he never drove in more than 75 runs. Platooned throughout his career, he had eight pinch-hit homers, two of which were grand slams. His career featured two very productive games (he hit three home runs in one 1956 game and drove in eight runs in a 1965 contest) and he made two unassisted double plays. When pitcher Jim Bailey was promoted to the 1959 Reds, Ed briefly became part of one of baseball's few "brother batteries." /(FK)

Howard Bailey — 1958– . LHP 1981–83 **Tigers** 119 ip, 6–9, 5.22

The Michigan native went from non-roster player to the Tiger starting rotation in April 1981, only to be sent down five starts later. He recorded four of his five 1983 wins in long relief. /(CC)

Mark Bailey — 1961– . C 1984– **Astros** 322 g, .223, 23 hr, 97 rbi

Signed as a third baseman, the 6'5" Bailey had been catching less than a year when he vaulted from Double-A to Houston in April 1984 to replace an injured Alan Ashby. He homered in three consecutive games from July 15 to 17, and homered from both sides of the plate September 16. His short apprenticeship as a catcher showed as time went on; he couldn't handle Joe Niekro's knuckleball, and had problems with his catching mechanics and throwing. His shoulder began troubling him in 1986. Although he was extremely patient at the plate (he had more walks than hits in 1986), he still struck out frequently. He began the 1988 season with Houston, but his declining batting average and increasing weight prompted a demotion to Tucson (Pacific Coast League), and in July he was traded to the Expos' organization for infielder Casey Candaele. /(JCA)

Bob Bailor — 1951– . OF-SS-2B-3B 1975–85 Orioles, **Blue Jays**, Mets, Dodgers 955 g, .264, 9 hr, 222 rbi. *1 LCS, 2 g, .000*

The Blue Jays made Bailor, a shortstop in the Orioles' organization, their first pick in the 1976 expansion draft. As a rookie, he hit .310, a record for a player on a first-year expansion franchise. Bailor was hustling, versatile, and injury-prone. After four years as a Toronto regular, he spent 1981–83 as a much-used Mets utility man. He was traded to the Dodgers with Carlos Diaz for Sid Fernandez and Ross Jones, a trade that helped the Mets more than Bailor ever did. /(TF)

Harold Baines (Hal) — 1959– . OF-DH 1980– **White Sox**, Rangers 1428 g, .288, 189 hr, 835 rbi. *1 LCS, 4 g, .125*
☛ *All-Star—85–87, 89.*

Baines was a 12-year-old little leaguer in Easton, MD when he caught the eye of White Sox owner Bill Veeck. When Chicago made him the first pick in the June 1977 draft, Paul Richards said Baines "was on his way to the Hall of Fame. He just stopped by Comiskey Park for 20 years or so." There was much pressure on the soft-spoken 20-year-old when he became a regular in 1980. It wasn't until 1982 that he began to produce, hitting 25 home runs with 105 RBI. With a batting style reminiscent of Mel Ott, the lefthanded hitter led the AL in 1983 with a then-ML record 22 game-winning RBI.

Baines's HR off Milwaukee's Chuck Porter on May 9, 1984 ended the major leagues' longest game ever by time (8:06) and the AL's longest game by innings (25). The bat went to the Hall of Fame. In 1986 Baines suffered a serious knee injury that required two operations, and forced him to DH. His 155th career HR in 1987 set the all-time White Sox record, and he became the first White Sox batter to hit 20 HR in six consecutive seasons. In mid-1989 he was traded to the contending Rangers to give him a chance at another pennant. /(RL)

Doug Bair — 1949– . RHP 1976–86, 89 Pirates, A's, **Reds**, Cardinals, Tigers 884 ip, 55–43, 3.60. *2 LCS, 2 ip, 0–1, 4.50. 2 WS, 3 ip, 0–1, 6.75*

The epitome of the longtime reliever with one supreme season, Bair had his in 1978 with the Reds. Theretofore an erratic hard thrower, he was suddenly brilliant, winning 7, saving 28, and posting a 1.98 ERA in 70 appearances. His ERA ballooned to 4.31 the next year, although he won 11 and saved 16. Although he would pitch well later in his career, he never again approached the numbers of his one great season. /(MC)

Doug Baird — 1891–1967. 3B-OF-2B 1915–20
Pirates, Cardinals, Phillies, Dodgers, Giants 617 g, .234,
6 hr, 191 rbi

Pittsburgh's Doug Baird and Max Carey were the
NL's best base-stealing tandem in 1915 and 1916.
But Baird batted just .218 over those two seasons
and fanned a league-high 88 times in '15. In 1921 he
broke an American Association record by stealing
72 bases for Indianapolis. /(ME)

Baker Bowl Philadelphia Phillies 1895–1938. LF-341,
CF-408, RF-281

Named for Phillies owner William F. Baker, the
Baker Bowl was a marvel when it opened with
18,000 seats on April 30, 1887, but was the most
outdated park in ML baseball when it was finally
abandoned. A simple wooden grandstand with a 40-
foot-high right-field wall (later increased to 60 feet),
it was badly damaged in an 1894 fire. During an
August 8, 1903 doubleheader the third base stands
collapsed, killing twelve people. The Phillies clung to
their decaying park until 1938, when they joined the
Athletics at Shibe Park, and in 1950 the Baker Bowl
was torn down. No ball ever cleared the 35′ wall of
the centerfield clubhouse. /(SCL)

Del Baker — 1892–1973. C 1914–16 **Tigers** 172 g,
.209, 0 hr, 22 rbi.
   Manager 1933, 38–42 **Tigers** 358–317, .530. _1 WS,
3–4, .429_

A catcher during his 22-year playing career, which
included only three ML seasons with the Tigers,
Baker became a minor league manager in 1927. A
Tiger coach, he replaced Mickey Cochrane as Detroit manager in 1938. An expert sign stealer, he
took the Tigers to the 1940 pennant but lost the WS
to the Reds in seven games. At the time of his death
he was a coach at Trinity College in San
Antonio. /(NLM)

Dusty Baker [Johnnie B., Jr.] — 1949– . OF-1B
1968–86 Braves, **Dodgers**, Giants, A's 2039 g, .278,
242 hr, 1013 rbi. _4 LCS, 17 g, .371, 3 hr, 13 rbi. 3 WS,
18 g, .232, 2 hr, 7 rbi_
☛ _All-Star—81–82. Gold Glove—81._

Hank Aaron said, "Dusty Baker has more potential
than any outfielder I've seen in all my seasons with
the Braves." Although only a 27th-round draft
choice, Baker seemed ready to realize that potential
when he batted .321 (third in the NL) in 1972, his
first full season in the ML. But after three straight
subpar seasons, he was traded to the Dodgers in
November 1975. Another poor season followed, but
in 1977 he rebounded (.291, 30 HR, 89 RBI). He set

Dusty Baker

a club record against San Diego with five RBI in one
inning, hit .357 with a four-game-record eight RBI
in the LCS, and batted .292 in the World Series. His
two-run homer off Steve Carlton provided the game-
winning RBI in the LCS. In three more LCS, he
never hit less than .316. In 1981, the muscular
leftfielder again finished third in batting (.320), won
a Gold Glove, and made an outstanding catch in the
All-Star Game at Cleveland. A prolonged contract
dispute sent him to the Giants on April 1, 1984; that
year, he hit .292 without the benefit of spring
training. /(ME)

Floyd Baker — 1916– . 3B-2B-SS 1943–55 Browns,
White Sox, Senators, Red Sox, Phillies 874 g, .251, 1 hr,
196 rbi

Baker turned down a football scholarship to sign
with the Browns. After an unimpressive beginning
epitomized by his two strikeouts as a pinch hitter in
the 1944 World Series, Baker developed into one of
the best fielders in the AL. His .317 mark for the
1950 White Sox marked the high point of the
taciturn Virginian's career. /(WB)

Frank Baker (Home Run) — 1886–1963. 3B 1908–14,
16–19, 21–22 **A's**, Yankees 1575 g, .307, 96 hr, 1013 rbi.
6 WS, 25 g, .363, 3 hr, 18 rbi
☛ _Led League—hr 11, 13–14. Led League—rbi 12–13..
Hall of Fame—1955._

A Maryland farm boy, Baker was a powerful slugger
in the dead ball era, leading or tying for the league
lead in homers four consecutive seasons (1911–14),
although 12 was his top total. Baker earned his
memorable nickname in the 1911 World Series,

when he hit game-winning home runs on successive days against the Giants' future Hall of Fame pitchers Rube Marquard and Christy Mathewson.

The lefthanded hitter was the third baseman in Connie Mack's fabled Philadelphia A's "$100,000 Infield," together in the years 1911–14. Teamed with him were Stuffy McInnis, Eddie Collins, and Jack Barry. Connie Mack broke his team up rather than pay the higher salaries brought on by Federal League competition, and after Baker sat out 1915 in protest, Mack sold him to the Yankees in 1916 for $35,000.

In 1920, Baker was again out of the game, due to the illness and subsequent death of his first wife. He returned to the Yankees as a part-time player and helped the team win its first two World Championships in 1921 and '22. His final at-bat was in the 1922 WS.

Baker managed in the Eastern Shore League in 1924–25 and discovered Jimmie Foxx, delivering him to Connie Mack after the 1924 season. He lived a quiet life on his farm near Trappe, MD, where he was born, making appearances at Old Timers' Games in New York and Philadelphia until his death in 1963. /(JK)

Frank Baker

Gene Baker — 1925– . 2B-3B 1953–58, 1960–61 **Cubs**, Pirates 630 g, .265, 39 hr, 227 rbi. *1 WS, 3 g, .000* ☛ *All-Star—55.*

An all-star shortstop in the Pacific Coast League, Baker switched to second base as a rookie with the Cubs in 1954 and, along with shortstop Ernie Banks, was named to the all-rookie team by *TSN*. Although he led NL second basemen in errors for three straight years, he had excellent range and his bat showed occasional home run power. In 1957, Baker was traded to the Pirates along with Dee Fondy for Dale Long and Lee Walls. Early the next season, he injured his knee. He missed all of 1959 and played only a few games in 1960–61 before turning to coaching and scouting for the Pirates. /(MN)

Steve Baker — 1956– . RHP 1978–79, 82–83 **Tigers**, A's, Cardinals 237 ip, 7–16, 5.13

With an explosive but uncontrolled fastball, Baker was 3–11 in parts of two seasons as a starter with the Tigers. He later returned to the ML as a reliever. /(MC)

Steve Balboni (Bones, Bye-Bye) — 1957– . 1B-DH 1981–Yankees, **Royals**, Mariners 842 g, .232, 164 hr, 461 rbi. *2 LCS, 10 g, .111, 1 rbi. 1 WS, 7 g, .320, 3 rbi*

A free-swinging power hitter, Balboni hit 152 HR in the minors from 1979 to 1983, leading his

league four straight years (1979–82). After three trials with the Yankees he was acquired by the Royals to replace Willie Aikens and averaged nearly 30 HR annually in four seasons, reaching a high of 36 in Kansas City's 1985 World Championship year. However, the streaky low-average hitter (he never batted above .240) set a team record with 166 strikeouts that year, leading the AL. At other times he struck out in nine consecutive plate appearances and in 13 straight games. He led league first basemen in errors in 1986 and tied for the lead in 1984, and became a DH after back trouble reduced his mobility. Released by the Royals in May 1988, he signed with the Mariners that June and resurrected his career with 21 HR and 61 RBI in 350 at-bats with Seattle. When he was awarded a big contract in arbitration that winter, he was traded to the Yankees just before the start of the 1989 season and hit 17 HR with 59 RBI in 300 at-bats, mostly as their DH. /(FO)

Jack Baldschun — 1936– . RHP 1961–67, 69–70 **Phillies**, Reds, Padres 704 ip, 48–41, 3.70

The red-haired screwballer was the workhorse of the Phillies bullpen from 1961 through 1965, saving 59 games, appearing in 65 or more games each year, and leading the NL with 12 relief wins in 1962. He won both ends of an April 14, 1962 doubleheader. /(JCA)

Dave Baldwin — 1938– . RHP 1966–70, 73 **Senators**, Brewers, White Sox 224 ip, 6–11, 3.09

A zoologist and anthropologist who later earned a Ph.D., this relief pitcher's wicked sidearm delivery was particularly effective against righthanded hitters.

His best year was as a rookie in 1967 when he saved 12 for the Senators and had a 1.70 ERA. /(JCA)

Lady Baldwin [Charles Busted] — 1859–1937. LHP 1884–90 Milwaukee (U), **Detroit (NL)**, Brooklyn, Buffalo (PL) 1017 ip, 73–41, 2.85. 20 wins: 86

In 1886, his one outstanding ML season, the Detroit ace led the NL with seven shutouts, tied for the league lead with 42 wins, and ranked second in strikeouts (323). Teammates gave him his odd nickname because he didn't smoke, curse, or join them in drinking bouts. /(FIC)

Mark Baldwin (Fido) — 1865–1929. RHP 1887–93 Cubs, Columbus (AA), Chicago (P), **Pirates**, Giants 2811 ip, 154–165, 3.36. 20 wins: 89–92

Baldwin's 34 losses led the American Association in 1889, but he also won 27 that year for sixth-place Columbus, and struck out 368 (a season high since topped only by Nolan Ryan and Sandy Koufax). The next year with Chicago his 32 wins tied for the Players' League lead. /(FIC)

Rick Baldwin — 1953– . RHP 1975–77 **Mets** 183 ip, 4–7, 3.59

The bible-toting sinkerballer led the Mets staff with 54 relief appearances as a rookie in 1975, when he had a respectable 3.34 ERA. After spending most of 1976 at Tidewater (International League), he earned only one win and one save in 40 appearances with the Mets in 1977. /(JCA)

Neal Ball — 1881–1957. SS-2B 1907–13 Yankees, **Indians**, Red Sox 496 g, .251, 4 hr, 151 rbi. *1 WS, 1 g, .000*

After leading AL shortstops with 80 errors in 1908, on July 19, 1909, the Cleveland infielder executed the major leagues' first unassisted triple play, catching a liner, doubling one Red Sox runner off second, and tagging another from first. He also hit an inside-the-park homer that inning. /(ADS)

Phil deCateesby Ball — 1864–1933. *Executive*

Ball became wealthy building refrigeration plants and, with Harry Sinclair, financed the St. Louis club in the Federal League. As part of the settlement with that league, the AL allowed him to buy the Browns in 1916 for $750,000. He remained owner until 1932. Ball became a strong supporter of Ban Johnson, opposed the hiring of Judge Landis, and for six years never voted in support of Landis. An early aviation enthusiast, he was director of several airplane companies and bought the factory where Lindbergh's plane was built. /(NLM)

Lee Ballanfant — 1895–Unk. *Umpire* NL 1936–57 *4 WS*
☛ *All-Star—4.*

A respected NL umpire for 22 years, Ballanfant had his most embarrassing moment in the heat of the 1940 pennant race. In the first inning of an important game between the Dodgers and Cardinals, he got in the way of a ball thrown to first base, preventing the Dodgers from completing an apparent double play. The ball remained in play, over the protests of the irate Dodgers. /(RTM)

Jeff Ballard — 1963– . LHP 1987– **Orioles** 438 ip, 28–28, 4.27

On the surprising 1989 Orioles, this finesse pitcher was 9–2 by the All-Star break. He finished 18–8, 3.43. /(WOR)

Jay Baller — 1960– . RHP 1982, 85–87 Phillies, **Cubs** 143 ip, 4–8, 4.85

Baller led the Eastern League with a 2.68 ERA at Reading in 1982 while striking out 155 batters in 151.1 innings, and was one of five players traded from the Phillies to the Indians for Von Hayes that December. The 6'6" reliever never pitched for the Indians, but resurfaced in the Cubs bullpen in 1985. In 1986 Baller recorded five of his six career saves. /(SCL)

Ed Ballinger — 1869–1966. *Writer*

Ballinger traveled a half-million miles covering the Pirates from the time he joined the Pittsburgh *Post* in 1903 until he retired 43 years later as sports editor of the *Post-Gazette*. /(NLM)

Win Ballou [Noble Winfield] (Old Pard) — 1897–1963. RHP 1925–27, 29 Senators, **Browns**, Dodgers 330 ip, 19–20, 5.11. *1 WS, 2 ip, 0–0, 0.00*

Ballou took credit for Washington's 1925 pennant when, in a crucial, late-season game with the Athletics, a ball hit up the middle caromed off his shin, resulting in a double play. His only solid ML season was 1926 with the Browns (11–10), but he pitched in the Pacific Coast League well into his forties. /(WAB)

Baltimore Orioles — 1954– . Team. 3059–2632, .538. *AL East Champions 69–71, 73–74, 79, 83 AL Champions 66, 69–71, 79, 83 World Champions 66, 70, 83*

In 1954 Bill Veeck sold the St. Louis Browns to a Baltimore-based group of investors, who moved the perpetual losers to their hometown. With Paul Richards at the helm both on the field and in the front office, the Orioles developed a highly productive farm system and by 1960 were contending for the pennant. The Orioles were built on the arms of the "Baby Birds," a group of young pitchers who included Wally Bunker and Milt Pappas, as well as the brilliant fielding of Brooks Robinson. The addition of Frank Robinson in 1966 brought Baltimore its first WS victory, a four-game sweep of the Dodgers. The Orioles soon became a mini-dynasty, reaching the WS three straight years (1969–71) with a lineup that included Boog Powell, Mark Belanger, and Paul Blair, and pitchers Mike Cuellar, Dave McNally, and Jim Palmer. Known for strong organizational unity and "The Oriole Way," which emphasized fundamentals and careful, measured development in the minor leagues, Baltimore has also produced a slew of pitching coaches (George Bamberger, Ray Miller, Wes Stock), managers (Earl Weaver, Frank Robinson), and front-office talent (Harry Dalton, Frank Cashen). A short period of decline in the 1980s was stemmed by Roland Hemond with a typical infusion of young pitching talent. /(SH)

Baltimore Orioles — 1882–1899. Team 1882–91 AA, 1892–99 NL 644–447, .590. *NL Champions 1894–96*

After an undistinguished run in the American Association that was actually interrupted in 1890, when the team chose to be a minor league club, the original Baltimore Orioles were absorbed by the National League after the AA fell apart following the 1891 season. Part-owner and manager Ned Hanlon built a dynasty around the Hall of Fame talents of John McGraw, Hughie Jennings, Willie Keeler, Joe Kelley, and Wilbert Robinson, and the team pioneered a cutthroat style of play that was simultaneously heady and dirty. The owners bought the Brooklyn club later in the decade and transferred most of the Orioles' best players to their new team, and when the NL dropped four teams after the 1899 season, the fabled Orioles were no more. /(SH)

George Bamberger (Bambi) — 1925– .
Manager 1978–80, 82–83, 85–86 **Brewers**, Mets
458–478, .489

The genial Bamberger recorded 213 victories in 18 years as a minor league pitcher but won more recognition as a ML pitching coach and manager. He was the Orioles pitching coach for a decade beginning in 1967. During that time, Baltimore had such standouts as Jim Palmer, Dave McNally, Mike Cueller, and Pat Dobson, all of whom won 20 games in 1971.

Offered the Milwaukee helm in 1978, Bamberger led the Brewers to a third-place finish and was named *TSN* and *UPI* Manager of the Year. In the spring of 1980, he underwent coronary bypass surgery but returned to manage from June 6 until his retirement in September. He was given a lifetime job in Milwaukee's front office but was lured away by the Mets. He managed New York from 1982 until he resigned voluntarily in June 1983, citing health reasons. In 1985 and '86 he managed the Brewers to sixth-place finishes. /(JCA)

Dave Bancroft (Beauty) — 1891–1972. SS 1915–30
Phillies, Giants, Braves, Dodgers 1913 g, .279, 32 hr,
591 rbi. *4 WS, 24 g, .172, 7 rbi.*
  Manager 1924–27 **Braves** 249–363, .407
☛ *Hall of Fame—1971.*

Bancroft was the classic shortstop. He had quick hands for a ground ball or a deft tag, quickness afoot for covering a middle infielder's territory, and quick-wittedness for lightning response to defensive opportunity. At bat, he was a dexterous switch-hitter,

Dave Bancroft with the Giants

ideal for the leadoff or second spot. In his time, he was considered by most to be better than Maranville, which meant he was the best.

The formidable Mickey Doolan had been the Phillies' shortstop for nine years before jumping to Baltimore of the Federal League in 1914, and the team floundered until Bancroft arrived from Portland (Pacific Coast League). A beauty from the start, he was a key player in the 1915 pennant drive and two subsequent second-place finishes. Thereafter, the team descended to the cellar, where owner William Baker's policy of selling stars for cash would keep it for a generation. For Bancroft, the Giants gave Baker plenty of money, 35-year-old Art Fletcher, and the first, and lesser, of two Giant pitchers named Hubbell.

Bancroft's three-plus years with the Giants were his best. He was McGraw's field leader and designated cutoff man. In 1921–22, he led the league in putouts, assists, and double plays. He became a .300 batter, had a six-for-six day in 1920, and hit for the cycle in 1921.

In late 1923, he was dealt to the Braves with Casey Stengel and Bill Cunningham for Billy Southworth and Joe Oeschger. McGraw, all heart, said he was giving up the league's best shortstop as a favor to Christy Mathewson (then fronting the listless Braves as their president) and to Bancroft, who would become their playing manager. The truth was that Bancroft was an aging 32, and New York had 20-year-old hotshot Travis Jackson with no place to put him.

A step slower in the field, Bancroft still was a class act, but he couldn't pry the Braves out of the second division. His fine career ended with two years at Brooklyn and a few games with the Giants as he made the inevitable transition to coaching. He ran a downhill course through the minors. Briefly, the old roughneck even managed a women's softball team.

Lifetime, Bancroft remains sixth in total chances for shortstops with 11,844, first in average putouts per game (2.5) and tied for second in average chances per game (6.3). /(ADS)

Frank C. Bancroft — 1846–1921. *Manager* 1880–85, 87, 89, 1902 Worcester (NL), Detroit (NL), Cleveland (NL), **Providence (NL)**, Philadelphia (AA), Indianapolis (NL), Reds 372–328, .531. First place: 84

Bancroft introduced baseball to Cuba in 1879 when he took a touring team to the Caribbean. He managed six ML clubs through the 1880s, including the 1884 Providence Grays, who won the first World Series. He spent 30 years as business manager for the Cincinnati Reds. /(JK)

Chris Bando (C.B.) — 1956– . C 1981–88 **Indians**, Tigers 497 g, .227, 27 hr, 141 rbi

Never the hitter brother Sal was, switch-hitting Cleveland native Chris Bando kept his job as the Indians' second-string catcher with his defense and uncomplaining attitude. He proved exceptional at handling the knuckleballs of Tom Candiotti and Phil Niekro. /(ME)

Sal Bando — 1944– . 3B 1968–1981 **A's**, Brewers 2019 g, .254, 242 hr, 1039 rbi. *5 LCS, 20 g, .270, 5 hrs, 8 rbi. 3 WS, 19 g, .206, 1 hr, 4 rbi*
☛ *All-Star—69, 72–74.*

Bando was a power-hitting third baseman and co-captain of the raucous Oakland A's dynasty that won five straight AL Western Division titles (1971–75) and three straight World Series (1972–74). He was the glue of the infield, although, characteristically for that team, he didn't always show respect for management. In June 1974, after a disappointing loss, he observed that A's manager Alvin Dark "couldn't manage a meat market." And although he was chosen for four All-Star teams, he never started, having the misfortune to play during Brooks Robinson's final years.

Bando managed to stick with colorful A's owner Charlie Finley for 11 seasons, including the last two years the franchise was in Kansas City. In both 1969 and 1971, Bando hit two grand slams. In the seventh game of the 1972 World Series, he knocked in a run with a double, then scored the eventual winning run on Gene Tenace's double in the sixth inning of a 3–2 A's victory.

Bando's best year came in 1973, when he led the league in doubles with 32 and hit a career-high .287 with 29 HR and 98 RBI. In the 1973 playoffs against Baltimore, he nearly hit three homers in the second game, a 6–3 Oakland win. In the third inning Al Bumbry made a spectacular leaping catch of Bando's first long drive. Following Game Two of the 1973 Series, he prompted the black armbands the players wore to show their feelings over the Mike Andrews incident, when Finley roasted the unfortunate second baseman's two-error performance. In the 1974 playoffs against Baltimore, Bando hit two homers. His solo homer off Jim Palmer in Game Three provided the game's only run, and in the fourth and final game Bando scored the eventual winning run on Reggie Jackson's seventh-inning double, the only hit for Oakland that afternoon.

Sal Bando

Bando escaped Finley in 1977 when he signed with the Brewers as a free agent, and stayed around long enough to see his younger brother, Chris, reach the majors in 1981 with Cleveland. /(SEW)

Eddie Bane — 1952– . LHP 1973, 75–76 **Twins** 168 ip, 7–13, 4.66

The curveballer was 40–4 in three years at Arizona State, and the Twins signed him for the largest bonus they had ever paid a pitcher. He debuted before 45,890 expectant Minnesota fans (7/4/73), but in three seasons he never lived up to their hopes. /(JCA)

Ed Bang — 1880–1968. *Writer*

After working for several newspapers in Ohio, Bang succeeded Grantland Rice as sports editor of the Cleveland *News* in 1907 and remained there for 53 years until the newspaper closed. In 1942, he estimated he'd written more than 50 million words for the *News*. Known for his distinctive foghorn voice and for answering every letter or call, whether from an important sports figure or only a fan, Bang was among those who once carried card No. 1 of the BBWAA and was a regular contributor to *The Sporting News.* /(NLM)

Dan Bankhead — 1920–1976. RHP 1947, 50–51 **Dodgers** 153 ip, 9–5, 6.52

Bankhead was the major leagues' first black pitcher, but enjoyed little success at that level. He pitched a no-hitter for Nashua in 1948, and, in his first big league at-bat, homered off Pittsburgh's Fritz Ostermueller. /(EGM)

Sam Bankhead — 1910–1976. SS-OF-2B-RHP-MGR Negro Leagues 1930–50 Birmingham Black Barons, Nashville Elite Giants, Louisville, Pittsburgh Crawfords, **Homestead Grays** statistics not available
☛ *All-Star—33–34, 36, 38, 42–44.*

The oldest of five brothers who played in the Negro Leagues, Sam Bankhead appeared in seven East-West all-star games between 1933 and 1946, during which time he played three different positions for three different teams and batted .346. He was an integral part of the Pittsburgh Crawfords and Homestead Grays of the 1930s and 1940s. He was known for his strong arm, consistent hitting, and versatility in the field. He interrupted his Negro National League career for several years to play in the Cuban winter league. In 21 documented games against white major leaguers, he batted .342. /(BP)

Scott Bankhead — 1963– . RHP 1986– Royals, **Mariners** 616 ip, 38–32, 4.03

Bankhead pitched for the 1984 U.S. Olympic team and appeared in only 31 games in the minors before being called up by the Royals. He was traded to Seattle in the deal for Danny Tartabull. In his first month with the Mariners, Bankhead went 4–1 with a 2.94 ERA, but he developed tendinitis and ended the season with a less impressive 9–8 record and 5.42 ERA. His usually sharp control and strikeout ability were established by 1988, but it wasn't until 1989, when he went on a hot streak after the All-Star break, that he proved himself a winning pitcher. He finished that year 14–6 with a 3.34 ERA. /(TF)

Ernie Banks (Mr. Cub) — 1931– . 1B-SS 1954–1971
Cubs 2528 g, .274, 512 hr, 1636 rbi
☛ *Most Valuable Player—58–59. Led League—hr 58, 60.
Led League—rbi 58–59. All-Star—55–62, 65, 67, 69.
Gold Glove—60. Hall of Fame—1977.*

He will always be "Mr. Cub," the most popular
player the Cubs ever had. His sunny personality is
legend, as is his refrain on a sunny day: "Let's play
two!" The first black player on the Cubs, Banks
came up as a shortstop, where he won consecutive
MVP awards, but actually played more games at
first base. He is also one of a handful of Hall of
Famers never to get into postseason play.

Growing up in Dallas, Banks had to be bribed
with nickels and dimes by his father to play catch.
Banks, more interested in softball than baseball, was
a high school star in both football and basketball,
and once ran a 52-second quarter mile. At the age of
17, he signed on to play baseball with a Negro
barnstorming team for $15 a game. Cool Papa Bell
later signed him for the Kansas City Monarchs. He

Ernie Banks

returned to them after two years in the army, and
the Cubs discovered him there at the end of the
1953 season. The 22-year-old went right to the Cubs
and hit his first homer on September 20, 1953, off
Gerry Staley in St. Louis. He quickly replaced Roy
Smalley, Sr., as the regular Cub shortstop in 1954.
Starting with his first game in 1953, he played 424
consecutive games until fracturing his hand midway
through the 1956 season.

Like his contemporary, Hank Aaron, Banks
didn't look like a power hitter. He was slim, with
powerful thighs, and he held his bat high, wiggling it
nervously while waiting for the pitch. Like Aaron he
got his power from amazingly quick and strong
wrists. A teammate of his once remarked that Banks
had "wrists right up to his armpits." An opposing
player noted that he often "hits the ball right out of
the catcher's mitt." In 1955, he switched to a lighter
bat, starting a trend. He then went out and smacked
44 HR, the most ever for a shortstop, including
three in one day at Wrigley against Pittsburgh and
an NL-record five grand slams. His best years were
his consecutive MVP years in 1958 and 1959. He
hit .313 and .304 respectively—his only full years
over .300 --and led the league in RBI both years,
with 129 and a career-high 143. He also hit a
league-leading and career-high 47 HR in 1958 and
added another 45 in 1959.

From 1955 to 1960, Banks hit more homers than
anyone in the majors, including Mantle, Mays, and
Aaron. At the end of the 1959 season, he was so
popular that the Cubs wanted to give him his own
day. The modest Banks gratefully declined, saying
that he hadn't been around long enough to be so
honored. By 1964, Banks had relented, and the
honorary day was held.

At first, Banks's fielding was erratic. He posted
error totals of 34, 22, and 25 early in his career,
culminating in a league-leading 32 in 1958. He
worked dilligently to cut his errors down to 12 in
1959, then a record for shortstops, and led NL
shortstops in fielding in both 1960 (he won a Gold
Glove) and 1961. Meanwhile, he kept hitting. In the
first 1960 All-Star game he had a two-run homer in
a 5–3 NL victory, and he ended the season leading
the league in HR for the second time, with 41.

Even though Banks had led the league in fielding
the previous two seasons, injuries to his legs had cut
down his range, so he accepted a move to first base
in 1962. When Leo Durocher took over the team in
1966, he kept bringing up young phenoms to replace
Banks, but none did. Banks won the fielding title at
his new position in 1969, and led NL first basemen

in assists five times. By 1970, his legs had begun to weaken from nagging injuries and arthritis. On May 12, 1970, he hit his 500th homer, the most avidly anticipated event in Wrigley Field history, with the possible exception of the first night game. After Banks's retirement in 1971, the Cubs hoisted a pinstriped pennant with his number 14 atop the left field foul pole at Wrigley Field. He was the first Cubs player to have his number retired. /(SEW)

Alan Bannister — 1951– . OF-2B-SS-DH 1974–85 Phillies, **White Sox**, Indians, Astros, Rangers 972 g, .270, 19 hr, 288 rbi

Highly touted in college, Bannister was the Phillies' first-round pick in the 1973 draft. Although versatile (he played every position but pitcher and catcher) he never lived up to his college raves and was rarely a regular. Only once, as the 1977 White Sox' shortstop, did he play in over 100 games at a position, and then he led all AL shortstops in errors (40). /(JCA)

Floyd Bannister — 1955– . LHP 1977– Astros, Mariners, **White Sox**, Royals 2,326 ip, 133–142, 4.03. *1 LCS, 6 ip, 0–1, 4.50*
☛ *Led League—k 82. All-Star—82.*

A standout at Arizona State, Bannister was named *TSN* College Player of the Year in 1976 and was the nation's first draft pick that June. He reached the Astros in 1977, but was ill and had blister problems in 1978 and was traded to the Mariners for Craig Reynolds. With his 90 mph fastball, sharp slider, and excellent curveball, Bannister notched many strikeouts but few wins. He fanned an AL-high 209 batters in 1982, but averaged just 10 wins a season in Seattle. Playing out his option, he signed with the White Sox for 1983. After losing nine of his first 12 decisions, he became the catalyst of Chicago's '83 pennant drive, going 13–1 (2.23) after the All-Star break. But, lacking the killer instinct and refusing to pitch inside, he was frequently victimized by the long ball, and was perceived as not living up to his potential. After he increased his value by going 16–11 in 1987, the White Sox traded him to the Royals for four young players, including pitching prospects Melido Perez and John Davis. /(RL)

Jack Banta — 1925– . RHP 1947–50 **Dodgers** 205 ip, 14–12, 3.78. *1 WS, 3 g, 3.18*

Banta, a sidearming reliever, had a 10–6 record for the 1949 Dodgers, winning the pennant-clinching game on the last day of the season. A 1950 arm injury ended his promising career. /(EGM)

Walter Barbare (Dinty) — 1891–1965. 3B-SS-2B 1914–22 Indians, Red Sox, Pirates, **Braves** 500 g, .260, 1 hr, 156 rbi

A light-hitting, long-armed infielder, Barbare went in a 1921 trade from Pittsburgh to the Braves for star shortstop Rabbit Maranville. He responded with his only solid season, batting .302. Barbare also managed and umpired in the minors. /(JK)

Red Barber [Walter] — 1908– . *Broadcaster 1934–66*

Barber was New York City's first baseball radio broadcaster, and the first baseball telecaster anywhere. He chronicled the rise of the Dodgers with phrases like "tearin' up the pea patch" and "the bases are FOB"—full of Brooklyns. The Mississippi-born Barber said, "(I) didn't broadcast with a Brooklyn accent, but I did broadcast with a Brooklyn heart." When fired by the Yankees, he ended his farewell interview by blowing a kiss to Brooklyn. /(TG)

Red Barber

Steve Barber — 1939- . LHP 1960–74 **Orioles**, Yankees, Pilots, Cubs, Braves, Angels, Giants 2000 ip, 121–106, 3.36. 20 wins: 63
☛ *All-Star—63, 66.*

One of the Orioles' "Baby Birds" (a group of promising young pitchers), Barber came up as a flame-thrower with a reputation for wildness. He led the AL in walks his rookie year, but by 1963 had settled down to become Baltimore's first modern-day ML 20-game winner. Tendinitis in his elbow sidelined him for the second part of 1966, and Barber missed pitching in the All-Star Game and World Series. He went 8–1/3 innings in his first start of 1967 before giving up a hit to Jim Fregosi, and threw a combined no-hitter with Stu Miller against Detroit two weeks later (Baltimore lost that game 2–1). He was traded to the Yankees in mid-'67. Problems with his elbow and his pitching mechanics limited his success with five more teams. /(JCA)

Turner Barber — 1893–1968. OF-1B 1915–23 Senators, **Cubs**, Dodgers 491 g, .289, 2 hr, 185 rbi. *1 WS, 3 g, .000*

Barber was a substitute except for 1921, when he and Cubs teammates George Maisel and Max Flack formed one of the least-renowned .300-hitting outfields. It was also Maisel's only season as a regular; Flack hit .300 three times. /(JK)

Curt Barclay — 1931- . RHP 1957–59 **Giants** 199 ip, 10–9, 3.48

After turning down a basketball contract with the Boston Celtics, the 6'3" Barclay joined the sixth-place Giants in their final year in New York. He posted a 9–9 rookie record, but the next season a shoulder injury ended his career. /(JK)

George Barclay (Deerfoot) — 1876–1909. OF 1902–05 **Browns**, Braves 401 g, .248, 4 hr, 140 rbi

Barclay never equalled his rookie season, when he hit .300 and stole 30 bases. /(WB)

Ray Bare — 1949- . RHP 1972, 74–77 Cardinals, **Tigers** 339 ip, 16–26, 4.80

Bare is remembered by Tiger fans for snapping a club-record 19-game losing streak in 1975 with a two-hit, 8–0 performance at California. /(CC)

Jesse Barfield — 1959- . OF 1981- **Blue Jays**, Yankees 1161 g, .263, 197 hr, 583 rbi. *1 LCS, .280, 1 hr, 4 rbi*
☛ *Led League—hr 86. All-Star—86. Gold Glove—86–87.*

Barfield has the best outfield arm of the 1980s. He led AL outfielders each year from 1985 to 1987 despite few runners being so foolhardy as to challenge him, and won Gold Gloves in 1986 and '87. He also has shown prodigious home run power, leading the ML with 40 HR in 1986, and was the Blue Jays' career HR leader as of the beginning of the 1988 season. Barfield was the first Blue Jay to hit a pinch grand slam, and the first to hit 20 homers and steal 20 bases in the same season. With George Bell and Lloyd Moseby, Barfield starred in what was considered by some the best outfield of the 1980s, but in early 1989 he was traded to the Yankees for pitching prospect Al Leiter. /(TF)

Clyde Barfoot — 1891–1971. RHP 1922–23, 26 **Cardinals**, Tigers 250 ip, 8–10, 4.10

Barfoot was in his early thirties before he got a chance as the second reliever in the Cardinals' bullpen. A longtime star in the Texas League, Pacific Coast League, and Southern Association, he won 314 minor league games in a career that spanned 25 years. /(FJO)

Cy Barger [Eros] — 1885–1964. RHP 1906–07, 10–12, 14–25 Yankees, **Dodgers**, Pittsburgh FL 975 ip, 47–62, 3.56

Barger's father wanted to give him an impressive-sounding Greek name, and chose Eros (the god of love) without knowing its source. Cy was sometimes impressive, as when he went 15–15 for the 1910 Dodgers, but he dropped to 1–9 two years later. He was 20–23 in two years with Pittsburgh of the Federal League. /(NLM)

Len Barker — 1955- . RHP 1976–85, 87 Rangers, **Indians**, Braves, Brewers 1322 ip, 74–76, 4.35
☛ *Led League—k 80–81.*

Flame-throwing Barker three-hit the White Sox in his first ML start with the Rangers, but his wildness caused his trade to Cleveland in 1979. There he learned to control his 96-mph fastball and posted a 19–12 mark in 1980 while leading the AL in strikeouts. He pitched a 3–0 perfect game against Toronto (5/15/81) and started that year's All-Star Game. He led in strikeouts again in 1981 and was 15–11 in 1982. The Braves gave up Brett Butler, Brook Jacoby and Rick Behenna to get him in late 1983, but he never managed a winning record for Atlanta. /(MC)

Al Barlick — 1915- . *Umpire* NL 1940–43, 46–55, 58–70 *7 WS, 7 ASU*

Al Barlick

A WWII Coast Guard veteran with a salty tongue, Barlick was firm and tough and demanded respect. He umpired a record seven All-Star Games, spanning four decades. He was the plate umpire in the 1970 game when Pete Rose flattened catcher Ray Fosse. A no-nonsense type, he stopped a game at Shea Stadium to have the coaching box rechalked and forfeited a game in Philadelphia when unruly fans hit him with a tomato and fellow ump Lee Ballanfant with a bottle. In 1949 his call of a trap by the Cubs' Andy Pafko produced one of the shortest home runs in history. While Pafko argued the call, batter Rocky Nelson circled the bases for a 220-foot homer. /(RTM)

Mike Barlow — 1948- . LHP 1975-81 Cardinals, Astros, **Angels**, Blue Jays 247 ip, 10-6, 4.63. *1 WS, 1 ip, 0.00*

The 6'6" reliever grew up near (but was no candidate for) Cooperstown, NY. He had a terrific September 1977 with the Angels, winning four games, more than he ever won again in a full ML season. /(JCA)

Ernest S. Barnard — Unk.-1931. *Executive.*

Barnard was sports editor of a Columbus, Ohio, newspaper when he joined the Indians as road secretary in 1904. He became president of the club in 1922 and in 1928 succeeded Ban Johnson as president of the AL, a position he held until his death. /(NLM)

Jesse Barnes — 1892-1961. RHP 1915-27 Braves, **Giants**, Dodgers 2569 ip, 153-149, 3.22. 20 wins: 19-20 *2 WS, 26 ip, 2-0, 1.71*
☛ *Led League—w 19.*

Barnes was a hard thrower who came to the ML with the Braves the year after their 1914 "miracle" pennant. By the time he became a regular starter, the team had strong pitching but little else. Barnes led the NL in losses (21) in 1917. After being traded to the Giants with Larry Doyle for aging Buck Herzog in January 1918, Barnes spent most of the season in the infantry but was 6-1 in nine starts for New York. The next year he was John McGraw's ace, leading the NL in wins with a 25-9 record and a 2.40 ERA. He was one of three Giants with 20 wins the following year with a 20-15 mark. In 1921 he contributed 15 wins to the Giants' pennant and won twice in the WS. Although his win total fell to 13 in 1922, one of the victories was a no-hitter against the Phillies (5/7/22). That fall he was on the mound for the Giants in the 10th inning of Game Two of the WS with the score tied at 3-3 when umpire George Hildebrand called the game because of darkness. Most observers insisted there was still plenty of light, and Commissioner Landis was so incensed he gave the gate receipts to charity. Barnes's younger brother Virgil pitched for the Giants during these years but did not become a regular starter until after Jesse was traded back to the Braves in 1923. They pitched against each other ten times, five as starters, with Jesse winning five and losing three. With the Braves, Jesse again led the NL in losses (20) in 1924. A lifetime .214 hitter, he is the only NL pitcher to walk twice in one inning (10/2/17). /(NLM)

Red Barnes [Emile Deering] — 1903-1959. OF 1927-30 **Senators**, White Sox 286 g, .268, 8 hr, 97 rbi

As a rookie centerfielder in 1928 Barnes formed part of the Senators' all-.300 outfield. Flanked by Hall of Famers Sam Rice (.328) and Goose Goslin (.379), Barnes hit .302 with 15 triples. /(JK)

Ross Barnes [Roscoe Charles] — 1850-1915. 2B-SS 1871-77, 79, 81 **Red Sox (NA)**, Cubs, Reds, Braves *NA:* 266 g, .379; NL: 234 g, .319, 2 hr, 111 rbi
☛ *Led League—ba 73, 75-76.*

The clever second baseman was the NL's first batting leader (.429) with Chicago in 1876. Having already won two National Association titles (1873, '75), he was also the first player to lead two different leagues in batting. He specialized in "fair-foul" hits—squibbed bunts that landed fair, rolled foul, but remained in play under the rules of the time. When the rules were changed before the 1877 season his BA plummeted. /(ADS)

Virgil Barnes (Zeke) — 1897–1958. RHP 1919–20, 22–28 **Giants**, Braves 1094, 61–59, 3.66. *2 WS, 17 ip, 0–1, 4.15*

Barnes joined the Giants after his older brother Jesse had become their star pitcher. Virgil did not establish himself until after Jesse was traded away. From 1924 to 1927 he won 53 games for New York. An injury to the deltoid and bursa tendons in his shoulder forced Barnes's retirement. /(NLM)

Walter S. Barnes — 1860–Unk. *Writer.*

A graduate of Harvard, Barnes began writing baseball for the Boston *Post* in 1880, then was sports editor of the *Journal, Herald,* and *Globe.* In 1939, he was the oldest member of the BBWA, holding card 1. /(NLM)

Barney Barnett (Larry) — 1945– *Umpire* AL 1968–87 *5 LCS 3 WS, 3 ASU*

Barnett was the plate ump in the third game of the 1975 WS when a controversial 10th-inning call took place. Reds batter Ed Armbrister bunted and seemed to interfere as Boston catcher Carlton Fisk went after the ball. Fisk's throw sailed into centerfield. Over Red Sox objections Barnett ruled no interference. The Reds later scored the winning run. /(RTM)

Rex Barney — 1924– . RHP 1943, 1946–50 **Dodgers** 598 ip, 35–31, 4.34. *2 WS, 9 ip, 0–2, 6.75*

Barney's fastball was unhittable but all too often unreachable. In six Dodger seasons of unfulfilled promise, only in 1948 did he strike out more batters than he walked (138 to 122). That season he went 15–13 with a 3.10 ERA and pitched a no-hitter against the Giants. After that he grew progressively wilder, to the frustration of Dodger boss Branch Rickey, who even tried a hypnotist on him. Barney later became a successful baseball broadcaster. /(JD)

Clyde Barnhart (Pooch) — 1895–1980. OF-3B 1920–28 **Pirates** 814 g, .295, 27 hr, 436 rbi. *2 WS, 11 g, .273, 9 rbi*

Barnhart was the Pirates' third baseman until Pie Traynor arrived, when he was moved to the outfield. Tough to strike out, he fanned only 149 times in 2673 at bats. He drove in a career-high 114 runs and hit .325 as the Pirates leftfielder in 1925. Lloyd Waner replaced Barnhart in 1927 but Waner moved to center when Kiki Cuyler fell into manager Donie Bush's doghouse and was benched. The slow-footed Barnhart went back to left and hit .319. In the four-game '27 WS, he drove in four of Pittsburgh's ten runs. His son, Vic, was a Pittsburgh shortstop in the 1940s. /(ME)

David Barnhill (Impo) — 1914–1983. RHP Negro Leagues 1937–49 Miami Clowns, Ethiopian Clowns, **New York Cubans**
☛ *All-Star—41–43.*

A small, fireballing strikeout artist, Barnhill was the ace of the New York Cubans' staff during the early 1940s, compiling an 18–3 record in 1941. He pitched in the 1941–43 East-West all-star games, defeating Satchel Paige in the 1942 contest. That year, the Pirates considered Barnhill for the role of breaking baseball's color line, but the opportunity did not materialize. In 1947, he shut out the Cleveland Buckeyes in the Negro World Series to help the Cubans to the championship. He was signed by the New York Giants in 1949, and in 1950 he compiled an 11–3 record for the AAA champion Minneapolis Millers (American Association). Since he was already 35, his age kept him from getting a shot at the majors. He continued to play in the Pacific Coast League and Florida International League until 1953. /(JR)

Bill Barnie (Bald Billy) — 1853–1900. C-OF 1883, 86 **Baltimore (AA)** 19 g, .180, 0 hr, inc rbi.
Manager **1883–94, 97–98 Baltimore** AA, Brooklyn-Baltimore (AA), Philadelphia (AA), Washington (NL), Louisville (NL), Dodgers 646–829, .438

Barnie was working in a brokerage office when he broke into baseball in 1871 as a catcher/outfielder. While managing Baltimore's American Association team in the 1880's, he occasionally caught for his team, but his .180 BA hardly indicated "leading by example." His third-place finish in 1887 was his best season, but "Bald Billy" managed for 14 ML seasons. In 1900, while managing Hartford of the Eastern League, he died in midseason from asthmatic bronchitis. /(NLM)

Salome Barojas — 1957– . RHP 1982–85 **White Sox**, Mariners 381 ip, 18–21, 3.85. *1 LCS, 2 ip, 0–0, 18.00*

On a scouting trip to Mexico during the 1981 players' strike, White Sox manager Tony LaRussa signed Barojas out of the Mexican League. In 1982, the rookie reliever, who spoke no English, won 6 and saved 21 for the Sox./(NLM)

George Barr — 1897–1974. *Umpire* NL 1931–49 *4 WS, 1 ASU*

Barr was the only modern umpire to be assigned consecutive WS (1948–49). As the plate umpire during a rainy 1949 game in Boston, Barr ejected the Braves' Connie Ryan after Ryan protested the decision not to call the game by kneeling in the on-deck circle wearing a raincoat./(RTM)

Jim Barr — 1948– . RHP 1971–80, 82–83 **Giants**, Angels 2064 ip, 101–112, 3.56. *1 LCS, 1 ip, 0–0, 9.00*

Barr signed with the Giants after starring for a University of Southern California team that included Bill Lee, Brent Strom, and Dave Kingman. Called up for long relief in August 1971, he helped the Giants to a Western Division title. The next August, he earned a starting slot after retiring 41 consecutive batters in relief. He won at least 11 games each season from 1973 through 1977, with a peak year of 15–12 in 1976. In 1974 he allowed only 1.76 walks per nine innings. He signed as a free agent with the Angels in 1979, but after arm trouble, returned to the Giants in 1982./(MC)

Bill Barrett (Whispering Bill) — 1900–1951. OF-SS 1921, 23–30 A's, **White Sox**, Red Sox, Senators 716 g, .288, 23 hr, 328 rbi

The gentlemanly, soft-spoken Barrett was primarily a singles hitter and batted .307 in 1926, his best full season. He was the league's worst fielding shortstop (.904) with the White Sox in 1924, after which he usually played right field./(EC)

Charles Barrett — 1871–1939. *Scout.*

Barrett was a mediocre minor league outfielder. He joined the St. Louis Browns as a scout in 1909 and worked one season for the Tigers before joining Branch Rickey's Cardinals from 1918 until his death. He helped Rickey develop the Cardinals' phenomenal minor league system, securing such players as Pepper Martin, Chick Hafey, and Jim Bottomley./(FVP)

Dick Barrett (Kewpie) — 1906–1966. RHP 1933–34, 43–45 A's, Braves, Cubs, **Phillies** 739 ip, 34–58, 4.30

This roly-poly wartime big leaguer was a Pacific Coast League standout, with seven 20-win seasons, 234 wins, and the league's most career strikeouts. After an 0–4 start with the Cubs in 1943, he was sold to the Phillies and responded with a 14-inning, 1–0 blanking of Cincinnati. His 20 losses led the NL in 1945./(JK)

Frank Barrett (Red) — 1913– . RHP 1939, 44–46, 50 Cardinals, **Red Sox**, Braves, Pirates 218 ip, 15–17, 3.51

Barrett was one of many career minor leaguers who played in the majors during WWII. As a 30-year-old rookie reliever, he won eight and saved eight for the 1944 Red Sox./(ME)

Jimmy Barrett — 1875–1921. OF 1899–1908 Reds, **Tigers**, Red Sox 865 g, .291, 16 hr, 255 rbi

A solidly built lefthanded hitter, Barrett had an exceptional arm and led outfielders in assists in three of the first four AL seasons. He twice led the league in drawing walks. A knee injury ended his career prematurely./(JK)

Johnny Barrett — 1915–1974. OF 1942–46 **Pirates**, Braves 588 g, .251, 23 hr, 220 rbi

The fleet lefthanded hitter led the NL in stolen bases (28) and triples (19) with the Pirates in 1944. Two years later, a knee injury diminished his speed and ended his ML career./(ME)

Marty Barrett — 1958– . 2B 1982– **Red Sox** 867 g, .281, 17 hr, 298 rbi. *2 LCS, 11 g, .267, 5 rbi. 1 WS, 7 g, .433, 4 rbi*

Steady but unspectacular both in the field and at the plate, Barrett starred in the 1986 postseason, winning ALCS MVP honors and setting a ML record with 24 hits in 14 postseason games. He hit a career-high .303 in his first full ML season (1984) and has remained an excellent number-two hitter. He rarely strikes out and is a skillful bunter, leading the AL in sacrifice hits three straight years from 1986 to 1988. Renowned for his savvy at second base, Barrett constantly confounds baserunners with decoys, bluffs, and an occasional hidden-ball trick. His younger brother Tom played 36 games for the Phillies in 1988./(SCL)

Red Barrett [Charles Henry] — 1915– . RHP 1937–40, 43–49 Reds, **Braves**, Cardinals 1263 ip, 69–69, 3.53. 20 wins: 45 *1 WS, 4 ip, 0.00*
☛ *Led League—w 45.*

With the Braves and Cardinals in 1945, Barrett led the NL in wins (23), complete games (24), innings pitched (284.2), and most hits allowed (287). On August 10, 1944, he threw just 58 pitches in defeating the Reds, 2–0. In 1947, Pirate slugger Ralph Kiner had hit seven homers in three games and faced Barrett the next day. "Barrett predicted that I wouldn't hit one off him," recalled Kiner. "I did, which made it eight homers in four games."/(RTM)

Francisco Barrios [born Francisco Javier Jimenez Jimenez] — 1953–1982. RHP 1974, 76–81 White Sox 717 ip, 38–38, 4.15

Big-city life was too much for Barrios, an excitable, gregarious Mexican. Possessing a 90-mph fastball, Barrios joined Chicago in 1976 and combined with Blue Moon Odom to no-hit Oakland on July 28. They walked 11, but prevailed 2–1. Barrios had a flush of success in 1977 with a 14–7 mark. But, bad tempered, he engaged umpires in verbal tirades, and once slugged it out with teammate Steve Trout in a Cleveland hotel. In 1981 he was arrested on a narcotics charge, and a year later he died of a drug overdose./(RL)

Ed Barrow (Cousin Ed) — 1868–1953. *Executive Manager* 1903–04, 18–20 Tigers, **Red Sox** 310–320, *.492. 1 WS, 4–2, .667*
☛ *Hall of Fame—1953..*

Ed Barrow

Ed Barrow was the man most responsible for the success of the New York Yankees between 1921 and 1945. With Barrow as general manager, the Yankees won 14 pennants and ten World Series, sweeping five of them. He achieved his foremost success by organizing and developing their farm system. After he became club president in 1939, he and George Weiss developed the Yankees into the most consistent pennant-winning organization in major league history.

Barrow worked for two newspapers in Des Moines, IA, before moving east in 1890. He formed a partnership with baseball concessioner Harry Stevens, and they got the scoreboard and pop concessions at the Pirates' Exposition Park. In 1894 Barrow became manager and GM at Wheeling, WV (International League). In 1895 he acquired the Paterson, NJ franchise in the Atlantic League, signed Honus Wagner, and served as president of the circuit from 1897 to 1899. He then purchased a part interest of the Toronto (International League) club, became its manager, and won a pennant in 1902. The Detroit Tigers then made him their manager, but he resigned during 1904 following a dispute with the GM. When two unsuccessful years of managing in the minors followed, Barrow left baseball.

Barrow returned in 1910 as president of the Eastern League. He was named manager of the Boston Red Sox in 1918 and immediately led them to the World Championship. That season, he acknowledged Babe Ruth's prowess as a hitter by increasingly working the ace pitcher into the lineup as an outfielder. The Red Sox sold Ruth to the Yankees in 1920, and at the close of the season, Barrow became the Yankee GM. In 1921–23, the Yankees won their first three pennants.

The forceful, straightforward Barrow possessed an explosive temper and once challenged Babe Ruth to a fight. He exercised strict discipline as manager and executive. In 1937 and 1941, he was named *TSN* Major League Executive of the Year. When the Yankees were sold to Larry McPhail, Dan Topping, and Del Webb in 1945, Barrow became chairman of the board, but he retired two years later. He was elected to the Hall of Fame by the Committee on Baseball Veterans in 1953, the year he died./(JLE)

Jack Barry — 1887–1961. SS-2B 1908–17, 19 **A's**, Red Sox 1222 g, .243, 10 hr, 429 rbi. *5 WS, 25 g, .241, 8 rbi.*

Manager 1917 **Red Sox** 90–62, .592

Barry spent most of his career with pennant-winning teams and was the shortstop in the Athletics' famous "$100,000 Infield." A key component of Connie Mack's first dynasty, Barry was signed off the campus of Holy Cross and helped the Athletics to World Championships in 1910–11 and '13. Observers considered Barry vital to the A's chances. Ty Cobb's spiking of Barry in the heat of the 1909 pennant race, depriving Philadelphia of his services, is often cited as the reason Detroit won the flag, even though Barry hit only .215 that season.

Not a great fielder, he was at least reliable, and he led AL shortstops in double plays in 1912. He was rated very highly by contemporaries, although he led in errors in 1910. That year he improved his batting to .259 with 60 RBI, 64 runs, and 52 walks in 487 at-bats. In the World Series, he had three runs scored and three RBI in the Athletics' 12–5 victory in Game Three. In 1911 he stole a career-high 30 bases and hit .368 in the World Series. The number-seven hitter's best year came in 1913, when he had career highs in batting (.275) and RBI (85). In 1914 he hit .071 in the World Series as Philadelphia was upset by the Miracle Braves. The disappointed and financially pressed Mack sold stars Barry and Eddie Collins to raise money to prevent further losses to defections to the Federal League.

New Red Sox owner Joe Lannin paid $8,000 for Barry in mid-1915. Used exclusively at second base, he hit .262 for Boston and proved to be the last piece in the pennant puzzle. Boston won consecutive World Championships in 1915 and 1916. Barry played only 94 games, hit just .203, and did not play in the World Series. His winning ways netted him $17,930 in WS shares over the course of his career.

Boston manager Bill Carrigan quit after the season to go into business, and Barry was named to replace him. He won 90 games, just one less than the 1916 team, but finished second to Chicago. As a player, he led AL second basemen in fielding but hit just .214. After spending all of 1918 in the military, he returned to a team, now managed by Ed Barrow, that was being sold off to bankroll new owner Harry Frazee's Broadway shows. When Barry hit .241 with only two RBI in 31 games, he was traded back to the Athletics in June. He chose to retire instead of reporting. /(SFS)

Shad Barry [John C.] — 1876–1936. OF-1B 1899–1908 Washington (NL), Braves, **Phillies**, Cubs, Reds, Cardinals, Giants 1099 g, .267, 10 hr, 390 rbi

Barry played every position except pitcher and catcher for seven teams in 10 years. He hit a career-high .304 as the Reds' first baseman in 1905, and during WWI was in charge of all baseball programs for the American Expeditionary Force. /(JK)

Dick Bartell (Rowdy Richard) — 1907– . SS 1927–43, 46 Pirates, Phillies, **Giants**, Cubs, Tigers 2016 g, .284, 79 hr, 710 rbi. *3 WS, 18 g, .294, 1 hr, 7 rbi* ☛ *All-Star—33, 37.*

"Rowdy Richard" battled rivals and umpires with his fists and mouth for 18 major league seasons. Although the 160-lb scrapper was best known for his aggressiveness, he was a good shortstop with occasional sting in his bat, six times batting over .300.

Dick Bartell

Nevertheless, his volatile personality wore out its welcome after a few seasons. He broke in with the Pirates (who kept him instead of young Joe Cronin), becoming the regular shortstop in 1928. In 1931, he was traded to the Phillies, and after four seasons there was traded again to the Giants. He helped New York win pennants in 1936 and '37. After a year with the Cubs, he was traded to Detroit just in time for their 1940 pennant. *Rowdy Richard*, his autobiography (with Norman Macht), was published in 1987. /(JD)

Tony Bartirome — 1932– . 1B 1952 **Pirates** 124 g, .220, 0 hr, 16 rbi

In his only ML season, the slick-fielding Pittsburgh native set a Pirate record by not hitting into a double play in 355 at-bats. His ML career was cut short by military service, but he played in the minors until 1963. After 19 years as the Pirate trainer, he moved with manager Chuck Tanner to the Braves as a coach in 1986. /(ME)

Bob Barton — 1941– . C 1965–74 Giants, **Padres**, Reds 393 g, .226, 9 hr, 66 rbi

Barton's most active year came in 1971 with the three-year-old Padres, when the strong thrower caught 119 games and set career highs in most offensive categories, but led NL catchers with 15 errors. It was his only season as anything but a reserve catcher. /(SFS)

Base Ball Writers Association of America — 1908–

Jack Rider of the Cincinnati *Enquirer* was traveling with the Reds in 1906 when he began discussing with other writers the need to improve working conditions. Sid Mercer of the New York *Globe* agreed. An earlier attempt to organize writers had failed; very few were on the road with teams. They enlisted Ernest Lanigan of the New York *Press* to do the missionary work because the *Press* had the most extensive baseball coverage.

According to a mistaken legend, the idea began when Hugh Fullerton of the Chicago *Examiner* found actor Louis Mann in his pressbox seat at the 1908 WS. Fullerton did indeed confront Mann, who often sat in the pressbox at the Polo Grounds, but that was a fairly common nuisance at the time.

The organization was formally constituted in Detroit on October 14, 1908, but a formative meeting of a few writers from New York, Brooklyn, Chicago, and Cincinnati had occurred in the NL offices in New York on August 11. NL president Harry Pulliam supported the idea.

In 1910, the New York teams gave the group a boost. At a city series they admitted only BBWAA members to the press box. As a result, the organization collected a high number of $2 annual dues. Among the goals of the BBWAA were better facilities, promoting uniform scoring, and acting with the leagues in making rules suggestions. Chapters were formed in most ML cities; their annual winter dinners have become big events. /(NLM)

Monty Basgall [Romanus] — 1922– . 2B 1948–49, 51 **Pirates** 200 g, .215, 4 hr, 41 rbi

Long a Los Angeles Dodger coach, Basgall originally signed with Brooklyn at age 19 in 1942, but he spent most of his playing career in the Pirates' organization. In 1949, he played in 107 games and hit .218 as Pittsburgh's sub for injured Danny Murtaugh. /(MC)

Eddie Basinski (Fiddler) — 1922– . SS-2B 1944–45, 47 **Dodgers**, Pirates 203 g, .244, 4 hr, 59 rbi

Basinski went straight from the University of Buffalo to the Dodgers, where he was the regular Brooklyn shortstop in 1945 while Pee Wee Reese was in the service. /(ME)

Kevin Bass — 1959– . OF 1982– Brewers, **Astros** 947 g, .275, 78 hr, 396 rbi. *1 LCS, 6 g, .292* ☛ *All-Star—86.*

One of three players the Brewers sent to Houston when they acquired veteran pitcher Don Sutton for their 1982 pennant drive, Bass was hitting .315 at Vancouver (Pacific Coast League) at the time of the trade, and has been with the Astros ever since. The switch-hitting Bass led the Astros in pinch hits in 1983 and 1984 before winning the starting centerfield job in 1985, then moved to right field when the club acquired Billy Hatcher. He has both power and speed, and was an NL All-Star in 1986 when he hit .311 with 20 HR and 22 stolen bases, helping the Astros to the NL West title. In the 1986 NLCS, Bass had three two-hit games. /(SCL)

Norm Bass — 1939– . RHP 1961–63 **A's** 253 ip, 13–17, 5.32

As a rookie, Bass hit his only ML home run, tossed two shutouts, and led the A's in wins with 11, but his ERA was an inflated 4.69. Lacking a reliable out pitch and consistent control, he faded from an improving Kansas City staff. /(FJO)

Johnny Bassler — 1895–1979. C 1913–14, 21–27 Indians, **Tigers** 811 g, .304, 1 hr, 318 rbi

Bassler was an excellent catcher and a steady .300 hitter with little power for the Tigers, finishing sixth, seventh, and fifth in AL MVP voting, 1922–24. He enjoyed the California lifestyle so much he cut short his ML career and spent many years playing and managing in the Pacific Coast League. /(JK)

Emil Batch (Heinie) — 1880–1926. 3B-OF 1904–07 **Dodgers** 348 g, .251, 7 hr, 98 rbi

Fans called this East New York boy "Ace" when he broke in at third base for Brooklyn late in 1904, but his NL-leading 57 errors the next year got him moved to the outfield for the rest of his career. /(TG)

John Bateman — 1942– . C 1963–72 **Astros**, Expos, Phillies 1017 g, .230, 81 hr, 375 rbi

Bateman battled weight problems throughout his career, paying over $2,000 in overweight fines. His best year was 1966, when he batted .279 and hit 17 homers for Houston. On September 29, 1970, he hit the final home run at Philadelphia's Connie Mack Stadium. During the late 1970s he traveled with Eddie Feigner's *King and His Court* four-man softball team. /(RTM)

Johnny Bates — 1882–1949. OF 1906–14 **Braves**, Phillies, Reds, Cubs, Baltimore FL 1163 g, .277, 25 hr, 417 rbi

Journeyman outfielder Bates hit .305 for the 1910 Phillies in his best year. He later became an off-season pool hall owner and breeder of show dogs. /(NLM)

Earl Battey — 1935– . C 1955–67 White Sox, **Senators/Twins** 1141 g, .270, 104 hr, 449 rbi. *1 WS, 7 g, .120, 2 rbi*
☛ *All-Star—62–63, 65–66. Gold Glove—60–62.*

From 1961 through 1966 the durable Battey played in 805 of the Twins' first 970 games despite injuries. Besides a perennial bad knee, several dislocated fingers, and a goiter problem (at times he ballooned to 60 pounds over his listed weight), he twice had cheekbones broken by pitched balls and wore a special helmet after 1962. In Game Three of the 1965 WS, he ran into a neck-high crossbar in Dodger Stadium while chasing a foul pop. He played the remainder of the series even though he could barely speak or turn his head.

A three-time Gold Glove winner, Battey topped all ML catchers in 1962 with a .280 BA, threw out 24 runners, and picked off 13. He had career highs of 26 homers and 84 RBI in 1963. He was the top vote-getter on the 1965 AL All-Star squad. /(JCA)

Matt Batts — 1921– . C 1947–56 Red Sox, Browns, **Tigers**, White Sox, Reds 546 g, .269, 26 hr, 219 rbi

A backup catcher, the husky Texan played ten years in the ML but only in 1953 with the Tigers did he appear in more than 100 games, hitting .278 with 42 RBI. /(CC)

Hank Bauer — 1922– . OF 1948–61 **Yankees**, A's 1544 g, .277, 164 hr, 703 rbi. *9 WS, 53 g, .245, 7 hr, 24 rbi.*
Manager 1961–62, 64–69 A's, **Orioles** 594–534, .527. First place: 66 *1 WS, 4–0, 1.000*
☛ *All-Star—52–54.*

One of Casey Stengel's favorites, Bauer didn't give away runs or make mental mistakes, and he had a fierce determination to win. He collected nine WS checks while with the Yankees and would snarl "Don't mess with my money!" to teammates who didn't hustle. The ex-Marine exuded authority; his face was likened to a clenched fist. Stengel platooned Bauer for much of his Yankee career, but he still emerged as a solid hitter with both power and speed. He started three straight All-Star games (1952–54) and hit 26 HR in 1956 and 18 first-inning leadoff HR in his career. He hit a three-run triple in the finale of the 1951 WS, and secured the 4–3 win over the Giants with a sliding catch in right field as the would-be tying run was streaking home. From 1956 to 1958 he set a WS record with a 17-game hitting streak. Bauer was eventually traded to the A's in the deal that brought Roger Maris to New York. He managed the Orioles to the 1966 World Championship. /(MG)

Russ Bauers — 1914– . RHP 1936–41, 46, 50 **Pirates**, Cubs, Browns 599 ip, 31–30, 3.53

Bauers led Pittsburgh starters in winning percentage (.684, 13–6) and ERA (2.88) as a rookie in 1937. He lost a one-hitter to Boston in 1938. He saw little major league action after a sore arm in 1939. /(ME)

Joe Bauman — 1922– . 1B *Minor League*.

Bauman was a minor league slugger who batted .337 and collected 337 home runs and 1057 RBI in 1019 games. First signed by the Braves, he lost four years to WWII, and held out from 1949–51. He won four HR titles in the nine years he played, but only once played above Class A. After hitting 103 HR for

Artesia in 1952–53, he won the Longhorn League (Class C) triple crown by batting .400 with 72 HR and 224 RBI for the Roswell Rockets in 1954. The 72 HR and .916 slugging average he achieved that season are all-time pro records. /(MC)

Frank Baumann (The Beau) — 1933– . LHP 1955–65 Red Sox, **White Sox**, Cubs 797 ip, 45–38, 4.11
☛ Led League—era 60.

Touted early as "a Herb Score with control," the burly lefthander received a $90,000 signing bonus from the Red Sox in 1952 and Sox owner Tom Yawkey nicknamed him "The Beau." His only good year was 1960, when he went 13–6 for the White Sox with an AL-best 2.67 ERA. /(JCA)

George Baumgardner — 1891–1970. RHP 1912–16 **Browns** 686 ip, 36–48, 3.22

Naive to a fault, Baumgardner never got paid what he was worth. The Browns paid the "rube" West Virginian in dollar bills to make his salary seem more substantial. His best record came when he was 14–13 in 1914 and led the AL in relief wins (6) and losses (5). /(WB)

Ross Baumgarten — 1955– . LHP 1978–82 **White Sox**, Pirates 496 ip, 22–36, 3.99

Baumgarten threw a shutout in his second ML start and authored two one-hitters (both against California, on 5/25/79 and 7/2/80). A series of ailments weakened his shoulder. His arm gone, he lost his last ten decisions. /(JCA)

Stan Baumgartner — 1894–1955. LHP 1914–16, 21–22, 24–26 Phillies, **A's** 506 ip, 27–21, 3.70

Baumgartner played on the University of Chicago's 1913–14 Big Ten football, baseball, and basketball champions; he later coached those three sports at the University of Delaware. In his only major league season of note, he went 13–6 for the 1924 Athletics. For 20 years he was a sportswriter for the Philadelphia *Inquirer*. /(NLM)

Frankie Baumholtz — 1918– . OF 1947–49, 51–57 Reds, **Cubs**, Phillies 1019 g, .290, 25 hr, 272 rbi

Baumholtz's career had a promising start when he finished fifth in the inaugural 1947 Rookie of the Year voting. He hit .283 with 32 doubles and a career-high 96 runs scored as the Reds' everyday right fielder and had 18 assists. His average rose to .296 in 1948, but his production fell off in all other categories. He was traded to the Cubs with Hank Sauer for Harry Walker and Peanuts Lowery in

1949 while batting .235. Baumholtz hit just .226 for Chicago and was out of the league the next year.

He made it back as the Cubs' centerfielder in 1951, and although he never equaled the production of his rookie season, he hit for a good average. His highest-average year, 1952, was interrupted by a broken hand; he finished at .325 while mostly playing right field. Back in centerfield in 1953, he had the arduous responsibility of covering most of the outfield between sluggardly sluggers Sauer and Ralph Kiner. Years later, Kiner would remember that all the centerfielder ever heard was, "You take it!"

In 1954 Baumholtz played part-time and began pinch hitting, although with little success (2-for-17). He grew into the role in 1954, leading the league in pinch hits (15-for-37). Sold to the Phillies after the season, he again led in pinch hits (14-for-52) in 1956, and played only 15 games in the outfield. He was out of the majors after only two at-bats in 1957.

Before breaking into the majors, Baumholtz played professional basketball for two seasons in the NBL and the BAA. /(JFC)

Ed Bauta — 1935– . RHP 1960–64 **Cardinals**, Mets 149 ip, 6–6, 4.35

The Pacific Coast League's top reliever in 1961 with Portland, this righthanded Cuban was the losing pitcher in the first game ever played at Shea Stadium, April 17, 1964, as the Mets bowed to Pittsburgh, 4–3. /(RTM)

Jose Bautista — 1964– . RHP 1988– **Orioles** 250 ip, 9–19, 4.61

After seven years in the Mets system, this Dominican was drafted by the Orioles and immediately moved into their rotation in 1988, posting a 6–15, 4.30 record. /(JFC)

Harry Bay (Deerfoot) — 1878–1952. OF 1901–08 Reds, **Indians** 673 g, .277, 5 hr, 141 rbi

Bay was the American League stolen base champion in 1903 with 45. He had 169 career stolen bases and remains among Cleveland's all-time leaders. He set a since-tied major league record with 12 outfield putouts in a July 19, 1904 game against Boston (12 innings). /(ME)

Don Baylor (Groove) — 1949– . DH-OF-1B 1970–88 Orioles, A's, **Angels**, Yankees, Red Sox, Twins 2292 g, .260, 338 hr, 1276 rbi. *7 LCS, 28 g, .271, 3 hr, 17 rbi. 3 WS, 10 g, .280, 1 hr, 4 rbi*
☛ Most Valuable Player—79. Led League—rbi 79. All-Star—79.

Don Baylor, batting

A durable power hitter, Don Baylor will probably be most noted as the major league record holder for being hit by a pitch. He was hit a major league-high 28 times in 1987, setting the career record (244) when plunked by Rick Rhoden on June 28. He was fast in the first half of his career, and retired with 285 stolen bases to go with his 338 HR.

Baylor was *TSN* Minor League Player of the Year in 1970. Part of the 1976 Reggie Jackson trade, Baylor stole a career-high 52 bases in his first season with Oakland, then signed with California as a free agent. He peaked in his 1979 MVP season, hitting .296 with 36 HR and leading the league with 139 RBI and 120 runs scored. After three successful but unhappy seasons in New York, he went to the Red Sox. He was voted the AL's top DH in 1985 and 1986, reaching the 2,000-hit plateau the latter year. Baylor received the Roberto Clemente Award for humanitarian service in 1985.

Known for his leadership, he played on seven first-place teams, and played in the World Series with three different teams in his last three seasons. /(ME)

Bill Bayne (Beverly) — 1899–1981. LHP 1919–24, 28–30 **Browns**, Indians, Red Sox 661 ip, 31–32, 4.82

Bayne had such a wicked curveball that it once led Ty Cobb to pinch-hit a righthanded hitter for himself. Bayne's best season was with the Browns in 1921, when he was 11–5, but he slumped to 4–5 during St. Louis's pennant run in 1922. He was a lifetime .290 hitter. /(WB)

Belve Bean [Beveric Benton] (Bill) — 1905–1988. RHP 1930–31, 33–35 **Indians**, Senators 235 ip, 11–7, 5.32

Used in relief and given a few starts by Cleveland, Bean was never able to establish himself. He won 17 of his last 20 decisions at Toledo (American Association) in 1932 to earn another shot. /(ME)

Dave Beard — 1959– . RHP 1980–85 **A's**, Mariners, Cubs 270 ip, 19–18, 4.69. *1 LCS, 0.2 ip, 0–0, 40.50*

Beard had only 21 innings of ML experience when he saved the deciding game of the 1981 AL Western Division playoff against the Royals. In the LCS, he retired two batters and surrendered a three-run home run to the Yankees' Lou Piniella. Beard led Oakland in saves in 1982 and 1983 with 11 and 10, then was traded to Seattle with catcher Bob Kearney for ace reliever Bill Caudill. He had a 5.80 ERA in 43 appearances for the Mariners in 1984, while Caudill saved 36 games for Oakland. /(SCL)

Mike Beard — 1950– . LHP 1974–77 Braves 118 ip, 4–2, 3.74

Beard's unhappiness at being farmed out to Richmond (International League) in 1976 sealed his fate with Atlanta manager Dave Bristol. "People who play baseball for a living never do grow up," groused Beard, a guitar-playing reliever. /(PB)

Gene Bearden (The Arkansas Traveler) — 1920– . LHP 1947–53 **Indians**, Senators, Tigers, Browns, White Sox 788 ip, 45–38, 3.96. 20 wins: 48 *1 WS, 11 ip, 1–0, 0.00*
☛ *Led League—era 48.*

The knuckleballer was a rookie sensation in 1948 when he went 20–7 and led the AL with a 2.43 ERA. His 20th win was the Indians' pennant-deciding playoff versus Boston. In the WS, he had a win and a save without giving up a run. He never again approached his rookie record. He winked at training rules, suffered a lingering thigh injury in 1949, and batters learned to lay off his nasty knuckler. /(JCA)

Gary Beare — 1952– . RHP 1976–77 **Brewers** 100 ip, 5–6, 5.13

A hard-luck hurler cut down by a sore arm in 1978, Beare got a 17-run explosion from the Brewers to beat the Indians in 1976. /(MC)

Larry Bearnarth — 1941– . RHP 1963–66, 71 **Mets**, Brewers 323 ip, 13–21, 4.13

Sinker-baller Bearnarth led the 1963 Mets with 58 appearances. Casey Stengel referred to the 6'2" 205-lb intellectual as "Big Ben." In the 1980s he was the Expo pitching coach. /(KT)

Jim Beattie — 1954– . RHP 1978–86 Yankees, **Mariners** 1149 ip, 52–87, 4.17. *1 LCS, 5 ip, 1–0, 1.69. 1 WS, 9 ip, 1–0, 2.00*

Beattie was a college basketball star at Dartmouth. He pitched brilliantly for the Yankees in the 1978 LCS and World Series, but the next season was on owner George Steinbrenner's shuttle to Triple-A, before being traded to Seattle as part of the deal for Ruppert Jones. In seven seasons with the Mariners, Beattie was a workhorse starter, setting club records (subsequently broken) for walks, runs, and earned runs allowed in a season. In 1982, Beattie set a club record for a starter by pitching 19 consecutive scoreless innings. On September 27, 1983, Beattie threw the first one-hitter in Mariners history, the only baserunner being the Royals' U.L. Washington, who singled in the third inning. He also surrendered Carl Yastrezemski's 3,000th hit. /(TF)

Jim Beauchamp — 1939– . 1B-OF 1963–65, 67–73 **Cardinals**, Astros, Braves, Reds, Mets 393 g, .231, 14 hr, 90 rbi. *1 WS, 4 g, .000*

In the minors, Beauchamp proved a good defensive outfielder and basestealer while hitting 186 home runs. The majority of his big league appearances came as a pinch hitter, and he collected 46 hits that way. His son, James, Jr., signed with Toronto in 1982. /(FJO)

Ginger Beaumont [Clarence] — 1876–1956. OF 1899–1910 **Pirates**, Braves, Cubs 1444 g, .311, 38 hr, 617 rbi. *2 WS, 11 g, .250*
☛ *Led League—ba 02.*

The first player ever to bat in a World Series was an outstanding leadoff hitter. Beaumont's chunky build (5'8", 190 lb) belied blazing speed that helped him beat out many infield hits. On July 22, 1899, at the Pirates' Exposition Park, he got six infield hits in six at-bats and scored six runs. Nicknamed for a shock of red hair, Beaumont batted .352 as a rookie and led the NL with .357 in 1902, and scored 100 or more runs each season from 1900 to 1903, with a league-high 137 in '03. /(ME)

Johnny Beazley (Beaz, Two-game Johnny) — 1918– . RHP 1941–42, 46–49 **Cardinals**, Braves 374 ip, 31–12, 3.01. *2 WS, 19 ip, 2–0, 2.37*

Beazley had a marvelous season in 1942, going 21–6 with a 2.13 ERA and finishing second in the NL in wins, winning percentage, and ERA. He capped it off with two wins in the Cardinals' World Series upset of the Yankees. While serving in the Air Force during WWII, the quiet Tennessean failed to warm up properly for an exhibition against his old teammates and severely hurt his arm. He tried in vain to regain his form after coming out of the service. /(WB)

Boom-Boom Beck [Walter William] — 1904–1987. RHP 1924, 27–28, 33–34, 39–45 Browns, Dodgers, **Phillies**, Tigers, Reds, Pirates 1034 ip, 38–69, 4.30

Boom-Boom Beck supposedly earned his nickname while pitching for Casey Stengel's Dodgers in 1934. Becoming upset when Stengel came out to remove him when the Dodgers still had a lead, Beck angrily threw the ball into right field at the old Baker Bowl in Philadelphia. The ball hit the tin-plated wall and caromed to center. The "boom-boom" of the rebound roused centerfielder Hack Wilson, who was relaxing during the pitching change and thought the game had resumed. Wilson pursued the ball and fired a strike back to the infield.

As an after-dinner speaker, the loquacious Beck later left audiences shaking their heads as he lamented that America was in danger of giving baseball back to the Indians. Pitching for atrocious teams but performing none too well himself, he had only two winning records in 12 major league seasons, a 1–0 mark in six games in 1927 and an 8–5 record split between the Reds and the Pirates in the war-weakened 1945 season, his last. He won his last game while coaching at Toledo (American Association) in 1951, pitching a 10–2 win over Minneapolis at the age of 46 to bring his total professional mark to an even 236–236. /(WB)

Clyde Beck (Jersey) — 1902– . 3B-2B-SS 1926–31 **Cubs**, Reds 468 g, .232, 12 hr, 162 rbi

When the Cubs hit four homers in the seventh inning on May 12, 1930, they were only the second team in history to accomplish the feat; utility man Beck hit the record-tying HR. He hit a career-high six HR in that rabbit-ball season but batted only .213, 90 points below the league average. /(WOR)

Fred Beck — 1886–1962. 1B-OF 1909–11, 14–15 Braves, Reds, Phillies, **Chicago (FL)** 635 g, .252, 34 hr, 251 rbi
☛ *Led League—hr 10.*

In 1910, Beck hit ten homers to tie for the NL lead. After dropping back to the minors, he returned as the Chicago Whales' (Federal League) regular first baseman for 1914–15. His long minor-league career ended in 1928. /(JK)

Beals Becker — 1886–1943. OF 1908–15 Pirates, Braves, Giants, Reds, **Phillies** 876 g, .276, 45 hr, 292 rbi. *3 WS, 7 g, .263*

Becker was a fair fielder and a lefthanded batter who had trouble with southpaw pitching. His top year was 1914, when he hit .325 with 9 homers and 66 RBI for the Phillies. He played better on the road than at home, reportedly because he had "rabbit ears" and reacted to hometown heckling. /(NLM)

Glenn Beckert (Bruno) — 1940– . 2B-3B 1965–75 **Cubs**, Padres 1320 g, .283, 22 hr, 360 rbi
☛ *All-Star—69–72. Gold Glove—68.*

The Cubs' regular second baseman for nine years, Beckert was a reliable contact hitter who hit second in the batting order for most of his career. He was the most difficult batter to strike out in the NL five times (in 1968 he whiffed only 20 times in 643 at-bats), and he walked only slightly more often, but nonetheless led the NL in runs scored with 98 in '68. Although never considered a power hitter, he had 20 or more doubles in six seasons.

Beckert was a minor league shortstop, but switched to second base after Ken Hubbs died. He won the Cubs' second-base job in 1965 and adjusted quickly to his new position, leading the NL in assists while finishing second in double plays and total chances per game. For his entire Cub career, he played alongside shortstop Don Kessinger (who often led off in front of Beckert), giving the Cubs an outstanding defensive keystone combo. Throughout Beckert's career, he was overshadowed by two of the greatest second basemen in baseball history. When he first came up, Bill Mazeroski was regularly leading the league in most defensive categories; after Maz faded, Joe Morgan grabbed the second-base spotlight. Beckert was second in the NL in assists from 1966 to 1969, and in 1971 he won a Gold Glove. He received his nickname, Bruno (after the wrestler Bruno Sammartino), from teammate Paul Popovich in the minor leagues, because Beckert frequently knocked down other infielders in pursuit of pop-ups.

Although he hit only .239 as a rookie, Beckert quickly improved and went on to hit .280 or better the next six seasons, peaking at .342 in 1971. On June 3, 1971, he drove in Ken Holtzman with the only run of the game in Holtzman's no-hitter against the Reds.

After his skills were eroded by knee and heel injuries over the next two seasons, Beckert was traded to the Padres for outfielder Jerry Morales. In San Diego, Beckert was a part-time infielder and pinch hitter limited again by ankle and finger injuries. /(SH)

Jake Beckley (Eagle Eye) — 1867–1918. 1B 1888–1907 **Pirates**, Pittsburgh (PL), Giants, Reds, Cardinals 2386 g, .308, 88 hr, 1575 rbi
☛ *Hall of Fame—1971.*

The lefthanded Beckley is first all-time in games played at first base. The powerful 5'10" 200-lb slugger hit .300 or better 13 times, including six straight years, 1899–1904. He had 2930 hits lifetime, and his 244 triples rank fourth on the career list. He scored 100 runs five times in the 1890s, and stole 315 bases in his career. On September 26, 1897 he hit three homers against the Cardinals while playing for the Reds. When on a hitting spree, his blood-curdling cry of "Chickazoola" rattled pitchers.

Jake Beckley

Beckley also won fame with his glove. His 25,000 chances and 23,696 putouts rank first all-time among first basemen. However, he had a notorious scatter-gun arm, and runners always took the extra base on him. He also had a unique hidden-ball trick: He hid the ball under one corner of the base. /(WB)

Bill Beckmann — 1907– . RHP 1939–42 **A's**, Cardinals 440 ip, 21–25, 4.79

Beckman first made the majors at age 32 in 1939 and enjoyed his best season the next year, going 8–4 with the A's. He was sent down to Rochester early in 1942, but earned a September call-up by the Cardinals. The Cards won the pennant by two games, one of which was Beckmann's clutch win in his last ML appearance. /(MC)

Joe Beckwith — 1955– . RHP 1979–80, 82–86 **Dodgers**, Royals 422 ip, 18–19, 3.54. *1 LCS, 2 ip, 0–0, 0.00. 1 WS, 2 ip, 0–0, 0.00.*

A freak spring-training eye injury caused Beckwith to sit out 1981. The situation was remedied by an equally unusual operation, which reduced the vision of his good eye to that of his bad eye. Beckwith was almost exclusively a reliever, and in 1984 he won a career-high eight games from the Royals' bullpen. /(TG)

John Beckwith (The Black Bomber) — 1902–1956. SS-3B-C-0F-MGR Negro Leagues 1919–38 Chicago Giants, Chicago American Giants, Baltimore Black Sox, Homestead Grays, Harrisburg Giants, New York Lincoln Giants, Bacharach Giants, New York Black Yankees, Newark Dodgers, Brooklyn Royal Giants 452 g, .348, 71 hr (inc.)
☛ *Led League—hr 30–31(NAL).*

Beckwith was a 230-lb righthanded slugger who smashed some of the longest and most memorable home runs in Negro League baseball during the 1920s and early 1930s. A pull hitter who swung a huge 38" bat, he hit against a severe fielder shift that did little to curtail his effectiveness. In 1921, as a 19-year-old rookie with the Chicago Giants, he became the first player, white or black, to hit a ball over the laundry roof behind Cincinnati's Crosley Field. His longest blast, according to Hosely Lee, who pitched against Beckwith in the Eastern Colored League, came at Washington's Griffith Stadium, which had the longest leftfield fence in the majors at the time. Beckwith's home run hit an advertising sign, approximately 460' from home plate and 40' above the ground, behind the leftfield bleachers. Negro

League great Ted Radcliffe said of Beckwith, "Nobody hit the ball any farther than him—Josh Gibson or nobody else."

Beckwith played several positions, yet, despite his great size, appeared most frequently at shortstop. The core of his career spanned 1921–31, for which time only partial statistics are available. Only twice during those years did he hit less than .322, but though he topped the .360 mark six times, he never won a batting title. He finished second three times—twice to Hall of Famer Oscar Charleston, and once to Chino Smith. In 1925, he hit .419 to Charleston's .430. He won two HR crowns, with nine in 1930 and seven in 1931, but lost two others to Charleston by one HR. He batted .398 as a rookie in 1921, and in 1924 batted .417 for the Baltimore Black Sox of the Eastern Colored League, hitting 40 HR against league and non-league competition. In 1927, he hit 12 HR in league competition, but reportedly hit an astounding 72 for the whole year. In 1930, with the N.Y. Lincoln Giants, he is said to have batted .546, including a documented .494 (40-for-81) in 20 league games.

Beckwith was temperamental, and had the reputation of being somewhat lazy and mean. He once punched out teammate Bill Holland, a pitcher, who had thrown his glove when Beckwith's fielding error cost him a game. Because of his fiery disposition, he was traded often. In his last appearance documented by a newspaper boxscore (1934), he went 1-for-3 against Hall of Famer Dizzy Dean. He played a handful of games from 1932 to 1934, and supposedly finished his career in 1938 with the Brooklyn Royal Giants, though no records of his last four years exist. /(JM)

Julio Becquer — 1931- . 1B 1955, 1957–61, 1963 **Senators**, Angels, Twins 488 g, .244, 12 hr, 114 rbi

Becquer had 63 career pinch hits and was the AL's top pinch hitter in 1957 and '59. He stole three bases for the 1957 Senators, a team which stole only 13. /(FK)

Hugh Bedient — 1889–1965. RHP 1912–15 **Red Sox**, Buffalo (FL) 937 ip, 58–53, 3.08. 20 wins: 12 *1 WS, 18 ip, 1–0, 0.50*

Bedient won 20 games as a Red Sox rookie in 1912 and another in the WS when he outpitched Christy Mathewson 2–1 in the fifth game. He also pitched the first seven innings of the final game, won by the Red Sox in the tenth. /(JK)

Steve Bedrosian (Bedrock) — 1957- . RHP 1981- **Braves**, Phillies, Giants 910 ip, 56–61, 3.23. *2 LCS, 4 ip, 0–0, 6.23. 1 WS, 3 ip, 0–0, 0.00*
☛ *Cy Young Award—87. All-Star—87.*

One of the NL's star relievers of the 1980s, Bedrosian was *TSN* NL Rookie Pitcher of the Year in 1982 and in 1987 won the NL Cy Young Award. He made only one relief appearance in four minor league seasons, and already had a hard slider and a good change of pace to go with his 96-mph fastball when he reached the ML. Encouraging him to throw as hard as possible, the Braves started him out in middle relief, and he led NL relievers with 123 strikeouts as a rookie, finishing with a 2.42 ERA and 11 saves. Bedrosian had continued success out of the bullpen in 1983–84, but in 1985 the Braves made him a starter. He didn't complete any of his 37 starts that year, and was 7–15. Before the 1986 season Bedrosian was traded to Philadelphia, where the Phillies made him their ace in the bullpen. He saved 29 games in 1986, and a ML-high 40 in 1987 to edge Rick Sutcliffe for the Cy Young Award. In 1988, he missed the first month of the season with walking pneumonia, but managed to save 28 of the Phillies' paltry 65 victories. In 1989 the Giants acquired Bedrosian for their successful pennant bid in exchange for three young prospects. /(SG)

Fred Beebe — 1880–1957. RHP 1906–11, 16 Cubs, **Cardinals**, Reds, Phillies, Indians 1294 ip, 63–84, 2.86
☛ *Led League—k 06.*

This workhorse led the NL in starts in 1909 while going 15–21 for the Cardinals. His rookie season was his best; he led the NL in strikeouts and was 16–10 overall, going 7–1 for the World Champion Cubs before being traded to St. Louis. /(WB)

Fred Beene — 1942- . RHP 1968–70, 72–75 Orioles, **Yankees**, Indians 288 ip, 12–7, 3.62

An excellent fielder and a fierce competitor, the 5'9" 155-lb Beene spent eight years in the Baltimore farm system. He was 6–0 with a 1.68 ERA with the 1973 Yankees. /(JCA)

Joe Beggs — 1910–1983. RHP 1938, 40–44, 46–48 Yankees, **Reds**, Giants 694 ip, 48–35, 2.96. *1 WS, 1 ip, 9.00*

Beggs failed as a starter with the Yankees in 1938 after a 21–4 record at Newark. Using his breaking ball and sinker, his strong relief pitching (12 wins, 7 saves) helped the 1940 Reds to the World Championship. /(JK)

Hank Behrman — 1921– . RHP 1946–49 **Dodgers**, Pirates, Giants 430 ip, 24–17, 4.40. *1 WS, 6 ip, 7.11*

The native Brooklynite went 11–5 his rookie season. Manager Burt Shotton said poor work habits kept Behrman from reaching his potential./(EGM)

Ollie Bejma [Aloysius Frank] (The Polish Falcon) — 1907– . 2B-SS 1934–36, 39 **Browns**, White Sox 316 g, .245, 14 hr, 117 rbi

The colorful 5'10" 115-lb infielder hit a home run in his first start that provided the winning margin over the Red Sox. In 1937, he was co-MVP of the American Association, just ahead of Ted Williams./(WB)

Mark Belanger (Blade) — 1944– . SS 1965–82 **Orioles**, Dodgers 2016 g, .228, 20 hr, 389 rbi. *6 LCS, 21 g, .200, 1 hr, 5 rbi. 4 WS, 22 g, .164, 2 rbi*
☛ *All-Star—76. Gold Glove—69, 71, 73–78.*

When the Orioles traded shortstop Luis Aparicio after the 1967 season, they replaced him with his roommate, Belanger. The slender "Blade" didn't relinquish the position until 1982. An eight-time Gold Glove winner, he played in 43 postseason games during a decade of strong Baltimore teams and holds several ALCS defensive records for shortstops. Seldom spectacular, Belanger rarely fielded a ball one-handed or sidearmed a throw, but he moved around short with sure-handed ease and grace. Although an unimpressive hitter, he had the distinction of swatting a home run in the first ALCS game played, versus Minnesota (10/4/69). That year was his best offensively, as he hit .287 with 50 RBI.

Granted free agency after 1981, Belanger signed with the Dodgers for his final season. A longtime player representative with Baltimore, he became a special assistant with the Major League Baseball Players' Association after retiring as a player./(JCA)

Wayne Belardi (Footsie) — 1930– . 1B 1950–51, 53–56 Dodgers, **Tigers** 263 g, .242, 28 hr, 74 rbi. *1 WS, 2 g, .000*

Belardi hit 11 homers in just 163 at-bats for the 1953 NL Champion Dodgers. After his trade to Detroit, "Footsie" had his most active season in 1954, hitting 11 HR in 99 games./(CC)

Tim Belcher — 1961– . RHP 1987– **Dodgers** 444 ip, 31–20, 2.82. *1 LCS, 15 ip, 2–0, 4.11. 9 WS ip, 1–0, 6.23*

Belcher began 1988 in the Dodger bullpen and earned a starting spot. His 12–6, 2.91 record helped the Dodgers to their storybook pennant, and he was named NL Rookie Pitcher of the Year by *TSN*. He was 3–0 in postseason play, but actually pitched rather poorly. In 1989 he led the NL with eight shutouts while going 15–12, 2.82, but when not pitching a shutout his ERA was 4.10.

Belcher was the center of controversy before he ever pitched in pro ball. Drafted by the Yankees in the January 1984 supplemental phase, he was taken by Oakland from the compensation pool after Baltimore signed Type A free agent Tom Underwood. The Yankees had not had a chance to protect him. The incident pointed up the inadequacy of the compensation system, which was abandoned soon thereafter. The Dodgers acquired Belcher in return for Rick Honeycutt./(SFS)

Bo Belinsky [Robert] — 1936– . LHP 1962–67, 69–70 **Angels**, Phillies, Astros, Pirates, Reds 666 ip, 28–51, 4.10

One of the most colorful players of the 1960s, the pool-hustling playboy was picked up from the Orioles organization by the Angels in the 1961 expansion draft. Undefeated in his first three ML starts, he pitched the first big-league no-hitter on the West Coast against the Orioles on May 5, 1962. Acting appearances in several TV shows, dates with Hollywood starlets Ann-Margaret, Connie Stevens, and Tina Louise, and a much-publicized romance with actress Mamie Van Doren helped keep Belinsky in the spotlight even after his pitching deteriorated./(RTM)

Beau Bell [Roy Chester] — 1907–1977. OF-1B 1935–41 **Browns**, Tigers, Indians 767 g, .297, 46 hr, 437 rbi
☛ *All-Star—37.*

For two seasons, 1936 and '37, Bell was one of the best righthanded hitters in the game. In 1936 he hit .344 with 123 RBI and 100 runs scored for the Browns, and he led the AL in hits (218) and doubles (51) in 1937 while hitting .340 with 117 RBI. Bell was a graduate of Texas A&M College, where he studied to be a teacher. When he batted .250 for the Browns in 1935, they farmed him out, calling him the "$17,500 Lemon." Following the advice of manager Rogers Hornsby, whose style Bell adopted, he raised his average nearly 100 points the next season. Alcohol problems hastened his decline, and he was out of the majors by 1942. He coached at the University of Texas for many years./(WB)

Buddy Bell [David Gus] — 1951– . 3B-OF-SS 1972–89 **Indians**, Rangers, Reds, Astros 2405 g, .279, 201 hr, 1106 rbi

☛ *All-Star—73, 80–82, 84. Gold Glove—79–84.*

Buddy and his father Gus hold the all-time father-son record for hits (4,337) and combined for 407 HR, tied for the second-best father-son total. A surehanded third baseman with enough range to play shortstop when needed, Buddy won six straight Gold Gloves and led AL third basemen five times in total chances per game, three times each in putouts and assists, and twice each in double plays and fielding.

Breaking in with the Indians in 1972 when Graig Nettles had third base locked up, Bell played outfield most of the season and was named to the *Baseball Digest* Rookie All-Star Team. Nettles was traded in the off-season, and in 1973 Bell showed himself to be among the league's best third base-

Buddy Bell with the Indians

man, leading in putouts and double plays. The Indians traded Bell to Texas in December 1978 for Toby Harrah. Bell responded with his best year to that point, hitting .299 with 18 HR, 101 RBI, and a league-leading 16 game-winning RBI, and won his first Gold Glove. The line-drive hitter eventually became the all-time Texas leader in doubles, RBI, extra-base hits, and total bases. A clutch hitter and smart baserunner, he also had a good batting eye.

A lackluster start in 1985, and the presence of prospect Steve Buechele, prompted Bell's trade to the Reds on July 19. The Cincinnati native filled a long-standing void at third. By joining the Reds, Bell gave the club five active members of the 2,000-hit club (with Pete Rose, Tony Perez, Dave Concepcion, and Cesar Cedeno). After weathering a lengthy adjustment to NL pitching and rumors that he was finished, Bell starred for the Reds in 1986 and '87, leading NL third basemen in fielding in '87. When he started 1988 on the disabled list, he lost his job to star rookie Chris Sabo, and was traded to the Astros in June. He returned to the Rangers as a free agent after the season and was projected as their DH, but injuries and what was becoming an annual first-half slump prompted him to retire./(ME)

Cool Papa Bell [James] — 1903– . OF Negro Leagues 1922–50 St. Louis Stars, Pittsburgh Crawfords, Homestead Grays, Kansas City Monarchs Statistics incomplete

☛ *Hall of Fame—1972.*

Bell was offered a chance to play for the Browns in 1951, but he turned it down; he was nearly 48 years old. He earned his nickname for his demeanor under pressure while pitching for the St. Louis Stars as a 19-year-old in 1922. A sterling fielder and an outstanding batter, what made Bell stand out more than anything else was his uncanny speed. Two exaggerated stories demonstrate the effect it had on his contemporaries. Satchel Paige often regaled audiences with the story that when he and Bell roomed together, Bell was so fast that he could turn out the light and be in bed before the room got dark. In truth, he did it one night, but only because there was a short in the wires. Another story has him hitting a ball up the middle and being struck by it as he slid into second base.

A verified story is that during an inter-racial all-star exhibition game on the West Coast, Paige laid down a bunt with Bell on first base. As catcher Roy Partee of the Indians set to throw to first, Bell brushed by him to score. By his own count, Bell once stole 175 bases in a 200-game season. The

Cool Papa Bell

scanty statistics of the Negro Leagues credit him with several years over .400.

There is little doubt that Bell could have starred in the major leagues had there been no color ban during his prime. An unselfish man off the field and on, in 1946 (Jackie Robinson's first year in white organized baseball), Bell deliberately forfeited the batting title to Monte Irvin to enhance Irvin's chance to follow Robinson to the majors. While

coaching and playing with the Monarchs, Bell demonstrated to the young Robinson that he would never make it with his weak arm at shortstop. Bell, in his forties, beat out everything hit to Robinson's right. /(WB)

Eric Bell — 1963– . LHP 1985–87 **Orioles** 194 ip, 11–15, 5.38

Bell was one of only two pitchers to last the entire 1987 season on the Orioles' roster (Mike Boddicker was the other), and he tied Boddicker for the club lead in wins with 10. Elbow surgery sidelined him for the entire 1988 season and left his career in jeopardy. /(ME)

Gary Bell (Ding Dong) — 1936– . RHP 1958–69 **Indians**, Red Sox, Pilots, White Sox 2015 ip, 121–117, 3.68. *1 WS, 5 ip, 0–1, 5.06*
☛ *All-Star—60, 66, 68.*

Bell used a blazing fastball to win 28 games in his first two ML seasons. He later learned to control his curve and developed a slider. In nine years at Cleveland he went through seven managers, who shifted him back and forth between starting and relieving. In 1962 he led the AL with nine relief victories, but he hated relieving, calling it a "rotten, thankless job." Starters received more money and prestige, and the wisecracking Bell preferred four days off to joke around on the bench. After saving 17 in 1965, he returned to starting and won 14 in 1966. Traded to the Red Sox early in 1967, he won 12 during their pennant drive. He had a loss and a save in the WS.

"Ding Dong" was drafted by the expansion Pilots in 1969 and won Seattle's home opener. As author Jim Bouton's roommate, he was prominently mentioned in *Ball Four.* /(JCA)

George Bell — 1959– . OF 1981, 83– **Blue Jays** 1039 g, .289, 181 hr, 654 rbi. *2 LCS, 12 g, .271, 1 hr, 3 rbi*
☛ *Most Valuable Player—87. Led League—rbi 87. All-Star—87.*

From 1984, when he became a regular in the Blue Jay lineup, through 1988, Bell averaged 31 home runs and 104 RBI per season to establish himself as one of the American League's dominant power hitters. Drafted by Toronto from the Phillies' organization at the end of 1980, he spent the next four seasons either on the Toronto bench or with the Blue Jays' Triple-A team at Syracuse. A torrid spring training served as a springboard for his 1984 season of 26 homers, 87 RBI, and a new team record of 69 extra-base hits, and established him as a regular, with Lloyd Moseby and Jesse Barfield, in perhaps baseball's finest outfield of the 1980s. His HR, RBI, and extra-base-hit totals climbed in each of his next three seasons. In August 1985 he clubbed homers in a Blue Jay-record four consecutive games. Two of the homers cleared the roof at Comiskey Park, and another landed in the centerfield bleachers. His high point as a slugger came in 1987 as he set team records with 47 home runs, 134 RBI (which led the AL), 16 game-winning RBI, 83 extra-base hits, 369 total bases, and a .605 slugging average.

Bell's selection as the 1987 American League MVP generated quite a bit of controversy in light of his poor performance in two crucial series at the end of the 1987 campaign against the Tigers, who defeated Toronto on the final day of the season to win the division. No stranger to discord, the hot-tempered native of San Pedro de Macoris in the Dominican Republic had incurred the hatred of Boston fans by directing a karate kick at Red Sox pitcher Bruce Kison, who seemed to be throwing at Blue Jay batters. His general surliness, lackadaisical defensive play, and team-record outfield errors incurred the wrath of Toronto management and fans, and prompted manager Jimy Williams's 1988 spring-training announcement that Bell would be moved to DH in order to improve team defense and save his knees. Bell bristled, then hit three home runs on Opening Day (the first player ever to do so). Nevertheless, a bitter, season-long feud with Williams ensued and played a decisive role in the downfall of the 1988 team. /(TF)

George Bell (Farmer) — 1874–1941. RHP 1907–11 **Dodgers** 1086 ip, 43–79, 2.85

Bell made his ML debut as a 32-year-old rookie, but was given little support by his team. In 1910 he led the NL in losses with 27 while winning only 10, yet posted an excellent 2.64 ERA. Nearly 40% of his wins came on 17 shutouts. /(TG)

Gus Bell [David Russell] — 1928– . OF 1950–64 Pirates, **Reds**, Mets, Braves 1741 g, .281, 206 hr, 942 rbi. *1 WS, 3 g, .000*
☛ *All-Star—53–54, 56–57.*

David Bell's parents so admired catcher Gus Mancuso they nicknamed their son Gus, but instead of a catcher, he became a power-hitting outfielder. Bell was hitting .400 at Indianapolis when he was called up to the Pirates in 1950, joining Ralph Kiner in the

Bucs' outfield. After two strong seasons, he spent part of 1952 back in the minors because of a dispute with the Pirate front office; he had wanted his family to travel with him, including his son Buddy, later an outstanding ML third baseman.

Traded to Cincinnati, Bell hit a career-high 30 homers in 1953. He had his best years with the Reds (1953–61), four times topping 100 RBI.

In the 1957 All-Star voting, Cincinnati fans sent in so many ballots they succeeded in having seven Reds named to the starting lineup. Commissioner Ford Frick removed Bell and Wally Post as starters, but Manager Walter Alston named Bell to the squad and he doubled in two runs in the seventh.

Selected by the Mets in the expansion draft, he collected the first Met hit, a single on April 11, 1962. /(RTM)

Hi Bell [Herman S] — 1897–1949. RHP 1924, 26–27, 29–30, 32–34 **Cardinals**, Giants 663 ip, 32–34, 3.69. *3 WS, 4 ip, 0–0, 4.50*

Bell was the last pitcher to start and win both games of a doubleheader. He did it for the Cardinals in 1924 and duplicated the feat for Rochester (International League) in 1928. He spent much of his career in relief and led the NL with eight saves in 1930, long before it was a statistic. /(WB)

Jay Bell — 1965– . SS-2B 1986– **Indians**, Pirates 194 g, .238, 7 hr, 65 rbi

Bell homered in his first big-league at-bat (9/29/86). He came to the majors as an error-prone shortstop coveted for his heavy hitting (17 HR in 362 at-bats for Buffalo, American Association, 1987) but proved to be an excellent fielder who just couldn't hit enough to keep his job.

Bell was the Twins' first-round pick in the June 1984 draft. He came to Cleveland as part of the package that sent Bert Blyleven to Minnesota. /(WOR)

Jerry Bell — 1947– . RHP 1971–74 **Brewers** 284 ip, 17–11, 3.27

Sinker-slider specialist Bell was 5–1 with a 1.65 ERA in 1972 and 9–9 in 1973, but a chronic back ailment shortened his career. /(JCA)

Kevin Bell — 1955– . 3B 1976–80, 82 **White Sox**, A's 297 g, .222, 13 hr, 64 rbi

Highly touted by White Sox manager Paul Richards, Kevin Bell proved a weak hitter and an average fielder. He hit an inside-the-park grand slam in

Royals Stadium on June 22, 1976 as the leftfielder was knocked unconscious in a collision with the wall. In June 1977 a knee injury ended his season, and he never won a regular job. /(RL)

Les Bell — 1901– . 3B 1923–31 **Cardinals**, Braves, Cubs 896 g, .290, 66 hr, 509 rbi. *1 WS, 7 g, .259, 1 hr, 6 rbi*

An early product of the Cardinals farm system, Bell led the American Association in BA in 1924 as a shortstop. Switched to third base, he helped the Cardinals win their first pennant in 1926 (.325, 17 HR, 100 RBI). With the Braves in 1928, he hit three homers and a triple in a single game. /(JK)

Rafael Belliard — 1961– . SS-2B 1982– **Pirates** 437 g, .219, 1 hr, 66 rbi

A fine-fielding shortstop, Belliard became Pittsburgh's starter midway through the 1986 season and hit a career-high .233. Returning to the Pirates in 1987 after being sent down midway through the season, he suffered a fractured left fibula, a recurrence of an injury he suffered twice in 1984. When Jose Lind slumped in 1989, Belliard won the second base job in the second half of the season. /(ME)

Harry Bemis — 1874–1947. C 1902–10 **Indians** 703 g, .255, 5 hr, 234 rbi

The 5'6" Bemis never hit higher than the .312 mark of his rookie 1902 season. In eight subsequent years with Cleveland, he shared catching duties as the lefthanded hitter. /(ME)

Johnny Bench — 1947– . C 1967–83 **Reds** 2158 g, .267, 389 hr, 1376 rbi. *6 LCS, 22 g, .253, 5 hr, 6 rbi. 4 WS, 23 g, .279, 5 hr, 14 rbi*
☛ *Rookie of the Year—68. Most Valuable Player—70, 72. Led League—hr 70, 72. Led League—rbi 70, 72, 74. All-Star—68–77, 80, 83. Gold Glove—68–77. Hall of Fame—1989.*

Considered by some the greatest catcher of all time, Bench got a "can't miss" tag when Peninsula of the Carolina League retired his uniform after he hammered 22 homers in 98 games as an 18-year-old in 1966. He spent the first four months of the 1967 season at Buffalo, then took over the Cincinnati catching job in August 1967. In spring training of 1968, Ted Williams autographed a baseball "To Johnny Bench, a Hall of Famer for sure." Bench met expectations quickly by catching a rookie-record 154 games that season, setting a record for catchers with 40 doubles, and becoming the first

catcher to win National League Rookie of the Year honors. He went on to become the National League's dominant catcher for nearly a decade and a half.

Bench batted either fourth or fifth for the Big Red Machine team that dominated the National League in the 1970s and won six division titles, four pennants, and two World Series. From 1970 to 1977, Cincinnati players won six of eight MVP awards; Bench won two of them. The first came in 1970 following his league-leading 45 home runs and 148 RBI, all-time records for catchers. After holding out and slumping somewhat in 1971, Bench rebounded in 1972 to win his second MVP award. That year, he had the hottest streak of his career, hitting seven homers in five straight games from May 30 through June 3, and he finished with 40 homers and 125 RBI, leading the league in both categories for the second time. He homered three times on July 26, 1970, en route to setting a record of 36 homers by July 31, and twice more had three-homer games, on May 9, 1973 and May 29, 1980. He won his third RBI crown in 1974, driving in 129 runs and leading the NL with 314 total bases.

Of partial Native American descent, Bench was named to the All-Star team in 13 consecutive seasons, and he faced fellow Native American catcher Bill Freehan in five of them. He batted .370 in All-Star competition, hitting homers in the 1969, 1971, and 1973 games and narrowly missing a second homer in 1969. His selection as an All-Star was based as much on his defensive abilities as his offensive skills. He won ten straight Gold Glove Awards and set a NL record by catching at least 100 games in each of his first 13 seasons. He established career records for putouts and chances. Blessed with exceptionally large hands, he was one of the first catchers after the Cubs' Randy Hundley to use a hinged mitt and a one-handed catching style. His throwing arm was unrivaled by catchers of his era.

Bench suffered his worst year as a regular in 1976 when he hit .234 with 16 homers, and some thought he was finished at the age of 29. But competing head-to-head in the World Series against Thurman Munson, the American League's best catcher, brought him alive. He outhit Munson .533 to .529 and won the Series MVP award. Bench recorded his last super season in 1977, hitting .275 with 31 home runs and 109 RBI.

Worn out by catching, Bench repeatedly requested a shift to another position, but the Reds lacked a suitable replacement, and were reluctant to

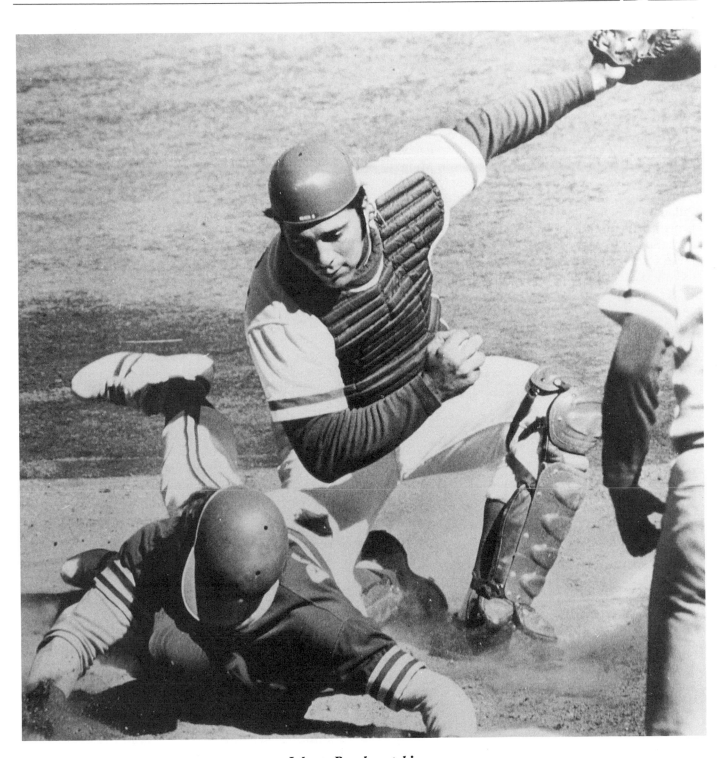

Johnny Bench, catching

accommodate him. They finally moved him to first base in 1981. On May 28, Bench fractured his ankle, with his batting average at .343. He missed two months and finished the season at .309, his only year over .293. Bench played primarily third base the next two seasons, but went back behind the plate for his last game at the end of 1983. He was elected to the Hall of Fame in his first year of eligibility and was inducted in 1989. /(MC/CR)

Chief Bender [Charles Albert] — 1883–1954. RHP
1903–17, 25 **A's**, Baltimore (FL), Phillies, White Sox
3017 ip, 210–127, 2.46. 20 wins: 10, 13 *5 WS, 85 ip, 6–4,
2.44*
☛ *Hall of Fame—53.*

Bender, for many years the only American Indian
elected to the Hall of Fame, boldly created his own
opportunities in a world still basically hostile toward
his race. His father was a German settler in Minnesota, his mother a Chippewa. He grew up on a
reservation, and was sent to a church-run school in
Philadelphia when he was eight. After being returned to his mother, he bolted the reservation at 13
to attend the Carlisle Indian School in Pennsylvania.

He accepted his Indian identity, stoically doffing
his cap to cheers for "The Chief," but signed

Chief Bender

autographs "Charley Bender." Being an Indian gave
him separate glamour among the sons of white
immigrants with whom he played, and small boys
whooped their admiration. But it was his pitching
skills that made him stand out.

Bender's career with the Athletics included two
seasons as league leader in winning percentage
(1910: 23–5; 1914: 17–3). He pitched a no-hitter
against Cleveland in 1910. In the 1905 World
Series, in which every game was a shutout, Bender
blanked the Giants 3–0 in Game Two, the only
game Connie Mack's club won. Christy Mathewson
dominated the Series with three shutouts, and Joe
McGinnity added his. Bender's 6–4 career WS
record included nine complete games, three coming
in 1911 when he twice came up against Mathewson,
and defeated him once. Bender jumped to the
outlaw Federal League for its final, 1915 season, and
experienced his most dismal record (4–16).

An all-around player, Bender appeared in several
games in the infield and outfield and pinch hit 29
times. He was an expert sign stealer, practicing his
art from the coaching box between starts. He steered
clear of temptations which wrecked others' careers,
such as that of the briefly phenomenal Louis Sockalexis, whose disastrous misadventures were used to
deny opportunity to other Native Americans. After
his playing career effectively ended with the Phillies
in 1917, Bender managed in the minors and
coached in the majors. He maintained a solid family
life in Philadelphia, based on values adopted while
living on a Quaker farm during his school boy
summers./(JK)

Bruce Benedict — 1955– . C 1978- **Braves** 982 g,
.242, 18 hr, 260 rbi. *1 LCS, 3 g, .250*
☛ *All-Star—81, 83.*

Benedict was Atlanta's starting catcher from 1980 to
1983, and made the NL All-Star team twice, but a
weak bat relegated him to backup status thereafter.
In 1982 he led NL catchers in fielding percentage
and hit .389 down the stretch as Atlanta won the AL
West. His .242 average in 1988 was his best since
1983, when he hit a career-high .298, and in 1989
starting catcher Jody Davis's poor hitting gave
Benedict increased playing time./(ME)

Ray Benge (Silent Cal) — 1902– . RHP 1925–26,
28–36, 38 Indians, **Phillies**, Dodgers, Braves, Reds
1875 ip, 101–130, 4.52

Although he spent only one of his nine full major
league seasons with a first-division team, Benge won

ten or more games six times. He was not a strikeout pitcher, but on June 16, 1929, he tied what was then a Phillies record with 13 strikeouts in a 7–2 victory at Chicago. /(AL)

Benny Bengough — 1898–1968. C 1923–32 **Yankees**, Browns 411 g, .255, 0 hr, 108 rbi. *2 WS, 6 g, .176, 1 rbi*

Born in Liverpool, England, Bengough came close to being a Catholic priest. A bullpen catcher in Buffalo, his mother insisted that the manager use him in a game. In his first start, he threw out four Browns baserunners in an exhibition game.

Bengough became a regular on the same day Lou Gehrig replaced Wally Pipp in the lineup in 1925; it was Bengough's only season of more than 58 games. A talkative catcher behind the plate, he would get laughs and distract hitters by running his fingers through his "imaginary" hair. He later coached the Browns, Senators, Braves, and Phillies. /(WB)

Juan Beniquez — 1950– . OF 1971–72, 74–88 Red Sox, Rangers, Yankees, Mariners, **Angels**, Orioles, Royals, Blue Jays 1500 g, .274, 79 hr, 476 rbi. *2 LCS, 5 g, .250, 1 rbi. 1 WS, 3 g, .125, 1 rbi*
☛ *Gold Glove—77.*

Versatile and dependable off the bench, Beniquez fared best late in his career, batting .300 four straight years (1983–86) when he was used primarily against lefthanded pitchers. He was a shortstop in the minors, and set a modern ML record with six errors there in two consecutive games for Boston in 1972. The Red Sox converted him to an outfielder, and he won a Gold Glove with Texas in 1977. Beniquez played for eight different AL clubs, an all-time record. /(ME)

Stan Benjamin — 1914– . OF 1939–42, 45 **Phillies**, Indians 242 g, .229, 5 hr, 41 rbi

Benjamin joined the Phillies in September of 1939 after batting .323 with Chattanooga (Southern Association). His only season as a major-league regular was 1941, when he hit just .235. /(AL)

Bennett Park — Detroit Tigers 1901–11

Named for Tiger catcher Charlie Bennett, the field was originally laid over cobblestones. It was rebuilt as Navin Field (now Tiger Stadium) in 1912, with the playing field turned 90 degrees. /(SCL)

Charlie Bennett — 1854–1927. C 1878, 80–93 Milwaukee (NL), Worcester (NL), **Detroit (NL)**, Braves 1062 g, .256, 56 hr, 420 rbi

Bennett's 15-year career as a part-time catcher was ended when he lost both legs in a train accident. He had been a fan favorite in Detroit, where he played from 1881 to 1888, and when the Tigers became an entry in the new American League in 1901, their new ballpark was named Bennett Park in his honor. It remained Bennett Park until 1912, when it became the site of the present Tiger Stadium. /(JK)

Dennis Bennett — 1939– . LHP 1962–68 **Phillies**, Red Sox, Giants, Angels 863 ip, 43–47, 3.69

An auto accident in Puerto Rico while playing winter ball after the 1962 season set the rangy Bennett back, and a sore left shoulder, incurred during his second straight 1–0 shutout in mid-September 1964, may have cost the Phillies the pennant. When Bennett went down, manager Gene Mauch went essentially to a two-man rotation, wearing out Jim Bunning and Chris Short in the stretch run. In subsequent seasons he never recovered his earlier form. /(AL)

Herschel Bennett — 1896–1964. OF 1923–27 **Browns** 317 g, .276, 7 hr, 104 rbi

A capable substitute outfielder, Bennett was hitting .330 in 1924 when a broken arm cost him the rest of the season. A later injury caused by crashing into a wall in Philadelphia hastened the end of his career. The son of a farmer, Bennett later served as the Springfield, Missouri, Commissioner of Revenue. /(WB)

Gene Benson — 1913– . OF Negro Leagues 1934–48 Bacharach Giants, Pittsburgh Crawfords, Newark Eagles, **Philadelphia Stars** statistics not available
☛ *All-Star—40, 46.*

Benson, an all-around performer in the Negro National League, was a 5'8" 185-lb outfielder who displayed great range in center while popularizing the basket catch. He was a starter on the 1940 and 1946 Eastern all-star squads. While he spent most of his career with the Philadelphia Stars, he was one of the players added to the Washington Elite Giants roster for the 1936 Black Title series with the Pittsburgh Crawfords, which was aborted when each club attempted to replace three defecting regulars. He also played winter ball in Venezuela (1945) and Cuba (1947–48). Available data places his lifetime batting average at more than .300, with a peak mark of .370, fifth-best in the NNL in 1945, when he shared the league lead with 57 hits. /(MFK)

Jack Bentley — 1895–1969. LHP-1B 1913–16, 23–27 Senators, **Giants**, Phillies 287 g, .291, 7 hr, 71 rbi; 714 ip, 46–33, 4.01. *2 WS, 10 g, .417, 1 hr, 2 rbi; 24 ip, 1–3, 4.94*

In Game Five of the 1924 World Series, Bentley pitched the Giants to a 6–2 win over the Senators and hit a two-run homer off Walter Johnson. However, he lost Game Two 4–3 and dropped the finale in relief when Earl McNeely's double-play grounder hit a pebble and bounced over third baseman Fred Lindstrom's head in the 12th inning after two other fielding blunders.

Bentley was an excellent hitter; while going 13–8 in 1923, his first year with the Giants, he hit .427 in 89 at-bats, including a league-leading 10 pinch hits in 20 pinch at-bats. He had been acquired after going 41–5 in three years with the Baltimore Orioles of the International League. Also playing in the outfield and at first base, he had hit .349 for Baltimore in 1922 and was considered "the next Babe Ruth." After going 16–5 in 1924, weight problems took their toll in 1925, as he went 11–9 with a 5.04 ERA, and he was traded to the Phillies. Playing first base in Philadelphia, he hit .258 in 75 games, pitching only eight times, and returned to the Giants near the end of the season. /(SH)

Joe Benz (Blitzen, Butcher Boy) — 1886–1957. RHP 1911–19 **White Sox** 1358 ip, 76–75, 2.42

Benz had a good spitter and knuckleball. In 1914, though he led the AL with 19 losses, he had one incredible stretch. On May 31, despite three White Sox errors, he no-hit Cleveland 6–1. Then, on June 6, he two-hit the Highlanders in a nine-inning 1–1 tie halted by rain. Six days later, he squared off against Walter Johnson, whom Benz had boasted he could beat. He held the Senators hitless for eight innings while the White Sox scored twice off the Big Train. In the ninth, Eddie Ainsmith hit a bounder toward Buck Weaver at short, but third baseman Scotty Alcock stuck his glove out and deflected the ball into left field, spoiling Benz's no-hitter. Nonetheless, he notched one of two wins he would get in ten lifetime decisions against Johnson. /(RL)

Todd Benzinger — 1963– . OF-1B 1987– **Red Sox**, Reds 354 g, .254, 38 hr, 189 rbi. *1 LCS, 4 g, .091*

A baby-faced switch-hitter with moderate power, Benzinger overcame an injury-riddled minor league career to make the Red Sox as an outfielder. He switched to to first base when Dwight Evans was returned to right field. The Red Sox traded him to Cincinnati with Jeff Sellers for Nick Esasky and Rob

Murphy, and he became the Reds' starting first baseman in 1989. He had seven RBI in one game against Detroit on September 15, 1987. /(SCL)

Johnny Berardino — 1917– . 2B-SS-3B 1939–42, 46–52 **Browns**, Indians, Pirates 912 g, .249, 36 hr, 387 rbi

After three years as a regular at the beginning of his career, including a 16-HR season in 1940, Berardino became a utility man who was called a "one-man infield" for his versatility. He hit a grand slam off Yankee relief ace Johnny Murphy in 1940. After playing for the Browns, Indians, and Pirates by the end of 1950, Berardino appeared with all three teams, in the same order, over the last two years of his career.

Following his release by Pittsburgh in 1952, Berardino had to hock his 1948 Indians World Series ring. He had appeared in a few of the "Our Gang" comedies as a child actor, and Bill Veeck once insured the infielder's face as a publicity stunt. Berardino dropped the second "r" from his name and returned to acting, spending over 25 years as Dr. Steve Hardy on the popular soap opera "General Hospital." /(WB)

Lou Berberet — 1929– . C 1954–60 Yankees, Senators, Red Sox, **Tigers** 448 g, .230, 31 hr, 153 rbi

One of only four regular catchers to field 1.000 for a full season, the stocky Berberet was perfect in 77 games for Washington in 1957 and made only one error in 59 games the year before. /(RM)

Juan Berenguer (Pancho Villa) — 1954– . RHP 1978– Mets, Royals, Blue Jays, Tigers, Giants, **Twins** 963 ip, 55–49, 3.93. *1 LCS, 6 ip, 0–0, 1.50. 1 WS, 4 ip, 0–1, 10.38*

A perennial prospect with the Mets, Berenguer had winning seasons as a part-time starter for Detroit in 1983–84 but found a true home in Minnesota in 1987. As set-up man for closer Jeff Reardon, he went 8–1 (3.94) for the '87 World Champions and 8–4 (3.96) in 1988. Extremely wild as a youngster, he learned to harness his 90-plus-mph fastball, which he liked to throw inside, and added a forkball. His effectiveness was aided by his intimidating appearance and disposition. A mean-looking, husky Panamanian with long hair and a mustache, he was called "Pancho Villa" by his teammates. "If I pulled up in front of a restaurant," said Giants catcher Bob Brenly, "and he came out to park my car, I'd eat somewhere else." /(JCA)

Bruce Berenyi — 1954– . RHP 1980–86 **Reds**, Mets 782 ip, 44–55, 4.03

A promising flamethrower whose career was cut short by injury, Berenyi came up to the Reds at the end of 1980 after leading the American Association in both strikeouts and walks. In strike-shortened 1981, he led the NL with 77 walks. Lack of control combined with the Reds' weak offense in 1982 (last in the NL in runs scored) resulted in a league-leading 18 losses despite a 3.36 ERA.

The Mets, contending for the pennant in 1984, traded Jay Tibbs, Eddie Williams, and pitcher Matt Bullinger to acquire Berenyi that June. He was 9–6 the rest of the way with a 3.76 ERA, and got off to an even better start in 1985. However, on April 24 he tore his rotator cuff while trying to pitch after his arm had tightened up during a rain delay.

Berenyi revealed later that his shoulder had hurt most of his career, but he'd gotten used to it; the trouble had first cropped up in 1978. Out for the rest of the year, he was unable to come back in 1986, contributing only two wins in the Mets' World Championship season. His uncle was former Browns' ace Ned Garver. /(SH)

Moe Berg [Morris] — 1902–1972. C-SS 1923, 26–39 Dodgers, **White Sox**, Indians, Senators, Red Sox 662 g, .243, 6 hr, 206 rbi

Among the most scholarly professional athletes ever, Berg was an alumnus of three universities, lawyer, mathematician, linguist, and poor hitter, eliciting the comment: "He can speak 12 languages but can't hit in any of them." His ability to handle young pitchers and his reputation as a bullpen mystic kept him in the majors, where his roommates wondered at his sacrosanct clutter of books and newspapers stacked in dozens of piles. He professed the belief that his newspapers were "alive" and could "die" from being looked at by someone else. On occasion he braved snowstorms to purchase replacements for "deceased" newspapers.

Casey Stengel called him "the strangest man ever to play baseball" even before it was known he had served America as a spy. Some may have wondered why a third-string catcher like Berg went to Japan in the early 1930s with the likes of Ruth and Gehrig on an all-star traveling team. In fact, Berg was assigned to take espionage photos. During WWII, he became one of America's most important atomic spies, gathering vital information on top German scientists and even performing some missions that might have required assassination. He declined the Medal of Merit for his wartime service and never wrote his memoirs after being angered by an assigned co-author who confused him with "Moe" of the Three Stooges.

Berg fit the classic spy image: dark, heavy-featured, mysterious, sybaritic, courageous, and impeccably mannered. Women were attracted to the cultured, lifelong bachelor. When he was criticized for "wasting" his intellectual talent on the sport he loved, Berg replied: "I'd rather be a ballplayer than a justice on the U.S. Supreme Court." /(DB)

Bill Bergen — 1873–1943. C 1901–11 Reds, **Dodgers** 947 g, .170, 2 hr, 193 rbi

The worst hitter ever to play regularly in the ML, his .170 career BA is 42 points below any other batter with 2500 or more at-bats. His .139 in 1909 is the lowest mark ever for a batting title qualifier. In the lineup for his arm, his 202 assists the same year are the ninth best by a catcher; that July 24, he set a 20th-century record by throwing out seven would-be basestealers. His brother Marty was also a ML catcher. /(TG)

Boze Berger [Louis William] — 1910– . 2B-SS-3B 1932, 35–39 Indians, **White Sox**, Red Sox 343 g, .236, 13 hr, 97 rbi

Berger was the MVP with New Orleans in 1934. He was Cleveland's starting second baseman in 1935, but was relegated to utility duty thereafter due to marginal hitting. When WWII started, Berger made a career of the military, staying in until 1962. /(LRD)

Heinie Berger [Charles] — 1882–1954. RHP 1907–10 **Indians** 609 ip, 32–29, 2.56

A spitball master, Berger made the majors after two 20-win seasons in the American Association. He twice won 13 for Cleveland, and established the club record for righthanders with 162 strikeouts in 1909. /(ME)

Wally Berger — 1905–1988. OF 1930–40 **Braves**, Giants, Reds, Phillies 1350 g, .300, 242 hr, 898 rbi. *2 WS, 7 g, .000, 1 rbi*
☛ *Led League—hr 35. Led League—rbi 35. All-Star—33–36.*

Had there been an award for Rookie of the Year in 1930, Wally Berger would have won it. He hit .310 that year for the Braves and established National League rookie records with 38 homers and 119 RBI. The powerfully built centerfielder was the heart of the Boston offense for seven seasons. Berger had torn up the Pacific Coast League with Los Angeles in 1929, establishing a club record with 40 HR, but he was the property of the Cubs, who in 1930 had the only all-100 RBI outfield ever, with Riggs Stephenson, Hack Wilson, and Kiki Cuyler. Berger was traded to Boston, where he batted over .300 in each of his first four seasons. In 1933 he led the Braves into the first division for the first time in 12 years. He hit .313, and though he missed nearly three weeks with illness, had 27 HR, exactly half his team's total, and second in the league to Chuck Klein. He was the NL's starting centerfielder in the 1933 and 1934 All-Star games. Berger's power statistics were not helped by his home ballpark. Still, he hit 105 home runs in Braves Field, more than any player in history. He had success with curveball pitchers, but his nemesis was Carl Hubbell, whose screwball would upset Berger's timing for several games. After his league-leading performances of 1935 (34 HR, 130 RBI), Berger suffered a shoulder injury in 1936. It worsened in 1937, when he was traded to the Giants, and he saw limited duty before being sent to the Reds, for whom he batted .307, in May 1938. Relegated to part-time play again in 1939, he was released to the Phillies in May 1940. Despite hitting .302 in 22 games, he was let go a month later. /(DBev)

Dave Bergman — 1953– . 1B-OF 1975, 77– Yankees, Astros, Giants, **Tigers** 1076 g, .260, 44 hr, 224 rbi. *3 LCS, 10 g, .375, 4 rbi. 1 WS, 5 g, .000*

Bergman was a batting champ and league MVP in each of his first two minor league seasons, but with little power has never been an everyday starter in the ML. He hit a career-high .294 for the Tigers in 1988, and his lefthanded bat and steady glove are assets on the bench. On March 24, 1984, he was traded twice; from the Giants to the Phillies, and then from the Phillies to the Tigers. /(SCL)

Jack Berly — 1903–1977. RHP 1924, 31–33 Cardinals, Giants, **Phillies** 215 ip, 10–13, 5.02

Berly suffered from poor control and was generally better as a reliever. He saw his most action in 1931 with the Giants, going 7–8 with a 3.88 ERA, both career bests, but even then he had a 2.88 ERA in 16 relief outings compared with 4.32 in his 11 starts. His career was ended in 1933 by a broken leg. /(WOR)

Chris Berman — 1955– . *Broadcaster.*

Well known as a co-host of ESPN's "SportsCenter," a nightly wrap-up of the day's sporting events, Berman has a memorable rapid-fire home run call ("Back, back, back, back, back, back . . .") and bestows humorous nicknames on players, like Bert "Be in" Blyleven and Dave "Parallel" Parker. /(SCL)

Dwight Bernard — 1952– . RHP 1978–79, 81–82 **Mets**, Brewers 176 ip, 4–8, 4.14. *1 LCS, 1 ip, 0.00. 1 WS, 1 ip, 0.00*

Bernard spent parts of two seasons in the Met bullpen with little success. A trade for Mark Bomback sent him to Milwaukee, where he won three and saved six for the 1982 pennant winners. /(GEB)

Tony Bernazard — 1956– . 2B 1979–87 Expos, White Sox, Mariners, **Indians**, A's 1065 g, .262, 75 hr, 391 rbi

Bernazard had an 0-for-44 streak at the plate with the 1984 Indians, finishing at .221. He peaked in 1986, when he batted .301 and set a club record for

Wally Berger

homers by a switch hitter (17). That July 1, he became the first Indian to homer from both sides of the plate in one game. Eventually, his bat could not compensate for his inadequacy as a fielder, and he was traded to Oakland in July of 1987. The next year he was playing in Japan. He was taught to play by Vic Power in his native Puerto Rico. /(ME)

Bill Bernhard (Strawberry Bill) — 1871-1949. RHP 1899-1907 Phillies, A's, **Indians** 1792 ip, 116-82, 3.04. 20 wins: 04

Bill Bernhard was the first Cleveland pitcher to lead the American League in winning percentage, with a .783 mark (18-5) in 1902. Like Nap Lajoie, Bernhard was barred from playing in Philadelphia after jumping from the Phillies to the Athletics in 1901. He joined Cleveland after one game in 1902. In 1904, after being slowed by a broken finger in 1903, he again led his staff in winning percentage, going 23-13. Bernhard later had a long managerial career in the Southern Association. /(ME)

Juan Bernhardt — 1953- . DH-3B-1B 1976-79 Yankees, **Mariners** 154 g, .238, 9 hr, 43 rbi

Bernhardt hit the first home run by a Mariner in the Kingdome, April 10, 1977. The Dominican played for his country's team in the 1971 Pan Am games. /(NLM)

Dale Berra — 1956- . SS-3B 1977-87 **Pirates,** Yankees, Astros 853 g, .236, 49 hr, 278 rbi

Yogi Berra's son was a highly-touted prospect from the time of his first-round selection by Pittsburgh in the 1975 draft. At first a utility infielder, Dale finally became a regular at shortstop in 1982. A productive bat (.263, 10 HR, 61 RBI) could not compensate for poor defense. Traded to the Yankees after drug problems, he played just 16 games with his father as manager before Yogi was fired. Dale was a spare part the rest of his career. He established a major league record in 1983 by reaching base seven times on catcher's interference. Dale and Yogi held the record for father-son home runs (407) until Bobby and Barry Bonds broke it in 1989. /(ME)

Yogi Berra [Lawrence Peter] — 1925- . C-OF 1946-63, 65 **Yankees**, Mets 2120 g, .285, 358 hr, 1430 rbi. *14 WS, 75 g, .274, 12 hr, 39 rbi.*
    Manager 1964, 72-75, 84-85 Yankees, **Mets** 484-444, .522. First place: 64, 73 *2 WS, 6-8, .429*
☛ *Most Valuable Player—51, 54-55 . All-Star—48-62. Hall of Fame—1972.*

Yogi Berra is known to millions who don't even follow baseball. His persona transcends the game. Berra is funny and, at a squat 5′8″, was a seemingly improbable star. But a star he was—a Hall of Famer. "To me," Casey Stengel said, "he is a great man. I am lucky to have him and so are my pitchers . . .He springs on a bunt like it was another dollar."

Through hard work and the help of Bill Dickey, Berra became a great catcher. He led the American

Yogi Berra

League in games caught and chances accepted eight times, and led the league in double plays six times. He is one of only four catchers to ever field 1.000 in a season (1958), and between July 28, 1957, and May 10, 1959, Berra set major league records by catching in 148 consecutive games and accepting 950 chances without making an error.

Yogi was a master at calling pitches and handling a pitching staff. He caught two no-hitters by Allie Reynolds in 1951 and Don Larsen's perfect game in the 1956 World Series. He treated every Yankee pitcher differently; some he goaded and some he babied, depending on their temperament. An excellent, cat-like athlete, he was also a good defensive left fielder late in his career.

As a slugger, he was feared throughout the league. Berra set American League records for home runs hit while playing catcher with his 30 home runs in both 1952 and 1956 and his 306 lifetime (these were later broken by Carlton Fisk). He also had five 100-RBI seasons. Between 1949 and 1955, when he was the heart of the Yankees' batting order, he led the club in RBI each season and won three MVP awards.

Berra was one of the greatest clutch hitters of all time—"the toughest man in the league in the last three innings," according to Paul Richards, a rival manager. Along with Roberto Clemente, Berra was probably the best bad-ball hitter in the game's history. He was skilled at golfing low pitches for deep home runs and chopping high pitches for line drives. Yet for all his aggressiveness at the plate, he was hard to strike out. In 1950, he fanned only 12 times in 597 at-bats.

As Lawrence Peter Berra had a way with the bat, so does he have a way with words. One of Berra's first notable quotes came in 1947, when the people of his hometown St. Louis threw Berra a "night" before a Yankees-Browns game. Grateful, Berra told the crowd: "I want to thank everyone for making this night necessary." He once said of a restaurant: "Nobody goes there anymore, it's too crowded." And as a veteran, he noted, "I've been with the Yankees 17 years, watching games and learning. You can see a lot by observing." "A nickel ain't worth a dime anymore," was his pithy comment on inflation. When asked as a child how he liked school he replied: "Closed." His colorful expressions that got to the heart of things became known as "Yogi-isms."

After playing briefly in the Yankee farm system, Berra enlisted in the navy in 1944. After his discharge in 1946 he reported to the Yankees'

Newark club in the International League. He had a great year (.314, 15 HRs, 59 RBI in only 277 at-bats) and was called across the Hudson.

Berra came up as an outfielder before being converted to catcher, and he shared New York's catching duties with Aaron Robinson at first, and later with Gus Niarhos, before becoming the Yankees' regular catcher from 1949 to 1959. Except for a few games with the Mets in 1965, Berra played his entire career as a Yankee, serving as an outfielder and pinch hitter as well as catcher in 1960–63.

When his career was over, Berra had played on a record ten World Series champions. He also played in an unmatched 14 World Series and holds WS records for games (75), at-bats (259), hits (71), and doubles (10).

Berra was named the Yankees' manager for the 1964 season, the final season of the mighty New York dynasty. The Yankees won the pennant but were defeated by St. Louis in a seven-game World Series. The day after the Series ended, the Yankees fired Berra and hired St. Louis Manager Johnny Keane. New York finished sixth in 1965.

Berra, meanwhile, rejoined Stengel with the Mets. He took over as the Mets' manager when Gil Hodges died suddenly in 1972 and led them to the NL pennant in 1973, thus joining Joe McCarthy as the second manager to win pennants in both leagues.

In 1976 Berra returned to the Yankees as a coach, and he managed the club again in 1984 and the beginning of 1985. He later coached for Houston. Wherever he goes, Berra remains one of baseball's most popular figures./(MG)

Ray Berres — 1908– . C 1934, 36–45 Dodgers, Pirates, **Braves**, Giants 561 g, .216, 3 hr, 78 rbi

Despite his weak bat, Berres's defense kept him in the majors for eleven seasons, usually in a backup role. He was a White Sox coach for more than 20 years. /(ME)

Charlie Berry [Charles Francis] — 1902–1972. C 1925, 28–36, 38 A's, **Red Sox**, White Sox 657 g, .267, 23 hr, 256 rbi.
Umpire AL 1942–62 5 WS, 5 ASU

Chosen at end on Walter Camp's last All-America team, Lafayette star Berry played both baseball and football on a ML level. In 1925–26 he starred for Pottsville of the NFL, leading the league in scoring in '25 with 74 points. His ML baseball career was longer but less distinguished, mostly as a reserve. He became an AL umpire in 1942 and remained for 21 years. At the same time he was a head linesman for the NFL, officiating in 12 championship games. In 1958, he umpired in the WS and later that year served as head linesman for the famous "Sudden Death" championship game between the Colts and Giants. His father, Charles Joseph Berry, played for three ML teams in 1884. /(RTM)

Joe Berry (Jittery Joe) — 1904–1958. RHP 1942, 44–46 Cubs, **A's**, Indians 294 ip, 21–22, 2.45

Jittery Joe was a fidgety righthander with a herky-jerky delivery who spent 18 years in the minors before leading the AL in relief wins (10) and saves (12) as a 39-year-old A's rookie in 1944. The 145-lb Berry was once blown off the mound by a gust of wind. /(JCA)

Ken Berry — 1941– . OF 1962–75 **White Sox**, Angels, Brewers, Indians 1383 g, .255, 58 hr, 343 rbi
☛ *All-Star—67. Gold Glove—70, 72.*

An extraordinary outfielder, Berry won two Gold Gloves. Leaping catches above the Comiskey Park fence became his trademark. An All-Star with the White Sox in 1967 when he had a 20-game hitting streak, Berry batted over .280 only twice, in 1972 and '73 with the Angels. From September 16, 1971 through July 27, 1973, he accepted a record 510 consecutive outfield chances without an error. /(JCA)

Neil Berry [Cornelius John] — 1922– . SS-2B 1948–54 **Tigers**, Browns, White Sox, Orioles 441 g, .244, 74 rbi

Sometimes called Connie, Berry was a reliable utility infielder with a weak bat. He played in more than 100 games only in 1949. /(RTM)

Damon Berryhill — 1963– . C 1987– **Cubs** 198 g, .255, 12 hr, 80 rbi

Berryhill relegated Jody Davis to the bench with a seven-HR, 38-RBI, .259 performance after being called up in 1988. He hit .257 with five HR and 41 RBI in 1989, but missed almost half the season with injuries. /(JFC)

Frank Bertaina — 1944– . LHP 1964–70 Orioles, **Senators**, Cardinals 413 ip, 19–29, 3.84

In his first ML game (9/12/64), Bertaina matched one-hitters with A's pitcher Bob Meyer. Known for his daffy behavior, he was dubbed "Toys in the Attic" by Moe Drabowsky. /(RTM)

Dick Bertell — 1935– . C 1960–65, 67 **Cubs**, Giants 444 g, .250, 10 hr, 112 rbi

Bertell hit .273 and .302 as a part-timer in 1961 and 1962. Catching a career-high 110 games for the Cubs in 1964, Bertell tied for the NL lead in errors (11). Traded to the Giants in May 1965, Bertell hit just .188 in 22 games for San Francisco. A knee injury kept him out for all of 1966, and a return to Chicago in 1967 was unsuccessful. /(SFS)

Reno Bertoia — 1935– . 3B-2B 1953–62 **Tigers**, Senators/Twins, A's 612 g, .244, 27 hr, 171 rbi

A Tiger bonus baby, the handsome, Italian-born infielder had speed and good hands but a light bat. In 1960, the only season in which he played in more than 100 games, he hit .265 as the Senators third baseman. /(GEB)

Bob Bescher — 1884–1942. OF 1908–18 **Reds**, Giants, Cardinals, Indians 1228 g, .258, 28 hr, 345 rbi

The 200-pound Bescher was a college football star at Wittenberg (Ohio). The winner of four consecutive stolen base titles (1909–12), he held the NL single-season record (81 in 1911) until Maury Wills broke it in 1962. A classic leadoff batter, he led the NL in runs (120) in 1912 and walks (94) in 1913. /(CG)

Herman Besse (Long Herm) — 1911–1972. LHP 1940–43, 46 **A's** 242 ip, 5–15, 6.97

Besse pitched one full season and parts of four others for Connie Mack's woebegone A's of the early 1940s. In 1942, his one year of steady work, he was 2–9 with a 6.50 ERA. /(MC)

Don Bessent (The Weasel) — 1931– . RHP 1955–58 **Dodgers** 211 ip, 14–7, 3.33. *2 WS, 13 ip, 1.35, 1–0*

A relief specialist, Bessent had an 8–1 record for the World Champion 1955 Dodgers and a staff-best 2.70 ERA. He was the winning pitcher in Game Two of the 1956 World Series. /(FK)

Takehiko Bessho — Unk.-Unk. P 1942–60 **Yomiuri Giants**

In 1949, his eighth season pitching, Bessho came to the fore by winning 42 games, a Japanese record equaled only by Iron Man Inao. He continued as Yomiuri's ace throughout the 1950s. With the Yakult Atoms in 1970, he became the first Japanese manager forced to resign in mid-season; previously, managers had only been sent away for periods of rest and meditation. /(MC)

Karl Best — 1959– . RHP 1983–86, 88 **Mariners**, Twins 92 ip, 5–6, 4.04

Best could never stick in the majors despite annual call-ups by the pitching-poor Mariners. The reliever's best stint by far came at the end of 1985, when he was 2–1 with a 1.95 ERA in 32 innings. /(SFS)

Larry Bettencourt — 1905–1978. OF-3B 1928, 31–32 **Browns** 168 g, .258, 8 hr, 53 rbi

A member of the College Football Hall of Fame, Bettencourt was a consensus All-America center at St. Mary's College in 1927 when he scored 12 touchdowns on intercepted passes, blocked punts, and recovered fumbles. He signed a baseball contract with the St. Louis Browns for $6,000, then the largest bonus ever paid a rookie just out of school, but failed to stick in three ML trials. In 1933 he played pro football for the Green Bay Packers. /(NLM)

Kaoru Betto — 1920– . 1B-OF 1948–57 **Yokohama Taiyo Whales**

☛ *Most Valuable Player—50. Led League—hr 50.*

One of Japan's first home run threats, Betto served in WWII and struggled at other jobs before turning to pro baseball at age 28. In 1950, he challenged Tomio Fujimara's Japanese HR record of 45, falling two short. Among the most flamboyant early Japanese stars, he married a beauty queen, and boasted that he never faced a pitcher he couldn't hit. As interim manager of the Taiyo Whales in 1967, he won ten games in a row before persuading the man he replaced to return. He did later become Taiyo's manager. /(MC)

Huck Betts [Walter Martin] — 1897–1987. RHP 1920–25, 32–35 **Phillies**, Braves 1366 ip, 61–68, 3.93

Betts was a curveballing righthander who was hampered by weak clubs and the lack of a fastball. The 5'11" 170-lb Huck (derived from his love for huckleberries) pitched mostly in relief for the Phillies, but had three solid seasons as a starter for the Braves. He won a career-high 17 games in 1934. /(FS)

Bruno Betzel — 1894–1965. 2B-3B-OF 1914–18 **Cardinals** 448 g, .231, 2 hr, 94 rbi

A light-hitting ML infielder, Betzel managed for 26 years in the minors (1928–56). He won seven pennants with seven different teams, the last with Toronto of the International League in his final managerial season. /(JK)

Kurt Bevacqua (Dirty) — 1947– . 3B-2B-1B-OF 1971–85 Indians, Royals, Brewers, Rangers, **Padres**, Pirates 970 g, .236, 27 hr, 275 rbi. *1 LCS, 2 g, .000. 1 WS, 5 g, .412, 2 hr, 4 rbi*

Bevacqua put in 15 ML years although he never played more than 64 games at any one position in a season. Nicknamed "Dirty" for his aggressive, diving, hard-sliding style, he pinch-hit more than 300 times. In 1980, he led the NL in both pinch hits and pinch at-bats. His career batting average as a pinch hitter was 30 points higher than his BA as a starter.

In the 1984 WS, manager Dick Williams surprised many by selecting Bevacqua as the DH for the Padres. He was a goat in Game One when he tripped and was thrown out trying to stretch a double in a 3–2 loss. But he blasted a game-winning homer in Game Two and kept the Padres' hopes alive for several innings with another homer in the fifth and final game. He won Topps' bubblegum-blowing contest in 1972 and was pictured on a special card in the following season's Topps set, with Joe Garagiola measuring the winning bubble. /(MC)

Bill Bevens — 1916– . RHP 1944–47 **Yankees** 642 ip, 40–36, 3.08. *1 WS, 11 ip, 0–1, 2.38*

Bevens pitched and lost one of the most famous games in baseball history, Game Four of the 1947 WS. Only 7–13 for the Yankees during the regular season, he survived a record 10 walks while holding the Dodgers hitless, and led 2–1 with two outs in the bottom of the ninth inning. Veteran Cookie Lavagetto's pinch-hit double off the right-field wall (his last major league hit) not only ended Bevens's bid for the first WS no-hitter, but also drove in the tying and winning runs for the Dodgers. /(GEB)

Buddy Biancalana [Roland Americo] — 1960– . SS-2B 1982–87 **Royals**, Astros 311 g, .205, 6 hr, 30 rbi. *2 LCS, 9 g, .211, 1 rbi. 1 WS, 7 g, .278, 1 rbi*

Biancalana made the majors with a strong arm and good glove. He battled Onix Concepcion for the Royals' shortstop job, but neither hit well enough. Lack of discipline at the plate handicapped Biancalana's hitting, but he started all 14 postseason games for the 1985 Royals and handled 55 chances flawlessly while making several dazzling plays. /(FJO)

Jim Bibby — 1944– . RHP 1972–81, 83–84 Cardinals, Rangers, Indians, **Pirates** 1723 ip, 111–101, 3.76. *1 LCS, 7 ip, 1.29. 1 WS, 10 ip, 2.61*

☛ *All-Star—80.*

Wildness, inconsistency, and injuries plagued the unusually muscular 6'5" 235-lb Bibby. Drafted first by the Mets and then by Uncle Sam, he spent two years in Viet Nam, one on the disabled list (after a spinal fusion operation), and five in the minors before reaching the majors in 1972. With Texas in 1973, he no-hit Oakland on July 30, and also pitched a one-hitter and a two-hitter. He went 12–4 with a 2.80 ERA for Pittsburgh in 1979 and pitched well in the LCS and WS. His .760 winning percentage (19–6) in 1980 was the NL's best. On May 19, 1981 the overpowering Bibby allowed a leadoff single to Atlanta's Terry Harper and then retired 27 Braves in a row. Shortly after that he suffered a rotator cuff injury that eventually ended his career. His brother, Henry, played in the NBA. /(JCA)

Vern Bickford — 1920–1960. RHP 1948–54 **Braves**, Orioles 1076 ip, 66–57, 3.71. *1 WS, 3 ip, 0–1, 2.70* ☛ *All-Star—49.*

The famous cliche about the 1948 Boston Braves NL championship team, "Spahn, Sain and two days of rain," did not do justice to Bickford's strong 11–5 record. His top season was 1950, when he went 19–14 and led the league in games started (39), complete games (27), and innings pitched (311 2/3). On August 11 of that year he no-hit the Dodgers, 7–0. In 1951, he broke a finger on his pitching hand and never regained his effectiveness. /(GEB)

Les Biederman — Unk.–1981. *Writer*

Biederman retired in 1969 after 39 years with the Pittsburgh *Press* and 20 years as a correspondent for *The Sporting News*. He ranked Harvey Haddix's 12-inning perfect game his greatest thrill in sports. A graduate of Ohio State, he was president of the BBWAA in 1959 and was credited with raising a half-million dollars for Children's Hospital in Pittsburgh. /(NLM)

Mike Bielecki (Bie) — 1959– . RHP 1984– **Pirates**, Cubs 505 ip, 30–26, 3.85. *1 LCS, 12 ip, 0–1, 3.72*

Baseball America's 1984 Minor League Player of the Year, Bielecki led NL rookies in starts and innings in 1986 but went winless in the second half (0–6) and spent most of 1987 in the minors. His 18–7, 3.14 record for the 1989 Cubs was a major factor in their surprising division title. He lost a heartbreaker in the LCS, dropping the final game after taking a 1–1 tie into the ninth inning. He had a no-decision in Game Two. /(ME)

Lou Bierbauer — 1865–1926. 2B 1886–98 Philadelphia (AA), Brooklyn (PL), **Pirates**, Cardinals 1383 g, .267, 33 hr, 706 rbi

Bierbauer jumped Philadelphia's American Association club to join the Players' League in 1890. When the PL folded, players were supposed to rejoin their previous clubs. Pittsburgh became known as the Pirates when they swiped Bierbauer from Philadelphia through a clerical error in 1891. Bierbauer tied a then-ML record with 12 putouts at 2B in an 1888 game. In 10 years as a regular, he led his league's second basemen in assists five times. /(ME)

Carson Bigbee (Skeeter) — 1895–1964. OF 1916–26 **Pirates** 1147 g, .287, 17 hr, 324 rbi. *1 WS, 4 g, .333, 1 rbi*

A reliable contact hitter, Bigbee peaked in 1922, when he scored 113 runs and hit .350 with 215 hits. Illness and poor vision handicapped the University of Oregon alumnus for the rest of his career. His brother Lyle played briefly in the ML. /(JK)

Craig Biggio — 1965– . C 1988– **Astros** 184 g, .247, 16 hr, 65 rbi

The Astros' first-round draft pick in June 1987, when Alan Ashby was hurt in 1988 Biggio was rushed and hit only .211. But in 1989 he hit .257 with 13 HR, 60 RBI, and 64 runs in 134 games. Unusually fast for a catcher, he often hit leadoff and stole 21 bases in 24 attempts, the second-best percentage in the NL. /(WOR)

Helene Hathaway Robinson Bigsby — 1878–1950. *Executive.*

The first woman club owner in the major leagues, she was president of the St. Louis Cardinals in 1916 while the wife of Schuyler P. Britton. /(NLM)

Larry Biittner — 1946– . OF-1B 1970–83 Senators/ Rangers, Expos, **Cubs**, Reds 1217 g, .273, 29 hr, 354 rbi

Biittner finished the 1980s tied for 12th on the all-time list for pinch hits with 95 (in 370 pinch at-bats). He was an inconsistent batter who sometimes had respectable averages, with a high of .315 in 1975 for Montreal. He showed power only in 1977, his first full season in Wrigley Field, when he hit .298 with career highs of 12 HR, 28 doubles, 62 RBI, and 74 runs. /(JFC)

Dann Bilardello — 1959– . C 1983–86, 89 **Reds**, Expos, Pirates 331 g, .212, 18 hr, 82 rbi

Bilardello struggled with injuries as a Dodger farm-hand before the Reds claimed him and made them their catcher for 1983. A dead-pull hitter, he batted .238 as a rookie and went downhill from there. His catching mechanics were excellent, but his game-calling was found lacking. He welcomed his trade to Montreal in 1986, but didn't last the season. He spent all of 1987–88 in the minors before resurfacing briefly with the Pirates in 1989 when Mike LaValliere missed half the season with a knee injury. /(JCA)

Steve Bilko — 1928–1978. 1B 1949–54, 58, 60–62 **Cardinals**, Cubs, Reds, Dodgers, Tigers, Angels 600 g, .249, 76 hr, 276 rbi

Bilko was a slugger who posted phenomenal numbers in the minor leagues but never met expectations in the majors. He got his first call-up with the Cardinals in 1949 after hitting 34 HR in 139 games at Rochester (International League), but didn't stick for a full season until 1953 (he had a broken arm in 1952). He played every game for St. Louis that year, but his 125 strikeouts, just 9 fewer than the ML record at the time, cut into his productivity. On May 28, 1953, he struck out five times in a ten-inning game. He hit .251, and his 21 HR, 84 RBI, 72 runs, and 70 walks were all career highs. He never played regularly again. Bilko was sold to the Cubs for $12,500 in April 1954 and was let go after the season.

In the next three years, Bilko built a legend. Playing for Los Angeles in the Pacific Coast League (which had an extended schedule due to the good weather—in 1955 he played 168 games), he led the league in HR each year, with totals of 37, 55, and 56. He won the Triple Crown in 1956 with a .360 batting average and 164 RBI while also leading the league with 163 runs scored, and he hit .300 all three seasons. This earned the 6′1″ slugger, charitably listed at just 240 pounds, another major league trial in 1958, with the Reds. He hit .264 with four HR in 31 games and was traded to the Dodgers with Johnny Klippstein for Don Newcombe in June. He hit just .208 with seven HR for Los Angeles. After spending 1959 at Spokane (Pacific Coast League), where he hit 26 HR and led with 92 RBI, he was picked up by Detroit for 1960 and recorded nine HR and a .208 average. In 1961 the expansion Angels were desperate enough to try Bilko, and he had his best season, hitting .279 with 20 HR (but 81 strikeouts) in 294 at-bats. He hit .287 in 1962, but a leg injury cut into his season. After one last tour with Rochester (International League) in 1963, he retired. He hit 313 HR and batted .312 in his minor league career. /(WOR)

Jack Billingham — 1943– . RHP 1968–80 Dodgers, Astros, **Reds**, Tigers, Red Sox 2231 ip, 145–113, 3.83. *2 LCS, 17 ip, 0–1, 4.32. 3 WS, 25 ip, 2–0, 0.36* ☛ *All-Star—73.*

Billingham, a distant relative of Christy Mathewson, was groomed as a reliever in the Dodger organization. He became a starter with Houston, and by 1972 was a mainstay in the rotation of Cincinnati's "Big Red Machine." The gentle, 6′4″ righthander won at least 10 games for 10 consecutive seasons (1970–79), with 19 victories in both 1973 and '74. He didn't miss a turn in '73 as he led the NL with 40 starts, 293 IP, and seven shutouts. In three World Series, Billingham allowed just one earned run in 25 1/3 innings; in Game Three of the 1972 WS, he threw eight shutout innings to defeat Oakland, 1–0.

In his first 1974 start, he gave up Hank Aaron's record-tying 714th home run. In 1978, after winning 87 games in six years with Cincinnati, Billingham was traded to Detroit. Two years later he finished with Boston. /(JCA)

Dick Billings — 1942– . C-OF 1968–75 **Senators/ Rangers**, Cardinals 400 g, .227, 16 hr, 142 rbi

Billings, who earned a B.S. degree at Michigan State, hit .305 in the minors but never hit higher than .254 in the major leagues. /(GEB)

George Binks (Bingo) [born George Binkowski] — 1914– . OF-1B 1944–48 **Senators**, A's, Browns 351 g, .253, 8 hr, 130 rbi

The speedy Binks got his ML opportunity at age 30 because of the World War II player shortage. He hit .278 with 81 RBI as centerfielder for the 1945 Senators, a team that missed the AL pennant by one game. His play earned him three more postwar seasons in the ML. /(MC)

Doug Bird — 1950– . RHP 1973–83 **Royals**, Phillies, Yankees, Cubs, Red Sox 1212 ip, 73–60, 3.99. *3 LCS, 8 ip, 1–1, 2.35*

Bird had a lively fastball, a nasty slider, and a palm ball. A reliever in five of his six years with Kansas City, he saved 20 as a rookie and went 11–4 with 14 saves in 1977. When he left KC after the 1978 season, he held the club's career marks in games pitched and saves. Over a three-year span with the Phillies, Columbus (International League), and the Yankees, Bird had an 18-game winning streak. The day after he finally lost (6/11/81), the Yankees traded him to the Cubs. /(JCA)

Mike Birkbeck — 1961- . RHP 1986- **Brewers** 236 ip, 12–17, 5.12

Birkbeck was 10–8 with a 4.72 ERA in 1988, but in 1989 he started the year 0–4 and went on the DL with a weakened rotator cuff. /(JFC)

Ralph Birkofer (Lefty) — 1908–1971. LHP 1933–37 **Pirates**, Dodgers 544 ip, 31–28, 4.19

The chunky Birkofer's excellent fastball and sharp-breaking curve stamped him an excellent prospect, but arm trouble forced his retirement after only five ML seasons. /(FS)

Joe Birmingham (Dode) — 1884–1946. OF 1906–14 **Indians** 772 g, .254, 6 hr, 265 rbi.
      Manager 1912–15 **Indians** 170–191, .471

A so-so hitter but an outstanding defensive centerfielder, Birmingham led AL outfielders with 33 assists in 1907. On October 2, 1908, he scored the only run in Addie Joss's perfect game against Ed Walsh. As the manager of the 1913 Cleveland team, then called the "Naps" in honor of second baseman Nap Lajoie, he caused a local furor by benching the star. /(CG)

Babe Birrer [Werner Joseph] — 1928- . RHP 1955–56, 58 **Tigers**, Orioles, Dodgers 120 ip, 4–3, 4.36

"Babe" earned his nickname on a July day in 1955 when, while working four innings in relief for Detroit, he smacked two three-run homers. He never hit another home run. /(CC)

Tim Birtsas — 1960- . LHP 1985–86, 88- **A's**, Reds 277 ip, 13–11, 4.12

After a 10–6 season as a rookie for Oakland in 1985, Birtsas spent most of 1986 disabled or in the minors. Originally drafted by the Yankees, he was part of the trade package that pried Rickey Henderson from the A's in 1984, and was sent to Cincinnati with Jose Rijo for Dave Parker in December 1987. /(ME)

Charlie Bishop — 1924- . RHP 1952–55 **A's** 294 ip, 10–22, 5.33

The swarthy fireballer threw a no-hitter in the Piedmont League in 1948. He pitched a shutout for the Athletics in his first big league start, but went 3–14 in 1953, his only full ML year. /(JCA)

Max Bishop (Tilly, Camera Eye) — 1899–1962. 2B 1924–35 **A's**, Red Sox 1338 g, .271, 41 hr, 379 rbi. *3 WS, 18 g, .182, 1 rbi*

Max Bishop

The leadoff man for Connie Mack's AL champions (1929–31), Bishop specialized in drawing walks in front of A's sluggers Al Simmons, Mickey Cochrane, and Jimmie Foxx. Seven times he topped 100 bases on balls, leading the AL with 128 in 1929. In one doubleheader, he walked eight times. He led AL second basemen in fielding four times. The quiet, gentlemanly Bishop later served 24 years as baseball coach at the U.S. Naval Academy, compiling a 306–143 record. /(JK)

Del Bissonette [Adelphia Louis] — 1899–1972. 1B 1928–31, 33 **Dodgers** 604 g, .305, 65 hr, 391 rbi.
      Manager 1945 **Braves** 25–36, .410

In his injury-shortened career, Bissonette set a Dodger rookie home run record with 25 in 1928 but led NL first basemen in errors in two of his three full seasons. A Brooklyn limerick of the time went: The Dodgers have Del Bissonette. No meal has he ever missed yet. The question that rises Is one that surprises: Who paid for all Del Bissonette? /(TG)

Hi Bithorn — 1916–1952. RHP 1942–43, 46–47 **Cubs**, White Sox 509 ip, 34–31, 3.16

Only 9–14 as a Cub rookie in 1942, the burly righthander blossomed to 18–12 the next year, fourth in the NL in wins. He led the league in shutouts (7) and posted a 2.60 ERA. He spent the next two seasons in military service, ballooning to 225. In 1946 he pitched mostly in relief with sporadic success. Sold to the Pirates, who released him in spring training, he pitched two innings for the White Sox in 1947 before a sore arm ended his ML career. He was shot to death on New Year's Day 1952 while attempting a comeback in the Mexican winter league. /(MC)

Jeff Bittiger — 1962– . RHP 1986– Phillies, Twins, **White Sox** 94 ip, 4–6, 4.77

Originally signed by the Mets in 1980, Bittiger couldn't balance strikeouts and control well enough to win in the majors. He was Texas League Pitcher of the Year in 1982. /(SFS)

Black Sox Scandal

The heavily favored Chicago White Sox were upset in the 1919 World Series by the Cincinnati Reds, five games to three. At the apex of the pennant race the following year, eight players were indicted for throwing the Series in return for payoffs from gamblers. Although they were all cleared by a conciliatory grand jury, newly appointed Commissioner Kenesaw Mountain Landis banned for life the eight so-called Black Sox—left fielder Shoeless Joe Jackson, first baseman and ringleader Chick Gandil, shortstop Swede Risberg, third baseman Buck Weaver, centerfielder Happy Flesch, pitchers Eddie Cicotte and Lefty Williams, and utility infielder Fred McMullin—from organized baseball. Only a handful of them actually received any payment, and Jackson hit .375 in the Series to lead both teams. Landis's office had been created because of the scandal, and he was chosen to fill it because he had shown a friendly attitude toward the baseball establishment when he was a judge. He justified banning all eight players on the grounds that not reporting the plot was as bad as actually taking part in the fix. The plan was apparently hatched by local Chicago gamblers, but New York gangster Arnold Rothstein was rumored to be its major backer. The players were easily tempted. They were not paid well by tight-fisted owner Charles Comiskey. Legend has it that upon Jackson's leaving the courthouse, a little boy cried, "Say it ain't so, Joe!" There have been

movements to have Jackson, who owns the third-highest batting average in baseball history, posthumously reinstated for election to the Hall of Fame. This revisionist sympathy has risen considerably with the release of two films connected to the scandal: "Eight Men Out" in 1988, based on the definitive Eliot Asinof book, and "Field of Dreams" in 1989, based on the W.P. Kinsella novel "Shoeless Joe." An off-Broadway play, "Out!" was also produced in New York in 1986./(SEW)

Bud Black [Harry Ralston] — 1957– . LHP 1981– Mariners, **Royals**, Indians 1260 ip, 70–71, 3.72. *2 LCS, 16 ip, 0–1, 3.45. 1 WS, 5 ip, 0–1, 5.06*

Black's effectiveness hinged on constantly mixing his fastball, curve, slider, and change-up to keep hitters guessing. Used initially as a middle reliever, he led Royals' starters in IP, wins, ERA, and strikeouts in 1984.

His fortunes fell in 1985, when he seemed to lose something off his set-up pitch, the fastball. The only Royal starter with a losing record in Kansas City's World Championship season, Black was put back in the bullpen in 1986 and was traded to the Indians in mid-1988. /(FO)

Don Black — 1916–1959. RHP 1943–48 **A's**, Indians 797 ip, 34–55, 4.35

After three years of trying to control Black's drinking problem, the A's suspended him in 1945, then sold him to Cleveland. Against the A's on July 10, 1947, he pitched the first no-hitter in Municipal Stadium before the largest crowd (47,871) ever to see a no-hitter up until then. The crowd was drawn by the expectation of the first appearance of Cleveland's Larry Doby, the AL's first black player, but Doby didn't play in the game. On September 13, 1948, Black collapsed at home plate after suffering a brain hemorrhage. While still in critical condition, he was given a night by Indians fans, who raised $40,000 for him. He recovered but never pitched again. /(NLM)

Joe Black — 1924– . RHP 1952–57 **Dodgers**, Reds, Senators 414 ip, 30–12, 3.91. *2 WS, 22 ip, 1–2, 2.82*

Joe Black, who began in the Negro Leagues, won Rookie of the Year honors as a 28-year-old reliever for the 1952 Dodgers. He won 14 in relief and added 15 saves, using a blazing fastball and tight curve. At season's end, Dodger manager Chuck Dressen started him twice (a win and a loss) to prepare him for starting the first game of the WS. He won 4–2, but then lost two close games (also starts) 2–0 and

4–2. His victory was the only one by a black pitcher in the WS until Mudcat Grant won in 1965.

In spring training the next year, Dressen insisted that Black learn several new pitches. He lost control of the two that had brought him success and was never effective again. /(GEB)

Ron Blackburn — 1935– . RHP 1958–59 **Pirates** 108 ip, 3–2, 3.50

An unheralded prospect at the Pirates' 1958 training camp, this righthanded reliever impressed the brass with his sinker and made the club. In 1959, he batted only five times, but his one hit was a homer against the Cubs. /(RTM)

Lena Blackburne [Russell Aubrey] (Slats) — 1886–1968. SS-3B-2B-RHP 1910, 12, 14–15, 18–19, 27, 29 **White Sox**, Reds, Braves, Phillies 548 g, .214, 4 hr, 139 rbi

Blackburne made an unusual contribution to baseball when he discovered and marketed the special mud from the Delaware River used by umpires to rub the gloss off new baseballs. His feminine nickname came from a leather-lunged minor league fan who compared him to another player, Cora Donovan, but Blackburne claimed it was because he had a "lean" physique. More successful as a minor league manager and coach, his term as White Sox skipper (1928–29) was most notable for his savage fistfight with one of his own players, Art (The Great) Shires. Blackburne's one outing as a pitcher came in his only appearance of 1929. /(JK)

Ewell Blackwell (The Whip) — 1922– . RHP 1942, 46–53, 55 **Reds**, Yankees, A's 1321 ip, 82–78, 3.30. 20 wins: 47 *1 WS, 5 ip, 7.20*
☛ *Led League—w 47. All-Star—46–51.*

A 6′6″ stringbean with a wicked sidearm delivery, Blackwell was virtually unhittable for righthanded batters as the ball seemed to explode at them from third base. As a Reds rookie in 1946 he had only a 9–13 record but a NL-leading six shutouts. In 1947 he was dubbed The Whip, as he led the NL in wins (22–8), complete games (23), and strikeouts (193) for the fifth-place Reds. His 16 consecutive wins set a NL mark for righthanders. He came very close to tying teammate Johnny Vander Meer's feat of back-to-back no-hitters. On the night of June 18, he no-hit the Braves; in his next outing he held the Dodgers hitless into the ninth before Eddie Stanky's one-out single.

Arm miseries the next couple of years took the snap out of "The Whip." In 1950 and '51, he came back partway with 17 and 16 wins, but his arm problems returned. He was 3–12 in 1952 when the Reds traded him to the Yankees on August 28. "I wish it could have been earlier in my career," he said later. "There was no great difference between the two leagues, but I'd have to say it was easier pitching in Yankee Stadium." He won a game down the stretch for New York and started the fifth game of the WS (no decision). The next season, he had two wins before his arm problems ended his career. /(RTM)

Tim Blackwell — 1952– . C 1974–83 Red Sox, Phillies, Expos, **Cubs** 426 g, .228, 6 hr, 80 rbi

The strong-armed receiver was usually a backup to better-known catchers. His only starting job came in 1980 with the Cubs when Barry Foote injured his back. Blackwell responded by hitting a career-high .272. /(JCA)

Ray Blades — 1896–1979. OF 1922–32 **Cardinals** 767 g, .301, 50 hr, 340 rbi. *3 WS, 8 g, .083.* *Manager* 1939–40 **Cardinals** 107–85, .557

Blades was an intelligent, aggressive reserve player for most of his 10 ML seasons, and he hit .300 in each of his three seasons as a starting outfielder for the Cardinals (1924–26). After managing in the Cardinals farm system in the mid-1930s, Blades managed the parent club to 92 wins and second place 1939, but was replaced when the Cardinals sputtered early in 1940. /(FS)

George Blaeholder — 1904–1947. RHP 1925, 27–36 **Browns**, A's, Indians 1914 ip, 104–125, 4.54

The hard-working Blaeholder was one of the original exponents of the slider, perfecting the "nickle curve" while pitching for the hapless St. Louis Browns. Although he never had a winning season for the Browns, he had ten wins or more for seven consecutive years. His four shutouts led the AL in 1929. /(JK)

Dennis Blair — 1954– . RHP 1974–76, 80 **Expos**, Padres 339 ip, 19–25 3.69

Called up to the Expos in 1974, the 6′5″ Blair beat the Phillies in his debut (on May 26), ten days before his 20th birthday. That season proved to be his best (11–7, 3.27). /(RM)

Footsie Blair [Clarence Vick] — 1900–1982. 2B-1B-3B 1929–31 **Cubs** 246 g, .273, 9 hr, 96 rbi. *1 WS, 1 g, .000*

In Blair's only season as a regular, he hit .273 with six HR and 97 runs scored in 1930. But in that rabbit-ball season, he was 30 points below the league average. /(SFS)

Paul Blair (Motormouth) — 1944- . OF 1964-80 **Orioles**, Yankees, Reds 1947 g, .250, 134 hr, 620 rbi. *7 LCS, 25 g, .238, 2 hr, 10 rbi. 6 WS, 28 g, .288, 1 hr, 5 rbi* ☛ *Gold Glove—67, 69-75.*

An intuitive centerfielder whose speed going back allowed him to play unusually shallow, the loquacious Blair won eight Gold Gloves. An Oriole from 1964 through 1976, he finished among Baltimore's all-time top five in a dozen offensive categories. His average was augmented by his bunting skills, and he had 171 career stolen bases. He had his best year in 1969 (.285, 26 HR, 76 RBI). In 1970, he suffered serious eye and facial injuries from a Ken Tatum beaning. Lingering fear at the plate caused him to seek help from a hypnotherapist. In 1971 he tried switch-hitting, but stopped after going 11-57.

Blair appeared in 53 postseason games with Baltimore and the Yankees. His 430-foot home run in Game Three of the 1966 WS gave the Orioles a 1-0 victory over the Dodgers, and he tied the record for most hits in a five-game WS, going 9-19 (.474) in 1970. He made several sensational catches in the '66 and '70 WS and '70 LCS./(JCA)

Walter Blair (Heavy) — 1883-1948. C 1907-11, 14-15 Yankees, **Buffalo (FL)** 442 g, .217, 3 hr, 106 rbi

A product of Bucknell University (as was Christy Mathewson before him), Blair hit .196 over five seasons as a Yankee reserve catcher. He was a regular for two seasons with Buffalo of the Federal League, hitting slightly better and filling in as a manager for two games. /(MG)

Sheriff Blake [John Frederick] — 1899-1982. RHP 1920, 24-31, 37 Pirates, **Cubs**, Phillies, Browns, Cardinals 1620 ip, 87-102, 4.13. *1 WS, 1 ip, 0-1, 13.50*

Blake was the second of three Cubs relievers (and the losing pitcher) during the famous seventh inning of Game Four of the 1929 WS, when the A's rallied for ten runs to overcome an 8-0 deficit. For most of his career he was a solid starter for the Cubs, with all but 6 of his 87 career wins coming in a Chicago uniform, including a 17-11 season in 1928. /(ME)

Johnny Blanchard — 1933- . C 1955, 59-65 **Yankees**, A's, Braves 516 g, .239, 67 hr, 200 rbi. *5 WS, 15 g, .345, 2 hr, 5 rbi*

Blanchard savored his position as the Yankees' third-string catcher for most of his career. A defensive liability, he nearly quit in 1960 when Casey

Stengel considered activating 40-year-old bullpen coach Jim Hegan to back up Yogi Berra while Elston Howard was injured. Stengel reconsidered, and Blanchard responded in 1961 with adequate defense and a career-best .305, 21 HR season. Blanchard holds the record with ten World Series pinch-hitting appearances. /(GDW)

Fred Blanding — 1888-1950. RHP 1910-14 **Indians** 814 ip, 45-46, 3.13

A former University of Michigan pitcher, Blanding made his ML debut against Washington (9/15/10) by defeating Walter Johnson, 3-0, on a six-hitter. Blanding had his best year in 1912, going 18-14 for the Indians. /(NLM)

Ted Blankenship — 1901-1945. RHP 1922-30 **White Sox** 1321 ip, 77-79, 4.32

Ted, brother of pitcher Homer (Si) Blankenship, was a stalwart Texan with the mediocre White Sox of the 1920s. In 1925, his best year, he was 17-8, and battled Grover Cleveland Alexander to a 19-inning, 2-2 tie in the Chicago City Series. He broke a finger in 1926 (13-10, 3.61) and was never the same after that. /(ADS)

Larvell Blanks (Sugar Bear) — 1950- . SS-2B 1972-80 Braves, **Indians**, Rangers 629 g, .253, 20 hr, 172 rbi

Called Sugar Bear after a cartoon character on a cereal box, Blanks was Atlanta's starting shortstop in 1975. He was traded twice in the same day (December 12, 1975): from the Braves to the White Sox to the Indians, with whom he was a utility man. /(JCA)

Cy Blanton [Darrell] — 1908-1945. RHP 1934-42 **Pirates**, Phillies 1218 ip, 68-71, 3.55 ☛ *Led League—era 35. All-Star—37, 41.*

Blanton broke into the majors as the top rookie pitcher of 1935. He was 18-13 with the Pirates, led the NL in ERA (2.58), and tied for the league lead in shutouts (4). Although he was named twice to the NL All-Star team in later years, he never pitched as well as in that first year. He died in 1945 in an Oklahoma state hospital for the mentally ill. /(ME)

Don Blasingame (The Blazer, The Corinth Comet) — 1932- . 2B 1955-66 **Cardinals**, Giants, Reds, Senators, A's 1444 g, .258, 21 hr, 308 rbi. *1 WS, 3 g, .143* ☛ *All-Star—58.*

A hustling everyday second baseman with four ML teams, Mississippi's "Corinth Comet" was a spray hitter and skillful bunter. As a rookie with St. Louis in 1956, he had 587 at-bats without once homering. He had eight HR the next year, but after that never hit more than two. Four times he spoiled no-hitters, twice in August 1963. "The Blazer" was particularly fast getting down the line, hitting into fewer double plays (one in every 123 at-bats) than anyone in history except Don Buford.

In 1960, he married the daughter of catcher Walker Cooper, a 1956–57 teammate. Blasingame later played, coached, and managed in Japan. /(JCA)

Wade Blasingame — 1943– . LHP 1963–72 **Braves**, Astros, Yankees 863 ip, 46–51, 4.52

The Braves gave Blasingame $100,000 to sign, and manager Bobby Bragan said the southpaw had the NL's best curveball when he went 9–5 in 1964. He was 16–10 at age 21 in 1965, but after a fractured finger and sore arm in 1966, he never had another winning season. /(JCA)

Steve Blass — 1944– . RHP 1964, 66–74 **Pirates** 1598 ip, 103–76, 3.63. *2 LCS, 23 ip, 1–1, 4.76. 1 WS, 18 ip, 2–0, 1.00*
☛ *All-Star—72.*

Blass presents one of baseball's great unsolved mysteries. Why did one of the NL's most consistent winners from 1968 through 1972 suddenly collapse? The slender, intelligent pattern pitcher with the jerky, unorthodox motion went 18–6 with a 2.12 ERA in 1968. His three-hit and four-hit victories in Games Three and Seven of the 1971 WS earned him the series MVP award. His 1972 season was his best: 19–8, 2.49 ERA.

Suddenly, in 1973, he couldn't cut his fastball loose and he was so wild he often threw behind batters. Yet there was no pain or stiffness in his arm. The once ebullient winner became emotionless on the mound. Teammates said he "looked relieved" when taken from a game. He struggled, going 3–9 with a 9.81 ERA. He pitched one game for the Pirates in 1974, walked seven and gave up five earned runs in five innings, and was sent to Charleston.

Everyone had a theory: "too nice a guy, afraid he'd hit a batter"; "his jittery motion finally let him down"; "he was afraid he couldn't duplicate his '72 record." Some said he was devastated by the tragic death of Roberto Clemente, whose eulogy he gave in Puerto Rico. He tried psychotherapy, transcendental meditation, optometherapy, and various mechanical experiments. Nothing helped. Blass later became a Pirate broadcaster. /(JCA)

Buddy Blattner [Robert Garnett] — 1920– . 2B-3B-SS 1942, 46–49 Cardinals, **Giants**, Phillies 272 g, .247, 16 hr, 84 rbi

A table tennis champion in his youth and a smooth-fielding, weak-hitting infielder over five ML seasons, Blattner became a baseball broadcaster after his playing career ended, working for the Cardinals, Angels, and Royals. As a player, his best season was 1946, when he hit .255 with 11 HR as the Giants' regular second baseman. /(FS)

Jeff Blauser — 1965– . 2B-SS-3B **Braves** 211 g, .260, 16 hr, 68 rbi

Blauser was a good-fielding shortstop in the minors, but was forced out of position by Andres Thomas. Hitting .270 in 1989, Blauser won back the short-stop job. /(WOR)

Marv Blaylock — 1929– . 1B 1950, 55–57 Giants, **Phillies** 287 g, .235, 15 hr, 78 rbi

Blaylock occasionally showed some power, particularly in 1956 when he batted .254 with 10 home runs, but he lost his first base spot to Ed Bouchee the next season. /(GEB)

Curt Blefary (Clank) — 1943– . OF-1B-C 1965–72 **Orioles**, Astros, Yankees, A's, Padres 974 g, .237, 112 hr, 382 rbi. *1 LCS, 1 g, .000. 1 WS, 4 g, .077*
☛ *Rookie of the Year—65.*

The Brooklyn-born Blefary originally signed with the Yankees, but was sold to Baltimore while still in the minors. He was named Rookie of the Year with the Orioles in 1965 when he hit .260 with 22 HR and 70 RBI. Nicknamed "Clank" by his teammates for his iron glove, Blefary was tried at first base and then catcher in an effort to keep his bat in the lineup. He caught Tom Phoebus's April 27, 1968 no-hitter. He blamed the constant defensive shuffling for his offensive decline. He was traded to Houston in 1969 as part of the deal that brought Mike Cuellar to Baltimore. /(JCA)

Cy Block — 1919– . 3B 1942, 45–46 **Cubs** 17 g, .302, 0 hr, 5 rbi. *1 WS, 1 g, --*

When spirited, determined Cy Block came up for nine games with the 1942 Cubs, he and Stan Musial were considered among the year's most promising rookies. Block then spent three seasons with the Coast Guard and appeared in only eight more ML games, but pinch-ran in the 1945 World Series. Trying the insurance business, he milked his brief ML career by renting a huge billboard on Broadway in New York City featuring himself in a Cub uniform and the slogan: "Life insurance is the home run investment, with it you can't strike out." Block became a millionaire businessman. /(DB)

Ron Blomberg — 1948– . DH-1B-OF 1969, 71–76, 78 **Yankees**, White Sox 461 g, .293, 52 hr, 224 rbi

The strapping, ebullient Southerner was the nation's and the Yankees' first draft pick in 1967. A powerful lefthanded hitter and terrible fielder, on Opening Day, 1973 he became baseball's first designated hitter; the irrepressible Blomberg commented: "I've been a DH all my life: Designated Hebrew." Accused of being a Designated Hypochondriac, the perennial prospect spent months and years sidelined with a variety of muscle injuries. Even when he was healthy, he was seldom permitted to face lefthanded pitching. In 1973 he hit a career-high .329 while playing in 100 games—for him, a full season. /(JCA)

Clifford Bloodgood — 1894–1957. *Writer*

Beginning in 1919 and for more than 30 years, readers of *Baseball Magazine* saw many articles by Bloodgood, who was the magazine's art and associate editor. /(NLM)

Jimmy Bloodworth — 1917– . 2B 1937, 39–43, 46–47, 49–51 **Senators**, Tigers, Pirates, Reds, Phillies 1002 g, .248, 62 hr, 453 rbi. *1 WS, 1 g, --*

Bloodworth was an adequate second baseman over eleven ML seasons but a subpar hitter. In 1943 with Detroit he set a since-broken AL record by grounding into 29 double plays. During one spring training game, he was credited with an "unpatriotic" base hit when he tapped the ball back to pitcher Elmer Riddle. Suddenly, the National Anthem blared forth from a loudspeaker, and, while Riddle stood at attention, Bloodworth scurried safely to first. /(GEB)

Lu Blue — 1897–1958. 1B 1921–33 **Tigers**, Browns, White Sox, Dodgers 1615 g, .287, 44 hr, 692 rbi

Blue broke in with the Tigers in 1921, hitting .308. Although he and manager Ty Cobb were less than friendly, he held the Detroit first base job for seven years. Small for a first baseman at 5'10", Blue fielded his position well. He was a switch-hitter, adept at drawing bases on balls. He finished second in the AL in drawing walks four times, and ended with a career on-base percentage near .400. His career totals included 1092 walks, 1151 runs scored, 109 triples, and 150 stolen bases. In six of his twelve years as a regular, he scored at least 100 runs. A

veteran of World War I, the Washington, D.C. native is probably the best-known former major leaguer to be buried in Arlington National Cemetery. /(LRD)

Vida Blue — 1949– . LHP 1969–83, 85–86 A's, Giants, Royals 3344 ip, 209–161, 3.26. 20 wins: 71, 73, 75 *5 LCS, 31 ip, 1–2, 4.60. 3 WS, 33 ip, 0–3, 4.05* ☛ *Most Valuable Player—71. Led League—era 71. Cy Young Award—71. All-Star—71, 75, 78, 81.*

Blue signed with the Athletics at age 19 instead of accepting one of numerous scholarship offers to become a major-college quarterback. He had his first wrangle with A's owner Charles O. Finley right away, when Finley wanted Blue to change his first name to "True."

Vida Blue

He was called up to the A's late in 1970. On September 21, 1970, he no-hit the Twins, who narrowly edged the Athletics for the division title. As a sophomore, Blue won 17 games by the All-Star break, then was the winning pitcher in the only All-Star game won by the American League between 1962 and 1983, when the NL was 19–1. Blue finished 1971 at 24–8, with 301 strikeouts in 312 innings. Though bombed in the ALCS by Baltimore, he was named both MVP and Cy Young Award winner.

Blue's prolonged holdout in 1972 was only resolved through the intervention of baseball commissioner Bowie Kuhn. Blue slumped to 6–10. Rumors flew that he'd hurt his arm by pitching without spring training and reporting overweight. Blue denied serious arm pain, but his strikeout record was never as spectacular the rest of his career as it was in 1971. Much later, he acknowledged that his drug problems had begun in 1972. As the Athletics won their first of their three straight World Championships, Blue contributed four shutout innings in relief of Blue Moon Odom to save the fifth and final playoff game.

He rebounded with 20–9 in 1973, when the Athletics had three 20-game winners, and was 17–15 in 1974, 22–11 in 1975, and 18–13 in 1976, as the Athletics chased the Royals to the wire in the last year the nucleus of their dynasty remained together. Already Finley had attempted to sell Blue to the Yankees in mid-season, for $1.5 million. Kuhn vetoed that deal. While most of the other Oakland stars departed through free agency, Finley tried to send Blue to the Reds for $1.75 million plus Dave Revering. Kuhn vetoed that, too. After suffering through a 14–19 season in 1977, Blue was finally traded to the Giants for eight players and $390,000. He gave the Giants an 18–10 season, becoming the first pitcher ever to start an All-Star game for each league, and earning NL Pitcher of the Year honors from *TSN*. Erratic pitching over the next few years continued after he was traded to the Royals after 1981. Drug rumors concerning Blue were confirmed in 1983. Blue was one of five members of the Kansas City Royals who eventually served prison time plus a suspension from baseball (a year in Blue's case) for cocaine use.

Given another chance by the Giants in the Bay Area where he remained popular, Blue was 18–18 in 1985–1986. The Athletics signed Blue for 1987, promoting a reunion with slugger Reggie Jackson, who also rejoined the club after 11 years away.

However, Blue flunked a urine test to detect cocaine use, and retired rather than face further scandal. /(MC)

Ossie Bluege — 1900– . 3B-SS-2B 1922–39 Senators 1867 g, .272, 43 hr, 848 rbi. *3 WS, 17 g, .200, 5 rbi.*
  Manager 1943–47 **Senators** 375–394, .488

"If it's a ground ball, I can field it," said the rookie shortstop in 1922 when asked if he could adjust to playing third. He spoke truly. Bluege (pronounced Blu-ghy) held down third base at Washington for much of the following 17 years. His numbers were modest, but he was consistent and mild. He neither smoke nor drank, and was an accountant in the off-season, with Washington's best hotels among his clients. Clark Griffith, the Senators' frugal owner, feared that poring over figures would ruin Bluege's batting eye, and ordered him to quit. As he never earned over $10,000, Bluege couldn't afford to.

Bluege was Griffith's organization man. After playing, he was a Senator coach (1940–42), manager (1943–47, including two well-handled second-place finishes), and farm director (1948–56). From 1957–71, for the Senators and Twins, he was club comptroller. Ossie's younger brother, Otto, or "Squeaky," had one season plus one game as a Cincinnati shortstop. /(ADS)

Jim Bluejacket — 1887–1947. RHP 1914–16 **Brooklyn (FL), Reds** 237 ip, 13–17, 3.46

Sportswriters disparaged the American Indian as an oddball redskin righthander, but despite eccentricities, he was no fool. After a marginal life in baseball, Bluejacket (born James Smith) had a successful career in the oil industry. /(ADS)

Bert Blyleven — 1951– . RHP 1970– **Twins**, Rangers, Pirates, Indians 4703 ip, 271–231, 3.22. 20 wins: 73 *3 LCS, 24 ip, 3–0, 2.59. 12 WS, 23 ip, 2–1, 2.35*
☛ *Led League—k 85. All-Star—73, 85.*

Possessing the premier curveball of his era, Bert Blyleven carved out a great career despite frequent accusations of underachievement. Born in the Netherlands, Blyleven was *TSN* AL Rookie Pitcher of the Year in 1970. His early career coincided with the collapse of the aging Minnesota club. Despite six straight years of better than 200 strikeouts and five of 15 or more wins with poor teams, more was expected of him. He was traded to the Rangers with Danny Thompson for Bill Singer, Roy Smalley, Mike Cubbage, Jim Gideon, and $250,000 on June 1, 1976. Blyleven pitched a no-hitter against California on September 22, 1977. He and John Milner

Bert Blyleven

46 in 1987. The homers were partially due to his outstanding control. He maintained a strikeout-to-walk ratio of nearly 3:1 while passing the 3000-strikeout mark in 1986. His eighth AL season with 200 or more strikeouts (1986) established a league record. Blyleven had 196 strikeouts in 1987, his ninth season of 15 or more wins (15–12) and turned in outstanding performances in postseason play, winning twice in the LCS and once in the World Series. After a mediocre 1988 season for the Twins, he moved on to the Angels and went 17–5 with a 2.73 ERA (fourth in the AL) in 1989. Leading the AL with five shutouts in '89, he finished the 1980s as the active career leader in that category and trailed only all-time leader Nolan Ryan among active players in strikeouts. /(ME)

Mike Blyzka — 1928– . RHP 1953–54 **Browns/ Orioles** 181 ip, 3–11, 5.58

The chunky reliever was included in the 18-player deal that sent Bob Turley and Don Larsen to the Yankees. /(GEB)

John Boccabella — 1941– . C-1B-OF 1963–74 Cubs, **Expos**, Giants 551 g, .219, 26 hr, 148 rbi

An original Expo after six part-time years with the Cubs, the versatile Boccabella hit two homers in one inning for Montreal (7/6/73). Expo Manager Gene Mauch called him "one of the most underrated players in the league." /(JCA)

Bruce Bochte — 1950– . 1B-OF 1974–82, 84–86 Angels, **Mariners**, A's 1538 g, .282, 100 hr, 658 rbi
☛ *All-Star—79.*

Bochte was an AL All-Star in 1979 when he hit .316 for the Mariners and his .300 the next season earned him the club MVP award. After hitting .297 in '82, he abruptly retired, explaining, "I was the Mariners' player rep for three years and became aware of a cold, impersonal attitude on the part of management, and wanted no part of that." Lured back to baseball by the A's in '84, he put in three more solid seasons. /(NLM)

Bruce Bochy — 1955– . C 1978–80, 82–87 Astros, Mets, **Padres** 358 g, .239, 26 hr, 93 rbi. *1 LCS, 1 g, .000. 1 WS, 1 g, 1.000*

Bochy was a backup catcher and pinch hitter with some power who never started more than 29 games behind the plate in one season. His bigger-than-normal hat size caused him trouble in 1982 when he was called up to the Mets. When he arrived in New

were traded to the Pirates for Al Oliver and Nelson Norman in another blockbuster deal on December 8, 1977.

Blyleven helped Pittsburgh to its 1979 World Series win, but he became increasingly unhappy with manager Chuck Tanner's strategy of going to the bullpen in close games. Openly admitting his pursuit of statistical goals, Blyleven announced his intention to retire, unless he was traded, on April 30, 1980. After being placed on the disqualified list, Blyleven agreed to rejoin the Pirates May 13. The slender righthander was virtually given to Cleveland in a six-player deal on December 9, 1980.

A severe elbow injury sidelined Blyleven for most of 1982. He struggled in 1983 but rebounded with one of his best seasons (19–7, 2.87) in 1984. Unhappy playing for a non-contender, he forced a trade back to Minnesota in 1985. His ERA skyrocketed in the Metrodome, but Blyleven continued to accumulate wins and strikeouts. He also surrendered a ML-record 50 homers in 1986 and a league-high

York, he could not find a helmet to fit him, and had to wait until his was rushed up from Tidewater (International League) before he could play. He became a minor league manager for the Padres when his playing days ended. /(JCA)

Hal Bock — 1939- . *Writer*

Bock has been covering baseball in New York for the Associated Press since 1963. His twice-weekly column, "Bock's Score," is published by 1700 newspapers. /NLM)

Eddie Bockman — 1920- . 3B 1946-49 Yankees, Indians, **Pirates** 249 g, .230, 11 hr, 56 rbi

After four years of military service during WWII, Bockman saw brief ML action as a reserve third baseman, and he has been a scout for the Phillies since 1960. His notable signees and discoveries include Bob Boone, Larry Bowa, Mark Davis, and Joe Charboneau. /(FVP)

Randy Bockus — 1960- . LHP 1986- **Giants** 56 ip, 2-1, 4.15

The injury-prone Giants staff afforded this reliever several opportunities in the majors. /(JFC)

Mike Boddicker — 1957- . RHP 1980- **Orioles**, Red Sox 1574 ip, 101-87, 3.70. 20 wins: 84 *2 LCS, 12 ip, 1-1, 4.63. 1 WS, 9 ip, 1-0, 0.00*
☛ *Led League—w 84. Led League—era 84. All-Star—84.*

Boddicker was outstanding in his first two ML seasons, baffling AL hitters with a collection of slow breaking balls. He was *TSN* AL Rookie Pitcher of the Year in 1983 and tied an LCS record with 14 strikeouts in a shutout win in the '83 ALCS. As a sophomore, he led the AL in both wins (20) and ERA (2.79). After three more seasons as Baltimore's most consistent starter, he was traded to the Red Sox in July 1988. He helped the Red Sox win the AL East by going 7-3 with a 2.63 ERA; he had been 6-12 with a 3.86 for the Orioles. He was 15-11, 4.00 in 1989 and gave up 217 hits in 211.2 innings, but won by holding opposing batters to a league-leading .212 batting average with runners in scoring position. /(ME)

Ping Bodie [Frank Stephan; born Francesco Stephano Pezzullo] — 1887-1961. OF 1911-14, 17-21 **White Sox**, A's, Yankees 1049 g, .275, 43 hr, 516 rbi

The burly, colorful, but modestly talented slugger took "Bodie" from the California town in which he once lived, while "Ping" approximated the sound of the ball off his bat. A fair hitter with a good arm (AL leader in outfield assists with 32 in 1917), Bodie was naturally funny and garrulous. Supposedly Ring Lardner blended elements of Bodie into the brash

ballplayer of his "You Know Me, Al" stories. Asked about rooming with the gallivanting Babe Ruth, Ping cracked: "I don't room with Ruth; I room with his suitcase!" When the slowfooted Bodie was out by yards in an attempted steal, columnist Bugs Baer wrote: "There was larceny in his heart, but his feet were honest." /(ADS)

Tony Boeckel (Elmer) — 1892-1924. 3B 1917, 19-23 Pirates, **Braves** 777 g, .282, 27 hr, 337 rbi

Before he died in an automobile crash at age 30, Boeckel was an aggressive if error-prone third baseman with occasional power. In his final season he hit .298. /(JK)

George Boehler — 1892-1958. RHP 1912-16, 20-21, 23, 26 **Tigers**, Browns, Pirates, Dodgers 201 ip, 6-12, 4.74

Although he didn't stick in the ML in nine tries, Boehler won 210 games in the minors during his 18-year career. Six times he won over 20, including a 38-13 mark with Tulsa of the Western League in 1922. /(NLM)

Joe Boehling — 1891-1941. LHP 1912-17, 20 **Senators**, Indians 925 ip, 55-50, 2.97

Although he never improved on his 17-7 rookie record in 1913, the slender Boehling turned in several solid seasons for Washington. He dropped out of baseball for several years, then returned for a lengthy minor league career. /(JK)

Joe Boever — 1960- . RHP 1985- Cardinals, **Braves** 159 ip, 5-14, 3.79

In 1989 Boever (pronounced BAY-vur) was the Braves' bullpen ace until a weight problem in the second half of the season. He saved 21 games but was 4-11, 3.94. /(SFS)

Dusty Boggess Lynton — 1904-1968. *Umpire* NL 1944-48, 50-62 *4 WS, 5 ASU*

Boggess spent 21 years in the minors, 16 as an infielder and catcher. His nickname stemmed both from his dusty red hair and his habit of scooping up dirt while he batted. A NL umpire for 18 years, he kept a souvenir ball autographed by every umpire he'd worked with. It was buried with him, as specified in his will. /(RTM)

Tommy Boggs — 1955- . RHP 1976-83 Rangers, **Braves** 577 ip, 20-44, 4.14

The second pick in the nation in June 1974, Boggs debuted with Texas at age 20. His record was 3-20 in parts of four seasons before he had his only winning year, 12-9 with Atlanta in 1980. /(JCA)

Wade Boggs — 1958– . 3B 1982– **Red Sox** 1183 g, .352, 64 hr, 523 rbi. *2 LCS, 11 g, .279, 5 rbi. 1 WS, 7 g, .290, 3 rbi*

☛ *Led League—ba 83, 85–88. All-Star—85–89.*

With an easy lefthanded stroke that sprays line drives to all fields, an outstanding eye for the strike zone, and a litany of routines that borders on the fanatical, Wade Boggs, the AL's perennial batting champion, has become a baseball anomaly, a player whose statistics are so staggering as to defy contemporary comparison. In the post-WWII era of declining batting averages, Boggs's .356 career mark through 1988 is the fourth-highest in ML history, behind Ty Cobb, Rogers Hornsby, and Joe Jackson. He has hit .349 or higher in six of his seven seasons (Rod Carew did so five times in 19 seasons), and in 1988 he became the only player in ML history with 200 or more hits in six consecutive seasons. As remarkable as his hitting ability is his patience at the plate. He routinely draws 100 walks in a season, leading the AL in both 1986 and '88, while his on-base percentage for his first seven seasons is a phenomenal .448. In 1985, Boggs reached base 340 times. Only Babe Ruth, Ted Williams, and Lou Gehrig have done better.

Still, Boggs is not without his detractors. He has a reputation as an egotistical statistics-minded player with little regard for his team's fortunes (although he did cry in the dugout after the Red Sox lost Game Seven of the 1986 WS to the Mets). He is criticized both for his lack of speed (12 career stolen bases) and an alleged lack of run-producing ability. Usually batting leadoff, Boggs finished the 1980s with 100 or more runs scored in seven consecutive seasons, and has rapped 40 or more doubles five times. In 1987, batting third most of the year, Boggs hit 24 HR and his .588 slugging percentage was third in the AL, but he has hit no more than eight HR in any other season.

Boggs's ML success did not come quickly. He toiled for six seasons in the Red Sox' minor league chain, always among his league's batting leaders, but stigmatized as an inadequate fielder. He reached the ML in 1982, and improved enough at third base to finish second in the AL Gold Glove voting in 1987. Boggs got his opportunity to play regularly when Carney Lansford injured his ankle in June 1982. He hit .349 the rest of the season to set an AL rookie record and finish third in the Rookie of the Year voting behind Cal Ripken and Kent Hrbek. The following season, Boggs won his first batting title with a .361 average and topped 200 hits and 100 runs for the first of six consecutive seasons. He

Wade Boggs

"slumped" to a career-low .325 in 1984, and has not hit below .357 since, winning the AL batting title every year.

To Boggs, perhaps the game's most superstitious player today, his cherished and obsessive rituals both before and during games are the keys to his consistency. His diet consists almost exclusively of chicken, and he runs pregame windsprints precisely at 7:17 each evening. He draws a Hebrew letter in the batter's box before each at bat, and his route to and from the playing field is so precise that by late summer his footprints are clearly visible in the grass in front of the Fenway Park dugout.

In 1988, the details of Boggs's long-term extramarital affair with Margo Adams became public, and Adams's lawsuit created dissension among the Red Sox, many of whom were asked to give depositions. Despite rumors he would be traded because of the scandal, Boggs remained in Boston through 1989. /(SCL)

Sammy Bohne [born Sammy Cohen] — 1896–1977. 2B-SS-3B 1916, 21–26 Cardinals, **Reds**, Dodgers 663 g, .261, 16 hr, 228 rbi

One of four Cincinnati infielders in the early 1920s who were graduates of the San Francisco sandlots, Bohne broke up Dodger Dazzy Vance's bid for a no-hitter with two outs in the ninth (6/17/23). That year a Chicago newspaper story implied that Bohne and Pat Duncan were associated with gamblers. The players were cleared by a federal judge, and later Bohne was awarded damages in a libel suit. /(NLM)

Bruce Boisclair — 1952– . OF 1974, 76–79 **Mets** 410 g, .263, 10 hr, 77 rbi

The lefty Met outfielder hit .287 in his rookie 1976 season, when he was the NL's best pinch hitter (12 for 21, .571). He was used mainly as a pinch hitter through 1979, when a broken wrist and a .184 BA ended his ML career. /(JCA)

Bernie Boland — 1892–1973. RHP 1915–21 **Tigers**, Browns 1063 ip, 68–53, 3.24

A regular starter for the Tigers for five years before suffering a broken arm, Boland had a top season of 16–11 in 1917. He used a sharply breaking curve ball to strike out Babe Ruth three times in one game. As a rookie in 1915 he came within one out of pitching a no-hitter against the Yankees. /(NLM)

Joe Boley [John Peter] — 1896–1962. SS 1927–32 **A's**, Indians 538 g, .269, 7 hr, 227 rbi. *3 WS, 12 g, .154, 2 rbi*

An exceptional fielder, steady hitter, and member of the Baltimore team that won seven consecutive International League championships (1919–25), Boley's reputed $100,000 price tag kept major-league bidders at bay for years. Connie Mack wrested him away for $60,000 in 1927, and the 28-year-old rookie batted .311 for the A's. Boley joined Jimmie Foxx, Max Bishop, and Jimmy Dykes in Mack's "Million Dollar Infield," which sparked the A's to three pennants and two world championships (1929–31). /(JL)

Jim Bolger (Dutch) — 1932– . OF 1950–51, 54–55, 57–59 Reds, **Cubs**, Indians, Phillies 312 g, .229, 6 hr, 48 rbi

Bolger couldn't stick with his hometown Reds, but he found a niche with the Cubs in 1957. He led the NL in pinch hits (17) and pinch at-bats (48), but that .354 pinch BA was followed by pinch averages of .196 and .125, ending his career. /(SFS)

Bobby Bolin — 1939– . RHP 1961–73 **Giants**, Brewers, Red Sox 1576 ip, 88–75, 3.40. *1 WS, 3 ip, 6.75*

The sidearming Bolin pitched two no-hitters in the minors and had a top ML mark of 14–6 in 1965. The next year he tied a then-ML record by striking out the first five Dodger batters he faced. He was the winning pitcher in the Milwaukee Brewers' first victory. /(GEB)

Frank Bolling — 1931– . 2B 1954, 56–66 **Tigers**, Braves 1540 g, .254, 106 hr, 556 rbi
☛ *Gold Glove—58.*

The younger brother of Milt Bolling, Frank twice hit 15 homers in a season. During his dozen ML years he never played an inning at any position other than second base. With the Tigers, he led AL second basemen in fielding in 1958. Traded to the Braves for centerfielder Billy Bruton after the 1960 season, he led NL second basemen in fielding in 1961, '62, and '64, finishing with a career mark of .982. /(GEB)

Milt Bolling — 1930– . SS-2B 1952–58 **Red Sox**, Senators, Tigers 400 g, .241, 19 hr, 94 rbi

The former Spring Hill college basketball star showed promise as a young shortstop, but injuries to his legs and elbows cost him first-string status. While with Detroit, he played a few games alongside brother Frank. Their uncle, John Bolling, played first base for the Phillies and Dodgers. /(EW)

Cliff Bolton — 1907–1979. C 1931, 33–37, 41 **Senators**, Tigers 335 g, .291, 6 hr, 143 rbi. *1 WS, 2 g, .000*

This North Carolina farm boy hit .304 for the Senators in 1935, the only year he played in more than 100 games. His small size and lack of power kept him in a backup role most of his career. /(GEB)

Tom Bolton — 1962– . LHP 1987– **Red Sox** 110 ip, 2–7, 5.10

Bolton's hittability confined him to middle relief in his short major league stints. /(WOR)

Mark Bomback — 1953– . RHP 1978, 80–82 Brewers, **Mets**, Blue Jays 314 ip, 16–18, 4.47

In his ninth minor league season, Bomback was named *TSN* 1979 Minor League Player of the Year with a 22–7 mark in the Pacific Coast League. He was 10–8 as a Met rookie the next year. /(GEB)

Tommy Bond — 1856–1941. RHP-OF 1874–82, 84 Brooklyn/Hartford (NA), Hartford (NL), **Boston (NL)**, Worcester (NL), Boston (UL), Indianapolis (AA) *NA*: 41–48; 126 g, .242; *ML*: 2780 ip, 193–115, 2.25; 361 g, .236, 0 hr, 121 rbi. 20 wins: 1874, 76–80
   Manager 1882 **Worcester (NL)** 5–22, .185
☛ *Led League—w 1877–78. Led League—k 1877–78. Led League—era 1877, 79.*

Bond became the first "triple crown" pitcher when he led the National League with 40 wins, 170 strikeouts, and a 2.11 ERA for Boston in 1877. In 1878 he repeated as leader in wins, strikeouts, shutouts, and winning percentage, while working more games and innings than any other NL pitcher. He won a career-high 43 games in 1879, again was the NL's ERA champion, and threw 12 shutouts while the entire league had only 42. In his first four NL seasons, he compiled a 154–68 record.

Bond was one of the first curveball pitchers. Born in Ireland, at age 18 he joined the 1874 National Association Brooklyn Atlantics. He remained with that team when it moved to Hartford in 1875 and became a pioneer entry in the NL in 1876. He was virtually his team's only pitcher for most of his career, particularly while with Boston. In 1880 Boston was shut out in eight of Bond's games, and Bond began phasing out his pitching career. He coached at Harvard and was a New England League umpire in 1882–83. He lived to be the last survivor of the National League's first season./(JK)

Walt Bond — 1937–1967. OF-1B 1960–62, 64–65, 67 Indians, **Astros**, Twins 365 g, .256, 41 hr, 179 rbi

This gigantic 6'7" 235-lb Kansas City Monarch and minor-league slugger battled leukemia as a player. During a four-year remission, he put together one productive major-league season, for the 1964 Colt .45's (20 HR, 85 RBI). Bond began 1967 with the Twins, but died in September./(JK)

Barry Bonds — 1964– . OF 1986– **Pirates** 566 g, .256, 84 hr, 223 rbi

Bobby Bonds's son came to the majors with talents similar to those of his father. Barry became the second 20-HR, 20-steal Pirate ever in 1987. He led 1986 NL rookies with 16 HR, 36 steals, 48 RBI, and 65 walks. Batting both third and leadoff, he started several games with home runs. Injuries slowed him from mid-1988 on, but he retained his 20-HR power. In 1989 he and Bobby took over the father-son HR title from the Berras./(ME)

Bobby Bonds — 1946– . OF-DH 1968–81 **Giants**, Yankees, Angels, White Sox, Rangers, Indians, Cardinals, Cubs 1,849 g, .268, 332 hr, 1,024 rbi. *1 LCS, 3 g, .250* ☛ *All-Star—71, 73, 75. Gold Glove—71, 73–74.*

The enigmatic Bonds, the quintessential 30–30 player, never quite lived up to his predicted potential and could never find a permanent home. After spending seven productive seasons with the Giants, most under the shadow of Willie Mays, he spent the final seven years of his career playing for seven different teams. He hit 30 homers for five different teams, a major league record. Bonds debuted auspiciously on June 25, 1968, hitting a grand slam in the seventh inning against the Dodgers in Candlestick, the only player in the 20th century to collect a grand slam as his first hit. In his first full season in 1969, he reached the 30–30 club with 45 stolen bases and 32 homers and led the league in runs, but also led the league in strikeouts, setting a major league record with 185. He repeated that feat the following year, setting a new strikeout record of 189. After Mays was dealt to the Mets, Bonds's career took off. He

Bobby Bonds

had his best year in 1973, narrowly missing the first 40-homer, 40-stolen base season with 39 dingers and 43 steals, but again leading the league in strikeouts. Bonds insists that he had five homers rained out, including two in a game against Atlanta. Against Pittsburgh, he led off consecutive games with homers on June 5 and 6, and set a then-ML record of 11 leadoff homers. He ended the 1973 season in a slump that carried into 1974, when he was benched and fined by Charlie Fox. He regained his batting eye, but was traded after the season to the Yankees for Bobby Murcer, starting his nomadic period. The Yankees made him their number three hitter, and Bonds responded with another 30-30 effort with 85 RBIs, and became the last NL outfielder to have an unassisted double play in a game against the Mets on May 31. But after the season, the Yankees traded him to California, where he played just 99 games because of an injured hand. He rebounded in 1977 for the Angels with his third 30-30 year, with 37 homers and 41 stolen bases and driving in a career high 115 runs. In a nine-game span from August 2 to 11, he smacked eight homers. Despite his fine season, he was traded in the off season to the White Sox, but played only 26 games before being shipped to the Rangers. His combined totals for the season gave him his second straight and fifth 30-30 season, yet he was again traded in the off season to the Indians. He had his last effective season, hitting 25 homers in spacious Municipal Stadium, and wanted his contract renegotiated. The Indians responded by trading him to the Cardinals, but he didn't hit well and was platooned. He was then sold to the Cubs, but appeared in just 45 games. Bonds was named batting coach of the Indians in 1984. In his career, he set a major league record of 35 leadoff homers, a mark eclipsed by Rickey Henderson in 1988. He and his son Barry are also the all-time leading father-son homer duo, passing the Bells and the Berras in 1989. /(SEW)

Bill Bonham — 1948- . RHP 1971-80 **Cubs**, Reds 1488 ip, 75-83, 4.00

Reliever Bonham was converted to starting midway through 1973, and the following season his 22 losses tied for the league lead despite his 7.07 strikeouts-per-nine-innings, third best in the NL. Plagued by wildness and playing for bad Cubs teams, he improved his record only marginally. On July 31, 1974, he struck out four batters in one inning; that season, his eight balks tied what was then the ML record. On August 5, 1975, he set a ML record when he allowed seven consecutive hits to start the game. A trade to the Reds for the 1978 season (for Woodie Fryman and Bill Caudill) turned his career around, and he finally had a winning season as a starter (11-5, 3.54). He contributed a 9-7 record to the 1979 Reds' division championship. /(JFC)

Ernie Bonham (Tiny) — 1913-49. RHP 1940-49 **Yankees**, Pirates 1551 ip, 103-72, 3.06. 20 wins: 42 *1 WS, 28 ip, 1-2, 3.21*
☛ *Led League—era 40. All-Star—42-43.*

Bonham was an important contributor to the 1941-43 Yankee pennants. The 6'2″ 215-lb hulk ("Tiny") was the first successful pitcher to use the forkball, and had excellent control. He led the AL with a 1.90 ERA as a rookie in 1940. In 1942 his .808 winning percentage (21-5), six shutouts, and 22 complete games were the league's best. Chronic back problems reduced his effectiveness his final five seasons, but he remained a tough competitor, winning his last six games. He died suddenly from appendicitis complications just two weeks after pitching his last game. /(GDW)

Bobby Bonilla — 1963- . 3B-OF 1986- White Sox, **Pirates** 601 g, .278, 66 hr, 306 rbi
☛ *All-Star—88-89.*

Pittsburgh's lost and found star was originally signed by the Pirates in 1981, but he was left unprotected and lost to the White Sox in 1985. Originally recommended to the Pirates by Syd Thrift, he was reacquired after Thrift became their GM in 1986. The powerful switch-hitter hit the seventh upper-deck HR in Three Rivers Stadium history on July 12, 1987 and hit a career-high .300 that year. In 1988 a hot first half had him leading the NL in HR and RBI and challenging for the Triple Crown, but he cooled off and finished with 24 HR and 100 RBI. Finally given a permanent position at third base in 1988, he was error-prone but showed fair range using an unusual sideways-facing stance in the field. /(ME)

Juan Bonilla — 1956- . 2B 1981-83, 85-87 **Padres**, Yankees, Orioles 429 g, .256, 7 hr, 101 rbi

Although he led NL second basemen with 13 errors in strike-shortened 1981, Bonilla made a good beginning with the Padres, hitting .290 in 99 games and showing good range afield. A broken wrist and rehabilitation from drug abuse shelved him for most of the 1982 season. In 1983 his BA skidded to .237. When he held out the following year, he was released. In subsequent tries with the Yankees and Orioles, he was unable to win a regular job. /(MC)

Barry Bonnell — 1953– . OF-3B 1977–86 Braves, **Blue Jays**, Mariners 976 g, .272, 56 hr, 355 rbi

Bonnell was a platoon outfielder with a good arm who would sometimes be among the league batting leaders during the season, but seldom at the end. An exception was 1983, when he hit .318 (10 HR and 54 RBI) for the Blue Jays. That December he was traded to Seattle for pitcher Bryan Clark. /(TF)

Zeke Bonura [Henry John] (Banana Nose) — 1908–1987. 1B 1934–40 **White Sox**, Senators, Giants, Cubs 917 g, .307, 119 hr, 704 rbi

A fans' delight and manager's nightmare, Bonura led AL first basemen in fielding in 1936 by refusing to become involved. As easy grounders bounded by untouched, Zeke waved his "Mussolini salute" with his glove. Known affectionately as "Banana Nose," the colorful and outspoken Bonura was the White Sox' first bona fide home run hitter, with 27 in his rookie year. He continued slugging, but his nonchalant fielding, aggravating annual hold-outs, and rumored interest in owner J. Lou Comiskey's daughter got him traded to Washington in 1938 in exchange for Joe Kuhel, the AL's top fielding first baseman. /(RL)

Greg Booker — 1960– . RHP 1983– **Padres** 253 ip, 5–7, 3.80. *1 LCS, 2 ip, 0–0, 0.00. 1 WS, 1 ip, 0–0, 9.00*

A 6′6″ reliever, Booker shuttled between San Diego and Las Vegas (Pacific Coast League) from 1983 to 1986 before finally spending full seasons with the Padres in 1987 and 1988. Originally drafted as a first baseman, he switched to pitching full-time in his second pro season (1982) and led the California League in losses, walks, and wild pitches. He still reached the ML at the tail end of the 1983 season, and in 1984 he pitched one inning in Game Three of the WS, walking four batters. Booker's father-in-law is Padres manager Jack McKeon. /(SCL)

Bob Boone — 1947– . C 1972–89 **Phillies**, Angels 2224 g, .254, 105 hr, 817 rbi. *6 LCS, 27 g, .310, 2 hr, 9 rbi. 1 WS, 6 g, .412, 4 rbi*
☛ *All-Star—76, 78–79, 83. Gold Glove—78–79, 82, 86–89.*

The most durable catcher in ML history, Boone had caught a ML-record 2066 games entering the 1990 season. The son of Tigers All-Star third baseman Ray Boone, Bob attended Stanford University before reaching the ML in late 1972, and although he had several good seasons at the plate, his value lay in his defensive skills and his handling of

Bob Boone

pitchers. In 1977, his eight errors and three passed balls were the lowest totals among NL catchers. He started for Philadelphia's three straight division champions (1976–78) as well as the World Championship club of 1980. After Boone's off-year in 1981 (.211, 4 HR, 24 RBI), the Phillies decided that Keith Moreland was ready to take over behind the plate, and Boone was traded to the Angels. He quickly proved the Phillies wrong. While Moreland struggled, Boone threw out 21 of the first 34 AL runners attempting to steal against him and steadied the Angels' pitching staff en route to the AL West title. He remained the Angels' starting catcher for seven years, but was let go after hitting a career-high .295 in 1988 at the age of 40. He signed with the Royals as a free agent and led them in 1989 with a .350 batting average with runners in scoring position. /(SG)

Ike Boone — 1897–1958. OF 1922–25, 27, 30–32 Giants, **Red Sox**, White Sox, Dodgers 356 g, .319, 26 hr, 192 rbi

A product of the University of Alabama, Boone hit well in several trials in the majors, but his lack of speed handicapped him in the field and on the bases. He had a career BA of .370 in the minor leagues, and in 1929 (over the course of 198 games in the Pacific Coast League), he set an organized baseball record with 553 total bases while batting .407 with 55 homers and 218 RBI. /(LRD)

Luke Boone (Danny) — 1890–1982. 2B-SS-3B 1913–16, 18 **Yankees**, Pirates 314 g, .209, 6 hr, 76 rbi

The regular second baseman for the Yankees in 1914–15, Boone's fielding couldn't make up for his poor hitting. The Pittsburgh native played in the American Association until 1936. /(ME)

Ray Boone (Ike) — 1923– . 3B-SS-1B 1948–60 Indians, **Tigers**, White Sox, A's, Braves, Red Sox 1373 g, .275, 151 hr, 737 rbi. *1 WS, 1 g, .000*
☛ *Led League—rbi 55. All-Star—54, 56.*

Boone was hitting .355 in the Texas League in late 1948 when Cleveland shortstop-manager Lou Boudreau was hurt. Boone, who had been converted from catcher to shortstop that year, was called up in time to earn a World Series share. Before long he forced Boudreau to switch to third base.

Boone had a powerful throwing arm, but bad knees and ankles limited his range. He led AL shortstops in errors in 1951. Traded to Detroit in an eight-player deal in 1953, he was switched to less-demanding third base, and his hitting improved. He more than doubled his HR and RBI output, hitting 26 HR, including four grand slams. A righthanded line-drive hitter who could handle the curveball, in 1955 he led the AL in RBI with 116.

Ray's son Bob Boone starred as a ML catcher. /(JCA)

John Boozer — 1939– . RHP 1962–64, 66–69 **Phillies** 394 ip, 14–16, 4.09

Boozer bounced between the minors and the Phillies five times on option, never able to keep a starting slot. Despite occasional streaks of wildness, he saved 11 games in relief for Philadelphia during his last two ML years. /(JK)

Pedro Borbon — 1946– . RHP 1969–80 Angels, **Reds**, Giants, Cardinals 1026 ip, 69–39, 3.52. *4 LCS, 14 ip, 1–0, 0.63. 3 WS, 11 ip, 0–1, 3.86*

An unabashed cockfighting enthusiast, macho Borbon reportedly could warm up faster and throw a ball farther than anyone else in the NL during the mid-1970s when he was a top reliever for Cincinnati's "Big Red Machine." He liked to show off by throwing strikes to home plate from the center field warning track during batting practice. His best seasons were 1973 (11–4 with 14 saves) and 1977 (10–5 with 18 saves). /(MC)

Frenchy Bordagaray [Stanley George] — 1910– . OF-3B 1934–39, 41–45 White Sox, **Dodgers**, Cardinals, Reds, Yankees 930 g, .283, 14 hr, 270 rbi. *2 WS, 3 g, --*

Frenchy fit Casey Stengel's Brooklyn Dodgers like fingers in a glove. Gifted but erratic, he mixed brilliant plays with bonehead ones. He ran when he wanted, failed to slide when he should have, and ignored signs. In 1935, he showed up at spring training with a mustache, a no-no in those days. They made him shave it off, which he blamed for a subsequent slump. With the Cardinals in '38, he led the league with 20 pinch hits in 43 at-bats. /(NLM)

Pat Borders — 1963– . C 1988– **Blue Jays** 150 g, .263, 8 hr, 50 rbi. *1 LCS, 1.000, 1 rbi*

Borders won platoon time with his bat, but poor throwing mechanics made this converted third baseman easy to steal on. /(JFC)

Rich Bordi — 1959– . RHP 1980– A's, Mariners, Cubs, **Yankees**, Orioles 371 ip, 20–20, 4.34

The 6'7" Bordi was the last player signed by A's owner Charley Finley. He made his ML debut with the A's in 1980 after pitching only 11 games in the minors. Traded or released six times thereafter, Bordi didn't spend a full season in the ML until 1984 with the Cubs, then appeared in 51 games for the Yankees in 1985 and 52 games for the Orioles in 1986. He was released by the Yankees after the 1987 season and made two starts for the World Champion A's in 1988, lasting less than eight innings total. /(SCL)

Glenn Borgmann — 1950– . C 1972–80 **Twins**, White Sox 474 g, .229, 16 hr, 151 rbi

Light-hitting but rifle-armed Borgmann set a Minnesota record when he led all ML catchers with a .997 fielding average in 1974, his first of two years as the Twins' regular catcher. Injuries, the emergence of Butch Wynegar, and Borgmann's poor hitting relegated him to reserve duty thereafter. /(MC)

Bob Borkowski (Bush) — 1926– . OF 1950–55 Cubs, **Reds**, Dodgers 470 g, .251, 16 hr, 112 rbi

Originally signed as a pitcher, "Bush" went 18–9 for Elizabethton, but his .384 BA convinced the Cubs to switch him to the outfield. Although he never earned a regular spot in the majors, he was a useful sub and righthanded pinch hitter, with a knack for hitting Giants and Phillies pitching. /(RM)

Steve Boros — 1936– . 3B-1B-2B 1957–58, 61–65 **Tigers**, Cubs, Reds 422 g, .245, 26 hr, 149 rbi.
Manager 1983–84, 86 **A's**, Padres 168–200, .457

Boros signed with Detroit for $25,000 while a student at the University of Michigan, where he received a B.A. in literature. He was voted American Association MVP with Denver in 1960 and had an excellent rookie season with the Tigers in 1961 until sidelined by a broken collarbone. After that the intellectual infielder was better known for his B.A. than his BA. Later a ML manager, in his only two full seasons (1983 A's and 1986 Padres) his teams finished with identical 74–88 records. He was considered a masterful teacher of baserunning. /(RM)

Hank Borowy — 1916– . RHP 1942–51 **Yankees**, Cubs, Phillies, Pirates, Tigers 1716 ip, 108–82, 3.50. 20 wins: 45 _3 WS, 29 ip, 3–2, 4.97_
☛ _Led League—era 45. All-Star—44._

Borowy pitched reliably for the Yankees during WWII, going 15–4 as a 1942 rookie and following with 14–9 and 17–12 years. After a 10–5 start in 1945, he was suddenly sold to the Cubs on July 27 for $97,000. He went 11–2 for the remainder of the season, leading the NL in winning percentage (.846) and ERA (2.14), as the Cubs won the pennant. In the WS, he shut out the Tigers in the first game, lost the fifth game, and then came back to win the sixth with four scoreless relief innings. He started the final game on one day's rest but gave up hits to the first three batters before leaving. _TSN_ named him to the all-star ML team for 1945. During the remainder of his career, he was plagued by finger blisters and a sore shoulder. /(ME)

Rick Bosetti — 1953– . OF 1976–82 Phillies, Cardinals, **Blue Jays**, A's 445 g, .250, 17 hr, 133 rbi. _1 LCS, 2 g, .250_

Bosetti was a flashy fielder who, with Toronto in 1979, led AL outfielders in putouts, assists, and errors. _The Rick Bosetti Baseball Book_ was the Blue Jays' first publication of tips from a big leaguer, though it was scarcely believable looking at the off-balance swings on Bosetti's bubblegum cards. Recognizing his own modest talents as a player, Bosetti had other goals—notably to urinate in the outfield of every major league park, a goal he was able to achieve. /(TF)

Chris Bosio — 1963– . RHP 1986- **Brewers** 621 ip, 33–37, 3.93

A hard thrower who can start or relieve, Bosio joined the Brewers' rotation midway through 1987 and tossed a two-hit shutout against Minnesota August 28. In 1988 he was 6–12 as a starter (despite a 3.36 ERA) and also saved six games. Bosio became the anchor of Milwaukee's staff in 1989 with a 15–10, 2.95 record. /(SCL)

Thad Bosley — 1956– . OF 1977- Angels, White Sox, Brewers, Mariners, **Cubs**, Royals 754 g, .274, 19 hr, 155 rbi. _1 LCS, 2 g, .000_

The often-injured Bosley usually hit well when given the chance, but never got more than 180 at-bats in any one season. He led the ML in pinch hits in both 1985 and 1987 and hit six pinch home runs for the Cubs in '85. He was on the DL seven different times in his career. Bosley led the California League with 90 stolen bases for Salinas in 1976. /(ME)

Dick Bosman — 1944– . RHP 1966–76 **Senators/Rangers**, Indians, A's 1591 ip, 82–85, 3.67. _1 LCS, 0.1 ip, 0.00_

A highly competitive control pitcher who told teammates, "If you don't hustle when I'm pitching, I'll kick your ass," Bosman was 14–9 with an AL-best 2.19 ERA for the 1969 Senators. He won a career-high 16 in 1970, and no-hit the A's while with Cleveland (7/19/74), losing a perfect game on his own error. Bosman won 11 to help Oakland to a division title in 1975, but the A's cut him in 1977. /(KT)

Lyman Bostock — 1950–1978. OF 1975–78 **Twins**, Angels 526 g, .311, 23 hr, 250 rbi

Bostock, the son of Negro League player Lyman Bostock, Sr., appeared headed for stardom before he was fatally wounded in 1978. In 1976, he hit .323 and received the Calvin R. Griffith Award for the most improved Twin. In 1977, he finished second to teammate Rod Carew in the AL batting race (.336 to Carew's .388). The well-liked Alabaman was shot in Gary, Indiana, in the back seat of a car driven by his uncle. Police later arrested the estranged husband of one of two women in the car. /(RM)

Boston Braves — 1871–1952. Team. 5118–5598, .478. *National Association Champions 72–75 NL Champions 1877–78, 83, 91–93, 97–98, 1914, 48, 57–58 World Champions 14, 57*

The franchise that is now the Atlanta Braves, after a 13-year stopover in Milwaukee, is the longest continuously active club in baseball history. A charter member of the National Association, the first professional league, the team called itself the Boston Red Stockings because manager Harry Wright and three other members of the Cincinnati Red Stockings, baseball's first pro team, were on the original club in 1871. They finished first four straight years (1872–75) and continued in the National League when that organization supplanted the NA in 1876.

Boston won eight NL pennants before the end of the 19th century, becoming known as the Beaneaters in the process. The 20th century wasn't as kind to the team, which finally assumed the familiar Braves name. Boston did make history in 1914 when the "Miracle Braves" took less than two months to go from last to first in the second half of the season and proceeded to stun the Athletics in the World Series, becoming in the process the first team to successfully utilize platooning. Financial difficulties took their toll over the next thirty years, as the Braves finished over .500 only five times from 1917 through 1945, but contractor Lou Perini bought the franchise for 1946. With a turnover of personnel on the field and in the front office, the team won the NL pennant in 1948, but declining attendance resulted in the move to Milwaukee only five years later. Babe Ruth hit his final home runs in a Boston Braves uniform in 1935, and Casey Stengel managed the club during the lean years of the late 1930s and early 1940s. /(SH)

The 1914 Boston Braves

Boston Red Sox [aka Puritans] (BoSox) — 1901– . 6996–6720, .510. *AL East Champions 75, 86, 88 AL Champions 03–04, 12, 15–16, 18, 46, 75, 86 World Champions 03, 12, 15–16, 18*

Red Sox fans like to moan about how their team always lets them down, but in fact it is one of the more successful franchises in the American League. It's just that they haven't won a World Championship since 1918 . . .

Originally called the Puritans, the franchise was quite successful in the first two decades of the American League. Their first pennant came in 1903, when Cy Young led the AL in wins and Buck Freeman led in HR and RBI, and they won the first World Series. They repeated in 1904, but Giants manager John McGraw refused to let his team play the WS. The Puritans were rebuilt over the rest of the decade, and when they won the AL flag in 1912, they featured Tris Speaker, who led AL outfielders with 35 assists and tied for the lead in HR, and

Smoky Joe Wood, who had a spectacular 34–5 record that included a string of 16 straight victories. Boston won the Series from the Giants in Game Seven on errors by Snodgrass and Merkle. The Red Sox then won back-to-back World Championships in 1915 and 1916, with Babe Ruth winning the ERA title in 1916. That year, he won a 14-inning 2–1 contest in Game Two. The Red Sox' fifth World Championship in as many chances came in 1918, and Ruth set a scoreless streak record of 29.2 innings dating back to 1916.

But owners Hugh Ward (largely an absentee owner) and Harry Frazee (unfortunately quite present) suffered losses on the New York stage and made up the difference by selling off the Red Sox' most talented players. Babe Ruth had been moved to the outfield in 1919 and proceeded to set a ML record with 29 HR. That winter he was sold to the Yankees in a complicated deal that included $100,000 cash and a $300,000 mortgage on Fenway

The 1908 Boston Red Sox

Park. He was only the first to go, and the Red Sox soon took up residence in the lower levels of the standings, finishing last nine times before Tom Yawkey bought the franchise in 1933 and brought in a new era.

Yawkey bought up established stars such as Lefty Grove, Joe Cronin, and Jimmie Foxx, who gave him an MVP season in 1938. Later in the decade GM Eddie Collins found Ted Williams and Bobby Doerr in the Pacific Coast League. These efforts produced an AL pennant in 1946 (when Ted Williams won the first of his two MVP awards) and a storied loss to the Cardinals in the World Series that began the legend of the Red Sox being fated to lose the big games. In the bottom of the eighth inning of Game Seven, Enos Slaughter scored the winning run from first on a single, while Red Sox shortstop Johnny Pesky supposedly held the ball. Actually, Pesky had his back to the play, which was fumbled by Leon Culberson; Pesky hesitated only slightly before relaying the ball to the plate, but it was too late.

The Red Sox contended for the next few seasons, losing a one-game playoff to the Indians in 1948, but by the mid-1950s slumped to mediocrity, and sometimes less than that. A continual cry for more pitching was unassuaged, and Boston fans had little to do but watch Williams, perhaps the greatest hitter of all time, until his retirement in 1960 took even that solace from them. But the rise of a younger set of stars in the 1960s, especially Carl Yastrzemski, brought the "Impossible Dream" pennant of 1967 after two straight ninth-place finishes. Yaz won the MVP award on the strength of a Triple Crown performance, the last in the majors. Once again it was the Cardinals who denied Yawkey's dreamed-of World Championship, as the Red Sox lost again in seven games.

The Red Sox once again entered a period of mediocrity, although they didn't suffer any losing seasons and contended occasionally. Once again it was the arrival of young blood that brought a pennant. Fred Lynn and Jim Rice had great rookie seasons in 1975, with Lynn capturing both MVP and Rookie of the Year honors, the only man ever to win the MVP in his first season. Rice succeeded Yastrzemski and Williams in the line of great Boston left fielders, and like them became the focus of the fans' love for and dissatisfaction with their team. Once again the Red Sox took the Series to seven games, getting there with a thrilling victory in Game Six (THE Game Six, in Boston; years later it was still referred to as such, with no confusion ever resulting from intervening sixth games of other

Series). Bernie Carbo's game-tying pinch-homer in the 8th inning and Carlton Fisk's dramatic, body-English-directed shot in the 12th inning were the main ingredients. But of course the Reds won Game Seven, and the fatalism of Boston rooters became legend. Tom Yawkey, who had often been accused of pampering and overpaying his favorite stars, died the following year without ever having achieved the World Championship he desired so ardently.

Another lost playoff game in 1978 varied the motif, harking back to the loss to the Indians 30 years earlier. Lost in the disapointment was a great Red Sox comeback at the end of the season after they had been overtaken by the Yankees. After that the triumvirate ownership of Mrs. Tom Yawkey, Haywood Sullivan, and Buddy LeRoux began feuding, and the team entered another fallow period. The arrival of Wade Boggs in 1982 and Roger Clemens in 1984 brought a pennant in 1986, with a dramatic Game Five HR by instant hero Dave Henderson turning the team around. But, one strike away from a World Championship in Game Six against the Mets, reliever Bob Stanley threw a wild pitch, and then Mookie Wilson hit a roller through Bill Buckner's legs at first base. Manager John MacNamara was criticized for not replacing Buckner with a defensive substitute for sentimental reasons. The speedy Wilson would have been safe anyway, but the error allowed the winning run to score, and the Red Sox once again lost in Game Seven. The inertial MacNamara was replaced in mid-1988 by Joe Morgan, nine and a half games back in fourth place at the All-Star break. Morgan led them on a hot streak that carried them to the division title. They won 19 of his first 20 games, and won an AL-record 24 straight games at home (the first five under MacNamara). They were swept by the overwhelming A's in the LCS. /(SH)

Daryl Boston — 1963– . OF 1984– **White Sox** 495, .239, 38 hr, 123 rbi

The lefthanded-hitting, 6'3" 185-lb Boston was the White Sox' first pick in the 1981 June draft. In 1984 he batted .312 in the American Association and led the league with 19 triples. In his debut with Chicago that May 13, he collected three hits before striking out. Over the next four seasons he shuttled between the majors and Triple-A, his occasional power not compensating for what was perceived as a lack of hustle in the outfield and aggressiveness at the plate. The White Sox' new batting coach in 1989, Walt Hriniak, helped him raise his average 30 points, but Boston lost his power in the process. /(RL)

Dave Boswell — 1945- . RHP 1964–71 **Twins,** Tigers, Orioles 1066 ip, 68–56, 3.52. *1 LCS, 11 ip, 0–1, 3.52. 1 WS, 3 ip, 3.38*

Pitching for the Twins in 1967, Boswell racked up 204 strikeouts as he, Jim Kaat, and Dean Chance became the first three pitchers on the same team to strike out 200 each in one season. In 1969 he went 20–12 and was involved in an off-the-field scuffle with teammate Bob Allison which resulted in Boswell getting punched by manager Billy Martin. In the 1969 LCS, he lost to the Orioles 1–0 in ten innings. /(RTM)

Ken Boswell — 1946- . 2B 1967–77 **Mets,** Astros 930 g, .248, 31 hr, 244 rbi. *2 LCS, 4 g, .308, 2 hr 5 rbi. 2 WS, 4 g, .667*

Known for his "bad hands" when he broke in with the Mets, Boswell made three errors on Opening Day, 1969. But in 1970, he set the major-league fielding mark for second basemen (.996) and played a then-record 85 consecutive errorless games. Always a platoon player, he tied a record with three pinch hits in the 1973 World Series. His career-high .279 BA came in the Mets' 1969 championship season. /(KT)

Tom Boswell — 1947- . *Writer.*

A writer and columnist for the Washington *Post* since 1969, Boswell has published two collections of baseball essays: *How Life Imitates the World Series* (1982); and *Why Time Begins on Opening Day* (1984). /(NLM)

Jim Bottomley (Sunny Jim) — 1900–1959. 1B 1922–37 **Cardinals,** Reds, Browns 1991 g, .310, 219 hr, 1422 rbi. *4 WS, 24 g, .200, 1 hr, 10 rbi.*
　Manager 1937 Browns 21–58, .266
☛ *Most Valuable Player—28 . Led League—hr 28. Led League—rbi 26, 28. Hall of Fame—1974.*

"Sunny Jim" was the first MVP to emerge from a team's own farm system. A product of Branch Rickey's Cardinal chain, he arrived at the parent club in 1922. Within a year, he replaced Jack Fournier at first base, as expected, and held the job until traded to Cincinnati after the 1932 season to make room for another farm boy, Ripper Collins.

A lefty cleanup man with a career slugging average of .500, Bottomley had a pleasant nature and smiling face, and the habit of wearing his cap tilted over his left eye. He batted his career-high .371 in his first full season (1923). On September 16, 1924, against the Dodgers, he drove in a record 12

Jim Bottomley

runs with two homers, a double, and three singles. The MVP in 1928, he batted .325, led the league in triples (20) and RBI (136), and tied Hack Wilson for the home run lead (31). He contributed mightily to the Cardinals' triumph in the 1926 WS, but did poorly in three others. In 1931, though limited by injury to 108 games, Bottomley finished third in the closest batting race in NL history (Chick Hafey—.3489; Bill Terry—.3486; Bottomley—.3482).

At 32 and no longer the .300 hitter he had been, the Cardinals sent Sunny Jim to Cincinnati for pitcher Ownie Carroll and outfielder Estel Crabtree—a trade of washed-up players. The Reds dealt him in 1936 to the Browns, where he was doing mostly pinch hitting when, in 1937, he was named to succeed his old friend, Rogers Hornsby, as manager. The hopeless Browns were last when he took over, and last when the season ended, eighty games later. He was bounced in favor of another old Card, Gabby Street.

Bottomley managed a bit in the minors, but no longer needed baseball. With savings from his salary ($15,000 tops) and World Series winnings (another

$22,000), he bought a Missouri cattle farm. Shortly before his death, he returned as a scout for the Cubs and manager in the Appalachian League. On the basis of strong career marks in doubles, hits, RBI, putouts, chances, and DP, he was posthumously elected to the Hall of Fame./(ADS)

Ed Bouchee — 1933- . 1B 1956–62 **Phillies**, Cubs, Mets 670 g, .265, 61 hr, 290 rbi

Bouchee peaked in his rookie 1957 season, batting .293 with 17 HR and 76 RBI. The husky lefthanded hitter was a Brave-killer, hitting 11 of his first 41 homers against Milwaukee. In 1958, illness kept him out until July./(AL)

Lou Boudreau — 1917- . SS 1938–52 **Indians**, Red Sox 1646 g, .295, 68 hr, 789 rbi. *1 WS, 6 g, .273, 3 rbi.*
  Manager 1942–50, 52–57, 60 **Indians**, Red Sox, A's, Cubs 1162–1224
☛ *Most Valuable Player—48. Led League—ba 44. All-Star—40–44, 47–48. Hall of Fame—1970 .*

A slick-fielding shortstop, steady hitter, and pennant-winning manager, Boudreau's career peaked in his fairy-tale 1948 season, but he was voted into the Hall of Fame for a career of distinguished play. He was captain of the basketball and baseball teams at the University of Illinois when he signed an agreement to join the Indians following graduation. Big Ten officials ruled him ineligible for amateur participation for the remainder of his college career. Free to work with the pros, he appeared in one ML game in 1938 as a pinch-hitter. He also played pro basketball with Hammond (IN) of the National Basketball League.

In 1939 he started with the Buffalo Bisons of the International League under manager Steve O'Neill. Originally a third baseman/catcher, Boudreau was moved to shortstop and teamed with second baseman Ray Mack. The young keystone combo gained attention for solid batting and adept fielding, particularly in turning double plays. Both were called up to Cleveland in the second half of the season.

In 1940, Boudreau's first full season, he was named to the AL All-Star team and hit .295 with 101 RBI. Boudreau played no part in the "Cleveland Crybabies" incident and the subsequent firing of manager Ossie Vitt. Cleveland struggled through a lackluster 1941 season, and in 1942 Boudreau was named player-manager. At 24, he was the youngest ever to manage a ML team from the outset of the season.

The innovative Boudreau oversaw the transformation of Bob Lemon from an infielder to a pitcher

Lou Boudreau

and created the "Williams Shift" and other tactics, but was unable to lift the Indians out of the middle of the pack. His shortstop play continued to win plaudits. He compensated for limited range by intelligent positioning and sure hands, and he led AL shortstops in fielding eight times. He won the 1944 AL batting title (.327) and led the league in doubles in 1941, 1944, and 1947.

When Bill Veeck purchased the Indians in 1946, he planned to replace Boudreau as manager. When word leaked out, a public clamor arose and Boudreau was retained. In 1948 Boudreau produced one of the greatest individual seasons ever. His team won the AL pennant and WS. He batted .355, hit 18 homers, batted in 106 runs, and scored 116. He was easily AL MVP. His play was inspirational. On August 8, he was sidelined with an ankle injury for a doubleheader with the Yankees before 73,484 Indian fans at Municipal Stadium. With the Tribe trailing 6–4, he limped to the plate and delivered a game-tying single. Cleveland swept the twin bill. The Indians and Red Sox ended the season tied for first. In the one-game playoff, Boudreau keyed the victory by going four-for-four with two homers.

Boudreau had little success in later seasons as a bench manager. He became a popular baseball broadcaster in Chicago. The greatest shortstop in Cleveland history, he saw his number 5 retired and the street bordering Municipal Stadium renamed Boudreau Boulevard. /(ME)

Jim Bouton (Bulldog) — 1939– . RHP 1962–70, 78 **Yankees**, Pilots, Astros, Braves 1239 ip, 62–63, 3.57. *2 WS, 24 ip, 2–1, 1.48*
☛ *All-Star—63.*

Bouton was a good pitcher before arm trouble deprived him of his fastball, but the personable nonconformist is best remembered for his book. *Ball Four*, a combination of his diary of the 1969 season (split between the expansion Pilots and the Astros) and his recollections of his Yankee career, broke baseball taboos by revealing the personal lives of his teammates past and present. Sometimes less-than-admirable but usually amusing details were included. Until then, the whole of baseball journalism had protected the public from such supposedly shocking knowledge as the drinking habits of Mickey Mantle and his Yankee buddies, the use of "pep pills," and the womanizing of most ballplayers on road trips. Commissioner Bowie Kuhn called it "detrimental to baseball."

Bouton first gained notice as an integral member of the Yankee staff in the final three seasons (1962–64) of the four-decade New York dynasty. His style was energetic, with his cap often flying off as he hurled both the ball and his body toward the plate. He was 7–7 as a rookie, then had an All-Star season in 1963. He was 21–7 with a 2.53 ERA and placed among the league leaders in most categories: second in winning percentage, shutouts (6), and fewest hits per nine innings (6.89), tied for second in wins, and fourth in ERA. He took a tough loss in Game Three of the World Series, opposing the Dodgers' Don Drysdale. Bouton surrendered the lone run of the game on a first-inning walk, a wild pitch, and a single; he tied a WS record with two wild pitches in the game.

Bouton was solid again in 1964, going 18–13 with a 3.02 ERA and leading the AL in starts. He had a fine World Series, winning Game Three 2–1 on a complete-game six-hitter (St. Louis's run was unearned) and also capturing Game Six, which was a 1–1 tie through six innings, by the score of 8–3.

But the Yankee dynasty and Bouton's career both came crashing down in 1965. He blew out his arm and the New York offense failed. He doggedly pitched through pain for two seasons, going 4–15, 4.82 in '65 and 3–8, 2.69 in 1966, the year the Yankees fell to last place.

Bouton spent most of the rest of his career in the bullpen, and began to throw a knuckleball in 1968. He retired after the 1970 season and spent some time as a TV sports reporter in New York. A successful minor league comeback in 1975 didn't lead to any offers, but he tried again in 1977; it was at this point that he said, "This winter I'm working out every day, throwing at a wall. I'm 11–0 against the wall." He was still unpopular among his ML peers, but he made it back with the Braves (owned by anti-establishment Ted Turner) in 1978 and went 1–3 in five starts. After finally calling it a career, he wrote about his comeback in an update of his first book called *Ball Five*. Since his retirement, he has gone into various baseball-related businesses and was one of the inventors of "Big League Chew," bubblegum shredded to resemble tobacco. /(SH)

Larry Bowa — 1945– . SS 1970–85 **Phillies**, Cubs, Mets 2247 g, .260, 99 hr, 525 rbi. *5 LCS, 21 g, .234, 3 rbi. 1 WS, 6 g, .375, 2 rbi.*
    Manager 1987–88 **Padres** 81–127, .389
☛ *All-Star—74–76, 78–79. Gold Glove—72, 78 .*

Fast feet, a strong arm, soft hands, a quick temper, and unlimited determination characterized Bowa's years as an outstanding ML shortstop. Often at odds with teammates, managers, and members of the media, Bowa never let distractions influence his play in the field. When he finished his playing career in 1985, he held the NL record for games played at shortstop (2,222), years leading NL shortstops in fielding (6), and for fewest errors in a season of 150 or more games (9). He also holds the ML record for highest fielding percentage for a career (.980) and for a season of over 100 games (.991).

A powerless switch-hitter early in his career, he developed into a tough out, hitting .280 or better four times, with a high of .305 in 1975, and seldom struck out. He was always a good basestealer, finishing with 318 for his career. With Bowa at

Larry Bowa

short, the Phillies won division titles from 1976 to 1978 and the world championship in 1980.

Bowa was named manager of the Padres before the 1987 season, but his aggressive and often angry style was ineffective, and he was fired after leading San Diego to a 16–30 start in 1988. /(AL)

Sam Bowens — 1939– . OF 1963–69 **Orioles**, Senators 479 g, .223, 45 hr, 143 rbi

Bowens hit 22 of his 45 homers in 1964, his first full season, tying an Oriole rookie HR record since surpassed by Cal Ripken, Jr. He was noted for his slow and easy lifestyle; when the Senators sent him to Buffalo in 1969, Sam took 13 days to report. /(RTM)

Frank Bowerman (Mike) — 1868–1948. C-1B 1895–1909 Baltimore (NL), Pirates, **Giants**, Braves 1045 g, .251, 13 hr, 392 rbi.
    Manager 1909 **Braves** 23–55, .295

Although overshadowed by Wilbert Robinson and Boileryard Clarke at Baltimore, and by Roger Bresnahan in New York, dour Frank was a capable backstop and the first to catch young Christy Math-

ewson. He also played 132 games at first, and a few at every other position, including one inning of pitching. Sent to Boston in the 1907 trade for Fred Tenney, he spent half a season managing the Doves. /(ADS)

Bob Bowman [Robert Leroy] — 1931– . OF 1955–59 **Phillies** 256 g, .249, 17 hr, 54 rbi

Husky and handsome, Bowman looked like a star, but his only real asset was a strong throwing arm. His hitting never measured up, and before leaving the Phillies he briefly tried pitching. /(AL)

Bob Bowman [Robert James] — 1910–1972. RHP 1939–42 **Cardinals**, Giants, Cubs 365 ip, 26–17, 3.82

As a Cardinal rookie in 1939, Bowman had a 13–5 record (including 7 relief wins) and tied for the NL lead in saves (9). Never effective after that, he is remembered for his near-fatal beaning of former teammate Joe Medwick after the two had argued in a hotel elevator before a game. /(JK)

Joe Bowman — 1910– . LHP 1932, 34–41, 44–45 A's, Giants, Phillies, **Pirates**, Red Sox, Reds 1466 ip, 77–96, 4.40

The 6'1" 190-lb Bowman was one of two 20-game losers with the last-place 1936 Phillies, and 33–38 in five years with stronger Pirate teams. After a sore arm and a sojourn in the minors, he bounced back with a 12–8 season for the wartime Red Sox. Often used as a pinch hitter, he twice batted over .300. /(ME)

Roger Bowman — 1927– . LHP 1949, 51–53, 55 Giants, **Pirates** 118 ip, 2–11, 5.81

A bright prospect in the Giants' system, a 1952 arm injury ruined the hard-throwing lefty's chances. He had a distinctive follow-through which left him vulnerable to ground balls up the middle. In 1954 he pitched a seven-inning perfect game for Hollywood (Pacific Coast League) on the last day of the season to clinch a tie for the pennant. /(DB)

Ted Bowsfield — 1936– . LHP 1958–64 Red Sox, Indians, **Angels**, A's 662 ip, 37–39, 4.35

In 1958, this Canadian had four wins, three against the Yankees. Casey Stengel called him, "that fella that throws them ground balls." Bowsfield won 11 games for the expansion Angels. /(RTM)

Bob Boyd (The Rope) — 1926– . 1B 1951, 53–54, 56–61 White Sox, **Orioles**, A's, Braves 693 g, .293, 19 hr, 175 rbi

Nicknamed "Rope" for his line-drive hitting, Boyd was the first Oriole regular to bat over .300 with .318 in 1957 and .309 the next year. Despite his high BA, he lacked the home run punch expected from a first baseman and was primarily a pinch hitter in his last seasons. /(RTM)

Oil Can Boyd [Dennis Ray] — 1959– . RHP 1982- **Red Sox** 1017 ip, 60–56, 4.16. *1 LCS, 14 ip, 1–1, 4.61. 1 WS, 7 ip, 0–1, 7.71*

One of 14 children of Negro Leaguer Willie James Boyd, the flamboyant, moody, and high-strung Oil Can is one of baseball's underachievers, plagued by a hot temper and persistent shoulder problems. Boyd emerged as one of the AL's top starters in 1985, pitching 272.1 innings despite an emaciated-looking 6′2″ 160-lb frame, fanning 12 batters in a game twice, and winning 15 games. At the same time, he became disliked around the league for his cocky demeanor and animated fist-pumping and finger-wagging on the mound. In 1986 Boyd had 11 wins by mid-July, but flew into a rage when he was left off the All-Star squad and was suspended by the Red Sox before checking into a hospital with emotional problems. He returned in August to add five more wins during Boston's pennant run, but a recurring blood clot in his right shoulder forced him onto the DL five times from 1987 to 1989 and has threatened to end his career. His nickname comes from his Mississippi hometown, where beer is called oil. /(SCL)

Clete Boyer — 1937– . 3B-SS 1955–57, 59–71 A's, **Yankees**, Braves 1725 g, .242, 162 hr, 654 rbi. *1 LCS, 3 g, .111, 3 rbi. 5 WS, 27 g, .233, 2 hr, 11 rbi*
☛ *Gold Glove—69.*

One of three Boyer brothers to reach the majors, Clete ranked as a top AL defensive third baseman during his eight years with the Yankees, overshadowed only by Baltimore's Brooks Robinson. In the 1962 World Series, he batted .318 against the Giants, including a home run in the opening game. When he homered in the seventh game of the 1964 WS two innings after his brother Ken had homered for the Cardinals, it marked the only time that brothers had connected for home runs in the same WS game. He holds the WS record for most career assists by a third baseman (66).

Traded to the Braves after the 1966 season, he enjoyed his best offensive year in 1967 with 26 homers and 96 RBI. He led NL third basemen in fielding in 1967 and 1969.

On August 31, 1969, as he approached the plate locked in a 1-for-17 batting slump, he fell "victim" to Morganna, a buxom blonde who'd earned notoriety by dashing on the field and kissing ballplayers. After the kiss, Clete got an RBI-single, two more hits in the game, and racked up eight hits in his next 15 at-bats.

After his release by the Braves in 1971, he played for Hawaii in the Pacific Coast League, where he became the first American professional to be traded to a Japanese league when he was dealt to the Tayio Whales for John Werhas.

Boyer coached for the A's and Yankees in the 1980s, often under his old teammate Billy Martin. /(RTM)

Cloyd Boyer (Junior) — 1927– . RHP 1949–52, 55 **Cardinals**, A's 396 ip, 20–23, 4.73

The older brother of Ken and Clete, Cloyd had less success as a pitcher than his siblings did at third base. He achieved consistency, however, by compiling winning percentages of exactly .500 in three different seasons. /(FK)

Ken Boyer — 1931–1982. 3B 1955–69 **Cardinals**, Giants, White Sox, Dodgers 2034 g, .287, 282 hr, 1141 rbi. *1 WS, 7 g, .222, 2 hr, 6 rbi.*
Manager 1978–80 **Cardinals** *166–191, .465*
☛ *Most Valuable Player—64. Led League—rbi 64. Gold Glove—58–61, 63.*

This quiet but dominant All-Star third baseman was a splendid fielder and consistently productive and clutch hitter. Signed as a pitcher by the Cardinals for $6,000, his poor pitching and strong hitting prompted his move to third base. He played brilliantly there for most of his 11 years in St. Louis. He won five Gold Gloves and led third basemen in double plays a record-tying five times. In eight different seasons, he hit over 20 homers, and combined with brother Clete for 444 HR. (Only the Aarons and DiMaggios hit more homers than the Boyers.) Ken's 255 as a Cardinal put him second only to Stan Musial.

After solid rookie and sophomore years, to Boyer's dismay he was sent to centerfield for most of the 1957 season, and GM Frank Lane criticized the soft-spoken Cardinal as an "unaggressive player." The arrival of Curt Flood in 1958 allowed Boyer to return to third base. It was during Solly Hemus's tenure as Cardinal manager that Boyer was named team captain. Hemus said, "Boyer is the guy everybody walks up to in the clubhouse and talks to." He led by example and through subtle prodding.

In 1959, Boyer went on a 29-game hitting streak,

Ken Boyer, running

the longest in the majors since Stan Musial's 30-game string in 1950. In 1960 and '61, he led the Cardinals in batting, HR, and RBI, hitting a career-high 32 homers in 1960. He twice hit for the cycle, once in 1961, and again in 1964. His 1964 MVP season (.295, 24 HR, 119 RBI) was climaxed by his clutch performance in the World Series against the Yankees. In Game Four, he stroked a grand slam off Al Downing to give the Cardinals a 4–3 win, and his

seventh-inning shot in Game Seven off Steve Hamilton catapulted the Cardinals to a 7–5 win and the world championship.

Boyer slumped in 1965 and was traded to the Mets for third baseman Charlie Smith and pitcher Al Jackson. His glittering career ended four years later with the Dodgers. He was a Cardinal coach in 1971–72, and took over as manager early in 1978. In 1979, he led the Redbirds to a third-place finish, but after winning only 18 of 51 in 1980, he was replaced by Whitey Herzog. Boyer died of lung cancer in 1982, and his uniform number 14 was retired by the Cardinals in 1984. /(RTM)

Buzz Boyle [Ralph] — 1908–1978. OF 1929–30, 33–35 Braves, **Dodgers** 366 g, .290, 12 hr, 125 rbi

The speedy rightfielder led NL outfielders in assists (20) in 1934 when he hit .305 for the Dodgers. His older brother Jim caught one game for the Giants in 1926. /(TG)

Gene Brabender — 1941– . RHP 1966–70 **Orioles**, Pilots/Brewers 621 ip, 35–43, 4.25

This mighty 6'5" 225-lb hurler would playfully bend the spikes used to fasten the tarpaulin. His busiest year was 1969, when he went 13–14 for the Pilots. Used in relief by the World Champion 1966 Orioles, the bespectacled Brabender was 4–3. /(RTM)

William G. Brabham — 1875–1947. *Executive.*

A lawyer from the University of North Carolina, Brabham was president of four different minor leagues at one time. In 1932, when the minors formed their own National Association, he was elected president and given powers over the minor leagues similar to those Judge Landis held for the majors. /(NLM)

Gib Brack (Gibby) — 1908–1960. OF 1937–39 Dodgers, **Phillies** 315 g, .279, 16 hr, 113 rbi

As a rookie outfielder with the Brooklyn Dodgers in 1937, Brack was among the top five NL hitters through May, but he slid back to mediocrity for the rest of his brief career. /(AL)

Buddy Bradford [Charles William] — 1944– . OF 1966–76 **White Sox**, Indians, Reds, Cardinals 697 g, .226, 52 hr, 175 rbi

Bradford provided speed, power, and defense, mostly as a fourth outfielder. On April 25, 1969, he became only the fourth White Sox player to hit a home run over the Comiskey Park roof, pounding one off the Twins' Tom Hall. Bradford hit a career-high 11 HR that season, during the first of his three stints with the White Sox. /(RL)

Larry Bradford — 1951– . LHP 1977, 79–81 **Braves** 104 ip, 6–4, 2.51

Returning from arm trouble, Bradford had an 0.95 ERA in 21 relief appearances in 1979. On his way to a 2.45 ERA in 56 appearances (with 4 saves) in 1980, he held opponents to 1.08 in his home park at

Atlanta, one of the best hitters' parks in the NL. /(MC)

Bill Bradley — 1878–1954. 3B 1899–1910, 14–15 Cubs, **Indians**, Brooklyn (FL), Kansas City (FL) 1461 g, .271, 33 hr, 552 rbi.
Manager 1914 **Brooklyn (FL)** 77–77, .500

Until he was injured in 1906, Bill Bradley was the greatest third baseman in the short history of the American League. In his first season as a regular, with the Cubs in 1900, the 22-year-old hit .282, but he showed a bit of what was to come by leading NL third basemen in total chances per game. When the AL declared itself a major league in 1901, Bradley jumped to his hometown Cleveland Blues (later the Indians). In the first seven years of the league, he led

Bill Bradley with Brooklyn of the Federal League

its third basemen in at least one fielding category every year except his injury-shortened season of 1906, and his .955 fielding average in 1904 set an AL record that stood for ten years. All told, he led AL third basemen four times in fielding, three times in double plays, twice in putouts, and once each in assists and errors. His AL career 3B marks in games, putouts, assists, double plays, total chances, and errors all stood until Frank "Home Run" Baker broke them.

But what also helped place Bradley above such contemporaries as Hall of Famer Jimmy Collins was his potent bat. In the first four years of the league, Bradley was consistently among the league's offensive leaders. His 29-game hitting streak in 1902 set an AL record that Ty Cobb broke in 1911. Bradley's streak helped him to his best season offensively, as he reached career highs in BA (.340, sixth in the AL), runs (104, fourth), doubles (39, tied for third), and HR (11, tied for second). On July 28, 1903 he hit three triples in a game, tying a still-standing AL record, and he hit for the cycle that September 24.

His hitting declined starting in 1905, and after 1907 his fielding slipped a bit; he hit .186 in 1909 and .196 in 1910, which cut down on his playing time. Managing the Brooklyn franchise in the Federal League in 1914, he hit .500 using himself as pinch hitter (3-for-6). The following season, 37 years old, he played 66 games for the FL's Kansas City team despite hitting .187. /(WOR)

George Bradley (Grin) — 1852–1931. RHP-3B-OF-SS 1875–1877, 79–84, 86, 88 St. Louis (NA) Cardinals, Cubs, Troy (NL), Providence (NL), **Cleveland (NL)**, Philadelphia (AA), Cincinnati (UA), Baltimore (AA) *NA:* 61 g, .268; 33–26; *ML:* 507 g, .228, 3 hr, 110 rbi; 2404 ip, 138–127, 2.50. 20 wins: 76, 84
☛ *Led League—era 76.*

On July 15, 1876, during the NL's first season, Bradley pitched the league's first no-hitter, defeating Hartford 2–0. That year, the perpetually grinning righthander pitched every one of St. Louis's 64 games and led them to a second-place finish with 45 wins. His 16 shutouts set a ML record tied only by Grover Alexander 40 years later. Brought to Chicago the next season to take over the pitching for Al Spalding, he was far less effective, and for the rest of his career played at third base as often as he pitched. /(FIC)

Phil Bradley — 1959– . OF 1983– **Mariners**, Phillies, Orioles 905 g, .290, 74 hr, 345 rbi

After an unsuccessful 1988 season with the Phillies distinguished only by his league-leading 16 HBP,

Bradley returned to the AL and became a key part of the resurgent 1989 Orioles. The former University of Missouri quarterback began his career with the Mariners. He hit 26 homers for them in 1985 but never hit more than 14 in any subsequent season, and he settled into his role as a hustling leadoff hitter with good extra-base-hit power and base-stealing ability. Despite hitting poorly at the start of most seasons and striking out frequently, Bradley batted at least .297 in each of his four full seasons with Seattle and is the only player to have a .300 batting average for his career as a Mariner. His complaints about the Mariners, their ballpark, and their fans led to his trade to Philadelphia. At the time of his departure, he held the Mariner season records for batting average, hits, total bases, and on-base percentage, and was tied for season team records for hits, consecutive hits, triples, and runs in a game. He was also the Mariners' career leader in triples and was second in career stolen bases. /(TF)

Scott Bradley — 1960– . C-3B-1B 1984– Yankees, White Sox, **Mariners** 413 g, .271, 17 hr, 144 rbi

Bradley had a finger broken in a home-plate collision in his first major league start as a catcher for the Yankees. He was traded to the White Sox and, after appearing in only nine games for Chicago, to the Mariners for Ivan Calderon. In his first season with Seattle, the hustling Bradley was the Mariners' top pinch hitter and the most difficult batter in the American League to strike out. Displaced by Dave Valle as the regular catcher, Bradley finished the 1980s as a backup catcher and designated hitter. /(TF)

Tom Bradley — 1947– . RHP 1969–75 Angels, **White Sox**, Giants 1017 ip, 55–61, 3.72

Behind Bradley's horn-rimmed glasses lurked an intellectual with a degree in Latin from the University of Maryland. The hard thrower fanned over 200 batters and won 15 games in each of his two seasons with the White Sox (1971 and 1972). /(RL)

Bobby Bragan — 1917– . SS-C 1940–44, 47–48 **Phillies**, Dodgers 597 g, .240, 15 hr, 172 rbi. *1 WS, 1 g, 1.000, 1 rbi.*
   Manager 1956–58, 63–66 Pirates, Indians, **Braves** 443–478, .481

Bragan served in almost every capacity in his lengthy baseball career. He was the Phillies' regular shortstop his first three years in the major leagues, then became a catcher. A minor-league manager for seven years, he attracted attention as a major-league skipper for wrangling with umpires. He made every sports section when, one day, he walked on the field sipping a soft drink through a straw, discussing the play in question with the umpires and offering each a taste of his drink. A scout and major-league coach, Bragan was also, for many years, president of the Texas League. /(AL)

Glenn Braggs — 1962– . OF 1986- **Brewers** 406 g, .256, 42 hr, 203 rbi

A swift, muscular outfielder, Braggs capped a stellar minor league career by hitting .360 in the Pacific Coast League in 1986 to win *Baseball America*'s Triple-A Player of the Year honors. He won Milwaukee's right field job in 1987 and was leading the Brewers with 42 RBI in July 1988 when a shoulder nerve problem ended his season. In 1989 he maintained the same level of play while adding high-percentage basestealing to his repetoire. /(JCA)

Dave Brain — 1879–1959. 3B-SS 1901, 03–08 White Sox, **Cardinals**, Pirates, Braves, Reds, Giants. 679 g, .252, 27 hr, 303 rbi

An unreliable fielder with good speed on the basepaths, the English-born Brain had power at the plate but no consistency. He cracked 15 triples for the Cardinals in 1903 and led the NL with 10 home runs in 1907 for the Braves. /(FJO)

Asa Brainard (Count) — 1841–1888. RHP-2B Washington (NA), Middletown (NA), **Lord Baltimores (NA)** 108 g, .239; 84 g, 24–56

In 1869 Brainard was brought to Cincinnati by Manager Harry Wright to pitch for the Cincinnati Red Stockings, baseball's first all-professional team. Paid $1,100 for his efforts, he was reportedly a "scientific" pitcher who succeeded by changing speeds with good control. The Red Stockings toured the country, taking on all challenges in 1869 and not losing a game until the following year. After the formation of the National Association in 1871, Brainard pitched for the Washington Olympians and then the Lord Baltimores but was unable to recapture the success of his Red Stocking days. In 1874, his final season, he was 5–24. When he died in 1888, he was the first of the old Red Stockings to pass on. /(BC)

Erv Brame — 1901–1949. RHP 1928–32 **Pirates** 791 ip, 52–37, 4.76

Brame was Pittsburgh's workhorse in 1929 and 1930, leading the club in complete games both years and tying for the NL high (22) in '30. Often used as a pinch-hitter, he hit .306 with eight homers during his career. /(ME)

Ralph Branca — 1926– . RHP 1944–54, 56 **Dodgers**, Tigers, Yankees 1484 ip, 88–68, 3.79. *2 WS, 17 ip, 1–2, 6.35*
☛ *All-Star—47–49.*

The fact that he threw the pitch Bobby Thomson hit for "the shot heard round the world" to win the 1951 playoff has obscured much of the rest of Branca's career. The one-time N.Y.U. basketball player was the starter and loser of the first two NL playoff games in 1946 and 1951. In 1947, he won 21 games for the Dodgers at age 21. In the WS that year, he won the Sixth Game, saved by Al Gionfriddo's famous catch of DiMaggio's drive. Before the '51 playoffs, Branca had worn number 13 and good-naturedly posed with black cats. Afterward, he changed his number, but not his luck. An off-season pelvis injury all but ended his career and he won only twelve more games over the next five years. He later became a broadcaster for the Mets. /(TG)

Ron Brand — 1940– . C-SS 1963, 65–71 Pirates, **Astros**, Expos 568 g, .239, 3 hr, 106 rbi

This 5'8" 175-lb catcher had a shotgun arm, and also played outfield, shortstop, third base, and second base. Brand collected Houston's first hit in the Astrodome, a triple off the Yankees' Mel Stottlemyre in an exhibition game. /(RTM)

Darrell Brandon (Bucky) — 1940– . RHP 1966–69, 71–73 Red Sox, Pilots, Twins, **Phillies** 590 ip, 28–37, 4.04

Brandon started 19 games for the AL champion 1967 Red Sox, but an arm injury shelved him for the World Series. He came back from the minors in 1971 for three moderately successful years in the Phillies' bullpen. /(PB)

Edgar G. Brands — 1888–1970. *Writer.*

A graduate of the U. of Illinois, Brands worked for newspapers in Illinois and Montana before becoming managing editor of Collyer Publishing Co., specialists in sports publications. In 1930, he joined *The Sporting News*, writing features, editorials, and a regular column, "Between Innings," and serving as editor until he retired in 1954. /(NLM)

Dr. William E. Brandt — Unk.–1963. *Writer.*

A practicing osteopathic physician, Dr. Brandt succeeded Ford Frick as manager of the NL Service Bureau and held the job for ten years until he resigned to do a daily radio show, "The Inside of

Sports." A graduate of Muhlenberg College, he began with the Philadelphia *Record* in 1912, and worked for the *Bulletin* and *Ledger* in that city and the *New York Times* before going to work for the NL. He wrote for several magazines and the *Encyclopaedia Britannica*. A 1921 graduate of Philadelphia College of Osteopathy, he was president of the school from 1953 to 1958. /(NLM)

Ed Brandt — 1905–1944. LHP 1928–38 **Braves**, Dodgers, Pirates 2268 ip, 121–146, 3.86

The forkballer led the NL in losses (21) as a rookie and was 21–45 in his first three seasons with the weak Braves. But he started 1931 with eight straight wins on his way to an 18–10 mark, and followed with several more strong seasons. He often pinch hit, and he led all pitchers in hitting with a .309 BA in 1933. /(ME)

Jackie Brandt — 1934– . OF 1956, 58–67 Cardinals, Giants, **Orioles**, Phillies, Astros 1221 g, .262, 112 hr, 485 rbi
☛ *All-Star—61.*

Some historians link the derivation of the baseball term "flake" to this nail-biting outfielder, since a teammate once commented that "things seem to flake off his mind and disappear." Brandt split his outstanding rookie season with the Cards and Giants, hitting a career-high .298 while leading the NL in fielding (.990). 1958 was spent in the military. He won a Gold Glove for his play in left field with San Francisco in 1959. /(RTM)

Kitty Bransfield [William Edward] — 1875–1947. 1B 1898, 1901–11 Braves, Pirates, **Phillies**, Cubs 1330 g, .270, 14 hr, 637 rbi. *1 WS, 8 g, .200, 1 rbi*

The slick-fielding Bransfield joined the Pirates in 1901 and was the regular first baseman on three straight pennant winners. Although he twice edged his BA over .300 (1902 and '08), his first season was the best overall performance of his career (.295, 92 runs, 91 RBI, 17 triples). He led NL first basemen in fielding in 1909 while with the Phillies. /(ME)

Mickey Brantley — 1961– . OF 1986– **Mariners** 302 g, .259, 32 hr, 125 rbi

Brantley hit .302 in 1987 while leading the Mariners with a club rookie-record 12-game hitting streak and tying team records with five hits and three home runs in one game against Cleveland September 14. Over the first half of the 1988 season, Brantley was among club leaders in hits and homers while playing centerfield for the Mariners. Brantley was world

heavyweight boxing champion Mike Tyson's "Big Brother" when Tyson was a youth in Catskill, New York. /(TF)

Steve Braun — 1948– . OF-3B-DH 1971–84 **Twins**, Mariners, Royals, Blue Jays, Cardinals 1361 g, .272, 51 hr, 382 rbi

After jumping to the Twins from Class A, Braun spent six seasons in Minnesota playing every infield and outfield position while batting .284. In August of 1978, he tied a Royal record by reaching base eleven consecutive times. Braun developed into a top pinch hitter with the Royals and Cardinals, retiring with 113 pinch hits, sixth on the all-time list. In 1986, Braun became a coach in the Cardinal farm system. /(FJO)

Braves Field Boston Braves 1915–52. LF-337, CF-370, RF-319

Braves Field was baseball's largest park at the time it opened, August 18, 1915, when over 40,000 fans jammed the single-decked grandstand to see the Braves defeat St. Louis 3–1 on a spacious field that was 402′ down the left-field line and 520′ to center. Those distances were shortened over the years, but the left-field fence remained 25′ high, and a 10′ wall in right guarded the "Jury Box," a small bleacher section with extremely boisterous fans. Home to the Braves until their move to Milwaukee, the park also hosted the Red Sox' home WS games in 1915 and 1916 and their Sunday games from 1929 to 1932, and was the scene of ML baseball's longest game, a 26-inning tie between the Dodgers and Braves on May 1, 1920. It is now the site of Boston University's Nickerson Field, and the seats along the right field foul line and the Gaffney Street entrance still stand. /(SCL)

Garland Braxton — 1900–1966. LHP 1921–22, 25–31, 33 Braves, Yankees, **Senators**, White Sox, Browns 938 ip, 50–53, 4.13
☛ *Led League—era 28.*

The lefthanded screwballer led the AL in relief appearances (56) and tied for the lead in saves (13) with the Senators in 1927. The next year, as a regular starter, he topped the league in ERA (2.51). A scratch golfer, he won senior titles in retirement. /(JK)

Al Brazle (Cotton, Ol' Boots and Saddles) —
1913–1973. LHP 1943, 46–54 **Cardinals**
1377 ip, 97–64, 3.31. *2 WS, 14 ip, 0–2, 4.50*

The side-arming Brazle spent eight years in the
minors before landing a job with the Cardinals in
1943 at age 28. In Game Three of the '43 World
Series, the sinkerballing rookie held a 2–1 lead over
the Yankees until the eighth, when New York
exploded for five runs. Exclusively a reliever his last
few years, Brazle led the NL in saves in 1952 and
'53./(RTM)

Sam Breadon — 1876–1949. *Executive.*

Breadon's first business venture was vending popcorn at the 1904 St. Louis World's Fair. He owned
an automobile agency until the 1930s. As a favor to
a friend, he invested $200 in the Cardinals, and 27
years later he controlled the team. Under Breadon,
the Cards won nine pennants and six WS. He
succeeded Branch Rickey as Cardinals president in
1920, but Rickey stayed on as GM. They began the
first farm system. At its peak, they owned 16 teams
outright and had 12 working agreements./(NLM)

Sid Bream — 1960– . 1B 1983– Dodgers, **Pirates**
562 g, .262, 45 hr, 240 rbi

The lanky, lefthanded first baseman came to Pittsburgh in the 1985 Bill Madlock deal. A career .329
hitter in the minors, Bream set a NL record with
166 assists at first base in 1986, his first full season,
and finished third in the league in doubles./(ME)

Harry Brecheen (The Cat) — 1914– . LHP 1940,
43–53 **Cardinals**, Browns 1908 ip, 132–92, 2.92. 20 wins:
48 *3 WS, 33 ip, 4–1, 0.83*
☛ Led League—era 48. Led League—k 48. All-
Star—47–48.

Brecheen became the first lefthander to record three
wins in a World Series, doing so against the Red Sox
in 1946. The screwballer blanked Boston 3–0 in
Game Two on a four-hitter. In addition, he singled
in the Cardinals' first run, and his sacrifice bunt set
up his team's two other runs. In Game Six, "The
Cat," named for his expert fielding and cat-like
movements, once again beat Mickey Harris. With
one day's rest, he pitched two innings of relief in
Game Seven to pick up his third win. He had a 0.45
ERA in the Series, and his lifetime WS ERA of 0.83
is the best ever.

　Brecheen's finest season came in 1948 when he
led the NL in winning percentage (.741, 20–7), ERA
(2.24), strikeouts (149), and shutouts (7). He was

Harry Brecheen

one of 61 players to play for both the Cardinals and
Browns./(RTM)

Hal Breeden — 1944– . 1B 1971–75 Cubs, **Expos**
273 g, .243, 21 hr, 76 rbi

The younger brother of former ML catcher Danny
Breeden, Hal had good power numbers in the
minors and the Cubs traded Hoyt Wilhelm to get
him from Atlanta. He was only used as a platoon
player and pinch hitter in the ML. With the Expos
in 1973, his most active season, he batted 258 times
and had 15 homers. On July 13 that year he became
only the second player to hit pinch homers in both
games of a doubleheader. From 1976 to 1978 he
played for the Nippon Ham Fighters of Japan's
Pacific League./(MC)

Marv Breeding — 1934– . 2B 1960–63 **Orioles**,
Senators, Dodgers 415 g, .250, 7 hr, 92 rbi

Breeding enjoyed a fine rookie season with Baltimore, batting a career-high .267. Though he led the
Pacific Coast League in stolen bases (27) in 1959

with Vancouver, he had only 19 in his ML career. /(RTM)

Fred Breining — 1955– . RHP 1980–84 **Giants**, Expos 437 ip, 27–20, 3.33

A throw-in to the Giants in the deal that sent Bill Madlock to the Pirates, Breining earned a spot in the San Francisco bullpen with a 2.54 ERA in 1981. He became a starter late the next season and finished 11–6. After an 11–12 year in '83, he was traded to the Expos for Al Oliver but reported with a career-ending rotator cuff injury. The Giants sent Andy McGaffigan to Montreal as a replacement. /(MC)

Ted Breitenstein — 1869–1935. LHP-OF 1891–1901 St. Louis (AA), **Cardinals**, Reds 2964 ip, 166–170, 4.04; 447 g, .216, 4 hr, 126 rbi. 20 wins: 94, 97–98
☛ *Led League—era 93.*

The handsome native St. Louisan dazzled hometown fans by tossing a no-hitter again Louisville in his first major league start (October 4, 1891). Seven years later, he no-hit Pittsburgh. The 5'9" lefty paired with St. Louis-born catcher Heinie Peitz, forming what fans called "the Pretzel Battery." Breitenstein twice led the NL in starts and complete games, but was a 20-game loser five straight seasons (1892–96) with weak Browns teams. He also played 65 games in the outfield. /(FJO)

Nick Bremigan — 1945– . *Umpire* AL 1974–87 *4 LCS 1 WS, 2 ASU*

Considered one of the top rule interpreters, Bremigan has been a syndicated columnist and given clinics to American armed forces in Spain, England, and Germany. He was one of the umpires involved in the famous George Brett pine tar incident. /(RTM)

Bob Brenly — 1954– . C 1981– **Giants**, Blue Jays 871 g, .247, 91 hr, 333 rbi. *1 LCS, 6 g, .235, 1 hr, 2 rbi*
☛ *All-Star—84.*

Brenly was the Giants' starting catcher from 1984 to 1987, averaging 18 home runs per season and providing steady defense. The burly righthanded hitter was signed as a third baseman out of Ohio University (where he tied Mike Schmidt's single-season HR record), then switched to catcher in 1979, his fourth pro season. He continued to fill in at third or first base when necessary in the ML, and played 45 games at third in 1986.

Brenly won the Giants' starting catching job in 1984, hitting .291 with 20 HR and 80 RBI. He

would never hit better than .267 again but he remained a consistent power threat. In Game Four of the 1987 NLCS he homered off the Cardinals' Danny Cox.

On September 14, 1986 against the Braves, in the fourth inning, Brenly tied a ML record with four errors at third base, booting three grounders and throwing wildly once to allow four unearned runs. In the fifth inning he hit a solo home run, and in the seventh he added a two-run single to tie the score, 6–6. In the bottom of the ninth with two out and the count full, he homered to win the game.

Brenly was released by the Giants after hitting only .189 in 1988. The Blue Jays signed him but released him in mid-1989. Popular in San Francisco, he was signed for their stretch drive. /(SCL)

Ad Brennan [Addison Foster] — 1881–1962. LHP 1910–15, 18 **Phillies**, Chicago (FL), Senators, Indians 677 ip, 38–35, 3.11

Although the Kansan had two double-digit winning seasons with the Phillies before he jumped to the Federal League in 1914, he is most often remembered for decking Giant Manager John McGraw in a fistfight beneath the stands. /(JK)

Don Brennan — 1903–1953. RHP 1933–37 Yankees, **Reds**, Giants 397 ip, 21–12, 4.19. *1 WS, 3 ip, 0–0, 0.00*

Burly Don Brennan showed early promise with his fastball as a starter for the Yankees, but control problems prompted his release, and he spent the remainder of his career working primarily from the bullpen. /(FS)

Tom Brennan (The Gray Flamingo) — 1952– . RHP 1981–85 **Indians**, White Sox, Dodgers 219 ip, 9–10, 4.40

Brennan was the Indians' first pick in the June 1974 draft. He finally reached Cleveland in 1981 and lasted one-plus season as a long reliever given an occasional start. "The Gray Flamingo" had an unorthodox delivery, pausing while standing on one leg. /(JCA)

Roger Bresnahan (The Duke of Tralee) — 1879–1944. C-OF-RHP 1897, 1900–15 Senators, Cubs, Orioles, **Giants**, Cardinals 1430 g, .279, 26 hr, 530 rbi; 50 ip, 4–1, 3.93. *1 WS, 5 g, .313, 1 rbi.*
   Manager 1909–12, 15 **Cardinals**, Cubs 348–432, .432
☛ *Hall of Fame—1945.*

Bresnahan was one of several players who became a close friend of John McGraw. With Christy Mathewson, another friend, it was an attraction of opposites. Roger could have been McGraw's twin:

Roger Bresnahan with the Giants

compact, pugnacious, fiercely concentrated on the game, and skilled in all the ways it takes to play it. Temperamental like his manager, he was an un-abashed Irish brawler, tough on teammates who did less than their best, tough on opponents, toughest on umpires, whom he baited and bedeviled. He was frequently ejected, fined and suspended, gave head-aches to League officials, and engaged in noisy confrontations with at least three club owners. He could play any position on the field.

Washington had him first as an 18-year-old pitcher who shut out the Browns, 3–0, on six hits in his major-league debut. His repertoire was dazzling. The papers credited him with "a speedy shoot, outcurve, inshoot, drop ball." Roger won three more games that season, but the Senators let him go the next spring when he insisted on more money than they would pay. The Cubs brought him up after two years in the high minors, played him for two innings, and lost him to McGraw's Orioles in 1901. Rapped hard in two outings, he was tried at second, third, the outfield, and when Wilbert Robin-son was hurt, behind the plate. He played well wherever they put him, but catching was his forte.

When McGraw departed the American League for the Giants at mid-year, Bresnahan made the leap with him. The Giants had Jack Warner and Frank Bowerman as their catchers, so Roger became the centerfielder. The season was a romp. Despite his hefty build, he was fast and agile enough not only to cover the outfield expanse, but to bat leadoff. He played 116 games, got 142 hits and batted a handsome .350, his career high and a mere .005 behind Honus Wagner.

By 1905 Bresnahan was the Giants' first-string catcher. Some say Mathewson urged McGraw to make the move, although Mac had known Roger's capabilities for years and could have figured it for himself, particularly now that he had acquired Turkey Mike Donlin for the outfield. Roger had another good year, hitting .302 and catching 87 games. He caught all five Series games against the Athletics, which meant Matty's three shutouts, Joe McGinnity's one, and Joe's shutout loss to Chief Bender. He also hit a sparkling .313.

Perhaps his most notable contributions to the game were in protective equipment. In 1905, after being hospitalized for a head injury from a beaning, he experimented with a batting helmet manufac-tured by the A.J. Reach Company. It was like the leather football helmet of the period sliced vertically: one half for covering the left side of a righthanded batter's head, the other for the lefty hitter. Although beanballs were frequent, the idea did not find favor. Two years later he devised catcher's shin guards. The first ones, evidently modeled after a cricketer's leg pads, were large and bulky, with a knee flap that came up to the thigh. They were greeted with ridicule and protest, but soon caught on. By 1909 they had more utilitarian shape and size, and were in general use. About 1908 he improved the flimsy wire catcher's mask with leather-bound rolls of padding to absorb the shock of foul-tips.

In winter that year, McGraw traded his friend to St. Louis. Roger had caught 139 games during the season, but he was 29 and slowing down. McGraw could afford to let him go. He had the young Chief Meyers on deck and the Cardinals eager to make a deal. Long a lackluster club and a cellar-dweller for two years, its owners thought a manager like the fiery Duke of Tralee might energize the players. To get him they gave up three of their few talents: Red Murray, a first-rate outfielder, Bugs Raymond, an eccentric but effective pitcher, and an experienced backup catcher, Admiral Schlei, acquired from Cincinnati.

Manager Bresnahan acquired some good players

and got them above .500 and in fifth place by 1911. The Cardinals' owner, Mrs. Schuyler Britton, who had recently inherited the club on the death of her uncle, Stanley Robison, was pleased with the improvement and rewarded Roger with a five-year contract at $10,000 per year, plus a percentage of the profits, if any. During the disappointing sixth-place season of 1912, however, Mrs. Britton, like owners before and since, second-guessed her manager publicly. Roger blistered her ears with some choice dugout repartee and was fired forthwith. Roger demanded to be paid as manager and player for the remaining four years of his contract. The Cardinals, unable to clear waivers for a trade, finally sold him to the Cubs. He backstopped Jimmy Archer in 1913, managed Chicago to a fourth-place finish in 1915, all the while continuing his contract fight with the Cardinals. He finally won a $20,000 settlement. His playing career ended in 1916. He was owner-manager of his hometown Toledo Mud Hens through 1923, then coached the Giants (1925–28) and Tigers (1930–31). /(ADS)

Rube Bressler [Raymond Bloom] — 1894–1966. OF-1B-P 1914–32 Phillies, **Reds**, Dodgers, Cardinals 1305 g, .301, 32 hr, 586 rbi; 540 ip, 26–32, 3.40

Nicknamed Rube in the tradition of more successful lefthanded pitchers (Waddell, Marquard), Bressler became a righthanded-hitting outfielder/first baseman in mid-career. He gripped the bat with his hands apart (as did Ty Cobb), and slap-hit his way to a .301 lifetime BA. Although he played for two pennant winners (1914 A's and '19 Reds), he never appeared in a WS game. /(JK)

Ed Bressoud — 1932– . SS-2B-3B 1956–67 Giants, **Red Sox**, Mets, Cardinals 1186 g, .252, 94 hr, 365 rbi. *1 WS, 2 g, --*
☛ *All-Star—64.*

Bressoud was a dependable shortstop whose arrival in 1956 allowed the Giants to send Alvin Dark to the Cardinals in a deal for Red Schoendienst. He spent just two of his six Giant seasons as their regular SS, but was successful in three years with the Red Sox because he adapted his swing to Fenway's leftfield wall; he hit 20 HR in 1963. Made expendable by Rico Petrocelli's emergence in 1965, Bressoud concluded his career against the Red Sox as a Cardinal utility man in the 1967 World Series. /(PB)

George Brett — 1953– . 3B-1B 1973- **Royals** 2137 g, .310, 267 hr, 1311 rbi. *6 LCS, 27 g, .340, 9 hr, 19 rbi. 2 WS, 13 g, .373, 1 hr, 4 rbi*
☛ *Most Valuable Player—80. Led League—ba 76, 80. All-Star—76–88. Gold Glove—85.*

If a player ever had claim to the title "The Franchise," it would be George Brett in Kansas City. He came from a baseball family. Older brother Ken pitched 13 years in the majors while two other brothers played minor league ball. Yet his beginnings in professional baseball were modest. He batted .281 over three-plus seasons in the minors. He led the California League in errors at third base in his second pro season. He hit only .125 in his first major league call-up and hit but two home runs with 47 RBI in his first full season with Kansas City.

Royals' batting coach Charlie Lau worked with Brett on hitting to all fields on every type of pitch. Brett learned to adapt to what pitchers offered instead of waiting for fastballs. Hal McRae, acquired by the Royals the year Brett came up, taught him

George Brett

resolute baserunning. In his second full season Brett led the AL in hits and triples while batting .308.

Season after season Brett put up star-studded batting statistics. From 1975 to 1988 he batted above .300 ten times, drove in over 100 runs four times, and topped 100 runs scored four times. In 1979 Brett tallied 85 extra-base hits and became the sixth player in history with 20 or more doubles, triples, and home runs in the same season.

Brett flirted with a .400 batting mark in 1980 and finished at .390, the highest major league average since Ted Williams's .406 in 1941. His incredible season included a 37-game hitting streak and Player of the Year Awards from *TSN*, *Baseball Digest*, UPI, and the Associated Press. One wonders what might have been had Brett been healthy. He suffered through a bruised heel, tendinitis, and torn ligaments that summer. However, the highlight of his season was capturing the AL pennant. "I know I captured a lot of the media's attention this past season," Brett explained, "but the Royals have a team built on teamwork, not on individuals."

George put together numbers in 1985 that rivaled 1979 and 1980. He surpassed the century mark in RBI, runs, and walks while hitting .335 with a career-high 30 HR.

Brett proved more than a one-dimensional player by continually improving his defense and baserunning. The most productive player in Royals' history, he was rewarded with a lifetime contract. He was a terror in postseason play as well. His nine career home runs and .728 slugging average are LCS records, as is his single-series slugging average of 1.056 (1978).

Brett had to overcome numerous injuries during his career that kept him on the disabled list more than 32 weeks from 1978 to 1989. He moved to 1B in 1987, opening up third base for rookie phenom Kevin Seitzer. The transition proved a success as George was named first baseman on *TSN*'s 1988 AL All-Star and Silver Slugger Teams. At 35 he showed no signs of slowing down, with 42 doubles, 24 home runs, and a .306 average.

Brett holds Royals' team records for career games, hits, runs, doubles, triples, home runs, runs batted in, and batting and slugging average. George and his three brothers own and operate the Spokane, WA franchise in the Northwest League. /(FO)

Ken Brett — 1948– . LHP 1967, 69–81 Red Sox, Brewers, Phillies, **Pirates**, Yankees, White Sox, Angels, Twins, Dodgers, Royals 1526 ip, 83–85, 3.93. *2 LCS, 5 ip, 3.86 1 WS, 1 ip, 0.00*
☛ *All-Star—74.*

Although later overshadowed by younger brother George, in 1967 Ken became the youngest pitcher (19 years, one month) to pitch in a WS game. He went on to tie the modern record for playing with the most teams (10). A three-time 13-game winner, the clever lefty was the winning pitcher while representing the Pirates in the 1974 All-Star Game at Pittsburgh. A good hitter (.262), he set a record for pitchers in 1973 by homering in four straight starts with the Phillies. /(ME)

Marv Breuer (Baby Face) — 1914– . RHP 1939–43 **Yankees** 484 ip, 25–26, 4.03. *2 WS, 3 ip, 0.00*

Breuer earned his engineering degree from the Missouri School of Mines, a college without a baseball team. The youthful, soft-spoken right-hander failed to live up to Yankee expectations after starring for Newark in the minors. /(JK)

Chet Brewer — 1907– . RHP Negro Leagues 1925–48 Kansas City Monarchs, Washington Pilots, Chicago American Giants, Philadelphia Stars, New York Cubans, Cleveland Buckeyes, Tennessee Rats 81–39 (inc.)
☛ *All-Star—34, 37, 48.*

Brewer was one of a stable of Kansas City Monarch pitchers that included the legendary Satchel Paige and Bullet Joe Rogan. He defeated some of the best hurlers of his day, both black and white—Willie Foster, Slim Jones, Smokey Joe Williams, Bob Feller, and Paige. He had a lively fastball and a devastating overhand "drop ball," which was especially tough on lefthanded hitters. He also threw a legal emery ball.

In 1926, his first full season with the Monarchs, Brewer went 12–1 with eight complete games. His .842 winning percentage (16–3) led the league in 1929; that season, he pitched 31 consecutive scoreless innings against league competition. One of his greatest performances came under the lights in 1930 against the Homestead Grays' Smokey Joe Williams. Brewer struck out 19, including 10 in a row, only to lose 1–0 in 12 innings on a fluke hit by Chaney White. Brewer won 30 games that year. He won 16 straight games in 1934 and finished the season with 33 victories against league and non-league opponents. Pitching in Mexico in 1939, he threw two no-hitters.

Brewer was a Pittsburgh Pirates scout from 1957 to 1974 and later worked for the Major League Scouting Bureau. /(LL)

Jack Brewer (Buddy) — 1919– . RHP 1944–46 **Giants** 217 ip, 9–10, 4.36

Brewer joined the Giants after his discharge from the Navy in 1944 and was an effective starter in 1945 (8–6, 3.83), but lost his job when the remaining ML players returned from WWII in 1946. /(FS)

Jim Brewer — 1937–1987 . LHP 1960–76 Cubs, **Dodgers**, Angels 1039 ip, 69–65, 3.07. *3 WS, 3 ip, 2.70* ☛ *All-Star—73.*

With a tip from Warren Spahn, Brewer developed a screwball in 1964, and became one of the most successful relievers in the NL. He averaged better than 19 saves a season for the Dodgers in the years 1968–73, with a career-high 24 in 1970. In 1972 his ERA was 1.26, and he averaged an outstanding 4.69 hits per nine innings. Dodger manager Walter Alston said, "We've had a lot of great relief pitchers, but I've never seen one better than Brewer."

In 1960 as a Cub rookie, the even-tempered lefty was the victim in a much-publicized mound altercation. Cincinnati's Billy Martin accused Brewer of throwing at him, charged the mound, and punched Brewer, breaking his jaw.

Brewer died at the age of 50 in an auto accident. /(JCA)

Tom Brewer — 1931– . RHP 1954–61 **Red Sox** 1509 ip, 91–82, 4.00 ☛ *All-Star—56.*

The Red Sox' most effective righthanded starter during the 1950s, Brewer pitched for teams that finished in the middle of the pack. His best year was 1956, when he finished 19–9 and pitched two innings of the All-Star Game. Throughout his career, he was especially tough on the Indians and A's. /(PB)

Fred Brickell — 1906–1961. OF 1926–33 **Pirates**, Phillies 501 g, .281, 6 hr, 131 rbi. *1 WS, 2 g, .000*

The Kansan reached the majors at age 19 and hit .312 during four-plus years as a Pirates sub. His BA dipped when the Phillies gave the him a chance to play regularly. His son Fritzie played briefly in the majors. /(ME)

Jack Brickhouse — Unk.– . *Broadcaster.*

Brickhouse began his radio career at the age of 18 in Peoria, Illinois. In 1940 he became the first radio broadcaster for both Cubs and White Sox games. He became the WGN telecaster when the station began its baseball coverage in 1948. He also broadcast Chicago Bears football for 21 years. In 1983, Brickhouse was given the Ford Frick Award and a place on the Hall of Fame Broadcasters' Honor Roll. /(NLM)

Jim Brideweser — 1927– . SS-2B 1951–57 Yankees, **Orioles**, White Sox, Tigers 329 g, .252, 1 hr, 50 rbi

Signed off the USC campus by the Yankees, Brideweser was mostly a backup shortstop. His busiest year came in 1957, when he batted .268 for the Orioles. /(RTM)

Marshall Bridges (Sheriff) — 1931– . LHP 1959–65 Cardinals, Reds, **Yankees**, Senators 345 ip, 23–15, 3.75. *1 WS, 4 ip, 0–0, 4.91*

A hard-throwing southpaw reliever, Bridges surprised everyone with his stellar Yankee performance in 1962 (8–4, 18 saves). "The Sheriff" lost his winning momentum after he was shot during a barroom incident the following winter. /(GDW)

Rocky Bridges [Everett Lamar] — 1927– . SS-2B-3B 1951–61 Dodgers, **Reds**, Senators, Tigers, Indians, Cardinals, Angels 919 g, .247, 16 hr, 187 rbi ☛ *All-Star—58.*

The wisecracking Bridges fashioned a second career as an eminently quotable minor league manager. Always chewing a huge wad of tobacco, he was responsible for such wry gems as "Tommy Lasorda's curve had as much hang time as a Ray Guy punt" and "There are three things the average man thinks he can do better than anybody else: build a fire, run a hotel, and manage a baseball team."

Before starting his minor league managing career, Bridges was a versatile utility man. In two rare seasons in which he held down just one position, he led NL second basemen (1953) and AL shortstops (1957) in total chances per game, but he never hit enough to be an everyday player. /(JFC)

Tommy Bridges — 1906-1968. RHP 1930-43,
45-46 **Tigers** 2826 ip, 194-138, 3.57. 20 wins: 34-36
4 WS, 46 ip, 4-1, 3.52
☛ *Led League—w 36. Led League—k 35-36..*

Bridges's victory totals fell tantalizingly short of
satisfying the demanding writers who elect players to
baseball's Hall of Fame. He had won 192 when, in
1943, at 37, he was called to military service. He
missed the soft pickings of wartime baseball in 1944
and rejoined the Tigers in 1945 to record a lone win.
The next year, when baseball resumed with its

Tommy Bridges

younger stars, there was no room for the veteran
who had helped the Tigers win four pennants. There
were victories remaining in him, but they were
gained in the Pacific Coast League where, at age 40,
Bridges led the league with a 1.64 ERA.

The son of a country doctor, Bridges graduated
from the University of Tennessee and was expected
to follow in his father's footsteps. He chose baseball
instead, and the only doctoring he did was intended
to induce sharp, breaking curves. Bridges's frail
appearance was deceptive. Though he had a blazing
fastball, his curve was the wonder of the AL for over
a decade. He once fanned 20 in a minor league
game, and led the AL in strikeouts in 1935 and
1936.

In 1932 Bridges lost a bid for a perfect game in
dramatic fashion that either proved the integrity of
the game, or was just poor sportsmanship. Walter
Johnson was the Washington manager, and his
Senators trailed Detroit, 13-0, with two out in the
ninth. Young Bridges was doing something Johnson
had never done: pitch a perfect game. The Washington pitcher, Bobby Burke, was due up. Instead,
Johnson sent gifted pinch hitter Dave Harris to bat.
Harris led the AL that season with 14 pinch hits. A
notoriously good curveball hitter, Harris out-dueled
Bridges, stroking a clean single to left to break up the
perfect game. The next batter was a routine out, and
Washington still lost by 13 runs.

Bridges won over 20 games for three straight
seasons (1934-36) and led the AL with 23 victories
in '36. Among his memorable feats was his clutch
performance in Game Six of the 1935 World Series.
With the score tied 3-3, Stan Hack opened the top
of the ninth with a triple. He remained there as
Bridges retired the next three batters. The Tigers
scored in the bottom of the inning, winning the
Series, and Bridges had his second victory.

During the 1930s, Bridges was named to the AL
All-Star staff six times, and gained a victory in 1939.
With 194 regular season victories, four in the WS,
and one in an All-Star game, Bridges had 199 career
wins. /(JK)

Al Bridwell — 1884-1969. SS-2B-3B 1905-15 Reds,
Braves, **Giants**, Cubs, St. Louis (FL) 1251 g, .255, 2 hr,
348 rbi

Bridwell was a useful lefthand-hitting infielder who
led NL regular shortstops in fielding in 1907 but is
chiefly remembered today for hitting the single that
began the infamous "Merkle Boner" rally in
1908. /(JK)

Bunny Brief [Anthony Vincent, born Antonio Bordetzki] — 1892–1963. 1B-OF 1912–13, 15, 17 **Browns**, White Sox, Pirates 183 g, .223, 5 hr, 59 rbi

Brief had 42 homers and 191 RBI for Kansas City (American Association) in 1921. He led his league in home runs eight times and twice led all minor leagues. He chose an apt alias, as his major-league career was just that. /(LRD)

Buttons Briggs [Herbert] — 1875–1911. RHP 1896–98, 1904–05 **Cubs** 855 ip, 44–47, 3.41

Briggs won 19 games for the 1904 Cubs but slumped to 8–8 the next year. By 1906 he was pitching semi-pro ball for Elyria of the Ohio Trolley League. His first pitch of that season was smashed for a homer by Wooster catcher Charles Follis, the first black pro football player. /(BC)

Dan Briggs — 1952– . 1B-OF 1975–79, 81–82 **Angels**, Indians, Padres, Expos, Cubs 325 g, .195, 12 hr, 53 rbi

Originally signed by the Angels as a pitcher, the mustachioed lefty hit well over .300 in several Triple-A seasons as a first baseman-outfielder, but never hit better than .226 in trials with five ML clubs. /(JCA)

John Briggs — 1944– . OF-1B 1964–75 **Phillies**, Brewers, Twins 1366 g, .253, 139 hr, 507 rbi

Perennial prospect John Briggs was a fast, well-built, lefthanded-hitting outfielder. Because of the rules regarding bonus players when he signed, Briggs spent only one season in the low minors, and then was retained by the Phillies in 1964. He only once hit over .270, and didn't play regularly until his trade to Milwaukee, where he hit a career-high 21 homers in 1971 and 1972. /(AL)

Johnny Briggs — 1934– . RHP 1956–60 **Cubs**, Indians, A's 165 ip, 9–11, 5.00

A promising youngster who never lived up to it, Briggs started 17 games for the 1958 Cubs with a 5–5 mark. He was 4–4 as a reliever with the Indians and A's in 1960, but his ERA was 6.42. /(FK)

Walter O. Briggs, Sr. — 1877–1952. Owner.

As a young man, Briggs was a vociferous Tiger fan; in 1902 he was nearly ejected from the ballpark by umpire Tom Connolly for loudly and vehemently castigating the ump. He made a fortune in the auto-body industry, and in 1920 he bought 25 percent of the Tigers. Later, he bought another 25 percent, and, when Frank Navin died in 1935, Briggs bought

Briggs Stadium, named for Walter Briggs and later renamed Tiger Stadium

the remainder of the club. He took no money out of the club, reinvesting profits (and adding his own money) to improve the team and the ballpark. In 1941 he was *TSN* Executive of the Year. On two occasions he bought each of his players a new suit and hat after outstanding victories, causing a league rule to be passed prohibiting such rewards for single-game efforts. /(NLM)

Harry Bright — 1929- . 1B-3B-C 1958–65 Pirates, **Senators**, Reds, Yankees, Cubs 336 g, .255, 32 hr, 126 rbi. *1 WS, 2 g, .000*

It took expansion to give versatile, tenacious Harry Bright his only season as a regular, as he hit 17 homers for the lackluster 1962 Senators. Pinch hitting for the Yankees in Game One of the 1963 WS, he became Sandy Koufax's 15th strikeout victim, then a WS record. /(JK)

Nellie Briles [Nelson] — 1943- . RHP 1965–78 **Cardinals**, Pirates, Royals, Rangers, Orioles 2112 ip, 129–112, 3.43. *1 LCS, 6 ip, 3.00. 3 WS, 31 ip, 2–1, 2.59*

A gritty control artist, Briles moved into the St. Louis starting rotation when Bob Gibson suffered a broken leg in 1967. He won nine straight games and led the NL in winning percentage (.737, 14–4) and the Cardinals in ERA (2.43). He was 19–11 in 1968, but slumped the next two years. Traded to the Pirates in 1971, he helped Pittsburgh to the pennant and pitched a two-hit shutout against Baltimore in Game Five of the WS. After winning 14 games in each of the next two seasons, he was traded to the AL, where he finished his career. Briles, who sang the National Anthem before Game Four of the 1973 WS, later became a TV baseball announcer. /(ME)

Jim Brillheart — 1903–1972. LHP 1922–23, 27, 31 **Senators**, Cubs, Red Sox 286 ip, 8–9, 4.19

Brillheart spent only parts of four seasons in the ML, but his career lasted from 1921 (with Greenville, SC of the Sally League) through 1946 (with San Diego of the Pacific Coast League). He is one of the few pitchers to work in over 1,000 games — 928 in the minors and 86 in the majors. /(NLM)

Ed Brinkman — 1941- . SS 1961–75 **Senators**, Tigers, Cardinals, Rangers, Yankees 1845 g, .224, 60 hr, 461 rbi. *1 LCS, 2 g, .250*
☛ *All-Star—73. Gold Glove—72.*

The wiry, durable Brinkman was a poor hitter until manager Ted Williams changed his batting style in 1969; his BA jumped nearly 80 points to .266. In 1972 with Detroit, he won a Gold Glove while

setting four single-season records for shortstops: consecutive errorless games (72), consecutive error-less chances (331), fewest errors (7), and best fielding percentage (.990). The older brother of ML catcher Chuck Brinkman, Ed was a teammate of Pete Rose at Cincinnati's Western Hills High. He joined the White Sox as a coach in 1983. /(JCA)

Joe Brinkman — 1944- . *Umpire* AL 1973–87 *3 LCS 2 WS, 2 ASU*

Brinkman, who for several years operated the Joe Brinkman Umpires' School in Cocoa, FL, was an All-Army baseball and football standout who hoped for a pro football career. He was chief of the umpiring crew that ruled George Brett out after he hit a home run with a bat deemed to have pine tar beyond the 18-inch limit. AL president Lee McPhail overturned the call. /(RTM)

Lou Brissie [Leland Victor] — 1924- . LHP 1947–53 **A's**, Indians 898 ip, 44–48, 4.07

Lou was the only survivor of his WWII infantry unit, which was wiped out in battle. However, an exploding shell shattered his left leg, causing him to wear a brace during his pitching career. The coura-geous 6′4″ southpaw went 16–11 in 1949 for the Athletics and helped himself by batting .267. Brissie later became the National Director of the American Legion baseball program. /(RM)

Dave Bristol — 1933- . *Manager* 1966–72, 76–77, 79–80 **Reds**, Brewers, Braves, Giants 658–764, .463

Bristol led the Reds to third place in 1969, but was replaced after the season by Sparky Anderson, who won the pennant in 1970. Bristol never again had a winning record, saddled as he was from then on with some of the worst teams in the majors. /(SH)

Jim Britt — 1911–1981. *Broadcaster.*

The voice of the Braves and Red Sox for ten years in the 1940s and '50s, Britt concentrated on the Braves when the Red Sox began airing road games. When the two Boston clubs decided to employ separate announcers, Britt was given his choice. He chose the Braves, and Curt Gowdy got the Red Sox job. When his team moved to Milwaukee in 1954, Britt went to Cleveland for four years, returning to Boston in 1958 to work TV news. He broadcast seven All-Star games and five WS, as well as doing football telecasts during the 1950s. /(NLM)

Jim Britton — 1944– . RHP 1967–69, 71 **Braves,** Expos 238 ip, 13–16, 4.01. *1 LCS, 0.1 ip, 0–0, 0.00*

The 6'5″ 215-lb Britton declined a football scholarship to Penn State and signed with the Orioles. Drafted by the Braves, he pitched a Texas League no-hitter against Little Rock on Opening Day, 1967. Atlanta used him as a spot starter in 1968–69, but he sat out 1970 with arm trouble. /(MC)

Johnny Broaca — 1909– . RHP 1934–37, 39 **Yankees,** Indians 674 ip, 44–29, 4.08

The bespectacled Yale graduate puzzled more than batters. He confused everyone by bolting the Yankees twice, taking up professional boxing when he could have been pitching in the World Series, and, eventually, rejecting a baseball career altogether. /(JK)

Pete Broberg — 1950– . RHP 1971–78 **Senators/ Rangers,** Brewers, Cubs, A's 963 ip, 41–71, 4.56

Broberg possessed great natural skills: "I thought we had another Bob Feller," said Ranger pitching coach Sid Hudson, "but he's a hardhead." In his best year, Broberg was 14–16 for the 1975 Brewers. /(KT)

Greg Brock — 1957– . 1B 1983– **Dodgers,** Brewers 859 g, .247, 102 hr, 406 rbi. *2 LCS, 8 g, .048, 1 hr, 2 rbi*

The man who replaced Steve Garvey at first base for the Dodgers had impossible press notices to live up to. Called "the best power hitting prospect the Dodgers have had since Duke Snider" after breaking home run records at Albuquerque and San Antonio, Brock most resembled Snider in his inability to hit lefthanded pitching. After being traded to the Brewers, Brock cut down his stroke and raised his average at the expense of some power. /(TG)

Lou Brock — 1939– . OF 1961–79 Cubs, **Cardinals** 2616 g, .293, 149 hr, 900 rbi. *3 WS, 21 g, .391, 4 hr, 13 rbi* ☛ *All-Star—67, 71, 74–75. Hall of Fame—1985.*

Signed out of Southern University for a $30,000 bonus in 1961, Brock moved up to the Cubs within one season. He hit only .263 and .258 in two full seasons with Chicago while showing flashes of both speed and power, including a 450-foot home run into the centerfield bleachers at the Polo Grounds, one of only four homers ever to land there. He came into his own after moving to St. Louis in a six-man trade on June 15, 1964. The deal was essentially Brock for pitcher Ernie Broglio, and is regarded as one of the worst the Cubs ever made. Brock averaged .348 in the 1964 stretch drive and finished

Lou Brock

the season at .315, with 111 runs scored, 200 hits, 30 doubles, 11 triples, and 43 stolen bases. In fourth place when Brock joined them, the Cardinals overtook the Phillies, Giants, and Reds to claim the pennant in the last week of the season. Brock then batted .300 with a homer as the Cardinals beat the Yankees in the World Series.

He scored 107 runs and stole 63 bases in 1965, then won his first of four straight and eight total stolen-base championships with 74 in 1966. Brock's greatest season was probably 1967, when he led the Cardinals to another World Championship with a league-leading 113 runs scored, 52 steals, and career highs of 21 homers, 76 RBI, and a .472 slugging average. Brock batted .414 with seven steals against Boston in the WS, breaking or tying four Series records. Although he slumped to .279 in 1968, Brock helped St. Louis win the pennant again by leading the NL in doubles (46) and triples (14) as well as steals (62). The Cardinals lost the World

Series to the Tigers in seven games, but Brock was sensational. He hit .464 to lead both clubs, with two homers and seven steals. At that time he had the highest average (.391) of any player in two or more World Series, along with a Series-record 14 steals. His .655 slugging average ranked fifth and his seven doubles ranked eighth.

Brock hit between .297 and .313 in each season from 1969 through 1976 and led the NL with 126 runs in 1971. Former teammate Bobby Tolan edged Brock, 57 to 51, for the 1970 stolen-base championship, but Brock then won four more titles in a row with 64, 63, 70 and 118.

Brock's 118 steals in 1974 shattered Maury Wills's major league record of 104, set in 1962, and remains the National League record through the 1980s (Rickey Henderson broke the ML record with 130 in 1982). At 35, Brock was by far the oldest man to steal 100 bases. "I figured it was now or never," he said.

He dropped off to "only" 56 steals in each of the next two seasons. Dipping to .221 and 17 steals in 1978, Brock lost his regular job and was urged to retire. Instead he rebounded to .304 with 21 steals, retiring first all-time in stolen bases with 938. He was elected to the Hall of Fame in 1985, his first year of eligibility.

Despite Brock's high averages and electrifying feats on the bases, his stature is disputed by baseball experts. He struck out over 100 times in nine seasons, over 90 times in 12 seasons, and fanned more often than he scored in 11 seasons. He also struck out 1,730 times career, the most all-time at his retirement, while walking only 761 times, a poor ratio for any player and horrendous for a leadoff man. Brock also led the NL in errors seven times, including five years consecutively, never committing fewer than 10 from 1964 through 1973. He was shifted from centerfield to right before settling in left in 1966, primarily because of his defensive shortcomings. /(MC)

Steve Brodie [Walter Scott] — 1868–1935. OF 1890–99, 1901–02 Boston (NL), Cardinals, Baltimore (NL), Pirates, Baltimore (AL), Giants 1438 g, .303, 25 hr, 900 rbi

Brodie was a solid, lefthanded-hitting outfielder who from 1893 to 1897 played 574 consecutive games. He batted .329 over those seasons. He was an important cog in the Baltimore Oriole machine that won National League pennants in 1894–96. Playing centerfield, he led NL outfielders in fielding with Pittsburgh in 1897 and with the Orioles in 1899. In

1900 he left the disbanded Baltimore franchise for the Chicago White Sox of the minor American League. In 1901 he was back in the majors with John McGraw's AL Baltimore Orioles. /(AJA)

Dick Brodowski — 1932– . RHP 1952, 55–59 **Red Sox**, Senators, Indians 215 ip, 9–11, 4.76

The baby-faced Brodowski reached Boston after less than two years of pro ball, then spent two years in the military, and was ineffective after his return. /(DB)

Bob Broeg — 1918– . *Writer.*

Broeg joined the *St. Louis Post-Dispatch* in 1945 and became sports editor in 1958. He is a member of the Board of Directors of the National Baseball Hall of Fame and the only person eligible to vote in the elections for the baseball, pro football, and college football Halls of Fame. He has authored nine books, including the popular *Redbirds: A Century of Cardinal Baseball*. In honor of his many contributions to baseball, the St. Louis chapter of SABR is named for him. /(FJO)

Ernie Broglio — 1935– . RHP 1959–66 **Cardinals**, Cubs 1337 ip, 77–74, 3.74

Broglio won 21 games, 7 in relief, for the 1960 Cardinals. Following an 18–8 record in 1963, he was dealt in June of 1964 for an unproven Cub outfielder, Lou Brock. Broglio won only seven more games in the majors. /(FJO)

Jack Brohamer — 1950– . 2B-3B 1972–80 **Indians**, White Sox, Red Sox 805 g, .245, 30 hr, 227 rbi

Small, gutsy, and bow-legged, Brohamer became Cleveland's second baseman in 1972 and was named to the *TSN* All-Rookie Team. He hit a career-high .270 in 1974. With the White Sox on September 24, 1977, he hit for the cycle. Brohamer, who started two ML triple plays, was a utility man for the second half of his career. /(JCA)

Tom Brookens — 1953– . 3B-2B-SS **Tigers**, Yankees 1272 g, .245, 70 hr, 411 rbi. *2 LCS, 7 g, .000. 1 WS, 3 g, .000*

Brookens first became Detroit's third baseman in 1980, and, as the decade progressed, alternately fended off challengers for his job and served in a utility role. A mediocre fielder, he led the AL in errors at 3B in 1980 and 1985, and tied an AL 3B record on September 6, 1980 with four errors in an inning. Though short on power and struggling to hit over .240, his clutch, heads-up play and team-first attitude kept him on Detroit clubs that saw post-season action in 1984 and 1987. Tom's twin brother, Tim, played in the Tigers organization, and their cousin, Ed "Ike" Brookens, pitched briefly with Detroit in 1975. /(JCA)

Brooklyn Dodgers [aka Bridegrooms, Trolley Dodgers, Superbas, Robins] (Daffiness Boys, Flock, Bums) — 1884–1957. Team AA 1884–89; NL 1890–1957 NL: 5214–4927, .514. *American Association Champions 1890 NL Champions 1899, 1900, 16, 20, 41, 47, 49, 52–53, 55–56 World Champions 55*

The only major league team whose named location was a borough (rather than a city or state), the Brooklyn Dodgers entered American mythology as a metaphor for lost innocence and community. They became a symbol of the decline of the eastern city. Many in Brooklyn agreed with columnists Pete Hamill and Jack Newfield when they named the three most evil men of the 20th century as "Hitler, Stalin, and Walter O'Malley." O'Malley moved the "Boys of Summer" to Los Angeles only ten years after their proudest moment, the breaking of the color barrier with Jackie Robinson, and two years

after their greatest triumph, beating the hated Yankees in the World Series after five losses.

The Dodgers are best remembered for their free-wheeling days as manager Wilbert Robinson's Daffiness Boys, for their legendary Ebbets Field fans, and for the cry of "Wait until next year." Brooklyn lost the only two league playoffs played during their tenure, in 1946 and 1951, and were the only major league team to finish in the cellar only once. They played the longest major league game ever, a 26-inning tie with the Braves in 1920. /(TG)

Hubie Brooks [Hubert] — 1956– . 3B-SS-OF 1980-Mets, **Expos** 1198 g, .276, 103 hr, 609 rbi
☛ *All-Star—86–87.*

Originally a third baseman, and the third player chosen in the June 1978 draft, Hubie Brooks was an early key to the rebuilt fortunes of the Mets. Though he gave the club its first real stability at third base, Brooks was shifted to shortstop in 1984 to make room for Ray Knight and was then traded with Floyd Youmans, Mike Fitzgerald and Herm Winningham to the Expos for Gary Carter after the season. An outstanding clutch hitter, in 1985 Brooks

The 1955 Brooklyn Dodgers

became the first NL shortstop since Ernie Banks (1960) to drive in 100 runs. Off to his greatest season in 1986, when he hit .340, Hubie was sidelined by a series of injuries, the most severe being torn ligaments and bone chips in his left thumb. His 1987 season was shortened by a broken wrist, suffered when he was hit by a Danny Darwin pitch. Brooks earned Silver Slugger Awards in 1985 and 1986.

Never a good fielder even at third base (he led NL third basemen in errors in 1981), Brooks's extreme lack of range at shortstop led the Expos to move him to right field in 1988. The move may have helped his durablity, but even in the outfield his defense proved barely adequate. /(ME)

Jim Brosnan (Professor) — 1929– . RHP 1954, 56–63 Cubs, Cardinals, **Reds**, White Sox 831 ip, 55–47, 3.54. *1 WS, 6 ip, 7.50*

Had pitching been his only talent, the 6′4″ 200-lb Brosnan would be recalled as a consistent reliever whose ERA for eight consecutive years never topped 3.79. Used exclusively in relief for the pennant-winning 1961 Reds, he compiled a 10–4 record and a 3.04 ERA in 53 appearances. But the spectacled and scholarly "Professor" became best known as the author of the autobiographical baseball book classics *The Long Season* and *Pennant Race.* /(FK)

Brotherhood of Ballplayers

In 1885 the owners put a $2,000 salary limit into the National Agreement. In response, John Montgomery Ward, star shortstop of the New York National League team, secretly formed the Brotherhood of Ballplayers. Its existence was announced in August 1886; in fall 1887 the Brotherhood demanded recognition by the owners, with members not signing contracts until it was granted. The Brotherhood Committee of Ward, Ned Hanlon, and Dan Brouthers held meetings with the NL, leading to a new form of contract that defined all relations between the league and its players, with no additional restrictions contained in outside documents. Section 18 of the new contract contained a clause allowing the club to reserve the player for the next season, provided that the full salary be written in the contract; a salary reduction constituted a release. Because of the $2,000 limit (broken by all teams in under-the-table deals with star players), the clause was not consistent with the status quo. The League Committee solved the problem by promising to strike the limit from the National Agreement. Players went ahead and signed contracts for the next season, but the limit wasn't stricken, "owing to the

alleged refusal of the other party to the agreement, the American Association [the other major league at the time], to consent," according to the Reach Guide. At this point, the American Association was in no position to buck the National League, so it was probably acting under NL orders. As a result, clubs were able to reserve players at reduced salaries the following fall.

At the same time, three NL clubs (Indianapolis, Pittsburgh, and Washington) stated that they needed a larger share of the gate receipts in big cities. The other owners voted down a change in the division of the gate, so John T. Brush of Indianapolis proposed a reduction of players' salaries on these clubs (despite the fact that these teams already paid lower salaries than other clubs). This was done by setting player ratings from "A" to "E" with prescribed salaries for each rating. This action was taken while Ward was overseas on tour with Al Spalding; Ward returned in April and insisted on the repeal of this rule, which would eventually reduce salaries throughout the league. Spalding, the chairman of the league committee appointed to deal with this controversy, stonewalled.

The Brotherhood, in a July 4, 1889 meeting in New York City, secretly organized the Players' League for the following season. Word leaked out in September, but all was denied until November. Chicago star Cap Anson was the only player who remained with the NL at first. The NL repealed the classification system, invoked the reserve clause, and moved Cincinnati and Brooklyn from the AA to the NL. In response to these moves and to generous contract offers, some players abandoned the new league. But a lawsuit against Ward failed when, in January 1890, it was ruled that the "contract was lacking in mutuality, unconscionable and inequitable." The National League transferred Indianapolis's players to New York, which had lost all but three of its members to the Players' League, and then bought out Indianapolis and Washington for $65,000. The NL played an eight-team schedule, with the former AA teams, Brooklyn and Cincinnati, carrying the NL at first. Pittsburgh played most of its games on the road. Although a good pennant race saved attendance after a bad slump in June, the NL as a whole lost $300,000 for the season, a tremendous sum at the time. On October 4, Cincinnati was lost to the Players' League, sold for $40,000. But the financial backers of the Players' League had also taken a licking and, unaware of the extent of the NL's losses, they caved in to the NL that winter. /(SH)

Mark Brouhard — 1956– . OF-DH 1980–85 **Brewers** 304 g, .258, 25 hr, 104 rbi. *1 LCS, 1 g, .750, 1 hr, 3 rbi*

Slow-footed slugger Brouhard was a reserve outfielder and DH for the Brewers. In the fourth game of the 1982 LCS, he played for injured Ben Oglivie after 28 days of inactivity. He had three hits, including a homer and three RBI, and tied an AL record with four runs scored. In 1986 he played for the Yakult Swallows of Japan's Central League (.258, 21 HR, 64 RBI) but was dropped from their roster in 1987 to make room for Bob Horner./(MC)

Heywood C. Broun — 1888–1939. *Writer.*

Broun was a copy reader, sports writer and editor, drama critic, war correspondent, and columnist in his 31-year career. He could reputedly bat out a column in 30 minutes. He was a big eater (6′3″, 250-lb) and a messy dresser who sported an old broad-brimmed hat. Broun attended Harvard but did not graduate before he began his journalism career in 1910 with the New York *Morning Telegraph*, a racing and theatrical paper. He moved to the *Tribune* in 1912, where he became drama critic in 1916. He began his column, "It Seems to Me," at the *World* in 1921. One of his most quoted lines appeared in 1915, when John McGraw frequently started pitcher Rube Schauer and relieved him with Ferdie Schupp: "It never Schauers but it Schupps."

Broun was the founder of the American Newspaper Guild in 1933. He moved to the *New York Post* in 1939, but died of pneumonia after writing only one column. His only baseball book, *The Sun Field*, was published in 1923. He received the J.G. Taylor Spink Award from the Hall of Fame in 1970./(NLM)

Dan Brouthers [Dennis Joseph] (Big Dan) — 1858–1932. 1B 1879–96, 1904 Troy (NL), **Buffalo (NL)**, Detroit (NL), Braves, Boston (PL), Boston (AA), Dodgers, Baltimore (NL), Louisville (NL), Phillies, Giants 1673 g, .343, 106 hr, 1056 rbi
☛ *Led League—ba 82–83, 89, 91–92. Led League—hr 81, 86. Led League—rbi 92. Hall of Fame—1945.*

Dan Brouthers was one of baseball's 19th-century superstars, a five-time batting champion who also led the NL in slugging percentage each of his first six full seasons. Particularly large for his era at 6′2″ and 205 lbs., mustachioed Big Dan sported a lusty lefthanded swing that produced a career .343 batting average, ninth-best of all time.

After parts of 1879–80 with Troy, which included two unsuccessful starts as a pitcher,

Brouthers became a regular in Buffalo in 1881 and led the NL in home runs and slugging percentage. He won his first batting title in 1882 with a .368 mark, and repeated the next season by batting .374. His average would not dip below .300 until his token appearence with the Giants in 1904, eight years after his initial retirement.

Brouthers joined Detroit in 1886 and hit .370 while leading the league in home runs (11), doubles (40), and, for the sixth consecutive season, slugging percentage. Although his average dropped to .338 and .307 the next two years, he led the league in doubles and runs each time, then moved on to Boston, where he regained the batting title with .373 in 1889. He jumped to the one-year Players League

Dan Brouthers

in 1890, helping Boston to the league championship, then joined Boston's American Association club in 1891, where he edged teammate Hugh Duffy for his fourth batting title. Back in the NL with Brooklyn in 1892, he led the league in hitting once again (.335) and also led in hits and RBI.

A capable barehanded fielder at first base, Brouthers made his best contributions at the plate. He went 6-for-6 on July 19, 1883, and on September 10, 1886, he blasted three home runs, a double, and a single for 15 total bases. When his ML career was done, he played in the Eastern League, winning a final batting title with a .415 average. He remained in baseball when former teammate and Giant manager John McGraw placed him in charge of the Polo Grounds press gate for many years. In 1945, when a dearth of turn-of-the-century stars was addressed by the Hall of Fame Veterans Committee, Big Dan Brouthers was among the eight inducted. /(JK)

Bob Brower — 1960– . OF 1986– **Rangers**, Yankees 256 g, .242, 17 hr, 60 rbi

Brower showed great promise in 1987, when he hit .261 with 14 HR as a part-time outfielder with Texas, but he dropped off to .224 with 1 HR in 1988 after starting the season on the DL. He replaced the injured Dave Winfield in the Yankee outfield in 1989, but erratic fielding and the acquisition of Jesse Barfield relegated Brower to Columbus. /(JFC)

Frank Brower — 1893–1960. OF-1B 1920–24 **Senators**, Indians 450 g, .286, 30 hr, 205 rbi

Signed as a pitcher by the Cardinals, Brower became an everyday player in the minors. He was called "The Babe Ruth of the Bushes" in 1920 when he hit .394 with 23 homers for Reading of the International League. The Senators purchased his contract but he produced no Ruthian ML stats. In 1923, his top year, he hit 16 homers for Cleveland. /(NLM)

Boardwalk Brown [Carroll] — 1889–1977. RHP 1911–15 **A's**, Yankees 731 ip, 38–40, 3.47

Brown got his nickname because he was discovered playing on the sandlots of Atlantic City by a scout for Connie Mack. He was 13–11 for the A's in 1912 and followed with 17–11 for the pennant winners of 1913, but was not used in the A's WS victory as Connie Mack used only three pitchers. After a 1–6 start in 1914, he was sold to New York. /(NLM)

Bob Brown — 1911– . RHP 1930–36 **Braves** 364 ip, 16–21, 4.48

Brown was a promising 14–7 (3.30) as a 21-year-old rookie in 1932, but only won two more games in four more seasons. /(JK)

Bobby Brown (Doc) — 1924– . 3B-SS-2B-OF 1946–52, 54 **Yankees** 548 g, .279, 22 hr, 237 rbi. *4 WS, 17 g, .439, 9 rbi*

After signing with the Yankees for a substantial bonus, Brown hit .300 in 1947 in 69 games and led the AL in pinch hits (9). The next year he again hit .300 in a career-high 113 games. Because he was a weak fielder, he was platooned at third base and occasionally used at other positions when his potent lefthanded bat was needed. After serving in the military for most of 1952 and all of '53, he retired from baseball in mid-1954 to practice medicine. He was a hitting star in four WS. His pinch-double tied the seventh game of the 1947 WS, he tripled with the bases loaded in the 1949 WS, and his double led to the only run in Game One of the 1950 WS. In 1984, Brown left a successful career as a surgeon and re-entered baseball as the successor to Lee MacPhail as president of the American League. /(FK)

Bobby Brown [Rogers Lee] — 1954– . OF 1979–85 Blue Jays, Yankees, Mariners, **Padres** 502 g, .245, 26 hr, 130 rbi. *3 LCS, 9 g, .067. 2 WS, 9 g, .063, 2 rbi*

The speedy Brown played in seven organizations, and in 1979 shared International League MVP honors (with Dave Stapleton), batting .349 for Columbus. While playing for Seattle on September 13, 1982, he broke up a Vida Blue no-hitter. /(NLM)

Buster Brown [Charles] — 1881–1914. RHP 1905–13 Cardinals, Phillies, **Braves** 1452 ip, 51–105, 3.20

Often disgruntled, saddled with poor teams, and plagued by wildness, Brown never had a winning ML season despite posting some good ERAs. In 1909, the former Ames College star kept his ERA for the Braves to 2.67 but went 9–23. /(NLM)

Chris Brown (Tin Man) — 1961– . 3B 1984– **Giants**, Padres, Tigers 449 g, .269, 38 hr, 184 rbi ☛ *All-Star—86.*

"Chris has the talent to be an MVP," said former teammate Mike Krukow in 1989, but the enigmatic Brown showed little desire to play like one, or often to play at all. Instead, he would infuriate both managers and teammates with a careless attitude and a litany of nagging, minor injuries that were usually described as imaginary. From 1984 to 1988, Brown missed over 250 games with ailments as ludicrous as a "bruised tooth," but was placed on the DL only once, when a Danny Cox pitch broke his jaw.

Brown made the *Topps* and *Baseball Digest* all-rookie teams in 1985 after hitting .271 with 16 HR, and in 1986 he was hitting .348 on June 25 and made the NL All-Star team. Brown had led the Giants in hitting in both 1985 and '86, but by July 4, 1987 the club was fed up with its moody third baseman and traded him to San Diego in a seven-player swap that brought Kevin Mitchell to San Francisco. Brown hit only .237 with 12 HR in 1987, and .235 in 80 games (though he was never on the DL) in 1988 before being traded to the Tigers in the off-season. Detroit manager Sparky Anderson believed he could motivate Brown, but Brown quickly came up with shoulder and back "problems" and was released in June. He then signed a minor league contract with the Pirates. Brown was called "Tin Man" by both teammates and opponents, a disparaging reference to the "Wizard of Oz" character who had no heart./(SCL)

Clint Brown — 1903–1955. RHP 1928–42 **Indians**, White Sox 1486 ip, 89–92, 4.26

One of the first relief aces, the righthanded junk-baller threw underhand, sidearm, and three-quarters. His 61 appearances in 1939 set the (since broken) ML record for relievers. A fair starter for the Indians from 1930 through 1933, with a 15–12 mark in 1932 his best, he was switched to relief in 1934 and then sold to the White Sox two years later. He led the AL in saves (18) in 1937 and relief wins (11) in 1939./(JK)

Darrell Brown — 1955– . OF-DH 1981–84 Tigers, A's, **Twins** 210 g, .274, 1 hr, 44 rbi

A singles hitter, Brown was a three-time first draft choice before signing with Detroit. He usually played centerfield and batted leadoff during his two years in Minnesota./(CC)

Dave Brown — 1896– . LHP Negro Leagues 1918–25 Chicago American Giants, New York Lincoln Giants statistics not available

To aquire Dave Brown for the Chicago American Giants, Rube Foster put up a $20,000 bond to get Brown a parole from a highway robbery conviction. While leading the 1920–22 team to three straight championships, Brown was generally considered the best lefthander in the Negro Leagues. In 1921 he

was 11–3 with five shutouts and a league-leading 2.47 runs per game (ERA unknown). For the four years for which league records are available, he was 41–18. He also played in the winter Cuban League, compiling a 17–12 record over four years. His career came to a sudden halt in 1925 when, sought in connection with a New York homicide, he disappeared./(BP)

Dick Brown — 1935–1970. C 1957–65 Indians, White Sox, **Tigers**, Orioles 641 g, .244, 62 hr, 223 rbi

A dependable catcher with occasional home run power, Brown's career ended in 1965 after surgery for a brain tumor. He scouted for the Orioles until his death five years later. His brother, Larry, played 12 years as a ML infielder./(JK)

Eddie Brown (Glass Arm Eddie) — 1891–1956. OF 1920–21, 24–28 Giants, Dodgers, **Braves** 790 g, .303, 16 hr, 407 rbi

The 6'3" 190-lb righthanded speedster lacked power and had a notoriously weak arm, but became a ML regular at age 31 and had four straight .300-plus seasons, with a career-high 99 RBI in 1925 and a NL-leading 201 hits in 1926./(JK)

Fred Brown — 1879–1955. OF 1901–02 **Braves** 9 g, .200, 0 hr, 2 rbi

His ML career consisted of only nine games, but Brown was far more successful in the political arena. In 1923 he became the first Democratic governor of New Hampshire in 65 years. He served as U.S. Senator from 1933 to 1939. In 1939 he was appointed Comptroller General of the United States./(BC)

Gates Brown [William James] — 1939– . OF-DH 1963–75 **Tigers** 1051 g, .257, 84 hr, 322 rbi. *1 LCS, 3 g, .000. 1 WS, 1 g, .000*

Brown never knew why his mother called him "Gates," but he preferred it to Billy, and the nickname stuck. In his first ML at bat (6/19/63), he hit a pinch homer, a fitting beginning for one of baseball's most successful pinch hitters. The squat, popular Brown had limited defensive skills and couldn't break into the regular Tiger outfield, but he collected 107 career pinch hits and 16 pinch homers. In both 1968 and 1974 he led the AL in total pinch hits./(JCA)

Hal Brown (Skinny) — 1924- . RHP 1951–64 White Sox, Red Sox, **Orioles**, Yankees, Astros 1680 ip, 85–92, 3.81

A knuckleball pitcher with outstanding control, Brown was both a starter and a reliever. With Houston in 1963, he walked just eight in 141 innings. Chunky as a youngster, his parents facetiously nicknamed him "Skinny." He was 12–5 with Baltimore in 1960, his best season, and pitched 36 consecutive shutout innings the next year to set the Oriole record. Although his ERAs with Houston in 1963–64 were as good as they had been with Baltimore, his record with the anemic Colt .45's (later the Astros) was 8–26./(JCA)

Ike Brown — 1942- . 2B-1B-OF 1969–74 **Tigers** 280 g, .256, 20 hr, 65 rbi. *1 LCS, 1 g, .500, 2 rbi*

Brown's first hit was a homer at Yankee Stadium. The stocky jack-of-all-trades was often called on to pinch-hit, batting .320 in that role in 1970–71. He hit eight homers in just 110 at-bats in '71./(CC)

Jackie Brown — 1943- . RHP 1970–71, 73–77 **Senators/Rangers**, Indians, Expos 893 ip, 47–53, 4.18

Curveball specialist Jackie Brown and his older brother Paul both signed with the Phillies after starring together in high school. Paul jumped to the majors as a phenom at 20 but was finished at 27, having gone 0–8 in four seasons. Jackie was 27 when he got his first shot at the majors in 1970. His best year was 1974, when he went 13–12 with a 3.57 ERA for the Rangers./(MC)

Jimmy Brown — 1910–1977. 2B-3B-SS 1937–43, 46 **Cardinals**, Pirates 890 g, .279, 9 hr, 319 rbi. *1 WS, 5 g, .300, 1 rbi*
☛ *All-Star—42.*

A product of the Cardinal farm system, the switch-hitting Brown was a leadoff hitter who seldom walked; he twice led the NL in at-bats (1939 and '42). He led Cardinal hitters with a BA of .300 in their 1942 WS win over the Yankees./(JK)

Jumbo Brown [Walter George] — 1907–1966. RHP 1925, 1927–28, 1932–33, 1935–41 Cubs, Indians, Yankees, Reds, **Giants** 598 ip, 33–31, 4.06

The 6'4" 295-lb giant fielded his position with surprising agility, but his fastball was ineffective after four innings. An undistinguished reliever throughout most of his career, he was most effective with the Giants in his final four seasons. He tied for the NL lead in saves in 1940 (7) and led in 1941 (8)./(JK)

Kevin Brown — 1965- . RHP 1986, 88- **Rangers** 219 ip, 14–10, 4.02

Brown was the fourth player taken in the June 1986 draft and was in the majors by the end of the year. He moved into the Rangers' rotation in 1989 and went 12–9 with a 3.35 ERA as their number-two starter./(SFS)

Larry Brown (Iron Man) — 1902–1972. C-MGR Negro Leagues 1919–49 Birmingham Black Barons, Pittsburgh Keystones, Indianapolis ABC's, **Memphis Red Sox**, Detroit Stars, Chicago American Giants, New York Lincoln Giants, New York Black Yankees, Cole's American Giants, Philadelphia Stars statistics not available
☛ *All-Star—33–34, 38–41.*

Recognized as one of the best defensive catchers in Negro League history, husky Larry Brown was known for his rifle arm and unusual habit of leaving his mask on when catching pop-ups. Referred to as "Iron Man," he prided himself on catching nearly every day, sometimes three games a day; in 1930, he caught 234 games. Though mediocre offensively, he excelled in his six all-star appearances, hitting .308. His best single season on record was 1928, when he batted .294 and led the Memphis Red Sox in games, at-bats, hits, and doubles. After starring for the Chicago American Giants in the early 1930s, he finished his career as player-manager for Memphis throughout the 1940s./(PG)

Larry Brown — 1940- . SS-2B-3B 1963–74 **Indians**, A's, Orioles, Rangers 1129 g, .233, 47 hr, 254 rbi. *1 LCS, 1 g, --*

An outstanding fielder, Brown was Cleveland's regular second baseman in 1964 and regular shortstop from 1965 to 1969. A confirmed .230 hitter, he showed some power with 12 homers in 1964, but his slugging declined after he suffered fractures of the skull, nose and cheekbone in a 1966 collision with another player. His brother Dick was an AL catcher for nine seasons./(MC)

Lloyd Brown (Gimpy) — 1904–1974. LHP 1925, 28–37, 40 Dodgers, **Senators**, Browns, Red Sox, Indians, Phillies 1693 ip, 91–105, 4.20

This Texan won 46 games over three years with Washington, 1930–32, after which he went 33–53. He is chiefly remembered as the pitcher who gave up the most home runs to Lou Gehrig (15), including two grand slams. Brown pitched for 30 years in pro ball, 1923–53, and scouted for the Phillies and Senators./(LRD)

Mace Brown — 1909– . RHP 1935–43, 46 **Pirates**, Dodgers, Red Sox 1075 ip, 76–57, 3.47. *1 WS, 1 ip, 0–0, 27.00*

One of the first relief specialists, Brown set a record in 1937 by making 50 appearances without recording a complete game. He led Pittsburgh in wins (15, all in relief) in 1938, in a major league high 51 appearances, but surrendered the "Homer in the Gloamin'" to Gabby Hartnett that propelled Chicago past Pittsburgh and on to the NL pennant. Brown again led the AL with 49 games in 1943. He is credited with 48 career saves. /(ME)

Mike Brown — 1959– . RHP 1982–87 **Red Sox**, Mariners 254 ip, 12–20, 5.75

After jumping directly from Class AA to the pitching-poor Red Sox in 1983, Brown warned, "I'm a rookie, not a savior." His six wins that season were a career high. /(SCL)

Mike Brown — 1959– . OF 1983–86 **Angels**, Pirates 297 g, .267, 23 hr, 110 rbi

The Angels' top minor leaguer in 1983, Brown hit .322 after a mid-1985 trade to the Pirates. He struggled as a platoon player in 1986, was farmed out, hit .379 in the Pacific Coast League, but was released prior to the 1987 season. /(ME)

Ollie Brown (Downtown) — 1944– . OF 1965–77 Giants, **Padres**, A's, Brewers, Astros, Phillies 1218 g, .265, 102 hr, 454 rbi. *2 LCS, 3 g, .000*

Brown earned the nickname "Downtown" by hitting 40 homers for Fresno in 1964, but he was disappointing in San Francisco. San Diego's first choice in the 1968 expansion draft, he hit 20 homers for the Padres in 1969 and had career highs of 23 homers and 89 RBI in 1970. Originally signed as a pitcher, his strong arm was an asset in the outfield. His older brother Oscar was a Braves outfielder, and another brother, Willie, played in the NFL. /(JCA)

Raymond Brown — 1908–before 1972. RHP-OF-MGR Negro Leagues 1930–53 Dayton Marcos, Indianapolis ABC's, Homestead Grays

Ray Brown played for Cum Posey's Homestead Grays from 1932–45 and married Posey's daughter before moving on to Mexico (1946–49) and the Canadian Provincial League (1950–53). He started the 1935 East-West all-star game, threw a no-hitter for Santa Clara (Cuban Winter League) in 1936, and pitched them to the 1938 Cuban crown. He was 9–3 for the 1944 Black World Champion Homestead Grays, and threw a one-hit shutout in the World Series. In 1945, he had a seven-inning perfect game for the Grays. He helped Sherbrooke to the 1951 Provincial title with an 11–10 record and a 3.31 ERA. A good batter who switch-hit at times, he often played the outfield and pinch hit. He was one of five players mentioned as being of major league caliber in a 1938 wire sent to the Pittsburgh Pirates by *The Pittsburgh Courier*. The other four were Hall of Famers Josh Gibson, Buck Leonard, Cool Papa Bell, and Satchel Paige. /(MFK)

Three-Finger Brown [Mordecai Peter Centennial](Miner) — 1876–1948 . RHP 1903–16 Cardinals, **Cubs**, Reds, St. Louis (FL),Brooklyn (FL), Chicago (FL) 3172 ip, 239–129, 2.06. 20 wins: 06–11 *4 WS, 58 ip, 5–4, 2.81.*
  Manager 1914 **St. Louis (FL)** 50–63, .442
☛ *Led League—era 06. Led League—w 09. Hall of Fame—1949.*

Some players overcome handicaps. Brown turned his to an advantage. As a seven-year-old boy he caught his right hand in a corn grinder on his uncle's

Three-Finger Brown

farm. It was necessary to amputate almost all the forefinger, and, although saved, the middle finger was mangled and left crooked. His little finger was also stubbed. Later, newspapers called him "Three-Finger," although to his teammates he was "Miner" because he'd worked several years in a coal mine before beginning in baseball at age 24. He started as an infielder, but when he learned to add spin to the ball by releasing it off his stub, he became a pitcher.

Brown was the pitching mainstay of the great "Tinker-to-Evers-to-Chance" Cub teams that won four pennants and two world championships, 1906–10. He won 20 or more games for six consecutive years, starting in 1906, and four of his five WS wins were shutouts.

The peak years of Brown's career coincided with those of Christy Mathewson, and they were often matched when the Giants and Cubs met. One game he lost to Mathewson was Matty's no-hitter in 1905. After that, Brown rolled off nine consecutive victories over Mathewson, the ninth coming in the playoff that decided the famous 1908 pennant race after the "Merkle Boner." In 1916, they faced each other for the final time, each with 12 wins. Mathewson beat Brown, in what turned out to be the last game for each.

Brown was a strong, durable pitcher, admired for his fitness. In 1914, *American Monthly*, a national magazine, published photos of his exercise program, a rugged series of body-building routines. Always in the starting rotation, he was still able to relieve frequently. He led the NL four times in saves and had 48 lifetime, in addition to his 239 career wins. /(JK)

Tom Brown — 1860–1927. OF 1882–98 Baltimore (AA), Columbus (AA), Pittsburgh (AA), Pirates, Indianapolis (NL), Braves, Boston (P), Boston (AA), **Louisville (NL)**, Cardinals, Washington (NL) 1786 g, .265, 64 hr, 528 rbi

When Brown reached England as one of the players on the 1888–89 World Tour, it was a homecoming for the Liverpool-born outfielder. A fleet ball hawk and basestealer, he usually batted leadoff although he led his league in striking out five times. In 1891 with Boston, he topped the American Association with 106 stolen bases and 177 runs scored. /(JK)

Tommy Brown [Thomas Michael] (Buckshot) — 1927– . SS-OF-3B 1944–45, 47–53 **Dodgers**, Phillies, Cubs 494 g, .241, 31 hr, 159 rbi. *1 WS, 2 g, .000*

Brown was just 16 when he broke in at shortstop with the wartime Dodgers in 1944, the youngest player ever to see regular action. On August 20,

1945, at age 17, he became the youngest player to homer in the majors. His weak hitting made him a utility infielder after the war. However, he hit three consecutive homers in a September 18, 1950 game. /(LRD)

Warren Brown — 1894–Unk. *Writer.*

A tall first baseman at the University of San Francisco, Brown once hit two bases-loaded triples in one inning. He signed with Sacramento of the PCL in 1914 but never went any higher. He became sports editor of the San Francisco *Call-Post*, then the New York *Evening Mail*. In 1923, he took over as sports editor of the Chicago *Herald Examiner*. He covered every World Series from 1920 to 1964. He was chairman of the Veterans Committee of the Hall of Fame. His books included *The Chicago Cubs, The Chicago White Sox*, and *Knute Rockne*. In 1973 he received the J.G. Taylor Spink Award from the Hall of Fame. /(NLM)

Willard Brown (Home Run, El Hombre) — 1913– . OF-SS Negro Leagues 1934–52 Monroe Monarchs, **Kansas City Monarchs** statistics not available; *ML:* OF 1947 **Browns** 21g, .179, 1 hr, 6 rbi
☛ *All-Star—37, 39–42, 46, 50.*

Brown was a longtime star with the Negro National League's Kansas City Monarchs. He was nicknamed "Home Run" by Hall of Famer Josh Gibson for out-slugging Gibson in their head-to-head confrontations. He began as a shortstop for the Monroe, LA Monarchs, and was later discovered by Kansas City Monarchs owner J.L. Wilkinson. Wilkinson offered Brown a $250 bonus, a $125-a-month salary, and $1 a day as meal money. Brown accepted the increase over his $10-a-week stipend in Monroe.

Brown matured into a complete and dangerous hitter. With Brown batting cleanup, the 1942 Monarchs routinely beat the Dizzy Dean All-Stars in exhibition games played in Chicago and Buffalo. Brown played in the 1942 and 1946 Negro World Series, and hit a combined .304 with three HR and 14 RBI.

Brown became a hero in Puerto Rico by winning three home run and three batting titles from 1946 through 1950, earning the nickname "El Hombre"—The Man. In 1947–48, he won the Triple Crown, hitting .432 with 27 HR and 86 RBI in 60 games.

While leading the NNL with a .372 average in the fall of 1947, the 34-year-old Brown signed with the St. Louis Browns. He became the first black player to hit a home run in the American League. But he felt the St. Louis club was not as talented as the Monarchs: "The Browns couldn't beat the Monarchs no kind of way, only if we was all asleep. That's the truth. They didn't have nothing. I said, 'Major league team? They got to be kidding'" After playing only 21 games, and frustrated with a .179 average, he quit the Browns because of racial pressures and the team's lack of a winning attitude, and rejoined the Monarchs./(LL)

Byron Browne — 1942– . OF 1965–72 Cubs, Astros, Cardinals, **Phillies** 349 g, .236, 30 hr, 102 rbi

A fleet, strong-armed outfielder with modest power, Browne struck out in more than a fourth of his at-bats, including a NL-high 143 in 1966 and a record-tying eight in two consecutive games that June. One of his 14 siblings was the ABA's Dennis Browne./(JCA)

George Browne — 1876–1920. OF 1901–12 Phillies, **Giants**, Braves, Cubs, Senators, White Sox, Dodgers 1102 g, .273, 18 hr, 303 rbi. *1 WS, 5 g, .182, 1 rbi*

Browne's speedy, aggressive play in right field and at the top of McGraw's batting order helped the Giants win pennants in 1904–05. The lefthanded hitter led the NL in runs scored in '04./(JK)

Jerry Browne (Guv'nor) — 1966– . 2B 1986– **Rangers**, Indians 370 g, .280, 7 hr, 103 rbi

A slightly built, slap-hitting Virgin Islander, Browne was the Rangers' 1987 Rookie of the Year, winning their second-base job and batting .271 with 27 stolen bases. He was hitting .197 in June 1988 when he was returned to the minors. Traded to the Indians in the Julio Franco deal, he had his best season in 1989, hitting .299 with 83 runs scored./(JCA)

Pete Browning (The Gladiator) — 1861–1905. OF 1882–94 **Louisville (AA)**, Cleveland (PL), Pirates, Reds, Louisville (NL), Cardinals, Dodgers 1185 g, .343, 47 hr, 352 rbi
☛ *Led League—ba 82, 85, 90.*

The famous Louisville Slugger line of baseball bats made by the Hillerich & Bradsby Company is named after the Louisville-born, bred, and employed Browning, who ordered the first customized bat in 1884. Browning himself was called "The Gladiator" for his desperate fights with fly balls. The epitome of the clumsy slugger (lifetime fielding average, .874), he was nearly deaf from mastoiditus, illiterate, and alcoholic. But he also compiled the

third-highest career BA for a righthanded batter and won three batting titles./(JK)

Tom Browning — 1960– . LHP 1984– **Reds** 1211 ip, 78–52, 3.73. 20 wins: 85

Browning broke into the ML with 20 wins for the Reds in 1985, becoming the first rookie to win 20 since the Yankees' Bob Grim in 1954, and on September 16, 1988 he pitched a perfect game against the Dodgers en route to an 18–5, 3.41 record. In between, he suffered through two weak seasons and one trip to the minors. His 11 straight wins in 1985 was the best streak by a Reds pitcher in 30 years./(ME)

Bill Brubaker — 1910–1978. 3B-2B 1932–40, 43 **Pirates**, Braves 479 g, .264, 22 hr, 225 rbi

Brubaker replaced Pie Traynor at third base for Pittsburgh in 1936. He had 102 RBI despite a league-leading 96 strikeouts. He slumped the next year and became the Pirates' utility man./(ME)

Bob Bruce — 1933– . RHP 1959–67 Tigers, **Astros**, Braves 1122 ip, 49–71, 3.85

The Detroit native spent a little over a year with the Tigers. Traded to Houston's expansion team, he was the leading winner in two of their first three years, with a career best of 15–9 in 1964./(JCA)

Mike Brumley — 1938– . C 1964–66 **Senators** 224 g, .229, 5 hr, 50 rbi

The lefthanded-hitting Brumley was an all-star three consecutive years in the minors, but hit only .244 as the Senators' regular catcher in 1964. His son, Mike, Jr., reached the majors with the Cubs in 1987./(JCA)

Tom Brunansky (Bruno) — 1960– . OF 1981– Angels, **Twins**, Cardinals 1228 g, .247, 208 hr, 639 rbi. *1 LCS, 5 g, .412, 2 hr, 9 rbi. 1 WS, 7 g, .200, 2 rbi*
☛ *All-Star—85.*

Chosen by California in the first round of the June 1978 draft, Brunansky exhibited consistent, if unspectacular, power throughout his career. He played just 11 games for the Angels in 1981 before being traded with pitcher Mike Walters for Doug Corbett and Rob Wilfong in May 1982. He was the rightfielder on the 1982 Major League All-Rookie team and set a club record with 15 game-winning RBI the following year. One of seven players with 20 or more homers each season from 1982 to 1987 and one of six to play 150 or more games each of those six years, Brunansky's power was hurt in the Metrodome, which favors left-handed pull hitters. He led all players in the 1987 ALCS in batting average, total bases, doubles, and RBI, and tied for the lead in runs, hits, and homers. He was Minnesota's active home run leader, fourth overall, when traded to St. Louis for Tommy Herr in 1988. /(ME)

George Brunet (Lefty) — 1935– . LHP 1956–57, 59–71 A's, Braves, Astros, Orioles, **Angels**, Pilots, Senators, Pirates, Cardinals 1432 ip, 69–93, 3.62

Brunet made over 30 minor and major league moves before sticking with the Angels for four-plus years starting in 1965. A hard-luck pitcher, he led the AL in losses in 1967 (19) and '68 (17) despite good ERAs of 3.31 and 2.85. In 15 of his losses in 1967, his teammates scored two runs or less. Brunet was still pitching in the Mexican League past age fifty. He holds the minor league strikeout record with more than 3100. /(JCA)

Tom Bruno — 1953– . RHP 1976–79 Royals, Blue Jays, **Cardinals** 123 ip, 7–7, 4.24

As a Royals farmhand, 6'5″ Tom Bruno threw seven-inning no-hitters in the Midwest League in 1972 and in the Southern League in 1974. An original Blue Jay, he was traded to St. Louis in 1978 and recorded a 1.98 ERA in 18 appearances, but was hit hard in 1979 and demoted. /(MC)

John T. Brush — 1845–1912. *Executive.*

One of the organizers of the original NL franchise in Indianapolis, where he owned a large clothing store, Brush became president of the club in 1887 and decided to become a leader in the game. The next year he pushed through the salary-limit rule, which helped spark the Players' League revolt in 1890. When his club dropped from the NL in 1889, Brush invested in the Giants, and in 1891 he was awarded the Cincinnati franchise in the reorganized, 12-team NL. He continued to own Indianapolis in the Western League. Ban Johnson, president of the league, accused him of using Cincinnati to draft players to send to Indianapolis. In 1902 he sold the Reds and bought control of the Giants. He tried to push through the idea of a trust holding all NL teams. The idea didn't get anywhere, and Brush made many enemies in the game. A diehard opponent of Ban Johnson, he fought the AL's attempts to put a team in New York and opposed the peace treaty between the AL and NL. Brush and his manager John McGraw refused to let the Giants play a WS in 1904. He won his fourth pennant with the Giants in 1912, then left for California to

recuperate from ill health after losing the WS to the Red Sox in seven games. He died on the train as it was passing through Missouri. /(NLM)

Warren Brusstar — 1952– . RHP 1977–84 **Phillies**, White Sox, Cubs 410 ip, 24–13, 3.05. *4 LCS, 13 ip, 1–0, 1.42. 1 WS, 2 ip, 0–0, 0.00*

A sinker-slider pitcher, Brusstar was a middle reliever who never started a game. Plagued by shoulder problems, he always pitched well in postseason play, and beat the Astros in Game Four of the 1980 LCS. /(AL)

Bill Bruton — 1929– . OF 1953–64 **Braves**, Tigers 1610 g, .273, 94 hr, 545 rbi. *1 WS, 7 g, .412, 1 hr, 2 rbi*

Bruton was a fleet centerfielder who led the NL in stolen bases in each of his first three seasons. His first ML homer (and his only one in 151 games in 1953) was the first home run hit at Milwaukee's County Stadium and gave the Braves a 3–2 victory over the Cardinals in ten innings.

Later his power output improved. Twelve times he led off games with home runs. In 1961, after being traded to the Tigers, he hit 17 homers. A knee injury cost him half of the 1957 season and a chance to appear in that year's WS. He came back strong the next season and hit .412 in the Series. His best season was probably 1960, his last with the Braves; he hit .286 and led the NL in runs scored (112) and triples (13). /(FK)

Billy Bryan — 1938– . C 1961–68 **A's**, Yankees, Senators 374 g, .216, 41 hr, 125 rbi

The 6'4″ Georgian was a backup most of his career. He caught 95 games for Kansas City in 1965 and achieved career highs of 14 homers, 51 RBI, and a .252 BA. /(JCA)

Clay Bryant — 1911– . RHP 1935–40 **Cubs** 543 ip, 32–20, 3.73. *5 WS ip, 0–1, 6.75*
☛ *Led League—k 38.*

Bryant spent 45 years in baseball as a pitcher, coach, and minor league manager. A .266 lifetime hitter, he won his own game on August 28, 1937 with a 10th inning grand slam. He went 19–11 for the 1938 pennant-winning Cubs, leading the NL in strikeouts (and walks). In his World Series start in Game Three, he pitched almost five hitless innings before Joe Gordon started a Yankee stampede with a home run. Bryant's career was ruined by arm trouble the next year. /(DB)

Ron Bryant — 1947- . LHP 1967, 1969-75 Giants, Cardinals 917 ip, 57-56, 4.02. *1 LCS, 2 ip, 0-0, 4.50.* 20 wins: 73
☛ *Led League—w 73.*

Bryant adopted a huge stuffed bear (that he called "Bear Bryant") as his lucky charm in 1972. It seemed to turn his fortunes around. From 7-10 in '71, his record improved to 14-7. In 1973 he led the NL in victories, compiling a 24-12 mark for the Giants. Unfortunately, a diving-board accident stemming from an alcohol problem caused him a serious back injury in the spring of 1974. He slumped to 3-15, was traded to the Cardinals, and was cut after 10 games. /(MC)

Steve Brye — 1949- . OF 1970-78 **Twins**, Brewers, Pirates 697 g, .258, 30 hr, 193 rbi

Brye was called up to the Twins after leading the Southern Association in batting in 1970, but he was seldom more than a platoon player in his nine ML years. In 1974, his most active season, he hit .283 in 135 games, but he had only two homers and 41 RBI. /(MC)

Jerry Buchek — 1942- . 2B-SS-3B 1961, 63-68 **Cardinals**, Mets 421 g, .220, 22 hr, 108 rbi. *1 WS, 4 g, 1.000*

Cardinals utility man Buchek pinch ran three times in the 1964 World Series, scoring a run in Game One as St. Louis's three-run ninth inning put the game out of the Yankees' reach. He also singled in his only WS at-bat. When Julian Javier was out with a broken finger in 1965, he filled in and hit a career-high .247. Traded to the Mets for 1967, Buchek saw his most action, playing in 124 games and hitting 14 HR, but he struck out 101 times in 411 at-bats. In 1968 he was moved from second base to third base, hitting only .182 in limited duty. /(WOR)

Jim Bucher — 1911- . 3B-2B-OF 1934-38, 44-45 **Dodgers**, Cardinals, Red Sox 554 g, .265, 17 hr, 193 rbi

The defensively versatile lefthanded hitter had his best season with the 1935 Dodgers, batting .302. In 1937, Brooklyn traded Bucher, Johnny Cooney, Joe Stripp and Roy Henshaw to the Cardinals for Leo Durocher. /(EGM)

Jack Buck — 1925- . *Broadcaster.*

Buck has been play-by-play announcer for the Cardinals since 1954. Virtually an institution in St. Louis, Jack is highly respected by his peers and has called NFL games for CBS and NBC since 1974. He received the Spink award in 1987. /(FO)

Al Buckenberger — 1861-1917. Manager 1889-90, 92-95, 02-04 Columbus (AA), Pirates, Cardinals, **Braves** 493-540, .477

Buckenberger was not a hard driver; he was a kind and tolerant leader who insisted that his players be sober gentlemen at a time when such conduct was not the rule. A light-hitting minor league infielder, he began managing in 1884 at Terre Haute in the Northwest League. His highest ML finish was second with Pittsburgh in 1893. After a seventh-place finish in 1894, he was replaced by Connie Mack. /(RLM)

Garland Buckeye (Gob) — 1897-1975. LHP 1918, 25-28 Senators, **Indians**, Giants 565 ip, 30-39, 3.90

A guard for the football Cardinals from 1921-24, the 260-lb southpaw cast the biggest shadow in baseball with Cleveland in 1925, and backed it up with a 13-8 record. In 1927 he was one of two pro footballers to surrender a homer to Babe Ruth (the other was Ernie Nevers). /(LRD)

Bill Buckner (Billy Bucks) — 1949- . 1B-OF-DH 1969- Dodgers, **Cubs**, Red Sox, Angels, Royals 2495 g, .289, 173 hr, 1205 rbi. *2 LCS, 11 g, .196, 3 rbi. 2 WS, 12 g, .212, 1 hr, 2 rbi*
☛ *Led League—ba 80. All-Star—81.*

Bill Buckner will forever be remembered for the Mookie Wilson ground ball that went through his legs in the sixth game of the 1986 World Series and cost Boston the championship, but he should be

Bill Buckner

remembered as an outstanding hitter and fielder who overcame serious injuries. A consistent outfielder with the Dodgers (1969–76), he went with Ivan DeJesus to the Cubs for Rick Monday. Shifting to first base, Buckner hit .300 with Chicago (1977–84), won the 1980 batting title and twice led the league in doubles (1981 and '83). Playing on gimpy ankles, Buckner had outstanding seasons at Boston in 1985 and 1986 after coming over for Dennis Eckersley. He tied a major league record by playing 162 games at first base in 1985 and broke the ML record he set in 1983 for assists at the position with 184. Entering the 1990 season, he led all active players with 2,707 career hits. /(ME)

Don Buddin — 1934– . SS 1956, 58–62 **Red Sox**, Astros, Tigers 711 g, .241, 41 hr, 225 rbi

Buddin, the regular Red Sox shortstop in 1956 and 1958–61, was often the target of Fenway Park fans because of his erratic fielding. He led AL shortstops in errors in '58 and '59. Only a fair hitter, he had 12 homers in '59 and a career-high BA of .263 in 1961, the season before the Sox traded him to Houston for Eddie Bressoud. /(RMu)

Steve Buechele (Boo) — 1961– . 3B-2B 1985- **Rangers** 668 g, .239, 69 hr, 242 rbi

Buechele became the Rangers' third baseman when Buddy Bell was traded to Cincinnati in mid-1985. A competent fielder and a righthanded hitter with some power, his failure to hit righthanded pitchers made him one of the players most pinch-hit-for in 1987. He roomed with quarterback John Elway at Stanford. /(JCA)

Fritz Buelow [Frederick William] — 1876–1933. C 1899–1907 Cardinals, **Tigers**, Indians, Browns 430 g, .192, 6 hr, 112 rbi

A dreadful hitter, Berlin-born Buelow was competent enough in the field to share catching duties on three AL teams. /(JK)

Charlie Buffinton — 1861–1907. RHP 1882–92 **Braves**, Phillies, Philadelphia (PL), Boston (AA), Baltimore (NL) 3404 ip, 231–151, 2.96. 20 wins: 83–85, 87–89, 91.
    Manager 1890 **Philadelphia (PL)** 21–25, .457

"Big Buff" was an ace in the days of minimal pitching staffs. A righthander noted for his "downer" (a sinking, overhand curve), Buffinton was key in Boston's 1883 pennant, combining with Grasshopper Jim Whitney for 61 of the team's 63 wins. Two years later, they were responsible for 59 of its 66 losses. Buff's best year came in between: 47

Charlie Buffinton with the Phillies

victories, 2.15 ERA, and 63 complete games. He struck out 17 Clevelanders in one game, eight of them in a row. For part of 1890, he managed Philadelphia's Players' League team. He led the American Association with a .757 winning percentage (28–9) in 1891, but retired with Baltimore in 1892 rather than take a NL-ordered mid-season salary cut. /(ADS)

Don Buford — 1937– . OF-2B-3B 1963–72 White Sox, **Orioles** 1286 g, .264, 93 hr, 418 rbi. *3 LCS, 7 g, .357, 1 hr, 4 rbi. 3 WS, 15 g, .207, 4 hr, 7 rbi*
☛ *All-Star—71.*

The compact, switch-hitting outfielder-handyman was a key member of the 1969–71 AL champion Orioles. After four years as a regular infielder with the White Sox, he went to Baltimore in the 1968 deal for Luis Aparicio. The 5'7" team player was a top leadoff man, drawing walks, stealing bases, and scoring runs (99 in three consecutive years, leading the AL in '71). He was also the most difficult man in modern baseball history to double up, grounding into only 33 double plays in 4553 at-bats. Buford led off the 1969 WS with a homer off Tom Seaver. After a disappointing 1972 season, he left the Orioles to play in Japan. Known there as "the greatest leadoff man in the world" for his heroics on the Orioles' 1971 tour of Japan, he hit .270 with 65 HR in 1973–76. /(JCA)

Bob Buhl — 1928– . RHP 1953–67 **Braves,** Cubs, Phillies 2587 ip, 166–132, 3.55. *1 WS, 3 ip, 0–1, 10.80* ☛ *All-Star—60.*

Although he won in double figures six times with the Braves, this fast worker pitched in the shadows of Warren Spahn and Lew Burdette in the 1950s. A paratrooper in Korea in 1952, Buhl broke in with the Braves in 1953 and went 13–8 (2.97).

In 1956 a fractured finger on his pitching hand in August kept him from winning 20; he finished 18–8. His herky-jerky motion caused arm problems, and though he missed a month in 1957, he went 18–7 (2.74 ERA) to help Milwaukee win the pennant.

Buhl was a famed Dodger-killer, beating them eight times in 1956 alone. After his April 1962 trade to the Cubs, his first Chicago victory came two days later against Los Angeles. He had a large repertoire of pitches and fielded well, but he was a notoriously poor hitter. In 1962 he went 0-for-70, the worst ML "0-fer" by a pitcher in a season. He hit .089 lifetime, striking out in 45% of his at-bats. /(JCA)

Jay Buhner — 1964– . OF 1987– Yankees, **Mariners** 150 g, .240, 22 hr, 72 rbi

Buhner's blond good looks, power, and daring outfield play evoked comparisons to Mickey Mantle in New York, but he had a big hole in his swing. He was the main player in the mid-1988 deal that brought Ken Phelps to the Yankees. Buhner played regularly for the Mariners the rest of the season, but ended with a .215 batting average for the year, although he did have 13 HR in 261 at-bats. The arrival of Jeff Leonard, Ken Griffey, Jr., and Darnell Coles reduced his playing time in 1989, but he greatly improved his average without losing any of his power. /(WOR)

DeWayne Buice — 1957– . RHP 1987– **Angels,** Blue Jays 172 ip, 9–11, 4.23

Buice had pitched ten years in the minors, including two in Mexico, before going 6–7 with a club-high 17

saves as a 29-year-old Angels rookie in 1987. He averaged almost a strikeout an inning. He was leading the staff in games but had a 5.11 ERA in June 1988 when he was disabled with a leg injury. /(JCA)

Bozeman Bulger — Unk.–Unk. *Writer.*

The clown prince of baseball writers during the early years of the century, Bulger was a witty, literate reporter whose work was mostly filed with the New York *Evening World.* He took a cavalier attitude toward his responsibilities as a statistics-keeping official scorer. He once balanced his boxscore by arbitrarily assigning an unaccounted-for hit to Larry Doyle of the Giants on the grounds that, "if anyone got it, he did it." Fortunately, Doyle's league-leading .320 average was five points better than anyone else's in 1915.

Bulger was commissioned a Lt. Col. during WWI and was Gen. Pershing's Press Officer in the AEF. /(JK)

Morgan G. Bulkeley — 1837–1922. *Executive.*

Bulkeley was elected to the Hall of Fame because he was the first president of the National League. Actually, it was William Hulbert who had the foresight and determination to create a strong league to replace the National Association, but Hulbert was from Chicago and the politics of the situation called for an Easterner to provide titular leadership for the new league. Insisting he could only serve for a year, Bulkeley accepted the position. He had been the principal backer of the Hartford team in the National Association, and continued to own the city's team during the National League's first season in 1876. He had no connection with baseball after 1876, a casual fan more interested in sulky races than pennant races (he was a member of the National Trotting Association for 30 years). Hulbert slipped into the president's chair the next year and directed the new league to its success. In 1937, when a Cooperstown committee decided whom to install for the 1939 opening ceremonies, an obvious choice was Ban Johnson, founder and president of the American League. It was necessary to equally represent the National League; thus Morgan Bulkeley, seemingly the logical counterpart of Johnson, was inducted.

Bulkeley's father had founded the Aetna Insurance Company, and when he died, Morgan gave up a prosperous merchandising business in New York to run Aetna. After his brief fling with baseball, he entered politics and served as alderman in Hartford

Morgan Bulkeley

Al Bumbry — 1947– . OF 1972–84 **Orioles** 1428 g, .283, 53 hr, 392 rbi. *4 LCS, 11 g, .156, 1 rbi. 2 WS, 11 g, .125, 2 rbi*
☛ *Rookie of the Year—73.*

The speedy Bumbry stole 254 bases during his career and set the Orioles' record with 252 lifetime. With 1403 Oriole hits, he left among the Birds' top five all-time. In 1973, he was the AL Rookie of the Year as he batted .337, and in 1980 became the first Oriole to get 200 hits in a season. The good defensive outfielder won a Bronze Star in Vietnam. /(EW)

Wally Bunker — 1945– . RHP 1963–71 **Orioles**, Royals 1085 ip, 60–52, 3.51. *1 WS, 9 ip, 1–0, 0.00*

In 1964, poised 19-year-old Wally Bunker burst into the ML with a one-hit shutout, victories in his first six starts, and a 19–5 rookie year with Baltimore. He developed a sore arm the next year and was only a part-time pitcher after that. He threw a six-hit shutout in the 1966 WS and won 12 games for the expansion Kansas City Royals in 1969 before arm miseries ended his career. /(JK)

Jim Bunning — 1931– . RHP 1955–71 **Tigers**, Phillies, Pirates, Dodgers 3760 ip, 224–184, 3.27. 20 wins: 57
☛ *Led League—w 57. Led League—k 59–60, 67.*

His career evenly split between the major leagues, Bunning was the first pitcher since Cy Young to win over 100 or to strike out over 1,000 in each league. He retired second only to Walter Johnson with 2,885 strikeouts. He pitched a no-hitter for Detroit in 1958 and a perfect game for the Phillies against the Mets in 1964.

The 6'3" righthander's unusual pitching style, a sweeping sidearm delivery that finished with his glove hand touching the ground well in front of the mound, made him especially difficult for right-handed batters.

Bunning was 20–8 for the Tigers in 1957 but never again won 20. He had 19 victories for Detroit in 1962; then, after being traded to the Phillies in 1964, he won 19 in each of his first three years in Philadelphia. In 1967, when he won 17, he set a ML record with five 1–0 losses.

After retiring as a player, Bunning managed in the minors for five years, then entered Kentucky politics. He was elected to the state legislature and ran unsuccessfully for governor. In 1986, he was elected to the U.S. House of Representatives as a Republican from a heavily Democratic district. /(AL)

before becoming a four-term mayor of the city starting in 1880. He next became governor of Connecticut, holding that office through a series of stormy administrations. A Republican, he was locked out of his office in the State Capitol by a Democratic legislature and became known as "The Crowbar Governor" when he pried the door open.

Bulkeley was elected to the United States Senate in 1904 and served one term, notable for his conflicts with President Theodore Roosevelt. He continued to direct the Aetna Insurance company, which became the nation's largest under his leadership, until his death at 84. /(JK)

Jim Bunning

Bill Burbach — 1947– . RHP 1969–71 **Yankees** 161 ip, 6–11, 4.48

Despite some erratic rookie pitching, this 6'4"fireballer was counted on in 1969 as a cornerstone of the Yankees' rebuilding plans. Ill with mononucleosis the next spring, he never regained his freshman form./(GDW)

Al Burch — 1883–1926. OF 1906–11 Cardinals, **Dodgers** 611 g, .254, 4 hr, 103 rbi

A stocky utility outfielder with a sub-.300 career slugging average, Burch had his only good season with Brooklyn in 1909, stealing 38 bases and batting .271./(JK)

Bob Burda — 1938– . 1B-OF 1962, 1965–66, 1969–72 Cardinals, **Giants**, Brewers, Red Sox 388 g, .224, 13 hr, 78 rbi

Burda's ten-year career was spent shuttling between the majors and minors. The lefthanded hitter led the NL with 14 pinch hits in 1971./(EW)

Lew Burdette — 1926– . RHP 1950–67 Yankees, **Braves**, Cardinals, Cubs, Phillies, Angels 3068 ip, 203–144, 3.66. 20 wins: 58–59 *2 WS, 49 ip, 4–2, 2.92* ☛ *Led League—w 59. Led League—era 56. Led League—k 59–61. All-Star—57, 59.*

On October 10, 1957, Burdette shut out the Yankees for the second time in four days. He was the first pitcher in 37 years to win three complete games in a single WS and the first since Christy Mathewson (1905) to throw two shutouts in a single Series. The win gave Milwaukee the world championship and earned Burdette Series MVP honors.

Lew Burdette

Hall of Fame lefty Warren Spahn and righthander Burdette gave the Braves a formidable one-two punch, with 443 victories between them in 13 seasons. A slider and sinkerball pitcher, Burdette was widely accused of throwing a spitball as well. His constant fidgeting on the mound fed that suspicion; it didn't indicate nervousness. Teammate Gene Conley said, "Lew had ice water in his veins. Nothing bothered him, on or off the mound. He was a chatterbox out there . . . He would talk to himself, to the batter, the umpire, and sometimes even to the ball."

Besides winning 20 games in 1958 and 21 in '59, Burdette won 19 twice and 18 once. His 2.70 ERA topped the NL in 1956. In two All-Star Games, he allowed only one run in seven innings. He no-hit the Phillies on August 18, 1960.

On May 26, 1959, he was the winning pitcher when Pittsburgh's Harvey Haddix hurled 12 perfect innings against the Braves, only to lose in the 13th. That winter, the puckish Burdette asked for a $10,000 raise, explaining: "I'm the greatest pitcher that ever lived. The greatest game that was ever pitched in baseball wasn't good enough to beat me, so I've got to be the greatest!"/(TJ)

Smoky Burgess [Forrest Harrill] — 1927- . C 1949, 51–67 Cubs, Phillies, Reds, **Pirates**, White Sox 1718 g, .295, 126 hr, 673 rbi. *1 WS, 5 g, .333*
☛ *All-Star—54, 55, 59–61, 64.*

Old Smoky, who inherited his name from his father, was a National League All-Star with three different teams. Built short and squat, he was a fine catcher and became of one of the best pinch hitters of his era. He retired with a record 507 pinch at-bats. Only Manny Mota has surpassed Burgess's 145 pinch hits.

Burgess batted .368 in 108 games for the Phillies in 1954. Always a strong, lefthanded hitter, he drove in nine runs for the Reds against Pittsburgh on July 29, 1955. Three of his four hits were home runs—one a grand slam off future batterymate Vern Law. He finished 1955 with a career-high 21 HR. He reported that his most satisfying pinch hit was his home run off Chicago's Sam Jones with two games left in the 1956 season. The Reds needed just one HR to equal the NL record of 221 set by the Giants. Manager Chuck Dressen ordered Burgess to hit for Roy McMillan, barking, "Make it a home run—or nothin'!" The ball landed on Sheffield Avenue. On May 26 of that season, he had caught a three-pitcher no-hitter when Johnny Klippstein, Hersh Freeman, and Joe Black combined to skunk the Braves. Exactly three years later, he was Harvey

Haddix's batterymate when the Pirate hurler pitched his famous 12-inning perfect game against the Braves.

After almost six seasons in Pittsburgh, Burgess was sold to the contending White Sox late in 1964. In his first AL appearance he hit a pinch homer off Detroit's Dave Wickersham to tie a crucial stretch-drive game. Much heavier than in his NL prime, Burgess almost seemed to roll out of the dugout for his frequent pinch-hitting appearances. From 1965 through 1967, he appeared in 237 games, catching only seven. He led the AL in pinch at-bats all three seasons, and in pinch hits the first two. He retired as a .286 lifetime pinch hitter. During the 1980s he coached in Atlanta's farm system./(RL)

Tom Burgmeier (Bugs) — 1943- . LHP 1968–84 Angels, Royals, Twins, **Red Sox**, A's 1258 ip, 79–55, 3.23
☛ *All-Star—80.*

A consistent and durable reliever until shoulder tendinitis ended his career at age 40, the savvy, fine-fielding Burgmeier had 102 lifetime saves. Signed by Houston, he debuted with California, and went to the Royals in the 1968 expansion draft. In 1971, he was 9–7 with 17 saves and a 1.74 ERA. He had a career-high 24 saves for Boston in 1980./(EW)

Si Burick — 1909–1986. *Writer.*

Sports editor of the Dayton *Daily News* for 54 years, Burick won the J.G. Taylor Spink Award in 1982, the first writer from a city with no ML team to be so honored. He covered his first opening game in Cincinnati in 1929 and never missed one until his death. Burick wrote *Alston of the Dodgers*; *The Main Spark*, a biography of Sparky Anderson; and *Byline: Si Burick*, an anthology of his columns./(NLM)

Bobby Burke (Lefty) — 1907–1971. LHP 1927–35, 37 **Senators**, Phillies 919 ip, 38–46, 4.29

A starter and reliever, Burke's best day came on August 6, 1931. After pitching a no-hitter to blank the Red Sox, he claimed to have thrown only six curves./(EW)

Glenn Burke — 1952- . OF 1976–79 **Dodgers**, A's 225 g, .237, 2 hr, 38 rbi. *1 LCS, 4 g, .000. 1 WS, 3 g, .200*

This speedster, who led three minor leagues in steals, is sometimes given credit for inventing the "high five." After his ML days, he participated in the Bay Area Gay Games./(TG)

Jimmy Burke (Sunset Jimmy) — 1874–1942. 3B 1898, 1901–05 Cleveland (NL), Milwaukee (AL), White Sox, Pirates, **Cardinals** 548 g, .244, 1 hr, 187 rbi.
Manager 1905, 18–20 Cardinals, **Browns** 189–213, .470

Burke was a St. Louis native who not only played in his hometown as a scrappy, light-hitting infielder (1903–05), but also managed both the Cardinals ('05) and Browns (1918–20). His ML teams never had a winning season, but he managed successfully in the minors and later coached for Joe McCarthy's 1929 Cubs pennant-winners and 1932 Yankee champions. A 1933 stroke left him an invalid. /(JK)

Tim Burke — 1959– . RHP 1985– **Expos** 479 ip, 37–19, 2.48
☛ *All-Star—89.*

Burke was a starter in the Pirates' and Yankees' organizations, but was brought to the majors as a reliever by Montreal's Buck Rodgers, who had managed Burke in Triple-A. A sinker-slider specialist with a back-to-the-batter delivery, Burke set an NL rookie record with a league-leading 78 appearances in 1985; as set-up man for Fireman of the Year Jeff Reardon, he won his first eight ML decisions, and finished 9–4 with eight saves. He became the leader of Montreal's fine bullpen-by-committee when Reardon was traded in 1987, going 7–0 with 18 saves and a 1.19 ERA, and walking fewer batters per inning than any other NL reliever (19 in 91 innings). He saved 28, went 9–3, and made the All-Star team in 1989. /(JCA)

Jesse Burkett (The Crab) — 1868–1953. OF 1890–1905 Giants, **Cleveland (NL)**, Cardinals, Browns, Red Sox 2072 g, .341, 75 hr, 952 rbi
☛ *Led League—ba 95–96, 01. Hall of Fame—1946.*

Burkett batted over .400 three times, a feat duplicated only by Ty Cobb and Rogers Hornsby. A lefthanded line-drive hitter and clever bunter, his ability to foul pitches off was one of the reasons for the introduction of the rule making foul balls strikes. He said he owed his success to "that old confeedence," but his speed helped him leg out many hits. He scored more than 100 runs in nine different seasons, twice topping the NL.

The 5'8" 155-lb Burkett starred in the outfield for the Cleveland Spiders during the 1890s and was one of the players switched to St. Louis in 1899 when the Cleveland franchise was stripped.

Called "The Crab" because of his caustic barbs and constant complaining, he insulted rivals, fans,

Jesse Burkett with the Cleveland Spiders

and teammates with equal venom. He was particularly sensitive to suggestions that he and Jack Glasscock, whom he resembled, were father and son, and would fight anyone who said so.

After leaving the ML, Burkett owned and managed the Worcester club of the New England League, 1906–13, making regular appearances in the outfield until he was 45. He later managed other minor league clubs and coached several college teams. In 1921, he coached for John McGraw's New York Giants, still as salty and bitter-tongued as ever. When the Giants won the WS, McGraw had to dig into his own pocket for a bonus for "The Crab"; the players refused to vote him a share. /(JK)

Ken Burkhart — 1916– . RHP 1945–49 **Cardinals**, Reds 519 ip, 28–20, 3.84.
Umpire NL 1957–73 *3 WS*
☛ *All-Star—4.*

Burkhart led the NL in winning percentage with a 19–8 (.704) mark as a Cardinals rookie in 1945. When the veteran players returned from WWII, he faded. Following an arm injury, he had to use an unusual shot-put delivery.

An excellent umpire, he umpired in back-to-back no-hitters in September 1968, Gaylord Perry on the 17th and Ray Washburn the next day. Burkhart was involved in a controversial play in the opening game of the 1970 WS when he became entangled with Orioles catcher Elrod Hendricks in a play at the plate. Burkhart called the Reds' Bernie Carbo out although replays showed Hendricks had tagged Carbo with his mitt while holding the ball in his other hand. /(RTM)

Ellis Burks — 1964- . OF 1987- **Red Sox** 374 g, .289, 50 hr, 212 rbi. *1 LCS, 4 g, .235, 1 rbi*

Tabbed a future MVP by Twins manager Tom Kelly, the speedy Burks earned the Red Sox' starting centerfield job at the age of 22, and as a rookie in 1987 became only the third player in club history to hit 20 HR and steal 20 bases in one season. He earned spots on both the *Baseball Digest* and *Topps* all-rookie teams, and in 1988 hit .294 with 92 RBI and 25 stolen bases. Defensively, Burks is one of the best centerfielders in the ML, with great range and a sure glove offsetting a somewhat erratic arm. His rise to stardom was interrupted by shoulder surgery in 1989. /(SCL)

Rick Burleson (Rooster) — 1951- . SS-2B 1974-84, 86-87 **Red Sox**, Angels, Orioles 1346 g, .273, 50 hr, 449 rbi. *2 LCS, 7 g, .350, 1 rbi. 1 WS, 7 g, .292, 2 rbi* ☛ *All-Star—77-79, 81. Gold Glove—79.*

Burleson sparked the Red Sox with his aggressive play at shortstop and as a lead-off hitter. He overcame a three-error debut in 1974 to become one of Boston's favorite players, relying on a tremendous arm to make up for anything he lacked in range. A Gold Glove winner in 1979, he set the ML record for double plays by a shortstop in 1980 with 147. Traded to the Angels in December of 1980, he injured the rotator cuff of his throwing arm in 1982, then retore it in '84. After a year off, he was voted AL Comeback Player of the Year in 1986, when he hit .284 in 93 games for the Angels. /(PB)

Johnny Burnett — 1904-1959. SS-3B-2B 1927-35 **Indians**, Browns 558 g, .284, 9 hr, 213 rbi

The Floridian had his first real shot with the Indians in 1930, and was hitting .312 on July 19 when he fractured a wrist, ending his season. He bounced back to bat .300 in 1931, and in an 18-inning game on July 10, 1932, set a single-game ML record with nine hits. The day before, he had had two hits, giving him 11, an AL record for most hits in two consecutive games. /(EW)

Wally Burnette — 1929- . RHP 1956-58 **A's** 262 ip, 14-21, 3.56

Burnette was 6-8 as a starter for the last-place 1956 A's but had a 2.89 ERA. Used mostly in relief the next year, his ERA ballooned to 4.30. /(FK)

Bill Burns (Sleepy Bill) — 1880-1953. LHP 1908-12 Senators, White Sox, **Reds**, Phillies, Tigers 725 ip, 30-52, 2.69

Burns was shuffled to five teams in his five ML seasons, and not only because he never had a winning year. He was a crap-shooting, card-playing gambler with good stuff but no ambition, known to read newspapers or doze on the bench during games. In 1919, while in Cincinnati selling oil stock, he reportedly learned of the Black Sox' World Series plans. He won $4,000 on the first two games, then lost it all when honest Dickie Kerr won the third game. /(NLM)

Britt Burns — 1959- . LHP 1978-85 **White Sox** 1095 ip, 70-60, 3.66. *1 LCS, 9 ip, 0-1, 0.96* ☛ *All-Star—81.*

Burns was actually discovered by *Chicago Tribune* book critic Bob Cromie. While in Birmingham in 1978, he read about a local whiz kid who had fanned 18 batters in one game. Cromie sent the clipping to his friend Bill Veeck, the White Sox owner. Later that season Burns made his Chicago debut at age 19. In 1980 the 6'5" Burns was named *TSN* Rookie Pitcher of the Year on the strength of a 15-13 (2.84 ERA) season. He pitched 30 consecutive scoreless innings in 1981, a year marred by his father's death two months after being hit by a car. Over the next three seasons, injuries set in, and Burns's ERA ballooned. But he pitched his heart out in the last game of the 1983 LCS, holding the powerful Orioles in check for nine innings. The White Sox could not score either, and Tito Landrum's tenth-inning home run beat Burns. After rebounding in 1985 to go 18-11, he was traded to the Yankees, for whom he never pitched: A chronic, degenerative hip condition ended his career. /(RL)

Ed Burns — 1891–1955. *Writer.*

Burns, who broke in with the Chicago *Herald* in 1914, joined the Chicago *Tribune* in 1925 and was also a longtime correspondent for *The Sporting News.* A large, round man, Burns wrote with an acerbic wit and could wield a sharp needle. More often, he was whimsical, as when he blamed the Cubs' loss of the 1930 pennant on a pair of peacocks manager Rogers Hornsby had purchased from owner William Wrigley. Peacocks were bad luck, he said. "Back in Indiana, we tolerated 'em only on millinery. And then only on certain folks." He was president of the BBWAA in 1947. /(NLM)

George Burns [George Joseph] — 1889–1966. OF 1911–25 **Giants**, Reds, Phillies 1853 g, .287, 41 hr, 611 rbi. *3 WS, 19 g, .257, 5 rbi*

Silent and self-effacing—the antithesis of hot-tempered mentor John McGraw—Burns was a country boy and pool shark from Utica, N.Y. An outstanding leadoff batter who led the NL five times in runs scored and walks, Burns twice topped the league in stolen bases, with a high of 62 in 1914. He had a special knack for playing the Polo Grounds' notorious sun field in left, abetted by a long-billed cap and

George J. Burns with the Giants

primitive sunglasses. He was beloved by the rooters in the left field bleachers, or "Burnsville." "Silent George" spent eleven seasons with the Giants, and was sent to Cincinnati after the 1921 World Series in a trade for third baseman Heinie Groh. On his first visit to the Polo Grounds with the Reds, Burns was honored with a day and given a diamond-studded watch. /(JK)

George Burns (Tioga George) — 1893–1978. 1B 1914–29 Tigers, A's, **Indians**, Red Sox, Yankees 1866 g, .307, 72 hr, 948 rbi. *2 WS, 6 g, .250, 3 rbi*
☛ *Most Valuable Player—26.*

Burns was in his thirteenth major league season in 1926 when he was named MVP, shining among the AL's greatest luminaries. Babe Ruth hit more home runs (47 to Burns's four), but Burns was second to Ruth in RBI, with 114. He tied Hall of Famer Sam Rice for most hits, 216, broke Tris Speaker's doubles record with 64, and batted .358.

Burns drove in the winning run for Cleveland in Game Seven of the 1920 WS, but the Indians traded him to Boston in 1921. Burns reciprocated by turning an unassisted double play against Cleveland in 1923. Somewhat error-prone, he led the AL in that category four of the 12 seasons in which he played over 100 games at first base. Slumping at bat after 1927, he hung on for two final lackluster seasons. He found rejuvenation, though, in the Pacific Coast League, where he played and managed for five more years, hitting .335. /(JK)

Jack Burns (Slug) — 1907–1975. 1B 1930–36 **Browns**, Tigers 890 g, .280, 44 hr, 417 rbi

A graceful, lefthanded-batting first baseman who rose rapidly on the strength of three high-average minor league seasons, Burns hit a career-high .305 for the Browns in 1932. He twice led AL first basemen in assists, three times in double plays. The Bostonian became a Red Sox coach and scout, covering New England until 1973. /(JK)

Oyster Burns [Thomas P.] — 1864–1928. OF-SS 1884–1885, 87–95 Wilmington (U), Baltimore (AA), Brooklyn (AA), **Dodgers**, Giants 1188 g, .301, 66 hr, 674 rbi
☛ *Led League—rbi 90.*

"Erster Boins" was a popular Brooklyn outfielder and utility man who led the NL with 123 RBI and finished second in HR (13) with the 1890 pennant winners. Burns reportedly earned his nickname selling shellfish in the off-season. /(JK)

George Burns with the Indians, batting

Todd Burns — 1963– . RHP 1988– **A's** 199 ip, 14–7, 2.71. *2 WS, 2 ip, 0–0, 0.00*

Burns proved to be a valuable man on the A's pennant-winning 1988 staff, relieving, filling in for injured rotation members when needed, and compiling an 8–2, 3.16 record. In 1989 he was effective replacing the injured Dennis Eckersley in the role of bullpen stopper. /(JFC)

Pete Burnside — 1930– . LHP 1955, 1957–63 Giants, Tigers, **Senators**, Orioles 567 ip, 19–36, 4.81

This well-traveled Dartmouth man won a career-high seven games for the 1960 Tigers as both a starter and reliever. /(CC)

Ray Burris — 1950– . RHP 1973–87 **Cubs**, Yankees, Mets, Expos, A's, Brewers, Cardinals 2189 ip, 108–134, 4.17. *1 LCS, 17 ip, 1–0, 0.53*

After two years in the Cubs' bullpen, Burris became Chicago's ace starter in 1975, going 15–10 for a mediocre team and following with a 15–13, 3.11 record in 1976. He dropped to 14–16 in 1977 and 7–13 in 1978. He was traded to the Yankees for Dick Tidrow in May 1979 and was sold to the Mets that August; he spent time on the DL in both 1979 and 1980. He recovered to help the Expos to their only division title with a 9–7, 3.04 record during the strike-shortened 1981 season and pitched well in the LCS. He pitched a five-hit shutout to beat the Dodgers in Game Two and left Game Five tied 1–1, only to see Steve Rogers give up a ninth-inning HR to lose the game and the series. He had only one more winning season after that, going 13–10 for Oakland in 1984. /(WOR)

Jeff Burroughs — 1951– . OF-DH 1970–84 **Senators/Rangers**, Braves, Mariners, A's 1603 g, .261, 234 hr, 854 rbi
☛ *Most Valuable Player—74. Led League—rbi 74.*

Burroughs was a top young power hitter, but by his late twenties had declined to the journeyman stage. The nation's first draft pick in 1969, he joined the Senators at 19. There, he often clashed with manager Ted Williams, though Burroughs later credited Williams for teaching him to concentrate. Burroughs hit 30 homers in 1973, his first season as the Rangers' regular right fielder. That set the stage for his MVP year in 1974, when he batted .301 with 25 homers and a league-leading 118 RBI. But the south wind at Arlington Stadium gave him fits (he fanned a league-high 155 times in 1976), and he profited from a trade to Atlanta, where he hit 41 homers with 114 RBI in 1977. Defensively, Burroughs was capable but slow. When he announced his goal was to win a Gold Glove, teammate Joe Lovitto said, "You won't make any errors. You don't get to a ball until it stops rolling." /(KT)

Dick Burrus [Maurice] — 1898–1972. 1B 1919–20, 25–28 A's, **Braves** 560 g, .291, 11 hr, 211 rbi

A three-sport star at North Carolina State, Burrus failed to stick in a trial with the A's. After four years in the minors, he returned to the ML to hit .340 for the 1925 Braves. However, he had little home run power, and when his batting average dropped to .270 he went on the bench. /(NLM)

Ellis Burton — 1936– . OF 1958, 60, 63–65 Cardinals, Indians, **Cubs** 215 g, .216, 17 hr, 59 rbi

Burton's only memorable season was 1963, when he tagged 13 home runs and drove in 42 runs while playing 26 games for the Indians and 93 for the Cubs. A switch-hitter, he twice homered from both sides of the plate in a game. /(FK)

Moe Burtschy [Edward] — 1922– . RHP 1950–51, 54–56 **A's** 185 ip, 10–6, 4.71

In 1954, his only full season in the majors, Burtschy was 5–4 with four saves in 46 appearances. The next year he had more luck than stuff before returning to the minors: despite a 10.42 ERA in 11 innings, his record was 2–0. /(MC)

Jim Busby — 1927– . OF 1950–62 White Sox, **Senators**, Indians, Orioles, Red Sox, Astros 1352 g, .262, 48 hr, 438 rbi
☛ *All-Star—51.*

Busby led AL outfielders twice in putouts and once in fielding percentage. He was among the top five stolen base leaders three times, and batted a career-high .312 for Washington in 1953. A cousin of pitcher Steve Busby, Jim coached for fellow Texan Paul Richards at Baltimore, Houston, Atlanta, and Chicago. /(TJ)

Steve Busby — 1949– . RHP 1972–76, 1978–80 **Royals** 1060 ip, 70–54, 3.72. 20 wins: 74
☛ *All-Star—74–75.*

Busby was the first pitcher to hurl no-hitters in each of his first two full major-league seasons (1973–74). The *TSN* AL Rookie Pitcher of the Year in 1973, he won 16 and no-hit Detroit on April 27. His second no-hitter came on June 19, 1974, as he retired the last 24 Milwaukee batters. During his next start, he retired the first nine, for an AL-record 33 straight. Over a 17-inning stretch he faced 54 batters, allowing no hits and three walks. A two-time All-Star, Busby set a Royal record with 22 wins in 1974. After three stellar seasons, knee and rotator cuff injuries ended his career. /(FJO)

Gussie Busch [August Anheuser, Jr.] — 1899–1989. *Executive.*

In 1953 Busch convinced the board of directors of the St. Louis-based brewery Anheuser-Busch to purchase the hometown Cardinals and renovate Sportsman's Park. Busch became president and chief executive officer of the team and rose to become one of the National League's most powerful owners. In the 1970s, when developers ran out of funds while building the new downtown stadium, he raised the final $3 million and the park was named Busch Stadium.

Referred to at his death as "the last of the old-time beer barons," Busch began working for his father, August Anheuser Busch, Sr., at the brewery started by his grandfather, Adolphus A. Busch, and Eberhard Anheuser. Control of the company passed to Gussie and his brother, Adolphus III, in 1934, and solely to Gussie on his brother's death in 1946. Busch built the ailing company into the largest brewery in the world by the time he retired from an active role in 1975. The brewery's ownership of the Cardinals led the team organist to use the Budweiser theme, and before each home game a team of Clydesdales, the symbol of Budweiser Beer, paraded around the playing field. /(SFS)

Busch Stadium

Busch Stadium St. Louis Cardinals 1966– . LF-330, CF-404, RF-330

A circular multi-purpose facility, Busch Stadium opened in 1966 with a natural grass field, but was converted to artificial turf in 1970. The infield dirt remained, however, until 1974, when it too was eliminated except for the areas around the bases. As with most modern parks, its outfield fences are symmetrical, but Busch's playing surface is extremely hard and fast, making it a haven for line-drive-hitting speedsters and dictating the makeup of recent Cardinals clubs. Named for the brewery family that owns the Cardinals, Busch has a small roof that is ringed with replicas of the famous St. Louis arch, which is only blocks away. The stadium has a capacity of 53,138 and was also home to the football Cardinals until their move to Phoenix in 1988. /(SCL)

Donie Bush [Owen Joseph] — 1887–1972. SS 1908–23 **Tigers**, Senators 1946 g, .250, 9 hr, 436 rbi. *1 WS, 7 g, .261, 2 rbi.*
  Manager 1923, 27–31, 33 Senators, **Pirates**, White Sox, Reds 497–539, .480. First place: 27 *1 WS, 0–4, .000*

The 5'6" 140-lb Tiger shortstop was a clever leadoff man who led the league in bases on balls five times. Despite a long, respectable playing career, Bush is best remembered as a manager. He led the Pirates to the World Series in 1927, where they were swept by the powerhouse Yankees. His vindictiveness may have been a factor; angry with future Hall of Famer Kiki Cuyler over a minor transgression, Bush benched him during the WS. After managing for seven major league seasons, Bush skippered in Triple-A, and became owner of the Indianapolis club. He later scouted for the Red Sox and worked for the White Sox to complete 65 years in organized baseball. /(JK)

Guy Bush (The Mississippi Mudcat) — 1901– . RHP 1923–38, 1945 **Cubs**, Pirates, Braves, Cardinals, Reds 2721 ip, 176–136, 3.86. 20 wins: 33 *2 WS, 17 ip, 1–1, 5.40*

One of the winningest Cubs pitchers (152–101), Bush did double duty throughout his career, starting 308 games and relieving in 234. He led the NL in either relief wins or saves in four different seasons (1925, 1926, 1929, 1935), yet started at least 15 times in each of those years. On May 4, 1927, he worked 18 innings as the Cubs outlasted the Braves 7–2.

Bush won 18 and saved eight for the 1929 Cub pennant winners, contributed 19 wins to the 1932 NL champs, and had his only 20-win season the next year.

He was traded to Pittsburgh in 1935. On May 25, Bush relieved against the Braves in a game at Forbes Field and gave up the last two home runs of Babe Ruth's career. /(ME)

Joe Bush (Bullet Joe) — 1892–1974. RHP 1912–28 **A's**, Red Sox, Yankees, Browns, Senators, Pirates, Giants 3092 ip, 194–183, 3.51. 20 wins: 22 *5 WS, 61 ip, 2–5, 2.67*

Because of veteran Jack Coombs's season-long illness, Connie Mack was forced to rush young pitchers into the breech in 1913. Twenty-year-old Joe

Donie Bush (l.) and Red Faber

Joe Bush

Bush was a good hitter (.253 BA) and was often used as a pinch hitter. He played a season as an outfielder in the Pacific Coast League after leaving the majors. /(JK)

Randy Bush — 1958– . OF-DH 1982– **Twins** 918 g, .252, 82 hr, 343 rbi. *1 LCS, 4 g, .250, 2 rbi. 1 WS, 4 g, .167, 2 rbi*

A lefthanded slugger who usually plays right field or is the Twins DH, Bush has reached double figures in home runs in five of his six full ML seasons despite never recording 400 at bats. As a rookie in 1982, he broke up Jim Clancy's perfect game with a ninth-inning single on September 28, and in 1986 he tied an AL record with two consecutive pinch-hit home runs. /(SCL)

Tom Buskey — 1947– . RHP 1973–80 Yankees **Indians**, Blue Jays 479 ip, 21–27, 3.66

As a rookie in 1974, Buskey was traded from the Yankees to the Indians and set a since-broken Cleveland record with 17 saves. After four seasons with Cleveland, he went to the minors, but re-emerged with the early Blue Jays, notching 7 of its staff's 11 saves during the dreadful 1979 season. Two of Buskey's three wins in 1980 came in a doubleheader against Cleveland. /(TF)

John Butcher — 1957– . RHP 1980–86 Rangers, **Twins**, Indians 833 ip, 36–49, 4.42

Sinker specialist Butcher was drafted four times before signing as a first-rounder with Texas. Although he one-hit the Royals (8/16/83), he did not establish himself as a regular starter until he was traded to the Twins in 1983 as part of the Gary Ward deal. He was 13–11 and 11–14 in two years in Minnesota before suffering a career-ending arm injury. /(MC)

Max Butcher — 1910–1957. RHP 1936–45 Dodgers, Phillies, **Pirates** 1786 ip, 95–106, 3.73

In mid-season 1939, the 6'2" 220-lb Butcher stood 2–13 with the Phillies when Pittsburgh acquired him in a trade for longtime Pirate first baseman Gus Suhr. Although the deal was unpopular in Pittsburgh at the time, by 1941 Suhr was out of the majors and Butcher was the staff ace at 17–12. A sore arm in 1942 reduced his effectiveness, but he posted three more winning seasons for the Pirates during the war years. /(MC)

Bush came through with a 14–6 mark to help the A's to the pennant, then added a five-hit win in the WS. Although plagued by wildness, the durable youngster continued to pitch well in the next few years, but Mack sold off most of his hitting stars and Bush's record slumped. In 1916 he pitched a no-hitter but led the AL in losses (24). Traded to the Red Sox in 1918, he helped them to a wartime pennant. In 1921, when he found his curve would no longer break, he developed a fork ball, then an almost unknown pitch. Traded to the Yankees for 1922, he had his best record, 26–7, for an AL-high .788 winning percentage.

Sal Butera — 1952- . C 1980- **Twins**, Tigers, Expos, Reds, Blue Jays 359 g, .227, 8 hr, 76 rbi. *1 LCS, 1 g, .667. 1 WS, 1 g, --*

The weak-hitting Butera played eight years in the Twins system before serving as Minnesota's backup catcher for 1980 through 1982. His experience as a batting practice pitcher paid off in the NL; he pitched a scoreless inning for the Expos in 1985, and one for the Reds in 1986. Released by Cincinnati, he re-signed with Minnesota to play for the 1987 World Champions. /(JCA)

Art Butler — 1887–1984. SS-2B 1911-16 Braves, Pirates, **Cardinals** 454 g, .241, 3 hr, 101 rbi

A utility infielder, in 1916 Butler led the NL with 54 pinch-hit appearances and 13 pinch hits. He roomed with Honus Wagner as a young Pirate, and was the oldest living ex-big leaguer before his death at 94. /(JK)

Bill Butler — 1947- . LHP 1969-72, 74-75, 77 **Royals**, Indians, Twins 592 ip, 23-35, 4.21

A Royals expansion draft pick from the Tigers, Butler was a Topps All-Star Rookie in 1969. Although his record was a modest 9–10, he struck out 156 in only 193 innings. He tumbled to 4–12 the next year as a sore elbow cost him his fastball. /(MC)

Brett Butler — 1957- . OF 1981- Braves, **Indians**, Giants 1200 g, .281, 36 hr, 318 rbi. *1 LCS, .211. 1 WS, 4 g, .286, 1 rbi*

The pint-sized, 160-lb Butler developed into one of baseball's surest and most wide-ranging centerfielders. He led the NL in triples in 1983, then was sent by the Braves to the Indians as part of a misguided trade for Len Barker. From 1984 through 1987, Butler was Cleveland's lefthanded leadoff hitter, drag-bunting and averaging 41 stolen bases. In 1985 he led AL outfielders with a .998 fielding percentage. His 14 triples in 1986 led the AL. After he jumped to his hometown Giants as a free agent for 1988, Cleveland's Andy Allanson called him a selfish player. /(ME)

Johnny Butler (Trolley Line) — 1894-1967. SS-3B 1926-29 **Dodgers**, Cubs, Cardinals 375 g, .252, 3 hr, 146 rbi

After 31-year-old shortstop Johnny Butler hit .339 and fielded sensationally in the American Association in 1925, the Dodgers sent seven players to Minneapolis for him, but he never topped .270 in the majors. /(JK)

Pee Wee Butts [Thomas] (Cool Breeze) — 1919–1973. SS Negro Leagues 1938-50 Atlanta Black Crackers, Indianapolis ABC's, **Baltimore Elite Giants** 203 g, .310, 3 hr (inc.)
☛ *Led League—ba 40.*

The 5'9" 145-lb Pee Wee Butts was one of the best shortstops in Negro League baseball of the 1940s. Lauded for his sure hands, exceptional range, and strong throwing arm, he combined with Baltimore Elite Giants teammate Junior Gilliam to form one of the great double play combinations in Negro League history, and Butts is credited with making the young Gilliam into a good infielder. Butts lacked power as a hitter but sprayed the ball to all fields, ringing up consistently high averages. He batted .308, .309, .287, and .321 in 1944–1947 (the only years of his career for which confirmed statistics exist) and was the Negro National League batting champion in 1940 with an unconfirmed .391 average. He appeared in six Negro League all-star games, starting five of them. /(JM)

John Buzhardt — 1936- . RHP 1958-68 Cubs, Phillies, **White Sox**, Orioles, Astros 1491 ip, 71-96, 3.66

The quiet South Carolinian broke in impressively, compiling a 3–0 record (1.85) in six games with the 1958 Cubs. The righthander hurled a one-hitter against the Phillies in 1959; after the season ended, the Phillies traded Richie Ashburn for Buzhardt, Alvin Dark, and Jim Woods. Buzhardt went 11–34 in two years with Philadelphia, but enjoyed a career-best 13–8 season with the 1965 Chisox. /(TJ)

Bud Byerly [Eldred] — 1920- . RHP 1943-45, 50-52, 56-60 Cardinals, Reds, **Senators**, Red Sox, Giants 491 ip, 22-22, 3.70. *1 WS, 1 ip, 0-0, 0.00*

Although he only once won as many as six games and never pitched more than 95 innings in a season, Byerly put in parts of 11 seasons in the majors. His top year came at age 36 when he was 6–6 with six saves for the 1957 Senators. /(FK)

Bill Byrd — 1907- . RHP Negro Leagues 1932-49 Columbus Turfs, Columbus Blue Birds, Cleveland Red Sox, Columbus Elite Giants, Washington Elite Giants, Nashville Elite Giants, **Baltimore Elite Giants** statistics not available
☛ *All-Star—36, 39, 41, 44-46.*

The 6'1" 210-lb Byrd was one of the last pitchers to legally throw the spitball, though he didn't depend on it entirely. He had excellent control and a repertoire of pitches that included the slider, fastball, curve, sinker, and two variations of the knuckler. A switch-hitter, he pinch-hit in one of his six East-West all-star game appearances, and batted .364 for the season with the 1934 Cleveland Red Sox. Although only partial statistics are available, it is known that he completed 56 of 85 league games he pitched between 1933–37 and 1944–47. His best year documented was 1945, when he was 10–6 with 79 strikeouts and 11 complete games. He played winter ball with Caguas in Puerto Rico in 1940–41, leading the league in wins (15). /(BP)

Harry Byrd — 1925– . RHP 1950, 52–57 **A's**, Yankees, Orioles, White Sox, Tigers 828 ip, 46–54, 4.35 ☛ *Rookie of the Year—52.*

Byrd, who wasn't afraid to throw a brushback pitch, earned AL rookie honors with 15 victories in 1952, when he and A's southpaw Bobby Shantz formed the league's winningest righty-lefty tandem (39). He lost a league-high 20 his sophomore year, and never again won more than 11. /(TJ)

Sammy Byrd (Babe Ruth's Legs) — 1906–1981. OF 1929–36 **Yankees**, Reds 744 g, .274, 38 hr, 220 rbi. *1 WS, 1 g, --*

Byrd earned his nickname during six years as a Yankee sub by often replacing the aging Babe Ruth in late innings. Byrd later became a professional golfer and won 23 tournaments. /(JK)

Bobby Byrne — 1884–1964. 3B-2B 1907–17 Cardinals, **Pirates**, Phillies, White Sox 1282 g, .254, 10 hr, 329 rbi. *2 WS, 8 g, .240*

Pittsburgh's August 1909 acquisition of the 5'7½" 145-lb infielder contributed key elements to the Pirates' pennant drive, including allowing Tommy Leach to stay in centerfield. Byrne had his best season in 1910, leading the NL in doubles (43) and tying teammate Honus Wagner in hits (178). /(JK)

Tommy Byrne — 1919– . LHP 1943, 46–57 **Yankees**, Browns, White Sox, Senators 1362 ip, 85–69, 4.11; .238, 14 hr, 98 rbi. *4 WS, 21 ip, 1–1, 2.53; .300, 2 rbi*

The slow-working southpaw and $10,000 Yankee bonus baby sometimes enjoyed informing batters what pitch was coming. Good thing, since he led the league in hit batsmen five times. He paced the AL in walks in 1949, '50, and '51, but triumphed despite his wildness, thrice winning 15 or more and leading the league with a .762 winning percentage (16–5) in 1955. A fine hitter who manager Joe McCarthy tried to talk into converting to first base, Byrne amassed 14 homers and pinch hit 80 times. /(TJ)

Milt Byrnes (Skippy) — 1916–1979. OF 1943–45 **Browns** 390 g, .274, 16 hr, 154 rbi. *1 WS, 3 g, .000*

Kept out of the service by bronchial asthma, Byrnes was a three-year wartime regular with the Browns, hitting a career-high .295 as centerfielder for the 1944 team that won the only pennant in Browns history. /(NLM)

Bill Byron — Unk.–Unk. *Umpire* NL 1913–19 *1 WS*

Byron was known as "The Singing Umpire" because he would sing some of his calls. His most famous rendition, to a rookie: "You'll have to learn before you're older, you can't get a hit with the bat on your shoulder." /(RTM)

Marty Bystrom — 1958– . RHP 1980–84 **Phillies**, Yankees 394 ip, 26–24, 4.11. *1 LCS, 5 ip, 0–0, 1.69. 2 WS, 6 ip, 0–0, 4.50*

The 6'5" righthander joined the Phillies in September of 1980 and seemed headed for stardom. He shut out the Mets in his first start, won his four others, and compiled a 1.50 ERA. He then started Game Five of the LCS and WS, and though Bystrom did not record a decision, Philadelphia won both games. Beleaguered by elbow and shoulder problems, Bystrom was traded to the Yankees in 1984. /(AL)

Putsy Caballero [Ralph Joseph] — 1927– . 2B-3B 1944–45, 47–52 **Phillies** 322 g, .228, 1 hr, 40 rbi. *1 WS, 3 g, .000*

A New Orleans schoolboy star, Caballero joined the Phillies at age 16 in wartime 1944, but only in 1948 and 1951 did he have over 150 at-bats. A utility infielder, he was often employed as a pinch-runner. /(AL)

Ramiro Caballero *Mexican Leagues*

Spending much of his career outside organized baseball, Caballero set a Mexican all-time record in 1962 with 59 home runs, adding 170 RBI and a .414 average for Guanajuato of the Mexican Central League. He won the Triple Crown in the same league for Leon two years later, hitting .380 with 35 HR and 145 RBI. After hitting .355 with 34 HR and 113 RBI in 1965, Caballero retired. /(MC)

Enos Cabell — 1949– . 3B-1B-OF 1972–86 Orioles, **Astros**, Giants, Tigers, Dodgers 1688 g, .277, 60 hr, 596 rbi. *3 LCS, 13 g, .184*

The angular Cabell found his path to the big leagues blocked by Baltimore regulars Brooks Robinson and Boog Powell. A deal to Houston gave him his opportunity at third base, a change he took advantage of to become a solid everyday performer. Combining line drive hitting with speed, Cabell stole over 30 bases every year between 1976 and '79, having his best year overall in 1977, when he hit .282 with career highs of 16 HR, 101 runs, and 42 stolen bases. This bad-ball hitter improved with age, hitting over .300 in 1983 with Detroit and again the following season in his second tour of duty with the Astros, this time as a first baseman. /(CC)

Greg Cadaret — 1962– . LHP 1987– **A's**, Yankees 231 ip, 16–9, 3.77. *1 LCS, 0.1 ip, 0–0, 27.00. 1 WS, 2 ip, 0–0, 0.00*

Cadaret was an effective set-up man for the pennant-winning 1988 A's. He was traded with Eric Plunk and Luis Polonia to the Yankees for Rickey Henderson in mid-1989 and was moved to the starting rotation. /(SFS)

Leon Cadore — 1890–1958. RHP 1915–24 **Dodgers**, White Sox, Giants 1257 ip, 68–72, 3.14. *1 WS, 2 ip, 0–1, 9.00*

On May 1, 1920, at Braves Field, Brooklyn's Cadore faced Joe Oeschger in the longest major league game ever played. Curveballer Cadore allowed 15 hits, walked five, and struck out seven. Brooklyn scored one run in the fourth; Boston answered with a run in the fifth. After 26 innings, with both starters still pitching despite the cold, damp weather, darkness fell, and the game was called, tied 1–1. Cadore went on to win a lifetime high of 15 that season. /(ADS)

Ray Cahill — Unk.–1952. *Scout.*

Cahill was a minor league catcher whose playing days ended during WWI when he was gassed while serving in France, and he suffered from chronic asthma thereafter. He scouted for the Browns from 1924 to 1941 and discovered Browns regulars Harlond Clift, Bob Muncrief, and Jack Kramer. /(FVP)

Les Cain — 1948– . LHP 1968, 1970–72 **Tigers** 374 ip, 23–19, 3.97

An impressive rookie in 1970, the hard-throwing Cain recorded 12 victories and 156 strikeouts, but was hindered thereafter by injuries and control problems. /(CC)

Sugar Cain [Merritt] — 1907–1975. RHP 1932–38 **A's**, Browns, White Sox 987 ip, 53–60, 4.83

Cain was a disappointment, having been hailed as the pitcher on whose broad shoulders Connie Mack would rebuild the A's staff after selling off Lefty Grove, Rube Walberg, and George Earnshaw in the early 1930s. A fastball that he couldn't control earned Cain the AL lead in walks in 1935, a year he spent with the A's and Browns. /(JK)

Ivan Calderon [born Ivan Calderon Perez] — 1962– . OF 1984– Mariners, **White Sox** 502 g, .273, 67 hr, 249 rbi

The injury-prone Calderon, a native Puerto Rican, was gunning for 1985 AL Rookie of the Year honors when he hurt his hand in August. Rated below-average defensively, he was sent by Seattle to the White Sox for catcher Scott Bradley the next June. In 1987 he hit 28 homers—many of them tape-measure shots—and led Chicago in 10 offensive categories. But his 1988 season, already marred by a ribcage pull, was ended in July by the need to have his chronically ailing shoulder repaired. /(RL)

Earl Caldwell (Teach) — 1905-1981. RHP 1928, 35-37, 45-48 Phillies, Browns, **White Sox**, Red Sox 587 ip, 33-43, 4.69

Caldwell shut out the Braves in his major league debut with the 1928 Phillies but did not win another ML game until called up by the Browns seven years later. His 7-16 (6.00) mark in 1936 resulted in banishment to the minors in 1937, where he pitched until his contract was purchased by the wartime 1945 White Sox. He threw fairly well as a 40-year-old that season, but, assigned to the bullpen in 1946, he became a sensation, winning an AL-high 13 in relief with eight saves. /(RL)

Mike Caldwell (Iron Mike, Mr. Warmth) — 1949- . LHP 1971-84 Padres, Giants, Reds, **Brewers** 2408 ip, 137-130, 3.81. 20 wins: 78 *1 LCS, 1 g, 3 ip, 0-1, 15.00 1 WS, 18 ip, 2-0, 2.04*

Caldwell leaped from Class A to the Padres in 1971, his first pro year. Swapped to the Giants for Willie McCovey and Bernie Williams, he blossomed with a 14-5 mark in 1974. He then underwent elbow surgery and had trouble regaining his form. The property of the Cardinals and Reds in 1977, he finally landed in Milwaukee. In 1978 he was AL Comeback Player of the Year, going 22-9 (2.36) with a league-high 23 complete games and shutting out the World Champion Yankees three times. In 1979 his .727 winning percentage (16-6) was the AL best; his eight consecutive victories set a Brewers record. After helping Milwaukee to the 1982 pennant with a 17-13 mark, he was pounded by the Angels in his LCS start, but shut out the Cardinals in the World Series opener and also won Game Five.

Caldwell used a three-quarters delivery, but threw sidearm to some lefties. His sinker was most effective, though he was accused of throwing a spitter. By 1984 his arm wore out, and he lost his fastball. Iron Mike retired as the Brewers' leader in complete games. /(MC)

Ray Caldwell (Slim) — 1888-1967. RHP 1910-21 **Yankees**, Red Sox, Indians 2242 ip, 133-120, 3.21. 20 wins: 20 *1 WS, .1 ip, 0-1, 27.00*

The 6'2" spitballer was once struck by lightning while pitching for the Yankees. He recovered, finished the game, and beat the Athletics 2-1. Caldwell won 19 for New York in 1915, and had his only 20-victory season with Cleveland in 1920. One of the veteran spitballers allowed to continue using the pitch after it was banned, he helped pitch the Indians to a pennant, but lost his only WS start. A lifetime .248 batter, Caldwell played 46 games in the outfield, and in 1915 led the AL with 33 pinch-hitting at-bats. /(JK)

Jeff Calhoun — 1958- . LHP 1984-88 **Astros**, Phillies 151 ip, 6-7, 2.51. *1 LCS, 1 ip, 0-0, 9.00*

A lefthanded, sinker-slider thrower, Calhoun proved an effective middle reliever, particularly against lefthanded hitters. He did not allow a run in his first six ML games for Houston in 1984, and in 1985 threw 20 consecutive scoreless innings. /(JCA)

California Angels — 1961- . Team. 2252-2381, .486. *AL West Champions 79, 82, 86*

Formed in the 1961 AL expansion, the Los Angeles Angels finished above .500 in their second season, faster than any other expansion team in the 20th century. After playing their first season in Wrigley Field, an old Pacific Coast League stadium, the club moved in with the Dodgers for four years, always calling their new home field Chavez Ravine rather than Dodger Stadium. The club changed its name to the California Angels in 1965 and moved to its own park in Anaheim in 1966. Bankrolled by Gene Autry, a cowboy-movie star, they spent freely when the free-agent era arrived in the mid-seventies, but have never gotten farther than the division championship. All three of their AL West titles have been followed by losing seasons. /(SFS)

Marty Callaghan — 1900-1975. OF 1922-23, 28, 30 Cubs, **Reds** 295 g, .267, 74 rbi

A reserve outfielder with little extra-base power, Callaghan tied a ML record with three at-bats in one inning (8/25/22) as the Cubs outslugged the Phillies 26-23. He had two singles and struck out. /(NLM)

Nixey Callahan — 1874-1934. OF-RHP-3B-2B-SS 1894, 1897-1905, 11-13 Phillies, Cubs, **White Sox** 923 g, .273, 11 hr, 394 rbi; 1063 ip, 99-73, 3.39. 20 wins: 1898-99
   Manager 1903-04, 12-14, 16-17 **White Sox**, Pirates 393-458, .462

Player-manager Callahan alternated among the mound, outfield, and infield. A two-time 20-game

The 1986 California Angels

winner with the Cubs, he could hit, field, and run, and was a crowd-pleaser. He continued as an outfielder after turning over the White Sox leadership to Fielder Jones in 1904, but he quit pitching. /(JK)

Johnny Callison — 1939– . OF 1958–73 White Sox, **Phillies**, Cubs, Yankees 1886 g, .264, 226 hr, 840 rbi ☛ *All-Star—62, 64–65.*

"He can run, throw, field, and hit with power," Gene Mauch said of Oklahoma-born Johnny Callison. "There's nothing he can't do well on a ball field." Playing for Mauch with Philadelphia, the lefthanded hitter batted as high as .300, hit as many as 32 HR, twice knocked in over 100 runs, and twice scored over 100. He led the NL with 40 doubles in 1966, and twice hit three homers in a game. In the 1964 All-Star Game, he hit a dramatic homer with two on and two out in the ninth off Dick Radatz to give the NL a 7–4 victory. That year, Callison finished second to Cardinal Ken Boyer in NL MVP balloting. /(TJ)

Paul Calvert — 1917– . RHP 1942–45, 49–51 **Indians**, Senators, Tigers 302 ip, 9–22, 5.31

A bespectacled French Canadian, the University of Montreal graduate was limited by a chronic sore arm. Usually a reliever, Calvert started 23 times for the 1949 Senators and led the league with 17 losses, including 14 in a row, the fourth longest streak in AL history. /(JK)

Ernie Camacho — 1955– . RHP 1980– A's, Pirates, **Indians**, Astros 248 ip, 10–20, 4.14

Camacho, a favorite of manager Pat Corrales, set an Indians record with 23 saves in 1984, though few came easy. Relying on a 90-mph fastball and little else, his career was derailed by a fragile arm and a psyche to match. He missed most of 1985 due to elbow surgery, but recovered in 1986 to save 20 games. His start in 1987 was so dreadful that he was booed even while warming up in the bullpen. He once said that he suffered headaches on the mound because he never blinked while pitching. /(ME)

Moises Camacho — 1933– . 2B 1951–75 Mexican Leagues

Considered the Rogers Hornsby of the Mexican League, Camacho batted more than .340 three straight seasons and twice topped 100 RBI for Mexicali in 1953–55, as remnants of the bankrupt Mexican circuit merged into the Class-C Arizona-Texas League. Returning to the Mexican League in 1957, he hit at least 20 homers three times, and .300 six times. Appointed Poza Rica's manager in 1971, he retired as a player, but couldn't resist re-activating himself to pinch hit until, at age 42, his lifetime average finally dipped below .300./(MC)

Ronaldo Camacho — 1935– . 1B-2B 1953–75 Minor and Mexican Leagues

Camacho struggled in the Cardinals chain as a middle infielder for several seasons before returning to his native Mexico in 1956 and becoming a first baseman. Over the next 20 years, he hit 317 homers, playing for nine Mexican League teams. He was the league's home run champion in 1962–63, and the RBI leader in 1963 and 1969./(MC)

Joseph Cambria (Papa Joe) — Unk.–1962. *Scout.*

Cambria was brought to the US from his native Italy when he was three months old, and was a minor league outfielder until he broke his leg in 1916. He owned several minor league clubs from 1929 to 1939, and became a scout for the Washington Senators, staying with the club when it moved to Minnesota as the Twins. Cambria signed Mickey Vernon, Early Wynn, and Ed Yost for the Senators, but was best known for his scouting in Cuba, signing over 400 Cuban players to pro contracts in his career./(FVP)

Dolf Camilli — 1907– . 1B 1933–43, 45 Cubs, Phillies, **Dodgers**, Red Sox 1490 g, .277, 239 hr, 950 rbi. *1 WS, 5 g, .167, 1 rbi*

☛ *Most Valuable Player—41. Led League—hr 41. Led League—rbi 41. All-Star—39, 41.*

Camilli combined graceful fielding with long ball power. When Larry McPhail assumed command of the decrepit Dodgers in 1938, Camilli was the first player he sought. A steady, low-key leader, Camilli became the Dodger captain, a counterbalance to excitable manager Leo Durocher. A former boxer whose brother had died in the ring fighting World Heavyweight Champion Max Baer, Camilli quelled clubhouse clashes with a quiet word and meaningful look. He also discouraged team veterans from hazing Dodger rookies Pee Wee Reese and Pete Reiser.

Camilli hit at least 23 HR eight straight seasons. He was named MVP in 1941 after leading Brooklyn to the pennant with league highs of 34 HR and 120 RBI. When Brooklyn traded him to the rival Giants in 1943, Camilli refused to report. His son Doug caught for the Dodgers and Senators in the 1960s./(JK)

Doug Camilli — 1936– . C 1960–67, 69 **Dodgers**, Senators 313 g, .199, 18 hr, 80 rbi

Camilli's father, Dolf, starred as a homer-hitting first baseman in the NL, but Doug couldn't match his father's bat. The high point of his nine ML seasons as a reserve was catching Koufax's 1964 no-hitter./(TG)

Ken Caminiti — 1963– . 3B 1987– **Astros** 254 g, .246, 14 hr, 102 rbi

Caminiti is an excellent fielder, but after a hot start in his first call-up, his hitting dropped off. He finally won the third base job in 1989, hitting .255 with 10 HR and 72 RBI./(WOR)

Howie Camnitz (Red, The Kentucky Rosebud) — 1881–1960. RHP 1904, 06–15 **Pirates**, Phillies, Pittsburgh (FL) 2085 ip, 133–106, 2.75. 20 wins: 09, 11–12 *1 WS, 4 ip, 0–1, 12.27*

"The Kentucky Rosebud" blossomed in 1909, tying Christy Mathewson for both the NL lead in winning percentage (.806), and second-most NL wins (25). Camnitz became Pittsburgh's sixth 100-game winner in 1912, en route to his third 20-win season in four years. Traded to the Phillies on August 20, 1913, after a 6–17 start, he pitched in just nine games for them, then jumped to Pittsburgh in the Federal League. His brother, Harry, pitched briefly for the 1909 Pirates and 1911 Cardinals./(ME)

Rick Camp — 1953– . RHP 1976–78, 80–85 **Braves** 942 ip, 56–49, 3.37. *1 LCS, 1 ip, 0–1, 36.00*

Arm trouble kept Camp out of the majors in 1979, but the sinkerballer returned in 1980 to save 22 games and set a Braves record with 77 appearances. He recorded a 1.78 ERA with 17 saves in 1981, and tied for the NL lead with nine relief wins. After that he was used in every pitching role, with mixed results. A notoriously poor hitter (.074), he surprised everybody with his only ML home run in the 18th inning of a July 4–5, 1985 marathon with the Mets; his post-3:00 AM blast with two out on an 0–2 pitch from Tom Gorman tied the game at 11–11, but he lost it 16–13 in 19 innings./(JCA)

Roy Campanella (Campy) — 1921– . C Negro
Leagues 1937–42, 1944–45 Baltimore Elite Giants
statistics not available *ML:* C 1948–57 **Dodgers** 1215 g,
.276, 242 hr, 856 rbi. *5 WS, 32 g, .237, 4 hr, 12 rbi*
☛ *All-Star—41, 44–45*
☛ *Most Valuable Player—51, 53, 55. Led League—rbi
53. All-Star—49–56. Hall of Fame—1969.*

Campanella, one of the five black players signed by
Brooklyn Dodgers owner Branch Rickey before the
1946 season, was the first catcher to break organized
baseball's color line. Just 5′9″ but solidly built, he
had already proven himself as a catcher during nine
years in the Negro National League, the winter
leagues, and Mexico. In 12 additional seasons, 10 in
the majors, he was one of the era's outstanding
players, and his leadership and indefatigable enthusiasm made him one of the most popular players in
the game.

Born in Philadelphia of a black mother and an
Italian father, Campanella began his baseball career
in 1937 with a hometown semi-pro team, the
Bacharach Giants. So impressive was his play that
the Baltimore Elite Giants of the Negro National
League offered him a uniform that year, though he
was only 15 years old. Still in school, he played only
on weekends and caught only to spell veteran Biz
Mackey. The next year, however, he left school and
joined the team full-time. He won the first-string job
in 1939 and led the Giants to playoff triumphs over
the Newark Eagles and the Homestead Grays. In
four games he collected five hits, including one HR,
and drove in seven runs.

Campanella soon challenged the aging Josh Gibson as the dominant Negro League catcher. He was
voted the MVP in the 1941 East-West all-star game,
but after a dispute with Baltimore owner Tom
Wilson, he jumped to the Mexican League for part
of 1942 and all of 1943. Rejoining the Giants, he led
the league in doubles in 1944 and in RBI in 1945.

In October 1945, Campanella caught for a black
all-star team in a five-game exhibition series against
a squad of white major leaguers managed by Charlie
Dressen. Dressen had orders to arrange an appointment for Campanella with the Brooklyn Dodgers,
who later signed the catcher for their Nashua, NH,
Class-B farm team (Eastern League), a club run by
Buzzie Bavasi and managed by Walter Alston.
Campanella, who roomed with pitcher Don Newcombe, hit .290, led the league in putouts, assists,
and errors, and won the MVP award. In 1947 he
advanced to Montreal, the Dodgers' International
League team, and again was named the MVP,
despite a season-ending slump that cut his average to

Roy Campanella

.273. Paul Richards, then the Buffalo manager,
called him "the best catcher in the business—major
or minor leagues."

Campanella made the Dodgers in 1948, but his
promotion to Brooklyn was delayed by Rickey's
plan to have him integrate the American Association. The owner forced manager Leo Durocher to
play the catcher in the outfield, where he was not
successful, and then sent him to St. Paul (AA) in
May. In 35 games, he had 40 hits (half for extra
bases) and 39 RBI and batted .325 before being
recalled.

Campanella returned to the Dodgers to stay. For
the next nine years, he caught for outstanding
Brooklyn teams whose members have been lionized
as "The Boys of Summer." They won National
League pennants in 1949, 1952, 1953, 1955, and
1956, narrowly missed two others, and climaxed

Brooklyn's baseball history with its only World Series triumph in 1955. Campanella's contributions to the Dodgers were remarkable. He won the MVP award three times in five years. In 1953, his best season, he batted .312, and scored 103 runs. Also, his 142 RBI (which led the league) and 41 HR set ML records for catchers (plus one HR as a pinch-hitter). He fielded with grace that belied his physique and handled with distinction a predominantly white pitching staff.

Like those of many catchers, Campanella's career was punctuated by injuries. In spring training of 1954, he chipped a bone in the heel of his left hand and damaged a nerve. It affected his hitting and limited him to 111 games. Surgery helped in 1955, but the problem returned the next year. Then, in January 1958, Campanella was permanently disabled in an automobile accident. Returning home from his liquor store, which he ran in the off-season, he lost control of his car on an icy street. The car slammed into a telephone pole and flipped over, pinning him behind the steering wheel. The crash fractured his fifth cervical vertebra and damaged his spinal cord. He survived and endured years of therapy, living far beyond the normal span for quadriplegics, but his career was over. He committed himself to decades of work in community relations for the Dodgers. /(SG)

Bert Campaneris (Campy) — 1942– . SS-3B-OF-2B 1964–81, 83 **A's**, Rangers, Angels, Yankees 2328 g, .259, 79 hr, 646 rbi. *6 LCS, 18 g, .221, 2 hr, 6 rbi. 3 WS, 19 g, .263, 1 hr, 5 rbi*
☛ *All-Star—68, 72–75, 77.*

Surrounded by superstars, Bert Campaneris was a key contributor to the great Oakland teams with his competitive spirit and superb play. His memorable debut with the Kansas City A's (July 23, 1964) included two home runs, one off the first major league pitch ever thrown to him. Bert became only the third player in big league history to hit two homers in his first game. He made headlines in one of club owner Charlie Finley's publicity stunts in 1965. On September 9, Campaneris played every position in a nine inning game. He also led the A's in hitting (.270), edged his cousin, Jose Cardenal, for the league lead in steals (51), and led the league in triples (12). Campy became one of baseball's all-time top base thiefs, stealing 649 bases to rank seventh all-time on his retirement and leading the American League six times, including his first four full seasons (1965–68).

When the A's moved to Oakland in 1968, Bert

Bert Campaneris

led the league in hits (177) and at-bats. Though he struck out more than some leadoff hitters and didn't walk much, he was a catalyst in the Oakland attack. Hitting from an extreme crouch, the Cuban right-hander would get on base and disrupt pitchers. He improved consistently on defense, leading AL short-stops with 795 chances in 1972. An adept bunter, he led the AL in sacrifice bunts in 1972 (20) and 1978 (40). Despite these credentials, Bert is most associated with an unfortunate incident in the 1972 American League Championship Series. In Game Two, he already had three hits, two steals and two runs scored as he faced Detroit hurler Lerrin LaGrow. When LaGrow's pitch hit Campaneris in the ankle, Bert flung his bat at the hurler. A near-riot ensued as Detroit manager Billy Martin charged Campaneris. The batter and pitcher were both ejected. Bert was suspended for the remainder of the playoffs, reinstated for the World Series (in which he was hit by pitches three times), and suspended for the first seven games of 1973. He was the shortstop on *TSN*'s post-season AL All-Star Team in 1973 and 1974. In 1976, his 52 steals helped the A's set an AL club record with 341 steals. Like most of the A's, Campaneris played out his option, moving to the Rangers. After a full season with Texas (1977), age and injuries limited Bert to part-time, utility duty. He spent 1982 in the Mexican League. In 1983, at the age of 41, Campaneris returned to the big leagues as a utility infielder with the Yankees, playing for Billy Martin. He responded with a career-high .322 batting average in 59 games and solid defense at second and third base. /(ME)

Al Campanis — 1916- . 2B 1943 **Dodgers** 7 g, .100, 0 hr, 0 rbi

Campanis worked for the Dodgers for 46 years, rising to vice-president in charge of player personnel. His career came to an unceremonious end early in 1987 when he made insensitive racial remarks in a network television interview.

He played seven games with the Dodgers in 1943 before leaving for WWII with the Navy, and when he returned he became a manager in the Dodgers' minor league system. Campanis became a scout in 1950 and director of scouting from 1957 to 1968, before finally settling in as a club vice-president in 1969. His son Jim was a ML catcher for parts of six seasons.

In the infamous 1987 interview, he provoked national ridicule by suggesting that black ballplayers lacked the "necessities" to become ML managers. /(FVP)

Bill Campbell — 1948- . RHP 1973-87 **Twins**, Red Sox, Cubs, Phillies, Cardinals, Tigers, Expos 1229 ip, 83-68, 3.55. *1 LCS, 2 ip, 0-0, .000. 1 WS, 4 ip, 0-0, 2.25*
☛ *All-Star—77.*

Like many relievers, Bill Campbell's career was marked by injury and a couple of brilliant seasons. Signed by the Twins in 1970, he was their bullpen ace in 1974 (19 saves) and 1976 (20 saves). He led the entire Minnesota staff with 17 wins in 1976, an AL relief record, also leading the league with a .773 winning percentage and 78 appearances. Signed by the Red Sox as a free agent, he again led his staff in wins (13), and he paced the AL with 31 saves to

become *TSN*'s Fireman of the Year for the second straight season. A severe elbow injury in 1978, probably caused by overwork, finished his career as a stopper. Still valuable, he found work with six teams from 1981 to 1987 and led the NL with 83 appearances for the 1983 Cubs. /(ME)

Billy Campbell — 1873-1957. LHP 1905, 07-09 Cardinals, **Reds** 408 ip, 23-25, 2.80

After going 3-0 in three starts for the Reds in 1907, Campbell followed with losing records the next two seasons. His ERAs (2.60, 2.67) were worse than average for those dead-ball years. /(SFS)

Bruce Campbell — 1909- . OF 1930-42 White Sox, Browns, **Indians**, Tigers, Senators 1360 g, .290, 106 hr, 766 rbi

Campbell beat the odds when he recovered from a 1935 bout with spinal meningitis. After leading the AL with 104 strikeouts as a rookie (1932), the lefthanded batter led the Browns with 106 RBI the following year. On November 20, 1934, Campbell came to Cleveland for Johnny Burnett, Bob Weiland, and cash. He quickly proved popular with the Tribe and was batting .325 in early August when he complained of a headache in Detroit. Soon he was in critical condition with cerebral spinal fever. Given a fifty-fifty chance to recover, Campbell was miraculously back in uniform in 1936. He collapsed again in May, but still batted a remarkable .372 in 76 games and was honored on Bruce Campbell Day at Cleveland's League Park. He had three hits that day and went 6-for-6 on July 2, 1936. Philadelphia writers honored Campbell as most courageous athlete of the year in 1936. /(ME)

Dave Campbell — 1942- . 2B-3B 1967-74 Tigers, **Padres**, Cardinals, Astros 428 g, .213, 20 hr, 89 rbi

Campbell's first ML hit was a home run for the World Champion 1968 Tigers. After three short trials, Detroit sent the 6'1" Michigan native to San Diego. In 1970, his only season as a regular, Campbell led NL second basemen in putouts, assists, and errors while hitting .219 with 12 HR for the Padres. /(TJ)

Dave Campbell (Chopper) — 1951- . RHP 1977-78 **Braves** 158 ip, 4-10, 3.82

Despite a 0-6 record, Campbell compiled 13 saves in 65 appearances as a rookie with the last-place 1977 Braves. Overworked and unappreciated, he developed arm trouble during 1978 and left the majors. /(PB)

Mike Campbell — 1964– . RHP 1987- **Mariners**
185 ip, 8–16, 5.74

Seattle native Campbell was the Mariners' first-round draft pick in June 1985, but was hampered by wildness. /(JFC)

Vin Campbell — 1888–1969. OF 1908, 10–12, 14–15 Cubs, Pirates, **Braves**, Indianapolis (FL), Newark (FL) 546 g, .310, 15 hr, 167 rbi

The Braves traded a worn Mike Donlin to get Campbell's bat into their lineup in 1912; Campbell led NL hitters in at-bats, and outfielders in errors. In 1914 he signed a three-year Federal League contract and had two .300-plus campaigns. When the Feds folded in 1916, he sued and won payment for the final year, but couldn't find work elsewhere. /(NLM/ ADS)

Casey Candaele — 1961– . 2B-OF-SS 1986- **Expos**, Astros 225 g, .244, 1 hr, 34 rbi

In 1987 the spunky, 5′9″ Candaele played six positions and finished fourth in NL Rookie of the Year balloting. His teammates had a pool to guess the date of his first home run; it came on July 19, and was the shortest ever to clear the fence at Olympic Stadium. A special yellow seat was set in the first row of bleachers to mark the shot. The switch-hitter was demoted and traded to Houston in mid-1988. Casey's mother, Helen Callahan St. Aubin, played in the professional All American Girls Baseball League of 1942–1954 and had 354 steals in 388 games. /(JCA)

John Candelaria (The Candy Man) — 1953– . LHP 1975-**Pirates**, Angels, Mets, Yankees, Expos 2368 ip, 167–107, 3.27. *3 LCS, 25 ip, 1–1, 2.13. 1 WS, 9 ip, 1–1, 5.00*
☛ *Led League—era 77. All-Star—77.*

Considered one of baseball's best "money" pitchers, Candelaria's toughest opponent was injury. From 1975 to 1988, he had only one losing season. His 1976 no-hitter was the first ever pitched by a Pirate in Pittsburgh. A gutsy competitor, Candelaria's biggest asset was great control of all his pitches from a tough three-quarter delivery. The 6′7″ 205-lb lefty helped Pittsburgh win the NL East as a rookie in 1975 and set a NLCS record with 14 strikeouts in Game Three. In 1977 he became the first NL pitcher since Sandy Koufax (in 1965) to win 20 games and lead in ERA (2.34) and winning percentage (.800, 20–5). He was Pittsburgh's first 20-game winner since 1960 and their first lefthander to win 20 since 1924. He led the 1979 World Champions with 14 wins and pitched shutout ball in the crucial sixth game of the World Series.

Candelaria overcame a severe arm injury in 1981. Plagued by chronic back problems, the already disgruntled Candelaria was moved to the bullpen in 1985 and traded to California in August as the Pirates dumped their high-salaried players after finishing last in 1984 despite leading the league in ERA. Candelaria was the AL Comeback Player of the Year in 1986 as the Angels won their division. He gave up only one earned run in his two LCS starts, winning one but losing Game Seven on errors. Near the end of another injury-plagued season in 1987, the Brooklyn, NY native was sent to the Mets, who had lost Ron Darling to injury, but Candelaria's 2–0 record wasn't enough to help them win their pennant race. Not wanting to return to the bullpen, he went to the Yankees after the season and was their best pitcher in 1988 (13–7, 3.38) but spent the last part of the year on the DL again, this time with knee ailments. More injuries cut into his 1989 campaign. /(ME)

Milo Candini — 1917– . RHP 1943-44, 46–51 **Senators**, Phillies 538 ip, 26–21, 3.92

After a 7–0 start with the Senators, Candini finished at 11–7 in 1943. Hard-throwing and occasionally wild, he spent all of 1945 in the army, and never again won more than three games in a season. /(EW)

Tom Candiotti (Candy) — 1957– . RHP 1983-84, 86- Brewers, **Indians** 970 ip, 56–64, 3.69

Candiotti was released by Milwaukee in 1985 after six years in the minors and two major league trials. He was in winter ball, working on a knuckler, when signed by the Indians. The surprise of their 1986 staff, he led with 16 wins and a 3.57 ERA, and topped the AL with 17 complete games. As the Indians fell in 1987, so did Candiotti, going 7–18 despite throwing two one-hitters; he lost one of them. /(JCA)

Candlestick Park (The Stick) San Francisco Giants 1960– . LF-335, CF-400, RF-335

Located on Candlestick Point, which juts into San Francisco Bay, Candlestick Park opened in 1960 as baseball's first truly "modern" stadium, only to quickly fall under criticism for its poor location. At first it was essentially round, but open in the outfield, and icy winds whipped in from the bay through the stadium's open end, often dropping the already cool temperatures an additional 15 to 20 degrees during the course of a night game. The most infamous incident occurred during the 1961 All-Star Game, when Giants pitcher Stu Miller was literally blown off the pitching rubber by a strong gust, forcing a costly balk. Originally natural grass, the stadium was converted to artificial turf and the open end enclosed for the NFL's 49ers in 1972, but it was converted back to grass in 1979. The additional seats made Candlestick the NL's largest park at the time and reduced the wind problem somewhat, but it remains the only uncovered stadium with a heating system. The field itself has substantial foul territory and a wire outfield fence well inside the permanent seats, and on home runs and deep fly balls dozens of fans leap from their seats to the field in hopes of catching a souvenir. /(SCL)

Eli Canel (Buck) — 1906–1980. *Broadcaster.*

Born in Buenos Aires of Scottish-Spanish descent, Canel worked as a reporter for the Associated Press in Latin America for seven years before moving to New York, where he broadcast Yankees home games in Spanish until 1972. Beginning in 1937, he broadcast 42 WS. His trademark line, translated, was "Don't go away, this game is really getting interesting." In 1985, the Hall of Fame voted him the Ford C. Frick Award for broadcasters. /(NLM)

John Cangelosi — 1963– . OF 1985– **White Sox,** Pirates 433 g, .242, 6 hr, 67 rbi

The 5'8" Cangelosi was the surprise of the White Sox' 1986 spring camp when he displaced Rudy Law and Daryl Boston to win the centerfield job. The spunky switch-hitter drew walks and stole 50 bases, an AL rookie record. But a 0-for-31 drought dropped his average below .230, and he was benched. Dealt to Pittsburgh in 1987, he batted .275, mostly pinch hitting, and on September 15 he became the first Pirate in 21 years to steal home. /(RL)

Chris Cannizzaro — 1938– . C 1960–65, 68–74 Cardinals, Mets, Pirates, **Padres,** Cubs, Dodgers 740 g, .235, 18 hr, 169 rbi
☛ All-Star—69.

Mispronouncing Cannizzaro's name, Casey Stengel said, "Canzoneri is the only defensive catcher who can't catch." In 1964, Cannizzaro batted .311, by far a career-high, in 60 games. Only with the 1969–70 expansion Padres was he a regular. /(TJ)

Jimmy Cannon — 1910–1973. *Writer.*

"Nobody asked me, but . . ." was Cannon's familiar lead. A protege of Damon Runyon and Mark Hellinger, Cannon's prose was admired by Ernest Hemingway. Cannon started as a copy boy for the New York *Daily News* in 1926 and joined the New York *American* as a sportswriter in 1936. In WWII he accompanied Gen. Patton's Third Army as a war correspondent. Cannon joined the New York *Post* in 1946 and, except for war correspondence duty in Korea, remained with the paper until hired away by the New York *Journal-American* in 1959; his $1,000 a week salary was believed to be the most in the country paid to a sports columnist. An early observer of the impact of black athletes on both sports and society, he made the immortal comment that boxer Joe Louis was a credit to his race—the human race. /(JK)

Jose Canseco — 1964– . OF 1985– **A's** 568 g, .270, 128 hr, 424 rbi. *2 LCS, 9 g, .303, 4 hr, 7 rbi. 2 WS, 9 g, .181, 2 hr, 8 rbi*
☛ *Rookie of the Year—86. Most Valuable Player—88. Led League—hr 88. Led League—rbi 88. All-Star—86, 88.*

Born in Havana, Cuba, Canseco became a baseball giant in both size and ability. The first-ever member of the "40–40" club with his 40 stolen bases and league-leading 42 HR in 1988, he also led with 124 RBI and won the MVP award in a landslide.

Canseco struck out in his first big-league at-bat and in 12 of his first 24 at-bats in 1985. Despite a club-record 175 strikeouts in 1986, his 33 HR earned him the Rookie of the Year award in a close decision over Wally Joyner. With great bat speed and power to all fields, he became the first Oakland player with back-to-back 100-RBI seasons and joined Dave Kingman as the A's only players with three straight 30-HR seasons. Two years of intense weight training improved his power, but he also improved greatly on defense and showed a strong arm, earning a move from left field to right field.

Canseco's three homers in the LCS matched George Brett's AL record, and his HR in Game Four went to dead center and dented a TV camera over 400' from the plate. In Game One of the WS, he hit his first major league grand slam in the second inning, the 16th slam in WS history, and just the second ever by a player in his first game (Dan Gladden had done it in 1987). But he went hitless for the rest of the Series as the Dodgers stunned the favored A's.

Canseco missed the first half of 1989 with a broken bone in his hand but stayed in the news with a string of speeding tickets that started before the season. His indentical twin brother, Ozzie, played in the Yankees' and A's systems. /(ME)

Ben Cantwell — 1902–1962. RHP 1927–37 Giants, **Braves**, Dodgers 1534 ip, 76–108, 3.91. 20 wins: 33

After Cantwell led NL relievers with 12 wins and 8 losses in 1932, Braves manager Bill McKechnie returned him to the rotation in 1933. Cantwell responded with a league-leading .667 winning percentage (20–10). But 1932–33 were by far his best years; in 1935, Cantwell suffered 25 losses, including 13 in a row. /(JK)

Doug Capilla — 1952– . LHP 1976–81 Cardinals, Reds, **Cubs** 293 ip, 12–18, 4.34

Not many pitchers have enjoyed the start that Capilla had breaking into professional ball. He struck out the first 21 batters he faced as a professional hurler while at Great Falls (Pioneer League). The Hawaiian was originally signed by San Francisco as an outfielder. The Cardinals drafted him from the Giants in 1973. At times he showed signs of being a standout, but he had control problems during his career. /(EW)

Buzz Capra [Lee William] — 1947– . RHP 1971–77 Mets, **Braves** 543 ip, 31–37, 3.88
☛ *Led League—era 74. All-Star—74.*

After being sold by the pitching-rich Mets, Capra earned a starter's role and turned in a stellar 1974 season in which he set an Atlanta Braves consecutive victory mark (9), won the league ERA crown (2.28), and averaged the fewest hits per nine innings of all NL pitchers. The following year he suffered the shoulder injury which drove him to early retirement. /(CR)

Pat Caraway — 1906–1974. LHP 1930–32 **White Sox** 478 ip, 22–40, 5.35

Caraway had a fair curveball and a bizarre, accordion-like windup, nearly doubling over his 6'4" frame before delivering. He went 10–10 as a rookie in 1930, but in 1931 came completely unglued. On July 23 in Boston, he pleaded in vain to be taken out after giving up 11 runs in 4-2/3 innings. Between innings, manager Donie Bush berated his pitcher unmercifully. Three days later in New York, Caraway was shelled 22–5, the worst loss in White Sox history. His 24 losses led the AL that year. Surpris-

ingly, he made the club the next spring, but was sent down in July. /(RL)

Harry Caray — 1920– . *Broadcaster.*

He has broadcast from the centerfield bleachers with a cooler full of beer. He sweeps foul balls from the backstop with a long fishing net. And he leads the most raucous choruses of "Take Me Out to the Ballgame," ever heard at the ballgame. Harry Caray is broadcasting's premier showman, as much an attraction at the ballpark as the teams for which he works.

He made his ML debut with the Cardinals in 1945, and by the mid-50s was heard across the Midwest on flagship station KMOX and baseball's largest radio network. Caray was fired in 1969 amid rumors of personal difficulties with the Busch family, then spent one season in Oakland before returning to the Midwest as the voice of the White Sox. From 1971 to 1981 his antics helped resurrect that nearly comatose franchise, but in 1982 he jumped to the Cubs. His fame reached new peaks with a national TV audience through superstation WGN and the natural affinity Wrigley Field has for his grandstanding antics.

At each stop, Caray has been an unapologetic homer, loudly cheering the locals while freely using "we" and "they" to describe the participants. But even his beloved hometown players are not exempt from the often caustic criticism he calls objectivity. As he put it, "If they're horseshit, there's nothing I can do about it." Caray fought off a stroke to continue in the Cubs' booth as the 1980s drew to a close, still barking his home run call, "It might be . . .It could be . . . It is!", and capping each victory with the simple and joyous exultation "Cubs win!" /(SCL)

Skip Caray — 1939– . *Broadcaster.*

The versatile son of Harry Caray became a Braves broadcaster in 1976 and has announced football, basketball, and hockey as well. Skip made his ML broadcasting debut on May 30, 1965, calling a Braves-Astros game for Atlanta TV station WSB as an emergency substitute for Mel Allen, who was attending his mother's funeral. /(SCL)

Bernie Carbo — 1947– . OF-DH 1969–80 Reds, Cardinals, **Red Sox**, Brewers, Indians, Pirates 1010 g, .264, 96 hr, 358 rbi. *1 LCS, 2 g, .000. 2 WS, 8 g, .200, 2 hr, 4 rbi*

The journeyman outfielder starred in the 1975 World Series, tying the Series record with two pinch homers; the second tied the score in the eighth inning of Game Six, setting the stage for Carlton Fisk's dramatic overtime home run. Carbo had been the Reds' number-one draft pick in the inaugural 1965 draft, ahead of Johnny Bench. He was *TSN* Rookie of the Year in 1970, batting .310 with 21 HR. But the lefthanded hitter slumped to .219 his sophomore year, and arrived in Boston in 1974. With the Red Sox, Carbo was given a giant stuffed animal for good luck. He tabbed it "Mighty Joe Young," and the beast became as well known in Boston as Bernie. His 1978 sale to Cleveland caused Boston pal Bill Lee to walk out (after the season, Lee was sent to the Expos); Lee claimed Carbo was "the best tenth man in baseball."/(EW)

Jose Cardenal — 1943– . OF-1B 1963–80 Giants, Angels, Indians, Cardinals, Brewers, **Cubs**, Phillies, Mets, Royals 2017 g, .275, 138 hr, 775 rbi. *1 LCS, 2 g, .167. 1 WS, 4 g, .200*

Colorful Cardenal played for nine teams in 18 ML seasons. The Cuban immigrant couldn't crack San Francisco's outfield and was traded to California following the 1964 season. He finished second in the AL in steals (37), showed good range and a strong arm in center field, but also developed a reputation as a moody player. After two subpar seasons, Cardenal was shipped to Cleveland. He led the Indians in steals twice and tied a ML record for outfielders by making two unassisted double plays in 1968. Traded to the Cardinals in 1970, he hit .293 with 74 RBI. In a 1971 season split between St. Louis and Milwaukee, he drove in a career-high 80 RBI. Finally reaching the Cubs in 1972, he stayed for six seasons. As the Cubs' right fielder in 1973, he led the team in hitting (.303), doubles (33), and steals (19). He was named Chicago Player of the Year by the Chicago baseball writers. In 1978–80, he played for the Phillies, Mets, and Royals, ending his ML career batting .340 down the stretch for Kansas City and starting two games in right field during the 1980 World Series. He is a cousin of longtime ML shortstop Bert Campaneris./(ME)

Leo Cardenas (Chico, Mr. Automatic) — 1938– . SS 1960–75 **Reds**, Twins, Angels, Indians, Rangers 1941 g, .257, 118 hr, 689 rbi. *2 LCS, 6 g, .167, 1 rbi. 1 WS, 3 g, .333*
☛ *All-Star—64–66, 68, 71. Gold Glove—65.*

Cardenas was one of baseball's best shortstops during the 1960s. The son of Rafael Cardenas, himself an outstanding pro shortstop in Cuba, Leo became known as "Mr. Automatic" for his fancy fielding. As a Cincinnati regular (1962–68), he won

a Gold Glove in 1965 and topped NL shortstops twice each in fielding and putouts and once in double plays. He hit 20 homers in 1966, a Reds record for shortstops. Traded to Minnesota for pitcher Jim Merritt in November 1968, Cardenas helped the Twins win a divisional championship in 1969, batting .280 and leading AL shortstops in assists, double plays, and putouts. His 570 putouts that year tied a 63-year-old league record. He led the AL in fielding again in 1971./(TJ)

Don Cardwell — 1935– . RHP 1957–70 Phillies, **Cubs**, Pirates, Mets, Braves 2123 g, 102–138, 3.92. *1 WS, 1 ip, 0–0, 0.00*

After three mediocre seasons in Philadelphia, Cardwell was traded to the Cubs in mid-1960 and pitched a no-hitter against St. Louis in his first start for his new team, the only pitcher ever to do so. The durable pitcher led the NL with 38 starts for the 1961 Cubs and won a career-high 15 games. He sandwiched two fine seasons in Pittsburgh around severe arm trouble in 1964. His 13–10 mark in 1965 was dragged down by six one-run losses. Cardwell was a valuable swingman for the Mets (1967–70) and helped them to their 1969 World Championship with his experience. After going 3–9 by late July, he won five straight, including a 1–0 game against the Pirates in which he drove in the only run./(ME)

Rod Carew — 1945– . 1B-2B 1967–85 **Twins**, Angels 2469 g, .328, 92 hr, 1015 rbi. *4 LCS, 14 g, .220, 1 rbi*
☛ *Rookie of the Year—67. Most Valuable Player—77. Led League—ba 69, 72–75, 77–78. All-Star—67–81, 83–84.*

"Carew had great hand action, probably as good as anyone who ever swung a bat. He always used the entire field. Because he could bunt so well, he brought the third baseman in close. He made the defense come to him instead of the other way around. He had a great sense of the strike zone, never chasing a bad ball, and had no fear at the plate," said Bill Rigney, one of Carew's managers.

Born on a train in the Panama Canal Zone, Carew moved with his mother to New York at age 17. After signing with the Twins a day out of high school in 1964, he played three minor league seasons before jumping from Class C to the majors in 1967. He got his first ML hit on Opening Day off Baltimore's Dave McNally; 18 years later, on August 4, 1985, with California, Carew singled off Minnesota's Frank Viola to become the 16th player to attain 3,000 hits.

Carew batted .292 in 1967 and was named AL Rookie of the Year. He hit .273 in 1968, but

Rod Carew

followed with 15 consecutive seasons over .300. Only Ty Cobb, Stan Musial, and Honus Wagner have exceeded that achievement. Carew won seven AL batting championships, and won them by consistently larger margins than anyone except Rogers Hornsby. In his MVP 1977 season, Carew's .388 was 50 points higher than the next-best average in ML baseball, Dave Parker's NL-leading .338. This was the largest margin in ML history.

In 1970 Carew was off to his best start when he injured his knee, and he played just 51 games. In 1972 he became the first player to win a batting crown without hitting a home run. After capturing three more straight championships (1973–75) Carew batted .331 in 1976, but lost the title on the last day, to George Brett (.333) and Hal McRae (.332). He came back in 1977 to lead with his .388, and in 1978 led for the final time with .333.

Hitting was Carew's trademark, but he was also

one of the game's best baserunners. Said Twins manager Frank Quilici, "There's nobody alive, nobody, who could turn a single into a double, a double into a triple the way Rod could. He may have been the most complete player of his time." Twins owner Calvin Griffith put Carew in the same class with Hall of Fame second basemen Hornsby and Charlie Gehringer.

Carew was moved from second to first base in 1975 to lengthen his career. After a dozen years with Minnesota, Carew forced a trade by announcing he would play out his option if the Twins did not deal him. (This was prompted in part by racist public statements by Griffith regarding black fans.) The club would receive nothing in return if he became a free agent. On February 3, 1979, he was traded to the Angels for Ken Landreaux, Dave Engle, Brad Havens, and Paul Hartzell. Carew, despite sitting out more than six weeks with a thumb injury that season, was instrumental in the Angels' drive to their first division title.

When Carew first came up, he was a loner—temperamental, often sullen—and didn't get along with his managers. He said in his autobiography, "I was always moody with managers . . .threatening to jump the club." Carew met with some racism in baseball, and following the announcement of his engagement to a Jewish woman, Marilynn Levy, he received death threats. As Carew matured, he became a family man, and a friendly, outgoing team leader.

Carew was on the losing club in four LCS, two with Minnesota and two with California. He would have played in 18 consecutive All-Star games, but was replaced due to injury in 1970 and 1979, and for the same reason was not chosen in 1982. In 1977 Carew received over four million All-Star votes, more than any other player ever. He established an All-Star record with two triples in the 1978 classic.

Always a base-stealing threat, Carew tied a ML record with seven steals of home in 1969, and amassed 348 career stolen bases. On May 18, 1969, he stole three bases in one inning. He led the league three times in base hits and once in runs scored, and led once and tied once in triples. He recorded 200 hits four times, and his 239 hits in 1977 was the highest total in the majors in 47 years. His 128 runs scored in '77 was the highest since 1961. Carew hit for the cycle in 1970, connected for five hits in a single game five times, and is 12th on the all-time hit list. His .339 average in 1983 set an Angels record, and he holds Twins season records for runs, hits, singles, triples, stolen bases, and batting average. /(JLE)

Andy Carey — 1931- . 2B 1952–62 **Yankees**, A's, White Sox, Dodgers 938 g, .260, 64 hr, 350 rbi. *4 WS, 16 g, .175, 2 rbi*

Carey was a $60,000 Yankee bonus baby out of St. Mary's College (CA). He was a notorious eater; because of him, the Yankees stopped allowing players to sign for meals. Carey became New York's regular third baseman in 1954, hitting .302. In July 1955 he helped turn four double plays in a game, tying a ML record for third basemen. The emergence of Clete Boyer made Carey expendable, and he was traded to Kansas City for Bob Cerv in 1960./(EW)

Max Carey [Maximilian Carnarius] (Scoops) — 1890–1976. OF 1910–29 **Pirates**, Dodgers 2476 g, .285, 69 hr, 800 rbi. *1 WS, 7 g, .458, 2 rbi.*
    Manager 1932–33 **Dodgers** 146–161, .476
☛ *Hall of Fame—1961.*

Carey was the best-fielding centerfielder of his era. For 9 of his 17 seasons with Pittsburgh, he topped the league in putouts and total chances, and his career totals are exceeded only by Mays and Speaker for putouts, and by Speaker, Mays, and Cobb for total chances. Four years he led in outfield assists, and his lifetime total of 339 is the modern NL record. Most impressive were the range and speed which took him to the most fielding chances per game seven times, and the best NL career total for double plays (86), again topped only by Speaker and Cobb.

He also used his speed on the bases, leading the NL in steals ten times, six times topping 50. In 1922, he stole 51 bases in 53 attempts. His 738 SB put him among the all-time leaders. A switch-hitting leadoff man, Carey scored 42% of the time he reached base by a hit or walk. Playing in cavernous Forbes Field, he had a total of 159 triples. His average rose after the shift to the lively ball, from .273 between 1910 and 1919 to .304 between 1920 and 1926.

Carey had turned to baseball when he no longer had the money to continue as a Lutheran divinity student. He joined the Pirates in 1910, played alongside player-manager Fred Clarke for a season, and took over left field when Clarke quit. In 1916, he moved back to centerfield.

Carey played vigorously and with flair. He was team captain in 1926 when Clarke returned to the Pirate bench to advise Manager Bill McKechnie. Carey, in a slump, heard that hard-nosed old Fred had urged McKechnie to bench him, saying that the batboy couldn't do worse at the plate. Ruffled,

Max Carey with the Pirates

Carey called a team meeting to protest Clarke's harsh judgment. The challenge backfired. There was more support for Clarke's position than Carey expected. In retaliation the front office released two Carey supporters outright and sold Carey himself to Brooklyn for $4,000.

He played through 1929, scouted for the Pirates in 1930, and managed the Dodgers to third- and sixth-place finishes in 1932 and 1933. He scouted and managed in the minors off and on through 1956, and was inducted into the Hall of Fame in 1961./(ADS)

Tom Carey (Scoops) — 1908–1970. 2B-SS 1935–37, 39–42, 46 **Browns**, Red Sox 465 g, .275, 2 hr, 169 rbi

Carey had never played second base until his debut with Rogers Hornsby's Browns in 1935; he made a league-high 25 errors while still learning the position in 1936. He became a utility infielder and, after WWII service, a Red Sox coach. /(JK)

Tex Carleton [James Otto] — 1906–1977. RHP 1932–38, 40 Cardinals, **Cubs**, Dodgers 1607 ip, 100–76, 3.91. *3 WS, 11 ip, 0–1, 5.06*

In the minors, Carleton once had 13 consecutive wins and threw a no-hitter. In the majors, he was at least a .500 pitcher in all but his first season, and he won at least ten games in all but his last. On May 30, 1940, he threw a no-hitter for Brooklyn, beating the Reds, 3–0. /(EW)

Cisco Carlos [Francisco] — 1940– . RHP 1967–70 **White Sox**, Senators 237 ip, 11–18, 3.72

Called up to the White Sox in the midst of a four-team 1967 pennant race, Carlos went 2–0 in seven starts with an 0.86 ERA. He dipped to 4–14 the following year because he could not keep the ball down, and he was sold to the Senators in 1969. /(RL)

Hal Carlson — 1892–1930. RHP 1917–30 **Pirates**, Phillies, Cubs 2002 ip, 114–120, 3.97. *1 WS, 4 ip, 6.75*

Carlson was in his fourteenth ML season when he died of a stomach hemorrhage in May 1930. He won a career-high 17 in 1926, and was 64–48 from 1925 until his death. He spent his first seven seasons with the Pirates. A respectable batter, Carlson delivered a pinch homer for the Phillies on May 30, 1925. /(ME)

Steve Carlton (Lefty) — 1944– . LHP 1965–88 Cardinals, **Phillies**, Giants, White Sox, Indians, Twins 5217 ip, 329–244, 3.22. 20 wins: 71, 72, 76, 77, 80, 82 *5 LCS, 53.2 ip, 4–2, 3.52. 4 WS, 31.2 ip, 2–2, 2.56*
☛ *Led League—w 72, 77, 80, 82. Led League—era 72. Led League—k 72, 74, 80, 82–83.. Cy Young Award—72, 77, 80, 82. All-Star—68, 69, 71, 72, 74, 77, 79–82.*

The second-winningest lefthander of all time behind Warren Spahn, Carlton is also second on the all-time strikeout list behind Nolan Ryan. He is the only pitcher ever to win four Cy Young Awards, and had six 20-win seasons.

When he had his first tryouts in 1963, scouts questioned whether he could throw hard enough to make the ML, but Carlton, a dedicated worker at

Steve Carlton

conditioning throughout his career, built himself up with weights and his fastball became his strikeout pitch. He also had a decent curveball with a sharp downward drop, and a sneaky pickoff move that tested the limits of the balk rule. In 1969, he began to develop his slider, a pitch that broke down and in to righthanded batters, and it became a devastating complement to his fastball in mid-career. Carlton was also dangerous at the plate, with a .201 career average and 13 HR.

Carlton had a respectable 1967 season (14–9, 2.98) to help the Cardinals win the WS, but began to earn national recognition in 1969. He started and won the All-Star Game and set a since-broken ML record with 19 strikeouts against the Mets on September 15. Ironically, he lost the game 4–3 on a pair of home runs by Ron Swoboda.

In 1970, a contract dispute kept him out of spring training, and he had trouble controlling his breaking pitches all season and lost 19 games. He went back to his fastball more the following year and won 20 games for the first time.

Carlton asked for a $10,000 raise to $65,000 in that off-season and the Cardinals' management balked. Instead, they traded him to the Phillies for Rick Wise, a deal that will always be one of the most notorious in Cardinals history. Carlton was phenomenal in 1972, pitching as well for an entire season as any pitcher ever. He went 27–10 for a Phillies club that won only 57 games. He led the league in wins, ERA (1.97), strikeouts (310, only the second lefthander ever to reach 300), and complete games, and enjoyed a 15-game winning streak. Of course, he won his first Cy Young Award.

He was less impressive in the three seasons that followed, partly due to occasional soreness in his left elbow. Two changes helped him regain his form in 1976. He adjusted his stance on the rubber, which improved his control, and he began pitching to his old friend and former Cardinal batterymate, Tim McCarver, though Bob Boone was the Phillies regular catcher. Carlton's slider was crackling, and his combination of power and finesse gave him 20 victories in 1976. The Phillies won their first NL East title. In 1977, he led the NL in wins (23–10) for the second time and the Phillies won another division title.

By this time, Carlton was working out with Phillies conditioning coach Gus Hoefling up to two hours a day. Always an intense competitor and a private, seemingly unemotional personality, Carlton took umbrage at some items in the Philadelphia newspapers, and in 1978 he stopped talking to the press altogether. He led the league in strikeouts and wins in 1980, and posted a 2.34 ERA, his best since 1972. In the postseason that year, he was nearly flawless, winning once in the LCS and beating the Royals twice in the WS. In 1982 he topped the NL in wins, strikeouts, and shutouts to earn his fourth Cy Young Award.

Carlton began to show signs of wear in 1983, despite leading the league in strikeouts for the fifth time. He began to have trouble completing and winning his starts, and he lost his role as the Phillies' ace to John Denny. In 1984, at the age of 39, Carlton was 13–7 for a .500 ballclub. But his ERA was up and his strikeout total well down, and he only completed one game. The following year he was only 1–8 after 16 starts before going on the DL. The Phillies asked him to retire in 1986, but Carlton refused and was released. He then broke eight years of silence in the media to voice his reasons and

thank the Philadelphia fans for their support. He finished his career in brief, desperate flings with the Giants, White Sox, Indians, and Twins, but his ERA stayed above 5.00./(SG)

Don Carman — 1959– . LHP 1983–89 **Phillies** 797 ip, 47–50, 4.04

Carman debuted as a reliever, earning a save in his first ML appearance, but was converted to a starter prior to the 1986 All-Star Break, and finished the season 10–5, 3.22. He broke his pitching thumb in a January 1987 auto accident and surrendered a club-record 34 HR the following season while winning a career-high 13 games./(SG)

John P. Carmichael — 1902–1986. *Writer.*

Fresh out of the University of Wisconsin, Carmichael joined the Chicago *Herald Examiner* in 1924 after a brief stint with the Milwaukee *Leader.* Five years later, he started a 43-year stand as columnist ("The Barber Shop") and later sports editor for the Chicago *Daily News.* Known for poking fun rather than malice, near the end of his career he said, "I take pride in the fact that never in my 40 years did I use my column to attack anyone." For many years he and his boss, Lloyd Lewis, jousted in print, Carmichael covering the Cubs and Lewis the White Sox. Carmichael was given the J.G. Taylor Spink Award in 1974./(NLM)

Pat Carney (Doc) — 1876–1953. OF-LHP 1901–04 **Braves** 338 g, .247, 3 hr, 131 rbi; 109 ip, 4–9, 4.69

As the Braves' regular right fielder in 1902, Carney hit .270 with 75 runs, 65 rbi, and 27 stolen bases. His average declined to .240 and then .204, ending his major league career. He sometimes pitched, but was always easy to hit and lacked control. He coached four years at his alma mater, Holy Cross, and later became a physician./(NLM)

Bill Carpenter — Unk.–1952. *Umpire* **NL**, AL 1897, 04, 06–07

Carpenter umpired in the NL as a 23-year-old in 1897, but the bulk of his career, 21 years, was spent in the International League. In 1933 he became chief of staff of the league office, with duties that included umpire supervision and schedule-making. He became so proficient at the latter that other leagues used his services./(RTM)

Bob Carpenter — 1917- . RHP 1940–42, 46–47
Giants, Cubs 399 ip, 25–20, 3.60

As a teenager, Carpenter persuaded his father, whose ill health required him to leave Chicago, to move to Pensacola. There, he knew, Bill Terry ran a baseball school. For $25, Carpenter was taught the curveball and was placed with a minor league team. He worked his way to Terry's Giants, had 11-win seasons in 1941 and 1942, and then spent three years in the military. When he returned, an injury limited his ability to play, and he retired. /(JK)

Cris Carpenter — 1965- . RHP 1988- **Cardinals**
116 ip, 6–7, 3.81

Carpenter signed for a $160,000 bonus after the Cardinals made him their first-round pick in the June 1987 draft. He showed good control but was too hittable. /(SFS)

Charlie Carr — 1876–1932. 1B 1898, 1901, 03–06, 14 Washington (NL), A's, **Tigers**, Indians, Reds, Indianapolis (FL) 507 g, .252, 6 hr, 240 rbi

A journeyman first baseman, Carr made contacts in his travels that were useful later for his successful sporting goods manufacturing business, Bradley & Carr, which supplied baseballs to several minor leagues. /(JK)

George Carr (Tank) — 1895-Unk. 1B-3B-OF-C Negro Leagues 1912–1934 Los Angeles White Sox, Kansas City Monarchs, Hilldale, Bacharach Giants, Philadelphia Stars 227 g, .318, 21 hr (inc.)

Carr was a hard-hitting Negro Leaguer whose surviving statistics show that he batted .339 in 1921, .300 in 1924, and .370 in 1925. He compiled a confirmed batting average of .318 over five documented seasons, and led the league with 23 stolen bases in 1925. He usually played winter ball in California. In one season in Cuba (1926–27), he batted a league-leading .416. He appeared in two Black World Series for Hilldale, hitting .316 in 1924 and .320 in 1925. /(JM)

Alex Carrasquel — 1921-1969. RHP 1939–45, 49 **Senators**, White Sox 861 ip, 50–39, 3.73

One of many fine Latin-American players imported by Washington owner Clark Griffith, Carrasquel had a fine fastball, which complemented well the famed Senator knuckle-ball staffs of the early 1940s. The tall Venezuelan became more of an asset to the Senators as his pitching savvy increased and he moved more into relief roles. All of his decisions came as a Senator and his brief fling with Chicago consisted of three appearances. /(EW)

Chico Carrasquel [Alfonso] — 1928- . SS-3B-2B 1950–59 **White Sox**, Indians, A's, Orioles 1325 g, .258, 55 hr, 474 rbi
☞ All-Star—51, 53–55.

Venezuelan Chico Carrasquel was signed in 1949 by the Dodgers, who then sold him to the White Sox. Carrasquel's inability to speak English may have caused Branch Rickey to move him. White Sox GM Frank Lane solved the communication problem by trading journeyman pitcher Alex Carrasquel—Chico's uncle—for reliever Luis Aloma, who served as the interpreter between Chico and man-

Chico Carrasquel

ager Paul Richards. Replacing Luke Appling, Carrasquel soon established himself as a top shortstop and batted .282 with a 24-game hitting streak as a rookie in 1950. He broke an AL record by accepting 297 chances (in 53 games) without an error in 1951, and beat out reigning MVP Phil Rizzuto as the AL's starting All-Star SS. But Carrasquel had trouble controlling his weight, and in 1952 he was benched for lethargic play. In October 1955 Chicago traded him with Jim Busby to Cleveland for Larry Doby. They had another Venezuelan SS waiting in the minors—Luis Aparicio. Carrasquel became a legend in his native Caracas, serving as play-by-play man on their Game of the Week. /(RL)

Cam Carreon [Camilo] — 1937–1987. C 1959–66 **White Sox**, Indians, Orioles 354 g, .264, 11 hr, 114 rbi

Platooning with J.C. Martin on the White Sox in 1963, Carreon tied Yogi Berra for the best fielding average among AL catchers. He had speed and good defensive skills, but he was unable to take control of a ballgame. As a result, the slow-footed Martin won the job in 1964. A year later, Carreon was traded to Cleveland in a deal that brought Tommy John to Chicago. His son, Mark, was signed by the Mets in 1981 and made his major league debut with them on September 8, 1987, six days after his father's death. /(RL)

Bill Carrick (Doughnut Bill) — 1873–1932. RHP 1898–1902 **Giants**, Senators 1325 ip, 63–89, 4.14

It is often said that a pitcher who loses 20 games in a season must be very good to be allowed to pitch so often. So Bill Carrick must have been a wonder. He lost 26 for the Giants in 1899, 22 in 1900, and 23 for Washington in 1901. /(JK)

Bill Carrigan (Rough) — 1883–1969. C 1906, 08–16 **Red Sox** 706 g, .257, 6 hr, 235 rbi. *3 WS, 4 g, .167, 1 rbi.* *Manager* 1913–16, 27–29 **Red Sox** 489–500, .494. First place: 15–16 *2 WS, 8–2, .800*

Carrigan was a dependable platoon catcher who took over a dissension-torn defending World Champion Red Sox team in 1913 as playing manager. He could not set things right until 1914, when he brought the team home second. In 1915 and 1916, with Babe Ruth added to his pitching rotation, Carrigan led Boston to two World Championships.

Carrigan quit at the peak of his success to become a banker in his native Maine. He made a surprise return as Red Sox manager in 1927, but the results were disastrous. The team finished last three straight seasons. While there was an absence of talent, it was

Bill Carrigan

also evident that the conservative Carrigan was out of his element in the free-swinging, lively-ball era. /(JK)

Don Carrithers — 1949– . RHP 1970–77 Giants, **Expos**, Twins 565 ip, 28–32, 4.46. *1 LCS, 0 ip, infinite*

A likable power pitcher, Carrithers never found consistency on the ML level. He went 9–1 in Phoenix in 1970 but in two-plus seasons with the Giants was 12–14 as a starter and reliever. Traded to Montreal, he split time between the Expos and Triple-A in 1974 and 1975. He appeared in only seven games for the Twins in 1977 after he was injured in a car accident. /(JCA)

Clay Carroll (Hawk) — 1941– . RHP 1964–78 Braves, **Reds**, White Sox, Cardinals, Pirates 1353 ip, 96–73, 2.94. *4 LCS, 12 ip, 2–1, 1.50. 3 WS, 20 ip, 2–1, 1.33*
☛ *All-Star—71–72.*

Carroll was the mainstay of the "Big Red Machine" bullpen. The chunky stopper recorded 88 relief wins and 143 saves, including 37 in 1972, then a single-season record. His performance won him the Fireman of the Year award.

Carroll came up through the Braves farm system and led the NL with 73 appearances in 1966. The good-natured country boy went to Cincinnati in a mid-1968 deal and never had a losing season. He threw mostly fastballs, and also had a variety of effective breaking pitches. Johnny Bench explained, "Clay tells you he can do the job and then he goes out and does it." Carroll appeared in more than 50 games in each of his eight seasons in Cincinnati, and led the NL with nine relief wins in 1970.

The Reds lost the 1970 WS to Baltimore in five games, but Carroll had Cincinnati's only win and appeared in four games without allowing a run. He maintained his WS effectiveness in 1975, winning the seventh game over Boston./(JCA)

Cliff Carroll — 1859–1923. OF 1882–88, 90–93 **Providence (NL)**, Washington (NL), Pirates, Cubs, Cardinals, Braves 991 g, .251, 31 hr, 346 rbi

A first baseman and catcher in the minors, Carroll played all his ML games in the outfield, three times leading NL left fielders in putouts. The Iowan quit baseball in 1889 to be a farmer, but missed the game and returned with Chicago in 1890 to enjoy his finest season, with career highs in three offensive and three defensive categories. His 134 runs scored ranked second in the NL./(FIC)

Ownie Carroll — 1902–1975. RHP 1925, 1927–34 **Tigers**, Yankees, Reds, Dodgers 1331 ip, 65–89, 4.43

A handsome, smiling pitcher, Carroll had a sensational college career at Holy Cross, going 50–2 in three seasons. Doomed to pitch for non-contenders, Carroll never reached ML stardom. He led the 1928 Tigers with a career-high 16 wins, but, in 1932, led the NL with 19 losses for the last-place Reds./(JK)

Tom Carroll — 1952– . RHP 1974–75 **Reds** 125 ip, 8–4, 4.18

Carroll went 3–0 in spot starts for the 1975 World Champion Reds, finishing 4–1 overall./(WOR)

Kid Carsey [Wilfred] — 1870–1960. RHP 1891–99, 1901 Washington (AA), **Phillies**, St. Louis (NL), Cleveland (NL), Washington (NL), Brooklyn (NL) 2222 ip, 116–138, 4.95. 20 wins: 1893, 95
Umpire 1894, 96, 1901 NL

As a 20-year-old rookie in 1891, Kid Carsey started 53 games for Washington, winning 14, but losing 37 to lead the American Association. He had four successive winning years with the Phillies, culminating with a career-best 24–16 in 1895./(AJA)

Gary Carter (The Kid) — 1954– . C 1974– **Expos**, Mets 2008 g, .265, 304 hr, 1,143 rbi. *3 LCS, 18 g, .243, 6 rbi. 1 WS, 7 g, .276, 2 hr, 9 rbi*
☛ *All-Star—75, 79–88. Gold Glove—80–82.*

The premier and most popular catcher of the late 1970s and early 1980s after Johnny Bench retired, Carter was known for his ebullience, durability, clutch hitting (10 career grand slams), and handling of pitchers and balls in the dirt. He was also accused by many of his teammates of being a camera hog and a publicity hound. The gung-ho Carter was an All-American quarterback in high school in California, captain of his baseball, football and basketball teams, and a member of the National Honor Society. He signed a letter of intent to play football at UCLA, but chose baseball after being picked by Montreal in the third round of the 1972 free agent draft. Montreal gradually converted Carter from an outfielder to a catcher with help from Norm Sherry. In 1975 Carter was named *TSN* Rookie of the Year, losing the baseball writers' award to John Montefusco. He missed the first 60 games of the 1976 season after running into a wall in spring training chasing a long line drive. He became a full-time catcher in 1977 and, on April 20, hit homers in three consecutive at-bats. Known equally for his defensive skills, Carter set a record for fewest passed balls in 150 or more games, with just one. Between 1977 and 1982, he led the NL in most chances six times, in putouts five times, assists four times, and double plays three times. The Expos of those years were filled with talent, and were always expected to win the pennant but never did. In 1979 Carter tore ligaments in his thumb in the final week of the season as the Pirates overtook the Expos. He hit .360 in 1980 and drove in 22 runs in September, but Mike Schmidt's homer in the 11th inning on the last day of the season gave the Phillies the NL flag. Carter won 1981 All-Star Game MVP honors on the strength of two homers. He had a career-high 106 RBI in 1984 to lead the league, and again won

Gary Carter

MVP honors in the 1984 All-Star Game with another homer. In that game, he caught Dwight Gooden for the first time. He caught Gooden on a regular basis the following year after being swapped for four players to the Mets. On Opening Day 1985, he hit a grand slam to win the game. On September 3, 1985, he had three consecutive homers in a game, and he finished the season with 18 game-winning RBI. After two seasons of 100-plus RBI, in 1986 his 105 RBI (tying the team record) led the Mets to the World Series. Carter contributed a single in the two-out, 10th inning rally in the sixth game of the 1986 World Series against the Red Sox, won by the Mets. His production started to fall off after the championship. He began the 1988 season by hitting eight homers in April to give him 299 homers, then went more than 230 at-bats before hitting number 300 in August in Chicago. In 1989 he hit below .200 before going down with a knee injury in May. After returning to action, he was relegated to backup duty and then released after the season. /(SEW)

Joe Carter — 1960– . OF-1B 1983– Cubs, **Indians** 862 g, .268, 151 hr, 531 rbi
☛ *Led League—rbi 86.*

Wichita State's Joe Carter was *TSN*'s 1981 College Player of the Year; the Cubs, choosing second, made him their number-one draft pick that June. He played briefly in Chicago before going to Cleveland in a major seven-player deal for Rick Sutcliffe in June 1984. A disappointment at first, he struggled with injuries until 1986, when he burst forth with a .302 average, 29 homers, and a ML-leading 121 RBI. Blessed with one of the best physiques in baseball, he missed the 30–30 club by one HR and one stolen base in having the best offensive year by an Indian in decades. He did reach 30–30 in 1987, overcoming a salary dispute in spring training and constant shifting between the outfield and first base. Carter defeated incumbent Brett Butler to become the Indians' player representative, and took over centerfield when Butler signed with the Giants for 1988. /(ME)

Paul Carter (Nick) — 1894–1984. LHP 1914–20 Indians, **Cubs** 480 ip, 21–25, 3.32

Carter spent most of his seven ML seasons in the bullpen, where his antics and capers entertained the fans. He insisted his nickname (Nick) came from his "cutting up" on the field. He was 4–1 for the pennant-winning Cubs in 1918 until he was sidelined by illness and forced to miss the World Series. /(BC)

Alexander Cartwright — 1820–1892. *Executive.*
☛ *Hall of Fame—1938.*

One spring day in 1845, New York bank teller Alexander Cartwright suggested to his ballplaying companions that they organize formally into a club. From that humble start grew America's national game. Versions of baseball had been played long before; varieties of the children's game known in England as "rounders" and in America as "base ball" or "town ball" were popular throughout the northeastern states. But when the Knickerbocker Base Ball Club organized that September, Cartwright and his friends transformed the children's game into an adult sport, chiefly by three innovations still in effect today.

First, they increased the distance between bases to an adult-length 90 feet. This was 50% to more than 100% longer than in earlier versions. Second, they brought the game an adult sense of order by dividing the field into fair and foul territory, narrowing the

Alexander Cartwright

hitter's range to the space between the foul lines, and reducing the number of defensive players needed. The number of players wasn't specified in the first rules, but by 1846 the club was playing with nine to a side, and that was later made official. And third, Knickerbocker rules forbade the practice, permitted in earlier versions, of putting out baserunners by throwing the ball at them. This change not only brought dignity to baseball but also made it safe to use a harder ball, which led to faster, sharper play.

This "manly" version of baseball quickly took hold throughout metropolitan New York, and by 1860 was established as far afield as New Orleans and San Francisco. Cartwright himself helped spread the game. In 1849 he left New York to seek gold in California, traveling overland with his baseball and Knickerbocker rules, teaching the game along the way. In California he was taken ill with dysentery and abandoned thoughts of gold for the healthful climate of Hawaii. There he introduced baseball in 1852, even before it had taken hold in Philadelphia.

Cartwright became one of Honolulu's leading merchants and bankers, founded its library and fire department (he was fire chief for ten years), and managed the finances of Hawaii's royal family. Although he died one of Hawaii's most respected citizens, his contribution to baseball was all but forgotten until 1938, when a review of his journals prompted his election to the Hall of Fame. /(FIC)

Rico Carty — 1941- . OF-DH 1963-67, 1969-70, 1972-79 **Braves**, Rangers, Cubs, A's, Indians, Blue Jays 1651 g, .299, 204 hr, 890 rbi. *1 LCS, 3 g, .300* ☛ *Led League—ba 70. All-Star—70.*

High on any list of the great natural hitters, the powerful Dominican called himself "the Big Boy." In 1960, as a naive youngster, he signed ten pro contracts. When the mess was straightened out, he became the property of the Milwaukee Braves, who converted the slow-footed catcher into a poor out-fielder. As a rookie in 1964 he hit .330, losing both the batting crown race (to Roberto Clemente) and the Rookie of the Year award (to Richie Allen). Tuberculosis sidelined him for the entire 1968 season; he spent five months in a sanitarium. Incredibly, he returned to hit .342 in 1969, despite seven shoulder dislocations. His .366 in 1970 (highest ML average since Ted Williams hit .388 in 1957) led the NL, and he started on the All-Star team as a write-in candidate. He broke his knee in a winter ball collision, costing him the 1971 season, and nearly his career. He was with three teams in 1973 and was playing in Mexico when the Indians signed him as a DH for 1974. His 31 home runs in 1978, with Toronto and Oakland, were a career high. /(JCA)

Bob Caruthers (Parisian Bob) — 1864-1911. OF-RHP 1884-93 **St. Louis (AA)**, Brooklyn (AA)/Dodgers, Cardinals, Cubs, Reds 705 g, .282, 29 hr, 213 rbi (inc.); 2829 ip, 218-97, 2.83. 20 wins: 85-90 ☛ *Led League—w 85, 89. Led League—era 85.*

Caruthers is among the all-time leaders in winning percentage at .692. He won 40 games twice, posting league-leading marks of 40-13 (1885) and 40-11 (1889) while pacing his teams to pennants. He pitched a four-hitter in his September 1884 major league debut with the St. Louis Browns of the American Association. Considered a heady pitcher who figured out batters' weaknesses, he helped the team to three straight pennants. He earned his nickname when he traveled to France after the 1885 season and engaged in a trans-Atlantic salary battle, settling for the then-huge sum of $3,200.

Caruthers also became a good hitter, and in 1887 he had an amazing season. Playing 54 games in the outfield and 7 at first base in addition to his 39 pitching appearances, he overcame malaria to hit .357 (fifth in the AA) and slug .547 (second) with eight HR (tied for fourth) and 59 stolen bases. He also went 29–9 as a pitcher and won four of St. Louis's five postseason victories in a traveling 15-game series. Despite all this, eccentric owner Chris von der Ahe sold him to the Brooklyn Bridegrooms of the AA after the season for $8,250. Von der Ahe blamed carousing and card playing for his team's defeat in the series, and Caruthers, an expert billiards and poker player, was just one of several scapegoats sold off.

Signing for a $5,000 salary that made him the highest-paid player in the AA, Caruthers earned it by helping the theretofore pathetic Bridegrooms to second place. In 1889, playing only five games elsewhere than the pitching box, his 40–11 season gave Brooklyn its first pennant.

Caruthers was the fourth pitcher in ML history to homer twice in one game, on August 16, 1886; in the same game, he got a triple and a double, to become the third pitcher with four extra-base hits in a game. He lost 11–9 when he was tagged out in the ninth inning trying to stretch his triple into a third HR. In 1893, when the pitching distance was moved back to 60′6″ from the former 50′, he had a sore arm and only played outfield. It was his last major league season, although he played until 1898 in the minors. /(SFS)

Chuck Cary — 1960– . LHP 1985– **Tigers**, Braves, Yankees 180 ip, 6–8, 3.51

Cary was a fair reliever until a 1988 injury cost him most of the season. He came back in 1989 with the pitching-poor Yankees after being released by the Braves. /(WOR)

Jerry Casale — 1933– . RHP 1958–62 **Red Sox**, Angels, Tigers 370 ip, 17–24, 5.08

The Brooklynite was 13–8 as a Boston rookie in 1959 but never won more than two in any other season. A decent hitter, Casale teamed with Don Buddin and Pumpsie Green to hit three consecutive homers on September 7, 1959. /(JCA)

Paul Casanova — 1941– . C 1965–74 **Senators**, Braves 859 g, .225, 50 hr, 252 rbi
☛ *All-Star—67.*

The rangy, cat-like Cuban refugee was named *TSN* AL all-star catcher as a Senators rookie in 1966. An enthusiastic, fun-loving spendthrift, he had a rifle arm and led AL catchers in double plays three times, but his hitting tailed off after his first two seasons. He caught all 22 innings and drove in the winning run against the White Sox in the longest night game in AL history (6/12/67). /(JCA)

Joe Cascarella (Crooning Joe) — 1907– . RHP 1934–38 **A's**, Red Sox, Senators, Reds 541 ip, 27–48, 4.84

In his rookie year with his hometown Philadelphia A's, he led the AL with seven relief wins, and was chosen for the all-star team which toured the Orient after the season. His fine tenor voice and a winning personality made him a popular figure on radio shows and in nightclubs. "Crooning Joe" later became operational vice president of Laurel Race Track. /(JK)

Charlie Case — 1879–1964. RHP 1901, 04–06 Reds, **Pirates** 396 ip, 24–18, 2.93

The Ohio native was the youngest member of Pittsburgh's pitching rotation in 1904–05. Case's .667 winning percentage (10–5) was second on the club in 1904. /(ME)

George Case — 1915– . OF 1937–47 **Senators**, Indians 1226 g, .282, 21 hr, 377 rbi
☛ *All-Star—39, 43–44.*

George Case is remembered as one of the greatest basestealers of all time, although his career was abbreviated by injuries. The Washington outfielder set a record by leading the ML in stolen bases five straight seasons (1939–43), and led again in 1945. Case's 61 stolen bases in 1943 was the highest ML single-season total in the period 1921–61. A three-time .300 hitter, Case scored an AL-leading 102 runs in 1943; that year, he was the AL's starting right fielder in the first night All-Star Game. In Bill Veeck's first ML promotion, Case raced Jesse Owens and lost. Case worked as a coach in the Mariner farm system. /(TJ)

Doc Casey [James Peter] — 1870–1936. 3B 1898–1907 Washington (NL), Dodgers, Tigers, **Cubs** 1114 g, .258, 9 hr, 354 rbi

Nap Lajoie credited Doc Casey for bringing him into pro ball. Lajoie, a Providence hack driver, was dubious about playing professionally until he saw the 5′6″ Casey catching for Pawtucket (New England League). Casey switched to third base, averaging 135 ML games a season from 1901 through 1907. He became a dentist and ran a Detroit drug store. /(JK)

Hugh Casey — 1913–1951. RHP 1935, 39–42, 46–49
Cubs, **Dodgers**, Pirates, Yankees 940 ip, 75–42, 3.45.
2 WS, 16 ip, 2–2, 1.72

Hugh Casey was on the mound in the ninth inning
of Game Four of the 1941 Yankee-Dodger World
Series. Brooklyn led, 4–3, with two out, nobody on,
and Tommy Henrich at bat. Henrich swung and
missed Casey's 3–2 pitch, but the third strike eluded
catcher Mickey Owen, and Henrich reached base,
beginning a game-winning rally. Owen became a
famous goat, and baseball historians since have
differed as to whether the elusive pitch was a
spitball.

Casey, who relieved in 287 of his 343 games, led
the NL in saves twice and relief wins three times. A
loner, a tough competitor, and a heavy drinker,
Casey became friends with Ernest Hemingway. At
Hemingway's house during spring training in Cuba,
the drunken pair once put on boxing gloves. Teammate Kirby Higbe later recalled, "Ernest would belt
Case one, and down he would go. Case would belt
old Ernest, and down he would go . . . The furniture
[really took] a beating." At age 37, allegedly despon-
dent over the breakup of his marriage, Casey committed suicide. /(TJ)

Dave Cash — 1948– . 2B 1969–80 Pirates, **Phillies**,
Expos, Padres 1422 g, .283, 21 hr, 426 rbi. *4 LCS, 14 g,
.288, 5 rbi. 1 WS, 7 g, .133, 1 rbi*
☛ *All-Star—74–76.*

The articulate Cash was an underrated second
baseman who hit .300 four times and set a number
of records, some significant and some trivial. His
lifetime .984 fielding average is the NL record for
second basemen.

Cash's career started slowly. In 1970 he hit .314
and showed fine range when filling in for aging All-
Star Bill Mazeroski. However, Cash's 1970–72
seasons were interrupted each July for two weeks of
military duty. Mazeroski didn't retire until after
1972, and Rennie Stennett appeared on the scene in
1971. Cash never became an everyday player with
Pittsburgh, although he averaged almost 450 at-bats
a year from 1971 to 1973 by occasionally playing
third base. His best moments with the Pirates were
in the 1971 LCS, when he hit .421, set a LCS record
with eight hits in a four-game series (his 19 at-bats
tied the record), and scored five runs, including the
series clincher in Game Four.

Finally, in October 1973 (with Willie Randolph
coming up through the farm system to compete with
Stennett and Cash), the Pirates traded Cash to the
Phillies for veteran pitcher Ken Brett. Cash played
in all the Phillies' games in 1974 and 1975 and
missed only two games in 1976. He set a since-
broken ML record of 699 at-bats in 1975, and set a
still-standing ML record for most at-bats with no
sacrifice hits. He also tied the ML record with three
consecutive seasons leading the majors in at-bats,
and set the NL record for consecutive games at
second base (443).

Cash not only played every day, he played well,
making the All-Star team each year. He hit .300 in
1974, scored 89 runs, stole 20 bases, and drove in a
career-high 58; in 1975 he upped his BA to .305
while leading the league with 213 hits, finishing
second in the NL with 40 doubles and a career-high
111 runs (only one behind Pete Rose). Although his
numbers fell off a bit in 1976 (.284, 92 runs), his 12
triples led the league, and he struck out only 13
times in 666 at-bats. To close out the year, he hit
.308 in the LCS while the Phillies were being swept
by the Reds. His weakness as a leadoff hitter was his
failure to walk more often, but he was nonetheless
one of the premier second basemen in the game. He
led NL second basemen in assists and double plays
in 1974, in putouts and double plays in 1975, and in
fielding average and double plays in 1976.

After the 1976 season, Cash declared free agency
and signed with the Expos. He maintained his level
of play in 1977, finishing second in assists and
batting .289 with 42 doubles (second in the NL), 91
runs, and a career-high 21 steals. But although his
defense remained strong in 1978, as he again led the
NL in putouts and fielding, his hitting declined
(.252, 66 runs). Manager Dick Williams replaced
Cash with Rodney Scott in 1979 despite the protests
of some players and the front office. Scott hit .238 to
Cash's part-time .321 that year, and although Scott
stole 39 bases and led the NL in total chances per
game, he was weak on the double play and scored
only 69 runs in 151 games. Williams's dismissal
during the 1981 season was ascribed by some to bad
feelings dating back to this controversy. Meanwhile,
Cash adjusted by becoming a valuable pinch hitter
(10-for-30). That November, Cash was traded to the
Padres for Bill Almon and Dan Briggs. He finished
his career with a disappointing .227 average for the
last-place Padres. After retirement he became the
Phillies' minor league fielding coach. /(SH)

Norm Cash — 1934–1986. 1B-OF 1958–74 White Sox, **Tigers** 2089 g, .271, 377 hr, 1103 rbi. *1 LCS, 5 g, .267, 1 hr, 2 rbi. 2 WS, 11 g, .333, 1 hr, 5 rbi* ☛ *Led League—ba 61. All-Star—61, 66, 71–72.*

Norm Cash had the greatest season of his career in 1961, but it was completely overshadowed by Roger Maris's 61 HR. Cash led the AL with 193 hits and a .361 batting average, 37 points ahead of the runner-up, teammate Al Kaline (they were only the eighth pair of AL teammates to finish one-two in a batting race). Only 12 players have topped his .488 on-base percentage that year, and none since. He had 132 RBI (fourth in the AL), 41 HR (sixth), eight triples (fourth), 119 runs (fourth), 11 stolen bases, 124 walks (second), a .662 slugging percentage (second, ahead of Maris), and 354 total bases (second). He finished fourth in the MVP voting, behind Maris, Mickey Mantle, and Jim Gentile.

Ironically, the season that was overlooked at the time was the apex of his career. All the performances cited were career highs. He dropped to .243 in 1962 and the 118-point drop is a record for a batting champ. Even on his own team, he was overshadowed by his roommate, Al Kaline. But although he never hit above .283 for the rest of his career, he was consistently one of the best first basemen in the majors. He hit 30 or more homers five times and 20 or more eleven times, including nine straight years (1961–69), and twice led the league in HR percentage (1965, 1971). He won *TSN* Comeback Player of the Year honors in 1965, finishing second in the AL in HR (30) and third in slugging (.512), then won the award again in 1971 when he hit 32 HR and slugged .531.

Cash never went on the DL, although some years he missed 20–40 games with minor injuries. His batting averages were actually well above average in the pitching-dominated late 1960s, and he walked frequently. Cash was a good fielder and at various times led the AL in putouts (1961), fielding average (1964, 1967), and assists (tied 1965, led 1966–67).

Cash was drafted in the 13th round by the NFL's Chicago Bears but he opted for baseball, beginning his career as an outfielder in the White Sox system. After missing 1957 for military service he made it to the majors briefly in 1958. He converted to first base and spent all of 1959 in the majors, although he played just 58 games in Chicago's AL championship season. In the off-season he was sent to Cleveland in the deal that brought Minnie Minoso back to Chicago, and then was picked up by Detroit in the most lopsided deal in their history: he was traded straight up for third baseman Steve Demeter, who had just five more at-bats in his ML career.

The genial, self-deprecating slugger tied two offbeat records. On June 27, 1963, he had no fielding chances at first base. And in the third inning of Game Six of the 1968 World Series, he had two hits as the Tigers scored 10 runs. He batted .385 for the Series, with five RBI and five runs, and hit a homer in Game Two. He also started the Series-winning rally in Game Seven with a two-out, seventh-inning single, and scored the first run of the game on Jim Northrup's triple. In the 1972 LCS,

Norm Cash after becoming Bob Gibson's record 16th strikeout victim in Game One of the 1968 World Series

Cash was part of the Tigers' "Over the Hill Gang". He homered in Game One in a losing cause and drove in the tying run of Game Four with a 10th-inning walk as the Tigers came from behind to force a fifth game.

Cash's 375 HR as a first baseman rank third in the AL, and his 377 HR overall were 30th all-time at the end of the 1980s. He and Kaline combined to hit 647 HR as teammates, the fourth-best AL total and eighth-best overall. His total of 317 hits and walks in 1961 is the 23rd-best in ML history; only seven people have bettered it, and only Wade Boggs has done it since Cash. He is seventh in lifetime assists among first basemen (1317) despite not being in the top ten in games at first base. Cash drowned in 1986 when he slipped on a boat, fell, and struck his head./(SH)

Joe Cashman — Unk.–Unk. *Writer.*

Cashman retired in 1970 after 53 years with the Boston *Record-American.* He was president of the BBWAA in 1953 and chairman of its Boston chapter for 22 years./(NLM)

Joe Cassidy — 1883–1906. SS-OF-3B 1904–05 **Senators** 303 g, .228, 2 hr, 76 rbi

A flashy fielder with cat-like agility, Cassidy was one of the first to play in the majors with no minor league experience. His 19 triples for the 1904 Senators tied him for the league lead and set a still-standing rookie record. He led AL shortstops with 520 assists and 66 errors in 1905, and was considered a top young shortstop when he died of malaria in the spring of 1906./(NLM)

George Caster — 1907–1955. RHP 1934–35, 37–46 **A's**, Browns, Tigers 1376 ip, 76–100, 4.54. *1 WS, 2/3 ip, 0–0, 0.00*

As a knuckleball starter for Connie Mack's hapless A's, Caster lost 19 games in 1937 and led the AL in losses in 1938 (20) and 1940 (19). Waived to the Browns after the 1940 season, he became an effective reliever, leading the AL in saves (12) in 1944 when the Browns won their only pennant./(NLM)

Pete Castiglione — 1921– . 3B-SS 1947–54 **Pirates**, Cardinals 545 g, .255, 24 hr, 150 rbi

In 1949, his first of two seasons as the Pirates' regular third baseman, he batted a career-high .268. The capable pinch hitter averaged .296 (16-for-54) lifetime in that role./(TJ)

Bob Castillo (Bobo) — 1955– . RHP 1977–85 **Dodgers**, Twins 688 ip, 38–40, 3.95. *2 LCS, 6 ip, 0–0, 2.84. 1 WS, 1 ip, 0–0, 9.00*

The Dodgers hoped Castillo, a three-time all-city player at Los Angeles's Lincoln High, would be their first star of Mexican origin. He wasn't. But he taught the screwball to Fernando Valenzuela, who was. In 1983, starting for Minnesota, he was 13–11 and voted Twins' Pitcher of the Year./(TG)

Carmen Castillo — 1958– . OF-DH 1982- **Indians**, Twins 558 g, .256, 55 hr, 185 rbi

Castillo, a fastball hitter, showed good power (11 HR in 184 at-bats in 1985), but could not win a regular job./(SFS)

Juan Castillo — 1962– . 2B-SS-3B 1986- **Brewers** 199 g, .215, 3 hr, 38 rbi

Another of the many middle infielders from San Pedro de Macoris in the Dominican Republic, Castillo is a fine fielder but has yet to hit consistently in the majors./(JFC)

Manny Castillo — 1957– . 3B 1980, 82–83 Royals, **Mariners** 236 g, .242, 3 hr, 73 rbi

The versatile Dominican was playing in the Mets organization at 16. In his ninth minor league season he hit .335 to earn a ML chance. As the Mariner third baseman in 1982, he set four team rookie records, hitting 29 doubles and striking out only 35 times in 506 at-bats./(JCA)

Marty Castillo — 1957– . 3B-C 1981–85 **Tigers** 201 g, .190, 8 hr, 32 rbi. *1 LCS, 3 g, .250, 2 rbi. 1 WS, 3 g, .333, 1 hr, 2 rbi*

A utility man for three complete seasons with the Tigers, Castillo hit his first ML homer to beat the Brewers in the ninth inning (6/28/83). His career highlight was a game-winning two-run homer in Game Three of the 1984 World Series./(MC)

John Castino — 1954– . 3B-2B-SS 1979–84 **Twins** 666 g, .278, 41 hr, 249 rbi
☛ *Rookie of the Year—79.*

Castino shared Rookie of the Year honors with Alfredo Griffin in 1979 when he hit .285 as the Twins' third baseman. He had career highs (.302, 13 HR, 64 RBI) the next season and led the AL in triples in 1981. Switched to second base in 1982 after the arrival of Gary Gaetti, Castino was hobbled by chronic back pain. A fused disc ended his career early in 1984./(MC)

Foster Castleman — 1931– . 3B-SS 1954–58 **Giants**, Orioles 268 g, .205, 20 hr, 65 rbi

Slick-fielding Castleman was the Giants' third baseman in 1956 and cracked 14 home runs, but his .226 batting average put him back on the bench the next year. Waived to the Orioles, he was handed the shortstop job in 1958, but his weak bat (.170) kept him from keeping it; Willie Miranda took it away by hitting .200. /(MC)

Slick Castleman [Clydell] — 1913– . RHP 1934–39 **Giants** 587 ip, 36–26, 4.25. *1 WS, 4 ip, 2.08*

Neat and well-groomed, "Slick" went 4–7 and 11–6 for the 1936–37 pennant-winning Giants. A 1937 arm injury shortened his career. /(JK)

Bill Castro [Williams Radhames] (Checo, Bills) — 1953– . RHP 1974–83 **Brewers**, Yankees, Royals 545 ip, 31–26, 3.33

The Dominican was an effective member of Milwaukee's bullpen for six years, beginning in 1975 when he led the Brewers staff with a 2.52 ERA. He specialized in getting the double-play ball and seldom allowed a home run. He left Milwaukee as a free agent in 1981 with a career 2.96 ERA. /(JCA)

Fidel Castro — 1926–

Castro was a star pitcher at Belen College and the University of Havana in Cuba and attracted the attention of several ML scouts with his wicked curveball. He turned down a $5,000 bonus from the Giants to pursue his law degree, and after graduating became a leader of Cuba's revolutionary movement. Although he never actually pitched in winter ball as is often claimed, he did once pitch to Don Hoak briefly during a game before being ejected from the ballpark. /(SCL)

Danny Cater — 1940– . 1B-OF-3B 1964–75 Phillies, White Sox, **A's**, Yankees, Red Sox, Cardinals 1289 g, .276, 66 hr, 519 rbi

The strong, silent Texan signed as a shortstop with the Phillies, but played first, third, and the outfield in his 12-year ML career. He had an unusual batting stance, with his feet close together, and a smooth, lazy-looking swing. Some thought him lackadaisical; he felt his low-key style was responsible for his being traded five times. One of baseball's great worriers, teammates said Cater could quote all his stats after each at-bat.

As Oakland's regular first baseman in 1968, he hit .290 to finish second to Carl Yastrzemski's .301

in an anemic AL batting race. Traded to the Yankees, he hit .301 in 1970 but had only 10 homers in two seasons, and he was shipped to Boston in 1972 for reliever Sparky Lyle. Lyle became a three-time All-Star; Cater hit an abysmal .237 that year. He rebounded in 1973 to hit .313 in 63 games. /(JCA)

Buster Caton [James Howard] — 1896–1948. SS 1917–20 **Pirates** 231 g, .226, 0 hr, 53 rbi

The 5'6" 165-lb Caton was one of several shortstops to bridge the gap between Honus Wagner and Rabbit Maranville in Pittsburgh. A WWI veteran, Caton was later a Dodger scout. /(ME)

Bill Caudill — 1956– . RHP 1979–87 **Cubs**, Mariners, A's, Blue Jays 667 ip, 35–52, 3.68
☛ *All-Star—84.*

Caudill was a fireballing reliever who saved 106 games while demonstrating pitching proficiency and a wonderful sense of fun. He was nicknamed "The Inspector" by his Mariners teammates when he "investigated" their bats, sleuthing for hits that were mysteriously missing. Caudill would come in from the bullpen to the Pink Panther theme. During a one-sided game against the Blue Jays, Caudill emerged from the dugout between innings with one-half of his beard shaved off. After setting franchise records for saves, Caudill was traded to a stronger Oakland team, where he had a 36-save season in 1984. Toronto traded Alfredo Griffin and Dave Collins for Caudill and signed him to a hefty long-term contract with the expectation that he would be Toronto's first genuine bullpen ace. But because Caudill's arrival in Toronto conicided with the sudden emergence of Tom Henke, he didn't get much opportunity to establish himself as a closer. He had shoulder problems that ended his career after a couple of seasons with the Blue Jays. His attempts to catch on with the A's and Indians were unsuccessful. /(TF)

Red Causey [Cecil Algernon] — 1893–1960. RHP 1918–22 **Giants**, Braves, Phillies 650 ip, 39–35, 3.59

The 6'1" 160-lb Causey had two stints with the Giants. Sent to Boston in a 1919 trade for Art Nehf, he was back for the Giants' championships in 1921 and 1922. /(JK)

Wayne Causey — 1936– . SS-2B-3B 1955–57, 61–68 Orioles, **A's**, White Sox, Angels, Braves 1105 g, .252, 35 hr, 285 rbi

Causey was a hard-playing, steady infielder who kept losing jobs to hotshot rookies. He was supposed to have been one himself. Signed for a $50,000 bonus in 1955, contemporary rules regarding "bonus babies" required his presence on the Baltimore roster until June 1957. After three years in the minors, he was traded to Kansas City in 1961 but lost his shot at shortstop to rookie Dick Howser. In mid-season he won the third base position, but injured his shoulder early in 1962. When he was ready to play again, Ed Charles had taken over at third base.

Causey's best years came in 1963–64, when he was finally the A's starting shortstop and led the team in hitting with .280 and .281 marks. But in spring 1965, by then the team captain, he dislocated his shoulder, opening the position for young Bert Campaneris. Causey was shipped to Chicago in May 1966, where he mostly played second base. /(JCA)

Phil Cavarretta — 1916– . 1B-OF 1934–55 **Cubs**, White Sox 2030 g, .293, 95 hr, 920 rbi. *3 WS, 17 g, .317, 1 hr, 5 rbi.*
   *Manager 1951–53 **Cubs** 169–213, .442*
☛ *Most Valuable Player—45 . All-Star—44, 46, 47.*

Cavarretta played 20 consecutive seasons with the Cubs. A lefthanded schoolboy pitcher for Lane Tech in Chicago, he signed a contract with Peoria (Central League) before he finished high school. He hit for the cycle as a right fielder in his first pro game in 1934. Brought up by the Cubs that September, he struck out as a pinch hitter in his debut, but homered in his first start for the only run of the game. He became the everyday first baseman for the 1935 NL champions as an 18-year-old.

In a May 1939 game against the Giants, Cavarretta broke an ankle sliding; 13 months later he repeated the same injury, also against New York. Exempt from military service because of an ear problem, he peaked during WWII. His 197 hits in 1944 tied with Stan Musial for the NL lead. In that year's All-Star Game, he reached base a record five times. He was the 1945 NL batting champion (.355), helping the Cubs to the pennant and winning MVP honors. He led all hitters in the 1945 WS with a .423 average (11 for 26).

Cavarretta was the Cubs' player-manager in 1951–53, and led the NL with 12 pinch hits in '51. Fired in spring training of 1954 because owner Phil

Wrigley bridled at Cavarretta's prediction of a second-division finish, he finished his playing career with the White Sox. He managed extensively in the minors, coached and scouted for the Tigers, and became an excellent batting instructor for the Mets' organization. /(NLM)

Ike Caveney (James) 1894–1949. SS 1922–25 **Reds** 466 g, .260, 13 hr, 196 rbi

Caveney was a Reds shortstop for four seasons in the 1920s. Later, as manager of the San Francisco Seals of the Pacific Coast League, he switched a young shortstop named Joe DiMaggio to the outfield. /(NLM)

O.P. Caylor — Unk.–Unk. *Writer.*

In 1880 Caylor organized the Cincinnati Reds and played a series against Spink's St. Louis Browns, a series that begat the American Association. A sedate, dignified man, not close to the players, he was baseball editor of the Cincinnati *Enquirer* for 20 years. Even though he was part owner and manager of the New York Mets, he was barred from the 1887 American Association meeting because he was also a writer. /(NLM)

Art Ceccarelli (Chic) — 1930– . LHP 1955–57, 59–60 **A's**, Orioles, Cubs 307 ip, 9–18, 5.05

Ceccarelli's best season was 1959, when he went 5–5 and threw two shutouts for the Cubs. /(TJ)

Cesar Cedeno — 1951– . OF-1B 1970–86 **Astros**, Reds, Cardinals, Dodgers 2006 g, .285, 199 hr, 976 rbi. *2 LCS, 8 g, .174, 1 rbi. 1 WS, 5 g, .133, 1 rbi*
☛ *All-Star—72–74, 76. Gold Glove—72–76.*

Cedeno's fine career pales only against the fact that he was billed by Astros manager Leo Durocher as "the next Willie Mays" (while the Cubs' manager, Durocher had similarly touted Adolfo Phillips). The comparisons to Mays were inevitable. Cedeno led the NL in doubles twice, stole over 50 bases six times, batted .320 twice, hit for the cycle twice, and won five Gold Glove awards. But for all he accomplished, he never came up to the "another Mays" prediction. He made something of a comeback in 1980 (.309, 10 HR, 73 RBI), helping Houston win its first division title and earning his fourth selection to *TSN*'s NL All-Star Team. Traded to the Reds after the 1981 season, he improved his play after he took a stress-relief course during the winter of 1983–84. On August 29, 1985, he was traded to the Cardinals, who were seeking a replacement for injured Jack Clark. He helped push St. Louis to the

Cesar Cedeno

home runs, 105 RBI, and .317. In 1961 he moved to first base, trading positions with Willie McCovey, and led the NL in home runs with 46 and RBI with 146, becoming more popular in San Francisco than teammate Willie Mays. Cepeda wrecked his knee in 1965, and was accused of malingering. Ultimately, he was traded to the Cardinals for Ray Sadecki. The 6′2″ 210-lb slugger led St. Louis to a pennant in 1967, topping the NL with 111 RBI and batting .325. Cepeda was nicknamed "The Baby Bull" after his father, "The Bull," an outstanding slugger sometimes called "The Babe Ruth of Puerto Rico." After his retirement as a player Cepeda served time in prison for marijuana smuggling. He admitted his guilt and served his time, but it is likely that the incident is a factor in his failure to gain election to the Hall of Fame. /(TJ)

Orlando Cepeda

pennant with a remarkable stretch drive: .434, 6 HR, 19 RBI in 28 games. However, after playing poorly in the postseason, he was released. /(ME)

Orlando Cepeda (The Baby Bull) — 1937– . 1B-OF
Giants, Cardinals, Braves, A's, Red Sox, Royals 1958–74
2124 g, .297, 379 hr, 1365 rbi. *1 LCS, 3 g, .455, 1 hr, 3 rbi.*
3 WS, 19 g, .171, 2 hr, 9 rbi
☛ *Rookie of the Year—58. Most Valuable Player—67.*
Led League—hr 61, rbi 61, 67. All-Star—1959–64, 67.

In his first ML game, the Giants' first regular-season game in San Francisco, Cepeda homered to help beat Don Drysdale and the Dodgers. It was a fitting beginning to a spectacular career that included nine .300 seasons and eight seasons with 25 or more homers. Bill Rigney, his manager for his first two ML seasons, called him "the best young righthanded power hitter I'd seen." He won Rookie of the Year honors in 1958 when he belted 25 homers, led the NL with 38 doubles, knocked in 96 runs, and batted .312. As a sophomore, he upped his figures to 27

Rick Cerone — 1954– . C 1975– Indians, Blue Jays, **Yankees**, Braves, Brewers, Red Sox 1257 g, .241, 54 hr, 402 rbi. *2 LCS, 6 g, .227, 1 hr, 2 rbi. 1 WS, 6 g, .190, 1 hr, 3 rbi*

Always a crowd favorite in New York, Cerone, a New Jersey native, was able to play near home when the Yankees acquired him from the Blue Jays after 1979. Cerone's finest season was 1980, when he finished seventh in AL MVP voting and had career highs in batting average (.277), home runs (14), and RBI (85).

Cerone earned the respect of his teammates by talking back to Yankees owner George Steinbrenner after the boss chewed out his team before the decisive Game 5 of the 1981 Divisional Playoffs. Cerone homered in that game, a 7–3 Yankees win.

Injuries hampered Cerone in 1982–84, and he was traded to Atlanta, where he played a year before being traded to Milwaukee. The Yankees signed him as a free agent before 1987, and he played in over 100 games for the first time since 1981. Twice he pitched, allowing no hits and only one walk in two innings, including a strikeout of Texas pitcher Bobby Witt, who was pinch hitting in a blowout. Let go by the Yankees in 1987, Cerone was picked up by the Red Sox and had renewed success sharing catching duties with Rich Gedman. /(EG)

John Cerutti — 1960– . LHP 1985– **Blue Jays** 632 ip, 37–28, 3.67

Cerutti was shuttled back and forth between the Blue Jay bullpen and starting rotation in his first several seasons. While he never showed overpowering stuff, he was effective when he overcame a tendency to allow home runs. On July 2, 1986, Cerutti threw a club-record four wild pitches against Boston. /(TF)

Bob Cerv — 1926– . OF 1951–62 Yankees, **A's**, Angels, Astros 829 g, .276, 105 hr, 374 rbi. *3 WS, 10 g, .258, 1 hr, 1 rbi*
☛ *All-Star—58.*

Cerv was sitting in the Yankee dugout one day in mid-1956 when manager Casey Stengel walked over and told him Enos Slaughter had been acquired from the A's. Casey said, "Nobody knows this, but one of us has been traded to Kansas City." Cerv looked around; he was the only player there. He had spent most of his first five years on the Yankee bench, but briefly became a star after going to the A's. In 1958 Cerv blasted 38 homers and was chosen over Ted Williams as the AL All-Star left fielder in the year of the Boston star's last batting

championship. He played a month of that season with his broken jaw wired shut. The Yanks reacquired Cerv in 1960 and, after the Angels claimed him in the expansion draft, traded for him again in 1961. /(JCA)

Ron Cey (Penguin) — 1948– . 3B 1971–87 **Dodgers**, Cubs, A's 2073 g, .261, 316 hr, 1139 rbi. *5 LCS, 22 g, .268, 4 hr, 14 rbi. 4 WS, 23 g, .253, 3 hr, 13 rbi* ☛ *All-Star—74–79.*

Cey filled a traditional trouble spot when he became the Dodgers' regular third baseman in 1973. He held the position for ten seasons and became the leading home run hitter in Dodger history. Six times an All-Star in the 1970s, Cey got his nickname from his stocky build, short legs, and choppy running style. In 1981 his string of eleven seasons with 20 or more homers was interrupted by the players' strike and a late-season broken arm. He returned in time to play in the WS, where he was beaned by a Goose Gossage

Ron Cey

fastball. Nevertheless, he was co-MVP in the Series. In 1983 he was traded to the Cubs. His 25 homers and 97 RBI helped them win the 1984 Eastern Division title. /(ME)

Elio Chacon — 1936– . SS-2B 1960–62 Reds, **Mets** 228 g, .232, 4 hr, 39 rbi. *1 WS, 4 g, .250*

The 5'9" Venezuelan batted .265 as a reserve second baseman with the NL Champion Reds of 1961. In Game Two of that World Series, Chacon hit a key bloop single off the Yankees' Ralph Terry, and scored the winning run in the Reds' only victory. In 1962 Chacon was the shortstop for the original Mets. /(TJ)

Chet Chadbourne (Pop) — 1884–1943. OF 1906–07, 14–15, 18 Red Sox, **Kansas City (FL)**, Braves 347 g, .255, 2 hr, 82 rbi

An institution in the Pacific Coast League, "Pop" collected 3,216 minor league hits over 21 years. A far-ranging outfielder, his only full ML seasons came in the Federal League, where he led in assists one year and fielding percentage the other. /(JK)

Henry Chadwick — 1824–1908. *Writer.*
☞ *Hall of Fame—1938.*

As an English schoolboy, Chadwick played rounders, a forerunner of baseball. In his early twenties (a decade after emigrating with his parents to Brooklyn), he played baseball, but remained indifferent to the new game for several years. Then, in 1856, while witnessing a well-played match between two of New York's better clubs, he became a fan, and decided to do everything he could to make baseball "a national sport for Americans" as cricket was for the English. He set out to persuade *The New York Times* (for which he reported cricket matches) and other major metropolitan dailies to cover baseball, offering to report the games himself.

By the time the last New York paper began reporting baseball in 1862, Chadwick had taken on his next task: promoting changes—through his writing and his membership on an early baseball rules committee—that would move the game toward more balanced offense and defense, and would make it a more "manly," "scientific" game, demanding mental as well as physical ability. He expanded the box score and developed a scoring system that enabled reporters to record every play, allowing them to describe games in greater detail. A modified version of his system is standard today.

In 1860 Chadwick prepared baseball's first guide; he edited one or more annually until his death,

Henry Chadwick

including the famous and respected Spaulding Guide from 1881–1908. Through his rules committee work, his books and pamphlets, and his contributions to more than 20 periodicals, he did more than any other writer to shape the game and spread its popularity, and earned himself the appellation "father of baseball." His decades of vociferous opposition to gambling were largely responsible for keeping the game freer from corruption than other major sports.

Besides baseball, Chadwick wrote about many other sports and games, from yachting to billiards to chess. He was also a pianist, songwriter, drama critic, and, briefly, during the Civil War, a news correspondent in Virginia. He was enshrined in baseball's Hall of Fame in 1938, the only writer elected to the Hall itself (as opposed to the Writers Wing). /(FIC)

Leon Chagnon (Shag) — 1902–1953. RHP 1929–30, 32–35 **Pirates**, Giants 393 ip, 19–16, 4.51

After two early flops, Shag stuck with the Bucs in 1932 (at age 29) and turned in three good years from the Pittsburgh bullpen. In 1931 he was a 20-game winner for Fort Worth (Texas League). /(ME)

Bob Chakales (Chick, The Golden Greek) — 1927– .
RHP 1951–57 Indians, Orioles, White Sox, **Senators**, Red
Sox 420 ip, 15–25, 4.54

Chakales jumped from A-ball to the majors and
won two of his three 1951 victories with his bat. In
parts of seven seasons, primarily in relief, he struggled with his control, but hit a solid .271./(JCA)

Dave Chalk — 1950– . 3B-SS 1973–81 **Angels**,
Rangers, A's, Royals 903 g, .252, 15 hr, 243 rbi. *1 WS,
1 g, --*
☛ *All-Star—74–75.*

The Angels' (and baseball's) number-one pick in the
1972 free agent draft, Chalk led AL shortstops with
29 errors as a rookie in 1974 but with Jim Sundberg
was one of two rookies to make the All-Star team.
He became an outstanding fielder at both short and
third base. A notoriously slow starter at bat, he often
didn't hit for average until August and never showed
much home run power. His top season was 1977,
when he hit .277 with 69 RBI. A 1979 knee injury
finished him as a regular./(MC)

George Chalmers (Dut) — 1888–1960. RHP
1910–16 **Phillies** 646 ip, 29–41, 3.41. *1 WS, 8 ip, 0–1,
2.25*

The Scottish-born spitballer went 25–6 for Scranton
(New York State League) in 1910, and was purchased by the Phillies. He was 13–10, his ML best,
in 1911. He pitched well in Game Four of the 1915
World Series, but lost to the Red Sox 2–1./(AL)

Cliff Chambers (Lefty) — 1922– . LHP 1948–53
Cubs, **Pirates**, Cardinals 897 ip, 48–53, 4.29

After a disappointing 2–9 debut in 1948 with the
last-place Cubs, Chambers was dealt to Pittsburgh,
where he led Pirate pitchers with 13 victories in
1949 and 12 in 1950. The 6'3" Oregonian won a
career-high 14 games in 1951; he started that season
with Pittsburgh, but went to the Cardinals in the
seven-player June trade that moved Joe Garagiola to
the Pirates./(TJ)

Chris Chambliss — 1948– . 1B 1971–86, 88 Indians,
Yankees, Braves 2173 g, .279, 185 hr, 972 rbi. *4 LCS,
17 g, .286, 2 hr, 10 rbi. 3 WS, 13 g, .275, 1 hr, 5 rbi*
☛ *Rookie of the Year—71. All-Star—76. Gold Glove—78.*

On October 14, 1976, Chambliss hit one of base-
ball's most dramatic home runs. His ninth-inning,
Game Five shot off Mark Littell decided the
Yankees-Royals LCS. It snapped a 6–6 tie, ended
New York's 12-year pennant drought, and made
Yankee Stadium go wild. In that Series, Chambliss

batted .524 and tied or broke five LCS records for
hits and RBI.

Chambliss was twice drafted by the Reds, in 1967
and in 1969, but continued school and attended
UCLA for a year. Signing with the Indians when he
was drafted a third time in 1970, he led the
American Association in hitting with a .342 mark at
Wichita in 1970. He was the first player to lead the
AA in batting in his first pro season, and is believed
to be the first "rookie" to have won a Triple-A
batting title. In only his second pro season, Chambliss was the 1971 AL Rookie of the Year, Cleveland's second ever (Herb Score was the first). It was
the first time a player won consecutive Rookie of the
Year honors on the minor and major league levels.
Called up that May, he batted .275 and played solid
defense at first base. He led Indian regulars in
batting the next two seasons.

Chris Chambliss

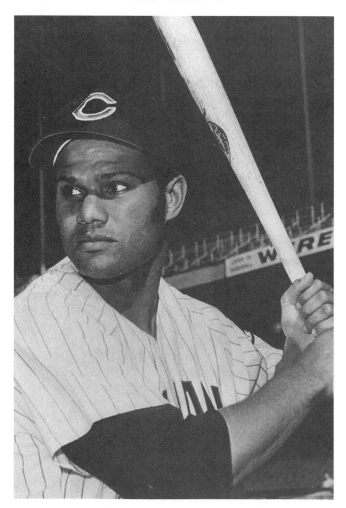

On April 27, 1974, Chambliss was sent to the Yankees in a seven-player deal. After struggling that year, he became a key part of the potent New York offense. In 1975 he batted .304, but he was most productive for New York's 1976–78 pennants. His consistent performance matched his temperament; he averaged 92 RBI over those years, and in 1978 won a Gold Glove as he led AL first basemen in fielding (.997). He was the quiet, steady exception on a loud and turbulent club.

Chambliss was traded to Toronto and on to Atlanta after the 1979 season. He prospered in the NL, hitting a career-high 20 HR in both 1982, when he helped the Braves to a division title, and 1983. After averaging 141 games in his first 14 seasons, he was switched primarily to bench duty in 1985, and in 1986 led the NL with 20 pinch hits. He was named the Yankee hitting coach for 1988 and was activated very briefly, striking out in his only at-bat. His cousin Jo-Jo White performed in the NBA. /(MG)

Billy Champion — 1947– . RHP 1969–76 Phillies, **Brewers** 805 ip, 34–50, 4.68

Champion was 15–5 with an International League-leading 2.03 ERA in 1968, and was 7–1, 1.66, before the Phillies called him up in 1969. Only 12–31 in four NL seasons, the 6'4″ redhead was considering quitting when he was traded to the Brewers. Originally a fastball-slider thrower, Champion added four more pitches and went 11–4 in 1974. An elbow injury sidelined him in August 1975 and forced him to retirement in 1976. /(JCA)

Mike Champion — 1955– . 2B 1976–78 **Padres** 193 g, .229, 2 hr, 49 rbi

Champion was the top-fielding Pacific Coast League second baseman in 1976 but hit only a weak .229 in his one year as the Padres' regular second baseman. /(MC)

Bob Chance — 1940– . 1B-OF 1963–67, 69 **Indians**, Senators, Angels 277 g, .261, 24 hr, 112 rbi

Chance won the Triple Crown with Charleston (Eastern League) in 1963 and followed with a strong 1964 rookie season with Cleveland (.279, 14 HR, 75 RBI), batting .340 versus Washington. The Senators traded for him and Manager Gil Hodges said he was "the kind of hitter who could wind up leading the league." But the unrelenting bench jockey had a tendency to gain weight and proved a disappointment. He split the 1965–67 seasons between Washington and Hawaii. /(JCA)

Dean Chance — 1941– . RHP 1961–71 **Angels**, Twins, Indians, Mets, Tigers 2148 ip, 128–115, 2.92. 20 wins: 64, 67 *1 LCS, 2 ip, 0–0, 13.50* ☛ *Led League—w 64. Led League—era 64, 67. Cy Young Award—64. All-Star—64, 67.*

Throwing hard from an unorthodox twisting windup, at the age of 23 in 1964 Chance won the Cy Young Award (when there was only one award including both leagues) in a landslide. Expectations were high, but he never evolved into a consistently dominant pitcher. With a touch of wildness and the disconcerting trait of never looking at home plate once he received the sign from his catcher, Chance would turn his broad back fully toward the hitter in mid-windup before spinning and unleashing a lively fastball, good sinker, or sidearm curve.

Chance was drafted by the Angels from the Orioles' organization in the 1960 expansion draft and as a rookie in 1962 was 14–10 with a 2.96 ERA starting in spots. He joined the rotation in 1963 and was 13–18 with meager support from his teammates. In 1964 he blossomed into the AL's most overpowering hurler. Pitching his home games in spacious Dodger Stadium (called Chavez Ravine by the Angels), Chance was 20–9 with a 1.64 ERA in '64 and tossed 11 shutouts, including 6 that he won 1–0. That June 6 he pitched 14 shutout innings against the Yankees, only to see the Angels lose 2–0 after he left the game. On September 10 he pitched a one-hitter against the Twins, allowing only an infield single to Zoilo Versalles in the eighth inning.

Chance slipped to 15–10 in 1965 and 12–17 in 1966 and began to berate his teammates for their poor play behind him. He was traded to Minnesota before the 1967 season and enjoyed a resurgence with the Twins, going 20–14 with a 2.73 ERA to win AL Comeback Player of the Year honors. He pitched a no-hitter against the Indians on August 25. On the final day of the season he faced the Red Sox with a chance to clinch the pennant. Chance lost, and Boston went to the World Series instead. Chance was 16–16 in 1968 and 5–4 in only 15 starts in 1969, then was traded to the Indians along with Graig Nettles in a six-player deal that brought Luis Tiant to the Twins. The Indians sold Chance to the Mets in mid-1970 and he spent his final season pitching mostly in relief with the Tigers in 1971.

Chance was a notoriously poor hitter, batting .066 in 662 career at-bats while striking out 353 times. /(SCL)

Frank Chance (Husk, The Peerless Leader) —
1877–1924. 1B-C-OF 1898–1914 **Cubs,**
Yankees 1286 g, .297, 20 hr, 596 rbi. *4 WS, 20 g, .310, 6 rbi.*

Manager 1905–14, 23 **Cubs,** Yankees, Red Sox
946–648, .593. First place: 06–08, 10 *4 WS, 11–9, .550*
☛ *Hall of Fame—1946.*

Chance was the first baseman in the double-play trio of "Tinker to Evers to Chance," immortalized by Franklin Adams in the poem "Baseball's Sad Lexicon." He was dubbed "The Peerless Leader" as he led the Cubs to pennants in 1906–08 and 1910 as their player-manager. Some called him "Husk" because he was husky, strong, and aggressive. He made his opinions known and never backed down from an argument. He ran his clubs with a clenched fist, coming down hard on any player who gave less than 100%. Eventually, he had trouble hearing criticism, or anything at all. Since he crowded the

Frank Chance

plate, he too often was beaned, and his hearing was eventually affected. As a result, he developed a peculiar whine which grated on his teammates and opponents.

Chance reached the majors as a catcher and part-time outfielder with Chicago, but when Johnny Kling came along, he shifted to first base. He led the NL with 67 stolen bases in 1903, and with 57 in 1906, when his 103 runs scored were also the league high. In only six seasons (1903–08) did he play in more than 100 games, but he batted better than .300 in the first four of them.

Chance's great success came as a young manager. He was 27 when he took over the Chicago club from Frank Selee in mid-1905; in seven full seasons, he won at least 100 games four times, and never finished lower than third. His .664 winning percentage (768–389) stands as the best in Cubs history. In 1906 the Cubs won 116 games—a major league record—while losing just 36. They lost to the White Sox in the '06 World Series, but defeated the Tigers in the next two. Chance led all participants in the '08 WS with a .421 batting average.

Chance moved to the Yankees in 1913, but ill health forced him to retire with New York in seventh place in 1914. He returned to his native California, and owned and managed the Los Angeles (Pacific Coast League) team in 1916–17. He returned East in 1923 to try to rebuild the Red Sox, decimated by the sale of stars (including Babe Ruth) to the Yankees, but finished in the cellar. He was to manage the White Sox in 1924, but his health worsened, and he died that September. In 1946 Chance, Joe Tinker, and Johnny Evers were inducted into the Hall of Fame./(JK)

Happy Chandler [Albert B.] — 1907– . Commissioner.
☛ *Hall of Fame—1982.*

Chandler was the second Commissioner, succeeding the legendary Judge Landis. He was elected in 1945, after having served as Governor of Kentucky for four years and U.S. Senator for six. He was perceived as a players' Commissioner, and he cautioned owners to be less stubborn to avoid later confrontations. His advice was ignored.

Despite the negative feelings of most club owners, he supported the entry of Jackie Robinson into the major leagues. When some players jumped to the Mexican League in 1946, he suspended them for five years (but gave them blanket amnesty in 1949). He suspended Dodgers manager Leo Durocher for one year for a series of actions detrimental to baseball's image, including consorting with gamblers. He was the first to put six umpires on the field for the World Series.

Having made some decisions that riled several owners, he was fired after one term, receiving only nine of the twelve votes necessary to continue. When he left, his reputation for being good-humored, iron-willed, and honest remained intact. He had put the players' pension fund on a sound footing, averted threats to the reserve clause, and helped open the ML door for black players. In 1982 he was named to the Hall of Fame. /(NLM)

Spud Chandler [Spurgeon Ferdinand] — 1907– . RHP 1937–47 **Yankees** 1485 ip, 109–43, 2.84. 20 wins: 43, 46
4 WS, 33 ip, 2–2, 1.62
☛ *Most Valuable Player—43. Led League—w 43. Led League—era 43, 47. All-Star—42–43, 46–47.*

When Chandler retired after the 1947 season, he possessed the highest winning percentage (.717) of any pitcher with 100 or more major league victories. In addition to his 109 regular-season triumphs, Chandler won the 1942 All-Star Game and recorded two victories, including the clincher, for the Yankees in the 1943 World Series. Chandler led AL pitchers in wins (20), winning percentage (.883), ERA (1.64), complete games (20), and shutouts (five) in 1943, capturing the MVP award. After time out for military service, he went 20–8 in 1946 and led the league in ERA (2.46) for a second time in 1947. Chandler, who played baseball and football for the University of Georgia, threw 26 shutouts during his ML career. /(TJ)

Darrel Chaney — 1948– . SS-2B-3B 1969–79 **Reds**, Braves 915 g, .217, 14 hr, 190 rbi. *2 LCS, 10 g, .120, 1 rbi. 3 WS, 9 g, .000*

Chaney led the Southern League in homers with 23 in 1968, but never hit more than 3 in a ML season. He spent seven years with the Reds, mostly as backup to shortstop Dave Concepcion. "There's a whole bunch of clubs in the majors on which he could play regularly," said manager Sparky Anderson. After Chaney was traded to the Braves in 1976, he became their starting shortstop and had his best year offensively (.252, 50 RBI), but his 37 errors led NL shortstops. /(JCA)

Tiny Chaplin [James Bailey] — 1905–1939. RHP 1928, 30–31, 36 Giants, **Braves** 371 ip, 14–24, 4.25

"Tiny" Chaplin was a hard-throwing 6'1" 195-lb righthander. He was an ineffective reliever with the Giants for three seasons, and returned to the minors

for five more years before resurfacing as a starter for the Braves in 1936. /(FS)

Ben Chapman (Chappy) — 1908– . OF-3B-2B-RHP 1930–41, 44–46 **Yankees**, Senators, Red Sox, Indians, White Sox, Dodgers, Phillies 1716 g, .302, 90 hr, 977 rbi; 141 ip, 8–6, 4.39. *1 WS, 4 g, .294, 6 rbi.*
  Manager 1945–48 **Phillies** 197–277, .416
☛ *All-Star—33–36.*

On a team best remembered for power, Chapman delighted Yankee fans with daring baserunning and fervent play from 1930 to 1936. An infielder in 1930, Chapman was moved to left field by new manager Joe McCarthy in 1931 to take advantage of his speed and throwing arm. Chapman led AL outfielders in assists in 1933 and 1935. He reached double figures in doubles, triples, HR, and steals in each of his first three seasons, and led the AL in stolen bases three straight years, 1931–33. He was the first batter for the AL in the inaugural 1933 All-Star Game.

Ben Chapman

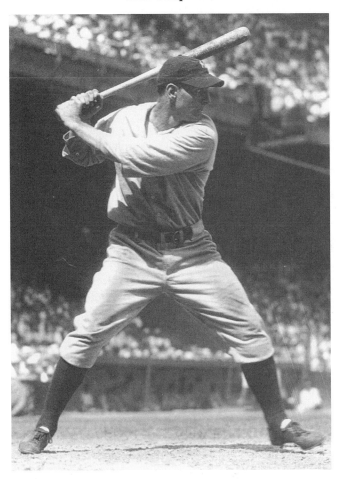

Chapman moved to center in 1934, but he and his temper were displaced by Joe DiMaggio in 1936. Traded to Washington in mid-1936, Boston in mid-1937, and (despite batting .340) Cleveland after 1938, Chapman was a regular through 1940. In 1942, as pitcher-manager for Richmond (Piedmont League), he punched umpire I.H. Case and was suspended from playing for a year. He returned as a pitcher with Brooklyn in 1944, and went 5–3 (3.40). Two weeks after his trade to the Phillies in 1945, Chapman was named their manager. His spirited leadership brought initial improvement, but soon his temper and poorly timed comments, especially his widely publicized vicious baiting of Jackie Robinson in 1947, exasperated owner Bob Carpenter. Chapman was fired in 1948. /(ME)

Charles Chapman — 1880–1941. *Scout.*

A catcher at Princeton and a graduate of Harvard Law School, Chapman scouted part-time for the Cardinals from 1921 to 1931 and full-time for the Reds from 1931 to 1941, discovering or recommending Chick Hafey, Dom DiMaggio, and Eddie Joost. He eventually became a history professor at the University of California, and authored *Play Ball! Advice for Young Ballplayers* with ex-ML catcher Hank Severeid. /(FVP)

Jack Chapman (Death to Flying Things) — 1843–1916. OF 1874–76 **Brooklyn (NA)**, St. Louis (NA), Louisville (NL) *NA:* 96 g, .253; NL: 17 g, .239, 0 hr, 5 rbi.
   Manager 1877–78, 82–85, 89–92 Louisville (NL), Milwaukee (NL), Worcester (NL), Detroit (NL), Buffalo (NL), **Louisville (NL)** 306–428, .417

Chapman was one of the foremost players of the 1860s. Although his services were much in demand, he played most seasons with the Brooklyn Atlantics, the team that broke the Cincinnati Red Stockings' two-year winning streak in an extra-inning game in 1871. For defeating Cincinnati, each Brooklyn player received $364 from the Atlantics' share of the gate receipts. In an age that admired fielding prowess more than hitting ability, Chapman became famous for his many long running catches, and was the first to receive the colorful nickname "Death to Flying Things." He later played two seasons in the National Association and one in the National League. A weight problem brought about his retirement as a player, but he became a highly respected manager for many years. His Louisville team won the 1890 American Association pennant. /(BC)

Ray Chapman — 1891–1920. SS 1912–20 **Indians** 1050 g, .278, 18 hr, 364 rbi

Ray Chapman is the only modern major leaguer to have died as a direct result of being hit by a pitch. At the Polo Grounds on August 16, 1920, Chapman, crowding the plate as usual, was struck in the temple by a pitch from Yankee submariner Carl Mays that barely missed the strike zone. Chapman was taken to a hospital, never regained consciousness, and died twelve hours later. Rookie Joe Sewell replaced Chapman at short, beginning a Hall of Fame career. Cleveland players wore black arm bands, and manager Tris Speaker rallied his dejected men to win the first World Championship in club history.

The popular Chapman led the Indians in stolen bases four times, setting a team record with 52 in 1917 that stood until 1980. He led the AL in runs scored and walks in 1918. He was hitting .303 with

Ray Chapman

97 runs scored when he died. It is baseball analyst Bill James's opinion that Chapman was "probably destined for the Hall of Fame had he lived." /(ME)

Sam Chapman — 1916– . OF 1938–41, 45–51 **A's**, Indians 1368 g, .266, 180 hr, 773 rbi
☛ *All-Star—46.*

Chapman went right to the majors from the University of California, where he had been an All-American football player. He had it all: speed, power, and a strong arm. He hit 20 or more homers five seasons, but struck out often, leading the AL with 96 in 1940. Chapman became a popular team leader, and batted .322 with 25 HR in 1941. By 1942, he was a Navy flier. After he returned at the end of 1945, he never again hit .300, but he had not lost his power, and in 1949 drove in 108 runs. He led AL outfielders in putouts four times, assists once, and errors twice. /(NLM)

Joe Charboneau — 1955– . OF-DH 1980–82 Indians 201 g, .266, 29 hr, 114 rbi
☛ *Rookie of the Year—80.*

They were writing songs in Cleveland about "Super Joe" when he was the 1980 AL Rookie of the Year (.289, 23 HR, 87 RBI). Then came one of the greatest downfalls in player history. He was sent down halfway through 1981 after hitting only .208. He underwent two back operations but never fully recuperated, and was released by the Indians' AA Buffalo affiliate in May 1983 after giving fans an obscene salute. A "flake" who would dye his hair exotic colors (or shave it off entirely), Charboneau impressed his teammates by opening beer bottles with an eye socket muscle. /(JCA)

Ed Charles (The Glider, Pops) — 1935– . 3B 1962–69 **A's**, Mets 1005 g, .263, 86 hr, 421 rbi. *1 WS, 4 g, .133*

Nicknamed "The Glider" for his graceful baserunning and third base play, Charles spent eight tough seasons with the Braves organization in the still-segregated South, and wrote published poetry concerning the universe, racism, and baseball. With Eddie Mathews at third, Milwaukee had no place for Charles and finally traded him to Kansas City. His 1962 rookie marks included career highs of .288 and 17 HR. He remained a steady contributor for five seasons, but his home run production was cut in half when owner Charlie Finley moved the fences back in 1965. Traded to the Mets in early 1967, he was their oldest regular and was waived in November. He re-made the club in the spring of 1968 and batted .276 with 15 homers. In the Mets' 1969

World Championship season, he shared third base duties with Wayne Garrett and Bobby Pfeil. /(JCA)

Oscar Charleston (The Hoosier Comet) — 1896–1954. OF-1B-MGR Negro Leagues 1915–54 Indianapolis ABC's, New York Lincoln Stars, Chicago American Giants, St. Louis Giants, Harrisburg Giants, Hilldale, Homestead Grays, **Pittsburgh Crawfords**, Toledo Crawfords, Indianapolis Crawfords, Philadelphia Stars, Brooklyn Brown Dodgers, Indianapolis Clowns statistics not available
☛ *Led League—ba 21(NNL). Led League—hr 21(NNL). All-Star—33–35. Hall of Fame—1976.*

Considered by many the greatest Negro League player of all, multi-talented Oscar Charleston was often compared with three great white contemporaries: his hitting and speedy, aggressive baserunning (and hard-sliding style) brought favorable comparison to Ty Cobb; his physique (he was barrel-chested, with spindly legs), power, and popularity, particu-

Oscar Charleston

larly with youngsters, were reminiscent of Babe Ruth; and his defensive style and skills, playing a shallow, far-ranging centerfield with a strong, accurate arm and excellent fly ball judgment, brought visions of Tris Speaker. The New York Giants' John McGraw, familiar with the untapped black talent available, considered the 6' 190-lb Charleston the best, and coveted him.

A native of Indianapolis, Charleston grew up serving as batboy for the local ABC's. At age 15, he joined the army and was stationed in the Philippines. The military gave the underage runaway the opportunity to display his abilities in track and baseball; he ran the 220-yard dash in 23 seconds, and played in the otherwise all-white Manila League. Entering big-time black baseball with the ABC's, he was a vital cog in their 1916 Black World Series triumph over the Chicago American Giants, batting .360 in seven of the 10 games played. After stints with the American Giants and New York Lincoln Stars, he rejoined Indianapolis when the Negro National League was organized in 1920.

Through 1923, the lefthanded-hitting and throwing Charleston posted a .370 batting average with the NNL ABC's and St. Louis Giants, and in 1921 led the league in hitting (.446), triples (10), HR (14), total bases (137), slugging (.774), and stolen bases (28), finishing second with 79 hits in 50 games. From 1922 to 1925, he was player-manager for the Eastern Colored League Harrisburg Giants, and, after a second-division finish in 1924, he led them to three consecutive second-place finishes. In 1925, he batted .424. From 1928 to 1931, he hit .347 in two-year stints with the Hilldale club and the Homestead Grays. The Grays won a 10-game Eastern Championship Series from the New York Lincoln Giants in 1930.

In 1932 Gus Greenlee persuaded Charleston to manage his Pittsburgh Crawfords. Josh Gibson, Judy Johnson, and Satchel Paige joined him to give the club four future Hall of Famers. Operating independently, they went 99–36 as their 36-year-old manager batted .363, second on the club to Gibson. Often considered black baseball's greatest team, the Crawfords became the dominant member of the tough National Negro Association, which operated from 1933 to 1936. Pittsburgh claimed the 1933 pennant, as did the Chicago American Giants, without resolution. In 1935 the Crawfords won the first NNL's only undisputed title. In 1936 they posted the best overall record, winning the second half of the split season. A title series with the first-half champion Washington Elite Giants was never completed, though the Giants won the only game played, 2–0.

Charleston remained with the Crawfords through 1940, following them in moves to Toledo and Indianapolis. He became manager of the NNL Philadelphia Stars in 1941 and the Brooklyn Brown Dodgers when Branch Rickey formed the United States League in 1945. He was thus put in a position to scout and evaluate players for organized baseball's integration. He managed through 1954, leading the Indianapolis Clowns to the '54 Negro American League title, but died after the season.

Statistics so far compiled show that Charleston batted .353 lifetime. He twice led the Cuban Winter League in SB, and had 31 during the 1923–24 campaign, setting a record that stood for more than 20 years. In 53 exhibition games against white major leaguers, he hit .318 with 11 HR.

Charleston had a famous temper, and enjoyed brawling, resulting in legendary encounters with umpires, opponents, agents raiding his teams, a Ku Klux Klansman, and, on one occasion, several Cuban soldiers. As his legs gave out, he moved from centerfield to first base, yet as long as he played, he never lost his home run power, nor his meanness on the basepaths. He was sympathetic toward young players, and was protective of rookie teammates. A demanding manager who expected his players to perform as well as he did, his strength as a pilot lay in his understanding of the intricacies of the game. He was elected to the Hall of Fame by the Committee on Negro Baseball Leagues in 1976. /(MFK)

Norm Charlton — 1963– . LHP 1988– **Reds** 157 ip, 12–8, 3.33

The skinny, hard-throwing Charlton was the Expos' first-round draft pick in June 1984. He joined the Reds' excellent middle-relief staff in 1988 and became effective with more work in 1989. /(SFS)

Mike Chartak (Shotgun) — 1916–1967. OF-1B 1940, 1942–44 Yankees, Senators, **Browns** 256 g, .243, 21 hr, 98 rbi. *1 WS, 2 g, .000*

The broad-shouldered ex-coal miner languished in the talent-rich Yankee organization, but became a spare outfielder and pinch hitter with the Browns, playing 35 games in 1944 for their only pennant winner. Chartak retired a year later after contracting tuberculosis. /(JL)

Hal Chase (Prince Hal) — 1883–1947. 1B 1905–19
Yankees, White Sox, Buffalo (FL), Reds, Giants 1917 g,
.291, 57 hr, 941 rbi.
    Manager 1910–11 **Yankees** 85–78, .521
☛ *Led League—ba 16. Led League—hr 15 .*

Among the most unsavory characters in the history
of the game, Chase was an oddly charismatic star.
He was considered by contemporary observers to be
the best-fielding first baseman ever, but he repeatedly threw games for the quick money he could
make betting against his own team, and he was
eventually banned for life.

He led his league's first basemen in errors seven
times, but only in 1911, as a playing manager, did he
lead in any positive fielding categories (putouts and
assists, but also errors once again). He holds the AL
career first baseman's mark for errors (285). On
September 21, 1906, he tied the ML record for
putouts by a first baseman in a nine-inning game
with 22; two other times he had 21.

The venal gate attraction jumped the Highlanders
(later the Yankees) after the 1907 season, demanding a $4,000 salary. Management gave in to him,
but he jumped anyway, playing for San Jose (California League) under an assumed name. He was
suspended, then reinstated; when he returned to

Hal Chase

New York, his teammates presented the redhead
with a silver loving cup. In 1910 manager George
Stallings accused Chase of throwing games. Chase
beat the charge and then used his popularity to take
over the managerial post himself at the end of the
season. In his first full year at the helm, the team
dropped from second place (88–63) to sixth
(76–76). Traded to the White Sox in June 1913
after his lackadaisical play became blatant, he
jumped to the Federal League a year later. Playing
in a small park, he hit an atypical 17 HR (his
previous high was four) to lead the league in 1915.
This made him much sought-after when the FL
folded, and he was signed by the Reds. He led the
NL in batting in 1916 with a career-high .339. He
hit .300 four times, but usually with very few walks.
He did steal as many as 40 bases (1910), and he
finished his career with 363 steals. However, Chase
never scored more than 85 runs or drove in more
than 89, both highs coming in 1915.

In 1918, playing under the scrupulously honest
Christy Mathewson, Chase was suspended for
throwing games. He was initially cleared by an
establishment eager to disbelieve Chase's accusers,
but the charge was later proven. John McGraw of
the Giants, always sure of his ability to reform the
wayward, tried Chase in 1919, but by the end of the
season wouldn't play him. Chase was implicated in
the Black Sox scandal when the World Series was
thrown at the end of the season, and thereafter he
was persona non grata. /(JFC)

Ken Chase (Lefty) — 1913– . LHP 1936–43 **Senators**,
Red Sox, Giants 1165 ip, 53–84, 4.27

Chase was a hard thrower who struggled with poor
teams and poor control. He allowed 143 walks in
1940 to lead the AL. Chase retired after 1943 to run
his family dairy farm near Cooperstown. /(JK)

Buster Chatham (Charles) — 1901–1975. 3B-SS
1930–31 **Braves** 129 g, .263, 6 hr, 59 rbi

The 5'5" 150-lb infielder played in more than 2,600
games, mostly in the minors, including a seven-
season stretch with Atlanta (Sally League) in which
he never missed a game. With Pueblo of the Western
League, he once made nine straight hits in a
doubleheader and hit two homers in his first two at-
bats the next day for 25 total bases on 11 hits.
Altogether he spent 53 years in baseball as player,
coach, scout, and manager. /(NLM)

Charlie Chech — 1879–1938. RHP 1905–06, 08–09 **Reds**, Indians, Red Sox 606 ip, 33–31, 2.52

Using a puzzling curve and good control, Chech won a career-high 14 games as a rookie with the 1905 Reds. After Chech's best season, 1908 (11–7, 1.74), the Indians traded him with Jack Ryan and $12,500 for 41-year-old Cy Young. Chech's 2.95 ERA in 1909 was the sixth-worst in the AL among pitchers with 100 or more innings. /(NLM)

Virgil Cheeves (Chief) — 1901–1979. RHP 1920–24, 27 **Cubs**, Indians, Giants 458 ip, 26–27, 4.73

Cheeves earned the name "Giant Killer" by beating the World Champion New Yorkers the first six times he faced them in 1921–22. He was much less effective against the rest of the NL, and a 12–11 mark in 1922 was his only winning season. /(NLM)

Larry Cheney — 1886–1969. RHP 1911–19 **Cubs**, Dodgers, Braves, Phillies 1881 ip, 116–100, 2.70. 20 wins: 12–14
☛ Led League—w 12.

Brought up by the Cubs at the end of the 1911 season, Cheney beat the Dodgers in an extra-inning game, but was literally knocked out of the box. Zack Wheat hit a line drive at Cheney's head which the pitcher deflected with his hand, driving his thumb into his nose, breaking both. The next year he couldn't grip the ball tightly and changed his delivery. He would dig his fingernails into the ball, creating a knuckler. With it, he went 26–10 as a rookie that season, tying for the league lead in wins and leading with 28 complete games.

The spitball, which he picked up from its master, Ed Walsh, became Cheney's most effective pitch. In 1913 the workhorse went 17–14 as a starter and 4–0 as a reliever, with NL highs of 11 saves and 54 appearances. That September 14 he shut out the Giants on 14 hits—the most ever given up by a ML pitcher in a nine-inning shutout. His 50 games, 40 starts, and 140 walks topped the league in 1914, his last 20-win season. /(JK)

Tom Cheney — 1934– . RHP 1957, 59–64, 66 Cardinals, Pirates, **Senators** 466 ip, 19–29, 3.77. *1 WS, 4 ip, 4.50*

Often spectacular when he was healthy, Cheney had eight shutouts among his 19 career wins. On September 12, 1962, he set a ML record with Washington by striking out 21 Orioles in a 16-inning 2–1 victory. A severe elbow injury suffered in July 1963 cut short his ML career. /(JCA)

Jack Chesbro (Happy Jack) — 1874–1931. RHP 1899–1909 Pirates, **Yankees**, Red Sox 2897 ip, 198–132, 2.68. 20 wins: 01–04, 06
☛ Led League—w 02, 04.

When Chesbro's spitball sailed over the catcher's head and the winning run scored from third on the last day of the 1904 season, the Highlanders (later the Yankees) lost the pennant. At the time, it overshadowed Chesbro's outstanding season of 41 wins, in which he completed his first 30 starts. He pitched 454 innings in 55 games.

Chesbro's career began slowly, with a minor league career plagued by the misfortune of being with shaky franchises that folded in mid-season. Finally he joined the Atlantic League, organized by Ed Barrow, and worked his way to the majors. He joined Pittsburgh mid-season of 1899.

Chesbro's fame as a pitcher began when he pitched the Pirates to their first pennants in 1901 and 1902. In 1902 he picked up the spitball, at a

Jack Chesbro with the New York Highlanders

time when its peculiar properties were first being discovered by a number of pitchers. He strung together enough starring seasons to offset his relatively short career. He had only 12 seasons in the major leagues, 9 as a regular starter. Still, with his extraordinary 1904 season, he gained election to the Hall of Fame in 1948.

After Chesbro's pitching skills had dried up and he left the major leagues, he began a prosperous career as a merchant in New England, running a saw mill and lumber yard in North Adams, MA. He continued to pitch, appearing with semi-pro teams, traveling to take on mill town teams who found the pitching of the former major league superstar easy to hit.

He was baseball coach at Amherst College in 1911, and in 1924 Clark Griffith, his manager in 1904, brought him back to the major leagues for a brief role as a coach for the Washington Senators. Although the team was to win the pennant, fans were slow to respond and Chesbro was dropped for payroll reasons. /(JK)

Bob Chesnes — 1921–1979. RHP 1948–50 **Pirates** 379 ip, 24–22, 4.66

The Pirates paid over $100,000 for a one-year phenom. Although he was 14–6 in his rookie 1948 season, he was considered an eccentric and a discipline problem. He slipped to 7–13 as a sophomore and was out of the majors by 1950. /(JCA)

Hilda Chester (Queen of the Bleachers, Howling Hilda) — Unk.–Unk

Chester may be the most famous sports fan ever. Beginning in the 1920s, she attended most Dodger games to support her favorites, razz the opposition, and lead the fans in snake dances through the Ebbets Field aisles. The stentorian bleacherite acquired her trademark brass cowbell from the Dodger players in the late 1930s. It replaced the frying pan which she banged with an iron ladle after her doctor forbade her to yell following a heart attack.

The plump, gray-haired Chester once influenced a game. She gave centerfielder Pete Reiser a note for manager Leo Durocher (a favorite of hers after he visited her in the hospital after her second heart attack), and Durocher mistakenly thought the message was from team president Larry McPhail. It said "Get Casey hot. Wyatt's losing it." In the eighth inning, soon after Durocher got the note, pitcher Whit Wyatt gave up a hit. Despite having pitched a

good game up to that point, Wyatt was relieved by Hugh Casey, who just barely saved the game. /(SH)

Shigeru Chiba (Buffalo) — Unk.–Unk. 2B 1938–56 **Yomiuri Giants**, Kintetsu Pearls

Considered the greatest second baseman in Japanese baseball before the arrival of American John Sipin, Chiba was a mainstay of the Yomiuri Giants. He managed the Kintetsu Pearls, who were renamed the Buffaloes in his honor. /(MC)

Chicago Cubs [aka White Stockings, Colts, Orphans] — 1874– . Team. 8620–7977, .519. *NL East Champions 84, 89 NL Champions 1876, 80–82, 85–86, 06–08, 10, 18, 29, 32, 35, 38, 45 World Champions 07–08*

The Cubs have played continuously in one city longer than any other franchise. Originally an amateur club, the team, then called the White Stockings, played in the National Association's inaugural season in 1871, but dropped out for two years after that. After rejoining in 1874, the franchise has continued to the present day. The National League was formed in 1876 by White Stockings president William Hulbert after four stars of the dynastic Boston club were lured to Chicago; Hulbert feared reprisals by the Red Stockings and the NA. The team won the pennant that year on the strength of the four Boston stars, especially the pitching of Al Spalding. Superstar Adrian Anson earned his nickname "Cap" when he was named manager in 1879. Often less than admirable (he was a major force in the creation of the color line), he was nonetheless one of the best players in the NL, winning three batting titles and leading in RBI four times. He spent 22 years playing in the NL, all for Chicago, and led the team to pennants in 1880–82 and 1885–86.

After the elimination of competing leagues and the adoption of a 12-team structure in 1892, the team, now called the Colts for their young players, was frequently below .500. Anson was fired in 1898, his only non-playing year as a manager. The team was rebuilt by Frank Selee and came to fruition under playing manager Frank Chance, "The Peerless Leader." He led the club, finally called the Cubs, to a ML-record 116 victories in 1906 (against 36 losses) as they won the first of three straight NL pennants. Featured was the immortal double-play combination of Joe Tinker, Johnny Evers, and leader Chance, with a pitching staff starring Three-Finger Brown. They beat the Tigers in the World Series in 1907 and 1908 and won another pennant in 1910. Contending for much of the following decade, the Cubs won again in 1918, mostly on the strength of a rotation of Hippo Vaughn, Lefty Tyler, Claude Hendrix, and Phil Douglas. The team had been invigorated by the absorption of much of the Chicago Whales' roster after the Federal League folded and by the purchase of the Cubs by Whales owner Charles Weeghman, who moved them into the Whales' ballpark. Chewing-gum mogul William Wrigley, Jr., already a shareholder, bought controlling ownership of the club in 1921 and renamed the park Wrigley Field.

The Cubs were again strong in the late 1920s, and won a pennant in 1929 under manager Joe McCarthy. A Hall of Famer himself, McCarthy had three other Hall of Famers on his roster: Rogers Hornsby, Hack Wilson, and Kiki Cuyler. Wilson set the NL RBI and HR records of 190 and 56 in 1930, but declined due to poor conditioning and was out of the majors four years later. Hornsby managed the club from the end of 1930 into the middle of 1932, but it took the relaxed leadership of "Jolly Cholly" Grimm, the team's first baseman, to bring another pennant in 1932. Wilson was gone and Hornsby semi-retired, but two other Hall of Famers took up the slack, Gabby Hartnett and Billy Herman. They were swept in an acrimonious World Series that featured Babe Ruth's "called shot" off Cub pitcher Charlie Root. That year, William Wrigley died and Philip Wrigley inherited the team. Another mid-season managerial change sparked the team to another pennant in 1935, as Hartnett took over the reins and the team won a NL-record 21 straight games (no ties). Hartnett won the NL MVP award, and Phil Cavaretta became a regular at the tender age of 18 and went on to become a Chicago institution, playing 20 seasons with the Cubs. Another pennant came in 1938, when Hartnett delivered his famous "Homer in the Gloamin'" off the Pirates' Mace Brown in a crucial late-season game. However, an ominous pattern developed as the club lost another World Series; they had not had a World Championship since 1908, despite their many pennants.

They would have far fewer chances from then on. A freak pennant in war-weakened 1945 led to another WS loss to Detroit, in a Series that led one reporter to express doubts that either team could win. The Cubs started building the losing reputation that is their latter-day heritage. From 1940 to 1966, the franchise had only three winning seasons (1945, 1946, and 1963) and finished last six times; they were lucky that first the Pirates and then the expansion Mets monopolized the cellar. Even Ernie Banks's consecutive MVP seasons in 1958 and 1959 could only lift them to sixth place. Banks took over from Cavaretta and Stan Hack as the fans' favorite and became known as Mr. Cub. His 47 HR in 1958

The 1938 Chicago Cubs

set the ML record for home runs by a shortstop and came among four straight seasons of 40 or more HR.

The Cubs' desperation led them to the infamous College of Coaches, a system of revolving managers. Used in 1961 and 1962, it "helped" them finish next-to-last both seasons. They went 82–80 in 1963, but blundered in June 1964 when they traded Lou Brock to the Cardinals in a six-player deal in which the best player they got was pitcher Ernie Broglio.

Leo Durocher took over in 1966, promising that "this is not a ninth-place club." He proved himself correct by finishing tenth, but the team contained the nucleus of a contender in regulars Banks, Billy Williams, Ron Santo, Don Kessinger, Randy Hundley, and Glenn Beckert. When Fergie Jenkins developed into a great pitcher in 1967, the Cubs moved up to third place for two years and looked like they'd win it all in 1969. Rooted on by the fanatical Bleacher Bums, they led the league for much of the season, but Durocher overworked his regulars and they wilted in the stretch, perhaps drained by being the only team that played all their home games in the day (when the temperature took more out of them than night games would). They finished second to the Miracle Mets that year, and second to the Pirates in 1970 and 1972; Durocher was replaced by Whitey Lockman in mid-1972. A fifth-place finish in 1973 signaled another era of losing ball. From 1973 through 1983 they had no winning seasons and finished last four times. Philip Wrigley died in 1977 and the Wrigley family sold the franchise to the Chicago *Tribune* in 1981.

GM Dallas Green, who came over from the Phillies, raided his old team for talent and came away with Ryne Sandberg as a throw-in in the swap of Larry Bowa for Ivan DeJesus. Just before the 1984 season, Green acquired outfielders Bob Dernier and Gary Matthews, and they combined with 90-RBI men Ron Cey, Jody Davis, and Leon Durham to put the club in contention. A midseason trade brought pitcher Rick Sutcliffe, who went 16–1 for the Cubs and led them to a division title as the Cubs beat out the equally surprising Mets. But the Padres upset the Cubs in the LCS after Chicago had won the first two games, and Jim Frey's managing was criticized by many observers. The Cubs returned to their losing ways in 1985 and dropped to last place again in 1987. The 1988 season was brightened only by the installation of lights at Wrigley Field, which offended baseball purists but may have saved Wrigley as the venue for future Cubs games. The talent developed under Green's administration (Mark Grace, Damon Berryhill, Jerome Walton, Greg Maddux, Dwight Smith) combined with Frey's acquisition of Mitch Williams and Mike Bielecki and the unorthodox managerial style of Don Zimmer to bring an unexpected division title in 1989. /(SFS)

Chicago White Sox — 1901– . Team. 6867–6810, .502. *AL West Champions 83 AL Champions 01, 06, 17, 19, 59 World Champions 06, 17*

White Sox fans have seen winners who couldn't hit and hitters who couldn't win, their team with short pants and opponents with long hits, scoreboards that exploded and phenoms who were duds, bright victories and baseball's blackest scandal, forty years mostly wandering in the wilderness of the AL second division, and some of the most glorious moments in American baseball history. They've often been frustrated but seldom bored.

The White Sox story began in St. Paul, Minnesota, where Charles Comiskey, a former first baseman and the son of a prominent Chicago politician, managed the Saints, one of the teams in Ban Johnson's successful but minor Western League. In 1900 Johnson and Comiskey, working in tandem, switched the Saints to Chicago's South Side as the first move in upgrading their circuit, which they renamed the American League.

Comiskey's nameless Chicago team won the 1900 AL pennant with a cast of former major leaguers and sandlot players. In 1901 Johnson broke away from the National Agreement and declared the AL a major league in open warfare with the established NL. The White Sox were quick to capitalize, signing such blue-chip players as Clark Griffith, Billy Sullivan, Sam Mertes, and Jimmy Callahan. They coasted to the 1901 title, their first ML pennant, and firmly established themselves in their tiny ballpark on 39th and Princeton Avenues. Comiskey added insult to injury by borrowing the former name of his crosstown rivals: "White Stockings" (shortened to "Sox" in 1902, reportedly to better fit headlines).

The 1906 "Hitless Wonders," short on hitting but very long on pitching and defense, earned the Sox' second AL pennant, then stunned the supposedly unbeatable Cubs of Tinker, Evers, and Chance by downing them in the first (and last) all-Chicago World Series. The next few years were highlighted by the pitching of "Big Ed" Walsh (40 wins in 1908) and the opening of Comiskey Park in 1910.

For all his demonstrated baseball smarts, Comiskey parted with dollars as readily as he parted with

The 1917 Chicago White Sox

blood, but the challenge of a Chicago Federal League franchise together with the presence of the Cubs forced him to revamp his ballclub in 1915. He acquired established stars Joe Jackson, Eddie Cicotte, and Eddie Collins to blend with rising youngsters like Buck Weaver, Red Faber, Lefty Williams, and Ray Schalk. By 1917, he had the best team in baseball, and one of the lowest-paid. His Sox won the world championship in 1917, slumped a year, then roared back stronger than ever in 1919. Surprisingly, they were upset by the Reds in the World Series that year, but they were well on their way to another pennant when the truth about their WS loss exploded. Eight players had conspired with gamblers to throw the Series. The eight "Black Sox"—Jackson, Cicotte, Williams, Hap Felsch, Swede Risberg, Chick Gandil, Fred McMullin, and Buck Weaver—were acquitted in court on technicalities, but new baseball Commissioner Kenesaw Mountain Landis banished them from organized baseball for life. Comiskey died in 1931, romantics insisted from a broken heart.

Stripped of their fallen stars, the Sox struggled for years despite occasional highlights from pitcher Ted Lyons, shortstop Luke Appling, and a few others. In 1936–37, under J. Louis Comiskey (Charles's son),

the team made serious pennant runs. But J. Louis's death in 1939, some catastrophic injuries (ace pitcher Monty Stratton lost his leg in a hunting accident), and WWII all combined to plunge the Sox to the bottom of the AL.

During the 1950s, a grab-bag aggregation built by frantic trader Frank Lane suddenly jelled into the "Go-Go Sox," an exciting contender fueled by Minnie Minoso, Nellie Fox, pitching, and aggressive baserunning. In 1959, shortly after Bill Veeck purchased controlling interest from the Comiskey family, the team won its first pennant in 40 years. Veeck's imaginative promotions, exploding scoreboard, and innovations (including players in short pants) helped take fans' minds off the Sox' slump in the 1960s.

The pennant drought continues, although there have been many outstanding players in White Sox stripes: Richie Zisk, Dick Allen, Wilbur Wood, Carlton Fisk, and Harold Baines, to name only a few. The team got as far as the AL West title in 1983. Owners have come and gone: Veeck to John Allyn, back to Veeck, and on to Jerry Reinsdorf and Eddie Einhorn. Attendance has sometimes dwindled, but hope springs from the promise of a new stadium in the 1990s. /(RL)

Floyd Chiffer — 1956– . RHP 1982–84 **Padres** 130 ip, 5–5, 4.02

Chiffer had a fine rookie 1982 season as a reliever with the Padres, compiling a 2.95 ERA in 51 games. He spent most of the next two seasons in Triple-A, had recurring arm trouble, and was traded to Minnesota. /(MC)

Rocky Childress [Rodney Osborne] — 1962– . RHP 1985–88 Phillies, **Astros** 108 ip, 2–3, 4.76

This finesse pitcher never stuck in the majors. His best and longest stint came in relief in 1987, when he was 1–2 with a 2.98 ERA for the Astros. /(WOR)

Cupid Childs [Clarence Algernon] — 1867–1912. 2B 1888, 90–1901 Phillies, Syracuse (AA), **Cleveland (NL)**, Cardinals, Cubs 1467 g, .306, 20 hr, 654 rbi

Childs hit .345 with a league-high 33 doubles in the 1890 American Association, setting a since-tied major league record with 18 chances accepted at second base in a nine-inning game that June 1. He joined the Cleveland Spiders (NL) in 1891 and became a vital cog in their offense, topping .300 in five of eight seasons and leading the league in runs scored in 1892 (136). His sharp batting eye made him an ideal lefthanded leadoff hitter; he walked 120 times while striking out only 12 in 1893. In 1894 he batted a career-high .353. /(AJA)

Rich Chiles — 1949– . OF-DH 1971–73, 76–78 Astros, Mets, **Twins** 284 g, .254, 6 hr, 76 rbi

Chiles set a team pinch-hitting record (11 hits) with Houston in 1971, and went to the Mets in a 1972 trade for Tommy Agee. His most productive season was 1977 with Minnesota (36 RBI), mostly as a DH/ pinch hitter. /(JCA)

Lou Chiozza — 1910–1971. 2B-3B-OF 1934–39 **Phillies**, Giants 616 g, .277, 14 hr, 197 rbi. *1 WS, 2 g, .286*

Chiozza became the first man to bat in a major league night game when he led off for the Phillies in Cincinnati on May 24, 1935. Lean, swift, and swarthy, he had steel-gray hair even as a rookie. His brothers Dino and Joe also played pro ball; Dino appeared in two games for the 1935 Phillies. /(JCA)

Bob Chipman (Mr. Chips) — 1918–1973. LHP 1941–52 Dodgers, **Cubs**, Braves 880 ip, 51–46, 3.72. *1 WS, 0.1 ip, 0–0, 0.00*

Chipman alternated between long relief and spot starts over his ML career. Never a hard thrower, he failed to impress Dodger manager Leo Durocher

although he did not allow an earned run in four appearances spread over three years (1941–43). Traded to the Cubs for Eddie Stanky in 1944, he went 12–10 that season, his career best. /(MC)

Harry Chiti — 1932– . C 1950–52, 55–56, 58–62 **Cubs**, A's, Tigers, Mets 502 g, .238, 41 hr, 179 rbi

The husky catcher broke in with the Cubs at age 17 and made infrequent appearances in 1950–52. After two years in the military he was handed the starting job in 1955, but hit only .231. The relaxed and flexible Chiti became an excellent knuckleball catcher, but after improving his hitting with Kansas City in 1958–59, he batted just .201 in 1960 and was out of the majors by age 30. /(JCA)

Neil Chrisley [Barbra O'Neil] — 1931– . OF 1957–61 Senators, **Tigers**, Braves 302 g, .210, 16 hr, 64 rbi

Chrisley was a lefthanded power hitter who had 60 homers over his last three minor league seasons and hit .343 at Indianapolis in 1957. He was used sparingly in parts of five ML seasons. /(JCA)

Larry Christenson — 1953– . RHP 1973–83 **Phillies** 1403 ip, 83–71, 3.79. *3 LCS, 14 ip, 0–1, 7.53. 1 WS, .1 ip, 0–1, 108.00*

The Phillies' first draft selection in June 1972, the 6'4″ Christensen won his ML debut in 1973 at age 19. He improved each year, and in 1977 went 19–6, winning 15 of his last 16. Hampered by injuries, he underwent three elbow operations and, in a 1979 charity bike-a-thon, broke his collarbone. He was knocked out in the first inning of Game Four of the 1980 WS, but won a divisional playoff game for the Phillies in strike-shortened 1981. He hit 11 career homers. /(JCA)

Mark Christman — 1913–1976. 3B-SS 1938–39, 43–49 Tigers, **Browns**, Senators 911 g, .253, 19 hr, 348 rbi. *1 WS, 6 g, .091, 1 rbi*

The older brother of NFL quarterback and TV football announcer Paul Christman, Mark was an ardent Cardinal fan who, spurned by Cardinal scouts, signed with Detroit but played most of his career with the Browns. A light hitter but a steady fielder, in his first year as a regular he led AL third basemen with a .972 fielding average in 1944. His career-high 83 RBI that year was more than twice his total for any other season. Sold to Washington in 1947, he played two seasons as the regular Senator shortstop. /(JCA)

Joe Christopher — 1935- . OF 1959-66 Pirates, **Mets**, Red Sox 638 g, .260, 29 hr, 173 rbi. *1 WS, 3 g, --*

The speedy and articulate Virgin Islander scored two runs without an at-bat as a pinch runner for the Pirates in the 1960 WS. An original Met, he had an outstanding 1964 season, hitting .300 with 16 HR and 76 RBI./(JCA)

Russ Christopher — 1917-1954. RHP 1942-48 **A's**, Indians 1000 ip, 54-64, 3.37. *1 WS, 0 ip, infinite*

The slim, 6'3" Christoper won in double figures three times, peaking with 14 victories for the 1944 A's. He pitched exclusively in relief in 1947-48, and his AL-leading 17 saves for Cleveland in his final year figured in the Indians' successful drive for the 1948 World Championship. His brother Lloyd played 16 ML games./(TJ)

Bubba Church [Emory Nicholas] — 1924- . RHP 1950-55 **Phillies**, Reds, Cubs 713 ip, 36-37, 4.10

In late July 1950, Church and Robin Roberts both pitched complete-game shutouts as the Whiz Kid Phillies swept a doubleheader from the Cubs. He was 8-6 as the Phils fought for their first pennant in 35 years but his season ended when he was struck in the face by a line drive off Ted Kluszewski's bat. In 1951 he bounced back with his top season, 15-11./(FK)

Nestor Chylak — 1922-1982. *Umpire* AL 1954-78 *3 LCS, 5 WS, 6 ASU*

Chylak, who "ate and lived umpiring," according to Dave Phillips, was an all-star among his peers. A fine teacher and technician, he set the standard for AL umps during much of his career. On June 14, 1974, unruly fans stormed the Cleveland field during the ninth inning of "Beer Night," when brew was available for 10 cents a cup. The game was tied 5-5 at the time, After several injuries, including a cut wrist for Chylak, peace was temporarily restored. But when another fan fight broke out near the pitcher's mound, Chylak declared visiting Texas the winner by forfeit./(RTM)

Al Cicotte (Bozo) — 1929-1982. RHP 1957-59, 61-62 Yankees, Senators, Tigers, Indians, **Cardinals**, Astros 260 ip, 10-13, 4.36

The grandnephew of Eddie Cicotte, Al spent three seasons with four AL clubs. Demoted to the International League in 1960, his 16-7 record with Syracuse earned him two more ML years. He was nicknamed "Bozo" after an ice cream he favored./(JCA)

Eddie Cicotte — 1884-1969. RHP 1905, 08-20 Tigers, Red Sox, **White Sox** 3224 ip, 208-149, 2.37. 20 wins: 17, 19-20 *2 WS, 45 ip, 2-3, 2.42*
☛ *Led League—w 17, 19. Led League—era 17.*

Had Eddie Cicotte not agreed to throw the 1919 World Series (and not been banned from baseball as a result), he would have been remembered as one of the game's greatest pitchers. He had a repertoire of deceptive pitches, and used pinpoint control and psychology.

In 1917 at age 33, Cicotte led the AL with 28 wins and a 1.53 ERA. He dropped to 12-19 in 1918, but led again in 1919 with a 29-7 mark. He walked few and fielded expertly, and the only time he "beat himself," he was paid $10,000 to do it. Though he took the bribe, he was not one of the disgruntled players at the core of the infamous "Black Sox." He was unhappy with his salary as his career wound down, and he wanted to buy a farm for security. "I did it for the wife and kiddies," he explained, but he had to work many years at Ford in Detroit before he could afford to retire./(JK)

Eddie Cicotte

Pete Cimino — 1942- . RHP 1965-68 Twins, **Angels** 161 ip, 5-8, 3.07

Cimino had only a blazing fastball when he struck out 20 in a minor league game. The one-pitch reliever worked to develop a curve and slurve (a slider-curve hybrid), but despite an excellent strike-out/innings-pitched ratio, he lasted just over two full ML seasons. /(JCA)

Gino Cimoli — 1929- . OF 1956-65 **Dodgers**, Cardinals, Pirates, Braves, A's, Orioles, Angels 969 g, .265, 44 hr, 321 rbi. *2 WS, 8 g, .250, 1 rbi* ☛ *All-Star—57.*

The strong-armed journeyman outfielder and opposite-field hitter had a career-high .293 BA for the Dodgers in 1957. Cimoli went to the Cardinals in December 1958 for Wally Moon and Phil Paine, but was traded to Pittsburgh after the 1959 season. A fourth outfielder for the Pirates, he was a valuable replacement, especially when Bob Skinner was hurt during the 1960 World Series. Cimoli's pinch-single in Game Seven sparked a five-run rally that preceded Mazeroski's dramatic Series-ending homer. Cimoli played regularly for the A's in 1962-63, and led the AL with 15 triples in 1962. /(ME)

Cincinnati Reds [aka Red Stockings, Redlegs] — 1882- . 7715-7537, .506. *American Association Champions 82 NL West Champions 70, 72-73, 75-76, 79 NL Champions 19, 39-40, 61, 70, 72, 75-76 World Champions 19, 40, 75-76*

The Red Stockings were charter members of the National League in 1876 but dropped out in 1881 because the NL banned beer sales at ballparks. They reappeared in the more liberal American Association in 1882, retaining only two players from the 1880 team, and captured the AA pennant on the strength of Will White's 40-win season and the best fielding in the league. They continued to contend in the AA until the franchise was switched to the NL for the 1890 season in an attempt to bolster the league's defense against the Players' League challenge. The club declined after that season and was sold by John T. Brush in 1902. He became famous later as the owner of the more lucrative Giants. The new owners were a group of city political bosses who named colleague August "Garry" Herrmann club president, a role he held until blindness forced him to retire in 1927. He was also the third member of the National Commission as long as that body existed. In 1905 Cy Seymour won the team's first batting title with a .377 average that still stands as the club record.

The Reds won their first NL pennant in 1919, only to have the Black Sox scandal taint their World Series victory. The team was built around Heinie Groh and Hall of Famer Edd Roush. A strong team, they were in contention through the end of Herrmann's tenure. Sidney Weil took over the club after Herrmann's resignation, but he was a victim of the Depression. Radio magnate Powel Crosley wanted to ensure the team would stay in town and bought the club in 1935, two years after Weil had had to turn over the club to the Central Trust Company, the bank that had held it for Weil after his financial collapse. Crosley was persuaded to buy by GM Larry McPhail, whom the bank had hired. Mc-Phail's innovative style led to the first night game in 1935 and a thriving minor league system developed by Frank Lane. When McPhail resigned in mid-1936, Warren Giles took over. The club won back-to-back pennants in 1939-40 and beat Detroit in the 1940 World Series. Stars on the club included Hall of Famer Ernie Lombardi, 1939 MVP Bucky Walters, 1940 MVP Frank McCormick, Paul Derringer, and Johnny "Double No-Hit" Vander Meer, who had pulled off his famous feat in 1938. The team contended through the end of WWII, but then fell to the second division. A bright spot on the weak post-war teams was feared sidearm pitcher Ewell Blackwell, who became the only man to pitch in six consecutive All-Star Games.

Giles was named NL president in 1951 and was replaced as Reds GM by Gabe Paul, who built a slugging team featuring Ted Kluszewski. At about this time the club began to call itself the Redlegs, due to the association of "Reds" with "Communists" during the Senator Joe McCarthy years. The Redlegs almost won a tight three-team race in 1956, but finished third, two games behind the Dodgers. They tied the NL HR record with 221 that season and Birdie Tebbetts won Manager of the Year honors.

Bill DeWitt succeeded Paul after the Reds had sunk to a 67-87 record in 1960, and DeWitt did a masterly job, instantly rebuilding the team with a series of brilliant moves and trades. Led by MVP Frank Robinson and ace Joey Jay, the team won a surprise pennant in 1961 under the direction of manager Fred Hutchinson, who would tragically die of cancer during the 1964 race. The season was chronicled in *Pennant Race* by pitcher Jim Brosnan, who had written *The Long Season* about the 1959 campaign.

The Reds were often contenders through the rest

The 1972 Cincinnati Reds

of the decade. The team was purchased in 1966 by a group headed by Francis Dale after rumors of a move. DeWitt's reputation was tarnished by the ill-advised trade of Robinson to Baltimore in exchange for Milt Pappas, and DeWitt was replaced by Bob Howsam in 1967. Sparky Anderson was named manager in 1970 and immediately won the NL pennant. The decade of the "Big Red Machine" was at hand. Featuring Rookies of the Year Johnny Bench (1968), Pete Rose (1963), and Tommy Helms (1966), other superstars such as Tony Perez, Davey Concepcion, and Lee May, and the young arms of Gary Nolan, Don Gullett, and Wayne Simpson, the team dominated the NL with 102 wins. With the addition of George Foster (acquired in exchange for Frank Duffy), Joe Morgan, Jack Billingham, Tom Seaver, and Ken Griffey, the offensive powerhouse won six division titles in the 1970s, with four NL pennants and back-to-back World Championships in 1975–76. They averaged 95 wins a season in the decade, and only in 1971 did they finish below second place. Bench was named MVP in 1970 and 1972, Rose won in 1973, Morgan took consecutive awards in 1975–76, and Foster won in 1977 with league-leading totals of 52 HR and 149 RBI.

John McNamara replaced Anderson as manager in 1979, and the Reds lost the LCS. The aging team dropped to third in 1980, and although it had the best record in the NL in the strike-split 1981 season, second-place finishes in both halves left the club out of postseason play. The Reds collapsed to last place in 1982 and 1983, with the emergence of Mario Soto as the staff ace the only high point. Howsam, who had moved up to club president, returned to the GM role in 1983, and brought back Rose to manage the team at the end of 1984. That year, colorful Marge Schott, who made her money in used cars, assumed control of the team. The Reds went on to finish second four years in a row (1985–88). The team played 1989 under the cloud of controversy regarding Rose's gambling. /(JFC)

Galen Cisco — 1937– . RHP 1961–65, 67, 69 Red Sox, **Mets**, Royals 659 ip, 25–56, 4.56

Co-captain and fullback for Ohio State's 1957 national collegiate football champs, the curveballing Cisco had little success with Boston and was released on waivers to the 1962 Mets. In the longest game, by time, in ML history (the 7:23, 23-inning Mets-Giants marathon of 5/31/64), he worked the last nine innings, shutting out San Francisco the first eight, then yielding two runs to lose 8–6. In three-plus years with the Mets, he was 18–43. He later became a respected ML pitching coach. /(JCA)

Bill Cissell (Spider Bill) — 1904–1949. 2B-SS 1928–34, 37–38 **White Sox**, Indians, Red Sox, A's, Giants 956 g, .267, 29 hr, 423 rbi

Chicago's Charles Comiskey paid $123,000 for Bill Cissell, who later said, "The ballyhoo I got when Portland sold me for that sum was the greatest burden any player ever carried to the majors." Cissell had six hits in his first 11 ML at-bats in 1928, then struggled. A poor-fielding shortstop, he was moved to second base in 1930. One writer described the double-play combo of Luke Appling and Cissell as the best "Alphonse and Gaston" act in baseball. Cissell's misfortunes in Chicago ended with his 1932 trade to Cleveland. Without the pressure, he batted a career-high .315 that season. Years later he worked as a Comiskey Park maintenance man. He died destitute at age 45; his funeral expenses were paid by Charles Comiskey's grandson, Chuck. /(RL)

Bud Clancy — 1900–1968. 1B 1924–30, 32, 34 **White Sox**, Dodgers, Phillies 522 g, .281, 12 hr, 198 rbi

Clancy's place in the record book came through no effort of his own: he is one of three first basemen to play a full nine innings without a putout or assist (4/27/30). /(JK)

Jim Clancy — 1955– . RHP 1977– **Blue Jays**, Astros 2353 ip, 135–154, 4.16. *1 LCS, 1 ip, 0–1, 9.00*
☛ *All-Star—82.*

The only player to play for the Blue Jays in each of their first 11 seasons, Clancy was the club's record-holder in both wins and losses when he joined the Astros as a free agent before the 1989 season. Selected from Texas in the 1976 expansion draft, he was a consistent starter for the Blue Jays in their wretched early years and joined Dave Steib as a cornerstone of the starting rotation that helped Toronto to prominence in the AL East in the mid-1980s. Clancy enjoyed his best season in 1982, winning a career-high 16 games with a 3.71 ERA for a last-place club, and on September 28 that year he was three outs from a perfect game against Minnesota when he surrendered a broken-bat single and settled for a one-hit shutout. /(TF)

Allie Clark — 1923– . OF 1947–53 Yankees, **Indians**, A's, White Sox 358 g, .262, 32 hr, 149 rbi. *2 WS, 4 g, .200, 1 rbi*

Despite some impressive early credentials, Clark never won a full-time outfield spot. He finished second to Jackie Robinson in the 1947 International League batting race and hit .322 in spot duty in his first two big league seasons, with the Yankees and Indians. /(ME)

Bobby Clark — 1955– . OF 1979–85 **Angels**, Brewers 396 g, .239, 19 hr, 100 rbi. *2 LCS, 3 g, .000, 0 hr, 0 rbi*

Clark was the Texas League MVP in 1978 when he led in home runs and RBI. He failed to hit with the Angels, and was often used as a late-inning defensive replacement for Reggie Jackson. /(MC)

Bryan Clark — 1956– . LHP 1981– **Mariners**, Blue Jays, Indians, White Sox 505 ip, 18–23, 4.17

Clark spent seven years in the minors before sticking with Seattle for all of 1981. Generally unimpressive, from 1984–87 he split time between the Triple-A affiliates and parent clubs of three AL organizations, then signed with Minnesota for 1988. /(JCA)

Earl Clark — 1907–1938. OF 1927–34 **Braves**, Browns 292 g, .291, 4 hr, 81 rbi

Although he hit over .300 three times with the Braves, Clark had no home run power and never played more than 84 games in a season. He suffered a broken hand on Opening Day 1929, but on May 10 of that year he set the ML record for most outfield chances accepted in a nine-inning game with 12 putouts and one assist. /(NLM)

Jack Clark (Jack the Ripper) — 1955– . OF-1B-DH 1975–**Giants**, Cardinals, Yankees, Padres 1658 g, .271, 282 hr, 998 rbi. *2 LCS, 7 g, .364, 1 hr, 4 rbi. 1 WS, 7 g, .240, 4 rbi*
☛ *All-Star—78–79, 85, 87.*

In his first 13 seasons, spent in the NL, this injury-prone slugger appeared in 140 or more games only three times. However, from the time he became a regular in 1977, he has had slugging percentages over .400 every year and five times has slugged better than .500, including a league-leading .597 in 1987. In '87 he led the NL in walks with 136 (while getting 120 hits) and HR percentage while hitting 35 HR with 106 RBI and 93 runs scored before an ankle injury ended his season on September 9. His inactivity probably cost him the MVP and the Cardinals the World Championship.

Clark missed most of 1986 with injuries after being the hero of the 1985 LCS with a dramatic ninth-inning three-run homer off Tom Niedenfuer in Game Six. Clark came to St. Louis prior to the 1985 season in exchange for David Green, Gary Rajsich, Dave LaPoint, and Jose Uribe; Clark had made clear his wish to escape both the Giants and Candlestick Park. In his nine years with San Francisco, Clark established himself as a superb clutch hitter, leading the NL in game-winning RBI (18) in 1980 and tying for the lead (21) in 1982. He led NL outfielders in assists in 1981, but was switched to first base to reduce the risk of injury.

After his career 1987 season, Clark got into a contract squabble with the Cardinals and signed as a free agent with the Yankees, who already had Don Mattingly at first base. He hit .242, his lowest average in a full season, and had 93 RBI, mostly as a DH. He escaped the "Bronx Zoo" to San Diego in return for Stan Jefferson, Lance McCullers, and Jimmy Jones in a blatant salary dump by management, but had his worst season in 1989. /(TF)

Mel Clark — 1926- . OF 1951-55, 1957 **Phillies**, Tigers 215 g, .277, 3 hr, 63 rbi

A slap-hitting outfielder, Clark hit .335 playing part-time for the 1952 Phillies. A 1953 knee injury took something away from his stroke, and his average declined sharply until his final appearances with Detroit in 1957. /(JD)

Rickey Clark — 1946- . RHP 1967-69, 71-72 **Angels** 432 ip, 19-32, 3.38

The sinkerballer joined Bill Rigney's Angels in 1967, going 12-11 with a fine 2.59 ERA. He fell to 1-11 the following year and never again had a season with more than four wins. /(TJ)

Ron Clark — 1943- . 3B-SS-2B 1966-69, 71-72, 75 **Twins**, Pilots/Brewers, A's, Phillies 230 g, .189, 5 hr, 43 rbi

The slim Texan was a rodeo rider, a Golden Gloves boxer, and a fine-fielding third baseman. But he hit only .185 in 1968, the only ML season in which he played more than 100 games. /(JCA)

Stephen C. Clark, Jr. — 1882-1960. *Executive.*

The founder of the National Baseball Hall of Fame, Clark was an heir to the Singer sewing machine fortune. He financed the building of the Hall of Fame Museum and was its president from 1939 until his death. In 1935 when an old baseball, reputed to have been used by Abner Doubleday, was found in a trunk stored in an attic on a farm in Fly Creek, NY, near Cooperstown, Clark bought the ball and exhibited it with other relics in the Village Club in Cooperstown. The small exhibit drew so much attention the idea of a larger museum was born. In 1937 NL president Ford Frick suggested a Hall of Fame be added to the plans. Frick helped get the support of AL president Will Harridge and Commissioner Landis. /(NLM)

Terry Clark — 1960- . RHP 1988- **Angels** 105 ip, 6-8, 5.06

Clark finally made it to the majors in 1988, while the Angels were looking for a fifth starter, and went 6-6 with a 5.05 ERA. The arrival of Bert Blyleven and Jim Abbott in 1989 pushed Clark off the staff. /(JFC)

Tom Clark — 1941- . *Writer.*

Tom Clark's poetic output includes paeans to Bill Lee, Amos Otis, the St. Louis Browns, and, especially, Roberto Clemente. He has written more than twelve books of poems, three novels, and four books on baseball, including an examination of the short, unhappy career of Shuffiin' Phil Douglas, *One More for the Shuffler*. Clark also edited the poetry section of *The Paris Review* for ten years. Born and raised in the Chicago area, he worked as a ballpark usher. /(SH)

Watty Clark [William Watson] — 1902-1972. LHP 1924, 27-37 Indians, **Dodgers**, Giants 1747 ip, 111-97, 3.66. 20 wins: 32

Clark peaked in 1932 with 20 wins for Brooklyn. He won in double figures five straight years (1928-32), but lost a NL-high 19 in 1929. Clark gave up as many or more hits as he had innings pitched in 11 of his 12 seasons. /(EW)

Will Clark (The Natural, Will the Thrill) — 1964- . 1B 1986- **Giants** 582 g, .304, 98 hr, 352 rbi. *2 LCS, 12 g, .489, 3 hr, 11 rbi. 1 WS, 4 g, .250*
☛ *Led League—rbi 88. All-Star—88-89.*

The most consistent NL slugger in the late 1980s, Clark was a member of the 1984 Olympic baseball team and was the second pick in the nation in the 1985 draft. He homered in his first pro at-bat with Fresno (Class A) and duplicated the feat in his first ML at-bat, facing Nolan Ryan in the Astrodome. In 1987 Clark tied a Giants record held by Willie Mays, Orlando Cepeda, and Willie McCovey by driving in runs in nine consecutive games. He led San Francisco to the NL West title with team highs of 35 HR, 91 RBI, and a .308 average while impressing with upper-deck smashes. He was the NL's starting All-Star first baseman in 1988 and 1989 and led the NL in '88 with 109 RBI and 100 walks. In 1989 he and Kevin Mitchell combined with Brett Butler and Rob Thompson to give the Giants the best top four of any lineup. Clark was the '89 LCS MVP, hitting .650 with two HR and 11 RBI. /(TF)

Boileryard Clarke [William Jones] (Noisy Bill) — 1868–1959. C-1B 1893–1905 Baltimore (NL), Boston (NL), **Senators**, Giants 950 g, .256, 21 hr, 431 rbi

Clarke shared catching duties with Wilbert Robinson on three consecutive first-place Baltimore (NL) teams (1894–96). In the American League's initial season, 1901, he was the Senators' first baseman. He later became the Princeton baseball coach. /(JK)

Fred Clarke (Cap) — 1872–1960. OF 1894–1911, 13–15 Louisville (NL), **Pirates** 2245 g, .315, 67 hr, 1015 rbi. *2 WS, 15 g, .245, 2 hr, 9 rbi.*
  Manager 1897–1915 Louisville (NL), **Pirates** 1602–1179, .576. First place: 01–03, 09 *2 WS, 7–8, .467* ☛ *Hall of Fame—1945.*

One of baseball's toughest competitors, a top hitter and daring baserunner, Clarke was the first successful boy manager. Discovered by Louisville owner Barney Dreyfuss in the minors, the lefthanded batter quickly dominated NL pitching to become one of the game's early stars. Clarke went 5-for-5 in his first game (6/30/1894), still a ML record. The leftfielder's playing style was compared to Ty Cobb's. Fearless and dynamic, he considered each season a war and each game a battle. In 1897 Clarke was made Louisville's manager. Despite the added responsibility, he batted a career-high .406.

After the 1899 season, Clarke was one of the 14 players who went to Pittsburgh when Dreyfuss virtually merged the Pirates and Colonels. With the best players from both teams, Clarke's powerhouse won 859 games in 1901–09 (.634 winning percentage). Clarke's strong leadership, potent bat, and a star-studded lineup accounted for three straight NL pennants, culminating with the first World Series in 1903, which the Pirates lost to the Boston Pilgrims (Red Sox).

In 1909 Clarke guided Pittsburgh to a club-record 110 wins and hit two homers against Detroit in the WS, which the Pirates won in seven games. That was Clarke's last great achievement. He had just completed four straight sub-.300 seasons as a hitter, after having hit over .300 ten times in his first 13 campaigns. Pushing sore, aging legs, Cap hit .324 in 1911, then virtually stopped playing, though he appeared in 12 games in 1913–15. After the 1915 season, he quit baseball and returned to his Kansas ranch.

Clarke retired among the all-time leaders in batting average, runs scored, hits, triples, and stolen bases. He was Pittsburgh's most successful manager in both wins (1,422) and percentage (.595) and

Fred Clarke

ranked among the all-time club leaders in games, at-bats, hits, triples, and stolen bases. In 1945 the Hall of Fame Veterans Committee enshrined him at Cooperstown. His brother Josh spent five years in the ML. /(ME)

Horace Clarke (Hoss) — 1940– . 2B-SS-3B 1965–74 **Yankees**, Padres 1272 g, .256, 27 hr, 304 rbi

Clarke, a native of St. Croix, Virgin Islands, took over for Bobby Richardson on the Yankees in 1967 and became one of the league's more surehanded second basemen. His .990 fielding average led the AL at second base in 1967, and he set an AL record by leading in assists at second base six consecutive years, through 1972. He also led in putouts from 1968 through 1971. A durable switch-hitter, he played in at least 143 games every year from '67 to

1973, and led the AL in at-bats in 1969–70. He had 151 career stolen bases. Though he never batted higher than .285, he was a pesky hitter; in 1970 he broke up three no-hitters in the ninth inning, thwarting bids by Joe Niekro, Sonny Siebert, and Jim Rooker. /(JJM)

Nig Clarke [Jay Justin] — 1882–1949. C 1905–11, 19–20 **Indians**, Tigers, Browns, Phillies, Pirates 506 g, .254, 6 hr, 127 rbi

Clarke, one of the first Canadian players to have an extended stay in the majors, was a highly rated defensive catcher hampered by arm problems. The Tigers' Germany Schaefer exploited Clarke's shortcoming in a tie game against Cleveland. Knowing the sore-armed catcher would have trouble throwing, Schaefer stole second, thinking the runner on third could score. When Clarke refused to throw, Schaefer "stole first base" and then, stealing second again, drew an errant throw from Clarke as the winning run scored. /(JK)

Tommy Clarke — 1888–1945. C 1909–18 **Reds**, Cubs 671 g, .265, 6 hr, 191 rbi

A native New Yorker who as a teenager played for George M. Cohan's semi-pro "Yankee Doodle Dandies," Clarke became a valued defensive catcher for the Reds. He was later a Giants coach under John McGraw and Bill Terry. /(JK)

John Clarkson — 1861–1909. RHP 1882, 84–94 Worcester (NL), Cubs, **Braves**, Cleveland (NL) 4536 ip, 326–177, 2.81. 20 wins: 85–92
☛ Led League—w 85, 87, 89. Led League—era 89. Led League—k 85–87, 89. Hall of Fame—1963.

Although never considered the premier pitcher of his day, Clarkson was highly regarded by teammates and opponents alike. He is still among the all-time leaders in wins, winning percentage, complete games, innings pitched, and several fielding categories.

Starting in an era of two-man rotations, Clarkson led the NL in wins, appearances, starts, complete games, innings, and strikeouts in 1885, 1887, and 1889; in shutouts in 1885 and 1889; and in strikeouts and ERA in 1889. As a result, the teams he pitched for during this period, the Chicago White Sox (later the Cubs) and the Boston Beaneaters (later the Braves), were consistently in contention, winning two pennants each. He accounted for 53 of the White Sox' 87 wins in 1885, and 49 of Boston's 83 victories in 1889. His win totals in those two years rank second and fourth on the all-time season list.

John Clarkson

On July 27, 1885, Clarkson hurled a no-hit, no-run game against the Providence Grays.

Manager Cap Anson proclaimed Clarkson "one of the greatest of pitchers," but complained about his ace's perpetual psychological demands, chiding that "he won't pitch if scolded." Clarkson was intelligent, sensitive, handsome, and generally subdued, but was not above certain acts of indiscretion on the field. In one game, he pitched a lemon instead of a ball to prove to the umpire that it was too dark to continue play. His contemporaries considered him a calculating, scientific pitcher who carefully analyzed every hitter's weaknesses. Peering out from deep-set dark eyes, his long, lean fingers cradling the ball, he had a slow, assured pace to his delivery, and he may well have dominated some hitters by intimidation alone.

The deal which sent Clarkson to Boston in 1888 rocked the baseball world, as he and teammate Mike "King" Kelly were sold outright to the Beaneaters for $10,000 apiece—an incredible sum at the time. After four years in Boston, a new manager, Frank Selee, traded Clarkson to also-ran Cleveland, where his talents faded. Along with pitching siblings Dad and Walter, John Clarkson shares third place in most career wins by brothers, behind the Niekros and Perrys (John and Dad both pitched for Boston in 1892). A business student before turning to pro ball, Clarkson purchased a cigar store in Cambridge upon retirement, and ran it until his death at age 47. He was inducted into the Hall of Fame 54 years later. /(AAs)

Walter Clarkson — 1878–1946. RHP 1904–08 **Yankees**, Indians 375 ip, 18–16, 3.17

The youngest of the pitching Clarkson brothers, Walter pitched for Harvard when the Ivy League school dominated college baseball. He was 9–4 with a 2.32 ERA for New York in 1906. /(JK)

Dain Clay (Ding-a-Ling) — 1919– . OF 1943–46 **Reds** 433 g, .258, 3 hr, 98 rbi

As players marched off to WWII, Clay moved from utility man to full-timer in the Reds' outfield. As his playing time increased, so did his defensive skills, and he showed some speed on the bases. /(EW)

Ken Clay — 1954– . RHP 1977–81 **Yankees**, Rangers, Mariners 354 ip, 10–24, 4.68. *1 LCS, 4 ip, 0.00. 2 WS, 6 ip, 6.00*

All but buried in the Yankee bullpen, the hard-throwing Clay starred in Game One of the 1978 AL LCS when he no-hit the Royals for 3-2/3 relief innings. New York sent Clay to Texas in a 1980 trade for Gaylord Perry. /(JCA)

Mark Clear — 1956– . RHP 1979–88 Angels, **Red Sox**, Brewers 797 ip, 71–49, 3.83. *1 LCS, 5.2 ip, 0–0, 4.76*
☛ *All-Star—79, 82.*

Clear's sweeping curveball was almost unhittable, but it didn't find the strike zone often enough to make him a dominating reliever. He still averaged more than one strikeout per inning over 10 ML seasons, and won 14 and saved 14 as the Red Sox' bullpen ace in 1982. /(SCL)

Doug Clemens — 1939– . OF 1960–68 Cardinals, **Cubs**, Phillies 452 g, .229, 12 hr, 88 rbi

A pinch-hitting specialist, Clemens went from the Cardinals to the Cubs as part of the Lou Brock deal in May 1964. He was platooned in centerfield and hit .279 in Chicago. After the Phillies acquired him for Wes Covington in 1966, he led the NL in pinch-hit at-bats in both 1966 and 1967. His career pinch-hit batting average of .229 matched his overall average. /(MC)

Roger Clemens (Rocket) — 1962– . RHP 1984- **Red Sox** 1285 ip, 95–45, 3.07. 20 wins: 86–87 *2 LCS, 30 ip, 1–1, 4.25. 1 WS, 12 ip, 0–0, 3.18*
☛ *Most Valuable Player—86. Led League—w 86–87. Led League—era 86. Led League—k 88. Cy Young Award—86–87. All-Star—86, 88.*

As a youngster, Clemens idolized all-time strikeout king Nolan Ryan, and in less than five full ML seasons he emerged as Ryan's rival as baseball's most overpowering pitcher. The physically imposing, 6'4" 220-lb Clemens has a confident attitude that borders on arrogance, impeccable mechanics, outstanding control, a good curveball, and a 95-mph fastball that can leave batters flailing helplessly. Clemens became only the fourth pitcher ever to win back-to-back Cy Young Awards, established a ML record with 20 strikeouts in a nine-inning game, and pitched 18 shutouts in his first 139 starts.

Originally drafted by the Mets out of high school, Clemens opted to pitch in college instead of signing, and in 1983 won the championship game of the College WS for the University of Texas. The Texas pitching staff included future major leaguers Greg Swindell, Calvin Schiraldi, and Bruce Ruffin. Drafted in the first round (19th overall) by the Red Sox that June, Clemens tore through Boston's minor league system. He fanned 36 batters in 29 innings at Class A Winter Haven and struck out 59 in 52 innings at Class AA New Britain before winning the Eastern League championship game with a three-hit shutout. In 1984, he began the season at Class AAA Pawtucket, struck out 50 in 39 innings, and was promoted to the ML in early May. On August 21, he fanned 15 Royals and walked none, and he finished the season 9–4. Shoulder troubles limited Clemens to a disappointing 15 starts in 1985, and he had surgery on his pitching shoulder on August 30.

At the start of 1986, Clemens's shoulder was still a question mark, but the 24-year-old responded with one of the finest pitching seasons in ML history. He won his first three starts and, on April 29, leaped into the national spotlight with 20 strikeouts in a 3–1 win over Seattle, breaking the record of 19 shared by Ryan, Steve Carlton, and Tom Seaver. In that game, Clemens tied an AL record with eight consecutive strikeouts and didn't walk a single batter. Red Sox manager John McNamara said afterwards, "I watched perfect games by Catfish Hunter and Mike Witt, but this was the most awesome pitching performance I've ever seen."

Clemens ran his record to 14–0 before losing to Toronto July 2, pitched three perfect innings to win the All-Star Game MVP award, and finished the season 24–4 with a 2.48 ERA. He won the AL Cy Young and MVP awards. In the postseason, however, he won only one of his four starts, and the Red Sox lost the WS in seven games.

Clemens skipped spring training in 1987 in a contract squabble, and was only 4–6 on June 12 that year, but went 16–3 the rest of the way to finish 20–9 with a league-leading seven shutouts and win his second consecutive Cy Young Award. In 1988, Clemens's 291 strikeouts were a Red Sox record, and he finished 18–12 with an AL-best eight shutouts. /(SCL)

Roberto Clemente (Bob) — 1934–1972. OF
1955–72 **Pirates** 2433 g, .317, 240 hr, 1305 rbi. *3 LCS, 12 g, .265, 1 hr, 7 rbi. 2 WS, 14 g, .362, 2 hr, 7 rbi*
☛ *Most Valuable Player—66. Led League—ba 61, 64–65, 67. All-Star—60–67, 69–72. Gold Glove—61–72. Hall of Fame—1973.*

Roberto Clemente left his mark on baseball with a style of play rarely seen in modern ML competition. In a combination of brilliant scouting and luck, the Pirates claimed the Puerto Rican-born 20-year-old from the Dodgers' Montreal farm club for $4,000 in the 1954 minor league draft.

Clemente came to a club that had suffered through three straight 100-loss seasons and was the laughingstock of baseball. He was not an immediate superstar, although his brilliant fielding ability and rifle arm were apparent from the beginning. He would eventually earn 12 Gold Gloves as a right fielder and set a ML record by leading the NL in assists five times.

In 1960 the righthanded hitter began a streak of eight consecutive seasons in which he batted no less than .312. He made the first of his 14 All-Star appearances in the two 1960 games. That year, Pittsburgh fielded its best team since Clemente's arrival, winning the NL pennant. He hit safely in every game of the World Series against the Yankees, batting .310. In Game Seven, he kept an eighth-inning rally alive with a hustling infield single, setting up a go-ahead homer by Hal Smith. But Clemente never wore his 1960 Championship ring. He finished eighth in the NL MVP voting, though he'd led the Pirates with 94 RBI; feeling snubbed, he wore his 1961 All-Star ring instead.

Clemente won the first of four NL batting titles with a .351 mark in 1961. For the next several years, he was consistently brilliant. In the outfield,

Roberto Clemente

he would track down every ball in range, often making spectacular diving or leaping catches. He played caroms out of the tricky right field corner at Forbes Field faultlessly. On routine flies, he used the basket catch made famous by his contemporary, Willie Mays. At bat, Clemente seemed forever uncomfortable, always rolling his neck and stretching his back. Standing deep in the box, he would pounce on inside pitches, or wait and drive outside deliveries to right field. Playing in spacious Forbes Field reduced his home run totals. His baserunning style was marked by effort and determination, with arms and legs pumping and helmet often flying off.

Despite his all-out play, Clemente was unjustly considered a hypochondriac. When he hurt, he said so, an uncommon practice in his day. Despite a severe back injury in 1954, an arm injury in 1959, and an attack of malaria in 1965, the label stuck, even though he played 140 or more games in eight straight seasons, 1960–67.

Clemente won two more batting titles in 1964 (.339) and 1965 (.329). Long overdue recognition finally came in 1966; though the Pirates finished third, and Clemente did not lead the league in any major offensive category, his career-high 29 HR and 119 RBI helped him win the MVP award. In 1967 he captured his fourth batting crown with a .357 average, his best ever. By then, he was becoming the elder statesman on a young Pittsburgh team. Indisputably one of baseball's greatest players, he still did not receive a great deal of national media attention until 1971, when Pittsburgh met Baltimore in the World Series. Clemente played like a man possessed, chasing down fly balls, unleashing great throws at every opportunity, batting .414 with 12 hits and two home runs, one in Pittsburgh's climactic Game Seven victory, and winning the Series MVP award.

On September 30, 1972, Clemente drove a double off Met pitcher Jon Matlack at Three Rivers Stadium for his 3,000th career hit. His .312 average that year marked his 13th .300 season and he was at or near the top of every batting category in Pirate history.

On New Year's Eve of 1972, Clemente boarded a DC-7 loaded with relief supplies for earthquake victims in Managua, Nicaragua. Shortly after take-off, the plane crashed into the Atlantic Ocean, a mile off the Puerto Rican coast. There were no survivors. The five-year mandatory waiting period for Hall of Fame eligibility was waived and Clemente was inducted in 1973. The Pirates retired his uniform number 21. /(ME)

Jack Clements — 1864–1941. C 1884–1900 Philadelphia (UL), **Phillies**, Cardinals, Cleveland (NL), Braves 1157 g, .286, 77 hr, 672 rbi

Clements was a lefthanded-throwing catcher, a squat, powerful man who hit home runs when they were a rarity. He caught 105 games in 1892, and was the last lefthanded catcher to play regularly. Righthanded batters learned to duck when a runner broke for second; Clements simply fired away. /(JK)

Pat Clements — 1962– . LHP 1985– Angels, **Pirates**, Yankees 285 ip, 12–10, 3.89

Because lefthanded relievers with control are a valued commodity, Clements was one of the players the Pirates asked for when they sent John Candelaria and George Hendrick to the Angels in 1985. Cle-

ments, a rookie, was 5–0 when traded. He went 0–6 in 92 appearances for Pittsburgh before he was sent to the Yankees with Rick Rhoden after the 1986 season. /(JCA)

Verne Clemons (Fats) — 1892–1959. C 1916, 19–24 Browns, **Cardinals** 474 g, .286, 5 hr, 140 rbi

A specialist in handling spitball pitchers, Clemons called Spittin' Bill Doak the most effective hurler he ever caught. In 1921 the stout backstop hit .320 in 117 games for the Cardinals. /(NLM)

Donn Clendenon — 1935– . 1B 1961–72 **Pirates**, Expos, Mets, Cardinals 1362 g, .274, 159 hr, 682 rbi. *1 WS, 4 g, .357, 3 hr, 4 rbi*

Football's Cleveland Browns, basketball's Harlem Globetrotters, and baseball's Pittsburgh Pirates all offered contracts to 6'4" Donn Clendenon. He chose the Pirates, and batted .302 for them in 80 games his rookie season (1962). In 1966 he hit 28 homers and drove in 98 runs, both career highs, while hitting .299. Clendenon twice topped NL batters in strikeouts. He led NL first basemen in errors three times, but he also paced them in double plays five times, and three times each in putouts and assists. The Expos took Clendenon in the October 1968 NL expansion draft, but dealt him to the Mets in June of 1969. Platooned with Ed Kranepool, Clendenon provided power that was critical to the team's surprising surge to a pennant. His home runs in Games Two, Four, and Five of the 1969 World Series meant the difference in each contest, and earned Clendenon the Series MVP award. He might never have played for the Mets had he not vetoed his trade from Montreal to Houston the previous January. /(TJ)

Cleveland Indians — 1901– . Team. 7061–6816, .509. *AL Champions 20, 48, 54 World Champions 20, 48*

As an American League charter franchise, the Cleveland Indians have a rich heritage overshadowed by a drought that began prior to the first expansion. First called the Blues, then the Bronchos, Cleveland became the Naps when Nap Lajoie was acquired in 1902. Pitching was an early and consistant club focal point. Addie Joss posted Hall of Fame credentials, including a perfect game during the heated 1908 pennant race. His career was tragically shortened by tuberculosis.

A new era dawned when Tris Speaker was acquired by the newly named Indians. After second place finishes in 1918 and 1919, Cleveland survived more tragedy to win its first pennant. Despite the loss of star shortstop Ray Chapman, killed by a Carl

The 1954 Cleveland Indians

Mays pitch, the Indians outlasted the scandal-ridden White Sox and the Yankees to reach a memorable World Series featuring the first grand slam in Series history (Elmer Smith), first homer by a pitcher (30-game winner Jim Bagby), and the only unassisted triple play in championship annals (Bill Wambsganss). Cleveland topped Brooklyn five games to two.

The next 28 pennant-less years were highlighted by near-misses in 1921 and 1926 and the Crybabies incident of 1940. Four years earlier, Bob Feller burst on the scene to begin a legendary career. Teamed with pitchers Mel Harder and Johnny Allen, plus young shortstop Lou Boudreau, Cleveland was the team to beat in 1940. Still, discord between players and manager Ossie Vitt increased to the point that club members petitioned owner Alva Bradley to replace the unpopular skipper. Bradley refused, the Indians were labeled Crybabies, and Detroit rallied to the pennant when unknown Floyd Giebel beat Feller in the season's final weekend.

The golden age of Cleveland baseball dawned on June 21, 1946, when Bill Veeck purchased the club from Bradley. Veeck made Larry Doby the first black to play in the American League in 1947. In 1948 he brought Negro League great Satchel Paige to the big leagues. Led by MVP player-manager Boudreau, the 1948 Indians topped the AL in batting average, fielding average, ERA, and drew a record home attendance of over 2.6 million fans. They beat the Boston Red Sox in the first-ever AL pennant playoff, then turned back the Braves in the World Series, four games to two. Feller suffered both losses, despite a brilliant two-hitter in the first game. Cleveland remained a contender for the next decade.

Following three straight second-place finishes (1951–53) under new manager Al Lopez, Cleveland posted the winningest regular season in ML history (111) in 1954, then failed to win once in the World Series against the Giants. Further tragedy occurred in the late 1950s. Herb Score's brilliant early career was ruined by a line drive off Gil McDougal's bat and by subsequent arm trouble. A young, contending club built by Frank Lane for 1959 was devastated by the most controversial trade in club history. Lane sent young, handsome home run champ Rocky Colavito to Detroit for batting champ Harvey Kuenn. Thirty years of frustration followed. Underfinanced ownership barely kept the club afloat. Rumors of a move to cities like New Orleans and Seattle were constant. What success there was usually came on the pitching mound. Sam McDowell was the AL Sandy Koufax, but alcoholism kept him from greater success. Luis Tiant was AL ERA king in the year of the pitcher (1968). Gaylord Perry, acquired in a trade for McDowell, was Cleveland's first Cy Young Award winner (1972).

The Indians made Frank Robinson the majors' first black manager in 1974. Players came and went, the best demanding trades or seeking free agency rather than play for a non-contender with poor attendance in the ancient and cavernous stadium. As a renaissance in both Cleveland and baseball took shape in the late 1980s, financially solid ownership, in the person of brothers Richard and David Jacobs, took over in December 1986. /(ME)

Cleveland Stadium (The Mistake on the Lake)
Cleveland Indians 1932– . LF-320, CF-400, RF-320

Currently the major league's largest stadium with a capacity of 77,797, Cleveland Stadium opened in 1932 for the Indians' Sunday and holiday games, while the remainder of their home schedule was played at League Park. By 1947 the entire schedule had been moved to this massive structure near the shore of Lake Erie. Originally called Lakefront and later Municipal Stadium, it has a circular, covered, double-decked grandstand that extends well beyond the foul poles before giving way to uncovered bleachers, which were originally 463' from home plate in right- and left-center fields. An inner fence was installed in April 1947, cutting the distance for a home run by over 40 feet, but to this date no ball has reached the centerfield bleachers. On September 12, 1954 the largest crowd in AL history (84,587) watched an Indians-Yankees game, but more recently poor Indians clubs and harsh winds from the nearby lake have often left the cavernous stadium depressingly empty. It is also home to the NFL's Cleveland Browns. /(SCL)

Reggie Cleveland — 1948– . RHP 1969–81
Cardinals, **Red Sox**, Rangers, Brewers 1809 ip, 105–106, 4.02. *1 LCS, 5 ip, 5.40. 1 WS, 7 ip, 0–1, 6.75*

This native Canadian was a durable starter and reliever who went 12–12 for St. Louis in 1971 to earn NL Rookie Pitcher of the Year honors. He won at least 10 games seven straight years, with 14 victories for the Cardinals in both 1972 and 1973. He was 46–41 in four-plus seasons with Boston. He was used mostly in relief with the Rangers and Brewers. /(EW)

Tex Clevenger [Truman Eugene] — 1932– . RHP
1954, 1956–62 Red Sox, **Senators**, Angels, Yankees
695 ip, 36–37, 4.18

Clevenger won a Boston roster spot after posting a 16–2 minor league record in 1953. He went to Washington, and was 9–9 in a league-leading 55 appearances in 1958. The Angels claimed Clevenger in the 1960 expansion draft, subsequently sending him and Bob Cerv to the Yankees in a trade for Ryne Duren. Clevenger closed his career with a 2–0 record and 2.84 ERA for the 1962 Yanks. /(TJ)

Stu Cliburn — 1956– . RHP 1984–85, 88 **Angels**
185 ip, 13–5, 3.11

Originally signed by Pittsburgh, Cliburn was picked up as a free agent by the Angels in 1982. He had a twin brother, Stan, who was an outfielder in the Angels' organization for six years. Stu relied upon a 90-mph fastball and a hard-breaking curve. He was named Angel "Rookie of the Year" in 1985, when he was 9–3 with six saves and a 2.09 ERA. /(EW)

Harlond Clift (Darkie) — 1912– . 3B 1934–45 **Browns**, Senators 1582 g, .272, 178 hr, 829 rbi
☛ *All-Star—37.*

In the years 1934–43, the St. Louis Browns' average season record was 62–90; in two of those seasons, they lost over 100 games. The rare good player on such a team is bound to go unrecognized. Harlond Clift was the most consistent power-hitting third baseman of his era, but was selected to the All-Star squad only once. When he hit 29 HR in 1937, it was a ML record for third basemen. He topped it the following year with 34 HR (third overall in the AL that season), and led the league's third basemen in HR four straight years, 1936–39. In his nine full seasons with the Browns he averaged 19 homers, 31 doubles, and 104 walks, hitting .300 twice and slugging .500 three times.

He was also one of the best fielders in the league; his 50 double plays and 405 assists in 1937 were records until Graig Nettles broke them in 1971, and Clift's 637 total chances in 1937 is still the second-best mark of this century. When he retired, his 309 double plays had broken Pie Traynor's career mark for third basemen.

Traded to the Senators in 1943, Clift missed the

Browns' one-shot championship the next year, and illness and injury ended his career in 1945. /(SH)

Ty Cline — 1939- . OF 1960-71 Indians, **Braves,** Cubs, Giants, Expos, Reds 892 g, .238, 6 hr, 125 rbi. *1 LCS, 2 g, 1.000. 1 WS, 3 g, .333*

An All-American at Clemson, Cline spent virtually all of his ML career as a reserve outfielder and pinch hitter. He scored the Reds' winning runs (after pinch hitting) in both the first and third games of the 1970 LCS. /(RMu)

Gene Clines (Roadrunner) — 1946- . OF 1970-79 **Pirates,** Mets, Rangers, Cubs 870 g, .277, 5 hr, 187 rbi. *3 LCS, 5 g, .167, 1 hr, 1 rbi. 1 WS, 3 g, .091*

Clines batted .405 in his 31-game 1970 ML debut. A fourth outfielder for Pittsburgh, he was noted for his defensive skills. Besides batting .308 in 1971, "Road Runner" stole 15 bases. After hitting .334 in 107 contests in 1972, his hitting declined. The Cubs made him a coach in 1979. /(TJ)

Billy Clingman — 1869-1958. 3B-SS-2B 1890-91, 95-1901, 03 Cincinnati (PL), Cincinnati-Milwaukee (AA), Pirates, **Louisville (NL),** Cubs, Senators, Indians 816 g, .246, 8 hr, 301 rbi

Clingman was considered the fastest infielder with the most accurate arm of the 1890s while with Louisville (NL). As a third baseman, Clingman led the NL in assists in 1896 and in fielding average in 1897. Moved to shortstop in 1898, he led AL shortstops in fielding average and assists in 1901. /(NLM)

Lu Clinton — 1937- . OF 1960-67 **Red Sox,** Angels, A's, Indians, Yankees 691 g, .247, 65 hr, 269 rbi

A good fielder with a strong and accurate throwing arm, Clinton could also be dangerous offensively. He had 52 extra-base hits for the Red Sox in both 1962 and 1963, including 22 HR (second on the club) in 1963. He had 77 RBI that year, but in four ensuing seasons with six clubs never again hit so productively. /(TJ)

Tony Cloninger — 1940- . RHP 1961-72 **Braves,** Reds, Cardinals 1768 ip, 113-97, 4.07. 20 wins: 65 *1 LCS, 5 ip, 3.60. 1 WS, 7 ip, 0-1, 7.36*

Raised on a North Carolina farm, the barrel-chested Cloninger usually got tougher as the game went on. He won 57 games in the 1964-66 seasons, peaking in 1965 with a 24-11 mark for Milwaukee. The $100,000 bonus baby was not only an effective, fireballing pitcher, but a dangerous batter as well. On July 3, 1966 against San Francisco, he hit two grand slams in one game, the only man—no less the only pitcher—in NL history to do so. His nine RBI that day are a one-game ML record for a pitcher. After a shoulder muscle pull and eye problems caused by a virus dropped his 1967 record to 4-7, he was traded to Cincinnati. Though he had mixed success there, he contributed nine wins to the Reds' 1970 NL pennant. /(JCA)

David Clyde — 1955- . LHP 1973-75, 78-79 **Rangers,** Indians 416 ip, 18-33, 4.63

Rangers owner Bob Short drafted Clyde number one in 1973, signed him for a $125,000 bonus, and rushed him to the majors against the advice of scouts. Clyde started 39 games in two years but developed arm trouble. His best season was 8-11 in 1978 after a trade to the Indians. /(MC)

Otis Clymer (Grump) — 1880-1926. OF 1905-09, 13 Pirates, **Senators,** Cubs, Braves 385 g, .267, 2 hr, 98 rbi

Clymer hit .296 his rookie year, but persistent leg injuries hampered the switch-hitter's career. /(JK)

Andy Coakley — 1882-1963. RHP 1902-09, 1911 A's, Reds, Cubs, Yankees 1072 ip, 60-59, 2.36. 20 wins: 05 *1 WS, 9 ip, 0-1, 2.00*

Coakley is best remembered as Lou Gehrig's coach at Columbia University, where he directed the baseball team, 1915-51. Years before that, he came to the Philadelphia A's from Holy Cross, a natty collegian considered the "Beau Brummel" of baseball. He won 20 games in 1905 but, in his only World Series appearance, became one of Christy Mathewson's victims when the Giants' superstar threw three shutouts against the Athletics. Columbia's baseball team currently plays at Andy Coakley Field. /(JK)

Gil Coan — 1922- . OF 1946-56 **Senators,** Orioles, White Sox, Giants 918 g, .254, 39 hr, 278 rbi

As a rookie, Coan took on five-time AL stolen-base champ George Case in a Griffith Stadium foot race. "Gil Coan was very fast, but I beat him," Case said years later. "It was a darn good promotion and pulled a lot of people into the ballpark, including General Eisenhower." With 23 stolen bases in 1948, Coan finished second in the AL. In 1950 and 1951 he put together back-to-back .303 seasons. /(TJ)

Pacific Coast League Minor League 1903- .

The Pacific Coast League has operated continuously since 1903, making it the second-oldest extant minor league. The original six-team membership consisted of San Francisco, Los Angeles, Oakland, Sacramento, Portland, and Seattle. During its early years the PCL battled several outlaw leagues for fan support; by 1909 it had established itself as the predominant Western baseball organization, and remained so until the arrival of NL teams in 1958.

Thriving under strong local ownership, the PCL expanded to eight teams in 1919. A 200-game March-to-October schedule was the PCL norm, producing extraordinary season statistics such as Tony Lazzeri's 60 home runs and 222 RBI for Salt Lake City in 1925.

In the years following WWII, supported by minor league attendance records set in 1946–47 at San Francisco, Oakland, and Los Angeles during close pennant races, a strong movement developed to grant the PCL major league status. Open Classification, just a step below major league level, was obtained in 1952. However, the transfer of the Dodgers and Giants in 1958 robbed the PCL of its largest cities and ended its major league aspirations./(DB)

Jim Coates — 1932– . RHP 1956, 59–63, 65–67 **Yankees**, Senators, Reds, Angels 683 ip, 43–22, 4.00. *3 WS, 13 ip, 0–1, 4.15*

"Coates," wrote Jim Bouton in *Ball Four* of his skeletal former teammate, "could pose as the illustration for an undertaker's sign. He has a personality to match . . . [and] was famous for throwing at people and then not getting into the fights that resulted." Regardless of Bouton's unflattering portrait, Coates was an effective pitcher for the Yankees in 1959–62, working both as a starter and reliever. He won 39 and lost only 15, with 15 saves. He benefited to an unusual extent from the strong offensive support the Yankees could offer./(MC)

Ty Cobb [Tyrus Raymond] (The Georgia Peach) — 1886–1961. OF 1905–1926 **Tigers**, A's 3034 g, .367, 118 hr, 1961 rbi. *3 WS, 17 g, .354, 11 rbi.*
    Manager 1921–26 **Tigers** 479–444, .519
☛ *Most Valuable Player—11. Led League—ba 05–15, 17–19. Led League—hr 09. Led League—rbi 07–09, 11. Hall of Fame—1936.*

Cobb has the highest career batting average in baseball history. When he retired after the 1928 season, he held 90 major league records. But his skill as a hitter is almost overshadowed by his reputation as the fiercest competitor ever, a reputation he encouraged. He would ceremoniously pick out a prominent location in the dugout and start sharpen-ing his spikes in full view of suddenly nervous opposing infielders.

One of the most vivid Cobb anecdotes is the half-true story of an interview that supposedly took place in the late 1950s. Cobb was asked how he would hit under "modern" conditions. Cobb answered, "Oh, I'd hit .310, .315." The interviewer was shocked. "But Mr. Cobb," he protested, "you hit over .400 three times! Why would you only hit .300 now?" Deadpan, Cobb replied, "Well, you have to remember. I'm 72 years old now." The other apocryphal stories about Cobb, a natural righthander who taught himself to hit lefthanded so he could be closer to first base, aren't as dubious. For instance: By mid-1925, he had finally had enough of reporters asking him about Babe Ruth's awesome home run prowess. Cobb, who had a split-handed grip that gave him more bat control but less power, had a well-known disdain for the long ball and the boisterous Babe, and told reporters that hitting home runs didn't take any special skill. To prove his point, he slid his hands down to the knob of the bat, Ruthian style, then hit three HR in that day's game against the Browns (5/5/25). To pound the point home, he hit two more the next day.

When the scrawny 18-year-old rookie joined the veteran Tigers in 1905, he was harassed regularly. Although the determined youngster doubled off Jack Chesbro in his first at-bat, he didn't hit well as a rookie. But in 1907 he became the youngest player ever to win a batting title. Cobb's own favorite moment came late in the 1907 season. The Tigers were only percentage points ahead over the Athletics for the league lead when the two teams met in Philadelphia on September 30. The A's took an 8–6 lead into the ninth, when Cobb smacked a two-run homer to tie the score. The two teams played 17 innings to a 9–9 tie, mathematically eliminating the A's and giving the Tigers their first pennant.

Cobb's batting title in 1907 was the first of 12, still a record, and first of nine in a row, also a record. He also established himself as a fine fielder. Cobb had 30 outfield assists in 1907, led the league in assists in 1908, and finished his career second all-time in assists and double plays among outfielders.

The Tigers took a third straight AL pennant in 1909, again stealing it from the A's, again with Cobb in the middle of things. In the first game of a three-game set against the A's in Detroit on August 24, Cobb's sharpened spikes opened up an ugly gash in third baseman Frank Baker's arm. Although the popular Baker finished the game, the Tigers swept the series to take first place and A's fans were

Ty Cobb, batting

incensed. The two teams met again in Philadelphia near the end of the season. Cobb had received telegraphed death threats that many, but not he, took seriously. Cobb got a police escort to and from the ballpark. Policemen ringed the field and plainclothesmen wandered the stands, but the only thing aimed at the hated Cobb was Philadelphia invective. The Tigers claimed their third pennant, and Cobb won his only Triple Crown, leading the league with 9 HR, 107 RBI, and a .377 average. The 1909 Series against the Pirates pitted AL batting champ Cobb against the NL's greatest star and batting champ, shortstop Honus Wagner. In the second game, after scoring the Tigers' first run on a steal of home, Cobb found himself on first. He yelled down at Wagner, "Watch out, Krauthead, I'm comin' down on the next pitch!" Sure enough, he took off. The 200-lb Wagner calmly took the throw and applied a none-too-gentle tag right in Cobb's mouth. The Tigers lost

their third straight Series, the first and only time a team has dropped three consecutive World Series.

It looked as if Cobb would win a fifth straight batting title in 1910, the year auto maker Chalmers decided to award the batting champ in each league with a new car. Cobb had a comfortable lead over the Indians' Nap Lajoie, but was sidelined the final game of the season. Lajoie was in St. Louis for a doubleheader, needing a perfect day to take the batting title. The Browns, like everyone else, wanted Lajoie to beat out the hated Cobb, and did all they could do to help Lajoie. In his first at-bat, Lajoie got a triple when his fly ball was "lost in the sun." Lajoie lined a clean single his next time up. Browns manager Jack O'Connor then ordered rookie third baseman Red Corrigan to play deep on the outfield grass, and the swift Lajoie exploited the alignment with six straight bunt singles. The final figures gave Cobb the title, .38415 to .38411, but Chalmers gave both players cars. O'Connor and Browns coach Henry Howell were later fired by the Browns. Ironically, later research revealed that record-keeping errors had denied Lajoie the title.

In 1911 Cobb set an AL record by hitting in 41 straight games, but Shoeless Joe Jackson was challenging Cobb for the batting title when the Tigers visited Jackson's Indians for a six-game set late in the season, the occasion of another apocryphal story. The young Jackson, batting over .400, was a great admirer of Cobb and tried hard to be friendly, but Cobb purposely ignored him. The slight supposedly flustered Jackson and affected his hitting. Cobb went on to win the title with a .420 average, while Jackson finished at .408. In 1912 Cobb was the unwitting catalyst to baseball's first strike. In a May 15 game against the Highlanders, Cobb's ears were burning from the continuous insults of a fan sitting behind the dugout. When Cobb could take no more, he charged into the stands and beat the fan senseless. Cobb was immediately suspended. The Tigers declared they would not play again until Cobb was reinstated. They were scheduled to play in Philadelphia the next day, and Tiger owner Frank Navin was notified he would be fined $5,000 if he didn't field a team. The players refused to play, so Navin and manager Hughie Jennings rounded up a group of amateurs to fill in. Needless to say, the ersatz Tigers were pounded 24–2. Cobb persuaded his teammates to go back before the next game. Jackson hit .395 that year, but Cobb ended up with his second straight .400 season, finishing at .410, which prompted the frustrated Jackson to publicly ponder just what it took to win a batting title.

Cobb's batting eye was certainly keen, but his baserunning won just as many games. Until Lou Brock half-a-century later, he was the career steal leader. He would steal second, then proceed directly to third as the throw came in behind him. A young catcher asked a veteran what to do when Cobb broke for second. "Throw to third," came the deadpan reply.

Cobb's batting reign finally ended in 1916, when Tris Speaker hit .386 to Cobb's .378, but Cobb won the next three years. In 1921 he was named player-manager of the Tigers, and responded with a career-high 12 HR. He got a taste of his own medicine in 1922, losing the batting title despite a .401 average when George Sisler batted .420.

Despite five straight winning seasons as manager, Cobb, followed a week later by Indians player-manager Speaker, suddenly retired after the 1926 season. The day after Christmas in 1926, the public found out why: Dutch Leonard, a disgruntled former player who had been released by both managers, accused Cobb and Speaker of fixing a game on September 24, 1919. Both stars, plus Cleveland outfielder Smokey Joe Wood, had allegedly agreed to let Detroit win the game to give the Tigers third place. Upon hearing the allegations, American League president Ban Johnson forced the two stars to quit. But Commissioner Kenesaw Landis cleared and reinstated both players when Leonard refused to leave California to testify. Cobb ended up in Philadelphia with Connie Mack, who defended the hated Cobb during the ordeal, and Cobb played two more years before retiring for good after a .328 season in 1928.

During his playing days, Cobb invested astutely in real estate, automobiles, and cotton, and bought a good-sized block of Coca-Cola stock at rock-bottom prices. By the time he retired, Coca-Cola had made Cobb one of the richest players in the game.

In 1936, despite an enduring reputation as the meanest player in the game, Cobb became the leading vote-getter among the first to be elected into the brand-new Hall of Fame. He received 222 of a possible 226 votes, seven ahead of Ruth and Wagner. Retirement didn't dull his competitive spirit, however. In 1941 Cobb beat Ruth in a well-publicized golf duel. In a 1947 old-timers game in Yankee Stadium, Cobb warned catcher Benny Bengough to move back since he hadn't swung a bat in almost 20 years. Bengough stepped back to avoid getting smacked by Cobb's unpracticed backswing. Cobb then laid a perfect bunt down in front of the plate, and easily beat the throw from a huffing and embarrassed Bengough.

The wealthy Cobb tried to clean up his image in his later years with philanthropy. In 1948 Cobb contributed $100,000 to a new hospital in his hometown of Royston, Georgia. He was the first witness in the 1951 congressional hearing on the reserve clause, testifying in favor of it. "Baseball," the fiery Cobb asserted, "is a sport. It's never been a business." /(SEW)

Gordon Cobbledick — 1899–1969. *Writer.*

A football player at Case University, Cobbledick became a baseball writer for the Cleveland *Plain Dealer* in 1928. After serving as a war correspondent, he was named sports editor in 1947. He also was a correspondent for *The Sporting News* until his retirement in 1964. He received the J.G. Taylor Spink Award in 1977. /(NLM)

Jaime Cocanower — 1957- . RHP 1983-86
Brewers 366 ip, 16-25, 3.99

Cocanower was voted the California League's best
pitching prospect after a stellar 1980 season but
faded quickly after starting for the Brewers for most
of 1984. His eight wins that year were a career
high. /(ME)

Mickey Cochrane [Gordon Stanley] (Black Mike) —
1903-1962. C 1925-37 **A's**, Tigers 1482 g, .320,
119 hr, 832 rbi. *5 WS, 31 g, .245, 2 hr, 6 rbi.*
     Manager 1934-38 **Tigers** 413-297, .582. First place:
34-35 *2 WS, 7-6, .538*
☛ *Most Valuable Player—28, 34 . All-Star—34-35. Hall
of Fame—1947.*

Cochrane's Hall of Fame plaque notes that he
"compiled a notable record as a player and manager. The spark of the Athletics' championship
teams of 1929-30-31, he had an average batting
mark of .346 for those three years. Led Detroit to
two league championships and a World Series title
in 1935." Cochrane's lifetime .320 average is the
highest of any ML catcher.
     Cochrane demonstrated his leadership and versa-
tility in his years at Boston University, where he was
not only a quarterback, punter, and running back,
but also at times the trainer and coach. Cochrane's
competitive nature secured him the sobriquet
"Black Mike." "Lose a one-to-nothing game," said
teammate Doc Cramer, "and you didn't want to get
into the clubhouse with Grove and Cochrane. You'd
be ducking stools and gloves and bats and whatever
else would fly." A natural leader, Mickey was also
quick enough of foot to occasionally be placed in the
leadoff spot, but more often he hit third in the order.
     Cochrane joined the A's in 1925 and hit .330 that
year, the first of his nine .300 seasons. On May 21,
1925, the lefthanded batter hit three home runs in a
single game. That season was the first of his four
campaigns as fielding leader among AL catchers.
During his career, Cochrane twice led in errors, but
led catchers six times in putouts and twice each in
double plays and assists. He caught over 100 games
in all but his final two seasons. Cochrane batted a
career-best .357 in 1930, and reached career highs
in homers (23), RBI (112), and runs scored (118) two
years later. He hit for the cycle twice in his career (7/
22/32, 8/2/33). He was named AL MVP in 1928
with Philadelphia and in 1934 with Detroit. Chosen
as a player to two All-Star teams, he also managed
the AL to victory in the 1935 contest.
     Cochrane played in five World Series. In his first,

Mickey Cochrane

1929, he scored the tying run in Game Four as the
A's overcame an 8-0 Cub lead with a 10-run
seventh inning. The A's won the game en route to
their first World Championship since 1913. In the

1930 WS, Cochrane hit an opening-game homer off Burleigh Grimes of the Cardinals, and a HR off Flint Rhem in Game Two. The A's won both contests. In 1935, on what he later called his "greatest day in baseball," Detroit's player-manager scored the run that beat the Cubs in the sixth and final Series game. Though he played in just 315 games over four seasons with the Tigers, Cochrane was chosen by Detroit fans in 1969 as the team's all-time catcher.

Black Mike's playing career ended abruptly on May 25, 1937, when his skull was fractured by a pitch from Yankee Bump Hadley. Cochrane, who had been the Tiger pilot since 1934, continued as manager until August 6, 1938. His .582 winning percentage (413–297) tops all who have spent at least one full season at the Detroit helm.

After WWII erupted, Cochrane was given a Navy commission to coach the Great Lakes Naval Base baseball team. In 1944, Great Lakes won 33 in a row, and beat the Cleveland Indians 17–4, to finish 48–2. Among his Great Lakes players were Tigers Barney McCosky, Schoolboy Rowe and Virgil Trucks, as well as John Mize, Billy Herman, and Gene Woodling. Following the 1944 season, the Navy assigned Lieutenant Commander Cochrane to the Pacific and replaced him at Great Lakes with Bob Feller. Cochrane eventually served as coach and GM for the A's, scout for the Yankees and Tigers, and VP of the Tigers. He and longtime batterymate Lefty Grove were elected to the Hall of Fame in 1947 by the BBWAA. Another Hall of Famer, Mickey Mantle, was named after Mickey Cochrane, his father's favorite player. /(TJ)

Phil Cockrell — 1898–1946. RHP-UMP Negro Leagues 1913–46 Hilldale, Bacharach Giants, Philadelphia Stars, Havana Red Sox, New York Lincoln Giants, Darby Daisies statistics not available

Cockrell began his career as a teenaged pitcher and eventually became a Negro National League umpire. During two years for which statistics are available, 1924–25, he won 25 games in leading Hilldale to Negro World Series matchups with the Kansas City Monarchs. He was the winning pitcher in the decisive sixth game in 1925. In the 1930s, Cockrell and Leon Day were Hilldale's only pitchers in a series of doubleheaders with the Brooklyn Bushwicks, an all-star team of major leaguers organized by Dizzy and Paul Dean. The major leaguers won only one of the 14 games. Cockrell was shot to death in Philadelphia in 1946. /(BP)

Chris Codiroli — 1958– . RHP 1982–88 **A's**, Indians 660 ip, 38–46, 4.80

Codiroli was Detroit's first pick in the 1978 June draft, but was plagued by elbow problems and released in 1981. Signed by the A's, he led Oakland with 12 wins as a rookie in 1983. Using a three-quarters and sometimes sidearm delivery, he worked painfully slowly, and was viewed as lacking confidence. He was demoted twice in 1984, but, working faster, came back in 1985 to go 14–14 and tie for the AL lead with 37 starts. His 1986 season was ended by elbow surgery, and, let go after 1987, he hooked on with Cleveland. /(JCA)

Dick Coffman — 1906–1972. RHP 1927–40, 45 Senators, **Browns**, Giants, Braves, Phillies 1460 ip, 72–95, 4.65. *2 WS, 6 ip, 12.00*

As a struggling starting pitcher for the lowly Browns, Coffman gained sudden recognition in August 1931 by pitching two 1–0 shutouts. He spent much of his later career in the bullpen, and was among the first to log over 300 games as a reliever. With the Giants, he led the NL in relief wins in both 1936 and 1937. His 51 appearances and 12 saves in 1938 were NL highs. Dick was a more successful big leaguer than brother George "Slick" Coffman. /(LRD)

Kevin Coffman — 1965– . RHP 1987–88 **Braves** 92 ip, 4–9, 5.46

Coffman was called up prematurely by the pitching-poor Braves and was extremely wild, averaging almost eight walks per nine innings in his first two years. He was traded to the Cubs with Kevin Blankenship for washed-up Jody Davis in September 1988. /(SFS)

Slick Coffman [George David] — 1910– . RHP 1937–40 **Tigers**, Browns 313 ip, 15–12, 5.60

Although Coffman had more self-confidence than stuff, in the cocky Alabaman's ML debut, he beat Lefty Grove 4–2. He was 7–5 as a Tiger rookie in 1937, but three straight seasons with ERAs over 6.00 followed. His brother, Dick, pitched 15 years in the majors. /(NLM)

Andy Cohen — 1904–1988. 2B 1926, 28–29 **Giants** 262 g, .281, 14 hr, 114 rbi.
    Manager 1960 **Phillies** 1–0, 1.000

When the Giants' John McGraw wanted a Jewish star and needed a second baseman to replace Rogers Hornsby, Cohen got the nod, but his .294 in 1929 couldn't compare with Hornsby. Cohen managed in the minors and coached for the Phillies, acting as manager for one game in 1960. Brother Syd pitched briefly for Washington and was the last AL pitcher to strike out Babe Ruth. /(NLM)

Rich Coggins — 1950– . OF 1972–76 **Orioles**, Expos, Yankees, White Sox 342 g, .265, 12 hr, 90 rbi. *2 LCS, 5 g, .200*

In 1973 the Orioles had the AL Rookie of the Year, Al Bumbry, and the runner-up, the short, slim, deceptively powerful Coggins, who hit .319 to Bumbry's .337. After a less impressive sophomore season and an 0-for-11 in the 1974 LCS, Coggins was traded with Dave McNally to Montreal for Ken Singleton and Mike Torrez. He developed a thyroid condition in the spring of 1975 and played his last ML season at age 25. /(JCA)

Jimmie Coker — 1936– . C 1958, 60–67 Phillies, Giants, **Reds** 233 g, .231, 16 hr, 70 rbi

This peppery third-string catcher, a rancher in Throckmorton, Texas, spent only two full seasons in the majors. Up with Cincinnati for all of 1965, Coker appeared in just 24 games. /(JCA)

Rocky Colavito [Rocco Domenico] (The Rock) — 1933– . OF 1955–68 **Indians**, Tigers, A's, Indians, White Sox, Dodgers, Yankees 1841 g, .266, 374 hr, 1159 rbi
☛ *Led League—hr 59. Led League—rbi 65. All-Star—59, 61, 62, 64–66.*

Few players captured the imagination of a town the way Rocky Colavito did Cleveland. The 6'3", boyishly handsome strongman from the Bronx had a charisma that made him the most memorable personality in Indians history; he was voted so in 1976. He reached 300 home runs faster than all but four players; he was 31 when he hit number 300.

Colavito came up with best buddy Herb Score in 1955, but stayed just five games. Called back to Cleveland in July 1956, he began a string of 11 straight seasons of more than 20 homers, averaging 32 a year. His numbers really soared when manager Joe Gordon convinced him to cut down his swing. Colavito made himself a complete player, a run-producing slugger and a right fielder with an arm comparable to that of Roberto Clemente. Colavito was prone to slumps, and the Cleveland fans would jump all over him. That's when one sportswriter first starting saying, "Don't knock the Rock."

In 1958 Colavito batted .303 with 41 homers and 113 RBI. In 1959 he became the first Indian to have two 40-HR seasons; his 42 tied him with Harmon Killebrew for the AL lead. That June 10, he hit four

Rocky Colavito

HR in consecutive at-bats in a game at Baltimore. Cleveland fans were stunned when GM Frank Lane sent him to Detroit for batting champion Harvey Kuenn the following April; Lane had actually had a clause in Colavito's 1959 contract that would have rewarded the slugger for hitting *fewer* than 40 homers. After a year of adjustment in Detroit in 1960 (he had only 87 RBI), Colavito had his greatest season, hitting .290 with 45 HR and 140 RBI.

Some still consider the Colavito-Kuenn trade highly responsible for the ensuing decades of baseball mediocrity in Cleveland. The error was corrected in 1965 when Colavito was re-acquired from Kansas City in a three-team deal by new Indians GM Gabe Paul. Colavito set a ML record by playing 162 errorless games in the outfield that year. He also led the league in walks (93) and RBI (108). In 1967 he accused Paul of forcing manager Joe Adcock to platoon him with Leon Wagner. He fell short of demanding a trade, but was sent to the White Sox. Though he played less than half his ML career with the Indians, when he left he was fifth on their all-time HR list (190). He had originally been signed as a pitcher-outfielder; he pitched one game for Cleveland in 1958, and beat the Tigers in relief for the Yankees in 1968, to record a career ERA of 0.00. The win with the Yankees, in which he hit a crucial home run, was the last win by a normally non-pitcher; since then, only Jose Oquendo, with a loss in 1988, has even had a decision. /(ME)

Nate Colbert — 1946- . 1B-OF 1966, 68-76 Astros, **Padres**, Tigers, Expos, A's 1004 g, .243, 173 hr, 520 rbi ☛ *All-Star—71-73.*

Colbert's name became synonymous with the young Padres. After coming through the St. Louis farm system and appearing with Houston, Colbert was San Diego's ninth selection in the 1968 expansion draft. A great fastball hitter with a strong, compact swing, Colbert devastated NL pitching, crashing 163 homers in his six seasons with San Diego. He led NL first basemen in assists in 1972 and 1973 and was an All-Star three times, 1971-73.

Colbert was the Padres' offense in 1972, driving in 111 of the 488 runs the club scored, and, for the second time, belting 38 homers, more than one-third of the Padres' total. On August 1, in Atlanta, he hit five homers in a doubleheader to tie the record set by Stan Musial, and drove in 13 runs, the most ever in a twin bill. Coincidentally, Colbert, a St. Louis native, recalls having been in the stands that day in 1954 when Musial hit the five homers.

Traded to Detroit in November 1974, back problems forced Colbert's retirement in 1976 at age 30. /(JCA)

Vince Colbert — 1945- . RHP 1970-72 **Indians** 249 ip, 9-14, 4.55

The Washington, D.C. native was Cleveland's only winning pitcher (7-6) with 10 or more starts in 1971. He was third on that staff with 50 total appearances, 40 in relief. Vince also excelled in track and basketball. /(ME)

Jim Colborn — 1946- . RHP 1969-78 Cubs, **Brewers**, Royals, Mariners 1597 ip, 83-88, 3.80. 20 wins: 73 ☛ *All-Star—73.*

In a 1966 College All-Star Game in the Netherlands, Colborn struck out 21. He attended the University of Edinburgh and was All-Scotland in basketball.

Success as a ML pitcher was harder to come by. As a young reliever in Chicago, Colborn found himself in Leo Durocher's doghouse and was shipped to Milwaukee. In 1973 he became the first Brewer to win 20 games. When three losing seasons ensued, Colborn went in a four-for-one trade to Kansas City for catcher Darrell Porter. On May 14, 1977, he tossed a 6-0 no-hitter against Texas, one of his 18 wins that year for the Royals. /(RMu)

Bert Cole — 1896-1975. LHP 1921-25, 27 **Tigers**, Indians, White Sox 605 ip, 28-32, 4.67

Scouted and signed out of the Pacific Coast League in 1920, Cole had his best year with the Tigers in 1923, 13-5. He later umpired in the PCL. /(NLM)

Dave Cole — 1930- . RHP 1950-55 **Braves**, Cubs, Phillies 237 ip, 6-18, 4.93

Good stuff and bad control kept Cole bouncing from ML bullpens to the minor leagues during his career. In 1954, the Cubs gave him 14 tries as a starter but he walked 62 in 84 innings en route to a 3-8 mark. /(FK)

King Cole [Leonard Leslie] — 1886-1916. RHP 1909-12, 14-15 **Cubs**, Pirates, Yankees 731 ip, 56-27, 3.12. 20 wins: 10 *1 WS, 8 ip, 3.38*

Cole's 20-4 record with the pennant-winning Cubs in 1910 gave him a league-leading .883 winning percentage. Ring Lardner gave King Cole literary immortality by writing about him in articles for *The Sporting News* which later emerged as the Alibi Ike stories. According to Lardner, Cole was a slow-thinking poker player who was threatened with a $50 fine by manager Frank Chance unless he quit spoiling poker games on train trips with his erratic playing. /(JK)

Bob Coleman — 1890-1959. C 1913-14, 16 **Pirates**, Indians 116 g, .241, 1 hr, 27 rbi.
  Manager 1944-45 **Braves** 107-138, .437

After brief service as a big-league backstop with a good arm but no speed, Coleman served 37 years as a manager, 24 of them in the Three-I League, sending stars ranging from Hank Greenberg to Felix Mantilla to the majors. He managed the Boston Braves in 1944 and part of 1945. /(ME)

Ed Coleman — 1901-1964. OF 1932-36 **A's**, Browns 439 g, .285, 40 hr, 246 rbi

Coleman was batting .342 in his first month with the A's in 1932 when he broke his ankle. The left-handed hitter was slow, but showed occasional power. In his final season, he led the AL in pinch at-bats and pinch hits (20-for-62, .323). /(JK)

Gordy Coleman — 1934– . 1B 1959–67 Indians, **Reds** 773 g, .273, 98 hr, 387 rbi. *1 WS, 5 g, .250, 1 hr, 2 rbi*

A football player at Duke, the 6'3" 210-lb left-handed hitter won the Triple Crown and was league MVP with Mobile (Southern Association) in 1959. He became Cincinnati's regular first baseman in the early 1960s. In his first year in the lineup, he hit 26 HR to play a key role in the Reds drive to the 1961 NL pennant. In 1962 he hit 28 in his only other productive season. /(RMu)

Jerry Coleman — 1924– . 2B-SS 1949–57 Yankees 723 g, .263, 16 hr, 217 rbi. *6 WS, 26 g, .275, 9 rbi.*
   Manager 1980 **Padres** 73–89, .451
☛ *All-Star—50.*

The graceful Coleman led AL second basemen in fielding his rookie year and was an All-Star in his second season, averaging .282 over the two years. However, a 1951 injury diminished his skills, and he will never realize the prediction of Hall of Famer Frankie Frisch that Coleman would eventually join him there. After his retirement, Coleman became a broadcaster for the Yankees and Padres (with a one-year sabbatical to manage San Diego). As an announcer, he earned the nickname "Master of the Malaprop" with such gems as "he slides into second with a standup double." /(TJ)

Joe Coleman [Joseph Patrick] — 1922– . RHP 1942, 46–51, 53–55 **A's**, Orioles, Tigers 1134 ip, 52–76, 4.38
☛ *All-Star—48.*

A less successful pitcher than son Joseph Howard Coleman, the senior Coleman won 14 games for the 1948 A's and 13 for both the 1949 A's and 1954 Orioles. He hurled three scoreless innings in the 1948 All-Star Game, won 5–2 by the AL. Coleman was brought to the attention of A's owner-manager Connie Mack by Brother Gilbert, the man who had alerted Orioles' owner Jack Dunn to Babe Ruth. /(TJ)

Joe Coleman [Joseph Howard] — 1947– . RHP 1965–79 Senators, **Tigers**, Cubs, A's, Blue Jays, Giants, Pirates 2571 ip, 142–135, 3.69. 20 wins: 71, 73 *1 LCS, 9 ip, 1–0, 0.00*
☛ *All-Star—72.*

Coleman overcame a 9–32 minor league record to twice win 20 games in the big leagues. The first player chosen by the Senators in the initial 1965 free agent draft, he had his best years after going to

Detroit in an eight-player deal for Denny McLain in 1970. He won 20 games in 1971, 19 in 1972, and a career-high 23 in 1973. In Game Three of the 1972 LCS, he shut out Oakland 3–0, striking out an LCS-record 14 batters. After going 10–18 (5.55) in 1975, Coleman worked for six teams in four years, mostly out of the bullpen.

The son of Joseph Patrick Coleman, the two rank third in father-son combined wins, their 194 victories placing them behind the Bagbys and the Trouts. /(RMu)

John Coleman — 1863–1922. OF-RHP 1883–90 Phillies, **Philadelphia (AA)**, Pirates 629 g, .257, 6 hr, 80 rbi; 843 ip, 23–72, 4.68

As a 20-year-old rookie, Coleman pitched hapless Philadelphia (NL) to 12 of its 17 victories in 1883, but he also lost 48 games, still the ML record. After that season, he was used mostly in the outfield. /(FIC)

Ken Coleman — Unk.– . *Broadcaster.*

A native Bostonian, Coleman edged out Lindsey Nelson for his first pro sports job as the Cleveland Browns radio announcer in 1952 and joined the Indians in 1954. He replaced Curt Gowdy as the voice of his hometown Red Sox in 1966 and, after a four-year hiatus in Cincinnati, remained the Red Sox' radio play-by-play man through the 1980s. He called the 1967 WS for NBC-TV. /(SL)

Ray Coleman — 1922– . OF 1947–48, 50–52 **Browns**, A's, White Sox 559 g, .258, 20 hr, 199 rbi

Traded five times in five seasons (each time involving the Browns), Coleman hit .271 in 1950 and .280 in 1951 with 76 RBI. The Dodgers acquired Coleman, a fine defensive player, after the 1952 season as insurance for Duke Snider but stashed him at the AAA level. /(MC)

Rip Coleman (Walter) — 1931– . LHP 1955–57, 59–60 Yankees, **A's**, Orioles 247 ip, 7–25, 4.58. *1 WS, 1 ip, 0–0, 9.00*

After two years of long relief and spot starts with the Yankees, Coleman filled the same slot for Kansas City in 1957 and 1959, compiling a woeful 2–17 mark. /(NLM)

Vince Coleman — 1960- . OF 1985- **Cardinals** 754 g, .261, 9 hr, 178 rbi. *2 LCS, 10 g, .275, 5 rbi. 1 WS, 7 g, .143, 2 rbi*
☛ *Rookie of the Year—85. All-Star—88–89.*

Coleman has led a league in stolen bases in each of seven professional seasons. In 1983 he set the professional record for stolen bases with 145 while playing for Macon in the South Atlantic League. He won NL Rookie of the Year honors in 1985 with 110 stolen bases and 107 runs scored, and went on to become the first player in history to steal 100 bases in each of his first three major league seasons. In 1989 he set a record by stealing 51 consecutive bases without being caught. Coleman considers third base easier to steal than second, and in 1987 he stole second and third in the same inning 13 times. The switch-hitter serves as St. Louis's leadoff batter but has trouble with breaking balls, averaging 112 strike-outs per season. With steady improvement in left field, he moved among the yearly leaders in assists. /(FO)

Darnell Coles — 1962- . 3B-OF-SS 1983- **Mariners**, Tigers, Pirates 606 g, .247, 57 hr, 271 rbi

Coles was Southern California's High School Athlete of the Year in 1980 and turned down a football and baseball scholarship at UCLA to sign with Seattle as the sixth overall selection in the 1980 draft. Traded to Detroit, he was part of an all-20 HR infield in 1986 as the Tigers' third baseman. An erratic hitter and a defensive liability, he went to the Pittsburgh outfield in 1987 and tied a club record with a three-HR game (9/30). He was traded back to Seattle in mid-1988 and was a regular OF in 1989. /(ME)

Dave Collins — 1952- . OF-DH-1B 1975- Angels, Mariners, **Reds**, Yankees, Blue Jays, A's, Tigers 1602 g, .273, 32 hr, 370 rbi. *1 LCS, 3 g, .357, 1 rbi*

A versatile, slap-hitting speedster with good defensive skills, Collins emerged as a base-stealing threat in spot duty with the Angels. He became a Mariner in the expansion draft, but was peddled to Cincinnati a year later. He became a fair leadoff hitter, usually platooned. He stole a career-high 79 bases in his only season as an everyday player, 1980, and hit .300 twice for the Reds. He became a free agent after 1981 and signed with the Yankees, who were briefly infatuated with speed. Except for a big 1984 season with Toronto, when he led the AL with 15

triples while hitting .308, he was an unspectacular performer, mostly used for his speed on the bases and in the field, for the rest of his career. /(ME)

Eddie Collins [Edward Trowbridge Sr.](Cocky) — 1887-1951. 2B 1906-30 A's, **White Sox** 2826 g, .333, 47 hr, 1299 rbi. *6 WS, 34 g, .328, 11 rbi.* Manager 1925-26 **White Sox** 160-147, .521
☛ *Hall of Fame—1939.*

Eddie Collins was one of the most accomplished all-around ballplayers ever to play the game. They called Collins "Cocky," not because he was arrogant, but because he was filled with confidence based on sheer ability. Bill James wrote, "Collins sustained a remarkable level of performance for a remarkably long time. He was past thirty when the lively ball era began, yet he adapted to it and continued to be one of the best players in baseball every year . . .his was the most valuable career that any second baseman ever had."

Collins played for 25 years, 20 of them as a regular. He won no batting titles because he played during the same time as Ty Cobb, but did lead the AL in stolen bases four times and in runs scored three consecutive seasons, 1912–14. Collins batted .333 lifetime, and stole 743 bases. He had 3,311 hits (eighth all-time) and was a superlative fielder, leading second basemen in fielding average nine times. He was an adroit bunter, a slashing, lefthanded-batting hit-and-run man, and a brilliant baserunner. In the dugout or on the coaching lines, he was a canny, sign-stealing, intuitive strategist.

Collins's background was atypical of a player of the early 1900s. He starred as captain of Columbia University's baseball team. Barred from playing his senior year because he had disguised himself as "Eddie Sullivan" to play professionally (even getting into a few games with the Athletics), Collins was named Columbia's coach, and stayed to get his degree.

Collins was one of the key young players on Connie Mack's great Athletic teams of 1909–14 that won pennants in all but 1912. He was the premier player in Mack's "$100,000 Infield," with Jack Barry at shortstop, Stuffy McInnis at first base, and Frank Baker at third base, a unit valued for its finely meshed teamwork as well as the players' great individual skills. Collins later attributed this harmony on the field to the personal relationships off it, which continued past playing days. The "$100,000 Infield's" exceptional defense had a big payoff in the dead ball era, when teams scrapped for one run at a time.

When Connie Mack disbanded his long-reigning

Eddie Collins (l.), Pants Rowland

"honest players," he was unforgiving of the eight who had sold out, yet described the team as the greatest on which he had played, winning despite hostility, feuds, and outright crookedness.

Collins continued to play season after season of superlative second base, always batting over .300. After the White Sox finished last in 1924, Collins was named manager. He led them for two seasons, winning more than he lost, but finished fifth both years. The White Sox judged that his days as an everyday infielder were ending, and released the $40,000-a-year player-manager.

Connie Mack invited his former star to return to his rebuilt Philadelphia A's. Collins played less and less, but took over more and more field duties from Mack. He was third-base coach and, unofficially, assistant manager, and turned down offers to manage other teams. The A's won three straight pennants (1929–31), with Collins pinch-hitting a few times in 1929 and '30. The promise of the Shibe brothers (the A's owners) and Mack that Collins would succeed old Connie (then 67) kept Collins on hand. Fortunately he didn't stay around long, since Mack didn't retire until age 88.

Instead, Collins's opportunity to run a team came with the Boston Red Sox. He and Tom Yawkey were alumni of the same prep school and became friends. The millionaire sportsman, on Collins's advice, purchased the Red Sox and brought Collins in as part-owner and GM. Collins began rebuilding a team that had never recovered from the sale of stars to the Yankees a decade earlier. Yawkey's money bought Joe Cronin from Washington to be player-manager, and pried loose stars Jimmie Foxx and Lefty Grove from the A's. Collins went on just one scouting trip for the Red Sox, to California, but came back with two extraordinary prospects, Bobby Doerr and Ted Williams.

Eddie Collins was elected to the Hall of Fame in 1939, the year Eddie, Jr. debuted with the Athletics as an outfielder. /(JK)

Hub Collins [George Hubbert] — 1864–1892. 2B-OF 1886–92 **Louisville (AA)**, Brooklyn (AA), Dodgers 680 g, .284, 11 hr, 242 rbi

Collins was the second baseman for successive Brooklyn pennant winners (American Association in 1889, NL in 1890). He led the AA in doubles (31) in 1888 and runs scored (148) in 1890, and stole 328 bases in his short career. Two seasons later, he died of typhoid fever. /(JK)

team in 1915, he sold Collins to the Chicago White Stockings. Collins starred in the 1917 World Series, hitting .409, and scoring a key run on one of his typical heads-up plays during a game-winning, Series-ending rally. Collins had maneuvered into a rundown between third and home to allow two other baserunners to get into scoring position. Seeing no one covering the plate, he wheeled past the catcher as he threw to third baseman Heinie Zimmerman, who unsuccessfully chased the fleet Collins home.

In 1918 Collins joined the Marines, but was back the next season on another pennant-winner, the infamous 1919 Chicago "Black Sox." As one of the

Jimmy Collins (Jaime) — Unk.– . OF 1978– Minor and Mexican Leagues

A light hitter in the Braves organization who never rose above Double-A, Collins joined Chihuahua (Mexican League) in 1978 and batted .350. Over the next decade, he played for six different Mexican League franchises, never falling below .302. His .438 mark in 1979 set a since-broken league record. He won another batting title with a .412 mark in 1984. /(MC)

Jimmy Collins — 1870–1943. 3B 1895–1908 Braves, Louisville (NL), **Red Sox**, A's 1728 g, .294, 64 hr, 982 rbi. *1 WS, 8 g, .250, 1 rbi.*
  Manager 1901–06 **Red Sox** 464–389, .544. First place: 03–04 *1 WS, 5–3, .625*
☛ *Led League—hr 1898. Hall of Fame—45.*

Until Pie Traynor came along in the 1920s, Jimmy Collins was universally considered baseball's greatest third baseman. Playing at the turn of the century, when the bunt was a big part of the game, Collins was the best at fielding them. His 601 chances accepted at 3B in 1899 remain a National League record. He led his league's third basemen in putouts five times, assists four times, double plays twice, and still stands second all-time in career putouts at 3B.

Collins was also outstanding at the plate. He topped the .300 mark five times, with a high of .346 for Boston (NL) in 1897. In 1898, he won the NL home run crown with 15, drove in well over 100 runs for the second consecutive season, and scored more than 100 runs for the third of four times.

Collins was player-manager of the Red Sox in the American League's first six seasons, leading Boston to a victory over Pittsburgh in the initial World Series in 1903. The Red Sox repeated in 1904, but interleague feuding cancelled the WS. Relieved of the managerial reins in 1907, Collins was traded to the Athletics, and he left the majors after batting .217 in 1908. He played and managed in the minors through 1911 before retiring to his native Buffalo. Wiped out by the Depression, he became a Buffalo parks employee. His 1945 election to the Hall of Fame preceded Traynor's by three years, though Traynor had been eligible before Collins's induction. /(JK)

Jimmy Collins with the Braves

Jocko Collins [John P.] — 1905–86. *Scout.*

Collins was the basketball captain at St. Joseph's University in Philadelphia and remained active in basketball as well as baseball He was an NBA referee and NBA supervisor of officials, and a scout for the Philadelphia 76ers.

As a baseball scout, he worked for the Phillies for 27 years, and briefly for the Astros, Giants, Orioles, and Mets before his retirement in 1980. His discoveries included Del Ennis, Dallas Green, and Tommy Lasorda. /(FVP)

Joe Collins [born Joseph Kollonige] — 1922– . 1B-OF 1948–57 **Yankees** 908 g, .256, 86 hr, 329 rbi. *7 WS, 36 g, .163, 4 hr, 10 rbi*

Collins hit four World Series homers. The first won Game Two of the 1951 classic; the second put the Yanks ahead to stay in the 1953 opener; the other two led New York to victory in Game One of the 1955 Series. In the seventh game of the 1952 WS (which followed an 18-homer season for Collins), the first baseman lost Jackie Robinson's pop fly in the Ebbets Field sun, which Billy Martin recovered to catch in a famous game-saving play. /(TJ)

Pat Collins — 1896–1960. C 1919–24, 26–29 **Browns**, Yankees, Braves 541 g, .254, 33 hr, 168 rbi. *3 WS, 6 g, .500*

An often forgotten member of the mighty 1927 Yankees, Pat Collins was the dependable catcher who batted eighth in the "Murderer's Row" lineup. /(JK)

Phil Collins (Fidgety Phil) — 1901–1948. RHP 1923, 1929–35 Cubs, **Phillies**, Cardinals 1324 ip, 80–85, 4.66

When Collins fidgeted on the mound, tugging his trousers and fingering the rosin bag, it was not a nervous affliction that delayed him; it was apprehension. Pitching in tiny Baker Bowl, he was backed by a team that was last in the league in fielding five of his six years with Philadelphia. Nonetheless, he achieved three winning seasons with them. /(JK)

Ray Collins — 1887–1970. LHP 1909–15 **Red Sox** 1345 ip, 84–62, 2.51. *1 WS, 14 ip, 0–0, 1.88.* 20 wins: 14

A lefty with excellent control, Collins was 19–8 for the 1913 Red Sox and 20–13 the next year. Ty Cobb said Collins gave him as much trouble as any pitcher he ever faced, and, on occasion, Collins was said to have walked a batter intentionally to pitch to Cobb. Collins must have liked Detroit, for he had doubleheader complete games against the Tigers on September 22, 1914, winning 5–3 and 5–0. A graduate of the University of Vermont, he later returned there as baseball coach. /(NLM)

Rip Collins [Harry Warren] — 1896–1968. RHP 1920–31 Yankees, Red Sox, **Tigers**, Browns 1712 ip, 108–82, 3.99. *1 WS, 2/3 ip, 0–0, 54.00*

Once described as a pitcher with a million dollars worth of talent and 25 cents worth of enthusiasm, Collins apparently played baseball only to support his real pleasures: hunting and fishing in the off-season, bright lights and parties during the season. He claimed to have become a beer drinker at age six, and his nickname came from a pre-Prohibition brand of whiskey. A four-sport star at Texas A & M, Collins won 14 games as a Yankee rookie in 1920, matched that figure with the Red Sox in 1922, and again with the Tigers in '24. He later became a law enforcement officer in Texas. /(NLM)

Ripper Collins [James Anthony] — 1904–1970. 1B 1931–38, 41 **Cardinals**, Cubs, Pirates 1084 g, .296, 135 hr, 659 rbi. *3 WS, 13 g, .277, 4 rbi*
☛ *Led League—hr 34. All-Star—35–37.*

Though the 5'9" 165-lb Collins was small for a first baseman, he was the most dangerous slugger on the Cardinal Gas House Gang, hammering 35 HR for the NL title in 1934. He was a fun-maker off the field, but he was relentlessly serious on it. He broke up four no-hitters in late innings. A one-time coal miner from Altoona, PA, a strike freed Collins to try pro ball. He spent 30 years as a player, coach, minor league manager, and sporting goods rep. A facile talker, he became a broadcaster. He said he got his nickname when, as a boy, he once hit the team's only ball and snagged it on a fence nail, ripping its cover. /(JK)

Shano Collins [John Francis] — 1885–1955. OF-1B 1910–25 **White Sox**, Red Sox 1798 g, .264, 22 hr, 705 rbi. *2 WS, 10 g, .270.*
    Manager 1931–32 **Red Sox** 73–136, .349

Collins was a versatile and cooperative team player. After making the White Sox in 1910, he was a disappointment at first base and was shifted to right field a few weeks into the season. By 1913 he had established himself as one of the AL's top defensive

Shano Collins

outfielders. He covered plenty of ground and had a strong arm. At the plate, his average suffered because of his tendency to overswing.

Collins was temporarily moved back to first base in 1915 when rookie Jacques Fournier proved to have an iron glove. When the White Sox captured the 1917 pennant on September 21, Collins delivered the game-winning hit. He was the team's senior player, platooned in right field with Nemo Leibold. Chicago won the World Series opener 2–1 thanks to Collins's 3-for-4 performance. He moved once more to 1B when Chick Gandil sat out the 1920 season. He finished his career as a regular outfielder with the talent-thin Red Sox of the early 1920s. His nickname, Shano, was a play on Sean, the Gaelic equivalent of John. /(RL)

Zip Collins [John Edgar] — 1892–1983. OF 1914–17, 21 **Pirates**, Braves, A's 286 g, .253, 2 hr, 63 rbi

Called "Zip" for his strong outfield throws, Collins's light hitting limited his ML career. A longtime minor league player and manager, he was active in efforts to establish a retirement home for former players. /(JK)

Jackie Collum — 1927– . LHP 1951–58, 62 Cardinals, **Reds**, Cubs, Dodgers, Twins, Indians 464 ip, 32–28, 4.15

Collum shut out the Cubs in his first ML game as a Cardinal rookie in 1951, and in 1956 he saved seven and won six out of the Cardinal bullpen. In between, he pitched nearly three full seasons for the Reds, winning 23 and losing 22. /(FK)

Nick Colosi — 1927– . *Umpire* NL 1968–82 *3 LCS 2 WS, 2 ASU*

Before turning to umpiring, Colosi was a maitre d' at the famous Copacabana night club in New York. His most famous call came in the 1975 WS. After much media hype on the legality of Red Sox pitcher Luis Tiant's hand movement as he came to a set position, Colosi called a balk (ironically, on Tiant's leg movement) in the fourth inning of the opening game. /(RTM)

Colt Stadium Houston Colt .45s 1962–64. LF-360, CF-420, RF-360

32,000-seat Colt Stadium housed the expansion Houston franchise until the Astrodome was completed in 1965, and was the site of two no-hitters. Renowned for its huge mosquitoes, it was located in what is now the Astrodome's north parking lot. /(SCL)

Bob Coluccio — 1951– . OF 1973–75, 77–78 **Brewers**, White Sox, Cardinals 370 g, .220, 26 hr, 114 rbi

Several athletes have been dubbed "The Italian Stallion," but Brewer broadcaster Merle Harmon labeled the 5'10" Coluccio "The Macaroni Pony." The speedy outfielder beat out Gorman Thomas for the Brewers' right-field job in 1973, but couldn't hit well enough to keep the position. /(RMu)

Earle Combs (The Kentucky Colonel) — 1899–1976. OF 1924–35 **Yankees** 1454 g, .325, 58 hr, 629 rbi. *4 WS, 16 g, .350, 1 hr, 9 rbi*
☛ *Hall of Fame—1970.*

A husky six-footer, the quiet leadoff man of the powerful 1927 Yankees covered Yankee Stadium's spacious center field, leading the league's centerfielders in putouts. Combs's specialty was the three-base hit; he had three in a 1927 game, led the AL in triples three times, and collected 154 in his career.

A cool, determined player, Combs was often overshadowed by his superstar teammates, but in nine seasons, he batted well over .300. In 1927 he

Earle Combs

hit .356, leading the AL with 231 hits (a team record until Don Mattingly broke it in 1986). He had a 29-game hitting streak in 1931.

The Kentucky Colonel's career came to an end in 1934 when, before the advent of warning tracks, he smashed into the wall at Sportsman's Park chasing a fly ball. His skull was fractured and his career virtually ended. After trying a comeback in 1935, and knowing that the Yankees would bring Joe DiMaggio up the next season, he accepted a coaching job. When DiMaggio arrived, Combs instructed him on the nuances of Yankee Stadium's outfield.

Combs left the Yankees during WWII. A good teacher, he returned to coach the Browns, Red Sox, and Phillies. He was inducted into the Hall of Fame in 1970 by the Veterans Committee. /(JK)

Steve Comer — 1954- . RHP 1978-84 **Rangers,** Phillies, Indians 701 ip, 44-37, 4.13

Comer was said to have three pitching speeds—slow, slower, and reverse. Relying on his changeup, Steve led all righthanded pitchers with 17 wins in 1979. A sore shoulder curtailed Comer in 1980, but he fashioned one more good season in relief the following year. Steve was handicapped by having no other pitches to complement his change. He became pitching coach of the Indians in 1987. /(ME)

Wayne Comer — 1944- . OF 1967-70, 72 Tigers, **Pilots/Brewers** 316 g, .229, 16 hr, 67 rbi. *1 WS, 1 g, 1.000*

The Virginian was the 25th player on the Tigers' 1968 championship squad. After the expansion draft, Comer took advantage of the friendly confines of Seattle's Sicks Stadium for 15 home runs and also stole 18 bases. A trade to Washington and a loss of power ended his career. /(CC)

Charlie Comiskey (Commy, The Old Roman) — 1859-1931. 1B 1882-94 **St. Louis (AA),** Chicago (PL), Reds 1385 g, .266, 29 hr, 883 rbi.
Manager 1883, 85-94 **St. Louis (AA),** Chicago (PL), Reds 824-533, .607. First place: 85-88
☛ *Hall of Fame—1939.*

Had the Black Sox scandal not exposed the pettiness that characterized most of Comiskey's later dealings, he might have been among the most respected elder statesmen of sport. Charles Comiskey was the son of a famous long-time Chicago alderman who represented the Irish ghettos of the near West Side. The boy rebelled against his father's plans to apprentice him to a plumber. Instead, he played semi-pro ball on the Chicago sandlots. In 1879 Comiskey hooked

Charlie Comiskey

up with baseball promoter Ted Sullivan, who taught him the art of playing first base. Until the 1880s, most first basemen started each play with a foot on the bag. Comiskey increased his range by playing off the bag, and his success popularized that style. As a player-manager for the St. Louis Browns of the American Association, Comiskey won four league titles (1885–1888).

Comiskey's greatest fame came not as a manager, but as a mogul. When Ban Johnson took over the fledgling Western League (formed November 21, 1893), few imagined that eight years later it would challenge the National League for baseball supremacy. Comiskey assisted Johnson by purchasing the Sioux City franchise, which he shifted to St. Paul, and in 1900, to Chicago, where it was christened the White Stockings. For the next 31 years "The Old Roman" was the driving force behind the White Sox, who won championships in 1901, 1906, 1917, and 1919.

Comiskey's own greed is considered to have been the real motivation for the "Black Sox" selling out to gamblers in 1919. When it was revealed that the players threw the Series for $10,000 because Comiskey had underpaid them for years, his sterling reputation was tarnished. Nonetheless, he was elected to the Hall of Fame in 1939, as an executive. /(RL)

Comiskey Park Chicago White Sox 1910- , American Giants (NAL)1941–50 LF-341, CF-401, RF-341

Comiskey Park stands on a piece of city landscape that once belonged to "Long" John Wentworth, Chicago's colorful mayor during the Civil War days. His South Side property later became the city dump before it was purchased by Charles Comiskey in 1909.

The ballpark constructed at 35th and Shields Avenue by the "Old Roman" has a troubled past and a questionable future. The so-called "curse" of Wentworth has nearly bankrupted several ownerships forced to deal with the old stadium's structural problems.

In 1910, construction workers rushed to finish the park before the scheduled unveiling on July 1. But a labor strike by the steel workers and the death of a carpenter who fell off a scaffold hours before the opener cast a pall over the festivities. Despite these setbacks, Comiskey Park opened for business on time, but the Sox lost the inaugural to the Browns 2–0.

The stadium was ideally suited for dead-ball-era play. Its spacious contours were influenced by pitcher Ed Walsh, who toured the major league parks with architect Zachary Taylor Davis. The thrifty Comiskey vetoed Davis's idea to build a cantilevered grandstand with ornate arches and cornices, and years later Comiskey Park suffered when compared to the great old stadiums of the past. But in the early years it was dubbed the "Baseball Capitol of the World," and the Cubs used it for the 1918 WS.

The changing nature of the game soon made Comiskey Park a relic. The long-ball hitting of Ruth, Gehrig, et al., during a time when the fans demanded high scores and prodigious home runs

Comiskey Park

from their heroes, was handicapped by a park the size of Comiskey. It wasn't until 1934, after Comiskey's death, that the ownership dealt with this problem. The plate was moved forward 14' to accommodate power hitter Al Simmons, but he never cared much for Comiskey Park, and was gone a year later; the plate was then moved back to its original location. In 1949 a chickenwire fence was installed by Frank Lane, but it was the opposition and not the White Sox who profited from the smaller dimensions, so he removed it after only a few games.

Comiskey was the site of the first All-Star game in 1933; it was also the permanent site of the Negro Leagues' yearly East-West all-star game, 1933–50. The infield was a hazard in those years. Once Luke Appling tripped over a piece of metal protruding near second base. It was a copper kettle that had surfaced after five decades. Night games beginning in 1939 helped bolster sagging attendance. In 1950 a scoreboard was built in center field, replacing the ones situated on the left and right field walls. Ten years later Bill Veeck added a final touch by adding fireworks to the scoreboard's capabilities. In 1968 artificial turf was installed in the infield, but it was removed in 1976.

Maintaining the nation's oldest park was beyond Veeck's limited budget during his second period of ownership. He was forced to sell the team to Jerry Reinsdorf and Eddie Einhorn, who installed a new Diamond Vision board, luxury suites, wider aisles, and improved front office facilities. However, the masonry and the infrastructure reputedly remain inadequate. The state legislature has voted to appropriate funds for the construction of a new stadium for the Sox across the street from Comiskey Park./(RL)

J. Louis Comiskey — 1885–1939. *Executive.*

The only son of Charles Comiskey, Lou was a shy and benevolent man who lived in the shadow of his illustrious father. He was appointed vice-president and treasurer of the White Sox in 1910. Two years later, he contracted scarlet fever and, for the rest of his life, had to maintain a hospital suite at St. Luke's in Chicago. Complicating his condition was his weight—300 lbs. In 1931, Charles Comiskey passed away, leaving the last-place White Sox to his son. Within a few years, Lou restored the club to respectability. He purchased Mule Haas, Al Simmons, and Jimmy Dykes from Philadelphia in 1932, and started the first White Sox farm system, which began yielding results by 1939. That year, Lou had

lights installed in Comiskey Park, but he did not live to see the first night game, passing away on July 18./(RL)

Adam Comorosky — 1904–1951. OF 1926–35 **Pirates**, Reds 813 g, .285, 28 hr, 417 rbi

A gritty player from the Pennsylvania coal mines, Comorosky had two .300 seasons with Pittsburgh, where he teamed with the Waner brothers in the outfield for four seasons./(JK)

Keith Comstock — 1955– . LHP 1984, 87– Twins, Giants, **Padres**, Mariners 97 ip, 3–3, 4.56

Comstock is a study in perseverance. Originally signed in 1976, he had a four-game stint with the Twins in 1984 but was released. He signed with the Yomiuri Giants in Japan to keep his career alive, but was 8–10 over two seasons and was released after 1986. He caught on with the Giants in 1987 and was traded to San Diego in the big deal that brought Kevin Mitchell to San Francisco. That season, his best in the majors, the reliever was 2–1 with a 4.61 ERA./(WOR)

Dave Concepcion — 1948– . SS-2B-3B-1B 1970–88 **Reds** 2488 g, .267, 101 hr, 950 rbi. *5 LCS, 15 g, .351, 1 hr, 1 rbi. 4 WS, 20 g, .266, 1 hr, 12 rbi* ☛ *All-Star—73, 75–82. Gold Glove—74–77, 79.*

Concepcion came out of Venezuela to become one of baseball's greatest shortstops. Wearing number 13, the lithe infielder won the position in 1972 after sharing it with Woody Woodward for two seasons. In 1973, Concepcion was named captain of the Reds. The winner of five Gold Gloves, he also started five All-Star Games from 1973 to 1982, more than any other NL shortstop during that period. He responded to his eighth straight selection (ninth overall) in 1982 by winning the Game's MVP award, hitting a two-run homer as the NL won its 11th straight game.

In 1978 Concepcion became the first Cincinnati shortstop to bat .300 since Joe Tinker in 1913. Hampered by an elbow injury in 1980, Concepcion took advantage of the Astroturf at Riverfront Stadium and developed the one-hop throw to first base to reduce arm strain. The winner of the Roberto Clemente award as the top Latin American ballplayer in the majors in 1977, he led the NL with 14 game-winning RBI in 1981, when he was the Reds' MVP. In four World Series, Concepcion hit better than .300 three times and topped .400 in the 1975 and '79 LCS. He played over 100 games at shortstop

Dave Concepcion forces the Cubs' Gary Martin

12 straight years (1974–85) and in 14 of 15 seasons, with an injury cutting into his 1973 season. Replaced by Barry Larkin in 1986, Concepcion became a dependable handyman working at all four infield positions. Only Pete Rose is ahead of him in doubles (389), games, hits (2,326), and at-bats in Reds history, and only Joe Morgan has more Reds stolen bases than Concepcion's 321. Concepcion also ranks in the Reds' top five in runs, RBI, and total bases. On his retirement, he was only 44 games away from Larry Bowa's NL record for shortstops. /(ME)

Onix Concepcion [born Onix Cardona Cardona] — 1957– . SS-2B-3B 1980–85, 87 390 g, .239, 3 hr, 80 rbi. *2 LCS, 7 g, .000. 2 WS, 6 g, --*

Groomed as the successor to U.L. Washington at shortstop, Concepcion was hampered by injuries and was unable to capitalize on his defensive and running talents enough to compensate for his lack of power and mediocre batting average. /(FO)

David Cone — 1963– . RHP 1986– Royals, **Mets** 573 ip, 39–17, 3.11. 20 wins: 88 *1 LCS, 12 ip, 1–1, 4.50* ☛ *All-Star—88.*

Cone was acquired in one of the Mets' best deals; the most important player they gave up was injury-prone catcher Ed Hearn. Cone himself spent much of 1987 on the DL, but when arm problems shelved starter Rick Aguilera early in 1988, Cone replaced him. He won his last eight starts of the season and led the NL in winning percentage (.870), the sixth-best mark ever for a 20-game winner. Going 20–3 with a 2.22 ERA, he finished third in Cy Young award voting. He was third in wins and second in a close ERA race, with Joe Magrane sitting out his last start of the season to protect a 0.04 point lead. Cone also tied for the NL lead in balks with 10, in a season known for strict enforcement. He had an odd group of rooters known as the "Coneheads" after the old *Saturday Night Live* routine. They wore traffic cones or alien makeup like that worn on the TV show.

Cone was the focus of controversy in Game Two of the LCS. A ghostwritten column under his name in a New York paper following the first game said that Orel Hershiser had been lucky to shut out the Mets for eight innings and called loser Jay Howell a "high school pitcher." The Dodgers used this as a rallying point and drove Cone out after just two innings. However, he came back strong in Game Six, going the distance in a 5–1 five-hit victory.

Cone struggled in 1989, but managed a 14–8, 3.52 mark and led the Mets with seven complete games. /(SH)

Bunk Congalton — 1875–1937. OF 1902, 1905–07 Cubs, Indians, **Red Sox** 310 g, .290, 5 hr, 128 rbi

The Canadian-born outfielder's major league career was brief, but he starred in the minors, twice leading the Western Association in batting. Congalton died of a heart attack while watching Bob Feller pitch in Cleveland Stadium. /(JK)

Billy Conigliaro — 1947– . OF 1969–73 **Red Sox**, Brewers, A's 347 g, .256, 40 hr, 128 rbi. *1 LCS, 1 g, .000. 1 WS, 3 g, .000*

Tony's brother and Boston's top 1967 draft choice hit 18 homers in 1970. A year later, he accused Carl Yastrzemski of running the Red Sox, and claimed that cliques kept him from being a regular. Traded to Milwaukee that October, Conigliaro retired after 52 games with the Brewers, but resurfaced with the 1973 World Champion Oakland A's. /(TJ)

Tony Conigliaro — 1945- . OF 1964-67, 1969-71, 1975 **Red Sox**, Angels 876 g, .264, 166 hr, 516 rbi
☛ *Led League—hr 65. All-Star—67.*

Tony Conigliaro hit .290 with 24 home runs in 1964, but broke his arm in August; Tony Oliva won the AL Rookie of the Year award. When the 20-year-old Conigliaro hit 32 HR in 1965, he became the youngest home run leader in AL history. The hometown hero was enjoying another standout year in 1967 when, on August 18, he was struck by a Jack Hamilton fastball that broke his cheekbone and so damaged his eyesight that he missed the entire 1968 season. He returned in 1969 to win Comeback of the Year honors, and in 1970 hit 36 HR. But his vision was still impaired, and he left the majors in July 1971, returning for a short comeback try in 1975. Further tragedy befell Conigliaro at age 37, when he suffered a heart attack (while riding in a car with brother Billy) that left him severely incapacitated. /(TJ)

Jocko Conlan (John) — 1899- . OF 1934-35 **White Sox** 128 g, .264, 0 hr, 31 rbi.
Umpire NL 1941-65 *5 WS, 6 ASU*
☛ *Hall of Fame—74.*

Conlan had a brief career as an AL outfielder but was elected to baseball's Hall of Fame in 1974 as an umpire. His first stint of umpiring came by accident. When regular AL umpire Red Ormsby was overcome by heat during a 1935 Browns-White Sox game, Conlan, a Chicago reserve, filled in. The next year, he launched his new career as an ump.

He umpired in the NL for 25 years, starting in 1941. His trademarks were his quick grin, polka dot tie, and balloon chest protector. He was allowed to continue using the outside protector for five years after the NL adopted the inside protector for its umps because he was at risk from being hit in the throat by pitches.

The spunky Irishman had many run-ins with NL managers, particularly firebrands Leo Durocher and Frankie Frisch. In a 1955 game he was suffering from an attack of arthritis and found it difficult to bend to see low pitches. When he called a strike on Jackie Robinson on a pitch nearly in the dirt, "Robinson seemed so honestly shocked over the call," Conlan said, "I figured I must have missed it. I didn't want any more like that." Rather than make another mistake, he left the field. /(RTM)

Jocko Conlan

Gene Conley — 1930- . RHP 1952, 54-63 **Braves**, Phillies, Red Sox 1589 ip, 91-96, 3.82. *1 WS, 2 ip, 10.80*
☛ *All-Star—54-55, 59.*

During baseball's off-season, 6'9" Gene Conley played basketball for the Boston Celtics. He won 14 for Milwaukee and finished second in NL Rookie of the Year balloting in 1954. In the 1955 All-Star Game, Conley struck out Al Kaline, Mickey Vernon, and Al Rosen in the top of the 12th. Moments later, Stan Musial homered for the NL, making Conley the winning pitcher. He won a career-high 15 for the Red Sox in 1962. That year, in a New York traffic jam, Conley and infielder Pumpsie Green deserted their team bus. Green reported to the team hotel the next evening, but Conley remained AWOL nearly three days, unsuccessfully trying to fly to Israel. "I don't know why I did it," he later said. /(TJ)

Sarge Connally [George Walter] — 1898–1978. RHP 1921, 23–29, 31–34 **White Sox**, Indians 994 ip, 49–60, 4.30

Connally picked up his nickname from WWI service. In baseball, he saw action as both a starter and reliever in twelve ML campaigns. /(JK)

Bob Connery — 1879–1967. *Scout.*

Connery discovered Rogers Hornsby for the Cardinals in 1915, purchasing him from the Denison, Washington club for $600. He was head scout for the Yankees from 1918 to 1924, and was part-owner and president of the St. Paul American Association club from 1925 to 1935. He was involved in securing Earle Combs, Lefty Gomez, and Tony Lazzeri for the Yankees. /(FVP)

Ed Connolly — 1939– . LHP 1964, 67 **Red Sox**, Indians 130 ip, 6–12, 5.88

The son of Ed Connolly, a Red Sox catcher in 1929–32, Ed, Jr., made the majors in 1964, the year after his father's death. He went 4–11 for Boston that year with a 4.91 ERA, mostly as a starter. The fireballer lacked control, and after resurfacing briefly with the 1967 Indians he faded. /(WOR)

Joe Connolly — 1888–1943. OF 1913–16 **Braves** 412 g, .288, 14 hr, 157 rbi. *1 WS, 3 g, .111, 1 rbi*

Platooned against righthanded pitching, Connolly was the leading hitter (.306) for the 1914 "Miracle Braves." He later served in the Rhode Island State Legislature. /(JK)

Tom Connolly — 1870–1963. *Umpire* NL 1898–1900, AL 1901–31 *8 WS*
☛ *Hall of Fame—1953.*

Born in England, Tom Connolly didn't want to play baseball; when his family settled in Natick, MA, and he learned about the game, Connolly wanted to be an umpire. The 5'7" 135-lb Connolly worked local games until he was spotted by Tim Hurst, a legendary National League umpire. Hurst recommended Connolly to sportswriter Tim Murnane, who was running the Class B New England League. Murnane hired Connolly in 1894, and in 1898 Connolly moved up to the National League. When the NL failed to support him in a showdown with a player, Connolly resigned midway through the 1900 campaign. Although Connie Mack had never seen Connolly umpire, he had heard enough about him to recommend Ban Johnson hire him for the new American League. Three of the inaugural 1901 season's openers were rained out, so when the lone game was played between Chicago and Cleveland, with Connolly its sole umpire, he could claim the distinction of having umpired the first AL game. He also umpired the first World Series in 1903.

Connolly earned a reputation for fearlessly ejecting hometown heroes when circumstances required. In his first AL season, he was challenged by Baltimore pitcher Joe McGinnity, who spit in his face. The league backed Connolly and suspended McGinnity. However, when Connolly failed to respond sufficiently after St. Louis outfielder Jesse Burkett punched a rival manager in the nose, he was reprimanded by Ban Johnson. Taking the hint, Connolly bounced ten players in his maiden season. After that, his reputation was enough to quell disturbances before they got out of hand. Ty Cobb said later that he learned to stop arguing when Tom's neck turned red. The last player Connolly tossed was Babe Ruth, in 1922. It was the last time Ruth was ejected. Ruth grew incensed by the taunts of a spectator, and started to climb into the stands. Connolly, nearly 100 pounds lighter and seven inches shorter than Ruth, blocked the Babe's path and scolded, "You should be ashamed of yourself," while escorting him off the field.

Connolly continued as an active umpire until 1931 when, at age 60, he became the chief of staff of American League umpires. He traveled the circuit evaluating and advising arbiters until he was 83. After retiring as Umpire-in-Chief, he served for many years on the Rules Committee. In 1953 Connolly and Bill Klem, his counterpart in the NL, became the first umpires named to the Hall of Fame. /(JK)

Roger Connor — 1857–1931. 1B-3B-2B-OF 1880–97 **Troy (NL)/Giants**, New York (PL), Phillies, Cardinals 1998 g, .318, 136 hr, 1078 rbi.
Manager 1896 **Cardinals** 9–37, .196
☛ *Led League—hr 90. Led League—rbi 89. Led League—ba 85 . Hall of Fame—1976.*

Connor's first major league team was the Troy Haymakers, when he was 23. Connor found a career and a wife in Troy when he went to a shirt factory where she worked; the long-torsoed Irishman had to be fitted with a special uniform and she took his measurements.

Connor was one of the greatest sluggers of the 19th century. His 136 career home runs stood as the record until Babe Ruth exceeded it in the lively ball era. A vivid image of the mustached Connor was written by veteran New York sportswriter Sam

Roger Connor

Crane, who claimed Connor was, "the best base runner I ever saw, excepting Bill Lange, and it behooved the baseman to give Roger a clear path. With his weight catapulting him, with speed and force, he slid feet first and, as he landed, could bob up, like a jack-in-the-box." Crane described Connor as a man with a tremendous reach and a good pair of hands who was exceedingly good on pickups, digging the ball out of the dirt. Although Roger

Connor could drive the ball for prodigious distances, his speed and line drives added up to triples and he is fifth on the all-time list with 233. His home runs could be awesome. He hit a magnificent shot in his first game with the Giants, in 1883, that caused jubilant patrons to pass the hat and buy a $500 gold watch in appreciation. He favored pitches down by his knees and would put his 220 pounds of farm-hardened muscle behind his hits.

After the Troy franchise moved to New York, Connor starred for the Giants until 1890, when he helped form the Players League and was its home run champion for its only season. His career continued after peace was made with the outlaws, alternating between the Giants, the Phillies, and the Cardinals until he retired from the ML after 1897. Back in his hometown of Waterbury he obtained a franchise in the tightly-knit Connecticut League, whose teams made one-day trolley jumps and slept at home every night. He hit .392 to lead his league in batting, his eye sharpened by spectacles that might have been laughed at in the big leagues. Later, he sold his Waterbury team and bought the franchise of the larger Springfield, MA entry. He played there until he was 46 in 1903, managing the team and saving himself, as owner, two salaries. He left baseball a prosperous man who could look back on his achievements in the earlier years of the game. He had six hits in six at-bats in an 1895 game against Jouett Meekin. He hit three home runs in succession in an 1888 game against Indianapolis and two home runs off Larry Corcoran in a game against Cap Anson's Chicago White Stockings when he was with Troy.

Roger Connor's case for the Hall of Fame election was argued strongly by Bill Klem, who held Connor in special esteem. In 1902, when Klem was breaking into professional umpiring in the Connecticut League, the young umpire gave several decisions against Connor's Springfield team. With the fans shouting for his blood, Klem was relieved when the huge playing manager of the home team put an encouraging arm across the young umpire's shoulders and assured everyone Klem had the right to call them as he saw them. /(JK)

Chuck Connors [Kevin] — 1921– . 1B 1949, 51 Dodgers, **Cubs** 67 g, .238, 2 hr, 18 rbi

The 6'7" Connors played pro basketball with the Boston Celtics after WWII before concentrating on baseball. In the Brooklyn organization he earned more applause for his spring training recitations of "Casey at the Bat" than for his hitting. He pinch-hit once for the Dodgers in 1949. The Cubs acquired him in 1951 and sent him to Los Angeles of the Pacific Coast League where he hit .321. A bit part in the Spencer Tracy—Katharine Hepburn movie "Pat and Mike" after the 1952 season convinced him to make acting his fulltime profession. In 1957 he landed the lead in the TV western series "The Rifleman," which aired through 1962. His second western series, "Branded," aired 1964–65. He has appeared in numerous movies and television dramas since, and won critical acclaim in the role of a slave owner in the television mini-series "Roots" (1977). /(MC)

Tim Conroy — 1960– . LHP 1978, 82–87 **A's**, Cardinals 467 ip, 18–32, 4.69

Conroy was Oakland's first pick in the 1978 June draft; Charley Finley brought the 18-year-old right to the majors, where he proved embarrassingly wild. Four years in Double-A and Class-A followed. He fought to control his 95-mph fastball and sharp-breaking curve, and returned to Oakland to go 7–10 in 1983. Back in the Pacific Coast League in 1985, he threw a seven-inning, 1–0 no-hitter against Tucson on May 14. He went to the Cardinals in the trade for Joaquin Andujar that December, but his flashes of brilliance were tempered by shoulder problems. /(JCA)

Wid Conroy [William Edward] — 1877–1959. 3B-SS-OF 1901–11 Milwaukee (AL), Pirates, Yankees, Senators 1377 g, .248, 22 hr, 452 rbi

Conroy picked up the nickname "Widow" for his solicitous concern for younger boys on his sandlot team and was known as "Wid" all his long life in organized baseball. He began as a shortstop, replacing Honus Wagner with Paterson in the Atlantic League, but was struck by malarial fever and dropped from the team. In 1900 Connie Mack invited him to try out for the Western Association team he would field in Milwaukee and transfer to Philadelphia when the American League began as a major circuit; Conroy won the last spot on the roster.

Conroy was the first-string shortstop of the NL champion 1902 Pirates, but became a third baseman when he returned to the AL with the Highlanders (later the Yankees) in 1903. He led AL third basemen twice in total chances per game. His 22-year career in pro baseball ended as a Phillies coach in 1922. /(JK)

Bob Considine — 1907–1975. *Writer.*

Author or co-author of 25 books and movie scripts, war correspondent, and syndicated columnist ("On the Line"), Considine wrote for the Hearst newspapers in Washington and New York, beginning in 1933. He was sports editor of the Washington *Herald* before writing for King Features. Among his books was a biography of Babe Ruth. /(NLM)

Billy Consolo — 1934– . SS-2B-3B 1953–62 **Red Sox**, Senators/Twins, Phillies, Angels, A's 603 g, .221, 9 hr, 83 rbi

Consolo went directly to the Reds from high school after signing for $60,000 in 1953. His .270 in 1957 was 41 points better than he hit in any other season. /(TJ)

Sandy Consuegra [Sandalio Simeon Castellon] — 1920– . RHP 1950–57 Senators, **White Sox**, Orioles, Giants 809 ip, 51–32, 3.37
☛ *All-Star—54.*

Consuegra's 16–3 record in 1954 produced an AL-best .842 winning percentage, and included a league-high eight relief wins (without a defeat). He pitched in the '54 All-Star Game, but yielded five earned runs on as many hits, retiring only one batter. The AL won despite him. /(TJ)

Dennis Cook — 1962– . LHP 1988– Giants, **Phillies** 143 ip, 9–9, 3.59

After an impressive debut in 1988 (2–1, 2.86 in four games), Cook was part of the package sent to the Phillies in mid-1989 for Steve Bedrosian, and Cook immediately moved into their rotation. /(JFC)

Doc Cook [Luther Almus] — 1886–1973. OF 1913–16 **Yankees** 286 g, .274, 3 hr, 75 rbi

The Yankees' regular right fielder in 1914–15, Cook had little extra-base power. His .283 was the best of any Yankee with over 100 games on the 1914 club, which was the worst-hitting team in the majors that year with a .229 team mark. /(MG)

Dusty Cooke [Allen Lindsey] — 1907– . OF 1930–36, 38 Yankees, **Red Sox**, Reds 608 g, .280, 24 hr, 229 rbi. *Manager* 1948 **Phillies**, 6–5, .545

Once a high-priced Yankee prospect, Cooke was slowed by a broken collarbone and a fractured leg. He played satisfactorily but not up to expectations with the Red Sox. He later became the Phillies trainer, and, forgetting his station, was thrown out of a game for making remarks from the bench. /(JK)

Duff Cooley [Dick Gordon] (Sir Richard) — 1873–1937. OF-1B 1893–1905 Cardinals, Phillies, Pirates, **Braves**, Tigers 1318 g, .294, 25 hr, 557 rbi

Cooley stood out among the rough types of turn-of-the-century baseball and was dubbed "Sir Richard" for his aristocratic manner. The lefthanded-hitting Texan played most in the outfield, but tried all positions except pitcher. When he retired, he had saved enough money to buy teams in Topeka and Salt Lake City, operating them profitably for many years. /(JK)

Danny Coombs — 1942– . LHP 1963–71 **Astros**, Padres 393 ip, 19–27, 4.08

A former Seton Hall basketball star, Coombs was initially unable to control his fastball-slider repertoire and was up and down with Houston for seven seasons. Sold to San Diego in 1970, he was 10–14 as a starter. /(MC)

Jack Coombs [John Wesley] (Colby Jack) — 1882–1957. RHP 1906–18, 20 **A's**, Dodgers, Tigers 2320 ip, 159–110, 2.78. 20 wins: 10–12 *3 WS, 53 ip, 5–0, 2.70.*
   Manager 1919 **Phillies** 18–44, .290
☛ *Led League—w 10–11.*

Colby Jack was signed by the Athletics off the campus of Colby College in Maine. On September 1, 1906, he pitched 24 innings to set an AL record tied only by his opponent that day, Boston's Joe Harris. Coombs's 13 shutouts in 1910 are an AL record. His 31 wins led the league that season, and he added three more victories in the World Series against the Cubs. Coombs was unbeaten in WS competition, winning another game in 1911 and one more for Wilbert Robinson's 1916 Brooklyn Dodgers. Coombs became a championship-winning coach at Duke University who sent many players to the majors. /(JK)

Jimmy Cooney (Scoops) — 1894– . SS 1917, 19, 24–28 Red Sox, Giants, Cardinals, **Cubs**, Phillies, Braves 448 g, .262, 2 hr, 150 rbi

Although he cracked 12 consecutive hits for Milwaukee of the American Association in 1923, the slick-fielding Cooney had trouble holding a ML job because of his weak bat. He made an unassisted triple play on May 30, 1927, for the Cubs against the Pirates. In the fourth inning he caught Paul Waner's liner, stepped on second to double Lloyd Waner, and tagged Clyde Barnhart coming down from first. He was the son of Jimmy Cooney, an 1890s NL shortstop, and his younger brother Johnny was a ML outfielder/pitcher for 20 years. /(BC)

Johnny Cooney — 1901– . OF-1B-LHP 1921–30, 1935–44 **Braves**, Dodgers, Yankees 1172 g, .286, 2 hr, 219 rbi; 795 ip, 34–44, 3.72

Johnny was the youngest of the "Cranston Cooneys," a Rhode Island ballplaying dynasty begun in the 1890s by James Joseph Cooney, whose four sons all played pro ball. Two brothers never got to the majors, but Johnny had two careers. As a pitcher who occasionally played first base or outfield, he had moderate success with the Braves in the 1920s. A sore arm forced him to give up pitching; after a four-year absence from the majors and an American Association batting title, he joined Casey Stengel's Dodgers in 1935. Cooney's best averages as a regular came with the Stengel-managed Braves, .318 in 1940 and .319 in 1941. Stengel later compared Cooney favorably to Joe DiMaggio as a fielder. /(JK)

Terry Cooney — 1933– . Umpire AL 1975–86 *2 LCS 1 WS, 1 ASU*

Ex-marine Cooney had some sensational confrontations with AL managers. In 1981 he endured a Billy Martin dirt attack (six kicks followed by a double handful fired at Cooney's mask) and in 1982 Earl Weaver attempted a punch, resulting in a week's suspension and $2,000 fine for Weaver. /(RTM)

Cecil Cooper — 1949– . 1B-DH 1971–1987 Red Sox, **Brewers** 1896 g, .298, 241 hr, 1125 rbi. *2 LCS, 8 g, .233, 5 rbi. 2 WS, 12 g, .191, 1 hr, 7 rbi*
☛ *Led League—rbi 80, 83. All-Star—79–80, 82–83, 85. Gold Glove—79–80.*

The smooth-fielding first baseman was one of the most consistent hitters of the late 1970s and early 1980s, always among the top batting and fielding leaders. But because he played at the same time as Rod Carew and George Brett, he never won a batting title.

Cooper was haunted by Carl Yastrzemski. As a young player in Boston, Cooper was forced to DH, and played first base only on the odd occasions when Yaz played the outfield or was rested. At the end of the 1976 season, the Red Sox realized they'd be better off with a power hitter than with Cooper, perceived as a singles hitter, so they swapped the lefty Cooper to get the powerful George Scott back from the Brewers. Cooper flourished, batting over .300 his first seven years in Milwaukee. He finished

Cecil Cooper

Claude Cooper — 1892–1974. OF 1913–17 Giants, **Brooklyn (FL)**, Phillies 373 g, .260, 4 hr, 104 rbi. *1 WS, 2 g, --.*

Cooper parlayed a sensational Texas League season, after which he was hailed as "another Speaker," into an invitation to join the pennant-bound Giants in 1913. He was voted a full World Series share and showed perverse appreciation by jumping to the outlaw Federal League.

Cooper broke his leg as soon as the Federal League opened its 1914 season. When the Federal League dissolved, Cooper and Bill Bradley retained John M. Ward as an attorney. Ward won a suit for the players, whom he had dealt with earlier as general manager of the BrookFeds, for another "bonus" based on presumed World Series entitlements due had they not jumped legal contracts.

Reinstated, Cooper played two seasons with the Phillies, failing to hit even .200, and returned to Texas./(JK)

Mort Cooper — 1913–1958. RHP 1938–47, 49 **Cardinals**, Braves, Giants, Cubs 1841 ip, 128–75, 2.97. 20 wins: 42–44 *3 WS, 45 ip, 2–3, 3.00* ☛ *Most Valuable Player—42. Led League—w 42–43. Led League—era 42. All-Star—42–43, 46.*

Cooper, whose brother Walker was his catcher during the early 1940s, went 22–7 with 10 shutouts and a 1.77 ERA and was the NL MVP for the 1942 World Champion Cardinals. In 1943 he led the NL in victories (21) for the second straight year, and followed with a 22-win 1944 campaign. The fastballer, who occasionally chewed aspirin on the mound for relief from an aching arm, started and lost the 1942 and 1943 All-Star Games. St. Louis traded Cooper to the Braves in May 1945 after suspending him for leaving the club over a salary dispute. Mort and Walker teamed again in 1947, when the fading pitcher appeared in eight games with the Giants./(TJ)

Walker Cooper — 1915– . C 1940–57 **Cardinals**, Giants, Reds, Braves, Pirates, Cubs 1473 g, .285, 173 hr, 812 rbi. *3 WS, 16 g, .300, 6 rbi* ☛ *All-Star—42–44, 46–50.*

"He was just about the strongest man I've ever known," said Ewell Blackwell. Enos Slaughter called him "one of the best behind the plate," adding, "He was a great guy . . .very good-natured." Walker Cooper was a 6'3" 210-lb heavy hitter and practical joker who was named to every NL All-Star squad 1942–50 (there was no game in 1945). After three World Series with St. Louis (where he was older brother Mort's batterymate), Walker was sold to the

second to Rod Carew in the All-Star balloting for first base in 1978, but when Carew got hurt, instead of Cooper taking his place, Yaz was brought in from the outfield to play first base.

Cooper had his best year in 1980. He led the league in RBI with 122 and hit a career-high .352, with 25 HR. But George Brett had his flirtation with .400 that year, finishing at .390 and spoiling Cooper's best shot at a batting title. Two years later, Cooper hit a career-high 32 HR and led Milwaukee to its comeback in the 1982 ALCS against the Angels. Down two games to none, the Brewers won three straight games at home, with Cooper singling in the tying and winning runs in the seventh inning of the final game. In 1983, he had his best power year, hitting .307, his last .300 season, with 30 HR and a league-leading and career-high 126 RBI./(SEW)

Walker Cooper

nor, would dive toward the bag as Cooper whipped a sidearm throw to third. Walter Schmidt caught him for most of his career with Pittsburgh and they knew each other so well that the battery wasted little time on signals. Cooper got a reputation as a fast worker.

A .239 lifetime batter, Cooper hit four homers in 1922, and hit .346 in 104 at-bats in 1924. /(JK)

Robert Coover — 1922– . *Writer.*

Novelist and playwright, and writer in residence at Brown University since 1979, Coover published *Universal Baseball Association, Inc., J. Henry Waugh, Prop.* in 1968. It depicts a statistics-obsessed loner compulsively playing a table baseball game and writing histories based on the results. /(NLM)

Wilbur Cooper

Giants in 1945. The Giants paid the then-princely sum of $175,000 while Cooper was still in the Navy. His best year was with the 1947 Giants, batting .305 with 122 RBI and contributing 35 of the club's 221 homers, a NL record. /(TJ)

Wilbur Cooper — 1892–1973. LHP 1912–26 **Pirates,** Cubs, Tigers 3480 ip, 216–178, 2.89. 20 wins: 20–22, 24 ☛ *Led League—w 21.*

Cooper won more games (202) than any other Pirate lefthander, at least 17 games a year from 1917 through 1924 with a career-high 24 in 1920 and a league-best 22 in 1921. The sinkerballer twice led the NL with 27 complete games, and led in two other seasons with 38 starts.

Cooper's fielding skills were exceptional, particularly his knack for picking runners off third base—seven in 1924 alone. His partner, Pie Tray-

Doug Corbett — 1952– . RHP 1980–87 Twins, **Angels**, Orioles 553 ip, 24–30, 3.32. *1 LCS, 7 ip, 1–0, 5.40*
☛ *All-Star—81.*

First signed by the Royals, Corbett was claimed by the Twins off Cincinnati's roster in the 1979 major league draft. In 1980, the sinkerballer set AL rookie records with 73 appearances and 23 saves. He saved 17 games with an AL-high 54 appearances in strike-shortened 1981. The Twins sent him to California in a 1982 trade for Tom Brunansky, but Corbett proved a disappointment. He spent parts of 1982 through 1985 in the minors, and did not record a save in 1983 or '85. His toughness was questioned; he would warn hitters, "Look out," when he'd accidently let loose inside. He made a comeback of sorts in 1986, saving 10 for the AL West Champion Angels, and winning LCS Game Four. /(JCA)

Joe Corbett — 1875–1945. RHP 1895–97, 1904 Washington (NL), **Baltimore (NL)**, Cardinals 482 ip, 32–19, 3.42. 20 wins: 97

The brother of World Heavyweight Boxing Champion "Gentleman Jim," Corbett won 24 games for the 1897 Orioles and added two more in a Temple Cup sweep. Later, as baseball coach at Santa Clara University, his star player was Hal Chase. /(JK)

Ray Corbin — 1949– . RHP 1971–75 **Twins** 652 ip, 36–38, 3.84

Corbin had eight wins and 83 strikeouts in each of his first three ML seasons. He recorded 14 of his 17 saves in 1973, but after elbow surgery in 1975 never again pitched in the majors. /(RMu)

Larry Corcoran — 1859–1891. RHP 1880–87 **Cubs**, Giants, Washington (NL), Indianapolis (NL) 2392 ip, 177–90, 2.36. 20 wins: 80–84
☛ *Led League—w 81. Led League—era 82.*

Corcoran was one of the best pitchers of the 1880s, winning 170 games and losing only 84 from 1880 through 1884 for the Chicago NL team. He pitched three no-hitters. According to historian Lee Allen, Corcoran was the first pitcher to work out a set of signals with his catcher. He invariably carried a huge chew of tobacco in his mouth and when he chewed it shifted visibly. His regular catcher, Silver Flint, suggested that he signal his curve by shifting his chew, and the idea worked perfectly. Overwork, dissipation, and Bright's disease ended his career, and he was dead by the age of 32. His .663 winning percentage is eighth all-time. A brother, Mike, pitched one losing game for Chicago in 1884. /(BC)

Tim Corcoran — 1953– . 1B-OF 1977–81, 83–86 **Tigers**, Twins, Phillies, Mets 509 g, .270, 12 hr, 128 rbi

The lefthanded Corcoran led the AL with 10 pinch hits as a rookie in 1977. He batted .322 in five Tiger spring trainings, but only in 1978 and 1980 did he spend full seasons in Detroit. An extra outfielder and backup first baseman, he batted .341 for Philadelphia in 1984, but was released after dropping to .214 in 1985. /(JCA)

Tommy Corcoran — 1869–1960. SS 1890–1907 Pittsburgh (PL), Philadelphia (AA), Dodgers, **Reds**, Giants 2201 g, .257, 34 hr, 1135 rbi

Originally a barehanded fielder, Corcoran successfully made the transition to gloves and the 20th century. In Cincinnati he played shortstop alongside Bid McPhee, whose career was coming to an end, and Miller Huggins, who was just beginning. In his final season, with the Giants, the 18-year veteran spelled rookie Larry Doyle at second.

Corcoran survived two collapsed leagues (the Players' League and the American Association) in his first two seasons, caught on with Brooklyn, and

Tommy Corcoran with the Reds

was traded to Cincinnati in 1897. There he excelled for a decade as shortstop and team captain. In 1903, he set a still-standing ML record for SS with 14 assists in a nine-inning game. Corcoran ranks high on the lifetime lists for putouts, assists, and total chances. A skillful sign stealer, he once uprooted an electric signaling device the Phillies had buried in their third base coaching box (a binocular-equipped observer in the scoreboard passed along catcher's signs to aid Phillie batters). Corcoran later umpired in several leagues, including the Federal League./(ADS)

Mike Corkins — 1946- . RHP 1969-74 **Padres** 459 ip, 19-28, 4.39

Taken from San Francisco by the Padres in the 1968 expansion draft, Corkins threw an Eastern League no-hitter in 1969, was called up, and on September 22 served up Willie Mays's 600th career home run. He was a lifetime .202 hitter with five HR in 119 at-bats. /(MC)

Pat Corrales — 1941- . C 1964-66, 68-73 Phillies, Cardinals, **Reds**, Padres 300 g, .216, 4 hr, 54 rbi. *1 WS, 1 g, .000.*
Manager 1979-80, 82-87 Rangers, Phillies, **Indians** 572-634, .474

Corrales, a poor hitter, spent much of his career as the backup catcher to Johnny Bench in Cincinnati. On September 29, 1965, he became one of only four ML players to reach base twice on catcher's interference in the same game. He skippered the Rangers for two seasons and then the Phillies, who made him the only manager to be fired with his team in first place (7/18/83). Thirteen days later, Corrales replaced Mike Ferraro as the Indians' manager. In 1986, Corrales charged Oakland pitcher Dave Stewart and tried to kick him but was quickly decked by a Stewart right to the jaw. Corrales was fired by Cleveland during the 1987 All-Star break, with the last-place Indians on their way to their second 100-loss season in three years. /(JCA)

Ed Correa — 1966- . RHP 1985-87 White Sox, **Rangers** 283 ip, 16-19, 5.16

First signed out of Puerto Rico by the White Sox, Correa, at age 20, was the youngest player in the AL as a Rangers rookie in 1986. He went 12-14 with a team-high 189 strikeouts, but a severe shoulder injury ended his 1987 season in July. A Seventh Day Adventist, Correa balked at pitching on Friday nights or Saturday afternoons. /(JCA)

Vic Correll — 1946- . C 1972, 74-80 Red Sox, **Braves**, Reds 410 g, .229, 29 hr, 125 rbi

Correll, a South Carolina native, was a favorite with Atlanta fans and owner Ted Turner as a part-time catcher from 1974 through 1977. After a short minor league stint as a player-coach, he spent three seasons with Cincinnati as the backup to Johnny Bench. /(PB)

Frank Corridon (Fiddler) — 1880-1941. RHP 1904-05, 07-10 Cubs, **Phillies**, Cardinals 1216 ip, 70-68, 2.80

Corridon is one of several who claim to have originated the spitball. With the International League Providence Grays, Corridon discovered that a ball which had landed in a puddle and was wet on one side did odd things when he threw it. A teammate suggested he wet the ball during games, and Corridon went on to have a respectable ML career. /(JK)

Jim Corsi — 1961- . RHP 1988- **A's** 60 ip, 1-3, 2.56

Corsi became an effective middle reliever for the A's in 1989. /(SFS)

Bill Corum — 1894-1958. *Writer.*

A graduate of the University of Missouri and Columbia University journalism school, Corum was a major in the AEF in WWI. He joined the New York *Times* in 1920 and moved to the New York *Journal* in 1925 and the Detroit *Evening Times* in 1935. He was a columnist for the New York *Journal-American* at the time of his death in 1958. Well liked and respected among writers, he was named president of Churchill Downs race track in 1949. /(NLM)

Al Corwin [Elmer Nathan] — 1926- . RHP 1951-55 **Giants** 289 ip, 18-10, 3.98. *1 WS, 2 ip, 0-0, 0.00*

As a rookie he mopped up in Game Five of the 1951 WS after the Giants fell behind the Yankees 13-1. On September 4, 1953 the spot starter hit the second of three consecutive Giants home runs between Wes Westrum and Whitey Lockman. /(JK)

Pete Coscarart — 1931- . 2B-SS 1938-46 Dodgers, **Pirates** 864 g, .243, 28 hr, 269 rbi. *1 WS, 3 g, .000* ☛ *All-Star—40.*

The brother of Braves' infielder Joe Coscarart was the outstanding rookie second baseman of 1939 and followed that season with an All-Star Game appearance the next year. As his hitting declined, Pete was replaced by Billy Herman in 1941 and then traded to Pittsburgh. He started at short for the 1942 Pirates and at second for the next three seasons. /(ME)

Howard Cosell — 1920– . *Broadcaster.*

Revolutionary in his work on ABC's boxing, "Wide World of Sports," and "Monday Night Football" telecasts, Howard Cosell was outspoken and opinionated, often insightful but annoyingly verbose. The overtly intelligent Cosell was never reverential toward the athletes he covered, but his shrill speaking style, incessant preaching, and overbearing manner were irritants that eventually got under the skin of his employers and co-workers, and much of his audience. He made no secret of his distate for baseball (he found it boring), and when he joined "Monday Night Baseball" in 1976 his lack of deep baseball knowledge was the subject of much criticism. When he retired from network television, he wrote a sports column for the New York *Daily News* through the late 1980s. /(SL)

Mike Cosgrove — 1951– . LHP 1972–76 **Astros** 275 ip, 12–11, 4.03

A hard-throwing reliever, Cosgrove was 7–3 for the Astros in 1974 and had five saves the next year, but when he switched to starting in '76, he developed arm trouble. /(MC)

John Costello — 1960– . RHP 1988– **Cardinals** 112 ip, 10–6, 2.65

Costello has been an effective set-up man in the Cardinals' bullpen, posting low ERAs. /(WOR)

Chuck Cottier [Charles Keith] — 1936– . 2B-SS-3B 1959–65, 68–69 Braves, Tigers, **Senators**, Angels 580 g, .220, 19 hr, 127 rbi.
  Manager 1984–86 **Mariners** 98–120

A good fielder but a weak hitter, Cottier had his best year at the plate with a .242 BA for the 1962 Senators. He tied a ML record that season with two doubles in one inning. The next year, he shocked Yankees' Hall of Famer Whitey Ford with two homers and four RBI in a game. As a manager, he once exhibited his temper by throwing bats and balls from the dugout after a call went against Seattle, finally uprooting first base and hurling it into the outfield. /(FK)

Henry Cotto — 1961– . OF 1984– Cubs, **Yankees**, Mariners 475 g, .258, 24 hr, 106 rbi. *1 LCS, 3 g, 1.000*

Cotto broke in with the Cubs as a defensive replacement for Gary Matthews, and in three seasons with the Yankees he shuttled between New York and Columbus (International League). He was traded to the Mariners along with Steve Trout for Lee Guetterman before the 1988 season, and hit .259 with 27 stolen bases for Seattle that year. /(TF)

Johnny Couch — 1891–1975. RHP 1917, 22–25 Tigers, Reds, **Phillies** 643 ip, 29–34, 4.63

In 1922, as a 31-year-old rookie with Cincinnati, Couch was a lucky 16–9. One writer stated, "If Couch allowed no runs, the Reds would make one. If he allowed five, his mates would make six." Couch's luck ran out; 1922 was his only winning season. /(AL)

Bill Coughlin — 1877–1943. 3B 1899, 1901–08 Washington (NL), Senators, **Tigers** 1050 g, .253, 15 hr, 380 rbi. *2 WS, 8 g, .214, 1 rbi*

Coughlin had a brief stay with Washington's NL club in 1899, and resurfaced there for the AL's inaugural 1901 season. Traded to Detroit in mid-1904, he captained the Tigers' first two pennant winners, 1907–08. Coughlin's best ML BA was .301 in 1902. /(JL)

Fritz Coumbe — 1889–1978. LHP 1914–21 Red Sox, **Indians**, Reds 761 ip, 38–38, 2.79

The slender junkballer won a career-high 13 with Cleveland in 1918. He played centerfield for the Reds in the major leagues' last triple-header (1920). /(ADS)

County Stadium Milwaukee Braves 1953–65, Milwaukee Brewers 1970– . LF-315, CF-402, RF-315

A publicly funded stadium built exclusively for baseball, County Stadium was also the first stadium built with lights included, rather than added at a later date. It opened for the Braves in 1953 with a capacity of 35,911, and the club drew a then NL-record 1.8 million fans after having drawn only 281,000 in Boston the season before. Now home to the Brewers, County Stadium has a natural grass field and extensive bleacher seating in left and center fields, as well as a reputation for the best bratwurst in the ML. Until recently, the Brewers' mascot, barrel-clad Bernie Brewer, would slide into a large beer stein in right-center field after each Brewer home run. /(SCL)

Clint Courtney (Scrap Iron) — 1927-1975. C 1951-61
Yankees, Browns/Orioles, White Sox, **Senators**, A's
946 g, .268, 38 hr, 313 rbi

The first catcher to wear glasses, Courtney was better
known as a fearless battler. Obtained by the Browns
at the request of manager Rogers Hornsby,
Courtney was *TSN* AL Rookie of the Year in 1952
(.286, 5 HR, 50 RBI, 116 G). He twice batted over
.300 as a platoon player. "Scrap Iron's" most
famous baseball brawl came in 1953 when the
Browns met the Yankees. Courtney and Phil Rizzuto collided at second base, and Billy Martin
jumped on Courtney in a wild melee that nearly
provoked a riot among the few fans at St. Louis. The
incident produced a then-AL record $850 in fines.
Courtney died on June 16, 1975 while manager of
Richmond (International League), exactly two years
to the day after he was hired for the position. /(ME)

Ernie Courtney — 1875-1920. 3B-1B-OF-SS
1902-03, 05-08 Braves, Orioles/Yankees, Tigers, **Phillies**
558 g, .245, 5 hr, 200 rbi

Reputed to have had the biggest hands in pro
baseball, Courtney played every infield position. The
lefthanded hitter enjoyed his best season in 1905
when he drove in 77 runs as the Phillies' regular
third baseman. /(AL)

Henry Courtney — 1898-1954. LHP 1919-22
Senators, White Sox 444 ip, 22-26, 4.90

After service as a WWI ambulance driver, Courtney
began pitching for New Haven of the Eastern
League. The Senators paid $7,500 for his contract,
and he threw three complete-game victories for
them at the end of the 1919 season. /(NLM)

Harry Coveleski (The Giant Killer) — 1886-1950. LHP
1907-10, 14-18 Phillies, Reds, **Tigers** 1248 ip, 81-55,
2.39. 20 wins: 14-16

Thrust into the midst of a furious pennant race
when he was called up by the Phillies in late
September 1908, Coveleski defeated the contending
Giants three times in five days, enabling the Cubs to
win the flag. Coveleski earned a $50 bonus and the
nickname "The Giant Killer." He slumped in 1909,
was traded, and returned to the minors. Resurfacing
with the Tigers in 1914, he put together three
straight 20-win seasons while losing no more than
13.

Coveleski and three brothers (including Hall of
Famer Stanley) came out of the Pennsylvania coal
fields to play pro ball. /(JL)

Stan Coveleskie [born Stanislaus Kowalewski, aka
Stan Coveleski] (Covey) — 1889-1984. RHP 1912, 16-28
A's, **Indians**, Senators, Yankees 3093 ip, 215-142, 2.88.
20 wins: 18-21, 25 *2 WS, 41 ip, 3-2, 1.74*
☛ Led League—era 23, 25. Led League—k 20. Hall of
Fame—1969.

Coveleskie always said it was the spitball that made
him a major-league pitcher. He had a three-hit
shutout in his debut with the A's in 1912, but was
returned to the minors for seasoning and learned the
spitter while with Portland (PCL), shortly before
being acquired by the Indians.

Despite the spitter's eccentricity, Coveleskie (as
the name was spelled during his playing days) was a
control pitcher who averaged one walk every 3.86
innings over fourteen years. His spitball broke three
ways—down, out, and down and out—and he said

Stan Coveleskie

he always could control its movement by the placement of his fingers on the ball. It was his bread and butter pitch, although he sometimes went two or three innings without throwing it and had the usual fastball and curve to mix things up.

He was equally sparing with strikeouts (981 lifetime). Because of his control many batters swung at his first pitch. A number of times he got out of an inning with three pitches, and on one occasion he went seven innings when every pitch was a strike, a foul, or a hit. He claimed success in fanning Ruth and in reducing Cobb's effectiveness by feeding him fastballs inside.

Overall, he had 39 shutouts, a streak of 13 wins in 1925 when he was 36 years old, and six consecutive seasons pitching more than 276 innings. His best years were with Cleveland, particularly the championship year of 1920 when he won three splendid five-hitters against Brooklyn in the Series. He allowed a total of two runs and two walks, struck out eight, and had an ERA of 0.67. After two under-.500 seasons, Cleveland traded him to Washington for two nonentities. His .800 (20–5) winning percentage and 2.84 ERA led the AL as the 1925 Senators repeated as AL champions. He lost two, however, in the Series against the Pirates.

A quiet, modest man, Covey was the youngest and most successful of five ball-playing brothers. Harry, the "Giant Killer" of 1908, was the only other one to reach the majors. /(ADS)

Wes Covington — 1932– . OF 1956–66 Braves, White Sox, A's, **Phillies**, Cubs, Dodgers 1075 g, .279, 131 hr, 499 rbi. *3 WS, 15 g, .235, 5 rbi*

A notorious time-waster at the plate, Covington used an unorthodox batting stance. The lefthanded hitter, who never had more than 373 at-bats in a season, hit 21 homers for the World Champion 1957 Braves and 24 HR (while batting .330) in 90 games in 1958. Although not highly regarded as an outfielder, Covington made two outstanding catches in the 1957 WS. In 1961, he played for four ML teams. He had a .320 pinch-hitting average for the 1963 Phils, batting .303 overall. /(TJ)

Billy Cowan — 1938– . OF 1963–65, 67, 69–72 **Cubs**, Mets, Braves, Phillies, Yankees, Angels 493 g, .236, 40 hr, 125 rbi

The Mississippi native totaled 35 homers and 122 RBI playing for two Cub farm teams in 1962. His only ML season as a regular was 1964, when he hit .241 with 19 HR and 50 RBI as the Cub centerfielder. /(TJ)

Al Cowens — 1951– . OF 1974–86 **Royals**, Angels, Tigers, Mariners 1584 g, .270, 108 hr, 717 rbi. *3 LCS, 14 g, .200, 1 hr, 6 rbi*
☛ *Gold Glove—77.*

A journeyman hitter through most of his career, soft-spoken Cowens had his best year for the Royals in 1977, hitting .312 with 14 triples, 23 HR, and 112 RBI. He finished second to Rod Carew in the MVP voting. A good defensive outfielder with a strong arm, his only other season with a batting average over .277 was 1979, when he managed .295 despite missing three weeks when a pitch broke his jaw. In 1982 for the Mariners, he hit 20 home runs and in both 1982 and 1984 he drove in 78 runs, his second-best totals. /(NLM)

Joe Cowley — 1958– . RHP 1982, 84–87 Braves, **Yankees**, White Sox, Phillies 469 ip, 33–25, 4.20

Cowley set an AL record by striking out the first seven Texas Rangers batters to start a game (5/28/86), and he threw a no-hitter with seven walks at California in a 7–1 win (9/19/86). Cowley spent eight seasons in the minors before earning a starting spot with the Yankees in July 1984. He won eight straight decisions that year, finishing 9–2. He was traded to the White Sox after a 12–6 record in 1985, then to the Phillies for Gary Redus before the 1987 season. Cowley was a huge bust for the Phillies, going 0–4 with 17 walks, 21 hits and a 15.43 ERA in just 11-2/3 innings. He was sent down, pitched just as poorly, and was sent home in July. /(EG)

Billy Cox — 1919–1978. 3B-SS 1941, 46–55 Pirates, **Dodgers**, Orioles 1058 g, .262, 66 hr, 351 rbi. *3 WS, 15 g, .302, 1 hr, 6 rbi*

Cox is considered by many the greatest fielding third baseman prior to Brooks Robinson. After a brief ML fling in 1941 and four years of military service, Cox became the Pirates' starting shortstop in 1946 and hit .290 to lead the club. Despite his career-high 15 HR in 1947, Cox was traded with Preacher Roe and Gene Mauch to Brooklyn for 37-year-old Dixie Walker and pitchers Hal Gregg and Vic Lombardi. It was one of Pittsburgh's worst trades, and Branch Rickey's and the Dodgers' best. Cox held down third base in Brooklyn for seven seasons and three NL Championships. Casey Stengel said of him, "That ain't a third baseman. That's a f----g acrobat." He led the NL in fielding percentage in 1950 and '52. /(ME)

Bobby Cox — 1941- . 3B 1968-69 **Yankees** 220 g, .225, 9 hr, 58 rbi.
Manager 1978-85 Braves, **Blue Jays** 621-615, .502 First place: 85 *1 LCS, 3-4, .429*

Signed in 1959 for a $40,000 bonus, Cox spent seven years in the Dodger farm system and was Atlanta property before coming up to the Yankees. In 1968 he was the Topps rookie all-star third baseman despite hitting .229 with only seven HR. He lost his job to Bobby Murcer the next spring. After bad knees forced his retirement in 1971, he managed six years in the Yankee organization, was a New York coach in 1977, and managed the Braves from 1978 through 1981. He moved to the Blue Jays, winning *TSN* Manager of the Year honors when he led Toronto to their first division title in 1985. But Cox's strict platooning style allowed Royals manager Dick Howser to outmaneuver him in the LCS. After the season, Ted Turner lured Cox back to Atlanta as GM. /(MC)

Casey Cox — 1941- . RHP 1966-73 **Senators/ Rangers,** Yankees 761 ip, 39-42, 3.70

After three years as an effective reliever, 6'5" Casey Cox went 8-12 as a starter in 1970. Off to a 0-3 start in 1971, Cox asked Washington manager Ted Williams to return to the bullpen. He won five and saved seven, and Williams declared that "Casey might be the best righthanded relief pitcher in the league." Cox was out of the majors two years later. /(TJ)

Danny Cox (Coxie) — 1959- . RHP 1983-88 **Cardinals** 986 ip, 56-56, 3.40. *2 LCS, 23 ip, 2-1, .235. 2 WS, 26 ip, 1-2, 4.21*

Cox was a key ingredient in the Cardinals' 1985 pennant as he went 18-9 in just his second full season. Possessing only an average fastball, he relied heavily on a great change-up. He spent stretches on the disabled list in 1986, '87, most of 1988, and all of 1989 with bone chips, a broken foot, and tendinitis. /(FO)

Larry Cox — 1947- . C 1973-75, 77-82 Phillies, **Mariners,** Cubs, Rangers 348 g, .221, 12 hr, 85 rbi

In 1977 Cox was one of the original Mariners, serving as a backup catcher. Traded to the Cubs in 1978, he returned to Seattle in 1979 and spent two years as the regular catcher, hitting .215 and .202. /(NLM)

Ted Cox — 1955- . 3B-OF-DH 1977-81 Red Sox, **Indians,** Mariners, Blue Jays 272 g, .245, 10 hr, 79 rbi

The Red Sox drafted Cox number one in June 1973, ahead of Fred Lynn. He was the International League's MVP and all-star third baseman in 1977. After Boston called him up, Cox tied an AL record with four hits in his first full game in Baltimore on September 18. He extended the streak to six the next day against the Yankees, to set the mark for "most consecutive hits, start of career." When the season ended, he had hit .362 in 13 games. The following spring, Boston included Cox in a trade with Cleveland for Dennis Eckersley. Cox hit .233 in 1970 and never played regularly in the majors. /(EW)

Bob Coyne — 1898-1976. *Cartoonist.*

Before retiring in 1975 after a 47-year career, Coyne drew over 15,000 sports cartoons for several Boston newspapers. /(NLM)

Estel Crabtree (Crabby) — 1903-1967. OF 1929, 31-33, 41-44 **Reds,** Cardinals 489 g, .281, 13 hr, 142 rbi

An everyday outfielder with the Reds in 1931-32, Crabtree was buried in the St. Louis farm system after 1933. He came back up in 1941 as a 4-F wartime player, having lost a kidney due to an outfield collision. Crabtree was born in Crabtree, Ohio. /(JK)

Harry Craft — 1915- . OF 1937-42 **Reds** 566 g, .253, 44 hr, 267 rbi. *2 WS, 6 g, .083.*
Manager 1957-59, 61-64 A's, Reds, **Astros** 360-485, .426

In his day, it was said nobody played centerfield better than Harry Craft. His bat was adequate and he had fair power, but his glove and arm made him valuable on a Cincinnati team that won titles in 1939 and 1940 with stellar defense and superb pitching. Craft's disputed home run in the Polo Grounds in 1939 hastened the advent of foul pole screens. He managed a series of unsuccessful major league teams, including the expansion Houston Colt .45's, and never finished higher than seventh in seven seasons. /(JK)

Roger Craig — 1931- . RHP 1955-66 **Dodgers,** Giants, Cardinals, Reds, Phillies, Mets 1536 ip, 74-98, 3.83. *4 WS, 26 ip, 2-2, 6.49.*
Manager 1978-79, 85- Padres, **Giants** 423-404, .511. First place: 87, 89 *2 LCS, 7-5, .583. 1 WS, 0-4, .000*

In 1986 *Sports Illustrated* called Roger Craig "the acknowledged maestro of the split-fingered fastball."

In 1985 he taught the split-finger to the Astros' Mike Scott, who won the 1986 Cy Young award. Craig had previously managed the 1978–79 Padres and served as a scout and pitching coach, notably in Detroit, where he taught Jack Morris the split-finger. As a manager, Craig is noted for one-run tactics and for calling lots of pitchouts. He won the NL West title in 1987 and the NL pennant in 1989.

With the fledgling Mets in 1962–63, Craig became the first pitcher to lead the NL in losses two straight years (24 in 1962, 22 in 1963). He tied a league record in 1963 by dropping 18 straight decisions. Conversely, he tied for the NL lead with four shutouts for Los Angeles in 1959, and won two World Series games, one each with Brooklyn and St. Louis. /(TJ)

Doc Cramer [Roger Maxwell] (Flit) — 1905– . OF
1929–48 A's, **Red Sox**, Senators, Tigers 2239 g, .296, 37 hr, 842 rbi. *2 WS, 9 g, .387, 6 rbi*
☛ *All-Star—35, 37–40.*

An agile, swift centerfielder, Cramer led the AL in putouts in 1936 and 1938. He was considered to be one of the best judges of fly balls in the ML, and also owned an excellent arm. Offensively, he was a leadoff hitter who specialized in singles, topping the AL five times and tying for the lead in total hits (200) in 1940. Twice, he collected six hits in a game. In his career, he had 2,705 hits. He led the league in at-bats in seven different seasons, the ML record. At age 40, he was a hitting star for the Tigers in the 1945 WS, batting .379, scoring seven runs, and batting in four. Later, as a White Sox coach, he was credited with developing Nellie Fox as a hitter.

Cramer was a semi-pro pitcher when discovered by Cy Perkins and signed by the Athletics. Sent to Martinsburg of the Blue Ridge League in 1929, he was locked in a close race with Joe Vosmik for the league batting title. On the final day of the season, he pitched against Vosmik's team and walked his rival four times. Cramer's .404 won the title.

Cramer tied a ML record by going 6-for-6 in a nine-inning game, and is the only American Leaguer to do it twice (6/20/32 and 7/13/35). Towards the end of his career, he was frequently used as a pinch-hitter, and led the AL with nine pinch hits in 1947. Sent up six times for Birdie Tebbetts, Cramer came through four times, and when the Tigers traded Tebbetts to Boston, Cramer complained, "It's like tearing up my meal ticket. A game is not official

Doc Cramer

until the announcement goes out 'Cramer for Tebbetts'."

Cramer gained medical knowledge before playing pro ball by observing a local doctor, and was therefore dubbed "Doc." Philadelphia sportswriter Jimmy Isaminger began calling him "Flit", after the insecticide, because the outfielder was death to fly balls. /(NLM/JK)

Del Crandall — 1930– . C 1949–50, 53–66 **Braves**, Giants, Pirates, Indians 1573 g, .254, 179 hr, 657 rbi. *2 WS, 13 g, .227, 2 hr, 4 rbi.*
    Manager 1972–75, 83–84 **Brewers**, Mariners 364–469, .437
☛ *All-Star—53–56, 58–60, 62. Gold Glove—58–60, 62 .*

"Crandall was a hell of a defensive catcher," Hank Aaron recalled. Joe Adcock said Crandall "couldn't hit with Campanella, but strictly as a catcher he was the best." Crandall replaced Walker Cooper as the Braves' regular catcher and captain and led NL backstops in fielding four times, winning four Gold Gloves. He appeared in eight All-Star games, homering in one; he also homered in both the 1957 and '58 WS, and three times collected over 20 HR in a season. After a shoulder problem sidelined him for most of 1961, Crandall batted a career-high .297 in 1962. Twenty years later, he managed Albuquerque (Pacific Coast League) to a remarkable 94–38 record, but in six years managing the Brewers and Mariners finished no higher than fifth. Crandall joined the White Sox broadcast team in 1985. /(TJ)

Doc Crandall [James Otis] — 1887–1951. RHP-2B 1908–16, 18 **Giants**, Cardinals, St. Louis (FL), Browns, Braves 1546 ip, 101–62, 2.92; 500 g, .285, 9 hr, 126 rbi. 20 wins: 15 *3 WS, 10 ip, 1–0, 1.69*

Crandall was the first pitcher to be used consistently as a reliever. Damon Runyon nicknamed him "Doc," calling him "the physician of the pitching emergency." Crandall started often, but led the league in relief appearances five seasons in a row with the Giants. He led in relief victories from 1910 through 1912, during which time he went 45–16 overall, helping the Giants win three pennants in 1911–13. A nimble fielder despite his bulky frame, he filled in at infield positions. The .285 lifetime hitter also pinch hit often. When he was sent to the Cardinals in 1913, the displeasure in New York was so great that the Giants repurchased him after two games. But he wound up in St. Louis the following year, in the Federal League, spending more games at second base than on the mound. He led the Federal League in 1915 with 6 relief wins among his 21 victories. /(JK)

Cannonball Crane [Edward Nicholas] — 1862–1896. RHP-OF-C 1884–86, 88–93 **Boston (UA)**, Providence (NL), Buffalo (NL), Washington (NL), Giants, New York (PL), Cincinnati-Milwaukee (AA), Reds, Dodgers 391 g, .238, 18 hr, 84 rbi; 1550 ip, 72–95, 3.99
☛ *Led League—era 91.*

As a rookie outfielder/catcher in 1884, Crane ranked second in the Union Association with 12 HR. By 1888 he had completed a transition to pitcher, and in 1891 led the American Association with a 2.45 ERA for Cincinnati/Milwaukee. Crane enjoyed only one winning season, and twice lost more than 20 games. He comitted suicide by drinking acid. /(FIC)

Sam Crane (Red) — 1894–1955. SS 1914–17, 20–22 A's, Senators, **Reds**, Dodgers 174 g, .208, 0 hr, 30 rbi

Crane was a light-hitting shortstop who continually impressed with brilliant play in the minors. He never won a permanent place until he was convicted of killing his girlfriend and her male companion in a hotel bar; he then secured a long-term position as SS on the prison team. /(JK)

Alfred R. Cratty — Unk.–Unk. *Writer.*

Cratty created the baseball and sporting department of the Pittsburgh *Chronicle-Telegraph* in 1885 and held that desk until he left in 1906 to enter medical school. He later returned to work for the Pittsburgh *Press.* He was an early correspondent for *The Sporting Life.* /(NLM)

Gavvy Cravath [Clifford Carlton] (Cactus) — 1881–1963. OF 1908–09, 12–20 Red Sox, White Sox, Senators, **Phillies** 1219 g, .287, 119 hr, 719 rbi. *1 WS, 5 g, .125, 1 rbi.*
    Manager 1919–20 **Phillies** 91–137, .399
☛ *Led League—hr 13–15, 17–19. Led League—rbi 13, 15.*

Cravath was the home run king of the deadball era. He set marks Babe Ruth would break soon after with the introduction of the lively ball. The tobacco-chewing, cussing bruiser was called "Cactus" for his prickly personality.
    Cravath was a sensation in the Pacific Coast League and the American Association. In between, he failed with the Red Sox, White Sox, and Senators. Given a second chance with the Phillies at age 31, he bloomed. In 1913 he led the NL with 19 HR and 128 RBI—35 more than runner-up Heinie Zimmerman. His league-high 179 hits gave him a .341 average, his career best. Over the next six years he won five more HR titles, with a high of 24 in 1915, when he repeated as RBI champ. That August 8, he tied a ML record with four doubles in a game. He won the 1919 NL HR crown with 12 in only 83 games.
    A gruff player, Cravath proved too easygoing as a manager, lasting just a season and a half at the Phillies helm. He frequently used himself off the

Gavvy Cravath with the Phillies

Jim Crawford (Catfish) — 1950– . LHP 1973, 1975–78 Astros, **Tigers** 432 ip, 15–28, 4.40

Crawford, most often used in relief, debuted with the 1973 Astros, saving six games. Traded to Detroit in a 1975 seven-player deal, he won a career-high seven games in 1977. /(TJ)

Sam Crawford (Wahoo Sam) — 1880–1968. OF-1B 1899–1917 Reds, **Tigers** 2517 g, .309, 97 hr, 1525 rbi. *3 WS, 17 g, .243, 1 hr, 6 rbi*
☛ *Led League—hr 01, 08. Led League—rbi 10, 14–15. Hall of Fame—1957.*

Crawford is most famous for hitting triples, 312 of them over a 19-year career, first on the all-time list. Second on the all-time triples list is Ty Cobb, who batted third in front of Crawford for the Tigers following the birth of the American League. The order is ironic because although the two were teammates, and often pulled off some uniquely synchronized double steals, the normally easy-going Crawford despised the fiery Cobb.

Crawford was nicknamed Wahoo Sam after his birthplace, Wahoo, Nebraska. A former barber, Crawford started out with the Cincinnati Reds in 1899 and hit a then-astounding total of 16 HR in 1901. In 1903 he jumped to the Tigers and led the American League in triples with 25. What is often forgotten about Crawford was his power to drive the ball over fences as well as between fielders; he hit 97 career HR, and at his retirement held the AL career record with 70. In 1908, Crawford led the AL in homers with seven, and so became the only player in baseball history to lead both leagues in homers.

Although they disliked each other, Cobb and Crawford worked closely together on the bases. Cobb, either by steals or by a triple, would often be standing at third when Crawford came to bat. Crawford was often walked. Crawford would jaunt easily to first and then, on cue from Cobb, switch into high gear and take off for second. At the same time, Cobb would break for home. "Sometimes they'd get him," Crawford would later recall, "sometimes they'd get me, and sometimes they wouldn't get either of us."

Once Cobb started winning batting titles regularly, fellow lefthanded hitter Crawford began to drive in more than 100 runs a season, leading the league three times in RBI in the 1910s. But, like Cobb, Crawford could find no success in the World Series. The duo's failures at the bat were the main reasons why the Tigers lost three straight Series in

bench, and had a league-high 12 pinch hits in 1920. The California native became a justice of the peace in Laguna, but lost his job for being too easygoing. /(JK)

Jerry Crawford — 1947– . *Umpire* NL 1977–87 *3 LCS*

A second-generation NL umpire, Jerry joined the NL staff in 1977, a year after his father, Shag Crawford, retired. Jerry's brother Joe umpired briefly in the minors before becoming an NBA referee. /(RTM)

Sam Crawford

1907, 1908, and 1909. Crawford's one shining World Series moment came in Game Five of the 1909 affair when he went 3-for-4 with a double and a homer, but the Tigers lost the game, 8–4, and the Series to Pittsburgh. Crawford ended his career 36 hits shy of 3,000 in 1917, then umpired in the Pacific Coast League for four years. /(SEW)

Shag Crawford — 1921– . *Umpire* NL 1956–75 *2 LCS 3 WS, 3 ASU*

Crawford caught briefly in the Phillies' organization, then umpired around the Philadelphia area to stay in the game. His slow, deliberate, strong calls and low crouch while touching the catcher's back with his hands characterized his umpiring style. One of the founders of the ML Umpires' Association, Crawford was asked to work the 1975 WS by umpire supervisor Fred Fleig. Shag refused because it had been agreed that the Series would use a rotation system for umpires. According to Crawford, he was fired for his refusal. "They said they retired me," he said, "but in my personal opinion, they dumped me." /(RTM)

Steve Crawford — 1958– . RHP 1980–82, 84–87, 89 **Red Sox**, Royals 436 ip, 22–17, 3.98. *1 LCS, 2 ip, 1–0, 0.00. 1 WS, 4 ip, 1–0, 2.63*

A 6′5″ 225-lb reliever with a menacing mustache but a straight fastball, Crawford won Game Five of the 1986 ALCS after escaping a bases-loaded, one-out jam in the bottom of the ninth, and won Game Two of the '86 WS in relief of Roger Clemens. /(SCL)

Willie Crawford — 1946– . OF 1964–77 **Dodgers**, Cardinals, Astros, A's 1210 g, .268, 86 hr, 419 rbi. *1 LCS, 2 g, .250, 0 hr, 1 rbi. 2 WS, 5 g, .375, 1 hr, 1 rbi*

Crawford never became the homegrown superstar the Dodgers anticipated when they signed him out of Los Angeles's Fremont High School for $100,000. In the majors at 17 and in the WS at 19, he struggled for consistency and eventually became a better-than-average player. In his best season, 1973, he hit .295, with 14 homers and 91 RBI. /(TG)

Robert Creamer — 1922– . *Writer.*

A senior editor at *Sports Illustrated* from 1954 to 1984, Creamer ghosted *Quality of Courage* for Mickey Mantle in 1964 and wrote *Jocko* with Jocko Conlan (1967), and *Rhubarb in the Catbird Seat* with Red Barber (1968). He was co-author of *The Yankees* (1979) and *Stengel: His Life and Times* (1984), and his 1974 book *Babe: The Legend Comes to Life* is considered the definitive biography of Babe Ruth. /(NLM)

Birdie Cree — 1882–1942. OF 1908–15 **Yankees** 742 g, .292, 11 hr, 332 rbi

The 5′6″ 150-lb Cree spent three seasons as the regular leftfielder for the Highlanders (later called the Yankees), but ultimately spurned baseball in favor of banking. /(JK)

Keith Creel — 1959– . RHP 1982–83, 85, 87 **Royals**, Indians, Rangers 203 ip, 5–14, 5.60

A strong prospect after a 24–12 record his first two years in the Royals' organization, Creel never developed one potent, reliable pitch. His best opportunity came with pitching-poor Cleveland in 1985, but he lost his first five decisions. /(FO)

James Creighton — 1841-1862. RHP statistics not available

In baseball's early days, when pitchers were required to toss the ball underhand and stiff-armed (with the pitching wrist facing up), Creighton puzzled batters with the speed of his delivery, gained by a sly snap of the wrist. Believed to be baseball's first professional player and acclaimed in his obituary as "one of the best players in the Union," he starred for two Brooklyn clubs, Star and Excelsior, before his death at 21 of "an internal injury occasioned by strain while batting." /(FIC)

Creepy Crespi [Frank Angelo Joseph] — 1918- . 2B-SS 1938-42 **Cardinals** 264 g, .263, 4 hr, 88 rbi. *1 WS, 1 g, --*

This St. Louis native climbed quickly up the Cardinal ladder. Crespi was among the top-rated second basemen in 1941, his first successful major league season. Unfortunately, an army camp accident put a sudden end to his promising career. In 1943 he broke his left leg playing army baseball, then broke it again in another place when he crashed into a wall in a wheelchair race. /(EW)

Tim Crews — 1961- . RHP 1987- **Dodgers** 162 ip, 5-2, 3.05

Crews came to the Dodgers with Tim Leary from Milwaukee in exchange for Greg Brock. The reliever's 4-0, 3.14 record helped the 1988 Dodgers win their World Championship. /(JFC)

Jerry Crider — 1941- . RHP 1969-70 Twins, **White Sox** 119 ip, 5-7, 4.51

Crider, a junkballer, was a mediocre spot starter and long relief man for the pitching-thin 1970 White Sox. In one performance against the Red Sox, Crider allowed a game-winning home run off the bat of Vicente Romo, Boston's relief pitcher. It was the only homer of Romo's eight-year career. /(RL)

Lou Criger — 1872-1934. C 1896-1910, 1912 Cleveland (NL), Cardinals, **Red Sox**, Browns, Yankees 1012 g, .221, 11 hr, 342 rbi. *1 WS, 8 g, .231, 4 rbi*

Small and agile, light-hitting Lou Criger lasted 16 years in the majors because of his ability as a catcher. Beginning in 1896, he was the batterymate of Cy Young in Cleveland and St. Louis of the National League, and Boston in the American League. Criger caught most of Young's 511 victories; the two played together until Criger's December 1908 trade to the Browns. During the first World

Series, played in 1903 between the Boston Pilgrims (later the Red Sox) and Pirates, gamblers offered Criger a bribe to throw the games. Criger spurned it, and caught every inning of the eight games in the Boston victory. /(JK)

Chuck Crim — 1961- . RHP 1987- **Brewers** 357 ip, 22-21, 3.16

Crim was a last-minute, non-roster invitee to the Brewers' 1987 camp, but made the club with a 1.08 spring ERA. He was a set-up man and spot starter until becoming a closer, saving 12 games, after Dan Plesac hurt his elbow. Back in middle relief thereafter, he led the AL in appearances in 1988 and 1989. /(JCA)

Jack Crimian — 1926- . RHP 1951-52, 56-57 Cardinals, **A's**, Tigers 160 ip, 5-9, 6.36

Crimian was the International League MVP in 1955 when he went 19-6 for Toronto. He then failed in his only real major league shot, going 4-8 (5.51) for the 1956 A's. /(NLM)

Hughie Critz — 1900-1980. 2B 1924-35 **Reds**, Giants 1478 g, .268, 38 hr, 531 rbi. *1 WS, 5 g, .136*

The son of respected professor Colonel Critz of Mississippi A&M, 5'8" 147-lb Hughie, like his father, captained the school's baseball team. In his first game with the Reds Critz had two hits against Grover Alexander and hit .322 in 102 games as a rookie. Critz topped NL second basemen in fielding four times and double plays three times. /(JK)

Warren Cromartie — 1953- . OF-1B 1974, 76-83 **Expos** 1038 g, .280, 60 hr, 371 rbi. *1 LCS, 5 g, .167, 2 rbi*

Cromartie, Ellis Valentine, and Andre Dawson formed what Expos announcer Duke Snider termed "the best young outfield" he'd ever seen in 1977-79. Only Dawson really lived up to Snider's billing. Cromartie always hustled but was erratic, prone to long slumps, and was not a power hitter. Extremely popular in Montreal, he hit .304 in 1981 as the Expos won their only division title, then skidded to .254 in '82. After being platooned in '83, he signed with the Yomiuri Giants of the Japan Central League. A great success in Japan, he hit over 30 home runs in each of his first three seasons while compiling good batting averages. /(MC)

Ray Crone — 1931- . RHP 1954-58 **Braves**, Giants 546 ip, 30-30, 3.87

A control pitcher, Crone beat the Cubs five times in going 10-9 for the 1955 Braves. He went to the Giants with Bobby Thomson in a 1957 trade for Red Schoendienst, but a sore arm finished him in 1958. /(MC)

Joe Cronin — 1906–1984. SS 1928–1945 Pirates, Senators, **Red Sox** 2124 g, .301, 170 hr, 1424 rbi. *1 WS, 5 g, .318, 2 rbi.*
  Manager 33–47, Senators, **Red Sox** 1236–1055, .540. First place: 33, 46 *2 WS, 4–8, .333*
☛ *All-Star—33–35, 37–39, 41. Hall of Fame—1956.*

For 14 years, Joe Cronin's signature appeared on all the baseballs used in the American League. But a far more interesting tidbit about this former American League president is that he was once sold by his uncle-in-law—not his father-in-law, as is often reported. Cronin was one of baseball's "boy wonder" managers when he piloted the 1933 Senators to an AL pennant at the age of 27, a year younger than Washington's first "boy wonder," Bucky Harris, was when he took Washington to its first pennant in 1924. It is often forgotten that the gentlemanly Cronin was one of the premier shortstops of his day, and knocked in more than 100 runs in a season eight times. He was also Carl Hubbell's fifth consecutive

Joe Cronin with the Senators

Hall of Fame strikeout victim in the 1934 All-Star game.

A former bank clerk, Cronin came up as a slow and clumsy shortstop for Pittsburgh. The Pirates had Arky Vaughan at shortstop, and in 1928 Cronin was dealt to Washington, where he bloomed. In 1930, his second full season, he had career highs in batting average (.346) and RBI (126), and *TSN* named him player of the year (1930 was the year before the baseball writers started electing regular MVPs). In 1933, Cronin was named player-manager by Washington owner Clark Griffith, and Cronin responded by guiding the Senators to their final World Series appearance. The Giants beat Cronin's club in five games, but Cronin batted .318.

The following year, Griffith introduced his young manager to his niece, Mildred Robertson, then a club secretary. The two were married later that year. But at the end of the 1934 season, Griffith sold his new nephew to the Red Sox for $225,000, the highest amount paid for a single player (Boston's sale of Babe Ruth was actually only for $125,000, with the remaining $300,000 being a personal loan from Yankee owner Ruppert to Red Sox owner Harry Frazee). Griffith arranged, however, for Cronin to receive a five-year contract good for $50,000 per year.

Cronin loved hitting in Fenway Park. Three times he registered slugging percentages over .500, with a career-high .536 in 1938, the year he led the AL in doubles with 51. He hit a career-high 24 HR in 1940, the year he also led the league in putouts and assists. Despite hitting .311 with 16 HR and 95 RBI in 1941, he took himself out of the regular lineup in 1942 to make room for a youngster named Johnny Pesky. He still pinch hit, though, setting a major league record of five pinch homers in 1943, including two in one day—one each in two ends of a doubleheader.

In early 1945 Cronin broke his leg, ending his playing career for good. He took the Red Sox to the World Series the following year, losing to the Cardinals on Enos Slaughter's dash home in the seventh game. He moved into the Red Sox front office in 1948 for 11 years, during which time he was elected to the Hall of Fame. In 1959, he was chosen American League president by the owners, the first former player so honored. In his two terms as AL president, he presided over the league's expansion from eight to ten teams in 1960, then to 12 teams in 1969. In 1970, he fired two umpires for "incompetency" when he learned they were trying to form a

union. In his final year as president, he blocked
George Steinbrenner's attempt to hire Dick Williams as manager, but allowed the Tigers to sign
Ralph Houk away from Steinbrenner's
Yankees. /(SEW)

John Cronin — 1874–1929. RHP 1895, 98–99, 01–04
Dodgers, Pirates, Reds, Tigers, Baltimore (AL), Giants
923 ip, 43–57, 3.40

Cronin pitched half of a rare doubleheader shutout
by the Dodgers in 1904 in his second tour with the
club. He retired when his 2.70 ERA that year,
slightly below the league average, brought him only
a 12–23 record. /(TG)

Ed Crosby — 1949– . SS-2B-3B 1970, 72–76
Cardinals, Reds, Indians 297 g, .220, 0 hr, 44 rbi. *1 LCS,
3 g, .500, 0 hr, 0 rbi*

Light-hitting Crosby played 101 games as a Cardinal
utility infielder in 1972, the only season in which he
played in more than half of his team's games. His
.217 batting average kept him on the bench. After a
trade to the Angels in December 1976, he refused to
report and was granted free agency. He signed with
the A's but was released before the '77 season
began. /(MC)

Frankie Crosetti (The Crow) — 1910– . SS-3B
1932–48 **Yankees** 1682 g, .245, 98 hr, 649 rbi. *7 WS,
29 g, .174, 1 hr, 11 rbi*
☞ *All-Star—36, 39.*

Anchoring the Yankee infield for most of his 17
seasons, Crosetti was always among the fielding
leaders. In 1938 and 1939 he led AL shortstops in
putouts and double plays. He topped the league with
27 stolen bases in 1938, and his 757 plate appearances that year set a ML record for a 154-game
season. He led the AL in HBP eight times.

One of the game's great sign-stealers, he was also
a master of the hidden ball trick. In his 17 playing
years, Crosetti was a member of nine AL Champion
teams and eight World Champions. After retiring in
1948, he was the Yankee third-base coach for 20
years, and participated in 15 more World Series. His
continuous Yankee service was the longest in the
team's history. /(EW)

Crosley Field Cincinnati Reds 1912–70. LF-328, CF-
387, RF-366

The scene of baseball's first ML night game on May
24, 1935, Crosley Field opened in 1912 as Redland
Field, but was renamed when Powell Crosley bought
the Reds in 1934. Originally 360′ down each line
and 420′ to center, the park was open almost a

Frankie Crosetti

decade before Pat Duncan hit the first over-the-
fence home run, on June 2, 1921. In January 1937
the park virtually disappeared when a massive flood
covered it with over 20′ of water, and Reds pitchers
Lee Grissom and Gene Schott posed for a wire-
service photo rowing a boat over the center field
fence. A billboard behind the left field fence advertised "Hit this sign and win a Seibler suit," which
the Reds' Wally Post did a record 11 times. Crosley
Field was abandoned by the Reds for Riverfront
Stadium. The city of Cincinnati impounded towed
cars there before it was torn down and then reconstructed on a Reds fan's farm in nearby
Kentucky. /(SCL)

Powell Crosley, Jr. — 1887–1961. *Executive*

At the urging of GM Larry MacPhail, Crosley, an
inventor and manufacturer of autos, refrigerators
and radios, bought the Reds in 1934 for $450,000

so the team would stay in Cincinnati. Redland Field, the home of the Reds from 1912 to 1970, was renamed Crosley Field in his honor. /(NLM)

Lave Cross [Lafayette Napoleon] — 1866–1927. 3B-C-OF-SS-2B 1887–1907 Louisville (AA), Philadelphia (AA), Philadelphia (PL), Phillies, St. Louis (NL), Cleveland (NL), Cardinals, Dodgers, **A's**, Senators 2275 g, .292, 47 hr, 1345 rbi. *1 WS, 5 g, .105.*
　　Manager 1899 **Cleveland (NL)**, 8–30, .211

Cross was a bowlegged wonder, cheered by Philadelphia fans in four different major leagues. He was primarily a catcher the first part of his career. When he switched to infield positions, he played them (until the rules were changed) using his catcher's mitt. With the Phillies on August 5, 1897, he set a still-standing ML record for most assists by a second baseman in a game, with 15 (12 innings).

Lave Cross

Cross left Philadelphia in 1898 to become the everyday third baseman for St. Louis (NL). For the first 38 games of 1899, he managed the Cleveland Spiders (NL), who compiled the worst record in ML history—20–134. He returned to Philadelphia as a member of the Athletics in 1901, the first AL season. From April 23, 1902 until May 8, 1905, he played in 447 consecutive games, all but one at third base. For seven straight seasons (1898–1904) he never batted below .290. Lave's brother, Amos, was a catcher for Louisville (AA) in 1885–87, and another brother, Frank, played one game for Cleveland (AL) in 1901. /(JK)

Monte Cross — 1869–1934. SS 1892, 1894–1907 Baltimore (NL), Pirates, Cardinals, Phillies, **A's** 1681 g, .234, 31 hr, 621 rbi. *1 WS, 5 g, .176*

After stints with the Orioles, Pirates, and Cardinals, Cross became the Phillies' regular shortstop in 1898. Connie Mack, his former Pirate manager, lured Cross to the A's in the fledgling American League. Cross topped AL shortstops in putouts in 1902 and 1903. In the NL, he had led shortstops four times in putouts, twice in assists, and three times in errors. /(TJ)

Frank Croucher (Dingle) — 1914–1980. SS-2B 1939–42 **Tigers**, Senators 296 g, .251, 7 hr, 86 rbi. *1 WS, 1 g, --*

A good fielder but a light hitter, Croucher missed the 1938 season with a broken leg but earned the Tigers' shortstop job in 1941 and hit a respectable .254. Traded to the Senators, he was out most of 1942 with a sore arm, then went into military service, ending his playing career. /(NLM)

Buck Crouse [Clyde] — 1897–1983. C 1923–30 **White Sox** 470 g, .262, 8 hr, 160 rbi

The tobacco-chewing, drawling Crouse was a reliable backup for Hall of Fame catcher Ray Schalk. It was Crouse who said to the scholarly Moe Berg, "Moe, I don't care how many of those degrees you got, they ain't learned you to hit the curveball no better than me." In 1937, Crouse was International League MVP, leading Baltimore to the playoffs as player-manager. /(DB)

General Crowder [Alvin] — 1899–1972. RHP 1926–36 **Senators**, Browns, Tigers 2344 ip, 167–115, 4.12. 20 wins: 28, 32–33 *3 WS, 26 ip, 1–2, 3.81* ☛ *Led League—w 32–33. All-Star—33.*

The 5'10″ Crowder topped the AL in winning percentage for the Browns in 1928 (21–5, .808). In

1930 St. Louis traded him with Heinie Manush for Goose Goslin of the Senators. Crowder led the AL in wins with Washington in 1932 (26–13) and 1933 (24–15). Selected to play in the first All-Star Game in '33, he hurled three innings for the victorious AL. Pitching for the Tigers in Game Four of the 1935 World Series, Crowder beat the Cubs 2–1; Detroit took the Series in six games. His nickname came from General Enoch Crowder, originator of America's WWI draft lottery. /(TJ)

George Crowe — 1923– . 1B 1952–53, 55–61 Braves, **Reds**, Cardinals 702 g, .270, 81 hr, 299 rbi ☛ *All-Star—58.*

This Negro Leaguer played pro basketball as a center and forward for Dayton of the NBL before joining the Boston Braves. The 6′2″ 210-lb left-handed batter supplied ten of Cincinnati's league record-tying 221 homers in 1956. As the Reds' regular first baseman, Crowe hit 31 HR in 1957, and was an All-Star in 1958. But Crowe was traded to St. Louis, where Stan Musial was manning first in 1959; Crowe, instead, led the NL with 17 pinch hits. /(TJ)

Terry Crowley — 1947– . DH-OF-1B 1969–83 **Orioles**, Reds, Braves, Expos 865 g, .250, 42 hr, 229 rbi. *3 LCS, 5 g, .250, 1 rbi. 3 WS, 8 g, .286, 2 rbi*

Crowley retired sixth all-time in both pinch hits (108) and pinch at-bats (419), with a .258 lifetime pinch average. The highlight of his career was a 9th-inning pinch grand slam against the Royals on August 8, 1982, giving the Orioles a 10–6 victory.

The lefthanded-hitting Crowley bounced between Baltimore and Rochester (International League) for his first five seasons, pinch hitting and filling in in the outfield. He moved increasingly to pinch hitting with the Reds in 1974. Back in Baltimore in 1977, Crowley hit .364 down the stretch. He pinch-hit .342 in 1978 and hit .317 in 1979. Crowley's best year, however, was 1980: 12 HR, 50 RBI, and a .288 average in 233 at-bats, including a .338 average with men in scoring position and a league-leading .297 pinch-hitting average. Crowley has worked as a major and minor league batting instructor. /(MC)

Walt Cruise — 1890–1975. OF 1914, 16–24 Cardinals, **Braves** 736 g, .277, 30 hr, 272 rbi

A journeyman major leaguer for parts of ten seasons, Cruise hit .346 in 108 games in 1921 and was the right fielder for the Braves in the 26-inning 1–1 tie played against Brooklyn on May 1, 1920. He scored the Boston run when his triple, his only hit in

nine at-bats, was followed by Tony Boeckel's single. Cruise was married at home plate in Cincinnati between games of a double-header. He did not play in the nightcap. /(NLM)

James Crusinberry — 1879–1960. *Writer*

Crusinberry broke in with the Chicago *Chronicle* in 1903 and worked for newspapers in Chicago, St. Louis, and New York before a long stay with the Chicago *Daily News*. While working for the Chicago *Tribune* in 1920, he played a considerable part in bringing to light the facts about the fixed World Series of 1919. A charter member of the BBWAA, he was its president in 1929–30. He was later a radio sports commentator for CBS until his retirement in 1948. /(NLM)

Jimmie Crutchfield [John W.] — 1910– . OF Negro Leagues 1930–45 Birmingham Black Barons, Indianapolis ABC's, **Pittsburgh Crawfords**, Newark Eagles, Toledo Crawfords, Indianapolis Crawfords, Chicago American Giants, Cleveland Buckeyes 315 g, .266, 5 hr (inc.) ☛ *All-Star—34–36, 41.*

The 5′7″ 150-lb righthanded-hitting Crutchfield was an excellent bat-handler, a fast runner, and a reliable outfielder. He batted .286 his rookie year for the 1930 Birmingham Black Barons, and in 1931 he moved to the Indianapolis ABC's and batted .330, believed to be his career high. When the financially troubled ABC's were unable to pay most of their players, Crutchfield jumped to the Pittsburgh Crawfords, with whom he stayed for five years, making the squad for the East-West all-star game three times. He played for the Newark Eagles in 1937, and though statistics are not available for his 1938–43 seasons, the hustling Crutchfield made the all-star team in 1941 as a member of the Chicago American Giants. /(JM)

Hector Cruz (Heity) — 1953– . OF-3B 1973, 75–82 **Cardinals**, Cubs, Giants, Reds 624 g, .225, 39 hr, 200 rbi. *1 LCS, 2 g, .200*

The younger brother of Jose and Tommy Cruz, who also wore Cardinal uniforms, Hector was signed out of Puerto Rico at age 17 and immediately heralded as the best of the three. In 1975 he was *TSN* Minor League Player of the Year, leading the American Association with 29 HR and 116 RBI. Converted from outfield to third base, he stuck with St. Louis in 1976 and led NL rookies with 13 HR and 71 RBI, but led NL third basemen with 26 errors. He never held another regular job. After bouncing around the NL, he played in Japan for Yomiuri in 1983. /(MC)

Jose Cruz — 1947– . OF-DH 1970–88 Cardinals, **Astros**, Yankees 2353 g, .284, 165 hr, 1077 rbi. *2 LCS, 11 g, .268, 6 rbi*
☛ *All-Star—80, 85.*

With quiet consistency and everyday play, Jose Cruz became one of the all-time Astro greats. Popular with Houston fans, he was one of three brothers to make the majors, along with Hector and Tommy. All three played in the St. Louis farm system, with Jose graduating to the Cardinals in 1970. He never blossomed alongside Lou Brock in the St. Louis outfield and was sold to Houston after the 1974 season. He became a fixture in the Astros' outfield and was their MVP in 1977, '80, '83, and '84. Hurt by the dimensions of the Astrodome and the fact that the ball doesn't carry well there, he led Houston in RBI seven times and in all Triple Crown catego-

Jose Cruz

ries in 1979 and '84 but received little recognition elsewhere.

Though he did not start on Opening Day in 1986 for the first time in a decade, Cruz was a key contributor to the Astros' division title, finishing second on the club in game-winning RBI. But he slumped badly in the LCS, a sharp contrast to his 1980 LCS performance which included a .400 average, four RBI, and eight walks. Few players appeared in more major league games without reaching the World Series than Cruz.

Cruz's reputation was dimmed by the effect of his home parks on his power stats; from 1975 through 1985, he had 80 HR on the road, but just 35 in the Astrodome. However, he hit .300 six times and stole as many as 44 bases (1977) while topping 30 steals in five years. And the lefthanded-hitting Puerto Rican had more games played, at-bats, hits, triples, and RBI than any player in Astros history. /(ME)

Julio Cruz — 1954– . 2B 1977–86 **Mariners**, White Sox 1156 g, .237, 23 hr, 279 rbi. *1 LCS, 4 g, .333*

Cruz was drafted by the expansion Mariners. A Gold Glove winner in 1978, he missed one-third of the next season with a torn ligament in his left thumb. Injuries also sidelined him for two months or more in '80 and '81, but he still stole more than 40 bases each year. With Willie Wilson, Cruz shares the AL record with 32 consecutive successful stolen base attempts. On June 7, 1981, he set an AL record for second basemen (and tied the ML record) with 18 total chances without an error in nine innings. The game went 11 innings and he handled one more chance to fall one short of the ML record. /(NLM)

Todd Cruz — 1955– . SS-3B 1978–80, 82–84 Phillies, Royals, Angels, White Sox, **Mariners**, Orioles 544 g, .220, 34 hr, 154 rbi. *1 LCS, 4 g, .133, 1 rbi. 1 WS, 5 g, .125*

Despite showing some home run power (16 homers in 1982), Cruz didn't hit enough to hold a regular ML job. A lower back injury and broken hand cost him the entire 1981 season. In 1982 and until they were both traded in mid-1983, he and unrelated Julio Cruz formed a "Cruz-and-Cruz" doubleplay combination for the Mariners. /(NLM)

Victor Cruz — 1957– . RHP 1978–81, 83 Blue Jays, **Indians**, Pirates, Rangers 271 ip, 18–23, 3.08

Cruz was Blue Jays Rookie of the Year and co-Rookie Pitcher of the Year in 1978 (7–3, 1.72, 9 saves). The pot-bellied righthander was then traded to Cleveland for infielders Alfredo Griffin and Phil Lansford. Continually fighting weight problems,

Cruz did not fulfill expectations in Cleveland and received little opportunity in Pittsburgh or Texas. /(ME)

Mike Cubbage (Cubbie) — 1950- . 3B-1B 1974-81 Rangers, **Twins**, Mets 703 g, .258, 34 hr, 251 rbi

After short trials with Texas, the bespectacled redhead went to Minnesota in a 1976 trade for Bert Blyleven. In 115 games at third base in 1978, Cubbage set a Twins fielding record (.971), batted a career-high .282, and hit for the cycle. He also filled in at first base, second base, and DH until 1980. Plagued by back miseries, Cubbage finished with the Mets as the NL's most active and successful pinch hitter in 1981 (12 for 44). He later became a manager in the Mets' farm system. /(MC)

Tony Cuccinello (Chick) — 1907- . 2B-3B 1930-40, 1942-45 Reds, **Dodgers**, Braves, Giants, White Sox 1704 g, .280, 94 hr, 884 rbi
☛ *All-Star—33, 38.*

As a rookie third baseman with Cincinnati, Cuccinello batted .312, and then spent nearly a decade as a regular at second base. He hit .300 four more times, and led NL second basemen in assists and double plays three times each. He pinch-hit for Carl Hubbell in the inaugural 1933 All-Star Game. "I'm the most surprised guy in baseball," said Cuccinello upon his release from the White Sox in January 1946, but with WWII over and younger players returning, Chicago cut the 38-year-old. He had finished the 1945 season at .308, one point behind NL leader Snuffy Stirnweiss's .309. Cuccinello did return to the Sox in 1957 as a coach under former teammate Al Lopez. Tony's younger brother, Al, spent one season with the Giants. /(TJ)

Mike Cuellar — 1937- . RHP 1959, 64-77 Reds, Cardinals, Astros, **Orioles**, Angels 2808 ip, 185-130, 3.14. 20 wins: 69-71, 74 *5 LCS, 44 ip, 2-2, 3.07. 3 WS, 41 ip, 2-2, 2.61*
☛ *Cy Young Award—69. All-Star—67, 71.*

Cuellar hurled a no-hitter for Cuban dictator Fulgencio Batista's Army team in 1955, at age 18. Allowed to sign with the Havana Sugar Kings of the International League two years later, he struck out seven straight batters in his very first game and had a 2.44 ERA.

Cuellar bounced from team to team in the high minors before he earned a promotion to the Cardinals and helped them win the 1964 pennant. He was on the World Series roster but did not get into a game. Back in the minors, Cuellar perfected a devastating palmball and was 9-1, 2.51 when dealt to Houston. In 1966, his first full year in the major leagues, Cuellar finished second in NL ERA, behind Sandy Koufax. He won a then-club-record 16 games in 1967, fanning 203. After the 1968 season, the Astros swapped Cuellar to Baltimore for Curt Blefary, at that point a highly regarded young power hitter.

Cuellar tied Denny McLain for AL Cy Young honors with a 23-11, 2.38 performance, then in the World Series was the only Oriole to beat the Mets. He led the AL with 24 wins and 21 complete games in 1970, capping the year by hitting a wind-blown grand slam off Jim Perry in the LCS against the Twins. Cuellar was 20-9 in 1971, as four Oriole starters won at least 20 that year. After winning 18 games in both 1972 and 1973, Cuellar enjoyed his last great season in 1974: 22-10, with a league-leading .688 winning percentage. At age 42 in 1979, two years after finishing up in the majors, Cuellar attempted a comeback, compiling a 7-6 record with three clubs in the Inter-American and Mexican Leagues. /(MC)

Leon Culberson — 1919- . OF 1943-48 **Red Sox**, Senators 370 g, .266, 14 hr, 131 rbi. *1 WS, 5 g, .222, 1 hr, 1 rbi*

Culberson had his highest BA in 1946 (.313) with the Red Sox. In that year's World Series, filling in for Dom DiMaggio, Culberson scooped up Harry Walker's single and threw it in to shortstop Johnny Pesky. When Pesky paused, Cardinal Enos Slaughter completed his dash home from first with the Series-winning run. /(TJ)

Tim Cullen — 1942- . 2B-SS 1966-72 **Senators**, White Sox, A's 700 g, .220, 9 hr, 134 rbi. *1 LCS, 2 g, .000*

On August 30, 1969 with the Senators, Cullen tied a ML record for second basemen by committing three errors in one inning. In 1970 he led AL second basemen with a .994 fielding percentage. The San Francisco native's best batting average came as a utility man in his last season, when he hit .261 across the bay in Oakland. /(TJ)

Roy Cullenbine — 1915- . OF-1B 1938-47 **Tigers**, Dodgers, Browns, Senators, Indians 1181 g, .276, 110 hr, 599 rbi. *2 WS, 12 g, .244, 6 rbi*
☛ *All-Star—41, 43.*

"Cullenbine wouldn't swing the bat," Bill Dewitt, a Browns official, later recalled. True, Cullenbine drew 852 walks in ten seasons, including an AL-leading 112 with Cleveland and Detroit in 1945. But he also swung well enough to twice bat .300, and hit 24 HR for the 1947 Tigers. Cullenbine was with three teams in 1942, ending up with the AL Champion Yankees. /(TJ)

Dick Culler — 1915–1964. SS-3B-2B 1936, 43–49 A's, White Sox, **Braves**, Cubs, Giants 472 g, .244, 2 hr, 99 rbi

An all-conference basketball player at High Point (NC) College, Culler became a good fielder but was a light hitter. His only service as a ML regular came with the Braves in 1945–46, when he also did his best hitting (.262, .255). /(NLM)

Nick Cullop [Henry Nicholas] (Tomato Face) — 1900–1978. OF 1926–27, 29–31 Yankees, Senators, Indians, Dodgers, **Reds** 173 g, .249, 11 hr, 67 rbi

Cullop was a good-fielding, power-hitting outfielder who set the minor league career record with 1857 RBI. In the best of his several ML trials, he hit eight homers in 104 games for Cincinnati in 1931; he also struck out 84 times to lead the league. He was *TSN* Minor League Manager of the Year in 1943 with Columbus and in 1947 with Milwaukee (both in the American Association). /(LRD)

Ray Culp — 1941– . RHP 1963–73 Phillies, Cubs, **Red Sox** 1897 ip, 122–101, 3.58
☛ *All-Star—63, 69.*

Culp signed with Philadelphia for $100,000 in 1959. As *TSN* NL Rookie Pitcher of the Year four years later, he led the Phillies with 14 victories, and posted a second 14-victory season in 1965. Often plagued by arm troubles, he slumped in 1966 and was traded to the Cubs. Dealt to Boston after one mediocre season, in 1968 he began using a palm ball and went 16–6, which included four straight shutouts. He won 17 games each of the next two seasons. On May 11, 1970, he struck out the first six batters he faced, tying the AL record. /(TJ)

George Culver — 1943– . RHP 1966–74 Indians, Reds, Cardinals, **Astros**, Dodgers, Phillies 788 ip, 48–49, 3.62

Signed by the Yankees, Culver struck out 18 in one of his first pro games. A starter with the Reds in 1968, he no-hit Philadelphia on July 29, walking five, to win 6–1. From 1970 on, he was a long reliever, and often led his club in appearances. Culver became a coach and manager in the Phillie system. /(MC)

John Cumberland — 1947– . LHP 1968–72, 74 Yankees, **Giants**, Cardinals, Angels 334 ip, 15–16, 3.82.
1 LCS, 3 ip, 0–1, 9.00

Cumberland came out of the Giants' bullpen in June 1971 to post a 9–6, 2.92 record as San Francisco's third starter in their drive to the division title. He was sold to St. Louis after starting 1972 0–4, and arm miseries ended his career. /(MC)

Candy Cummings [William Arthur] — 1848–1924. RHP 1872–77 **New York (NA)**, Baltimore (NA), Philadelphia (NA), Hartford (NA), Hartford (NL), Cincinnati (NL) *NA:* 124–72; *ML:* 372 ip, 21–22, 2.78
☛ *Hall of Fame—39.*

Cummings is generally credited with having invented the curveball. He maintained he came up with the idea as a 14-year-old in 1863 while watching the flight of clam shells he was throwing on a New England beach. Years of experimentation followed as he perfected the twisting pitch, and discovered that it worked best when thrown into the wind. He wore a kid glove on his pitching hand to prevent blisters, and once broke his wrist throwing the pitch. The 5'9" 120-lb Cummings felt he needed the advantage of the deceptive curveball because he was small even as an adult. His fame spread on the amateur diamond as he earned the nickname "Candy," a term of admiration.

Widely sought after by National Association clubs, Cummings performed for four different teams in as many years. In the NA, he never won fewer than 28 games a season. When the National League was formed in 1876, Cummings won 16 games for the Hartford Blues, and on September 9 he became the first major leaguer to pitch two complete games in one day. In 1877 he was appointed president of baseball's first minor league, the International Association, and performed as player-president. Pitching for Cincinnati (NL), he had lost his stuff and was soundly criticized by the press and fans.

The often conflicting testimony of 19th-century pitchers adds to the mystery surrounding the curveball's origin. One pitcher would claim to be the inventor, only to credit someone else years later. Because of Candy's 1908 article, "How I Pitched the First Curve," and the support of highly respected baseball writer Henry Chadwick, Cummings's claim has gained greatest backing. Another pitcher receiving support has been major leaguer Fred Goldsmith, who made the first recorded public demonstration of the curveball on August 16, 1870. Legend has it that Goldsmith, embittered at not receiving "official"

Candy Cummings with the Brooklyn Star

credit as the pitch's inventor, was found on his deathbed clutching a faded newspaper clipping of his demonstration. The heartbroken Goldsmith died in 1939—the year Cummings joined the Hall of Fame. /(DB)

Joseph Cummings — Unk.-Unk. *Writer.*

One of the first baseball writers to travel with a club, Cummings covered the Orioles of the 1890s for several Baltimore papers before succeeding Joe Flanner as editor of *The Sporting News.* /(NLM)

Bert Cunningham [Ellsworth Elmer] — 1865-1952. RHP 1887-91, 1895-1901 Brooklyn (AA), Baltimore (AA), Philadelphia (PL), Buffalo (PL), **Louisville (NL)**, Cubs 2727 ip, 142-167, 4.22. 20 wins: 88, 98

On August 20, 1890, Cunningham pitched two complete games for last-place Buffalo (Union Association), defeating Chicago 6-2 and 7-0. He went 28-15 as Louisville's top starter in 1898. /(JK)

Bill Cunningham — 1896-1960. *Writer.*

Cunningham, a popular radio commentator and after-dinner speaker throughout New England, served two 19-year hitches as a sportswriter and columnist in Boston. He was with the *Post* from 1922 to 1941, and then the *Herald* until 1960. /(NLM)

Bill Cunningham — 1895-1953. OF 1921-24 **Giants**, Braves 318 g, .286, 9 hr, 112 rbi. *2 WS, 8 g, .176, 3 rbi*

Cunningham was a gifted defensive centerfielder who patrolled the deep reaches of the Polo Grounds in the early 1920s. His acrobatic catch of Babe Ruth's 450-foot drive, after circling the Eddie Grant monument, saved Art Nehf's 1-0 shutout in Game Three of the 1923 WS. /(JK)

Bruce Cunningham — 1905-1984. RHP 1929-32 **Braves** 382 ip, 13-24, 4.64

Cunningham spent four mediocre seasons with the second-division Boston Braves. When a pinched nerve halted his pitching career, he became a homicide inspector, and later a private detective. /(JK)

George Cunningham — 1894-1972. RHP-OF 1916-19, 21 **Tigers** 162 g, .224, 1 hr, 13 rbi; 477 ip, 16-25, 3.13

As a young pitcher prone to shoulder trouble, Cunningham complained so much about the slump-ridden, injury-depleted Tiger outfield of 1918 that manager Hughie Jennings gave him the right-field job for three weeks. He did no better than the regulars. After his arm problems ended his pitching career in 1920, Cunningham worked on his hitting in the minors and returned to the Tigers as an outfielder for one game in 1921. /(MC)

Joe Cunningham — 1931- . 1B-OF 1954, 1956-66
Cardinals, White Sox, Senators 1141 g, .291, 64 hr,
436 rbi
☛ *All-Star—59.*

The articulate, lefthanded Cunningham hit three
homers in his first two ML games. In his All-Star
1959 season, his .345 BA was second in the NL to
Hank Aaron's .355. Describing Cunningham's 1962
season, when he led AL first basemen in fielding,
Richard Lindberg wrote, "The balding first baseman
made plays not seen since Joe Kuhel's time (1930s
and '40s) . . .after a game, Cunningham sat in a
corner updating a little black book that he kept on
each American League pitcher."/(TJ)

Mario Cuomo — 1932- . OF

Before entering law school and embarking on a
political career, Cuomo played centerfield for the
Class D Brunswick (Georgia) Pirates in 1952. He
was hitting .353 when he injured his wrist in a
collision with the outfield fence, and later spent two
weeks in the hospital after being hit in the head with
a pitch. He finished the season hitting .244 with one
home run and 26 RBI in 81 games and retired from
professional baseball. In 1976 Cuomo was elected
Governor of New York, and in the late 1980s he was
a proponent of bringing an expansion ML franchise
to Buffalo./(SCL)

Nig Cuppy [George Joseph, born George Maceo
Koppe] — 1869-1922. RHP 1892-1901 **Cleveland (NL)**,
Cardinals, Braves, Red Sox 2284 ip, 162-98, 3.48. 20
wins: 92, 94-96

Cuppy and Cy Young provided a one-two punch
that kept the Cleveland (NL) Spiders competitive
during the mid-1890s. Cuppy was at his best as a
rookie in 1892, going 28-13 (2.51). He was a 20-
game winner again from 1894 through 1896, compiling a 75-43 record. He led the NL with three
shutouts and eight relief wins in 1894. In those days,
players who had dark skin were sometimes tagged
with racist nicknames; Nig Cuppy may have been
one./(AJA)

Clarence Currie — 1878-1941. RHP 1902-03 Reds,
Cardinals, Cubs 364 ip, 14-23, 3.46

The Cardinals purchased Currie from the Reds in
August of 1902, and he went 6-5 the rest of the
season with the best ERA on the staff. In 1903 he
struggled to 4-12 by mid-season and was sold to the
Cubs./(FJO)

Cliff Curtis — 1883-1943. RHP 1909-13 **Braves**,
Cubs, Phillies, Dodgers 745 ip, 28-61, 3.31

A starter with erratic control, Curtis began promisingly in his debut 1909 season, with a 1.41 ERA,
eight complete games in nine starts, and the best
winning percentage (.444) on the last-place Braves.
The following year, he went 6-24./(MC)

Jack Curtis — 1937- . LHP 1961-63 **Cubs**, Braves,
Indians 279 ip, 14-19, 4.84

Curtis finished third (behind Billy Williams and Joe
Torre) in 1961 Rookie of the Year voting following
his 10-13 season. Traded to Milwaukee for Bob
Buhl the next year, Curtis finished with Cleveland in
1963./(TJ)

John Curtis — 1948- . LHP 1970-84 Red Sox,
Cardinals, **Giants**, Padres, Angels 1641 ip, 89-97, 3.96

Curtis threw three no-hitters as a Clemson University freshman, and in the 1967 Pan American games
he became the first U.S. pitcher to defeat Cuba.
After going 11-8 and 13-13 for the Red Sox in
1972-73, he was traded to the Cardinals, who were
in need of a lefthanded starter. He lasted another
decade in the majors because of his adaptability; he
started and worked in long and short relief, three
times winning 10 games a season. While still active
he worked as a sportswriter for the San Francisco
Examiner./(FJO)

Robert W. Curtis — 1867-1939. *Writer.*

Curtis joined the sports department of the New
York *Sun* in 1889 and was assigned to investigate
the Brotherhood war and the Players' League. He
scooped other reporters on the collapse of the league
a year later. Before joining the *New York Times* in
1922, he worked for the *Recorder* and
Herald./(NLM)

Guy Curtright — 1912- . OF 1943-46 **White Sox**
331 g, .276, 9 hr, 108 rbi

After earning his master's degree during a nine-year
minor league apprenticeship, Curtright batted .291
and hit safely in 26 straight games as a rookie in
1943, his only season as a ML regular./(TJ)

George Cutshaw (Clancy) — 1887-1973. 2B
1912-23 **Dodgers**, Pirates, Tigers 1516 g, .265, 25 hr,
653 rbi. *1 WS, 5 g, .105, 2 rbi*

Cutshaw was voted the top defensive second baseman of 1910-20 by the Society for American
Baseball Research. He led in putouts five times,

assists four times, double plays twice, and fielding percentage three times. He batted cleanup and finished in the top ten in stolen bases seven years in a row (271 career). Cutshaw was tough to strike out, fanning only 10 times in 488 at-bats in 1920. /(CG)

Kiki Cuyler [Hazen Shirley] — 1899–1950. OF 1921–38 Pirates, **Cubs**, Reds, Dodgers 1879 g, .321, 127 hr, 1065 rbi. *3 WS, 16 g, .281, 2 hr, 12 rbi* ☛ *All-Star—34. Hall of Fame—1968.*

Curly-haired, hazel-eyed Kiki Cuyler played with competitive zeal, yet was admired amidst rough and tumble teammates for his gentlemanly qualities. He hit .300 ten times in his major league career. When the Pirates benched this superstar late in their 1927 pennant-winning year and kept him out of the World Series with the Yankees, the general public was mystified and Pittsburgh fans were outraged. When the 27-year-old Cuyler was traded for journeyman infielder Sparky Adams and rookie outfielder Pete Scott after the season, it created one of the mysteries of baseball history. That he became an even greater star for the Chicago Cubs removed suspicions that Cuyler's skills had lessened.

Cuyler, a hard-swinging batter who hit line drives to all fields and led the NL with 26 triples in 1925, had protested being moved from third to second in the lineup by Pirates first-year manager Donie Bush, who wanted Cuyler to replace Hall of Famer Max Carey, Pittsburgh's longtime number-two hitter (Carey had been traded the year before). Like Carey, Cuyler could steal bases. Carey had won ten titles; Cuyler would retire with four (and lead the NL twice in runs scored). However, where Carey was an adept bunter and sliced hits behind the runner, Cuyler swung from the heels, struck out more often than the average player of the era, and was not suited to bat second. Cuyler accepted his manager's decision but it rankled him. He chafed under Bush's expectations and batted below his usual level, dropping to .309 after seasons of .354, .357 and .321.

Cuyler, who ran the bases with abandon, was benched after he went into second base standing up in a risky effort to block a double play relay to first. When the baseman bobbled the ball, but managed to tag out Cuyler, Bush fumed that Cuyler would have been safe if he had slid. Cuyler had also angered Pittsburgh owner Barney Dreyfuss by winning a salary dispute before the season. When Lloyd Waner joined his brother Paul on the 1927 Pirates, the owner apparently feared the payroll impact of three superstar outfielders more than he appreciated

Kiki Cuyler

the distinction and success they could bring.

Cuyler had become a Pittsburgh favorite in 1925 when he finished a close second to triple crown winner Rogers Hornsby for MVP. He also became the hero of the World Series that year against Washington. Walter Johnson had won Game One 4–1 and shut out Pittsburgh 4–0 in Game Four. Johnson began the eighth inning of Game Seven with a 7–6 lead. Cuyler came to bat with the bases loaded and two out. He hit a tremendous drive to the right centerfield wall, clearing the bases with an apparent inside-the-park home run. However, the umpires ruled the ball had become entangled in a tarpaulin rolled up against the wall. Cuyler was given a ground rule double but the score was now 9–7 and the demoralized Senators were blanked in the top of the ninth.

Cuyler was called "Cuy" by his school teammates. It was while winning the MVP title of the Southern Association with Nashville in 1923 that he acquired the euphonious Kiki nickname. Fans heard the players shout for him to take the ball when he rushed in a short fly. The shortstop would yell, "Cuy," and the second baseman would echo the call. In the pressbox the writers turned this into "Kiki." Older fans wince to hear him called "Keekee."

Like Rogers Hornsby, whose batting style he copied, Cuyler didn't drink or smoke. After attending West Point during WWI, Cuyler returned home and married his high school sweetheart. He found a job in the Buick plant in Flint, Michigan, and switched to Chevrolet to play on the company's baseball team in the fast Detroit Industrial League. Soon the professional scouts found him. He kept his contacts with the automotive industry and between seasons served as athletic director for a 12,000-man program.

When a broken foot in 1932 and the passing of seasons slowed Cuyler, his final averages fell below his eventual lifetime .321 mark. He played his final years with second-division teams in Cincinnati and Brooklyn, serving as a playing coach. He returned to the Southern Association to manage and was called back to coach the Cubs early in the 1940s. He was a Boston Red Sox coach when he died suddenly, only 50 years old, before the 1950 season began. Cuyler was elected to the Baseball Hall of Fame by the Veterans Committee in 1968. /(JK)

Mike Cvengros — 1901–1970. LHP 1922–25, 27, 29 Giants, **White Sox**, Pirates, Cubs 552 ip, 25–40, 4.58. *1 WS, 2 ip, 0–0, 3.86*

This modestly talented pitcher of Slavic descent pitched one game for the 1922 World Championship Giants and, after bouncing back from the minors twice, collected losing World Series shares from the 1927 Pirates and 1929 Cubs. Cvengros was the victim of a three-run Babe Ruth homer in the 1927 WS. /(DB)

Cy Young Award

Commissioner Ford Frick pushed the idea of an MVP-type award for pitchers, and the BBWAA approved the idea in 1956. The Cy Young Memorial Award commemorated the career of baseball's all-time career victory leader, who had died the previous year. Part of Frick's rationale was that pitchers rarely won the MVP award, but in the award's inaugural season, Brooklyn's Don Newcombe won both. The NL and AL shared the award at first (also at Frick's insistence) rather than having separate winners in each league, but this was changed in 1967, two seasons after Frick's retirement. Sandy Koufax had won the award in three of the previous four seasons. The voting system originally had each writer voting for just one pitcher, but after Denny McLain and Mike Cuellar tied for the award in 1969, the rules were changed to allow each writer to cast weighted votes for first, second, and third. /(JFC)

John D'Acquisto — 1951– . RHP 1973–82 **Giants**, Cardinals, Padres, Expos, Angels, A's 780 ip, 34–51, 4.56

In 1974 *TSN* named D'Acquisto NL Rookie Pitcher of the Year when he went 12–14 with a 3.77 ERA for the fifth-place Giants, but he missed most of the next season after elbow surgery. Always wild, he was easier to hit afterwards, and was no longer a good starter. He tied an NL record with three wild pitches in the seventh inning on September 24, 1976. The San Diego native made a comeback with the Padres in 1978 by switching to the bullpen (10 saves, 2.13 ERA) but declined in subsequent years. /(SH)

Lonnie Paul Dade — 1951– . OF-3B-DH 1975–80 Angels, **Indians**, Padres 439 g, .270, 10 hr, 107 rbi

A good-fielding third baseman in the minors, Dade played out his option with the Angels and became the Indians' regular leftfielder in 1977 (Buddy Bell was established at 3B). He hit a powerless .291 with 65 runs and 16 steals in 134 games. Traded to the Padres in June 1979 for Mike Hargrove, he moved back to 3B, but hit .189 in 1980 while sharing 3B with Luis Salazar, Tim Flannery, and Aurelio Rodriguez. /(WOR)

Bill Dahlen (Bad Bill) — 1870–1950. SS-3B-OF 1891–1911 **Cubs**, Dodgers, Giants, Braves 2443 g, .274, 84 hr, 1233 rbi. *1 WS, 5 g, .000, 1 rbi.*
   Manager 1910–13 **Dodgers** 251–355, .414
☛ *Led League—rbi 1904.*

Dahlen played shortstop for a National League-record 20 years. His specialty was fielding, to which his NL-record 7,500 SS assists and ML-record 13,325 chances attest. Yet he lasted long enough to make 972 errors at SS, the most by a player at any position in a single league. He was also a consistent hitter with considerable power for the deadball era.

Dahlen broke in as a fleet-footed 21-year-old with the 1891 Chicago Colts (later the Cubs), playing third base and the outfield. By 1895 he was the everyday shortstop. Like many players of the era, he had his best season in 1894 (the year after pitchers were moved back), reaching personal highs of 15 HR, 107 RBI, and a .362 average. He set a record from June 20 through August 6 with a 42-game hitting streak that Willie Keeler exceeded three years later. After failing to hit on August 7, he reeled off a 28-game streak, thus hitting in 70 of 71 games. Twice in his career, in 1896 and 1898, he tripled three times in a game, and in 1900 tripled twice in one inning.

Dahlen played for Brooklyn from 1899 through 1903, then achieved his lifelong dream of playing for the Giants when Brooklyn dealt him for pitcher John Cronin and shortstop Charlie Babb. It was one of the worst trades in Brooklyn history, as Cronin lasted one season, Babb two. Meanwhile, Dahlen led the NL with 80 RBI in 1904, and was the SS for the 1905 World Champion Giants. After a stint with the 1908–09 Braves, he returned to Brooklyn and managed the club for four seasons, never finishing higher than sixth. He was replaced by Wilbert Robinson in November of 1913. /(AJA)

Babe Dahlgren [Ellsworth Tenney] — 1912– . 1B-3B 1935–46 Red Sox, **Yankees**, Braves, Cubs, Browns, Dodgers, Phillies, Pirates 1139 g, .261, 82 hr, 569 rbi. *1 WS, 4 g, .214, 1 hr, 2 rbi*

Dahlgren was the Red Sox' first baseman as a rookie in 1935, but was displaced in 1936 when Boston acquired Jimmie Foxx. He dropped to the minors, and in 1937 played third base for the championship Newark (International League) club. On May 2, 1939, he played first base for the Yankees in place of the ailing Lou Gehrig, whose consecutive-game string thus ended at 2,130. Dahlgren homered that day, and he remained the Yankee first baseman for two seasons. He saw regular action, mostly in the NL, through the end of WWII. /(JK)

Bill Dailey — 1935– . RHP 1961–64 Indians, **Twins** 185 ip, 10–7, 2.76

Despite excellent minor league seasons and effective pitching in two brief trials with Cleveland, Dailey wasn't handed the stopper's role until 1963 with the Twins. In 66 games, he had six wins and 21 saves, with a 1.99 ERA. The next season he couldn't lift his arm without pain and his career was over. /(MC)

Bill Dahlen

One Arm Daily [Hugh Ignatius, born Harry Criss] — 1857–Unk. RHP 1882–87 Buffalo (NL), Cleveland (NL), **Chicago-Pittsburgh (UA)**, Washington (UA), St. Louis (NL), Washington (NL), Cleveland (AA) 1415 ip, 73–89, 3.05. 20 wins: 83–84
☛ *Led League—k 84.*

Daily's nickname was an exaggeration of his physical handicap. Before the start of his major league career, he lost his left hand in a gun accident. He compensated by fashioning a pad covering his wrist; he would trap the ball between the pad and his good hand. He was able to play three games in the outfield, two at second base, and one at shortstop in his major league career, and he hit as high as .214 with six doubles in 1884.

Daily pitched well at times, especially in the beginning of his career. For the Cleveland Spiders (NL), the surly hurler threw a 1–0 no-hitter against Philadelphia on September 13, 1883. He was the first pitcher in ML history to toss consecutive one-hitters, striking out 19 in the first of the pair to tie a

ML record that stood for over a century. This came in the Union Association, in that league's only year. At the end of the season, he had struck out 483, the second-best season total ever, although pitching conditions were to change greatly, and permanently, within a decade. His only winning seasons came in his first two years, as he went 15–14 and 23–19, fairly ordinary marks for the time. He went 28–30 for three UA teams in 1884 and was never again a good pitcher. He vanished from the scene after his last year in the majors. /(SFS)

Bruce Dal Canton — 1942– . RHP 1967–77 Pirates, **Royals**, Braves, White Sox 930 ip, 51–49, 3.68

Desperate for pitching, the Pirates in 1965 signed several mature semi-professionals who'd been by-passed by scouts when younger. One was Woody Fryman, 25; another was Dal Canton, 24. Both had settled down to teaching high school and coaching. Both had been passed over earlier because of control problems. Both jumped to the ML in their second year and became effective spot starters/long relievers. Dal Canton had a career-best 9–4 mark in 1970, helping Pittsburgh to a division title. He later returned to teaching as a pitching coach. /(MC)

Gene Dale — 1889–1958. RHP 1911–12, 15–16 Cardinals, **Reds** 442 ip, 21–28, 3.60

In 1915 Dale gave up the most walks of any pitcher in the NL but was 18–17 with a 2.46 ERA for the seventh-place Reds. The next year, after pitching less effectively early in the season, he was suspended by the Reds and left baseball. /(NLM)

Jerry Dale — 1933– . *Umpire* NL 1970–84 *3 LCS 1 WS, 2 ASU*

Dale was umpiring the sixth game of the 1977 WS when Reggie Jackson homered three times. A former pitcher in the Senators' organization, Dale was a NL umpire for 15 seasons before being dismissed, over his bitter objections, for "lack of mobility" resulting from a knee injury. Dale earned his Ph.D. from Pepperdine University. His masters thesis examined personality differences between 92 student umpires and active ML umpires. He began leading yearly photographic safaris to Kenya in 1972. /(RTM)

Arthur Daley — Unk.–1974. *Writer.*

A graduate of Fordham, Daley joined the *New York Times* in 1926. Ten years later he covered the Olympics in Berlin, the first *Times* sportswriter to get a foreign assignment. In 1942 he began 31 years as a columnist for the *Times*, and, in 1973, became the first sportswriter to win a Pulitzer Prize. Daley's books include *The Story of the Olympic Games* (with John Kieran) and *Times at Bat*. /(NLM)

Buddy Daley [Leavitt Leo] — 1932– . LHP 1955–64 Indians, **A's**, Yankees 967 ip, 60–64, 4.03. *2 WS, 1–0, 8 ip*
☛ *All-Star—59–60.*

This courageous southpaw was a natural righthander who contracted polio as a child. Though one arm was shorter than the other, Daley taught himself to throw lefthanded. A starter for the A's, he won 16 in both 1959 and '60, but mostly relieved with Cleveland and New York. Daley's specialties were a roundhouse curve and a knuckler. /(GDW)

Pete Daley — 1930– . C 1955–61 **Red Sox**, A's, Senators 391 g, .239, 18 hr, 120 rbi

Daley backed up defensive whiz Sammy White in Boston for five seasons, never getting 200 at-bats. He was taken by the "new" Washington Senators in the 1961 expansion draft, but lasted only one more season. /(JK)

Dom Dallessandro (Dim Dom) — 1913–1988. OF 1937, 40–44, 46–47 Red Sox, **Cubs** 746 g, .267, 22 hr, 303 rbi

Dom Dallesandro was a squat, colorful Cubs outfielder during WWII. The powerfully-built line-drive hitter batted .304 in 1944 but was called into the service in 1945 and missed the only Cubs pennant of the era. His nickname was short for "Diminutive Dominick," a reference to his 5'6" height. /(BC)

Abner Dalrymple — 1857–1939. OF 1878–88, 91 Milwaukee (NL), **Cubs**, Pirates, Cincinnati-Milwaukee (AA) 951 g, .288, 43 hr, 298 rbi
☛ *Led League—hr 1885.*

Dalrymple was the leadoff man for Cap Anson's Chicago White Stockings (later to become the Cubs), a team that won five National League pennants in seven seasons (1880–82, 85–86). In 1884 he hit 22 homers for the Chicago team that, benefiting from a short rightfield fence, amassed 140—a single-season club record that stood until the 1927 Yankees hit 158. Dalrymple led the NL in at-bats four times, in hits in 1880, and in homers, with 11, in 1885. He was credited with the 1878 batting crown until research in the 1960s dropped him to .354 while Providence's Paul Hines' average was elevated to .358. Dalrymple's four doubles in a game (7/3/1883) still tie him with many others for the ML record. /(JK)

Clay Dalrymple — 1936– . C 1960–71 **Phillies**, Orioles 1079 g, .233, 55 hr, 327 rbi. *1 WS, 2 g, 1.000*

Remembered mainly for his strong-armed defense, Dalrymple actually won the Phillies' regular catching job in 1960 with his bat, pinch-hitting 12-for-42, with an overall batting average of .272. Not a power threat, though a lefthanded dead pull hitter, Dalrymple had his best hitting year in 1962 (.276, 11 homers, and 54 RBI). He led NL catchers in assists in 1963, '65 and '67, and set a league record with 99 consecutive errorless games (and 628 chances) during 1966 and 1967. Traded to the Orioles in 1969, Dalrymple suffered a broken ankle in 1970, hastening his retirement. /(MC)

Dalton Gang

The Dalton Gang is the team of executives supporting Brewer GM Harry Dalton in the late 1970s and 1980s. They include: Walter Shannon, Senior Advisor, Baseball Operations; Bruce Manno, Assistant GM and Farm Director; Dee Fondy and Sal Bando, Special Assistants; Ray Poitevint, Vice President, International Baseball Operations; Dick Foster, Scouting Director; and Walter Youse, Eastern Scouting Supervisor. /(SOM)

Jack Dalton — 1885–Unk. OF 1910, 14–16 **Dodgers**, Buffalo (FL), Tigers 345 g, .286, 4 hr, 112 rbi

Dalton distinguished himself in his second ML game with four hits off Christy Mathewson (1910). He returned in 1914 to provide great fielding in an all-.300 Brooklyn outfield with Zack Wheat and Casey Stengel. /(TG)

Tom Daly [Thomas Peter] (Tido) — 1866–1939. 2B-C-3B 1887–96, 1898–1903 Cubs, Washington (NL), **Dodgers** 1564 g, .278, 49 hr, 811 rbi

Daly was the lone catcher on the Chicago club that made the world tour of 1888–89. Although he was considered a good receiver, his arm was suspect, and Chicago dealt him to Washington. He moved to the infield with Brooklyn and played mostly second base after 1892. He went on to manage in the high minor leagues and scout for the Indians and Yankees. /(JK)

Ray Dandridge (Hooks) — 1913– . 3B-2B-SS Negro Leagues 1933–49 Detroit Stars, Newark Dodgers, Newark Eagles, New York Cubans (NNL), Nashville Elite Giants statistics not available
☛ *Hall of Fame—1987.*

Ray Dandridge was a masterful third baseman, a stylist who could make all the plays. He was smooth and relaxed, with soft hands, a strong arm, and the versatility to excel at any infield position. "People would pay their way in to the game just to see him field," claimed Monte Irvin. Roy Campanella said, "I never saw anyone better as a fielder." Hoyt Wilhelm, who played against Dandridge in Cuba and with him in Minneapolis (American Association), asserted, "No matter how the ball was hit, he always made the throw so that he just did get the man at first." Others observed that a train could go through Dandridge's bowlegs, but that a baseball never did.

Dandridge started his pro career with the 1933 Detroit Stars and moved to the Negro National League's Newark Eagles, for whom he starred throughout the remainder of the 1930s. A spray hitter with good bat control, he seldom struck out, and skillfully executed the hit-and-run. In 1935, he hit .368. Looking for more money in 1939, he opted to play in Latin America. He went to Mexico in 1940, and spent most of the decade there. When he came back for a year in Newark in 1944, he batted .370, leading the NNL in hits, runs, and total bases. In 1945 he set a Mexican League record for hitting safely in the most consecutive games and managed his team to a pennant. In nine Mexican League seasons, he compiled a .343 average. Following the 1948 season, he returned to the States as player-manager of the New York Cubans.

During his time in the NNL, Dandridge registered a lifetime .355 average, and played in three East-West all-star games, hitting .545. He played winter ball in Mexico, Venezuela, Puerto Rico, and Cuba; in 11 seasons of Cuban Winter League action, he batted .282.

Soon after Jackie Robinson signed with the Brooklyn Dodgers, Bill Veeck contacted Dandridge about playing with the Cleveland Indians, but Dandridge refused to leave Mexico without a bonus. Later, in 1949, at age thirty-five, he was signed by the New York Giants and assigned to their Triple-A farm club at Minneapolis. He batted .363 his first year there, and won the league's MVP award in 1950, when he led Minneapolis to the league championship. Despite his achievements, the Giants would not promote him to the parent club.

While at Minneapolis, Dandridge provided advice and assistance to a young Willie Mays, who never forgot the help or the man. Returning to Cooperstown for Dandridge's induction into the Hall of Fame (he was elected by the Committee on Baseball Veterans in 1987), Mays stated, "Ray Dandridge helped me tremendously when I came through

Minneapolis. Sometimes you just can't overlook those things. Ray was a part of me when I was coming along." /(JR)

Dave Danforth (Dauntless Dave) — 1890–1970. LHP 1911–12, 16–19, 22–25 A's, **White Sox**, Browns 1186 ip, 71–66, 3.89. *1 WS, 1 ip, 0–0, 18.00*

Danforth was called Dauntless Dave because he pitched with a constantly pain-racked left arm. He used his large, strong hands to loosen the covers on baseballs, adding to the break on his curveball. In 1917 he recorded AL highs of 50 appearances, six relief wins, and nine saves for Chicago. He left the majors just in time to avoid involvement with the 1919 Black Sox, returning in 1922 for several strong seasons with the Browns. /(JK)

Dan Daniel [born Daniel Moskowitz] — 1890–1981. *Writer.*

Daniel, a raspy-voiced, round-shouldered hulk of a man, was still pecking out copy at the age of 91. Refused a byline early in his career because of his Jewish name, Moskowitz, Daniel made his first name do double duty from then on. The prodigious writer had long stints with *Baseball Magazine* and *The Sporting News* when they were the lone baseball publications. He also co-founded and edited *Ring Magazine*, covering boxing.

A resource of fact as well as acerbic opinion, Daniel conducted the "Ask Daniel" feature in the New York *World-Telegram* sports section at the peak of that paper's fame. /(JK)

Bennie Daniels — 1932– . RHP 1957–65 Pirates, **Senators** 997 ip, 45–76, 4.44

Daniels, a regular starter for the expansion Senators of the early 1960s, received little support, but was 12–11 for the last-place 1961 team. The next year he became the first pitcher to win a game at D.C. (now RFK) Stadium. /(FK)

Bert Daniels — 1882–1958. OF 1910–14 **Yankees**, Reds 523 g, .255, 5 hr, 130 rbi

An early itinerant college athlete, Daniels played football and baseball under his own name at Villanova, Notre Dame, and Bucknell while playing semi-pro and minor league ball under aliases. He led the AL in hit-by-pitch three times. New York led the AL in stolen bases in 1910 with 288; Daniels led the team with 41. /(CG)

Kal Daniels [Kalvoski] — 1963– . OF 1986– **Reds**, Dodgers 377 g, .302, 54 hr, 168 rbi

A young, fast power hitter, Daniels hit .334 with 26 HR and 26 stolen bases in 1987, despite missing a month on the DL, and in 1988 he led the NL in on-base percentage as the Reds' starting left fielder. Often temperamental, Daniels was suspended briefly in September 1988 for throwing a bat into the dugout. The erratic fielder missed most of 1989 with a variety of physical problems, and in midseason he was traded to the Dodgers with Lenny Harris for Tim Leary and Mariano Duncan. Only 25, he had his sixth knee operation near the end of the 1989 season. /(ME)

Harry Danning (Harry The Horse) — 1911– . C 1933–42 **Giants** 890 g, .285, 57 hr, 397 rbi. *2 WS, 5 g, .214, 2 rbi*
☛ *All-Star—38–41.*

Danning, whose brother Ike caught two games for the 1928 Browns, backed up Gus Mancuso for the 1936 pennant-winning Giants, then took over as the regular for the 1937 NL Champions. He earned a reputation (and nickname) for durability. The Horse hit 46 homers and averaged .303 in the period 1937–40. Playing with injuries in the next two seasons, his hitting suffered. He retired after WWII military service. /(MC)

Pat Darcy — 1950– . RHP 1974–76 **Reds** 187 ip, 14–8, 4.14. *1 WS, 4 ip, 0–1, 4.50*

Intermittent arm trouble caused the Astros to give up on Darcy after five years in their farm system. Dealt to the Reds, he was a one-year wonder, going 11–5 with a 3.57 ERA for the 1975 World Champions. The next year his arm problems returned and he was soon out of the majors. /(MC)

Alvin Dark (Blackie) — 1922– . SS-3B 1946, 48–60 Braves, **Giants**, Cardinals, Cubs, Phillies 1828 g, .289, 126 hr, 757 rbi. *3 WS, 16 g, .323, 1 hr, 4 rbi.*
   Manager 1961–64, 66–71, 74–75, 77 **Giants**, A's, Indians, Padres 994–954, .510. First place: 62, 74–75 *2 LCS, 3–4, .429. 2 WS, 7–5, .583*
☛ *Rookie of the Year—48 . All-Star—51–52, 54.*

In 1969 fans chose Alvin Dark as the top shortstop in Giants' history. He won the 1948 Rookie of the Year award, hit .300 four times, led the NL in doubles once, led league shortstops three times each in putouts and double plays, and hit 20 or more home runs and scored over 100 runs twice each. Dark's single in the ninth inning of the third 1951 NL playoff game started the rally that culminated in Bobby Thomson's famous pennant-winning homer. As a manager, Dark won the 1962 NL pennant for

Alvin Dark

San Francisco and the 1974 World Championship with Oakland. While leading San Francisco, he once tore off a finger at the joint throwing a metal chair after a loss. After finding religion, his calmer personality enabled him to work two tours for A's owner Charlie Finley. /(TJ)

Ron Darling — 1960– . RHP 1983– **Mets** 1392 ip, 87–55, 3.38. *2 LCS, 12 ip, 0–1, 7.50. 1 WS, 18 ip, 1–1, 1.53*
☛ *All-Star—85. Gold Glove—89.*

Darling, the Rangers' first pick in the June 1981 draft, came to the Mets with Walt Terrell in return for Lee Mazzilli in 1982. In his rookie 1984 season he went 12–9, quickly gaining a reputation for picking up hard-luck no-decisions, and was overshadowed by Dwight Gooden's amazing rookie year. Darling made the 1985 All-Star team and finished 16–6. He had perhaps his best start ever opening a crucial late-season series against the Cardinals, pitching nine shutout innings as the Mets won in the 11th inning on October 1. Earlier that year in his only ML relief appearance, he finished the Mets' 19-inning, 16–13 victory over the Braves by striking out Rick Camp at 3:55 am, the latest-ending game in baseball history.

The Hawaiian also led the NL in walks in 1985, with 114 in 248 innings, the second year in a row he topped 100. Some said he thought too much and was too much of a perfectionist. His control improved in 1986 (81 walks in 237 innings) and he posted a career-best 2.81 ERA as the Mets won the World Championship. He went 15–6, and the Mets were 27–8 in his starts. He was hit hard in his LCS start. Starting the World Series opener, he lost a 1–0 three-hitter on an unearned run. He came back to win Game Four with seven shutout innings. In the Mets' Game Seven victory, he was knocked out early.

Darling's worst season was 1987, when he posted a 4.29 ERA and missed September on the DL. The split-finger fastball artist came back in 1988, going 17–9 with a 3.25 ERA. In the LCS he took a no-decision in Game Three and lost Game Seven. He set a NLCS record for most runs allowed in a seven-game series (9). He struggled with his control through most of 1989.

Darling is an excellent fielder and has one of the best pick-off moves among righthanders. He is sometimes used as a pinch runner, and in 1989 he hit homers in two consecutive starts. His brother Eddie was in the Yankee system in 1981–82.

While at Yale, Darling faced St. John's pitcher Frank Viola in an NCAA playoff game, no-hitting them for 11 innings but losing in 1–0 in the 12th inning. It is the longest no-hitter in NCAA history. /(SH)

Bobby Darwin — 1943– . OF-DH-RHP 1962, 69, 71–77 Angels, Dodgers, **Twins**, Brewers, Red Sox, Cubs 646 g, .251, 83 hr, 328 rbi; 7 ip, 0–1, 10.29

Darwin signed with the Angels as a pitcher in 1962. That year with San Jose (California League) he struck out 202 and walked 149 in 153 innings. His control problems and disabling injuries contributed to his gradual switch to the outfield starting in 1966.

The Twins made Darwin their regular centerfielder in 1972, and although he showed good power over the next three seasons (22, 18, and 25 HR), he led the AL in strikeouts each year (145, 137, 127) and had fewer fielding chances than any other centerfielder. In 1974 he tied for fourth in HR and was fifth in RBI (94). Traded to Milwaukee in 1975 while hitting .219, he was never again a regular, and he finished his career with more strike-outs than hits. /(SH)

Danny Darwin — 1955– . RHP 1978– **Rangers**, Brewers, Astros 1750 ip, 100–105, 3.51

A Texan, Darwin went undrafted and was signed by the Rangers. Throwing in the 94-mph range, he fanned the first four Mariners he faced in his ML debut (9/24/78). In 1980 he went 13–4 (2.62) with eight saves but broke a knuckle on his right hand when aiding Mickey Rivers in a scuffle with fans outside Comiskey Park on June 4 and was disabled for three weeks. Moved into and out of the rotation, he was a .500 pitcher before his 1985 trade to Milwaukee. That year he went 8–18, despite a staff-best 3.80 ERA. He lost 10 consecutive games to set a Brewers record; it took a one-hitter against the Twins to halt the streak. Becoming more of a finesse pitcher, he was traded to Houston for their 1986 pennant drive and went 5–2. /(JCA)

Frank Dascoli — 1915– . *Umpire NL 1948–62 3 WS, 2 ASU*

Dascoli, a respected NL umpire for 15 years, effected a baseball oddity. On September 27, 1951 he cleared the Dodger bench after a disputed play. On the bench was Boston Celtics basketball star Bill Sharman, who was also a recently-recalled Dodger farmhand. Thus, Sharman became the only player ever kicked out of a ML game without ever appearing in one. In the off-season Dascoli was a Connecticut state trooper. /(RTM)

Jake Daubert — 1884–1924. 1B 1910–24 **Dodgers**, Reds 2014 g, .303, 56 hr, 722 rbi. *2 WS, 12 g, .217, 1 rbi* ☛ *Led League—ba 13–14.*

In his day, Daubert was the National League's best all-around first baseman. The lefthander was a two-time NL batting champion and steady .300 batter for ten years of the dead ball era. He escaped the Pennsylvania coal mines and the minor leagues in 1910, taking over first base for Brooklyn at age 26. He was a model of consistency, fielding within a .989-.994 range for 15 years, and was mobile enough to average 10.5 chances per game and take part in 1199 double plays. A chop hitter, he twice led the league in triples and had 165 lifetime. He also had a NL record 392 sacrifices, 4 in one 1914 game for another record.

Daubert was modest, polite, and colorless, though a tiger about money. WWI and competition with the Federal League raised salary levels generally, and Daubert's went from $5,000 to $9,000. Charles Ebbets probably guaranteed his 1916 Dodger pennant by extending Daubert's $9,000 another four years (and treating Zack Wheat and Nap Rucker liberally as well).

Jake Daubert

When the major leagues shortened the 1918 season and tried to prorate salaries, Daubert sued Ebbets for the unpaid balance ($2,150) and got most of it in a settlement. Furious at this, Ebbets traded him to Cincinnati in 1919 for the less-talented Tommy Griffith. Daubert helped lead the Reds to a pennant and a tarnished World Championship in the Black Sox WS.

Daubert benefited from the change to the lively ball. In 1922, at age 38, he had 205 hits for a .336 average, scored 114 runs, and hit 12 HR. Late in the 1924 season he became ill, and a month later died from complications after an appendectomy. /(ADS)

Rich Dauer — 1952– . 2B-3B 1976–85 **Orioles** 1140 g, .257, 43 hr, 372 RBI. *2 LCS, 8 g, .080, 1 rbi. 2 WS, 11 g, .250, 1 hr, 4 rbi*

After leading the International League with a .336 BA, Dauer replaced Bobby Grich at second base for the Orioles. He never hit up to expectations—.284 in 1980 was his best—but he seldom struck out and was a reliable fielder. His homer in the seventh game of the 1979 WS gave the Orioles a brief lead. He set

ML records in 1978 by playing 86 straight errorless games at second and handling 425 chances without an error. /(MC)

Darren Daulton — 1962– . C 1983, 85–89 **Phillies** 329 g, .206, 24 hr, 101 rbi

The Phillies traded away Bo Diaz and then Ozzie Virgil to make room for the Daulton–John Russell catching platoon, but injuries limited Daulton's playing time in 1984–85. A home-plate collision with Mike Heath ended his 1986 season in June. Thereafter, the resulting knee injury prevented him from crouching as low as other catchers. In 1987 the Phillies signed Lance Parrish, and Daulton remained the backup until 1989. /(SG)

Hooks Dauss [George August, born George August Daus] — 1889–1963. RHP 1912–26 **Tigers** 3391 ip, 221–183, 3.32. 20 wins: 15, 19, 23

Detroit's six long-term, one-team-only players is the most of any franchise; the first of them was Hooks (or Hookie) Dauss. A stocky righthander with nicknames deriving from his assortment of sharp-breaking curves, Dauss won 221 games in a fifteen-year career, the most for any pitcher while wearing a Tiger uniform. It is a record easily overlooked, for Dauss toiled mostly in the second division. Still, he achieved ten winning seasons and a winning percentage considerably better than his team's.

He was a friendly, good-natured fellow; some thought that with more aggression he might have won more games. Still, Hookie led the league in hit batsmen three times and is tenth on the lifetime list. /(ADS)

Dauvray Cup

In 1887 Giants shortstop Monte Ward's wife, actress Helen Dauvray, donated a cup that would be held by the winner of the yearly postseason series between the National League and American Association champions, a series which had been played (with one interruption) since 1882. The Cup would become the property of whichever team won it three times. However, the war between the leagues in 1891 resulted in an end to postseason play before any team had won three series. The Cup has been lost. /(SH)

Vic Davalillo — 1939– . OF 1963–74, 77–80 **Indians**, Angels, Cardinals, Pirates, A's, Dodgers 1458 g, .279, 36 hr, 329 rbi. *4 LCS, 8 g, .545, 1 rbi. 4 WS, 14 g, .200, 1 rbi*

☛ *All-Star—65. Gold Glove—64.*

Davalillo, whose older brother Yo-Yo played briefly for the Senators in 1953, started his pro career in 1958 as a pitcher. Called up to the Indians after only one full season as an outfielder, the Venezuelan missed two months in 1963 with a broken right wrist (hit with a pitch by Hank Aguirre) but still hit .292. He was Cleveland's regular centerfielder for the next four seasons. In 1964 the 5'7" 150-lb lefthander won a Gold Glove and led the league's outfielders in double plays (5) and finished third in stolen bases (21). In his All-Star year, 1965, his .301 BA was the third-best in the AL, he finished fifth in stolen bases (26), and he led outfielders in total chances per game. However, he lost much of his range in subsequent years, and he was a poor-percentage basestealer. He was also hindered by his lack of power and his impatience at the plate. The Indians experimented with him as a pinch hitter in 1966 and '67, but he was a poor 7-for-38 (.184) over that period.

After Davalillo bounced around for several years, the pinch-hitting experiment finally worked in St. Louis, where he led the NL in 1970 with 24 pinch hits and 73 pinch at-bats (.329). Traded to the Pirates with Nellie Briles for Matty Alou and George Brunet for 1971, he played outfield and pinch hit .333 for the World Champions. Pittsburgh's regular left fielder in 1972, he hit .318, but he slumped the next two seasons (.184, .174), although he hit .625 for the A's in the 1973 LCS. In Game Five, his RBI triple in the fourth (he scored when Jesus Alou singled) helped drive Doyle Alexander out of the game as Oakland clinched the series against the Orioles.

Davalillo went to the Mexican League early in 1974 and remained there until the Dodgers picked him up in August 1977 for their pennant drive (he hit .313). He became the first player to play for three different teams in the LCS, his only appearance being a crucial one. With the Phillies up 5–3 in Game Three, Davalillo beat out a drag bunt with two out in the ninth. He scored on Manny Mota's double, and the Dodgers rallied to win the game. They took the series the next day. Davalillo stayed with the Dodgers as a pinch hitter and reserve outfielder/first baseman for the next three seasons and retired with 95 pinch hits, which at that time tied him for sixth on the all-time list. /(SH)

Dave Davenport — 1890–1954. RHP 1914–19 Reds, St. Louis FL, **Browns** 1537 ip, 74–83, 2.93. 20 wins: 15
☛ *Led League—so 15.*

After ten games for the Reds in 1914, the 6'6" Davenport jumped to the Federal League. In 1915

he won 22 for the St. Louis Feds, led the league in games pitched, innings pitched, complete games, strikeouts, and shutouts, and pitched a no-hitter. When the FL folded, he joined the Browns, where Manager Fielder Jones called him the best pitching prospect he'd ever worked with. Although he had a couple of effective seasons with the Browns, including a 17–17 year in 1917, Davenport was out of the ML by 1920, the year his brother Claude pitched in one game for the Giants. /(NLM)

Jim Davenport (Peanut, Golden Glove) — 1933– . 3B-SS-2B 1958–70 **Giants** 1501 g, .258, 77 hr, 456 rbi. *1 WS, 7 g, .136, 1 rbi.*
    Manager 1985 **Giants** 56–88, .389
☛ *All-Star—62. Gold Glove—62 .*

His first big league manager, Bill Rigney, called Jim Davenport "the greatest third baseman I ever saw—at least the only one I'd compare with Billy Cox." Davenport, who played every infield position as well as the outfield during his 13-year ML tenure, led NL third basemen in fielding three times and won a Gold Glove in 1962. Also in '62, Davenport reached career-high figures in batting (.297) and home runs (14) and played in an All-Star Game. In 1967 the 5'11" 180-lb Davenport played errorless ball in 65 straight games and averaged .370 as a pinch hitter. After many years as a Giants coach, he became their manager in 1985, 27 years after his ML playing debut in the team's first San Francisco game. Davenport relinquished the managerial reins before the season ended. In 1987 he became a Phillies coach. /(TJ)

L. Robert Davids — 1926– . *Writer.*

Bob Davids calls himself a statistorian. He is a longtime government employee, and his interest in the use of statistics in analyzing political and military history prepared him for baseball research. His digging turned up interesting sidelights on the game that appeared regularly in *The Sporting News* between 1951 and 1965. Davids began circulating his own newsletter, *Baseball Briefs*, and gathered a group of 16 like-minded individuals at Cooperstown on August 10, 1971, where they founded the Society for American Baseball Research. Davids was SABR's first president and served two later terms as well. /(NLM)

Mark Davidson — 1961– . OF 1986– **Twins** 271 g, .216, 3 hr, 31 rbi. *1 LCS, 1 g, --. 1 WS, 2 g, .000*

Davidson's best season came as an extra outfielder on the 1987 World Championship Twins. He hit

.267 and played errorlessly in the outfield. His father, Max, was a minor league outfielder from 1947 to 1954. /(SFS)

Satch Davidson (Dave) — 1936- . *Umpire* NL 1969-84 *2 LCS 2 WS*

Davidson, who was given the nickname Satch by schoolmates because he was a fan of that Bowery Boy, is an example mentioned by umpires who oppose instant replays on stadium TV. A replay in Cincinnati so excited one fan that he threw an unopened can of beer which struck Davidson. Two games as a catcher for Columbus (International League) were the extent of Davidson's pro playing career. /(RTM)

Ted Davidson — 1939- . LHP 1965-68 **Reds**, Braves 195 ip, 11-7, 3.69

Davidson was a stylish reliever with a good fastball who admitted to using a spitter now and then. He also had an excellent curveball, which he threw sidearm to lefthanded batters. In 1966 he made 54 appearances for the Reds. Prior to the 1967 season, he was at a bar when his estranged wife shot him in the stomach and chest with a .25 caliber pistol. He pitched only parts of two seasons after his recovery. /(RTM)

Alvin Davis — 1960- . 1B 1984- **Mariners** 881 g, .290, 131 hr, 530 rbi
☛ *Rookie of the Year—84. All-Star—84.*

The AL Rookie of the Year in 1984, Alvin Davis was the only Mariner to win a major award in the first dozen years of the franchise. In 1984 Davis set or tied franchise records for most RBI, game-winning RBI, walks, and intentional walks, as well as home runs by a rookie. Hitting most of his homers in the Kingdome, Davis is the Mariners' career home run leader, with a high of 29 in 1987. Davis is also the franchise leader in RBI (the Mariners' only player to have two 100-RBI seasons), total bases, extra-base hits, and walks. His sharp batting eye helps raise his on-base percentage almost 100 points above his batting average, making up for occasional fielding deficiencies and slow baserunning. /(TF)

Bob Davis — 1952- . C 1973, 75-81 **Padres**, Blue Jays, Angels 290 g, .197, 6 hr, 51 rbi

A backup catcher for five years in San Diego, Davis had a weak bat that kept him on the bench. In 1980 he appeared in 91 games for Toronto but hit only .216 with 19 RBI. /(MC)

Brock Davis [Bryshear Barnett] — 1943- . OF 1963-64, 66, 70-72 Astros, **Cubs**, Brewers 242 g, .260, 1 hr, 43 rbi

At age 19, Davis opened in centerfield for Houston, but he was soon in the minors, where he struggled for eight seasons. In 1971, he was platooned in the Cubs' outfield but hit a soft .256. Swapped to Milwaukee, he hit .318 in 85 games, 36 as a pinch hitter. /(MC)

Chili Davis [Charles Theodore] — 1960- . OF 1981- **Giants**, Angels 1186 g, .268, 144 hr, 601 rbi. *1 LCS, 6 g, .150*
☛ *All-Star—84, 86.*

The native of Kingston, Jamaica was another in the long line of outfielders developed by the Giants. The switch-hitter set a NL career record with three games in which he homered from both sides of the plate. Two of those games came in 1987, his best season, when he hit a career-high 24 HR. He signed with the Angels as a free agent after the season to escape Candlestick Park, which he hated. He had a career-high 93 RBI with California in 1988, but shattered the Angels team record for outfielders errors with a league-leading 19, fielding just .942. He did lead NL outfielders in assists in 1982, and when he led in errors in 1986, his nine errors tied the ML record for fewest errors by a league leader.

Davis's nickname was originally Chili Bowl, resulting from a bad haircut in his childhood. /(SH)

Curt Davis (Coonskin) — 1903-1965. RHP 1934-46 Phillies, Cubs, Cardinals, **Dodgers** 2325 ip, 158-131, 3.42. 20 wins: 39 *1 WS, 5 ip, 0-1, 5.06*
☛ *All-Star—36, 39.*

Curt Davis, a 6'2" 185-lb native of Greenfield, Missouri, pitched in a NL-leading 51 games, winning 19, as a Phillies rookie in 1934. Davis won 15 or more three additional times during his career: 1935 (16) for the Phillies, 1939 (22) for the Cardinals, and 1942 (15) for the Dodgers. Davis was named to the 1936 and 1939 NL All-Star teams; he surrendered three runs in 2/3 of an inning as Carl Hubbell's reliever in the 1936 game and did not play in the 1939 game. Davis was the Dodgers' starting and losing pitcher in the opening game of the 1941 World Series; the winner of that 3-2 contest was future Hall of Famer Red Ruffing. Davis was one of three players traded, along with cash, by the Cubs to the Cardinals for Dizzy Dean in 1938. /(TJ)

Dick Davis — 1953- . OF-DH 1977-82 **Brewers**, Phillies, Blue Jays, Pirates 403 g, .265, 27 hr, 141 rbi

Davis had his best season in part-time duty with the Brewers in 1979, when he had career highs in HR (12), runs (51), and RBI (41) while hitting .266. A terrible defensive liability, he was usually a DH until traded to the Phillies in 1981 for Randy Lerch. After his ML career, he became a star for Japan's Kintetsu Buffalos. He is a cousin of Enos Cabell. /(SFS)

Dixie Davis [Frank Talmadge] — 1890–1944. RHP 1912, 15, 18, 20–26 Cubs, White Sox, Phillies, **Browns** 1319 ip, 75–71, 3.97

After a decade of pitching in the minors, Davis became an effective pitcher for the Browns in 1920 with an 18–12 season. On August 9, 1921 he pitched a complete 19-inning game against the Senators, finally won by the Browns, 8–6. In the last nine innings, he did not allow a hit. Davis hit an inside-the-park home run in the 16th inning but was called out for failing to touch first base. /(NLM)

Eric Davis — 1962– . OF 1984– **Reds** 640 g, .275, 142 hr, 413 rbi
☛ *All-Star—87–89. Gold Glove—87–89.*

Davis seemed to have unlimited potential in 1987, when he hit .293 with 37 HR and 50 stolen bases and made numerous breathtaking catches in centerfield for the Reds. But he has also been prone to both strikeouts (at least 100 in each of his years as a regular) and nagging injuries. He has already hit three home runs in a game twice (9/10/86 and 5/3/87). /(ME)

George Davis — 1870–1940. SS-3B-OF 1890–1909 Cleveland (NL), **Giants**, White Sox 2377 g, .297, 73 hr, 1435 rbi.
    Manager 1895, 1900–01 **Giants** 108–139, .437
☛ *Led League—rbi 97 .*

Davis began his career as an outfielder in Cleveland, but was traded to the Giants in 1893 for future Hall of Famer Buck Ewing. Primarily a third baseman his first four years in New York, he became a full-time shortstop in 1897. He was the Giants' player-manager for part of 1895, and again from mid-1900 through 1901.

His anti-establishment stance in 1903 may have cost Davis consideration for the Hall of Fame. Davis was an outstanding hitter (he batted over .300 for nine consecutive seasons with the Giants), and an even better fielder, during a time when the National League was bitterly divided and corrupt. His problems began after the 1902 season, his first with the White Sox. Dissatisfied with Charles Comiskey's pay structure, Davis elected to jump back to the National League Giants. When peace was declared

George Davis

between the two warring leagues early in 1903, Davis was "awarded" to the White Sox, but he had other ideas. He sat out the season until John Brush, president of the National League, sanctioned an illegal scheme hatched by the Giants to regain Davis. After four games in a Giant uniform, Davis was served with an injunction. John Montgomery Ward, the famous baseball lawyer, represented Davis in court, and his efforts were supported by Brush, who filed a counter-suit to keep Davis in the NL. On July 15, 1903 the case was thrown out, and peace was restored in baseball. Years later, Ban Johnson punished Ward for his impertinence by seeing to it that he was not appointed NL president. As for Davis, he went on to play six more seasons with the White Sox, though he never again batted over .278. /(RL)

Glenn Davis — 1961– . 1B 1984– **Astros** 737 g, .264, 144 hr, 454 rbi. *1 LCS, 6 g, .269, 1 hr, 3 rbi*
☛ *All-Star—86, 89.*

Davis has been one of the NL's premier power hitters since his 1985 rookie season, despite playing half his games in the spacious Houston Astrodome where fly balls historically do not carry well. The strapping first baseman began the 1985 season in Tucson (Pacific Coast League), hitting .305 in 60 games there before being called up to Houston when

Terry Puhl was injured in June, and he hit 20 HR for the Astros, earning a spot on the *Topps* All-Rookie Team. 1986 was Davis's first full season in the ML, and the 25-year-old hit .265 with 32 doubles, 31 HR, and 101 RBI to finish second behind Mike Schmidt in the NL MVP voting as the Astros won the NL West. In the NLCS, he homered off Dwight Gooden in his first at bat to give the Astros a 1–0 win in Game One. Davis, a notorious streak hitter, added 27 HR in 1987 (including 3 in one game September 10) and 30 in 1988, and in 1989 became the first player in Astros history to hit 20 or more home runs in five consecutive seasons. As a child, he was adopted by the family of future ML pitcher Storm Davis. /(SCL)

Harry Davis (Jasper) — 1873–1947. 1B-OF-3B 1895–99, 1901–17 Giants, Pirates, Washington NL, **A's**, Indians 1757 g, .277, 74 hr, 952 rbi. *3 WS, 16 g, .246, 7 rbi.*
    Manager 1912 **Indians** 54–71, .432
☛ *Led League—hr 04–07. Led League—rbi 05–06.*

The gentlemanly Davis was an outstanding slugger for Connie Mack's Philadelphia teams in the early 20th century. In the A's 1911 WS victory over the Giants, he and Frank "Home Run" Baker each drove in five runs. Only Davis, Baker, Babe Ruth, and Ralph Kiner have led a ML in home runs four or more years in a row. Davis accomplished the feat 1904 through 1907 and also led in doubles in 1902, '05, and '07 and in RBI in '05 and '06. The native Philadelphian was named the A's first captain and managed whenever Connie Mack was absent. The highly regarded sign stealer remained with the team as a player or coach until 1927, except for 1912, when he became manager of Cleveland. His strict disciplinary tactics failed to help the Indians and he quit after 127 games with the team in sixth place. From 1913 to 1917 he made token appearances in the A's lineup. While still with the A's, he became a Philadelphia city councilman. /(ME/JK)

Jim Davis — 1924– . LHP 1954–57 **Cubs**, Cardinals, Giants 406 ip, 24–26, 4.01

A nephew of his contemporary, pitcher Marv Grissom, Davis was the best pitcher (11–7, 3.52) on the lowly 1954 Cubs. He never matched his freshman success. /(TJ)

Jody Davis — 1956– . C 1981– **Cubs**, Braves 1075 g, .246, 127 hr, 489 rbi. *1 LCS, 5 g, .389, 2 hr, 6 rbi*
☛ *All-Star—84, 86. Gold Glove—86.*

A fine catcher both offensively and defensively for the Cubs from 1981 to 1987, Davis became expend-

Harry Davis

able in 1988 when Damon Berryhill emerged as a capable ML player, and he was traded to the Braves on September 29 after hitting a career-low .230. Davis was originally drafted by the Mets, and he was traded to the Cardinals organization for Ray Searage after 1979. He played only 58 games in 1980 after losing 50 pounds while being treated for an ulcer, then was drafted by the Cubs following the season. As a rookie with Chicago in 1981, Davis grabbed the starting catching job by hitting .389 in May, but lost it the following spring to Keith Moreland before regaining it during the 1982 season. In 1983 Davis hit .271 with 24 HR and 84 RBI, and in 1984 he made the NL All-Star team for the first time as the Cubs won the NL East. Davis starred in the '84 NLCS, with seven hits in five games and home runs in Games Four and Five, but the Cubs lost the final three games to the Padres after taking a 2–0 series lead. He won a Gold Glove in 1986, throwing out 78 would-be basestealers, and hit 21 HR, but in 1987 his durability and consistency began to lapse. He had caught at least 138 games each of the previous four seasons, and had never gone on a ML disabled list, but in 1988 an early-season stint on the DL forced the promotion of Berryhill from the minors, and Davis would catch only 76 games. /(SCL)

Joel Davis — 1965– . RHP 1985–88 **White Sox** 248 ip, 8–14, 4.91

The White Sox made the 6'5" Davis their first pick and the 13th player chosen overall in the June 1983 draft. The Red Sox, with the 19th pick, took Roger Clemens. Davis was rushed from high school through the minors and arrived ill-prepared in the majors at age 20. Each year his ERA rose while his confidence dwindled. In his one brief shining ML moment, Davis was the winning pitcher on April 21, 1987, when the White Sox ended Milwaukee's 13-game winning streak to open the season. /(RL)

John Davis — 1963– . RHP 1987– Royals, **White Sox** 113 ip, 7–8, 4.84

The 6'7" 215-lb Chicago native came to the White Sox in the Floyd Bannister deal after going 5–2 with a 2.27 ERA in 1987. The reliever fell off to 2–5 with a 6.64 ERA in 1988 and pitched only briefly in 1989 before being sent back down. /(WOR)

Lefty Davis — 1875–1919. OF 1901–03, 07 Dodgers, **Pirates**, Yankees, Reds 348 g, .261, 3 hr, 110 rbi

Davis became the Pirate right fielder in 1901 when Honus Wagner moved to shortstop. A solid hitter with a strong arm, Davis never regained his form after he suffered a broken leg at the Pirates' Exposition Park in 1902. /(ME)

Mark Davis — 1960– . LHP 1980– Phillies, **Giants**, Padres 858 ip, 40–65, 3.76
☛ *Cy Young Award—89. All-Star—88–89.*

This stocky curveballer spent five seasons, split between the bullpen and the starting rotation, with the Giants before he blossomed as a relief stopper with the Padres in 1988. Originally signed by the Phillies, Davis was traded to the Giants with Mike Krukow for Joe Morgan and Al Holland before the 1983 season.

Davis was exclusively a starter in 1983 and was the Giants' Opening Day starter in 1984, but he spent almost all of 1985–86 in the bullpen, where he struck out over a batter an inning but saved only 11 games in two years. In a game against the Mets in 1985 he threw 23 straight curveballs.

Davis rejoined the Giants' rotation in 1987 before he was traded to San Diego in July, part of a seven-

player deal that included Kevin Mitchell, Craig Lefferts, Dave Dravecky, and Chris Brown. Handed the stopper role for the first time in his career, Davis emerged as an overpowering reliever in 1988. He was the Padres' lone All-Star, posting 28 saves, a career-best 2.01 ERA, and 102 strikeouts in 98.1 innings. He won the NL Cy Young Award in 1989 with a 44-save season, posting a 1.85 ERA and striking out 92 batters in 92.2 innings. /(SCL)

Mike Davis — 1959– . OF-DH 1980– A's, Dodgers 963 g, .259, 91 hr, 371 rbi. *2 LCS, 5 g, .333. 1 WS, 4 g, .143, 1 hr, 2 rbi*

A speedy but unexceptional outfielder with a strong arm, Davis won Oakland's right field job in 1983 and batted .275 with 32 stolen bases. A first-ball, fastball hitter, he slumped to .230 in 1984 before adjusting in 1985, hitting .287 with 24 HR and 82 RBI. Just after the 1987 All-Star break, he kicked a dugout door in anger, injuring his knee, and fell into a prolonged slump. He signed as a free agent with the Dodgers for 1988, but failed to hit and lost his job. He found room in the lineup in the World Series as a DH, and his two-run homer in Game Five proved the winning margin as the Dodgers clinched their unlikely World Championship. In Game One, Davis pinch hit with two out in the ninth inning, drew a walk from the A's Dennis Eckersley, stole second, and scored on Kirk Gibson's dramatic game-winning homer. /(JCA)

Peaches Davis [Ray Thomas] — 1905– . RHP 1936–39 **Reds** 542 ip, 27–33, 3.87

Davis reached the ML at age thirty-one after developing an effective sinker. He split time between starting and relieving for the Reds, with a career-high 11 wins in 1937. /(NLM)

Piper Davis [Lorenzo] — 1917– . 1B-2B-SS-MGR Negro Leagues 1943–50 **Birmingham Black Barons** statistics not available
☛ *All-Star—46–48.*

Although he never played in the white major leagues, Davis teamed with future major leaguer Artie Wilson to form one of the outstanding double play combinations in Negro League ball. He hit a team-leading .353 and led the Negro National League in RBI as player-manager of the 1948 Birmingham Black Barons, leading them to the World Series. At Birmingham from 1948 to 1950, he managed Willie Mays. In 1951 Davis became the first black signed by the Red Sox. An outstanding all-around athlete, he also played basketball for the Harlem Globetrotters. /(BP)

Ron Davis — 1955– . RHP 1978–88 **Yankees**, Twins, Cubs, Dodgers, Giants 746 ip, 47–53, 4.05. *2 LCS, 7.1 ip, 0–0, 1.23. 1 WS, 2.1 ip, 0–0, 23.14*
☛ *All-Star—81.*

Davis never started a ML game, but was often outstanding in relief, especially as a set-up man for Rich Gossage with the Yankees. He had an AL rookie-record 14 relief wins in 1979, three seasons with 25 or more saves, and on May 4, 1981 he fanned eight consecutive Oakland batters. He also had little to offer besides a hard fastball, and was ineffective when it failed him. /(ME)

Spud Davis [Virgil Lawrence] — 1904–1984. C 1928–41, 44–45 Cardinals, **Phillies**, Reds, Pirates 1458 g, .308, 77 hr, 647 rbi. *1 WS, 2 g, 1.000, 1 rbi.*
Manager 1946 **Pirates** 1–2, .333

Virgil Lawrence Davis batted .300 in 9 of his 16 seasons. In 1933 his .349 average was second in the NL to future Hall of Famer Chuck Klein's .368. Davis led NL catchers in assists in 1931, double plays in 1932, and total chances per game in 1934, years in which rival catchers included future Cooperstown enshrinees Gabby Hartnett and Al Lopez. Davis later backed up Ernie Lombardi at Cincinnati, and Lopez at Pittsburgh.

As a member of the 1935 Cardinals, Davis feuded with Dizzy Dean. Dean accused him of not hustling after a foul during a loss to Cincinnati, and insisted on a different catcher the next time out. Teammates sided with Davis, but manager Frankie Frisch complied with Dean's demand. Davis managed the Pirates briefly in 1946. /(TJ)

Storm Davis [George Earl] — 1961– . RHP 1982– **Orioles**, Padres, A's 1319 ip, 92–62, 3.86. *3 LCS, 19 ip, 0–1, 2.41. 2 WS, 13 ip, 1–2, 9.00*

Once a promising young starter for the Orioles (14–9, 3.12 as a 22-year-old in 1984), Davis seemed washed up with the Padres in 1987. He rallied in Oakland to win the AL Comeback Player of the Year award with a 16–7 record for the 1988 AL champions and was 19–7 (4.36) in 1989. He grew up with Astro Glenn Davis, who was raised by Storm's parents and adopted the family name. /(ME)

Tommy Davis — 1939– . OF-DH-3B 1959–76 **Dodgers**, Mets, White Sox, Pilots, Astros, A's, Cubs, Orioles, Angels, Royals 1999 g, .294, 153 hr, 1052 rbi. *3 LCS, 12 g, .295, 3 rbi. 2 WS, 8 g, .348, 2 rbi*
☛ *Led League—ba 62–63. Led League—rbi 62. All-Star—62–63.*

Tommy Davis

In 1981, Tommy Davis (then the Mariner batting coach) said, "They used to call me lazy or lackadaisical, but the lazier I felt the better I'd hit." Before playing pro ball, the 6'2" 195-lb Davis had been a high school basketball standout and teammate of future NBA great Lenny Wilkens. Jackie Robinson had helped convince Davis to sign a baseball pact with his hometown Brooklyn club in 1956. However, by the time Davis made the big leagues in 1959, the Dodgers had forsaken his borough for Los Angeles. Playing outfield and some third base, the line-drive hitter topped the NL in hits (230), and BA (.346) in 1962; his league-leading 153 RBI were the most in the NL in 25 years. The following year Davis won his fourth pro batting title (he'd captured crowns in the Midwest and Pacific Coast leagues), hitting .326. He was the first National Leaguer to capture successive batting crowns since Stan Musial (1950–52). He was the starting left fielder for the NL All-Stars in '62, and paced all hitters with a .400 average in the '63 World Series as the Dodgers swept the Yankees in four games.

Davis slipped to .275 in 1964, and a broken ankle in 1965 limited him to 17 games. He rebounded in 1966, enjoying the third of his six .300 ML seasons (.313), but when the Los Angeles-Baltimore World Series ended, the Dodgers sent Davis to the Mets in a trade for Ron Hunt. After one year in New York,

Davis went to the White Sox in a six-player deal that brought Tommie Agee to the Mets. From 1969 through 1972, Davis played with five teams, starting with the Seattle Pilots, who had taken him in the expansion draft. He landed in Baltimore in late '72, where he served primarily as DH for three seasons and in two LCS. Davis ended his playing days with the highest career pinch-hitting average (.320, 63-for-197) in baseball history. /(TJ)

Willie Davis — 1940– . OF 1960–76, 79 **Dodgers**, Expos, Cardinals, Rangers, Padres, Angels 2429 g, .279, 182 hr, 1053 rbi. *1 LCS, 2 g, .500. 3 WS, 15 g, .167, 3 rbi*
☛ *All-Star—71, 73. Gold Glove—71–73.*

Davis was named *TSN* Minor League Player of the Year in 1960, and was generally considered the fastest man in baseball. The Dodgers' regular centerfielder for 13 years, Davis ranks high in virtually every all-time Dodger offensive category. His 31-game hitting streak in 1969 was the longest in 24 years, and he later had another streak of 25 games. A three-time Gold Glove winner, Davis also twice led the NL in errors. He committed a WS-record three errors, all in the fifth inning of Game

Willie Davis

Two in 1966. In 1965, he set a WS record with three stolen bases in a game, and in '62, he and Maury Wills set a new NL record for stolen bases by two teammates with 136 (Wills had 104, Davis 32). Traded four times between December 1973 and October 1975, Davis played in Japan before a brief final tour as an Angel. /(TG)

Bill Dawley — 1958– . RHP 1983–88 **Astros**, White Sox, Cardinals, Phillies 462 ip, 27–30, 3.41
☛ *All-Star—83.*

Acquired from the Reds by Houston in 1983, Dawley was an All-Star as a rookie that year, saving 14 games. An imposing 6′4″ 240-lb fastball-slider pitcher, he followed with a league-high 11 relief wins and a 1.93 ERA in 1984. But he suffered with tendinitis in 1985, was released the following spring, and spent each of the next three years with different clubs. /(JCA)

Andre Dawson (Hawk, Awesome) — 1954– . OF 1976- **Expos**, Cubs 1871 g, .281, 319 hr, 1131 rbi. *2 LCS, 10 g, .128, 3 rbi*
☛ *Rookie of the Year—77. Most Valuable Player—87. Led League—hr 87. Led League—rbi 87. All-Star—81–83, 87–89. Gold Glove—80–85, 87–88.*

After a decade of stardom with Montreal, Dawson reached new heights with the Cubs. A free-swinging righthanded batter susceptible to being hit by pitches, Dawson was a complete player with the Expos, outstanding at bat, in the field, and on the bases. Still, he was largely overshadowed by the popular Gary Carter. Dawson led NL outfielders in chances three straight seasons (1981–83), but the artificial surface at Olympic Stadium took its toll on his knees. By 1986 he was determined to play on grass. Despite the collusively-limited free agent market, he went to the Cubs by signing a blank contract, getting a 1987 salary far below market value ($500,000). Rejuvenated by natural grass and day baseball, and helped statistically by the move to the league's best offensive park after ten years in one of its worst, he turned in an MVP season in 1987, leading the NL with 49 HR and 137 RBI. He was the first player on a last-place team ever to win the MVP. /(ME)

James P. Dawson — 1896–1953. *Writer.*

Dawson began a 45-year career with the *New York Times* as a copy boy in 1908. Eight years later, he became boxing editor and covered boxing and baseball until his death during spring training in 1953. The annual award presented to the top rookie in the Yankees' training camp is named in his honor. /(NLM)

Andre Dawson

Joe Dawson — 1897–1978. RHP 1924, 27–29
Indians, **Pirates** 238 ip, 11–17, 4.15. *1 WS, 1 ip, 0.00*

Dawson led the Pirates with 24 relief appearances in 1928, garnering 7 of his 11 career victories. /(ME)

Boots Day [Charles Frederick] — 1947– . OF 1969–74
Cardinals, Cubs, **Expos** 471 g, .256, 8 hr, 98 rbi

Sure-handed and quick, Day was one of the smaller modern players at 5'9", 160 lb. Platooned by the Expos, he hit .283 in 1971 and .275 two years later. He was 30-for-129 as a ML pinch hitter. After being sent down to the minors he tried unsuccessfully to make a comeback as a pitcher. /(MC)

John B. Day — Unk.–Unk. *Executive.*

Founder of the New York Giants in the NL in 1883, Day began with the New York Mets of the American Association, with Jim Mutrie. He formed the Giants by bringing most of the Troy club to New York and won two pennants. A year after moving

into the Polo Grounds site he lost most of his players to the Brotherhood's New York club in 1890 and went broke, holding various jobs with the NL thereafter. /(NLM)

Leon Day — 1916– . RHP Negro Leagues 1934–50
Baltimore Black Sox, Brooklyn Eagles, **Newark Eagles**, Baltimore Elite Giants (NNL) statistics not available
☛ *All-Star—35, 37, 39, 42–43, 46.*

Day was the most outstanding pitcher in the Negro National League during the late 1930s and early 1940s. A heady pitcher, he was the Newark Eagles' ace. He had a sneaky fastball, which he delivered with a no-windup, sidearm motion and complemented with a good curve and change-of-pace to set impressive strikeout records.

Day was also a good hitter and baserunner. When not pitching, he often played second base or the outfield, or pinch-hit.

Day's best season was 1937, when, backed by the Eagles' "million-dollar infield," he was 13–0 in league play and batted .320. In 1940 he established the Puerto Rican record of 19 strikeouts while locked in an 18-inning marathon with spitballer Bill Byrd; the game was called with the score tied 1–1. He also played two winters in Cuba and one in Venezuela (going 12–1), and three summers in Mexico.

Day appeared in a record seven East-West all-star games from 1935 through 1946, winning his only decision and setting an all-star record by striking out a total of 14 batters. In the 1942 game, he struck out five of the seven he faced without giving up a hit. That year he set a Negro League record when he struck out 18 Baltimore batters in one game, including Roy Campanella three times. For post-season play, he was recruited by the Homestead Grays to oppose Satchel Paige in the Negro World Series; he struck out 12 batters in a 4–1 victory.

Day served in the army during WWII, was discharged in February 1946, and threw an Opening Day no-hitter against the Philadelphia Stars. He recorded a 9–4 record that year, led the league in strikeouts, and started two games in the Negro World Series, in which the Eagles defeated the Kansas City Monarchs.

After pitching for the 1949 champion Baltimore Elites, Day left to play in Canada in 1950. Then, well past his prime, he entered organized baseball, pitching for Toronto (International League) in 1951 and Scranton (Eastern League) in 1952 before returning to Canada, where he finished his career in 1955. /(JR)

Ken Dayley — 1959– . LHP 1982– Braves, **Cardinals** 495 ip, 29–41, 3.63. *2 LCS, 10 ip, 0–0, 0.00. 2 WS, 10 ip, 1–0, 0.84*

Dayley used a snappy curve and fastball to become the Cardinals' top lefthanded reliever. He recovered from career-threatening ligament damage in his left elbow in 1986 to win a personal-best nine games in '87. /(FJO)

Mike de la Hoz — 1939– . 3B-2B-SS 1960–69 Indians, **Braves**, Reds 494 g, .251, 25 hr, 115 rbi

A handy utility infielder, de la Hoz never had 200 at-bats in a season. The hustling Cuban pinch hit in 40% of his games. As a Milwaukee Brave on July 8, 1965, he hit a pinch-homer in the eighth inning, singled to tie the game in the ninth, and singled and scored in the 12th to give his club a 9–8 victory over the Astros. /(RTM)

Don De Mola — 1952– . RHP 1974–75 **Expos** 156 ip, 5–7, 3.75

After he was signed and released by the Yankees, the Expos rediscovered De Mola pitching amateur ball in New York. He rose quickly to the majors, and worked 60 games in relief in 1975, but his arm blew out in 1976. /(MC)

Charlie Deal — 1891–1979. 3B 1912–21 Tigers, Braves, St. Louis (FL), Browns, **Cubs** 850 g, .257, 11 hr, 318 rbi. *2 WS, 10 g, .152*

When regular Braves third baseman "Red" Smith broke his leg in one of the last regular-season games in 1914, Deal took over at third and helped Boston sweep the WS in four games. His $2,400 season salary was nearly matched by his $2,200 Series share. When the Braves denied him a $500 raise the next year, he jumped to the Federal League for $4,500 and a $3,000 bonus. From 1917 to 1921 he was the Cubs' regular third baseman. /(BC)

Chubby Dean [Alfred Lovill] — 1916–1970. LHP-1B 1936–43 A's, Indians 533 g, .274, 3 hr, 128 rbi; 686 ip, 30–46, 5.08

Dean went right from Duke University -where his coach was former Philadelphia hurler Jack Coombs—to the Athletics. He played first base and pinch-hit often his first two seasons before Connie Mack, desperate for pitchers, put him on the mound. He was an unspectacular but useful starter, reliever, and pinch hitter for the A's and Indians. He went into the military in 1943 and never returned to ML baseball. /(JK)

Dizzy Dean [Jay Hanna] — 1911–1974. RHP 1930, 32–41, 47 **Cardinals**, Cubs, Browns 1966 ip, 150–83, 3.03. 20 wins: 33–36 *2 WS, 34 ip, 2–2, 2.88* ☛ *Most Valuable Player—34. Led League—w 34–35. Led League—k 32–35. All-Star—34–37. Hall of Fame—1953.*

Dizzy Dean actually had only six full seasons in the majors, but no player packed more accomplishments, excitement, and shenanigans into a shorter time.

Dean was given his nickname by his sergeant in the army, where he picked up the basics of pitching. He was pitching for a semi-pro team in San Antonio when a manager in the Cardinals' farm system spotted him at a tryout camp. The Cardinals signed him, and he split 1930 between St. Joseph, Missouri, and Houston, rolling up a combined 25–10 minor league record before pitching a three-hitter for St. Louis on the last day of the season. Returned to Houston for the 1931 campaign, Dean struck out 303 batters on his way to 26 victories.

As a rookie in 1932, the 21-year-old Dean was joining the "Gas House Gang" World Champions. He won 18 and led the NL in strikeouts, shutouts, and innings pitched. He helped his own cause repeatedly with superb fielding, a .258 batting average, and fine speed on the bases. From 1933 to 1936 Dean absolutely dominated batters. During this stretch he won 102 games, led the league in complete games each year, and averaged 50 games and more than 300 innings per season. He was the unquestioned ace of the Cardinal staff and would often come in from the bullpen between starts. In 1933 he struck out 17 Cubs in a game, a major league record at that time.

During spring training in 1934, Dizzy proudly predicted that he and his brother Paul would win 45 games that season. The incredible prediction seemed ludicrous because Paul had never pitched a game in the majors. Yet Dizzy's boast proved conservative; he won 30 and Paul won 19. Dizzy led the league in wins, strikeouts, shutouts, and complete games, was second to Carl Hubbell for the ERA crown, and batted .246. He easily outdistanced Paul Waner for the MVP award. He capped off his spectacular year with two wins over the Tigers in the World Series, including a shutout in the seventh game.

The 1935 season proved a virtual carbon copy of 1934 as the Deans won 47. Dizzy slipped to 28 victories but still led the league in many pitching categories. This time he was edged out by Gabby Hartnett for MVP. Dean won 24 and saved 11 the next year and again narrowly missed the MVP award, losing to Carl Hubbell.

Dizzy Dean with the Browns

In 1937 Dean appeared headed for another 25-win season by the All-Star break. Exhausted from the toll of so many innings, he asked to sit out the All-Star Game but went at the urging of Cardinal owner Sam Breadon. As the starter for the NL, Dean suffered a broken toe when he was struck by an Earl Averill line drive. Dean tried to come back before it had fully healed, altering his pitching motion to favor the injured foot, but the change brought on bursitis in his valuable right arm.

Traded to the Cubs for three players and $185,000 just before the start of the 1938 season, he replaced his blazing fastball and dazzling curve with a changeup and slow curve. Dean was able to chip in a 7–1 mark with a 1.81 ERA in 13 games, helping Chicago to the NL pennant. Over the next three years Dean appeared in only 30 games. At age 30 he retired and became a broadcaster for the St. Louis Browns. In 1947, after frequent criticism of Browns hurlers all year, Dean took the mound himself three times. In the last game of the season he shut out the White Sox for four innings and got a base hit in his only at-bat.

Dean's meteoric pitching career provided ample reason to immortalize him. His bold and zany antics on and off the field have made him one of the most recognizable characters in American folklore. He loved to challenge and bait opposing players before and during games. He was a relentless braggart; fortunately he was as good as he said he was. He gambled and was pretty good at that too. Dean and Pepper Martin formed the core of the Gas House Gang. Whether in the dugout, clubhouse, or hotel, Dean and Martin could be expected to be up to some sort of prank. His popularity and colorful approach to the game continued unabated when he entered the radio broadcaster's booth. His malapropisms and blatant avoidance of the rules of grammar were legendary, and fans loved it. In 1950 he began doing baseball's Game of the Week on national television. He remained in sportscasting for more than 20 years. /(FO)

Paul Dean (Daffy) — 1913–1981. RHP 1934–41, 43 **Cardinals**, Giants, Browns 787 ip, 50–34, 3.75. *1 WS, 18 ip, 2–0, 1.00*

When Paul joined his famous brother Dizzy on the Cardinals' pitching staff, Dizzy predicted, "Me 'n Paul will win 45 games." They won 49, 19 by Paul, and put the Cards in the World Series, where they each won 2 more. During the September pennant drive, Dizzy shut out the Dodgers on three hits in the first game of a double-header; Paul pitched a no-hitter in the nightcap. "I wished I'da known Paul was goin' to pitch a no-hitter," Dizzy said. "I'da pitched one, too." Paul was dubbed "Daffy" by sportswriters but he was actually shy and rather serious. In 1935, he again won 19 for the Cardinals. The next year, he held out for more money. After signing, he tried to pitch too soon, hurt his arm, and never regained his form. /(FJO)

Tommy Dean — 1945– . SS 1967, 69–71 Dodgers, **Padres** 215 g, .180, 4 hr, 25 rbi

A high school basketball All-American, Dean signed with the Dodgers in 1964 for a $60,000 bonus. A reliable fielder, he was a poor hitter. In 101 games with the Padres in 1969, his most active ML season, he hit only .176. /()

Wayland Dean — 1902–1930. RHP 1924–27 **Giants**, Phillies, Cubs 446 ip, 24–36, 5.31

Wayland Dean was only 28 when he died of tuberculosis, two years after an arm problem halted his career. He was a fine batter and was 6-for-26 as a pinch hitter in 1926. /(JK)

Hank DeBerry — 1893–1951. C 1916–17, 22–30 Indians, **Dodgers** 648 g, .267, 11 hr, 234 rbi

After brief trials with the Indians, DeBerry had a great season in the Southern Association. Dodger scout Larry Sutton urged owner Charlie Ebbets to buy DeBerry and his batterymate, the almost 30-year-old Dazzy Vance. DeBerry's subsequent value was mostly as Vance's personal catcher. /(JK)

Dave DeBusschere — 1940– . RHP 1962–63 **White Sox** 102 ip, 3–4, 2.90

In his first summers as a White Sox minor league pitcher, DeBusschere was impressive, posting a 10–1 record with Savannah (Sally League) in 1962. In the winters, the 6'6" Detroit native won fame as a dominating forward for the NBA's Detroit Pistons. The White Sox, who had given him a $75,000 signing bonus, were encouraged when he threw a ML shutout in 1963, but the Pistons upped the ante by naming him player-coach, at age 24 the youngest coach in NBA history. DeBusschere gave up baseball, going on to a Hall of Fame basketball career (1963–72). Disciplined, unselfish, and dedicated to defense, he was considered the ultimate team player, and was a catalyst on two New York Knicks World Championship teams. He wore number 22 during his entire pro career. He served one year as GM of the American Basketball Association Nets before becoming the ABA's commissioner. He later returned to the Knicks for a term as their GM. He was elected to the NBA Hall of Fame in 1982. /(DB)

Art Decatur — 1894–1966. RHP 1922–27 **Dodgers**, Phillies 549 ip, 23–34, 4.47

Usually a reliever, Decatur led the NL with seven relief wins for Brooklyn in 1924. Born in Ohio, he developed a fondness for Alabama while pitching in the minors and later became president of the Georgia-Alabama League. /(JK)

Doug DeCinces — 1950– . 3B 1973–87 **Orioles**, Angels, Cardinals 1649 g, .259, 237 hr, 879 rbi. *3 LCS, 16 g, .297, 1 hr, 6 rbi. 1 WS, 7 g, .200, 1 hr, 3 rbi*
☞ *All-Star—83.*

DeCinces had the impossible task of replacing Brooks Robinson at third base for the Orioles. Actually, his talents were similar to Robinson's. Slow afoot, DeCinces gained a reputation for good hands and as a clutch hitter. Battling back problems throughout his career, he became expendable with the arrival of Cal Ripken, Jr., who started his career at third base. Dealt to the Angels for 1982,

DeCinces responded with his best season, reaching career highs with 30 HR, 97 RBI, and a .301 average. He hit .316 in the LCS and won regard as the AL's best all-around third baseman. He averaged over 21 HR a season during his California career, which ended in late September of 1987 when he was traded to the Cardinals to make room for Jack Howell. DeCinces played only four games for St. Louis, which won the NL pennant, and went to Japan after being released following the season. /(ME)

Joe Decker — 1947– . RHP 1969–76, 79 Cubs, **Twins**, Mariners 710 ip, 36–44, 4.17

Decker threw hard but had streaks of wildness. In spring training, his own teammates sometimes refused to bat against him. He struggled unsuccessfully for four years to win a spot with the Cubs, then became a regular starter with the Twins in 1973 and 1974. After his 16–14 season in '74, he explained his success: "I try to tranquilize myself when I pitch. If I'm lethargic, I have better stuff." /(MC)

Jeff Dedmon — 1960– . RHP 1983–88 **Braves**, Indians 394 ip, 20–16, 3.84

Dedmon was drafted four times before signing with Atlanta. Throwing a sinker and adding a knuckle curve, he averaged 56 games a year as a long reliever in 1984–87, but lacked the control and consistency to be a stopper, and was traded to Cleveland in 1988. /(JCA)

Bill Deegan — 1935– . *Umpire* AL 1970–80 *3 LCS 1 WS, 1 ASU*

In 1977, Deegan was behind the plate for two AL no-hitters, a rare occurrence for any umpire. The year before, he was on the spot for an unusual play at Yankee Stadium when Red Sox first baseman Carl Yastrzemski lost his glove leaping for a high pickoff throw. The Yankees argued to invoke the rule that all runners advance two bases when a fielder throws his glove at a ball. Not so on two counts, ruled Deegan at first base. The glove did not touch the ball and the fielder's action was unintentional. /(RTM)

Rob Deer — 1960– . OF 1984– Giants, **Brewers** 624 g, .229, 121 hr, 339 rbi

A hacking, heavyset, righthanded slugger, Deer's prodigious home runs are matched by equally prodigious strikeout totals. He came up through the Giants minor league chain, winning three minor league home run crowns (one at each level), but also leading his league in strikeouts four times. Deer was with the Giants for all of 1985, but was traded to the Brewers after hitting only .185 with eight home runs in 78 games, and he won Milwaukee's right field job in 1986. He belted 33 HR in his first AL season, but also fanned a whopping 179 times, then set an AL record with 186 strikeouts the following season (breaking Pete Incaviglia's year-old mark by 1). He led the league again in 1988 with 153 strikeouts, hitting a career-high .252 as his home run output fell to 23./(SCL)

Ivan DeJesus — 1953- . SS 1974–88 Dodgers, **Cubs**, Phillies, Cardinals, Yankees, Giants, Tigers 1371 g, .254, 21 hr, 324 rbi

Signed by the Dodgers in 1969 as a high school student in Puerto Rico, DeJesus got his break in 1977 when he was traded to the Cubs. Filling the gap left by Don Kessinger, he scored a league-high 104 runs in 1978, and in 1980 set a record for Cubs shortstops with 44 stolen bases. His poor attitude and unhappiness with the trade of friend and double-play partner Manny Trillo resulted in a disastrous 1981 season (.194); the Cubs made a splendid move by sending him to the Phillies for Larry Bowa and rookie Ryne Sandberg. In 1982, former Cub teammate Jody Davis accused DeJesus of intentionally allowing Latin opponents to slide in safely at second. In the 1983 World Series, DeJesus batted an anemic .125 and became the goat when his error in Game Three allowed Baltimore's winning run to score./(DB)

Ed Delahanty (Big Ed) — 1867–1903. OF-IF 1888–1903 **Phillies**, Cleveland (PL), Senators 1834 g, .345, 100 hr, 1464 rbi
☛ *Led League—ba 99, 02. Led League—hr 93. Led League—rbi 93, 96, 99. Hall of Fame—1945.*

One of seven brothers from Cleveland, five of whom played ML baseball, Ed Delahanty was a premier 19th-century slugger. The 6'1" 190-lb righthander made his pro debut in 1887 with Mansfield of the Ohio State League, batting .355. The next year, he was at .408 after 21 games with Wheeling of the Tri-State League when the Phillies bought his contract for $1,500. He arrived in Philadelphia in time to play 74 games, mostly at second base, but hit only .228.

He jumped to the Players' League in 1890, but returned to the Phillies the next year. After a .306 year in 1892 with a league-leading 21 triples, he blossomed in 1893, narrowly missing the triple crown (.368, 19 HR, 146 RBI). The next year he hit

Ed Delahanty

.400, but he needed .408 in 1899 to win his first batting title. Delahanty collected six-hit games in 1890 and '94 and had ten consecutive hits in 1897. His four doubles in one game tied the record in 1899, and on July 13, 1896 he hit four home runs—the second man to do so—and a single in a losing cause at Chicago.

After switching to the new AL, he won a second batting title with the Senators (.376) in 1902. He also led in slugging average, a feat he'd accomplished three times in the NL. His disdain for training rules got him suspended in June 1903, and he left his club in Detroit to take a train to New York. At International Bridge near Niagara Falls, the conductor put him off the train for being drunk and disorderly. Staggering along the tracks in the dark, he fell through an open drawbridge and was swept over the falls to his death./(AL)

Jim Delahanty — 1879–1953. 2B-3B-OF-1B 1901–02, 04–12, 14–15 Cubs, Giants, Braves, Reds, Browns, Senators, **Tigers**, Brooklyn (FL) 1186 g, .283, 18 hr, 489 rbi. *1 WS, 7 g, .346, 4 rbi*

Jim Delahanty, a versatile player, was one of five brothers who played major league ball, including Big Ed, a Hall of Famer. Jim had the next-best career, finishing in the Federal League and going to their outlaw minor, the New England Colonial League, in 1915 to lead the league in batting while managing Hartford to the championship. /(JK)

Bill DeLancey — 1901–1946. C 1932, 34–35, 40 **Cardinals** 219 g, .289, 19 hr, 85 rbi. *1 WS, 7 g, .172, 1 hr, 4 rbi*

Branch Rickey once gave DeLancey a place on his all-time team, even though the lefthanded-hitting catcher played in only 219 ML games. Thirty-one when he joined the Cardinals for a brief trial late in 1932, he returned in 1934 to platoon with Spud Davis for the World Champion "Gas House Gang," hitting .316 with 13 home runs and 40 RBI. He was particularly adept at handling the Cardinals' eccentric pitchers. In 1935, he slumped at the plate and appeared tired. At the end of the season he was discovered to be suffering from tuberculosis. He missed four years, then hit .222 in a comeback attempt in 1940. /(MC)

Art Delaney [born Arthur Helenius] (Swede) — 1895–1970. RHP 1924, 28–29 Cardinals, **Braves** 287 ip, 13–22, 4.26

After three strong years at Oakland of the Pacific Coast League, Delaney received a second ML trial with the Braves in 1928. Despite a fair 3.79 ERA, his record was 9–17. /(NLM)

Jose DeLeon [born Jose Chestaro] — 1960– . RHP 1983– **Pirates**, White Sox, Cardinals 1234 ip, 61–77, 3.70 ☛ *Led League—k 89.*

A fireballing Dominican with a good forkball, DeLeon flirted with no-hitters in his second and third ML starts in 1983, carrying one into the seventh against the Padres, and the other into the ninth against the Mets. But he went 2–19 for Pittsburgh in 1985, leading the NL in losses—and received a raise. He was traded to the White Sox for Bobby Bonilla in 1986, went 11–12 in 1987, and was sent to the Cardinals for Lance Johnson and Ricky Horton. He eventually blossomed under Whitey Herzog, going 16–12, 3.05 in 1989 and leading the NL in strikeouts. /(RL)

Luis DeLeon — 1957– . RHP 1981–85, 87 Cardinals, **Padres**, Orioles 330 ip, 17–19, 3.14

Obtained as part of the deal that sent Ozzie Smith to the Cardinals, DeLeon gave the Padres two excellent seasons of relief until overwork caught up with him. In 1982 he was 9–5 with 15 saves in 61 appearances and the next year 6–6 with 13 saves. His strength was his control, as he walked only 43 batters in 223 innings during those seasons. /(MC)

Bobby Del Greco — 1933– . OF 1952, 56–58, 60–63, 65 Pirates, Cardinals, Cubs, Yankees, Phillies, **A's** 731 g, .229, 42 hr, 169 rbi

Plucked off the Pittsburgh sandlots, Bobby was part of the Pirates' youth parade in the early 1950s. Considered one of the top defensive outfielders of his era, the speedy Del Greco made a great catch for the Cardinals late in the 1956 season against the Braves that aided the Dodgers in winning the pennant. /(RM)

Wheezer Dell [William George] — 1887–1966. RHP 1912, 15–17 Cardinals, **Dodgers** 430 ip, 19–23, 2.55. *1 WS, 1 ip, 0.00*

Dell led the Dodgers in strikeouts as a rookie, but the acquisition of Rube Marquard and Larry Cheney limited him to a marginal role with the 1916 pennant winners. /(TG)

Ike Delock — 1929– . RHP 1952–53, 55–63 **Red Sox**, Orioles 1238 ip, 84–75, 4.03

Delock had several above-average seasons for the Red Sox in the 1950s. He led the AL with 11 relief wins in 1956 while tying for fourth with nine saves (then not an official statistic). In general, he was better coming out of the bullpen, compiling a 3.08 ERA lifetime in that role. But as his career went on, he was used less and less as a reliever. His record as a starting pitcher was 50–60. A 1962 knee injury hastened the end of his career. /(JFC)

Jim Delsing — 1925– . OF 1948–56, 60 White Sox, Yankees, Browns, **Tigers**, A's 822 g, .255, 40 hr, 286 rbi

The Browns' pinch-runner in 1951 for midget Eddie Gaedel, Delsing hit .300 several times in the minors and made the Northern League, Pacific Coast League, and American Association all-star teams. His top ML BA was .288 with the 1953 Tigers. His son Jim is a member of the PGA tour. /(RTM)

Joe DeMaestri (Oats) — 1928– . SS 1951–61 White Sox, Browns, **A's**, Yankees 1121 g, .236, 49 hr, 281 rbi. *1 WS, 4 g, .500* ☛ *All-Star—57.*

DeMaestri was drafted by the White Sox out of the Red Sox organization before being shuffled from Chicago to St. Louis, back to Chicago, and on to Philadelphia. He began a seven-year stretch as the Athletics' starting shortstop in 1953. On July 8, 1955 DeMaestri went 6-for-6. As a utility infielder finishing up with the Yankees, he roomed with Yogi Berra. /(RL)

Al Demaree — 1886–1962. RHP 1912–19 **Giants**, Phillies, Cubs, Braves 1424 ip, 80–72, 2.77. *1 WS, 4 ip, 0–1, 4.50*

Demaree was most effective early in the season, and 14 of his 80 career wins were shutouts. He was 13–4 for the Giant pennant winners in 1913 and 14–11 for the Phillies when they won the 1915 pennant. In 1916 he won 19, including both games of a September 20 doubleheader against the Phillies. Demareee later became a sports cartoonist, syndicated in over 200 newspapers. His work appeared in *The Sporting News* for over 30 years./(NLM)

Frank Demaree [born Joseph Franklin Demaria] — 1910–1958. OF 1932–33, 35–44 **Cubs**, Giants, Braves, Cardinals, Browns 1155 g, .299, 72 hr, 591 rbi. *4 WS, 12 g, .214, 3 hr, 6 rbi*
☛ *All-Star—36–37.*

After hitting .272 in 1933 as the Cubs' centerfield replacement for injured Kiki Cuyler, who broke his leg in spring training, Demaree was sent to Los Angeles of the Pacific Coast League and responded with an MVP year (.383, 45 homers, 190 RBI, and 45 stolen bases in 186 games). Regaining the Cubs job in 1935, he had three consecutive excellent seasons, hitting .325, .350, and .324, with highs of 17 homers and 115 RBI in 1937. He was the starting centerfielder for the NL in the 1936 and 1937 All-Star games. In seven more ML seasons, he slipped to the status of journeyman reserve./(ME)

Larry Demery — 1953– . RHP 1974–77 **Pirates** 445 ip, 29–23, 3.72. *2 WS, 3 ip, 21.00*

Son of Negro League outfielder/pitcher Artist Demery, Larry broke into the Pirate rotation a few days after turning 21. He was 7–5 (2.90) in 1975, mostly in long relief, and 10–7 (3.17) in 1976. A 1977 arm injury ended his career./(MC)

Don Demeter — 1935– . OF-3B-1B 1956, 58–67 Dodgers, **Phillies**, Tigers, Red Sox, Indians 1109 g, .265, 163 hr, 563 rbi. *1 WS, 6 g, .250*

The slim, 6'4" righthanded slugger hit more than 20 HR each year from 1961 through 1964 and twice hit 3 homers in a game, with the Dodgers in 1959 and the Phillies in 1961. In his best offensive season, playing mostly third base for the '62 Phillies, Demeter batted .307 with 29 HR and 107 RBI. He set a ML record for outfielders with 266 consecutive errorless games, from September 1962 with the Phillies through July 1965 with the Tigers./(AL)

Ray Demmitt — 1884–1956. OF 1909–10, 14–15, 17–19 Yankees, **Browns**, Tigers, White Sox 498 g, .257, 8 hr, 165 rbi

After graduating from the University of Illinois, Demmitt broke in with Ottawa in 1906 under the name of Ray. He was a regular in only three ML seasons; his best effort came in 1918, when he hit .281 with 61 RBI in 405 at-bats for the Browns./(NLM)

Gene DeMontreville — 1874–1962. 2B-SS 1894–1904 Pirates, **Washington (NL)**, Baltimore (NL), Cubs, Dodgers, Braves, Senators, Browns 922 g, .306, 17 hr, 497 rbi

Eugene Napolean DeMontreville, the elegantly-named son of French parents, appeared in boxscores mostly as plain Gene Demont due to the space limitations of the typesetters. He finished his career with 228 stolen bases and was the master of the delayed steal. A younger brother, Lee, appeared briefly with the Cardinals. Ill health shortened DeMontreville's playing career./(JK)

Bingo DeMoss [Elwood] — 1889–1965. 2B-SS-MGR Negro Leagues 1905–43 Topeka Giants, Kansas City Giants, **Chicago American Giants**, Indianapolis ABC's, Detroit Stars, Cleveland Giants, Chicago Brown Bombers, Brooklyn Brown Dodgers 462 g, .247, 4 hr (inc.)

DeMoss, a 6'2" 175-lb righthanded hitter and a smart, aggressive fielder, was considered the best second baseman of his day in Negro League baseball. He began as a shortstop in 1905 with the Topeka Giants, the first full-time black semi-pro team in the Midwest. After hurting his arm while pitching in an emergency, he moved to second base. DeMoss spent his prime years with the Chicago American Giants, and as a player-manager for the Indianapolis ABC's and Detroit Stars. From 1920 through 1930, he batted .247, including highs of .314 for the 1929 Detroit Stars and .292 for the 1920 Chicago American Giants.

DeMoss was a proficient bunter and hit-and-run man, making him an ideal second-place hitter. Jelly Gardner, who batted ahead of DeMoss on the American Giants, said of his teammate, "If he thought you'd be out trying to steal, he'd foul off the pitch if he couldn't hit it well. He could hit 'em anywhere he wanted to.

DeMoss retired as a player after 1930, but continued to manage through 1943. His last assignment was with the Brooklyn Brown Dodgers of the

United States Baseball League, a circuit organized by Branch Rickey to scout players for possible signing by the Brooklyn Dodgers. The league lasted only one full season, 1945. /(JM)

Rick Dempsey — 1949– . C 1969– Twins, Yankees, **Orioles**, Indians, Dodgers 1635 g, .234, 90 hr, 435 rbi. *3 LCS, 11 g, .296, 4 rbi. 3 WS, 14 g, .308, 1 hr, 3 rbi*

A flaky individual but a take-charge catcher, Rick Dempsey's break came on June 15, 1976 when he went from the Yankees to the Orioles in a ten-player deal. When he left Baltimore, signing as a free agent with Cleveland in 1987, he had caught more games than anyone for the Orioles. His greatest moment came as MVP of the 1983 World Series. He had the game-winning RBI in Game Two and homered and doubled in the Game Five clincher, hitting .385 overall.

Dempsey led AL catchers in fielding in 1981 and 1983 and in assists in 1979. He sacrificed batting average for added power in his last years at Baltimore (1984–86). Expected to stabilize a young Cleveland club, Dempsey suffered on both offense and defense. His 1987 season was curtailed by a broken left thumb suffered in a home plate collision with Bo Jackson. Dempsey rebounded in a reserve role with the 1988 Dodgers. /(ME)

Bill Denehy — 1946– . RHP 1967–68, 71 **Mets**, Senators, Tigers 105 ip, 1–10, 4.56

When Denehy led the rookie New York-Penn League in wins and shutouts, he was ranked as a top prospect. His tendency to surrender homers curtailed his success in the majors. He was traded with $100,000 to Washington for manager Gil Hodges in 1967. /(MC)

Don Denkinger — 1936– . *Umpire* AL 1968, 77–87 *2 LCS 2 WS, 2 ASU*

Denkinger was at the center of the most controversial play of the 1985 WS. The Cardinals led in the Series 3–2 and led in the ninth inning of the sixth game, 1–0. Denkinger called the Royals' Jorge Orta safe at first on a grounder to the Cardinals' Jack Clark. TV replays showed pitcher Tod Worrell had beaten Orta to the bag. Kansas City went on to rally for two runs, averting elimination, and the next day they won the Series. /(RTM)

Don Dennis — 1942– . RHP 1965–66 **Cardinals** 115 ip, 6–5, 3.69

Dennis's 1.47 ERA at Jacksonville in 1965 was his ticket to the majors. Brought in from the bullpen to protect a Cardinal lead in the ninth inning, the 6'2" fastballer served up a home run which tied the score. But when teammate Bill White homered in the Cardinals' next at-bat, it made a winner out of Dennis. Undaunted, he did not allow a run in his next nine appearances and finished the year at 2–3 with six saves. His efforts gained him St. Louis rookie-of-the-year honors. /(RM)

Jerry Denny [born Jeremiah Dennis Eldridge] — 1859–1927. 3B 1881–91, 93–94 **Providence (NL)**, Cardinals, Indianapolis (NL), Giants, Cleveland (NL), Phillies, Louisville (NL) 1237 g, .260, 74 hr, 512 rbi

Denny set ML career records for third basemen that still stand: 4.2 total chances per game and 1.6 putouts per game. Though he also holds the NL career record for errors at third base (553), for five seasons he ranked first or second in fielding average. On October 24, 1884 Denny hit the only home run in the first post-season series (a forerunner of the World Series) to defeat the New York Metropolitans and win the game and the Series for the Providence Grays. /(FIC)

John Denny — 1952– . RHP 1974–86 **Cardinals**, Indians, Phillies, Reds 2149 ip, 123–108, 3.58 *1 LCS, 6 ip, 0–1, 0.00. 1 WS, 13 ip, 1–1, 3.46*
☛ *Led League—w 83. Led League—era 76. Cy Young Award—83. All-Star—83.*

Denny had an excellent curve and changeup, but only an average fastball. Control was all-important for his success. He helped himself considerably with fine fielding and passable batting for a pitcher. A temperamental sort, he suffered from weak ankles throughout much of his career.

A hot and cold pitcher, he led the NL in ERA with the Cardinals in 1976 but was only 11–9 on the season. Two years later, he won 14, but when he fell off to 8 wins in 1979, St. Louis traded him to Cleveland. Late in 1982 the Indians dealt him to Philadelphia.

Denny had by far his best season in 1983 with the Phillies. His 19–6 mark gave him league highs in wins and percentage. His 2.45 ERA was his personal best. The Phillies won the pennant, and Denny received the Cy Young Award. /(FJO)

Bucky Dent [Russell Earl] — 1951– . SS 1973–84 White Sox, **Yankees**, Rangers, Royals 1392 g, .247, 40 hr, 423 rbi. *3 LCS, 12 g, .200, 6 rbi. 2 WS, 12 g, .349, 9 rbi.*
 Manager 1989 **Yankees** 18–22, .450
☛ *All-Star—75, 80–81.*

In 1978 Dent was the unlikely hero in the playoff game against Boston when his short three-run homer over Fenway's Green Monster, off Mike Torrez, changed the course of the game as the Yankees went on to win 5–4. His fine play continued as he was named WS MVP as the Yankees won their second straight championship with Dent at shortstop.

Dent, a promising White Sox shortstop, came to the Yankees in a much-heralded deal in April 1977. He was touted as the final piece in the great Yankee team. Dent was a natural with his boyish good looks, the perfect foil for the Yankees' rough and abrasive identity. He became an instant idol with legions of adoring teenage girls to cheer him on. He remained popular even as his skills eroded; in 1982 he narrowly missed being voted starting All-Star shortstop while hitting .200 even as Robin Yount was tearing up the league en route to an MVP award. Dent played two years for Texas and finished his career in Kansas City in 1984. He constructed a baseball training school in Florida featuring a replica of the Green Monster, and replayed the feat with an obliging Mike Torrez at the opening of the field in 1989. Dent replaced Dallas Green as Yankee manager in August 1989. /(TJG)

Sam Dente (Blackie) — 1922– . SS-3B 1947–55 Red Sox, Browns, **Senators**, White Sox, Indians 745 g, .252, 4 hr, 214 rbi. *1 WS, 3 g, .000*

This modestly talented infielder joined the Senators' starting lineup in 1949, and hit a career-high .273. The slogan "We'll win plenty with Dente" circulated through the stands at Griffith Stadium early in the campaign when the team led the league, but the catchy rhyme became more famous than the player. After the 1951 season, Dente was relegated to a utility role with the White Sox and Indians. /(RL)

Bob Dernier — 1957– . OF 1980– Phillies, **Cubs** 904 g, .255, 23 hr, 152 rbi. *2 LCS, 6 g, .235, 1 hr, 1 rbi. 1 WS, 1 g, --*
☛ *Gold Glove—84.*

A leadoff man, Dernier set a Phillies' rookie record in 1982 with 42 stolen bases. But he showed little progress as a hitter, batted .231 in 1983, and tried unsuccessfully to learn to switch-hit. Traded to Chicago with Gary Matthews in 1984, he became the first Cubs outfielder to win a Gold Glove; a far-ranging centerfielder, he compensated for slow teammates Matthews in left and Keith Moreland in right. His 45 stolen bases in '84 were the most by a Cub in 77 years. Slowed by injuries in 1985–86, he eventually lost his job to Dave Martinez, and re-signed with the Phillies as a free agent for 1988. /(JCA)

Paul Derringer

Paul Derringer (Duke, 'Oom Paul) — 1906–1988. RHP 1931–45 Cardinals, **Reds**, Cubs 3645 ip, 223–212, 3.46. 20 wins: 35, 38–40 *4 WS, 53 ip, 2–4, 3.42*
☛ *All-Star—35, 38–42.*

Derringer won 40 games at Rochester in the International League and led them to two pennants in 1929 and 1930. He helped the Cardinals win the pennant with an 18–8 mark in 1931, but was traded to the Reds in 1933 for Leo Durocher. He started and won the first major league night game at Cincinnati in 1935. Hurling three consecutive 20-win seasons (1938–40) and going 25–7 in 1939, Derringer led the Reds to two successive pennants and the World Championship in 1940. He was the winning pitcher in the 1940 All-Star Game and had two one-hit games that same season.

Derringer led the league in winning percentage in 1931 and 1939, games lost in 1933, games started in 1936, 1938, and 1940, and complete games and innings pitched in 1938. He had 32 career shutouts, won ten 1–0 complete games, and had a 1.88 walk ratio. He was sold to the Cubs in 1943 and helped them capture the pennant in 1945. /(JE)

Gene Desautels (Red) — 1907– . C 1930–33, 37–43, 45–46 Tigers, **Red Sox**, Indians, A's 712 g, .233, 3 hr, 186 rbi

While playing at Holy Cross under coach Jack Berry, Desautels was a peppy, rah-rah catcher adept at encouraging and supporting young pitchers. He spent four seasons as a backup catcher for the Tigers and then returned to the minors for three seasons. He joined the Red Sox in 1937 and played regularly for four years. In 1938, his best season, he caught 108 games and hit .291. After the 1940 season, he was traded to the Indians and returned to his backup role. /(NLM)

Jim Deshaies — 1960– . LHP 1984– Yankees, **Astros** 738 ip, 49–36, 3.42

One of several promising young pitchers traded away by the impatient Yankees in the 1980s, Deshaies pitched a no-hitter for Nashville (Southern League) in 1984 before leading the International League in ERA at Columbus the same season, and became the 1,000th player ever to play for the Yankees that September. He was shelled in his two ML starts, however, then struggled at Columbus in 1985, and was traded to Houston for 40-year-old Joe Niekro in the last two weeks of the season.

Deshaies was 12–5, 3.25 as a rookie with the Astros in 1986, and on September 23 he set a ML record by striking out the first eight Dodgers he faced before journeyman Larry See popped out. As the Astros' fourth starter, however, he did not pitch in the LCS against the Mets. Deshaies struggled in 1987, but still posted an 11–6 record, and in 1988 he lowered his ERA to a career-best 3.00, while his record slipped to 11–14. /(SCL)

Jimmie DeShong — 1909– . RHP 1932, 34–39 A's, Yankees, **Senators** 873 ip, 47–44, 5.08

Notoriously wild, DeShong was a reliever for the 1934–35 Yankees before being dealt to Washington. He posted an 18–10 mark in 1936, but slumped in 1938, and was waived back to the Yankees early in 1939. He finished his career in the minors. /(MC)

Detroit Tigers — 1901– . Team. 7133–6613, .519. *AL East Champions 72, 84, 87 AL Champions 07–09, 34–35, 40, 45, 68, 84 World Champions 35, 45, 68, 84*

The Tigers rival any team in baseball for the distinction as most conservative. Authoritarian ownership through the years resisted change (night baseball, the hiring of black players and free agents) while fielding teams that have been generally re-

The 1935 Detroit Tigers

spectable, sometimes outstanding, rarely just bad. Detroit was a charter member of the American League in 1901. The city was at first an indifferent baseball town; AL president Ban Johnson considered moving the Detroit team to Pittsburgh in 1903. But the NL blocked the move at the same time it granted recognition to the American League. The automobile industry spurred growth in Detroit and support for the Tigers followed. That support has rarely slipped. Tiger baseball became big business under the ownership of Frank Navin (1907–35). The team won five pennants during that period, and its first World Series in 1935, shortly before Navin's death. Walter O. Briggs Sr., the new owner, enlarged the home stadium, Navin Field (dating to 1912) in 1938 to 56,000 seats and renamed it after himself.

In 1940, major league baseball Commissioner Landis awarded free agency to 91 Tigers players, ruling that general manager Jack Zeller had violated baseball's working agreement with the minor leagues by making secret deals with players on different teams in the same leagues. Forty-eight years later, an arbitrator freed Tigers star Kirk Gibson after finding the Tigers guilty of collusion in restricting the free agent market. Only the Cubs held out longer against night baseball than the Tigers, who added lights in 1948. Detroit signed no black players until after Briggs died in 1952 and his son, Walter Jr., succeeded him. Third baseman Ossie Virgil (June 6, 1958) was the first black to play for the Tigers. From 1951 to 1960, Detroit never finished better than 17 games out of first place. Briggs' heirs sold the team to his partners in 1960. John Fetzer and general manager Jim Campbell built strong teams based on pitching, defense, and left-handed power. In a key move, they hired Sparky Anderson to manage in mid-1979. Pizza magnate Tom Monaghan purchased the team in October 1983, and his new willingness to spend money helped Anderson acquire the right players to operate his incomparable platoon system. Anderson's tenure peaked with a World Series victory in 1984 over the San Diego Padres. /(KT)

Tom Dettore — 1947– . RHP 1973–76 Pirates, **Cubs** 179 ip, 8–11, 5.21

Dettore never spent a full season in the ML. In 1975, he was 5–4 as a reliever for the pitching-poor Cubs, but his 5.40 ERA showed his ineffectiveness in the bullpen. /(MC)

Mike Devereaux — 1963– . OF 1987– Dodgers, **Orioles** 171 g, .248, 8 hr, 52 rbi

Devereaux unexpectedly made the Dodgers with a hot spring training in 1987, but soon played himself back to the minors. He went to Baltimore after 1988 in the Eddie Murray deal and finally hit well at the major league level in 1989 as a part-time outfielder. A .300 hitter with power in the minors, in the majors he is more valuable for his speed. /(JFC)

Adrian Devine — 1951– . RHP 1973, 1975–80 **Braves**, Rangers 387 ip, 26–22, 4.21

Signed by Atlanta, swapped to Texas, returned to Atlanta, and traded back to Texas in some complicated deals, Devine rebounded after 1975 arm surgery and set a Ranger record with 15 saves in 1977. Arm trouble ultimately ended his career after 1980. /(MC)

Joe Devine — 1895–1951. *Scout.*

From 1923 to 1930 Devine was the Pirates scout on the West Coast, where he discovered Paul and Lloyd Waner, Joe Cronin, and Arky Vaughan. After managing in the Pacific Coast League for two years, he joined the Yankees' scouting staff, and discovered or purchased Joe DiMaggio, Billy Martin, and Jackie Jensen. /(FVP)

Art Devlin — 1879–1948. 3B 1904–13 **Giants**, Braves 1301 g, .269, 10 hr, 504 rbi. *1 WS, 5 g, .250, 1 rbi*

Famed sportswriter Grantland Rice named Devlin third baseman on his all-time Giants team. After

Art Devlin with the Giants

two minor league seasons at Newark, Devlin joined New York in 1904. In three of his eight Giant seasons, he led NL third basemen in assists; in 1908 he also led in putouts and fielding average. Alert and speedy, he had good range at third base (he ranks 15th all-time in chances per game) and stole more than 20 bases six times, tying for the league lead with 59 in 1905. Devlin's best batting average was .299 in 1906. He averaged only one HR per year but his first HR came in his first ML at bat, with the bases loaded. After finishing his NL career with two seasons in Boston, Devlin played four additional years in the minors. /(FIC)

Jim Devlin — 1849-1883. RHP-1B 1873-77 Philadelphia (NA), Chicago (NA), **Louisville (NL)** NA: 136 g, .275; 6-16; NL: 129 g, .293, 1 hr, 55 rbi; 1181 ip, 65-60, 1.89. 20 wins: 76-77
☛ Led League—k 76.

Devlin was the workhorse of the NL in its first two seasons, pitching nearly all of Louisville's games and logging 1,181 innings. Late in 1877, he was implicated with three teammates in throwing games that denied the Colonels what had seemed a sure pennant. He was expelled from baseball and died nearly destitute six years later. /(FIC)

Josh Devore — 1887-1954. OF 1908-14 **Giants**, Reds, Phillies, Braves 601 g, .277, 11 hr, 149 rbi

An expert bunter and baserunner who was adept at drawing walks, Devore was an effective leadoff man for the Giants' pennant-winners of 1911 and 1912. In a 21-12 win over the Braves (6/20/12), he stole four bases in one inning, reaching first twice in the ninth and stealing second and third each time. His spectacular catch of a fly ball in deep right center with two men on in Game Three of the 1912 WS preserved a 2-1 victory for the Giants. His last ML appearance was as a WS pinch hitter for the "Miracle Braves" of 1914. /(NLM)

Charlie Dexter — 1876-1934. OF-C-3B-1B 1896-1903 **Louisville (NL)**, Cubs, Braves 771 g, .261, 16 hr, 346 rbi

Dexter did everything but pitch, and six times stole over 20 bases. In 1898, his .314 BA was Louisville's second-highest, and his 44 stolen bases ranked fourth in the NL. /(FIC)

Lou Dials [Alonzo Odem] — 1904- . 1B-OF-MGR Negro Leagues 1925-46 Chicago American Giants, Memphis Red Sox, Detroit Stars, Hilldale, Columbus Blue Birds, Akron, New York Black Yankees, Cleveland Giants, Homestead Grays statistics not available
☛ All-Star—36.

An outstanding outfielder and first baseman, Dials broke in with one of Negro baseball's most powerful teams, the Chicago American Giants, in 1925. Unconfirmed statistics show Dials winning the 1931 Negro National League batting title with a .382 average for the Detroit Stars. Returning to Chicago, he was an all-star in 1936. With the Negro Leagues on shaky financial ground, Dials went to the North Mexican League, where he managed Torrion to two championships and continued to hit well over .300.

Had the Pacific Coast League owners had the strength to oppose Commissioner Landis, in 1943 Dials could have been the first black signed into organized ball. Dials and Chet Brewer were set to become members of the Los Angeles Angels (PCL) until Chicago Cubs owner Phil Wrigley vetoed the plan. They later were denied a chance by the Oakland owner as well, who said, "The other owners would crucify me if I let you play." Dials continued to barnstorm against white major leaguers until his retirement. He became a scout and an outstanding speaker on behalf of the Negro Leagues. /(DC)

Bo Diaz — 1953- . C 1977-89 Red Sox, Indians, Phillies, **Reds** 993 g, .255, 87 hr, 452 rbi. 1 LCS, 4 g, .154. 1 WS, 5 g, .333
☛ All-Star—81.

Diaz had only one at-bat with the Red Sox in 1977 and played sporadically for Cleveland as the backup to Ron Hassey until an injury to Hassey made him the Indians' starting catcher early in 1981. He hit .356 with 25 RBI in the first half of that strike-interrupted season but sprained his wrist as the season resumed and missed the rest of the year. After he was traded to Philadelphia for 1982, his first NL season was his best, as he hit .288 with 18 HR and 85 RBI, but in 1984 he lost his job to Ozzie Virgil. Diaz became a starter again with the Reds in 1986-87, but hit only .219 in 92 games in 1988. In 1989, he shared the Reds' catching job with Jeff Reed. /(SG)

Carlos Diaz — 1958- . LHP 1982-86 Braves, Mets, **Dodgers** 258 ip, 13-6, 3.21. 1 LCS, 3 ip, 0-0, 3.00

Diaz, who relied primarily upon a hard slider, was almost exclusively used as a set-up man. He was involved in a rare Hawaiian-for-Hawaiian trade when the Mets included him in the package to secure Sid Fernandez from the Dodgers. /(TG)

Mike Diaz (Rambo) — 1960- . 1B-OF-C 1983, 86-
Cubs, **Pirates**, White Sox 293 g, .247, 31 hr, 102 rbi

The muscular Diaz could play first base, outfield,
catcher, or third base, but always seemed best-suited
for DH. He was popular and a good pinch hitter.
His 12 HR in 1986 were second to teammate Barry
Bonds among NL rookies. He tied a ML record with
no putouts at first base in a nine-inning game on
June 26, 1987./(ME)

Rob Dibble — 1964- . RHP 1988- **Reds** 158 ip, 11-6,
1.99

An extremely hard thrower with a phenomenal
strikeout ratio, Dibble came into his own in the first
half of 1989 as a set-up man for John Franco,
although he injured his shoulder in a fight after
hitting the Mets' Tim Teufel with a pitch. /(SFS)

Leo Dickerman — 1896–1982. RHP 1923–25
Dodgers, **Cardinals** 436 ip, 19–27, 3.95

Dickerman, a 6'4" power pitcher, debuted at age 27
with the 1923 Dodgers. Traded to the Cards for
veteran pitcher Bill Doak, Dickerman went 7–4
(2.84) in 1924. His 4–11 record and 5.58 ERA in
1925 meant the end of his ML career./(DQV)

Bill Dickey — 1907- . C 1928-43, 46 **Yankees**
1,789 g, .313, 202 hr, 1,209 rbi. *8 WS, 38 g, .255, 5 hr,
24 rbi*
☛ *All-Star—33–34, 36–43, 46. Hall of Fame—1954.*

The premier catcher of the late 1930s and early
1940s, the lefthanded-hitting Dickey was the soul of
the Yankee dynasty bridging the Ruth, Gehrig and
DiMaggio eras as a player, and the Mantle era as a
coach. He was a keen handler of pitchers, especially
the erratic Lefty Gomez, as quiet as his roommate,
Gehrig, consistent, setting a major league record for
catching 100 or more games in 13 straight seasons,
and never played another game at another position.
He was the first Yankee to find out about Gehrig's
illness and was the only active player to play himself
in the Gary Cooper movie "Pride of the Yankees."
The Yankees retired his number 8, but ironically
Dickey didn't wear that number at the start or the
end of his Yankee days. When Dickey first came up,
Benny Benbaugh wore number eight. When he came
back to coach, Yogi Berra was wearing it.

Dickey's quiet demeanor off the field belied fiery
behavior behind the plate. On July 4, 1932 he was
suspended for 30 days and fined $1,000 for breaking
the jaw of the Senators' Carl Reynolds with one
punch, after a collision at home plate. In the 1934
All-Star Game, Dickey broke Carl Hubbell's strikeout string with a single. After six straight .300-plus
seasons, Dickey dipped to .279 in 1935, but came
back the next season with a fury. From 1936 to
1939, Dickey, who had never hit more than 14
homers in a season, belted 102 in four years. He had
a career high of 29 in 1937, including grand slams
on consecutive days, August 3 and 4. His batting
average bloomed as well, with a career-high .362 in
1936, followed by a .332 mark in 1937.

Dickey continued his batting onslaught in the
second game of the 1936 World Series against the
crosstown Giants when he hit a two-run homer and
knocked in five runs. On July 26, 1939 he slammed
three straight homers against the Browns in a 14–1
win. In the four-game World Series sweep that year
against the Reds, Dickey slammed two homers and
drove in five runs, including the winning run in the
bottom of the ninth in Game One. Dickey also

Bill Dickey

caught more World Series games than any catcher, 38.

Both Dickey's average and power dropped drastically in 1940 and 1941, totaling only 16 homers in two years. In 1942, Dickey caught only 82 games, and only 85 in 1943, but drove in the only two runs with a homer in the fifth and final game of the World Series against the Cardinals, avenging the Yankees' loss the year before. At the end of the season, at age 36, Dickey enlisted in the Navy. He came back for a final go-round in 1946, but appeared in only 54 games. Midway through the season, he took over the managerial reins from Joe McCarthy, who had gone to manage the Red Sox. He guided the Yankees to a 57–48 mark, but resigned right after the season. He came back as a coach under Casey Stengel from 1947 to 1957, passing along his knowledge to Berra. He scouted for the Yankees in 1959 before retiring. /(SEW)

George H. Dickinson — Unk.-1937. *Writer.*

Dickinson was sports editor of the New York *Herald* in its heyday, and his support in publicizing the Brotherhood helped get the Players' League off the ground in 1890. His knowledge of telegraphy helped him to a scoop when he picked up news of a big deal going over the wire in a hotel lobby. He was later managing editor of the New York *Evening Telegram.*/(NLM)

Emerson Dickman — 1914–1981. RHP 1936–41 **Red Sox** 349 ip, 22-15, 5.33

The two-sport star at Washington and Lee University was regularly ribbed for his resemblance to movie star Robert Taylor. His career in the Red Sox bullpen was curtailed by military service in WWII. He later coached at Princeton. /(NLM)

Johnny Dickshot [born John Oscar Dicksus] — 1910- . OF 1936-39, 44-45 Pirates, Giants, **White Sox** 322 g, .276, 7 hr, 116 rbi

A part-timer until 1945, Dickshot was Chicago's everyday left fielder that season; he batted .302, third-best in the AL, and finished fifth with 18 stolen bases./(TJ)

Jim Dickson — 1938- . RHP 1963-66 Astros, Red, **A's** 142 ip, 5-3, 4.36

Although Dickson came up briefly in 1963 with Houston, his first full season was 1965 with the A's. The hard thrower came out of the bullpen 68 times that summer to establish an AL rookie record. His 5.35 ERA in 1966 ended his ML career. /(RTM)

Murry Dickson — 1916- . RHP 1939-40, 42-43, 46-59 Cardinals, **Pirates**, Phillies, A's, Yankees 3052 ip, 172-181, 3.66. 20 wins: 51 *3 WS, 19 ip, 0-1, 3.86* ☛ *All-Star—53.*

Since his six-pitch repertoire required much experimentation, Dickson came to be called "the Thomas Edison of the mound." He pitched in the 1943 WS while on furlough from the army. Topping the NL with a .714 winning percentage in 1946, his 15–6 record included the Cardinals' pennant-clinching playoff victory over Brooklyn. Sold to Pittsburgh in January 1949, Dickson had a career-high 20 wins in 1951. He led the league in losses three straight years (1952–54), losing 60 games over that span. Dickson received credit for the save in the 1953 All-Star Game. /(TJ)

Walt Dickson (Hickory) — 1878-1918. RHP 1910, 12-15 Giants, Braves, **Pittsburgh (FL)** 700 ip, 25-52, 3.60

Dickson had little success in either the National or Federal Leagues. He was 3–19 for the 1912 Braves and led the Feds with 21 losses for Pittsburgh in 1914. He led the Texas League in ERA (1.06) in 1916. /(ME)

Bob Didier — 1949- . C 1969-74 **Braves**, Tigers, Red Sox 247 g, .229, 0 hr, 51 rbi. *1 LCS, 3 g, .000*

The switch-hitting son of longtime baseball scout Mel Didier, Bob was named to the Topps ML rookie all-star team in 1969, when he hit .256 for Atlanta in his only season as a regular. He became an Oakland coach in 1984./(TJ)

Chuck Diering [Charles Edward Allen] — 1923- . OF 1947-52, 54-56 **Cardinals**, Giants, Orioles 752 g, .249, 14 hr, 141 rbi

Signed by his hometown Cardinals in 1941, Diering's most active year with St. Louis was 1949, when he hit .263 in 131 games. In December 1951, Diering and Max Lanier were traded to the Giants for Eddie Stanky. A late-inning defensive replacement in New York, Diering had only 23 at-bats in 1952. In 1954, Baltimore's first season, Diering was named the most valuable Oriole, batting .258./(RTM)

Larry Dierker — 1946- . RHP 1964-77 **Astros**, Cardinals 2334 ip, 139-123, 3.30. 20 wins: 69 ☛ *All-Star—69, 71.*

Larry Dierker used his fastball, curveball, screwball, slider, and changeup to reach double figures in victories nine times, and in 1969 became the first Astro to win 20. Coveted by 18 ML teams, the 6'4" Hollywood, CA native signed with Houston and debuted on his 18th birthday. His 1967 campaign was shortened by military service, and in 1973 he suffered a shoulder injury. On July 9, 1976 Dierker no-hit the Expos; the Montreal manager was Karl Kuehl, who had signed him. "I didn't think I would ever do it," exclaimed Dierker upon finally pitching a no-hitter after four near-misses. He left the Astros in 1976 as their career leader in virtually every pitching department. /(TJ)

Bill Dietrich (Bullfrog) — 1910–1978. RHP 1933–48 A's, Senators, **White Sox** 2004 ip, 108–128, 4.48

Though Dietrich was a Philadelphia product, the Athletics' Connie Mack waived him to Washington in 1936, believing he would never gain control. Unable to see without his glasses, Dietrich was a stubborn fireballer with streaks of wildness. He often hurt himself by getting frustrated by late-inning walks and hits, or by teammates' errors. He improved his control in his 10-plus seasons with the White Sox, but was never a strikeout pitcher, and rarely a winner. Yet on June 1, 1937 he no-hit the Browns, 8–0. Believing a seventh-inning error had been ruled a hit, he did not know what he had accomplished until his teammates mobbed him after the last out. He won a career-high 16 games in 1944 while losing 17, tops in the AL. /(DB)

Dick Dietz (Mule) — 1941– . C 1966–73 **Giants**, Dodgers, Braves 646 g, .261, 66 hr, 301 rbi. *1 LCS, 4 g, .067*
☛ *All-Star—70.*

Signing for $90,000 in 1963, Dietz and his roommate, fellow bonus catcher Randy Hundley, became known as "The Gold Dust Twins." Called up late in 1966, he hit a 410-foot homer off Sandy Koufax. Playing just 56 games in 1967, he was named the Topps all-star rookie catcher, but didn't become a regular until 1970. That year, he peaked in every offensive category (.300, 22 HR, 107 RBI), and homered in the ninth inning of the All-Star Game. Beaned in mid-1971, Dietz played down the stretch in a tight race with L.A. with his head heavily bandaged. When the Giants clinched, Dietz grabbed a radio microphone to shout, "The Dodgers can go to hell!" Because of a clerical error, the Giants lost Dietz to the Dodgers in 1972, but he broke his finger in his first start for Los Angeles. /(MC)

Dutch Dietz — 1912–1972. RHP 1940–43 **Pirates**, Phillies 295 ip, 14–16, 3.87

The reliever led Pittsburgh in winning percentage (.778, 7–2) and ERA (2.33) as a 29-year-old rookie in 1941. Dietz was the most active Pirate reliever in '41 and '42. /(ME)

Martin Dihigo

Martin Dihigo — 1905–1971. 2B-RHP-OF-SS-3B-1B-C-MGR Negro Leagues 1923–36, 45 Cuban Stars (East), New York Cubans, Homestead Grays, Philadelphia Hilldale, Darby Daisies 405 g, .297, 62 hr (inc.); 218–106
☛ *Led League—hr 26 (ECL), 35 (NNL). All-Star—35, 45. Hall of Fame—1977.*

Martin Dihigo, a 6'3" 210-lb righthanded Cuban, was one of the most versatile players of all time. His incredible skills gained him the unique honor of being elected to the Mexican, Cuban, and American Halls of Fame. Endowed with great speed and an exceptionally strong arm, Dihigo was a star performer at every position.

Dihigo began his American career in 1923 at the age of 18, playing first base with the touring Cuban Stars. He played in America from 1923 until 1936. After 1936 he played his summer ball in Mexico, except in 1945 when he was the player-manager of the New York Cubans. He reportedly continued to play in the Mexican Leagues until the 1950s, although his statistics are available only through 1947.

Statistics documenting Dihigo's American career exist for 1923–31, 1935–36, and 1945. In those 12 years, Dihigo hit over .300 six times, including .325 in 1926 with a league-leading 11 home runs in 40 games, and .333 in 1935 with a league-leading 9 home runs in 42 games. His overall American statistics show a .295 career batting average and a 6–1 record as a pitcher in 1931.

Dihigo was primarily a pitcher in Latin America, where he was known for his blazing fastball. His Mexican League totals show a lifetime .317 batting average in 10 seasons (1937–44, 1946–47), including a league-leading .387 in 1938. He was 119–57 as a pitcher in Mexico, going 18–2 with a 0.90 ERA in 1938 and 22–7 with a league-leading 2.53 ERA in 1942. He threw the first no-hitter in Mexican League history, and also had no-hitters in Venezuela and Puerto Rico.

Dihigo played for 24 seasons in Cuba (1922–29, 1931–46). The record of his Cuban career is somewhat fragmentary, but for the years which are documented (1922–29, 1931, 1935–46), he hit over .300 nine times, finishing with a lifetime .291 batting average. As a pitcher he was 93–48 in 1935–46.

Statistics exist for one year of play in the Dominican Republic (1937), when Dihigo hit .351.

Combining his Dominican, American, Cuban and Mexican statistics results in a lifetime .302 batting average with 130 home runs (11 seasons worth of home run totals are missing) and a 218–106 (.673) pitching mark. Dihigo often showed his versatility in Negro League competition by playing all nine positions in the course of a single game.

Known for his warm, friendly personality, Dihigo was a national hero in his native Cuba, where he served as Minister of Sport in his later years. He was elected posthumously to the American baseball Hall of Fame in 1977. In a poll conducted in the early 1980s among ex-Negro League players and other experts on black baseball, Dihigo gathered votes as best all-time outfielder and third baseman, and was voted to the first team all-time black all-star team as a second baseman. /(JJM)

Steve Dillard — 1951– . 2B-3B-SS 1975–82 Red Sox, Tigers, **Cubs**, White Sox 438 g, .243, 13 hr, 102 rbi

A good-fielding utility man, Dillard never played more than 60 games at one position in a season. /(JFC)

Bob Dillinger — 1918– . 3B 1946–51 **Browns**, A's, Pirates, White Sox 753 g, .306, 10 hr, 213 rbi
☛ *All-Star—49.*

Dillinger led the AL in hits in 1948 and in stolen bases three consecutive years (1947–49). After batting .292 in 1951, Dillinger retired at age 33, claiming to have lost interest in the game. /(DQV)

Bill Dillman — 1945– . RHP 1967, 70 **Orioles**, Expos 155 ip, 7–12, 4.53

Dillman pitched five no-hit innings for Baltimore versus the A's in his ML debut, and won his first four decisions before the hitters caught up with his strictly fastball-curveball repertoire. /(MC)

Frank Dillon (Pop) — 1873–1931. 1B 1899–1902, 04 Pirates, Tigers, Orioles, **Dodgers** 312 g, .252, 1 hr, 116 rbi

On opening day of the AL's first season (4/25/01), Dillon led the Tigers to their first victory by becoming the first AL batter to hit four doubles in one game. Early in the 1902 season, he was sent to Los Angeles of the Pacific Coast League, where he became a hitting star. The adept hit-and-run man was captain of the Brooklyn Dodgers in 1904, then returned to Los Angeles to become player-manager for 11 seasons. In 2,175 minor league games, he averaged .295. /(TG)

Miguel Dilone [born Miguel Angel Reyes Reyes] — 1954– . OF 1974–85 Pirates, A's, **Indians**, White Sox, Expos, Padres 800 g, .265, 6 hr, 129 rbi

This free-swinging Dominican singles hitter stole 267 bases in his career, with a season-best 61 for the Indians in 1980, third in the AL. Dilone (pronounced de-lo-NAY) spent four seasons trying unsuccessfully to break into the Pirates' outfield. In 1977 he set a since-broken NL record for the most steals in a season without being caught, 12. He finally got some playing time with the A's in 1978, and he stole 50 bases, fourth in the AL. He was also caught stealing 23 times. Dilone hit just .229 that year and scored 34 runs in 258 at-bats. He was sold to the Cubs in mid-1979 and Cleveland bought him at the end of the season.

Dilone's stolen base percentage in 1980 was much better (61-for-79), and he had career highs in BA (.341, third in the AL) and runs (82), but walked only 28 times in 528 at-bats. He never again got as much playing time. /(WOR)

Dom DiMaggio (The Little Professor) — 1917– . OF 1940–42, 46–53 **Red Sox** 1,399 g, .298, 87 hr, 618 rbi.
1 WS, 7 g, .259, 3 rbi
☛ *All-Star—41–42, 46, 49–52.*

The youngest and smallest of the three DiMaggio brothers, the bespectacled centerfielder was a perennial All-Star with the Red Sox for 11 seasons, missing three years of his prime because of WWII. Twice DiMaggio, together with Ted Williams, was part of a .300-hitting outfield, once in his rookie year of 1940 with Doc Cramer in right field, and

Dom DiMaggio with the San Francisco Seals of the Pacific Coast League

again 10 years later in 1950 with Al Zarilla in right. A slick fielder, fans used to yell that he played his own position as well as the slow-footed Williams's spot in left field. DiMaggio set the pace for consistency, hitting in 34 straight games in 1949, and another 27 straight in 1951, and scored more than 100 runs seven times. In the 1946 Series, he scored the deciding run in Game Five to give the Red Sox a 3–2 edge in the Series, eventually lost in seven games to the Cardinals on Enos Slaughter's dash for home. Twice DiMaggio led the league in at-bats from his leadoff spot, and twice in runs scored. He shared the outfield with brother Joe in three All-Star games, and drove him in with a single in the 1941 game. /(SEW)

Joe DiMaggio (Joltin' Joe, The Yankee Clipper) — 1914– . OF 1936–42, 46–51 **Yankees** 1736 g, .325, 361 hr, 1537 rbi. *10 WS, 51 g, .271, 8 hr, 30 rbi* ☛ *Most Valuable Player—39, 41, 47. Led League—ba 39–40. Led League—hr 37, 48. Led League—rbi 41, 48. All-Star—36–42, 46–51. Hall of Fame—1955.*

During the centennial celebration of professional baseball, Joe DiMaggio was named the game's greatest living player. Since that 1969 assessment,

DiMaggio's legend has grown with the fans who made it. He remained a top-drawer celebrity almost 40 years after playing his final game.

The Yankee Clipper could do everything well. He may have been the best all-around player ever, with a generous dash of class added in. His natural talent became apparent in 1933 when he batted safely in 61 consecutive games playing for his hometown San Francisco Seals in the Pacific Coast League. Scouts flocked to see him, but they shied away when DiMaggio injured a knee. The Yankees' interest continued, however, and a deal was arranged in 1934 that allowed DiMaggio to play one more year with the Seals. He came to New York in 1936 and set AL rookie records for runs (132) and triples (15), besides hitting .323 with 29 HR and 125 RBI. He was an instant star.

DiMaggio was a beautiful hitter with a classic swing. He had an exceptionally wide stance that gave him a controlled short stride, strong wrists that generated enormous power, and the ability to wait until the last instant before lashing into a pitch. His 46 homers in 1937, including a ML-record 15 in July, remain a Yankee record for a righthanded hitter. What makes his HR total more impressive is that he played half his games at Yankee Stadium, then the toughest power park in baseball for righties. At the time left-centerfield, known as "Death Valley", extended 457 feet from the plate. DiMaggio also hit as high as .381 in 1939, and struck out only 369 times in his career while hitting 361 homers, a phenomenal ratio for a power hitter.

But DiMaggio was more than a hitter. He was a splendid defensive outfielder with a great throwing arm. He made tough plays look easy. He was graceful and free of theatrics, and he was positioned correctly all the time. He was studious. His positioning encompassed the batter, the pitcher, and the count. He was always alert to the game situation, and always threw to the correct base. He was virtually flawless in 1947, making one lone error on the year. And to his manager, Joe McCarthy, he was "the best base runner I ever saw." DiMaggio was the quiet, undemonstrative type McCarthy liked. He was introspective, sometimes stoic. But he was a leader all the same, steering the Yankees to nine World Championships.

DiMaggio had two major league careers, one before World War II and the other after it. In each year of the former (1936–42) he hit over .300 and exceeded 100 RBI. This was the time of his magical 56-game hitting streak. The "impossible" streak—traveling a dozen games beyond Wee Willie Keeler's 1897 consecutive-game record of 44 and 15

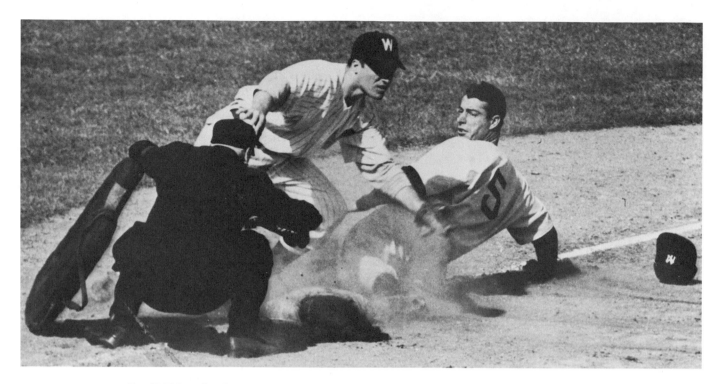

Joe DiMaggio, Senators third baseman Eddie Yost, umpire George McQuinn

games beyond what had been the modern record, George Sisler's 41-game string of 1922—began on May 15, 1941. It kept an entire nation enthralled through June and half of July, before two great plays by Cleveland third baseman Ken Keltner ended it on July 17. DiMaggio hit .407 during the streak and edged Boston's Ted Williams for the AL MVP award, even though Williams hit .406 that year.

The war took three prime years from DiMaggio's baseball life. His second career was beset by injuries and then eroding skills. But he was still DiMaggio. Boston claimed an easy pennant in 1946, but there would be no Red Sox dynasty. The Yankees were World Champions in 1947, 1949, 1950, and 1951. Even while playing most of 1948 with a painful heel injury, DiMaggio almost brought the Yankees home. The Yankees lost out to the Red Sox and Indians on the next-to-last day of the season, but DiMaggio led the league in home runs (39) and RBI (155).

DiMaggio's career seemed over in 1949. He was unable to stand on his sore heel without pain and, of course, was unable to play. One miraculous June morning, the pain was gone, and DiMaggio made a spectacular return. After missing the season's first 65 games, he led the Yankees to a three-game sweep of

the Red Sox at Fenway Park with four homers and nine RBI. His brother Dom, a Red Sox star, witnessed the display (another brother, Vince, also was a major leaguer).

Many experts consider Joe DiMaggio the best player in the history of the game. He is admired not only for his achievements but for his refusal to rest on his natural skills, working instead to constantly improve his play. He was responsible to himself, his teammates, and his fans. He had pride. He was more than an exceptional athlete; he was the consummate professional. /(MG)

Vince DiMaggio — 1912– . OF 1937–46 Braves, Reds, **Pirates**, Phillies, Giants 1110 g, .249, 125 hr, 584 rbi ☞ *All-Star—43–44.*

The oldest of the three DiMaggios, Vince was a good fielder and baserunner, but could not hit like Joe or Dom. Six times he led the league in striking out, and in 1938 set a ML record by fanning 134 times (a mark frequently surpassed since). He reached highs of 21 HR and 100 RBI for the Pirates in 1941, and hit four grand slams for the Phillies in 1945. He played in two All-Star Games and collected a homer, triple, and single in the 1943 contest. As a centerfielder, he led the NL in assists three times and putouts twice. Vince had a long minor league career, including four years as a player-manager. /(LRD)

Lou DiMuro — 1931–1982. *Umpire* AL 1963–80, 82 *3 LCS 2 WS, 4 ASU*

Affectionately called "Pops" by those who knew him, DiMuro was struck by a car and killed in Arlington, Texas, shortly after umpiring a twi-nite White Sox-Rangers game. He was beset by accidents throughout his career. In May 1979 the Yankees' Cliff Johnson crashed into him in a play at the plate and sidelined him for most of the season. Two years later he suffered a sprained back and severe bruises when he slipped and fell in the Milwaukee visitors' dugout during a rain delay. Ironically, his umpiring career began due to an injury; he had broken a finger while playing baseball in the Air Force and turned to umpiring to remain active. /(RTM)

Bill Dineen (Big Bill) — 1876–1955. RHP 1898–09 Washington NL, Braves, **Red Sox**, Browns 3074 ip, 171–177, 3.01. 20 wins: 00, 02–04 *1 WS, 35 ip, 3–1, 2.06.*
    Umpire AL 1909–37 *8 WS, 1 ASU*

Dineen won 20 games for the 1900 Braves but really came into his own when he jumped to the Red Sox in 1902. He had three straight seasons of 21 or more wins. The hero of the 1903 WS, he won three of four decisions. Two of his victories, including the final game, were shutouts. In 1905, he pitched a no-hitter against the White Sox. Dineen went directly from pitching in the AL to umpiring in the league. During his 29 years as an AL umpire, he worked in 45 WS games. During the early 1930s, the AL gave a cash prize to the umpire with the lowest average time for his games. The winner was Dineen. /(RTM)

Frank DiPino — 1956– . LHP 1981– Brewers, **Astros**, Cubs, Cardinals 592 ip, 29–35, 3.69

DiPino threw a seven-inning, Eastern League no-hitter for Holyoke as a Milwaukee farmhand on June 8, 1980. Acquired in a 1982 trade for Don Sutton, DiPino led the Astros in saves in 1983 (20) and 1984 (14). He struggled with control in 1985, and, with Dave Smith's emergence as a closer, was dealt to the Cubs for Davey Lopes in 1986. He went 9–0 in 1989 as a middle reliever for the Cardinals. /(JCA)

Dizzy Dismukes [William] — 1890–1961. RHP-MGR Negro Leagues 1913–50 Philadelphia Giants, Brooklyn Royal Giants, Mohawk Giants, **Indianapolis ABC's**, Chicago American Giants, Dayton Marcos, Pittsburgh Keystones, Memphis Red Sox, St. Louis Stars, Cincinnati Dismukes, Detroit Wolves, Homestead Grays, Columbus Blue Birds, Birmingham Black Barons, Kansas City Monarchs 26–22 (inc.)

Dismukes had a 37-year career in Negro League baseball that spanned all aspects of the game. He began in 1913 as a submarine pitcher with the Philadelphia Giants and played until the early 1930s. He then spent 20 years as a coach, manager, team business manager, and, ultimately, secretary of the Negro National League. While overseas during WWI, he reputedly taught major leaguer Carl Mays how to pitch.

   One of the top black pitchers of the 1910s, Dismukes pitched the Brooklyn Royal Giants to the Eastern Negro Championship in 1914, then started three times in the four-game Black World Series against the Chicago American Giants. The Royal Giants lost the series, but no record of Dismukes's efforts remain. His most productive years as a pitcher were spent with the Indianapolis ABC's. He appeared with them in three games of the 1916 Black World Series, starting two and going 1–1. He was 11–6 for the ABC's in 1920, the first year of his career. The five-time 20-game winner notched a creer-high 30 victories in 1961. From 1958 through 1964, he never worked fewer than 44 games or 263 innings a season. /(MC)

Art Ditmar — 1929– . RHP 1954–62 A's, **Yankees** 1268 ip, 72–77, 3.98. *3 WS, 11 ip, 0–2, 3.18*

After leading the AL with 22 losses with the 1956 A's, the rubber-armed Ditmar went to the Yankees in a nine-player deal. He won 28 games for the 1959–60 Yankees, then unexpectedly plummeted.

   Manager Casey Stengel's decision to start Ditmar over ace Whitey Ford in Game One of the 1960 World Series has been second-guessed by many, since Ditmar retired only one batter while giving up three runs in the Pirates' 6–4 win. Deprived of the chance to pitch three times, Ford threw shutouts in the third and sixth games, but Pittsburgh triumphed in seven. Ditmar was bombed again in Game Five. When a Budweiser TV commercial of the mid-1980s incorporated the original radio broadcast of Game Seven, with announcer Chuck Thompson erroneously naming Ditmar instead of Ralph Terry as the pitcher off whom Bill Mazeroski hit his famous home run, Ditmar sued Anheuser-Busch for $500,000, saying his reputation was tarnished. /(RTM)

Jack Dittmer — 1928- . 2B 1952-57 **Braves**, Tigers 395 g, .232, 24 hr, 136 rbi

A hot lefthanded-hitting minor leaguer, Dittmer reached his ML peak batting .266 as the 1953 Braves' regular second baseman, but was a part-timer thereafter. /(RTM)

Ken Dixon — 1960- . RHP 1984-87 **Orioles** 482 ip, 26-28, 4.66

Dixon looked to have a long future with the Orioles after his 8-4 (3.67) rookie 1985 season. He had a 90-mph fastball and a major league curve. But after being hit hard in 1987, falling to 7-10 (6.43), he was dealt to Seattle for Mike Morgan in a trade of two disappointing righthanders. The Mariners were unhappy with Dixon's velocity when they released him in spring training of 1988. Dixon filed a grievance against the club, saying he was released after he hurt his shoulder that spring. The Mariners said Dixon was injured before joining them. /(JCA)

Rap Dixon [Herbert Albert] — 1902-1945. OF 1922-37 Harrisburg, Baltimore, Chicago, Darby, Pittsburgh, Philadelphia, Brooklyn, New York Cubans, Newark, Homestead, Washington statistics not available

Dixon was a slugging outfielder who played on many of the great Negro League teams of the 1920s and 1930s. He combined power, average, and speed to pose a triple threat. His range and fine throwing arm made him a top defensive outfielder. He played hard and was known as a ferocious slider.

In 1929 Dixon played with the Baltimore Black Sox, Negro American League champions. He batted .382 with seven home runs, and led the league with six triples. In 1930, taking part in the first game played between black teams in Yankee Stadium, Dixon launched three HR into the right field seats. In 1932, he became part of one of the finest black teams ever assembled, Gus Greenlee's barnstorming Pittsburgh Crawfords. Playing beside Hall of Famers Satchel Paige, Oscar Charleston, Judy Johnson, Josh Gibson, and Cool Papa Bell, Dixon held his own, batting .343 with 15 HR.

Dixon was selected to the inaugural East-West all-star game, in 1933, and in it stole a base, scored two runs, and had an RBI. He helped the Philadelphia Stars capture the Negro National League championship in 1934. He hit .344 in 1935, his last year as a regular. In 26 games against white major leaguers, he compiled a .372 average. /(ETW)

Sonny Dixon [John Craig] — 1924- . RHP 1953-56 **Senators**, A's, Yankees 263 ip, 11-18, 4.17

Dixon, mainly a relief pitcher, led the AL in appearances (54) in a 1954 campaign split between Washington and Philadelphia. /(WOR)

Tom Dixon — 1955- . RHP 1977-79, 83 **Astros**, Expos 200 ip, 9-14, 4.33

Dixon debuted with a five-hitter over the Cardinals on August 6, 1977. He was 7-11 in 30 games for Houston in 1978, but erratic control shortened his ML stay. /(MC)

Bill Doak (Spittin' Bill) — 1891-1954. RHP 1912-24, 1927-29 Reds, **Cardinals**, Dodgers 2783 ip, 170-157, 2.98. 20 wins: 14, 20
☛ *Led League—era 14, 21.*

Doak joined St. Louis at age 22 and spent over 11 years as a dependable pitcher with generally lackluster Cardinal teams. In his sophomore 1914 season, he went 20-6 with a NL-low 1.72 ERA, boosting the Cards to their best record up to that time. The spitballer's 20 wins in 1920 weren't enough to keep St. Louis from finishing fifth. The next year, Doak's .714 winning percentage (15-6) and 2.59 ERA led all NL hurlers. When Doak followed with losing seasons in 1922-23, Branch Rickey dealt the veteran to Brooklyn in mid-1924. Doak went 11-5 the remainder of that campaign, then voluntarily retired. He returned in 1927, and posted an 11-8 record with the Dodgers before fading and ending his career back with St. Louis in 1929. Doak remains among the Cardinals' top ten all-time in eight pitching categories, with his 32 shutouts ranking second only to Bob Gibson's 56. /(DQV)

Masayuki Dobashi — 1938- . P 1956-68 **Toei Flyers** 162-162, 2.64

Pitching for Tokyo's "other" team, the lackluster Toei Flyers, Dobashi never received the publicity accorded to stars of the crosstown rival Giants. That's how the shy and guarded hurler preferred it. A deadpan stoic on the mound, the five-time 20-game winner notched a career-high 30 victories in 1961. From 1958 through 1964, he never worked fewer than 44 games or 263 innings a season. /(MC)

John Dobbs — 1876-1934. OF 1901-05 Reds, Cubs, **Dodgers** 582 g, .263, 7 hr, 207 rbi

A strong-armed centerfielder with a weak bat, Dobbs had a short ML career. He managed 25 years in the minors, 23 in the Southern Association, and compiled a .563 winning percentage and six league championships. He was co-owner of the Charlotte team of the Piedmont League at his death. /(TG)

Chuck Dobson [Charles Thomas] — 1944– . RHP 1966–71, 73–75 **A's**, Angels 1258 ip, 74–69, 3.78

Kansas City scout Whitey Herzog had only to look in the A's backyard to find Dobson, a 6'4" fireballer. Dobson threw a Northwest League no-hitter his first pro season (1965), but was disabled much of his rookie 1966 season with a rotator cuff strain. He returned to win in double figures for five straight ML seasons. In 1970, Dobson led the AL with 40 starts, going 16–15. He was on his way to 20 wins in 1971 with a 15–5 record in August, but recurring shoulder problems cut short his season, and eventually ended his career. /(MC)

Joe Dobson (Burrhead) — 1917– . RHP 1939–43, 46–54 Indians, **Red Sox**, White Sox 2170 ip, 137–103, 3.62. *1 WS, 12.2 ip, 1–0, 0.00*
☛ *All-Star—48.*

The youngest of 14 children, Dobson grew up in the heart of the Depression dustbowl in Durrant, Texas. At the age of nine, he lost his thumb and left forefinger playing with a dynamite cap. He began his ML career with the Indians and was traded in December 1940 to Boston, where he had his best years. In 1947, he won a career-high 18, with a 2.95 ERA. Over the period 1941–50, with time out in 1944–45 for the military, Dobson was 106–72 for Boston. Traded to the White Sox in December 1950, Dobson turned in his final winning season in 1952 with a 14–10 mark. He finished his steady, unspectacular career with the Red Sox in 1954. /(RL)

Pat Dobson — 1942– . RHP 1967–77 Tigers, Padres, Orioles, Braves, **Yankees**, Indians 2120 ip, 122–129, 3.54. 20 wins: 71 *2 WS, 11 ip, 0–0, 3.97*
☛ *All-Star—72.*

Dobson used a big curveball to become one of the quartet of 20-game winners on the 1971 Orioles, when he went 20–8 with a 2.90 ERA in his first winning season in the majors. He signed with Detroit for a reported $35,000 bonus in 1959 and spent three years with the parent club, pitching mostly in relief. He was traded to the Padres in December 1969 with Dave Campbell for Joe Niekro and attracted the attention of the Orioles by going 14–15 as the ace for last-place San Diego.

Dobson's strong 1971 season earned him a start in Game Four of the World Series, but he gave up 10 hits in 5–1/3 innings, getting a no-decision in the loss, and was in the bullpen for the rest of the Series. Dobson's 2.65 ERA in 1972 was an improvement from his 20-win season, but he went 16–18 and tied for the AL lead in losses (only one member of the quartet, Jim Palmer, repeated as a 20-game winner). Traded to the Braves with Davey Johnson after the season, he was then sent to the Yankees in mid-1973 and in 1974 went 19–15 with a 3.07 ERA as the ace of second-place New York. After an off-year in 1975 (11–14, 4.07) he was traded to the Indians for Oscar Gamble and recovered with a 16–12, 3.48 season. But his 3–12, 6.16 record in 1977 ended his career. /(SFS)

Larry Doby — 1923– . OF 1947–59 **Indians**, White Sox, Tigers 1533 g, .283, 253 hr, 969 rbi. *2 WS, 10 g, .237, 1 hr, 2 rbi.*
    Manager 1978 **White Sox** *37–50, .425*
☛ *Led League—hr 52, 54. Led League—rbi 54. All-Star—49–55.*

In August 1947, four months after Jackie Robinson had broken the National League's color line, Larry Doby was signed for the Indians by Bill Veeck (whom he affectionately called his "godfather") and was the first black ballplayer in the American League. "The only difference [was] that Jackie Robinson got all of the publicity," Doby later recalled. "You didn't hear much about what I was going through because the media didn't want to repeat the same story." On the field, Doby noted, "I couldn't react to (prejudicial) situations from a physical standpoint. My reaction was to hit the ball as far as I could." Born in South Carolina, Doby grew up in New Jersey. He attended Long Island University and played in the Negro National League.

In 1948, his first full season, Doby hit 16 HR and contributed a .301 batting average to Cleveland's successful World Championship drive. He batted a team-leading .318 in the 1948 World Series, winning the fourth game with a 400-foot home run off Braves star Johnny Sain. Although he led league outfielders with 14 errors in 1948, he became a good enough fielder to be named by *TSN* as the top centerfielder in the majors in 1950, ahead of Joe DiMaggio and Duke Snider. In 1952 the lefthanded hitter led the AL with 32 HR, 104 runs, and a .541 slugging percentage. Doby topped AL batters in strikeouts two years running (111 in 1952 and 121 in '53).

He played in every All-Star Game from 1949 through 1954, hitting a key homer as a pinch-hitter

Larry Doby

in his last All-Star at-bat. In the Indians' 1954 record-setting 111-win season, his 32 HR and 126 RBI paced the league.

After his ML playing career, he played in Japan and coached for the Expos, Indians, and White Sox. He managed the White Sox for most of 1978; one of his catchers was his namesake, Cleveland native Larry Doby Johnson. /(TJ)

John Dodge — 1889–1916. 3B 1912–13 Phillies, **Reds** 127 g, .215, 4 hr, 48 rbi

Dodge was a fine-fielding third baseman whose hitting was too weak to keep him in the majors. He was playing for Mobile (Southern Association) against Nashville in June 1916 when he was hit in the face with a Tom Rogers pitch. He died the next night. /(JK)

Dodger Stadium [aka Chavez Ravine] Los Angeles Angels 1962–1965, Los Angeles Dodgers 1962– . LF-330, CF-400, RF-330

Built by Dodger owner Walter O'Malley in Chavez Ravine, overlooking downtown Los Angeles,

Dodger Stadium was the last baseball stadium constructed with team capital, and is one of the few modern stadiums to retain some of the atmosphere of smaller classic ballparks. Although it is large (56,000 capacity), Dodger Stadium was built exclusively for baseball, with the multi-decked grandstand extending along the foul lines to provide the best sight lines. The grandstand extends slightly beyond each foul pole before giving way to separate bleacher sections, called pavilions, in both left and right fields, distinctive for their unusual zigzag roofs. In the infield, Dodger Stadium offers some unique field-level box seats, which provide a dugout-level view of the game, and the infield dirt is a mixture of crushed brick and clay with an unusual reddish hue. The outfield fences are symmetrical, and the field is natural grass.

Originally, Dodger Stadium was home to both the Dodgers and the Angels, who called it Chavez Ravine to avoid publicizing their NL rivals, but the Angels moved to Anaheim in 1966, leaving the Dodgers as sole occupants. Deep power alleys (385') and substantial foul territory make Dodger Stadium a pitcher's park, and Dodger pitching staffs are routinely among the NL's best in ERA. In 1963 the unusually high mound was lowered five inches because it gave pitchers too much of an advantage. On September 9, 1965 Sandy Koufax pitched his then-record fourth no-hitter here, a 1–0 perfect game against the Cubs. Only two home runs have ever been hit completely out of the stadium, both by the Pirates' Willie Stargell.

Outside, Dodger Stadium is ringed with massive parking lots, reflecting its Southern California location, where all travel is done by freeway. The Dodgers routinely draw 40,000 fans to a game here, and were the first ML team ever to top three million in total attendance for one season. /(SCL)

Dodger Sym-Phony

The Brooklyn Dodgers, their fans, and their opponents were serenaded for more than twenty years by a small but faithful group of amateur ragtime musicians. Louis "Brother Lou" Soriano, the founder and conductor, played snare drum, Paddy Palma beat the bass drum with "Dodgers Sym-Phony Band" emblazoned on the drumhead, Phil Caccavale played trumpet, Al Alfano was the trombonist, and Pete Della Iacono was on cymbals. Della Iacono, later a deputy New York State boxing commissioner, said the group "moved up and down the aisles, but we always started in Section 8. I think they put us there because in the army, Section 8 was the classification for the guys who were crazy." The group mocked umpires with "Three Blind Mice" (in the days when only three umpires worked a game), played "Who's Sorry Now" or "The Worms Crawl In, the Worms Crawl Out" when opposing pitchers were knocked out, and, for each opposing player who made an out, provided a cymbal crash as he sat down. /(SH)

Bobby Doerr — 1918– . 2B 1937–44, 46–51 **Red Sox** 1865 g, .288, 223 hr, 1247 rbi. *1 WS, 6 g, .409, 1 hr, 3 rbi* ☛ *All-Star—41–44, 46–48, 50–51. Hall of Fame—1986.*

Owner Tom Yawkey had recently spent thousands of dollars to purchase established stars like Joe Cronin, Jimmy Foxx, and Lefty Grove in an effort to rebuild the forlorn Red Sox. But future Hall of Famer Bobby Doerr arrived as a 19-year-old rookie in 1937, having played pro ball since 1934. He was signed by Eddie Collins on the same scouting trip that netted Ted Williams. As the team's established second baseman in 1938, Doerr batted .289 and

never hit below .270 in his next 13 seasons with the Red Sox, his only ML team. In those years Doerr thrice topped .300 and led the league in slugging in 1944. Doerr played in eight All Star games. During his career his chief rivals in all-round second base play were the fading Charlie Gehringer of the Tigers and Joe Gordon of the Yankees.

Although generally ineffective at bat in All-Star play, Doerr was a tower of strength in his only World Series appearance. Returning from military service, Doerr helped the Red Sox land the 1946 pennant by batting .271 with 18 homers and 116 RBI. In the World Series that year, Doerr batted .406 with a homer and three RBI to pace the Red Sox in their losing seven-game struggle with the Cardinals.

Retiring after the 1951 season, Doerr later served the Red Sox as a coach and was still active as a coach with the 1980 Toronto Blue Jays. In 1986 Doerr was voted into the Hall of Fame by the Veterans Committee. /(DV)

Bobby Doerr making a force play

Ed Doheny — 1874–1916. LHP 1895–1903 **Giants,** Pirates 1393 ip, 75–83, 3.75

A Boston writer earned $100 in 1895 for tipping off Giants owner Andrew Freedman about Doheny, who was pitching for St. Albans, VT (Northern League). In seven seasons, Doheny was never a winner for New York, as the club only once finished higher than seventh. Traded to the Pirates in mid-season 1901, he overcame his control problems and went 16–4 for the 1902 pennant winners; his .800 winning percentage was the second-best in the NL. The Pirates repeated in 1903, and his 16–8, .667 mark was the fifth-best NL winning percentage. /(NLM)

Cozy Dolan [Patrick Henry] — 1872–1907. OF-LHP 1895–96, 1900–06 **Braves,** Cubs, Dodgers, White Sox, Reds 830 g, .269, 10 hr, 315 rbi; 255 ip, 12–13, 4.44

Dolan was dropped to the minors after failing as a Braves pitcher in 1895–96, but resurfaced as an outfielder in 1900. He was sold back to Boston in 1905, and died of typhoid on a spring training trip in 1907, prompting the cancellation of the remainder of the Braves' camp. /(JK)

Cozy Dolan [Albert J, born James Alberts] — 1889–1958. OF-3B 1909, 11–15, 22 Reds, Yankees, Phillies, Pirates, **Cardinals,** Giants 378 g, .252, 7 hr, 111 rbi

Dolan was a utility man who played most regularly in the outfield of the 1914–15 Cardinals. He was a Giants coach in 1924 when he was banned from baseball for game-fixing. New York outfielder Jimmy O'Connell accused him of instigating O'Connell's attempt to bribe Philadelphia shortstop Heinie Sand. /(TJ)

Joe Dolan — 1873–1938. SS-2B-3B 1896–97, 1899–1901 Louisville (NL), **Phillies,** A's 323 g, .214, 6 hr, 122 rbi

Utility infielder Dolan played a career-high 108 games for both Philadelphia clubs in 1901, but hit only .203 and was gone from the ML the next year. He became a railroad flagman in Omaha. /(JK)

Jiggs Donahue — 1879–1913. 1B-C 1900–02, 04–09 Pirates, Brewers, Browns, **White Sox,** Senators 813 g, .255, 5 hr, 327 rbi. *1 WS, 6 g, .333, 4 rbi*

Released by the Browns as a catcher in 1902, Donahue held the Chicago first base job for five seasons, three times leading the AL in fielding, 1905–1907. Though a notoriously poor hitter, Jiggs was one of only three White Sox starters to bat over

.250 for the 1906 World Champion "Hitless Wonders," and paced all batters with a .333 mark in the WS. In Detroit on May 31, 1908 the fancy fielder recorded 21 putouts in a nine-inning game. Donahue contracted syphilis, and died in 1913. He was survived by a brother, Pat, an AL catcher in the years 1908–10. /(RL)

Red Donahue [Francis Rostell] — 1873–1913. RHP 1893, 1895–1906 Giants, Cardinals, **Phillies,** Browns, Indians, Tigers 2975 ip, 167–173, 3.61. 20 wins: 99, 01–02

Donahue led the NL in games, starts, and complete games for last-place St. Louis in 1897 and lost a league-high 33 games with a bloated 6.13 ERA. With the Phillies the next year he no-hit the Braves 5–0 on July 8 and then won 20 games three times between 1899 and 1902. /(JK)

Tim Donahue — 1870–1902. C 1891, 95–1900, 02 Boston (AA), **Cubs,** Senators 466 g, .236, 2 hr, 163 rbi

Donahue, who played all but seven of his ML games with Chicago, led NL catchers with 16 double plays in 1898. However, his fielding throughout his career averaged 35 points lower than that of league leaders. /(FIC)

Atley Donald (Swampy) — 1910– . RHP 1938–45 **Yankees** 932 ip, 65–33, 3.52. *2 WS, 7 ip, 0–1, 7.71*

Donald was the Yankees' number-four or -five starter for most of his career. He was blessed with the support of New York's tremendous offense and sparkling defense, but was also a good pitcher in his own right. His only losing record, 0–1, came in his two-game call-up in his first season, 1938. In 1939 he was 13–3 with a 3.71 ERA that was nearly a run lower than the league average. His 3.03 ERA in 1940 would have been the third-best in the AL had he been used enough to qualify. He continued to pitch effectively until 1945, when eye and elbow injuries ended his career.

In his only World Series start, Game Four of the 1941 WS, Donald took a no-decision, surrendering four runs in four innings. Nonetheless, the Yankees took a 3–1 Series lead when the Dodgers' Mickey Owen committed his famous passed ball in the ninth inning, allowing a Yankee rally to erupt. Donald took a loss in relief in Game Four of the 1942 Series as the Cardinals handed the Yankees their first losing World Series in 20 years. /(SFS)

John Donaldson — 1943– . 2B 1966–70, 1974 **A's,** Pilots 405 g, .238, 4 hr, 86 rbi

Donaldson pushed Dick Green aside as the A's regular second baseman in 1967, batting a team-high .276 as a 160-lb cleanup hitter. Traded to the Pilots in June 1969, he returned in 1970 and finished as a reserve in Oakland. /(MC)

John Donaldson — 1892–1970. LHP-OF Negro Leagues 1912–32 Tennessee Rats, All-Nations, Chicago American Giants, Indianapolis ABC's, Kansas City Monarchs, Detroit Stars, Brooklyn Royal Giants, Donaldson All-Stars, Los Angeles White Sox .248 (inc.)

In 1915, New York Giants manager John McGraw saw John Donaldson pitch for the All-Nations and remarked, "If Donaldson were a white man, or if the unwritten law of baseball didn't bar Negroes from the major leagues, I would give $50,000 for him and think I was getting a bargain." Donaldson had a sharp-breaking curveball, a lively fastball, and excellent control. He hit his peak with the All-Nations just before WWI. The club, founded in 1912 by J.L. Wilkinson and J.E. Gall, was composed of blacks, whites, Latins, Japanese, Hawaiians, and Native Americans. But it was more than a novelty—it was a competitive, successful team.

Donaldson was reported to have struck out more than 240 batters over a 12-game span in 1916. In one 18-inning game, he struck out 35; in a 12-inning contest, he fanned 27 more. He threw three consecutive no-hitters against semi-pro teams. He led the All-Nations to three victories in four games against that year's Black World Champions, the Indianapolis ABC's. In the fall, the All-Nations beat Rube Foster's Chicago American Giants two games out of three, with Donaldson earning both wins.

The All-Nations disbanded in 1918 when most of their quality players were drafted for WWI. Donaldson went to play for the Detroit Stars. Wilkinson regrouped his troops after the war, renamed them the Kansas City Monarchs, and entered the newly formed Negro National League. Donaldson rejoined the team as a centerfielder and pitcher. The solid rotation of Donaldson, Bullet Rogan, Jose Mendez and Rube Currie formed one of the most feared pitching staffs in the annals of black baseball.

After leaving the Monarchs in 1923, Donaldson formed the John Donaldson All-Stars and toured the Midwest against local and semi-pro teams. He went on to scout for the Chicago White Sox. /(LL)

Augie Donatelli — 1914–Unk. *Umpire* NL 1958–73 *5 WS*

Donatelli flew 18 missions as a tailgunner before being shot down over Europe. While a POW in a German Stalag, he began umpiring softball games. He reached the ML in 1958 and stayed for 24 years. Donatelli was one of the leaders in the formation of the Umpires' Association. He was the plate umpire in Game Four of the 1957 WS when the Braves' Nippy Jones insisted a called ball had really hit him in the foot. Jones proved his case by showing Donatelli the shoe polish on the baseball and was awarded first base. /(RTM)

Mike Donlin (Turkey Mike) — 1878–1933. OF 1899–1906, 08, 11–12, 14 Cardinals, Orioles, Reds, **Giants**, Braves, Pirates 1050 g, .333, 51 hr, 543 rbi. *1 WS, 5 g, .316, 1 rbi*

Donlin became the idol of Giants fans after coming to New York in 1904. A superb hitter, he topped .300 ten times in 12 ML seasons. He hit .356 and scored a league-high 124 runs in 1905, then paced the Giants with six hits in their World Series victory over the Athletics. A broken leg limited him to 37 games in 1906, and he was a season-long holdout the next year. After another strong season in 1908 (.334, 106 RBI), Donlin left baseball for a fling at a vaudeville and movie career. Donlin again announced his retirement when Pittsburgh sold him to the Phillies in 1912, but returned as a pinch hitter with the Giants in 1914. /(DQV)

Blix Donnelly [Sylvester Urban] — 1914–1976. RHP 1944–51 Cardinals, **Phillies**, Braves 692 ip, 27–36, 3.49. *1 WS, 6 ip, 1–0, 0.00*

The highlight of Donnelly's career came in his first major league season when he entered Game Two of the 1944 WS in the eighth inning and pitched four scoreless innings, striking out seven and getting the win when the Cardinals scored in the 11th. Sixty percent of his career appearances came in relief. /(WOR)

Jim Donohue — 1938– . RHP 1961–62 Tigers, **Dodgers**, Twins 155 ip, 6–8, 4.29

Donohue was a Cardinal and Dodger farmhand before Detroit drafted him. Primarily a reliever, he was 5–7 with six saves as a rookie, and 1–1 in his second and final season. /(TJ)

Pete Donohue — 1900–1988. RHP 1921–32 **Reds**, Giants, Indians, Red Sox 2112 ip, 134–118, 3.87. 20 wins: 23, 25, 26
☛ *Led League—w 26.*

Donohue, credited with perfecting the changeup, led the NL once each in wins, starts, complete games, and shutouts, and twice in innings. He beat the Phillies 20 consecutive times between 1921 and August 1925. /(TJ)

Dick Donovan (Tricky Dick) — 1927- . RHP 1950-52, 1954-65 Braves, Tigers, **White Sox**, Senators, Indians 2017 ip, 122-99, 3.67. 20 wins: 62 *1 WS, 8 ip, 0-1, 5.40* ☞ *Led League—era 61.*

A late bloomer, the 6'3" Donovan didn't win a game in four short ML trials with the Braves and Tigers. Traded to the White Sox in 1955, his mastery of the slider made him a 15-game winner. His .727 winning percentage (16-6) led the AL in 1957. With the expansion Senators, his 2.40 ERA was the league low in 1961, but Washington sent him to the Indians in an October trade for Jimmy Piersall. Donovan went 20-10 for Cleveland in 1962, his last winning season. /(DQV)

Patsy Donovan [Patrick Joseph] — 1865-1953. OF 1890-1904, 06-07 Braves, Dodgers, Louisville (AA), Washington (AA), Washington (NL), **Pirates**, Cardinals, Senators 1821 g, .300, 16 hr, 736 rbi.
    Manager 1897, 99, 1901-04, 06-08, 10-11 Pirates, Cardinals, Senators, **Dodgers**, Red Sox 683-878, .438

Born in County Cork, Ireland, Donovan joined the National League in 1890, the year the Players' League incursion created a player shortage. He was

Patsy Donovan

with Louisville and Washington of the American Association in that major league's final season, 1891. After a brief stint with Washington's NL entry in 1892, he starred with the Pirates for eight seasons, notching six consecutive .300 seasons and serving as player-manager in 1897 and 1899.

Dealt to the Cardinals in 1900, Donovan was their player-manager in 1901-03. A good base-stealer, his 45 swipes in 1900 led the NL, and he stole 518 bases lifetime. Being traded to Washington of the American League in 1904 gave him the distinction of playing for three Washington clubs in three major leagues. In 1906-08 he managed the Dodgers, appearing in eight contests in '06 and '07. His last years at the helm came with the 1910-11 Boston Red Sox. Donovan was never on a pennant winner, and his best managerial effort was the 1910 Red Sox' 81 wins, good for fourth place. /(DQV)

Wild Bill Donovan [William Edward] — 1876-1923. RHP 1898-1912, 15-16, 18 Washington (NL), Dodgers, **Tigers**, Yankees 2967 ip, 186-139, 2.69. 20 wins: 01, 07 *3 WS, 50 ip, 1-4, 2.70.*
    Manager 1915-17, 21 **Yankees**, Phillies 251-310, .447
☞ *Led League—w 01.*

Donovan was durable, and needed to be; due to wildness, he threw more pitches than most hurlers. While he led the NL with 25 wins for Brooklyn in 1901, he also led with 152 walks. Wild Bill starred in both major leagues, jumping to Detroit in 1903. His best season (25-4, AL-high .862 winning percentage) turned the Tigers into pennant-winners in 1907, and they repeated in 1908 and '09. But Donovan's results in WS starts were poor, and he won only one of five decisions.

After going 10-9 in 1911, Donovan continued his career in the minor leagues, as a pitcher, coach, and manager. He piloted the Yankees from 1915 to 1917, appearing in several games, and pitched two final games for Detroit in 1918. He also skippered the Phillies for part of 1921. He was killed in a train wreck while riding in a sleeper. As manager of his minor league team, he had claimed a lower berth. Above him slept the business manager, George Weiss, who was uninjured in the wreck, and who became a Hall of Famer as GM of the Yankees and Mets. /(JK)

Red Dooin [Charles Sebastian] — 1879-1952. C 1902-16 **Phillies**, Reds, Giants 1290 g, .240, 10 hr, 344 rbi.
    Manager 1910-14 **Phillies** 392-370, .514

Wild Bill Donovan (l.), Clark Griffith

Dooin was an outstanding defensive catcher for the Phillies during the first decade of the 20th century. Reportedly the first to use papier-mache shin guards, he wore them under his stockings. In 1908, he led all NL catchers in assists. That same year, he was offered a bribe to throw a series to the Giants; he reported it. Named the Phillies' player-manager in 1910, he suffered a broken ankle that season and a broken leg in 1911, ending his days as a regular. He shepherded the Phillies to second place in 1913. A fine singer, he performed with the Dumont Minstrels in Philadelphia. /(NLM)

Mickey Doolan — 1880–1951. SS 1905–16, 1918 **Phillies**, Baltimore (FL), Chicago (FL), Cubs, Giants, Dodgers 1728 g, .230, 15 hr, 554 rbi

Doolan, a dentist, served as Phillie captain and V.P. of the Players' Fraternity, a major leaguers' union. A regular shortstop for 11 seasons, he spent two years in the Federal League with Baltimore and Chicago. /(TJ)

John Dopson — 1963– . RHP 1985, 88– Expos, **Red Sox** 351 ip, 15–21, 3.79

Dopson went 3–11 in 1988 for the Expos despite a fine 3.04 ERA. Traded to the Red Sox after the season in the Spike Owen deal, he received better support and proved to be a good, if inconsistent, number-three starter. He had balk trouble in the American League. /(WOR)

Bill Doran — 1958– . 2B 1982– **Astros** 1056 g, .265, 63 hr, 372 rbi. *1 LCS, 6 g, .222, 1 hr, 3 rbi*

Doran led NL second basemen in assists in his rookie 1983 season and quickly established himself as one of the league's best both defensively and offensively. The pouty-lipped fan favorite proved a consistent offensive threat, with career highs of 16 HR (1987) and 42 steals (1986). His 92 runs in 1986, matching his personal best, helped the Astros win the division title. He had arm troubles in 1988, but nonetheless led NL second basemen in fielding. /(SH)

Harry Dorish (Fritz) — 1921– . RHP 1947–56 Red Sox, Browns, **White Sox**, Orioles 834 ip, 45–43, 3.83

One of the first relief specialists in the post-WWII era, Dorish recorded 44 lifetime saves. He led the league in 1952 with 11 saves for the 1952 White Sox. He bettered that in 1953, when he won 10 and saved 18, but Ellis Kinder led with 27. /(DQV)

Gus Dorner — 1876–1956. RHP 1902–03, 06–09 Indians, Reds, **Braves** 894 ip, 37–69, 3.33

Pitching for the Reds and Braves in 1906, Dorner had a decision in each of his 33 starts, and completed 30 of them; he still led the NL with 26 losses. He later managed in the minors. /(NLM)

Rich Dotson (Dot) — 1959– . RHP 1979– **White Sox**, Yankees 1828 ip, 111–109, 4.16. 20 wins: 83 *1 LCS, 5 ip, 0–1, 10.80*

At the 1977 winter meetings, the Angels sent Dotson, their first-round pick that June, to the White Sox in a headline-grabbing, six-player deal for Brian Downing. Dotson reached Chicago late in 1979, but was unimpressive until 1983, when he became the youngest White Sox pitcher in 70 years to record 20 victories; his 22–7 mark helped Chicago to a division title. Between the '83 and 1984 All-Star Games, he went 25–6. But he missed most of 1985 with a circulatory problem near his right shoulder that required surgery. He struggled back in 1986, did not miss a start, but lost a league-high 17 games with a 5.48 ERA. During the 1987 winter meetings, Chicago sent him to the Yankees for outfielder Dan Pasqua, whom they had long coveted. /(RL)

Abner Doubleday — 1819–1893

In 1905, a commission headed by Al Spalding wrongly credited Doubleday with inventing the game of baseball in in Cooperstown, New York in 1839. Doubleday was actually a cadet at West Point when he was alleged to have mapped out the first baseball diamond, and after graduating in 1842 he enjoyed a distinguished military career. He fought in Mexico as well as the Civil War, eventually becoming a major general.

The commission was convinced of Doubleday's role by the testimony of an elderly gentleman named Abner Graves, who claimed to be a childhood playmate of Doubleday's and present when the game was invented. Graves's story was later "verified" by the discovery of a rotting baseball among his personal effects. That ball became known as "The Doubleday Baseball" and remains on display at the Hall of Fame. Doubleday left behind numerous diaries and never claimed to have invented baseball, yet he remains one of the game's great mythological figures. The annual Hall of Fame Game is played each summer at Doubleday Field in Cooperstown. /(SCL)

Patsy Dougherty [Patrick Henry] — 1876–1940. OF 1902–11 Red Sox, Yankees, **White Sox** 1233 g, .284, 17 hr, 413 rbi. *2 WS, 14 g, .185, 2 hr, 6 rbi*

The brawling Irishman was the first player to hit two home runs in a World Series with a pair for the Red Sox in 1903. After Dougherty engaged in a fistfight with Highlanders Manager Clark Griffith, New York placed him on waivers. White Sox Manager Fielder Jones, who'd earlier discovered Dougherty as a semi-pro, claimed him to bolster the "Hitless Wonders," the 1906 Sox who won the World Championship. He led the AL in stolen bases in 1908 with 47. /(RL)

Phil Douglas (Shufflin' Phil, The Shuffler) — 1890–1952. RHP 1912, 14–15, 17–22 White Sox, Reds, Dodgers, Cubs, **Giants** 1708 ip, 93–93, 2.80

When he was sober and when his spitter was dancing, Douglas was one of the NL's better right-handers. His high point was two sterling Giant victories over the Yankees in the 1921 World Series. His low was banishment from baseball for life by Judge Landis. Befuddled first by a taxing drying-out

regimen and then by a relapse, and demoralized by a John McGraw tongue-lashing, Douglas had written a Cardinals outfielder about an ambiguous offer to quit the Giants in the heat of the 1922 pennant race in return for "an inducement." /(ADS)

Klondike Douglass [William Bigham] — 1872–1953. 1B-C-OF 1896–1904 Cardinals, **Phillies** 747 g, .274, 10 hr, 275 rbi

Douglass came to the majors in 1896 as the Cardinals' left fielder, but fielded only .894, low even for those days, and had poor range. He was primarily a catcher in 1897, and hit .329. He was the everyday first baseman for the Phillies in 1898, and hit .258 with 105 runs scored in his best season. Moved back and forth between catcher and 1B in subsequent seasons, he was never again an everyday player. /(JFC)

Taylor Douthit — 1901– . OF 1923–33 **Cardinals**, Reds, Cubs 1074 g, .291, 29 hr, 396 rbi. *3 WS, 13 g, .140, 1 hr, 3 rbi*

One of Branch Rickey's farm system products, Douthit joined the Cardinals in 1923 and spent nine seasons with St. Louis before finishing with the Reds and Cubs. A wide-ranging centerfielder, Douthit led NL outfielders in putouts three times, and twice in errors. He had little power (914 of his 1201 hits were singles) but he topped .300 three times. Over or near .300 in each of St. Louis' 1926, '28, and '30 pennant-winning seasons, he faltered in World Series play, going just 7-for-50. /(DQV)

Tommy Dowd [Thomas Jefferson] (Buttermilk Tommy) — 1869–1933. OF-2B 1891–99, 1901 Boston (AA), Washington (AA), Washington (NL), **St. Louis (NL) [Perfectos]**, Phillies, Cleveland (NL), Red Sox 1320 g, .271, 23 hr, 501 rbi.
    Manager 1896–97 **St. Louis (NL)**, 30–63, .323

Dowd came up as a second baseman, but spent the heart of his career as the right fielder for the 1893–95 St. Louis Perfectos (NL). He managed St. Louis for the last 62 games of 1896, and was fired after a 6–25 start in 1897. He was dealt to the Phillies a few days later, only to be reacquired by St. Louis for the following season. /(AJA)

Tom Downey — 1884–1961. SS-2B-3B 1909–12, 14–15 **Reds**, Phillies, Cubs, Buffalo FL 651 g, .240, 7 hr, 188 rbi

Although he was a versatile infielder for four years in

the NL and two in the Federal League, his weak bat kept him from holding down a regular position. /(NLM)

Al Downing — 1941– . LHP 1961–77 **Yankees**, A's, Brewers, Dodgers 2268 ip, 123–107, 3.22 20 wins: 71 *1 LCS, 4 ip, 0–0, .000. 3 WS, 16 ip, 0–3, 6.06*
☛ *All-Star—67.*

Al Downing, who gave up Hank Aaron's record-breaking 715th homer, entered baseball loaded with potential. His fastball exploded and his curveball danced. Called by some "the black Sandy Koufax," he never lived up to that billing, partly because of control problems and inconsistency and later because of arm miseries, but for four seasons he was excellent.

Recalled from the minors to the Yankees for good in June 1963, Downing maintained a summer-long electric pace of low-hit games. The first black starting pitcher in club history allowed a scant 5.84 hits per nine innings and finished with a 13–5 record. In 1964 he led the league with 217 strikeouts. Downing in 1967 became a complete pitcher, cutting down on his walks, mastering a changeup and mixing up his pitches. He finished 14–10 with the ninth-place Yankees.

Pitching for the Dodgers in 1971, Downing reached the pinnacle, winning 20 games, including a league-leading five shutouts. /(MG)

Brian Downing — 1950– . OF-C-DH 1973– White Sox, **Angels** 2018 g, .266, 234 hr, 934 rbi. *3 LCS, 16 g, .197, 1 hr, 8 rbi*
☛ *All-Star—79.*

Downing transformed himself, through hard work, weight training (before it was common), and experimentation, from an inconsistent, weak-hitting catcher to a reliable clutch-hitting slugger who set the AL record for consecutive errorless games by an outfielder (244 games, from May 25, 1981 through July 21, 1983, second game).

Downing showed the intensity that would characterize his play throughout his career literally from the first pitch of his first game. Playing third base, he raced after a short foul pop-up that was apparently out of reach. He dived and caught it, but bruised his leg so severely that he was out for nearly six weeks. In his second day after coming back, he got his first ML hit, an inside-the-park HR off Mickey Lolich. In his first full season, 1974, Downing showed good power with 10 HR in 293 at-bats, but hit only .225. The White Sox' number-one catcher in 1975, he hit .240 with seven HR in 420 at-bats. Traded with two

pitchers to California after the 1977 season in return for Bobby Bonds, Rich Dotson, and Thad Bosley, he was their regular catcher for the next two seasons. In 1978 he set the club mark for fielding average by a catcher, .993. After the season he had bone chips removed from his right elbow. He made the All-Star team in 1979, hitting a career-high .326 with 12 HR and 75 RBI as the Angels won their first division title.

After missing most of 1980 with a broken ankle, he spent most of 1981 in the outfield and never caught again after that season. He began his errorless streak in the OF, but did not compile it at the expense of his aggressive style of play, which compensated for his below-average speed. His 330 errorless chances in 1982 set the AL mark for most chances in an errorless season. Downing hit 28 HR, 16 better than his previous high, and scored 109 runs while driving in 84. Manager Gene Mauch used him as both a leadoff hitter for his ability to get on base (86 walks), and as a cleanup hitter for his power and clutch hitting. The Angels won another division title, but once again Downing hit poorly in the LCS. He missed five weeks in 1983 with a broken left wrist, but otherwise continued his consistent production. Although he is a streaky hitter within each season, at the end of the year he has posted his usual 20 HR, 85 RBI and runs, and .275 BA. His career-high 95 RBI in 1986 helped the Angels to another division title, and although he hit only .222 in the LCS, he drove in seven runs to lead both teams. He utilized another of his talents, getting hit by a Calvin Schiraldi pitch with the bases loaded in the ninth inning of Game Four to send the contest into extra innings. His intense play and his unusually wide, open batting stance, as well as his clutch performance, finally gained him national notice. Angels owner Gene Autry earlier in the year had, as part of California's 25th anniversary, named Downing the left fielder on the franchise's all-time team.

Downing switched to DH in 1987 to lessen the wear on his body. He had his best season, reaching career highs with 29 HR, 110 runs, and 106 walks (tied for the AL lead). He spent three weeks on the DL near the start of the 1988 season and hit just .242, his lowest average since 1975, although he hit 25 HR in 484 at-bats. He recovered in 1989 and completed his domination of the Angels' all-time offense totals. He is first in home runs, RBI, runs, extra base hits, total bases, hits, doubles, games, and at-bats. He is in the top ten in most Angels' season records. /(SH)

Kelly Downs — 1960– . RHP 1986– **Giants** 525 ip, 33–30, 3.57. *2 LCS, 10 ip, 1–0, 2.70. 1 WS, 5 ip, 0–0, 7.71*

A tall control specialist, Downs spent six full seasons in the minors before finally reaching the Giants in 1986. He has been plagued by misfortune throughout his brief ML career. He posted a 2.75 ERA in 14 starts as a rookie in 1986 and was one of the Giants' top starters for most of 1987, but he was relegated to the bullpen when San Francisco acquired Rick Reuschel for its successful pennant drive. Downs rejoined the rotation in 1988 and was 13–9, 3.32 before spending the last month of the season on the DL with shoulder problems that plagued him through 1989. Originally with the Phillies organization, Downs was one of two pitchers traded to San Francisco for Al Oliver in 1984. His older brother, Dave, was 1–1 in four starts for the Phillies in 1972, including a 3–0 shutout against the Braves in his ML debut./(SCL)

Billy Doyle — 1881–1939. *Scout.*

Doyle signed Branch Rickey out of Ohio Wesleyan University to play for the Texas League Dallas Steers. He later scouted for the Browns, Indians, and Phillies. He joined the Tigers in 1919 and stayed until his death in 1939. Eventual stars he scouted included Sad Sam Jones and Rick Ferrell./(FVP)

Carl Doyle — 1912–1951. RHP 1935–36, 39–40 **A's**, Dodgers, Cardinals 223 ip, 6–15, 6.95

Doyle pitched five games for the 1939 Dodgers, one as a starter; it was the only shutout of his career. He suffered a broken arm in 1940, and later scouted for the Tigers./(NLM)

Danny Doyle — 1917– . C 1943 **Red Sox** 13 g, .209, 0 hr, 6 rbi

Doyle played only 13 games for the Red Sox at catcher during WWII, but has been a full-time scout for Boston almost continuously since 1949. His signees and discoveries include Roger Clemens, Jim Lonborg, and Ellis Burks./(FVP)

Hugh Doyle — 1876–1925. *Writer.*

Doyle was sports cartoonist for the Philadelphia *Press* for 25 years, then the *Ledger* until he retired in 1921./(NLM)

Jack Doyle (Dirty Jack) — 1869–1958. 1B-C-OF-2B-SS-3B 1889–1905 Columbus (AA), Cleveland (NL), **Giants**, Baltimore (NL), Washington (NL), Cubs, Senators, Dodgers, Phillies, Yankees 1564 g, .301, 25 hr, 924 rbi.

Manager 1895, 98 **Giants**, Washington (NL) 51–55, .481.

Umpire NL 1911

Ireland native Jack Doyle is one of 20 major leaguers to have played 100 games at four different positions. He was also reputedly baseball's first pinch hitter, coming off the bench to single for the Giants in 1892. In five consecutive years, 1893 through 1897, and seven in all, he topped the .300 mark. He had three stints with the Giants, and from 1898 through 1900 was their starting first baseman. He was the second of three managers for the 1895 Giants, and the second of four with the 1898 Senators./(AJA)

Larry Doyle (Laughing Larry) — 1886–1974. 2B 1907–20 **Giants**, Cubs 1765 g, .290, 74 hr, 793 rbi. *3 WS, 19 g, .237, 1 hr, 5 rbi*

☛ *Most Valuable Player—12. Led League—ba 15.*

Doyle was a nervous youngster in June 1907 when he took the wrong ferry across the Hudson River and arrived late for his first ML game. Giants manager John McGraw started the scrappy prospect at second base, a position unfamiliar to Doyle. The

Larry Doyle with the Giants

game was close, coming down to a crucial ninth-inning grounder which Doyle booted. Certain Mc-Graw would send him down, Doyle sheepishly confronted him, only to receive words of encouragement and, the following season, the Giants' captaincy. He became a five-time .300 hitter.

Doyle's hitting and solid defense helped New York to three straight pennants, starting in 1911, when he led the NL in triples and said, "It's great to be young and a Giant." He scored the famous "phantom" run that forestalled the Athletics' victory in the 1911 World Series. In the dusk of Game Five's 10th inning, Doyle came home on an outfield fly but did not touch the plate, umpire Bill Klem later admitted, saying he would have called Doyle out had the A's tried to tag him.

Doyle led the NL with 172 hits in 1909, and batted a high of .330 in 1912. He won the NL batting title in 1915 with a .320 mark and league highs of 189 hits and 40 doubles. He stole 297 career bases, swiping home 17 times. His eight errors tie him with Eddie Collins for most in total World Series at 2B./(ASN)

Slow Joe Doyle [Judd Bruce] — 1881–1947. RHP 1906–10 **Yankees**, Reds 436 ip, 22–22, 2.85

When his team was at bat on hot days, Doyle would sometimes lie down on the tarpaulin and nap, but he earned his nickname by being one of the slowest workers ever to take the mound. In addition to stalling, he relied on a "drop" (a sinker), a "raise ball," and a spitter. Although he threw shutouts in his first two ML starts, 11 wins in 1907 was his career high./(NLM)

Doug Drabek — 1962– . RHP 1986– Yankees, **Pirates** 771 ip, 47–39, 3.35

Drabek became a top pitching prospect with his strikeout ability. Despite a terrible first half (1–8) in 1987, he led the Pirates in starts and strikeouts and was NL Pitcher of the Month for August. He was acquired from the Yankees in the Rick Rhoden deal as part of Pittsburgh's rebuilding program./(ME)

Moe Drabowsky — 1935– . RHP 1956–72 **Cubs**, Braves, Reds, A's, Orioles, Royals, Cardinals, White Sox 1641 ip, 88–105, 3.71. *2 WS, 10 ip, 1–0, 0.90*

Born in Ozanna, Poland, Drabowsky came to the U.S. with his parents in 1938, fleeing the Nazi invasion. He accepted a reported $50,000 bonus to sign with the Cubs after fanning 16 in a no-hitter for Trinity College of Hartford. Joining the Cubs' rotation immediately, Drabowsky managed a 2.47 ERA

as a rookie. Inclined to work inside, he led the NL with 10 hit batsmen in 1957, hitting a record four men on June 2, 1957. He finished second in the league with 170 strikeouts, going 13–15 for a seventh-place club. A sore arm cost Drabowsky his fastball in 1958, when he yielded Stan Musial's 3,000th hit. Drabowsky struggled, pitching for eight clubs in four years. The Orioles drafted him for 1966 and Drabowsky turned his career around with a 6–0, 2.81 record and seven saves for the 1966 World Champions. Relieving Dave McNally with one out and the bases loaded in the third inning of Game One of the World Series, Drabowsky gave up just one hit, no earned runs, and struck out 11 to earn the win as he finished the game. He had a WS-record six strikeouts in a row. He won his first 12 Baltimore decisions, achieving ERAs of 1.60 and 1.91 in '67 and '68. Doing it all, Drabowsky also batted .364, .350, and .286 in 1966–1968. Selected by the Royals in the 1969 expansion draft, Drabowsky led the AL with 11 relief wins, saving 11 with a 2.94 ERA in 52 games. He returned to Baltimore to post a 4–2 record down the stretch in 1970, climaxed with two more clutch relief performances in that World Series. He returned to Poland in 1987 as a baseball ambassador, helping the Poles form their first team for Olympic competition.

A well-known flake, he was once rolled to first base in a wheelchair after being hit by a pitch and specialized in bullpen pranks./(MC)

Delos Drake — 1886–1965. OF 1911, 14–15 Tigers, **St. Louis (FL)** 331 g, .263, 5 hr, 119 rbi

Drake's efforts to break into the Detroit lineup were hampered by a broken leg in 1905. A consistent .300 hitter in the minors, he never rose above a utility role in the majors. He was a prize-winning trap shooter and worked as a cowboy./(NLM)

Dick Drago — 1945– . RHP 1969–81 **Royals**, Red Sox, Angels, Mariners 1876 ip, 108–117, 3.62. *1 LCS, 5 ip, 0–0, 0.00. 1 WS, 4 ip, 0–1, 2.25*

Drago made the majors when he was picked by the Royals in the expansion draft, and he became the ace of their struggling staff. Improving with the rest of the team, he had his best season in 1971 (17–11, 3.01), but his record suffered when the team declined in 1972 (12–17 despite a 2.99 ERA). Boston acquired him for 1974, and in their AL championship season in 1975 he was their bullpen ace with 15 saves. He saved Games Two and Three as the Red Sox swept the A's in the ALCS, but lost Game Two of the World Series in the ninth inning on a Ken

Griffey double. His three scoreless innings of one-hit ball in Game Six kept Boston in the game, and they won on Carlton Fisk's famous homer in the 12th inning.

Traded to California for 1976 and then to Baltimore in mid-1977, he returned to the Red Sox for 1978 and had his last good season in 1979, going 10–6 with 13 saves. /(SFS)

Dave Dravecky — 1956– . LHP 1982– **Padres**, Giants 1063 ip, 64–57, 3.13. *2 LCS, 21 ip, 1–1, 0.43. 1 WS, 5 ip, 0–0, 0.00*
☞ *All-Star—83.*

A consistently effective starter and occasional reliever for the Padres for over five seasons, Dravecky was traded to the Giants in mid-1987 in a seven-player swap that included Mark Davis, Kevin Mitchell, and Craig Lefferts. He was outstanding in the 1987 LCS, tossing a two-hit shutout in Game Two and running his LCS scoreless-inning string to a record-tying 16, but he made only seven starts in 1988 before going on the DL with what turned out to be a career- and life-threatening cancerous tumor in his pitching arm. He made a surprisingly successful comeback attempt in mid-1989, winning two games before his weakened arm snapped as he threw a pitch. He rebroke it during the Giants' LCS victory celebration. /(ME)

John Drebinger — Unk.–Unk. *Writer*

A high school track star and son of a violinist in the Metropolitan Opera orchestra, Drebinger was the oldest writer traveling the baseball circuit when he retired at age 73. He began with the weekly Staten Island *Advance* and joined the *New York Times* in 1923. He covered every WS for the *Times* from 1929 to 1963. In 1973 he received the J.G. Taylor Spink Award from the Hall of Fame. /(NLM)

Chuck Dressen [Charles Walter] — 1898–1966. 3B 1925–31 **Reds**, Giants 646 g, .272, 11 hr, 221 rbi.
   Manager 1934–37, 51–53, 55–57, 60–61, 63–66 **Reds**, Dodgers, Senators, Braves, Tigers 1037–993, .511. First place: 52–53 *2 WS, 5–8, .385*

Dressen never doubted his own baseball savvy. "Hold them, boys," he often told his team. "I'll think of something." The 5'5" 146-lb extrovert took up diverse challenges: picking racetrack winners, quarterbacking George Halas's Decatur Staleys (forerunner of the Chicago Bears) and the Racine Legion of the early NFL, and playing eight years as a NL third baseman.

He is most famous as a ML manager. He managed successive pennant winners for the Dodg-

ers in 1952–53, but bucked owner Walter O'Malley's policy by asking for a multi-year contract. O'Malley replaced him with Walter Alston. Dressen spent a year at Oakland of the Pacific Coast League, then returned to the majors with the talentless Senators. Two seasons after leading Brooklyn to 105 victories, the same tactician took Washington to 101 losses. A second losing season and a poor 1957 start cost Dressen his job.

In 1960, he took over the Milwaukee Braves. Late in 1961, with the team in third place, he was summoned to the front office. Expecting photographers to record his signing of a new contract, he dressed in his best suit. Instead, he was told he was being let go.

Dressen managed Toronto in the minors the next season, then joined the Dodgers as a special scout in 1963. In June, he received his fourth ML command, with the ninth-place Tigers. He brought them in fifth and followed with two straight fourth-place finishes. On May 15, 1966 the 67-year-old Dressen managed his last victory. The next day he checked into a hospital. Twelve weeks later he died of a heart attack.

Dressen had a gambler's love for number 7 and wore it whenever he could. When the Dodgers acquired star Joe Medwick from St. Louis in 1940, he asked for 7, then worn by Dressen as a coach. Chuck agreed; the next day he went to his coach's box sporting his new number: 77. As usual, he'd "thought of something." /(JK)

Rob Dressler — 1954– . RHP 1975–76, 78–80 Giants, Cardinals, **Mariners** 390 ip, 11–23, 4.18

Dressler signed out of high school as San Francisco's first-round pick in the June 1972 draft. He had good control but was hit hard, going 3–10 with the 1976 Giants and 4–10 with the 1980 Mariners. /(KC)

Karl Drews — 1920–1963. RHP 1946–49, 1951–54 Yankees, Browns, **Phillies**, Reds 827 ip, 44–53, 4.76. *1 WS, 3 ip, 3.00*

The 6'4" Drews came through the Yankee organization slowly, and was 6–6 for the 1947 world champs. When he unexpectedly won 14 for the Phillies in 1952, including five shutouts, his 2.72 ERA was by far his best. Brother Roy was a catcher in the Giants' organization. /(RTM)

Dan Driessen — 1951– . 1B-3B-OF 1973–87 **Reds**, Expos, Giants, Astros, Cardinals 1732 g, .267, 153 hr, 763 rbi. *4 LCS, 13 g, .162, 2 rbi. 3 WS, 10 g, .276, 1 hr, 2 rbi*

Overshadowed on the star-studded "Big Red Machine," Driessen gave the Reds valuable versatility for his first four seasons. He hit a career-high .301 in his rookie season and then was Cincinnati's starting third baseman in 1974. Pete Rose moved to third base in 1975, but Driessen replaced Tony Perez at first base from 1977 to 1981, one of the longest tenures at first base in Reds history. The uncle of Gerald Perry, Driessen led NL first basemen in fielding three times. A smart, steady hitter, he led the NL with 93 walks in 1980 and generally walked more than he struck out.

In 1976, Driessen was the NL's first DH in the World Series. He hit .357, the only good average he had in post-season play. Traded in mid-1981, he wandered the league until his retirement, finishing his career filling in at first base for the 1987 NL champion Cardinals after first Jack Clark and then Cesar Cedeno were injured. /(ME)

John Drohan — 1890–1969. *Writer.*

Drohan retired in 1955 after covering baseball for the Boston *Traveler* from 1919. He was a frequent contributor to magazines and *The Sporting News.* /(NLM)

Walt Dropo (Moose) — 1923– . 1B 1949–61 Red Sox, **Tigers,** White Sox, Reds, Orioles 1288 g, .270, 152 hr, 704 rbi

☛ *Rookie of the Year—50. Led League—rbi 50. All-Star—50.*

The 6'5" 220-lb Moose, from Moosup, CT, was the embodiment of his era. He was the strong, silent type, slow afoot but a deadly power hitter. He hit 152 career home runs, but had only five stolen bases.

Dropo turned down an offer from football's Chicago Bears to sign with the Red Sox in 1947. He came up sensationally in 1950, starting on the All-Star team and winning AL Rookie of the Year honors with 34 homers, a .322 average, and a league-leading 144 RBI. Dropo's next best was 29 HR and 97 RBI two years later, but he never again had over 19 HR or hit over .281. In one brilliant stretch in July 1952, after being traded to Detroit, he collected 12 consecutive hits to tie a ML record. Included in the streak was a 7-for-7 performance in a doubleheader against Washington. /(RL)

Dick Drott (Hummer) — 1936–1985. RHP 1957–63 **Cubs,** Astros 688 ip, 27–46, 4.78

When Dick Drott won 15 games for the seventh-place Cubs in 1957, he seemed headed for stardom.

He was wild enough to lead the league in walks, but his fastball intimidated batters at first. Then, his career floundered because of arm problems and he passed to the expansion Houston team in the draft.

On April 27 of his rookie season, Drake was ejected from a game for borrowing a wheelchair from a crippled fan and wheeling fellow flake Moe Drabowsky to first base after Drabowsky was hit on the foot by a pitch. /(JK)

Louis Drucke — 1888–1955. RHP 1909–12 **Giants** 317 ip, 18–15, 2.90

Hailed as a wonder find by John McGraw when the Giants signed him out of TCU in 1909, Drucke was 12–10 in 1910. He struck out 151 in 215 innings but was wild. His career was cut short when he ruptured an arm muscle in a subway accident. /(NLM)

Cal Drummond — 1917–1970. *Umpire* AL 1960–69 *1 WS, 1 ASU*

Drummond was plagued with ill health late in his career. After brain surgery in 1969, he was working his way back to the majors when he died while umpiring a minor league game in 1970. He was a member of the umpiring crew that called a balk on Stu Miller during the 1961 All-Star Game at Candlestick Park when the little pitcher was blown off the mound by the wind. /(RTM)

Charles Dryden — 1869–1931. *Writer.*

A charter member of the BBWAA, Dryden's turns of phrase are often repeated. His assessment of the futile Senators, "Washington: first in war, first in peace, and last in the American League," is a classic. Of Ed Walsh, he wrote, "He's the only man who can strut standing still." He named Frank Chance "The Peerless Leader," Charles Comiskey "The Old Roman," Phil Douglas "Shuffin' Phil," and the 1906 White Sox "The Hitless Wonders." Dryden left grade school to work in a foundry before joining the San Francisco *Examiner* in the early 1890s. By 1893, he was sports editor of the San Francisco *Chronicle.* In 1900 he joined Hearst's New York *American.* When he began poking fun at Andrew Freedman, the Giants' owner barred him from the Polo Grounds. Dryden continued to write humorous accounts of games by perching on a telephone pole outside the park. After brief stints with the *Evening World* and Philadelphia *North American*, he joined the Chicago *Examiner* for what was then the highest salary of any baseball writer. He later worked for the *Herald Examiner* and *Tribune.* Dryden, who wrote all his copy in longhand until near the end of his career, retired in 1921 after a stroke left him paralyzed and nearly speechless. He was voted the J.G. Taylor Spink Award in 1965./(NLM)

Don Drysdale — 1936– . RHP 1956–68 **Dodgers**
3432 ip, 209–166, 2.95. 20 wins: 62, 65 *5 WS, 39 ip, 3–3, 2.95*
☞ *Led League—w 62. Cy Young Award—62. All-Star—59, 61–65, 67–68. Hall of Fame—1984.*

A tall, charismatic sidearmer, Drysdale combined an explosive fastball with great control to become one of baseball's premier power pitchers. His greatest personal achievement came in 1968, "the year of the pitcher." He logged six consecutive shutouts en route to a since-broken record 58.2 consecutive scoreless innings. He pitched his record-tying fifth shutout on the day of the California presidential primary and was congratulated by Robert Kennedy in the speech he gave just before he was assassinated.

Drysdale's real glory days were earlier, when he was paired with Sandy Koufax as the most feared pitching duo of the 1960s. The Dodgers finished the regular season in first place in four out of five years from 1962 to 1966 without an overwhelming offense. The two staged a highly publicized joint holdout following their combined 49–20 record in 1965. They sought a three-year, $1.05 million contract to be divided evenly. Drysdale eventually signed for $110,000, quite a bit better than the $35,000 he made when he won 25 in 1962. He summed up his persepective in 1980: "When we played, World Series checks meant something. Now they just screw up your taxes."

Don Drysdale

Drysdale was a workhorse, leading the NL in games started every year from 1962 to 1965, as well as in innings pitched in 1962 and 1964. He never missed a start. He also led in shutouts in 1959. One of the best-hitting pitchers of his day, he led NL pitchers in homers four times, twice tying the NL record of seven. His career total of 29 ranks second to Warren Spahn's in NL history. In 1965 he hit .300 and slugged .508, pinch hit frequently, and achieved the rare feat of winning 20 and hitting .300 in the same year. In 1958 he slugged .591.

Drysdale's tenure spanned Dodger eras. He won 17 in their last year in Brooklyn, and pitched the team's first West Coast game (a loss at San Francisco). When he retired, he was the last Brooklyn player left on the Dodgers. He had the longest career played under a single manager—13 years with Walter Alston. When Drysdale came up, he played with Duke Snider and the "Boys of Summer." He retired from a staff that included Don Sutton, who pitched through the 1980s.

Knocking down hitters was a major tool in Drysdale's pitching repertoire. He set the 20th-century NL career record by hitting 154 batters, and led the NL in that category a record five times. His philosophy on the knockdown pitch was simple—"If one of our guys went down, I just doubled it. No confusion there. It didn't require a Rhodes scholar."

A fixture at All-Star time, Drysdale holds All-Star records with eight games pitched, five starts, 19.1 innings, and 19 strikeouts. He went 2–1, 1.40, allowing only 10 hits.

Drysdale was one of the most appealing Dodgers to the Hollywood entertainment community. He appeared on numerous TV shows including "You Bet Your Life," "The Donna Reed Show," and "The Brady Bunch." After his playing days, Drysdale became an announcer for the Angels and the White Sox before returning to the Dodgers. "Interviews were the hardest thing for me at first," he said. "I felt so damn funny asking players questions when I already knew the answers." /(TG)

Monk Dubiel [Walter John] — 1919–1969. RHP 1944–45, 48–52 Yankees, Phillies, **Cubs** 879 ip, 45–53, 3.87

Dubiel was a competent wartime Yankee pitcher, exempted from military service because of an eye problem. He went 13–13 as a rookie in 1944, 10–9 in 1945, then was demoted. Later toiling unspectacularly in the NL, he was hampered by a hip injury, an ear infection, and a chronic back ailment. /(JL)

Jean Dubuc (Chauncey) — 1888–1958. RHP 1908–09, 12–16, 1918–19 Reds, **Tigers**, Red Sox, Giants 1444 ip, 86–76, 3.04

Dubuc twice won 17 games for Detroit, and in 1919 led the NL with six relief victories. Used 93 times as a pinch hitter, he belted two homers during the dead ball season of 1913. His career ended when he was banned for life in connection with the Black Sox scandal. /(TJ)

Jim Duckworth — 1939– . RHP 1963–66 **Senators**, A's 267 ip, 7–25, 5.26

Pitching for Washington in a 1965 game, Duckworth struck out eight of the first nine Tigers he faced. Plagued by a fear of flying, he once went on the disabled list to seek help in overcoming it. /(RTM)

Clise Dudley — 1903– . RHP 1929–33 **Dodgers**, Phillies, Pirates 420 ip, 17–33, 5.03

Dudley hit the first major league pitch he saw over the Ebbets Field wall (4/27/29). He became a .333 pinch hitter. Unfortunately, he was a pitcher who was often pounded. In the one-third inning he worked in 1933, he allowed six hits and a walk for a 135.00 ERA. /(JK)

Hal Dues — 1954– . RHP 1977–78, 80 **Expos** 134 ip, 6–8, 3.09

Dues recorded a 2.36 ERA in his rookie 1978 season with Montreal, then had elbow surgery from which he could not recover. /(KC)

Jim Duffalo — 1935– . RHP 1961–65 **Giants**, Reds 298 ip, 15–8, 3.39

Duffalo twice recorded ERAs under 3.00 as a Giant reliever, but never appeared in over 35 games. He had a good fastball, and over his career averaged better than six strikeouts per nine innings. /(RTM)

Frank Duffy — 1946– . SS-3B-2B 1970–79 Reds, Giants, **Indians**, Red Sox 915 g, .232, 26 hr, 240 rbi. *1 LCS, 1G, .000*

The freckle-faced, sure-handed Duffy was Cleveland's starting shortstop from 1972 through 1977. A Stanford graduate drafted by Cincinnati, in May 1971 he went to the Giants with Vern Geishert for George Foster in a notoriously uneven trade, and that November he was dealt to the Indians with Gaylord Perry for Sam McDowell. He led AL shortstops in fielding in 1973 and 1976. /(JCA)

Hugh Duffy

Hugh Duffy — 1866–1954. OF 1888–1901, 04–06
Cubs, Chicago (PL), Boston (AA), **Braves**, Milwaukee (AL),
Phillies 1736 g, .328, 103 hr, 1299 rbi.
  Manager 1901, 04–06, 10–11, 21–22 Milwaukee (AL),
Phillies, White Sox, Red Sox 535–671, .444
☛ *Led League—ba 94. Led League—hr 94, 97. Led
League—rbi 94 . Hall of Fame—1945.*

Owner of the highest single-season batting average in
ML history (.438 in 1894), Duffy was one of the
game's early stars. He was an outstanding outfielder
for Boston in the 1890s, and later, as a Red Sox
coach, was a tutor to the young Ted Williams.

Originally an infielder in the New England
League, Duffy idolized Cap Anson and signed with
Anson's Chicago White Stockings (later the Cubs)
for the 1888 season despite being offered more
money by the local Boston club. Only 5'7", Duffy
replaced Billy Sunday, soon to be a world-famous
evangelist, as Chicago's right fielder. Duffy was sold
to Boston (American Association) after three seasons, and then became a Brave when the AA broke

up. With Duffy now patrolling centerfield, he and
right fielder Tommy McCarthy became known as
the "Heavenly Twins."

Duffy hit over .300 in nine of his ten seasons in
Boston, but 1894 was his best year by far. Not only
did he hit .438, but he won baseball's first Triple
Crown with 18 HR and 145 RBI as well. He also led
the NL with 236 hits, 50 doubles, and a .679
slugging percentage. He never approached those
numbers again, although he did win another home
run crown in 1897. Duffy was not successful as a
manager; in eight seasons, he finished over .500 only
twice, never higher than fourth, and three times in
the cellar. Still, as a Red Sox coach emeritus, he
patiently indulged reporters' requests for tales of the
good old days, while maintaining that his rookie
pupil, Ted Williams, was the best hitter he had ever
seen. In 1945 Duffy was elected to the Hall of Fame
by the Veterans Committee./(JK)

Joe Dugan (Jumping Joe) — 1897–1982. 3B-SS-2B
1917–29, 31 A's, Red Sox, **Yankees**, Braves, Tigers
1446 g, .280, 42 hr, 571 rbi. *5 WS, 25 g, .267, 1 hr, 8 rbi*

While he may have deserved it for his prowess afield,
Joe Dugan earned his nickname for being AWOL
from his first big league club as a youngster.

The tall, rangy infielder went directly from the
campus of Holy Cross to the Athletics in 1917. A
shortstop in his first three seasons, Dugan became
one of the finest all-around third basemen of his era.
After batting .194 and .195 in his first two seasons
he found his stroke and developed into a timely
hitter, reaching a high of .322 in 1920.

Best known for his six and one half years with the
Yankees, Dugan was a key member of five pennant
winners including the fabled 1927 World Champion
"Murderer's Row."

Dugan's controversial trade from the Red Sox to
the Yankees in late July 1922, during a heated
pennant race, caused an uproar which helped to
bring about a June 15 trading deadline the following
year./(JL)

Bill Duggleby (Frosty Bill) — 1874–1944. RHP 1898,
1901–07 **Phillies**, A's, Pirates 1732 ip, 92–104, 3.19

On April 21, 1898 Duggleby became the very first
player to homer in his first ML at-bat, and remains
the only man to accomplish the feat with a grand
slam. Called Frosty Bill because he spurned the
companionship of his teammates and dressed in a
heavy black suit even in summer, Duggleby went
19–12 for the Phillies in 1901. When he and Nap

Lajoie jumped the team to join the Athletics of the second-year American League, they were both enjoined in a lawsuit. Unlike Lajoie, Duggleby jumped back to the Phillies after just two appearances with Connie Mack's Athletics. /(JK)

Tom Dukes — 1942- . RHP 1967–72 Astros, **Padres**, Orioles, Angels 216 ip, 5–16, 4.37. *1 WS, 4 ip, 0.00*

First signed by the Yankees, Dukes saved 10 of the 1970 Padres' 63 wins. He was 1–5 for the 1971 AL champion Orioles and went with them on their postseason tour of Japan. /(MC)

Bob Duliba (Ach) — 1935- . RHP 1959–60, 62–65, 67 Cardinals, **Dodgers**, Red Sox, A's 257 ip, 17–12, 3.47

Duliba's first ML hit helped seal his first ML victory, with St. Louis in 1960. The righthander with the musical nickname pitched solely in relief, at his best going 6–4 with nine saves with the 1964 Angels. /(JL)

George Dumont (Pea Soup) — 1895–1956. RHP 1915–19 **Senators**, Red Sox 347 ip, 10–23, 2.85

As a 19-year-old Washington rookie in 1915, Dumont threw successive two-hit shutouts and lost a 10-inning complete game to compile a 2–1 record. He never pitched that well again. In 1917, his only year as a regular starter, he was 5–14. /(NLM)

Dave Duncan — 1945- . C 1964, 67–76 **A's**, Indians, Orioles 929 g, .214, 109 hr, 341 rbi. *2 LCS, 4 g, .375, 2 rbi. 1 WS, 3 g, .200*
☛ *All-Star—71.*

Signed for a reported $65,000 bonus in 1963, Duncan hit for power, not average (46 HR, California League, 1966) and didn't win a job with the A's until they moved to Oakland in 1968. Batting just .126 in 1969, and often on Marine reserve duty, Duncan finally became a regular in 1971. After his military duty was over, Duncan grew his hair down his back. Following a career-high 19 HR (batting .218) for the A's in 1972, he was traded to Cleveland. After knee injuries forced his retirement, he became a continually-employed ML pitching coach. /(MC)

Frank Duncan — 1901–1973. C-OF-MGR Negro Leagues 1920–48 Chicago Giants, **Kansas City Monarchs**, New York Black Yankees, Pittsburgh Crawfords, Homestead Grays, New York Cubans, Chicago American Giants 517 g, .252 (inc.)
☛ *All-Star—38.*

Duncan was a top defensive catcher and a successful playing manager in the Negro Leagues. He was a hardnosed competitor who played on the great Kansas City Monarch teams of the 1920s and managed the Monarchs in the 1940s, guiding such stars as Satchel Paige, Josh Gibson, and Jackie Robinson. Kansas City teammate Newt Allen said Duncan was a "great receiver and thrower—one of the greatest," but "wasn't much of a hitter." He ran the bases with reckless abandon and earned a reputation as a hard-sliding competitor. /(PG)

Mariano Duncan — 1963- . SS-2B 1985–87, 89- **Dodgers**, Reds 421 g, .235, 23 hr, 108 rbi. *1 LCS, 5 g, .222, 1 rbi*

A surprise 1985 Opening Day starter at second base, Duncan took over at shortstop and placed third in the NL Rookie of the Year voting. But some criticism apparently shook his confidence and his batting average plummeted, leading to a demotion in 1987. He returned as a utility man in 1989 and went to the Reds in the Kal Daniels trade. /(TG)

Pat Duncan — 1893–1960. OF 1915, 19–24 Pirates, **Reds** 727 g, .307, 23 hr, 374 rbi. *1 WS, 8 g, .269, 8 rbi*

Duncan had three .300 seasons during his five-year tenure as Cincinnati's regular left fielder. In the fourth game of the tainted 1919 World Series, "Black Sox" conspirator Eddie Cicotte deliberately mishandled Duncan's grounder, beginning a game-winning rally for the Reds. /(TJ)

Vern Duncan — 1890–1954. OF 1913–15 Phillies, **Baltimore (FL)** 311 g, .279, 4 hr, 97 rbi

Duncan was the regular centerfielder for Baltimore in his, and the Federal League's, only two full seasons. /(TJ)

Sam Dungan — 1866–1939. OF 1892–94, 1900–01 **Cubs**, Louisville (NL), Senators 382 g, .301, 3 hr, 197 rbi

After a five-year absence from the National League, Dungan won the American League batting title in 1900, when the AL was still a minor league. He batted .320 as the Senators' right fielder in 1901, then retired. /(AJA)

Davey Dunkle (Edward) — 1872–1941. RHP 1897–99, 1903–04 Phillies, Washington (NL), White Sox, **Senators** 421 ip, 17–30, 5.02

After winning five of seven decisions for the 1897 Phillies, Dunkle lost his effectiveness. His 9–13 with a 4.16 ERA for the 1903 Senators was his best full season in the majors. /(BC)

Fred Dunlap (Sure Shot) — 1859–1902. 2B 1880–91 **Cleveland** (NL), St. Louis (UA)/Cardinals, Detroit (NL), Pirates, New York (PL), Washington (AA) 965 g, .292, 41 hr, 299 rbi (inc.)
☛ Led League—hr 84. Led League—ba 84.

In ten NL seasons, the slick-fielding Dunlap at various times led NL second basemen in all fielding categories and twice batted over .300. But his greatest year was 1884 when, playing for power-house St. Louis in the short-lived Union Association, he led UA second basemen in all five fielding categories while leading the league in BA (his .412 was 52 points above that of the next-best hitter), slugging (.621), runs (160), and HR (13). His 160 runs scored set a new ML record, and still rank fourteenth-best of all time. /(FIC)

Jack Dunn — 1872–1928. 3B-RHP-SS-OF 1897–1904 Dodgers, Phillies, Baltimore (AL), **Giants** 490 g, .245, 1 hr, 164 rbi; 1077 ip, 64–59, 4.11

Jack Dunn was a pitcher and infielder who won 23 games for the pennant-winning Dodgers in 1899. He managed Providence (Eastern League) to a pennant in 1905, then had his greatest success in Baltimore (Eastern League/International League) starting in 1907 where, as owner-manager, he built the most successful minor league franchise in history. After winning a pennant in 1908 he bought the team from his former manager Ned Hanlon. Known for his ability to size up young players, he never forgot a player or a play. He found and developed players like Lefty Grove, Babe Ruth, Joe Boley, Jack Bentley, Ernie Shore and sold them for $50,000 to $100,000. On the field the Orioles once posted a 27-game winning streak. In 1914 he fielded the greatest team in the minors. They were 15 games in front when competition from the crosstown Federal League team forced him to sell off his 12 top stars to the majors and temporarily move to Richmond. Starting in 1919, they won seven International League pennants in a row. Dunn declined an offer to manage the Braves in 1928, and that fall had a fatal heart attack while on horseback watching bird dog field trials. /(NLM)

Mike Dunne — 1962– . RHP 1987– **Pirates**, Mariners 433 ip, 23–27, 3.97

TSN NL Rookie Pitcher of the Year in 1987, Mike Dunne led the NL in winning percentage (.684), had the league's second-best ERA (3.03), and led all rookies in wins (13–6). He was the Cardinals' first draft choice in June 1984 and a member of the '84

U.S. Olympic baseball team. He went to Pittsburgh in the Tony Pena deal. /(ME)

Steve Dunning — 1949– . RHP 1970–74, 76–77 **Indians**, Rangers, Angels, Expos, A's 613 ip, 23–41, 4.57

Dunning, Stanford's MVP and *TSN* College Player of the Year in 1970, became Cleveland's first pick in that June's draft. He went right to the majors, but never met expectations. He even fooled Ted Williams, whose Senators Dunning one-hit on April 18, 1971. Williams said "he's going to be some pitcher some day." But Dunning went 8–14 in '71, and had little success with four other clubs. /(KC)

Shawon Dunston — 1963– . SS 1985– **Cubs** 612 g, .256, 44 hr, 224 rbi. *1 LCS, 5 g, .316*
☛ *All-Star—88.*

The Cubs made Dunston the first pick in the nation in the 1982 June draft after he batted .790 as a senior at Brooklyn's Thomas Jefferson High. A raw talent with a rifle arm, he was Chicago's Opening Day shortstop in 1985, but hit .194 before being sent down on May 15; he was obviously unprepared as a fielder, and made glaring baserunning mistakes. Some felt the Cubs had rushed the wild-swinging youngster. But Dunston was handed back his job when Larry Bowa was released in August. In 1986, he led NL shortstops in putouts, assists, double plays, errors, and home runs (17). He drew only 21 walks in more than 600 plate appearances. Injuries kept him out two months of 1987, but he was hitting .287 in mid-1988 and won an All-Star spot. He was pulled out of the last game before the break by manager Don Zimmer for reportedly missing three hit-and-run signs. /(JCA)

Ryne Duren (Blind Ryne) — 1929– . RHP 1954, 57–65 Orioles, A's, **Yankees**, Angels, Phillies, Reds, Senators 589 ip, 27–44, 3.83. *2 WS, 5 g, 13 ip, 1–1, 2.03*
☛ *All-Star—58–59, 61.*

Duren came to the Yankees in 1958 at age 29 with a blazing 95-mph fastball. He quickly became the most feared reliever in the league. "Blind Ryne," who had uncorrected vision of 20/70 and 20/200, would frighten hitters when he entered the game, squinting toward home through bottle-thick glasses. He enhanced the effect by intentionally throwing his first warm-up pitch back to the screen. Initially, it may not have always been planned; while in the minors his control was so erratic that he once hit the on-deck batter.

Duren's career peaked quickly. In 1958 he won

six and saved a league-high 20 games in just 44 appearances. He was often brilliant in New York's World Series victory over the Braves, going 1–1 (1.93) with a save. He saved 14 in 1959, at one point going 18 games—36 innings—without allowing a run. In those two seasons he allowed only 89 hits, fanning 183 in just 151 innings. But drinking did Duren in. Though he continued to record more strikeouts than innings, his downhill slide was swift, as his records show. His decline, despair, and hard-won recovery are chronicled in his autobiography, *The Comeback*. He retired with 57 career saves./(GDW)

Ed Durham (Bull) — 1907–1976. RHP 1929–33 **Red Sox**, White Sox 642 ip, 29–44, 4.45

The curveballing South Carolinian used good control to win a career-high 10 games for the White Sox in 1933. Illness ended his ML career the following spring./(JK)

Leon Durham (Bull) — 1957– . 1B-OF 1980-Cardinals, **Cubs**, Reds 1067 g, .277, 147 hr, 530 rbi. *1 LCS, 5 g, .150, 2 hr, 4 rbi*
☛ *All-Star—82–83.*

A promising outfielder and first baseman with St. Louis, Durham was the bait that, with Ken Reitz, brought Bruce Sutter and a pennant to the Cardinals. Durham finished third in the 1982 NL batting race at .312 and became the Cubs' first 20-HR 20-steal player since 1911. He played outfield for the Cubs until replacing Bill Buckner at first base in 1984, when his career-high 96 RBI helped Chicago to a division title. Aided by Wrigley Field, but troubled by inside pitches, Durham joined the Cubs' all-time HR leaders but never fulfilled expectations. He was traded to his hometown Reds early in 1988 and missed most of the season with drug rehabilitation. He came back with the Cardinals in 1989 as a late-inning defensive replacement for Pedro Guerrero, but was again suspended for drug use./(ME)

Leo Durocher (The Lip) — 1905– . SS-2B 1925, 28–41, 43, 45 Yankees, Reds, **Cardinals**, Dodgers 1637 g, .247, 24 hr, 567 rbi. *2 WS, 11 g, .241.*
　Manager 1939–46, 48–55, 66–73 **Dodgers**, Giants, Cubs, Astros 2010–1710, .540. First place: 41, 51, 54 *3 WS, 15 g, 7–8, .467*
☛ *All-Star—36, 38, 40.*

Durocher had many adjectives applied to him during his colorful career, both kind and unkind. He was a brash, abrasive, hustling, light-hitting, slick-fielding, umpire-baiting bench jockey who was in

baseball for nearly five decades as a player, manager, coach, and commentator.

Durocher spent his first full major league season with the 1928 World Champion Yankees, and became New York's starting shortstop in 1929. He moved on to the Reds in 1930, and the Cardinals in 1933, becoming captain of the "Gashouse Gang" in 1934. His last season as a first-stringer came with the 1939 Dodgers. Never much of a hitter, he topped .260 only five times in 17 years, with a high of .286 in 1936. He became an All-Star mostly on the strength of his glovework; a flashy, acrobatic SS, he led the NL in fielding in '36 and 1938.

Durocher went on to a long, distinguished, and tumultuous career as a manager. He was player-manager of the Dodgers in 1939–41, 1943, and 1945, though he played only a few games in the latter three years. He guided the Dodgers to the NL pennant in 1941, and to second-place finishes in 1940, 1942, and 1946. Perhaps his finest moment as Dodger manager came in spring training of 1947 when he personally quashed a rebellion by players who were protesting the presence of Jackie Robinson.

Durocher's tenure in Brooklyn was marked by—among other things—feuds with GM Branch Rickey, who could not always tolerate Durocher's antics and managing style. Durocher lived life in the fast lane. He was a pro at the card table, and favored the horse track. Stories emerged that he was friendly with such characters as Bugsy Siegel. In 1945, he was indicted for assaulting a fan under the stands. His problems reached a peak in 1947, when he was suspended for the season for reputed association with gamblers. The Dodgers won the pennant with Burt Shotton at the helm instead.

Durocher returned in 1948, gave rookie Roy Campanella the catching job, and moved young Gil Hodges to first base. But the Dodgers fell to last place on July 7. Eight days later, Rickey fired Durocher and rehired Shotton, as the rival Giants fired their manager, Mel Ott, and hired Durocher. Durocher guided the Giants to a pennant in 1951, overtaking the Dodgers in a spectacular race and defeating them in the subsequent playoff, thanks to Bobby Thomson. In 1954, Durocher led New York to his only WS victory. After the 1955 season, he became a TV commentator.

Durocher returned to manage the Cubs from 1966 until late in 1972, and the Astros through 1973, finishing second several times. Toward the end, his players were aware that he was becoming

Leo Durocher, umpire Art Gore

senile; some were with Durocher for weeks before the manager knew who they were. He retired among the all-times leaders in games managed (3740), wins (2010), and losses (1710). His life story was told in his autobiography, *Nice Guys Finish Last*, co-written with Ed Linn. The phrase (or something to that effect) was one that had been attributed to Durocher in '47, referring to Ott, whose Giants had been losing. /(JJM)

Melvin Durslag — Unk.- . *Writer.*

After writing for Hearst newspapers for 26 years, Durslag was named executive sports editor of the Los Angeles *Herald Examiner* in 1964. His byline continued to appear in *TV Guide* and *The Sporting News*, and he was a Hearst syndicated columnist through the 1980s. /(NLM)

Cedric Durst — 1896–1971. OF-1B 1922–23, 26–30 Browns, **Yankees**, Red Sox 481 g, .244, 15 hr, 122 rbi. *2 WS, 5 g, .333, 1 hr, 2 rbi*

Durst's most important contribution to the Yankees came when they traded him and $50,000 to Boston for Red Ruffing early in the 1930 season. Durst had been a reserve outfielder on the great 1927 Yankees. Legend says that even the Yankee subs would have been stars for other teams. In truth, Durst had been only a utility player in three seasons with the Browns before coming to New York, and when the Red Sox played him regularly in 1930, he hit only .240, well below the AL average of .288. /(NLM)

Erv Dusak (Four Sack) — 1920- . OF-RHP 1941–42, 46–52 **Cardinals**, Pirates 413 g, .243, 24 hr, 106 rbi; 54 ip, 0–3, 5.33. *1 WS, 4 g, .250*

Tagged Four Sack after a game-winning homer early in his pro career, Dusak stuck with the 1946 World Championship Cardinals following WWII service. When his average dropped from .284 in 1947 to .209 in '48, Dusak became a pitcher, but he never won and never stayed a full season. /(MC)

Frank Dwyer — 1868–1943. RHP 1888–99 Cubs, Chicago (PL), Cincinnati-Milwaukee (AA), **Reds** 2810 ip, 176–152, 3.85. 20 wins: 1892, 96
   Manager 1902 **Tigers** 52–83, .385.
   Umpire 1889, 93–97, 99, 1901 NL, 1904 AL

Dwyer debuted with Cap Anson's powerhouse Chicago (NL) team, and in 1890 jumped to the Players' League, though he missed most of the season. He went 21–18 in 1892, toiling in the NL for St. Louis and Cincinnati. When the pitching mound was moved from 50' to 60'6" from the plate in 1893 and the league ERA ballooned, Dwyer survived the transition much better than many pitchers. He went 18–15 in '93, though his ERA rose from 2.98 to 4.13. Peaking in 1896, he compiled a 24–11 (3.15) mark. In 1899 he became a NL umpire, and, after managing the 1902 Tigers to seventh place, umpired in the AL in 1904. He later became the New York State Boxing Commissioner. /(AJA)

Jim Dwyer — 1950- . OF-DH-1B 1973- Cardinals, Expos, Mets, Cardinals, Giants, Red Sox, **Orioles** 1189 g, .257, 73 hr, 319 rbi. *1 LCS, 2 g, .250. 1 WS, 2 g, .375, 1 hr, 1 rbi*

After six years roaming the NL and two with the Red Sox, Dwyer found a home in Baltimore in 1981. A DH, extra outfielder, and lefthanded pinch hitter, he set the Orioles' career record for pinch homers. In his first World Series plate appearance, he homered off Philadelphia's John Denny for Baltimore's only run of Game One in 1983. /(JCA)

Jerry Dybzinski (Dybber) — 1955- . SS-3B-2B 1980-85 **Indians**, White Sox, Pirates 468 g, .234, 3 hr, 93 rbi. *1 LCS, 2 g, .250*

Dybzinski helped the AL West title-bound 1983 White Sox with clutch hitting and solid defense at shortstop, but committed a key baserunning gaffe in Chicago's Game Four LCS loss to Baltimore. Dybzinski was inserted in the lineup to replace regular shortstop Scott Fletcher, who was 0-for-7 in the Series at that point. With two on in the seventh inning of a scoreless tie at Comiskey Park, Dybzinski bunted into a force play. Julio Cruz followed with a sharp single to left, and lead runner Vance Law was held at third base. Dybzinski steamed around second with his head down before realizing third base was occupied. During the ensuing rundown, Law tried to score and was thrown out, effectively ending the rally; Baltimore won in the tenth inning.

Dybzinski, a Cleveland native, spent three seasons as an Indians utility man. /(ME)

Jim Dyck — 1922- . OF-3B 1951-56 **Browns/Orioles**, Indians, Reds 330 g, .246, 26 hr, 114 rbi

Dyck's all-around effective play for the Browns in 1952 earned him a spot on the ML rookie all-star team. He made a leaping catch at the left-field wall in Bobo Holloman's 1953 no-hitter against the A's, but played little after hitting .213 that season. /(RTM)

Duffy Dyer — 1945- . C 1968-81 **Mets**, Pirates, Expos, Tigers 722 g, .221, 30 hr, 173 rbi. *1 LCS, 1 g, --. 1 WS, 1 g, .000*

Dyer caught for the Arizona State 1965 and 1966 College World Series champs as a teammate of Reggie Jackson, Sal Bando, and Joe Keough. A poor hitter, he was a backup for Jerry Grote on the 1969 World Champion and 1973 NL champion Mets, and for Manny Sanguillen on the division-winning

1975 Pirates. Dyer caught a career-high 93 games for Pittsburgh in 1977. He later became a minor league manager and ML coach. /(MC)

Eddie Dyer — 1900-1964. LHP 1922-27 **Cardinals** 256 ip, 15-15, 4.75.
   Manager 1946-50 **Cardinals** 446-325, .578. First place: 46 *1 WS, 4-3, .571*

Dyer, a genteel southerner, was a marginal pitcher for parts of six seasons with the Cardinals, becoming a manager in that organization after pitching just one inning in 1927. He managed nine minor league champions between 1928 and 1942, and was named *TSN* Minor League Manager of the Year for his leadership at Columbus (American Association) in 1942. Dyer headed the St. Louis farm operation while Billy Southworth took the Cardinals to three straight wartime pennants. When Southworth left to manage the Braves, Dyer replaced him, and won the 1946 pennant and the World Series against the Red Sox. Despite his successful debut, when the team finished second the next three seasons, Dyer's reputation as a gifted leader and developer of talent was not enough to quiet critics. After a fifth-place finish with a 78-75 record in 1950, Dyer was offered just a one-year contract extension; the Rice alumnus instead chose the business world in booming Houston. /(JK)

Jimmy Dygert (Sunny Jim) — 1884-1936. RHP 1905-10 **A's** 986 ip, 57-49, 2.65. 20 wins: 07

Dygert appeared with the pennant-winning Athletics of 1905 and 1910. He won 21 games in 1907, but poor control of his spitball (he walked a league-leading 97 in 1908) diminished his effectiveness. /(JK)

Jimmy Dykes — 1896-1976. 3B-2B-1B-SS 1918-39 **A's**, White Sox 2282 g, .280, 109 hr, 1071 rbi. *3 WS, 18 g, 1 hr, 11 rbi*.
   Manager 1934-46, 51-54, 58-61 **White Sox**, A's, Orioles, Reds, Tigers, Indians 1407-1538, .478
☛ *All-Star—33* .

Jimmy Dykes averaged 125 games in 13 full seasons with the Athletics, but only once played the same position all year -second base in 1921. He had big, strong wrists from working as a pipefitter, and reputedly threw harder than any other non-pitcher in the game. He did everything but pitch and catch, prompting Connie Mack to call him his most valuable player. "Having one Dykes is like having five or six players and only one to feed, clothe, and pay," said Mack in 1929.

Jimmy Dykes

A Philadelphia native, Dykes was bought by the Athletics to take over second base in 1918 when regular Maury Shannon was drafted. Dykes played the season out before he too went into the army. Heavy-chested, heavy-legged, and wide in the rear, he returned in the spring of 1919 overweight and out of shape. He was sent down to play 2B with first baseman Ivy Griffin and shortstop Chick Galloway. In the fall they all joined the A's to stay.

In 1924, Dykes was given a Flint sedan for being named team MVP. He topped the .300 mark five times between '24 and 1930, and played third base in the 1929–31 World Series. In September of 1932, he was sold with Al Simmons and Mule Haas to the White Sox for $100,000. In the first All-Star Game, played at Comiskey Park in 1933, Dykes had two hits.

Dykes replaced Lew Fonseca as White Sox manager in 1934 and stayed until early in 1946. He was a player-manager until 1939. A chirping, joshing, noisy character and an accomplished bench jockey, he kept his calm in arguing with umpires as a player, but as a manager was frequently fined, and sometimes suspended, for letting loose volleys of strong language.

Dykes joined the Athletics as a coach in 1949, and was Mack's choice to manage the club in 1951.

After three poor finishes, he took over the Orioles in 1954, their first year in Baltimore after moving from St. Louis. He coached for the Reds, leading them for part of 1958, and managed the Tigers until August of 1960, when he was sent to the Indians for Joe Gordon in a rare trade of managers. He also coached the Braves and Kansas City A's. Gene Mauch broke Dykes's record of managing 21 years without winning a pennant. Dykes's highest finish was third place. /(NLM)

Lenny Dykstra (Nails) — 1963– . OF 1985- **Mets**, Phillies 634 g, .268, 34 hr, 172 rbi. *2 LCS, 13 g, .351, 2 hr, 6 rbi. 1 WS, 7 g, .296, 2 hr, 3 rbi*

Dykstra is thought of as a speedy singles hitter, but after breaking in with a home run in his first game he went on to surprise with some of the most memorable homers in recent Mets history. In Game Three of the dramatic 1986 LCS, his two-run ninth-inning HR off Astros relief ace Dave Smith gave the Mets a 6–5 victory. He also starred in the Mets' clinching victory in Game Six. His pinch-triple leading off the ninth started a game-tying rally, and he drove in the last run in the three-run rally in the 16th inning that led to the Mets' 7–6 win. After New York lost the first two games of the World Series, Dykstra's leadoff HR in Game Three sparked them to a 7–1 victory, and he hit a two-run shot that went off Boston right fielder Dwight Evans's glove and over the wall in Game Four as the Mets evened the Series. Dykstra also hit .429 in the Mets' 1988 LCS loss to the Dodgers, including a three-run HR in Game Five.

Dykstra's rally-starting triple in the '86 LCS was more typical of what was expected of him. As the Mets' leadoff hitter against righthanded pitchers, he teamed with number-two hitter Wally Backman to ignite the Mets' offense. The pair's all-out style of play earned them the nickname "The Partners in Grime." Dykstra had career highs of 31 stolen bases, a .295 average, and 58 walks in '86. It was his ability to draw more walks than the Mets' former regular leadoff man, switch-hitter Mookie Wilson, that won Dykstra the larger part of the centerfield platoon. He also was a surer fielder than Wilson; Dykstra's diving, sliding catches made him a favorite of the fans, but he rarely took a chance that backfired. Dykstra had his most productive year in 1987 with career highs of 10 HR, 37 doubles, and 86 runs scored in 431 at-bats. He declined in 1988, and was traded to the Phillies in mid-1989 with Roger McDowell for Juan Samuel in a much-criticized move. /(SH)

Arnie Earley — 1933- . LHP 1960-67 **Red Sox**, Cubs, Astros 381 ip, 12-20, 4.48

The bespectacled Earley was often the set-up man for Dick Radatz with the 1962-65 Red Sox. In 1965 Earley made a career-high 57 appearances, but went 0-1 without a save. Seldom used for more than an inning, he was generally the first lefthander called in from the bullpen. /(PB)

Tom Earley (Chick) — 1917-1988. RHP 1938-42, 45 **Braves** 359 ip, 18-24, 3.78

Earley wanted a tryout with the Red Sox but settled for signing with the Braves. After pitching for them for parts of five seasons, he went into the military, where he damaged his arm irreparably, tearing ligaments playing first base. /(NLM)

Jake Early — 1915- . C 1939-43, 46-49 **Senators**, Browns 747 g, .241, 32 hr, 264 rbi
☛ *All-Star—43.*

While Early was the second-string catcher, he learned to handle the Senators' four knuckleballers by watching Rick Ferrell. When Ferrell spent a couple of years with the Browns, Early took over and he caught the entire 1943 game for the AL All-Stars. He was an exuberant chatterbox behind the plate, singing and doing mock pitch-by-pitch broadcasts to distract hitters. /(JK)

George Earnshaw (Moose) — 1900-1976. RHP 1928-36 **A's**, White Sox, Dodgers, Cardinals 1915 ip, 127-93, 4.38. 20 wins: 29-31 *3 WS, 63 ip, 4-3, 1.58*
☛ *Led League—w 29.*

Moose, a genial 6'4" 210-lb righthander from Swarthmore College, teamed with Lefty Grove on the Philadelphia A's to form the game's premier pitching duo for the years 1929-31 (79 wins by Grove, 67 by Earnshaw). He won a league-high 24 in 1929, but twice led the league in walks. A basic fastball and curveball pitcher, Earnshaw said, "I didn't fool around with those junk pitches." He won a Bronze Star as a WWII naval officer, then scouted and coached for the Phillies. /(TJ)

Mike Easler — 1950- . OF-DH 1973-77, 79-87 Astros, Angels, **Pirates**, Red Sox, Yankees, Phillies 1151 g, .293, 118 hr, 522 rbi. *1 LCS, 1 g, .000. 1 WS, 2 g, .000*

Mired in the minor leagues for a decade, Easler finally won a job with the Pirates in 1980, hitting .338 with 21 HR and 74 RBI (in 393 at-bats) after spending the previous season as their primary pinch hitter. Most effective against righthanded pitchers, he moved from the outfield to first base when traded to Boston for John Tudor in 1984 but his all-around poor defense made him a DH. He had career highs of 27 HR and 91 RBI. The lefthander was traded to the Yankees after the season for righthanded slugger Don Baylor, another DH, in an attempt to match the hitters to their most compatible ballparks. Successful in New York, Easler was traded, reacquired, and released within one year despite continuing to hit for average. /(ME)

Mal Eason (Kid) — 1879-1970. RHP 1900-03, 05-06 Cubs, Braves, Tigers, **Dodgers** 944 ip, 36-75, 3.39. *Umpire* NL 1901-02, 10-15

Eason posted his only winning record during his rookie season (1-0 in one start in 1900). Before hurting his arm in 1906, an injury that ultimately ended his career, Eason pitched a 2-0 no-hitter for the Dodgers against the Cardinals on July 20.

Eason became a Southern League umpire in 1910, then joined the National League. Eason's umpiring career lasted longer than his playing career, ending in 1922 in the Pacific Coast League. /(MA)

Luke Easter — 1915-1979. 1B 1949-54 **Indians** 491 g, .274, 93 hr, 340 rbi

The 6'4" 240-lb Negro League veteran was 34 when the Indians promoted him from the minors. In 1950, they thought so highly of the lefthanded hitter that they traded Mickey Vernon, a once and future AL batting champ, making Easter their everyday first baseman. He hit 28 home runs as a rookie; one, a 477-foot shot, is considered the longest ever hit at Cleveland Municipal Stadium. In 1952, he hit 31

Luke Easter

homers (his ML career high), one less than the AL leader, teammate Larry Doby; however, Easter's 7.1 HR percentage topped the AL. He continued playing Triple-A ball into his late forties. Working as a bank messenger in 1979, he was shot to death by holdup men. /(TJ)

Howard Easterling — Unk.–Unk. 3B-2B-SS Negro Leagues 1936–43, 46–49 Cincinnati Tigers, Chicago American Giants, **Homestead Grays**, New York Cubans statistics not available

Easterling was the third baseman for the 1940 through 1943 Negro National League pennant-winning Homestead Grays. A 5'9" 175-lb switch-hitter, he generally batted fifth behind power hitters Buck Leonard and Josh Gibson. He hit approximately .315 lifetime. In 1941, he went 6-for-10 in a doubleheader sweep as the Grays defeated the New York Cubans in the league championship series. He hit .333 in the 1942 Black World Series, and partial data on the 1943 BWS shows he batted .280. He started at third base for the East in the 1940, 1943, 1946, and 1949 all-star games, and at shortstop for

the West in 1937, compiling a .320 average. He led the 1949–50 Venezuelan Winter League in doubles (16) and home runs (nine) in closing out his career. /(MFK)

Jamie Easterly (The Rat) — 1953– . LHP 1974–79, 81–87 Braves, Brewers, **Indians** 613 ip, 23–33, 4.61

In nine full and four partial seasons in the majors, the 5'9", sneaky-fast Easterly managed 23 wins and 14 saves. After he posted his career-best 4–1 record in 1985, the long reliever re-signed with the Indians under a lucrative, two-year contract, but spent the bulk of that time disabled with shoulder problems. While on loan to the Expos organization on July 14, 1979, he threw a seven-inning perfect game for Denver (American Association). /(JCA)

Ted Easterly — 1885–1951. C-OF 1909–15 **Indians**, White Sox, Kansas City (FL) 704 g, .300, 7 hr, 261 rbi

A lefthanded-hitting catcher, Easterly had three AL years over .300 and led the league in pinch hits (13) in 1912 while playing for both Cleveland and Chicago. He jumped to the Federal League in 1914 and finished third in batting (.335). /(ME)

Rawley Eastwick — 1950– . RHP 1974–81 **Reds**, Cardinals, Yankees, Phillies, Royals, Cubs 526 ip, 28–27, 3.30. *3 LCS, 8 ip, 2–0, 5.87 1 WS, 8 ip, 2–0, 2.25*

Eastwick was a rookie sensation in 1975, tying for the NL lead with 22 saves, with a 2.60 ERA. He then won three and saved two in post-season play as the Reds became the '75 World Champions. The 6'3" fireballer saved a league-high 26 in 1976, which, with his 11 relief wins, earned him the NL Fireman of the Year award. After being traded to St. Louis during a 1977 salary dispute, Eastwick parlayed free agency into a $1.1 million five-year pact in 1978 with the Yankees. They shipped him to the Phillies that June 14. Eastwick set a NL fielding record for pitchers by going 274 consecutive error-less games. /(MC)

Ebbets Field Brooklyn Dodgers 1913–57. LF-348, CF-384, RF-297

Cramped but colorful Ebbets Field, in the Flatbush section of Brooklyn, was home to the Dodgers in their lean times and glory years, until the franchise was transplanted to Los Angeles. Built by Dodger owner Charlie Ebbets for the 1913 season, the widely anticipated park opened without a press box, and no one brought the key to the bleachers for the first game. Originally the double-decked grandstand stood only along the foul lines, leaving the left field

Ebbets Field

corner 419' distant, and center 477'. The grandstand was extended to left and center in the 1930s, however, making the park a hitter's paradise. The left-field power alley was 351' and center became a very comfortable 388', made even shorter by the upper deck, which hung over the playing field. The right field wall was a sight in itself. A patchwork collection of local advertisements, a scoreboard, and a large black screen that was in play, it was 38' high and abutted Bedford Avenue. The screen made up the top 19', sending balls rebounding at unpredictable angles, while the wall itself was concave, angled in the middle. The large black scoreboard featured the famous Abe Stark "Hit sign, win suit" advertisement on the bottom, and a Schaefer beer ad on top which gave the official scorer's ruling on hits and errors by lighting up the appropriate letter (h or e).

Renowned for its laughable Dodgers in the 1920s and 1930s, Ebbets Field was also known for its vocal and boisterous fans. Hilda Chester would attend each game with her clanging cowbell, while the Dodgers Sym-Phony, a collection of musically inclined fans, played other instruments. In the 1940s, the Reds' Lonny Frey hit an inside-the-park home run when his drive to right hit the screen and fell straight down, coming to rest on top of the lower half of the wall, 19' above the field. And on October 3, 1947 Cookie Lavagetto broke up Bill Bevens's World Series no-hit bid with two out in the ninth.

By 1957, however, Ebbets Field had grown too old to satisfy Dodger owner Walter O'Malley, and in 1958 Brooklyn's beloved Dodgers were in Los Angeles. Only 6,673 fans attended the final game, and the park was demolished in 1960. The Jackie Robinson apartment complex now stands on the site. /(SCL)

Charlie Ebbets — 1859–1925. Owner.
Manager 1898 **Dodgers** 38–68, .358

Ebbets joined the Brooklyn club as a bookkeeper in 1883, gradually began buying shares in the team, and became president in 1898. He never played the game, but tried his hand at managing in 1898, finishing tenth. Ned Hanlon, the owner-manager of the Baltimore Orioles, bought some of the remaining Brooklyn stock after the '98 season, moved the best Baltimore players to Brooklyn, and won pennants in 1899 and 1900. However, when Hanlon wanted to move the team to Baltimore after the 1905 season, Ebbets bought him out.

Ebbets is sometimes credited with inventing the rain check and with suggesting that teams with the worst records should draft first, long before there was a draft. He had a deserved reputation for honesty and was popular in Brooklyn.

He financed the building of a new ball park for his team in 1912 by selling half of the club to the McKeever Brothers, contractors in Brooklyn. When the park was opened the next year, it was named Ebbets Field by a vote of sportswriters. Ebbets's Dodgers won pennants in 1916 and 1920. At the turn of the century, the prescient Ebbets was widely quoted when he said, "Baseball is in its infancy." /(NLM)

Dennis Eckersley (The Eck) — 1954– . RHP 1975– Indians, **Red Sox**, Cubs, A's 2742 ip, 165–138, 3.56. 20 wins: 78 *3 LCS, 17 ip, 0–1, 3.18. 2 WS, 3 ip, 0–1, 5.41*
☛ *All-Star—77, 82, 88.*

After an early career as a brash young flamethrower and a seven-year spell as a mediocre starter, The Eck was reborn in Oakland as a dominating bullpen stopper. In 1988, he led the AL with 45 saves, one shy of the ML record.

Eckersley broke into the ML with the Indians in 1975 as a cocky 20-year-old with shoulder-length hair and an explosive fastball. He fanned 200 batters in 1976, no-hit the Angels 1–0 on May 30, 1977 (part of a 22.1-inning hitless string), and was 20–8, 2.99 with the Red Sox in 1978. By 1980, however, his fastball had shortened, and he was 74–78 as a starter from 1980 to 1986.

Eckersley was traded to Oakland at the start of the 1987 season and was sent to the bullpen. He regained his effectiveness and fanned 113 batters in 116 innings. In 1988, he emerged as baseball's best reliever and he saved all four Oakland wins in the ALCS, but his season ended on a sour note when he surrendered a two-out, two-run home run to a hobbling Kirk Gibson in the bottom of the ninth inning of Game One of the WS. /(SCL)

William Eckert (Spike) — 1909–1971. Commissioner.

Eckert was a retired Air Force general, a supply officer who specialized in negotiating defense contracts. When he was elected commissioner in 1965, he knew nothing about baseball's inner workings and had not attended a game in ten years. At the time every baseball man nominated had too many enemies to gain enough votes. Eckert was quiet, bright, honest, and willing, but he was in a situation for which he had neither preparation nor aptitude. Lee McPhail was appointed administrator to help him, but Eckert became a symbol of executive futility. He incurred the public's ire by refusing to cancel games after the assassinations of Robert Kennedy and Martin Luther King and the owners' disdain because he refused to deal forcefully with substantive business issues. Anticipating a players' strike and having no confidence in Eckert's ability to handle the situation, the owners voted him out in early 1969 although he still had three years on his contract. /(NLM)

Ox Eckhardt [Oscar George] — 1901–1951. OF 1932, 36 Braves, **Dodgers** 24 g, .192, 1 hr, 7 rbi

Eckhardt averaged .367 over 13 seasons lifetime as one of the greatest minor league hitters ever. The 6'1" 190-lb Texan led the Pacific Coast League in batting four times. /(TJ)

Bruce Edwards (Bull) — 1923–1975. C 1946–52, 54–56 **Dodgers**, Cubs, Senators, Reds 591 g, .256, 39 hr, 241 rbi. *2 WS, 9 g, .241, 2 rbi*
☛ *All-Star—47, 51.*

A solid catcher with warning track power, Edwards hit .295 for Brooklyn in 1947 and led NL catchers that year in putouts and double plays. Following the season, the 5'8" 180-lb Bull hurt his arm throwing during an exhibition game against the inmates at Folsom Prison. His damaged arm and the emergence of Roy Campanella put him on the bench for the rest of his career. /(RTM)

Dave Edwards — 1954– . OF 1978–82 **Twins**, Padres 321 g, .238, 14 hr, 73 rbi

Bigger than older brothers Mike and Marshall Edwards, Dave had the best arm and power of the three, but struck out almost as often as he got a hit. /(MC)

Doc Edwards [Howard] — 1937– . C 1962–65, 70 Indians, **A's**, Yankees, Phillies 317 g, .238, 15 hr, 87 rbi. *Manager* 1987–89 **Indians** 173–207, .455

The ex-Navy medic applied solid defensive skills as a backup catcher in the bigs, followed by a career as a coach with the Phillies and Indians and as a minor league manager. Edwards's 1981 Charleston Charlies played Pawtucket in a 33-inning marathon, the longest game in professional history. He replaced Pat Corrales as the Indians' manager in July 1987 and was dismissed in September 1989./(JCA)

Hank Edwards (Henry) — 1919–1988. OF 1941–43, 46–53 **Indians**, Cubs, Dodgers, Reds, White Sox, Browns 735 g, .280, 51 hr, 276 rbi

Edwards hit .301 and led the AL in triples (16) with the Indians in 1946. A series of injuries, the worst when he dislocated his shoulder landing on a fence while making a leaping catch, ended his days as a regular./(ME)

Henry P. Edwards — 1873–1948. *Writer.*

An early dean of baseball writers, Edwards became sports editor of the Cleveland *Recorder* in 1898. In 1901 he joined the Cleveland *Plain Dealer*. He was credited with helping several sandlot players be discovered by ML teams, including Rube Marquard and Roger Peckinpaugh. In 1928 he organized the AL service bureau, which he managed from its beginning until 1942. One of the founders of the BBWAA, he served as secretary-treasurer for 15 years./(NLM)

Jim Joe Edwards [James Corbette] — 1894–1965. LHP 1922–26, 28 **Indians**, White Sox, Reds 580 ip, 26–37, 4.41

Edwards was most productive in 1923, going 10–10 for Cleveland. With the White Sox three years later, three of his six wins were shutouts./(TJ)

Johnny Edwards — 1938– . C 1961–74 **Reds**, Cardinals, Astros 1470 g, .242, 81 hr, 524 rbi. *2 WS, 4 g, .333, 2 rbi*
☛ *All-Star—63–65.*

Edwards was a durable, strong-armed, take-charge catcher whose intelligence matched his fine physical ability. A 6'4" 220-lb graduate of Ohio State, he set a ML season record for catcher's total chances (helped by a pitching staff of strikeout artists) with 1,221 in 1969, his first year with Houston. When he retired five years later, he held the NL career record for total chances by a catcher (9,745), since broken by Johnny Bench. Edwards won two Gold Gloves. As a rookie playing in the 1961 New York-Cincinnati World Series, he hit .364. He batted a career-high .281 for the 1964 Reds and had his best HR season in 1965 with 17./(TJ)

Mike Edwards — 1952– . 2B 1977–80 Pirates, **A's** 317 g, .250, 2 hr, 49 rbi

Edwards won a regular job with Oakland in 1978, when he had a 17-game hitting streak. On August 8 of that year he set an AL record with two unassisted double plays in one game. He lost his job after leading the league in errors in both '78 and '79. Mike's twin, Marshall, and their younger brother, Dave, also played ML baseball./(MC)

Dick Egan — 1884–1947. 2B-SS 1908–16 **Reds**, Dodgers, Braves 917 g, .249, 4 hr, 292 rbi

Egan hit over .250 only once in four years as the Reds' regular second baseman, but stole 141 bases, often teaming on double steals with Bob Bescher, who led the NL each year./(JK)

Dick Egan — 1937– . LHP 1963–64, 66–67 **Tigers**, Angels, Dodgers 101 ip, 1–2, 5.15

In 1962, Egan led the Pacific Coast League in wins (17) and strikeouts (201) pitching for Hawaii. Used exclusively in relief in the ML, the southpaw picked up two saves./(RTM)

Tom Egan — 1946– . C 1965–72, 74–75 **Angels**, White Sox 373 g, .200, 22 hr, 91 rbi

A high school All-American in baseball and football, the 6'4" Egan signed for $100,000 with California, and was converted from third base to catcher as a 19-year-old rookie in 1965. Egan allowed five passed balls in one game (7/28/70), then an AL record, but none the rest of the year. Always a backup, he had some power, but struck out once every three at-bats. In 1971, Egan was featured in a national ad campaign for life insurance that never mentioned that he played baseball./(MC)

Wish Egan [Aloysius Jerome] — 1881–1951. RHP 1902, 05–06 Tigers, **Cardinals** 279 ip, 8–26, 3.83

Egan was 6–15, 3.58 as a starter for the Cardinals in 1905 before an arm injury ended his playing career. He signed on to scout for Detroit in 1910, and remained with the Tigers until 1950, sometimes doubling as a coach. His discoveries included Hal Newhouser, Dizzy Trout, and Hoot Evers, and it was at his insistence that the Tigers traded Barney McCosky for George Kell in 1946./(FVP)

Howard Ehmke (Bob) — 1894–1959. RHP 1915–17, 19–30 Buffalo (FL), **Tigers**, Red Sox, A's 2820 ip, 166–166, 3.75. *1 WS, 12 ip, 1–0, 1.42.* 20 wins: 23

Ehmke broke in with the Federal League but was grabbed by Detroit when the Feds folded and twice won 17 games for them. Traded to the Red Sox in 1923, he pitched a no-hitter that would have been a one-hitter had not an Athletics' runner failed to touch first base on an apparent double. Four days later he pitched a one-hitter against the Yankees, the only hit being a ground ball that bounced off the third baseman's chest. Ehmke won 20 games for the Red Sox in '23 and 19 the next season. By 1929, he seemed nearly washed up, having won only seven games for the pennant-winning Athletics. It came as a shock when Connie Mack started him in the World Series opener against the Cubs. Mack reasoned that the sidearming Ehmke had the perfect mix of control and slow stuff to keep the predominantly righthand-hitting Cubs off balance, and gave Ehmke time off near the end of the season to personally scout the Cubs. Ehmke struck out a then-record 13 in pitching an eight-hit, 3–1 victory. /(NLM)

Howard Ehmke

Rube Ehrhardt [Welton Claude] — 1894–1980. RHP 1924–29 **Dodgers**, Reds 587 ip, 22–34, 4.15

Ehrhardt finessed batters with curves and change-ups, but manager Wilbert Robinson preferred big fastballers who overpowered hitters. Banished to the bullpen, Ehrhardt was called on so often that he twice led the NL in relief appearances and innings. /(JK)

Juan Eichelberger — 1953– . RHP 1978–83, 88 **Padres**, Indians, Braves 603 ip, 26–36, 4.10

The hard thrower with an unusual short-arm delivery had control problems, walking 273 while striking out 268 in the majors. Eichelberger was the staff ace of the last-place 1981 Padres, with eight victories. /(MC)

Mark Eichhorn — 1960– . RHP 1982, 86– **Blue Jays**, Braves 457 ip, 29–23, 3.19

Mark Eichhorn is a relief pitcher with a sidearm delivery who was the AL Rookie Pitcher of the Year in 1986, when he disdained the opportunity to pitch five meaningless extra innings at the end of the season in order to win the AL ERA title that went to Roger Clemens (whose ERA was 2.48 compared with Eichhorn's 1.72). As well as ERA, Eichhorn set Blue Jay rookie records for games, wins, saves, strikeouts and hit batters. In 1987 Eichhorn tied the AL record for appearances (89), being used mainly as a set-up man for fireballer Tom Henke. Eichhorn's effectiveness declined as he attempted to change his delivery so he wouldn't be so easy to steal on and as righthanded batters learned to lay off his wicked breaking ball. /(TF)

Dave Eilers — 1936– . RHP 1964–67 Braves, Mets, Astros 123 ip, 8–6, 4.45

Eilers's minor league record was 33–7 from 1963 to 1965. In the International League in 1964, he made 18 straight relief appearances without allowing a run. Used by Houston in 35 games in 1967, he went 6–4. /(RTM)

Eddie Einhorn — 1936– . *Executive.*

The colorful Einhorn was always in the midst of a controversy, be it the struggle to establish a United States Football League franchise in Chicago or answering his critics concerning the White Sox' new stadium. The former executive of CBS Sports began by selling hot dogs at Comiskey Park during the 1959 World Series. In 1981, former law school classmate Jerry Reinsdorf invited him to join the limited partnership which bought the club from Bill Veeck. Einhorn later founded Sportsvision, the Chicago cable outlet airing White Sox, Bulls, Sting, and Blackhawk games. He was instrumental in finalizing the six-year, multi-million-dollar pact between baseball and TV in 1981. In 1983, when the Chisox won the AL West division title, fans were treated to the sight of Einhorn jumping up and down in unabashed joy, wearing his Sox hat and warm-up jacket. /(RL)

Charles Einstein — 1926- . *Writer.*

A graduate of the University of Chicago and the son of radio comedian Harry (Parkyakarkas) Einstein, Charles Einstein worked for INS (1945–1953), San Francisco newspapers, and *Sport Magazine*, and edited the first wire-service news reports especially for television. In addition to novels, he has published four books with or about Willie Mays, and also co-authored books with Juan Marichal and Orlando Cepeda. /(NLM)

Jim Eisenreich — 1959- . OF-DH 1982–84, 87- Twins, **Royals** 308 g, .268, 16 hr, 111 rbi

Eisenreich vaulted through the minors to the Twins, but after a .303 beginning, he experienced Tourette's Syndrome, a nervous disorder that causes uncontrollable tics, sidelining him for most of 1982–84, and prompting an early retirement. His problems under control, he signed with the Royals in a comeback bid and batted .382 at Omaha (AAA) in 1987 after nearly three years away from pro ball. He joined Kansas City as a designated hitter and pinch hitter, better able to control himself when not in the field, but was able to play 64 games in the outfield in 1988. /(FO)

Harry Eisenstat — 1915- . LHP 1935–42 Dodgers, **Tigers**, Indians 479 ip, 25–27, 3.84

Primarily a reliever, the Brooklyn-born Eisenstat went 9–6 with the 1938 Tigers. Rather than return to baseball after 1942, Eisenstat felt it his patriotic duty to retain his defense plant job. /(TJ)

Kid Elberfeld (The Tabasco Kid) [Norman Arthur] — 1875–1944. SS-3B-2B 1898–99, 1901–11, 14 Phillies, Reds, Tigers, **Yankees**, Senators, Dodgers 1293 g, .271, 10 hr, 535 rbi.
   Manager 1908 **Yankees** 27–71, .276

The 5'5" Elberfeld played a fiery brand of baseball, challenging baserunners to slash him out of their way, living up to the title "The Tabasco Kid." His legs were badly scarred, and he grimly poured raw whiskey into spike wounds to cauterize them. He hit .310 as Detroit's shortstop his first full season, 1901, and was the Highlanders' everyday shortstop from mid-1903 through 1907. After a short, unsuccessful stint as New York's manager for part of 1908, he went back to playing full time the following year. He remained in baseball for decades, battling umpires and foes as a hotheaded minor league manager. /(JK)

Al Munro Elias — 1872–1939. *Statistician.*

In 1913 Al Elias and his brother Walter established their Bureau of Statistics. Their first production was scorecards featuring the latest team and individual statistics, which they peddled in saloons and other haunts of baseball fans. But newspapers refused to consider the use of their stats until three years later, when Elias sold their first weekly compilation of batting and pitching averages to the New York *Telegram*. Three years later the brothers were the official statisticians for the NL and International League. Other minor leagues soon signed up. In 1937 they took over publication of the *Little Red Book*, and for many years published the official *Green Book*, the NL's annual summary. /(NLM)

Hod Eller [Horace Owen] — 1894–1961. RHP 1917–21 **Reds** 863 ip, 61–40, 2.62. 20 wins: 19. *1 WS, 18 g, 2–0, 2.00*

Eller was an effective pitcher in his first four years with the Reds, peaking in the pennant-winning season of 1919, when he went 20–9 with a 2.39 ERA. That fall he threw a shutout in Game Five of the WS, with six consecutive strikeouts in the second and third innings, and a complete-game victory in the finale. But his WS achievements were tainted: the Reds' opponents were the infamous "Black Sox," bribed to throw the Series. /(JK)

Frank Ellerbe (The Governor) — 1895–1988. 3B-SS 1919–24 Senators, **Browns**, Indians 420 g, .268, 4 hr, 152 rbi

The last surviving member of the 1922 St. Louis Browns (the winningest team in the 52-year history of that franchise), The Governor from South Carolina was the only son of a state governor to play in the majors. /(WAB)

Hal Elliott (Ace) — 1899–1963. RHP 1929–32 **Phillies** 322 ip, 11–24, 6.95

Elliott led the NL in games pitched (48) as a starter and reliever for the last-place Phillies in 1930. The league as a whole batted a record .306 that year, and Elliott's ERA was 7.67. /(JK)

Jumbo Elliott [James Thomas] — 1900–1970. LHP 1923, 25, 27–34 Browns, Dodgers, **Phillies**, Braves 1206 ip, 63–74, 4.24
☛ *Led League—w 31.*

At one time the biggest man in the majors, Elliott stood 6'3" and his weight sometimes ballooned to 245. In 1931, he tied for the NL lead with 19 wins while pitching for the sixth-place Phillies. /(NLM)

Dock Ellis — 1945– . RHP 1968–79 **Pirates**, Yankees, A's, Rangers, Mets 2129 ip, 138–119, 3.45. *5 LCS, 30 ip, 2–2, 2.43. 2 WS, 6 ip, 0–2, 12.71*
☛ *All-Star—71.*

Flamboyant righthander Dock Ellis was among the most controversial players on the tempestuous Pirate teams of the early 1970s. An outspoken and political Afro-American, he antagonized the Pittsburgh front office by dressing colorfully and sometimes wearing his hair in curlers in the clubhouse. On June 12, 1970 in San Diego, he threw a no-hitter while under the influence of a hallucinogen, according to his autobiography (with Donald Hall) *Dock Ellis in the Country of Baseball.* And on May 1, 1974, in what he claimed was an attempt to rouse his teammates from lethargy, Ellis tied a major league record by bouncing baseballs off the first three Cincinnati batters he faced.

Ellis was 14–3 at the All-Star Break in 1971, but said he wouldn't start against the AL's Vida Blue in the All-Star Game because baseball would never start "two soul brothers" against each other. Ellis and Blue did start, and Ellis lost, the only loss for the NL between 1963 and 1982. He finished the season with a career-high 19 wins, and added another victory in Game Two of the NLCS against the Giants.

Ellis was traded to the Yankees with Willie Randolph and Ken Brett for Doc Medich after the 1975 season, and in 1976 he won Comeback Player of the Year honors with a 17–8, 3.19 record for the AL champions. He also won Game Three of the LCS against the Royals. In 1977, Ellis was traded to Oakland for Mike Torrez, then was sold to Texas six weeks later, and he finished the season 12–12. He retired after going 4–12 for the Rangers, Mets, and Pirates in 1979. /(TF)

John Ellis — 1948– . 1B-C-DH 1969–81 Yankees, **Indians**, Rangers 883 g, .262, 69 hr, 391 rbi

A competent hitter, the ungraceful 6'2" 225-lb Ellis played most regularly for the Indians in 1973–74, hitting career highs of 14 HR and 68 RBI in '73. He

came to Cleveland in the six-player 1972 deal that sent Graig Nettles to the Yankees. In May 1976 with Texas, Ellis suffered a broken leg, dislocated ankle, and torn ligaments sliding into second. He returned in 1977 to play part-time and, for a while, coach for the Rangers. /(TJ)

Rube Ellis [George William] — 1885–1938. OF 1909–12 **Cardinals** 555 g, .260, 14 hr, 199 rbi

Ellis stole 25 bases as the Cardinals' regular left fielder in 1910. Just before his death in 1938, he was an unsuccessful candidate for secretary of the Association of Professional Ball Players of America. /(WAB)

Sammy Ellis — 1941– . RHP 1962, 64–69 **Reds**, Angels, White Sox 1004 ip, 63–58, 4.15. 20 wins: 65
☛ *All-Star—65.*

Commenting on the 1965 season, when he went 22–10 for Cincinnati, Ellis said, "The Reds scored a lot of runs for me. I thought the year before was a better year (10–3) as far as being an asset to the team." In subsequent seasons, his blazing fastball and dancing knuckleball were weakened by arm problems. Ellis later became a Yankee pitching coach. /(RTM)

Dick Ellsworth — 1940– . LHP 1958, 60–71 **Cubs**, Phillies, Red Sox, Indians, Brewers 2156 ip, 115–137, 3.72. 20 wins: 63
☛ *All-Star—64.*

As a rookie, Dick Ellsworth paced NL pitchers in fielding. The lanky lefthander won 22 games for the 1963 Cubs. He lost 22, to lead the league and tie a Cub record, in 1966. Ellsworth twice led the NL in hits surrendered. He was tagged for 34 homers, most among NL hurlers, in 1964. Four years later, Ellsworth compiled a .696 (16–8) NL winning percentage. Like fellow big league hurlers Tom Seaver and Jim Maloney, Ellsworth attended Fresno (California) High School. /(TJ)

Don Elston — 1929– . RHP 1953, 57–64 **Cubs**, Dodgers 755 ip, 49–54, 3.69
☛ *All-Star—59.*

Hard-throwing Elston started 14 games for the Cubs in 1957 but switched to relief and became one of the NL's best. In 1958 he set a Cub record (since broken) with a league-leading 69 appearances. The following year, he and bullpen mate Bill Henry tied for the appearance lead with 65. Elston was picked for the 1959 NL All-Star team. In the eight seasons he relieved, Elston saved 63 games for Cub teams that seldom won very many games. "The most important asset of a reliever is his temperament," he said. "I wasn't too crazy about the term 'ice water in his veins,' but that is a good description." /(MC)

Bones Ely [Frederick] — 1863-1952 SS-OF 1884, 86, 90-02 Buffalo NL, Louisville AA, Syracuse AA, Dodgers, Cardinals, **Pirates**, A's, Senators 1341 g, .258, 24 hr, 585 rbi

Ely was the regular Pittsburgh shortstop from 1896 until early in 1901, when he was dismissed from the team for allegedly trying to persuade players to jump to the rival American League. His replacement was converted outfielder Honus Wagner. Half of Ely's career homers came in 1894. /(ME)

Elysian Fields

This unenclosed field in Hoboken, New Jersey, was the site of the first organized baseball game June 19, 1846, when the New York Base Ball Club defeated Alexander Cartwright's New York Knickerbockers 23-1 in four innings. /(SCL)

Red Embree [Charles Willard] — 1917- . RHP 1941-42, 44-49 **Indians**, Yankees, Browns 707 ip, 31-48, 3.72

The red-haired Embree pitched in 20 games for the Indians before retiring to become a farmer in 1943. He returned to lead the International League with 19 wins in '44, and rejoined the Tribe rotation to win eight games in each of 1946 and '47. His only winning record came with the 1948 Yankees, when he went 5-3 as a spot starter and reliever. /(ME)

Bob Emslie — 1859-1953. RHP 1883-85 **Baltimore AA**, Philadelphia AA 792 ip, 44-44, 3.19.
Umpire AA, NL 1890-24

Emslie's three-year ML pitching career was highlighted by his 32-17 season for Baltimore in 1884, a year of unusual records because talent was stretched thin with three major leagues operating. He became a ML umpire in 1890 and remained on the job for 35 years. Emslie was working the bases in the famous "Merkle Boner Game," but when he admitted he hadn't seen whether Merkle had touched second or not, fellow ump Hank O'Day was forced to make the call. According to a famous story, Emslie, irritated that Giants' manager John McGraw had called him a "blind robber," showed up at a Giants' practice with a rifle, placed a dime on the pitching mound, and then with a shot fired from behind home plate sent the coin spinning into the outfield. Reportedly, McGraw never again challenged his eyesight. /(RTM)

Yutaka Enatsu — 1949- . LHP 1967-84 **Hanshin Tigers**, Hiroshima Carp, Seibu Lions 206-158, 2.49

Highly touted as a rookie fresh from high school, the sidearming Enatsu won 12 games for the Hanshin Tigers. He followed with 25 victories, a Japanese record 401 strikeouts, and a 2-1, 10-inning loss to the powerful Yomiuri Giants in the game that decided the 1968 pennant. In 1969 he pitched 34 consecutive shutout innings against Yomiuri for six of his 15 victories in a season shortened by elbow pain. He rebounded to go 21-14 in 1970 but was suspended for two weeks over alleged involvement with gamblers. When he again lost the game that meant the pennant, he became Japan's leading target of fan abuse and media criticism. He openly feuded with manager and fellow star pitcher Minoru Murayama over his workload.

Handicapped by arm trouble and a heart condition aggravated by chain-smoking, Enatsu still won 20 games in 1972 and 1973. Slumping the next two seasons, he was pronounced washed up at age 27. He scored a brilliant comeback following his trade to Hiroshima, becoming the first player to be named MVP in both Japanese major leagues. Working mainly in relief, he contributed a 9-5, 2.66 record to Hiroshima's 1979 championship.

Enatsu was the winningest and highest-paid active pitcher in Japan when he was released by the Seibu Lions in 1984 after a shoving match with the manager. In 1985, at age 36, he signed a minor league contract with the Milwaukee Brewers, hoping to make the major league team in spring training. He didn't, amid intense publicity. He refused a minor league assignment and returned to Japan. /(MC)

Bob Engel — 1933- . *Umpire* NL 1965-87 *7 LCS 3 WS, 3 ASU*

Engel, a highly respected NL umpire, has worked more than a third of the NL LCS since their inauguration in 1969. /(RTM)

Joe Engel — 1893-1969. RHP 1912-15, 17, 19-20 **Senators**, Reds, Indians 407 ip, 17-23, 3.38

Engel's ML pitching career was ordinary, but it launched him into a baseball role he filled joyously: minor league team owner. Starting in 1930, he was a one-man scouting system and his Chattanooga team (Southern Association) was the top farm club for the Senators. He became the most colorful baseball promoter of his time. He staged elephant hunts, hired a female pitcher to strike out Babe Ruth and Lou Gehrig in an exhibition game, and gave away bizarre and valuable gifts, all to pack people into his ball park. /(JK)

Clyde Engle (Hack) — 1884–1939. OF-1B-3B-2B 1909–16 Highlanders, **Red Sox**, Buffalo (FL), Indians 831 g, .265, 12 hr, 318 rbi. *1 WS, 3 g, .333, 2 rbi*

Engle, a run-of-the-mill utility man, was involved in one of the most celebrated plays in World Series history. Pinch hitting for the Red Sox in the tenth inning of the 1912 Series' final game, he lofted an easy fly ball which was muffed by Giants centerfielder Fred Snodgrass. Tris Speaker, getting a second chance after his foul pop fell uncaught, singled in Engle for the tying run. Boston then won it all on Larry Gardner's long outfield fly. /(JK)

Dave Engle — 1956– . C-OF-DH-1B 1981– **Twins**, Tigers, Expos 594 g, .262, 31 hr, 181 rbi
☛ *All-Star—84.*

Like brother-in-law Tom Brunansky, Engle was drafted by the Angels in 1978. He went to the Twins in the 1979 trade for Rod Carew, and hit the first official home run in the Metrodome (4/6/82). Converted from outfield to catcher for 1983, he batted .305, and in 1984 was the Twins' only All-Star. Never developing good catching skills, he became a reserve, and in 1987 was Montreal's top righthanded pinch hitter. /(JCA)

Gil English — 1909– . 3B-SS-2B 1931–32, 36–38, 44 Giants, Tigers, **Braves**, Dodgers 240 g, .245, 8 hr, 90 rbi

Reportedly the last player personally scouted by John McGraw, English was a strong-armed third baseman who kept up a steady stream of chatter. McGraw watched him for two weeks at Durham before signing him. Unfortunately, English could neither strong-arm nor chatter his way on base, and he never played a full season as a ML regular. /(NLM)

Woody English [Elwood George] — 1907– . SS-3B 1927–38 **Cubs**, Dodgers 1261 g, .286, 32 hr, 422 rbi. *2 WS, 9 g, .184, 1 rbi*
☛ *All-Star—33.*

English batted a career-best .335 in 1930 and was among the NL leaders in runs scored, triples, and walks. He hit .319 in 1931 while leading NL

shortstops in putouts, and paced NL third basemen in fielding (.973) in 1933. /(TJ)

Del Ennis — 1925– . OF 1946–59 **Phillies**, Cardinals, Reds, White Sox 1903 g, .284, 288 hr, 1284 rbi. *1 WS, 4 g, .143*
☛ *All-Star—46, 51, 55.*

The Philadelphia Irishman was the original *TSN* Rookie Award winner in 1946; he hit a career-high .313, and was among the NL top five in batting, HR, slugging percentage, and total bases. Ennis twice hit over .300 again, surpassed 30 HR twice, and knocked in more than 100 runs seven times, peaking with a NL-leading 126 RBI for the pennant-winning 1950 Phillies. That year Ennis set a team record by grounding into 25 double plays. He had three homers in one game (7/23/55) and was a no-hit spoiler three times in his career. In the Phillies' 100th anniversary year, 1983, Ennis was chosen for their "Centennial team." /(TJ)

James Enright — 1912–1982. *Writer.*

Enright covered baseball for the Chicago *Evening American* for 20 years, starting in 1944, and later for the Chicago *American* and Chicago *Today* before he retired in 1974. He was co-author of *Ernie Banks: Mr. Cub*. A tall man who weighed over 260 pounds, Enright was a basketball official in the Big Ten and worked several NCAA finals. He is a member of the Basketball Hall of Fame as an official. /(NLM)

Mike Epstein (Superjew) — 1943– . 1B 1966–74 Orioles, **Senators**, A's, Rangers, Angels .244, 130 hr, 380 rbi. *2 LCS, 7 g, .190, 1 hr, 1 rbi. 1 WS, 6 g, .000*

Epstein was dubbed Superjew by rival manager Rocky Bridges after he led the California League in batting and home runs in 1965, and was *The Sporting News* Minor League Player of the Year in 1966 when he won International League MVP honors at Rochester (.309, 29 HR, 102 RBI). The burly, lefthanded slugger arrived at spring training in 1967 as baseball's most-heralded prospect, but after the Orioles tried in vain to convert him to the outfield (they already had Boog Powell at first base), they demoted him to Rochester again. The outspoken Epstein refused to report, going home to California instead, and did not play again until the end of May, when he was traded to the Senators with Frank Bertaina for Pete Richert. Later that season, in his first at-bat against the Orioles, Epstein hit a grand slam.

Epstein was a capable power hitter in the ML, but

never hit quite well enough to offset his frequent strikeouts, poor defense, and big mouth. He hit .278 with 30 HR for the Senators in 1968, but slipped to .256 with 20 HR in 1970 and was one of four players traded to Oakland for Darold Knowles before the 1971 season. With the A's, Epstein hit .270 with 26 HR in 1972, but was 0-for-16 in the WS and was traded back to the Rangers (formerly the Senators) for relief pitcher Horacio Pina in November. He played only 27 games with Texas in 1973, then was traded to the Angels, and after hitting .161 in 18 games for California in 1974 Epstein was out of the ML for good. /(SCL)

Eddie Erautt [Joseph Michael] — 1924-1976. RHP 1947-51, 53 **Reds**, Cardinals 380 ip, 15-23, 4.86

Erautt, used mainly in long relief, and his older brother Joe (with the White Sox briefly in 1950-51) were trained as a battery by their father, a Saskatchewan semi-pro. /(MC)

Eric Erickson (The Swatting Swede) — 1892-1965. RHP 1914, 16, 18-22 Giants, Tigers, **Senators** 822 ip, 34-57, 3.85

Born in Sweden, Erickson was a semi-pro star whose bat was as feared as his fastball. He won 31 games in the Pacific Coast League in 1917, but never had a winning ML season. /(JK)

Paul Erickson (L'il Abner) — 1915- . RHP 1941-48 **Cubs**, Phillies, Giants 814 ip, 37-48, 3.86. *1 WS, 7 ip, 0-0, 3.86*

This 6'2" product of smalltown Zion, IL, was called "Li'l Abner" after Al Capp's hillbilly comic strip character. A fireballer who walked as many as he struck out, he both started and relieved. His most famous appearance was his pennant-clinching victory in relief for the Cubs in 1945. He entered the game with two on and two out, and a one-run lead. With the count 0-1, he threw a wild fastball from which Pittsburgh batter Tommy O'Brien ducked—but the ball hit the bat for a foul. Expecting another fastball, O'Brien looked at a sweeping curve for strike three. /(DB)

Roger Erickson — 1956- . RHP 1978-83 **Twins**, Yankees 799 ip, 35-53, 4.14

Erickson made the Twins after just one year in the minors and went 14-13 with a 3.96 ERA in 1978. It was his only winning season. /(JFC)

Dick Errickson (Lief) — 1914- . RHP 1938-42 **Braves**, Cubs 736 ip, 36-47, 3.85

A moderately successful pitcher with some poor Braves teams, Errickson peaked at 12-13 with a 3.16 ERA for the seventh-place 1940 club. It was said he was sometimes rattled by rival coaches who claimed he was tipping his pitches. /(NLM)

Carl Erskine (Oisk) — 1926- . RHP 1948-59 **Dodgers** 1719 ip, 122-78, 4.00. 20 wins: 53 *5 WS, 42 ip, 2-2, 5.83*
☛ *All-Star—54.*

Carl Erskine, who teamed with Don Newcombe to anchor the pitching staff for the powerful post-WWII Brooklyn teams, won 61% of his decisions in 12 years with the Dodgers. The 5'10" righthander injured his shoulder during his rookie season and pitched with pain most of his career. Because he couldn't throw a lot between starts, he never developed any specialty pitches. He remained a fastball/curveball/changeup pitcher who was able to change speeds on the curve. "Oisk" went 20-6 in 1953 to lead NL pitchers in winning percentage (.769). His 14 strikeouts as the winner of Game Three of the '53 WS set a Series record that stood for 14 years. He had two no-hitters: on June 19, 1952 against the Cubs, and on May 12, 1956 against the Giants. /(TJ)

Nick Esasky — 1960- . 1B-3B 1983- **Reds**, Red Sox 801 g, .251, 122 hr, 427 rbi

Esasky replaced Johnny Bench at third base for the Reds in 1983 and made the *Topps* all-rookie team with a .265 average and 12 HR. The strikeout-prone slugger was converted to first base full-time in 1987, and was traded to Boston with Rob Murphy for Todd Benzinger and Jeff Sellers before the 1989 season. /(ME)

Nino Escalera — 1929- . OF-1B 1954 **Reds** 73 g, .159, 0 hr, 3 rbi

Escalera was a scout for the Mets from 1966 to 1981 and for the Giants from 1982 to the present. His ML career consisted mostly of pinch hitting for the Reds in 1954. He discovered Jose Oquendo and Juan Berenguer. /(FVP)

Jimmy Esmond — 1889-1948. SS 1911-12, 14-15 Reds, Indianapolis FL, **Newark FL** 461 g, .264, 9 hr, 162 rbi

Esmond had a great arm and good range but frequent injuries and illnesses hampered him throughout his career. He played regularly in the Federal League's two seasons, and in 1914 led the FL in triples with 15. /(NLM)

Hector Espino — 1939- . 1B-OF 1960-84 Mexican Leagues

A symbol of Mexican pride, the slugging Espino declined offers from the Cardinals, Mets, and Padres while playing 25 seasons with San Luis de Potosi, Monterrey, and Tampico. He did play 32 games for Jacksonville (International League) in 1964, batting .300, but was offended by racial discrimination and swore he would never again play in the United States. He led the Mexican League in batting in 1964 and in 1966–68; in home runs in 1964 and 1972; and in RBI in 1962 and 1973. His Mexican League record of 46 HR, set in 1964, stood until 1986. He retired at age 45 with the career record for minor league home runs, 484. /(MC)

Nino Espinosa — 1953–1988. RHP 1974–81 **Mets**, Phillies, Blue Jays 821 ip, 44–55, 4.17

The Dominican was the ace of the miserable Mets of 1977–78. He beat the Phils 1–0 on a three-hitter, driving in the only run on September 14, 1977. Philadelphia traded for him in 1979, and he had a career-best 14–12. Bothered by arm trouble early in the Phillies' 1980 World Championship season, he returned to the minors, missing post-season play. /(MC)

Sammy Esposito — 1931– . 3B-SS-2B 1952, 55–63 **White Sox**, A's 560 g, .207, 8 hr, 73 rbi. *1 WS, 2 g, .000*

A career utility man from Chicago's South Side, Esposito was beloved by White Sox fans. On September 7, 1960, he started in place of Nellie Fox, ending Fox's consecutive-game streak at 798—a ML record for second basemen. When Esposito booted a cinch double play ball, an enraged fan, who had bet heavily on the game, charged onto the field and began punching the 5'9" infielder. /(DB)

Chuck Essegian — 1931– . OF 1958–63 Phillies, Cardinals, Dodgers, Orioles, A's, **Indians** 404 g, .255, 47 hr, 150 rbi. *1 WS, 4 g, .667, 2 hr, 2 rbi*

Essegian, a member of Stanford's 1952 Rose Bowl team, is one of two players to hit two pinch hit home runs in a World Series. In the 1959 WS, his sixth-inning pinch homer tied Game Two for Los Angeles and the Dodgers went on to win. With the Dodgers safely ahead in the sixth and final game, he batted for Duke Snider in the ninth inning and homered again. Essegian added a postscript by pinch-homering on Opening Day in 1960. /(RTM)

Jim Essian — 1951– . C 1973–84 Phillies, White Sox, **A's**, Mariners, Indians 709 g, .244, 33 hr, 206 rbi

Strong-armed Essian was the regular catcher for the White Sox in 1977, when he hit .273 with a good

batting eye and had career highs of 10 HR, 50 runs, and 44 RBI. Traded to the A's for 1978, he slumped to .223 and was never first-string again. /(WOR)

Bill Essick (Vinegar Bill) — 1881–1951. RHP 1906–07 **Reds** 61 ip, 2–3, 2.95

After a nine-game ML career with the Reds, Essick became a minor league owner and manager, leading Vernon to three consecutive Pacific Coast League pennants. As the PCL scout for the Yankees from 1926 to 1950, Essick signed Joe DiMaggio after other scouts had given up on him because of his leg injuries. His nickname was derived from his surname, which sounds like the German word for vinegar. /(FVP)

Bobby Estalella — 1911– . OF-3B 1935–36, 39, 41–45, 49 Senators, Browns, **A's** 680 g, .282, 44 hr, 308 rbi

The chunky native Cuban became a starter as a draft-exempt wartime player. He was suspended from 1946 to 1948 for trying to jump to the Mexican League and appeared in only eight more ML games. /(JK)

Chuck Estrada [Charles Leonard] — 1938– . RHP 1960–64, 66–67 **Orioles**, Cubs, Mets 764 ip, 50–44, 4.07
☛ *Led League—w 60. All-Star—60.*

A hard thrower but often wild, Estrada was one of the brightest of several young Orioles pitchers who arrived in the ML about the same time. His 18 wins as a rookie topped the AL in 1960. He won 15 the next season but led only in walks. His 17 losses were the most in the AL in 1962. He never recovered from an elbow injury in 1963. After his retirement he found frequent employment as a pitching coach. /(CR)

Andy Etchebarren — 1942– . C 1962, 65–78 **Orioles**, Angels, Brewers 948 g, .235, 49 hr, 309 rbi. *5 LCS, 12 g, .2121, 1 hr, 4 rbi. 4 WS, 9 g, .074* ☛ *All-Star—66–67.*

Etchebarren became the Orioles' number-one catcher in 1966 when regular Dick Brown retired on account of a brain tumor. Etchebarren hit only .221 with 11 HR and 50 RBI while striking out 106 times in 412 at-bats, but the Orioles won the World Championship with him behind the plate. He caught every inning of their sweep of the Dodgers in the World Series as Jim Palmer, Wally Bunker, and Dave McNally tossed shutouts in the last three games. Known for his bushy eyebrows, Etchebarren was gradually supplanted by the better-hitting Elrod

Hendricks but remained with Baltimore as a back-up until 1975. Finishing his career with the Brewers, he later became a Milwaukee coach. /(SH)

Shinichi Eto — 1937- . OF 1959-76 **Chunichi Dragons**, Lotte Orions
☛ *Led League—ba 64-65, 71.*

An all-star Japanese left fielder, Eto hit between 20 and 30 home runs most seasons, collected 2,057 hits, and batted .300 for much of his career. He won batting titles in 1964 (.323) and 1965 (.336). Rebelling against Chunichi's team curfew in 1970, he threatened to retire if not traded. Shipped inter-league to the Lotte Orions for 1971, he bested American teammate George Altman for his third batting crown—in somewhat tainted fashion. As Altman recalled, Eto, a righthanded batter, was an opposite-field hitter. With the title on the line, Nankai manager Katsuya Nomura positioned his infield so as to leave the right side open, and Eto went 4-for-4. Nomura had won the HR title over American Daryl Spencer through similar collusive measures six years earlier. /(MC)

Nick Etten — 1913- . 1B 1938-39, 41-47 A's, Phillies, **Yankees** 937 g, .277, 89 hr, 526 rbi. *1 WS, 5 g, .105, 2 rbi*
☛ *Led League—hr 44. Led League—rbi 45.*

Upon being dealt to the Yanks in 1943 after two seasons with the lowly Phillies, Etten exclaimed, "Imagine a man in that environment hearing that he had been sold to the Yankees!" The lefthanded batter thrived briefly in Yankee pinstripes, leading the AL with 22 HR and 97 bases on balls in 1944, and with 111 RBI the following year. /(TJ)

Al Evans — 1916-1979. C 1939-42, 44-51 **Senators**, Red Sox 704 g, .250, 13 hr, 211 rbi

Evans's defensive ability gradually won him more playing time with the Senators despite his largely unproductive bat. His best year was 1949, the only season in which he caught more than 100 games, when he hit .271 with 42 RBI. /(MC)

Barry Evans — 1956- . 3B-2B 1978-82 **Padres**, Yankees 224 g, .251, 2 hr, 41 rbi

After Evans led the Northwest League in hits and RBI in his 1977 pro debut, the Padres traded incumbent third baseman Doug Rader to make room for a budding star. But tantrums and injuries kept him from ever winning an everyday ML job. /(MC)

Billy Evans — 1884-1956. *Umpire* AL 1906-27 *6 WS*
☛ *Hall of Fame—1973.*

One of the foremost umpires in baseball history, Evans was refined and fastidious. He substituted diplomacy for belligerency during baseball's rowdier days. He began as a sportswriter but took up umpiring after he substituted for an absent arbiter in a game he was covering. He was only 22 when he was promoted from a Class C league to the AL, the youngest man ever to be employed as a ML umpire and the only one ever promoted all the way from Class C.

In his 22 years as an AL umpire, he achieved a reputation for fairness and unquestioned integrity. In Game Two of the 1909 WS, played in Pittsburgh, the Pirates' Dots Miller hit a low line drive along the foul line in the direction of temporary right-field bleachers that rested in part in fair territory. As the ball sailed over the stands the fans stood and obstructed the views of Evans and the other umpire, Bill Klem. Neither saw the ball land. Both marched to the outfield and Evans began questioning the bleacherites as to whether the ball was fair or foul. On their testimony Evans decided the ball had

Billy Evans

landed fair and skipped into the crowd. Miller, who had circled the bases, was sent back to second with a ground-rule double.

Although he was a diplomat, Evans once fought Ty Cobb under the grandstand after Cobb challenged Evans over two close out calls at the plate. Al Schacht, baseball's "Clown Prince," described the fight: "When the game ended they both went under the grandstand while the members of both teams became spectators. Billy posed like a real fighter while Ty stalked him like a Tiger and then suddenly hit him in the jaw. Down went Evans with Ty on top of him. With his knee on Evans' chest, Ty held Billy by the throat and tried to choke him. We finally got him off Billy and that was the end of the fight."

Evans continued his writing career, authoring many articles and a book: *Umpiring from the Inside.* From 1920 to 1927 he wrote a syndicated column, "Billy Evans Says." In later years Evans served as GM for Cleveland (1927–36) and Detroit (1947–51), farm director for Boston (1936–40), GM of the NFL's Cleveland Rams (1941), and president of the Southern Association (1942–46). In 1973 he was elected to baseball's Hall of Fame./(RTM)

Darrell Evans — 1947– . 3B-1B-DH 1969– Braves, **Giants,** Tigers 2687 g, .248, 414 hr, 1354 rbi. *2 LCS, 8 g, .296, 1 rbi. 1 WS, 5 g, .067, 1 rbi* ☛ *All-Star—73.*

During the early 1970s, Evans was considered to be the premier third baseman behind Mike Schmidt in the National League. The only player to hit 40 homers in each league, he is the oldest player to win a home run title, hitting 40 with the Tigers at the age of 38 in 1985.

Evans credits Ted Williams's book for teaching him how to hit; Eddie Mathews taught him how to pull. Originally drafted by the A's in 1968, Evans started wearing contact lenses in 1971 and started hitting for power regularly. Hitting third in front of Aaron, Evans saw plenty of good pitches and, in 1973, was one of a record three Braves players to crack 40 homers: Aaron had 40, Evans 41, and Davey Johnson had 43. Even though he preceded Aaron in the lineup, he led the league in walks with 124, and again the following year with 126. He finished his career 10th all-time in walks. Evans was on first base when Aaron hit number 715 on April 8, 1974. In June 1976, Evans was traded in a six-player deal to San Francisco. Although he was productive for seven years, Candlestick Park was not suited for his power. In 1983, he switched to first

Darrell Evans

base. On June 15, he hit three homers in a game. After the season, he signed on as a free agent with the Tigers.

The Tigers got immediate dividends when Evans hit a three-run homer Opening Day to spark the Tigers to a 35–5 start as they coasted to the American League pennant and World Series championship, despite Evans's 1-for-15 performance against the Padres. In 1985, he led the league in homers for the only time in his career to begin the most productive power phase of his career, hitting 29 homers in 1986 and 34 in 1987 at the age of 40. As a full-time DH in 1988, he managed 22 homers, but hit only .208, and was traded by the Tigers back to the Braves during the off-season. He saw considerable action in 1989 due to the demotion of third baseman Ron Gant and the season-ending injury of first baseman Gerald Perry, and continued to show good power while hitting for a low average./(SEW)

Dwight Evans (Dewey) — 1951– . OF-DH 1972- **Red Sox** 2382 g, .273, 366 hr, 1283 rbi. *3 LCS, 14 g, .180, 1 hr, 6 rbi. 2 WS, 14 g. .300, 3 hr, 14 rbi* ☛ *Led League—hr 81. All-Star—78, 81, 87. Gold Glove—76, 78–79, 81–85.*

In the strike-shortened 1981 season, Evans suddenly arrived as a slugger. He hit .296, shared the AL HR title with 22, and led the league in what would become his specialty, bases on balls. Evans walked 85 times in 1981 (he had never drawn more than 69 walks before) and 112 in 1982, and led the AL twice more in '85 and '87 with 114 and 106. Along with his improved patience at the plate, Evans unveiled a new batting stance—a deeper crouch with his weight shifted drastically onto his back foot. The improvements were swift and dramatic. He hit .292 with 32 HR, 98 RBI, and 122 runs scored in 1982, and had a virtually identical season in 1984 (.295, 32 HR, 104 RBI, 121 runs scored). His average slumped in 1985–86, but he still slugged 55 HR and drew 211 walks over the two seasons, and in 1987, at the age of 35 and in his 16th ML season, Evans recorded career highs in batting average (.305), HR (34), and RBI (123).

The Red Sox shifted Evans to first base in July 1987. He never adjusted to the infield, and in mid-1988 he returned to right field, where his play declined appreciably. In mid-1989 he became Boston's regular DH. Still, Evans has retained his reputation as an outstanding clutch hitter, and his careful pitch selection makes him particularly dangerous batting with a 3–0 count (he has eight career HR in that situation). Only Carl Yastrzemski has played more games for the Boston Red Sox. /(SCL)

Dwight Evans

Evans had already become a regular in the Boston outfield when he was joined by sensational rookies Jim Rice and Fred Lynn in 1975. As the 1980s ended, Rice and Lynn were clearly at the ends of their careers, while Evans remained among the best in the game. Number 24 made his reputation as a strong-armed outfielder who froze baserunners in their tracks, and later blossomed into one of the AL's better hitters, averaging 28 HR per year after the age of 30.

After winning International League MVP honors at Louisville in 1972 (.300, 17 HR, 95 RBI), Evans joined the Red Sox for good in 1973 but hit only .223. His offensive contributions were unexciting for several seasons, but he excelled defensively. He mastered Fenway Park's tricky right-field corner and employed the strongest outfield throwing arm in the AL. His lunging catch in the 11th inning of Game Six of the 1975 WS robbed Joe Morgan of a Series-winning HR, started an inning-ending double play, and set the stage for Carlton Fisk's famous HR in the 12th. In 1976, he won the first of his eight Gold Gloves, fourth-best all-time among outfielders behind Willie Mays, Roberto Clemente, and Al Kaline.

Jim Evans — 1946– . *Umpire* AL 1971–87 *4 LCS 3 WS, 1 ASU*

As a political science major at the University of Texas, Evans was a member of the debating team. He was the plate umpire in the longest AL game by time (8 hours, 6 minutes) in Chicago on May 8, 1984 (finished May 9), when the White Sox beat the Brewers 7–6. /(RTM)

Joe Evans (Doc) — 1895–1953. OF-3B 1915–25 **Indians**, Senators, Browns 732 g, .259, 3 hr, 209 rbi. *1 WS, 4 g, .308*

Converted from third base to the outfield in 1920, Evans alternated with left fielder Charlie Jamieson for Cleveland in that year's World Series, and had three hits in Game Six. He was a physician after leaving baseball. /(ME)

Roy Evans — 1874–1915. RHP 1897–99, 02–03 Cardinals, Louisville NL, Washington NL, Giants, **Dodgers**, Browns 614 ip, 28–42, 3.66

Evans pitched with only occasional success for six teams in five ML seasons. In 1902, in a season split between the Giants and Dodgers, he had his best ERA, 3.00, but led the NL in losses with 19. /(BC)

Steve Evans — 1885–1943. OF 1908–15 Giants, **Cardinals**, Brooklyn (FL), Baltimore (FL) 978 g, .287, 32 hr, 466 rbi

Evans had his best year in 1914 with fifth place Brooklyn of the Federal League, finishing second in the league in batting (.348), homers (12), RBI (96), and doubles (41). One of baseball's funniest clowns, his antics got him traded to the Cardinals after just two games with the Giants in 1909. /(WAB)

Bill Everett — 1868–1938. 1B-3B-OF 1895–1901 **Cubs**, Senators 698 g, .317, 11 hr, 341 rbi

An accomplished bunter and basestealer, Everett was a good leadoff man who topped 100 runs scored three times. His fielding, charitably described by one reporter as "always honest," was poor. /(BC)

Hoot Evers [Walter Arthur] — 1921– . OF 1941, 46–56 **Tigers**, Red Sox, Giants, Orioles, Indians 1142 g, .278, 98 hr, 565 rbi
☛ *All-Star—48, 50.*

An outstanding prospect, Evers never achieved the stardom predicted for him. After his career was delayed four years by WWII, he returned as the Tigers' starting centerfielder in 1946, only to miss half the season with a broken ankle. He played his first full season in 1947, hitting .296, then hit over .300 three straight years. He peaked in 1950, making his second All-Star appearance, leading AL outfielders in fielding (.997), and hitting .323 with 21 homers, 103 RBI, and a league-leading 11 triples. He also hit for the cycle September 7. He slumped badly the next year. In 1952, as the Red Sox' left fielder while Ted Williams was in the military, a broken finger hampered Evers's batting grip and he never regained his stroke. A fine defensive player, Evers bounced from team to team until 1956 but never hit higher than .264. /(JK)

Johnny Evers (The Trojan, The Crab) — 1883–1947. 2B 1902–1917, 22 **Cubs**, Braves, Phillies, White Sox 1783 g, .270, 12 hr, 538 rbi. *4 WS, 20 g, .316, 6 rbi.*
    Manager 1913, 21, 24 **Cubs**, White Sox 196–208, .485
☛ *Most Valuable Player—14 . Hall of Fame—1946.*

A Franklin P. Adams poem immortalized a snappy-fielding Cub infield that was primarily responsible for three straight NL pennants starting in 1906, and World Series victories in 1907 and 1908, with Evers its brainy center. The play that earned Evers

Johnny Evers

(rhymes with "beavers," not "feathers") his reputation as a quick-witted infielder came on September 23, 1908, in an afternoon at the Polo Grounds in the thick of a tight pennant race. Al Bridwell had singled in Mike McCormick from third with two out in the bottom of the ninth to give the Giants an apparent 2–1 victory. But Giants' rookie third baseman Fred Merkle, the runner at first base, didn't advance all the way to second on the play. As was the custom of the day, Merkle saw the run score, then turned and headed into the clubhouse. Evers, standing at second, called for the ball, and touched second for the force. Umpire Hank O'Day called Merkle out and declared the game a tie. When the two teams ended the season tied for the NL pennant, the game was replayed as a playoff, which the Cubs won.

The slightly-built but tempermental Evers was nicknamed "The Crab" for the way he sidled up to grounders. He joined the established Tinker and Chance full-time in 1903. Evers had identical .350 World Series averages in 1907 and 1908, knocking in the winning run in the fifth and final game. Ironically, 1910, the year Adams fashioned his poem, was the final season that the trio played together. Evers was hurt for most of 1911, and player-manager Chance had retired as a player to devote his full energies to managing. Evers and Tinker, despite their on-field teamwork, didn't speak to each other their final years together, the result of some imagined slight, and often traded punches in the clubhouse. Despite the fighting, Evers enjoyed his best season in 1912, when he hit a career high .341, and replaced Chance as manager in 1913. In February 1914, he was traded to Boston, where he formed another slick double-play combination with shortstop Rabbit Maranville. In the Miracle Braves sweep of the Athletics in the 1914 Series, Evers batted .438 and drove in the winning runs in the final 3–1 victory.

When Evers came back from Europe and WWI, he coached briefly for former enemy John McGraw on the Giants and was assistant manager for the Cubs in 1921. In 1923, he joined the crosstown White Sox as a coach, and managed the team in 1924. He entered the Hall of Fame six months before his death, and was the last surviving member of the double-play combo. /(SEW)

Bob Ewing (Long Bob) [George Lemuel] — 1873–1947. RHP 1902–12 **Reds**, Phillies, Cardinals 2301 ip, 128–118, 2.49. 20 wins: 05

A spitball pitcher, Ewing was a workhorse for the Reds in the century's first decade, topping 300 innings three times. He was 20–11 in 1905 and twice won 17. His 1907 ERA was 1.73. Traded to the Phillies in 1910, he pitched a two-hitter and two three-hitters while winning 16. /(NLM)

Buck Ewing [William] — 1859–1906. C-1B-OF-3B-2B-SS 1880–97 Troy (NL), **Giants**, New York (PL), Cleveland (NL), Reds 1315 g, .303, 70 hr, 733 rbi.
    Manager 1890, 95–1900 New York (PL), **Reds**, Giants 489–395, .553
☛ *Led League—hr 83 . Hall of Fame—1939.*

When the doors of the Baseball Hall of Fame were first opened, in 1939, Buck Ewing's plaque was ready to go up on the wall. Elected by the Committee on Baseball Veterans, Ewing had simply been baseball's best catcher and, according to his contemporaries, was unequaled as an all-around player in the 19th century. Until Mickey Cochrane, Bill Dickey, and Gabby Hartnett came along, Ewing was listed as the catcher on virtually everyone's all-time team.

A lifetime .303 hitter with a high of .344 in 1893,

Buck Ewing

Ewing was also a dead-ball-era NL home run champ, hitting 10 for New York in 1883. He topped the NL with 20 triples in 1884, and hit 15 triples four other times. In a June 9, 1883 game, he hit three triples. When stolen bases started being tallied, Ewing averaged 37 a season, with a high of 53 for the 1888 Giants.

Ewing played during a time when catchers did not catch every day. He never caught more than 97 games a season, and only once caught more than 80. He was said to have been a master at throwing out baserunners; he led NL catchers in assists three times in the 1880s, and in double plays twice. He spent few games behind the plate after 1890. Instead, he was stationed mostly in the outfield and at first base. He also pitched 47 innings.

Buck's brother John, a pitcher, compiled a 53–63 career record. He pitched for Buck in the 1890 Players' League, when Buck caught for and managed New York. John led the NL with a .724 winning percentage (21–8) and a 2.27 ERA as Buck's batterymate with the 1891 Giants. John then retired, and Buck went on to Cleveland in 1893. Buck returned to his hometown of Cincinnati as a first baseman-manager in 1895, and played one final game in 1897. Managing the Reds through 1899, he never finished higher than third. He piloted the Giants for part of 1900, and died six years later. /(JK)

Exhibition Stadium Toronto Blue Jays 1977–1989. LF-330, CF-400, RF-330

Exhibition Stadium was built for football in 1959 and was modified for the expansion Blue Jays. Home plate lay near the corner of one end zone, and the main seating areas, along each sideline of the football field, extended down the first-base line and behind the left-field fence. The best seats, both because they were the only roofed section and because they offered the best view of the game, were the left-field general admission seats, paradoxically the cheapest tickets. Originally there were no seats at all along what is now the third-base line (behind the end zone), and a number of seats in deep centerfield and down the right-field line were rarely sold due to poor sight lines. The artificial-turf playing field was contained by a temporary blue fence inside the permanent seating, and home runs to right field bounced across the unused portion of the football field. The Blue Jays' April 30, 1984 game was postponed due to heavy winds. The open end of the field faced Lake Ontario, and metal seats compounded the problems with cold weather. The discomfort led the team to move to the indoor Skydome in 1989. /(SCL)

Exposition Park — Pittsburgh Pirates 1891–1909, Pittsburgh (PL) 1890, Pittsburgh (FL) 1914–15

Home of the Pirates until Forbes Field was completed, Exposition Park twice had its roof ripped off by strong winds, in 1900 and 1901, and no ball ever cleared the original left and center field fences. Today, Three Rivers Stadium stands on the site. /(SCL)

Red Faber [Urban Clarence] — 1888–1976. RHP 1914–33 **White Sox** 4088 ip, 254–212, 3.15. 20 wins: 15, 20–22 *1 WS, 27 ip, 3–1, 2.33*
☛ *Led League—era 21–22. Hall of Fame—1964.*

Faber was a steady, even-tempered spitballer whose long life in the second division probably kept him from the select 300-win club. With Chicago's lineup decimated by the loss of the Black Sox stars, Faber endured 13 seasons in or below fifth place, and only three at .500 or above. His lifetime winning percentage of .545 was achieved mostly with teams below .500.

Faber acquired his spitter in 1911, after a sore arm ruined early tryouts with the Pirates. Sold to Des Moines (Western League), he had two sterling seasons, and was purchased by the White Sox for $3,500. The Sox and Giants scheduled a world tour after the 1913 season. Faber, who had not yet pitched an inning of major league ball, was loaned to the Giants when Christy Mathewson declined to take the trip. Faber won four exhibitions against his future teammates, and began his 20-year, one-team career in 1914.

He was the pitching star of the 1917 Series win over the Giants, missed most of 1918 in the Navy, and returned to help win the 1919 pennant with 11 victories. He was on the bench for the scandalous Series, however, with recurring arm trouble and the flu.

Faber's peak years were 1921 and 1922, when he won 25 and 21 games while the Sox were finishing seventh and fifth. He led the league in ERA and complete games both years. From 1914 through 1923, he had ten consecutive winning seasons. But he was not overpowering. His 1,471 strikeouts are far down the all-time list, yet he always claimed success against Ruth and Cobb. Like many spitballers, he threw the spitter sparingly, for contrast, and with a variety of motions. Always poised, the excellent control pitcher became increasingly sager. In his 4,087 innings, he allowed only 110 HR (one every 37 innings), and hit only 104 batters (one every 39).

His oddest statistical feats came as a batter. A .134 switch hitter, in 1915 he walked seven times in a row. Twice, he made the most of his rare on-base appearances by stealing home.

Faber served several seasons as a White Sox coach. After baseball, he worked until his eighties on a Cook County Highway Department survey team. /(ADS)

Roy Face — 1928– . (The Baron) RHP 1953, 55–69 **Pirates**, Tigers, Expos 1375 ip, 104–95, 3.48. *1 WS, 10 ip, 0–0, 5.23*

"Considered by many to be the best relief pitcher in history, [Face] confronted all types of jams in his career," wrote Edward Kiersh. "Relying mainly on a forkball, he squelched so many rallies in 1959, en route to his record winning percentage of .947 (18–1), that manager Danny Murtaugh tagged him Sam Spade." The shy, gutsy, 5′8″ righthander was twice drafted by Branch Rickey, first for the Dodgers, then, in 1952, for Pittsburgh. Face recorded 96 career relief wins (fifth all-time), 193 saves (sixth), and holds the ML mark for most relief wins in a season, 18 (17 consecutive for another record). He owns the NL career records for most games finished (574) and most games pitched for one club (802, for Pittsburgh). Face led the NL three times each in saves and relief losses, and twice in appearances. He saved three games of the 1960 World Series. /(TJ)

Len Faedo — 1960– . SS 1980–84 **Twins** 174 g, .251, 5 hr, 52 rbi

Faedo seemed the heir apparent to the Twins' shortstop job despite a history of injuries in the minors. He was hitting .277 in 1983 when a leg injury put him out again. He came back overweight and played only 16 games in 1984. /(MC)

Bill Fahey — 1950– . C 1971–72, 74–77, 79–83 **Senators/Rangers**, Padres, Tigers 383 g, .241, 7 hr, 83 rbi

Always a backup catcher, Fahey saw his most action sharing duty with Gene Tenace for the Padres in 1979–80. In 1980 Fahey had career highs of 93 games and 22 RBI. The Detroit native then finished his career backing up Lance Parrish on the Tigers. The 1978 gap in his ML career came after he was called up by the Rangers but spent the rest of the season on the DL. /(SFS)

Red Faber

Roy Face

Ferris Fain (Burrhead) — 1921– . 1B 1947–55 **A's**, White Sox, Tigers, Indians 1151 g, .290, 48 hr, 570 rbi
☛ *Led League—ba 51–52. All-Star—50–54.*

Ferris Fain won consecutive AL batting titles in 1951 (.344, when a broken foot held him to 117 games) and 1952 (.327). Although those were the only two full seasons in which he hit .300, he also hit .302 in 1954, when a knee injury limited him to 65 games and started the decline that cut off his career a year later after just nine seasons. His career high in HR was just 10 (1950), but he led the AL in doubles in 1952. However, his greatest value lay in his ability to get on base: his on-base percentage was above .400 every year of his career, finishing at .425 lifetime. He walked 100 times in five seasons, and was in the AL top five every season he was healthy; only once did he strike out more than 37 times in a season.

Fain was considered the best-fielding first baseman in the league until Vic Power came up. Although he tied the AL record by leading in errors five times, he was a daring, far-ranging fielder who

was the first first baseman to regularly field bunts on the third base line. He holds the ML record for double plays in a season with 194 in 1949; it broke the previous record by 31 (his 192 in 1950 is second). He set the since-tied AL record for double plays in a nine-inning game (six on September 1, 1947 in the second game). He led the league four times in assists and twice each in total chances per game and double plays, and ranks third all-time among first basemen in assists per game. /(JFC)

Jim Fairey — 1944– . OF 1968–73 Dodgers, **Expos** 399 g, .235, 7 hr, 75 rbi

Despite his excellent arm, Fairey became typecast as a lefthanded pinch hitter after smacking a pinch homer for Los Angeles in 1968. Taken by the Expos in the expansion draft, Fairey hit .254 lifetime in the pinch, and led the NL with 55 pinch-hitting appearances in 1972. /(MC)

Ferris Fain (sliding) and Roy Campanella in the 1951 All-Star Game

Ron Fairly — 1938– . 1B-OF-DH 1958–78 **Dodgers,** Expos, Cardinals, A's, Blue Jays, Angels 2442 g, .266, 215 hr, 1044 rbi. *4 WS, 20 g, .300, 2 hr, 6 rbi* ☛ *All-Star—73, 77.*

In a ML career that spanned 21 seasons, Fairly was a good hitter whose talents were sometimes overshadowed by a stunning lack of speed. When asked in his final season if he'd lost any speed, he replied, "There was nothing to lose." In both 1963 and 1967 he tied a ML record by having no triples in 150 or more games. A consistent hitter who hit at least 10 home runs 14 times, Fairly also walked often enough to post good-to-excellent on-base averages. DHing for the 1977 expansion Blue Jays, he hit a career-high 19 HR. Versatile enough to play the outfield despite his lumbering style, the steady Fairly was better suited to first base, leading NL first

basemen in fielding in 1963. He took over at first base for the Dodgers in 1962, but surrendered the position to Gold Glover Wes Parker in 1966. Fairly returned to the outfield.

After several years of declining batting averages, Fairly was traded to the expansion Expos in 1969 in the deal that returned Maury Wills to Los Angeles. After he escaped the vastness of Dodger Stadium, Fairly's batting average and power rebounded. Starting in 1974 he was less of a full-time player; only with Toronto in 1977 did he play more than 110 games again. /(JFC)

Pete Falcone — 1953– . LHP 1975–84 Giants, Cardinals, **Mets,** Braves 1435 ip, 70–90, 4.07

The swarthy southpaw went 12–11 his rookie season with the Giants (1975), but lost to teammate John

Ron Fairly

Montefusco in Rookie Pitcher of the Year voting. Traded to the Cardinals for Ken Reitz, Falcone repeated as a 12-game winner in 1976. After two losing seasons with the Mets (1979–80), he was moved out of the rotation. He signed as a free agent in 1983 with Atlanta, whose skipper was Joe Torre—fellow Brooklynite and Falcone's manager in New York. /(TJ)

Bibb Falk (Jockey) — 1899– . OF 1920–31 **White Sox**, Indians 1354 g, .314, 69 hr, 785 rbi

The University of Texas southpaw was a versatile athlete, undefeated in three years of varsity pitching and an All-Conference tackle in football. He succeeded the banished Joe Jackson in left field at Comiskey Park, and gave the Sox nine strong seasons, averaging .315 and three times topping 90 RBI. Traded to Cleveland for catcher Chick Autry in 1929, he had three more .300-plus seasons, the last two as the AL's most productive pinch hitter.

From 1940 to 1967 (except for three years as an Air Force sergeant during WWII), he was the aggressive, witty, sharp-tongued baseball coach at his alma mater. His 468–176 record earned 20 Southwest Conference titles and two national championships.

His younger brother Chet pitched for the Browns. /(ADS)

Cy Falkenberg [Frederick Peter] — 1880–1961. RHP 1903, 05–11, 13–15, 17 Pirates, Senators, **Indians**, Indianapolis (FL), Newark (FL), Brooklyn (FL), A's 2275 ip, 131–123, 2.68. 20 wins: 13–14
☛ *Led League—k 15.*

The 6'5" pitcher was already a veteran in 1913 when he reached his AL peak at 23–10 for Cleveland. Falkenberg was a prize recruit of the outlaw Federal League, jumping for a lucrative contract in 1914. He was worth the money, leading Indianapolis to the pennant by winning 25 and leading the league in games (49), starts (43), shutouts (9), innings pitched (377), and strikeouts (236). /(JK)

Joe Falls — 1928– . *Writer.*

Falls broke in as a copyboy for the Associated Press in 1946, then went on to cover baseball for three Detroit newspapers, the most recent being the *News*. Falls was a longtime *Sporting News* correspondent, and his writing reflects a sympathetic personality and a willingness to reveal his own emotions. /(NLM)

Cliff Fannin (Mule) — 1924–1966. RHP 1945–52 **Browns** 733 ip, 34–51, 4.85

Fannin pitched a shutout in his first ML start in 1946, beating the White Sox, 1–0. He is best remembered as the losing pitcher for the Browns in their 29–4 loss to the Red Sox on June 8, 1950, the most lopsided score in baseball history. /(WAB)

Frank Fanovich (Lefty) — 1922– . LHP 1949, 53 Reds, **A's** 105 ip, 0–5, 5.49

A New York City native and bullpen denizen, Fanovich failed to record a win or save in his two ML seasons. He lost his only start for the 1949 Reds, and two out of three for Jimmy Dykes's 1953 A's. /(TJ)

Carmen Fanzone — 1941– . 3B-1B-2B-OF 1970–74 Red Sox, **Cubs** 237 g, .224, 20 hr, 94 rbi

Fanzone reached the majors at age 29 after a largely undistinguished minor league career. From 1971 to 1974 he was an effective utility man with the Cubs, versatile and with good long-ball power. /(MC)

Ed Farmer — 1949- . RHP 1971-74, 77-83 Indians, Tigers, Phillies, Orioles, Brewers, Rangers, **White Sox**, A's 624 ip, 30-43, 4.30
☛ *All-Star—80.*

Farmer's best stint came as the bullpen ace of the White Sox; in the years 1979-81 he had 14, 30, and 10 saves. When he signed with the Phillies as a free agent following the 1981 season, Chicago picked Joel Skinner from the compensation pool. Farmer was property of the Yankees for three days during spring training in 1974 before being sold to the Phillies./(JFC)

Steve Farr — 1956- . RHP 1984- Indians, **Royals** 500 ip, 24-28, 3.67

After languishing over eight seasons in the minors, Farr capitalized on a trial with the Royals in 1985. Relying on a baffling slider and fine curveball, he eventually replaced Dan Quisenberry as the Royals' closer. In 1988 Farr saved 20 games and led Kansas City pitchers with a 2.50 ERA./(FO)

Dick Farrell (Turk) — 1934-1977. RHP 1956-69 **Phillies**, Dodgers, Astros 1704 ip, 106-111, 3.45
☛ *All-Star—58, 62, 64-65.*

The 6'4" 215-lb Farrell lost his major league debut as a starter in 1956, then relieved in his next 258 appearances. He overpowered hitters with his sinking fastball and led the NL with ten relief wins his rookie 1957 season with Philadelphia. In the 1958 All-Star Game, he struck out four of the seven batters he faced, including Ted Williams. Selected by Houston from Los Angeles in the 1961 expansion draft, Farrell became a starter and lost 20 for the original Colt .45s. Returned to the bullpen when the Phillies reacquired him in 1967, he again led the NL with ten relief wins. Farrell retired with 83 career saves. He worked on an offshore oil rig in Great Britain and was killed in a 1977 auto accident in Yarmouth, England./(AL)

Doc Farrell [Edward Stephen] — 1901-1966. SS-2B-3B 1925-30, 32-33, 35 Giants, **Braves**, Cardinals, Cubs, Yankees, Red Sox 591 g, .260, 10 hr, 213 rbi

The former captain of the University of Pennsylvania's baseball team played baseball in the summers and was a dentist in the off-season. He became a much-traveled utility player, with six ML teams in nine seasons. He hit a career-high .316 while playing three infield positions for the 1927 Giants and Braves. The next year the Braves gave him the shortstop job, the only season he played

over 100 games at a single position. He hit .215./(JK)

Duke Farrell [Charles Andrew] — 1866-1925. C-3B 1888-1905 Cubs, Chicago (PL), Boston (AA), Pirates, Washington (NL), Giants, **Dodgers**, Red Sox 1563 g, .275, 51 hr, 912 rbi. *1 WS, 2 g, .000, 1 rbi*
☛ *Led League—hr 91. Led League—rbi 91.*

A versatile switch-hitter, Farrell broke in as a protege of Cap Anson, who discovered him as a semi-pro player while the White Stockings were barnstorming New England. With Boston of the American Association in 1891, Farrell had league highs of 12 HR and 110 RBI. He later led the NL in pinch hits three times, and pinch hit for the Boston Puritans (later Red Sox) in the first World Series in 1903. He was a Boston Brave scout until his death./(JK)

John Farrell — 1876-1921. 2B-OF 1901-05 Senators, **Cardinals** 541 g, .261, 4 hr, 141 rbi

Farrell's rookie 1901 season was his best offensively, as he batted .272, scored 100 runs, and stole 25 bases for the Senators. With the Cardinals, he led the league in assists at second base in 1902, and in double plays from 1902-04./(WAB)

John Farrell — 1962- . RHP 1987- **Indians** 487 ip, 28-25, 3.86

Farrell was the best the Indians' farm system had when he was called up to Cleveland on August 18, 1987, despite his 24-41 minor league mark. Eight days later he stopped Paul Molitor's hitting streak at 39 games. He turned out to be one of Cleveland's most pleasant surprises, finishing the year at 5-1 and following with a 14-10 record in 1988. Elbow problems cropped up toward the end of 1988 and he was less effective in 1989./(JCA)

Kerby Farrell — 1913-1975. 1B-LHP 1943, 45 Braves, **White Sox** 188 g, .262, 0 hr, 55 rbi; 23 ip, 0-1, 4.30.
Manager 1957 **Indians** 76-77, .497

Farrell was a singles hitter who made it to the majors during the talent-poor WWII years. He succeeded Hall of Fame manager Al Lopez as the Indians' pilot in 1957 and Cleveland fell from second place to sixth./(JFC)

Bill Faul — 1940- . RHP 1962-66, 70 Tigers, **Cubs**, Giants 262 ip, 12-16, 4.71

The stocky righthander had an auspicious debut with two three-hit victories in his first three starts for the Tigers in 1963. Among his six triumphs for the 1965 Cubs, Faul tossed three shutouts. /(CC)

Charlie Faust [Charles Victor] (Victory) — 1880–1915. RHP 1911 **Giants** 2 ip, 0–0, 4.50

Giants manager John McGraw wrote, "I give Charlie Faust full credit for winning the pennant for me—the National League pennant of 1911." Faust had approached McGraw before the season and explained that a fortune teller told him if he pitched for the Giants, they would win the pennant. Faust became a good luck charm, traveling with the team and warming up to pitch every game. He hurled an inning against the last-place Dodgers on the final day, shutting them out on one hit. He also reached base by getting hit by a pitch, and was allowed to steal second and third, and score. "Who's loony now?" he asked teammates as the crowd cheered. Faust was committed to an institution in 1914. When he died in 1915, the Giants finished last. /(KT)

Federal League — 1914–1915. League.

Sure that the growing popularity of baseball could support a third major league, John T. Powers of Chicago brought together a group of entrepeneurs in 1913 and founded the Federal League. In its first year of existence the six-team circuit made no pretentions to major league status and respected major league contracts. Only a few faded major leaguers were in the league that season, although all six managers were former players of note, including Cy Young, who piloted Cleveland. Following the season, in which only one team folded, the owners ousted the cautious Powers and replaced him as president with James Gilmore, one of the Chicago owners.

The league expanded to eight teams and put franchises in Eastern cities for 1914, posing more direct competition to the major leagues. Some prominent players were signed, including Three Finger Brown and Joe Tinker. Officially, the FL was still respecting contracts, but as the majors began to play tough following some contract disputes with players who played the leagues against each other, open warfare erupted in the signing of players and in court. Walter Johnson almost signed with the upstart league, but Senators owner Clark Griffith convinced the AL to pay for Johnson's salary increase for the good of the league.

A close pennant race gave the FL fair attendance figures in most of its cities, but large financial losses were suffered due to extensive litigation. Even though the Feds won most of the cases, the NL and AL continued to file suits in an attempt to drain the coffers of the Federal backers. In January 1915 the Federal League filed an antitrust suit against major league baseball, hoping for a ruling against the reserve clause that would give the FL protection against further such harassment. They chose to enter their case before Judge Kenesaw Mountain Landis, who was known for his hard line against monopolies. But Landis felt differently about baseball, and put off a decision. After a season of declining attendance despite having signed more stars and another close pennant race, talk of a "peace settlement" became common. The major leagues had also suffered, but were better able to sustain themselves.

That winter, the "peace treaty" was announced. The majors partially compensated the debt-ridden Federal League owners; the FL withdrew its lawsuit, still being sat on by Judge Landis; and FL owners Phil Ball and Charles Weeghman bought, respectively, the Browns and the Cubs. The grateful major leagues appointed Judge Landis to the new office of Commissioner five years later. /(SH)

Mike Felder (Tiny) — 1961– . OF 1985- **Brewers** 334 g, .240, 6 hr, 72 rbi

The 5'8", switch-hitting Felder won four straight minor league stolen-base titles (1982–85). The Brewers' left fielder at the start of 1986, he pulled a hamstring in May and was disabled and sent down. As Milwaukee's fourth outfielder in 1987, he stole 34 bases. /(JCA)

Harry Feldman — 1919–1962. RHP 1941–46 **Giants** 666 ip, 35–35, 3.80

A wartime pitcher, Feldman was the winner for his hometown Giants in the most lopsided victory in franchise history, 26–8 over the Dodgers (4/30/44). In 1946 Feldman jumped to the Mexican League, which was raiding major league rosters for experienced players. /(JK)

Gus Felix — 1895–1960. OF 1923–27 **Braves**, Dodgers 583 g, .274, 12 hr, 230 rbi

Strong, likable Felix led his team's outfielders three times in RBI, and twice in fielding. He peaked with the 1925 Braves, hitting .307. /(EC)

Bob Feller (Rapid Robert) — 1918- . RHP 1936–41, 45–56 **Indians** 3837 ip, 266–162, 3.25 20 wins: 39–41, 46–47, 51 *1 WS, 14 ip, 0–2, 5.02*
☛ *Led League—w 39–41, 46–47, 51. Led League—era 40. Led League—k 38–41, 46–48. All-Star—38–41, 46–48, 50. Hall of Fame—1962..*

The winningest pitcher in Cleveland Indians history, in 1962 Feller became the first pitcher since charter member Walter Johnson to be elected to the Hall of Fame in his first year of eligibility. Though regarded as the fastest pitcher of his day, he himself attributed his strikeout records to his curve and slider. Blessed with a strong arm and an encouraging father, young

Bob Feller (r.) and Jim Hegan after Feller's third no-hitter

Feller pitched to a makeshift backstop on the family farm near Van Meter, Iowa. Cleveland scout Cy Slapnicka signed him for one dollar and an autographed baseball.

His velocity became an immediate legend when he struck out eight Cardinals in a three-inning exhibition stint. He came up as a 17-year-old at the end of 1936 and fanned 15 Browns in his first ML start and 17 Athletics shortly thereafter. But he was extremely wild. In 1938 he became a regular starter for the Indians. He won 17 and led the AL in strikeouts with 240. He also set a ML record with 208 walks. Although he led the AL in walks three more times, his control progressively improved. Meanwhile, he led the AL in both strikeouts and wins from 1939 to 1941.

In 1940 he won his personal high with 27, including an Opening Day no-hitter against the White Sox. Yet the year was tarnished, first when Cleveland veterans, including Feller, earned the nickname Crybabies by asking Cleveland owner Alva Bradley to replace stern manager Ossie Vitt. Then Feller lost the season's climactic game and the pennant to Tigers unknown Floyd Giebell, despite pitching a three-hitter.

He lost nearly four seasons to the Navy during WWII, earning eight battle stars. When he returned, he was better than ever, rejoining a powerful pitching staff that would soon include Bob Lemon, Mike Garcia, and Early Wynn. He won 26 games in 1946 and broke Rube Waddell's strikeout record with 348 (later research indicated Waddell may have fanned 349). He also threw his second no-hitter, against the Yankees. All told, Feller threw three no-hitters and 12 one-hitters.

In 1948 he started to decline, although he led the AL in strikeouts for the seventh and final time. He salvaged his season with six straight wins down the stretch to help the Indians to their first pennant in 28 years. He opened the WS against the Braves, but lost 1–0 on a controversial call. He'd apparently picked Boston's Phil Masi off second base, but the Braves' catcher was called safe. Masi then scored the game's only run when Tommy Holmes singled.

After two mediocre years, he bounced back with a 22–8 season in 1951 to lead the AL in wins for the sixth time and in winning percentage for the only time. He spent his final seasons as a highly effective spot starter, but was not used in the 1954 WS.

One of the first of the modern businessman-players, he was incorporated (Ro-Fel, Inc.) and made nearly as much money from barnstorming and endorsements as from playing. In 1957 his number 19 was the first to be retired by the Indians. And in 1969 he was voted baseball's greatest living righthanded pitcher in ceremonies for professional baseball's centennial. Always outspoken, and a natural promoter, he remains a popular ambassador for baseball. /(ME)

Happy Felsch [Oscar Emil] — 1891–1964. OF 1915–20 **White Sox** 749 g, .293, 38 hr, 446 rbi. *2 WS, 14 g, .229, 1 hr, 6 rbi*

Broad and powerful, Felsch was a natural at playing the game. A superb centerfielder with exceptional range and a rifle arm, Felsch still shares the records for double plays by an outfielder in a season (15) and assists in a game (4). Warm, smiling, and amiable, he loved silly riddles, whiskey, ribald jokes, and playing baseball.

On the White Sox, the fun-loving Felsch gravitated to the more raucous members of the team, who included the ringleaders of the Black Sox conspiracy. Years later, Felsch told author Eliot Asinof, "There was so much crookedness around, you sort of fell into it. I was dumb, all right. We started out talking about all the big money we would take, like a bunch of kids pretending to be big shots. I never really believed it would happen . . . and the next thing we knew, we were all tied up in it." Once he agreed to the sinister plot, this simple man found himself in a situation he couldn't control. The gamblers had a hold on him. Through threats, they forced him to throw more games during the 1920 season.

When the Black Sox scandal came out and he was barred from baseball, he was just emerging as a top power hitter, with 14 home runs in 1920. /(DB)

John Felske — 1942– . C-1B 1968, 72–73 Cubs, **Brewers** 54 g, .135, 1 hr, 9 rbi.
Manager 1985–87 **Phillies** 190–194, .495

Felske came up with his hometown Cubs but never won a job in the majors. After Phillies GM Paul Owens decided to stop managing, he hired organization man Felske. Philadelphia finished second under Felske in 1986 but was 21-1/2 games behind the Mets. He was fired while at 29–32 in 1987 after another slow start by the Phillies. /(JFC)

Terry Felton — 1957– . RHP 1979–82 **Twins** 138 ip, 0–16, 5.53

Winless with three losses in brief appearances for the Twins from 1979 to 1981, Felton made 48 appearances in 1982 and went 0–13, setting ML records for most career losses without a victory and most

consecutive losses from the beginning of career. He did collect three saves toward the end of 1982. /(MC)

Fenway Park Boston Red Sox 1912– , Boston Braves 1914–15. LF-315, CF-390, RF-302

Home of the Boston Red Sox since April 20, 1912, Fenway Park is one of baseball's last remaining classic ballparks, with a single-level grandstand, wildly asymmetrical fences intersecting at crazy angles, and extremely close seating that allows many fans to be nearer to home plate than any infielder. Built to conform to the surrounding streets near Boston's Kenmore Square, Fenway Park's wooden grandstand was converted to concrete and steel for the 1934 season by new owner Tom Yawkey, and the basic structure of the park has remained unchanged since. Its most distinctive feature is the Green Monster, a 37-foot-high wall that extends straight from the left field corner to almost dead centerfield. Once plastered with advertisements, it is now solid green, only 315′ down the line (but rumored to be even shorter) and 379′ to the intersection of the left and center field fences. From the plate, the wall seems to loom invitingly behind the shortstop, but while it does turn many routine fly balls into home runs, at the same time it knocks deep line drives back toward the infield for the longest singles in the majors. Outside, it runs along Lansdowne Street, and the 23′ net atop it hangs over the sidewalk to protect pedestrians from falling baseballs, while inside it holds one of the major league's three remaining manually operated scoreboards. Originally, left field also included a 10′ incline, known as Duffy's Cliff for Red Sox left fielder Duffy Lewis, but the hill was eliminated in the 1934 renovations.

The centerfield wall is 17′ high and extends from the Monster to the right field bullpens, where it angles sharply toward the infield. The deepest part of the park, a triangle next to the Red Sox bullpen, is 420′ from the plate. The bullpens were known as Williamsburg when they were added in 1940 to shorten the fences for young slugger Ted Williams, but are still 380′ away in the right field power alley. The fence curves suddenly in toward the right-field foul pole (302′), creating another set of extremely tricky caroms. Balls hit down the line, if not cut off quickly, will hug the fence and roll all the way into right center for triples or even inside-the-park home runs. In this corner, the fence is the shortest in the ML, ranging from three to five feet high.

Like the playing field, the seating areas have

Fenway Park

changed little since 1934. The grandstand is still essentially a single deck, although some roof seats and luxury boxes have been added, and there is a massive bleacher section in center and right fields. Fenway Park has almost no foul territory, and fans along the left field line can literally reach into the outfield or hold conversations with obliging players. No ball has ever cleared the right field roof, but one red seat deep in the right field bleachers marks the landing spot of Ted Williams's longest home run here. Steel girders supporting the roof do create many obstructed-view seats, and several sections in deep right field do not even face home plate, but Fenway's seats are generally the best in the ML. Despite the park's small capacity (less than 34,000, lowest in the ML) and complete absence of parking facilities, the Red Sox frequently top two million in total attendance.

Fenway Park has hosted its share of memorable baseball moments. It was the scene of the AL's only two one-game playoffs, in 1948 and 1978, as well as what has been called the greatest WS game ever, Game Six in 1975. Carl Yastrzemski collected his 3,000th hit here, and Ted Williams homered in his final ML at-bat. On the lighter side, on May 17, 1947 a seagull dropped a three-pound fish on the Fenway Park mound during a game, leaving Browns' pitcher Ellis Kinder dumbfounded. /(SCL)

Alex Ferguson [James Alexander] — 1897–1976. RHP 1918, 21–29 Yankees, **Red Sox**, Senators, Phillies, Dodgers 1236 ip, 61–85, 4.91. *1 WS, 14 ip, 1–1, 3.21*

Forkball artist Ferguson had his winningest season for the seventh-place 1924 Red Sox, when he won 14 while losing a league-high 17. Traded twice in 1925, he joined the Senators in late August, went

5–1 down the stretch, and pitched well in the World Series. /(EW)

Bob Ferguson (Fighting Bob, Death to Flying Things) — 1845–1894. 2B-3B-SS 1871–84 New York (NA), Brooklyn (NA), Hartfords (NA), Hartford (NL), Cubs, **Troy (NL)**, Phillies, Pittsburgh (AA) *NA:* 259 g, .243, *ML:* 562 g, .271, 1 hr, 178 rbi (inc).

Manager 1871–84, 86–87 New York (NA), Brooklyn (NA), Hartfords (NA), Hartford (NL), Cubs, **Troy (NL)**, Phillies, Pittsburgh (AA), New York (AA) *NA:* not available; *ML:* 292–351, .454

One of the most outstanding and influential ballplayers of the 19th century, Ferguson first attracted national attention in 1870 when, as captain of the Brooklyn Atlantics, he drove in the tying run and scored the winning run as the Atlantics handed the Cincinnati Red Stockings their first loss in two years. An outstanding leader, he managed every team he played for from 1871 through 1884. Baseball's first switch-hitter, he was only ordinary with the bat but was considered an outstanding fielder (although the quaint nickname Death to Flying Things, signifying stellar play on fly balls, was first given to Atlantics teammate Jack Chapman). Ferguson's primary contribution to baseball was his forthright character and unquestioned honesty in a time when many baseball players had low morals and were often the pawns of gamblers. In 1872 he was elected president of the National Association of Professional Baseball Players and held that position for several years, leading the fight for honest baseball that resulted in the establishment of the National League in 1876. Quick-tempered and hot-headed, he became an umpire in his later years, and once broke a player's arm with a bat to finish an argument. /(BC)

George Ferguson — 1886–1943. RHP 1906–11 Giants, **Braves** 698 ip, 31–46, 3.34

Ferguson was 12–11 for the 1908 Braves but injured his arm. The next year he suffered through a 5–23 season, leading the NL in losses. /(NLM)

Joe Ferguson — 1946– . C-OF **Dodgers**, Cardinals, Astros, Angels 1013 g, .240, 122 hr, 445 rbi. *2 LCS, 6 g, .200, 2 rbi. 2 WS, 7 g, .200, 1 hr, 2 rbi*

Ferguson became the Dodgers' regular catcher in 1973 and set a ML catcher record by committing only three errors (700 or more chances), leading the league's catchers in fielding average and double plays. He hit .263 and reached career highs with 25 HR, 26 doubles, 88 RBI, 84 runs, and 87 walks (for an on-base percentage of .376), despite spending

three weeks on the DL in the middle of the season. He also played 20 games in the outfield, and would continue to play both catcher and outfield throughout his career.

In 1974 Steve Yeager, better defensively, took over more of the catching duties. Ferguson hit 16 HR, but gained more attention for his playoff exploits, as the TV announcers were taken with the idea of a strong-armed catcher playing right field. Ferguson hit only .231 but drew five walks, scored three runs, and drove in two in the four-game series. In the World Series he hit a two-run homer off Vida Blue for what proved to be the winning margin in the Dodgers' only victory over the A's.

After spending the second half of 1975 on the DL and starting slowly in 1976, Ferguson was traded with two minor players to the Cardinals for Reggie Smith and was sent on to Houston after the season. As the Astros' primary catcher, Ferguson had another fine season (16 HR, 61 RBI, 85 walks) before the Dodgers reacquired him in July 1978 for Jeff Leonard and Rafael Landestoy. Ferguson helped Los Angeles to another NL pennant. In 1979, again splitting time between catching and the outfield, he hit 20 HR with 69 RBI in 122 games, but he finished his career as a part-timer. He ended the 1980s as a coach with the Dodgers. /(SH)

Chico Fernandez [Humberto Perez] — 1932– . SS 1956–63 Dodgers, Phillies, **Tigers**, Mets 856 g, .240, 40 hr, 259 rbi

Fernandez was a bright prospect who could not displace Pee Wee Reese at shortstop for the Dodgers, and the Phillies traded five players to get him for 1957. He was their regular shortstop for two seasons. After starting off adequately with the bat (.262 with 51 RBI in 1957), the native Cuban fell off over the next two seasons and saw limited time in 1959, hitting .211. The Tigers gave him the shortstop job in 1960, and although he led the AL in errors that season, he surprised in 1962 with 20 HR (half his career total). After starting 1963 with a .143 BA, he was traded to the Braves and then the Mets in just one day. The Mets traded him to the White Sox in 1964 for Charley Smith, but Fernandez didn't see any more major league action. /(WOR)

Frank Fernandez — 1943– . C-OF 1967–72 **Yankees**, A's, Senators, Cubs 285 g, .199, 39 hr, 116 rbi

A backup catcher his entire career, Fernandez never played in more than 94 games a year during his six seasons in the majors. His two best years were 1969 for the Yankees, when he hit a career-high .223 with

12 home runs, and 1970 for the A's, when he belted 15 homers.

Nanny Fernandez [Froilan] — 1918– . 3B-SS-OF 1942, 46–47, 50 **Braves**, Pirates 408 g, .248, 16 hr, 145 rbi

The dark, stocky Fernandez was of Castilian descent, his parents having left Spain for California shortly before his birth. He drove in 55 runs his first season but was not the same after losing three prime years to military service. /(JK)

Sid Fernandez (El Sid) — 1962– . LHP 1983- Dodgers, **Mets** 1033 ip, 69–45, 3.22. *2 LCS, 10 ip, 0–2, 8.10. 1 WS, 7 ip, 0–0, 1.35*
☛ *All-Star—86–87.*

A native Hawaiian who wears number 50 to honor his home state, Fernandez was given up on by the Dodgers because of his weight problems (despite two minor league no-hitters in 1982). Obtained by the Mets with infielder Ross Jones for Bob Bailor and Carlos Diaz, he blossomed in 1985, striking out 180 batters in 170 innings while going 9–9 with a 2.80 ERA. Fernandez has been inconsistent due to his widely fluctuating weight, which when high reduces his stamina. It has also caused him knee problems (which put him on the DL in August 1987) and makes him a poor fielder who's slow to cover first base.

Fernandez uses a herky-jerky motion, seemingly throwing the ball entirely with his arm after finishing his stride. It's hard for batters to pick up the ball coming out of his uniform, and his rising fastball is deceptive and effective. He led the NL in strikeouts per inning in 1985, and on July 14, 1989 he struck out 16 Braves (but lost, 3–2), setting a franchise record for lefthanders. At home games, fans in the right field upper deck post an "S" for each strikeout.

Fernandez's 16–6 record in 1986 helped the Mets to a pennant, but he didn't start in the World Series (after losing Game Four of the LCS 3–1 to Mike Scott) because manager Davey Johnson didn't want to use the lefthander in Fenway. But he had a 1.35 ERA out of the bullpen, and his 2–1/3 hitless innings in Game Seven, including four strikeouts, kept the Mets in the game after they had gone down by three runs early. New York rallied to win the Series.

Through the 1980s, Fernandez did not pitch to his potential for an entire season. He was bombed in Game Five of the 1988 LCS by the Dodgers and took the loss. /(SH)

Tony Fernandez — 1962– . SS 1983- **Blue Jays** 867 g, .292, 36 hr, 338 rbi. *2 LCS, 12 g, .341, 3 rbi*
☛ *All-Star—86–87, 89. Gold Glove—86–89.*

After becoming a regular with the Blue Jays midway into the 1984 season, Fernandez challenged Cal Ripken and Alan Trammell as the American League's best shortstop. A great defensive player, he led AL shortstops in putouts and fielding percentage in 1986. Rarely walking or striking out, Fernandez averaged around 600 at-bats per season. The speedy switch-hitter from San Pedro de Macoris, Dominican Republic, showed good extra-base power. His career average, close to .300, is nearly the same from both sides of the plate. He holds most Blue Jay records for switch-hitters. In 1986 he became the first Blue Jay to record a 200-hit season, and he set a major league record for most hits by a shortstop in this century, collecting 212 of his 213 hits at that position.

Fernandez showed toughness, playing with injuries. In one stretch he played in a Blue Jay-record 403 consecutive games. The elbow injury he sustained on a slide by Detroit's Bill Madlock with a week to go in the 1987 season was a turning point in the AL East pennant race, and the injury affected his play for the first half of the 1988 season. Fernandez was beaned by Cecilio Guante in April 1989 after hitting a grand slam earlier in the game. He returned to the Blue Jay lineup following reconstructive face surgery and hit a career-high 11 HR. /(TF)

Al Ferrara (The Bull) — 1939– . OF 1963, 65–71 **Dodgers**, Padres, Reds 574 g, .259, 51 hr, 198 rbi. *1 WS, 1 g, 1.000*

As a youngster, Ferrara appeared as a solo pianist at Carnegie Hall. Because of his muscular frame, a teammate once quipped, "He says he was a piano player, but more than likely he was a piano mover." Generally a fourth outfielder, with the Dodgers in a 1965 game against the Cubs, Ferrara broke up a Dick Ellsworth no-hitter with an eighth-inning, three-run pinch-homer. In 1967 he was Dodger of the Year, batting .277 with 16 homers. /(RM)

Don Ferrarese (Midget) — 1929– . LHP 1955–62 **Orioles**, Indians, White Sox, Phillies, Cardinals 507 ip, 19–36, 4.00

Like most little pitchers, the 5'9" 170-lb Midget struggled to make the majors. Used as a starter and reliever, he never won more than five games a season with his assortment of breaking balls. /(AL)

Mike Ferraro — 1944– . 3B 1966, 68–69, 72 **Brewers** 162 g, .232, 2 hr, 30 rbi.
   Manager 1983, 86 **Indians**, Royals 76–98

Although he was voted the top Yankee farmhand in 1966, Ferraro did not gain a regular ML job until the Brewers handed him third base in 1972. He hit .255 with only two homers and the next year turned to coaching. As the Indians' manager in 1983, he left after 100 games with the team in seventh place. He was interim manager of the Royals in 1986. /(MC)

Rick Ferrell — 1905– . C 1929–45, 47 **Browns**, Red Sox, Senators 1884 g, .281, 28 hr, 734 rbi
☛ *All-Star—33–38, 44. Hall of Fame—1984.*

A North Carolina farmboy and one of seven brothers, Rick Ferrell saved pennies to buy his first catcher's mitt for $1.50. Over 60 years later, the Veterans Committee elected him to the Hall of Fame. Although he played chiefly with second-division teams, Ferrell is always included among the greatest catchers of his age.

Blessed with a strong, durable physique and a placid yet determined personality, for 18 seasons Ferrell was a fine all-around receiver. In two stints each with the Browns and Senators, with three-plus years in Boston sandwiched between, he ultimately established the AL record with 1,805 games behind the plate.

At the plate, Ferrell had a fine eye and was remarkably selective. He coaxed 931 walks while fanning only 277 times, and achieved an impressive .433 career on-base percentage. Nineteen percent of his hits were doubles.

With St. Louis, he batted .290 over the years 1929–32, and caught the eye of Red Sox owner Tom Yawkey, who was trying to rebuild. Boston had had a .300-hitting catcher in only 1901 and 1919. In the years 1933–36, Ferrell broke Red Sox catchers' records in batting, doubles, HR, and RBI. His .302 average with the Red Sox is 12th on the club's all-time list. Rick's brother Wes joined him in Boston in 1934. Though a pitcher, Wes hit more career HR (38) than Rick (28). In June 1937, the brothers were packaged in a trade to Washington for Ben Chapman and Bobo Newsom.

Ferrell was back with the Browns in 1941–43. Then, during his second tour with Washington, he met the unprecedented challenge of handling four knuckleball pitchers in the starting rotation. In 1945 the Senators just missed the pennant, and their knuckle quartet amassed 60 wins.

Rick Ferrell with the Red Sox

After his playing days, Ferrell served as a Senators coach for four seasons. He followed with many years in the Tiger organization, as a coach, scout, GM, and, at over 80, executive consultant. In 1987 manager Sparky Anderson commented, "I hope I'm like Rick when I am his age!" /(EC)

Wes Ferrell — 1908–1976. RHP 1927–41 **Indians**, Red Sox, Senators, Yankees, Dodgers, Braves 2623 ip, 193–128, 4.04. 20 wins: 29–32, 35–36
☛ *Led League—w 35.*

"Wes was a marvelous character," recalled Bill Werber of teammate Wes Ferrell. "I've seen him, after being removed from a ball game, hit himself in the jaws with both fists and nearly knock himself out . . . jump in the air and crunch the face out of an expensive watch . . . tear card deck after card deck to pieces because he wasn't getting good hands. He hated to lose, at anything. He was a very determined competitor, the kind you like to have on your side."

Ferrell, an alumnus of Guilford College in his native North Carolina, set a ML record by posting 20 or more victories in each of his first four seasons (1929–32, with Cleveland). With Boston, the 6′2″ righthander also won a league-high 25 games in 1935, and was 20–15 in 1936. On his way to a .601 career winning percentage, he led AL pitchers four times in complete games, and three times in innings pitched. In 1931 Ferrell won 13 consecutive decisions, and no-hit the Browns (4/29). Two years later, he was named to the original AL All-Star team.

Ferrell was one of the best-hitting pitchers baseball has known. He set records for most single-season HR (nine, in 1931) and career HR (38) by a pitcher, and averaged .280 lifetime. "I didn't see any big deal in being a good hitter as well as a good pitcher," said Ferrell, a two-time minor league batting champion as an outfielder after his ML playing days. "A lot of guys could do it if they tried."

Ferrell's older brother and sometime batterymate, Rick, is enshrined in Cooperstown. (A third Ferrell brother, George, had a 20-year minor league career.) Journalist Bob Broeg suggested that Wes, too, could have made the Hall of Fame if arm trouble (which changed him from a blinding fastballer into a curveball and off-speed specialist) hadn't curtailed his career. Broeg also wrote, "If . . . there was one major difference between [Wes and Rick] Ferrell, it was in their temperament. Wes was a prima donna and hotheaded. Rick, though he lost his cool occasionally, was . . . a soft-spoken team man." Wes's Cleveland manager, Roger Peckinpaugh, fined and suspended him for refusing to leave a 1932 game. His Bosox skipper, Joe Cronin, fined him for leaving a 1936 game without permission. Later, as a minor league manager, Ferrell was slapped with suspensions for belting an umpire, and removing his team from the field. /(TJ)

Wes Ferrell with the Indians

Tom Ferrick — 1915– . RHP 1941–42, 46–52 A's, Indians, Browns, **Senators**, Browns, Yankees, Senators 674 ip, 40–40, 3.47. *1 WS, 1 ip, 1–0, 0.00*

A 6′2″ 220-lb reliever, Ferrick saved 56 games in a career interrupted by three years of service in WWII. For the 1947 Senators, he led the AL with seven relief losses. In 1950 his nine relief wins topped the AL. Joining the Yankees that June, he was the man Casey Stengel turned to when the manager lost faith in bullpen ace Joe Page. On the way to the pennant, Ferrick won eight games and saved nine in just 30 appearances. Working one inning in relief, he won Game Three of New York's World Series sweep of the Phillies. /(JJM)

Hobe Ferris [Albert Sayles] — 1877–1938. 2B-3B 1901–09 **Red Sox**, Browns 1286 g, .239, 39 hr, 550 rbi. *1 WS, 8 g, .290, 7 rbi*

A spirited competitor and skillful second baseman, Ferris was the hero of the final game of the first

World Series (1903), as he batted in all three Boston runs for the shutout victory over Pittsburgh. /(EW)

Boo Ferriss [David Meadow] — 1921– . RHP 1945–50 **Red Sox** 880 ip, 65–30, 3.64. 20 wins: 45–46 *1 WS, 13.1 ip, 1–0, 2.03*
☛ *All-Star—46.*

Just out of the military, in 1945 Ferriss was the sensation of the American League. The 6'2" 208-lb rookie went 21–10 and defeated all seven opponent clubs the first time he faced them. Supported by a powerful Red Sox lineup, he went 25–6, for a league-high .806 winning percentage, on the way to the 1946 pennant, and shut out St. Louis in World Series Game Three. A .250 lifetime hitter, he had 19 RBI in both 1945 and 1947, and was used 41 times as a lefthanded pinch hitter. Ferriss's career was cut short by asthma and arm trouble. He served as a coach for the Red Sox and at Delta State in Mississippi. /(EW)

Lou Fette — 1907–1981. RHP 1937–40, 45 **Braves**, Dodgers 691 ip, 41–40, 3.15. 20 wins: 37

Fette astounded the baseball world when he and fellow rookie teammate Jim Turner each won 20 games in 1937. More remarkable was that both of the Braves' "ancient rookies" topped 30 years of age. Fette was a quiet, hard-working, poised pitcher who shared the league lead in shutouts in 1937 with five, and led in 1939 with six. /(EW)

John Fetzer — 1901– . Owner.

As a developer of radio and TV stations, Fetzer's strength was in creating new concepts for packaging radio and television coverage of ML baseball after he became owner of the Tigers in 1962. He was a member of the ML executive council, and was active on expansion and planning committees. /(NLM)

Chick Fewster [Wilson Lloyd] — 1895–1945. 2B-OF-SS-3B 1917–27 **Yankees**, Red Sox, Indians, Dodgers 644 g, .258, 6 hr, 167 rbi. *1 WS, 4 g, .200, 1 hr, 2 rbi*

Despite an 11-year career, Fewster is chiefly remembered for one play: Brooklyn's "three-men-on-third" muddle of 1926 against the Braves. Actually, Fewster never made it to third. Babe Herman, whose base hit to right set things in motion, passed him between second and third, thereby becoming an automatic (second) out. With cautious Dazzy Vance clinging to third, Fewster's only option was to return to second. But, bemused by events, he fled into the outfield, where he was tagged out to end the inning. /(ADS)

Mark Fidrych (The Bird) — 1954– . RHP 1976–80 **Tigers** 412 ip, 29–19, 3.10
☛ *Rookie of the Year—76. Led League—era 76.*

Fidrych had "a talent that was exceptional and an approach to his game that was both uninhibited and refreshing," said author Donald Honig, noting that Fidrych "talked to the ball, shook hands with his infielders after good plays, cavorted with the pure joy and unrestrained enthusiasm of a Little Leaguer." The 6'3" righthander with flowing, blond curls was the talk of baseball in 1976, starting and losing the All-Star Game, and going 19–9 for the Tigers with 24 complete games and a 2.34 ERA—both AL-bests. Arm trouble limited him to just ten ML wins after his Rookie of the Year showing. /(TJ)

Cecil Fielder (Big Daddy) — 1963– . DH-1B 1985- **Blue Jays** 220 g, .243, 31 hr, 84 rbi. *1 LCS, 3 g, .333*

Despite his name, Fielder reached the ML on the strength of his bat, not his glove. He hit .311 in a brief trial with the Blue Jays in 1985 and hit .269 with 14 HR in 1987, but was never more than a part-time player. Fielder was sold to Japan's Hanshin Tigers after the 1988 season. /(TF)

Ed Figueroa (Figgy, Eduardito) — 1948– . RHP 1974–81 Angels, **Yankees**, Rangers, A's 1309 ip, 80–67, 3.51. 20 wins: 78 *3 LCS, 17 ip, 0–2, 8.10. 2 WS, 15 ip, 0–2, 6.75*

After a solid 1975 season (2.91 ERA, fifth-best in the AL) with the last-place Angels, he was traded with Mickey Rivers to the Yankees for Bobby Bonds. He was the Yankee staff's biggest winner over three AL-championship seasons, winning 55 from 1976 to 1978. In 1978 Figueroa became the first native Puerto Rican to win 20 games in the majors (he had been close two years earlier, but a rainout on the last day of the season deprived him of his chance). After elbow surgery in 1979, he did not pitch effectively; leaving the majors, he continued pitching in Mexico. /(EW)

Tom Filer — 1956– . RHP 1985, 88- Blue Jays, **Brewers** 263 ip, 20–13, 4.27

After bouncing around the minors for seven years, Filer came up with the Blue Jays in mid-1985 and helped them to their only division title with a 7–0, 3.88 record. The starter spent all of 1986 on the DL but made it back to the majors with Milwaukee in 1988, going 5–8 with a 4.43 ERA. /(WOR)

Dana Fillingim — 1893–1961. RHP 1915, 18–23, 25 A's, **Braves**, Phillies 1076 ip, 43–73, 3.56

Righthander Fillingim was one of eight NL spitballers permitted to continue throwing the pitch after it was outlawed in 1920. He had two good years with the Braves of 1920–21, but thereafter was afflicted with a sore arm that led to rising ERAs. /(ADS)

Pete Filson — 1958– . LHP 1982–87 **Twins**, White Sox, Yankees 357 ip, 15–14, 4.01

First signed by the Yankees, Filson won his first 12 pro decisions, including seven-inning no-hitters in the 1979 Appalachian League and the 1980 South Atlantic League. Traded to the Twins in 1982, he proved to have only a mediocre major league fastball. Used mostly in long relief, he became known as an inconsistent, flaky lefthander who thought too much. The Yankees reacquired him in 1987. /(JCA)

Rollie Fingers [Roland Glen] — 1946– . RHP 1968–85 **A's**, Padres, Brewers 1701 ip, 114–118, 2.90. *5 LCS, 19 ip, 1–2, 3.72. 3 WS, 33 ip, 2–2, 1.35* ☛ *Most Valuable Player—81. Cy Young Award—81. All-Star—73–76, 78, 81–82.*

Almost as famous for his handlebar mustache as his pitching, the lanky righthander is the greatest relief artist in baseball, lasting 17 years and compiling the most career saves (341) and World Series saves (7).

Known for his control and durability, Fingers made it a point never to pitch more than two innings at a time in order to maintain his strength. Like many relievers, Fingers began his career as a starter. He began the 1969, 1970, and 1971 seasons as a starter, but finished all three seasons in the bullpen. In 1972 he finally became a full-time reliever, winning 11 games in relief and saving 21 to lead Oakland to its first-ever World Series appearance. In the decisive seventh game against the Reds, Fingers worked out of a bases-loaded, one-out jam in the eighth inning to preserve the 3–2 victory and the championship. He piled up another 22 saves with a 1.92 era in 1973 with two World Series saves, and led the AL in games in 1974 with 76.

In 1974 Fingers pitched the final two innings of the only four-pitcher no-hitter in baseball history as he, Vida Blue, Glenn Abbott, and Paul Lindblad combined to blank the California Angels 5–0. Fingers shone in the World Series that year, earning the victory in Game One, then saved Oakland's

Rollie Fingers

other three victories over the Dodgers to win Series MVP honors. Fingers led the AL in appearances in 1975 with 75, but lost 11 games in relief in 1976.

Like many Oakland players, Fingers fled Charlie Finley, and signed on with San Diego as a free agent in 1977. He promptly led his new league in appearances with 78, and also led the league for the first time in saves with 35. He followed with 37 saves in 1978 to tie the then-ML record, even though he also lost 13 games in relief. He slumped to just 13 saves and a 4.50 ERA in 1979, then came up with a forkball to supplement his sinker and slider. In 1980 he saved 23 games and won 11 more games in relief.

After the season, San Diego believed Fingers, now 34, was past his prime and, in an 11-player deal, swapped Fingers and former Oakland teammate Gene Tenace to the Brewers. Fingers showed he still had plenty of arm left, though, leading the AL in saves with 28 with a 1.04 ERA and the 1981 Brewers to their first post-season appearance. Fingers figured in 55 percent of his team's victories, and won both the MVP and the Cy Young awards. He pitched much of the 1982 season in pain, saving 29 games, but missed the entire 1983 season.

At the age of 38, Fingers came back in 1984 to post a 1.96 ERA and compiled 23 saves for a team that won only 67 games. In 1985 age finally caught up to Fingers, who slumped to a 5.04 ERA, and he was released by the Brewers at the end of the year. /(SEW)

Jim Finigan — 1928–1981. 3B-2B 1954–59 **A's,** Tigers, Giants, Orioles 512 g, .264, 19 hr, 168 rbi

Finigan had a banner rookie year in 1954. He led the league in double plays at third base, and his .302 batting average made him the last regular to hit over .300 for the Athletics in Philadelphia. /(RM)

Herman Fink — 1911–1980. RHP 1935–37 **A's** 284 ip, 10–20, 5.22

A hefty North Carolina farmboy, Fink maximized his minimal salary by living on drugstore snacks and milkshakes on the road, pocketing most of his meal money. In the starting rotation only in 1936, Fink went 8–16. /(NLM)

Charles O. Finley (Charley O) — 1918– . Owner.

One of the most flamboyant, innovative, and controversial baseball club owners ever, Finley began as a semi-pro first baseman-manager in Indiana. Near-fatal tuberculosis in 1946 ended his playing career but inspired him to found a life insurance empire. Outbid for the Kansas City A's in 1960 by Arnold Johnson, Finley acquired the team a few months later when Johnson died. The A's had been sending such stars as Roger Maris, Clete Boyer, and Ralph Terry to the Yankees in exchange for washed-up journeymen; Finley immediately suspended dealings with New York and, as his own general manager, soon established a knack for acquiring unheralded talent like Ed Charles and Jose Tartabull.

Finley's first of many feuds with players and managers commenced at the 1962 All-Star break when he ordered Manny Jimenez, who was leading the AL with a .350 average, to start hitting home runs. Manager Hank Bauer took Jimenez's side and was fired after the season. Jimenez slumped and was sent down in 1963. In mid-1967, Finley fined and suspended young pitcher Lew Krausse for "rowdyism," and publicly berated his players over an insignificant airplane incident. A near-mutiny by the players followed. Finley fired manager Alvin Dark,

then released Ken Harrelson, the team's best hitter, who had been quoted as saying that Finley was "a menace to baseball." Signed by the Red Sox, Harrelson helped them to the pennant, and won the AL RBI title the following year.

Finley had already established a reputation as a cantankerous buffoon by trading for sluggers Jim Gentile and Rocky Colavito, then building a bizarre "pennant porch" designed to increase their home run production. He later paraded a mule named Charley O about the field, into cocktail parties, and even through hotel lobbies. He relocated the A's Double-A franchise to Birmingham because he was born there. He introduced orange baseballs, ball girls, and a mechanical rabbit that gave baseballs to the umpires. He advocated night World Series games in an effort to boost fan interest.

Meanwhile, Finley signed Jim Hunter and dubbed him Catfish to give him press appeal, concocting a story set in Hunter's childhood to justify the nickname. Finley also signed Reggie Jackson, Sal Bando, Vida Blue, Bert Campaneris, and a host of others who became the nucleus of his Oakland dynasty. He shifted the club from Kansas City to Oakland after the 1967 season in a move he later acknowledged as his one big mistake. In a half-empty stadium, the A's were contenders during 1969 and 1970, then won five straight division titles in 1971–75 and World Championships in 1972–74.

Finley was named *TSN* Man of the Year for 1972, but continued having disputes with players. After Reggie Jackson hit 47 HR in 1969, Finley, during a prolonged contract dispute, threatened to send him back to the minors. Similar bitterness followed when Vida Blue won the Cy Young Award in his first full season, 1971. Both times, Commissioner Bowie Kuhn intervened to help bring about a resolution. In the 1973 World Series, Finley fired Mike Andrews after the reserve infielder committed two consecutive errors in the 12th inning of Oakland's Game Two loss to the Mets. Other A's and manager Dick Williams rallied to Andrews's defense. Kuhn forced Finley to reinstate the player. Williams resigned after winning the Series, and Finley replaced him with Alvin Dark.

Under Dark, the A's won another World Championship in 1974. But after the season, Catfish Hunter was declared a free agent by arbitrator Peter Seitz because Finley had failed to make contractually stipulated payments for Hunter into an insurance annuity fund. Even without Hunter, the A's easily won their division in 1975. In the spring of 1976, Finley traded Jackson to the Orioles. During the season, he tried to sell Joe Rudi and Rollie Fingers to the Red Sox and Vida Blue to the Yankees, and did sell Paul Lindblad to the Rangers. In desperate financial trouble because of low attendance, Finley claimed he needed the money to sign free agents and rebuild. Kuhn disagreed, voiding the sales of Rudi, Fingers, and Blue as not being "in the best interests of baseball." Kuhn later voided another sale of Blue, to the Reds. Meanwhile, major league players won the right to play out their options, and seven A's did so in 1976. Despite the uncompensated losses, Finley rebuilt, and the A's were en route to yet another division title in 1981 when he sold the club to the Levi-Strauss company. /(MC)

Chuck Finley — 1962- . LHP 1986- **Angels** 531 ip, 30-32, 3.58. *1 LCS, 2 ip, 0-0, 0.00* ☛ *All-Star—89.*

The 6'6" Finley pitched only 41 innings in the minors before joining the Angels as a reliever in 1986, and became a starter at the tail end of 1987. He was 9-15, 4.17 in 1988. In 1989 he harnessed his strikeout potential to go 16-9 with a 2.57 ERA as the Angels contended. /(ME)

Mickey Finn [Cornelius Francis Neal] — 1904-1933. 2B-3B 1930-33 **Dodgers**, Phillies 321 g, .262, 3 hr, 102 rbi

Finn was a scrapper from New York. While in the Pacific Coast League, he once punched out pitcher Duster Mails, who had thrown at Finn. As a Dodger, Finn drew a sneering comment from the Cubs' Rogers Hornsby and challenged him. Hornsby backed down, but his pugnacious teammate, Billy Jurges, got into the fight. Finn was traded to the Phillies, but died after complaining of stomach pains and undergoing an operation during the 1933 season. /(JK)

Happy Finneran [Joseph Ignatius] (Smokey Joe) — 1891-1942. RHP 1912-15, 18 Phillies, **Brooklyn (FL)**, Tigers, Yankees 570 ip, 27-34, 3.30

Finneran won 24 games in two seasons with the BrookFeds. Happy may have needed a change in demeanor in his later career as a funeral home director. /(JK)

Lou Finney — 1910-1966. OF-1B 1931, 33-42, 44-47 **A's**, Red Sox, Browns, Phillies 1270 g, .287, 31 hr, 494 rbi ☛ *All-Star—40.*

When Connie Mack broke up his champion Athletics, he hoped Finney would replace Al Simmons in the outfield and in the hearts of Philadelphia fans.

Lou did neither, but he provided 15 steady, dependable ML seasons. With Boston, he spelled strongman Jimmie Foxx at first base and, in 1939, collected a league-leading 13 pinch hits.

After managing in the low minors, he and his brother Hal, a reserve catcher for five seasons with the Pirates, ran a feed store in Alabama. /(JK)

Mike Fiore (Lefty) — 1944- . 1B-OF 1968-72 Orioles, **Royals**, Red Sox, Cardinals, Padres 254 g, .227, 13 hr, 50 rbi

Originally signed by the Mets, the Brooklynite was taken by the Orioles in the first-year draft. An excellent fielder, he had a good eye at the plate, and surprising power. /(EW)

Bill Fischer — 1891-1945. C 1913-17 Dodgers, Chicago (FL), Cubs, **Pirates** 412 g, .274, 10 hr, 115 rbi

The lefthanded-hitting Fischer struggled in the National League, but led the 1915 Federal League champion Chicago club by hitting .329 while sharing catching duties with Art Wilson. /(ME)

Bill Fischer — 1930- . RHP 1956-64 White Sox, Tigers, Senators, **A's**, Twins 831 ip, 45-58, 4.34

A former Marine drill instructor, Fischer established a ML record in 1962, pitching 84-1/3 consecutive innings for the A's without giving up a base on balls, surpassing Christy Mathewson's mark of 68. That season, Fischer walked only eight batters, covering 127-2/3 innings. He became a pitching coach for the Reds and Red Sox. /(RM)

Carl Fischer — 1905-1963. LHP 1930-35, 37 **Senators**, Browns, Tigers, White Sox, Indians 823 ip, 46-50, 4.63

The 6' 180-lb Fischer won 13 games for Walter Johnson's 1931 Senators, and was 11-15 for the 1933 Tigers. Among his batterymates were Hall of Famers Mickey Cochrane and Rick Ferrell. /(TJ)

Hank Fischer (Bulldog) — 1940- . RHP 1962-67 **Braves**, Reds, Red Sox 547 ip, 30-39, 4.23

Fischer was signed to a Braves contract in 1959 by John "Honey" Russell, his basketball coach at Seton Hall who doubled as a baseball scout. Bulldog had his best season in 1964, winning 11 for Milwaukee and recording all five of his career shutouts. /(RM)

Rube Fischer — 1916- . RHP 1941, 43-46 **Giants** 383 ip, 16-34, 5.10

Noted for his high, overhand delivery, the Giants considered the 6'4" Fischer a top prospect. His career all but ended in 1944 when he had an operation transplanting part of his shin bone to his spine. /(EW)

Mike Fischlin — 1955– . SS-2B-3B 1977–78, 80–87 Astros, **Indians**, Yankees, Braves 517 g, .220, 3 hr, 68 rbi

Fischlin hit a career-high .268 as Cleveland's regular shortstop in 1982 but spent the rest of his career as a journeyman utility infielder. In 1978 for the Astros, he tied an odd NL record by handling just one chance in two consecutive games at shortstop (June 18, 20). /(MM)

Bob Fishel — 1914–1988. *Executive.*

Fishel was Bill Veeck's publicity man at Cleveland and St. Louis, and was the man who signed midget Eddie Gaedel to a Browns contract. Later, he was promotion director for the Yankees for 20 years. At the time of his death, he was AL vice-president for public relations. An award named in his honor is given to the outstanding baseball publicist each year. /(NLM)

Bob Fisher — 1887–1963. SS-2B 1912–16, 18–19 **Dodgers**, Cubs, Reds, Cardinals 503 g, .276, 11 hr, 170 rbi

A regular shortstop in only two seasons, Fisher did not hit well enough to compensate for his errors and lack of range; in 1913 with Brooklyn, he led the NL with 52 errors. Bob's brother, Newt Fisher, was a longtime minor league catcher, manager, and umpire. /(JK)

Brian Fisher — 1962– . RHP 1985– Yankees, **Pirates** 544 ip, 32–31, 4.34

Fisher was a surprising relief star for the 1985 Yankees, leading AL rookies with 14 saves while posting a 2.38 ERA. He declined in effectiveness in 1986 and was traded to Pittsburgh. Becoming a starter in 1987 after 126 straight relief appearances, he proceeded to finish among the league leaders in complete games and shutouts. /(ME)

Chauncey Fisher (Peach) — 1872–1939. RHP 1893–94, 96–97, 1901 Cleveland (NL), **Reds**, Dodgers, Giants, Cardinals 436 ip, 21–27, 5.37

Chauncey was the older brother of Tom Fisher (1902 Tigers, 1904 Braves). He broke into the majors in 1893 with the Cleveland Spiders and tossed two complete-game losses. He was sent to Cincinnati in mid-1894. He finished the season with a dismal 2–10 record and an ERA of 7.76. He bounced back in 1896–97 for Cincinnati and Brooklyn, winning 19 games in the two years. He returned to the major leagues in 1901, when he

threw a game for the Giants and one for the Cardinals. He also pitched for the Chicago White Sox championship team of 1900, the year before they attained major league status. /(AJA)

Eddie Fisher — 1936– . RHP 1959–73 Giants, **White Sox**, Orioles, Indians, Angels, Cardinals 1538 ip, 85–70, 3.41

The 6'2″ 200-lb University of Oklahoma graduate learned the knuckleball from Hoyt Wilhelm, and in 1965 the two teamed in the Chicago bullpen that set a record with 53 saves. That year Fisher led AL pitchers with 82 relief appearances and 15 relief wins, and saved 24, all career highs. He also pitched two shutout innings in the All-Star Game. Fisher again led the AL with 67 appearances in 1966, but he split the season between Chicago and Baltimore. Fisher had come to the White Sox in a 1961 trade that sent Billy Pierce and Don Larsen to San Francisco.

Fisher was known for his great Donald Duck impersonation. /(TJ)

Jack Fisher (Fat Jack) — 1919– . RHP 1959–69 Orioles, Giants, **Mets**, White Sox, Reds 1976 ip, 86–139, 4.06

With Baltimore in 1960, Fisher enjoyed his only winning season, going 12–11. That year he faced Ted Williams on September 28, allowing the Splendid Splinter to homer in his final ML at-bat. Almost a year later, on September 26, 1961, Fisher surrendered Roger Maris's 60th homer of the 1961 season. He pitched the Mets' first game at Shea Stadium (4/17/64), but was not involved in the decision as the Pirates won, 4–3. Fisher lost NL-highs of 24 in 1965 and 18 in 1967 for the Mets. /(RM)

Ray Fisher — 1887–1982. RHP 1910–17, 19–20 **Yankees**, Reds 1756 ip, 100–94, 2.82. *1 WS, 7.2 ip, 0–1, 2.35*

Fisher was a competent, consistent pitcher for the Yankees before the Babe Ruth era. The poised, studious righthander is best remembered as a college coach at Michigan University, and for the circumstances under which he left organized baseball. Fisher coached baseball (and, at first, freshman football, and young Gerald R. Ford) for 38 years, winning nine Big Ten championships.

He became the victim of the petulance and pettiness of Cincinnati owner Garry Herrman, and Commissioner Landis, often a capricious tyrant. Fisher, whose salary disputes had made him a target of the owners, asked to be released by the Reds so he could accept an offer from Michigan. Instead, he was blacklisted, dumped into the same group of suspended players as the Black Sox. Fisher was not accepted back into pro ball until late in life, becoming a spring training pitching instructor for the Braves in 1960, and the Tigers for 1963–65. /(JK)

Carlton Fisk (Pudge) — 1947– . C 1969, 71- **Red Sox**, White Sox 2141 g, .271, 336 hr, 1166 rbi. *2 LCS, 7 g, .276, 2 rbi. 1 WS, 7 g, .240, 2 hr, 4 rbi*
☛ *Rookie of the Year—72. All-Star—72–74, 76–78, 80–82, 85. Gold Glove—72.*

One of the AL's premier catchers for almost two decades, Carlton Fisk overcame a series of serious injuries early in his career to establish himself as a marvel of durability at baseball's most taxing position. At the start of the 1989 season, Fisk's 1,838 games caught trailed only Bob Boone and Al Lopez

in ML history, and his 282 HR as a catcher were exceeded only by Johnny Bench and Yogi Berra.

A true New Englander, Fisk was born in Vermont, attended the University of New Hampshire, and in January 1967 was the first-round draft choice of the Boston Red Sox, the fourth player chosen in the nation. When he arrived as Boston's full-time catcher in 1972, he already had a nickname (Pudge, from his childhood), and a trademark wad of tobacco that bulged inside one cheek. On the field, Fisk was an immediate star. He hit .293 with 22 HR and a league-leading nine triples in '72, won a Gold Glove, and became the first player ever to win the Rookie of the Year award unanimously. His average slipped to .246 in 1973 as he belted 26 more HR, and in 1974 he suffered the first major injury of his career, landing on the DL from June 28 until the end of the season with a broken collarbone. In 1975

Carlton Fisk (l.) with Boston, Roy Howell of the Blue Jays

Fisk reinjured himself in spring training and did not play until June, but he hit .331 in 79 games to help the Red Sox to the World Series.

Fisk found himself in the spotlight twice in the WS. In the 10th inning of Game Three, he collided with Ed Armbrister while chasing a bunt in front of home plate, but no interference was called, and the Reds rallied for the winning run. In Game Six, Fisk got his revenge, drilling a Pat Darcy pitch off the left-field foul pole for a 12th-inning, game-winning home run in what many consider the most dramatic game in WS history. Fisk's leaping gyrations down the first base line as he urged the ball to stay fair were recorded by NBC's television cameras, and placed the "reaction shot" into the vocabulary of baseball TV producers.

In 1977 Fisk hit .315 with 26 HR and 102 RBI and committed only four passed balls as he battled the Yankees' Thurman Munson for the distinction of being the AL's best catcher. Fisk started the All-Star Game in both 1977 and 1978, but the Yankees edged the Red Sox for the pennant and went on to win the WS each year. Injuries again curtailed Fisk's 1979 season (he played 91 games, mostly as a DH), and after a decent 1980 (.289, 18 HR) he stunned Boston fans by signing with the Chicago White Sox. The Red Sox' front office had blundered by failing to postmark his new contract in time, and Fisk became a free agent. With his change of Sox, Fisk flip-flopped his uniform number from 27 to 72, and in fairy-tale fashion, Chicago opened the 1981 season at Fenway Park. Playing against the Red Sox for the first time, Fisk hit a three-run, eighth-inning HR to win the game, 5–3.

In Chicago, Fisk has defied the aging process, accepting occasional assignments in the outfield, at first base, or as a DH, but playing most of his games at catcher. He hit .289 with 26 HR in 1983 to help the White Sox to their only AL West title, but hit only .176 in the ALCS as Chicago lost to Baltimore in four games. In 1984 he hit 21 HR but drove in only 43 runs, the fewest RBI ever for a player with 20 HR. Fisk hit only .238 in 1985, but recorded career bests in both HR (37) and RBI (107). Thirty-three of his 37 HR came as a catcher, eclipsing Lance Parrish's year-old AL record for the position. As a 40-year-old in 1988, he hit .277 with 19 HR in only 76 games. He missed much of the first half of 1989, but hit .293 with 13 HR and 68 RBI in 103 games. /(SCL)

Ed Fitz Gerald — 1924– . C 1948–59 Pirates, **Senators**, Indians 807 g, .260, 19 hr, 217 rbi

With the Senators in 1959, Fitz Gerald became the first ML player to hit into a triple play on Opening Day. In a 1953 game, the catcher turned a rare unassisted double play. He was one of seven brothers who barnstormed as the Traveling Fitz Gerald Basketball Team. /(RM)

Mike Fitzgerald — 1960– . C 1983– Mets, **Expos** 571 g, .241, 29 hr, 207 rbi

Fitzgerald homered off the Phillies' Tony Ghelfi in his first major league at-bat (9/13/83). As the Mets' starting catcher in 1984, he tied Jerry Grote's club record .995 fielding percentage and was named the Topps all-star rookie catcher. That December, the Mets sent him to the Expos with Hubie Brooks, Floyd Youmans, and Herm Winningham in the blockbuster trade for Gary Carter. Fitzgerald had trouble staying healthy as Carter's replacement in Montreal. He had shoulder and knee problems in 1985. He was batting a career-high .282 on August 1, 1986 when he broke a finger during a game at Shea Stadium—an injury that ended his season and bothered him for several years. /(JCA)

Al Fitzmorris — 1946– . RHP 1969–78 Royals, Indians, Angels 1277 ip, 77–59, 3.65

This switch-hitter began his career as an outfielder, and he hit a respectable .242 in the majors before the DH was introduced. The Royals took Fitzmorris from the White Sox in the expansion draft, and after four seasons of work as a reliever and spot starter, the good-fielding pitcher was sent down in 1973. Called back up in mid-season, he became a starter and went 8–3 with a 2.83 ERA. Fitzmorris was a reliable number-two starter for the next three seasons, winning 44 games as the Royals finally achieved respectability and won their first AL West title (1976). He was selected by the Blue Jays in the expansion draft after the 1976 season and was traded to the Indians for Alan Ashby and a minor leaguer. /(WOR)

Freddie Fitzsimmons (Fat Freddie) — 1901–1979. RHP 1925–43 **Giants**, Dodgers 3224 ip, 217–146, 3.51. 20 wins: 28 *3 WS, 25.2 ip, 0–3, 3.86.*
  Manager 1943–45 **Phillies** 102–179, .363

Fat Freddie Fitzsimmons "was from the old school," wrote Joe McGuff. "He knocked down line drives with his feet and legs, challenged batters and umpires and withstood the verbal explosions of John McGraw, the terrible-tempered manager of the New York Giants." The knuckle-curveballer led the NL with a .731 (19–7) winning percentage for the 1930 Giants. He again topped the league (and set a Dodger record) with an .889 (16–2) percentage in 1940.

Fred Fitzsimmons

each year. In 1915, when the Whales were league champions, that total ranked fourth in the league, and Flack's career-high .314 was fifth-best. The Cubs bought out the Whales after the FL folded. Flack spent the next six seasons as the Cubs' regular leadoff hitter, scoring 85 runs in 1920 for his personal NL high. He twice led NL outfielders in fielding, with very high averages for the time: .991 (1916) and .989 (1921).

When the Cubs lost the 1918 World Series, it was Flack's error in the third inning of the final game that let in the Red Sox' only two runs. Contrary to his record as listed in Macmillan's *Baseball Encyclopedia*, he did not have an RBI in the Series. /(SFS)

Ira Flagstead (Pete) — 1893–1940. OF 1917, 19–30 Tigers, **Red Sox**, Senators, Pirates 1218 g, .290, 40 hr, 450 rbi

A 5′9″ righthanded batter who hit for average more than power, Flagstead batted over .300 five times. A skillful fielder, he spent most of his career in centerfield, though the Tigers tried him at shortstop and second base in 1921. Flagstead holds the AL record, and is tied for the ML record for the most double plays started by an outfielder in a game, with three (4/19/26). /(EW)

Patsy Flaherty — 1876–1968. LHP-OF 1899–1900, 03–05, 07–08, 10–11 Louisville (NL), **Pirates**, White Sox, Braves, Phillies 1303 ip, 66–84, 3.10; 235 g, .197, 6 hr, 70 rbi. 20 wins: 04

Flaherty didn't stay long with any ML club, making seven moves in nine seasons. He lost a league-leading 25 games for the White Sox in 1903, giving up 338 hits. Chicago released him with a 1–2 record during the 1904 season. Picked up by the Pirates, he went 19–9, thus finishing 20–11 in his only winning season. Flaherty had dead ball era power and was sometimes used as a pinch hitter or in the outfield. /(JK)

Red Flaherty [John] — 1918– . *Umpire* AL 1953–73 *2 LCS 4 WS, 3 ASU*

An AL umpire for 21 years, Flaherty became involved in perhaps his most heated argument in Fenway Park in 1960 when he called Red Sox runner Don Buddin safe at the plate after the Tigers seemingly had caught him in a rundown. Flaherty ruled that the catcher had missed the tag. The Tigers countered that Buddin had run out of the baseline. Cal Hubbard, AL supervisor of umpires, happened to be in the stands that day. He supported Flaherty's call completely. /(RTM)

As manager from mid-1943 to mid-1945, Fitzsimmons's Phillies were a flop. His *TSN* obit recalled that "he was one of the principals in the great tampering uproar in 1949 when he was a coach for the Giants and his old pal, Leo Durocher. The Braves claimed tampering, because the discussion of the Giants' job occurred while Fitzsimmons was still under contract to the Braves." Fitzsimmons and Durocher were fined by Commissioner Happy Chandler, who also suspended Fitzsimmons for a month. Fitzsimmons spent three years as GM of the National Football League Brooklyn Dodgers. /(TJ)

Max Flack — 1890–1975. OF 1914–25 Chicago (FL), **Cubs**, Cardinals 1411 g, .278, 35 hr, 391 rbi. *1 WS, 6 g, .263*

Flack's .974 lifetime fielding average was the best ever for a right fielder when he retired, and was only a point behind the record for all outfielders. He made it to the majors with the Chicago Whales of the Federal League in 1914–15, stealing 37 bases

Vincent X. Flaherty — 1912–1977. *Writer.*

A nattily dressed night person, Flaherty worked for the Washington *Times-Herald* before going to the West Coast as a columnist for the Los Angeles *Examiner*. In the 1940s he was an early advocate of bringing a ML team to Los Angeles. /(NLM)

Mike Flanagan — 1951– . LHP 1975– **Orioles,** Blue Jays 2617 ip, 163–134, 3.89. *3 LCS, 16 ip, 2–1, 5.51. 2 WS, 19 ip, 1–1, 3.32*
☛ *Led League—w 79. Cy Young Award—79.*

After losing his first five major league decisions, Flanagan achieved a decade of dependable pitching. From 1977 to 1987, no AL pitcher started more games (334). His record was .500 or better each season from 1977 to 1984. His Cy Young season included the ML lead in wins (23–9). He tied for the league lead in shutouts, finished sixth in MVP voting, and was honored as Graduate of the Year by the Junior American Legion and Babe Ruth programs. He won the first game of the World Series, but lost Game Five when he was moved up in the rotation in a controversial move by manager Earl Weaver. Armed with a big-breaking curveball, an underrated fastball, and a great pickoff move, Flanagan suffered a severe knee injury in 1983 and a torn Achilles tendon in 1985. Struggling in Baltimore, Flanagan found new life after being acquired by Toronto during the 1987 stretch run. He had more wins (17) and innings pitched (208) against the Blue Jays than any other hurler. /(ME)

Joseph Flanner — Unk.–1924. *Writer.*

Flanner was editor of *The Sporting News* until he was named secretary to August Herrmann, chairman of the National Commission. He held his position until Judge Landis became baseball's first Commissioner in 1921. /(NLM)

Tim Flannery — 1957– . 2B-3B 1979–89 **Padres** 972 g, .255, 9 hr, 209 rbi. *1 LCS, 3 g, .500. 1 WS, 1 g, 1.000*

Flannery reached the Padres as a utility man in 1979, his second pro season. An intelligent and reliable player who made the most of limited ability, he was primarily a pinch hitter for the 1984 NL Champions; it was his grounder that eluded Cubs first baseman Leon Durham to start San Diego's winning rally in the deciding game of the LCS. Flannery batted .280 as a starter at second in 1985–86, but lost his job to Joey Cora in 1987, and Roberto Alomar in 1988. /(JCA)

Fred Fleig — 1908–1979. *Executive.*

Fleig broke into baseball in 1937 as business manager of a Cincinnati farm club for Warren Giles. He followed Giles into the NL and was secretary-treasurer of the league when he retired in 1978 after 28 years. /(NLM)

Bill Fleming [Leslie Fletchard] — 1913– . RHP 1940–44, 46 Red Sox, **Cubs** 442 ip, 16–21, 3.79

Effectively mixing his fastball and nice curve, the 6′ righthander won 18 at Hollywood and led the Pacific Coast League in strikeouts in 1940. But Fleming was a marginal wartime major leaguer, who in 1944 had a NL-high ten relief losses. /(EW)

Les Fleming (Moe) — 1915–1980. 1B 1939, 41–42, 45–47, 49 Tigers, **Indians,** Pirates 434 g, .277, 29 hr, 199 rbi

In his rookie 1942 season, Fleming hit .292 with 14 HR and 82 RBI as Cleveland's everyday first baseman, then took a job in a war-related industry. Expected to become a full-fledged star upon his return, he never matched his successful rookie year. /(EW)

Art Fletcher — 1885–1950. SS 1909–20, 22 **Giants,** Phillies 1529 g, .277, 32 hr, 675 rbi. *4 WS, 25 g, .191, 8 rbi.*
Manager 1923–26, 29 **Phillies,** Yankees 237–383, .382

Fletcher was John McGraw's shortstop for over a decade, providing the Giants with brilliant fielding, dependable hitting, and on-field leadership. A caustic, belligerent copy of McGraw during the game, off the field he was a non-profane, churchgoing family man. As the frustrated manager of four second-division Phillies teams, Fletcher's final gesture was the drawing of a caricature of umpire Bill Klem as a catfish, a comparison the jowly, heavy-lidded Klem loathed. Fletcher became Miller Huggins's assistant in 1927, and remained a Yankee coach until 1945. When Huggins died in 1929, Fletcher took over as interim manager, but refused all other offers to manage again. /(JK)

Elbie Fletcher — 1916– . 1B 1934–35, 37–43, 46–47, 49 Braves, **Pirates** 1415 g, .271, 79 hr, 616 rbi
☛ *All-Star—43.*

Line-drive-hitting, fancy-fielding, lefthanded Elbie Fletcher debuted with the 1934 Braves; he had attracted their attention by organizing a newspaper write-in campaign on his own behalf. Traded to Pittsburgh in June 1939, Fletcher batted .290 that

Art Fletcher

Elmer Flick — 1876–1971. OF 1898–1910 Phillies, A's, **Indians** 1484 g, .315, 47 hr, 756 rbi
☛ *Led League—rbi 00. Led League—ba 05. Hall of Fame—63.*

Largely unknown by modern fans, Flick was one of the great all-around performers at the turn of the century. In 1905 he won the AL batting title with a .306 average, the lowest mark to take the crown until Carl Yastrzemski's .301 in 1968. Flick narrowly missed the NL title in 1900, batting .378 to Honus Wagner's .381. After compiling a .344 lifetime average in the NL (1898–1901), Flick jumped to the Philadelphia Athletics, following Nap Lajoie, who'd gone a year earlier. When the Phillies obtained an injunction barring the jumpers from playing in Philadelphia, both Lajoie and Flick, an Ohioan, wound up in Cleveland.

Elmer Flick

year, had 104 RBI in 1940, drew the most walks in the NL in 1940 and 1941, and started in the 1943 All-Star Game. In 1944 Fletcher paced the Bainbridge, MD Naval Training Station team (which included ML veterans Dick Bartell and Buddy Blattner) in batting./(TJ)

Scott Fletcher — 1958– . SS-2B-3B 1981– Cubs, White Sox, **Rangers** 997 g, .268, 17 hr, 302 rbi

Fletcher was considered a utility infielder by the Cubs, and was traded to the White Sox in 1983. Given the shortstop job in 1984, he batted .250 and played a solid defense. But with the arrival of Ozzie Guillen in 1985, Fletcher was left to shuttle around the infield, and was traded to Texas in November. He amazed skeptics in 1986 by putting together a 19-game July hitting streak, batting .300 for the season, and leading the Rangers with 34 doubles. He again topped Texas regulars in batting in 1987 (.287)./(RL)

In his first six seasons in Cleveland, Flick never batted below .297. The 5′6″, lefthanded-hitting right fielder used a thick-handled bat, enabling him to get solid hits on inside pitches. On July 6, 1902, Flick became the first American Leaguer to hit three triples in one game, a feat he repeated in the NL. The speedster set a ML record by leading the AL in triples three consecutive seasons (1905–07). He also led the circuit in stolen bases twice (1904, 1906) and runs scored once (1906).

Following the 1907 season, Detroit manager Hughie Jennings offered Ty Cobb to Cleveland for Flick, but Cleveland declined the offer. The 21-year-old Cobb had just won his first batting title (.350), while the 31-year-old Flick managed .302. Cobb, however, was despised by his teammates. The likable Flick stayed in Cleveland. The rest of his career was plagued by a mysterious stomach ailment. He played just 99 more games over three seasons, but dragged down his lifetime average. Flick was elected to the Hall of Fame by the Veterans Committee in 1963. /(ME)

Curt Flood — 1938– . OF-3B 1956–69, 71 Reds, **Cardinals**, Senators 1759 g, .293, 85 hr, 636 rbi. *3 WS, 21 g, .221, 8 rbi*
☛ *All-Star—64, 66, 68. Gold Glove—63–69.*

Flood had a marvelous career that will always be marred by his misjudging of a fly ball in the seventh game of the 1968 World Series, and his suit against baseball that eventually led to free agency. The 5′9″ Houston native played just eight games with Cincinnati before beginning his stellar 12-year stay with St. Louis in 1958. In 1964 he led the NL with 211 hits. He batted a career-high .335 in 1967.

In an act that Flood felt was "impersonal," the Cardinals traded him, Tim McCarver, Byron Browne, and Joe Hoerner to the Phillies on October 7, 1969, for slugger Dick Allen, Cookie Rojas, and Jerry Johnson. Flood balked at his trade to Philadelphia, which had a poor team and played its games in an old stadium, before usually belligerent fans in 1969. Flood fought the reserve clause. He first asked Commissioner Kuhn to declare him a free agent, and was denied. He filed suit on January 16, 1970, stating that baseball had violated the nation's antitrust laws. Even though he was making $90,000 at the time, Flood likened "being owned" to "being a slave 100 years ago." The case went to the Supreme Court, with former Supreme Court Justice Arthur Goldberg pressing his case. Goldberg agreed to work for expenses, which totaled nearly $200,000, before judgment was finally rendered. The Supreme Court

Curt Flood

upheld the District Court and Court of Appeals rulings favoring organized baseball.

Flood sat out 1970, but signed with the Senators in 1971 for $110,000. To get the rights to Flood, who was still bound by the reserve clause, Washington had to part with marginal players Greg Goossen, Jerry Terpko, and Gene Martin, none of whom would ever appear with Philadelphia. Flood played 13 games for Washington, hit a paltry .200, and retired in April. He later spent the 1978 season in the A's broadcasting booth with Bud Foster. /(WAB)

Jesse Flores — 1914- . RHP 1942-47, 50 Cubs, **A's**, Indians 973 ip, 44-59, 3.18

Released by the Cubs in 1942 because he had "nothing but a dink screwball," Flores pitched regularly for the A's in 1943-47. The Mexican's best game was an Opening Day two-hitter, which he lost 1-0. /(NLM)

Ben Flowers — 1927- . RHP 1951, 53, 55-56 **Red Sox**, Tigers, Cardinals, Phillies 168 ip, 3-7, 4.49

Flowers was a star athlete in the military during WWII, and had a brilliant minor league career. He set a since-surpassed AL record by relieving in eight consecutive Red Sox games in 1953. /(EW)

Jake Flowers [D'Arcy Raymond] — 1902-1962. 2B-SS-3B 1923, 26-34 Cardinals, **Dodgers**, Reds 583 g, .256, 16 hr, 201 rbi. *2 WS, 8 g, .071*

Flowers was a dangerous man to trade. When the Cardinals sent him to Brooklyn, his homer off Wee Willie Sherdel won his new team's first game against his former mates. Traded back to St. Louis, he homered off Brooklyn's Dazzy Vance the first time the clubs met. Sent back to Brooklyn, he hit a first-game homer off the Cardinals' Dizzy Dean. His ML career ended when a Paul Dean pitch broke his arm. *TSN* named him Minor League Manager of the Year in 1937. /(JK)

Doug Flynn — 1951- . 2B-SS-3B 1975-84 Reds, **Mets**, Rangers, Expos 1267 g, .238, 7 hr, 282 rbi. *1 LCS, 1 g, --*
☛ *Gold Glove—80.*

A weak hitter whose glove kept him in major league lineups for ten years, Flynn was one of four young Cincinnati players for whom the Mets traded Tom Seaver on June 15, 1977. /(CR)

Lee Fohl (Leo) — 1870-1965. C 1902-03 Pirates, **Reds** 5 g, .294, 0 hr, 3 rbi.
  Manager 1915-19, 21-26 **Indians**, Browns, Red Sox 713-792, .474

A catcher in only five ML games, Fohl was the owner and playing manager of Waterbury in the Eastern Association when the Indians hired him as manager in 1915. He finished second to the Red Sox by 2-1/2 games in 1918, but the next year, with the team in third place, he let his pitcher pitch to Babe Ruth instead of walking him. Ruth homered to win the game and Fohl was fired the next day. He was hired in 1921 by Bob Quinn to manage the Browns and came within one game of winning the 1922 pennant. George Sisler, the Browns' best player, missed the entire 1923 season, but Fohl still had the club in third place when he was fired after 101 games. Quinn, then president of the Red Sox, hired him in 1924, but the Sox had sold off their best players and Fohl finished seventh once and last twice. /(NLM)

Hank Foiles — 1929- . C 1953, 55-64 Reds, Indians, **Pirates**, A's, Tigers, Orioles, Dodgers 608 g, .243, 46 hr, 166 rbi
☛ *All-Star—57.*

Foiles rode to the majors on the coattails of Herb Score, his Indianapolis batterymate in 1954. He batted .332 in the American Association that year. Foiles was a first-string ML catcher in only two seasons, including 1957, when he played a career-high 109 games and represented the last-place Pirates in the All-Star Game. /(ME)

Tom Foley — 1959- . SS-2B-3B 1983- Reds, Phillies, **Expos** 621 g, .254, 26 hr, 192 rbi

In high school, ambidextrous Tom Foley played shortstop righthanded and quarterback lefthanded. Unable to win an everyday job in the majors, his ability to play second, third, and short (though unspectacularly), and his value as a lefthanded pinch hitter got him into at least 100 games in four of his first six seasons. In spring training with the 1986 Phillies, he was knocked out cold sliding into a base on March 16 and had his wrist broken by a Roger McDowell pitch the next day, disabling him for more than a month. /(EW)

Tim Foli — 1950- . SS 1970-84 Mets, **Expos**, Giants, Pirates, Angels, Yankees 1677 g, .251, 25 hr, 499 rbi. *2 LCS, 8 g, .214, 4 rbi. 1 WS, 7 g, .333, 3 rbi*

The bespectacled Foli led NL shortstops in fielding as a Pirate in 1980, and AL shortstops as an Angel two years later. He paced NL shortstops twice each in double plays and total chances, and once in putouts. In 1982 his 14 walks set an AL record for the fewest received by a player in 150 or more games (broken by Ozzie Guillen three years later). Foli was the Mets' first draft pick in June 1968, and was traded with Ken Singleton and Mike Jorgensen to Montreal for Rusty Staub in 1972. The fiery Foli became the first Expo ever to hit for the cycle (4/21/76). He batted .333 in ten LCS and WS games for the World Champion 1979 Pirates. His older brother, Ernie, played minor league ball. Foli was a Ranger coach from 1985 to 1987. /(TJ)

Rich Folkers — 1946- . LHP 1970, 72-77 Mets, **Cardinals**, Padres, Brewers 422 ip, 19-23, 4.11

Folkers was best when used exclusively as a reliever, and his career year came with the 1974 Cardinals, when he went 6-2 with a 3.00 ERA. Traded to the Padres after the season in a three-way deal that also involved the Tigers, he became the subject of one of San Diego broadcaster Jerry Coleman's famous malaprops when Coleman reported that "Rich Folkers is throwing up in the bullpen." /(JFC)

Dee Fondy — 1924- . 1B 1951-58 **Cubs**, Pirates, Reds 967 g, .286, 69 hr, 373 rbi

The 6'3" lefthanded first baseman batted .376 to lead the Pacific Coast League in 1951, and thrice batted .300 in the majors. In July 1953, Fondy struck out six times in a Cubs' doubleheader, five times in one game. /(EW)

Lew Fonseca — 1899-1989. 1B-2B-OF 1921-25, 27-33 Reds, Phillies, **Indians**, White Sox 947 g, .316, 31 hr, 485 rbi.
   Manager 1932-34 **White Sox** 120-198, .377
☛ *Led League—ba 29 .*

Though the 1929 AL batting champ had a distinguished playing career, his long-term contribution to baseball was pioneering the use of film to analyze and promote the game. Fonseca became interested in cameras while acting in "Slide, Kelly, Slide," a 1927 comedy starring Joe E. Brown. He used film to detect flaws in his players as manager of the Chicago White Sox (1932-34). Fonseca became director of promotions for both the AL and NL.

   Versatile in the field and spectacular at the plate, Fonseca's only season as a regular at one position (first base with Cleveland) was 1929, and he responded by hitting .369. He topped the .300 mark six times, but had trouble staying healthy. He suffered a broken leg in 1928, and a broken arm in 1930. A torn ligament in his leg ended his career. /(ME)

Ray Fontenot — 1957- . LHP 1983-86 Yankees, **Cubs**, Twins 494 ip, 25-26, 4.03

Fontenot went 8-2 filling in for the injured Ron Guidry as a rookie on the 1983 Yankees, and the two Louisiana natives would often converse in French. The soft thrower was often injured himself, however, and never fulfilled the promise he had shown. /(ME)

Barry Foote — 1952- . C 1973-82 **Expos**, Phillies, Cubs, Yankees 687 g, .230, 57 hr, 230 rbi. *2 LCS, 3 g, .500. 1 WS, 1 g, .000*

Foote was Montreal's strong-armed starting catcher from his rookie 1974 season (when he recorded career highs of 60 RBI and .262) until 1977. On April 22, 1980, playing for the Cubs against the Cards, he had eight RBI, including a game-winning grand slam. Following his playing career he managed in the Yankee farm system. /(EW)

Forbes Field Pittsburgh Pirates 1909-1970. LF-365, CF-435, RF-300

Forbes Field was named for a British general of the French and Indian War, and most of its 35,000 seats were in a covered grandstand that extended from third base around home plate and into right field, while unfortunate fans in the upper left corner of the bleachers along the left field line could not see the batter. The park featured a huge foul territory behind home plate, an extremely hard infield, and spacious left and center fields contained by an ivy-covered brick wall. Lights were added in 1940, and during WWII a 32-foot-high Marine towered over the left field wall. Left field bullpens were added briefly to reduce the handicap facing Pirate sluggers Hank Greenberg and Ralph Kiner, and the area became known as both Greenberg Gardens and Kiner's Korner. No no-hitters were pitched at Forbes Field in 68 seasons, but it was the scene of Bill Mazeroski's Game Seven home run in the 1960 WS, and on May 25, 1935 Babe Ruth's final career home run was the first ball ever to clear the right field roof. The field is now the site of a University of Pittsburgh library and dorms, but home plate remains on display in its final location. /(SCL)

Dale Ford — 1942- . *Umpire* AL 1975-87 *2 LCS 1 WS*

Ford, who has also officiated basketball, was involved in two large controversies. During the 1981 season, he threatened to forfeit the second game of a White Sox-Angels doubleheader at Comiskey Park because of comments made by Chicago broadcaster Jimmy Piersall, which Ford said were inciting the 40,248 in attendance. In 1983 through union counsel Richie Phillips, Ford filed a lawsuit for an unspecified amount against Billy Martin for calling him "a stone liar" in an interview. /(RTM)

Dan Ford [Darnell Glenn, Sr.] (Disco Dan) — 1952- . OF-DH 1975-85 **Twins**, Angels, Orioles 1153 g, .270, 121 hr, 566 rbi. *2 LCS, 6 g, .273, 2 hr, 4 rbi. 1 WS, 5 g, .167, 1 hr, 1 rbi*

Unable to break into the A's outfield of Reggie Jackson, Joe Rudi, and Bill North, Ford was traded to the Twins after the 1974 season and immediately

Forbes Field

became a regular. His best season for Minnesota came in 1976, when he hit .267 with 20 HR, 86 RBI, 87 runs, and 17 steals. Traded to the Angels for 1979, he had his best season, with career highs of .290, 21 HR, 101 RBI, and 100 runs. He also homered in Games One and Two of the Angels' first LCS appearance, and batted .294 in the series.

Poor defensively, the right fielder led AL outfielders in errors in 1981 and was traded to the Orioles for Doug DeCinces. Ford was a semi-regular for two more years despite declining production. He came up lame after Game One of the 1983 LCS and had only one pinch-hit at-bat for the rest of the series. He played poorly in the World Series, but produced the winning run in Game Three when, with runners on first and third, Ivan DeJesus booted Ford's grounder.

Ford finished out his career with two more seasons as a Baltimore utility player. /(SFS)

Dave Ford — 1956- . RHP 1978-81 **Orioles** 155 ip, 5-6, 4.01

A solidly built, 6'4" Cleveland native, Ford threw a fastball, knuckle curve, changeup, and slider. In his ML debut, he shut out Chicago for 8-1/3 innings and won 1-0. Primarily a long reliever who'd get a spot start, he appeared in a career-high 25 games in 1980. /(EW)

Hod Ford [Horace Hills] — 1897-1977. SS-2B 1919-33 Braves, Phillies, Dodgers, **Reds**, Cardinals 1446, .263, 16 hr, 494 rbi

Ford broke in with the Braves in 1919 while still attending Tufts University, foregoing his final year of college eligibility. A smooth fielder and timely hitter, he set the record (since broken) for double plays by a shortstop (128) with the Reds in 1928, as the team set a record for double plays (194) that lasted for 30 years. /(NLM)

Russ Ford — 1883-1960. RHP 1909-15 **Yankees**, Buffalo (FL) 1487 ip, 98-71, 2.59. 20 wins: 10-11, 14

While a semi-pro pitcher, Ford accidentally discovered that a scuffed baseball could be made to break sharply. He began intentionally doctoring the ball using emery paper, and disguised his pitches as spitballs, which were legal. The Canadian was brilliant as a New York rookie, going 26-6 in 1910. He followed with a 22-11 mark, but his effectiveness waned and chronic arm soreness developed. In 1912 he lost an AL-high 21. He had one resurgent season in 1914, leading the outlaw Federal League with a

.769 winning percentage (20–6). His brother Gene pitched seven games for the 1905 Tigers. /(JK)

Ted Ford — 1947– . OF 1970–73 Indians, **Rangers** 240 g, .219, 17 hr, 68 rbi

After failing to crack .200 in two trials with the Indians, Vietnam veteran Ford was installed as a regular in the Rangers' outfield in 1973. His 14 homers and 50 RBI did not make up for his .235 BA. /(MC)

Whitey Ford [Edward Charles] (The Chairman of the Board) — 1926– . LHP 1950, 1953–67 **Yankees** 3170 ip, 236–106, 2.75. 20 wins: 61, 63. *11 WS, 146 ip, 10–8, 2.71*

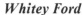 *Led League—w 55, 61, 63. Led League—era 56, 58. Cy Young Award—61. All-Star—54–56, 58–61, 64. Hall of Fame—1974.*

They called Ford "The Chairman of the Board" for good reason. He was for more than a decade the star pitcher of a team that operated with corporate

Whitey Ford

efficiency, and his intelligence and confidence were on display whenever he was on the mound. In contrast to pitchers who dominated hitters with overpowering physical abilities, the 5′10″ 180-lb lefthander controlled games with his mastery of the mental aspects of pitching and pinpoint control. Batters had to deal with his assortment of pitches: He mixed splendid changeups, marvelous curves, and a good fastball. He had one of the league's best pickoff moves, and he was an excellent fielder. And, like most successful businessmen, he was at his best when the pressure was greatest.

His most eye-catching statistics are his consistently low ERAs and his high winning percentage. In 11 of 16 seasons he was under a 3.00 ERA, and his worst was 3.24. His .690 winning percentage ranks third all-time and first among modern pitchers with 200 or more wins. Of course, he benefited from strong Yankee bat support, defense, and relief pitching, but his winning percentage was usually higher than the team's. He allowed an average of only 10.94 baserunners per nine innings and posted 45 career shutouts, including eight 1–0 victories.

After joining the Yankees in mid-season 1950, he won nine straight before a home run by Philadelphia's Sam Chapman gave him his only loss. In the WS, he pitched 8–2/3 innings without allowing an earned run to win the fourth game of a Yankee sweep. He spent 1951 and 1952 in the service, but returned to post 18–6 and 16–8 marks in 1953 and 1954.

His 18–7 record in 1955 tied him for most AL wins. He led in complete games (18) and was second in ERA (2.63). *TSN* named him to its annual ML all-star team. In the final month of the season, he pitched consecutive one-hitters. The following year he was even better, going 19–6, to lead the AL in winning percentage and ERA (2.47). Again he was named to the *TSN* all-star team. He won his second ERA crown in 1958 (2.01).

Through 1960, Yankee manager Casey Stengel limited Ford's starts, often resting him at least four days between appearances, and aiming him for more frequent use against better teams. In 1961 new manager Ralph Houk put him in a regular four-man rotation, and Ford led the AL in starts (39) and innings pitched (283) and earned the Cy Young Award with a 25–4 record, leading the ML in wins and percentage. Two years later, he again led in wins, percentage, starts, and innings pitched, with a 24–7 mark. At the time there was only a single Cy Young award for both leagues. Sandy Koufax won for 1963, but Ford was voted the top AL pitcher by

TSN. They opposed each other in both the first and fourth games of the '63 WS, with Koufax winning both times. In Game Four Ford lost a two-hitter on an unearned run.

The Yankees won 11 pennants in Ford's years with them. He ranks first all-time in WS wins (10), losses (8), games and games started (22), innings pitched, hits, bases on balls, and strikeouts. In the 1960, '61, and '62 Series, he pitched 33 consecutive scorelesss innings, breaking Babe Ruth's WS record of 29–2/3.

A fun-loving native New Yorker, Whitey formed a curious odd couple with Oklahoman Mickey Mantle. The two were a familiar duo in the Big Apple's nightclubs. They were inducted into the Hall of Fame together in 1974./(FK)

Frank Foreman — 1863–1957. RHP 1884–85, 89–96, 1901–02 Chicago (UA), Kansas City (UA), Baltimore (AA), **Reds**, Washington (NL), Baltimore (NL), Giants, Red Sox, Baltimore (AL) 1726 ip, 97–93, 3.94. 20 wins: 89

Foreman won 23 games for Baltimore in 1889 and 97 over his 11-year ML career, throwing mostly fastballs. His main claim to fame was that he discovered future Hall of Fame lefthander Eddie Plank pitching at Gettysburg College. Foreman's brother, Brownie, pitched briefly in the ML./(BC)

Mike Fornieles [Jose Miguel Torres] — 1932– . RHP 1952–63 Senators, White Sox, Orioles, **Red Sox**, Twins 1157 ip, 63–64, 3.96
☛ *All-Star—61.*

Fornieles had a spotty career as a starter/reliever, with a lifetime 18–31 record as a starter. But when the Cuban was used exclusively in relief by the Red Sox, he achieved success. In 1960 he went 10–5 and led the league with 14 saves (not then an official statistic) and an AL-record 70 appearances, and in 1961 he had a career-high 15 saves and made the All-Star team./(SH)

Bob Forsch — 1950– . RHP 1974–88 **Cardinals**, Astros 2795 ip, 168–136, 3.76. 20 wins: 77. *3 LCS, 15 ip, 2–1, 3.52. 3 WS, 22 ip, 1–3, 7.36*

Only Hall of Famers Bob Gibson and Jesse Haines pitched more years or won more games for the Cardinals than Forsch. He won 20 games in 1977 and led the Cardinals staff in victories six times. Converted from a third baseman, he threw two no-hitters in the minors, then no-hit the Phillies in 1978 and the Expos in 1983. He and his brother, Ken, were the first brothers to toss ML no-hitters.

A power pitcher early in his career, Bob later

relied on a deliberate delivery, pinpoint control, and a changeup, mixed with a sinker and occasional fastball. He helped himself with his bat by becoming an excellent bunter with some home run power. He won *TSN*'s Silver Slugger Award in 1980 and 1987. /(FJO)

Ken Forsch — 1946- . RHP 1970-84, 86 **Astros**, Angels 2126 ip, 114-113, 3.37. *1 LCS, 8 ip 0-1, 4.15* ☛ *All-Star—76, 81.*

Ken Forsch and his brother Bob are the only brothers to hurl no-hitters (Ken's coming on April 7, 1979, against Atlanta) and only the third pair of brothers to win more than 100 games each. Ken coupled a forkball with his fastball to fashion a 16-year ML career. In 1976 he was named to the NL All-Star team as a reliever and finished the season with 19 saves for the Astros. In 1981 he was named to the AL team for his work as a starter with the Angels. /(FJO)

Terry Forster (Trees) — 1952- . LHP 1971-86 **White Sox**, Pirates, Dodgers, Braves, Angels 1105 ip, 54-65, 3.23. *2 LCS, 1 ip, 1-0, 0.00. 2 WS, 6 ip, 0-0, 0.00*

Forster was a phenom at 18, a glutton at 34. In between he notched 127 saves. Signed out of high school, he pitched just 10 games in A-ball in 1970, and was so impressive he made the White Sox the following April. In 1972 he broke a club record with 29 saves. In that last year before the DH rule, he batted .526; he was a .397 lifetime hitter. From 1971 to 1973 he hurled 138-1/3 innings without surrendering a home run. He was the AL Fireman of the Year in 1974, saving a league-high 24 games. His fastball was clocked at 94.9 mph that September 7, but by the next season he was on the shelf with a bad arm; most felt he had been overworked by manager Chuck Tanner. After going 2-12 in 1976, mostly as a starter, he was traded to Pittsburgh with Rich Gossage (whom Chicago had also made a starter) for Richie Zisk and Silvio Martinez.

In November of 1977, Forster became the first free agent ever signed by the Dodgers. He rebounded with 22 saves and a 1.94 ERA for the 1978 pennant winners, but had bone chips removed from his elbow after the World Series. He was sometimes effective from 1982 through 1986, constantly battling weight problems. His eating habits began attracting national attention. He was with the Braves when, in June 1985, *Late Night* host David Letterman made Forster a national celebrity by calling him "a fat tub of goo." /(RL)

Ray Fosse (Mule) — 1947- . C 1967-77, 79 **Indians**, A's, Indians, Mariners, Brewers 924 g, .256, 61 hr, 324 rbi. *3 LCS, 10 g, .200, 1 hr, 6 rbi. 2 WS, 12 g, .152, 1 hr, 1 rbi* ☛ *All-Star—70, 71. Gold Glove—70-71.*

Fosse was involved in one of the most celebrated plays in All-Star Game history. In 1970, his first season as a Cleveland regular, he established himself as one of baseball's best catchers, earning a spot on the All-Star team. With the score tied 4-4 in the 12th inning, Fosse blocked home plate with Pete Rose charging in. Rose barreled Fosse over to score the winning run. Never one to be stopped by injuries, Mule continued to play that year (though X-rays later revealed he had a fractured shoulder) until a broken index finger finally ended his season.

Fosse never again displayed the power and consistency he had shown in '70 (.307, 18 HR). He had been Cleveland's number-one pick in the first-ever June free agent draft (1965), chosen before Johnny Bench. Fosse was disabled five times in his career: while still in the minors in 1967; for most of 1969; for most of 1974 (hit by a pitch, pulled a side muscle, and then suffered a pinched nerve in his neck trying to break up a clubhouse fight); twice in 1976; and for all of 1978. And although it didn't put him on the DL, there was an odd incident in 1970: A cherry bomb thrown from the stands blew up by his foot, badly burning the arch of his foot and causing a shock. Always tough and determined, he stayed in the game, limping, was hit by a pitch, but played the next day.

Fosse, who had huge hands that were compared to ham hocks, was a Gold Glove winner in 1970 and 1971. He went on to catch for the 1973-75 pennant-winning A's, but the injuries took their toll and forced an early retirement. He later became an Oakland executive and broadcaster. /(ME)

Alan Foster — 1946- . RHP 1967-76 Dodgers, Indians, Angels, **Cardinals**, Padres 1026 ip, 48-63, 3.73

With Spokane of the Pacific Coast League in 1967, the Dodger bonus-baby pitched 1-0 no-hitters in consecutive appearances against Seattle and was tabbed "can't miss." After failure with the Dodgers and a trip to the AL, he had his most successful season with St. Louis in 1973 (13-9, 3.14). /(JCA)

Bill Foster [Willie] — 1904-1978. LHP-MGR Negro Leagues 1923-37 Memphis Red Sox, **Chicago American Giants**, Birmingham Black Barons, Homestead Grays, Kansas City Monarchs, Cole's American Giants 1544 ip, 150-70 ☛ *All-Star—33-34.*

Bill Foster—the younger half-brother of the Father of Negro Baseball, Rube Foster—was one of the finest lefthanded pitchers in Negro League history. He played most of his career with Rube's Chicago American Giants, and was an intelligent power pitcher with near-perfect control and a variety of pitches, all delivered with the same fluid motion. Occasionally, he would use a hesitation wind-up. Black all-star third baseman and manager Dave Malarcher once said, "Willie Foster's greatness was that he had this terrific speed and a great, fast-breaking curveball and a drop ball, and he was really a master of the change-of-pace. He could throw you a real fast one and then use the same motion and bring it up a little slower, and then a little slower yet. And then he'd use the same motion again, and Zzzz. He was really a great pitcher."

After a brief stay with the Memphis Red Sox in 1923, brother Rube enticed Willie to join his Chicago American Giants. For three years under Rube's tutelage, Willie learned the art of pitching. In 1926 he won 26 consecutive games, leading the Giants to the playoffs against the Kansas City Monarchs. He won the last two games 1–0 and 5–0 to win the league championship. In the Black World Series finale against the Bacharach Giants, he threw a 1–0 shutout.

In 1927 Foster posted a Negro League record of 18–3, and went 14–1 in the California Winter League. In a repeat BWS appearance against the Bacharach Giants, he won the opener 6–2, lost the fifth game (shortened to 6–1/2 innings due to darkness), lost the eighth game because of four fielding errors, and came back in the ninth game to win the championship.

After the 1929 season, Foster pitched a two-game series against an American League all-star team composed of players from the Tigers, Browns, Indians, and White Sox. He struggled in the first game, but followed with a shutout in the second contest, pitching eight innings of no-hit ball and striking out nine. Detroit slugger Charlie Gehringer told Foster after the series, "If I could paint you white I could get $150,000 for you right now."

Available box scores show Foster winning 11 of 21 confrontations with the legendary Satchel Paige. He also won six of seven games against white major leaguers. In 1933 he posted a complete-game victory in the first East-West all-star game, giving up seven hits and seven runs while striking out four. His last year in baseball was spent with a white semi-pro team in Elgin, IL, and a black team called the Washington Browns in Yakima, WA. He later returned to his alma mater, Alcorn College, as baseball coach and dean of men./(LL)

Eddie Foster (Kid) — 1888–1937. 3B-2B 1910, 12–23 Yankees, **Senators**, Red Sox, Browns 1498 g, .264, 6 hr, 446 rbi

The 5'6" Foster was widely regarded as the best hit-and-run man of his day. His clutch hitting deprived Eddie Plank of his last bid for a no-hitter. In Plank's final season, with the 1917 Browns, the 42-year-old pitcher had gone 8–2/3 innings without allowing Washington a hit. He walked a batter, and Foster doubled him home to end Plank's bid. /(JK)

George Foster — 1949– . OF 1969–86 Giants, **Reds**, Mets, White Sox 1977 g, .274, 348 hr, 1239 rbi. *4 LCS, 10 g, .242, 3 hr, 6 rbi. 3 WS, 13 g, .326, 6 rbi* ☛ *Most Valuable Player—77. Led League—hr 77–78. Led League—rbi 76–78. All-Star—76–79, 81.*

Foster excelled in track, football, and baseball at El Camino College in California, drawing the attention of the Giants, who made him their third pick in the January 1968 draft. It took seven seasons in the majors and minors, with two organizations, before Foster arrived with Cincinnati to stay. The 6'1" 180-lb outfielder soon became an important cog in the Big Red Machine of the 1970s.

Foster became a regular in 1975. A mediocre fielder at best, Foster had a strong but inaccurate arm. He was a better than average baserunner. But he made a name for himself as a powerful, productive hitter who had five of the best seasons of any player of his time. Foster's three consecutive RBI championships (1976–78) tied a ML record. In 1977, his MVP year, he hit .320 with 149 RBI and 124 runs and blasted 52 HR to become only the seventh NL player to hit 50 or more in a season. He hit three straight homers in a July 14 game that season, and his 31 road homers set the ML record for righthanded batters. In 1978 Foster again led the NL with 40 HR.

After eleven seasons and three World Series with Cincinnati, Foster was traded to the Mets in 1982. Signing him to a five-year contract worth over $10 million, the team's new owners, Nelson Doubleday and Fred Wilpon, showed their willingness to spend money to rebuild the Mets. He hit just 13 HR that year, 28 the next, and was considered a disappointment. Word got around among NL pitchers that he wouldn't lay off low curveballs, and he regularly struck out on curves in the dirt. Foster was released by the Mets in August of their World Championship 1986 season. The struggling veteran, hitting .227 at

George Foster

the time, claimed he was the victim of racism, but he failed to regain his stroke after the White Sox picked him up. He retired tied for tenth in career grand slams with 13. /(EW)

John B. Foster — 1863–1941. *Writer.*

Foster succeeded Henry Chadwick as editor of *Spalding's Guide* in 1908. He had been the state editor of the Cleveland *Press* until 1888. When the sports editor of the *Leader* became ill, Foster replaced him. In 1896 he moved to New York, where he worked for the *Evening Telegram* and *The Sun* and for the Consolidated Press Association. He served as sports editor of the *Telegram* for 15 years. He was secretary of the New York Giants from 1913 to 1919, then returned to *The Sun* until 1931. A

member of the original rules committee, he was an authority on baseball rules, law, and administration. He was said to have answered more than 500,000 questions by mail on all phases of the game. /(NLM)

Pop Foster (Clarence) — 1878–1944. OF 1898–1901 **Giants**, Senators, White Sox 262 g, .281, 10 hr, 136 rbi

After a short ML career, Foster turned to coaching and physical education, where he achieved nation-wide fame. He was director of athletics in army camps during WWI, physical director at Brooklyn Polytechnic Institute for five years, and in the physical education department at Princeton from 1924 until his death. /(BC)

Roy Foster — 1945– . OF 1970–72 **Indians** 337 g, .253, 45 hr, 118 rbi

A one-year wonder, Foster was second to Thurman Munson in 1970 AL Rookie of the Year voting, but was *TSN*'s AL Rookie Player of the Year (268, 23 HR, 60 RBI). He then played just two more mediocre seasons. /(ME)

Rube Foster [Andrew] — 1878–1930. RHP-MGR Negro Leagues 1902–26 Chicago Union Giants, Cuban Giants, Cuban X-Giants, Philadelphia Giants, Chicago Leland Giants, **Chicago American Giants** statistics not available
☛ *Hall of Fame—1981.*

Foster overcame childhood illness to become an outstanding pitcher, a shrewd manager, and the dominant executive in black baseball. As a 6'4" 200-lb teenager, he joined the Yellow Jackets, a traveling black team in Texas. John McGraw saw Foster during spring training of 1901 (or thereabouts) and wanted him and other blacks for his New York Giants. But, unable to use them, he instead asked Foster to tutor the Giants' pitchers. Christy Mathewson reportedly learned his "fadeaway" pitch (a screwball) from Foster.

Foster then joined the Chicago Union Giants, pitched a shutout in his first start, but soon lost his effectiveness. He regained his form while with a white semi-pro club in the Michigan State League, and defeated every team in the circuit. Because of his difficulties, he had become a keen student of the game, and a wily pitcher. By 1902 he was with the black Cuban Giants.

In 1903 Foster was the top black pitcher in the country. He pitched the Cuban X-Giants to the black championship, and was the winner in four of their five victories over the Philadelphia Giants in the Black World Series. The following year, he

Rube Foster

pitched the Philadelphia Giants to the title, and recorded both victories in a best-of-three series against the Cuban X-Giants.

It is difficult to distinguish fact from fiction in Foster's pitching career; he is credited with a 51–4 season early on. Documentation does exist for a 1904 no-hitter he tossed against the Camden, NJ team. He reportedly gained his nickname by defeating the Athletics' Rube Waddell in 1902, and is reputed to have fared well in duels with major league pitchers Chief Bender, Mordecai Brown, and Cy Young. Frank Chance called him "the most finished product I've ever seen in the pitcher's box," and Honus Wagner said he was "one of the greatest pitchers of all time . . .smartest pitcher I've ever seen . . ."

Foster began managing in 1907, when he guided the Chicago Leland Giants to a 110–10 record. Their record was 64–21–1 in 1908. In 1909 Foster challenged the Chicago Cubs to a series, which the Cubs won in three close games. Foster pitched the

second game and took a 5–2 lead into the ninth inning, but lost 6–5. Mordecai Brown won the first and third contests. There is no record of any major league club coming forth to answer Foster's challenge in 1910, when his team went 123–6.

In 1911 Foster left the Lelands to form a partnership with Chicago businessman John C. Schorling. From this union came one of black baseball's strongest teams, the Chicago American Giants. They dominated both the Chicago semi-pro scene (regularly winning the championship) and national black baseball, capturing Negro League titles in 1914 and 1917 and sharing the 1915 championship with the New York Lincoln Stars. Competing against white major leaguers following the 1915 season, they won the California Winter League crown.

In the winter of 1919 Foster organized the first viable black major league, the Negro National League, which operated in the Midwest and the South from 1920 through 1931. He served as president of the new league until 1926, and ruled it completely. An Eastern counterpart was organized in 1923 and Black World Series between the two leagues were held from 1924 through 1927.

Foster continued to manage through 1925, and won the Negro National League's first three pennants (1920–22). He made use of psychology and speed, invented the bunt-and-run, and intimidated opponents. White major leaguers often attended his games to learn his tactics. Though he made few rules, he expected his players to follow them. He ran the games as he ran the NNL -in total control—and once hit a player across the head with his pipe for tripling after he was given the bunt sign.

Foster's last known public meeting was in 1926 with lifelong friends Ban Johnson and John McGraw, through whom it is believed he was trying to schedule white major league teams to play his American Giants. Shortly thereafter he began to lose his mind, and spent his last four years in the Kankakee, Illinois State Hospital. /(MFK)

Rube Foster [George] — 1889–1976. RHP 1913–17 **Red Sox** 843 ip, 58–34, 2.35. *2 WS, 21 ip, 2–0, 1.71*

After Boston teammate Smoky Joe Wood taught him how to throw a fastball, the 5'7" Foster went 14–8 (1.65) in 1914 and 19–8 in 1915. He won two games and went 4-for-8 at the plate in the 1915 WS. Foster no-hit New York on June 21, 1916. /(EW)

Bob Fothergill (Fat) — 1897–1938. OF 1922–33
Tigers, White Sox, Red Sox 1105 g, .326, 36 hr, 582 rbi

Fothergill was an outstanding line-drive hitter more famous for his girth than his hits. Charitably listed at 230, the 5'10"outfielder was sensitive about his size and preferred Bob or Roy (his middle name) to Fat. The stories were told in every dugout: Leo Durocher once complained it was illegal to have two men in the batter's box; during a crash fasting program, Fothergill supposedly bit an umpire after a called third strike; there were several accounts of his shattering outfield fences in pursuit of fly balls. But he could hit. In 1927, his top year, he batted .359 with 114 RBI for the Tigers. Eventually relegated to pinch hitting, he led the AL with 19 in 1929. Of those with more than 200 pinch-hit at-bats, only Fothergill has posted a .300 career average. /(DB)

Steve Foucault — 1949– . RHP 1973–78 **Rangers**, Tigers, Royals 496 ip, 35–36, 3.21

A catcher in the minors, Foucault switched to pitching after suffering a knee injury. Hurling side-arm, overhand, and underhand, he was Texas's top reliever from 1973 to 1975, recording all 12 Ranger saves in 1974 and 52 lifetime. /(JCA)

Jack Fournier [Jacques Frank] — 1892–1973. 1B-OF 1912–18, 20–27 White Sox, Yankees, Cardinals, **Dodgers**, Braves 1530 g, .313, 136, 859 rbi
☛ *Led League—hr 24.*

Purchased by the White Sox from the Red Sox in 1912, Fournier presented Clarence Rowland and a half-dozen other managers with the dilemma of what to do with this inept-fielding pure hitter. Rowland solved that problem in 1916, a year after Fournier had led the AL in slugging, by replacing him at first base with the marginal Jack Ness. Fournier hit .350 for the Yankees in limited duty in 1918 before they passed him off to the Cardinals. Fournier led NL first basemen with 25 errors in 1920. After three productive years in St. Louis, Fournier was dealt to Brooklyn on February 15, 1923. Fournier said he would quit the game rather than leave St. Louis, but he ended his holdout and reported to the Dodgers. Fournier had found his spot, among an offensive unit that included Zack Wheat, Milt Stock, and Zack Taylor. He turned in a six-for-six performance on June 29 of that year, hit .351, and made a league-high 21 errors. In 1924 Fournier led the NL with 27 HR, and in 1925 was second to Rogers Hornsby with 130 RBI. /(RL)

Jack Fournier with the Braves

Dave Foutz (Scissors) — 1856–1897. RHP-1B-OF 1884–96 St. Louis (AA), Brooklyn (AA), **Dodgers** 1997 ip, 147–66, 2.84; 1135 g, .277, 32 hr, 547 rbi. 20 wins: 85–87
   Manager 1893–96 **Dodgers** 264–257, .507
☛ *Led League—w 86. Led League—era 86.*

Chris Von der Ahe, bumptious owner of the American Association St. Louis Browns, acquired Foutz by buying the entire Bay City, MI franchise. Paired with Bob Caruthers, the slender, 6'2" Scissors pitched the Browns to American Association championships from 1885 to 1887. Parisian Bob contributed 99 wins in those three seasons, Foutz 98. Foutz won a league-leading 41 in 1886 (his third straight year with an over-.700 winning percentage), in 504 innings, and recorded 11 shutouts. In 1887 Foutz managed a mere 25 wins, but hit .357 in 65 games as an outfielder and first baseman, positions he played more frequently for the rest of his career.

Cashing in on his investment, Von der Ahe sold his ace righthanders to Brooklyn in 1888 for $13,500. With the hard-hitting Foutz at first base, Brooklyn won the 1889 Association championship, switched to the National League, and won another pennant in 1890. Foutz pitched more in 1892, recording his last 13 wins. In 1893 he became a playing manager, but in four years never moved the team higher than fifth.

As a pitcher, Foutz's .690 winning percentage is the second-highest career mark (tied with Whitey Ford) among retired pitchers, just behind the .692 of Bob Caruthers. /(ADS)

Art Fowler — 1922– . RHP 1954–57, 59, 61–64 **Reds**, Dodgers, Angels 1024 ip, 54–51, 4.03

As a 48-year-old player-coach on Billy Martin's 1970 Denver (American Association) team, Fowler saved 15 games and won 9, with a 1.59 ERA. He subsequently followed Martin as a pitching coach to several ML cities, including New York. Mostly a reliever during his playing days, Fowler won a career-high 12 games for the 1954 Reds. His brother, Jesse, pitched with the Cardinals 30 years before Art's ML debut. /(TJ)

Dick Fowler — 1921–1972. RHP 1941–42, 45–52 **A's** 1303 ip, 66–79, 4.11

Fowler anchored the Philadelphia Athletics' pitching staff in the late 1940s, but despite his splendid fastball and fine curve, he never had more than 15 wins. In 1945 he returned from the Canadian Army to no-hit St. Louis on September 9. Fowler was one of three A's pitchers to lose an AL-high 16 in 1946. /(EW)

Charlie Fox (Irish) — 1921– . C 1942 **Giants** 3 g, .429, 0 hr, 1 rbi.
Manager 1970–74, 76, 83 **Giants**, Expos, Cubs 377–369, .505. First place: 71 *1 LCS, 1–3, .250*

Fox caught only three games for the Giants but began managing in their farm system at Class-D level and worked his way up to Triple-A. He served as a scout for the Giants and ML coach before replacing Clyde King as Giants manager early in the 1970 season. He led San Francisco to the Western Division championship the next year and was voted *TSN*'s ML Manager of the Year. A traditionalist with a fiery temper, Fox was later both GM and interim manager of the Expos and interim manager of the Cubs. /(BC)

Howie Fox — 1921–1955. RHP 1944–46, 48–52, 54 **Reds**, Phillies, Orioles 1108 ip, 43–72, 4.33

The 6'3" Fox attended the University of Oregon on a basketball scholarship for a year before signing with the Reds in 1943. His one winning season, 1950, came a year after his 6–19 mark made him the losingest pitcher in the majors. In December 1951 he was sent to the Phillies with Smoky Burgess in a seven-player deal. After pitching in the Texas League in 1955, he was stabbed to death while bouncing three young men from his tavern near San Antonio. /(NLM)

Nellie Fox [Jacob Nelson] — 1927–1975. 2B 1947–65 A's, **White Sox**, Astros 2367 g, .288, 35 hr, 790 rbi. *1 WS, 6 g, .375*
 Most Valuable Player—59. All-Star—51–61, 63. Gold Glove—57, 59–60.

The 5'10" 160-lb Fox was long one of the top AL second basemen. After an unimpressive 1948 rookie season, Fox was traded to the White Sox for catcher Joe Tipton. He became a vital member of the Go-Go Sox for 14 seasons, noted for his tobacco-chewing and aggressive play. He withstood injury and illness to establish a record for consecutive games at second base, playing 798 straight (August 7, 1956 through September 3, 1960). Teaming first

Nellie Fox

with Chico Carrasquel and then with Luis Aparicio, he gave the team strength up the middle. Hard work made him a reliable hitter (six .300-plus seasons) who rarely struck out. He led the AL in fewest strikeouts 11 times and he struck out only 216 times in 9232 career at-bats, the third-best percentage in ML history. In 1959, when the Sox won their first pennant in 40 years, he was AL MVP. The White Sox retired his uniform number, 2./(RL)

Pete Fox [Ervin] — 1909-1966. OF 1933-45 **Tigers**, Red Sox 1461 g, .298, 65 hr, 694 rbi. *3 WS, 14 g, .327, 6 rbi*

Fox was one of the AL's better outfielders, both offensively and defensively, and a mainstay of the strong Detroit teams of the mid-1930s. A semi-pro pitcher when the Tigers first spotted him, he was advised to concentrate on the outfield. Within three seasons, Fox had led the Texas League by hitting .357, and had arrived in Detroit. Always dangerous on the bases, he became a steady fielder with a good arm, and a good doubles hitter with occasional home run power. He hit over .300 each year from 1935 through 1937, had six doubles in the 1934 World Series, and was the top batter in the 1935 WS, getting ten hits (.385)./(EW)

Terry Fox — 1935- . RHP 1960-66 Braves, **Tigers**, Phillies 397 ip, 29-19, 2.99

A reliever with 59 career saves, Fox never had a losing ML season. He compiled a 1.41 ERA in 39 games for Detroit and surrendered Roger Maris's 58th homer in 1961. He recorded a 1.71 ERA in 1962./(TJ)

Bill Foxen — 1884-1937. LHP 1908-11 **Phillies**, Cubs 326 ip, 16-20, 2.56

Foxen's 7-7 as a rookie with the Phillies in 1908 turned out to be his best ML season. He annoyed umpires with his constant, open bickering during games. /(NLM)

Jimmie Foxx (Double X, The Beast) — 1907-1967. 1B-3B-C 1925-42, 44-45 **A's**, Red Sox, Cubs, Phillies 2317 g, .325, 534 hr, 1921 rbi; 23 ip, 1-0, 1.59. *3 WS, 18 g, .344, 4 hr, 11 rbi*
☛ *Most Valuable Player—32-33, 38. Led League—ba 33, 38. Led League—hr 32-33, 35, 39. Led League—rbi 32-33, 38. All-Star—33-41. Hall of Fame—1951.*

One of the greatest power hitters in major league history, Foxx broke in as a catcher, won fame as a first baseman, and filled in elsewhere, including several turns on the mound.

Jimmie Foxx

Born at Sudlersville, MD, Foxx grew strong doing chores on his father's farm. At age ten, he had had enough of farm life, and tried to join the army. Rejected by the military, he turned to sports, especially his first love, track. He played high school baseball and was soon demonstrating the power which would make him famous. His power displays caught the attention of Frank "Home Run" Baker, who was managing Easton of the Eastern Shore League. After being invited for a tryout, Foxx soon became Baker's protege. Baker owed a favor to his old boss, Connie Mack, and recommended the youngster. Mack took the 17-year-old Foxx in 1925 and sat him next to him on the Athletics' bench for several seasons. Mack had the young Mickey Cochrane at catcher, so he converted Foxx to first base, where he became a regular in 1928.

Before long, Foxx was being called "the right-handed Babe Ruth." In virtually every AL park, there was a story to tell about a mighty Foxx homer. In Chicago, he hit a ball over the double-decked stands at Comiskey Park, clearing 34th Street. His gigantic clout in Cleveland won the 1935 All-Star Game. In Yankee Stadium, his blast high into the left field upper deck had enough power to break a seat. In St. Louis, his ninth inning blast in Game Five of the 1930 Series just about clinched it for the A's. In Detroit, he hit one of the longest balls ever, way up into the left field bleachers.

At bat, Foxx presented a menacing picture. A strong, powerful man, he held the bat at the end and stood fairly deep in the batter's box, using a wide stance and a full stride into the ball. As the pitch approached, his powerful arm muscles flexed visibly before he hit the ball. Like many sluggers, Foxx struck out often, and he led the AL seven times.

Perhaps more impressive than his homers was his record as an RBI man. Like Babe Ruth and Lou Gehrig, he drove in over 100 runs in 13 seasons. Also hitting for average, he won the Triple Crown in 1933 (.356, 48 HR, 163 RBI), one of three seasons he led the league in RBI; his best RBI mark was 175 in 1938, when he would have captured his second Triple Crown if not for Hank Greenberg's 58 HR. He was the HR champ four times despite competition from Ruth, Gehrig, Greenberg, and DiMaggio.

In 1932 Foxx hit 58 homers; he might have hit more than 60 if not for a spell in August when he suffered from an injured wrist. Five times he hit the right field screen in St. Louis; the screen was not there when Ruth hit 60 HR in 1927. Also in 1932, a screen that Ruth hadn't had to contend with was erected in left field in Cleveland. Reportedly, Foxx hit that at least three times.

Foxx never made big money with the financially troubled Athletics, and he had to be unloaded to Tom Yawkey's Boston Red Sox, where he was paid well. A good-natured and well-liked man, he became an immediate favorite. He also took a young slugger under his wing. "I truly loved Foxxie," said Ted Williams some 40 years later.

Foxx was sent to the Cubs in 1942. He retired in 1943, but came back to play a few games during WWII with the Cubs and Phillies. His exceptionally strong throwing arm even enabled him to pitch in nine games for the Phillies in 1945, including two starts. The BBWAA elected him to the Hall of Fame in 1951.

A friend to all, Double X was always picking up the check. He drank heavily, saw several business ventures fail, and what little money he had made in baseball disappeared. He managed in the minors, coached at Minneapolis (American Association), and took a turn in the Red Sox radio booth in 1946. In July 1967, at age 59, he choked to death on a piece of meat while dining with his brother. Foxx is still ninth on the all-time HR list (534), sixth in RBI (1921), and fourth in slugging percentage (.609). /(EW)

Joe Foy — 1943–1989. 3B 1966–72 **Red Sox**, Royals, Mets, Senators 716 g, .248, 58 hr, 298 rbi

Foy was *TSN* Minor League Player of the Year and International League MVP in 1965. A hustling infielder with fair home run power, he twice led AL third basemen in double plays while with Boston but also twice led them in errors. The World Champion Mets traded the promising Amos Otis to secure Foy as their regular third baseman in 1970, but his skills eroded prematurely, due in part to a substance abuse problem. /(JCA)

Paul Foytack — 1930– . RHP 1953, 55–64 **Tigers**, Angels 1498 ip, 86–87, 4.14

Though the strong-armed Foytack had control problems early on, he ultimately became a mainstay of the Tiger staff. From 1956 through 1959, he twice won 15, and twice 14. In '56 he led the AL with 142 walks, but also struck out a career-high 184. Traded to the Angels in mid-1963, Foytack set a ML record against the Indians on July 31 when he allowed four consecutive home runs to Woodie Held, Pedro Ramos, Tito Francona, and Larry Brown in one inning. /(JL)

Ken Frailing — 1948– . LHP 1972–76 White Sox, **Cubs** 218 ip, 10–16, 3.96

Frailing appeared briefly with the White Sox before going to the Cubs in a 1973 trade for Ron Santo. He was a reliever and spot starter for two seasons prior to a career-ending 1976 shoulder injury. /(JCA)

Earl Francis — 1936– . RHP 1960–65 **Pirates**, Cardinals 406 ip, 16–23, 3.77

Francis was born in Slab Fork, WV. His career was delayed four years by Air Force service. He won nine and was second to Bob Friend on the Pirates with 121 strikeouts in 1962, his best ML year. /(ME)

Ray Francis — 1893–1934. LHP 1922–23, 25
Senators, Tigers, Yankees, Red Sox 337 ip, 12–28, 4.65

In 1922 Francis went 7–18 for the sixth-place Senators (including an 0–3 relief mark); his 4.28 ERA was the best of his career. /(JFC)

John Franco — 1960– . LHP 1984– **Reds** 528 ip, 42–30, 2.49
☛ *All-Star—86–87, 89.*

Franco only had one ERA below 4.00 in the minors, but the hard-throwing Brooklyn native advanced to the ML nonetheless, where he emerged as an overpowering bullpen stopper for the Reds. Originally drafted by the Dodgers, Franco was traded to the Reds with one other minor leaguer for Rafael Landestoy in 1982. He debuted in 1984, posting a 2.64 ERA in 54 appearances for Cincinnati, and in 1985 Franco was the lefthanded set-up man for Ted Power, leading the NL with 12 relief wins and saving 12 more games on his own. Franco has been the Reds' lone closer since 1986, recording 29, 32, and 39 saves in 1986–88, and, thanks to the presence of Rob Murphy and later Rob Dibble in the Reds bullpen, seldom enters a game before the ninth inning. In 1989 Franco enjoyed yet another outstanding season, although he tailed off in the second half. /(SCL)

Julio Franco — 1961– . SS-2B 1982– Phillies, **Indians**, Rangers 1064 g, .298, 58 hr, 524 rbi
☛ *All-Star—89.*

One of five players sent from Philadelphia to Cleveland for Von Hayes in 1982, Franco became one of the best offensive middle infielders of the 1980s. Some said the Dominican's immaturity made him a divisive presence during his six years with the Indians, but he was an easy target on losing teams with his weak defense and flamboyant style. Hitting from a distinctive knock-kneed stance with his bat wrapped high behind his ear, he earned raves in 1985 when he drove in 90 runs, taking advantage of a very high 244 opportunities with runners in scoring position. Franco batted .303 or better in 1986–88, but the Indians continued to lose despite high expectations (one national magazine picked them to win the WS in 1987).

Franco led AL shortstops in errors in 1984 and 1985, but made fewer after his fielding percentage was used against him in arbitration hearings. His powerful bat only partly compensated for his lack of range, and he gained a reputation of being unable to make the big play defensively. On April 20, 1985, he disappeared for two days in the Bronx, later saying he had been ill at the home of a friend who had no phone. On June 8, 1986, he left Cleveland Stadium without permission just before a game after fighting with his wife. "I would have let him go if he had asked," said manager Pat Corrales, always a Franco booster.

In May 1985 the Indians acquired shortstop Johnnie LeMaster and asked Franco to move to second base. Franco balked at taking the job from his friend Tony Bernazard, and LeMaster was sent packing three weeks later. Franco was finally moved to second base in 1988 after Corrales was fired and Bernazard was traded. Franco was traded to Texas for Pete O'Brien, Jerry Browne, and Oddibe McDowell before the 1989 season. He emerged as a Rangers team leader and mentor to Rafael Palmeiro and Ruben Sierra. Franco hit .316 with 92 RBI and stole 21 bases in 24 attempts. /(JCA)

Terry Francona — 1959– . 1B-OF 1981– **Expos**, Cubs, Reds, Indians 705 g, .274, 16 hr, 143 rbi. *1 LCS, 2 g, .000*

The son of long-time ML player Tito Francona, Terry was *The Sporting News* College Player of the Year at the U. of Arizona in 1980, and was the Expos first-round draft pick in the 1980 free agent draft. A line drive hitter with little power, Francona played less than two seasons in the minors, and hit .352 at Denver (American Association) in 1981 to earn a promotion to Montreal. With the Expos, he spent half of 1982 and half of 1984 on the DL, and hit .267 in 1985 before being released. He played single seasons with the Cubs and Reds in 1986–87, then signed a minor league contract with the Indians for 1988, and hit .311 after joining the parent club in mid-season. /(SCL)

Tito Francona — 1933– . OF-1B 1956–70 Orioles, White Sox, Tigers, **Indians**, Cardinals, Phillies, Braves, A's, Brewers 1719 g, .272, 125 hr, 656 rbi

The standout mark in Francona's career is his .363 average in 1959. Platooned with Jimmy Piersall in the outfield and Vic Power at first base, and often used as a pinch hitter, the lefthanded batter did not qualify for the batting title. He was later a full-time starter in the outfield and at first base for the Indians. He led the AL with 36 doubles in 1960. After leaving Cleveland following the 1964 season, Francona journeyed through baseball as a "supersub." He led the AL with 15 pinch hits in 1970. His son Terry also played for the Indians, among others. /(ME)

Fred Frankhouse — 1904– . RHP 1927–39 Cardinals, **Braves**, Dodgers 1888 ip, 106–97, 3.92
☛ *All-Star—34.*

Frankhouse won ten or more games each year from 1933 through 1937. In 1934, his All-Star year, Frankhouse notched a career-high 17 victories for the Braves. With Brooklyn in 1937, the curveballer outdueled Carl Hubbell to snap the latter's record 24-game winning streak. /(TJ)

Herman Franks — 1914- . C 1939-41, 47-49 Cardinals, **Dodgers**, Phillies, Giants 190 g, .199, 3 hr, 43 rbi. *1 WS, 1 g, .000.*
   Manager 1965-68, 77-79 **Giants**, Cubs 605-521, .537

A graduate of the University of Utah, Franks was a weak-hitting backup catcher for several NL teams. He scouted for the Giants for a dozen years, then became manager of their Salt Lake City club in 1961. He managed the Giants to four straight second-place finishes, 1965-68. He was also credited with straightening Willie Mays's financial affairs, which were a mess when Franks arrived in San Francisco. After leaving the Giants, he had a successful business career and formed a group that tried to buy the Yankees in 1972. He came out of retirement to manage the Cubs for three seasons beginning in 1977 as a favor to his friend, Cubs GM Bob Kennedy. /(NLM)

Chick Fraser [Charles Carrolton] — 1871-1940. RHP 1896-1909 Louisville (NL), Cleveland (NL), **Phillies**, A's, Braves, Reds, Cubs 3356 ip, 177-212, 3.68. 20 wins: 99, 01

Fraser was a hawk-nosed pitcher who threw a no-hitter in 1903 for the Phillies. He twice won 20 games, but he also led his league in walks three times. He became a coach with masterful control of the fungo bat. Fraser was the brother-in-law of Hall of Famer Fred Clarke; while with Louisville, the two had taken sisters as brides. They were reunited in Pittsburgh when Clarke signed Fraser as a scout. Fraser later scouted for the Dodgers and Yankees. /(JK)

Willie Fraser — 1964- . RHP 1986- **Angels** 467 ip, 26-30, 4.45

Fraser was the Angels' first-round selection in the June 1985 draft. He joined their starting rotation when Kirk McCaskill and John Candelaria were sidelined in 1987, and went 10-10 (3.92). His 5.41 ERA in 1988 was largely attributable to the 33 home runs he allowed -the most by any AL pitcher. The Yankees reached him for five HR that August 16, though California held on to win the game 15-6. On August 10, 1988, Fraser pitched a one-hitter against Seattle, winning 2-1. The one hit was a homer, by Alvin Davis. /(JCA)

Harry Frazee — 1881-1929. *Executive.*

The man who sold Babe Ruth to the Yankees for $100,000 and a $300,000 loan, Frazee was a theatrical producer who bought the World Champion Red Sox for $400,000 in 1917 and sold the last-place team for $1.5 million in 1923. Often when he needed money to cover his theatrical investments, he would sell off his best players, frequently to the Yankees. In the middle of the 1919 season, he sold pitcher Carl Mays, who had left the team, to New York. AL president Ban Johnson voided the deal, insisting Mays should have been suspended and not available for sale or trade. The Yankees went to court and won, causing a rift between club owners that was not healed until Johnson resigned nine years later. Meanwhile, Frazee had contributed Everett Scott and Herb Pennock to the budding Yankee dynasty. /(NLM)

George Frazier — 1954- . RHP 1978-87 Cardinals, **Yankees**, Indians, Cubs, Twins 676 ip, 35-43, 4.20. *2 LCS, 7 ip, 1-0, 2.45. 2 WS, 6 ip, 0-3, 11.12*

Frazier, who spent most of his career as a set-up reliever, is best known for tying the World Series record for losses with three for the Yankees in 1981. He also pitched in the 1984 LCS for the Cubs and the 1987 WS for the Twins. Frazier had a career-high eight saves for the 1983 Yankees. /(EG)

Vic Frazier — 1904-1977. RHP 1931-34, 37, 39 **White Sox**, Tigers, Braves 579 ip, 23-38, 5.77

Frazier's 1937 homesickness created a roster spot for Braves rookie Jim Turner. Turner responded with 20 wins, seven more than Frazier had collected in his top season (1931 with Chicago). /(TJ)

Johnny Frederick — 1902-1977. OF 1929-34 **Dodgers** 805 g, .308, 85 hr, 377 rbi

Frederick had a great rookie season in 1929, hitting .328, with 24 homers and a rookie record 52 doubles. Known for his extraordinary pinch hitting, in 1932 he connected for six pinch homers, breaking a 19-year-old record. /(WAB)

Roger Freed — 1946- . OF-1B 1970-72, 74, 76-79 Orioles, **Phillies**, Reds, Expos, Cardinals 344 g, .245, 22 hr, 109 rbi

The renowned minor league slugger hit 42 home runs for Denver (American Association) in 1976 but only 22 in parts of eight ML seasons. In 1971 with the Phillies, his only season as a ML regular, Freed hit .221. /(JCA)

Andrew Freedman — Unk.–1915. *Executive.*

Perhaps the most hated team owner in baseball history, Freedman owned the New York Giants from 1895 to 1902. He conspired unsuccessfully with John T. Brush in 1901 to create a trust in which all NL teams would be pooled and owned through shares held by the club owners. Upon his death, *The Sporting News* said, "He had an arbitrary disposition, a violent temper, and an ungovernable tongue in anger which was easily provoked and he was disposed to be arbitrary to the point of tyranny with subordinates." The Giants floundered during his regime and attendance dwindled. An influential Tammany Hall politician, he used his political clout to tie up possible sites where an AL team might play in New York until the peace treaty between the leagues in 1902./(NLM)

Bill Freehan — 1941– . C-1B 1961, 63–76 **Tigers** 1774 g, .262, 200 hr, 758 rbi. *1 LCS, 3 g, .250, 1 hr, 3 rbi. 1 WS, 7 g, .083, 2 rbi*
☛ *All-Star—64–73, 75. Gold Glove—65–69.*

The Tigers signed Freehan, a University of Michigan baseball and football star, for a $100,000 bonus in 1961. Two years later the Detroit native became their regular catcher and held the position for 14 seasons.

Freehan showed signs of becoming the league's top catcher in 1964, his first and only season as a .300 hitter, and his first as an All-Star. That began a streak of ten straight years representing the AL, seven of those as a starter. After two seasons of hitting .234, the righthanded hitter matured in 1967, finishing third in MVP voting after leading the Tigers to within one game of the AL title. In 1968 the quiet leader reached career highs with 25 HR and 84 RBI, capping off the season by catching Tim McCarver's foul pop for the final out in Game Seven of the World Series triumph in St. Louis. A batter who crowded the plate, he was hit by pitches 24 times that year—then a league record—including three HBP in one game on August 16.

Freehan never matched his 1968 offensive stats, though he had a three home run game in Boston in August 1971. Freehan was outstanding behind the plate. The five-time Gold Glove recipient tied a record with 19 putouts in a 1965 contest. In 1968 he set an AL record for most putouts and chances in a year. When he retired, Freehan held the ML career marks for most chances, most putouts, and highest fielding average for a catcher. He is among the Detroit top ten in six offensive categories. He wrote *Behind the Mask*, a diary of the 1969 season./(CC)

Bill Freehan

Buck Freeman [John Frank] — 1871–1949. OF-1B 1891, 98–1907 Washington (AA), Washington (NL), Braves, **Red Sox** 1126 g, .294, 82 hr, 713 rbi. *1 WS, 8 g, .281, 4 rbi*
☛ *Led League—hr 99, 03. Led League—rbi 02–03.*

This 5'11" 160-lb slugger preceded Babe Ruth by a generation, but could have been the prototype for the future home run champion. A lefthanded pitcher converted to the outfield because of his outstanding hitting, Freeman was one of the premier power hitters of baseball's dead-ball era.

In his first full ML season, 1899, Freeman hit 25 home runs for Washington to lead the National League. This total, only two fewer than Ned Williamson's record of 27 in 1884, was not surpassed until Ruth hit 29 in 1919. Moving to the Red Sox of the newly formed American League in 1901, he finished second in HR for two years before leading with 13 in 1903. (Freeman and Sam Crawford are the only players to have led both the AL and NL in home runs.) In both 1902 and 1903, Freeman was the AL leader in RBI.

Buck Freeman

Strong-armed but erratic in the field, Freeman was tried at first base, but was at his best in right field. His heavy hitting, especially in clutch situations, carried the Red Sox to two pennants (1903–04), and victory in the first modern World Series, in 1903. /(JL)

Hersh Freeman (Buster) — 1928– . RHP 1952–53, 55–58 Red Sox, **Reds**, Cubs 359 ip, 30–16, 3.74

Like many relievers, Freeman shone briefly, then faded. The big fireballer failed in three trials with the Red Sox but became a star in the Reds' bullpen. In 1956 he saved 18 and led the NL with 14 relief wins. That season he won three games within a 24-hour period, receiving credit for both victories in a twi-night doubleheader and then winning an afternoon game the next day. /(JK)

Marvin Freeman (Starvin' Marvin) — 1963– . RHP 1986, 88– **Phillies** 71 ip, 4–3, 5.22

The 6′6″ 200-lb Freeman looked promising in his 1986 call-up, going 2–0 with a 2.25 ERA. He has pitched poorly at every level since then, although he

threw a 6–0 no-hitter against Richmond on July 28, 1988 for the Maine Guides (International League). He went on the DL early in 1989 with a strained right triceps muscle. /(JFC)

Gene Freese (Augie) — 1934– . 3B-2B 1955–66 **Pirates**, Cardinals, Phillies, White Sox, Reds, Astros 1115 g, .254, 115 hr, 432 rbi. *1 WS, 5 g, .063*

Rookie siblings Gene and George Freese teamed up on the 1955 Pirates and even battled for the same position. Both played third base, while Gene, seven years the junior, also played second base and turned in the better season (.253, 14 HR, 44 RBI). Shaky fielding offset his powerful bat. He played for five teams in four years (1958–61), and had his best season (.277, 26 HR, 87 RBI) for the 1961 NL Champion Reds. Freese lost everyday status after suffering a broken ankle in March 1962. He ranks among the all-time leaders with nine pinch homers, including two consecutive in April 1959. /(ME)

Jim Fregosi — 1942– . SS-3B-1B 1961–78 **Angels**, Mets, Rangers, Pirates 1902 g, .265, 151 hr, 706 rbi.
 Manager 1978–81, 86–87 **Angels**, White Sox 359–385, .483. First place: 79 *1 LCS, 1–3, .250*
☛ *All-Star—64, 66–70. Gold Glove—67* .

Fregosi was the premier power-hitting shortstop in the AL during the 1960s and the first and only star of the expansion California Angels in the late 1960s. During his playing days, he was known as a cheerleader and was pegged as a future manager by many observers. In New York, however, Fregosi was simply the disappointing player the Mets received in the Nolan Ryan trade. Fregosi is one of the few players to hit for the cycle twice, once on July 28, 1964, and again on May 20, 1968. He had his best year in 1970, when he hit established career highs for homers (22), RBI (82), and runs (95) while hitting .278. He never regained his earlier form. After being sent to the Mets for four players, including Ryan, in December of 1971, Fregosi spent time with the Rangers and the Pirates. After 20 games with the Pirates in 1978, he was offered the manager's job with the Angels. In his first full season at the helm in 1979, he guided the Angels to the AL West title, the first pennant in their history. He later managed the White Sox in 1986–87. /(SEW)

Howard Freigau (Ty) — 1902–1932. 3B-SS-2B 1922–28 Cardinals, **Cubs**, Dodgers, Braves 579 g, .272, 15 hr, 226 rbi

Freigau was an early Big Ten basketball star at Ohio State. A utility man for the most part, he spent one year, 1926, as the Cubs' third baseman. /(JK)

Dave Freisleben — 1951– . RHP 1974–79 **Padres,** Indians, Blue Jays 866 ip, 34–60, 4.29

Freisleben was the Padres' top pitching prospect when he joined them in 1974 after compiling a 40–20 record in three minor league seasons. Though he pitched well in his first few ML years, he never had a winning record. He retired with 430 strikeouts and 430 walks. /(JCA)

Tony Freitas — 1908– . LHP 1932–36 A's, **Reds** 518 ip, 25–33, 4.48

The 5'8" southpaw had a 12–5 rookie year with the A's in 1932. With the Reds on July 1, 1934, he lost a thrilling 17-inning duel to Dizzy Dean of the Cardinals. Freitas was the winningest lefthander in minor league history, with 342 career victories, mostly for Sacramento (Pacific Coast League), and was selected by the Society of American Baseball Research in 1984 as the all-time best minor league pitcher. /(LRD)

Jim French — 1941– . C 1965–71 **Senators** 234 g, .196, 5 hr, 51 rbi

French was a light-hitting backup catcher whose fine batting eye and ability to throw out baserunners weren't enough to keep him in the lineup. He was hampered by a 1966 leg injury, and was most used in 1969 and 1970, when he had more walks than hits each season. A horse named after French finished second in the 1971 Kentucky Derby and Belmont Stakes. /(WOR)

Larry French — 1907– . LHP 1929–42 Pirates, **Cubs,** Dodgers 3152 ip, 197–171, 3.44. *3 WS, 15 ip, 0–2, 3.00* ☛ *All-Star—40.*

In the 1930s, only Carl Hubbell worked more innings than Larry French's 2,481. The rugged lefthander appeared in more than 40 games seven straight years, beginning with a league-high 47 in 1932. He led the NL in starts the next season, his third straight as league leader in hits allowed. French recorded 40 career shutouts, leading the NL in 1935 and 1936, his first two seasons with the Cubs. He ignited Chicago's 21-game winning streak to capture the 1935 NL pennant, winning five in that stretch. He won 18 games three times, and lost 19 for the 1938 Cubs. French finished his career brilliantly, leading the NL in winning percentage for the 1942 Dodgers (15–4, .789). He joined the Navy in 1943, retiring in 1969 as a captain. /(ME)

Larry French

Walter French (Fitz) — 1899–1984. OF 1923, 25–29 **A's** 398 g, .303, 2 hr, 109 rbi. *1 WS, 1 g, .000*

An All-American halfback at West Point, French left in 1922 to play with the Rochester Jeffersons of the NFL. He tried baseball the next year, and spent six seasons as a substitute outfielder and pinch hitter/runner. In 1925 he played both football (Pottsville Maroons) and baseball at the major league level. /(LRD)

Benny Frey — 1906–1937. RHP 1929–36 **Reds,** Cardinals 1160 ip, 57–82, 4.50

A sidearm pitcher with a sweeping motion that was effective against righthanded hitters, Frey spent all but one month (in 1932) of his ML career with the Reds. He led the NL in losses (18) as a rookie in 1930. When the Reds sent him down to Nashville in 1937, the moody Frey refused to report and asked to be put on the voluntarily retired list. He committed suicide that November. /(JK)

Jim Frey — 1931- . *Manager* 1980-81, 84-86 Royals, **Cubs** 323-287, .530. First place: 80, 84 *2 LCS, 5-3, .625. 1 WS, 2-4, .333*

Frey led the Royals to the AL pennant in his first year as a major league manager, 1980, but was fired before the end of the 1981 season. His abilities as a judge of talent and as a leader were not questioned, but he was considered deficient in tactical judgment. Reappearing with the Cubs in 1984, he led them to a surprising division title, but they were upset by the Padres when Frey left his ace, Rick Sutcliffe, in Game Five a bit too long. The Cubs had won the first two games of the series. Again falling below .500 the following season, he was fired in mid-1986 but moved to the front office, replacing Dallas Green as GM. Frey's judgment of minor league talent and several astute trades were instrumental in Chicago's 1989 title. /(SH)

Lonny Frey [Linus Richard] (Junior) — 1910- . 2B-SS 1933-43, 46-48 Dodgers, Cubs, **Reds**, Yankees, Giants 1535 g, .269, 61 hr, 549 rbi. *3 WS, 8 g, .000, 1 rbi*
☛ *All-Star—39, 41, 43.*

Frey played in three All-Star Games and three World Series, and in 1939 batted .291 and scored 95 runs to help Cincinnati into the WS. Pitcher Bucky Walters remembered teammates Frey, Myers, and third baseman Bill Werber as "good, fast, smart ballplayers." Indeed, Frey was fast enough to lead the NL with 22 stolen bases for the Reds in 1940. Although he twice topped NL shortstops in errors, Frey led the league's second basemen twice each in fielding percentage and double plays. /(TJ)

Pepe Frias [Jesus] — 1948- . SS-2B-3B 1973-81 **Expos**, Braves, Rangers, Dodgers 723 g, .240, 1 hr, 108 rbi

One of the many latter-day shortstops from San Pedro de Macoris in the Dominican Republic, Frias was a light hitter but earned his pay with his glove. In 1978 he played 73 games at short and second without making an error. /(MC)

Barney Friberg [Augustaf Bernhardt] — 1899-1958. 3B-2B-OF-SS 1919-20, 22-33 Cubs, **Phillies**, Red Sox 1299 g, .281, 38 hr, 471 rbi

The versatile Friberg went from the Massachusetts sandlots to the Cubs before his twentieth birthday. A regular at second base, third base, and in right field, Friberg played every position during his career. The Phillies started to make him a pitcher during the early 1930s (he had pitched once in 1925), but

injuries to his teammates forced him to remain in the infield. /(JL)

Marion Fricano — 1923-1976. RHP 1952-55 **A's** 387 ip, 15-23, 4.32

Fricano made a promising 9-12, 3.88 ERA start as a 30-year-old rookie with the seventh-place A's in 1953. The next year, erratic control dropped him to 5-11 and 5.16. /(MC)

Ford Frick — 1895-1978. *Executive.*
☛ *Hall of Fame—1970.*

It was fitting that the ultimate tribute to Ford Frick was his election to the Hall of Fame. He was president of the National League when the shrine was proposed, and he gave the idea his fullest support.

Frick began his career as a midwestern sports writer and moved to New York with the Hearst papers. He pioneered the nightly radio sports report,

Ford Frick

giving scores and news. In 1934 he became NL public relations director and succeeded the ailing William Heydler as NL president the next year. In 1951 he replaced Happy Chandler as Commissioner as the owners sought a less stubbornly independent figure at the helm than Chandler or the untameable Judge Landis. Much-derided for his controversial decision to attach an asterisk to Roger Maris's record 61 HR in the new 162-game season in 1961 (Frick had been Babe Ruth's ghostwriter), he saw his resourceful administration and gentle guidance of the owners away from their instinct for self-destruction overshadowed by the asterisk issue. In Frick's wake have come General Eckert, Bowie Kuhn, and Peter Ueberroth, and a trend toward baseball as a billion-dollar business perhaps too willing to shed its old values, values the traditionalist Frick revered. /(JK)

Bob Friend (Warrior) — 1930- . RHP 1951–66 **Pirates**, Yankees, Mets 3611 ip, 197–230, 3.58. 20 wins: 58
1 WS, 6 ip, 0–2, 13.50
☛ *Led League—w 58. Led League—era 55. All-Star—56, 58, 60.*

In 15 seasons with Pittsburgh, Friend pitched on five last-place teams and is the only pitcher to have lost more than 200 (230) while winning fewer than 200 (197). In 1955 he became the first to lead a major league in ERA (2.83) while pitching for a last-place team. Friend twice topped the NL in hits allowed, and lost a league-high 19 in both 1959 and 1961. But he paced the NL in starts each season from 1956 through 1958, innings in 1956 and 1957, and tied with Warren Spahn for the NL lead with 22 wins in 1958. Friend shares the NL record with two All-Star Game victories (1956 and 1960), and lost the 1958 All-Star Game as a reliever. Friend lost Games Two and Six in the dramatic 1960 Yankee-Pirate World Series. A Purdue graduate, Friend served as Pittsburgh and NL player representative. /(TJ)

Owen Friend (Red) — 1927- . 2B-3B-SS 1949–50, 53, 55–56 **Browns**, Tigers, Indians, Red Sox, Cubs 208 g, .227, 13 hr, 76 rbi

Friend was a utility man whose early ability prompted comparison to Rogers Hornsby at the plate and Eddie Stanky in the field. He modeled himself after Joe Gordon. The result was still Owen Friend, and that was less than major league caliber. /(WAB)

Frankie Frisch (The Fordham Flash) — 1898–1973. 2B-3B 1919–37 Giants, **Cardinals** 2311 g, .316, 105 hr, 1244 rbi. *8 WS, 50 g, .294, 10 rbi.*
Manager 1933–38, 40–46, 49–51 Cardinals, **Pirates**, Cubs 1137–1078, .513. First place: 34 *1 WS, 4–3, .571*
☛ *Most Valuable Player—31 . All-Star—33–35. Hall of Fame—1947.*

Frisch graduated from Fordham University in 1919 after starring there in baseball, football, basketball, and track. He joined the Giants without playing a game in the minors. A natural athlete with great speed and dexterity, Frisch was tutored long and hard by manager John McGraw on batting and sliding technique. The youthful Frisch quickly became a favorite of McGraw, who named him team captain. He played second base, third base, and occasionally shortstop, wherever his talents were most needed. Although his first two seasons produced only modest offensive results, his fielding was superb and his speed spectacular. He also rarely struck out, an ability Frisch became legendary for. In 17 full seasons, only twice did he fan more than 18 times. From 1921 to 1926 Frisch averaged over 100 runs scored per season, never batted below .324, and stole bases with abandon. He was instrumental in four consecutive Giants pennants and batted .363 in those four World Series (1921–1924).

When the Giants faded in 1925 and 1926, McGraw vented much of his frustration on Frisch. After exactly 1,000 games as a Giant, Frankie was dealt to the Cardinals with pitcher Jimmy Ring for the dominant NL hitter of the 1920s, second baseman and manager Rogers Hornsby, who had had a falling-out with St. Louis owner Sam Breadon.

The extremely competitive, switch-hitting Frisch was saddled with the almost impossible task of making fans in St. Louis forget Hornsby, a man who had just won six straight batting titles with a six-season average of .397. As longtime St. Louis *Post-Dispatch* sportswriter Bob Broeg said, "Frisch didn't make them forget the Rajah, but he made them remember the Flash." In his first season in St. Louis, Frisch hit .337 and finished second in the MVP voting. He also had 641 assists and 1,059 chances at second base, season records which have endured, and he led the league in fielding average.

By the early 1930s, Branch Rickey's farm system had surrounded the veteran second baseman with hungry, talented youngsters, and the Gas House Gang was born. Frisch's zest for the game was contagious. He went on to bat .312 in a decade as a Cardinal and played on four more pennant winners.

Frankie Frisch

He batted over .300 thirteen times in his career. From 1933 to 1938 he managed the Cardinals. Ironically, Frisch was united with Rogers Hornsby in 1933 when Hornsby served as a pinch hitter and backup second baseman. Shortly after Frisch assumed the helm of the Cardinals in mid-season, Hornsby was released so he could accept the same position with the St. Louis Browns.

Frisch managed with the same fire with which he had played. He loved to argue with, show up, and humor umpires. He directed the 1934 Cardinals, one of the most raucous conglomerations of baseball characters, including the Dean brothers, Pepper

Martin, Leo Durocher, Joe Medwick, and Ripper Collins, to a World Championship. After he left the Cardinals, Frisch managed 10 more years with the Pirates and Cubs. He did radio play-by-play for the Boston Braves in 1939 and for the Giants in 1947 and was a Giants coach in 1948. /(FO)

Danny Frisella (Bear) — 1946–1977. RHP 1967–76 **Mets**, Braves, Padres, Cardinals, Brewers 611 ip, 34–40, 3.32

The swarthy forkballer won 8 and saved 12 with a 1.98 ERA for the Mets in 1971, his best year. He had 57 saves in his career, and was coming off a strong five-win, nine-save season with the Brewers when he was killed in a dune buggy accident on New Year's Day, 1977. /(JCA)

Doug Frobel — 1959– . OF 1982–85, 87– **Pirates**, Expos, Indians 268 g, .201, 20 hr, 58 rbi

Nurtured in the Pittsburgh farm system, Canadian-born Frobel proved unable to replace Dave Parker when handed the right field job in 1984. His long, looping swing produced homers in the minors, strikeouts in the majors. /(ME)

Sam Frock — 1882–1925. RHP 1907, 1909–11 **Braves**, Pirates 343 ip, 14–24, 3.23

Frock pitched in eight games for the 1909 World Champion Pirates and was eligible for but did not appear in the WS that year. Traded to the last-place Braves in 1910, he was 11–20. /(NLM)

Bruce Froemming — 1939– . *Umpire* NL 1971–87 *5 LCS 2 WS, 2 ASU*

In a 1986 *TSN* poll of its 26 correspondents, Froemming was voted the best all-around umpire in the NL and also the umpire with the quickest thumb. On September 2, 1972, the Cubs' Milt Pappas was one pitch away from a perfect game. The 3–2 pitch to the Padres' 27th batter was called a ball by Froemming. Pappas pitched his no-hitter, but sulked for years that the call cost him a perfect game. Froemming simply explained that he had to call it a ball or he would have no integrity. The rotund arbiter was behind the plate when Nolan Ryan pitched his record fifth no-hitter. /(RTM)

Todd Frohwirth — 1962– . RHP 1987– **Phillies** 86 ip, 3–2, 3.78

This 6'4″ 195-lb reliever was 1–0 with a 0.00 ERA in his 10-game call-up in 1987, but has since suffered from wildness. /(SFS)

Art Fromme — 1883-1956. RHP 1906-15 Cardinals, **Reds**, Giants 1438 ip, 80-90, 2.90

After two consecutive 5-13 seasons for the Cardinals, Fromme was traded to the Reds and blossomed with a 19-13 mark and 1.90 ERA in 1909. Illness ruined his 1910 season, but he came back to win 16 in 1912. Early in 1913 he was traded to the Giants with Eddie Grant for Josh Devore, Red Ames, Heinie Groh, and $20,000. Although he was 20-11 for New York in 1913-14, he was regarded as a disappointment, and manager McGraw did not use him in the 1913 World Series./(NLM)

Dave Frost — 1952- . RHP 1977-82 White Sox, **Angels**, Royals 550 ip, 33-37, 4.11. *1 LCS, 4 ip, 0-1, 18.69*

The 6'6" Frost went 16-10 with a staff-best 3.58 ERA for the 1979 AL West champion Angels. Elbow problems then made him less effective; he recorded ERAs of 5.31 and higher in each of his final three seasons./(JCA)

Woodie Fryman — 1940- . LHP 1966-83 Pirates, Phillies, Tigers, **Expos**, Reds, Cubs 2411 ip, 141-155, 3.77. *2 LCS, 13 ip, 0-2, 6.08*
☛ *All-Star—68, 76.*

The Kentucky tobacco farmer didn't sign a pro contract until age 25. After only 12 minor league games, he started the 1966 season with Pittsburgh and hurled three consecutive shutouts. In his career, he threw four one-hitters. In 1972 he was 4-10 with the Phillies when he was sent to Detroit, where he went 10-3 to help the Tigers to a divisional title.

During his second stint with Montreal, he became a dependable reliever, racking up 24 wins and 46 saves in 1979-82. Modest and uncomplaining, Fryman pitched much of his career with severe arthritis in his elbow, yet stayed in the ML to age 43./(JCA)

Tito Fuentes [Rigoberto Peat] — 1944- . 2B-SS-3B 1965-67, 69-78 **Giants**, Padres, Tigers, A's 1499 g, .268, 45 hr, 438 rbi. *1 LCS, 4 g, .313, 1 hr, 2 rbi*

The nimble Cuban was a flamboyant fielder who was often called a hot dog. Fuentes was San Francisco's regular second baseman in the early 1970s and set a NL record by committing just six errors (.993 fielding average) in 1973 after leading NL second basemen in errors the previous two seasons. A productive, punch-type switch-hitter, he drove in 78 runs for the Giants in 1973, and 83 for the Tigers in 1977 when he batted a career-high .309. On

September 13, 1973, he was hit by three pitches in one game, a ML record./(JCA)

Tomio Fujimura — Unk.-Unk. 1B-OF **Hanshin Tigers**
☛ *Led League—ba 49. Led League—hr 50.*

Fujimura was a Japanese slugger, a macho WWII veteran who disdained the use of a glove and refused the opportunity to switch teams for more money. He raised the single-season Japanese home run record from 25 to 45 in 1949. He also briefly held the national record for single-season batting average, hitting .362 in 1950. His career total of 224 HR was a Japanese record when he retired./(MC)

Yutaka Fukumoto — 1947- . OF **Hankyu Braves**

Japanese baseball emphasizes power rather than speed; only 10 or 12 players steal more than 20 bases in any given year. Fukumoto, however, stole 106 bases in 1972, a Japanese record. His 95 stolen bases the following year have been the only serious challenge to the mark. At age 33, in 1979, he again led Japanese baseball in stolen bases, with 60. A centerfielder and leadoff hitter, he typically batted about .290./(MC)

John Fulgham — 1956- . RHP 1979-80 **Cardinals** 231 ip, 14-12, 2.84

Fulgham's very promising career was cut short by a rotator cuff injury. He was 10-6 (2.53) as a rookie in 1979 but was plagued by the arm problem in 1980. All of his 14 ML wins were complete games./(JCA)

Vern Fuller — 1944- . 2B-3B 1964, 66-70 **Indians** 325 g, .232, 14 hr, 65 rbi

Fuller was a steady fielder with a little power. He was mostly a backup, but played 102 games at second and hit .236 for Cleveland in 1969, his busiest season. Though a food connoisseur, the angular-featured infielder was always slender./(JCA)

Curt Fullerton — 1898-1975. RHP 1921-25, 33 **Red Sox** 423 ip, 10-37, 5.11

Fullerton came down to Boston from his native Maine to struggle through six seasons with some of the worst Red Sox clubs ever assembled. He walked twice as many as he struck out./(EW)

Hugh S. Fullerton, Jr. — 1904-1965. *Writer.*

A graduate of Princeton, Fullerton was on the New York sports desk of the Associated Press for his entire 38-year career./(NLM)

Hugh S. Fullerton, Sr. — 1873–1935. *Writer.*

For the first 25 years of the 20th century, Fullerton was the best-known baseball writer in the country and a titan of the Chicago press box, along with Lardner, Sanborn, and Dryden. After graduating from Ohio State, he began in 1889 in Cincinnati. In 1896 he moved to the Chicago *Record* as baseball writer and then on to the *Tribune*. Fullerton was instrumental in exposing the Black Sox scandal in 1919. In the 1920s he moved to New York and was later editor of *Liberty Magazine* for six years. He also wrote for the Bell syndicate, the Columbus *Dispatch* and the Philadelphia *Inquirer*. He was one of the first to write stories on inside baseball for top mass-circulation magazines. Reportedly the first to use the slang word "dope" for baseball information, Fullerton also wrote fiction and a book on the science of baseball with Johnny Evers. One of the founders of the BBWAA, he was awarded the J.G. Taylor Spink Award in 1964. /(NLM)

Chick Fullis [Charles Philip] — 1904–1946. OF 1928–34, 36 **Giants**, Phillies, Cardinals 590 g, .295, 12 hr, 167 rbi. *1 WS, 3 g, .400*

In his only season as an everyday outfielder (Phillies, 1933), this speedy line-drive hitter had 200 hits to bat .309, and led the NL in at-bats and putouts. Briefly a member of the Cardinals' famed Gas House Gang, Fullis retired early due to eye trouble. /(JL)

Dave Fultz — 1875–1959. OF 1898–99, 1901–05 Phillies, Baltimore (NL), **A's**, Yankees 645 g, .271, 3 hr, 223 rbi

A Brown graduate with a law degree from Columbia, Fultz was a useful outfielder who led the AL in 1902 with 109 runs for Philadelphia. In 1903 he had the Highlanders' (Yankees) first extra-base hit. A practicing attorney, Fultz organized the Player's Fraternity in 1912. Ty Cobb and Christy Mathewson were among its officers, but it achieved little and folded in 1918. After service as a WWI aviator, Fultz became president of the International League. /(JK)

Frank Funk — 1935– . RHP 1960–63 **Indians**, Braves 248 ip, 20–17, 3.01

Funk was Cleveland's ace reliever in 1961, despite an AL-high 11 relief losses. He also won 11 and saved 11 that year. Funk became a minor league manager and ML coach. /(ME)

Liz Funk [Elias Calvin] — 1904–1968. OF 1929–30, 32–33 Yankees, **Tigers**, White Sox 273 g, .267, 6 hr, 105 rbi

Funk was a 5'8", lefthanded contact hitter. After a solid but unspectacular 1930 campaign with Detroit, he was sent down. In need of a leadoff hitter in 1932, the White Sox acquired him. They liked the centerfielder's speed and desire, but by 1933 they had better hitters. /(RL)

Carl Furillo (Skoonj, The Reading Rifle) — 1922– . OF 1946–60 **Dodgers** 1806 g, .299, 192 rbi, 1058 rbi. *7 WS, 40 g, .266, 2 hr, 13 rbi*
☛ *All-Star—52–53.*

Furillo was one of Roger Kahn's famed Boys of Summer. Kahn described him as The Hard Hat Who Sued Baseball. He sued the Dodgers in 1960 for dropping him while he was hurt. He was awarded $21,000 as a settlement. From then on, Furillo couldn't find a job in baseball. He contended

Carl Furillo

that he had been blackballed. Kahn found him years later, installing Otis elevators at the World Trade Center.

Furillo had his best season in 1953, when he hit .344 to win the NL batting title. A volatile and intense competitor, Skoonj (short for scungili, Italian for snail) broke his hand during a September brawl with Leo Durocher and the Giants, and missed most of the rest of the season. The Reading Rifle had a gun for an arm, and read the tricky, 40'-high right field wall in Ebbets Field masterfully. His career highlights include a miraculous catch of Johnny Mize's bid for a home run in Game Five of the 1952 World Series; a game-tying, ninth-inning homer in Game Six of the 1953 WS; and throwing Reds pitcher Mel Queen out at first on a 300' shot hit into the right field gap at Ebbets Field. /(WAB)

Fred Fussell (Moonlight Ace) — 1895–1966. LHP 1922–23, 28–29 Cubs, **Pirates** 295 ip, 14–17, 4.86

The 5'10" 156-lb lefthander had two unsuccessful trials in the majors. He was given his unusual nickname in 1933 after pitching the first International League twilight no-hitter. /(JK)

Frank Gabler (The Great Gabbo) — 1911–1967. RHP 1935–38 **Giants**, Braves, White Sox 376 ip, 16–23, 5.26. *1 WS, 5 ip, 0–0, 7.20*

The Great Gabbo was known for sounding off, and for fistfights on the mound with Tex Carleton. In the minors, his skull was fractured by a line drive. In 1936 Gabler boasted he'd win ten games. Eddie Brannick, the Giants' secretary, offered him a $100 suit if he won eight. Gabler helped his team to the NL pennant by winning nine, and collected on the bet. /(NLM)

John Gabler (Gabe) — 1930– . RHP 1959–61 Yankees, **Senators** 164 ip, 7–12, 4.39

A fringe major leaguer, Gabler had brief stints with the Yankees and the expansion 1961 Senators. He failed to finish any of his 14 ML starting assignments. /(DQV)

Ken Gables — 1919–1960. RHP 1945–47 **Pirates** 240 ip, 13–11, 4.69

Pittsburgh's youngest pitcher (26) in wartime 1945, the rookie was 11–7. Gables pitched in one final ML game in 1947 and worked in the Pacific Coast League, mostly with Sacramento, until 1954. /(ME)

Len Gabrielson — 1940– . OF-1B 1960, 63–70 Braves, Cubs, Giants, Angels, **Dodgers** 708 g, .253, 37 hr, 315 rbi

Gabrielson got a $75,000 bonus to sign with the Braves in 1960. He had fair power but never won an everyday job. He played the most in 1965, when he hit a career-high .293 for the Cubs and Giants. He was a below-average outfielder. Used often as a pinch hitter, his best season in that role was 1969 (13-for-36) for the Dodgers. He is the son of Len Gabrielson, who played first base in five games for the 1939 Athletics. /(WOR)

Eddie Gaedel — 1925–1961. PH 1951 **Browns** 1 g, --

The most publicized stunt in baseball history took place August 18, 1951, at Sportsman's Park in St. Louis, when, to the surprise of 18,369 fans, 3'7" 65-lb midget Eddie Gaedel emerged from a seven-foot

birthday cake between games of a Browns-Tigers doubleheader. Browns owner Bill Veeck concocted the idea to boost attendance, and to help celebrate the 50th anniversary of both the American League and the Falstaff Brewing Co., radio sponsor of the Browns.

Gaedel, a stage performer, was wearing a Browns uniform with the number 1/8, and little slippers turned up at the end like elf's shoes. In the bottom of the first, St. Louis manager Zach Taylor sent Gaedel to the plate to pinch hit for Frank Saucier. Veeck had instructed the diminutive Brownie to crouch low, and not swing his toy-like bat. Detroit skipper Red Rolfe protested Gaedel's presence, but Taylor produced a legitimate contract, filed with the AL and cleared by umpire Ed Hurley.

In his stance, Gaedel's strike zone measured 1-1/2 inches. Detroit pitcher Bob Cain walked the midget, throwing four straight balls. When Jim Delsing went in to run for him, the crowd gave Gaedel a standing ovation. The Browns lost, 6–2, despite Gaedel's instant offense. AL president Will Harridge was furious with Veeck's burlesque and unsuccessfully tried to strike Gaedel's name from the record books. Gaedel was paid $100 for his appearance, and was insured for $1 million by Veeck. In future years Veeck used him in a few other promotions. /(RTM)

Gary Gaetti — 1958– . 3B 1981– **Twins** 1207 g, .259, 185 hr, 673 rbi. *1 LCS, 5 g, .300, 2 hr, 5 rbi. 1 WS, 7 g, .259, 1 hr, 4 rbi*
☛ *All-Star—89. Gold Glove—86–89.*

Gary Gaetti overcame a slow start to gain recognition as the AL's premier third baseman by 1988. The 1980 Midwest League home run champ, Gaetti became the 47th major leaguer to homer in his first big league at-bat, September 20, 1981 off Charlie Hough in Texas. In 1982 he replaced former co-Rookie of the Year John Castino at third for the Twins. An outstanding defensive player with multiple league leaderships in putouts, assists, and double plays, Gaetti's offense finally caught up in 1986 (.287, 34 HR, 108 RBI) and 1987 (31 HR, 109 RBI). In the 1987 LCS he became the first player ever to hit two home runs in his first two at-bats of postseason play. He was the LCS MVP, won his second straight Gold Glove, and set a Twins third base record with a .973 fielding average in 1987.

Gaetti gained notoriety in the 1989 All-Star Game when he displayed a religious slogan written on his batting gloves to the TV cameras during the pregame introductions. /(ME)

James A. Gaffney — Unk.–1932. *Executive.*

A successful New York contractor and politician with Tammany Hall connections, Gaffney was instrumental in putting together the 1914 Miracle Braves and bringing about a settlement of the Federal League war. He bought the Braves in 1911 and named John Montgomery Ward as president, but soon fired him and took over the operation himself. Gaffney set out to build a winner faster than his old friend Frank Farrell, the Yankees' owner. He hired George Stallings as manager and paid to keep Johnny Evers, the key man on the '14 team, from the Federal League. During the 1915 WS, Gaffney arranged a peace conference between the National Commission and the upstart Federal League. That fall he sold the Braves to a syndicate that included Harvard football coach Percy Haughton. /(NLM)

John Gaffney — Unk.–Unk. *Umpire* **NL**, AA, PL 1884–95

One of the first to be dubbed King of Umpires, Gaffney controlled the game through tact and diplomacy. At a time when umpires worked games alone, he popularized the technique of working behind the plate until a man reached base, then moving behind the pitcher. He also began the practice of calling a ball "fair" or "foul" at the point where it left the park, rather than where it was last seen. In 1888 he was the highest paid umpire in baseball, earning $2,500 a year plus expenses on the road. /(RTM)

Phil Gagliano — 1941– . 2B-3B-OF-1B 1963–74 **Cardinals**, Cubs, Red Sox, Reds 702 g, .238, 14 hr, 159 rbi. *1 LCS, 3 g, .000. 2 WS, 4 g, .000*

Gagliano was a solid utility player who spent his first seven-plus seasons with the Cardinals. He appeared in a career-high 122 games in 1965, hitting eight homers with 53 RBI. Developing into a top pinch hitter, he batted .354 in that role with the 1971–72 Red Sox, .366 for Cincinnati in 1973. He played with future St. Louis teammates Tim McCarver and Mike Shannon, and ML pitcher Jim Donahue, at Christian Brothers High School in Memphis, Ten-

nessee. His brother Ralph appeared in one game with the 1965 Indians. /(MC)

Greg Gagne — 1961– . SS 1983– **Twins** 717 g, .250, 47 hr, 216 rbi. *1 LCS, 5 g, .278, 2 hr, 3 rbi. 1 WS, 7 g, .200, 1 hr, 3 rbi*

Acquired from the Yankees in a 1982 deal for Roy Smalley, Gagne won Minnesota's shortstop job in 1985. He hit two inside-the-park homers in the Metrodome on October 4, 1986. Though he led AL shortstops with 26 errors that year, in 1987 he set a club shortstop record with 47 straight errorless games, and helped the Twins to their first World Championship. He hit solo homers in Games Three and Four of the LCS and in WS Game Four, and singled in the winning run in WS Game Seven. /(JCA)

Joe Gaines [Arnesta Joe] — 1936– . OF 1960–66 Reds, Orioles, **Astros** 362 g, .241, 21 hr, 95 rbi

The speedy Gaines enjoyed several .300 seasons in the minors, including a .315 year at Indianapolis (American Association) in 1961. Used mainly as a reserve in the majors, his top average was .286 with the 1963 Orioles. /(RTM)

Del Gainor (Sheriff) — 1886–1947. 1B 1909, 11–17, 19, 22 Tigers, **Red Sox**, Cardinals 546 g, .272, 14 hr, 185 rbi. *2 WS, 2 g, .500, 1 rbi*

Gainor's 14th-inning pinch single in Game Two of the 1916 World Series drove in Boston's winning run, ending the longest game in WS history and sealing Babe Ruth's first postseason pitching victory. /(JL)

Augie Galan — 1912– . OF 1934–49 **Cubs**, Dodgers, Reds, Giants, A's 1742 g, .287, 100 hr, 830 rbi. *3 WS, 10 g, .138, 2 rbi*
☛ *All-Star—36, 43–44.*

Galan was an injury-prone outfielder who had a good career despite the mishaps. He was the first everyday major leaguer to play an entire season without hitting into a double play, as well as the first to homer from both sides of the plate in the same contest (6/25/37). Having shattered his right elbow playing ball as a child, Galan had a deformed arm. He broke into the majors as a Cub infielder in 1934, and was a star outfielder by the following year, batting .314 and leading the league with 133 runs and 22 stolen bases to help Chicago to the pennant. In 646 at-bats, he did not hit into a single double play, although he did hit into a triple play. In 1936 Galan became the first Cub to homer in the All-Star Game.

After batting .304 for the Cubs in 1939, he broke his right knee in 1940. The Cubs gave up on Galan and his injuries, dealing him to the Dodgers in 1941. Two years later, he was back in the starting lineup, hitting over .300 each season from 1944 through 1947 before the years caught up with him. From 1945 on, he batted exclusively lefthanded. /(ARA)

Andres Galarraga (Big Cat) — 1961– . 1B 1985-
Expos 585 g, .282, 77 hr, 313 rbi
☛ *Gold Glove—89.*

Andres Galarraga was signed by the Expos, at the recommendation of Felipe Alou, as a 17-year old power prodigy. Given the first-base job for 1986, he had a terrible spring training (.107, no extra base hits) and was assigned to platoon with Jason Thompson. The platoon ended quickly as Galarraga caught fire early in the regular season. The Venezuelan missed much of the 1986 season with a right knee injury and right rib cage pull, but gave better evidence of his skills in 1987 (.305, 13 HR, 90 RBI), finishing second in the NL in doubles. Capable of awesome power, Galarraga sacrificed some distance for batting average, but continued to post high strikeout numbers. He combined average and power in 1988, hitting .302 with 29 HR, leading in doubles (42) but also in strikeouts (153). He was nicknamed for his defensive quickness at first base. /(ME)

John W. Galbreath — 1898–1988. *Executive.*

A breeder of champion racehorses, Galbreath, with Bing Crosby and two other partners, bought the Pirates in 1946. He was president from 1950 to 1969, when his son succeeded him. The family sold the team in 1985. /(NLM)

Rich Gale — 1954– . RHP 1978–84 **Royals**, Giants, Reds, Red Sox 971 ip, 55–56, 4.53. *1 WS, 6 ip, 0–1, 4.26*

Gale was *TSN* Rookie Pitcher of the Year in 1978, with a 14–8, 3.09 record that remained his career best. His 13–9, 3.91 performance in 1980 was his only other winning season and helped the Royals to the AL pennant. He was hit hard by the Phillies in his two WS starts and lost the sixth and deciding game. /(SFS)

Denny Galehouse — 1911– . RHP 1934–44, 46–49 Indians, Red Sox, **Browns** 2003 ip, 109–118, 3.98. *1 WS, 18 ip, 1–1, 1.50*

During much of the 1944 campaign, Galehouse served the St. Louis Browns as a Sunday pitcher while working weekdays in an Akron, Ohio war plant. He relinquished his factory job late in the season. After posting several stretch drive victories, Galehouse beat Mort Cooper and the Cardinals in the 1944 World Series opener, but lost, 2–0, in a Game Five rematch. During his second stint with the Red Sox, Galehouse lost the 1948 pennant playoff game to Cleveland 8–3 as a surprise starter. It was his last major league decision. /(TJ)

Alan Gallagher (Dirty Al) — 1945– . 3B 1970–73 **Giants**, Angels 442 g, .263, 11 hr, 130 rbi. *1 LCS, 4 g, .100*

Gallagher's mother wanted many sons, but having just one, gave him all their names. Alan Mitchell Edward George Patrick Henry Gallagher, a self-proclaimed marginal player, lasted four seasons in the majors on sheer hustle. Dirty Al never looked good in a uniform. He was once the subject of a *New York Times Magazine* article on journeymen players. /(DQV)

Dave Gallagher — 1960– . OF 1987- Indians, **White Sox** 277 g, .273, 6 hr, 78 rbi

The White Sox signed Gallagher after the 1987 season, when he was released by the Mariners. He won the centerfield job in Chicago with his errorless fielding and a .303 average in 1988. /(WOR)

James Gallagher — 1904– . *Writer-Executive*

After twelve years as a baseball writer for the Chicago *American*, Gallagher moved to the front office of the Cubs as GM and later vice president in 1940. He spent 1957 heading an advertising and public relations agency with Bill Veeck, then joined the Phillies in 1958. He planned to retire in 1962, but was convinced to work part-time for Commissioner Ford Frick instead. He worked in the Commissioner's office until 1974. /(NLM)

Bert Gallia — 1891–1976. RHP 1912–20 **Senators**, Browns, Phillies 1277 ip, 65–58, 3.14

After winning 26 at Kansas City in the American Association, Gallia was bought by Washington for pitcher Jim Vaughn, outfielder Clarence Walker, and cash. Starting and relieving, he had seasons of 17–11 (1915) and 17–12 (1916). After the 1917 season he was traded to the Browns with $15,000 for Burt Shotton and Doc Lavan. /(NLM)

Paul Gallico — 1898–1976. *Writer.*

Gallico was the highest-paid sports editor in the country in the 1930s, earning $25,000 a year for the New York *Daily News* from 1923 to 1936. Then he

asked for a $70-a-week city-desk job, which enabled
him to turn to free-lance writing. He authored 41
books. As a columnist, he fought one round with
Jack Dempsey and tried to catch Dizzy Dean's
curveball so he could tell his readers what it was like.
Gallico created the Golden Gloves boxing
tournament. /(NLM)

Chick Galloway [Clarence Edward] — 1896–1969.
SS 1919–28 **A's**, Tigers 1076 g, .264, 17 hr, 407 rbi

Galloway was the Athletics' everyday shortstop in
1921–26. His playing days ended when a pitch
thrown by Haskell Billings in batting practice fractured his skull. A Presbyterian College (SC) grad, he
returned to coach there, and later scouted for the
Reds, A's, and Braves. /(NLM)

Pud Galvin [James Francis] (Gentle Jeems, The Little
Steam Engine) — 1856–1902. RHP 1879–92 **Buffalo (NL)**,
Pittsburgh (AA), Pirates, Pittsburgh (PL), Cardinals
5941 ip, 361–310, 2.87. 20 wins: 79–84, 86–89
   Manager 1885 **Buffalo (NL)** 8–22, .267
☛ *Hall of Fame—1965.*

A stocky pitcher with a blinding fastball, Pud Galvin
racked up phenomenal totals in the early days of
major league baseball. Galvin was 37–27 for Buffalo
in 1879, his rookie season and the first of six straight
20-win campaigns. Though he never pitched for a
club that finished better than third, Galvin became
one of baseball's all-time winningest pitchers.

His best seasons came with Buffalo in 1883 and
1884. In the former, Galvin was 46–22 and led the
NL in games (76), starts (75), complete games (72),
innings pitched (656–1/3) and shutouts (5). His
1884 achievements (46–22, 12 shutouts) were overshadowed by Hoss Radbourn's 60 wins for Providence. Galvin had ended Radbourn's 18-game
winning streak, and a 20-game Providence win
streak, with a 2–0 victory on September 9. He threw
three shutouts against Detroit between August 2 and
August 8, including a no-hitter on August 4, becoming the second pitcher in ML history with two or
more no-hitters. (He had no-hit Worcester in 1880.)
His 396 strikeouts in 1884 were a career high, and
one of the highest pre-1900 single season totals.

In 1885 Galvin jumped from Buffalo (NL) to
Allegheny (American Association), the club that
joined the NL in 1887 as Pittsburgh. From 1886
through 1889, Galvin notched another four straight
20-win seasons. Galvin jumped to the Players'
League in 1890. He returned to the Pirates in 1891,

Pud Galvin

but was released during the following season. He
finished his ML career in his native St. Louis.

Galvin retired as one of baseball's all-time leaders
in wins (sixth), losses (second), complete games (639,
second), innings pitched (second), and shutouts (57,
tied for tenth). On July 21, 1892, Galvin faced Tim
Keefe in the last battle of 300-game winners until
Don Sutton met Phil Niekro in 1986. Galvin and
Keefe met four times as 300-game winners from
1890 to 1892, the first such meetings in ML history.

Galvin died, penniless, in a Pittsburgh rooming house. Fan contributions paid for his burial. His brother, Lou, pitched two games for St. Paul (Union Association) in 1884. Pud was inducted into the Hall of Fame in 1965 by the Veterans Committee./(ME)

Oscar Gamble — 1949– . OF-DH 1969–85 Cubs, Phillies, Indians, **Yankees**, White Sox, Padres, Rangers 1584 g, .265, 200 hr, 666 rbi. *3 LCS, 8 g, .211, 2 rbi. 2 WS, 6 g, .214, 2 rbi*

Gamble was the Cubs' best prospect when he was traded to Philadelphia after the 1969 season with Dick Selma for Johnny Callison. His low batting average prevented him from winning a job in his three years with the Phillies, despite flashes of power. He had the last hit and the last RBI in Philadelphia's Connie Mack Stadium. Only after his trade to Cleveland for 1973 did the lefthanded batter finally blossom. As a platoon DH and occasional outfielder, he hit 20 HR in 390 at-bats.

After two more solid seasons, Gamble went to the Yankees for Pat Dobson in December 1975. He played right field, and helped New York to its first AL pennant in 12 years with 17 HR and 57 RBI in 340 at-bats. His wife, Juanita, sang the national anthem at Yankee Stadium several times that season, including once before a playoff game. However, the Yankee front office had her in tears when they forced Oscar to cut off his luxuriant Afro, the largest in baseball. It added more than four inches to his height and sometimes popped his batting helmet off.

Traded before the start of 1977 with LaMarr Hoyt, then a minor leaguer, and $200,000 for the White Sox' Bucky Dent, Gamble had his best season. He hit .297 with career highs of 31 HR, 83 RBI, 75 runs, and 22 doubles (in 408 at-bats), and the White Sox contended, improving to 90–72 from 64–97 the previous season. He opted for free agency after the season and signed a lucrative deal with San Diego. Slowed by minor injuries, he hit only seven HR and was traded to Texas after the season. He returned to the Yankees in August 1979 in a deal that also sent Mickey Rivers to the Rangers. Gamble was hitting .335 at the time of the trade, then caught fire. He hit .389 in his two months with the Yankees and finished with a career-high .358 mark that was by far the best in the league. But Gamble's 274 at-bats weren't close to qualifying him for the batting title. He spent the next five years in New York, finally accepting his career-long platoon role, and providing vital lefthanded power. He helped the Yankees to their last two titles as they won their division in 1980 and took the AL pennant in the 1981 strike season. In that year's Eastern Division playoff, Gamble's two-run homer in the opener sparked New York to a 5–3 victory, and he also homered in the 7–3 clincher over Milwaukee. He hit .556 for the series, platooning with Lou Piniella at DH. In the LCS, he had only one hit, but walked five times in 11 plate appearances and scored the second run, after walking, of New York's 3–1 victory in the opener. Gamble finished with a return to the White Sox in 1985./(SH)

Chick Gandil [Charles Arnold] — 1888–1970. 1B 1910, 12–19 White Sox, **Senators**, Indians 1147 g, .277, 11 hr, 557 rbi. *2 WS, 14 g, .245, 10 rbi*

At age 17, Gandil ran away from home to play ball in the rough-and-tumble towns along the Arizona-Mexico border. He supplemented his income by boxing in the local heavyweight division, picking up $150 a fight. He joined the White Sox in 1910, lasted part of a year, and was sold to Washington, where he remained until 1916. Gandil made the acquaintance of Sport Sullivan, a sports gambler and bookie. Sullivan had rich and powerful friends, and his friendships with ballplayers like Gandil were crucial to a World Series fixing scheme he planned to pull off.

Gandil rejoined the White Sox in 1917 as their regular first baseman, but he was a malcontent, and was later considered to be the ringleader of the 1919 WS fix. His contacts with Sullivan, Abe Attell, and Billy Maharg paved the way for the 1920 scandal. In that 1919 Series, Gandil batted a paltry .233 but committed only one error. Gandil refused to play for Charles Comiskey in 1920, due to a salary dispute with the penurious owner. In 1921 he was banned from baseball by Commissioner Landis./(RL)

Bob Ganley — 1875–1945. OF 1905–09 Pirates, **Senators**, A's 572 g, .254, 2 hr, 123 rbi

Ganley's best season was 1907, when he hit .273 and had career highs of 73 runs and 40 stolen bases as the Senators' everyday right fielder, but he led AL outfielders in errors. His hitting declined thereafter, and when he hit .197 in 80 games with the Athletics in 1909, it ended his career./(JFC)

Ron Gant — 1965– . 3B-2B 1987– **Braves** 242 g, .236, 30 hr, 94 rbi

Gant became the Braves' starting second baseman at the age of 23 in 1988, replacing Damaso Garcia only two weeks into the season, and he enjoyed a solid year at the plate, leading all ML rookies in HR (19) and RBI (60) while batting .259. In the field, however, Gant was dreadful, letting ground ball after ground ball scoot through his legs as he led NL second baseman with 26 errors. The Braves shifted Gant to third base late in 1988, but it did little good, and he began the 1989 season in an awful batting slump, hitting below .200 into June. He was then sent down to the low minors to learn to play the outfield. /(SCL)

Jim Gantner (Gumby) — 1953- . 2B-3B 1976- **Brewers** 1472 g, .275, 44 hr, 478 rbi. *1 LCS, 5 g, .188, 2 rbi. 1 WS, 7 g, .333, 4 rbi*

Gantner is unheralded despite more than a decade of dependable performances that put him among the Brewers' all-time leaders in almost every offensive category. He became Milwaukee's starting second baseman in 1981 and has led the AL in chances at the position three times. He hit .282 with career highs in HR (11) and RBI (74) in 1983, and was the Brewers' MVP in 1984. He suffered a career-threatening knee injury in a 1989 collision with Yankee outfielder Marcus Lawton. /(ME)

John Ganzel — 1874-1959. 1B 1898, 1900-01, 03-04, 07-08 Pirates, Cubs, Giants, **Yankees**, Reds 747 g, .251, 18 hr, 336 rbi.
Manager 1908, 15 **Reds**, Brooklyn (FL) 90-99, .476

Ganzel led NL first basemen in putouts, fielding, and total chances per game in 1901 with the Giants, but hit a mere .215. He improved to career bests of .277, 71 RBI, and 61 runs with the Highlanders (later the Yankees) in 1903 and again led league first basemen in fielding and total chances per game. After another good year in 1904, when his six HR tied for fourth in the AL and the Highlanders lost the pennant on the last day of the season, he bought the Grand Rapids (Western League) club, and the next winter he paid the Highlanders (later the Yankees) $3,000 for his release so he could play for it. Returning to the majors in 1907, he led the NL with 19 triples for Cincinnati. He was player-manager for the 1908 Reds, and again led NL first base in fielding. While in the International League he was, at one time, the highest-paid minor league manager, earning $7,000 and a part of the profits.

John Ganzel was one of five brothers to play pro ball; one, Charlie, was a 14-year ML catcher. John's nephew, Charlie's son Babe Ganzel, played briefly for Washington in 1927-28. /(NLM)

Joe Garagiola

Joe Garagiola — 1926- . C 1946-54 **Cardinals**, Pirates, Cubs, Giants 676 g, .257, 42 hr, 255 rbi. *1 WS, 5 g, .316, 4 rbi*

The jokes in Garagiola's best-seller, *Baseball Is a Funny Game* (1960), helped foster his image as a marginal player. In truth, his career was no joke. Signed by the Cardinals' Branch Rickey for $500 off the sandlots of St. Louis, Garagiola (Yogi Berra's boyhood pal) began his pro baseball career at 16. After two years in the minors and two in the military, the catcher reported to the Cardinals in 1946. In the opening game of the '46 playoffs, Garagiola's three hits and two RBI helped the Cardinals to a 4–2 win over the Dodgers. In the World Series with Boston, he collected six hits, including four in Game Four.

In mid-June of 1950, Garagiola was hitting .347. During a game against the Dodgers, he laid down a bunt and raced to first. Brooklyn second baseman Jackie Robinson went to take the throw, but had trouble finding the bag with his foot. Garagiola, trying to avoid colliding with Robinson, broke stride and fell. He suffered a shoulder separation, caught only 30 games that year, and was traded to the Pirates in 1951. He played in a career-high 118 games and hit .273 for the last-place Pirates in 1952.

His broadcasting career began in 1955 with the Cardinals. In 1961 he began working for NBC's "Major League Baseball," where he continued until the end of 1988. In 1965 he replaced Mel Allen on Yankee broadcasts, then in 1969 moved to hosting NBC's daily "Today Show" until 1973. He remains a national celebrity known for one-liners, reminiscences of his days as a Pirate, and Yogi Berra anecdotes. His first book, *Baseball Is a Funny Game*, remains one of the best-selling baseball books ever. /(RTM)

Gene Garber — 1947– . RHP 1969–70, 72–88 Pirates, Royals, Phillies, **Braves** 1509 ip, 96–113, 3.34. *3 LCS, 9 ip, 1–3, 5.79*

Garber's corkscrew motion helped make him one of baseball's all-time leaders in saves, games pitched, and relief wins. He pitched in 249 games for Philadelphia, including a NL-high 71 in 1975, teaming with Tug McGraw for a great lefty-righty combination. Traded to the Braves on June 15, 1978 for Dick Ruthven, Gene set Atlanta records with 558 relief appearances and 141 saves. He also set club records with 56 games finished and 30 saves in 1982 as the Braves went to the playoffs and the bullpen won the Rolaids awards as the outstanding relief corps. The sidearmer ended Pete Rose's 44-game hit streak of 1978 with a memorable strikeout. A crafty pitcher relying on a change-up among a variety of pitches, Garber was unable to post consistently outstanding seasons, doing best in 1978, 1982 and 1986. /(ME)

Barbaro Garbey — 1956– . 1B-DH-OF-3B 1984–85, 88 **Tigers**, Rangers 196 g, .275, 11 hr, 81 rbi. *1 LCS, 3 g, .333. 1 WS, 4 g, .000*

A member of the Cuban national team, Garbey fled to the U.S. in the 1980 "Freedom Flotilla." While hitting .321 for Evansville (American Association) in 1983, he was suspended for a month during an investigation of charges that he had fixed games while in Cuba, but was exonerated. He was suspended a second time in 1983 after threatening a heckling fan with a bat.

He joined the Tigers in 1984 and batted .287 for the World Champions. He was an aggressive, line-drive hitter, but could not play any position well. His temperamental behavior led to his November 1985 trade to the A's, with whom he never appeared. He played in Mexico before resurfacing with the Rangers in 1988. /(MC)

Chico Garcia — 1924– . 2B 1954 **Orioles** 39 g, .113, 0 hr, 5 rbi

Garcia's career was a microcosm of Mexican League history. The Pascual brothers were just beginning their effort to turn the Mexican League into a third major league when Garcia broke in with Mexico City. He and Vern Stephens were supposed to form the double play combo for San Luis Potosi in 1946, but Stephens reneged on his contract, returning instead to the majors. After Garcia hit over .300 there and with Puebla through 1948, he joined the Juarez franchise, jumping from the financially struggling Mexican League into the Arizona-Texas League for 1949. He led the league in runs, hits, triples, and batting (.377), then spent most of four years at Shreveport before finally teaming with Stephens in Baltimore.

Garcia enjoyed his best seasons after returning to Mexico with Monterrey in 1960–1965, averaging .351, .346, .342, and then .368 at age thirty-eight, plus a career-high 21 homers as he won his second batting title. He finished, still a .300 hitter, with Vera Cruz, Aguila, and the Mexico City Tigers, retiring at age 46. His career totals show a .306 average over 2,803 minor league games. /(MC)

Damaso Garcia — 1957– . 2B-SS 1978–86, 88– Yankees, **Blue Jays**, Braves, Expos 1032 g, .283, 36 hr, 323 rbi. *1 LCS, 7 g, .233, 1 rbi* ☛ *All-Star—84–85.*

A surly second baseman who rarely drew walks, Garcia was a good fielder when he hustled, but he was unwilling to dive for balls. Garcia hit above .300 in both 1982 and 1983, but later got into a power struggle with Toronto management, insisting he should be the leadoff batter. Toronto fans were particularly harsh with Garcia, especially after he burned his uniform in the clubhouse after one of his poorer performances.

After 29 games in two seasons for the Yankees, Garcia spent seven seasons with the Blue Jays, where he became the club's career leader in at-bats, hits, and stolen bases. In 1982 Garcia became the first Blue Jay to steal 50 bases in a season, and in 1986 he became the first player to collect 1,000 hits as a Blue Jay. Garcia's 21-game hitting streak in 1983 tied teammate Lloyd Moseby for the team record, and on June 27, 1986, he tied a ML record by hitting four doubles in a game against the Yankees. He was traded to Atlanta before the 1987 season, then was released after hitting only .117 in 21 games in 1988. He caught on with the Expos in 1989. /(TF)

Dave Garcia — 1920– . *Manager 1977–82 Angels,* **Indians** 307–310, .498

A minor league infielder for 20 years, Garcia never played in a ML game. After managing in the minors and coaching for the Padres, Indians, and Angels, he became California manager in July 1977 and held that position until May of the next season. He rejoined the Indians as a coach in 1979 and was named manager later that season. In four full seasons, he finished as high as fifth only once. Garcia was liked for his fairness and decency, but he was sometimes criticized for lacking the toughness to inspire his players. /(BC)

Kiko Garcia [Alfonso Rafael] — 1953– . SS-2B-3B 1976–85 **Orioles**, Astros, Phillies 619 g, .239, 12 hr, 112 rbi. *1 LCS, 3 g, .273, 2 rbi. 1 WS, 6 g, .400, 6 rbi*

Garcia saw more and more action at shortstop with Baltimore from 1976 through 1979 as Mark Belanger's career began to wind down. He played 126 games for the '79 pennant winners, then tied or set three ALCS chances and assists records at shortstop. An unlikely hero in the Orioles' Game Three, 8–5 World Series victory over Pittsburgh, he went 4-for-4, driving in four runs—three with a bases-loaded triple. He had had only 24 RBI all season. Injuries sidelined him three times in 1980–82. He was a utility man for the 1983 pennant-winning Phillies, but did not play in the WS against his former Baltimore teammates. /(MC)

Mike Garcia (The Big Bear) — 1923–1986. RHP 1948–61 **Indians**, White Sox, Senators 2175 ip, 142–97, 3.27. 20 wins: 51–52 *1 WS, 5 ip, 0–1, 5.40* ☛ *Led League—era 54. All-Star—52–54.*

Garcia was part of the great Indian pitching staff that included Bob Feller, Early Wynn, and Bob Lemon. Signed in 1942, The Big Bear spent three years in the military. He went 14–5 in his rookie year (1949). The hard-throwing Californian of Mexican-Indian descent posted his second straight 20-win season in 1952, leading the AL in starts and hits

allowed, and tying for most shutouts (6). He again tied for the shutout lead (5) with an AL best 2.64 ERA in 1954 and was 19–8 as Cleveland set an AL record with 111 wins and ended the Yankees' pennant string at five. Garcia lost Game Three of the World Series in which Giants routed the Indians in four straight.

The championship season was Garcia's last good campaign. After three subpar years, he hurt his back in 1958. Cut and resigned, he won three final games in 1959. He left among the Indians' top ten all-time in wins, losses, games pitched, shutouts, winning percentage, and strikeouts. /(ME)

Pedro Garcia — 1950– . 2B 1973–77 **Brewers**, Tigers, Blue Jays 558 g, .220, 37 hr, 184 rbi

As a rookie with the 1973 Brewers, Garcia tied for the AL lead with 32 doubles and was runner-up to Al Bumbry in AL Rookie of the Year voting. The native Puerto Rican hit just .199 as Milwaukee's everyday second baseman in 1974. /(DQV)

Rich Garcia — 1942– . *Umpire AL 1975–87 3 LCS 2 WS 1 ASU*

Garcia's common-sense approach put him in the wrong on the rules during his second ML season. When a pitch bounced in the dirt, hit A's catcher Tim Hosley in the throat, and lodged between his uniform and chest protector, Garcia called time and advanced runners on first and third one base. Actually rule 509-g states: "If the ball lodges in the catcher's mask, protector or uniform, it is a live ball and in play." Although he had grounds, A's manager Chick Tanner did not file a protest. /(RTM)

Danny Gardella — 1920– . OF-1B 1944–45, 50 **Giants**, Cardinals 169 g, .267, 24 hr, 85 rbi

Gardella was a shipyard worker in 1944 when he joined the wartime Giants. He and brother Al, both lefthanded New Yorkers, were with the Giants in 1945 when 5'7" Danny hit 18 homers. Refusing the Giants' $4,500 contract offer in 1946, Gardella jumped to Vera Cruz of the Mexican League for $10,000. Suspended for five years by Commissioner Chandler along with the other Mexican League jumpers, Gardella sued baseball, claiming he had been bound only by the controversial reserve clause, not a contract. This celebrated antitrust case against baseball, Gardella *v.* Chandler, was dismissed by a district court in 1948, but Gardella's attorney, Frederic Johnson, won an appeal before the Second Circuit Court in 1949. Fearful of this significant threat to the reserve clause, baseball officials settled

Danny Gardella

out of court for $29,000 and lifted Gardella's suspension. Gardella joined the Cardinals in 1950 but was dropped after one at-bat. Nevertheless, his victory was the only successful challenge to base-ball's reserve clause in the federal courts. Though his cause was much maligned by players and the press, his challenge was a stepping-stone to free agency. /(DQV)

Ron Gardenhire — 1957– . SS-2B 1981–85 **Mets** 285 g, .232, 4 hr, 49 rbi

Gardenhire batted .240 as the Mets shortstop in 1982, but then was a utility man and shuttled between Triple-A and New York. A recurring ham-string injury in 1984–85 finished him with the Mets. The Twins made him a minor league manager after he played in their system. /(JCA)

Billy Gardner (Shotgun) — 1927– . 2B-SS-3B 1954–63 Giants, **Orioles**, Senators/Twins, Yankees, Red Sox 1034 g, .237, 41 hr, 271 rbi. *1 WS, .000.*
    Manager 1981–85, 87 **Twins**, Royals 330–417, .442

Ticketed to be the Royals' third-base coach in 1987, Gardner instead became the team's manager when terminally ill Dick Howser resigned during spring training. But Gardner was fired that August. He had piloted the Twins from May 1981 until June 1985, with a second-place finish in 1984. His pro playing career touched four decades (1945–71) and in-cluded ten ML seasons. He was Baltimore's regular second baseman from 1956 to 1959, and in 1957 he led the AL in doubles and at-bats. He was in Minnesota's original Opening Day lineup, and played briefly later that season for the powerful 1961 Yankees. /(TJ)

Jelly Gardner [Floyd] — 1895– . OF-1B Negro Leagues 1919–33 Detroit Stars, **Chicago American Giants**, Homestead Grays, New York Lincoln Giants 567 g, .286, 1 hr (inc.)

Gardner was a 5'6" 160-lb lefthanded line-drive hitter who batted leadoff for the powerful Chicago American Giant teams in the 1920s. An outstand-ing, far-ranging centerfielder, he was one of the era's fastest runners.
    Gardner played his first full season with Chicago in 1920. He batted a career-high .367 in 1924 and .333 in 1926. The Giants won four pennants during Gardner's first seven-year tour with them (1920–26), and triumphed in the '26 Black World Series. Gardner played in all 11 games of the series, batted just .222, but stole three bases and scored eight runs.
    Gardner went to the New York Lincoln Giants in 1927 after a salary dispute, but returned to Chicago in 1928 and batted .307 in 1929. He returned to his first team, the Detroit Stars, in 1931 and closed out his career with them. /(JM)

Jim Gardner — 1874–1905. RHP 1895, 97–99, 1902 **Pirates**, Cubs 423 ip, 25–22, 3.85

Gardner had Pittsburgh's best winning percentage (.800, 8–2) in 1895, but only pitched in home games so he could attend law school. Most used in 1898, he was 10–13. Born in Pittsburgh, Gardner died there at age 30. /(ME)

Larry Gardner — 1886–1976. 3B-2B 1908–24 **Red Sox**, Athletics, Indians 1922 g, .289, 27 hr, 929 rbi. *4 WS, 25 g, .198, 3 hr, 11 rbi*

Gardner was a steady third baseman and an above-average dead-ball era hitter. The lefthanded batter joined the Red Sox out of the University of Vermont in 1908, and was their regular third baseman from 1912 through 1917, including three World Champi-onship seasons. Gardner's sacrifice fly in the tenth inning of the final game of the 1912 WS finished the Giants. In early 1918, the Red Sox sent him in a package to the A's for standout first baseman Stuffy McInnis. After a year in Philadelphia, Gardner joined Cleveland and his former teammate, manager Tris Speaker. He cashed another WS check with the Indians in 1920, and hit a career-high .319 in 1921. Gardner later returned to his alma mater as baseball coach and athletic director. /(EW)

Rob Gardner [Richard Frank] — 1944– . LHP 1965–68, 70–73 **Mets**, Cubs, Indians, Yankees, A's, Brewers 331 ip, 14–18, 4.35

Gardner's only good ML season came with the Yankees in 1972 (8–5, 3.06). He had a complex trade history. Originally sent to Oakland by the Yankees in April 1971 with Ron Klimkowski for Felipe Alou, he was reacquired by New York in May for Curt Blefary. The A's got him back after the 1972 season with Rich McKinney in return for Matty Alou and sold Gardner to Milwaukee in May 1973, but the deal was canceled and Gardner returned in July. /(SFS)

Wes Gardner — 1961– . RHP 1984– Mets, **Red Sox** 363 ip, 15–22, 4.83. *1 LCS, 5 ip, 0–0, 5.79*

Gardner led the International League in saves at Tidewater in 1984 and 1985, but couldn't earn a spot on the Mets' pitching staff. He was dealt to Boston with Calvin Schiraldi for Bob Ojeda. He pitched only one inning in 1986 before tearing cartilage in his right shoulder, but his 10 saves in 1987 led the Red Sox. In 1988 and 1989, he was used as an occasional starter. /(SCL)

Wayne Garland — 1950– . RHP 1973–81 Orioles, **Indians** 1040 ip, 55–66, 3.89. 20 wins: 76 *1 LCS, 0.2 ip, 0–0, 0.00*

After three years in the Baltimore bullpen, Garland became a starter in 1976 and went 20–7 with a 2.68 ERA, ranking third in the league in wins (and second in winning percentage with .741). He had played out his option, and he became a free agent after the season. After signing a lucrative long-term contract with the Indians, in 1977 Garland went 13–19 with a 3.59 ERA for fifth-place Cleveland, tying for the AL lead in losses. On May 5, 1978, he had to have surgery for a rotator cuff tear. He never had another winning season, and he is remembered whenever the supposed evils of free agency and long-term contracts are discussed. /(SH)

Mike Garman — 1949– . RHP 1969, 71–78 Red Sox, **Cardinals**, Cubs, Dodgers, Expos 434 ip, 22–27, 3.63. *1 LCS, 1.1 ip, 0–0, 0.00. 1 WS, 4 ip, 0–0, 0.00*

Boston's number-one pick in the June 1967 draft, the 6'3" Garman had an outstanding fastball and good curve. He pitched sparingly for the Red Sox but blossomed as a reliever with St. Louis. He saved 12 for the 1977 NL champion Dodgers, and 42 lifetime. Garman's father was in the Pirate farm system, brother Steve in the Giants'. /(EW)

Debs Garms — 1908–1984. OF-3B 1932–35, 37–41, 43–45 Browns, **Braves**, Pirates, Cardinals 1010 g, .293, 17 hr, 328 rbi. *2 WS, 4 g, .000*
☛ Led League—ba 40.

Slightly built Debs Garms, a lefthanded-hitting Texan, led the NL with a .355 batting average with Pittsburgh in 1940. Two years earlier, when he batted .315 for the Braves, Garms broke Johnny Vander Meer's string of 21-1/3 hitless innings, which included two consecutive no-hit games. At age 37, Garms was cut by the Cardinals after hitting .336 in 74 games in 1945. /(TJ)

Phil Garner (Scrap Iron) — 1949– . 2B-3B 1973–88 A's, Pirates, **Astros**, Dodgers, Giants 1845 g, .260, 109 hr, 839 rbi. *3 LCS, 9 g, .269, 1 hr, 3 rbi. 1 WS, 7 g, .500, 5 rbi*
☛ All-Star—76, 80–81.

A gritty infielder who got by as much on determination as talent, Garner established himself as a second baseman with the A's under manager Chuck Tanner. When Tanner moved to Pittsburgh, he promptly traded for Garner, who was used at third, then at second after the Pirates acquired Bill Madlock. In 1978 Garner tied a ML record with grand slams in consecutive games (September 14 and 15). An important member of the 1979 World Champion Pirates, he was sometimes called "the best number-eight hitter in baseball." His .500 batting average in the 1979 WS, with at least one hit in each of the seven games, underlined the contention. He was traded to Houston in mid-1981 for the younger Johnny Ray, and Garner, platooned at third base, helped the Astros win the NL Western Division in 1986. /(ME)

Ralph Garr (Roadrunner) — 1945– . OF 1968–80 **Braves**, White Sox, Angels 1317 g, .306, 75 hr, 408 rbi
☛ Led League—ba 74. All-Star—74.

A Grambling football star, Garr reached the Braves briefly in 1968 (his second pro season) and stole home for the first of 172 steals. Unable to crack the

Braves' talent-laden outfield, the lefthanded hitter spent 1969 and 1970 with Richmond (International League), winning back-to-back batting titles. Finally given a job in Atlanta in 1971, he batted .343, with 219 hits, 101 runs, and 30 stolen bases. In 1974 Garr's .353 took the NL batting crown, and he led the league with 214 hits and 17 triples. The free-swinging leadoff man repeated as triples leader in 1975, and hit .300 twice again with the White Sox (1976 and 1977). Among baseball insiders, Garr was known as much for his squeaky voice, Hank Aaron imitations, and nonstop comic monologues as for his bat. He later became a hitting and baserunning instructor. /(MC)

Scott Garrelts — 1961– . RHP 1982- **Giants** 758 ip, 56–41, 3.01. *2 LCS, 14 ip, 1–0, 5.65. 1 WS, 7 ip, 0–2, 9.82*
☛ *Led League—era 89. All-Star—85.*

The hard-throwing Garrelts was the best member of the Giants' bullpen from 1984 to 1988, leading the club in saves each year despite never posting more than 13. He was made a starter in 1989 as the Giants experimented with Mike LaCoss in relief; Garrelts led the NL in ERA (2.28) as the Giants won the division title. He was the Giants' first-round pick in the June 1979 free agent draft, and led the Midwest League in both strikeouts and walks in 1980. In 1985 he led the last-place Giants in both wins (9) and saves (13). /(SCL)

Wayne Garrett — 1947– . 3B-2B 1969–78 **Mets**, Expos, Cardinals 1092 g, .239, 61 hr, 340 rbi. *2 LCS, 8 g, .194, 1 hr, 4 rbi. 2 WS, 9 g, .161, 2 hr, 2 rbi*

The redheaded Garrett played mostly third base, and hit .385 for the Mets in the 1969 LCS. He led 1973 World Series players with 11 strikeouts (tying a seven-game Series futility record) and two HR. Brother Adrian spent small parts of eight seasons in the majors. After losing a game to the 1969 Mets, Cub Ron Santo—referring to rookie Garrett at second base, Ed Kranepool at first base, Al Weis at shortstop, and Bobby Pfeil at third base—remarked, "It's a shame losing to an infield like that . . .I wouldn't let that infield play in Tacoma." /(TJ)

Gil Garrido — 1941– . SS-2B-3B 1964, 68–72 Giants, **Braves** 334 g, .237, 1 hr, 51 rbi. *1 LCS, 3 g, .200*

The Panamanian was first called to the majors in 1961 at age 20, but, knowing no English, couldn't find Candlestick Park and was returned to the minors without getting to play. In the Pacific Coast League he set records at shortstop for fielding percentage and errorless games. He appeared briefly with the Giants, and eventually won a platoon job

with the Braves. Garrido never did master English, and finished in the Mexican League. /(MC)

Ned Garver — 1925– . RHP 1948–61 **Browns**, Tigers, A's, Angels 2477 ip, 129–157, 3.73. 20 wins: 51
☛ *All-Star—51.*

Garver became the only 20th century pitcher to win 20 games in a season for a team which lost 100 when he went 20–12 for the 1951 Browns. He led the AL in complete games (24) that season, as he had the previous year (22). His $25,000 contract in 1952 made him the highest-paid Brown in history. Garver had batted .407 in the Ohio State League in 1944, so it was no surprise when he batted .305 in 1951 to pace the Browns. He hit sixth on occasion, and had a .218 lifetime BA with seven HR. His zeal for hitting was arrested midway through his career when Early Wynn nearly beaned him. Garver lost a league-high 17 with St. Louis in 1949. He had very little trouble getting Mickey Mantle out, but found Vic Wertz a particular thorn in his side. /(WAB)

Steve Garvey (Senator) — 1948– . 1B-3B 1969–87 **Dodgers**, Padres 2332 g, .294, 272 hr, 1308 rbi. *5 LCS, 22 g, .356, 8 hr, 21 rbi. 5 WS, 28 g, .319, 1 hr, 6 rbi*
☛ *Most Valuable Player—74. All-Star—74–81, 84–85. Gold Glove—74–77.*

The most durable player of his era, Garvey played a NL-record 1,207 consecutive games. Originally a third baseman with a suspect arm, he became part of baseball's longest-running infield when he moved to first base. Ron Cey took over at third, and they flanked Davey Lopes and Bill Russell from 1973 to 1981.

Garvey projected his Mr. Clean image to the nation in a TV interview before the 1974 World Series when he explained that "I always try to act as though there is a little boy or a little girl around, and I try never to do anything that would give them a bad example." His nickname, Senator, referred to his post-baseball political aspirations.

Garvey exploded as a NL star in 1974. He was elected to the All-Star team as a write-in candidate that year, and was voted MVP of the game. He followed this up by winning the NL MVP award, capping a nearly perfect season for the man whose father used to drive the Dodgers' bus at Vero Beach during spring training.

Garvey's name would not be left off the All-Star ballot again, and he was elected as a starter the next six years. In 1978 he became the first player to receive more than four million All-Star votes, and he was named MVP of the game that year as well. In ten All-Star Games he hit .393, and his slugging

Steve Garvey

average of .955 is the highest of any player with more than 20 at-bats.

One of the great clutch players of his time, he retired with the NLCS career records for HR (8) and RBI (24) and was named LCS MVP in 1978 and 1984. He also hit .368 in the 1981 divisional series.

The winner of four Gold Gloves, Garvey retired with a .996 fielding average. In 1977 he hit a Los Angeles Dodgers-record 33 HR, the only time in a seven-year period when he failed to better .300 and 200 hits. With Cey, Reggie Smith, and Dusty Baker, Garvey was one of a record four Dodgers to hit 30 homers that year. He led the NL in hits twice and games played six times.

A tremendous Los Angeles favorite who had a junior high school named after him while still an active player, Garvey traumatized fans by signing with the Padres as a free agent in December 1982. On his first trip to Los Angeles as a Padre, he took out a full-page newspaper ad thanking fans for their past support. By the end of his career, lacking protection in the Padres' lineup, Garvey's unwillingness to take bases on balls and a parallel propensity for chasing bad pitches had taken their toll on his

yearly statistics. Following the expiration of his five-year contract with San Diego, he discussed returning to the Dodgers, but an arm injury caused him to retire.

Garvey's Mr. Clean image was tarnished two years after his retirement, when he admitted fathering the children of different women. He had earlier suffered the embarassment of a tell-all book by his ex-wife Cyndy. /(TG)

Jerry Garvin [Theodore Jared] — 1955– . LHP 1977–82 **Blue Jays** 607 ip, 20–41, 4.42

The 6'3" Garvin was taken by Toronto from Minnesota in the 1976 expansion draft. Going 10–18 in 1977 and picking off an unofficial record 22 baserunners, he was named to several all-rookie teams. A reliever after a 1979 arm injury, he set a club record with 61 appearances in 1980. /(EW)

Ned Garvin [Virgil Lee] — 1874–1908. RHP 1896, 99–1904 Phillies, Cubs, Brewers, White Sox, **Dodgers**, Yankees 1401 ip, 57–97, 2.72

Garvin had 13 shutouts among his 57 victories. With Chicago (NL) on September 22, 1899, Garvin allowed 13 hits, yet pitched a complete game shutout to beat the Braves 3–0. /(ARA)

Harry Gaspar — 1883–1940. RHP 1909–12 **Reds** 825 ip, 44–48, 2.69

Gaspar broke in with Duluth in 1905 and after playing with three other minor league teams was drafted by the Reds in 1908. He was released to Toronto in mid-1912 but refused to report and was suspended. Gaspar remained out of the game until 1914 when he joined Sioux City (Western League). He was named manager of Sioux City in mid-1915. He retired from the game in 1919. /(MA)

Pilo Gaspar [Miguel] — 1930– . C 1950–76 Minor and Mexican Leagues

Gaspar caught a record 2,291 minor league games. He hit 44 homers for Laredo (Rio Grande Valley League) in 1950–51, but had only 29 more in the 15 seasons that followed. Though Mexican-born, he didn't play professionally in Mexico until age 28. He batted as high as .330 with Vera Cruz, and caught regularly until age 44. /(MC)

Tommy Gastall — 1932–1956. C 1955–56 **Orioles** 52 g, .181, 0 hr, 4 rbi

Gastall followed in Harry Agganis's tragic footsteps as star quarterback at Boston College. Signed to a $40,000 bonus by the Orioles, he was used sparingly and died at the age of 24 on September 20, 1956 when he crashed while flying a light plane. /(SFS)

Clarence Gaston (Cito) — 1944– . OF 1967, 69–78 Braves, **Padres**, Pirates 1026 g, .256, 91 hr, 387 rbi.
  Manager 1989– **Blue Jays** 77–49, .611. First place: 89 *1 LCS, 1–4, .200*
☛ *All-Star—70 .*

San Diego took Gaston from the Braves in the 1968 expansion draft. In his 1970 All-Star season, he hit .318 with 29 HR and 93 RBI. The 6′3″ Texan returned to Atlanta in 1975 as a backup and became a Blue Jays coach in 1982. Named Toronto's manager in mid-1989, he turned the team around and became the first black manager in post-season play./(TJ)

Milt Gaston [Nathaniel Milton] — 1896– . RHP 1924–34 Yankees, **Browns**, Senators, Red Sox, White Sox 2105 ip, 97–164, 4.55

A winner only in his first two seasons, Gaston led the league in losses with 18 for the Browns in 1926, and 20 with the Red Sox in 1930. He was one of the few players of his day to go straight to the majors. He threw a moving forkball that caused his catchers problems; it was rumored he was traded to Washington because Browns owner Phil Ball was tired of ducking his wild pitches. Milt's brother, Alex, was a ML catcher./(WAB)

Aubrey Gatewood — 1938– . RHP 1963–65, 70 **Angels**, Braves 178 ip, 8–9, 2.78

Gatewood debuted with the Angels, four-hit the Red Sox in his first ML start, and continued to look promising through 1965. Arm trouble sent him back to the minors, except for three games in 1970 with Atlanta./(MC)

Doc Gautreau [Walter Paul] — 1904–1970. 2B 1925–28 A's, **Braves** 261 g, .257, 0 hr, 52 rbi

Gautreau's fine career at Holy Cross made him a favorite in Boston. The 5′4″ 129-lb backup second baseman spent a lifetime in organized ball as a scout and minor league manager./(JK)

Joe Gedeon — 1893–1941. 2B 1913–14, 16–20 Senators, Yankees, **Browns** 581 g, .244, 2 hr, 171 rbi

Gedeon was a fringe character in the 1919 Black Sox scandal. Not part of the principal activities, he was a light-hitting second baseman for the uninvolved Browns. He had, according to Commissioner Landis, "guilty knowledge" of the White Sox' intentions of throwing the Series. Banned from organized ball, Gedeon played independent West Coast baseball, causing a problem for other players who were forbidden to play in games when he appeared./(JK)

Rich Gedman — 1959– . C 1980– **Red Sox** 896 g, .260, 83 hr, 356 rbi. *2 LCS, 11 g, .357, 2 hr, 7 rbi. 1 WS, 7 g, .200, 1 hr, 1 rbi*
☛ *All-Star—85–86.*

Gedman was *TSN* AL Rookie Player of the Year in 1981 and by the age of 25 had become one of baseball's top catchers, but was plagued by injuries, holdouts, and inconsistency thereafter. With a wide-open, weight-back batting stance, Gedman hit 24 HR in 1984 and followed with career highs in average (.295) and RBI (80) in 1985 while throwing out nearly half of opposition basestealers. His average dipped to .258 in 1986, and in 1987 he remained unsigned until May 1, then hit only .205 before injuring his thumb in mid-July. In 1988 and 1989, he platooned with Rick Cerone./(SCL)

Lou Gehrig [born Ludwig Heinrich Gehrig] (Columbia Lou, The Iron Horse, Larrupin' Lou, Buster) — 1903–1941. 1B 1923–39 **Yankees** 2164 g, .340, 493 hr, 1990 rbi. *7 WS, 34 g, .361, 10 hr, 35 rbi*
☛ *Most Valuable Player—27, 36. Led League—ba 34. Led League—hr 31, 34, 36. Led League—rbi 27–28, 30–31, 34. All-Star—33–38. Hall of Fame—1939.*

Lou Gehrig was the greatest first baseman ever and a key component in the Yankee legend. He and Cy Young hold the last two "unbreakable" records; Gehrig's 2,130 consecutive games played has never been approached, and in fact the two longest such streaks since then, combined, don't even match his mark. Because he was also handsome, a native New Yorker, and eventually a tragic figure, he became as glamorous as a retiring "mama's boy" could be.

Born in a German neighborhood, Gehrig began his legendary career at Columbia University. Freshmen weren't eligible for varsity play, but in his sophomore season Gehrig set multiple school records, most notably season marks of seven HR, a .444 batting average, and a .937 slugging average. Also a pitcher, he still holds the Columbia record for strikeouts in a game, fanning 17 Williams batters in a game he lost. It is rumored that Columbia coach Andy Coakley, a former major leaguer, was paid $500 by the Yankees to convince the youngster to sign with the Yankees. By the way, although Gehrig did hit some prodigious shots at Columbia, he never hit one through a window in the athletic office in Low Library, as depicted in *The Pride of the Yankees*—nobody could.

Lou Gehrig

Gehrig played two seasons with Hartford of the Eastern League and debuted in the majors four days short of his 20th birthday. He had brief but successful stints with the Yankees in 1923 and 1924. He started his famous streak on May 31, 1925, pinch hitting for Pee Wee Wanninger. (Earlier that year, Wanninger had replaced Everett Scott at shortstop, breaking Scott's much-remarked-upon string of 1,307 consecutive games.) The next day, regular first baseman Wally Pipp sat out a game with a headache, and Gehrig started in his place. The team was in seventh place at the time, and Babe Ruth was sick, so some experimentation was in order. Hindsight makes it seem as though the rookie then monopolized the position, but in fact Gehrig's

position was still somewhat tenuous. He was pinch hit for three times that month, and didn't start on July 5, although he came into the game later. Gehrig had a good season, certainly, hitting .295 with 20 HR and 68 RBI in 126 games. But it was in 1927, when he was moved to the cleanup spot and had Bob Meusel protecting him in the order that became known as Murderer's Row, that Gehrig put up big numbers for the first time. He won the MVP award (then given by the league and not awarded to repeat winners) and led the AL with 175 RBI, 52 doubles, and 447 total bases. He finished behind Ruth with 47 HR, 149 runs, a .765 slugging average, and 109 walks. His .373 batting average also ranked second.

Gehrig was overshadowed by Ruth for as long as

Ruth was a Yankee. Gehrig was great, Gehrig was consistent, Gehrig was a role model—but Ruth was larger than life. However, it is Gehrig who owns the AL season record for RBI, with 184 in 1931, and who hit a ML-record 23 grand slams lifetime. Gehrig and Rocky Colavito are the only AL players to hit four homers in a nine-inning game, and Gehrig hit for the cycle twice; Ruth never did. He had at least 100 RBI and 100 runs every full season of his career, 13 straight years, and led the AL five times in RBI and four times in runs. In fact, he topped 150 RBI seven times, also a ML record, and is third all-time on the RBI list. His .632 slugging average also ranks third, and when he retired, only Ruth had hit more home runs.

Ruth pursued media attention and made great copy, but Gehrig led a quiet married life. For a while the two were friends, but a coolness developed between them, variously ascribed to Ruth making a pass at a female friend of Gehrig's or making a derogatory comment about Mom Gehrig, whom Lou always worshiped. Nonetheless, Ruth and Gehrig had a cordial professional relationship until Ruth left the team after the 1934 season. In 1931, the year they tied for the AL HR lead, Gehrig lost a home run passing Ruth on the bases.

Ruth and Gehrig carried the Yankees, but there were some years when they just weren't enough. Connie Mack's Athletics won three straight years, 1929–31, before the Yankees came back in 1932 for another World Championship. In the following seasons, it became clear that Ruth was fading. In their last year together, 1934, Gehrig won the Triple Crown with 49 HR, 165 RBI, and a .363 BA; in 1935 he dropped off to .329 with 30 HR and 119 RBI. He was also bothered more and more by lumbago; in 1934 he had suffered an attack on the field and had to be carried off. He was quite aware of his consecutive games streak, as were manager Joe McCarthy and the writers. The next day he was penciled in the lineup as the leadoff hitter, listed at shortstop. Hardly able to stand, he singled, and Red Rolfe pinch ran for him and finished the game at shortstop. He kept his string going through the years despite a broken thumb, a broken toe, back spasms, and lumbago, stoically, in fact proudly, playing through the pain.

The arrival of Joe DiMaggio in 1936 made enough of a difference that Gehrig had his last two great seasons in 1936 and 1937 as the Yankees won World Championships. The Giants managed something no other team had done since 1926: they won a World Series game from the Yankees. But Gehrig homered in close contests in Games Three and Four.

He was always a good World Series hitter, with 10 HR lifetime, including a record-setting four in the four-game 1928 WS.

The Yankees repeated in 1938, but Gehrig dropped below .300 for the first time since his rookie season. In 1939 he was obviously enfeebled, and on May 2 he took himself out of the lineup. He was hitting just .143, and was quite clumsy afield. Many players were afraid he would injure himself, but nobody would suggest that he sit down, not even manager McCarthy. Gehrig had to take the initiative himself. He never played again, and although, in his capacity as team captain, he continued to carry the lineup card out every day, eventually even that proved more than he could handle. He was diagnosed as having a rare, almost unknown, and incurable disease, amyotrophic lateral sclerosis, forever after known as Lou Gehrig's disease. It was not announced that he was doomed, although many suspected it and Gehrig knew. On July 4, 1939, Lou Gehrig Day was held at Yankee Stadium. It may be the most famous ceremony in baseball history, with Gehrig's assertion that "today, I consider myself the luckiest man on the face of the earth" an unforgettable statement. The waiting period for the new Hall of Fame was waived, and he was admitted the year it opened, in 1939. He spent his last two years of life working for New York Mayor Fiorello LaGuardia, and died on June 2, 1941. /(SH)

Charlie Gehringer (The Mechanical Man) — 1903– . 2B 1924–42 **Tigers** 2323 g, .320, 184 hr, 1427 rbi. *3 WS, 20 g, .321, 1 hr, 7 rbi*
☛ *Most Valuable Player—37. Led League—ba 37. All-Star—1933–38. Hall of Fame—49.*

One of baseball's most surehanded second basemen and a dependable hitter, the taciturn and undemonstrative Gehringer was called The Mechanical Man. "You wind him up Opening Day and forget him," teammate Doc Cramer said. Detroit manager Mickey Cochrane explained, "Charlie says 'hello' on Opening Day, 'goodbye' on closing day, and in between hits .350." His silence and lack of color were legendary. During a game in the 1930s Detroit shortstop Bill Rogell captured a windblown pop fly well on the second-base side of the infield and accidentally spiked Gehringer. "I can catch those too," Gehringer said mildly and limped back to his position.

He covered second base in a smooth, seemingly effortless style. He had quick hands and rarely lost a ball he got his glove on. Gehringer led all AL second basemen in fielding percentage nine times, led or

Charlie Gehringer

In 1926 Gehringer became the Tigers' regular second baseman.

A reliable hitter with good power, he led the AL in batting in 1937 with a .371 mark. He was chosen MVP that season. He had more than 200 hits in seven different seasons and led the league in hits and runs scored in 1929 and 1934. He led once in triples and twice in doubles, ranking tenth all-time in two-base hits. Seven times he had more than 100 RBI. In 1929 he topped the AL in stolen bases. His controlled, lefthanded batting swing made him difficult to strike out. In 16 full seasons, his strikeouts ranged from 16 to 42.

Gehringer starred for Tigers pennant winners in 1934, 1935, and 1940. He slumped badly in 1941, then entered the Navy for three years. In 1949 he was elected to Baseball's Hall of Fame. From 1951 through 1953 he served as Detroit's GM and vice president, continuing in the latter position through 1959. At the time of baseball's centennial celebration in 1969, a special committee of baseball writers named him the game's greatest living second baseman. /(FS)

Phil Geier (Little Phil) — 1875–1967. OF-2B 1896–97, 1900–01, 04 Phillies, Reds, A's, Milwaukee (AL), **Braves** 349 g, .249, 2 hr, 102 rbi

Geier won the American Association batting championship in 1903, hitting .362 to earn a third ML trial. His .243 BA as a regular with the 1904 Braves sent him back down. /(BC)

Gary Geiger — 1937– . OF 1958–67, 69–70 Indians, **Red Sox**, Braves, Astros 954 g, .246, 77 hr, 283 rbi

After coming up through the Indians' system and playing in Cleveland in 1958, Geiger was traded to the Red Sox with the fading Vic Wertz in return for Jimmy Piersall. In 1959 Geiger played centerfield between the previous year's MVP, Jackie Jensen, and batting champ, Ted Williams. A lefthanded hitter playing in Fenway Park, Geiger was batting .302 in 1960 when he went down with a collapsed lung, missing the rest of the season. He hit 50 HR over the next three seasons, but never hit near .300 again. He did hit .385 in 1964, but in only five games; he missed most of the season due to illness that extended into 1965, when he also suffered a fractured skull. The Red Sox gave up on him, and comebacks with the Braves and Astros as a reserve outfielder and pinch hitter proved disappointing. /(SH)

tied for the lead in assists seven times, and had the most putouts three times. Baseball authority H.G. Salsinger wrote: "He lacks showmanship, but he has polish that no other second baseman, with the exception of the great Napoleon Lajoie, ever had. He has so well-schooled himself in the technique of his position that he makes the most difficult plays look easy."

Following one year at the University of Michigan, Gehringer was signed by the Tigers in 1924 on the recommendation of former Tigers star Bobby Veach. The legend persists that then-manager Ty Cobb doubted the slim youngster's ability to hit ML pitching. Cobb later said, "I knew Charlie would hit and I was so anxious to sign him that I didn't even take the time to change out of my uniform before rushing him into the front office to sign a contract."

Dave Geisel — 1955– . LHP 1978–79, 81–85 **Cubs,** **Blue Jays,** Mariners 208 ip, 5–5, 4.02

Geisel was a reliever with no outstanding pitch who was primarily used to get out lefthanded hitters. He had trouble staying healthy, broke an ankle in 1980 and a collarbone in 1981, and spent only one full season in the majors—1983 with Toronto (0–3, five saves). /(MC)

Harry Geisel — 1888–1966. *Umpire* AL 1925–42 *3 WS 2 ASU*

Geisel's complaints in 1937 about the slickness of new baseballs led to the ML adopting the special deglossing mud with which all balls are now rubbed before they go into play. On April 16, 1940, Geisel was behind the plate as Bob Feller blanked Chicago in the only Opening Day no-hitter. /(RTM)

Charley Gelbert — 1906–1967. SS-3B 1929–32, 35–37, 39–40 **Cardinals,** Reds, Tigers, Senators, Red Sox 876 g, .267, 17 hr, 350 rbi. *2 WS, 13 g, .300, 5 rbi*

A superb fielder with a lively bat, Gelbert was four years into a bright career with St. Louis when an off-season hunting accident nearly cost him his left leg. After sitting out two years, he returned to the majors in 1935 as a utility man. In 1931 Gelbert set records for shortstops in a seven-game World Series with 42 chances, 29 assists, 6 double plays, and a 1.000 fielding average. /(JL)

John Gelnar — 1943– . RHP 1964, 67, 69–71 Pirates, **Pilots/Brewers** 230 ip, 7–14, 4.19

In 1969 the expansion Pilots traded Lou Piniella, who won the Rookie of the Year award that season, to the expansion Royals for Gelnar and outfielder Steve Whitaker. Gelnar compiled a 3–10, 3.31 record starting and relieving. When the team moved to Milwaukee in 1970, he had his only winning season, going 4–3 with four saves. /(JFC)

Joe Genewich — 1897–1985. RHP 1922–30 **Braves,** Giants 1402 ip, 73–92, 4.29

Genewich was a $5-a-game sandlot pitcher with no college or minor league experience when the Braves signed him. As a rookie in early 1923, he outpitched the Giants' Jack Bentley, for whom John McGraw had just paid $65,000. Genewich had had limited success in five-plus Boston seasons (57–76) when McGraw traded four players for him in mid-1928. He went 11–4 the rest of the season, then faded. /(NLM)

Jim Gentile (Diamond Jim) — 1934– . 1B 1957–58, 60–66 Dodgers, **Orioles,** A's, Astros, Indians 936 g, .260, 179 hr, 549 rbi
☛ *All-Star—60–62.*

Since there was no room for a rookie first baseman on a team that already had Gil Hodges, Diamond Jim (so nicknamed by Roy Campanella, who considered the young lefthanded slugger a diamond in the rough) languished for eight years in the Dodger farm system. Finally traded to Baltimore, in 1961 the temperamental San Francisco native batted .302 with 46 HR and—on only 147 hits—a club record 141 RBI. His five '61 grand slams, including two straight in one game, set an AL record that stood until 1987. /(TJ)

Gary Gentry — 1946– . RHP 1969–75 **Mets,** Braves 903 ip, 46–49, 3.56. *1 LCS, 2 ip, 0–0, 9.00. 1 WS, 7 ip, 1–0, 0.00*

As a hard-throwing rookie, Gentry was an effective starter (13–12) for the 1969 Miracle Mets. With defensive help from Tommie Agee in centerfield, Gentry and Nolan Ryan combined to shut out Baltimore in Game Three of the '69 WS. His November 1972 trade to Atlanta was followed by a ruinous elbow injury. /(CR)

Rufe Gentry [James Rufus] — 1918– . RHP 1943–44, 46–48 **Tigers** 243 ip, 13–17, 4.37

Workhorse Gentry pitched 300 innings and won 20 games for Buffalo (International League) in 1943. For Detroit in 1944 he was 12–14, with an AL-high 108 walks. A holdout in 1945, he was placed on the voluntary retired list, but pitched ten innings for Detroit from 1946 to 1948. /(EW)

Wally Gerber (Spooks) — 1891–1951. SS 1914–15, 17–29 Pirates, **Browns,** Red Sox 1522 g, .257, 7 hr, 476 rbi

The Browns' aggressive everyday shortstop from 1919 through 1927, Gerber led AL shortstops in errors in 1919 and 1920, but settled down to lead in double plays four times. He had quick hands for everything, except (his teammates said) picking up the check, but when the Depression rolled around, Gerber, who had invested well, became a source of financial help for former teammates. /(JK)

Ken Gerhart — 1961– . OF 1986–88 **Orioles** 215 g, .221, 24 hr, 64 rbi

The injury-plagued Gerhart had his best year in 1987, reaching career highs with a .243 average, 14

HR, and 34 RBI before going on the DL in mid-August and missing the rest of the year. /(JFC)

Al Gerheauser (Lefty) — 1917–1972. LHP 1943–46, 48 **Phillies**, Pirates, Browns 643 ip, 25–50, 4.13

Gerheauser lost two of every three decisions as a wartime starter in Philadelphia and was mostly a reliever with Pittsburgh and St. Louis. Wildness was his primary handicap. /(EW)

Dick Gernert — 1928– . 1B-OF 1952–62 **Red Sox**, Cubs, Tigers, Reds, Astros 835 g, .254, 103 hr, 402 rbi. *1 WS, 4 g, .000*

Gernert was a power hitter out of Temple University. He hit 19 HR as a Boston rookie and 21 as a sophomore in the only years he was a regular. The off-season schoolteacher pinch hit four times for the Reds in the 1961 World Series. /(EW)

Cesar Geronimo — 1948– . OF 1969–83 Astros, **Reds**, Royals 1522 g, .258, 51 hr, 392 rbi. *5 LCS, 17 g, .095, 1 hr, 4 rbi. 3 WS, 18 g, .246, 2 hr, 7 rbi* ☛ *Gold Glove—74–77.*

Geronimo, the outstanding defensive centerfielder of five divisional champions and the 1975–76 World Champion Reds teams, was first signed by the Yankees, who briefly tried to make a pitcher out of him. The lefthanded Dominican made his ML debut with Houston, and went to Cincinnati in the November 1971 deal that also moved Joe Morgan to the Reds. Geronimo was the 3,000th strikeout victim of both Bob Gibson and Nolan Ryan. "I was just in the right place at the right time," he joked. /(TJ)

Doc Gessler [Harry Homer] — 1880–1924. OF-1B 1903–06, 08–11 Tigers, Dodgers, Cubs, Red Sox, **Senators** 880 g, .281, 14 hr, 363 rbi. *1 WS, 2 g, .000.* *Manager* 1914 **Pittsburgh (FL)** 6–12, .333

A fine batter but never a great outfielder, Gessler was known as the strong man of baseball for his feats of physical strength. One of three doctors in the 1906 World Series (with Doc White and Frank Owen), Gessler became a physician, graduating from Johns Hopkins Medical School. /(EW)

Al Gettel — 1917– . RHP 1945–49, 51, 55 **Yankees**, Indians, White Sox, Senators, Giants, Cardinals 734 ip, 38–45, 4.28

Gettel recorded a 2.97 ERA for the 1946 Yankees and won 11 games for the 1947 Indians. Later, with Oakland (Pacific Coast League), Gettel pitched and won a 22-inning marathon. /(TJ)

Gus Getz (Gee Gee) — 1889–1969. 3B-2B 1909–10, 14–18 Braves, **Dodgers**, Reds, Indians, Pirates 339 g, .238, 2 hr, 93 rbi. *1 WS, 1 g, .000*

A good glove man, Getz was the third baseman for the 1915 Dodgers. He played just seven games for the Reds in 1917, but one was the May 2, Fred Toney-Hippo Vaughn double no-hitter. He later managed and umpired in the minors. /(NLM)

Charlie Getzein (Pretzels) — 1864–1932. RHP 1884–92 **Detroit (NL)**, Indianapolis (NL), Braves, Cleveland (NL), Cardinals 2539 ip, 145–139, 3.46. 20 wins: 86–87, 90

Getzein was an outstanding pitcher of the 1880s. In 1886 he was 30–11 for the Detroit NL team. The following season, he was 29–13 and led the NL in winning percentage (.690) as Detroit won the pennant. In the 15-game postseason championship series between the NL winner and the American Association champion, he posted four wins. Getzein and catcher Charlie Ganzel became known as the Pretzel Battery because they both were of German extraction. /(BC)

Rube Geyer [Jacob Bowman] — 1885–1962. RHP 1910–13 **Cardinals** 412 ip, 17–26, 3.67

Geyer was a winner only in his rookie Cardinal season, going 9–6 in 1911. He was a minor league manager when his playing days ended. /(NLM)

Patsy Gharrity — 1892–1966. C-1B 1916–23, 29–30 **Senators** 679 g, .262, 20 hr, 249 rbi

A roommate and favorite catcher of Walter Johnson, Gharrity became a coach when Johnson managed the Senators and Indians. The versatile Gharrity also played first base and outfield. He hit .310 as Washington's regular catcher in 1921. /(JK)

A. Bartlett Giamatti (Bart) — 1938–1989. *Executive.*

Giamatti, a lifelong Red Sox fan, came to prominence as the president of Yale University, where his tough dealing with the college's union favorably impressed baseball's owners. Also appreciated was his devotion to baseball's tradition. Named president of the NL in December 1986, he gained attention for his 30-day suspension of Pete Rose in 1988 after Rose, the Reds' manager, shoved umpire Dave Pallone. After succeeding Peter Uebberoth as Commissioner in April 1989, Giamatti's most famous decision once again involved Rose, whom he suspended for life for gambling. A week later, Giamatti died of a massive heart attack.

Giamatti received his B.A. (English) and Ph.D. (Comparative Literature) from Yale and, after teaching at Princeton in 1964–66, returned to Yale in 1966. He became Yale's president in July 1978 and served for eight years. He wrote many books and articles on Renaissance literature as well as a number of baseball essays. /(SH)

Joe Giard (Peco) — 1898–1956. LHP 1925–27 **Browns,** Yankees 278 ip, 13–15, 5.96

As a rookie, Giard went 10–5 despite a 5.04 ERA and twice as many walks as strikeouts for the slugging 1925 Browns. He slipped to 3–10 (7.00) in 1926 and was traded to the Yankees. /(WAB)

Joe Gibbon — 1936– . LHP 1960–72 **Pirates,** Giants, Reds, Astros 1119 IP, 61–65, 3.52. *1 LCS, 0.1 ip, 0–0, 0.00. 1 WS, 3 ip, 0–0, 9.00*

A 6′4″ University of Mississippi basketball All-American, Gibbon looked like the emerging star of Pittsburgh's staff in 1961 (13–10, 3.32). After an injury-plagued 1962, he bounced back in 1964 to go 10–7. He went to the Giants in a 1965 trade for Matty Alou, who then won the 1966 batting title. By 1968 Gibbon was solely a reliever. /(ME)

Jake Gibbs [Jerry Dean] — 1938– . C 1962–71 **Yankees** 538 g, .233, 25 hr, 146 rbi

This University of Mississippi All-American quarterback and third baseman was drafted by the AFL Oilers and the NFL Browns. A $105,000 Yankee bonus-baby, Gibbs was thought to be in the Dickey-Berra-Howard mold, but he had a weak bat and an injury-prone body, and spent most of his career as a platoon player. He returned to coach at Ole Miss. /(GDW)

Bob Gibson [Robert Louis, Jr.] — 1957– . RHP 1983–87 **Brewers,** Mets 270 ip, 12–18, 4.24

Gibson was a wild power pitcher with no effective breaking pitches. He was a middle reliever and sometimes starter except for the second half of 1985, when he bolstered a failing Rollie Fingers in Milwaukee's bullpen and finished 6–7 with 11 saves. /(JCA)

Bob Gibson (Hoot) — 1935– . RHP 1959–75 **Cardinals** 3885 ip, 251–174, 2.91. 20 wins: 65–66, 68–70 *3 WS, 81 ip, 7–2, 1.89*
☛ *Most Valuable Player—68. Led League—w 70. Led League—era 68. Led League—k 68. Cy Young Award—68, 70. All-Star—62, 65–70, 72. Gold Glove—65–73. Hall of Fame—1981.*

Bob Gibson getting his record 24th strikeout of the 1964 World Series

There have been few pitchers more intimidating or more dominating than Bob Gibson. His great physical stamina and tremendous concentration gave him an enormous edge enhanced by his willingness to pitch inside and sometimes hit batters. His 1968 season is one of the very best ever turned in by a pitcher, and his stellar World Series performances made him the toughest pitcher in the Fall Classic since Whitey Ford and brought him Hall of Fame election in 1981. With a blazing fastball, darting slider, good curve, and pinpoint control, from 1963 to 1972 Gibson averaged better than 19 wins per season. He struck out more than 200 batters nine times and led the NL four times in shutouts. In 1971 he no-hit the Pirates.

Two aspects of Gibson's career demand special mention. In 1968 he pitched 13 shutouts on his way to a 1.12 ERA, the second-lowest since 1893 in 300 innings. During one stretch Gibson allowed only two runs over 92 innings. His strikeouts to innings ratio approached 1.0, while he walked only 62 batters all season. At one point he won fifteen games in succession.

The second area in which Gibson proved phenomenal was World Series play. He won seven consecutive games and pitched eight straight complete games in World Series competition. Only Whitey Ford owns more World Series victories than Gibson, who is also second all-time in WS strikeouts. In the opening match of the 1968 classic, Gibson beat 30-game winner Denny McLain 4–0 and set a Series record by fanning 17 Tigers. His 35 total strikeouts in the 1968 WS were also a record. He won Game Four 10–1, but lost Game Seven 4–1, on two days' rest, to Mickey Lolich. Gibson lost a shutout in the seventh inning when Curt Flood uncharacteristically misjudged a routine fly ball.

Gibson won the clinchers in both the 1964 and 1967 Series. In Game Two of the 1964 Series against the Yankees, he lost 8–3 but kept it close until he was knocked out in the ninth inning. He won Game Five 5–2 in ten innings, taking a shutout into the ninth. Coming back on two days' rest for Game Seven, he won 7–5. In 27 innings, he had 31 strikeouts and a 3.00 ERA. In 1967 he beat Boston's Jose Santiago in the opener, 2–1, and in Game Four, 6–0, and bested Jim Lonborg 7–2 in the finale.

A sickly child who almost died, Gibson was found to have a heart murmur but went on to excel in basketball and baseball in high school. He accepted a basketball scholarship to Creighton University and was the first person inducted into the school's Sports Hall of Fame. In 1957 Bob agreed to sign with the Cardinals for $4,000 and reported to the Omaha farm club. After the baseball campaign was complete, he joined the Harlem Globetrotters for a season. His Omaha manager, Johnny Keane, had great confidence in him, but two trials with the Cardinals had produced a 6–11 record and not much of an impression on the St. Louis manager, Solly Hemus. However, when Keane replaced Hemus in 1961, he put Gibson in the starting rotation to stay. Gibson blossomed in 1963, going 18–9, as the Cardinals contended following the acquisition of fine-fielding shortstop Dick Groat.

Gibson retired as the winningest pitcher in Cardinals history. He became the second pitcher in history to fan 3,000 batters and also hurled 56 shutouts. His incredible career was accomplished despite a fractured leg (1962), a severely strained elbow (1966), a broken leg (1967), and badly torn ligaments and knee surgery (1973). After struggling through the 1975 campaign on bad legs, Gibson decided in early September that it was time to retire when light-hitting Pete LaCock powered a grand-slam home run off him.

Gibson proved quickly and repeatedly there simply wasn't an element of the game he hadn't mastered. From 1965 to 1973 he won nine consecutive Gold Gloves for fielding excellence. He often helped his cause with the bat, laying down a successful bunt or hitting up the middle. He had 24 regular-season home runs plus a pair in World Series play. In 1970 he batted .303 and was occasionally employed as a pinch hitter.

After serving as former teammate Joe Torre's pitching coach with the Mets and Braves, Gibson returned to St. Louis as a baseball radio commentator and sports show host. /(FO)

Frank Gibson — 1890–1961. C 1913, 21–27 Tigers, **Braves** 468 g, .274, 8 hr, 146 rbi

A switch-hitting catcher and frequent pinch hitter, Gibson played pro ball for 21 years, mostly in the minors. He once held out with the Braves—not for more money, but for more work. /(NLM)

George Gibson (Moon) — 1880–1967. C 1905–18 **Pirates**, Giants 1213 g, .236, 15 hr, 345 rbi. *1 WS, 7 g, .240, 2 rbi.*
    Manager 1920–22, 1925, 1932–34 **Pirates**, Cubs 413–344, .546

For 11 years, Gibson was a full-time or platooned Pirate catcher. He set a Pittsburgh record with 1,113 games caught from 1905 through 1916. The burly Canadian was a surprisingly light hitter. Named Pirate manager by owner Barney Dreyfus in 1920, the team folded down the stretch in 1921 and Gibson quit in mid-1922. He was rehired by new owner Bill Benswanger ten years later, guided the Pirates to second-place finishes in 1932–33, but was fired after a slow start in 1934. Though he compiled a .546 career winning percentage, Gibson reputedly was unable to maintain discipline. /(ME)

Josh Gibson

Josh Gibson — 1911–1947. C-OF Negro Leagues 1930–46 Homestead Grays, Pittsburgh Crawfords 508 g, .384, 142 hr (inc.)
☛ *Led League—ba 38, 42–43, 45. Led League—hr 32, 34, 36, 38–39, 42, 44–46. Hall of Fame—1972.*

The warm, fun-loving, well-liked Gibson was a 6'1" 215-lb catcher who was considered by many the greatest Negro League player of all time and the best hitter of his era.

Gibson's pro career began in 1930 at the age of 18. He was watching a game between the Homestead Grays and the Kansas City Monarchs, who had brought along their new lighting system. It was the first night baseball game played in Pittsburgh. The lighting was poor, and Grays pitcher Smokey Joe Williams and catcher Buck Ewing got their signals crossed. Williams threw a fastball and split Ewing's hand. Grays manager Judy Johnson, who knew of Gibson's reputation as an outstanding semi-pro player, recalled, "I called time and Josh was sitting up there in the stands and I asked him if he wanted to catch and he said 'yes sir,' so we had to hold up the game while he went and put Buck Ewing's uniform on. We signed him the next day."

Gibson played for the Grays in 1930–31, then jumped to the Crawfords in 1932 and won three home run titles (1932, 1934, and 1936). In '36 he hit 20 HR in only 38 games. He batted .385 in 1933, and .457 in 1936. He began 1937 in the Dominican Republic, where he hit .453. Returning to the Grays in July, when the Dominican season ended, he batted .435. He won the HR title in 1938 and 1939, and won his first batting title in '38 with a .440 mark; he had just missed in '36 (.457) and '37 (.435).

Gibson joined Vera Cruz of the Mexican League and hit .467 in an abbreviated 1940 season. In 1941 he batted .374 and led the league with 33 HR and 124 RBI in 94 games. He also won the Puerto Rican Winter League batting title in '41 with a .480 mark, and was named the league's MVP.

Gibson returned to the Homestead Grays in 1942 and led the league with 20 HR in only 42 games while batting a league-high .452. On January 1, 1943, he suddenly fell into a coma that lasted for a day. Doctors told him he had a brain tumor, but Gibson refused to let them operate, fearing that surgery would leave him a vegetable. He continued to play, winning HR titles in 1944–46 and batting crowns in 1943 and 1945.

On January 20, 1947, Gibson told his mother that he was going to die that night. She laughed, but told him to go to bed and that she would call a doctor. With his family gathered around him, Gibson asked for his baseball trophies to be brought to his bedside. He was laughing and talking when he suddenly sat straight up, had a stroke, and died. He was 35 years old.

Not only did Gibson hit home runs with amazing frequency, he hit them astounding distances. He blasted one in Monessen, PA, that was measured at 575′. *The Sporting News* of June 3, 1967, credits him with a homer in a Negro League game at Yankee Stadium that hit two feet from the top of the wall circling the bleachers in centerfield, about 580′ from home plate. It was estimated that had the drive had cleared the wall, it would have traveled 700′. And, although it never has been conclusively verified, Jack Marshall, of the Chicago American Giants, claims that Gibson did smash a ball over the stadium's triple deck next to the bullpen in left field, the only fair ball ever hit out of the House That Ruth Built.

Regarding Gibson's defensive skills, Walter Johnson said he was as good as Bill Dickey. Roy Campanella called him "not only the greatest catcher, but the greatest ballplayer I ever saw." Cool Papa Bell said Gibson was merely a "good" catcher who had a strong arm, was a good handler of pitchers, but was poor on pop-ups. Jimmie Crutchfield, Gibson's teammate on the 1932–36 Crawfords, offered this assessment: "I can remember when he couldn't catch this building if you threw it at him . . .And I watched him develop into a very good defensive catcher. He was never given enough credit for his ability as a catcher."

In 13 complete seasons in the Negro Leagues, Gibson won nine HR titles and four batting crowns. His lifetime average of .384 was the highest in Negro League history. In a poll conducted in the early 1980s among experts on black baseball, Gibson was named the Negro Leagues' greatest catcher. He was elected to the Hall of Fame by the Committee on Negro Baseball Leagues in 1972. /(JM)

Kirk Gibson — 1957– . OF-DH 1979– **Tigers**, Dodgers 1114 g, .274, 184 hr, 603 rbi. *3 LCS, 15 g, .254, 2 hr, 12 rbi. 2 WS, 6 g, .368, 3 hr, 9 rbi*
☛ *Most Valuable Player—88.*

Coming to the Dodgers as a free agent in 1988, Gibson's intensity spurred the team to a World Championship highlighted by his dramatic game-winning home run in the Series opener. Kept out of the lineup by a leg injury, he pinch hit with two out in the bottom of the ninth with Mike Davis on base and the Dodgers down 4–3. Visibly wincing on each swing, he fouled off four pitches before he hit a slider out off A's relief ace Dennis Eckersley and limped around the bases. It was his only at-bat in the Series.

Gibson was also a hero in the LCS, with a 12th-inning solo shot to beat the Mets in Game Four. He hit a three-run homer in Los Angeles' 7–4 victory in Game Five and got the game-winning RBI in the clincher with a first-inning sacrifice fly. Not a good fielder, his approach was displayed in Game Three when, playing on a sloppy field, the gimpy Gibson made a crucial slipping, lunging catch in the mud despite nearly falling down three times in pursuit of the fly ball.

An All-America football flanker and baseball outfielder at Michigan State University, Gibson was Detroit's number-one pitck in the June 1978 draft. His raw power and speed led Sparky Anderson to dub him "the next Mickey Mantle." Injuries restricted his progress until 1984, when he became the first Tiger ever to hit 20 home runs and steal 20 bases in the same season, the first with at least 10 doubles, triples, homers, and steals since Charlie Gehringer in 1930, and dominated postseason play. He was the MVP of the LCS, then led the Tigers with seven RBI and three steals in the World Series. He hit two homers and scored the winning run in the fifth, and final, game. In 1986 Gibson set a major league record with five consecutive game-winning RBI and was honored as AL Player of the Week three times. An extremely intense player, with awesome power resulting in several tape-measure home runs, Gibson's below-average defense resulted in a shift from right field to left in 1987. His home run and game-winning single at Toronto on September 27, 1987 enabled the Tigers to avoid a sweep, recover, and wrest the division title from the Blue Jays.

A year after his 1988 MVP award, injuries limited Gibson to 71 games and a .213 batting average. /(ME)

Norwood Gibson — 1877–1959. RHP 1903–06 **Red Sox** 609 ip, 34–32, 2.93

A 1901 Notre Dame graduate with a degree in chemistry, the spitballing Gibson was the number-four starting pitcher on both the 1903 and 1904 pennant-winning Red Sox. /(CG)

Paul Gibson — 1960– . LHP 1988– **Tigers** 224 ip, 8–10, 3.94

Both a starter and reliever, Gibson pitched well in his rookie season, going 4–2 with a 2.93 ERA, but experienced control problems in 1989. /(SFS)

Russ Gibson — 1939– . C 1967–72 **Red Sox**, Giants 264 g, .228, 8 hr, 78 rbi. *1 WS, 2 g, .000*

Gibson spent ten years in the minors, and in his first major league game, April 14, 1967, caught fellow rookie Billy Rohr as the latter came within one out of a no-hitter. Gibson caught the first game of that year's World Series. /(RMu)

Sam Gibson — 1899–1983. RHP 1926–28, 30, 32 **Tigers**, Yankees, Giants 594 ip, 32–38, 4.24

The sidearming Gibson was only moderately successful in the majors but was a legend in the Pacific Coast League. He had six 20-win seasons for San Francisco and won 307 minor league games, the last at age 47. /(JK)

Floyd Giebell — 1909– . RHP 1939–41 **Tigers** 68 ip, 3–1, 3.99

Giebell's meteoric career peaked on September 27,

1940, when he beat Cleveland ace Bob Feller and won the AL pennant for Detroit with a fine six-hitter that proved to be his last ML victory. /(EW)

Paul Giel — 1932– . RHP 1954–55, 58–61 **Giants**, Pirates, Twins, A's 240 ip, 11–9, 5.39

Reliever Giel hurled for the original editions of both the San Francisco Giants (1958) and Minnesota Twins (1961). He later became the athletic director at his alma mater, the University of Minnesota, where he had been an All-American single-wing tailback. /(TJ)

Billy Gilbert — 1876–1927. 2B-SS 1901–06, 08–09 Brewers, Baltimore (AL), **Giants**, Cardinals 850 g, .247, 5 hr, 237 rbi. *1 WS, 5 g, .235, 1 rbi*

Gilbert, a scrappy John McGraw-type player, was the keystone star of the Giants infield when they won pennants in 1904 and 1905. McGraw, managing Baltimore, had purchased Gilbert in 1902 to play shortstop. When McGraw took over the Giants in 1903, Gilbert came along and took charge of second base. Gilbert later managed in the minors and coached for the Boston Braves. /(JK)

Charlie Gilbert — 1919–1983. OF 1940–43, 46–47 Dodgers, Cubs, **Phillies** 364 g, .229, 5 hr, 55 rbi

This injury-plagued, fleet outfielder had a weak bat, but nonetheless led the NL with 40 pinch at-bats for the Phillies in 1947. His father, Larry, was a Braves outfielder in 1914–15, and his brother, Tookie, was a Giants first baseman in 1950 and 1953. /(EW)

Wally Gilbert — 1901–1958. 3B 1928–32 **Dodgers** 591 g, .269, 7 hr, 214 rbi

An adventurous third baseman, Gilbert led the NL in errors in 1930 and assists in 1931, when he got six hits in a game and went homerless in 552 AB. /(TG)

Rod Gilbreath — 1952– . 2B-3B 1972–78 **Braves** 500 g, .248, 14 hr, 125 rbi

In seven years with the Braves Gilbreath performed as a utility infielder, mainly at second base. A light hitter, Gilbreath augmented his limited offensive ability by drawing 147 walks in his career. /(DV)

Brian Giles — 1960– . 2B-SS 1981–83, 85–86 **Mets**, Brewers, White Sox 242 g, .228, 6 hr, 39 rbi

Giles was the Mets' regular second baseman in 1983 and hit .245 with 17 steals and 39 runs in 400 at-bats. /(WOR)

George Giles — 1909– . 1B Negro Leagues 1927–38 Philadelphia Stars, Kansas City Monarchs, St. Louis Stars, Detroit Stars, Homestead Grays, Baltimore Elite Giants, Brooklyn Eagles, New York Black Yankees, Kansas City Royal Giants, Gilkerson Union Giants, Pittsburgh Crawfords, Satchel Paige All-Stars .312 (inc.) ☛ *All-Star—35.*

Giles was a superb Negro League first baseman and a lifetime .300 hitter. Black all-star Ted "Double Duty" Radcliffe called Giles "the best colored first baseman I ever saw . . ." Giles played for the St. Louis Stars, one of the Negro Leagues' greatest teams, from 1929 through 1931. In a 1930 eight-game series against major league all-stars, the Stars won six games against the pitching of Willis Hudlin, George Uhle, and Earl Whitehill. The Stars won the Negro National League pennant in 1930 and 1931. In the twilight of his career, Giles played for the Satchel Paige All-Stars. His final contribution to pro baseball was as manager of the 1935 Brooklyn Eagles. /(LL)

Warren Giles — 1896–1979. *Executive.* ☛ *Hall of Fame—1979.*

Back home in Moline, Illinois, from the army in WWI, Giles went to a meeting about the future of the local Three-I League team, and was elected

Warren Giles

president of the club. After success with Moline, he moved to front-office positions in the St. Louis Cardinals' farm system, eventually becoming GM at Rochester, the Cardinals' top minor league club. In 1937 he took over as GM of the Cincinnati Reds; two years later, the team won the NL pennant and in 1940 they became World Champions. Giles was elected club president in 1948.

In 1951, during the owners' voting for a new Commissioner, Giles and Ford Frick stalemated through 17 ballots until Giles withdrew his name. The following year, he was elected president of the NL. During his 18-year tenure, the affable Giles presided over historic franchise shifts, including those of the Dodgers and Giants to the West Coast and the Boston Braves to Milwaukee and then Atlanta. New NL franchises were added with the Mets, Astros, Padres, and Expos. He was elected to the Hall of Fame in 1979. His son, Bill, is president and part owner of the Phillies. /(NLM)

Frank Gilhooley (Flash) — 1892–1959. OF 1911–19 Cardinals, **Yankees**, Red Sox 312 g, .271, 2 hr, 58 rbi

Gilhooley was a reserve outfielder who, in his one season as a regular (1918), led AL outfielders by participating in eight double plays, tying a Yankee record. /(EW)

George Gill — 1909– . RHP 1937–39 **Tigers**, Browns 395 ip, 24–26, 5.05

In May 1939, Gill was one of six Detroit players sent to the Browns in a trade for legendary hurler Bobo Newsom. He then went 1–12 for the worst Browns team in history (43–111). /(TJ)

Carden Gillenwater — 1918– . OF 1940, 43, 45–46, 48 Cardinals, Dodgers, **Braves**, Senators 335 g, .260, 11 hr, 114 rbi

Gillenwater was a glittering defensive outfielder with speed and a strong arm, but a disappointing bat. A regular only with the 1945 Braves, he hit a career-high .288, and in 1946 he tied a major league OF record with 12 putouts in a game. /(EW)

Bob Gillespie (Bunch) — 1918– . RHP 1944, 47–48, 50 Tigers, **White Sox**, Red Sox 202 ip, 5–13, 5.07

Purchased by the White Sox in 1947 after a strong year in the Texas League, Gillespie completed only 1 of 17 starts (5–8, 4.73). /(DB)

Ray Gillespie — Unk.–1979. *Writer.*

A sports writer for 55 years, Gillespie eventually carried BBWAA card No. 1, signifying seniority

among active writers. He was with the St. Louis *Star* until it folded in 1951 and he became associate editor of *The Sporting News*. His biggest scoop was the $5,000 fine and indefinite suspension of Babe Ruth by Yankees manager Miller Huggins in 1925. Friendly with the Pasqual brothers of Mexico, he scored many inside stories when they raided ML teams to stack their Mexican League in 1946. /(NLM)

Jim Gilliam (Junior) — 1928–1978. 2B-3B-OF 1953–66 **Dodgers** 1956 g, .265, 65 hr, 558 rbi *7 WS, 39 g, .211, 2 hr, 12 rbi*
☛ *Rookie of the Year—53. All-Star—56, 59.*

Nicknamed Junior as the youngest member of the Baltimore Elite Giants, Gilliam and shortstop Pee Wee Butts formed one of the great double play combos in Negro National League history during the 1940s. The Tennessean was named to the Negro NL East All-Star team three straight years (1948–50). Finally signed by the Dodgers and sent to Montreal, Gilliam twice led the International League in runs scored (117 in 1951, and 111 in 1952). He also led in fielding in 1952, convincing the Dodgers to shuttle Jackie Robinson between second base and third base and Gilliam between the infield and outfield to get him into the lineup.

As Dodger second baseman in 1953, Gilliam set a league rookie record with 100 walks, led the NL with 17 triples, scored a career-high 125 runs, and

Jim Gilliam

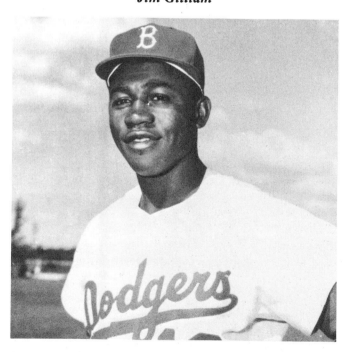

was named Rookie of the Year. He switch-hit homers in the 1953 World Series. In 1956, 1957, and 1959, Gilliam finished second to Willie Mays in stolen bases. He scored at least 100 runs in each of his first four seasons, and hit .300 for the only time in 1956.

Gilliam became a fan favorite in the Dodgers' first season in Los Angeles (1958) by leading the club in hits, doubles, steals, walks, and fielding. Switched to third base, he homered in the second 1959 All-Star Game. He retired after 1964 to become Los Angeles's third base coach, but he came out of retirement in 1965 to hit .280 for the World Champion Dodgers and join first baseman Wes Parker, second baseman Jim Lefebvre, and short-stop Maury Wills in the major leagues' first switch-hitting infield. He retired again and then returned once more to help the Dodgers repeat as NL champions in 1966. Gilliam coached until his sudden death of a brain hemorrhage just before the start of the 1978 World Series. The Dodgers retired his uniform number 19. /(MC)

James A. Gilmore — 1870–Unk. *Executive.*

A former coal company salesman, Gilmore was president of a company manufacturing ventilating machines when he organized and headed the Federal League. After two years of work and one year of operating the league, he received nothing in the settlement that ended the war with the National and American Leagues. /(NLM)

Joe Ginsberg [Myron Nathan] — 1926– . C 1948, 50–54, 56–62 **Tigers**, Indians, A's, Orioles, White Sox, Red Sox, Mets 695 g, .241, 20 hr, 182 rbi

The well-traveled Ginsberg was a second- or third-string catcher except for 1951–52 with Detroit. Yankee Vic Raschi wasn't amused when Ginsberg, a clubhouse comedian, homered to spoil his June 13, 1952 no-hit bid. He was the starting catcher in the Mets' first home game; as a result, his name has been in the "How to Score" section of Shea Stadium programs for over twenty years. /(EW)

Al Gionfriddo (The Little Italian) — 1922– . OF 1944–47 **Pirates**, Dodgers 228 g, .266, 2 hr, 58 rbi. *1 WS, 4 g, .000*

The 5'6" Gionfriddo pressed the best accomplishments of his career into the 1947 Dodger-Yankee World Series. In Game Four, he walked and scored on Cookie Lavagetto's two-run, ninth-inning single, the only hit off the Yankees' Bill Bevens. In Game Six, Gionfriddo went "back, back, back" (as called by announcer Red Barber) to make a crucial, one-handed catch of Joe DiMaggio's 415-foot shot. After the Series, neither Gionfriddo, Bevens, nor Lavagetto played another ML game. /(ME)

Dave Giusti — 1939– . RHP 1962, 64–77 Astros, Cardinals, **Pirates**, Cubs, A's 1717 ip, 100–93, 3.60. *5 LCS, 15 ip, 0–2, 6.60. 1 WS, 5.1 ip, 0–0, 0.00* ☛ *All-Star—73.*

Palmball master Dave Giusti ranks among the best relievers in Pirate history. He began as a starter, leading Houston with 15 wins in 1966 and 186 strikeouts in 1968. After one disappointing season with the Cardinals (1969), he was obtained by Pittsburgh GM Joe L. Brown in a four-player deal. Moved to the bullpen, Giusti led the NL with nine relief wins in 1970, and was named NL Fireman of the Year in 1971 when his 30 saves led the league. He became the first NL pitcher to appear in every game of a four-game LCS (1971), and notched a record three saves. One of the first consistent relief aces, he had four more double-figure save years for Pittsburgh, and in 1974 set the since-broken NL lifetime record for saves with 110. He finished out his career with the A's and Cubs in 1977, and retired with 145 saves. /(ME)

Dan Gladden — 1957– . OF 1983– Giants, **Twins** 731 g, .276, 43 hr, 256 rbi. *1 LCS, 5 g, .350, 5 rbi. 1 WS, 7 g, .290, 1 hr, 7 rbi*

Gladden was hitting .397 at Phoenix (Pacific Coast League) in 1984 when he was promoted to the Giants, and the speedy outfielder maintained his torrid pace in San Francisco, batting .351 with 31 stolen bases in 86 games as the Giants centerfielder. He earned spots on both the Topps and *Baseball Digest* all-rookie teams that year, but has hit no higher than .276 since. Traded to Minnesota before the 1987 season, Gladden was switched from centerfield to left, where he started regularly for the World Champion Twins. In the '87 WS, his grand slam off Bob Forsch broke open Game One. /(SCL)

Fred Gladding — 1936– . RHP 1961–73 **Tigers**, Astros 601 ip, 48–34, 3.13

A product of the majors' bullpen revolution, Gladding was groomed as a relief specialist. In his 13 years in the majors, he started only one game. He also managed only one hit in 63 career at-bats. But Gladding saved 109 games, and with the 1969 Astros the portly reliever's 29 saves led the National League. /(DV)

Fred Glade — 1876–1934. RHP 1902, 04–08 Cubs, **Browns,** Yankees 1072 ip, 52–68, 2.62

After a strong 18–15 rookie year with a 2.27 ERA, Glade, a durable Browns righthander with good control, plummeted to an AL-high 25 losses as St. Louis crashed to the cellar in 1905. He bounced back with winning seasons in the next two years. /(FJO)

Jack Glasscock (Pebbly Jack) — 1859–1947. SS-2B 1879–95 **Cleveland (NL),** Cincinnati (UA), St. Louis (NL) [Browns], Indianapolis (NL), Giants, St. Louis (NL) [Perfectos], Pirates, Louisville (NL), Washington (NL) 1736 g, .290, 27 hr, 752 rbi.
    Manager 1889 **Indianapolis (NL)** 34–33, .507
☛ *Led League—ba 1890* .

Glasscock was one of the National League's premier 19th-century shortstops. He was called "Pebbly Jack" for his habit of groundskeeping at his position, picking up and tossing away pebbles, which some baseball historians claim were imaginary. He played bare-handed, was one of the first to use a signal to inform his catcher which middle infielder would cover second on a steal, and was one of the first shortstops to back up throws to the second baseman. He managed Indianapolis for part of 1889, while leading the NL with 205 hits, and discovered 18-year-old farmboy Amos Rusie in the nearby countryside. In 1890 he replaced shortstop Monte Ward on the Giants when Ward led the defection of talent to the Players' League. Glasscock won the NL batting title that year, hitting .336, and had six singles in six at-bats on September 27. He topped the .300 mark five times. /(JK)

Tommy Glaviano (Harpo, The Rabbit) — 1923– . 3B-OF-2B 1949–53 **Cardinals,** Phillies 389 g, .257, 24 hr, 108 rbi

A favorite of Cardinal owner Sam Breadon, Glaviano was a wild dresser and clubhouse comedian. Errant throws kept the infielder from regular status. In a light rain at Ebbets Field on May 18, 1950, he made four errors at third base for the Cardinals. Three came on successive plays in the ninth inning, allowing the Dodgers to rally and win. /(FJO)

Tom Glavine — 1966– . LHP 1987– **Braves** 432 ip, 23–29, 4.29

The Braves rushed Glavine to the majors, and he led the NL in losses in 1988, going 7–17 with a 4.56 ERA. He started 1989 as one of the hottest pitchers in the league, showing excellent control, but then dropped off in effectiveness later in the season.
    Glavine was the fourth pick of the NHL's Los Angeles Kings in the 1984 draft. /(WOR)

Ralph Glaze — 1882–1968. RHP 1906–08 **Red Sox** 340 ip, 14–21, 2.89

A graduate of Dartmouth, Glaze was picked up by the Red Sox in 1906 from Savannah of the South Atlantic League for $300. Used as a part-time starter and sometimes-reliever, he was a strikeout artist. Glaze became baseball coach at Baylor, Drake, and the University of Southern California, where he also served as athletic director. /(EW)

Whitey Glazner [Charles Franklin] — 1893– . RHP 1920–24 **Pirates,** Phillies 784 ip, 41–48, 4.21

Glazner turned in a brilliant rookie season (14–5, 2.77), then faltered and went to the Phillies in a 1923 deal that brought future Pirate star Lee Meadows to Pittsburgh. /(ME)

Jack Glasscock

Kid Gleason

Kid Gleason [William] — 1866–1933. 2B-RHP 1888–1908, 1912 Phillies, Cardinals, Baltimore NL, **Giants**, Tigers, White Sox 1966 g, .261, 15 hr, 823 rbi; 2389 ip, 134–134, 3.79. 20 wins: 90–91, 93
  Manager 1919–23 **White Sox** 392–364, .519 *1 WS, 3–5, .375*

Best known today as the betrayed manager of the infamous Black Sox, Gleason was a star player of the 1890s. He began as a pitcher with the Phillies. After two losing seasons, he blossomed with a 38–17 mark in 1890 when desertions to the Players' League stripped the Phillies of their regular starters. He never approached that level again, although he twice more topped 20 wins. When the distance from the mound to the plate was increased in 1894, he lost his effectiveness.

A timely hitter and heady player, Gleason switched to second base, helping the Orioles win a pennant in 1895. He was traded the next year to the Giants, where he was named team captain. According to some reports, he was the first to order an intentional base on balls as a way to bypass a strong hitter. In 1897 he had his best offensive year, hitting .319 with 106 RBI. He jumped to the AL in 1901, then returned to the Phillies in 1903 for four more years as the regular second baseman. He stole 328 career bases.

After retiring as a player, he served first as a coach, then as the manager of the White Sox. Nicknamed Kid in part because he was 5'7" but mostly for his enthusiasm, his heart was broken by his players' sellout of the 1919 WS. He continued as manager of the crippled team through 1923, then became a coach for Connie Mack in Philadelphia. /(JK)

Jerry Don Gleaton — 1957– . LHP 1979–83, 84–85, 87-Rangers, Mariners, White Sox, **Royals** 258 ip, 10–18, 4.72

Gleaton was the Rangers' first-round draft pick in June of 1979, signed out of the University of Texas. After the 1980 season, he was included in an 11-player trade to Seattle that featured Rick Honeycutt and Richie Zisk. Gleaton was released by the White Sox before finding a home as a set-up man in the 1987 Royals bullpen. /(NLM)

Jim Gleeson (Gee Gee) — 1912– . OF 1936, 39–42 Indians, **Cubs** Reds 392 g, .263, 16 hr, 154 rbi

Gleeson, a switch-hitter, hit .313 for the 1940 Cubs in his one solid season. He met Yogi Berra while in the Navy and coached under him with the Yankees in 1964. He also managed in the Yankee system and was a Brewers scouting supervisor. /(NLM)

Marty Glickman — 1907– . *Broadcaster.*

An All-East football tailback at Syracuse University and a sprinter on the 1936 U.S. Olympic team, Glickman broadcast games from the Western Union ticker on WHN in New York before WWII, and broadcast a nightly re-creation of a New York game from 1940 to 1953. When night baseball took over and the Dodgers moved to Los Angeles, Glickman concentrated on New York pro football broadcasts. /(NLM)

Al Glossop — 1912– . 2B-SS-3B 1939–40, 42–43, 46 Giants, Braves, **Phillies**, Dodgers, Cubs 309 g, .209, 15 hr, 86 rbi

The switch-hitting infielder was the Phillies' regular second baseman in 1942. Sold by the Dodgers to the Cubs in September 1943, he spent the 1944–45 seasons in the military and appeared in only four ML games after his return. /(EGM)

Bill Glynn — 1925- . 1B 1949, 52-54 Phillies, **Indians** 310 g, .249, 10 hr, 56 rbi

Glynn became Cleveland's first baseman when Luke Easter suffered a broken foot in 1953. He lost the job on June 1, 1954, when the Indians acquired Vic Wertz. However, in a July 5 game against Detroit, he hit three of his 10 ML home runs. /(ME)

Ed Glynn (The Flushing Flash) — 1953- . LHP 1975-83 **Tigers**, **Mets**, Indians 262 ip, 12-17, 4.12

A good strikeout pitcher, The Flushing Flash was a Shea Stadium hot dog vendor before Detroit signed him in 1971. Only one of the reliever's nine seasons was spent entirely in the majors (1980, with the Mets). /(JCA)

Larry Goetz — 1900-1962. *Umpire* NL 1936-57 *3 WS 2 ASU*

Goetz umpired in the NL for 22 years. A typical instance of his firm handling of dissenters came in 1956 when the Reds' Frank Robinson disputed a strike call longer than Goetz thought appropriate. The ump ordered the Giants' Steve Ridzik to pitch and called strike three while Robinson was still arguing. /(RTM)

Bill Gogolewski — 1947- . RHP 1970-75 **Senators/ Rangers**, Indians, White Sox 502 ip, 15-24, 4.02

Except for a pair of saves recorded with the 1975 White Sox, journeyman starter Gogolewski's decisions came with the moribund Senators and Rangers. His best year was 6-5 (2.76 ERA) in 1971 for Washington. /(DV)

Jim Golden — 1936- . RHP 1960-63 Dodgers, **Astros** 208 ip, 9-13, 4.54

A marginal pitcher with the 1960-61 Dodgers, Golden posted his best mark in a one-year stint with the expansion Houston Colt .45s in 1962. He went 7-11 and batted .222. /(DV)

Gordon Goldsberry — 1927- . 1B 1949-52 **White Sox**, Browns 217 g, .241, 6 hr, 56 rbi

The matinee idol Californian led the AL in pinch hits with 12 for the 1950 Chisox. He later became the Cubs' director of minor leagues and scouting. /(RL)

Peter Golenbock — 1946- . *Writer.*

In 1972 Golenbock was a lawyer with Prentice-Hall, checking reports, when he induced them to publish his book about the Yankees, *Dynasty*. In 1978 *The Bronx Zoo*, written with Sparky Lyle, sold 220,000 hardcover copies. His other baseball books include *Guidry*, with Ron Guidry, *Number 1*, with Billy Martin, and *Bums*, about the Brooklyn Dodgers. /(NLM)

Mike Goliat — 1925- . 2B 1949-52 **Phillies**, Browns 249 g, .225, 20 hr, 99 rbi. *1 WS, 4 g, .214, 1 rbi*

Despite never having played second base in the minors, Goliat started there for the 1950 NL Champion Whiz Kids. He struggled defensively, and his .234 average that year was his career best. /(JK)

Dave Goltz — 1949- . RHP 1972-83 **Twins**, Dodgers, Angels 2039 ip, 113-109, 3.69. 20 wins: 77 *1 LCS, 4 ip, 0-0, 7.36. 1 WS, 3 ip, 0-0, 5.40*
☛ *Led League—w 77.*

The 6'4" Goltz, the first native Minnesotan originally signed by the Twins to reach their major league roster, was throwing in his parents' backyard when he was discovered by a Twins scout in 1966. In his eight years with the Twins, Goltz became the fourth winningest pitcher in club history, never having a losing season. His ascent to the majors was thwarted by arm trouble and a stint in Vietnam. He rebounded for a combined 14-3 mark and a seven-inning no-hitter for Lynchburg (Carolina League) in 1971, his last full minor league season. Though a notoriously slow starter (he didn't win a game in April until 1979), he won 14 or more games five straight times (1975-79) for Minnesota. He peaked at 20-11 in 1977, tying for the AL lead in victories and starts, and one-hitting the powerful Red Sox on August 23.

Goltz opted for free agency and signed a six-year, multimillion contract with the Dodgers for 1980. He shut out the Giants twice that April, then struggled. Los Angeles released him in May 1982. He managed an 8-5 comeback with the '82 division champion Angels, but was finished by a torn rotator cuff in 1983. /(MC)

Lefty Gomez [Vernon Louis] (Goofy, The Gay Castillion) — 1908-1988. LHP 1930-43 **Yankees**, Senators 2503 ip, 189-102, 3.34. 20 wins: 31-32, 34, 37 *5 WS, 50 ip, 6-0, 2.86*
☛ *Led League—w 34, 37. Led League—era 34, 37. Led League—k 33-34, 37. All-Star—33-39. Hall of Fame—1972.*

Remembered mainly for his colorful personality, Lefty Gomez was also one of baseball's greatest winners, ranking third in Yankee history in regular-season wins with 189. His 6–0 World Series record gave him the most wins without a loss in World Series history. His three victories in All-Star Game competition (against one loss) also are a record.

Gomez's zaniness set him apart from the decorous Yankees of the 1930s. He once held up a World Series game, exasperating manager Joe McCarthy (as he did with some frequency), to watch an airplane pass by. Gomez got away with needling his buddy, Joe DiMaggio, because DiMaggio, like everyone else, enjoyed the Gomez wit, which produced such statements as: "I've got a new invention. It's a revolving bowl for tired goldfish."

The Yankees purchased Gomez from his hometown San Francisco Seals in 1929 for $35,000. Two years later he won 21 games for them. His smoking fastball belied his slender frame. He was a nail, with a whiplash arm and a high leg kick.

Lefty Gomez

Gomez and righthander Red Ruffing formed the lefty-righty pitching core for the great New York teams of the 1930s. In 1934 he led the league in seven major categories, including wins (26), ERA (2.33), and strikeouts (158), the pitching equivalent of the Triple Crown. He led the league again in the top three pitching categories in 1937.

Arm miseries hounded him throughout his career. As his fastball lost its effectiveness, Gomez moved from power pitcher to finesse pitcher. "I'm throwing as hard as I ever did," he quipped, "the ball's just not getting there as fast." Gomez fooled hitters and made a beautiful, slow curve work for him. He had a great comeback in 1941 (15–5) after a 3–3 mark in 1940, leading the league in winning percentage (.750).

Gomez threw a shutout in 1941 while issuing 11 walks, the most walks ever allowed in a shutout. And though a notoriously poor hitter, he produced the first RBI in All-Star history and singled home the winning run in the 1937 World Series clincher.

After pitching one game for Washington (he lost) in 1943, Gomez retired, later to hook up with the Wilson sporting goods company as a goodwill ambassador. He was asked on joining Wilson why he had left his last position. Gomez, who never took himself seriously, responded that he left because he couldn't "get the side out." /(MG)

Luis Gomez [born Luis Gomez Sanchez] — 1951– . SS-2B-3B 1974–81 **Twins**, Blue Jays, Braves 609 g, .210, 0 hr, 90 rbi

Born in Mexico and raised in Los Angeles, the 5′9″ Gomez played freshman basketball at UCLA with Bill Walton. Gomez was a reserve in Minnesota before becoming Toronto's shortstop for 1978. He set an Atlanta record in 1980 with a .968 fielding percentage at shortstop and strung together 42 consecutive errorless games. But, batting .191, he lost his job to Rafael Ramirez. /(MC)

Preston Gomez — 1923– . 2B-SS 1944 **Senators** 8 g, .286, 0 hr, 2 rbi.
Manager 1969–72, 74–75, 80 **Padres**, Astros, Cubs 346–529, .395

Gomez played eight games for the Senators in 1944 without having any minor league experience. He was sent down the following spring and did not return as a player. After a long minor league apprenticeship, the personable Cuban was named Padres manager in 1969 and remained until eleven games into the 1972 season. His 1974 Astro team finished fourth at 81–81, the only time a Gomez-managed team finished out of last place. Twice in his managerial career he pinch hit for pitchers who had no-hitters going, Clay Kirby (with the Padres) and Don Wilson (Astros). /(BC)

Ruben Gomez — 1927- . RHP 1953-60, 62, 67 **Giants**, Phillies, Indians, Twins 1454 ip, 76-86, 4.09. *1 WS, 7.1 ip, 1-0, 2.45*

Puerto Rican-born Ruben Gomez was an erratic starter, given to wildness, who went 17-9 for the 1954 World Champion Giants despite a league-leading 109 walks. Late in his rookie 1953 season, Gomez hit Carl Furillo with a pitch, and the Dodger outfielder went at Giant manager Leo Durocher, who the Dodgers accused of ordering beanballs. Furillo broke his hand in the ensuing melee, ending his season, while his .344 batting average stood to cop the NL crown.

The Braves' Joe Adcock had hit seven HR in nine games coming into a night game at Milwaukee on July 18, 1956. Gomez hit him on the wrist in his first at-bat and they exchanged remarks as Adcock went to first base. Adcock charged the mound; Gomez threw the ball, hitting him in the thigh, and then ran for the safety of the Giants' dugout. Gomez was fined $250. He also had a beanball war with Cardinals pitcher Sam Jones in 1957, and that July 16, Gomez put Frank Robinson in the hospital, hitting him in the head with a pitch. /(JK)

Jesse Gonder — 1936- . C 1960-67 Yankees, Reds, **Mets**, Braves, Pirates 395 g, .251, 26 hr, 94 rbi

The burly receiver was the 1962 Pacific Coast League batting champ and RBI leader. Defensive deficiencies and his lack of speed kept him a backup. Nearly 20 percent of his ML at-bats were as a pinch hitter. /(CR)

Hiroshi Gondo — 1940- . P 1961-64 **Chunichi Dragons**

Virtually a one-man staff, Gondo won 35 games and worked 429 innings as rookie for the Chunichi Dragons. But he was finished at age 24, the victim of a torn rotator cuff. Elder brother Masatochi pitched nearly 15 seasons for the Hanshin Tigers, but never with spectacular success. /(MC)

Mike Gonzales — 1890-1977. C 1912, 14-21, 24-29, 31-32 Braves, Reds, **Cardinals**, Giants, Cubs 1042 g, .253, 13 hr, 263 rbi. *1 WS, 2 g, .000.* Manager 1938, 40 **Cardinals** 9-13

Gonzales coined a standard phrase with his pithy assessment of the abilities of a player he scouted:

"Good field, no hit." That could also describe the playing career of the Cuban-born catcher. Although he played for five NL teams, he is most often associated with the Cardinals, for whom he served as regular catcher (1916-18 and 1924), longtime coach, and twice as interim manager. /(JK)

Pedro Gonzales — 1938- . 2B-3B 1963-67 Yankees, **Indians** 407 g, .244, 8 hr, 70 rbi. *1 WS, 1 g, .000*

One of the many ML infielders from San Pedro de Macoris, Dominican Republic, Gonzalez couldn't dislodge Bobby Richardson in New York and failed to hit enough to hold his job in Cleveland. He was suspended in 1965 for swinging his bat at pitcher Larry Sherry. /(ME)

Fernando Gonzalez — 1950- . 2B-3B 1972-74, 77-79 Pirates, Royals, Yankees, **Padres** 404 g, .235, 17 hr, 104 rbi

A lifetime .302 pinch hitter, the squat, hard-swinging Gonzalez was a utility infielder and outfielder until the Padres made him their second baseman for 1978-79. He opened the "Fernando Gonzalez Escuela de Beisbol" in his native Puerto Rico. /(JCA)

Julio Gonzalez [aka Julio Cesar Hernandez Hernandez] — 1959- . 2B-SS-3B 1977-83 **Astros**, Cardinals, Tigers 370 g, .235, 4 hr, 66 rbi

Signed out of Puerto Rico by the Cubs, Gonzalez went to Houston for Greg Gross in 1976. He was most active in his rookie 1977 season, hitting .245 as a shortstop and third baseman. /(MC)

Tony Gonzalez — 1936- . OF 1960-71 Reds, **Phillies**, Padres, Braves, Angels 1559 g, .286, 103 hr, 615 rbi. *1 LCS, 3 g, .357, 1 hr, 2 rbi*

Gonzalez spent his best years with the Phillies (mid-1960 through 1968). The Cuban led NL outfielders in fielding average three times, including 1962, when he had no errors in 276 chances. He was the first regular centerfielder ever to field 1.000, and only the third outfielder overall.

In 1967 Gonzalez's career-high .339 batting average was second in the NL and the majors. He was a reliable hitter for average, drew walks, and at times showed good power. He hit a career-high 20 HR in 1962 and in 1963 his career highs of 36 doubles and 12 triples tied for third and finished second in the NL, respectively.

Gonzalez was taken by the Padres in the expansion draft, but was traded to the Braves in June 1969 and helped them to their division title with a .294

average, 10 HR, and 50 RBI in 89 games for Atlanta. He homered off the Mets' Tom Seaver in Game One of the LCS but also made the final error of the Braves' blunder-filled eighth inning. With two out and the bases loaded, he let J.C. Martin's single get past him in centerfield and three runs scored to put the game out of reach. Gonzalez's .357 average in the series tied him with Hank Aaron to lead Braves batters, and his four runs scored tied him with Rico Carty. Gonzalez was sold to the Angels in mid-1970, and when he dropped to a career-low .245 average in 1971, it ended his major league career. /(JFC)

Johnny Gooch — 1897–1975. C 1921–30, 33 **Pirates**, Dodgers, Reds, Red Sox 815 g, .280, 7 hr, 293 rbi. *2 WS, 6 g, .000*

Gooch was a dependable switch-hitter and slick-fielding catcher for Pittsburgh from 1922 through 1927 who platooned first with Walter Schmidt and then with Earl Smith. He hit .329 as a rookie, and was part of a Pirate youth movement that made them a powerhouse in the 1920s. Gooch was later a successful minor league manager and a Pittsburgh coach in 1937–38. /(ME)

Wilbur Good (Lefty) — 1885–1963. OF 1905, 08–16, 18 Yankees, Indians, Braves, **Cubs**, Phillies, White Sox 750 g, .258, 9 hr, 187 rbi

An extra outfielder most of his career, the 5′6″ Good was responsible for two events of some small significance in Cub history. On June 19, 1913, he hit the first pinch homer in Cub annals, and on August 18, 1915, he became the only Cub player to steal second, third, and home in the same inning. /(ARA)

Gladys Gooding — 1893–1963. Organist.

Larry MacPhail discovered Gladys Gooding at a hockey game at Madison Square Garden, where she played the organ for the New York Rangers and, later, the basketball Knickerbockers. He thought organ music might be a fine thing for Ebbets Field. Beginning in 1942, she was a favorite of Dodger fans and a celebrity in her own right until the team went west in 1958. She wrote the words and music for "Follow the Dodgers," the team's fight song even after the move to Los Angeles. /(NLM)

Dwight Gooden (Doc, Doctor K) — 1964– . RHP 1984– **Mets** 1291 ip, 100–39, 2.64. 20 wins: 85 *2 LCS, 35 ip, 0–1, 1.06. 1 WS, 9 ip, 0–2, 8.00* ☛ *Rookie of the Year—84. Led League—w 85. Led League—era 85. Led League—k 84–85. Cy Young Award—85. All-Star—84–86, 88.*

Gooden had a record-breaking Rookie of the Year season in 1984 after jumping straight to the majors from Lynchburg of the Class-A Carolina League. The Mets' number-one pick in the June 1982 draft (the fifth player taken) had led the league in wins, ERA, and strikeouts in 1983, fanning 300 in 191 innings, and Davey Johnson had sworn that wherever he was managing in 1984, he would have Gooden. But after he was named the Mets' manager, he discovered that GM Frank Cashen wanted to bring the 19-year-old Gooden along slowly; Cashen remembered the case of Tim Leary, once a hot Mets prospect, who blew out his arm in his 1981 debut on a cold, windy day at Wrigley after concealing pain. Gooden made his debut indoors, on April 7, in the Astrodome. He went on to set a ML rookie record with 276 strikeouts in only 218 innings. The strikeouts earned him the nickname Doctor K and a rooting section in the upper deck that hung out a red K for each strikeout during his starts. He tied the ML mark for strikeouts in two consecutive games, with 32 in starts on September 12 and 17, which, combined with his September 7 start, gave him a record 43 in three straight games. Going 17–9 with a 2.60 ERA, he instantly became the Mets' ace and made them overnight contenders. He was the youngest All-Star ever, and he and Fernando Valenzuela combined to strike out six consecutive batters, between them breaking Carl Hubbell's record.

Gooden reached new heights in 1985, winning the Cy Young award with the "pitcher's Triple Crown," leading the NL in wins (24–4), ERA (1.53), and strikeouts (268). His 16 complete games also led the league, and his rising fastball and snapping curve dominated NL hitters. Curveballs are referred to by ballplayers as "Uncle Charley," but Gooden's is called "Lord Charles." The shy but poised Gooden was the toast of New York; the only fault that could be found with him was that his big motion meant he had trouble holding runners close to first base. But the Mets, trying to protect their young superstar's future health, gave pitching coach Mel Stottlemyre the assignment of making Gooden less reliant on throwing hard. Perhaps it was that; perhaps it was hitters learning to lay off his rising fastball, which was often above the strike zone. Whatever it was, Gooden after 1985 was never the totally dominating strikeout king he had been. He went 4–0 in April 1986, but the question in every newspaper's sports section was "What's wrong with Gooden?" after he surrendered a home run to the first batter he faced that year, Pittsburgh's R.J. Reynolds. In contrast to his fine performance in the 1984 All-Star Game, in the 1986 game he gave up a two-run homer to Lou Whitaker and took the loss. No longer overpowering, he finished with 200 strikeouts in 250 innings, a 17–6 record, and a 2.84 ERA. The Mets won the World Championship, but Gooden went without a postseason win. He took a tough 1–0 loss in the LCS opener as the Astros' Mike Scott overwhelmed the Mets; the Astros' run came on a Glenn Davis home run. Gooden pitched masterfully in the Mets' Game Five victory, surrendering only one run in 10 innings in a matchup against Nolan Ryan; the Mets won in the 12th inning. It was the first time that Davey Johnson had ever let Gooden pitch beyond the ninth inning. Gooden set NLCS records for a seven-game series with 20 strikeouts and eight walks. He pitched less well in the World Series, and lost two games; he has rarely pitched well on three days' rest.

In 1987, following winter problems in his hometown Tampa that included a police beating of Gooden and his nephew Gary Sheffield, who would later be signed by the Brewers, Gooden went into a drug rehabilitation program just before the start of the season. He went 15–7 with a 3.21 ERA after coming back, but the club blamed his absence in the first two months for the Mets' narrow division title loss. In 1988 he declared that he wanted to be called Doc instead of Doctor K now that he was a different kind of pitcher. His 18–9, 3.19 record led the Mets to a division title, but he again lost the All-Star Game, tying the record for lifetime losses in the mid-summer classic. And again he pitched well in the LCS, but not well enough to win. He took no-decisions in the Mets' Game One victory and their 12th-inning loss in Game Four, giving up a game-tying solo homer to the Dodgers' Mike Scioscia in the ninth inning of the latter contest. He suffered his first injury in 1989, going down with a sore shoulder in the middle of the year, exactly the sort of injury the Mets had sought to prevent with their change of his pitching style. At the time, he was 9–4 with a 2.99 ERA and was the only consistently good starter in the Mets' rotation; his loss doomed the team's pennant hopes. He came back briefly in relief at the end of the season./(SH)

Billy Goodman — 1926–1984. 2B-1B-3B-OF **Red Sox**, Orioles, White Sox, Astros 1623 g, .300, 19 hr, 591 rbi. *1 WS, 5 g, .231, 1 rbi*
☛ *Led League—ba 50. All-Star—49, 53.*

The versatile Goodman led the AL in batting with a .354 mark in 1950, one of five times he hit .300. He hit .290 or better 11 straight years (1948–58). But despite his steady hitting and versatile fielding, Goodman never quite achieved stardom.

Starting out as the regular first baseman for the powerful 1948 Red Sox, he led AL first basemen in total chances per game in 1948 and in fielding in 1949 while hitting .298. Because the lefthanded batter had no home run power and was capable at almost every position, he moved aside to accommodate the arrival of slugging first baseman Walt Dropo in 1950. Goodman won his batting championship that season while playing the outfield and all four infield positions. He took over as the regular at second base in 1952 after Bobby Doerr retired, and he led AL second basemen in total chances per game. He kept the job through 1956, finishing third in the AL in batting in 1953 (.313) and second in walks in 1955 (99). After leading the league's second basemen in errors in 1956 and starting out batting .063 in 1957, he was traded to the Orioles for Mike Fornieles. From then on, he played mainly third base, backing up George Kell for a year and then moving on to the White Sox in 1958. He was a dependable reserve on the White Sox' 1959 pennant-winners. /(WOR)

Ival Goodman (Goodie) — 1908–1984. OF 1935–44 **Reds**, Cubs 1107 g, .281, 95 hr, 525 rbi. *2 WS, 11 g, .295, 6 rbi*
☛ *All-Star—38–39.*

En route to the Cincinnati Reds Hall of Fame, Goodman led the NL in triples his first two seasons, set a since-broken Reds' season homer mark (30 in 1938), and played in two All-Star Games and World Series. In the 1939 Series opener, right fielder Goodman and centerfielder Harry Craft let Charlie Keller's fly ball drop between them for a triple; Keller soon scored the Yankees' winning run./(TJ)

Ed Goodson — 1948– . 1B-3B 1970–77 **Giants**, Braves, Dodgers 515 g, .260, 30 hr, 170 rbi. *1 LCS, 1 g, .000. 1 WS, 1 g, .000*

Goodson's pure, lefthanded swing was at its best in 1973, his first full ML season. As the Giants' most-used third baseman he batted .302 with 12 homers in 102 games. With the Dodgers, he was almost exclusively a pinch hitter./(JCA)

Danny Goodwin — 1953- . DH-1B 1975, 77-82 Angels, **Twins**, A's 252 g, .236, 13 hr, 81 rbi

Twice baseball's number-one draft pick, the intelligent catcher opted for pre-med studies in 1971, then accepted a six-figure bonus from the Angels upon graduation. However, he damaged his throwing arm early, and saw only limited ML action as a DH and first baseman. /(JCA)

Marv Goodwin — 1893-1925. RHP 1916-17, 19-22, 25 Senators, **Cardinals**, Reds 447 ip, 21-25, 3.30

Goodwin had just pitched his way back to the majors in 1925 when he died in an off-season plane crash on an Air Reserve training flight. Goodwin was one of the spitballers permitted to openly continue using the pitch after 1919. /(JK)

Don Gordon — 1959- . RHP 1986-88 Blue Jays, **Indians** 132 ip, 3-8, 4.72

Gordon came to Cleveland as part of the deal that sent Phil Niekro to the Blue Jays in August 1987. The reliever never got his ERA below 4.00 in the majors, but led the International League in ERA in 1985 with a 2.07 mark for Syracuse. /(JFC)

Joe Gordon (Flash) — 1915-1978. 2B 1938-43, 46-50 **Yankees**, Indians 1566 g, .268, 253 hr, 975 rbi. *6 WS, 29 g, .243, 4 hr, 16 rbi.*
   Manager 1958-61, 69 **Indians**, Tigers, A's, Royals 305-318, .490
☛ *Most Valuable Player—42 . All-Star—39-43, 46-49.*

The acrobatic Joe Gordon would be remembered for his defensive skills alone, but he was also a powerful and timely hitter. He holds the AL second basemen's records for career HR (246) and HR in a season (32 in 1948). The low-key, humorous player emerged from the Yankee system to take Tony Lazzeri's place. He hit for the cycle on September 8, 1940. In the 1941 World Series Gordon snuffed out Dodger rallies with his glove and went 7-for-14 with a .929 slugging average.

In 1942 Gordon was the AL MVP, hitting .322 with 103 RBI. The eight-time All-Star missed two seasons for army service. He hit just .210 when he returned in 1946, and after exactly 1,000 games and 1,000 hits for the Yankees, was traded to Cleveland for Allie Reynolds. His hitting form returned, with career highs of 32 HR and 124 RBI in 1948, as he teamed with Lou Boudreau for a pennant and Gordon's sixth World Series.

Gordon was named Cleveland manager in 1958 and the Indians finished second in 1959. In 1960 he was part of baseball's most unusual trade when the Indians and Tigers swapped managers, with Gordon and Jimmy Dykes trading places. Gordon managed the Kansas City A's for part of 1961, and the Kansas City Royals for all of their maiden 1969 season. /(JK)

Sid Gordon — 1917-1975. OF-3B 1941-43, 46-55 **Giants**, Braves, Pirates 1475 g, .283, 202 hr, 805 rbi
☛ *All-Star—48-49.*

Gordon became one of Manhattan's most popular players, after being born and raised in Brooklyn. A reliable outfielder who could play acceptably at third base, the stocky righthanded hitter hit .251 as a Giants rookie in 1943, then spent two years in the service. In 1947 the Giants broke the single-season home run record, and Gordon hit 13 of their 221. In 1948 he blossomed with 30 homers, 107 RBI, and a .299 batting average. He held out in the spring of 1949 but finally settled for $2,500 less than he'd asked for. After the season he was sent to the Braves in a multiplayer deal that brought Alvin Dark and Eddie Stanky to the Giants. A check for $2,500 from Giants owner Horace Stoneham underscored the esteem in which Gordon was held. /(FS)

Tom Gordon (Flash) — 1967- . RHP 1988- **Royals** 179 ip, 17-11, 3.78

A starter in the minors, Gordon came up to the Royals as a reliever. The 5'9" 160-lb flamethrower was 10-2 in July as a set-up man, with 78 strikeouts in 66 innings (twice as many strikeouts as hits allowed), when he was moved into the rotation. He finished the year 17-9. /(SFS)

George Gore (Piano Legs) — 1857-1933. OF 1879-92 **Cubs**, Giants, New York (PL), Cardinals 1310 g (1301 N/C), .301 (.303 N/C), 46 hr, 526 rbi (617 N/C)
☛ *Led League—ba 1880.*

Gore was signed by Chicago's Cap Anson after playing for a local New England team in an exhibition against the White Stockings (later the Cubs). In 1880, his second season, Gore won the NL batting crown with a .360 mark (Anson's .337 was second) and also led in slugging percentage (.463). Anson claimed that Gore was too much the playboy, however, and when Chicago lost the postseason championship series with St. Louis, the American Association pennant-winners, Gore was dispatched to the Gothams (later renamed the Giants).

Gore led the NL in runs scored in 1881-82, and in walks three times. Scoring over 100 runs seven times, with a high of 150 (1886), he finished his career with 1,327 runs in 1,310 games. Gore, Harry Stovey, and Billy Hamilton are the only players

George Gore

(4,000 at-bats) with more runs scored than games. Gore set a ML record on June 25, 1881, when he had seven stolen bases in a game. On July 9, 1885, he hit two doubles and three triples to set a since-tied ML record of five extra-base hits in a game, and he went 6-for-6 on May 7, 1880. He was called Piano Legs for his bulging calf muscles. /(JK)

Tom Gorman — 1925- . RHP 1952–59 Yankees, **A's** 689 ip, 36–36, 3.77. *2 WS, 3.2 ip, 0–0, 2.45*

Gorman was about to be sent to the minors in 1952 when the Yankees gave him one more chance in relief against Washington. He responded by pitching nine innings of no-hit, no-run ball. Gorman went on to save 18 games for the A's in 1955, one behind the league leader. /(RTM)

Tom Gorman (Big Tom) — 1916–1986. LHP 1939 **Giants** 5 ip, 0–0, 7.20.
   Umpire NL 1951–76 *2 LCS 5 WS 5 ASU*

Gorman spent three years pitching in the Giants' organization before enlisting in the army in 1941. Upon his return in 1946, an arm injury curtailed his pitching career, and he turned to umpiring in 1947 in the New England League. He was promoted to

the NL in 1951 and quickly became one of its most respected arbiters. In the heat of the 1962 pennant race, Gorman discovered the San Francisco groundskeepers had heavily watered the infield to slow down Dodger base-stealing star Maury Wills. Gorman held up the start of the game for an hour and a half until the basepaths dried out. In the 1968 WS, Gorman was behind the plate when Bob Gibson struck out 17 Tiger batters. After retiring as a field ump, Gorman served as a NL supervisor of umpires. The entertaining after-dinner speaker's autobiography, *Three and Two*, was published in 1979. /(RTM)

Tom Gorman [Thomas Patrick] — 1957- . LHP 1981–87 Expos, **Mets**, Phillies, Padres 214 ip, 12–10, 4.34

The 6'4" Gorman failed to become the ace reliever the Expos had hoped for. He developed a forkball, which kept him in the majors for three seasons as a Mets middle reliever. He went 6–0 (2.97) in 1984, but lost the good forkball in 1985 (4–4, 5.13). /(JCA)

Hank Gornicki [Frank Ted] — 1911- . RHP 1941–43, 46 Cardinals, Cubs, **Pirates** 285 ip, 15–19, 3.38

Gornicki pitched a shutout in his first major league start, but could not stick with a talented St. Louis club. He led the Pirates with a 2.57 ERA in 1942 and in appearances (42) in 1943. /(ME)

Johnny Gorsica [born John Gorczyca] — 1915- . RHP 1940–44, 46–47 **Tigers** 724 ip, 31–39, 4.18. *1 WS, 11 ip, 0–0, 0.79*

Gorsica started out playing first base, but made the Tigers in 1940 after just two seasons as a pitcher. Relying on an overhand sinkerball, he both started and relieved. Provided great relief work in 1940 WS, going 4.2 innings in Game Two, 6.2 innings in Game Six after starters were knocked out. Both games were losses, but he compiled a 0.79 ERA. /(NLM)

Johnny Goryl — 1933- . 2B-3B-SS 1957–59, 62–64 Cubs, **Twins** 276 g, .225, 16 hr, 48 rbi.
   Manager 1980–81 **Twins** 34–38, .472

The low-key Goryl spent 20 consecutive years with the Twins organization as a utility infielder, a minor league player and manager, a major league coach, and, finally, the Twins' manager when Gene Mauch resigned in August 1980. Replaced by Billy Gardner in 1981, Goryl became Cleveland's third base coach. /(JCA)

Jim Gosger — 1942- . OF-1B 1963, 65–71, 73–74 Red Sox, **A's**, Pilots, Mets, Expos 705 g, .226, 30 hr, 177 rbi

The hustling, lefthanded outfielder spent only three full seasons in the majors. Though he started the season as an original Seattle Pilot, he played in 10 games for the 1969 Mets, enough to earn a $100 World Series check. /(JCA)

Goose Goslin [Leon Allen] — 1900–1971. OF 1921–1938 **Senators**, Browns, Tigers 2287 g, .316, 248 hr, 1609 rbi. *5 WS, 32 g, .287, 7 hr, 18 rbi* ☛ *Led League—ba 28. Led League—rbi 24. Hall of Fame—1968.*

Although the sweet-hitting Goslin played for the usually mediocre Senators (in three separate tours) and Browns for much of his career, he managed to squeeze his way into five World Series, making the most of each appearance. In the 1924 Series, the Senators won their first and only world title, with Goslin batting .344 and contributing three HR and seven RBI. The following year he hit another three HR, although the Senators lost to Pittsburgh. After a subpar Series in 1933 back with the Senators, he drove in the winning run in Game Two of the 1934 Series for his new team, the Tigers, who lost to the Cardinals in seven games. The Tigers beat the Cubs in six games in 1935, thanks to Goslin's game-winning RBI single in the bottom of the ninth of the final game.

Clark Griffith almost didn't sign the powerful left fielder. When Griffith went to scout him in a Sally League game in South Carolina, Goslin managed to get hit on the head by a fly ball. But he also hit three HR in the game. Goslin's career was true to that good-hit, no-field pattern. Opposing players often described the arm-waving Goslin chasing a fly ball as a bird with wings flapping, giving further meaning to his nickname. As a young player, one defensive asset was a strong arm, but he ruined even that during one spring training with an ill-advised attempt to learn to put the shot.

Between 1924 and 1928, Goslin's lowest average was .334, yet his only batting title came in a rather unusual finish in 1928. He was tied with Heinie Manush on the last day of the season, and coincidentally, the Senators were playing Manush's Browns. Goslin went into his last at-bat leading Manush, but didn't want to bat for fear of making an out and losing the precarious lead. His teammates goaded him to bat. Goslin then tried to get himself thrown out of the game. He ended up with

Goose Goslin with the Browns

an infield hit and the batting title, having gone 7 for his final 15 to bat .379. Goslin would later join Manush in St. Louis for the 1930 through 1932 seasons.

Goslin was also responsible for the first fine levied against an umpire. In the 1935 fall classic, Goslin got into a heated discussion with Hall of Fame arbiter Bill Klem, during which Klem lost his temper and used what Goslin later described as "overripe language." Commissioner Landis then fined Klem, not Goslin.

Goslin spent his final years running a boat-rental concession in Bridgeton, New Jersey, his native state, and died just three days after his 1928 batting rival Manush. /(SEW)

Howie Goss — 1934- . OF 1962–63 Pirates, **Astros** 222 g, .216, 11 hr, 54 rbi

The 6'4" outfielder showed power during his nine-year minor league career by hitting 172 home runs. With the 1963 Colt .45's, Goss managed nine HR in 133 games. /(RTM)

Goose Gossage [Richard Michael] — 1951– . RHP 1972– White Sox, Pirates, **Yankees**, Padres, Cubs, Giants 1636 ip, 113–98, 2.92. *4 LCS, 11 ip, 1–1, 4.91. 3 WS, 13.2 ip, 1–0, 2.63*
☛ *All-Star—75–78, 80–82, 84–85.*

Gossage was one of the most consistent relief pitchers ever, and is second on the all-time save list with 302 (entering 1989) and fourth in relief victories (101). The hard thrower had three mediocre seasons with the White Sox, but broke through in 1975, when he saved 26 games and won 9. The White Sox made him a starter in 1976, but Gossage went 9–17 and never started another game. The Pirates traded for him the following year, and he went 11–9 with 26 saves and a 1.62 ERA, his lowest for a full season. Gossage became a free agent and

Goose Gossage

signed with the Yankees, taking over the stopper role from the previous year's Cy Young winner, Sparky Lyle, as New York won its second straight World Championship. Gossage went 10–11 with 27 saves and pitched 134 innings, fourth-highest on the staff. He saved the AL East playoff game against the Red Sox, and was on the mound when New York clinched the pennant and World Championship.

Gossage's 1979 season was cut short following a clubhouse scuffle with Cliff Johnson, but he came back to save a career-high 33 games in 1980. He allowed George Brett's LCS-clinching home run in Game Three. Gossage was extremely effective during the strike-shortened 1981 season, allowing just 22 hits in 47 innings to go with 48 strikeouts and 20 saves. He saved all three wins over Milwaukee during the divisional playoffs and both Yankees wins over the Dodgers in the World Series. Following two more seasons in New York (30 saves in 1982, 13–5 with 22 saves in 1983), he signed with the Padres as a free agent and helped them reach the World Series in 1984. Gossage compiled 72 saves during his first three seasons with the Padres, but slumped in 1987 and 1988 (with Chicago Cubs) and was released. He signed with San Francisco for the 1989 season, was released, and signed with the Yankees. /(EG)

Julio Gotay — 1939– . SS-2B-3B 1960–69 Cardinals, Pirates, Angels, **Astros** 389 g, .260, 6 hr, 70 rbi

This extremely superstitious native Puerto Rican, who feared touching the cross, had a ML career interrupted by several trips to the minors. In his only season as a regular, as the Cardinals' shortstop in 1962, Gotay hit .255. /(RTM)

Jim Gott — 1959– . RHP 1982– **Blue Jays**, Giants, Pirates 749 ip, 35–48, 4.17

Gott is a pitcher with impressive stuff, but not always the greatest consistency. Drafted by the Blue Jays from the St. Louis organization, as a 22-year old rookie he won a 10-inning complete game 1–0 victory over the Detroit Tigers. In his three seasons in Toronto, Gott was shuttled between the bullpen and the starting rotation. In 1985 he was traded to San Francisco (for Gary Lavelle), where he learned the split-fingered fastball from manager Roger Craig and was used mainly as a starter. In 1987 Gott went to the Pirates in the late-season deal that sent Rick Reuschel and Don Robinson to the Giants. In Pittsburgh Gott emerged as the Pirates' late-inning stopper, but missed practically all of 1989 after being injured in the Pirates' opener. When trying to convince people that Dwight Gooden wasn't unhittable, Chili Davis remarked, "He ain't Gott, man."/(TF)

Curt Gowdy — 1919– . *Broadcaster.*

Smooth, steady, and always well-prepared, Curt Gowdy announced Super Bowls, Olympic Games, and NCAA basketball championships along with his record 12 World Series and two decades as host of television's "The American Sportsman." Gowdy joined Mel Allen on Yankee broadcasts in 1949. He became a New England institution as the radio voice of the Red Sox from 1951 to 1965. Gowdy left Boston to join the fledgling NBC "Game of the Week" on TV, and was baseball's lone national voice from 1966 to 1975, providing the play-by-play for every WS and All-Star Game in that span. He was named National Sportscaster of the Year three times, and in 1984 he was named to the writers and broadcasters wing of the Hall of Fame./(SCL)

Hank Gowdy — 1889–1966. C 1910–17, 19–25, 29–30 Giants, **Braves** 1050 g, .270, 21 hr, 322 rbi. *3 WS, 14 g, .310, 1 hr, 4 rbi*

Gowdy joined the 1910 Giants at age 20, was dealt to the Braves in 1911, and spent the next twelve seasons in Boston. The 6'2" righthander was a starting catcher from 1914 through 1916 and batted .545 with a homer and three RBI to lead the "miracle" Braves to a 1914 World Series sweep over the Athletics. He caught the no-hitters of George Davis (9/9/1914) and Tom Hughes (6/16/1916). Gowdy was the first ML player to enlist for WWI and saw considerable action in France. After he returned in 1919, he shared Boston's catching duties before he was reacquired by the Giants in 1923. Gowdy was a goat in the Giants' 1924 WS loss to Washington; he tripped over his mask and missed a pop-up, which led to the Series-winning run. Dropped by the Giants in 1925, Gowdy returned to the Braves for limited duty in 1929–30./(DQV)

Billy Grabarkewitz (Bulldog, Grabby) — 1946– . 3B-2B-SS 1969–75 **Dodgers**, Angels, Phillies, Cubs, A's 466 g, .236, 28 hr, 141 rbi
☞ *All-Star—70.*

The injury-prone Grabarkewitz was in the minors when he said, "I was X-rayed so often I glow in the dark." As a rookie, he led the 1970 Dodgers with 17 HR and 92 runs scored, and was named to the All-Star team./(TG)

Johnny Grabowski (Nig) — 1900–1946. C 1924–29, 31 White Sox, **Yankees**, Tigers 296 g, .252, 3 hr, 86 rbi. *1 WS, 1 g, .000*

Grabowski shared catching duties with Pat Collins and Benny Bengough on the 1927 Yankees. He later became an umpire in the International League./(JK)

Earl Grace — 1907–1980. C 1929, 31–37 Cubs, **Pirates**, Phillies 627 g, .263, 30 hr, 251 rbi

Grace was a platoon catcher at Pittsburgh in 1931–35. In 1932 he set NL records with 110 consecutive errorless games (400 chances) and fewest errors (one) in 100 or more games (114)./(ME)

Joe Grace — 1914–1969. OF 1938–41, 1946–47 Browns, Senators 484 g, .283, 20 hr, 172 rbi

The Browns first wanted the lefthanded line-drive hitter to catch, but manager Luke Sewell preferred Grace in the outfield. Grace hit .309 as a fourth outfielder in 1941. He spent 1942–45 in the Navy./(WAB)

Mark Grace (Amazing Grace) — 1964– . 1B 1988– **Cubs** 276 g, .305, 20 hr, 136 rbi. *1 LCS, 5 g, .647, 1 hr, 8 rbi*

Only a 24th-round pick in the 1985 draft, Grace was the *TSN* NL Rookie of the Year in 1988, hitting .296 with seven HR and 57 RBI in 486 at-bats. However, he tied for the NL lead in errors by a first baseman. In 1989 he hit .314 and led the Cubs with 79 RBI, and led Chicago regulars in the LCS with 8 RBI and a .647 batting average./(WOR)

Mike Grady — 1869–1943. C-1B-3B-OF 1894–1901, 1904–06 Phillies, **Cardinals**, Giants, Senators 919 g, .294, 35 hr, 459 rbi

Grady could not field any position well. Once, playing third base for the 1899 Giants, he bobbled a ground ball, overthrew first, and when the batter advanced all the way to third base, dropped the throw from the first baseman. As the runner headed home, Grady launched the ball over the catcher's head./(AJA)

Bill Graham — 1884–1936. LHP 1908–10 **Browns** 348 ip, 14–29, 2.90

A hard-luck pitcher, Graham managed to compile a career 2.90 ERA, yet win less than a third of his decisions. In 1910 Graham was 0–8 with a poor 3.56 ERA for the last-place 47–107 Browns./(WAB)

Kyle Graham (Skinny) — 1899–1973. RHP 1924–26, 29 **Braves**, Tigers 278 ip, 11–22, 5.02

Graham had just purchased a hot dog when called in to relieve for Detroit in a 1929 game against the A's. Told that Mickey Cochrane, Al Simmons, and Jimmie Foxx were coming to bat, Graham said, "Leave this hot dog alone. I'll be right back."/(NLM)

Alex Grammas — 1926– . SS-3B-2B 1954–63 **Cardinals**, Reds, Cubs 913 g, .247, 12 hr, 163 rbi
Manager 1969, 76–77 Pirates, **Brewers** 137–191, .418

The good-fielding Grammas barely hit enough to stay in the lineup, but was the Cardinals' everyday shortstop in 1954, 1955, and again in 1959. In between, he was a reserve with the Reds. His best average as a regular was .269 in 1959. He was the Pirate coach chosen to manage the last five games in 1969 after Larry Shepard was fired, and he piloted the Brewers to the basement in 1976 and 1977. He coached for Sparky Anderson in Cincinnati and Detroit./(MC)

Jack Graney — 1886–1978. OF-LHP 1908, 10–22 **Indians** 1403 g, .250, 18 hr, 420 rbi; 3 ip, 0–0, 5.40. *1 WS, 3 g, .000*

The stocky, 5′9″ Graney, a sharp-eyed leadoff man, played his full 14-year career for Cleveland. The converted pitcher led the AL in doubles in 1916, and in walks in 1917 and 1919. When his playing days ended he became the first ex-major leaguer to move to the broadcasting booth. Graney became a popular Indians play-by-play announcer./(JK)

Wayne Granger — 1944– . RHP 1968–76 Cardinals, **Reds**, Twins, Yankees, White Sox, Astros, Expos 640 ip, 35–35, 3.14. *1 LCS, 1 ip, 0–0, 0.00. 2 WS, 3 ip, 0–0, 13.50*

Teammates said that 6′2″ 165-lb Wayne Granger could "shower in a shotgun barrel." As a rookie Cardinals reliever in 1968, the sinkerballer recorded a 2.25 ERA. Swapped to the Reds with Bobby Tolan for Vada Pinson, in 1969 he went 9–6 (2.79) with 27 saves in a then-NL-record 90 appearances, winning his first of two straight Fireman of the Year awards. His 35 saves in 1970 set a since-broken NL mark. After yielding a grand slam to Orioles pitcher Dave McNally in Game Three of the '70 WS, Granger was never again as effective, though his 70 appearances in 1971 were again the NL high. He saved 19 games in 1972 for the Twins before arm trouble curtailed his effectiveness. He retired with 108 saves./(MC)

Charles Grant (Chief Tokohama) — Unk.–1932. 2B Negro Leagues 1896–1910 Page Fence Giants, Columbia Giants, Cuban X Giants, Philadelphia Giants, New York Black Sox

When John McGraw took his Baltimore Orioles to Hot Springs, Arkansas for spring training in 1901, he saw that a bellboy at their hotel was a particularly fine second baseman. McGraw wanted to sign him for the Orioles, but Charles Grant was black. McGraw decided to sidestep the color line by composing an elaborate fiction that Grant, who was rather light-skinned, was Charlie Tokohama, a full-blooded Cherokee Indian. Grant went along with the ruse, and the sporting papers of the day were filled with news of McGraw's sensational new find. The plot was eventually exposed when Charles Comiskey, president of the Chicago White Sox, recognized Grant as the second baseman of the Columbia Giants, a Chicago-area black team.

McGraw dropped Grant from the Orioles' roster, and Chief Tokohama never played in the majors. No statistics survive from his 15 seasons in Negro baseball, though he was the starting second baseman for the black championship teams of 1903 and 1904, the Cuban X Giants and the Philadelphia Giants, respectively. Grant was killed in Cincinnati in a freak accident in July 1932 when a passing auto blew a tire and jumped the curb, striking him while he was relaxing in front of his apartment house./(JJM)

Eddie Grant (Harvard Eddie) — 1883–1918. 3B-SS 1905, 07–15 Indians, **Phillies**, Reds, Giants 960 g, .249, 5 hr, 277 rbi. *1 WS, 2 g, .000*

Grant graduated from Harvard in 1905 and was given a tryout by Cleveland. He got three hits his first game, but was hitless the next day against Cy Young and was dropped to the minors. He reappeared with the 1907 Phillies, and took over as leadoff batter in 1908, leading the NL in at-bats in 1908 and 1909. Grant became a fine-fielding third baseman, fast on the bases and dependable in the clutch. After two-and-a-half seasons with the Giants, he retired in 1915 to practice law in New York City.

In World War I, he led a mission in the Argonne Forest offensive to rescue the "Lost Battalion" trapped behind German lines. When he met with machine gun fire, he became the only ML player killed in wartime action. A monument to his memory was placed in the Polo Grounds' deep centerfield, and each Memorial Day there was a wreath-laying ceremony at his plaque./(JK)

Frank Grant — 1868–1937. 2B-SS Negro Leagues 1886–1903 Meriden (EL), Buffalo (IL), **Cuban X Giants**, Harrisburg (EL), Lansing, Colored Capital All-Americans, New York Gorhams, Philadelphia Giants statistics not available

The most accomplished black baseball player of the 19th century, Grant joined Buffalo (International League) in 1886 and became the first black to play on the same team in organized baseball for three consecutive seasons. With his extraordinary range and strong arm, he was compared favorably with the best second basemen of his era. One Buffalo writer asserted that Grant was the best all-around player Buffalo had ever seen; four future Hall of Famers had played in Buffalo prior to Grant. Though just 5'7" 155-lb, he had surprising power at the plate; one-fourth of his hits in the International League were for extra bases. He led his team and/or league in various offensive categories, including batting average, stolen bases, total bases, and home runs. During the 1887 season, he hit for the cycle in one game and stole home twice in another. By the late 1880s, black players were banished from organized baseball. Grant went on to play for such strong independent Negro teams as the Cuban X Giants, Big Gorhams, and Philadelphia Giants through 1903./(JMa)

George Grant — 1903– . RHP 1923–25, 27–29, 31 Browns, **Indians**, Pirates 346 ip, 15–20, 5.64

Grant earned 10 of his 15 wins in 1928, when he led a weak Indians squad in winning percentage (.556) despite an ERA of 5.04./(ME)

Mark Grant — 1963– . RHP 1984, 86– Giants, **Padres** 441 ip, 18–28, 4.12

The 10th player in the nation selected in the June 1981 free agent draft, Grant twice led his league in wins in the minors, and was Midwest League MVP at Clinton in 1982 (16–5, 2.36 ERA, 243 strikeouts). He has struggled both as a starter and in relief in the ML./(ME)

Mudcat Grant [James Timothy] — 1935– . RHP 1958–71 **Indians**, Twins, Dodgers, Expos, Cardinals, A's, Pirates 2441 ip, 145–119, 3.63. 20 wins: 65 *1 LCS, 2 ip, 0–0, 0.00. 1 WS, 23 ip, 2–1, 2.74*
☛ *Led League—w 65. All-Star—65.*

Colorful Mudcat Grant was not only a 14-year ML pitcher, but a broadcaster and entertainer. He spent his first seven-plus seasons with the Indians, compiling a 67–63 record. He then reached his pinnacle

with the 1965 pennant-winning Twins, leading the AL in victories and winning percentage (21–7, .750) and in shutouts (six). He defeated the Dodgers in the World Series opener 8–2, lost Game Four 7–2, and won Game Six 5–1, helping himself with a three-run homer. He worked mostly in relief after his trade to the Dodgers in November of 1967, and in 1969 recorded the expansion Expos' first win. With Oakland and Pittsburgh in 1970, he went 8–3 (1.87) with 24 saves. Sporting muttonchop sideburns, he was the lead singer of a group called "Mudcat and the Kittens."/(ME)

George Grantham (Boots) — 1900–1954. 2B-1B 1922–34 Cubs, **Pirates**, Reds, Giants 1444 g, .302, 105 hr, 712 rbi. *2 WS, 8 g, .231*

After driving in 160 runs for Tacoma (Western League) in 1922, Grantham became the Cubs' starting second baseman. He struck out more than any NL player in 1923 and 1924, but was the run producer Pittsburgh needed. In a major postseason deal in 1924, the Bucs sent Rabbit Maranville, Charlie Grimm, and Wilbur Cooper to the Cubs for Grantham, Vic Aldridge, and Al Niehaus. Some Pittsburgh fans criticized trading three popular players for an erratic fielder (Grantham) and two unknowns, but the trade paid off for the Pirates. Grantham, switched from second base to first base, batted a career-high .326 and dramatically reduced his strikeouts in 1925. Pittsburgh won the World Series, and the Cubs finished last. Grantham batted over .300 in each of his seven seasons with Pittsburgh, splitting time between first base and second base./(ME)

Mickey Grasso [Newton Michael] — 1920–1975. C 1946, 50–55 Giants, **Senators**, Indians 322 g, .226, 5 hr, 87 rbi. *1 WS, 1 g, --*

Nicknamed Mickey because of his remarkable resemblance to Hall of Fame catcher Mickey Cochrane, Grasso homered for Trenton in 1941 in his first at-bat in organized baseball. A former WWII prisoner of the Germans in North Africa, he batted .287 as a part-time catcher with the Senators in 1950./(RM)

Stephen O. Grauley (Sog) — 1879–1958. *Writer.*

In nearly 60 years with the Philadelphia *Inquirer*, Grauley covered Connie Mack's Athletics from their inception until after Mack's retirement. At the 1951 A's home opener, Mack chose Grauley as his box-seat companion for the first Athletics game without Mack as manager. Sog (his initials) played on the first baseball team fielded by Temple University, in the 1890s. As a sportswriter, he was known for his factual and accurate writing in an age of flamboyant phrasing. He became sports editor of the *Inquirer* in 1924. He was a charter member of the BBWAA. /(NLM)

Dolly Gray [William] — 1878–1956. LHP 1909–11 **Senators** 568 ip, 15–51, 3.52

Nicknamed for "Goodbye, Dolly Gray," a popular Spanish-American War ballad, Gray had a record worse than that of his doormat team. He lost a one-hitter when, after a two-out error, he walked seven straight on 3–2 counts. /(JK)

Gary Gray — 1952– . 1B-DH 1977–82 Rangers, Indians, **Mariners** 211 g, .240, 24 hr, 71 rbi

In his one full ML season, Gray had 13 HR — 10 by June 1 — in 69 games for the 1981 Mariners. In 12 minor league seasons, including many in the Mexican League, he never hit below .300. /(JCA)

John Gray (Mitty) — 1927– . RHP 1954–55, 57–58 **A's**, Indians, Phillies 169 ip, 4–18, 6.18

Gray had the top ERA (2.72) in the American Association with Indianapolis in 1956. Pitching for Cleveland in 1957, he hurled his only shutout, for his final ML victory. /(RTM)

Pete Gray — 1917– . OF 1945 **Browns** .218, 0 hr, 13 rbi

Despite losing his right arm in a childhood truck accident, Gray became a major league ballplayer. The naturally righthanded youngster learned to throw and bat from the opposite side. Batting with one arm, Gray sprayed line drives around the field. On the basepaths, he displayed speed and daring, and fielding was a study in agility and dexterity. After catching a fly ball, Gray would tuck his thinly padded glove under his stump, roll the ball across his chest, and throw, all in one fluid motion.

Gray was a semi-pro star in the coal towns of his native Pennsylvania and with the famed Brooklyn Bushwicks. He entered pro ball in 1942 with Three Rivers (Canadian-American League) and hit .381 in 42 games. In the Southern Association in 1943, Gray hit .289 in a full season with Memphis. He won national attention in 1944 when he batted .333 for Memphis, hit five HR, tied a league record by stealing 68 bases, and was named the Southern Association's MVP. This outstanding showing earned Gray a spot with the 1945 St. Louis Browns.

Even with the quality of major league play at an all-time low due to the WWII player shortage, Gray was overmatched. But he was capable of remarkable performances. In a doubleheader at Yankee Stadium in May, Gray had four hits, scored twice, drove in two, and handled nine chances in the outfield. When baseball returned to full strength in 1946, the Browns sent Gray down. He continued to play in the minors and barnstorm with exhibition teams until the early 1950s. Gray retired to his hometown of Nanticoke, PA, and became a recluse. /(JL)

Sam Gray (Sad Sam) — 1897–1953. RHP 1924–33 A's, Browns 1951 ip, 112–115, 4.20. 20 wins: 28

Gray once started off a game for the 1926 Athletics by throwing 15 straight balls. He eventually won the game with a two-hitter, 3–1. In 1925 a series of misfortunes kept him from an outstanding record. He won his first eight, but a pitched ball broke his right thumb. Later that season, his wife died suddenly. He still finished 16–8. Two years later, Gray went a career-best 20–12 for the Browns. The eccentric curveballer led the AL with 37 starts, 305 innings, and four shutouts in 1929, and with 37 starts and 24 losses in 1931. /(WAB)

Ted Gray — 1924– . LHP 1946, 48–55 **Tigers**, White Sox, Indians, Yankees, Orioles 1134 ip, 59–74, 4.37 ☛ *All-Star—50.*

Signed off the Detroit sandlots, Gray was a hard-throwing star in WWII service ball. In the majors, the forkballer was hindered by chronic blisters and he held his ERA below 4.00 only once in nine seasons. After eight seasons with the Tigers, he appeared with four different teams in 1955. /(JK)

Harry M. Grayson — 1894–1968. *Writer.*

Grayson retired in 1964 after 30 years as sports editor of *NEA*. It was said of him that he never went to bed; he was one of the few nightlifers who could outlast Casey Stengel. His book, *They Played the Game*, was published in 1944. /(NLM)

Eli Grba — 1934– . RHP 1959–63 Yankees, **Angels** 536 ip, 28–33, 4.48

On Opening Day, 1961, the bespectacled Grba defeated Baltimore in the first game ever played by the expansion Angels. The ex-Yankee reliever used a good fastball to win 19 games for the Angels in two years, 17 as a starter. /(RTM)

Dallas Green — 1934– . RHP 1960–67 **Phillies**, Senators, Mets 562 ip, 20–22, 4.26.

Manager 1979–81, 89 **Phillies**, Yankees 225–195, .536. First place: 80 *1 LCS, 3–2, .600. 1 WS, 4–2, .667*

After a pitching career in which he recorded all his ML decisions for the Phillies, Dallas Green managed two Phillies farm clubs, served as an assistant director and director of their minor league system, and managed the parent club for over two years. In 1980 the 6'5" 245-lb Green guided the Phillies to their first World Championship since 1915. "I express my thoughts," he said. "I'm a screamer, a yeller and a cusser. I never hold back." At the 1981 press conference marking his appointment as the Cubs' GM, Green remarked, "I'm no Messiah, but I'll guarantee no one will ever outwork us. When I hire someone he better work at it or hear from me." In 1984 the Cubs won the NL East title, their first championship in nearly 40 years, based largely on strong years from former Phillies Gary Mathews, Bob Dernier, and MVP Ryne Sandberg. Green resigned after a 1987 last-place finish, but his rebuilding of the Chicago farm system paid off with a pennant in 1989.

Hired by George Steinbrenner to manage the Yankees in 1989, Green rebuilt the team with GM Syd Thrift but was fired before the end of the season for referring to Steinbrenner as Manager George. /(TJ)

Danny Green — 1876–1914. OF 1898–1905 Cubs, **White Sox** 923 g, .293, 29 hr, 422 rbi

Green was a foolhardy baserunner and a .304 hitter for the Chicago Colts (Cubs) in 1898–1901. When American League raiders offered lucrative contracts to unhappy National League stars, Charles Comiskey landed Green, who became the White Sox right fielder in 1902. In 1906, with Green's throwing arm burning out, Comiskey let him manage half the club in split-squad spring training. Green had his players roller-skating, believing it was better than jogging, but his training ideas did not please Comiskey. After Green's spring squad lost most of its games, Green was outrighted to the American Association. He died in 1914 of complications from a beaning. /(RL)

David Green — 1960– . OF-1B 1981–85, 87 **Cardinals**, Giants 489 g, .268, 31 hr, 180 rbi. *1 LCS, 2 g, 1.000. 1 WS, 7 g, .200*

Green was a highly touted young talent, showing speed, power, and excellent defensive ability. He hit .283 in 76 games in 1982 and .284 with 34 stolen bases in 1983. The Giants obtained him with Jose Uribe, Dave LaPoint, and Gary Rajsich for Jack Clark, and hoped he would be a capable successor to Clark at first base. He wasn't. Personal problems, including fear for his family in strife-torn Nicaragua, led to his decline. After flings in the Mexican and Japanese leagues (1986–87), a glimmer of his potential shone again in September 1987. The Cardinals recalled him during their successful pennant drive to substitute for the injured Clark, and Green hit .267 and slugged .500 in limited action. /(FO)

Dick Green — 1941– . 2B 1963–74 **A's** 1288 g, .240, 80 hr, 422 rbi. *4 LCS, 17 g, .162, 1 rbi. 3 WS, 19 g, .149, 2 RBI*

Green was a superb-fielding, light-hitting second baseman, whose glove work was a key to Oakland's three straight World Championships (1972–74) and a highlight of the 1974 WS. In the clincher, he was the pivot man in an exciting eighth-inning double play that preserved the A's 3–2 victory over the Dodgers. The Iowan led AL second basemen in fielding in 1969 (.986). Usually a second baseman during his 12 years in Kansas City and Oakland, Green played every infield position and even caught two games. He had some power, reaching double figures in homers four times. His best year offensively was 1969, when he hit .275, with career highs of 64 RBI and 43 extra-base hits. /(TJ)

Freddie Green — 1933– . LHP 1959–62, 64 **Pirates**, Senators 142 ip, 9–7, 3.48. *1 WS, 4 ip, 0–0, 22.50*

Out of nowhere, Green became the ace lefthander in the 1960 Pirate bullpen (8–4, three saves) and even hit two HR. But he lost his battle with his control problems and never notched another win or save. /(ME)

Gene Green — 1933–1981. OF-C 1957–63 **Cardinals**, Orioles, Senators, Indians, Reds 408 g, .267, 46 hr, 160 rbi

Overlooked by the scouts, the strong-armed outfielder had to ask for a tryout in 1952. Green took up catching, but sat on the bench most of his short career. "If baseball ever adopted the two platoon system," he once quipped, "I'd get $50,000: 25 for hitting, and 25 for sitting." /(WAB)

Lenny Green — 1934– . OF 1957–68 Orioles, **Senators/Twins**, Angels, Red Sox, Tigers 1136 g, .267, 47 hr, 253 rbi

Twice in his career, Green was traded to a club against which his team was playing its next game.

The Twins' everyday centerfielder in their first two seasons, Green had a 24-game hitting streak in 1961, a club record until Ken Landreaux broke it in 1980. /(RTM)

Pumpsie Green [Elijah Jerry] — 1933– . 2B-SS 1959–63 **Red Sox**, Mets 344 g, .246, 13 hr, 74 rbi

In 1959 Pumpsie became the first black player on the Red Sox, the major leagues' last integrated team. The switch-hitter's brother, Cornell Green, was a Dallas Cowboys defensive back. /(RMu)

Hank Greenberg (Hammerin' Hank) — 1911–1986. 1B-OF 1930, 33–41, 45–47 **Tigers**, Pirates 1394 g, .313, 331 hr, 1276 rbi. *4 WS, 23 g, .318, 5 hr, 22 rbi*
☛ *Most Valuable Player—35, 40. Led League—hr 35, 38, 40, 46. Led League—rbi 35, 37, 40, 46. All-Star—37–40. Hall of Fame—1956.*

Although he missed time through injuries, military service, and early retirement, Greenberg still ranks as one of the most fearsome sluggers in baseball history. The powerful righthander played only the equivalent of nine-and-a-half seasons, yet produced outstanding career totals as well as exceptional season marks.

A native New Yorker, Greenberg was the son of Rumanian-born Jewish immigrants who owned a successful cloth-shrinking plant. Hank graduated from James Monroe High School in the Bronx, then attended New York University on an athletic scholarship for one semester before beginning his professional baseball career. The 6'4″215-lb Greenberg's athletic success stemmed from size, strength, and hard work, more than native talent. His high school coach explained: "Hank was so big for his age and so awkward that he became painfully self-conscious. The fear of being made to look foolish drove him to practice constantly and, as a result, to overcome his handicaps."

Greenberg tried out for the New York Giants but Giants Manager John McGraw, although constantly on the lookout for a Jewish star to attract New York's large Jewish population and impressed by Greenberg's powerful hitting, decided Hank was too clumsy and uncoordinated to help the Giants. Hank turned down a lucrative offer from the Yankees, realizing there would be little chance of making the ML with Lou Gehrig on first for the Bombers. He also rejected overtures from the Senators, who had Joe Judge. In January 1930 he signed with the Tigers.

After several minor league stops, he was called up to the Tigers in 1933. Still awkward in the field,

Hank Greenberg

though quick on his feet, he showed line-drive power, with 33 doubles, 12 homers, and a .301 batting average. In 1934 he cracked a league-leading 63 doubles and batted .339 with 26 homers and 139 RBI as the Tigers won the AL pennant. In the WS loss to the Gashouse Gang Cardinals, he hit .321 but struck out nine times.

The Tigers repeated as AL champs in 1935, spurred by Greenberg's league-topping 36 homers and 170 RBI. He was named AL MVP. He suffered a broken wrist in the second game of the WS and watched from the sideline as the Tigers defeated the Cubs. Off to an excellent start in 1936, with 16 RBI in 12 games, he broke the same wrist in a collision at first base and missed the rest of the season, amid speculation that his career was over.

Instead, he rebounded with 183 RBI in 1937, the third-highest total ever. He also hit 40 homers and batted .337. The next season he made a determined assault on Babe Ruth's 60 home run record. With five games to go, he had 58, to tie Jimmie Foxx's record for righthanded hitters, but he was unable to add to that total. He set a record for most multi-homer games in a season, with eleven.

In 1940, Greenberg shifted from his hard-won first base position to left field to enable the Tigers to find a regular lineup spot for hard-hitting but poor-fielding Rudy York. The result was a Detroit pennant, breaking the Yankees' streak of four straight pennants. Many credited Greenberg's willingness and ability to learn a completely new position as the key factor in Detroit's success. He hit .340 and led the AL in doubles (50), home runs (41), and RBI (150), and earned his second MVP award.

Greenberg, then a bachelor, was one of the first major leaguers inducted into the service, entering 19 games into the 1941 season. He was discharged from the army on December 5, 1941, two days before the Japanese attack on Pearl Harbor. He immediately enlisted as an officer candidate in the Air Corps. Hank served with distinction in the Far East until his discharge in mid-1945. He returned with a bang, with a home run in his first game. His grand slam on the final day of the season won the pennant for the Tigers. In the WS win over the Cubs, he hit two more homers and batted in seven runs.

He led the AL in homers (44) and RBI (127) again in 1946, but a salary dispute developed with the Tigers during the season. Rather than raise his salary, Detroit waived him out of the AL to Pittsburgh. Greenberg deeply resented learning of the deal from the radio rather than being informed in advance of the public announcement. The Pirates coaxed him into playing the 1947 season with a complicated contract that netted him between $100,000 and $145,000, making him the NL's first $100,000 player. A bullpen was built in front of Forbes Field's distant left field wall and fans quickly labeled it "Greenberg Gardens." Although he hit a disappointing .249, he contributed 25 home runs and served as a gate instructor. More important, he served as hitting instructor and advisor to his protege and friend, young Ralph Kiner. When Greenberg retired after the 1947 season, the left field bullpen became known as "Kiner's Korner."

In 1948 Cleveland owner Bill Veeck hired Greenberg as farm system director. He became general manager in 1950 and built the team that derailed the Yankees' string of pennants in 1954. Unable to purchase stock in the Indians, he moved to the White Sox as part owner and vice president as that team won the 1959 pennant. He retired from baseball in 1963 to become a successful investment banker. /(FS)

Joe Greene [James Elbert] — 1911- .C-1B-OF Negro Leagues 1932–48 Atlanta Black Crackers, **Kansas City Monarchs**, Cleveland Buckeyes statistics not available

Greene caught for the perennial Negro American League champion Kansas City Monarchs from 1939 through 1947. Strong pitching was a Monarch trademark; Greene handled some of the best, including Satchel Paige. His career opened with the Atlanta Black Crackers, and ended there with a NAL title series in 1938, canceled after the Memphis Red Sox won two games. He was the starting catcher for the West in the 1940 and 1942 East-West all-star games, and in the Monarchs' 1942 Black World Series triumph he batted .444 with a home run and eight RBI. He was decorated for combat service in WWII. In 1947 he hit a long home run off Bob Feller in an exhibition game. In his last three years in the NAL, Greene batted .293. /(MFK)

Kent Greenfield — 1902–1978. RHP 1924–29 **Giants**, Braves, Dodgers 775 ip, 41–48, 4.54

Greenfield, a rangy curveballer, pitched creditably for the Giants in 1925–26 before being traded to the Braves. Hampered by recurring control problems, he was less effective from then on. /(FS)

Jim Greengrass — 1927- . OF 1952–56 **Reds**, Phillies 504 g, .269, 69 hr, 282 rbi

The husky righthanded hitter joined the Reds in September 1952, more than eight years after his pro debut. He had 100 RBI his first full season, 27 HR his second, then faded, hampered by phlebitis. /(AL)

Gus Greenlee [William Augustus] — 1897–1952. *Executive.*

The owner of the Pittsburgh Crawfords, 1931–38, in 1933 Greenlee organized the National Negro Association, commonly known as the second Negro National League, into which it evolved. He served as its president with absolute power, awarding the first pennant to his own Crawfords. This claim was disputed by the Chicago American Giants, since the schedule had not been completed. The circuit survived until being absorbed by the Negro American League in 1949. Greenlee also initiated the East-West all-star game in 1933. The Negro Leagues' showcase event, it annually drew crowds approaching 50,000 to Comiskey Field.

In addition to the Crawfords, he also owned his

own ballpark, a famous nightclub (the Crawford Bar & Grill), and a stable of boxers including light-heavyweight champion John Henry Lewis. Greenlee was a power in black Pittsburgh's racketeering and politics. /(MFK)

Tom Greenwade — 1904–1986. *Scout.*

A scout for the Browns and Dodgers before beginning a 40-year stint with the Yankees in 1945, Greenwade gave Dodger owner Branch Rickey favorable reports on Jackie Robinson and Roy Campanella, and signed Mickey Mantle and Bobby Murcer for the Yankees. /(FVP)

Mike Greenwell — 1963– . OF 1985– **Red Sox** 476 g, .320, 59 hr, 315 rbi. *2 LCS, 6 g, .250, 1 hr, 3 rbi. 1 WS, 4 g, .000*
☛ *All-Star—88–89.*

The heir to Ted Williams, Carl Yastrzemski, and Jim Rice in left field for the Boston Red Sox, Greenwell rapidly established himself as one of baseball's best hitters. With a smooth lefthanded batting stroke modeled after George Brett's, he finished third in the 1987 AL Rookie of the Year voting (behind Mark McGwire and Kevin Seitzer) and in 1988 beat out Jim Rice for the leftfield job, hitting .325 with 22 HR, 119 RBI, and only 38 strikeouts. His first three ML hits were home runs, the first a 13th-inning game-winner at Toronto September 25, 1985. /(SCL)

Eric Gregg — 1951– . *Umpire* NL 1977– *2 LCS 1 ASU*

The roly-poly Gregg gained off-season recognition with a TV sports show on "Evening Magazine." He was perhaps the only ump ever to call interference on himself. In 1978 he bumped Cardinal catcher Ted Simmons in the act of throwing and subsequently nullified a Dodgers double steal. /(RTM)

Hal Gregg — 1921– . RHP 1943–50, 52 **Dodgers**, Pirates, Giants 827 IP, 40–48, 4.54. *1 WS, 12.2 ip, 0–1, 3.55*

Gregg led the NL in walks in 1944 and 1945, and walked 11 batters in one 15-inning game (6/15/44). He went 18–13 (3.47) to lead Dodger pitchers in '45, but a sore arm held him to just 13 more victories. /(ME)

Tommy Gregg — 1963– . OF-1B 1987– Pirates, **Braves** 137 g, .250, 7 hr, 30 rbi

Gregg led the Eastern League in batting in 1987 with a .371 mark. When Pirates GM Syd Thrift sent him

to the Braves as the player to be named later in return for Ken Oberkfell in September 1988, it contributed to Thrift's firing in the off-season. Gregg started 1989 as one of the Braves' hottest hitters, but was disabled early. When he returned, he was moved to first base part-time to replace Gerald Perry, who was out for the rest of the year. /(JFC)

Vean Gregg [Sylveanus Augustus] — 1885–1964. LHP 1911–16, 18, 25 **Indians**, Red Sox, A's, Senators 1392 ip, 91–63, 2.70. 20 wins: 11–13
☛ *Led League—era 11.*

Gregg had a great 1910 season in the Pacific Coast League, throwing 14 shutouts. He continued his success in his rookie season with the Indians in 1911, going 23–7 to lead the AL with a .767 winning percentage and a 1.81 ERA. The powerful left-hander followed with two more 20-win seasons before suffering a sore arm which reduced his effectiveness. Traded to the Red Sox in mid-1914, he never again had a successful ML season, though he was a big winner after he returned to the minors. Younger brother Dave had a one-inning ML pitching career with Cleveland in 1913. /(JK)

Paul Gregory (Pop) — 1908– . RHP 1932–33 **White Sox** 221 ip, 9–14, 4.72

Gregory bore an uncanny resemblance to and copied the delivery of White Sox ace Ted Lyons. He became Lyons' protege and constant companion. After pitching well late in 1932, he was slated to be Chicago's third starter in 1933, but reported overweight and was ineffective. /(RL)

Bill Greif — 1950– . RHP 1971–76 Astros, **Padres**, Cardinals 716 ip, 31–67, 4.41

As a starter for the last-place 1972–74 Padres, 6'4" Bill Greif suffered through records of 5–16, 10–17, and 9–19. He was traded from St. Louis to Montreal in 1976, but was released without appearing in a game. /(MC)

Ed Gremminger (Battleship) — 1874–1942. 3B 1895, 1902–04 Cleveland (NL), **Braves**, Tigers 383 g, .251, 7 hr, 165 rbi

Playing for the Braves, Gremminger led NL third basemen in putouts and fielding in 1902 and in putouts, assists, and double plays in 1903; those were his only years as a regular, despite respectable hitting. He managed in the minors from 1908 to 1912. /(NLM)

Zane Grey — 1875–1939. *Writer.*

A star outfielder while studying dentistry at the University of Pennsylvania, Grey was signed by Ed Barrow for Wheeling in the Interstate League in 1895. He got as far as Toronto of the Eastern League in 1899 before beginning his dental practice in New York. His brother, Romer, played briefly with the Pirates. Grey wrote 86 books, mostly westerns, but three were baseball novels: *The Shortstop*, *The Redheaded Outfield*, and *The Young Pitcher*. /(NLM)

Bobby Grich — 1949– . 2B 1970–86 Orioles, **Angels** 2008 g, .266, 224 hr, 864 rbi. *5 LCS, 24 g, .182, 3 hr, 9 rbi* ☛ *Led League—hr 81. All-Star—72, 74, 76, 79–80, 82. Gold Glove—73–76.*

An excellent fielder with a surprisingly powerful bat, Grich was one of the AL's best all-around second basemen for over 15 seasons with the Orioles and Angels, earning All-Star recognition six times. The 6′2″ 180-lb Grich was big for a middle infielder, but as a converted minor league shortstop he had plenty of range in the field, and he generated considerable power with a strong-wristed righthanded batting stroke.

Grich was *TSN* Minor League Player of the Year at Rochester (International League) in 1971, hitting .336 with 32 HR and leading the league's shortstops in fielding, and as a 23-year old rookie with the Orioles in 1972, he played shortstop for the AL in the All-Star Game, finishing the season at .278 with 12 HR. Grich moved to second base full-time in 1973 and promptly set a ML record for that position with a .995 fielding percentage, and from 1973–76 he reached double figures in home runs and stolen bases each year while hitting near .260.

Grich became a free agent after the 1976 season and signed with the Angels for 1977, only to spend most of the year on the DL. He then had a miserable year offensively in 1978, but rebounded in 1979 to hit .294 with career highs in HR (30) and RBI (101) as the Angels won the AL West. In the strike-shortened 1981 season, Grich was one of four AL players to tie for the league home run title with 22, and also led the league with a .543 slugging percentage while batting a career-high .304. In the field, Grich had lost some range, but was still sure-handed, and in 1985 he regained his ML fielding record (which had been broken by Rob Wilfong in 1980) with a .997 percentage, committing only two errors at second base all season.

Bobby Grich

Grich played in the ALCS five times, yet never reached the WS. He came closest in his final ML season (1986), when the Angels blew a 5–2 lead to the Red Sox in the ninth inning of Game Five, then lost Games Six and Seven as well. Grich is second behind Brian Downing on the Angels all-time home run list. /(SCL)

Bill Grieve — 1900–1979. *Umpire AL 1938–55 3 WS 2 ASU*

Grieve was known for two things among AL players: his many little fears and phobias, and for showing favoritism to the Yankees. Although the latter charge was without merit, some players called him the Number One Yankee Fan. /(RTM)

Tom Grieve — 1948– . OF-DH 1970, 72–79 **Senators/Rangers**, Mets, Cardinals 670 g, .249, 65 hr, 254 rbi

Grieve has spent almost all of his two-plus decades in professional baseball with the Senators-Rangers organization. He played two errorless seasons (1973–74) in the Rangers' outfield in limited duty, and saw his most activity in 1976 as a DH, reaching career highs of 20 HR, 23 doubles, 81 RBI, and 57 runs while batting .255. In December 1977 he went to the Mets in a four-team deal that netted Texas Jon Matlack, and one year later he was dealt to St. Louis for Pete Falcone. The Cardinals released him in May and he finished the season with the Rangers' Triple-A Tucson club, then joined the Texas front-office in 1980. In 1984, at age 36, he became the youngest GM in the ML. /(JFC)

Ken Griffey, Jr. — 1967- . OF 1989- **Mariners** 127 g, .264, 16 hr, 61 rbi

Griffey was off to a Rookie of the Year season in 1989 before injury ended his season right after the All-Star break. He and his father, Ken Sr., are the first father-son duo to play in the majors at the same time. /(JFC)

Ken Griffey, Sr. — 1950- . OF-1B 1973- **Reds**, Yankees, Braves 2000 g, .297, 147 hr, 824 rbi. *3 LCS, 9 g, .313, 6 rbi. 2 WS, 11 g, .186, 5 rbi*
☛ *All-Star—76-77, 80.*

An unsung star of the 1975-81 Reds, Ken Griffey hit .307 in nine years in his first stint with Cincinnati and challenged for the NL batting title in 1976 and 1977. The right fielder was a heads-up, all-around player, but was most proficient at the plate. Hailing from Donora, Pennsylvania, like Stan Musial, the lefthanded Griffey's career slumped after he moved to the Yankees in a 1981 transaction. Used in a platoon role at first base and in the outfield, Griffey's entire game suffered. Injuries also slowed him, but Ken was rejuvenated upon joining the Braves. Rejoining the Reds in 1989, he and his son, Ken Jr., made history as the first father and son to play in the major leagues at the same time. /(ME)

Alfredo Griffin — 1957- . SS 1976- Indians, **Blue Jays**, A's, Dodgers 1603 g, .253, 23 hr, 452 rbi. *1 LCS, 7 g, .160, 3 rbi. 1 WS, 5 g, .188*
☛ *All-Star—84. Gold Glove—85.*

Griffin was co-winner of the 1979 AL Rookie of the Year award, along with Minnesota's John Castino. As a steady, everyday shortstop, he spent six years with the Blue Jays, playing in 392 consecutive games. Griffin was traded after the 1984 season to Oakland, where, despite his reluctance to draw walks and a tendency to be overaggressive on the basepaths, he began to harness the offensive promise he showed in 1980 when he set an AL record for most triples by a switch-hitter with a league-leading 15. After establishing personal bests in most offensive categories with the Athletics, Griffin was traded to the Dodgers for Bob Welch prior to the 1988

season in a move that helped both teams to league championships. A Dwight Gooden fastball broke his hand in May 1988, and he was disabled for much of 1988 and 1989. /(TF)

Doug Griffin — 1947- . 2B 1970-77 Angels, **Red Sox** 632 g, .245, 7 hr, 165 rbi. *1 WS, 1 g, .000*
☛ *Gold Glove—72.*

Tony Conigliaro went to the Angels in a 1971 deal that brought this Pacific Coast League All-Star to Boston. The injury-plagued 1972 Gold Glove second baseman was beaned by a Nolan Ryan fastball on April 30, 1974. /(RMu)

Mike Griffin — 1865-1908. OF 1887-98 Baltimore (AA), Philadelphia (PL), **Dodgers** 1511 g, .299, 41 hr, 625 rbi.
Manager 1898 **Dodgers** 1-3, .250

In 1887, playing centerfield for Baltimore of the American Association, Griffin stole 94 bases to set a ML rookie record that stood until Vince Coleman stole 110 in 1985. In 1889 he led the AA in runs scored. He led the NL in doubles in 1891, his first season in CF for the Brooklyn Bridegrooms (later called the Dodgers), where he remained through 1898. He retired with 473 stolen bases. /(AJA)

Mike Griffin — 1957- . RHP 1979-82, 87 Yankees, Cubs, Padres, **Orioles** 199 ip, 7-15, 4.44

Texas traded the 6'4" Griffin to the Yankees with Dave Righetti in a 1978, 10-player deal. Griffin was New York's best rookie in the spring of 1980, then went 2-4 and was sent down. He pitched for seven organizations without a full or winning season in the majors. /(MC)

Tom Griffin — 1948- . RHP 1969-82 **Astros**, Padres, Angels, Giants, Pirates 1493 ip, 77-94, 4.07

Griffin struggled through three minor league seasons before going 11-10 for Houston in 1969, winning *TSN* NL Rookie Pitcher of the Year honors. He struck out 200 batters in 188 innings. On April 19, 1970, he one-hit the Padres, but slipped to 3-13 and spent time in Triple-A. He battled back from arm trouble and worked mostly out of the Astros bullpen until late in 1973. On May 7, 1974, he one-hit the Pirates en route to a career-best 14-10 mark. A good-hitting pitcher, he managed 10 HR in 405 career at-bats. /(MC)

Griffith Stadium Washington Senators 1911–61. LF-388, CF-421, RF-320

Built for Clark Griffith's Senators when National Park burned down during spring training in 1911, the original concrete and steel grandstand took only 18 days to construct, but when the double-decked stands were extended from the bases to the foul poles in 1920, the roofs of the new sections were considerably higher than the originals, giving the stadium a makeshift appearance. While Griffith Stadium's left field fence was usually over 380′ away, right field was never more than 330′, but it was guarded by a 30′ wall that extended all the way to the centerfield bleachers, jutting in dramatically in deep right-center to allow for a large tree on the outside. It was the AL's lowest-capacity park (27,410) for many years, and the president traditionally threw out the first ball each Opening Day. It was demolished in 1965 and is now the site of Howard University Hospital. /(SCL)

Clark Griffith (The Old Fox) — 1869–1955. RHP 1891, 93–1907, 09–10, 12–14 St. Louis (AA), Boston (AA), **Cubs**, White Sox, Yankees, Reds, Senators 3386 ip, 240–141, 3.31. 20 wins: 94–99, 01
    Manager 1901–20 White Sox, Yankees, Reds, **Senators** 1491–1367, .522 First place: 01
☛ *Led League—era 98. Hall of Fame—1946.*

A native of the prairie, Griffith was a professional trapper at age ten, emulating his father, a commercial hunter. When the Griffiths relocated to Bloomington, IL, young Clark discovered organized baseball. He signed his first pro contract in 1888 with Milwaukee of the Western League, and jumped to the American Association, pitching for both St. Louis and Boston in 1891 before the league collapsed.

In 1893 Griffith assembled a 30–18 record for the Oakland Oaks (Pacific Coast League). When the Oaks' owners, in mid-season, did not come up with back pay owed the players, Griffith organized his

Griffith Stadium

teammates to strike. Needing employment, several of them, including Griffith, audaciously found work as itinerant vaudevillians in San Francisco's Barbary Coast district. When the owners found enough money, the greasepaint was abandoned and the season was completed.

Griffith was signed by Cap Anson for his NL Chicago Colts (later Cubs) in 1893. Griffith's eight years in Chicago were the high point of his playing career, and Anson's tutelage added a dimension to his ambitious personality. The Old Fox earned his nickname by utilizing a six-pitch arsenal, including the screwball (which he claimed to have invented), a silencing quick-pitch delivery, and the ruse of hiding the ball in the plane of his body before delivering. Griffith scuffed, scratched, cut, and spit upon nearly every pitch without hesitation, yet when the call came to make these tactics illegal in 1920, Griffith led that bandwagon. Young Clark claimed it was bad luck to pitch a shutout, and avoided doing so until 1897.

Griffith served as vice president of the League Protective Players' Association, and in 1900, he led the members in baseball's first universal strike. The players wanted the minimum salary raised to $3,000 and their uniforms paid for by the owners. Honorable demands aside, The Old Fox had the ulterior motive of helping old friend Ban Johnson establish his rival American League. He contrived to get every player to pledge not to sign a new contract without LPPA approval. This tactic crippled NL owners. Griffith persuaded 39 NL stars to jump to the AL; for his efforts, he was rewarded with the player/managership of the new Chicago franchise in 1901 and 1902, before moving on to the same duties with the newborn New York Highlanders (later Yankees) from 1903 to 1908. A tremendous animosity grew between Griffith and the New York owners. Oddly enough, the NL took him back with open arms to manage the Cincinnati Reds from 1909 to 1911. But when Johnson convinced him to rebuild the ailing franchise in Washington, Griffith had a home for life.

Placing himself in debt (a position from which he never strayed far), Griffith purchased control of the lackluster Senators over the years 1912–20. His financial ills forever kept him at odds with his players. It was probably an economic motivation that brought about a change in his racial views. As early as 1911, with the Reds, Griffith began signing Cuban ballplayers, the first to do so. The often-broke Griffith sometimes combined sentimentality with a nose for box-office attractions. During the

Clark Griffith

Depression, Griffith sold star outfielder Goose Goslin to Detroit, asserting he could no longer afford him. But when the aging Goslin was released by the Tigers some years later, Griffith found a spot for him on the Senators' roster. War hero Bert Shepard had potential as a pitcher, but lost a leg in combat. Griffith signed him anyway. Wartime blackout restrictions did not prevent him from obtaining government approval to hold more night games than other franchises in order to provide more "R-and-R" for the dayworkers of the Washington bureaucracy. The ex-vaudevillian always knew what drew a crowd. In 1946 he installed the first device to record pitch speed (borrowed from the U.S. Army) so that visiting flamethrower Bob Feller could give the fans a pre-game thrill.

Griffith's major strategic contribution to the game was the development of the relief pitcher. While in New York, he yielded to the pressures from his Tammany Hall owners and pitched his two premier starters, Jack Chesbro and Jack Powell, a staggering 845 combined innings in 1904. In 1905 both were markedly less effective, and completed many fewer games. The Old Fox finished many games for them personally, making a career-high 18 relief appearances that season. Along with John McGraw, Griffith revolutionized baseball with his reliance on the bullpen. He subsequently developed the first great relievers, Allan Russell and Fred Marberry. He turned relief strategy into a weapon against McGraw's Giants in the 1924 World Series. In Game Seven, Griffith sent in a succession of relief pitchers that led McGraw, committed to the lefty-righty percentages, to remove star first baseman Bill Terry from the game. When Griffith finished up with the great Walter Johnson, the Senators went on to win the Series with a 12-inning triumph. /(ASN)

Tommy Griffith — 1889–1967. OF 1913–25 Braves, Reds, **Dodgers**, Cubs 1401 g, .280, 52 hr, 619 rbi. *1 WS, 7 g, .190, 3 rbi*

Griffith was a swift right fielder with one of the best arms in the NL. He was consistently in double figures in assists and topped 20 three times. A favorite with Dodger fans from 1919 to 1924, he was an occasional .300 hitter. His best all-around year was 1921, when he hit .312 with a dozen homers and drove in 71 runs for Brooklyn. /(TG)

Art Griggs — 1883–1938. 1B-OF-2B 1909–12, 14–15, 18 **Browns**, Indians, Brooklyn (FL), Tigers 442 g, .277, 5 hr, 152 rbi

Griggs was a football star at Kansas University and the University of Pittsburgh. In his baseball career, he was a steady hitter who played on 15 clubs in ten leagues throughout a 27-year pro career. In his best ML performance, he hit .364 in 28 games with Detroit in 1918. He was also a respected minor league manager. /(WAB)

Hal Griggs — 1928– . RHP 1956–59 **Senators** 347 ip, 6–26, 5.50

Griggs was a 21-year-old bellhop in a Miami hotel when the owner of a minor league team invited him to try out. He once lost 18 straight in the minors, and he fared poorly with Washington. /(RTM)

Steve Grilli — 1949– . RHP 1975–77, 79 **Tigers**, Blue Jays 148 ip, 4–3, 4.51

The slender Grilli was the righthanded complement to John Hiller in the Detroit bullpen of 1976. Control problems limited his effectiveness, and he was sold to Toronto in 1978. /(CC)

J. Ed Grillo — 1870–1920. *Writer.*

One of the most famous sportswriters of his time, Grillo was a sports editor in Cincinnati in the 1890s, where he became a confidant of Ban Johnson. When the American Association was reorganized in 1904, he became league president. He returned to sports writing a few years later with the Washington *Post*, and was with the Washington *Star* when he retired in 1917. /(NLM)

Bob Grim — 1930– . RHP 1954–60, 62 **Yankees**, A's, Indians, Reds, Cardinals 760 ip, 61–41, 3.61. 20 wins: 54 *2 WS, 11 ip, 0–2, 4.91*
☞ *Rookie of the Year—54. All-Star—57.*

In 1954 Grim became the first Yankee rookie since Russ Ford in 1910 to win 20 games. He won a league-leading eight in relief to compile the only 20-win season ever of fewer than 200 innings (199). Coupled with his blazing fastball was a biting slider which damaged his arm and reduced his ability in subsequent years. In the 1955 WS he saved Game One, but in Game Five he gave up three Dodger homers to lose his only WS start.

Grim's arm troubles forced him solely into relief by 1957, when he led AL relievers with 12 wins, eight losses, and 19 saves. In Game Four of the '57 WS, he relieved Tommy Byrne in the bottom of the tenth after Byrne had hit Milwaukee's Nippy Jones with a pitch. Grim surrendered a double that tied the game, and then gave up a home run to Eddie Mathews. Grim was generally mediocre after leaving New York in 1958. /(GDW)

Burleigh Grimes (Ol' Stubblebeard) — 1893–1985. RHP 1916–34 Pirates, **Dodgers**, Giants, Braves, Cardinals, Cubs, Yankees 4180 ip, 270–212, 3.53. 20 wins: 20–21, 23–24, 28 *4 WS, 56.2 ip, 3–4, 4.29.*
Manager 1937–38 **Dodgers** 130–171, .432
☞ *Led League—w 21, 28. Led League—k 21. Hall of Fame—1964.*

Burleigh Grimes was the last legal spitball pitcher in the majors. In a 19-year career that ended in 1934, he often faked the spitter to keep batters guessing.

Grimes never shaved on days he pitched, because the slippery elm he chewed to increase saliva irri-

Burleigh Grimes

tated his skin. His growth of stubble added to his ominous mound presence and led to his nickname, Ol' Stubblebeard. The belligerent pitcher never permitted a batter to dig in at the plate. It was said Grimes's idea of an intentional pass was four pitches at the batter's head.

During the 1920s, Grimes was a standout, twice leading the league in victories and five times topping the 20-win mark. He was durable, leading the league four times in starts and three times in innings pitched. After five straight winning seasons for Brooklyn, his 19 losses in 1925 topped the NL. Following a 12–13 mark in 1926, he was traded to the Giants and was 19–8 in his one season for New York. He peaked as a 25-game winner for Pittsburgh in 1928.

Grimes carried his cantankerous ways with him as manager of the Dodgers, though the team was rarely in a game long enough to make battling tactics pay off. He took over a bedraggled club that had frustrated Casey Stengel in 1937. His chances of developing a winner were undermined when new boss Larry McPhail brought shortstop Leo Durocher to the team. Grimes and Durocher were both battlers, but Durocher was brash and charming, while Grimes was simply pugnacious. Grimes was also frustrated when McPhail signed Babe Ruth as a first base coach and batting practice attraction. Ruth would belt ball after ball over the screen into Bedford Avenue, but his attention span would lapse in the first base coaching box. By 1939 Burleigh and the Babe were gone. Durocher began his managerial career and a new era came to Brooklyn.

A decade of minor league managing followed for Grimes, during which he never ceased his aggressive baseball behavior. Although he was a genial companion off the field, he raged at every close decision against his team. He was suspended in 1940 while managing Grand Rapids (Michigan State League) for an altercation with an umpire. He died of cancer at age 92, twenty-one years after the Veterans Committee selected him for Cooperstown. /(JK)

Oscar Grimes — 1915– . 3B-2B-1B-3B 1938–46 Indians, **Yankees**, A's 602 g, .256, 18 hr, 200 rbi

After parts of five seasons as a Cleveland utility infielder, Grimes was handed the third base job for the Yankees in 1944. He made three errors in one game in 1944 and led AL third basemen with 31 errors in 1945. His father, Ray Grimes, was a NL first baseman in the 1920s. /(MG)

Ray Grimes — 1893–1953. 1B 1920–24, 26 Red Sox, **Cubs**, Phillies 433 g, .329, 27 hr, 263 rbi

Ray Grimes was a Cub hero of the early 1920s whose twin brother Roy had a brief trial with the Giants, and whose son Oscar was a ML infielder. Ray had two fine seasons for the Cubs in 1921 and 1922, batting .321 and .354 (second in the NL). During one stretch in 1922, he drove in at least one run for 17 consecutive games, a ML record. A slipped disc in June 1923 shortened his promising career. /(ARA)

Charlie Grimm (Jolly Cholly) — 1898–1983. 1B 1916, 18–36 A's, Cardinals, Pirates, **Cubs** 2164 g, .290, 79 hr, 1078 rbi. *2 WS, 9 g, .364, 1 hr, 5 rbi.*
Manager 1932–38, 44–49, 52–56, 60 **Cubs**, Braves 1287–1069, .546 First place: 32, 35, 45 *3 WS, 5–12, .294*

Jolly Cholly was an ebullient, fun-loving fellow who frolicked through 20 seasons as a player. He was also a tolerant manager who could coax career-best performances from mediocre players and gave free rein to his stars.

Charlie Grimm

Grimm was the most skillful first baseman of his era. He won nine fielding titles wearing a small mitt and ranging wide of the bag. He broke in with the Athletics in 1916 and won his first regular job with the 1920 Pirates. In Pittsburgh, he teamed with fellow free spirits Rabbit Maranville and Cotton Tierney, to the despair of owner Barney Dreyfuss. The vaudeville team of Gallagher and Shean had a patter song which Grimm, a lefthanded banjo player, appropriated. Once, Grimm snared a sharp grounder, and instead of simply stepping on first, threw the ball to Cotton, shouting, "Have we got him, Mr. Tierney?" "Absolutely, Mr. Grimm," came the rejoinder as the ball was thrown back to Charlie for the putout. Grimm had a 23-game hitting streak in 1923.

Grimm and Maranville were traded to the Cubs after the 1924 season, and continued their fun-loving ways. In 1932, his eighth year as Chicago's first baseman, Grimm became manager of a Cub team that had responded badly to Rogers Hornsby's stern direction, and captured the pennant with a 14-game September winning streak. They won again in 1935, but in mid-1938 Grimm resigned, saying he couldn't relate to or control his players. Gabby Hartnett stepped in, and the team rallied to the pennant while Grimm called the games from the broadcasting booth.

Grimm gave up sportscasting in 1941 to return as a Cubs coach, and then had what he described as the most fun of his career, managing Milwaukee of the American Association for Bill Veeck. After three successful seasons, Grimm was back at the helm in Wrigley Field. In 1945 his Cubs won another pennant, one which would have to last Cub fans for decades.

After being relieved as manager in 1949, Grimm moved to the front office, but in 1950 he returned to the minors, again leading Milwaukee to win the Little World Series. Braves owner Lou Perini invited him to manage in Boston in 1952, and when Perini shifted the franchise to Milwaukee the next year, the established local hero, Charlie Grimm, went along to manage. He remained for over three seasons, twice finishing second.

Grimm had a final fling leading the Cubs in 1960, but, after 17 games, swapped jobs with broadcaster Lou Boudreau. He stayed with the Cubs in various front office jobs another 15 seasons. After his death, his widow was allowed to scatter his ashes over Wrigley Field. /(JK)

Ross Grimsley — 1950– . LHP 1971–80, 82 Reds, **Orioles**, Expos, Indians 2039 ip, 124–99, 3.81. 20 wins: 78 *3 LCS, 18 ip, 1–1, 3.50. 1 WS, 7 ip, 2–1, 2.57* ☛ *All-Star—78.*

Although his pitching speeds ranged from slow to slower, Grimsley was effective for the powerful Reds of 1971–75. He was named lefthander on the *Baseball Digest* 1971 All-Star Rookie team, pitched a two-hitter in Game Four of the 1972 NLCS, and won a pair in the WS. Handsome, with wild, curly hair and piercing green eyes, he was also a free spirit. His refusal to conform to the Reds' short-hair policy helped hasten a trade to Baltimore. The son of Ross Sr., who pitched briefly in the ML, Grimsley signed with Montreal as a free agent in 1978. That year he became the Expos' first 20-game winner and was named Montreal Player of the Year and Tennessee's top pro athlete. /(ME)

Dan Griner (Rusty) — 1888–1950. RHP 1912–16, 18 **Cardinals**, Dodgers 674 ip, 28–55, 3.49

Griner never had a winning major league season; with the 1913 Cardinals, he topped the NL with 22 losses. Back with St. Paul (American Association) in 1919, relying on his "mudball," he did not allow an earned run in winning three complete games in the playoffs against Vernon (Pacific Coast League). /(NLM)

Lee Grissom (Lefty) — 1907– . LHP 1934–41 **Reds**, Yankees, Dodgers, Phillies 702 ip, 29–48, 3.89. *1 WS, 1.1 ip, 0–0, 0.00*
☛ *All-Star—37.*

The loss of the brother of ML pitcher Marv Grissom might have cost the 1938 Reds a pennant. He had won 12 in 1937 and was counted to contribute again, but early in '38 he tried to steal a base, broke his ankle, and was out for the season. When Grissom returned in 1939 to win nine, Cincinnati won the pennant by 4–1/2 games. /(JK)

Marv Grissom — 1918– . RHP 1946, 49, 52–59 **Giants**, Tigers, White Sox, Red Sox, Cardinals 810 ip, 47–45, 3.41. *1 WS, 3 ip, 1–0, 0.00*
☛ *All-Star—54.*

The 6'3" 190-lb Grissom was 12–10 in 1952, his first full season in the majors. He starred as a reliever for the Giants from mid-1953 to 1958, winning 10 games and saving 19 in 1954, and also winning the first game of the WS that year. He registered his career-low ERA of 1.56 in 1956. He served as the A's pitching coach after his retirement as an active player. His brother Lee pitched in the majors from 1934 to 1941. /(JJM)

Dick Groat — 1930– . SS 1952, 55–67 **Pirates**, Cardinals, Phillies, Giants 1929 g, .286, 39 hr, 707 rbi. *2 WS, 14 g, .204, 3 rbi*
☛ *Most Valuable Player—60. All-Star—59–60, 62–64.*

Groat was an All-American basketball player at Duke and averaged 12 points per game with the Fort Wayne Pistons in the NBL (52–53). However, it was at shortstop in double play combinations with Bill Mazeroski and later with Julian Javier that Groat excelled. A natural athlete, he never played minor league ball. The slick ball-handler was at or near the top of the league each year in assists, putouts, and double plays.

Groat was the complete ballplayer. He batted over .300 four times, and in 1960, Phillies manager Gene Mauch said, "He holds the Pirates together," as Pittsburgh won a World Championship over the Yankees. Traded to St. Louis, he solved the Cardinals' shortstop problem (there had been a different regular shortstop every year since 1956). With Groat, the Cardinals finished second in 1963

Dick Groat

and were World Champions the following season. /(FO)

Heinie Groh — 1889–1968. 3B-2B 1912–27 Giants, **Reds**, Pirates 1676 g, .292, 26 hr, 566 rbi. *5 WS, 21 g, .264, 4 rbi.*
   Manager 1918 **Reds** 7–3, .700

Famous for his unique "bottle bat," with a non-tapered barrel and thin handle, the 5'8" 158-lb third baseman was an outstanding leadoff man. He deftly dropped bunts from his peculiar wide-open stance, used his keen eye and short stature to draw walks, and kept his BA in the .280–.320 range. He had played only 31 games for the Giants when he was traded to Cincinnati, where he starred for eight seasons. He hit for the cycle on July 5, 1915. After a bitter holdout in 1921, he signed in June only on the promise that he would be traded. He was immediately swapped to New York but Commissioner Landis canceled the deal. In December, the Giants finally reacquired him and the still-peppery Groh helped them win three straight pennants. His older brother Lew played two games for the A's in 1919 as a 36-year-old rookie. /(JK)

Heinie Groh

Steve Gromek — 1920– . RHP 1941–57 **Indians**, Tigers 2065 ip, 123–108, 3.41. *1 WS, 9 ip, 1–0, 1.00*

Gromek had pitched mostly in relief for the 1948 Indians, going 9–3 (2.84), but started the pivotal fourth game of the '48 World Series against the Braves, and threw a complete-game, 2–1 victory. The picture of Gromek hugging teammate Larry Doby, who had homered, is a landmark in the annals of baseball's battle to integrate successfully. Gromek relied on a fastball, change, and knuckle-curve. He played his first two pro seasons as an infielder, but made it to Cleveland in his first year pitching, 1941, by going 14–2 in the Michigan State League. He led the Indians with a 19–9 record in 1945. Traded to Detroit in 1943, the native of Hamtramck (just a few miles from Tiger Stadium) led the 1954 Tigers with 18 wins. /(ME)

Bob Groom — 1884–1948. RHP 1909–18 **Senators**, St. Louis (FL), Browns, Indians 2336 ip, 120–150, 3.10. 20 wins: 12

From June 19 through September 25, 1909, Washington rookie Bob Groom set a since-tied major

league record by losing 19 consecutive games. He finished the season at 7–26, tying the AL mark for losses. A wild fireballer, he also led the league with 105 walks for the 42–110 Senators. He finally found success in 1912, going 24–13. Jumping to the Federal League in 1914, he did atypically poorly for a ML veteran, losing 20 games. As a St. Louis Brown, Groom no-hit the White Sox in the second game of a May 6, 1917 doubleheader, a day after teammate Ernest Koob had no-hit them. While Chicago went on to win the pennant, Koob went 6–14, and Groom's 8–19 tied him for the league lead in losses. /(NLM)

Don Gross — 1931– . LHP 1955–60 **Reds**, Pirates 398 ip, 20–22, 3.73

Gross became a lefthanded pitcher through an accident. As a seven-year-old he caught his right arm in his mother's washing machine wringer. He learned to throw lefthanded while his arm mended but in everything else he remained righthanded. /(BC)

Greg Gross — 1952– . OF 1973– Astros, Cubs, **Phillies** 1809 g, .287, 7 hr, 308 rbi. *2 LCS, 8 g, .333, 1 rbi. 2 WS, 6 g, .000*

An excellent contact hitter who rarely struck out, Gross had at least 39 pinch-hit at-bats in each of his nine seasons in Philadelphia, and through 1988 was the third leading pinch hitter in ML history, with 136 hits. He hit .314 for Houston in 1974 to win *The Sporting News* NL Rookie Player of the Year honors, but it would be his only ML season as a full-time starter, as his weak arm, little speed, and no power came to be seen as liabilities. He still got over 400 AB in two more seasons in Houston, and after a 1979 trade sent him from the Cubs to the Phillies, Gross became a pinch hit specialist. He returned to Houston in 1989. /(SG)

Kevin Gross — 1961– . RHP 1983–89 **Phillies**, Expos 1306 ip, 71–78, 3.95
☛ *All-Star—88.*

Plagued by back troubles most of his career, the 6'5" Gross pitched most of 1987 with a herniated disc. He was suspended for 10 days in August when he was caught using sandpaper to scuff the ball on the mound. He started fast in 1988, earning a spot on the All-Star team, but slumped to 12–14 by the end of the year. Gross was traded to Montreal for Floyd Youmans and Jeff Parrett before the 1989 season. /(SG)

Milt Gross — 1912–1973. *Writer.*

Gross was a humorist and humanist whose column, "Speaking Out," appeared in the New York *Post* and other papers for 24 years. He was one of the first to interview athletes and write about them as people with human emotions and frailties. Gross wrote numerous magazine articles and books on boxing and golf, and a baseball book, *Yankee Doodles.* /(NLM)

Wayne Gross — 1952– . 3B-1B 1976–86 **A's**, Orioles .233, 121 hr, 396 rbi. *1 LCS, 3 g, .000*
☛ *All-Star—77.*

A stocky lefthanded hitter with good power and little speed, Gross was the A's starting third baseman as a rookie in 1977, and with 22 HR was the last-place club's lone representative at the All-Star Game that year. He hit only .233, though, and began the 1978 season at Vancouver (Pacific Coast League) before rejoining the A's for good after 17 games. Gross played regularly with Oakland, either at third or first, until he was traded to the Orioles for Tim Stoddard after the 1983 season. He hit .216 as Baltimore's third baseman in 1984, and matched his rookie year and career-high HR output with 22. /(SCL)

Jerry Grote — 1941– . C-3B 1963–64, 66–78, 81 Astros, **Mets**, Dodgers, Royals. 1421 g, .252, 39 hr, 404 rbi. *4 WS, 15 g, .240, 1 rbi. 4 LCS, 11 g, .194, 3 rbi*
☛ *All-Star—68, 74.*

Success came, but not easily or early for Jerry Grote. After hitting .181 in 100 games for the 1964 Colt .45s (later the Astros), he returned to the minors. The Mets purchased his contract, but in his first two years in New York Grote hit poorly, was mediocre behind the plate, and blamed it on the umpires, manager, and teammates. Manager Wes Westrum said, "If he ever learns to control himself, he might become the best catcher in baseball." Grote learned, becoming a key ingredient on Met teams for a dozen years. Lou Brock once said that Grote was the toughest catcher in the league to steal against. Grote was behind the plate on his birthday when the Mets won their first pennant in 1969. He caught every inning of the 1969 and 1973 LCS and WS, setting three WS fielding records in 1973. Though he played only 61 games with the Dodgers, he appeared with them in the 1977 and 1978 WS. The Royals, short of catching, lured him out of retirement in 1981. /(FJO)

Johnny Groth — 1926– . OF 1946–60 **Tigers**, Browns, White Sox, Senators, A's 1248 g, .279, 60 hr, 486 rbi

Time, Collier's, The Saturday Evening Post, and *Life* all tabbed Groth for superstardom in 1949 after he hit .340 with 30 home runs for Buffalo (International League) in 1948. He hit .293 as the Tigers' regular centerfielder, and in 1950 hit .306 with 12 homers and 85 RBI, at one point banging eight consecutive hits. Groth played 10 more seasons, but never equaled his 1950 totals. /(JK)

Lefty Grove [Robert Moses] (Mose) — 1900–1975. LHP 1925–41 **A's**, Red Sox 3941 ip, 300–140, 3.06. 20 wins: 27–33, 35 *3 WS, 51 ip, 4–2, 1.75*
☛ *Most Valuable Player—31. Led League—w 28, 30–31, 33. Led League—era 26, 29–32, 35–36, 38–39. Led League—k 25–31. All-Star—33, 35–39. Hall of Fame—1947.*

Lefty Grove had a blazing fastball and a temper to match. By the time he had pitched 17 seasons, eking out a 300th win in his last appearance, both were gone. He arrived with a reputation for wrath, and led the American League in strikeouts seven consecutive years, victories four times (including 31 wins in 1931), ERA nine times (no one else ever did more than five), and winning percentage five times. Grove also led in shredded uniforms, kicked buckets, ripped-apart lockers, and alienated teammates.

Grove tested the saintly patience of Connie Mack, a placid patriarch who won his last three pennants mostly by handing Grove the ball. Eventually, Grove gained control over himself and the ball. As a rookie, he led the league in walks as well as strikeouts. Later, he learned to win with pinpoint control and guile. Connie Mack explained, "Groves was a thrower until after we sold him to Boston and he hurt his arm. Then he learned to pitch."

Mack called his star "Groves," for that's how Lefty's name appeared in box scores while pitching for Baltimore in the International League. He arrived there in the midst of a string of seven consecutive pennants, and Baltimore was not required to sell its stars to the majors. Grove was 25 before he could reach the Athletics, after Mack paid $100,600 for him, topping the flat $100,000 the Yankees had paid the Red Sox for Babe Ruth.

The nine seasons Grove pitched for Philadelphia were his best. The team won three pennants, but crowds dwindled, tiring of victory and pinched by the ongoing Depression. Grove was sold to the suddenly rich Red Sox, whose new owner, Tom Yawkey, was buying up star players. Though Grove had led the league with 24 wins in 1933, his first year with Boston, 1934, was a sore-armed struggle.

Lefty Grove

He bounced back in 1935 with his final 20-victory season, but won by craftily working hitters.

Grove had largely overcome his uneasiness with strangers. He came, with a limited education, from a hard life in the bituminous hills of western Maryland. It took him time to adjust to being a national celebrity. When he had a rubber stamp made with his facsimile autograph, so as to accommodate as many fans as possible, he was branded an illiterate who couldn't write his name. If there was one thing he could write, it was his signature; it appeared on a string of lucrative contracts, first with Mack, then topped by Yawkey.

Grove went home between seasons to the hard-scrabble town of Lonaconing, MD, and opened a bowling alley that became the social center of the region. He retired to become a genial townsman, his hair turning white, weight added to his 6′3″ frame. He would smile when reminded of stories of his once-terrible temper. He'd shake his head when someone spoke of the game he lost while trying for an AL record-breaking 17th consecutive victory in

1931. The A's failed to get him a run, and, after the game's only hit (a bloop single), a substitute outfielder misjudged an ordinary line drive, and the winning run scored. In later years, Grove would have forgiven the player who misjudged the ball, if he could have remembered his name. He never forgot, or forgave, star fielder Al Simmons, who had taken the day off to visit a doctor. Despite missing that record, Grove left behind a bevy of honors, including a batting record: he fanned 593 times, the most ever by a pitcher. His ultimate honor came with his 1947 induction into Cooperstown. /(JK)

Orval Grove — 1919- . RHP 1940-49 **White Sox** 1177 ip, 63-73, 3.78

Grove was one of the first pitchers to come out of the White Sox farm system, established in 1939. Invited to camp in 1943 with a $1 contract, having missed most of 1942 following knee surgery, he made the club and was given his first start in June. He then set a White Sox season record by winning his first nine decisions. On July 8, he took a no-hitter into the ninth inning against the Yankees. With one out, Joe Gordon broke it up with a double to left that was fair by inches. Grove ended the year at 15-9, but proved a winner only during the war years. /(RL)

Johnny Grubb — 1948- . OF-DH 1972-87 **Padres**, Indians, Rangers, Tigers 1424 g, .278, 99 hr, 475 rbi. *2 LCS, 5 g, .455, 2 rbi. 1 WS, 4 g, .333* ☞ *All-Star—74.*

Naturally a righthanded batter, Grubb learned to hit lefthanded by emulating his hero, Mickey Mantle. He batted .311 as a Padres rookie in 1973, and in 1975 set a then-club record of 36 doubles. His 21-game hitting streak with Texas tied for the longest in the AL in 1979. He had nine stints on the DL; in 1981 surgeons removed a rib to relieve a circulatory problem. He became a key Tiger DH, extra outfielder, and pinch hitter. His 11th-inning double won Game Two of the 1984 LCS. /(JCA)

Frank Grube (Hans) — 1905-1945. C 1931-36, 41 **White Sox**, Browns 394 g, .244, 1 hr, 107 rbi

When Moe Berg held out in 1931, White Sox scouts combed the minors for another catcher, coming up with Grube. In 1932 Chicago acquired Charlie Berry, who had beaten out Grube for the first-string catching job at Lafayette College and did so again with the White Sox. On the football field, Grube succeeded Berry as star end at Lafayette College and then followed him into the NFL for a season (1928) before turning to baseball. /(RL)

John Gruber — Unk.–1932. *Writer.*

The official scorer for the Pittsburgh Pirates for 40 years until the early 1930s, Gruber was honored with a plaque put up in the Forbes Field press box in 1933. /(NLM)

Kelly Gruber — 1962– . 3B 1984– **Blue Jays** 538 g, .263, 52 hr, 208 rbi. *1 LCS, 5 g, .294, 1 rbi*
☛ *All-Star—89.*

Gruber emerged in 1988 as a key player for the Blue Jays, hitting .278 with 16 home runs and 81 RBI. Primarily a third baseman, he made appearances at second base and shortstop and in the outfield as well. Gruber was acquired by Toronto from Cleveland in the major league draft, which required him to spend time on the Blue Jays' bench during the 1984 season before being sent to the minors. In 1986 Gruber was expected to take the third base job from the aging platoon of Rance Mulliniks and Garth Iorg, but he had a disappointing season after minor injuries and was used mainly as a utility player. When Mulliniks was injured in the first inning of the 1988 home opener, Gruber took over for him in dramatic fashion, with a 4-for-6 game featuring two home runs and an RBI double. He became the full-time third baseman, showed promise of becoming a fine all-around player, and was named to the 1989 AL All-Star team. /(TF)

Joe Grzenda — 1937– . LHP 1961, 64, 66–67, 69–72 Tigers, A's, Mets, Twins, **Senators**, Cardinals 308 ip, 14–13, 4.01. *1 LCS, 0.2 ip, 0–0, 0.00*

A reliever in all but three of his ML appearances, Grzenda, a nervous chain-smoker, was known as Shaky Joe. He threw the last pitch for the Senators in 1971 before the fans swarmed the field and the team (sans Grzenda) moved to Texas. /(JL)

Cecilio Guante — 1960– . RHP 1982– **Pirates**, Yankees, Rangers 548 ip, 27–31, 3.35

The hard-throwing, injury-prone Dominican led the 1985 Pirates in appearances and games finished. The tall, slender pitcher was a career reliever, delivering from all angles, but throwing more than pitching. /(ME)

Mark Gubicza — 1962– . RHP 1984– **Royals** 1313 ip, 84–67, 3.51. *1 LCS, 8 ip, 1–0, 3.24*
☛ *All-Star—88–89.*

Gubicza fired a 93-mph fastball and 90-mph slider, but wildness was his early nemesis. Equipped with better control and an improved changeup and slider, he was the ace of the Royals' staff in 1988. /(FO)

Mike Guerra [Fermin Romero] — 1912– . C 1937, 44–51 Senators, **A's**, Red Sox 565 g, .242, 9 hr, 168 rbi

Guerra was one of 10 Latins signed by Joe Cambria to play for the Senators during WWII. His best years, though, came with the 1949 and 1950 Athletics. He managed his hometown Havana club in the Florida International League and scouted for the Tigers. /(NLM)

Mario Guerrero — 1949– . SS-2B 1973–80 Red Sox, Cardinals, Angels, A's 697 g, .257, 7 hr, 170 rbi

In his only season of everyday play, this error-prone Dominican hit .275 but drew only 15 walks in 505 at-bats, scoring just 27 runs. /(SH)

Pedro Guerrero — 1956– . OF-3B-1B 1978– **Dodgers**, Cardinals 1242 g, .308, 193 hr, 732 rbi. *3 LCS, 15 g, .196, 1 hr, 8 rbi. 1 WS, 6 g, .333, 2 hr, 7 rbi*
☛ *All-Star—81, 83, 85, 87, 89.*

Writer Bill James called Guerrero "the best hitter God has made in a long time." Originally signed as a free agent by the Indians, Guerrero was virtually stolen by the Dodgers after his first pro season, acquired in exchange for pitching flop Bruce Ellingsen. He first hit the limelight when his five RBIs in the final game of the 1981 World Series gave him a piece of the first three-way Series MVP award. In 1982 he became the first Dodger to hit 30 HR and steal 20 bases in a season, and he did it again the following year.

In 1985 Guerrero tied a major league record with 15 HR in June, en route to tying the Los Angeles record of 33. He also reached base 14 consecutive times that year, two shy of Ted Williams's record, and led the league in both slugging and on-base percentage.

Although an aggressive baserunner, he is considered a poor slider; he ruptured a tendon sliding in spring training and missed most of the 1986 season. His basestealing was subsequently curtailed. His .338 BA in 1987 was the highest for a Dodger since Tommy Davis's .348 in 1962 and earned him UPI's Comeback of the Year award.

Dodger management appeared to believe him

capable of any athletic feat, and they thought nothing of shifting him to third base in mid-career, and in and out as the need arose. Although he gained a reputation for being shaky at third, statistics show that he was about as good as anyone in the league at getting to the ball. In the minors he made all-star teams at both first base and third base, and he broke into the Dodger lineup as a replacement for the injured Davey Lopes at second base. Guerrero was traded to the Cardinals for pitcher John Tudor during the 1988 season and missed out on the Dodgers' World Championship that fall. /(TG)

Lee Guetterman — 1958– . LHP 1984– **Mariners**, Yankees 337 ip, 17–15, 4.30

The 6′8″ Guetterman is the third-tallest player in major league history. Showing a pattern of near-invincibility in the beginning of the season but inconsistency the rest of the time, the reliever won his first five games for the Mariners in 1987 and was 8–1 at the All-Star break, but finished 11–4 with a 3.81 ERA. In 1989 he set the Yankee record for scoreless innings from the start of a season with 29, but was hit hard for much of June and July before regaining his touch. /(TF)

Ron Guidry (Gator, Louisiana Lightning, The Ragin' Cajun) — 1950– . LHP 1975–88 **Yankees** 2392 ip, 170–91, 3.29. 20 wins: 78, 83, 85 *3 LCS, 22 ip, 2–1, 4.03. 3 WS, 32 ip, 3–1, 1.69*
☛ *Led League—w 78, 85. Led League—era 78–79.. Cy Young Award—78. All-Star—78–79, 82–83. Gold Glove—82–86.*

Although Guidry won over 20 games three times in his career, he is remembered for having one of the greatest single seasons ever. He was 25–3 with a 1.74 ERA in 1978, won the Cy Young Award unanimously, and finished second to Boston's Jim Rice in AL MVP voting. Guidry set club records that year in strikeouts (248) and consecutive wins at the start of a season (13). He called his Yankee-record 18 strikeouts against California on June 17 of that year "perhaps my greatest single thrill." He started the AL East playoff game on October 2, 1978 against Boston and won 5–4 in what was "probably the most tension-packed game I ever played in." Guidry was named *TSN* Player of the Year and Man of the Year and the Associated Press's Male Athlete of the Year, and he made every all-star team. His nine shutouts tied Babe Ruth's AL record for a lefthander.

During the 1970s, Yankee management made a policy of acquiring pitchers through trades and free agent signings. As a result, Guidry did not find a regular place in the Yankee rotation until 1977, when he was 26 years old. Even then, there were those who felt that the 5′11″ 160-lb lefty was too small to pitch effectively and last in the major leagues. Guidry dispelled the notion by going 16–7 that year and perfecting the wicked slider that became his bread and butter pitch. He went on to lead the majors in victories from 1977 through 1987 with 168, posting records of 18–8 (1979), 21–9 (1983), and 22–6 (1985). He is fourth on the all-time Yankee victory list (170), second in strikeouts (1,778), sixth in games and innings, and tied for sixth in shutouts (26). Guidry compiled a 5–2 postseason record, 3–1 in World Series play.

Guidry's success and durability were attributable in part to the fact that he was an outstanding athlete. He won five straight Gold Glove awards (1982–1986) and was twice used briefly in the outfield.

Guidry was slow to recover from elbow surgery following the 1988 season, and he started 1989 on the disabled list before beginning a rehabilitation assignment in June at Triple-A. When he didn't impress the Yankee management with his performance at Columbus, he retired from baseball on July 12, 1989.

Guidry was a good amateur drummer who kept a trap set at Yankee Stadium and once played with the Beach Boys during a postgame concert. /(EG/CR)

Ozzie Guillen [born Oswaldo Jose Guillen Barrios] — 1964– . SS 1985– **White Sox** 769 g, .263, 6 hr, 224 rbi
☛ *Rookie of the Year—85. All-Star—88.*

The White Sox drew criticism for trading LaMarr Hoyt to the Padres in December of 1984 in a seven-player deal that yielded them prospect Ozzie Guillen. But the highly rated, 21-year-old Venezuelan shortstop easily outdistanced Milwaukee's Ted Higuera to capture 1985 AL Rookie of the Year honors. Guillen committed just 12 errors to lead AL shortstops in fielding and set a record for White Sox shortstops. His .273 batting average was higher than expected. He was right when he predicted he would drive in the winning run in Tom Seaver's first attempt to win his 300th game that August 4. While his bubbly, gregarious personality became interpreted by opponents as hot-dogging, by 1988 he established himself as an All-Star. /(RL)

Don Gullett — 1951– . LHP 1970–78 **Reds**, Yankees 1391 ip, 109–50, 3.11. *6 LCS, 41 ip, 2–3, 3.98. 5 WS, 52 ip, 2–2, 3.61*

Hailed by Sparky Anderson as a sure Hall of Famer and the next Sandy Koufax, this Kentucky farm boy was a vital part of the Big Red Machine in the early 1970s. The 19-year-old rookie flamethrower struck out six Mets in a row on August 23, 1970 (2nd game), tying a relief record, and Willie Stargell said Gullett "throws nothing but wall-to-wall heat." Moved into the rotation in 1971, Gullett went 16–6 (2.64) and led the NL in winning percentage (.727). He usually had a high winning percentage; from 1973 through 1976 he was 61–26. He was named to *TSN*'s postseason all-star team in 1974.

Gullett signed with the Yankees as a free agent for 1977 and went 14–4 to help New York to a World Championship, but it would be his last good season. Persistent shoulder problems, perhaps caused by his pitching motion, led to rotator cuff damage that ended his career. /(KC)

Bill Gullickson — 1959– . RHP 1979–87 **Expos**, Reds, Yankees 1644 ip, 101–86, 3.61. *1 LCS, 14 ip, 0–2, 2.51*

Gullickson was the second player taken in the June 1977 draft, and his 10–5, 3.00 record in 1980 earned him *TSN* NL Rookie Pitcher of the Year honors. He finished second (behind Steve Howe) in the NL Rookie of the Year voting. In 1981 he helped the Expos to their only division title with a 7–9, 2.81 record and beat the Phillies 3–1 in Game Two of the divisional playoff necessitated by the split-season format used after the players' strike. In the LCS, he lost Games One and Four to the Dodgers when Montreal could muster only one run each game for him.

With the exception of the strike season, the consistent Gullickson was in double figures in wins every season from his rookie year on. Acquired by the Reds for 1986, he went 15–12. The Yankees traded Dennis Rasmussen to get Gullickson, in the last year of his contract, for their 1987 pennant drive, but he was unhappy with the atmosphere in the Bronx and accepted a $2 million offer to pitch in Japan the following season.

In an April 10, 1982 game, Gullickson tied the modern ML record with six wild pitches. /(JFC)

Harry Gumbert (Gunboat) — 1909– . RHP 1935–44, 46–50 **Giants**, Cardinals, Reds, Pirates 2157 ip, 143–113, 3.68. *3 WS, 4 ip, 0–0, 27.00*

The 6'2" 185-lb Gumbert began his fifteen-year career as a starter. He reached double figures in wins from 1936 to 1941 and again in 1943–1944, including an 11–3 mark in 1936 and an 18–11 record in 1939. He spent 1945 in the military and by 1947 was strictly a reliever, totaling 48 saves over his career.

Gumbert appeared in WS for the Giants in 1936 and 1937 and the Cardinals in 1942. He pitched in a total of six games, allowing 12 hits and five walks with a 27.00 ERA.

Gumbert led the NL in games pitched in 1948 (61), relief wins in 1947 (10) and 1948 (10), relief loses in '47 (10) and '48 (8), and saves in '48 (17). /(JJM)

Dave Gumpert — 1958– . RHP 1982–83, 85–87 Tigers, **Cubs**, Royals 136 ip, 3–2, 4.31

A Michigan native who grew up idolizing Detroit's Al Kaline, Gumpert was signed by the Tigers in 1980. At his peak, he recorded a 2.64 ERA relieving in 26 games in 1983 and was voted the Detroit Sports Broadcasters Association's Rookie of the Year. /(JCA)

Randy Gumpert — 1918– . RHP 1936–38, 1946–52 A's, Yankees, **White Sox**, Red Sox, Senators 1053 ip, 51–59, 4.17
☛ *All-Star—51.*

As a teenager, Gumpert threw batting practice for the A's at Shibe Park for two years before signing in 1936 for $300 a month. He was 11–3 (2.31) at his best in 1946 for the Yankees, for whom he became a scout. /(NLM)

Larry Gura — 1947– . LHP 1970–85 Cubs, Yankees, **Royals** 2046 ip, 126–97, 3.76. *4 LCS, 28 ip, 2–2, 4.18. 1 WS, 12.1 ip, 0–0, 2.19*
☛ *All-Star—80.*

An All-American at Arizona State, in 1968 Gura pitched two no-hitters in the National Baseball Congress tournament. Drafted by the Cubs, he saw limited ML duty from 1970 to 1973 and was then dealt to Texas and sold to the Yankees. In New York, Gura posted a 12–9 record over two seasons, but new manager Billy Martin didn't like him and sent him to the Royals for catcher Fran Healy. Healy played only 74 games for the Yankees, while Gura blossomed as a crafty starter with the Royals, going 88–49 from 1976 through 1982. He was the Royals' Pitcher of the Year in 1978 (16–4, 2.72), won 18 in both 1980 and 1982, and was on four Royals division winners. The fine-fielding Gura went through both 1980 and 1981 without an error. He was known as a fitness fanatic who pursued a strict diet and conditioning regimen. In 1983 he slumped to a league-leading 18 losses. Gura finished where he had started, pitching briefly with the Cubs in 1985./(DQV)

Frankie Gustine — 1920– . 2B-3B-SS 1939–50 **Pirates**, Cubs, Browns 1261 g, .265, 38 hr, 480 rbi ☛ *All-Star—46–48.*

Gustine was signed by Pie Traynor as a 16-year-old prospect and was 19 when he joined the Pirates as a third baseman in Traynor's last season as manager. With his mentor gone, Gustine was shifted between second base and shortstop. His progress was also hindered by a chronic double hernia and assorted injuries. Finally, in 1947, he returned to Traynor's old position and led NL third basemen in putouts, assists, errors, and double plays while he had his best season offensively (.297, nine HR, 67 RBI, 102 runs). He was an All-Star at second base in 1946 and at third base in 1947–48./(JK)

Bill Guthrie — Unk.–1950. *Umpire* NL, **AL** 1913–15, 22, 28–32

Guthrie was one of the few umpires to work in both the National and American leagues. On the last day of the 1928 season, Goose Goslin, knowing he could lock up the AL batting title by avoiding his final at-bat, attempted to get himself thrown out of the game by constantly arguing Guthrie's calls. The umpire understood Goslin's intent and refused to be ruffled. The frustrated Goslin swung away and got a hit./(RTM)

Cesar Gutierrez (Cocoa) — 1943– . SS 1967, 69–71 Giants, **Tigers** 223 g, .235, 0 hr, 26 rbi

The quintessential "good field, no hit" shortstop, Gutierrez nevertheless made baseball history with his bat. In the second game of a June 21, 1970 doubleheader, he had six singles and a double in seven at-bats in a 12-inning game to set the AL record (and tie the ML mark) for hits in a game without making an out. But 1970 was the Venezuelan's only season as a regular; he hit a career-high .243 and led AL shortstops in errors./(SH)

Jackie Gutierrez — 1960– . SS-2B 1983–88 **Red Sox**, Orioles, Phillies 356 g, .237, 4 hr, 63 rbi

Gutierrez hit a career-high .263 as the Red Sox' rookie shortstop in 1984, but set ML records for the fewest assists and total chances by a shortstop in a full season. He hit only .218 the following year, lost his job back to Glenn Hoffman, and was traded to

Baltimore. His father and brother competed in track and field in, respectively, the 1936 and 1964 Olympics./(SCL)

Don Gutteridge — 1912– . 2B-3B 1936–40, 1942–48. Cardinals, **Browns**, Red Sox, Pirates 1151 g, .256, 39 hr, 391 rbi. *2 WS, 9 g, .192, 1 rbi.* *Manager* 1969–70 **White Sox** 109–172, .388

The high point of Gutteridge's career came on his second day as a Cardinal, in 1936. In a doubleheader in Ebbets Field, the rookie got six hits, including an inside-the-park HR, and stole home twice. One of 70 players to play for both the Cardinals and Browns, Gutteridge was a pepperpot second baseman on the Browns' lone pennant-winner in 1944. On June 30, 1944, Gutteridge took part in five double plays in one game, setting a since-surpassed AL second basemen's record. Coaching for the White Sox when Al Lopez retired on May 4, 1969, Gutteridge replaced him and stayed at the helm until he was fired in September 1970./(WAB)

Joe Guyon — 1892–1971. OF *Minor Leagues.*

A Chippewa Indian, Guyon was Jim Thorpe's football teammate at Carlisle and later an All-America at Georgia Tech (named as a tackle even though he was a triple-threat halfback). He played professional football from 1919 through 1926, often in the same backfield with Thorpe. He was named to both the National College Football Hall of Fame and the Pro Football Hall of Fame. But he preferred baseball and hit .329 over twelve summers, mostly with Atlanta (Southern Association) and Louisville (American Association) in the high minors. He stole 203 bases for his career, with a high of 45 in 1921 for Atlanta. Four times he scored over 100 runs, including 152 in 1925, his best year overall. He hit .363 that year, with 38 doubles, 17 triples, and 106 RBI, all full-season career highs. His football career and his hopes of making the ML in baseball were both ended by a knee injury sustained when he ran into an outfield fence in May 1928./(MC)

Jose Guzman — 1963– . RHP 1985–88 **Rangers** 620 ip, 37–44, 4.21

Guzman has shown flashes of great talent in four ML seasons, but it has been tempered by injuries and poor pitching. He was 14–14 in 1987 and fanned 157 batters in 206.2 innings in 1988. Arm trouble caused him to miss all of 1989./(ME)

Tony Gwynn — 1960– . OF 1982– **Padres** 1060 g, .332, 45 hr, 416 rbi. *1 LCS, 5 g, .368, 3 rbi. 1 WS, 5 g, .263*

 Led League—ba 84, 87–89. All-Star—84–89. Gold Glove—86–89.

By 1988 Tony Gwynn had established himself as the outstanding average hitter in the National League. San Diego's third-round choice in the June 1981 draft, Gwynn quickly moved to the majors after a batting title and Most Valuable Player honors at Walla Walla (Rookie Northwest League). Despite a broken left wrist in 1982, Gwynn's batting prowess improved at the big league level. He became the first Padre to reach 200 hits and captured the first batting title for the frachise in 1984. Gwynn was voted into the All-Star Game, finished third in the NL MVP voting, and delivered the game-winning RBI in the fifth game of the Championship Series that sent San Diego to its first World Series. Tony also earned the first of three Padres MVP awards. The wrist injury hampered Gwynn in 1985, but he led the NL in hits the following two years. His 1987 season was the greatest offensive show in Padres history. His .370 batting average was the best in the NL since Stan Musial's .376 in 1948. He became San Diego's career leader in batting average and was among the all-time club leaders in runs scored, hits and doubles. He added another title in 1988 despite a terrible first half, coming on to win with a .313 mark that is the lowest ever to lead the NL. Originally a deficient outfielder, Gwynn improved to Gold Glove quality in 1986. A tough batter to strike out, Gwynn tied a record with five stolen bases on September 20, 1986 in Houston. He was also part of the first trio to hit consecutive home runs to start a major league game, in 1987. Tony was also a draft choice of the San Diego Clippers of the National Basketball Association. His brother Chris played with the Dodgers./(ME)

Bert Haas — 1914- . 1B-3B-OF 1937-38, 42-43, 46-49, 51 Dodgers, **Reds**, Phillies, Giants, White Sox 723 g, .264, 22 hr, 263 rbi
☞ *All-Star—47.*

When Haas arrived in the majors with Brooklyn, he pinch-hit four days in a row, collecting a single and three doubles. Haas served in Italy during WWII. Aggressive and hard-hitting, he hit a career-high .286 in 1947. /(EW)

Moose Haas [Bryan Edmund] — 1956- . RHP 1976-87 **Brewers**, A's 1655 ip, 100-83, 4.01. *1 LCS, 7 ip, 1-0, 4.91. 1 WS, 7 ip, 0-0, 7.36*

Finesse pitcher Haas employed pinpoint control in 1980 to go 16-15 with a 3.11 ERA. In the 1981 strike season, he was 11-7, but lost his two starts in the divisional playoff as the Brewers lost to the Yankees. He had better luck in 1982, defeating the Angels 9-5 in Game Four of the LCS, although he was hit hard in two appearances in the World Series. His best season came in 1983 as his 13-3 mark gave him a league-leading .814 winning percentage. The A's gave up four players to get Haas for 1986, but after a 7-2 start, arm trouble ended his season and, eventually, his career. On April 12, 1978 he set a Brewers record with 14 strikeouts against the Yankees. /(WOR)

Mule Haas [George William] — 1903-1974. OF-1B 1925, 28-38 Pirates, **A's**, White Sox 1168 g, .292, 43 hr, 496 rbi. *3 WS, 18 g, .161, 2 hr, 9 rbi*

Haas had a great outfield tutor in Tris Speaker with the Athletics in 1928. He adopted Speaker's style of playing shallow, loping back to catch fly balls over his shoulder or dashing in for shoetop grabs. He learned bench jockeying from another master, Eddie Rommel. Haas, Al Simmons, and Jimmy Dykes were sold to the White Sox for $100,000 in 1932. /(JK)

John Habyan — 1964- . RHP 1985- **Orioles** 160 ip, 9-10, 4.61

Pitching for Charlotte (Southern League) on May 13, 1985, Habyan no-hit Columbus in a 6-0

victory. He went from the Instructional League to Baltimore that September. In spending most of 1987 with the Orioles, he posted a 6-7 record. /(JCA)

Stan Hack (Smiling Stan, Stanislaus) — 1909-1979. 3B 1932-47 **Cubs** 1938 g, .301, 57 hr, 642 rbi. *4 WS, 18 g, .348, 5 rbi.*
    Manager 1954-56, 58 **Cubs**, Cardinals 199-272, .423
☞ *All-Star—38-39, 41, 43.*

Genial Stan Hack, with his famous smile, was one of the most popular players of his day. He batted .352 in 1931, his first year in pro ball, and William Veeck personally went to Sacramento to sign him to a Cubs contract. By 1934 Hack was a fixture at third base in Wrigley Field. He exhibited a smooth, easy style, twice leading the NL in fielding and assists, and five times in putouts. At bat, he slashed singles and doubles, rarely swinging for the fences. He topped the 100 mark in runs scored seven times (six consecutive), had league-high stolen base totals in 1938 and 1939, and league-high hit totals in 1940 and 1941.

Hack retired in 1943, in part because he didn't get along with Cubs manager Jimmy Wilson. When Wilson was fired early in 1944, Charlie Grimm returned and coaxed Hack out of retirement. In 1945 Hack hit a career-high .323 in helping the Cubs to a pennant for a fourth time. When he finished playing in 1947, he had tied the then-record for most years as a NL third baseman (16). He began managing the Cubs in 1954, in three years never finishing higher than sixth. He coached for the Cardinals, and managed in the minors until 1966.

An opposing player once said that Hack "has more friends than Leo Durocher has enemies." Hack was known to party in his early career, and reportedly was often carried home by drinking partner Pat Malone. Bill Veeck turned Hack's captivating smile into a promotion; he once walked the Wrigley bleachers selling an item featuring a grinning picture of Hack on the back of a mirror, with the slogan, "Smile with Stan Hack." The fans began shining the mirrors into opposing batters' eyes, which prompted the umpires to confiscate the gimmicks and threaten to forfeit the game. /(DB)

Stan Hack

Warren Hacker — 1924– . RHP 1948–58, 61 **Cubs**, Reds, Phillies, White Sox 1283 ip, 62–89, 4.21

As a boy, Hacker wanted to be a coal miner like his father, who insisted he pursue baseball instead. Hacker followed a 15–9, 2.58 1952 season with a league-leading 19 defeats in 1953, and had three more losing seasons with poor Cub teams. The righthander relied mostly on knucklers and sinkers. He came within two outs of a no-hitter versus the Braves on May 21, 1955./(AA)

Harvey Haddix (The Kitten) — 1925– . LHP 1952–65 Cardinals, Phillies, Reds, **Pirates**, Orioles 2235 ip, 136–113, 3.63. 20 wins: 53 *1 WS, 7 ip, 2–0, 2.45* ☛ *All-Star—53–55. Gold Glove—58–60.*

Haddix will always be remembered for his performance on the night of May 26, 1959. Though he didn't feel well, he took his turn against Lew Burdette and the Braves. Haddix retired 36 consecutive batters, pitching 12 perfect innings, but his Pirate teammates didn't score. In the 13th, Milwaukee's leadoff batter, Felix Mantilla, reached first on third baseman Don Hoak's error and was then sacrificed to second. The tiring Haddix intentionally walked Hank Aaron, and Joe Adcock followed with a home run. Adcock passed Aaron on the basepath (making the final score 1–0), but the no-hitter and the game were lost. Haddix's 12–2/3-inning, one-hit complete game was the majors' longest ever.

Haddix led the American Association in ERA, wins, strikeouts, and complete games in 1950. After serving in the military in 1951, and pitching briefly in 1952, the wiry southpaw had a brilliant 20–9 rookie season with the Cardinals, leading the NL with six shutouts. Basically a .500 pitcher after his sophomore season, Haddix went to the Pirates from Cincinnati with Hoak and Smoky Burgess in a seven-player deal. He was in the spotlight in the 1960 World Series. After winning Game Five as a starter, he relieved in Game Seven and won when Bill Mazeroski hit his famous homer. Nicknamed "the Kitten" at St. Louis for his resemblance to Harry "the Cat" Brecheen, Haddix finished as an effective reliever for the Orioles. He later served as pitching coach for several big league clubs. /(ME)

George Haddock (Gentleman George) — 1866–1926. RHP-OF 1888–94 Washington (NL), Buffalo (PL), Boston (AA), **Dodgers**, Phillies 1580 ip, 95–87, 4.07. 20 wins: 91–92
☛ *Led League—w 91.*

In 1891, a year after losing a league-high 26 games for Buffalo (Players' League), Haddock snapped back to lead Boston (American Association) to a pennant with 34 wins, tying Baltimore's Sadie McMahon for the league lead. /(FIC)

Bump Hadley [Irving Darius] — 1904–1963. RHP 1926–41 **Senators**, White Sox, Browns, Yankees, Giants, A's 2945 ip, 161–165, 4.25. *3 WS, 3 g, 2–1, 4.15*

The chunky curveballer was 14–6 as a rookie (1927), but generally had mediocre records with the Senators. Things got worse with the second-division Browns; in 1932, he led the AL with 21 losses. In 1932 and 1933 he led the league in walks, and retired third on the all-time walks list. After being traded to the powerful Yankees, he achieved consistent success and played on four straight pennant winners (1936–39). Hadley fractured Mickey Cochrane's skull with a pitch in 1937, ending the great catcher's career. Bump came by his nickname as a child when his short, heavy build was likened to that of a children's book character, Bumpus. /(JK)

Mickey Haefner — 1912– . LHP 1943–50 **Senators**, White Sox, Braves 1467 ip, 78–91, 3.50

Haefner was one of the Senators' four wartime knuckleballers, whose butterfly pitches brought out the best in Hall of Fame catcher Rick Ferrell and 1943 All-Star catcher Jake Early. In 1945, the chunky lefthander won 16, his ML high, but had losing records from 1947 on. /(JK)

Chick Hafey [Charles James] — 1903–1973. OF 1924–35, 37 **Cardinals**, Reds 1283 g, .317, 164 hr, 833 rbi. *4 WS, 23 g, .205, 2 rbi*
☛ *Led League—ba 31. All-Star—33. Hall of Fame—1971.*

One of the hardest-hitting righthanded batters in the game, Hafey had his best years with the Cardinals. It is difficult to assess how great Hafey might have been if not for his ill health, poor eyesight, and constant salary disputes. Hafey had a chronic sinus condition that required several operations and affected his vision. After beanings in 1926, a doctor advised him to wear glasses, and since his eyesight would vary from day to day, he used three different pairs. He became one of the first bespectacled outfielders.

Chick Hafey

Hafey was known for his rifle arm and his line drives. He started as a pitcher, but switched to everyday play under Branch Rickey. He was regarded by many as the second-best righthanded hitter of his day, behind Rogers Hornsby. A quiet man, he was somewhat overshadowed by the more colorful individuals who played on the Cardinals' championship teams of the 1920s and early 1930s.

In 1929 Hafey tied a National League record with ten successive hits. After batting .336 in 1930, he held out for $15,000, reporting ten days late to spring training. He eventually signed for $12,500, but Rickey fined him $2,100 for not being in playing shape. Hafey responded by winning the 1931 batting title with a .349 mark. He then demanded $17,000 for 1932, including a return of the $2,100. Rickey offered him $13,000, a raise of just $500. Incensed, Hafey drove home to California and waited until April 11, when he found out he had been traded to the Reds for Bennie Frey, Harvey Hendrick, and $50,000; Rickey had Joe Medwick waiting in the wings.

Hafey was happy to join the Reds, who paid him $15,000, though they were a last-place club. Battling the flu and his sinus condition, Hafey played just 84 games, but hit .344. In 1933 he hit .303, making the first All-Star team (and getting the first hit in All-Star history, a single in the second inning), but his health was not good. His last campaign as an everyday player was 1934. He hurt his shoulder in 1935, but on May 24, played in the first-ever regular season night game. The evening's dampness aggravated his sinuses. He saw the future of night baseball, and realized his career was ending. He retired, sitting out the rest of 1935 and all of 1936, but attempted a comeback in '37, playing in 89 games. He then quit for good, at the age of 34. He was elected to the Hall of Fame 34 years later by the Veterans Committee. /(WB)

Rip Hagerman (Zeriah) — 1888–1930. RHP 1909, 14–16 Cubs, **Indians** 431 ip, 19–33, 3.09

A minor league whiz (30–17 with Topeka of the Western Association in 1908), the fastballer was too wild for consistent ML success, averaging nearly five walks per nine innings. /(ME)

Joe Hague — 1944– . 1B-OF 1968–73 **Cardinals**, Reds 430 g, .239, 40 hr, 163 rbi. *1 LCS, 3 g, .000. 1 WS, 3g, .000*

Hague peaked in 1970, hitting .271. Traded to the Reds for Bernie Carbo in 1972 after publicly blaming Cardinal president Gussie Busch for the team's demise, he batted .270 lifetime (24-for-89) as a lefthanded pinch hitter. /(WAB)

Don Hahn — 1948– . OF 1969–75 Expos, **Mets**, Phillies, Cardinals, Padres 454 g, .236, 7 hr, 74 rbi. *1 LCS, 5 g, .235, 1 rbi. 1 WS, 7 g, .241, 2 rbi*

Hahn alternated in centerfield with an aging Willie Mays on the 1973 pennant-winning Mets. /(FSt)

Ed Hahn — 1875–1941. OF 1905–10 Yankees, **White Sox** 553 g, .237, 1 hr, 122 rbi. *1 WS, 6 g, .273*

Hahn's keen eye and speed made him a valuable leadoff man for the White Sox during their "Hitless Wonders" years. He still holds the AL season records, set in 1907, for fewest putouts (182) and fewest chances (206) for a full-time outfielder. /(DBing)

Noodles Hahn [Frank] — 1879–1960. LHP 1899–1906 **Reds**, Yankees 2012 ip, 129–92, 2.55. 20 wins: 99, 01–03

At the turn of the century, Noodles was Cincinnati's best pitcher. A splendid 23–7 in his rookie season, he was the only lefthander until Steve Carlton to win 20 games for an eighth-place team. He also led the league in strikeouts. He no-hit the Phillies in 1900, completed 41 games in 42 1901 starts, a year in which he fanned 19 Bostons, and he achieved his fourth 20-win record in five seasons in 1903. In 1905 his arm gave out. Over his career he had 210 complete games in 229 starts, threw 25 shutouts, and issued only 379 walks, about 1.7 per nine innings. After baseball he was a Cincinnati meat inspector and stayed in good physical condition by working out afternoons with the Reds until he was 67. /(ADS)

Hinkey Haines [Henry Luther] — 1898–1979. OF 1923 **Yankees** 28 g, .160, 0 hr, 3 rbi. *1 WS, 2 g, .000*

Haines was a member of both the Yankees' first World Championship team (1923) and the first NFL championship team of the New York Giants (1927). The exciting running back from Penn State was the darling of Giants fans. /(MG)

Jesse Haines (Pop) — 1893–1978. RHP 1918, 20–37 Reds, **Cardinals** 3208 ip, 210–158, 3.64. 20 wins: 23, 27, 28 *4 WS, 32 ip, 3–1, 1.67*
☛ *Hall of Fame—1970.*

Haines pitched more years (18) in a Cardinals uniform than anyone in history, and only Bob Gibson won more games for the club. Although originally signed by the Tigers, he played his entire ML career, except one game, with St. Louis. In 1920, with the Cardinals desperately short of starting pitching, field manager and president Branch Rickey coaxed the team directors into borrowing $10,000 to buy the 26-year-old Haines from Kansas City (American Association), where he'd gone 21–5 in 1919. He immediately became the St. Louis workhorse, throwing more than 300 innings in his first year.

Jesse Haines

Haines had a blazing fastball and acquired a knuckleball that extended his career. He learned it from Eddie Rommell, who had been very successful with the pitch for the Athletics. Haines actually gripped the ball with his knuckles, rather than the fingertips, as do most knuckleball pitchers. This allowed him to fire his knuckler with more speed than most.

A pleasant and kind fellow off the field, Haines couldn't stand defeat and was known to lose his temper at teammates when poor defense cost him a game. He won 20 games for the first time in 1923 but stumbled to an 8–19 record the next year. One of his eight wins was a 5–0 no-hitter against Boston on July 17, making him the first Cardinal pitcher to throw a no-hitter since 1876.

The Cardinals won the 1926 pennant as Haines went 13–4. In the WS, he shut out the Yankees 4–0 in Game Three, hitting a two-run homer to help his own cause. He started the seventh game and allowed only two runs through six innings. But he'd developed a blister from throwing his knuckler and in the seventh inning he loaded the bases with two out. In came Grover Alexander to strike out New York's Tony Lazzeri for one of the great moments in Series history. Haines received credit for the win that made the Cardinals World Champions, but Alexander was the hero. In the movie *The Winning Team*, with Ronald Reagan as Alexander, Haines was played by Bob Lemon.

The 1927 season was Haines's finest, as he rolled up 24 victories and led the NL with six shutouts and 25 complete games. He followed with a 20–8 season in 1928, as the Cardinals won their second pennant. He pitched for three more pennant-winners: 1930, 1931, and 1934. In WS play he was 3–1, with a 1.67 ERA.

As he put on years and saw his hair thin, Haines picked up the nickname "Pop." The label accurately described his fatherly treatment of younger players. His knuckleball remained intimidating, and he continued as an effective reliever and spot starter past his forty-fourth birthday. He served as the Dodgers' pitching coach in 1938. In 1970 the Veterans Committee named him to the Hall of Fame. /(FJO)

Jerry Hairston (Popeye) — 1952– . OF-DH-1B 1973–77, 81–89 **White Sox**, Pirates 859 g, .258, 30 hr, 205 rbi. *1 LCS, 2 g, .000*

Jerry's father, Sam Hairston, was the first American-born black player signed by the White Sox; he caught two games in 1951. Working for Chicago as a scout in 1970, Sam signed his son. Jerry proved adequate at the plate, but his outfielding was suspect. After four unproductive seasons, he was sold to Pittsburgh in 1977, then drifted to Mexico. Re-acquired by Chicago late in 1981, Hairston led the AL in pinch at-bats each year from 1982 to 1985, and in pinch hits in 1983–85. On April 15, 1983, his two-out, ninth-inning pinch hit ended a perfect-game bid by Detroit's Milt Wilcox. Hairston switch-hit, but was stronger from the left side. When released in 1988, his 93 career pinch hits put him in a tie for 12th all-time; he came back in 1989 to get his 94th pinch hit. His brother John played briefly for the 1969 Cubs. /(RL)

George Halas (Papa Bear) — 1895–1983. OF 1919 **Yankees** 12 g, .091, 0 hr, 0 rbi

Although Halas played only 12 games with the Yankees—six in the outfield—the myth persists that he was Babe Ruth's predecessor as Yankee rightfielder. Ruth actually replaced Sammy Vick in 1920. Soon after Halas's demotion that season, he helped establish the National Football League. For over 60 years, he operated the Chicago Bears, playing end through 1929, and coaching through 1968. He is a member of the Pro Football Hall of Fame. /(MG)

Bob Hale — 1933– . 1B 1955–61 **Orioles**, Indians, Yankees 376 g, .273, 2 hr, 89 rbi

Hale was called up after his three hits led the Orioles' Piedmont League team to an upset of the parent club in an exhibition game. His 19 pinch hits (an Indian record) and 63 pinch at-bats in 1960 led the AL. 40% of his ML at-bats came as a pinch hitter. /(RTM)

John Hale — 1953– . OF-DH 1974–79 **Dodgers**, Mariners 359 g, .201, 14 hr, 72 rbi

Hale had four hits in four at-bats in 1974; one drove in the winning run to clinch the NL West title for Los Angeles. /(EW)

Odell Hale (Bad News, Chief) — 1908–1980. 2B-3B 1931, 33–41 **Indians**, Red Sox, Giants 1062 g, .289, 73 hr, 573 rbi

Hale was named Bad News by enemy pitchers. A good RBI man, twice exceeding 100 in a season, he hit for the cycle on July 12, 1958. He made the most errors among AL second basemen in 1934 and third basemen in 1935, but he led third basemen in assists in 1935 and 1936. One peculiar assist in 1935 came when the Red Sox loaded the bases against the Indians. Joe Cronin hit a line drive that conked Indians third baseman Hale in the head. Deflected to the shortstop on the fly, the ball was relayed to second base and on to first for a triple play. /(EW)

Sammy Hale — 1896–1974. 3B-OF 1920–21 23–30 Tigers, **A's**, Browns 883 g, .302, 30 hr, 392 rbi

As a Tiger rookie in 1920, Hale led the AL with 17 pinch hits in 52 at-bats, but he failed to stick, and the A's bought him from Portland for $75,000 in 1923. At Philadelphia, he played third base whenever Jimmy Dykes was playing another position. Hale was a smart fielder reputed to have the smallest hands in the game. /(NLM)

Ed Halicki — 1950– . RHP 1974–80 **Giants**, Angels 1063 ip, 55–66, 3.62

The 6'7" Halicki ascended quickly through the Giants system, and in his sophomore ML season, he

no-hit the Mets 6–0 (8/24/75). He won a career-high 16 in 1977, and in May 1979, he pitched back-to-back two-hitters. /(EW)

Albert Hall — 1958– . OF 1981– **Braves** 375 g, .251, 5 hr, 53 rbi

The switch-hitting, 155-lb Hall was a four-time minor league basestealing champion who stole 100 bases in the Carolina League in 1980. He was a 10-year veteran of the Braves organization in 1987 when he finally had a 200 at-bat season with Atlanta, hitting .284 in a part-time role. That September 23 he became the first Atlanta Brave ever to hit for the cycle. /(JCA)

Bob Hall — 1923–1983. RHP 1949–50, 53 **Braves**, Pirates 276 ip, 9–18, 5.40

Hall's best season was as a rookie reliever with the 1949 Braves (6–4, 4.36). Born in the Pittsburgh suburb of Swissvale, Hall finished his ML career with the Pirates, his arm having been ruined in a 21-inning stint in a Pacific Coast League game. /(ME)

Charley Hall [born Carlos Clolo] (Sea Lion) — 1885–1943. RHP 1906–07, 09–13, 16, 18 Reds, **Red Sox**, Cardinals, Tigers 911 ip, 53–45, 3.08. *1 WS, 11 ip, 3.38*

Among the first pitchers to specialize in relief, Hall started only 81 games in 188 appearances. He led the AL with six relief wins for Boston in both 1910 and 1912. /(EW)

Dick Hall — 1930– . RHP-OF 1952–57, 59–71 Pirates, A's, **Orioles**, Phillies 669 g, .210, 4 hr, 56 rbi; 1259 ip, 93–75, 3.32. *2 LCS, 5 ip, 2–0, 0.00. 3 WS, 3 ip, 0–1, 0.00*

A Little All-American football end at Swarthmore College, the 6'6" Hall went straight to the Pirate outfield after signing for a substantial bonus. When he failed to hit well, he switched to pitching. Hall struggled with his new craft in the minors and missed the 1958 season with hepatitis, before emerging to lead the Pacific Coast League in wins, winning percentage, and ERA in 1959. After marginal success as a ML starter, he became one of the top relievers of the 1960s, exhibiting exceptional control despite an awkward-looking herky-jerky motion. In his last 462 ML innings, he unintentionally walked only 23 batters. He led the AL in relief wins in 1970. /(ME)

Donald Hall — 1928– . *Writer.*

A prolific writer of poetry and children's fiction, and professor of English at the University of Michigan from 1957 to 1976, Hall wrote *Fathers Playing Catch with Sons* (1985) and *Dock Ellis in the Country of Baseball* (1976)./(NLM)

Drew Hall — 1963- . LHP 1986- **Cubs**, Rangers 137 ip, 5-5, 5.26

The hard-throwing Hall, the third player in the nation selected in the June 1984 draft, has been hampered by control problems. He was traded to the Rangers with Rafael Palmiero and Jamie Moyer for Mitch Williams and five other players after the 1988 season./(SFS)

Halsey Hall — 1899-1978. *Writer-Broadcaster*

"Mr. Baseball" in Minneapolis, Hall was a sportswriter and broadcaster in the Twin Cities for 45 years. His first radio work was covering the Dempsey-Gibbons fight in 1923. After 35 years with the Minneapolis *Star*, he left in 1961 to become a full-time member of the Twins' broadcasting team until his retirement in 1972. A chain smoker of cigars, he was doing a Twins game one day when some ashes ignited a pile of papers. His coat was soon in flames, but he shed it without missing a play. Fans sent him an asbestos jacket./(NLM)

Irv Hall — 1918- . 2B-SS 1943-46 **A's** 508 g, .261, 0 hr, 168 rbi

Despite 40 errors as a wartime rookie shortstop, Hall was known as a heads-up fielder. He became a player-manager in the Browns' and A's farm systems./(EW)

Jimmie Hall — 1938- . OF 1963-70 **Twins**, Angels, Indians, Yankees, Cubs, Braves 968 g, .254, 121 hr, 391 rbi. *1 WS, 2 g, .143*
☛ *All-Star—64-65.*

Hall's career-high 33 HR in his rookie season ranked fourth in the AL in 1963. The Twins' centerfielder by default, he didn't cover enough ground but gave Minnesota a powerful outfield trio when he played with Bob Allison and Harmon Killebrew or Tony Oliva. His best year came in the Twins' 1965 AL championship season, when he reached career highs in BA (.285), RBI (86), steals (14), and doubles (25). After dropping to .239 in 1966, he was traded to the Angels, for whom he had one more decent season before declining. He played for five teams in his last three seasons./(SFS)

Marc Hall — 1887-1915. RHP 1910, 13-14 Browns, **Tigers** 302 ip, 15-25, 3.25

Hall won 10 games for the 1913 Tigers and had a 2.69 ERA the following season until rheumatism and Bright's disease ended his career. He died less than a year later./(NLM)

Mel Hall — 1960- . OF 1981- Cubs, **Indians**, Yankees 845 g, .278, 88 hr, 408 rbi

After hitting 17 HR in his first full season in 1983 for the Cubs, Hall was traded in mid-1984 in the deal that brought Rick Sutcliffe and a division title to Chicago. He was hitting a career-high .318 in 1985 when he broke his collarbone running into an outfield wall. He rebounded to hit 18 HR in both 1986 and 1987, but dropped off to 6 HR in 1988. The Yankees traded Joel Skinner for Hall shortly after Dave Winfield's back problem became known in spring training of 1989, but Hall slumped, was injured, and found himself in part-time duty as a DH and left fielder on his return to the lineup, the Yankees having acquired Jesse Barfield in the interim./(SFS)

Tom Hall (The Blade) — 1947- . LHP 1968-77 Twins, **Reds**, Mets, Royals 853 ip, 52-33, 3.27. *5 LCS, 14 ip, 1-1, 6.28. 1 WS, 8 ip, 0-0, 0.00*

The 6' 150-lb frame that earned him the sobriquet The Blade didn't stop Hall from being one of the hardest throwers in the majors (he averaged nearly a strikeout per inning). Used for starting and relief by Twins teams that won divisional championships in 1969 and 1970 (Hall lost his Game Two start in the 1970 LCS), he came into his own after being acquired by the Reds for the 1972 season. Getting plenty of work in the deep bullpen employed by manager Sparky "Captain Hook" Anderson, Hall was 10-1 with eight saves (3-0 in seven spot starts) for the NL champs. He won Game Two of the LCS after entering in the fifth inning with two out and two runners on and a two-ball, no-strike count on the Pirates' Willie Stargell. Hall fanned Stargell on a called third strike and finished the game, allowing only one run. He also contributed three innings of scoreless, one-hit relief in Game Five to keep the Reds in the game for their ninth-inning, come-from-behind, pennant-clinching victory. He continued his fine work in the World Series, saving Game Six and throwing 8-1/3 scoreless innings overall in the Reds' losing effort against the A's. After two more solid seasons with Cincinnati, Hall was dealt to the Mets early in 1975 and then was picked up by the Royals in May 1976 as Kansas City went on to win its first division title. /(SH)

Bill Hallahan (Wild Bill) — 1902–1981. LHP 1925–26, 29–38 **Cardinals**, Reds, Phillies 1740 ip, 102–94, 4.03. *4 WS, 40 ip, 3–1, 1.36*
☛ *Led League—w 31. Led League—k 30–31. All-Star—33.*

Hallahan was not called Wild Bill because of his temperament, but because his fastball produced league-leading totals in walks (1930–31, '33), and strikeouts (1930–31). Until Dizzy Dean emerged, he was the star of the Cardinal staff, and he led them to pennants in 1930–31. He threw two WS shutouts. The NL's starting pitcher for the first All-Star Game in 1933, Wild Bill lived up to his name. After walking five batters, he was lifted in the third inning and was the losing pitcher. /(JK)

Bill Haller — 1935– . *Umpire* AL 1961, 63–82 *4 WS*

Haller was "an umpire's umpire," according to fellow ump Dave Phillips. One of the last to wear an outside chest protector, Haller was assistant supervisor of AL umpires in 1983–85, but was fired, he believes, because of his refusal to work a game during the 1984 umpires' strike. His brother Tom was a ML catcher. /(RTM)

Tom Haller — 1937– . C 1961–72 **Giants**, Dodgers, Tigers 1294 g, .257, 134 hr, 504 rbi. *1 LCS, 1 g, .000. 1 WS, 4 g, .286, 1 hr, 3 rbi*
☛ *All-Star—66–68.*

After a career at quarterback for the University of Illinois, the 6'4″ Haller signed with the Giants in 1958. In their pennant-winning 1962 season, he hit 18 HR as a platoon catcher. He was San Francisco's first-string receiver in the years 1964–67, and hit 27 HR in 1966. He went to the Dodgers in a 1968 trade for Ron Hunt and Nate Oliver, the first trade between the two clubs since 1956. In a ML first, on July 14, 1972, Tom was the Tiger catcher while his brother, Bill, umpired behind the plate. The durable Haller caught all 23 innings of a May 31, 1964 Mets-Giants game, and set the NL record for most double plays by a catcher in a season (23, in 1968). After serving as a Giant coach from 1977 to 1979, he was their vice president of baseball operations from mid-1981 until September 1986. /(RTM)

Jack Hallet — 1913–1982. RHP 1940–43, 46, 48 Cubs, **Pirates**, Giants 277 ip, 12–16, 4.05

A borderline major leaguer for five of his six seasons, Hallet's best season was 1946 with the Pirates when he struck out 64 in 115 innings with a 3.29 ERA. /(ME)

Bill Hallman — 1876–1950. OF 1901, 03, 06–07 **Milwaukee (AL)**, White Sox, Pirates 319 g, .235, 3 hr, 86 rbi

Hallman was the first outfielder to lead the American League in errors, committing 26 for Milwaukee in 1901, the AL's initial season. He was never again a major league regular, but had a long minor league career. /(NLM)

Bill Hallman — 1867–1920. 2B-3B-SS-OF-C 1888–98, 1901–03 **Phillies**, Philadelphia (PL), Philadelphia (AA), Cardinals, Dodgers, Indians 1503 g, .272, 20 hr, 769 rbi.
Manager 1897 **Cardinals** 13–46, .220

This 5'8″ Pittsburgh native played every position during his 14-year major league carer, although he was primarily a second baseman. He batted over .300 for four straight seasons in the mid-1890s and had three stints with the Phillies. /(AL)

Billy Hamilton (Sliding Billy) — 1866–1940. OF 1888–1901 Kansas City (AA), **Phillies**, Braves 1593 g, .344, 40 hr, 736 rbi
☛ *Led League—ba 91, 93. Hall of Fame—1961.*

One of only three players in ML history with more runs scored than games played, Hamilton was perhaps the best player of the 1890s. Seven times a stolen-base champion, he combined raw speed, daring baserunning, patience at the plate, and a .344 career average (sixth-best all-time) to become the game's first great leadoff hitter. In a period when stolen bases were also credited when baserunners gained more bases than a batter earned on a hit, Hamilton compiled phenomenal stolen base totals.

After 35 games with Kansas City in 1888, Hamilton won a starting spot the next year and hit .301 with a league-leading 117 stolen bases. He would not fall below .300 again until his final ML season. In 1890 Hamilton brought his head-first slides to the NL's Phillies, where he led the league with 102 steals in 1890 and 115 in 1891, the year he won his first batting title with a .340 mark. Following an off-year in 1892, he moved from left field to center in 1893 and hit .380 to edge teammate Sam Thompson for his second batting championship.

Sliding Billy continued his record-setting basepath feats in 1894 with the help of his fellow Phillies, who hit a ML-record .343 as a team that year. Playing in 131 of his club's 132 games, Hamilton scored 196 runs, by far the best ML season total ever. He accomplished this by leading

Billy Hamilton

the league in walks (126) and stolen bases (99), including 7 steals in one game on August 31. He also strung together a 36-game hitting streak, the sixth-longest in NL history, and had career highs of 87 RBI, 223 hits, 15 triples, 25 doubles, and a .399 batting average. After leading the league once again in runs, walks, and stolen bases in 1895, he was traded to the Braves for third baseman Billy Nash. In Boston, he continued to terrorize opposing in-fields, leading the NL in stolen bases twice more in 1896 and 1898. But knee and leg injuries in 1898 and 1899 finally began to slow him down, and he retired after hitting only .287 in 1901.

In addition to his lofty batting average, Hamilton finished his career with a .455 on-base percentage, 1,187 walks, 1,692 runs scored, and 937 stolen bases. He was elected to the Hall of Fame by the Veterans' Committee in 1961./(AJA)

Dave Hamilton — 1947- . LHP 1972-80 **A's**, White Sox, Cardinals, Pirates 704 ip, 39-41, 3.85. *1 LCS, 0 ip, 0-0, 0.00. 1 WS, 1 ip, 0-0, 27.00*

Hamilton was the fifth starter on the A's teams that won three consecutive World Championships, 1972-74. Traded to the White Sox with Chet

Lemon for Stan Bahnsen and Skip Pitlock in June 1975, he was used almost exclusively in relief. In 1976 he was made the stopper of the bullpen, collecting 10 saves while Chicago made an ill-advised attempt to convert Goose Gossage into a starter./(SH)

Earl Hamilton — 1891-1968. LHP 1911-24 **Browns**, Tigers, Pirates, Phillies 2343 ip, 116-147, 3.16

The 5'8" 160-lb Hamilton no-hit the Tigers 5-1 on August 30, 1912, and used his good changeup to become the Browns' leading winner from 1912 to 1914. After going 0-9 in 1917, he was sold to the Pirates. He completed all six of his starts for a perfect 6-0 (0.83) record in 1918 before military service shortened his season. Two years later he and the Giants' Rube Benton matched shutouts for 16 innings before New York prevailed in the 17th. Hamilton later owned the St. Joseph's franchise in the Western League./(NLM)

Jack Hamilton (Hairbreadth Harry) — 1938- . RHP 1962-69 Phillies, Tigers, **Mets**, Angels, Indians, White Sox 612 ip, 32-40, 4.53

Hamilton led the NL in walks in his rookie 1962 season and was 7-12 as a starter. His 1.95 ERA in 15 relief appearances showed promise, so he saw most of his subsequent action out of the bullpen. After spending most of 1965 on the DL with the Tigers, he was sold to the Mets for 1966 and had a career-high 13 saves. That May 4, he pitched an 8-0 one-hitter against the Cardinals; the only hit was a third-inning single by the opposing pitcher, Ray Sadecki. Traded to the Angels in mid-1967, he returned to starting and went 9-6, 3.25 for them the rest of the way. It was his best season, but it was marred in August when he hit Tony Conigliaro in the face with a pitch, nearly blinding him and curtailing a great career./(SFS)

Jeff Hamilton — 1964- . 3B 1986- **Dodgers** 368 g, .237, 23 hr, 109 rbi. *1 LCS, 7 g, .217, 1 rbi. 1 WS, 5 g, .105*

Hamilton had his best season for the 1988 World Champion Dodgers, reaching career highs with a .236 average, six HR, and 33 RBI but spending all of August on the DL./(WOR)

Steve Hamilton (Hambone) — 1935- . LHP 1961-72 Indians, Senators, **Yankees**, White Sox, Giants, Cubs 664 ip, 40-31, 3.05. *1 LCS, 1 ip, 9.00. 2 WS, 3 ip, 3.00*

An important Yankee reliever who had played pro basketball with the Minneapolis Lakers, the 6'6" Hamilton threw a nasty slider with a three-quarter sidearm motion that froze lefthanded hitters. He saved the sixth game of the 1964 World Series. In 1965, he recorded a 1.39 ERA in 46 games, and in 1968 saved a career-high 11. Late in his career he added a blooper pitch, thrown with a hesitation delivery, fashioned after Rip Sewell's "Eephus" ball. Hamilton called it the "Folly Floater," and it helped extend his career. He recorded 42 ML saves./(GDW)

Ken Hamlin — 1935- . SS-2B 1957, 59-62, 65-66 Pirates, A's, Angels, **Senators** 468 g, .241, 11 hr, 89 rbi

A product of Western Michigan University, Hamlin was a fine fielder with good speed and a strong arm. His best offensive year came in 1965, when he hit .273 for the Senators./(RTM)

Luke Hamlin (Hot Potato) — 1906-1978. RHP 1933-34, 37-42, 44 Tigers, **Dodgers**, Pirates, A's 1405 ip, 73-76, 3.77. 20 wins: 39

Hamlin got his nickname because he juggled the ball while getting ready to pitch. Hamlin led the NL with 36 starts and won 20 in 1939, but Dodger manager Leo Durocher subsequently became disenchanted with the pitcher's inability to hold leads. Once, when Durocher saw an old political campaign poster for the Abe Lincoln-Hannibal Hamlin ticket, he commented, "It proves Lincoln was a great man; he could win even with Hamlin."/(JK)

Atlee Hammaker — 1958- . LHP 1981- Royals, **Giants** 980 ip, 55-57, 3.54. *2 LCS, 9 ip, 0-1, 7.00. 1 WS, 2 ip, 0-0, 15.43*
☛ *Led League—era 83. All-Star—83.*

One of three pitchers acquired from the Royals for an aging Vida Blue in 1982, Hammaker seemed headed for stardom in 1983 when he made the NL All-Star team, led the league in ERA (2.25) and fanned 14 Astros on September 11, but has been plagued by arm woes ever since. Hammaker's troubles seemed to begin in the 1983 All-Star Game. He entered in the third inning and retired only two batters, surrendering a home run to Jim Rice, a grand slam to Fred Lynn, and seven runs altogether as the NL lost for the first time since 1971. He went on the DL for a month later in '83, and had surgery twice in 1984, once on his shoulder and once on his elbow, limiting him to only six starts. He then missed all of 1986 recovering from a second shoulder operation. Since 1988, Hammaker has been used more often in relief than as a starter./(SCL)

Granny Hamner [Granville] — 1927- . SS-2B-3B-RHP 1944-59, 62 **Phillies**, Indians, A's 1531 g, .262, 104 hr, 708 rbi. *1 WS, 4 g, .429*
☛ *All-Star—52-54.*

An All-Star at shortstop and second base, Hamner was 17 when he made his ML debut in 1944. He stuck for good in 1949. Hamner played a key role on the 1950 pennant-winning club and hit well in the four-game WS loss to the Yankees. Regarded as one of the NL's best clutch hitters, Hamner rapped 30 or more doubles four times. He was also a superb relay man with a very strong arm. He took brief turns on the mound in 1956-57. When his career as an infielder ended after his trade to Cleveland in 1959, he joined the A's as a minor league manager and honed his knuckleball sufficiently to pitch three AL games in relief for Kansas City in 1962. Granny's brother, Garvin (Wes) Hamner, played infield with the Phillies in 1945./(AL)

Ralph Hamner (Bruz) — 1916- . RHP 1946-49 White Sox, **Cubs** 220 ip, 8-20, 4.58

Hamner started and relieved for both Chicago clubs, but never had a winning season. His most active season was 1948 with the Cubs when he went 5-9, allowing nearly a hit an inning and walking more batters than he struck out./(JFC)

Garry Hancock — 1954- . OF-DH-1B 1978, 80-84 **Red Sox**, A's 273 g, .247, 12 hr, 64 rbi

Drafted six times while in school, Hancock finally signed with Cleveland in 1976. After being traded to Boston, he won the International League batting championship for Pawtucket in 1979, but he never cracked the Red Sox all-star outfield of Jim Rice, Fred Lynn, and Dwight Evans./(RMu)

Rich Hand — 1948- . RHP 1970-73 **Indians**, Rangers, Angels 488 ip, 24-39, 4.00

A standout college pitcher at the University of Puget Sound, Hand signed with the Indians in 1969 and jumped into the Cleveland rotation after less than a season in the minors. He was 8-19 in a year and a half and gained a reputation for being hard to coach. He was returned to the minors, then swapped to the Rangers. In 1972, he was 10-14 with a 3.32 ERA for Texas but developed a sore arm and was through at 26./(MC)

Lee Handley (Jeep) — 1913-1970. 3B-2B 1936-41, 44-47 Reds, **Pirates**, Phillies 968 g, .269, 15 hr, 297 rbi

Handley was a rookie Pirate regular at second base in 1937, and a full- or part-time third baseman from 1938 through 1941, tying for the NL lead in steals (17) in 1939. The flashy 5′7″ infielder suffered a serious beaning in 1939 and was hurt in an auto accident after the 1941 season. He recovered and platooned at third base for Pittsburgh in 1945–46. Brother Gene was an A's infielder, 1946–47. /(ME)

Bill Hands — 1940– . RHP 1965–75 Giants, **Cubs,** Twins, Rangers 1951 ip, 111–110, 3.35. 20 wins: 69

In the Cubs clubhouse, Hands was the undisputed chess champion. He also had some fine years as a pitcher. In 1968 he was 16–10. Hands won 20 games and led the staff with a 2.49 ERA when the Cubs contended in 1969. Hands was the stopper, halting several losing streaks to keep the Cubs in the race against the Mets.

He was 18–15 in 1970, but back ailments and muscle spasms in his pitching arm limited his effectiveness in later years. His finest outing came August 3, 1972, when he one-hit the Expos. A .078 lifetime hitter, Hands set a ML record by fanning in 14 straight official at-bats in 1968. /(AA)

Fred Haney (Pudge) — 1898–1977. 3B-2B 1922–27, 29 **Tigers,** Red Sox, Cubs, Cardinals 622 g, .275, 8 hr, 228 rbi.
 Manager 1939–41, 53–59 Browns, Pirates, **Braves** 629–757, .454. First place: 57, 58 *2 WS, 7–7, .500*

Following a career spent mostly as a Tiger third baseman and a long stint in Triple-A, Haney began managing at Toledo (American Association) in 1936. He was elevated to the Browns in 1939, but guided them to a club-record 111 losses. Replaced early in 1941, he went back to Toledo. He turned to broadcasting games for Hollywood (Pacific Coast League) in 1943–48, then managed the club to two pennants in four seasons. That success earned him the job in Pittsburgh, where he finished last three years in a row (1953–55). Taking over the Braves in June 1956, he led them to a world championship in 1957 and a pennant in 1958. Despite finishing second in 1959, he was fired. He was called a conservative manager and was once hung in effigy by Milwaukee fans during a pennant-winning campaign. He later broadcast NBC-TV's Game of the Week, and served as GM of the expansion Los Angeles Angels. /(ME)

Larry Haney — 1942– . C 1966–70, 72–78 Orioles, Pilots, **A's,** Cardinals, Brewers 480 g, .215, 12 hr, 73 rbi.
 1 WS, 2 g, --

Although he hit a game-winning two-run homer in his first ML game, Haney's weak bat kept him from being more than a reserve catcher throughout his career. With the division- winning A's in 1974, he played in 76 games but hit just .165. Two years later, in his most active season, he batted .226 in 88 games. /(MC)

Ned Hanlon — 1857–1937. OF 1880–92 Cleveland (NL), **Detroit (NL),** Pirates, Pittsburgh (PL), Baltimore (NL) 1267 g, .260, 30 hr, 406 rbi.
 Manager 1889–1907 Pirates, Pittsburgh (PL), **Dodgers,** Reds 1315–1165, .530. First place: 1894–96, 99, 1900

Hanlon had a longer and more illustrious career as a manager than as a player. Though never much of a hitter, he was the centerfielder for the National League Detroit club from 1881 through 1888. In

Ned Hanlon

1889 he went to the Pirates, and by season's end he was their manager. In 1890 he was one of the discontented players that formed the Players' League, but when the league folded he was taken back by the Pirates. He lasted for 78 games as their manager, and took over the Baltimore Orioles in 1892. There he remained through 1898.

In Baltimore, Hanlon put together one of the most famous 19th-century teams. They finished first in 1894–96, becoming known for their temperament, aggressive tactics, and heads-up play. Hanlon was partially responsible for the widespread use of the hit-and-run, fielders covering each other on plays, and the full-time use of a groundskeeper. His cunning rubbed off on such future managers as John McGraw, Hughie Jennings, Wilbert Robinson, Kid Gleason, and Miller Huggins. He was such an autocrat that Orioles owner Harry Vonderhorst wore a button that said "Ask Hanlon."

With owners having a hand in more than one club, it was decided in 1899 that Hanlon and his top players go to the Brooklyn Superbas (later known as the Dodgers), which had more drawing power; Baltimore folded after the season. In Brooklyn, Hanlon led his team to two consecutive pennants in 1899 and 1900. Let go after a last-place finish in 1905, he was picked up by Cincinnati, which placed sixth in Hanlon's two final years as a ML manager./(AJA)

Bill Hanna — 1862–1930. *Writer.*

A baseball writer in New York for 42 years, Hanna graduated from Lafayette in 1878 and began his career with the Kansas City *Star*. In 1888, he moved to New York with the *Herald*, spent many years with the *Sun*, and then returned to the *Herald* in 1920. One of the best-informed writers of his time, Hanna disliked slang and jargon. He wrote in simple, terse, but well-chosen and informative phrases, and helped make sportswriting a respected profession./(NLM)

Preston Hanna — 1954– . RHP 1975–82 **Braves**, A's 436 ip, 17–25, 4.62

The Braves' top draft choice (and 11th in the nation) in 1972, Hanna never blossomed due to injuries and an inability to control his knuckle curve. He was 7–13 in 1978, his only year as a regular starter./(MC)

Jim Hannan — 1940– . RHP 1962–71 **Senators**, Tigers, Brewers 822 ip, 41–48, 3.88

Notre Dame graduate Hannan's 254 strikeouts (in only 196 innings) in his first pro season led the New York-Penn League in 1961, but he was always plagued by control problems. Taken from the Red Sox organization by the Senators in the second expansion draft, his best year was 1968, when he went 10–6 for the 65–96 Washington team. The lifetime .091 hitter struck out in 13 consecutive at-bats in 1968, an AL record. Hannan was a player representative, and his master's thesis on the Major League pension plan was used by Marvin Miller to acquaint himself with baseball's benefit system. Hannan became a stockbroker in the Washington area./(CG)

Andy Hansen (Swede) — 1924– . RHP 1944–45, 47–53 **Giants**, Phillies 618 ip, 23–30, 4.22

This thin, 6'3" blond sinkerballer was generally used in middle relief. He had a career-high 100 innings in 1948, coming out of the Giants' bullpen 27 times and going 5–3 with a 2.97 ERA./(RTM)

Ron Hansen — 1938– . SS-3B-2B 1958–72 Orioles, **White Sox**, Senators, Yankees, Royals 1384 g, .234, 106 hr, 501 rbi
☛ *Rookie of the Year—60. All-Star—60.*

The uncommonly tall (6'3") shortstop missed the 1957 season with a slipped disc, and went 0-for-19 in his 1958 Orioles debut. He returned to Baltimore in 1960, and his career-high 22 HR and 86 RBI won him AL Rookie of the Year honors. He led AL shortstops in double plays in 1961, spent six months of 1962 in the Marines due to the Cuban Missile Crisis, re-injured his back, and was traded to the White Sox in a January 1963 deal for Luis Aparicio. Hansen led the league twice more in double plays and four times in assists. On August 29, 1965 he tied an AL record with 18 chances in the first game of a doubleheader, and added 10 more in the second for a total of 28, setting another record. Out again with back problems in 1966, he was swapped to the Senators in a 1968 deal for Tim Cullen. Hansen turned the majors' first unassisted triple play in 41 years on July 30, 1968 against the Indians. He was then shipped back to the White Sox for Cullen, making them the only two players to be traded for one another twice in the same season. Hansen finished his career as a utility man, and became a coach and minor league manager./(MC)

Erik Hanson — 1965– . RHP 1988– **Mariners** 155 ip, 11–8, 3.19

Hanson was the Mariners' top pitching prospect at the start of 1989 after going 2–3 with a 3.24 ERA in a September call-up the year before. He was 9–5 with a 3.18 ERA—the lowest for a Seattle starter that year—but missed almost half of 1989 on the DL. He pitched a 5–0 no-hitter for Calgary (Pacific Coast League) against Las Vegas on August 21, 1988 (seven innings)./(SFS)

Mel Harder (Chief, Wimpy) — 1909– . RHP 1928–47
Indians 3426 ip, 223–186, 3.80. 20 wins: 34–35
    Manager 1961 **Indians** 0–1, .000
☛ *All-Star—34–37.*

Only Bob Feller won more games for the Indians than Mel Harder, who spent 36 years with the club as a pitcher and coach. His 582 appearances and 186 losses set Cleveland records. Only Walter Johnson and Ted Lyons pitched more seasons with one club than Harder's 20 with Cleveland. Harder pitched the first game ever in Cleveland Municipal Stadium, losing 1–0 to Philadelphia's Lefty Grove on July 31, 1932.

Nearsighted, Harder wore thick glasses. Joe DiMaggio said that he gave him more trouble than just about any pitcher, wasting his fine curveball outside, then coming in tight with the fastball. Harder held DiMaggio to a .180 average against him lifetime, and struck him out three times in a 1940 game.

By today's rules, Harder would have been the ERA leader in 1933, when he posted a 2.95 mark. But he was a .500 pitcher until 1934, when he went 20–12. He followed with a 22–11 season, but came down with bursitis in his shoulder and a sore elbow. He nevertheless won an average of 15 games a season from 1936 through 1940. He was released late in 1941, but was given another chance after having elbow surgery. Though he won 47 more games over the next six seasons, he did not regain his old form.

Harder is the only pitcher to work 10 or more All-Star innings without allowing an earned run. Though overshadowed by Carl Hubbell, he won the 1934 All-Star Game, finishing it with five shutout innings. Using today's standards, he would have been awarded saves in the 1935 and 1937 contests.

Harder became one of the first coaches to be exclusively a pitching coach, and lasted through 12 Cleveland managers. Under Harder, seven different Indians won 20 games, for a total of 17 times. Two others led the AL in wins with fewer than 20. He was credited with changing Bob Lemon from a poor-hitting infielder to a Hall of Fame pitcher. He

Mel Harder

left Cleveland in 1964, going on to coach for the Mets, Cubs, Reds, and Royals through 1969./(ME)

Jim Hardin — 1943– . RHP 1967–72 **Orioles,** Yankees, Braves 751 ip, 43–32, 3.18

Originally signed by the Mets, Hardin was drafted by Baltimore and went 18–13 (2.51) in 1968, his second ML year. He failed to win more than six in any of his remaining four seasons./(JCA)

Carroll Hardy — 1933- . OF 1958–64, 67 Indians, **Red Sox**, Astros, Twins 433 g, .225, 17 hr, 113 rbi

Hardy was the only man ever to pinch hit for Ted Williams; after Williams fouled a pitch off his foot in a 1960 game, Hardy finished the at-bat. A reserve for most of his ML baseball career, he saw the most action in 1962 (362 at-bats for the Red Sox) but hit only .215. He was also a defensive back with the NFL's San Francisco 49ers in 1955. /(JCA)

Larry Hardy — 1948- . RHP 1974–76 **Padres**, Astros 127 ip, 9–4, 5.24

As a rookie in 1974, Hardy worked 76 games (second in the NL only to Mike Marshall) in going 9–4 for the last-place Padres. Arm trouble finished the sinker-slider pitcher's career. /(MC)

Steve Hargan — 1942- . RHP 1965–72, 74–77 **Indians**, Rangers, Blue Jays, Braves 1632 ip, 87–107, 3.92
☛ All-Star—67.

Hargan had a roller coaster career. He was an All-Star in 1967, his second full season with Cleveland (14–13, 2.62, six shutouts). After elbow surgery in 1968, he struggled until 1970, when he bounced back to go 11–3 (2.90). In the three seasons that followed, he went 1–16 and spent more than a year in the minors. He again rebounded, posting a 12–9 mark with the Rangers in 1974. /(JCA)

Alan Hargesheimer — 1956- . RHP 1980–81, 83, 86 **Giants**, Cubs, Royals 111 ip, 5–9, 4.70

A sub-.500 pitcher in the minors, the strong right-hander was capable of working a lot of innings. The starter was most active with the 1980 Giants, going 4–6 with a 4.32 ERA. /(FO)

Bubbles Hargrave [Eugene Franklin] — 1892–1969. C 1913–15, 21–28, 30 Cubs, **Reds**, Yankees 852 g, .310, 29 hr, 376 rbi
☛ Led League—ba 26.

When Hargrave hit .353 in 1926, he became the first full-time catcher to lead his league in batting; only Ernie Lombardi ever matched the feat. It was the first time that decade that Rogers Hornsby, who slumped to .317 that year, didn't win the crown. Hargrave had only 326 at-bats, but at the time the percentage title qualification was 100 games; Hargrave caught 93 games, but pinch-hitting appearances brought his total to 105 games. The primitive state of catchers' protective gear made it fairly common for first-string catchers to play fewer than 100 games. It wasn't until 1951 that the require-ment was changed to 400 at-bats, but the statistical record book *Total Baseball* doesn't list him as the league leader in 1926.

Hargrave hit .300 six straight years (1922–27). His best season was 1923, when he caught the most games of his career (109) and reached personal highs in HR (10), RBI (78), runs (54), and doubles (23) while batting .333. He had failed his first major league trial, hitting .207 in parts of three seasons with the Cubs. He was the Reds' primary catcher in the years he was a .300 hitter, and in 1924 he led NL receivers in double plays. His last season was spent as a backup catcher for the Yankees. His younger brother was Pinky Hargrave. /(JFC)

Pinky Hargrave (William) — 1896–1942. C 1923–26, 28–33 Senators, Browns, **Tigers**, Braves 650 g, .278, 39 hr, 265 rbi

Not as good a hitter as his older brother Bubbles, Pinky batted righthanded in his first four ML seasons, switch-hit from 1928 to 1932, and batted only lefthanded in 1933. His flaming red hair inspired his nickname and his defensive ability earned him ten years as a ML catcher, mostly as a backup. /(JK)

Charlie Hargreaves — 1896–1979. C 1923–30 **Dodgers**, Pirates 421 g, .270, 4 hr, 139 rbi

Though Hargreaves only once caught as many as 70 games for the Dodgers, Brooklyn fans liked him enough to pelt Phillies outfielder George Harper with soda bottles for colliding with him. /(TG)

Mike Hargrove [Dudley Michael] (The Human Rain Delay, Grover) — 1949- . 1B-OF 1974–85 **Rangers**, Padres, Indians 1559 g, .290, 79 hr, 659 rbi
☛ Rookie of the Year—74. All-Star—75.

Nicknamed The Human Rain Delay for his deliberate preparation in the batter's box as he analyzed each situation, the lefthanded Hargrove ranks 16th in career on-base percentage and twice led the AL in walks. He was named 1974 AL Rookie of the Year, hitting a career-high .323 with the Rangers. He led AL first basemen in assists twice and errors three times. Traded to the Padres in 1979, he slumped to .192 in 52 games and was waived back to the AL, hitting .325 in 100 games for the Indians. He followed with two more .300 seasons, but slowly lost his job to Pat Tabler. Hargrove became a minor league manager for the Indians. /(MC)

Isao Harimoto — 1935– . OF 1959–81 **Toei Flyers/ Niitaku Home Flyers/Nippon Ham Fighters,** Yomiuri Giants, Lotte Orions .319 (inc)
☛ *Led League—ba 67–68.*

Considered the greatest ballplayer ever to emerge from Korea, Harimoto retired with a Japanese baseball record 3,085 hits and the second highest lifetime batting average in Japanese history. He hit between 23 and 30 home runs a season until late in his career.

Several times, Harimoto attracted tentative interest from American teams who hoped that, as a Korean (though of Japanese ancestry), Harimoto would not feel bound to remain in Japan. After the 1968 season and a second batting title, he qualified for free agency, an option Japanese players rarely exercise. Though he did not declare interest in signing with other teams, he did threaten to retire if not given a 10-year bonus by the Toei Flyers, who were not financially sound. The San Francisco Giants and Los Angeles Dodgers were rumored to be ready to make offers when Harimoto finally accepted more than double the Flyers' initial offer. This episode, a drinking problem, and alleged lack of hustle made Harimoto a leading target of fan abuse for the rest of his career. /(MC)

Mike Harkey — 1966– . RHP 1988- **Cubs** 35 ip, 0–3, 2.60

The fourth pick overall in the June 1987 draft, Harkey was the Cubs' best pitching prospect coming off his 1988 call-up when he was 0–3 but had a 2.60 ERA. However, in Spring Training in 1989 he had lost more than 10 mph off his fastball, and was sent down. /(WOR)

Tim Harkness — 1937– . 1B 1961–64 Dodgers, **Mets** 259 g, .235, 14 hr, 61 rbi

After signing a pro hockey contract with the Montreal Canadiens organization, this Quebec native opted to play baseball. Harkness unseated Marv Throneberry as the Mets' first baseman in 1963, only to be replaced shortly thereafter by bonus baby Ed Kranepool. /(CR)

Dick Harley — 1872–1952. OF 1897–1903 **Cardinals,** Cleveland (NL), Reds, Tigers, Cubs 740 g, .262, 10 hr, 236 rbi

Georgetown University graduate Harley was a journeyman outfielder for seven ML seasons. Later he became a highly respected college baseball coach at Pitt, Penn State, and Villanova. /(BC)

Larry Harlow — 1951– . OF 1975, 77–81 Orioles, Angels 449 g, .248, 12 hr, 72 rbi. *1 LCS, 3 g, .125, 1 rbi*

In his first (and only) season as a regular, Harlow had just 26 RBI for the 1978 Orioles, and was traded to California. In a ninth-inning rally in 1979 ALCS Game Three, Harlow doubled off Baltimore's Don Stanhouse to drive in Brian Downing for the Angels' first-ever playoff victory. /(JCA)

Bob Harmon (Hickory Bob) — 1887–1961. RHP 1909–16, 18 **Cardinals,** Pirates 2054 ip, 107–133, 3.33. 20 wins: 11

Bought by the Cardinals after pitching a no-hitter for Shreveport (Texas League) early in 1909, Harmon hurled a 16-inning victory over the Phillies that year. After winning 23 games in 1911 and 18 in 1912, he lost his effectiveness and was traded to Pittsburgh. /(NLM)

Chuck Harmon — 1926– . 3B-OF-1B 1954–57 **Reds,** Cardinals, Phillies 289 g, .238, 7 hr, 59 rbi

Harmon hit over .300 five consecutive years in the minors but never approached such numbers in the majors. As a star basketball player at the University of Toledo, he led the school to the 1943 NIT finals. /(RTM)

Terry Harmon — 1944– . 2B-SS-3B 1967, 69–77 **Phillies** 547 g, .233, 4 hr, 72 rbi. *1 LCS, 1 g, --*

The versatile infielder set a NL record when he successfully accepted 18 chances at second base in a game (6/12/71). He was also the Phillies' player representative and a regular member of their winter basketball team. /(JCA)

Brian Harper — 1959– . OF-C-DH 1979, 81– Angels, Pirates, Cardinals, Tigers, A's, **Twins** 393 g, .282, 22 hr, 127 rbi. *1 LCS, 1 g, .000. 1 WS, 4 g, .250, 1 rbi*

After wandering through six organizations in eleven years (he was 7-for-26 as a pinch-hitter for the NL-champion 1985 Cardinals), Harper finally found a home in 1988 platooning at catcher for the Twins. He hit .295 in 166 at-bats, his most playing time to that point at the major league level, and earned more playing time. He responded by hitting .325 in 1989 as the Twins' primary catcher, with career highs of eight HR and 57 RBI. /(JFC)

George Harper — 1892–1978. OF 1916–18, 22–29 Tigers, Reds, **Phillies,** Giants, Cardinals, Braves 1073 g, .303, 91 hr, 528 rbi. *1 WS, 3 g, .111*

A good hitter with decent power, Harper hit three home runs in the first game of a September 20, 1928 doubleheader. After 11 ML seasons he continued in the minors during the Depression and was still a player-manager at the age of 44. /(JK)

Harry Harper — 1895–1963. LHP 1913–21, 23 **Senators**, Red Sox, Yankees, Dodgers 1256 ip, 57–76, 2.87. *1 WS, 1 ip, 0–0, 20.25*

Harper spent seven years with the luckless Senators, with a 6–21 record in 1919 to lead the AL in losses. He later made a fortune as a New Jersey industrialist. /(JK)

Jack Harper [Charles William] — 1878–1950. RHP 1899–1906 Cleveland (NL), Cardinals, Browns, **Reds**, Cubs 1207 ip, 79–63, 3.58. *20 wins: 01, 04*

Called up for his first major league start at age 21, Harper halted the National League-record 24-game losing streak of the 1899 Cleveland Spiders by winning 5–4. When the NL was cut from twelve teams to eight in 1900, he was transferred to the Cardinals, for whom he went 23–13 in 1901, finishing second in the NL in wins and winning percentage. After two more average years, he again won 23 (losing 9) with a career-low 2.37 ERA for the Reds and was third in the NL in wins and winning percentage. After missing most of 1906 with a finger injury and bone chips in his elbow, he was traded to the Cubs in October. A holdout the following year ended his major league career. /(NLM)

Terry Harper — 1955– . OF 1980–87 **Braves**, Tigers, Pirates 540 g, .253, 36 hr, 180 rbi. *1 LCS, 1 g, .000*

A Georgia native signed by the Braves as a pitcher in 1973, Harper was made an everyday player in 1976, but it was 1983 before he spent a full season in Atlanta. In July of 1982 he dislocated his left shoulder while standing by the plate and enthusiastically waving a runner home. In his one solid season, 1985, he hit 17 HR. He played in Japan after his 1987 release by Pittsburgh. /(JCA)

Tommy Harper — 1940– . OF-3B 1962–76 **Reds**, Indians, Pilots/Brewers, Red Sox, Angels, A's, Orioles 1810 g, .257, 146 hr, 567 rbi. *1 LCS, 1 g, .000*
☛ *All-Star—70.*

Blending speed and power, Harper became only the fifth member of the "30–30 Club," hitting 31 HR and stealing 38 bases for the 1970 Brewers. As a young, highly touted outfielder with the Reds in 1965, he hit 18 homers and led the NL with 126 runs scored. After a disappointing 1967 season (.217), he was traded to Cleveland, where he continued to slump in a platoon role. Rescued by the Seattle Pilots in the 1968 expansion draft, he led the

ML with 73 stolen bases in 1969, the highest AL total since Ty Cobb's 96 in 1915.

Although he preferred the outfield, Harper played mostly at third base (and 82 games at second base) for the Pilots and Brewers. Traded to Boston before the 1972 season, he returned to the outfield. In 1973 he was the Red Sox' MVP, hitting 17 HR, scoring 71 runs, and stealing an AL-high 54 bases. /(JCA)

Toby Harrah [Colbert Dale] — 1948– . 3B-SS-2B 1969, 71–86 **Senators/Rangers**, Indians, Yankees 2155 g, .264, 195 hr, 919 rbi
☛ *All-Star—72, 75–76, 82.*

Harrah was a power-hitting infielder who spent most of his 17-year career on second-division teams. He was the Senators' primary shortstop in their last season of existence and remained there for the franchise's first five seasons in Texas. Coming up straight from Double-A ball in 1971, he was over-matched at first, hitting .230 and slugging .290. He improved as a batter and fielder in 1972 after spending the winter studying with Chico Carrasquel in South America. Harrah hit .259 with 10 HR despite missing time with an appendectomy and a shoulder injury; the injury forced him out of the All-Star Game.

He came into his own in 1974, hitting 21 HR with 74 RBI and 79 runs. It was the first of his five 20-HR seasons. He also showed range in the field, leading AL shortstops in putouts and tying in errors. Manager Billy Martin said, "I don't know how a guy could cover more ground, and he also has that great arm." In 1975 Harrah improved further, hitting .293 and drawing 98 walks while driving in a career-high 93 runs. It was the first of his .400 on-base percentage seasons; his .406 was fourth in the AL. *TSN* named him the shortstop on its postseason AL all-star team. In 1976 he had his best year defensively, leading AL shortstops in putouts and total chances per game (and errors). He also established the first of his two odd fielding records, accepting no chances at shortstop in a June 25 doubleheader. On September 17 the following year, he set another record by playing 17 innings at third base without recording an assist.

Harrah's best year offensively came in 1977, when he was moved to third base after Bert Campaneris was signed as a free agent. Harrah led the AL with 109 walks and hit 27 HR, both career highs, and stole 27 bases. He and Bump Wills hit back-to-back inside-the-park home runs at Yankee Stadium, only the second time that was ever accomplished. In 1978 he stole a career-high 31 bases but slumped to .229. He moved back to shortstop at mid-season as Campaneris hit .186.

After the season Harrah was traded to the Indians for Buddy Bell and he replaced Bell at third base. Although the Rangers often had losing records, they had contended in 1974, 1977, and 1978. In Cleveland, Harrah's talents were buried on a perennial sixth-place finisher that dropped another notch when the expansion Blue Jays finally improved. In his five years with the Indians, Harrah scored 100 runs twice (his career high, in 1980 and 1982). In his only .300 season, .304 in 1982, he also hit 25 HR and finished second in the AL with a .400 on-base percentage. He led AL third basemen in fielding in 1983. At third, he almost always guarded the line, which cut down on his range; he maintained that it was more important to cut off potential doubles than singles. He played in 476 consecutive games before a Dennis Martinez pitch sidelined him with a broken hand in April 1983.

The Yankees acquired Harrah in a five-player deal in February 1984. By the end of spring training, Graig Nettles had been traded to San Diego for panning the club's planned third-base platoon, and Harrah was not only faced with the pressure of replacing the popular Nettles, but was also blamed for causing his departure. He slumped horribly, lost the job to rookie Mike Pagliarulo, and hit just .217. After the season he was traded back to the Rangers for Billy Sample and a minor league pitcher. Happy to be back in Texas, he was the regular second baseman (Buddy Bell was at 3B) and rebounded to .270. Drawing a career-high 113 walks (second in the majors), he finished third in the AL with a .437 on-base average, behind Wade Boggs and George Brett. He retired after hitting .218 in 1986. /(SH)

Ray Harrell (Cowboy) — 1912–1984. RHP 1935, 37–40, 45 **Cardinals**, Cubs, Phillies, Pirates, Giants 330 ip, 9–20, 5.70

Harrell was unimpressive in a 1935 trial with St. Louis, but Branch Rickey, trying to bolster a sagging Cardinal pitching staff, gave him another shot in 1937 as a reliever and spot starter. Hit hard, Harrell was sold to the Cubs after the 1938 season. /(FJO)

Bud Harrelson [Derrel McKinley] — 1944– . SS-2B 1965–80 **Mets**, Phillies, Rangers 1533 g, .236, 7 hr, 267 rbi. *2 LCS, 8 g, .172, 5 rbi. 2 WS, 12 g, .220, 1 rbi* ☛ *All-Star—70–71. Gold Glove—71.*

Harrelson grew up in California wanting to play for the Giants, who rejected him as too small. He signed with the Mets, and on September 16, 1966, stole home in the ninth to cost the Giants a key game in a pennant race they lost by one and a half games. That same week, he stole home to beat the Pirates, who finished two out. After a .108 debut in 1965, he learned to switch-hit.

Between recurring back problems and weekend duty in the National Guard Reserve, he missed considerable playing time, but when he was in the lineup, he sparked the Mets. His excellent fielding kept him in the lineup no matter what his average, but he also contributed with his speed on the basepaths and by drawing more than his share of walks. His best year was 1970, when he reached career highs in five offensive categories and tied the since-broken NL shortstop record of 54 consecutive errorless games (6/24–8/19). In 1971 he won a Gold Glove and led the Mets with 28 stolen bases. Harrelson is second on the Mets' all-time list in games and at-bats (to Ed Kranepool) and triples, and ranks high in hits, runs, and stolen bases. He became a minor league manager and ML coach for the Mets. Pete Rose is still booed in Shea Stadium for his hard collision with Harrelson while trying to break up a double play in the 1973 New York-Cincinnati LCS. Released after 1977, Harrelson turned to softball, but was picked up by the Phillies on their way to the division title. /(MC)

Ken Harrelson (Hawk) — 1941– . 1B-OF 1963–71 **A's**, Senators, Red Sox, Indians 900 g, .239, 131 hr, 421 rbi. *1 WS, 4 g, .077, 1 rbi* ☛ *All-Star—68.*

The big and powerful Harrelson was baseball's 1960s flower child. He wore his blond hair long and sported Nehru jackets, beads, bell bottoms, and no socks. Catcher Duke Sims dubbed him "Hawk" for his aquiline nose, and he had that emblazoned on the back of his uniform. A careless-fielding power hitter, he hit 23 homers for Kansas City in 1965. Late in 1967, Harrelson was quoted as saying, "Charlie Finley is a menace to baseball." The angered A's owner released him. Seven teams approached Harrelson; the Red Sox, in the thick of a pennant race, won him with a $73,000 bonus, and Harrelson helped them to the '67 pennant. In 1968, he hit 35 homers and led the AL with 109 RBI. Boston fans picketed Fenway Park early in 1969 when Harrelson was traded to Cleveland. He missed most of 1970 with a broken leg and played grudgingly for the Indians until 1971, when he quit to become a pro golfer, something he had threatened for years. When that failed, he became an outspoken broadcaster, and, for 1986, was the White Sox' much-criticized GM. /(JCA)

Will Harridge — 1883–1971. *Executive.*
☛ *Hall of Fame—1972.*

As a Wabash Railroad ticket agent, Harridge handled travel arrangements for the AL until Ban Johnson hired him as his private secretary, a position he held from 1911 to 1927. When Johnson resigned as AL president, Harridge became league secretary. When Johnson's successor, E.S. Barnard, died in 1931, Harridge became the third AL president.

Softspoken, reserved, and iron-willed, he remained for 28 years. He avoided the spotlight, preferring to handle league matters discreetly behind closed doors. He always said his most difficult moment came in 1931 when he fined Yankees catcher Bill Dickey $1,000 and suspended him for 30 days during a hot pennant race. Dickey had slugged White Sox outfielder Carl Reynolds and broke his jaw in an unprovoked attack.

Will Harridge

Although Harridge advocated the establishment of an annual All-Star Game, which began in 1933, he generally supported the status quo in baseball. He originally opposed night baseball. He was persuaded during WWII that night games enabled more families to attend games, and he became a supporter of baseball under lights. After retiring as league president in 1958, he served as chairman of the board until his death in 1971. In 1972, he was elected to the Hall of Fame. /(NLM)

Bill Harrington — 1927– . RHP 1953, 55–56 **A's** 116 ip, 5–5, 5.03

After two innings with the 1953 Philadelphia Athletics, Harrington moved with the franchise to Kansas City. The wild reliever compiled records of 3–3 and 2–2 with the lowly 1955–56 clubs. /(FK)

Bill Harris — 1900–1965. RHP 1923–24, 31–34, 38 Reds, **Pirates**, Red Sox 434 ip, 24–22, 3.92

From 1921 to 1945, Harris won 257 minor league games, including two no-hitters for Buffalo in 1936. The righthander had one decent ML season (10–9, 3.64) for the 1932 Pirates. /(ME)

Bob Harris [Robert Ned] — 1916–1976. OF 1941–43, 46 **Tigers** 262 g, .259, 16 hr, 81 rbi

A good hitter and a decent fielder, Harris did well enough at the plate and in the outfield with Buffalo to earn a promotion to Detroit. He played most in 1942 and 1943 before entering military service. /(EW)

Bob Harris [Robert Arthur] — 1916– . RHP 1938–42 Tigers, **Browns**, A's 646 ip, 30–52, 4.96

A fur trapper in Nebraska between seasons, Harris pitched valiantly for poor Browns' and A's teams before leaving for army service, 1943–45. Released by the Athletics upon his return, he demanded compensation for this shoddy treatment, and settled for an undisclosed sum with Connie Mack. /(JK/ EW)

Bucky Harris [Stanley Raymond] — 1896–1977. 2B 1919–29, 31 **Senators**, Tigers 1264 g, .274, 9 hr, 506 rbi. *2 WS, 14 g, .232, 2 hr, 7 rbi.*
   Manager 1924–43, 47–48, 50–56 **Senators**, Tigers, Red Sox, Phillies, Yankees 2159–2219, .493. *3 WS, 11–10, .523*
☛ *Hall of Fame—1975.*

"First in war, first in peace, and last in the American League," ran the old saw about Washington, but in

Bucky Harris

1924 the perennial AL tail-ender Senators were World Champions. In his first season at the helm was 27-year-old Bucky Harris, the youngest regular ML manager and the team's second baseman. Washington's rugged "Boy Manager" led by example and earned the respect of such veterans as Walter Johnson, Sam Rice, and Roger Peckinpaugh.

In the 1924 World Series against the Giants, Harris batted .333 and hit two home runs. He also set records for chances accepted, double plays, and putouts in the exciting seven-game affair. His base hit in the eighth inning of the deciding contest tied the score, and the Senators rallied in the twelfth to clinch Washington's one and only World Championship. It was in that contest that Harris the manager won acclaim. His strategy of replacing righthanded starter Curly Ogden with lefthander George Mogridge after only two batters forced the Giants' hard-hitting Bill Terry out of the lineup.

Harris learned baseball in the mining region of northeastern Pennsylvania. After leaving school at 13, he worked in a local colliery. Hughie Jennings, another future Hall of Famer from Harris's home town of Pittston, arranged for the scrappy youngster's first job in pro ball, in 1915. Harris reached the majors in 1919.

An exceptional fielder, he topped AL second basemen in putouts four times and in double plays a record five straight times (1921–25). An adequate hitter with base stealing ability, Harris had a knack for being hit by pitches. An outstanding basketball player, he played professionally with local Pennsylvania teams during the off-season, until concerned Washington officials ordered him to cease.

Under Harris, the Senators repeated as AL champs in 1925, but lost a hard-fought seven-game Series to the Pirates. After suffering his first losing season in 1928, he was traded to, and named manager of, the Tigers. Except for a few appearances at second base, Harris was a bench manager from then on. He spent five unsuccessful seasons directing the Tigers, one with the Red Sox, and then eight more with the Senators, never finishing higher than fourth. Despite the many losing campaigns, Harris was regarded as a knowledgeable manager and was extremely popular with his players. His patient, gentlemanly manner inspired such loyalty that when the Phillies fired Harris in mid-1943, his players threatened to strike.

Between ML jobs, Harris managed in the International and Pacific Coast leagues. In 1947, he led the Yankees to a World Series victory, and was named *TSN* Manager of the Year. He was dropped abruptly a year later after a 94–60 third-place finish. Though he managed for another seven years, Harris never again landed in the first division.

Harris also served as assistant GM of the Red Sox and scouted for the White Sox. Named a special assignment scout with the expansion Washington Senators in 1963, he finished where he had begun his ML career a half century earlier. Harris, the youngest man to lead a major league team to a World Series victory, was elected, as a manager, to the Hall of Fame in 1975 by the Veterans Committee. /(JL)

Charlie Harris (Bubba) — 1926– . RHP 1948–49, 51 **A's**, Indians 186 ip, 6–3, 4.84

Harris came out of the bullpen 45 times as a rookie for the 1948 A's and went 5–2 with five saves. /(RTM)

Dave Harris (Sheriff) — 1900–1973. OF 1925, 28, 30–34 Braves, White Sox, **Senators** 542 g, .281, 32 hr, 247, rbi. *1 WS, 3 g, .000*

Never a regular, Harris hit .310 as a pinch hitter. On August 5, 1932, with the Senators trailing Detroit 13–0 and two outs in the ninth inning, Harris's pinch single ruined Tommy Bridges's perfect game. /(NLM)

Gail Harris — 1931– . 1B 1955–60 Giants, **Tigers** 437 g, .240, 51 hr, 190 rbi

Harris was a power hitter but lacked consistency. In 1958 for the Tigers, his best season, he had 20 home runs and 83 RBI but led AL first basemen in errors. /(BC)

Greg Harris — 1955– . RHP 1981– Mets, Reds, Expos, Padres, **Rangers**, Phillies 791 ip, 35–45, 3.52. *1 LCS, 2 ip, 0–0, 31.50. 1 WS, 5 ip, 0–0, 0.00*

The curveballing, ambidextrous Harris bounced around the NL before landing with the 1984 NL champion Padres. Roughed up by the Cubs in the playoff opener, he allowed a NLCS-record six earned runs in one inning. He came into his own after his 1985 sale to Texas, leading AL relievers with 111 strikeouts and posting a 2.47 ERA. He went 10–8 (2.83) with a staff-high 20 saves in 1986, but in 1987 he both started and relieved, went 5–10 without a save, and was released. He had missed some games that season after injuring his elbow flicking sunflower seeds to a friend in the stands. /(JCA)

Greg Harris [Greg Wade] — 1963– . RHP 1988– **Padres** 153 ip, 10–9, 2.47

Harris has one of the best curves in the league and will use it repeatedly. In 1989 he established himself as the number-two man out of the Padres' bullpen. /(SFS)

Joe Harris (Moon) — 1891–1959. 1B-OF 1914, 17, 19, 22–28 Yankees, Indians, **Red Sox**, Senators, Pirates, Dodgers 971 g, .317, 47 hr, 517 rbi. *2 WS, 11 g, .350, 3 hr, 7 rbi*

Harris batted over .300 each of his full seasons except his last. A starting outfielder for the Red Sox in 1922–23 before moving to first base in 1924, Harris was traded to Washington in 1925 and hit .323 to help the Senators to the pennant. He batted .440 with three HR in the seven-game WS loss to Pittsburgh. /(ME)

Joe Harris — 1882–1966. RHP 1905–07 **Red Sox** 317 ip, 3–30, 3.35

In 1906, the luckless Harris compiled one of the worst records ever by a ML hurler. His 2–21 record for the error-prone last-place Red Sox included 14 straight losses and eight shutouts pitched against him. He set an AL record going the route in a 24-inning loss to Philadelphia's Jack Coombs (4–1, on September 1). Boston-area native Harris suffered again in 1907, going 0–7. /(EW)

Lum Harris [Chalmer Luman] — 1915– . RHP 1941–44, 46–47 A's, Senators 820 ip, 35–63, 4.16.
    Manager 1961, 64–65, 68–72 Orioles, Astros, **Braves** 466–488, .488. First place: 69 *1 LCS, 0–3, .000*

Harris had a good fastball and a fair knuckler, but he pitched for poor A's clubs. His 21 losses (including 13 straight) in 1943 were the most in the AL. In the most successful of his years as manager of the Braves, he led Atlanta to the 1969 NL West title. The Mets swept the LCS. /(EW)

Mark Harris — 1922– . *Writer.*

A novelist, playwright, and English professor at San Francisco State, Purdue, and Arizona State, Harris is known among baseball fans for his series of novels about Dizzy Dean-esque flake Henry Wiggen: *The Southpaw* (1953), *Bang the Drum Slowly* (1956), *A Ticket for a Seamstitch* (1959), and *It Looked Like Forever* (1979). Harris also did the screenplay for the Robert De Niro film of *Bang the Drum Slowly*, considered by many critics to be among the best baseball movies ever. /(NLM)

Mickey Harris — 1917–1971. LHP 1940–41, 46–52 **Red Sox**, Senators, Indians 1050 ip, 59–71, 4.18. *1 WS, 10 ip, 0–2, 3.72*
☛ *All-Star—46.*

Harris's 17–9 record in 1946 (after four years in the army) contributed to a Red Sox pennant. Though plagued by arm problems most of his career, his 53 relief appearances and 15 saves for the 1950 Senators led the AL. /(EW)

Spence Harris — 1900–1982. OF 1925–26, 29–30 White Sox, Senators, A's 164 g, .249, 3 hr, 46 rbi

Harris was unimpressive in several trials in the majors but had a long and productive career in the minors (1921–48), setting all-time minor league career records for hits (3,617), runs (2,287), doubles (743), and total bases (5,434). /(LRD)

Vic Harris — 1905–1978. OF-MGR Negro Leagues 1923–50 Cleveland Tate Stars, Toledo Tigers, Chicago American Giants, **Homestead Grays**, Detroit Stars, Pittsburgh Crawfords, Cleveland Browns, Baltimore Elite Giants, Birmingham Black Barons statistics not available ☛ *All-Star—38, 42–43, 47.*

Unlike many Negro League players who flitted from team to team, Harris spent most of his career (23 of 28 years) with one club—the Homestead Grays—as a strong-hitting outfielder and manager. He started playing as a 17-year-old with the Cleveland Tate Stars, and settled in with the Grays during their strong independent years. He was an aggressive baserunner and could "undress an infielder, cut the uniform right off his back," according to one contemporary.

Harris managed the Grays during their years in league play, from 1936 through 1948, winning nine consecutive pennants (1937–45) and two Black World Series titles (1943 and 1944). In 1938, when the Grays dominated the league and won the first half with an .813 winning percentage, Harris reportedly hit .380. In the waning days of the Negro Leagues, he coached for the Baltimore Elite Giants in 1949 and managed the Birmingham Black Barons in 1950. /(BP)

Vic Harris — 1950– . 2B-OF-3B-SS 1972–78, 80 **Rangers**, Cubs, Cardinals, Giants, Brewers 579 g, .217, 13 hr, 121 rbi

Harris batted .249 with eight homers for Texas in 1973, his only season as a regular. Because he switch-hit and could play the infield and the outfield, he was a valuable utility man. /(JCA)

Chuck Harrison (Charles William) — 1941– . 1B 1965–69, 71 **Astros**, Royals 328 g, .238, 17 hr, 126 rbi

The Texas Tech linebacker was a tenacious first baseman who could hit home runs in the minors (40 at San Antonio in 1964). He was Houston's regular first baseman only for 1966, as he had trouble hitting the curveball. /(JCA)

Roric Harrison — 1946– . RHP 1972–75, 78 Orioles, **Braves**, Indians, Twins 590 ip, 30–35, 4.24

Harrison was the property of nine organizations. He led the International League with 15 wins in 1971, but a wrenched knee in the playoffs cost him a promotion to the Orioles. He underwent several knee operations, the first in 1969. At his best, he went 11–8 for the 1973 Braves. /(MC)

Slim Harriss [William Jennings Bryan] — 1896–1963. RHP 1920–28 **A's**, Red Sox 1750 ip, 95–135, 4.25

Slim was a 6'6" 180-lb, hard-throwing Texan. Pitching for the A's against the White Sox, he gave up singles to the first 2 hitters, then retired 27 in a row. While teammate Eddie Rommel was winning an AL-high 27 games in 1922, Harriss was losing a league-high 20. His only winning season was 1925 (19–12). He again led the AL in losses in 1927, with 21 for the Red Sox. /(NLM)

Earl Harrist (Irish) — 1919– . RHP 1945, 47–48, 52–53 Reds, **White Sox**, Senators, Browns, Tigers 384 ip, 12–28, 4.34

On July 5, 1947 Harrist faced pinch hitter Larry Doby, the AL's first black player, in Doby's first ML appearance, and struck him out. The mediocre reliever won that game, but only 11 others. /(JK)

Jack Harshman — 1927– . LHP-1B, 1948, 50, 52, 54–60 Giants, **White Sox**, Orioles, Red Sox, Indians 258 g, .179, 21 hr, 65 rbi; 1169 ip, 69–65, 3.50

Harshman began his pro career as a slugging first baseman, leading the Southern Association in HR (47) and RBI (141) in 1951; he went on to hit 21 ML homers. In 1952 he began the transition to the mound. Harshman set the White Sox team record for strikeouts in a single game with 16 at Boston on July 25, 1954. /(EW)

Bill Hart — 1865–1936. RHP-OF 1886–87, 92, 95–98, 1901 Philadelphia (AA), Dodgers, Pirates, **Cardinals**, Indians 229 g, .207, 4 hr, 66 rbi; 1582 ip, 66–120, 4.65

In 1896, pitching for the Cardinals, Hart led the NL in losses with 29, but he won over 250 minor league games. He pitched for 25 seasons in the ML and minors, beginning and ending with Chattanooga of the Southern Association. When he retired as a player in 1910 after winning his last start, he turned to umpiring. /(BC)

Jim Ray Hart — 1941– . 3B-OF-DH 1963–74 **Giants**, Yankees 1125 g, .278, 170 hr, 578 rbi. *1 LCS, 3 g, .000* ☛ *All-Star—66.*

Bob Gibson welcomed Jim Ray to the big leagues in 1963 by breaking his shoulder blade with a fast ball in the back. A few days after Hart's return, he was beaned by Curt Simmons and missed the rest of the season. But in 1964, his first full year, the stocky strongman proved he wasn't gun-shy with a San Francisco-rookie record 31 homers. Until a 1969 shoulder injury made him a part-timer, he averaged

28 homers a season. On September 8, 1970 he hit for the cycle and tied a ML record with six RBI in one inning. Although the former North Carolina cotton picker was so quiet it was said a soft chuckle was a whole conversation for him, he was vocal about his hatred of playing third base: it was "just too damn close to the hitters."/(JCA)

Chuck Hartenstein (Twiggy) — 1942– . RHP 1965–70, 77 **Cubs**, Pirates, Cardinals, Red Sox, Blue Jays 297 ip, 17–19, 4.52

A sinkerballing reliever, the slender Hartenstein was nicknamed Twiggy by teammate Billy Williams. At his best as a rookie with the 1967 Cubs, he was 9–5 with ten saves. Hartenstein became a ML pitching coach with Cleveland and Milwaukee./(AA)

Grover Hartley (Slick) — 1888–1964. C 1911–17, 24–27, 29–30, 34 Giants, **St. Louis (FL)**, Browns, Red Sox, Indians 569 g, .268, 3 hr, 144 rbi

The well-traveled catcher was a master with young pitchers. Hartley's only year as a regular came in 1915 with St. Louis of the Federal League. He was a minor league manager and a coach with the Browns and Pirates./(EW)

Fred Hartman (Dutch) — 1868–1938. 3B 1894, 1897–99, 1901–02 Pirates, Cardinals, **Giants**, White Sox 580 g, .278, 10 hr, 332 rbi

After two-plus National League seasons, Hartman played for Chicago in 1900, when the American League was a minor league. When the AL became a major league in 1901, Hartman batted .309 as the third baseman on the league's first pennant-winner./(AJA)

Harry Hartman — Unk.–Unk. *Broadcaster.*

A Cincinnati sports broadcaster and Reds' P.A. announcer in the 1930s, Hartman was voted the most popular ML sports announcer in a 1933 *Sporting News* poll. Supposedly, he was the first to call a home run with "Going, going, gone!"/(NLM)

Gabby Hartnett [Charles Leo] — 1900–1972. C 1922–41 **Cubs**, Giants 1990 g, .297, 236 hr, 1179 rbi. *4 WS, 16 g, .241, 2 hr, 3 rbi.*
    Manager 1938–40 **Cubs** 203–176, .536. *1 WS, 0–4, .000*
☛ *Most Valuable Player—35. All-Star—33–38. Hall of Fame—1955.*

Hartnett was the oldest of 14 children. His father Fred was a semi-pro catcher who had an exceptional

Gabby Hartnett

throwing arm. Millville, MA, oldtimers still talk about "the Hartnett arm"—Fred's, four of his sons', and three of his five daughters' who barnstormed with a women's team.

Gabby broke his arm as a child. It didn't knit properly, and his mother insisted he carry a pail of stones or sand wherever he went, to exercise it. His father held backyard baseball clinics for four sons, all of whom played amateur or semi-pro ball. Chickie, a catcher, once signed a pro contract, but was homesick and returned to Millville before ever playing. Gabby completed eight years of schooling, went to work in the U.S. Rubber shop, and caught for the plant nine and any other team his father could get him on. He spent a year and a half at a junior college, and in 1921 signed with the Eastern League's Worcester Boosters. He batted .264, and was purchased by Chicago for $2,500. As a shy rookie, his reticent personality led to his ironic nickname.

Hartnett became Chicago's catcher by 1924, batting .299, and in 1925 hit 24 HR, though he struck out 77 times to lead the NL. In 1929, his arm went mysteriously dead in spring training, where he had reported with his new bride, Martha. Nothing helped the arm, and during a Cubs' series in Boston, he went to see his mother in Woonsocket, RI, after the games. She predicted that his arm would be better as soon as his pregnant wife delivered their child. Hartnett caught just one game that season. Junior was born December 4, and within two weeks, Gabby's arm soreness was gone.

Hartnett followed in 1930 with his best season ever, hitting .339 with career highs of 37 HR and 122 RBI. An All-Star six straight years, in the 1934 game he was the catcher when Carl Hubbell fanned Ruth, Gehrig, Foxx, Simmons, and Cronin in succession. He was named NL MVP in 1935, batting .344 (third in the league), topping NL catchers in assists, double plays, and fielding average, and led the Cubs to the pennant.

His finest day came on September 28, 1938. He had become the Cubs' manager in mid-season, and had his team within a half game of the first-place Pirates. With darkness and haze rapidly enveloping Wrigley Field in the ninth, and the score 5–5, two out, no one on, down 0–2 in the count, Hartnett slammed his "Homer in the Gloamin'." Three days later, the Cubs clinched the pennant.

Hartnett managed the Cubs to fifth place in 1940, was fired, and hit .300 as a 40-year-old catcher/ pinch hitter for the Giants in 1941. He retired as a player, having four times led NL catchers in putouts, six times in assists, and seven in double plays. Though he topped the league in errors three of his first four seasons, he later led in fielding average six years, including a record-tying four straight from 1934–37.

After an often hectic five seasons managing in the minors, Hartnett quit baseball after 1946, opening a recreation center and bowling alley in Lincolnwood, IL. He sold it in 1964 to join Kansas City as a coach, scout, and troubleshooter for two years, but relations with manager Alvin Dark were not good, and Hartnett was dropped.

Joe McCarthy, who saw much of Mickey Cochrane and managed both Bill Dickey and Hartnett, called Gabby "The Perfect Catcher." He is widely considered the greatest NL catcher before Johnny Bench. His 20 years and 1,790 games behind the plate put him among the all-time leaders in service, and he is among the Cubs' all-time top ten in nine offensive categories. The BBWAA inducted him into Cooperstown in 1955. /(JK)

Topsy Hartsel [Tully Frederick] — 1874–1944. OF 1898–1911 Louisville (NL), Reds, Cubs, **A's** 1354 g, .276, 30 hr, 341 rbi. *2 WS, 6 g, .273*

The 5'5" Hartsel used his size to work pitchers for walks, five times leading the league. The lefthanded leadoff man played for four pennant winners in his ten seasons with the Athletics. The dependable leftfielder led the AL in stolen bases and runs scored in 1902. /(JK)

Roy Hartsfield — 1925– . 2B 1950–52 **Braves** 265 g, .273, 13 hr, 59 rbi.
  Manager 1977–79 **Blue Jays** 166–318, .343

A competent second baseman whose playing career was curtailed by injuries, Hartsfield became the first-ever manager of the Toronto Blue Jays, directing them to three consecutive last-place finishes in 1977–79. /(FS)

Clint Hartung (Floppy, The Hondo Hurricane) — 1922– . RHP-OF 1947–52 **Giants** 511 ip, 29–29, 5.02; 196 g, .238, 14 hr, 43 rbi, *1 WS, 2 g, .000*

Hartung is a baseball metaphor for a player with apparently unlimited talent who is never able to harness it. The 6'5", 210-lb Hondo, Texas, native joined the Giants with a fabulous record as a pitcher and hitter while on WWII service teams against ML-caliber competition. Contemporary cynics said he should "not bother playing, just get ready for the Hall of Fame," and he struggled for six unproductive seasons. He lacked the control to be an effective pitcher, and he struck out too much to play regularly. /(FS)

Paul Hartzell (Tall Paul) — 1953– . RHP 1976–80, 84 **Angels**, Twins, Orioles, Brewers 703 ip, 27–39, 3.90

After just one season of Class A ball, the 6'5" flame-thrower went 7–4 (2.77) with the Angels in 1976, but followed with two losing seasons. One of four players dealt to Minnesota for Rod Carew in 1979, Hartzell went 6–10 that season and returned to the minors. /(JCA)

Roy Hartzell — 1881–1961. OF-3B-SS-2B 1906–16 Browns, **Yankees** 1288 g, .252, 12 hr, 397 rbi

The lefthanded hitter shuttled among second base, third base, shortstop, and outfield each season. His 595 at-bats for the Browns led the AL in 1909, and his 91 RBI for New York in 1911 were the most by a player in the Yankees' first 13 years. /(FS)

Bryan Harvey — 1963– . RHP 1987- **Angels** 136 ip, 10–8, 2.58

Harvey was named *TSN* Rookie Pitcher of the Year for 1988 when he had 17 saves and a 2.13 ERA to establish himself as the ace of the Angels' bullpen. /(WOR)

Doug Harvey — 1930– . *Umpire* NL 1962–87 *6 LCS 4 WS 5 ASU*

One of the most respected umpires of his time, Harvey says of his profession: "Umpires are necessary evils. That's just the nature of the beast. For years people have looked on umpiring as a job they could get any postman to do." He first got the urge to become an umpire while watching Don Larsen's perfect game in the 1956 WS on TV. In a 1978 game, Harvey collected three scuffed baseballs, then ejected Dodger pitcher Don Sutton for apparently doctoring the balls. The league decided not to penalize Sutton after he threatened to sue the NL if he was suspended. /(RTM)

Ernie Harwell — 1918– . *Broadcaster.*

A talented writer and accomplished lyricist and composer outside the broadcast booth, Harwell has been the immensely popular voice of the Tigers for almost three decades. In 1934, as a 16-year-old Georgia high school student, Harwell became *The Sporting News*'s Atlanta correspondent. His work would eventually appear in *Collier's*, *Reader's Digest*, and *The Saturday Evening Post*, but he chose to make his living as a broadcaster.

Harwell was broadcasting for the Atlanta Crackers when his work caught the attention of Dodgers owner Branch Rickey, and Rickey traded minor league catcher Cliff Dapper to the Crackers to bring Harwell to Brooklyn in 1948. He later worked briefly with the Giants and Orioles before settling in Detroit in 1960. Harwell originally worked on both TV and radio, but after 1965 his endearing, friendly voice was heard exclusively on radio. His 1955 baseball essay, "A Game for All America," is displayed in baseball's Hall of Fame. /(SL)

Tufie Hashem — Unk.–1968. *Scout.*

Hashem began his baseball career as GM of Mexicali in 1949, and began scouting for the Cardinals in 1954 when he steered Ruben Amaro their way. He also worked briefly for the Pirates and Angels, and made numerous scouting trips to Mexico and Latin America, but his most prominent discoveries were American-born players like Jay Johnstone, Rudy May, Doug Griffin, and Roy White. /(FVP)

Mickey Haslin — 1910– . SS-2B-3B 1933–38 **Phillies**, Braves, Giants 318 g, .272, 9 hr, 109 rbi

Haslin was a 5'8" utility infielder who led the Phillies in pinch hits in 1934. In the first ML night game (5/24/35), Haslin drove in Philadelphia's only run in a 2–1 loss at Cincinnati. /(GEB)

Buddy Hassett — 1911– . 1B-OF 1936–42 **Dodgers**, Braves, Yankees 929 g, .292, 12 hr, 343 rbi. *1 WS, 3 g, .333, 2 rbi*

The steady-hitting first baseman was stuck in the Yankee farm system while Lou Gehrig was in his prime. Sold to Brooklyn, Hassett hit .310 his rookie year. Gehrig retired, and the Yankees traded top prospect Tommy Holmes to the Braves in 1942 to retrieve Hassett. His appearance with the Yankees in the 1942 WS, before entering the military, marked the end of his career. /(JK)

Ron Hassey (Babe) — 1953– . C-DH 1978- **Indians**, Cubs, Yankees, White Sox, A's 1046 g, .272, 65 hr, 402 rbi. *2 LCS, 6 g, .537, 1 hr, 4 rbi. 1 WS, 5 g, .250, 1 rbi*

The good-hitting, burly Hassey was Cleveland's primary catcher from mid-1979 to 1984. He led all major league catchers by batting .318 in 1980. A decent defensive catcher, he caught Len Barker's perfect game in 1981. The lefthanded hitter was proficient as a pinch hitter and was a strong finisher. He was traded between Chicago and New York four times from 1984 to 1986. Bad knees limited him, especially on defense. He was a backup on championship A's teams in 1988 and 1989. /(ME)

Andy Hassler — 1951– . LHP 1971, 73–85 **Angels**, Royals, Red Sox, Mets, Pirates, Cardinals 1123 ip, 44–71, 3.83. *3 LCS, 16 ip, 0–2, 4.60*

The 6'5" Hassler recorded a pair of one-hitters, one with the 1974 Angels, the other with the 1977 Royals. In 1975–76, Hassler lost an Angel-record 17 straight decisions. /(EW)

Bob Hasty — 1896–1972. RHP 1919–24 **A's** 752 ip, 29–53, 4.65

Before improving his fielding, Hasty was in danger of being bunted out of baseball. The finesse pitcher never had an ERA below 4.25. /(NLM)

Billy Hatcher — 1960– . OF 1984- Cubs, **Astros**, Pirates 609 g, .263, 30 hr, 212 rbi. *1 LCS, 6 g, .280, 1 hr, 2 rbi*

The Astros left fielder was ejected from a September 1, 1987 game against Chicago when the barrel of his bat split, revealing it had been corked. Hatcher claimed he had no idea the bat had been doctored, that he had borrowed it from pitcher Dave Smith, who had used it only during batting practice. Hatcher received a 10-day suspension. That year, the year of the rabbit ball, was the most successful of Hatcher's first four (.296, 11 HR, 63 RBI). His 53 stolen bases ranked third in the NL. A catalyst on Houston's 1986 division-winner, Hatcher hit a dramatic, 14th-inning home run to tie Game Six of the LCS at 4–4; it took 16 innings for the Mets to win the game, clinching the pennant. /(JCA)

Mickey Hatcher — 1955– . OF-3B-1B 1979– Dodgers, **Twins** 1044 g, .283, 38 hr, 362 rbi. *1 LCS, 6 g, .238, 3 rbi. 1 WS, 5 g, .368, 2 hr, 5 rbi*

This clubhouse comic and team energizer sometimes wears a batting helmet with a propeller on it. He became the nation's darling with his 1988 postseason play. After hitting only one HR all year, he homered in the first inning of the first and final WS games and made the finest defensive plays of the Series. An enthusiastic, hustling player, he would have been WS MVP but for Orel Hershiser. Hatcher spent six seasons with the Twins as an effective utility player, then was released during the spring of 1987 before signing with the Dodgers. /(TG)

Fred Hatfield — 1925– . 3B-2B-SS 1950–58 Red Sox, **Tigers**, White Sox, Indians, Reds. 722 g, .242, 25 hr, 165 rbi

In only two seasons did the versatile utility infielder play 100 games at any one position. Hatfield was twice involved in trades involving future Hall of Famers, first George Kell and later Early Wynn. He was a direct descendant of the Hatfields who feuded with the McCoys. /(GEB)

Joe Hatten — 1916–1988. LHP 1946–52 **Dodgers**, Cubs 1087 ip, 65–49, 3.87. *2 WS, 11 ip, 8.44*

After four years in the minors and several in the service, Hatten reached the majors at the age of twenty-nine. The Dodger starting pitcher in Jackie Robinson's first ML game in 1947, Hatten went on to a career-best 17–8 that year. /(EGM)

Lou Hatter — 1920–1988. *Writer.*

Hatter was a baseball writer for 40 years for the Baltimore *Sun*, and covered the Orioles from 1954 until he retired in 1984. /(NLM)

Grady Hatton — 1922– . 3B-2B 1946–56, 60 **Reds**, White Sox, Red Sox, Cardinals, Orioles, Cubs 1312 g, .254, 91 hr, 533 rbi.
Manager 1966–68 **Astros** 164–221, .426
☛ *All-Star*—52 .

Hatton jumped straight to the Reds from military service in 1946, hitting .271 with 14 HR and 69 RBI. He followed in 1947 with 16 HR, 77 RBI, 91 runs, and a .281 average, but tailed off thereafter. He managed the Oklahoma City 89ers to two pennants in three years and then managed the Astros from 1966 to 1968. He finished eighth, ninth, and last, despite the presence of Rusty Staub, Jim Wynn, Bob Watson, Nate Colbert, Mike Cuellar, Larry Dierker, Don Wilson, Doug Rader, and Joe Morgan (whom he tried to turn into an outfielder). /(MC)

Arnold Hauser (Pee Wee) — 1888–1966. SS 1910–13, 15 **Cardinals**, Chicago (FL) 433 g, .238, 6 hr, 137 rbi

Called "The Midget" by Cardinal manager Roger Bresnahan, the 5'7" Hauser was actually a half-inch taller than his double-play partner, Miller Huggins. /(JK)

Joe Hauser (Unser Choe) — 1899– . 1B 1922–24, 26, 28–29 **A's**, Indians 629 g, .284, 79 hr, 356 rbi

The lefthanded-hitting Hauser batted .323 as a rookie in 1922, and in 1924 led the A's with 27 HR (second to Ruth) and 115 RBI. He broke his kneecap in 1925, missing the entire season. Following his ML career, he became a minor league slugger. He is the only player in professional ball to twice hit 60 home runs in a season, with 63 for Baltimore (International League) in 1930 and 69 for Minneapolis (American Association) in 1933. /(LRD)

Tom Hausman — 1953– . RHP 1975–76, 78–82 Brewers, **Mets**, Braves 441 ip, 15–23, 3.79

Chronic back problems and ulcers headed a long list of maladies that sidelined Hausman year after year. In 1980, his healthiest season, he appeared in 55 Met games, mostly in middle relief. /(JCA)

Clem Hausmann — 1919–1972. RHP 1944–45, 49 **Red Sox**, A's 263 ip, 9–14, 4.21

The slim Texan used an effective curveball in a brief ML career during WWII. /(EW)

George Hausmann — 1916- . 2B 1944-45, 49 **Giants** 301 g, .268, 3 hr, 78 rbi

At 5'5" 145-lb, Hausmann was the Giants' regular second baseman during the last years of WWII. He was suspended for jumping to the outlaw Mexican League in 1946. After the suspension was lifted, he played a few games in 1949. /(FS)

Brad Havens — 1959- . LHP 1981-83, 85- **Twins**, Orioles, Dodgers, Indians, Tigers 591 ip, 24-37, 4.81

After leading the Twins' 1982 pitching staff in starts (32) and strikeouts (129), Havens was their Opening Day pitcher in 1983, but he was twice sent down, and finished with an 8.18 ERA. The International League strikeout leader in 1984 and 1985, he returned to the majors as a middle reliever. /(JCA)

Andy Hawkins — 1960- . RHP 1982- **Padres**, Yankees 1311 ip, 75-73, 4.00. *1 LCS, 4 ip, 0-0, 0.00. 1 WS, 12 ip, 1-1, 0.75*

The Padres' first pick in the 1978 June draft, Hawkins showed few signs of living up to expectations until the 1984 postseason, when he allowed just one earned run in 15.2 innings of relief and was the winner in San Diego's only World Series victory. In 1985 he picked up where he had left off, becoming the first NL pitcher in 26 years to win his first 11 decisions, breaking the Padres' record for consecutive wins by a starter. Hampered in the second half by a circulatory problem in his left index finger (caused by throwing the slider), he finished the season at 18-8. He recovered from 1987 shoulder problems to go 14-11 (3.35) in 1988. Signed by the Yankees after the season to a big free agent contract, he became their number-one pitcher and had another hot streak in the middle of the season after a bad start. /(JCA)

Wynn Hawkins (Hawk) — 1936- . RHP 1960-62 **Indians** 203 ip, 12-13, 4.17

The 6'3" Hawkins came out of Baldwin-Wallace University as their all-time leading basketball scorer. On June 17, 1960 he surrendered Ted Williams's 500th home run. He later served the Indians as a scout and as their traveling secretary. /(RTM)

Pink Hawley [Emerson P.] — 1872-1938. RHP 1892-01 Cardinals, **Pirates**, Reds, Giants, Milwaukee (AL) 3012 ip, 168-177, 3.96. 20 wins: 95, 96, 98

After suffering a NL-high 26 losses with St. Louis in 1894, Hawley rebounded for the Pirates in 1895 with a 32-21 year, including a league-leading 444

innings pitched. He topped 300 innings in five other seasons. /(ME)

Ben Hayes — 1957- . RHP 1982-83 **Reds** 115 ip, 6-6, 4.70

The inconsistent reliever had a 1.97 ERA in 26 appearances in 1982. The next year he allowed only one earned run in 18 appearances during June and July, but collapsed to finish 4-6, 6.49, and never appeared again in the ML. /(JCA)

Frankie Hayes (Blimp) — 1914-1955. C 1933-34, 36-47 **A's**, Browns, Indians, White Sox, Red Sox 1364 g, .259, 119 hr, 628 rbi
☛ *All-Star—39-41, 44, 46.*

Hayes was a highly-regarded defensive catcher and a five-time All-Star. He led the AL three times in total chances per game, twice each in fielding, putouts, double plays, and errors, and once in assists. His 29 double plays in 1945 is the second-highest total ever for a catcher. When he caught 155 games in 1944, he set a still-standing AL record.

He failed in his first trial in the majors, batting just .226 in 1934, but he came back up in 1936 to spend six seasons as the Athletics' primary catcher. His best offensive season was 1939, when he hit .283 and had career highs of 20 HR and 83 RBI; he hit a career-high .308 in 1940 (with 61 walks in 465 at-bats). On July 25, 1936 he tied the major league record with four doubles in a game. /(WOR)

Jackie Hayes [Minter Carney] — 1906-1983 2B-3B-SS 1927-40 Senators, **White Sox** 1091 g, .265, 20 hr, 493 rbi

Joe Cronin called second baseman Hayes "the best double play artist in the league." Hayes and shortstop Luke Appling formed a fine double play combination while Hayes was the White Sox' regular at second base for much of 1932-37. In 1937 Hayes's 115 double plays led AL second basemen. He had career highs of 84 RBI in 1936, and .328 average in 1938. /(EW)

Von Hayes — 1958- . OF-1B 1981-89 Indians, **Phillies** 1195 g, .274, 122 hr, 573 rbi. *1 LCS, 2 g, .000. 1 WS, 4 g, .000*
☛ *All-Star—89.*

Tall and reed-thin, with great speed and deceptive strength, Hayes is a natural outfielder, but has spent much of his playing time at first base. The Indians touted him as their best prospect in a decade, and he made his ML debut after only one season in the minors. His first full ML season, 1982, produced a .250 average, 14 HR, 82 RBI, and 32 stolen bases.

The Phillies were sufficiently impressed to send five players, including Julio Franco, to Cleveland in exchange for Hayes. Hayes never lived up to the "five-for-one" expectations he faced in 1983, but in 1984 he hit .292 with 16 HR and 46 stolen bases, and on June 11, 1985 he homered twice in the first inning against the Mets, a ML first. Faced with a surplus of outfielders, the Phillies switched Hayes to first base in 1986, and he hit .305 with 19 HR, 98 RBI, and 24 steals, leading the NL in doubles and tying for the lead in runs scored. He made the All-Star team in 1989, hit a career-high 26 HR, and was second in the NL with 101 walks. /(SG)

Joe Haynes — 1917–1967. RHP 1939–52 Senators, **White Sox** 1581 ip, 76–82, .401

Haynes sandwiched eight years with the White Sox between two stints with the Senators. He was Chicago's ace reliever in 1942 (8–5, 2.62, six saves), leading the AL with 40 appearances. His best season came as a starter in 1947 (14–6, 2.42). Haynes was married to Thelma Griffith, adopted daughter of Washington owner Clark Griffith, who brought Joe back home in a December 1948 trade with Cleveland. Haynes later became a Senators coach, GM, and vice president, moving with the franchise to Minnesota. /(GB)

Ray Hayworth — 1904– . C 1926, 29–39, 42, 44–45 **Tigers**, Dodgers, Giants, Browns 698 g, .265, 5 hr, 238 rbi. *1 WS, 1 g, --*

A fine defensive catcher but only an ordinary hitter, Hayworth lost his job as the regular Tiger backstop in 1934 when Mickey Cochrane became player-manager. Hayworth was Cochrane's sub as Detroit won pennants in 1934 and 1935 and continued as a backup for the remainder of his career. His brother Red caught for the Browns during WWII. /(JK)

Bob Hazle (Hurricane) — 1930– . OF 1955, 57–58 Reds, **Braves**, Tigers 110 g, .310, 9 hr, 37 rbi

A lefthanded streak hitter, Hazle was called up by the Braves when outfielder Bill Bruton was injured in July 1957. Red hot, he batted .403 in 41 games and helped Milwaukee win the pennant. /(NLM)

Ed Head — 1918–1980. RHP 1940, 42–44, 46 **Dodgers** 465 ip, 27–23, 3.48

After spending the 1945 season in the military, he no-hit the Braves at Ebbets Field on April 23, 1946. Shortly thereafter, Head suffered a career-ending arm injury. /(EGM)

Fran Healy — 1946– . C 1969, 71–78 **Royals**, Giants, Yankees 470 g, .250, 20 hr, 141 rbi

The son of 1930s NL catcher Francis Healy, Fran was regarded as a potential star in 1974, when he hit .252 for the Royals with 53 RBI. Unusually fast for a catcher, he had 16 stolen bases that season, the most by a ML catcher in 37 years. He caught both of Steve Busby's no-hitters. His career sank with a shoulder injury in 1975. Traded to the Yankees, he backed up Thurman Munson and was a valuable mediator in the Reggie Jackson-Billy Martin feuds of 1977–78. He later became a broadcaster for a NY cable sports network. /(MC)

Bunny Hearn [Bunn] — 1891–1959. LHP 1910–11, 13, 15, 18, 20 Cardinals, Giants, **Pittsburgh (FL)**, Braves 400 ip, 13–24, 3.56

Hearn never earned more than a temporary spot on a ML roster, but he was baseball coach at the University of North Carolina for 27 years. /(ME)

Jim Hearn — 1921– . RHP 1947–59 Cardinals, **Giants**, Phillies 1703 ip, 109–89, 3.81 *1 WS, 8 ip, 1–0, 1.04* ☛ *Led League—era 50. All-Star—52.*

After a promising 12–7 rookie year with the Cardinals in 1947, Hearn went into a tailspin, engendered in part by a chronic lack of confidence. The Giants were able to purchase him cheaply in July of 1950. He was 0–1 with a 10.00 ERA when he arrived in New York, but for the remainder of the season he went 11–3 and brought his ERA down to a league-leading 2.49. His five shutouts tied for the league lead. The next season, he was 17–9 as the third starter on the staff behind aces Sal Maglie and Larry Jansen, as the Giants swept to the "miracle" pennant of 1951. Hearn was a sinkerball pitcher. Although he had fairly good control, his walks often outnumbered his strikeouts, but he was excellent at throwing double play pitches. /(FS)

Jeff Heath — 1915–1975. OF 1936–49 **Indians**, Senators, Browns, Braves 1383 g, .293, 194 hr, 887 rbi ☛ *All-Star—41, 43.*

Heath twice led the AL in triples, and averaged 18 HR and over 81 RBI in ten seasons as a regular. He hit a career-high .343 in 1938, his first year as Cleveland's everyday left fielder. In Bob Feller's 1940 Opening Day no-hitter, Heath scored the game's only run. In 1947 with the Browns he hit career highs of 27 HR and 87 RBI. Bought by the 1948 pennant-bound Boston Braves, Heath responded with a .319 average and 20 HR, but in the final week of the season, he broke his leg sliding and missed the WS against the Indians. Heath remains among Cleveland's top ten in triples, HR, and slugging percentage. /(GEB)

Mike Heath — 1955- . C-OF 1978- Yankees, **A's**, Cardinals, Tigers 1153 g, .252, 78 hr, 419 rbi. *2 LCS, 6 g, .308, 1 hr, 2 rbi. 1 WS, 1 g, --*

Heath was the A's starting catcher in the early 1980s, but the veteran righthander has been a part-time player and valuable reserve for most of his career, and has played every position but pitcher in the ML. Heath was a shortstop when signed by the Yankees in 1973, and did not begin catching until 1976. Two years later, at the age of 23, he caught one inning in Game Five of the WS after the Yankees had called him up in the latter half of the season. Heath was traded to the Rangers in the deal that made Dave Righetti a Yankee in November 1978, and was still in the minors when the Rangers traded him to Oakland. He became Oakland's starting catcher in strike-shortened 1981, and caught over 100 games in both 1984 and 1985, hitting exactly .250 with 13 HR each year. After 65 games with the Cardinals in 1986, Heath returned to the AL with the Tigers, where he has shared the catching chores with Matt Nokes. /(SCL)

Jeff Heathcock — 1959- . RHP 1983, 85, 87-88 Astros 158 ip, 9-9, 3.76

A 6'4" sinkerballer, Heathcock was one of the Astros' most highly regarded prospects when, while with Tucson (Pacific Coast League) in April 1984, he tore up his right knee while covering first base. He missed the rest of that season, and through 1988 was shuttled between Tucson and Houston. /(JCA)

Cliff Heathcote — 1898-1939. OF-1B 1918-32 Cardinals, **Cubs**, Reds, Phillies 1415 g, .275, 42 hr, 448 rbi. *1 WS, 2g, .000*

Heathcote was part of an unusual trade on May 30, 1922. Swapped from the Cardinals to the Cubs between games of a doubleheader for outfielder Max Flack, he and Flack were hitless in the morning but collected hits with their new teams that afternoon as the Cubs took a pair. On August 25, 1922 the lefthanded-hitting Heathcote was 5-for-5 with four RBI and five runs scored in the major leagues' biggest slugfest ever: Cubs 26, Phillies 23. Usually a regular through 1926, he hit a career-high .313 in 82 games in 1929 as the Cubs won the pennant. /(AA)

Neal Heaton — 1960- . LHP 1982- **Indians**, Twins, Expos, Pirates 1223 ip, 61-83, 4.46

Heaton was the pearl of a Cleveland farm system that produced little in the early 1980s. He went 11-7 as a rookie in 1983, but was having his third straight losing season when traded to Minnesota for John Butcher in 1986. The move proved folly for Cleveland that winter when they released Butcher, and the Twins sent Heaton to Montreal in a deal for Jeff Reardon. Heaton was 10-4 at the 1987 All-Star break, then skidded to finish 13-10. Reardon's 31 saves helped the Twins to the World Championship. /(JCA)

Dave Heaverlo — 1950- . RHP 1975-81 **Giants**, A's, Mariners 539 ip, 26-26, 3.41

A jokester who shaved his head and insisted on keeping his non-roster number 60 as a rookie, Heaverlo relieved in all his 356 ML appearances. After he went 5-1 (2.55) in 1977, the Giants sent him to Oakland with six other players, plus $390,000, for Vida Blue. He earned 19 saves in two years with the A's. /(JCA)

Wally Hebert (Preacher) — 1907- . LHP 1931-33, 43 **Browns**, Pirates 484 ip, 21-36, 4.63

The sidearmer insisted his name be pronounced "Ay-bare." After three poor seasons with the Browns, he reemerged during WWII to go 10-11, 2.98 for the 1943 Pirates. /(JK)

Richie Hebner — 1947- . 3B-1B 1968-85 **Pirates**, Phillies, Mets, Tigers, Cubs 1908 g, .276, 203 hr, 1890 rbi. *8 LCS, 26 g, .284, 3 hr, 12 rbi. 1 WS, 3 g, .167, 1 hr, 3 rbi*

An off-season gravedigger at a cemetery run by his father, Hebner signed for $40,000 and made the Pirates two seasons later despite losing playing time to military reserve duty. He led NL rookies with a .301 average in 1969, and hit a career-high 25 HR for Pittsburgh in 1973. After seven years and five division championships as the Pirate third baseman, Hebner played out his option, and spent two seasons at first base helping the Phillies win NL East titles in 1977 and 1978. Ousted by the 1979 arrival of free agent Pete Rose, he led the Mets with 79 RBI that season, was swapped to the Tigers, and had a career-high 82 RBI in only 104 games in 1980. After a second tour with the Pirates, he became the top pinch hitter for the division-winning 1984 Cubs. He set the ML record for most times on the losing club in the LCS (7) and the NL record for most LCS played in (8). /(MC)

Guy Hecker (Blond Guy) — 1856–1938. RHP-1B-OF 1882–90 **Louisville (AA)**, Pirates 709 g, .284, 19 hr, 102 rbi; 2906 ip, 177–150, 2.92.
　　Manager 1890 **Pirates** 23–113, .169
☛ *Led League—ba 86. Led League—era 84. Led League—w 84. Led League—k 84 .*

Hecker is the only pitcher ever to win a ML batting title. A hard thrower (when the regulation pitching distance was 50 feet), he often played first base or outfield for his mediocre Louisville team when he wasn't pitching. Appearing in only 84 of the Colonels' 136 games in 1886, he hit .342 to top Pete Browning by .002 and lead the league. In a game against Baltimore that year, he went 6-for-7, a record for pitchers; his seven runs scored in that game is still a record for any player. Three of his hits that day were inside-the-park home runs; this was the first three-homer game by a pitcher and the only three-homer game for any player in the American Association's ten-year existence as a major league. Hecker also won 27 games for sixth-place Louisville that year, but by then he was on the downgrade, each year slipping farther from his phenomenal 52–20 season of 1884, when he completed 72 games in 73 starts, pitched 670.2 innings, had 385 strikeouts, and compiled an estimated ERA of 1.80, all league-leading statistics. /(ADS)

Mike Hedlund (Red) — 1946– . RHP 1965, 68–72 Indians, **Royals** 466 ip, 25–24, 3.55

Hedlund signed with Cleveland for a significant bonus after throwing a no-hitter in the 1963 Connie Mack World Series. In 1969 he went to Kansas City in the expansion draft. He was 15–8, 2.71 in 1971 but spent the rest of his career fighting a sore arm. /(MC)

Danny Heep — 1957– . OF-1B 1979– Astros, **Mets**, Dodgers, Red Sox 828 g, .259, 30 hr, 218 rbi. *3 LCS, 13 g, .167, 1 rbi. 2 WS, 8 g, .158, 2 rbi*

Heep was an extra lefthanded bat when the Astros sent him to the Mets for pitcher Mike Scott in December 1982. His four pinch-hit home runs in 1983 led the majors and set a Mets record. Heep was the top pinch hitter (9-for-30) for the 1986 World Champion Mets. He had career highs of 320 at-bats, 49 RBI, and a .300 batting average in 1989 for the Red Sox when they lost several outfielders to injury. /(JCA)

Bob Heffner (Butch) — 1938– . RHP 1963–66, 68 **Red Sox**, Indians, Angels 353 ip, 11–21, 4.51

On June 28, 1963 with Boston, Heffner became only the second ML pitcher to record three putouts in an inning. /(GEB)

Don Heffner (Jeep) — 1911– . 2B-SS-3B 1934–44 Yankees, **Browns**, A's, Tigers 743 g, .241, 6 hr, 248 rbi.
　　Manager 66 **Reds** 37–46, .446

Although he played 11 years as a ML infielder, Heffner's proudest moment came as a 19-year-old minor leaguer. He pitched for an all-star team of ML players against the Baltimore Black Sox, a top Negro team, and beat star pitcher Pud Flornoy 1–0 in a five-inning game. After several seasons as a Yankee utility man, he was a regular with the Browns for four years before WWII. /(JK)

Jim Hegan (Shanty) — 1920–1984. C 1941-42, 46–50 **Indians**, Tigers, Phillies, Giants, Cubs 1666 g, .228, 92 hr, 525 rbi. *2 WS, 10 g, .188, 1 hr, 5 rbi*
☛ *All-Star—47, 49–52.*

This superb defensive catcher spent more than a decade as a Cleveland regular, catching 20-game winners Feller, Lemon, Wynn, Garcia, Score, and Bearden. Although he hit 14 home runs in both 1948 and 1950, he never had a batting average

Jim Hegan

higher than .249. But Cleveland fans never booed the likable Hegan, no matter how low his average dropped. As Bill Dickey commented, "When you can catch like Hegan, you don't have to hit." Lithe, quick, and graceful, the durable Hegan was artful on pop-ups and balls in the dirt and was respected by baserunners. He received much of the credit for Cleveland's pitching success; fellow catcher Joe Tipton said, "Hitters who strike out against the Indians cuss Hegan." Hegan caught no-hitters by Don Black (7/10/1947), Bob Lemon (6/30/1948), and Bob Feller (7/1/1951). His catching was a key to the Indians' 1948 and 1954 pennants. When he retired in 1960, his 1,629 games caught was seventh on the all-time list. Mike Hegan is his son. /(JCA)

Mike Hegan — 1942– . 1B-OF-DH 1964, 66–67, 69–77 Yankees, **Pilots/Brewers**, A's 965 g, .242, 53 hr, 229 rbi. *2 LCS, 4 g, .000. 2 WS, 9 g, .167*
☛ *All-Star—69.*

Hegan grew up shagging flies with dad Jim at Cleveland's Municipal Stadium, and came up only four years after his father's last season. Although in only five games with the 1964 Yankees, he appeared in the WS that year. In 1969 the strapping left-hander led Seattle with a .292 mark. A popular, all-out player, Hegan took pride in his defense; he set a ML record by playing 178 consecutive errorless games at first base from 1970 to 1973. He retired to become a Milwaukee broadcaster. /(JCA)

Jack Heidemann — 1949– . SS-3B-2B 1969–72, 74–77 **Indians**, Cardinals, Mets, Brewers 426 g, .211, 9 hr, 75 rbi

Cleveland's first-round draft pick in 1967, Heidemann became the Indian shortstop in 1970 at age 20, but hit only .211. In two separate mishaps the next year, he suffered a concussion and a knee injury. After that he was limited to a utility role. /(JCA)

Emmet Heidrick (Snags) — 1876–1916. OF 1898–1904, 08 Cleveland (NL), Cardinals, **Browns** 757 g, .300, 16 hr, 342 rbi

Heidrick was transferred from Cleveland to St. Louis after 1898 by Frank and Stanley Robison, who owned both teams. He stole 55 bases for the Cardinals in 1899, and in 1901 hit a career-high .339 as part of their all-.300 outfield. /(WAB)

Harry Heilmann (Slug) — 1894–1951. OF-1B 1914, 16–30, 32 **Tigers**, Reds 2146 g, .342, 183 hr, 1551 rbi
☛ *Led League—ba 21, 23, 25, 27. Hall of Fame—52.*

Heilmann was a 6'1" 200-lb righthanded hitter who captured four American League batting titles in 15 seasons with the Tigers. Heilmann is among Detroit's all-time leaders in every major hitting category. He was working as a bookkeeper when he was offered his first baseball job. In 1913 he hit .305 for Portland (Northwest League) and was purchased by the Tigers for $1,500. He first joined Detroit in 1914, but stayed from 1916 through 1929, with only two gaps; he missed half of 1918 while on a Navy submarine, and several weeks of 1922 with a broken collarbone.

Harry Heilmann

A fair outfielder, Heilmann was moved to first base for 1919 and 1920 and led the AL in errors at that position both seasons. During the 1920s, he was a part of .300-hitting Tiger outfields in seven seasons. Joining him, at various times, were Hall of Famers Ty Cobb and Heinie Manush, and Detroit stars Bobby Veach and Bob Fothergill. Disgruntled pitcher Dutch Leonard wrote to Heilmann in December 1926, telling him of the two letters Leonard had sent to Ban Johnson implicating Joe Wood and Ty Cobb in betting on games. Heilmann showed the letter to Tigers owner Frank Navin and the story came out into the open.

Heilmann was involved in many close batting races. In 1921, he topped Ty Cobb by five points by hitting .394 with a league-high 237 hits. His .403 mark in 1923 bested Babe Ruth's .393. In 1925 he caught and passed Tris Speaker with a few games to go; he refused to come out of the lineup, and won the title, .393 to .389. He trailed Al Simmons by one point going into the last day of the 1927 season; in a doubleheader at Cleveland, he had four hits in the first game, and three in the second, finishing at .398—six points above Simmons.

Arthritis in his wrists began bothering Heilmann in 1929. He was sold to the Reds after the '29 season, but was unable to play in 1931. He came back as a player-coach in 1932, appearing in 15 games. Popular with fans and players, with a keen sense of humor and a trove of stories, he was the radio voice of the Tigers for 17 years. During WWII, he traveled to the Middle East as part of a baseball group entertaining troops. He died of lung cancer at age 56 in 1951, and was elected to the Hall of Fame the following year. /(NLM)

Fred Heimach (Lefty) — 1901–1973. LHP 1920–26, 28–33 **A's**, Red Sox, Yankees, Dodgers 1289 ip, 62–69, 4.46

Heimach helped himself. His fielding skill made him a "fifth infielder," and his .236 lifetime average included 52 pinch-hit appearances in which he hit .385. When a broken ankle finished him in 1933, he had run up a string of errorless games that went back to 1926, covering 171 chances. /(JK)

Don Heinkel — 1959– . RHP 1988– **Tigers**, Cardinals 63 ip, 1–1, 4.74

When Heinkel finally made the majors in 1988 with the Tigers as a relief pitcher, his season was interrupted for a month and a half by injury. Released at the end of the season, he was picked up by the Cardinals and was used as a starter in 1989 to fill in on their injury-prone staff. /(JFC)

Ken Heintzelman — 1915– . LHP 1937–42, 46–52 Pirates, **Phillies** 1502 ip, 77–98, 3.93. *1 WS, 8 ip, 1.17*

Twelve years after his ML debut, Heintzelman had sudden success in 1949 (17–10, 3.02) with a NL-high five shutouts and a nine-game winning streak for the Phillies. His son Tom was an infielder for the Cardinals and Giants in the 1970s. /(ME)

Bob Heise — 1947– . SS-2B-3B 1967–77 Mets, Giants, **Brewers**, Cardinals, Angels, Red Sox, Royals 499 g, .247, 1 hr, 86 rbi

Heise was a utility man his entire career. He hit .323 in his first call-up, a 62 at-bat stint, but never again hit higher than .268 in more than 10 at-bats and hit as low as .204. /(SFS)

Woodie Held [Woodson George] — 1932– . SS-OF-2B-3B 1954, 57–69 Yankees, A's, **Indians**, Senators, Orioles, Angels, White Sox 1390 g, .240, 179 hr, 559 rbi

As an outfielder with Kansas City in 1957, his rookie year, Held hit 20 HR. He was Cleveland's starting shortstop from 1959 through 1962. He hit a career-high 29 homers in 1959 and averaged 21 a year in six seasons with the Indians. He struck out often, nearly once in every four at-bats. Though easy-going off the field, he was notorious for his tantrums after striking out. A versatile and reliable fielder, he remained a valuable utility man after his days as a regular. /(JCA)

Al Helfer — 1912–1975. *Broadcaster.*

In 1935, while playing first base for Washington & Jefferson University, Helfer was offered a contract by Connie Mack, but he was set on a career in radio. During his career, he traveled five million miles and broadcast more Rose Bowl and WS games than anyone before or since. He worked on local broadcast teams in Pittsburgh, Cincinnati, Brooklyn, New York, and Oakland, and in 1950 began calling the Mutual Network's Game of the Day. He was also a television announcer on non-sports shows. "Red Barber and I were the first play-by-play team," he once claimed. "Before that, one man would do the first half of the game and then disappear. We interacted during the entire game." /(NLM)

Tommy Helms — 1941- . 2B-3B-SS-DH 1964-77 **Reds**, Astros, Pirates, Red Sox 1435 g, .269, 34 hr, 477 rbi. *1 LCS, 3 g, .273. 1 WS, 5 g, .222.*
Manager 1988- **Reds** 26-36, .419
☛ *Rookie of the Year—66. All-Star—67-68. Gold Glove—70-71.*

The NL Rookie of the Year in 1966 as a third baseman, Helms became one of the best second basemen of the 1960s. The excellent fielder led the NL in fielding percentage and double plays three times. Noted more as a hit-and-run man than a power hitter, he hit the first HR by a Red at Riverfront Stadium. Helms went to Houston with Lee May in the blockbuster November 1971 trade that brought Joe Morgan, Jack Billingham, and Cesar Geronimo to Cincinnati.

A longtime Reds coach, Helms filled in for manager Pete Rose during Rose's 30-day suspension in 1988 and replaced him after Rose was banned in 1989. /(GEB)

Roland Hemond (Rollie) — 1929- . *Executive.*

After a successful career as director of the Angels' farm system, 1961-70, developing such players as Clyde Wright and Jim Spencer, Hemond was hired in 1971 as director of player personnel by the White Sox (and later became GM) to reverse their fortunes. At the winter meetings that year, he moved 16 players within 18 hours. Chuck Tanner was brought in to manage, and the team won 23 more games than in 1970. Hemond traded for Dick Allen, who became the AL MVP in 1972. Richie Zisk, Rich Dotson, Rudy Law, and Bob James were just a few of his other productive acquisitions. Hemond was the architect of the 1983 Division Champions, for which he won UPI's Executive of the Year award. /(RL)

Charlie Hemphill (Eagle Eye) — 1876-1953. OF 1899, 1901-04, 06-11 Cleveland (NL), Cardinals, Red Sox, Indians, **Browns**, Yankees 1242 g, .271, 22 hr, 421 rbi

Hemphill was with the Cleveland Spiders when the best members of that team were transferred to St. Louis in 1899 by owners who controlled both teams at once. He managed the Yankees briefly when Hal Chase was ill, and later was a playing manager at Atlanta. His brother, Frank, played briefly for the White Sox and Senators. /(NLM)

Harry Hempstead — 1869-1938. *Executive.*

The son-in-law of John T. Brush, Hempstead took over the Giants in 1912 when Brush died, and ran the club until 1919, winning three pennants. He then sold the team to Charles A. Stoneham. /(NLM)

Rollie Hemsley [Ralston Burdett] — 1907-1972. C 1928-44, 46-47 Pirates, Cubs, Reds, **Browns**, Indians, Yankees, Phillies 1593 g, .262, 31 hr, 555 rbi. *1 WS, 3 g, .000*

Hemsley drank himself off four clubs before whipping alcoholism with the help of Alcoholics Anonymous. Early on, his speed was above average for a catcher. Platooned in Pittsburgh, he was traded to the Cubs in 1931 to back up Gabby Hartnett, and then to the Reds in 1933. Waived to the Browns in 1933, he became a top AL receiver, hitting .309 in 1934. Despite a .222 batting average in 1937, Cleveland traded three players to get him, and he handled the bulk of the Indians' catching chores in 1939 after an injury to Frank Pytlak. He caught Bob Feller's 1940 Opening Day no-hitter, and drove in the game's only run with a triple. He became a backup after his December 1941 sale to the Reds. Hemsley was *TSN* Minor League Manager of the Year in 1950 and 1963. /(ME)

Solly Hemus — 1923- . SS-2B-3B 1949-59 **Cardinals**, Phillies 969 g, .273, 51 hr, 263 rbi.
Manager 1959-61 **Cardinals** 190-192, .497

A consistent performer with a good eye at the plate, Hemus led the NL three times in HBP. Aided by 20 HBP and 96 walks in 1952, Hemus scored 105 runs to tie teammate Stan Musial for the NL lead. The regular Cardinals shortstop from 1951 through 1953, in 1954 Hemus batted a career-high .302.

Since 1959 there have been only five ML playing managers: Pete Rose, Frank Robinson, Joe Torre, Don Kessinger, and Hemus. As the Cardinals skipper in 1959, he played 24 games, mostly pinch hitting, as St. Louis finished seventh. In 1960 he managed the team to third place. With the Cardinals in sixth place midway through the 1961 season, Hemus was replaced. He later coached for the Mets and Indians. /(RTM)

Dave Henderson — 1958- . OF 1981- **Mariners**, Red Sox, Giants, A's 1078 g, .260, 127 hr, 474 rbi. *3 LCS, 14 g, .273, 3 hr, 9 rbi. 3 WS, 16 g, .345, 4 hr, 10 rbi*

The Red Sox acquired Henderson for their 1986 stretch run. He hit a two-out, two-run homer for Boston in the top of the ninth inning of Game Five of the 1986 LCS with the California Angels one strike away from their first World Series appearance. The game was won on Henderson's sacrifice fly in the 11th inning and also featured a home run by

Bobby Grich that popped out of Henderson's glove and over the outfield wall.

Traded to the Giants on September 1, 1987 to make room for rookie Ellis Burks, Henderson helped the Giants to a division title and then signed as a free agent with Oakland that winter. The centerfielder posted career-high totals of 24 homers, 38 doubles, 100 runs, 94 RBI, and a .304 batting average, (.051 above his previous career average) for the AL champion 1988 A's. In the 1989 WS, he hit home runs in consecutive innings in Game Three after just missing one in the first inning (a double off the railing).

Henderson was the Mariners' first pick in the 1977 free-agent draft. At the time of his trade to Boston, Henderson was Seattle's career leader in home runs and was tied for the team lead in extra-base hits. He is the nephew of Joe Henderson, a pitcher with the White Sox and Reds in the 1970s. /(TF)

Ken Henderson — 1946– . OF 1965–80 **Giants**, White Sox, Braves, Rangers, Mets, Reds, Cubs 1444 g, .257, 122 hr, 576 rbi. *1 LCS, 4 g, .313, 2 rbi*

Touted at 19 as Willie Mays's successor, Henderson was a regular in only four of his eight years with the Giants. He hit a career-high .294 with 17 home runs and 20 stolen bases as San Francisco's left fielder in 1970, but his average dropped the next two years and he was traded to the White Sox. Henderson was shocked by the trade, but recovered to hit .292 with 20 HR and 95 RBI for Chicago in 1974. /(FS)

Rickey Henderson (The Man of Steal, Style Dog) — 1957– . OF 1979– **A's**, Yankees 1472 g, .290, 138 hr, 561 rbi. *2 LCS, 8 g, .385, 2 hr, 6 rbi. 1 WS, 4 g, .474, 1 hr, 3 rbi*
☛ *All-Star—80, 82–88. Gold Glove—81.*

Baseball's most brilliant leadoff man came to quick prominence. The speedy switch-hitter set the AL season steal record with 100 in 1980, his second ML season. Responding to the leadership of manager Billy Martin (1980–82), Henderson's remarkable 130 steals in 1982 broke Lou Brock's ML record. The Martin-Henderson combination was reunited following a December 5, 1984 trade that sent Stan Javier and Jay Howell, Jose Rijo, Eric Plunk and Tim Birtsas to Oakland for Henderson and pitcher Bert Bradley. He returned to the A's in 1989, while in the last year of his contract, in return for Eric Plunk, Greg Cadaret, and Luis Polonia. The MVP of the 1989 LCS, he set a LCS (and postseason) record with eight steals and tied the LCS record for

Rickey Henderson

runs with eight. He hit .400, had a .609 on-base average, and led both teams with five RBI in the five-game series. He then hit .474 in the WS and led off Game Three with a HR as the A's swept the Giants.

In 1985 Henderson became the first AL player ever with a 20 homer-50 steal season (24, 80), a feat he repeated in 1986. He broke Bobby Bonds's career record for leadoff home runs (35) in 1989. Henderson has led the AL three times in runs scored, tied for the lead once, and scored 100 runs in nine seasons. His 146 runs scored in 1985 were the most in the majors since 1949 and his average of over a run scored per game was the best since 1939. Though teammate Don Mattingly won the 1985 AL MVP Award, Henderson may have been more valuable, scoring on 56 of Mattingly's 145 RBI. Rickey was a close second in the 1981 MVP voting, but a distant third in 1985.

A Gold Glove winner in 1981, Henderson moved from left field to centerfield in 1985, returning to left, which he preferred, in 1988. He became notorious for his snatch catch on easy fly balls, swatting his glove from over his head to his side. Henderson's 1985 achievements came despite missing the first 15 games of the season with a sprained ankle. Hamstring injuries (his "hammies," as he called them) slowed Henderson in 1987 and 1988. Already possessing the all-time stolen base records for the Yankees and the Oakland A's, Henderson seems certain to top Lou Brock's all-time career stolen base record. He had nearly twice as many steals as Brock over a comparable number of games. Henderson chose number 24 after his idol, Willie Mays. The ultimate leadoff hitter led the AL in steals in each of his first eight seasons with over 100 games played (1980–86, '88). His three singles in the 1982 All-Star game tied a record. /(ME)

Steve Henderson (Hendu) — 1952– . OF-DH
1977–88 **Mets**, Cubs, Mariners, A's, Astros 1085 g, .280, 68 hr, 428 rbi

Henderson was one of four young players the Reds traded to the Mets for Tom Seaver on June 15, 1977. Though he played in only 99 games that year, he led the last-place Mets with 65 RBI and lost by one vote to Andre Dawson in Rookie-of-the-Year balloting. His nine triples in 1978 tied a club record, and his .306 average in 1979 and .290 in 1980 led the Mets. Traded to the Cubs for Dave Kingman in 1981, he had one more solid season, hitting .294 with 32 doubles for the 1983 Mariners. /(JCA)

Bob Hendley — 1939– . LHP 1961–67 **Braves**, Giants, Cubs, Mets 879 ip, 48–52, 3.97

On September 9, 1965 Hendley one-hit the Dodgers for the Cubs, but opposing pitcher Sandy Koufax threw a perfect game for a 1–0 Dodger victory. Five days later, the two hurlers met again and Hendley pitched a four-hitter to beat Koufax, 2–1. /(RTM)

George Hendrick (Silent George) — 1949– . OF-1B
1971–88 A's, Indians, Padres, **Cardinals**, Pirates, Angels 2048 g, .278, 267 hr, 1111 rbi. *3 LCS, 11 g, .188, 2 rbi. 2 WS, 12 g, .256, 5 rbi*
☛ *All-Star—74–75, 80, 83.*

Hendrick gave credit to Joe Rudi for enabling him to become a complete player in Oakland. Hendrick had an easy style that seemed too casual to some, but he averaged 22 homers annually in four campaigns with Cleveland. Traded to San Diego, he responded with a .311 season. Hendrick blossomed with the Cardinals, reaching the .300 plateau three times while driving in over 100 twice. Although Silent George had long refused to speak to the press, he was well-liked by his teammates and the fans in St. Louis. He was a very capable right fielder and

later assumed duties at first base when Keith Hernandez was dealt. *TSN* awarded Hendrick Silver Slugger Awards at each position. /(FO)

Harvey Hendrick (Gink) — 1897–1941. 1B-OF-3B
1923–25, 27–34 Yankees, Indians, **Dodgers**, Reds, Cardinals, Cubs, Phillies 922 g, .308, 48 hr, 413 rbi. *1 WS, 1 g, .000*

The 6'2″ Vanderbilt graduate played every position but catcher and pitcher. In his one full season at a single position, Hendrick led the NL with 18 errors and 147 double plays at first base for the 1931 Reds. He was traded frequently, as most teams found his poor defense outweighed his .300 bat. /(JK)

Ellie Hendricks [Elrod Jerome] — 1940– . C
1968–79 **Orioles**, Cubs, Yankees 711 g, .220, 62 hr, 230 rbi. *5 LCS, 10 g, .333, 1 hr, 5 rbi. 4 WS, 14 g, .238, 1 hr, 5 rbi*

Hendricks became famous in Game One of the 1970 World Series for a defensive play that he didn't really make. Attempting to tag out Bernie Carbo of the Reds in the sixth inning after Ty Cline hit a chopper in front of the plate, Hendricks collided with umpire Ken Burkhart while "tagging" Carbo with his mitt and holding the ball in his throwing hand. The bowled-over Burkhart couldn't see the play and called Carbo out. Hendricks had hit the game-tying HR in the previous inning. The next day, his two-run double in the fifth inning drove in the winning runs; he had four RBI in the Series.

The ever-smiling Hendricks was a favorite of Earl Weaver's for his steady fielding and because left-handed-hitting catchers were hard to come by. Twice Baltimore traded and reacquired him. Hendricks had back-to-back 12 HR seasons in 1969–70 while platooning with Andy Etchebarren, but never started more than 95 games in a season. The native Virgin Islander did lead AL catchers in fielding in 1969. His .250 average in 1971 was a career high. He spent much of the 1980s as the Orioles' bullpen coach. /(SH)

Jack Hendricks — 1875–1943. OF 1902–03 Giants, Cubs, **Senators** 42 g, .207, 0 hr, 4 rbi.
Manager 1918, 24–29 Cardinals, **Reds** 520–528, .496

After an undistinguished ML trial as an outfielder, Hendricks began managing in the minors in 1906. Beginning in 1910, he won three straight pennants with Denver in the Western League, then managed at Indianapolis in the American Association for four years. When Miller Huggins was fired by the Cardinals, Hendricks signed a two-year contract to replace him, finished last in 1918, and resigned to become athletic director for the Knights of Columbus. He went to France in 1919, then spent five more years as manager at Indianapolis. When Reds manager Pat Moran died in March of 1924, Hendricks took over the Cincinnati job. He finished second, only two games behind the Cardinals in 1926. Educated as a lawyer at North Christian University, he never practiced. /(NLM)

Claude Hendrix — 1889–1944. RHP 1911–20 Pirates, Chicago (FL), **Cubs** 2371 ip, 143–117, 2.65. 20 wins: 12, 14 *1 WS, 1 ip, 0.00*
☛ *Led League—w 14.*

A 24-game-winner for the Pirates in 1912, Hendrix's best season came with the Chicago Whales of the Federal League in 1914, when he went 29–11 with a 1.69 ERA and led the league in wins, appearances, and complete games. He also batted .322 that season and was a lifetime .241 hitter, with 13 HR and 97 RBI. On May 15, 1915 he pitched a 10–0 no-hitter over Pittsburgh (FL). Following the Federal League's demise, Hendrix went to the Cubs in 1916. His 19–7 record tied for the league lead in winning percentage (.727) in 1918 and helped the Cubs capture the pennant. Hendrix's career ended under suspicious circumstances in February of 1921. The Cubs released him for having allegedly bet against his teammates in a game he was scheduled to pitch the previous August, but in which he was replaced at the last moment by Grover Alexander. /(AA)

Tim Hendryx — 1891–1957. OF 1911–12, 15–18, 20–21 Indians, **Yankees**, Browns, Red Sox 414 g, .276, 6 hr, 191 rbi

A depleted 1917 Yankee outfield afforded Hendryx his first regular major league job. Another OF spot opened up with the 1920 Red Sox when Babe Ruth was sold to New York, and Hendryx, filling in, batted .328. /(MG)

Tom Henke (The Terminator) — 1957– . RHP 1982- Rangers, **Blue Jays** 442 ip, 27–22, 2.81. *2 LCS, 9 ip, 2–0, 3.00*
☛ *All-Star—87.*

One of the most overpowering relievers of the late 1980s, Henke combined a 95-mph fastball with an effective forkball to average more than a strikeout per inning. After appearing in 41 games over three seasons for the Rangers, Henke was selected by the Blue Jays as compensation when Texas signed free agent Cliff Johnson. He pitched impressively at Syracuse (International League) before being called up to Toronto on July 28, 1985. In his first month, Henke recorded eight saves; prior to 1985, the most saves by a Blue Jay reliever in an entire season was 11. Henke converted 13 of his 15 opportunities into saves in 1985, and by the time of the 1985 LCS, "The Ballad of Tom Henke" was being played over loudspeakers outside Exhibition Stadium.

In 1986 Henke's 27 saves set a new Blue Jay record, which he broke in 1987 with a league-leading 34. In 1987 Henke allowed fewer hits (5.9) and recorded more strikeouts (12.3) per nine innings than any other AL pitcher. /(TF)

Weldon Henley — 1880–1960. RHP 1903–05, 07 A's, Dodgers 32–43, 2.94

Henley pitched for Connie Mack's Athletics shortly after the turn of the century, posting his only winning record (12–9) in his first season. One of Henley's four victories in the 1905 season was a 6–0 no-hitter against the Browns on July 22. /(MA)

Butch Henline [Walter John] — 1894–1957. C-OF 1921–31 Giants, **Phillies**, Dodgers, White Sox 740 g, .291, 40 hr, 268 rbi.
Umpire NL 1945–48

The Phillies were roundly criticized for trading .300 hitter Irish Meusel to the Giants for an unproven rookie, but Henline became Philadelphia's most-used catcher from 1922 to 1926. In 1922 he batted a career-high .316 and led NL receivers in fielding. /(GB)

Mike Henneman — 1961– . RHP 1987- Tigers 278 ip, 31–13, 2.85. *1 LCS, 5 ip, 1–0, 10.80*
☛ *All-Star—89.*

When Detroit reliever Guillermo Hernandez faltered in 1987, 6'4″ rookie Mike Henneman took up the slack, going 11–3 with seven saves. He scored two wins and a save in the last four meetings with Toronto as the Tigers overtook the Blue Jays for the division title. *TSN* named Henneman AL Rookie Pitcher of the Year. He recorded 10 saves in the first month of the 1988 season before his arm tightened up. Disabled for a time, he finished at 9–6 (1.87) with 22 saves. He was 11–4 with a 3.70 ERA in 1989. /(JCA)

Phil Hennigan — 1946– . RHP 1969–73 **Indians**, Mets 281 ip, 17–14, 4.26

Hennigan's progress was delayed by a year in Vietnam, where he won a medal for valor. From 1970 through 1972, he posted winning records in relief for losing Cleveland clubs, and led the staff with 14 saves in 1971. /(ME)

Pete Henning — 1887–1939. RHP 1914–15 **Kansas City (FL)** 345 ip, 14–28, 3.83

Henning's only major league experience came in the Federal League, where he went 6–12 and 8–16 and led the league in relief losses with 11 in 1914. /(SFS)

Tommy Henrich (Old Reliable) — 1913– . OF-1B 1937–42, 46–50 **Yankees** 1284 g, .282, 183 hr, 795 rbi. *4 WS, 21 g, .262, 4 hr, 8 rbi*
☛ *All-Star—42, 47–50.*

Along with Joe DiMaggio and Charlie Keller, Henrich formed one of baseball's most acclaimed outfields for the Yankees before and after WWII. Commissioner Landis ruled Henrich a free agent in April 1937 after he had been illegally hidden in the Indians' farm system, and he signed with the Yankees, hitting .320 as a part-timer. He helped the team to six pennants, and although he played in only four WS because of injury and military service, he was a key figure in two of the most famous Series games. In 1941, he was the man whose third strike skipped past Mickey Owen, leading to a legendary Yankee rally. In 1949 he homered off Don Newcombe in the ninth inning of the first game to give Allie Reynolds a 1–0 victory.

An excellent fielder, Henrich lived up to his "Old Reliable" nickname with his bat, hitting 22 homers in 1938 and 31 in 1941. After the war, he had his greatest season statistically in 1948, leading the AL in triples and runs scored, and batting .308 with 25 homers and 100 RBI. But he was probably more valuable in 1949, when his consistent clutch hitting helped keep the injury-racked Yankees in the pennant race. In 115 games, he hit 24 homers, batted in 85, and scored 90. He finished sixth in the MVP voting. /(MC)

Bill Henry — 1927– . LHP 1952–55, 58–69 Red Sox, Cubs, **Reds**, Giants, Pirates, Astros 913 ip, 46–50, 3.26. *1 WS, 2.1 ip, 0–0, 19.29*
☛ *All-Star—60.*

Henry blossomed as an outstanding lefthanded reliever in 1959, when he led NL pitchers with 65 appearances. In 1961, his 16 saves were instrumen-

tal in helping the Reds win the National League pennant. He had five straight seasons in double figures in saves and retired with 90. /(GB)

Dutch Henry [Frank John] — 1902–1968. LHP 1921–24, 27–30 Browns, Dodgers, **Giants**, White Sox 646 ip, 27–43, 4.39

The slender curveballer, primarily a reliever, had his career year for the 1927 Giants, with an 11–6 record and a league-high six wins out of the bullpen. Henry was handicapped by poor control. /(FS)

Dwayne Henry — 1962– . RHP 1984– **Rangers**, Braves 78 ip, 3–6, 5.33

Henry looked promising in his 1985 call-up, when he was 2–2 with three saves and a 2.57 ERA. But after his 1986 season was interrupted by injury, he never had an ERA below 4.66 at any level. /(SFS)

John Henry (Bull) — 1889–1941. C-1B 1910–18 **Senators**, Braves 683 g, .207, 2 hr, 171 rbi

Henry was Walter Johnson's catcher during the pitcher's peak years. A smart baseball man, this Amherst alumnus subsequently coached at Cornell before becoming a minor league umpire. /(JK)

Roy Henshaw — 1911– . LHP 1933, 35–38, 42–44 **Cubs**, Dodgers, Cardinals, Tigers 742 ip, 33–40, 4.16

Henshaw's best record was 13–5 for the Cubs in his second year. In 1937 he went from Brooklyn to the Cardinals in the trade for Leo Durocher. /(GEB)

Ron Herbel — 1938– . RHP 1963–71 **Giants**, Padres, Mets, Braves 894 ip, 42–37, 3.82

The powerfully-built Herbel was a part-time starter who won a career-high 12 games with the 1965 Giants. Hampered by arm problems, he pitched mostly in long relief, leading the NL in 1970 with 76 appearances and nine relief wins for the Padres and Mets. He was the worst-hitting pitcher ever (minimum 100 at-bats), batting a mere .029 (6-for 206). /(FS)

Ray Herbert — 1929– . RHP 1950–51, 53–55, 58–66 Tigers, **A's**, White Sox, Phillies 1881 ip, 104–107, 4.01. 20 wins: 62
☛ *All-Star—62.*

In his tenth ML season, with the White Sox in 1962, the durable Herbert went 20–9 for a league-leading .690 winning percentage. Though he dropped to 13–10 in 1963, his seven shutouts led the AL. Herbert gave up Carl Yastrzemski's first base hit, in 1961, and holds Kansas City Athletic records for most innings, most earned runs, and most games lost./(GB)

Babe Herman [Floyd Caves] — 1903–1987. OF-1B 1926–37, 45 **Dodgers**, Reds, Cubs, Pirates, Tigers 1552 g, .324, 181 hr, 997 rbi

As the lefthanded-batting Herman put it, "I wasn't the world's greatest fielder, as a lot of stories will attest, but I was always a pretty fair country hitter." Having led the NL in errors in consecutive seasons

Babe Herman

(at first base in 1927, outfield in 1928), Herman often had to deny having once been hit on the head by a fly ball.

Only he and Bob Meusel have hit for the cycle three times. The .393 batting average (second to Bill Terry's .401), 416 total bases, 241 hits, and 143 runs he amassed in 1930 still stand as Dodger records. He also reached a high of 35 HR in 1930, and, with the Reds in 1932, led the NL with 19 triples. On July 10, 1935 at Cincinnati, he hit the first home run in a night game. The "headless horseman of Ebbets Field," as Dazzy Vance called Herman, once "tripled" into a double play (Herman got a double on the play), as three Dodgers wound up on third base, leading to the greatest of all the "Daffiness Boys" quips: "The Dodgers have three men on base." "Oh yeah, which base?"/(TG)

Billy Herman [William Jennings Bryan] (Bryan) — 1909– . 2B-3B 1931–47 **Cubs**, Dodgers, Braves, Pirates 1922 g, .304, 47 hr, 839 rbi. *4 WS, 18 g, .242, 1 hr, 7 rbi.*
    Manager 1947, 64–66 Pirates, **Red Sox** 189–274, .408
☛ *All-Star—34–43. Hall of Fame—75.*

Herman was the finest National League second baseman of the 1930s and early 1940s. He batted more than .300 eight times in his 15-year career, and scored at least 100 runs five times. His top years came as a Cub. In 1935 he led the NL with 227 hits and 57 doubles, and reached career highs with a .341 average and 113 runs scored. His 18 triples in 1939 led the league.

A starter at 2B from 1932 to 1943, in several seasons he played in every one of his team's games. He tied the NL record at 2B for most years leading in putouts (seven). He led the NL in 2B assists three times, errors four times, and fielding average three times. On June 28, 1933 he tied the ML record for most 2B putouts in a doubleheader (16), and tied the NL record for most 2B putouts in a game (11); an acknowledged master at playing the hitters, that season he set the NL season record for putouts (466). He appeared in 10 All-Star games, batting .433 (13-for-30). A member of three Cubs pennant-winners, he led all participants in the 1935 World Series with six RBI. After a slow start in 1941, he was traded to the Dodgers for two mediocrities and $65,000, supposedly because Cub manager Jimmie Wilson saw Herman as a threat to his job.

Kirby Higbe, a teammate in Chicago and Brooklyn, said that Herman "stood out at second base over any other second baseman I ever saw . . . he was the greatest hit-and-run man in baseball then or now." Leo Durocher agreed, saying Herman was

Billy Herman

"... universally accepted as the classic number-two hitter ... an absolute master at hitting behind the runner."

Herman managed extensively in the minors, coached for the Dodgers, Braves, Red Sox, Angels, and Padres, and also scouted. He managed the 1947 Pirates for all but the last game of the season; winning the season finale under replacement Bill Burwell, they moved into a tie for seventh place. Herman took over the Red Sox in October 1964 and lasted through 146 games of 1966, never finishing higher than eighth. /(JJM)

Gene Hermanski — 1920– . OF 1943, 46–53 **Dodgers**, Cubs, Pirates 739 g, .272, 46 hr, 259 rbi. *2 WS, 11 g, .219, 3 rbi*

Hermanski batted .295 for the 1948–50 Dodgers, but his fielding deficiencies kept him from being a regular outfielder. In 1948 he hit a career-high 15

home runs—three coming in consecutive at-bats in an August 5 game. /(JJM)

Enzo Hernandez — 1949– . SS 1971–78 **Padres**, Dodgers 714 g, .224, 2 hr, 113 rbi

Acquired from the Orioles, Hernandez was installed as a Padres regular in 1971 and led NL shortstops with 33 errors. He had only 12 RBI in 549 times at bat. More or less the regular through 1976, he improved his defense but never hit well. Only in 1976 did his RBI outnumber his stolen bases (24 to 12). /(MC)

Jackie Hernandez — 1940– . SS-3B 1965–73 Angels, Twins, **Royals**, Pirates 618 g, .208, 12 hr, 121 rbi. *1 LCS, 4 g, .231, 1 rbi. 1 WS, 7 g, .222, 1 rbi*

Originally signed as a catcher, the Cuban native was converted to shortstop. In 1965, he was voted the best-throwing shortstop in the Pacific Coast League. In the 1971 WS, Hernandez fielded flawlessly for the Pirates. /(RTM)

Keith Hernandez (Mex) — 1953- . 1B 1974-
Cardinals, Mets 2045 g, .298, 161 hr, 1063 rbi. *3 LCS, 16 g, .281, 1 hr, 9 rbi. 2 WS, 14 g, .245, 1 hr, 12 rbi* ☛ *Most Valuable Player—79. Led League—ba 79. All-Star—79-80, 84, 86-87. Gold Glove—78-88.*

Hernandez was indisputably the best-fielding first baseman of his time, winning eleven straight Gold Gloves and setting major league records for most seasons leading league first basemen in double plays (six) and lifetime assists by a first baseman. He revived Ferris Fain's practice of charging to the third base line on bunts and made the technique his own; trying for the force in such situations is usually a risky proposition, but Hernandez's judgment was rarely wrong. His great range helped him lead NL first basemen in assists five times, putouts four times, and fielding average twice. Twice he tied for

Keith Hernandez

the lead in errors with 13; it is the lowest total ever to lead the NL, and he never made more errors than that in a season.

Hernandez led the NL in batting in 1979 with the Cardinals, winning the only shared MVP award in history that year (Willie Stargell was the other recipient) as well as *TSN* NL Player of the Year. He also had career highs with 48 doubles and 116 runs, both league-leading totals, and 105 RBI. His .344 BA, also a career high, marked the first time he had hit .300; he went on to top .300 five other times. But while with the Cardinals, he had a reputation as a carefree, unintense player. Manager Whitey Herzog traded him to the last-place Mets for journeyman relief pitcher Neil Allen in mid-1983 after becoming convinced that Hernandez was using drugs. When Herzog defended the trade by hinting as much, Hernandez threatened a libel suit, but the 1985 Pittsburgh drug trials revealed it was true.

With the Mets, it seemed that Hernandez was trying to live down his old reputation. From the first day, he was the team's most intense player. Usually the Mets' number-three hitter, he became a great clutch hitter who worked the count and fouled off pitches until he got the offering he wanted. In the short lifetime of the game-winning RBI as an official statistic, he set ML records for most in a season (24 in 1985) and most lifetime (129). Always selective, he led the NL with 94 walks in 1986. His on-base percentage was above .400 seven times during his career, and he led the league in 1979 and 1980. His clubhouse leadership was acknowledged in 1987, when he was named the team captain. It was his last good season. After missing much of 1988 (hamstring troubles) and 1989 (knee problems), he was released. /(SH)

Ramon Hernandez — 1940- . LHP 1967-68, 71-77 Braves, Cubs, **Pirates**, Red Sox 430 ip, 23-15, 3.03. *3 LCS, 8 ip, 0-1, 3.24*

First signed in 1959, the sidearming screwballer peaked with the Pirates, teaming with righthander Dave Giusti to give Pittsburgh an exceptional bullpen from 1972-75. The Puerto Rican-born reliever was brilliant in 1972 (5-0, 1.67, 14 saves). /(ME)

Willie Hernandez [Guillermo Villanueva] — 1954- . LHP 1977- Cubs, Phillies, **Tigers** 1045 ip, 70-63, 3.38. *2 LCS, 4 ip, 0-0, 4.08. 2 WS, 9 ip, 0-0, 0.96* ☛ *Most Valuable Player—84. Cy Young Award—84. All-Star—84-86.*

Willie Hernandez was a fine, but unsung, reliever until 1984. He had been among the NL leaders in appearances with the Cubs in 1982 and the Cubs and Phillies in 1983. Traded to Detroit March 24, 1984, Hernandez quickly became manager Sparky Anderson's stopper. His phenomenal season (9–3, 1.92, 32 saves in 33 chances, 80 games, 112 strikeouts in 140 innings) earned both the MVP and Cy Young awards. He appeared in every non-complete postseason game for Detroit, with three saves in as many chances. In 1985 he became the first Tiger with back-to-back 30-save seasons, but he lost 10 games and gradually fell into disfavor with the fans. Stating a preference to be called Guillermo (his given first name), the mustachioed screwballer took a back seat to Mike Henneman in Detroit's bullpen in 1987 and 1988. /(ME)

Larry Herndon — 1953– . OF-DH 1974, 76–88 Cardinals, Giants, **Tigers** 1537 g, .273, 107 hr, 550 rbi. *2 LCS, 5 g, .286, 1 hr, 3 rbi. 1 WS, 5 g, .333, 1 hr, 3 rbi*

Herndon was *TSN* NL Rookie Player of the Year as the Giants' centerfielder in 1976, hitting .288 in 337 at-bats. His batting average fell as his playing time increased in San Francisco, and he was traded to the Tigers after the 1981 season. In cozy Tiger Stadium Herndon found his home run stroke, belting a career-high 23 (including three in one game May 18) in 1982 and 20 more in 1983. In 1987, platooning against lefthanded pitchers, he hit a career-high .324. /(SCL)

Eddie Herr — 1872–1943. *Scout.*

Herr was a minor league pitcher and manager who joined the Cardinals as a scout in 1913, and also scouted for the Tigers, Yankees, and Indians. He secured Bill Doak for the Cardinals and Bill Dickey for the Yankees, and unsuccessfully tried to get Carl Hubbell a tryout with the Tigers. /(FVP)

Tom Herr — 1956– . 2B 1979– **Cardinals**, Twins 1262 g, .275, 22 hr, 493 rbi. *3 LCS, 16 g, .262, 1 hr, 9 rbi. 3 WS, 21 g, .190, 1 hr, 6 rbi* ☛ *All-Star—85.*

Herr took over as St. Louis's second baseman in 1980. With Ozzie Smith, he formed one of the best double play combinations in baseball, three times leading the NL in twin killings. He made only six errors at second base in 1984, nine in 1986, and seven in 1987. Not known for power, the selective switch-hitter did not get his first home run until his 337th major league game. Nonetheless, his speed and ability to make contact made him an excellent third-place hitter, especially in Busch Stadium with its distant fences and Astroturf. In 1981 and 1982 he did not go hitless more than two games in a row

and in 1985 and 1986 he led Cardinals batters in RBI. He drove in 110 runs in 1983, becoming only the seventh second baseman in history to reach the century mark.

Herr was traded to the Twins for Tom Brunansky early in the 1988 season and was a disappointment for Minnesota. They traded him to the Phillies for Shane Rawley after the season. /(FO)

Pancho Herrera — 1934– . 1B-2B-3B 1958, 60–61 **Phillies** 300 g, .271, 31 hr, 128 rbi

In 1960 the 6'3" 220-lb Cuban set a NL record for a 154-game season by striking out 136 times. He led NL first basemen in assists and tied for the lead in errors that year. /(GEB)

Art Herring (Sandy) — 1907– . RHP 1929–34, 39, 44–47 **Tigers**, Dodgers, White Sox, Pirates 698 ip, 34–38, 4.32

The wiry, 5'7" Herring was at his best in relief. After his first ML tour, he slipped back to the minors. He resurfaced with Brooklyn at age 37, during the war-caused player shortage, to have his best seasons. /(EW)

Ed Herrmann — 1946– . C 1967, 69–78 **White Sox**, Yankees, Angels, Astros, Expos 922 g, .240, 80 hr, 320 rbi ☛ *All-Star—74.*

Herrmann was a hard working White Sox catcher in the early 1970s, gutsy in blocking the plate and knocking down Wilbur Wood's knuckleballs. Thanks mainly to Wood, Herrmann led the AL in passed balls four times. Although his batting averages were generally low, he had some power. In 1970, when he hit a career-high .283 with 19 homers in 96 games, he spent his bench time during home games in the bullpen helping restore a 1929 Ford. After infrequent Chicago victories, he'd delight fans by riding the smoking "Big White Machine" around the park. His grandfather Marty pitched for the Dodgers in 1918. /(DB)

Garry Herrmann [August] — 1859–1931. *Executive.*

Herrmann was president of the Cincinnati Reds from 1902 until illness forced his retirement in 1927. He began as a printer's devil and acquired the nickname "Garibaldi," later shortened to "Garry," but rose to a position of prominence through Cincinnati ward politics. In addition to his duties as Reds president, Herrmann served as president of the National Commission, the governing body of major league baseball, from its creation in 1903 until 1920. Sometimes called "The Father of the World

Series," he was influential in reestablishing the event in 1905 after the Giants had refused to participate in 1904. /(BC)

Mike Hershberger — 1939– . OF 1961–71 White Sox, **A's**, Brewers 1150 g, .252, 26 hr, 344 rbi

Quick and strong-armed, Hershberger was called up to the White Sox in late 1961 and hit .309 down the stretch. Once he became a regular, however, his hitting tailed off. His .279 in 1963 was his career best for any season as a regular. Despite his so-so bat, his defensive ability kept him in the majors for eleven seasons. He led AL outfielders with 17 assists in 1967. /(MC)

Willard Hershberger — 1910–1940. C 1938–40 **Reds** 160 g, .316, 0 hr, 70 rbi. *1 WS, 3 g, .500*

Hershberger's suicide during the 1940 season ended a frustrated career. A farmhand in the player-rich Yankee system, he shared a catching future with Buddy Rosar, judged the better defensive player. Bill Dickey was the Yankee catcher, a lefthanded hitter. Both Hershberger and Rosar were righthanded, and Rosar was chosen as Dickey's backup. Hershberger was sold to Cincinnati, and had to settle in behind another future Hall of Fame catcher, Ernie Lombardi. /(JK)

Orel Hershiser (Bulldog) — 1958– . RHP 1983- **Dodgers** 1457 ip, 98–64, 2.69. 20 wins: 88 *2 LCS, 40 ip, 2–0, 2.03. 1 WS, 18 ip, 2–0, 1.00*
☛ *Led League—w 88. Cy Young Award—88. All-Star—87–89. Gold Glove—88.*

No pitcher ever finished a season the way Hershiser finished 1988. After pitching five consecutive shutouts, the sinkerballer broke former Dodger Don Drysdale's record 58-inning scoreless streak by one with a ten-inning scoreless, no-decision effort in his final start of the season at San Diego. With his eight shutout innings in the LCS opener against the Mets, he went 67 innings without being scored upon. He picked up a save against the Mets in Game Four the day after a start, finished the Mets off with a shutout in Game Seven, and followed with another against the A's in the WS en route to becoming the first NL player to win the MVP in both postseason series. In the one WS game he batted in (Game Two), he went 3-for-3 with two doubles, a run, and an RBI while surrendering only three hits, all to Dave Parker.

Hershiser averaged 15 wins a season in the four years prior to 1988, and was 19–3, 2.03 in 1985, including an 11–0, 1.08 record at Dodger Stadium.

In 1989 lack of support left him with a 15–15 record despite a 2.31 ERA, second-best in the NL.

Nicknamed Bulldog by Dodger manager Tom Lasorda, the devoutly religious Hershiser has said, "You don't have to be a wimp to be a Christian." He played defense and left wing for the Philadelphia Flyers' Junior A hockey team. He is the fourth in his family to bear the name Orel, and his son is the fifth. /(TG)

Buck Herzog [Charles Lincoln] — 1885–1953. 2B-3B-SS 1908–20 **Giants**, Braves, Reds, Cubs 1493 g, .259, 20 hr, 445 rbi. *4 WS, 25 g, .245, 6 rbi.*
Manager 1914–16 **Reds** *165–226, .422*

Giants manager John McGraw traded away the aggressive Herzog three times. The second trade, in 1913, came after Herzog played third base on three straight Giants pennant winners and hit .400 in the 1912 WS. McGraw brought Herzog back a third time, and in 1917, Herzog was on another New York pennant-winner, this time playing second base. The much-traveled University of Maryland graduate found an appropriate second career as the general athletic passenger agent for the B&O Railroad. /(JK)

Whitey Herzog [Dorrel Norman Elvert] (The White Rat) — 1931– . OF 1956–63 Senators, A's, **Orioles**, Tigers 634 g, .257, 25 hr, 172 rbi.
Manager 1973, 75– Rangers, Royals, **Cardinals** *1248–1078, .537. First place: 76–78, 82, 85, 87 6 LCS, 16–14, .533. 3 WS, 10–11, .476*

Affectionately called The White Rat, Herzog has earned respect in baseball for his superb managerial skills. He has had five division winners and one World Champion (the 1982 Cardinals). Herzog was named Manager of the Year in 1976 by UPI, and in 1982 by *TSN* and UPI. He was also voted Manager of the Year by the BBWAA in 1985 for leading St. Louis to the NL pennant. In 1981 and 1982, when he was also GM, the UPI named him Executive of the Year as well. He is one of 37 managers to collect over 1,000 victories. Columnist Larry King says, "Every game is like a chess match with Whitey, and other managers must feel like they are playing against 10 guys when they go up against him."

Signed by the Yankees out of high school, Herzog reported to McAlester in the Sooner State League in 1949. It was there that sportscaster Bill Speith nicknamed the chunky spray hitter Whitey for his light-colored hair. As a member of the Athletics in 1960, Herzog hit into an all-Cuban triple play

Whitey Herzog

against Washington. The Senators involved were pitcher Camilio Pascual, first baseman Julio Becquer, and shortstop Jose Valdivelso. /(RTM)

Joe Hesketh (Fungo) — 1959- . LHP 1984- **Expos** 433 ip, 28-19, 3.37

Teammates dubbed Hesketh Fungo because his 6'2" 170-lb build reminded them of the long, thin bat. The American Association Pitcher of the Year for 1984 (12-3), in his ML debut that August he was called for a balk before ever throwing a pitch. He was 10-5 in 1985 before fracturing his shin in a collision with Dodger catcher Mike Scioscia, and in 1986 he underwent surgery for an impinged shoulder nerve. He returned to Montreal as a reliever late in 1987. /(JCA)

Otto Hess — 1878-1926. LHP-OF 1902, 04-08, 12-15 **Indians**, Braves 1418 ip, 70-90, 2.98; 279 g, .215, 5 hr, 58 rbi. 20 wins: 06

Hess was born in Berne, Switzerland, and reached the majors after serving with the army in the Philippines. He was unhittable at times, erratic at

others, and had a reputation for having one bad inning in each game. He had one big season, going 20-17 for Cleveland in 1906. /(NLM)

Johnny Hetki — 1922- . RHP 1945-48, 50, 52-54 **Reds**, Browns, Pirates 525 ip, 18-26, 4.39

After spending parts of five seasons with the Reds, in 1951 Hetki went 19-10 for Toronto (International League). He was the relief ace of the 1953-54 last-place Pirates. /(ME)

Ed Heusser (The Wild Elk of the Wasatch) — 1900-1956. RHP 1935-36, 38, 40, 43-46, 48 Cardinals, Phillies, A's, **Reds** 1087 ip, 56-57, 3.69
☛ *Led League—era 44.*

The Utah native was generally a reliever until 1944 when, as a Reds' starter, he led the NL with a 2.38 ERA. A switch hitter, it was said Heusser could also throw with either arm, and may have in the minors. /(EW)

Joe Heving — 1900-1970. RHP 1930-31, 33-34, 37-45 Giants, White Sox, **Indians**, Red Sox, Braves 1038 ip, 76-48, 3.90

The brother of catcher Johnnie Heving, Joe was a sinkerballer who led his league three times in relief wins and twice in relief losses. In 1944 he was the only grandfather playing ML baseball, but still topped the AL with 63 appearances for Cleveland, and had a career-best 1.96 ERA. Heving finished in 1945 with 63 lifetime saves. /(GEB)

Johnnie Heving — 1896-1968. C 1920, 24-25, 28-32 Browns, **Red Sox**, A's 398 g, .265, 1 hr, 89 rbi. *1 WS, 1 g, .000*

Heving was winding up his major league career as a non-power hitting backup catcher as his younger brother Joe, a ML reliever, was breaking in with the Giants. /(EW)

John A. Heydler — 1869-1956. *Executive. Umpire* 1895-98 NL

Heydler was a government printer in Washington in the 1880s. His interest in baseball led him into umpiring and later sportswriting. He became secretary to NL president Harry Pulliam and became interim president after Pulliam's suicide. He became secretary-treasurer under president John K. Tener, and succeeded Tener as NL president in 1918. Heydler was not very energetic in investigating scandal or in opposing league owners, but he was innovative in his thinking. He supported the selection of Judge Kenesaw Landis as Commissioner of

Baseball in 1920, helped establish the Baseball Hall of Fame, and proposed the designated hitter as early as 1929. After resigning as president in 1934, he served as NL chairman of the board until his death. /(NLM)

Jack Hiatt — 1942– . C-1B 1964–72 Angels, **Giants**, Expos, Cubs, Astros 483 g, .251, 22 hr, 154 rbi

A second-string catcher and fill-in first baseman with the Giants in 1968, Hiatt figured in Don Drysdale's record scoreless inning streak. When Dick Dietz flied out after being refused first base despite being hit by a pitch with the bases loaded, Hiatt followed by popping up for the last out of Drysdale's fifth straight shutout. /(GEB)

Kevin Hickey — 1956– . LHP 1981–83, 89 **White Sox**, Orioles 192 ip, 7–11, 3.38

Hickey was a softball pitcher signed out of a public tryout by the White Sox in 1978. Arm trouble interrupted his career after three years, but he made a successful comeback with the 1989 Orioles. His herky-jerky motion made him effective in both long and short relief. /(RL)

Jim Hickman — 1937– . OF-1B-3B 1962–74 Mets, Dodgers, **Cubs**, Cardinals 1421 g, .252, 159 hr, 560 rbi
☛ *All-Star—70.*

This original New York Met was both the first member of the franchise to hit for the cycle (8/7/63) and the first to hit three home runs in a game (9/3/65). During his first seven ML seasons Hickman was considered a clumsy outfielder whose occasional power insufficiently compensated for frequent strikeouts. The Cubs acquired him from the Dodgers in 1968, and he batted a paltry .223. On August 1, 1969, he was down to .216 on the first-place Cubs. While his teammates faltered in the stretch, Hickman came off the bench to hit .301 for August, with 10 HR and 25 RBI. He kept hitting well the next year with a .315 average, 32 HR, 115 RBI, and 13 game-winning hits. In the 1970 All-Star Game, his 12th-inning single drove in Pete Rose for the game-winning run. He was slowed in ensuing years by various ailments. /(AA)

Piano Legs Hickman (Charles) — 1876–1934. 1B-OF-2B-3B Braves, Giants, Red Sox, **Indians**, Tigers, Senators, White Sox 1,080 g, .301, 59 hr, 614 rbi

An early slugger, Hickman was the first player to lead a league while playing for two teams (Boston and Cleveland) with 194 in 1902. That year, he approached a triple crown season when he was second in the AL home runs (11) and RBI (110), and

third in BA (.363). On June 30, 1902 Nap Lajoie, Hickman, and Bill Bradley became the first trio to hit consecutive home runs in this century. With the 1900 Giants, he set an NL record for errors by a third baseman with 91, after which he was usually stationed in the outfield or at first base. His nickname described his massive limbs which supported his 5'9" 215-lb frame. /(ME)

Kirby Higbe [Walter Kirby] — 1915–1985. RHP 1937–43, 46–50 Cubs, Phillies, **Dodgers**, Pirates, Giants 1952 ip, 118–101, 3.69. 20 wins: 41 *1 WS, 4 ip, 0–0, 7.36*
☛ *Led League—w 41. Led League—k 40. All-Star—40, 46.*

The title of Higbe's autobiography, *The High Hard One*, describes his pitching style. He led the NL in walks four times (1939–41 and '47). He also led with 137 strikeouts in 1940. After he went 14–19 for the last-place Phillies in 1940, both the Giants and Dodgers were after the young flamethrower. Brooklyn's Larry MacPhail snatched Higbe by giving the financially troubled Phillies $100,000 and three players in return. Higbe was worth the price, joining teammate Whit Wyatt atop the NL with 22 wins in 1941 and leading the league with 48 games and 39 starts for the NL champs.

Higbe was ambivalent concerning the addition of Jackie Robinson to the Dodgers. Higbe had spent many hours throwing rocks at blacks while growing up in South Carolina, and he believed in segregation, telling Branch Rickey he preferred not to have to play with a "negruh." But Higbe's competitive nature made him respect the fiery Robinson. He didn't have to worry about Robinson for long; he was traded to Pittsburgh on May 3, 1947. /(ME)

Dennis Higgins — 1939– . RHP 1966–72 White Sox, **Senators**, Indians, Cardinals 410 ip, 22–23, 3.42

Higgins had a herky-jerky motion and a live fastball, and was among the AL's best relievers during his two years with the Senators. In 1968 he was 4–4 with 13 saves, and he finished third in the 1969 Fireman of the Year balloting with a 10–9 record and 16 saves. /(JCA)

Pinky Higgins [Michael Franklin] — 1909–1969. 3B 1930, 33–44, 46 A's, Red Sox, **Tigers** 1802 g, .292, 141 hr, 1075 rbi. *2 WS, 14 g, .271, 1 hr, 8 rbi.*
Manager 1955–62 Red Sox 543–541, .501
☛ *All-Star—34, 36, 44.*

Signed out of the University of Texas, for a dozen years Higgins was a hard-hitting, steady-fielding third baseman. Especially dangerous with men on base, he twice drove in 106 runs. Higgins set a ML record when he hit safely in 12 consecutive at-bats in 1938. He hit .333 in the 1940 World Series with the Tigers and handled a record ten chances at third base in Game Four. After playing in all seven games of the 1946 WS with the Red Sox, Higgins retired.

A low-key approach and patience with young players made Higgins a popular manager in the minors and later with the Red Sox. In 1955, his first of eight seasons managing Boston, he was named *TSN* Manager of the Year. His best showings were third-place finishes in 1957–58. Higgins also served as Red Sox vice president and GM, and later was an Astro scout./(JL)

Andy High (Handy Andy) — 1897–1981. 3B-2B-SS 1922–34 **Dodgers**, Braves, Cardinals, Reds, Phillies 1314 g, .284, 44 hr, 482 rbi. *3 WS, 9 g, .294, 1 rbi*

The best of the three lefthanded-hitting High brothers played in the daffier days of Wilbert Robinson's Dodgers and was dubbed "Handy Andy" for his competent versatility. The Cards used him mostly at third base, and he was with them for pennants in 1928, '30, and '31. In only three seasons did he appear in over 100 games at a single position./(JK)

Hugh High (Bunny, Lefty) — 1887–1962. OF 1913–18 Tigers, **Yankees** 504 g, .250, 3 hr, 123 rbi

Oldest of the three High brothers, Hugh couldn't break into the Tiger outfield of Cobb, Sam Crawford, and Bob Veach. He was a regular with the Yankees for three years./(JK)

Dick Higham — 1851–1905. OF 1871–76, 78, 80 New York (NA), Lord Baltimores (NA), Chicago (NA), **Hartford (NL)**, Providence (NL), Troy (NL) *NA: 239 g, .288; ML: 130 g, .323, 1 hr, 64 rbi.*
Umpire NL 1881–82

Higham was the only ML umpire ever dismissed for cheating. When he was a hard-hitting outfielder in the National Association and early NL, the English-born Higham was the subject of rumors that his play was not always on the level. Even though he led the NL in doubles in 1876 and 1878 and in runs scored in '78, his reputation for shady dealings curtailed his ML career. Nevertheless, the NL hired him as an umpire after his playing days ended, apparently because he had sometimes umpired in the NA. In 1882 William Thompson, the mayor of Detroit and president of the Wolverines baseball team, became convinced that Higham was consistently calling close decisions against Detroit. Thompson hired a private detective who turned up a letter that Higham had mailed to a well-known gambler in which he

outlined a simple telegram code on how and when to bet. "Buy all the lumber you can!" meant bet on Detroit. No telegram meant bet against them. Thompson and the other owners confronted Higham and he was banished from baseball. Reportedly, the crooked ump went back to Chicago and became a bookkeeper./(RTM)

Ted Higuera — 1958– . LHP 1985- **Brewers** 1085 ip, 78–44, 3.28. 20 wins: 86
☛ *All-Star—86.*

Signed by the Brewers after a great year at Juarez in the Mexican League (league leader in wins, complete games, innings pitched and strikeouts), Higuera posted the best rookie record in the Milwaukee club's history (15–8), finished second in Rookie of the Year balloting, and was *TSN* AL Rookie Pitcher of the Year in 1985. The following season, Higuera became Milwaukee's first 20-game winner of the 1980s (and the first Mexican-born 20-game winner, beating Fernando Valenzuela by a matter of days) and finished second in the Cy Young Award voting. His 240 strikeouts in 1987 were the most by any Milwaukee pitcher, surpassing Tony Cloninger's 211 with the 1965 Braves./(ME)

George Hildebrand — 1878–1960. OF 1902 **Dodgers** 11 g, .220, 0 hr, 5 rbi.
Umpire AL 1912–34 *4 WS*

Some historians credit Hildebrand with inventing the spitball. Supposedly, while playing catch as a minor league outfielder in 1902, he discovered what a ball dampened by dew on the grass could do. Subsequently, he taught the pitch to Elmer Stricklett, who taught it to Ed Walsh. Of all his calls in 23 years as a ML umpire, the most controversial came in Game Two of the 1922 WS between the Giants and Yankees when he stopped play because of darkness in the 10th inning of a 3–3 tie. He was criticized at the time by many who believed the game could have been continued for several more innings. Commissioner Landis, sensitive to WS scandal two years after the Black Sox, turned the game receipts over to charity./(RTM)

Oral Hildebrand — 1907–1977. RHP 1931–40 **Indians**, Browns, Yankees 1430 ip, 83–78, 4.35. *1 WS, 4 ip, 0–0, 0.00*
☛ *All-Star—33.*

The rangy righthander was a star basketball player at Butler University before turning to baseball. His best season, (16–11, 3.76) in 1933 with the Indians, earned him a spot on the AL's first All-Star Game roster. /(ME)

Tom Hilgendorf — 1942– . LHP 1969–70, 72–75 Cardinals, **Indians**, Phillies 313 ip, 19–14, 3.04

After a decade spent mostly in the minors, the father of six led the Indians 1973 bullpen with six saves in 48 appearances. In 1975 with Philadelphia, the forkballer had his best and last ML season, 7–3 with a 2.13 ERA. /(JCA)

Carmen Hill (Specs, Bunker) — 1895– . RHP 1915–16, 18–19, 22, 26–30 **Pirates**, Giants, Cardinals 787 ip, 49–33, 3.44. 20 wins: 27 *1 WS, 6 ip, 4.50*

In 1915 Hill and Lee Meadows were the first two pitchers to wear glasses in the majors. After winning 22 for Pittsburgh in 1927, Hill started Game Four of the WS against the Yankees and gave up the home run that Babe Ruth is shown hitting on the Ruth 20-cent stamp issued in 1983. /(NLM)

Donnie Hill — 1960– . 2B-SS-3B 1983–88 **A's**, White Sox 551 g, .257, 22 hr, 174 rbi

The A's had optioned the ambidextrous, switch-hitting Hill to Triple-A in spring training of 1985 when Tony Phillips broke his foot. Hill took Phillips's second base job and, changing from a pull hitter to a spray hitter, improved his average from .230 in 1984 to a career-high .285. His 1987 season with the White Sox was marred by conjunctivitis, caused by his contact lenses. /(JCA)

Hunter Hill — 1879–1959. 3B 1903–05 Browns, **Senators** 325 g, .216, 1 hr, 80 rbi

Hill missed the first month of the 1904 season with the mumps and led AL third basemen in errors. Traded by the Browns that July, he batted .197 for the 38–113 Senators. He spent 20 years in the Texas League, managing Houston and umpiring. /(NLM)

Jesse Hill — 1907– . OF 1935–37 Yankees, **Senators**, A's 295 g, .289, 6 hr, 108 rbi

Hill was an Olympic hopeful in track and a football star at the University of Southern California. The fleet fielder hit a pinch homer in his first pro game. /(JK)

Ken Hill — 1965– . RHP 1988– **Cardinals** 211 ip, 7–16, 3.89

Despite only one winning record and one ERA below 4.50 in seven stops before 1989, St. Louis called up Hill when their staff was stricken with multiple injuries. After a good start, he found himself overmatched, and finished 7–15, 3.80. /(WOR)

Marc Hill — 1952– . C 1973–86 Cardinals, **Giants**, Mariners, White Sox 737 g, .223, 34 hr, 198 rbi

A sound defensive catcher, the solidly built Hill served as a backup nearly all of his 14 ML seasons. His only time as a regular came with the Giants in 1977–78, when he hit .250 and .243. /(FS)

Pete Hill [J. Preston] — 1880–1951. OF-2B-MGR Negro Leagues 1904–25 Philadelphia Giants, Leland Giants, Chicago American Giants, Detroit Stars, Philadelphia Madison Stars, Cleveland Tate Stars, Milwaukee Bears, Baltimore Black Sox statistics not available

Hill was one of the outstanding players in Negro League history. He was a lefthanded line-drive batter who hit to all fields, and an excellent defensive outfielder with great range and a strong accurate arm.

Hill was the cornerstone of three of the most talented teams in the pioneer years of black baseball. From 1904 through 1907, he was the star left fielder for Sol White's powerhouse Philadelphia Giants. Rube Foster took over as manager of Frank Leland's Giants in 1907, reorganized the team, and brought Hill to the club for his leadership ability. For three seasons beginning in 1908, Hill was Foster's field general. The 1910 Leland Giants posted a 123–6 record, including 21 shutouts against the best talent in the Midwest. In 1911, Foster formed a new team, the Chicago American Giants, consisting mostly of former Leland players. He made Hill the team captain the following year.

Hill was always his team's premier slugger. In 1911, as an American Giant, only once in 116 games did he fail to get a hit. He accomplished this feat against pitchers of the Tri-State League and against many white major leaguers, including Nap Rucker, Eddie Plank, Chief Bender, and Mordecai Brown. Cum Posey, owner of the Homestead Grays, called Hill "the most consistent hitter of his time. While a lefthanded batter, he hit both lefthanders and righthanders equally well. He was the backbone, year in and year out, of great ball clubs."

When Foster organized the Detroit Stars in 1919, he asked Hill to become the team's player-manager. At the age of 41 in 1921, Hill led the Stars in batting with a .388 average. He went on to play with the Madison Stars of Philadelphia, the Cleveland Tate Bears, and the Milwaukee Bears. He also played in

Cuba, compiling a .307 average in six seasons. He led the Cuban Winter League with a .365 average for Habana in '10–11. His final position in pro baseball was as the business manager of the 1924–25 Baltimore Black Sox. /(LL)

Shawn Hillegas — 1964– . RHP 1987– Dodgers, **White Sox** 274 ip, 17–20, 4.13

Hillegas (pronounced HILL-uh-gus) pitched well after joining the White Sox in a September 1988 trade, going 3–2 with a 3.15 ERA. But he pitched so badly at the start of 1989 that he was relegated to the bullpen. /(JFC)

Chuck Hiller (Iron Hands) — 1934– . 2B 1961–68 **Giants**, Mets, Phillies, Pirates 704 g, .243, 20 hr, 152 rbi. *1 WS, 7 g, .269, 1 hr, 5 rbi*

Iron Hands Hiller led NL second basemen with 29 errors playing for the 1962 NL champion Giants. He was the first NL player to hit a World Series grand slam, connecting off Marshall Bridges in the seventh inning of San Francisco's 7–3, Game Four victory over the Yankees. Later used extensively as a pinch hitter by the Mets, he led the NL with 15 pinch hits in 1966. /(CR)

Frank Hiller — 1920–1987. RHP 1946, 48–53 Yankees, **Cubs**, Reds, Giants 533 ip, 30–32, 4.42

The top pitcher in Lafayette College history, going 22–2, Hiller was a hot prospect in the Yankee farm system before he hurt his arm. After surgery, he became the forgotten man in the New York bullpen. Sold to the Cubs in 1950, he was 12–5 with the help of a forkball he'd learned from former major leaguer Joe Bush. /(BC)

John Hiller — 1943– . LHP 1965–70, 72–80 **Tigers** 1241 ip, 87–76, 2.83. *1 LCS, 3 ip, 1–0, 0.00. 1 WS, 2 ip, 0–0, 13.50*
☛ *All-Star—74.*

Hiller nearly died when he suffered a massive stroke in 1971, but after a miraculous recovery he was pitching again for the Tigers by the end of 1972. He posted 38 saves in 1973 to set a ML record and win Comeback Player of the Year and Fireman of the Year honors. He was also 10–5 with a 1.44 ERA and led the AL with 65 appearances.

After a moderately successful career as a reliever and occasional starter (he tied a since-broken ML record for consecutive strikeouts from the start of a game with six on August 6, 1968) Hiller missed all of 1971 after being stricken. He came back as a batting-practice pitcher in June 1972 and returned

to action a month later, helping Detroit to the division title and winning Game Four of the LCS. Hiller set some more relief marks in 1974, the year after his save record, when his 17–14 record (13 saves) tied both the AL mark for relief wins and the ML standard for relief losses. The Canadian had several more seasons as the ace of the Tigers' bullpen and retired with a club-record 125 saves. /(JFC)

Dave Hillman — 1927– . RHP 1955–62 **Cubs**, Red Sox, Reds, Mets 624 ip, 21–37, 3.87

Hillman and the Cubs defeated the Dodgers 12–2 on September 26, 1959, forcing Los Angeles into the pennant playoff in which they beat the Braves. /(AA)

Hilltop Park New York Yankees 1903–12, New York Giants 1911. LF-365, CF-542, RF-400

Hilltop Park's single-decked wooden grandstand provided a scenic view of the nearby Hudson River and New Jersey Palisades from behind home plate. Its upper-Manhattan site is now occupied by Columbia-Presbyterian Hospital. /(SCL)

Dave Hilton — 1950– . 3B-2B 1972–75 **Padres** 161 g, .213, 6 hr, 33 rbi

Hilton was San Diego's Opening Day third baseman in both 1973 and '74, but his weak bat sent him back to Hawaii both times. After four games in 1975, he was stricken with hepatitis and never again appeared in a ML game. /(JCA)

Bill Hinchman — 1883–1963. OF 1905–09, 15–18, 20 Reds, Indians, **Pirates** 908 g, .261, 20 hr, 369 rbi

Hinchman failed to hit as a regular Cleveland outfielder (1907–09) but won a second chance at the majors by setting American Association records for hits, doubles, and total bases at Columbus in 1914. In both 1915 and '16 he topped .300 for the Pirates. A broken leg in 1917 ended his productivity. As a Pittsburgh scout, he discovered Arky Vaughan, Lloyd Waner, and Billy Cox, among others. His brother Harry played briefly with Cleveland in 1907. /(ME)

Paul Hines — 1852–1935. OF-1B-2B-3B-SS 1872–91 Washington (NA), Chicago (NA/NL), **Providence (NL)**, Washington (NL), Indianapolis (NL), Pirates, Braves, Washington (AA) *NA: 178 g, .302; ML: 1481 g, .301, 56 hr, 631 rbi*
☛ *Led League—ba 78. Led League—hr 78. Led League—rbi 78.*

With Providence in 1878, Hines's career-high .358 average, four HR, and 50 RBI in 62 games were enough to earn him baseball's first triple crown. He hit over .300 eleven times. Rarely ranked among the leaders in fielding, he was famous for his running outfield catches. One such catch in 1878 began a triple play. Boston runners on first and third took off on a short fly over the shortstop's head which seemed a sure hit. Hines charged in from centerfield to make a spectacular shoestring catch, ran to third base to double off one runner, then threw to second base to catch the other and complete the triple play. Some of the game's participants later argued that both runners had rounded third before Hines tagged the base, thereby giving him an unassisted triple play. But newspaper accounts agree that Hines's contribution was two putouts and an assist. /(FIC)

Chuck Hinton [Charles Edward] — 1934– . OF-1B 1961–71 Senators, **Indians**, Angels 1353 g, .264, 113 hr, 443 rbi
☛ *All-Star—64.*

Grabbed from Baltimore by Washington in the 1960 expansion draft, the graceful Hinton became a regular outfielder and infield fill-in for the Senators. He had an excellent 1962 season (.310, 17 HR, 75 RBI, 28 steals) and was an All-Star in 1964. Traded to Cleveland for Woody Held and Bob Chance, Hinton played six years for the Indians, interrupted by one disappointing season (.195) with California in 1968. Nominally an outfielder/first baseman, the versatile Hinton played every defensive position during his ML career. /(JCA)

Rich Hinton — 1947– . LHP 1971–72, 75–76, 78–79 **White Sox**, Yankees, Rangers, Reds, Mariners 250 ip, 8–17, 4.86

This native Tucsonan and University of Arizona product pitched three Triple-A seasons in front of his hometown fans while he was a White Sox farmhand. Traded five times, he never won or saved more than two games in any ML year. /(JCA)

Al Hirshberg — 1910–1973. *Writer.*

The author of the Jim Piersall biography, *Fear Strikes Out*, Hirshberg also wrote books about Carl Yastrzemski, Frank Howard, and Bob Cousy. A Boston University graduate, he worked for the Boston *Post* and *Herald* before becoming a book and magazine writer. /(NLM)

Larry Hisle — 1947– . OF-DH 1968–71, 73–82 Phillies, **Twins**, Brewers 1197 g, .273, 166 hr, 674 rbi
☛ *Led League—rbi 77. All-Star—77–78.*

Hisle, a soft-spoken orphan, was recruited for Ohio State University by the governor of Ohio, and signed with the Phillies while still enrolled. Despite tying the then-ML rookie record by striking out 152 times, Hisle was a Topps Rookie All-Star (.266, 20 HR) in 1969 even though he was still weak from a 1968 hepatitis infection. He had an abysmal sophomore season, batting .205 and fanning once every three at-bats. Traded and returned to the minors, he resurfaced with Minnesota in 1973 and blossomed. Fleet afoot, with a strong arm and excellent power, he became a top run producer in five seasons as a Twins regular, culminating in 1977 with a league-leading 119 RBI (.302, 28 HR). He didn't get along with parsimonious Twins owner Calvin Griffith; as a free agent, Hisle signed a $3.2 million package with Milwaukee in 1978 and delivered 34 homers and 115 RBI to finish third in the AL MVP balloting. Brewer manager George Bamberger called him "the kind of player kids should look up to" and "without a doubt one of the nicest men I've ever known." In April 1979, Hisle tore his rotator cuff making a throw and played just 79 games in four more ML seasons. /(JCA)

Billy Hitchcock — 1916– . 3B-2B-SS 1942, 46–53 Tigers, Senators, Browns, Red Sox, **A's** 703 g, .243, 5 hr, 257 rbi.
Manager 1960, 62–63, 66–67 Tigers, **Orioles**, Braves 274–261, .512

Hitchcock was the Tigers' primary shortstop in his first season, but spent 1943–45 in the Army Air Force, receiving the Bronze Medal for his service in the Pacific. The only team for which he played more than a hundred games in a season was the Athletics, in 1950 (second base) and 1952 (third base); he led AL third basemen in errors in 1952. He later managed, finishing highest with the fourth-place 1963 Orioles. He was also a coach and a scout, and was president of the Southern Association from 1971 to 1980. His brother, Jim, played briefly with the Braves in 1938. /(NLM/MA)

Lloyd Hittle (Red) — 1924– . LHP 1949–50 **Senators** 152 ip, 7–11, 4.43

Casey Stengel's redheaded ace at Oakland (Pacific Coast League), Hittle earned five of his seven ML victories against the White Sox. /(JK)

Myril Hoag — 1908-1971. OF 1931-32, 34-42, 44-45 **Yankees**, Browns, White Sox, Indians 1020 g, .271, 28 hr, 401 rbi. *3 WS, 8 g, .320, 1 hr, 3 rbi*

Journeyman Hoag served as a reserve on four Yankee pennant-winners. He had extremely small feet which required special shoes, and somehow supported a 5'11" 180-lb body. In a career-high 129 games as the 1939 Browns' right fielder, Hoag hit .295 with 10 HR. /(JK)

Don Hoak (Tiger) — 1928-1969. 3B 1954-64 Dodgers, Cubs, Reds, **Pirates**, Phillies 1263 g, .265, 89 hr, 498 rbi. *2 WS, 10 g, .231, 3 rbi*
☛ *All-Star—57.*

Hoak was an outspoken, brawling firebrand, the spiritual leader of the 1960 World Champion Pirates. A pro boxer as a teenager, he lost seven straight knockouts before giving it up. He carried his pugnacity to the ballfield. He broke in sharing third base in Brooklyn with Billy Cox and Jackie Robinson. As a Cub on May 2, 1956, he set a NL record by striking out six times in a game (17 innings). In 1957, he led the NL with 39 doubles for the Reds and earned an All-Star Game berth in the Cincinnati ballot-box-stuffing incident. Traded to Pittsburgh, he led the Pirates in walks in 1959-61, and paced the 1960 championship team with 97 runs scored.

In a Braves-Reds game on April 21, 1957, Hoak was on second and Gus Bell was on first when Wally Post grounded to shortstop. Hoak fielded the ball himself, flipping it to a stunned Johnny Logan at short. Hoak was out for getting hit by a batted ball, but the Reds still had two on and Post was credited with a single. The third such incident involving the Reds that season, it moved league presidents Warren Giles and Will Harridge to jointly announce a rule change that declared both the runner and the batter out if the runner intentionally interfered with a batted ball, with no runners allowed to advance.

Hoak later managed in the Pittsburgh system. He died of a heart attack chasing his brother-in-law's stolen car on October 9, 1969, the day Danny Murtaugh was rehired as Pirates manager—a position Hoak had openly sought. /(ME)

Ed Hobaugh — 1934- . RHP 1961-63 **Senators** 212 ip, 9-10, 4.34

The captain of the 1954 Big Ten champion Michigan State baseball team had his most active ML season as a rookie seven years later. He was 7-9 for the last-place Senators. /(RTM)

Glen Hobbie — 1936- . RHP 1957-64 **Cubs**, Cardinals 1263 ip, 62-81, 4.20

The Cub ace from 1958 to 1960, Hobbie peaked in 1959, going 16-13. Included was a 1-0 one-hitter over the Cardinals April 22 in which Stan Musial spoiled a perfect game by doubling with two out in the seventh. Hobbie's 20 losses in 1960 led the league. A strained shoulder in 1961 ended his effectiveness. /(AA)

Dick Hoblitzell — 1888-1962. 1B 1908-18 **Reds**, Red Sox 1317 g, .278, 27 hr, 619 rbi. *2 WS, 10 g, .273, 3 rbi*

A consistent first baseman for the Reds, Hoblitzell was sold to the Red Sox in the middle of 1914 and assigned to room with rookie pitcher Babe Ruth. A starter for Boston's World Champions in 1915 and '16, he retired two years later at the age of 29 to practice dentistry. He later returned to baseball as a minor league manager and umpire. /(JK)

Butch Hobson [Clell Lavern] — 1951- . 3B-DH 1975-82 **Red Sox**, Angels, Yankees 738 g, .248, 98 hr, 397 rbi

The former University of Alabama football star's all-out play caused him many injuries throughout his baseball career. He became a Red Sox regular in 1977, setting team records for third basemen with 30 home runs and 112 RBI. His 43 errors in 1978 were the most by any AL fielder, and his .899 fielding average was the first below .900 by a regular in 62 years. The hard-nosed slugger suffered through elbow problems and, after a trade to California in 1981, a shoulder separation. He played 30 games for the Yankees in 1982 before being sent down to Columbus (International League). /(JCA)

Oris Hockett — 1909-1969. OF 1938-39, 41-45 Dodgers, **Indians**, White Sox 551 g, .276, 13 hr, 214 rbi

After failing in a trial with Brooklyn, Hockett won a second ML chance with strong years at Nashville (Southern Association). He played regularly for four wartime years, with a top mark of .293 for the White Sox in 1945. /(ME)

Johnny Hodapp — 1905-1980. 2B-3B 1925-33 **Indians**, White Sox, Red Sox 787 g, .311, 28 hr, 429 rbi

As Cleveland's starting second baseman, Hodapp hit .300 four straight seasons, climaxing with .354 in 1930, when he led the AL in hits (225) and doubles (51), batted in 121 runs and scored 111. He also topped AL second basemen in putouts. A knee injury the next season hampered him on both offense and defense, shattered his confidence, and finally ended his career. /(ME)

Shovel Hodge [Clarence Clement] — 1893–1967. RHP 1920–22 **White Sox** 301 ip, 14–15, 5.17

Hodge stood 6′4″ and was dubbed Shovel for his big feet. In his September 6, 1920 debut, he held the Tigers hitless for 7–1/3 innings. When the Black Sox scandal decimated Chicago's pitching staff in 1921, Hodge proved an inadequate replacement. /(RL)

Gil Hodges [born Gilbert Ray Hodge] — 1924–1972. 1B-OF-C-3B 1943, 47–63 **Dodgers**, Mets 2071 g, .273, 370 hr, 1274 rbi. *7 WS, 39 g, .267, 5 hr, 21 rbi.*
    Manager 1963–71 **Senators**, Mets 660–754, .467. *1 LCS, 3–0, 1.000. 1 WS, 4–1, .800*
☛ *All-Star—49–55, 57. Gold Glove—57–59 .*

Known as the "Miracle Worker" when he piloted the 1969 Mets to the World Championship, Hodges was a slugging, eight-time All-Star first baseman. A dead-pull hitter who always looked for the inside pitch, Hodges was a model of consistency, collecting over 100 RBI for seven consecutive years (1949–55) and hitting 20 or more HR 11 straight seasons (1949–59). His lifetime 14 grand slams established the NL mark, since eclipsed by Willie McCovey (18) and Hank Aaron (16).

Hodges was nineteen when he played third base for one game with the Dodgers in late 1943. He struck out twice and walked, then joined the Marines. He returned in 1947 as a catcher, but with the emergence of Roy Campanella, he was moved to first base. Manager Leo Durocher said, "With my catching set, I put a first baseman's glove on our other rookie catcher, Gil Hodges, and told him to have some fun. Three days later, I looked up and, wow, I was looking at the best first baseman I'd seen since Dolf Camilli."

Hodges was the Dodgers' Lou Gehrig—big, strong, and gentle. The three-time Gold Glove winner played first base gracefully. His hands were so large that teammates joked he didn't even need a glove. His quick footwork provoked the allegation that he rarely had his foot on the bag for his putouts.

On August 31, 1950 against the Braves, Hodges hit four homers. His 40 HR in 1951 were second only to Ralph Kiner's 42, but he struck out a league-high 99 times. He reached career highs in 1954, hitting .304 with 42 HR and 130 RBI (second to Ted Kluszewski's 49 and 141). During the 1952 WS loss to the Yankees, Hodges went a dreadful 0-for-21, and prayers were said for the beloved Dodger in

Gil Hodges

churches all across Brooklyn. In the following year's Series he hit .364. Hodges homered in each of his last four World Series, his shots winning 1956's Game One and 1959's Game Four for the Dodgers.

Ending his playing career with the Mets, Hodges hit the first homer in their history, on April 11, 1962 at St. Louis. Though he began 1963 with the Mets, he was sent to Washington for Jimmy Piersall, and took over as manager of the struggling Senators, who were 14–26 under Mickey Vernon. In five seasons, the best Hodges could do was a sixth-place finish in 1967.

Hodges was traded back to the Mets as manager in exchange for pitcher Bill Denehy and cash. His 1968 club finished ninth, but the following season, Hodges took the Mets to the pennant, skillfully platooning at five positions. The Mets swept the Braves in the LCS, then took the WS from Baltimore in five games. Hodges managed the Mets to two third-place finishes in 1970 and '71. He died suddenly of a heart attack after a spring training golf game on April 2, 1972, two days before his 48th birthday. The Mets retired his number 14. /(RTM)

Ron Hodges — 1949– . C 1973–84 **Mets** 666 g, .240, 19 hr, 147 rbi. *1 WS, 1 g, --*

No relation to the great Gil Hodges, Ron roomed with Gil Hodges, Jr., in the minor leagues. A reliable backup catcher and lefthanded pinch hitter, Ron's patience at the plate allowed him to draw enough walks to make him more effective than his BA indicated. He caught a career-high 96 games in 1983. /(JCA)

Russ Hodges — 1910–1971. *Broadcaster.*

When Bobby Thomson stunned the Dodgers with his "Shot Heard 'Round the World" to win the 1951 NL playoff series, Russ Hodges delivered what has become the most famous call in ML history, repeatedly crying "The Giants win the pennant! The Giants win the pennant!" as bedlam reigned in the Polo Grounds. Raised in Kentucky, Hodges broadcast for the White Sox, Cubs, Reds, Senators, and Yankees before settling for two decades as the voice of the Giants. He would salute each Giants home run with his trademark "Bye, bye baby!" and was heard on New York's WMCA and San Francisco's KSFO until his sudden death of a heart attack in 1971. /(SCL)

Ralph Hodgin — 1916– . OF-3B 1939, 43–44, 46–48 Braves, **White Sox** 530 g, .285, 4 hr, 188 rbi

Hodgin batted .314 for the 1943 White Sox, but became one of the few players to bat .300 as a rookie but never repeat the feat. On April 21, 1947 he suffered a concussion when a fastball from Tiger ace Hal Newhouser glanced off his skull. After that he lost his aggressiveness at the plate. /(RL)

Billy Hoeft — 1932– . LHP 1952–66 **Tigers**, Red Sox, Orioles, Giants, Braves, Cubs 1847 ip, 97–101, 3.94. 20 wins: 56
☛ *All-Star—55.*

Hoeft was a mainstay in the Tigers starting rotation in the 1950s, then embarked on a second career as an itinerant lefthanded reliever, changing teams six times between 1959 and 1966. He spent most of his rookie season in the Detroit bullpen, then struggled as a starter in 1953–54, winning only 16 games over the two seasons. In 1955 Hoeft was still only Detroit's third starter in terms of starts and innings, but he led the AL with seven shutouts on his way to a 16–7, 2.99 record and a spot on the AL All-Star team. In 1956 Hoeft became the first Tiger lefthander since Hal Newhouser to win 20 games, posting a 20–14 mark, but after mediocre seasons in 1957–58, Hoeft returned to the bullpen for the balance of his career.

He was traded to the Red Sox for Ted Lepcio and Dave Sisler in May, 1959, then shipped to Baltimore for Jack Harshman six weeks later. Hoeft enjoyed his best seasons in relief with the Orioles, recording a 2.02 ERA in 1961 and four wins plus seven saves in 1962, then was traded to the Giants and later to the Braves, spending single seasons with each club. On July 14, 1957 Hoeft hit two of his three career home runs. /(SCL)

Joe Hoerner — 1936– . LHP 1963–64, 66–77 Astros, **Cardinals**, Phillies, Braves, Royals, Rangers, Reds 563 ip, 39–34, 2.99. *2 WS, 5 ip, 0–1, 8.44*
☛ *All-Star—70.*

A clubhouse prankster and top short reliever, Hoerner blossomed after a weak heart forced him to switch to a less taxing sidearm delivery. His highest ERA in the years 1966–71 was 2.89. He recorded career bests of 17 saves and a 1.47 ERA for the Cardinals in 1968; on June 1, he tied a NL record for consecutive strikeouts by a relief pitcher, with six. In 1969 Hoerner was involved in the celebrated Curt Flood trade. Though Flood did not report to the Phillies, Hoerner did, and led the NL with nine relief wins in 1970. He retired with 99 career saves, and Hank Aaron never got a hit off him in 22 career at-bats. /(JCA)

Frank Hoerst (Lefty) — 1917– . LHP 1940–42, 46–47 **Phillies** 348 ip, 10–33, 5.17

Hoerst went 3–10 in 1941, but two of the victories came over the pennant-winning Dodgers. In 1944 he broke an ankle while coaching a high school basketball team. /(NLM)

Fred Hoey — 1885–1932. *Broadcaster.*

In 1926 the president of the Yankee Radio Network decided that every major sporting event in New England should be broadcast by a recognized authority. Hoey, who saw his first baseball game in the 1897 Temple Cup Series, worked all Boston home games until he died. During winters he held an executive position at the Boston Garden. In 1931 Fenway Park fans honored him with a special day. /(NLM)

Bill Hoffer — 1870–1959. RHP 1895–99, 1901 **Baltimore (NL)**, Pirates, Indians 1254 ip, 91–47, 3.75. 20 wins: 1895–97

Baltimore's Bill Hoffer led the National League with winning percentages of .811 (30–7) in 1895 and .781 (25–7) in 1896. When the American League was recognized as a major league in 1901, Hoffer became the AL's first pitcher; he issued the first walk, got the first strikeout, and was tagged with the first loss as Cleveland dropped an 8–2 decision to Chicago on April 24, 1901. He won just three games in that, his final ML season. /(ME)

Danny Hoffman — 1880–1922. OF 1903–11 A's, **Yankees**, **Browns** 828 g, .256, 13 hr, 235 rbi. *1 WS, 1 g, .000*

The lefthanded-hitting Hoffman was considered a top A's prospect in 1904 when a pitch from Boston southpaw Jesse Tannehill hit him in the eye. He never recovered enough vision to stand in against lefthanded pitching. He was the American League's 1905 stolen-base champ, with 46, and stole 185 bases in his career. /(NLM)

Glenn Hoffman — 1958– . SS-3B 1980–87 **Red Sox**, Dodgers 718 g, .244, 22 hr, 207 rbi

After hitting .285 in 114 games as a rookie third baseman in 1980, Hoffman was shifted to shortstop in 1981 when the Red Sox acquired Carney Lansford. He started at shortstop in Boston in 1982–83 and again in 1985, but he spent almost all of 1986 on the DL and didn't make the Red Sox' postseason roster. /(SCL)

Guy Hoffman — 1956– . LHP 1979–80, 83, 86–88 **White Sox**, Cubs, Reds, Rangers 339 ip, 17–17, 4.25

Just 5'9", Hoffman was not drafted after college but was signed by the White Sox in 1978 while playing in a Peoria, IL weekend league. He went 8–0 in the minors, was promoted to Chicago in less than a year, and was 0–5 as a rookie reliever. After spending much of 1981–85 in Triple-A, he went 6–2 for the 1986 Cubs and, despite elbow problems, produced a 9–10 mark for the 1987 Reds. /(JCA)

Bobby Hofman — 1925– . 2B-1B-3B-C 1949, 52–57 **Giants** 341 g, .248, 32 hr, 101 rbi

Hofman, the nephew of Circus Solly Hofman, had nine career pinch HR. A useful utility infielder who even made 26 appearances at catcher, he continued to show versatility later when, as a coach for budget-minded Charles O. Finley, he doubled as the Oakland A's traveling secretary. /(RTM)

Solly Hofman [Arthur Frederick] (Circus Solly) — 1894–1956. OF-2B-1B-SS 1903–16 Pirates, **Cubs**, Brooklyn (FL), Buffalo (FL), Yankees 1194 g, .269, 19 hr, 495 rbi. *3 WS, 16 g, .298, 8 rbi*

Hofman was the slick centerfielder and general handyman for the four Cub pennant-winners of 1906–08 and 1910. His teammates called him Circus Solly because of his many "circus" catches in the outfield. Hofman was a timely hitter and good baserunner. His best season was 1910 when he hit .325 and had 86 RBI.

In the "Merkle Boner" game of 1908 against the Giants, it was Hofman who retrieved Al Bridwell's single and called to second baseman Johnny Evers that Merkle had failed to touch second. His throw from the outfield sailed over Evers' head but was eventually retrieved for the forceout that ended the game in a tie. The Cubs won the makeup game and the pennant. According to baseball historian Paddy Keough, a friend of Hofman, the throw got past Evers because Circus Solly could not resist clowning, even on that crucial play, and threw a curveball to Evers. /(BC)

Fred Hofmann (Bootnose) — 1894–1964. C 1919–25, 27–28 **Yankees**, Red Sox 378 g, .247, 7 hr, 93 rbi. *1 WS, 2 g, .000*

Hofmann's 36 years in organized baseball started as the Yankees' backup catcher at the beginning of their dynasty. He was a pennant-winning minor league manager and coached 12 years for the Browns. When the team moved to Baltimore, he went along as a scout. /(JK)

Shanty Hogan [James Francis] — 1906–1967. C 1925–37 Braves, **Giants**, Senators 989 g, .295, 61 hr, 474 rbi

Nicknamed for his physical resemblance to a small hut, the 6'1" 240-lb Hogan was an excellent target behind the plate as well as a solid hitter. Traded to the Giants with Jimmy Welsh for Rogers Hornsby in January 1928, Hogan hit .333, the first of four consecutive .300 seasons, and was one of seven Giants regulars to hit .300 that year. Sold back to the Braves for the 1933 season, he shook off public criticism of his weight to record 120 consecutive errorless games, 18 shy of the NL record for catchers. /(JK)

Bill Hogg (Buffalo Bill) — 1880–1909. RHP 1905–08 **Yankees** 730 ip, 37–50, 3.06

The Highlanders' number-three or number-four starter for his entire stay in the majors, Hogg was wild with above-average ERAs. He had two winning records, 14–13 in 1906 and 10–8 in 1907. /(JFC)

Brad Hogg — 1888–1935. RHP 1911–12, 15, 18–19 Braves, Cubs, **Phillies** 448 ip, 20–29, 3.70

Seven years after his first of three short major league trials, Hogg won 13 games for the 1918 Phillies, tying for the staff high. A graduate of Mercer University, Hogg was a lawyer. /(NLM)

Chief Hogsett [Elon Chester] — 1903– . LHP 1929–38, 44 **Tigers**, Browns, Senators 1222 ip, 63–87, 5.02. *2 WS, 8 ip, 0–0, 1.08*

Dubbed with the nickname accorded anyone with Indian ancestry, the half-Cherokee was a successful reliever for the Tigers during the early 1930s, twice leading the AL in relief wins (1932, 1935). His work helped Detroit to pennants in 1934 and '35. He left the majors after 1938 and pitched six years of AAA ball before being recalled by the Tigers for a brief wartime stint. /(JK)

Bobby Hogue — 1921– . RHP 1948–52 **Braves**, Browns, Yankees 327 ip, 18–16, 3.97. *1 WS, 3 ip, 0–0, 0.00*

Hogue compiled an 8–2 record as a relief pitcher for the pennant-winning 1948 Boston Braves. He saw no action in the World Series that year, but he did appear twice for the Yankees in the 1951 Series. /(FK)

Cal Hogue — 1927– . RHP 1952–54 **Pirates** 114 ip, 2–10, 4.91

From 1945 to 1953, Hogue pitched for 10 different teams in 10 different leagues, only once winning as many as 10 games. In three trials with Pittsburgh, he walked almost twice as many batters as he struck out. /(ME)

Ken Holcombe — 1918– . RHP 1945, 48, 50–53 Yankees, Reds, **White Sox**, Browns, Red Sox 375 ip, 18–32, 3.98

Holcombe showed promise as a reliever with the Yankees in 1945 but bursitis sent him back to the minors. He reemerged as the White Sox' fourth starter in the 1950s and posted an 11–12 mark in 1951. The bursitis reappeared the next season and eventually ended his career. /(RL)

Fred Holdsworth — 1952– . RHP 1972–74, 76–78, 80 Tigers, **Orioles**, Expos, Brewers 183 ip, 7–10, 4.38

Control artist Holdsworth was an effective relief pitcher in a partial season for Baltimore in 1976, winning four and saving two with a 2.03 ERA. /(MC)

Walter Holke (Union Man) — 1892–1954. 1B 1914, 16–25 Giants, **Braves**, Phillies, Reds 1212 g, .287, 24 hr, 487 rbi. *1 WS, 6 g, .286, 1 rbi*

A sure-handed first baseman with a reliable bat, Holke played most of his career with losing teams. In the Braves' 26-inning tie with Brooklyn in 1920, he made 42 putouts at first base. Though he played at a time when players often tried to intimidate umpires with aggressive arguing, the mild-mannered Holke played 11 ML seasons without being thrown out of a game and stretched his record to 20 pro seasons before he was given the boot as a manager in the Three-Eye League. /(JK)

Al Holland — 1952– . LHP 1977, 79–87 Pirates, **Giants**, Phillies, Angels, Yankees 646 ip, 34–30, 2.98. *1 LCS, 3 ip, 0–0, 0.00. 1 WS, 4 ip, 0–0, 0.00* ☛ *All-Star—84.*

"Gimme the ball!" is what Al Holland wants his epitaph to say. A career reliever with an excellent fastball, he finished his rookie season with a 1.76 ERA and seven saves for the Giants in 1980, but was always part of a bullpen-by-committee in San Francisco.

Traded with Joe Morgan to the Phillies for Mark Davis and Mike Krukow, Holland became their stopper in 1983. His 25 saves plus two more in the postseason helped them to the World Series, where they lost to the Orioles. He saved a career-high 29 games in 1984, but also lost 10, as his ERA jumped to 3.39 and his fastball grew more hittable. He would notch only five more saves before being released by the Yankees early in 1987. /(SG)

Bill Holland — 1901–Unk. RHP-MGR Negro Leagues 1920–41 Detroit Stars, Chicago American Giants, New York Lincoln Giants, Brooklyn Royal Giants, **New York Black Yankees**, Philadelphia Stars statistics not available
☛ *All-Star—39.*

Holland was the mainstay of the New York Black Yankees' pitching staff in the 1930s. Of his 22 years in baseball, 18 were spent in New York. He was the first black pitcher to pitch in Yankee Stadium when he beat the Baltimore Elite Giants before a crowd of 15,000 in 1930.

The 5'8" 175-lb Holland joined his first pro team, the Detroit Stars, in 1920. In 1922 he led the league with 16 wins. Hall of Famer Cool Papa Bell ranked Holland with Satchel Paige, Smokey Joe Williams, and Bullet Joe Rogan as the best pitchers in the Negro Leagues. Though he relied mainly on the fastball, he also expertly mixed in a curve, a drop, a changeup, and an occasional emery ball. /(PG)

Ed Holley — 1899–1986. RHP 1928, 32–34 Cubs, **Phillies**, Pirates 548 ip, 25–40, 4.40

Holley led the 1932–33 Phillies pitching staff in starts and complete games and won a club-high 13 in 1933. He was sold to Pittsburgh after a 1–8 start in 1934. /(ME)

Bug Holliday [James Wear] — 1867–1910. OF 1889–98 Cincinnati (AA), **Reds** 929 g, .316, 65 hr, 617 rbi. *Umpire* NL 1903
☛ *Led League—hr 1889, 92 .*

Holliday tied for the 1889 American Association home run title, with 19, while batting .343 as a rookie for Cincinnati. From 1890 to 1894 he was the Reds' centerfielder, and in 1892 he captured the National League HR crown, with 13. His last season as a regular, '94, was his finest, as he again hit 13 HR, batted a career-high .383 and drove in 119 runs. He returned to the NL as an umpire in 1903. /(AJA)

Al Hollingsworth (Boots) — 1908– . LHP 1935–40, 42–46 Reds, Phillies, Dodgers, Senators, **Browns**, White Sox 1520 ip, 70–104, 3.99. *1 WS, 4 ip, 0–0, 2.25*

Hollingsworth split 11 seasons between starting and relieving, never winning more than a dozen games. On May 28, 1938 he hit a grand slam off the Cardinals' Lon Warneke. He later became a minor league manager and served two stints as a Cardinals coach. /(WAB)

Charlie Hollocher — 1896–1940. SS 1918–24 **Cubs** 760 g, .304, 14 hr, 241 rbi. *1 WS, 6 g, .190*

When healthy, Hollocher was a first-rate shortstop. He took part in two triple plays and twice led the league in fielding average. The lefthanded hitter batted second and seldom struck out. He led the NL with 161 hits and 509 at-bats as a rookie in 1918, and his .340 in 1922 was the highest mark for a shortstop since Honus Wagner's .354 in 1908. He never fulfilled his great promise due to recurrent illness, and committed suicide at age 44. /(ADS)

Bobo Holloman [Alva Lee] — 1925–1987. RHP 1953 **Browns** 65 ip, 3–7, 5.23

Holloman was the third pitcher in major league history, after Charlie Jones and Ted Breitenstein, to throw a no-hitter in his first start. After he had bounced around the Cubs' farm system, Holloman's contract was purchased by the lowly St. Louis Browns prior to the 1953 season. His early appearances with them, all in relief, yielded an ERA close to 9.00. Undaunted, the confident Holloman pestered manager Marty Marion to give him a chance as a starter. He took the mound in that capacity for the first time on the rainy night of May 6, 1953 before a hometown crowd of 2,473 and no-hit the Athletics 6–0. The 29-year-old rookie embellished his performance with three RBI and his only two hits in the majors. He never pitched another complete game in his major league career, which was over before the end of 1953.

Holloman was a colorful personality who stopped at the foul line each time he pitched to scratch the initials of his wife and son in the dirt. Brown's owner Bill Veeck said of him, "He had charm and he had humor and he had unlimited confidence in himself." /(CR)

Ken Holloway [born Kenneth Eugene Hollaway] — 1897–1968. RHP 1922–30 **Tigers**, Indians, Yankees 1160 ip, 64–52, 4.40

"As a handler of men, Ty Cobb is cruel, autocratic, and entirely without sympathy," said Holloway, a Tiger curveballer. "Cobb made his pitchers throw a beanball. One day I ignored his order to throw at Joe Judge. Even though I got Judge to pop up, it cost me a hundred dollar fine." Holloway's best seasons were 1924 (14–6), when his nine relief wins led the AL, and 1925 (13–4). /(NLM)

Wattie Holm [Roscoe Albert] — 1901–1950 OF-3B-C 1924–29, 32 **Cardinals** 436 g, .275, 6 hr, 174 rbi. *2 WS, 8 g, .136, 2 rbi*

Holm was signed as a schoolboy by the Cardinals. Normally an outfielder, he eventually played every position during his pro career. One of his three home runs in 1928 was a pinch hit grand slam. /(JL)

Brian Holman — 1965– . RHP 1988– **Expos**, Mariners 132 ip, 5–10, 3.61

One of several Expos rookies in 1988 who had a losing record despite pitching well, Holman was traded to the Mariners in May 1989 and moved into the Mariners' rotation. /(SFS)

Scott Holman — 1958– . RHP 1980, 82–83 **Mets** 134 ip, 3–8, 3.34

The muscular Californian was a power pitcher with chronic shoulder problems. He was 1–7 in 35 appearances for the Mets in 1983, his only complete ML season. /(JCA)

Ducky Holmes [James William] — 1869–1932. OF 1895–99, 1901–05 Louisville (NL), Giants, Cardinals, **Baltimore (NL)**, Tigers, Senators, White Sox 932 g, .282, 17 hr, 374 rbi

The chunky Iowan insulted a Jewish club owner with an ethnic slur, leading to a lengthy clash between NL owners. One of his suspensions, for verbal abuse of an umpire, is cited as the start of the feud between AL founders Ban Johnson and Charles Comiskey. A fine hitter and basestealer, he once played for four teams in two years because he was such a troublemaker. /(DB)

Tommy Holmes (Kelly) — 1917– . OF 1942–52 **Braves**, Dodgers 1320 g, .302, 88 hr, 581 rbi. *2 WS, 9 g, .185, 1 rbi.*
    Manager 1951–52 **Braves** 61–69, .469
☛ *Led League—hr 45.*

Braves right fielder Holmes hit safely in a 20th-century NL record 37 straight games, from June 6 through July 8 of his 1945 *TSN* MVP season. That year, he hit .352 with 117 RBI, 125 runs, and 15 stolen bases, and had league highs of 47 doubles, 224 hits, a .577 slugging average, and 28 HR; he is the only player ever to lead a league in home runs and fewest strikeouts (9) in the same season. But these totals were all career highs, and though he batted over .300 in his next three seasons, he never

again managed more than nine homers or 79 RBI. Appointed the Braves' manager in mid-1951, Holmes was fired early in 1952, finishing up as a Dodger pinch hitter. When Pete Rose broke his hitting-streak record in 1978, a tearful Holmes thanked him "for making people remember me." /(MC)

Tommy Holmes — 1904–1975. *Writer.*

Holmes, who was handicapped by the loss of an arm as a youth, became one of the foremost baseball writers in the country. He covered the Dodgers for over 30 years, starting with the Brooklyn *Eagle* in 1926 and later moving to the New York *Herald-Tribune*. He was president of the BBWAA in 1947 and wrote several books, including *The Dodgers*. He was given the J.G. Taylor Spink Award in 1979. /(NLM)

Jim Holt — 1944– . OF-1B 1968–76 **Twins**, A's 707 g, .265, 19 hr, 177 rbi. *3 LCS, 8 g, .125. 1 WS, 4 g, .667, 2 rbi*

After hitting .266 and .259 as a platoon player for Minnesota in 1970–71, Vietnam veteran Holt was sent down to the Pacific Coast League. Recalled in '73, he hit .297 and knocked 11 homers in 132 games. When he slumped the next year, he was traded to the A's. At Oakland he was mainly a pinch hitter, leading the AL in pinch at-bats and hits in 1975. /(MC)

Brian Holton — 1959– . RHP 1985– **Dodgers**, Orioles 313 ip, 18–16, 3.45. *1 LCS, 4 ip, 0–0, 2.25. 1 WS, 2 ip, 0–0, 0.00*

Curveballer Holton spent nine seasons in the minors, including six at Albuquerque (Pacific Coast League), before finally reaching the ML, and found his niche as a middle-inning reliever in the Dodgers' 1988 World Championship season. He saved Game Five of the NLCS against the Mets and pitched two scoreless innings in the World Series opener, helping the Dodgers to stay close in the game won by Kirk Gibson's famous ninth-inning pinch homer. The Dodgers quickly converted his newly-established value and traded him to the Orioles that winter in the Eddie Murray deal. /(TG)

Jerome Holtzman — 1926– . *Writer.*

Senior baseball writer and columnist for the Chicago *Sun-Times* and a weekly contributor the *The Sporting News* for many years, Holtzman has written more than 100 articles for other publications. He is baseball advisor for the *Encyclopaedia Britannica* and sports editor for the *Britannica Yearbook*. For the *Official Baseball Guide*, Holtzman writes a 25,000-word review of the year, intended as a historical record. His books include *No Cheering in the Press Box*, *Three and Two* (a biography of umpire Tom Gorman), and *Fielder's Choice*, an anthology of baseball fiction. /(NLM)

Ken Holtzman — 1945- . LHP 1965–79 **Cubs**, A's, Orioles, Yankees 2867 ip, 174–150, 3.49. 20 wins: 73 *4 LCS, 35 ip, 2–3, 2.06. 3 WS, 35 ip, 4–1, 2.55* ☛ *All-Star—72, 73.*

Holtzman was christened "The New Koufax" as a 20-year-old rookie in 1966, and Cubs fans hoped their hard-throwing, Jewish lefthander would rival the achievements of the retiring Dodger ace. Holtzman never did, of course, but he did pitch two no-hitters with the Cubs and was an excellent ML starter for over a decade, helping the A's to three consecutive World Championships in 1972–74. He had outstanding control as well as a lively fastball, and he preferred inducing batters to hit the ball into outs rather than simply trying to overpower them.

Holtzman brought the Koufax comparisons upon himself on September 25, 1966, when he squared off against the Hall of Famer for the first and only time. Holtzman was on his way to an 11–16 rookie season while Koufax was in the final weeks of his career, and on that day Holtzman took a no-hitter into the ninth inning before settling for a 2–1 win. He was a perfect 9–0 in 1967, but spent most of the season in military service. He was a disappointing 11–14, 3.35 in 1968. Still only 23 in 1969, Holtzman was 17–13 for the second-place Cubs and tossed six shutouts, including a 3–0 no-hitter against the Braves August 19. Less than two years later he pitched a second no-hitter, beating the Reds 1–0 on June 3, 1971, but he finished the season 9–15, 4.48 and was traded to the A's for outfielder Rick Monday.

Joining a rotation that already included Catfish Hunter, Blue Moon Odom, and Vida Blue, Holtzman helped Oakland over the top in 1972, going 19–11, 2.51 as the A's won the first of three consecutive WS. In 1973 he was 21–13, 2.97, won Game Three of the LCS 2–1 with an 11-inning complete game, and won Game Seven of the WS against the Mets. And in 1974 he was 19–17, 3.07, tossed a shutout in the LCS, and won Game Four of the WS. He won 18 games in 1975, but lost twice in the LCS as Oakland was swept by Boston, and in 1976 he was traded with Reggie Jackson to the Orioles for Don Baylor, Mike Torrez, and Paul Mitchell. He lasted less than half a season in

Baltimore before being traded to the Yankees in a 10-player blockbuster that brought Rudy May, Tippy Martinez, Scott McGregor, and Rick Dempsey to the Orioles in exchange for Doyle Alexander, Elrod Hendricks, and Grant Jackson. In 1978 the Yankees dealt him back to the Cubs for reliever Ron Davis. /(SCL)

John Holway — 1929- . *Writer.*

A graduate of the University of Iowa and Georgetown, Holway has worked for the U.S. Information Agency since 1956. A historian of black baseball, he wrote *Voices of the Great Black Baseball Leagues* (1975). /(NLM)

Rick Honeycutt — 1954- . LHP 1977- Mariners, Rangers, **Dodgers**, A's 1858 ip, 95–125, 3.76. *4 LCS, 7 ip, 1–0, 16.19. 2 WS, 6 ip, 1–0, 3.00* ☛ *Led League—era 83. All-Star—80, 83.*

Honeycutt began his roller-coaster ML career as a bright young prospect for the Mariners, then was traded to the Rangers in an 11-player deal before the 1981 season. He collapsed from 11–6, 3.30 in 1981 to 5–17, 5.27 in 1982, but won the AL Comeback of the Year award in 1983, leading the AL in ERA even though he finished the season with the NL Dodgers. A control pitcher, Honeycutt enjoyed three solid seasons in Los Angeles before beginning the 1987 season 2–12 and being traded to Oakland for Tim Belcher. He reestablished himself as a set-up man in the A's bullpen, and in 1988 he won Game One of the LCS and Game Two of the WS in relief.

Honeycutt was an All-American first baseman at the University of Tennessee, and hit .301 in his first pro season while playing first base and shortstop in addition to pitching. In 1980 he was ejected from a game when an umpire found a tack inside a bandage on his finger. /(TG)

Donald Honig — 1931- . *Writer.*

Novelist Honig is among the most prolific factual baseball book writers ever. His publications include: *Baseball When the Grass Was Real* (1975), *Baseball Between the Lines* (1976), *Man in the Dugout* (1977), *The Last Great Season* (1979), *October Heroes* (1979), *Image of Their Greatness* (1979), and *100 Greatest Baseball Players of All Time* (1980). In the 1980s, he has focused on coffee table-style illustrated histories, producing over a dozen. /(NLM)

Jim Honochick — 1917– . *Umpire AL 1949–73*
1 LCS 6 WS 5 ASU

A sore arm caused Honochick to turn from being a
minor league outfielder to umpiring in 1946. The
highlight of his 25 ML seasons, he claims, was
working behind the plate in the Seventh Game of
the 1955 WS when Brooklyn's Johnny Podres beat
the Yankees, 2–0. Honochick gained fame in the
1980s for his myopic self-portrayal in a Miller Lite
beer commercial with Boog Powell. /(RTM)

Don Hood — 1949– . LHP 1973–80, 82–83 Orioles,
Indians, Yankees, Cardinals, Royals 847 ip, 34–35, 3.79

Hood was Baltimore's number-one draft selection in
June 1969. He allowed just one HR in 57 innings in
1974. Both a starter and reliever, he worked a
career-high 155 innings with Cleveland in
1978. /(JCA)

Jay Hook [James Wesley] — 1936– . RHP 1957–64
Reds, Mets 752 ip, 29–62, 5.23

A bonus player signed by the Reds out of Northwestern, he seemed to be hitting his stride until
mumps laid him low in 1960. Ineffective the next
year, he was acquired by the expansion Mets in
1962 and pitched the first game won by the team
(after they'd lost their first nine). After receiving his
masters degree in thermodynamics, he retired at
twenty-eight to take a job with Chrysler. /(JK)

Harry Hooper — 1887–1974. OF 1909–25 **Red Sox**,
White Sox 2308 g, .281, 75 hr, 817 rbi. *4 WS, 24 g, .293,
2 hr, 6 rbi*
☛ *Hall of Fame—1971.*

Hooper prided himself on being a college man of
high ideals during an era when most ballplayers
weren't, and he nearly became a civil engineer
before the lure of big money led him to sign with the
Red Sox for $2,850 in 1909. Extremely popular
with teammates, fans, and even opponents, he was
the right fielder in the fabled "Million Dollar
Outfield" with Tris Speaker and Duffy Lewis. He
taught himself to play the difficult sun field and
invented the famous rump slide to snare short flies
and stop with his body those he could not reach. His
strong, accurate arm accounted for 150 of the trio's
455 assists. Hooper never led the American League
in any of the important offensive categories, but he
did compile a valuable .403 on-base average as the
Red Sox leadoff hitter from 1909 to 1920, and

Harry Hooper

became the Red Sox' all-time leader in triples with
130 and in stolen bases with 300. He went on to
collect 2,466 hits over 17 seasons.

The strongly religious Hooper was reputed to
have prayed for a Boston victory in the final game of
the 1912 Series and to have attributed to divine
intervention his bare-handed, game-saving catch off
Larry Doyle which prevented victory by the Giants.
Years later at an old-timers' game, Doyle was asked
if he remembered Hooper and replied, "How in hell
can I ever forget him!" In 1915 Hooper became the
first player to hit two homers in a single World
Series game.

Recalling his years with the Red Sox, Hooper told
Lawrence Ritter that it was he who convinced
manager Ed Barrow to move young Babe Ruth to
the outfield on the days when Ruth was not pitching
in order to exploit Ruth's crowd appeal and ability
as a slugger. That was in 1919, shortly before owner
Harry Frazee sold off his best players, including
Ruth, for cash. Disgusted by the sales, Hooper held

out for a salary of $15,000. Frazee dealt Hooper for cash and two reserve outfielders to the Chicago White Sox, whose owner, Charlie Comiskey, hoped that the acquisition of a big-name player would restore credibility to his franchise, which had been shattered by the Black Sox scandal. The unhappy Hooper threatened to retire, but finally joined the White Sox for a salary of $13,250 which he told Comiskey he would accept as a goodwill gesture toward the new club. Five years later, when the White Sox had seemingly righted themselves with an influx of young talent, Comiskey reduced Hooper's salary to a stingy $7,000.

Hooper retired to enter the booming real estate market. He later coached baseball at Princeton and was the postmaster of Capitola, California. In 1971 Hooper was elected to the Hall of Fame by the Veterans Committee. /(CR)

Bob Hoopere — 1922-80. RHP 1950-55 **A's**, Indians, Reds 621 ip, 40-41, 4.80

Canadian-born Hoopere won 15 games as a rookie with the last-place 1950 Philadelphia Athletics, who won only 52 games that year. After one more good season in 1951 (12-10), Hoopere developed arm trouble. He spent two more seasons with the A's before becoming a relatively obscure member of the great 1954 Cleveland pitching staff. /(MA)

Burt Hooton (Happy) — 1950- . RHP 1971-85 Cubs, **Dodgers**, Rangers 2651 ip, 151-136, 3.38. *3 LCS, 21 ip, 2-0, 3.00 3 WS, 32 ip, 3-3, 3.69* ☛ *All-Star—81.*

Hooton acquired the ironic nickname Happy from Tommy Lasorda for never looking the part. After going 35-3 for the University of Texas, he signed with the Cubs for $50,000 in 1971 and went straight to Tacoma, where his 19-strikeout game tied a 66-year-old Pacific Coast League record. In his first three ML games, in September of that year, he held opposing hitters to a .111 average and struck out 15 in one game. The following April 16, he no-hit the Phillies in his fourth ML start. His performance steadily declined with the Cubs, but he responded to a 1975 trade to the Dodgers by winning his final 12 decisions, finishing 18-9. His unusual knuckle curve made him a mainstay of baseball's best rotation through nine seasons and three pennants. He peaked at 19-10 in 1978. During the prolonged 1981 postseason he went 4-1 with a 0.82 ERA and defeated the Yankees in the final game of the WS. /(TG)

Joe Hoover — 1915-1965. SS 1943-45 **Tigers** 338 g, .243, 5 hr, 84 rbi. *1 WS, 1 g, .333*

Hoover was the Tigers shortstop in 1943-45 while all three Detroit shortstops from 1942—Billy Hitchcock, Johnny Lipon, and Murray Franklin -were in the military. His last ML appearance came in Game Six of the 1945 World Series. Hoover drove a run in during that game, which Detroit won 8-7 in extra innings. /(JCA)

Gail Hopkins — 1943- . 1B 1968-74 **White Sox**, Royals, Dodgers 514 g, .266, 25 hr, 145 rbi

Signed as a catcher, the stocky contact hitter mostly played first base and pinch hit during his seven ML seasons, then pursued a medical career. The left-handed hitter was tough to strike out, fanning only 83 times in 1,219 at-bats (6.8%). /(JCA)

Johnny Hopp (Cotney, Hippity) — 1916- . OF-1B 1939-52 **Cardinals**, Braves, Pirates, Dodgers, Yankees, Tigers 1393 g, .296, 46 hr, 458 rbi. *5 WS, 16 g, .160* ☛ *All-Star—46.*

Hopp's cotton-colored hair led to the nickname Cotney, used by friends and teammates; the press preferred the alliterative Hippity. He played with abandon typical of the Cardinals Gashouse Gang, diving into bases head first as Pepper Martin had before him. 1941 was Hopp's first season as a regular, when he subbed at first base for an injured Johnny Mize. Hopp was so successful (.303) that St. Louis traded Mize to the Giants. Hopp hit .336 as the 1944 World Champion Cardinals' centerfielder, leading NL outfielders with a .997 fielding percentage. He batted a career-high .339 in 1950 with Pittsburgh and the Yankeees. /(JK)

Tsuneo Horiuchi (Bad Boy Taro) — 1948- . P 1966-81 **Yomiuri Giants**

One of the Yomiuri Giants' top pitchers throughout the late 1960s and 1970s, Horiuchi became better known for his mouth and flamboyance than for his arm. Winning 12 consecutive games as an 18-year-old rookie, he proclaimed himself a superstar, refused to bow respectfully to elder players, argued with management, goofed off in exhibition games, spat while on television, and shamefully let his cap fall off during his follow-through. He went on to taunt rivals and discuss their shortcomings with uncommon candor throughout his career. He pitched his way back into the good graces of Japanese fans in a disastrous 1971 postseason series against the Baltimore Orioles as one Japanese pitcher with whom the Orioles had trouble. /(MC)

Joe Horlen [Joel Edward] — 1937- . RHP 1961-72 **White Sox**, A's 2001 ip, 116-117, 3.11. *1 LCS, 0 ip, 0-1, 1 WS, 1 ip, 0-0, 6.75*
☛ *Led League—era 67. All-Star—67.*

Tobacco made Horlen sick. The cure was a wad of Kleenex; Horlen swirled the stuff around in his mouth the day he no-hit the Tigers, September 10, 1967. Four years earlier, against Washington on July 29, 1963, he had carried a no-hitter into the ninth. With one out, Chuck Hinton dribbled a single into center, and with two out, Don Lock drilled a hanging curve to the outer reaches of RFK Stadium. The memory of that game seemed to cast a pall on "Hard Luck Horlen," who posted a 1.88 ERA the next season, but had to settle for a 13-9 record. His glory year was 1967, but even a 19-7 record with the AL's highest winning percentage (.731) and lowest ERA (2.06) did not translate into a Cy Young award. The honor went to Jim Lonborg (22-9, 3.16) of the pennant-winning Red Sox. /(RL)

Bob Horner — 1957- . 3B-1B 1978-86, 88 **Braves**, Cardinals 1020 g, .277, 218 hr, 685 rbi. *1 LCS, 3 g, .091*
☛ *Rookie of the Year—78. All-Star—82.*

Bob Horner went straight from Arizona State University to Atlanta's starting line-up with impressive but ultimately disappointing results. He was a second baseman on *TSN*'s College All-America team in 1977 and 1978, signed for a $175,000 bonus with the Braves, hit a home run in his first major league game, and won Rookie of the Year honors. A steady home run hitter, Horner fought weight and injury problems. Slow, with poor range, he moved from third to first in 1985. A dead-pull streak hitter and slow starter, Horner played for the Yakult Swallows of Japan in 1987 after playing out his option with the Braves. He was signed by the Cardinals in 1988 to replace their departed slugger Jack Clark. Horner tied a major league record with a four-home run game in 1986. /(ME)

Rogers Hornsby (Rajah) — 1896-1963. 2B-SS 1915-37 **Cardinals**, Giants, Braves, Cubs, Browns 2259 g, .358, 301 hr, 1584 rbi. *2 WS, 12 g, .245, 5 rbi.*
    *Manager 1925-26, 28, 30-37, 52-53 Cardinals, Braves, Cubs, **Browns**, Reds 680-798, .460. 1 WS, 4-3, .571*
☛ *Most Valuable Player—25, 29. Led League—ba 20-25, 28. Led League—hr 22, 25. Led League—rbi 20-22, 25. Hall of Fame—1942.*

Baseball's greatest righthanded hitter always stood in the far back corner of the batter's box and strode into the pitch with a perfectly level swing. Catchers frequently called low and away against him, but his diagonal stride brought those pitches comfortably within reach. High and inside, he said, was hardest to hit, because his move edged him so close to the pitch. Often he simply leaned away, and umpires who respected his judgment of the strike zone would call a ball.

At the plate, Hornsby was imperturbable. He never argued with umpires, and was never thrown out of a game. He hit line drives to all fields, and was swift down to first and going for extra bases. His power was formidable; he led his league four times in doubles, once in triples, and twice in home runs, and his 289 HR as a second baseman are an all-time record. He hit safely in 33 consecutive games in 1922. Only thirteen players have amassed more than his 1,011 extra-base hits, and just six have topped his .577 career slugging average. Only Ty Cobb exceeded his .358 lifetime batting average, and no modern player (four did it before 1900) ever hit higher than his .424 in 1924. Since he could hit them all, he feared no pitcher. He disdained golf, he once explained, because when he hit a ball, he wanted someone else to chase it.

Hornsby came to the Cardinals as a shortstop, but was tried at third, and even in the outfield. By 1920 he was settled at second. No disgrace in the field, he led the NL in various categories, ending with a .957 career fielding average. As a shortstop in 1917 he tied a ML record with 14 assists in a game. He was known for the difficulty he had with pop flies, due to a balance problem when going back and looking up.

Outwardly, Hornsby was clearly made in the heroic mold. Handsome, dimpled, rosy-cheeked, forthright, professional, spirited, and motivated, he had the statistics to prove his preeminence. When Sam Breadon traded him to the Giants in 1926, following his first MVP year and at the height of his popularity as a World Series-winning player-manager, St. Louis rocked in a hurricane of protest. But

Rogers Hornsby

it, too. He received $100,000 even though every club in the league had to ante up to pay for it.

In New York, Hornsby had grudging admiration for manager John McGraw, and served as deputy manager in his absence. He won few friends among the players, however, and had no admiration at all for the management. Owner Charles Stoneham and his subordinates suffered the rough edge of Hornsby's tongue in public, and Stoneham was so angry that he took a fraction of the hero's value from the Braves to get rid of him after one season.

Boston liked him, and his .387 average, but could not refuse the Cubs' offer of $200,000 and five players in a trade after the 1928 season. The Rajah won his second MVP award in 1929 (.380, 39 HR, 149 RBI, and a league-leading 156 runs scored) as the Cubs took their first pennant since 1918. Hornsby was cool, distant, and professional with everyone, though still outspoken. A broken leg kept him out of action in 1930, and shortly before season's end he replaced Joe McCarthy as manager.

He led the Cubs to third place in 1931, batting .331, but was fired in mid-1932. A heel spur had kept him from playing much, but the club was doing well. Again, it was front-office trouble that got him ousted. Gambling on horses, a lifelong compulsion, had him in debt. Even scoldings by Commissioner Landis were received in chill silence or were bluntly rebuffed. Under Charlie Grimm, the club clinched the pennant, and its smoldering dislike for Hornsby ignited when the team did not vote him a World Series share.

Hornsby played out his career as a pinch hitter, hitting .300 for both St. Louis teams. He then managed the Browns and a succession of minor league teams. Bill Veeck brought him back in 1952 to manage the Browns again, and Gabe Paul gave him a shot with Cincinnati. In 1961 he scouted for the about-to-be New York Mets, and then he coached for them in 1962. Through it all, he never changed. He didn't smoke or drink, not even coffee. To preserve his unparalleled batting eye, he refused to read or go to the movies. He was an old-time lobby-sitter, and would talk endlessly about hitting to anyone who wanted to learn, though he never understood why ordinary players didn't become Hornsbys by heeding his instructions. /(ADS)

Rick Horton — 1959– . LHP 1984– **Cardinals**, White Sox, Dodgers 631 ip, 31–26, 3.68. *3 LCS, 10 ip, 0–0, 2.61. 2 WS, 7 ip, 0–0, 6.43*

In four years with the Cardinals, Horton was successful in long and short relief and starting. The soft

Breadon had had a bellyful of Hornsby. The other side of the man was a barbed-wire personality, cold, contentious, and brutally frank. He had a big problem dealing with authority. Owners and front-office men invariably saw him at his most belligerent. His hazel eyes locking into theirs, he told them to get out of his clubhouse, stop harassing his players, mind their own business, and leave him alone or get someone else to do the job.

For Breadon, already infuriated by his employee's verbal abuse, the last straw was a contract dispute. Hornsby wanted three years at $50,000 each. Breadon, always nervous about money, offered one year, lost patience with the impasse, and dealt him away for Frank Frisch and Jimmy Ring, a better trade for St. Louis than it first seemed. The Rajah then added insult to injury by pushing Breadon for top dollar for the 1,167 shares of Cardinal stock he had acquired at Branch Rickey's departure. He got thrower was best at working the corners and holding runners. His speed made him valuable as a pinch runner. /(FO)

Tony Horton — 1944– . 1B 1964–70 Red Sox, **Indians** 636 g, .268, 76 hr, 297 rbi

After hitting .278 with 27 HR and 93 RBI in 1969, the career of this promising hitter ended at age 25 the following year when a batting slump and booing fans led to such emotional distress that he had to be hospitalized. Horton hit three homers for Cleveland on May 24, 1970, but was reportedly upset because the Indians lost when he failed to hit a fourth. /(JCA)

Willie Horton — 1942– . OF-DH 1963–80 **Tigers**, Rangers, Indians, A's, Blue Jays, Mariners 2028 g, .273, 325 hr, 1163 rbi. *1 LCS, 5 g, .100. 1 WS, 7 g, .304, 1 hr, 3 rbi*
☛ *All-Star—65, 68, 70, 73.*

A short, squat, but immensely strong righthanded slugger, Horton battled weight problems throughout his ML career but was always one of the AL's most dangerous long-ball threats, hitting two home runs in a game 30 different times. He was the Tigers left fielder from 1965 to 1974, then became a designated hitter as he added both years and pounds, and in his final four ML seasons he played for six different AL clubs.

Horton stood barely 5'11", and early in his career he often reported to spring training weighing 220–230 lbs., where he would attempt to shed 20 lbs. to reach his playing weight. He was an All-Star in his first full ML season (1965), hitting .273 with 29 HR and 104 RBI, and hit 27 HR with 100 RBI the following year. An ankle problem hampered him in 1967, but he recovered from off-season surgery to hit .285 with 36 HR in 1968 as the Tigers captured the AL pennant. In the WS, he showed a surprisingly strong throwing arm, nailing Cardinals speedster Lou Brock at home plate on a key play in Game Five on the way to a seven-game Detroit victory. And in 1969 three of his 28 HR were grand slams.

Horton's home run production tailed off considerably from 1970 to 1974, but he hit .305 in 1970 and a career-high .316 in 1973. Then, in 1975, he became Detroit's full-time designated hitter and belted 25 HR. The Tigers traded Horton to Texas for Steve Foucault at the beginning of the 1977 season, and the Rangers shipped him to Cleveland with aborted phenom David Clyde for Tom Buskey and John Lowenstein before 1978. Horton was the DH for the Indians, A's, and Blue Jays at various times in 1978, then signed with the Mariners as a

free agent and played all 162 games in 1979, slugging 29 HR with 106 RBI. He retired after the 1980 season, fourth on the Tigers all-time home run list. /(SCL)

Al Horwits — 1903–Unk. *Writer.*

Horwits went from high school in 1920 to the baseball beat for the Philadelphia *Public Ledger*. His biggest scoop came in 1933, when he broke the story of the A's stars being sold three weeks before the official announcement. The *Public Ledger* folded in 1942, and Horwits worked for the Athletics for a few years. In 1945 he was president of the BBWAA. Later he worked in Hollywood as a publicist for Universal Pictures. /(NLM)

Dave Hostetler — 1956– . 1B-DH 1981–84, 88 Expos, **Rangers**, Pirates 255 g, .229, 37 hr, 124 rbi

Hostetler hit .232 with 22 HR and 67 RBI as the Rangers' primary first baseman in 1982, but struck out 113 times in 418 at-bats and saw less playing time thereafter. /(WOR)

Byron Houck — 1891–1969. RHP 1912–14, 18 **A's**, Brooklyn (FL), Browns 531 ip, 26–24, 3.30

With the Athletics, Houck was sometimes unbeatable, and sometimes walked virtually every batter he faced. He led the AL with eight relief wins in 1913, earning $2,100, and jumped to the Federal League in 1914. /(NLM)

Charlie Hough — 1948– . RHP 1970– Dodgers, **Rangers** 2888 ip, 174–157, 3.60. *3 LCS, 6 ip, 0–0, 5.68. 3 WS, 12 ip, 0–0, 4.38*
☛ *All-Star—86.*

Almost exclusively a reliever with the Dodgers, Charlie Hough became one of the greatest starting pitchers in Texas Rangers history. The knuckleballer led Texas in wins, complete games, and innings pitched each year from 1982 to 1987, winning a higher percentage of his club's victories than any other major league hurler those six years, and became the club's all-time leader in strikeouts, games pitched, wins, losses, innings pitched, and walks. In 1987 Charlie became the oldest pitcher in American League history to lead the league in starts and innings pitched, achieving career highs in wins, strikeouts, starts and innings at age 39. He also helped the Rangers set a major league record with 73 passed balls, contributing to 65 of them.

Originally signed as a third baseman, Hough learned the knuckler from Los Angeles scout Goldie Hold, with help from Hoyt Wilhelm, Jim Brewer, and Tom Lasorda. A middle-innings reliever with the Dodgers, Hough led the NL with 12 relief wins in 1976. He started just once from 1970 to 1978. /(ME)

Frank Hough — Unk.–1913. *Writer.*

Hough was a baseball writer for the Philadelphia *Inquirer* when Connie Mack arrived to launch the A's in 1901, and was one of two newspapermen given 25 percent of the team to help get it started. He later sold his interest in the club to Mack and became sporting editor of the *Inquirer.* /(NLM)

Ralph Houk (Major) — 1919– . C 1947–54 **Yankees** 91 g, .272, 0 hr, 20 rbi. *2 WS, 2 g, .500.*
    Manager 1961–63, 66–78, 81–84 **Yankees**, Tigers, Red Sox 1619–1531, .514. First place: 61–63 *3 WS, 8–8, .500*

After WWII combat duty, Houk debuted with the 1947 Yankees, hitting .272 in 41 games, before the arrival of Yogi Berra sent Houk back to the minors. He played only 50 more games in seven seasons as Berra's back-up. Following three years managing Denver (American Association) and three as a Yankee coach, he replaced Casey Stengel as Yankee manager in 1961, winning World Championships his first two seasons and adding a pennant in 1963. Kicked upstairs after the Dodgers swept the '63 WS, Houk served as Yankee vice president and general manager until May 1966. During that time, critical mistakes were made, notably keeping declining veterans until their trade value dissipated. Back on the field, Houk managed the Yankees (1966–73), the Tigers (1974–78), and the Red Sox (1981–84). After 20 years of managing, he stood tenth in games, wins, and losses, with a .514 winning percentage. A player favorite, Houk was never fired. Houk was named a Twins' vice president in November 1986, and his advice helped build the Twins' 1987 World Champions. /(MC)

Frank House [Henry Franklin] (Pig) — 1930– . C 1950–51, 54–61 **Tigers**, A's, Reds 653 g, .248, 47 hr, 235 rbi

This bonus baby was the Tigers' most active catcher from 1954 to 1957. The chunky, lefthanded-hitting Alabaman peaked in 1955 with 15 HR and 53 RBI in 102 games. He earned his nickname as a baby, when his family used to say he was "big as a house" and he twisted "big" into "pig." /(CC)

Tom House — 1947– . LHP 1971–78 **Braves**, Red Sox, Mariners 536 ip, 29–23, 3.79

The bespectacled reliever led Atlanta with 11 saves in both 1974 and '75. An extra in several movies and TV shows, House had his biggest moment in the spotlight on April 8, 1974, when he caught Hank Aaron's 715th home run in Atlanta's bullpen. He became the Rangers' pitching coach in 1985 and gained notoriety for having his pitchers throw footballs as a training routine. /(JCA)

Paul Householder — 1958– . OF 1980–87 **Reds**, Cardinals, Brewers, Astros 466 g, .236, 29 hr, 144 rbi

A switch-hitter with power in the minors who was said to have had all the tools, Householder was continually expected to blossom, but never did. With the Reds in 1983, his .991 fielding percentage led all NL outfielders. When Milwaukee's Robin Yount had surgery in September 1985, Householder, given a last chance to play every day, hit eight homers for the month. /(JCA)

Houston Astros [aka Colt .45s] — 1962– . Team. 2167–2306, .484. *NL West Champions 80, 86*

The Astros gave their name to Astroturf, the plastic grass that came into baseball because the real thing died indoors. It was a new problem, for the Astrodome was the first domed baseball park (opened in 1965), an attempt to avoid the Texas heat. The stadium was the brainchild of Astros owner Roy Hofheinz, who had a Texan's sense of size and spectacle.

    The club was originally to be in the proposed Continental League, an operation forestalled by the major leagues with the old tactic of offering the soundest owners new ML franchises. Unlike the Mets, the Astros (then called the Colt .45s) immediately went with youth under the direction of GM Paul Richards, a master talent evaluator. Products of the Astros' farm system in the 1960s included Joe Morgan and Rusty Staub. The strategy didn't make them instant contenders, like the AL's Angels, but it kept them above the Mets. The club reached the .500 level in the first year of divisional play, 1969, and contended off and on through the 1970s, which featured Cesar Cedeno, called "The New Willie Mays" by manager Leo Durocher. The arrival of overpowering pitcher J.R. Richard in 1976 made the team even stronger. He suffered a career-ending stroke in 1980, but the club went on to its first division title that year, led by franchise favorite Jose Cruz, the reacquired Morgan, and 20-game-winner

The 1980 Houston Astros

Joe Niekro. They finished in a tie with the Dodgers but won the one-game playoff. The team won the second half of the 1981 strike-split season, but this time the Dodgers prevailed in postseason play. Led by Cy Young winner and split-finger fastballer Mike Scott, the Astros captured another division title in 1986, but lost to the Mets in a storied LCS that featured Scott's MVP performance in a losing cause, Nolan Ryan's nine innings of two-hit, 12-strikeout pitching to a no-decision in Game Five as the Astros lost in 12 innings, and the climactic Game Six, a 16-inning topsy-turvy marathon won by New York./(WOR)

Art Houtteman (Hard Luck) — 1927– . RHP 1945–50, 52–57 **Tigers**, Indians, Orioles 1555 ip, 87–91, 4.14. *1 WS, 2 ip, 0–0, 4.50*
☛ *All-Star—50.*

Signed off the Detroit sandlots, Houtteman first appeared with the Tigers at 17. A fast learner with a sharp curve and deceptive sinker, he came back from a 2–16 season in 1948 to win 15 in 1949. He suffered a fractured skull that year but recovered to win 19 games in 1950. After a year in the army, and the death of his baby in a car crash, he struggled to

an 8–20 record in 1952. Traded to Cleveland, he was 15–7 for the 1954 pennant-winners./(JCA)

Steve Hovley — 1944– . OF 1969–73 **Pilots/ Brewers**, A's, Royals 436 g, .258, 8 hr, 88 rbi

The free-spirited Stanford graduate once quipped, "Billy Graham is a cracker." Hovley debuted with the one-year Pilots in 1969. Starting the season with a crewcut, he wouldn't cut his hair, not wanting to discriminate against any particular hairs. A line-drive hitter with good speed, Hovley was generally a fourth outfielder and led the AL in pinch-hit appearances with Kansas City in 1972./(JCA)

Bruce Howard — 1943– . RHP 1963–68 **White Sox**, Orioles, Senators 528 ip, 26–31, 3.18

Because of roster limits, the White Sox had to decide which of two young pitchers to keep at the beginning of the 1963 season. They squared off in an intra-squad game. Howard won and remained with the team, becoming a spot starter from 1965 to 1967. He used a slip pitch and sinker effectively, but was troubled by wildness and eventually left the majors. The other young pitcher, after being released by the Sox, signed with the Tigers. His name was Denny McLain./(RL)

Del Howard (George) — 1877–1956. OF-1B-2B Pirates, Braves, **Cubs** 536 g, .263, 6 hr, 193 rbi. *2 WS, 3 g, .167*

Howard played regularly for the Pirates and Braves before coming to the Cubs in 1907. Although he could not break into the strong Chicago lineup, he was a useful backup on the 1907 and '08 championship teams. His younger brother Ivan played in the AL from 1914 to 1917. /(BC)

Elston Howard — 1929–1980. C-OF 1955–68 **Yankees**, Red Sox 1605 g, .274, 167 hr, 762 rbi. *10 WS, 54 g, .246, 5 hr, 19 rbi*
☛ *Most Valuable Player—63. All-Star—57–65. Gold Glove—63–64.*

The Yankees' first black player, Howard was forced to play the outfield through much of his first five seasons because Yogi Berra was behind the plate. By 1960, Howard was the starting catcher and Berra was more often in the field. Howard was an exceptional defensive catcher; his .993 career fielding average is one of the highest ever, and he pioneered

Elston Howard

the use of a hinged catcher's mitt that led to the modern one-handed catching techniques. He was also highly regarded as a handler of pitchers. He was named to the AL All-Star team nine consecutive years.

Howard was a strong hitter, three times topping .300, with a high of .348 in 1961. He hit from an exaggerated spread stance when he came up, which he modified later in his career. He was AL MVP in 1963, as much for his leadership as for his .287 BA, 28 homers, and 85 RBI. He led the Yankees to their fourth straight pennant in a year when Maris and Mantle were often out with injuries.

After playing in nine WS with the Yankees, he was traded to the Red Sox in August of 1967 and helped Boston to that season's pennant. In 1969, he returned to the Yankees, where he served as a coach for eleven years. Howard and Pee Wee Reese share the record for playing on the most WS losers. /(GDW)

Frank Howard (The Capital Punisher, Hondo) — 1936–OF-1B 1958–73 Dodgers, **Senators**, Rangers, Tigers 1902 g, .273, 382 hr, 1119 rbi. *1 WS, 3 g, .300, 1 hr, 1 rbi.*
Manager 1981, 83 Padres, **Mets** 93–133, .412
☛ *Rookie of the Year—60. Led League—hr 68, 70. Led League—rbi 70. All-Star—68–71.*

The 6'8" 275-lb Howard captured NL Rookie of the Year honors in 1960 with the Dodgers, batting .268 with 23 HR and 77 RBI in 117 games. He hit 31 HR in 1962, but was traded to Washington in a December 1964 deal that brought Claude Osteen to Los Angeles. The Senators' behemoth slugger went on a rampage in May 1968, hitting a ML record 10 HR in 20 at-bats over a stretch of six consecutive games. He finished the year with 44 HR, leading the AL. He hit a career-high 48 in 1969, but Harmon Killebrew beat him by one. Howard recaptured the HR crown (44) and added the RBI title (126) in 1970. In 1974 he went to Japan to play for Taiheiyo, but he hurt his back striking out in his first game and never played again.

A warm and upbeat character, Howard coached for the Brewers and was the Padres' manager for the 1981 season. A coach with the Mets, he took over as interim manager for 116 games in 1983 when George Bamberger resigned. He began coaching first base for the Mariners in 1987.

A college All-American at Ohio State in both baseball and basketball, Howard still holds two Madison Square Garden Holiday Festival Tournament rebounding records. /(RTM)

Frank Howard

Wilbur Howard — 1947– . OF 1973–78 Brewers, **Astros** 466 g, .250, 6 hr, 71 rbi

Howard spent his first year in the minors as a pitcher, but reached the ML as a good defensive outfielder and pinch hitter. In by far his busiest season (121 games, Houston, 1975), he hit .283 with 32 steals and 67 runs. /(JCA)

Art Howe — 1946– . 3B-2B-1B 1974–82, 84–85 Pirates, **Astros**, Cardinals 891 g, .260, 43 hr, 293 rbi. *2 LCS, 6 g, .188, 2 rbi.*
    Manager 1989– **Astros** 86–76, .531

A handyman in the Astros' infield from 1977 to 1982, Howe's .432 average in May 1981 earned NL Player of the Month honors. He hit a career-high .296 that year. After five years as a Rangers coach, Howe was named the Astros manager for 1989. /(FJO)

Irwin M. Howe — 1866–1934. *Statistician.*

After 20 years as a printing salesman, Howe began compiling and distributing baseball records. In 1911 he formed the Howe News Bureau and became official statistician for the American League and many minor leagues. He designed the official scoring blank still in use. /(NLM)

Steve Howe — 1958– . LHP 1980–83, 85, 87 **Dodgers**, Twins, Rangers 379 ip, 29–31, 2.70. *1 LCS, 2 ip, 0–0, 0.00. 1 WS, 7 ip, 1–0, 3.86*
☛ *Rookie of the Year—80. All-Star—82.*

Howe broke Joe Black's club rookie record for saves with 17 for the 1980 Dodgers. The hard-throwing reliever enjoyed four sparkling seasons in Los Angeles, concluding with 18 saves and a 1.44 ERA in 1983. Howe unraveled quickly, however, when he admitted using cocaine during games the previous year, and after he failed drug tests, Commissioner Bowie Kuhn suspended him for the 1984 season to protect the "image of baseball." Comeback attempts in 1985 and 1987 failed as Howe kept reverting to drug use, but in 1989 he claimed once again to have finally beaten his addiction and announced plans to return to the ML in 1990. /(TG)

Dixie Howell [Millard] — 1920–1960. RHP 1940, 49, 55–58 Indians, Reds, **White Sox** 226 ip, 19–15, 3.78

Howell labored in the minors for 18 years before earning a spot in the White Sox bullpen in 1955 at age 35. In three years of short relief, he won 19 and saved 19. /(RL)

Dixie Howell [Homer Elliott] — 1919– . C 1947, 49–53, 55–56 Pirates, **Reds**, Dodgers 340 g, .246, 12 hr, 93 rbi

After performing part-time duty behind the plate for the 1947 Pirates and for the Reds, Howell closed out his career in Brooklyn as a seldom-seen backup to the great Roy Campanella. /(FK)

Harry Howell (Handsome Harry) — 1876–1956. RHP 1898–1910 Dodgers, Baltimore (NL), Baltimore (AL)/ Yankees, **Browns** 2568 ip, 131–146, 2.74

An early spitballer, Howell was the workhorse of the 1904–08 Browns pitching staff, averaging 308 innings and 15 wins a season. In three of those years, his ERA was 1.98 or less. He lost his job as a

Browns scout when he tried to pressure the St. Louis official scorer to give an extra hit to Cleveland's Nap Lajoie on the last day of the 1910 season. Lajoie and Ty Cobb were in a tight race for the batting title; Lajoie had eight hits against the Browns that day, but Cobb took the title by a point. Howell became a minor league umpire. /(NLM)

Jack Howell — 1961- . 3B-OF 1985- **Angels** 542 g, .241, 68 hr, 218 rbi. *1 LCS, 2 g, .000*

The Angels released veteran third baseman Doug DeCinces late in 1987 to give a position to left-handed-hitting Jack Howell, who had spent that season playing third, second, and the outfield and had hit 23 HR. One of those homers was a broken-bat shot in Yankee Stadium that confirmed for many that the 1987 ball was juiced up. Bothered by a thumb injury for much of 1988, Howell put up only mediocre numbers (.254, 16 HR, 63 RBI). /(JCA)

Jay Howell — 1955- . RHP 1980- Reds, Cubs, **Yankees**, A's, Dodgers 579 ip, 39-36, 3.58. *1 LCS, 0.2 ip, 0-1, 27.00. 1 WS, 3 ip, 0-1, 3.38*
☛ *All-Star—85, 87, 89.*

Howell was one of the hardest-throwing relief pitchers of the 1980s, despite an up-and-down career. He led the AL in strikeouts per inning in 1984 with the Yankees and became the stopper for the A's and the Dodgers. He had his best season in 1989 (5–3, 1.58 ERA, 28 saves). In between, he endured horrible collapses, with ERAs above 5.00 in both 1983 and 1987. He was the losing pitcher in the 1987 All-Star Game.

Howell achieved national notoriety with the Dodgers in the 1988 LCS against the Mets. In Game Three, played in a cold rain, he was ejected for having pine tar on his glove. He was suspended: at first for the next three LCS games, but ultimately, after an appeal, for two. He had already lost Game One in the ninth inning on the first run he had surrendered since August 11. In the World Series, his inconsistency continued; he surrendered a game-losing ninth-inning homer to the A's Mark McGwire in Game Three, but came back the next day to save Game Four with 2–1/3 innings of scoreless relief. /(TG)

Ken Howell — 1960- . RHP 1984- **Dodgers**, Phillies 303 ip, 18-29, 4.04. *1 LCS, 2 ip, 0-0, 0.00*

One of the hardest throwers in baseball, Howell once struck out 14 consecutive batters in winter ball. He enjoyed uncharacteristically good control when he

came up in 1984, but reverted to form in subsequent years. He was traded from the Dodgers to the Orioles in the Eddie Murray deal December 4, 1988, then was dealt to the Phillies in a package for Phil Bradley four days later. Made a starter, he went 12–12 with a 3.44 ERA for last-place Philadelphia and was the ace of their rotation. /(TG)

Roy Howell — 1953- . 3B 1974-84 Rangers, **Blue Jays**, Brewers 1112 g, .261, 80 hr, 454 rbi. *1 LCS, 1 g, .000. 1 WS, 4 g, .000*
☛ *All-Star—78.*

Drafted from the Rangers in 1977, the red-haired Howell became a local star for the brand-new expansion Blue Jays. In September of that year, he had a team-record nine RBI as Toronto thrashed the Yankees 19–3 at Yankee Stadium. He held team career records in hits, total bases, RBI, and strikeouts when he left as a free agent to sign with Milwaukee in 1981. /(TF)

Bill Howerton (Hopalong) — 1921- . OF 1949-52 **Cardinals**, Pirates, Giants 247 g, .274, 22 hr, 106 rbi

Wild horses couldn't keep Howerton from a professional baseball career. The California cowboy overcame a severe ankle injury in a childhood riding accident to be named to *TSN*'s 1950 All-Rookie team, hitting .281 with 10 HR and 59 RBI. /(JL)

Dan Howley (Dapper Dan) — 1885-1944. C 1913 **Phillies** 26 g, .125, 0 hr, 2 rbi.
Manager 1927-32 **Browns**, Reds 397-524, .431

Howley broke in as a catcher with Indianapolis of the American Association in 1906 and appeared briefly with the Phillies in 1913. He managed at Montreal for four years, then moved to Toronto (International League), where he won a pennant in 1918. He was a coach for the Tigers in 1919 and 1921–22. He returned to Toronto, and in 1926 won a pennant to break Baltimore's streak of seven straight flags. A combative manager known for his ability to develop young pitchers, he managed the Browns and Reds for three seasons each. In 1928 he brought the Browns in third, his best ML finish. /(NLM)

Dick Howser — 1937-1987. SS-2B 1961-68 A's, **Indians**, Yankees 789 g, .248, 16 hr, 165 rbi.
Manager 1978, 80-86 Yankees, **Royals** 507-425, .544. First place: 80-81, 84-85 *3 LCS, 4-9, .308. 1 WS, 4-3, .571*
☛ *All-Star—61.*

A feisty, quick infielder with good bat, Howser later became respected as a successful manager, but died tragically on the heels of his greatest personal triumph: leading the Royals to the 1985 World Championship.

The 5'8″ 155-lb Howser signed with the Athletics for a reported $21,000 bonus and had two outstanding seasons. In 1961 he hit .280, stole 37 bases, scored 108 runs, and was named *TSN* AL Rookie of the Year. He also led AL shortstops in putouts and errors. His only other year as a regular was 1964, when he hit .258 with 101 runs and 20 steals.

Howser won an AL East title for the Yankees his first full year as manager (1980), but was sacked by George Steinbrenner when the Yankees lost the LCS. He returned to the majors in late 1981 to lead the Royals to the AL West title. He won the division again in 1984 and the WS in 1985. But two days after he managed the AL to an All-Star Game victory in 1986, it was discovered that he had a brain tumor. He retired during spring training of 1987 and succumbed shortly afterward. /(JM)

Dummy Hoy [William Ellsworth] — 1862–1961. OF 1888–99, 1901–02 **Washington (NL)**, Buffalo (PL), St. Louis (AA), Reds, Louisville (NL), White Sox 1798 g, .288, 40 hr, 726 rbi

Hoy was the reason umpires adopted hand signals to go along with the vocal calls of "out," "safe," and "strike." The 5'4″ 148-lb outfielder was a deaf-mute, but he overcame adversity to have the greatest career of any seriously handicapped player, accumulating 2,054 hits. He hit .300 three times and scored 100 runs eight times. He also stole 30 or more bases in his first twelve ML seasons, and totaled 597 in an era when runners were credited with stolen bases for taking an "extra base" (going from first to third on a single, for example). Hoy led the NL with 82 steals in his first season and set NL rookie records for games, at-bats, hits, singles, and walks. He walked frequently, leading his league with 119 in 1891 and 86 in 1901. His on-base average topped .400 four times. In the field, the centerfielder led NL outfielders in putouts and total chances per game in 1897. On June 19, 1889, he threw out three runners at the plate in one game—one of only three players ever to do that.

Hoy, one of 29 players to play in four major leagues, was a regular until his last season. He began with perennially bad Washington, jumped to the Players' League for its one season (1890), and had his first experience with a winning team playing for the Browns (AA) in 1891. When the AA folded, he was returned to Washington, but the Ohio native

Dummy Hoy with Washington of the NL

joined Cincinnati for 1894. After two seasons with the feeble Louisville franchise, he left the majors for the new Chicago White Sox of the American League. He remained with the team in 1901, the AL's first major league season. He closed out his major league career with one last season in Cincinnati in 1902, but hung on for another year with Los Angeles (Pacific Coast League), playing all of the team's 211 games and stealing 46 bases at the age of 42. He lived longer than any major league player before him, which earned him the honor of throwing out the first ball of Game Three of the 1961 World Series, at Cincinnati, at the age of 99. /(WOR)

LaMarr Hoyt [Dewey LaMarr] — 1955– . RHP
1979–86 **White Sox**, Padres 1311 ip, 98–68, 3.99. 20
wins: 83 *1 LCS, 9 ip, 1–0, 1.00*
☛ *Led League—w 82–83. Cy Young Award—83. All-Star—85.*

Hoyt was an unknown pitcher struggling in the
Yankee farm system sent to the White Sox along
with Oscar Gamble and Bob Polinsky on April 5,
1976. In return the Yanks received Bucky Dent. The
deal was roundly criticized in Chicago, but it ultimately paid dividends. Hoyt began his ML career in
1980 in Chicago's bullpen. In 1982 he was put into
the rotation with startling success. He won his first
nine decisions to equal a White Sox record set by
Lefty Williams in 1917 and Orval Grove in 1943,
and finished 19–15, leading the AL in wins. As a
starter, his already sharp control became almost
unbelievable; he walked only 48 batters in 239.2
innings.

As good as he'd been, Hoyt improved in every
way to lead Chicago to the AL West title in 1983.
He was 15–2 after the All-Star break, en route to a
landslide Cy Young Award. Hoyt walked just 31
batters that year, four of which were intentional.
The total was just three more than Cy Young's
record of 28, set in 1904. His 24 victories paced the
AL for the second year in a row, and in the ALCS he
tossed a five-hitter against Baltimore in the opener
to claim Chicago's only win.

Hoyt faltered along with the rest of the White Sox
team in 1984. He did fire a one-hitter against the
Yankees on May 2 in Comiskey Park, allowing only
a scratch single to Don Mattingly. Hoyt gave up 31
homers in 1984, second-highest in the league, and
after the season he was traded to San Diego with two
minor leaguers for Tim Lollar, Ozzie Guillen, Bill
Long, and Luis Salazar.

Hoyt was 16–8 in his first season with the Padres,
and started the 1985 All-Star Game for the NL. By
1986, however, a lingering drug problem came to
light, and he was suspended by Commissioner Peter
Uebberoth for one year in 1987. Hoyt was invited to
try out for the White Sox in 1988 following his 45-
day stay in prison, but he was arrested again after
law-enforcement officials uncovered a cache of marijuana and cocaine in his Columbia, South Carolina
apartment. He began his second prison term on
February 21, 1988./(NLM)

Waite Hoyt (Schoolboy) — 1899–1984. RHP 1918–38
Giants, Red Sox, **Yankees**, Tigers, A's, Dodgers, Pirates
3763 ip, 237–182, 3.59. 20 wins: 27–28 *7 WS, 84 ip,
6–4, 1.83*
☛ *Led League—w 27. Led League—era 27. Hall of
Fame—1969.*

Hoyt was a mainstay on the pitching staff of the
great Yankee teams of the 1920s. The righthander
pitched for New York from 1921 to early 1930 and
had a record of 157–98 in pinstripes. He was 23–7
in 1928 and also led the AL with eight saves. In
1927 he was 22–7, and he won 19 in 1921 and '22.
In 1927 he led the AL in wins (22), ERA (2.63), and
winning percentage (.759). He reached double
figures in wins from 1921 to 1931 and in 1934. He

Waite Hoyt

spent the last seven years of his career in the NL, which he led in relief wins in 1934 (7) and 1935 (5).

Hoyt appeared in seven WS (1921–23, '26–28 with the Yankees and 1931 with the A's). He was 2–0 in 1928, and 2–1 in 1921, tying Christy Mathewson's record with a 0.00 ERA in three games started. He ranks high in numerous WS lifetime categories, including wins (6 for fifth), losses (4 for seventh), strikeouts (49 for eighth), games (12 for seventh), and innings pitched (84 for fifth). In 1941 Hoyt moved to the broadcast booth. He was the voice of the Reds until his retirement in 1965. He was elected to the Hall of Fame in 1969. /(JM)

Al Hrabosky (The Mad Hungarian) — 1949– . LHP 1970–82 **Cardinals**, Royals, Braves 721 ip, 64–35, 3.11. *1 LCS, 3 ip, 0–0, 3.00*

A blazing fastball, used 90 percent of the time, made Hrabosky one of the most effective relievers of the 1970s. The chunky southpaw's nickname, The Mad Hungarian, came from his nationality, Fu Manchu mustache and long hair, and angry stomping to the back of the mound to psych himself up. He was *TSN* NL Fireman of the Year in 1975 with St. Louis (13–3, 1.67, 22 saves). When he wasn't selected to the All-Star team in 1974, St. Louis fans rallied behind him, honoring him with a "We Hlove Hrabosky Hbanner Hday." Traded in December 1977 to the Royals for reliever Mark Littell, in 1979 he signed a multi-million-dollar contract with the Braves via free agency, but recorded only 7 of his lifetime 97 saves with Atlanta. He became a Cardinal broadcaster. /(FJO)

Kent Hrbek (Herbie) — 1960– . 1B-DH 1981– **Twins** 1156 g, .290, 201 hr, 724 rbi. *1 LCS, 5 g, .150, 1 hr, 1 rbi. 1 WS, 7 g, .208, 1 hr, 6 rbi*
☛ *All-Star—82.*

Born in Minneapolis, Minnesota, Kent Hrbek was an instant fan favorite when he joined the Twins in 1982, following a .379 batting average in the California League, best among all pro hitters in 1981. He hit the first home run in the Hubert H. Humphrey Metrodome on April 3, 1982 in an exhibition game against the Phillies. He was second to Cal Ripken, Jr. in the 1982 AL Rookie of the Year vote. The Twin MVP in 1984, Hrbek was the senior member (Minnesota service) on the 1987 World Champion Twins. Kent made the final putouts in the game that clinched the Western Division and in the final games of the LCS and World Series. He hit the 14th grand slam in World Series history in Game Six. He set club records with 20 homers in

the Metrodome and a .996 fielding percentage in 1987. With batting championship skills, the burly, sometimes overweight Hrbek sacrificed some batting average for power, but also exhibited improved discipline at the plate through his career. /(ME)

Cal Hubbard [Robert] — 1900–1977. *Umpire* AL 1937–51 *4 WS 3 ASU*
☛ *Hall of Fame—1976.*

The only man to be elected to the baseball, college football, and pro football halls of fame, Hubbard was a huge man, 6'3" and 250 lbs. At little Centenary and Geneva colleges, he won nationwide fame as a bone-crushing tackle. In his professional football career, he played end and linebacker in addition to tackle for the 1927 champion New York Giants and the 1929–31 Green Bay Packers champions. He was named at tackle on the first three official All-NFL teams, 1931–33.

He began umpiring minor league games during the summers while he was playing pro football, and

Cal Hubbard

the year after he retired from the gridiron, he became an AL umpire. In 1944, Hubbard gained notoriety as the first umpire to eject a pitcher (the Browns' Nels Potter) for throwing a spitball. Hubbard's imposing size and keen eyesight made him one of the best at his trade. He was once examined at the Boston Optical Lab and was found to have 20–10 vision, the strongest ever recorded—even better than Ted Williams.

Ironically, a hunting accident in 1951 affected the sight in his left eye and led to his retirement from the field. He served as supervisor of AL umpires for 15 years. He was elected to the Baseball Hall of Fame in 1976, the year before his death. /(RTM)

Glenn Hubbard — 1957– . 2B 1979–89 **Braves**, A's 1354 g, .244, 70 hr, 448 rbi. *1 LCS, 3 g, .222, 1 rbi. 1 WS, 4 g, .250*
☞ *All-Star—83.*

Hubbard led NL second basemen in double plays three times and assists twice, but his offensive skills gradually eroded from their 1983 peak (.263, 12 HR, 70 RBI) and his range in the field shrank as well. An aggressive, fearless player, he started at second base for Oakland's 1988 AL Champions after spending 10 seasons with Atlanta. /(ME)

Bill Hubbell — 1897–1980. RHP 1919–25 Giants, **Phillies**, Dodgers 931 ip, 40–63, 4.68

Hubbell was the cause of a baseball rules change. With the Phillies in 1925, he walked a batter intentionally by throwing four times to first base, as there was no rule against it. When he did it again several weeks later, league president John Heydler threatened to suspend him. The following year the rule was changed, requiring that the pitches be made to the catcher. /(NLM)

Carl Hubbell (King Carl, The Meal Ticket) — 1903–1988. LHP 1928–43 **Giants** 3589 ip, 253–154, 2.97. 20 wins: 33–37 *3 WS, 50 ip, 4–2, 1.79*
☞ *Most Valuable Player—33, 36. Led League—w 33, 36–37. Led League—k 37. Led League—era 33–34, 36. All-Star—33–38, 40–42. Hall of Fame—1947.*

With his slow, cartwheel-like delivery of the screwball, the lefthander off the Oklahoma oil fields recorded five consecutive 20-win seasons for the Giants and helped propel his team to World Series competition in 1933, 1936, and 1937. He was the only peacetime pitcher ever to win two MVP awards (Hal Newhouser won two during the talent-poor years of WWII) and was a true workhorse; in 1934, while winning 21 games, pitching 313 innings, and

Carl Hubbell

leading the league with a 2.30 ERA, Hubbell also paced NL hurlers with eight saves. With his gaunt, smiling face, big, floppy ears, and an arm permanently turned completely around from the strain of tens of thousands of screwballs, King Carl appeared unlikely to strike fear in the hearts of opposing batters.

Hubbell was obtained by Detroit from Oklahoma

City (Western League) in 1925, but performed unspectacularly in their farm system. Manager Ty Cobb wouldn't let him throw his screwball in spring training trials, and Hubbell was outrighted to Beaumont (Texas League) in 1928. That season, a Giants' scout convinced John McGraw to acquire him. McGraw encouraged his young southpaw to utilize his best pitch at will, and Hubbell went 10-6 after his promotion in 1928. The following May 8, he no-hit the Pirates. In sixteen years with New York, he had only one losing record (11-12 in 1940) and established himself as the premier NL pitcher of his era, though he was never as colorful as his archrival, Dizzy Dean.

Hubbell's preeminence shone through most strikingly in 1933 and 1936, his MVP seasons. In '33, he led the AL with 23 wins, a 1.66 ERA, ten shutouts, and 308.2 IP. Typical of his performance was a July 2 game against the powerful Cardinals. Through eighteen innings, he controlled his singular pitch so masterfully as not to allow a walk, while striking out 12. In his two WS starts that year against the Senators, Hubbell pitched 20 innings, striking out 15, and did not allow an earned run.

The feat that Hubbell will always be remembered for took place in New York's Polo Grounds, in the second ML All-Star Game, July 10, 1934. Matched against his crosstown rival, Lefty Gomez, Hubbell allowed a single to Charley Gehringer, then walked Heinie Manush. Babe Ruth went down on five pitches, taking a screwball for a called third strike. Next, Lou Gehrig, in his prime, struck out swinging on four pitches. The baserunners pulled off a double steal, but could not break the southpaw's concentration. Jimmie Foxx fanned on three screwballs to end the first-inning threat. Handed a one-run lead, in the second, Hubbell continued his amazing streak, striking out Al Simmons and Joe Cronin. Bill Dickey managed a sharp single to center, but Hubbell came back to strike out Gomez, going on to complete three scoreless innings and establishing the All-Star record of six strikeouts.

Over the course of the 1936-37 seasons, Hubbell accomplished another incredible achievement. On July 17, 1936, with a record of 10-6, he began a streak of 16 consecutive wins through the end of the season, then picked up with eight victories to open 1937, establishing the ML record of 24 consecutive wins. His 26 victories, .813 winning percentage, and 2.31 ERA in '36 led the NL, and his 1937 numbers, 22 wins, .733, and 159 strikeouts, did the same.

After undergoing elbow surgery following the 1938 campaign, Hubbell won 11 games a season,

1939-42. He retired from play in 1943, and was named the Giants' director of minor league operations. He joined the immortals of Cooperstown in 1947, and worked for the Giants until 1977, when a stroke relegated him to part-time scouting duties. The Giants retired his number 11. /(AAs)

Ken Hubbs — 1941-1964. 2B 1961-63 **Cubs** 324 g, .247, 14 hr, 98 rbi
☛ *Rookie of the Year—62. Gold Glove—62.*

The 1962 NL Rookie of the Year set a ML record with 78 consecutive errorless games. He handled 418 chances over that stretch, also a record. "Hubbs of the Cubs" was the first rookie to win a Gold Glove, and also set a NL rookie record with 661 at-bats. Hubbs died in February 1964, when a private plane he was piloting crashed in Utah. /(DS)

Clarence Huber (Gilly) — 1897-1965. 3B 1920-21, 25-26 Tigers, **Phillies** 254 g, .263, 6 hr, 93 rbi

Huber broke in with Mexia in the West Texas League in 1915, and spent most of his career in the Texas League and Southern Association. He saw the most major league action with the 1925-26 Phillies, hitting a career-high .284 in '25 but dropping off to .245 in '26. /(NLM)

Hubert H. Humphrey Metrodome (The Homer Dome) Minnesota Twins 1982- . LF-343, CF-408, RF-327

Located just east of downtown Minneapolis, the Metrodome features a distinctive air-supported fiberglass roof, a 23' canvas fence in right field, and the liveliest artificial turf in the ML. It was dubbed the Homer Dome in its inaugural season when 191 home runs were hit there, but with the addition of air conditioning in 1984 and the gradual raising of the fences (left field is now 13' high), it has become a largely neutral home run park. The white roof, which makes it difficult to see fly balls, collapsed during the fall of 1982, but was quickly reinflated. And on May 4, 1984 Dave Kingman was awarded a double when his towering infield pop-up hit the roof and never came down. The Twins thrive on the support of an often deafening crowd in the Metrodome, and were 56-25 at home in 1987 (85-77 overall) before becoming the World Champions with the worst regular-season record when they swept four home WS games against the Cardinals. The Metrodome also houses football's Minnesota Vikings. /(SCL)

Rex Hudler — 1960– . 2B-SS 1984–86, 88– Yankees, Orioles, **Expos** 212 g, .247, 10 hr, 28 rbi

After bouncing around for ten years, Hudler won a platoon job at second base and shortstop with the 1988 Expos and reached new highs in every category, hitting .273 and stealing 29 bases. /(WOR)

Willis Hudlin (Ace, Hud) — 1906– . RHP 1926–40, 44 **Indians**, Senators, Browns, Giants 2613 ip, 158–156, 4.41

Hudlin and his sidearm sinker accounted for the seventh-most wins (157) and third-most losses (151) in Indian history. His work was overshadowed by teammates Mel Harder and Bob Feller, the only pitchers to work more games for Cleveland than Hudlin's 475. For three years, 1927–29, he was Cleveland's Yankee-killer, with 14 wins against New York. The scholarly-looking Hudlin was a Detroit coach, 1957–59. /(ME)

Charles Hudson — 1959– . RHP 1983– **Phillies**, Yankees, Tigers 1008 ip, 50–60, 4.14. *1 LCS, 9 ip, 1–0, 2.00. 1 WS, 8 ip, 0–2, 8.64*

Hudson made an immediate impact when the Phillies brought him up from Triple-A in June 1983. Inserted into the starting rotation, he posted an 8–8 record in 26 starts. He took a no-hitter into the ninth inning on July 20 against Houston before Craig Reynolds broke it up with a one-out bloop single. Hudson helped the Phillies reach the World Series by defeating the Dodgers in Game Three of the LCS. But he lost two games during the Series to the Orioles, never lasting through the fifth inning and tying a five-game Series record by allowing four home runs. He never reached .500 again with the Phillies and was traded to New York in 1987, where he won his first six decisions. A month-long slump led to a brief demotion to Columbus, but he recovered to finish 11–7 in 16 starts and 19 relief appearances. After a 6–6 1988 season, the Yankees traded him to Detroit. /(EG)

Johnny Hudson (Mr. Chips) — 1912–1970. 2B-SS-3B 1936–41, 45 **Dodgers**, Cubs, Giants 426 g, .242, 4 hr, 96 rbi

Hudson became a favorite in Brooklyn for his clutch hitting. Later a Giant scout, he remained on their staff from 1945 until his death. /(JK)

Sid Hudson — 1915– . RHP 1940–42, 46–54 **Senators**, Red Sox 2181 ip, 104–152, 4.28
☛ *All-Star—41–42.*

The 6'4" Hudson jumped to the Senators after two years in the Florida State League, going 24–4 in the latter. His best major league mark was 17–16 as a rookie in 1940, and he pitched an inning in the 1941 All-Star Game. After military service (1943–45), Hudson resumed his place in the Senators' rotation, tying for the AL lead with 17 losses in 1949. A good-hitting pitcher, he batted .220 lifetime, .308 in 1947. Active until age 39, he became a longtime pitching coach, instructor, and scout. /(MC)

Frank Huelsman — 1874–1959. OF 1897, 1904–05 Cardinals, White Sox, Tigers, Browns, **Senators** 240 g, .258, 5 hr, 97 rbi

Huelsman played for three other AL teams in 1904 before landing a regular position for the Senators, but after hitting .271 for Washington in 1905 he returned to the minors. He was a star in the minor leagues, compiling a .342 batting mark over nearly 20 years and winning five batting crowns and six RBI titles. /(BC)

Phil Huffman — 1958– . RHP 1979 **Blue Jays** 173 ip, 6–18, 5.77

In 1979 the pitching-poor Blue Jays rushed the 21-year-old into their starting rotation after only 34 games in the minors. He led the AL in losses (18) in a one-season career highlighted by a one-hitter against Oakland. /(TF)

Miller Huggins (Hug, The Mighty Mite) — 1879–1929. 2B-3B 1904–16 Reds, **Cardinals** 1585 g, .265, 9 hr, 318 rbi.
    Manager 1913–1929 Cardinals, **Yankees** 1413–1134, .555. First place: 21–23, 26–28 *6 WS, 18–15, .545*
☛ *Hall of Fame—1964.*

The smart, scrawny 5'6" Huggins was a first-rate second baseman before he became famous for managing the Yankees to their first six pennants and three World Championships. He was fast and sure-handed afield; his record is dotted with games in which he handled 15 chances, or figured in three double plays. He led the league in putouts, assists, double plays, and fielding once each, and twice in errors. The Mighty Mite was the ideal leadoff man, a switch-hitter who coaxed 1,002 career walks (four times leading the league) and stole some 50 bases a season (though stolen bases were not tabulated during his six early years with Cincinnati). Not a long-ball hitter, he did have three triples in a game in 1904.

The Cardinals acquired Huggins in 1910. By 1913 he was player-manager, and by 1917 had retired to the bench. He prodded two third-place

Miller Huggins

and bad actors until an appalling slump in 1925 and the $5,000 fine and nine-day suspension of Babe Ruth. With Ruppert's backing, Huggins brought his unruly crew to heel, and established himself as boss, beginning the club's tradition of Yankee pride. Though history recalls the pillage of Harry Frazee's Red Sox as the making of the Yankees, Gehrig, Earle Combs, and Tony Lazzeri were discovered elsewhere, and others (Bob Meusel and Herb Pennock, for example) blossomed under Huggins's encouragement and handling. When he died of erysipelas in 1929, at age 50, judgment was nearly universal that Huggins was in a managerial class by himself. A plaque in his honor was placed in Yankee Stadium's centerfield in 1932. /(ADS)

Dick Hughes — 1938– . RHP 1966–68 **Cardinals** 307 ip, 20–9, 2.79. *2 WS, 9 ip, 0–1, 4.82*

When Bob Gibson suffered a broken ankle with the pennant-bound 1967 Cardinals, Hughes, a 29-year-old rookie, made up for the loss by going 16–6 for a league-leading .727 winning percentage. Arm trouble ended his short career. /(FJO)

Jim Hughes — 1951– . RHP 1974–77 **Twins** 441 ip, 25–30, 4.31

Hughes's only winning season was 1975, when he was 16–14 with a 3.82 ERA. He pitched a seven-inning perfect game for Lynchburg in the Carolina League against Rocky Mount on July 30, 1972. /(SFS)

Jim Hughes [James Jay] — 1874–1924. RHP 1898–99, 1901–02 Baltimore (NL), **Dodgers** 1097 ip, 83–41, 3.00. 20 wins: 98–99
☛ *Led League—w 99.*

Hughes gained fame in 1897 when he shut out the famous Baltimore Orioles on three hits during a West Coast exhibition. Orioles Manager Ned Hanlon hired him and brought him east, where he had four excellent seasons, including a league-leading 28–6 mark with the 1899 Dodgers. Preferring to play in California, he joined the Pacific Coast League in 1903 and pitched there until a back injury ended his career. His older brother Mickey won 25 games for the 1888 Brooklyn team. /(BC)

Long Tom Hughes — 1878–1956. RHP 1900–09, 11–13 Cubs, Orioles, Red Sox, Yankees, **Senators** 2644 ip, 131–174, 3.09. 20 wins: 03 *1 WS, 2 ip, 0–1, 9.00*

Nicknamed for his height, a then-impressive 6'1", Hughes completed 32 starts as a Cubs rookie while striking out 225, the third-best NL rookie total ever.

finishes out of his nondescript team, and guided a green and awkward Rogers Hornsby through his first ML seasons. Holder of a law degree (though he never practiced) and a shrewd investor in the stock market, Huggins was businessman enough to think he could buy the St. Louis club. His bid rebuffed, he resigned. Ban Johnson, the opportunistic president of the American League, promptly urged Jacob Ruppert, the Yankees' principal owner, to grab Huggins. The manager's record was not distinguished, but he was a sound baseball man, and Johnson was happy to help steal him from the NL.

Together with imperious Ed Barrow, the GM, Huggins developed the slugging Yankee teams that ended the dead-ball era forever. A mediocre lot when he arrived, they were among the all-time greats at his death. They were a bunch of carousers

He jumped to the AL the following year, and helped the Red Sox to the first World Series with a 20–7, 2.57 mark as their third starter in 1903, behind Cy Young and Bill Dineen. He was the only Boston pitcher besides Young and Dineen to appear in the WS, losing Game Three. /(JK)

Roy Hughes (Jeep, Sage) — 1911- . 2B-3B-SS 1935–39, 44–46 **Indians**, Browns, Phillies, Cubs 762 g, .273, 5 hr, 205 rbi. *1 WS, 6 g, .294, 3 rbi*

A much-used utility infielder, in 1936 Hughes hit a career-high .295 as Cleveland's regular second baseman. Nicknamed Jeep because of his speed, Hughes was the Cubs shortstop in the 1945 World Series. /(DS)

Sammy Hughes — 1910–1981. 2B Negro Leagues 1930–46 Louisville White Sox, Washington Pilots, Nashville Elite Giants, Columbus Elite Giants, Washington Elite Giants, **Baltimore Elite Giants** statistics not available

Generally considered black baseball's premier second baseman, Hughes was a crack defensive player with wide range and a strong arm. The 6'3" 190-lb righthanded batter was a solid contact hitter and a proficient hit-and-run man who had occasional power. His good baserunning and tough, intelligent style of play made him a complete ballplayer.

A native of Louisville, KY, Hughes began his pro career with the local black White Sox in 1930. After spending 1932 with the Washington Pilots, he joined the Elite Giants in 1933. With the exception of 1941, which he spent in Mexico, Hughes stayed with the Elites until his retirement.

From 1930 through 1937, Hughes batted .333. In the 1937 Denver Post Baseball Tournament, he batted .379. In 10 exhibition games with white major leaguers, he collected 16 hits for a .390 average.

Hughes started the 1934 and 1935 East-West all-star games for the West, and the 1936, 1938, and 1939 contests for the East. He batted .263 (5-for-19) in his five all-star appearances.

Two things eluded Hughes. The first was a Negro League championship. The closest he came was 1936, when his Washington Elite Giants won the NNL first-half crown and faced the second-half winners, the Pittsburgh Crawfords. The league championship series was canceled after one game. The Giants won that contest, 2–0.

The second thing to elude Hughes was an opportunity to enter organized baseball. In 1943, Hughes and Roy Campanella were to receive tryouts with the Pittsburgh Pirates, but the opportunity never

materialized. Along with Larry Doby, Monte Irvin, Sam Jethroe, and others who eventually made the major leagues, Hughes was promoted by Negro League sportswriters as a candidate for the integration of baseball. By the time Branch Rickey tabbed Jackie Robinson, Hughes was long past his prime. /(MFK)

Tom Hughes — 1884–1961. RHP 1906–07, 09–10, 14–18 Yankees, **Braves** 863 ip, 55–39, 2.56

On August 30, 1910 Hughes didn't allow Cleveland a hit or a walk for 9 innings, but lost 5–0 in the 11th. He resurfaced for the Braves in 1914 and won 16 games in both 1915 and 1916, leading the NL in relief wins each year. On June 16, 1916 he pitched a second no-hitter, winning 2–0 over Pittsburgh and striking out Honus Wagner to end the game. /(JK)

Tommy Hughes — 1919- . RHP 1941–42, 46–48 **Phillies**, Reds 688 ip, 31–56, 3.92

Hughes was the fireballing ace of two of the worst teams in Phillies history (1941–42). On June 3, 1941 he one-hit the Cubs, retiring the first 21 batters. /(JL)

Jim Hughey (Cold Water Jim) — 1869–1945. RHP 1891, 93, 96–1900 Cincinnati-Milwaukee (AA), Cubs, Pirates, **Cardinals**, Cleveland (NL) 1007 ip, 29–80, 4.87

After going 7–24 with the last-place Cardinals of 1898, Hughey led the NL in losses with a 4–30 mark for the incredible Cleveland Spiders of 1899, generally considered the worst team ever in the NL. His nickname referred to his hometown, Coldwater, Michigan. /(BC)

Tex Hughson [Cecil Carlton] — 1916- . RHP 1941–44, 46–49 **Red Sox** 1376 ip, 96–54, 2.94. 20 wins: 42, 46 *1 WS, 14 ip, 0–1, 3.14*
☛ *Led League—w 42. Led League—k 42. All-Star—42–44.*

The Texan was a fastballer with a sharp curve. Going 22–6 in 1942, he led the AL in wins, complete games (22), innings (281), and strikeouts (113). He again led in complete games (20) in 1943, and his .783 winning percentage (18–5) in 1944 was the AL's best. After spending 1945 in the military, Hughson returned in good form, going 20–11 in 1946. Arm problems prematurely ended his successful career. /(EW)

Mark Huismann — 1958- . RHP 1983- **Royals**, Mariners, Indians, Tigers, Orioles 288 ip, 12–11, 4.31. *1 LCS, 3 ip, 0–0, 10.13*

A career reliever, Huismann won the Allie Reynolds Award as the top pitcher in the American Association with 34 saves and a 2.04 ERA at Omaha in 1985. He was traded to Seattle in May 1986 and then to Cleveland a year later, and was released by the Indians in the spring of 1988 before signing a minor league contract with the Tigers. /(SCL)

William Hulbert — 1832–1882. *Executive.*

A Chicago businessman who owned the Chicago White Stockings of the National Association, Hulbert induced several stars from eastern teams, including Philadelphia's Cap Anson and Boston's Al Spalding, to jump to his team for the 1876 season. The NA was a weak league, beset by gamblers, failing franchises, and rowdy and drunken behavior among players. Hulbert avoided any action by the

William Hulbert

NA over his pirating of players by convening several responsible team owners and founding the National League. Although Hartford owner Morgan Bulkeley was the figurehead president in the NL's first year, Hulbert was actually in charge. In 1877, he officially took over as president. He introduced regular schedules (and expelled New York and Philadelphia for failing to fulfill theirs), banned alcoholic beverages from ball parks, and worked to eliminate gambling on games. In 1877, when the Louisville club began to fritter away a 3–1/2 game lead in August, Hulbert supported an investigation that uncovered evidence of game-fixing. Four players were banned for life. When Hulbert died in 1882, he left a league firmly established. /(NLM)

Tim Hulett — 1960- . 3B-2B 1983–87 **White Sox** 373 g, .239, 29 hr, 108 rbi

A brash, hard-nosed player in the old mold, Hulett was not afraid of anyone. In one game Hulett was berated by Tom Seaver for making an error at second base. Unintimidated, Hulett blasted Seaver in no uncertain terms. He played regularly at second and third with the White Sox in 1985–86, hitting 17 HR in '86, but he slumped in June 1987 and lost his job. /(RL)

Rudy Hulswitt — 1877–1950. SS 1899, 1902–04, 08–10 Louisville (NL), **Phillies**, Reds, Cardinals 644 g, .253, 3 hr, 203 rbi

In his first full ML season, 1902, Hulswitt hit .272 for the Phillies and led NL shortstops in putouts. The next season was his best, as he had career highs in games (138), doubles (22), and RBI (58) and again led in putouts. However, he set the post-1900 National League record by making 81 errors. A bad shoulder ended his playing days. He had a long managing career in the minors and scouted for the Red Sox and Braves. /(NLM)

Tom Hume — 1953- . RHP 1977–87 **Reds**, Phillies 1086 ip, 57–71, 3.85. *1 LCS, 4 ip, 0–1, 6.75* ☛ *All-Star—82.*

In 1980, his first season exclusively as a reliever, the mild-looking, bespectacled Hume was named co-winner (with Rollie Fingers) of the NL Fireman of the Year Award (9–10, 2.56, 78 games, 25 saves). That off-season, he and Reds teammate Bill Bonham and their wives were trapped in a Las Vegas hotel fire and had to be rescued from the roof.

Hume's nine relief wins in 1981 led the NL. Forced out for two months of the 1982 season after he injured his knee by catching his foot in a turf seam in Montreal, he never again recorded more than nine saves in a season, and was generally reduced to the role of set-up man. Hume's first ML hit was a home run. In 183 more at-bats, he never hit another. /(JCA)

John Hummel (Silent John) — 1883–1959. 2B-OF-1B 1905–15, 18 **Dodgers**, Yankees 1161 g, .254, 29 hr, 394 rbi

Hummel spent 12 seasons in the majors, two of them as the Dodgers' starting second baseman. He led NL second basemen in fielding both years (.965 and .972). Hummel also led the league in strikeouts (81) in 1910. Hummel's career in organized baseball spanned 24 years. After his playing career in the majors, Hummel coached in the minors. Hummel managed minor league teams in Saskatoon, Binghamton, Harrisburg, Scranton, and Wheeling, and finished his career managing Springfield in 1927. /(MA)

Terry Humphrey — 1949– . C 1971–79 Expos, Tigers, **Angels** 415 g, .211, 6 hr, 85 rbi

Hitting was not Humphrey's strong point. A smart, 6'3" catcher with a rifle arm, he suffered several injuries with Montreal and Detroit, but was California's regular receiver in 1977, before Brian Downing's arrival. /(EW)

Bob Humphreys — 1935– . RHP 1962–70 Tigers, Cardinals, Cubs, **Senators**, Brewers 566 ip, 27–21, 3.36. *1 WS, 1 ip, 0–0, 0.00*

Noted for his "side-saddle" delivery, reliever Humphreys joined the pennant-winning Cardinals in 1964 in time to contribute two wins and two saves down the stretch. The next year, he was part of an unusual Cubs staff that also included submariner Ted Abernathy and sidearmer Bill Faul. He pitched well for the Senators in the late 1960s but made frequent brief trips to the minors to correct his mechanics. /(MC)

Bert Humphries — 1880–1945. RHP 1910–15 Phillies, Reds, **Cubs** 798 ip, 50–43, 2.79

Already 30 years old when he broke into the majors, Humphries had one outstanding season, leading the NL with an .800 winning percentage (16–4) for the 1913 Cubs. /(AA)

John Humphries — 1915–1965. RHP 1938–46 Indians, **White Sox**, Phillies 1002 ip, 52–63, 3.78

The smoke-throwing righthander from the University of North Carolina went 20–7 for New Orleans in 1937, including a no-hitter. He jumped to Cleveland in 1938, leading the AL with 45 appearances and eight relief wins as the Indians' Rookie of the Year. All four of Humphries's 1941 White Sox victories were shutouts. /(EW)

Randy Hundley — 1942– . C 1964–77 Giants, **Cubs**, Twins, Padres 1061 g, .236, 82 hr, 381 rbi
☛ *All-Star—69. Gold Glove—67.*

In December 1965 the Cubs made one of their best deals of the decade, acquiring two unproven players, Hundley and pitcher Bill Hands, from the Giants for Don Landrum, Lindy McDaniel, and Jim Rittwage. Hands became a 20-game winner, and Hundley turned out to be the best Cub catcher since Gabby Hartnett.

In the years 1966–69, Hundley caught nearly every Cub game. He set a ML record with 160 games behind the plate (147 complete) in 1968, and became the first player in history to catch 150 or more games for three consecutive years (1967–69). This iron man accomplishment stems in part from his own stamina, but was also a result of manager Leo Durocher's reluctance to play the second-stringers. When he won the Gold Glove in 1967, he committed just four errors for a NL record. Hundley popularized a new hinged glove that permitted a one-handed catching style, protecting his throwing hand. His arm was strong and accurate, he called pitches well, and hit with power. When the Cubs made their unsuccessful run for the flag in 1969, Hundley's fielding and 18 HR were key contributions, but he was thoroughly worn out by season's end.

The effects of overwork began to show the following April when Hundley injured his left knee and missed more than half the season. The right knee popped in 1971, limiting his action to nine games. Never the same after that, he drifted to the Twins in 1973, the Padres in 1974, and returned to finish with 15 games for the Cubs in 1976–77. /(AA)

Bill Hunnefield (Wild Bill) — 1899–1976. SS-2B-3B 1926–31 **White Sox**, Indians, Braves, Giants 511 g, .272, 9 hr, 144 rbi

An off-season accountant, Hunnefield often reported late to spring training because it coincided with tax season. An infielder with an erratic arm, he twice played on the winning side in no-hitters (Ted Lyons, 1926, and Wes Ferrell, 1931) and made a total of four errors in the two games. /(DB)

Ken Hunt — 1934– . OF 1959–64 Yankees, **Angels**, Senators 310 g, .226, 33 hr, 111 rbi

Hunt came up as a slick fielder, but was unable to crack the powerful Yankee lineup. His only year as a regular came with the 1961 expansion Angels. He hit .255 with 25 HR and 84 RBI, but struck out 120 times in 479 at-bats and led AL outfielders in errors. He played only 13 games in 1962 due to an arm injury and military service; from then on he never reached .200. /(SFS)

Ron Hunt (Zeke) — 1941– . 2B-3B 1963–74 Mets, Dodgers, Giants, **Expos**, Cardinals 1483 g, .273, 39 hr, 370 rbi
☛ All-Star—64, 66.

Hunt once said, "Some people give their bodies to science; I give mine to baseball." He retired with three major league records for HBP: most times in a career (243); in a season (50, 1971); and in a game (three, tied). For seven straight years he led the NL in HBP. He had other ways to get on, as two .300 seasons and good walk totals showed. He set Expo team records for fewest strikeouts in a season (19, 1973) and fewest times hitting into double plays (one, 1971). Though he played on the early, horrid Met teams, he was heartbroken when he was traded to the Dodgers in November 1966. After retiring, Hunt went into ranching outside St. Louis. /(FJO)

Billy Hunter — 1928– . SS-2B 1953–58 **Browns/ Orioles**, Yankees, A's, Indians 630 g, .219, 16 hr, 144 rbi.
Manager 1977–78 **Rangers** 147–108, .576
☛ All-Star—53 .

A flashy fielder, Hunter was an All-Star as a Browns rookie. He was hitting .252 at the time, but finished the season at .219. As the Orioles' third base coach, he was renowned for his frenetic, arm-wheeling "Go!" signal. /(WAB)

Catfish Hunter [James Augustus] — 1946– . RHP 1965–79 **A's**, Yankees 3448 ip, 224–266, 3.26. 20 wins: 71–75 6 LCS, 69 ip, 4–3, 3.25. 6 WS, 63 ip, 5–3, 3.29
☛ Led League—w 74–75. Led League—era 74. Cy Young Award—74. All-Star—66–67, 70, 72–76. Hall of Fame—1987.

Nicknamed Catfish for effect by A's owner Charles O. Finley when Hunter was signed for $75,000, other stories about the origin of the humble North Carolina farmboy's moniker are apocryphal. He was 26–2 with five no- hitters in high school, but nearly lost his chance to play pro ball when he suffered a foot wound in a hunting accident. He missed the 1964 season due to surgery, and made the A's in 1965. From then until 1977, Hunter didn't miss a start. Named to the All-Star team for the first of eight times in 1966, he first participated in '67, yielding only one run in five innings, but lost. On May 8, 1968 against Minnesota, he pitched the AL's first regular-season perfect game in 46 years. (Charlie Robertson in 1922 was the last; Don Larsen's came in the World Series in 1956.) Hunter received a $5,000 raise on the spot from Finley.

In 1970, his first season over .500 (18–14), Hunter tied for the AL lead with 40 starts. He then won 21 games each season from 1971 to 1973; his .750 winning percentage (21–7) in 1972 and .808 (21–5) in 1973 led the AL. In 1974 he won the Cy Young Award; his 25 wins tied him with Fergie Jenkins for the AL lead, and his 2.49 ERA stood alone at the top. In each of those four seasons, Oakland won their division, and three times were World Champions. Hunter was 4–0 with one save in seven A's WS appearances.

Hunter was declared a free agent for 1975 by arbitrator Peter Seitz when Finley failed to pay $50,000, half of Hunter's salary, to a life-insurance fund. Hunter signed with the Yankees for $3.5 million, by far the largest amount ever paid a player to that point, inspiring others, especially A's stars, to seek free agency. In 1975, his first season in New York, Catfish went 23–14, tying with Jim Palmer for the league lead in wins and topping the AL in complete games and innings pitched. However, he took the loss in the '75 All-Star Game. He helped the Yankees to three straight pennants (1976–78) despite declining effectiveness due to arm strain and diabetes. After going 2–9 in 1979, Hunter retired at age 33. Though continuing to assist the Yankees in spring training, his priorities remained on his farm in Hertford, NC.

Catfish Hunter

A good hitting pitcher, Hunter batted .350 in 1971 (36-for-103) and .226 lifetime, with six home runs. He holds Oakland's all-time top spots in wins (161), starts (340), innings (2,456), shutouts (31), and strikeouts (1,520). His World Series marks in five categories rank him among the top ten in history. Soft-spoken and humble, with a dose of country charm, Catfish was inducted into the Hall of Fame in 1987./(MC)

Willard Hunter — 1934– . LHP 1962, 64 Dodgers, **Mets** 114 ip, 4–9, 5.68

Hunter contributed a 1–6 record to the worst team in ML history, the 1962, 40–120 Mets. Hunter was 3–3 as a reliever in 41 games in '64, but overwork blew out his arm./(MC)

Huntington Avenue Grounds Boston Red Sox 1901–11. LF-440, CF-635, RF-280

A huge field that hosted circuses and carnivals, the Huntington Avenue Grounds were the site of the first World Series game, October 1, 1903, and are now part of Northeastern University. /(SCL)

Steve Huntz — 1945- . SS-3B-2B 1967, 69–71, 75 Cardinals, **Padres**, White Sox 237 g, .206, 16 hr, 60 rbi

The Cardinals drafted Huntz from the Orioles' organization in December 1964 after he showed fine fielding skills in his first pro season, but he broke a leg in spring training and missed all of 1965. His only significant ML action came with the Padres in their sophomore season, 1970, when he had career highs of .219, 11 HR, and 54 runs. /(WOR)

Tom Hurd (Whitey) — 1924–1982. RHP 1954–56 **Red Sox** 186 ip, 13–10, 3.96

Hurd spent seven years in the White Sox system before reaching the majors with the Red Sox. The first team he beat was the White Sox. In 1955 he led the AL with eight relief wins. /(NLM)

Clint Hurdle — 1957- . OF-1B 1977–83, 85–87 **Royals**, Reds, Mets, Cardinals 515 g, .259, 32 hr, 193 rbi. *2 LCS, 7 g, .300, 1 rbi. 1 WS, 4 g, .417*

A Royals number-one draft pick, Hurdle was American Association Rookie of the Year and MVP in 1977 but never reached the ML stardom many predicted for him. As the regular right fielder for the 1980 Royals pennant winners, he hit .294, with 10 homers and 60 RBI. A back injury put him out most of the next season, and he never regained his batting stroke. A positive clubhouse attitude and a willingness to play anywhere, even catch, extended his career. /(FJO)

Ed Hurley — 1910–1969. *Umpire* AL 1947–65 *4 WS 3 ASU*

The plate umpire at one of baseball's most bizarre moments, Hurley called four straight balls in 1951 when the Browns sent 3′7″ midget Eddie Gaedel to bat. When Hurley was retired by the AL in 1965 because of age, he fought the action in court but lost. /(RTM)

Bruce Hurst — 1958- . LHP 1980- **Red Sox**, Padres 1704 ip, 103–84, 4.01. *2 LCS, 28 ip, 1–2, 2.57. 1 WS, 23 ip, 2–0, 1.96* ☛ *All-Star—87.*

Keeping righthanded sluggers at bay with a mix of slow breaking pitches and a sneaky fastball, Hurst was a rare lefthander who excelled at Fenway Park. He was 33–9 there from 1986 to 1988, and his 56 Fenway wins are second only to Mel Parnell's among lefthanders. His pickoff move to first base is a weapon as well (he caught 15 baserunners in 1984), but he has never excelled consistently over a full season. Hurst had a 2.99 ERA in 1986, a year in which he spent six midsummer weeks on the DL with a pulled groin, and 1984 (3.92) and 1988 (3.62) are the only other years in Boston his ERA was below 4.00. He baffled the Mets in the 1986 WS, winning Game One 1–0 and Game Four 4–2, prompting Darryl Strawberry to remark, "Clemens is tough, but he's no Hurst." He had been voted WS MVP before the Mets rallied to win Game Six with three runs in the bottom of the 10th, and the award was given to Ray Knight when the Mets won Game Seven as well. Hurst became baseball's most coveted free agent after a career-best 18–6 record in 1988, and he accepted less money from the Padres than the Red Sox had offered so he could pitch in San Diego, closer to his Utah roots. He went 15–11 with a career-best 2.69 ERA in 1989. /(SCL)

Don Hurst — 1905–1952. 1B-OF 1928–34 **Phillies**, Cubs 905 g, .298, 115 hr, 610 rbi ☛ *Led League—rbi 32.*

This strong lefthanded hitter came into the majors when offense was at its peak. In four of his first five years with the Phillies, he batted over .300. In 1932, his best all-around season, he hit .339 with 24 HR, and led the NL with 143 RBI. Traded to the Cubs during the 1934 season, he failed to hit, and his ML career ended. /(AL)

Tim Hurst — 1865–1915. *Umpire* NL, AL 1891–97, 00–09 *Manager* 1898 **Cardinals** 39–111, .260

Pugnacious Tim Hurst had a reputation for settling arguments over disputed calls by striking arguing players on their heads with his mask or his fists. In 1897 an irate fan tossed a beer stein at Hurst. The umpire threw it back, hit the wrong fan, and was fined $100 and dismissed by the NL. Hired to manage the Cardinals, he took them to a last-place finish while reputedly leading the league in umpire-baiting. After another stormy five years as a NL ump, Hurst joined the AL. In one game, after an argument with New York manager Clark Griffith, he followed Griffith to the dugout and knocked him cold. On August 4, 1909, he spit in the eye of Athletics second baseman Eddie Collins, ending an argument and igniting a riot. Hurst was fired by the AL, after which he became a boxing referee. /(RTM)

Hy Hurwitz — 1910–1966. *Writer.*

Hurwitz was a baseball writer for the Boston *Globe* for 40 years and secretary-treasurer of the BBWAA for eight years until his death. /(NLM)

Ted Husing — 1901–1961. *Broadcaster.*

Husing was a top radio personality for 30 years. In 1924, he won an announcing audition that had 600 competitors. Three years later he joined CBS, doing all sports, including several WS. His rapid delivery was once measured at 400 words-per-minute. A colorful, outspoken, sometimes imaginative announcer, Husing was banned from Harvard's football games for calling the play of their All-America quarterback "putrid." Three years later he was temporarily suspended from doing the 1934 WS by Judge Landis for allegedly second-guessing the umpires in previous broadcasts. Husing left CBS in 1946 to become one of the first disc jockeys. /(NLM)

Bert Husting (Pete) — 1878–1948. RHP 1900–02 Pirates, **Milwaukee AL**, Red Sox, A's 437 ip, 24–21, 4.16

A fullback in the same University of Wisconsin backfield with the legendary Pat O'Dea, Husting pitched his college team to the 1898 Western Conference championship. After a strong 14–5 with the 1902 A's, he left baseball to pursue a law career. /(BC)

Johnny Hutchings — 1916–1963. RHP 1940–42, 44–46 Reds, **Braves** 471 ip, 12–18, 3.96. *1 WS, 1 ip, 9.00*

The tireless, 6'2" 250-lb Hutchings made a career-high 57 appearances in 1945. Following his ML days, he pitched, coached, and managed in Indianapolis from 1946 through 1960. /(JK)

Bill Hutchinson (Wild Bill) — 1859–1926. RHP 1889–95, 97 **Cubs**, Cardinals 3066 ip, 182–158, 3.59. 20 wins: 90–92
☛ *Led League—w 90–92. Led League—k 92.*

Yale grad Hutchinson played weekend ball as a hobby and from there went straight to the majors. Pitching for average Cubs teams, he led NL hurlers three straight years in wins, complete games, and innings pitched, despite competition from Amos Rusie, Cy Young, and Kid Gleason. His worst ERA in that stretch was 2.81, but he was out of the ML four years later. /(JK)

Fred Hutchinson (Moose, The Bear, The Great Stone Face) — 1919–1964. RHP 1939–41, 46–53 **Tigers** 1464 ip, 95–71, 3.73. *1 WS, 1 ip, 0–0, 9.00.*
   Manager 1952–54, 56–64 Tigers, Cardinals, **Reds** 830–827, .501. First place: 61 *1 WS, 1–4, .200*

One writer said Hutchinson looked like a man who had just lost an argument to an umpire—something Hutchinson often did. He was hot-tempered, given to tossing furniture about the clubhouse and smashing light bulbs after frustrating defeats. But he was extremely well-liked as a player, and as a manager, commanded love and veneration from his players.

Hutchinson was an aggressive, relentless, and smart pitcher, but did not have overwhelming speed. His career with Detroit was interrupted by four years

Fred Hutchinson

in the Navy, but he returned in 1946 and had five consecutive winning campaigns, averaging 15 victories a season. A lifetime .263 hitter, he was used 91 times in the pinch, with four home runs—one of them his last hit, in 1953. For several years he was the AL player representative.

Hutchinson replaced Red Rolfe as Detroit manager in mid-1952. He left after the 1954 season because the Tigers would not give him more than a one-year contract. From 1956 through 1958, he managed the Cardinals. Cincinnati's Frank Lane explained why he hired Hutchinson in 1959: "When I was general manager of the White Sox and Hutch was at Detroit, I went looking for him in Chicago one night to talk about something. I found him in a hotel room with several players, explaining the cutoff play on a blackboard. He was the first manager I ever knew who believed in night school. That impressed me."

Hutchinson won one pennant with the Reds, in 1961, but lost the World Series to the Yankees. He battled cancer until he was forced to resign in August of 1964. Named as a coach for the '64 All-Star Game, he moved with great effort and pain, but would not miss it. The Reds went on to finish second. When Hutchinson died at age 45 that November 12, he was voted Most Courageous Athlete and was honored by several chapters of the Baseball Writers Association with fundraising events for cancer research. /(NLM)

Ira Hutchinson — 1910–1973. RHP 1933, 37–41, 44–45 White Sox, **Braves**, Dodgers, Cardinals 611 ip, 34–33, 3.76

In 1933 Hutchinson was shelled in his lone appearance for his hometown White Sox, but he found a home in the NL four years later, pitching capably in relief for seven seasons. /(JK)

Tom Hutton — 1946– . 1B-OF 1966, 69, 72–81 Dodgers, **Phillies**, Blue Jays, Expos 952 g, .248, 22 hr, 186 rbi. *2 LCS, 4 g, .000*

This slick-fielding lefthanded first baseman and fill-in outfielder excelled as a late-inning defensive replacement. He hit .700 against Tom Seaver and batted .269 lifetime as a pinch hitter. He had three game-winning pinch homers during his career with the Phillies. The brother-in-law of pitcher Dick Ruthven, he was a guitar player who played professionally in Las Vegas. Hutton later became a ML broadcaster. /(AL)

Dick Hyde — 1928– . RHP 1955, 57–61 **Senators**, Orioles 298 ip, 17–14, 3.56

The bespectacled, submariner was the AL's top reliever in 1958. He led in relief wins (10) and saved 18 to account for 46% of the last-place Senators' victories. His 1.75 ERA was Washington's best since Walter Johnson's 1.49 in 1919. Back problems the next season ended his effectiveness. /(MC)

Iron Man Inao [Kasuhisa] — 1938– . P 1956–1969 Nishitetsu Lions 276–137, 1.98
☛ *Rookie of the Year—56 Sawamura Award 57–58, 61, 63.*

With a 276–137 lifetime record, and a career ERA of 1.98, Iron Man Inao is widely regarded as the greatest of all Japanese pitchers. He broke in with a 21–6 record and 1.06 ERA at age 18, pacing the Lions to their second pennant and first Japan Championship as both ace starter and top clutch reliever. Inao earned his nickname Iron Man two years later, as the Lions made it four pennants in five years and three Japan Championships in a row. Either starting or relieving in all the Lions' last nine regular-season games to put them into the Japan Series, Inao then started five of seven games against the Yomiuri Giants. He lost once as a starter and once in relief as the Giants took a 3–0 lead.

Pitching the last six innings of the fourth game, Inao homered in the 10th to keep the Lions alive. He then tossed three complete-game victories in a row, including a 26-inning scoreless streak, to beat the Giants in the greatest comeback in baseball history, Japanese or American. After his sensational debut, Inao posted records of 35–6, 33–10, 30–15, 20–7, 42–14, 25–18, and 28–16. His ERA climbed above 1.69 only once in his first five years, and never topped 2.54 in any year he pitched more than half a dozen games. Most incredibly, Inao appeared in 61, 68, 72, 75, 39, 78, 57, and 74 games over his first eight years, working 262, 374, 373, 402, 243, 404, 321, and 386 innings. In the seven years following his rookie season, Inao never completed fewer than 19 games. Not since the pitching distance was increased to 60′ 6″ has any American pitcher handled a comparable workload. Inao struck out 182, 288, 334, 321, 179, 353, 228, and 226 batters during his eight-year streak of dominance, totals even more impressive considering that Japanese batting styles then stressed contact over power. A complete player, he often kept himself in close games with excellent hitting and fielding, as well as his arm. The arm gave out in 1964. Appearing in

only two games, Inao came back to handle a more normal workload in 1965 and 1966, averaging "only" 200 innings with ERAs of 2.38 and 1.79, in a "mere" 38 and 54 games, many in relief. Retiring as an active player three years later when only 31, Inao managed the Lions to five straight second-division finishes, 1970–74. /(MC)

Pete Incaviglia (Inky) — 1964– . OF-DH 1986– Rangers 541 g, .252, 100 hr, 303 rbi

Incaviglia is one of the few players to jump directly from college ball—he was *Baseball America*'s NCAA Player of the Year at Oklahoma State in 1985—to the ML. His slugging prowess has been offset by defensive failings and enormous strikeout totals. He was the Expos' first- round draft choice in June 1985, but refused to sign until a trade with Texas had been negotiated. In 1986, he tied the Rangers' single-season home run record with 30 as a rookie, but he also struck out 185 times, four shy of Barry Bonds's ML record. In three ML seasons through 1988, Incaviglia had 506 strikeouts and 377 hits. Injuries slowed him in 1989. /(ME)

Jeff Innis — 1962– . RHP 1987– Mets 84 ip, 1–3, 2.88

Despite pitching well in his call-ups, Innis was stuck behind fellow submarine reliever Terry Leach until Leach was traded to the Royals in mid-1989. /(JFC)

International League — 1883– . *Minor League.*

The International League, the oldest minor league in existence, was founded in 1883 as the Interstate League, either the second or the fourth minor league formed, depending on the definition. It was reorganized as the Eastern League in 1884 and took the name International League in 1913. Usually one of the strongest minor leagues, it has boasted some legendary teams. The Baltimore Orioles of the 1910s and 1920s, owned by Jack Dunn, developed such stars as Babe Ruth (who hit only one HR in his short time in the minors), Lefty Grove, Max Bishop, and George Earnshaw. They won seven straight pennants (1919–25) by keeping many of those stars for years after they were ready for the majors. Minor league teams were still mostly independent then, not tightly controlled by major league teams. The late 1930s Newark Bears, referred to as the Yankee B-team, featured future stars Joe Gordon and Charlie Keller. Clubs in Toronto and Montreal justified the International name, and it was in Montreal, where Branch Rickey judged that racial prejudice would be less of a problem than in the States, that Jackie Robinson made his organized-baseball debut in 1946.

In 1988 the International League combined with the American Association in the "Triple-A Alliance", playing interleague games and a postseason series. /(SFS)

Dane Iorg — 1950– . OF-1B 1977–86 Phillies, **Cardinals**, Royals, Padres 743 g, .276, 14 hr, 216 rbi. *2 LCS, 6 g, .500, 1 rbi. 2 WS, 7 g, .526, 3 rbi*

A contact hitter without power or speed, Iorg excelled in the post-season. He hit .529 as the Cardinals' designated hitter in the 1982 WS and won Game Six of the 1985 WS for the Royals with a two-run pinch single in the bottom of the ninth against the Cardinals. Garth Iorg is his brother. /(FJO)

Garth Iorg — 1954– . 3B-2B 1978, 80–87 **Blue Jays** 931 g, .258, 20 hr, 238 rbi. *1 LCS, 7 g, .133*

Iorg was a solid utility player who spent most of his career as the righthanded half of a third-base platoon with Rance Mulliniks. He was most recognizable for his strange batting stance, on the toes of his front foot and leaning back toward the catcher as the ball was being pitched.

Selected by the Blue Jays from the Yankee organization in the 1976 expansion draft, Iorg spent his entire nine-season ML career with the Blue Jays. In his final ML plate appearance, Iorg made Toronto's last out of the 1987 season when a hit would have tied the Blue Jays with Detroit for the AL East title. At the time of his retirement, Iorg was the Blue Jay career leader in pinch hits. Usually a singles hitter, Iorg hit well enough (with batting stats aided by judicious platooning) to have the highest batting average (.313) on the Blue Jays in their division-winning 1985 season, along with a .469 slugging percentage. Garth is the brother of Dane Iorg. /(TF)

Monte Irvin — 1919– . OF-1B 1949–56 **Giants**, Cubs 764 g, .293, 99 hr, 443 rbi. *2 WS, 10 g, .394, 4 rbi* ☛ *Led League—rbi 51. Hall of Fame—1973.*

After baseball's color line was broken in 1947, Monte Irvin was one of the first black players signed

Monte Irvin with the Newark Eagles

by the Giants. He could run, throw, field, hit, and hit with power, all brilliantly. He earned 16 letters and all-state honors in four sports at East Orange (NJ) High School. His outstanding athletic career was almost prematurely ended in 1938 when he scratched his hand in a basketball game; the resulting infection kept him near death for seven weeks. He recovered and returned to the Orange Triangles, a semi-pro team that he had joined in 1932. He began playing for the Newark Eagles on weekends under the name "Jimmy Nelson" to protect his amateur standing, a practice he continued while attending Lincoln University.

Irvin became one of the brightest stars in the Negro Leagues, playing in four East-West all-star games. After hitting league highs of .422 in 1940 and .396 in 1941, he won the triple crown in Mexico with a .398 average and 30 home runs in 68 games. Many Negro League owners felt Irvin was the best-qualified candidate to break the major league color line, but Irvin was drafted in 1942 and spent the next three years in the army.

Upon his return from the service, Irvin was tentatively contacted by the Dodgers' Branch Rickey, but felt he needed to play himself back into shape. He earned MVP honors in the 1945–46 Puerto Rican Winter League. He then led the Negro National League in RBI and hit .389, taking the Eagles to a victory over the Kansas City Monarchs in the 1946 Negro World Series. Irvin hit .462, slammed three HR, and scored the winning run in the seventh game. He was ready for the majors, but Rickey did not want to pay Eagles owner Effa Manley for the rights to Irvin's contract. Irvin remained with the Eagles and proceeded to lead the NNL in HR and RBI.

After Irvin spent the 1948–49 winter in Cuba, Rickey relinquished his claim, and the New York Giants paid Manley $5,000 for Irvin's contract. Assigned to Jersey City (International League), he batted .373. He debuted with the Giants on July 27, 1949 as a pinch hitter. Back with Jersey City in 1950, he was called up after hitting .510 with 10 HR in 18 games. He batted .299 for the Giants that season, playing first base and the outfield. In 1951 Irvin emerged as a star, hitting .312 with 24 HR, leading the National League with 121 RBI, and finishing third in MVP balloting. He hit .458 in the 1951 World Series and stole home off Yankee pitcher Allie Reynolds in the second game.

During an exhibition game in April 1952, Irvin broke his ankle sliding into third. He reinjured the leg in August 1953 and never regained his earlier form. He was sent down in mid-1955, and spent his final ML season with the Cubs. He scouted for the Mets in 1967–68, then joined the Commissioner's office as a public relations representative. The Committee on Negro Baseball Leagues elected him to the

Hall of Fame in 1973; he later became a member of that body and of the Hall of Fame Committee on Baseball Veterans. /(JR)

Charlie Irwin — 1869–1925. 3B-SS-2B-OF 1893–1902 Cubs, **Reds**, Dodgers 989 g, .267, 16 hr, 488 rbi

A sure-handed fielder and one of the fastest third basemen of his day, Irwin was always among the 1890s' NL defensive leaders. He showed a flash of power in 1894, with eight home runs for Chicago. /(DAS)

James C. Isaminger — 1881–1946. *Writer.*

The rotund Isaminger broke in with the Cincinnati *Times-Herald*. In 1905, he was recommended by Ban Johnson for a job with the Philadelphia *North American*, where he remained until the paper was sold in 1925. He moved to the *Inquirer*, where he remained until his death. Isaminger was credited with investigative reporting second only to Hugh Fullerton in exposing the Black Sox of 1919. His columns "Under the Spotlight" and "Tips from the Sporting Ticker" were widely read, as were his reports in *The Sporting News*. He edited the Reach Guides from 1928 until they were discontinued just before WWII. President of the BBWAA in 1946, Isaminger was voted the J.G. Taylor Spink Award in 1974. /(NLM)

Frank Isbell (Bald Eagle) — 1875–1941. 1B-2B-OF-3B 1898, 1901–09 Cubs, **White Sox** 1119 g, .250, 13 hr, 455 rbi. *1 WS, 6 g, .308, 4 rbi*

The leading hitter (.279) on the 1906 "Hitless Wonder" White Sox, Isbell was a versatile player who at one time or another played every position, including pitcher (4–7, 3.59). He joined the White Sox as a first baseman in 1900, the year before the AL declared itself a major league. Totally bald, he was upset when the team picture was taken without caps. The next year he led the new major league in stolen bases (52). When his hitting declined, he moved to second base, where he played when the weak-hitting White Sox won the World Championship in '06. Ironically, Isbell set several WS offensive records that still stand: most hits, two consecutive games (7); and most doubles and extra base hits in a game (4). He also held the record for most errors in a WS by a second baseman until 1981, when Davey Lopes took that dubious distinction. /(DB)

Mike Ivie (Poison Ivie) — 1952– . 1B-3B-DH-C 1971, 74–83 **Padres**, Giants, Astros, Tigers 857 g, .269, 81 hr, 411 rbi

Padres manager John McNamara said Ivie, San Diego's number-one draft choice in 1970, "was born to catch." But Ivie hated catching and preferred first base; the Padres tried him at third base too, including 61 games there in 1975. When he was moved again to third base in 1977, he jumped the team for several days. It looked as though he would live up to his promise as a hitter in 1976, when he hit .291 with 70 RBI in 405 at-bats. But San Diego tired of his attitude and traded him in February 1978 for Derrel Thomas.

Ivie hit a career-high .308 for the Giants in 1978 when he backed up the aging Willie McCovey at first base. Ivie showed little range but was a useful pinch hitter. He went 12-for-31 in the pinch and tied a major league record with two pinch grand slams that season. That performance won him more playing time in 1979, and he had career highs of 27 HR and 89 RBI in 402 at-bats. He also had a clause written into his contract specifying that he would not have to catch.

His power vanished in 1980 (four HR in 286 at-bats) and Ivie once again wore out his welcome. He was traded to Houston in April 1981 for Jeff Leonard and Dave Bergman, and his career petered out thereafter. Rick Monday summed it up best when he said, "Mike Ivie is a forty-million-dollar airport with a thirty-dollar control tower." /(JFC)

Jerry Izenberg — 1930– . *Writer.*

A graduate of Rutgers, Izenberg joined the Newark *Star-Ledger* in 1963 and is a columnist for the Newhouse syndicate. He has published several collections of columns and essays and has written and produced over 30 television shows, including documentaries on manager Johnny Keane, the New York Mets, and Roberto Clemente. /(NLM)

J

Ray Jablonski (Jabbo). — 1926–1985. 3B-OF-1B 1953–60 **Cardinals**, Reds, Giants, A's 808 g, .268, 83 hr, 438 rbi
☛ *All-Star—54.*

In the mid-1950s, the Cardinals had a group known as the Polish Falcons; Ray Jablonski, Rip Repulski, and Steve Bilko. Jablonski debuted as the Cards' regular third baseman in 1953, hitting 21 HR and collecting 112 RBI. He developed an exuberant following, with a large section of Sportsmans Park frequently yelling, "Go-Go Jabbo." An All-Star in 1954, Jablonski peaked at the plate, hitting .296, but his league-high 34 errors at 3B and .925 FA (worst in the AL for regulars at all positions) made him expendable. Traded to the Reds, he was replaced in St. Louis by rookie Ken Boyer. Jablonski's glove kept him from further success. /(RTM)

Jack Murphy Stadium San Diego Padres 1969– . LF-329, CF-405, RF-329

An attractive modern facility with natural grass and good sight lines, Jack Murphy Stadium opened as San Diego Stadium in 1967, and did not have a tenant until the Padres were created in the NL's 1969 expansion. Renamed in 1981, the stadium was originally three-sided, open in right field with only a small bleacher section there, as opposed to five seating levels around the rest of the field. The right-field bleachers were recently expanded, however, enclosing the field fully and bringing the capacity up to its current 59,022. The Padres share the stadium with the NFL's San Diego Chargers. /(SCL)

Fred Jacklitsch — 1876–1937. C-1B-2B 1900–05, 07–10, 14–15, 17 **Phillies**, Dodgers, Yankees, Baltimore (FL), Braves 490 g, .243, 5 hr, 153 rbi

Except for 1914, when he jumped to Baltimore of the Federal League, this native Brooklynite spent his ML career as a second-string catcher, filling in a few times in the outfield and at every infield position. /(AL)

Bill Jackowski (Jack) — 1914– . *Umpire* NL 1952–68 3 WS 3 ASU

Jackowski was the plate umpire on September 18, 1968 when the Cardinals' Ray Washburn pitched a no-hitter against the Giants the day after San Francisco's Gaylord Perry no-hit St. Louis, the first consecutive game no-hitters in history. It was the second no-hitter called by Jackowski that season, making him one of ten umpires to have worked the plate for two no-hitters in one season. /(RTM)

Al Jackson — 1935– . LHP 1959–69 Pirates, **Mets**, Cardinals, Reds 1389 ip, 67–99, 3.98

Former Reds outfielder Vada Pinson described this 5'10" Texan as "Very competitive, small, big heart—he knew how to pitch. He fought you every kind of way to help beat you." Although Jackson went 8–20 for the fledgling Mets in both 1962 and 1965, the gutty southpaw threw all four of the Mets' shutouts in 1962. His 43 career victories were a pre-Seaver Met high. Jackson went 9–4 with the World Champion '67 Cards but did not appear in the World Series. /(RTM)

Bo Jackson [Vincent Edward] — 1962– . OF 1986- **Royals** 400 g, .244, 81 hr, 235 rbi
☛ *All-Star—89.*

After winning the Heisman Trophy and *TSN* College Football Player of the Year in 1985, Jackson opted to sign with the Royals instead of Tampa Bay in the NFL. He joined the Royals after just 53 games in the minors and, while showing speed and power, he struck out frequently and displayed questionable defense.

After showing improvement in 1987 with 22 HR despite 158 strikeouts, Bo announced his plan to play football in the off-season with the Raiders as "a hobby," a move initially not appreciated by Kansas City players or fans. In 1988 Jackson slammed 25 homers and stole 27 bases but still struck out 146 times. However, in 1989 he finally raised his batting average, to .256, hit 32 HR with 105 RBI, and used his speed and strong arm to become one of the most exciting left fielders in baseball. /(FO)

Danny Jackson — 1962– . LHP 1983– **Royals**, Reds 1089 ip, 66–68, 3.66. *1 LCS, 10 ip, 1–0, 0.00. 1 WS, 16 ip, 1–1, 1.69*
☛ *Led League—w 88.*

Jackson was a member of a cast of talented pitchers the Royals developed in the early 1980s. After some early successes, Danny fought through an 18-loss season in 1987. The Royals, desperate for a short-stop, dealt him to the Reds for Kurt Stillwell.

In 1988 Jackson dominated NL hitters with a moving fastball and wicked slider on his way to a league-leading 23 victories. He finished second in the Cy Young balloting only because of Orel Hershiser's record-setting scoreless innings streak. Injuries limited him to a 6–11, 5.60 record in only 20 starts in 1989. /(FO)

Darrell Jackson — 1956– . LHP 1978–82 **Twins** 411 ip, 20–27, 4.38

This Arizona State product started 15 games for Minnesota in his first pro year (1978). He was 9–9 (3.87) in 1980; then, chemical dependency and shoulder problems cut short his career. /(JCA)

Darrin Jackson — 1963– . OF 1985, 87–88 **Cubs** 112 g, .270, 6 hr, 20 rbi

Jackson saw the most action in 1988, hitting .266 with six HR in 188 at-bats. /(SFS)

Grant Jackson (Buck) — 1942– . LHP 1965–82 Phillies, Orioles, Yankees, **Pirates**, Expos, Royals 1359 ip, 86–75, 3.46. *4 LCS, 9 ip, 2–0, 3.12. 3 WS, 9 ip, 1–0, 2.00*
☛ *All-Star—69.*

Jackson, a quality reliever for much of his 18-year career, got his greatest attention as a member of Pittsburgh's World Champion "Family" in 1979. The number-two man in the bullpen behind Kent Tekulve, Jackson went 8–5 with a career-high 14 saves and finished third in the NL in appearances, behind teammates Tekulve and Enrique Romo. Jackson gave up no runs and only two hits in his six postseason appearances in '79, winning Game One of the LCS and the World Series clincher as the Pirates completed their dramatic seven-game comeback. He was only the sixth black pitcher to win a WS game.

Jackson didn't have a winning record in six seasons for the Phillies at the start of his career. An attempt to use him as a starter looked promising in 1969 (14–18, 3.34) but fell apart in 1970 (3–15, 5.28, plus two relief wins). Traded to the Orioles for 1971, he became an important member of the Orioles' bullpen-by-committee arrangement and never again had a losing season. In 1973 he was 8–0, tied for sixth all-time for most wins in a season without a loss, and won Game Four of the LCS over the A's. Traded to the Yankees in the 10-player June 1976 deal that brought Rick Dempsey, Rudy May, and Scott McGregor to Baltimore, Jackson was the only new Yankee who didn't disappoint, going 6–0 the rest of the way to help New York to its first AL pennant in 12 years. /(WOR)

Jim Jackson — 1877–1955. OF 1901–02, 05–06 Orioles, Giants, **Indians** 347 g, .236, 4 hr, 132 rbi

Jackson followed manager John McGraw from the original Orioles to the Giants in 1902 but was released after hitting .182. In Cleveland he served under another Hall of Famer, Nap Lajoie, then played and managed in the minors until 1917. /(ME)

Joe Jackson (Shoeless Joe) — 1887–1951. OF 1908–1920 A's, **Indians**, White Sox 1330 g, .356, 54 hr, 785 rbi. *2 WS, 14 g, .345, 1 hr, 8 rbi*

Jackson was supremely gifted in his baseball ability and supremely limited in his ability to deal with real life. He could hit, run, and throw with the best but he lacked education, judgment, and character. When his limitations overcame his gifts, it was a tragedy of both baseball and American life.

Joe was an illiterate son of the cotton-town South, ignorant of city ways, easy to ridicule for everything but his baseball talent. The Athletics, his first ML team, turned him sullen and ineffective with their cruel, mocking humor. Manager Connie Mack gave up on him and shipped him to Cleveland for a mediocre outfielder, Bris Lord.

His Cleveland teammates accepted Jackson as he was and treated him well. He responded with the great years of his career. A graceful natural hitter (supposedly Babe Ruth patterned his batting stance on Jackson's), he hit for power in an age of slap hitters, yet kept his BA near the top. In 1911, his first full season, he hit .408, then followed with .395, .373, and a mere .338 in 1914. He was unerring in the field, had a powerful and accurate arm, and ran the bases with savvy.

Money troubles forced Cleveland to trade him to the White Sox in 1915 for three undistinguished players and $31,500. He hit less well for the Sox but still reigned as the star of the powerful team Comiskey had assembled. He contributed an uncharacteristically low .301 to the championship 1917 Sox but hit .351 with 96 RBI for the 1919 pennant winners. In 1920, he had one of his greatest seasons (.392, 12

Shoeless Joe Jackson

HR, 121 RBI), but everything crashed with the revelation of the Black Sox scandal.

Friends pointed to his .375 WS average as evidence that he'd played on the square, but Jackson had undoubtedly accepted the promise of $5,000 to fix the games. Banned from baseball for life, he returned to his small South Carolina town, started a dry-cleaning business, and prospered. Occasionally he swung "Black Betsy," his famous bat, in sandlot and outlaw games. In time, he retrieved some of his dignity if not the glory. Locally, he was warmly regarded at his death. /(ADS)

Joe S. Jackson — Unk.–Unk. *Writer.*

Jackson was the founder of the BBWAA and its first and only president from 1907 to 1919. He became sports editor of the Detroit *Free Press* in 1901. In 1910, he joined the Washington *Post* as sports editor, remaining for three years. /(NLM)

Larry Jackson (Hot Potato) — 1931– . RHP 1955–68 **Cardinals**, Cubs, Phillies 3262 ip, 194–183, 3.40. 20 wins: 64
☛ *Led League—w 64. All-Star—57–58, 60, 63.*

In his second year of pro ball, Jackson dominated the California League, striking out 351 batters while posting a 28–4 record. A reliever early on with the Cardinals, the strong-armed workhorse averaged 259 innings over his last ten campaigns while winning 13 or more each of his final 12 years. After leading the NL with 38 starts and 282 innings in 1960, Jackson suffered a broken jaw in spring training of 1961 when hit by Duke Snider's shattered bat. He recovered, winning 11 of his last 12 decisions and the St. Louis baseball writers' Comeback of the Year Award. In October 1962, Jackson and Lindy McDaniel were traded to the Cubs in a complicated three-team deal. Jackson pitched nearly 300 innings in 1964 and won a league-high 24 games, accounting for almost one third of the Cubs' victories. Rather than report to the expansion Expos in 1969, Jackson returned to his native Idaho, becoming a sportswriter and state legislator. /(FJO)

Mike Jackson — 1964– . RHP 1986– Phillies, **Mariners** 321 ip, 13–21, 3.36

In parts of two seasons with the Phillies, Jackson was 3–10 with a 4.12 ERA, mainly in relief. After being traded to Seattle along with Glenn Wilson in exchange for Phil Bradley, he emerged as a fine reliever. In his first season with the Mariners, Jackson had the lowest ERA on the club. /(TF)

Randy Jackson [Ransom Joseph] (Handsome Ransom) — 1926– . 3B 1950–59 **Cubs**, Dodgers, Indians 955 g, .261, 103 hr, 415 rbi. *1 WS, 3 g, .000*
☛ *All-Star—54–55.*

A Texas Christian University football player, Jackson played in the 1945 and '46 Cotton Bowls. He hit 19, 19, and 21 homers in 1953–55 with the Cubs. In 1955 he led NL third basemen in double plays. The Dodgers traded Walt Moryn, Don Hoak, and Russ Meyer to the Cubs for Jackson and pitcher Don Elston in expectation that the slugger would succeed Jackie Robinson at third base, but after a serious knee injury in 1957, Jackson never again played regularly. /(MC)

Reggie Jackson (Mr. October) — 1946– . OF-DH
1967–1987 **A's**, Orioles, Yankees, Angels 2820 g, .262,
563 hr, 1702 rbi. *11 LCS, 45 g, .227, 6 hrs, 20 rbi. 5 WS,
27 g, .357, 10 hr, 24 rbi*
☛ *Most Valuable Player—73. Led League—hr 73, 75, 80,
83. Led League—rbi 73. All-Star—69, 71–75, 77–84.*

Jackson became the first player to have a candy bar
named after him, predicting that this would happen
if he played in New York. Reggie could talk and
Reggie could hit: a sportswriter's dream. The peak
of his career came in a boisterous five-year stint with
the Yankees, which he began by asserting that he
was "the straw that stirred the drink," a statement
that drew the ire of new teammate Thurman Munson and manager Billy Martin. But the outspoken,
flamboyant, muscular outfielder was a winner wherever he went.

In 21 seasons, Jackson played on 11 divisional
winners, six pennant winners, and five World Cham-

pions. He has a .357 lifetime World Series average,
nearly 100 points above his lifetime regular-season
average, and the best career World Series slugging
average at .755. His total of 563 HR was sixth all-
time when he retired. His 2,597 strikeouts, however,
are first all-time.

If the Mets had been wiser, Jackson actually
would have started his career in New York after
playing at Arizona State. But the Mets selected a
catcher, Steve Chilcott, with the first pick in the
1967 amatuer draft, and the A's got Jackson. Joe
DiMaggio was a batting instructor with the A's in
those years, and tried unsuccessfully to get the
youngster to cut down his swing to reduce his
strikeouts. In 1968 Jackson came close to setting an
all-time strikeout mark, fanning 171 times. In 1969
he set career highs in HR with 47, RBI with 118,
slugging average at .608, runs with 123, and walks
with 114, leading the league in the last two catego-

Reggie Jackson

ries. He also led the league in strikeouts for the second of four straight years with 142.

His success in 1969 was haunted by what could have been. In a weekend series in June in Boston, he had 15 RBI in 14 at-bats, including 10 with two homers on Saturday the 15th. On July 2, he hit three HR in Oakland against Seattle. By July 29, he had 40 HR and was 23 games ahead of Ruth's 1927 pace. He then stopped hitting. The slump lasted throughout the 1970 season and practically until the All-Star game in Detroit in 1971, where his mammoth blast over the right-field roof at Tiger Stadium would have left the stadium completely had it not struck a light tower. He made the 1971 All-Star squad only because of an injury to Tony Oliva.

Jackson was as aggressive on the bases and in the field as he was at the plate. In the 1972 LCS against Detroit, he twisted his knee sliding home, and he was forced to watch the World Series in street clothes. He came back with a vengeance in 1973. He won the MVP award with a .293 average and league-leading figures in HR (32), RBI (117), runs (99), and slugging average (.531). In the World Series against the Mets, Jackson was helpless in the three night games, getting only one hit in 10 at-bats. During the day, however, he was 8-for-17. In Game Six, he drove in two runs with a double, then scored the third Oakland run in the A's 3-1 victory over Tom Seaver. He hit his first Series homer in the third inning of the seventh game, a two-run shot that proved to be the difference in the clincher, and led the right-field bleachers in cheers throughout the game. He was named the Series MVP.

Jackson sometimes revealed surprising humility. He once admitted that he'd settle for being "one half the player Willie Mays is." Modest or not, he led the A's to their third straight world title in 1974. But regular clashes with owner Charlie Finley in 1975 prompted Jackson to seek greener pastures. Finley swapped him to Baltimore in 1976, where he led the league in slugging for the third time. But the pull of the New York media circus was strong to Jackson, and in 1977 he set up his permanent press conference in the Bronx. There were continual fights and headlines, but also the first World Championships in Yankee Stadium in over a decade.

Game Six of the 1977 Series was Jackson's shining moment. He had already homered in each of the previous two games. In the fourth inning, he hit a two-run shot into the right-field seats on Burt Hooton's first pitch to him to give the Yankees a 4-3 lead. The following inning, he hit Elias Sosa's first offering into an identical location for another

two runs and a 7-3 lead. In the eighth, when he knocked the first pitch he saw from Charlie Hough into the bleachers, he became the first player besides Babe Ruth to homer three times in a Series game, and the first ever to hit five home runs in one Series.

Jackson's dugout fights with Martin and the clash of personalities with owner George Steinbrenner drove him to California in 1982, where he led the league in HR with 39 and the Angels to a division title. He also led the league in strikeouts, with 156, for the first time in 11 years. His final years with the Angels were spent in the pursuit of Mickey Mantle's career home run total of 536, which he finally surpassed in 1986. He ended his career back in Oakland in 1987. He announced his intentions to retire before the season began, which created a grand farewell tour. /(SEW)

Ron Jackson — 1953- . 1B-3B 1975-84 **Angels**, Twins, Tigers, Orioles 926 g, .259, 56 hr, 342 rbi. *1 LCS, 1 g, 1.000*

One of thirteen children, Jackson was a third baseman/handyman through 1978. Traded to Minnesota, he was the Twins' regular first baseman for 2-1/2 years, hitting 14 home runs in 1979. /(JCA)

Roy Lee Jackson — 1954- . RHP 1977-86 Mets, **Blue Jays**, Padres, Twins 559 ip, 28-34, 3.77

Toronto obtained Jackson from the Mets in a trade for Bob Bailor, the Blue Jays' first pick in the expansion draft, and Jackson became a competent reliever for a poor team. With fairly modest accomplishments, Jackson was able to make entries in the Blue Jay record book that would stand until the emergence of Tom Henke. Jackson's 10 saves in 1984 tied the Blue Jay single-season high at that time, and his 30 career saves had him one behind club leader Joey McLaughlin at the time of Jackson's release. In May 1984, Jackson set a club record for wins in a month with six, all in relief. /(TF)

Sonny Jackson [Roland Thomas] — 1944- . SS-OF 1963-74 Astros, **Braves** 936 g, .251, 7 hr, 162 rbi. *1 LCS, 1 g, --*

Jackson was a 150-lb lefthanded batter who hit .292 and stole a post-1900 NL rookie record 49 bases in 1966. He and Joe Morgan were supposed to be Houston's double-play combo of the future, but Jackson hit just .237 his sophomore season and was traded to Atlanta. There he had injury problems, and never played more than 97 games at shortstop. He spent the 1971 season in the outfield. /(PB)

Travis Jackson (Stonewall) — 1903–1987. SS-3B 1922–36 **Giants** 1656 g, .291, 135 hr, 929 rbi. *4 WS, 19 g, .149, 4 rbi*

☛ *Hall of Fame—1982.*

Jackson was the first of John McGraw's final generation of great rookies. Succeeding Dave Bancroft at shortstop in 1924, the 5′10″ 160-lb Arkansan was soon joined by Bill Terry, Freddie Lindstrom, and Mel Ott as key players on Giant pennant winners of the 1930s. Jackson was a strong-armed SS with good range, as indicated by rankings in the top dozen for lifetime per-game putouts, assists, and chances. He led NL shortstops with 58 errors as a rookie in 1924, but twice led in fielding average, twice in double plays, and four times in assists. In 1934, with knee injuries lessening his mobility, he played his last season at SS, leading the NL with 43 errors. He moved to third base for his last two seasons.

Though generally batting around the sixth spot in the Giants' lineup, he was a keen bunter and a consistent righthanded hitter who had the measure of the short Polo Grounds fences. He batted over .300 six times, peaking at .339 in 1930. His 21 HR in 1929 were a career high, as were his 101 RBI in 1934. After his playing days, he coached for the Giants and managed a dozen minor league clubs. /(ADS)

Elmer Jacobs — 1892–1958. RHP 1914, 16–20, 24–25, 27 Phillies, **Pirates**, Cardinals, Cubs, White Sox 1189 ip, 50–81, 3.55

Jacobs had one winning year, going 9–6 in 1918, having been swapped from Pittsburgh to the Phillies in July for former 20-game winner Erskine Mayer. Never an overpowering pitcher, he walked more than he struck out. /(DAS)

Spook Jacobs [Forrest Vandergrift] — 1925– . 2B 1954–56 **A's**, Pirates 188 g, .247, 0 hr, 33 rbi

After years of minor league apprenticeship, the frail infielder was the regular A's second baseman in 1954, but his good glove couldn't compensate for his light bat. He later produced baseball card and autograph shows. /(JK)

Travis Jackson

Baby Doll Jacobson [William Chester] (Jake) — 1890–1977. OF 1915, 17, 19–27 Tigers, **Browns**, Red Sox, Indians, A's 1472 g, .311, 84 hr, 819 rbi

At Mobile (Southern League) in 1912, the grandstand band played "Oh, You Beautiful Doll" after Jacobson's Opening Day homer, and the next day's paper captioned his photo, "Baby Doll." After a decade in the minors, he spent 1917 in the majors, served a year in the military, and returned as a Browns' regular at 28. The best of Jacobson's ML career was contained in seven straight years over .300 (1919–25), five of them with Ken Williams and Jack Tobin flanking him in the Browns' best-remembered outfield. A burly righthander who swung a light bat, he hit well for average, if not for power. For all his heft (at 6'3" and 215-lb, he was the league's biggest man), he was also a capable fielder. At one time he held 13 fielding marks; his 484 putouts in 1924 stood as a record for 24 years. In 1927 he played seven consecutive games for the Red Sox without a putout or assist. /(ADS)

Beany Jacobson [Albert L.] — 1881–1933. LHP 1904–07 **Senators**, Browns, Red Sox 612 ip, 25–47, 3.19

Jumped all the way from Decatur of the Three-I League to the majors in 1904, Jacobson went 6–23 for the Senators despite a respectable 3.55 ERA. /(BC)

Merwin Jacobson (Jake) — 1894–1978. OF 1915–16, 26–27 Giants, Cubs, **Dodgers** 133 g, .230, 0 hr, 24 rbi

Jacobson, a great minor league hitter, played on seven straight International League Baltimore Oriole championship teams (1919–25). He hit .404 to lead the league in batting in 1920. He made the equivalent of major league wages and pocketed postseason shares with the independently owned team. His few major league opportunities came before he reached his peak and after he had passed it. /(JK)

Brook Jacoby (Jake) — 1959– . 3B 1981, 83-Braves, **Indians** 914 g, .273, 98 hr, 390 rbi
☛ All-Star—86.

In one of the worst trades in Atlanta history, Jacoby, Brett Butler, and Rick Behenna were sent to Cleveland for Len Barker in 1983. Jacoby had spent five years in the Braves system, hitting with power. He quickly became the Indians' hardy, everyday third baseman. An exceedingly quiet, unaggressive player, he proved a calm and sure-handed fielder, good on

fielding the bunt and going to his left, but hesitant to dive for a ball. A poor baserunner and a streaky hitter, he peaked in 1987 (the year of the rabbit ball) when he cut way down on his strikeouts. He batted .300 but managed just 69 RBI; 27 of his 32 homers were solo shots, and he hit just .225 with runners in scoring position. /(JCA)

Sig Jakucki [Sigmund] (Jack) — 1909–1979. RHP 1936, 44–45 **Browns** 411 ip, 25–22, 3.79. *1 WS, 3 ip, 0–1, 9.00*

After an unsuccessful stint in 1936, Jakucki resurfaced during WWII and clinched the Browns' only pennant with a 5–2 win over the Yankees on the last day of the 1944 season. His heavy drinking resulted in his suspension the following year. /(WAB)

Bill James (Big Bill) — 1887–1942. RHP 1911–12, 14–19 Indians, Browns, **Tigers**, Red Sox, White Sox 1180 ip, 65–71, 3.20. *1 WS, 4.2 ip, 0–0, 5.79*

Big Bill's nickname reflected his 6'4" frame and differentiated him from the contemporary Braves pitcher of the same name. James went 15–14, 2.85 for the Browns in 1914 and earned a spot on an AL all-star squad that barnstormed the country in a 32-game series against NL stars. He was sold to the White Sox in August 1919, just in time for the tainted World Series. He made his final ML appearance in the deciding game, relieving intentional loser Lefty Williams with only one out in the first inning and the White Sox already trailing 4–0. /(JK)

Bill James (Seattle Bill) — 1892–1971. RHP 1913–15, 19 **Braves** 542 ip, 37–21, 2.28. 20 wins: 14 *1 WS, 11 ip, 2–0, 0.00*

James was brilliant for one season, helping pitch the 1914 Miracle Braves to a World Championship with 26–7 record and 1.90 ERA. In the WS he shut out the Giants 1–0 on two hits in Game Two and won Game Three in relief. He won only five games in 1916, entered the military for WWI, and got no decision in his one postwar appearance. /(JK)

Bill James — 1949– . *Writer.*

A former high school English teacher in Kansas, Bill James delved into the study of baseball statistics, publishing a series of "baseball abstracts" each season from 1977 through 1988 and *The Bill James Historical Baseball Abstract* in 1985. One of the primary developers of modern sabermetrics, he is largely responsible for the newfound popularity of statistical analyses of baseball questions. His writing is accessible and often acerbic. James is also a contributing editor to *Inside Sports*./(NLM)

Bob James — 1958– . RHP 1978–79, 82–87 Expos, Tigers, **White Sox** 407 ip, 24–26, 3.80

An intimidating 6'4" 230-lb power pitcher, James was the Expos' first-round pick in the 1976 June draft. After saving 10 games for Montreal in 1984 (his first full ML season), he was traded to the White Sox and earned a club-record 32 saves in 1985. But he essentially ended his 1986 season, and his career, that August 4 by tearing a muscle in his pitching arm. Disabled for more than two months of 1987, the bearded reliever could not regain his 92-mph fastball and was released. He recorded 73 career saves./(JCA)

Charlie James — 1937– . OF 1960–65 **Cardinals**, Reds 510 g, .255, 29 hr, 172 rbi. *1 WS, 3 g, .000*

The Texas League rookie of the year in his first pro season (1958) and an International League all-star the following year, James was a platoon player with the Cardinals, splitting leftfield duty with Stan Musial in 1963./(MC)

Chris James — 1962– . OF-3B 1986– **Phillies**, Padres 413 g, .256, 50 hr, 190 rbi

James was a promising young hitter with great speed before he missed most of the 1986 season with a broken ankle. He rebounded in 1987 to hit .293 with 17 HR while playing only part-time in the crowded Phillies outfield. As a starter in 1988, he tried to hit home runs, and his average fell 50 points. He played third base when Mike Schmidt went on the DL for rotator cuff surgery and was announced as Schmidt's successor when the Hall of Famer retired in 1989, but he was traded to San Diego within a month. His brother Craig was a running back for the New England Patriots./(SG)

Dion James — 1962– . OF 1983–85, 87– Brewers, **Braves**, Indians 557 g, .285, 19 hr, 165 rbi

James was the Brewers' Rookie of the Year in 1984, when he won the centerfield job and batted .295. The following spring he twice dislocated his right shoulder diving for fly balls. After spending 1986 in the minors, James (Milwaukee's first-round pick in 1980) was traded for Brad Komminsk (Atlanta's top pick in 1979). The slap-hitter switched from a straight-up stance to an open crouch, giving him new power; he hit .312 with 37 doubles and 10 HR in 1987. On April 13 against the Mets, his routine fly ball hit a dove and fell uncaught. James was a

major disappointment in Atlanta's dismal 1988 season and was criticized for erratic fielding. He was traded to the Indians in mid-1989 for Oddibe McDowell, the Rangers' number-one pick in 1984./(JCA)

Jeff James (Jesse) — 1941– . RHP 1968–69 **Phillies** 147 ip, 6–6, 4.51

James earned a spot with the Phillies after winning 11 straight for their San Diego (Pacific Coast League) farm club in 1967. The highlight of his brief ML career was a four-hit shutout of Chicago in July of his rookie season./(AL)

Johnny James — 1933– . RHP 1958, 60–61 Yankees, **Angels** 119 ip, 5–3, 4.76

A career reliever, James earned a spot with the Yankees in 1960 by pitching part of a team no-hitter in spring training. He contributed a 5–1 mark to the pennant winners but was dropped from the roster before the WS./(MC)

Charlie Jamieson (Chuck, Jamie, Hawk) — 1893–1969. OF-LHP 1915–32 Senators, A's, **Indians** 1779 g, .303, 18 hr, 550 rbi; 48 ip, 2–1, 6.19. *1 WS, 6 g, .333, 1 rbi*

Jamieson was a late bloomer. He had been in the majors for four years before Cleveland manager Tris Speaker bamboozled Connie Mack into adding him to an already unbalanced 1919 trade in the Indians' favor. From 1920 to 1931, he owned left field at League Park. Jamieson started as a pitcher, and he took to the mound in five of his ML seasons. By the time he reached Cleveland, he was clearly a superbly athletic outfielder and a swift, hard-hitting leadoff man. He had nine full seasons over .300, including .359 in 1924. In 1923, he had a 23-game hitting streak and led the AL with 222 hits and 644 at-bats. Defensively, he made spectacular diving catches and powerful, accurate throws. In 1928 his 22 outfield assists were tops, and in a 17-day span he started two triple plays. Jamieson was a frequent MVP candidate, though never a winner./(ADS)

Gerry Janeski — 1946– . RHP 1970–72 **White Sox**, Senators/Rangers 281 ip, 11–23, 4.71

Janeski tied for the International League lead with 15 wins at Louisville in 1969. When the White Sox traded Gary Peters and Don Pavletich to the Red Sox for Syd O'Brien and pitcher Billy Farmer that December, Janeski replaced Farmer when the latter was discovered to have a sore arm. Farmer was

10–17 for the White Sox in 1970, earning Chicago Rookie of the Year honors. Local sportswriters dubbed him The Wheat Germ Kid because his locker resembled a health food store. /(RL)

Vic Janowicz (Crash) — 1930– . C-3B 1953–54 **Pirates** 83 g, .214, 2 hr, 10 rbi

From Ohio State, the 1950 Heisman Trophy winner was the first to ever play ML baseball. One of several bonus baby busts for Pittsburgh in the 1950s, Janowicz returned to the NFL Redskins after 1954, but his career was tragically ended by a 1956 car accident. /(ME)

Larry Jansen — 1920– . RHP 1947–54, 56 **Giants** 1765 ip, 122–89, 3.58. 20 wins: 47, 51. *1 WS, 10 ip, 0–2, 6.30*
☛ *Led League—w 51. All-Star—50–51.*

The lantern-jawed Jansen was nearing his 27th birthday when he arrived in the NL, but for five seasons he was one of the league's best righthanders. After being purchased from the Pacific Coast League, he had a magnificent rookie year in 1947, going 21–5 and leading the league in winning percentage. He threw an outstanding overhand curve and a good fastball, and had excellent control. After one of his ten consecutive complete-game wins, Giants catcher Walker Cooper commented, "I don't believe he missed the target (catcher's mitt) by more than two inches all day." He won 18 in 1948 and 19 in 1950, while tying for the league lead with five shutouts. In 1951, the mild-mannered Jansen combined with Sal Maglie as the Giants' one-two pitching punch in winning the "miracle" pennant. They tied for the league lead in victories with 23 each.

Later, as pitching coach for the Giants, he helped develop Juan Marichal and Gaylord Perry. /(FS)

Hal Janvrin (Childe Harold) — 1892–1962. SS-2B-1B-3B-OF 1911, 13–17, 19–22 **Red Sox**, Senators, Cardinals, Dodgers 756 g, .232, 6 hr, 210 rbi. *2 WS, 6 g, .208, 1 rbi*

A teenager when he joined his hometown Red Sox in 1911, Childe Harold was nicknamed for the hero of Byron's epic poem. Janvrin demonstrated versatility but never held a steady job at any one position. /(JK)

Jarry Park (Le Parc Jarry) Montreal Expos 1969–76. LF-340, CF-420, RF-340

Cozy but often cool Jarry Park, site of the first ML games played outside the United States, had a capacity of 28,000 and featured hearty fans and ML

baseball's first bilingual public address announcements. Home runs to right field occasionally landed in an adjacent public swimming pool. /(SCL)

Pat Jarvis — 1941– . RHP 1966–73 **Braves**, Expos 1284 ip, 85–73, 3.58. *1 LCS, 4 ip, 0–1, 12.46*

Hard-nosed Pat Jarvis was the Braves' number-three starter behind Phil Niekro and Ron Reed in the late 1960s. He won between 13 and 16 games a year from 1967 to 1970 and had just one losing ML season (1971, 6–14). In the 1969 LCS, Jarvis started and lost the final game to the Mets. He was a rodeo rider before playing baseball. /(PB)

Ray Jarvis — 1946– . RHP 1969–70 **Red Sox** 116 ip, 5–7, 4.64

Signed by Boston out of the Cape Cod summer league, the sinkerballing native of Providence pitched in two ML seasons before succumbing to arm injuries. Jarvis tied a ML record by striking out five times in a nine-inning game. /(RMu)

Larry Jaster — 1944– . LHP 1965–70, 72 **Cardinals**, Expos, Braves 597 ip, 35–33, 3.65. *2 WS, 0.1 ip, 0–0, 81.00*

Called up to the Cardinals late in 1965, Jaster threw three complete-game victories in three starts. In 1966 he threw five shutouts, all against the pennant-bound Dodgers, to set a major league record for most consecutive shutouts won from one club in a season. He finished the year with a career-high 11 victories.

Relieving in the third inning of Game Six of the 1968 World Series, Jaster pitched to three batters without retiring any, surrendering a grand slam to Jim Northrup, as the Tigers scored a Series-record 10 runs. He threw the first ML pitch in Canada, pitching for the Expos in their 1969 home opener. /(FJO)

Al Javery (Bear Tracks) — 1918–1977. RHP 1940–46 **Braves** 1143 ip, 53–74, 3.80
☛ *All-Star—43–44.*

A wartime workhorse for the Braves (he was deferred for varicose veins), Javery had four straight seasons with double-figure wins and earned spots on two All-Star teams, but had only one winning record (17–16 in 1943). /(JK)

Julian Javier (Hoolie, The Phantom) — 1936- . 2B-3B 1960-72 **Cardinals**, Reds 1622 g, .257, 78 hr, 506 rbi. *4 WS, 19 g, .333, 1 hr, 7 rbi*
☛ *All-Star—63, 68.*

The Dominican Javier was dealt from the Pirate farm system to the Cardinals in a May 1960 trade for popular pitcher Vinegar Bend Mizell. His range and speed quickly enabled him to establish himself as the everyday second baseman for a dozen seasons in St. Louis. In 1963, Javier and teammates Ken Boyer, Dick Groat, and Bill White made up an all-Cardinal starting All-Star infield. Javier was so good covering ground, pivoting on the double plays, and going back for pop-ups that GM Bing Devine proclaimed him better defensively than Frankie Frisch, Rogers Hornsby, or Red Schoendienst.

Javier hit .360 in the 1967 WS against Boston, including a three-run homer in Game Seven to help Bob Gibson win his third Series game and bring the World Championship to St. Louis. He is the father of Stan Javier. /(FJO)

Stan Javier — 1965- . OF 1984, 86- Yankees, **A's** 384 g, .236, 5 hr, 80 rbi. *2 LCS, 3 g, .333, 1 rbi. 1 WS, 3 g, .500, 2 rbi*

Javier was part of the package Oakland received for Rickey Henderson in December 1984. He became a semi-regular in the A's 1988 AL pennant-winning season after they became dissatisfied with Luis Polonia's fielding. Javier hit .257 with 20 steals and 49 runs in 397 at-bats. In Game Five of the 1988 World Series, he drove in the only two runs the A's scored against Orel Hershiser in the whole Series. /(WOR)

Joey Jay — 1935- . RHP 1953-55, 57-66 Braves, **Reds** 1546 ip, 99-91, 3.77. 20 wins: 61-62 *1 WS, 9 ip, 1-1, 5.59*
☛ *Led League—w 61. All-Star—61.*

Late in 1953 at the age of eighteen, Jay hurled a three-hit shutout for the Braves to beat the Reds in his first ML start. A $20,000 bonus baby, Jay was the first graduate of the Little League program to reach the majors. Ironically, he had been the subject of a petition attempting to bar him from Little League at age twelve because of his advanced size. While in the majors, he wrote an article entitled "Don't Trap Your Son in Little League Madness."

But Jay didn't blossom with Milwaukee, who still had Warren Spahn and Lew Burdette winning 20 a year. He went 7-5 (2.14) in 1958, but missed the World Series with a broken finger. Traded to Cincinnati in December 1960, he flourished, in 1961 tying Spahn for the league lead in wins (21) and shutouts (4), and beating the Yankees in Game Two of the WS. He won 21 again in 1962, but dropped to 7-18 the following year and was finished by 1966. /(RTM)

Hal Jeffcoat — 1924- . OF-LHP 1948-59 **Cubs**, Reds, Cardinals 918 g, .248, 26 hr, 188 rbi; 697 ip, 39-37, 4.22

One of a family of pro ballplayers (older brother George pitched in the NL), fast, smooth-fielding Hal Jeffcoat broke in with the 1948 Cubs as an outfielder. His light hitting forced him into a backup role by 1950, and he converted to pitching in 1954 to utilize his strong arm. He became a top reliever, making 50 appearances (2.95 ERA) in 1955 and, after his trade to the Reds, went 8-2 in 1956. /(DAS)

Mike Jeffcoat — 1959- . LHP 1983-85, 87 **Indians**, Giants, Rangers 287 ip, 15-16, 4.01

Jeffcoat spent one full season in the majors, as a long reliever for the 1984 Indians (5-2, 2.99). He saw little ML action after his 1985 trade to the Giants. /(JCA)

Gregg Jefferies — 1967- . 2B-3B 1987- **Mets** 176 g, .271, 18 hr, 75 rbi. *1 LCS, 7 g, .333, 1 rbi*

Jefferies was the Mets' first-round pick in the 1985 June draft and was a minor league MVP each of his first three seasons. He had an outstanding late-season call-up in 1988, hitting .321 with six HR in 109 at-bats, and Mets manager Davey Johnson deliberately held him out of some games so that he would qualify for Rookie of the Year in 1989. Jefferies pushed the slumping, injured Howard Johnson off third base for the LCS and hit well, but his inability to bunt may have cost the Mets Game Five. In Game Seven he made a crucial error in the Dodgers' five-run second inning, completely muffing an easy double play ball.

Jefferies was given the second base job from the start of the 1989 season, but went through a horrible slump in the first two months, showing very little selectivity at the plate. Manager Johnson stuck with him, and he eventually came around, hitting .258 in 1989. Johnson, a Gold Glove second baseman in his playing days, also worked with him on turning the double play.

The intense scrutiny of Jefferies extended to his father's training regimen for him while he was growing up, which included unusual exercises such as building strength by swinging a bat underwater. /(JFC)

Jesse Jefferson — 1949– . RHP 1973–81 Orioles, White Sox, **Blue Jays**, Pirates, Angels 1086 ip, 39–81, 4.81

The hard-throwing but often wild Jefferson had his only winning season (6–5) as an Oriole rookie in 1973. The 24th pick of the Blue Jays in the 1976 expansion draft, he was an abysmal 22–56 in four years in Toronto. Jefferson's two-hitter against the Mariners on July 27, 1980 demonstrated that he could be a brilliant pitcher at times. There were other times when he was terrible. He set a Blue Jay franchise record with nine walks in a game against Baltimore on June 18, 1977, and he allowed 10 earned runs (with four homers) against Chicago on April 11, 1978. Jefferson's best full season came in 1977, when he went 9–17 with a 4.31 ERA. /(TF/JCA)

Stan Jefferson — 1962– . OF 1986– Mets, **Padres**, Yankees, Orioles 224 g, .218, 14 hr, 57 rbi

This native New Yorker was the Mets' first-round pick in the June 1983 draft. Sent to San Diego in the Kevin McReynolds-Kevin Mitchell deal after the 1986 season, Jefferson was a regular in the Padres' outfield in 1987, although he spent much of the first half on the DL. He stole 34 bases but hit just .230, although that remained a career high. /(SFS)

Steve Jeltz — 1959– . SS 1983- **Phillies** 653 g, .213, 5 hr, 120 rbi

Jeltz beat out Luis Aguayo for the Phillies' starting shortstop job in 1986 but hit only .219. The Phillies signed Dickie Thon for 1989, and Jeltz and Thon shared the job. Jeltz hit three homers in a 17-game span after hitting one in six previous seasons and became the first Phillie ever to homer from both sides of the plate in one game. /(SG)

Fats Jenkins [Clarence] — 1898–1968. OF-MGR Negro Leagues 1920–40 New York Lincoln Giants, Harrisburg Giants, Bacharach Giants, Baltimore Black Sox, **New York Black Yankees**, Philadelphia Stars, Brooklyn Eagles, Brooklyn Royal Giants statistics not available

Fats Jenkins was a wiry, 5'7" outfielder who inherited his nickname from a plump older brother. A great all-around athlete who played professional basketball with the Renaissance team, he was a good hitter and a fast runner.

Statistics documenting Jenkins's career are sketchy; none exist for his first four years (1920–23).

He batted .319 in 1924 and .307 in 1925 for the Harrisburg Giants, and .358 for the 1929 Atlantic City Bacharachs. He played in the 1933 and 1935 East-West all-star games. At the age of 37, Jenkins hit .305 for the 1935 Brooklyn Eagles and stole nine bases in 42 games to lead the league.

Though his name is most often linked with the New York Black Yankees, virtually no recorded statistics remain of Jenkins's years with them. Fragmentary evidence gives him a lifetime average of .319 in the Negro Leagues, while black-baseball historian James Riley credits him with a .331 mark. His last job in black baseball was as manager of the 1940 Brooklyn Royal Giants. /(JM)

Ferguson Jenkins — 1943– . RHP 1965–1983 Phillies, **Cubs**, Rangers, Red Sox 4500 ip, 284–226, 3.34. 20 wins: 67–72, 74

☛ *Led League—w 71, 74. Led League—k 69. Cy Young Award—71. All-Star—67, 71.*

Jenkins never received the fame his accomplishments warrant. He racked up 284 victories, had six consecutive 20-win seasons paired with 200-plus strikeouts, pitched more than 300 innings five times, and is high on the all-time strikeout list with 3,192. He never pitched on a pennant winner, though, and was usually on teams that were known more for hitting than pitching.

When the Cubs acquired Jenkins midway through the 1966 season, manager Leo Durocher converted the hard-throwing 6'5" 200-lb righthander into a starter. Beginning in 1967 and continuing through 1972, Jenkins won at least 20 games every year. He set a modern Cubs record with 236 strikeouts in 1967, then raised the record each of the next three seasons to 260, 273, and 274. In the 15-inning 1967 All-Star game, Jenkins equaled Carl Hubbell's 1934 strikeout numbers, fanning six in three innings, but he gave up a sixth-inning homer to Brooks Robinson that tied the score at 1–1. He gave up another homer, to Harmon Killebrew, in his only other All-Star appearance (1971). He led the NL in 1971 with a 24–13 record with 263 strikeouts, a 2.77 ERA, and 30 complete games to win the Cy Young award. He also hit .243 with six homers.

After failing to win 20 games in 1973, and because of Ron Santo's diminishing skills at third base, the Cubs traded Jenkins to the Texas Rangers for Bill Madlock. In his first start in a Ranger uniform, he shut out the World Champion A's on one hit. He led the AL with a 25–12 record, the seventh and last time he would win 20 games. He fell to 17–18 in 1975 and was traded to Boston. He

Ferguson Jenkins

Hughie Jennings (Ee-Yah) — 1869–1928. SS-1B-2B 1891–1903, 07–09, 12, 18 Louisville (AA)/(NL), **Baltimore (NL)**, Dodgers, Phillies, Tigers 1285 g, .312, 18 hr, 840 rbi.
Manager 1907–20 **Tigers** 1131–972, .538. First place: 07–09 *3 WS, 4–12, .250*
☛ *Hall of Fame—1945.*

One of baseball's most colorful and best-loved characters, Jennings rose from breaker boy in the Pennsylvania anthracite fields to the Hall of Fame. The redheaded, freckled firebrand wore a major league uniform for more than three decades as a player, coach, and manager. He also earned a law degree and built a successful off-season legal practice. Jennings's best years came as captain of the powerful, brawling Baltimore Orioles, National League champions in three straight years, 1894–96 and winners of the 1897 Temple Cup. Operating within and outside the rules, Jennings and teammates John McGraw, Willie Keeler, Joe Kelley, and Wilbert Robinson were the scourge of opponents and umpires. During his five full seasons in Baltimore, Jennings never batted below .328 and achieved a high of .398 in 1896, the ML record for shortstops. In addition, he stole as many as 70 bases in a season and was the leader in fielding average and putouts three times each.

His hitting declined in later years, and a sore arm forced a move back to first base, but Jennings's superior skills as a strategist and field leader kept him steadily employed. He played for pennant winners in Brooklyn in 1899 and 1900, and later captained the Phillies before embarking on a managing career in the minors. Purchased by the Tigers in 1907, Jennings guided the team to pennants in his first three years at the helm. The Tigers lost all three World Series, however, and never again won a pennant under Jennings, who remained on the job through 1920. From the third base coaching box, the hyperactive skipper prodded his charges, among them the young Ty Cobb, and taunted the opposition with shouts, whistles, and gyrations. His piercing yell of "Ee-Yah" became a trademark. Upon leaving the Tigers, Jennings was signed by former Oriole teammate John McGraw as a coach and assistant manager with the Giants. In the role of right-hand man, Jennings was a part of four consecutive pennant-winning clubs (1921–24).

Though durable, Jennings suffered an incredible string of mishaps on and off the field. He was often hit by pitches; a then-record 49 times in 1896 alone. Two skull fractures, one the result of an accidental dive into an empty swimming pool, slowed but did

was going to Fenway Park with high expectations for 1976, joining a Red Sox team that had come within one win of a world title the previous year. But the fire had gone out of Jenkins's arm. He could not win more games than he lost. By late 1977, Red Sox manager Don Zimmer was fed up with Jenkins's inconsistency and banished him to the bullpen. On September 18 in Baltimore, Brooks Robinson Night, Jenkins supposedly fell asleep (Jenkins said he simply had his feet up in the cart) in the bullpen and had to be woken up to warm up. Zimmer was livid, and Jenkins didn't pitch again in a Boston uniform. At the end of the year, Jenkins headed back to Texas, where he partially regained his form and won 18 games. Jenkins was reacquired by the Cubs in 1982 and led the club in innings pitched and ERA with a 14–15 record at the age of 38. /(SEW)

Hughie Jennings

than predicted, career up the coast in Boston. Jensen played just 11 years, his career cut short by a fear of flying. Ted Williams called his right-field partner the best outfielder he ever saw. A steady RBI man, Jensen drove in 100 or more runs five of his seven years with the Red Sox and led the league three times with 116 in 1955, 122 in 1958, and 112 in 1959. He hit over .300 only once, in 1956, a season highlighted on August 2, when he drove in nine runs. Although the speedy Jensen led the league in stolen bases with 22 in 1954 and in triples with 11 in 1956, he also had a proclivity for grounding into double plays, hitting into 185 over his career (once every 28 at-bats)./(SEW)

Woody Jensen [Forrest Docenus] — 1907– . OF 1931–39 **Pirates** 738 g, .285, 26 hr, 235 rbi

In the mid-1930s, Jensen teamed with Paul and Lloyd Waner in the Pittsburgh outfield. He was called Woody as a play on Forrest, and because (from Bremerton, Washington) he once played in the Timber League. The lefthanded hitter rarely walked and set a ML record with 696 at-bats in 1936, batting leadoff with Lloyd dropping to second./(ME)

John Jeter (The Jet) — 1944– . OF 1969–74 Pirates, **Padres**, White Sox, Indians 336 g, .244, 18 hr, 69 rbi. *1 LCS, 3 g, .000*

The speedy Jeter spent his first two seasons as a late-inning defensive substitute for Willie Stargell in the Pirates' outfield. He couldn't produce consistently when given more playing time by the Padres in 1972 (.221) and the White Sox in 1973 (.240)./(SFS)

Sam Jethroe (Jet) — 1922– . C-OF Negro Leagues 1942–49 Cincinnati Buckeyes, Cleveland Buckeyes statistics not available; *ML*: OF 1950–52, 54 **Braves**, Pirates 442 g, .261, 49 hr, 181 rbi
☛ *Rookie of the Year—50.*

After stealing 89 bases in the International League in 1949, Jethroe became the first black to play for the Braves. The twenty-eight-year-old switch-hitter was the 1950 NL Rookie of the Year, hitting .273 with 18 HR, 100 runs scored, and a major league-leading 35 stolen bases. His numbers were virtually identical in 1951 and he again won the major league stolen base title with 35. The centerfielder slumped to .232 in 1952, struck out 112 times, fielded poorly (leading NL outfielders in errors for the third straight

not stop him. A nervous breakdown after the 1925 season, however, brought his baseball days to an end. He was elected to the Hall of Fame in 1945./(JL)

Jackie Jensen — 1927–1982. OF 1950–61 Yankees, Senators, **Red Sox** 1,438 g, .279, 199 hr, 929 rbi. *1 WS, 1 g, .000*
☛ *Most Valuable Player—58. All-Star—52, 55, 58. Gold Glove—59.*

The blond Golden Boy, a product of the Yankee farm system of the 1940s, was heralded as DiMaggio's heir as a rookie in 1950. But he hit only .171 in 45 games, and Mickey Mantle assumed that role the following year. Jensen, freed from the pressures of following a legend, enjoyed a solid, if less productive season, and reportedly had vision trouble (his 28 steals was second in the NL and the majors). Amid rumors he was older than listed, he spent 1953 in Toledo, batting .307. Acquired by Pittsburgh, he played just two games for the Pirates. He spent five more seasons with Toronto (International League).

But Jethroe's best years had been spent in the Negro Leagues with the Cleveland Buckeyes, for whom he batted .342 in six seasons. He was selected to the Negro Leagues' East-West all-star game four times. He is the only player to have hit a ball over the 472-foot leftfield fence at Toledo's Swayne Field and into the coal piles of the Red Man Tobacco Factory. In the spring of 1945, he was selected with Jackie Robinson and Marvin Williams for an unsuccessful tryout with the Red Sox. Boston coach Hugh Duffy said, "There is no doubt about it that they are ballplayers. They look good to me." Robinson said that at that tryout, Jethroe "looked like a gazelle in the outfield." But the Red Sox would be the last major league team to integrate, while Jethroe went on to star for their crosstown rivals. /(LL/ME)

Houston Jimenez [Alfonso] — 1957– . SS-2B 1983–84, 87–88 **Twins**, Pirates, Indians 158 g, .185, 0 hr, 29 rbi

Jimenez spent much of his career in the Mexican League. He saw the most major league action with the 1984 Twins, hitting a ML-career-high .201 in 298 at-bats. He received his nickname as a child after a television Western character. /(WOR)

Manny Jimenez — 1938– . OF 1962–64, 66–69 **A's**, Pirates, Cubs 429 g, .272, 26 hr, 144 rbi

Jimenez looked promising when he hit .301 with 11 HR and 69 RBI in his rookie 1962 season. But he lost his power in reduced playing time in 1963 and, regaining it in 1964, saw his BA plummet to .225. He resurfaced with the Pirates, leading the NL in pinch hits in 1967 and in pinch at-bats the following year, when he went 10-for-53 in that role. He hit .303 overall that year by going 10-for-13 in his only non-pinch at-bats. /(JFC)

Tommy John — 1943– . LHP 1963–74, 76–89 Indians, White Sox, **Dodgers**, Yankees, Angels, A's 4707 ip, 288–231, 3.34. 20 wins: 77, 79–80 *5 LCS, 48 ip, 4–1, 2.08. 3 WS, 34 ip, 2–1, 2.67*
☛ *All-Star—68, 78–80.*

A sinkerballer with impeccable control, John's major league career spanned 26 seasons and seven U.S. presidents, both ML records. In mid-career, he

Tommy John

made history by becoming the game's first "right-handed southpaw" when he had a tendon transplanted from his right forearm to his left elbow to remedy a tear that threatened to drive him from baseball.

After breaking in with the Indians, John became an effective starter for the mediocre White Sox from 1965 to 1971, leading the AL in shutouts in 1966 and 1967. He was traded to the Dodgers for Dick Allen before the 1972 season, and in 1973 he led the NL in winning percentage with a 16–9 record. John seemed to be embarking on his best season in 1974, posting a 13–3 mark before injuring his pitching elbow in July.

Dr. Frank Jobe performed the revolutionary surgery that saved John's career, and it was amazingly successful. The soft-throwing John joked that he told Jobe to "put in a Koufax fastball. He did, but it was Mrs. Koufax's." He underwent rehabilitation for a year and a half, missing the entire 1975 season, and his 10–10 record in 1976 earned him the Comeback Player of the Year Award. He then won

20 games in three of the next four seasons. John was 20–7 for the Dodgers in 1977 and 17–10 in '78, helping them to the World Series each year. But the Dodgers lost to the Yankees both times. John then signed with the Yankees as a free agent before the 1979 season and won 21 and 22 games in his first two seasons in New York.

John was traded to the Angels for Dennis Rasmussen late in the 1982 season and was released in 1985 at the age of forty-two, but after a brief stint with Oakland he returned to the Yankees in 1986 and led the club in innings pitched as a 44-year-old in 1987. He often explained his unusual durability by pointing out that his pitching arm was much younger than his chronological age.

John's excellent sinker induced numerous ground balls and double plays throughout his career, and he was usually a fine fielder himself, setting club records with errorless seasons for both the Dodgers and White Sox. On July 27, 1988, however, John tied a ML record by committing three errors on one play. In the fourth inning against the Brewers, John muffed a ground ball for one error and threw wildly past first base for a second. Then, inexplicably, he intercepted the throw home from right field and threw wildly past the catcher.

He was released by the Yankees early in the 1989 season. /(TG)

Adam Johnson (Tex) — 1888–1972. RHP 1914–15, 18 Red Sox, **Chicago (FL)**, Baltimore (FL), Cardinals 450 ip, 23–30, 2.92

Johnson was 4–9, 3.08 with the Red Sox, earning $400 a month in his rookie 1914 season, when he was traded to the Indians. He jumped to the Chicago Whales of the Federal League and went 9–5, 1.58 the rest of the way to lead the FL in ERA. It was his only successful season. His son Adam Jr. pitched briefly for the 1941 Athletics. /(NLM)

Alex Johnson — 1942– . OF 1964–76 Phillies, Cardinals, **Reds**, Angels, Indians, Rangers, Yankees, Tigers 1322 g, .288, 78 hr, 525 rbi
☛ Led League—ba 70. All-Star—70.

No one could quite figure how to motivate Johnson, a surly yet talented hitter with a great arm who never achieved popularity despite his skills. He is best remembered for edging the popular Carl Yastrzemski in the AL batting race in 1970, .3289 to .3286. Known as an aggressive contact hitter who didn't strike out much and who hated to walk or talk, Johnson admitted that he never gave 100% and never hustled. He once told a reporter, "I'm just

paid to hit." As a result of this lackadaisical attitude, he spent time with eight different teams in his 13-year career. Called the fastest righthanded hitter from home plate to first, Johnson had his first success with the Reds in the late 1960s, hitting over .300 both seasons he spent in Cincinnati. His fine play in 1970 was quickly forgotten the next season when Angels manager Lefty Phillips suspended him for being "a bad influence." After leaving California, he never again hit .300. /(SEW)

Ban Johnson [Byron Bancroft] — 1864–1931.
Executive

The American League is Johnson's gift to baseball. Others were present at the creation, but it was Johnson's driving force, shrewd business sense, rigorous standards, and lively imagination that made the league a success.

He gave form and definition to the emerging role of baseball executive. After studying law but falling short of a degree at Marietta (Ohio) College, he became sports editor for the Cincinnati *Commercial-Gazette*. After Johnson's friend Charlie Comiskey was fired as Reds manager after the 1894 season, they took over the faltering Western League, with Ban as president. It soon became known as the best-run circuit in baseball. A name change (to the American League) in 1900, combined with a series of swift, opportunistic maneuvers, outflanked the established NL, and by 1901 Johnson's league claimed major status. After some fine-tuning of franchises, the AL achieved the structure it held until 1954. In 1903 the NL was forced to accept its parity and agree to a World Series between league champions.

As boss, Johnson found no task too large or too small to merit his attention. He located millionaires to bankroll his teams, came down hard on rowdies and roughhousing on the field, appointed managers, arranged trades, and apportioned players. He arranged schedules to spread travel costs equitably, interpreted rules, levied fines and suspensions, issued statistics, and even recruited William Howard Taft as the first president to throw out an Opening Day ball. One of his most important contributions was to enforce respect for umpires as symbols of baseball's integrity.

He did it all with little grace and no humor. Johnson was hot-tempered, bullheaded, imperious, and uncompromising, not unlike many other tycoons of his time. But he was successful. His owners voted him $25,000 a year and his presidency for life.

During his term on the National Commission (the triumvirate, including the AL and NL presidents,

Ban Johnson

that ruled ML baseball from 1903 until 1920), he was thought of as baseball's czar, but his downfall was inevitable. New AL owners were less willing to accept his high-handed decisions affecting their investments. Old friends were angered. Comiskey had once said, "Ban Johnson IS the American League!" But when he lost pitcher Jack Quinn to the Yankees on a Johnson ruling, the White Sox owner thundered: "I made you, and by God I'll break you!"

Indirectly, he did. The Black Sox scandal caused the abolition of the National Commission and the establishment of Judge Landis as Commissioner of Baseball. Johnson's era had ended. He remained AL president, but Landis limited his duties, curtailed his power, and ultimately humiliated him. After promoting an investigation concerning charges that Ty Cobb and Tris Speaker had been involved in gambling fixes in 1919, he was persuaded to resign on October 17, 1927./(ADS)

Bart Johnson [Clair Barth] — 1950- . RHP 1969–74, 76–77 **White Sox** 810 ip, 43–51, 3.95

Dogged by injuries throughout his career (he missed all of the 1975 season with an ailing back), the 6'5" power pitcher had two good seasons. In 1971 he went 12–10, with 14 saves, and in 1974 he was 10–4 with a 2.73 ERA. He hit .329 in 50 games as an outfielder with Appleton (Midwest League) in 1972./(JCA)

Billy Johnson (Bull) — 1918- . 3B 1943, 46–53 **Yankees**, Cardinals 964 g, .271, 61 hr, 487 rbi. *4 WS, 18 g, .237, 5 rbi*
☛ *All-Star—47.*

Johnson caught manager Joe McCarthy's attention in the Yankees' wartime 1943 Asbury Park, New Jersey, training camp by taking infield practice while it was snowing. Johnson took over the Yankee third base job from Red Rolfe that season and had a great rookie year, hitting .280 with 94 RBI (third in the league) and leading AL third basemen in putouts, assists, and double plays. His bases-loaded triple in the eighth inning of Game Three of the 1943 WS overcame a 2–1 deficit to win the game. He spent 1944–45 in the military and had an off-year in 1946, but came back strong in 1947 to tie for fourth in the AL with 95 RBI. He set a record for a seven-game Series that fall with three triples; his four overall tied the lifetime WS record. He also led the Yankees with eight runs in the '47 Series, twice as many as runner-up Joe DiMaggio.

In 1948 he hit a career-high .294 with 12 HR while leading AL third basemen in total chances per game, but dropped off in overall production. The arrival of Casey Stengel in 1949 cut into his playing time and his effectiveness, as Stengel platooned him with Bobby Brown, used him as a defensive replacement, and played him at first base. When Gil McDougald arrived in 1951, Johnson was traded in May to the Cardinals for Don Bollweg and $15,000. In his last full-time season, he led NL third basemen in fielding and hit a career-high 14 HR./(SH)

Bob Johnson [Robert Lee] (Indian Bob) — 1906- . OF-1B-2B-3B 1933–45 **A's**, Senators, Red Sox 1863 g, .296, 288 hr, 1283 rbi
☛ *All-Star—35, 38–40, 42–44.*

Indian Bob, half Cherokee, had speed and power. When the Athletics sold Al Simmons after the 1932 season and Lou Finney, tabbed as his replacement in left field, didn't measure up, Johnson won the job. An A's regular for a decade, Johnson hit .307 with a

Indian Bob Johnson

career-high 34 HR his second year and batted a peak .338 in 1939. For seven straight seasons, he drove in over 100 runs. He had a 26-game hitting streak in 1934. On June 16, 1934 Johnson went six-for-six with two homers and two doubles, and on August 29, 1937 he set a ML record with six RBI in one inning on a grand slam and a double. He got the only hit in three one-hitters, once with a home run off Lefty Gomez in 1937. But Johnson was one of the few players to have serious difficulties with Connie Mack; he felt he was underpaid, and eventually demanded to be traded. He went to the Senators in 1943, and then to the Red Sox, where he hit .324 in 1944, his seventh and final All-Star season. He then spent five more seasons in the minors. Brother Roy played from 1929–38 with four major league teams. /(NLM)

Bob Johnson [Robert Wallace] — 1936– . SS-2B-3B-1B 1960–70 A's, Senators, **Orioles**, Mets, Reds, Braves, Cardinals 874 g, .272, 44 hr, 230 rbi

This versatile infielder only once appeared in more than 100 games in a season: in 1962, when he had career highs of 112 HR, 58 runs, and 43 RBI for the Senators. He led his league in pinch hits three times (1964, 1967, and 1969). In the years 1967–1969 he played with six teams, two each season, returning finally to the A's, with whom he had begun his career. /(JFC)

Bob Johnson [Robert Dale] — 1943– . RHP 1969–74, 77 Mets, Royals, **Pirates**, Indians, Braves 692 ip, 28–34, 3.48. *2 LCS, 14 ip, 1–0, 1.29. 1 WS, 5 ip, 0–1, 9.00*

In his one season with Kansas City (1970), 6'4" Bob Johnson struck out 206, the third-highest total ever for a rookie and a Royal record. He was second to Bert Blyleven in *TSN* AL Rookie Pitcher of the Year voting. Johnson went 9–10 with a 3.45 ERA for the World Champion 1971 Pirates. When Nellie Briles pulled a hamstring warming up for Game Three of the LCS, Johnson was his emergency replacement and pitched five-hit ball for eight innings, surrendering only an unearned run and winning a 2–1 duel against the Giants' Juan Marichal. He lost his Game Two World Series start, however, giving up four runs in 3–1/3 innings.

Johnson followed up his triumph with his best season in 1972 (4–4, 2.96), relieving more, as the Pirates won the division title, and in 1973 had his only winning record (4–2), coming almost exclusively out of the bullpen. /(SFS)

Chappie Johnson [George] — 1875–Unk. C-1B-MGR Negro Leagues 1896–1921 Page Fence Giants, Columbia Giants, Chicago Union Giants, Brooklyn Royal Giants, Leland Giants, Philadelphia Giants, Chicago Giants, St. Louis Giants, Dayton Chappies, Custer's Baseball Club of Columbus, Philadelphia Royal Giants, Norfolk Stars statistics not available

Johnson was one of the best black catchers during the two decades before the Negro National League was formed. He also played first base, starting his career there with the Columbia Giants of Chicago in 1896. As he developed as a catcher, he became known not only as an excellent handler of pitchers but also as a coach. He reportedly was hired by the white St. Paul club of the American Association to work with young catchers for several years in the early 1900s. He later became a highly successful manager. /(BP)

Chief Johnson [George Howard] — 1886–1922. RHP 1913–15 Reds, **Kansas City (FL)** 688 ip, 41–43, 2.95

Johnson was a Winnebago Indian from Nebraska who went to the Carlisle Indian School in Pennsylvania. He was earning $3,200 a year with the Reds in 1914 when he jumped to Kansas City of the Federal League. Johnson's best season came in his last, 1915, as he went 18–17 with a 2.75 ERA in the Federal League, beefing up his record with a 4–0 mark in relief. /(NLM)

Cliff Johnson [Clifford, Jr.] (Heathcliff) — 1947– . DH-1B-C-OF 1972–86 Astros, Yankees, Indians, Cubs, A's, **Blue Jays**, Rangers 1369 g, .258, 196 hr, 699 rbi. *4 LCS, 15 g, .317, 1 hr, 4 rbi. 2 WS, 4 g, .000*

A powerful righthanded slugger whose bat often sailed across the infield as he swung at pitches and missed, Johnson holds the ML record for pinch home runs with 20, including an Astro-record 5 in his first full season. Without the designated hitter rule, Johnson struggled in the NL, never settling at a defensive position and leading the ML in passed balls in 1976 in only 66 games at catcher. Traded to the Yankees on June 15, 1977, Heathcliff blasted three home runs against the Blue Jays 15 days later, including two in the 8th inning. In 1979 he broke the thumb of teammate and Yankee bullpen ace Rich Gossage in a locker room scuffle and was traded to Cleveland. After 1980 the smart, patient hitter was primarily a DH. /(TF)

Connie Johnson [Clifford] — 1922– . RHP 1953, 55–58 White Sox, **Orioles** 716 ip, 40–39, 3.44

Johnson led the 1957 Orioles starters in wins (14), innings pitched (242), and ERA (3.20). He teamed with George Zuverink to match the one-hitter thrown by Chicago's Jack Harshman, but the Orioles lost 1–0. /(FK)

Darrell Johnson — 1928– . C 1952, 57–58, 60–62 Browns, White Sox, **Yankees**, Cardinals, Phillies, Reds, Orioles 134 g, .234, 2 hr, 28 rbi. *1 WS, 2 g, .500.*
Manager 1974–80, 82 Red Sox, **Mariners**, Rangers 472–590, .444. First place: 75 *1 LCS, 3–0, 1.000. 1 WS, 3–4, .429*

Johnson spent six seasons in the major leagues as a reserve catcher with seven different teams, developing the patience and perspective needed to manage. After success in the Red Sox farm system, he was named Boston manager in 1974. The following season the Sox won the pennant and took the WS to seven games before losing. Fired in July 1976,

Johnson became manager of the expansion Mariners in 1977 and piloted them through their first three and a half seasons. /(BC)

Dave Johnson — 1948– . RHP 1974–75, 77–78 Orioles, **Twins** 108 ip, 4–10, 4.64

Groomed as a reliever by the Orioles, Johnson broke his wrist in a 1975 motorcycle accident but became the "original" Mariner when Seattle purchased him (9/29/1976). Sold to the Twins, he made 30 appearances in 1977. /(EW)

Davey Johnson — 1943– . 2B-1B-3B 1965–75, 77–78 **Orioles**, Braves, Phillies, Cubs 1435 g, .261, 136 hr, 609 rbi. *4 LCS, 10 g, .289, 2 hr, 6 rbi. 4 WS, 21 g, .192, 6 rbi.*
Manager 1984– **Mets** 575–395, .593. First place: 86, 88 *2 LCS, 7–6, .538. 1 WS, 4–3, .571*
☛ *All-Star—68–70, 73. Gold Glove—69–71.*

Johnson was a three-time Gold Glove winner for the Orioles at second base (1969–71) and a good enough fielder to play 43 games at shortstop, filling in for Mark Belanger. But he is known as a home run hitter and as a manager. In 1973 his 43 HR, one behind the NL leader, set the ML record for second basemen as the Braves became the only team ever to have three 40-HR men: Johnson, Hank Aaron, and Darrell Evans. Johnson hit .270 that year, with career highs of 99 RBI, 84 runs, and 81 walks, and was *TSN*'s NL Comeback Player of the Year.

The Orioles had traded him because manager Earl Weaver felt that Johnson had lost too much range afield by bulking up for power; Bobby Grich took over the job. Prior to that Johnson had led AL second basemen in putouts (1970), double plays (1971), fielding (1972), and errors (1966, his rookie season). Even before his surprising power in 1973, he'd been a useful hitter, finishing fourth in the AL in doubles in 1967 and third in 1969. That year, when the Orioles lost to the Miracle Mets in the World Series, Johnson's fly ball to Cleon Jones was the final out. He had better luck in 1970, hitting two homers in the LCS as Baltimore swept the Twins. His best offensive figures for Baltimore came in 1971, when he hit .282 with 18 HR and 72 RBI. After he dropped off to .221 with five HR in 1972, he was traded to Atlanta with Pat Dobson, Roric Harrison, and Johnny Oates for Earl Williams and a throw-in. Besides his record-setting power performance, Johnson tied for the NL lead in double plays by a second baseman, but he also led in errors and couldn't cover as much ground as he once had. He split 1974 between first and second and fell off to

Davey Johnson

.251 with 15 HR, and after one pinch at-bat in 1975 he signed with the Yomiuri Giants for two years. In Japan, he became the only player to be a teammate of both Hank Aaron and Sadaharu Oh. He was a disappointment in his first year overseas (.197, 13 HR), but he improved to .275 with 26 HR in 1976.

Johnson made it back to the majors with the division-winning 1977 Phillies as a utility man and pinch hitter (9-for-26), hitting .321 with eight HR in 156 at-bats. In 1978 he tied a ML record with two pinch grand slams. But although he hit .333 in the pinch, his overall average dropped to .232.

Johnson began his managerial career in 1979. He won pennants in each of his three seasons in the minors and advanced quickly through the Mets' system, jumping over more experienced managerial candidates. Mets GM Frank Cashen had been the GM at Baltimore during Johnson's time there. Johnson, who earned a mathematics degree from Trinity (Texas) University, gained immediate atten-

tion for his use of computers to compile player data. His attention to batter-pitcher matchups for platooning and in-game switches was learned from Earl Weaver. Johnson's strategy also owes much to his former manager. He dislikes the bunt and manages according to the credos of "pitching and three-run homers" and "play for one run, lose by one run." Johnson took over a team that hadn't won a pennant since 1973 but was ready to win after being rebuilt from the minors up by Cashen and the Mets' new owners. Johnson went on to become the first NL manager to win at least 90 games in each of his first five seasons, winning the World Championship in 1986 and the NL East in 1988 and finishing second in the other years. /(SH)

Deron Johnson — 1938– . 1B-3B-DH-OF 1960–62, 64–76 Yankees, A's, **Reds**, Braves, Phillies, Brewers, Red Sox, White Sox 1765 g, .244, 245 hr, 923 rbi. *1 LCS, 4 g, .100. 1 WS, 6 g, .300*
☛ *Led League—rbi 65.*

Johnson was a muscular, strikeout-prone, right-handed slugger who didn't play regularly in the ML until his ninth professional season, but still hit 245 home runs in the ML after belting 162 in the minors. He was dubbed "another Mickey Mantle" by the overreactive New York press after hitting .329 with 24 HR and 78 RBI in only 63 games in the lowly Nebraska State League in 1956, but he played only 19 games for the Yankees before being traded to the A's in 1961. He was purchased by the Reds after spending most of 1962 in the military, and in 1963 he led the Pacific Coast League with 33 HR at San Diego.

Johnson hit 21 HR for the Reds in 1964, and no longer tried to pull every pitch over the left-field fence, although he still struck out often. In 1965 he led the NL with 130 RBI while batting .287 with 32 HR, and he added 24 HR in 1966. Defensively, Johnson was bouncing from first base to third base to the outfield, rarely remaining at one position for more than a season. The Braves traded three players to get Johnson after the 1967 season, but sold him to Philadelphia after he hit only .208 in 1968, and with the Phillies he tied a ML record with home runs in four consecutive at-bats, July 10 and 11, 1971. After Johnson's average dipped again to .213 in 1972, the Phillies traded him to the A's for a single minor leaguer, and he spent 1973–76 shuttling around the AL as a designated hitter and occasional first baseman. /(SCL)

Don Johnson (Pep) — 1911– . 2B-3B 1943–48 **Cubs** 511 g, .273, 8 hr, 175 rbi. *1 WS, 7 g, .172*

Don was born in Chicago the winter before his father, shortstop Ernie Johnson, debuted with the White Sox. Pep, a journeyman minor leaguer, joined the Cubs in 1943 at age thirty-one, became a regular at second base in 1944, and hit a high of .302 for the 1945 pennant winners. /(DAS)

Don Johnson — 1926– . RHP 1947, 50–52, 54–55, 58 Yankees, Browns, **Senators**, White Sox, Orioles, Giants 631 ip, 27–38, 4.78

Johnson contributed a 4–3 mark to the Yankees' 1947 pennant winners but was not used in the WS. Bouncing between the majors and minors for the next decade, he had his best season with the 1954 White Sox, going 8–7 with a 3.13 ERA. /(MC)

Earl Johnson (Lefty) — 1919– . LHP 1940–41, 46–51 **Red Sox**, Tigers 546 ip, 410–32, 4.30. *1 WS, 3 ip, 1–0, 2.70*

The "smiling Swedish southpaw" spent two seasons with the Red Sox before enlisting in the Army right after Pearl Harbor. He returned with a Silver Star, Bronze Star, and a cluster for heroism earned during the Battle of the Bulge. Back to the baseball wars, Johnson won the opening game of the 1946 WS in relief and in 1948 won an AL-high nine out of the bullpen. His brother Chet pitched briefly with the Browns in 1946. /(JK)

Ernie Johnson — 1888–1952. SS-2B 1912, 15–18, 21–25 **White Sox**, St. Louis (FL), Browns, Yankees 809 g, .265, 19 hr, 256 rbi. *1 WS, 2 g, --*

Johnson was given the White Sox' starting shortstop job in 1921 when Swede Risberg was banned for fixing the 1919 WS. He hit .295 that year, but clumsy fielding and a 1923 salary holdout prompted his sale to the Yankees. His son Don was a Cubs second baseman. /(RL)

Ernie Johnson — 1924– . RHP 1950, 52–59 **Braves**, Orioles 575 ip, 40–23, 3.27. *1 WS, 7 ip, 0–1, 1.29*

A Braves reliever for eight of his nine ML seasons, Johnson pitched well in the 1957 WS but lost Game Six when he surrendered a solo home run to the Yankees' Hank Bauer. Johnson has been with the Braves organization more than forty years and has been a fulltime broadcaster since 1966. /(FK)

Grant Johnson (Home Run) — 1874–Unk. SS-2B-MGR Negro Leagues 1894–1921 Page Fence Giants, Columbia Giants, Brooklyn Royal Giants, Cuban X-Giants, Philadelphia Giants, New York Lincoln Giants, Lincoln Stars, Pittsburgh Colored Stars, Pittsburgh Stars of Buffalo statistics not available

Dubbed "Home Run" for his power hitting during the turn-of-the-century dead-ball era, the right-handed-hitting Johnson was one of the pioneers of black baseball. His first team, the Page Fence Giants, which he formed with fellow pioneer Bud Fowler, played for a time in a white league in Michigan. Johnson moved on to play for what was regarded as the best black team of the early 1900s, the 1906 Philadelphia Giants, managed by Hall of Famer Rube Foster. Foster then took Johnson and five other players with him to form the Chicago American Giants of 1910, which Foster said was his best team ever. Playing in Cuba that winter, Johnson hit .412 against top competition that included the Detroit Tigers with Ty Cobb. In five years in the Cuban Winter League, he batted .319 in 156 games.

A star shortstop, Johnson moved to second base with the New York Lincoln Giants in 1912 to make room for future Hall of Fame SS John Henry Lloyd. Johnson finished his career as a playing manager in Buffalo, retiring at the age of fifty-eight. /(PG)

Hank Johnson — 1906–1982. RHP 1925–36, 39 **Yankees**, Red Sox, A's, Reds 1066 ip, 63–56, 4.75

A starter and reliever during a career hampered by illness, Johnson had several victorious seasons as a Yankee; in 1928 he was 4–0 against the Athletics' Lefty Grove (14–9 overall), and in 1930 he led the AL with nine relief wins. /(EW)

Harold Johnson (Speed) — 1884–Unk. *Writer*

The editor of *Who's Who in Major League Baseball* in 1933, Johnson had begun his career with the Columbus (Ohio) *Citizen* in 1906. For the next ten years, he covered the Cubs and White Sox for the Chicago *Record-Herald*. After a year as sports editor for NEA in Cleveland, he returned to Chicago with the *Evening American* from 1919 to 1932. /(NLM)

Howard Johnson (HoJo) — 1960– . 3B-SS Tigers, **Mets** 869 g, .258, 136 hr, 422 rbi. *2 LCS, 8 g, .050. 2 WS, 3 g, .000*
☛ *All-Star—89.*

When finally given a chance to play regularly, Johnson established himself as one of the most well-rounded hitters in the game. In 1987 he and Darryl Strawberry became the first teammates to both hit

30 HR and steal 30 bases, and Johnson's 36 HR set a NL record for a switch-hitter.

Johnson's first full season came with the World Champion 1984 Tigers. He hit 12 HR with 50 RBI in 355 at-bats, but manager Sparky Anderson chose to use Dave Bergman, Marty Castillo, and Tom Brookens in the postseason rather than Johnson, who got only one pinch at-bat in the World Series. Detroit's disbelief in his potential led them to trade him to the Mets that December for Walt Terrell. In New York Johnson found himself in a platoon with Ray Knight. His ability to play shortstop, although without much range, got him in the lineup sometimes; manager Davey Johnson was quite willing to stack his lineup offensively at the cost of weaker defense. But it wasn't until after Knight left as a free agent that Johnson played every day, staving off the challenge of the promising Dave Magadan.

Usually hitting sixth or seventh, Johnson was easy to pitch around in 1987, but still hit .265 with 36 HR (fifth in the league) and 99 RBI. Opposing managers, especially Whitey Herzog of the rival Cardinals, repeatedly had Johnson's bat confiscated to check for cork. Eventually Herzog realized that Johnson's power was for real; two years later he suggested that Johnson's arms should be checked instead. Johnson fell off to 24 HR and 23 steals in 1988, playing the second half of the season with a sore right shoulder; he hit very poorly in the LCS. Over the winter, he was the center of many trade rumors, with hot rookie Gregg Jefferies supposedly ready to take over third base. The Mets were glad they kept him. At the All-Star break, Davey Johnson said, "the Mets' season [was] a Howard Johnson highlight film." HoJo moved to third in the lineup but continued to draw walks, showing both that he was a patient hitter and that NL pitchers would rather pitch to anybody else, even Darryl Strawberry. Johnson finished with career highs of 101 RBI (tied for fourth in the NL), 104 runs (tied for the NL lead), and 41 steals (tied for third) while batting .287 with 36 HR (second in the NL). He was only the third player ever to have two 30–30 seasons in HR and steals.

A dead fastball hitter in his first few seasons, Johnson used a high-tech reflex program to learn to wait better. But his ability to hit even the best fastballs gave him many clutch late-inning home runs against opponents' ace relievers, who tend to be fireballers. A favorite victim is the Cardinals' Todd Worrell, who surrendered five home runs lifetime to Johnson before Whitey Herzog finally wouldn't let Worrell pitch to Johnson in vital situations.

Johnson's major weakness is his fielding. He has a strong but erratic arm, and his range is generally poor. Davey Johnson tends to use him at shortstop when fly-ball pitchers are on the mound, with Sid Fernandez being the best example. Johnson sometimes seems not to know all the duties of a shortstop and has been known to forget to take throws from the outfield. However, he does have a third baseman's reflexes and can leap well for liners over his head. /(SH)

Jerry Johnson — 1943- . RHP 1968–77 Phillies, Cardinals, **Giants**, Indians, Astros, Padres, Blue Jays 770 ip, 48–51, 4.31. *1 LCS, 1 ip, 0–0, 13.50*

Originally a third baseman in the Mets' system, Johnson's longest ML stint without a trip to the minors was 1970–73. With the division-winning 1971 Giants, he led NL relievers with 12 wins and 9 losses and recorded 18 saves. He retired with 41 lifetime saves. /(JCA)

Jing Johnson [Russell Conwell] — 1894–1950. RHP 1916–17, 19, 27–28 A's 539 ip, 24–37, 3.35

A research chemist out of Ursinus (PA) College, where he later served as athletic director, Johnson was 9–12 for the A's in 1917 and 9–15 in 1919, serving in the military in between. He also coached at Bucknell and Lehigh. /(NLM)

Joe Johnson — 1961- . RHP 1985–87 **Braves**, Blue Jays 327 ip, 20–18, 4.48

Johnson won 13 games as a starting pitcher in 1986 while spending time with the Braves and Blue Jays. He failed to make the Blue Jays out of spring training in 1987, but he joined them later in the season and posted a 3–5 record and 5.13 ERA. Selected by the Angels in the December 1987 major league draft, he spent the 1988 season with California's Triple-A team at Edmonton. /(TF)

John Henry Johnson — 1956- . LHP 1978–81, 83–84, 86–87 A's, **Rangers**, Red Sox, Brewers 603 ip, 26–33, 3.89

After coming from the Giants to Oakland in a seven-for-one trade for Vida Blue in 1978, the rookie Johnson went 11–10 to lead the A's in wins. Possessing a fine fastball and little else, he was 2–8 the following June when he was sent to the Rangers. He played out his ML career in middle relief. Pitching for Hawaii (Pacific Coast League) on May 2, 1985, he no-hit Calgary. /(JCA)

Judy Johnson [William Julius] — 1899–1989. 3B Negro Leagues 1921–38 Hilldale, Homestead Grays, Darby Daisies, Pittsburgh Crawfords 615 g, 19 hr (inc.) ☛ *All-Star—33, 36. Hall of Fame—1975.*

Connie Mack once told Judy Johnson, "If you were

a white boy you could name your own price."
Johnson was considered the Negro Leagues' top
third baseman in the 1920s and 1930s. Because of
his defensive abilities, he was known as "the black
Pie Traynor."

When Johnson was a child growing up in Wilmington, DE, his father set up a "fitness center" for
the neighborhood children, complete with barbells,
monkey bars, and the like. "My Daddy liked
physical fitness and wanted me to be a prizefighter,"
Johnson recalled. He was exposed to baseball at an
early age, serving as batboy for his father's local
team. He realized then that his "greatest ambition
was to play baseball." He quite school after tenth
grade and went to work on the New Jersey docks
during WWI.

After the war, Johnson caught on with the Chester Giants, playing on weekends. He then signed a
pro contract with the Atlantic City Bacharach Giants, who paid him $5 per game. In 1919, he played
for the semi-pro Madison Stars of Philadelphia,
which served as a sort of minor league team for the
Hilldale club. Hilldale purchased Johnson for $100
in 1920, and in 1921 gave him $150 a month to be
their starting third baseman. While with Hilldale,
Johnson acquired the nickname Judy, because he
resembled a Chicago American Giants player, Judy
Gans.

Hilldale won a championship in 1921 and played
in the first two Negro League World Series, in 1924
and 1925, winning the latter. In the 1924 NLWS,
lost to the Kansas City Monarchs, Johnson led both
teams in hitting (.341) and had five doubles, a triple,
and a home run. Hilldale and Kansas City met again
in the 1925 NLWS, and though Johnson batted just
.250, he singled and later scored the winning run in
the tenth inning of a 1–1 tie in Game Three. Hilldale
won, five games to one.

By the mid-1920s, Johnson had established himself as a top third baseman and a dangerous clutch
hitter, with a career average of over .300. Hall of
Famer John Henry Lloyd had great influence on
him. Said Johnson of Lloyd, "He's the man I give
the credit for polishing me; he taught me how to
play third base." Johnson was not a particularly fast
runner, but he meticulously studied opposing pitchers and took every advantage on the basepaths. He
often stole third base. He played winters in Florida
or Cuba (where he compiled a .334 average in six
seasons) but never again set foot on a boat after his
return voyage from Cuba in 1931.

In 1929, his final season with Hilldale, Johnson
batted .401—believed to have been his career high.
The Eastern Colored League folded in 1930 as a
result of the Depression, and Johnson joined the

Judy Johnson

Homestead Grays as a player-coach. One night,
when the Grays' catcher was injured during a game,
Johnson pulled from the stands and signed 18-year-
old catcher Josh Gibson, who became a Hall of
Famer.

Johnson returned to Hilldale (which had become
the Darby Daisies) in 1931 and remained there until
mid-1932, when he jumped to the Pittsburgh
Crawfords. The Crawfords' lineup, which included
Gibson and fellow Hall of Famers Cool Papa Bell
and Oscar Charleston, was often compared to the
New York Yankees' "Murderers Row." He played
in his last NLWS in 1935 when the Crawfords faced
the New York Cubans. He got a clutch hit in the
ninth inning of the sixth game, with the bases
loaded, the score tied 6–6, and the Crawfords

behind three games to two in the series. His sharp single down the first base line won the game for them and they went on to win the series the next day.

After baseball's color barrier was broken, Johnson scouted and coached for the Philadelphia Athletics. He worked for the Phillies from 1959 to 1973 and helped sign Richia Allen. In 1975 he was elected to the Hall of Fame by the Committee on Negro Baseball Leagues. /(TB)

Ken Johnson [Kenneth Wandersee] (Hooks) — 1923–. LHP 1947–52 Cardinals, **Phillies**, Tigers 269 ip, 12–14, 4.58

The rangy Johnson's wildness impeded his career, though he had flashes of brilliance; he pitched a one-hitter for the Cardinals in his first ML start. Traded to the Phillies in April 1950, Johnson went 4–1 on the way to the pennant. /(AL)

Ken Johnson — 1933–. RHP 1958–70 A's, Reds, Astros, **Braves**, Yankees, Cubs, Expos 1737 ip, 91–106, 3.46. *1 WS, 0.2 ip, 0–0, 0.00*

Johnson was the ultimate hard-luck pitcher: He pitched a no-hitter against the Reds on April 24, 1964 but lost 1–0 on two walks and two errors. He first gained notice when he was acquired by the Reds in July 1961 and went 6–2 for them (6–6 on the season) as they won a surprise pennant. He had his first winning season in 1965 when he was traded to the Braves in May; he finished at 16–10, 3.42, and followed up with 14–8 and 13–9 seasons before falling below .500 for the rest of his career. /(WOR)

Lamar Johnson — 1950–. 1B-DH 1974–82 **White Sox**, Rangers 792 g, .287, 64 hr, 381 rbi

A 6'2" offensive player who hit for power and average, as he ballooned to 232 pounds Johnson's speed, fielding, and numbers suffered. He batted .309 for the 1979 White Sox, including a 19-game hitting streak. A choir singer, in 1977 he sang "The Star Spangled Banner" before a Chicago game, then had two homers and a double, the White Sox' only hits in their 2–1 victory. /(EW)

Lou Johnson (Slick, Sweet Lou) — 1934–. OF 1960–62, 65–69 Cubs, Angels, Braves, **Dodgers**, Indians 677 g, .258, 48 hr, 232 rbi. *2 WS, 11 g, .286, 2 hr, 4 rbi*

Johnson spent almost a decade in the minors and failed to stick after brief stints with the Cubs, Angels, and Braves. The Dodgers acquired him from Detroit in exchange for Larry Sherry before the 1964 season, and in their 1965 World Series victory he hit two homers, including the winning shot in the clincher. In the 1966 Series against the Orioles, Johnson's .267 average led the otherwise baffled Los Angeles offense, and his one run scored was half the Dodgers' total. He was the Dodgers' regular left fielder in 1965–67 and one of the few power sources the team had. In 1965 his 12 HR tied for the team lead, and he was second on the club in 1966 (17) and 1967 (11). A broken leg in 1967 reduced his playing time, and he was traded after the season. He split 1968 between the Cubs and the Indians in his last season as a regular. /(JFC)

Randy Johnson — 1963–. RHP 1988– Expos, **Mariners** 187 ip, 10–13, 3.34

The tallest major leaguer ever, 6'10" 225-lb, hard-throwing Randy Johnson had an excellent September stint with the Expos in 1988, going 3–0 with a 2.42 ERA in four starts. But he started poorly in 1989 and ascribed it to being rattled by taunts about his size; he was moved to relief and then sent down. One of the three pitchers sent to Seattle in May 1989 for Mark Langston, he went 7–9 with a 4.40 in the Mariner rotation, showing below-average control. /(JFC)

Roy Johnson — 1903–1973. OF 1929–38 Tigers, **Red Sox**, Yankees, Braves 1153 g, .296, 58 hr, 556 rbi. *1 WS, 2 g, .000.*
    Manager 1944 **Cubs** 0–1, .000

Roy and his brother, the A's "Indian Bob" Johnson, were part-Indian, from Oklahoma. A strong-armed outfielder, Roy twice led the league in assists and twice in errors; as a Tiger rookie in 1929, he set the still-standing AL record of 31 outfield errors. Also in 1929, he led the league with 640 at-bats and tied for the top spot with 45 doubles. He led the AL with 19 triples for the 1931 Tigers and often finished among the league leaders in stolen bases. A four-time .300 hitter, he became a genuine team leader. Johnson, Smead Jolley, and Earl Averill formed one of the all-time great-hitting minor league outfields with the Pacific Coast League San Francisco Seals. /(EW)

Si Johnson — 1900–1985. RHP 1928–43, 46–47 **Reds**, Cardinals, Phillies, Braves 2281 ip, 101–165, 4.09

Pitching almost exclusively for second-division clubs, Johnson won only 101 games in 17 seasons. He led the NL in losses twice and in 1933 lost 12 straight for the last-place Reds. He spent 1944–45 in the Navy, avoiding two more last-place finishes by the Phillies. /(JK)

Steamboat Johnson [Harry] — Unk.–1951. *Umpire* NL 1914

Although he umpired only one year in the ML, Johnson became famous for his work in the minors, including 28 years in the Southern Association. Fittingly, he was behind the plate for the longest Southern Association game, a 23-inning tie between Atlanta and Chattanooga in 1919. Johnson, who received his nickname for a voice that "resembled the blast of a Mississippi River side-wheeler," published a book about umpiring called *Standing the Gaff* in 1935. /(RTM)

Syl Johnson — 1900–1984. RHP 1922–40 Tigers, Cardinals, Reds, **Phillies** 2165 ip, 112–117, 4.06. *3 WS, 16 ip, 0–1, 4.50*

Syl Johnson's injury-plagued career extended for 19 unspectacular seasons as a starter and workhorse reliever. At various times, line drives broke his cheekbone, ribs, big toe, and three fingers on his pitching hand. He did have six consecutive healthy seasons, in which time he compiled almost half his career wins and appeared in three Cardinals World Series. /(JK)

Tim Johnson — 1949– . SS-2B-3B 1973–79 **Brewers**, Blue Jays 516 g, .223, 0 hr, 84 rbi

The light-hitting motorcycle enthusiast was given the Brewers shortstop job in 1973 but hit only .213. He was primarily a utility player for the remainder of his ML career. /(JCA)

Tom Johnson — 1951– . RHP 1974–78 **Twins** 273 ip, 23–14, 3.39

After three undistinguished seasons, Johnson emerged as the Twins' bullpen ace in 1977, with 15 saves and a ML-high 16 relief wins. But his 71 appearances took their toll, and Johnson vanished after an ineffective 1978 season. /(JCA)

Wallace Johnson (Wally) — 1956– . 1B-2B 1981–84, 86–**Expos**, Giants 381 g, .263, 4 hr, 54 rbi

With the exception of seven games in 1983 with the Giants, Johnson has spent his entire ML career with Montreal. He came up as a second baseman and has played first base in recent years, but he is primarily a pinch hitter. He led the NL in pinch hits in 1987 (17-for-61, .279) and 1988 (22-for-64, .344), and in pinch at-bats in '89. /(SFS)

Walter Johnson (The Big Train, Barney) — 1887–1946. RHP 1907–27 **Senators** 5923 ip, 416–279, 2.17. 20 wins: 10–19, 24–25 *2 WS, 50 ip, 3–3, 2.34.*
   Manager 1929–35 **Senators**, Indians 530–432, .551 ☛ *Most Valuable Player—13, 24 . Led League—w 13–16, 18, 24. Led League—k 10, 12–19, 21, 23–24. Hall of Fame—1936.*

Ty Cobb is supposed to have said that his greatest embarrassment was batting against Walter Johnson on a dark day in Washington. An uncommonly mellow acknowledgment of human frailty by cranky Ty, it was surely God's truth about gentle Walter. In an era lacking electronic speed guns, Johnson was generally thought to throw the fastest ball in the game. A 6'1" righthander with long arms, he threw his hummer with an easy sidearm motion. Contemporaries recalled his pitches as nearly invisible, arriving with a "swoosh" and smashing into the catcher's mitt like a thunderclap. In 21 seasons with the Washington Senators (10 in the second division), Johnson won 416 games. Only Cy Young won more (and only Young and Pud Galvin lost more). There was no pitching category in which he did not excel. In 1914, for example, he led the AL in wins, games, starts, complete games, innings, strikeouts, and shutouts. He eventually amassed 110 shutouts, the most ever. His 38 1–0 wins are, by far, an all-time record.

Among his accomplishments were 16 straight wins (1912); a string of 56 scoreless innings, and a 36–7 (1.09) mark in 1913; five wins, three of them shutouts, in nine days (1908); 66 triumphs over Detroit, the most for any AL pitcher against any one team; 200 victories in eight seasons, 300 in 14. He had his disappointments: 65 of his losses were by shutouts, 26 of them by 1–0 scores (both records); he lost six of eight duels with formidable Red Sox lefty Babe Ruth; and for all of Ty Cobb's dark-day embarrassments, he batted .335 in 67 games against Johnson.

Forgetting the numbers, what pleased people most was that Johnson combined extraordinary baseball talent with a wholly admirable character. In a rowdy game, he was mild, modest, decent, friendly, and forbearing. Across the nation, beyond the confines of baseball, he personified values that Americans respected. He persisted into the lively ball era and the Jazz Age with his old-fashioned, almost Lincolnesque virtues intact. Sportswriters rarely found him less than chivalric and dubbed him "Sir Walter" and the "White Knight."

He was Kansas-born of a farm family which ventured West to try its luck in the California oil

Walter Johnson

starter and relief ace. Ultimately, he was 40–30 in relief, with 34 saves. The legend grew with him. He acquired nicknames deriving from the machinery that best exemplified the overwhelming speed of his fastball: "Barney," for Oldfield, the mile-a-minute auto racer; and "Big Train," for America's impressive, highballing railroads. Still, the image of the kindly fellow prevailed; one who, comfortably ahead in a late inning, might ease up to allow a weak batter or an old friend a hit; who never blamed teammates for losses, however grievously they erred; who never drank, cussed, or argued with umpires; who never deliberately threw at hitters, although his long career contributed to his setting the ML career mark with 206 hit batsmen. Cobb said he'd move up in the box and crowd the plate knowing he would never get a brush-back pitch from Sir Walter.

Johnson's control was exemplary. His catchers swore by him. In 802 games, he gave up a mere 1,405 walks, less than one every 4.1 innings. But he had wild streaks and still has a piece of the AL record for wild pitches in one season (21).

As the years wore on, Johnson became a Washington landmark. He was tempted during the Federal League uproar, and actually signed with the Chicago Whales, but revoked the contract when penny-pinching Clark Griffith made an emergency trip to Kansas to up the ante and restore him to his pedestal. Finally, in 1924, with the shrewdest trades of his life, Griffith put together Washington's first pennant winner. Going 23–7 at age thirty-seven, Johnson was finally in a World Series. His performance against the Giants in the seventh game is one of baseball's favorite stories. Appearing in relief, two days after pitching a complete game, he held the Giants scoreless for four innings until Early McNeely's 12th-inning grounder deflected off a pebble, over Freddie Lindstrom's head, allowing Washington's winning run to score. In 1925, with another 20 wins from Johnson, the Senators repeated. This time, after winning two from the Pirates, Johnson lost Game Seven. Rain and Roger Peckinpaugh's errors helped, but he was rapped for 15 hits and deserved the 9–7 loss.

When his glorious career wound down, Johnson tried his hand at managing: Newark for a season, Washington (1929–32), and Cleveland (1933–35). His .551 winning percentage was respectable, but the manager never measured up to the player. He was considered too easygoing. But he was among the select group admitted to the Hall of Fame when it first opened. /(ADS)

fields. When Washington got him, he was going on twenty, and burning up a semi-pro league in southwestern Idaho. The story has, variously, a fan, a traveling liquor salesman, or an old-time umpire writing east about the young phenom, but only purse-poor Washington and its manager, Joe Cantillon, acted in time. Already interested in a fleet Western Association outfielder named Clyde Milan, Cantillon sent an injured catcher west to scout the pair. He corralled them both; Johnson signed for a $100 bonus, train fare, and a big league salary of $350 a month.

He was not an overnight success. The fastball was undeniable, but he was susceptible to the bunt and to the confusions of inexperience and an eighth-place club. After going 13–25 his third season (1909), he turned things around and became the AL's premier pitcher. For the Senators he was both

Doc Johnston [Wheeler Roger] — 1887–1961. 1B 1909, 12–16, 18–22 Reds, **Indians**, Pirates, A's 1055 g, .263, 14 hr, 379 rbi. *1 WS, 5 g, .273*

When Doc's Indians met younger brother Jimmy's Dodgers in the 1920 World Series, Doc outhit his sibling, though Jimmy finished with the higher career mark. In 1919, Doc had nine consecutive hits in a four-game stretch. /(JL)

Jimmy Johnston — 1889–1967. 3B-OF-2B-SS-1B 1911, 14, 16–26 White Sox, Cubs, **Dodgers**, Braves, Giants 1377 g, .294, 22 hr, 410 rbi. *2 WS, 7 g, .250*

No star, Johnston was a hustler who would play anywhere and always to the outer limits of his abilities. He was well-traveled in the minors, hiring on with seven clubs in four leagues before finding a home in 1916 with Brooklyn, where he was a fan favorite for a decade. Essentially an outfielder, he finally played the most games at third, a significant number at second and short, and 49 at first. He was a solid righthanded hitter, even in the dead-ball days, and eventually achieved .325 averages in the two years (1921 and 1923) when he had 203 hits. In a 1922 game, he hit for the cycle. The Dodgers used him in the leadoff spot, as he could wait out a pitcher, run the bases cleverly, and steal. In 1920 he and brother Doc, of the Indians, were the first family pair to face each other in a World Series (beating the Meusels by a year). After his playing days, the Tennessean coached the Dodgers and managed a number of minor league teams. /(ADS)

James Johnstone — Unk.–Unk. *Umpire* AL, **NL**, FL 1902–12, 14–25

Johnstone, who umpired in three different major leagues, angered the Giants with some of his calls in a 1906 game. The next day, August 7, he was denied entry to the ballpark. Bob Emslie, the second umpire, refused to start the game without him, and the game was forfeited to the Cubs as one of their record 116 wins. /(RTM)

Jay Johnstone — 1945– . OF 1966–85 Angels, White Sox, A's, **Phillies**, Yankees, Padres, Dodgers, Cubs 1748 g, .267, 102 hr, 531 rbi. *4 LCS, 8 g, .471, 2 rbi. 2 WS, 5 g, .667, 1 hr, 3 rbi*

Johnstone earned a deserved reputation as a flake who kept his teammates entertained with his uninhibited clubhouse antics, but he was also a fine lefthanded hitter who managed to last 20 seasons in the ML despite playing over 130 games only once (1969 with the Angels). He was originally a speedy, switch-hitting centerfielder, but abandoned hitting from the right side after his rookie season. Only two years after hitting a career-high 16 HR for the White Sox in 1971, Johnstone was released outright and his career seemed doomed. He came back with the Phillies, however, and in the 1976 LCS he was phenomenal in a losing effort. He was seven-for-nine in the series, but the Reds swept the Phillies in three. Johnstone starred again in the 1981 WS for the Dodgers, belting a pinch two-run HR as Los Angeles came back from a 6–3 deficit to win Game Four 8–7. After finishing his career as a reserve outfielder and pinch hitter, Johnstone became a baseball broadcaster. /(SCL)

Smead Jolley (Smudge) — 1902– . OF-C 1930–33 White Sox, **Red Sox** 473 g, .305, 46 hr, 313 rbi

The 6'3" Jolley had over 100 RBI in two of his four ML seasons, but his fielding was subject to ridicule. However, the story about a line drive going through his legs, bouncing off the wall and again threading his wickets, then him throwing wildly, adding up to three errors, is undocumented. His fielding lapses were tolerated in the minors, where he led his league in batting six times. /(LRD)

Dave Jolly (Gabby) — 1924–1963. RHP 1953–57 **Braves** 291 ip, 16–14, 3.77

Jolly had horrible control, walking 6.1 batters per nine innings pitched. In 1954, his best season, he won 11 and saved 10 with a 2.43 ERA out of the Braves' bullpen. /(FK)

Barry Jones — 1963– . RHP 1986– **Pirates**, White Sox 193 ip, 11–13, 3.40

Jones was traded to the White Sox for Dave LaPoint in August 1988 and was effective the rest of the season as Bobby Thigpen's set-up man. He slumped in 1989. /(WOR)

Bob Jones (Ducky) — 1889–1964. 3B 1917–25 **Tigers** 853 g, .265, 7 hr, 316 rbi

Jones hit .303 with 72 RBI as the Tigers' third baseman in 1921, easily his best season. After nine underproductive years in Detroit he returned to the Pacific Coast League, where he had starred before reaching the majors. /(JK)

Bobby Jones — 1949– . OF-DH-1B 1974–77, 81, 83–86 **Rangers**, Angels 314 g, .221, 20 hr, 86 rbi

Jones was 34 years old when he finally spent a full season in the majors, as an extra lefthanded bat with the 1984 Rangers. First signed by the Washington Senators in 1967, he became deaf in one ear during 14 months of combat in Vietnam. A standout hitter year after year in Triple-A, he left to play in Japan for 1979 and 1980. Two of his 17 ML doubles came in the 12-run 15th inning of a July 3, 1983 game between Texas and Oakland. /(JCA)

Charley Jones [born Benjamin Wesley Rippay] (Long Charley) — 1850–Unk. OF 1875–80, 83–88 Keokuk (NA), Reds, Cubs, Braves, **Cincinnati (AA)**, New York (AA), Kansas City (AA) *NA:* 12 g, .250; *ML:* 882 g, .299, 55 hr, 219 rbi (inc)
☛ *Led League—hr 79. Led League—rbi 79.*

Jones was an outstanding but often controversial slugger during the 1870s and 1880s. With Cincinnati from 1876 to 1878, he became the Reds' most popular player but was sometimes criticized in the press for carousing. In 1877, he caused a furor by signing a contract with the Cubs when he believed that his Cincinnati team was about to fold. After two games with Chicago, he returned to the still-struggling Reds. However, in 1879 he was able to sign a three-year contract with Boston. He led the NL in home runs (9) and RBI (62) in 1879 for the Braves. The next year he became the first player to hit two homers in one inning (6/10/80). But after the 1880 season he was suspended by the club and blacklisted for refusing to play. He countered that he had not been paid and sued for his salary. A jury sided with the club and Jones stayed out of baseball until 1883 when the blacklisting was lifted and he signed with Cincinnati of the American Association. In 1884, he became the third man to hit three triples in one game. /(BC)

Charlie Jones (Casey) — 1876–1947. OF 1901, 05–08 Red Sox, **Senators**, Browns 478 g, .233, 5 hr, 143 rbi

Jones was a smart, strong-armed outfielder and an adept basestealer who collected 84 stolen bases in three seasons as a Senators regular. He was replaced in Washington's outfield by Clyde Milan, who remained for 15 years. Jones lasted one more year after his 1907 trade to the Browns. /(NLM)

Cleon Jones — 1942– . OF 1963, 65–76 **Mets**, White Sox 1213 g, .281, 93 hr, 524 rbi. *2 LCS, 8 g, .353, 1 hr, 7 rbi. 2 WS, 12 g, .234, 1 hr, 1 rbi*
☛ *All-Star—69.*

Jones was a major ingredient in the 1969 Mets' World Championship. His career-high .340 average was third in the NL, the highest a Met has ever finished in that category. He led the Mets with 10 game-winning RBI (not an official statistic at the time) and established personal bests with 92 runs and 75 RBI as one of the few offensive forces on a team that did it with pitching and mirrors. At the start of the year he was 26 years old, but he was the oldest regular on the team.

Jones figures especially prominently in Mets history as a pivotal figure in the turning points of the 1969 and 1973 seasons. In 1969, manager Gil Hodges removed Jones from left field after Jones had not hustled after a hit during the first game of a doubleheader on July 30 against the Astros; it signaled to the players that Hodges would accept only 100% effort and helped the Mets take themselves more seriously in their suprising pennant contention. In 1973, it was a fielding play that Jones did make that suggested that another miracle season was in the making. The evening Willie Mays announced that he would retire at the end of the season, September 20, the Mets were in the middle of a three-game series with the first-place Pirates. With the game tied 3–3 in the ninth inning, the Pirates had Richie Zisk on at first when Dave Augustine hit what seemed to be a certain home run. But the ball hit the top of the fence and bounced back into Jones's glove. Jones threw a strike to third baseman Wayne Garrett, whose relay caught Zisk at the plate. The Mets won in the thirteenth inning, and took over first place the next day. /(SH)

Cowboy Jones (Albert, Bronco) — 1874–1958. LHP 1898–01 Cleveland NL, **Cardinals** 526 ip, 25–34, 3.61

Jones was a second-line Cleveland Spiders pitcher in 1898 but good enough to be switched to the Cardinals in 1899 when owner Frank Robison, who owned both clubs, stripped the Cleveland roster in a vain attempt to build a St. Louis powerhouse. In 1900, Jones's only year of regular starting, he was 13–19. /(BC)

Dalton Jones — 1943– . 2B-3B-1B 1964–72 **Red Sox**, Tigers, Rangers 907 g, .235, 41 hr, 237 rbi. *1 WS, 6 g, .389, 1 rbi*

Jones was a utility infielder, but he contributed several key hits to the Red Sox' "Impossible Dream" pennant of 1967. On September 18, in the heat of a tight four-team race, he hit a game-winning tenth-inning homer at Tiger Stadium. The left-handed batter led the AL with 13 pinch hits that season. He started at third base in four games of the World Series and batted .389 (7-for-18). A .261 lifetime pinch hitter, he got more than one third of his ML at-bats off the bench. Dalton hit a grand slam for Detroit on July 9, 1970 but passed Don Wert between first and second base, making it a single./(PB)

Davy Jones (Kangaroo) — 1880–1972. OF 1901–04, 06–15 Milwaukee (AL), Browns, Cubs, **Tigers**, White Sox, Pittsburgh (FL) 1085 g, .270, 9 hr, 289 rbi. *3 WS, 15 g, .265, 1 hr, 2 rbi*

Davy Jones was the third or fourth outfielder, with Ty Cobb and Sam Crawford, during the Tigers' years of early AL dominance. A speedy leadoff man, he was sure-handed afield and a settling influence on the volatile Cobb and the sometimes surly Crawford./(JK)

Doug Jones — 1957– . RHP 1982, 86– Brewers, **Indians** 276 ip, 17–19, 2.67
☛ *All-Star—88–89.*

Jones had spent seven years in the Milwaukee organization and was recovering from shoulder problems when the Indians gave him a chance in 1985 at Double-A. There he took on an austere attitude and learned a new pitch, the circle change, which behaves like a screwball. With it he became a 30-year-old rookie with the 1987 Indians. In 1988 he was among baseball's elite relievers, setting a ML mark by recording saves in 15 consecutive appearances and breaking the Indians record for saves in a season./(JCA)

Fielder Jones — 1874–1934. OF 1896–08, 14–15 Dodgers, White Sox, St. Louis (FL) 1794 g, .285, 22 hr, 632 rbi. *1 WS, 6 g, .095.*
Manager 1904–08, 14–18 **White Sox**, St. Louis (FL), Browns 685–582, .541. First place: 06 *1 WS, 4–2, .667*

Prophetically named, Jones became an outstanding centerfielder (first AL outfielder to execute an unassisted double play) as well as a top-notch slap-hitter who six times batted over .300. However, he's most

Fielder Jones with the St. Louis Terriers of the Federal League

remembered as the manager of the 1906 White Sox, the "Hitless Wonders." Jones led this group of powder-puff hitters to a surprise AL pennant and then won the only all-Chicago World Series from the favored Cubs. When he threatened to quit, he drew a $10,000 contract from miserly White Sox owner Charles Comiskey. The sullen-faced Jones brought the Sox to within a few games of the pennant in each of his other four years as their manager.

A stern taskmaster, Jones routinely suspended players for drinking, being out of shape, or making bonehead plays, but he was also an early champion of players' rights and often argued with Comiskey on their behalf. He would charge in from his centerfield position to berate umpires and was often banished from games for kicking and swearing. An innovative tactician, he is credited with inventing the "motion infield" and was one of the first to position his outfielders according to the hitter.

He quit the White Sox after a controversy. He lost the final game of the 1908 season and the pennant when he started a weary Doc White in place of a rested Frank Smith. Personal motives may have been involved: Jones and Smith despised each other. Coaxed back to baseball by a fat Federal League contract in 1914, he guided a last-place St. Louis team to within a percentage point of the pennant the next year. Named manager of the Browns, he had three also-ran finishes with them. /(DB)

Gordon Jones — 1930- . RHP 1954-62, 64-65 **Cardinals**, Giants, Orioles, A's, Astros 378 ip, 15-18, 4.16

Jones was 4-4 with two shutouts and a 2.00 ERA after his 1954 call-up by the Cardinals. He was traded with Red Schoendienst in one of GM Frank Lane's many unpopular trades, a six-for-three deal with the Giants. Jones later scouted for the Yankees. /(FO)

Jake Jones — 1920- . 1B 1941-42, 46-48 White Sox, **Red Sox** 224 g, .229, 23 hr, 117 rbi

Jones played briefly with the White Sox before entering WWII and returned to play a full season only once, hitting .237 with 19 HR and 96 RBI for the White Sox and Red Sox in 1947. /(FS)

Jeff Jones — 1956- . RHP 1980-84 **A's** 205 ip, 9-9, 3.96. *1 LCS, 2 ip, 0-0, 4.50*

The 6'3" reliever was unscored upon in his first seven ML games and peaked with Billy Martin's AL West champion A's in 1981 (4-1, 3.39). He then suffered arm problems and his ERA ballooned to over 5.00. /(JCA)

Jimmy Jones — 1964- . RHP 1986- **Padres**, Yankees 391 ip, 22-22, 4.04

The third choice overall in the 1982 June draft (two picks before Dwight Gooden), Jones suffered injuries in three of five unspectacular minor league seasons. San Diego's choice seemed vindicated when he one-hit the Astros in his ML debut (9/21/86), but the inconsistent Jones endured the tirades of impatient manager Larry Bowa in 1987 and fell to 9-14 in 1988. Sent to the Yankees in the Jack Clark trade, he didn't make the team in the spring and appeared in only 11 games, with a 5.25 ERA. /(JCA)

Lynn Jones — 1953- . OF 1979-86 **Tigers**, Royals 527 g, .252, 7 hr, 91 rbi. *2 LCS, 8 g, .200. 1 WS, 5 g, .667*

A career backup player (he had trouble hitting the curveball), Jones proved most valuable to the 1985 World Champion Kansas City Royals as a late-inning defensive replacement for left fielder Lonnie "Skates" Smith. In the 1985 World Series, he doubled and tripled in two pinch-hitting appearances. His brother Darryl was a DH-outfielder for the 1979 Yankees. /(JCA)

Mack Jones (Mack the Knife) — 1938- . OF 1961-63, 65-71 **Braves**, Reds, Expos 1002 g, .252, 133 hr, 415 rbi

Jones broke in with four hits in his first game, tying the post-1900 NL mark. He hit 31 HR in his first full season (1965), finishing third in the NL in home run percentage. He teamed that year with Hank Aaron, Eddie Mathews, Joe Torre, Felipe Alou, and Gene Oliver as the Braves set a NL record with six 20-HR men in one season. When the Braves moved to Jones's native Atlanta in 1966 he hit 23 HR despite a shoulder injury, but his power gradually dropped off until 1969. Playing for the expansion Expos in cozy Jarry Park, he hit 22 HR and batted a career-high .270, and on April 14 he hit the first ML home run in Canada off Nelson Briles. /(JFC)

Mike Jones — 1959- . LHP 1980-81, 84-85 **Royals** 226 ip, 11-10, 4.42. *1 LCS, 1 ip, 0-0, 6.75*

Undisciplined and wild in the minors, Jones sparkled with a 6-3 mark after a mid-season call-up by the Royals in 1981. He fought back from a fractured neck sustained in an 1981 auto accident but never completely recovered his velocity. /(FJO)

Nippy Jones [Vernal Leroy] — 1925- . 1B-2B 1946-52, 57 **Cardinals**, Phillies, Braves 412 g, .267, 25 hr, 209 rbi. *2 WS, 4 g, .000*

In his final ML appearance of a career plagued by back problems, Jones batted in the bottom of the 10th inning of Game Four of the 1957 WS, with his Braves trailing the Yankees 5-4. After appearing to have avoided a wild Tommy Byrne pitch, Jones successfully argued that the pitch had struck his foot by pointing to a polish smudge on the ball. He took first base and the Braves rallied for three runs to win the game. /(FJO)

Odell Jones — 1953- . RHP 1975, 77-79, 81, 83-84, 86, 88 Pirates, Mariners, **Rangers**, Orioles, Brewers 549 ip, 24-35, 4.42

A fastball alone wasn't enough to keep Jones in the ML. He had brief success with the 1983 Rangers in relief (10 saves) by adding a submarine motion to his normal overhand delivery. /(ME)

Oscar Jones (Flip Flap) — 1879-1946. RHP 1903-05 **Dodgers** 875 ip, 45-46, 3.20. 20 wins: 03

A 20-game winner as a rookie, Jones flip-flopped his record to 17–25 in his sophomore year to lead the NL in losses, even though he lowered his ERA from 2.94 to 2.75. He threw 324 innings with 31 complete games in 1903 and 377 innings with 38 complete games the next year, all among the highest figures for post-1900 pitchers. /(BC)

Percy Jones — 1899-1979. RHP 1920-22, 25-30 **Cubs**, Braves, Pirates 1028 ip, 53-57, 4.33

Jones pitched mostly in relief for his nine ML seasons, with a top year of 12–7 for the 1926 Cubs. In 1928, he was the talk of the baseball world when he reportedly inherited $500,000. Three years later, while on the Columbus Redbirds roster, he fell from a third-story window and broke his back. He spent the rest of his life in a wheelchair. /(BC)

Randy Jones — 1950- . LHP 1973-82 **Padres**, Mets 1931 ip, 100-123, 3.42. 20 wins: 75-76
☛ *Led League—w 76. Led League—era 75. Cy Young Award—76. All-Star—75-76.*

A poised, fast-working control pitcher and a master of the slider and sinker, Jones won the 1976 NL Cy Young Award, going 22–14 for the Padres with league highs in wins, starts, complete games, and innings. That year, he tied Christy Mathewson's NL record of 68 innings without issuing a walk and became the first NL pitcher since WWII to win 20 and not strike out 100. With a 20–12 record and an ERA title (2.24) the previous season, Jones finished second to Tom Seaver in Cy Young voting, making him only the second pitcher to be runner-up one year and win the award the next (Mike Marshall was the other). He tied for most losses in the NL in 1974, when he went 8–22, and his 1975 performance won him *TSN*'s NL Comeback Player of the Year Award. He stopped the AL in the ninth inning of the 1975 All-Star Game and was the starter and winner in the 1976 contest. The owner of two one-hitters, Jones established a Padre record by hurling three consecutive shutouts in May 1980. He was often injured and generally ineffective after his trade to the Mets following the 1980 season, and he had trouble winning at Shea Stadium even in periods when he was pitching well on the road.

Jones established the ML season record for most chances accepted by a pitcher without an error (112 in 1976), tied ML pitchers' records for highest season fielding percentage (1.000, 1976) and most

assists in an inning (3, 9/28/75), and tied the NL pitchers' season record for the most double plays (12, 1976). /(EW)

Rick Jones [Thomas Frederick] — 1955- . LHP 1976-78 **Red Sox**, Mariners 158 ip, 6-9, 4.04

The 1975 Carolina League Pitcher of the Year (13–3), the 6'5" Jones came up with the Red Sox, was drafted by the expansion Mariners, and had a short and unimpressive ML stay. His father and brother both played minor league ball. /(MC)

Ron Jones — 1964- . OF 1988- **Phillies** 45 g, .290, 10 hr, 30 rbi

Jones showed power beyond any of his minor league numbers when the Phillies called him up in 1988; he hit eight homers in 124 at-bats. However, he spent most of 1989 on the DL. /(JFC)

Ruppert Jones — 1955- . OF 1976-87 Royals, **Mariners**, Yankees, Padres, Tigers, Angels 1331 g, .250, 147 hr, 579 rbi

Seattle made Jones the first player selected in the 1976 expansion draft, which created the Mariners and Blue Jays. A lefthanded hitter with good speed early in his career, Jones hit 24 home runs in Seattle's inaugural season and 21 in 1979, then was traded away to become an extra outfielder and spare bat for several other teams. With the Angels in 1985, he slugged 21 home runs in only 389 at-bats. Jones holds the Mariner record for most runs scored in a season (109 in 1979) and is tied for club records for runs and walks in a single game. Against Detroit on May 16, 1978, Jones tied a major league record for most putouts by an outfielder in an extra-inning game. Jones was a favorite with Seattle fans, and after being traded he was still greeted with cries of "Rupe! Rupe!" when he visited the Kingdome. /(TF)

Sad Sam Jones (Horsewhips Sam) — 1892-1966. RHP 1914-35 Indians, Red Sox, **Yankees**, Browns, Senators, White Sox 3883 ip, 229-217, 3.84. *4 WS, 22 ip, 0-2, 2.05*

Sad Sam's 22 consecutive seasons pitching in one league (the American) is a ML record shared with Herb Pennock, Early Wynn, Red Ruffing, and Steve Carlton. The native Ohioan was sent from Cleveland to the Red Sox in a 1916 trade for Tris Speaker, who was in his prime. In 1918, Jones's first season in a starting rotation, he went 16–5 (league-best .762 winning percentage). He won 23 games for the fifth-place 1921 Red Sox, with a league-high five shutouts. But his finest season may have been 1923, when he was 21–8 as the Yankees' ace, hurling a September 4 no-hitter against the Athletics and leading New York to their first World Championship. His relief work in the final game of the Series clinched it for the Yanks.

Bill McGeehan of the New York *Herald-Tribune* dubbed him Sad Sam because, to him, Jones looked downcast on the field. Jones told Lawrence Ritter that the reason he looked downcast was because, "I would always wear my cap down real low over my eyes. And the sportswriters were more used to fellows like Waite Hoyt, who'd always wear their caps way up so they wouldn't miss any pretty girls." Jones' sharp-breaking curve also earned him the name Horsewhips Sam. Like most pitchers of his day, Jones relieved as well as started, and his eight saves in 1922 led the AL. He lost a league-high 21 in 1925 as the Yanks dropped to seventh. Waived from St. Louis to Washington in 1927, Jones rebounded to top the 1928 Senators' staff with a 17–7 record. His 15–7 finish in 1930 marked his last outstanding season. /(EW)

Sam Jones (Toothpick Sam, Sad Sam, Red) — 1925–1971. RHP 1951–52, 55–64 Indians, Cubs, Cardinals, **Giants**, Tigers, Orioles 1643 ip, 102–101, 3.59. 20 wins: 59

☛ *Led League—w 59. Led League—k 55–56, 58. Led League—era 59. All-Star—55, 59.*

Known as Red in the Negro leagues for his reddish complexion, in the majors Jones became Sad Sam, after the original Sad Sam Jones, and Toothpick Sam for the toothpick he always chewed on the mound. Jones pitched the Cleveland Buckeyes to the Negro World Series in 1947. He signed with the Cleveland Indians in 1950 but never got a chance in the rotation of Bob Feller, Bob Lemon, Early Wynn, and Mike Garcia, spending most of five years in the minors. Swapped to the Cubs in a deal for Ralph Kiner, on May 12, 1955 Jones no-hit Pittsburgh, walking seven in the process. He led the NL in losses (20), strikeouts, and walks (185, while allowing only 175 hits). He repeated as strikeout and walk leader in 1956, and again in 1958 after his trade to the Cardinals. With the Giants in 1959, he was both a leading starter and most effective reliever in a tight race. On June 30 of that year, at Los Angeles, a bobble by Giant shortstop Andre Rodgers was scored a single, depriving Jones of a second no-hitter; he got it instead on September 26, though it

was a rain-shortened, seven-inning one against St. Louis. His 21 wins in 1959 led the NL, as did his 2.83 ERA and 109 walks. After an 18–14 1960 season, Jones was hampered by arm trouble, winning 12 more over four seasons.

Recalled Hobie Landrith, who caught Jones with the Cubs, Cards, and Giants, "You've never seen a curveball until you've seen Sam Jones's curveball. If you were a righthanded hitter that ball was a good four feet behind you. It took a little courage to stay in there because he was wild and he could throw a fastball very hard. He wasn't very expressive, he wasn't the gregarious type (but) he injected humor." /(MC)

Sheldon Jones (Available) — 1922– . RHP 1946–53 **Giants**, Braves, Cubs 920 ip, 54–57, 3.96. *1 WS, 4 ip, 0–0, 2.08*

Jones' nickname, Available, came from a character in the Li'l Abner comic strip, but it suited the hard-throwing righthander during his days with the Giants. He both started and relieved on a regular basis from 1948 to 1951. He was most effective in 1948, when he went 16–8, with five saves, but for the four-year period, he started 88 games and relieved in 90 others. /(FS)

Sherman Jones (Roadblock) — 1935– . RHP 1960–62 Giants, **Reds**, Mets 110 ip, 2–6, 4.73. *1 WS, 1 ip, 0–0, 0.00*

Hard-throwing but wild, the 6'4" Jones was one of a record eight pitchers used by the Reds against the Yankees in the fifth and final game of the 1961 World Series. The Mets' starter in their first-ever home game (4/13/62), he was 0–4 that year before recurring arm problems finished him. /(MC)

Slim Jones [Stuart] — 1913–1938. LHP Negro Leagues 1933–38 Baltimore, Philadelphia statistics not available

☛ *All-Star—34–35.*

Jones was the 6'6" 185-lb ace of the Negro National League's Philadelphia Stars. His blistering fastball consistently put him among NNL leaders in strikeouts. His league-high 11 victories helped the Stars capture the 1934 NNL championship. He was the starting pitcher for the East in the all-star games of 1934 and 1935. Duels between Jones and Satchel Paige at Yankee Stadium were a major attraction during the 1930s. Jones's career was ended by arm trouble in 1938. He died later that year. /(ETW)

Tom Jones — 1877–1923. 1B-2B 1902, 04–10 Baltimore (AL), **Browns**, Tigers 1058 g, .251, 3 hr, 336 rbi. *1 WS, 7 g, .250, 2 rbi*

Outstanding fielding and clever baserunning made Jones a regular for seven seasons. His 22 putouts at first base in a nine-inning 1906 Browns game set a longstanding AL record. Jones homered just three times in 3,847 at-bats, one of the ten worst HR percentages in ML history. /(JL)

Tracy Jones — 1961– . OF 1986– **Reds**, Expos, Giants, Tigers 339 g, .280, 18 hr, 116 rbi

Comparisons were quickly drawn between the aggressive, solid-hitting, high-strung Jones and his manager in Cincinnati, Pete Rose. "I like aggressiveness," Rose said in 1987, "but Tracy has to learn to control his . . .He has to learn you don't have to swing at the first pitch every time . . .He never quits moving . . .He gets just enough of a lead so he has to dive back into first and get his uniform dirty. Then his night is complete." Often injured, and unable to find a permanent place in the Reds' talent-laden outfield, the outspoken Jones was traded to Montreal in 1988. /(JCA)

Willie Jones (Puddin' Head) — 1925–1983. 3B 1947–61 **Phillies**, Indians, Reds 1691 g, .258, 190 hr, 812 rbi. *1 WS, 4 g, .286*
☛ *All-Star—50–51.*

Signed off the sandlots of South Carolina, the 6′2″ 205-lb Jones became the Phillies' regular at third base in 1949 and remained there for a decade. As a rookie, he tied a major league record with four straight doubles in a game at Boston (4/20/1949) and, for the only time in his career, led NL third basemen in errors. In five seasons the durable Jones had the league's best fielding percentage, and his seven years leading the NL in putouts at 3B tied a record. A dependable hitter with power, he had a career-high 25 HR as a key member of the 1950 pennant-winning "Whiz Kids." He stands in Philadelphia's all-time top ten in six offensive categories, and his six career Phillie grand slams ties him for second behind Mike Schmidt. Traded to Cleveland in 1959, he ended with Cincinnati in 1961. /(AL)

Bubber Jonnard [Clarence James] — 1897–1977. C 1920, 22, 26–27, 29, 35 White Sox, Pirates, **Phillies**, Cardinals 103 g, .230, 0 hr, 20 rbi

Bubber and his twin brother, Claude, formed a rare brother battery in Nashville in 1920–21, but neither one enjoyed much ML success. After spreading 103 ML games over six seasons and 15 years, Jonnard worked as a scout and coach for the Giants for almost 20 years and later scouted for the Kansas City A's, the Orioles, and the Mets. He landed Ken Singleton and Ed Kranepool for the Mets. /(FVP)

Claude Jonnard — 1897–1959. RHP 1921–24, 26, 29 **Giants**, Browns, Cubs 349 ip, 14–12, 3.79. *2 WS, 2 ip, 0–0, 0.00*

A slender, curveballing reliever, Jonnard led the NL in saves in 1922 and 1923 and tied Giant teammate Rosy Ryan for the league lead in appearances (45) in 1923. With those two in the bullpen, New York won pennants from 1922 through 1924. An .056 lifetime hitter, the Tennessean's twin brother was Clarence "Bubber" Jonnard. /(FS)

Eddie Joost — 1916– . SS-2B-3B 1936–37, 39–43, 45, 47–55 Reds, Braves, **A's**, Red Sox 1574 g, .239, 134 hr, 601 rbi. *1 WS, 7 g, .200, 2 rbi.*
   Manager 1954 **A's** 51–103, .331
☛ *All-Star—49, 52.*

Joost became the Reds' regular shortstop in 1941 and committed 45 errors. After his 45 errors in '42 led the league, he was traded to the Braves. There, Joost suffered further ignominy in 1943, setting a record by hitting just .185, the lowest batting average ever for a player with 400 or more at-bats. He then retired voluntarily but gained a second life with the Athletics beginning in 1947. Though his hitting improved, he found a better way to reach base: walking. From 1947 through 1952, he walked more than 100 times a season, twice gaining more walks than hits. He was an All-Star in 1949 (reaching highs of 23 HR and 81 RBI), and again in '52, after having led AL shortstops in putouts four times to tie the league record. Joost was the A's manager in 1954 but led his untalented crew to a last-place finish. /(EW)

Lou Jorda — 1893–1964. *Umpire* NL 1927–31, 40–52 *2 WS 2 ASU*

Jorda was immortalized in the famous Norman Rockwell painting which appeared on the April 23, 1949 cover of *The Saturday Evening Post*, depicting three umpires and two managers. Beans Reardon is flanked by Larry Goetz and Jorda, who is standing behind Reardon's left shoulder and staring into a rainy sky. Two years later, Jorda was the home plate umpire as Bobby Thomson hit the three-run homer in the playoff to win the 1951 pennant for the Giants. /(RTM)

Buck Jordan [Baxter Byerly] — 1907– . 1B-3B 1927, 29, 31–38 Giants, Senators, **Braves**, Reds, Phillies 811 g, .299, 17 hr, 281 rbi

A reliable contact hitter, Jordan compiled high averages in the minors, but his way to the majors was blocked by first basemen with more powerful bats. Finally a regular with the Braves in the mid-1930s, he twice topped .300, with a career-high .323 in 1936, and twice had eight hits in a doubleheader (8/25/35 and 6/26/38). /(JK)

Jimmy Jordan (Lord) — 1908–1957. 2B-SS-3B 1933–36 Dodgers 376 g, .257, 4 hr, 118 rbi

Jordan won the Central League batting crown in 1928 and was the Sally League MVP in 1930. Originally in the Cardinal chain, he was sold to the Dodgers and became a much-used utility infielder. /(EW)

Pat Jordan — 1941– . *Writer.*

A minor league player for four years, an auto racer, and an English teacher, Jordan is a contributor to *Sports Illustrated* and published the book *A False Spring* in 1975. /(NLM)

Ricky Jordan [Paul Scott] — 1965– . 1B 1988- **Phillies** 213 g, .293, 23 hr, 118 rbi

Philadelphia's first-round pick in the June 1983 draft, Jordan was called up in mid-1988 when Von Hayes went on the DL. He won the first base job (with Hayes moving to the outfield on his return) by hitting .308 with 11 HR in 273 at-bats. In his first full season as the Phillies' regular first baseman, he hit .285 with 12 HR and 75 RBI despite an injury early in the season. /(SH)

Tim Jordan — 1879–1949. 1B 1901, 03, 06–10 Senators, Yankees, **Dodgers** 540 g, .261, 32 hr, 232 rbi
☛ *Led League—hr 06, 08.*

The popular Jordan was one of the few players to live up to the Brooklyn team's nickname, Superbas. A feared lefthanded slugger, he led the NL with 12 HR in 1906 and 1908, but ailing knees forced his premature retirement. /(JL)

Arndt Jorgens — 1905–1980. C 1929–39 **Yankees** 306 g, .238, 4 hr, 89 rbi

The Norwegian-born Jorgens filled in especially well when Bill Dickey was supended in 1932. His brother Orville pitched for the Phillies. /(EW)

Orville Jorgens — 1908– . RHP 1935–37 **Phillies** 496 ip, 21–27, 4.70

Unlike older brother Arndt, Orville was born in the U.S. Obtained by the Phillies after winning 14 for Galveston (Texas League) in 1934, he led the NL with 53 appearances as a rookie in '35, going 10–15 for a seventh-place team. /(AL)

Mike Jorgensen — 1948– . 1B-OF 1968, 70–85 Mets, **Expos**, A's, Rangers, Braves, Cardinals 1633 g, .243, 95 hr, 426 rbi. *1 LCS, 2 g, .000. 1 WS, 2 g, .000* ☛ *Gold Glove—73.*

Jorgensen was always an asset due to fine defensive skills (he won a Gold Glove at first base in 1973), a team-first attitude, and an ability to draw walks, despite being a modest batsman. Originally a Met, he was traded to Montreal in 1972 with Tim Foli and Ken Singleton for Rusty Staub. He had career highs of 18 HR and 144 games as the Expos' first baseman in 1975. Mostly a lefthanded pinch hitter and defensive replacement in later years, after appearing in the 1985 WS with the Cardinals he became a manager in their farm system. /(FJO)

Spider Jorgensen [John Donald] — 1919– . 3B-OF 1947–51 **Dodgers**, Giants 267 g, .266, 9 hr, 107 rbi. *2 WS, 11 g, .194, 3 rbi*

As a rookie in 1947, the wiry Jorgensen was the Dodgers' clutch third baseman. He bruised his throwing arm by hunting that winter, injured it further in spring training, and his career collapsed. /(EW)

Rick Joseph [Ricardo Emelino] — 1940–1979. 3B-1B-OF 1964, 67–70 A's, **Phillies** 270 g, .243, 13 hr, 65 rbi

A strong, 6'1" 190-lb Dominican, Joseph was mostly a Phillies fill-in. When the team, beset by injuries, won nine in a row in mid-1969, Joseph batted .368 with 12 RBI. That year, he hit safely in 16 straight games. Joseph died at age 39 of a kidney ailment. /(AL)

Duane Josephson (Josie) — 1942– . C-1B 1965–72 **White Sox**, Red Sox 470 g, .258, 23 hr, 164 rbi
☛ *All-Star—68.*

A Southern League All-Star and Pacific Coast League MVP, Josephson had the reputation of being injury-prone, though his bruises resulted from his hard-nosed play. The White Sox' regular catcher in 1968, a heart problem forced his retirement. /(EW)

Addie Joss [Adrian] — 1880–1911. RHP 1902–1910
Indians 2336 ip, 160–97, 1.88. 20 wins: 05–08
☛ *Led League—w 07. Led League—era 04, 08. Hall of Fame—1978.*

Contemporaries of 6′3″ Addie Joss admired him as much as almost anyone who ever put on a major league uniform. His untimely death from an attack of tubercular meningitis in April 1911 shocked the baseball world; Cleveland's opener in Detroit was

Addie Joss

postponed due to funeral services in Toledo. So well thought of was Joss that the top AL players of the day formed an all-star team to play the Indians for the benefit of his widow.

After winning 25 games in his second pro season at Toledo (Western Association), Joss pitched a one-hitter in his 1902 debut. He led the AL with five shutouts that season, and he won at least 20 games each year from 1905 through 1908. His career-high 27 victories in 1907 tied him for the AL lead with Chicago's Doc White. Joss used a good fastball and an exceptional curve to five times record ERAs of 1.83 or less. His 1908 league-leading ERA of 1.16 is the eighth-lowest ever. On October 2, 1908 Joss and Chicago's 40-game winner, Big Ed Walsh, squared off in one of the game's most memorable pitching duels. Cleveland, Chicago, and Detroit (who ultimately prevailed) were locked in a pennant race, adding to the tension of the contest. Walsh tossed a four-hitter, striking out 15 and allowing only one run. Joss, however, was even better, setting down 27 straight for a perfect game. Two years later, he no-hit the White Sox again.

Perhaps most remarkable of Joss's feats was his completion of 234 of his 260 starts. In his final season he was plagued by arm injuries, making just 13 appearances. His lifetime 1.88 ERA ranks second all-time to Ed Walsh's 1.82. Joss pitched only nine years; it was his ERA that convinced the Veterans Committee to bend the 10-year career minimum rule and let him into the Hall of Fame. /(EW)

Bill Joyce (Scrappy Bill) — 1865–1941. 3B-1B
1890–92, 94–98 Brooklyn (PL), Boston (AA), Dodgers, Washington (NL), **Giants** 905 g, .294, 71 hr, 607 rbi.
Manager 1896–98 **Giants** 177–122, .592
☛ *Led League—hr 96 .*

Scrappy Bill Joyce bounced from team to team in the 1890s, intimidating opponents with his ready fists and pitchers with his potent blue-tipped bat. After three undistinguished seasons in three different leagues, Joyce sat out 1893 in a contract dispute but returned with Washington in 1894 to hit a career-high .355, the first of four consecutive .300 seasons. Joyce's 17 home runs in both '94 and '95 were one shy of the league lead, but he won the HR crown in 1896, edging Ed Delahanty 14–13. He hit three homers in one game August 20, 1894, hit for the cycle May 30, 1896, and set a ML record with four triples in a game May 18, 1897. He was also partly responsible for the term "Texas Leaguer"—a shallow pop fly that falls for a hit—when he and fellow

Texas League alumnus Arthur Sunday debuted in Toledo with back-to-back bloopers. /(JK)

Wally Joyner (Wally World) — 1962– . 1B 1986-
Angels 620 g, .288, 85 hr, 381 rbi. *1 LCS, 3 g, .455, 1 hr, 2 rbi*

A baby-faced lefthanded hitter, Joyner replaced Rod Carew as the Angels' first baseman in 1986. He became the first rookie to start an All-Star Game since fan balloting returned in 1970 and finished a close second to Jose Canseco in AL Rookie of the Year balloting. After a brilliant first half, he struggled during the second half and missed four games of the LCS with a staph infection. In 1987 Joyner was California's MVP, set a club record for HR by a first baseman (34), and became the ninth player in ML history with back-to-back 100-RBI seasons as a rookie and sophomore. His power declined in 1988 (13 HR), as the ball was deadened, but he still managed 85 RBI. After a slow start in 1989 he finished with 16 HR and 79 RBI while batting .282. /(ME)

Oscar Judd (Lefty, Ossie) — 1908– . LHP 1941-48 Red Sox, **Phillies** 771 ip, 40–51, 3.90
☞ *All-Star—43.*

The Canadian-born Judd was a hard worker and a good hitter (.262 lifetime) and pinch hitter. Towards the end of his career he was afflicted with a sore arm. He was 11–6 (2.90) at his best for the 1943 Red Sox. /(EW)

Joe Judge — 1894–1963. 1B 1915-34 **Senators**, Dodgers, Red Sox 2170 g, .298, 71 hr, 1034 rbi. *2 WS, 14 g, .286, 1 hr, 4 rbi*

Agile and diminutive, Judge set fielding standards for first basemen with graceful sure-handedness. He played from the dead-ball era to the rabbit-ball era of the 1920s and 1930s and led or tied AL first basemen in fielding six times, still an AL record. He compiled a brilliant lifetime fielding average of .993, an AL record that stood for more than 30 years. At his retirement, he also held AL career first base marks for games, putouts, double plays, and total chances, and his 131 double plays in 1922 set a since-broken AL season record.

A lefthanded thrower and hitter, his batting average topped .300 in nine full seasons. Judge was a perennial Washington favorite who, in 1924, with Bucky Harris at second base, Ossie Bluege at third base, and MVP Roger Peckinpaugh at shortstop, formed a defensive unit which is thought by many to be the best ever assembled. Judge was the baseball

coach at Georgetown from 1937 to 1958, except for 1945–46, when he helped coach the Senators. /(JK)

Walt Judnich — 1917–1971. OF-1B 1940-42, 46–49 **Browns**, Indians, Pirates 790 g, .281, 90 hr, 420 rbi. *1 WS, 4 g, .077, 1 rbi*

While advancing through the Yankee farm system, the 6'1", nervously charged outfielder reminded scouts of Joe DiMaggio. Judnich's problem was the Yankees already had DiMaggio in centerfield; that was solved by Judnich's sale to the Browns. While never "another DiMaggio," he led AL outfielders in fielding three times and had an arm like DiMaggio's. A lefthanded power hitter who debuted in 1940 with 24 HR, he lost three prime years to military service. /(JK)

Howie Judson — 1926– . RHP 1948-54 **White Sox**, Reds 615 ip, 17–37, 4.29

A courageous man, Judson pitched his final seasons knowing he might be going blind from a retina infection. Though he never had a winning season, he was a highly respected hurler. /(EW)

Billy Jurges — 1908– . SS-3B 1931-47 **Cubs**, Giants 1816 g, .258, 43 hr, 656 rbi. *3 WS, 13 g, .156, 2 rbi.* *Manager 1959–60* **Red Sox** *78–83, .484*
☞ *All-Star—37, 39–40.*

After attending Richmond Hill High School in Brooklyn, where Phil Rizzuto went a decade later, the fiery Jurges came up to the Chicago Cubs in 1931. His fine defensive skills prompted the Cubs to move Woody English from shortstop to third base, despite Jurges's .201 batting average. Jurges and second baseman Billy Herman, a fellow rookie and former Louisville teammate, became the league's premier double-play combination and teamed in three World Series during the 1930s. Jurges went on to patrol National League infields for 17 seasons, four times leading the league's shortstops in fielding percentage. An adequate hitter, Jurges once rapped nine consecutive hits, one shy of the NL record.

Jurges's solid, steady career started off with a bang. On July 6, 1932 Violet Valli (dubbed Violet Popovitch Heindel Valli by Cubs player/manager Charlie Grimm) called Jurges on the telephone, then entered his hotel room with a gun to attempt suicide. Jurges intervened and took a bullet in the hand and another through the ribs. This episode may have served as the prototype for *The Natural*, rather than the shooting of Eddie Waitkus by a crazed female fan in 1949. Although Jurges wound up missing only three weeks of action, the contending Cubs signed ex-Yankee shortstop Mark Koenig, who hit .353 for them. Because the Cubs voted Koenig a one half Series share, they were ridden by the Yankees that year's World Series, highlighted by Ruth's "called" home run.

Although Jurges was an unexceptional Red Sox manager for parts of two seasons, 1959–60, his tenure is worth noting. Under Jurges, infielder Pumpsie Green ended the Red Sox' status as the only team in the majors without a black player. /(JC/CR)

Al Jurisich — 1921–1981. RHP 1944–47 **Cardinals**, Phillies 388 ip, 15–22, 4.24. *1 WS, 0.2 ip, 0–0, 27.00*

Effective as a rookie spot-starter and long reliever for the 1944 champion Cardinals, the Louisianan lost his job to returning veterans after WWII ended. Injuries curtailed Jurisich's time with the Phillies. /(MC)

Skip Jutze [Alfred Henry] — 1946– . C 1972–77 Cardinals, **Astros**, Mariners 254 g, .215, 3 hr, 51 rbi

Good defense kept this poor-hitting backup catcher in the majors. In his most active season, he caught 86 games for the 1973 Astros, batting .223. He hit his three career homers with the Mariners in 1977, his final year. /(JCA)

Jim Kaat (Kitty) — 1938– . LHP 1959–83 **Senators/ Twins**, White Sox, Phillies, Yankees, Cardinals 4528 ip, 283–237, 3.45. 20 wins: 66, 74–75 *2 LCS, 8 ip, 0–1, 4.50. 2 WS, 17 ip, 1–2, 3.78*
☛ *Led League—w 66. All-Star—62, 66, 75. Gold Glove—62–77.*

The square-shouldered, 6′4″ Kaat is one of a hand-ful of major leaguers to play in four decades. His 25 years of pitching was a major league record. The last active original Washington Senator, Kaat moved like a cat around the mound, winning 16 consecu-tive Gold Gloves. He won 18 games for the AL champion Twins in 1965, then had his best season in 1966, going 25–13 and leading the league with 41 starts, 19 complete games, and 304 innings. That year only one Cy Young trophy was awarded for both leagues, to the Dodgers' Sandy Koufax, but *TSN* selected Kaat as AL Pitcher of the Year.

Following five more seasons with victories in double figures, Kaat was 10–2 in 1972 when he sprained his left wrist and missed the remainder of the season. He was 11–12 in August 1973 (including a one-hitter at California on July 1) when, thinking Kaat's best days were behind him, the Twins sold him to the White Sox. In Chicago, Kaat was reunited with his former Minnesota pitching coach and mentor, Johnny Sain. In his two full seasons in the Chicago stable, Kaat won 41 games, often using a quick-pitch delivery.

Despite his 20–14 record with over 300 innings pitched in 1975, Kaat, age thirty-seven, was sent to the Phillies in a trade for Alan Bannister, Dick Ruthven, and Roy Thomas, the oldest of whom was twenty-four. In his first tour of duty in the NL, Kaat was 26–30 in three seasons. In May 1979, he was sold to the Yankees and, for the first time, relieved in more games than he started. He spent most of his final four ML years working out of the bullpen, and pitched in relief in four games of the 1982 World Series for St. Louis against Milwaukee.

A good all-around athlete, Kaat also hit 16 homers in his career, with a .185 lifetime batting average. He stands as the Twins' all-time winningest pitcher, with 189 victories. After retiring as a player,

he was the Reds' pitching coach in 1986. He has also worked as a TV announcer for the Yankees. /(RM)

Clifford Kachline — 1922– . *Writer.*

An associate editor of *The Sporting News*, Kachline edited the *Spink Baseball Guide* and *Dope Book* for 20 years until 1967. He was the historian at the Hall of Fame from 1969 to 1982, when he became the first full-time executive director of SABR. He retired in 1985. /(NLM)

Harold Kaese — 1909–1975. *Writer.*

Kaese began as sport editor for the Boston *Tran-script* after graduating from Tufts University. He was a sportswriter and columnist for the Boston *Globe* for 32 years until his 1973 retirement. In 1976 he was given the J.G. Taylor Spink Award (admittance to the Writers Wing of the Hall of Fame). /(NLM)

Oscar Kahan — 1910–1981. *Writer.*

A 1930 graduate of the University of Missouri, Kahan broke in with the St. Louis *Star-Times*, then went to the Associated Press, where he gained a reputation for accurate and authoritative writing. He became assistant managing editor of *The Sporting News* and remained for 32 years, specializing in developing news of the minor leagues. /(NLM)

George Kahler (Krum) — 1889–1924. RHP 1910–14 **Indians** 627 ip, 32–41, 3.17

The hard-throwing Kahler led the AL in walks (121) and went 12–19 in 1912, his only season as a regular ML starter. /(ME)

Roger Kahn — 1927– . *Writer.*

A premier baseball essayist, the Brooklyn-born Kahn at twenty-five began covering the Dodgers for the New York *Herald Tribune*. He later wrote for *Sports Illustrated* and *Newsweek*. His 1972 best-seller, *The Boys of Summer*, an account of the great Brooklyn teams of the 1950s, is a recognized classic. It was followed by *Season in the Sun* (1977) and *The Seventh Game* (1982). Kahn bought the Utica club in the New York-Penn League and in 1985 wrote

Jim Kaat

Good Enough to Dream based on that experience. Kahn and Pete Rose wrote *Pete Rose: My Story* in 1989. /(NLM)

Mike Kahoe — 1873–1949. C, 1895, 99–1905, 07–09 Reds, Cubs, **Browns**, Phillies, Senators 410 g, .212, 4 hr, 105 rbi

One of the first catchers to wear shin guards, Kahoe joined the Browns in their inaugural season (1902) and won the starting job from Joe Sugden the following year. He promptly gave it back by hitting .189. /(WAB)

Don Kaiser (Tiger) — 1935– . RHP 1955–57 **Cubs** 240 ip, 6–15, 4.15

Kaiser was one of many young players hurt by the rule of the 1950s that forced bonus signees to rust on the ML roster instead of playing in the minors. He won 49 of 50 high school games, including seven no-hitters and two perfect games. In his first start with the Cubs he pitched a two-hitter, but his lack of seasoning made him generally ineffective. /(BC)

Ken Kaiser — 1945– . *Umpire* AL 1977–87 *2 LCS 1 WS*

Voted the Most Colorful Umpire in the AL in a 1986 *TSN* poll, Kaiser is a former bar bouncer and pro wrestler. In the ring he wore a black hood, carried an ax, and was billed as "The Hatchet Man." In 1981, when Billy Martin was suspended but still telephoning instructions to the dugout, Kaiser took the phone from a player's hand, said, "You're disconnected, Billy!" and ripped the instrument from the dugout wall. He was a strict enforcer of the balk rule even before the leagues toughened enforcement in 1988. He was behind the plate for Gaylord Perry's 300th win on May 6, 1982. /(RTM)

George Kaiserling — 1893–1918. RHP 1914–15 Indianapolis (FL), **Newark (FL)** 537 ip, 30–23, 2.68

Kaiserling spent his ML career in the Federal League, winning 17 games for league champion Indianapolis in 1914 after pitching in the same city's American Association franchise in 1913. When the league collapsed he was sold to the Tigers, spent two years in the minors, and died in March 1918. /(JK)

Al Kaline (Mr. Tiger) — 1934– . OF 1953–74 **Tigers** 2834 g, .297, 399 hr, 1583 rbi. *1 LCS, 5 g, .263, 1 hr, 1 rbi. 1 WS, 7 g, .379, 2 hr, 8 rbi*
☛ *Led League—ba 55. All-Star—55–67, 71, 74. Hall of Fame—1980.*

Al Kaline is Mr. Tiger, not only because he played in more games as a Tiger than anyone else and hit more home runs than any Tiger, but also because he gave his Detroit teammates and fans his classiest best in baseball skill, leadership, and determination each inning he played.

Kaline was born into a sports-minded family that included a father and two uncles who played semi-pro baseball. Though smaller than most boys his age and somewhat shy, he became a top-notch player by sheer practice and playing time. He enrolled in several organized leagues each season, being transported from field to field by family members. Young Al possessed a great arm, developed solid hitting skills, and had great infielder quickness.

Scout Ed Katalinas signed Kaline ($35,000 bonus) right off the Baltimore sandlots and Al never played one inning in the minor leagues. On June 25, 1953, his first game, he played right field for the first time in his life. He was used sparingly by Manager Fred Hutchinson, usually as a pinch runner. His first homer came off Dave Hoskins (Cleveland) and he

As a perennial All-Star, Kaline homered off Lew Burdette (1959) and Bob Buhl (1960) while hitting .324 in All-Star 16 games. In 1962 Kaline was having a fantastic year (.336, 13 HR, 38 RBI) when on May 26 he fractured his right collarbone diving for the last-out catch in a 2–1 Hank Aguirre win at New York. Two months later he reentered the race with a game-winning, two-run single in a 4–3 Aguirre win. In a mere 100 games that year he hit 29 HRs with 94 RBI. Proportionately, had he played the entire season, he would have eclipsed 30 homers and possibly 40 for the only time in his career. That injury certainly cost him the opportunity to later become the first American Leaguer to collect 400 homers and 3,000 hits in a career. Various injuries removed Kaline from some 200 games during his 15 "prime" years. In 1963 Kaline again finished second to a Yankee catcher, Elson Howard, in the MVP balloting.

After missing a third of the 1968 season, Kaline was fit into manager Mayo Smith's World Series lineup by playing centerfielder Mickey Stanley at shortstop. In the seventh inning of Game Five, the bases were full and the Tigers were down 3–2 in score and 3–1 in games. Kaline singled home two runs to win the game and ignite Detroit's comeback for the World Championship.

Kaline made playing right field into an art form. He won 10 Gold Gloves in 11 years (1957–59, 61–67). All comparisons to his glove work eventually fell short because he was so graceful and quick. Never a wasted motion, never a wrong decision. Kaline has said, "When I first came up to the Tigers I was scared stiff, but I had desire. Desire is something you must have to make it in the majors. I was never satisfied with just average." Though he was not spectacular, he was as close to perfect as a player could be. All of his baseball skills were impeccably honed: hitting for power and average, speed, throwing, and fielding judgment.

Always a Detroit hero, Al Kaline joined the Tiger broadcasting crew after his retirement from the field. /(RT)

Rudy Kallio — 1892–1979. RHP 1918–19, 25 **Tigers,** Red Sox 222 ip, 9–18, 4.17

Kallio failed both his ML trials, but the native Oregonian found a home in the Pacific Coast League, winning 211 games in 20 seasons. /(JK)

Al Kaline

singled off Satchel Paige before that first season ended.

In his rookie year of 1954 Kaline hit a modest .276 with four HR and was part of an outfield corps that included Don Lund, Bob Nieman, Bill Tuttle and highly touted Jim Delsing. By 1959 all of these phenom outfielders were gone in favor of Charlie Maxwell, Harvey Kuenn, and Kaline. Kaline's second career homer in 1954 was a grand slam, making him the second youngest ever to have hit one. (Eddie Onslow of the 1912 Tigers was the youngest until Boston's Tony Conigliaro moved him back in 1964.) Red Sox legend Ted Williams told Kaline to build his wrist strength up over the winter by squeezing baseballs as hard as he could. Though the slender rookie's glove was never in doubt, his power was. Those doubts were laid to rest early in 1955 as Kaline hit in 23 of his first 24 games, including seven home runs—three at Kansas City in one game (his only three-homer game), two in one inning. Ending at .340, 27 HR, 102 RBI, and 121 runs, he was the youngest AL batting champ, shading the immortal Ty Cobb for the honor. It was the only time he would amass 200 hits in a season. He finished second in MVP voting, just 17 points behind Yogi Berra.

Willie Kamm — 1900–1988. 3B 1923–35 **White Sox,** Indians 1692 g, .281, 29 hr, 826 rbi

After two years of stopgap at third base, for the 1923 season, the White Sox found Willie Kamm to replace the banished Buck Weaver. He cost them $100,000, then the highest price ever paid for a rookie. Kamm never had Weaver's flair, but he was a more polished third baseman. He had exceptional hands and good instincts, and got his throws away quickly. He led his league in fielding eight times in a 13-year career. He was also adept at the hidden-ball play, claiming success once or twice a season. Kamm attributed his high number of fielding chances to canny White Sox pitchers Ted Lyons and Red Faber; Lyons's low curves and Faber's spitballs induced hitters to top the ball, often to third. Kamm was not as successful as a hitter, although he had a reputation for coming through in the clutch. In 1931 he was sent to Cleveland for first baseman Lew Fonseca. In 1936–37 he managed the San Francisco Missions (Pacific Coast League). Although his highest baseball salary was $13,500, he retired in comfort, having survived the 1929 crash to make a substantial gain in the stock market. /(ADS)

Alex Kampouris — 1912– . 2B 1934–39, 41–43 **Reds,** Giants, Dodgers, Senators 708 g, .243, 45 hr, 284 rbi

The Chicago Hellenic Society, hungering for a countryman to honor in 1937, assembled at Wrigley Field one day to salute the Reds' second baseman. Kampouris was given a car and extolled before the game, then proceeded to commit three errors in one inning. Kampouris hit .316 in 16 games for the Dodgers in 1941, but never hit better than .249 in any other season. /(JK)

Masanichi Kaneda (Golden Arm, Emperor) — 1930– . LHP 1951–70 **Kokutetsu Swallows,** Yomiuri Giants, Lotte Orions 400 wins, 2.24 (inc). 20 wins: 1950–64

Kaneda, a fastballer born of Korean parents, won at least 20 games in Japan each year from 1950 through 1964, twice winning 30. While going 30–17 in 1963, he refused to pitch without three days' rest, causing a national uproar as the first pitcher to violate the ironman "Code of the Samurai." In 1964, he became the first Japanese star to play out his option and switch teams, leaving Kokutetsu for Yomiuri. There, he immediately rejected strict and strenuous team discipline, choosing to train himself, inciting another uproar. /(MC)

Rod Kanehl (Hot Rod) — 1934– . 2B-OF-3B 1962–64 **Mets** 340 g, .241, 6 hr, 47 rbi

The Mets picked up Kanehl, who spent eight years in the Yankee farm system, in the minor league draft. Manager Casey Stengel remembered the hustling utility man who vaulted a fence to catch a fly ball in the Yankees' 1954 instructional camp. The fan favorite hit the Mets' first grand slam on July 6, 1962, in the first Met victory witnessed by owner Joan Payson. /(SH)

Kansas City Athletics — 1955–1967. Team. 829–1222, .404

The Athletics had operated in Philadelphia for 54 years, but attendance and better Phillies teams prompted the shift to Kansas City, which had not seen major league baseball since the Federal League (1914–15). Blues Stadium was expanded and renamed Municipal Stadium to accommodate the Athletics. Their maiden year in Missouri produced a sixth-place finish under manager Lou Boudreau, the highest the Athletics would ever place in Kansas City. In 13 seasons they compiled an unenviable 829–1,222 record under ten managers.

In 1960 insurance and real estate magnate Charlie Finley purchased controlling interest in the club. He took a strong role in the daily operations of the club, often usurping his manager's function. Finley tried numerous promotions, moved the fences in and out, fired managers and broadcasters yearly, and traded players in an attempt to produce a winner and maintain fan interest. After a 13th consecutive losing season in Kansas City, Finley moved the Athletics to Oakland without realizing the great baseball potential the Royals would later discover. /(FO)

Kansas City Royals — 1969– . Team. 1922–1734, .526. *AL West Champions 76–78, 80, 84–85 AL Champions 80, 85 World Champions 85*

In 1968 Ewing Kauffman purchased an AL expansion franchise that took the field the following year as the Kansas City Royals. In 1971, only their third season, the Royals finished second. Never has an expansion team fared so well so quickly. Three factors contributed to the rapid and sustained success. First, their farm system quickly produced a number of stars, including George Brett, Willie Wilson, and Frank White, and pitchers Paul Splittorff, Steve Busby, Dennis Leonard, and Dan Quisenberry. Second, the Royals' front office made

The 1977 Kansas City Royals

several trades that brought pivotal players to Kansas City, such as Hal McRae, Amos Otis, Freddie Patek, John Mayberry, and Cookie Rojas. And finally, the team employed highly competent field bosses like Jack McKeon, Whitey Herzog, Jim Frey, and Dick Howser, who molded youth and veterans into winning combinations. In their first twenty campaigns, the Royals won a World Championship (1985), two AL pennants, six AL Western Division titles, and had seven second-place finishes. They lost three straight bitterly contested LCS to the Yankees from 1976 to 1978 before finally reaching the WS with a sweep of the Yankees in the 1980 playoffs. /(FJO)

Erv Kantlehner — 1892– . LHP 1914–16 **Pirates**, Phillies 399 ip, 13–29, 2.84

Kantlehner struck out 253 batters for Victoria (Northwestern League) in 1913. Despite a 2.26 ERA in 1915, he was 5–12 for Pittsburgh; in 8 of those 12 losses, Pittsburgh was shut out. /(ME)

Ed Karger (Loose) — 1883–1957. LHP 1906–11 Pirates, **Cardinals**, Reds, Red Sox 1088 ip, 48–67, 2.79

Karger's most successful season was with the Red Sox in 1910, when he was 11–7 with a relatively

high 3.19 ERA. Before that he compiled losing records despite better ERAs for second-division Cardinals teams. /(WOR)

Ron Karkovice — 1963– . C 1986– **White Sox** 193 g, .204, 12 hr, 53 rbi

The White Sox' first draft pick in 1982 hit four HR in 97 at-bats in his 1986 call-up. The strong-armed catcher was handed Carlton Fisk's job in 1987 but hit just .071 in 39 games, struck out 40 times in 85 at-bats, and was sent down. Under new batting coach Walt Hriniak, he improved to .264 in 1989, although at the expense of his power. Karkovice has been used as a pinch runner, unusual for a catcher. /(SFS)

Andy Karl [Anton Andrew] — 1914– . RHP 1943–47 Red Sox, **Phillies**, Braves 422 ip, 19–23, 3.51

Though lackluster in Louisville (American Association) in 1942 in his sixth season in the Red Sox farm system, Karl made the ML with the 1943 Red Sox because of the WWII player shortage. His 67 appearances and 15 saves for the 1945 Phillies were NL highs. /(AL)

Benn Karr (Baldy) — 1893–1968. RHP 1920–22, 25–27 **Red Sox**, Indians 780 ip, 35–48, 4.60

Handy Benn Karr both started and relieved; a .245 batter, he also pinch-hit 79 times. With Boston he had AL highs of six relief losses in 1920 and five relief wins in 1921./(JK)

Max Kase — 1898–1974. *Writer*

Kase was sports editor and columnist ("Brief Kase") for the New York *Journal American* from 1938 until the paper folded in 1966. He won the Pulitzer Prize in 1950 for exposing the college basketball scandal. Kase's career began in 1917 with International News Service. He was sports editor of the Havana *Telegram* and Boston *American* before moving to New York, where he also operated two restaurants./(NLM)

Eddie Kasko — 1932– . SS-3B-2B 1957–66 Cardinals, **Reds**, Astros, Red Sox 1077 g, .264, 22 hr, 261 rbi. *1 WS, 5 g, .318, 1 rbi.*
    Manager 1970–73 **Red Sox** 346–295, .540
☛ *All-Star—61 .*

Kasko, a reliable ML infielder for ten years, was named the NL All-Star shortstop in 1961 when the Reds won the pennant. The year before, he set career highs by hitting .292 with 51 RBI. With Houston in 1964, he led NL shortstops in fielding percentage. He was known as a laid-back practical joker who could keep a clubhouse loose. After managing for three years in the International League, he led the Red Sox for four seasons. Although he brought them in third twice and second twice, his soft-spoken, unflappable approach was deemed too placid by the front office./(BC)

Ed Katalinas — Unk.–1988. *Scout.*

Katalinas was a member of the Detroit Tigers organization for over four decades, joining as a part-time scout in 1940 and rising to scouting director in 1956 and scouting coordinator in 1975. He first spotted Al Kaline as a Baltimore grade-school player, and signed him in 1953 just after his high-school graduation. In 1963 Katalinas's recommendation brought Denny McLain from the White Sox on waivers when Chicago failed to protect him, and he also helped sign Ray Oyler and Jim Northrup./(FVP)

John Katoll (Big Jack) — 1872–1955. RHP 1898–1902 Cubs, **White Sox**, Baltimore (AL) 361 ip, 17–22, 3.22

The 6'4" 200-lb Big Jack won 16 games, including six shutouts, for the 1900 White Sox when the AL was still a minor league. On August 21, 1901 he threw a baseball at umpire Jack Haskell, instigating a brawl in which Haskell's lip was split by Chicago shortstop Frank Shugart. Both Katoll and Shugart were arrested and then suspended./(RL)

Ray Katt — 1927– . C 1952–59 **Giants**, Cardinals 417 g, .232, 32 hr, 120 rbi

A sound catcher but a weak hitter, Katt was a regular only once, for the 1955 Giants. He set the NL record with four passed balls in one inning on September 10, 1954; knuckleballer Hoyt Wilhelm was the pitcher./(FS)

Benny Kauff — 1890–1961. OF 1912, 14–20 Yankees, Indianapolis (FL), Brooklyn (FL), **Giants** 859 g, .311, 49 hr, 454 rbi. *1 WS, 6 g, 2 hr, 5 rbi*
☛ *Led League—ba 14–15.*

"The Ty Cobb of the Federal League" led the FL in batting and stolen bases in both its seasons. When it disbanded, Kauff was the plum picked by John McGraw for the Giants. In 1917 the lefthander batted .308 and hit two HR in the World Series. Kauff began running with a suspect crowd, and in 1920 was ruled ineligible for major league play by Commissioner Landis, not for throwing games, but for being implicated in a stolen car ring. Kauff was cleared of criminal charges in court, but his entreaties for readmission to baseball failed./(JK)

Tony Kaufmann — 1900–1982. RHP 1921–31, 35 **Cubs**, Phillies, Cardinals, Giants 1086 ip, 64–62, 4.18

Pitching for the Cubs in the early 1920s, Kaufmann was tutored by Grover Alexander. He was 14–10 in 1923 and 16–11 the next year, his best seasons. A good hitter, his two home runs on the Fourth of July, 1925 made him one of a handful of pitchers to homer twice in one game. From 1938 to 1961 he worked for the Cardinals as a minor league manager, ML coach, and scout./(BC)

Marty Kavanagh — 1891–1960. 2B-1B-OF 1914–18 **Tigers**, Indians, Cardinals 369 g, .249, 10 hr, 122 rbi

The Tigers starting second baseman as a rookie, Kavanagh lost his job to Ralph Young in 1915 but remained a handy backup, playing every position except pitcher and catcher. After leading the AL with 10 pinch hits in 1915 he was given 46 pinch at-bats in 1916, but hit only .152. /(JK)

Tetsuharu Kawakami (The God of Batting) — Unk.–Unk. 1B 1938–39, 46–58 **Yomiuri Giants** .313 (inc)

For many years, Kawakami had the highest lifetime average in Japanese baseball history. He was the first Japanese to hit 20 home runs in a season, and his .377 average in 1950 set a single-season Japanese record. The icy and aloof Kawakami attributed his success to winters spent in Zen meditation at remote mountain temples, and to a distinctive red bat.

Kawakami became the Yomiuri Giants' manager in 1961 and promptly released longtime batting rival Wally Yonamine, a Nisei. He built an all-Japanese team that won 11 pennants and nine consecutive championships (1965–73) in 14 years. When Yomiuri beat the 1968 National League champion St. Louis Cardinals twice in three games on a goodwill tour, Kawakami argued that his club was the best in baseball. Irritated, the Cardinals came back to pummel Yomiuri seven games in a row. After a period of humility, Kawakami proclaimed superiority to the visiting American League champion Baltimore Orioles in the fall of 1971. In 11 confrontations, the Orioles scored eight convincing wins and three ties. /(MC)

Eddie Kazak [born Edward Tkaczuk] — 1920– . 3B 1948–52 **Cardinals**, Reds 218 g, .273, 11 hr, 71 rbi

Kazak hit .304 with occasional power as a Cardinal rookie in 1949, but was injured and lost his third base job to Tommy Glaviano. Relegated to pinch hitting, he led the NL with 42 pinch at-bats in 1950. /(MC)

Ted Kazanski — 1934– . 2B-SS-3B 1953–58 **Phillies** 417 g, .217, 14 hr, 116 rbi

One of the most highly rated schoolboy players of his time, this rangy infielder was given a reported $100,000 bonus to sign with the Phillies and debuted at nineteen. Only in 1956 did he play in over 100 games, batting just .211, and he was through by the age of twenty-four. /(AL)

Steve Kealey — 1947– . RHP 1968–73 Angels, **White Sox** 214 ip, 8–5, 4.28

Kealey was an undistinguished reliever who was most active with the 1971 White Sox, going 2–2 with six saves and a 3.86 ERA. /(SFS)

Johnny Keane — 1911–1967. *Manager* 1961–66 Cardinals, Yankees 398–350, .532. First place: 64 *1 WS, 4–3, .571*

After 31 years in the Cardinals organization, Keane replaced Solly Hemus as manager midway through 1961. He led St. Louis to a World Championship in 1964 but, upset that friend and GM Bing Devine had been fired, resigned to manage the Yankees in 1965 in an arrangement made months prior to beating New York in the Series.

He took over a deteriorating Yankee team that finished below .500 for the first time since 1925. He was fired the next season after a 4–16 start. /(FJO)

Bob Kearney (Sarge) — 1956– . C 1979, 81–87 Giants, A's, **Mariners** 479 g, .233, 27 hr, 133 rbi

Kearney was a take-charge guy and a good enough defensive catcher to entice the Mariners to trade relief ace Bill Caudill for him. He never hit well enough in Seattle to secure the starting catching job. /(TF)

Ray Keating — 1891–1963. RHP 1912–16, 18–19 **Yankees**, Braves 751 ip, 30–51, 3.29

Keating was one of the pitchers allowed to continue throwing the spitball after it was banned in 1919. The amnesty did Keating no good, as he was dropped by the Braves before the 1920 season. He kept throwing his pet pitch in the Pacific Coast League, using it successfully until he retired in 1932. /(JK)

Cactus Keck [Frank Joseph] — 1899–1981. RHP 1922–23 **Reds** 218 ip, 10–12, 3.51

Sidearmer Keck got his nickname by pitching in the West Texas League after WWI, after having served in the army as an underage volunteer. /(JK)

Harry Keck — 1897–Unk. *Writer.*

Keck at fifteen had his first byline, with the Philadelphia *Evening Times* in 1912. Two years later, he moved to Pittsburgh with the *Post*. He became sports editor for the Pittsburgh *Gazette-Times* in 1919, then for the Baltimore *American* from 1923 to 1925 before beginning a stay at the Pittsburgh *Sun-Telegraph* from 1927 to 1960. /(NLM)

Bob Keefe — 1882–1964. RHP 1907, 1911–12 Yankees, **Reds** 361 ip, 16–21, 3.14

The closest Keefe came to a winning season was 12–13 in 1911 for the sixth-place Reds. /(JFC)

Dave Keefe — 1897–1978. RHP 1917, 19–22 **A's**, Indians 354 ip, 9–17, 4.15

Keefe is credited with originating the forkball, which came naturally to him—he lost the middle finger on his pitching hand in a childhood accident. In his one respectable year, with the Athletics in 1920, he was 6–7 (2.97), with half his wins coming in relief. He continued in the minors until 1932, when he went to Philadelphia's Shibe Park to pitch batting practice for the exercise; he stayed for 19 years, 7 as a coach, and he pitched batting practice for the AL at nine All-Star games. In 1950 he became the Athletics' traveling secretary. /(NLM)

Tim Keefe (Sir Timothy) — 1857–1933. RHP 1880–93 Troy (NL), New York (AA), **Giants**, New York (PL), Phillies 5072 ip, 344–225, 2.62. 20 wins: 83–89, 92
☛ *Led League—w 88. Led League—era 80, 85, 88. Hall of Fame—1964.*

Keefe was one of the iron-armed marvels of 19th-century baseball. He flourished in the days of two- or four-man pitching staffs, and threw mostly from 50', although his rookie year was the last at 45' and his final one the first at 60'6″. Scarcely a season went by without an impressive, league-leading performance in one statistical category or another. In 1880, though pitching only 12 games for Troy (NY), he had an ERA of 0.86. In 1883, when the franchise collapsed and was moved to New York as Jim Mutrie's Metropolitans, he pitched 68 complete games in 68 starts for a total of 619 innings, won 41 and struck out 361. On July 4, he won a doubleheader against Columbus (OH), throwing a one-hitter in the morning game, a two-hitter after lunch. Two years later, John B. Day, who owned both the Mets and the Giants, shifted Keefe and manager Mutrie to the National League team. Keefe's colleagues were Buck Ewing, Monte Ward, and Roger Conner, as well as his Troy pitching mate, Mickey Welch.

Shoulder-high overhand pitching was now permitted and coming into vogue. Keefe had his doubts about the effectiveness of full overhand pitching, but was strong for fundamentals, first of all control. He threw a fastball, curve, and a change-up. In 1886 Keefe had 62 complete games and won 42, his career high, although 1888, when the Giants achieved their first pennant, was his finest season. He led the league in seven categories: 51 complete games, 35 victories (for a winning percentage of .745), a 1.74 ERA, 333 strikeouts, eight shutouts, and the fewest average hits per nine innings (6.55).

Tim Keefe

Nineteen of his wins were consecutive, a record that would stand for 24 years. In postseason play he scored four more over the St. Louis Browns of the American Association. Keefe even designed and sold to the Giants their famous "funeral" uniforms of that year, all-black with "New York" in white letters across the shirt front.

His 1889 contract paid him $4,500, more than any other Giant. Yet for all his star status, Keefe fought actively for ballplayers' welfare. He helped his brother-in-law Monte Ward to establish the Players League and served as secretary for the Brotherhood. He protested player salary ceilings and was among those who won court tests of the reserve clause. He was a quiet, gentle man. In 1887 he had a nervous breakdown after skulling a batter with a fastball.

With the collapse of the Brotherhood, he signed with the Phillies for his final three years, enjoying an outfield of Ed Delahanty, Billy Hamilton, and Sam Thompson behind him. Finished as a player after 1893, he umpired in the National League for two years, then left the game for the real-estate business and occasional coaching duties at Harvard, Princeton, and Tufts. /(ADS)

Bob Keegan (Smiley) — 1920– . RHP 1953–58 **White Sox** 645 ip, 40–36, 3.66
☛ *All-Star—54.*

After years as a Yankee farmhand battling injuries and criticism of his unorthodox delivery, Keegan made it to the ML as a 32-year-old rookie with the White Sox in 1953. In 1954 he was 12–3 by mid-season and was named to the All-Star team. A knee injury handicapped his next two seasons, but in 1957 he came back to win ten games, including a no-hitter. Keegan credited a slowed delivery for his renewed success. He was called Smiley because, according to Billy Pierce, "it always looked like he was smiling, even when he wasn't." /(DB)

Willie Keeler (Wee Willie) — 1872–1923. OF 1892–1910 Giants, Dodgers, Baltimore (NL), **Yankees** 2124 g, .345, 34 hr, 810 rbi
☛ *Led League—ba 97–98. Hall of Fame—1939.*

Wee Willie had a catchy nickname, extraordinary statistics, membership on one of the game's great teams, and a formula for success that became baseball's classic axiom. A two-time batting champion as the Baltimore Orioles' right fielder, Keeler advised simply, "Keep your eye on the ball and hit 'em where they ain't."

Keeler arrived from Binghamton (Eastern League) as a hard-hitting lefthanded third baseman in 1892, the last year pitchers threw from 50 feet. But it was not until Ned Hanlon acquired him for Baltimore in 1894 that he blossomed into an excellent outfielder. The 5'4-1/2" 140-lb Keeler was Hanlon's leadoff man through nine glorious years in Baltimore and Brooklyn, five as pennant winners, three in second place. He was a consistent contributor to those successes, batting .378 over the nine-year period and averaging 215 hits and 134 runs. While there was a surge of high-average hitting as pitchers adjusted to the new 60'6" distance to the plate, Keeler hit .355 or better until 1902 and did not drop below .300 until 1907.

In 1897, at age twenty-five, Wee Willie enjoyed his finest season. He batted .432, the third-highest mark in ML history, and led the league with 243 hits in only 128 games. He also hit safely in 44 consecutive games, an NL record since equaled by only Pete Rose.

Although the native Brooklynite jumped to the New York Highlanders in 1903, becoming one of few to play for three New York teams, he is best remembered for his years in Baltimore. His contemporaries recognized him as one of the game's great

Willie Keeler

bat handlers, a precise bunter, and place hitter as well as a master of the "Baltimore chop" off the hardened dirt in front of home plate. He choked his short bat almost halfway up, and with a quick wrist snap would punch the ball over the infielders' heads. He was extremely fast down the line and worked the hit-and-run expertly with teammate John McGraw. Aggressive and opportunistic, Keeler remained cheerful and friendly, without a trace of McGraw's unpleasant anger. A bachelor who prospered in real estate when his playing days ended, he was elected to the Hall of Fame in 1939. /(ADS)

Vic Keen — 1899–1976. RHP 1918, 21–27 A's, **Cubs**, Cardinals 748 ip, 42–44, 4.11. *1 WS, 1 ip, 0–0, 0.00*

When he pitched at the University of Maryland, 15 teams offered Keen contracts. He was never more than a journeyman ML pitcher, with a top season of 15–14 in 1924 for the Cubs, but his ten wins two years later helped the Cardinals win their first pennant. /(BC)

Sid C. Keener — 1888–Unk. *Writer.*

Director of the Hall of Fame from 1952 to 1963, Keener started as a copyboy with the St. Louis *Star* in 1902. He saw his first byline with the St. Louis *Times* in 1907. After a year in Chicago, he returned to the *Times* as assistant sports editor and succeeded Harry Neily as sports editor in 1914. He rejoined the *Star* in 1929 and continued as sports editor when the *Star* and *Times* merged. /(NLM)

Bill Keister (Wagon Tongue) — 1874–1924. SS-2B-OF-3B 1896, 98–1903 **Baltimore (NL)**, Braves, Cardinals, Baltimore (AL), Senators, Phillies 621 g, .312, 18 hr, 400 rbi

Keister holds the record for the lowest season fielding average for a shortstop in 100 or more games with a butterfingered .861 for Baltimore of the AL in 1901. In 114 games he made 97 errors. From 1898 through 1903 he hit .300 or better each season (and each with a different team), but even batting .320 in '03 could not keep him in the majors. /(BC)

Mike Kekich — 1945– . LHP 1965, 68–75, 77 Dodgers, **Yankees**, Indians, Rangers, Mariners 861 ip, 39–51, 4.59

Occasionally brilliant but more often erratic, Kekich was a hard-throwing lefthander who is best remembered for swapping families with Yankees teammate Fritz Peterson. He came up with the Dodgers but couldn't crack their tough staff, and he spent his most active years with the Yankees. He was 10–9, 4.08 for New York in 1971 and 10–13, 3.70 in 1972. His American career was ended by a shoulder injury in 1977, though he later pitched in Mexico and Japan. /(JJM)

Charles Kelchner (Pop) — Unk.–1958. *Scout.*

Kelchner was a professor of languages and athletic director at Albright College, and a scout for the A's, Browns, and Cardinals, working for the last for 40 years. He signed Joe Medwick and Rip Collins. /(FVP)

George Kell — 1922– . 3B 1943–57 A's, **Tigers**, Red Sox, White Sox, Orioles 1795 g, .306, 78 hr, 870 rbi
☛ *Led League—ba 49. All-Star—47–54, 56–57. Hall of Fame—1983.*

Easily the best player to emerge during the WWII player shortage, Kell remained the AL's premier third baseman long after the war had ended, and eventually earned a spot in the Hall of Fame.

George Kell

After two seasons as the Athletics' third baseman, Kell was traded to Detroit for Barney McCosky in May 1946 and became a perennial All-Star. He finished the 1946 season at .322, his first of eight consecutive .300 seasons. He missed 57 games in 1948 due to injuries. He first suffered a broken wrist when hit by a Vic Raschi pitch, and then several weeks later a Joe DiMaggio line drive fractured his jaw.

In 1949, Kell won his only batting title, and in the process denied Ted Williams his third triple crown. Williams had led the batting race until the final week of the season, but Kell came back from an injury to have a hot streak. When Williams went hitless in the season finale, Kell snatched the title, .3429 to .3428. Kell hit .340 the following year, leading the AL with 218 hits and 56 doubles, but lost the batting title to

Boston's Billy Goodman. After leading the league in hits and doubles once again in 1951, Kell was sent to Boston in June 1952 as part of a nine-man deal that included Dizzy Trout, Hoot Evers, Walt Dropo, and Johnny Pesky. His brother, Skeeter, played for the Athletics that season.

George Kell was as gifted in the field as he was at the plate, leading AL third baseman seven times in fielding and four times each in assists and total chances/game. After concluding his career as Baltimore's third baseman, he was succeeded there by Brooks Robinson. Kell became a Tigers play-by-play man and was inducted into the Hall of Fame by the Veterans Committee in 1983. /(JK)

Hal Kelleher — 1913- . RHP 1935-38 **Phillies** 135 ip, 4-9, 5.95

Kelleher shut out the Reds 1-0 in his September 17, 1935 debut for his hometown Phillies. He only won three more games after that. /(JK)

Mick Kelleher — 1947- . SS-3B-2B 1972-82 Cardinals, Astros, **Cubs**, Tigers, Angels 622 g, .213, 0 hr, 65 rbi

Kelleher was a good-fielding shortstop who saw the most action when acquired by the Cubs for 1976, stepping into Don Kessinger's shoes. He hit .228 in 124 games and thereafter was a utility infielder. /(SFS)

Charlie Keller (King Kong) — 1916- . OF 1939-43, 45-52 **Yankees**, Tigers 1170 g, .286, 189 hr, 760 rbi. *4 WS, 19 g, .306, 5 hr, 18 rbi* ☛ *All-Star—40-41, 43, 46-47.*

Keller's black, bushy brows and muscular body inspired his alliterative nickname. The talent-laden Yankees kept the lefthanded slugger in Newark (International League) the season after he was the league batting champion and *TSN* Minor League Player of the Year for 1937. A place was made for him in 1939, and he hit .334 with the first of six Yankee pennant winners for which he would play. He was a five-time All-Star and reached highs of 33 HR and 122 RBI in 1941. He led the AL in walks with 106 in both 1940 and 1943. Keller's career was interrupted for maritime service in WWII. He had chronic back problems which eventually relegated him to pinch hitting, and he led the league in that department (9-for-38) in 1951, his final full season. Keller coached for the Yankees before retiring to rural Maryland to run a horse farm. His brother Hal caught briefly for the Senators and spent over 20 years as a front-office man for the Senators, Rangers,

and Mariners. His son, Charlie Jr., led the Eastern League in hitting with a .349 average before being sidelined by the same congenital back problem that had plagued his father. /(JK)

Dick Kelley — 1940- . LHP 1964-69, 71 **Braves**, Padres 520 ip, 18-30, 3.39

Kelley's only winning record came with the 1966 Braves when he went 7-5 with a 3.22 ERA, mostly as a starter. /(SFS)

Harry Kelley — 1906-1958. RHP 1925-26, 36-39 Senators, **A's** 676 ip, 42-47, 4.86

Breaking in with the Senators at nineteen, Kelley spent a decade in the minors before the A's brought him back in 1936. His 21 losses in 1937 led the AL. He won 265 games in the minors. /(JK)

Joe Kelley — 1871-1943. OF-1B 1891-1908 Braves, Pirates, **Baltimore (NL)**, Dodgers, Reds 1845 g, .317, 65 hr, 1194 rbi. *Manager* 1902-05, 08 **Reds**, Braves 337-321, .512 ☛ *Hall of Fame—71.*

A turn-of-the-century star, Kelley was an outfielder for the Baltimore Orioles dynasty in the 1890s, and a player-manager in the first decade of the 20th century. A 19-year-old rookie for Boston and Pittsburgh in 1891, Kelley bounced to Baltimore by the end of 1892 and was starting in center field in 1893. Switched to left in 1894, Kelley had his best season as the Orioles won the first of four consecutive league championships. He hit .393 with 167 runs scored, the second-best run total in NL history, but also only the second-best that season, as Philadelphia's Billy Hamilton scored an amazing 196 times. Kelley went a perfect 9-for-9 in a September 3 doubleheader that year, including a ML-record-tying four doubles in one game. From 1895 to 1897, his average never dipped below .364.

After the 1898 season, Kelley moved to the Brooklyn Dodgers along with manager Ned Hanlon and Orioles stars Dan McGann, Hughie Jennings, Willie Keeler, Jim Hughes, and Doc McJames. The Dodgers won pennants in 1899 and 1900. Kelley moved to first base in 1901 and returned to the Orioles, now in the fledgling AL, in 1902. With the club headed for a last-place finish, he left in mid-season to become Cincinnati's player-manager. By 1906, Kelley's average had crashed to .228 and the Reds let him go, but he resurfaced for a final season, managing the Braves to a sixth-place finish in 1908 while batting .259. The Veterans Committee elected him to the Hall of Fame in 1971. /(AJA)

Joe Kelley

Tom Kelley — 1944– . RHP 1964–67, 71–73 Indians, **Braves** 408 ip, 20–22, 3.75

Kelley was given a chance with Cleveland after going 16–3 for Portland (Pacific Coast League) in 1965, including a no-hitter against Spokane on May 29. Back in the minors by 1967, he had shoulder surgery but returned with the Braves in 1971 to post a 9–5 (2.96) mark./(PB)

Alex Kellner — 1924– . LHP 1948–59 **A's**, Reds, Cardinals 1849 ip, 101–112, 4.41. 20 wins: 49
☛ *All-Star—49.*

Noted for his roundhouse, off-speed curve, Kellner was 20–12 as a rookie in 1949 despite walking 129 batters while fanning only 94. He led the AL with 20 losses the next year and tied for the 1951 loss lead (14) as the A's plummeted into the second division. He never again won more than 12. Like longtime teammate and pal Bobby Shantz, Kellner worked

hard at hitting and fielding to help his cause, batting .215 lifetime. He remained with the A's (joined briefly in 1952–53 by brother Walt, a pitcher) until waived to the Reds in mid-1958. His 7–3 record, 2.30 ERA, and .282 average the rest of the way helped his former A's manager Jimmy Dykes keep the Reds in distant contention. Kellner was swapped to the Cardinals after the season, and recurring shoulder trouble ended his career./(MC)

Win Kellum [Winford Ansley] — 1876–1951. LHP 1901, 04–05 Red Sox, **Reds**, Cardinals 347 ip, 20–16, 3.19

Kellum went 15–10, 2.60 for the third-place 1904 Reds and was then sold to the Cardinals./(WOR)

Bob Kelly — 1927– . RHP 1951–53, 58 **Cubs**, Reds, Indians 362 ip, 12–18, 4.50

Kelly posted his only winning record (7–4) as a rookie and occasional starter with the last-place Cubs in 1951./(FK)

George Kelly (Highpockets) — 1895–1984. 1B-2B 1915–17, 19–30, 32 **Giants**, Pirates, Reds, Cubs, Dodgers 1622 g, .297, 148 hr, 1020 rbi. *4 WS, 26 g, .248, 1 hr, 10 rbi*
☛ *Led League—hr 21. Led League—rbi 20, 24. Hall of Fame—1973.*

Kelly flourished in an era of weak first basemen in the National League. Though his credentials for entry into the Hall of Fame may be marginal, he had respectable talents afield and at bat, and he joined Frank Frisch, Dave Bancroft, and Heinie Groh in what many consider the best Giant infield of all time.

A nephew of outfielder Bill Lange, one of Cap Anson's Colts (later the Cubs) of the 1890s, and a brother of Ren Kelly, who pitched one game with the 1923 A's, George was shuffled about for five years before becoming the Giants' regular first baseman in 1920. Tall for his time (6'4"), he was nicknamed Highpockets and Long George by the press; to his teammates he was Kell, a reserved and even-tempered fellow.

Kelly excelled in the field, setting single-season marks for putouts, assists, double plays, and total chances, in part because shortstop Bancroft was also setting marks for assists. A righthander, he had a powerful and accurate arm. In 1921 against the Yankees, he made a brilliant first-to-third throw to nip Aaron Ward for a game-ending, Series-winning double play. He was John McGraw's preferred cutoff man, dashing into the outfield on long hits to handle the relay. Despite his size, he played a creditable second base for most of 1925, when

George Kelly as a coach

McGraw wanted Kelly's bat in the lineup while trying young Bill Terry at first base. He even won his only game as a pitcher, beating the Phillies and Joe Oeschger in five innings of relief.

He batted over .300 for six consecutive seasons (1921–26) and was intermittently impressive as a long-ball hitter. Twice he hit three home runs in one game, the splurge in 1924 accounting for all eight Giant runs, the National League record for most RBIs in a game while batting in all the club's runs. The same year, he set another NL record by hitting seven homers in six games, with at least one in each. He also knocked in 100 or more runs four years in a row, capped by a league- and career-high 136 in 1924. Even so, his lifetime slugging average was an unspectacular .452. This evidently did not worry his manager. Over the years, McGraw said, the placid, reliable Kelly made more important hits than any player he ever had.

Displaced by Terry in 1927, Kelly was traded to the Reds for Edd Roush. Released in 1930, he returned briefly to the majors with the Cubs and Dodgers when Charlie Grimm and Del Bissonette were injured. When his playing days were over, he coached the Reds and Braves for 11 years and scouted for several teams. /(ADS)

Joe Kelly — 1886–1977. OF 1914, 16–19 Pirates, Cubs, **Braves** 376 g, .224, 6 hr, 117 rbi

Kelly was the everyday centerfielder for the 1914 Pirates, hitting .222 with career highs of 48 RBI, 47 runs, 21 steals, and 19 doubles, but he was a poor fielder. In his next-most-active season, 1917, he led NL outfielders in errors while again hitting .222. /(SFS)

John Kelly (Honest John, Diamond John, Kick) — 1856–1926. C 1879 **Syracuse NL**, Troy NL 16 g, .155, 0 hr, 2 rbi.
　　Manager 1887 **Louisville** 76–60, .559.
　　Umpire **AA**, NL, PL 1882–88, 90, 97

Kelly, a robust 6-footer, became an umpire because of his weak hitting and proneness to injuries. He worked in both the NL and American Association in 1884 and was requested by the owners of the AA Browns and Union Association Maroons when they agreed to play a seven-game series at the end of the season. The following year he was selected to umpire the "world championship" series between Chicago of the NL and St. Louis of the AA. In 1887 he managed the Louisville Eclipse of the AA, where he introduced the "Hurrah Plan" with the players sprinting to and from their positions, even in practice. At the end of the season he umpired his third world championship series. Eventually, he was dismissed from umpiring as "unjustly severe." He turned first to refereeing boxing and worked three championship bouts. He later opened a gambling house in New York. /(RTM)

King Kelly [Michael Joseph] — 1857–1894. OF-C 1878–93 Reds, **Cubs (NL)**, Braves, Boston (PL), Cincinnati-Milwaukee (AA), Boston (AA), Giants 1463 g, .307, 69 hr, 794 rbi.
　　Manager 1890–91 **Boston (PL)**, Cincinnati-Milwaukee (AA) 124–105, .541
　🐾 *Led League—ba 84, 86 . Hall of Fame—1945.*

Kelly, who played every position, was one of the greatest players of his era. Beginning his career with the Reds in 1878, he soon was given the title King of Baseball, and became the number one idol of the nation. Joining Chicago in 1880, Kelly sparked Cap Anson's team to five NL titles. He performed on

King Kelly

eight pennant winners in 16 seasons and hit .300 or better eight times. His .354 in 1884 and .388 in 1886 led the NL. He led the league three times each in doubles and runs scored, and he is one of ten NL players to have scored a league-record six runs in one game. Kelly won renown for his daring baserunning, stealing at least 50 bases for four successive years, with a high of 84 for the Braves in 1887. He once stole six bases in one game. His sensational baserunning and sliding led fans to cheer him on, yelling, "Slide, Kelly, slide!"

After Kelly was traded to the Braves for a record $10,000 in one of the biggest deals in baseball's early history, Chicago fans were so upset they boycotted their team, except when Boston played there. Joining the Players' League in 1890 as Boston's player-manager, Kelly's team captured the league championship by posting an 81–48 record.

After serving as player-manager for Cincinnati-Milwaukee of the American Association for part of 1891, Kelly returned to Boston and helped the Braves win titles in 1891 and 1892. He played a few games for the Giants in 1893, then drifted to the minors, managing Allentown in the Pennsylvania State League and Yonkers in the Eastern League.

Imaginative and quick-thinking, Kelly was credited by Cap Anson with devising the hit-and-run play, although this is disputed. He studied the rules and found ways to get around them, causing the league to make changes. Colorful both on and off the field, Kelly acted with flair and was admired and adored by fans. He wore the finest tailored clothes and the most current styles. American billboards featured the handsome, happy-go-lucky Irishman as the nation's best-dressed man. Kelly supplemented his income with off-season stage appearances and wrote *Play Ball*. Following his retirement from baseball, he opened a saloon in New York. In 1894, en route to Boston to appear at the Palace Theater, he died of pneumonia at age thirty-six. /(JE)

Ray Kelly — 1914–1988. *Writer.*

Kelly spent 50 years with the Philadelphia *Bulletin*, beginning at sixteen as a copyboy. For the last few years he formed a rare father-and-son combination, covering the Phillies with Ray W. Kelly of the Camden (New Jersey) *Post*. Kelly was a semi-pro soccer player in the 1930s who once covered a game in which he scored the winning goal. In his story for the *Bulletin* he gave credit for the goal to another player. Following his retirement he wrote for a weekly paper and did publicity for Philadelphia Park racetrack. /(NLM)

Roberto Kelly — 1964– . OF 1985– **Yankees** 198 g, .291, 11 hr, 62 rbi

This speedy Panamanian won the Yankee's centerfield job in 1989 after Claudell Washington wasn't signed and hit a surprising .302 with 35 steals. /(WOR)

Tom Kelly — 1950– . 1B 1975 **Twins** 49 g, .181, 1 hr, 11 rbi.
   Manager 1986– **Twins** 268–241, .527

Longtime Twins organization man Kelly was the surprise choice to manage the club at the end of 1986. His low-key style helped him lead the underdog club to a World Championship in 1987 despite an 85–77 mark. Improving to 91–71 in 1988, the Twins finished second. /(SFS)

Bill Kelso — 1940– . RHP 1964, 66–68 **Angels**, Reds 201 ip, 12–5, 3.13

Kelso spent four years catching in the minors before converting to pitcher. His best effort was a 5–3, 11-save season for the 1967 Angels. /(RM)

Ken Keltner — 1916– . 3B 1937–44, 46–50 **Indians**, Red Sox 1526 g, .276, 163 hr, 852 rbi. *1 WS, 6 g, .095* ☛ *All-Star—40–44, 46, 48.*

Keltner earned recognition as Cleveland's all-time greatest third baseman for his 11 seasons there. A timely hitter, the seven-time All-Star was a fabulous fielder known for going to his right. He ended Joe DiMaggio's record hit streak at 56 on July 17, 1941 before a then-record night crowd (67,468) in Cleveland. Keltner made two stops of DiMaggio line drives, one a brilliant backhanded stab. On October 4, 1948, in the first playoff in AL history, Keltner's single, double, and three-run homer helped the Indians defeat the Red Sox at Fenway Park. That season, Keltner reached career highs of 31 HR (third in the AL) and 119 RBI (sixth). When he left Cleveland, he was among the club's all-time leaders in games played, doubles, HR, RBI, and hits. /(ME)

Russ Kemmerer (Rusty, Dutch) — 1931– . RHP 1954–55, 57–63 Red Sox, **Senators**, White Sox, Astros 1067 ip, 43–59, 4.46

Hard-throwing Kemmerer was 5–3 down the stretch for the Red Sox as a rookie in 1954. He was swapped to the Senators in 1957, spending three losing seasons in their rotation, and he finished as a long reliever with the Colt .45s (later the Astros). /(MC)

Steve Kemp — 1954– . OF 1977–86, 88 **Tigers**, White Sox, Yankees, Pirates, Rangers 1168 g, .278, 130 hr, 634 rbi ☛ *All-Star—79.*

A highly touted hitter while at the University of Southern California, Kemp was the first player chosen in the nation in the January 1976 draft. After only one season in the minors he was the Tigers' starting left fielder in 1977. He had a looping, lefthanded batting stroke and was neither fast nor graceful in the field, but he made the AL All-Star team in 1979 when he hit .318 with 26 HR and 105 RBI. Kemp was traded to the White Sox for outfielder Chet Lemon after the 1981 season and spent only one season in Chicago before signing with the Yankees as a free agent. His batting average wilted to .241 under the pressure of high expectations in New York, and after the 1984 season he was

traded with Tim Foli to the Pirates for Dale Berra and Jay Buhner. Battling vision problems, he hit only three home runs in 105 games with Pittsburgh in 1985–86 before retiring. /(SCL)

Fred Kendall — 1949– . C 1969–80 **Padres**, Indians, Red Sox 877 g, .234, 31 hr, 244 rbi

Kendall became a San Diego favorite as their regular catcher for much of 1972–76 and was named Most Valuable Padre in 1973 when he hit a career-high .282. Randy Jones credited Kendall with much of his success, and Kendall caught all of Jones's league-leading 22 victories in 1976. The last original Padre when sent to the Indians in December 1976, he returned as a backup in 1979. /(JCA)

Bill Kennedy (Lefty) — 1921–83. LHP 1948–53, 56–57 Indians, **Browns**, White Sox, Red Sox, Reds 465 ip, 15–28, 4.71

Kennedy struck out 456 for Rocky Mount in the Western Carolinas League in 1946. He went 8–8 his rookie year with Cleveland and St. Louis, but wildness dogged his career. As a White Sox reliever in 1952, he led the AL with 47 appearances, but his record was otherwise undistinguished. /(BC)

Bob Kennedy — 1920– . OF-3B 1939–42, 46–57 White Sox, **Indians**, Orioles, Tigers, Dodgers 1483 g, .254, 63 hr, 514 rbi. *1 WS, 3 g, .500, 1 rbi.* *Manager 1963–65, 68* **Cubs**, A's 264–278, .487

Blessed with a strong, accurate throwing arm, Bob Kennedy was one of the first rookie prospects to come out of the newly developed White Sox farm system. The night before he signed in 1937, he was working as a popcorn vendor at Comiskey Park for the Louis-Braddock boxing match. He moved into the starting lineup in 1940, but he committed a league-leading 33 errors at third base. After missing three seasons in military service, he returned to play mostly outfield. Dealt to the Indians in June 1948, he batted .301 the rest of the way and became a member of the last World Championship Indians team. He hit a career-high .291 as their right fielder in 1950.

Kennedy managed the Cubs from 1963 to early 1965, never finishing higher than seventh, and the A's in their first year in Oakland (1968). In subsequent years he was the GM of the Cubs and Astros. His son, Terry, became a star catcher. /(RL)

Brickyard Kennedy [William P.] (Roaring Bill) — 1867–1915. RHP 1892–1903 **Brooklyn (NL)**, Giants, Pirates 3021 ip, 184–160, 3.96. 20 wins: 93–94, 99–1900 *1 WS, 7 ip, 0–1, 5.14*

A prototype of all the Daffy Dodgers to come, Roaring Bill, who conversed at the top of his lungs, was a lovable, eccentric illiterate. He once left the team, misdirected by a policeman who thought Bill wanted to go home to Ohio, rather than find his way from Brooklyn to the Polo Grounds. His restaurant misadventures became legendary, as he always waited until a teammate ordered, then asked for the same, though he wasn't always sure what he was getting. Once, when he reached the hotel dining room as the others were leaving, he asked, "Did you have a good dinner?" Told by one departing diner he had, Bill said to the waiter, "I'll have what he had." Later he complained to the player who had bequeathed him his dinner selection, "It was all right, except for that newfangled dessert." Bill had encountered his first charlotte russe, served in a cardboard cone. "It was that Charley Ross, the waiter called it, the crust was so tough I could hardly eat it."

Kennedy was a winner his first four years with Brooklyn and went 26–20 in 1893. After three losing seasons, he rebounded to go 22–8 in 1899 and 20–13 in 1900. As a spot starter with the Pirates, he pitched in the first World Series in 1903. Up 3–1 in games, Pittsburgh pitted Kennedy against Boston's Cy Young. They matched zeros for five innings until Pittsburgh fell apart, making four errors, losing 11–2. It was Kennedy's last game. Boston won the next three to become World Champions./(JK)

John Kennedy — 1941– . 3B-SS-2B 1962–67, 69–74 Senators, Dodgers, Yankees, Pilots/Brewers, **Red Sox** 856 g, .225, 32 hr, 185 rbi. *2 WS, 6 g, .167*

Kennedy was the model good-field, no-hit utility infielder. He pinch-homered in his first major league at-bat, for the Senators on September 5, 1962. He shared the birthdate of May 29 with President John F. Kennedy./(BC)

Junior Kennedy — 1950– . 2B-SS-3B 1974, 78–83 **Reds**, Cubs 447 g, .248, 4 hr, 95 rbi

After ten years in the minors, Kennedy filled in as Cincinnati's second baseman in 1978–79 while Joe Morgan was hurt. After Morgan signed with Houston as a free agent, Kennedy lost the second base job in 1980 to Ron Oester. His brother Jim was a Cardinal infielder in 1970./(JCA)

Monte Kennedy (Lefty) — 1922– . LHP 1946–53 **Giants** 961 ip, 42–55, 3.84. *1 WS, 3 ip, 0–0, 6.00*

Kennedy came to the Giants in 1946 after three years in the army. Wildness curtailed his effectiveness and he led the NL in walks his rookie year. He won a career-high 12 in 1949./(JK)

Terry Kennedy — 1956– . C 1978– Cardinals, **Padres**, Orioles, Giants 1315 g, .264, 108 hr, 589 hr. *2 LCS, 10 g, .206, 1 rbi. 2 WS, 9 g, .194, 1 hr, 5 rbi* ☛ *All-Star—81, 83, 85, 87.*

Kennedy was stuck behind catcher Ted Simmons at St. Louis until the 11-player deal on December 8, 1980 that sent Kennedy to San Diego and brought Rollie Fingers, briefly, to the Cardinals. From 1981 to 1987, only Gary Carter (940) caught more major league games than Kennedy (934). Terry was San Diego's MVP in 1982, tying Johnny Bench's catchers' record of 40 doubles. Kennedy had 42 doubles overall and led all catchers with 64 extra-base hits. He lost his job to Benito Santiago late in 1986 but set a Padres record by batting .478 as a pinch hitter. Traded to Baltimore for 1987, Kennedy became the second catcher to start All-Star games for both leagues and set club records in starts (135) and total games (142) as a catcher. The strikeout-prone, 6'4" 224-lb lefthanded batter never produced the power expected to go with his size. A prime target for basestealers due to a suspect throwing arm, Kennedy compensated with great knowledge of hitters and ability to handle pitchers.

Terry and his father, Bob Kennedy, are one of only four father-son duos to both play in the World Series. Acquired by the Giants in 1989 while his father was a Giants executive, Terry helped them to the NL pennant./(ME)

Vern Kennedy [Lloyd Vernon] — 1907– . RHP 1934–45 **White Sox**, Tigers, Browns, Senators, Indians, Phillies, Reds 2026 ip, 104–132, 4.67. 20 wins: 36 ☛ *All-Star—36, 38.*

Vern Kennedy pitched a no-hitter for Chicago against Cleveland in his first full season in 1935. He followed with a 21–9 record in 1936, but he led the league with 147 walks. A sore arm slowed him down after 1937, and in 1939 with Detroit he lost an AL-high 20 games./(JK)

Jerry Kenney — 1945- . 3B-SS 1967, 69-73 **Yankees**, Indians 465 g, .237, 7 hr, 103 rbi

Kenney, a tall, slender (6'1" 170-lb) lefthanded-hitting third baseman, was part of the trade that brought Graig Nettles to the Yankees in 1973. He was the Yankee third baseman from 1969 to 1971, and had career highs in 1971 with a .262 average, 56 walks, and 50 runs, in 325 at-bats. /(JM)

Joe Keough — 1946- . OF 1968-73 A's, **Royals**, White Sox 332 g, .246, 9 hr, 81 rbi

Keough played semi-pro ball in Canada before signing with Oakland in 1966, the last year in the majors for his brother Marty. Joe homered in his first ML at-bat but rarely thereafter. In 1971 he hit .248 in 110 games for the Royals in his best season. /(FJO)

Marty Keough — 1935- . OF-1B 1956-66 Red Sox, Indians, Senators, **Reds**, Braves, Cubs 841 g, .242, 43 hr, 176 rbi

Marty, older brother of outfielder Joe Keough, spent his 11 ML seasons as a part-timer. In 1962, his first year in Cincinnati, he hit a personal-best .278 with seven HR in 111 games. His son Matt pitched for Oakland. /(BC)

Matt Keough — 1955- . RHP 1977-83, 85-86 **A's**, Yankees, Cardinals, Cubs, Astros 1190 ip, 58-84, 4.17. *1 LCS, 8 ip, 0-1, 1.08*
☛ *All-Star—78.*

Signed as an infielder, Keough was heralded by A's owner Charley Finley as Sal Bando's successor at third base. But when Keough hit .210 in Double-A in 1976, Finley put him on the mound. He joined Oakland a year later, and as a sophomore in 1978 was the A's only All-Star. He remained in the rotation on Finley's orders in 1979 despite a 2-17 record; he lost his first 14 decisions to tie the ML record for most consecutive losses at the start of a season. But his 16-13 mark in 1980 won him AL Comeback Player of the Year honors. He slumped to 11-18 (5.72) in 1982, tying for the AL lead in losses. Nursing a sore arm, he bounced around before landing in Japan, where his father, major leaguer Marty Keough, had played in 1968. His uncle, Joe Keough, spent most of his six-year career with the A's. /(MC)

Kurt Kepshire — 1959- . RHP 1984-86 **Cardinals** 270 ip, 16-15, 4.16

After a promising rookie season, Kepshire became very inconsistent, with excellent control and velocity one game and neither the next. He was so unpredictable the Cardinals left him off their 1985 postseason roster despite his 10-9 record. /(FJO)

Charlie Kerfeld — 1963- . RHP 1985-87 **Astros** 168 ip, 15-6, 3.70. *1 LCS, 4 ip, 0-1, 2.25*

Kerfeld was a breath of fresh air as an enthusiastic, wisecracking, and obese 6'6" righthander who won 11 games and saved seven for the 1986 NL West champion Astros. But his weight problems forced him back to the minors after a horrendous start in 1987, and elbow trouble has put his pitching career in jeopardy. /(ME)

Jim Kern (Emu) — 1949- . RHP 1974-86 **Indians**, Rangers, Reds, White Sox, Phillies, Brewers 793 ip, 53-57, 3.33
☛ *All-Star—77-79.*

The eccentric, intelligent 6'5" prankster was nicknamed Emu because he looked and acted like a big bird. Kern and Sparky Lyle, in the Rangers' bullpen for two seasons, were known as Craziness, Inc. for their antics and off-the-field misadventures. Kern was hit in the mouth with a throw from his catcher while watching a foul ball in Texas in August 1980. He fell backward off the mound, suffering a concussion. The temporary amnesia he reportedly suffered may have been the result of an opportunistic sense of humor.

His overpowering fastball and lunatic reputation made him an intimidating short reliever; he averaged 8.6 strikeouts per nine innings, 1976-79, when he won 41 games and saved 75. Though he lost an AL-high 10 in relief for Cleveland in 1977, he turned it around in 1979 with Texas, where he was 13-5 with 29 saves and a 1.57 ERA, earning him Fireman of the Year cohonors with Mike Marshall. That was his last effective season, as he injured his elbow in 1980. Unhappy in Cincinnati, Kern forced the Reds to trade him in 1982 by regrowing his scraggly beard, breaking the Reds' unwritten "no facial hair" rule. /(BC)

Buddy Kerr [John Joseph] — 1922- . SS 1943-51 **Giants**, Braves 1067 g, .249, 31 hr, 333 rbi
☛ *All-Star—48.*

Kerr was a slick, wide-ranging shortstop for the otherwise lumbering Giants of the 1940s. Although a less-than-average hitter, he led NL shortstops in assists, putouts, and double plays in 1945, and he had a top .982 fielding average in 1946. When the

Giants hit a NL record 221 home runs in 1947, Kerr's contribution was a mere 7, though he managed a career-high .287 batting average./(BC)

Dickey Kerr — 1893–1963 . LHP 1919–21, 25 **White Sox** 811 ip, 53–34, 3.84. 20 wins: 20 *1 WS, 19 ip, 2–0, 1.42*

Kerr was the one honest starter employed by the White Sox in the scandalous 1919 World Series. He won his two starts against the Reds, one by shutout, while the corrupt star pitchers, Ed Cicotte and Lefty Williams, each dumped their first two assignments. Kerr was 21–9 in 1920 and, after the guilty players were purged, went 19–17 for the demoralized, seventh-place 1921 White Sox. Denied a $500 raise, he decided to pitch for independent teams rather than for tightfisted Charley Comiskey.

Kerr had a long career as a minor league manager. He converted the 19-year-old Stan Musial from a pitcher to an outfielder. The Kerrs befriended the Musials, whose first son was born while Dickey Kerr drove through red lights to get Lil Musial to the hospital; the boy was named Richard in his honor. When Stan achieved stardom with the Cardinals, the Musials repaid the Kerrs' kindness by giving them a house in Houston./(JK)

John Kerr — 1898–1980. 2B-SS 1923–24, 29–34 Tigers, **White Sox**, Senators 471 g, .266, 6 hr, 145 rbi. *1 WS, 1 g, .000*

A native of San Francisco, Kerr was a favorite in the Pacific Coast League. He was the White Sox regular second baseman in 1929 and 1931. With Washington, Kerr was the roommate and inseparable companion of Moe Berg./(JK)

Joe Kerrigan — 1954– . RHP 1976–78, 80 **Expos**, Orioles 219 ip, 8–12, 3.90

As a rookie in 1976, Kerrigan won both games of a doubleheader against St. Louis, his only two wins that season. The 6'5" forkballer shared Montreal bullpen duties with Don Stanhouse in 1977, making 66 appearances and saving 11. The two were then shipped to Baltimore. Kerrigan returned as the Expos' bullpen coach in 1983. His brother Tom was a catcher in the Phillies organization in the 1960s./(MC)

Don Kessinger — 1942– . SS 1964–79 **Cubs**, Cardinals, White Sox 2078 g, .252, 14 hr, 527 rbi.
   Manager 1979 **White Sox** 46–60, .434
☛ *All-Star—68–72, 74 .*

Kessinger accepted a $25,000 bonus to sign out of the University of Mississippi. With Ernie Banks, Glenn Beckert, and Ron Santo, he gave Chicago an all-star infield. Though he led the NL in errors in his first season as a regular (1965), Kessinger quickly established himself as an outstanding fielder, leading league shortstops in putouts three years, assists four years, double plays four years, and fielding average once. He played 54 straight errorless games in 1969, then the record for shortstops, and started for the NL in five All-Star games. He was a pesky, reliable hitter, with a top average of .274 in 1966 and 1972. On July 17, 1970 he went 6-for-6 in a 10-inning game. The clean-living Kessinger served as player-manager for the White Sox in 1979./(BC)

Jimmy Key — 1961– . LHP 1984– **Blue Jays** 1115 ip, 74–49, 3.36. *2 LCS, 15 ip, 1–1, 4.91*
☛ *Led League—era 87. All-Star—85.*

Key bounced back from 1988 arm trouble but could not reestablish himself as one of the AL's top lefthanders in 1989. When Key began with the Blue Jays in 1984, the franchise had never enjoyed good lefthanded pitching. Key set a club rookie record for saves (10), as well as a club mark for appearances with 63. In 1985 Key joined the starting rotation and became the first lefthanded starter to win a game for Toronto since 1980 (a 614-game dry spell) on his way to a 14–6 record with a 3.00 ERA. On May 22, 1986 Key threw a one-hitter against the White Sox (the only hit a fifth-inning single by Ozzie Guillen). In 1987 Key was the AL ERA leader (2.76) while tying the Blue Jay record with 17 wins. In his eight defeats, his teammates scored only 12 runs, and he had seven no-decisions in which he held the opposition to two runs or less. Key's most heartbreaking loss was a 1–0 defeat in the final game of the 1987 season in Detroit, with the division championship on the line. He is the Blue Jays' career leader in ERA and ranks third in wins, strikeouts, and shutouts./(TF)

John Kibler — 1929– . *Umpire* NL 1963–86 *5 LCS 4 WS 4 ASU*

A 24-year veteran umpire, Kibler seldom made a mistake. One of those rare occasions came on June 16, 1986, his final season, when, as crew chief, he called a rainy Pirates-Cardinals game without waiting the stipulated amount of time. NL president Chub Feeney upheld the protest./(RTM)

Leo Kiely — 1929–1984. LHP 1951, 54–56, 58–60 **Red Sox**, A's 523 ip, 26–27, 3.37

After a 7–7 rookie half season with Boston in 1951, Kiely went into the army. Returning in 1954, he was demoted to the bullpen. Kiely led Pacific Coast League relievers in 1957, going 21–6, and saved 12 for the Red Sox in 1958. /(JK)

John Kieran — 1882–1981. *Writer.*

The son of the first president of Hunter College, Kieran had the mind of a college professor and the voice of a New York taxi driver. An amateur naturalist, he was an expert in several subjects on the radio program *Information, Please* for ten years beginning in 1938. He started his newspaper career in 1915, writing at space rates for the sports section of *The New York Times*, then moved to the *Herald Tribune* in 1922. After two years with the Hearst papers (1925–26), he returned to the *Times* to begin the paper's first bylined sports column, "Sports of the Times," starting January 1, 1927. In 1943, he went to the New York *Sun* and wrote a general column. His columns often included bits of poetry. Among his books are *Not Under Oath*, *The Story of the Olympics* (with Arthur Daley), and *The Natural History of New York*. He received the J.G. Taylor Spink Award from the Hall of Fame in 1973. /(NLM)

Pete Kilduff — 1893–1930. 2B-SS-3B 1917–1921 Giants, Cubs, **Dodgers** 428 g, .270, 4 hr, 159 rbi. *1 WS, 7 g, .095*

Kilduff would unknowingly tip off Dodger team-mate Burleigh Grimes's spitter by tossing dirt into his glove. He was also one of the baserunners erased by Bill Wambsganss's unassisted triple play in the 1920 Brooklyn-Cleveland WS. /(JK)

Paul Kilgus — 1962– . LHP 1987– **Rangers**, Cubs 438 ip, 20–32, 4.23. *1 LCS, 3 ip, 0–0, 0.00*

After two losing seasons in which he showed glimmers of talent (three shutouts in 1988) but had control problems, Kilgus went to the Cubs in the Rafael Palmiero-Mitch Williams trade and struggled, going 6–10 with a 4.39 ERA. /(JFC)

Mike Kilkenny — 1945– . LHP 1969–73 **Tigers**, A's, Padres, Indians 410 ip, 23–18, 4.44

Kilkenny signed off the Toronto sandlots, choosing baseball over hockey. He was voted Tiger Rookie of the Year in 1969, with eight wins and four shutouts,

but was inconsistent after that. He was traded three times between May 9 and June 11, 1972. /(CC)

Harmon Killebrew (Killer) — 1936– . 1B-3B-OF-DH 1954–1975 **Senators/Twins**, Royals 2435 g, .256, 573 hr, 1584 rbi. *2 LCS, 6 g, .211, 2 hr, 4 rbi. 1 WS, 7 g, .286, 1 hr, 2 rbi*
☛ *Most Valuable Player—69. Led League—hr 59, 62–64, 67, 69. Led League—rbi 62, 69, 71. All-Star—59, 61, 63–71. Hall of Fame—1984.*

In the mid-1960s, it wasn't Aaron or Mays or Mantle but Harmon Killebrew who seemed to have the best shot at Ruth's lifetime homer record. At the end of 1967, the 31-year-old Killer, a nickname that contradicted his gentle nature, had hit 380 home runs, more than Ruth had at the same age. But in 1968 he was out much of the year with an injury, and after 1970 his enormous power dissipated quickly. Killebrew finished fifth in HR all-time, and third in home run frequency, and left behind a legacy of pure power.

Killebrew was the Senators' first "bonus baby" in 1954, signing a week before his 18th birthday on the recommendation of a U.S. Senator from his home state of Idaho. He shuttled between the majors and minors for five years before finally getting a legitimate shot. He made the starting lineup for good in 1959 when second baseman Pete Runnels got spiked and Killebrew came through with two HR. He finished the season with a league-leading 42, the first of eight times he would top 40.

Throughout his career, Killebrew changed positions frequently. He came up as a second baseman, was soon moved to third, then to left field for a few seasons, over to first base for a while, then back to third, back to first, and finally off the field altogether to DH. He would often shift between two positions in the same game. But Killer never groused and his lack of a permanent defensive spot never seemed to affect his power. In 1962, the second year after the original Senators moved to Minnesota and became the Twins, Killebrew hit a ball completely over the left-field roof at massive Tiger Stadium. On May 2, 1964 he was the fourth straight Twin to homer in the eleventh inning against the Angels to tie a ML record. On June 3, 1967 against the Angels, Killebrew rifled a three-run shot six rows into Metropolitan Stadium's upper deck in left field, shattering two seats. The shot was estimated to have gone 530 feet. The splintered seats were painted orange and never sold again. The next day he hit another shot to

Harmon Killebrew

almost the same spot, the ball pounding off the upper deck facing.

All-Star games brought out the best and worst in Killebrew. He homered in three contests. His first came in the first game in 1961 and provided the AL with its first run in an eventual 5–4 loss. In the 1965 game, his sixth-inning two-run homer in front of his home fans tied the game at 5–5 in another one-run AL loss. In 1968, he overstretched for a throw for an error that led to the only run of the game. The stretch also caused him to pull his hamstring, and he was out for the rest of the season, effectively ruining his chance to catch Ruth. In the homer-rich contest at Tiger Stadium in 1971, his two-run shot in the sixth provided the eventual winning runs in a 6–5 AL victory to snap an eight-game AL slide.

Killebrew, who never drank and was never thrown out of a game, came back from his All-Star hamstring injury to have his best season in 1969. He had career highs with 49 HR and 140 RBI and was selected the AL MVP. He hit another 41 HR in 1970 but saw his home run total slide to only 28 in 1971, although he did lead the league in RBI with 114. His home run totals slid further to 26 in 1972, to 5 in an injury-plagued 1973, and to 13 in 1974. The press reported acrimony between Killebrew and Twins owner Cal Griffith when Killer was released after the 1974 season, which Killebrew denied. But it was obvious that his eroding skills could no longer help Minnesota. He signed on with Kansas City for a final season in 1975. After retirement, he became a Twins broadcaster. He was elected to the Hall of Fame in 1984./(SEW)

Bill Killefer (Reindeer Bill) — 1887–1960. C 1909–21 Browns, **Phillies**, Cubs 1035 g, .238, 4 hr, 240 rbi. *2 WS, 7 g, .111, 2 rbi.*
  Manager 1921–25, 30–33 **Cubs**, Browns 523–623, .456

Bill Killefer was Grover Alexander's batterymate, first with the Phillies and then with the Cubs, to whom the two were traded in 1917. He became the Cubs' manager during the 1921 season, led them until 1925, and managed the Browns in 1930–33.

In nine years he had just one first-division finish, when the Cubs came in fourth in 1923. Killefer fared better in developing catchers, bringing Bob O'Farrell and Gabby Hartnett to stardom with the Cubs. Bill was the younger brother of utility player Red Killefer. /(JK)

Red Killefer [Wade] (Lollypop) — 1884–1958. OF-2B 1907–10, 14–16 Tigers, Senators, **Reds**, Giants 467 g, .248, 3 hr, 116 rbi

Journeyman brother of catcher Bill Killefer, Red played every infield position during his career. He was a regular only once, in the outfield of the 1915 Reds. He had a long and successful career managing in the Pacific Coast League. /(JK)

Frank Killen (Lefty) — 1870–1939. LHP 1891–1900 Cincinnati-Milwaukee (AA), Washington (NL), **Pirates**, Braves, Cubs 2511 ip, 161–124, 3.78. 20 wins: 1892–93, 96
☛ *Led League—w 1893.*

Pittsburgh workhorse Killen won 34 games in 1893, his first year with the Pirates. Connie Mack, Killen's manager and batterymate, said the primary reason the Pirates did not win the 1895 pennant was that Killen was injured. The hurler came back strong in 1896, leading the NL in games, starts, complete games, and innings pitched, and winning 29 games in his last big season. A lifetime .241 hitter, he had 11 home runs in 998 at-bats. /(ME)

Ed Killian (Twilight Ed) — 1876–1928. LHP 1903–10 Indians, **Tigers** 1598 ip, 102–78, 2.38. 20 wins: 05, 07
2 WS, 6 ip, 0–0, 4.26

A hero in Detroit when he won both games of a doubleheader against Boston to clinch the 1907 pennant, Killian was the hardest pitcher to homer against in ML history. Pitching in the dead-ball era, he allowed only nine HR in his career—one every 178 innings—and once went almost four full seasons (1,001 innings) without surrendering one. Acquired by Detroit after one season in Cleveland, Killian won 23 games in his second year as a Tiger, and in 1907 wents 25–13 with a 1.78 ERA and .320 batting average. /(JK)

Matt Kilroy (Matches) — 1866–1940. LHP-OF 1886–94, 98 **Baltimore (AA)**, Boston (PL), Cincinnati-Milwaukee (AA), Washington (NL), Louisville (NL), Cubs 330 g, .222, 1 hr, 66 rbi, 2436 ip, 142–134, 3.47. 20 wins: 86–87, 89
☛ *Led League—w 87. Led League—k 86.*

Although Kilroy lost an American Association-high 34 games as a rookie in 1886, he also led last-place Baltimore with 29 wins and struck out 513 batters (in 583 IP) for a ML record that has never been equaled. In 1887, though striking out "only" 217, Kilroy led the AA with 46 wins to boost Baltimore to third place. Younger brother Mike joined him to pitch one game in 1888 and later appeared with the Phillies. /(FIC)

Newt Kimball — 1915– . RHP 1937–38, 40–43 Cubs, **Dodgers**, Cardinals, Phillies 235 ip, 11–9, 3.78

Blond, broad-shouldered Newt Kimball went 9–3 in four part-time seasons for the Dodgers. Sold to the Cardinals in 1940, he was returned to Brooklyn after pitching two games when Commissioner Landis voided the transaction due to a mishandling of the waiver process. /(JK)

Henry Kimbro — 1912–Unk. OF-MGR Negro Leagues 1937–50 Washington Elite Giants, Homestead Grays, **Baltimore Elite Giants**, New York Black Yankees statistics not available
☛ *All-Star—41, 43–44, 46–47.*

A good all-around ballplayer, Kimbro hit for consistently high averages and was noted for his defensive ability and baserunning. At various times in the 1940s he led the league in runs scored, doubles, and triples. He batted .371 in 1946 and .363 in 1947, finishing third each season. He appeared in six East-West all-star games. Playing for Havana in the Cuban Winter League during the 1947–48 season, he won the batting crown with a .346 average, and set a league record with 104 hits. /(BP)

Chad Kimsey [Clyde Elias] — 1905–1942. RHP 1929–33, 36 **Browns**, White Sox, Tigers 509 ip, 24–29, 5.07

This burly, 6'3" reliever had strong arms and hands from milking cows. With the Browns, Kimsey's five relief losses in 1929, and seven in 1930, were AL highs. The lifetime .282 batter was sometimes used to pinch-hit. /(JK)

Jerry Kindall (Slim) — 1935– . 2B-SS 1956–58, 60–65 **Cubs**, Indians, Twins 742 g, .213, 44 hr, 198 rbi

After three seasons below .170, Kindall tried switch-hitting to win the Cubs' second base job, but he was traded to Cleveland when Ken Hubbs arrived. He was the Twins' 2B for most of their AL Championship 1965 season, but he hit only .196 and was released before the WS. /(MC)

Ellis Kinder (Old Folks) — 1914–1968. RHP 1946–57 Browns, **Red Sox**, Cardinals, White Sox 1479 ip, 102–71, 3.43. 20 wins: 49

Old Folks Kinder didn't pitch in the majors until he was over thirty, but he went on to an occasionally spectacular 12-year career. After two ordinary years with the Browns, he was traded to the Red Sox following the 1947 season. In 1949 he was a sensational starter, going 23–6 with league highs of six shutouts and a .793 winning percentage. With the Red Sox and Yankees tied before the last game of the season, Kinder vowed to win if given three runs. He left after eight innings, trailing 1–0, and New York bombed his relief to take the game 5–4 and win the pennant. He became a top reliever in 1951, saving 14 and winning 10 out of the bullpen, both top AL marks. In 1953 he made a then-record 69 appearances, again leading in relief wins (10) and saves (27). He retired with 102 career saves. /(BC)

Ralph Kiner — 1922– . OF-1B 1946–1955 **Pirates**, Cubs, Indians 1472 g, .279, 369 hr, 1015 rbi
☛ Led League—hr 46–52. Led League—rbi 49. All-Star—48–53. Hall of Fame—1975..

Kiner was baseball's greatest home run hitter during the years after WWII. Although his career was curtailed by a bad back, the powerful righthanded slugger had a ratio of homers to at-bats exceeded only by Babe Ruth.

Signed by the Pirates for an $8,000 bonus, Kiner hit 27 home runs in two minor league seasons before the war. Following military service (1943–45), he became Pittsburgh's starting left fielder in 1946. Despite starting slowly, he hit 23 homers to tie the club record and lead the NL, the lowest total to lead the league since 1921. Kiner was the Pirates' first home run champion since 1906, and home attendance rose to its highest level since the pennant year of 1927 even though the team tumbled to seventh place.

In 1947, the Pirates obtained Hank Greenberg, the '46 AL home run champ, and tailored Forbes Field to the two righthanded power hitters. A double bullpen, 30 feet wide by 200 feet long, significantly cut the distances in left field. "Greenberg Gardens" (later "Kiner's Korner") reduced the left-field line from 365 to 335 feet and the left-center power alley from 406 to 355 feet. The two sluggers became roommates and Kiner credited Greenberg with his continued success. Greenberg managed only 25 homers in his final season, but Kiner blasted 51 to tie Johnny Mize for the NL lead. Finishing strong, he set a ML record with eight homers in four games

Ralph Kiner

from September 10 to 12. His batting average jumped to a career-high .313 and he led the NL with a slugging percentage of .639.

Meanwhile, attendance boomed at Forbes Field despite the Pirates' poor record. Fans would stay in the stands until Kiner had his final at-bat, then file for the exits. More than five million fans paid to watch losing Pirates teams from 1947 to 1950.

In 1948, Kiner again tied Mize for the NL homer championship, hitting 40. The following year, a stretch drive of 16 September homers brought him to 54, only two shy of Hack Wilson's NL record. He also became the first player to hit 50 homers twice in the NL. His 47 home runs in 1950 established a league record of 102 in two consecutive seasons, and he was named *TSN* Player of the Year.

Kiner was sometimes mistakenly labeled a poor outfielder. He lacked speed, but he was sure-handed and had an accurate (but weak) arm. He led the NL in HR in 1951 and 1952 to run his streak to seven consecutive titles, but the Pirates around him were in shambles. His back problems were also beginning to plague him. On June 3, 1953 he was traded to the Cubs in a famous "we finished last with you, we can finish last without you" deal. In Chicago, Kiner teamed in the outfield with the equally slow and powerful Hank Sauer, with whom he had shared the NL home run title the year before. Before the 1955 season, Cleveland GM Greenberg acquired him for the Indians. He hit 18 homers for the Tribe in his final season. Only thirty-three when his bad back ended his career, Kiner retired having hit a home run in every 14.1 at-bats.

After his retirement, he served briefly as GM of the San Diego Padres in the Pacific Coast League, then launched a broadcasting career. Since 1962, he has done play-by-play for the Mets. In 1975 Kiner was named to Baseball's Hall of Fame. /(ME)

Clyde King — 1925– . RHP 1944–45, 47–48, 51–53 **Dodgers**, Reds 496 ip, 32–25, 4.14.
Manager 1969–70, 1974–75, 82 **Giants**, Braves, Yankees 235–231, .504

King was a righthanded reliever who started only 21 of the 200 games in which he appeared. He was the star of the Dodger bullpen in 1951, going 14–7 with six saves and leading the NL in relief wins (13). King managed three major league teams: the Giants in 1969–1970, the Braves in 1974–1975, and the Yankees in 1982. His best managerial record was 90–72 with the Giants in 1969, good for second place in the AL West. After his dismissal as Yankees manager, he remained part of owner George Steinbrenner's brain trust through the 1980s. /(JJM)

Eric King — 1964– . RHP 1986– **Tigers**, White Sox 482 ip, 30–24, 3.79. *1 LCS, 5 ip, 0–0, 1.69*

Acquired from the Giants in a six-man 1985 trade, King was Tiger Rookie of the Year in 1986 when he replaced injured starter Dan Petry and went 11–4 (6–0 at Tiger Stadium). He moved to the bullpen when Petry returned in 1987, saving nine games for Detroit's AL East Champions. Traded to the White Sox for 1989, he returned to starting and was 9–10 with a 3.39 ERA. /(JCA)

Hal King — 1944– . C 1967–68, 70–74 Astros, **Braves**, Rangers, Reds 322 g, .214, 24 hr, 82 rbi. *1 LCS, 3 g, .500*

Never a regular, King saw the most action when he platooned with Bob Tillman in 1970. King had career highs in batting (.260), HR (11), and RBI (30) that year. Over the course of his career, he struck out more often than he got a hit. /(WOR)

Jim King — 1932– . OF 1955–58, 61–67 Cubs, Cardinals, Giants, **Senators**, White Sox, Indians 1125 g, .240, 117 hr, 401 rbi

A steady, strong-armed right fielder for a decade, the lefthanded-hitting King had home run power, though he seldom topped .250 in batting average. He had personal highs of 24 HR and 62 RBI for the 1963 Senators. /(BC)

Joe King — 1909–1979. *Writer.*

A sportswriter and columnist ("Clouting 'Em") for 40 years with the New York *Telegram* and its successors, King left in 1969 to become an assistant managing editor in Ridgewood, New Jersey. A longtime correspondent for *The Sporting News*, he wrote eleven books, including *Batboy of the Giants.* /(NLM)

Lee King — 1892–1967. OF 1916–22 Pirates, **Giants**, Phillies 411 g, .247, 15 hr, 144 rbi. *1 WS, 2 g, 1.000, 1 rbi*

John McGraw waived King, a substitute outfielder, to the Phillies in 1921 but reacquired him in 1922. As a late-inning replacement in the final game of the '22 WS, King singled home the insurance run that wrapped up a 5–3 win and a four-game sweep for the Giants over the Yankees. /(JK)

Nellie King — 1928– . RHP 1954–57 **Pirates** 173 ip, 7–5, 3.58

The 6'6" King displayed uncanny control in the minors. He was effective out of the Pirate bullpen before a sore arm forced an early retirement. /(JL)

Silver King [born Charles Frederick Koenig] — 1868–1938. RHP 1886–93, 96–97 Kansas City (NL), **St. Louis (AA)**, Chicago (PL), Pirates, Giants, Reds, Washington (NL) 3191 ip, 206–152, 3.18. 20 wins: 87–90, 92
☛ *Led League—w 88, 90. Led League—era 88, 90.*

Before he was twenty-one, King had helped pitch St. Louis to two AA pennants (1887 and 1888) and recorded the first two of four consecutive seasons in which he would win more than 30 games. His finest—and busiest—year was 1888, when he led the AA with personal bests in complete games (64), innings pitched (586), wins (45), shutouts (6), and ERA (1.64). His 258 strikeouts in 1888, also a personal high, were second best in the AA.

This fastball pitcher played as Silver King: "King" from the translation of the German, "Koenig;" "Silver" for a thatch of hair that resembled burnished silver. Wide-shouldered, with long, pow-

Silver King with Chicago of the Players' League

erful arms and tremendous hands, King is credited with being the first to use a sidearm delivery. He mixed fastballs, curves, and changes, using just one motion, disdaining a windup. /(JK/FIC)

Mike Kingery — 1961– . OF 1986– Royals, **Mariners** 270 g, .256, 15 hr, 81 rbi

Six-and-a-half seasons in the minors as a non-drafted free agent earned Mike Kingery spot duty in the outfield for the 1986 Royals, and he hit safely in each of his first nine games. He was traded (with Scott Bankhead and Steve Shields) to Seattle for Danny Tartabull after the season. In 1987, his first full major league season, Kingery hit .280 and played excellent, hustling defense, leading Mariner outfielders in assists with 15. His average fell off to .203 in 1988, however, and a crowd of young, talented, Seattle outfielders pushed him back to the minors. /(TF)

Brian Kingman — 1954– . RHP 1979–83 **A's**, Giants 551 ip, 23–45, 4.13. *1 LCS, 0.1 ip, 0–0, 81.00*

Despite Kingman's leading the AL in losses in 1980 with his 8–20 mark for Oakland, his 3.84 ERA showed enough capability to keep him in the majors. But he was a combined 7–18 in 1981–82, his last full seasons. /(BC)

Dave Kingman (Kong, Sky, Big Bird) — 1948– . OF-1B-3B-DH 1971–86 Giants, **Mets**, Padres, Angels, Yankees, Cubs, A's 1941 g, .236, 442 hr, 1210 rbi. *1 LCS, 4 g, .111*
☛ *Led League—hr 79, 82. All-Star—76, 79–80.*

Kingman could hit baseballs great distances, but disdained defense, the fans, and sportswriters—female writers in particular. He was a pitcher at USC before coach Rod Dedeaux converted him to the outfield. He played mostly third base and first base with the Giants, pitching in a couple of games, played outfield and first base with the Mets and Cubs, and became a DH in the American League.

Kong's tremendous home runs (he retired 20th on the all-time list) and sweeping strikeouts (he led the NL three times), after which he'd sometimes fall in a 6'6" tangle of arms and legs, brought him unwanted attention. People admired his strength, laughed at his awkwardness. In 1979 he tied a ML record for HR in two consecutive games (five), and most times hitting three or more HR in a game in one season (two). On the other hand, in 1982 he tied a ML record by striking out five times in a nine-inning game.

Kingman was a smart and, at one time, fast baserunner, and he had a lightning-quick swing with a home run uppercut. He shortened his stroke while with the Cubs in 1979 (in the "friendly confines" of Wrigley Field) and set career marks in batting average (.288) and home runs (a league-high 48). He led the NL in HR with 37 for the 1982 Mets but batted just .204. His average dropped to .198 in 1983; with Oakland in 1984, his 35 homers, career-high 118 RBI, and .268 average won him AL Comeback Player of the Year honors. Kingman's unpredictable, often antisocial behavior and one-dimensional game got him traded often; he tied a modern record by playing with four different clubs during the 1977 season. While with Oakland in 1985, he sent a rat to a female sportswriter. In 1986, though he had just come off a 35-HR season, the free agent found no takers. /(KT)

Dennis Kinney — 1952- . LHP 1978-82 Indians, Padres, Tigers, A's 155 ip, 4-9, 4.53

In 1980, his only full major league season, Kinney relieved in 50 games for the Padres, recording his four career wins. /(BC)

Walt Kinney — 1893-1971. LHP 1918-20, 23 Red Sox, **A's** 291 ip, 11-20, 3.59

Kinney had poor control and went 9-15 while walking 91 in 202 innings in his most active season, 1919 with the Athletics. /(JFC)

Richard Kinsella (Sinister Dick) — 1862-1939. *Scout.*

Never a player, Kinsella was a Springfield, Illinois businessman and a powerful local Democrat. He was friends with Giants manager John McGraw and steered Fred Merkle, Rube Marquard, and Ross Youngs to New York. /(FVP)

W.P. Kinsella — Unk.- . *Writer.*

A Canadian English professor at the University of Calgary, Kinsella's baseball fiction includes *Shoeless Joe* (1982), and *The Iowa Baseball Confederacy* (1985), fantasies that show imagination and a fan's love for the game. *Shoeless Joe* was the basis for the hit movie *Field of Dreams* (1989). /(NLM)

Sachio Kinugasa — 1947- . 3B 1964- **Hiroshima Toyo Carp**

Kinugasa made headlines wherever people follow baseball on June 13, 1987 when he played in his 2,131st consecutive game to break the record held for 48 years by New York Yankees great Lou Gehrig. A few weeks later, Kinugasa became the third Japanese player to crack 500 career home runs, following Sadaharu Oh and Katsuya Nomura. At long last he became a fan favorite, overcoming years of abuse endured because his father was a black American soldier. Kinugasa struck out often, in contrast to most Japanese players, and did not hit for a high average. Some typical Kinugasa seasons were 30 HR, 72 RBI, and .271 for Hiroshima's 1979 pennant winners, and 20 HR, 57 RBI, and .278 for the 1981 winners. /(MC)

Fred Kipp — 1931- . LHP 1957-60 **Dodgers**, Yankees 113 ip, 6-7, 5.08

Kipp's only full year was 1958, when he appeared in 40 games for the Dodgers, 31 in relief, and went 6-6 with a 5.01 ERA. /(BC)

Bob Kipper — 1964- . LHP 1985- Angels, **Pirates** 401 ip, 17-30, 4.49

Born with spondylitis (inflamation of the vertebrae), Kipper was California's first choice in the June 1982 draft. The youthful-looking, inconsistent lefthander was California League Pitcher of the Year in 1984 and jumped up to the Angels in 1985. He suffered from shoulder trouble in 1986. /(ME)

Clay Kirby — 1948- . RHP 1969-76 **Padres**, Reds, Expos 1549 ip, 75-104, 3.83

Saddled with little support at San Diego, Kirby lost 20 games (the league high) as a rookie in 1969, and 18 in 1973, but registered a fine 15-13 (231 strikeouts) with the last-place Padres in 1971. He was 12-9 and 10-6 with the heavy-hitting Reds in 1974 and 1975.

On July 21, 1970 manager Preston Gomez of the Padres pinch hit for Kirby in the eighth inning of a game against the Mets in which he had not allowed a hit, but was losing 1-0. On September 4, 1974 Kirby was in the Reds' dugout when the Astros' Don Wilson was losing a no-hitter 2-1 after eight innings. Kirby's teammate Don Gullett asked what the odds were that Gomez, managing the Astros, would pinch hit for Wilson; Kirby replied, "I guarantee he will." He was right. /(BC)

Jay Kirke [Judson Fabian] — 1888-1968. OF-1B-3B 1910-15, 18 Tigers, Braves, **Indians**, Giants 320 g, .301, 7 hr, 148 rbi

Kirke was legendary as an eccentric who lived for his base hits. His fearsome hitting offset his poor defense, about which he was unconcerned. The despair of four ML teams who tried to fit him into their lineups, Kirke collected over 3,000 hits in his 1906-35 minor league career. /(JK)

Willie Kirkland (Boom Boom) — 1934- . OF 1958-66 Giants, **indians**, Orioles, Senators 1149 g, .240, 148 hr, 509 rbi

Though he possessed power, a strong arm, and defensive skill, Kirkland never fully capitalized on his talent. A starting outfielder for three years with both the Giants (1958-60) and the Indians (1961-63), the lefthanded slugger amassed 91 HR in 1959-62. In 1961 he hit three straight homers on July 9 off Chicago's Cal McLish (all on two-strike pitches), then walked and sacrificed in two more plate appearances. Following the All-Star break, he homered in his first official at-bat against the Twins, tying the major league record with four consecutive home runs. That season Kirkland led the Indians with 27 HR and 95 RBI and tied for the AL lead in double plays by an outfielder. He had led NL outfielders in double plays in 1958. Kirkland later played in Japan, hitting .241 with 126 HR for Hanshin, 1968–73. Unlike many former ML players in Japan, Kirkland adjusted well, learning to speak Japanese, and married a Japanese woman. /(ME)

Ed Kirkpatrick (Spanky) — 1944– . OF-C-1B 1962–77 Angels, **Royals**, Pirates, Rangers, Brewers 1311 g, .238, 85 hr, 424 rbi. *2 LCS, 5 g, .000*

Popular Ed Kirkpatrick earned his keep with versatility and occasional power. Debuting at age seventeen, he spent seven years up and down with the Angels before he was traded in 1968 to Kansas City, where he played more or less regularly for five seasons. Most productive in his first two years with the Royals, he had 14 HR in 1969. As Kansas City's regular catcher (a position he preferred not to play) in 1970, he hit 18 HR with 62 RBI. A 1981 car accident left Kirkpatrick in a wheelchair. /(BC)

Don Kirkwood — 1950– . RHP 1974–78 **Angels**, White Sox, Blue Jays 374 ip, 18–23, 4.37

Twins Don and Ron Kirkwood signed with the Angels in 1972, but only Don reached the majors. He was 6–5 with seven saves as a rookie in 1975, his best year. Arm trouble ended his career prematurely. /(MC)

Bruce Kison (Buster) — 1950– . RHP 1971–85 **Pirates**, Angels, Red Sox 1809 ip, 115–88, 3.66. *5 LCS, 29 ip, 4–0, 1.21 2 WS, 6 ip, 1–1, 5.40*

Slender, 6'4", baby-faced Bruce Kison gained quick notoriety in Game Four of the 1971 World Series, the first night game in Series history. The rookie Pirate relieved Luke Walker in the first inning with two out and three runs in. He hit a Series record three batters but allowed the Orioles only one hit in 6-1/3 innings to win 4–3. The injury-prone pitcher became known both for brushback pitches and quality stretch-run performances. He tied a record with four wins in LCS play. /(ME)

Frank Kitson — 1872–1930. LHP 1898–1907 Baltimore (NL), **Dodgers**, Tigers, Senators, Yankees 2215 ip, 128–118, 3.17. 20 wins: 99

Kitson was a top lefthander at the turn of the century, winning 22 games for Baltimore in 1899 and 19 for Brooklyn in both 1901 and 1902. He jumped to the AL in 1903 but was less successful.

Friends blamed overwork; from 1899 through 1903 he never pitched fewer than 253 innings. /(BC)

Ron Kittle — 1958– . OF-DH 1982– **White Sox**, Yankees, Indians 721 g, .241, 156 hr, 407 rbi. *1 LCS, 3 g, .286*
☛ *Rookie of the Year—83. All-Star—83.*

This strongboy from nearby Gary, Indiana, was an instant hit in Chicago. Kittle had been released by the Dodger organization after a spinal fusion operation in 1978 and was working in iron construction when invited to Comiskey Park for a tryout. His combined output for two minor league seasons, 1981 and 1982, was 90 homers. As the White Sox left fielder in 1983, he batted .254 with 35 HR and 100 RBI, combining with Greg Luzinski to form the most potent HR duo in club history. He played in the All-Star Game and the LCS, and he won AL Rookie of the Year honors. But he also struck out a league-high 150 times. In 1984 his average dropped to .215, and his 32 HR did not compensate for his failure to advance runners and hit in the clutch. He was hampered by a shoulder injury in 1985 and was batting .213 in 1986 when he was traded to the Yankees. He hit 12 HR in 159 at-bats in 1987, spent 40 days on the disabled list, and was released. The Indians picked him up in 1988, and he returned to the White Sox for 1989 but spent much of the season on the DL after a good start. /(RL)

Malachi Kittredge — 1869–1928. C 1890–99, 1901–06 **Cubs**, Louisville (NL), Washington (NL), Braves, Senators, Indians 1215 g, .219, 17 hr, 390 rbi

Kittredge caught for the Chicago NL team through most of the 1890s. Although he was a poor hitter, he was steady and reliable behind the plate and an accurate thrower. In 1904 he was made manager of the hapless Washington Senators, but after the team led off the season at 1–16, he relinquished the reins to Patsy Donovan. /(BC)

Billy Klaus — 1928– . SS-3B 1952–53, 55–63 Braves, **Red Sox**, Orioles, Senators, Phillies 821 g, .249, 40 hr, 250 rbi

After seven years in the minors, Klaus hit a career-high .283 with 7 HR as the Red Sox' rookie shortstop in 1955. His brother Bobby played briefly with the Reds and Giants. /(JK)

Bobby Klaus — 1937– . 2B-3B-SS 1964–65 Reds, **Mets** 215 g, .208, 6 hr, 29 rbi

The younger brother of Billy Klaus briefly replaced Pete Rose at second base for the Reds in 1964. A utility infielder good at turning the double play, he hit .244 as a Met later that season, but just .191 in 119 games the next. /(KT)

Chuck Klein — 1904–1958. OF 1928–44 **Phillies**, Cubs, Pirates 1753 g, .320, 300 hr, 1201 rbi. *1 WS, 5 g, .333, 1 hr, 2 rbi*
☛ *Most Valuable Player—32. Led League—ba 33. Led League—hr 29, 31–33. Led League—rbi 31, 33. All-Star—33–34. Hall of Fame—1980.*

One of the most prodigious sluggers of the late 1920s and early 1930s, Chuck Klein was a star from the day he joined the Phillies in July 1928. The short right-field fence at Baker Bowl (280 feet) contributed

Chuck Klein

to the lefthanded-hitting Klein's slugging records and high batting average. He collected more than 200 hits for five straight seasons (1929–33), leading the NL the last two. With 250 hits in 1930, he batted .386 but still finished third in the league behind Bill Terry (.401) and Babe Herman (.393). It was a hitter's year, but Klein's average was 83 points above the league mark.

Klein led the league in total bases for four consecutive years (1930–33), leading in doubles in two of them and HR in three. He led in runs scored three straight years, powered six HR in four straight games in 1929, and twice hit five in three games. Unlike most sluggers, he was a competent baserunner, topping the circuit in 1932 with 20 steals and hitting 15 triples. His league-leading numbers of outfield assists in 1930 (44, a modern NL record), 1932, and 1933 were largely a product of his skill at fielding the strange caroms off the corrugated tin wall at Baker Bowl.

The NL MVP in 1932, Klein won the Triple Crown in 1933 (28 HR, 120 RBI, .368), though Carl Hubbell took MVP honors. During his first six years, Klein hit 191 HR and collected 1,209 hits, 699 runs, and 727 RBI. Traded to the Cubs for the 1934 season, Klein was a disappointment in Chicago by his previous standards. Many Baker Bowl home runs turned into long outs at Wrigley Field. Even so, he hit 20 and 21 HR in two seasons and batted .301 and .293. The Phillies reacquired him in May 1936, and Klein had his greatest game when he smashed four homers in a 10-inning contest on July 10. Klein was elected to the Hall of Fame by the Veterans Committee in 1980. /(AA)

Lou Klein — 1918–1976. 2B-SS 1943, 45–46, 49, 51 **Cardinals**, Indians, A's 305 g, .259, 16 hr, 101 rbi. *1 WS, 5 g, .136.*
*Manager 1961–62, 65 **Cubs** 65–83, .439*

Klein unexpectedly fought his way into the Cardinal lineup in 1943, playing every inning of every game, batting .287. After losing almost two years to WWII, he returned to lose second base in a three-way battle with Red Schoendienst and Emil Verban. Disgusted, he jumped to the Mexican League, was barred from organized baseball, and later signed to play in the outlaw Quebec Provincial League. Before playing an inning in Canada, he was reinstated in 1949 and became the first jumper to return to the big leagues. But he still couldn't beat Schoendienst out of a job. Klein was one of the Cubs' "College of Coaches," managing in 1961–62, and again, by himself, for most of 1965. /(MC)

Ted Kleinhans — 1899–1985. LHP 1934, 36–38 Phillies, **Reds**, Yankees 143 ip, 4–9, 5.27

After a career spent largely in the minors, Kleinhans found his niche in baseball as the coach for Syracuse, his alma mater, and later was that city's commissioner of parks and recreation. /(JK)

Red Kleinow [John Peter] — 1879–1929. C 1904–11 **Yankees**, Red Sox, Phillies 584 g, .213, 3 hr, 135 rbi

In 1904 the Highlanders (later the Yankees) came within one pitch of winning their first pennant. Forty-one-game winner Jack Chesbro sailed a spitball well over Kleinow's head which was ruled a wild pitch, but Kleinow took criticism for failing to catch it. /(JK) R

Bill Klem (The Old Arbitrator) — 1874–1951. *Umpire 1905–40 NL 18 WS 2 ASU*
☛ *Hall of Fame—1953.*

Generally regarded as the greatest umpire in the game's history, Klem umpired exclusively behind the plate his first 16 years because of his acknowledged superiority in calling balls and strikes. As a plate umpire, he pioneered the inside chest protector. Until Klem, all plate umpires wore the outside protector, commonly called the "balloon." Klem said the inside protector gave him a better look at the pitch because he could move in closer behind the catcher. He took a catcher's protector, added shoulder pads, and wore it under his shirt instead of outside. Since he was the dean of NL umpires, the senior circuit adopted the inside protector years before the AL.

Klem worked a record 18 WS, a total of 104 games, including five straight assignments from 1911 to 1915. His first WS was 1908 (Cubs-Tigers) and his last 1940 (Reds-Tigers). Klem also umpired the first All-Star Game in 1933. In 36 years, he was behind the plate for five no-hitters, the last being Paul Dean's over Brooklyn (9/21/34). He even officiated a race around the bases between Hans Lobert and a horse in 1914 at Oxnard, California. He declared the horse the winner by a nose.

Among the many memorable games Klem umpired was Opening Day at the Polo Grounds in 1907. A winter storm left piles of snow around the field. In the eighth inning, with New York leading the Phillies 3–0, spectators began bombarding the visting Phillies, umpires, and each other with snow-

Bill Klem

balls. Klem forfeited the game to Philadelphia because it was up to the home team to keep order.

He could be stubborn. He reportedly once started to call a runner out at the plate, then signaled safe when a ball rolled loose. The catcher showed him he still held the ball; the loose ball had apparently fallen from one of Klem's pockets. He refused to change his call.

He adored the nickname The Old Arbitrator but despised being called Catfish. In Lawrence Ritter's *The Glory of Their Times*, Chief Meyers said, "All you had to do was call him Catfish and out of the game you'd go. Maybe it was because he had rather prominent lips, and when he'd call a ball or a strike he'd let fly a rather fine spray from his mouth. Sort of gave the general impression of a catfish, you know."

Early in Klem's career, Giants manager John

McGraw threatened to get him fired. Klem replied: "Mr. Manager, if it's possible for you to take my job away from me, I don't want it." His integrity helped secure the reputation of umpires as honest and impartial. He brought dignity to the game, along with competence and pride. Shortly before he died, he described the last game he ever worked. "I walked away from the beefing ballplayer, saying to myself, 'I'm almost certain Herman tagged him.' Then it came to me and I almost wept. For the first time in my career, I only 'thought' a man was tagged." Klem retired that afternoon.

He always maintained, "I never called one wrong," though in later years he would place his hand over his heart and add, "from here." After his retirement, he served as Chief of NL Umpires until his death. Klem was elected to the Hall of Fame in 1953./(RTM)

Ed Klepfer (Big Ed) — 1888–1950. RHP 1911, 13, 15–17, 19 Yankees, White Sox, **Indians** 448 ip, 22–17, 2.81

Spitballer Klepfer went to Cleveland in the 1915 deal that sent Joe Jackson to Chicago and was 14–4, 2.37 with the 1917 Indians. He spent 1918 in the military and apparently lost his stuff afterward. His career .048 batting average is the second-worst ever for a pitcher with at least 100 at-bats./(ME)

Eddie Klieman (Babe) — 1918–1979. RHP 1943–50 **Indians**, Senators, White Sox, A's 542 ip, 26–28, 3.49. *1 WS, 0 ip, 0–0, infinite*

Klieman pitched well despite fits of wildness as a part-time starter for Cleveland in 1944–45, but he was gradually forced to the bullpen, and then the minors, by veterans returning from WWII. He came back in 1947 to lead the AL with 17 saves and 58 appearances and posted a 2.60 ERA for the 1948 World Champion Indians./(MC)

Lou Klimchock — 1939– . 3B-2B-1B A's, Braves, Senators, Mets, **Indians** 318 g, .232, 13 hr, 69 rbi

Klimchock won two minor league batting titles, but his indifferent defense kept him on the bench in the ML. In 1969 with the Indians, he hit .287 in a career-high 90 games./(JCA)

Ron Klimkowski — 1945– . RHP 1969–72 **Yankees**, A's 188 ip, 8–12, 2.92

After leading the International League with 15 wins and a 2.18 ERA in 1969, the junkball specialist pitched in 45 games for the Yankees in 1970, mostly in middle relief, going 6–7 (2.66)./(JCA)

Bob Kline (Junior) — 1909– . RHP 1930–34 **Red Sox**, A's, Senators 441 ip, 30–28, 5.05

Alternating a fastball with a sinker he learned from roommate Wilcy Moore, Kline won 11 games for the hapless 1932 Red Sox. In 1934, he led the AL in relief wins (7) despite a 7.21 ERA./(JK)

Ron Kline — 1932– . RHP 1952, 55–70 Pirates, Cardinals, Angels, Tigers, **Senators**, Twins, Giants, Red Sox, Braves 2077 ip, 114–144, 3.75

A starter the first half of his career, Kline was converted to relief and collected 108 saves. As a Pirate starter, his 18 losses in 1956 and 16 in 1958 were NL highs. In 1965 he led the AL with 29 saves and was second with 74 appearances, giving him the single-season Senator club records for saves, games pitched, and games finished. Returning to the Pirates in 1968, Kline had 12 relief wins (10 in succession) to lead the NL.

Kline had one of the most peculiar pitching rituals in baseball, touching his cap, belt, and shirt before each pitch. One of the poorer-hitting pitchers in the game, Kline managed only a lifetime .092 average./(JLE)

Steve Kline — 1947– . RHP 1970–74, 77 **Yankees**, Indians, Braves 749 ip, 43–45, 3.27

Kline, a control pitcher, had a banner year in 1972, going 16–9 for the Yankees with a 2.40 ERA. After injuring his arm the next year, he went to Cleveland in the 1974 deal that brought Chris Chambliss to the Yankees./(JCA)

Johnny Kling (Noisy) — 1875–1947. C 1900–08, 10–13 **Cubs**, Braves, Reds 1260 g, .272, 20 hr, 513 rbi. *4 WS, 21 g, .185, 3 rbi.*
   Manager 1912 **Braves** 52–101, .340

The catcher of Frank Chance's great Cub teams of 1906–10, Kling was the NL's premier defensive catcher and a capable hitter. Batterymate Ed Reulbach called him "one of the greatest catchers who ever wore a mask." In the years 1902–08, Kling led the league in fielding four times, putouts six, assists twice, and double plays once. On June 21, 1907, he threw out all four Cardinal runners who attempted to steal second base. In the WS that fall, Kling nabbed seven Tigers in 14 tries, with Ty Cobb unable to steal a single base. In the winter of 1908–09, Kling won the world pocket billiard championship and decided to forsake the baseball diamond for the pool table. Defeated in his attempt to retain the title, he rejoined the Cubs in 1910 but

Johnny Kling

when Enos Slaughter made his fabled mad dash home to win Game Seven of the '46 WS. /(ME)

Johnny Klippstein — 1927– . RHP 1950–67 **Cubs**, Reds, Dodgers, Indians, Senators, Phillies, Twins, Tigers 1967 ip, 101–118, 4.24. *2 WS, 5 ip, 0–0, 0.00*

Klippstein was sometimes called "the wild man of Borneo" because of his frequent control troubles. The journeyman was used in both starting and relief assignments in his early days, but in 1958 was made almost exclusively a reliever by Dodger manager Walter Alston. Though he never won more than 12 games in a season, there was always a team willing to take him. With the Indians for one season, he had a league-leading 14 saves in 1960. Five years later, teaming in the Minnesota bullpen with ace Al Worthington, Klippstein went 9–3 with five saves to help the Twins to their first pennant. He finished with 66 career saves. He is the son-in-law of former pitcher Emil "Dutch" Leonard. /(ARA)

Fred Klobedanz — 1871–1940. LHP 1896–99, 1902 **Braves** 702 ip, 53–25, 4.12. *20 wins: 97*

Although Boston fans said Klobedanz "was as hard to hit as he was to pronounce," he profited from the fact that the 1897–98 NL-champion Braves had by far the league's best run-scoring machine. In 1897 he went 26–7 and led the NL in winning percentage. The next year he was 19–10. But in both seasons, his ERA was higher than the league average, he gave up more hits than innings pitched, and he walked many more than he struck out. When the Braves' hitters tailed off in 1899, he ceased to win. /(BC)

Ted Kluszewski (Klu) — 1924–1988. 1B 1947–61 **Reds**, Pirates, White Sox, Angels 1718 g, .298, 279 hr, 1028 rbi. *1 WS, 6 g, .391, 3 hr, 10 rbi*
☛ *Led League—hr 54. Led League—rbi 54. All-Star—53–56.*

The sleeveless Cincinnati uniforms of the 1950s were made to allow Kluszewski's bulging muscles room to move, but he was more than a slugger. The former University of Indiana football star hit with marked consistency and awesome power and fielded his position smoothly. He led the NL with 49 homers and 141 RBI in 1954 and averaged 43 HRs and 116 RBIs from 1953 to 1956. He also hit .300 seven times. In 1955 he led in hits (192) and set a modern NL record by scoring runs in 17 straight games. Starting in 1951, he topped NL first basemen in fielding five straight years, a ML record. Injuries eventually cut into his skills, and he spent his last

was a part-timer thereafter. His brother Bill pitched briefly in the NL during the 1890s. /(ARA)

Bob Klinger — 1908–1977. RHP 1938–43, 46–47 **Pirates**, Red Sox 1090 ip, 66–61, 3.68. *1 WS, 0.2 ip, 0–1, 13.50*

The Pirates' leading winner in 1939, when he went 14–17 and led the NL in losses, Klinger returned from WWII Navy duty to lead the AL with nine saves for the 1946 Red Sox. He was the pitcher

Ted Kluszewski

five seasons pinch-hitting nearly as often as he started, but with the White Sox in the six-game 1959 WS, he banged three homers and drove in 10 runs./(ME)

Mickey Klutts [Gene Ellis] — 1954- . 3B-SS-2B 1976-83 Yankees, **A's**, Blue Jays 199 g, .241, 14 hr, 59 rbi. *1 LCS, 3 g, .429*

Klutts was disabled at least ten times; he suffered one injury when he ran into a tarp. In 1981 with Oakland, the round-faced infielder hit five homers in just 15 games./(JCA)

Clyde Kluttz — 1917-1979. C 1942-48, 51-52 **Braves**, Giants, Cardinals, Pirates, Browns, Senators 656 g, .268, 19 hr, 212 rbi

A journeyman ML catcher for nine seasons, Kluttz spent 42 years in professional baseball. As a scout for the Yankees, he convinced free agent Catfish Hunter to sign with New York. Later, Kluttz served as Baltimore's Director of Player Development./(JCA)

Otto Knabe [Franz Otto] (Dutch) — 1884-1961. 2B 1905, 07-16 Pirates, **Phillies**, Baltimore (FL), Cubs 1285 g, .247, 8 hr, 364 rbi.
Manager 1914-15 **Baltimore (FL)** 131-177, .425

With Knabe on one side of second base and shortstop Mickey Doolan on the other, opposing baserunners entered this territory at considerable physical risk. The roughhousing second baseman jumped the Phillies to become a player-manager in the Federal League./(JL)

Chris Knapp [Robert Christian] — 1953- . RHP 1975-80 White Sox, **Angels** 603 ip, 36-32, 5.00. *1 LCS, 2 ip, 0-1, 7.71*

Knapp was 12-7 after his promotion to the White Sox in 1977, then was traded to the Angels. He jumped the club for three weeks in mid-1978 over a contract dispute but finished 14-8. Knapp slipped on a wet Yankee Stadium mound in May 1979, rupturing a disc, and was through after a 2-11 record in 1980./(MC)

Bob Knepper — 1954- . LHP 1976- Giants, **Astros** 2663 ip, 143-152, 3.64. *1 LCS, 15 ip, 0-0, 3.52* ☛ *All-Star—81.*

Knepper stepped into San Francisco's starting rotation, replacing injured John Montefusco, in 1977. The following year, Knepper led NL lefthanders in ERA, led the entire league in shutouts, and won a career-high 17 games. Two straight off-years resulted in a trade to Houston for Enos Cabell, where Knepper became the winningest lefthander in Astros history. He was the NL Comeback Player of the Year in 1981 (9-5, 2.18), finishing second to Nolan Ryan in the ERA race. From 1984 to 1986 Knepper was one of the NL's best lefties. His 17 wins in 1986 tied the Houston record for lefthanders. He also tied teammate Mike Scott for the league lead with five shutouts. Knepper took leads to the ninth inning in Games Three and Six of the 1986 LCS, but New York rallied to win both, and the series. Knepper dipped to a league-high 17 losses in 1987, but in 1988 a great start propelled him to a 14-5, 3.14 record. He returned to the Giants in 1989 after a terrible start and finished 7-12, 5.13./(ME)

Lou Knerr [Wallace Luther] — 1921-1980. RHP 1945-47 **A's**, Senators 287 ip, 8-27, 5.04

Knerr managed records of only 5-11 and 3-16 in his two years with the Athletics; in 1946 he was one of three last-place A's pitchers to lose a league-high 16. He finished his career in 1949 in the outlaw Quebec Provincial League, filling in for Mexican League jumpers who had returned to the majors after their suspensions were lifted in mid-season. /(MC)

Elmer Knetzer (Baron) — 1885–1975. RHP 1909–12, 14–17 **Dodgers**, Pittsburgh (FL), Braves, Reds 1267 ip, 68–69, 3.15

Knetzer played a long time as a journeyman pitcher, compiling his best record with the Pittsburgh Federal League club in 1914 (19–11) after missing the entire 1913 season as a holdout. He continued pitching after leaving the majors and finished his career with Springfield of the Mid-Atlantic League in 1934 at the age of forty-nine. /(MA)

Bill Knickerbocker (Knick) — 1911–1963. SS-2B 1933–42 **Indians**, Browns, Yankees, White Sox, A's 907 g, .276, 28 hr, 368 rbi

Knickerbocker was Cleveland's regular shortstop from 1934–36, and though he hit well (.317 in '34), he had difficulties in the field. /(RL)

Jack Knight [Elmer Russell] — 1895–1976. RHP 1922, 25–27 Cardinals, **Phillies**, Braves 255 ip, 10–18, 6.85

On a personal eight-game losing streak in his last full ML season, Knight came on in relief against the Giants on June 24, 1926. He hit his only two career homers, in innings five and six, but Philadelphia still lost to New York 12–7. /(AL)

John Knight (Schoolboy) — 1885–1965. SS-3B-1B-2B 1905–07, 09–13 A's, Red Sox, **Yankees**, Senators 767 g, .239, 14 hr, 270 rbi

Signed out of high school, this native of Philadelphia was nineteen when he found himself in the Athletics' 1905 Opening Day lineup because shortstop Monte Cross broke a hand. Knight was hitting .400 in mid-June but finished the season at .203. Eager to win a pennant in 1907, Connie Mack traded Knight to the Red Sox for veteran third baseman Jimmy Collins. Mack later said Knight was the only young player he ever regretted letting go. /(NLM)

Ray Knight — 1952– . 3B-1B 1974, 77–88 **Reds**, Astros, Mets, Orioles, Tigers 1495 g, .271, 84 hr, 595 rbi. *2 LCS, 9 g, .211, 2 rbi. 1 WS, 7 g, .391, 1 hr, 5 rbi* ☛ *All-Star—80, 82.*

The man who replaced Pete Rose as Cincinnati's third baseman in 1979 later became the first World Series MVP to join a new team the next season. After three seasons at Cincinnati, Knight was traded to Houston, making way for another Cincinnati legend, Johnny Bench. Knight saw extensive duty at first base for the Astros before going to the Mets, for

three minor leaguers, in 1984. After a poor 1985 season, New York coach Bill Robinson changed Knight's batting stance from a crouching to a straight-up position. Ray earned Comeback Player of the Year honors for his 1986 season (.298, 11 HR, 76 RBI) while platooning with Howard Johnson. Knight hit the decisive homer in the Game Seven of the World Series after scoring the winning run in Game Six on Mookie Wilson's grounder through Bill Buckner's legs. Knight had nearly been the goat of Game Six for his fielding miscues, but the Mets' win wiped that out. Following a contract dispute, Knight went to Baltimore as a free agent in 1987, allowing Johnson to emerge as a star on the Mets. Knight is married to golf star Nancy Lopez, and caddied for her briefly after his retirement. /(ME)

Bobby Knoop — 1938– . 2B-3B 1964–72 **Angels**, White Sox, Royals 1153 g, .236, 56 hr, 331 rbi ☛ *All-Star—66. Gold Glove—66–68.*

A superlative second baseman, Knoop (pronounced "Kuh-NOP") won three Gold Gloves and was voted the Angels' Owner's Trophy for "inspirational leadership, sportsmanship and professional ability" four times. Called "the Nureyev of second base" by sportswriters, the acrobatic introvert established an AL second base record with 12 putouts in a nine-inning game (8/60/66). Knoop and his roommate, shortstop Jim Fregosi, turned an AL-record six double plays in a May 1, 1966 game. Usually a poor hitter, he hit 17 home runs in 1966, including a home run and double in the same inning (April 30). He became an Angel coach in 1979. /(JCA)

Jack Knott [John Henry] — 1907–1981. RHP 1933–42, 46 **Browns**, White Sox, A's 1557 ip, 82–103, 4.97

In eleven ML seasons, Knott only once pitched for a team that reached the first division, the fourth-place White Sox of 1939. Playing during a high-scoring era, he never finished with an ERA under 4.15 but still produced winning records in five seasons. /(JK)

Darold Knowles — 1941– . LHP 1965–80 Orioles, Phillies, **Senators**, A's, Cubs, Rangers, Expos, Cardinals 1092 ip, 66–74, 3.12. *1 LCS, 1/3 ip, 0–0, 0.00. 1 WS, 6 ip, 0–0, 0.00* ☛ *All-Star—69.*

The fast-working reliever earned 143 career saves. In his rookie year, while Knowles was saving 13 for the Phillies, manager Gene Mauch said, "He's got the courage of a daylight burglar." Pitching for the last-place Senators in 1970, he lost a ML-record 14 in relief yet saved 27 with a 2.04 ERA. In 54 games with Oakland in 1972 he registered a superb 1.36 ERA. He became the only pitcher ever to appear in all seven games of a World Series, saving two in Oakland's victory over the Mets in 1973. On his retirement, he was tied for 13th in career saves. /(JCA)

Mark Knudson — 1960- . RHP 1985- Astros, **Brewers** 273 ip, 13-17, 4.32

Despite unimpressive minor league credentials, Knudson pitched in the ML briefly each season from 1985 to 1988, and 1989 was the first time he began the season on a ML roster. He was 11-8, 3.40 with Denver (American Association) in '88. /(ME)

Kevin Kobel — 1953- . LHP 1973-74, 76, 78-80 Brewers, **Mets** 475 ip, 18-34, 3.88

Kobel debuted with Milwaukee before his 20th birthday. He pitched one full season, going 6-14 in 1974, before arm trouble forced him to the minors for most of 1975 through 1977. Given a second chance by the Mets, he pitched respectably in 1978-79. /(JCA)

Alan Koch — 1938- . RHP 1963-64 Tigers, **Senators** 128 ip, 4-11, 5.41

A flamethrower who also swung a mean bat (.286), Koch lacked control and returned to the minors after spending most of 1964 in the Senators' starting rotation. /(MC)

Len Koenecke — 1904-1935. OF 1932, 34-35 Giants, **Dodgers** 265 g, .297, 22 hr, 114 rbi

Koenecke hit .320 with 14 HR for Brooklyn in 1934. Dismissed by Casey Stengel for erratic play and behavior in September 1935, Koenecke chartered a plane home. A fight broke out on board the small plane, supposedly after the drunken Koenecke made improper advances to the pilot and copilot. Koenecke was hit on the head with a fire extinguisher by the copilot and killed. /(TG)

Mark Koenig — 1902- . SS-3B-2B 1925-36 **Yankees**, Tigers, Cubs, Reds, Giants 1162 g, .279, 28 hr, 443 rbi. *5 WS, 20 g, .237, 5 rbi*

In 1926 Koenig and Tony Lazzeri became the Yankees' double play combination. Switch-hitter Koenig batted second. He had a shaky rookie year afield with a league-leading 52 errors during the season and 4 more in the 1926 World Series, one of which opened the door to the Cardinals' winning rally in Game Seven. He batted .500 in the 1927

Series, and in 1928 again led the AL in errors, but hit a career-high .319. In 1929 Leo Durocher played more games at shortstop than he did, and the following year, Koenig was traded to Detroit, where he played some short, some second, and pitched unsuccessfully. Released to the San Francisco Missions (Pacific Coast League) in 1932, he was called up by the Cubs in August when Billy Jurges was shot, hit .353 in a 33-game dash for the pennant, and was awarded an ungenerous one half Series share. The Cubs' WS opponents were his old teammates, the Yankees, who reacted hotly to this supposed mistreatment. Some accounts say that Ruth's "called shot" HR was an indirect result, with Ruth razzing Cubs pitcher Root. With Cincinnati in 1934, old-timers Koenig and Jim Bottomley refused to fly on road trips, taking the train instead. /(ADS)

Jack Kofoed — 1894-Unk. *Writer.*

Kofoed was one of America's most prolific magazine writers, contributing articles and fiction to 200 magazines. He did movie and radio writing as well. He began in 1912 with the Philadelphia *Ledger and Record*, then moved to New York, where he was a columnist for the *Post* from 1924 to 1933. He later was a feature columnist for the Miami *Herald*. /(NLM)

Dick Kokos [born Richard Jerome Kokoszka] — 1928-1986. OF 1948-50, 53-54 **Browns/ Orioles** 475 g, .263, 59 hr, 223 rbi

As a Browns rookie at twenty, Kokos showed power, but his play was erratic. In 1949 he led AL outfielders in assists and double plays, hit 23 HR, but struck out a league-high 91 times. He led the AL in errors in 1950, and was returned to the minors, reappearing as a platoon player in '53. He was able to throw from the outfield to home plate while on his knees. /(MC)

Don Kolloway (Butch, Cab, The Blue Island Flash) — 1918- . 2B-1B 1940-43, 46-53 **White Sox**, Tigers, A's 1079 g, .271, 29 hr, 393 rbi

Brought up to the White Sox in 1940, the infielder from Chicago's South Side moved into the second base spot in 1942. A line drive hitter with exceptional speed, Kolloway led the league in doubles that year and is one of only a handful of AL players to steal second, third, and home in one game (6/28/41 vs. Cleveland). /(RL)

Ray Kolp (Jockey) — 1894–1967. RHP 1921–24, 27–34 Browns, **Reds** 1688 ip, 79–95, 4.08

After a 14–4 sophomore season with the 1922 Browns, who lost the pennant to the Yankees by one game, Kolp had just one more year over .500. He was nicknamed Jockey for his ability to badger opponents with a salty tongue and loud mouth. /(ADS)

Brad Komminsk — 1961– . OF 1983–87, 89 **Braves**, Brewers, Indians 298 g, .219, 20 hr, 95 rbi

Komminsk was the Braves' greatest disappointment of the 1980s. A first-round pick in June 1979, he homered in his first pro at-bat and reached double figures in homers for four consecutive minor league seasons. But he hit just .227 with four HR in spending all of 1985 with Atlanta. The Braves gave up on him in 1987, sending him to Milwaukee for Dion James. He resurfaced with the 1989 Indians, hitting .237 but driving in 33 runs in 198 at-bats. /(JCA)

Ed Konetchy (Big Ed) — 1885–1947. 1B 1907–21 **Cardinals**, Pirates, Pittsburgh (FL), Braves, Dodgers, Phillies 2083 g, .281, 74 hr, 992 rbi. *1 WS, 7 g, .174, 2 rbi*

Konetchy began playing first base for the Cardinals in 1907, had a 20-game hitting streak in 1910, and in 1911 led the NL with 38 doubles. He was one of very few players to hit a ball out of old Robinson Field in St. Louis. Sent to the Pirates in a December 1913 trade, in 1915 he jumped to Pittsburgh of the Federal League. With the Dodgers in 1919, Konetchy became the third of eight NL players to collect a record ten consecutive hits. He also played the entire major-league-record 26-inning game in 1920 between the Dodgers and Braves. Batting over .300 four times, Konetchy compiled 100 or more hits in 14 consecutive seasons and broke up four no-hitters. After his ML days, he played with Fort Worth (Texas League) in 1922–27, batting .345 with 41 HR in 1925. /(JLE)

Doug Konieczny — 1951– . RHP 1973–75, 77 **Astros** 221 ip, 7–18, 4.93

Konieczny struck out a Southern League-leading 222 for Columbus in 1973. He was 6–13 in 1975, his only full year in the Astros' rotation, but suffered arm trouble throughout his career. /(MC)

Jim Konstanty [Casimir James] — 1917–1976. RHP 1944, 46, 48–56 Reds, Braves, **Phillies**, Yankees, Cardinals 945 ip, 66–48, 3.46. *1 WS 15 ip, 0–1, 2.40*
☛ *Most Valuable Player—50. All-Star—50.*

Ed Konetchy

Jim Konstanty

An all-around athlete from Syracuse University, Konstanty had brief trials with the Reds and Braves before finally developing a palmball and sticking with the Phillies in 1949, at age thirty-two. In 1950 he led Philadelphia to the pennant with 16 wins and 22 saves (both NL highs) in a then-record 74 appearances, all NL highs. He was the first relief pitcher to win the MVP award. After having relieved in 133 straight games for the Phillies, he started Game One of the 1950 WS and lost to the Yankees 1–0. Konstanty dropped a league-high 10 out of the bullpen in 1951, started 19 games in 1953, and saved 11 for the 1955 pennant-winning Yankees, but he never again approached the success of his MVP season. /(AL)

Ernie Koob — 1893–1941. LHP 1915–17, 19 **Browns** 500 ip, 23–30, 3.13

In 1916 Koob pitched a 17-inning scoreless tie against the Red Sox, losing a win when he failed to touch third while rounding the bases in the 15th inning. The next year, he won a 1–0 no-hitter against the White Sox. /(JK)

Cal Koonce — 1940– . RHP 1962–71 **Cubs**, Mets, Red Sox 970 ip, 47–49, 3.78

In mid-season of 1962, Cub rookie Koonce looked like a new Cy Young with a 9–1 mark. He finished the year 10–10 and never again reached double figures in wins. /(ARA)

Jerry Koosman — 1943– . LHP 1967–85 **Mets**, Twins, White Sox, Phillies 3839 ip, 222–209, 3.36. 20 wins: 76, 79 *3 LCS, 14 ip, 1–0, 6.43 2 WS, 26 ip, 3–0, 2.39*
☛ *All-Star—68–69.*

Known for his control throughout his career, Koosman led the International League in strikeouts in 1967, and in 1968 emerged as the Mets' lefthanded ace. He was NL Rookie Pitcher of the Year and

Jerry Koosman

runner-up to Johnny Bench for Rookie of the Year. He broke club records with 19 wins, seven shutouts, and a 2.08 ERA (all set by Tom Seaver the year before). All are still Met rookie records. He also fanned 62 times (in 91 at-bats), the most by a NL pitcher since 1900.

Seaver and Koosman became one of the league's top righty/lefty starting combos. As a sophomore, Koosman was 17–9 for the 1969 World Champions, and he beat Baltimore twice in the Series. He overcame arm problems in 1971 and was a hard-luck 14–15 (2.84) for the '73 pennant winners. Peaking in 1976, he recorded a 21–10 mark. But in 1977, Seaver was traded to the Reds, the Mets deteriorated, and Koosman went 8–20 to tie Phil Niekro for the league lead in losses. Koosman left the Mets as runner-up to Seaver or all-time club leader in ten pitching categories. Sent to the Twins in a December 1978 trade for Jesse Orosco, Koosman rebounded for a 20–13 record in 1979. In the strike-shortened 1981 season, his 13 losses for the Twins and White Sox were enough to tie for the AL lead. Recurring arm and shoulder trouble ended his career after two seasons with the Phillies. /(MC)

Larry Kopf [William Lorenz] — 1890–1986. SS-2B 1913–17, 19–23 Indians, A's, **Reds**, Braves 850 g, .249, 5 hr, 266 rbi. *1 WS, 8 g, .222, 2 rbi*

Kopf never hit .300 at any professional level, but on May 2, 1917 his 10th-inning single off Hippo Vaughn broke up the double no-hit duel between Vaughn and Fred Toney. Kopf came around to score the game's only run on Jim Thorpe's scratch single. Brother Wally Kopf played two games at third for the Giants. /(LRD)

Howie Koplitz — 1938– . RHP 1961–62, 64–66 Tigers, **Senators** 175 ip, 9–7, 4.21

The Tigers promoted Koplitz after his 23–3 performance with a no-hitter for Birmingham (Southern Association) in 1961. He won his first seven big league decisions, spanning 1961–65, but injured his shoulder in 1966. /(KT)

Joe Koppe [born Joseph Kopchia] — 1930– . SS-2B 1958–65 Braves, Phillies, **Angels** 578 g, .236, 19 hr, 141 rbi

In his rookie 1959 season, Koppe showed good range at shortstop and hit .261 with seven HR, seven triples, and 68 runs. They were to be career highs; he missed much of the next season with a wrist injury and never hit as well afterward. Traded to the expansion Angels in May 1961, he was their

regular shortstop for two seasons, before he lost the job to Jim Fregosi in 1963. Koppe spent the rest of his career as a utility infielder. /(SFS)

Leonard Koppett — 1923– . *Writer.*

Born in Moscow, Russia, Koppett came to the United States at age five and grew up one block from Yankee Stadium. His sportswriting career began with the New York *Herald-Tribune* in 1948. In 1954, he moved to the *Post* and in 1963 the *Times*. In 1975, Koppett left daily sportswriting to live in Palo Alto, California. In addition to many magazine articles, he wrote *Thinking Man's Guide to Baseball* in 1967. /(NLM)

Andy Kosco — 1941– . OF-1B 1965–74 Twins, Yankees, **Dodgers**, Brewers, Angels, Red Sox, Reds 658 g, .236, 73 hr, 267 rbi. *1 LCS, 3 g, .300*

Originally a Tiger bonus baby, the slugging outfielder played for seven other ML teams in ten years, usually as a part-timer. In 1969, his best year, he led the Dodgers with 19 homers and 74 RBI. He hit .300 for the Reds in the '73 NLCS. /(JCA)

Dave Koslo [born George Bernard Koslowski] — 1920–1975. LHP 1941–42, 46–55 **Giants**, Orioles, Braves 1591 ip, 92–107, 3.68. *1 WS, 15 ip, 1–1, 3.00*
☛ *Led League—era 49.*

After spending 1943–45 in the military, Koslo returned to the Giants in '46 to lead the NL with 19 losses, 35 starts, and 251 hits allowed. In 1949, he became the only pitcher to lead the league in ERA (2.50) without recording a shutout. Kelso beat the Yankees, 5–1, in the 1951 World Series opener, but lost the sixth and final game 4–3. /(RMu)

Sandy Koufax — 1935– . LHP 1955–66 **Dodgers** 2324, 165–87, 2.76. 20 wins: 63, 65–66 *4 WS, 57 ip, 4–3, 0.95*
☛ *Most Valuable Player—63. Led League—w 63, 65–66. Led League—era 62–66. Led League—k 61, 63, 65–66. Cy Young Award—63, 65–66. All-Star—61–66. Hall of Fame—1972.*

Koufax packed a Hall of Fame career into the final six of his dozen ML seasons. He was always a hard thrower, but control problems hobbled him during his early years. A Brooklyn high school baseball and basketball star, Koufax played both sports as a freshman at the University of Cincinnati, then signed a bonus contract with the Dodgers. Under the rules of the time, the club was forced to keep the 19-year-old on its ML roster.

Used little while the team was in Brooklyn,

Sandy Koufax

Koufax began to show flashes of brilliance once the Dodgers reached the West Coast. He was 11–11 in 1958 and tied the then-ML strikeout mark with 18 against the Giants on August 31, 1959. That season he lost a 1–0 game to the White Sox in the WS. Although only 8–13 in 1960, he struck out 197 batters in 175 innings.

Whether it was following the advice of part-time Dodger catcher Norm Sherry to ease up on his speed to achieve control or simply the maturing of a pitcher with great stuff, almost overnight Koufax became overpowering. In 1961, he went 18–13 and led the NL in strikeouts with 269. Between 1961 and 1966, he led the NL in wins and shutouts three times each, complete games twice, and strikeouts four times. His 382 strikeouts in 1965 set a new ML record. He led in ERA a record five consecutive years, with his best mark 1.73 in his final year. He pitched a no-hitter each season from 1962 to 1965, with the last a 1–0 perfect game against the Cubs on September 9, 1965. He led the Dodgers to pennants in 1963, 1965, and 1966, and won the NL Cy

Young Award each year. His 25–5 mark in 1963 also won him the MVP. Koufax and Don Drysdale formed one of baseball's all-time great lefty-righty duos. They held out as a "package" in 1966, forcing the Dodgers to meet their terms.

Koufax achieved success despite physical problems. A mysterious circulatory ailment in his pitching arm cost him half a season in 1962. Another arm injury in 1964 shortly led to an arthritic pitching elbow. After a 27–9 record in 1966, he retired at age thirty-one rather than risk crippling his arm. Five years later he became the youngest man to be elected to the Baseball Hall of Fame and only the sixth to achieve the honor in his first year of eligibility. /(JL)

Lou Koupal — 1898–1961. RHP 1925–26, 28–30, 37 Pirates, **Dodgers**, Phillies, Browns 335 ip, 10–21, 5.58

Koupal was not an overpowering pitcher, and he became accustomed to working with runners on base. He left the majors in 1930 and resurfaced at age thirty-eight with the pitching-poor 1937 Browns, going 4–9 with six complete games. /(FJO)

Ernie Koy (Chief) — 1909– . OF 1938–42 **Dodgers**, Cardinals, Reds, Phillies 556 g, .279, 36 hr, 260 rbi

Chief Koy, of Indian ancestry, was a powerfully built righthanded hitter with blazing speed. A Dodger regular in 1938 and 1939, he homered in his first ML at-bat (4/19/38). A son, Ernie Jr., played for the pro football Giants, 1965–70. /(LAW)

Masayaki Koyama — Unk.–Unk. P 1952–75 **Hanshin Tigers**

Koyama enjoyed the longest career of any Japanese pitcher by combining bull's-eye control with a baffling variety of motions, ranging from straight over-the-top to deep submarine. He "could throw strikes blindfolded," said Daryl Spencer. Nonetheless, Koyama walked Spencer four times on 16 consecutive balls in late 1965 to ensure that Katsuya Nomura, and not the American Spencer, would win the home run title. /(MC)

Al Kozar — 1922– . 2B 1948–50 **Senators**, White Sox 285 g, .254, 6 hr, 94 rbi

Kozar was the everyday second baseman of the Senators in his first season and hit .250 with 25 doubles. Batting just .200 in May 1950, he was a throw-in in a deal with the White Sox but was blocked by Nellie Fox's presence. /(SFS)

Joe Krakauskas — 1915-1960. LHP 1937-42, 46 **Senators**, Indians 583 ip, 26-36, 4.53

Among the few Quebecers to make the majors, Krakauskas was 11-17 at his most active, with the 1939 Senators. Traded to Cleveland for Ben Chapman after the 1940 season, he couldn't break into the deep Indians' rotation./(MC)

Jack Kralick — 1935- . LHP 1959-67 Senators/ Twins, **Indians** 1218 ip, 67-65, 3.56
☛ *All-Star—64.*

On August 26, 1962, pitching for Minnesota, Kralick no-hit the Athletics 1-0, retiring the first 25 batters. Traded to Cleveland for Jim Perry the following year, he recorded a career-high 14 wins./(JCA)

Jack Kramer — 1918- . RHP 1939-41, 43-51 **Browns**, Red Sox, Giants, Yankees 1637 ip, 95-103, 4.24. *1 WS, 11 ip, 1-0, 0.00*

Flunking in four shots with the Browns due to poor control, Kramer got a fifth chance, thanks to the WWII player shortage. He went 17-13 (2.49) for the 1944 pennant winners, adding a complete game victory in Game Three of the WS against the Cardinals. Traded to the Red Sox after 1947, he enjoyed an 18-5 season in '48, with an AL-best .783 winning percentage. Though he pitched with both pennant-winners in 1951, the Yankees and Giants, he didn't last to the Series with either./(MC)

Randy Kramer — 1960- . RHP 1988- **Pirates** 121 ip, 6-11, 4.08

Kramer struggled with his control when moved into the Pirates' rotation in 1989./(SFS)

Ed Kranepool (Krane) — 1944- . 1B-OF 1962-79 **Mets** 1853 g, .261, 118 hr, 614 rbi. *2 LCS, 4 g, .286, 3 rbi. 2 WS, 5 g, .143, 1 hr, 1 rbi*
☛ *All-Star—65.*

Kranepool signed with the Mets out of James Madison High in the Bronx for $85,000. Asked why the 6'3", lefthanded first baseman was being kept on the bench in 1962, manager Casey Stengel replied, "Listen. He's only seventeen and he runs like he's thirty." When, by nineteen, Kranepool hadn't developed as expected, a New York newspaper headline asked, "Is Ed Kranepool Over the Hill?" He en-

dured such taunts but later enjoyed glory. After six years, including the 1969 World Championship season, as the Mets' most regular first baseman, in 1970 hefty number 7 was sent to the minors, and considered retiring. But in 1971, he hit .280 with career highs in HR, RBI, and runs scored, and led the league with a .998 fielding average. He flowered as a pinch hitter late in his career, batting a ML-record .486 in 1974 (with a league-leading 17 pinch hits) and hit .396 in the role from 1974 through 1978. Kranepool played in each of the Mets' first 18 seasons, retiring as the all-time club leader in eight offensive categories. He made money away from baseball as a stockbroker and restaurateur./(KT)

Gene Krapp (Rubber, Rubber Arm) — 1887-1923. RHP 1911-12, 14-15 Indians, **Buffalo (FL)** 757 ip, 38-47, 3.23

Krapp led AL pitchers with 136 walks (in 215 innings) in his rookie 1911 season, but was the third-hardest to hit and went 13-9. His control worsened in 1912 (42 BB in 59 innings) and he was out of the majors until coming back in the Federal League, going 14-14 and 9-19 for the BufFeds./(JFC)

Harry Krause (Hal) — 1887-1940. LHP 1908-12 **A's**, Indians 525 ip, 37-26, 2.50
☛ *Led League—era 09.*

Krause won his first ten starts as a rookie in 1909; six of the ten wins were shutouts, and four of those were 1-0. He finished the season 18-8 with an AL-best 1.39 ERA, the ninth-best AL ERA ever and a record low for AL rookies. He still had to scrape for work on a staff that featured Jack Coombs and Hall of Famers Chief Bender and Eddie Plank, and he was 6-6 and 12-8 the following two seasons as the Athletics won consecutive World Championships. He didn't pitch in either WS. Krause was sent to the minors with a sore arm in 1912 and found a home in the Pacific Coast League, winning 249 games there in 16 seasons. Overall, he won 337 games in his professional career./(NLM)

Lew Krausse [Lewis Bernard, Jr.] — 1943- . RHP 1961, 64-74 **A's**, Brewers, Red Sox, Cardinals, Braves 1284 ip, 68-91, 4.00

Krausse was signed by his father, an A's scout and a former Philadelphia Athletics pitcher, for a $125,000 bonus in 1961. Just days out of high school, the raw youngster was immediately brought to Kansas City by A's owner Charlie Finley. Krausse shut out the Angels in his first pro start, but after 12 ML games he was sent to the minors for seasoning. Krausse wasn't a ML winner until 1966 (14–9, 2.99). Known as a rowdy playboy, he was a leading figure in the "war" between Finley and his players in 1967, and his record dropped to 7–17. /(JCA)

Ken Kravec — 1951– . LHP 1975–82 **White Sox**, Cubs 859 ip, 43–56, 4.46

Kravec led White Sox pitchers in strikeouts from 1977 to 1979. He was 15–13 in 1979, his best season. Back problems reduced his effectiveness from 1980 through the end of his career. /(JCA)

Danny Kravitz (Dusty, Beak) — 1930– . C 1956–60 **Pirates**, A's 215 g, .236, 10 hr, 54 rbi

A lefthanded-hitting defensive specialist, Kravitz was a third-string catcher with the Pirates and, in 1960, the A's. His first ML homer came with the bases filled to seal a 6–5 Pirate win in 1956. /(JL)

Mike Kreevich (Iron Mike) — 1908– . OF-3B 1931, 35–45 Cubs, **White Sox**, A's, Browns, Senators 1238 g, .283, 45 hr, 514 rbi. *1 WS, 6 g, .231*
☛ *All-Star—38.*

There were two outstanding AL rookies in 1936. Joe DiMaggio was the other. Kreevich, originally signed by the Cubs, quietly hit .307 for the White Sox that year. His 16 triples in 1937 were the league high. He was a consistent .300 hitter early on, with stellar defensive work in centerfield. Thanks to his powerful throwing arm, he led NL outfielders with 18 assists in 1939. But after a two-year slump at the plate, Kreevich was sent to the A's in a December 1941 deal for Wally Moses. Kreevich was only the second player in history to ground into four double plays in a game, on August 4, 1939 against the Senators. /(RL)

Ray Kremer [Remy Peter] (Wiz) — 1893–1965. RHP 1924–33 **Pirates** 1954 ip, 143–85, 3.76. 20 wins: 26, 30 *2 WS, 26 ip, 2–2, 3.12*
☛ *Led League—w 26, 30. Led League—era 26–27.*

An immediate success in 1924, Kremer went 18–10 for Pittsburgh, tying for the NL lead with 41 appearances and four shutouts. He later tied for the league high in wins with 20 in both 1926 and 1930, led the NL in ERA in 1926 and '27, and in starts (38), innings (276) and hits (366) in 1930. A two-fisted drinker, Kremer was known to tear up a Pullman car and throw his teammates' shoes out the

window en route to the next city. But he had 15 or more wins for seven straight years. After pitching a complete game victory in Game Six of the 1925 WS, he returned to defeat the Senators in the clincher with four innings of relief work. /(NLM)

Wayne Krenchicki (Chick) — 1954– . 3B-1B-2B-SS 1979–86 Orioles, **Reds**, Tigers, Expos 550 g, .266, 15 hr, 124 rbi

A strong defensive player trained at three infield positions in the Orioles organization, the lefthanded-hitting Krenchicki never was a front-liner because he couldn't handle lefthanded pitching. He batted just .188 lifetime against lefties, with no extra-base hits. /(JCA)

Red Kress [Ralph] — 1907–1962. SS-3B-1B-OF-2B 1927–36, 38–40, 46 **Browns**, White Sox, Senators, Tigers, Giants 1391 g, .286, 89 hr, 799 rbi

Ebullient Red Kress led AL shortstops in fielding in 1929, but in errors in 1930. The Browns moved him off SS so Jim Levey could move in; Levey, in turn, led the league in errors. The next season, St. Louis traded Kress (after three seasons of hitting over .300 with over 100 RBI a year) to the White Sox, who were unveiling Luke Appling at SS. Kress therefore adapted to whatever position he had to, even pitching, to the detriment of his batting average. The Senators got him next and he competed with Joe Cronin, who was not only the shortstop but the manager; Cronin released Kress. After he spent 1937 in Minneapolis (American Association), hitting .330 and leading shortstops in total chances, the Browns reacquired him. Played at short, he responded by hitting .302 and leading the league in fielding. Traded to Detroit in 1939, he broke his leg during the season. In 1940, the pennant-bound Tigers released the hard-luck Kress. He loved baseball enough to quit after coaching for the hapless 1962 Mets. That November, his heart gave out. /(JK)

Lou Kretlow — 1923– . RHP 1946, 48–56 Tigers, **Browns/Orioles**, White Sox, A's 785 ip, 27–47, 4.87

The Tigers gave Kretlow a $35,000 bonus to sign in January 1946, but he never managed more than a half-dozen wins in any of his ten ML seasons. /(FK)

Frank Kreutzer — 1939– . LHP 1962–66, 69 White Sox, **Senators** 210 ip, 8–18, 4.40

First signed by the Red Sox, Villanova's Kreutzer was in and out of the Senator rotation from 1964 to 1966, struggling with control. He then spent two disappointing years with hometown Buffalo (International League). /(MC)

Paul Krichell — 1882–1957. C 1911–12 **Browns** 85 g, .222, 0 hr, 16 rbi

Krichell had fewer than 250 ML at-bats as a reserve catcher with the Browns, but he became one of the greatest scouts in ML history. After coaching for the Red Sox in 1919, Krichell was hired by Ed Barrow to scout for the Yankees in 1920 and remained with them until his death in 1957. He was director of scouting and chief scout beginning in 1946. He discovered Yankee Hall of Famers Lou Gehrig and Whitey Ford, as well as standouts like Tony Lazzeri, Mark Koenig, and Vic Raschi. /(FVP)

Howie Krist (Spud) — 1916– . RHP 1937–38, 41–43, 46 **Cardinals** 444 ip, 37–11, 3.32. *1 WS, 0 ip, 0–0, --*

Krist's 10–0 record in 1941, his first full season, is the third-best undefeated season ever. Usually a reliever, he threw three shutouts in 1943, but arm trouble and a two-year army hitch ended his effectiveness. /(FJO)

Gary Kroll — 1941– . RHP 1964–66, 69 Phillies, **Mets**, Astros, Indians 159 ip, 6–7, 4.24

A fireballing giant with a deceptive motion, Kroll pitched two no-hitters in the minors and once struck out 309 batters in a season. As a nervous ML rookie, however, he committed a league-leading four balks in just 24 innings. /(JL)

Bill Krueger — 1958– . LHP 1983– **A's**, Dodgers, Brewers 541 ip, 30–33, 4.44

A 6'5" basketball player at Portland (Oregon) University, Krueger did not begin pitching until his junior year. He joined the A's rotation in 1983 and was 6–5 on June 25 when he strained a forearm muscle; scouts said he lost his best stuff with the injury. Traded to the Dodgers in 1987, he threw a seven-inning no-hitter for Albuquerque (Pacific Coast League) against Phoenix that August 14. /(JCA)

Ernie Krueger — 1890–1976. C 1913, 15, 17–21, 25 Indians, Yankees, Giants, **Dodgers**, Reds 318 g, .263, 11 hr, 93 rbi. *1 WS, 4 g, .167*

A backup receiver, the native of Illinois had better than average speed and power. He appeared with Brooklyn in the 1920 WS against Cleveland. /(EM)

Otto Krueger [Arthur William] (Oom Paul) — 1876–1961. SS-3B-OF 1899–1905 Cleveland (NL), **Cardinals**, Pirates, Phillies 507 g, .251, 5 hr, 196 rbi

Krueger was a regular infielder for two years with the Cardinals before being traded in 1903 to the pennant-winning Pirates, where he was used as a utility man. He missed the 1903 World Series, the first between the NL and AL, because he was in the hospital after being beaned in a late-season game against his former Cardinal teammates. /(BC)

Art Kruger — 1881–1949. OF 1907, 10, 14–15 Reds, Indians, Braves, **Kansas City (FL)** 365 g, .232, 6 hr, 115 rbi

Kruger failed to hit in the National and American leagues and was earning $275 a month with Los Angeles (Pacific Coast League) when he joined the Kansas City Packers of the newly formed Federal League to have his only respectable season in 1914. /(NLM)

John Kruk — 1961– . 1B-OF 1986– **Padres**, Phillies 492 g, .290, 41 hr, 217 rbi

The 5'10" 195-lb Kruk looks quite unathletic but hit over .300 his first two seasons. His best season was 1987, when he hit .313 with 20 HR, 91 RBI, and 18 stolen bases. He slumped to .241 in 1988 but rebounded to .300 in 1989 and was traded to the Phillies in mid-season. /(WOR)

Mike Krukow — 1952– . RHP 1976– Cubs, Phillies, **Giants** 2190 ip, 124–117, 3.90. 20 wins: 86 *1 LCS, 9 ip, 1–0, 2.00*
☛ *All-Star—86.*

After nine seasons as a consistent but unspectacular starter, Krukow starred for the Giants in 1986, recording career bests in wins (20), ERA (3.05), and strikeouts (178) and finishing third in the NL Cy Young balloting. Prior to 1986 the 6'5" curveballer rarely completed games and had never won more than 13 games despite making regular starts for whichever team he played for. In 1987–89 he was hampered by injuries, winning only 16 games. Krukow's 20 wins in 1986 were the most by a Giants pitcher since Ron Bryant won 24 in 1973. /(SCL)

Dick Kryhoski — 1925– . 1B 1949–55 Yankees, Tigers, **Browns/Orioles**, A's 569 g, .265, 45 hr, 231 rbi

Kryhoski and Roy Sievers shared first base for the Browns in 1953, the last year of the team's existence. Kryhoski was involved in baseball's biggest trade ever, a 17-player, two-part 1954 deal between the Orioles and Yankees. /(RM)

Tony Kubek — 1936– . SS-OF 1957–65 **Yankees** 1092 g, .266, 57 hr, 373 rbi. *6 WS, 37 g, .240 2 hr, 10 rbi* ☛ *Rookie of the Year—57. All-Star—58, 59, 61.*

Kubek was the AL Rookie of the Year in 1957, hitting .297 and showing amazing versatility as he spent substantial time in the outfield, at shortstop, and at third base, with brief early stints at second base and first base as well. He displaced Gil McDougald and became the Yankees' regular shortstop in 1958. For eight seasons he and second baseman Bobby Richardson formed one of baseball's best double-play combinations. In 1961, Kubek cracked 38 doubles (a Yankees record for shortstops), and in his first at-bat after returning from the army late in 1962, he delivered a three-run home run. Kubek appeared in six WS with the Yankees. Playing in his hometown of Milwaukee, he hit a pair of homers in Game Three of the 1957 Series against the Braves. And in Game Seven of the 1960 WS he was victimized by one of the most famous bad hops in history. An apparently tailor-made double-play ball skipped up and hit Kubek in the throat, prolonging a five-run eighth-inning Pittsburgh rally that set the stage for Bill Mazeroski's Series-winning home run in the bottom of the ninth. A dangerous neck and back condition forced Kubek to retire at the age of twenty-nine, but he quickly became one of television's most successful baseball announcers. Kubek remained extremely friendly, popular, and respected long after his playing days ended. /(MG)

Ted Kubiak — 1942– . 2B-SS-3B 1967–76 **A's,** Brewers, Cardinals, Rangers, Padres 977 g, .231, 13 hr, 202 rbi. *2 LCS, 7 g, .333, 1 rbi. 2 WS, 8 g, .167*

Kubiak four times led his minor league in putouts, assists, and double plays at shortstop, prompting A's owner Charles O. Finley to shift All-Star shortstop Bert Campaneris to the outfield. After Campaneris balked, Kubiak was traded to the Brewers before the 1970 season. He returned to Oakland to become their infield reserve for three World Championships (1972–74). /(MC)

Johnny Kucab (Yats) — 1919–1977. RHP 1950–52 **A's** 152 ip, 5–5, 4.44

Kucab made just three starts in his 59 major league appearances, but one, on the final day of the 1950 season, was his first win, and Connie Mack's last game as a ML manager. /(LAW)

Jack Kucek [John Andrew] — 1953– . RHP 1974–80 **White Sox**, Phillies, Blue Jays 206 ip, 7–16, 5.10

A 90-mph fastball vaulted the articulate speech major to the majors for nine games in his first pro season but couldn't keep him there. Impressive minor league ERAs and a 1978 Iowa no-hitter won him yearly trials with the White Sox from 1974 to 1979. /(JCA)

Johnny Kucks — 1933– . RHP 1955–60 **Yankees,** A's 938 ip, 54–56, 4.10. *4 WS, 19 ip, 1–0, 1.89*

A 6'3" sidearmer, Kucks had a sensational sophomore year in 1956, going 18–9 for the Yankees with a spectacular, three-hit shutout of the Dodgers in Game Seven of the World Series. He never had another winning season. /(GW)

Harvey Kuenn — 1930–1988. OF-SS-3B 1952–66 **Tigers**, Indians, Giants, Cubs, Phillies 1833 g, .303, 87 hr, 671 rbi. *1 WS, 4 g, .083.*
   Manager 1975, 82–83 **Brewers** 160–118, .576. First place: 82 *1 LCS, 3–2, .600. 1 WS, 3–4, .429*
☛ *Rookie of the Year—53. Led League—ba 59. All-Star—53–60.*

The unassuming, broad-faced Tiger bonus baby reached the majors in his first pro season after just 63 games in the low minors. En route to the 1953

Harvey Kuenn

Rookie of the Year Award, Kuenn hit .308 with a league-leading 209 hits, setting a ML rookie record with 679 at-bats and an AL rookie record with 167 singles. Smooth and consistent, Kuenn was Detroit's shortstop from 1953 to 1957 and then switched to the outfield. A line-drive hitter, he led the AL in hits four times and won the league batting title in 1959 with a .353 mark. Traded to Cleveland the next year for home run champion Rocky Colavito, he was booed by Indian fans who blamed him for Colavito's departure. Nevertheless, Kuenn hit .308. He spent the remainder of his playing career in the NL and retired after the 1966 season with 2,092 hits.

Made a Brewer coach in 1972, the native of Milwaukee overcame heart and stomach surgery and the amputation of his right leg below the knee. In June 1982 he took over as manager of the fifth-place Brewers. He took the team, known as "Harvey's Wallbangers" for their heavy hitting, to the 1982 World Series, where they lost in seven games to St. Louis. Kuenn was named Manager of the Year./(JCA)

Joe Kuhel — 1906–1984. 1B 1930–47 **Senators,** White Sox 2105 g, .277, 131 hr, 1049 rbi. *1 WS, 5 g, .150, 1 rbi.*
Manager 1948–49 **Senators** 106–201, .345

The Comiskeys took a lot of heat for trading away colorful Zeke Bonura in 1938, but the deal brought the AL's best-fielding first baseman to the White Sox for the worst. Whatever Joe Kuhel lacked in flamboyance, he made up for with his steady, reliable defense. In time, Chicago fans accepted him.

Kuhel moved into the Senators' lineup in 1931. In the pennant year of 1933, he enjoyed his finest season, hitting .322 and leading AL first basemen in putouts. He never batted that high with Chicago, but he did hit 27 HR in 1940 (by far his most) and continued to excel with the glove. In a July 20, 1941 doubleheader against the Athletics, he recorded 17 putouts in the first game, and 23 in the second, eclipsing a 35-year-old record held by Hal Chase. He was a fearless player, who once took on Eldon Auker and the entire Browns team after being skulled by a high hard one. Kuhel managed the Senators to seventh- and eighth-place finishes in 1948 and 1949./(RL)

Bowie Kuhn — 1926– . *Executive*

As baseball's Commissioner from 1969 to 1984, Kuhn presided over the sport's period of greatest affluence but also, paradoxically, one of its most strife-ridden eras. With the major leagues threatened by a players' strike before the 1969 season and with

the office of the Commissioner vacant after the firing of General Eckert in December 1968, the owners hired Kuhn, a lawyer for the National League and a favorite of Dodgers owner Walter O'Malley. In the style that he would use throughout his three terms, Kuhn verbally placated the owners and then gave in to all the Players Association demands. He dealt with the controversial Curt Flood case at the end of the year, denying Flood's request to overturn the reserve clause and, more specifically, allow Flood to circumvent a trade that had sent him from the contending Cardinals to the cellar-dwelling Phillies.

Kuhn went on to withstand a spring training strike in 1972 that cut into the start of the season, and he forced the owners to abandon a pre-season lockout in 1976 following a pro-player decision by

Bowie Kuhn

an independent arbitrator in the Messersmith-Mc-Nally challenge to the reserve clause. Kuhn had advised against the use of an arbitrator in the case, his law background perhaps leading him to realize what shaky ground the owners were on. Kuhn forestalled a player strike in 1980, but was unable to prevent the mid-season strike of 1981, when the owners stood firm in an ultimately unsuccessful rear-guard action against free agency.

Despite his frequent, albeit forced, accomodations of player demands, Kuhn was perceived as a tool of the owners and as overmatched by the head of the Players Association, Marvin Miller. Kuhn regularly chided the players for their demands, called them overpaid, and preached of the potential evils of free agency, all stances pleasing to his employers, the owners. But Kuhn's officious, pompous manner gained him enemies beyond the ranks of the players. His handling of an investigation of Cubs manager Leo Durocher ended in personal, although largely private, embarrassment. Writer Red Smith excoriated Kuhn in many columns, producing such bon mots during the 1981 strike as "this strike wouldn't have happened if Bowie Kuhn were alive today" and "an empty car pulled up and Bowie Kuhn got out." Kuhn also feuded with A's owner Charlie Finley, who referred to Kuhn as a "village idiot" and then apologized for the offense to village idiots. Kuhn vetoed some of Finley's innovations, and in 1973 he prevented Finley from vindictively placing second baseman Mike Andrews on the DL during the World Series following a costly error. Their biggest clash came when Kuhn voided the sales, and lopsided trades involving cash, of A's stars Vida Blue, Joe Rudi, and others. The players were going to leave Oakland as free agents to escape Finley's tyrannical ownership, and Finley was trying to get some value for them. Many owners in the past had sold off their stars; Connie Mack, who had guided the A's for a half-century, was famous for breaking up his great teams. But Kuhn ruled that Finley's deals were not "in the best interests of baseball." Kuhn also suspended Yankees owner George Steinbrenner for a year after he was convicted of perjury and making illegal contributions to the election campaign of Richard Nixon, and suspended Braves owner Ted Turner for tampering.

Kuhn may ultimately be remembered for the spectacular growth of baseball in the 1970s and 1980s, a period that began with expansion in 1969, the same year Kuhn became Commissioner. Attendance in 1980 was more than triple what it had been in 1968, and television revenue was up more than $10 million dollars in the same period. But the eagerness of baseball to bow to the demands of network TV resulted in concessions criticized by purists. The most notable of these concessions was night baseball during the World Series. The first such game, in 1971, found Kuhn attending bareheaded and coatless despite the cold weather, with the cameras frequently focusing on him in an attempt to deny the effects of the temperature. /(WOR)

Duane Kuiper — 1950- . 2B 1974-85 **Indians**, Giants 1057 g, .271, 1 hr, 263 rbi

An outstanding fielder who twice led AL second basemen in fielding percentage, Kuiper's disciplined hitting style made him a fine spoiler: three times (against Andy Hassler, Nolan Ryan, and Ron Guidry), he was the only man to get a hit. On August 29, 1977 after 1,381 ML at-bats without a home run, he finally popped one, off Steve Stone. In his remaining 1,997 plate appearances, the lean infielder managed (intentionally, he contends) to not hit another one. The clowning Kuiper took a warped pride in his accomplishment, saying: "One is better than none, but any more than that and people start expecting them." /(JCA)

Won Kuk Lee (Ernesto) — Unk. - . P, Minor and Mexican Leagues

A Korean, Kuk Lee was signed in 1964 by the San Francisco Giants organization, who also signed Masanori Murakami that year. He pitched ambidextrously, earning brief looks in spring training. After the Giants released him, he concentrated on pitching righthanded, changed his name to Ernesto, married a Mexican woman, grew a handlebar mustache, and, playing into the 1980s, won more than 150 Mexican League games. /(MC)

Bill Kunkel — 1936-1985. RHP 1961-63 A's, Yankees 142 ip, 6-6, 4.29.
Umpire AL 1968-85 *4 LCS 2 WS 2 ASU*

Kunkel had a brief fling as a ML reliever. His most active year was 1961, when he appeared in 58 games for the A's. He turned to umpiring and reached the ML in 1968. It was Kunkel who discovered pitcher Rick Honeycutt doctoring the baseball with a tack wedged inside a Band-Aid on his right hand. "I grabbed his hand and got stuck," Kunkel explained. Honeycutt received a 10-day suspension. During 1984 spring training, Kunkel's son Jeff, a member of the Rangers, brought the lineup card to the plate the only time father and son have appeared in the same ML game as umpire and player. Kunkel was also a college basketball referee for 20 years. /(RTM)

Jeff Kunkel — 1962– . SS-2B-3B-OF 1984– **Rangers** 238 g, .241, 15 hr, 55 rbi

Kunkel is the son of Bill Kunkel, whose umpiring career overlapped the first season of Jeff's ML career. Jeff was the third pick in the nation in the June 1983 draft, but his offense was too weak for a regular job and he became a utility man. /(JFC)

Whitey Kurowski [George John] — 1918– . 3B-SS-2B 1941–49 **Cardinals** 916 g, .286, 106 hr, 529 rbi. *4 WS, 23 g, .253, 1 hr, 9 rbi*
☛ *All-Star—43–44, 46.*

A stocky, thick-legged infielder with surprising speed, Kurowski overcame childhood osteomyelitis (which made his right arm shorter than his left) to become one of the finest third basemen of the 1940s. Kurowski led the NL three times in putouts, twice in fielding average, and once each in assists and double plays. He displayed power, hitting 20 or more home runs in three different seasons. His ninth-inning homer off Yankee pitcher Red Ruffing in Game Five of the 1942 World Series broke a 2–2 tie to clinch the championship for the Cardinals.

Kurowski reached career highs of 27 HR and 104 RBI in 1947, his last season playing regularly, and batted over .300 three times (1945–47). An arm injury in 1948 and an elbow injury in 1949 combined to end his career. /(LAW)

Emil Kush — 1916–1969. RHP 1941–42, 46–49 **Cubs** 346 ip, 21–12, 3.48

Kush "had a natural sidearm sinker and a pretty good curve," according to Cubs manager Charlie Grimm, who recommended Chicago sign him after he tried out on a whim. He pitched mostly in relief and was 9–2 in 1946 and 8–3 the next year before arm trouble and an operation curtailed his career. Considered something of a jinxed pitcher, he often spoke of a 1948 incident. With the Cubs leading by two runs in the ninth with two out and two on, his centerfielder knocked himself cold crashing into the wall pursuing a fly ball. Before another outfielder recovered the ball, the batter circled the bases for a game-winning homer. /(BC)

Craig Kusick — 1948– . 1B-DH 1973–79 **Twins**, Blue Jays 497 g, .235, 46 hr, 171 rbi

A brawny long-ball hitter and a slow, deficient fielder, Kusick split his time among first base, DH, and pinch hitter. He saw the most action in 1977, when he posted career highs of 12 homers and 45 RBI in 115 games. /(JCA)

Randy Kutcher — 1960– . OF-SS 1986– **Giants**, Red Sox 181 g, .227, 9 hr, 35 rbi

Alaskan-born Kutcher saw the most action in 1986, when he hit .237 in 71 games as a utility man for the Giants. He went to the Red Sox after the 1987 as the player to be named later in return for Dave Henderson. /(SFS)

Marty Kutyna — 1932– . RHP 1959–62 A's, **Senators** 290 ip, 14–16, 3.88

Kutyna was 14–10 for Portland (Pacific Coast League) as a starter in 1959, then allowed no earned runs in his four-game debut as an Athletics reliever. He appeared in at least 50 games in each of his three remaining seasons. /(MC)

Bob Kuzava (Sarge) — 1923– . LHP 1946–47, 49–55, 57 Indians, White Sox, Senators, **Yankees**, Orioles, Phillies, Pirates, Cardinals 862 ip, 49–44, 4.05. *3 WS, 4 ip, 0–0, 2.08*

Kuzava rose to sergeant during WWII, then tried unsuccessfully to crack the Indians rotation. Traded to the White Sox, he went 10–6 as a rookie in 1949. By mid-1951, he was a Yankee spot starter and long reliever, going 11–7. In the final game of the '51 WS, he retired the Giants with the bases loaded to record a save, and in Game Seven of the '52 Series, set down the last eight Dodgers for another. The latter performance was especially notable; lefthanders weren't supposed to be able to beat the Dodgers, who featured a righthanded lineup with the exception of Duke Snider, especially not in Ebbets Field. But manager Casey Stengel played his hunch and proved correct.

In a rare 1953 start, he lost a no-hitter against the White Sox with one out in the ninth. /(MC)

Chet Laabs — 1912–1983. OF 1937–47 Tigers, **Browns**, A's 950 g, .262, 117 hr, 509 rbi. *1 WS, 5 g, .200* ☛ *All-Star—43.*

The stocky Laabs was a wartime hero for the St. Louis Browns when they won their only pennant in 1944. Used sparingly all season, he had only three home runs before he hit two against the Yankees on the season's last day to win the pennant-clinching game.

Laabs had good power, finishing second in the AL in 1942 with 27 HR. He had a knack for timely hits, leading the AL in pinch hits in 1940. But he was strikeout prone and led the AL (105) in 1943. In 1938, when Cleveland's Bob Feller struck out 18 Tigers, Laabs was a five-time victim. /(JK)

Clem Labine — 1926– . RHP 1950–62 **Dodgers**, Tigers, Pirates, Mets 1079 ip, 77–56, 3.63. *5 WS, 31 ip, 2–2, 3.16* ☛ *All-Star—56–57.*

The free-spirited sinkerballer was one of baseball's premier relievers in the 1950s. The durable Labine helped the Dodgers to four pennants in Brooklyn and another in Los Angeles. Labine was 13–5 in a NL-leading 60 appearances for the 1955 World Champions and led the league in saves the next two seasons. He retired Dodger-killer Stan Musial 49 consecutive times. After leaving the Dodgers, Labine pitched for the Pirates in the 1960 WS.

Two of Labine's brightest moments came in the unaccustomed role of a starter, a 10–0 victory over the Giants in the second game of the 1951 NL playoff and a 1–0 10-inning shutout of the Yankees in Game Six of the 1956 WS. Although never a threat at bat, Labine's three hits in 1955 were all home runs. /(LAW)

Coco Laboy [Jose Alberto] — 1939– . 3B 1969–73 **Expos** 420 g, .233, 28 hr, 166 rbi

As a 29-year-old rookie, Laboy led the Expos with 83 RBI in the team's inaugural season. After a second-year slump (.199), the popular Puerto Rican was relegated to the bench. /(LAW)

Bob Lacey — 1953– . LHP 1977–81, 83–84 **A's**, Indians, Rangers, Angels, Giants 451 ip, 20–29, 3.67

The 6'5" Lacey debuted with Oakland in 1977 and worked 33 innings before allowing an earned run. In 1978 he led the American League with 74 appearances. He was used only 47 times by manager Billy Martin in 1980 but recorded a 2.93 ERA. On the last day of the '80 season, he was given his first ML start, pitched a complete-game shutout, and apparently ruined his arm. He bounced around, was often disabled, and was never again consistent. /(MC)

Candy LaChance [George Joseph] — 1870–1932. 1B 1893–99, 1901–05 **Dodgers**, Baltimore NL, Indians, Red Sox; 1263 g, .280, 39 HR, 690 RBI. *1 WS, 8 g, .222*

A bull-like man who prided himself on his strength, LaChance belied his nickname with a sour disposition. He once challenged Rube Waddell to a wrestling match before a game. After an hour, Waddell pinned him, then went out and pitched a shutout while LaChance recuperated on the bench. /(JK)

Marcel Lachemann — 1941– . RHP 1969–71 **A's** 101 ip, 7–4, 3.45

A pitching star at the University of Southern California, in the majors Lachemann was used exclusively in relief. His brother Rene was a ML player, coach, and manager. /(LAW)

Pete LaCock — 1952– . 1B-OF 1972–80 Cubs, **Royals** 715 g, .257, 27 hr, 224 rbi. *3 LCS, 6 g, .333, 1 rbi. 1 WS, 1 g, --*

The son of TV game-show host Peter Marshall, LaCock was the American Association MVP in 1974 (.327, 23 HR, 91 RBI). The 6'2" lefthander hit .364 in the 1978 LCS. He left the majors in 1981 to play in Japan. /(TL)

Frank LaCorte — 1951– . RHP 1975–84 Braves, **Astros**, Angels 490 ip, 23–44, 5.01. *1 LCS, 3 ip, 1–1, 3.00*

This curveballer had chronic arm trouble, spending parts of four seasons and all of one (1985) on the disabled list. A starter with Atlanta, he was demoted after going 1–8 in 1977. Traded to the Astros in

1979, he became a reliever, and he excelled in 1980. He was 5–0 with eight saves and a 0.90 ERA at the All-Star break, but tendinitis in his shoulder (which eventually ended his career) caused a second-half slump; he finished 8–5, with 11 saves and a 2.82 ERA. /(MC)

Mike LaCoss (Buffy) — 1956– . RHP 1978– Reds, Astros, Royals, **Giants** 1615 ip, 91–94, 3.93. *3 LCS, 8 ip, 0–1, 5.63. 1 WS, 4 ip, 0–0, 6.23*
☛ *All-Star—79.*

A resilient, versatile finesse pitcher, LaCoss was waived by the Reds after 1981 and released by the Royals after 1985 before making the Giants staff as a nonroster invitee to spring training in 1986. He led San Francisco's 1987 NL West champions with 13 wins, and after an injury-plagued 1988, began the 1989 season as the Giants' bullpen stopper. The success of Craig Lefferts in relief and injuries to many starters moved LaCoss into the rotation; he finished 10–10 with a 3.17 ERA as the Giants won the NL pennant.

LaCoss enjoyed his best season at age twenty-three, going 14–9 with the NL West champion Reds in 1979 and pitching in the All-Star Game. But by 1983 he was a struggling reliever and occasional starter with the Astros, and he posted a 5.09 ERA in 1985. In 1985 he hit his only two ML home runs in consecutive at-bats. /(SCL)

Lee Lacy — 1948– . OF-2B 1972–87 Dodgers, Braves, **Pirates**, Orioles 1523 g, .286, 91 hr, 458 rbi. *3 LCS, 4 g, .333. 4 WS, 13 g, .231, 3 rbi*

Lee Lacy was a utility man for years before getting steady outfield play. A dependable pinch-hitter, Lacy hit five pinch home runs in 1978, including a ML record-tying three in a row. The free swinger was a fair number-two batter with his speed and hitting prowess. He was briefly the starting second baseman of the 1973 Dodgers until Davey Lopes took over. Full-time duty seemed to beckon in 1976, after a trade to Atlanta, but Lacy was dealt back to Los Angeles in June. He went to Pittsburgh as a free agent in 1979. The righthander batted .304 in six seasons with Pirates, with extensive playing time from 1982 to 1984. The final year included a NL-high .996 fielding percentage in the outfield. Defensively, his speed and strong arm were his best assets. /(ME)

Pete Ladd (Bigfoot) — 1956– . RHP 1979, 82–86 Astros, **Brewers**, Mariners 287 ip, 17–23, 4.14. *1 LCS, 3 ip, 0–0, 0.00. 1 WS, 1 ip, 0–0, 0.00*

Ladd was a one-year phenom. A hard-throwing

sinker-slider pitcher with a herky-jerky motion, he was an intimidating presence with his long hair, beard, and 6'3″ 240-lb physique. He saved 25 games for the 1983 Brewers, replacing the injured Rollie Fingers, but was hit hard in 1984 (5.24 ERA). By the end of 1985 he was back in the minors. In the 1982 LCS, he saved two games and was runner-up in the series MVP voting. /(JCA)

Doyle Lade (Porky) — 1921– . RHP 1946–50 **Cubs** 537 ip, 25–29, 4.39

The corpulent Cub was 11–10 as a rookie in 1947 but never won more than five or had an ERA under 4.00 after that. A switch-hitter in his first two seasons, he had a lifetime .220 BA and was considered a good-hitting pitcher. /(AA)

Ed Lafitte (Doc) — 1886–1971. RHP 1909, 11–12, 14–15 Tigers, **Brooklyn (FL)**, Buffalo (FL) 647 ip, 35–36, 3.34

After an 11–8 season with the 1911 Tigers, Lafitte told manager Hugh Jennings that he wanted to leave early the following season to resume dental school. Jennings told him if he left early to keep on going. Lafitte did. He became a dentist, but also pitched in the Federal League. With the Brooklyn Tip-Tops, he pitched the Feds' first no-hitter, defeating Kansas City 6–2 on September 19, 1914 (walking seven), and went 16–16 with a 2.63 ERA but led the league in walks (127 in 291 innings). /(NLM)

Lerrin LaGrow — 1948– . RHP 1970, 72–80 **Tigers**, Cardinals, White Sox, Dodgers, Phillies 779 ip, 34–55, 4.11. *1 LCS, 1 ip, 0–0, 0.00*

LaGrow earned his first call-up to the majors by being named Southern League Player of the Year in 1970. In his only two seasons as a starting pitcher, he went 8–19 (1974) and 7–14 (1975), prompting the Tigers to give up on him. After returning to the AL with the White Sox in 1977, he was the ace of their bullpen for two seasons; he finished third in the AL with 25 saves in '77. /(WOR)

Joe Lahoud (Duck) — 1947– . OF-DH 1968–78 **Red Sox**, Brewers, Angels, Rangers, Royals; 791 g, .223, 65 hr, 218 rbi. *1 LCS, 1 g, .000*

Lahoud was rushed to the Red Sox from Class A in 1968 to replace the injured Tony Conigliaro in right field, but had trouble hitting curves. Although he surpassed the league BA only once (in 1974 with .271) in 11 seasons of platooning, his power produced seasons of 14, 12, and 13 homers in 1971–74. He hit three in one game for the Red Sox on June 11, 1969. /(MC)

Jeff Lahti — 1956- . RHP 1982-86 **Cardinals** 286 ip, 17-11, 3.12. *1 LCS, 2 ip, 1-0, 0.00. 2 WS, 5 ip, 0-0, 11.81*

With the pennant-bound 1985 Cardinals, Lahti was brilliant with 19 saves and a 1.84 ERA. He retired 27 consecutive batters during one stretch, and he was the winner in Game Five of the LCS. Recurring shoulder damage ended his career. /(FO)

Nap Lajoie (Larry) — 1874-1959. 2B-1B-SS 1896-16 Phillies, A's, **Indians** 2475 g, .339, 82 hr, 1599 rbi.
   Manager 1905-09 **Indians** 397-330, .546
☛ *Led League—ba 01, 04-05. Led League—hr 01. Led League—rbi 98, 01, 04 . Hall of Fame—1937.*

One of the most powerful and consistent right-handed hitters of the dead-ball era, Lajoie is often rated the greatest second baseman in baseball history. Handsome, graceful, talented, and popular with both fans and teammates, he was an important figure in the launching of the AL and the survival of the Cleveland franchise. In 1937, he became the sixth player elected to the Hall of Fame.

Lajoie joined the NL Phillies during the 1896 season and played first base in 39 games. The following year he became a regular, hit .363, and led the NL in slugging percentage (.578). He moved to second base in 1898 and led the league in RBI (127) and doubles (40).

In 1901 he jumped across town to the new AL Athletics of Connie Mack, giving the fledgling league instant credibility. Although the young AL was not yet on a par with the established NL, Lajoie's batting marks were nevertheless exceptional. He led in hits (229), doubles (48), home runs (14), runs scored (145), and RBI (125). His .422 batting average still stands as a league record.

The next year the Phillies obtained an injunction forbidding Lajoie from playing in Pennsylvania. As a defense against unpredictable court proceedings, AL president Ban Johnson transferred Lajoie's contract to Cleveland, where his arrival instantly invigorated a moribund franchise.

Although Lajoie led the AL in batting twice more, hitting .355 in 1903 and .381 in 1904, the race he lost to Ty Cobb in 1910 is a piece of baseball legend. The 1910 batting title was hotly contested, with a Chalmers automobile to go to the leading batter. Most of the baseball world rooted for the popular Lajoie and against the hotheaded Cobb, who had won the three previous titles. On the final day of the season, Lajoie bunted for seven infield

Nap Lajoie

hits and swung for a triple in a doubleheader at St. Louis. St. Louis manager Jack O'Connor was ultimately fired when it was revealed that he had ordered his third baseman to play deep against Lajoie. Lajoie finished second by a point despite the machinations but received an auto anyway. Later historical research by *The Sporting News* revealed Lajoie's .384 average actually should have won the title. Cobb's official average of .385 was inflated because one of his games was inadvertently counted twice. In a dispute that rose to the highest baseball levels, Commissioner Bowie Kuhn ruled in 1981 that the mistake would not be corrected.

Playing in the dead-ball era, Lajoie was not a home run hitter. He was, however, a powerful, righthanded pull hitter and his smashes down the left-field foul line were legendary. His 648 doubles rank tenth all-time and he hit ten or more triples in seven seasons. He finished his career with 3,251 hits. In the field, the 6′1″195-lb Lajoie was known for his grace despite being considerably bigger than most infielders of his day. He had excellent speed and good hands.

He managed the Cleveland team from 1905 to 1909 and during that time the club was called the Naps in his honor. He stepped down voluntarily because he believed his managing duties were hurting his play and ultimately hurting the team. His only sub-.300 batting marks (until his final three seasons) came while he was the Cleveland manager./(JM)

Eddie Lake — 1916- . SS-2B 1939-41, 43-50 Cardinals, Red Sox, **Tigers** 835 g, .231, 39 hr, 193 rbi

Although a weak bat kept him in a utility role most of his career, Lake had a knack for drawing walks and topped 100 in each of the three years he played regularly, 1945–47. He led AL shortstops in assists and double plays in '45 for the Red Sox and scored 105 runs for the 1946 Tigers./(LAW)

Joe Lake — 1881-1950. RHP 1908-13 Yankees, **Browns**, Tigers 1318 ip, 62-90, 2.85

Lake lost a league-leading 22 games for the 1908 Highlanders with a high 3.17 ERA (third-worst in the league). His ERA fell to 1.88 in 1909 and he was 14-11. He was 15-9 lifetime in relief./(WAB)

Steve Lake — 1957- . C 1983- Cubs, **Cardinals**, Phillies 325 g, .239, 11 hr, 76 rbi. *1 LCS, 1 g, 1.000. 1 WS, 3 g, .333, 1 rbi*

Lake played in the Orioles, Brewers, and Astro systems before joining the Cubs. Well-liked for his team-first attitude, he was excellent at gunning down runners. He was a boon to the NL champion 1987 Cardinals, filling in for the injured Tony Pena./(FO)

Al Lakeman (Moose) 1918-1976. C 1942-49, 54 **Reds**, Phillies, Braves, Tigers 239 g, .203, 15 hr, 66 rbi

Lakeman was a backup catcher for parts of nine ML seasons but never caught even half of his team's games. In 76 games for the 1945 Reds, he hit a career-high .256. Later, he managed in the minors for ten years, nine in the second division./(MC)

Jack Lamabe — 1936- . RHP 1962-68 Pirates, **Red Sox**, Astros, White Sox, Mets, Cardinals, Cubs 711 ip, 33-41, 4.24. *1 WS, 3 ip, 0-1, 6.75*

Lamabe was successful in his first two seasons, going 7-4, 3.15, with six saves for the 1963 Red Sox. A conversion to starting failed, however, and he bounced around the majors for the rest of his career. He was acquired by the Cardinals in July 1967 and made eight appearances in August without allowing a run, helping St. Louis to the NL pennant. He lost Game Six of the World Series as the Cardinals used eight pitchers that day, tying the record./(SFS)

Al LaMacchia — 1921- . RHP 1943, 45-46 **Browns**, Senators 31 ip, 2-2, 6.46

LaMacchia was 15-2 for San Antonio (Texas League) in 1942 but appeared in only 16 ML games, mostly as a wartime reliever. He scouted briefly for the Phillies before working for the Braves from 1961 to 1975. He has been with the Blue Jays since their inception in 1977. His signees and discoveries include Rick Mahler and Bruce Benedict./(FVP)

Ray Lamanno — 1919- . C 1941-42, 46-48 **Reds** 442 g, .252, 18 hr, 150 rbi
☛ *All-Star—46.*

In 1942 Lamanno replaced his boyhood idol and fellow native Oaklander Ernie Lombardi as the Reds' starting catcher and hit .264 with 12 home runs. He lost the next three seasons to WWII./(JK)

Bill Lamar (Good Time Bill) — 1897-1970. OF 1917-21, 24-27 Yankees, Red Sox, Dodgers, **A's** 550 g, .310, 19 hr, 245 rbi. *1 WS, 3 g, .000*

As Lamar's nickname indicates, he often tested his managers' patience. Two years after he hit .356 for the A's they traded him to Washington. When he refused to report without a raise, he was suspended for the season and never again played in the majors./(JK)

Wayne LaMaster — 1907- . LHP 1937-38 **Phillies**, Dodgers 295 ip, 19-27, 5.82

LaMaster was drafted by the Phillies after two winning seasons in the American Association. Although he led the NL with 19 defeats as a rookie in 1937, he won 15 for the seventh-place Phillies. In August of his poor second season, he was traded to the Dodgers, who used him in three games and then sent him back to the minors./(AL)

Ray Lamb — 1944– . RHP 1969–73 Dodgers, **Indians** 424 ip, 20–23, 3.54

This high-kicking curveballer was overshadowed at the University of Southern California by teammate Tom Seaver. Signed by the Dodgers in 1966, Lamb was a Hollywood movie extra in the off-season. Though generally used in relief, he started 30 games for Cleveland in 1971–72. /(ME)

Dennis Lamp — 1952– . RHP 1977– **Cubs**, White Sox, Blue Jays, A's, Red Sox 1605 ip, 86–87, 3.81. *2 LCS, 11 ip, 0–0, 0.00*

A jack-of-all-trades, Lamp was an effective starter early in his career, led the White Sox in saves in 1983, and has pitched middle-relief almost exclusively since 1985. He joined the Cubs' rotation in 1978 and pitched a one-hitter against San Diego June 9, finishing 7–15 with a 3.29 ERA. After a rocky 1980, in 1981 Lamp was traded to the White Sox; his 2.41 ERA was third-best in the AL. He also settled for a second one-hitter when Robin Yount led off the ninth inning with a double on August 25. Lamp was pitching in relief as well as starting for the White Sox, and in 1983 he saved 15 games for the AL West champions, then signed with the Blue Jays. At the time, the White Sox were entitled to compensation for losing a Type A free agent, and they selected the Mets' Tom Seaver from the compensation pool in a move that stunned New York fans. In 1985 Lamp went 11–0 in relief for the Blue Jays, but his ERA swelled to 5.05 in 1986. He made the Red Sox' pitching staff as a non-roster invitee to spring training in 1988. /(SCL)

Les Lancaster — 1962– . RHP 1987– **Cubs** 291 ip, 16–11, 3.68. *1 LCS, 6 ip, 1–1, 6.35*

Lancaster started 18 games as a rookie for the Cubs in 1987 but was dispatched to the bullpen the following year. He played a vital role in the Cubs' 1989 NL East championship, saving eight games with a 1.36 ERA (4–2) behind stopper Mitch Williams. He won Game Two of the LCS against the Giants 9–5 with four innings of relief, although he gave up three runs. He came into the seventh inning of Game Three with a runner on, the Cubs winning 4–3, and a 1–0 count on Robby Thompson, who had homered off him the previous day. Thinking the count was 2–0, he threw another ball, then grooved what he thought was a 3–0 fastball; Thompson hit another HR, and the Giants won 5–4. /(SCL)

Stan Landes — 1923– . *Umpire* NL 1955–72 *3 WS 2 ASU*

Landes was the first president of the Umpires'

Association but states his union efforts were not the cause of his firing in 1972. His weight had ballooned to 360 pounds (before he lost 75 on a crash diet). He was also deeply in debt, which made him a potential target for gamblers. /(RTM)

Rafael Landestoy — 1953– . 2B-SS 1977–84 Dodgers, **Astros**, Reds 596 g, .237, 4 hr, 83 rbi. *2 LCS, 7 g, .182, 2 rbi. 1 WS, 1 g, .000*

Signed out of the Dominican Republic as an outfielder, the speedy Landestoy became a utility man in the majors. In his best season, he hit .270 for the Astros as their regular second baseman for most of 1979. He followed in 1980 with 23 stolen bases, again in a utility role. /(MC)

Bill Landis — 1942– . LHP 1963, 67–69 A's, **Red Sox** 170 ip, 9–8, 4.46

Despite a record of 40–69 over six minor league seasons, Landis joined the 1967 World Champion Red Sox and went 1–0 in 18 appearances. The reliever missed the World Series due to an army commitment. /(PB)

Jim Landis — 1934– . OF 1957–67 **White Sox**, A's, Indians, Astros, Tigers, Red Sox 1346 g, .247, 93 hr, 467 rbi. *1 WS, 6 g, .292, 1 rbi*
☛ *All-Star—62. Gold Glove—60–64.*

The swift, graceful fielder was the White Sox' center fielder for 8 of his 11 seasons. In 1959 Landis scored six runs in the six-game WS for the "Go-Go Sox." Although his batting average was usually low, as a regular he averaged 67 walks a season, showed occasional power, and had 14 or more stolen bases six straight times in a nonrunning era. By far his best year was 1961, when he hit .283 with 22 HR and 85 RBI, all career highs. His .989 fielding average at retirement was second all-time among outfielders. /(CC)

Kenesaw Mountain Landis — 1866–1944. *Executive.*
☛ *Hall of Fame—1939.*

Landis was granted absolute power over the game as commissioner in 1920 after the Black Sox scandal had tainted the game. He exercised his authority tyrannically until his death in 1944, with no recourse from his decisions available or public criticism of them permitted. Although he was harsh and narrow-minded, and often arbitrary and inconsistent, he persuaded most Americans that the integrity of the national pastime had been restored.

Landis was a judge in an Illinois federal district court when he came to the attention of baseball's

Judge Landis

years as commissioner he banished 15 players, including the eight Black Sox, and at one time had 53 players ineligible. Though he did not treat his victims equally or, in some cases, fairly, the numerous bribe offers, thrown games, and betting plots that arose showed baseball's corruption to be far deeper than once believed, and his no-mercy stance was accepted, if not applauded.

Landis was opposed to the development of farm systems and made free agents of numerous players he decreed to have been "covered up" in the minor leagues, but he was unable to eradicate the practice, which preserved many of the faltering leagues. He loved the World Series, conducted it personally, and was constantly photographed at games with his chin on the railing of a front row box. He was also a strong supporter of both the Hall of Fame and the All-Star Game, pushing hard to continue the midsummer exhibitions during WWII. Landis was inducted to the Hall of Fame himself in 1939, and no commissioner since has enjoyed such power. /(ADS)

Ken Landreaux — 1954– . OF 1977–87 Angels, Twins, **Dodgers** 1264 g, .268, 91 hr, 479 rbi. *3 LCS, 14 g, .238, 3 rbi. 1 WS, 5 g, .167*
☛ *All-Star—80.*

Landreaux was *TSN* Minor League Player of the Year in 1977 with a .359 average at Salt Lake City (Pacific Coast League) and broke in with the Angels late that year. He threw out three baserunners from the outfield in his first ML game. He was traded to the Twins when the Angels acquired Rod Carew before the 1979 season, and in 1980 he set a Minnesota record with a 31-game hitting streak, the longest in the AL since Dom DiMaggio's 34 in 1949. He also tied a ML record with three triples in one game that July 3. Landreaux was traded to the Dodgers for three prospects in 1981 and was their starting centerfielder through 1985. He enjoyed his best season in 1983 (.281, 17 HR, 66 RBI), and in the strike-shortened 1981 season he did not make a single error. /(TG)

Hobie Landrith [Hobert Neal] — 1930– . C 1950–63 Reds, Cubs, Cardinals, **Giants**, Mets, Orioles, Senators 772 g, .233, 34 hr, 203 rbi

Landrith is perhaps best known as the Mets' first pick in the expansion draft; manager Casey Stengel explained the choice by saying, "You gotta have a

establishment during the Federal League's antitrust suit, which was heard in his court. A Federal League victory would have destroyed baseball's unique monopoly status, and Landis won the owners' gratitude by stalling his decision until the Feds had collapsed and their suit was withdrawn. The three-man National Commission, which had ruled baseball since 1903 under the leadership of Ban Johnson, had been weakened by owner disputes and grievances, and collapsed in the aftermath of the Series scandal. Judge Landis was the first and only choice for commissioner.

Named after a Civil War battle, young Kenesaw was meagerly educated and minimally trained for the law. Still, his craggy face, shock of white hair, and flamboyant style were captivating. In his first catcher or you're gonna have a lot of passed balls.'' Landrith had been a backup for the Reds (1950–55) but was traded after the 1955 season, when he had missed time with a broken collarbone. He was a regular for a weak Cubs team in 1956 and hit .221 while leading the league's catchers in errors. As a regular on the 1959 Giants, he had his best season, hitting .251 with 29 RBI and 30 runs in 283 at-bats./(JFC)

Bill Landrum — 1957– . RHP 1986– Reds, Cubs, **Pirates** 172 ip, 6–5, 3.51

Landrum bounced around for a decade before catching fire with the Pirates in 1989. Picked up in desperation to replace injured bullpen stopper Jim Gott, Landrum had a 0.21 ERA in his first 28 appearances. He finished the year with 26 saves and a 1.67 ERA. His father, Joe Landrum, pitched for the Dodgers in 1950 and 1952./(WOR)

Don Landrum — 1936– . OF 1957, 60–66 Phillies, Cardinals, **Cubs**, Giants 456 g, .234, 12 hr, 75 rbi

A lefthanded hitter with outstanding speed but not much else, Landrum hit .282 in a platoon role for the 1962 Cubs. Half of his career homers came in 1965 when the Cubs used him regularly in centerfield./(LAW)

Tito Landrum — 1954– . OF 1980–88 **Cardinals**, Orioles, Dodgers 607 g, .249, 13 hr, 111 rbi. *2 LCS, .333, 1 hr, 1 rbi. 2 WS, 10 g, .360, 1 hr, 1 rbi*

Landrum's surprising 10th-inning home run off Britt Burns in Game Four of the 1983 LCS broke up a scoreless tie and clinched the series for the Orioles. A utility player always in top physical condition, Tito batted .391 and .333 as a pinch hitter in 1984–85. With the 1985 Cardinals he batted .429 in the LCS and .360 in the WS, with a HR in Game Four./(FO)

F.C. Lane [Ferdinand] — 1885–Unk. *Writer.*

A biologist trained at Boston University and MIT, Lane wrote extensively about baseball. He was editor of *Baseball Magazine* for 27 years./(NLM)

Frank Lane (Trader Frank, Frantic Frank, The Wheeler Dealer) — 1896–Unk. *Executive.*

Lane played a little minor league ball and was a minor league executive and president of the American Association, but gained fame as general manager of the White Sox, Cardinals, and Indians. He traded stars like Red Schoendienst, Rocky Colavito, and Roger Maris with abandon. Cardinal owner

Gussie Busch blocked Lane's attempted trade of Stan Musial. Lane became business manager of the Athletics in 1961 and later scouted for the Orioles and Brewers./(FJO)

Al Lang — Unk.–Unk

A Pittsburgh laundry owner and Florida real estate investor, Lang was the mayor of St. Petersburg when he persuaded the Yankees to come there for spring training in 1925, three years after the Boston Braves had made it their headquarters. Since then, Florida has remained the center of spring training activity./(NLM)

Jack Lang — 1921– . *Writer.*

The secretary of the BBWAA makes the phone call to notify players when they are named MVP or Cy Young Award winner or have been elected to the Hall of Fame. Since 1966 that has been Jack Lang's pleasure, first as secretary-treasurer of the writers' organization and, since 1988, as executive secretary.

Lang made his debut on the baseball beat in 1946 covering the Dodgers for the Long Island *Press*. When the Dodgers left town, he switched to the Yankees. Out of that came his first book, *The Fighting Southpaw* (1962), with Whitey Ford. That year the Mets were born and Lang covered them for the *Press* until that paper closed in 1977, then for the New York *Daily News* until he left in 1987 to join *SportsTicker* as a contributing editor and columnist. He received the J.G. Taylor Spink Award in 1986. Lang also wrote *Baseball Basics for Teenagers* (1981) and *The New York Mets: 25 Years of Baseball Magic* (1986)./(NLM)

Bill Lange (Little Eva) — 1871–1950. OF 1893–99 **Cubs** 811 g, .330, 40 hr, 578 rbi

Later described by A.H. Spink, founder and editor of *The Sporting News*, as "Ty Cobb enlarged, fully as great in speed, batting skill and base running," the legendary Chicago outfielder quit baseball at his peak to wed the daughter of a San Francisco real estate magnate, who forbade her to marry a ballplayer. The exceptionally popular Lange set the Cub season batting record with .389 in 1895 (still unbroken) and had a string of six consecutive .300 seasons when he quit. He was famous as a reveler while with the Cubs, but he also discovered Frank Chance and recommended him to the team. Fables grew around his career. For many years he was credited as the last player before Maury Wills to steal 100 bases in a season, but later research reduced his 1896 total to 84. The next season Lange led the NL with 73. His

Bill Lange

defense was so sensational that a story grew up that he once crashed through a wooden outfield fence making a catch. Again, later research has restored the boards (though the catch was remarkable, according to eyewitnesses). A huge man for his time, the 6'1" 190-lb Lange refused all comeback offers once he left the game, although the marriage for which he quit the game ended in divorce. /(ARA)

Dick Lange — 1948- . RHP 1972-75 **Angels** 277 ip, 9-15, 4.46

Lange was a star in the Angel farm system: 13-0 in 14 starts for Idaho Falls in 1970 and the top ERA in the Pacific Coast League in 1972. He was never consistent in four ML seasons. /(MC)

Frank Lange (Seagan, Bill) — 1883-1945. RHP 1910-13 **White Sox** 498 ip, 28-25, 2.96

The Chicago press labeled Lange "Bill" after the popular Chicago NL outfielder of the 19th century. The White Sox curveballer battled arm problems

but fanned 13 against New York on September 20, 1910. He compiled a .500 record over the next two years but was released in mid-1913. /(RL)

Rick Langford — 1952- . RHP 1976-86 Pirates, **A's** 1491 ip, 73-106, 4.01. *1 LCS, 7 ip, 1-0, 1.23*

Langford, who had tied for the AL lead with 19 losses in 1977, had his first of two winning seasons when Billy Martin arrived in Oakland in 1980. Langford went 19-12 that year with league highs of 290 innings pitched and 28 complete games—22 of them consecutive, setting an A's record. In 1981 he again led the AL in complete games (18) and won the clincher in the AL Western Division playoffs. He was a fast-working finesse pitcher and an excellent fielder; his first major league error (10/2/80) broke a streak of 230 consecutive chances accepted—an AL record for pitchers. When he developed elbow trouble in 1983 after leading the A's in innings and complete games a fourth straight year, many—but not Langford—blamed Martin for having overworked his starters. Langford struggled to come back through the last four years of a six-year contract and went 1-10 (7.36) in a final try in 1986. /(JCA)

Mark Langston — 1960- . LHP 1984- **Mariners**, Expos 1374 ip, 86-76, 3.80
☛ *Led League—k 84, 86-87. All-Star—87. Gold Glove—87-88.*

One of the most overpowering lefthanders of his day, Mark Langston ended the 1989 season with the likelihood of becoming the highest-paid pitcher of all time. Traded to contending Montreal for three pitching prospects during the 1989 season by a Seattle club that feared losing him to free agency, Langston quickly established that he could strike out batters in either league.

Langston was *TSN* AL Rookie Pitcher of the Year in 1984, the fourth rookie to lead the league in strikeouts, and he set a Mariners record with 17 wins. Injuries hampered him in 1985 and kept him below 200 strikeouts for the only time in the 1980s. But he came back to lead the AL in strikeouts in 1986 and 1987. In 1987 Langston set a new Mariner record with 19 wins and became the first Mariner to win a Gold Glove. He set team season records for innings, complete games, strikeouts, and shutouts. On May 10, 1988 Langston broke his own team record by striking out 16 Blue Jays. Langston complements a blazing fastball with an effective assortment of other pitches. /(TF)

Hal Lanier — 1942– . SS-2B-3B 1964–73 **Giants**, Yankees 1196 g, .228, 8 hr, 273 rbi. *1 LCS, 1 g, .000.*
   Manager 1986–88 **Astros** 254–232, .523. First place: 86 *1 LCS, 2–4, .333*

Signed for a $50,000 bonus, Lanier made a successful ML debut, batting a career-high .274 and gaining a spot on the 1964 Topps All-Star Rookie team. A serious beaning in 1965 left him with epilepsy, and he never hit above .233 again. He spent seven seasons as a Giants regular, moving from second base to shortstop, and finally to third base. In 1968 Lanier led all NL shortstops in putouts and fielding average. After his playing days, he managed in the minors and coached in the majors. In 1986, as the rookie manager of the Astros, he led Houston to the NL West title and was named Manager of the Year. His father, Max, was an NL pitching star./(LAW)

Max Lanier — 1915– . LHP 1938–46, 49–53 **Cardinals**, Giants, Browns 1618 ip, 108–82, 3.01. *3 WS, 32 ip, 2–1, 1.71*
   All-Star—43–44.

Although he became a lefthander only because he broke his right arm twice as a child, Lanier was the top-winning southpaw for three consecutive Cardinal pennant winners, 1942–44. He was 6–0 in 1946, then jumped to the Mexican League, causing his suspension from organized baseball. He was reinstated in 1949 and won 11 games for the Cardinals in both 1950 and '51. Lanier's son Hal became a major league player, coach, and manager./(LAW)

Ernest J. Lanigan — 1873–1962. *Writer*

Shortly after *The Sporting News* was launched, 15-year-old Lanigan went to work for his uncles, the Spink brothers. He worked for the New York *Press* until 1911, when he became secretary of the International League under Ed Barrow. He served stints as baseball editor for the Cleveland *Leader*, business manager of several Cardinals farm teams, and press information director for the International League. His frail health was a factor in his frequent job changes. In 1946, he was named curator of the Hall of Fame and later served as its historian.

   Lanigan is a titan of baseball record keeping. He was among the first to advocate the formation of the BBWAA and published *The Baseball Cyclopedia* in 1922, an early model for today's *The Baseball Encyclopedia* and *Total Baseball*. He was instrumental in making the RBI an official statistic and the unofficial lists he compiled for years are a valuable resource. Called Figure Filbert by Damon Runyon, he once confided: "I really don't care much about baseball, or looking at ball games, major or minor. All my interest in baseball is in its statistics."/(NLM)

Johnny Lanning (Tobacco Chewin' Johnny) — 1910– . RHP 1936–43, 45–47 Braves, **Pirates** 1071 ip, 58–60, 3.58

Lanning gained attention in his first ML year when he defeated the Cardinals, Cubs, and Giants in succession in September 1936, when the three teams were fighting for the pennant. Although a consistent pitcher for eleven ML seasons, he never met the expectations he raised as a rookie. His brother Tom pitched three games for the Phillies in 1938./(ME)

Carney Lansford — 1957– . 3B-1B 1978– Angels, Red Sox, **A's** 1588 g, .294, 141 hr, 748 rbi. *3 LCS, 11 g, .333, 1 hr, 9 rbi. 2 WS, 9 g, .294, 1 hr, 5 rbi*
   Led League—ba 81.

An often-overlooked outstanding natural hitter, Lansford was the Angels Rookie of the Year in 1978, third in the overall AL vote. Traded to Boston in December 1980, in 1981 Lansford became the first righthanded hitter since 1970 to lead the AL in hitting (.336). He went to Oakland in December 1982 in a deal for Tony Armas. A superb fielder despite a lack of range, Carney appeared headed to first base until the emergence of Mark McGwire. Slowed by wrist and ankle injuries in 1983 and a broken right wrist in 1985, the streaky Lansford was healthy over the next four years and was usually the leadoff or number-two hitter. He stole a career-high 29 bases in 1988 and was second in the AL with a .336 batting average as Oakland won AL pennants both years. He is Oakland's all-time leading hitter (.296) entering the 1990 season and among its all-time leaders in runs, hits, doubles, and slugging percentage. A quietly intense player, Lansford became recognized as a team leader on the Athletics.

   Carney's younger brother Joe played 25 games for the Padres in 1982–83./(ME)

Paul LaPalme (Lefty) — 1923– . LHP 1951–57 **Pirates**, Cardinals, Reds, White Sox 616 ip, 24–45, 4.42

LaPalme pitched a shutout in his first ML game but suffered for much of his career with some of baseball's worst teams, the 1952–54 Pirates. The knuckleballer led the NL with eight wild pitches in '54. Despite his wildness, he had seven saves for the White Sox in 1957./(ME)

Dave LaPoint — 1959- . LHP 1980- Brewers, **Cardinals**, Giants, Tigers, Padres, White Sox, Pirates, Yankees 1324 ip, 73-75, 3.96. *1 WS, 8 ip, 0-0, 3.24*

LaPoint joined the Cardinals in a blockbuster deal that sent Ted Simmons and Rollie Fingers to Milwaukee. A finesse pitcher with good control who relied on making batters hit his pitch, LaPoint had three winning years with the Cardinals. Then, in a series of rapid moves, he played for seven teams between 1985 and 1989. Popular with his team-mates for his good humor and upbeat attitude, LaPoint was the White Sox' best starter in 1988 until he was acquired for the stretch run by the Pirates that August. The following winter he signed with the Yankees as a free agent, but missed most of 1989 on the DL./(FO)

Frank LaPorte (Pot) — 1880-1939. 2B-3B-OF 1905-15 **Yankees**, Red Sox, Browns, Senators, Indianapolis (FL), Newark (FL) 1193 g, .281, 14 hr, 560 rbi
☛ *Led League—rbi 14.*

LaPorte was a quiet player who split most of his seasons among several positions. In 1911 he batted a career-high .314 with 37 doubles and 82 as the Browns' second baseman, leading AL second base-men in assists, double plays, and errors. He was pushed out by Del Pratt in 1912 and sold to the Senators. He could hit line drives as hard as any AL player when he jumped to the Federal League, which he led with 107 RBI in 1914 while batting .311 for the first-place Indianapolis Hoosiers in 1914. He bowed out after a 1915 season in which his average dropped to .253, although he did lead league second basemen in putouts, assists, and double plays./(NLM)

Jack Lapp — 1884-1920. C 1908-16 **A's**, White Sox 565 g, 5 hr, 166 rbi. *4 WS, 5 g, .235, 1 rbi*

Lapp was a platooned or backup catcher on four Philadelphia A's pennant winners in five seasons (1910-11, 13-14). In 1911 he was the top-hitting AL catcher, with a .353 mark in 68 games. He died of pneumonia at age thirty-five./(NLM)

John Lardner — 1912-1960. *Writer.*

One of Ring Lardner's four sons, John continued the family tradition of superb sports journalism and is best remembered for his weekly column in *News-week*, where he observed with wry humor events in the sports world. He also served as TV critic for *The New Yorker* and was drama critic for the New York daily *The Star*./(JK)

Ring Lardner — 1885-1933. *Writer.*

Ring Lardner was regarded as unusual when he made the switch from writing baseball humor to being the prolific author of witty essays and short stories. No writer had ever examined baseball as a source for serious literary material until Lardner did it with his stories about Jack Keefe, the prototype of all eccentric rookies, in *You Know Me, Al*. Lardner based his fictional character and the events of his baseball stories on his experiences covering the Chicago teams for the *Tribune*, and his series "Pullman Tales" delighted readers of *The Sporting News*. He eventually gave up beat coverage, confin-ing his reporting to the coverage of annual events such as the World Series. His sardonic outlook is best exemplified by a comment directed at overly inquisitive children. "Shut up, I explained," he wrote.

Lardner suspected the White Sox of throwing the 1919 World Series from the start and walked through the team's train car during the Series singing a self-penned ditty, "I'm Forever Blowing Ball-games," to the tune of "I'm Forever Blowing Bubbles," a popular song of the day./(JK)

Roy Largent — 1879-1943. *Scout.*

Roy and his wife, Bessie, formed a unique husband-and-wife scouting tandem for the White Sox from 1924 to 1939. Roy was totally deaf, and Bessie would read his lips, serve as his ears, and drive the car on scouting trips. She eventually became a shrewd judge of talent herself. The Largents discov-ered over 100 eventual ML players, including Luke Appling, Zeke Bonura, and Lon Warneke./(FVP)

Norm Larker — 1930- . 1B-OF 1958-63 **Dodgers**, Astros, Braves, Giants 667 g, .275, 32 hr, 271 rbi. *1 WS, 6 g, .188*
☛ *All-Star—60.*

The hustling lefthander, who overcame the loss of a kidney, was considered as a fine fielder but an ordinary hitter until 1960. Suddenly, his line drives fell in, and he finished with a .323 batting average, within one hit of the NL batting crown won by Dick Groat. He never came close to matching his '60 season and was out of the majors three years later./(LAW)

Barry Larkin — 1964- . SS 1986- **Reds** 414 g, .289, 31 hr, 154 rbi
☛ *All-Star—88-89.*

Like many of his companions on the 1984 U.S. Olympic baseball team, Larkin sped to the majors.

The Reds made the native Cincinnatian their first pick in the June 1985 draft; 14 months later, they made him their shortstop. Larkin gave them a leadoff hitter with good power for a middle infielder. He homered on Opening Day of 1987 but was hampered by a hyperextended knee for the first half of the year. In 1988 he became an All-Star and led the Reds with a .296 batting average. Larkin was hitting .340 at the All-Star break in 1989, but tore ligaments in his elbow during an outfield-to-home relay contest the day before the All-Star Game. When he returned in September he could only pinch hit. /(JCA)

Gene Larkin — 1962- . DH-1B 1987- **Twins** 370 g, .267, 18 hr, 144 rbi. *1 LCS, 1 g, 1.000, 1 rbi. 1 WS, 5 g, .000*

Larkin surpassed all of Lou Gehrig's school batting records as a switch-hitting third baseman at Columbia, and never hit below .302 in the minors. The line-drive hitter splits his time between DH and first base, where he backs up Kent Hrbek. Larkin was hit by 15 pitches in 1988 to lead the AL. /(SCL)

Dave LaRoche — 1948- . LHP 1970-83 **Angels**, Twins, Cubs, Indians, Yankees 1049 ip, 65-58, 3.53. *1 LCS, 1 ip, 0-0, 6.75. 1 WS, 1 ip, 0-0, 0.00* ☛ *All-Star—76-77.*

LaRoche gained notoriety for his blooper pitch, called the LaLob. Almost exclusively a reliever (he lost all six decisions in his 15 career starts), he saved 126 games lifetime. His best season was 1978, when he saved 25 while going 10-9 with a 2.81 ERA for the Angels. He had five other seasons in double figures in saves. /(SFS)

Don Larsen — 1929- . RHP 1953-65, 67 Browns/ Orioles, **Yankees**, A's, White Sox, Giants, Astros, Cubs 1548 ip, 81-91, 3.78 *5 WS, 36 ip, 4-2, 2.75*

Though he had a mediocre career record, Larsen was immortalized by his World Series perfect game of October 8, 1956. He had gone 11-5 for the Yankees that year and, after being knocked out in the second inning of Game Two, started Game Five. He set down 27 Dodgers in a row, outdueling Sal Maglie and winning 2-0 for the first no-hitter in Series history. The last batter Larsen faced was Dale Mitchell, who was declared out by umpire Babe Pinelli on a called third strike. Mitchell and others, including Mickey Mantle in centerfield, thought the ball a bit outside, but mayhem had erupted and catcher Yogi Berra had jumped into Larsen's arms before Mitchell could argue.

Before joining the Yankees, Larsen had a 3-21

Don Larsen

record for the 1954 Orioles to lead the AL in losses. But two of his wins came against New York, who took him as part of an 18-player deal that winter. One early morning in spring training of 1956, Larsen, who had a reputation as a partier, crashed his car into a telephone pole, prompting manager Casey Stengel to say, "He was probably mailing a letter." But he was a capable pitcher who, like Yankee teammate Bob Turley, adopted a no-windup delivery. His 11 wins in 1956 were his season high. He went 1-10 with the A's in 1960 and bounced around before receiving his last ML chance with the Cubs in 1967. He was the last active former St. Louis Brown. A lifetime .242 batter, he had 14 career home runs and was used 66 times as a pinch hitter. /(GDW)

Dan Larson — 1954- . RHP 1976-82 **Astros**, Phillies, Cubs 324 ip, 10-25, 4.39

Larson went 5-8 and 1-7 for the Astros and then was traded before 1978 to the Phillies. He was then included in a package with Keith Moreland and Dickie Noles to get Mike Krukow from the Cubs. /(JFC)

Tony LaRussa — 1944- . 2B-SS 1963, 68-71, 73 **A's**, Braves, Cubs 132 g, .199, 0 hr, 7 rbi.
Manager 1979- **White Sox**, A's 752-683, .524. First place: 83, 88 *2 LCS, 5-3, .625. 2 WS, 5-4, .556*

LaRussa had managed less than two full seasons in the minors when he replaced Don Kessinger as the White Sox manager on August 2, 1979 at the age of thirty-four. Extremely bright and articulate, LaRussa led the White Sox to the AL West title with a ML-high 99 wins in 1983, winning several Manager of the Year awards. The White Sox stumbled in 1984-85, however, and after a 26-38 start in 1986 LaRussa was fired June 19, only to sign as the manager of the A's three weeks later. He managed the A's to third place finishes in 1986 and 1987, then took them to the WS in 1988, where they lost to the Dodgers in five games. As a player, LaRussa made his ML debut with the Kansas City A's at the age of eighteen, but spent most of his career in the minors, where he played until 1977. LaRussa received a law degree from Florida State in 1978, making him the fifth lawyer/manager in baseball history. The other four are in the Hall of Fame /(SCL)

Frank Lary (Mule, The Yankee Killer) — 1930- . RHP 1954-65 **Tigers**, Mets, Braves, White Sox 2162 ip, 128-116, 3.49 20 wins: 56, 61
☛ *Led League—w 56. All-Star—60-61. Gold Glove—61.*

Frank Lary and older brother Al, a Cubs pitcher, both debuted in 1954. Al's major league career was short, but in 1956, the fireballing Frank emerged as the ace of a strong Tiger staff, leading the American League with 21 wins. He was especially tough on the perennial pennant-winning Yankees, going 5-1 against them in 1956 and 7-0 in 1958—the first time since 1916 that New York had been beaten seven times in one season by one pitcher. Lary defeated them five times in a row in 1959, making it 13 wins in 14 decisions. Lifetime against the Yankees, Lary was 27-13. His best season was 1961, when he was 23-9, threw a one-hitter, and led the league with 22 complete games. In his three All-Star appearances, he didn't allow an earned run. He developed a sore arm in 1962 and changed teams four times during 1964 and 1965. As late as the 1970s, while coaching and scouting for various organizations, he was trying to convince teams he could pitch again. /(MC)

Lyn Lary (Broadway) — 1906-1973. SS-3B 1929-40 **Yankees**, Red Sox, Senators, Browns, Indians, Dodgers, Cardinals 1302 g, .269, 38 hr, 526 rbi

In 1928 the Yankees paid Oakland (Pacific Coast League) the then-exorbitant sum of $125,000 for their sensational double-play combo, Lyn Lary and Jimmy Reese. Shortstop Lary was a Yankee until May 1934. In 1931 Lary had 107 RBI, the most ever by a Yankee shortstop, and was one of six Yankees to score 100 runs. He also cost Lou Gehrig that season's home run title when, incorrectly thinking a ball Gehrig hit out had been caught, Lary left the basepath and was passed by Gehrig, who was declared out. Playing for the 1936 Browns, Lary led the AL with 37 stolen bases. /(MG)

Fred Lasher (Whip) — 1941- . RHP 1963, 67-71 Twins, **Tigers**, Indians, Angels 202 ip, 11-13, 3.88. *1 WS, 2 ip, 0-0, 0.00*

This sidearming reliever appeared in 34 games for the 1968 World Champion Tigers and a career-high 55 for Detroit and Cleveland in 1970. /(FK)

Bill Laskey — 1957- . RHP 1982-86, 88 **Giants**, Expos, Indians 745 ip, 42-53, 4.14

A soft-throwing righthander with excellent control, Laskey made the Topps and *Baseball Digest* All-Rookie teams as a starting pitcher in 1983, going 13-12, 3.14 for the Giants. His ERA rose and his strikeout total fell each year until 1986, when he was sent to the bullpen, and he spent all of 1987 working in relief for the Tigers AAA Toledo club. In 1988, Laskey posted a 5.18 ERA in 17 relief appearances with the Indians and was released August 21. /(SCL)

Tommy Lasorda — 1927- . LHP 1954-56 Dodgers, A's 26 ip, 0-4, 6.48.
Manager 1976- **Dodgers** 1099-957, .535. First place: 77-78, 81, 83, 85, 88 *6 LCS, 16-14, .533. 4 WS, 12-11, .522*

"My heart bleeds Dodger blue," Lasorda has claimed, during his 35-plus years in the Dodger organization. He looked like a promising pitcher on June 1, 1948 when, in a 15-inning game for the Schenectady Blue Jays (Canadian-American League, Class C), he struck out 25 Amsterdam Rugmakers, setting a since-broken pro record. He even drove in the winning run with a single. In his next two starts, he struck out 15 and 13, gaining the attention of the Dodgers, who signed him for their Montreal club. Lasorda compiled a 98-49 record in nine years with Montreal of the International

Tommy Lasorda

League, the Dodgers' top farm club, 1950–1955 and 1958–1960. His best records were 17–8 in 1953 and 18–6 in 1958, when he led the league in victories, complete games, and shutouts. Lasorda helped Montreal to the International League championship five times. He received only two brief trials with the Dodgers, and on May 5, 1955 he tied a ML record with three wild pitches in one inning. Lasorda was demoted in 1955 to make room for bonus baby Sandy Koufax, then sold to Kansas City in 1956, but couldn't stick with the Athletics or Yankees either. Stuck in the high minors, Lasorda moved to Los Angeles a year before the Dodgers did, with the Angels of the Pacific Coast League.

After his second stint in Montreal, Lasorda became a Dodger scout in 1961 and then a minor league manager in 1965. He won five pennants and finished second twice and third once through 1972, with only one record below .500.

Promoted to the Dodgers as a coach, Lasorda served as Walter Alston's understudy until September 29, 1976, when Alston retired. He inherited the infield of Steve Garvey, Davey Lopes, Bill Russell, and Ron Cey that he had helped assemble in the minor leagues, and he reacquired catcher Joe Ferguson, another of his proteges, to alternate with Steve Yeager. In 1977–78, he became the first NL manager to win pennants his first two seasons, but the Dodgers lost the WS to the Yankees in six games each time. After the 1981 player strike, Lasorda's Dodgers defeated the Astros in the divisional playoff; beat the Expos in the LCS on Rick Monday's two-out, ninth-inning homer; and then crushed the Yankees with a power display in the World Series. Lasorda managed the Dodgers to division titles in 1983 and 1985, but lost both times in the LCS. In 1988, he shared NL Manager of the Year honors with the Pirates Jim Leyland and took the Dodgers to an upset win over the Mets in the LCS and a shocking WS upset of the A's. A media favorite, Lasorda is noted for his good humor and his love of Italian cooking. /(MC)

Arlie Latham [Walter Arlington] (The Freshest Man on Earth) — 1859–1952. 3B 1880, 83–96, 99, 1909 Buffalo (NL), **St. Louis (AA)**, Chicago (PL), Reds, Cardinals, Washington (NL), Giants 1627 g, .269, 27 hr, 398 rbi (inc.). *Manager* 1896 **Cardinals** 0–2, .000

The impish Latham laughed his way through baseball. A dandy third baseman and leadoff hitter for the St. Louis Browns of the then-major league American Association when they won four straight pennants in the 1880s, he scored 100 or more runs nine times, leading the AA in 1886 (152). In 1888 he led with 109 stolen bases under the more liberal scoring rules of the time.

He was equally famous for his comedy in the coach's box, taunting rivals while amusing the crowd with his antics. He was probably the first clown in baseball to develop an act and certainly the first to be hired exclusively as a baseline coach, by John McGraw of the Giants.

Eventually he and his wife moved to England, returning only when WWII seemed imminent. The Giants made a place for him as an attendant in the press box, where the still spry Latham amused writers with his witty observations and reminiscences. /(JK)

Barry Latman (Shoulders) — 1936– . RHP 1957–67 White Sox, **Indians**, Angels, Astros 1219 ip, 59–68, 3.91 ☛ *All-Star—61.*

The broad-shouldered, hard-throwing Latman was considered an outstanding prospect, yet his only successful year was 1961, when he went 13–5 for

Cleveland and was named to the AL All-Star squad for the second game. /(ME)

Charlie Lau — 1933–1984. C 1956, 58–67 Tigers, Braves, **Orioles**, A's 527 g, .255, 16 hr, 140 rbi

Except for catching Warren Spahn's 1961 no-hitter, Lau's playing career was relatively uneventful; he gained his notoriety as the most respected batting coach of his time. He was a lifetime .180 hitter until 1962, when he radically changed his batting style to win a job with the Orioles. He adopted a contact hitter's stance, straight out of the 19th century: feet wide apart, bat held almost parallel to the ground. He had two hits in an inning he entered as a pinch hitter on June 23 and doubled four times in a game on July 13, 1962, tying a ML record. His average jumped to .294. Slow afoot, with a weak arm, he caught less and pinch hit more each season. After 1966 arm surgery, he only pinch hit. At a team party in August 1966, he saved MVP Frank Robinson from drowning after a swimming pool accident.

Lau taught his hitting technique to the Orioles, A's, Royals, Yankees, and White Sox. His book *How to Hit .300* supplanted Ted Williams's *The Science of Hitting* as the "Bible of Batting." Most of the Royals adopted his spray-hitting style: Hal McRae, George Brett, Amos Otis, and Willie Wilson all used the Lau approach during their most successful seasons. In 1983 Lau voluntarily gave up his spot on the White Sox coaching staff to enable scout Loren Babe, who was dying of lung cancer, to qualify for his ten-year pension. Babe died in February 1984. Lau died from cancer of the colon in March. /(MC)

Billy Lauder — 1874–1933. 3B 1898–99, 1901–03 **Phillies**, A's, Giants 483 g, .261, 6 hr, 254 rbi

A steady third baseman but an average runner, Lauder had his best year with the 1899 Phillies, when he had career highs of 90 RBI and 74 runs while hitting .268. /(DAS)

Tim Laudner — 1958– . C 1981– **Twins** 734 g, .224, 77 hr, 263 rbi. *1 LCS, 5 g, .071, 2 rbi. 1 WS, 7 g, .318, 1 hr, 4 rbi*
☛ *All-Star—88.*

Laudner was the Southern League MVP in 1981, hitting .284 with 42 HR at Orlando to earn a September promotion to the Twins. He was the Twins starting catcher in 1982, then shared with job with Dave Engle and Mark Salas until 1987 when he became the starter once again. A strong righthanded

batter, Laudner hit only .191 in 1987, but he made the AL All-Star Team in 1988 with a .251 average and 13 HR and doubled in his only at-bat in the All-Star Game. /(SCL)

France Laux — Unk.–Unk. *Broadcaster.*

A pioneer sports announcer in St. Louis, Laux worked most World Series and All-Star games between 1929 and 1939, when he moved to WABC in New York. /(NLM)

George Lauzerique — 1947– . RHP 1967–70 **A's**, Brewers 113 ip, 4–8, 5.00

Lauzerique never had a winning season in his short ML career, suffering from control problems. The native Cuban was 13–4, 2.30 in 1967 for a Birmingham (Southern League) team that included Reggie Jackson, Joe Rudi, and Rollie Fingers. On July 6 that year, he pitched a seven-inning perfect game. /(WOR)

Cookie Lavagetto [Harry Arthur] — 1912– . 3B-2B 1934–41, 46–47 Pirates, **Dodgers** 1043 g, .269, 40 hr, 486 rbi. *2 WS, 8 g, .118, 3 rbi.*
        Manager 1957–61 **Senators/Twins 276–393, .413**
☛ *All-Star—38–41.*

A dependable regular, Cookie Lavagetto's moment of fame came in Game Four of the 1947 World Series. Yankee pitcher Bill Bevens had walked two batters in the ninth inning but was one out away from a no-hitter when Lavagetto pinch hit a game-winning double off the right-field wall, beating Bevens 2–1. /(JK)

Mike LaValliere (Spanky) — 1960– . C 1984- Phillies, Cardinals, **Pirates** 437 g, .269, 8 hr, 142 rbi
☛ *Gold Glove—87.*

LaValliere helped make the trade of Pittsburgh favorite Tony Pena look good with a .300 bat and Gold Glove fielding in 1987. He excelled in throwing out potential basestealers and earned a starting spot on the 1986 Cardinals, starting a club rookie record 108 games behind the plate. Signed as a third baseman by the Phillies, the squat LaValliere moved to catcher in 1982. He was MVP in the 1976 Babe Ruth World Series. /(ME)

Doc Lavan [John Leonard] — 1890–1952. SS 1913–24 Browns, A's, Senators, **Cardinals** 1162 g, .245, 7 hr, 377 rbi

A light-hitting shortstop, Lavan was error-prone, booting the ball for both St. Louis teams. He made 75 errors in 1915 for the Browns and later twice led

NL shortstops in miscues while with the Cardinals. /(JK)

Gary Lavelle — 1949– . LHP 1974–85, 87 **Giants**, Blue Jays, A's 1086 ip, 80–77, 2.93. *1 LCS, 0 ip, 0–0. 0.00*
☛ *All-Star—77, 83.*

Lavelle's 136 career saves ranked him third among lefthanded relievers on his retirement. He spent 7–1/2 seasons in the minors before being called up by the Giants in mid-1974, but he remained a fixture in San Francisco for the next decade. In 11 seasons with the Giants, his ERA only once was above 3.42. In 1977 he set team records for games (73) and saves (20), and by 1984 he was the Giants' all-time leader in those categories (breaking Christy Mathewson's games mark). Lavelle led NL relievers with 13 wins in 1978. Greg Minton took over as the Giants' main closer in 1980, and in 1983 he and Lavelle became the NL's first relief duo to each post at least 20 saves in a season.

Lavelle was traded to Toronto for Jim Gott and two minor leaguers before the 1985 season and led the AL East champions with 69 appearances that season. Chronic elbow problems forced him to sit out the 1986 season. Toronto released him in early 1987, and an attempted comeback with the A's failed. /(TF)

Jimmy Lavender — 1884–1960. RHP 1912–17 **Cubs**, Phillies 1207 ip, 62–76, 3.09

Lavender was a spitballer who won ten or more games in five seasons. His two career highlights came against the Giants. On July 8, 1912 he won the game that ended Rube Marquard's record 19-game winning streak, and on August 31, 1915 he hurled a 2–0 no-hitter against New York. /(ARA)

Rudy Law (Lawman) — 1956– . OF 1978, 80, 82–86 Dodgers, **White Sox**, Royals 749 g, .271, 18 hr, 198 rbi. *1 LCS, 4 g, .389*

Law set a since-surpassed Los Angeles Dodger rookie record by stealing 40 bases in 1980 but, failing to hit in the second half, was returned to the minors. The White Sox acquired him in 1982 and made him their leadoff man. In 1983 he was the catalyst in Chicago's division championship; he led AL outfielders in fielding average and eclipsed Luis Aparicio's club stolen base record, with 77. He was forced to give up his uniform 11 in 1984 when it was retired in honor of Aparicio. Signed as a free agent by the Royals in 1986, he injured a knee and soon left the majors. /(RL)

Vance Law — 1956– . 3B-2B-SS-1B 1980– Pirates, **White Sox**, Expos, Cubs 1138 g, .257, 71 hr, 433 rbi. *1 LCS, 2 g, .000*
☛ *All-Star—88.*

The son of Vern Law, Vance was drafted by Pittsburgh in 1978, traded to the White Sox in March 1982 and became Chicago's everyday third baseman in 1983. On May 8 and 9, 1984 against the Brewers, he played all 25 innings of the longest game in AL history, establishing the AL record for the longest errorless game by a third baseman. He erupted with 17 homers in 1984 but then was traded to Montreal for Bob James. Manager Buck Rodgers made good use of Law's talents in 1985–87, even using him as a relief pitcher six times. Law signed with the Cubs as a free agent for 1988, had a productive first half, and made the NL All-Star team. A bad back limited him in 1989, and he struck out in all three of his LCS at-bats. /(RL)

Vern Law (Deacon) — 1930– . RHP 1950–51, 54–67 Pirates 2672 ip, 162–147, 3.77. 20 wins: 60 *1 WS, 18 ip, 2–0, 3.44*
☛ *Cy Young Award—60. All-Star—60.*

Law was largely responsible for the Pirates' World Championship in 1960, when he captured the Cy Young Award with a 20–9 record and a league-high 18 complete games. Despite nursing a late-season sprained ankle, he won the first and fourth games of the Series and had a no-decision in the famed seventh game, won by the Pirates on Bill Mazeroski's ninth-inning homer.

Idaho Senator Herman Welker recommended favorite son Law to former classmate Bing Crosby, part owner of the Pirates. Signed by the Pirates in 1948, Law, a control pitcher with a classic, straight-up motion, reached Pittsburgh in 1950 but spent 1952 and 1953 in the military. He and Bob Friend anchored a young pitching staff on last-place teams in 1954, 1955, and 1957. But both blossomed in 1958 and the Pirates rose to second place. Though Friend slumped in 1959, Law went 18–9.

After reaching the top in 1960, Law missed most of 1961 with a torn rotator muscle. Pitching in pain throughout 1962, he rebounded to go 10–7, but more physical problems in 1963 forced him on to the voluntary retired list. He made a surprising comeback in 1964 (12–13, 3.61) and in 1965, at age thirty-five, led the Pirates with 17 wins and a 2.15 ERA. He was honored with the Lou Gehrig Memorial Award as comeback player of the year. After more injuries his last two years, he retired among Pittsburgh's all-time pitching leaders. Vern and his wife, VaNita, had six children: Veldon, Veryl,

Vern Law

Vaughn, Varlin, VaLynda, and major league infielder Vance. /(ME)

Tom Lawless — 1956- . 2B-3B 1982, 84- Reds, **Cardinals**, Blue Jays 328 g, .210, 2 hr, 23 rbi. *1 LCS, 3 g, .333. 2 WS, 4 g, .100, 1 hr, 3 rbi*

Lawless was the unlikely hero of Game Four of the 1987 World Series. With the Twins and Cardinals tied 1–1 in the fourth inning, he hit a three-run homer off Frank Viola as the Cardinals went on to win 7–2. The speedy utility man was playing only because third baseman Terry Pendleton's rib injury hindered his righthanded hitting. Lawless had had only two hits in 25 at-bats the entire season (.080), and at that point in his career he had one HR in 215 at-bats and hadn't homered in the last three years. /(JFC)

Brooks Lawrence (Bull) — 1925- . RHP 1954–60 Cardinals, **Reds** 1041 ip, 69–62, 4.25

As a 29-year-old rookie seasoned in the Negro National League, Lawrence went 15–6, starting and relieving for the 1954 Cardinals. Hit hard in 1955, he was demoted to Oakland (Pacific Coast League), where he earned a second chance by going 5–1 down the stretch. Acquired by the Reds, he opened 1956 with 13 straight victories, among them two two-hitters. He finished 19–10, then went 16–13 in 1957. He won only eight games in 1958 and seven in 1959, when he threw a third two-hitter. /(MC)

Earl Lawson — Unk.-Unk. *Writer.*

President of the BBWAA in 1976 and longtime correspondent for *The Sporting News*, Lawson covered the Reds for 34 years for the Cincinnati *Star* and *Post*. He retired in 1984 and received the J.G. Taylor Spink Award in 1985. /(NLM)

Roxie Lawson [Alfred Voyle] — 1906–1977. RHP 1930–31, 33, 35–40 Indians, **Tigers**, Browns 852 ip, 47–39, 5.37

After three ML trials with ERAs over 6.00, Lawson had three wins for the 1935 World Champion Tigers, including a shutout over Lefty Grove. In 1937 he managed 18 wins with a whopping 5.26 ERA. /(JK)

Bill Laxton — 1948- . LHP 1970–71, 74, 76–77 Phillies, **Padres**, Tigers, Mariners, Indians 244 ip, 3–10, 4.72

Laxton's only winning record came when the wild reliever was 3–2 for the 1977 expansion Mariners. He had a 7-inning, 2–1 no-hit win on August 25, 1967 for Clinton (Midwest League). /(SFS)

Johnny Lazor — 1912- . OF 1943–46 **Red Sox** 223 g, .263, 6 hr, 62 rbi

Lazor played centerfield for the Red Sox while Dom DiMaggio was in the military. He hit .310 in 1945 but was out of work the next year. /(JK)

Jack Lazorko — 1956– . RHP 1984–88 Brewers, Mariners, Tigers, **Angels** 222 ip, 5–8, 4.22

Drafted five times before signing with the Astros, Lazorko relieved his way through seven organizations and temporarily filled gaps in a few major league bullpens. Given a chance to start by the disappointing 1987 Angels, the 31-year-old recorded all five of his ML wins. /(JCA)

Tony Lazzeri (Poosh 'Em Up) — 1903–1946. 2B-3B-SS 1926–39 **Yankees**, Cubs, Dodgers, Giants 1739 g, .292, 178 hr, 1191 rbi. *7 WS, 32 g, .262, 4 hr, 19 rbi* ☛ *All-Star—33.*

Lazzeri was a prominent member of the 1927 Yankees' "Murderers' Row" lineup and the second baseman on five World Championship Yankee clubs. He had seven 100-RBI seasons and four times hit as many as 18 home runs. His excellent glove, driving leadership, and superior baseball instincts made him the hero of Italian-Americans, as their first superstar. He was known as "the quiet man of the Yankees." Though an epileptic, he never had an on-the-field seizure in his 12 Yankee seasons.

Playing for Salt Lake City (Pacific Coast League) in 1925, assisted by the altitude and a 200-game schedule, Lazzeri set since-broken pro baseball records for HR (60) and RBI (222) and a still-standing record for runs (202). The following year, he played 155 games for New York. With two out and the bases loaded in the seventh inning, he struck out against Grover Cleveland Alexander in the Game Seven of the 1926 World Series, won by the Cardinals 3–2. The famous incident damaged Lazzeri's reputation as a clutch hitter. Yet Miller Huggins, his manager, said: "Anyone can strike out, but ballplayers like Lazzeri come along once in a generation."

From 1927 through 1930, and again in 1932, Lazzeri batted .300 or better; his .354 in 1929 put him among the league leaders. On May 24, 1936 he became the first major leaguer to hit two grand slams in one game and set a still-standing AL record with 11 RBI. /(MG)

Charlie Lea — 1956– . RHP 1980–84, 87–88 **Expos**, Twins 923 ip, 62–48, 3.54 ☛ *All-Star—84.*

An excellent young starter for the Expos for several seasons, Lea was the NL's starting and winning pitcher in the 1984 All-Star Game, then saw his career ruined by arm problems that forced him to miss the entire 1985 and 1986 seasons. He began

Tony Lazzeri

the 1980 season at Memphis (Southern League) for the third consecutive year, but after a 9–0, 0.84 start he was in Montreal by mid-season, where he went 7–5. Lea won only five games in the strike-shortened 1981 season, but one of them was a 4–0 no-hitter against the Giants May 10, and in 1982 he cracked double figures in wins for the first time in his pro career, finishing 12–10. In 1983 Lea won a career-high 16 games, and in 1984 he was 15–10, 2.89 to earn his All-Star Game start but was hurt shortly thereafter. He could not pitch at all in 1985 or 1986. Lea spent most of 1987 rehabilitating in the minors and endured one dreadful inning with the Expos before his comeback as a starter for the Twins in 1988, finishing 7–7 with a 4.85 ERA. /(SCL)

Freddy Leach — 1897–1981. OF 1923–32 **Phillies**, Giants, Braves 991 g, .307, 72 hr, 509 rbi

Leach was a railroad telegrapher playing for town baseball teams in the Ozarks in 1922 when he decided to try professional baseball. After leading the Missouri Valley League in hitting (.383) in his first year, he finished the season with George Stallings's independent Rochester team in the International League, and by 1923 he was with the Phillies. The stocky, thick-eyebrowed Leach bounced up and down between the majors and minors for several years before establishing himself as a steady-hitting, strong-armed outfielder with the Phillies. In 1927 he led NL outfielders in assists. The Giants traded Lefty O'Doul and cash for Leach's contract in October 1928. The deal was widely regarded as a mistake by Giants manager John McGraw when O'Doul hit .398, 108 points higher than Leach, to win the 1929 NL batting title, but McGraw announced he was satisfied that Leach was more versatile and far better defensively. Leach contributed two .300-plus seasons before retiring. /(JK)

Rick Leach — 1957– . OF-1B 1981– Tigers, **Blue Jays**, Rangers 721 g, .265, 16 hr, 167 rbi

Leach was a star quarterback at the University of Michigan from 1976 to 1978 and was a local hero when he signed with the Tigers rather than play pro football. After several seasons as a utility outfielder with Detroit, Leach was released and picked up by Toronto, where he was a star in the minors and a role player with the Blue Jays. Although his role was limited to that of backup outfielder and lefthanded bat off the bench, Leach demonstrated the psychological makeup that made him a winner in football, diving for balls a faster outfielder would have caught easily or a lazier outfielder would have let drop. /(TF)

Terry Leach — 1954– . RHP 1981–82, 85– **Mets**, Royals 461 ip, 29-15, 3.28. *1 LCS, 5 ip, 0-0, 0.00*

This control pitcher uses a low sidearm motion. Bending to his right as he throws, he scrapes his padded right knee on the mound. Leach had a career season (11-1) in 1987, when numerous injuries to the Mets staff gave him more chances to

pitch. After three straight wins in relief, he became a starter and won another seven in a row, for a Met-record 10 consecutive wins from the beginning of the season.

Leach set another record in his first stint with the Mets. His 10-inning, 1–0 one-hitter against the Phillies on October 1, 1982 is the only extra-inning one-hitter in club history. His NL career record as a starter is 11–2 with a 2.82 ERA, but the Mets' rotation was so deep that he only saw emergency work in that role. He was a valuable long-relief man on two pennant winners. In 1989 he was traded to Kansas City. /(SH)

Tommy Leach — 1877–1969. OF-3B-SS 1898–1915, 18 Louisville (NL), **Pirates**, Cubs, Reds 2155 g, .269, 62 hr, 810 rbi. *2 WS, 15 g, .293, 9 rbi*
☛ *Led League—hr 02.*

A 5'6" speedster, Leach was Pittsburgh's third baseman in the first World Series, played in 1903 against the Red Sox. He specialized in triples and hit four in the '03 WS—two in one game—to set still-

Tommy Leach

standing Series records. Of his 62 major league home runs, 49 were inside the park; none of his seven 1903 homers were hit over the fence. He led the National League with six home runs in 1902 and twice topped the league in runs scored—with Pittsburgh in 1909 and with Chicago in 1913. /(JK)

League Park Cincinnati Reds 1894–1901. LF-253

In 1895 the Reds created the first "batter's eye" by painting the centerfield wall black, making it easier to see incoming pitches. Erected on the site of Cincinnati's original League Park, which saw its grandstand collapse on Opening Day 1884, killing one spectator, the second League Park burned down in 1901 and was rebuilt as Crosley Field. /(SCL)

League Park Cleveland (NL) 1891–99, Cleveland Indians 1901–32, 34–46. LF-375, CF-420, RF-290

Converted to baseball's fourth concrete-and-steel park in 1910, Cleveland's League Park never had lights, and after 1932 the Indians played many of their home games at the colossal new Municipal Stadium. The scene of Bill Wambsganss's unassisted triple play in the 1920 WS, League Park had its stands torn down in 1950 and it is now a public park. /(SCL)

Luis Leal — 1957– . RHP 1980–85 **Blue Jays** 947 ip, 51–58, 4.14

The chunky starter from Venezuela showed flashes of brilliance for the Blue Jays within a mediocre career. Leal was erratic, with a five-game winning streak in 1983 that was followed by a four-game losing streak the same season. On June 2, 1980 Leal gave up an AL-record five consecutive hits to start a game. On August 15, 1984 in a doubleheader with Cleveland, Leal was allowed to stay in the game to give up a team-record 10 runs (all earned). At the time of his release, Leal ranked behind only Jim Clancy and Dave Stieb as Blue Jays' career leader in starts, innings, wins, losses, strikeouts, and walks. /(TF)

Tim Leary — 1958– . RHP 1981, 83– Mets, Brewers, **Dodgers**, Reds 831 ip, 45–56, 3.77. *1 LCS, 4 ip, 0–1, 6.23. 1 WS, 7 ip, 0–0, 1.35*

One of several successful reclamation projects of Dodgers pitching coach Ron Perranoski, Leary posted a 17–11, 2.91 record for the World Champion Dodgers in 1988 after winning a total of 20 games in six previous ML seasons. Leary was a college All-American at UCLA and was the second pick overall in the June 1979 free-agent draft, and in 1980 he was Texas League MVP, leading the league

in wins and shutouts for Jackson. Leary made the Mets in 1981, only to be injured in his first start on a cold April day at Wrigley Field, then missed all of 1982 with an injured nerve. He moved to Milwaukee in a six-player, four-team trade in 1985 and was 12–12 for the Brewers in 1986 before being traded to Los Angeles with Tim Crews for slugger Greg Brock. Leary started and lost Game Six of the 1988 LCS for the Dodgers, but he pitched well out of the bullpen in the World Series. After the season he received the NL Comeback Player of the Year Award. He was traded to the Reds in mid-1989. /(TG)

Bevo LeBourveau [DeWitt Wiley] — 1894–1947. OF 1919–22, 29 **Phillies**, A's 280 g, .275, 11 hr, 69 rbi

LeBourveau was the scourge of American Association pitching, twice winning the batting championship, and he hit .349 in 1,584 minor league games. His hitting skills resisted transfer to the majors, and he never had a 100-game season. /(JK)

Bill Lee (Spaceman) — 1946– . LHP 1969–82 **Red Sox**, Expos 1945 ip, 119–90, 3.62 *1 LCS, 1 ip, 0–0, 0.00. 1 WS, 14 ip, 0–0, 3.14*
☛ *All-Star—73.*

Lee's colorful personality sometimes overshadowed his excellent pitching. He earned his Spaceman nickname when, on his first view of Fenway's left field wall, he asked, "Do they leave it there during games?" Always willing to speak his mind, he led a Red Sox revolt against manager Don Zimmer (whom he called "the gerbil"); criticized domed stadiums, artificial turf, and the designated hitter rule; and admitted to marijuana use, but only "sprinkled on cereal." He ultimately left the ML when he walked off the Expos in protest of the release of friend Rodney Scott. He was the victim of freak accidents, including one where he was nearly killed by a taxi that ran him down while he was jogging. In between the oddities, he was a fine control pitcher who won 17 games three straight seasons for Boston (1973–75) and 16 for the Expos in 1979. /(MC)

Bill Lee [William Crutchfield] (Big Bill, General) — 1909–1977. RHP 1934–47 **Cubs**, Phillies, Braves 2864 ip, 169–157, 3.54. 20 wins: 35, 38 *2 WS, 21 ip, 0–2, 2.95*
☛ *Led League—w 38. Led League—era 38. All-Star—38–39.*

General Lee was a 6'3" Louisianan whose extremely high leg kick deceived batters and gave his fastball added speed. He was buried in the Cardinals system despite a 71–31 record over four seasons. Branch

Rickey made a choice between Paul Dean and Lee in 1934, bringing Dean to the majors and selling Lee to the Cubs. Lee shut out the Phillies in his first ML start (5/7/34). In his sophomore season, 1935, he led the NL with a .769 winning percentage (20–6), recorded five victories during the Cubs' 21-game winning streak, and won the pennant clincher.

Lee was positively intimidating in 1938, helping the Cubs to another World Series by leading the league with 22 wins, a .710 winning percentage, a 2.66 ERA, 37 starts, and nine shutouts. During one period he reeled off 32 consecutive scoreless innings and yielded only one run in 47 innings; the lone run was driven in by a pitcher and prevented Lee from hurling five straight shutouts. In September he racked up a streak of 37–1/3 scoreless innings, which included a flawless relief job between four shutouts.

Lee lost his touch in 1940. His eyes began to fail, and he had trouble seeing his catcher's signals. The high point of his 8–14 season in 1941 came on May 7, when he hit two home runs in a game. With the help of eyeglasses, he went 13–13 in 1942, then bounced from team to team, twice winning 10 games. After he retired, he underwent delicate surgery for two detached retinas and eventually lost his sight. /(DB)

Bob Lee (Moose, Horse) — 1937– . RHP 1964–68 **Angels**, Dodgers, Reds 492 ip, 25–23, 2.71

Lee was the ace of the Angels' bullpen for three years, finishing fifth in the AL with 19 saves his rookie year (1964) and fourth with 23 in 1965 (before the save was an official statistic). His 1.51 ERA in 1964 was the second-lowest ever in the AL for a rookie. He faded after being traded to the NL following the 1966 season. /(JFC)

Cliff Lee — 1896–1980. OF-1B 1919–26 Pirates, **Phillies**, Reds, Indians 521 g, .300, 38 hr, 216 rbi

Cliff's bat earned him one season (1923) as an outfield regular with the cellar-dwelling Phillies, but essentially he was a utility man who had catching, outfield, and first base skills. /(ADS)

Don Lee (Moose) — 1934– . RHP 1957–58, 60–66 Tigers, Senators/Twins, **Angels**, Astros, Cubs 828 ip, 40–44, 3.61

The son of 16-year veteran Thornton Lee, Don was an occasional starter who won a career-high 11 games in 1962, 8 for the expansion Angels. /(FK)

Hal Lee (Sheriff) — 1905– . OF 1930–36 Dodgers, Phillies, **Braves** 752 g, .275, 33 hr, 323 rbi

Discovered as a college star for the University of Mississippi, Lee was a graceful fielder who twice hit .303. Yet he never lived up to early promise, reportedly because he lacked ambition. /(JK)

Leron Lee — 1948– . OF 1969–76. Cardinals, **Padres**, Indians, Dodgers 614 g, .250, 31 hr, 152 rbi

A top high school football player, Lee refused numerous scholarship offers to sign with the Cardinals for an estimated $50,000. His only good year came with the Padres in 1972 when he batted .300 in 101 games, only the second Padre ever to hit that mark. /(BC)

Manny Lee — 1965– . 2B-SS 1985– **Blue Jays** 370 g, .265, 7 hr, 90 rbi. *2 LCS, 2 g, .250*

Lee's natural position is shortstop, but at Toronto he found himself behind fellow San Pedro de Macoris, Dominican Republic native Tony Fernandez. In 1988, between the departure of Damaso Garcia and the ascendance of Nelson Liriano, Lee was the Blue Jays' primary second baseman, and hit a career-high .291. /(SFS)

Mark Lee — 1953– . RHP 1978–81 **Padres**, Pirates 176 ip, 7–8, 3.63

Lee's only winning record came in his rookie 1978 season, when the 6'4" 225-lb reliever went 5–1 with a 3.28 ERA. /(WOR)

Thornton Lee (Lefty) — 1906– . LHP 1933–48 Indians, **White Sox**, Giants 2331 ip, 117–124, 3.56. 20 wins: 41

☛ *Led League—era 41. All-Star—41.*

Lee reached the major leagues in 1933 at age twenty-seven and struggled for four years with Cleveland. His fortunes changed when White Sox manager Jimmy Dykes saw something in the left-hander and obtained him in a three-way deal. Relying on fine control and a sinking fastball, he blossomed under the tutelage of coach Muddy Ruel and became one of baseball's top lefthanders from 1937 to 1941. But little offensive support left him on the losing end of many close decisions. In 1941 he had a great year, leading the league with 30 complete games and a 2.37 ERA, and collecting a $2,500 bonus for winning more than 20. Three years of misery followed; he broke his arm and underwent two bone chip removals and a neck operation. He bounced back in 1945, going 15–12, and was still pitching at age forty-two, nine years before his son, pitcher Don Lee, broke in with the

Tigers. Ted Williams homered off both of them, the only man to hit a HR off a father and son. /(DB)

Watty Lee [Wyatt Arnold] — 1879–1936. OF-LHP 1901–04 **Senators**, Pirates 235 g, .242, 4 hr, 70 rbi; 549 ip, 30–37, 4.29

Lee divided his playing time between the mound, where he was 16–16 as a rookie, and the outfield, where he hit .256 as a regular the next year. /(JK)

Sam Leever (The Goshen Schoolmaster) — 1871–1953. RHP 1898–1910 **Pirates** 2661 ip, 193–101, 2.47. 20 wins: 99, 03, 06 *1 WS, 10 ip, 0–2, 6.30*
☛ *Led League—era 03.*

A righthander of quiet ways, sober temperament, and sharp-breaking curveball, Leever was a mainstay of the Pirate pitching staff during the heyday of Honus Wagner. Born in Goshen, Ohio, and a former teacher (hence his nickname), Leever was not colorful, just consistent, posting 11 consecutive winning seasons. In 1903, his best year, he led the NL in winning percentage (.781), ERA (2.06) and shutouts (7). Two of his 25 wins came in a string of six consecutive shutouts, still the ML record. Near the end of that season he injured his shoulder while trapshooting, a second sport at which he excelled. As a result he had a sore arm during the 1903 WS and lost twice to the Red Sox. His lifetime winning percentage of .656 is third (after Christy Mathewson and Sal Maglie) among NL pitchers in the 20th century and tenth all-time. /(ADS)

Jim Lefebvre (Frenchy) — 1943– . 2B-3B 1965–72 **Dodgers** 922 g, .251, 74 hr, 404 rbi. *2 WS, 7 g, .273, 1 hr, 1 rbi.*
    Manager 1989– **Mariners** 73–89, .451

Part of the Dodgers' switch-hitting infield of the mid-1960s with Jim Gilliam, Maury Wills, and Wes Parker, Lefebvre homered from both sides of the plate in one game on May 7, 1966. His 12 HR as a rookie in 1965 was the lowest total to lead a pennant winner since 1947, and he homered off Dave McNally in the 1966 WS opener, providing one of the two runs the Dodgers would score all series in a four-game sweep by the Orioles. He played in Japan in 1973–76 and later coached the Dodgers, Giants, and A's. He was named the Mariners' manager in the winter of 1988 after gaining respect as the batting coach of the AL champion A's. /(TG)

Joe Lefebvre — 1956– . OF-3B 1980–84, 86 Yankees, **Padres**, Phillies 447 g, .258, 31 hr, 130 rbi. *2 LCS, 3 g, .000. 1 WS, 3 g, .200, 2 rbi*

Lefebvre (pronounced "luh-FAY") was a promising power hitter who homered in his first two major league games for the Yankees, tying a record. After being traded to the Padres, he was unsuccessfully converted to third base (and even caught some games). On September 13, 1982 he had six hits in a 16-inning game.

Lefebvre seemed finally ready to fulfill his promise after hitting .310 following a May 1983 trade to the Phillies, finishing at .306 for the year with eight HR and 20 doubles in 278 at-bats and helping Philadelphia win the NL pennant. But he was felled by back trouble in June 1984 and missed all of 1985 too; a comeback attempt in 1986 failed. /(SFS)

Craig Lefferts — 1957– . LHP 1983– Cubs, **Padres**, Giants 683 ip, 32–39, 3.00. *3 LCS, 7 ip, 2–0, 1.29. 2 WS, 9 ip, 0–0, 1.04*

A career reliever, the German-born Lefferts was a set-up man for six years before emerging as the Giants' closer in the first half of 1989. After Steve Bedrosian was acquired, the two shared the role. Lefferts pitched 10 shutout innings in the 1984 postseason for the Padres, winning the final two games of the LCS and saving San Diego's lone victory in the WS, and in 1986 led the ML with 83 appearances (breaking Rollie Fingers's Padres record). He was traded to San Francisco in the seven-player, July 4, 1987 deal that also involved Kevin Mitchell and Mark Davis. /(SCL)

Ron LeFlore — 1948– . OF 1974–82 **Tigers**, Expos 1099 g, .288, 59 hr, 353 rbi
☛ *All-Star—76.*

Ron LeFlore first played baseball while serving a 5-to-15-year sentence for armed robbery. The native of Detroit, who first claimed to have been born in 1952, then 1950, and finally admitted to 1948, was discovered when Tiger manager Billy Martin visited Jackson State Prison. Signed to a contract in July 1973, he made the majors a year later and was made Detroit's regular centerfielder by manager Ralph Houk to take advantage of LeFlore's blinding speed. Possibly the fastest man in baseball during his prime, he hit .316 with 93 runs and 58 stolen bases in 1976 despite a season-halting leg injury late in the year. He had a 30-game hitting streak, the longest in the AL in 27 years. He added power with 16 HR in 1977 and was the first Tiger since Al Kaline, 22 years earlier, to get more than 200 hits. LeFlore also led AL righthanded batters with a .325 average after a slow start that saw him hitting .230 at the end of May. His life story was published in *Breakout*, later made into the movie *One in a Million*.

In his best season, 1978, he led the AL with 126 runs and 68 stolen bases, had a career-high 62 RBI despite being a leadoff batter, and hit in 27 straight games. After reaching a new personal high of 78 steals in 1979, also hitting .300 with 100 runs scored, he was sent to Montreal in a salary dispute. He led the NL with 97 steals but dropped to .257 with four HR. He retired after two part-time seasons with the White Sox. /(SH)

Ken Lehman — 1928- . LHP 1952, 56-58, 61 Dodgers, **Orioles**, Phillies 265 ip, 14-10, 3.91. *1 WS, 2 ip, 0-0, 0.00*

As a rookie, Lehman mopped up in the Dodgers' Game Two loss in the 1952 WS. An ineffective reliever in Brooklyn, he was sold to Baltimore in 1957 and had his best season, 8-3 with six saves and a 2.52 ERA. /(FK)

Paul Lehner — 1920-1967. OF 1946-52 **Browns**, A's, White Sox, Indians, Red Sox 540 g, .257, 22 hr, 197 rbi

Lehner was an average outfielder with a weak bat for the Browns during his first four ML seasons. Suddenly, after a trade to Philadelphia in 1950, he hit .309 with nine homers, far beyond his previous highs. Believing Lehner had hit his stride, the White Sox insisted he be included in the three-team deal that brought Minnie Minoso to Chicago. Lehner's batting average sank and he was out of the majors by 1952. /(RL)

Nemo Leibold [Harry Loran] — 1892-1977. OF 1913-25 Indians, **White Sox**, Red Sox, Senators 1258 g, .266, 4 hr, 283 rbi. *4 WS, 13 g, .161, 2 rbi*

The 5'7" 157-lb Leibold, nicknamed for the comic strip character Little Nemo, hit only four homers in 13 ML seasons but played on four pennant winners. He was a reliable fielder and a pesky hitter, particularly when platooned against righthanded pitchers. As a longtime minor league manager, he was notoriously bellicose. In 1946 he was suspended for the season after a shoving match with a minor league umpire. When he was reinstated before the end of the season, several umpires quit in protest. /(JK)

Charlie Leibrandt — 1956- . LHP 1979-82, 84- Reds, **Royals** 1573 ip, 92-78, 3.77. *3 LCS, 24 ip, 1-3, 3.80. 1 WS, 16 ip, 0-1, 2.76*

The Leibrandt for Bob Tufts deal remains one of the Royals' best trades. While Tufts never pitched

another game, Charlie established himself as the paradigm of reliability in the Kansas City rotation. Not equipped with one outstanding pitch, he mastered the talent of painting the edge of the strike zone while never coming down the center. Overshadowed by Saberhagen and Gubicza, he posted the most Royals victories from 1985 to 1988. /(FJO)

Lefty Leifield [Albert Peter] — 1883-1970. LHP 1905-13, 18-20 **Pirates**, Cubs, Browns 1838 ip, 124-96, 2.47. 20 wins: 07 *1 WS, 4 ip, 0-1, 11.25*

Leifield was an outstanding starter for the Pirates until a sore arm all but ended his career at age twenty-eight. He won 20 games in 1907 and 19 for the 1909 pennant winners. He threw three one-hitters, but in one, he got his team's only hit and lost to the Cubs' Three Finger Brown. /(JK)

Dave Leiper — 1962- . LHP 1984, 86- **A's**, Padres 190 ip, 9-4, 3.94

The Padres took Leiper from Oakland in a 1987 trade for Storm Davis. Leiper recorded a 2.17 ERA in 35 games of middle relief for San Diego in 1988. /(JCA)

Al Leiter — 1965- . LHP 1987- **Yankees**, Blue Jays 114 ip, 7-8, 4.92

The Yankees' second-round pick in the June 1984 draft, Leiter came up in 1987 hailed as the trade-decimated farm system's best pitching talent. Put into the rotation in 1988, he was frequently unable to pitch due to a recurring blister. Traded to Toronto early in the 1989 season for Jesse Barfield, he went on the DL with tendinitis shortly thereafter. His brothers Kurt and Mark pitched in the Orioles organization. /(WOR)

Larry LeJeune [Sheldon Aldenbert] — 1885-1952. OF 1911, 15 Dodgers, **Pirates** 24 g, .167, 4 rbi

On October 12, 1910, Field Day in Cincinnati, LeJeune threw a baseball a record 426 feet 9 inches. Although he never hit well in the ML, he was a five-time minor league batting champion. /(ME)

Jack Lelivelt — 1885-1941. OF 1909-14 **Senators**, Yankees, Indians 381 g, .301, 2 hr, 126 rbi

Lelivelt was a bulky, slow-footed outfielder who became an outstanding minor league manager. He compiled a .331 minor league batting average from 1906 through 1925, the last five seasons as a playing manager. Over 21 seasons, his teams won 1861 games for a .564 percentage, including three Pacific Coast League titles. /(JK)

Dave Lemanczyk (Tarzan) — 1950– . RHP 1973–80 Tigers, **Blue Jays**, Angels 920 ip, 37–63, 4.62
☛ *All-Star—79.*

Lemanczyk was a workhorse starter for the Blue Jays in their expansion years. His 13 wins in 1977 tied a record for a first-year expansion team. A dozen seasons later, Lemanczyk remained on the franchise record books for his 1977 totals for wild pitches, hits, and runs allowed. On April 24, 1979 against the Rangers, Lemanczyk threw the Blue Jays' first one-hitter, on his way to an All-Star selection and a career-best 3.71 ERA. After his playing career, Lemanczyk became a player agent, and became engaged in acrimonious litigation with Dave Stieb. /(TF)

Denny Lemaster — 1939– . LHP 1962–72 **Braves**, Astros, Expos 1788 ip, 90–105, 3.58
☛ *All-Star—67.*

Lemaster seemed on the brink of stardom through most of his 11-season ML career but never quite fulfilled his early promise. Signed by the Braves for a $60,000 bonus in 1958, the hard-throwing lefty fanned 11 straight batters for Jacksonville in 1959 and led the Texas League in strikeouts the next year. After going 10–4 in half a season at Louisville and apparently overcoming his early control problems, he joined the Braves' rotation in mid-season. He struck out 190 with a 3.04 era in 1963 and went 17–11 in 1964. The next year he developed a sore arm which bothered him intermittently through the rest of his career. Traded to Houston in 1968, he continued to show flashes of brilliance and record excellent strikeout totals until his arm problems ended his effectiveness in 1971. /(MC)

Johnnie LeMaster — 1954– . SS 1975–85, 87 **Giants**, Indians, Pirates, A's 1039 g, .222, 22 hr, 229 rbi

LeMaster was the 43rd player to hit a home run in his first ML at-bat, but he hit very little after that. As the Giants' regular shortstop from 1978 through 1985, the slender infielder was a sometimes competent fielder. /(FS)

Dick LeMay (Lefty) — 1938– . LHP 1961–63 **Giants**, Cubs 108 ip, 3–8, 4.17

Known for his weird, leg-kicking, arm-flailing, hip-swiveling, shoulder-dipping windup, LeMay depended on his screwball. Recommended to the Giants by famed screwballer Carl Hubbell, LeMay

enjoyed strong International and Pacific Coast league years after leaving the majors. /(BC)

Bob Lemon — 1920– . RHP-3B 1941–42, 46–58 **Indians** 615 g, .232, 37 hr, 147 rbi; 2850 ip, 207–128, 3.23. 20 wins: 48–50, 52–54, 56 *2 WS, 30 ip, 2–2, 3.94.*
   Manager 1970–72, 77–79, 81–82 **Royals**, White Sox, Yankees 432–401, .519. First place: 78, 81 *2 LCS, 6–1, .857. 2 WS, 6–6, .500*
☛ *Led League—w 50, 54–55. Led League—k 50. All-Star—48–54. Hall of Fame—1976.*

The easygoing Lemon learned to pitch in the major leagues and went on to become one of the most successful righthanders of the post-WWII period. He was enshrined in the Hall of Fame in 1976. In two trials as a third baseman before the war he failed to stick with the Indians because of his mediocre hitting. He showed a strong arm in the field, but his throws had a natural sinking effect. Upon his return to Cleveland after three years in the Navy, he turned to pitching at age twenty-six.

Bob Lemon

Although bothered by wildness, he showed enough promise in his first season on the mound (2.49 ERA in 94 innings) to continue the experiment. In 1947 he was 11–5 and became the Indians' second most effective starter behind Hall of Famer Bob Feller.

Cleveland won the 1948 pennant, as Feller, Lemon, and rookie Gene Bearden combined for 59 wins. Lemon, at 20–14, led the AL in shutouts (10), complete games (20), and innings pitched (294). On June 30, he threw a no-hitter to top the Tigers 2–0. In the World Series, he picked up two wins (1.65 ERA) as the Indians defeated the Braves.

Lemon became the leader of the outstanding Indians pitching staffs of the 1950s that also included Feller, Early Wynn, Mike Garcia, and later Herb Score. In a remarkably consistent nine-year stretch (1948–56), Lemon won 20 or more games seven times. He missed the magic number only in 1951 with 17 victories and 1955 when his 18 wins topped the league. A workhorse, he led in complete games five times and innings pitched four. *TSN* named him the Outstanding AL Pitcher three times (1948, 50, 54).

The 1954 Indians set an AL record with 111 victories (in 154 games) as Lemon led the pitching staff with a 23–7 mark. He opened the World Series against the Giants and took a 2–2 tie into the tenth inning before giving up a three-run home run to pinch hitter Dusty Rhodes. When the Indians lost the next two, manager Al Lopez brought Lemon back on two days' rest, but he was shelled early as the Giants swept the Series.

Lemon's money pitch was his sinking fastball. He led the AL in strikeouts with 170 in 1950, but he was most effective when opposing batters were beating the ball into the dirt. Always slightly wild, his season bases on balls and strikeout marks were usually similar, as were his career bases totals of 1,251 walks and 1,277 strikeouts.

Lemon was considered to be one of the best-hitting pitchers of his time and was often used as a pinch hitter, totaling 31 hits in 109 pinch-hit appearances (.284). His 37 home runs lifetime is just one behind Wes Ferrell's record for pitchers, and his 7 HR in 1949 ties him for second on the pitchers' season list.

After leaving the majors, Lemon pitched briefly in the Pacific Coast League, then turned to scouting, coaching, and managing. In 1966 *TSN* named him Minor League Manager of the Year when his Seattle team won the PCL championship. From 1970–72 he managed the Kansas City Royals, with a 1971

second place the team's best mark, earning him Manager of the Year honors. He took over the Chicago White Sox in 1977, managing another mediocre team to a strong finish, and again won Manager of the Year. But Lemon was replaced the next season with the team in fifth place.

A few weeks later, Lemon began a bewildering series of ups and downs with the New York Yankees. First, he succeeded fiery Billy Martin as skipper of the third-place Yankees. The team responded to his relaxed leadership and finished the regular schedule tied with the Red Sox for the division title. New York won the one-game playoff on Bucky Dent's home run. After taking the LCS, Lemon's Yankees went on to a World Series win over the Dodgers.

Midway through the 1979 season, Martin replaced him as Yankee manager. In 1981, when the player strike split the season into two parts, Gene Michael managed the Yankees to a first-half division lead, but when the team faltered in the second half after the strike, Lemon returned as manager. He took the Yankees to victory in the divisional playoff between the Yankees and second-half winner Milwaukee and then a three-game sweep of Oakland in the LCS. The Yankees lost the World Series to the Dodgers in six games. When New York started slowly in 1982, Lemon was again replaced as manager, this time by Michael. /(BC)

Chet Lemon — 1955– . OF 1975– White Sox, **Tigers** 1884 g, .274, 210 hr, 852 rbi. *2 LCS, 8 g, .161, 2 hr, 4 rbi. 1 WS, 5 g, .294, 1 rbi*
☛ *All-Star—78–79, 84.*

Lemon first signed with the A's but was acquired by the White Sox in a June 1975 trade for Stan Bahnsen. A third baseman in the minors, he became Chicago's center fielder in 1976. He made a hustling, aggressive style of play his trademark, with headfirst slides into first base and his willingness to be hit by a pitch. Getting great jumps on the ball, he broke two AL records in 1977: most chances for an outfielder (524) and most putouts (512). From 1978 through 1981, he batted .304, with a high of .318 in 1979, when he tied for the AL lead with 44 doubles.

After the '81 season, Lemon was traded to Detroit for Steve Kemp. Leaving spacious Comiskey Park for smaller Tiger Stadium, his home run production went up, but his average dipped. He matured as a player, becoming a smarter baserunner and a key contributor to Detroit's perennially strong teams. /(RL)

Jim Lemon — 1928- . OF-1B 1950, 53-63 Indians, **Senators/Twins**, Phillies, White Sox 1010 g, .262, 164 hr, 529 rbi.

Manager 1968 **Senators** 65-96, .404

☛ *All-Star—60* .

Combining power, speed, and an exceptional arm, Lemon joined the Indians in 1950 but lost 1951 and 1952 to the Korean War. Sold to the Senators in May 1954, in 1956 he hit 27 home runs and led the AL in triples and in double plays by an outfielder. That August 31 he became the first Senator to hit three consecutive home runs. Lemon led the AL in strikeouts three years in a row (1956–58); his 138 strikeouts in 1956 (in a 154-game season) set a record. On September 5, 1959 he tied two ML records by hitting two homers and driving in six runs in one inning. He had 100 RBI in both 1959 and 1960. In 1960 he chased Mickey Mantle and Roger Maris for the AL home run crown, losing to Mantle 40 to 38. Slowed by injuries in 1961 and 1962, he attempted a comeback as a first baseman with the Phillies in 1963. He coached for the Twins from 1965 to 1967 and managed the Senators to their usual last-place finish in 1968. Replaced by Ted Williams for 1969, he remained in baseball as a batting coach, mainly with the Twins. /(MC)

Mark Lemongello — 1955- . RHP 1976-79 Astros, Blue Jays 537 ip, 22-38, 4.06

After breaking in impressively with Houston late in the 1976 season with a 3–1 record and a 2.79 ERA, Lemongello slipped once he was placed in the regular rotation. His trade to Toronto brought catcher Alan Ashby to the Astros. /(BC)

Don Lenhardt — 1922- . OF-1B-3B 1950-54 **Browns**, White Sox, Tigers, Orioles 481 g, .271, 61 hr, 239 rbi

Footsie (because of his narrow shoe size) was a rangy power hitter whose slow drawl matched his running speed. Despite 22 home runs as a rookie, he was dealt five times in five years, including the nine-player swap that sent George Kell to the Red Sox. A broken leg in 1954 ended his career. /(BC)

Ed Lennox (Eggie) — 1885-1939. 3B 1906, 09–10, 12, 14–15 Phillies, **Dodgers**, Cubs, Pittsburgh (FL) 448 g, .274, 18 hr, 185 rbi

A journeyman infielder, Lennox led NL third basemen in fielding average in 1909 as a Dodger rookie. He hit best in the Federal League. His 1914 totals (.312, 11 HR, 84 RBI) were all career highs. /(JK)

Eddie Leon — 1946- . SS-2B 1968-75 Indians, White Sox, Yankees 601 g, .236, 24 hr, 159 rbi

Leon was a college baseball All-American at the University of Arizona in 1966 with a .378 batting average and 74 RBIs, but he showed little hitting ability in his eight-year ML career. /(BC)

Max Leon — 1950- . RHP 1973-78 **Braves** 311 ip, 14-18, 3.70

Leon began pitching professionally in his native Mexico, joining the Braves organization in 1973 after a 17-7 season at Jalisco. A starter in Mexico, he was used mainly in long relief once he reached the majors. After suffering arm trouble, he returned to Mexico and again became a consistent winner, including an 18-2 record in 1983-84. /(MC)

Buck Leonard [Walter Fenner] — 1907- . 1B-OF Negro Leagues 1933-50 Brooklyn Royal Giants, Homestead Grays statistics not available

☛ *Hall of Fame—1972.*

Leonard is the only Negro League first baseman enshrined in Cooperstown. A lefthanded power hitter, he teamed with legendary slugger Josh Gibson to lead the Homestead Grays to nine consecutive Negro National League championships from 1937 through 1945. The duo was dubbed the "Thunder Twins" by the black press. Leonard was called a black Lou Gehrig, Gibson a black Babe Ruth. While Gibson slugged tape measure home runs, the pull-hitting Leonard, who feasted on fastballs, demonstrated his smooth, powerful stroke by hitting line drives off and over the walls. Leonard was equally smooth and consistent at first base. His sure-handed glove work was compared with that of Hal Chase and George Sisler. He was a smart fielder who always made the right play. Dependable and respected by his teammates, he was a steadying influence on the Grays.

Leonard began his career in 1933 with the semi-pro Elks and Black Swans in his native Rocky Mount, NC, after he lost his job due to the Depression. After being picked up by the Portsmouth, VA Firefighters, he was soon signed by the Baltimore Stars. When the Stars broke up later that season, he finished with the Brooklyn Royal Giants. The next spring, he was recruited by former Homestead ace Smokey Joe Williams for Cum Posey's Grays. For the next 17 years, Leonard was the Grays' first baseman.

Beginning in 1942, when Leonard hit 42 HR, the Grays appeared in four consecutive Black World

Buck Leonard

Series and won championships in 1943–44. Leonard tied Gibson for the '44 HR title, and in the BWS he batted .500. He hit .375 in 1945, finishing behind Gibson in the HR race. Leonard tied for the HR lead and won his third batting title with a .395 mark in 1948. Under Leonard's inspirational leadership, the Grays won their 10th pennant that year and a record third BWS.

Years before Branch Rickey brought Jackie Robinson to the Dodgers, Senators owner Clark Griffith approached Leonard and Gibson about playing in the majors. But Griffith backed down,

deciding not to disturb the status quo. When the color line was finally broken, Bill Veeck contacted Leonard about playing in the majors, but the veteran felt he was too old. He said he "didn't want to embarrass anyone or hurt the chances of those who might follow." His only appearance in organized ball came at age forty-six, in 1953, when he played 10 games for Portsmouth (Piedmont League) and batted .333.

Leonard compiled a lifetime .341 average in the Negro National League and a .382 mark in exhibitions against major leaguers. He made a record 12 appearances in the annual East-West all-star game, hitting .317 with an all-star record three HR.

After the Grays disbanded, Leonard played in Mexico from 1951 to 1955. He liked the warm climate, having spent winters on the diamonds of Cuba, Puerto Rico, and Venezuela. In 1962 he helped organize the Rocky Mount (Carolina League) club and served as its vice-president. Leonard and Gibson were inducted into the Hall of Fame by the Committee on Negro Baseball Leagues in 1972. /(JR)

Dennis Leonard — 1951– . RHP 1974–83, 85–86 **Royals** 2187 ip, 144–106, 3.69. 20 wins: 77–78, 80 *4 LCS, 31 ip, 2–3, 4.31. 1 WS, 11 ip, 1–1, 6.75*
☛ *Led League—w 77.*

The redhead was the Royals' Pitcher of the Year in 1975, 1977, and 1979. He employed a hard fastball, curve, and slider to average 18 wins a year, 1975–80. His philosophy: "Win or lose, take something out of a game that will help me next time." In 1982 he missed half the season after suffering a broken finger from a line drive. Torn knee ligaments cost him nearly all of the next three seasons. In 1986 Leonard returned to honor the final year of his contract. He made the starting rotation, and though his record was only 8–13, he pitched several strong games in the first half of the season, including two shutouts. Before coming to the Royals, he hurled two no-hitters in the minors. /(FO)

Dutch Leonard [Emil] — 1909–1983. RHP 1933–36, 38–53 Dodgers, **Senators**, Phillies, Cubs 3218 ip, 191–181, 3.25. 20 wins: 39

Emil "Dutch" Leonard was one of the first pitchers to rely heavily on the knuckleball. Pitching almost exclusively for losing teams during his 20 years in the ML, he nevertheless won 191 games. His success with what was until then considered a trick pitch inspired a whole generation of knuckleball specialists, including Hoyt Wilhelm.

After his 14–11 year with the Dodgers in 1934, a sore arm threatened Leonard's career. Eventually he was sent to Atlanta of the Southern Association where, with the help of the knuckleball, he posted two strong seasons. He returned to the majors with Washington in 1938 and the next year enjoyed a 20–8 year with the sixth-place Senators.

Although Leonard occasionally mixed in a fastball or slip pitch to keep hitters off-balance, the knuckler was his primary out pitch. He had exceptional control of all his pitches, averaging only 2.06 walks per nine innings pitched.

After an 18–13 season in 1941, Leonard missed almost all the next year with a broken ankle, but he came back to post double-digit win totals for the Senators through 1946, including a 17–7 mark in 1945. An oddity that season, aside from Washington's uncharacteristic second-place finish, was that three other regular Senator hurlers—Roger Wolff, Mickey Haefner, and Johnny Niggeling—were knuckleballers.

Leonard was sold to the Phillies after the 1946 season and was traded with Monk Dubiel to the Cubs for Eddie Waitkus and Hank Borowy two years later. Though he had always been a starting pitcher, he became an outstanding reliever with the Cubs. He once cited as one of his greatest thrills a game in which he was called in against the powerful Dodgers to protect a one-run lead in the ninth inning with the bases loaded and no outs. He retired Jackie Robinson, Gil Hodges, and Roy Campanella without a run scoring. /(BC)

Hub Leonard (Dutch) — 1892–1952. LHP 1913–21, 24–25 **Red Sox**, Tigers 2190 ip, 139–112, 2.77. *2 WS, 2–0, 1.00*

☛ *Led League—era 14.*

Hub was a sterling lefthander in the days of Red Sox greatness, although he never achieved a 20-win season. He threw two no-hitters and his 1.01 ERA in 1914 is the all-time top mark. In 1927, then a successful California grape grower, he made public two letters implicating Ty Cobb, Tris Speaker, and himself in a possibly fixed game in 1919. Other than resentment of his two former managers, his motive was unclear. When he refused to leave California to press his case, the two Hall of Famers were exonerated by Judge Landis. /(ADS)

Jeffrey Leonard (Hac-Man) — 1955– . OF-DH 1977– Dodgers, Astros, **Giants**, Brewers, Mariners 1281 g, .268, 134 hr, 648 rbi. *2 LCS, 10 g, .310, 4 hr, 5 rbi*

☛ *All-Star—87, 89.*

Called Hac-Man for his aggressiveness at the plate and Penitentiary Face for his perpetual scowl, Leonard escaped the streets of Philadelphia to become a dangerous, free-swinging ML hitter. He led all minor leaguers with a .365 average at Albuquerque (Pacific Coast League) in 1978 and was *TSN* NL Rookie Player of the Year when he hit .290 with 23 steals for the Astros in 1979. Traded to the Giants with Dave Bergman for Mike Ivie in late 1981, the sullen-looking slugger injured his hand diving for a ball in 1982 but rebounded with 21 HR in both 1983 and 1984, and his .302 average in 1984 was a career high. A sizzling start in 1987 (he was hitting .374 on May 27) earned Leonard an All-Star appearance, and in the 1987 LCS he became only the third player in postseason history to win the MVP award while his team lost the series. Leonard hit home runs in each of the first four games, taunting the Cardinals with his slow, deliberate "one-flap-down" trot, with one arm held against his side and the other arm extended. He hit .417 for the series. He was traded to Milwaukee for Ernest Riles in June 1988, and after the season signed as a free agent with Seattle, where he resurrected his career. A foot injury confined him to DHing, but he nonetheless reached career highs with 24 HR and 93 RBI. /(SCL)

Joe Leonard — 1894–1920. 3B-2B-1B 1914, 16–17, 19–20 Pirates, Indians, **Senators** 269 g, .226, 2 hr, 61 rbi

Utility man Leonard of the Senators fell ill in Boston early in 1920 and was sent back to Washington, where he died of a ruptured appendix. /(JK)

Dave Leonhard — 1942– . RHP 1967–72 **Orioles** 337 ip, 16–14, 3.15. *2 WS, 18 ip, 0–0, 3.00*

A perpetual prospect, college-trained Leonhard (degree in history from Johns Hopkins) used good control of his slow ball to teeter just short of the brink of blossoming. Seven wins in 1968 and again in '69 were his best marks. /(BC)

Ted Lepcio — 1930– . 2B-3B-SS 1952–61 **Red Sox**, Tigers, Phillies, White Sox, Twins 729 g, .245, 69 hr, 251 rbi

Although his 1960 manager, Eddie Sawyer, labeled him "the worst player I ever saw," Lepcio was a competent utility man with occasional power (15 home runs in 1956) for ten ML seasons. A bonus baby out of Seton Hall College, he reportedly signed for $60,000. /(BC)

Don Leppert — 1931– . C 1961–64, Pirates, **Senators** 190 g, .229, 15 hr, 59 rbi

The burly backup catcher, known as a handy man in a brawl, became the 20th player to hit a home run in his first ML at-bat (June 18, 1961). At Wabash College, he starred with the shotput and discus. /(BC)

Randy Lerch — 1954– . LHP 1975–86 **Phillies**, Brewers, Expos, Giants 1100 ip, 60–64, 4.52. *1 LCS, 5 ip, 0–0, 5.06*

Known nearly as well for his hitting as for his pitching, Lerch had a lifetime batting average of .206, with 56 base hits. In 1978 his three home runs led all NL pitchers. Two of those came in a crucial September 30 game against the Pirates to help edge the Phillies past Pittsburgh for the division crown.

He started the fourth and final game of the 1978 LCS, but was tagged for three runs and seven hits in 5–1/3 innings, as the Phillies lost to the Dodgers. The 6'5" lefthander enjoyed three seasons in double-figure wins but was less effective after breaking a bone in his wrist in 1979. /(BC)

Walt Lerian (Peck) — 1903–1929. C 1928–29 **Phillies** 201 g, .246, 9 hr, 50 rbi

The Phillies' starting catcher in 1929, Lerian was killed during the off-season when he was struck by an out-of-control automobile that ran up onto the sidewalk. /(JK)

Barry Lersch — 1944– . RHP 1969–74 **Phillies**, Cardinals 570 ip, 18–32, 3.82

Blond, fun-loving Lersch featured a good curve with excellent control and added a knuckleball late in his career. In 1971, he suffered through a personal 11-game losing streak, one less than the Phillie record. /(BC)

Sam Leslie (Sambo) — 1905–1979. 1B 1929–38 **Giants**, Dodgers 822 g, .304, 36 hr, 389 rbi. *2 WS, 5 g, .500*

Leslie was a solid hitter but mediocre fielder, leading one writer to comment: "He could hit if you woke him up at two in the morning but couldn't field if you played him at two in the afternoon." A top pinch hitter with the Giants (22 for 72 in 1932), he was traded to the Dodgers for Lefty O'Doul and Watty Clark in 1933. After four years as a regular, he was sold back to the Giants, where his pinch hitting contributed to pennants in 1936 and 1937. /(FS)

Walt Leverenz (Tiny) — 1887–1973. LHP 1913–15 **Browns** 323 ip, 7–31, 3.15

Leverenz had two dismal seasons for the Browns, going 6–17 as a rookie in 1913 and 1–12 in 1914. His downfall was the base on balls; he averaged almost five walks and only three strikeouts a game. /(WAB)

Dixie Leverett [Gorham Vance] — 1894–1957. RHP 1922–24, 26, 29 **White Sox**, Braves 638 ip, 29–34, 4.50

Leverett was impressive as 1922 White Sox rookie, going 13–10 with four shutouts. When he reported to camp 10 pounds overweight in 1925, he was sent down. He shed the weight but couldn't do the job after making the club in 1926. /(RL)

Jim Levey — 1906–1970. SS 1930–33 **Browns** 440 g, .230, 11 hr, 140 rbi

Discovered while playing for the Marines, Levey made 147 errors in three years as the Browns' regular shortstop, hitting .280 in 1932 but under .210 in all his other seasons. In 1934 he joined Pittsburgh of the NFL and played three seasons at halfback. /(JK)

Dutch Levsen [Emil Henry] — 1898–1972. RHP 1923–28 **Indians** 404 ip, 21–26, 4.17

Levsen registered 16 of his 21 major league wins in 1926. That August 28, he became the last pitcher to record complete game victories in both ends of a doubleheader, as he tossed a pair of four-hitters against the Red Sox. /(ME)

Allen Lewis — 1916– . *Writer.*

Lewis was with the Philadelphia *Evening Ledger* before starting 33 years as a baseball writer for the *Inquirer* in 1946. For 16 years he wrote a weekly column on baseball and was a *Sporting News* correspondent. He covered 24 WS and was a member of the scoring-rules committee from 1958 to 1972. Lewis wrote *This Date in Philadelphia Phillies History* and *Phillies Pictorial History*. He received the J.G. Taylor Spink Award in 1981. /(NLM)

Buddy Lewis [John Kelly] — 1916– . 3B-OF 1935–41, 45–47, 49 **Senators** 1349 g, .297, 71 hr, 607 rbi
☛ *All-Star—38, 47.*

One of several stars who lost the peak years of their careers to military service, Lewis joined the Senators for eight games as an 18-year-old in 1935. The next season, when second baseman Buddy Myer was injured, the Washington infield was reshuffled and Lewis took over at third base. Myer was the defending AL batting champ, but Lewis hit a very respectable .291 and scored 100 runs. Myer became Lewis's mentor and the veteran's nickname was given to the youngster.

In the years before WWII, Lewis hit over .300 three times and scored 100 or more runs four times, with a high of 122 in 1938. He led the AL in triples (16) in 1939. In 1940 he moved to right field, allowing longtime Senator shortstop Cecil Travis, who was slowing down, to move to third. After returning from the service, he hit .333 at the end of the 1945 season and .292 in 1946. He had an off-year in 1947, then missed all of 1948 with an injury. When he could not regain his earlier form in a 1949 comeback bid, he retired. /(MC)

Duffy Lewis [George Edward] — 1888–1979. OF 1910–17, 19–21 **Red Sox**, Yankees, Senators 1459 g, .284, 38 hr, 793 rbi. *3 WS, 18 g, .284, 1 hr, 8 rbi*

Lewis was the left fielder in the famous Red Sox outfield that included Tris Speaker and Harry Hooper. He became so adept at fielding along the steep incline in front of Fenway Park's left-field fence that it became known as "Duffy's Cliff." Despite being one of the few players apparently liked by Ty Cobb, Lewis's fondest memories included throwing out Cobb as he attempted to stretch hits. At bat, he was a reliable line-drive hitter and good RBI man, with a personal high of 109 in 1912. In 1914 he became the first ML player to pinch hit for Babe Ruth, then a Red Sox rookie pitcher. The next season, he saw Ruth's first homer; in 1935, as traveling secretary for the Braves, a post he held for 30 years, he saw Ruth's last. /(EC)

Johnny Lewis — 1939– . OF 1964–67 Cardinals, **Mets** 266 g, .227, 22 hr, 74 hr

Shy and quiet, Lewis played in a shell, never realizing the stardom predicted for him. His career highlight came on June 14, 1965 when he homered leading off the 10th inning at Crosley Field to break up Jim Maloney's no-hitter and win the game 1–0 for the Mets. That was his only year as a regular; he hit .245 with 15 HR, 45 RBI, and 64 runs. /(BC)

Phil Lewis — 1883–1959. SS 1905–08 **Dodgers** 508 g, .242, 4 hr, 130 rbi

The 6' 195-lb Lewis was big for a turn-of-the-century shortstop, yet he was no slugger, and in four years as Brooklyn's shortstop was found lacking

defensively. He later became a logger in the Adirondacks. /(JK)

Ted Lewis (Parson, The Pitching Professor) — 1872–1936. RHP 1896–1901 **Braves**, Red Sox 1405 ip, 94–64, 3.53. 20 wins: 97–98

Born in Wales, Lewis signed with the Boston Nationals in 1896 after graduating from Williams College. He won 21 games that season and went 26–8 in 1897, both pennant-winning years for Boston. On June 22, 1898 he won a marathon game in relief and did not walk a batter in 13-2/3 innings. He continued his education during the off-season and coached baseball at Harvard, 1897–1901. After the 1901 season, he retired from baseball to teach full-time at Columbia and later at Williams. He became a prominent educator, eventually serving as president of Massachusetts State College, 1926–27, and the University of New Hampshire from 1927 until his death. /(LRD)

Jim Leyland — 1944– . *Manager* 1986- **Pirates** 303–343, .469

Leyland won Manager of the Year honors for leading the Pirates to a surprising second-place finish in 1988. A patient teacher, he worked well with Pittsburgh's young stars. /(JFC)

Sixto Lezcano — 1953– . OF 1974–85 **Brewers**, Cardinals, Padres, Phillies, Pirates 1291 g, .271, 148 hr, 591 rbi. *1 LCS, 4 g, .308, 1 hr, 2 rbi. 1 WS, 4 g, .125* ☛ *Gold Glove—79.*

Lezcano led both leagues in outfielder assists, with the Brewers in 1978 and the Padres in 1983. Erratic at bat, Lezcano had his best year in 1979 with the Brewers when he hit .321, with 28 homers (10 in August) and 101 RBI. /(MC)

Al Libke (Big Al) — 1918– . OF 1945–46 **Reds** 254 g, .268, 9 hr, 95 rbi

Libke was a top prospect during WWII when he hit .309 and won several games as a pitcher in the Pacific Coast League. He started in right field for the Reds for two seasons but couldn't hold his job when the talent supply improved after the war. /(JK)

Don Liddle (Little) — 1925– . LHP 1953–56 Braves, **Giants**, Cardinals 428 ip, 28–18, 3.75. *1 WS, 7 ip, 1–0 1.29*

The 160-lb lefthander was inevitably Little Liddle. Traded to the Giants as part of the Braves' deal for Johnny Antonelli and Bobby Thomson, he started and won the final game of the 1954 World Series four-game sweep of the Indians. /(BC)

Fred Lieb — 1888–1980. *Writer.*

Lieb was working as a clerk for the Norfolk & Western Railroad in 1909 when he began submitting biographies of players to *Baseball Magazine*. That led to a job with the Philadelphia News Bureau, and in 1911 he moved to New York, joined the new Base Ball Writers Association, and held honorary card No. 1. During the next 20 years he worked for the New York *Sun*, *Evening Telegraph*, and *Post*. In 1931 the cigar- and pipe-smoking Lieb took a team to Japan for a profitable tour. That and other profitable investments allowed him to retire in 1934. The following year Taylor Spink induced him to write a regular column and the most important obituaries for *The Sporting News*, which he did from his home in St. Petersburg, Florida, for 35 years. He also did a weekly Hot Stove League column for the St. Petersburg *Times*. His books include the classic *Baseball As I Have Known It*; *Connie Mack, Grand Old Man of Baseball*; and team histories of the Tigers, Red Sox, Cardinals, Pirates, Orioles, and Phillies. He received the J.G. Taylor Spink Award from the Hall of Fame in 1972. /(NLM)

Hank Lieber — 1911– . OF 1933–42 **Giants**, Cubs 813 g, .288, 101 hr, 518 rbi. *2 WS, 5 g, .235, 2 rbi*
 All-Star—38, 40–41.

Leiber was a 6'1-1/2" 205-lb, righthanded outfielder who was a starter with the Giants in 1935, '36, and '38 and the Cubs in 1939–1940. He hit over .300 three times (.331 in 1935, .310 in '39 and .302 in '40). His best year was 1935 when he had 203 hits, 22 home runs, 110 runs scored, 107 RBI, and a career-high .331 batting average. In 1942 he had a complete-game loss as a pitcher. /(JM)

Glenn Liebhardt (Sandy) — 1883–1956. RHP 1906–09 **Indians** 613 ip, 36–35, 2.17

Liebhardt had two solid seasons, going 18–14 (2.05) for Cleveland in 1907 and 15–16 (2.20) in 1908. His son of the same name pitched briefly for the A's and Browns in the 1930s. /(WAB)

Derek Lilliquist — 1966– . LHP 1989- **Braves** 166 ip, 8–10, 3.97

Lilliquist was the sixth selection nationwide in the June 1987 draft. He was one of several young Braves pitchers to do well at the start of 1989 and showed good control. /(JFC)

Bob Lillis (Flea) — 1930– . SS-2B-3B 1958–67 Dodgers, Cardinals, **Astros** 817 g, .236, 3 hr, 137 rbi. *Manager 1982–85* **Astros** 276–261, .514

A native of Los Angeles, Lillis signed with Brooklyn in 1951 and appeared to be ready to replace Pee Wee Reese at shortstop in 1958, the year the Dodgers moved to Los Angeles. After injuries delayed his debut, he batted .391 in 20 games in 1958, but he lost the shortstop job to rookie Maury Wills in 1959. He was swapped to the Cardinals in mid-1961, drafted by the expansion Colt .45s that winter, and was the team's MVP in its inaugural season. He batted a career-high .268 in 1964 and remained a Houston regular until 1966. A scout and instructor in the Astros organization from 1968 to 1972, he joined their major league coaching staff in 1973 and replaced Bill Virdon as manager on August 10, 1982. Leading the Astros to third place in 1983, Lillis finished second in NL Manager of the Year voting. After an 83–79 record in 1985, he was replaced by Hal Lanier. /(MC)

Lou Limmer — 1925– . 1B 1951, 54 **A's** 209 g, .202, 19 hr, 62 rbi

Limmer suffered a broken neck in 1948 but led the American Association in home runs and RBI the next year. Despite outstanding minor league stats, he failed two ML trials because of his low batting average and indifferent fielding. /(BC)

Rufino Linares — 1955– . OF 1981–82, 84–85 **Braves**, Angels 207 g, .270, 11 hr, 63 rbi

One of many Dominicans from the little town of San Pedro de Macoris to reach the majors, Linares hit .298 in 1982. But that winter a devastating broken ankle while playing winter ball kept him out for a year and took away his speed. /(BC)

Carl Lind — 1904–1946. 2B-SS 1927–30 Indians 256 g, .272, 1 hr, 74 rbi

As a rookie in 1928, Lind batted .294 with a league-high 650 at-bats and led the Indians with 42 doubles and 102 runs scored. After a postseason illness, he was never again a regular. /(ME)

Jose Lind — 1964– . 2B 1987- **Pirates** 342 g, .255, 4 hr, 108 rbi

The acrobatic Lind is famous for his ability to jump over any teammate from a standing start. In his first full season in 1988 he quickly established himself as one of the best-fielding second basemen in the league and just missed leading NL second basemen in fielding average and putouts. The Pirates traded Johnny Ray near the end of the 1987 season to make room for Lind, who hit .322 in his call-up. In 1988 he hit .262, stole 15 bases, and scored 82 runs.

Lind is a cousin of Onix Concepcion and has a brother, Orlando, who pitches in the Pirates system. /(SFS)

Vive Lindaman [Vivian Alexander] — 1877–1927. LHP 1906–09 **Braves** 904 ip, 36–60, 2.92

Lindaman kept in shape by walking 17 miles a day as a mail carrier. He shut out Brooklyn 1–0 in his first ML start on April 14, 1906. Despite throwing 32 complete games (third in the league) as a rookie, he finished 12–23; his Braves teammates were shut out in eight of his losses. /(NLM)

Paul Lindblad — 1941– . LHP 1965–78 **A's**, Senators, Rangers, Yankees 1214 ip, 68–63, 3.28. *1 LCS, 5 ip, 0–0, 0.00. 1 WS, 6 ip, 1–0, 4.76*

Lindblad was a useful AL lefthander for 14 seasons, working mainly in middle relief. Although he never won more than nine games in a single season, he had 64 career saves in addition to his 68 wins (61 in relief). He received credit for the win in the Athletics' third-game, 11-inning World Series victory in '73 by working two scoreless innings. A strong fielder, he set a record by going from 1966 through 1974 (385 appearances) without making a single error. /(BC)

Johnny Lindell — 1916–1986. OF-1B-RHP 1941–50, 53–54 **Yankees**, Cardinals, Pirates, Phillies 854 g, .273, 72 hr, 405 rbi; 252 ip, 8–18, 4.47. *3 WS, 12 g, .324, 7 rbi*

Johnny Lindell made the transition from a pitcher to an outfielder in the major leagues, then battled back to the majors again as a pitcher near the end of his career. After signing with the Yankees while at the University of Southern California, he posted outstanding minor league pitching marks, including 23–4 at Newark in 1941. He was called up to the majors at the end of that season and spent '42 on the Yankee staff. He threw a knuckleball and curve, but Yankee manager Joe McCarthy did not believe he had a major league fastball and switched him to the outfield in 1943. In his best season, 1944, he hit .300 with 18 home runs and 103 RBI. After WWII ended, he was used mostly as a reserve. All told, he played on three pennant winners (1943, '47, '49).

Sold to the Cardinals in May 1950, he managed only a .186 batting average. At the end of the season, he was sold again, this time to Hollywood of the PCL, where manager Fred Haney put him back on the pitching mound. In 1952 he posted a 24–9 pitching record, batted fourth, and occasionally played the outfield. He was easily the league MVP. At age thirty-six he returned to the majors, pitching for the Pirates and Phillies in 1953 for a combined 6–17 mark. He had trouble putting his knuckleball over (his 139 bases on balls led the league) and hitters sat on his fastball. /(BC)

Jim Lindsey — 1898–1963. RHP 1922, 24, 29–34, 37 Indians, **Cardinals**, Reds, Dodgers 431 ip, 21–20, 4.70. *2 WS, 8 ip, 0–0, 3.38*

After a couple of awful trials with Cleveland, Lindsey became the Cardinals' most-used reliever in 1930–31. During those two pennant-winning seasons, he won 9 and saved 12. His 2.77 ERA in '31 led the staff. /(FJO)

Freddie Lindstrom (Lindy) — 1905–1981. 3B-OF-2B 1924–36 **Giants**, Pirates, Cubs, Dodgers 1438 g, .311, 103 hr, 779 rbi. *2 WS, 11 g, .289, 4 rbi*
☛ *Hall of Fame—76.*

Lindstrom joined the Giants in 1924 and that fall became the youngest player (18 years, 10 months, 13 days) to appear in a World Series. In Game Five, he had four hits against Washington's Walter Johnson, but Lindstrom is best remembered for his part in the seventh and deciding game. In the bottom of the 12th, Earl McNeely's grounder took a wild hop (blamed on a pebble) over third baseman Lindstrom's head, allowing the Series-winning run to score.

Lindstrom hit .300 or better in seven of his 13 ML seasons. In 1928 he batted .358 with a league-leading 231 hits; he had 231 hits again in 1930, reaching career highs of .379 and 22 home runs. He drove in more than 100 runs in both seasons.

He was never outstanding at 3B, and when he suffered back problems in 1931, Lindstrom was moved to the outfield. Bill Terry was made Giants manager in 1932 when John McGraw retired. Lindstrom was bitter that he was not the choice and asked Terry to trade him. He was obliged in a three-team deal that sent him to Pittsburgh that December. But 1933 was his last year as a regular. In 1935 he helped the Cubs to a pennant by filling in at 3B and in the OF. He retired while with Brooklyn in 1936. He finally got his chance to manage, in the minors, from 1940 through 1942, and he coached at Northwestern University in the early 1950s. His son, Charlie, caught one game with the 1958 White Sox. Despite being an everyday player in only seven seasons, Lindstrom was elected to the Hall of Fame

Freddie Lindstrom

by the Committee on Baseball Veterans in 1976. /(JJM)

Dick Lines — 1938– . LHP 1966–67 **Senators** 169 ip, 7–7, 2.83

A native of Quebec, Canada, Lines relieved in 53 and 54 games for the 1966–67 Senators, winning seven, losing seven, and saving six. /(FK)

Ed Linke — 1911– . RHP 1933–38 **Senators**, Browns 449 ip, 22–22, 5.61

In 1935 a line drive by the Yankees' Jesse Hill rebounded off Linke's head to catcher Jack Redmond on the fly, and Ben Chapman was caught off second base for a rally-killing double play. Linke was hospitalized for three days but returned to win his next eight starts. /(JK)

Larry Lintz — 1949– . SS-2B-3B 1973–78 **Expos**, Cardinals, A's, Indians 350 g, .227, 0 hr, 27 rbi

In 1976 Lintz's stat line included 21 runs scored, 31 stolen bases, and one official at-bat. For his career, nearly a third of his appearances were as a pinch runner. He stole 128 bases, but he couldn't steal first. /(BC)

Phil Linz (Supersub, Mr. Laffs) — 1939– . SS-2B-3B-OF 1962–68 **Yankees**, Phillies, Mets 519 g, .235, 11 hr, 96 rbi. *2 WS, 10 g, .235, 2 hr, 2 rbi*

In spring training of 1962, rookies Phil Linz and Tom Tresh battled for the Yankee shortstop job. Linz was a feisty singles hitter, but the more powerful Tresh won the contest, and thereafter Linz filled in capably at three infield positions. The humorous Linz was the protagonist in the famed "Harmonica Incident" of late August 1964. The third-place Yankees, who had just lost four straight in Chicago, were in the team bus, stuck in traffic. Linz began playing "Mary Had a Little Lamb" on his harmonica, enraging manager Yogi Berra. A ruckus ensued. The event may have galvanized the successful stretch run for a pennant, but the publicity sealed Berra's dismissal after the season. /(GDW)

Frank Linzy — 1940- . RHP 1963, 1965–74 **Giants**, Cardinals, Brewers, Phillies 516 g, 817 ip, 62–57, 2.85

Sinkerball specialist Linzy totaled 111 saves in 11 ML seasons. In 1965, he was named *TSN* NL Rookie Pitcher of the Year when he won 9 and saved 21 (his top total) for the Giants. The stocky righthander led the NL in relief wins with 14 in 1969, adding 11 saves. Traded (for relief pitcher Jerry Johnson) in 1970, he appeared in 67 games but his ERA ballooned to 4.66. The next year, after a good start, he was injured in a collision with first baseman Bob Burda and underwent facial surgery, returning before the end of the season. The Brewers acquired him for a minor leaguer in 1972, and after two moderately successful seasons in Milwaukee, he was dealt to the Phillies for his final year./(BC)

Johnny Lipon — 1922- . SS-3B 1942, 46, 48–54 **Tigers**, Red Sox, Browns, Reds 758 g, .259, 10 hr, 266 rbi.
    Manager 1971 **Indians** 18–41, .305

As the Tigers' regular shortstop from 1948–51, Lipon was more adequate than outstanding. But after his playing career, he became a highly respected minor league manager, often rumored to be in line for a major league job. His only opportunity came when he replaced Alvin Dark at Cleveland for the last 59 games of the 1971 season./(BC)

Nelson Liriano — 1964- . 2B 1987- **Blue Jays** 268 g, .259, 10 hr, 86 rbi. *1 LCS, 3 g, .429, 1 rbi*

Liriano was handed Toronto's second base job at the beginning of 1988 but slumped badly at first and lost playing time to Manny Lee. He won it back in 1989 after Lee temporarily replaced injured shortstop Tony Fernandez. That April 22, Liriano broke up Nolan Ryan's bid for a sixth no-hitter with a ninth-inning triple; a week later, he broke up a Kirk McCaskill no-hitter in the ninth./(SOM)

Joe Lis — 1946- . 1B-OF 1970–77 **Phillies**, Twins, Indians, Mariners 356 g, .233, 32 hr, 92 rbi

Lis led two minor leagues in home runs, but struck out too often to stay in the major leagues. In the only season he approached regular status (253 at-bats as the Twins' first baseman in 1973), he had career highs of nine HR, 25 RBI, and 37 runs, batting just .245./(WOR)

Hod Lisenbee [Horace Milton] — 1898–1987. RHP 1927–32, 36, 45 Senators, **Red Sox**, A's, Reds 969 ip, 37–58, 4.81

In his 1927 rookie year with Washington he was 18–9 with an AL-leading four shutouts. He beat the "Murderers' Row" Yankees five times that season (and gave up Babe Ruth's 58th HR). After that Lisenbee was a journeyman pitcher in both the majors and minors. Following his retirement in 1942, he came back in 1944 with Syracuse (International League) and pitched a no-hitter at the age of forty-five. The next year, he pitched 31 games for the Reds, mostly in relief. After the war, he continued to pitch in his native city of Clarksville, TN (Kitty League) until he was fifty./(LRD)

Ad Liska [Adolph James] — 1906- . RHP 1929–33 **Senators**, Phillies 351 ip, 17–18, 3.87

A submarine pitcher who suffered a boyhood injury that prevented him from throwing overhand, Liska had a brief major league career. He excelled in the Pacific Coast League, where, from 1936 to 1949, he won 248 games for Portland./(JK)

Mark Littel — 1953- . RHP 1973, 75–82 Royals, **Cardinals** 532 ip, 32–31, 3.32. *2 LCS, 7 ip, 0–1, 2.35*

Big (6'3" 210-lb) Littel was the American Association Pitcher of the Year in 1973. The strikeout pitcher used his blazing fastball to become bullpen ace for the Royals and later the Cardinals, but in the 1976 ALCS he surrendered a pennant-winning home run to the Yankees Chris Chambliss in the bottom of the ninth inning of Game Five. He saved 56 games from 1976 to 1981 until elbow spurs cut short his career./(FJO)

Bryan Little — 1959- . 2B-SS 1982–86 **Expos**, White Sox, Yankees 327 g, .245, 3 hr, 77 rbi

Little was the Expos' starting shortstop in the first part of 1983 but was otherwise a utility man. He led the NL with 24 bunt hits in 1983 and was voted the major leagues' best bunter in two separate polls. His father and two brothers, Tom and Grady, all played minor league ball./(JCA)

Dick Littlefield — 1926- . LHP 1950–58 Red Sox, White Sox, Tigers, Browns/Orioles, **Pirates**, Cardinals, Giants, Cubs, Braves 762 ip, 33–54, 4.71

Littlefield was dealt 10 times during his nine-year career, in trades involving 38 other players. He lasted longest with the Pirates—almost two years—winning a career-high 10 games in 1954. Pittsburgh then stole Bill Virdon from the Cardinals for Littlefield and Bobby Del Greco in a May 1956 trade. The Giants traded him to the Dodgers for

Jackie Robinson in December 1956, but the deal was voided when Robinson retired. /(ME)

John Littlefield — 1954- . RHP 1980-81 **Cardinals**, Padres 130 ip, 7-8, 3.39

Called up during the 1980 season, reliever Littlefield led the Cards in appearances (52), relief wins (5), and saves (9). That winter he was one of seven players dealt to the Padres in the Rollie Fingers deal. /(FJO)

Danny Litwhiler — 1916- . OF 1940-44, 46-51 **Phillies**, Cardinals, Braves, Reds 1057 g, .281, 107 hr, 451 rbi. *2 WS, 10 g, .229, 1 hr, 3 rbi*
☛ *All-Star—42.*

Litwhiler had to overcome serious knee injuries in the minor leagues. Called up by the Phillies late in the 1940 season, he batted .345, hitting in 21 straight games. The following year he had a career-high 18 home runs, collecting one in every NL park. In 1942 he became the first major league outfielder to play at least 150 games in a season without making an error. He was traded in 1943 to the Cardinals, who won pennants in 1943 and 1944. His was one of two Cardinal homers hit in their 2–0 victory over the Browns in Game Five of the '44 World Series. Because of his badly damaged knee, Litwhiler was originally classified 4F, but in 1945 the Selective Service began targeting ballplayers. After spending 1945 in the military playing baseball at Fort Lewis, Litwhiler was solely a platoon player for the rest of his ML career. /(JK)

Bud Lively [Everett Adrian] (Red) — 1925- . RHP 1947-49 **Reds** 249 ip, 8-13, 4.16

Lively spent 19 months fighting in Europe before getting a shot with the Reds in 1947. His father Jack was 7-5 for the 1911 Tigers. /(JK)

Mickey Livingston [Thompson Orville] — 1914-1983. C 1938, 41-43, 45-49, 51 Senators, **Phillies**, Cubs, Giants, Braves, Dodgers 561 g, .238, 19 hr, 153 rbi. *1 WS, 6 g, .364, 4 rbi*

A career backup, Livingston caught more than 100 games only in 1943, split between the Phillies and Cubs. Then, after military service, he was a surprise hero in the Cubs' WS loss in 1945, with three doubles and four RBI. /(ARA)

Winston Llenas — 1943- .2B-OF-3B 1968-69, 72-75 **Angels** 300 g, .230, 3 hr, 61 rbi

Llenas interrupted his career as one of the Mexican League's greatest third basemen to spend five seasons with the Angels, primarily as a pinch hitter. In 1973, he led the AL in pinch hit at-bats (56) and hits (16), with a .269 batting average overall. A top slugger in the Mexican League before his ML stint, he returned there in 1977 for seven more seasons, including three .300 years. /(MC)

Nelson Lloyd — 1851-1925. *Executive.*

As a part owner of the Reds and Giants, Lloyd was not known to the public. He was often credited with being a behind-the-scenes peacemaker in the many bitter battles that were fought among the owners over control and direction of the game in the early years of the century. /(NLM)

Pop Lloyd [John Henry] (El Cuchara) — 1884-1964. SS-1B-2B-C Negro Leagues 1905-31 Macon Acmes, Cuban X-Giants, Brooklyn Royal Giants, Philadelphia Giants, Leland Giants, New York Lincoln Giants, Chicago American Giants, Columbus Buckeyes, Hilldale, Bacharach Giants, Atlantic City Bacharachs, New York Black Yankees .342, 26 hr (inc.)
☛ *Led League—ba 10, 15, 28. Hall of Fame—1977.*

Pop Lloyd, premier Negro League shortstop and baseball nomad, was promoted by many as the greatest player of all time. He played on at least a dozen different teams in his 26-year career. When asked why so many teams, Lloyd replied, "Where the money was, that's where I played." A tall, angular man with a Dick Tracy profile, Lloyd was a nondrinking, soft-spoken gentleman who seldom cursed. He was a complete professional, on and off the field.

Lloyd was a lefthanded line-drive hitter who used a closed stance. He held the bat in the cradle of his left elbow, and would uncoil to unleash a controlled attack on the baseball. A gifted runner with long, smooth strides, he deceived opponents into under-rating his speed. He was often compared to Honus Wagner. Connie Mack of the Philadelphia A's, who spent 50 years in the game, said, "Put Lloyd and Wagner in the same bag and whichever one you pulled out, you wouldn't go wrong."

Lloyd began as a catcher in 1905 with the Macon Acmes, who could not provide him with a mask. After one season, he moved to the Cuban X-Giants as an infielder. He helped the Philadelphia Giants to a league championship the following year and stayed

.329 batting average and twice led the league in triples. He excelled in a 1910 series played in Havana against the Detroit Tigers. The Tigers won 7 of the 12 games, with Ty Cobb hitting .369 in five contests. But Cobb's average was only good enough for fourth place; Lloyd batted .500 in 12 games and added insult to injury by tagging Cobb out on three consecutive basestealing attempts. In 29 recorded games against white major leaguers, Lloyd batted .321.

As Lloyd's legs began to go, he moved from SS to first base. Approaching age thirty-five, he signed with the Brooklyn Royal Giants as player-manager, and was active for three abbreviated seasons before going to the Columbus Buckeyes in 1921. Then thirty-eight, Lloyd led the Buckeyes in games, hits, doubles, and stolen bases while batting .337. Rejuvenated, he topped the .320 mark for Hilldale in 1923 and for the Bacharach Giants in 1924–25. He was forty-four when he hit a league-leading .564 for the New York Lincoln Giants in 1928; he also led with 11 HR and 10 SB in a 37-game schedule.

When Babe Ruth was interviewed by pioneering announcer Graham McNamee, he was asked who was the greatest player of all time. Ruth asked, "You mean major leaguers?" "No," replied McNamee, "the greatest player anywhere." "In that case," responded Ruth, "I'd pick John Henry Lloyd." Lloyd was elected to the Hall of Fame by the Committee on Negro Baseball Leagues in 1977. /(LL)

Hans Lobert [John Bernard] (Honus) — 1881–1968. 3B-SS 1903, 05–17 Pirates, Cubs, **Reds**, Phillies, Giants 1317 g, .274, 32 hr, 482 rbi.
Manager 1938, 42 **Phillies** 42–111, .275

A four-time .300 hitter, Lobert was a top NL third baseman in the days before WWI. Bearing a slight physical and facial resemblance to Honus Wagner, the speedy, bowlegged Lobert stole 30 or more bases seven times in 1907–14. His six steals of home as a Phillie tie him for second on their all-time list. He stole second, third, and home on September 27, 1908 and he once raced a horse around the bases following an exhibition game. On October 12, 1910 at Field Day in Cincinnati, he was clocked rounding the bases in 13.8 seconds. Following his playing days, Lobert coached at West Point (1918–25), spent nearly two decades as a minor league manager and ML coach, and managed the Phillies for two games in 1938 and all of 1942. He was influential in transforming Bucky Walters from a marginal ML

Pop Lloyd

two more. He spent 1910 with the Leland Giants, who posted a 123–6 record, before moving on to the New York Lincoln Giants, for whom he hit .475 in 1911 and .376 in 1912.

Rube Foster enticed Lloyd to join his Chicago American Giants, and from 1914 through 1917 Lloyd batted cleanup for the four-time Western League champions. His teammates there included such greats as Oscar Charleston, Bingo DeMoss, Louis Santop, Smokey Joe Williams, and Cannonball Dick Redding. Chicago won world championships in '14 and '17.

Lloyd played 12 seasons in Cuba, where he earned the nickname El Cuchara—The Shovel. He was known for scooping up handfuls of dirt while adeptly fielding his position. In Cuba, he compiled a

Hans Lobert

infielder into a star pitcher. His brother Frank played 11 games in the Federal League. /(ME)

Don Lock — 1936- . OF 1962-69 **Senators**, Phillies, Red Sox 921 g, .238, 122 hr, 373 rbi

The Senators traded the aging Dale Long for Lock before he had played a single ML game, and six days later Lock homered in his debut to give Washington a 1-0 win over Chicago. Always a home run threat when he made contact, Lock was plagued by strike-outs, fanning once every four plate appearances. He hit 27 and 28 HR in 1963-64 but also struck out 151 and 137 times. /(FK)

Larry Locke (Bobby) — 1934- . RHP 1959-1965, 67-68 **Indians**, Cardinals, Phillies, Reds, Angels 417 ip, 16-15, 4.02

The flaky Locke, a hairstylist, spent just one full season in the majors—with the Indians in 1961. From November 1961 through April 1962, he was alternately the property of the Indians, Cubs, Cardinals, and Phillies. /(ME)

William H. Locke — 1869-1913. *Executive.*

Locke was sports editor of the Pittsburgh *Press* for ten years until 1903, when he was named secretary of the Pirates. In January 1913 he headed a group including W.F. Baker and Governor Tener of Pennsylvania that bought the Phillies. He was named president but died suddenly on August 14 of that year. /(NLM)

Bob Locker (Foot) — 1938- . 1965-73, 75 **White Sox**, Pilots/Brewers, A's, Cubs 879 ip, 57-39, 2.76. *2 LCS, 3 ip, 0-0, 10.13. 1 WS, .1 ip, 0-0, 0.00*

In 1965 sinkerballer Bob Locker joined knuckleballers Hoyt Wilhelm and Eddie Fisher in the White Sox bullpen. Locker led the American League with 77 appearances and saved 20 games in 1967. When asked about his success, the geology major explained that he derived his powers from consuming honey—nature's essence. Locker was traded to the Pilots in 1969 and sold to Oakland a year later. He went 7-2 in 1971, and 6-1 with 10 saves for the 1972 World Champion A's. When Rollie Fingers established himself as Oakland's ace reliever, Locker was traded to the Cubs, for whom he won 10 and saved 18 in 1973. He retired with 95 career saves. /(RL)

Gene Locklear — 1949- . OF 1973-77 Reds, **Padres**, Yankees 292 g, .274, 9 hr, 66 rbi

A full-blooded Cherokee, the lefthanded batter had 150 pinch-hit at-bats in 292 ML appearances. Locklear had a .321 batting average for the Padres in 1975, his only 100-game season. After a .240 season for the Nippon Ham Fighters of Japan in 1978, he retired to pursue a career as an artist. /(MC)

Whitey Lockman [Carroll Walter] — 1926- . 1B-OF 1945, 47-60 **Giants**, Cardinals, Orioles, Reds 1666 g, .279, 114 hr, 563 rbi. *2 WS, 10 g, .186, 1 hr, 4 rbi.*
    Manager 1972-74 **Cubs** 157-162, .492
☛ *All-Star—52.*

Lockman homered in his first ML at-bat, July 5, 1945 and once led off consecutive games with home runs, but he was never a feared power hitter. He hit a career-high 18 homers in 1948, his first full season, and had his only .300 season in 1949. Still, he was a consistent contributor and one of the hardest men to double up in ML history, hitting into one double play every 87 at-bats. In the Giants-Dodgers playoff series in 1951, his ninth-inning double drove Don Newcombe from the game and set the stage for Bobby Thomson's famous home run. /(FK)

Skip Lockwood [Claude Edward, Jr.] (Jaws) — 1946– . RHP 1965, 69–80 A's, Pilots/Brewers, Angels, **Mets**, Red Sox 1236 ip, 57–97, 3.55

Lockwood received a $100,000 bonus to sign with the A's as a third baseman in 1964, but he didn't hit and converted to pitching in 1968. He failed again, as a starting pitcher, and began the switch to relieving in 1973, his last year with Milwaukee. He finally achieved a modicum of success as the ace of the Mets' bullpen in the late 1970s; his 19 saves in 1976 tied him for second in the NL and 20 saves in 1977 (when he set a since-broken Met record with 63 appearances) was good for a tie for fifth. He got his nickname of Jaws (after the shark movie) at this time for "chewing up" batters. But in 1978 he dropped off to 15 saves and tied Rollie Fingers for the league lead with 13 relief losses, the third-worst NL mark ever. In June 1979 he went on the DL with tissue tears in his shoulder and missed the rest of the season; a comeback attempt with Boston in 1980 failed. /(SH)

Dario Lodigiani (Lodi) — 1916– . 3B-2B 1938–42, 46 **A's**, White Sox 405 g, .260, 16 hr, 156 rbi

When Lodigiani played second base at San Francisco's Lowell Junior High, his double play partner was Joe DiMaggio. He missed 1943–45 in military service, and an elbow injury in 1946 hindered his comeback. He had a long career in the Pacific Coast League and as a White Sox scout. /(NLM)

Billy Loes — 1929– . RHP 1950, 52–61 **Dodgers**, Orioles, Giants 1190 ip, 80–63, 3.89. *3 WS, 22 ip, 1–2, 4.91*
☛ *All-Star—57.*

Renowned for his wacky reasoning, Loes advised against becoming a 20-game winner, because "If you win 20 games, they expect you to do it every year." Loes never did win 20, but was 50–25 over four seasons in Brooklyn. /(FK)

Tom Loftus — 1856–1910. OF 1877, 83 St. Louis NL, **St. Louis AA** 9 g, .182, 0 hr, inc rbi.
Manager 1884, 88–91, 00–03 Milwaukee (UA), Cleveland (AA), Cleveland (NL), Reds, **Cubs**, Senators 455–583, .438

Loftus's career as a ML manager was far longer than his ML playing career. He often had a part ownership in the clubs he managed. He did not believe in changing pitchers during a game, and in 1890 he worked to change the rule prohibiting a manager from being a third base coach. For a time he was president of the Three-I League. /(NLM)

Bob Logan (Lefty) — 1910–1978. LHP 1935, 37–38, 41, 45 Dodgers, Tigers, Cubs, Reds, **Braves** 223 ip, 7–15, 3.15

Logan spent most of 1932 through 1943 with Indianapolis (American Association), starting more openers for them than any pitcher in their history. His only major league wins came at age thirty-five with the war-decimated 1945 Braves. /(NLM)

Johnny Logan (Yatcha) — 1927– . SS-3B 1951–63 **Braves**, Pirates 1503 g, .268, 93 hr, 547 rbi. *14 WS g, .154, 1 hr, 4 rbi*
☛ *All-Star—55, 57–59.*

Scrappy Johnny Logan never backed down from a fight and never lost one. His quick hands compensated for an average arm at shortstop and were an asset when, outraged by beanballs, he took on opponents as big as Don Drysdale. In Milwaukee, he was a minor league star for four years and a major league standout when he moved there with the Braves in 1953. He was the shortstop for the 1957 and 1958 NL pennant winners; in '57, he led the league with 37 doubles and reached career highs with 83 RBI and a .297 batting average. Traded to Pittsburgh for Gino Cimoli in 1961, he served the Pirates as a backup infielder and pinch hitter through 1963. /(JK)

Lucky Lohrke [Jack Wayne] — 1924– . 3B-2B-SS 1947–53 **Giants**, Phillies 354 g, .242, 22 hr, 96 rbi. *1 WS, 2 g, .000*

Lohrke gained the nickname Lucky when he was called off the Spokane (Western International League) team bus 15 minutes before its departure. Lohrke was headed for Triple-A; the bus was headed for disaster. It crashed into a ravine, killing eight players. Lohrke went on to become the Giants regular third baseman in 1947 and a utility man thereafter. /(JK)

Bill Lohrman — 1913- . RHP 1934, 37-44 Phillies, **Giants**, Cardinals, Dodgers, Reds 990 ip, 60-59, 3.69

According to some historians, Lohrman invented the slider. Others merely credit him as one of the first to use the pitch extensively. A Giants starter from 1938 to 1941, he was traded to the Cardinals in December 1941 as part of the deal that brought Johnny Mize to New York, but after pitching five games for St. Louis in 1942 he was sold back to the Giants. Lohrman went on to have his best season, 14-5 and a 2.48 ERA. /(BC)

Mickey Lolich — 1940- . LHP 1963-76, 78-79 **Tigers**, Mets, Padres 3639 ip, 217-191, 3.44. 20 wins: 71-72 *1 LCS, 19 ip, 0-1, 1.42 1 WS, 18 ip, 3-0, 1.67*
☛ *Led League—w 71. Led League—k 71. All-Star—69, 71-72.*

Portly lefty Lolich stole the spotlight from teammate Denny McLain in 1968, despite McLain's 31-win season. Lolich won three games in the 1968 World Series, giving up only five runs in his three complete games, including a 4-1 victory in the seventh game

Mickey Lolich

against Bob Gibson on two days' rest. In the sixth inning of that victory, he picked off both Curt Flood and Lou Brock. A notoriously poor hitter (a career .110 average), Lolich cracked his only major league homer in Game Two of the Series off Nelson Briles.

The picture of consistency throughout his career, Lolich struck out 200-plus seven times and finished 12th all-time in strikeouts with 2,832, second only to Steve Carlton among lefties. Lolich was not a natural lefthander. A childhood run-in with a motorcycle left him with a broken left collarbone. Rehabilitating his left arm actually made it stronger than his right. Lolich came up the same year as McLain but was far more consistent, never winning fewer than 14 games in his 11 full years in a Tiger uniform. In 1968, while McLain piloted planes and played the organ, Lolich rode motorcycles and played the drums on his way to 17 wins, going 10-2 over the last two months of the season. In 1971 he had a league-leading 25 victories and 308 strikeouts. He would have won the Cy Young Award but for Vida Blue's spectacular rookie season. Lolich won 22 the following year with a career-best 2.50 ERA and again felt he deserved the Cy Young Award, but he lost a close vote to Gaylord Perry.

Lolich was traded to the Mets for Rusty Staub after the 1975 season, then "retired" after going 8-13 for New York in 1976. He sat out the entire 1977 season to get out of his contract, then signed with San Diego for two final seasons. /(SEW)

Sherm Lollar — 1924-1977. C 1946-63 Indians, Yankees, Browns, **White Sox** 1752 g, .264, 155 hr, 808 rbi. *2 WS, 8 g, .308, 1 hr, 6 rbi*
☛ *All-Star—50, 54-56, 58-60. Gold Glove—57-59.*

Lollar, a quiet workhorse who led by example, was the White Sox' catcher through the "Go-Go" years. This was ironic, since he was painfully slow. But he was a dangerous hitter with good power and was outstanding on defense. He led AL backstops four times in fielding and his .992 career average ranks in the top five all-time. In 1962 he equaled the ML record by catching six pop-ups in one game.

Lollar came up with the Indians in 1946 but was traded to the Yankees that December in the deal that sent Gene Bearden to Cleveland. After he put in two years of backup work in New York, the Browns acquired him in one of their many deals with the Yankees. In 1952 an eight-player deal brought him to Chicago, where he appeared in over 100 games for ten straight seasons.

On April 23, 1955 he became the third major leaguer in history to collect two hits in one inning

Sherm Lollar

twice in the same game. He slugged a pair of homers and had five RBI as the Sox defeated Kansas City 29–6. His best season was 1959. He hit 22 homers and had 84 RBI while handling Sox pitchers fault- lessly as Chicago won its first pennant in 40 years. /(RL)

Tim Lollar — 1956– . LHP 1980–86 Yankees, **Padres**, White Sox, Red Sox 906 ip, 47–52, 4.27. *1 LCS, 4 ip, 0–0, 6.23. 1 WS, 2 ip, 0–1, 21.60*

Lollar looked like one of the NL's up-and-coming lefthanders when he went 16–9 for the 1982 Padres. He had a 90-mph fastball and was extremely tough on lefthanded hitters. Troubled by a bad elbow in 1983, he dropped to 7–12 and quickly faded. He didn't survive the second inning of his 1984 WS start, allowing the Tigers four runs on four hits and four walks in Game Two. Lollar played first base as well as pitcher in his first two minor league seasons,

and he was one of baseball's best-hitting pitchers during his ML stint (.234). He hit three homers in both 1982 and 1984 and came through with a pinch hit when given one at-bat by the 1986 Red Sox. /(JCA)

Stan Lomax — 1899–1988. *Broadcaster.*

After graduating from Cornell, Lomax wrote for the Bronx *Home News* and the New York *Journal- American* and shared a 15-minute nightly sportscast with Ford Frick. When Frick became NL president in 1932, Lomax left the newspaper to do the radio show full-time and was heard on WOR from 1932 until his retirement in 1978. /(NLM)

Ernie Lombardi (Schnozz, Bocci) — 1908–1977. C 1931–47 Dodgers, **Reds**, Braves, Giants 1853 g, .306, 190 hr, 990 rbi. *2 WS, 6 g, .235, 2 rbi*
☛ *Most Valuable Player—38. Led League—ba 38, 42. All-Star—36–40, 42–43. Hall of Fame—1985.*

Famed for his long hits, lead feet, and large nose, Lombardi was one of baseball's top catchers during the 1930s and 1940s. The only catcher to win two batting titles, his consistently high batting averages were achieved despite his legendary lack of speed. Contemporary Billy Herman said later: "I don't think anybody could top him. But he was so slow afoot that those infielders could play him so deep that he just didn't have any place to hit the ball. He had to hit it over the fence or against the fence or just too hard for anybody to be able to make a play." Lombardi's powerful line smashes were leg- endary; he hit with his fingers interlocked so he could grip his bat, the league's heaviest, closer to the end.

Lombardi broke into baseball with Oakland of the Pacific Coast League at age eighteen. After being sent out to Ogden for seasoning, he had three outstanding seasons, catching 120, 164, and 146 games and hitting .377, .366, and .370. The Dodg- ers bought his contract in 1931, but though he hit a strong .297, they traded him to Cincinnati in a six- player deal in March 1932.

His greatest years were with the Reds, catching over 100 games for ten straight seasons and hitting .300 in seven. Twice he led NL catchers in fielding. In 1938, he won the NL MVP award by becoming only the second catcher to ever lead a major league in hitting (.342), while cracking 19 homers and driving in 95 runs. That season he caught Johnny Vander Meer's consecutive no-hitters. He was a mainstay for the 1939 Reds pennant winners and 1940 World Champions.

Ernie Lombardi

The 1939 WS saw an incident that haunted his career. In the 10th inning of the fourth and final game, Yankee Charlie Keller crashed into him in a close play at the plate. Lombardi was stunned and another Yankee run scored while he lay on the ground. Newspapers unfairly called it "Lombardi's Swoon."

Sold to the Braves in 1942, he won his second batting title (.330) and then spent his final five ML seasons with the Giants.

In his later years, he was bitter because he was not named to baseball's Hall of Fame. Eight years after his death, he was enshrined by the Veterans Committee. /(MC)

Vic Lombardi — 1922– . LHP 1945–50 **Dodgers**, Pirates 945 ip, 50–51, 3.68. *1 WS, 7 ip, 0–1, 12.15*

Lombardi fanned 19 batters in a game twice in one week in the 1941 Penn State Association. Scouts who went to check him out were surprised to find he was just 5'7" and 158 pounds. But by the last year of WWII, with talent scarce, Lombardi's size was overlooked. Given a chance, he won between 10 and 13 games a season as a .500 pitcher for the 1945–47 Dodgers and the 1948 Pirates. /(JK)

Steve Lombardozzi — 1960– . 2B 1985– **Twins**, Astros 444 g, .233, 20 hr, 107 rbi. *1 LCS, 5 g, .267, 1 rbi. 1 WS, 7 g, .412, 1 hr, 4 rbi*

Lombardozzi was the second baseman for the 1987 World Champion Minnesota Twins, batting just .238 for the season but .412 (7 for 17) to lead all hitters in the World Series. As a rookie in 1986, he led AL second basemen with a .991 fielding percentage. But the Twins wanted more run production, and in April 1988 they traded slugger Tom Brunansky for the Cardinals' Tommy Herr. When Herr did not pan out, the Twins acquired Wally Backman for 1989 and traded Lombardozzi to the Astros. /(JCA)

Jim Lonborg — 1942– . RHP 1965–79 **Red Sox**, Brewers, Phillies 2,465 ip, 157–137, 3.86. *2 LCS, 9 ip, 0–2, 5.79 1 WS, 24 ip, 2–1, 2.63*
☛ *Led League—w 67. Cy Young Award—67. All-Star—67.*

Gentleman Jim is mainly remembered for his gutsy performance in the 1967 World Series, after a Cy Young 22–9, 246-strikeout career season. The tall and articulate Lonborg had compiled just a 19–27 record in his first two seasons before leading the Red Sox to their first pennant in 31 years. He ensured the pennant by beating the Twins and Dean Chance on the last day of the season, the only time the Red Sox were in first place in a wild three-team race between the Red Sox, Tigers, and Twins. Four days later in the World Series, he beat the heavily favored Cardinals with a one-hitter 5–0 to knot the Series at one game each. He lost the perfect game when he walked Curt Flood with two out in the sixth on a 3–2 pitch, then lost the no-hitter when Julian Javier doubled with two out in the eighth. Lonborg then tossed a three-hit, 3–1 victory in Game Five to give Boston a 3–2 Series edge. A Roger Maris homer in the ninth spoiled the shutout and Lonborg's 17-

inning scoreless skein. By the seventh game and on only two days' rest, however, Lonborg finally gave out, losing a 7–2 decision to Bob Gibson, who won his third Series game. After the dream season, Lonborg was largely ineffective, winning just 27 more games for the Red Sox in the next four years. He won 14 games after being traded to Milwaukee in 1972, then spent the remaining seven years of his career in Phildelphia. In 1974 he won 17 games, but the highlight of his season was a grand slam he hit on June 29 against Montreal, only his third career homer. He won 18 games in 1976 and went 11–4 in 1977 before fading out two seasons later. /(SEW)

Bill Long — 1960– . RHP 1985, 87– **White Sox** 456 ip, 21–25, 4.33

A product of the San Diego farm system, Long was a throw-in on the 1984 deal that sent Ozzie Guillen to the White Sox for LaMarr Hoyt. He was twenty-seven when he got his first ML win, a two-hit shutout against the Yankees on May 5, 1987. He became a long reliever and an adequate starter. /(RL)

Dale Long — 1926– . 1B 1951, 55–63 Pirates, Browns, **Cubs**, Giants, Yankees, Senators 1013 g, .267, 132 hr, 467 rbi. *2 WS, 5 g, .250, 1 rbi*
☛ *All-Star—56.*

The 6'4" 205-lb Long turned down a contract from the NFL Green Bay Packers to play pro baseball. He stuck with the Pirates in 1955 after 11 minor league seasons (2 as a home run champ) and led the NL in triples. In May 1956, he hit eight homers in eight consecutive games, a record equaled by Don Mattingly in 1987. Traded to the Cubs in 1957, he found cozy Wrigley Field to his liking, hitting 55 HR over the next three seasons. In 1958 he caught two games using his first baseman's mitt, becoming the first lefthanded catcher since 1906. In 1959 he tied a then-NL record by hitting back-to-back pinch homers. He also helped the Yankees down the stretch in 1963 with timely pinch hits. After his playing career, he worked as a minor league umpire. /(DB)

Herman Long (Germany) — 1866–1909. SS 1889–1904 Kansas City (AA), **Braves**, Yankees, Tigers, Phillies 1872 g, .279, 92 hr, 1052 rbi
☛ *Led League—hr 1900.*

With a powerful arm, a quick release, and outstanding range, speed, and agility, Long played shortstop, according to the Boston *Globe*, "like a man on a flying trapeze." He joined Fred Tenney, Bobby Lowe, and Jimmy Collins in the Braves' (then called

Herman Long with the Braves

the Beaneaters) infield that was probably the best of the 19th century. His career chances-per-game (6.4) tops all shortstops.

One of three Beaneaters to play on five NL pennant winners in the 1890s, he was a strong run producer, twice knocking in over 100 and scoring over 100 seven times. His 149 runs scored led the NL in 1893 and his 12 home runs led in 1900. Noisy and uncouth on the field, he urged teammates to greater efforts, ragged opponents, and stirred up fans. He always played all out, once breaking Pittsburgh catcher Connie Mack's leg with a ferocious slide when there was no play at the plate.

After his playing days, he managed in the minors. However, he contracted tuberculosis, moved far from the scenes of his success to Colorado, and died broke and friendless. /(ADS)

Tommy Long — 1890–1972. OF 1911–12, 15–17
Senators, **Cardinals** 418 g, .269, 6 hr, 140 rbi

Long led the NL by cracking 25 triples for the
Cardinals in 1915, the most by a rookie in this
century and the second highest rookie total ever.
After hitting .294 and .293 in his first two seasons as
a Cardinal, he slumped badly in 1917 and disappeared from the majors. /(BC)

Ed Lopat [born Edmund Walter Lopatynski] (Steady
Eddie, Junk Man) — 1918– . LHP 1944–55 White Sox,
Yankees, Orioles 2439 ip, 166–112, 3.21. 20 wins: 51
5 WS, 52 ip, 4–1, 2.60.
    Manager 1963–64 **A's** *90–124, .421*
☛ *Led League—era 53. All-Star—51.*

To frustrated hitters he was the Junk Man. Lopat
turned his lack of a fastball into an advantage,
keeping hitters off stride with an assortment of slow
breaking pitches thrown with cunning and accuracy.
Free-swinging teams like the Indians became easy
victims; Lopat was 40–12 lifetime against
Cleveland.

After four seasons with the White Sox, Lopat was
traded to his hometown Yankees in February 1948,
and manager Casey Stengel pitched him between
flamethrowers Allie Reynolds and Vic Raschi, the
contrast making Lopat's slow stuff all the more
unhittable. He averaged 16 wins a year in the World
Championship seasons of 1949–53, won a career-
high 21 games in 1951, and led the AL in ERA
(2.42) and winning percentage (.800, 16–4) in 1953.
In the 1951 WS, he pitched a pair of complete
games, beating the Giants 3–1 in Game Two and
13–1 in Game Five. When his playing days were
over, Lopat remained in baseball as a coach, manager, general manager, and scout. /(MG)

Stan Lopata — 1925– . C 1948–60 **Phillies**, Braves
853 g, .254, 116 hr, 397 rbi. *1 WS, 2 g, .000*
☛ *All-Star—55–56.*

A decorated WWII veteran and the first NL catcher
to wear glasses, Lopata didn't see much action
behind Andy Seminick and Smokey Burgess until he
assumed a deep crouch at the plate at the urging of
Rogers Hornsby. He then hit .290 with 14 home
runs in 1954 and belted 22, 32, and 18 HR the next
three seasons before a dwindling batting average put
him back on the bench. /(JK)

Davey Lopes — 1946– . 2B-OF 1972–87 **Dodgers**,
A's, Cubs, Astros 1812 g, .263, 155 hr, 614 rbi. *6 LCS,
22 g, .282, 2 hr, 11 rbi. 4 WS, 23 g, .211, 4 hr, 11 rbi*
☛ *All-Star—78–81. Gold Glove—78.*

One of the most effective thieves in a basestealing
era, Lopes stole five in a game on August 24, 1974
to tie a 70-year-old NL record and in 1975 he set a
since-broken ML record with 38 consecutive successful steals. He was the league leader in 1975 (77)
and 1976 (63), and he stole five in the 1981 LCS and
added four more in the World Series. He set the
NLCS career record of nine, and his ten in the WS
ranks third. He stole 47 bases at age thirty-nine and
25 at forty. His career total of 557 stolen bases
ranked 10th all-time as the 1980s ended.

Perhaps the best moments in Lopes's career came
in the 1978 World Series against the Yankees. He
hit two HR and drove in five runs in Game One, and
added another HR in the sixth and final game. In a
losing cause, he hit .308 with two steals for the
Series.

When the Dodgers traded Lopes to the A's
following the 1981 World Series, they broke up the
longest-running infield ever. Lopes has played with
Steve Garvey, Bill Russell, and Ron Cey for nine
seasons. Lopes won the 1978 Gold Glove at
second base and had excellent power for his posi-

Davey Lopes

tion. He hit a career-high 28 HR in 1979 and hit 17 twice. He coached for the Rangers following his playing career in the late 1980s. /(TG)

Al Lopez — 1908– . C 1928, 30–47 **Dodgers**, Braves, Pirates, Indians 1950 g, .261, 52 hr, 652 rbi.
   Manager 1951–65, 68–69 Indians, **White Sox** 1422–1026, .581. First place: 54, 59 *2 WS, 2–8, .200* ☞ *All-Star—33, 41. Hall of Fame—1977.*

The 5'11" 165-lb Lopez had a long and distinguished career as a catcher and manager and was enshrined in the Hall of Fame in 1977.

Not much of an offensive threat, Lopez hit higher than .275 only three times in his 19-year career. His career high in home runs was eight (1936 and 1939) and in RBI was 57 (1930). His great value was as an extremely durable receiver. For many years he held the record for most games caught in the major leagues (1,918) and the NL (1,861), and for most years in the NL catching 100 or more games (12). These endurance marks were somewhat inflated by the fact that he was largely a defensive replacement the last two and a half seasons of his career. He tied the record for most games caught in the NL without a passed ball (114 games in 1941) and led NL catchers in assists three times (1932–33, 1936) and fielding average three times (1940, 1943–44).

Lopez also left his mark as a manager. He led the Indians from 1951 to 1956 and the White Sox from 1957 to 1965 and 1968 to 1969. He was the only AL manager to finish ahead of the Yankees in the 1950s, winning pennants with the Indians in 1954 and the White Sox in 1959. He finished second every other year that decade, and nine times overall. His record as a manager was 1,422–1,026, with a .581 winning percentage that is ninth on the all-time list.

In a poll taken among retired major leaguers in the mid-1980s, Lopez was rated the seventh-best defensive catcher as well as the seventh-best manager of all time. /(JJM)

Aurelio Lopez — 1948– . RHP 1974, 78–87 Royals, Cardinals, **Tigers**, Astros 910 ip, 62–36, 3.56. *2 LCS, 6.1 ip, 1–1, 4.26. 1 WS, 3 ip, 1–0, 0.00* ☞ *All-Star—83.*

Dubbed Senor Smoke for his lively fastball, the portly veteran of 12 seasons in Mexico was one of the AL's top relievers for several years with Detroit, all after the age of thirty. Lopez had pitched professionally in his native Mexico for nine years before joining the Royals at the tail end of 1974 but returned to his longtime team, the Mexico City Reds, the following season, and in 1977 was the Mexican League MVP with a 19–8, 2.01 record. The Cardinals purchased his contract that fall and traded him to Detroit a year later, where Lopez quickly became the Tigers' bullpen stopper. He saved 21 games in 1979 and 21 more in 1980 while leading the AL with 13 relief wins. He recorded only six saves in 1981–82 but rebounded with 18 in 1983, then added 10 wins and 14 saves in 1984 working primarily as a set-up man for Cy Young Award winner and MVP Willie Hernandez. Lopez won the deciding fifth game of the WS against the Padres with two innings of relief, then suffered an off-year in 1985 and signed with the Astros as a free agent. He pitched exclusively in relief for Houston in 1986–87, saving eight games. /(SCL)

Carlos Lopez [born Carlos Antonio Morales Morales] — 1950– . OF 1976–78 Angels, Mariners, Orioles 237 g, .260, 12 hr, 54 rbi

Lopez played five years in his home country Mexican leagues before being purchased by the Angels' organization after the 1973 season. The Mariners

Al Lopez

selected him in the expansion draft, and he had his best season in 1977, batting .283 with 16 steals, eight HR, and 34 RBI in 297 at-bats (all career highs). He slumped to .238 with the Orioles in 1978, his last year in the majors. /(WOR)

Hector Lopez — 1932- . OF-3B-2B 1955-66 A's, **Yankees** 1451 g, .269, 136 hr, 591 rbi. *5 WS, 15 g, .286, 1 hr, 7 rbi*

The versatile Panamanian was traded from the A's to the Yankees during the 1959 season and was with New York for five straight pennants (1960-64). He played mostly third base for Kansas City, mostly outfield for New York, and he provided timely hitting as both a regular and pinch hitter. In the 1961 World Series against Cincinnati, he drove in seven runs—five in the final game, a 13-5 Yankee victory. /(JK)

Marcelino Lopez — 1943- . LHP 1963, 65-67, 69-71 Phillies, **Angels**, Orioles, Brewers, Indians 653 ip, 31-40, 3.62. *1 LCS, .1 ip, 0.00. 1 WS, .1 ip, 0.00*

The tall Cuban was named to the Topps All-Star Rookie team in 1965 after a 14-13, 2.93 ERA season with the Angels. Often wild, the next year he slumped to 7-14 while leading the AL in hit batsmen. Arm problems over the next few years handicapped his ML career. /(MC)

Bris Lord [Bristol Robotham] (The Human Eyeball) — 1883-1964. OF 1905-07, 09-13 **A's**, Indians, Braves 741 g, .256, 13 hr, 236 rbi. *3 WS, 16 g, .159, 4 rbi*

Signed off the sandlots by the A's 1905 pennant winners when their regular centerfielder was injured, Lord was a stocky journeyman with a fine arm. Later, the A's reacquired him in one of the all-time lopsided trades: even-up for Shoeless Joe Jackson. /(ADS)

Harry Lord — 1882-1948. 3B 1907-15 Red Sox, **White Sox**, Buffalo (FL) 972 g, .278, 14 hr, 294 rbi. *Manager* 1915 **Buffalo (FL)**, 59-48, .551

At times, Lord inspired his teammates with his hustle, earning the White Sox captaincy; at other times, it seemed he didn't want to play. The two years he batted more than .310 (1909 and 1911), he followed with marks of .267. He excelled at stretching doubles into triples. But as a fielder, he was virtually immobile. In 1913, he set single-season AL records for fewest chances accepted (364) and fewest assists (221) by a third baseman in 150 or more games. He jumped the White Sox in 1914, returned only to demand his release, and disappeared again

when Charles Comiskey turned him down. Ten days later, Buffalo (Federal League) announced they had signed Lord, who didn't show up until the next year to serve as player-manager. /(DB)

Los Angeles Dodgers — 1958- . Team. 2866-2389, .545. *NL West Champions 74, 77-78, 81, 83, 85, 88 NL Champions 59, 63, 65-66, 74, 77-78, 81, 88 World Champions 59, 63, 65, 81, 88*

When Dodger fans stopped dodging the Brooklyn trolleys that gave the team its name and started dodging traffic on the notorious Los Angeles freeways (eventually starting a local tradition of leaving the ballpark early to beat the traffic) America entered a new era.

"Dem Bums" had gone Hollywood. Leaving behind revered Ebbets Field, considered too small by owner Walter O'Malley, they wound up in the stadium considered by many the best ever built, and became the most successful sports franchise ever fielded, setting the ML single-season attendance record several times. They also became known for a succession of great pitching staffs starting with Koufax and Drysdale; bringing back the running game with Maury Wills; and the long tenures of their managers, Walter Alston and Tommy Lasorda. Los Angeles continued the Brooklyn tradition of appearing in every NL playoff, winning in 1959 and losing in 1962 and 1980. The 1959 win followed a seventh-place finish, a record comeback. /(TG)

Los Angeles Memorial Coliseum Los Angeles Dodgers 1958-61. LF-252, CF-420, RF-300

Expanded to 105,000 seats for the 1932 Olympics, the Coliseum was easily baseball's largest stadium, but was structurally incapable of containing a normal baseball field. Its oval-shaped playing area created 250' and 302' foul lines in its first season, and 120' of unused space between the centerfield fence and the seats. A 42' screen was erected in the left-field corner in an attempt to reduce the number of pop fly home runs, while the right-field fence shot sharply out to an almost unreachable 440' in 1958. That year, 193 home runs were hit in the Coliseum: 182 to left, 3 to center, and 8 to right. In only four seasons the Dodgers set several attendance records at the Coliseum, including 92,706 for Game Five of the 1959 WS against the White Sox and 93,103 for a May 7, 1959 exhibition against the Yankees on Roy Campanella Night. /(SCL)

The 1966 Los Angeles Dodgers

Baldy Louden [William] — 1885–1935. 2B-SS-3B 1907, 12–16 Yankees, Tigers, **Buffalo (FL)**, Reds 599 g, .261, 12 hr, 202 rbi

Louden was earning $2,700 a year with the Tigers when he chose to join Buffalo of the Federal League in 1914; he batted .313 as their shortstop. When the Feds folded in 1916, he hit .219 for the Reds while leading NL second basemen in fielding average. /(NLM)

Slim Love [Edward Haughton] — 1890–1942. LHP 1913, 16–20 Senators, **Yankees**, Tigers 119 g, 517 ip, 28–21, 3.04

Although he never had a losing ML season, wildness kept the 6'7" lefty from real success. In 1918, the only season he pitched regularly, Love was 13–12 for the Yankees but led the AL in walks. /(JK)

Joe Lovitto — 1951– . OF-3B 1972–75 **Rangers** 306 g, .216, 4 hr, 53 rbi

Lovitto hit .300 in the minors the season before he was called up, but his best major league mark was .224 in his rookie 1972 season. /(JFC)

Grover Lowdermilk (Slim) — 1885–1968. RHP 1909, 11–12, 15–20 Cardinals, Cubs, **Browns**, Tigers, Indians, White Sox 590 ip, 23–39, 3.58. *1 WS, 1 ip, 0–0, 9.00*

Grover and his brother Lou Lowdermilk both pitched for the 1911 Cardinals. Grover was 6'4" and lean, with long fingers, and was favorably compared to Walter Johnson—except that he couldn't control his blazing fastball. He was a member of the 1919 Black Sox but was not involved in the scandal. /(WAB)

Bobby Lowe (Link) — 1868–1951. 2B-OF-3B-SS 1890–07 **Braves**, Cubs, Pirates, Tigers 1824 g, .273, 70 hr, 984 rbi.
Manager 1904 **Tigers** 30–44, .405

A righthanded-batting leadoff man with fair power, the handsome, mustachioed Bobby Lowe (along with Kid Nichols and Herman Long) starred on all five Beaneater (later known as the Braves) pennant winners of the 1890s, playing second base in an infield that has been called the 19th century's best. On Decoration Day 1894, Lowe became the first

Bobby Lowe

major leaguer to homer four times in one game, doing it off Cincinnati's Elton "Iceberg" Chamberlain. The home runs came consecutively, in six at-bats, all over the 250-foot left-field wall of Boston's Congress Street Grounds, the Beaneaters' temporary home while their regular park was under repair. After the 20–11 Boston victory, the crowd showered Lowe with $160 in silver coins. /(ADS)

John Lowenstein — 1947– . OF-DH-3B-2B 1970-85 **Indians**, Rangers, Orioles 1368 g, .253, 116 hr, 441 rbi. *2 LCS, 6 g, .167, 1 hr, 5 rbi. 2 WS, 10 g, .308, 1 hr, 4 rbi*

After spending eight of his first nine ML seasons as a utility man with the Indians (1970–77) and the Rangers (1978), Lowenstein was picked up on waivers by Baltimore. The lefty was platooned against righthanded pitchers and became a favorite of manager Earl Weaver for his intelligence and attitude. Lowenstein reached his peak in 1982 when, platooning in left field, he hit .320 with 24 HR, 66 RBI, 69 runs, and 54 walks (all career highs) in just 322 at-bats (122 games). His .602 slugging average and 7.5 HR percentage would have led the majors if he had had enough at-bats to qualify. And he led all outfielders in fielding, going the entire season (111 games) without an error.

Even when not posting such spectacular numbers, Lowenstein was consistently valuable for the Orioles. In 1979, he missed much of the stretch run with a badly sprained ankle, but in Game One of the LCS he pinch hit. In the bottom of the tenth inning with the score tied 3–3 with two out and two on, he hit an opposite field homer off the Angels' John Montague. Lowenstein followed this in the World Series with a pinch two-run double in the eighth inning of Game Four as the Orioles rallied for six runs after being down 6–3. In 1983 he hit a WS homer in Game Two to tie the game in an eventual 4–1 victory as Baltimore won the first of four straight to become World Champions. /(WOR)

Turk Lown [Omar Joseph] — 1924– . RHP 1951-54, 56-62 **Cubs**, Reds, White Sox 1032 ip, 55–61, 4.12. *1 WS, 3 ip, 0–0, 0.00*

Lown was a hard-throwing but very wild starter with few successes in his first three years with the Cubs. Switched to relief, he blossomed into a star. His top season was 1959, when he helped the White Sox to their first pennant in 40 years with a 9–2 mark, an AL-leading 15 saves, and a 2.89 ERA. His nickname came from his fondness for turkey. /(AA)

Peanuts Lowrey [Harry Lee] — 1918–1986. OF-3B 1942-43, 45-55 **Cubs**, Reds, Cardinals, Phillies 1401 g, .273, 37 hr, 479 rbi. *1 WS, 7 g, .310* ☛ *All-Star—46.*

Lowrey came to the Cubs during the war years. When Chicago won its last pennant in 1945, he contributed a .283 BA and 89 RBI. But after several years of steady play, he was traded with Harry Walker to the Reds in 1949 for Frank Baumholtz and Hank Sauer in one of the best deals the Cubs ever made. Lowrey slumped in Cincinnati, but upon his sale to the Cardinals in 1950, his career enjoyed a rebirth. He batted a career high .303 in 1951 and led the NL in pinch hits with 13 in 1952 and 22 in 1953.

His nickname stemmed from the fact that his grandfather described the infant Lowrey as "no bigger than a peanut." Later, when he performed in child bit parts in silent films, actress Thema Todd reportedly gained his good behavior with promises to buy him peanuts. He also had a speaking part in *The Winning Team*, which starred Ronald Reagan as Grover Cleveland Alexander. /(ARA)

Mike Loynd — 1964– . RHP 1986–87 **Rangers** 111 ip, 3–7, 5.82

Loynd tied an NCAA record with 20 wins for Florida State in 1986 and defeated Cleveland in his debut with the Rangers that July 24 after just five minor league starts. He was sent to Houston after being hit hard in 1987. /(JCA)

Tony Lucadello — Unk.–1989. *Scout.*

Lucadello became a full-time scout with the Cubs in 1948 after part-time scouting during WWII. He joined the Phillies' scouting staff in 1957. He discovered Mike Schmidt, Ferguson Jenkins, Alex Johnson, and Toby Harrah, and he signed 50 major leaguers. His brother Johnny was an infielder for the Browns and the Yankees. /(FVP)

Gary Lucas — 1954– . LHP 1980–87 **Padres**, Expos, Angels 669 ip, 29–44, 3.01. *1 LCS, 2 ip, 0–0, 11.57*

Normally a good control pitcher, Lucas entered Game Five of the 1986 LCS with a 5–4 lead and no one on base, needing just one out to send the Angels to the WS. He promptly hit Rich Gedman with his first pitch (his first hit batsman since 1982), setting up Dave Henderson's home run off Donnie Moore in the next at bat. The lanky lefthander debuted with San Diego in 1980, and from 1981 to 1983 he saved 13, 16, and 17 games, leading the NL with 57 appearances in 1981 while posting a career-best 2.00 ERA. He was traded to the Expos for Scott Sanderson after the 1983 season, and then to the Angels two years later. /(SCL)

Red Lucas [Charles Fred] (The Nashville Narcissus) — 1902–1986. RHP-PH 1923–24, 26–38 Giants, Braves, **Reds**, Pirates 907 g, .281, 3 hr, 190 rbi; 396 g, 2542 ip, 157–135, 3.72

Lucas broke in as a pitcher but lacked a good fastball, so efforts were made to convert him into an infielder to take advantage of his hitting ability. His exceptional control eventually made him a top NL righthander, but his reputation as a good-hitting pitcher far overshadowed his accomplishments on the mound. He won 109 games for the perennial second-division Reds from 1926 through 1933, with highs of 18 in 1927 and 19 in 1929. In 1933 he walked only 18 in 220 innings, and his 1.61 bases on balls per nine innings places him 20th all-time.

In 1929, '31, and '32 he led the NL in complete games and in one stretch in 1931–32 completed 27 consecutive starts, a modern record. For his career he completed 68% of 301 starts. Among his best-pitched games were a 15-inning, 1–0 win over the

Giants (7/16/33) and a 3–0 win over the Dodgers (7/22/27) in which he issued no walks, faced the minimum 27 batters, and gave up only one scratch hit.

His career batting average was .281 and his 114 pinch hits and 437 pinch at-bats (a .261 average) were ML records for many years. He still ranks in the top ten in both categories. /(LRD)

Frank Lucchesi — 1926– . *Manager* 1970–72, 75–77, 87 **Phillies**, Rangers, Cubs 316–399, .442

A light-hitting minor league outfielder, Lucchesi first became a manager in the low minors at age twenty-three. After 19 years, he received his first ML assignment with the Phillies in 1970. He later managed the Rangers from mid-1975 until mid-1977 and ten years later finished the 1987 season as interim manager of the Cubs. With the Rangers in spring training in 1977, he was physically attacked on the field by Texas second baseman Lenny Randle, who was outraged at being benched. Lucchesi suffered a black eye, fractured cheekbone, and other injuries. He had Randle arrested a month later after turning down a settlement (Randle was also fined by the team for Lucchesi's medical expenses). The bad publicity led to Lucchesi's June firing. Randle was later found guilty of assault, and Lucchesi sued him for $200,000, saying that the incident cost him his job. It was finally settled two years later. /(BC)

Ron Luciano — 1937– . *Umpire* AL 1968–80 *3 LCS 1 WS 1 ASU*

"I was an umpire, but beneath my chest protector beat the heart of a fan," said Luciano. He applauded great plays, shook hands with home run hitters, and congratulated players after a good game. His on-the-field histrionics delighted the fans but were often frowned upon by players and fellow umpires. In 1975 Cleveland manager Frank Robinson levied $200 fines against Indians caught talking to Luciano during a game.

The only things that bothered Luciano were long games and making decisions. Boredom and the pressures of his profession often spawned his theatrics. He would frequently render an out call by pumping his arm several times or with a mock shooting gesture with his right hand.

Luciano's clashes with Baltimore manager Earl Weaver were legendary. The first time the two met was in Rochester (International League), and Luciano ejected the feisty manager in four straight games. In the majors, Luciano ejected Weaver eight times. The feud between the two was so severe that the AL took Luciano off Baltimore games.

Upon his resignation, the comic ump worked as a color commentator for the NBC Game of the Week for two seasons. His three books (with David Fisher), *The Umpire Strikes Back*, *Strike Two*, and *The Fall of the Roman Umpire*, have all been highly successful.

A football standout at Syracuse University, the burly 6′4″ 260-lb tackle played in the 1959 Pro-College All-Star Game and briefly with the Buffalo Bills in the AFL before becoming an umpire. /(RTM)

Fred Luderus — 1885–1961. 1B 1909–20 Cubs, **Phillies** 1346 g, .277, 84 hr, 647 rbi. *1 WS, 5 g, .438, 1 hr, 6 rbi*

Luderus was Grover Cleveland Alexander's first baseman in the Phillies' few strong years before 1920. By the standards of the time, he was a power hitter, batting fifth behind NL HR leader Gavvy Cravath to give the Phillies their middle-of-the-order punch. A lefthanded batter who threw right-handed, he was the first to hit two over-the-fence homers at Baker Bowl in a single game, long clouts even in that stadium's modest confines.

He came up with the Cubs, filled in for the ailing Frank Chance for a few games, and was traded for Bill Foxen, an undistinguished pitcher. He captained the pennant-winning 1915 Phillies and was their only strong hitter in the losing WS with the Red Sox, batting in six of his team's meager total of ten runs. An iron man, he played 533 consecutive games and was proud of never having been lifted for a pinch hitter. /(ADS)

Steve Luebber — 1949- . RHP 1971–72, 76, 79, 81 **Twins**, Blue Jays, Orioles 206 ip, 6–10, 4.62

Luebber never overcame control problems. In his best season, 1976, he went 4–5 with a 4.00 ERA while walking 62 in 119 innings. /(SFS)

Urbano Lugo [Rafael] — 1962- . RHP 1985- **Angels**, Expos 138 ip, 4–7, 5.01

The son of a Venezuelan pitching great of the same name, Lugo was rated the Eastern League's top pitching prospect in 1984 and was 3–4 while spending most of 1985 with the Angels. He won just one more ML game after a January 1986 elbow operation. /(JCA)

Fred Luderus

Mike Lum — 1945- . OF-1B 1967–81 **Braves**, Reds, Braves, Cubs 1517 g, .247, 90 hr, 431 rbi. *2 LCS, 3 g, .667*

The Hawaiian hit three HR against the Padres on July 3, 1970. He was most productive with the 1973 Braves, hitting .294 with 16 HR and 82 RBI as a first baseman and outfielder. But he achieved his greatest success as a lefthanded pinch hitter. His 103 career pinch hits and 418 pinch at-bats put him among the all-time leaders. In his second stint with the Braves, in 1979, he led the NL with 17 pinch hits in 52 tries, and pinch homered in consecutive games on September 4 and 5. He left in 1981 standing second to Hank Aaron in games played by for the Atlanta Braves. /(PB)

Harry Lumley — 1880-1938. OF 1904-10 **Dodgers** 730 g, .274, 38 hr, 305 rbi.
 Manager 1909 **Dodgers** 55-98, .359
☛ *Led League—hr 04* .

The Dodgers drafted Lumley after he led the Pacific Coast League in batting in 1903. As a rookie rightfielder, he led the NL in triples (18) and homers (9). Named Dodger player-manager in 1909, he guided the team to a sixth-place finish. /(AL)

Jerry Lumpe — 1933- . 2B-3B-SS 1956-67 Yankees, **A's**, Tigers 1371 g, .268, 47 hr, 454 rbi. *2 WS, 12 g, .231, 2 rbi*
☛ *All-Star—64.*

A line-drive hitter but a defensive liability at third base and shortstop for the Yankees, Lumpe was traded to the A's in 1959 and became a steady second baseman. In 1962 he reached career highs in average (.301), HR (10), and RBI (83) and put together a 20-game hitting streak. /(FK)

Don Lund — 1923- . OF 1945, 47-49, 52-54 Dodgers, Browns, **Tigers** 281 g, .240, 15 hr, 86 rbi

Five of Lund's seven seasons consisted of fewer than 55 at-bats. He hit .257 as the Tigers' right fielder in 1953, his only year as a regular. /(FK)

Carl Lundgren — 1880-1934. RHP 1902-09 **Cubs** 1322 ip, 90-55, 2.42

Lundgren was a starting pitcher on three successive Cub pennant winners (1906-08), but despite going 17-6 (2.21) in 1906 and 18-7 (1.17) in 1907, he was never used in a World Series; always, there were even better pitchers ahead of him. He later replaced Branch Rickey as baseball coach at the University of Michigan. /(JK)

Dick Lundy (The King) — 1899-1965. SS-2B-3B-MGR Negro Leagues 1916-48 Bacharach Giants, New York Lincoln Giants, Hilldale, Baltimore Black Sox, Philadelphia Stars, Newark Dodgers, New York Cubans, Newark Eagles, Jacksonville Eagles statistics not available

Lundy was one of the top shortstops in Negro League history, a great star and showman respected for his quiet professionalism, leadership qualities, and ability to perform suberbly under pressure. An exceptional fielder, he had great range and an outstanding throwing arm. He was a consistent, powerful switch-hitter who posed a threat on the basepaths.
 Lundy moved north with his hometown Jacksonville, FL team in 1915 when they became the Atlantic City Bacharach Giants. In 1921, he led the club with a .484 batting average. His 13 home runs in 1924 led the Eastern Colored League. He became the Bacharach Giants' player-manager in 1925 and led them to pennants in 1926 and 1927. In the 1926 Black World Series against the Chicago American Giants, Lundy hit .325 with six RBI, four runs scored, and six stolen bases in a losing cause.
 Lundy joined the Baltimore Black Sox in 1929 and became part of their "million-dollar infield" with Oliver Marcelle, Frank Warfield, and Jud Wilson. The Black Sox were Negro American League champions that year. In 1933 Lundy moved to the Philadelphia Stars, and though he was no longer in his prime, he was selected to play in the first East-West all-star game.
 Lundy played eight years in the Cuban Winter League, compiling a .341 average; he led the league in stolen bases in 1924. In 33 games against white major leaguers, he hit .289. He retired as an active player in 1937, after 22 seasons in the Negro Leagues. /(ETW)

Tony Lupien [Ulysses John] — 1917- . 1B 1940, 42-45, 48 **Red Sox**, Phillies, White Sox 614 g, .268, 18 hr, 230 rbi

A Harvard graduate, Lupian succeeded Jimmie Foxx as Red Sox first baseman during WWII, but he carried a better glove than bat. After leaving the ML, he managed in the minors, coached at Dartmouth, and wrote a book about baseball's reserve clause. /(EW)

Al Luplow — 1939- . OF 1961-67 **Indians**, Mets, Pirates 481 g, .235, 33 hr, 125 rbi

Luplow's ML career as a journeyman outfielder was highlighted by his selection to the Topps Rookie All-Star team in 1962 and a brilliant catch for the Indians at Fenway Park (6/27/63). He raced head-long toward right-center, grabbed Dick Williams's drive backhand, and flipped over the fence into the bullpen. /(EW)

Dolf Luque (The Pride of Havana) — 1890-1957. RHP 1914-15, 18-35. Braves, **Reds**, Dodgers, Giants 3220 ip, 193-179, 3.24. 20 wins: 23 *2 WS, 9 ip, 1-0, 0.00*
☛ *Led League—w 23. Led League—era 23, 25.*

One of the first Cubans to succeed in the majors, Luque came to the U.S. in 1912 to pitch for Long Branch (NY-NJ League) and was 22-5 in 1913. After a couple of unsuccessful trials with the Braves, he caught on with the Reds during WWI and stayed for 12 seasons. In the 1919 WS, he relieved twice

Dolf Luque

without allowing a run, and the next year he became a regular Cincinnati starter. He led the NL in losses (23) in 1922 but had his career year the next season, leading the league in wins (27), winning percentage (.771), and ERA (1.93). Although he never again topped 20 wins, Luque led again in ERA with 2.63 in 1925. In the 1930s he turned to relief pitching for the Giants. His 4-1/3 shutout innings earned him the win in the 10-inning fifth and final game of the 1933 WS./(EW)

Billy Lush — 1873-1951. OF 1895-97, 1901-04 Washington (NL), Braves, Tigers, **Indians** 489 g, .249, 8 hr, 152 rbi

Lush was a fast but unproductive switch-hitter. Playing for Washington in 1896, he compiled an .885 fielding percentage, the worst among National League outfielders. His brother Ernie played one game for the 1910 Cardinals. /(DAS)

Johnny Lush — 1885-1946. LHP-OF-1B 1904-10 Phillies, **Cardinals** 369 g, .254, 2 hr, 94 rbi; 1239 ip, 66-85, 2.68

As an 18-year-old first baseman/outfielder with the Phillies, Lush was the youngest regular ML player of the 20th century. He became a full-time pitcher for

Philadelphia in 1906, when he had a career-high 18 wins and a no-hitter against the Dodgers, but he had only one more winning season. /(JK)

Rube Lutzke [Walter John] — 1897-1938. 3B 1923-27 **Indians** 572 g, .249, 4 hr, 223 rbi

A gifted fielder, Lutzke was weak at the plate and was often removed for pinch hitters. He led American League third basemen in putouts, assists, and errors in 1923. /(ME)

Greg Luzinski (The Bull) — 1950- . OF-DH 1970-84 **Phillies**, White Sox 1821 g, .276, 307 hr, 1128 rbi. *5 LCS, 20 g, .274, 5 hr, 12 rbi. 1 WS, 3 g, .000*
☛ *Led League—rbi 75. All-Star—75-78.*

Luzinski earned the nickname The Bull with his bulging arms, thick neck, massive body, and vicious righthanded batting stroke. As the Phillies' left fielder in the 1970s, he teamed with third baseman Mike Schmidt to form a potent slugging combination and help the Phillies to four NL East championships in five years.

The 6'1" 220-lb Luzinski reached the ML for good in 1972, with two minor league home run crowns, one minor league batting championship, and three minor league strikeout titles on his resume. He hit .281 with 18 HR as a rookie, and .285 with 29 HR and 97 RBI in 1973, the year Schmidt joined the lineup. From 1975 to 1980, the pair averaged nearly 66 HR a year. Luzinski was hobbled by knee surgery in 1974 but rebounded in 1975 to hit .300 with 34 HR and a NL-best 120 RBI. The Bull still routinely struck out 100 times a season, yet pushed his average up to .304 the following year as the Phillies won the first of three consecutive division titles, and in 1977 he logged career highs in all three Triple Crown catagories, batting .309 with 39 HR and 130 RBI. In LCS play, Luzinski was just as dangerous, slugging home runs in Game Two in 1976, Game One in 1977, and Games Three and Four in 1978, but the Phillies lost all three series. Luzinski's production fell off badly in 1979, and in 1980 his average dropped to .228, but the Phillies finally advanced past the LCS with a five-game victory over the Astros, as Luzinski homered to win Game One. In the WS, the Phillies used the clumsy-fielding Luzinski primarily as the designated hitter and he failed to get a single hit, but the Phillies beat the Royals in six games.

Luzinski was sold to the White Sox before the 1981 season and he immediately became Chicago's full-time DH, where he no longer had to endure criticism for his wretched defense. He played four seasons in Chicago, helping them to the AL West title in 1983 with 32 HR and 95 RBI, then retired after hitting .238 with 13 HR in 1984. The Bull is fourth on the Phillies all-time home run list, behind Schmidt, Del Ennis, and Chuck Klein. /(SCL)

Sparky Lyle [Albert Walter] — 1944- . LHP 1967-82 Red Sox, **Yankees**, Rangers, Phillies, White Sox 1391 ip, 99-76, 2.88. *3 LCS, 11.2 ip, 2-0, 2.31. 2 WS, 7.1 ip, 1-0, 1.23*
☛ *Cy Young Award—77. All-Star—73, 76, 77.*

Lyle was one of the AL's best relievers for over a decade with the Red Sox and Yankees, leading the league in saves in 1972 and 1976, and in 1977 he became the first reliever ever to win the AL Cy Young Award. A wisecracking lefthander with a sizable paunch visible beneath his uniform, Lyle relied on a crackling slider almost exclusively in his heyday but also possessed a good fastball and a capable curve. He never started a ML game.

Lyle pitched briefly for the Red Sox as a rookie in 1967, but not at all in the WS, and in 1968 he began to emerge as their bullpen ace, finishing 6–1 with 11 saves and a 2.74 ERA. He saved 17 games in 1969 (third in the AL), 20 in 1970, and 16 in 1971, but before the 1972 season he was traded to the rival Yankees even-up for first baseman Danny Cater, one of the worst trades in Red Sox history. Lyle immediately led the AL with 35 saves for the Yankees in 1972 while recording a 1.91 ERA, and he added 27 saves in 1973, a career-low 1.66 ERA in 1974, and an AL-best 23 saves in 1976 as the Yankees won the AL championship. In 1977 Lyle was even better, winning 13 games and saving 26 (second in the AL), then adding a win in the WS as the Yankees beat the Dodgers in six games and Lyle captured the AL Cy Young Award.

By the spring of 1978, however, Lyle was feuding with Yankee management, irked over owner George Steinbrenner's decision to sign relief aces Rich Gossage and Rawley Eastwick as free agents despite the presence of Lyle in the club's bullpen. Gossage became the club's closer, and after the season Lyle was traded to Texas in a 10-player-deal that brought Dave Righetti to the Bronx. By 1980, Lyle's slider had lost its snap, and he saved only 15 games in three final seasons with the Rangers, Phillies, and White Sox. He made his feelings about playing for the Yankees known in *The Bronx Zoo*, a book he wrote with Pete Golenbock in 1979. /(SCL)

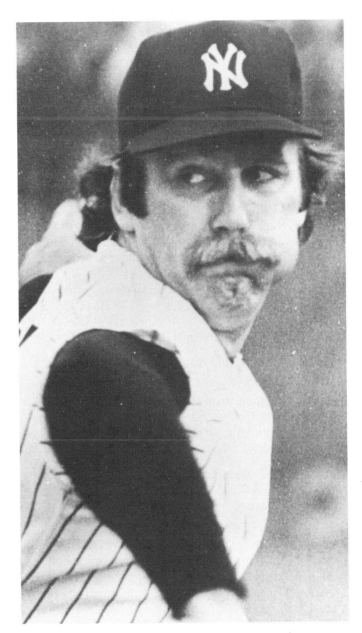

Sparky Lyle

Ed Lynch — 1956- . RHP 1980-87 **Mets**, Cubs 940 ip, 47-54, 4.00

After pitching for the lowly Mets of the early 1980s, Lynch was 10-8, 3.44 as their third starter when they finished second in 1985, but he was traded to the Cubs for a pair of minor leaguers in the middle of 1986 as the Mets were storming toward a World Championship. Lynch had excellent control (2.2 walks per nine innings in the ML) and could pitch in relief as well as start, but a 2-9, 5.38 record with Chicago in 1987 ended his ML career. /(SCL)

Jerry Lynch — 1930– . OF 1954–66 Pirates, **Reds** 1184 g, .277, 115 hr, 470 rbi. *1 WS, 4 g, .000*

Lynch's outstanding pinch hitting (19-for-47, .404) was a major factor in the 1961 Reds' surprising NL pennant. Overall, he had career-high averages of .315 (batting) and .624 (slugging) for the season, with 13 HR and 50 RBI in only 181 at-bats. When he retired, the poor-fielding outfielder ranked first all-time in pinch HR (18) and second in pinch hits (116) and was tied for first in pinch at-bats (447). The lefthanded-hitting Lynch led the NL in pinch hits twice (19 in both 1960 and 1961).

Lynch joined the Reds after missing most of the 1956 season due to illness. With Pittsburgh, he had been a part-time outfielder and occasional catcher, but not a very successful pinch hitter (9-for-49, .184, over three seasons). He was a semi-regular outfielder in 1958 and '59, reaching bests of 17 HR (1959, 379 at-bats) and 68 RBI (1958, 420 at-bats). He returned to the Pirates in mid-1963./(SFS)

Mike Lynch — 1880–1927. RHP 1904–07 **Pirates**, Giants 655 ip, 43–32, 3.05

A crafty collegian from Brown University, Lynch won 32 games for Pittsburgh in his first two seasons. He led the Pirates in strikeouts in 1904 but tended to walk as many as he whiffed. /(ME)

Thomas J. Lynch (King of the Umpires) — 1859–1924. *Umpire* NL 1888–99, 1902

Lynch was a National League umpire known for his honesty. He was instrumental in increasing the prestige of umpires through such actions as leaving the field rather than continue the game in face of heavy fan abuse. He became National League president in 1910 as a compromise candidate and served until 1914. Although his tenure was largely uneventful, his brusque manner and forthright opinions offended several club owners and brought about his replacement./(BC)

Fred Lynn — 1952– . OF 1974– **Red Sox**, Angels, Orioles, Tigers 1879 g, .284, 300 hr, 1088 rbi. *2 LCS, 8 g, .517, 1 hr, 8 rbi. 1 WS, 7 g, .280, 1 hr, 5 rbi*
☛ *Rookie of the Year—75. Most Valuable Player—75. Led League—ba 79. All-Star—75–83. Gold Glove—75, 78–80.*

Despite ten 20-HR seasons, one batting title, and All-Star appearances in each of his first nine seasons, Fred Lynn always fell short of expectations--betrayed by a fragile body and burdened with one of the finest rookie seasons in ML history.

In 1975, Lynn captivated Boston with his effort-

Fred Lynn

less lefthanded swing, ringing line drives, and almost daily sprawling catches in centerfield as he led a young Red Sox club to within one win of the World Championship. On June 18 he bombed the Tigers with 3 HR, 10 RBI, and 16 total bases in one game, and by season's end Lynn had hit .331, led the AL in runs and doubles, and became the only player ever to be named Rookie of the Year and MVP in the same season. In 1979, he was even better, leading the AL in batting (.333) with 39 HR and 122 RBI. Lynn, however, longed to play in his native California, and the Red Sox obliged by trading him to the Angels in January 1981. Away from Fenway Park, Lynn would never hit .300 again.

He remained one of the AL's better-fielding outfielders when healthy, and had six consecutive 20 HR seasons (1982–88). His grand slam in the 1983 All-Star Game (the only grand slam in All-Star play) was his fourth All-Star Game home run, second only to Stan Musial in ML history. But he was never the Hall of Famer he had appeared destined to be in 1975, and the main culprit was injuries. While some were the result of reckless play (he broke a rib crashing into an outfield fence and twice tore up his knee breaking up double plays), more often it was nagging strains and sprains that kept him off the field. The only year in which he played 150 games was 1978. /(SCL)

Barry Lyons — 1960– . C 1986– **Mets** 188 g, .241, 7 hr, 64 rbi

Lyons finally got a chance to play regularly when Gary Carter had knee surgery early in the 1989 season. Lyons was hot at first, hitting two HR in his first week as a regular, but soon he slumped and then went on the DL with a broken foot. He came off the DL the same time as Carter. /(WOR)

Denny Lyons — 1866–1929. 3B 1885–97 Providence (NL), **Philadelphia (AA)**, St. Louis (AA), Giants, Pirates, Cardinals 1121 g, .310, 62 hr, 569 rbi

A fine righthanded hitter and remarkable fielder for those gloveless days, Lyons ranks second among ML third basemen in putouts per game. His best seasons were 1887, when he hit a career-high .367 and set the ML record for putouts at third base (255); and 1890, when he hit .354, led the AA in slugging (.531), and led league third basemen in fielding. /(FIC)

Jimmy Lyons — Unk.–Unk. OF-MGR Negro Leagues 1911–32 New York Lincoln Giants, St. Louis Giants, Chicago Giants, Brooklyn Royal Giants, Indianapolis ABC's, **Chicago American Giants**, Detroit Stars, Cleveland Browns, Louisville Black Caps statistics not available

Jimmy Lyons was a vital cog on Rube Foster's great Negro League Chicago American Giants of the early 1920s. Winners of pennants in each of the first three years of the Negro National League (1920–22), the Chicago American Giants relied on the swift, left-handed outfielder for his defensive skill, speed on the bases, hitting, and expert drag bunting. Teammate Willie Powell noted that Lyons "didn't know what it was to get up to bat and take his full swing, 'cause Rube always had him put it here, lay it down there." According to Powell, the 5′6″ Lyons was faster than Hall of Famer Cool Papa Bell—a statement naturally disputed by Bell. Lyons was a feared baserunner known to sharpen his spikes. He led the NNL with 22 steals and a .394 batting average in 1920. He finished his career as manager of the Louisville Black Caps in 1932. /(PG)

Steve Lyons (Psycho) — 1960– . OF-3B-2B 1985– Red Sox, **White Sox** 596 g, .262, 14 hr, 164 rbi

Lyons was Boston's first pick in the June 1981 draft. Though signed as an infielder, he played 88 games in centerfield as a Red Sox rookie in 1985. Known as Psycho because of his reckless hustle and flakiness, he became a Boston fan favorite and hosted a local call-in show. On June 29, 1986 the White Sox accommodated Tom Seaver's desire to play for an East Coast team by shipping him to Boston for Lyons. Relegated to a utility role, Lyons became an attitude problem and was sent down in 1987. He later returned to bat .280 and was made Chicago's third baseman two months into the 1988 season. /(RL)

Ted Lyons — 1900–1986. RHP 1923–42, 46 **White Sox** 4161 ip, 260–230, 3.67. 20 wins: 25, 27, 30
  Manager 1946–48 **White Sox** 185–245, .430
☛ Led League—w 25, 27. Led League—era 42. All-Star—39. Hall of Fame—1955.

Lyons never pitched in the minor leagues and never pitched in a World Series, but 21 seasons of yeoman work for the seldom-contending White Sox earned his 1955 election by the BBWAA to the Hall of

Ted Lyons

Fame. He attended Baylor University with plans for a law career, but his college pitching made him a sought-after prospect. Upon graduation in 1923, he turned down an offer from the A's to sign with Chicago for $300 a month and a $1,000 bonus. He joined the team in St. Louis on July 2 and relieved in the first ML game he ever saw, retiring the three Browns he faced.

By the next season he was a regular starter, and in 1925 he led the AL in victories (21) for a fifth-place team. He repeated as AL win leader in '27 and won 22 in 1930. In 1925–30, he averaged nearly 19 wins a season, although the White Sox never finished in the first division. Late in 1925, in a game that Chicago uncharacteristically won 17–0, he held the Senators to no hits for 8–2/3 innings. On August 21, 1926 he no-hit the Red Sox, winning 6–0.

Then, in 1931, he injured his arm and lost his fastball. His manager, Donie Bush, pronounced his arm "dead." But Lyons developed a knuckleball and was soon pitching effectively again. In 1936, he helped pitch the club to its first finish in the AL first division (third) since he had joined the team 14 years earlier.

His most important weapon was excellent control. Never a strikeout pitcher, he walked only 1,121 batters in 4,161 innings pitched over his career, and at one point in 1939 he hurled 42 consecutive innings without issuing a base on balls.

In 1939 White Sox Manager Jimmie Dykes began pitching him once a week, always on Sunday, to save his arm and to take advantage of Lyons's tremendous popularity to draw large crowds. The Sunday-only pattern continued through 1942, with Lyons's .634 winning percentage (52–30) the best for any four-year section of his career. In 1942 he led the AL in ERA (2.10) while completing all 20 of his starts and winning 14.

In the fall of '42, the 41-year-old lifelong bachelor joined the U.S. Marines, spending part of his three-year hitch in combat. In 1946 he returned to the White Sox and pitched five more complete games, winning only one, his 260th. Thirty games into the season he replaced Dykes as White Sox manager. His managerial record through 1948 was 185–245, with the main criticism being that he was too easy-going to enforce discipline. He later coached and scouted before retiring in 1966 to help his sister manage a Louisiana rice plantation. /(RL)

Rick Lysander — 1953– . RHP 1980, 83–85 A's, **Twins** 257 ip, 9–17, 4.31

Signed by Oakland, Lysander bounced around the minors for six seasons until a 10–3 season of relief for Ogden of the Pacific Coast League earned him a short trial in 1980. He was traded to the Astros and then to the Twins. In 1983 he pitched in 61 games with a 3.38 ERA but his performance later suffered because of overwork. /(MC)

Jim Lyttle — 1946– . OF 1969–76 **Yankees**, White Sox, Expos, Dodgers 391 g, .248, 9 hr, 70 rbi

Lyttle hit .310 in 126 at-bats for the 1970 Yankees in his most active season. He was a good outfielder, but had little power and lacked consistency. /(JFC)

Duke Maas [Duane Frederick] — 1929–76. RHP 1955–61 Tigers, A's, **Yankees** 735 ip, 45–44, 4.19. *2 WS, 2 ip, 0–0, 15.43*

Maas figured in one of the largest trades of the 1950s. In November 1957 the Tigers traded him with Bill Tuttle, Jim Small, John Tsitouris, Frank House, Kent Hadley, and Jim McManus to Kansas City for Billy Martin, Gus Zernial, Lou Skizas, Tom Morgan, Mickey McDermott, and Tim Thompson. The next year Maas went to the Yankees with Virgil Trucks for Bob Grim and Harry Simpson. In 1959, his best season, Maas was 14–8 with a 4.43 ERA and four saves, going 5–0 in relief. /(NLM)

Bob Mabe — 1929– . RHP 1958–60 **Cardinals**, Reds, Orioles 142 ip, 7–11, 4.82

Mabe lost the sight in his right eye in a childhood accident. After flunking out of the Cardinals' rotation in 1958 (3–9) he earned two more chances, but never had a full major league season. /(MC)

Bill Macdonald — 1929– . RHP 1950, 53 **Pirates** 160 ip, 8–11, 4.66

Macdonald was Pittsburgh's first bonus player. He shut out Philadelphia in his first major league start (5/23/50) and finished the year at 8–10. After losing 1951 and 1952 to military duty, he made just four ML appearances. /(ME)

Mike Macfarlane — 1964– . C 1987– **Royals** 147 g, .245, 6 hr, 48 rbi

Macfarlane platooned with Jamie Quirk in 1988, hitting .265. He saw less regular action in 1989, when the Royals acquired Bob Boone. /(SFS)

Danny MacFayden (Deacon Danny) — 1905–1972. RHP 1926–41, 43 **Red Sox**, Yankees, Reds, Braves, Pirates, Senators 2706 ip, 132–159, 3.96

Bespectacled, quiet Danny MacFayden lasted 17 years in the majors, averaging less than eight wins a season. He compiled losing records with four straight last-place Red Sox teams before going 16–12 to help them out of the cellar in 1931. After beginning the 1932 season 1–10, he was sold to the Yankees. He was waived by Cincinnati to the Boston Braves in 1935. With ERA of 2.95 and under for the Braves, he won a career-high 17 games in 1936, and 14 in both 1937 and 1938. After his playing career, MacFayden was a longtime coach at Bowdoin College. /(EC)

Ken Macha — 1950– . 3B-1B 1974, 77–81 Pirates, **Expos**, Blue Jays 180 g, .258, 1 hr, 35 rbi

A power-hitting catcher in the minors, Macha became a defensive swinger as a ML reserve. He regained his punch playing in Japan, hitting 82 HR for the Chunichi Dragons from 1982 through 1985, with a high of 31 in 1984. His brother Mike played briefly for the Braves and Blue Jays in 1979–80. /(MC)

Norman L. Macht — 1929– . *Writer.*

A graduate of the University of Chicago and a former minor league general manager, Macht is a freelance baseball historian. He published *Rowdy Richard: A Firsthand Account of the National League Baseball Wars of the 1930s and the Men Who Fought Them*, with Dick Bartell (1987). He is currently working on a biography of Connie Mack. /(NLM)

Connie Mack — 1862–1956. C-1B 1886–96 Washington (NL), Buffalo (PL), **Pirates** 723 g, .245, 5 hr, 265 rbi
  Manager 1894–96, 1901–50 Pirates, **A's** 3776–4025, .484. First place: 02, 05, 10–11, 13, 14, 29–31 *8 WS, 24–19, .558*
☛ *Hall of Fame—1937.*

The U.S. Supreme Court ruled in 1922 that baseball was a sport, not a business. But Connie Mack always saw it as a business first. Like any business, it had to show a profit to keep going. "It is more profitable for me to have a team that is in contention for most of the season but finishes about fourth," he once confided. "A team like that will draw well enough during the first part of the season to show a profit for the year, and you don't have to give the players raises when they don't win." But of course Mr. Mack—as he was universally addressed—liked winners. He had nine of them, and won five World Series. He also holds the managerial record for most wins lifetime with 3776—but he attained it through longevity. With it came the records for most losses (4,025) and most games managed (7878).

For 50 of his 60 years in baseball, he had an ownership interest in the team he managed, the Philadelphia Athletics. He started in 1901 with a 25 percent piece of the team and eventually became sole owner. Baseball was his only business. Gate receipts and concessions sales were the only sources of capital he had to work with. He never had any corporate coffers to tap and never took much money out of the game. It was financial realities that forced him to break up two of the greatest teams ever put together. After winning four pennants in five years from 1910 to 1914, he lost some of his stars to the Federal League's higher salaries, and sold off his other top players. The Athletics fell from first to last and stayed there for seven years.

Gradually he built another winner. From 1925 through 1933 the Athletics finished no lower than third, dethroning the Yankees in 1929–30–31 with a team that rivals the 1927 Yankees for all-time honors. Once again, squeezed between declining attendance brought on by runaway pennant races, the Great Depression, and higher salary demands of his champion players, Mack sold his stars and dismantled his last winning team. For the last 17 years, until he retired at 88 in 1950, the Athletics had only one first-division finish, fourth in 1948.

Behind the saintly, grandfatherly appearance of the 6'1"150-lb, ramrod-straight, blue-eyed Mr. Mack, there was a complex personality, a blend of patience and impetuosity, kindness and stubbornness, tightfistedness and generosity. He never raised his voice and seldom confronted a player in front of his teammates, but he could put a man in his place with a cutting sarcastic comment. He disdained swearing, but did sometimes cut loose with a salty barrage. To strangers of any age who approached him in a hotel lobby or dining room, he was invariably courtly and pleasant. Despite a tendency to mispronounce some names and forget others, he had an unfailing memory for the faces of old friends from his hometown, East Brookfields, Massachusetts, and gave them a genuinely warm welcome whenever they came to Boston to see the Athletics play.

From the beginning in Philadelphia he never wore a uniform on the bench, and rarely went into the clubhouse except for a pre-game meeting, a practice he inaugurated in the major leagues. He was called the tenth man on the field for his ability to move his fielders, using his scorecard, into the proper positions. He liked tall, strong pitchers and considered pitching eighty percent of the game.

Mack was born to Irish immigrants, the third of seven children. He was attracted to the early forms of baseball at a young age, and played infield and outfield positions before becoming the town team's regular catcher. After they won the state championship in 1883, Mack offered his services to several teams in the Connecticut State League, and was signed by Meriden (with his battery mate and later brother-in-law Willie Hogan) for the 1884 season, at $90 a month. He played for Hartford the next two years (in the Eastern League in 1886) and was sold at the end of the season to Washington in the National League.

In 1890 Mack was an avid supporter of the revolt that led to the formation of the Players' League. He signed with Buffalo and got his first taste of club ownership, investing his life savings of $500 in the team. He lost it all.

Assigned to Pittsburgh in 1891, he replaced Al Buckenberger as manager toward the end of the 1894 season. By 1896 front office interference caused him to look elsewhere. The Milwaukee club in Ban Johnson's Western League was making a change, and in 1897 Mack began four years of managing and running the business affairs of the team. They were years in which he learned more about the game than at any other time. Mack's connection with Johnson led to an offer to organize and manage the Philadelphia entry in the new American League in 1901. With the financial backing of sporting goods maufacturer Ben Shibe, Mack began his 50-year reign in the dugout and front office. The Athletics were the dominant team in the young league, winning 6 of the first 14 pennants. In 1933 he managed the American League in the first All-Star Game.

Four years after he retired, the Athletics were sold to Arnold Johnson and moved to Kansas City in 1955.

As a player, Mack played every position in the majors except third base and pitcher, but he was primarily a brainy, wily, sometimes rule-bending catcher. He distracted batters with his chatter, was not above tipping a hitter's bat just before a swing, and learned to make a slapping sound as a batter swung and missed that made it sound like a foul tip. He was a .245 lifetime hitter; his best season was 1893 (the first year the pitcher was moved to 60'6" from the former distance of 50'), when he hit .293.

Mack's first wife died in 1892, leaving three children. His sons, Roy and Earle, were active in the

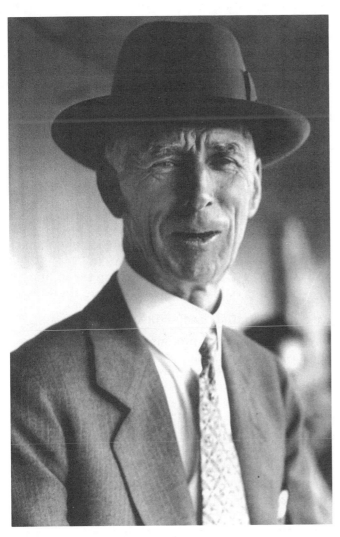

Connie Mack

team's operation. He remarried in 1910 and had a son, Connie, Jr., who was also involved in the team, and four daughters. From the start Connie Mack was the most popular player with the fans wherever he played. Meriden fans gave him a gold watch in 1884. Washington fans gave him a silver tray. For the first half of the 20th century he was probably the best-loved and most respected man in any field in America. /(NLM)

Gene Mack [McGillicuddy] — Unk.–1953. *Cartoonist.*

Mack, a relative of Connie Mack, was a Boston cartoonist enduringly known for intricate sketches of ball parks, filled with illustrations of odd or famous incidents at the spots where they happened. Many of his works hang in the Hall of Fame museum. They were collected into a book in 1950. /(NLM)

Ray Mack [born Raymond James Mickovsky] — 1916–1969. 2B 1938–44, 46–47 **Indians,** Yankees, Cubs 791 g, .232, 34 hr, 278 rbi

A tough and brilliant second baseman, Cleveland native Ray Mack teamed with Lou Boudreau as the Indians' double play combo in the early 1940s. He saved Bob Feller's Opening Day no-hitter in 1940 with a diving stop for the final out. Mack had passed up football for baseball, but his son Tom played for the NFL Rams. /(JK)

Shane Mack — 1963– . OF 1987–88 **Padres** 161 g, .241, 4 hr, 37 rbi

Mack was a member of the 1984 U.S. Olympic baseball team and was the Padres' first-round pick in the June '84 draft. He has failed all his major-league trials. /(WOR)

Pete Mackanin — 1951– . 2B-SS-3B 1973–81 Rangers, **Expos**, Phillies, Twins 548 g, .226, 30 hr, 141 rbi

Mackanin was traded to Montreal in 1975 and hit 12 homers—second among NL second base-man—but batted just .225. Bone chips in his elbow sidelined him with the Phillies in 1979. /(NLM)

Gordon MacKay — 1878–1941. *Writer.*

After working for Boston and Cleveland newspapers, MacKay was sports editor for several papers in Philadelphia, the last of which was the *Inquirer.* He was also a contributor to the *Reach Guide.* /(NLM)

Ken MacKenzie — 1934– . LHP 1960–65 Braves, **Mets,** Cardinals, Giants, Astros 208 ip, 8–10, 4.80

Canadian reliever MacKenzie saw his only signifi-cant action with the expansion Mets, and he was the only pitcher on their 1962 staff to post a winning record (5–4). The Yale graduate once pointed out to manager Casey Stengel that he was the lowest-paid member of his graduating class; Stengel replied that MacKenzie had the highest ERA. /(JFC)

Biz Mackey [Raleigh] — 1897–1959. C-SS-3B-MGR Negro Leagues 1918–47 San Antonio Giants, Darby Daisies, Indianapolis ABC's, Hilldale, Baltimore Elite Giants, Philadelphia Stars, Washington Elite Giants, Nashville Giants, Newark Eagles 654 g, .312, 46 hr (inc.) ☛ *All-Star—33, 35–36, 38, 47.*

Considered by many the greatest catcher in Negro League history, Mackey was a master practitioner behind the plate. He possessed a powerful arm, and used the current standard "snap throw." He was strong enough to throw to second base from a sitting position, which he customarily did in between-inning warm-ups. He was a switch-hitter who batted for power and a high average.

Homestead Grays manager Cum Posey rated Mackey as his number-one all-time catcher: "Mackey was a tremendous hitter, a fierce competitor; although slow afoot he is the standout among catchers who have shown their wares in this nation." Roy Campanella was a 15-year-old with the Baltimore Elite Giants when Mackey taught him the fine points of catching. Campanella said, "I gathered quite a bit from Mackey, watching how he shifted his feet for an outside pitch, how he threw with a short, quick accurate throw without drawing back.

After two seasons with the San Antonio Giants, Mackey joined the Indianapolis ABC's and hit .352 in 1922 before being traded to the Hilldale team. He led Hilldale to their first title in 1923, batting .364. The next year he hit .325, helping Hilldale earn an invitation to the first Black World Series, against the Kansas City Monarchs. From 1922 through 1931, Mackey compiled a .327 average, with a high of .365 in 1930. In the first East-West all-star game, he was chosen over Hall of Fame teammates Josh Gibson and Oscar Charleston to bat cleanup.

Mackey's cherubic face and jolly nature never failed to delight fans and teammates. He completed his brilliant career as player-manager for the Newark Eagles. There he prepared Larry Doby, Don Newcombe, and Monte Irvin for the major leagues. Irvin called Mackey "the dean of teachers." /(LL)

Felix Mackiewicz — 1917- . OF 1941-43, 45-47 A's, **Indians**, Senators 223 g, .259, 2 hr, 55 rbi

After short trials with the A's from 1941-43, Mackiewicz gained a spot in Cleveland's outfield in 1945 due to the WWII talent shortage; he played in over half his ML games that season, batting .273. /(ME)

Macmillan Baseball Encyclopedia (Big Mac) — 1969- .

The first choice of baseball aficionados, this seven-pound reference is subtitled *The Complete and Official Record of Major League Baseball*. Originally the product of Information Concepts, Inc. (ICI), headed by David Neft, it was produced in conjuction with Lee Allen, the long-time historian of the Hall of Fame. Starting in 1967, the records of every player who could be found were completely recalculated from original box scores; official league records were error-riddled and untrustworthy. Some records thus revamped proved too controversial; right away, an official rules committee of Major

League Baseball overthrew the decision to give Babe Ruth an additional home run, and in the years since many changes in well-known and revered career and season totals have gradually been restored to their more well-known state, occasioning a break between Macmillan and ICI. But with the help of the Society for American Baseball Research, and especially the Biographical Committee, the accuracy of the encyclopedia overall has been vastly improved in the many editions since the first one in 1969. /(SH)

Max Macon — 1915- . LHP-1B-OF 1938, 40, 42-44, 47 Cardinals, Dodgers, **Braves** 297 ip, 17-19, 4.24; 226 g, .265, 3 hr, 46 rbi

Macon was a marginally talented pitcher who found greater success as a first baseman for the 1944 Braves, batting .273. After two years in the military, he appeared in only one more ML game. /(EGM)

Larry MacPhail [Leland] — 1890-1975. *Executive.*

Few executives had as profound an impact on the game as Larry MacPhail. In Cincinnati (1934-36) MacPhail introduced night baseball and commercial air travel to the majors. He laid the groundwork for the Reds' 1939-40 pennant winners, and he departed in controversy before they won, a trademark of his career. He went to Brooklyn in 1938. In his first year, the franchise made money for the first time since 1920. MacPhail hired Babe Ruth as coach to generate interest and, anticipating Charlie Finley years later, brought the "stitched lemon," a yellow baseball, to spring training. MacPhail's presence inaugurated the modern era of Brooklyn baseball. In the 38 years before MacPhail, the Dodgers had won three pennants; in the 20 years following his arrival they won seven and lost in playoffs two times after finishing tied for first. MacPhail also brought Red Barber with him from Cincinnati to introduce daily game broadcasts in New York, ending a gentleman's agreement among the three local clubs not to do so.

In 1941, there was jubilation following the Dodgers' clinching of their first pennant in 21 years. In the excitement, MacPhail was left on a platform at the 125th Street Station, expecting to board the team train to meet a jubilant crowd at Grand Central Station. Manager Leo Durocher had decided to skip the stop in an attempt to keep the players on board. A furious MacPhail fired Durocher on the spot, something he did numerous times, many of which he seemed not to remember later. According to Durocher, "There is a thin line between genius and insanity, and in Larry's case it was sometimes so

Larry MacPhail

thin you could see him drifting back and forth."

MacPhail began as a protege of Branch Rickey, and Rickey replaced him in Brooklyn when MacPhail went into the army in 1942. MacPhail was a veteran of WWI as well, and had been in a group of plotters who had nearly succeeded in kidnapping Kaiser Wilhelm.

After the war, MacPhail joined the Yankees, and he had three managers (Joe McCarthy, Bill Dickey, and Johnny Neun) quit on him in 1946. He also came close to arranging what would have been one of the biggest trades in ML history while drinking with Red Sox owner Tom Yawkey. The pair allegedly agreed to swap Ted Williams for Joe DiMaggio, but when they sobered up Yawkey asked for Yogi Berra as well, and the deal was nixed.

Following the Yankees' victory over Rickey's Dodgers in the exciting 1947 Series, MacPhail upstaged the clubhouse victory party by unleashing

a barrage of insults, punching a writer, and announcing his resignation in a drunken stupor. Topping Webb bought him out the next day.

The innovative, tempestuous MacPhail started a family baseball tradition. His son Lee became president of the American League, and his grandson Andy was general manager of the 1987 World Champion Minnesota Twins. /(TG)

Lee MacPhail — 1917– . *Executive.*

Lee's quiet, soft-spoken, introverted personality contrasted sharply with that of his explosively extroverted father, Larry MacPhail. After graduating from Swarthmore College, he began his baseball career as business manager at Reading in the Interstate League in 1941. He became director of player personnel for the Yankees from 1948 through 1958, helping to produce the team that won nine pennants in those years. He moved to Baltimore as president and GM in '58, building the team that won the 1966 world championship. In 1965, MacPhail became chief administrative assistant to Commissioner William Eckert. He was named *TSN*'s Executive of the Year in 1966. In October of that year, he returned to the Yankees as executive vice-president and GM, serving until 1973, when he was elected president of the AL. During his ten years in that post, he directed expansion to Toronto and Seattle, helped develop the designated hitter rule, and was known as a voice of reason and moderation. He was possibly the only AL president to have seen symphony orchestras perform in every league city. He resigned in 1983 to become president of the ML Player Relations Committee, representing the owners in negotiations with the players' association.

Lee's son, Andy, is the GM of the Minnesota Twins. /(NLM)

Mike Madden — 1957– . LHP 1983–86 **Astros** 194 ip, 12–10, 3.94

Madden was one of three players acquired by Houston from Milwaukee for Don Sutton in 1982. His career was marred by a series of hand and arm injuries, a serious one (elbow) coming after his first ML start -a 1–0 combined shutout of the Cubs (5/25/83). /(JCA)

Elliott Maddox — 1947– . OF-3B 1970–80 Tigers, Senators/Rangers, Yankees, Orioles, **Mets** 1029 g, .261, 18 hr, 234 rbi. *1 LCS, 3 g, .222, 1 rbi. 1 WS, 2 g, .200*

Maddox relocated frequently after reaching the ML as a pesky utility player for the Tigers in 1970, but started regularly only once in 11 ML seasons, hitting

.303 as the Yankees centerfielder in 1974. He was traded to the Senators with Denny McLain after the 1970 season, moved with the club to Texas in 1972, was sold to the Yankees before 1974, traded again to the Orioles after 1976, and finally signed as a free agent with the Mets before the 1978 season. /(SCL)

Garry Maddox — 1949- . OF 1972-86 Giants, **Phillies** 1749 g, .285, 117 hr, 754 rbi. *5 LCS, 19 g, .286, 9 rbi. 2 WS, 10 g, .235, 1 hr, 2 rbi*
☛ *Gold Glove—75-82.*

Dubbed "The Secretary of Defense," Maddox had such range in the outfield that Mets broadcaster Ralph Kiner commented, "Two-thirds of the earth is covered by water, the other one-third is covered by Garry Maddox." Maddox's speed and ability to go back on the ball enabled him to play shallow and catch many short flies that would otherwise have been hits. Using an unorthodox, spread-out batting stance, he established himself as a low-ball hitter who would seldom walk. When rookie Gary Matthews joined Maddox and Bobby Bonds in 1973, San Francisco had one of baseball's best outfields. Maddox batted .319 in 1973, reached double figures in doubles, triples, HR, and steals, and had a career-high 76 RBI.

In 1975 Maddox was dealt to the Phillies for Willie Montanez and won the first of eight straight Gold Gloves; only Roberto Clemente and Willie Mays won more in the OF. For the following decade, Maddox was the centerfielder for one of baseball's most dominant teams. Through 1980, he had to compensate for slow-footed left fielder Greg Luzinski. In 1976 he batted a career-high .330, and led the NL in outfield putouts (he led again in 1978). His 10th-inning, game-winning double in Game Five of the 1980 LCS put Philadelphia in the World Series for the first time since 1950. Injuries, particularly a bad back, curtailed his playing time beginning in 1982. He retired in May 1986. /(ME)

Nick Maddox — 1886-1954. RHP 1907-10 Pirates 605 ip, 43-20, 2.29. 20 wins: 08 *1 WS, 9 ip, 1-0, 1.00*

On September 20, 1907, the 20-year-old rookie hurled Pittsburgh's first no-hitter, beating Brooklyn 2-1. He was 23-8 in 1908 and won the third game of the 1909 World Series over Detroit, but was released after posting just two wins in 1910. /(ME)

Greg Maddux — 1966- . RHP 1986- Cubs 674 ip, 45-38, 3.77
☛ *All-Star—88.*

Maddux was the surprise of National League pitchers in 1988. Coming off a 6–14 rookie season, he was 15–3 by the '88 All-Star break, but the baby-faced 22-year-old tired in the second half and finished at 18–8. On September 9, 1986, Greg took on and defeated his older brother, Phillies pitcher Mike Maddux, to mark the first time rookie brothers ever pitched against each other. /(JCA)

Mike Maddux — 1961- . RHP 1986- **Phillies** 227 ip, 10–13, 4.51

The older brother of Cubs pitcher Greg Maddux, Mike went 3–7, 5.42 as a rookie in 1986 and spent most of 1987 at Maine (International League). He relieved more often than he started in 1988, compiling a respectable 3.76 ERA. When he pitched against Greg on September 29, 1986, it marked the first time in ML history that brothers had faced each other as rookies. /(SG)

Dave Madison — 1921-1985. RHP 1950, 52-53 Yankees, Browns, **Tigers** 158 ip, 8-7, 5.70

Madison was part of the eight-man trade that featured Vic Wertz for Ned Garver in August 1952. The 6'3" middle reliever went 3–4 (6.82) for the Tigers in 1953, his final year. /(MC)

Ed Madjeski — 1909- . C 1932-34, 37 A's, **White Sox**, Giants 166 g, .241, 5 hr, 56 rbi

Desperate for catching, the 1934 White Sox signed Madjeski, just released by the A's, after he convinced them his arm was sound. But catching his first series, Madjeski caused a Chicago loss with a bad throw and allowed Boston 11 stolen bases in three games. For the last-place 1934 White Sox, he was the best of five who shared catching duty. /(RL)

Bill Madlock (Mad Dog) — 1951- . 3B-2B-DH-1B 1973-87 Rangers, Cubs, Giants, **Pirates**, Dodgers, Tigers 1806 g, .305, 163 hr, 860 rbi. *3 LCS, 10 g, .268, 4 hr, 9 rbi. 1 WS, 7 g, .375, 3 rbi*
☛ *Led League—ba 75-76, 81, 83. All-Star—75, 81, 83.*

The first player in major league history to win a pair of batting crowns with two different teams, Bill Madlock's bat sparked three different teams to post-season play. After outstanding performances at Spokane (Triple-A) and Texas in 1973, Madlock was traded to the Cubs with Vic Harris for Ferguson Jenkins. Madlock replaced Ron Santo at third base and hit .313, the highest average for a Cubs third baseman since 1945. The 5'11" 190-lb Madlock had a compact swing, one of the prettiest in baseball, and scattered line drives throughout the National

Bill Madlock

League. He easily won the 1975 batting title and edged Ken Griffey in 1976. A sometimes moody player who earned a reputation early in his career for sitting down against tough pitchers, Madlock was dealt to San Francisco on February 11, 1977 with Rob Sperring for Bobby Murcer, Steve Ontiveros, and Andy Muhlstock. The Giants moved Madlock, at best an adequate fielder, from third base to second, and his batting tailed off.

The unhappy infielder was rescued by Pittsburgh on June 28, 1979. Madlock and Len Randle came to the Pirates for Ed Whitson, Al Holland, and Fred Breining and brought a pennant to Pittsburgh. Madlock returned to third base, batted .328 during the season, and hit .375 in the World Series. He solidified both the offensive and defensive lineups of the World Champions. After two more batting titles, his play mirrored the decline of the Pirates. Again a pennant contender, this time the Dodgers, was willing to trade young prospects for a proven bat.

Madlock went to Los Angeles on August 31, 1985 and batted .360 in a successful stretch run. He hit three HR in the Dodgers' LCS loss. In 1987 Madlock filled Detroit's void at third base and earned a third trip to postseason play. The 37-year old became a free agent following the 1987 season and played in Japan in 1988. From 1971 through 1989, Madlock was the only righthanded batter to lead the NL in batting average. /(ME)

Dave Magadan — 1962- . 1B-3B 1986- **Mets** 334 g, .293, 8 hr, 103 rbi. *1 LCS, 3 g, .000*

Magadan, a lefthanded line-drive hitter, has shown the same skills as cousin Lou Piniella. The Mets' second-round pick in the June 1983 draft, he was the offensive hero of the Mets' division-clinching game in 1986 during a late-season call-up. His playing time was restricted by the presence of Keith Hernandez and Howard Johnson, but he hit .300 while filling in for the injured Hernandez in 1989, and manager Davey Johnson often moved Howard Johnson to shortstop to get Magadan's bat into the lineup. /(JFC)

Bill Magee [born William Fitzgerald] — 1864–1922. RHP 1897–99, 1901–02 **Louisville (NL)**, Phillies, Washington (NL), Cardinals, Giants 743 ip, 29–51, 4.93

Magee posted a 16–15 record for the second-division 1898 Louisville Colonels (NL), then found little success in toiling for five NL teams in four more seasons. He walked more than twice as many as he struck out. /(DAS)

Lee Magee [born Leopold Christopher Hoernschemeyer] — 1889–1966. OF-2B-1B-3B 1911–19 **Cardinals**, Brooklyn (FL), Yankees, Reds, Dodgers, Cubs 1034 g, .275, 12 hr, 277 rbi.
Manager 1915 **Brooklyn (FL)** 53–64, .453

Magee batted a career-high .323 as player-manager for Brooklyn's 1915 Federal League entry. His career came to a turbulent end when a jury found him guilty of having bet against his own team, the Dodgers, in 1919. /(JK)

Sherry Magee [Sherwood Robert] — 1884–1929. OF-1B 1904–19 **Phillies**, Braves, Reds 2085 g, .291, 83 hr, 1182 rbi. *1 WS, 2 g, .500.*
Umpire NL 28
☛ *Led League—ba 10. Led League—rbi 07, 10, 14, 18.*

Magee was one of the great players of the dead-ball era, 1900–1919. He could hit, run, field, and throw with the best, and played intelligently and aggressively. He was critical of sloppy play and unimagina-

Lee Magee

85 RBI in 1907 were the league high. In 1910 he led the NL in batting (.331), slugging average (.507), runs scored (110), and RBI (123), and stole 49 bases. Over his career he had 441 stolen bases, including 23 steals of home. On July 12, 1906, he stole second, third, and home in the ninth inning against St. Louis. During a July 20, 1912 game with the Cubs, he stole home twice. In 1914 he led the NL in hits (171), doubles (39), RBI (103), and slugging average (.509).

When Magee was not named Philadelphia's player-manager for 1915, he asked to be traded. He was sold to the Braves, who finished second while the Phillies won their first pennant. He played center in Boston until he was waived to Cincinnati in August 1917. He led the NL in RBI a final time in the war-shortened 1918 season, and concluded his ML career by pinch hitting twice in the 1919 World Series.

Magee played in the minors from 1920 to 1926, then took up umpiring. In light of his misbehavior in 1911, he was watched closely while officiating in the NL in 1928, and he performed very well. But he contracted pneumonia and died the following March. /(LRD)

George Magerkurth — 1888–1966. *Umpire* NL 1929–47 *2 ASU 4 WS*

In Magerkurth's first game in the Polo Grounds in 1929, he ejected Giants' manager John McGraw. The warning flags were out for what was to come as the 6'3" 225-lb "Mage" circled NL parks with his short fuse. He would go into orbit when called his hated nickname "Meathead." His encounters with Leo Durocher and the Dodgers are legendary. Magerkurth was a hated man among Dodger fans during the 1940s. In a Dodger victory parade after they won the 1941 pennant, a coffin labled "Magerkurth" was carried down Fulton Street. A couple of years later, an irate Dodger fan leaped from the Ebbets Field stands, tackled Magerkurth at home plate, and began punching him on the ground.

On July 15, 1939, the Reds' Harry Craft homered into the upper deck in left field at the Polo Grounds. The Giants screamed that the ball was foul and an argument developed. Magerkurth was at first base and had nothing to do with the call, but somehow he and New York shortstop Billy Jurges ended up in a fistfight. NL President Ford Frick fined each $250 and suspended them for ten days. The fiasco led to the installation of nets running the length of both Polo Grounds foul poles to determine fair and foul balls; today all ball parks are so equipped. /(RTM)

tive management, and occasionally his temper got the best of him. On July 10, 1911 his one-punch knockout of umpire Bill Finneran, who had ejected Magee for arguing a called third strike, led to his suspension for the rest of the season; however, he was reinstated after five weeks.

Magee was Philadelphia's left fielder for a decade. In his second year, 1905, he played 155 games. His

Sal Maglie

Sal Maglie (The Barber) — 1917- . RHP 1945, 50-58 **Giants**, Indians, Dodgers, Yankees, Cardinals 1723 ip, 119-62, 3.15. 20 wins: 51 *3 WS, 29 ip, 1-2, 3.41*
☛ *Led League—w 51. All-Star—51-52.*

Maglie was one of the lesser-known players barred from organized baseball in 1946 by Commissioner Chandler for jumping to the Mexican League, but he became the most successful returnee when the suspension was lifted. In 1950, he went 18-4 for the Giants and led the NL in winning percentage. His 23-6 mark the next year helped New York to the pennant won in a playoff on Bobby Thomson's home run.

Although he had an ever-present "five o'clock shadow," Maglie was called "The Barber" for his practice of throwing close to (shaving) the batter's chin. "When I'm pitching," he explained, "I own the plate."

A back ailment reduced Maglie's effectiveness in 1955. He was waived to Cleveland and eventually the Dodgers picked him up for $1,000 in mid-1956. He pitched magnificently down the stretch to help the Dodgers to a pennant, going 13-5 and pitching a

no-hitter on September 25, in a key game against the Phillies. /(FS)

Jim Magnuson — 1946- . LHP 1970-71, 73, **White Sox**, Yankees 102 ip, 3-7, 4.57

During a 1966 NCAA tournament game Magnuson reputedly hit the longest home run in the history of the University of California, Berkeley's Clint Evans Field (built in 1913). A pitcher as a pro, he never spent a full season in the majors. /(MC)

George Magoon (Topsy Maggie) — 1875-1943. SS-2B 1898-99, 1901-03 Dodgers, Baltimore (NL), Cubs, **Reds**, White Sox 522 g, .239, 2 hr, 201 rbi

Magoon was a good-fielding, light-hitting shortstop and second baseman who played the major part of his career with Cincinnati. He had his best year in 1901, batting .252 with 53 RBI. /(DAS)

Joe Magrane — 1964- . LHP 1987- **Cardinals** 570 ip, 32-25, 2.89. *1 LCS, 4 ip, 0-0, 9.00. 1 WS, 7 ip, 0-1, 8.59*
☛ *Led League—era 88.*

A first-round draft pick in 1985, the fireballer overwhelmed opponents in two-plus minor league seasons with a 1.89 ERA. Despite time out for a sore elbow his rookie season, Magrane was 9–7 and finished third in NL Rookie of the Year balloting. The quotable media favorite employed excellent control, and a great curve and changeup in 1988 to win the ERA crown (2.18) but at 5–9 was the first ERA leader with a losing record. He again missed time that year on the DL, and he sat out his last start of the season to protect his ERA crown, which he won by four points. He was 18–9 with a 2.91 ERA in 1989. /(FO/SH)

Freddie Maguire — 1899–1961. 2B 1922–23, 28–31 Giants, Cubs, **Braves** 618 g, .257, 1 hr, 163 rbi. *1 WS, 2 g, --*

Maguire hit .279 as the Cubs' second baseman in 1928 and was one of five players sent with $200,000 to Boston for Rogers Hornsby that November. He lasted three more seasons with his hometown Braves as Hornsby's replacement at 2B. /(JK)

Art Mahaffey — 1938– . RHP 1960–66 **Phillies**, Cardinals 999 ip, 59–64, 4.17

Mahaffey had an unusually effective pickoff move. Called up to the Phillies in 1960, he vowed to pick off his first baserunner. He picked off his first three: the Cardinals' Curt Flood and Bill White during one relief appearance, and the Giants' Jim Marshall in the next. His move toward second was also deceptive, because no one would be covering the bag. He would whirl and fake a throw so convincingly that the runner would either freeze or set out for third. On April 23, 1961, Mahaffey fanned 17 Cubs (winning 6–0) to tie the since-broken NL record for strikeouts in a day game. He finished the year with a league-high 19 losses. He went 19–14 in 1962, but lost his fastball to an arm injury in 1963. /(NLM)

Roy Mahaffey (Popeye) — 1903–1969. RHP 1926–27, 30–36 Pirates, **A's**, Browns 1056 ip, 67–49, 5.01. *1 WS, 1 ip, 0–0, 9.00*

The quiet Mahaffey was at his best as the fourth starter for the 1931 AL champion Athletics, going 15–4 (4.21) and finishing third in the AL in winning percentage. His ERA seem high by modern standards, but in the explosive offensive times he pitched in, they were usually average or better.

In five years of regular appearances against the Yankees, he never gave up a home run to Babe Ruth. /(NLM)

Mickey Mahler — 1952– . LHP 1977–82, 85–86 **Braves**, Pirates, Angels, Expos, Tigers, Rangers, Blue Jays 406 ip, 14–32, 4.68

Like his brother Rick, Mickey first signed with Atlanta. He threw seven-inning no-hitters for Savannah (Southern League) in 1974 and for Richmond (International League) in 1977. He was a Braves starter in 1978–79 but was released in 1980. With the Expos on June 5, 1985 in his first ML start in six years, he one-hit the Giants; then he went 0–4. The winningest American pitcher in Dominican Winter League history, he compiled 41 victories through 1986. /(PB)

Rick Mahler — 1953– . RHP 1979– **Braves**, Reds 1751 ip, 87–101, 3.95. *1 LCS, 2 ip, 0–0, 0.00*

Rick Mahler was the workhorse of Atlanta's staff in the 1980s. He did not stick for good until a surprising 1984 season. He tied a modern NL record with three Opening Day shutouts (1982, '86, '87). The streaky hurler led the NL in starts in 1985 and 1986 but also in hits allowed and, in 1986, in losses (14–18). He was demoted to partial relief duty in 1987. Still, Mahler ranked among Atlanta's all-time leaders in wins, starts, innings, and strikeouts after he went to the Reds as a free agent following the 1988 season. In 1989 he was again demoted to relief. /(ME)

Neil Mahoney — Unk.–1973. *Scout.*

Mahoney, never a pro player, joined the Red Sox as a scout in 1939 and served as head scout from 1960 to 1973. His discoveries for the Red Sox included Jimmy Piersall, Walt Dropo, Wilbur Wood, and the club's eventual GM and CEO, Haywood Sullivan. /(FVP)

Duster Mails [John Walter] (The Great) — 1895–1974. LHP 1915–16, 20–22, 25–26 Dodgers, **Indians**, Cardinals 516 ip, 32–25, 4.10. *1 WS, 15 ip, 1–0, 0.00*

Self-proclaimed "The Great," Mails was, when not plagued by arm problems. Called up to the Indians in August of 1920, he won seven straight, including a pennant-clinching shutout over Chicago, then did not allow a run in his two World Series starts. /(JK)

Miles Main (Alex) — 1884–1965. RHP 1914–15, 18 Tigers, **Kansas City (FL)**, Phillies 403 ip, 21–22, 2.77

The 6'5" Main's career began and ended with WWI. He jumped to the Federal League from Detroit and won 13 but was not claimed when the league collapsed. He returned briefly to the Phillies, then dropped from sight. /(ADS)

Woody Main [Forrest Harry] — 1922– . RHP 1948, 50, 52–53 **Pirates** 205 ip, 4–13, 5.14

Groomed as a relief pitcher, Main had one full major league season and little success. In 1952 he led the 42–112, last-place Pirates with 48 appearances but he was 2–12, including an 0–7 mark in relief. /(ME)

Fritz Maisel [Frederick Charles] (Flash) — 1889–1967. 3B-2B-OF 1913-18 **Yankees**, Browns 591 g, .242, 6 hr, 148 rbi

Maisel held the Yankee team record with 74 steals in a season (1914) until Rickey Henderson stole 80 in 1985. He was the Yankees' everyday third baseman in 1914, led the AL in steals, and reached career highs in runs (78), RBI (47), walks (76), and doubles (23). He improved to .281 in 1915 and stole second, third, and home in one game on April 17. After suffering a broken collarbone in 1916, Maisel never again hit better than .232. He stole home 14 times in his career, which ties him for 16th all-time. His younger brother, George, spent four years in the majors. /(SFS)

George Maisel — 1892–1968. OF 1913, 16, 21–22 Browns, Tigers, **Cubs** 167 g, .282, 0 hr, 50 rbi

The kid brother of Yankee stolen base champ Fritz Maisel, George persevered in baseball long enough to win a regular spot with the 1921 Cubs. Though the speedy centerfielder hit .310, his total lack of power made him expendable. /(DB)

Hank Majeski [Heeney] — 1916– . 3B-2B 1939–41, 46–55 Braves, Yankees, **A's**, White Sox, Indians, Orioles 1069 g, .279, 57 hr, 501 rbi. *1 WS, 4 g, .167, 1 hr, 3 rbi*

From 1947 to 1951, Hank Majeski was a leading AL third baseman. His .988 fielding percentage for the 1947 A's set a ML record. A two-time minor league batting champ, he established a record by hitting six doubles in a doubleheader, August 27, 1948, during his peak season (.310, 12 HR, 120 RBI). Following an off-year in 1949, he was traded to the White Sox, but he was reacquired by Philadelphia in 1951. Concluding his career as a backup in Cleveland, he replaced Al Rosen at third base in Game Three of the 1954 World Series and delivered a pinch-hit home run in Game Four. /(ME)

Major League Players Association — 1953– .

The organization that came to prominence in the rapidly changing game in the 1970s appeared 20 years earlier out of the ashes of the short-lived American Baseball Guild, which had a similar structure. When the pension won by that group was threatened by the owners in 1953, the player repre-

sentatives of the 16 teams hired attorney J. Norman Lewis to fight the threat. That battle was won, but the new union was largely neglected until Marvin Miller revamped it starting in 1966.

Within two years the Association had signed the first Basic Agreement with the owners. Progress at first was cautious; for instance, the union advised Curt Flood against challenging baseball's reserve clause. But an unprecedented, albeit brief, strike at the beginning of the 1972 season gave notice that the players had a unity not seen since the 1890 Players' League revolt, and when the owners tried to fight back in 1981, a longer strike in mid-season forever changed the image of the game. The concessions made by the owners in the face of these two strikes revamped player-owner relations completely: arbitration, free agency, the right of veterans to veto trades, and vastly higher salaries. Miller trained his assistant and eventual successor, Donald Fehr, before retiring in 1984; Fehr chose as his assistant former player Mark Belanger. /(WOR)

Dave Malarcher [Gentleman Dave] — 1894–1982. 3B-OF-2B-MGR Negro Leagues 1916–34 Indianapolis ABC's, Detroit Stars, Chicago American Giants .267, 5 hr (inc.)

Malarcher was a speedy, switch-hitting Negro Leaguer, particularly effective in the clutch. A smart, disciplined, and well-conditioned athlete, he was called "Gentleman Dave" because of his gentle, cultured, soft-spoken nature. He never smoked or drank alcohol, never argued with umpires, and was never ejected from a game. His philosophy was, "Education should discipline the mind, and the mind should discipline the body."

Malarcher was born and raised in Louisiana, the youngest of ten children. His mother was a former slave who learned to read and write despite having no formal education, and emphasized the importance of education to her children. Malarcher graduated from the University of New Orleans (now Dillard), where he played third base and captained and managed the baseball team. He performed for the black semi-pro New Orleans Eagles before joining the Indianapolis ABC's in 1916.

In 1918 Malarcher served in France and then played in the American Expeditionary Force's league. Upon discharge he joined the Detroit Stars, and in 1920 he became a member of Rube Foster's Chicago American Giants in the newly formed Negro National League. He remained with the American Giants as a player and manager until his retirement. Generally regarded as the NNL's premier third baseman during his playing days, the 5'7" 145-lb Malarcher became its top manager after replacing Foster in 1926.

Statistics available show that Malarcher batted .250 in postseason championship play and scored 26 times on 31 hits. He scored 16 runs on 15 hits in Black World Series play. He was the leading run scorer for the 1926 and 1927 Black World Champion American Giants, and he topped the team in stolen bases four consecutive seasons (1923–26). He led his club with a .326 batting average in 1925. In six exhibition games played in 1917 and 1923, he hit white major league pitchers for a .368 average.

Malarcher was truly a clutch player. In what he described as his greatest thrill in baseball, before a crowd of 10,000 in Chicago on August 16, 1922, Malarcher singled home Christobel Torriente in the bottom of the 20th inning to give his club a 1–0 win over Atlantic City's Bacharach Giants. And in another clutch moment, in the seventh game of the 1926 Black World Series with the score tied in the bottom of the ninth, he beat out an infield hit, stole second, took third on a passed ball, and scored the game-winning run on John Hines's two-out single. In the ninth inning of the final game, he sacrificed Jelly Gardner into position to score the series-winning run on Sandy Thompson's single. He also scored game-winners in two 1927 BWS contests as Chicago took their second straight title.

In 1928, Malarcher managed his club to the 1928 NNL title series, where they lost to the St. Louis Stars, five games to four. He sat out for two years before returning to the American Giants in 1931, and led them to the 1932 Negro Southern League pennant.

In Malarcher's final two seasons, championship claims were marked by controversy. The 1933 NNL schedule was not completed. Chicago won the first half and defeated the NSL New Orleans Crescent Stars in a set of games billed as the Black World Series. However, NNL president Gus Greenlee later awarded the pennant to his own Pittsburgh Crawfords. In 1934, the Philadelphia Stars were awarded the NNL crown after beating Chicago, four games to three, in the championship series. The American Giants disputed this claim because of a protested loss upon which no action was ever taken.

Malarcher initiated the use of black umpires in NNL contests. A real estate broker, he was also a published poet who wrote about baseball, mankind, and history. After his wife's death in 1946, he wrote a tribute to their love, one of three book-length poems he penned. At the age of 52, he returned to school to learn more about real estate. He formed a scholarship fund for his parents' descendants, naming it after his mother. /(MFK)

John Malarkey — 1872–1949. RHP 1894–96, 99, 1902–03 Washington (NL), Cubs, **Braves** 566 ip, 21–38, 3.64

Malarkey posted an 0–8 record with the 43–85 Washington (NL) team of 1895, putting on an average of almost two runners an inning. He won a career-high 11 games, but lost 16 for Boston in 1903. /(DAS)

Candy Maldonado — 1960– . OF 1981– Dodgers, **Giants** 818 g, .251, 70 hr, 332 rbi. *4 LCS, 14 g, .161, 4 rbi. 1 WS, 4 g, .091*

Maldonado won the Giants' right-field job in 1986 with a .425 average as a pinch hitter, winning team MVP honors and hitting 18 HR despite not cracking the starting lineup until August. He followed with his best season in 1987, hitting .292 with 20 HR and 85 RBI for the NL West champs, but the free-swinging Puerto Rican native has struggled since. The error-prone outfielder rarely walks, and he slumped badly in 1989, finishing at .217 and losing his regular status. /(SCL)

Les Mallon — 1905– . 2B-3B 1931–32, 34–35 **Phillies**, Braves 383 g, .283, 8 hr, 119 rbi

Mallon's rookie 1931 season with Philadelphia was his best; he batted .309 in 122 games. But an injury suffered toward the end of that year kept him from greater success. /(NLM)

Pat Malone [Perce Leigh] — 1902–1943. RHP 1928–37 **Cubs**, Yankees 1915 ip, 134–92, 3.74. 20 wins: 29–30 *3 WS, 21 ip, 0–3, 3.05*
☛ *Led League—w 29–30. Led League—k 29.*

After losing his first seven decisions in his rookie year, Malone recovered to post an 18–13 record. He led the Cubs to the pennant in 1929, going 22–10 and leading the NL in wins, shutouts, and strikeouts. However, he lost two games in the World Series, getting knocked out in the fourth inning of Game Two and dropping Game Five 3–2, after taking a shutout into the ninth inning, as the Athletics clinched the Series.

Malone tied for the NL lead in wins in 1930 (20–9). He continued to be a solid pitcher, but his promising career never really developed, supposedly because of his love of the night life. After 1934 he was traded to the Cardinals for Ken O'Dea, and before the start of the 1935 season he was sold to the

Yankees for $15,000. Used moderately often in relief by the Cubs, Malone spent most of the rest of his career coming out of the Yankee bullpen, and went 12–4 in 1936, leading the AL in relief wins (8) and saves (9). He saved Game Three of that year's World Series, but lost Game Five in the tenth inning on a double and two sacrifices after three innings of scoreless relief.

A good-hitting pitcher in his prime, in 1930 he hit four HR while batting .248. /(DAS)

Billy Maloney — 1878–1960. OF-C 1901–02, 05–08 Milwaukee (AL), Browns, Reds, Cubs, **Dodgers** 696 g, .236, 6 hr, 177 rbi

Maloney went straight from the campus of Georgetown University to catching for Milwaukee of the AL in the league's first year. He hit .293 but his work behind the plate was unsatisfactory. In 1904 he led the NL in stolen bases (59) while an outfielder with the Cubs. Traded with three others to the Dodgers for Jimmy Sheckard the next season, he failed to hit above .229 in three years as a regular. /(BC)

George Maloney — 1928– . Umpire AL 1969–84

While working in the Class D Florida State League, Maloney and his fellow umpire once ejected so many players the game ended in a forfeit. His most controversial ML call came in 1975 when two Yankees, Graig Nettles and Sandy Alomar, ended on third base at the same time. The Cleveland catcher tagged Alomar and Maloney called him out. Then Nettles was tagged as he stepped off the base, but Maloney said he had called time. The argument erupted over whether the ball was still in play or not so that Nettles could ask for time out. /(RTM)

Jim Maloney — 1940– . RHP 1960–71 **Reds**, Angels 1849 ip, 134–84, 3.19. 20 wins: 63, 65 *1 WS, 1 ip, 0–0, 27.00*

With a fastball timed at 99.5 mph in 1965, Maloney won in double figures for the Reds each year from 1963 to 1969. He went 23–7 in 1963, and was 20–9 in 1965 while pitching two of his three no-hitters. His first, on June 14 against the Mets, lasted ten innings; he struck out 18, but Johnny Lewis hit a leadoff homer in the 11th (and Roy McMillan singled later in the inning), and Maloney lost 1–0. On August 19, he again pitched ten no-hit innings, this time completing a hitless, 1–0 victory over the Cubs. His third no-hitter was an easy 10–0 victory against the Astros on April 30, 1969. Maloney also threw five one-hitters. The strikeout pitcher fanned

eight Braves in a row on May 21, 1963, tying what was then a modern NL record. That year, he struck out a career-high 265 in 250 innings. A damaged Achilles tendon and a shoulder injury shortened his career. /(JK)

Gordon Malzberger (Maltzy) — 1912–1974. RHP 1943–44, 46–47 White Sox 293 ip, 20–13, 2.70

One of fourteen children, Malzberger was a control pitcher, a Texas League standout who got his chance with the wartime White Sox. His ability to pitch frequently led manager Jimmy Dykes to put him in the bullpen. His 14 saves in 1943 and 10 relief wins and 12 saves in 1944 were league highs; in '44, he racked up a 10–2 record including seven relief wins in a row by July 15, but finished 10–5. He spent 1945 in the military, and was off the roster by 1948. /(RL)

Frank Malzone — 1930– . 3B 1955–66 **Red Sox**, Angels 1441 g, .274, 133 hr, 728 rbi
☛ *All-Star—57–60, 63. Gold Glove—57–59.*

Dependable third baseman Frank Malzone averaged over 152 games and 83 RBI a year for the Red Sox, 1957–64. His best season came as a rookie in 1957 when he drove in a career-high 103 runs. That year he became the first player in modern baseball history to lead his position in games played, putouts, assists, errors, double plays, and fielding percentage and earned the first of three consecutive Gold Gloves. He tied an American League record with 10 assists on September 24.

In 1958, he led the AL with 627 at-bats and hit a career-high .295. Through 1961, he tied a record by leading AL third basemen in double plays five straight seasons. Malzone had made his Boston debut in 1955, going 6-for-10 in a doubleheader against Baltimore. After 11 seasons with the Red Sox, he finished up with the Angels in 1966. /(ME)

Al Mamaux — 1894–1963. RHP 1913–24 Pirates, **Dodgers**, Yankees 1293 ip, 76–67, 2.90. 20 wins: 15–16 *1 WS, 4 ip, 0–0, 4.50*

Pittsburgh native Al Mamaux was the Pirates' ace in 1914 and 1915, winning 21 games each season. He was called "the new Christy Mathewson" in 1915, but dropped to 2–11 in 1916 and was traded to Brooklyn in 1918. He managed Newark to International League pennants in 1930 and 1931. A vaudeville singer during and after his playing days, he was dubbed "The Golden-Voiced Tenor." /(ME)

Frank Mancuso — 1918- . C 1944-47 **Browns,** Senators 337 g, .241, 5 hr, 98 rbi. *1 WS, 2 g, .667, 1 rbi*

The younger brother of NL catcher Gus Mancuso, Frank suffered a leg injury during WWII paratrooper training that knocked him out of the service and hampered his career. He caught for the Browns' only pennant-winner, in 1944./(NLM)

Gus Mancuso (Blackie) — 1905-1984. C 1928, 30-45 Cards, **Giants,** Cubs, Dodgers, Phillies 1460 g, .265, 53 hr, 543 rbi. *5 WS, 18 g, .173, 0 hr, 4 rbi*
☛ *All-Star—35, 37..*

Buried in the Cardinal farm system for five years, Mancuso was rescued in 1930 by Judge Landis, who told St. Louis to keep him on the ML club or lose him. The stocky catcher went on to become one of the top NL catchers of the 1930s. After working as a backup for two Cardinal pennant winners (1930-31), Mancuso was traded to the Giants in 1933. Manager Bill Terry credited his acquisition as the major factor in moving New York from sixth in 1932 to the '33 pennant. A fine defensive receiver,

Gus Mancuso

the swarthy Mancuso handled a pitching staff that included Carl Hubbell, Fred Fitzsimmons, and Hal Shumacher. He continued as the Giants' regular through the pennant seasons of 1936-37 and later shared catching duties on other NL clubs until the end of WWII. Although he admitted, "I was so slow-footed I could be a real rally-stopper on the bases," Mancuso hit a respectable .265 for his career. In 1936, his best all-around season, he batted .301 and drove in 63 runs.

His younger brother, Frank, caught four years in the AL during the mid-1940s./(FS)

Angel Mangual — 1947- . OF-DH 1969, 71-76 Pirates, **A's** 450 g, .245, 22 hr, 125 rbi. *4 LCS, 10 g, .143, 2 rbi 3 WS, 10 g, .176, 1 rbi*

One of several Puerto Rican spray hitters developed by the Pirates in the 1960s, Mangual was a fourth outfielder and pinch hitter for Oakland's championship clubs of 1971-75. Angel's brother Pepe was a NL outfielder./(ME)

Pepe Mangual [Jose Manuel Guilbe] — 1952- . OF 1972-77 **Expos,** Mets 319 g, .242, 16 hr, 83 rbi

The speedy Puerto Rican was the Expos' everyday centerfielder in 1975 and hit only .245, but he walked 74 times, scored 84 runs, and stole 33 bases. He tied a ML record on August 11 when he struck out five times in a nine-inning game. Mangual was hitting better in 1976 (.260) when he was traded to the Mets, but he lost his stroke in New York (.186 the rest of the way) and was out of the majors after one more year. It was while Mangual was with New York that Mets-beat writer Jack Lang said of him, "Pepe Mangual can drop anything he gets his hands on." His older brother was Angel Mangual of the A's./(SFS)

Leo Mangum (Blackie) — 1896-1974. RHP 1924-25, 28, 32-35 White Sox, Giants, **Braves** 258 g, 11-10, 5.37

Swarthy Blackie Mangum won impressively in Triple-A but did little with his seven major league opportunities. Primarily a reliever, he won a career-high five games for the 1934 Braves./(JK)

Clyde Manion (Pete) — 1896-1967. C 1920-24, 26-30, 32-34 **Tigers,** Browns, Reds 477 g, .217, 3 hr, 112 rbi

A light-hitting catcher, Manion's defensive skills and ability to handle pitchers kept him in the majors as a backup. In parts of six seasons with the Tigers, he never hit a ball out of the park—not even in practice. With the Browns in 1928, in his first at-bat against his former team, he homered. /(JK)

Phil Mankowski — 1953- . 3B 1976-80, 82 **Tigers**, Mets 269 g, .264, 8 hr, 64 rbi

Mankowski was never a regular, but he platooned with Aurelio Rodriguez at third base for the Tigers in 1977-78, hitting .276 and .275. /(FK)

Effa Manley (The First Lady of Black Baseball) — 1897 or 1902-1981. Owner Negro Leagues 1935-48 Brooklyn Eagles, Newark Eagles

Effa Manley was the brains of the Negro League's Newark Eagles. Effa and her husband Abe organized the Brooklyn Eagles in 1935, but bought the Newark Dodgers the following year and renamed them the Eagles. Under her watchful eyes, the well-paid Eagles became one of the best-known Negro League teams as they traveled proudly in their $15,000 Flexible Clipper bus. The Eagles won the league championship and Black World Series in 1946 under the guidance of player-manager Biz Mackey. Soon after Jackie Robinson broke the color line in 1947, Manley lost the services of Larry Doby, Monte Irvin, and Don Newcombe. She spoke out against the raiding of Negro League teams by major league clubs without compensation, but despite her efforts, the Eagles had to disband in 1948. /(LL)

Les Mann — 1893-1962. OF 1913-28 **Braves**, Chicago (FL), Cubs, Cardinals, Reds, Giants 1493 g, .282, 44 hr, 503 rbi. *2 WS, 9 g, .241, 3 rbi*

Mann was platooned in the outfield of the 1914 World Champion Braves; the next year he jumped to the Federal League and led that circuit with 19 triples. He headed a player revolt for better shares in the 1918 WS as a member of the pennant-winning Cubs. He batted over .300 six times, mostly as a reserve; in his three seasons with the Cardinals (1921-23), he hit .328, .347, and .371. He turned in Giant pitcher Phil Douglas for writing him a letter inviting a bribe in 1922. After his playing days, Mann formed the National Amateur Baseball Association. In 1936, he persuaded the World Olympic Committee to add baseball as an exhibition event; two American teams puzzled a throng of Germans, who formed a larger crowd than had ever attended a World Series game. /(JK)

Rick Manning — 1954- . OF 1975-87 **Indians**, Brewers 1555 g, .257, 56 hr, 458 rbi
☛ *Gold Glove—76.*

Defensive prowess ultimately prolonged a career that seemed headed for better things when Manning broke in with Cleveland at age 20. The fast, left-handed-hitting centerfielder hit .285 as a rookie in 1975 and .292 in 1976, when he won a Gold Glove. He was among the very best defensive outfielders, but he never hit for power, and his average dropped. Increasingly frustrated playing for the non-contending Indians, Manning campaigned for a trade. On June 6, 1983, he and Rick Waits went to the Brewers for Gorman Thomas, Jamie Easterly, and Ernie Camacho. He led ML outfielders with 478 chances in 1983 and tied a record for centerfielders by accepting 12 chances in a 15-inning game, but the Brewers were eventually unable to carry Manning's weak bat. /(ME)

Rube Manning [Walter S.] — 1883-1930. RHP 1907-10 **Yankees** 502 ip, 22-32, 3.14

Manning saw the most action in 1908, when he was 13-16 with a 2.94 ERA (55 points above the league average) with the last-place Highlanders (later the Yankees). /(SFS)

Fred Manrique — 1961- . 2B-SS 1981, 84- Blue Jays, Expos, Cardinals, **White Sox**, Rangers 420 g, .260, 15 hr, 122 rbi

Manrique joined shortstop Ozzie Guillen in 1987 to continue a White Sox tradition of slick, Venezuelan double-play combos begun by Luis Aparicio and Chico Carrasquel. Manrique had had trials with three other ML teams, and had played for Jim Fregosi in Louisville (American Association) in 1986. Fregosi was named White Sox manager that June, and had Chicago acquire Manrique from St. Louis in December. /(RL)

Felix Mantilla (The Cat) — 1934- . 2B-SS-OF-3B 1956-66 **Braves**, Mets, Red Sox, Astros 969 g, .261, 89 hr, 330 rbi. *2 WS, 8 g, .000*
☛ *All-Star—65.*

On May 26, 1959, Mantilla led off the 13th inning by reaching first on Don Hoak's throwing error, ruining Harvey Haddix's perfect game, and eventually scoring the game's only run. A utility man for six seasons with the Braves, he was selected by the Mets in the expansion draft and became their most regular third baseman in 1962, hitting .275 with 11 home runs. The Red Sox traded three players to acquire him the following winter, and in Fenway Park his offensive production jumped considerably. He hit a career-high .315 in 1963 and belted 30 homers in 1964, 19 more than his previous best.

Playing second base in 1965 he drove in 92 runs, but his average plummeted to .219 in 1966 after he was traded to Houston. /(FK)

Mickey Mantle (The Commerce Comet) — 1931– . OF-1B 1951–68 **Yankees** 2401 g, .298, 536 hr, 1509 rbi. *12 WS, 65 g, .257, 18 hr, 40 rbi*
☛ *Most Valuable Player—56–57, 62. Led League—ba 56. Led League—hr 55–56, 58, 60. Led League—rbi 56. All-Star—52–65, 67–68. Gold Glove—62. Hall of Fame—1974.*

Mickey Mantle was a baseball star of the highest magnitude. When Detroit great Al Kaline was taunted by a youngster who said, "You're not half as good as Mickey Mantle," he replied, "Son, nobody is half as good as Mickey Mantle."

Mantle was a multi-talented offensive threat. He drove in runs with enormous power from either side of the plate. He got on base by hitting well for average and drawing more than 100 walks in each of 10 seasons. And he scored runs with his excellent speed, stealing as many as 21 bases in a season (1959). Overall, he scored more runs than he drove in (1,677 to 1,509), a rarity among power hitters.

Mantle, out of Commerce, Oklahoma, arrived in New York in a whirl of unbridled expectations. He made headlines with great play at an "instructional school" the Yankees conducted in 1951 and then in spring training, which included a highly publicized barnstorming tour of the West Coast. Only 19, Mantle was hot, but he fizzled in New York. The Yankees sent him to their top farm club at Kansas City, but he continued to struggle until his father, Mutt Mantle, came for a visit. After the brief family reunion, Mantle lifted his average to .361 and, in only 166 at-bats, hit 11 homers with 50 RBI. He returned to New York and played alongside the soon-to-retire Joe DiMaggio, and ended up with a respectable (.267,13 HR, 65 RBI) rookie season.

When DiMaggio retired Mantle took over in centerfield, and he played the position from 1952 to 1966. To reduce his outfield running when his injuries—which were many—were severe, he would occasionally play in left or right field. In 1967–68, his final seasons, he played first base to ease the burden on his aching legs.

Mantle and Yogi Berra were the Yankees' twin engines in Mantle's early years (1951–55). The centerfielder and catcher each hit 25 homers per season and together produced from 150 to 225 RBI. Then, in 1956, Mantle emerged as a superstar, the greatest switch-hitter in the history of baseball and one of its biggest drawing cards. He hit .353 that year with 52 home runs and 130 RBI to win the

Mickey Mantle

Triple Crown. It was the first of three straight years that he led the league in runs scored (132). He received numerous awards for his accomplishments, including the Hickock Belt as the top professional athlete of the year. Mantle capped the year with three homers in the World Series, one in Don Larsen's perfect game, in which he also made a saving defensive play.

Even though he was not quite 5'11", Mantle hit some tremendous home runs. He reached the gothic wrought-iron facade that hung from the old stadium's roof five times. In addition to his widely remembered shots of May 30, 1956, when only the top 18 inches of the right-field facade kept the ball in the park, and May 22, 1963, when the ball was still rising when it hit the facade a few feet from the top, Mantle struck the same right-field facade on August 7, 1955, against Detroit; on May 5, 1956, against Kansas City; and on June 23, 1957, against the White Sox.

Born to be a ballplayer (he was named after the great catcher Mickey Cochrane), Mantle was the first power-hitting switch-hitter. He also hit for average, peaking at .365 in 1957. He was always a better hitter from the right side, but was capable enough from the left to hit 373 of his 536 career homers. He also used a drag bunt from the left side that made it nearly impossible to throw him out, and he was once clocked at 3.1 seconds from home to first base.

When slugging outfielder Roger Maris joined the Yankees, he and Mickey became known as the "M & M Boys." The two got into a friendly home run duel in 1961, which culminated in Maris breaking Babe Ruth's 60-homer record by one. Mantle had 54, but again, as happened frequently in his career, physical problems hampered him. In the final month of the 1961 campaign he pulled an arm muscle, contracted a virus infection and developed an abscess inside his hip.

During the first years of his career, Mantle was treated harshly by the fans and press in New York, but in 1960, thanks in part to the press, a different perception of him emerged. He was suddenly seen as someone who played through pain and played to win. Already popular with his teammates, he became enormously popular with the fans.

Mantle's drawing power was due to his hitting, but when he was healthy he was also an excellent defensive outfielder. He was lightning-fast, with a strong and accurate arm.

Mantle played on 12 pennant winners and seven World Championship clubs. He holds World Series records for home runs (18), RBI (40), runs (42),

walks (43), extra-base hits (26), and total bases (123). In his final World Series in 1964 he had three homers and eight RBI and batted .333.

He was inducted into the Hall of Fame in 1974 in his first year of eligibility. /(MG)

Heinie Manush [Henry Emmett] — 1901–1971. OF 1923–39 Tigers, Browns, **Senators**, Red Sox, Dodgers, Pirates 2009 g, .330, 110 hr, 1173 rbi. *1 WS, 5 g, .111* ☛ *Led League—ba 26. All-Star—34. Hall of Fame—1964.*

Overshadowed by Hall of Famers Ty Cobb and Harry Heilmann in Detroit, feisty Heinie Manush found the limelight in St. Louis and Washington. A lefthanded, line-drive-hitting outfielder, he broke in with player-manager Cobb's 1923 Tigers and batted .334. He lost his job to Al Wingo in 1925, but came back strong in 1926. Replacing the 39-year-old Cobb in centerfield, Manush battled Babe Ruth and teammates Heilmann and Bob Fothergill down to the wire for the batting title. On the final day of the season, Manush went 6-for-9 in a doubleheader to overtake Ruth and win the crown at .378.

Manush slumped to .298 under new Tiger manager George Moriarty in 1927 and was traded to the Browns. The move agreed with him. Playing left field in 1928, he again batted .378, but finished one point behind Washington's Goose Goslin. He led the AL with 241 hits, and tied for the lead in doubles that year and the next. In 1929, his .355 was good for third in the AL batting race.

In a blockbuster trade made on June 13, 1930, Goslin and Manush exchanged uniforms, with pitcher Alvin Crowder also going to the Senators. Manush batted .342 in 1932. In 1933 he hit .336 to finish second behind Jimmie Foxx, batting safely in 33 consecutive games from July 22 to August 25. He also led the circuit in hits and triples in pacing Washington to its last World Series appearance. When President Roosevelt threw out the first pitch before Game Three, Manush captured the ball in the ensuing scramble for it among the players. After the game, he presented it to winning pitcher Earl Whitehill. In Game Four, Manush made history as the first player ever ejected from a Series game. Protesting when umpire Charley Moran called him out, Manush pulled on the ump's bow tie, held in place with an elastic band, and then let the tie snap back.

A third-place finish in the 1934 AL batting race marked Manush's last outstanding year in Washington. In 1937, his first NL season, he batted .333 for Brooklyn. He finished with Pittsburgh in 1939, and played and managed in the minors until 1945. He

Heinie Manush

scouted for the Braves and Pirates, was a Senators coach in 1953–54, and served Washington as a scout through 1962. His brother Frank played third base for the Philadelphia Athletics in 1908. Manush was elected to the Hall of Fame by the Committee on Baseball Veterans in 1964. /(ME)

Kirt Manwaring — 1965– . C 1987- **Giants** 131 g, .223, 1 hr, 33 rbi. *1 LCS, 3 g, .000. 1 WS, 1 g, 1.000*

The Giants' second-round pick in the June 1986 draft, Manwaring was projected to be their regular catcher in 1988 and 1989, but didn't hit well enough to keep the job. /(WOR)

Cliff Mapes (Tiger) — 1922– . OF 1948–52 **Yankees**, Browns, Tigers 459 g, .242, 38 hr, 172 rbi. *2 WS, 5 g, .071, 2 rbi*

In the minors, Mapes pitched, caught, and played first base and the outfield. A part-time player with decent power for the Yankees, in 1948 he had to give up his uniform number 3 when it was retired to honor Babe Ruth, then became the first Yankee to wear number 13. Later he wore number 7, now retired in honor of Mickey Mantle. /(GDW)

Georges Maranda — 1932– . RHP 1960, 62 Giants, **Twins** 123 ip, 2–7, 4.52

Maranda went 18–6 as one of a trio of Quebecois pitchers at Louisville (American Association) in 1959, with Ron Piche and Claude Raymond. The Giants then drafted him from the Braves, but sent him down to make room for rookie Juan Marichal. Maranda appeared in 32 games for the Twins in 1962. /(MC)

Rabbit Maranville [Walter James Vincent] — 1891–1954. SS-2B 1912–33, 35 **Braves**, Pirates, Cubs, Dodgers, Cardinals, Braves 2670 g, .258, 28 hr, 884 rbi. *2 WS, 8 g, .308, 3 rbi.*
  Manager 1925 **Cubs**, 23–30, .434
☛ *Hall of Fame—1954.*

Rabbit Maranville was a 5′5″ baseball clown with a goblin face full of laugh lines. His humor was antic and visible to the fans: handing an umpire a pair of glasses or mocking slow pitchers and ponderous batters in pantomime. Photographers loved him. He would pull the bill of his cap over one ear—baseball's oldest comic gesture—and jump into the arms of his biggest teammate. He was an after-hours roisterer, too. After a few drinks with kindred souls like banjo-playing Jolly Cholly Grimm, he became the hotel ledge walker, the goldfish swallower, the practical joker.

Nicknamed for his speed and rabbit-like leaps, he was always a superior fielder, famous for his unique basket catch of high infield flies. Consistency was his hallmark and greatest virtue. During his first tour with Boston, he led NL shortstops in putouts each year from 1914 to 1919 (except for 1918, which he spent in the Navy), assists twice, double plays three times, and fielding average once.

Although a well-established Boston favorite, he was traded to Pittsburgh in 1921 for outfielders Billy Southworth and Fred Nicholson, shortstop Walter Barbare, and $15,000. With the Pirates, he led shortstops in fielding average in 1923. When young Glenn Wright took over at short in 1924, Maranville shifted to second and again had the league's best fielding average. He was dealt to the Cubs after the 1924 season, but alcohol nearly did him in. He failed in a managerial opportunity with Chicago and was relieved of duties with his club in eighth place after 53 games.

Due to his instability, he moved around the

Rabbit Maranville

consistent. From 1929 to 1933, despite aging, he never played fewer than 142 games a season. He was the league's top fielding shortstop in 1930, and second baseman in 1932.

During a spring training game against the Yankees in 1934, Maranville, a spry 42, was on the front end of a double steal. The throw went to second, and Maranville, trying to score from third, had Frank Crosetti's return throw beaten, but he slid into the rookie catcher blocking the plate and snapped the tibia and fibula in his left leg. The breaks took most of the season to mend, and when he tried to play in 1935, he was clearly not his old self. But he batted .323 in 123 games for Elmira (New York-Penn League) while managing in 1936, and played six games while skippering Albany (Eastern League) three years later, at 47.

Maranville stands first among all shortstops in putouts (5,139), third in assists (7,534), and second in total chances (13,124). He hit a creditable .251 in the dead-ball years from 1914–20 and improved to .265 in the lively-ball era thereafter. In two World Series (1914 and 1928), he had identical .308 averages. He was the cleanup hitter for the 1914 Braves. He hit 177 triples lifetime, which ties him with Stan Musial at 20th on the all-time list. Of his 28 home runs, 22 were inside the park, and in 1922, he set a still-standing ML record by going to the plate 672 times (the league high) without homering. Maranville was elected to the Hall of Fame in 1954, the year of his death. /(ADS)

Firpo Marberry [Frederick] — 1898–1976. RHP 1923–36 **Senators**, Tigers, Giants 2067 ip, 147–89, 3.63. *3 WS, 12 ip, 0–1, 3.75*

Marberry's physique and dark, scowling look suggested boxer Luis Firpo, "The Wild Bull of the Pampas," who had once knocked Jack Dempsey out of the ring. The nickname suited the pitcher. He was one of the first pitchers to be used almost exclusively in relief, leading the American League five times in saves. He was even more successful when he started, winning 94 games in that role for a .644 percentage. His 53 relief wins yielded a .589 percentage.

In the final stages of his career he was offered an umpiring job by the American League and retired from the pennant-bound Detroit Tigers to call balls and strikes the rest of the year. He was never assigned to games involving his former teammates. /(JK)

league despite his star status. The Cubs waived him to Brooklyn. The Dodgers, who suffered many eccentrics gladly in their time, released him unconditionally halfway through 1926. The Cardinals, always bargain hunters, picked him up and optioned him to Rochester (International League), where he got his drinking under control. In 1928, with the Cardinals in trouble at shortstop, Branch Rickey brought Maranville back to bolster the infield in a pennant-winning season. Charley Gelbert arrived in 1929, and Maranville was sold back to the Braves. As always, his play in the field was remarkably

Firpo Marberry

Ghost Marcelle [Oliver] — 1897–1949. 3B-SS Negro Leagues 1918–30 Brooklyn Royal Giants, **Bacharach Giants**, New York Lincoln Giants, Detroit Stars, Baltimore Black Sox 413 g, .315, 11 hr (inc.)

Marcelle was the finest-fielding third baseman in Negro League baseball during the 1920s. A Creole from New Orleans, he was a righthanded slash hitter who was most dangerous in the clutch. Hall of Fame Negro League third baseman Judy Johnson admitted that Marcelle was better than he was defensively, although not offensively.

Nearly complete statistics indicate that Marcelle batted .315 from 1919 to 1930. He hit a career-high .379 for the 1922 Bacharach Giants, .352 in 1924 with the Bacharach and New York Lincoln Giants, and .324 for Bacharach in 1927. He also hit well in the Cuban Winter League, compiling a lifetime average of .305 from 1923 through 1930. In the 1923–24 season he batted .393 to lead the league.

In 17 exhibition games against major league competition, Marcelle hit .365 (23-for-63). He played in two Black World Series for the Bacharach Giants, hitting .293 with six RBI in 11 games in 1926 and .235 with two RBI in nine games in 1927.

Marcelle was known for his uncontrollable temper. He would fight with umpires, opponents, and his own teammates. Marcelle reputedly once became so enraged that he struck Hall of Famer Oscar Charleston in the head with a bat. His temper may have led to his premature retirement. Bill Yancey, a teammate of Marcelle's, said, "What got [Marcelle] out of baseball, he and [teammate] Frank Warfield had a fight in Cuba [probably in the winter of 1927–28, over a dice game]and Warfield bit his nose off. He was a proud, handsome guy, you know, and then he used to wear a black patch across his nose and he got so he couldn't play baseball anymore."/(JM)

Phil Marchildon — 1913– . RHP 1940–42, 45–50 **A's**, Red Sox 1214 ip, 68–75, 3.93

A fiery and outspoken Ontario native, Marchildon went 17–14 for the 1942 Athletics. He became a gunner in the WWII Royal Canadian Air Force, was shot down on his 26th mission in 1944, and lost forty pounds during a nine-month ordeal as a POW in Germany. He returned to baseball in 1945 after recuperating at home. Teammate George Kell said later that "[W]hen he came back he was very quiet and very serious about everything he did. Mr. Mack said he'd really changed. He'd been through a lot. But he said very little about it."

Marchildon led the last-place 1946 A's with 13 wins, but tied two teammates with an AL-high 16 losses. In 1947 he helped pull his club out of the cellar with a 19–9 record. He had a perfect game with two outs in the eighth inning in a game against Cleveland when he walked Ken Keltner. Marchildon gave up two singles that tied the score in the ninth, but won his own game with a double in the 12th. /(NLM)

Johnny Marcum (Footsie) — 1909–1984. RHP 1933–39 A's, **Red Sox**, Browns, White Sox 1099 ip, 65–63, 4.66

Marcum was the A's ace during his two full years with them, and won 17 for their last-place 1935 club. He then went the way of most of Connie Mack's best—sold to the Red Sox, with Jimmie Foxx. Called "Footsie" for his big feet, Marcum was a lifetime .265 batter, used 99 times as a lefthanded pinch hitter. /(JK)

Joe Margoneri — 1930– . LHP 1956–57 **Giants** 126 ip, 7–7, 4.29

Margoneri was working in the Pennsylvania coal mines and playing semi-pro ball when signed by the

Giants. He both started and relieved in his 36-game ML stint. /(NLM)

Juan Marichal (Manito, The Dominican Dandy) — 1937- . RHP 1960-75 **Giants**, Red Sox, Dodgers 3509 ip, 243-142, 2.89. 20 wins: 63-66, 68-69 *1 LCS, 8 ip, 0-1, 2.25 1 WS, 4 ip, 0-0, 0.00*
☛ *Led League—w 63, 68. Led League—era 69. All-Star—62-69, 71. Hall of Fame—1983.*

When he was signed out of the Dominican Air Force at age 19, high-kicking Juan Marichal already had pinpoint control of his curve, slider, screwball, and blinding fastball, all thrown with a variety of motions. He led the 1958 Midwest League and the 1959 Eastern League in wins and ERA. When he debuted with the Giants on July 19, 1960, he shut out the Phillies on one hit—Clay Dalrymple's eighth-inning pinch single. Four days later, he four-hit the World Championship-bound Pirates.

Marichal started the Giants toward their 1962 pennant by shutting out the Cardinals on Opening Day (Marichal eventually recorded six Opening Day victories, setting an NL mark). He was 18-8 in early September when he injured his foot; he missed several starts and lost his last three decisions. The Giants and Dodgers finished in a tie, forcing a playoff. Marichal started the deciding third game, but was behind when he reinjured the foot and had to be relieved in the eighth by eventual winner Don Larsen. He managed one start in the World Series, coming out after four shutout innings when he smashed his finger trying to bunt.

From 1962 through 1971, San Francisco averaged 90 wins per year, with Marichal averaging 20. He led the NL in wins in 1963 (25-8) and 1968 (26-9); in shutouts in 1965 (10) and 1969 (8); and in ERA in 1969 (2.10). A workhorse, he topped the league in innings pitched in 1963 and '68 and in complete games in '64 and '68. Pitching in eight All-Star Games, he compiled a 2-0 record and a 0.50 ERA in 18 innings. On June 15, 1963, he no-hit Houston 1-0. That July 2, he beat Warren Spahn and the Braves 1-0 in 16 innings. Even without his best stuff, Marichal could pull out a victory, once blanking the Dodgers on 12 hits.

On August 22, 1965, Marichal faced Sandy Koufax at Candlestick Park in the heat of a tight pennant race. The Giants and Dodgers had come close to a brawl two days earlier over catcher's interference calls. Los Angeles's Maury Wills had allegedly tipped Tom Haller's mitt with his bat on purpose, and Marichal's best friend, Matty Alou, retaliated by tipping John Roseboro's face mask.

Juan Marichal

Roseboro nearly beaned Alou with his return throw to the mound. In the August 22 game, Marichal had flattened Wills and Ron Fairly with pitches when Roseboro purportedly asked Koufax to hit Marichal. When Koufax refused, Roseboro's return throw came close to Marichal's head. Name-calling ensued, until Roseboro suddenly ripped off his mask and stood up. Marichal rapped the catcher on the head with his bat. What followed was one of the most violent brawls in major league history. Willie Mays led away Roseboro, who had suffered a concussion, while Dodger Bob Miller tackled Marichal, Alou slugged Miller, and Tito Fuentes menaced the Dodgers with his bat. Roseboro sued Marichal, but eventually dropped the suit. Marichal was fined $1750, was suspended for a week, and missed two starts as the Giants finished two games behind the Dodgers. Years later, Marichal said, "I feel sorry that I used the bat."

In the spring of 1970, Marichal suffered a severe reaction to penicillin that led to chronic arthritis and a back injury when he tried to return too soon. Having lost much of his former stuff, he pitched with guile. He won 18 for the Giants in 1971, including the division clincher on the last night of the season. After going 6-16 in 1972 and 11-15 in

1973, he was sold to the Red Sox, and managed a 5–1 record in spot starts. After he was released, he tried to catch on with the Dodgers, of all teams, in 1975. Roseboro asked Los Angeles fans to support Marichal; they did, but Marichal, ineffective in two starts, retired. Also retired, by the Giants, was Marichal's number 27. When the Dominican was not named to the Hall of Fame in his first two years of eligibility, Roseboro campaigned for his election, and received a special thanks at Marichal's induction ceremony in 1983. /(MC)

Marty Marion (Slats, The Octopus) — 1917– . SS 1940–50, 52–53 **Cardinals**, Browns 1572 g, .263, 36 hr, 624 rbi. *4 WS, 23 g, .231, 1 hr, 11 rbi.*
    Manager 1951–56 Cardinals, Browns, **White Sox** 356–373, .488
☛ *Most Valuable Player—44. All-Star—43, 44, 46–50.*

Marion was the premier defensive NL shortstop of his day, named to seven successive NL All-Star squads. With Marion at SS, the Cardinals won four

Marty Marion

pennants, three World Championships, and, from 1941 through 1949, never finished lower than second. Nicknamed "Slats" by Burt Shotton, who managed him in the minors, the 6'2" 170-lb Marion disproved the theory that shortstops had to be small men. His unusually long arms, which reached for ground balls like tentacles, prompted writers to dub him "The Octopus."

Marion was a consistent hitter who generally batted toward the bottom of the order. His 38 doubles led the NL in 1942. Deferred from military service because of a trick knee, he was the NL MVP in 1944, when he helped the Cardinals to a World Championship with his glove, winning his first of four fielding titles.

A back injury cut Marion's career short, and he managed the Cardinals from the bench in 1951, finishing third. Replaced by Eddie Stanky, he moved crosstown to the Browns, and took over for manager Rogers Hornsby early in the 1952 season. He played 67 games that season, three the next, and was let go after a last-place finish in 1953. He managed the White Sox for two-plus seasons, always coming in third. His brother, John "Red" Marion, played briefly for the 1935 and 1943 Senators. /(JK)

Roger Maris — 1934–1985. OF 1957–68 Indians, Athletics, **Yankees**, Cardinals 1463 g, .260, 275 hr, 851 rbi. *7 WS, 41 g, .217, 6 hr, 18 rbi*
☛ *Most Valuable Player—60–61. Led League—hr 61. Led League—rbi 60–61. All-Star—60. Gold Glove—60.*

When Maris hit his record 61st home run of the 1961 season, he became the owner of the most glamorous of all baseball standards, a mark he has held for nearly as long as his predecessor Babe Ruth did before Maris broke it. A great outfielder with a fine arm, an adept baserunner, and a team player willing to move baserunners and slide hard to break up double plays, Maris was a winner in two cities, appearing in more World Series than any other player in the 1960s and establishing himself as one of the dominant players of the first half of the decade.

In 1953 Maris signed with the Indians out of high school for a $5,000 bonus after turning down an athletic scholarship from the University of Oklahoma. He hit .325 at Fargo-Moorhead. Fargo today houses a Roger Maris museum. At Keokuk in 1954 manager Jo Jo White taught him to pull, and Maris hit 32 home runs. Using a 35-inch, 33-ounce bat, he broke into the major leagues with the Indians by going 3-for-5 on Opening Day 1957 against the White Sox, and the next day he hit his first big league home run, a grand slam game winner, in the top of the 11th inning. His 14 rookie homers were followed by 28 in his second season, which he started with Cleveland and finished with Kansas City. The Athletics acquired him along with Preston Ward and Dick Tomanek for Vic Power and Woody Held.

Seeking to restructure their team after finishing third in 1959, the Yankees, who had traded frequently with the Athletics in the late 1950s, obtained Maris from Kansas City with Kent Hadley and Joe DeMaestri for Don Larsen, Hank Bauer, Marv Throneberry, and Norm Siebern. In his first game as a Yankee, he hit two home runs, a double and a single, and he wound up with 39 home runs for the year, one behind Mantle's league-leading 40. He topped the league with a .581 slugging percentage and beat out Mantle for MVP honors by three points in the weighted voting. Although New York lost the 1960 World Series on Bill Mazeroski's home run in the bottom of the ninth inning of the seventh game, prompting the firing of manager Stengel, a new Yankee dynasty marked by five consecutive AL crowns had begun.

Under new manager Ralph Houk in 1961, the Yankees fielded a set lineup, usually batting Maris third and Mantle fourth. The two preyed on American League pitchers, including the weak-armed staffs of Los Angeles and Washington, the league's two expansion franchises. Neck-and-neck with Mantle through September until Mantle was felled by an injury, the nation watched as Maris hit his 59th homer in the 155th game of the year, his 60th in game 159, and his 61st in the final and 163rd game of the season at Yankee Stadium off Tracy Stallard of the Red Sox in a 1–0 Yankee victory. The home run ball was caught by a 21-year-old truck driver, Sal Durante, who sold it to Sam Gordon, a Sacramento restaurant owner. Gordon displayed it for a while, then gave it to Maris.

Controversy surrounded the feat. There were those who claimed that Maris's achievement was tainted, because Maris, who played in 161 of the Yankees' 163 games that season, had more games to break the total of 60 that Ruth had accumulated in 1927 playing in 151 of the team's 155 games. (Each team played one tie game.) Commissioner Ford Frick ordered an asterisk attached to the record. With time, however, his ruling has been dwarfed by the feat itself and survives only as a piece of trivia surrounding the lore of Maris's chase of the record. Maris's great season included AL-leading totals of 142 RBI and 132 runs scored, and it led the Yankees to a World Series victory over Cincinnati.

Roger Maris

In addition to winning his second consecutive MVP award, Maris was awarded the Hickock Belt as best professional athlete of the year, and was named Catholic Athlete of the Year. He won numerous other plaques, as well as a Gold Glove.

The quest for the home run record weighed heavily on Maris, and the hair of his famed crew cut began to fall out from tension in the stretch run of the chase. The pressure he felt was exacerbated by his accurate assessment that he was never as popular with fans as he thought he should have been. A private man who seldom showed emotion, he irritated many reporters with his angry stubbornness and his fierce, combative integrity. "I'm impatient," he said of himself. "When I think something isn't right, I want it to be made right then and there. I don't believe in holding things in. When I'm impatient or dissatisfied I say something." Much of his impatience was aimed at himself. "You can always do better than you're doing," he said. "You have to try all the time." Shortly before his death from lymph-gland cancer in 1985, he said, "I always come across as being bitter. I'm not bitter. People were very reluctant to give me any credit. I thought hitting 60 home runs was something. But everyone shied off. Why, I don't know. Maybe I wasn't the chosen one, but I was the one who got the record."

The four intentional walks Maris drew in a 12-inning game in 1962 were indicative of the respect accorded him around the league following his 1961 season. Maris had his last great season as a Yankee in 1962. He had more than 30 homers and more than 100 RBI for the third year in a row, and the Yankees defeated San Francisco in the World Series. A hand injury plagued him in 1963 and robbed him of his power, and he never fully regained his home run form, despite making a partial comeback in 1964. Batting in a game in June 1965, he took a swing and felt something pop in his right hand. He was sidelined the rest of the year, but did not submit to surgery until the season was over. His 1965 injuries were a portent of the future for an aging Yankee team, which slid to a last-place finish in 1966. Maris played in only 95 games, pinch hitting in 20 more, and hit 13 homers.

In December 1966 Maris was traded to the Cardinals for Charley Smith, a much-traveled third baseman with a .240 career average. St. Louis moved Mike Shannon from the outfield to third base and played Maris in right field. The change was the only alteration of the lineup the Cardinals fielded in 1966 when they finished in sixth place, 12 games behind the Dodgers, but it was a significant one, as they won consecutive National League championships in 1967 and 1968 with Maris. He batted .385 for their 1967 World Championship team. / (NLM/CR)

Cliff Markle — 1894–1974. RHP 1915–16, 21–22, 24 Yankees, **Reds** 235 ip, 12–17, 4.10

Markle was a marginal righthander whose best year was 4–5 (3–3 in relief) with the second-place Reds of 1922. In a career total of 235 innings, he allowed exactly one hit per inning. /(ADS)

Dick Marlowe — 1929–1968. RHP 1951–56 **Tigers**, White Sox 243 ip, 13–15, 4.99

Pitching for Buffalo on August 15, 1952, Marlowe hurled the International League's first nine-inning perfect game in 42 years, a 2–0 victory over Baltimore. He spent virtually all of his ML career with the Tigers, working mostly in relief. /(FK)

Rube Marquard [Richard William] — 1889–1980. LHP 1908–25 **Giants**, Dodgers, Reds, Braves 3306 ip, 201–177, 3.08. 20 wins: 11–13 *5 WS, 58 ip, 2–5, .532* ☛ *Led League—w 12. Hall of Fame—1971.*

Most players nicknamed Rube got the name because they came from farms or small country towns. But Marquard grew up in Cleveland, where his father was the city engineer. After making a name for himself as a sandlot pitcher, Marquard signed for $200 a month with Indianapolis in 1907. They optioned him to Canton in the Central League, where he won 23 and lost 13. After he won the Indianapolis home opener, 2 to 1, against Kansas City in 1908, a newspaper account said, "He is so tall and skinny (6'3" 180-lbs) he looks like a big number one when he stands on the mound, but he pitches like Rube Waddell." They called him Rube ever after.

After he won 20 for Indianapolis and pitched a perfect game, the New York Giants paid a then-record $11,000 for his contract. At 18 he reported to the Giants in mid-September, just in time to see the game with the Cubs in which Fred Merkle failed to touch second base. New York was still in an uproar

Rube Marquard

over the incident a few days later when Marquard made his big league debut against Cincinnati. Somewhat panicked by the size of the crowd, Marquard hit lead-off batter Miller Huggins in the ribs, then walked the next two batters. After a visit from catcher Chief Myers, the nervous rookie decided to "let up a little." "I let up, all right," Marquard later admitted. "Hans Lobert hit the next pitch right out of the park." As he departed for the clubhouse, the bleacher fans labeled him the "$11,000 Lemon."

After two mediocre seasons, Marquard blossomed in 1911, going 25-7. In the World Series against the Athletics, he was instrumental in the coining of another immortal's nickname. In Game Two he was locked in a 1-1 tie with Eddie Plank in the sixth inning when he threw a high, inside fastball to Frank Baker with a man on. Baker hit a game-winning homer, and was known thereafter as Home Run Baker.

Marquard and Christy Mathewson were writing daily commentaries on the games for rival newspapers. The next morning Mathewson's column criticized Marquard for the pitch he threw to Baker. That afternoon Baker hit a game-tying homer in the top of the ninth off Matty; the A's won in the 11th. Marquard had the last word in his column.

Marquard won 19 straight from Opening Day to July 3 in 1912, tying a mark set by Tim Keefe. Under present rules it would have been 20; he was not credited with a 4-3 win over Brooklyn when he relieved in the eighth inning with the score tied. That historic streak plus two 1912 World Series victories brought him a flock of show-business offers. He had made his vaudeville debut the previous winter, and after the 1912 season made a movie with Alice Joyce called "19 Straight." He teamed up with Blossom Seeley, a headliner, in a skit, "Breaking the Record," and later married her. They did a dance called the Marquard Glide. Rube was at home on stage. He'd say to the audience, "You wished it on yourselves, and I got nerve enough to sing it," and did. In 1913 they did an act, "The Suffragette Pitcher," in which Rube put on a dress and pitched for Blossom's all-girl team. Later Rube did singing and talking acts with other headline performers.

Marquard relied more on control and a forkball changeup than his fastball. "Any hitter can hit a fast one," he said. "But not many can hit slow ones." In 1914 Marquard and Babe Adams pitched 21 innings, Rube getting the win. Three days later Marquard shut out the Reds. He claimed he never had a sore arm. In 1915 he pitched a no-hitter against

Brooklyn in one hour, 16 minutes. But he missed his old coach, Wilbert Robinson, now manager of the Dodgers, and was getting tired of McGraw's riding. With McGraw's permission, he arranged his own sale to Brooklyn for $7,500. He got into two more World Series with the Dodgers but never won a Series ring.

Marquard led the NL with 18 losses in 1918 despite a 2.64 ERA. Then, on June 9, 1919, he broke his left leg sliding into third base and was out the rest of the year. He returned in 1920 to go 10-7 for Brooklyn's NL champions, then spent a season with the Reds before finishing his career in Boston with the Braves. He missed most of 1924 with various illnesses and pitched mostly in relief in 1925.

Marquard managed Providence in the Eastern League in 1926, spent part of 1927 with Baltimore, managed Jacksonville in the Southeastern League, did a little umpiring, and was a scout and coach for Atlanta in the Southern Association. He worked for many years at mutuel windows at racetracks in Florida and Maryland. /(NLM)

Connie Marrero — 1917- . RHP 1950-54 **Senators** 735 ip, 39-40, 3.67
☛ *All-Star—51.*

Nearly 33 when his ML career began, the native Cuban was a capable starter for mediocre Senators teams, twice winning 11 games. On April 26, 1951 Marrero one-hit the A's, allowing only a Barney McCosky home run. /(FK)

Bill Marriott — 1893-1969. 3B-2B 1917, 20-21, 25-27 Cubs, Braves, **Dodgers** 264 g, .266, 4 hr, 95 rbi

Marriott was the regular Dodgers third baseman in 1926. He played seven years of minor league ice hockey. /(BC)

Armando Marsans — 1887-1960. OF-1B 1911-18 **Reds**, St. Louis (FL), Browns, Yankees 655 g, .269, 2 hr, 221 rbi

Marsans was not the first Cuban in the major leagues, but he was the first successful and highly popular one. Half black, he was light-skinned enough to cross baseball's rigid color line, and could be considerd the first black in 20th-century major league ball. He was discovered by Clark Griffith, Cincinnati manager and the principal exploiter of the world of inexpensive Latino players. A swift outfielder, Marsans could also play the infield when needed. Though only an average hitter, he was an audacious baserunner. His slide was a thing of beauty. He was also an early challenger of baseball's restrictive contracts, giving Cincinnati ten days' notice in 1914 and jumping to the Federal League. An injuction barring him from playing for the St. Louis Feds was eventually dismissed, but by the time he was free to play again, he was nearing the end of the trail. /(ADS)

Freddie Marsh — 1924– . 3B-SS-2B 1949, 51–56 Indians, **Browns/Orioles**, Senators, White Sox 465 g, .239, 10 hr, 96 rbi

Marsh was the Browns' third baseman in 1951, but in 1952 was traded to the Senators in May, back to the Browns in June, and on to the White Sox after the season. A utility man thereafter, he missed half of 1955 with the Orioles because of a broken elbow and a leg injury. /(NLM)

Cuddles Marshall [Clarence Westly] — 1925– . RHP 1946, 48–50 **Yankees**, Browns 185 ip, 7–7, 5.98

Marshall was dubbed Cuddles while with the 1946 Yankees because the rookie with matinee-idol looks was, at twenty-one, the team's youngest member. That May 28, he started the first night game played at Yankee Stadium. Wildness and a sore arm limited his career. /(WAB)

Dave Marshall — 1943– . OF 1967–73 Giants, **Mets**, Padres 490 g, .246, 16 hr, 114 rbi

The defensively deficient Marshall was a singles hitter who was used as a backup outfielder throughout his career. /(JFC)

Jim Marshall — 1932– . 1B-OF 1958–62 Orioles, **Cubs**, Giants, Mets, Pirates 410 g, .242, 29 hr, 106 rbi. *Manager* 1974–76, 79 **Cubs**, A's 229–326, .413

Marshall was a lefthanded-hitting first baseman and admitted "fringe" player. His biggest day at the plate was his first with the Cubs, in 1958, when he hit three home runs in a doubleheader. Traded six times, in 1962 he played 17 games for the expansion Mets. He spent the next three years in Japan, hitting 78 HR for Chunichi. After managing in the minors, he became a Cubs coach in 1974, took over for manager Whitey Lockman in mid-season, and had three losing years. He led the A's to a 54–108 mark in 1979 before the arrival of Billy Martin. /(NLM)

Max Marshall — 1913– . OF 1942–44 **Reds** 329 g, .245, 15 hr, 105 rbi

Marshall saw all of his major league action during WWII. He was the only one of 12 outfielders used by the 1942 Reds to bat as high as .250. /(NLM)

Mike Marshall — 1960– . OF-1B 1981- **Dodgers** 928 g, .271, 137 hr, 484 rbi. *3 LCS, 17 g, .206, 2 hr, 10 rbi. 1 WS, 5 g, .231, 1 hr, 3 rbi*
☛ *All-Star—84.*

Injuries became Marshall's biggest impediment to matching his extraordinary minor league success. In 1981, the 6′5″ 215-lb slugger was named *TSN* Minor League Player of the Year for winning the first Pacific Coast League triple crown in 25 years (.373, 34 HR, 137 RBI). Handed the Dodgers' right-field job in 1983, he was beaned by Jeff Reardon on April 9, and took two months to start hitting. A foot operation cost him part of 1984. Healthy (except for an appendectomy) in 1985, he had 28 HR and 95 RBI. He was leading the NL with 17 HR in June of 1986 when back strain set in; he finished with 19. His problems in 1987 included a wart removal, food poisoning, and back, wrist, and ankle injuries.

He hit what appeared to be a home run in his first ML at-bat in September 1981, but the umpires missed the call and he wound up with a double; Giants right fielder Jack Clark later admitted the ball had landed in the stands and bounced out. While still single, Marshall's friendship with Belinda Carlisle of the rock group The Go-Go's was the talk of Tinsel Town. /(TG)

Mike Marshall — 1943– . RHP 1967, 69–81 Tigers, Pilots, Astros, **Expos**, Dodgers, Braves, Rangers, Twins, Mets 1386 ip, 97–112, 3.14. *1 LCS, 3 ip, 0–0, 0.00 1 WS, 9 ip, 0–1, 1.00*
☛ *Cy Young Award—74. All-Star—74, 75.*

Marshall wanted to play regularly when he signed with the Phillies, and spent four years in their system as a shortstop. But three seasons of league-leading marks in errors and a chronic back problem forced him to the mound. He wound up getting into more games as a relief pitcher than he probably would have as a shortstop. He set single-season records for relief appearances in both the National and American Leagues. "At times with the Dodgers I would have to crawl into the trainer's room," he said. "He would twist and turn me to get my back in shape to pitch that day."

Marshall earned three degrees at Michigan State, including a Ph.D. in kinesiology. He made his own decisions as to his training and pitching methods and was much disliked by his teammates, who saw him as an egomaniacal individualist who looked down upon them and would not take advice, but always had plenty to give. He clashed with many of his managers, who saw him as a smart-aleck college boy. Those disagreements slowed his progress, and

Pitcher Mike Marshall

record 92 games in 1973, he led in saves (31) and in relief wins and losses (14–11), and was named NL Fireman of the Year.

Afraid that Marshall had thrown too much, and in need of a centerfielder, the Expos traded him to the Dodgers for Willie Davis. Marshall helped L.A. to the 1974 pennant. He broke his own mark with 106 appearances, and established ML records for most relief innings pitched (208) and most consecutive games pitched in a season (13). In postseason play, he allowed one run in 12 innings, and became the first pitcher to finish every game of a World Series. He again was named NL Fireman of the Year, and became the first reliever to win a Cy Young Award.

Marshall's theories fell through in 1975, when he was beset by injuries. He lost 14 in relief to set a since-broken NL mark, and in 1976 was traded to Atlanta. There he was once suspended for refusing to suit up for a game after voicing objections to his handling by manager Dave Bristol. He continued to have injury and personal problems until the Twins, managed by Gene Mauch, took a chance on the free agent in May 1978. Marshall shared the 1979 AL Fireman of the Year Award with Jim Kern, worked a AL-record 90 games, saved a league-high 32 games, and lost 14 games in relief to tie an AL record. But Mauch felt Marshall's vociferous involvement with the Players Association in 1980, when a strike was threatened, was affecting his pitching. Let go on June 6, Marshall filed a grievance, contending he was released because of his union activities. He made a final stop with the 1981 Mets, and retired among the all-time leaders in saves (188) and relief wins (92)./(NLM)

Willard Marshall — 1921– . OF 1942, 46–55 **Giants,** Braves, Reds, White Sox 1246 g, .274, 130 hr, 604 rbi ☛ *All-Star—42, 47, 49..*

A slow-footed but sure-handed outfielder, Marshall had one of the most powerful throwing arms in the league. At the Giants' spring training camp in 1942, the polite, unheralded youngster so impressed manager Mel Ott that he started the season as the Giants' regular left fielder. After a slow start, the lefthanded-hitting rookie came on strong, finishing with a .257 batting average and 59 RBI in 116 games. Following a three-year stint in the Marines, Marshall rejoined the Giants in 1946. He had his best season the next year, contributing 36 home runs to the club's NL record total of 225, and driving in 107 runs. Although he never approached that homer or RBI figure again, he hit a career-high .307 for the Giants

resulted in many of his nine organization changes. Among other things, he believed in long-distance running for pitchers instead of wind sprints, and that by properly training specific muscles, a pitcher can throw every day. His screwball was his most effective pitch; he publicly complained about some of his managers and pitching coaches who didn't want him to use it. In 1969 Pilots manager Joe Schultz objected to Marshall's unorthodox pickoff move (he turned clockwise, rather than counter-clockwise), but it worked for Marshall. He was sold to Houston after the season.

Marshall finally found a home in Montreal, managed by an accepting Gene Mauch. He saved 23 games in 1971, and in 1972 led the NL with 65 appearances and 14 relief wins. In working a ML-in 1949, and later had several solid seasons with the Braves and Reds. /(FS)

Billy Martin [Alfred Manuel] — 1928–1989, 2B-SS 1950–53, 55–61 **Yankees**, A's, Tigers, Indians, Reds, Braves, Twins 1021 g, .257, 64 hr, 333 rbi. *5 WS, 28 g, .333, 5 hr, 19 rbi.*
   Manager 1969, 71–83, 85, 88 Twins, Tigers, Rangers, **Yankees**, A's 1249–1004, .554. First place: 69, 72, 76–77, 81 *5 LCS, 8–13, .381. 2 WS, 4–6, .400*
☛ *All-Star—56.*

Billy Martin was one of baseball's most fascinating characters from the time he left the tough side of Berkeley, California, and entered pro ball in 1946 until his tragic death in an auto accident near his home in Fenton, New York, on Christmas 1989. Martin played for Casey Stengel with the Oakland Oaks in 1948. Stengel loved him like the son he never had and admired his aggressive play. When Stengel became manager in New York, he had the Yankees obtain Martin.

Martin's Yankee career began in 1950 and ended abruptly on June 15, 1957, and Stengel couldn't do anything to save him. The trading of Martin and several other players to Kansas City on that date followed a highly publicized nightclub scuffle involving several Yankee stars, including Mickey Mantle and Hank Bauer. Martin was blamed for the mess.

Martin was a fine Yankee second baseman and Stengel's sparkplug. He lacked the ability of close friends Mickey Mantle and Whitey Ford, but he did whatever it took to win. The only year New York didn't win the pennant while Martin was a Yankee was the year he was in the Army, 1954. His alertness saved the seventh game of the 1952 World Series for New York, 4–2. With two outs in the seventh and the bases full of Dodgers, Jackie Robinson lifted a pop-up near the pitcher's mound that seemed to freeze the Yankee infield—until Martin raced in to make a lunging catch.

In the Yankees-Dodgers rematch in 1953, Martin was the World Series MVP. He hit .500, set a six-game Series record with 12 hits, and singled home the winning run in the bottom of the ninth in the finale.

He enjoyed his best season in 1956, making the All-Star team and setting personal highs in homers (15) and RBI (75). He bounced around—and brawled around—the majors for four years after his 1957 Yankee departure. While playing for the Reds in 1960, Martin attacked Cubs rookie Jim Brewer during a game and broke Brewer's cheekbone.

Martin was with Minnesota when he retired as a player. He remained in the Minnesota organization,

Billy Martin

becoming the Twins' third-base coach and then, in 1969, their manager. He beat up Twins pitcher Dave Boswell and ignored owner Calvin Griffith, and he got himself fired in spite of winning the AL West title.

Martin repeated the pattern with Detroit (1971–73), winning the AL East in 1972, and Texas (1973–75), where he finished an amazing second in 1974 to capture the first of his four Manager of the Year awards. But maintaining the affection of management was a problem for him.

By the time Martin got to New York in August 1975, he was recognized as one of the best managers in the game, and he led the Yankees to a surprisingly easy 1976 pennant. Then owner George Steinbrenner signed Reggie Jackson, and the relative peace of the Yankee clubhouse became imperiled. During a series in Boston, Martin and Jackson almost came to blows as a national TV audience watched. But the Yankees won the 1977 World Championship all the same.

In July 1978, however, Martin suspended Jackson for bunting against orders, and later told the press that Jackson and Steinbrenner were liars. Martin was forced to resign. He returned to the Yankee helm in July 1979, only to be fired again in October after punching out a marshmallow salesman.

Martin then managed at Oakland (1980–82), where his "Billy Ball"—characterized as featuring the running game, the hit-and-run, and the suicide squeeze, but also including a league-leading total of home runs—revived an A's franchise that in 1981 won the AL West.

Martin was fired by the A's, hired by the Yankees (1983), fired by the Yankees, hired by the Yankees (1985), fired by the Yankees, hired by the Yankees (1988), and—after yet another nightclub brawl—fired by the Yankees once again. The five terms managing one club tied the major league record./(MG)

Freddie Martin — 1915–1979. RHP 1946, 49–50 **Cardinals** 162 ip, 12–3, 3.78

Martin was one of the first pro players to enter WWII service, and among the last to come out. In 1946 he reached the Cardinals, but left to play in the Mexican League. Reinstated in 1949, he went 6–0./(NLM)

Herschel Martin — 1909–1980. OF 1937–40, 44–45 **Phillies**, Yankees 607 g, .285, 28 hr, 215 rbi

Martin developed his back muscles swinging a sledge in Oklahoma's oil fields. The switch-hitter scored 102 runs as a Phillies rookie in 1937. He batted a career-high .302 for the 1944 Yankees. He was a Mets scout from their inception in 1961 until 1979./(NLM)

J.C. Martin [Joseph Clifton] — 1936– . C-1B-3B 1959–72 **White Sox**, Mets, Cubs 905 g, .222, 32 hr, 230 rbi. *1 LCS, 2 g, .500, 2 rbi. 1 WS, 1 g, --*

After Martin failed as both a first and third baseman, he was converted by the White Sox to a fine-fielding catcher. He particularly excelled at handling the floating knuckleballs of Hoyt Wilhelm. On September 10, 1967, he caught Joel Horlen's no-hitter. That winter, the Mets acquired him to back up Jerry Grote.

Though a weak hitter, Martin is best remembered for two pinch-hitting appearances for New York. In the 1969 LCS opener, he delivered a key bases-loaded single. When he came off the bench in the bottom of the 10th in Game Four of the World Series, he triggered one of the most controversial plays in post-season history. He bunted to Baltimore pitcher Pete Richert, whose throw to first struck Martin on the wrist and ricocheted into short right, allowing pinch runner Rod Gaspar to score the winning run from second. Orioles manager Earl Weaver, who had been ejected earlier, saw the play and protested after the game that Martin had run illegally inside the foul line. Umpire Shag Crawford thought otherwise./(DB)

Jerry Martin — 1949– . OF 1974–84 **Phillies**, Cubs, Giants, Royals, Mets 1018 g, .251, 85 hr, 345 rbi. *3 LCS, 8 g, .143, 1 hr, 2 rbi*

Martin was a valuable fourth outfielder and pinch hitter on three consecutive Phillies division championship clubs (1976–78). He hit three pinch homers in 1978 and added another in the LCS. He then spent two seasons as a Cubs regular, hitting 42 HR. He was a streaky hitter, his power coming in bursts. Following a contract dispute, he was traded to the Giants in December of 1980, and to the Royals a year later. The free-swinging Martin didn't adapt well to the AL, where he saw more breaking pitches. A wrist injury and his 1984 suspension for involvement with drugs led to his premature exit from baseball. With ex-teammate Willie Wilson, he served a three-month sentence in the Fort Worth Correctional Institute. His father, Barney, pitched two innings for the 1953 Reds./(DB)

John Martin — 1956– . LHP 1980–83 **Cardinals**, Tigers 290 ip, 17–14, 3.93

Martin's best stretch of pitching came after he was recalled by the Cardinals in 1981. He outdueled Nolan Ryan and Steve Carlton enroute to an 8–5 record./(FJO)

Morrie Martin — 1922– . LHP 1949, 51–59 Dodgers, **A's**, White Sox, Orioles, Cardinals, Indians, Cubs 605 ip, 38–34, 4.29

Martin persevered despite calamity. He began his pro career in 1941, but was wounded as a combat engineer in WWII. In spring training of 1949, a death in the family took him away for three weeks; he lasted just 10 games in his debut with Brooklyn. The next spring he sprained his ankle and was sent down. Drafted by the Athletics, he went a career-best 11–4 in 1951, beating every AL club at least once before suffering a season-ending collision with Cleveland catcher Jim Hegan. He sat out most of 1952 after breaking a finger. /(NLM)

Ned Martin — Unk.– . *Broadcaster.*

Martin has been heard on Red Sox radio and television broadcasts since 1961, acknowledging outstanding plays with a subdued "Mercy!" Originally paired on radio with Curt Gowdy and then Ken Coleman, he was at his best with Jim Woods until 1978, when the pair were let go, and Martin moved into the Red Sox television booth the following season. /(SCL)

Pepper Martin (Johnny) — 1904–1965. OF-3B 1928, 30–40, 44 **Cardinals** 1189 g, .298, 59 hr, 501 rbi. *3 WS, 15 g, .418, 1 hr, 8 rbi*
☛ *All-Star—33–35, 37.*

Martin, labeled "The Wild Horse of the Osage" by a Rochester sportswriter for his aggressive play, was the personification of the Cardinals' Gashouse Gang. He played every facet of the game with passion. His bellyflop slides helped him to lead the NL in stolen bases and score more than 120 runs in each of three seasons. He dashed for every batted ball as if it were the seventh game of the World Series. In lopsided games, he would reportedly throw at batters who bunted instead of throwing them out at first. He got along well with manager Frankie Frisch, although his horseplay could exasperate the skipper.

In the 1931 WS, Martin batted .500, with five extra-base hits and five stolen bases. His career WS batting average of .418 is the highest among players with 50 or more at-bats. /(FJO)

Renie Martin — 1955– . RHP 1979–84 **Royals**, Giants, Phillies 508 ip, 24–35, 4.27 *1 WS, 9 ip, 0–0, 2.79*

A sharp-breaking curve and above-average fastball earned Martin a spot in the Royals' bullpen in 1979. He was 10–10 in 1980, when he started 20 games. Not a strikeout pitcher, he relied on keeping the ball low and nibbling at the corners. Traded to the Giants in 1982, he failed to become a regular starter. /(FJO)

Speed Martin [Elwood Goode] — 1893–1983. RHP 1917–22 Browns, **Cubs** 592 ip, 30–42, 3.78

Martin joined the Cubs late in 1918 and contributed six quick victories—three in relief—to help clinch the pennant. He had limited success in three more ML seasons and finished in the Pacific Coast League. /(JK)

Pepper Martin

Stu Martin — 1913– . 2B-3B 1936–43 **Cardinals**, Pirates, Cubs 722 g, .268, 16 hr, 183 rbi

Martin was brought up to ease Cardinal manager Frankie Frisch into retirement as a player. He platooned with Frisch at second base as a rookie in 1936, hitting .298. In 1939, he led NL second basemen in fielding. /(FJO)

Joe Martina (Oyster Joe) — 1889–1962. RHP 1924 **Senators** 125 ip, 6–8, 4.67. *1 WS, 1 ip, 0–0, 0.00*

A wild fireballer, Martina won 121 games in seven seasons at Beaumont (Texas League), and 133 more in seven years with his hometown New Orleans (Southern Association) club en route to a minor league mark of 349–277. In 1980, George Brunet broke Martina's record of 2,770 minor league career strikeouts. /(MC)

Buck Martinez [John Albert] — 1948– . C 1969–71, 73–86 Royals, Brewers, **Blue Jays** 1049 g, .225, 58 hr, 321 rbi. *1 LCS, 5 g, .333, 4 rbi*

Originally signed by the Phillies, Martinez fashioned a seventeen-season career on defensive talents. Although a .283 hitter in five minor league campaigns, he hit over .250 only twice in the majors. He was slow afoot and hit with power infrequently. He was, however, excellent at blocking home plate, had an accurate arm, and handled pitchers well. Martinez was most productive in platoon situations, first with Bob Stinson at Kansas City, then with Charlie Moore in Milwaukee, and finally paired with Ernie Whitt for Toronto. In 1976 he tied Jim Sundberg for best fielding average (.991) among AL receivers.

Martinez never fully recovered from a fractured leg and dislocated ankle sustained while blocking home plate in July 1985. After tagging out the lead runner and suffering the broken leg, he threw to third from the ground. It was a bad throw, and that runner came home too; Martinez managed to take the throw and tag him out too. /(FO)

Carmelo Martinez — 1960– . OF-1B 1983– Cubs, **Padres** 812 g, .249, 88 hr, 353 rbi. *1 LCS, 5 g, .176. 1 WS, 5 g, .176*

After homering in his first ML at-bat with the Cubs in September 1983, Martinez was traded to San Diego with Craig Lefferts and infielder Fritz Connally for Scott Sanderson, and in 1984 he started in left field for the NL champion Padres, teaming with Kevin McReynolds to give the Padres a promising young outfield duo. Martinez led San Diego with 21 HR in 1985, then was hampered by tendinitis in one knee in 1986, hitting only .238 with nine home runs. A heavy, slow-footed righthanded hitter, Martinez rebounded with a .273 average and 15 HR in 1987, but struggled in 1988, hitting only .236. His cousin Edgar Martinez played 27 games with the Mariners in 1987–88. /(SCL)

Dave Martinez — 1964– . OF 1986– **Cubs**, Expos 459 g, .264, 18 hr, 116 rbi

Martinez batted .292 as a Cubs rookie in 1987 and had become a favorite at Wrigley Field when he was suddenly sent to Montreal for Mitch Webster in a July 1988 swap of underachieving centerfielders. The Cubs felt Martinez was not selective enough at the plate and not aggressive enough on the

basepaths. In 1989 he platooned in centerfield with light-hitting Otis Nixon. /(JCA)

Dennis Martinez — 1955– . RHP 1976– **Orioles**, Expos 2485 ip, 153–123, 3.90. *1 LCS, 8 ip, 0–0, 3.24. 1 WS, 2 ip, 0–0, 18.00*
☛ *Led League—w 81.*

Developed in the Baltimore system, Dennis Martinez was a star with the Orioles, then overcame alcoholism in a successful comeback with the Expos. Using a basic repertoire of pitches, Martinez was the International League Pitcher of the Year in 1976. He averaged 15 wins a year from 1977 to 1982, excepting an injury-interrupted 1980. From 1983 to 1985, he was simply a hard thrower. Traded to Montreal in 1986, he learned to cope with alcoholism, but still found himself out of a job in May 1987. Given a last chance by Montreal, Martinez led NL pitchers with a .733 winning percentage (11–4) in 1987 and became the staff ace by pitching, not just throwing. His 16–7 record (3.18 ERA) in 1989 helped the Expos contend for the title. /(ME)

Fred Martinez [Alfredo] — 1957– . RHP 1980–81 **Angels** 155 ip, 7–9, 4.47

This Los Angeles native was the number-two starter on a weak Angels staff in 1980, going 7–9 with a 4.53 ERA. /(WOR)

Marty Martinez [Orlando Oliva] — 1941– . SS-3B-2B-C 1962, 67–72 Twins, Braves, **Astros**, Cardinals, Rangers, A's 436 g, .243, 0 hr, 57 rbi

Martinez was a utility man who over the course of his career played the outfield, every infield position, and 30 games as a catcher. In the season in which he was most used, 1968, he hit .230 with a career-high 34 runs scored in 356 at-bats. /(SFS)

Ramon Martinez — 1968– . RHP 1988– **Dodgers** 134 ip, 7–7, 3.35

Martinez was a member of the 1984 Dominican Republic Olympic baseball team. He came up at the age of 20 in 1988 and impressed observers, although he went only 1–3. He began fulfilling his promise in 1989, after the Dodgers' trade of Tim Leary made room for Martinez in the rotation. /(JFC)

Silvio Martinez — 1955– . RHP 1977–81 White Sox, **Cardinals** 583 ip, 31–32, 3.87

Three days after no-hitting Omaha for Springfield (American Association) on May 26, 1978, this Dominican was called up to the Cardinals, and one-hit the Mets at Shea Stadium in his first ML start.

He went 15–8 in 1979, adding two more one-hitters and two two-hitters. Elbow problems set in during 1980, and he was dumped on the Indians the following November. /(NLM)

Teddy Martinez [Teodoro Noel Encarncion] — 1947– . SS-2B-3B 1970–75, 77–79 **Mets**, Cardinals, A's, Dodgers 657 g, .240, 7 hr, 108 rbi. *1 LCS, 3 g, --. 1 WS, 2 g, --*

Martinez was a career utility man. In the only season the Dominican played more than 50 games at a single position (75 out of 116 games at shortstop for the Mets in 1974), he hit .219 with career highs of two HR and 43 RBI. In 1977 with the Dodgers he tied a NL second base record with five double plays in a game on August 21. /(JFC)

Tippy Martinez [Felix Anthony] — 1950– . LHP 1974–86, 88 Yankees, **Orioles**, Twins 835 ip, 55–42, 3.45. *1 LCS, 6 ip, 1–0, 0.00. 2 WS, 4 ip, 0–0, 4.15* ☛ *All-Star—83.*

Martinez was a mainstay of the Orioles bullpen for nearly 10 seasons, leading the club in saves five times and saving at least 10 games each year from 1980 to 1984, with a career-high 21 in 1983. Originally drafted by the Senators, Martinez reached the ML with the Yankees in 1974, then was traded to the Orioles on June 15, 1976 in a 10-player deal that sent Rudy May, Scott McGregor, and Rick Dempsey to Baltimore in exchange for Ken Holtzman, Doyle Alexander, Grant Jackson, and Elrod Hendricks. Martinez was primarily a set-up man for Dan Stanhouse in 1978–79, then became Baltimore's lefthanded closer in 1980, teaming with Tim Stoddard and later Sammy Stewart to give the Orioles an effective lefty-righty bullpen combination. He won the final game of the 1983 ALCS with four shutout innings in relief and saved 17 more games in 1984, but his ERA swelled to 5.40 in 1985 and 5.63 in 1986. A comeback with the 1988 Twins lasted only four innings. /(SCL)

Joe Marty — 1913–1984. OF 1937–41 Cubs, **Phillies** 538 g, .261, 44 hr, 222 rbi. *1 WS, 3 g, .500, 1 hr, 5 rbi*

The 1936 Pacific Coast League batting champion with San Francisco, Marty was sold to the Cubs and was the first Cub to homer in a night game (7/1/38 at Cincinnati). He drove in five of their nine runs in the 1938 World Series loss to the Yankees. He was a regular with the Phillies in 1939–41 before his career was ended by four years in the military. /(JK)

Randy Martz — 1956– . RHP 1980–83 **Cubs**, White Sox 290 ip, 17–19, 3.78

Martz was named 1977's Most Valuable College Player, going 14–0 for South Carolina. He was 11–10 for the 1982 Cubs, but he returned to the minors after one game with the 1983 White Sox. /(JCA)

Phil Masi — 1917– . C 1939–52 **Braves**, Pirates, White Sox 1226 g, .264, 47 hr, 417 rbi. *1 WS, 5 g, .125, 1 rbi* ☛ *All-Star—46–48.*

Masi was one of the National League's top defensive receivers, and uncommonly fast for a catcher. A weak bat held him back initially, but he became a first-stringer due to his fine handling of Braves pitchers, from knuckleballer Jim Tobin to stars Warren Spahn and Johnny Sain.

As a pinch runner in the first game of the 1948 World Series, Masi was safe on a controversial call on a pickoff attempted by Cleveland pitcher Bob Feller and shortstop Lou Boudreau. He subsequently scored the game's only run. In 1949, during his 11th season with the Braves, he was traded to the Pirates, who sold him to the White Sox that winter. In his first season in the AL, he led the league's catchers in fielding. /(ME)

Don Mason — 1944– . 2B 1966–73 **Giants**, Padres 336 g, .203, 3 hr, 27 RBI

Mason was a marginal performer who played all or parts of eight ML seasons despite being a poor hitter. In his only extended period as a regular, he hit .212 as the Padres' second baseman in 1971. /(FS)

Jim Mason — 1950– . SS 1971–79 Senators/Rangers, **Yankees**, Blue Jays, Rangers, Expos 633 g, .203, 12 hr, 114 rbi. *1 LCS, 2 g, 0 at-bats. 1 WS, 3 g, 1.000, 1 hr, 1 rbi*

Mason had the lowest batting average in the 1970s of any player with at least 1500 at-bats. He hit below .200 in six of his eight seasons (not counting his nine at-bats in 1971) with a career high of .250 in 1974, his only year as a regular. That August 8, he tied a ML record with four doubles in a game. In the 1976 World Series for the Yankees he earned a unique distinction. After he came in for defense in Game Three, he hit a solo homer in the seventh inning in his only WS at-bat, the only man in history to do so. He was the Blue Jays' starting shortstop in their first game. /(WOR)

Mike Mason — 1958– . LHP 1982–88 **Rangers**, Cubs, Twins 606 ip, 29–39, 4.53

Mason, a surprise addition to the starting rotation of the last-place 1984 Rangers, went 9–13 with the second-lowest ERA among AL rookies—3.61. He never improved, and he missed time with hamstring and elbow injuries. He was a control pitcher with unspectacular stuff who, his critics said, too often lacked concentration and gave up too many hits when ahead in the count. He spent 1989 in the Astros organization. /(JCA)

Roger Mason — 1958– . RHP 1984–87 Tigers, **Giants** 137 ip, 6–9, 4.02

The 6'6" Mason made two starts for the 1984 World Champion Tigers, then was traded to San Francisco before the 1985 season. As a Giant, Mason won only five games in three years, spending most of his time in the minors. /(SCL)

Walt Masterson — 1920– . RHP 1939–42, 45–53, 56 **Senators**, Red Sox, Senators, Tigers 1650 ip, 78–100, 4.15
☛ *All-Star—47, 48.*

As a 20-year-old, Masterson lost 12 games in a row for the 1940 Senators, finishing 3–13. His 5–9 record in 1942 included four shutouts. The bespectacled hurler spent almost three years in the military, mostly playing for naval teams. He won a career-high 12 games in 1947. As the AL's starting pitcher in the 1948 All-Star Game, he gave up a first-inning, two-run homer to Stan Musial, but the AL won 5–2. He finished the year 8–15. Masterson struck out Mickey Mantle five straight times in 1951, which contributed to Mantle's being sent back down. The Senators later made Masterson their pitching coach. /(NLM)

Tommy Matchick — 1943– . SS-3B-2B 1967–72 **Tigers**, Royals, Red Sox, Brewers, Orioles 292 g, .215, 4 hr, 64 rbi. *1 WS, 3 g, .000*

Matchick hit only .203 in 80 games for the 1968 World Champion Tigers, but on July 19 his two-run home run off Moe Drabowsky with two outs in the ninth inning gave Detroit a 5–4 win. /(FK)

Joe Mathes (The Old Hustler) — 1891–1978. 2B-3B 1912, 14, 16 A's, **St. Louis (FL)**, Braves 32 g, .273, 0 hr, 6 rbi

Mathes spent 68 years in professional baseball, calling everyone he met along the way "Hustler." He joined the Cardinals' scouting staff in 1936 after

an inconsequential ML playing career and two decades in the minors as a player and manager. Mathes convinced Branch Rickey to make an out-fielder out of sore-armed pitcher Stan Musial. He remained with the Cardinals until 1958, and returned from 1964 to 1976, after brief stints with the Tigers, Giants, and Mets. He signed Red Schoendienst after he had been overlooked at a tryout camp. /(FVP)

Bobby Mathews — 1851–1898. RHP 1871–77, 79, 81–87 Ft. Wayne (NA), Lord Baltimores (NA), New York (NA), New York (NL), Reds, Providence (NL), Braves, **Philadelphia (AA)** *NA*: 253 g, 132–111; *ML*: 2734 ip, 166–138, 3.00. 20 wins: 1872–76, 83–85

Mathews, who played five seasons each in the National Association, National League, and American Association, is the only player ever to pitch 100 games or to win at least 50 in three different major leagues. In 1868 as an innovative 16-year-old, Mathews pitched baseball's first recorded spitball. The next season, he threw the first "out-curve" tossed in a manner permitted by the rules. On May 4, 1871, he pitched Ft. Wayne (NA) to a 2–0 victory over Cleveland (NA) in baseball's first professional league game. Pitching all 65 of the New York Mutuals' (NA) games in 1874, he won a career-high 42. In three successive seasons, 1883–85, he won 30 games for the Philadelphia Athletics (AA), leading them to a pennant in 1883. /(FIC)

Eddie Mathews — 1931– . 3B 1952–68 **Braves**, Astros, Tigers 2388 g, .271, 512 hr, 1453 rbi. *3 WS, 16 g, .200, 1 hr, 7 rbi.*
    Manager 1972–74 **Braves** 149–161, .481
☛ *Led League—hr 53, 59. All-Star—53, 55–62. Hall of Fame—1978.*

A natural athlete blessed with tremendous power, a rifle arm, and a durable body, Mathews was the premier third baseman of his era, overshadowing Clete Boyer, the young Brooks Robinson, and Al Rosen. A key member of the excellent Braves teams of the late 1950s, he was elected to the Hall of Fame in 1978 on his fifth try. His 512 homers ties him with Ernie Banks; and his 486 homers hit as a third baseman were a record until surpassed by Mike Schmidt.

Heavily scouted in high school, Mathews signed with the Boston Braves in 1949 on the night of his high school graduation. He and his father had scouted major league rosters and had decided that

Eddie Mathews

Boston's Bob Elliott was the third baseman most likely to be replaced in a few years. In less than three years Mathews was starting at third for the Braves; he kept the job for fifteen years and two franchise shifts. Ironically, Mathews played for minor league teams in Atlanta and Milwaukee on his way up.

Mathews's ascension in the majors coincided with the decline of the Boston Braves. A shy twenty-year-old, he grew up quickly in the empty confines of Braves Field, and while the team slumped to seventh place, he provided one of the few bright spots for the future along with shortstop Johnny Logan and pitcher Lew Burdette. Mathews's 25 HR (and only 58 RBI) in 1952 included tape measure shots in Philadelphia, St. Louis and Cincinnati, plus three homers on September 27 in Ebbets Field off Joe Black and Ben Wade. His hustle and determination attracted attention throughout the league—particularly in spring training when he bowled over Com-

missioner Ford Frick and Braves publicist Billy Sullivan while running down a foul fly.

In 1953 the depressed Boston franchise was uprooted to Milwaukee in spring training. The Braves quickly became the darlings not only of the city but the entire upper Midwest region in a brief but intense romance unparalleled in baseball history. Coinciding with the deliverance from Boston was a dramatic improvement in talent as Adcock, Bruton, and Conley, and later Aaron, Buhl, and Covington joined the roster. Sparked by the new surroundings, Mathews improved from .242 with 25 HR and 58 RBI in 1952 to .302 with 47 HR and 135 RBI and became a star virtually overnight. Both of his power categories were career highs. The Braves shot to second place and were contenders through the rest of the decade.

Mathews had a remarkable physique, and his powerful stroke and bat speed were marveled at by opponents. "He swings the bat faster than anyone I ever saw," commented Carl Erskine. "You think you've got a called strike past him and he hits it out of the catcher's glove." Even Ty Cobb, not known for his appreciation of the modern ballplayer, was impressed. "I've only known three or four perfect swings in my time. This lad has one of them."

The fast start enjoyed by Mathews is still unsurpassed in baseball history. He hit 190 home runs in his first five seasons, putting him far ahead of Ruth at age 25, and piled up impressive RBI totals, although his average remained below .300 in most seasons. Mathews' World Series and All-Star statistics belie his excellence. In 10 All-Star games Mathews had three times as many errors (6) as hits. His lifetime All-Star average was .080 and he fielded just .647, but both of his hits were home runs. In three World Series he averaged but .200.

After losing the pennant to the Dodgers by a single game in 1956, the Braves came back the following year with a seven-game World Series triumph over the Yankees. Mathews won Game Four with a 10th-inning homer off Bob Grim, and his backhanded grab of Bill Skowron's shot down the line closed off the Yankees in Game Seven. Despite hitting only .227, four of Mathews's five hits were for extra bases. His .292 average, 32 homers and 94 RBIs contributed greatly to the Braves' regular season success.

In 1958 Mathews suffered through a subpar season at the bat, hitting only .251, and the Braves' one-year reign as World Champions ended with a Yankee win in seven games. Mathews could only manage a .160 average and struck out 11 times. Although he rebounded to a career high of .306 with a league-leading 46 HR and 114 RBI in 1959, the Braves were beaten by a rejuvenated Los Angeles Dodgers team in a two-game playoff series. Mathews contributed a second-game homer off Don Drysdale.

From 1959 on, Mathews's home run totals steadily declined. With one exception—the last Milwaukee year (1965), when he belted 32—they dropped from 46 down to 10 in his last season as a regular, and his batting average, while never high, also showed his diminishing skills. He continued to play third base regularly but he reflected the Braves team as a whole: respectable, but not good enough to contend.

A final 1966 season with the Braves permitted Mathews to play in Atlanta, thus becoming the only three-city ballplayer with the same franchise. After Mathews hit .250 with 16 HR he was shipped to Houston for Dave Nicholson. He had little success in the Astrodome and in July 1967 he was traded to Detroit, which hoped he would regain his former

power down the short right-field line in Tiger Stadium, but Mathews produced just nine homers in a year and a half.

Mathews coached for the Braves in the early 1970s and served as manager in 1972–74. His 1973 team featured slugging from former teammate Hank Aaron, Davey Johnson, and Darrell Evans, the first trifecta of 40-HR-season teammates. /(PB)

Greg Mathews — 1962– . LHP 1986–88 **Cardinals** 411 ip, 26–25, 3.79. *1 LCS, 10 ip, 1–0, 3.48. 1 WS, 4 ip, 0–0, 2.45*

A 13–1 record with a 1.11 ERA in Class A in 1985 earned Mathews a midseason promotion to AAA. His eleven victories in 1986 were the most by a Cardinal rookie pitcher in fifteen years. He spent half of the 1988 season disabled with a strained quadricep; more injuries caused him to miss all of 1989. /(FO)

Nelson Mathews — 1941– . OF 1960–65 Cubs, **A's** 306 g, .223, 22 hr, 98 rbi

Called "another Earle Combs" by Charlie Grimm for the way he got a jump on the ball, Mathews signed with the Cubs for a $25,000 bonus. Traded to the A's after trials in 1960–63, he was their centerfielder only for 1964, striking out an AL-high 143 times and leading AL outfielders in putouts and errors. /(NLM)

Christy Mathewson (Big Six, Matty) — 1878–1925. RHP 1900–16 **Giants**, Reds 4782 ip, 372–187, 2.13. 20 wins: 01, 03–14 *4 WS, 101.2 ip, 5–5, 1.15.* *Manager* 1916–18 **Reds** 164–176, .482 ☛ *Led League—w 05, 07–08, 10. Led League—era 05, 08–09, 11, 13. Led League—k 03–05, 07–08. Hall of Fame—1936.*

The dominant pitcher of his era and one of five all-time greats originally inducted into the Hall of Fame, Mathewson looked like the classic American hero: tall, blond, and blue-eyed, with a reputation for clean living and good sportsmanship that was often held up as a splendid example for the nation's youth. While those virtues were surely exaggerated, his pitching skills were not. He retired with 372 wins (fourth all-time), 78 shutouts (third), and a 2.13 ERA (fifth).

The son of a gentleman farmer, Mathewson attended Bucknell University, where he was class president, an excellent field goal kicker, and, of course, star pitcher. Leaving Bucknell in 1899 to pitch for Taunton (New England League), he advanced to Norfolk (Virginia League) the following year and went 20–2. The Giants bought him for

$1,500, but returned him to Norfolk when he lost his first three decisions, declaring the deal cancelled and demanding their money back. He was then drafted by the Reds for $100 and traded to the Giants for sore-armed Amos Rusie, who had not pitched since 1898. Reds' owner John T. Bush was about to buy the Giants and wanted a promising pitcher when he got there.

In 1901 Mathewson won 20 games with a 2.41 ERA for the Giants, but manager Horace Fogel still did not believe his young star would win consistently, and had him practice at first, shortstop, and in the outfield. John McGraw arrived in mid-1902 to quickly put a stop to such experiments, and from 1903 to 1914 Mathewson never won fewer than 22 games.

Mathewson's pitching was marked by intelligence, good mechanics, and outstanding control (he walked only 1.6 batters per nine innings), but he also had a magic pitch. Today's screwball, he called it his "fadeaway," a reverse curve that broke in to right-handed batters. Thrown with an extremely unnatural twist of the arm, he rarely threw more than a dozen a game, but the threat was always there. Combined with his other outstanding pitches, it made him one of baseball's rare masters. He could breeze through a game on 75 or 80 pitches, often holding something back for what he called "pitching in a pinch" (the name of his book).

Mathewson was only 14–17 in his second full season, but led the NL with eight shutouts and posted a fine 2.11 ERA. The following year he won 30 games and led the league in strikeouts, feats he would repeat in 1904 and 1905. In the 1905 World Series, Matty turned in one of baseball's best post-season performances, shutting out the Athletics in Games One, Three, and Five, allowing only 14 total hits, as the Giants took the Series 4–1. In 1906–07 Christy's brother Henry pitched three games for the Giants, going 0–1; until Gaylord and Jim Perry broke their record, Christy and Henry held the record for wins by brothers.

Mathewson's finest regular season was 1908, as he led the league in wins (37), ERA (1.43), strikeouts (259), and shutouts (12), but the Giants finished a game behind the Cubs. Between 1911 and 1914 Mathewson won 98 games to young Grover Alexander's 96, but when Matty slipped to 8–14 in 1915 Alexander won 31, and the mantle of the league's best pitcher was passed. In 1916 he was traded to the Reds, where he won the one game he pitched before leading them to two fourth-place finishes as manager. When he retired, Matty had won the ERA title and the strikeout crown five times each and had led the NL in wins and shutouts four times each.

Christy Mathewson

Off the field, public reputation aside, some found him brusque and stand-offish, others said he had a swelled head. He was also known to break a contract, once signing with the Philadelphia Athletics before changing his mind and jumping back to the Giants. Still, he lent considerable prestige to the players' unionizing efforts in 1912, and while managing once suspended Hal Chase for "indifferent playing." He was also one of the few to publicly state he thought the White Sox were throwing the 1919 WS.

Enlisting as an Army captain in 1918, he served overseas and was gassed in a training exercise, thereafter suffering from tuberculosis. He coached with the Giants in 1919–20, but spent much of his time upstate, fighting TB. He served as part-time president of the Braves in 1923, and died two years later at the age of 47./(ADS)

Verdell Mathis (Lefty) — 1913– . LHP-OF-1B Negro Leagues 1940–50 **Memphis Red Sox** statistics not available
☛ *All-Star—41, 44–45..*

Slender Lefty Mathis spent his entire career with the Memphis Red Sox, earning a reputation as one of the best pitchers in Negro League baseball during the 1940s. A protege of veteran catcher and Memphis manager Larry Brown, Mathis received pitching advice from his idol, Satchel Paige, and learned his great pickoff move from Luis Tiant, Sr.

Mathis pitched in three East-West all-star games, and was the only pitcher other than Paige to win two such contests. He was overpowering in the 1944 East-West game, quieting the bats of the East's Hall of Fame sluggers Josh Gibson, Roy Campanella, Buck Leonard, Cool Papa Bell, and Ray Dandridge.

Mathis pitched year-round, often playing in Mexico in the off-season, and toured with Paige's All Stars versus Bob Feller's All Stars in 1946. He was a good lefthanded hitter and usually played the outfield or first base when not on the mound./(PG)

Jon Matlack — 1950– . LHP 1971–83 **Mets**, Rangers 2363 ip, 125–126, 3.18. *1 LCS, 9 ip, 1–0, 0.00. 1 WS, 17 ip, 1–2, 2.16*
☛ *Rookie of the Year—72. All-Star—74–76.*

Matlack, another in the long line of good pitchers developed by the Mets, won the Rookie of the Year award in 1972 by going 15–10 with a 2.32 ERA (fourth in the NL). He had been their first pick in the June 1967 draft. The offense-deficient Mets won the NL pennant in 1973, but Matlack had a 14–16 record despite 205 strikeouts (third in the league) and a 3.20 ERA. A Marty Perez line drive fractured Matlack's skull, but he was back in the rotation in 11 days. Matlack threw a two-hit, nine-strikeout shutout in Game Two of the LCS; it matched the LCS record for fewest hits allowed in a game. In Game One of the World Series he gave up only two unearned runs (on third-inning errors by Felix Millan and Willie Mays), but lost 2–1. He won Game Four 6–1, giving up three hits in eight innings, but was knocked out in the third inning of Game Seven, taking the loss.

In 1974 his support was even worse: he led the NL with seven shutouts and his 2.41 ERA was third,

but he went 13–15. He went 16–12 in 1975 and won the All-Star Game with four strikeouts in two innings. His finest season was 1976, when he went 17–10 with a 2.94 ERA, tied for the NL lead with six shutouts, and finished third with 16 complete games. His effectiveness dropped drastically the next year, as he went 7–15 with a 4.21 ERA and was traded to the Rangers after the season in a four-team deal. He rebounded to finish second in the AL with a 2.27 ERA and went 15–13. He missed two-thirds of 1979 with elbow surgery, and never matched his earlier success. Plagued through much of his career by shoulder problems, he was so protective of his pitching arm that he wouldn't draw blinds with his left hand during the season./(SH)

Al Mattern — 1883–1958. RHP 1908–12 **Braves** 844 ip, 37–58, 3.37

A workhorse who pitched 316 innings as a rookie in 1909, Mattern twice won 16 games for Braves teams that were losing over 100 games and leading the league in errors in four of his five seasons. In 1910 Mattern pitched six shutouts./(ADS)

Gary Matthews (Sarge) — 1950– . OF 1972–87 **Giants**, Braves, Phillies, Cubs, Mariners 2033 g, .281, 234 hr, 978 rbi. *2 LCS, 9 g, .310, 5 hr, 13 rbi. 1 WS, 5 g, .250, 1 hr, 1 rbi*
☛ *Rookie of the Year—73. All-Star—79.*

"An aggressive, hustling ballplayer with a great attitude" was Wes Westrum's description of Gary Matthews as a young outfielder with San Francisco, and the description fit until his retirement 16 seasons later. Matthews teamed with Garry Maddox and Bobby Bonds with the Giants to form one of the best NL outfields in the 1970s. Matthews hit .300 with 10 triples and 17 stolen bases to win the NL Rookie of the Year Award in 1973, and was an amazingly consistent hitter throughout his career, never hitting below .278 or above .304 until 1985. His aggressive playing style was evident on the basepaths, where he grabbed extra bases and up-ended fielders with a formidable takeout slide, and in the outfield, where he was only average overall, but still made many astonishing catches. The Giants switched him from leadoff to cleanup hitter in 1975, but he broke his thumb and missed 50 games. Then, after a contract dispute to start the '76 season, he hit .279 with 20 HR and was traded to the Braves.

He had his best season in Atlanta in 1979 (.304, 27 HR, 90 RBI, 97 runs) and made the All-Star team for the only time in his career. He slumped early in 1980 but recovered to post respectable numbers, and when he was traded to Philadelphia in March 1981, he was reunited in the outfield with

Gary Matthews

Garry Maddox. Matthews hit .301 in his first year in Philadelphia, and was brilliant in the 1983 LCS, winning MVP honors with a .429 average, three HR and eight RBI. He homered in each of the final three games, including a three-run shot off Jerry Reuss in the first inning of the finale, which the Phillies won 7–2. The Phillies began to unload their aging veterans in the off-season, and Matthews was dealt to Chicago, where the Cubs hoped he would provide inspired leadership. He led the NL in walks in 1984 as the Cubs won the NL East, and he quickly became a favorite of the Wrigley Field bleacher fans. After 1984 his contributions diminished. He was released by the Cubs in mid-1987, and played 45 games with the Mariners before he retired. /(SG)

Wid Matthews — 1896–1965. OF 1923–25 **A's**, Senators 192 g, .284, 1 hr, 39 rbi

Matthews was a spring phenom for the Athletics in 1923, winning the centerfield job, but finished the season leading AL outfielders in errors. He rode the bench for Senators pennant-winners in 1924–25 and later became a scout. /(ADS)

Bobby Mattick — 1915– . SS 1938–42 **Cubs**, Reds 206 g, .233, 0 hr, 64 rbi.
  Manager 1980–81 **Blue Jays** 104–164, .388

The son of outfielder Wally Mattick (White Sox, 1912–13, Cardinals, 1918), Bobby played only one season as a regular, with the Cubs in 1940. He became an incomparable longtime scout and player development specialist with many organizations, signing such stars as Frank Robinson, Vada Pinson, Curt Flood, Rusty Staub, Don Baylor, and Gary Carter. Mattick helped draft the expansion Blue Jays, and managed them to last-place finishes in 1980 and 1981. /(ARA)

Don Mattingly — 1961– . 1B 1982– **Yankees** 1015 g, .323, 164 hr, 717 rbi
☛ *Most Valuable Player—85. Led League—ba 84. Led League—rbi 85. All-Star—84–89. Gold Glove—85–89.*

After becoming a regular in 1984, Mattingly established himself as one of the preeminent stars of the 1980s. He hit for average and power, fielded his position at first base with brilliance, and displayed a work ethic and charisma reminiscent of Yankee greats of the past.

In 1982 Mattingly joined a Yankee team that was reluctant to play kids from its farm system, preferring to trade them for proven players or let them languish on the bench as insurance against injury to regulars. Mattingly saw limited action through 1983, playing primarily in the outfield, the position at which the Yankees originally drafted him. Although his career minor league batting average was .332, there was little in Mattingly's minor league performance to indicate that he might emerge as a power hitter. However, Mattingly used those first two years in the majors to become a smart two-strike hitter and learned to look for the inside pitch that he might drive into Yankee Stadium's short right-field porch. The result was his fine 1984 season, in which he took over the first-base job and hit 23 homers en route to capturing the batting title on the last day of the season with a .343 average that edged teammate Dave Winfield's .340. He became the first Yankee lefthanded hitter to bat over .340 since Lou Gehrig hit .351 in 1937.

Despite often starting the season abysmally, Mattingly established himself as a dominant hitter from 1984 through 1989. In each of those seasons, he hit over .300, collected more than 186 hits, and, except for 1988, drove in 100 or more runs. During that league record for total homers in an eight-game streak, and his concurrent streak of 10 games with at least one extra-base hit broke Babe Ruth's 1921 AL record. The power streak ended on July 20, the night Mattingly tied the major league record of 22 putouts by a first baseman in a nine-inning game.

Mattingly matched his hitting with outstanding defense. From 1985 through 1988, he won four consecutive Gold Glove awards at first base. Along with Chick Gandil (1916–1919), Mattingly (1984–1987) holds the record of leading AL first basemen in fielding percentage for four consecutive years. His skills allowed him to play second base and third base on a few occasions despite throwing lefthanded. /(EG/CR)

Rick Matula — 1953– . RHP 1979–81 **Braves** 355 ip, 19–23, 4.41

Sinkerballer Matula won a spot in the Braves' rotation as a non-roster invitee to spring training in 1979. He went 8–10 that season and 11–13 the next. /(PB)

Len Matuszek — 1954– . 1B-OF-DH 1981–87 **Phillies**, Blue Jays, Dodgers 379 g, .234, 30 hr, 119 rbi. *1 LCS, 3 g, 1.000*

Matuszek had decent power but a low batting average, and spent most of his career as a backup first baseman and a valuable pinch hitter. He shared the Phillies' first base job with Tim Corcoran in 1984 and had career highs of 12 HR and 43 RBI in only 262 at-bats. /(SCL)

Gene Mauch (Skip) — 1925– . 2B-SS 1944, 47–52, 56–57 Dodgers, Pirates, Dodgers, **Cubs**, Braves, Cardinals, Red Sox 304 g, .239, 5 hr, 62 rbi.
Manager 1960–82, 85–87 **Phillies**, Expos, Twins, Angels 1901–2037, .483. First place: 82, 86 *2 LCS, 5–7, .417*

When he retired in spring training of 1988, Gene Mauch had managed more games and for more years (26) than anyone in major league history but Connie Mack, John McGraw, and Bucky Harris. He also managed the longest without winning a pennant; he came close three times. Leading by 6-1/2 games with two weeks to go, his 1964 Phillies collapsed, finishing in a tie for second. Many said he overworked his three best pitchers at the end of the race. His Angels won two divisions titles, but suffered heartbreaking losses in the ALCS. They needed to win one of the final three games in 1982 against Milwaukee, but failed to do so. In 1986,

Don Mattingly

period, no major league player had more RBI than his 684, and only Wade Boggs (1,269) had more hits than Matingly's 1,219. Mattingly displayed his power in 1985 when, batting third in the Yankee lineup, he amassed career highs of 35 home runs and a league-leading 145 RBI en route to being named AL MVP.

In 1986 Mattingly set new Yankees marks for doubles (53) and hits (238) in a season, becoming the first Yankee since Lou Gehrig with three consecutive 200-hit seasons. During the 1987 season, Mattingly set or tied five remarkable major league records. He hit six grand slams to set a new single-season mark. (He had never hit one prior to 1987.) He tied Dale Long's 1956 record by homering in eight consecutive games from July 8 through July 18. His 10 homers during that period were a major

Gene Mauch

California was one strike away when Boston's Dave Henderson homered to win Game Five; the Red Sox then easily took the final two contests. When asked by brave reporters how he could deal with those memories, Mauch replied, "I have an amazing ability to forget."

Mauch's playing career began in 1943 in the Dodger organization. He relied more on brains than on brawn. He had had trials with five NL teams in 1953 when he became the 28-year-old playing manager of the Southern Association's Atlanta Crackers. "I really wasn't ready," he later admitted. He had a low boiling point, often fought with umpires, and expected too much of his players. With an eye on again playing in the majors, he gave up managing. He batted .348 as the 1956 Pacific Coast League's All-Star second baseman, then spent all of 1957 with the Red Sox.

Testy and combative as a player, Mauch mellowed in his second chance as a manager, beginning in 1958 with Minneapolis (American Association). He took the Phillies' helm in 1960, survived 23

consecutive losses in 1961 (a modern NL record), and was named NL Manager of the Year in 1962 (81–80, seventh place) and 1964 (92–70, second). He was thrown out by umpires only three times in his first five seasons. When he left Philadelphia in 1968, he had compiled 645 wins—second most in franchise history.

Mauch was chosen to be the expansion 1969 Expos manager, and lasted through 1975, winning a third Manager of the Year Award in 1973 (79–83, fourth). He guided the Twins (including his nephew, Roy Smalley, Jr.), from 1976 until his resignation in late August of 1980, when he tired of having teams in the rebuilding stage. He vowed not to manage any club but a contender. The following May, he replaced Jim Fregosi in California. He resigned after the 1982 LCS loss, moved up to become Director of Player Personnel for two years, and returned to the Angels dugout in 1985.

Mauch was known as a sharp tactician who loved the sacrifice bunt and the pinch hitter. His detractors faulted him for overmanaging and for giving more signs than the Coast Guard. He liked to make use of his entire roster. "I want everybody to feel he has a chance to get into a game when he comes to the ballpark," he said. "I play guys when I want to so they'll be ready when I have to. I don't consider myself a motivator of players. I think it's an insult to a ballplayer to have to be motivated."/(NLM)

Al Maul (Smiling Al) — 1865–1958. RHP 1884, 1887–91, 93–1901 Philadelphia (UA), Phillies, Pirates, Pittsburgh (PL), **Washington (NL)**, Baltimore (NL), Dodgers, Giants 1431 ip, 84–78, 4.43. 20 wins: 98

Maul hit his peak with a 20–6 year for the 1898 Baltimore Orioles but was a disappointment for most of his career. When he was sold by Nashville to Philadelphia in 1887, the $2,500 price was reported to be the most ever paid for a minor leaguer up to that time./(BC)

Dick Mauney — 1920–1970. RHP 1945–47 **Phillies** 229 ip, 12–14, 2.99

Mauney joined the Phillies after WWII service and turned in two respectable seasons as an occasional starter before arm problems ended his career in 1947./(FS)

Carmen Mauro — 1926– . OF 1948, 50–51, 53 **Cubs**, Dodgers, Senators, A's 167 g, .231, 2 hr, 33 rbi

Mauro was a high school track star and strong-armed outfielder. His first major league hit was an inside-the-park home run for the 1948 Cubs. He played in the minors until a crushed disc forced him to quit in 1959. /(NLM)

Dal Maxvill — 1939– . SS-2B 1962–75 **Cardinals**, A's, Pirates 1423 g, .217, 6 hr, 252 rbi. *2 LCS, 6 g, .111. 4 WS, 23 g, .115, 2 rbi*
☞ *Gold Glove—68.*

Maxvill, whom sportswriter Bob Broeg called "the thin man" and "silhouette shadow," had great range and a rubber arm. He was the Cardinals' starting shortstop from 1966 until his trade to Oakland in August 1972. He retired with a .973 fielding average at short, then the NL's best career mark. Never a threat at the plate, in 1970 he set major league records for fewest hits (80), doubles (5), and total bases (89) for 150 or more games, and in 1968 he established the World Series mark for futility, going 0-for-22. However, on April 14, 1969, against the Expos, his grand slam was the first ever hit in ML play in Canada. Maxvill was a coach for the A's, Mets, Braves, and Cardinals before being named Cardinal GM in 1985. /(FJO)

Charlie Maxwell (Smokey) — 1927– . OF 1950–52, 54–64 Red Sox, Orioles, **Tigers**, White Sox 1133 g, .264, 148 hr, 532 rbi
☞ *All-Star—56–57.*

Maxwell achieved an odd measure of success as a player who hit especially well on Sundays. And for a five-year stretch (1956–60), he also hit well on most of the other days. Maxwell finished 1956 with 28 HR (fifth in the AL) and set career highs by batting .326 (fourth) and slugging .534 (third). The Tigers had made him a regular that season for the first time in his career; his performance earned him a starting spot on the All-Star team.

Maxwell's batting average slipped in later seasons but he retained his power, with four 20-HR seasons. In 1959 he tied for fourth in the AL with 31 HR and was fifth in RBI with 95. He averaged nearly 72 walks a year in his five seasons as a regular, and as a left fielder led AL outfielders in fielding in 1957 and 1960, showing good range. /(JFC)

Tiny Maxwell [Robert W.] — 1884–1922. *Writer.*

Sports editor of the Philadelphia *Evening Public Ledger* from 1916 until his untimely death in an auto accident at age 38, Maxwell had been a star football lineman at the University of Chicago and Swarthmore. A photo of the battered 250-pound Maxwell leaving the field after the University of Pennsylvania team had concentrated its efforts on him was said to have been influential in bringing reforms to football, including the legalization of the forward pass in 1906. Maxwell played pro football in 1906 with the champion Massillon (Ohio) Tigers, and later became a famous game official. He entered newspaper work in 1906 with the Chicago *American* and moved to Philadelphia six years later. Maxwell was vice-president of the BBWAA. The Maxwell Club, which gives annual awards to the the nation's outstanding football stars, was founded in his honor in 1937. /(NLM)

Carlos May — 1948– . OF-DH-1B 1968–77 **White Sox**, Yankees, Angels 1165 g, .274, 90 hr, 536 rbi. *1 LCS, 3 g, .200. 1 WS, 4 g, .000*
☞ *All-Star—69, 72.*

May was perhaps the only player in baseball history to wear his birth date on the back of his uniform—May 17. In 1969 he was an All-Star and the leading candidate for Rookie of the Year when, on Marine reserve duty at Camp Pendleton in August, a mortar misfired and blew off part of his right thumb. He was hitting .281 at the time, with 18 home runs and 62 RBI. May showed determination through several painful skin graft operations and was named *TSN* Rookie of the Year, but lost the BBWAA vote to Lou Piniella (.282, 11 HR, 68 RBI). He returned in 1970, and while he never posted the numbers his older brother Lee did, Carlos was always a good contact hitter. He reached career highs of .308 in 1972, and 20 HR and 96 RBI in 1973. Occasionally criticized in Chicago for lackadaisical outfield play, he was traded to the Yankees in May 1976, and shared DH duty with Piniella in the '76 LCS and WS. /(RL)

Dave May — 1943– . OF 1967–78 Orioles, **Brewers**, Braves, Rangers, Pirates 1253 g, .251, 96 hr, 422 rbi. *1 LCS, 1 g, .000. 1 WS, 2 g, .000*
☞ *All-Star—73.*

May stagnated on the Orioles' bench in his first three seasons, seeing action as a backup outfielder and an unsuccessful pinch hitter. Acquired by Milwaukee in mid-1970 and made a regular, he had his best season in 1973, with career highs of 25 HR, 93 RBI, 96 runs, and a .303 average. He tied for the league lead in total bases with 295. After a disappointing 1974 season (.226, 10 HR), he was traded to Atlanta with a minor league pitcher in the deal that brought Hank Aaron back to Milwaukee. May had a good year in part-time duty in 1975, hitting 12 HR in just 203 at-bats, but dropped off again in 1976 and was part of the deal that brought 1974 AL MVP Jeff Burroughs from the Rangers. /(WOR)

Jakie May [Frank Spruiell] — 1895–1970. LHP
1917–21, 24–32 Cardinals, **Reds**, Cubs 1562 ip, 72–95,
3.88. *1 WS, 5 ip, 0–1, 11.57*

At the end of his career as an intermittently sore-armed pitcher for second-division clubs, May wound up as a Cubs reliever. His final game came in the 1932 World Series. The Yankees swept the Cubs in four straight, and May was hit hard, taking the loss in Game Four. However, he had the satisfaction of twice striking out Babe Ruth that day, after Ruth had humbled the Cubs with his "called home run" in Game Three. /(JK)

Jerry May — 1943– . C 1964–73 **Pirates**, Royals,
Mets 556 g, .234, 15 hr, 130 rbi

Never much of a hitter, May earned the catching job in Pittsburgh in 1967 with his strong defense. He kept it until July 14, 1969, when he crashed into the dugout in Montreal's Jarry Park. On the way to the hospital, his ambulance was hit by another vehicle, and his right shoulder was injured. Replaced by rookie Manny Sanguillen, May was subsequently sent to Kansas City with shortstop Freddie Patek and pitcher Bruce Dal Canton in a six-player deal following the 1970 season. Often disabled, he struggled against AL pitchers in part-time duty, but fielded .997 in 1971. /(ME)

Lee May — 1943– . 1B-DH 1965–1982 Reds, Astros,
Orioles, Royals 2071 g, .267, 354 hr, 1244 rbi. *2 LCS, 5 g,
.158, 3 rbi. 2 WS, 7 g, .368, 2 hr, 8 rbi*
☛ *Led League—rbi 76. All-Star—69, 71–72.*

One of the most consistent power hitters of his time, the hulking May hit 20-plus HR and 80-plus RBI in 11 seasons, but always seemed about to be replaced by "the future." First, Tony Perez's emergence as an RBI threat prompted the Reds to trade May to the Astros in an eight-player deal in 1971, with Joe Morgan the primary acquisition. After May spent three years in Houston, the emergence of Bob Watson prompted a trade to Baltimore in 1975. After six seasons with the Orioles, Eddie Murray came up to prompt May's final move, to Kansas City in 1981. His expendability may have been caused by his average fielding ability and his tendency to strike out: he fanned 1,570 times in 18 years, high on the all-time list. Ten times he struck out more than 100 times in a season.

May, whose younger brother Carlos came up with the White Sox, reached the majors with the Reds in 1965, but didn't become a regular until 1967. He was an early cog in the Big Red Machine, hitting

Lee May

.290 in 1968, and had his best season in 1969, with 38 HR and a career-high 110 RBI. Brooks Robinson stole the 1970 World Series for the Orioles, but May hit two HR and drove in eight runs in the five-game series. His second homer was a clutch three-run shot in the eighth inning to give the Reds their lone victory, 6–5, and snapped the Orioles' 17-game winning streak. /(SEW)

Milt May — 1950– . C 1970–84 Pirates, Astros, Tigers,
White Sox, **Giants** 1192 g, .263, 77 hr, 443 rbi. *2 LCS, 2 g,
.333, 1 rbi. 1 WS, 2 g, .500, 1 rbi*

Son of Phillies third baseman Pinky May, Milt was signed as an infielder by the Pirates, who made him a catcher. He was a good handler of pitchers and a lefthanded line-drive hitter who rarely swung at a bad pitch, but also was reputedly the slowest runner in the majors for much of his career. At age 21, he drove in Pittsburgh's winning run in Game Four of the 1971 World Series. The Astros gave up Jerry Reuss for May after the 1973 season, making him their everyday catcher. On May 4, 1975, he drove in Bob Watson for ML baseball's one millionth run. Traded to Detroit, he played six games in 1976 before a broken ankle sidelined him for the season. With the 1981 Giants, he batted .310—the highest mark ever for a San Francisco catcher. He was re-acquired by the Pirates late in 1983, and was made a coach for 1987./(AJA)

Pinky May [Merrill] — 1911– . 3B 1939–43 Phillies 665 g, .275, 4 hr, 215 rbi
☛ *All-Star—40.*

The father of major league catcher Milt May, Pinky led NL third basemen in fielding three times in his five ML seasons. In May's first four seasons, the Phillies finished last; in 1943, his final year before the military ended his career, they climbed to seventh./(EW)

Rudy May — 1944– . LHP 1965, 69–83 **Angels,** Yankees, Orioles, Expos 2622 g, 152–156, 3.46. *2 LCS, 11 ip, 0–1, 4.76. 1 WS, 6 ip, 0–0, 2.84*

May spent the most time with the Angels, but it was with contending Yankees and Orioles clubs that his contributions gained the most attention. He had only one winning season with the Angels, 1972, when he was 12–11 with a 2.94 ERA. However, he showed good skills, and the Yankees, looking to start contending again under new owner George Steinbrenner, purchased May in June 1974. May went 8–4 for second-place New York and finished the year with a 3.19 ERA, then went 14–12 in 1975. In June 1976 he was part of a blockbuster 10-player deal that sent him with Tippy Martinez, Scott McGregor, and Rick Dempsey to the Orioles. He went 11–7 the rest of the way and 18–14 in 1977, and was traded with Bryn Smith in the six-player deal that brought Don Stanhouse from the Expos. A slump to 8–10 in 1978 led to a switch to relief in 1979; he went 10–3 with a 2.30 ERA in both roles that year.

May returned to the Yankees as a free agent after that season and had his best year in 1980. Used as a starter and a reliever, he led the league with a 2.47 ERA and went 15–5, second in winning percentage behind Cy Young winner Steve Stone. He took a complete-game, 3–2 loss in Game Two of the LCS against the Royals. May was less effective thereafter./(WOR)

John Mayberry — 1949– . 1B-DH 1968–82 Astros, **Royals,** Blue Jays, Yankees 1620 g, .253, 255 hr, 879 rbi. *2 LCS, 9 g, .200, 2 hr, 6 rbi*
☛ *All-Star—73–74.*

Mayberry was a slugging first baseman who topped 20 HR eight times (30 twice) and 100 RBI three

times, and led the AL in walks in 1973 (122) and 1975 (119). He hit three homers in a game twice (7/1/1975 vs. Rangers, 6/1/1977 vs. Blue Jays) and hit for the cycle on August 5, 1977. *TSN* named him AL all-star first baseman in 1973 and 1975.

Mayberry showed power in four trials with the Astros but never hit higher than .216 for them and was traded to the Royals for 1972. Kansas City made him its regular first baseman, and he responded by hitting a career-high .298 with 25 HR, 100 RBI (second in the AL), and a league-leading 122 walks. A pulled hamstring in July and a broken wrist in August accounted for his mediocre 1974 performance (.234, 22 HR, 69 RBI). His best season came in 1975, when he hit .291 and reached career highs with 34 HR (third in the AL) and 106 RBI (second). He was considered one of the AL's most feared sluggers, and other teams began shifting their defenses to the right to counter his powerful pull hitting. He slumped to .232 with 13 HR in 1976, but did drive in 95 runs as the Royals won their first division title. He homered in the last game of the LCS as the Royals lost to the Yankees.

He hit .230 in 1977, although he did have 23 HR. He also made himself unpopular in Kansas City by sitting out the last game of the LCS with a toothache as the Royals lost to New York again (he homered in Game One). Kansas City then sold the man who stood as the club's career leader in HR and RBI to the year-old Blue Jays. He led Toronto in RBI and HR each of his four seasons there, rebounding to 30 in 1980 and setting since-broken HR and RBI career marks for the young franchise, but he never totally regained his former productivity. Three times he had the Blue Jays' only hit in a game. Traded to the Yankees in May 1982 for two prospects, he slumped abysmally, batting only .209 for his new team, and his career ended.

Mayberry is the Royals' season record holder in walks (122) and double plays by a first baseman (156) and still ranks in their top ten in most career offensive categories. Although the 6'3"220-lb Mayberry was a very slow runner, he was quite agile around the bag and led AL first basemen three times in putouts, twice in fielding, and twice in double plays./(JFC)

Lee Maye — 1934– . OF 1959–71 **Braves,** Astros, Indians, Senators, White Sox 1288 g, .274, 94 hr, 419 rbi

Maye was a solid line-drive hitter throughout his ML career, but found himself stuck in platoon situations for most of his 11 seasons. He started regularly around the Braves outfield early in his career, and in 1964 hit a career-high .304 while leading the NL with 44 doubles, but a trade to Houston in 1965 and then to Cleveland in 1967 relegated him to part-time status. In his spare time, Maye was an accomplished singer, starring in the group Arthur Lee Maye and the Crowns and occasionally singing with The Platters. /(SCL)

Erskine Mayer [James Erskine] — 1891–1957. RHP 1912–19 **Phillies**, Pirates, White Sox 1427 ip, 91–70, 2.96. 20 wins: 14–15 *2 WS, 12 ip, 0–1, 2.19*

Although overshadowed by Grover Alexander, Mayer had two big winning seasons with the wartime Phillies. Thereafter, he was a spot pitcher with a good winning percentage, but half as many innings pitched. He had 14 victories in relief and six saves. /(ADS)

Eddie Mayo [born Edward Joseph Mayoski] — 1910– . 2B-3B 1936–38, 43–48 Giants, Braves, A's, **Tigers** 834 g, .252, 26 hr, 287 rbi. *2 WS, 8 g, .241, 2 rbi*

Mayo failed to hit in major league trials during the 1930s, but later benefited from the WWII player shortage. Returning in 1943 with the Athletics, he led AL third basemen in fielding average. He had never played a ML game at second base until he joined the 1944 Tigers, but he led the position in double plays that year and in fielding the next. Detroit won the 1945 World Series with 35-year-olds at shortstop and second base—Skeeter Webb and Mayo. Mayo hit .285 that year, and he remained with the Tigers well after the younger players returned from the war. /(JK)

Carl Mays (Sub) — 1891–1971. RHP 1915–29 **Red Sox**, Yankees, Reds, Giants 3020 ip, 208–126, 2.92. 20 wins: 17, 18, 20, 21, 24 *4 WS, 57 ip, 3–4, 2.20*
☛ *Led League—w 21.*

Carl Mays had to live with the very sad fact that his fast-rising submarine ball had caused modern major league baseball's first fatality. Pitching for the Yankees on August 16, 1920, decades before the advent of the batting helmet, Mays cracked the skull of Cleveland's Ray Chapman; Chapman, crowding the plate, froze in the path of the pitch. He died the next day. Ty Cobb, in particular, made life as miserable as he could for Mays over the tragedy, but the pitcher learned to live with it. He had remarkable self-confidence, especially under stress.

Mays was occasionally used as a reliever (31–13, 27 saves). He actually pitched mostly in relief as a 1915 Boston rookie, leading the AL with five relief wins and seven saves. He followed his 22–9 (1.74)

record in 1917 with a 21–13 mark in 1918, tying for the league lead in complete games and shutouts. That August 30, he threw two complete-game victories over Philadelphia, allowing only one run. In the 1918 World Series, he went the distance in winning a pair of 2–1 games over the Cubs. But in 1919, disgruntled over what he thought was lack of support from his teammates (he was 5–11), he demanded a trade. Thus began the great parade of Red Sox players to the Yankees.

Mays went 26–11 with a league-best six shutouts for New York in 1920. In 1921, he led the AL in games and innings pitched, victories and winning percentage (27–9, .750), and tied for the lead in saves. He also batted .343. Though he pitched well in the WS, he went 1–2 in the Yankees' loss to the Giants. After going 5–2 in 1923, he was sold to the Reds, for whom he went 20–9 in 1924, and 19–12, with a league-high 24 complete games, in 1926. He finished his ML career as a reliever with the Giants, going 7–2. His lifetime batting average of .268 made him one of the best-hitting pitchers ever. He went on to scout for the Indians, A's, and Braves. /(EC)

Carl Mays

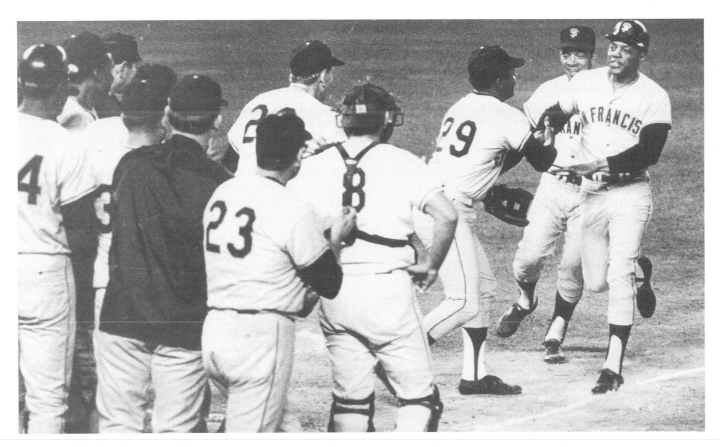

Willie Mays, far right, after his 600th home run

Willie Mays (The Say Hey Kid) — 1931– . OF
1951–52, 54–73 **Giants**, Mets 2992 g, .302, 660 hr,
1903 rbi. *2 LCS, 5 g, .278, 1 hr, 4 rbi. 4 WS, 20 g, .239,
6 rbi*
☛ *Rookie of the Year—51. Most Valuable Player—54,
65. Led League—ba 54. Led League—hr 55, 62, 64–65.
All-Star—54–73. Gold Glove—57–68. Hall of
Fame—1979.*

Considered by many the greatest player of all time,
Mays was the prototype of the complete player; he
hit for average and power, ran the bases with
intelligence and speed, played a spectacular
centerfield, and possessed a great arm. He was also
remarkably durable, playing in at least 150 games
for 13 consecutive seasons.

Mays starred in baseball, basketball, and football
at Birmingham, Alabama's Fairfax Industrial High
School before joining the Birmingham Barons of the
Negro National League at age 17. The New York
Giants purchased his contract in 1950, and he
played for Trenton of the Interstate League, then
joined the Triple-A Minneapolis Millers of the
American Association in 1951. In his 35-game stay
at Minneapolis, he hit a sizzling .477, and the Giants
called him up in late May 1951.

Mays had a discouraging 0-for-12 start with the
struggling Giants. Manager Leo Durocher kept his
spirits up by declaring that despite his poor start,
Mays was and would remain the Giants' full-time
centerfielder that season. His first hit was the first
home run of his ML career, off Warren Spahn. It
helped Mays to end his slump, and he became one
of the sparks that ignited the Giants in their classic,
come-from-behind pennant chase, climaxed by
Bobby Thomson's dramatic ninth-inning playoff
home run that beat Brooklyn for the NL championship. Mays was on deck when Thomson hit it out.
His World Series debut saw him play opposite future
cross-river rival Mickey Mantle, who was also a
rookie. The meeting foreshadowed the debate of
nearly a decade about who among Mays, Mantle,
and Brooklyn's Duke Snider was the greatest New
York centerfielder of the 1950s.

Mays served in the army in 1952 and 1953, and
the Giants finished second and fifth, respectively. He
returned to the Polo Grounds in 1954, leading the
NL with a .345 batting average with 41 homers and
110 RBI to help the Giants to the NL flag. The 1954

World Series is most often remembered for a marvelous outfield play by Mays in the first game. With the score tied late in the game, Indians first baseman Vic Wertz clubbed a long drive to deep centerfield at the Polo Grounds. At the crack of the bat, Mays turned his back to the plate, raced for the outfield wall, glanced up at the last minute, and pulled the ball in over his shoulder. Nearly 430 feet from the plate, he whirled and threw on a line to the infield. The play killed the Indians' threat, and the Giants won the game and swept the Series.

In 1955, his last season under manager Durocher, Mays led the league with 13 triples, 51 home runs, and a .659 slugging average. He won four consecutive stolen-base titles from 1956 through 1959. He stole 338 bases in his career and might have had more had he and the Giants not elected to minimize his chance of injury on the basepaths. His unique 1957 performance of 20 or more doubles, triples, homers, and stolen bases established his claim as one of the game's greatest all-around offensive threats.

Mays had a habit of addressing his fellow players with a high-spirited "say hey" salutation, prompting New York sportswriter Barney Kremenko to call him the Say Hey Kid. An exuberant figure during his earlier days in New York, he became a folk hero by playing stickball with children in Harlem streets bordering the Polo Grounds. He was embraced lovingly by New Yorkers, who were heartbroken when the Giants moved to San Francisco following the 1957 season, but his reception in the Bay Area was lukewarm by comparison, and he was never shown the affection accorded to Orlando Cepeda and Willie McCovey, who debuted there. Some writers ascribed Mays's limited popularity to his New York affiliation. Other writers found Mays to be aloof from the fans as well as the media, and there were rumors that he demanded special treatment from his managers. Nevertheless, he continued to shine. He cracked 49 home runs in 1962 as the Giants tied the Dodgers for first place on the last day of the season and captured the pennant in a three-game playoff before losing the World Series to the Yankees in a seventh-game 1–0 squeaker.

Along with Mantle and Aaron, Mays was the dominant slugger of the 1950s and 1960s. From 1958 through 1966, he produced eight consecutive seasons of over 100 runs and RBI. He collected four home runs in a game in Milwaukee on April 30, 1961, and he hit three homers in a game on two other occasions. He hammered 52 homers in 1965 to join Ruth, Foxx, Kiner, and Mantle as the only players with more than one 50-home run season. He hit 30 or more homers in each of 11 seasons. On May 4, 1966, Mays passed Mel Ott's 19-year-old record of 511 National League home runs and finished his career with a total of 660, ranking him third on the all-time list behind Henry Aaron's 755 and Babe Ruth's 714.

Mays's preeminence as a centerfielder is supported statistically by his career total of 7,095 putouts, the most in major league history. He used his patented basket catch on routine fly balls, and he regularly dumbfounded onlookers by making seemingly impossible plays. After a particularly astonishing display in which Mays raced to his left, speared a fly ball, spun 360 degrees counterclockwise, and threw the ball on a 325-foot line to nail a tagging Dodger baserunner at the plate, Brooklyn manager Charlie Dressen commented, "I won't believe that play until I see him do it again."

In May 1972, the fading Mays was traded to the Mets. With them, he played his final season and made his final World Series appearance on a 1973 team that had finished the year with a record just slightly over .500. The ten-year contract he signed as a goodwill ambassador and part-time coach for the Mets took effect after his retirement as a player. Shortly after Mays's election to the Hall of Fame in 1979, Commissioner Bowie Kuhn issued a controversial order requiring Mays to choose between his employment by the Mets and his job as a greeter for a hotel casino. Mays chose employment by the casino, and he was barred from his baseball duties in October 1979. However, the edict was lifted in 1985 by new commissioner Peter Uberroth. Mays then retained his job as greeter while serving as a part-time hitting coach for the Giants. /(FS/CR)

Bill Mazeroski — 1936– . 2B 1956–72 **Pirates** 2163 g, .260, 138 hr, 853 rbi. *3 LCS, 4 g, .400. 2 WS, 8 g, .308, 2 hr, 5 rbi*
☛ *All-Star—58–60, 62–64, 67. Gold Glove—58, 60–61, 63–67.*

Not only was Mazeroski the greatest second baseman in Pirate history, he was also very likely the best defensive second basemen of all time. Yet he achieved instant fame with one swing of the bat on October 13, 1960. He had already made his mark in that World Series against the Yankees with a two-run homer in the opener. Batting in the bottom of the ninth in the seventh game, he drove Ralph Terry's second pitch over the left field wall at Forbes Field to give Pittsburgh a 10–9 win and its first World Championship since 1925. That dramatic

Bill Mazeroski

fielder that his name peppers the record books. An eight-time Gold Glove winner, he set ML second base records with 1,706 career double plays and 161 double plays in a season (1966, when the Pirates set a NL record with 215 total double plays). He led NL second basemen in double plays a record eight seasons (1960–67); in chances accepted a record eight; and in assists a record nine, including five straight (1960–64) for another NL mark. His 163 games at second base in 1967 set the ML record, and he tied the NL record of five seasons with more than 500 assists. /(ME)

Lee Mazzilli (Maz) — 1955– . OF-1B 1976- **Mets**, Rangers, Yankees, Pirates, Blue Jays 1475 g, .259, 93 hr, 460 rbi. *3 LCS, 11 g, .133. 1 WS, 4 g, .400* ☛ *All-Star—79.*

Brooklyn native Mazzilli was heavily promoted by the star-hungry Mets in the late 1970s, not only as a prospect but also as a sex symbol. The ambidextrous son of pro welterweight boxer Libero Mazzilli was an all-around athlete, winning eight national speed-skating championships. The Mets' first-round draft selection in June 1973, he set what is believed to be a professional record when he stole seven bases in a seven-inning game for Visalia against San Jose on June 8, 1975.

He broke into the majors with a splash in a September 1976 call-up, pinch hitting a three-run homer off the Cubs' Darold Knowles in his second plate appearance and hitting a game-winning two-run off Kent Tekulve with two out in the ninth inning twelve days later to knock the Pirates out of contention. In 1978 he became the first Met to hit home runs from both sides of the plate in one game. But after being compared by the Mets public relations department to the earlier New York centerfield trio of Mays, Mantle, and Snider, Mazzilli was bound to disappoint.

With speed and a good batting eye, Mazzilli might have been an ideal leadoff batter, but the Mets needed him to drive in runs from the middle of the lineup. Surrounded by a weak offense in his first stint in New York, he had more walks than RBI every season. His best season came in 1979, when he had a 19-game hitting streak and hit .303 with 16 HR, 34 doubles, 79 RBI, 78 runs, and 34 steals. He tied a Mets record with five runs scored in a game against the Braves on August 18, and was the hero of the All-Star Game, tying the score in the eighth inning with a two-run pinch homer and then walking with the bases loaded in the ninth to drive in the winning run. Mazzilli was moved to first base in 1980, but the simultaneous arrival of Dave King-

shot helped earn him the Babe Ruth Award as outstanding player in the Series, and *TSN*'s ML Player of the Year Award.

Signed out of an Ohio high school in 1954, the West Virginia native advanced to Pittsburgh in 1956. With shortstop Dick Groat, Mazeroski cemented a rebuilt Pirate infield that formed the base of the 1960 champions. He replaced the departed Groat as team captain, paired with shortstop Dick Schofield in 1963–64, then spent the rest of his career turning double plays with Gene Alley. Leg injuries began to take their toll in 1969; he soon turned over second base to young Dave Cash.

Mazeroski was a fine offensive performer, one of the top home run hitters among NL second basemen despite the spacious dimensions of his home park. He hit as many as 19 HR in 1958. But it is as a man and Mookie Wilson in 1981 forced him back to left field. He hit only .228 while experiencing back and elbow problems.

The Mets traded Mazzilli to Texas for Ron Darling and Walt Terrell just before the start of the 1982 season. He disappointed Texas too, suffering shoulder and wrist injuries and spending six weeks on the disabled list. Texas traded him to the Yankees for Bucky Dent that August, and he was passed on to the Pirates in the off-season. Only a part-time player in Pittsburgh, he led NL pinch hitters in plate appearances (72) in 1985 and hit .286 with an on-base percentage of .437 in that role. When the Pirates released him in 1986, the Mets reacquired him for their pennant drive and he hit .276 for the eventual World Champions. Mazzilli's five pinch-hit at-bats set an LCS record. In the World Series, he led off the eighth inning of Game Six with a pinch single off Cal Schiraldi and scored the tying run, permitting the Mets to win in extra innings. In Game Seven he again started a tying rally with a sixth-inning pinch single off Bruce Hurst.

In 1987 Mazzilli continued his pinch-hit success, tying for the NL lead with 17 pinch hits, but in subsequent years he declined. When he joined the Blue Jays in mid-1989 after being released by New York, he ranked in the top ten in most Mets career offensive categories. /(SH)

Jimmy McAleer — 1864–1931. OF 1889–98, 1901–02, 07 **Cleveland (NL)**, Cleveland (PL), Indians, Browns 1021 g, .255, 15 hr, 469 rbi.
Manager 1901–11 Indians, **Browns**, Senators 736–889, .453

A stylish and graceful outfielder for the old Cleveland Spiders, McAleer came out of retirement to help form the new American League's St. Louis franchise. He successfully raided the Cardinals for players such as Hall of Famers Jesse Burkett and Bobby Wallace and managed the Browns for eight years. He was part owner of the Red Sox in 1912–13. /(ADS)

Sport McAllister [Lewis William] — 1874–1962. OF-C-1B-SS-RHP 1896–99, 1901–03 **Cleveland (NL)**, Tigers, Baltimore (AL) 418 g, .247, 5 hr, 164 rbi; 113 ip, 4–7, 5.32

As versatile as they came, McAllister switch-hit and played every position at least seven times. He was a .300 batter with the Tigers in 1901, the first American League season. /(JK)

Ernie McAnally (Mac) — 1946– . RHP 1971–74 **Expos** 624 ip, 30–49, 4.02

McAnally, who started in the minors as an outfielder, was picked out of the Mets' system by Montreal in the expansion draft. His best season was his first, when he went 11–12 with a 3.89 ERA; he never had a winning season. /(SFS)

Jim McAndrew (Mac, Moms) — 1944– . RHP 1968–74 **Mets**, Padres 771 ip, 37–53, 3.65

McAndrew was called up by the Mets in July 1968 when the Mets were short of pitching for a doubleheader. In the words of reporter Jack Lang, he was a "sacrificial lamb": he opposed the Cardinals' Bob Gibson, that season's Cy Young winner, and lost 2–0. McAndrew then proceeded to set new standards for bad luck, with considerable help from the Mets' weak offense. He lost five of his first seven starts by shutout, including a ML-record four in a row. He had to shut out St. Louis and Steve Carlton, 1–0, to record his first win, but Carlton returned the favor in McAndrew's next start, beating the Mets 2–0. McAndrew finished the year 4–7 with a 2.28 ERA. Despite generally respectable pitching through most of his career, his only winning season came in 1972 (11–8, 2.80), and although he was on the postseason roster in both 1969 and 1973, he wasn't used. /(SH)

Dick McAuliffe — 1939– . 2B-SS-3B 1960–75 **Tigers**, Red Sox 1763 g, .247, 197 hr, 697 rbi. *1 LCS, 5 g, .200, 1 hr, 1 rbi 1 WS, 7 g, .222, 1 hr, 3 rbi* ☛ *All-Star—65–67.*

Known for his wide-open batting stance and Mel Ott-style leg kick, McAuliffe was a rarity in the 1960s, a middle infielder with power, three times topping 20 homers. One of the best leadoff men of his era, he tied a ML record by going the entire 1968 season without grounding into a double play. The Tigers' catalyst in their 1968 World Championship year, leading the AL with 95 runs scored, the gritty McAuliffe was suspended for five days during the stretch drive for charging Chicago's Tommy John during a brushback war. He showed his fortitude again the following season, hitting a pinch homer in his last at-bat before being forced onto the disabled list with a knee injury. He was the AL's starting shortstop in the 1965 and 1966 All-Star games, and was an All-Star second baseman in 1967. He retired among Detroit's all-time top ten in five offensive categories. /(CC)

Al McBean — 1938- . RHP 1961-70 **Pirates**, Padres, Dodgers 1072 ip, 67-50, 3.13

Born in St. Thomas, Virgin Islands, McBean was photographing a Pirates tryout camp in 1957, tried out himself, and earned a ticket to professional baseball. He graduated to the big leagues in 1961 and fashioned Pittsburgh's second-best record (15–10) in 1962. Thin, loose-jointed, and cat-like on the mound, he found even more success as a reliever. He was *TSN* NL Fireman of the Year in 1964, when he had 22 saves and led the league with eight relief wins. Known for his flashy attire and expensive wardrobe, he returned to starting in 1968 and went to the Padres in the expansion draft after the season. /(ME)

Algie McBride — 1869-1956. OF 1896, 98-1901 Cubs, **Reds**, Giants 403 g, .292, 12 hr, 179 rbi

McBride was a good fielder whose best year came with Cincinnati in 1898 when he batted .302 and stole sixteen bases. He was basically a utility player. /(DAS)

Bake McBride [Arnold Ray] — 1949- . OF 1973-83 Cardinals, **Phillies**, Indians 1071 g, .299, 63 hr, 430 rbi. *3 LCS, 12 g, .229, 2 hr, 3 rbi. 1 WS, 6 g, .304, 1 hr, 5 rbi* ☛ *Rookie of the Year—74. All-Star—76.*

McBride hit .300 seven times, including the first five years of his career. He was named Rookie of the Year in 1974 when he hit .309 with 81 runs and 30 steals as the second-place Cardinals' centerfielder. He missed time with injuries the next two seasons (although he was named to the All-Star team in 1976) and was traded to the Phillies in June 1977. Moving from spacious Busch Stadium to Veterans Stadium, he hit a career-high 15 HR while batting .316 and stealing a personal-best 36 bases, and started the winning ninth-inning rally in Game One of the LCS. In 1978 he slumped to .269 but led NL outfielders in fielding, tied a ML record for right fielders with 10 chances in a game (September 8), and pinch hit a game-tying HR in the seventh inning of the Phillies' LCS loss in Game Four. He tied for second in the NL with 12 triples in 1979.

McBride rebounded to .309 (fourth in the NL) in the Phillies' 1980 World Championship season, setting career highs of 87 RBI and 33 doubles. He went on to belt a game-winning three-run HR in the Series opener and singled in the tying run and scored the game winner in the Phillies' eighth-inning rally in their Game Two victory.

After limited time in 1981, McBride was traded

to the Indians and finished with two years of part-time duty. /(WOR)

George McBride (Pinch) — 1880-1973. SS 1901, 05-06, 08-20 Milwaukee (AL), Pirates, Cardinals, **Senators** 1658 g, .218, 7 hr, 447 rbi. *Manager* 1921 **Senators** 80-73, .523

McBride was the American League's premier defensive shortstop of his day. With Washington, he led the league in fielding four straight years (1912–15), in double plays six times between 1908 and 1915, and in putouts three times. Though he didn't hit for a high average, he was known as Pinch for coming through in the clutch. While managing the Senators in 1921, he was hit in the face by a ball in batting practice, paralyzing one side of his face. He suffered a nervous breakdown and retired at the end of the season, but he later coached for Ty Cobb in Detroit. /(JK)

Ken McBride — 1935- . RHP 1959-65 White Sox, **Angels** 808 ip, 40-50, 3.79

McBride looked promising in the expansion Angels' inaugural season, finishing 12–15 with a 3.65 ERA in 1961, and was a regular starter for the club in each of its first four seasons. His best season was 1962, when he was 11–5, 3.50, with four shutouts, despite losing time to a back injury. His career was ended in 1965 by a sore arm. /(JFC)

Tom McBride — 1914- . OF 1943-48 **Red Sox**, Senators 408 g, .275, 2 hr, 141 rbi. *1 WS, 5 g, .167, 1 rbi*

Playing for Boston, McBride tied a major league record with six RBI in an inning on August 4, 1945, and made the first and final outs of the 1946 World Series. With Washington on July 2, 1948 he set the ML record of 12 putouts in left field in an extra-inning game. /(EW)

Bill McCahan — 1921-1986. RHP 1946-49 **A's** 291 ip, 16-14, 3.84

Athletics manager Connie Mack paid this Philadelphia native's way through Duke University. McCahan joined the Athletics after serving as a test pilot during WWII and tossed a 2–0 seven-inning shutout against the Indians in his first major league game. He also played guard for Syracuse in the NBL in 1946–47. McCahan was 10–5 with a 3.32 ERA in 1947 and pitched a 3–0 no-hitter against Washington September 3. It was only the fifth rookie no-hitter in AL history, and the only Senators baserunner reached on an error. His only bad season came when he had a sore arm in 1948. The Athletics had forbidden him to play basketball in the off-season, and he switched to moving oil drums and hurt his arm. /(NLM)

Windy McCall [John William] — 1925– . LHP 1948–50, 54–57 Red Sox, Pirates, **Giants** 253 ip, 11–15, 4.22

McCall failed in his first two ML tries because of poor control, but he gained a reputation for constantly talking. After a good season in the Pacific Coast League, the Giants bought his contract for $65,000 in 1954, and he gave them three seasons of adequate relief pitching. /(BC)

Alex McCarthy — 1888–1978. 2B-SS-3B 1910–17 **Pirates**, Cubs 432 g, .229, 5 hr, 122 rbi

Notre Dame's Alex McCarthy joined South Bend of the Central League in 1910, forcing their shortstop, Max Carey, to the outfield. By the end of the season, both were in Pittsburgh, McCarthy as the backup for shortstop Honus Wagner. His best year was 1912, when he hit .277 as the Pirates' second baseman. /(CG)

Jack McCarthy — 1869–1931. OF 1893–94, 1898–1907 Reds, Pirates, **Cubs**, Indians, Dodgers 1091 g, .287, 7 hr, 474 rbi

McCarthy led the 1901 Cleveland Blues (later the Indians) with a .321 batting average. With the Cubs on April 26, 1905, he became the only NL outfielder ever to start three double plays in a game, throwing out three Pirates at the plate. /(DAS)

Joe McCarthy (Marse Joe) — 1887–1978. Manager 1926–46, 48–50 Cubs, **Yankees**, Red Sox 2126–1335, .614. First place: 29, 32, 36–39, 41–43 *9 WS, 30–13, .698*
☞ *Hall of Fame—1957.*

Joe McCarthy managed in the major leagues for 24 seasons. His winning percentage of .614 is the highest in baseball history. His seven World Championships are a record shared only with another Yankee manager, Casey Stengel. He was elected to the Hall of Fame in 1957.

McCarthy never played in the majors. He grew up in Germantown, Pennsylvania, and broke into pro ball in 1906. He got a taste of managing at Wilkes-Barre, Pennsylvania, in 1913 and a few years later made a name for himself as a manager in Louisville, where he developed outfielder Earle Combs. In 1926 McCarthy was named manager of the Chicago Cubs and he led them to the National League pennant in 1929.

Fired by the Cubs following the 1930 season, McCarthy in 1931 assumed the helm of a Yankee

Joe McCarthy

team that regarded him as a National League interloper; many of the rollicking Yankee veterans thought Babe Ruth should be the manager, a point of view that Ruth himself did not discourage. McCarthy never won Ruth over, but he did win the other players' loyalty and slowly molded his kind of undemonstrative and proficient team.

In 1932 McCarthy became the first manager to capture pennants in both leagues. In the ensuing World Series the Yankees beat the Cubs in four games, a great moment of revenge for their manager. Then came three consecutive second-place finishes—and the unkind tag of Second-Place Joe—before the Yankees' four consecutive World Championships in 1936–39. The late-1930s teams were arguably the most powerful ever, and their manager was a great proponent of power baseball. In 1941 McCarthy won his sixth World Series in six tries as the Yankees' manager, but the following year his streak was broken by the Cardinals. The Yankees won the rematch 1943 Series in five games.

McCarthy's teams were outstanding. They seldom had a difficult pennant race and, by and large, they overwhelmed their World Series foes. They were so good that some believed the batboy could have taken them to pennants, an insinuation that McCarthy hated. His temper flared when it was suggested he had only to push buttons to win. Many experts consider McCarthy the greatest manager of all time. He was a great double-play teacher, but his real strengths lay in his mental alertness. He seldom made the same mistake twice, missed little on the field, and had an amazing memory for minute details. Joe DiMaggio said, "Never a day went by when you didn't learn something from McCarthy."

McCarthy's players respected him, most liked him, and some were devoted to him. But he was perceived by the public as dull. Take away the fat little cigars and the long-sleeved uniforms and you were left with air. Squatty, square-jawed, tenacious—there was a sour side to this spike-fisted disciplinarian. Yet his heart almost broke when Lou Gehrig became fatally ill.

The war years were tough on McCarthy, and when Larry MacPhail became his boss in 1945, he didn't have the same rapport he had enjoyed with Ed Barrow. On May 24, 1946, McCarthy resigned. He became the Red Sox' manager in 1948 and came within a hair of winning a pennant that year and again in 1949, before retiring for good early in the 1950 season. McCarthy died January 13, 1978 at the age of 90. /(MG)

Johnny McCarthy — 1910–1973. 1B 1934–41, 43, 46, 48 Dodgers, **Giants**, Braves 542 g, .277, 25 hr, 209 rbi. *1 WS, 5 g, .211, 1 rbi*

Before he signed, the lefthanded McCarthy hoped to pitch in pro ball. He took over first base for the Giants in 1937 when manager Bill Terry retired as a player. In 1940, and again with the Giants in 1948, McCarthy led the league in pinch hits and pinch at-bats. /(EW)

Tommy McCarthy — 1863–1922. OF 1884–96 Boston (UA), **Braves**, Phillies, St. Louis (AA), Dodgers 1275 g, .292, 44 hr, 666 rbi.
Manager 1890 **St. Louis (AA)** 13–13, .500
☛ *Hall of Fame—1946.*

McCarthy's statistics are unimpressive for a Hall of Famer, but his creative innovations left an indelible mark on the game. He hit .300 only four times in 13 seasons and had a lifetime fielding percentage of .897, and was at his best from 1892 to 1895 when he and Hugh Duffy were "the Heavenly Twins" in the Boston outfield. McCarthy had played for manager Frank Selee's Oshkosh champions in the North Western League in 1887, and after four years in the American Association was reunited with Selee in Boston. Selee encouraged innovative baseball, and McCarthy is credited with perfecting, if not inventing, the hit-and-run; runner-to-batter signals; and an outfield trap, designed to freeze forced baserunners, where if the runner stayed on base McCarthy would trap the ball and get at least a forceout and possibly a double play. After retiring as a player, McCarthy scouted, coached several colleges, and ran a bowling alley and saloon with Duffy. The Veterans Committee elected him to the Hall of Fame in 1946. /(ADS)

Tommy McCarthy as a Dodger coach

Lew McCarty — 1888–1930. C 1913–21 Dodgers, **Giants**, Cardinals 532 g, .266, 5 hr, 137 rbi. *1 WS, 3 g, .400, 1 rbi*

McCarty, an adequate receiver and above-average hitter, was never more than a platooned catcher in nine ML seasons. He was traded from the Dodgers to the Giants for Fred Merkle in August 1916 and hit .339 for the year. /(FS)

Tim McCarver (Buckethead) — 1941– . C-1B 1959–80 **Cardinals**, Phillies, Expos, Red Sox 1909 g, .271, 97 hr, 645 rbi. *3 LCS, 7 g, .071, 1 rbi. 3 WS, 21 g, .311, 2 hr, 11 rbi*
☞ *All-Star—66–67.*

McCarver appeared in eight games with the Cardinals in 1959 at the age of 17 and in six games with the Phillies in 1980 to become a four-decade player. In the intervening years, McCarver established himself as one of the top defensive catchers of the 1960s and 1970s. He became the Cardinals' regular catcher in 1963 and was a key component in the emergence of pitching star Bob Gibson with whom he helped the 1964 Cardinals to the team's first World Series since 1946. McCarver won Game Five with a three-run homer in the top of the tenth inning to give the Cardinals a 3–2 lead in the Series. He was the Series' leading hitter with a .478 average on 11 hits. McCarver's 13 triples in 1966 made him the only catcher to lead a league in that category, and he went on to have his best season in 1967. Although he faded after leading the NL with a .355 average at mid-season, he finished with career highs in average (.295), homers (14), and RBI (69). The Cardinals won the World Series, and McCarver placed second in the MVP balloting to teammate Orlando Cepeda.

McCarver hit only 12 homers in the next two seasons and was traded, at the end of 1969, with would-be free agent Curt Flood to the Phillies for Dick Allen in a seven-player swap. He spent over two years with the Phillies before a series of trades sent him to the Expos, back to the Cardinals, and on to the Red Sox. During his travels, McCarver caught two no-hitters: the gem thrown by the Phillies' Rick Wise against the Reds on June 23, 1971 in which Wise hit two homers, and the no-hitter that Bill Stoneman of the Expos pitched against the Mets on October 2, 1972, the last day of the season.

In spring training of 1965, the stubborn Mc-Carver got into an argument with the equally stubborn rookie Steve Carlton over pitch selection. The two went on to make Cardinals history as batterymates. In mid-1975, at the behest of Carlton,

Tim McCarver

McCarver was reacquired by the Phillies. He spent the rest of his career with them as Carlton's personal catcher. McCarver's quip that when he and Carlton die, they'll be buried 60 feet six inches apart is indicative of the folksy, talkative style that characterized him as a Mets broadcaster. /(SEW/CR)

Kirk McCaskill — 1961– . RHP 1985- **Angels** 869 ip, 56–44, 3.90. *1 LCS, 9 ip, 0–2, 7.71*

An All-American in ice hockey at the University of Vermont, McCaskill was runner-up for the Hobey Baker award (college hockey's player of the year) in 1981 and played professional hockey for the Sherbrooke Jets (American Hockey League) in 1983–84. He began to concentrate on baseball full-time in the summer of 1984 and was promoted to the Angels in 1985, finishing 12–12 in his rookie season. McCaskill blossomed in 1986, with a 17–10 record, 202 strikeouts, and a 3.36 ERA for the AL West champion Angels, but he lost Games Two and Six to the Red Sox in the LCS. He missed most of 1987 after surgery to remove bone chips from his pitching elbow and was only 8–6 in 1988, but in 1989

McCaskill reestablished himself as one of the AL's top pitchers as the resurgent staff of the Angels carried them to contention. /(SCL)

Steve McCatty (Cat) — 1954– . RHP 1977–85 **A's** 1189 ip, 63–63, 3.99. *1 LCS, 3 ip, 0–1, 13.50*
☛ *Led League—w 81. Led League—era 81.*

McCatty was one of the five Oakland starters whose burnout was blamed by some on overuse by manager Billy Martin. The five threw 93 of the A's modern-day-record 94 complete games in 1980, though McCatty had just 11. In strike-shortened 1981, when Oakland won the AL West title, the 6'3" power pitcher had a league-best 2.32 ERA and tied for the AL lead with 14 wins and 4 shutouts. He finished second to Rollie Fingers in Cy Young voting. He had a complete-game victory in the divisional playoff series against the Royals.

Of McCatty's 22 games, 16 were complete. His arm miseries began in 1982. He lost his fastball, wasn't very effective as a finesse pitcher, and in 1985 suffered through a final, 4–4, 5.57 season. /(JCA)

Joe McClain — 1933– . RHP 1961–62 **Senators** 236 ip, 8–22, 4.42

McClain was a regular starter for the 1961 expansion Washington Senators, the team that replaced the former Senators who'd moved to Minnesota. His 3.86 ERA was better than his 8–18 record. /(BC)

Dan McClellan — Unk.–Unk. RHP Negro Leagues 1903–30 Cuban X-Giants, **Philadelphia Giants, Smart Set, New York Lincoln Giants, Quaker Giants** statistics not available

McClellan is credited with pitching the first perfect game in black baseball history. He did so in 1903 with the Cuban X-Giants, the most successful black team of the time. Generally considered one of the best black pitchers prior to the establishment of the Negro National League in the 1920s, he later became a highly successful manager. No statistical data are available on his playing career. /(BP)

Harvey McClellan (Little Mac) — 1894–1925. SS-3B-2B-OF 1919–24 **White Sox** 344 g, .221, 4 hr, 98 rbi

Little Mac was one of the most popular White Sox of his era. He debuted the day after the Black Sox clinched the 1919 pennant and was a smooth glove man who never hit well. During the summer of 1924, he underwent two painful gallstone operations that forced his retirement. He died a year later. /(RL)

Lloyd McClendon — 1959– . C-OF-1B 1987– **Reds,** Cubs 209 g, .254, 17 hr, 67 rbi. *1 LCS, 3 g, .667*

McClendon spent his first two seasons as a backup to Bo Diaz on the Reds. He was part of the package that brought Tom Seaver back to the Mets after the 1982 season. McClendon was a major factor in the 1989 Cubs' surprising NL East title, hitting .300 with nine HR in his first three months with the club and filling in at first base, third base, catcher, and in the outfield. /(SFS)

John McCloskey (Honest John) — 1862–1940. *Manager* 1895–96, 1906–08 Louisville (NL), **Cardinals** 197–434, .312

McCloskey was a catcher in the semi-pro Texas League who helped organize the professional Texas League in 1888. It was the first of five minor leagues he founded. He spent 36 seasons managing 30 different clubs, and, including his time as a player and umpire, he logged 44 years in organized ball. /(MC)

Bob McClure — 1952– . LHP 1975–88 Royals, **Brewers**, Expos, Mets 1007 ip, 56–52, 3.88. *1 LCS, 2 ip, 1–0, 0.00. 1 WS, 4 ip, 0–2, 4.15*

Primarily a reliever, McClure made his ML debut with the Royals in 1975 and was traded to Milwaukee in the spring of 1977 as the player-to-be-named-later in a deal that sent Jim Colborn and Darrell Porter to Kansas City. McClure pitched well in the Brewers' bullpen from 1977 to 1980, leading the club in saves twice, then spent almost all of 1981 on the DL with arm problems. In 1982 McClure was moved to the starting rotation and went 12–7 for the AL champion Brewers, but with Rollie Fingers unavailable for the postseason, McClure returned to the bullpen and saved Games Four and Five of the WS, but lost Games Two and Seven. McClure started again in 1983–84 before returning to the bullpen for good in 1985, and in 1986 he was sold to the Expos, who released him in July 1988. McClure signed with the Mets two weeks later, where he was reunited with former Little League and high school teammate Keith Hernandez and pitched occasionally for the NL East champions before being released once again following the season. He is second on the Brewers all-time games pitched list. /(SCL)

Amby McConnell [Ambrose Moses] — 1883–1942. 2B 1908–11 **Red Sox**, White Sox 409 g, .264, 3 hr, 119 rbi

McConnell contributed 26 of the 1909 Red Sox' club-record 215 stolen bases and was one reason they were called The Speed Boys. He later managed in the minors and owned a club in the Canadian-American League. /(EW)

George McConnell — 1877–1964. RHP-1B 1909, 12–16 **Yankees**, Cubs, Chicago (FL) 842 ip, 41–51, 2.60; 196 g, .229, 1 hr, 33 rbi
☛ *Led League—w 15.*

McConnell started out as a first baseman, but became a spitballing pitcher. He won 30 games for Rochester (International League) in 1911, then had little success with the Highlanders. He topped the Federal League with 25 wins and a .714 winning percentage in 1915, but returned to mediocrity with the Cubs. /(NLM)

Billy McCool — 1944– . LHP 1964–70 **Reds**, Padres, Cardinals 529 ip, 32–42, 3.59

McCool's 21 saves in 1965 and 18 in 1966 out of the Reds' bullpen tied him for the second-best NL total both years, although his eight relief losses in '65 led the league. In 1967 Ted Abernathy won the stopper role from him, and in 1968 McCool suffered a wrist injury. /(SFS)

Barry McCormick [William] — 1874–1956. 3B-2B-SS 1895–1904 Louisville (NL), **Cubs**, Browns, Senators 989 g, .238, 16 hr, 418 rbi

McCormick was a jack-of-all-trades infielder who appeared in over 100 games for eight straight seasons. On June 29, 1897, he went 6-for-8, including a triple and a home run, and scored five times as Chicago humiliated Louisville, 36–7. The 36 runs remain the most ever scored in a game by a major league team. /(ARA)

Bill McCormick — Unk.–Unk. *Umpire* FL, AL, **NL** 1914–15, 17, 19–29 *2 WS*

In 1925 McCormick took part in one of the most unusual innings in World Series history. In the top of the eighth of Game Three, the Pirates Earl Smith hit a long drive which Senators outfielder Sam Rice seemed to catch while falling into the bleachers. McCormick huddled with fellow umps Brick Owens, George Moriarty, and Cy Rigler to review the play before it was ruled a catch. Then in the bottom of the inning, the Senators inadvertently batted out of order, but the Pirates didn't notice. In the absence of an appeal and in accordance with the rules, McCormick and the other umpires remained mute. /(RTM)

Frank McCormick (Buck) — 1911–1982. 1B 1934, 37–48 **Reds**, Phillies, Braves 1534 g, .299, 128 hr, 954 rbi. *3 WS, 14 g, .271, 1 rbi*
☛ *Most Valuable Player—40. Led League—rbi 39. All-Star—38–44.*

A native New Yorker, 6'4″ Frank McCormick went to a tryout at the Polo Grounds, but was turned down because at the time the Giants were disinclined to use righthanded first basemen. He instead went on to be a seven-time All-Star for Cincinnati. In 1938 he became only the eighth ML player to have more than 200 hits in his first full season. His 128 RBI in 1939 led the league. He was voted the NL's MVP in 1940 when he topped the circuit in hits for a third consecutive season, led in doubles and at-bats, drove in 127 runs, and led Cincinnati to its first World Championship in 21 years. Deferred from military service due to a disc problem, he averaged 149 games a season between 1938 and 1945. He set a NL first basemen's record by playing in 652 consecutive games, from April 1938 until May 1942.

McCormick was a dedicated first-ball hitter. "I learned early that pitchers tried to sneak a good one by you to get ahead in the count. I didn't let it go by." He didn't try to outguess the pitcher, and therefore was rarely fooled; he struck out only once in every 30 at-bats. He was sold in December of 1945 to the Phillies; when they released him during 1947, he was picked up by the Braves, and led the NL with 13 pinch hits. His final ML appearance came in the 1948 World Series. He returned to the Reds as a minor league manager, ML scout, coach, and broadcaster. /(NLM)

Jim McCormick — 1856–1918. RHP-OF 1878–87 Indianapolis (NL), Cleveland (NL), Cincinnati (UA), Providence (NL), Cubs, Pirates 4276 ip, 264–214, 2.43; 534 g, .236, 4 hr, 139 rbi. 20 wins: 1879–86
    Manager 1879–80 **Cleveland (NL)** 74–92, .446
☛ *Led League—w 1880, 82. Led League—era 1883, 84.*

McCormick was a burly, Scottish-born, underhand pitcher during baseball's pioneering era, when most teams carried only two or three pitchers. As a 23-year-old playing manager in 1879, he recorded a National League-high 40 wins, starting 60 of Cleveland's 82 games. The following year, he led the league with 45 wins, working 657 innings. He then relinquished his managing job to concentrate on pitching. In 1882, as he had in 1880, he recorded league highs in wins (36), appearances, starts, innings pitched, hits allowed, and—for the third consecutive season—complete games. His 466 career complete games put him among the all-time leaders.

In 1883 and 1884, McCormick led the NL in ERA (1.84 and 2.37) and winning percentage (.675 and .615). His 40–25 mark in '84 included ten shutouts, and was bolstered by a 21–3 record in the short-lived Union Association. His final winning campaign came with Chicago in 1886, when he won 16 straight to finish 31–11. McCormick's teams were shut out in 43 of his 214 career losses. In 1880 he was on the losing end of ten shutouts, including a 1–0 loss to Worcester's Lee Richmond, who threw a perfect game. /(JK)

Mike McCormick [Myron Winthrop] — 1917–1976. OF 1940–43, 46–51 **Reds**, Braves, Dodgers, Giants, White Sox, Senators 748 g, .275, 14 hr, 215 rbi. *3 WS, 14 g, .288, 4 rbi*

McCormick helped the Reds to a pennant by batting .300 as a rookie in 1940 and set a World Series record with 24 outfield assists in seven games. He lost almost three seasons to naval duty, but he was with the Braves for their 1948 championship season, and he made another WS appearance for the 1949 Dodgers. He twice broke his leg sliding. /(JK)

Mike McCormick — 1938– . LHP 1956–71 **Giants**, Orioles, Senators, Yankees, Royals 2381 ip, 134–128, 3.73. 20 wins: 67

☛ *Led League—era 60. Led League—w 67. Cy Young Award—67. All-Star—60–61.*

In 1956 every major league club was after this overpowering 17-year-old who had posted a 49–4 American Legion record, including four no-hitters and a 26-strikeout performance. The Giants signed McCormick for a reported $60,000 bonus and, under the rules of the time, had to bring him right to New York. Scared and wild, he lasted just three innings in his first start. In 1957, pitching mostly in relief, he became the youngest modern NL pitcher (18) to record three wins.

As McCormick matured, he gained greater success. On June 12, 1959, he threw a five-inning no-hitter against Philadelphia. He was the NL ERA leader in 1960 (2.70) when he went 15–12. But he dropped to 13–16 in 1961 when he allowed a league-high 33 home runs. He was plagued by arm trouble through 1962, and the hot-tempered pitcher was traded to Baltimore.

McCormick was returned to the minors before rebounding with the 1965 Senators. He recorded marks of 8–8 and 11–14 and was reacquired by the Giants in December 1966. He had lost his blazing fastball, but had mastered his breaking pitches and developed a screwball. In 1967 he went 22–10 (2.85), leading the NL in wins, and won the Cy Young and Comeback Player of the Year awards. Over the next two-plus seasons, he went 26–27 for San Francisco. He finished up in the Pacific Coast League. /(NLM)

Moose McCormick [Harry Elwood] — 1881–1962. OF 1904, 08–09, 12–13 **Giants**, Pirates, Phillies 418 g, .285, 6 hr, 133 rbi. *2 WS, 7 g, .333, 1 rbi*

McCormick was one of the game's first and best pinch-hit specialists. He batted .301 (28-for-93) off the bench and led the NL with 11 hits in 30 pinch at-bats for the Giants in 1912.

McCormick was the runner on third base whose run didn't count because of Fred Merkle's famous "Bonehead Play" (September 23, 1908, Giants versus Cubs). He left baseball several times to work as an engineer in the steel industry and coached at Bucknell (his alma mater) and at the U.S. Military Academy. Called "Moose" for his eight-foot stride, as an old-timer McCormick would ink-stamp a little moosehead under his autograph. /(JK)

Barney McCosky — 1918– . OF 1939–42, 46–48, 50–53 **Tigers**, A's, Reds, Indians 1170 g, .312, 24 hr, 397 rbi. *1 WS, 7 g, .304, 1 rbi*

McCosky hit .300 in six of his first seven seasons and was an integral part of the Tigers' drive to the 1940 AL pennant. The league's finest leadoff hitter in his first two seasons, he hit .311 with 120 runs (fourth in the AL), 14 triples (second), and 20 steals (fourth, and caught only four times) in his 1939 rookie season and led AL outfielders in putouts. In his career season in 1940, he reached career highs with a .340 batting average (sixth in the AL), 123 runs (third), 19 triples (first), 200 hits (tied for first), and 39 doubles. In the World Series, he hit .304 and scored five runs as Detroit lost to the Reds in seven games. He declined to .324 and .293 in the next two seasons, and then lost three years in the military (1943–45). When he returned in 1946, he hit just .198 for the Tigers, who traded him to the Athletics that May for George Kell. He rebounded, hitting .354 the rest of the way, and had two more .300 seasons (95 runs in 1948). But he lost all of 1949 to a back injury and was never the same afterwards. /(WOR)

Willie McCovey (Stretch) — 1938– . 1B-OF 1959–80
Giants, Padres, A's 2588 g, .270, 521 hr, 1555 rbi. *1 LCS,
4 g, .429, 2 hr, 6 rbi. 1 WS, 4 g, .200, 1 hr, 1 rbi*
☛ *Rookie of the Year—59. Most Valuable Player—69.
Led League—hr 63, 68–69. Led League—rbi 68–69. Hall
of Fame—1986.*

On October 16, 1962 at Candlestick Park, McCovey
came within inches of being a World Series hero.
The Giants trailed the perennially powerful Yankees
1–0 with runners at second and third and two out in
the bottom of the ninth inning of the seventh game.
McCovey hit a line drive toward right field that
second baseman Bobby Richardson speared to end
the Series. The play has been discussed by fans ever
since. It even became a running element of Charles
Schulz's "Peanuts" comic strip, a moment in life
that Charlie Brown could relate to with complete
empathy.

   After belting 29 homers in three months in the
Pacific Coast League in 1959, McCovey joined the
Giants in the middle of the season and debuted by
going 4-for-4 with two singles and two triples against
Robin Roberts. He hit .354 that year and, despite
playing in only 52 games, won NL Rookie of the
Year honors. McCovey slumped badly in 1960 and
spent time in the minor leagues at Tacoma. The stay
was a short one, for the Giants, headed toward a
fifth-place finish, sorely needed his bat in their
lineup. McCovey was a first baseman by trade, but
he spent three seasons in the early 1960s primarily
in the outfield in deference to smoother-fielding
Orlando Cepeda. When Cepeda was felled by a knee
injury in 1965, first base became McCovey's.

   Since he was a soft-spoken man playing on a star-
studded Giants team, McCovey's talents were not as
often heralded by the media and fans as those of
teammates Mays, Cepeda, and Marichal. However,
his opponents respected the devastating dead-pull
power that was his majestic personal trademark and
made him one of the most feared home run hitters
of his time. McCovey first led the NL in homers in
1963, with 44, and won the title again in 1968, with
36, and in 1969, with 45. For four consecutive
seasons, 1967–1970, he led the NL in home run
percentage. In 1970 the slugger homered in all
twelve parks, one of the few players ever to accomplish that feat. Toward the end of his career, on June
27, 1977, McCovey hit a grand slam and a solo
home run in the same inning against the NL
champion Cincinnati Reds, becoming the only
player in history to hit two home runs in one inning
twice; his first such effort came on April 12, 1973.

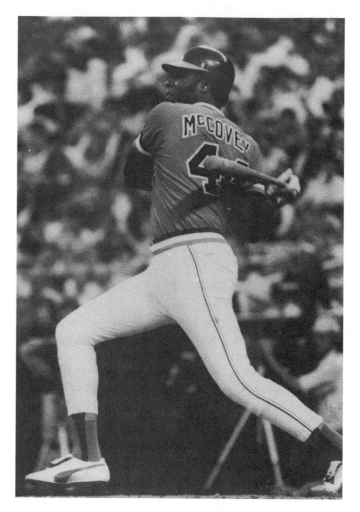

Willie McCovey

   McCovey had his banner year in 1969 and won
the MVP award. In addition to leading the NL with
45 homers, 126 RBI, and a .656 slugging percentage, he drew a record 45 intentional walks and
finished fifth with a .320 batting average. His 9.2
home run percentage that year is one of the highest
ever. McCovey's appearance in the 1969 All-Star
Game was his third of six, and he paced the NL to a
9–3 victory with two home runs. McCovey was an
integral part of an ever-changing Giants team that
contended for a decade, reaching the World Series in
1962 and the NL playoffs in 1971. Giants owners
devastated Bay Area fans by sending McCovey, their
favorite player, to the upstart San Diego Padres
prior to the 1974 season. Tagged Big Mac in
deference to Padres and McDonald's owner Ray
Kroc, McCovey had two good seasons and one poor
one before the Padres sold him to the Oakland

Athletics, the Giants' cross-bay competition. He played in only 11 games for the A's, who released him at the end of the season. McCovey was invited by new Giants ownership to San Francisco's spring training camp in 1977, and he responded with a 28-homer, 86-RBI comeback at the age of 39.

The final hurrah of McCovey's career came in 1980 when he hit his only home run of the season and the 512th and final one of his career, which then tied him with Eddie Mathews for tenth place all-time in home runs. Having played during four decades, he retired during the season and joined the Giants' public- and community-relations staff. McCovey was inducted into the Hall of Fame in 1986. /(AA/CR)

Benny McCoy — 1915– . 2B 1938–41 Tigers, **A's** 337 g, .269, 16 hr, 156 rbi

McCoy was the prize among 91 Detroit farmhands set free by Commissioner Landis in 1939. He had just been sent to the Philadelphia A's in a trade for star outfielder Wally Moses, angering Detroit fans who believed McCoy, a Michigan native, belonged on their team. With the deal canceled, ten teams bid for McCoy. Connie Mack paid him an announced $45,000 bonus to sign with the A's and gave him a two-year contract at $10,000 a season. McCoy played in 1940 and 1941, spent the next four years in the Navy, and his baseball career ended. /(JK)

Larry McCoy — 1941– . *Umpire* AL 1970–87 *2 ASU 4 LCS 1 WS*

McCoy was an occasional prankster. For example, on Easter Sunday, 1987, in Milwaukee, Brewers catcher B.J. Surhoff stuck his mitt behind his back to get a new ball, only to discover the ump had popped an egg into it. /(RTM)

Les McCrabb (Buster) — 1914– . RHP 1939–42, 50 **A's** 210 ip, 10–15, 5.96

In McCrabb's only full ML season, he went 9–13 (5.49) for the last-place 1941 A's. He returned in 1950 after an eight-year absence from the majors, but allowed four earned runs in just 1–1/3 innings. /(FK)

Tom McCraw — 1941– . 1B-OF 1963–75 **White Sox**, Senators, Indians, Angels 1468 g, .246, 75 hr, 404 rbi

McCraw was a journeyman hitter with speed who won the 1962 American Association batting crown (.326). He joined the White Sox in June 1963 when first baseman Joe Cunningham broke his collarbone. Much heralded as a rookie, McCraw struggled at the plate for most of his eight seasons with Chicago, only once topping the .260 mark. On May 24, 1967, he hit three home runs in one game at Minnesota, and almost had a fourth when he sent a Jim Kaat fastball to the warning track. He tied a ML first base record by committing three errors in one inning on May 3, 1968, but that year he led AL first basemen in assists, double plays, total chances per game, and errors. Ted Williams taught him to hit the ball with more authority as his manager with the 1971 Senators, and McCraw used his training as a batting coach for the Indians and Giants. /(RL)

Tom McCreery — 1874–1941. OF-1B 1895–1903 Louisville (NL), Giants, Pirates, **Dodgers**, Braves 799 g, .290, 26 hr, 387 rbi

McCreery was an unsuccessful pitcher who became a switch-hitting outfielder with decent power. His first full season was his best. Only 21, he hit .351 for 12th-place Louisville, slugged .546, and tied for the league lead with 21 triples. On July 12, 1897, he hit three home runs in one game. /(ADS)

Lance McCullers — 1964– . RHP 1985– **Padres**, Yankees 477 ip, 25–31, 3.25

A starter in the minors, the hard-throwing McCullers was the Padres' Rookie of the Year in 1985 when, filling in for an ailing Goose Gossage, he recorded saves in his first three ML appearances and compiled a 2.31 ERA in 23 games. In 1987 he was San Diego's stopper (8–10, 3.72, 16 saves) and led NL relievers in innings pitched (123.1). But he faltered in 1988 and, with the emergence of Mark Davis, became expendable. He went to the Yankees in a trade for Jack Clark after the season. /(JCA)

Clyde McCullough — 1917–1982. C 1940–43, 46–56 **Cubs**, Pirates 1098 g, .252, 52 hr, 339 rbi. *1 WS, 1 g, .000*
☛ *All-Star—48.*

Though he was platooned for much of his career, the rugged, strong-armed McCullough was considered a top defensive catcher, and is reputed to have been the last catcher to play without a chest protector. Though he had only five home runs in 1942, he hit three in a row on July 26, all solo shots, as his Cubs lost to the Phillies 4–3. Following two years in the Navy, he returned to the Cubs just in time to pinch hit in the final game of the 1945 World Series, one of only two players ever to appear in a WS game without a regular-season appearance. After batting .209 in 1948, he was swapped to the Pirates, where he hit .297 in 1951 for a career high. Returned to the Cubs two years later, he caught Sam Jones's no-hitter against the Pirates on May 12, 1955. It was the first no-hitter by a black pitcher, and the first in Wrigley Field in 38 years. McCullough coached one season each for the Senators, Twins, Mets, and Padres, and managed and instructed in the Mets' farm system. /(ARA)

Harry McCurdy — 1900–1972. C 1922–23, 26–28, 30–34 Cardinals, White Sox, **Phillies**, Reds 543 g, .282, 9 hr, 148 rbi

McCurdy was a slow-footed backup catcher and a respected lefthanded batter. A frequent pinch hitter, he led the NL with 15 pinch hits in 52 at-bats for the 1933 Phillies. /(JK)

Lindy McDaniel — 1935– . RHP 1955–75 **Cardinals**, Cubs, Giants, Yankees, Royals 2140 ip, 141–119, 3.45 ☛ All-Star—60.

Tall, lanky, and durable, McDaniel pitched mostly in relief for 21 ML seasons and retired with 987 appearances, second only to Hoyt Wilhelm in ML history. A righthander with splendid control, McDaniel was rarely overpowering and recorded 20 or more saves in a season only three times, but his quiet consistency was welcome in any bullpen. Off the field McDaniel was deeply religious (he was an ordained minister in the Church of Christ) and in great demand as an off-season speaker, but he avoided preaching to his teammates directly, instead confining his thoughts to a monthly newsletter, "Pitching for The Master."

McDaniel bypassed the minor leagues completely after signing with the Cardinals in 1955, and in 1957 he was 15–9, 3.49 as a 21-year-old starter. His ERA swelled to a career-worst 5.80 in 1958, however, and he was demoted briefly to the American Association, and in 1959 he became a reliever almost exclusively and led the NL with 15 saves while also winning 13 games in relief. McDaniel led the NL in saves again the following year with 26, and after an October, 1962 trade sent him to the Cubs he led the NL in saves for the third time in five seasons, posting 22 in 1963. He pitched for the Cubs and Giants from 1963 to 1967, but was no longer used to finish games as frequently, and in mid-season 1968 he was traded to the Yankees for Bill Monbouquette. McDaniel enjoyed a resurgence with the Yankees in 1970, finishing second in the AL with 29 saves while posting a career-best 2.01 ERA, but by 1974 he had been traded a final time, to the Royals for Lou Piniella and pitcher Ken Wright. When he

retired, McDaniel's 172 career saves placed him fourth all-time, but he has since fallen out of the top ten. /(SCL)

Von McDaniel — 1939– . RHP 1957–58 **Cardinals** 89 ip, 7–5, 3.45

The younger brother and teammate of Lindy McDaniel, Von was an 18-year-old phenom in 1957. He shut out the Dodgers 2–0 in his first ML start June 26, allowing only two infield hits, and one-hit the Pirates July 28. A sore shoulder ended his career the following year. /(FK)

Mickey McDermott [Maurice Joseph] — 1928– . LHP 1948–58, 61 **Red Sox**, Senators, Yankees, A's, Tigers, Cardinals 1317 ip, 69–69, 3.91. *1 WS, 3 ip, 0–0, 3.00*

McDermott threw an Eastern League no-hitter for Scranton as a 17-year-old on July 14, 1946, and first joined the Red Sox at 19. The strikeout pitcher had not had a losing year and was coming off an 18–10 season when he was sent to Washington in a December 1953 trade for outfielder Jackie Jensen—much to the dismay of Boston's many Irish fans, with whom the colorful McDermott had become a favorite. He liked to sing, and had done so in Boston nightclubs and with Eddie Fisher at Grossinger's in the Catskills. McDermott tailed off after the trade, while Jensen became a star. A lifetime .252 batter who had 127 pinch-hit at-bats, McDermott had nine career home runs—four with the 1957 A's, for whom he played two games at first base. /(JK)

Danny McDevitt — 1932– . LHP 1957–62 **Dodgers**, Yankees, Twins, A's 456 ip, 21–27, 4.40

On September 24, 1957, rookie McDevitt, a native New Yorker, shut out the Pirates in the Dodgers' last game at Brooklyn's Ebbets Field. He won 10 games for Los Angeles' 1959 NL champions. /(FK)

Jim McDonald (Hot Rod) — 1927– . RHP 1950–58 Red Sox, Browns, **Yankees**, Orioles, White Sox 468 ip, 24–27, 4.27. *1 WS, 8 ip, 1–0, 5.87*

Spot-starting and working in long relief, McDonald contributed to Yankee pennants in 1952 and 1953. He yielded six runs in Game Five of the 1953 World Series, but won 11–7, thanks to Mickey Mantle's grand slam plus homers by Billy Martin, Gene Woodling, and Gil McDougald. /(MC)

Tex McDonald [Charles C., born Charles C. Crabtree] — 1891–1943. OF-SS-2B-3B 1912–15 Reds, Braves, Pittsburgh (FL), **Buffalo (FL)** 357 g, .298, 13 hr, 135 rbi

McDonald earned $2,100 while hitting .359 in 62 games for the 1913 Braves. The Texan moved on to the Federal League, where he batted .307 as a utilityman in 1914. /(NLM)

Webster McDonald — 1900–1982. RHP-MGR Negro Leagues 1918–1945 Philadelphia Giants, Richmond Giants, **Chicago American Giants**, Hilldale, Wilmington Potomacs, Darby Daisies, Washington Pilots, Philadelphia Stars, Detroit Stars 59–38 (inc.)

McDonald was a 6′ 180-lb submarine-style pitcher in the Negro Leagues from 1918 until the late 1930s. Little is known of the first seven years of his career, but in his two best-documented seasons he went 11–3 in 1926 and 10–5 in 1927 for the Chicago American Giants. In four games of the Black World Series of those years, he went 1–1. In 1933 he helped organize the Philadelphia Stars and, as player-manager in 1934, won a critical playoff game to help take the Negro National League championship from his former team, the American Giants. The control pitcher is credited with an as-yet undocumented 86–42 lifetime mark in the Negro Leagues, and a 14–4 record in exhibition games against major league teams. /(JM)

Gil McDougald — 1928– . 2B-3B-SS 1951–60 **Yankees** 1336 g, .276, 112 hr, 576 rbi. *8 WS, 53 g, .237, 7 hr, 24 rbi*
☛ *Rookie of the Year—51. All-Star—52, 56–59.*

Mickey Mantle joined the Yankees to great fanfare in 1951, but teammate Gil McDougald, who batted .306 with 14 HR, was AL Rookie of the Year. He used an open batting stance with his feet far apart, and dangled the head of his bat below the plane of his hands. On May 3, McDougald tied a major league record with six RBI in one inning. He capped the year by becoming the first rookie to hit a grand slam in the World Series (Game Five). An All-Star in 1952, playing mostly third base, McDougald shifted to second in 1954 when Billy Martin was drafted. When Martin returned, McDougald replaced 37-year-old Phil Rizzuto in 1956 to become an All-Star shortstop. He was successful at whichever infield position the Yankees needed him to play. He batted a career-high .311 in 1956 and led the AL with nine triples in 1957. His pinch single won the 1958 All-Star Game. A member of eight Yankee pennant-winners, McDougald ranks among the leaders with 53 WS games and 190 WS at-bats. At age 33, though he may have had several good years left, he retired rather than join the Washington Senators, who selected him in the 1961 expansion

Gil McDougald

draft. To this day, he is remembered as much for hitting the line drive that ruined Herb Score's career as he is for his own accomplishments. /(MC)

Jack McDowell — 1966– . RHP 1987– **White Sox** 187 ip, 8–10, 3.66
In 1987 the 6′5″ 180-lb McDowell led Stanford to the College World Series title, was Chicago's top pick in June, helped Birmingham capture the South-

ern League crown, and joined the White Sox in September. He began his major league career with 13 scoreless innings, and went 3–0 with a 1.93 ERA. But he missed several turns with a tired arm in 1988, and found wins hard to come by. /(RL)

Oddibe McDowell — 1962– . OF 1985– **Rangers**, Indians, Braves 658 g, .253, 66 hr, 226 rbi

McDowell was a two-time All-American at Arizona State, a starter on the 1984 U.S. Olympic team, and the Rangers' first pick in the June 1984 draft. Brought up to much fanfare in 1985, the 5'9" centerfielder wore number 0 and led AL rookies with 18 HR and 25 stolen bases. Against Cleveland on July 23, he hit for the cycle. He matched his rookie performance in 1986 and 1987 and even set a Ranger record for runs scored with 105 in 1986, but did not become the superstar Texas expected. He did not hit lefthanders well, and baserunners were taking advantage of his weak arm. He had slumped to .205 in June 1988 when he was optioned to Oklahoma City. He returned and finished at .247, but the Rangers included him with Pete O'Brien and Jerry Browne in a December trade for Cleveland shortstop Julio Franco. A similar lack of success for the Indians prompted them to trade him to Atlanta for Dion James in July 1989. /(JCA)

Roger McDowell — 1960– . RHP 1985– **Mets**, Phillies 525 ip, 36–32, 2.91. *2 LCS, 13 ip, 0–1, 2.08. 1 WS, 7 ip, 1–0, 4.91*

After missing almost all of 1984 for elbow surgery, McDowell discovered that he had acquired a sinking fastball. He made the Mets in spring training and shared stopper status in the bullpen with Jesse Orosco, recording 17 saves and a 2.83 ERA. In 1986 he set a short-lived Mets record by winning seven straight games from the start of the season and finished 14–9 (his 14 relief wins led the NL) with 22 saves as the Mets won the World Championship. In the famous 16-inning Game Six of the 1986 LCS, he pitched five innings of one-hit relief to help the Mets beat the Astros, and although he pitched poorly, he won Game Seven of the World Series as the Mets came back to defeat the Red Sox.

He began the 1987 season on the DL with a hernia, and although he had a career-high 25 saves, he was inconsistent. He returned to form in 1988 while sharing the bullpen stopper role with Randy Myers, and the Mets won the division title. He then surrendered a homer to Kirk Gibson in the 12th inning of Game Four in the LCS and took the loss.

McDowell became known as the chief prankster of the Mets, setting off firecrackers in the bat rack to "wake up" the bats and wearing his uniform upside down in the dugout during a nationally televised game, with his pants over his head and shoes on his hands. Traded to the Phillies with Len Dykstra for Juan Samuel in 1989, he left the Mets ranking second on the team's career saves list. /(SH)

Sam McDowell (Sudden Sam) — 1942– . LHP 1961–75 **Indians**, Giants, Yankees, Pirates 2493 ip, 141–134, 3.17. 20 wins: 70
☛ *Led League—era 65. Led League—k 65–66, 68–70. All-Star—65–71.*

McDowell seemed capable of becoming the greatest strikeout pitcher the game had ever known, but by 1976 he was out of baseball, a victim of alcoholism.

A lanky 6'5" lefthander with a ferocious fastball, a good changeup, and just enough wildness to keep hitters nervous, McDowell was overwhelming from 1965 to 1970, winning five strikeout titles and twice fanning over 300 batters by the age of 28 (only Sandy Koufax, Nolan Ryan, Walter Johnson, and J.R. Richard have struck out 300 batters as many times). McDowell started one game for the Indians as a 19-year-old in 1961, and found little success in

Sam McDowell

Cleveland in 1962–63, walking almost seven batters per nine innings. By 1964 he was beginning to harness his tremendous talent, and in 1965 he dominated AL hitters. McDowell led the AL with a 2.18 ERA, despite walking a league-high 132 batters, and allowed only 178 hits in 273 innings while striking out 325, at the time the fourth-best total in modern ML history. He struck out 15 Tigers in 10 innings June 5, and his 10.71 strikeouts per nine innings set a ML record broken by Dwight Gooden in 1984.

Sudden Sam continued to terrorize AL hitters in 1966, leading the league in strikeouts and shutouts and pitching back-to-back one-hitters. After losing the strikeout title to Jim Lonborg in 1967, he regained it in 1968, with 283, and recorded a 1.81 ERA (second-best in the AL). He also walked a league-high 110. He struck out 279 in 1969, and in 1970 McDowell was *TSN* Pitcher of the Year with 20 wins and 304 strikeouts. He fanned 16 Angels on May 1, 1968, and 15 batters three more times.

His biggest problem was not batters. "I was the biggest, most hopeless, and most violent drunk in baseball," McDowell would admit later. He won only 13 games in 1971, walking a career-high 153, as his drinking began to affect his on-field performance. He was traded to the Giants for 1972, winning 10 games for the last time. He finished in the Pirates' bullpen in 1975.

McDowell struck out 2,453 batters in his career. His total of 74 games with 10 or more strikeouts is fourth behind Ryan, Koufax, and Steve Carlton, and his career average of 8.86 strikeouts per nine innings trails only Ryan and Koufax. He led the league in walks five times and wild pitches three times, but averaged only seven hits allowed per nine innings for his career. McDowell has been employed by the Texas Rangers as a counselor to drug- and alcohol-addicted players. /(FK)

Terris McDuffie — 1910– . RHP-OF Negro Leagues 1930–45 Birmingham Black Barons, Brooklyn Eagles, Newark Eagles, Baltimore Black Sox, New York Black Yankees, Homestead Grays, Philadelphia Stars statistics not available
☛ *All-Star—41, 44.*

McDuffie was successful as an outfielder early in his career, hitting .297 and leading the league with 18 stolen bases with the Birmingham Black Barons in 1930. He became a strong pitcher with good control; with the Newark Eagles in 1938, he completed all 27 of the games he started. He was 27–5 in 1941, leading the Homestead Grays to the pennant. He

was also the winning pitcher in his first East-West all-star game in '41.

In 1945 McDuffie and Dave "Showboat" Thomas had tryouts with the Brooklyn Dodgers, largely as a publicity stunt forced on Branch Rickey by Joe Bostic, sports editor of the black newspaper *People's Voice.* Both players were in their late thirties, past their prime. Rickey signed Jackie Robinson later that year. /(BP)

Will McEnaney — 1952– . LHP 1974–79 **Reds,** Expos, Pirates, Cardinals 350 ip, 12–17, 3.75

McEnaney's one outstanding season came as the number-two man out of the 1975 World Champion Reds' bullpen. He was 5–2 with 15 saves and a 2.47 ERA, all career bests, and his 70 appearances were second in the NL. He capped it off by saving Game Seven of the World Series against the Red Sox, getting Carl Yastrzemski to fly to center for the final out in a 4–3 win. In 1976 he tied a World Series record with two saves, closing out Games Three and Four as Cincinnati swept the Yankees. He never started a game in the ML, after being a starter through most of his minor league career. /(SFS)

Chappie McFarland (Charles) — 1875–1924. RHP 1902–06 **Cardinals,** Pirates, Dodgers 841 ip, 34–59, 3.35

McFarland was a consistent loser for the weak Cardinals of 1903–05. His best season was 14–17 in 1904. His older brother, Monte, pitched briefly for the Cubs in the 1890s. /(BC)

Ed McFarland — 1874–1959. C 1893, 1896–1908 Cleveland (NL), Cardinals, **Phillies,** White Sox, Red Sox 887 g, .275, 12 hr, 383 rbi

McFarland was a fine fielder, leading NL catchers in assists and fielding percentage in 1900 while batting .305. He jumped to the AL White Sox in 1902 and shared catching duties with Billy Sullivan. /(ADS)

Herm McFarland — 1870–1935. OF 1896, 98, 1901–03 Louisville (NL), Reds, White Sox, **Baltimore (AL)/Yankees** 354 g, .266, 13 hr, 167 rbi

The hustling, 5'6" McFarland hit the White Sox' first-ever grand slam, on May 1, 1901. He had a close call the following spring training in Excelsior Springs, MO, when manager Clark Griffith took his players on a 10-mile run. Griffith, McFarland, and two others were halfway over a train trestle high over a ravine when they heard a train approaching. With no time, Griffith ordered his men to grab a railroad tie and dangle over the river. After the train rumbled past, teammates ran to pull them up. /(RL)

Andy McGaffigan — 1956– . RHP 1981– Yankees, Giants, **Expos**, Reds 742 ip, 34–30, 3.31

A much-traveled hard-throwing righthander, Mc-Gaffigan was the Southern League Pitcher of the Year at Nashville in 1980 (15–5, 2.38) and made his ML debut with the Yankees in 1981 before becoming one of two prospects traded to the Giants for Doyle Alexander in the spring of 1982. McGaffigan started occasionally for the Giants in 1983, then was traded twice in 1984, first to Montreal and then to Cincinnati, where he started exclusively in 1985 and fanned 11 Astros on August 1. He was traded back to Montreal after the season in a six-player swap and has been an effective set-up man for bullpen ace Tim Burke since 1987. In 1986–88, McGaffigan was 16–3 in relief with 18 saves. /(SCL)

Dan McGann [Dennis Lawrence] (Cap) — 1871–1910. 1B 1895–96, 1898–1908 Louisville (NL), Braves, Baltimore (NL), Dodgers, Washington (NL), Cardinals, Baltimore (AL), **Giants** 1459 g, .286, 42 hr, 736 rbi. *1 WS, 5 g, .235, 4 rbi*

McGann followed manager John McGraw from Baltimore to the New York Giants in the middle of the 1902 season and started at first base for Giant pennant winners in 1904 and 1905, the team McGraw insisted was his best ever. On May 27, 1904, McGann became the first modern player to steal five bases in one game. /(ADS)

Bill McGee (Fiddler Bill) — 1909–1987. RHP 1935–42 **Cardinals**, Giants 853 ip, 46–41, 3.74

Called up by the Cardinals for one start late in 1935, McGee defeated the Cubs 2–1 on a three-hitter. He went 16–10 in 1940. Traded to the Giants in May of 1941, he had 11 starts before finally winning a game that August; he finished 2–10. He had suffered a similar drought in 1938, losing nine a row. McGee was called Fiddler Bill because he played the violin. /(NLM)

Willie McGee — 1958– . OF 1982– **Cardinals** 1039 g, .292, 49 hr, 483 rbi. *3 LCS, 16 g, .292, 1 hr, 10 rbi. 3 WS, 20 g, .291, 3 hr, 11 rbi*
☛ *Most Valuable Player—85. Led League—ba 85. All-Star—83, 85, 87. Gold Glove—83, 85–86.*

Acquired from the Yankee farm system for Bob Sykes in one of the Cardinals' best moves, McGee immediately took over centerfield. He was a bad-ball hitter, swinging at anything thrown, yet he got results year after year. In 1985 his .353 average was the highest in history for a switch-hitter and led the NL, and he reached other career highs with 114

runs, 56 stolen bases, and a league-leading 18 triples. Hitting behind Jack Clark, the 1987 NL leader in on-base percentage, McGee responded with a career-high 105 RBI.

The pigeon-toed McGee is a good basestealer due to sheer speed rather than ability to read pitchers. McGee's speed gave him enormous range in the field and, coupled with a strong arm, won him three Gold Gloves. Although criticized at times for lack of concentration at the plate and in the field, McGee was still regarded as one of the best outfielders of the 1980s until a variety of injuries kept him out for much of the 1989 season. /(FO)

Ed McGhee (Maggie) — 1924–1986. OF 1950, 53–55 White Sox, **A's** 196 g, .246, 3 hr, 43 rbi

McGhee played in 104 games and was a steady outfielder with the A's in 1953, but he hit .263 without power and never again was a regular. /(MC)

Dan McGinn — 1943– . LHP 1968–72 Reds, **Expos**, Cubs 409 ip, 15–30, 5.10

A punter and pitcher at Notre Dame, McGinn was the first pick by Cincinnati in the 1966 draft. He set a rookie record pitching in 74 games for the Expos in 1969. That year, his only ML homer (off Tom Seaver) was the first for an expansion team. A week later, he was the winning pitcher in the first ML game ever played on foreign soil. In 1970 manager Gene Mauch pulled him out of the bullpen, for only his second ML start, to oppose Seaver, who had won 16 straight. McGinn shut out the Mets on three hits. /(CG)

Joseph McGinn — 1861–1922. *Writer.*

Born in Ireland, McGinn came to the U.S. in 1884 and worked on several New York newspapers before becoming a sportswriter for Associated Press in 1893. Late in his career, he was known as the dean of New York sportswriters. McGinn was also an expert on boxing. He remained with AP until he became ill in 1921. /(NLM)

Joe McGinnity (Iron Man) — 1871–1929. RHP 1899–1908 Baltimore (NL), Dodgers, Baltimore (AL), **Giants** 3459 ip, 247–144, 2.64. 20 wins: 1899–1906 *1 WS, 17 ip, 1–1, 0.00*
☛ *Led League—w 1899, 1900, 03, 04, 06. Led League—era 04. Hall of Fame—1946.*

McGinnity did not get to the majors until he was 28, then lasted only 10 seasons, but earned his sobriquet, Iron Man, by his frequent appearances. He often pitched both halves of doubleheaders. He had had two inauspicious years in the minors, and was dropping Baltimore, and McGinnity was awarded to Brooklyn. He again topped the NL in wins, going 29–9, and earned the Iron Man nickname by winning five games in six days. When John Mc-Graw, for whom had he pitched in 1899, beckoned, McGinnity jumped to the new American League. In July 1902, they both went back to the NL, with McGraw taking the Giants' helm.

From 1902 through 1908, McGinnity and Christy Mathewson formed a dynamic duo, with one or the other topping the league in victories every year. McGinnity led with 31 in 1903, when he pitched 434 innings—the most in a season by any 20th century pitcher. Three times that August he threw complete games victories in both ends of doubleheaders. His 35 wins led the NL in 1904, when his .814 winning percentage (35–8) and 1.61 ERA were also the NL best. He won 27 in 1906 to again lead the circuit.

McGinnity was a rough, tough player who, when he ran a saloon, never had to hire a bouncer. He welcomed diminutive umpire Tom Connolly into the majors by spitting in the future Hall of Famer's face. His durability was remarkable. With the exception of 1902, he led his league in games pitched every year from 1900 to 1907, and in innings from 1899 to 1904. He started and went the route more times than any AL pitcher in 1901, and any NL pitcher in 1904. Decades before there were bullpen specialists, he often led or tied for the lead in relief wins, relief losses, and saves. In his two World Series starts, in 1905, he did not allow an earned run.

McGinnity left the majors after the 1908 season to pitch for and manage Newark (Eastern League). He went on for years in the minors, a steady winner, still throwing underhand and mixing in a spitball. He had racked up 171 minor league wins when he last took the mound at age 54. He returned to the Dodgers for a time as a coach. In 1946 he was elected to the Hall of Fame by the Veterans Committee. /(JK)

Lynn McGlothen — 1950–1984. LHP 1972–82 Red Sox, Cardinals, Giants, **Cubs**, White Sox, Yankees 1498 ip, 86–93, 3.98
☛ *All-Star—74.*

McGlothen was the Louisiana high school tennis champion for three years and then attended Grambling State College. He came up with the Red Sox but had his first full major league season (1974) with the Cardinals, pitching in the All-Star Game and finishing at 16–12 (2.70). He won 15 games in 1975, and, on August 19 against Cincinnati, struck

Joe McGinnity

pitching semi-pro ball when he developed an underhand delivery and change of pace which, in one season, vaulted him to the majors. As a rookie with the 1899 Baltimore Orioles, he led the National League with 28 victories.

The NL cut back from 12 teams to eight in 1900,

out the side on nine pitches. He spent much of 1977 on the Giants' disabled list with a bad shoulder, but won 13 for the Cubs in 1979 and 12 in 1980. McGlothen was killed in a fire at age 34. /(ARA)

Jim McGlothin (Red, Mac) — 1943–1975. RHP 1965–73 **Angels**, Reds, White Sox 1301 ip, 67–77, 3.61. *1 LCS, 1 ip, 0–0, 0.00. 2 WS, 7 ip, 0–0, 9.82* ☛ *All-Star—67.*

McGlothin was the Angels' number-two starter for three seasons (1967–69) and made the All-Star squad in 1967, when he tied for the AL shutout lead (6) while going 12–8, 2.96. Traded to the Reds with pitchers Pedro Borbon and Vern Geishert after the 1969 season for Alex Johnson and Chico Ruiz, he and Borbon proved valuable additions, helping Cincinnati to NL pennants in 1970 and 1972. McGlothin went 14–10 and 9–8 those years, but was hit hard in both his World Series starts. /(JFC)

Stoney McGlynn [Ulysses Simpson Grant] — 1872–1941. RHP 1906–08 **Cardinals** 476 ip, 17–33, 2.95

As a rookie, McGlynn led the NL in starts, complete games, innings pitched, hits allowed, and walks while pitching for the last-place 1907 Cardinals, who sported the weakest offense and the worst defense in the league. Despite tossing three shutouts and compiling 14 wins, McGlynn lost a league-leading 25 games. /(FJO)

Bill McGowan — 1896–1954. *Umpire AL 1925–54 4 ASU 8 WS*

In 1933 McGowan was one of that "great clan of probity," in the words of Yale professor Billy Phelps, who were given the honor of working the first All-Star Game. In a 16-plus year period, McGowan reportedly worked 2,541 consecutive games. An AL umpire for 30 years, he never shrank from making the tough calls. One of his decisions cost Lou Gehrig sole possession of the 1931 home run title. That April 26, Gehrig hit the ball into the centerfield bleachers in Washington, but the ball popped back out of the stands and into the out-fielder's hands, confusing baserunner Lyn Lary, who slowed down. Gehrig kept running and accidentally passed Lary on the basepaths, and McGowan called Gehrig out to end the inning. At season's end, Gehrig's total of 46 home runs left him tied for the league lead with teammate Babe Ruth. /(RTM)

Frank McGowan (Beauty) — 1901–1982. OF 1922–23, 28–29, 37 **A's**, Browns, Braves 375 g, .262, 6 hr, 108 rbi

McGowan excelled in the majors only in 1928, when he batted .363 in 168 at-bats with the Browns. His best years came in the International League, where the popular lefthanded hitter was the 1936 MVP (.356, 23 HR, 111 RBI). He managed Baltimore in 1932–33, and earned his way into the International League Hall of Fame. He was the Orioles' New England scouting supervisor from 1954 through 1973. /(NLM)

Roscoe McGowen — 1886–1966. *Writer.*

A longtime correspondent for *The Sporting News*, McGowan sprinkled his writing with quotes from Shakespeare and the literary classics. At age 11 he was a reporter and printer's devil for an Iowa weekly. Later he moved to the Walnut Grove (Illinois) *Banner* for $15 a month, and then became a railroad telegrapher and wire reporter for the AP. While he was with the Rock Island *Argus*, his contributions to the Chicago *Tribune* led to a job with the New York *Daily News* in 1922. A 30-year stay with the *New York Times* began in 1929. It was McGowan who asked Giants' manager Bill Terry about the Dodgers' chances in 1934 and received the famous answer, "Is Brooklyn still in the league?," a remark that returned to haunt the Giants at season's end. McGowan was president of the BBWAA in 1949. /(NLM)

Bob McGraw — 1895–1978. RHP 1917–20, 25–29 Yankees, Red Sox, Dodgers, Cardinals, **Phillies** 591 ip, 26–38, 4.89

Signed by the Yankees out of Colorado University in 1917, McGraw had his best years at Minneapolis (American Association). With the 1928 Phillies, he lost a NL-high eight games in relief. /(NLM)

John McGraw (Little Napoleon) — 1873–1934. 3B-SS 1891–1906 Baltimore (AA), **Baltimore (NL)**, Cardinals, Baltimore (AL), Giants 1099 g, .334, 13 hr, 462 rbi.
Manager 1899, 1901–32 Baltimore (NL), Baltimore (AL), **Giants** 2840–1984, .589. First place: 04–05, 11–13, 17, 21–24 *9 WS, 26–28, .481* ☛ *Hall of Fame—1937.*

For many years John McGraw was the dominant figure in American baseball. He was an excellent player—certainly the best ever to become a great manager—yet his success derived from more than athletic talent. He had a profound understanding of

John McGraw

began his professional career at Olean (New York-Penn League) in 1890 and within a year had jumped to the American Association's Baltimore club. When the American Association collapsed after 1891, Baltimore was absorbed into the National League and McGraw became a member of the soon-to-be-legendary Orioles.

Although his ML playing career spanned 16 seasons, McGraw was at his best as Ned Hanlon's fiery third baseman in Baltimore, a star on a team that won three consecutive titles from 1894 to 1896. A lefthanded batter, he was an adroit bat handler who could hit for average, batting over .321 nine consecutive seasons. He twice led the league in runs and walks and stole 436 bases. He and Willie Keeler were experts at the hit-and-run play.

McGraw was notorious for blocking, tripping, or otherwise obstructing the baserunners while the lone umpire watched the flight of the ball. Some say his shenanigans prompted the stationing of additional umpires on the basepaths.

There then began a period in which he successfully opposed the baseball "establishment" at every opportunity. Barely 26 in 1899, he refused to be shifted to Brooklyn, which the Baltimore club partially owned and wanted to strengthen. While manager Hanlon and five Orioles starters led Brooklyn to the championship in 1899 and 1900, McGraw and catcher Wilbert Robinson remained behind in Baltimore, where they owned a profitable saloon together. McGraw was named manager of the leftover Orioles and led them to third place. The Orioles were disbanded when the NL reduced to eight teams in 1900, and McGraw and Robinson were sold to St. Louis. They agreed to go only on the condition that the reserve clause be removed from their contracts, an unheard-of concession. In 1901 he became player-manager of the new American League's Baltimore franchise, but after frequent run-ins with league president Ban Johnson, a man as intractable as himself, he jumped in mid-1902 to the NL's New York Giants.

McGraw brought Robinson, Roger Bresnahan, Dan McGann, and Joe McGinnity with him to New York, and found Christy Mathewson already there. With the ample financial resources of new owner John T. Brush, McGraw quickly turned a floundering second-division team into a contender, winning a then-record 106 games and the pennant in 1904. McGraw and Brush refused to allow the club to meet the AL champion Red Sox in the WS (the first Series had been played the year before), however. In 1905 McGraw's Giants won a second consecutive

the game and was alert to all the opportunities each inning offered. "The main idea," he always said, "is to win."

His personality was indeed that of a "Little Napoleon": arrogant, abrasive, and pugnacious. He outgeneraled his opponents while abusing them verbally and, sometimes, with his fists. His players suffered his tyranny as the price of victory, proud to be Giants. In his 29 full seasons as Giants manager he finished first or second 21 times, winning 10 pennants and three World Series.

McGraw's rise to prominence was swift. A scrawny youngster from Truxton, New York, he

NL pennant, finishing 105–48, and this time they did play the WS. They whipped the Athletics in five games behind Mathewson's three shutouts.

McGraw's managerial style was reminiscent of his antics as a player. He swaggered through every city in the league, battling opposing teams, managers, owners, umpires, and league officials. He had a genius for inciting crowds and the Giants quickly became the most despised team in the league, often dodging rocks and bottles as they left enemy ballparks. In 1906 McGraw arrogantly had "Champions of the World" emblazoned across the front of the team's jerseys.

Strategically, McGraw favored the hit-and-run and disdained the sacrifice bunt. He had a sharp eye for playing talent and traded daringly, getting useful work from drinkers and neurotics other clubs had given up on. And with tips from his many friends in bush leagues across the country, he found bright young stars to replace fading older ones.

McGraw's Giants won three consecutive pennants from 1911 to 1913, but lost the WS all three years, twice to the Athletics and once to the Red Sox. The 1912 WS featured Fred Snodgrass's famous dropped fly ball, which allowed the Red Sox to rally for two runs in the 10th inning of the final game. McGraw lost another WS to the White Sox in 1917, then rattled off four consecutive pennants beginning in 1921. By then, the Yankees were emerging as an AL dynasty, but the Giants beat their Bronx rivals in 1921 and 1922, before the Yankees returned the favor in 1923.

McGraw unwittingly hastened his own demise by urging wealthy Jake Ruppert to buy the Yankees, ushering in the Ruthian long-ball era. The Yankees quickly established themselves as the city's dominant team, and the Giants were overtaken by the Pirates, Cardinals, and Cubs in their own league. In 1932 McGraw surrendered the manager's reins to Bill Terry, retiring with 2,840 victories. He returned in 1933 to manage the NL squad in the inaugural All-Star Game. /(ADS/SCL)

Tug McGraw [Frank Edwin] — 1944– . LHP
1965–1984 Mets, **Phillies** 1516 ip, 96–92, 3.13. *6 LCS, 27 ip, 0–2, 2.67 2 WS, 21 ip, 2–1, 2.11*
☛ *All-Star—72, 75.*

"You Gotta Believe," the rallying cry for the Mets' miracle pennant drive in 1973, was coined by flaky lefthanded reliever Tug McGraw. Sixteen times in the last month of the season, he would charge off the mound slapping his glove on his right thigh, screaming at no one in particular while racking up 11 saves

Tug McGraw

and four victories. While McGraw, a bullpen mainstay of the Mets for nine seasons and the Phillies for ten, was one of the main reasons the Mets were able to capture the NL flag, he was also one of the reasons they had to catch up. He was going through a horrible slump, blowing leads and getting his pitching and pride pounded. The Mets, ultimately the only team to finish over .500 for the season in the NL East, began their climb in last place, 12–1/2 games out. By August 30, they were 6–1/2 out and McGraw was 0–6. McGraw returned to form, and the Mets reached first place to stay on September 21. McGraw finished the season with 25 saves.

McGraw's best year was actually 1972, when he posted an 11–4 record with 27 saves and a 1.70 ERA. He also was credited with the victory in the 1972 All-Star Game, giving up only one hit and striking out four in working the final two innings.

His shining moment as a Phillie came in the 1980 World Series. In the fifth game, McGraw struck out the Royals' Amos Otis with the bases loaded in the bottom of the ninth to preserve a 4–3 victory. In the sixth and final game, in Philadelphia, McGraw squeezed out of bases-loaded jams in the final two innings and got the save to give the Phillies their first World Championship. It was his third WS save lifetime, and his five LCS saves is a record. He retired with 180 saves.

McGraw was given the nickname Tug by his mother, because he used to tug when she breast-fed him. /(SEW)

Scott McGregor — 1954– . LHP 1976–88 **Orioles** 2141 ip, 138–108, 3.99. 20 wins: 80 *2 LCS, 16 ip, 1–1, 0.57. 2 WS, 24 ip, 2–2, 2.12*
☛ *All-Star—81.*

A curveballing control specialist with an outstanding pickoff move, McGregor was a prize obtained by Baltimore in a 10-player deal with the Yankees on June 15, 1976. One of the winningest pitchers of the 1980s, he joined Mike Flanagan as the lefthanders in Baltimore's starting rotation in 1978. The next year McGregor won the deciding game of the LCS, but lost Game Seven of the World Series on Willie Stargell's dramatic home run. In 1980 McGregor reached 20 wins on the final day of the season. He rebounded from injuries in 1982 to lead Baltimore starters in wins (18), percentage (.720), starts (36), complete games (12), and innings pitched (260) in 1983. He won the fifth, and final, game of the World Series with a five-hit, 5–0 shutout of the Phillies. From 1978 to 1985, McGregor was the only major league pitcher to finish with a winning record each season. He was New York's first pick in the June 1972 draft and a teammate of George Brett at El Segundo High School. /(ME)

Harry McGrew (Ted) — Unk.–1969. *Umpire/Scout* NL 1930–34

McGrew hit only .194 in 12 seasons as a minor league infielder, and was best known as a longtime scout. He scouted first for the Dodgers in 1938, and at various times worked for the Phillies, Pirates, Red Sox, and Braves, before returning to the Dodgers from 1963 to 1968. His discoveries and/or signees include Rico Carty, Alvin Dark, Pee Wee Reese, and Pete Reiser. /(FVP)

Fred McGriff — 1963– . 1B-DH 1986– **Blue Jays** 425 g, .269, 90 hr, 217 rbi. *1 LCS, 5 g, .143, 3 rbi*
☛ *Led League—hr 89.*

McGriff was a throw-in in a 1982 deal between the Blue Jays and Yankees. He created an annual stir in spring training with tape-measure home runs before making the team as a platoon DH in 1987, when he broke Jesse Barfield's team rookie record for HR. In his first visit to Yankee Stadium, McGriff hit an upper-deck home run. Although he tends to strike out a lot, McGriff has a good batting eye and draws many walks, and his on-base averages and slugging percentages are high. In 1988, his first season as Toronto's everyday first baseman, McGriff's fielding was erratic, but he also finished second in the AL in both HR (34) and slugging (.552). His league-leading 36 HR in 1989 (.269, 92 RBI, 98 runs, 119 walks) helped Toronto to the division title. /(TF)

Deacon McGuire [James Thomas] — 1865–1936. C-1B 1884–88, 1890–1908, 1910, 12 Toledo (AA), Detroit (NL), Philadelphia (NL), Cleveland (AA), Rochester (AA), Washington (AA), **Washington (NL)**, Dodgers, Tigers, Yankees, Red Sox, Indians 1781 g, .278, 45 hr, 787 rbi.
Manager 1898, 1907–11 Washington (NL), **Red Sox**, Indians 208–289, .419

McGuire appeared in more major league seasons than any catcher in baseball history—26. He caught 1,611 games, most coming during the 19th century. He reached his peak with the National League Washington club, topping the .300 mark each year

Deacon McGuire

from 1894 through 1897, and never again. At a time when pinch hitters were rarely used, he was a good one (14-for-41 lifetime). Though he managed in six different years, only the 1910 Indians were his for an entire season, and he never had a winning record. /(JK)

Bill McGunnigle (Gunner) — 1855-1899. OF-RHP 1879-80, 82 **Buffalo (NL)**, Worcester (NL), Cleveland (NL) 56 g, .173, 0 hr, 6 rbi; 157 ip, 11-8, 2.81.
Manager 1880, 88-91, 96 Buffalo (NL), **Brooklyn (AA)**, Dodgers, Pirates, Louisville (NL) 324-244, .570

Sometimes identified as the first catcher to wear a glove in a game (against Harvard in 1875), McGunnigle became a pitcher and then an outfielder in the NL. As a manager, he used a tin whistle to signal his men. He compiled a unique record, winning pennants in two consecutive years (1889-90) in two different leagues (AA and NL) with the same team, Brooklyn. /(NLM)

Mark McGwire — 1963- . 1B 1986- **A's** 467 g, .259, 117 hr, 321 rbi. 2 LCS, 9 g, .364, 2 hr, 6 rbi. 2 WS, 9 g, .176, 1 hr, 2 rbi
☛ Rookie of the Year—87. Led League—hr 87. All-Star—87-89.

A member of the 1984 U.S. Olympic baseball team and Oakland's first-round draft choice in the 1984 free agent draft, McGwire shattered the ML rookie home run record with 49 in 1987 (the old record was 38) and was unanimously chosen AL Rookie of the Year. Standing 6'5" with an immensely strong righthanded stroke and a freckled, boyish-looking face, the redhead began the 1987 season backing up Rob Nelson at first base, but moved into the starting lineup within three weeks. He belted three home runs against Cleveland June 27 and two more the next day to tie the ML record for home runs in consecutive games, and by the All-Star break he had 33 HR and was on pace to break Roger Maris's single-season record. McGwire's bat cooled considerably in August (only three home runs), but he still led the AL in both HR and slugging percentage while batting .289 with 118 RBI. In 1988 McGwire "slipped" to .260 with 32 HR and 99 RBI but the A's still took the AL pennant. In the WS, McGwire's solo home run in the bottom of the ninth won Game Three, 2-1, but that was his only hit as the A's lost to the Dodgers in five games. /(SCL)

Marty McHale — 1888-1979. RHP 1910-11, 13-16 Red Sox, **Yankees**, Indians 358 ip, 12-30, 3.57

Marty was an undistinguished righthander who did much better as a vaudevillian (with Turkey Mike Donlin), newspaperman, and stockbroker. Variety, admiring his fine Irish tenor, called him "the Baseball Caruso." /(ADS)

Austin McHenry (Mac) — 1895-1922. OF 1918-22 **Cardinals** 543 g, .302, 34 hr, 286 rbi

Rated by Branch Rickey as one of the best left fielders ever, McHenry had good speed and a strong arm, and hit for average and power. He batted .350 in 1921, third-best in the league, and was fourth in HR (17), tied for third in RBI (102), and second in slugging average (.531). He hit .303 in 64 games in 1922; the falloff was due to a brain tumor. He died that November. /(FJO)

Stuffy McInnis [John Phalen] — 1890-1960. 1B-SS-3B, 1909-27 **A's**, Red Sox, Indians, Braves, Pirates, Phillies 2128 g, .308, 20 hr, 1060 rbi. 5 WS, 20 g, .200, 4 rbi.
Manager 1927 **Phillies** 51-103, .331

Wearing the small, rounded mitt of his day, Stuffy McInnis set still-standing fielding records for first basemen: in 1921, playing for the Red Sox, he made only one error in 152 games for a .9993 fielding average; with the Red Sox and Indians over the course of 163 games in 1921-22, he accepted 1,700 chances without an error; his 1,300 errorless chances in 1921 set the record for a season. His reputation for skillful defensive play developed with the Athletics, with whom he first appeared as a shortstop in 1909. In 1911 he replaced Harry Davis at first base in the "$100,000 Infield," hooking up with Frank Baker, Eddie Collins, and Jack Barry for three pennant winners (1911, 1913, and 1914). He appeared with six league champions altogether; the Red Sox were AL champs his first year with them in 1918, and, when the Pirates picked him up in 1925 as an extra, they won the championship. McInnis batted over .300 in 12 of his 19 seasons, and in each year from 1910 to 1915. A righthanded line-drive pull hitter, he could punch the ball to the opposite field as well. He gained his nickname as a youngster in the Boston suburban leagues, where his spectacular playing brought shouts of "that's the stuff, kid." He quit as manager of the Phillies after one last-place season in 1927, and coached at Harvard for five years. /(JK)

Stuffy McInnis

A righthander, Rocks lost 20 games or more in three seasons with Brooklyn's miserable turn-of-the-century teams. For the Cubs he pitched decent relief in Game One of the 1910 Series, but was blasted in a third of an inning in Game Three. /(ADS)

Matty McIntyre — 1880–1920. OF 1901, 04–12 Athletics, **Tigers**, White Sox 1068 g, .269, 4 hr, 319 rbi. *2 WS, 9 g, .190*

One of baseball's forgotten men, Matty was a left-handed thrower and leadoff hitter who played more than 550 games as Detroit's left fielder with Cobb and Crawford, while the well-remembered Davy Jones sat on the bench. /(ADS)

Doc McJames [James McCutchen, born James McCutchen James] — 1873–1901. RHP 1895–99, 1901 **Washington (NL)**, Baltimore (NL), Dodgers 1361 ip, 79–80, 3.43. 20 wins: 1898

McJames was among the National League leaders with 27 wins and a 2.36 ERA for Baltimore in 1898, but a month-long attack of malaria curtailed his 1899 season with Brooklyn. He pitched 13 games in 1901, and died that September. /(DAS)

Archie McKain (Happy) — 1911–1985. LHP 1937–41, 43 Red Sox, **Tigers**, Browns 486 ip, 26–21, 4.26. *1 WS, 3 ip, 0–0, 3.00*

McKain went 8–8 as a Red Sox rookie in 1937, and 5–0 in relief for the 1940 AL Champion Tigers. When the Browns traded him to Brooklyn in July 1943, he quit the game and returned to his native Kansas to farm. /(NLM)

Hal McKain — 1906–1970. RHP 1927, 29–32 Indians, **White Sox** 381 ip, 18–23, 4.93

When the Indians tried to protect Hal McKain from the free agent draft by temporarily promoting him to the major league roster, Commissioner Landis turned McKain loose. McKain had won 20 games in the Three-I League in 1928, and the White Sox signed him the next spring. But he wrenched his back in 1930, developed arm problems, and lost a league-high six games in relief in 1931. /(RL)

Dave McKay — 1950– . 2B-3B-SS 1975–82 Twins, **Blue Jays**, A's 645 g, .229, 21 hr, 170 rbi. *1 LCS, 3 g, .273, 1 hr, 1 rbi*

Canadian Dave McKay was the Blue Jays' starting third baseman in their first-ever game in 1977. McKay was a dependable fielder at second, third, or shortstop, and holds Blue Jay records for putouts, assists, and chances in a game for a second baseman.

Joe McIntosh — 1951– . RHP 1974–75 **Padres** 220 ip, 8–19, 3.68

The ambidextrous McIntosh went 8–15 as the Padres' number-two starter in 1975. /(WOR)

Harry McIntyre [John Reed] (Rocks) — 1879–1949. RHP 1905–13 **Dodgers**, Cubs, Reds 1650 ip, 71–117, 3.22. *1 WS, 5 ip, 0–1, 6.75*

In 1978 McKay had a (since broken) team-record hitting streak of 16 games. He was a switch hitter without much power or speed, and finished the 1980s as a coach for Oakland. /(TF)

Ed McKean (Mack) — 1864–1919. SS 1887–99 Cleveland (AA), **Cleveland (NL)**, Cardinals 1654 g, .302, 66 hr, 1070 rbi

One of the better-hitting shortstops of his era, McKean spent a dozen seasons as a regular in his hometown Cleveland, playing in both the American Association and the NL. He hit a career-high .357 in 1894 and twice led the NL in at-bats. /(JK)

Ed McKean

Jim McKean — 1945– . *Umpire* AL 1974–87 *2 ASU 3 LCS 2 WS*

McKean played Canadian League football with the Montreal Alouettes and was named to the Canadian Football Hall of Fame. His most ticklish call as a ML umpire came on Opening Day in 1976. With the Brewers trailing the Yankees 9–6 in the bottom of the ninth, Don Money apparently hit a grand slam home run to win the game. But the homer was negated because a moment before the pitch, New York's Chris Chambliss had asked for and been granted time by first base umpire McKean. The Yankees won the game. /(RTM)

Bill McKechnie (Deacon) — 1886–1965. 3B-2B-1B-SS 1907, 10–18, 20 **Pirates**, Braves, Yankees, Indianapolis (FL), Newark (FL), Giants, Reds 845 g, .251, 8 hr, 240 rbi.
    Manager 1915, 22–26, 28–46 Newark (FL), Pirates, Cardinals, Braves, **Reds** 1898–1724, .524. First place: 25, 28, 39–40 *4 WS, 8–14, .364*
☛ *Hall of Fame—1962.*

Deacon Bill was what is known as "a sound baseball man." He was an unexceptional player; his knowledge of the game exceeded his physical ability. In 1913 Yankee manager Frank Chance played him at second base despite his deficiencies because, he said, McKechnie "knew more baseball than all the rest of my team put together." McKechnie had a checkered career as a utility infielder. Between 1912 and 1916, he played for eight teams, including a one-game stint with the Braves. His two Federal League seasons (1914–15) were his most productive. Sold to the Giants when the Feds collapsed, he was included in the July 1916 trade that sent Hall of Famers Edd Roush and worn-out Christy Mathewson to the Reds for Buck Herzog and Wade Killefer.

Managing was his forte. He won pennants in three cities—a record that has never been matched. His first trial as a manager came at age 29, with the Newark Peps (FL) for 102 games in 1915. He succeeded George Gibson at Pittsburgh in mid-1922 and brought the club from fifth place to a tie for third. In 1925 he won his first pennant and defeated the Senators in the World Series, but was fired a year later when the appointment of former Pirate skipper Fred Clarke as a management consultant in the dugout led to confusion and a player revolt. After moving to St. Louis as a coach, McKechnie took the reins when Bob O'Farrell was removed for failing to win the 1927 pennant. McKechnie obliged Cardinal

Bill McKechnie

McKechnie followed with eight years as the Braves' manager, never finishing higher than fourth. In 1935 Boston lost a club-record 115 games, but McKechnie remained through 1937. He spent nine seasons managing at Cincinnati, winning pennants in 1939 and 1940. In the 1939 WS he was swept by the Yankees again, but in 1940 his Reds beat the Tigers in seven.

A baseball conservative, Deacon Bill was more effective with pitchers than hitters, although his shrewd coaching of Larry Doby at Cleveland (1947–49) hastened the youngster's adjustment to the major leagues. He was strict with players, but his quiet self-discipline and fairness won their respect. McKechnie was money-conscious, and his moves to Boston and Cincinnati were for lucrative, long-term contracts. He was a churchgoer and family man, which earned him his nickname. /(ADS)

Jack McKeon (Trader Jack) — 1930– .
Manager 1973–75, 77–78, 88– **Royals**, A's, Padres
442–431, .506

McKeon managed in the minors for 15 years with success and a sense of humor. He once fired blanks at a player who ran through a stop sign at third. In his first year with the Royals, he brought them home second, but they slumped to fifth the next year. Although he had them back in second in 1975, he was fired after 96 games. After managing Oakland, he became general manager of the Padres and acquired the nickname Trader Jack because of his many deals. In 1988 he returned to the dugout when San Diego fired Larry Bowa. /(BC)

Bill McKinley — 1910– . *Umpire* AL 1946–65 *3 ASU 4 WS*

McKinley ranked high among AL umpires for two decades, but because he had the surname as the former president, he also endured 20 years of angry players and fans barking, "They shot the wrong McKinley!" /(RTM)

Rich McKinney — 1946– . 3B-2B-OF-1B-DH
1970–75, 77 **White Sox**, Yankees, A's 341 g, .225, 20 hr, 100 rbi

After batting a career-high .271 for the White Sox in 1971, McKinney, a utility man, was traded to the Yankees for Stan Bahnsen. The Yankees hoped he would be their everyday third baseman, but while Bahnsen won 21 games for Chicago the following year, McKinney hit .215 in 37 games for New York and tied an AL record with four errors at third April 22. /(JCA)

owner Sam Breadon by managing the Cardinals to first place in 1928, but the four-game World Series loss to the Yankees led to his 1929 demotion to Rochester (International League), while Rochester's manager, Billy Southworth, took over the Cardinals. Late in the season, Breadon decided he had made a mistake, and switched them back; combined, Southworth and McKechnie managed a fourth-place Cardinal finish.

Denny McLain (Sky King) — 1944- . RHP 1963–1972
Tigers, Senators, A's, Braves 1886 ip, 131–91, 3.39. 20
wins: 66, 68–69 *1 WS, 17 ip, 1–2, 3.24*
☛ *Led League—w 68–69. All-Star—66, 68–69.*

He was brash. He was flamboyant. He had a lounge
act in Las Vegas. He performed on TV shows,
including Ed Sullivan's. He paraded about in a white
mink coat. He was Hall of Fame shortstop Lou
Boudreau's son-in-law. He was also convicted of
racketeering and smuggling cocaine and spent time
in jail. And, for a while, Denny McLain was one of
the finest pitchers in baseball.

In 1968 McLain was the league MVP and a
unanimous Cy Young Award winner, going 31–6
with a 1.96 ERA, 28 complete games, and 280
strikeouts. He was the first 30-game winner since
Dizzy Dean in 1934, and helped the Tigers to their
first World Championship since 1945.

McLain first came up in 1963 and he showed
early flashes of brilliance, winning 16 games in
1965, 20 in 1966, and 17 in 1967. He might have
won 20 in 1967, if not for an unexplained accident
at home where he hurt his toe and missed his last six
starts. His teammates, manager, and Tiger fans
thought he was dogging it, and he was blamed for
the Tigers' close second-place finish in a wild, four-
team scramble for the AL pennant.

Starting 1968, he could do nothing to erase the
fans' memory of the previous season. He was booed
at home after commenting that Detroit's fans were
"the world's worst." But soon the victories started to
pile up. He won nine straight starts from mid-June
to mid-July to stretch his record to 18–2. On
September 1, he converted a Boog Powell line drive
into a triple play to preserve his 27th victory. He
was in the dugout when he won his 30th, a 5–4
come-from-behind victory over Oakland. In his 31st
victory, he had a 6–1 lead over the Yankees, so he
grooved a pitch to Mickey Mantle in Mantle's last
game in Tiger Stadium. Mantle crashed what would
be his next-to-last career homer, passing Jimmie
Foxx on the all-time home run list. McLain would
have won 33 games if not for two consecutive 2–1
losses.

In the 1968 World Series, McLain lost both starts
in which he opposed the Cardinals' Bob Gibson,
who had won 22 games and set a major league
record with a 1.12 ERA. But McLain won Game Six
on two days' rest, setting up teammate Mickey
Lolich to beat Gibson in the seventh game.

Many thought that his nonstop off-season party-
ing would adversely affect McLain, but his lifestyle

Denny McLain

didn't stop Tiger management from awarding their
cocky ace the team's first $100,000 contract. Mc-
Lain responded by winning a second Cy Young
Award (he shared it with the Orioles' Mike Cuellar)
with a 24–9 mark and a team-record nine shutouts.
But things started to unravel midway through the
1969 season. He angered manager Mayo Smith by
not showing up until the fourth inning of the All-
Star Game, which Smith wanted him to start. Then
Sky King left before the game was over, flying out in
his private Cessna.

In 1970 things fell apart. On April 1, Commissioner Bowie Kuhn suspended McLain for three
months for a 1967 bookmaking incident. In August

McLain filed for bankruptcy, then dumped ice water on a couple of Detroit writers. On September 9, Kuhn suspended him for the rest of the season for gun possession. Finally, on October 9, after a dismal 3–5, 4.65 season, he was traded to the Senators. Amid constant run-ins with no-nonsense Washington manager Ted Williams, McLain lost 22 games in 1971. He spent the 1972 season in Oakland and Atlanta. At the age of 28, his fastball and money were gone and his career was over. He put on weight. He tried several businesses, all of which failed. In the early 1980s, he spent over two years in jail before being granted a new trial and being released early in 1989. As he began to reassemble his life, he played the organ in a Michigan bar where Leon Spinks was the bartender, while listening to offers from promoters looking to get him back in the spotlight. /(SEW)

Bo McLaughlin [Michael Duane] — 1953– . RHP 1976–79, 81–82 **Astros**, Braves, A's 313 ip, 10–20, 3.73

McLaughlin was 4–5, 2.85 as a starter for the 1976 Astros, but was switched to relief thereafter. He never again had an ERA below 4.00. /(SFS)

Byron McLaughlin — 1955– . RHP 1977–80, 82–83 **Mariners**, A's, Angels 427 ip, 16–29, 5.08

After being released by two organizations, McLaughlin went 18–13 (1.84) in the Mexican League in 1977 to earn a shot with Seattle. Mediocre as a starter, he had his only ML success there in 1979, going 6–2 in relief (7–7 overall) with 14 saves. /(JCA)

Joey McLaughlin — 1956– . RHP 1977, 79–84 Braves, **Blue Jays**, Rangers 449 ip, 29–28, 3.85

At the time of his release by the Blue Jays in 1984, Joey McLaughlin was their only reliever ever to have saved 10 games in a season, and his 31 career saves as a Blue Jay were surpassed only by Tom Henke over the franchise's first dozen seasons. His 2.85 ERA in 1981 and 3.21 in 1982 were bright spots on teams that had yet to make the transition from expansion team to contender. McLaughlin then had the misfortune of pitching poorly down the stretch in 1983, the first year in which the Blue Jays contended for the AL East title. /(TF)

Larry McLean [John Bannerman] — 1881–1921. C-1B 1901, 03–04, 06–15 Red Sox, Cubs, Cardinals, **Reds**, Giants 862 g, .262, 6 hr, 298 rbi. *1 WS, 5 g, .500, 2 rbi*

This 6'5" 225-lb catcher was reportedly a man of gentle disposition—when sober. He left behind a trail of barroom brawls, the last of which ended when he was shot to death at age 39 by an alarmed Boston saloonkeeper.

McLean played eight seasons with Cincinnati, and went 6-for-12 for the Giants in the 1913 World Series. He left the majors in the wake of a drunken encounter with New York manager John McGraw. McGraw and his coaches were sitting outside a St. Louis hotel when McLean staggered up and challenged them to a fight. Scout Dick Kinsella broke a chair over McLean's head, and McGraw cut the catcher from the team. /(JK)

William McLean — Unk.–Unk. *Umpire* NA, **NL**, AA 1872–80, 82–85, 89–90

McLean, an ex-prizefighter, deserves the title as the first truly professional umpire. He demanded that he be paid the then-unheard-of sum of $5 per game. So great were his talents and reputation for fairness that NL officials not only met his demands but also sent him on an expense-paid tour of every city in the league. McLean lived in Boston but often umpired games in Providence. He made the trip on foot, rising at 4:00 A.M. /(RTM)

Mark McLemore — 1964– . 2B 1986– **Angels** 252 g, .238, 5 hr, 71 rbi

McLemore was the Angels' regular second baseman in 1987, hitting .236 with 25 steals. He spent over two months on the DL in 1988, and Johnny Ray returned to his natural position in his absence, winning the job. /(JFC)

George McLinn (Stony) — 1884–Unk. *Writer.*

Sports editor of the Pittsburgh *Gazette-Times* in 1906, McLinn moved to the Philadelphia *Press* and was sports editor from 1908 until the paper closed in 1922. He was an original member of the BBWAA. /(NLM)

Cal McLish [Calvin Coolidge Julius Caesar Tuskahoma](Buster) — 1925– . RHP 1944, 46–49, 51, 56–64 Dodgers, Pirates, Cubs, **Indians**, Reds, White Sox, Phillies 1609 ip, 92–92, 4.01
☛ *All-Star—59.*

"There were eight kids in my family, and I was the only one my father was permitted to name, so I guess he figured he'd make up for the situation." That is how Cal McLish explains his long string of given names. He went right from American Legion ball to the Dodgers at age 18 in talent-scarce 1944, but didn't spent a full season in the majors until 1951. Four years in the Pacific Coast League followed before he found success with the Indians; he went 16–8 in 1958, and 19–8 in 1959. He had a nightmarish outing on May 21, 1957 at Boston: in one inning, he walked Jackie Jensen and allowed home runs to Gene Mauch, Ted Williams, Dick Gernert, and Frank Malzone. A lifelong friend of Mauch, McLish broke in with him in 1944, pitched for him in Philadelphia until arm trouble hit in 1964, and was Mauch's pitching coach on the Phillies (1965–66) and Expos (1969–75). /(NLM)

Don McMahon — 1930–1987. RHP 1957–74 **Braves**, Astros, Indians, Red Sox, White Sox, Tigers, Giants 1311 ip, 90–68, 2.96. *1 LCS, 3 ip, 0–0, 0.00. 3 WS, 10.1 ip, 0–0, 4.35*
☛ *All-Star—58.*

A relief pitcher who didn't rely on gimmicks, the well-traveled McMahon threw a fastball and a simple overhand curve for 18 ML seasons, and when he retired, only Hoyt Wilhelm, Lindy McDaniel, and Cy Young had pitched in more games. McMahon played before the dominating bullpen closer had emerged as a baseball position, and he never saved more than 19 games in a single season, but the stocky righthander was always in demand as durable, hard-throwing reliever.

McMahon was converted to relief pitching in the minors by manager Whitlow Wyatt after he had gone 2–13, 5.01 as a starter for Toledo (American Association) in 1955, and in 1957 he reached the ML, posting a 1.54 ERA in 32 appearances for the World Champion Braves. He led the NL with 15 saves in 1959, then in 1962 he began a sojourn that took him to seven different clubs in eight seasons. The Braves sold him to the Astros in 1962 (where he made his only two ML starts, both losses), who sold him to the Indians after 1963. McMahon saved 27 games in two seasons with the Indians, then switched teams in mid-season each year from 1966 to 1969, yet still posted a 1.98 ERA in 1967 and again in 1968. The Indians traded McMahon to the Red Sox with Lee Stange for Dick Radatz in 1966, and the Red Sox shipped him to the White Sox for Jerry Adair in 1967. Chicago traded him to Detroit for Dennis Ribant the following year, and in 1969 the Tigers sold him to San Francisco, where he spent his final six seasons. In 1971 McMahon led the NL with nine relief wins and recorded a career-high 19 saves for the Giants. /(SCL)

Marty McManus — 1900–1966. 2B-3B-1B-SS 1920–34 **Browns**, Tigers, Red Sox, Braves 1831 g, .289, 120 hr, 996 rbi.
Manager 1932–33 **Red Sox** 95–151, .386

McManus played every infield position with gritty determination. A Browns regular from 1921 to 1926, mostly at second base, he batted a high of .333 in 1924 and led the AL with 44 doubles in 1925. With the Tigers in 1930, his 23 stolen bases topped the league. He was player-manager in the last doleful days of the Red Sox before Tom Yawkey bought the team, then played for the Braves for 1934, and he managed in the minors for many years. /(JK)

Norm McMillan (Bub) — 1895–1969. 3B-2B-SS-OF 1922–24, 28–29 Yankees, Red Sox, Browns, **Cubs** 413 g, .260, 6 hr, 147 rbi. *2 WS, 6 g, .091*

McMillan was a widely traveled, 33-year-old utilityman when he surprised everyone by winning the Cubs' third base job in spring training of 1929. He remained at third base through the last game of the World Series, which was his final ML contest. /(DB)

Roy McMillan — 1930– . SS 1951–66 **Reds**, Braves, Mets 2093 g, .243, 68 hr, 594 rbi.
Manager 1972, 75 Brewers, **Mets** 27–28, .491
☛ *All-Star—56–57. Gold Glove—57–59.*

When *The Sporting News* began awarding Gold Gloves for fielding excellence in 1957, Roy McMillan received the first three for shortstops. A gutsy professional, universally respected by his peers, McMillan teamed with second baseman Johnny Temple to hold together the infield of the hard-hitting Reds for most of the 1950s. On a team that routinely hit for power in tiny Crosley Field, McMillan's weak bat was an affordable luxury. A strong arm, exceptional range and durability, and an astute sense of the game belied his bespectacled, mild-mannered appearance.

In 1954 McMillan set a since-surpassed NL record with 129 double plays. His career was spent away from the national spotlight, as he never played for a Cincinnati pennant winner. Ironically, McMillan's trade to Milwaukee for Joey Jay—who was to lead the NL in wins—brought the 1961 Reds the pitching needed to win their first league title in 21 years. McMillan's two All-Star Game starts were somewhat tainted by Cincinnati's ballot-stuffing campaign.

After three years with the Braves, McMillan concluded his playing career with the 1964–66

Roy McMillan

John McMullen (Lefty) — 1849–1881. OF-P 1871–75 Troy Haymakers (NA), New York Mutuals (NA),**Philadelphia Athletics (NA)**, Philadelphia White Stockings (NA) 244 g, .281; 15–16
☛ *Led League—ba 1874.*

After a season as a lefthanded pitcher—a rarity in the National Association—McMullen switched to the outfield. A .248 hitter over four of his five NA seasons, he exploded in 1874 to lead the circuit at .387./(FIC)

Ken McMullen — 1942– . 3B-1B-DH-OF 1962–77 Dodgers, **Senators**, Angels, A's, Brewers 1583 g, .248, 156 hr, 606 rbi. *1 LCS, 1 g, .000*

Signed by the Dodgers for $60,000 in 1960, McMullen got his first real shot at third base when Jim Gilliam moved to second for the 1963 Dodgers. But McMullen hit only .236 and in 1964 Gilliam was moved back to third. That winter McMullen had been part of a blockbuster deal with Washington that sent him, along with Frank Howard, Dick Nen, Phil Ortega, and Pete Richert, to the Senators for Claude Osteen, John Kennedy, and $100,000.

Finally a regular, he hit 18 HR with a .263 average and proved to be a good fielder at third base, finishing just behind AL leader Clete Boyer in total chances per game (but McMullen led in errors). He was the Senators' everyday third baseman for four more seasons and developed a good batting eye, reaching a career-high .272 in 1969.

McMullen also led the league in total chances per game three straight seasons with Washington (1967–69), in double plays ('67), and in putouts ('69), and tied ML third basemen's records for assists in a nine-inning game (11 on 9/26/66) and double plays started in a nine-inning game (4 on 8/13/65). After a slow start in 1970, McMullen was sent to the Angels at the end of April for Rich Reichardt and Aurelio Rodriguez, and led for the fourth straight season in total chances per game (although he slumped to .229 with 14 HR). He never won a Gold Glove because he played in the same era as Brooks Robinson.

McMullen's last good season came in 1971, when he reached a career high in HR (21). Dropping off to nine HR in 1972, he went back to the Dodgers in another big deal, going with Andy Messersmith in exchange for Frank Robinson, Bill Singer, Bobby Valentine, and two others. After three years spent backing up Ron Cey and pinch hitting, he signed with the A's for 1976 and was a utility man, leading the league in pinch hits (9-for-31). Sold to the

Mets. His presence brought New York's previously chaotic infield immediate respectability; he eventually groomed Bud Harrelson to take his place. He started a triple play against the Giants in the May 31, 1964 23-inning marathon that lasted a NL-record seven hours and 23 minutes.

Also significant was McMillan's durability. His 584 consecutive games at shortstop from 1951 to 1955 set a NL record. He played 150 or more games in eight different seasons—six in a row—including 157 games for the Mets at age 35. He went on to manage in the minors, coach for Milwaukee and the Mets, and scout. McMillan replaced Yogi Berra as Mets manager for 53 games in 1975./(PB)

Brewers for 1977, he finished his career as a DH/utility man. /(JFC)

Fred McMullin — 1891–1952. 3B 1914, 16–20 Tigers, **White Sox** 304 g, .256, 1 hr, 70 rbi. *2 WS, 8 g, .154, 2 rbi*

This least significant of the Black Sox had little opportunity to throw games, pinch hitting twice in the tainted Series, singling once. A capable backup third baseman, McMullin was aware of the fix, and was banned from baseball for life. /(ADS)

Craig McMurtry — 1959– . RHP 1983–86, 88– **Braves**, Rangers 616 ip, 28–38, 4.01

TSN's NL Rookie Pitcher of the Year in 1983, the skinny, bespectacled Texan debuted with a 15–9, 3.08 ERA mark to lead the Braves staff. He slumped to 9–17 in 1984, and 1985 included elbow problems. He was moved to the bullpen in 1985, and he never had a winning record after his rookie season. /(PB)

Eric McNair (Boob) — 1909–1949. SS-2B-3B 1929–42 **A's**, Red Sox, White Sox, Tigers 1251 g, .274, 82 hr, 633 rbi. *2 WS, 3 g, .000*

McNair was called Boob after the Rube Goldberg cartoon character Boob McNutt. A utility infielder on the 1930 and 1931 pennant-winning A's, he became Philadelphia's regular shortstop in 1932, hitting 18 HR and a league-high 47 doubles. He led AL shortstops in errors and double plays in 1934, and, after his power dropped off, Connie Mack sold him to the Red Sox in 1935. McNair was Boston's second baseman in 1937 and the White Sox' third baseman in 1939, when he hit a career-high .324 with a 20-game hitting streak. /(JLE)

Hurley McNair (Mack) — 1888–1948. OF-RHP-UMP Negro Leagues 1912–42 Gilkerson's Union Giants, Chicago Giants, Chicago American Giants, Detroit Stars, Chicago Union Giants, Cincinnati Tigers, Kansas City Monarchs 509 g, .314, 40 hr (inc.)

McNair was a solid lefthanded hitter with speed to burn. Like many other Negro League stars, he played for the 25th Infantry Wreckers, based at Fort Huachuca, AZ. In 1915 he was a member of the champion Chicago American Giants. From 1920 through 1927, he batted .320 with the Kansas City Monarchs, playing on the 1923–25 champions, and leading the team in home runs in 1927. Upon retiring as a player, he became a Negro National League umpire, earning about $140 a month. /(LL)

Dave McNally — 1942– . LHP 1962–1975 **Orioles**, Expos 2729 ip, 184–119, 3.24. 20 wins: 68–71 *5 LCS, 40 ip, 3–2, 2.68. 4 WS, 50 ip, 4–2, 2.34* ☛ *Led League—w 70. All-Star—69–70, 72.*

An unflappable lefthander with great control, McNally was the first of Baltimore's "Big Four" 20-game winners, joined later by Mike Cuellar, Jim Palmer, and Pat Dobson on the 1971 Baltimore staff. But McNally's place in baseball history may have less to do with how well he labored than with his impact on baseball's labor relations. He and the Dodgers' Andy Messersmith became baseball's first two legal free agents in 1975.

Even before he won 20 games, McNally was a hero in Baltimore. He outpitched Don Drysdale to win the fourth and final game of the 1966 Series 1–0 on a four-hitter, bringing Baltimore its first World Championship. Though he led the AL with 24 wins in 1970, his best overall season was 1968, when he posted a 22–10 record, with career bests of a 1.95

Dave McNally

ERA and 202 strikeouts. He helped the Orioles win the 1969 AL playoffs with an 11-inning, 11-strikeout, 1–0 victory against Minnesota in Game Two. However, he failed to hold a 3–0 lead in the fifth and final game of the 1969 Series against the Mets.

McNally's shining World Series moment came in the batter's box, not on the pitcher's mound. In the sixth inning of Game Three of the 1970 Series against the Reds, he became the only pitcher ever to hit a grand slam in a World Series. Ironically, the blast came off Tony Cloninger, who once hit a record two grand slams in a game while pitching for the Braves.

After the Curt Flood case and a short players' strike in 1972 failed to resolve the free agency issue, McNally and Messersmith decided to test the reserve clause and played their 1974 seasons without a contract. After the season, arbitrator Peter Seitz declared both players free agents. McNally signed with the Expos, but won only three games while losing six and registering a 5.26 ERA, prompting his retirement. /(SEW)

Mike McNally — 1893–1965. 2B-3B-SS 1915–17, 19–25 **Red Sox**, Yankees, Senators 492 g, .238, 1 hr, 85 rbi. *3 WS, 9 g, .200, 1 rbi*

A clever reserve infielder on five pennant winners, McNally stole home for the Yankees in the first game of the 1921 World Series. He became a minor league manager and scout, and the Indians' farm director. /(JK)

John McNamara — 1932– . *Manager* 1969–70, 74–77, 79–88, 90 A's, Padres, Reds, Angels, **Red Sox**, Indians 1048–1078, .493. *2 LCS, 4–6, .333. 1 WS, 3–4, .429*

A minor league catcher, McNamara never made it to the majors as a player, but his baseball knowledge gave him steady employment as a ML manager. A quiet man who did his job with little fanfare, he was sometimes criticized by fans who wanted a more colorful manager. In 1970 he was fired from the A's as being "too nice." Nevertheless, his teams usually finished as well or better than predicted. In 1986, when his Red Sox won the AL pennant, he was chosen co-Manager of the Year, along with Houston's Hal Lanier. Boston fired McNamara in mid-1988 and went on to win their division under his replacement, Joe Morgan. /(BC)

Tim McNamara — 1898– . RHP 1922–26 **Braves**, Giants 395 ip, 14–29, 4.78

A boyhood batterymate of Gabby Hartnett, McNamara went from Fordham College to the Boston Braves in 1922 and won three games in a row, pitching 26 straight scoreless innings. Hit hard the next two years, he recorded his last ML victory in 1924. /(JMu)

Graham McNamee — Unk.–Unk. *Broadcaster.*

Called "the greatest announcer we ever had," by Red Barber, McNamee abandoned a professional singing career in favor of radio announcing in May 1923 and by October was broadcasting the World Series. McNamee teamed with Grantland Rice for the 1923 WS, the first to be broadcast in its entirety. His vivid play-by-play prompted a deluge of fan mail, and his voice graced the World Series for the next decade. /(SL)

Earl McNeely — 1898–1971. OF-1B 1924–31 **Senators**, Browns 683 g, .272, 4 hr, 213 rbi. *2 WS, 11 g, .222, 1 rbi*

The Senators' Clark Griffith sent three players and $40,000 to Sacramento (Pacific Coast League) for McNeely in 1924. One of the players was Wid Matthews, a favorite with Washington fans. The fans protested so loudly that Griffith tried to cancel the deal, but Sacramento refused and Commissioner Landis upheld Sacramento. McNeely was not made welcome in Washington until he hit the ball that hopped over Freddie Lindstrom's head to give the Senators the victory over New York in the '24 World Series. /(NLM)

Jerry McNertney (Mac) — 1936– . C 1964, 66–73 **White Sox**, Pilots/Brewers, Cardinals, Pirates 590 g, .237, 27 hr, 163 rbi

McNertney began as a first baseman in the minors in 1958, but converted to catcher starting in 1961 and made the White Sox for 1964 after leading International League catchers in fielding in 1963. A backup through 1968 (he spent almost all of 1965 on the DL), he was chosen by the Seattle Pilots in the expansion draft and had his only season as a regular in 1969, batting .241 with career highs of eight HR and 55 RBI. He coached for the Yankees in the 1980s. /(WOR)

Pat McNulty — 1889–1963. OF 1922, 24–27 Indians 308 g, .290, 6 hr, 84 rbi

McNulty was a Cleveland native and Ohio State multi-sport star for whom the Indians had high hopes. He proved a disappointment, though he batted .314 in 1925. /(JK)

Bid McPhee [John Alexander] (King Bid) —
1859–1943. 2B 1882–99 Cincinnati (AA), **Reds**
2138 g, .275, 52 hr, 726 rbi.
Manager 1901–02 **Reds** 79–124, .389
☛ *Led League—hr 1886 .*

Over a career of 18 years, played entirely for
Cincinnati teams in the 19th century, Bid McPhee
was the best second baseman in the game. He was
deservedly called King Bid. Only four men have
played more games at 2B. Only Eddie Collins made
more career putouts or handled more chances; only
Frankie Frisch topped his record for total chances in
a season, and no one has yet exceeded the 529
putouts he achieved in 1886. In an era when fine
fielding was highly prized, he led his league in
double plays in 11 seasons and had the best fielding
average in nine. His .978 mark in 1897 was the
highest of any second baseman in his time. And he
did it all barehanded. Gloves were in general use by
1886, but McPhee resisted their use until 1897,
when his career was winding down.

The righthanded leadoff batter was a consistent
run producer, scoring more than 100 runs a season
ten times. He hit with fair power, leading the league
with seven HR in 1886, and he had 189 career
triples, including a league-high 19 in 1887. That was
impressive long-ball hitting for the dead-ball era. In
his rookie year in the American Association (1882),
color-coded uniforms were introduced to help new
fans learn the players' positions (the players called
them "clown suits"). McPhee wore orange and
black, the designation for second base. Throughout
his career, fundamental changes were made in
baseball's rules. Pitchers threw underhand from 45'
when he broke in, and it took seven balls to earn a
walk. He adjusted to overhand pitching for the next
nine seasons, and to the modern distance of 60'6"
thereafter.

McPhee was a sober and sedate man, never fined
or ejected from a game, and always in condition. He
performed without flair, but his excellence thrilled
the fans. He retired as a player while still command-
ing respect. /(ADS)

Mike McQueen — 1950– . LHP 1969–72, 74 **Braves**,
Reds 218 ip, 5–11, 4.67

At one time touted as "the next Warren Spahn,"
McQueen reached the Braves at age 19. After going
0–5 in 1972, he and teammate Jim Breazeale were
injured in a head-on car wreck. McQueen spent two
months in the hospital with a dislocated hip and sat
out the 1973 season. He was unsuccessful in a
comeback try with Cincinnati. /(PB)

George McQuillan — 1885–1940. RHP 1907–11,
13–16, 18 **Phillies**, Reds, Pirates, Indians 1576 ip, 85–89,
2.38. 20 wins: 08
☛ *Led League—era 10.*

A Phillies standout, McQuillan was 23–17 (1.53) in
1908, his first full season, and led the NL with a
1.60 ERA two years later. He was called "The Giant
Killer" for his domination over New York. After
illness and arm problems caused his drop to the
minors, he survived a fearful blow to the head by a
line drive off the bat of Tiger slugger Claude
Rossman. Reacquired from Pittsburgh by the 1915
Phillies as pennant insurance, he contributed four
vital victories late in the season. /(JK)

Hugh McQuillan (Handsome Hugh) — 1897–1947.
RHP 1918–27 **Braves**, Giants 1561 ip, 88–94, 3.83.
3 WS, 25 ip, 1–1, 3.60

The Giants paid the Braves $100,000 for McQuil-
lan. As a third starter, he helped New York capture
three consecutive NL pennants (1922–24). The
deal, made on July 30, 1922, a few days after a
controversial Yankee-Red Sox trade, led to the
adoption of a June 15 trading deadline which stood
for decades. /(JL)

George McQuinn — 1910–1978. 1B 1936, 38–48
Reds, **Browns**, A's, Yankees 1550 g, .276, 135 hr, 794 rbi.
2 WS, 13 g, .256, 1 hr, 6 rbi
☛ *All-Star—39, 40, 42, 44, 47, 48.*

McQuinn was a solid-hitting, excellent-fielding, lefthanded first baseman who spent seven years in the
Yankee farm system while Lou Gehrig reigned in
New York. Drafted by the Browns in 1937, he put
together a 34-game hitting streak in 1938, finishing
at .324. He remained a St. Louis regular for eight
years, leading AL first basemen in fielding three
times and in assists twice. In 1944 his opening game
home run gave the Browns their first-ever World
Series victory.

McQuinn was 4F in the WWII draft because of a
bad back, but was reclassified in 1945 when 4F
athletes were targeted for service. Through the
intervention of Illinois congressman Melvin Price
(requested by the Browns) and Happy Chandler,
McQuinn and others who were legitimately unable
to meet combat requirements were allowed to stay
with their teams.

With Gehrig long gone, McQuinn played first
base for the Yankees in 1947–48, and was a starting

All-Star both seasons. He set All-Star records with 14 putouts and 14 total chances accepted at first base in the 1948 contest. He went on to manage in the minors and scout for the Senators and Expos. /(NLM)

Hal McRae — 1945– . DH-OF 1968, 70–87 Reds, **Royals** 2084 g, .290, 191 hr, 1097 rbi. *8 LCS, 28 g, .261, 1 hr, 9 rbi. 4 WS, 17 g, .400, 0 hr, 6 rbi*
☛ *Led League—rbi 82. All-Star—75–76, 82.*

McRae came up as a good-hitting but poor-fielding platoon partner for Bernie Carbo in Cincinnati, but he found a home in Kansas City as a DH. Famed batting coach Charlie Lau helped him hone his batting talents, and he developed into a remarkably consistent hitter. His aggressive style of play and team-first spirit made him a natural leader.

McRae batted over .300 six times and led the AL twice in doubles. His 133 RBI in 1982 topped the league and set a Royals record. In 1976 he was edged for the batting title by teammate George Brett, .333 to .332, on Brett's controversial inside-the-park home run in his final at-bat. Charges that racism led Minnesota outfielder Steve Braun to intentionally misplay Brett's fly ball surfaced, but

Hal McRae

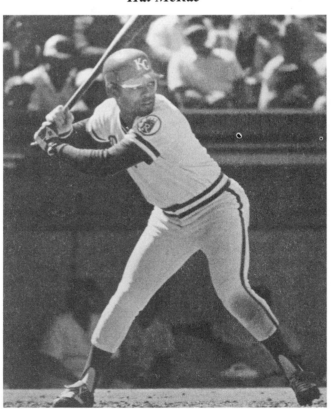

were never proven. McRae was named Designated Hitter of the Year three times by *TSN*.

McRae's career almost ended before it began when he broke his leg in four places while playing winter ball in Puerto Rico after the 1968 season. In June 1985, Hal's son Brian, a shortstop, was selected in the first round of the free agent draft by the Royals. This is thought to be the first time a father and son played for the same organization at the same time. /(FJO)

Kevin McReynolds (Big Mac) — 1959– . OF 1983– **Padres**, Mets 942 g, .270, 143 hr, 539 rbi. *2 LCS, 11 g, .263, 3 hr, 8 rbi*

McReynolds was the sixth player in the nation taken in the June 1981 draft, and made it to the major at the end of 1983 after being named Player of the Year in his minor leagues in both 1982 and '83 as well as *TSN* Minor League Player of the Year in '83. The Padres' regular centerfielder in their 1984 NL pennant season, he led NL outfielders in putouts that year and the next. He tied for the team lead with 20 HR while batting .278 with 75 RBI. His three-run homer powered the Padres to their Game Three 6–2 comeback victory against the Cubs in the LCS after he had scored the go-ahead run earlier in the game.

McReynolds dropped off to .234 with 15 HR in 1985, and, never outwardly demonstrative, he was accused of a lack of drive. Spurred on by such comments, he came back in 1986 with 26 HR and 96 RBI while batting .288, but was part of a seven-player deal that sent him to the World Champion Mets after the season. He hit .276 with 26 HR and 95 RBI in the middle of the Mets' powerful offense, but he hit only .213 with runners in scoring position. He improved that mark by more than .100 in the Mets' 1988 division title season, but was still prone to long slumps. But he showed a new talent, setting a major league record for most steals in a season, 22, without being caught. He also became the first player ever to have three straight seasons of 95 or more RBI without topping 100. The Mets were also happy with his fine defense in left field. He even led NL outfielders in assists in 1988, a relative rarity for leftfielders.

In 1989 McReynolds extended his stolen base streak to a ML-record 33 (dating back to 1987) before he was finally caught. Vince Coleman shattered the record later the same season. /(SH)

Robert B. McRoy — 1882–1917. *Executive.*

McRoy spent half his life as an executive in baseball, serving as secretary of the AL for the league's first 11 years. In 1911 he was part-owner of the Red Sox for a year, and in 1915 he was named vice president and treasurer of the Indians. One of his first acts was to close the deal that brought Tris Speaker to Cleveland from the Red Sox. From 1909 to 1917 McRoy was the business manager of the WS with John Heydler. /(NLM)

John McSherry — 1944- . *Umpire* NL 1971-87
2 ASU 4 LCS 2 WS

The 300-pound McSherry once called Pete Rose out on strikes. "That ball was low," insisted Pete. "You missed it. If it had been a hamburger, you wouldn't have missed it!" Despite cracks about his size, McSherry earned respect for his expert knowledge of the rules. He has served as an umpiring school instructor and as the executive director of the New York School of Umpiring. /(RTM)

Cal McVey — 1850-1926. 1B-3B-C-RHP 1876-79
Cubs, **Reds** 265 g, .328, 3 hr, 172 rbi;165 ip, 9-11, 3.76.
Manager 1878-79 **Reds** 72-52, .581

An excellent hitter who could play any position, including pitcher, McVey was only 18 when he joined Harry Wright's Cincinnati Red Stockings, the first professional team, which barnstormed to a 56-0-1 record in 1869. When the first professional league, the National Association, was formed in 1871, McVey followed Wright to the Boston Red Stockings and hit .419. The NL replaced the NA in 1876, and Iowa native McVey joined the White Stockings (later the Cubs), batting .347 and collecting six hits in one game twice in four days (July 22 and 25). He returned to Cincinnati in 1878 as the Reds' player-manager but left for California after a fifth-place finish in 1879. He was involved in Pacific Coast League baseball for many years. /(JK)

Doug McWeeny (Buzz) — 1896-1953. RHP 1921-22, 24, 26-30 White Sox, **Dodgers**, Reds 948 ip, 37-57, 4.17

The 6'2" 190-lb McWeeny had his best years for the Dodgers in the late 1920s. He was 11-13 in 1926 with a 3.04 ERA and 14-14 in 1928 with a 3.17 ERA. He led the NL in walks (114) and shutouts (4) in 1928. He was suspended by the White Sox for part of 1922 and all of 1923. /(JM)

Larry McWilliams — 1954- . LHP 1978- Braves, **Pirates**, Cardinals, Phillies, Royals 1550 ip, 78-90, 3.95

The lanky McWilliams won his first seven big league decisions, including August 1, 1978 when his surprising catch helped stop Pete Rose's 44-game

hitting streak. Following arm trouble, his delivery was revamped by coach Johnny Sain from a slow motion to an accelerated, whip-like delivery. Mc-Williams peaked as *TSN* NL All-Star lefthanded pitcher for 1983. He was fifth in the Cy Young voting and had more strikeouts (199) than any Pittsburgh pitcher since 1969. He was relegated to relief and spot-start duty after further arm trouble in 1985. /(ME)

Bobby Meacham — 1960- . SS-2B 1983-88
Yankees 457 g, .236, 8 hr, 114 rbi

A highly thought-of switch-hitter in the Yankee organization for years, Meacham was the everyday shortstop only in 1985. Injuries and inconsistent overall play relegated him to utility play and time in the minors. Meacham hit just .218 in 1985 and led the major leagues with 23 sacrifice hits. He was traded to the Rangers for Bob Brower before the 1989 season, but was cut by Texas. /(EG)

Louis Meacham — Unk.-1910. *Writer.*

Meacham was the first booster of baseball in the Chicago press, as a reporter on the *Tribune* in the 1860s. For a time, he was the only Chicago reporter to keep a scorecard and print accounts of the games. Eventually other papers began to give baseball space. /(NLM)

Lee Meadows (Specs) — 1894-1963. RHP 1915-29
Cardinals, Phillies, Pirates 3151 ip, 188-180, 3.38. 20
wins: 26 *2 WS, 14 ip, 0-2, 6.28*
☛ Led League—w 26.

The first modern major leaguer to wear glasses, nearsighted Lee Meadows led the National League with 23 losses, winning only 12, as a sophomore for the last-place 1916 Cardinals. But he proved to be a workhorse, making a league-high 51 appearances in 1916 and averaging 241 innings a year for his first 13 seasons. He suffered another NL-high 20-loss season with St. Louis and Philadelphia in 1919. He fared better after he was traded to Pittsburgh in May 1923. He went 88-52 as a Pirate, tied teammate Ray Kremer and the Reds' Pete Donohue for the NL lead with 20 wins in 1926, and led the league in starts and complete games in 1927, going 19-10. He opened both the 1925 and 1927 World Series, losing each time. A sore arm in 1928 finished his ML career. /(ME)

Dave Meads — 1964- . LHP 1987-88 **Astros** 88 ip, 8-4, 4.48

Meads did a fair job as a middle reliever in two call-ups by the Astros in 1987 and 1988. /(SFS)

Tom Meany — 1903–1964, Writer.

Meany started with the Brooklyn *Daily Times* in 1923, beginning a stream of bubbly, fact-laden prose that ceased only when he died as the publicist of the Mets in 1964. The largest part of his sports writing career was spent covering the Brooklyn Dodgers for the New York *World-Telegram*. He also wrote numerous baseball articles for *Colliers* and was their sports editor at his death. Possessed of a fabulous memory and a quick wit, he assessed clumsy slugger Rudy York, who boasted of Cherokee ancestors, as "part Indian and part first baseman." /(JK)

Charlie Meara (Goggy) — 1891–1962. OF **Yankees** 4 g, .286, 0 hr, 1 rbi

Meara came down with jaundice in his only major league season and had to leave the team. Ownership accused him of going to play elsewhere while on leave, and he had to sue to recover his salary. /(SFS)

Doc Medich [George Francis] — 1948– . RHP 1972–82 Yankees, Pirates, A's, Mariners, Mets, **Rangers**, Brewers 1996 ip, 124–105, 3.78. *1 WS, 2 ip, 0–0, 18.00*

In Medich's first major league game (9/5/72 against Baltimore), he drew a walk as the starting pitcher when the Yankees batted around in the top of the first. In the bottom of the inning he failed to retire a batter, and the next day he began his first year of medical school at Pitt. Medich did better in 1973 (14–9, 2.91), and after two more solid years he was traded to his hometown Pirates in the deal that brought the Yankees Willie Randolph, Dock Ellis, Ken Brett, and several pennants. Following a rocky 1976 (8–11, 3.51) and an itinerant 1977 split between three clubs, he settled down in Texas and provided the Rangers with five workmanlike seasons before the Brewers acquired him for their 1982 stretch drive. Medich then retired to practice sports medicine near Pittsburgh. His medical training came in handy before a 1978 game in Baltimore when he saved the life of a stricken fan by performing heart massage. /(FDS)

Joe Medwick (Ducky-Wucky, Muscles) — 1911–1975. OF 1932–48 **Cardinals**, Dodgers, Giants, Braves 1984 g, .324, 205 hr, 1383 rbi. *2 WS, 12 g, .326, 1 hr, 5 rbi* ☛ *Most Valuable Player—37. Led League—ba 37. Led League—hr 37. Led League—rbi 36–38. All-Star—34–42, 44. Hall of Fame—1968.*

Medwick's reputation as a bad-ball hitter who slashed doubles to all fields got him into the Hall of Fame, but he is most often remembered for his

unusual removal from Game Seven of the 1934 World Series. With the Cardinals winning a blowout in Detroit, he slid hard into Tiger third baseman Marv Owen on his sixth-inning triple, even though the throw hadn't come in yet. When Medwick went out to left field with the score 9–0, Detroit fans threw bottles, food, and garbage at him. Commissioner Landis, in attendance as always at the Series game, ordered Medwick from the field for his own safety so the game could be resumed, and Chick Fullis replaced him in left field. Medwick hit .379 with five RBI for the Series, including four hits, one a HR, in the opener.

Medwick came up in September 1932 and hit .349 to win the job. He hit .300 his first 11 seasons, and won the NL's last Triple Crown in 1937 with career highs of 31 HR, 154 RBI, and a .374 BA. He was NL MVP that year, also leading in slugging, runs, and doubles. For three straight years, 1936–38, he led the NL in both RBI and doubles. He drove in at least 100 runners six straight seasons (1934–39), scored 100 runs six times, including five consecutive years (1934–38), hit 40 doubles seven straight years (1933–39), and had seven seasons of 10 or more triples.

His prime seasons came with the Cardinals. After

Joe Medwick

dropping off slightly in 1939, he was sold to the Dodgers in mid-1940 for the then-astronomical sum of $125,000. He helped Brooklyn to their first pennant in over 20 years in 1941 with his last great season, but suffered a life-threatening beaning by former teammate Bob Bowman after quarreling with him in an elevator; Branch Rickey thought it was an attempt by St. Louis to ruin Medwick. He had decent seasons in 1942 and, after a trade to the Giants, in 1944, but was never the same after the beaning. The Hall of Fame Veterans Committee selected him in 1968. /(WOR)

Jouett Meekin — 1867–1944. RHP 1891–1900 Louisville (AA), Louisville (NL), Washington (NL), **Giants**, Braves, Pirates 2603 ip, 156–134, 4.07. 20 wins: 94, 96–97
☛ *Led League—w 94.*

Hard-throwing Meekin teamed with Amos Rusie to give the pre-McGraw Giants their best pitching staffs, tying for the NL lead with 36 wins each in 1894. A lifetime .243 hitter, Meekin hit three triples in one game on July 4, 1894, and belted 15 career home runs. /(ADS)

Ernest Mehl — 1900–1986. *Writer.*

Considered the father of ML baseball in Kansas City, Mehl went to work for the Kansas City *Star* in 1920 and was sports editor from 1950 until he retired in 1965. He worked for years to bring a ML franchise to the city, finally achieving success with the A's in 1955. When A's owner Arnold Johnson died in 1960, Mehl was part of the group that tried to buy the team, and when the A's moved to Oakland in 1968, he started the fight for an expansion team, ultimately the Royals. Mehl was an ordained minister who appeared in many pulpits on Sunday mornings while traveling as a baseball writer. /(NLM)

Heinie Meine [Henry William] (The Count of Luxemburg) — 1896–1968. RHP 1922, 29–34 Browns, **Pirates** 999 ip, 66–50, 3.95
☛ *Led League—w 31.*

Meine's career was handicapped by the outlawing of the spitball, his out pitch. Adjusting to life without it, Meine appeared once for the 1922 Browns, pitched well in the minors, and then retired to operate a tavern in 1927. Egged on by his patrons, he made his comeback as a junkballer. As a Pirate in 1931, he tied for the NL lead with 19 wins, and lead the league in starts (35) and innings (284). /(ME)

Roman Mejias — 1930– . OF 1955, 57–64 **Pirates**, Astros, Red Sox 627 g, .254, 54 hr, 202 rbi

Mejias left the sugar cane fields of Cuba when signed by the Pirates. He hit in 54 consecutive games at Waco (Big State League) in 1954. The fast Mejias saw only part-time duty in Pittsburgh but seemed to blossom with Houston in 1962, hitting .286 with 24 HR and 76 RBI. Acquired by Boston for his righthanded power, he could not match his 1962 efforts. /(ME)

Sam Mele [Sabath Anthony] — 1923– . OF-1B 1947–56 Red Sox, **Senators**, White Sox, Orioles, Reds, Indians 1046 g, .267, 80 hr, 544 rbi.
Manager 1961–67 **Twins** 518–427, .429. First place: 65 *3 WS–4, .429*

Mele was a basketball star at NYU in the early 1940s, but pursued a pro baseball career. A journeyman player with a respectable bat, he played for seven teams in eight years. He tied for the AL lead with 36 doubles as Washington's right fielder in 1951. After the Senators moved to Minneapolis in 1961, Mele replaced Cookie Lavagetto as manager mid-season. He brought the Twins in second in 1962, and in 1965 he took them to the World Series, which they lost to the Dodgers in seven games. /(JK)

Sam Mele

Luis Melendez — 1949- . OF 1970-77 **Cardinals**, Padres 641 g, .248, 9 hr, 122 rbi

Melendez was called up along with Jose Cruz in 1970 to form an outfield with Lou Brock that Cardinals fans expected to last for years. Luis was unable to duplicate his strong minor league marks and spent his career platooning and pinch hitting. A pinch grand slam in 1972 was perhaps the high point of his eight ML years. /(FJO)

Oscar Melillo (Spinach, Ski) — 1899-1963. 2B-3B 1926-37 **Browns**, Red Sox 1377 g, .260, 22 hr, 548 rbi

Melillo's career, and life, were threatened by Bright's disease, an often fatal kidney inflammation, and he doggedly stuck to a doctor's prescribed diet of spinach, and nothing but spinach, until cured. A smooth-fielding second baseman, he was a Browns regular for nearly a decade. He became a popular coach and was a loyal lieutenant to Lou Boudreau with the Indians, Red Sox, and A's. /(JK)

Bill Melton — 1945- . 3B-DH-OF-1B 1968-77 **White Sox**, Angels, Indians 1144 g, .253, 160 hr, 591 rbi
☛ *Led League—hr 71. All-Star—71.*

Going into the last day of the 1971 season, Bill Melton found himself in a three-way tie with Reggie Jackson and Norm Cash for the AL home run lead, with 32. A dead-pull hitter, he sent a breaking ball from Milwaukee's Bill Parsons into the left-field stands, becoming the first White Sox player to win a home run title. It was his second straight 33-HR year. But for much of his time in Chicago, he was the target of broadcaster Harry Caray, who drew attention to the third baseman's fielding inadequacies. Melton took the criticisms to heart, and when his production fell off after missing most of 1972 with a herniated disc, he was berated in Chicago. Thankful for his December 1975 trade to the Angels, he left the White Sox as their all-time HR leader, with 154. In 1970 he became the first AL player to strike out ten times over three consecutive games. /(RL)

Cliff Melton (Mountain Music) — 1912-1986. LHP 1937-44 Giants 1454 ip, 86-80, 3.42 20 wins: 37 *1 WS, 11 ip, 0-2, 4.91*

Friends dubbed the guitar-playing balladeer from the hills of North Carolina "Mountain Music." Others taunted the gentle, 6'5" giant because of his large, floppy ears. He blew a chance with the Yankees when he couldn't ignore the Cubs' Gabby Hartnett's needling during an exhibition game. After Melton was returned to Baltimore, GM Jack Ogden gave him a bonus every time he went after his tormentors. Twice, the huge lefthander charged into enemy dugouts.

He was 20-9 and had a league-high seven saves as a Giants rookie in 1937, but was beaten twice by the Yankees in the World Series. He was an under-.500 pitcher from 1939 on, and left the majors in 1944 after an arm injury and conflicts with management. /(JK)

Rube Melton [Reuben Franklin] — 1917-1971. RHP 1941-44, 46-47 Phillies, **Dodgers** 704 ip, 30-50, 3.62

An independent, 6'5" country boy, Melton jumped the Cardinals organization and played two years of semi-pro ball before being reinstated in 1940. When St. Louis forgot to protect him in the draft, he was plucked by the Phillies. He led NL pitchers in bases on balls in 1942, when he went 9-20. He was a cousin of Cliff Melton. /(JK)

Bob Melvin — 1961- . C 1985- Tigers, **Giants** 391 g, .225, 25 hr, 119 rbi. *1 LCS, 3 g, .429*

Excellent defensively, Melvin has struggled at the plate in each of his five ML seasons. In 1987 he threw out 40% of the opposition's would-be base-stealers (second-best in the NL) as the Giants' part-time catcher, nailing Tim Raines and Vince Coleman twice each. He also hit a career-high 11 HR that year, but batted just .199. /(SCL)

Memorial Stadium Baltimore Orioles 1954- . LF-309, CF-405, RF-309

Originally a 30,000-seat minor league park, Memorial Stadium was built in 1949 to replace Oriole Park, home of the local International League club, which had burned down five years earlier. When the Browns moved from St. Louis and became the ML Orioles in 1954, an unusual uncovered second deck was added to the stadium, increasing the park's capacity by 50% but also creating numerous obstructed-view seats in the lower level with its bulky support columns. The exterior is red brick and the playing field remains natural grass with a large foul territory. And while the corners are only 309' away, the fences shoot out sharply to 360' before sloping more gradually toward center. On May 8, 1966, Frank Robinson hit the only home run to leave the stadium completely when he drove a Luis Tiant pitch over the left field bleachers. Today, Memorial Stadium concession stands serve the only crab cakes in ML baseball. /(SCL)

Jose Mendez (Joe) — 1888 or 1889–1928. RHP-SS-3B-2B-MGR Negro Leagues 1908–26 Cuban Stars, Stars of Cuba, All-Nations, Los Angeles White Sox, Chicago American Giants, Detroit Stars, **Kansas City Monarchs** statistics not available

New York Giants manager John McGraw said that lean, long-armed pitcher Jose Mendez was worth $50,000 — but in his day there was no market in organized baseball for a Cuban with coal-black skin. Mendez is generally regarded as one of the greatest Cuban ballplayers who did not play in the American major leagues.

Mendez was a smart pitcher who changed speeds well and had a rising fastball and sharp-breaking curve. Hall of Famer John Henry Lloyd said that he never saw any pitcher superior to Mendez. Arthur Hardy, another contemporary, said that Mendez threw harder than the legendary Smokey Joe Williams.

Mendez compiled a 15–6 record his first year in the Cuban Winter League. He came to America in 1908 and went 44–2 for the 1909 Cuban Stars (some games were played against semi-pro teams). He spent all of 1910 in Cuba, playing both summer and winter, going 18–2. By 1914 he had compiled a 62–17 record in Cuba, but he developed arm trouble and never again pitched there regularly.

Mendez played for the All-Nations of Kansas City from 1912 to 1916. The team was the most racially mixed of all time, carrying blacks, whites, Japanese, Hawaiians, American Indians, and Latin Americans on its roster. A barnstorming rather than a league club, the All-Nations played a high caliber of baseball, in 1916 going 3–1 against the powerful Indianapolis ABC's and splitting a series with the Chicago American Giants.

Mendez's greatest success came as a playing manager with the Kansas City Monarchs in 1920–26. Occasionally pitching and playing the infield, he led the Monarchs to three straight Negro National League pennants (1923–25). His pitching record was 20–4, with seven saves. In the 1924 Black World Series against Hilldale of the Eastern Colored League, Mendez was 2–0 with a 1.42 ERA in four games, including a shutout in the only game he started. In the 1925 BWS, also against Hilldale, he was 0–1.

Mendez was 8–7 in exhibition games against major league competition. He defeated Jack Coombs in 1908 and Hall of Famer Eddie Plank in 1909, and split two games with Christy Mathewson. /(JM)

Mario Mendoza [born Mario Aizpuro Aizpuru] — 1950– . SS 1974–82 **Pirates**, Mariners, Rangers 686 g, .215, 4 hr, 101 rbi. *1 LCS, 3 g, .200, 1 rbi*

George Brett coined the phrase "Mendoza line" to describe the point in the Sunday-paper batting statistics where the batters' averages were below Mendoza's. This was usually at about .200. Mendoza was considered a good-fielding shortstop, but the Mexican hit below .200 three straight seasons (1975–77) and five times in his nine-year career. He played most regularly in 1979 after being traded to the Mariners, hitting .198 in 148 games (373 at-bats). His career-high BA was .245 in 1980. /(SFS)

Jock Menefee [John] — 1868–1953. RHP-OF 1892–95, 98, 1900–03 Pirates, Louisville (NL), Giants, **Cubs** 1111 ip, 58–69, 3.81; 221 g, .222, 0 hr, 57 rbi

Unimpressive in stints with Pittsburgh, Louisville, and the Giants, Menefee had his best season at 12–10, 2.42 for the 1902 Cubs. He played the outfield as often as he pitched in 1901–02, but couldn't hit better than .257. /(ADS)

Denis Menke — 1940– . SS-3B-2B-1B 1962–74 **Braves**, Astros, Reds 1598 g, .250, 101 hr, 606 rbi. *2 LCS, .240, 1 hr, 1 rbi. 1 WS, 7 g, .083, 1 hr, 2 rbi* ☛ All-Star—69–70.

Menke was a hard-nosed shortstop with some power who played every infield position. He was a key member of the 1969 Astros who challenged the Braves for the division flag, and played a minor role at the beginning of the Big Red Machine.

Menke arrived with the Braves in the early 1960s and showed early power, reaching 20 HRs in 1964. His production declined after the Braves moved to Atlanta and he was sent to Houston with Denny Lemaster for Sonny Jackson. Menke made the All-Star team two years with the Astros, and was part of the Joe Morgan-Lee May trade that created Cincinnati's dynasty of the 1970s. A 1972 Series homer off Catfish Hunter in Game Five was a final career highlight. /(PB)

Mike Menosky (Leaping Mike) — 1894–1983. OF 1914–17, 19–23 Pittsburgh (FL), **Senators**, Red Sox 809 g, .278, 18 hr, 250 rbi

An all-out player, Menosky was called Leaping Mike for his daring, fence-crashing catches. Signed by the Federal League and sent to its minor league (the Colonial), he saw most of his action in the AL, and in 1921 he hit .300 for Boston. /(JK)

Rudi Meoli — 1951- . SS-3B-2B 1971, 73–75, 78–79 **Angels**, Cubs, Phillies 310 g, .212, 2 hr, 40 rbi

In Meoli's only season as a regular, he led AL shortstops in errors with 27 in only 95 games at the position, hitting .223. /(JFC)

Orlando Mercado — 1961- . C 1982–84, 86- **Mariners**, Rangers, Tigers, Dodgers, A's, Twins 203 g, .196, 4 hr, 38 rbi

A career backup catcher, this Puerto Rican saw the most action with the 1983 Mariners, batting .197 in 178 at-bats. /(JFC)

Sid Mercer — Unk.–1945. *Writer*.

One of the founders of the BBWAA, the tall, slender Mercer worked to keep the press boxes free of outsiders. Raised on an Illinois farm, Mercer attended Dixon College for two years. He was a baseball writer for the St. Louis *Republic* and *Post-Dispatch* when he was hired by the Browns as road secretary in 1906. A year later he joined the New York *Evening Globe*.

In 1917 John McGraw was suspended for 17 days after he blasted league president John Tener in an interview with Mercer. McGraw later denied the quotes, and when he questioned Mercer's veracity, the writer suggested they "step outside." Tener fined McGraw $1,000 and the Giants' manager didn't speak to Mercer for ten years. Mercer was president of the BBWAA in 1940 and was with the New York *Journal-American* when he died in 1945. He was posthumously awarded the J.G. Taylor Spink Award by the Hall of Fame in 1969. /(NLM)

Win Mercer — 1874–1903. RHP-3B-OF-SS 1894–1902 **Washington (NL)**, Giants, Senators, Tigers 2466 ip, 131–164, 3.98; 561 g, .285, 7 hr, 197 rbi. 20 wins: 1896, 97

The 5′7″ 140-lb Mercer was the ace of the lowly Washington (NL) club at the end of the 19th century; he went 25–18 in 1896 and 20–20 in 1897. A .285 hitter, he often played the infield or outfield when not pitching. He joined the Tigers in 1902 and went 15–18 with a career-best 3.04 ERA. The following winter, Detroit appointed the 28-year-old their player-manager for 1903. But that January 12, Mercer checked into a San Francisco hotel room and killed himself by inhaling poison gas. He left a suicide note warning of the evils of women and gambling. /(AJA)

Fred Merkle — 1888–1956. 1B 1907–20, 25–26 **Giants**, Dodgers, Cubs, Yankees 1637 g, .273, 61 hr, 733 rbi. *5 WS, 27 g, .239, 1 hr, 8 rbi*

Fred Merkle is forever famous for his bonehead play on September 23, 1908, resulting in a playoff game for the NL pennant in which the Cubs beat Merkle's Giants. The play itself was clouded by contradictory affidavits by players, conflicting opinions by various baseball officials, and protests lodged by both teams over the umpires' handling of the incident.

The confusion started when Merkle, the runner on first, failed to touch second after an apparent game-winning base hit. Instead, he turned back toward the dugout, as was customary at the time, when he saw the run cross the plate. As the happy Polo Grounds crowd filed across the field towards the centerfield gate, second baseman Johnny Evers got the ball and stepped on second, claiming a forceout which negated the winning run. With the fans already crowding the field, the game could not be played to a decision, and had to be replayed.

Fred Merkle

When the season ended with the two teams tied, a group of Giants, led by Christy Mathewson, went to owner John T. Brush. They claimed they shouldn't have to play another game for something they had already won. The gravely ill Brush expressed disappointment at their attitude, and they played and lost. Whatever the merits of the case, it was one of baseball's most controversial plays and it haunted Merkle not just for the rest of his playing days, but all his life. He bitterly refused requests for interviews in later years because he didn't want to relive the incident.

He was 19 at the time and had played in only 35 games that season; after the loss of the playoff game, he intended to quit the game, but McGraw persuaded him to come back. He was still affected by the incident in 1909, hitting just .187, but McGraw stayed with him.

Merkle cost the Giants $2,500. The 6'1" 190-lb righthanded first baseman was one of the fastest big men the game had seen. In eight different years he stole 20 or more bases, with a career high of 49 in 1911, when the Giants stole a record 347. He was the cleanup hitter, but not a long-ball threat.

Merkle was involved in another crucial lapse in the last game of the 1912 World Series. After Fred Snodgrass dropped a fly ball in the 10th inning, Tris Speaker popped up foul between home and first. Merkle and catcher Chief Meyers let it drop between them. Speaker then singled in the tying run and the Red Sox went on to win the game and the Series.

Merkle was one of the first to take up bridge and golf, when those games were unknown to most players. In 1913 he fell into two batting slumps. McGraw discovered he had been playing golf with reporters before going to the Polo Grounds. He stopped Merkle's golfing, and golf was taboo on the Giants during the remainder of McGraw's tenure. But Merkle, McGraw, and Mathewson continued to play bridge.

In late 1916 the Dodgers' first baseman, Jake Daubert, injured an ankle. The Dodgers wanted Merkle, and McGraw traded him for catcher Lew McCarty. He would end up in another World Series. Traded to the Cubs in 1917, he got into his fifth World Series the next year; every one of them had been with a losing team. As a coach with the Yankees in 1926 he was again on the losing side in a Series.

He played in the International League 1921–25 and managed in the low minors for a few years. /(NLM)

Durwood Merrill — 1938– . *Umpire* AL 1977–87
1 ASU 3 LCS

During the off-season, Merrill hosts a daily radio talk show in Texas and at Christmas plays Santa Claus. He is generally friendly, jovial, and considered fun to be around. Nevertheless, in a 1986 *TSN* poll, he was voted the AL ump with the quickest thumb. At one time he served as head football coach and athletic director at East Texas State University. /(RTM)

Lloyd Merriman (Citation) — 1924– . OF 1949–51, 54–55 **Reds**, White Sox, Cubs 455 g, .242, 12 hr, 117 rbi

Merriman was a war hero, an All-American, and a college graduate at a time when most athletes disdained the academic life. In between his WWII hitch in the Marines and his aerial dogfights in Mig Alley during the height of the Korean War, Merriman was an All-American fullback for Stanford in 1946. His gridiron heroics earned him an invitation to the Chicago Bears training camp, but he opted to finish his schooling. In 1948 the Cincinnati Reds paid him a large bonus, and he joined the parent club a year later. He had four seasons of part-time duty for Cincinnati before being sold to the White Sox and then the Cubs in 1955. Merriman had twelve outfield put-outs against the Cubs on September 7, 1951, his career highlight. /(RL)

Jim Merritt — 1943– . LHP 1965–75 **Twins**, Reds, Rangers 1483 ip, 81–86, 3.65. 20 wins: 70 *1 LCS, 5 ip, 1–0, 1.69. 2 WS, 5 ip, 0–1, 9.00*

Noted for his pinpoint control, Merritt debuted with the 1965 pennant-winning Twins and tied a since-broken AL record when he fanned seven consecutive batters on July 21, 1966. He was traded to Cincinnati after the 1968 season for Leo Cardenas. Backed by the league's best offense and bullpens that led the NL in saves, Merritt went 17–9 in 1969 and 20–12 for the 1970 league champion Reds. Bothered by a sore arm in the World Series, he went 1–11 the following year, and finished, unsuccessfully, with the Rangers, where he was fined $250 after admitting to using some of teammate Gaylord Perry's K-Y jelly on the ball. /(JLE)

Sam Mertes (Sandow) — 1872–1945. OF-2B-1B-SS Phillies, Cubs, White Sox, **Giants**, Cardinals 1190 g, .279, 40 hr, 721 rbi. *1 WS, 5 g, .176, 3 rbi*
☛ *Led League—rbi 03.*

With the 1902 White Sox, Mertes led AL outfielders in assists, played at least one game at every position, and won the only game he ever pitched. The following year, as a Giants outfielder, he was the NL RBI champ, tied for the league lead in doubles, and led outfielders in fielding. His 108 RBI, 17 triples, and 52 stolen bases in 1905 put him near the top of the NL and helped New York to a World Championship. He was nicknamed Sandow after a renowned strongman of the day. /(NLM)

Lennie Merullo — 1917– . SS 1941–47 **Cubs** 639 g, .240, 6 hr, 152 rbi. *1 WS, 3 g, .000*

Merullo was a wartime shortstop who did his battling on the diamond. In 1946 he tangled with Eddie Stanky of the Dodgers during a game and the next day accepted a challenge from Dixie Walker before the game in a fight unusually serious by baseball standards. After his playing career he spent 25 years as the Cubs' chief scout. He nicknamed his son Boots because, the day the boy was born, Lennie made four errors. /(JK)

Steve Mesner — 1918–1981. 3B-SS 1938–39, 41, 43–45 Cubs, Cardinals, **Reds** 451 g, .252, 2 hr, 167 rbi

Mesner signed a contract at age 16 in 1934, and the next year hit .331 for Los Angeles (Pacific Coast League). He served as Cincinnati's third baseman during WWII, never batting higher than .272. He led NL third basemen in errors in 1943 and 1945 and in assists in 1945. /(NLM)

Andy Messersmith [John Alexander] — 1945– . RHP 1968–79 **Angels**, Dodgers, Braves, Yankees 2230 ip, 130–99, 2.86. *1 LCS, 7 ip, 1–0, 2.57. 1 WS, 14 ip, 0–2, 4.50*
☛ *All-Star—71, 74–76. Gold Glove—74–75.*

Messersmith was a good pitcher who spent more than a decade in the majors, but his mound performances will forever be overshadowed by the role he played in the advent of free agency. Both he and Dave McNally tested the reserve clause by playing the 1975 season without contracts in their option years. The players' contention was that this freed them from their contracts; the reserve clause would bind them beyond their contracts for the option year and no further. The owners insisted that the reserve clause was automatically and perpetually renewed. Arbitrator Peter Seitz ruled for the players, and a new era in baseball's labor relations was inaugurated.

When he made his decision to challenge the reserve clause, Messersmith was coming off a strong 1974 season. He was 20–6 with a 2.59 ERA, leading the NL in winning percentage and tying for first in wins for a pennant-winning Dodger team. He

won Game Two of the LCS 5–2 but lost the World Series opener 3–2 and also failed in Game Five, 5–2. He made himself attractive in his contractless 1975 season by leading the NL in starts (40), complete games (19), innings (322), shutouts (7), and fewest hits per nine innings (6.8). He went 19–14 with a 2.29 ERA to finish third in wins and second in ERA, and his 213 strikeouts ranked third. He made the All-Star team and won the Gold Glove Award both years.

He was not the first free agent (Catfish Hunter had been released from his contract by Commissioner Bowie Kuhn the year before, after owner Charlie Finley refused to honor a bonus in the contract), but Messersmith's precedent was more important. He was signed by the Braves for an estimated $1.75 million after owner Ted Turner won a furious month-long bidding war. Signed on April 10, Messersmith missed spring training and proved to be the first in another category: the disappointing free agent. He pitched well enough, going 11–11 with a 3.04 ERA for last-place Atlanta. He was even named to the All-Star team for the third straight season (although he was replaced due to injury), but more was expected of the newly minted baseball millionaire. He lost most of 1977 to injuries and was sold to the Yankees for 1978. He made the rotation with an impressive spring training, but he hurt his shoulder a week before the season started when he stumbled while covering first base. He made only six appearances that year and failed in a comeback in 1979 with the Dodgers.

Before becoming a baseball pioneer, Messersmith spent five seasons as Anaheim's hometown hero with the Angels. He pitched well for mediocre teams, never posting an ERA higher than 3.00, and went 20–13 in 1971 for the sub-.500 Angels, making the All-Star team for the first time. He joined the Dodgers for 1973 with Ken McMullen as part of the blockbuster deal that sent Frank Robinson, Bill Singer, Mike Strahler, Bobby Valentine, and Billy Grabarkewitz to the Angels. /(SFS)

Bill Messman — Unk.–1984. *Scout.*

The longtime Midwest scouting supervisor for the Minnesota Twins began his scouting career with the Reds in 1954 and joined the Senators in 1959, following them to Minnesota. Messman remained with the Twins until his death in 1984, and his top discoveries included Graig Nettles, Tim Laudner, and Gary Gaetti. /(FVP)

Bud Metheney [Arthur Beauregard] — 1915- . OF 1943-46 **Yankees** 376 g, .247, 31 hr, 156 rbi. *1 WS, 2 g, .125*

The Yankees' right fielder while Tommy Henrich was serving in WWII, Metheny hit a career-high .261 for the 1943 World Champions and committed the most errors (11) by an AL outfielder in 1944. /(JLE)

Catfish Metkovich [George Michael] — 1921- . OF-1B 1943-47, 49, 51-54 **Red Sox**, Indians, White Sox, Pirates, Cubs, Braves 1055 g, .261, 47 hr, 373 rbi. *1 WS, 2 g, .500*

The clean-shaven Metkovich was nicknamed by Casey Stengel when he injured himself trying to pull a hook from a catfish. The Ted Williams look-alike played outfield for the Red Sox while Williams was fighting WWII, and Metkovich batted .277 with a 25-game hitting streak in 1944. /(JK)

Metropolitan Stadium (The Met) Minnesota Twins 1961-1981. LF-343, CF-402, RF-330

Designed to be expanded when it opened for the Minneapolis Millers (American Association) in 1956, the Met had its capacity more than doubled to 45,919 when the Twins arrived. Three separate seating areas, all unconnected to the original structure, were added in the outfield and along the left field line, including a huge double-decked grandstand behind the left field fence. The Met had a grass field and relatively short power alleys (usually 360'-365'), but a deep centerfield until 1975. It hosted one no-hitter and one World Series in its 21 seasons, and on August 25, 1970 a mid-game bomb scare sent fans spilling into the outfield for safety. The Twins abandoned their poorly maintained ballpark in favor of the new Metrodome in 1982, and in 1984-85 the stadium was razed to clear space for a convention center and amusement park. /(SCL)

Butch Metzger [Clarence Edward] — 1952- . RHP 1974-78 Giants, **Padres**, Cardinals, Mets 294 ip, 18-9, 3.74
☛ *Rookie of the Year—76.*

Metzger was 11-4 with 16 saves (fifth in the NL) and a 2.92 ERA for the Padres in 1976 to win NL Rookie of the Year honors. His 77 appearances (tied for second in the NL) set a ML rookie record, and his 10 straight wins tied the ML mark for a rookie reliever. Coming as it did at the start of the season, the streak combined with his 1-0 records in 1974 and 1975 to set another ML relief record: 12 straight wins at the beginning of a career. Metzger was

traded to St. Louis in May 1977 for John D'Acquisto and Pat Scanlon (the Padres had signed free agent Rollie Fingers in December 1976), and was 4-2 with seven saves for the Cardinals. His meteoric career was ended by arm trouble after he was sold to the Mets for 1978. /(SFS)

Roger Metzger — 1947- . SS 1970-80 Cubs, **Astros**, Giants 1219 g, .231, 5 hr, 254 rbi
☛ *Gold Glove—73.*

A speedy, switch-hitting shortstop who started for the Astros from 1971 until 1978, Metzger never hit better than .251 in the ML and had little power, but he led the NL in triples twice while playing his home games on the hard, spacious Astrodome turf. Acquired from the Cubs in exchange for Hector Torres, Metzger led NL shortstops in fielding percentage in 1973 and 1976, then was sold to the Giants during the 1978 season. /

Alex Metzler — 1903-1973. OF 1925-30 Cubs, A's, **White Sox**, Browns 560 g, .285, 9 hr, 207 rbi

Metzler became a regular with the White Sox in 1927 and batted over .300 that year and the next. He crashed into a wall in 1930, suffering a shoulder injury that ended his ML career. /(JLE)

Bob Meusel (Long Bob, The Rifle) — 1896-1977. OF-3B 1920-30 **Yankees**, Reds 1407 g, .309, 156 hr, 1067 rbi. *6 WS, 34 g, .225, 1 hr, 17 rbi*
☛ *Led League—hr 25. Led League—rbi 25.*

Though Bob Meusel had numbers superior to some Hall of Famers, he could have done even better, according to manager Miller Huggins and others, had it not been for his indifferent attitude. The younger brother of NL star Irish Meusel, Bob was a solid, all-around player, capable of hitting with power and for high average, and of stealing a base. Long Bob, at 6'3", was the tallest member of the great 1927 Yankees, a muscular outfielder with one of the strongest throwing arms in the game.

Meusel batted .313 or better in seven of his first eight seasons. He struck out a league-high 88 times in 1921, and was one of the all-time strikeout victims in World Series play (24). He became the first Yankee to win a HR title batting righthanded exclusively, with 33 in 1925, the year Babe Ruth missed 50 games after his "big bellyache." Meusel was also the 1925 AL RBI champ, with 138.

When pals Meusel and Ruth took part in a 1921 barnstorming tour against the wishes of Commissioner Landis, both were suspended for the first 39 days of the 1922 season. Meusel was a grim, unpopular character. In 1924, bat in hand, he charged Detroit pitcher King Cole following a close pitch. The ensuing riot was called one of the worst in modern baseball history, and resulted in a forfeit and heavy fines for the participants.

Meusel led the Yankees in stolen bases five times, with a high of 26 in 1924. He stole second, third, and home in a May 16, 1927 game, and pilfered home twice in WS play. He and Babe Herman are the only players to hit for the cycle three times. On September 5, 1921, he tied a ML record with four outfield assists in one game. He ranks among the all-time Yankee leaders in doubles (338), triples (87), RBI (1,005), and batting average (.311). /(ME)

Irish Meusel [Emil Frederick] — 1893–1963. OF 1914, 18–27 Senators, Phillies, **Giants**, Dodgers 1294 g, .310, 106 hr, 819 rbi. *4 WS, 23 g, .276, 3 hr, 17 rbi*
☛ *Led League—rbi 23.*

Irish was the older brother of Bob Meusel, also a star outfielder. The two faced each other in three successive World Series (1921–23), Irish playing for the Giants, Bob for the Yankees. Though of Alsatian heritage, Irish got his nickname because he looked Celtic. He had seemed lackadaisical as a .300-hitting

Bob Meusel

Irish Meusel (r.) with brother Bob and Bob's wife

Phillies outfielder. John McGraw obtained him in July 1921 and made him the cleanup batter for the Giants team that won four straight pennants, 1921–24. Irish hustled in the field for the acerbic McGraw. He had over 100 RBI each year from 1922 to 1925, with a career-high 132 in 1922, and a league-high 125 in 1923. /(JK)

Mexican League — 1955– . League.

Now classified as Triple-A, the Mexican League is regarded in Mexico as the domestic major league. There have actually been six Mexican leagues of note. The first was an outlaw circuit directed by Jorge Pasquel from the late 1930s until 1953. Having major league ambitions, Pasquel stocked his teams with Negro League greats, then raided the U.S. major leagues for additional talent when a player surplus and pay cuts there followed the WWII player shortage. Pasquel's raids netted 23 ML regulars, most of whom jumped to the Quebec Provincial League in 1948–49, and were reinstated by the majors in June 1949. Struggling financially, Pasquel's league dissolved in 1953. The northern clubs merged into the Arizona-Texas and Arizona-Mexico leagues of 1953–57. The Mexican League proper reorganized in 1955, and has operated continuously since.

The Mexican Central League, recognized as Class-A, formed in 1960, and was joined during the decade by the short-lived Mexican Northern League, Mexican Pacific League, and Mexican Rookie League. All were based on previously existing outlaw circuits. The last three were acknowledged farm leagues for the Mexican League, but the Mexican Central League, while hosting some farm clubs, had aspirations to equal status. The Mexican and Central leagues finally merged into a single 20-team circuit with four divisions in 1979. A players' strike curtailed the 1980 season, but six clubs broke the strike to play a 40-game schedule. Following numerous bankruptcies, the Mexican League dwindled to 14 teams in two divisions.

Long known as a last stop for over-the-hill major leaguers, the Mexican League has swung back and forth between dead-ball and lively-ball eras. A new lively-ball era commenced in 1984: In 1983 no player hit 20 home runs; in 1986 14 hit more than 30. /(MC)

Benny Meyer [Earache] — 1888–1974. OF 1913–15, 25 Dodgers, **Baltimore (FL)**, Buffalo (FL), Phillies 310 g, .265, 7 hr, 84 rbi

Opponents claimed that Meyer gave them an earache by shouting incessantly while a coach with the Phillies and Tigers. He played all but 29 of his major league games in the Federal League. For 60 years he was a minor league player, coach, and manager, and a scout. His brother, Lee, was a Brooklyn shortstop for seven games in 1909. To wring a signing bonus from the Dodgers, Benny brazenly faked a letterhead for his modest farm and invited Brooklyn owner Charlie Ebbets to visit. He rounded up cows from every farm in the range and put them in his pastures, telling Ebbets he couldn't abandon his herd for the paltry amount he had been offered. He extracted a $1,000 bonus, but played in only 38 games for Brooklyn, hitting .195. /(JK)

Bill Meyer — 1892–1957. C 1913, 16–17 White Sox, **A's** 113 g, .236, 1 hr, 21 rbi.
Manager 1948–52 **Pirates** 317–452, .412

A catcher, Meyer broke in with Knoxville in the Southeastern League in 1910 and was up briefly with the White Sox and A's in 1916–17. He played eight years at Louisville (American Association). In 1926 he succeeded Joe McCarthy as Louisville manager and won a pennant in his first year. He managed 16 years in the Yankees organization, won pennants in the International League, New York-Penn League, Eastern League, and American Association, and was named minor league manager of the year in 1939 at Kansas City. He was offered the Yankees job in 1946, but he had suffered a heart attack and did not think he was up to it. He returned to Kansas City and won another pennant. He went to the Pirates in 1948 and was named *TSN* Manager of the Year for a fourth-place finish. He later scouted for the Pirates. /(NLM)

Bob Meyer — 1939– . LHP 1964, 69–70 Yankees, Angels, A's, **Pilots/Brewers** 129 ip, 2–12, 4.40

Meyer was wild, leading more than one minor league in hit batsmen and wild pitches. He worked for three AL clubs in 1964, and lost his best-pitched game that September 12, a one-hitter for Kansas City against Baltimore. Frank Bertaina also threw a one-hitter, beating him 1–0. /(NLM)

Dan Meyer (Whitey) — 1952– . 1B-OF-3B-DH, 1974–85 Tigers, **Mariners**, A's 1118 g, .253, 86 hr, 459 rbi

Meyer was a minor league batting champ who hadn't blossomed with the Tigers when chosen by Seattle in the 1976 expansion draft. The lefthanded hitter was the Mariners' first-ever first baseman and had career highs of 22 HR and 90 RBI in their inaugural 1977 season. In 1979 an injury to Bill Stein forced Meyer to move to third base, a position he had not played in the majors, but his hitting was not affected; he earned Player of the Month honors in June with a 21-game hitting streak. He played left field in 1980 but was traded to the A's after a disappointing 1981. He left the Mariners as their all-time leader in seven offensive categories, including HR (64) and RBI (313). With Oakland, Meyer was a handyman and pinch hitter until his release in May 1985. /(JCA)

Dutch Meyer [Lambert Daniel] — 1915- . 2B 1937, 40-42, 45-46 Cubs, Tigers, **Indians** 286 g, .264, 10 hr, 93 rbi

In his one full major league season (1945), Meyer played second base for Cleveland and batted .292 while Ray Mack served in the military. In 1950 he led the East Texas League with a .375 batting average as Gladewater's player-manager. /(ME)

Jack Meyer (Whitey, Monk) — 1932-1967. RHP 1955-61 **Phillies** 455 ip, 24-34, 3.92

Meyer was a much-used Phillies reliever for five seasons, but was a stopper only as a rookie in 1955, when he led the NL with 16 saves and seven relief losses. In a September 22, 1958 game against the Pirates, he set a since-tied NL record for relievers by striking out six consecutive batters. /(FK)

Joey Meyer — 1962- . DH-1B 1988-89 **Brewers** 156 g, .251, 18 hr, 65 rbi

Meyer won the Midwestern League Triple Crown in his first pro season, one of two 30-HR, 100-RBI seasons he had in the minors. The 6'3" 260-lb Hawaiian struck out 88 times in 327 at-bats in his first ML season. On September 20, 1988 he tied the ML record by striking out five times in a nine-inning game. After limited playing time in 1989, he signed with Japan's Taiyo Whales. /(SFS)

Russ Meyer (The Mad Monk) — 1923- . RHP 1946-57, 59 Cubs, **Phillies**, Dodgers, Reds, Red Sox, A's 1531 ip, 94-73, 3.99. *3 WS, 12 ip, 0-1, 3.09*

The flamboyant Russ Meyer was a rabid bench jockey who had an explosive temper and relished the title, The Mad Monk. He frequently angered his teammates, opponents, and the umpires, often to his own detriment. He would lose his cool on the mound after a base hit or an infielder's error. Once, with the Phillies, after being knocked out of a game, he took off his spikes and hurled them into the shower ceiling, where they stuck. Despite his tantrums, he was often effective. He went 17-8 for Philadelphia in 1949. In 1952 he won 13 games and was coveted by the Dodgers, who, in desperate need

of another solid starter, purchased him from the Braves in a four-team deal. He helped them to the 1953 pennant with a 15-5 mark and followed with an 11-6 record in 1954. In June of 1955 he broke his shoulder blade in a collision, and he never returned to winning form. /(JK)

Levi Meyerle (Long Levi) — 1845-1921. 3B-2B-OF-SS-1B 1871-77, 84 Philadelphia Athletics (NA), **Philadelphia White Stockings (NA)**, Chicago (NA), Phillies, Reds, Philadelphia (UA) *NA: 221 g, .353. ML: 85 g, .329, 0 hr, 49 rbi*
☛ *Led League—ba 1871. Led League—hr 1871.*

Meyerle was an awesome hitter in the earliest days of professional baseball. He won the first batting championship of the first recognized league, with a lofty .488 in 26 games for the National Association's Philadelphia Athletics, and his four home runs also led the league. He played all five years of the NA's existence, and was in the Athletics' (later named the Phillies) lineup for the first scheduled game of the National League in 1876. A quiet gentleman, he was a longtime favorite in Philadelphia, where he played most. Although not an adept fielder, he was versatile, seeing action at every position except catcher. He excelled with the bat, in part because of his impressive, muscular, 6'1" frame which, in an era of much smaller players, earned him the nickname Long Levi. Despite his past popularity, his death went unremarked by all the Philadelphia newspapers. /(ADS)

Chief Meyers [John Tortes] — 1880-1971. C 1909-17 **Giants**, Dodgers, Braves 992 g, .291, 14 hr, 363 rbi. *4 WS, 18 g, .290, 6 rbi*

A Cahuilla Indian from California, Meyers was the New York Giants' star catcher when they won three straight pennants from 1911 to 1913; he batted .332, .358, and .312 in those years. Slowed by catching more than 100 games in six straight seasons (1910-15), he retired at age 37 in 1917. He was booed while managing in a semi-pro game in 1920 and, disgusted, quit baseball. Educated at Dartmouth, he was employed by the Department of the Interior as an Indian supervisor. He scoffed at his nickname, Chief, bestowed on virtually every athlete of Indian ancestry. /(JK)

Red Meyers [Ray C.] — Unk.-1987. *Scout.*

Meyers was a sandlot baseball and football coach before he became a scout in 1943 for the Cubs. He switched to the White Sox in 1947 and worked briefly for the Yankees before catching on with the Tigers, for whom he would scout from 1954 to 1975. /(FVP)

Gene Michael (Stick) — 1938– . SS-2B 1966–75 Pirates, Dodgers, **Yankees**, Tigers 973 g, .229, 15 hr, 226 rbi.
    Manager 1981–82, 86–87 Yankees, **Cubs** 204–199, .506. First place: 81

The 6′2″ Michael was dubbed Stick for his long, lean look. As a Kent State basketball star, he was coveted by several NBA teams, but chose to play baseball. After a season each with the Pirates and Dodgers, he found a home with the Yankees in 1968. Eager to please, he even pitched that year, hurling three shutout innings. A notoriously poor hitter, he remained the everyday Yankee shortstop for five years because of his smooth glovework and heads-up play; he became noted for pulling off the hidden-ball trick.

Michael became a minor league manager, a coach, and a GM for the Yankees. He was soon caught in the revolving door of Yankee skippers. Though he led the team to a first-half title in the 1981 split season, George Steinbrenner replaced him with Bob Lemon on September 6. Michael replaced Lemon the next April, registered a 44–42 record, and was fired in August.

In June 1986, Cub GM Dallas Green chose Michael as manager. In his first game, Michael was automatically ejected when his pitcher, after being warned, threw too close to a batter. By the end of the season, Green was openly criticizing Michael for not being tough enough. Late in 1987, Michael told a reporter he was not returning in 1988; he soon resigned before he could be fired. /(DB)

Al Michaels — 1944– . *Broadcaster.*

Identified immediately as a Vin Scully sound-alike when he started broadcasting the Giants from 1974 to 1976, Michaels has become nationally recognized and popular for his own accomplishments. He became ABC's number-one Monday Night Baseball announcer in 1983 after seven seasons working backup games. His most famous call, however, remains his countdown to the gold medal for the underdog U.S. hockey team in the 1980 Olympics, concluding with a joyous "Do you believe in miracles? Yes!" /(SL)

Cass Michaels [aka Casimir Eugene Kwietniewski] — 1926–1982. 2B-SS-3B 1943–54 **White Sox**, Senators, Browns, A's 1288 g, .262, 53 hr, 501 rbi ☛ *All-Star—49–50.*

Playing under the name Cass Kwietniewski in 1943–44, Michaels reached the ML for two games as a 17-year-old third baseman in 1943, and was the White Sox' regular shortstop in 1945. Bumped to a utility position by Luke Appling in 1946–47, Michaels played all 154 games at second base in 1948, hitting a career-high .308 with 83 RBI. When a 1954 beaning impaired his vision and ended his 12-year career, he was only 28. /(FK)

Eddie Mifflin — 1923–1971. Fan.

Eddie Mifflin was a salesman, businessman, and Pennsylvania state legislator who stands as the fan with the greatest impact on the history of baseball. Mifflin's encyclopedic knowledge of baseball statistics, his salesmanship, and serendipity helped give us the greatest hitter of all time.

Ted Williams announced that his retirement would follow the 1954 season in a three-part article in *The Saturday Evening Post* that April. It made sense. The Red Sox slugger was 36 years old, coming off a succession of seasons interrupted by injuries and military service. The broken elbow he suffered in the 1950 All-Star Game had, he felt, robbed him of power permanently. When he came back from the Korean War in June 1953, only a genuine need for money had compelled him to sign through the end of 1954. And a broken shoulder in spring training had cemented his resolve just before the *Post* articles ran.

Near the end of the 1954 season, Eddie Mifflin encountered Williams in the Baltimore train station after a Red Sox-Orioles series. He introduced himself and said, "You're not really going to retire, are you? You can't, you know. Your numbers aren't good enough." Williams was intrigued. "What do you mean my numbers aren't good enough? I've got a lifetime batting average over .350. I've hit home runs and knocked in 100 every year of my career. How can my numbers not be good enough? Good enough for what?"

Mifflin explained. The success of Williams's career would be measured one definitive way: Would he be elected to the Hall of Fame in the first year he became eligible? Williams had missed so much playing time in WWII and Korea that his career totals weren't yet impressive enough. And baseball writers were the voters for the Hall of Fame. "Ted, you barely have 350 home runs. You don't have 1,500 rbi. You don't even have 2,000 hits. And these writers hate your guts; they didn't even vote you the MVP twice when you won the Triple Crown. You needs stats that are undeniable. These aren't."

Ted arranged to meet Mifflin again in New York later in the road trip. They stayed up all night discussing Williams's lifetime stats, where he stood in relation to Ruth, Cobb, Foxx, and Gehrig. Finally, Ted said, "What do I have to do?" Said Mifflin, "You've got to hit 500 home runs. Only three guys have done it: Ruth, Foxx, and Ott. Hit 500 home runs and they'll have to put you in on the first ballot."

In May 1955 Williams rejoined the Red Sox. He went on to compile the most amazing statistics in baseball history for a hitter over 35. He won two more batting championships. And he had his new friend, Eddie Mifflin, encouraging him and marking his progress with telegrams and phone calls. "Congratulations, those two RBI yesterday moved you past Foxx."

Williams had the only off-year of his big league career in 1959. At age 41, he suffered from a painful neck throughout the season and slumped to .254. Yawkey wanted him to retire. But he finished the season with 492 home runs. Mifflin's vision for Williams was fulfilled with his triumphant final 1960 season: a .316 farewell average, soaring past Mel Ott's 511 home runs, and capping his career with the 521st in his last at-bat. And five years later, on the first ballot, Williams was elected to the Hall of Fame. /(MS)

Pete Mikkelsen — 1939– . RHP 1964–72 Yankees, Pirates, Cubs, Cardinals, **Dodgers** 653 ip, 45–40, 3.38. *1 WS, 5 ip, 0–1, 5.79*

Mikkelsen was a durable sinkerballer who filled various relief roles for several ML clubs. As a Yankee rookie in the 1964 World Series, he was the victim of Cardinal Tim McCarver's game-winning three-run homer in the tenth inning of Game Five. At his best, he appeared in 71 games with nine wins and 14 saves for the 1966 Pirates. He finished with 49 career saves. /(GDW)

Eddie Miksis — 1926– . 2B-OF-3B-SS 1944, 46–58 Dodgers, **Cubs**, Cardinals, Orioles, Reds 1042 g, .236, 44 hr, 228 rbi. *2 WS, 8 g, .273*

Miksis was one of many teenagers to make the majors during WWII, arriving a few months shy of his 18th birthday. A utility man with every other team he played for, Miksis was a regular only on the second-division Cubs in 1951–56.

As a Dodger in Game Four of the 1947 WS, pinch running for Pete Reiser, he scored the winning run from first base when Cookie Lavagetto's two-out ninth-inning double ended Bill Bevens's bid for the first WS no-hitter. /(AA)

Bob Milacki — 1964– . RHP 1988– **Orioles** 268 ip, 16–12, 3.46

Milacki was superb in his 1988 trial, going 2–0 with a 0.72 ERA in three starts, including a shutout. He was 14–12 (3.74 ERA) in his first full season in 1989. /(WOR)

Clyde Milan (Deerfoot) — 1887–1953. OF 1907–22 Senators 1981 g, .285, 17 hr, 617 rbi.
  Manager 1922 **Senators** 69–85, .448

In 1912 Clyde Milan stole 88 bases to top Ty Cobb and lead the American League, breaking Cobb's single-season record of 83 stolen bases set the previous year. He beat Cobb and Eddie Collins again in 1913, leading with 75 stolen bases, but Cobb regained the title and the record with 96 steals in 1915. Milan stole 495 bases lifetime. According to longtime owner Clark Griffith, he was the best centerfielder the Senators ever had. He played shallow, using his speed to catch up with deep fly balls. He was signed on the same scouting trip that netted Washington Walter Johnson, and the pair were

Clyde Milan

roommates—well matched because of their gentle temperaments—for the next 15 years. Milan was the Senators' player-manager in 1922 but was considered too easygoing. He managed in the minors until 1937, when he returned to Washington as a coach. He was 65 when, hitting fungos in the heat of spring training, he had a fatal heart attack. His brother Horace was also a Senators outfielder in 1915 and 1917./(JK)

Larry Milbourne — 1951- . 2B-SS-3B 1974–84 Astros, **Mariners**, Yankees, Twins, Indians, Phillies 989 g, .254, 11 hr, 184 rbi. *1 LCS, 3 g, .462, 1 rbi. 1 WS, 6 g, .250, 3 rbi*

Milbourne spent his whole career as a utility man. In 1979 he led the AL with 12 pinch hits (in 30 at-bats) in his only successful season in that role. He excelled in the 1981 postseason for the Yankees, playing every game in place of the injured Bucky Dent at shortstop. Milbourne hit .316 with four runs scored in the five-game divisional playoff against Milwaukee. In the LCS against the A's, he scored the first run of the series in Game One and tied Game Two with a fourth-inning RBI single, batting .462 with four runs as New York swept in three. He dropped off to .250 in the World Series as the Yankees lost to Los Angeles, but he drove in the first run of New York's Game Two victory with the only extra-base hit of the game, a fifth-inning double./(JFC)

Dee Miles [Wilson Daniel] — 1909–1976. OF 1935–36, 39–43 Senators, **A's**, Red Sox 503 g, .280, 2 hr, 143 rbi

Miles was a lefthanded line-drive hitter whose inadequate fielding kept him from winning a regular job. He began as a pitcher in the Cardinals chain, was a .293 batter for the A's from 1939 to 1942, and led the AL with 15 pinch hits in 45 attempts in 1941./(JK)

Johnny Miljus (Big Serb) — 1895–1976. RHP 1915, 17, 20–21, 27–28 Pittsburgh (FL), Dodgers, **Pirates**, Indians 457 ip, 29–26, 3.92. *1 WS, 7 ip, 0–1, 1.35*

Miljus, a Pirate reliever who served honorably in WWI, is one of those unfortunates whose career compresses to a single play: the Game Four ninth-inning wild pitch that escaped Johnny Gooch and allowed the Yankees to sweep the 1927 World Series./(ADS)

Felix Millan (The Cat) — 1943- . 2B 1966–77 **Braves**, Mets 1480 g, .279, 22 hr, 403 rbi. *2 LCS, 8 g, .323, 2 rbi. 1 WS, 7 g, .188, 1 rbi*
☛ All-Star—69–71. Gold Glove—69, 72.

A two-time Gold Glove second baseman, Millan was a dependable cog in both Atlanta's 1969 divisional championship and the Mets' 1973 pennant. Signed out of Puerto Rico by Kansas City in 1964, he was drafted by the Braves and took over at second base in 1968. In 1970 he hit .310 and went 6-for-6 on July 6. Despite three All-Star berths, he was traded after his one poor season at the plate (.257 in 1972). In one of the Mets' best trades ever, they acquired Millan and George Stone for Gary Gentry and Dan Frisella, sparking New York to a World Series and heralding the decline of the Braves. Choking way up on the bat, Millan was the NL's toughest man to strike out in 1973–75. He had a 19-game hitting streak in 1975 and set Met single-season marks with 162 games, 676 at-bats, 191 hits, and 37 doubles./(PB)

Bill Miller (Hooks) — 1926- . LHP 1952–55 **Yankees**, Orioles 131 ip, 6–9, 4.24

Miller was a minor league strikeout leader who had difficulty with control in the majors. He was sent from the Yankees to the Orioles in an 18-player trade in 1954./(JL)

Bing Miller [Edmund John] — 1894–1966. OF 1921–36 Senators, **A's**, Browns, Red Sox 1821 g, .312, 117 hr, 990 rbi. *3 WS, 18 g, .258, 8 rbi*

Bing Miller was a dependable, hard-hitting, graceful outfielder whom Connie Mack dealt to the Browns in 1926 but reacquired following the 1927 season. Miller joined with Mule Haas and Al Simmons in the Athletics' outfield for Mack's last champions of 1929–31. He batted over .300 in nine seasons, with a high of .342 for Philadelphia in 1924. In 1934 with the A's, and 1935 with the Red Sox, he led the AL in pinch hits and pinch at-bats. He was a contact hitter who considered it a disgrace to take a called third strike; when he did so in 1936, he knew it was time to retire. Miller became a coach with the Red Sox, Tigers, White Sox, and A's. His brother Ralph was an infielder with the Phillies in 1920–21 and the Senators in 1924./(JK)

Bob Miller [Robert Gerald] — 1935- . LHP 1953–56, 62 **Tigers**, Reds, Mets 189 ip, 6–8, 4.72

Miller signed with Detroit for $60,000 in 1953, debuted with the Tigers at age 17, but never had success with them. In 1962 he became the first Met to lose a game on his first pitch when he came on in the 12th inning of a 4–4 game and threw a screwball that the Braves' Del Crandall crushed for a home run. He was one of two Bob Millers with the 1962 Mets; they roomed together on the road./(NLM)

Bob Miller [Robert John] — 1926- . RHP 1949-58 **Phillies** 822 ip, 42-42, 3.96. *1 WS, 0.1 ip, 0-1, 27.00*

Miller stumbled while carrying a suitcase during his rookie year with the Phillies, causing a chronic sacroiliac problem. He nevertheless finished 11-6 for the 1950 Whiz Kids, then in the World Series was knocked out by the Yankees in the first inning of his Game Four start. He remained with Philadelphia for almost a decade, working mostly in relief. /(NLM)

Bob Miller [Robert Lane] (R.B.) — 1939- . RHP 1957, 59-74 Cardinals, Mets, **Dodgers**, Twins, Indians, Cubs, White Sox, Padres, Pirates, Tigers 1551 ip, 69-81, 3.37. *3 LCS, 6 ip, 0-1, 4.76. 3 WS, 9 ip, 0-1, 2.00*

Forever to be remembered as one of two Bob Millers on the 1962 Mets (they even roomed together), this Bob Miller was distinguished by his nickname R.B., which stood for Righty Bob. Used mostly as a starter that year, he pitched better than his 4.89 ERA would indicate, but lost lots of close games. On the next-to-last day of the season, he could have made the record books; he was 0-12, and only one pitcher had ever lost as many as 13 games without a win. But that afternoon, Miller beat the Cubs 2-1. The half-dozen sportswriters who followed the Mets that year had always crowded around his locker after his tough losses and no-decisions to get his reaction, but that day there was only one sportswriter on hand, and he was so busy covering for four papers that he didn't make it to the clubhouse.

Miller had his greatest success after being traded to the Dodgers following the 1962 season. Converted to relief, he posted good ERA and led the NL in appearances in 1964 (74). After a 2-9 record in 1967, he was traded to the Twins. From 1970 through 1973, he played on seven teams, and in each of three of those four years, he played for three teams. He returned to the Mets at the end of '73 and finished his career with them in 1974. /(SH)

Bruce Miller — 1949- . 3B-2B 1973-76 **Giants** 196 g, .246, 1 hr, 51 rbi

Miller was a slap-hitting infielder who never became a regular in four seasons with the Giants. In his busiest season, 1975, he played 99 games and hit .239. /(FS)

Doc Miller [Roy Oscar] — 1883-1938. OF 1910-1914 Cubs, **Braves**, Phillies, Reds 511 g, .295, 12 hr, 235 rbi

The Canadian-born Miller lost the 1911 batting race to Honus Wagner, who had 100 fewer at-bats, by just one point. Miller did lead the NL with 192 hits and also finished second with 36 doubles. In 1913, no longer a regular, he led the NL with 20 pinch hits and 56 pinch at-bats. /(WOR)

Dots Miller [John] — 1886-1923. 1B-2B-SS-3B 1909-17, 19-21 **Pirates**, Cardinals, Phillies 1589 g, .263, 32 hr, 715 rbi. *1 WS, 7 g, .250, 4 rbi*

Second baseman Miller was Honus Wagner's double-play partner in Pittsburgh from 1909 to 1911, then moved to first base. He was used all over the Cardinals' infield from 1914 to 1919, playing virtually every day. As a rookie manager, he led San Francisco to the 1922 Pacific Coast League championship, but took ill and died in September 1923, four days before his 37th birthday. /(ME)

Dyar Miller — 1946- . RHP 1975-81 Orioles, **Angels**, Blue Jays, Mets 465 ip, 23-17, 3.23

Miller began his career in 1968 as a catcher in the Phillies' organization but switched to pitching almost immediately. He pitched a seven-inning no-hitter in the Texas League in 1970, but came to the majors as a reliever and started only one game in his ML career. His best season was his first; he went 6-3 with eight saves after being called up in 1975. /(JFC)

Eddie Miller (Eppie) — 1916- . SS-2B 1936-37, 39-50 Braves, **Reds**, Phillies, Cardinals 1512 g, .238, 97 hr, 640 rbi
☛ *All-Star—41-44, 46-47.*

As a young, slick-fielding Cincinnati shortstop, Miller could not supplant Billy Myers (who hit for a better average), and he was traded to the Braves in 1938. A broken leg cut short his 1939 season, but he returned in 1940 to bat a lifetime-best .276. He led league shortstops in fielding each year from 1940 through 1943 and again in 1945. Reacquired by the Reds after the 1942 season, he was their regular shortstop through 1947, when he topped the NL with 38 doubles and reached career highs of 19 HR and 87 RBI. A six-time All-Star shortstop, he played second base for the Phillies in 1949. /(JK)

Elmer Miller — 1890-1944. OF 1912, 15-18, 21-22 Cardinals, **Yankees**, Red Sox 413 g, .243, 16 hr, 151 rbi. *1 WS, 8 g, .161, 2 rbi*

Miller, after playing with a host of teams in several leagues, returned to the Yankees in the middle of 1921. He played centerfield in all the World Series games in 1921, although he hit only .161. Miller was traded in mid-July 1922 to the Red Sox. The next year Miller jumped to the outlaw Mid-West League, joining the Beloit Fairies. Miller played with the team until 1927 and later managed a team in Fremont, Montana. /(MA)

Frank Miller (Bullet) — 1886–1974. RHP 1913, 16–19, 22–23 White Sox, **Pirates**, Braves 1010 ip, 52–66, 3.01

Miller earned his nickname with 265 strikeouts for Des Moines (Western League) in 1909 and 279 for San Francisco (Pacific Coast League) in 1912. He was a Pittsburgh starter in 1916–19, and was 11–13 as last-place Boston's ace in 1922. /(ME)

Hack Miller [Lawrence] — 1894–1971. OF 1916, 18, 22–25 Dodgers, Red Sox, **Cubs** 349 g, .323, 38 hr, 205 rbi. *1 WS, 1 g, .000*

After brief trials with the Dodgers and Red Sox, Chicago native Miller had a spectacular rookie season with the 1922 Cubs, batting .352 with 78 RBI. He followed with 20 homers, 88 RBI, and a .301 average in 1923. The son of a circus strong man, the 5′9″195-lb Miller generally used a 47-oz bat. He entertained fans and teammates with such feats of strength as bending iron bars with his hands and pounding spikes into wood with his fist protected only by a baseball cap. Ironically, his muscle-bound physique handicapped him defensively, and by May 1925 he was gone from the majors. /(ARA)

Jake Miller — 1897–1975. LHP 1924–31, 33 **Indians**, White Sox 1070 ip, 60–59, 4.09

Miller led the 1927 Indians with a 3.21 ERA, though he won more in 1929 (14–12, 3.58). Although inconsistent and injury-prone, he won ten or more games every other season, 1925 to 1929. /(ME)

John Miller — 1941– . RHP 1962–63, 65–67 **Orioles** 227 ip, 12–14, 3.89

Miller was 4–8 as a spot starter for the 1966 World Champion Orioles. Sold to the Mets after pitching only six innings in 1967, he never made a NL appearance. /(FK)

Marvin Miller — 1917– . *Executive.*

Marvin Miller never played the game, but he may have had more influence on baseball than anyone else in this half of the century. Hired by the players in 1966, he brought a wealth of experience garnered in the tough steelworkers' union to bear on baseball labor relations, and his knowledge, organizational ability, and resolve completely overmatched the owners and their representatives, particularly Commissioners Bowie Kuhn and Spike Eckert. In a time

of baseball prosperity which saw manifold increase in the value of franchises, his tough tactics finally got the players not only a "bigger piece of the pie" but also greater, if grudging, respect for their wishes in regard to trades and other matters.

Miller made himself unpopular with fans as well as owners by leading two strikes, at the beginning of 1972 and in the middle of 1981. But he always compromised with the owners in some way; the great progress he made came over the course of five contract negotiations and 18 seasons. Retiring in 1984, he had achieved more than could have been imagined when he took office: an end to the reserve clause, with free movement from team to team through free agency, resulting in a hundredfold increase in the highest salaries; arbitration in labor disputes; the right for veteran players to veto trades; a vastly improved pension plan funded largely through percentages of television revenue; and, first, recognition of the players' union, the right to bargain collectively, and the use of agents to negotiate individual contracts. He may be reviled for having made baseball a business, but it had been since 1876; he made the business pay off for the 600-odd players active each year instead of just their 26 bosses. /(WOR)

Norm Miller — 1946– . OF 1965–74 **Astros**, Braves 540 g, .238, 24 hr, 159 rbi

Miller was a spare outfielder for most of his career, with military service interrupting his 1967, '70, and '71 seasons. He saw the most action in 1969 and hit .264 with career highs of 50 RBI, 58 runs, and 21 doubles in 119 games. Traded to Atlanta on April 22, 1973 for Cecil Upshaw, Miller spent practically the entire season on the DL. /(WOR)

Otto Miller (Moonie) — 1889–1962. C 1910–22 **Dodgers** 927 g, .245, 5 hr, 231 rbi. *2 WS, 8 g, .136*

From 1910 to 1922, round-faced Moonie Miller caught nearly half of Brooklyn's games. In 1920 he peaked with a .289 batting average and a league-leading .986 fielding average. Miller lumbered into Wambsganss's tag for the third out of the only unassisted triple play in World Series history. /(ADS)

Rick Miller — 1948– . OF 1971–85 **Red Sox**, Angels 1482 g, .269, 28 hr, 369 rbi. *1 LCS, 4 g, .250. 1 WS, 3 g, .000*
☛ *Gold Glove—78.*

Miller was a singles-hitting reserve outfielder in Boston for most of 1971–77, trapped behind Carl

Yastrzemski, Jim Rice, Fred Lynn, and Dwight Evans. Named the Red Sox' Unsung Hero in 1972 and Man of the Year in 1974, Miller married teammate Carlton Fisk's sister, played out his option in 1977, and signed with California. Happy to be playing every day, Miller's sliding catches and solid outfield performance in 1978 won him a Gold Glove. He batted a career-high .293 as leadoff man for the 1979 AL West champion Angels, and returned to Boston as part of a five-man trade in December 1980. Again the Unsung Hero in 1981, in a May 11 game he hit four doubles to tie an ML record. Used less in his last three seasons, Miller became a dependable lefthanded pinch hitter./(EW)

Roscoe Miller (Roxy, Rubberlegs) — 1876–1913. RHP 1901–04 **Tigers**, Giants, Pirates 773 ip, 39–46, 3.45. 20 wins: 01

Miller went 23–13 as a Detroit rookie in 1901, but the next year was on his way to a 7–20 record when he was traded to the Giants. He never again won more than seven games./(DAS)

Roy Miller (Doc) — 1183–1938. OF 1910–14 Cubs, **Braves**, Phillies, Reds 511 g, .295, 12 hr, 235 rbi

Doc's short, peripatetic career peaked in 1911. His .333 batting average was only .001 behind league leader Honus Wagner, his 192 hits led the NL. The lefthander topped NL pinch hitters in 1913 with .357 and hit .325 lifetime./(ADS)

Stu Miller — 1927– . RHP 1952–54, 56–68 Cardinals, Phillies, **Giants**, Orioles 1693 ip, 105–103, 3.24. *1 WS, 2 g, 0–0, 0.00*
☛ *Led League—era 58.*

When Miller was called up by the Cardinals in mid-1952 and manager Eddie Stanky first saw the harmless-looking, 165-lb pitcher, he asked the clubhouse man, "Who's that stenographer?" In his initial start that August 12, Miller shut out the Cubs 1–0. When he first faced the Dodgers, he no-hit them into the eighth inning. But he struggled after his rookie season and spent time in the minors before emerging as one of baseball's best relievers.

It was said that Miller threw at three speeds—slow, slower, and slowest; that "he threw a pitch that stopped"; and that "if you wait five minutes, the ball gets to you fairly fast." He got by on a variety of curveballs and by changing speeds on his changeup. With his herky-jerky windup, he baffled hitters in both leagues. With the Giants in 1958, he recorded a league-best 2.47 ERA, starting

and relieving. He was the NL Fireman of the Year in 1961, when he registered league highs of 17 saves and 14 relief wins. Well-remembered for being literally blown off the mound by a gust of wind at Candlestick Park in the '61 All-Star Game, he won the contest, striking out Mickey Mantle, Roy Sievers, and Elston Howard in succession.

Miller saved 27 games to win his second Fireman of the Year Award in 1963, his first season as an Oriole; he broke the AL record by appearing in 71 games. That April 30, he combined with Steve Barber to no-hit the Tigers, though the Orioles lost 2–1 because of walks, a wild pitch, and an error. When Miller retired in 1968, he was third, behind Hoyt Wilhelm and Roy Face, in career saves and in wins plus saves. He has since been passed by more than a dozen relievers./(NLM)

Ward Miller (Windy) — 1884–1958. OF 1909–10, 12–17 Pirates, Reds, Cubs, **St. Louis (FL)**, Browns 769 g, .278, 8 hr, 221 rbi

Miller hit .327 lifetime as a lefthanded pinch hitter, and had his best seasons as the starting left fielder for the St. Louis Federal League franchise./(ADS)

Randy Milligan — 1961– . 1B-DH 1987– Mets, Pirates, **Orioles** 167 g, .259, 15 hr, 53 rbi

Milligan struggled in his 1988 trial with the Pirates, but cut down his strikeouts platooning with the 1989 Orioles and was a factor in their surprising second-place finish./(JFC)

Bob Milliken (Bobo) — 1926– . RHP 1953–54 **Dodgers** 180 ip, 13–6, 3.59. *1 WS, 2 ip, 0–0, 0.00*

A reliever and spot starter, Milliken contributed an 8–4 mark toward the Dodgers' 1953 NL pennant in his rookie season. He had made the team, at the age of twenty-seven, with a great spring training. He had almost come up in 1950 off a 12–5, 2.65 record for Fort Worth in 1949, but he missed the whole season after injuring his arm and spent the next two years in the army. His arm problems returned in 1954. Milliken was a Cardinals coach, 1965–70./(MC)

Buster Mills [Colonel Buster] — 1908– . OF 1934–35, 37–38, 40, 42, 46 Cardinals, Dodgers, **Red Sox**, Browns, Yankees, Indians 415 g, .287, 14 hr, 163 rbi.
Manager 1953 **Reds** 4–4, .500

Often used as a leadoff man because of his good speed, Mills was a regular for only the 1937 Red Sox and the 1938 Browns. He later became a coach and managed eight games for the 1953 Reds./(EW)

Lefty Mills [Howard Robinson] — 1910–1982. LHP 1934, 37–40 **Browns** 435 ip, 15–30, 6.06

A teenaged mechanic aboard the aircraft carrier *Lexington*, Miles never played baseball until joining the ship's team to get shore leave. He quit the service for a pitching career and went 10–12 at his best for the 1938 Browns. /(JK)

Al Milnar (Happy) — 1913– . LHP 1936, 38–43, 46 **Indians**, Browns, Phillies 996 ip, 57–58, 4.22

For three years, 1939–41, Milnar was Cleveland's number-two pitcher behind Bob Feller. He peaked at 18–10 in 1940. Control problems were his undoing; in 1942 he walked 85 while striking out 35. /(ME)

Eddie Milner — 1955– . OF 1980–88 **Reds**, Giants, Reds 804 g, .253, 42 hr, 195 rbi. *1 LCS, 6 g, .143*

A cousin of NL first baseman/outfielder John Milner, Eddie was one of the swiftest and surest centerfielders of the 1980s. Playing regularly for Cincinnati from 1982 through 1986, he stole as many as 41 bases and scored as many as 82 runs a year. He was coming off his best season (15 HR and a 20-game hitting streak) when he was traded to San Francisco in January of 1987. That spring, his teammates noted he was behaving erratically; on April 17 he was voluntarily admitted to a drug rehabilitation center. The Giants released him after the season, but Cincinnati gave him another chance late in 1988. /(JCA)

John Milner (The Hammer) — 1949– . 1B-OF 1971–82 **Mets**, Pirates, Expos 1215 g, .249, 131 hr, 498 rbi. *3 LCS, 9 g, .111, 1 rbi. 2 WS, 10 g, .306, 3 rbi*

Milner was a talented prospect for whom the Mets had high expectations, but his recurring hamstring problems often caused him to miss time. He was a native of Atlanta who grew up as a fan of Hank Aaron, appropriated his idol's nickname, and appeared to imitate his batting stance. Breaking in as an outfielder, he batted only .238 in his rookie year (1972), but hit 17 HR in 362 at-bats and showed a good eye at the plate.

Milner hit a career-high 23 HR in 1973, with 72 RBI, 69 runs, and a .252 average in 451 at-bats as the NL champion Mets' primary first baseman. His power dropped off after 1974, and the Mets traded him with Jon Matlack as part of a four-way deal that sent Milner to Pittsburgh as New York got Willie Montanez, Ken Henderson, and Tom Grieve.

Milner played less for the Pirates, but in 1979 he contributed 16 HR in 326 at-bats while hitting a career-high .276 as the Pirates' "Family" won a World Championship. He was picked up by the Expos for their 1981 pennant drive as they took the only division title in their history, and he finished his career in 1982 with the Pirates.

Milner had ten career grand slams, including three for the Mets in 1976 and pinch hit grand slams for the Pirates in 1979 and 1982 (both in August pennant races). Eddie Milner of the Reds is his cousin. /(SFS)

Milwaukee Braves — 1953–1965. Team. 1446–890, .563. *NL Champions 57–58 World Champions 57*

It could be said that the modern baseball era began in 1953, when the Braves moved from Boston to Milwaukee. It was the first major league franchise move in fifty years, and began the westward movement of baseball as it followed the shifting population of the country.

From 1948 to 1952 Lou Perini's Boston Braves suffered a devastating 80% drop in attendance from their 1948 pennant-boosted figures. Unhappy competing with the Red Sox for fan loyalty and dollars, Perini moved his team to Milwaukee, a town that for years had supported a minor league franchise. At first, the move succeeded beyond all expectations. Braves attendance in 1953 was more than 1.8 million and set a National League record. The Braves' young talent included Hank Aaron and Eddie Mathews, and the team contended throughout the rest of the decade. They won the WS in 1957 and followed it with a NL pennant in 1958, but attendance had already begun to drop somewhat. This trend was accelerated when the team failed to contend in the early 1960s, and by 1966 Milwaukee had lost to Atlanta the team it had greeted so enthusiastically in 1953. /(SH)

Milwaukee Brewers (The Brew Crew, Harvey's Wallbangers) — 1970– . Team. 1542–1633, .486. *AL East Champions 82 AL Champions 82*

The Brewers appeared on the scene when the expansion Seattle Pilots moved to Milwaukee after just one season, seeking better attendance. The Brewers maintained the Pilot's dismal level of performance for their first eight seasons (switching to the Eastern Division in 1972), but the hiring of Harry Dalton as GM after the 1977 season produced immediate results. He appointed former Baltimore colleague George Bamberger manager, and Bamberger, a successful pitching coach, made Mike Caldwell into a 20-game winner. First-round 1977 draft pick Paul Molitor made the team in spring training and was *TSN* AL Rookie of the Year. Larry Hisle was signed as a free agent. Ben Oglivie was acquired in exchange for two mediocre pitchers. Slugging outfielder Gorman Thomas was purchased from the Rangers in February 1978. They all joined a core of Robin Yount, Sixto Lezcano, and Cecil Cooper in propelling the Brewers to their first winning season, a 93–69 mark good for third place. The Brewers contended the next two years, and won the second-half crown in the strike-split 1981 season, but lost to the Yankees in the divisional playoff. The key to this success was a seven-player deal that brought Rollie Fingers, Ted Simmons, and Pete Vuckovich from the Cardinals in December 1980. Fingers won the MVP and Cy Young awards for his 28 saves and 1.04 ERA, and Vuckovich led the league in winning percentage.

The Brewers won the AL pennant in 1982 after Harvey Kuenn took over from Buck Rodgers when the team was 23–24; they went 72–43 the rest of the way. Stretch-drive acquisition Don Sutton beat the Orioles on the final day of the season to win the division title by one game. Yount ran away with the MVP award, Vuckovich was the Cy Young winner, and Molitor led the AL with 136 runs. In the LCS, Milwaukee came back from a 2–0 deficit to sweep the last three games and defeat the Angels. The Brewers took the Cardinals to seven games in the World Series before losing. In subsequent years, they declined, but a bright spot was the outstanding performance of rookie Ted Higuera in 1985.

In 1987 the Brewers got off to a record-tying start when they won their first 13 games of the season. A short while later they had a 12-game losing streak after Paul Molitor went on the DL. His 37-game hitting streak was the highlight of the second half of the season. /(WOR)

Rudy Minarcin (Buster) — 1930– . RHP 1955–57 **Reds**, Red Sox 170 ip, 6–9, 4.66

Minarcin was a wild starter with the Reds in early 1955 but spent the rest of his brief career as a long reliever. /(MC)

Don Mincher (Minch, Mule) — 1938– . 1B 1960–72 **Senators/Twins**, Angels, Pilots, A's, Senators/Rangers 1400 g, .249, 200 hr, 643 rbi. *1 LCS, 1 g, .000. 2 WS, 10 g, .167, 1 hr, 2 rbi* ☛ All-Star—67, 69.

Mincher was a backup for Vic Power and Bob Allison at the beginning of his career, and gradually won more playing time. He hit 23 HR in just 287 at-bats in 1964 and earned the lead position in a first-base platoon for the pennant-winning 1965 team. He hit .251 with 22 HR and 66 RBI in 346 at-bats. In Game One of the World Series, he homered in his first WS at-bat, off Don Drysdale in the second inning, to give the Twins a lead they never surrendered. He tied a WS record for first basemen with four assists in Game Two as the Twins won again. However, he hit only .130 for the Series.

On June 9, 1966, Mincher contributed one of the Twins' AL-record five homers in one inning. But Mincher's power dropped off in 1966 (14 HR in 431 at-bats), and Minnesota traded him to the Angels after the season. He rebounded in 1967 with 25 HR (tied for fifth in the AL) and 81 runs, but on April 11, 1968 Mincher was beaned by Sam McDowell and suffered dizzy spells all season. Hitting only 13 HR, he was left unprotected in the expansion draft. Picked by the Pilots, he came back once again with 25 HR and a career-high 78 RBI, and the A's traded four players to acquire him and a throw-in for 1970. He hit a personal-best 27 HR that year, but led AL first basemen in errors.

Mincher's power dropped in the next two seasons as he was dealt to the Senators, who then moved to Texas (he is the only person to play for both Senators teams and the Twins and Rangers). The A's reacquired him for their 1972 pennant drive, and although he hit only .148, there was one moment of glory left for him. In Game Four of the World Series against the Reds, the A's trailed 2–1 in the ninth inning with one out and two on. Mincher's pinch-hit single off Reds bullpen ace Clay Carroll tied the score as the A's went on to win the game and the Series. It was Mincher's final major league at-bat. /(SH)

Mutsuo Minegawa — 1935– . P 1954–Unk. **Nankai Hawks**

Japan's version of Hoyt Wilhelm or Roy Face, Minegawa was mostly a reliever but could start when necessary. He specialized in a submarine curve, delivered with precise control. From 1956 through 1966, he never had a losing record or an ERA over 2.91. Eight times he pitched at least 50 games, usually working close to 200 innings. At his best, he went 19–7 (1.97) in 1961. /(MC)

Craig Minetto [aka Craig Stephen Briceno] — 1954– . LHP 1978–81 **A's** 145 ip, 1–7, 5.40

Released after one season in the Expos organization, Minetto starred in the Italian pro league in 1975. Signed by the A's in 1977, he became the first product of Italian baseball to play in the U.S. major

The 1969 Minnesota Twins

leagues, but was limited by chronic wildness and a 1980 arm injury. /(MC)

Steve Mingori (Mingo) — 1944– . LHP 1970–79 Indians, **Royals** 584 ip, 18–33, 3.04. *3 LCS, 8 ip, 0–0, 4.32*

Reliever Mingori's sidearm delivery and excellent screwball were equally tough on right- and left-handed batters. Although usually employed to get only one or two batters out, he retired 16 Red Sox in a row in a 1975 appearance. /(FJO)

Paul Minner (Lefty, Tall Paul) — 1923– . LHP 1946, 48–56 Dodgers, **Cubs** 1310 ip, 69–84, 3.94. *1 WS, 1 ip, 0–0, 0.00*

The 6'5" Minner saw limited action as a Dodger reliever, but in his one mop-up inning against the Yankees in the 1949 WS, the stadium lights were turned on, and he became the first to pitch under artificial lighting in the World Series. He was sold to the talent-poor Cubs, and joined their starting rotation in 1950. He tied for the NL lead in losses in 1951, when he was 6–17 for last-place Chicago. He came back in 1952 with a career-best 14–9 mark. A Cardinal-killer, Minner was 21–8 against St. Louis lifetime, 5–0 in his 9–9 1955 season. A severe back injury in 1956 ended his career. /(ARA)

Minnesota Twins — 1961– . Team. 1545–1630, .487. *AL West Champions 69–70, 87 AL Champions 65, 87 World Champions 87*

When the American League expanded in 1961, Calvin Griffith seized the opportunity to move his Washington Senators to what he hoped would be a better region. An expansion Senators franchise filled the gap left by his move, placating the congressmen who insisted on a franchise in Washington. Griffith was unhappy with Washington as a baseball town and felt that the neighborhoods away from the Capitol were declining. In Minnesota the team was renamed the Twins for Minneapolis-St. Paul, the Twin Cities.

Griffith may have been tighter with his money than many other owners, but he was always a good judge of talent. With Tony Oliva and, later, Rod Carew joining the likes of Harmon Killebrew and Bob Allison, the Twins won their first AL pennant in 1965 and won consecutive division titles in 1969–70. But Griffith's fiscal policies could not work in the free agency era. When other owners started to bid competitively for free agents, Minnesota was doomed to lose most of its good players, sooner or later. Griffith certainly wasn't going to replace them by signing free agents himself. After nearly a decade of losing teams and declining attendace, he sold the franchise in 1984 to local banker Carl Pohlad. Subsequently the Twins revived, due largely to the talent Griffith had signed, such as Kent Hrbek, Gary Gaetti, Tom Brunansky, Kirby Puckett, and Frank Viola. Minnesota surprised the baseball world in 1987 with its first World Championship. /(SH)

Doug Minor — Unk.–1959. *Scout.*

A scout for the White Sox from 1935 until his death in 1959, Minor served in both WWI and WWII, and was cited for heroism three times. His notable signees included Alex Grammas and Bob Kennedy. /(FVP)

Minnie Minoso [Saturnino Orestes Arrieta Armas] — 1922– . OF-3B 1949, 51–64, 76, 80 Indians, **White Sox**, Cardinals, Senators 1841 g, .298, 186 hr, 1023 rbi
☛ *All-Star—51–54, 57, 60. Gold Glove—57, 59–60.*

Minoso debuted in 1949, but he was still officially a rookie when obtained by the White Sox in a three-team deal involving the Indians and A's on April 30, 1951. On May 1, in a game against the Yankees in Comiskey Park, the young Cuban speedster became the first black player to don a White Sox uniform. In the very first inning, Minoso homered off Vic Raschi. (Mickey Mantle hit his first ML home run in the sixth inning of the same game.) Minoso finished his rookie year as the AL leader in stolen bases (31) and triples (14); his .326 batting average was second only to Philadelphia's Ferris Fain's .344, and his 112 runs fell one short of Dom DiMaggio's league-leading 113. Though the Yankees' Gil McDougald won the baseball writers' Rookie of the Year honors, Minoso was *TSN's* Rookie of the Year. He led the AL in stolen bases again in 1952 and 1953 and in triples in 1954, and tied for the league lead in steals in 1956 and in doubles in 1957. He would do whatever was necessary to get on base, including getting in the way of fastballs. In 16 AL seasons, he set the league record by being hit by a pitch 189 times. Traded with Fred Hatfield to Cleveland in December 1957 for Early Wynn and Al Smith, he was not around when the Go-Go White Sox won the 1959 AL pennant; Bill Veeck awarded him an honorary championship ring anyway. With Cleveland, Minoso hit a career-high 24 home runs in 1958, and he batted .302 in both 1958 and 1959 before the White Sox reacquired him. In 1960 he led the AL with 184 hits, was second to Roger Maris with 105 RBI, and batted over .300 for his eighth and final time. Following stints with the Cardinals and Senators, he retired after spending 1964 as a White Sox pinch hitter. Twelve years later, during the second Veeck ownership, Minoso was brought out of retirement and went hitless as Chicago's DH against the Angels' Frank Tanana on September 11, 1976. "It's been many years since I face pitching like this," he explained. "I hope they [the fans] forgive me." The next day, he collected his last ML hit. He

Minnie Minoso

was a White Sox coach from 1976 to 1978, and in 1980, when he was again activated, joining Nick Altrock as the only five-decade major leaguers; he went 0-for-2 as a pinch hitter. Ever popular in Chicago, he became a team goodwill ambassador. /(RL)

Greg Minton — 1951– . RHP 1975– **Giants**, Angels 1116 ip, 58–64, 3.11
☛ *All-Star—82.*

The sinkerballing Minton was one of the NL's better relievers from 1980 to 1984, saving at least 19 games each year for the Giants. Originally drafted by the Royals, he was traded to the Giants in 1973 for catcher Fran Healy, and from 1975 to 1978 he shuttled between San Francisco and Phoenix (Pacific Coast League). He spent his first full season with the Giants in 1979, recording a 1.80 ERA in 46 relief appearances, and in 1980 he saved 19 games as San Francisco's new bullpen ace. Minton finished second in the NL in saves (to Bruce Sutter) each of the next two seasons, with 21 in the strike-shortened 1981 campaign and 30 in 1982. In 1983 he and Gary Lavelle became the first NL teammates to each save 20 games in a season.

Minton lost his closer's role to Scott Garrelts in 1985. After undergoing elbow surgery before the 1987 season, he was released by San Francisco in May. The thirty-five-year-old signed with the Angels five days later, saved 10 games for California that season, and remained an effective member of their bullpen through the 1980s. /(SCL)

Paul Mirabella — 1954- . LHP 1978- Rangers, Yankees, Blue Jays, Orioles, **Mariners**, Brewers 441 ip, 15-27, 4.51

Mirabella set a Blue Jays record with 10 consecutive losses in 1980. After a decade of shuttling between the minors and majors, he finally stuck in the Brewers' bullpen in 1988. In only his second full ML season, he had a 1.65 ERA and four saves. A sore left shoulder interrupted his progress and shelved him for most of the 1989 season. /(TF)

Willie Miranda — 1926- . SS 1951-59 Senators, White Sox, **Browns/Orioles**, Yankees 824 g, .221, 6 hr, 132 rbi

In 1953 Miranda became the first Cuban to play for the Yankees since Armando Marsans in 1918. Quick and sure-handed, he led AL shortstops in every fielding category but average for Baltimore in 1955. He had good range and a strong arm that enabled him to throw out runners from deep in the hole. In 1959 he fled Cuba by hiding in the cockpit of a Pan Am plane; he returned two decades later to help family members escape by boat. /(NLM)

Bobby Mitchell — 1943- . OF-DH 1970-71, 73-75 Yankees, **Brewers** 273 g, .235, 21 hr, 91 rbi

Mitchell's most playing time came as the Brewers' fourth outfielder in 1975, when he hit career highs of .249 and nine HR in his last season. /(WOR)

Bobby Mitchell — 1955- . OF 1980-83 Dodgers, **Twins** 202 g, .243, 3 hr, 43 rbi

Mitchell was the Twins' regular centerfielder in 1982 and hit .249 with two HR, 48 runs, and 28 RBI. /(JFC)

Clarence Mitchell — 1891-1963. LHP-1B-OF 1911, 16-32 Tigers, Reds, Dodgers, **Phillies**, Cardinals, Giants 649 g, .252, 7 hr, 133 rbi; 2217 ip, 125-139, 4.12. *2 WS, 10 ip, 0-0, 0.87*

The NL's only lefthanded legal spitballer after 1920, Mitchell was a starter in all or parts of 18 ML seasons, but not until 1931 with the Giants, at age 40, did he win as many as 13 games. Often used in the field and as a pinch hitter, in 1922 he played 42 games at first base for Brooklyn, pitched in only five, and batted .290. Mitchell was the ill-fated Dodger whose liner started Bill Wambsganss's unassisted triple play in the 1920 World Series; two innings later, he hit into a double play, thus accounting for five outs in two at-bats. /(ADS)

Dale Mitchell — 1921-1987. OF 1946-56 **Indians**, Dodgers 1127 g, .312, 41 hr, 403 rbi. *3 WS, 13 g, .138, 1 hr, 1 rbi*
☛ *All-Star—49, 51-52.*

A splendid hitter for over a decade in Cleveland, Mitchell is best remembered for one of his few at-bats with the Dodgers. Despite being one of the toughest batters to fan in ML history (only 119 strikeouts in 3,984 at-bats), on October 8, 1956, he took a called third strike for the final out in Don Larsen's perfect game in Game Five of the 1956 World Series.

After hitting .432 in 11 games for the Indians in 1946, Mitchell became their starting left fielder in 1947 and hit .316. He hit over .300 six of his seven seasons as a regular, with a career-high .336 in 1948 as Cleveland won the World Series. Mitchell led the AL with 203 hits and 23 triples in 1949, and hit .300 with 13 home runs in 1953, but in 1954 he was relegated to pinch-hitting duties after the arrival of Al Smith. His last ML home run, on September 18, 1954, clinched the pennant for the Indians. He was sold to the Dodgers in July 1956, and his final ML at-bat was his pinch-hitting appearance against Larsen. He always maintained that the third strike he took was really a ball. /(FK)

Fred Mitchell [born Frederick Francis Yapp] — 1878-1970. RHP-C-1B 1901-05, 10, 13 Red Sox, A's, **Phillies**, Dodgers, Yankees, Braves 202 g, .210, 0 hr, 52 rbi; 718 ip, 31-48, 4.10.
Manager 1917-23 **Cubs**, Braves 494-543, .476. First place: 18 *1 WS, 2-4, .333*

The brainy Mitchell began as a pitcher, relieving Cy Young in his and the Red Sox' first-ever game, in 1901. Only moderately successful, he remained a ML pitcher until 1905 and resurfaced as a catcher with New York in 1910. He managed the Cubs from 1917-20, leading them to the 1918 pennant, and managed his hometown Boston Braves, 1921-23, before moving into the front office and coaching for 30 years at Harvard. /(JK)

John Mitchell — 1965– . RHP 1986– **Mets** 126 ip, 3–8, 4.08

Acquired from the Red Sox with Bob Ojeda for Calvin Schiraldi and Wes Gardner in an eight-player trade after the 1985 season, Mitchell started 19 games for the Mets in 1987 when the club's pitching staff was riddled with injuries. He spent most of 1988 at Tidewater (International League), where he was 10–9, 2.84 and led the league in innings pitched. His brother Charlie appeared in 12 games in relief for the Red Sox in 1984–85. /(SCL)

Johnny Mitchell — 1894–1965. SS 1921–25 Yankees, Red Sox, **Dodgers** 329 g, .245, 2 hr, 63 rbi

The 5'8" 155-lb Mitchell, a light-hitting switch-hitter, was the starting shortstop for the Red Sox in 1923 and the Dodgers in 1925, though he hit his career-high .263 in 1924. He was part of the July 1922 trade that brought Joe Dugan to New York. /(JM)

Kevin Mitchell (Mitch, World, Boogie Bear) — 1962– 3B-OF 1984– Mets, Padres, **Giants** 548 g, .275, 100 hr, 319 rbi. *3 LCS, 14 g, .291, 3 hr, 9 rbi. 2 WS, 9 g, .280, 1 hr, 2 rbi*

☛ *Most Valuable Player—89. Led League—hr 89. Led League—rbi 89. All-Star—89.*

"Hitting is easy for me," Mitchell once said, and in his 1989 MVP season he demonstrated it. Batting cleanup behind Will Clark for the Giants, the strong, squat (5'11" 210 lb), righthander had 31 HR and 81 RBI by the All-Star break and finished with ML-leading totals of 47 HR and 125 RBI. In the LCS, he hit .353 with two HR and seven RBI.

Raised by his grandmother, Mitchell used baseball to escape the San Diego street gangs of his youth, but not before collecting three gunshot wounds. In the minors, Mitchell's sullen, street-wise attitude often overshadowed his obvious talent, and in 1981 he brawled with teammate Darryl Strawberry during a pickup basketball game.

Mitchell played six positions for the World Champion Mets as a rookie in 1986, including 24 games at shortstop, and hit .277 to finish third in NL Rookie of the Year voting. In the off-season, he was traded to San Diego with a slew of prospects for Kevin McReynolds, and the Padres made him their starting third baseman. Faced with hometown distractions, Mitchell's play suffered, and on July 4, 1987 he was traded to San Francisco. He was hitting only .247 with seven HR at the time, but he hit a pair of home runs in his Giants debut and hit .306

the rest of the season as the Giants won the NL West.

Mitchell slumped to .251 in 1988, then was switched to left field in 1989, began wearing contact lenses, and started getting hitting advice from coach Dusty Baker. In the field, Mitchell is competent but rarely spectacular at virtually any position. In early 1989, however, he earned notoriety when he over-ran a fly ball in the left-field corner and reached back to catch it bare-handed. /(SCL)

Mike Mitchell — 1879–1961. OF 1907–14 **Reds**, Cubs, Pirates, Senators 1133 g, .278, 27 hr, 514 rbi

A steady fielder and solid hitter for the Reds from 1907 to 1912, Mitchell twice led the NL in triples and hit for the cycle August 11, 1911. He was part of the trade that pried Joe Tinker from the Cubs in December 1912. /(ADS)

Paul Mitchell — 1950– . RHP 1975–80 Orioles, A's, **Mariners**, Brewers 621 ip, 32–39, 4.45

Mitchell starred in the Baltimore system and beat Oakland's Vida Blue, 3–2, for his first ML win in 1975. That winter, he was traded to the A's with Don Baylor and Mike Torrez for Reggie Jackson and Ken Holtzman. Mitchell went 9–7 in 1976, was waived to Seattle in 1977, and was the best starter for the last-place 1978 Mariners, going 8–14. /(JCA)

Roy Mitchell — 1885–1959. RHP 1910–14, 18–19 **Browns**, White Sox, Reds 676 ip, 32–37, 3.42

In his only year in a rotation, Mitchell went 13–16 for the 1913 Browns. His four saves in 1914 were enough to tie him for the AL lead. He pitched briefly for the 1919 pennant-winning Reds, but not in the World Series. /(WAB)

Willie Mitchell — 1889–1973. LHP 1909–19 **Indians**, Tigers 1632 ip, 84–92, 2.86

At age 20 in 1910, Mitchell was one of the American League's top lefthanders, going 12–8 (2.60) for Cleveland. When he went 14–8 in 1913, his 1.74 ERA was third-best in the league. He led the Indians in wins and losses (12–17), games, complete games, and strikeouts in 1914. /(ME)

George Mitterwald — 1945– . C 1966, 68–77 **Twins**, Cubs 887 g, .236, 76 hr, 301 rbi. *2 LCS, 5 g, .333, 2 rbi*

Mitterwald backed up Johnny Roseboro on the Twins' 1969 division-winning team and became the primary catcher in 1970 when they repeated. He hit .222 with 15 HR and 46 RBI in 1970 and hit .500

in Minnesota's losing effort in the LCS. He played the most in 1973, catching 122 games and reaching career highs of 16 HR, 64 RBI, 50 runs, and .259. He was traded to the Cubs for Randy Hundley after the season and spent four years backing up Steve Swisher. Mitterwald hit three homers in an April 17, 1974 game against the Pirates. After Swisher was traded, Mitterwald was the Cubs' number-one catcher in 1978, his last season. /(SFS)

Johnny Mize (The Big Cat) — 1913– . 1B 1936–42, 46–53 **Cardinals**, Giants, Yankees 1884 g, .312, 359 hr, 1337 rbi. *5 WS, 18 g, .286, 3 hr, 9 rbi*
☛ *Led League—ba 39. Led League—hr 39, 40, 47–48. Led League—rbi 40, 42, 47. All-Star—37, 39–42, 46–49, 53. Hall of Fame—1981.*

Mize, a dependable but slow-moving first baseman, left the game with some remarkable achievements. The burly, red-faced slugger is the only man to hit three home runs in a game six times; in 30 games he homered twice; he had seven pinch-hit home runs, and he homered in all of the 15 ML parks in use during his career. A remarkable slugger who was also a contact hitter, he struck out only 524 times while hitting 359 home runs. He was a student of hitting who relied as much on knowledge of the pitchers and an extremely graceful, well-balanced hitting style as he did on his considerable strength.

Successful surgery to correct an upper-leg bone spur saved Mize's career in 1935 and he hit .329 in his rookie year with the Cardinals in 1936. From 1937 through 1941, he powered the Cardinals' attack with more than 100 RBI each season. He was traded to the Giants after the 1941 season and gave them four excellent seasons around three years spent in the Navy during WWII. He tied Ralph Kiner for the NL home run title with 51 in 1947, when the Giants set a since-broken ML record with 221, and again with 40 in 1948. In August 1949 he was sold to the Yankees for $40,000. From 1949 through 1953, he was a part-time first baseman and pinch hitter deluxe for five Yankees championship teams. He led the AL in pinch hits three straight years, 1951–53. He was the WS MVP in 1952, hitting .400 with three home runs in the seven-game series.

Former Cardinals teammate Stan Musial said of Mize during Mize's 1981 induction into the Hall of Fame: "Did you ever see a pitcher knock him down at the plate? Remember how he reacted when brushed back? He'd just lean back on his left foot, bend his body back and let the pitch go by. Then he'd lean back into the batter's box and resume his stance, as graceful as a big cat." /(FS)

Johnny Mize

Vinegar Bend Mizell [Wilmer David] — 1930– . LHP 1952–53, 56–62 **Cardinals**, Pirates, Mets 1529 ip, 90–88, 3.85. *1 WS, 2.1 ip, 0–1, 15.43*
☛ *All-Star—59.*

A big starter with control problems, Mizell was consistent but unspectacular. He led the NL in walks as a rookie, and from 1952 to 1960 he never won 15 games despite only one ERA above 3.75. On September 1, 1958, he shut out the Reds on four hits despite allowing nine walks and five stolen bases. Mizell was traded to Pittsburgh in May 1960 and helped the Pirates to the pennant with a 13–5 mark, but retired only one batter in his lone WS start in Game Three, surrendering five runs and taking the loss. He later served several terms as a Republican congressman from Mississippi. /(FK)

Danny Moeller — 1885–1951. OF 1907–08, 12–16 Pirates, **Senators**, Indians 704 g, .243, 15 hr, 192 rbi

A switch-hitting right fielder, Moeller hit exactly 10 triples in each of his four seasons as a regular. On

July 19, 1915 he stole second, third, and home in the first inning against Cleveland, as the Senators stole a ML-record eight bases that inning. /(ADS)

Joe Moeller (Skeeter) — 1943- . RHP 1962, 64, 66-71 **Dodgers** 583 ip, 26-36, 4.02. *1 WS, 2 ip, 0-0, 4.50*

The 6'5" 195-lb Moeller was plagued by injuries while trying to find steady work with the pitching-laden Dodgers. He was 7-13, 4.21 in 24 1964 starts, and 7-9, 3.93 in 1970, his most productive seasons. /(FK)

Ron Moeller (The Kid) — 1938- . LHP 1956, 58, 61, 63 Orioles, **Angels**, Senators 153 ip, 6-9, 5.78

Bonus-baby Moeller never stuck with Baltimore, but finally made it with the expansion 1961 Angels. He went 4-8 with a 5.83 ERA, mostly as a starter. /(WOR)

Randy Moffitt — 1948- . RHP 1972-83 **Giants**, Astros, Blue Jays 782 ip, 43-52, 3.65

The brother of tennis great Billie Jean King, Moffitt averaged 58 games a year out of San Francisco's bullpen from 1972 through 1978. A sinkerballer with good control, he threw his fastball and slider with overhand, three-quarter, and sidearm deliveries. He was second in the NL with 15 saves in 1974, and sixth in 1976 with 14. He missed much of 1980 and 1981 with a mysterious stomach ailment that turned out to be a fungus so rare that his was only the world's third known case. Doctors finally burned it out. Moffitt retired with 96 career saves. /(NLM)

Herb Moford — 1928- . RHP 1955, 58-59, 62 Cardinals, **Tigers**, Red Sox, Mets 157 ip, 5-13, 5.03

Moford spent each of his four seasons with a different team. His only significant action came in 1958 with Detroit, when he went 4-9 with a 3.61 ERA as a starter and reliever. /(JFC)

George Mogridge — 1889-1962. LHP 1911-12, 15-27 White Sox, Yankees, **Senators**, Browns, Braves 2275 ip, 133-130, 3.20. *1 WS, 12 ip, 1-0, 2.25*

Long, lean George was a control pitcher who gave up few walks, generally achieved a good ERA, and until Dave Righetti in 1983, was the only Yankee to pitch a regular season no-hitter (against the Red Sox in 1917). He was traded to Washington in 1921, as the Yankees were entering their first great years, served with Walter Johnson as a bellwether of the Senators' staff, and pitched five innings of the famous seventh game of Washington's winning 1924 Series.

For his times, he was also active in relief, winning 20, losing 21, and earning 21 saves.

When resin was banned by the American League in 1920, George worked the powder into the underside of the bill of his cap: convenient, effective, and never discovered. /(ADS)

Kid Mohler [Ernest Follette] — 1874-1961. 2B 1894 **Washington (NL)** 3 g, .111, 0 hr, 0 rbi

Originally a righthanded pitcher, 5'4" Kid Mohler became a lefthanded second baseman because of an injury to his right arm as a teenaged pro rookie. From 1891 through 1914, he played a pro baseball record of 2,871 games at second base—all but three of them in the minors. He attributed his renowned sure-handedness to never wearing a glove. /(MC)

Dale Mohorcic (Horse) — 1956- . RHP 1986- **Rangers**, Yankees 311 ip, 15-19, 3.53

Mohorcic was a 30-year-old rookie when he reached the Rangers in 1986 and tied a ML record for relief pitchers by appearing in 13 consecutive games that August. Manager Bobby Valentine let him pitch to one batter with a six-run lead in the 13th game. Mohorcic led the Rangers with 16 saves and a 2.99 ERA in 1987, in 74 games. He underwent elbow surgery in March 1988, and was 0-6 (7.67) in his last 30 appearances when he was traded to the Yankees for Cecilio Guante that August 30. The Cleveland native was named after Indians outfielder Dale Mitchell. /(JCA)

John Mokan — 1895-1985. OF 1921-27 Pirates, **Phillies** 582 g, .291, 32 hr, 273 rbi

The swift, 5'7" 165-lb Mokan reached the majors in 1921 after two seasons as a top minor league basestealer. He batted better than .300 in three of his five seasons with the Phillies. /(NLM)

Bob Molinaro (Molly) — 1950- . OF-DH 1975, 77-83 Tigers, **White Sox**, Orioles, Cubs, Phillies 401 g, .264, 14 hr, 90 rbi

Molinaro was a speedy extra outfielder and left-handed-hitting DH. Of his last 142 at-bats, 122 came as a pinch hitter; his 9-for-35 off the bench for the 1981 White Sox led the AL, and he pinch hit a NL-high 67 times for the Cubs and Phillies in 1982. He considered leaving pro ball after spending the 1975 off-season dealing blackjack in Las Vegas. /(JCA)

Paul Molitor (Molly) — 1956– . 3B-2B-DH-SS-OF
1978–Brewers 1437 g, .300, 119 hr, 581 rbi. *1 LCS, 5 g,
.316, 2 hr, 5 rbi. 1 WS, 7 g, .355, 2 rbi*
☛ *All-Star—80, 85.*

A largely unheralded performer, Paul Molitor received due recognition by challenging baseball's great hitting streaks in 1987. A solidly built right-hander with especially strong legs but weak hamstrings, Molitor overcame two trips to the disabled list in 1987 to lead the American League in runs scored (114) and doubles (41) while finishing second in the batting race (.353). His hit streak was the talk of baseball when it ended at 39 games. The Brewers were 76–41 with him in the lineup, 22–23 without.

Molitor was *TSN* AL Rookie of the Year in 1978, playing shortstop (while Robin Yount was injured) and second base. Voted into the 1980 All-Star Game at second base, Molitor moved to centerfield in 1981, then to right after surgery repaired torn left ankle ligaments. He moved to third base in 1982 and played brilliantly in the regular season, with a league-high and club-record 136 runs scored, and in the postseason, including a World Series-record five hits in one game. Another severe setback was a 1984 elbow injury that required surgery. He was Milwaukee's Comeback Player of the Year in 1985. The leadoff batter's prime position since 1982 was third base, but he was also used extensively as a designated hitter, not because of any fielding deficiency but to protect him from injury. /(ME)

Fritz Mollwitz [Frederick] (Zip) — 1890–1967. 1B
1913–19 Cubs, **Reds**, Pirates, Cardinals 534 g, .241, 1 hr,
158 rbi

The only major leaguer born in Kolberg, Germany, was a regular in only two seasons: with the Reds in 1915 and the Pirates in 1918. /(ARA)

Joe Monahan — 1918–1973. *Scout.*

Monahan scouted for the Cardinals from 1947 until his death in 1973, signing eventual ML players Nate Colbert, Gary Geiger, Dal Maxvill, and the older Dick Schofield. His father, Pat, was also a longtime ML scout. /(FVP)

Bill Monboquette (Monbo) — 1936– . RHP 1958–68
Red Sox, Tigers, Yankees, Giants 1961 ip, 114–112, 3.68.
20 wins: 63
☛ *All-Star—60–63.*

The ace of weak Red Sox teams in the early 1960s, Monboquette won at least 14 games four straight years, peaking in 1963 with a 20–10 mark. A four-time All-Star, in 1960 he started the year's first All-Star Game for the AL, but allowed three home runs in two innings to take the loss. Monboquette relied on changing speeds with good control, but on May 12, 1961, he fanned 17 Senators in a nine-inning game (at the time the second-best effort in AL history). He no-hit the White Sox on August 1, 1962, defeating Early Wynn 1–0, and had a second no-hit bid foiled by a Zoilo Versalles home run in September 1964. /(FK)

Rick Monday — 1945– . OF-1B 1966–84 A's, **Cubs**,
Dodgers 1986 g, .264, 241 hr, 775 rbi. *5 LCS, 11 g, .241,
1 hr, 1 rbi. 3 WS, 14 g, .184*
☛ *All-Star—68, 78.*

Monday, the first player ever taken in the draft, had a long, solid career but had chronic back problems and never achieved at the level first expected of him.

After being picked in June 1965 by the A's and signing for a $104,000 bonus, he became a semi-regular in 1967. For the A's, Monday hit as high as .290 (1970) and as many as 18 HR (1971). His five strikeouts on April 19, 1970 tied the ML record for a nine-inning game.

After the 1971 season he was traded straight-up for Cub pitcher Ken Holtzman. Moving from the spacious Oakland Coliseum to cozy Wrigley Field, and playing more often, he increased his production: He hit 26 HR in 1973, 20 in 1974 while batting .294, and a career-high 32 in 1976. In 1976, probably his best year overall, the leadoff batter scored a career-high 107 runs, fifth in the NL. In a game on May 16, 1972, he homered in three consecutive at-bats.

In January 1977 Monday went to the Dodgers in a five-player deal that sent Bill Buckner and Ivan DeJesus to Chicago. Monday had two more good seasons before a 1979 injury limited him to 12 games. Thereafter he was an extra outfielder and a not especially successful pinch hitter. He earned national notoriety with the Dodgers when he dashed from his position in centerfield and snatched an American flag from a fan who was about to burn it. He was also the hero of the 1981 LCS, hitting a two-out, ninth-inning two-run homer off Expos ace Steve Rogers to win the clincher 2–1.

A centerfielder until his injury, Monday was a good fielder with an accurate arm; he led NL outfielders in fielding in 1972 and twice led his league in outfield double plays. He hit 16 leadoff home runs lifetime. He hit into only 71 double plays in his career, an excellent average of one every 86.4 at-bats. He was the sixth-easiest player in history to strike out and ranks 16th in career strikeouts. He made up for it by walking fairly often, with a high of 92 walks in 1973, fifth in the NL that season. /(SFS)

Don Money (Brooks) — 1947– . 3B-2B-DH-SS-1B-OF 1968–83 Phillies, **Brewers** 1720 g, .261, 176 hr, 729 rbi. *1 LCS, 4 g, .182, 1 rbi. 1 WS, 5 g, .231, 1 rbi*
☛ *All-Star—74, 76–78.*

Money's nickname, Brooks, is a tribute to his fielding prowess but, like Robinson, he was also a productive hitter whose offensive capabilities were often overlooked because of his excellent glove work.

Originally signed by the Pirates' Syd Thrift, Money was traded to Philadelphia with Woody Fryman and two other pitchers in return for Jim Bunning. In his rookie 1969 season, he was the Phillies' regular shortstop. Larry Bowa came up in 1970 and Money moved to third base, batting a career-high .295 with 14 HR and 66 RBI in 120 games. He saw his average drop into the .220s in the next two seasons, but he started playing every day in 1972 and led NL third basemen in putouts, double plays, and fielding. He was sent to the Brewers in a seven-player deal after the season to make room for Mike Schmidt.

In Milwaukee, his average rebounded to the .280s as the Brewers' leadoff batter, and he stole a career-high 22 bases in 1973 (and 19 in 1974). He led AL third basemen in fielding in 1973 and 1974. Willingly moved to second base in 1977 after the Brewers got Sal Bando, Money had his best year, reaching career highs in HR (25), RBI (83), and runs (86). After that he was an "expensive utility man" (his own phrase), kept not only for his versatility afield but also for his power. He was primarily a DH for several seasons, including 1982 when the Brewers were AL champions. /(WOR)

Sid Monge [Isidro] — 1951– . LHP 1975–84 Angels, **Indians**, Phillies, Padres, Tigers 764 ip, 49–40, 3.53
☛ *All-Star—79.*

Cleveland traded Dave LaRoche to California in 1977 to acquire the Mexican-born Monge, who replaced LaRoche as the Indians' lefthanded relief ace. With excellent control, and above-average fastball, slider, and screwball, Monge led the Indians in ERA in 1978 and 1979. He set club records with 76 appearances and 12 relief wins, and recorded 19 saves in 1979, his All-Star year. After slumping in 1980 and 1981, he was traded to the Phillies for Bake McBride. Though he recorded few saves, he rebounded with a 7–1 record in 1982, and, with the Phillies and Padres in 1983, was 10–3. Monge and

Jim Kern share second place on the Indians' all-time save list with 46. /(ME)

Bill Monroe (Uncle Bill) — 1877–1915. 2B-1B-3B-SS Negro Leagues 1896–1914 Chicago Union Giants, Chicago Unions, Philadelphia Giants, New York Quaker Giants, **Brooklyn Royal Giants**, Chicago American Giants statistics not available

Monroe was a star infielder during black baseball's early years. An exciting second baseman, he played regularly for top teams, including the Philadelphia Giants (1903–06), losers of the 1903 Black World Series, winners of the 1904 BWS, and the top black club in the East in 1905 and 1906. His stint with the Brooklyn Royal Giants (1906–10) included the 1909 Eastern title. He was with Rube Foster's Chicago American Giants when they claimed the 1913 and 1914 black Western crowns. Chicago then swept Monroe's former Brooklyn team in four straight in the 1914 BWS. Monroe paced a 7–6 third game victory with four hits.

A strong hitter, Monroe usually hit in the middle of the order on strong clubs. He batted .333 in the 1907–08 Cuban Winter League. Rube Foster and Philadelphia Giants manager Sol White considered Monroe capable of stardom in the white major leagues. John McGraw of the New York Giants echoed their sentiments. Monroe died at the age of 38. /(MFK)

Ed Montague (Fast Eddie) — 1948– . *Umpire* NL 1976–87 *1 ASU 3 LCS 1 WS*

Montague was reportedly fined $500 in 1982 when he grabbed the shirt of Mets third baseman Hubie Brooks during an argument. Montague's father played four seasons with Cleveland but was best known as the scout who signed Willie Mays. /(RTM)

Eddie Montague — 1905–1988. SS-3B 1928, 30–32 **Indians** 220 g, .262, 2 hr, 69 rbi

Montague was a backup shortstop for the Indians for four seasons, then found his niche as a scout for the Giants from 1942 to 1981, signing Willie Mays. He later landed Ron Bryant and Bob Knepper for the Giants. In one season (1941), scouting for the Red Sox, he signed Mel Parnell. His son, Ed Montague, Jr., is a NL umpire. /(FVP)

John Montague — 1947– . RHP 1973–75, 77–80 Expos, Phillies, **Mariners**, Angels 547 ip, 24–26, 4.76. *1 LCS, 4 ip, 0–1, 9.00*

Montague saved the expansion Mariners' first-ever victory, on April 9, 1977. Over two relief appearances that July, he tied an AL record by retiring 33 consecutive batters. He was sidelined with hip pain in 1978; a benign tumor was found and removed after the season. In his first 10 days after being acquired by the Angels in late August 1979, Montague won two games and saved five, playing a key role in California's division title. /(NLM)

Willie Montanez [Guillermo Naranjo] — 1948– . 1B-OF 1966, 70–82 Angels, **Phillies**, Giants, Braves, Mets, Rangers, Padres, Expos, Pirates 1632 g, .275, 139 hr, 802 rbi
☛ *All-Star—77.*

Signed as a first baseman by St. Louis in 1965, lefthanded Willie Montanez was lost to the Angels in that November's draft, but was returned to the Cardinals in mid-1966. On April 8, 1970, he was sent to the Phillies with pitcher Bob Browning as compensation for Curt Flood's failure to report the previous October. Used in centerfield in lieu of Flood, Montanez hit a career-high 30 homers and drove in 99 runs as a rookie in 1971. He led the NL with 39 doubles and 22 outfield assists the following year. Returning to first base, he became the flashiest fielder at that position since fellow Puerto Rican Vic Power; famous for his snap catches, Montanez was widely considered a hot dog. He led NL first basemen in assists with the Phillies and Giants in 1975; with the Giants and Braves in 1976; and with the Mets in 1978. His wide-ranging, aggressive play also led to a league-leading 22 errors in 1976. He batted more than .300 each year from 1974 to 1976, but hit .287 in his All-Star 1977 season with Atlanta. He was traded nine times; twice the deals involved John Milner. /(MC)

Aurelio Monteagudo (Monty) — 1943– . RHP 1963–67, 70, 73 **A's**, Astros, White Sox, Royals, Angels 132 ip, 3–7, 5.06

Son of major leaguer Rene Monteagudo, Aurelio developed an effective screwball. After the Cuban recorded two of his three ML wins in 1973, California traded him to the Phillies. He returned to the Angels as a minor league instructor. /(NLM)

Rene Monteagudo — 1916–1973. OF-LHP 1938, 40, 44–45 Senators, **Phillies** 156 g, .289, 0 hr, 21 rbi; 168 ip, 3–7, 6.42

A 5'7" Cuban signed by the Senators, Monteagudo failed in two trials as a pitcher, suffered a sore arm, and resurfaced four years later as a Phillies outfielder. In 1945 he was the NL's most used and most successful pinch hitter (18-for-52) and worked 14 games in relief. His son, Aurelio, also pitched in the majors. /(NLM)

John Montefusco (The Count) — 1950– RHP 1974–86 **Giants**, Braves, Padres, Yankees 1651 ip, 90–83, 3.54
☛ *Rookie of the Year—75. All-Star—76.*

The flamboyant Count of Montefusco took San Francisco by storm in the mid-1970s. Reminiscent of Dizzy Dean, he made predictions and backed them with sensational performances. He made a sparkling debut with the Giants in September of 1974, defeating the arch-rival Dodgers in relief and hitting a home run in his first ML at-bat. In 1975 the fastballer predicted a shutout over the Dodgers and then delivered, 1–0. His 1975 record of 15–9, with a 2.88 ERA and the second-highest strikeout total in the league (215), earned him the NL Rookie of the Year Award. In 1976 he was 16–14, with a 2.84 ERA and a NL-topping six shutouts. He no-hit the Braves, 9–0, on September 29.

As injuries affected his performance, his antics lost their charm. A fistfight with Giants manager Dave Bristol hastened his exit from San Francisco. In a brief 1983 comeback, he had a combined 14–4 mark with the Padres and Yankees. /(FS)

Rich Monteleone — 1963– . RHP 1987– Mariners, **Angels** 51 ip, 2–2, 3.35

Monteleone, the Tigers' first-round pick in the June 1982 draft, pitched better with the 1989 Angels (3.18 ERA) than he ever had even at his lowest level in the minors. His strong showing as a set-up man was a factor in the Angels' contention. /(SFS)

Bob Montgomery — 1944– . C 1970–79 **Red Sox** 387 g, .258, 23 hr, 156 rbi. *1 WS, 1 g, .000*

Montgomery labored nine years in the minors before a .324 batting average and 14 home runs at Louisville earned him a ML spot with the Red Sox. As Boston's backup catcher for 10 years, he averaged fewer than 40 games a season. /(BC)

Jeff Montgomery — 1962– . RHP 1987– Reds, **Royals** 174 ip, 16–7, 2.69

Montgomery took over the bullpen stopper role for the Royals in 1989 after Steve Farr went on the DL.

Montgomery saved 18 games with a 1.37 ERA and had a 7–3 record. He struck out 94 in 92 innings. /(WOR)

Montreal Expos — 1969– . Team. 1611–1724, .483.
NL East Champions 81

The Expos came into being in the 1969 expansion that split the leagues into divisions. They finished last their first two seasons, but bright spots included Coco Laboy being named *TSN* NL Rookie of the Year in 1969 and Carl Morton winning the BBWAA's Rookie of the Year award in 1970. Expo Bill Stoneman pitched the first ML no-hitter outside the United States in 1972, and the club contended in 1973 under manager Gene Mauch. The team dropped back to the 100-loss level in 1976 after Mauch left. The development of stars Andre Dawson, Gary Carter, and Larry Parrish led to the team's first winning season in 1979 when they won a franchise-record 95 games and finished second. In the strike-split 1981 season, the Expos won their division, but through the first half of the decade they earned a reputation as a club that was great on paper but just above average on the field.

The Expos' principal owner and chairman of the board, Charles Bronfman of Seagram's, has held his position since the team's inception; only two other principal executives in the NL have a longer tenure. /(SFS)

Ray Monzant — 1933– . RHP 1954–58, 60 **Giants** 317 ip, 16–21, 4.38

Monzant was a curveballer who seemed unable to decide whether to pitch for the Giants or stay home in Venezuela. He was consistently late in reporting, claiming a variety of excuses, and finally sat out the entire 1959 season. After a comeback attempt in 1960, he retired for good. /(BC)

Wally Moon — 1930– . OF-1B 1954–65 Cardinals, **Dodgers** 1457 g, .289, 142 hr, 661 rbi. *2 WS, 8 g, .240, 1 hr, 2 rbi*
☛ *Rookie of the Year—54. All-Star—57, 59. Gold Glove—60.*

"Moon shots" were what they called the home runs that lefthanded-batting Wally Moon golfed over the 42-foot wall a mere 250 feet down the Los Angeles Coliseum's left field line with his inside-out swing. Though he didn't hit many of them, the newly arrived Moon hit them early in 1959, and his ingenuity seemed to capture the spirit of the ragtag bunch that took the Dodgers from seventh place to the World Championship. Appropriately, he scored the last run ever in the Coliseum.

Moon homered in his first major league at-bat, as a Cardinal in 1954, en route to batting .304 and winning the Rookie of the Year award over Hank Aaron. He peaked with 24 HR in 1957, but was traded to the Dodgers after a .238 showing in 1958. A fine defensive outfielder, he won a Gold Glove in 1960. /(TG)

Jim Mooney — 1906–1979. LHP 1931–34 Giants, **Cardinals** 356 ip, 17–20, 4.25. *1 WS, 1 ip, 0–0, 0.00*

In a primitively lit night game played in the Southern Association in 1930, this lefthander struck out 23 batters. Brought up to the Giants in August 1932, Mooney went 7–1, but wildness made him a loser after that. /(JK)

Balor Moore — 1951– . LHP 1970, 72–74, 1977–80 Expos, Angels, **Blue Jays** 719 ip, 28–48, 4.51

Moore, who debuted at 19, was the fledgling Expos' first pick in the June 1969 draft. An overpowering young pitcher, the Texan was called a lefthanded Nolan Ryan and went 9–9 in 1972, averaging almost 10 strikeouts a game. That winter he pitched a perfect game for San Juan in Puerto Rico, the first nine-inning perfect game in that league's 36-year history. Wild in 1973, he fell to 7–16. After being demoted and disabled in 1974, Moore underwent elbow surgery in 1975 and left the Montreal organization with a French-Canadian wife, but without a fastball. He didn't win another ML game until 1978, with Toronto, for whom he went 12–17 over three seasons. /(JCA)

Barry Moore — 1943– . LHP 1965–70 **Senators**, Indians, White Sox 600 ip, 26–37, 4.16

Moore's only winning record came in 1969, when he went 9–8 with a 4.30 ERA in his last season with the Senators. /(WOR)

Charlie Moore — 1953– . C-OF 1973–87 **Brewers**, Blue Jays 1334 g, .261, 36 hr, 408 rbi. *1 LCS, 5 g, .462. 1 WS, 7 g, .346, 2 rbi*

Moore was a good contact hitter with little power who backed up Darrell Porter at catcher for the Brewers for three seasons, then started from 1977 to 1980 before being forced back to the bench by the acquisition of Ted Simmons in 1981. In 1982 the strong-armed Moore shifted to right field, where he led AL outfielders with six double plays, and he remained there until 1985, when he moved back behind the plate. Moore hit .300 in 1979 and .301 in 1981 (in only 48 games), but usually batted near the bottom of the order, and never drove in more than 49 runs in a season. /(SCL)

Cy Moore — 1905-1972. RHP 1929-34 **Dodgers**, Phillies 466 ip, 16-26, 4.86

Dodger manager Wilbert Robinson couldn't bring himself to use a pitcher who didn't have a curveball, so he kept the fastballing Moore on the 1930 staff as a batting practice pitcher. Moore did relieve some in 1931-32, then got a chance to start in two mediocre seasons with the Phillies. /(JK)

Dobie Moore [Walter] — 1893-Unk. SS-OF Negro Leagues 1920-26 **Kansas City Monarchs** .359, 34 hr (inc.)
☛ Led League—ba 24.

Casey Stengel once said, "That Moore was one of the best shortstops that will ever live!" A superb fielder with outstanding range and a rifle-like arm, Moore joined the Negro League Kansas City Monarchs from the legendary 25th Infantry Wreckers Army team. In his six years with the Monarchs, he batted a cumulative .359 and helped them to three pennants (1923-25). He batted .300 in the 1924 Black World Series and .364 in the 1925 BWS. His brief career was ended in 1926 when he was injured in an accidental shooting. /(LL)

Donnie Moore — 1954-1989. RHP 1975, 77-88 Cubs, Cardinals, Brewers, Braves, **Angels** 656 ip, 43-40, 3.66. *2 LCS, 8 ip, 0-1, 4.70*
☛ All-Star—85.

Donnie Moore's up-and-down career was most notable for one pitch. One strike away from putting California in the World Series, he allowed a Dave Henderson home run in Game Five of the 1986 LCS. Henderson's game-winning sacrifice fly off Moore then turned the series in favor of victorious Boston. Moore's shocking suicide less than a year after the end of his major league career was partially a result of his brooding on this failure; he said he had become another Ralph Branca, doomed to be remembered for just one pitch and one failure. His career was ended by a string of injuries, and he was also dismayed by his inability to continue playing; shortly before his death he had been released by a minor league team.

After signing a $3 million contract with the Angels in 1985, Moore set a club record with 31 saves, surpassing his entire previous major league total, and was named club MVP. Trying to justify his big contract, Moore tried to pitch despite a sore shoulder in 1986 and succumbed to nerve irritation in his right rib cage in 1987.

More effective against lefthanders than righthanders, the righthanded Texan led the 1978 Cubs in games pitched, but was overshadowed by Bruce Sutter and Willie Hernandez. He tied for the Atlanta lead in games pitched in 1983 and led the club in 1984. /(ME)

Earl Moore (Crossfire) — 1878-1961. RHP 1901-14 **Indians**, Yankees, Phillies, Cubs, Buffalo (FL) 2767 ip, 161-153, 2.78. 20 wins: 10
☛ Led League—k 10. Led League—era 03.

A strikeout pitcher with streaks of wildness, Moore whipped the ball in with an intimidating, sweeping sidearm motion. With Cleveland on May 9, 1901, he pitched the AL's first no-hitter, but lost it, and the game, in the tenth, allowing Chicago two hits. In 1903 he led the league with a 1.77 ERA, going 19-9. He was a stubborn holdout for almost all of 1906 and was traded to New York in 1907. He won a career-high 22 games for the Phillies in 1910, leading the league in strikeouts, but his 19 losses the next year tied for the league's most. /(JK)

Eddie Moore — 1899-1976. 2B-OF-SS-3B 1923-30, 32, 34 **Pirates**, Braves, Dodgers, Giants, Indians 748 g, .285, 13 hr, 257 rbi. *1 WS, 7 g, .231, 1 hr, 2 rbi*

A consistent singles-hitter, the 5'7" Moore replaced Rabbit Maranville in 1925 as second baseman for the Pirates, hit .298 in the leadoff spot, and helped Pittsburgh win the World Championship. To make room for a high-priced bust named Hal Rhyne, Moore was sold to the Braves in 1926. He remained as a valuable utility man for seven more ML seasons. /(ME)

Euel Moore (Chief) — 1908- . RHP 1934-36 **Phillies**, Giants 225 ip, 9-16, 5.48

A Chickasaw Indian, Moore developed a sore arm when Phillies manager Jimmie Wilson tried unsuccessfully to change him from an overhand pitcher to a sidearmer. /(NLM)

Gene Moore (Rowdy) — 1909-1978. OF Reds, Cardinals, **Braves**, Dodgers, Senators, Browns 1042 g, .270, 58 hr, 436 rbi. *1 WS, 6 g, .182*

Moore's father, Eugene Sr., pitched briefly for the Pirates (1909-10) and the Reds (1912). Eugene Jr. became the Braves' regular right fielder in 1936 and led NL outfielders with 32 assists. He hit .290 with 13 HR, 38 doubles, 91 runs, and 67 RBI in his rookie season. He reached highs of 16 HR and 70 RBI in 1936, again leading the NL in assists. His power dropped off thereafter, and he was never again an everyday player. He did make the World Series with the Browns in 1944, and scored the first run in Game One, the only game they won. /(SFS)

Joe Moore (Jo-Jo, The Gause Ghost) — 1908– . OF 1930–41 **Giants** 1335 g, .298, 79 hr, 513 rbi. *3 WS, 16 g, .274, 1 hr, 3 rbi*

Moore was the Giants' left fielder and, despite drawing few walks, leadoff man for much of 1932–41. A lefthanded slap-hitter, he batted over .300 five times, and led the NL in at-bats in 1935. Because Moore was a notorious first-ball hitter, some managers insisted their pitchers start him off with a ball outside the strike zone, fining those who allowed Moore a first-pitch hit. Often, Moore had to duck an opening delivery. When Hank Leiber was Moore's roommate, he told Dizzy Dean to quit throwing at Joe or he'd break every bone in Dean's body. Moore tied a record with nine hits in a five-game World Series (1937), and with two hits in one inning in the 1933 WS. /(NLM)

Johnny Moore — 1902– . OF 1928–29, 31–37, 45 Cubs, Reds, **Phillies** 846 g, .307, 73 hr, 452 rbi. *1 WS, 2 g, .000*

Lefthanded-batting Johnny Moore was a satisfactory fielder who hit wherever he went. In Chicago, he competed with .336 hitter Riggs Stephenson and Hall of Famers Hack Wilson and Kiki Cuyler before securing a job when Wilson was traded in 1932; he batted .305 that pennant-winning season. He reached a high of .330 with the Reds and Phillies in 1934 and played ten years in the Pacific Coast League—all with Los Angeles—hitting .326. /(JK)

Junior Moore [Alvin Earl] — 1953– . 3B-OF-DH 1976–80 Braves, **White Sox** 289 g, .264, 7 hr, 73 rbi

Moore hit .300 in four of six minor league seasons before starting at third base in 1977 for Atlanta. But through a contractual loophole he was made a free agent by an arbitrator that winter. He signed with the White Sox, for whom he played three seasons as a handyman. /(JCA)

Marianne Moore — 1888–1972. Poet.

Moore, the 1952 Puliter Prize-winning poet, was an avid Dodgers fan until they left Brooklyn. She switched her allegiance to the Yankees and threw out the first ball in their 1968 opener. A Bryn Mawr graduate, she taught English at Carlisle Indian School, where Jim Thorpe was one of her students. One of her favorite players was Whitey Ford: "Like Whitey's three kinds of pitch and prediagnosis with

pickoff psychosis . . ." She liked the precision positions of pitcher and catcher: "It's a pitcher's battle all the way, a duel; a catcher's, as with cruel puma paw Elston Howard lumbers lightly back to plate." And she described a catch by Mickey Mantle: "Mickey, leaping like the devil, why gild it, although deer sound better, shares what was beating toward its treetop nest, one-handing a souvenir to be, meant to be caught by you and me." /(NLM)

Mike Moore — 1959– . RHP 1982– **Mariners**, A's 1699 ip, 85–107, 4.13. *1 LCS, 7 ip, 1–0, 0.00. 1 WS, 13 ip, 2–0, 2.08*
☛ *All-Star—89.*

The Mariners selected Moore first overall in the 1981 draft, ahead of Tony Gwynn, Joe Carter, Frank Viola, and Kevin McReynolds. In 1985 Moore was 17–10 (setting the Mariners' season record for winning percentage, .630) with a 3.46 ERA in a hitter's park without much support. He showed flashes of brilliance in 1987 and 1988, although he went 9–19 and 9–15. On August 21, 1988 Moore struck out 16 Yankees to tie Mark Langston's club record for strikeouts in a game.

The defending AL champion A's signed Moore as a free agent before the 1989 season, and he led the rotation with a 2.61 ERA while going 19–11. He continued to excel in the postseason, winning all three of his starts and hitting a two-run double in Game Four. /(TF)

Randy Moore — 1905– . OF-1B-3B-C 1927–28, 30–37 White Sox, **Braves**, Dodgers, Cardinals 749 g, .278, 27 hr, 308 rbi

Primarily an outfielder, Moore could fill in anywhere, and even caught when necessary. A steady performer with the Boston Braves, he reached highs of 135 games and a .302 batting average in 1933. A Texan, he made a fortune in the oil business after his playing career ended and made wealthy men of former Braves teammates by tipping them off to investments. /(JK)

Ray Moore (Farmer) — 1926– . RHP 1952–53, 55–63 Dodgers, **Orioles**, White Sox, Senators/Twins 1073 ip, 63–59, 4.06. *1 WS, 1 ip, 0–0, 9.00*

Moore was a righthanded fastballer who walked almost as many as he fanned. Offensively, he hit six home runs despite a .187 batting average. In December 1957 he was traded with Billy Goodman and Tito Francona to the White Sox for lefthander Jack Harshman and Larry Doby. /(NLM)

Roy Moore — 1898–1951. LHP 1920–23 **A's**, Tigers 407 ip, 11–26, 4.98

After the Athletics paid Waco (Texas League) $5,000 for Moore in 1920, he lost his first 13 decisions before recording his sole win of the season. He went 10–10 in 1921, but walked almost twice as many as he struck out. He was a good hitter for a pitcher, batting .257 with three HR in 1921 and hitting .239 lifetime; Connie Mack used him as a pinch hitter on five occasions, but he went 0-for-5./(NLM)

Terry Moore — 1912– . OF 1935–42, 46–48 Cardinals 1298 g, .280, 80 hr, 513 rbi. *2 WS, 12 g, .205, 4 rbi.*
   Manager 1954 **Phillies** 35–42, .455
☛ *All-Star—39–42.*

A popular and classy centerfielder with speed and a strong arm, Moore was considered among the league's best. Underrated because he was overshadowed by more colorful teammates, he was captain of two Cardinal World Championship teams (1942 and 1946). As a rookie in 1935, he hit two doubles and two homers in one game, and a few weeks later went 6-for-6 in another. He was an All-Star from 1939 through 1942, a stretch during which he hit .295. Moore put together a 20-game hitting streak in 1942 and entered the military that fall. He seemed to have lost his batting eye, but not his fielding flair, when he returned in 1946. He was kept out of the lineup by an old knee injury. He had nine consecutive hits and rebounded for a .283 average in 1947. Retiring after 1948, he was a Cardinals coach in 1949–52, and again in 1956–58 after managing the Phillies for part of 1954./(EW)

Whitey Moore [Lloyd Albert] — 1912– . RHP 1936–42 **Reds**, Cardinals 513 ip, 30–29, 3.75. *2 WS, 11 ip, 0–0, 2.38*

Despite throwing a no-hitter for Syracuse (on July 25, 1937, against Jersey City, a 1–0 win in nine innings) and leading the International League in strikeouts, Moore came up to the Reds as an unheralded rookie. He went 13–12 at his best for Cincinnati's 1939 pennant winners./(NLM)

Wilcy Moore (Cy) — 1897–1963. RHP 1927–29, 31–33 **Yankees**, Red Sox 692 ip, 51–44, 3.69. *2 WS, 16 ip, 2–0, 0.56*

Though occasionally used as a starting pitcher, Wilcy Moore was among the first to gain fame as a reliever. He developed a sidearm sinkerball after hurting his shoulder in the Sally League. As a 30-year-old rookie with the 1927 Yankees, he went

19–7 and led the league with 13 relief wins and 13 saves (his 2.28 ERA would also have led, had he qualified with the then-necessary ten complete games). After saving the opener of the 1927 World Series against the Pirates, he started and won the fourth and final game. He later claimed that overwork in 1927 caused the arm problems which sidelined him in 1928 and hampered his career. Even so, his 10 saves for the Red Sox in 1931 were the AL high. He returned to the Yankees in 1932, his relief win in the WS closing out another four-game sweep, this time of the Cubs./(JK)

Bob Moorhead — 1938– . RHP 1962, 65 Mets 119 ip, 0–3, 4.51

Moorhead allowed five runs in three innings of work in the Mets' first-ever relief appearance on April 11, 1962. After another bad outing, he broke his fist punching a locker. He came back in 1965 as a knuckleballer./(KT)

Bob Moose — 1947–1976. RHP **Pirates** 1304 ip, 76–71, 3.50. *3 LCS, 10 ip, 0–2, 6.10. 1 WS, 10 ip, 0–0, 6.52*

Moose figure in two of the most memorable moments in Pirates history. He pitched a 1969 no-hitter against the Mets, and in Game Five of the 1972 LCS Moose's wild pitch allowed George Foster to score the run that sent the Reds to the World Series in Roberto Clemente's last game.

The hard thrower was an established starter when injury intercepted. In 1974 Moose underwent surgery for a blood clot in his right shoulder. Removal of a rib was necessary to free up a vein causing the problem. He missed more action in 1975 with a badly bruised thumb, but made a successful move to relief the next season. He led the 1976 Pirates in saves (10) and appeared ready to inherit Dave Giusti's role as stopper, but he died in a vehicular accident in Martin's Ferry, Ohio, on October 9, 1976./(ME)

Jake Mooty [J T] — 1913–1970. RHP 1936–37, 40–44 Reds, **Cubs**, Tigers 434 ip, 16–23, 4.03

Called Jake because his parents failed to provide more than the initials J T, Mooty was pitching for the Cubs in 1940 when he beaned Pee Wee Reese, putting him in the hospital for 18 days and cutting short his rookie season./(JK)

Andres Mora [born Andres Ibara Ibarra] — 1955– . OF-DH 1976–78, 80 **Orioles**, Indians 235 g, .223, 27 hr, 83 rbi

A slugging outfielder who struck out as often as he hit safely, Mora led the Mexican League in home runs and RBI for his hometown Saltillo team in 1974. In his second ML game (4/17/76, versus Oakland), Mora homered to break Paul Lindblad's streak of 91 homerless innings. He spent much of 1976–78 with Baltimore and hit six HR in one seven-game stretch in August of 1977./(JCA)

Jerry Morales [Julio] — 1949– . OF 1969–83 Padres, **Cubs**, Cardinals, Tigers, Mets 1441 g, .259, 95 hr, 570 rbi ☛ *All-Star—77.*

Puerto Rico's Jerry Morales was taken from the Mets organization by the Padres in the 1968 expansion draft, but had his most productive seasons with the Cubs, 1974–77. He had career highs of 91 RBI in 1975, 16 homers in 1976, and a .290 average in 1977, his All-Star year./(ARA)

Jose Morales — 1944– . DH-1B-C 1973–84 A's, **Expos**, Twins, Orioles, Dodgers 733 g, .287, 26 hr, 207 rbi. *1 LCS, 2 g, .000*

Morales set season records of 25 pinch hits and 78 pinch at-bats in 1976 and ranks third all-time with 123 pinch hits and fifth with 445 pinch at-bats. He led his league three times each in pinch hits and pinch at-bats. He hit .323 in 1978 to lead AL DHs in batting, and he hit .300 five times overall, but never had more than 242 at-bats in a season. A catcher in the minors, he led four leagues in errors and didn't make the majors until his tenth pro season./(WOR)

Rich Morales — 1943– . SS-2B-3B 1967–74 **White Sox**, Padres 480 g, .195, 6 hr, 64 rbi

Morales was an embarrassment at the plate; his glove kept in the majors. In 1972 the White Sox utility man was the only AL infielder to play at least 10 games at three positions, but he batted .206, and just .161 the next year. He managed in the Cubs' and A's farm systems, scouted for the White Sox, and served as the Braves' bullpen coach./(RL)

Billy Moran — 1933– . 2B-3B 1958–59, 61–65 Indians, **Angels** 634 g, .263, 28 hr, 202 rbi

Moran failed in his first trial, hitting .226 in 115 games for the Indians in 1958. Catching on with the expansion Angels, he won the second base job in 1962, leading AL second basemen in assists and total chances per game while reaching career highs with 17 HR, 74 RBI, 90 runs, and a .282 average. He had another strong season in 1963, leading AL second basemen in putouts, assists, and total chances per game (and errors), but fell off a bit

offensively (7 HR, 65 RBI, 67 runs). He was traded to Cleveland next June when he had hit no HR, and spent the rest of his career as a utility man./(WOR)

Charley Moran (Uncle Charley) — 1878–1949. C 1903, 08 **Cardinals** 25 g, .221, 0 hr, 3 rbi. *Umpire NL 1917–39 4 WS*

Moran played briefly in the NL and umpired there for 23 years, but he is better known for his football career. A fullback with the Massillon Tigers in 1905, he went on to become a highly successful coach at many schools, including Texas A&M, Carlisle, and Bucknell. In 1921 his Centre College Praying Colonels, featuring All-America Bo McMillin, handed Harvard its first defeat in three years. In 1927, he coached the Frankford Yellow Jackets of the National Football League./(RTM)

Harry Moran — 1889–1962. LHP 1912, 14–15 Tigers, Buffalo (FL), **Newark (FL)** 374 ip, 24–19, 3.34

Moran was a mediocre pitcher whose only significant action came in the Federal League. He went 11–8, 4.27 in 1914 for the BufFeds, and improved to 13–10, 2.54 for the Newark Peps in 1915./(SFS)

Herbie Moran — 1884–1954. OF 1908–10, 12–15 Athletics, Braves, **Dodgers**, Reds 595 g, .242, 2 hr, 135 rbi. *1 WS, 3 g, .077*

Moran was a peppery little lefthanded leadoff hitter who had two seasons as a regular at Brooklyn, then became one of the 11 who played George Stallings's weak outfield in the Braves' miracle year of 1914./(ADS)

Pat Moran — 1876–1924. C-3B 1901–14 **Braves**, Cubs, Phillies 819 g, .235, 18 hr, 262 rbi. *2 WS, 3 g, .000. Manager* 1915–23 Phillies, **Reds** 748–586, .561. First place: 15, 19 *2 WS, 6–7, .462*

During his playing days, Moran was mostly a backup catcher, but he had the highest HR percentage in the NL as a 1903 Boston Beaneater (Brave), with seven homers in 389 at-bats. A successful manager, he led the 1915 Phillies to a pennant in his first try, and he was the Reds' skipper for their 1919 World Series victory over the Black Sox./(ARA)

Dave Morehead (Moe) — 1943– . RHP 1963–70 **Red Sox**, Royals 820 ip, 40–64, 4.15. *1 WS, 3 ip, 0–0, 0.00*

Morehead was 19 when he shut out the Senators in his major league debut with Boston on April 13, 1963. He tied for the league lead with 18 losses in 1965, but on September 16 he pitched a no-hitter against Cleveland, allowing just one walk. He won only 12 games from 1966 through 1970, but he did contribute five victories to the 1967 AL champion Red Sox. /(EW)

Seth Morehead (Moe) — 1934– . LHP 1957–61 **Phillies**, Cubs, Braves 318 ip, 5–19, 4.81

Morehead was used most often in 1960, when he went 2–4 with four saves and a 2.80 ERA in relief for the Cubs, but was 0–5, 6.35 as a starter. /(JFC)

Keith Moreland — 1954– . OF-3B-C-1B 1978– Phillies, **Cubs**, Padres, Tigers, Orioles 1306 g, .279, 121 hr, 674 rbi. *2 LCS, 7 g, .316, 3 rbi. 1 WS, 3 g, .333, 1 rbi*

Originally a third baseman, and most valued for his offense, Keith Moreland was moved to catcher in 1977. After two seasons as a part-timer in Philadelphia, he was traded to Chicago. Found wanting defensively, he was moved to the outfield. Moreland was the Cubs' leading batter (.302) in 1983 and peaked in 1985 (.307, 14 HR, 106 RBI) while becoming a respectable, if slow, right fielder. He moved back to third base in 1987, replacing Ron Cey, and struggled defensively. However, he hit a career-high 27 homers. Traded to San Diego for Goose Gossage in 1988, he played outfield and first base. He moved on to Detroit for 1989 and was traded in mid-season to the contending Orioles. /(ME)

Lew Moren (Hicks, The Million Dollar Kid) — 1883–1966. RHP 1903–04, 07–10 Pirates, **Phillies** 878 ip, 48–57, 2.95

Moren was dubbed The Million Dollar Kid because his father, a wealthy steamboat and coal-barge operator, gave him $100 every time he won a game. Moren spent four years in the Phillies' rotation. He went 11–18 in 1907 with a 2.54 ERA, slightly worse than the league average of 2.46. His best year was 1909, when he had his only winning record, 16–15. He threw out his arm one wet, chilly day, and quit rather than go back to the minors. /(NLM)

Julio Moreno — 1921–1987. RHP 1950–53 **Senators** 337 ip, 18–22, 4.25

This 5'8" Cuban came to the Senators from Havana late in 1950 as a poised, 29-year-old rookie. He used a good fastball to go 9–9 in 1952. /(EW)

Omar Moreno (Omar the Outmaker) — 1953– . OF 1975–86 **Pirates**, Astros, Yankees, Royals, Braves 1382 g, .252, 37 hr, 386 rbi. *1 LCS, 3 g, .250. 1 WS, 7 g, .333, 3 rbi*

Moreno, the fleet leadoff man of the 1979 World Champion Pirates, was an offensive and defensive threat when at the top of his game. The great speed that allowed him to rob opponents of extra-base hits was also his greatest offensive weapon. When hitting instructor Harry Walker convinced Moreno to chop the ball in 1979, he hit a career-high .282. All too often, though, the strikeout-prone, rarely walking Panamanian swung for the fences. He led the NL in steals in 1978 and '79, and set a Pittsburgh record with 96 steals in 1980, but scored just 87 runs, 23 fewer than 1979. He also led in triples in 1980 and in at-bats in '79 and '80. He left Pittsburgh after 1982 as a free agent and thereafter bounced around the majors. He finished his career with 487 steals, 14th on the career list at the time. /(ME)

Roger Moret [Rogelio Torres] — 1949– . LHP 1970–78 **Red Sox**, Braves, Rangers 722 ip, 47–27, 3.67. *1 LCS, 1 ip, 1–0, 0.00. 1 WS, 2 ip, 0–0, 0.00*

The sidearming Moret's aim for the strike zone was as erratic as his personality, but when he had control of both he was a capable winner. He led the AL in winning percentage twice for the Red Sox, going 13–2 in 1973 and 14–3 for the AL champions in 1975. Otherwise, he was 20–22 in a nine-year ML career. Moret won the second game of the 1975 ALCS against the A's by pitching a scoreless sixth inning. He gave up the winning hit to Joe Morgan in WS Game Three, but was not charged with the loss. /(MS)

Bobby Morgan — 1926– . 2B-SS-3B 1950, 52–58 Dodgers, **Phillies**, Cardinals, Cubs 671 g, .233, 53 hr, 217 rbi. *2 WS, 3 g, .000*

After Morgan was named International League MVP in 1949 (.337, 112 RBI), the Dodgers put a $250,000 price tag on him, and he moved to the head of a long line of heirs apparent to Pee Wee Reese's shortstop spot. When Reese's tenure prevented that, he was projected as the next Dodger third baseman. Neither his batting nor his fielding was sufficient, and in 1954 he was traded to Philadelphia. /(BC)

Cy Morgan [Harry Richard] — 1878–1962. RHP 1903–05, 07–13 Browns, Red Sox, **A's**, Reds 1445 ip, 78–78, 2.51

Morgan, a spitballer, was 31 when Connie Mack acquired him from the Red Sox to help the A's win championships in 1910 and 1911. Morgan went 18–12 and 15–7, but with 20-game winner Jack Coombs and Hall of Famers Eddie Plank and Chief Bender on the A's staff, he was not used in either World Series. /(JK)

Ed Morgan — 1904–1980. 1B-OF 1928–34 **Indians**, Red Sox 771 g, .313, 52 hr, 473 rbi

Playing out of position in the outfield in 1929, Morgan fielded only .908 but hit .318. Made the Indians' regular first baseman in 1930, he slugged .601 (tied for fifth in the AL) with 26 HR and 47 doubles (tied for third), all career highs, while hitting .349 (he did lead the AL with 66 strikeouts). He hit a career-high .351 in 1931, walking 83 times as well, but his power gradually dropped off over the rest of his career. He led AL first basemen in errors twice and putouts once. /(SFS)

Joe Morgan — 1930– . 3B-2B 1959–61, 64 Braves, A's, Phillies, **Indians**, Cardinals 88 g, .193, 2 hr, 10 rbi.
   Manager 1988– **Red Sox** 129–110, .534. First place: 88 *1 LCS, 0–4, .000*

Morgan was named interim manager of the Red Sox when John McNamara was fired during the 1988 All-Star break, and he led Boston from third place, 9-1/2 games out, to its second AL East championship in three seasons. A native of nearby Walpole, Massachusetts, he starred in baseball and ice hockey at Boston College before spending 31 seasons in the minors as both a player and manager. The "interim" was dropped from his title when the Red Sox won 19 of the first 20 games he managed. /(SCL)

Joe Morgan (Little Joe) — 1943– . 2B 1963–1984 Astros, **Reds**, Giants, Phillies, A's 2650 g, .271, 268 hr, 1134 rbi. *7 LCS, 27 g, .135, 2 hr, 5 rbi. 4 WS, 23 g, .235, 3 hr, 8 rbi*
☛ *Most Valuable Player—75–76. All-Star—66, 72–79. Gold Glove—73–77.*

Morgan was a rare commodity, a speedy second baseman with power. The 5'7" 150-lb Little Joe was also one of the smallest number-three hitters in recent baseball history. Morgan ranks third all-time in walks behind Babe Ruth and Ted Williams. He is also the only second baseman to win consecutive MVP awards, in 1975 and 1976. In the batter's box, Morgan would flap his back elbow distinctively as a

Joe Morgan and Rennie Stennett, runner

timing device, and he was a major component of the Big Red Machine, the first National League team to win consecutive World Series since the 1921–22 New York Giants.

Morgan started his career in the spacious Astrodome, and actually spent more years with Houston than with Cincinnati. He was the main player acquired by the Reds in a nine-player swap that sent Lee May to the Astros. Morgan's power was shown to better advantage in Riverfront Stadium, helped by coaching from Ted Kluszewski. Morgan doubled his home run output in two seasons. His first year in Cincinnati, he made the All-Star team for only the second time, and was named the game's MVP when he singled in the winning run in the bottom of the tenth. He ended up leading the league in walks with 115 and runs scored with 122.

In 1975 Morgan led the NL in walks for the third time with 132, while combining a .327 BA with 17 HR, 94 RBI, and 67 stolen bases. Morgan's MVP season sparked the team into the 1975 World Series against the Red Sox, one of the most exciting Series ever played. Morgan, as usual, was in the thick of the excitement. In Game Three, Morgan knocked in the winning run with a single in the 10th inning. In Game Four, he made the last out in a 5–4 Boston victory. In Game Five, he drew 16 pickoff throws at first just prior to a single by Bench and a three-run homer by Perez. In the seventh and deciding game, Morgan's RBI single in the top of the ninth gave the Reds their first World Championship.

In 1976 Morgan topped his previous power totals with a career-high 27 HR, became only the fifth second baseman to drive in more than 100 runs (111), and led the league in slugging average at .576. He also batted .320, stole 60 bases, and had an on-base average of .516 to earn his straight second MVP. The Reds then swept the Yankees in the Series.

In 1980 he went back to Houston, where he helped the Astros to a division title, and spent two years in San Francisco, almost leading the untalented Giants to a surprise pennant in 1982. Still productive, even if unable to match his earlier high standards, Morgan ended up on a geriatric Phillies team in 1983 with fellow Reds alumni Pete Rose and Tony Perez, making it as far as the World Series but losing in five games to Baltimore. He ended his playing career in Oakland in 1984 and then became an announcer for the A's and for ABC. /(SEW)

Mike Morgan — 1959– . RHP 1978– A's, Yankees, **Mariners**, Orioles, Dodgers 938 ip, 42–79, 4.51

Encouraged by Dodger pitching coach Ron Perranoski, who changed the grip he used for his fastball, Morgan suddenly became effective in the first half of 1989, although he was moved to the bullpen after a slump. He was a high school phenom (and the fourth pick overall in the June 1978 free agent draft), rushed directly to the majors by the A's, only to be sent to the minors and then to the Yankees and Blue Jays for a season with each. Injuries disabled him and he spent over a year with the Blue Jays' Syracuse farm club before being drafted by the Mariners. Morgan was a regular starter for Seattle in 1986 and 1987 seasons, losing 17 games each year. After the 1987 season, Morgan was traded to Baltimore for Ken Dixon, an exchange of failed prospects. On occasion, Morgan would show flashes of the promise that made him a high school star, but he would get shelled at least as often. /(TF)

Ray Morgan — 1889–1940. 2B-3B-SS 1911–18 **Senators** 739 g, .254, 4 hr, 254 rbi

Morgan was the spark plug of the 1912 Senators, who won 17 games in a row and climbed from the cellar to second place. His leadoff walk on June 23, 1917, was protested by Red Sox pitcher Babe Ruth, who was ejected from the game. Ernie Shore relieved Ruth, picked off Morgan, and retired the next 26 batters to pitch a perfect game. /(JK)

Tom Morgan (Plowboy) — 1930–1987. RHP 1951–52, 54–63 **Yankees**, A's, Tigers, Senators, Angels 1023 ip, 67–47, 3.61. *3 WS, 10 ip, 0–1, 5.59*

Morgan made the jump from Class A to the Yankees as a 21-year-old in 1951. Used as a spot starter and middle reliever, he went 9–3 to help win a pennant. He pitched mostly in relief for three more Yankee pennant-winners before being traded to Kansas City in 1957. Known as Plowboy because of his stooped walk, exhibited in his frequent trips from the bullpen to the mound, Morgan went 8–2 as a reliever for the expansion 1961 Angels and retired in 1963 with 64 lifetime saves. He scouted, managed in the minors, and was an Angels pitching coach. /(BC)

George Moriarty — 1884–1964. 3B-1B 1903–04, 06–15 Cubs, Yankees, **Tigers**, White Sox 1071 g, .251, 5 hr, 376 rbi. *1 WS, 7 g, .273, 1 rbi.*
   Manager 1927–28 **Tigers** 150–157, .489.
   Umpire AL 1917–26, 29–40 *5 WS*

Moriarty spent fifty years in baseball, making his most indelible contribution as a tough and colorful American League umpire for 22 years. As a player, he was a good fielder but only ordinary at bat. His strength was his baserunning. He accumulated 248 lifetime thefts, with a season high of 34 for the AL 1909 champion Tigers, and stole home 11 times in his career. He joined the AL umpiring staff two years after he retired. In 1927 he took time off to manage the Tigers, succeeding his former teammate Ty Cobb. He led Detroit to fourth place in his first season but after they dropped to sixth in 1928, he returned to umpiring.

While wearing the blue, he was the object of one of Jimmy Dykes's most famous jibes. He called a third strike on Dykes, who then asked: "How do you spell your name?" Moriarty spelled it out. "That's what I thought," said Dykes. "Only one 'i.'" When the White Sox disputed his decisions one day, Moriarty challenged them all to a fight under the stands. He decked the one player who dared step forward, breaking his hand on the player's jaw. He retired as an umpire in 1940 and joined the AL public relations staff. His final job in baseball was as a Tigers scout. His brother Bill was a Reds shortstop for six games in 1909. /(RTM/JK)

John Morlan — 1947– . RHP 1973–74 Pirates 106 ip, 2–5, 4.16

Morlan switched from outfielder to pitcher in 1971, and in 1973 tied for the International League lead with a .688 winning percentage (11–5). Each of his first four pro seasons was delayed by his teaching job in Columbus, OH. /(ME)

Ed Morris — 1899–1932. RHP 1922, 28–31 Cubs, **Red Sox** 674 ip, 42–45, 4.19

The ace of the last-place 1928–29 Red Sox, this fireballer later injured his arm during a scuffle in a St. Louis hotel elevator. He was stabbed to death at a Florida fish fry before spring training in 1932. /(EC)

Jack Morris — 1955– . RHP 1977– **Tigers** 2794 ip, 183–132, 3.66. 20 wins: 83, 86 *2 LCS, 15 ip, 1–1, 4.20. 1 WS, 18 ip, 2–0, 2.00*
☛ *Led League—w 81. Led League—k 83. All-Star—81, 84–85, 87.*

A streaky pitcher within the season, Jack Morris was consistent from year to year and was the winningest pitcher of the 1980s. He became Detroit's top winner in 1979 and led the club in wins each of the next eight seasons, a stretch unprecedented in Tigers

history. Using a fastball, split-finger fastball, and slider, from 1980 to 1988 he made 33 or more appearances every season, except for strike-shortened 1981. He pitched into the seventh inning in 26 straight starts in 1983. Morris's 1984 no-hitter at Chicago matched the earliest, by date (April 7), in major league history. At the other end of the season, Morris was undefeated in three postseason appearances; two complete game triumphs in the World Series and a LCS win.

Morris is among Detroit's all-time leaders in wins, games, starts, complete games, innings pitched, strikeouts and shutouts. His three straight shutouts in 1986 was a first for a Detroit right-hander. Following that season, free agent Morris appeared headed back to his home state of Minnesota. However, his price was too high for the Twins, who were, like all the clubs, in a period of collusion on free agent signings, so Morris re-signed with the Tigers. A proud, determined, competitive, and sometimes angry individual, Morris exhibited complete athletic skills. He set a record in the 1984 World Series for most putouts (5) by a pitcher in a five-game series. Although he gave up plenty of

Jack Morris

home runs, many were with the bases empty. Along with the keystone combination of Alan Trammell and Lou Whitaker and manager Sparky Anderson, Morris was a cornerstone of the rebuilding project that turned Detroit into a contending team for most of the 1980s. /(ME)

John Morris — 1941– . LHP 1966, 68–74 Phillies, Orioles, **Pilots/Brewers**, Giants 232 ip, 11–7, 3.96

Morris's best season came in relief for Baltimore in 1968, when he went 2–0 with a 2.56 ERA (his lowest). He saw more action, with less success, for the Brewers in 1970–71. /(JFC)

Jim Morrison — 1952– . 3B-2B 1977–88 Phillies, White Sox, **Pirates**, Tigers, Braves 1089 g, .260, 112 hr, 435 rbi. *2 LCS, 3 g, .333*

A solid performer, especially on offense, Morrison had a career season with the 1986 Pirates (.274, 23 HR, 88 RBI). He set a major league record that year for fewest chances accepted by a third baseman (150 games) in a season. With the 1980 White Sox, he led American League second basemen in assists and errors. However, his versatility and offense made him a valued performer; he played every position except catcher in his career. /(ME)

Johnny Morrison [Jughandle Johnny] — 1895–1966. RHP 1920–27, 29–30 **Pirates**, Dodgers 1535 ip, 103–80, 3.65. 20 wins: 23 *1 WS, 9 ip, 0–0, 2.89*

Morrison's nickname, Jughandle Johnny, was a tribute to his sweeping curveball, considered among the best ever. He was 25–13 for the Pirates in 1923, and, as a workhorse starter and reliever, tied for the NL lead in games pitched in 1924 and led in 1925. A heavy drinker, he was suspended by Pittsburgh at times in 1926 and 1927, when, claiming illness, he went home to the hills of Kentucky. Dodger manager Wilbert Robinson had tolerance for wayward imbibers; after the sobering experience of being sent to the minors, a repentant Morrison was welcomed to Brooklyn in 1929. Robinson's reclamation project was a one-year success, as Morrison was the NL's best reliever, with eight saves and ten wins out of the bullpen. But, early in 1930, he failed to report for a game, was deemed "out of shape" and fined $200, and left Brooklyn for good. His brother Phil pitched in one game for the Pirates in 1921. /(JK)

Jo-Jo Morrissey — 1904–1950. 2B-SS-3B 1932–33, 36 **Reds**, White Sox 254 g, .232, 0 hr, 45 rbi

Morrissey had hard luck. Soon after the rookie joined the 1932 Reds, his child died. In 1933 he

played 148 games (by far his most), though hampered by a finger injury. He suffered a broken cheekbone in 1936. He was in the minors in 1939 when he snapped an Achilles tendon, ending his career. /(NLM)

Jacob C. Morse — 1860–1937. *Writer.*

Beginning in 1889, Morse was one of four men (Tim Murnane, Ed Stevens, and Walter Barnes were the others) who controlled the destiny of baseball in Boston during his 25 years with the Boston *Herald*. He was secretary of the New England League and the founder and first editor of *Baseball Magazine* in 1907. In later years he wrote for the Boston *Traveler*. /(NLM)

Bubba Morton [Wycliffe Nathaniel] — 1931– . OF 1961–63, 66–69 Tigers, Braves, **Angels** 451 g, .267, 14 hr, 128 rbi

Morton was a light-hitting backup outfielder who saw considerable action with the Angels (1966–69), hitting a career-high .313 in 1967. He showed some power with seven HR in 1969, but his average dropped to .244. He made only one error in his last three seasons. /(WOR)

Carl Morton — 1944–1983. RHP 1969–76 Expos, **Braves** 1649 ip, 87–92, 3.73
☛ *Rookie of the Year—70.*

Morton compiled an 18–11 record for the Expos in 1970 and was voted NL Rookie of the Year. He began as an outfielder in the Braves' organization, became a success when converted to the mound, and was taken by the Expos in the 1968 expansion draft. After he slipped to 7–13 in 1972, Morton was traded back to Atlanta, where he strung together three winning seasons for mediocre Braves teams. He won only four games in 1976 and finished in the minors. Morton was only 39 when he died of a heart attack after jogging. /(JK)

Guy Morton (Alabama Blossom) — 1893–1934. RHP 1914–24 **Indians** 1630 ip, 98–88, 3.13

Morton overcame a nightmarish beginning to forge a solid major league career with the Indians. He lost his first 13 games in 1914, a ML record for consecutive losses at the start of a career that was broken by Terry Melton in 1982. Morton finally notched his only win of the year in September. The following season, he led Cleveland with a career-high 16 wins, losing 15. On June 11, 1916, he struck out four A's in one inning. His son, Guy Jr., reached the majors for one pinch at-bat with the 1954 Red Sox. /(ME)

Walt Moryn (Moose) — 1926– . OF 1954–61 Dodgers, **Cubs**, Cardinals, Pirates 785 g, .266, 101 hr, 354 rbi

Moryn had his best seasons for the Cubs, knocking in 88 runs in 1957 and hitting 26 home runs in 1958. That season he had three homers in one game (5/30/58) against the Dodgers. Moryn was never a gazelle in the field, but his outstanding shoestring catch with two outs in the ninth saved Don Cardwell's no-hitter against the Cardinals in 1960. /(BC)

Lloyd Moseby (Shaker) — 1959– . OF 1980- **Blue Jays** 1392 g, .257, 149, 652 rbi. *2 LCS, 12 g, .255, 1 hr, 6 rbi* ☛ *All-Star—86.*

Moseby was the second player chosen in the 1978 free agent draft. He was rushed to the majors by the talent-hungry Blue Jays faster than the development of his considerable potential would have warranted with an established franchise. A talented center-fielder, Moseby combined with Jesse Barfield and George Bell to form what was sometimes called the best outfield in baseball in the late 1980s. Moseby is the Blue Jays' career leader in games, at-bats, runs, hits, doubles, total bases, extra-base hits, stolen bases, strikeouts, being hit by the pitch, and sacrifice flies. In 1983 he became the first Blue Jay to score 100 runs in a season, and he tied teammate Damaso Garcia for a team-record (and league-leading) 21-game hitting streak. In 1984 Moseby tied with teammate Dave Collins for the AL lead in triples.

By the end of the decade, the "best outfield" was being dismantled. Barfield was traded to the Yankees, and Moseby was being pushed by emerging star Junior Felix. /(TF)

Earl Moseley — 1884–1963. RHP 1913–16 Red Sox, **Indianapolis/Newark (FL)**, Reds 856 ip, 50–49, 3.01 ☛ *Led League—era 15.*

Moseley made the majors at the age of 28 and went 9–5. Jumping to the Federal League in 1914, he went 18–18 and 16–16 for the Indianapolis-Newark franchise, leading the league in ERA (just ahead of Hall of Famers Eddie Plank and Three Finger Brown) in 1915 and tying for fifth in strikeouts. He failed to continue his success with Cincinnati in 1916, going 7–10 with a 3.89 ERA to close out his ML career. /(SFS)

Gerry Moses — 1946– . C 1965, 68–75 **Red Sox**, Angels, Indians, Yankees, Tigers, White Sox, Padres 386 g, .251, 25 hr, 109 rbi ☛ *All-Star—70.*

The baby-faced Moses posed a long-ball threat, though his season high was only six. After 1970, when he made the All-Star squad, he bounced around the American League and generally served as a backup or platoon catcher. /(PB)

John Moses (Holy) — 1957– . OF 1982- **Mariners**, Twins 620 g, .263, 10 hr, 129 rbi

Moses has been an excellent pinch runner and utility outfielder who plays good, hustling defense. A 16th-round draft choice out of the University of Arizona in 1980, Moses had 25 stolen bases in 1986 and 23 in 1987, and raised his average to .316 for the 1988 Twins. /(TF)

Wally Moses — 1910– . OF 1935–51 **A's**, White Sox, Red Sox 2012 g, .291, 89 hr, 679 rbi. *1 WS, 4 g, .417* ☛ *All-Star—37.*

Moses was a swift young outfielder in the Palmetto League when approached by a Giants scout under

Wally Moses

orders to find a Jewish player. "But I'm Irish, Scotch, and English," Moses told him. The scout didn't sign him. Moses debuted with the A's in 1935, batted over .300 each of his seven years with them, and then never did so again. In 1937 he had by far his most productive season, hitting 25 home runs (his next best total was nine) with 86 RBI (20 above his next best mark). He missed a World Series chance when his 1939 trade to Detroit for Benny McCoy was nullified by Commissioner Landis, who made McCoy and 96 other Tigers free agents. Through years of second-division finishes in Philadelphia, Moses had little chance to display his speed on the basepaths. But with the 1943 White Sox, who led the league in stolen bases, he had 56, and a league-high 12 triples. In the field, he had a strong arm but was weak on ground balls. He led the AL in putouts (329) in 1945. With the Red Sox in 1946, he tied a World Series record with four hits in a game (the 23rd player to do so). He finished with the A's, and later coached for them. /(NLM)

Paul Moskau — 1953- . RHP 1977–83 **Reds**, Pirates, Cubs 634 ip, 32–27, 4.22

Moskau was a mediocre starter who won more often than not with the powerful Big Red Machine behind him. His lowest ERA was 3.91 in 1979. /(JFC)

Les Moss — 1925- . C 1946–58 **Browns/Orioles**, Red Sox, White Sox 824 g, .247, 63 hr, 276 rbi.
   Manager 1968, 79 White Sox, **Tigers** 39–52, .429

Moss spent virtually his entire major league career fighting Sherm Lollar for playing time, first with the Browns and later with the White Sox. With St. Louis in 1948, before Lollar arrived from the Yankees, Moss reached career highs with 107 games, 14 home runs, and 46 RBI. He scouted, coached, and managed in the White Sox and Tiger organizations for nearly 30 years. He was interim manager of the White Sox while Al Lopez was hospitalized in 1968, and he managed the Tigers for the first third of 1979 before being replaced by Sparky Anderson. /(MC)

Ray Moss — 1901- . RHP 1926–31 **Dodgers**, Braves 416 ip, 22–18, 4.95

Used mostly in relief, at his best Moss had 20 starts and went 11–6 despite a 5.04 ERA for the 1929 Dodgers. /(EGM)

Don Mossi (The Sphinx) — 1929- . LHP 1954–65 **Indians**, Tigers, White Sox, A's 1548 ip, 101–80, 3.43.
   1 WS, 4 ip, 0–0, 0.00

A master of control, as a rookie reliever for the 1954 American League champion Indians, Mossi was 6–1 with a 1.94 ERA and was unscored upon in three World Series appearances against the Giants. From 1954 to 1958 (except for 1957, when he was a starter) Mossi and righthander Ray Narleski formed one of baseball's best bullpen pairs. In November 1958, Cleveland sent them both to Detroit to acquire Billy Martin and Al Cicotte. Moved into the Tigers' rotation, Mossi was 17–9 with 15 complete games in 1959. On a team that won 101 games in 1961, he led Tiger starters with a 2.96 ERA while going 15–7. After relief stints with the White Sox in 1964 and the A's in 1965, he retired with what was then the best-ever fielding average for a pitcher

Johnny Mostil (Bananas) — 1896–1970. OF 1918, 20–29 **White Sox** 972 g, .301, 23 hr, 376 rbi

Fleet-footed Johnny Mostil was one of the premier AL outfielders of the 1920s. He led the league in stolen bases in 1925 and 1926 and in runs scored in '25, and four times batted over .300. In a 1925 spring training game, Mostil snared a foul fly down the left-field line while playing center. Though he hit a career-high .328 in 1926, on March 9, 1927, he tried to kill himself in his Shreveport hotel room, inflicting 13 razor cuts to his wrist, neck, and arms. The press reported that Mostil suffered from neuritis, but rumors circulated that Mostil was having an affair with the wife of teammate Red Faber, and attempted suicide when Faber found out and threatened to kill him. Mostil recovered and returned by the end of the season, but played less than two more years. Later, he became a minor league manager and White Sox scout. /(RL)

Most Valuable Player Award (MVP) — 1931- .

The Most Valuable Player Award has been given each year since 1931 to the best player from each league, as voted by selected members of the Base Ball Writers Association of America (BBWAA). Predecessors using quite similar voting structures existed intermittently before 1931.
   In 1910 the Chalmers auto company had promised one of their cars to the major leaguer with the highest batting average that season. After a scandal in which Napoleon Lajoie was allowed to go 8-for-8 on the last day of the season to overtake the unpopular Ty Cobb in the batting race, the Chalmers people awarded both players cars. To avoid such problems in the future, they decided not to base subsequent awards on raw statistics (which, at the time, were of dubious accuracy anyway). In-

stead, they set up a panel of respected sportswriters, one from each major league city. Using a weighted ballot on which first place was worth eight points, second was worth seven points, and so on through eight places, one writer per team in each league voted on that league's best player. Upon winning the car, a player was no longer eligible in later years.

The Chalmers award lasted only four years, 1911–14, but when the American League revived the idea in 1922, they used the same voting system, and many of the same writers. This was the first award to use the title "Most Valuable Player"; rather than awarding a car, they planned to build a monument on which winners' names would be carved. The National League joined in two years later, awarding a trophy and a $1,000 bond, with these changes: There would be ten places on the ballot, and there could be repeat winners. Rogers Hornsby was the first to repeat, winning in 1925 and 1929. The AL discontinued their award after 1928, and the NL dropped the idea after 1929.

In 1931 the BBWAA took over, using the voting structure the NL had used. In 1938 they switched to three voters per team and a more heavily weighted ballot on which first place counted for 14 points. This basic structure has lasted to the present day. /(JFC)

Manny Mota — 1938– . OF 1962–80, 82 Giants, Pirates, Expos, **Dodgers** 1536 g, .304, 31 hr, 438 rbi. *3 LCS, 6 g, .600, 1 rbi. 2 WS, 4 g, .000*
☛ *All-Star—73.*

Baseball's all-time pinch-hit leader, with 150, it was said Mota could wake up on Christmas morning, step into the box, and rip a single to right. Pittsburgh's fourth outfielder from 1963 to 1968, the Dominican blossomed under manager Harry Walker's tutelage to hit .332 in 1966, his first of seven .300 seasons in eight years. Hindered by a lack of power and fielding ability, Mota's only season of more than 400 at-bats came with the 1970 Dodgers. Amid a 1974 youth movement, he emerged as a pinch hitter extraordinaire. He had ten or more pinch hits six straight seasons; 250 of his last 309 at-bats came off the bench. One of his greatest moments came in the ninth inning of Game Three of the 1977 LCS at Philadelphia. Down two strikes, he hit an RBI double, and the Dodgers rallied for three runs and a 6–5 victory. Near the end of his career, he often began the season as a coach, only to be activated each year for the stretch drive. He finally retired with a .297 pinch-hitting average. His .315

batting average is the best (1,800 or more at-bats) in Los Angeles Dodger history. /(ME)

Darryl Motley — 1960– . OF 1981, 83–87 **Royals**, Braves 413 g, .243, 44 hr, 159 rbi. *2 LCS, 5 g, .200, 2 rbi. 1 WS, 5 g, .364, 1 hr, 3 rbi*

Motley made the Royals and won a regular job through determination and tireless effort. In 1984 he produced his best season, finishing second or third on the Royals in most offensive categories. He had power, but lack of patience at the plate kept him from becoming a much more productive hitter. A 62-point drop in batting average in 1985 caused his relegation to platooning. /(FO)

Curt Motton — 1940– . OF 1967–74 **Orioles**, Brewers, Angels 316 g, .213, 25 hr, 89 rbi. *3 LCS, 4 g, .500, 2 rbi. 1 WS, 1 g, .000*

Motton was a backup outfielder and pinch hitter whom Orioles manager Earl Weaver kept around for his power. In 1968, the only season he had more than 90 at-bats, Motton hit .198 but had a career-high eight HR in 216 at-bats, including a since-broken ML record-tying two consecutive pinch homers on May 15 and 17. He hit .303 in limited duty in 1969, including 8-for-25 pinch hitting, and won Game Two of the LCS with an 11th-inning pinch single off Ron Perranoski that drove in the only run of the game. He delivered again in Game One of the 1971 LCS with a fifth-inning pinch double off Vida Blue that tied the game. The winning pitcher in both cases was Dave McNally. /(WOR)

Mike Mowrey — 1884–1947. 3B 1905–17 Reds, **Cardinals**, Pirates, Pittsburgh (FL), Dodgers 1275 g, .256, 7 hr, 461 rbi. *1 WS, 5 g, .176, 1 rbi*

Husky Mike brought hot grounders under control by slapping them with his glove hand to subdue the bounce, then barehanding the pickup and throw. He had the prototypical third baseman's virtues: a strong and accurate arm, consistency afield, and a reliable, if not potent, bat. He led the Federal League for average at his position in 1915 and the National in 1916, while helping Brooklyn to its first pennant in the modern era. /(ADS)

Jamie Moyer — 1962– . LHP 1986– **Cubs**, Rangers 566 ip, 32–43, 4.48

A slender but durable starter, Moyer pitched over 200 innings for the Cubs in 1987 and 1988, then was traded to the Rangers before the 1989 season in a nine-player deal that also brought Rafael Palmeiro to Texas. On April 13, 1987 he took a no-hitter into the ninth inning against Philadelphia before Juan Samuel singled, and he finished the game with 12 strikeouts, a record for Cub lefthanders. Moyer was 12–15, 5.10 in 1987, and 9–15 in 1988, but lowered his ERA to 3.48./(SCL)

Don Mueller (Mandrake the Magician) — 1948– . OF 1948–59 **Giants**, White Sox 1245 g, .296, 65 hr, 520 rbi. *1 WS, 4 g, .389, 0 hr, 1 rbi*
☛ *All-Star—54, 55.*

Nicknamed Mandrake the Magician because of the frequency with which his hits found holes in the infield defense, the heavy-legged Mueller joined the Giants full-time in 1949 and became the club's regular right fielder in 1950, hitting .291. One of his greatest disappointments came in 1951, when he was unable to play in the WS after injuring his ankle in the last inning of the Giants' "miracle" playoff game victory to win the 1951 pennant.

He hit .333 in 1953 (fifth in the NL), and then had his career year in 1954. He led the NL in hits with 212 and hit .342, just barely losing the batting title to Willie Mays. In the WS sweep over the Indians, he hit .389 and scored four runs.

Mueller did not hit well after 1955 and he retired after 1959 at age 32. He was the son of Walter Mueller, a Pirate outfielder in the 1920s./(FS)

Emmett Mueller (Heinie) — 1912–1986. 2B-3B-OF 1938–41 **Phillies** 441 g, .253, 17 hr, 127 rbi

A 5'6" switch-hitter, Mueller was playing minor league ball at age 16, two years before he finished high school. He hit a home run off Brooklyn's Van Lingle Mungo in his first major league at-bat (4/19/38). His playing days ended when he entered the military in 1942./(NLM)

Heinie Mueller [Clarence Francis] — 1899–1975. OF-1B 1920–29, 35 **Cardinals**, Giants, Braves, Browns 693 g, .282, 22 hr, 272 rbi

Mueller was one of Cardinals manager Branch Rickey's favorite players, though his baserunning exploits turned all his managers gray. He missed half of 1925 because of a broken foot, and in 1926 he was traded to the Giants. There he told manager John McGraw he wasn't used to being chewed out, and was soon dealt to the Braves. Entering both games of a 1927 doubleheader as a pinch hitter, Mueller drove in eight runs in three at-bats. His brother Walter was an extra outfielder with the Pirates in the 1920s, and his nephew, Don, played 10 years for the Giants./(NLM)

Ray Mueller (Iron Man) — 1912– . C 1935–40, 43–44, 46–51 Braves, Pirates, **Reds**, Giants 982 g, .252, 56 hr, 373 rbi
☛ *All-Star—44.*

Mueller's first major league hit was a home run off Carl Hubbell for the Braves in 1935. A second-string catcher until his return to the minors in 1940, he resurfaced with Cincinnati in 1943 and responded to the WWII baseball manpower shortage by catching 233 consecutive games. He and Frankie Hayes of the A's each caught 155 games in 1943, setting a ML record. The feat earned him the nickname Iron Man but didn't exempt him from military service in 1945./(JK)

Billy Muffett (Muff) — 1930– . RHP 1957–62 Cardinals, Giants, **Red Sox** 376 ip, 16–23, 4.33

Muffett pitched 14 minor league seasons, and all or parts of six in the majors. He no-hit San Antonio for Shreveport in the 1955 Texas League playoffs. He wound up seeing more major league time as a coach than he had as a player; he served the Cardinals for four years, beginning with their 1967 World Championship season, spent much of the 1970s with the Angels, and succeeded Roger Craig as Tiger pitching coach in 1985./(NLM)

Hugh Mulcahy (Losing Pitcher) — 1913– . RHP 1935–40, 45–47 **Phillies**, Pirates 1161 ip, 45–89, 4.49
☛ *All-Star—40.*

Mulcahy was called Losing Pitcher by scribes who noted how often the initials "L.P." followed his name in the box scores. He led the National League in losses for last-place Phillies teams in 1938 and 1940 but was selected to the 1940 NL All-Star squad. In 1941 he became the first major leaguer drafted by the army, and he missed the 1941–44 seasons, returning for a few appearances in 1945–47./(JK)

Ren Mulford — 1859–1932. *Writer.*

Mulford was a baseball writer for Cincinnati newspapers in the 19th century before entering the advertising field. As a promoter of the game in its earliest days, he fought to keep baseball clean./(NLM)

Terry Mulholland — 1963– . RHP 1986, 88– **Giants**, Phillies 216 ip, 7–15, 4.67

Mulholland was called up by the Giants in mid-1988 after a spate of injuries struck their rotation and went 2–1, with uncharacteristically excellent control, before he went down with a broken arm. He missed the last two months of the season and it was feared he might never pitch again, but he came back in 1989 and was one of the players sent to Philadelphia in return for Steve Bedrosian. /(JFC)

Tony Mullane (Count, The Apollo of the Box) — 1859–1944. R/LHP-OF 1881–84, 86–94 Detroit (NL), Louisville (AA), St. Louis (AA), Toledo (AA), **Cincinnati (AA)**, Reds, Baltimore (NL), Cleveland (NL) 4540 ip, 285–215, 3.05;784 g, .243, 8 hr, 128 rbi. 20 wins: 82–88, 91–92
☛ *Led League—k 82.*

Mullane was a multi-talented marvel, baseball's first ambidextrous pitcher. He played without a glove, facing the batter with both hands on the ball before throwing it with either one. Handsome and muscular, with a reputation as a dandy, Mullane was also a skilled boxer, skater, and musician, as well as one of the better pitchers of his day. He twice led his league in shutouts, once in strikeouts, and once in winning percentage while regularly pitching over 400 innings. Despite his sober demeanor off the field (he did not drink, smoke, or gamble), Mullane was a free spirit who routinely ignored the game's reserve clause. He jumped to the Union Association and then to Toledo after winning 35 games for the Browns in 1883 without stopping to play in the UA. He was suspended for all of 1885 when he signed

Tony Mullane

with Cincinnati after Toledo had resold him to the Browns. And in 1892 he sat out half the season to protest the NL's pay cuts. When he wasn't pitching, Mullane played every position except catcher, and switch-hit his way to a .243 batting average in 2,720 at-bats. /(ADS)

Eddie Mulligan — 1894–1982. 3B-SS 1915–16, 21–22, 28 Cubs, **White Sox**, Pirates 351 g, .232, 1 hr, 88 rbi

Mulligan spent 17 years in the Pacific Coast League and 20 years as president of the California League. His only seasons as a ML regular were 1921–22 as the third baseman succeeding banned Black Sox player Buck Weaver with Chicago. Mulligan never used profanity, and his only ejection in his 25 seasons as a ballplayer came when he called an umpire "a snot." During most of his career he also played professional soccer in the fall and winter. Upon his retirement as California League president, the league established a rookie of the year award in his honor. /(BC)

George Mullin (Wabash George) — 1880–1944. RHP **Tigers**, Senators, Indianapolis (FL), Newark (FL) 3686 ip, 228–196, 2.82. 20 wins: 05–07, 09–10 *3 WS, 58 ip, 3–3, 2.02*
☛ *Led League—w 09.*

A powerfully built fastballer, Mullin's semi-pro years brought him to Wabash, IN, where he won a bride and two major league contracts. In 1901 he signed with both the Dodgers and Tigers. Forced to choose, Wabash George took the team closer to his new home and won 13 games for the seventh-place 1902 Tigers. Mullin led the AL in walks while pitching more than 300 innings each year from 1903 to 1906. But he and the Tigers improved, running off consecutive pennants from 1907 to 1909. His .784 winning percentage and 29 wins were league highs in '09. On July 4, 1912, his birthday, Mullin no-hit the Browns. A .263 lifetime hitter, he was used 101 times as a pinch hitter. /(JK)

Pat Mullin — 1917– . OF 1940–41, 46–53 **Tigers** 864 g, .271, 87 hr, 385 rbi
☛ *All-Star—47–48.*

Detroit's number 6 before Al Kaline, Mullin batted .345 in 54 games as a Tiger rookie in 1941, then served four years in WWII. He was an All-Star in 1947 and in 1948—his best year—when he batted .288 with 23 HR and 80 RBI. After that he was a reserve, and made 57 appearances as a lefthanded pinch hitter in his final year, 1953. /(CC)

Willard Mullin — 1902-1978. *Cartoonist.*

Mullin was a jovial, party-loving artist, and his lifetime output of more than 10,000 illustrations appeared in the New York *World-Telegram* six days a week from 1934 until the paper closed in 1966, and in ads, books, magazines, and programs. His first job was with the Los Angeles *Herald.* He pictured teams in clever personifications: the Brooklyn Bum, St. Louis Swifty (the Cardinals' riverboat gambler), and others. In 1971 he was cited by the cartoonists' association as the sports cartoonist of the century./(NLM)

Rance Mulliniks — 1956- . 3B-SS-DH-2B 1977- Angels, Royals, **Blue Jays** 1168 g, .273, 69 hr, 394 rbi. *2 LCS, 6 g, .333, 1 hr, 3 rbi*

Mulliniks has been a steady role player for the Blue Jays. Originally a shortstop with the Angels and Royals, Mulliniks was the lefthanded component of a Blue Jay third-base platoon (with Garth Iorg) in the 1980s. When Mulliniks was injured during the home opener of the 1988 season, Kelly Gruber proved he was ready to become an everyday third baseman, and Mulliniks gracefully adapted to a reduced role as a lefthanded DH when he returned from the disabled list. Not blessed with great defensive skills, Mulliniks had been steady, leading AL third basemen in fielding percentage three straight seasons, 1984-86. He has set several Blue Jay club records at the plate, including the highest single season batting average (.324 in 1984), most doubles by a lefthanded batter (34 in 1983), most seasons leading the club in pinch hits (3), most consecutive hits (8), and most consecutive times on base (10). His father, Harvey, a former pitcher in the Yankee organization, proved a useful advisor to break Mulliniks out of batting slumps./(TF)

Jerry Mumphrey — 1952- . OF 1974-88 **Cardinals,** Padres, Yankees, Astros, Cubs 1585 g, .289, 70 hr, 575 rbi. *1 LCS, 3 g, .500 1 WS, 5 g, .200*
☛ *All-Star—84.*

A speedy switch-hitter who hit at least .277 with occasional power for nine straight seasons (1979-87), Mumphrey was a defensive liability. He played his first full ML season in 1976, and in 1977 he hit .287 with 22 stolen bases as the Cardinals' centerfielder but also committed nine errors. He was traded to Cleveland with John Denny for Bobby Bonds after hitting .295 in 1979, then was traded to the Padres before the 1980 season began. Mumphrey hit .298 with a career-high 52 stolen bases in 1980, but he led NL outfielders with 11 errors and went to the Yankees in a six-player deal that brought Ruppert Jones and Tim Lollar to the Padres. Mumphrey led AL outfielders with eight errors in 1981 while hitting .307, and in 1982 hit .300 with nine home runs, then was traded to Houston for Omar Moreno. He hit .290 and .277 in two seasons with the Astros before a final trade sent him to the Cubs for Billy Hatcher. Mumphrey became an accomplished pinch hitter and hit .304 as a part-time player in 1986 and .333 with a career-high 13 HR in only 309 at-bats in 1987, but was released after hitting .136 in 1988./(SCL)

Bob Muncrief — 1916- . RHP 1937, 39, 41-49, 51 **Browns,** Indians, Pirates, Cubs, Yankees 1401 ip, 80-82, 3.80. *2 WS, 9 ip, 0-1, 1.04*

Muncrief won 13 games four times for the Browns, his 13-8 mark in 1944 contributing to the only pennant winner in franchise history. He dropped to 3-12 in 1946, and he was traded to Cleveland after going 8-14 in 1947. He contributed five wins to the Indians' 1948 championship and pitched two scoreless innings in Bob Feller's Game Five WS victory./(JK)

George Munger (Red) — 1918- . RHP 1943-44, 46-52, 56 **Cardinals,** Pirates 1229 ip, 77-56, 3.83. *1 WS, 9 ip, 1-0, 1.00*
☛ *All-Star—44, 49.*

Munger reached St. Louis during the WWII player shortage in 1943 and went 9-5 as a rookie and 11-3 (1.34) as a sophomore before entering the military in mid-1944. He returned to beat the Red Sox 12-3 in Game Four of the 1946 WS, backed by the Cardinals' Series record-tying 20 hits. He was 16-5 with six shutouts in 1947 and 15-8 in 1949 before arm problems reduced his effectiveness./(MC)

Van Lingle Mungo — 1911-1985. RHP 1931-43, 45 **Dodgers,** Giants 2113 ip, 120-115, 3.47
☛ *Led League—k 36. All-Star—34, 36, 37.*

In the mid-1930s, Mungo was considered to have the talent of contemporaries Dizzy Dean and Carl Hubbell, but he pitched for losing Dodger clubs and made matters worse by being easily upset by his teammates' ineptitude. Accused of wasting his strength by compiling strikeouts early in his games, he believed the only sure way to retire batters was to

Van Lingle Mungo

fan them. He was the 1936 National League strike-out leader, with 238. He also led the NL in walks three times. In an era when starters were expected to go the distance, Mungo, who led the NL in games started in 1934 and 1936, only finished 47% of his career starts. But between 1932 and 1936, he averaged 16 wins a year.

Mungo was wild and mean, a high-kicking fireballer with a fierce temper. He was known as a drinker, and was involved in some bizarre off-the-field incidents. He once had to be smuggled out of Cuba to escape the machete-wielding husband of a nightclub dancer with whom he'd been caught in bed. His career went downhill after he injured his arm in the 1937 All-Star Game. He won only 13 ML games over his next six seasons. Becoming a junkballer, he went 14–7 in 1945. The lifetime .221 hitter sometimes pinch-hit. In 1970 his colorful name was prominently used in a nostalgic bossa nova ballad. /(JK)

Municipal Stadium Kansas City A's 1955–67, Kansas City Royals 1969–72. LF-369, CF-421, RF-338

Built in 1923 and known as Ruppert Stadium and later Blues Stadium before being sold to the city, it was home to the Negro League Kansas City Monarchs and the minor league Kansas City Blues until the Athletics moved from Philadelphia. The arrival of ML baseball prompted the addition of a tall second deck to the grandstand and the centerfield scoreboard came from Boston's Braves Field. Eccentric A's owner Charlie Finley later installed a host of unique features and gadgets, including a small zoo behind the right-field fence that housed a mule named Charlie O. (the team mascot), a compressed-air device that blew dirt off the plate from below, and a mechanical rabbit that rose out of the ground with new baseballs for the umpire. /(SCL)

Victor Munoz — Unk.–1922. *Writer.*

Sports editor of *Diario de la Marina* of Havana, Cuba, Munoz was the best-known and most widely quoted Latin American baseball writer of his time. He was one of the first members of the BBWAA, and covered every WS from 1905 to his death. /(NLM)

Thurman Munson — 1947–1979. C 1969–79
Yankees 1423 g, .292, 113 hr, 701 rbi. *3 LCS, 14 g, .339, 2 hr, 10 rbi. 3 WS, 16 g, .373, 1 hr, 12 rbi*
☛ *Rookie of the Year—70. Most Valuable Player—76. All-Star—71, 73–78. Gold Glove—73–75.*

After fewer than 100 minor league games, Munson became the Yankees' starting catcher in 1970. The Yankees went from a mediocre team to back-to-back World Championships and Munson rivaled Fisk in the AL as the decade's top catcher.

The gruff Munson immediately established his ability to handle veteran pitchers, but had a terrible start as a rookie. Manager Ralph Houk, a former catcher, stuck with him and was vindicated when Munson came around (.302) and captured AL Rookie of the Year honors. Munson's power was slow to develop, but he hit for average and usually batted second in his early years. He was an outstanding fielder, with perhaps the league's quickest release in throwing out basestealers. A sore shoulder later reduced his accuracy.

During the Yankees' mini-dynasty of 1976–78 Munson was at his peak. Off the field, he was a leader in the team's vicious clubhouse humor. On the field, he piled up his career-best offensive statistics (even a surprising 14 stolen bases in 1976). He hit over .300 with 100 or more RBI three years in a row (1975–77), won the MVP Award in 1976, and hit .529 in the 1976 WS and .320 in the 1977 and 1978 WS. Munson deserves much of the credit for

Thurman Munson

the late-season surge by a shaky Catfish Hunter during the Yankees' 1978 comeback.

During the Yankees' rebuilding years, Bobby Murcer and Munson were the stars around whom the team was constructed, and they were close. Murcer was traded in 1975, but the pair were reunited briefly in 1979. Munson had a more volatile relationship with Reggie Jackson. Initially resented in 1977 for his big free-agent contract, Jackson was shunned by his new teammates. It was Munson, the team captain, who broke the ice and worked to include Jackson in team banter. But then a pre-season interview was published in which Jackson claimed that he was "the straw that stirs the drink. It all comes down to me. Maybe I should say Munson and me, but he really doesn't enter into it. Munson thinks he can be the straw that stirs the drink but he can only stir it bad." Later in the season things were smoothed over, but the relationship was never again more than professional.

Eventually the strain of catching 130 games a year began to show, and Munson started playing the outfield and DHing more. However, on August 2, 1979, Munson died as the private plane he was flying crashed in Canton, Ohio. /(FDS)

Edgar Munzel — 1907–Unk. *Writer.*

After two years at Northwestern, Munzel joined the Chicago *Herald-Examiner* in 1929. There, and later with the *Sun-Times*, he covered more than 9,000 games until 1973. A former president of the BBWAA, he was given the J.G. Taylor Spink Award in 1977. /(NLM)

Steve Mura — 1955– . RHP 1978–83, 85 **Padres,** Cardinals, White Sox, A's 634 ip, 30–39, 3.99

Mura was a mediocre pitcher who was the last-place Padres' number-two starter in 1980–81. He tied for the NL lead with 14 losses in 1981. /(SFS)

Masanori Murakami — 1944– . LHP 1964–65 **Giants** 89 ip, 5–1, 3.43

Murakami is the only native product of the Japanese leagues to play in the major leagues. He was successful in limited use as a reliever for the Giants, but his U.S. career was cut short when the Japanese government, afraid that its country's teams would be decimated should others follow Murakami's path, demanded that he be returned. Since then, only a few veterans whose Japanese careers were nearly over have been allowed to try out for American teams. None have made it to the majors.

His unique status made Murakami the focus of outlandish expectations on the resumption of his Japanese career. The tremendous pressure affected his performance at first. Although he eventually settled down, he never became the superstar that the public expected. /(JFC)

Minoru Murayama — 1936– . P 1959–72 **Hanshin Tigers**

Murayama recorded the lowest career ERA in the history of Japanese baseball. He went 18–10 with a 1.19 ERA as a rookie, and registered a 1.20 ERA in 1962. He again kept his ERA under 2.00 in 1965 and 1966. A workhorse, he topped 290 innings five times in his first eight seasons, while completing as many as 26 games a year. Yet, unlike fellow iron man and rival Tadashi Sugiura, Murayama was not a strikeout pitcher. In between bouts with arm trouble, he won 24 or 25 games four times. Apparently washed up at age 32, he was appointed Hanshin's player-manager for 1970, and was expected to ease himself out of the rotation. Instead, he picked his spots and posted a 14–3 mark with a Japanese record 0.98 ERA. Feuding with ace Yutaka Enatsu, Murayama won only seven games in 1971, and was fired. /(MC)

Bobby Murcer — 1946– . OF-DH 1965–66, 69–1983 **Yankees**, Giants, Cubs 1,908 g, .277, 252 hr, 1,043 rbi. *2 LCS, 2 g, .143. 1 WS, 4 g, .000*
☛ *All-Star—71–75. Gold Glove—72.*

In 1965 Murcer joined a veteran Yankee team with 31 World Series rings among them. Like Maris, his lefthanded power stroke was suited to Yankee Stadium's short porch. Like Mantle, he was signed by scout Tom Greenwade as a shortstop out of an Oklahoma high school. Murcer's legacy was clear; but the nineteen-year-old rookie couldn't seem to handle major league pitching, especially lefthanders, in brief stints with the Yankees in 1965 and 1966. After two maturing years in the army, Murcer returned to New York in 1969 to find a barely recognizable Yankee team. Gone were Richardson, Clete Boyer, Maris, Howard, and Ford. Gone was Mantle, who had retired at the end of the previous season. Murcer was given the Mick's locker and, after an aborted experiment at third base, took over Mantle's position in centerfield as well and was asked by management and fans alike to fill Mantle's shoes.

The gentlemanly Murcer took the inevitable comparisons in stride. Although he lacked Mantle's awesome power and struck out often in his early years, the line-drive hitter possessed a good Stadium stroke. Beginning with the last at-bat of the first game of a doubleheader against the Indians at Yankee Stadium on June 24, 1970, he hit home runs in four consecutive at-bats, the only Yankee other than Gehrig to accomplish that feat. During the 1971 season, Murcer began to hit more regularly to left field, cut his strikeouts by 40, boosted his average by 80 points to .331, and finished second in the batting race. His great season solidified his popularity in New York and marked his arrival as a star. Murcer hit at least 22 homers in each of his first five full seasons, with a career-high 33 in 1972. He drove in a league and career-high 102 runs that year and won a Gold Glove. In 1973, he became the youngest AL player to earn $100,000, and responded with his second and final .300 season, hitting .304.

With the Yankees' playing home games at Shea Stadium during 1974, Murcer's "Stadium stroke" resulted in numerous warning-track drives but only 10 actual home runs. The Yankees traded him straight-up at the end of the season for the Giants' Bobby Bonds, who was considered a superstar.

Bobby Murcer

Candlestick Park was no friendlier to Murcer than Shea. Not until he was sent to the Cubs and Wrigley Field in a five-player deal that included Bill Madlock did Murcer find another home ballpark suited to his home run stroke. He responded with his last great season, hitting 27 homers and driving in 90 runs.

A subpar performance in 1978 led the Cubs to trade him to the Yankees during the 1979 season for a minor league pitcher, and he was reunited with Piniella, Chambliss, Nettles, and his close friend Thurman Munson, who came up at the end of 1969. Murcer homered at the Stadium on the night of August 2 shortly after learning that Munson had died that day in a plane crash.

The popular Murcer was a productive part-timer for two seasons and lingered for two more before moving to the Yankee broadcast booth following his retirement early in the 1983 season. /(SEW/CR)

Tim Murnane (The Silver King) — 1852–1917. 1B-OF-2B 1872–78, 84 Middletown Mansfields (NA), Philadelphia Athletics (NA), Philadelphias (NA), **Braves**, Providence (NL), Boston (UA) *NA:* 154 g, .263; *ML:* 229 g, .258, 3 hr, 63 rbi.
> *Manager* 1884 Boston (UA) 8–17, .320

Murnane's baseball career ran the gamut. He began playing before pro teams were organized, joined the National Association, and was a member of Harry Wright's 1877–78 National League champion Boston clubs. He managed Boston's entry in the ill-fated Union Association, scouted, and served as president of the New England League. Becoming a widely read sportswriter, he rose to the post of sports editor of the Boston *Globe*. The highly opinionated, jovial, white-haired bon vivant defended players' rights, deplored high salaries, and criticized umpires. When he died at age 64 in 1917, leaving a widow and four young children, his grief-stricken colleagues organized a fund-raising game. The Red Sox donated the use of Fenway Park, and pitcher Babe Ruth shut out an all-star team directed by Connie Mack; the event raised $10,000. /(ADS/JK)

Charles W. Murphy — Unk.–1931. *Executive.*

Murphy began as a baseball writer for the Cincinnati *Enquirer*, then went to the New York Giants as publicist. When he heard the Chicago NL club was for sale, he got backing from Charles Taft of Cincinnati and bought it. His teams won four pennants and the World Series in 1907 and 1908. His style antagonized the more conservative NL owners, and when John Tener became NL president,

Murphy was urged to dispose of his team, the most profitable of the time. He sold out to Charles Weeghman as part of the settlement of the Federal League war. /(NLM)

Dale Murphy — 1956– . OF-1B-C 1976- **Braves** 1829 g, .270, 354 hr, 1088 rbi
☛ *Most Valuable Player—82–83. Led League—hr 84–85. Led League—rbi 78, 80, 82–83. All-Star—80, 82–87. Gold Glove—82–86.*

An embodiment of the All-American athlete, Dale Murphy was a shining star for Atlanta clubs, both pennant contenders and cellar-dwellers. Murphy was actually signed by the Braves as a catcher. His arm was so erratic that he had trouble throwing the ball back to the pitcher. Equally unsettled offensively, he led the NL in strikeouts in 1978 (145) and 1980 (133). The Mormon was Atlanta's starting first baseman in 1978 and shared the position with Bob Horner in 1979. When the Braves traded Barry Bonnell for Chris Chambliss, Murphy found a home in the outfield and Atlanta had a base for pennant contention.

Proving to be one of baseball's most durable players, Murphy reached stardom in 1982, leading the Braves to a pennant with Gold Glove defense

Dale Murphy

and All-Star offense. The following year, Murphy became the youngest of the four players in National League history to win back-to-back MVP awards. Possessing great opposite-field power, he also led the NL in slugging percentage for the first of two straight seasons.

Murphy played centerfield in 1981, moved to left for two seasons, returned to center for three years, and shifted to right in 1987. As the Braves drifted from contention, he continued his superb play. He was the top vote-getter for the 1985 All-Star Game and winner of the Lou Gehrig Award. Murphy was in Atlanta's Opening Day lineup each year from 1978 to 1988 and played more games than any other Atlanta Brave. From September 27, 1981 to July 9, 1986, Murphy played 740 consecutive games, one of the longest streaks in baseball history. The skein should have ended after 676 games when Murphy received a nine-stitch wound after his right palm got caught in a seam of Atlanta's outfield fence. But the next day, he hit a dramatic pinch home run to keep the streak alive. A complete player, Murphy won five straight Gold Glove awards and joined the elite 30-homer, 30-stolen-bases club in 1983. Always a streak hitter, with hot and cold usually balancing over a season, Murphy came back from poor numbers in 1986 with a career-high 44 homers in 1987. He did not find enough hot streaks in 1988, but remained one of the most respected players in baseball, with even his off-seasons producing numbers most would envy. /(ME)

Danny Murphy — 1876–1955. 2B-OF 1900–15 Giants, **A's**, Brooklyn (FL) 1518 g, .288, 44 hr, 708 rbi. *3 WS, 16 g, .288, 1 hr, 10 rbi*

A second baseman for the Athletics' early champions, Murphy yielded the position to Eddie Collins in 1909. He batted a career-high .329 in 1911. An expert sign stealer, he was a favorite of Connie Mack and his hometown Philadelphia fans, but he deserted them as his career was ending to join the Federal League. /(JK)

Danny Murphy — 1942– . OF-RHP 1960–62, 69–70 Cubs, **White Sox** 117 g, .177, 4 hr, 13 rbi; 112 ip, 4–4, 4.65

A highly regarded high school star, Murphy signed for a $125,000 bonus and began his career as an 18-year-old outfielder with the Cubs, but saw little action. Converted to pitching to save his career, he made it back to the majors in 1969 with the crosstown White Sox and had some success as a reliever, garnering nine saves in two seasons. /(JFC)

Dwayne Murphy — 1955– . OF 1978– **A's**, Tigers, Phillies 1360 g, .246, 166 hr, 609 rbi. *1 LCS, 3 g, .250, 1 rbi*
☛ *Gold Glove—80–85.*

Injuries, and a long-ball love affair, curtailed the outstanding promise of Dwayne Murphy's career. Foremost a defensive star, with six straight Gold Gloves (1980–85), the lefthanded hitter showed surprising power with 27 home runs in 1982 and 33 in 1984. Part of Oakland's dream outfield (with Rickey Henderson and Tony Armas) from 1980 to 1982, Murphy was most effective as a line-drive hitter behind Henderson and least effective when consistently trying to hit for power. A severe back injury, suffered in 1986, and chronic foot problems slowed the righthanded fielder. Murphy's diminished, but still outstanding, defensive ability kept him in the major leagues. /(ME)

Ed Murphy — 1877–1935. RHP 1898, 1901–03 Phillies, **Cardinals** 465 ip, 24–26, 3.64

Murphy was a good-hitting pitcher (.246 lifetime) who struck out few batters, but didn't walk many, either. At his best, he went 10–9 as the 1901 Cardinals' fourth starter. /(DAS)

Eddie Murphy (Honest Eddie) — 1891–1969. OF 1912–21, 26 **A's**, White Sox, Pirates 760 g, .287, 4 hr, 195 rbi. *3 WS, 12 g, .200*

Murphy was an everyday outfielder on the 1913 and 1914 pennant-winning A's and led the AL with eight pinch hits as a member of the 1919 Black Sox; Honest Eddie was not tempted by the fixers. /(JK)

Johnny Murphy (Fordham Johnny, Grandma, Fireman) — 1908–1970. RHP 1932, 34–1947 **Yankees**, Red Sox 1045 ip, 73–42, 3.50. *6 WS, 16 ip, 2–0, 1.10*
☛ *All-Star—37–39.*

This curveballing righthander held the lifetime record for saves (107) and wins in relief (73) until the spate of relievers in the 1960s. A control pitcher, he began his career as a starter with the Yankees, starting 20 games as a rookie in 1934. After being switched to the bullpen the following season, he started only 20 more games in his 13-year career. Despite being a reliever, he had losing records in only two seasons, and led the majors in saves in four seasons, with a high of 19 in 1939 for one of the most powerful of all Yankee teams. He also set then-records of 12 wins in relief in 1937 and 1943. His best overall season was 1941, when he had 15 saves

Johnny Murphy

and a 1.98 ERA and an 8–3 record. Lefty Gomez, when asked to predict how many games he (Gomez) would win, replied "Ask Murphy." /(SEW)

Morg Murphy — 1867–1938. C 1890–98, 1900–01 Boston (PL), Boston (AA), **Reds**, Cardinals, Pirates, Phillies, A's 566 g, .225, 10 hr, 227 rbi

Murphy was a light-hitting catcher who played in four major leagues, one of 29 to do so. He is best remembered for the time when, after his playing days were over, he was caught red-handed stealing opponents' signals. The Reds' third base coach, Tom Corcoran, had unlodged some dirt in the coach's box and found a wire that led to Murphy in the clubhouse. He was using an electrical buzzer to relay stolen signals back to his club's third base coach. /(AJA)

Rob Murphy — 1960– . LHP 1985– **Reds**, Red Sox 344 ip, 19–18, 2.64

The heavyset fastballer joined the Reds in mid-1986 and posted a microscopic 0.72 ERA in 34 relief appearances. Murphy became the set-up man for relief ace John Franco in 1987–88, appearing in 163 games over the two seasons, including a NL-high 76 in 1988, averaging nearly a strikeout an inning, but saving only six games. Murphy was traded to the Red Sox with Nick Esasky for Todd Benzinger and Jeff Sellers, and in 1989 he had nine saves behind Lee Smith in the Boston bullpen. /(SCL)

Tom Murphy — 1945– . RHP 1968–79 **Angels**, Royals, Cardinals, Brewers, Red Sox, Blue Jays 1443 ip, 68–101, 3.78

Murphy began his career as a starter for the Angels and was 16–13, 4.24 in 1970 on the only winning team California had during his tenure. The Brewers switched him to relief in 1974, and he had two 20-save seasons (second in the AL in '74 and third in '75) but his nine relief losses in 1975 led the league. He was traded with Bobby Darwin to the Red Sox for Bernie Carbo in the mid-1976 deal that led Bill Lee to leave the Red Sox in protest. /(WOR)

Dale Murray — 1950– . RHP 1974–85 **Expos**, Reds, Mets, Blue Jays, Yankees, Rangers 901 ip, 53–50, 3.86

Murray was an outstanding Expo rookie in 1974, using his exploding fastball and diving forkball to record a 1.03 ERA and ten saves in 32 games. Despite missing a month of the 1975 season with hepatitis, he led NL relievers with 15 wins, and in 1976 he led the league with 81 appearances. He ran up a streak of 247.1 innings without allowing a home run, between August 18, 1974 and August 20, 1976—the longest such streak since WWII. He was durable yet inconsistent after leaving Montreal, as overwork took the bite from his fastball. He spent much of 1980–81 and 1984–85 in Triple-A, but amassed 60 ML saves before a sciatica condition ended his career. /(GDW)

Eddie Murray — 1956– . 1B-DH 1977– **Orioles**, Dodgers 1980 g, .291, 353 hr, 1278 rbi *2 LCS, .333, 2 hr, 8 rbi. 2 WS, 12 g, .196, 3 hr, 5 rbi* ☛ *Rookie of the Year—77. Led League—hr 81. Led League—rbi 81. All-Star—78, 81–86. Gold Glove—82–84.*

From his Rookie of the Year start as a 21-year-old with just a half-season of Triple-A baseball under his belt in 1977 until 1986, Murray was a model of consistency. He became the first player to win the rookie award as a designated hitter. He earned a trip to Baltimore with a brilliant spring training in 1977 and replaced the departed Reggie Jackson in the Orioles' offense. Moving to first base in 1978, Eddie soon proved a brilliant defensive player and won

Eddie Murray

three straight Gold Gloves. Though he never won the MVP, he was in the running each year from 1981 to 1985 and was the Most Valuable Oriole each of those years.

A perennial slow starter, Murray still led the Orioles in Triple Crown stats four times and became the first AL player with 100 game-winning RBI. He slumped badly in the 1979 World Series (4-for-26). He fared better in 1983, hitting two homers in the decisive fifth game of the World Series.

Murray is among baseball's all-time leaders in grand slam home runs. He hit at least one slam in each season from 1980 to 1986. He is Baltimore's all-time home run leader and among its all-time leaders in all other offensive categories. A natural righthanded hitter, Murray ranks second only to Mickey Mantle on the switch-hitters home run list.

The great numbers were eventually overshadowed by an attitude summed up when the low-key but professional Murray said that baseball was "just a job" in 1987. He was labeled as a player who played only as well as he had to without consistently giving his all. Criticism to that effect from the late Orioles owner, Edward Bennett Williams, angered Murray, possibly contributing to the first baseman's poor 1986 season. As Murray went, so went the Orioles. Baltimore took a nose dive that began when the switch-hitting slugger went on the disabled list, for the first time in his career, on July 10, 1986.

The native of Los Angeles was traded to the Dodgers for 1989 and led the team with 20 HR and 88 RBI, although he hit only .247. /(ME)

George Murray (Smiler) — 1898–1955. RHP 1922–24, 26–27, 33 Yankees, **Red Sox**, Senators, White Sox 416 ip, 20–26, 5.38

Finishing only 10 of 43 starts in an era when greater endurance was expected, Murray was often relegated to middle relief. He won a career-high seven games for the 1923 Red Sox. /(EW)

Ray Murray (Deacon) — 1917– . C 1948, 50–54 Indians, **A's**, Orioles 250 g, .252, 8 hr, 80 rbi

Murray was a backup catcher who had career highs of 268 at-bats, six HR, 41 RBI, and a .284 BA in 1953. /(SFS)

Red Murray [John Joseph] — 1884–1958. OF 1906–15, 17 Cardinals, **Giants**, Cubs 1264 g, .270, 37 hr, 579 rbi. *3 WS, 19 g, .206, 6 rbi*
☛ *Led League—hr 09.*

Murray's seven home runs with New York in 1909 won him the NL crown, and he finished second each year in stolen bases from 1908 to 1910. Playing in right, he led NL outfielders in assists in 1909 (30) and 1910 (26). In 1912 Murray made a game-saving catch for Christy Mathewson that has been called the greatest catch in Forbes Field history. Mathewson later recalled that heavy thunderclouds threatened throughout the game. At the moment of the leaping, fingertip catch, blinding lightning lit up the sky, and "the accompanying crash of thunder fairly jarred the earth." /(CG)

Ivan Murrell [Augustus Peters] — 1945– . OF 1963–64, 67–74 Astros, **Padres**, Braves 564 g, .236, 33 hr, 123 rbi

Murrell saw little action before being chosen by San Diego in the expansion draft. In his best season, 1970, he had career highs of 347 at-bats, 12 HR, 35 RBI, and 41 runs while hitting .245. /(JFC)

Danny Murtaugh — 1917–1976. 2B-SS-3B 1941–43, 46–51 Phillies, Braves, **Pirates** 767 g, .254, 8 hr, 219 rbi.
Manager 1957–64, 67, 70–71, 73–76 Pirates 1115–950, .540. First place: 60, 70–71, 74–75 *4 LCS, 4–10, .286. 2 WS, 8–6, .571*

Unflappable Danny Murtaugh parlayed charm, confidence, and intelligence into a lengthy, highly successful managerial career. As a player, the Irishman batted over .270 only three times. He led the NL in stolen bases as a Phillies rookie in 1941, and led league second basemen in putouts, assists, and double plays for the Pirates in 1948, his first of four seasons playing in Pittsburgh. He began managing in the Pirates' system in 1952, and in 1957 took the helm of the parent club from Bobby Bragen. He upset Casey Stengel and the Yankees in the seven-game 1960 World Series, and was named *Sport Magazine*'s "Man of the Year." Due to ill health, Murtaugh resigned in 1964, but he served as interim manager in 1967. He retook the reins for 1970 and 1971, guiding a rebuilt Pirate club to two NL East titles and the 1971 World Championship. He returned again, with his familiar rocking chair, in 1973, to become only the second man to manage one club four times (Billy Sharsig did it five times with Philadelphia of the American Association). After winning NL East pennants in 1974 and 1975, Murtaugh retired for good as Pittsburgh's second-winningest manager. His number 40 was retired by the Pirates. /(ME)

Tony Muser — 1947– . 1B 1969, 71–78 Red Sox, White Sox, **Orioles**, Brewers 663 g, .259, 7 hr, 117 rbi

Muser was a good defensive first baseman whose best season offensively came in 1973 with the White Sox, when he hit .285 with career highs of four HR, 30 RBI, and 38 runs in 309 at-bats. That July 3, he walked five times in a game to tie the AL record. He became a Brewers coach after finishing his career with them. /(WOR)

Stan Musial (Stan the Man, The Donora Greyhound, Banj) — 1920– . OF-1B 1941–44, 46–63 **Cardinals** 3,026 g, .331, 475 hr, 1,951 rbi. *4 WS, 23 g, .256, 1 hr, 8 rbi*

☛ *Most Valuable Player—43, 46, 48. Led League—ba 43, 46, 48, 50–52, 57. Led League—rbi 48, 56. All-Star—43–44, 46–63. Hall of Fame—1969.*

Few players in the history of baseball have matched the accomplishments and consistency of Stan Musial. Even fewer so engendered the admiration and affection of fans, not only at home but in every ballpark on the circuit, as did this Polish-American from a steel-mill town in Pennsylvania.

Signed as a pitcher when he was seventeen, Musial was 15–8 in two seasons with Williamson, West Virginia, but the scouting report filed on the young southpaw recommended his release because he was wild and inconsistent. Despite the report, he was sent to Daytona Beach as a pitcher for the 1940 season and, under the tutelage of former White Sox great Dickie Kerr, he compiled an 18–5 record. Kerr, who often had as few as 15 players on his roster, also played Musial in the outfield. Stan responded by batting .352. Late in the season, he made a diving catch in the outfield, crashing on his left shoulder, and the consequent injury finished him as a pitcher. Musial was convinced by Kerr to remain in baseball as an outfielder. The next year he ripped through Class C and the International League before hitting .426 in a September call-up with the Cardinals.

That was the beginning of a love affair with St. Louis that would keep Musial a Cardinal for 22 seasons, a team record. After his playing days he served as general manager, and senior vice president of the Cardinals for more than 25 years.

The lefthanded-hitting Musial had good speed and was famous for his compressed, closed batting crouch, from which he appeared to be peering at the pitcher around a corner. He won his first NL batting title in his second full year and led the NL in hits six times, doubles eight times, triples five times, runs five times, while winning five more batting titles. Preacher Roe claimed to have the best way to pitch Musial: "I throw him four wide ones and then I try to pick him off first base." Although not initially expected to be a long-ball hitter, Musial developed his power without increasing strikeouts, and averaged 31 home runs per season from 1948 to 1957. Musial once told Roger Kahn that he hit so well because he always knew what the pitch was by seeing the rotation of the ball as it approached the plate. When he retired, Musial owned or shared 29 NL records, 17 ML records, 9 All-Star records, including most home runs (6), and almost every Cardinals career offensive record. In 1956 *TSN* named Musial its first Player of the Decade.

For one who played so long, Musial was unbelievably consistent. He smacked 1,815 hits at home and the same number on the road. He scored 1,949 runs and drove in 1,951. He batted .310 or better 16 straight seasons and added a .330 season just short of his 42nd birthday. Over 21 full seasons he averaged a remarkable 172 hits, 92 runs scored, 92 RBI, 34 doubles, and 23 home runs per year. His best offensive season was 1948, when he hit a career-

Stan Musial

high .376 and missed the NL Triple Crown by a single homer. That year he led the NL in batting average, slugging, hits, doubles, triples, runs, and RBI. On May 2, 1954, he set a ML record with five home runs in a doubleheader. And on July 12, 1955 his 12th-inning home run won the All-Star Game for the NL. Brooklyn fans labeled him "Stan the Man" for the havoc he wreaked on Dodger pitching every time he came to Ebbets Field. Musial rarely experienced long slumps; he put together strong starts, solid mid-seasons, and great finishes. He hit .323 or better in every month of the season, with September-October his best stretches. He was also the first man to play more than 1,000 games each at two positions.

Immediately following Musial's retirement as an active player in 1964, President Johnson named him director of the National Council on Physical Fitness. For a single season, 1967, Musial was St. Louis's general manager. With Musial's longtime roommate and close friend Red Schoendienst as field manager,

the Cardinals romped to a pennant and beat the Red Sox in the World Series.

On or off the field he wore a smile and meant it. Although he obviously did not always agree with umpires or managers, he did not argue calls or tactical moves. He made time for his family, fans, church, and civic organizations. A bronze statue stands in front of Busch Stadium in St. Louis as a permanent tribute to the greatest Cardinal, Stan the Man. And in 1972 he achieved the unique distinction of becoming the first foreigner to receive the Polish government's Merited Champions Medal, their highest sports award. /(FO)

Jeff Musselman — 1963– . LHP 1986– **Blue Jays**, Mets 217 ip, 23–13, 4.11

Harvard graduate Musselman's budding career as a lefthanded spot-starter and set-up man was interrupted in 1989 when he lost time to personal problems and then was traded to the Mets for Mookie Wilson. His 68 appearances in 1987 were the fifth-most ever by a rookie pitcher. He developed a muscle tear in his pitching shoulder, had off-season surgery, and did not rejoin the Blue Jays until midway through the 1988 season, at which time he was used as a starter. /(TF)

Jim Mutrie (Truthful James) — 1851–1938. *Manager* 1883–91 New York (AA), **Giants** 658–419, .611. First place: 1884, 88–89

Sporting a tall stovepipe hat and a magnificent handlebar mustache, Mutrie arrived in New York in 1880 determined to create a great baseball team. By 1883, with the backing of John B. Day, he was able to gain admission to the American Association for the New York Metropolitans with himself as manager. At the same time, he organized a National League New York team. After the Metropolitans won the AA pennant in 1884, Mutrie became manager of the NL team, taking several Metropolitan players with him. He built the NL team into a powerhouse by adding such stars as future Hall of Famers Buck Ewing, Tim Keefe, and Mickey Welch. The team was unusually tall, and Mutrie's repeated references to "his giants" evolved into the accepted name for the team. The Giants won NL pennants in 1888 and 1889. Defections to the Players' League in 1890 depleted the team, and after 1891 Mutrie was forced out as manager. /(BC)

George Myatt (Mercury, Stud, Foghorn) — 1914– .
2B-3B-SS-OF 1938–39, 43–47 Giants, **Senators** 407 g,
.283, 4 hr, 99 rbi.
    Manager 1968–69 **Phillies** 21–35, .375

Myatt was a speedy basestealer, hence the nickname
Mercury. A steady hitter with little power, he played
sparingly with the Giants in 1938–39, was sent to
the minors, and returned as a wartime regular with
the Senators. He was the Phillies' interim manager
for two games in 1968 and for the last 54 games of
1969. /(EW)

Glenn Myatt — 1897–1969. C-OF 1920–21, 23–36
A's, **Indians**, Giants, Tigers 1004 g, .270, 38 hr, 387 rbi

Myatt reached the A's after spending 1919 in the
Navy, and after two seasons was shipped to Cleveland. He batted .342 as the Indians' starting catcher
in 1924, but backed up Luke Sewell for much of
1926–33. /(EW)

Buddy Myer [Charles Solomon] — 1904–1974. 2B-SS-
3B 1925–41 Red Sox, **Senators** 1923 g, .303, 38 hr,
850 rbi, *2 WS, 8 g, .286, 2 rbi*
☛ *Led League—ba 35. All-Star—35, 37.*

The Senators' Clark Griffith moaned that it was "the
dumbest deal I ever made," after he traded Buddy
Myer to the Red Sox for shortstop Topper Rigney in
1927. Rigney lasted for 45 games, while Myer led
the league with 30 stolen bases and batted .313 in
1928; Griffith had to give up five players to get Myer
back after the season. Myer became Washington's
solid second baseman for a decade, leading the
league in fielding in 1931 and 1938, and winning the
AL batting crown in 1935 with a last-day splurge of
base hits. He edged Joe Vosmik, .3495 to .3489,
when the Cleveland outfielder tried to nurse his lead
by sitting out a game on the last day of the season.
Myer was a lefthanded batter so adept at dragging
the ball that he beat out 60 bunts in one season. He
batted over .300 nine times, and retired at the start
of WWII. /(JK)

Billy Myers — 1910– . SS 1935–41 **Reds**, Cubs 738 g,
.257, 45 hr, 243 rbi. *2 WS, 11 g, .200, 2 rbi*

The 1939–40 Reds were low-scoring teams. Myers,
their shortstop, was valuable for his expertise at
reading the intent of baserunners and picking up hit-
and-run and steal signs. His sacrifice fly drove in the
winning run in the seventh game of the 1940 World

Series. Billy's brother, Lynn, was a Cardinal infielder
in 1938–39. /(NLM)

Elmer Myers — 1894–1976. RHP 1915–22 **A's**,
Indians, Red Sox 1101 ip, 55–72, 4.06

Arriving in Philadelphia as Connie Mack was dismantling a dynasty, Myers shut out the Senators
4–0 in his first ML game (10/6/15) and pitched 315
innings as a rookie in 1916. He won 28 games for
four last-place Athletics teams before being traded
to Cleveland. /(ADS)

Hap Myers [Ralph Edward] — 1888–1967. 1B
1910–11, 13–15 Red Sox, Browns, Braves, **Brooklyn (FL)**
377 g, .268, 4 hr, 116 rbi

Myers was purchased by the Braves after he stole 77
bases in the Western League in 1912. He had 57
stolen bases for Boston in 1913, earning $2,250 as
their everyday first baseman, then jumped to the
Federal League. /(NLM)

Hy Myers [Henry Harrison] — 1889–1965. OF-2B-3B-
1B 1909, 11, 14–25 **Dodgers**, Cardinals, Reds 1310 g,
.281, 32 hr, 559 rbi. *2 WS, 12 g, .208, 1 hr, 4 rbi*
☛ *Led League—rbi 19.*

Hy Myers had several outstanding years for the
Dodgers, batting over .300 three times and recording league highs of 14 triples and 73 RBI in 1919
and 22 triples in 1920. He played in the longest ML
game ever, a 26-inning tie with the Braves on May
1, 1920. /(JK)

Randy Myers (Wojo) — 1962– . LHP 1985– **Mets**
240 ip, 17–13, 2.74. *1 LCS, 5 ip, 2–0, 0.00*

Myers has a fastball that has been timed at nearly
100 mph, and he became the Mets' bullpen stopper
in 1988 with 26 saves in 29 opportunities to place
second in the NL with an .897 save percentage. He
became known for self-effacing humor, describing
himself as "the set-up man for Roger [McDowell]"
and "just another control pitcher." He won Games
One and Three of the LCS in the Mets' losing effort
against the Dodgers. /(SH)

Bob Myrick — 1952– . LHP 1976–78 **Mets** 140 ip,
3–6, 3.47

Myrick is the grandnephew of former All-Star
infielder Buddy Myer. The mediocre reliever was
traded to Texas with pitcher Mike Bruhert in June
1979 for Dock Ellis. /(JFC)

Jack Nabors [Herman John] — 1887–1923. RHP
1915–17 **A's** 270 ip, 1–25, 3.87

Nabors tied the ML record for consecutive losses
with 19 for the 1916 Athletics, the worst team of the
20th century (36–117, .235). In 14 of those losses,
the A's scored 2 runs or less, and Nabors finished
1–20 with a 3.47 ERA, the fifth-highest ERA in the
league among pitchers with 150 innings. /(NLM)

Shigeo Nagashima — 1937– . 3B 1958–74 **Tokyo
Yomiuri Giants** .305, 444 hr
☛ *Rookie of the Year—58. Led League—ba 59–61, 63,
73. All-Star—58–74.*

Nagashima, who usually batted fourth behind home
run champ Sadaharu Oh, was Japan's most popular
and highest-paid player in his time. After a spectacular career at Rikkyo University, he signed with the
Giants for a then-record $48,000 bonus. His 9th-
inning homer to win the 1959 Emperor's Game is
generally regarded as the greatest moment in Japanese baseball history. Upon retirement, he became
the Giants' manager, winning the Japan Series in
1976. He was promoted to GM when Oh retired and
was named manager in 1981. /(MC)

Mike Nagy — 1948– . RHP 1969–74 **Red Sox,**
Cardinals, Astros 419 ip, 20–13, 4.15

Nagy was *TSN* AL Rookie Pitcher of the Year with
a 12–2 record for the 1969 Red Sox, but because of
arm troubles never pitched a full season again. /(PB)

Sam Nahem (Subway) — 1915– . RHP 1938, 41–42,
48 Dodgers, Cardinals, **Phillies** 224 ip, 10–8, 4.69

Nahem went 2-for-5 in his ML debut, a complete
game win for the Dodgers in 1938. /(NLM)

Bill Nahorodny — 1953– . C 1976–84 Phillies, **White
Sox,** Braves, Indians, Tigers, Mariners 308 g, .241, 25 hr,
109 rbi

Nahorodny's only season as a regular came in his
rookie year, 1978, when he caught 104 games for
the White Sox and reached career highs of eight HR
and 35 RBI while batting .236. /(WOR)

Futoshi Nakanishi — 1931– . OF-1B 1952–69
Nishitetsu Lions
☛ *Led League—hr 53–56.*

The 5'8" 180-lb Nakanishi could reportedly hit a
ball 500 feet, but burned out early due to injuries
and scandal. He won four consecutive Japanese
home run titles from 1953 through 1956, hitting as
many as 36 HR in 1953. Through 1958, his average
never dipped below .296. He played his last full
season at age 27, but after missing most of two
years, rebounded in 1961 with 21 HR in 99 games.
Appointed the Nishitetsu Lions' manager for 1963,
he remained a part-time player and led his club to
the Japan Series. He continued to pinch hit effectively for another four seasons. Upon retiring, he
became a commentator, but his broadcast career
ended abruptly when three Lions were among six
players barred for life for fixing games. Although not
directly implicated, Nakanishi proclaimed himself
responsible, and vowed to break all contact with
baseball. /(MC)

Dick Nallin — Unk.–1956. *Umpire* AL 1915–32 *4 WS*

Nallin was the first umpire to call no-hitters in
consecutive appearances behind the plate. On May
5, 1917 in St. Louis, he called a 1–0 no-hitter by the
Browns' Ernie Koob against the White Sox. The
next day he went behind the plate for the second
game of a doubleheader between the same two
clubs, and Bob Groom no-hit Chicago 3–0. Five
years later in 1922, he was the plate umpire when
Charlie Robertson of the White Sox threw a perfect
game against the Tigers. /(RTM)

Larry Napp — 1919– . *Umpire* AL 1951–74 *4 ASU
2 LCS 4 WS*

Napp served as the assistant supervisor of AL
umpires following 24 years as an ump. When he
called a strike, his leg would come up as fast as his
arm. He worked two perfect games; he was at third
base when Don Larsen threw his WS perfect game in
1956 and at first base when Catfish Hunter pitched
his in 1968. The judo expert also worked as both a
boxing instructor and referee. /(RTM)

Hal Naragon — 1928- . C 1951, 54-62 **Indians**, Senators/Twins 424 g, .266, 6 hr, 87 rbi. *1 WS, --*

Naragon was backup to Jim Hegan at Cleveland and to Earl Battey at Washington and Minnesota, never playing enough to establish himself. He and Johnny Sain coached together on the Twins and Tigers in the 1960s. /(ME)

Ray Narleski — 1928- . RHP 1954-59 **Indians**, Tigers 702 ip, 43-33, 3.60. *1 WS, 4 ip, 0-0, 2.25*
☛ *All-Star—56, 58.*

Overshadowed on an all-star Cleveland pitching staff, Narleski used a blazing fastball and excellent control to lead the 1954 AL champions with 13 saves as a rookie. In 1955, he led the league with 19 saves, eight relief wins, and 60 appearances. He gradually drew more starting assignments, then was sent to Detroit with bullpen companion Don Mossi in a November 1958 trade for Billy Martin. Expected to be the Tigers' relief ace, Narleski was 4-12 with a 5.78 ERA in 1959. Ray's father, Bill Narleski, was a Red Sox infielder in 1929-30. /(ME)

Jerry Narron — 1956- . C 1979-81, 83-87 Yankees, Mariners, **Angels** 392 g, .211, 21 hr, 96 rbi. *1 LCS, 4 g, .500*

The light-hitting Narron was released by the Mariners after batting .222 with 17 RBI in 76 games in 1981, then was signed by the Angels and spent most of 1982-83 in the Pacific Coast League. He hit .301 with 27 HR and 102 RBI for Edmonton in 1983 to earn a promotion to the Angels, and spent the next three seasons as Bob Boone's backup in California, never hitting higher than .247. /(SCL)

Buster Narum (Leslie) — 1940- . RHP 1963-67 Orioles, **Senators** 396 ip, 14-27, 4.45

Wildness and lack of support plagued Narum in his two seasons as a regular starter for the Senators (1964-65). Although his .059 batting average is one of the ten worst ever for a batter with over 100 at-bats, he hit a home run the first time he came to the plate in the ML and three of his seven ML hits were home runs. /(BC)

Billy Nash — 1865-1929. 3B 1884-98 Richmond (AA), **Braves**, Boston (PL), Phillies 1549 g, .275, 61 hr, 977 rbi.
Manager 1896 **Phillies** 62-68, .477

As Philadelphia's player-manager in 1896, Nash left the team briefly to scout a player in Fall River, MA, and returned with Nap Lajoie. Before managing the Phillies, Nash was a consistent third baseman in Boston for 11 seasons, twice hitting 10 home runs. /(JK)

Jim Nash (Jumbo) — 1945- . RHP 1966-72 **A's**, Braves, Phillies 1107 ip, 68-64, 3.59

The 6'5" 225-lb Nash was named AL Rookie Pitcher of the Year by *TSN* in 1966 when he broke in with a 12-1 record for the seventh-place A's. His .923 winning percentage would have led the majors, but he didn't have enough decisions to qualify. Likewise, his 2.06 ERA would have been second in the AL, but he pitched only 127 innings. He fell to 12-17, 3.76 in 1967 as the A's dropped to last place, but rebounded in 1968 as the A's rose to sixth, going 13-13 with a 2.28 ERA and six shutouts. He also struck out 50 times in 74 at-bats, the seventh-worst percentage among pitchers in the modern era. He was 13-9, 4.08 with the Braves in 1970 after being traded for Felipe Alou. His career ended with a 1-9 mark in 1972. /(SFS)

Phil Nastu — 1955- . LHP 1978-80 **Giants** 114 ip, 3-5, 4.50

Nastu was a curveballing lefthander whose early promise was not realized in three years with the Giants. Given 14 starts in 1979, he went 3-4. /(FS)

National Association — 1857-Unk.

The National Association was founded in 1857 and consisted of 16 New York clubs; it was the first organization of its kind in baseball. It became truly national in December 1865 when 91 clubs attended the New York convention. The Association's functions were to sanction rules and preserve amateur status. /(SH)

National Association of Professional Base Ball Players — 1871-1875. League.

A loosely organized league recognized by some as the first major league (although in 1969 the rules committee rejected this claim), the National Association of Professional Base Ball Players was the first professional league. Although it included the best teams and players of its time, it admitted any club that could pay a ten-dollar entry fee. Although it was not descended from the old amateur National Association, its structure was based on that of the older organization, which may have been its greatest problem. Scheduling was not fixed in advance, and many teams simply dropped out when they discovered they were losing money. Additionally, only pro ballplayers were allowed to hold office (the first president was Robert Ferguson), and some charged that discipline was lax; gambling pervaded the sport. The NA ceased to exist after the organization of the National League in 1876./(SH)

National Base Ball Reporters Association — 1887–1890.

A local organization of baseball writers in Philadelphia in 1885 led to the founding of the National Base Ball Reporters Association on December 12, 1887 in Cincinnati. George Mumford of St. Louis was the first president, with Henry Chadwick serving as vice-president. The 29 members made playing and scoring-rules recommendations, including the definitions of stolen bases and earned runs, the inclusion of strikeouts in box scores, and crediting the batter with a hit when a baserunner was struck by a batted ball. The group fell apart in 1890 after dividing over the Players' League controversy./(SH)

National Commission — 1903–1920.

When the National and American leagues drew up their "peace treaty" following two years of cutthroat competition for star players after the American League declared itself a major league in 1901, a governing body was formed to oversee baseball. The three members were NL president Henry Pulliam, AL president Ban Johnson, and Cincinnati owner Garry Herrmann. Herrmann, widely-respected enough to be considered impartial despite his NL affiliation, served for the life of the National Commission, as did Johnson; Pulliam was followed by his successors as NL president. The Commission saw baseball through a growth in popularity that brought with it a successfully withstood challenge from the Federal League, but the triumvirate foundered on the Black Sox scandal. Herrmann's resignation in 1920 broke up the Commission, and its function was replaced by the new office of Commissioner, filled by Judge Landis./(SH)

National League — 1876– . League.

The National League grew out of the first professional league, the National Association. Depending on which source (or which motive) one chooses to believe, William Hulbert, the owner of the Chicago franchise in the Association, founded the new league because the disorganized, undisciplined NA was a hotbed of rowdyism, drunkenness, and gambling, or because he had just stolen the four best players of the championship Boston club for his own use the following season and wanted to preempt any move to expel him from the NA. What matters is that the league Hulbert founded, whether from high-mind-

edness or necessity, has lasted to the present day and is largely responsible for baseball's having retained its integrity and popularity through its early troubled history.

Hulbert did have the diplomacy to make Morgan Bulkeley, the owner of the Hartford team in the Association, the president. The new league consisted of four western teams (Chicago, Cincinnati, St. Louis, and Louisville) and four eastern teams (Hartford, New York, Boston, and Philadelphia). The inaugural year featured such innovations as a set number of franchises limited to cities big enough to fiscally support a team (populations not less than 75,000), regular schedules arranged in advance (70 games, 10 against each team), teams that actually played all the games on those schedules, and enforceable contracts; the first pennant was won by Hulbert's Chicago White Stockings (now known as the Cubs), who were led by Hulbert's confidant and co-conspirator Al Spalding, one of the league's best pitchers (and one of the players taken from Boston). The league met over the winter and elected Hulbert president (Bulkeley didn't come to the meeting). He proceeded to expel the New York Mutuals and the Philadelphia Athletics for not having honored their entire schedules when doing so would have been financially difficult; the NL played with six teams in 1877 (and a 60-game schedule). A gambling scandal involving second-place Louisville, which had looked like a pennant-bound team until it began losing in unlikely ways in the second half of the season, led to the banning for life of four players, showing the new league was serious about its integrity. The most powerful teams were Boston, Providence (which joined in 1877), and Chicago (soon managed by Cap Anson, as Spalding went into the business end of the game and started his famous sporting goods company).

Hulbert continued as a strong president until his death in 1882. The league had remained unprofitable for most of that time, and various austerity measures were adopted by the teams, most notably lower salaries and greater use of the reserve clause (first thought of by Boston owner Arthur Soden in 1879). But the nation experienced an economic boom centered in urban areas, and the effects boosted pro ball's popularity and profitability, allowing the annual schedule to be lengthened over the course of the century. The advent of a second major league in 1883, the American Association, provided a popular two-league format. Beginning in 1884, that format included loosely organized postseason series between the two league winners, the precursor of the World Series. The NL and the AA between them crushed the fledgling Union Association, which lasted for just one year, 1884. Following that season, the short reign of A.G. Mills as NL president ended and the strong-willed Nick Young took over through 1902. As business picked up, Chicago remained a league power under Anson, and the New York Giants joined them at the top of the standings.

The NL and the AA continued to work together until the fateful 1890 season, when the Players' League revolt turned the baseball world upside down. In the 1884 "war" with the UA, relations between the NL and the AA had been strained by such NL actions as persuading the AA to expand to counter the new league (a move which was a financial disaster for the AA) and the purchase of the champion New York Mets of the AA by the NL New York Giants, who annexed much of the Mets' roster in the following year. But the NL reached new heights of ruthlessness in the Players' Revolt by persuading the AA's two best franchises, Brooklyn and Cincinnati, to move to the NL. Of the three leagues operating in 1890, the AA suffered the most, and collapsed after the 1891 season. The NL took in four AA franchises and spent the rest of the century with an unwieldy 12-team format in which most teams spent the majority of the season out of contention and post-season play was meaningless (and unprofitable).

The 1890s were dominated by Boston, led by Frank Selee and starring Hugh Duffy, Billy Hamilton, Jimmy Collins, and Kid Nichols, and the famous Baltimore Orioles, managed by Ned Hanlon and featuring John McGraw, Hughie Jennings, Willie Keeler, and Wilbert Robinson. Cleveland often finished a strong second under player-manager Patsy Tebeau, thanks to the strong arm of Cy Young. But the controversial result of the 12-team structure was the concept of syndicatism, used in 1899, wherein two teams could be owned by the same people. In a farcical pennant race, Brooklyn freely plundered sister team Baltimore's roster and won. A similar move by the St. Louis club, which picked the best players off the Cleveland roster, resulted in only a fifth-place finish, and a disastrous 20–134 last place finish for the hapless Spiders. The NL returned to the eight-team format for the 1900 season, paring down both for maximum profitability and in preparation for another baseball war.

The American League, which was the old Western League with a name change, spent the 1900 season gearing up for battle and declared war in 1901, raiding NL rosters for stars. The AL proved to be a better-organized, better-financed, and more determined foe than previous rivals, and the NL gave up the fight after two seasons. The two leagues began cooperating in 1903 as the NL acquired a new president, Harry Pulliam. The return to a two-league format allowed the resumption of postseason play with the World Series of 1903, and after a one-year hiatus due to McGraw's continuing feud with AL president Ban Johnson, the Series resumed in 1905 and has continued to the present day.

By this point baseball had come to closely resemble the current-day game. Foul balls were strikes, the pitcher threw overhand from a mound 60' 6" away from home plate, gloves were in universal use, and the franchises were all in familiar cities. The situation at the top of the league was also stable, with the Pirates, Giants, and Cubs dominating. Fred Clarke and Honus Wagner led Pittsburgh to consecutive pennants in 1901–03, and slipped in another title in 1909. John McGraw's Giants then won in 1904–05 on the strong arm of Christy Mathewson. Frank Chance's Cubs, celebrated in "Tinker to Evers to Chance," then set the major league victory record in 1906, winning 116 games in the first of three straight pennants. They won again in 1910, and then the Giants took over again for three years. The "Miracle Braves" surprised in 1914, the year the Federal League presented a new challenge. The American and National leagues outwaited the upstart, with the help of Judge Landis in the courts. But the subsequent realignment of rosters and salaries evened competition, and from 1914 through 1920 no team repeated. John McGraw had rebuilt the Giants by the beginning of the 1920s (also winning in 1917) and won four straight pennants, 1921–24. The Pirates won in 1925 and 1927, but a new era in team development was previewed by the Cardinals, who won their first pennant in 1926 and upset the Yankees in the World Series. Rather than relying exclusively on trades and purchases to build his team, GM Branch Rickey began putting together the "farm system" as we have come to know it, featuring exclusive working agreements with minor league teams. The concept was resisted at first by some minor league owners and by organized baseball; Commissioner Landis several times released minor league players from their contracts and criticized the new structure as being anti-competitive. But it worked, as the Cardinals became the next NL dynasty, and success as usual brought imitation. But the Cardinals had not only gotten there first, they also carried the concept to its broadest use, with the most far-flung organizational structure in the history of baseball. The Cardinals won additional pennants in 1928, 1930–31, and '34 and later became known as the "Gas House Gang" for the players' brash, all-out style of play. Although the stars included such untutored personalities as Dizzy Dean and Pepper Martin, they were led by the educated Frankie Frisch, the "Fordham Flash."

The Cubs, with Gabby Hartnett behind the plate, won in 1929, 1932, 1935, and 1938, while the Giants, now led by Bill Terry and featuring the slugging of Mel Ott and the screwball of Carl Hubbell, won in 1933 and 1936–37. The Reds closed out what many consider the Golden Era of baseball with consecutive flags in 1939–40. However, the AL had dominated the past two decades in the World Series and philosophically by developing the home-run-dominated game that the fans liked best. The NL tried to join in by juicing up the ball to unprecedented levels in 1930, producing a season in which the league average was .303 and Terry led with a .401 average, the last National Leaguer to hit .400. But despite such stars as Rogers Hornsby, Chuck Klein, Mel Ott, and Ernie Lombardi, it was the AL that featured the big boppers who stood out above their peers. But the balance of power would shortly begin a slow but steady shift.

First came World War Two. World War One had led to a shortened season in 1918, but President Roosevelt felt that baseball was good for the nation and the restrictions this time were largely travel-related. However, the rosters were weakened to a much greater extent by the length of United States involvement as players were drafted or volunteered. The years 1941–45 featured increasingly weaker teams, although certainly not at first as Branch Rickey and Larry McPhail worked their respective magic on the laughingstock Dodgers to bring the "Bums" their first pennant since 1920. The 1941 Dodgers were largely McPhail's creation, but Rickey was responsible for the future success of the franchise. Unlike many owners, he signed players regardless of their draft status (Pee Wee Reese being the best example) and once again built a formidable farm system. By the end of the war the Dodgers were poised on domination. Meanwhile, the Cardinals' system at first ensured them a steadier supply of replacements for lost regulars, as St. Louis won three straight pennants, 1942–44. The Cubs had their last gasp in 1945. The team with the longest record of

success in the league would thereafter win nothing but a pair of divisional titles 40 years later.

St. Louis won again in 1946, beating the Dodgers in a three-game playoff, but that year Branch Rickey had taken the most significant step of the century when he signed Negro Leaguer Jackie Robinson to the Dodgers' minor league Montreal club, opening up a vast new source of talent. NL president Ford Frick, who reigned from 1934 to 1951, was instrumental in quashing player protests against Robinson's move to the majors in 1947. Robinson immediately led Brooklyn to a pennant. He was soon followed to Ebbets Field by Roy Campanella, Don Newcombe, and others, and the Dodgers won in 1949, 1952–53, and 1955–56, never finishing lower than third place in the other seasons. Not only the Dodgers, but the NL in general signed black ballplayers more willingly than AL clubs, and although the Yankees continued AL superiority in the World Series, the NL caught up in the All-Star game. The Giants signed Willie Mays and Monte Irvin and became instant winners, beating the Dodgers in the spectacular 1951 playoff. New York won again in 1954 in Mays's first full season after losing much of 1952–53 in the military.

Former Reds GM Warren Giles became NL president in 1951 and reigned until 1969, overseeing major changes in the league. The Boston Braves became the Milwaukee Braves in 1953, the league's first franchise shift of the 20th century but hardly the last. New York's two NL clubs moved to the West Coast after the 1957 season, when Milwaukee won the first of two straight pennants on the strength of Hank Aaron's youthful talents. And the Yankees finally lost some World Series, to Brooklyn in 1955 and to Milwaukee in 1957. The Dodgers won in 1959, finally taking a playoff series (from Milwaukee). They signaled another shift, to a more varied offense that relied less on home runs. This change was aided by a move away from the old bandbox ballparks into newer and larger stadiums. Sluggers such as the Dodgers' Gil Hodges and Duke Snider found that this hastened the ends of their careers, and soon the Dodgers' stars were pitchers Sandy Koufax and Don Drysdale and speedsters Maury Wills and Willie Davis.

The two leagues expanded to undercut a proposed third circuit, Branch Rickey's Continental League. The NL added the New York Mets and the Houston Astros in 1962. The Pirates in 1960 and the Reds in 1961 won one-shot pennants, and then it was back to the Dodgers, Giants, and Cardinals. The Giants beat the Dodgers in a playoff yet again in 1962, but Los Angeles won in 1963 and 1965–66. St. Louis, led by Bob Gibson and Lou Brock, won in 1964 and administered the coup de grace to the Yankee dynasty in the World Series. They put together back-to-back titles in 1967–68, and then came something completely different.

The 1969 expansion, in which the NL and AL both became 12-team leagues, resulted in a new structure in which the leagues were divided into divisions. It prevented the problem of earlier 12-team leagues, where too many teams suffered bad attendance after being eliminated from the pennant race early on. The once-lowly Mets beat the Braves in the first League Championship Series, and the new franchises, the Montreal Expos and the San Diego Padres, both finished last in the new format. Expansion mirrored the growing popularity of the game.

The 1970s were largely dominated by the Reds and the Dodgers in the Western Division, and by the Pirates and the Phillies in the Eastern Division. The "Big Red Machine" won six division titles, with Los Angeles taking the rest of the Western crowns; Pittsburgh also won six division titles, with Philadelphia winning three and the Mets sneaking in at .509 in 1973, the lowest winning percentage ever for a division winner. The big winners based their strength on imposing offenses. The Reds featured Johnny Bench, George Foster, Tony Perez, and Pete Rose, while Pittsburgh had Willie Stargell, Dave Parker, Bill Madlock, and, at the beginning of the decade, Roberto Clemente. The Dodgers and Phillies mixed in pitching, with Philadelphia led by Mike Schmidt and Steve Carlton while Los Angeles had Don Sutton, Tommy John, and the longest-lasting infield ever: Steve Garvey, Davey Lopes, Bill Russell, and Ron Cey. The Mets got by on pitching, and were eliminated from contention by the 1977 trade of Tom Seaver to the Reds. Free agency in general had less of an influence in the NL, perhaps because the Reds eschewed it.

The NL by this point had settled in as the more traditional of the two leagues, choosing not to adopt the designated hitter rule and not expanding in 1977. However, Astroturf became much more common in the NL, with seven teams installing fake grass (although San Francisco later returned to the real thing). This and more big parks increased the NL's reputation as the speed league. Manager Whitey Herzog relied on speed to make the Cardinals an oddly dominant team in 1980s. They won the NL flag in 1982, 1985, and 1987, but

finished out of contention (and usually below .500) in all other years except 1981, when they had the best record in the division but did not win either half of the strike-split season. A similar fate befell the Reds that season, their last good effort until four straight second-place finishes, 1985–88, under manager Pete Rose.

No NL team repeated, even as division titlists, in the 1980s. Houston finally won in 1980, beating the Dodgers in a playoff, but lost to the Phillies in the LCS. Philadelphia went on to finally capture its first World Championship that year, and won the pennant in 1983, but have declined ever since. Houston also won a division title in 1986 on the strong right arm of Mike Scott. The Dodgers won division titles in 1981, 1983, 1985, and 1988, winning the pennant and World Championship in 1981 and 1988. They still relied on pitching above all; the new stars were Fernando Valenzuela and Orel Hershiser. The hapless Mets were rebuilt completely and established something of a dynasty in the second half of the decade. They were World Champions in 1986, won the East in 1988, and finished second in 1984, 1985, and 1987. But stars such as Darryl Strawberry and Kevin McReynolds, and the team in general, were accused of playing below their potential. Dwight Gooden anchored their pitching staff starting in 1984, when he had one of the greatest rookie pitching seasons ever. The 1969 expansion teams finally won, the Expos in 1981 and the Padres in 1984. San Diego upset the Cubs, who won another surprising division title in 1989. And split-finger fastball guru Roger Craig led the Giants to a division titles in 1987 and 1989 despite a perpetually injured pitching staff.

Bart Giamatti became NL president in 1987 and immediately faced controversies ranging from brawls and knockdown pitches to Pete Rose pushing an umpire to redefinitions of the balk and the strike zone. Perhaps the biggest issue arose early in the season, when Dodger GM Al Campanis gave an interview on nationwide TV in which he impugned the qualifications of blacks to manage or otherwise take part in the business end of baseball. When Giamatti moved up to become Commissioner in 1989, he was replaced by Bill White, the first black to hold that high an office and also the first ex-major leaguer to be NL president. /(SH)

Julio Navarro (Whiplash) — 1936– . RHP 1962–66, 70 **Angels**, Tigers, Braves 212 ip, 7–9, 3.65

The Puerto Rican reliever's best season came in 1963, when he saved 12 games while going 4–5, 2.89. /(JFC)

Frank Navin (Lucky Frank) — 1871–1935. *Executive.*

Navin was president of the Detroit Tigers for 32 years. Although trained in the law, he worked as a bookkeeper for S.F. Angus, the Tigers' second owner. When the club was sold to William Yawkey in 1903, Navin purchased $5,000 worth of stock, reportedly with money won in a card game. Elevated to club president, he brought in Hughie Jennings, Ty Cobb, and others, who helped lead the Tigers to consecutive pennants in 1907, 1908, and 1909. The grateful Yawkey gave Navin half ownership of the team. The baseball park (now Tiger Stadium) was called Navin Field from 1912 through 1937. Attendance grew in Detroit even though the team went more than two decades before its fourth pennant. Navin became rich and a civic leader, but was nearly ruined in 1931 by the Depression and his own racetrack losses. He was forced to sell most of his Tiger stock to William O. Briggs, although he remained team president. In 1934 the Tigers won their fourth pennant, and shortly before Navin's death in 1935 they defeated the Cubs in the World Series. /(BC)

Rollie Naylor — 1892–1966. RHP 1917, 19–24 **A's** 1011 ip, 42–83, 3.93

Naylor lost 23 games for the 48–106 Athletics in 1920 despite a 3.47 ERA (well below the league average of 3.79). His playing career was shortened by a 1923 leg injury, but he umpired in the minors until 1943. /(NLM)

Charlie Neal — 1931– . 2B-SS-3B 1956–63 **Dodgers**, Mets, Reds 970 g, .259, 87 hr, 391 rbi. *2 WS, 7 g, .323, 2 hr, 6 rbi*
☛ *All-Star—59–60. Gold Glove—59.*

Neal was one of the heroes of the 1959 World Series, hitting two home runs for the Dodgers in Game Two at Comiskey Park and driving in the winning run with the second, a two-run shot. For the Series, he hit .370 and slugged .667.

The versatile Neal came up as a second baseman in 1956, was a shortstop and occasional third baseman in 1957, and finally won the second-base job in 1958. He led NL second basemen in double plays that year and the next, also leading in putouts and fielding average in 1959. The Dodgers moved in 1958 to Los Angeles, where they played at the oddly shaped Coliseum, and that stadium's 251' left-field line accounted for Neal's jump from 12 HR in 1957 to 22 (in 473 at-bats) in 1958. His best season came in 1959, when he made the All-Star team for the

first time, hit 19 HR, and reached career highs in triples (11, tied with teammate Wally Moon for the NL lead), doubles (30), runs (103), RBI (83), steals (17), batting average (.287), and slugging average (.464). His offense and playing time declined after that, and he was obtained by the expansion Mets for the 1962 season, serving as their best infielder (no matter where he played) until he was traded to the Reds in mid-1963, his last season. /(WOR)

Greasy Neale [Alfred Earle] — 1891–1973. OF 1916–22, 24 **Reds**, Phillies 768 g, .259, 8 hr, 200 rbi. *1 WS, 8 g, .357, 4 rbi*

A member of the Pro Football Hall of Fame, Neale is the only man to play in a World Series, coach a football team in the Rose Bowl (Washington and Jefferson, 1922), and win an NFL title (two in 10 years with the Philadelphia Eagles). The highlight of his baseball career came in the tainted 1919 WS, when he led the Reds with ten hits. /(NLM)

Ron Necciai (Rocket Ron) — 1932– . RHP 1952 **Pirates** 55 ip, 1–6, 7.08

The 6'5" 19-year-old Necciai received nationwide attention after his remarkable 27-strikeout, no-hit game of May 13, 1952, pitching for Bristol against Welch (Appalachian League). His performance was marred only by a walk, a hit batsman, a dropped third strike, and an error. His next start was a 24-strikeout two-hitter. That season he fanned 109 batters in 43 innings at Bristol and a Carolina League-high 172 in 126 innings at Durham before getting the call to Pittsburgh. Branch Rickey said, "There have been only two young pitchers I was certain were destined for greatness . . . .One of those boys was Dizzy Dean. The other is Ron Necciai." Rocket Ron went 1–6. Plagued by ulcers and arm trouble, he soon was out of baseball. /(ME)

Johnny Nee — 1890–1957. *Scout.*

Nee was a player-manager in the minor leagues at Terre Haute in 1912 at the age of 22, and managed in the minors until 1926, when he joined the Yankees' scouting staff. He remained with the Yankees until 1946, when he began a decade as the Phillies' chief scout. He was an unsuccessful candidate for governor of Missouri in 1949. /(FVP)

Tom Needham (Deerfoot) — 1879–1926. C 1904–14 **Braves**, Giants, Cubs 523 g, .209, 8 hr, 117 rbi. *1 WS, 1 g, .000*

Irish-born Tom Needham was a clever handler of pitchers who caught half of the Braves' games in

1904–07, but batted .196 or less in seven of his 11 seasons. He coached and scouted for the White Sox. /(NLM)

Cal Neeman — 1929– . C 1957–63 **Cubs**, Phillies, Pirates, Indians, Senators 376 g, .224, 30 hr, 97 rbi

Neeman was a regular only as a rookie for the 1957 Cubs, when he led NL catchers in putouts and double plays. He was then relegated to backup duty, and thrown in with Tony Taylor on a 1960 trade to Philadelphia for Don Cardwell and Ed Bouchee. /(DB)

Ron Negray — 1930– . RHP 1952, 55–56, 58 Dodgers, **Phillies** 163 ip, 6–6, 4.04

Negray had his only winning season in 1956 with Philadelphia, going 4–3 with a 3.52 ERA as a starter and reliever. /(JFC)

The Negro Leagues — 1920–1960. League.

The first successful attempt to establish a major Negro baseball league came in 1920, with the founding of the Negro National League. The circuit operated through 1931, with clubs located in the Midwest and the South. The Eastern Colored League was formed in 1923, and survived into the spring of 1928. Eastern teams played as the American Negro League in 1929.

The East-West League folded in the season it was founded, 1932; that year, the Negro Southern League was the only major circuit to complete its schedule. The NSL was a minor league before and after the 1932 season. From 1933 through 1936, the second Negro National League ran unchallenged as a black major league. It included teams from the East and Midwest, and from Nashville in 1933–34. By 1936, the NNL was operating exclusively in the East. In 1937 midwestern and southern franchises formed the Negro American League. The NAL and the NNL co-existed through 1948; in 1949, the NAL absorbed the NNL, and survived as the last major black circuit through 1960.

Negro leagues generally contained six teams, though it was not uncommon for them to have a few more or less. Baltimore, Chicago, Kansas City, New York, and Philadelphia were usually represented. Among other cities fielding teams were Atlantic City, Birmingham, Cleveland, Detroit, Indianapolis, Memphis, Newark, Pittsburgh, St. Louis, and Washington. The schedules were set up to allow member teams to play against other competition, primarily white semi-pro opponents. As a result, it was common for the black clubs to play more non-league than league contests. Teams normally played from 50 to 80 league games a season.

Over the years, 11 inter-league Black World Series were held. The NNL and ECL titlists played from 1924 through 1927. Champions from the NAL and NNL met from 1942 through 1948. In 1933 club owners initiated the East-West all-star game. Into the 1950s, the contest was played each summer at Chicago's Comiskey Park. Bringing the best black players together, the East-West game would attract from 20,000 to 50,000 fans, and provided an important source of revenue for the black teams. /(MFK)

Art Nehf — 1892–1960. LHP 1915–29 Braves, **Giants**, Reds, Cubs 2708 ip, 184–120, 3.20. 20 wins: 20, 21 *5 WS, 79 ip, 4–4, 2.16*

Just 5'9" and 176 lbs, Nehf joined the Braves late in 1915 after leading the Central League with 218 strikeouts and a 1.38 ERA. The crafty southpaw went 17–8 in 1917 and in 1918 topped the National League in complete games. He pitched a 21-inning game that season against the Pirates, only to lose 2–0. He had compiled a 52–41 record for the light-hitting Braves when, on August 15, 1919, he was traded to the Giants for four players and cash. He went 9–2 the rest of the way, but the Giants still couldn't catch the Reds and finished second.

In 1920, Nehf won a career-high 21 games. From 1921 through 1924 he helped the Giants to four consecutive pennants. Following a 20–10 season in 1921, he lost his first two World Series starts (the Giants scored a mere one run—unearned—in those games), but defeated the Yankees 1–0 in the final game. In the 1922 WS rematch, Nehf again won the decisive contest. He pitched another 1–0 shutout against the Yankees in Game Three of the 1923 Series. In the 1924 Series opener, he beat the Senators' Walter Johnson in 12 innings, but Nehf lost Game Six 2–1. Washington took the title the following day.

Nehf won 107 while losing only 60 in seven years with the Giants. Sold to the Reds in 1926, he pitched infrequently, and he was released in August 1927. He rebounded with 13 wins for the Cubs in 1928. His last major league appearance came with Chicago in Game Four of the 1929 World Series, when he failed to retire a batter.

During his 15 ML seasons, Nehf recorded 30 shutouts. He participated in 12 double plays in 1920, equaling the NL record for a pitcher. In 12 World Series games, he placed himself among the all-time WS leaders in seven pitching categories. A

Art Nehf

competent, lifetime .210 batter, he hit five home runs in 1924, including two in one game. /(JLE)

Gary Neibauer — 1944– . RHP 1969–73 **Braves**, Phillies 149 ip, 4–8, 4.77. *1 LCS, 1 ip, 0–0, 0.00*

Neibauer spent only one full season in the majors; he spent a career shuttling back and forth between Richmond (International League) and Atlanta. Arm trouble and wildness forced him out of the majors. /(PB)

Harry Neily — 1884–1948. *Writer.*

Neily worked for 17 newspapers from his start in 1898. His last stop was the *Chicago American*, where he remained for 17 years until his retirement in 1933. A charter member of the BBWAA, he resigned as sports editor of the St. Louis *Times* in

1914 to become business manager of the St. Louis Feds. He was later responsible for building Wrigley Field on Catalina Island, where the Cubs trained. /(NLM)

Bernie Neis — 1895–1972. OF 1920–27 **Dodgers**, Braves, Indians, White Sox 677 g, .272, 25 hr, 210 rbi. *1 WS, 4 g, .000*

The switch-hitting, 5'7" 160-lb Neis was a part-time outfielder for most of his career. He hit a career-high .303 in 80 games in 1924 and was a starter for the Dodgers in 1923 and the Braves in 1925. /(JM)

Bots Nekola [Francis Joseph] — 1906–87. LHP 1929, 33 **Yankees**, Tigers 20 ip, 0–0, 5.85

Nekola scouted for the Boston Red Sox for 27 seasons, signing or discovering Carl Yastrzemski, Rico Petrocelli, and Ben Oglivie. He was a pitching star at Holy Cross. /(FVP)

Dave Nelson — 1944– . 2B-3B 1968–77 Indians, **Senators/Rangers**, Royals 813 g, .244, 20 hr, 211 rbi. *1 LCS, 2 g, .000*
☛ *All-Star—73.*

When Dave Nelson stole a career-high 51 bases in 1972, he always had the green light from manager Ted Williams, who rarely allowed any player such free rein. Nelson's best season, in 1973, was the only time he was an everyday player; he had career highs in batting average (.286) and home runs (7) and made the All-Star team. It was his second and last season above .240. He later became a baserunning coach for several teams. /(SH)

Gene Nelson — 1960– . RHP 1981– Yankees, Mariners, **White Sox**, A's 844 ip, 46–50, 4.14. *2 LCS, 6 ip, 2–0, 0.00. 2 WS, 7 ip, 0–0, 8.59*

First signed by the Rangers, Nelson jumped from the Florida State League (20–3 in 1980) to the Yankees in 1981; at 20, he was the youngest player in the majors. In 1982 he was traded to Seattle, but failed to impress the Mariners and was drafted off their Triple-A roster by the White Sox, who used him as a setup man and spot starter. Chicago manager Tony LaRussa liked Nelson's work habits. After LaRussa took over at Oakland in 1986, he had the A's acquire Nelson, who won Games Two and Three of the 1988 LCS with scoreless relief. /(RL)

Jim Nelson — 1947- . RHP 1970-71 **Pirates** 103 ip, 6-4, 3.06

A palmball pitcher, Nelson faded after winning his first four major league decisions, including the last game played at Forbes Field, June 28, 1970. /(ME)

Lindsey Nelson — 1919- . *Broadcaster.*

An overworked national star in the late 1950s on NBC's college football, NBA basketball, and ML baseball broadcasts, Nelson surprisingly accepted a job with the expansion New York Mets in 1962 and became their top announcer for 19 seasons. He worked with Ralph Kiner and Bob Murphy throughout his Mets career. Nelson's garish plaid sports coats matched the colorfully inept early Mets beautifully, and in 1965 he broadcast a Mets-Astros game from a gondola suspended from the Astrodome roof. Equally adept at television and radio, Nelson also broadcast Notre Dame football games from 1967 to 1979, and after three seasons with the San Francisco Giants, taught broadcasting seminars at his alma mater, the University of Tennessee. Twice named National Sportscaster of the Year, Nelson also broadcast 26 Cotton Bowls. He was inducted into the Writers Wing of the Hall of Fame in 1988. /(SL)

Lynn Nelson (Line Drive) — 1905-1955. RHP 1930, 33-34, 37-40 Cubs, **A's**, Tigers 268 g, .281, 5 hr, 55 rbi; 677 ip, 33-42, 5.25

Dubbed Line Drive by opposing batters who enjoyed facing him, Nelson had more success as a hitter than as a pitcher. With the A's in 1937, he batted .354 (40-for-113) with four home runs, and led the AL with nine pinch hits and 38 pinch at-bats. He wrestled professionally as the Masked Marvel. /(EW)

Mel Nelson — 1936- . LHP 1960, 63, 65, 67-69 **Cardinals**, Angels, Twins 173 ip, 4-10, 4.41. *1 WS, 1 ip, 0-0, 0.00*

Although he pitched parts of six ML seasons, Nelson did his best work after a late call-up to the Cardinals in 1968. He won two starts, pitched well in middle relief, and compiled a 2.91 ERA, as the Cardinals won the pennant. /(FJO)

Rocky Nelson [Glenn Richard] — 1924- . 1B 1949-52, 54, 56, 59-61 Cardinals, **Pirates**, White Sox, Dodgers, Indians 620 g, .249, 31 hr, 173 rbi. *2 WS, 8 g, .250, 1 hr, 2 rbi*

Legendary minor league slugger Nelson won the Triple Crown at Montreal in 1955 (.364, 37 HR, 130 RBI) and Toronto in 1958 (.326, 43 HR, 120 RBI). Three times the International League MVP, he finally stuck in the majors in 1959 on his second go-round with Pittsburgh. Platooned with the iron-gloved Dick Stuart, Rocky provided better fielding while batting .291 in 1959 and .300 in 1960. Nelson was known for his oversized tobacco chaw, continuous chatter, and an odd, open batting stance, with both feet pointed at the pitcher. The Portsmouth, Ohio native was inducted into the International League, the Ohio Baseball, and the Canadian Baseball halls of fame. /(ME)

Roger Nelson (Spider) — 1944- . RHP 1967-74, 76 White Sox, Orioles, **Royals**, Reds 636 ip, 29-32, 3.06. *1 LCS, 2 ip, 0-0, 0.00*

After a promising 4-3, 2.41 season for Baltimore in 1968, Nelson was the Royals' first pick in the expansion draft. He was 7-13 despite a 3.31 ERA as their number-four starter in 1969 and then spent most of 1970 on the DL with shoulder trouble. He made it back in 1972, and was 11-6 with the fifth-best ERA (2.08) in the AL. On August 23 he pitched a one-hitter against the Red Sox (Ben Oglivie singled in the seventh inning). That winter he was traded with Richie Scheinblum to Cincinnati for Hal McRae and Wayne Simpson. Nelson sat out much of the rest of his career with injuries, pitching well when healthy. /(WOR)

Dick Nen — 1939- . 1B 1963, 65-70 Dodgers, **Senators**, Cubs 367 g, .224, 21 hr, 107 rbi

Nen had only one hit in eight at-bats for the 1963 World Champion Dodgers, but it was a monstrous home run over the right field roof in St. Louis on September 18 as the Dodgers and Cardinals battled for the pennant. Nen's home run tied the game, which the Dodgers went on to win in 13 innings, and he received a $1,000 WS share from his grateful teammates after they swept the Yankees in October. The husky first baseman didn't reach the ML again until 1965 with the Senators, and hit above .218 only once in four seasons as a part-time player. /(SCL)

Graig Nettles (Puff) — 1944- . 3B-OF 1967-88 Twins, Indians, **Yankees**, Padres, Braves, Expos 2700 g, .248, 390 hr, 1,314 rbi. *7 LCS, 24 g, .259, 5 hr, 19 rbi. 5 WS, 24 g, .225, 7 rbi*
☛ *Led League—hr 76. All-Star—75, 77-80, 85. Gold Glove—77-78.*

Graig Nettles

Nettles's moment in the sun came in Game Three of the 1978 World Series against the Dodgers when he made four dazzling stops, twice robbing Reggie Smith of hits. Nettles's fielding enabled New York to win its first of four straight games, after losing the first two games in Los Angeles, to win the Series.

Nettles was a power-hitting third baseman in the mold of Eddie Mathews, and his 319 homers as an AL third baseman are the record. He played mainly the outfield for the Twins in his first three seasons (Harmon Killebrew was at third), but switched permanently to third base when he joined Cleveland in 1970 in a six-player deal in which he was the only non-pitcher. In 1971 he set AL records with 412 assists and 54 double plays, and he led the league in assists in 1972, as well as errors. After the 1972 season, he was swapped to New York, but had trouble adapting and suffered a poor year defensively in 1973, and hit just .234. He rebounded the following year, however. In April, he clubbed 11 homers, half his total for the year, including four in a doubleheader on April 14. On September 14, both he and his brother Jim, playing for the Tigers, homered in the same game.

Nettles led the league in homers in 1976 with 32, but had his best season in 1977. He won the Gold Glove, slammed 37 homers, drove in a career-high 107 runs, and scored 99 runs to lead the Yankees to the first of two World Championships, both over the Dodgers. His power production dropped off during the next two seasons. After committing seven errors in his first 20 games in 1980, he was diagnosed with hepatitis in July and was out for 67 games, but came back to play in the Yankees' playoff loss to the Royals.

Nettles was traded to San Diego in 1984 and was a key figure with ex-teammate Goose Gossage and ex-Dodger Steve Garvey in the Padres' first pennant. He was dealt to the Braves in 1987 and the Expos in 1988, for whom he mainly pinch hit. In 1989, he was involved in the new over-35 "senior" league of former major leaguers started in Florida. /(SEW)

Jim Nettles — 1947- . OF 1970-72, 74, 79, 81 **Twins**, Tigers, Royals, A's 240 g, .220, 16 hr, 57 rbi

Jim Nettles and his brother Graig became only the fourth set of brothers to homer in the same game in the AL on September 14, 1974 when Graig was with the Yankees and Jim was with Detroit. They rank fifth all-time among brother combinations in HR with 406. Jim saw his most action in 1972 with the Twins, hitting .204 in 235 at-bats with four HR and 15 RBI. He played in Japan and Mexico after his ML days ended, and later became a minor league manager. /(SFS)

Jerry Neudecker — 1930- . *Umpire* AL 1965-86

Neudecker's balloon chest protector was sent to the Baseball Hall of Fame in Cooperstown. After the outside protector was disallowed in the AL, a grandfather clause left him the last ML umpire to wear the balloon. Neudecker was the plate umpire for Catfish Hunter's perfect game on May 8, 1968. /(RTM)

Johnny Neun — 1900- . 1B 1925–28, 30–31 **Tigers**, Braves 432 g, .289, 2 hr, 85 rbi.
Manager 1946–48 Yankees, **Reds** 125–143, .466

Never a regular, the speedy, slick-fielding Detroit first baseman entered the record books on May 31, 1927. With two Cleveland runners on, Neun nabbed Homer Summa's line drive and tagged Charlie Jamieson off first. Then, ignoring his shortstop's shouts to throw the ball, he dashed toward second and tagged the bag before Glenn Myatt could get back. Neun had executed the major leagues' seventh unassisted triple play. The sixth had been turned the day before, by Cubs shortstop Jimmy Cooney.

Switch-hitter Neun led the AL with 12 pinch hits in 42 tries in 1926. He became a player, coach, and manager for the Yankees' Newark (International League) farm team, a dynasty in the 1930s and early 1940s. In 1946, he was New York's interim manager for 14 games, replacing Bill Dickey. He skippered the Reds from 1947 through 100 games in 1948./(JK)

Ernie Nevers — 1903–1976. RHP 1926–28 **Browns** 178 ip, 6–12, 4.64

One of two pro footballers to give up a homer to Babe Ruth in 1927 (the other was Garland Buckeye), Nevers's heroics against the Four Horsemen of Notre Dame while playing for Stanford in the 1925 Rose Bowl made him a box-office draw upon his arrival in the major leagues in 1926. Pushed too quickly to succeed as a pitcher, he switched back to football to become a pioneer fullback star in the NFL./(JK)

New York Giants [aka Gothams, Green Stockings] — 1883–1957. Team. 6067–4898, .553. *NL Champions 1888–89, 1904–05, 11–13, 17, 21–24, 33, 36–37, 51, 54 World Champions 05, 21–22, 33, 54*

A New York team under the ownership of factory owner John B. Day and local sports figure Jim Mutrie replaced the Troy, NY team in the NL in 1883. The two also entered a team called the Metropolitans in the American Association that

The 1922 New York Giants

same year. Mutrie managed the Mets and John Clapp was the first manager of the NL team, then called the Gothams or Green Stockings. The NL team's original stars were Buck Ewing, Roger Connor, and Mickey Welch, who'd been with Troy, and former Providence pitcher-turned-shortstop John Montgomery Ward. At first, the Mets, with former Troy pitcher Tim Keefe, were more successful, winning the AA pennant in 1884. The following year, Mutrie moved over to manage the NL team, bringing Keefe and several other Mets with him. The team, which included a number of six-footers, received its name from Mutrie's habit of referring to his charges as "My boys, my giants!" Mutrie's Giants won NL pennants in 1888 and 1889.

Under unpopular owner Andrew Freedman, the Giants experienced mediocre seasons through the 1890s despite the excellent power pitching of right-hander Amos Rusie. Freedman changed managers 12 times in eight years before he hired John McGraw to lead his team in 1902. The next year he sold the team to John T. Brush, who let McGraw control the on-field operation. The Giants dominated the National League in 30 years under McGraw, winning ten pennants and finishing second 11 times. The 1905, 1921, and 1922 teams won World Championships. During the first quarter of the 20th century, the Giants were baseball's most successful franchise both on the field and at the box office. Among the great players under McGraw were Christy Mathewson, Roger Bresnahan, Joe McGinnity, Frankie Frisch, Mel Ott, Travis Jackson, and Bill Terry.

Brush died in 1912 and his son-in-law, Harry Hempstead, took over the team. In 1919, the Giants were purchased by a syndicate headed by New York stockbroker Charles Stoneham, the beginning of a powerful baseball family. After Stoneham's death in 1936, his son Horace replaced him as team president.

McGraw retired in 1932. Spearheaded by first baseman-manager Terry, home run champ Ott, and lefthander Carl Hubbell, the Giants won three pennants and one World Championship in the 1930s, then slipped into the doldrums through the 1940s.

Manager Leo Durocher and star centerfielder Willie Mays brought a pennant in 1951 and a WS victory in 1954, but sharply declining attendance and the growing inadequacy of the Polo Grounds threatened the team's survival. After the 1957 season, Stoneham moved the team to San Francisco. /(FS)

New York Mets — 1962– . Team. 2073–2392, .464. *NL East Champions 69, 73, 86, 88 NL Champions 69, 73, 86 World Champions 69, 86*

The Mets began as a franchise in the Continental League proposed by Branch Rickey. When the major leagues absorbed this potential rival, as they had so many others, by selling ML franchise rights to some of its sounder backers, the gap that had been left in New York City by the departure of the Dodgers and Giants after 1957 was filled by the expansion Mets. Chief owner Joan Payson, a millionaire, had been a Giants fan, and her team consciously played to the nostalgia of veteran fans. Before their first season, the Mets hired Casey Stengel and George Weiss, both recently let go by the Yankees, as manager and general manager. Gil Hodges, Don Zimmer, Gus Bell, Roger Craig, Clem Labine, Richie Ashburn, Frank Thomas, Gene Woodling, Duke Snider, Jimmy Piersall, Roy McMillan, Yogi Berra, Warren Spahn, and Joe Pignatano, all local favorites or former stars who would be remembered, played for the Mets in their first four seasons. (Johnny Antonelli and Billy Loes were purchased, but decided they would rather retire than play for the ragtag team.) The tactic was a bigger success as a promotional device than as a plan to win ballgames. The Mets, playing at the old Polo Grounds, went 40–120 in their first year, the worst record in the 20th century. But the fans, referred to as the "New Breed," were in the mold of the old Brooklyn Dodger fans, taking their team to heart as much for its faults as for its virtues, and in their enthusiasm introduced banners at the ballpark. At first, the painted bedsheets were quickly confiscated by park security, but local sportswriters pressured George Weiss, whose dignified Yankee sensibilities were offended by such unserious behavior, into allowing this new splash of color to thrive. The Mets became the first club to have an official Banner Day promotion.

Casey Stengel was largely responsible for the new team's image. He could see from the beginning that the Mets weren't going to win, so he clownishly played to the writers, providing a constant flow of funny quotes and stories and diverting attention from the cold facts.

George Weiss did his best to find promising young players, coming up with All-Star Ron Hunt in 1963 (he finished second to Pete Rose in Rookie of the Year voting). The club moved into Shea Stadium in 1964 and outdrew the pennant-bound Yankees. By the late 1960s the club, guided by GM Johnny

The 1986 New York Mets

Murphy and director of player development Whitey Herzog, had developed some of the best pitchers in the league. In the storied 1969 season a homegrown rotation anchored by Tom Seaver, Jerry Koosman, and Gary Gentry, with Nolan Ryan as a spot starter and Tug McGraw in the bullpen, took the "Miracle Mets" to a completely unexpected World Championship under manager Gil Hodges. The pattern was set for the 1970s: great pitching, below-average hitting. In mid-1972, in a move reminiscent of their earliest years, the Mets acquired Willie Mays, a favorite of Mrs. Payson's, so the Hall of Famer could finish his ML career in the city where it had started. During this time the Mets became known for their bad trades, most often ascribed to chairman of the board M. Donald Grant. The two worst trades shipped Nolan Ryan to the Angels for Jim Fregosi, and Amos Otis to the Royals for Joe Foy.

The Mets finished in third place for three years (1970–72) and then had another surprise pennant in 1973 under new manager Yogi Berra. Their record of 82–79 (.509) is the worst ever for a league champion. But they beat the 99–63 Reds in the NLCS, and took the A's to seven games in the World Series.

In September 1975 Joan Payson died. The loss of her financial resources relegated the team to an era of penny-pinching. They remained respectable through 1976 but then collapsed into the cellar for three straight seasons.

In 1980 the team was purchased for $21.3 million by Fred Wilpon, a real-estate magnate who had pitched for Brooklyn's Lafayette High School while Sandy Koufax played first base, and Nelson Doubleday of the publishing family. They appointed former Orioles GM Frank Cashen executive vice president and general manager, and he rebuilt the team from the bottom up. The team finished fifth in 1980 and '81, and last in 1982 and '83, but contended in 1984 under new manager Davey Johnson, finishing second. Once again, the Mets' success was based on pitching, with Rookie of the Year Dwight Gooden leading a staff that included Ron Darling, Sid Fernandez, and Jesse Orosco. But this time the Mets had an offense too. Darryl Strawberry, the number-one pick in the nation in 1980, won the Rookie of the Year award in 1983, the same season the Mets acquired clutch-hitting Gold Glove first baseman Keith Hernandez from the Cardinals. Howard Johnson and Gary Carter were added in 1985. Bob Ojeda joined in 1986 as the Mets dominated, going 108–54. They won a dramatic LCS over the Astros, winning a 16-inning clincher called by some the greatest game ever played, and came back in the World Series to beat the Red Sox in seven. They remained the favored team in the NL through 1989, but won only the 1988 NL East title in the three seasons following their World Championship. /(SH)

New York Yankees [aka Highlanders] (Bronx Bombers, Murderers' Row) — 1903- . Team. 7641-5788, .569. *AL East Champions 76-78, 80-81 AL Champions 21-23, 26-28, 32, 36-39, 41-43, 47, 49-53, 55-58, 60-64, 76-78, 81 World Champions 23, 27-28, 32, 36-39, 41, 43, 47, 49-53, 56, 58, 61-62, 77-78*

The Yankees are without dispute the most successful franchise in baseball history. They have won a record 22 World Series and 33 AL pennants and totally dominated the sport in the 1940s and, especially, the 1950s. They have won more games than any franchise, even though they are in the younger American League.

The club came to New York when AL president Ban Johnson moved the Baltimore franchise to compete with the Giants for attendance. The club cost owners Frank Farrell and Bill Devery $18,000. Playing in Hilltop Park in upper Manhattan, the club was named the Highlanders, until they moved into the Polo Grounds (shared with the Giants) and became the Yankees. The club almost won the 1904 pennant on the strength of Jack Chesbro's 41-12 record, but lost on the last day of the season when Chesbro wild-pitched in the losing run in the ninth inning. The team remained respectable for several years and then declined. In January 1915 Colonel Jacob Ruppert and Colonel Tillinghast L'Hommedieu Huston bought the franchise for $460,000. That season the famous Yankee pinstripes were seen for the first time. The new owners began buying talent almost immediately, picking up Bob Shawkey in 1916 as Connie Mack finished breaking up the Athletics.

But the deal that made the Yankees into a powerhouse came in January 1920, when they bought Babe Ruth from the Red Sox as Boston owner Harry Frazee sold off his stars to finance his Broadway shows. Ruth changed baseball history by hitting 54 HR in 1920, breaking the record of 29 that he had set the previous year. At the end of the 1920 season the Yankees hired Boston manager Ed Barrow to be their general manager. Knowing the Boston players well, he continued the Yankees' stripping of the Red Sox roster by acquiring Wally

Schang and Waite Hoyt a few months later, Joe Bush, Everett Scott, and Joe Dugan after the 1921 season, and Herb Pennock in 1923. The Yankees had just won their first pennant, and although they lost to their Polo Grounds landlords, John McGraw's Giants, that year and the next, they outdrew them. The popularity of the team, especially Ruth, helped finance the building of Yankee Stadium, hence its nickname of "The House That Ruth Built." In May 1922, two weeks after construction of the park was begun, Ruppert bought out Huston for $1.5 million.

Moving into their new home in 1923, the Yankees celebrated by finally besting the Giants in the 1923 WS, the Yankees' first World Championship. After a two-year hiatus, the Yankees resumed their pennant-winning ways with another three straight, 1926-28. The 1927 team has become symbolic of overwhelming strength. Nicknamed Murderer's Row, the offense posted the highest team slugging percentage in history, .489. The Yankees won 110 games and finished 19 games ahead of the Athletics, who had Hall of Famers Ty Cobb, Al Simmons, Mickey Cochrane, and Lefty Grove, and won 91 games. Ruth set another, nearly unbreakable record by hitting 60 home runs, and had 164 RBI, second in the league. The man who finished ahead of him, Lou Gehrig, drove in 175 and finished second to Ruth with 47 HR while batting .373 (third in the AL). Ruth, Gehrig, and Earle Combs finished 1-2-3 in runs scored, and it was Gehrig, Ruth, and Combs atop the total bases list. Tony Lazzeri finished third behind Ruth and Gehrig in home runs. This powerhouse, which led in every major offensive category but doubles and steals, might have won with the worst pitching staff in the league, but instead it had the best, with Hoyt leading the league in ERA and winning percentage and tying in wins. Teammate Urban Shocker followed him on the ERA list. The Pirates were swept in four games in the World Series, supposedly demoralized just by watching the Yankees take batting practice. The Yankees had another Series sweep in 1928, of the Cardinals.

In 1929 the Yankees wore numbers on their backs, the first team to do so on a permanent basis. Bill Dickey took over behind the plate, and the Yankees finished second; manager Miller Huggins died in September of that year. Shawkey led the team to a third-place finish in 1930, and Joe McCarthy took over in 1931, when Lefty Gomez had the first of his four 20-win seasons. McCarthy

The 1927 New York Yankees

ended the three-year reign of the Athletics in 1932 and once again the Yankees swept the Series. They had won 12 consecutive WS games. The team finished second the next three seasons, with Ruth being let go after 1934.

But a new era of domination was coming, presaged by the November 1934 purchase of Joe DiMaggio from the San Francisco Seals of the Pacific Coast League. An agreement between the two teams allowed him to play one last season for the Seals, which had the effect of creating great anticipation in New York. His rookie season in 1936 certainly did not disappoint the Yankees, as he was the team's second-best hitter, behind Gehrig, in the three major categories, hitting .323 with 29 HR and 125 RBI. Red Ruffing, picked up from Boston in mid-1930 after leading the league in losses the previous two seasons, had the first of four straight 20-win seasons in 1936. The Giants managed to end the Yankees' WS consecutive game-winning streak in the first game, but the Yankees beat them that year and the next. In 1938 it was the Cubs' turn to lose, as New York swept them. Joe Gordon was now the Yankee second baseman, having pushed Lazzeri aside, and that helped compensate for the reduced effectiveness of Gehrig. Col. Ruppert died in January 1939, and GM Barrow succeeded him as club president. Later that year, when Gehrig ended his monumental 2,130 consecutive-game streak by sit-

ting himself down, it was discovered that he had amyotrophic lateral sclerosis. He never played again and died two years later. His spot was taken by Babe Dahlgren, and the Yankees swept the Reds in the Series. McCarthy had led them to World Championships in four consecutive seasons, then a record.

After a third-place finish in 1940, the Yankees had a memorable season in 1941. DiMaggio hit in a record 56 games, and rookie Phil Rizzuto took over shortstop from the aging Frankie Crosetti. Their Game One victory in the WS gave them another consecutive-victory streak, of ten games. The first of the fabled Yankee-Dodger matchups, the 1941 World Series was effectively decided in Game Four. The Dodgers were ahead 4–3 in the ninth inning with two out, and were about to even the Series at two games apiece. But Hugh Casey's third strike got past Mickey Owen, and, given that reprieve, the Yankees came back with four runs and clinched the Series the next day. They hadn't lost a WS since 1926, to the Cardinals; their triumph in eight Series without an intervening loss was yet another record. The string was snapped in 1942 when the Cardinals triumphed again, but the Yankees came back to beat them in 1943 despite the loss of DiMaggio, Rizzuto, and others to military service. Spud Chandler helped compensate with a 20–4 season. But so many players were lost to military service in the next two years that the Yankees slipped to third, and then fourth, place. In January 1945 Dan Topping and Del Webb purchased the club for $2.8 million. They replaced Barrow with Larry McPhail, giving him a third of the club. He brought night baseball, his innovation in Cincinnati, to Yankee Stadium after the war ended. But McCarthy, who had completely rebuilt the image of the Yankees from the team of carousers it had been during Ruth's time, did not get along with the unstaid McPhail, and quit in early 1946. Bill Dickey and Johnny Neun also managed the team that year, and the Yankees finished third.

In 1947 the Yankees had a new manager, Bucky Harris; a new catcher, Yogi Berra (he shared duties with Aaron Robinson); a new staff ace, Allie Reynolds; and a new bullpen ace, Joe Page. They ran away with the flag and beat the Dodgers in a memorable World Series that included a near-no-hitter by Bill Bevens. McPhail proved too much of an embarrassment, and was replaced by director of minor league operations George Weiss. When the Yankees finished third in 1948, Harris was fired, despite winning 94 games. Weiss convinced the owners to bring in Casey Stengel, whom he knew from Stengel's time managing the Oakland Oaks of the Pacific Coast League. Many were surprised and disappointed with the choice of a manager who had lost in a big way in both his previous major league assignments, and who had developed a reputation as a clown, but Stengel would go on to win with the Yankees to an extent unmatched by any before or since.

Stengel inherited a "Big Three" of Reynolds, Eddie Lopat, and Vic Raschi on the pitching staff and an offense that, though it included Tommy Henrich, Joe DiMaggio, and Phil Rizzuto, reminded no one of the Bronx Bombers of seasons past. He compensated by raising platooning to a new level of complexity, and he made Berra the regular catcher (he led the team in RBI the next seven seasons and won three MVP awards), gave more playing time to Bobby Brown, Jerry Coleman, Hank Bauer, and Gene Woodling, and began a practice of late-season pick-ups of veterans by buying slugger Johnny Mize, then 36 years old, from the Giants at the end of August 1949. DiMaggio was injured for much of that season, but came back cold off the DL to ravage the Red Sox in an important series at Fenway Park. Stengel finished one game ahead of Joe McCarthy's Red Sox, but had an easier time of it in the World Series as the Yankees beat the Dodgers in five games. In 1950 Whitey Ford began making the "Big Three" into the "Big Four" and the Phillies were swept in the Series. DiMaggio passed the torch to

rookie Mickey Mantle in 1951, Gil McDougald won Rookie of the Year, and Johnny Sain was picked up at the end of August as the Yankees won their third straight World Championship. Mantle took over in centerfield in 1952 and Stengel installed Billy Martin, a favorite of his from Oakland, as the regular second baseman. The Dodgers fell in a seven-game Series, and Stengel had equalled McCarthy's four straight World Championships, and more important to him personally, his mentor John McGraw's four straight pennants.

Oddly, Yankee Stadium was sold to Earl and Arnold Johnson of Kansas City at the beginning of the 1953 season, presaging the close link that would develop between New York and Kansas City after the Athletics moved there in 1955 (previously it was a Yankee minor league outpost). Mantle hit his famous 565-foot home run in Washington that April 17, and Whitey Ford came back from two years of military service to become the staff ace as the Yankees coasted to another title. Stengel got his record fifth consecutive World Championship as Martin hit .500 in the Series against the Dodgers, equaling the Series record with 12 hits.

The Indians managed to interrupt the Yankees in 1954 by winning an AL-record 111 games; Stengel's personal high of 103 games was good enough for second place. Bill Skowron came up and began winning time at first base, and Bob Grim won the Rookie of the Year award with a 20–6 mark, although he proved to be a one-year wonder. Don Larsen and Bob Turley were picked up from the Athletics in December in the first of many similar transactions. A month later John Williams Cox bought Yankee Stadium and sold the grounds to the Knights of Columbus; in 1962 he left the facilities to Rice University. In 1955 Mantle led the AL in home runs for the first of four times and Ford led in wins for his first time. New York returned to the top of the standings. But the Dodgers finally triumphed in the Fall Classic, beating the Yankees in seven games. Mantle had his finest season in 1956, winning the first of his three MVP awards with league highs of 52 HR and 130 RBI in his finest season. The World Series featured Larsen's perfect game as the Yankees won in seven games.

In June 1957 Martin was traded to Kansas City, over Stengel's objections, in a deal that brought Ryne Duren to the Yankees. Martin had supposedly been involved in a brawl at a New York nightclub, and although he was not a major figure in the incident, Weiss considered him a bad influence. Bobby Richardson took over at second base. The

Braves defeated New York in the World Series in 1957, but the Yankees revenged themselves in a 1958 rematch after cruising to a third straight easy pennant. Tony Kubek won the shortstop job and Rookie of the Year honors, Turley was the Cy Young winner, and Duren took over as the bullpen ace. But in 1959 the team stumbled, finishing in third with a 79-75 record. It was the first time since 1946 that they hadn't won at least 90 games, and their worst season since 1925. The truth was that the talent was running out, partly because of the Yankees' early failure to sign gifted black players. Aside from Ford, the pitching staff was not dominating. Stengel had maneuvered spot starters in and out for years, but for one year, it didn't work. Even so, the Yankees had dominated the decade in unprecedented fashion. But the owners decided that Stengel was getting too old.

Another raid on the Athletics' roster brought Roger Maris to New York for 1960, and he won the first of his back-to-back MVP awards. Defensive whiz Clete Boyer took over third base, moving butcher Hector Lopez into the outfield to share time with Berra, who relinquished the majority of the catching duties to Elston Howard, who had patiently played out of position in the outfield and at first base for five years. The Yankees rebounded to 97-57 and won by eight games, but lost to the Pirates in a wild, seesaw World Series that saw Pittsburgh outscored 55-27, outhit .338-.256, and outpitched 3.54-7.11. But the Pirates won the close games, and Bill Mazeroski's climactic Game Seven home run in the bottom of the ninth inning cost Stengel and Weiss their jobs as club president Topping forced them out in the name of a supposed youth movement.

Former third-string catcher Ralph Houk took over the reins in 1961 as two teams and eight games were added in expansion. Maris and Mantle chased Ruth's 60 home runs all season, with Maris topping it in the final game and winning his second MVP award. Ford had his best season, going 25-4 and winning Cy Young honors, as Houk stabilized the rotation for the first time in years and Luis Arroyo saved 29 games (then a record, although it was not yet a statistic). The surprise NL winners, the Reds, were disposed of in five games in the Series. The Yankees repeated easily in 1962 as Ralph Terry had a career year, going 23-12 and winning two games in the Yankees' seven-game triumph over San Francisco. Mantle won his final MVP award, and Tom Tresh was named Rookie of the Year in his best season after temporarily pushing Kubek aside.

Skowron was traded after the Series, and Joe Pepitone took over first base in 1963. Tresh spent the whole season in the outfield as Mantle was sidelined most of the season. Howard captured MVP honors as the Yankees won their third straight pennant for Houk. But the superior pitching of the Dodgers swept New York in the World Series. Houk moved to the front office after the season and Berra took over in the dugout. The Yankees won the best AL pennant race in over a decade in 1964 to again win five straight AL titles. Topping had been disappointed by the team's showing in the early part of the season, though, and it was already arranged that Berra would be fired after the season, with Cardinals manager Johnny Keane to replace him. The fact that New York lost the World Series to the Cardinals in seven games was enough justification for Topping; the odd turn of events went through. Berra was luckier than he realized.

Topping had arranged during the season to sell the team to CBS. Following the World Series, they purchased 80% of the franchise for $11.2 million, buying the remaining 20% later. Their investment fell apart on them as the Yankees had their first losing season since 1925 in 1965 and then dropped to last place in 1966. Kubek and Ford had retired, Maris had lost most of his power, Mantle was deteriorating physically, and Tresh hit home runs but contributed little else. Houk took over in 1966 after the team started the year 4-16. The team improved only marginally in 1967, as Mantle and Pepitone switched positions; Mantle's knees were no longer able to handle outfield play. Howard and Tresh lost their skills, and the mediocre Horace Clarke became the symbol, fairly or unfairly, of a new Yankee era. The team rebounded to an 83-79 fifth-place finish in 1968, Mantle's last season. But the years 1965-71 are perhaps best summed up in the current Yankee media guides, where the only highlights listed in that time period are the painting of Yankee Stadium after the 1966 season and Mickey Mantle Day in 1969. Mel Stottlemyre won 20 games three times, and Thurman Munson came up in 1970. The Yankees even finished second that year, although they were 15 games back. But the club remained mediocre for several more years.

A large group of businessmen bought the Yankees from CBS in January 1973. Principal owner George Steinbrenner, who made his money in shipbuilding, claimed he was going to be a silent partner, but Houk resigned after the season over Steinbrenner's meddling in decision-making. It was the first indication of a coming managerial carousel unmatched in instability and surprising twists. Playing at Shea Stadium while Yankee Stadium was renovated by the City of New York, the Yankees were led by low-key Bill Virdon to a second-place finish in 1974, just two games out. The team featured Graig Nettles, Bobby Murcer, and Chris Chambliss. Virdon was replaced with the volatile Martin after going 53–51 in the first two-thirds of 1975. Catfish Hunter was the ace of the pitching staff, the first of Steinbrenner's blockbuster free-agent signings. The owner's willingness to spend freely proved to be his best quality.

The remodeled Yankee Stadium was opened in 1976, and a revamped team that now included Willie Randolph at second base and Mickey Rivers in centerfield, and Ed Figueroa and Dock Ellis on the mound, finished first for the first time in 12 years. Munson won MVP honors, Nettles led the AL in homers, and Sparky Lyle emerged as the bullpen ace with 23 saves. Chambliss's dramatic ninth-inning home run clinched the LCS. New York was swept by the Reds in the World Series, but the Yankees had reestablished themselves as a dynasty. Superstar Reggie Jackson was Steinbrenner's next headline-grabbing free-agent acquisition; Don Gullett was also picked up for 1977. Jackson alienated many Yankees with an undiplomatic, bragging interview, and Martin was unhappy that he hadn't gotten the hit-and-run man he wanted. But with Munson leading the Yankees in the clubhouse and on the field, and Jackson leading them statistically, the club captured its first World Championship in 15 years. Lyle captured Cy Young honors. Jackson's remarkable performance in the final game of the Series, in which he hit three consecutive homers, all on the first pitch, clinched the Series and earned him the nickname Mr. October. The 1978 season topped 1977 in all respects. The new free-agent arrival was Goose Gossage, who won the stopper role from Lyle. Martin and Jackson and Steinbrenner feuded openly, with Martin getting the ax while 52–42 for calling Steinbrenner and Jackson liars. Officially, he retired for health reasons. After interim manager Dick Howser lost one game, Chicago manager Bob Lemon took over the Yankees. But there was a startling twist to his situation, as it was announced just four days later (at Old- Timers Day) that Martin would return in 1980. Under Lemon's calm guidance and masterful handling of the pitching staff, helped by the return of several injured Yankees, the club went 48–20 the rest of the way to tie the Red Sox. Ron Guidry won the climactic playoff game, running his record to 25–3, on Bucky Dent's home run. Guidry won the Cy Young Award, and Ed Figueroa became the first Puerto Rican 20-game winner. Kansas City fell to the Yankees again in the LCS, and the Yankees won their second straight World Championship, the most recent team to repeat. Dent continued his improbable heroics to win the Series MVP award; Nettles's spectacular fielding might have won it for him if he had only hit better than his feeble .160. Tommy John and Luis Tiant were signed as free agents over the winter; John led the staff in wins in 1979. Martin's return came sooner than expected when he replaced Lemon on June 18 with the Yankees at 34–30. But the team was stunned by the August death of the irreplaceable Munson in a plane crash. They finished in fourth place.

Martin was replaced after the season by Dick Howser, who led the Yankees to a 103-victory division title. Newest free-agent acquisition Rudy May led the league in ERA, and Jackson led in HR. But the team was swept by the Royals in the LCS, and Steinbrenner forced Howser to "retire" in a charade that fooled no one. Gene Michael was named as Howser's replacement in an effort to use his popularity as a former Yankee star to offset outrage at the dismissal of Howser. Steinbrenner's biggest free-agent signing came that December when he signed Dave Winfield to a 10-year contract. Dave Righetti won the Rookie of the Year award. In a season broken into two parts by a mid-season players' strike, the Yankees won the first half easily and then coasted, finishing under .500 in the second half of the season. Steinbrenner's unhappiness with this situation, which emphasized the unimportance of the second half and threatened attendance, led to the firing of Michael in the beginning of September. He was replaced by Lemon, who led the Yankees past the Brewers (in the divisional playoff) and the A's. But the Yankees' World Series loss elicited Steinbrenner's outrageous "apology" to New York fans that was an implicit criticism of Winfield's 1-for-22 performance. It would prove to be the Yankees' last postseason appearance for quite a while.

Lemon was fired again after starting the 1982 season 6–8. Gene Michael replaced him for 86 games and was in turn replaced after he attempted to stand up for the players during a disappointing 79–83 fifth-place finish (the team was at .500 at the time). Clyde King lasted to the end of the season and Martin was rehired for 1983. The Yankees finished third that year, and third under Berra in 1984 as Don Mattingly and Winfield battled down to the last

Don Newcombe

day of the season before Mattingly won the batting title. Berra was fired while 6–10 in April 1985, with Martin once again taking over. He drove the team to a second-place finish as Mattingly won the MVP and Guidry went 22–6. After the season Lou Piniella, another popular ex-Yankee, replaced Martin as manager. He lasted through a second-place finish in 1986, but finished in fourth in the tough 1987 AL East despite an 89–73 record. Martin spent the whole summer sniping at Piniella's managerial expertise from the Yankee broadcast booth, and replaced Piniella, who was made GM, after the season. In Martin's fifth term, a record for times managing one team for a non-owner (Bill Sharsig named himself manager of the Philadelphia club in the American Association), his erratic and violent behavior once again embarrassed the team, and he was fired and replaced by Piniella. Dallas Green was named manager for 1989 and began rebuilding the team with GM Syd Thrift, but was unsurprisingly fired that August; 1978 playoff hero Bucky Dent replaced him. It was the 17th managerial change in Steinbrenner's 17 years of ownership. /(SH)

Don Newcombe (Newk) — 1926– . RHP 1949–51, 54–60 **Dodgers**, Reds, Indians 2155 ip, 149–90, 3.56. 20 wins: 51, 55–56 *3 WS, 22 ip, 0–4, 8.59*
☛ *Rookie of the Year—49. Most Valuable Player—56. Led League—w 56. Led League—k 51. Cy Young Award—56. All-Star—49–51, 55.*

The first outstanding black pitcher in ML history, Newcombe is the only player to have won the Rookie of the Year, MVP, and Cy Young awards. Physically imposing, the 6'4" 220-lb Newk was sometimes criticized as lethargic, but his explosive fastball was likened by Ted Williams to those of AL stars Bob Feller and Virgil Trucks. He anchored the pitching rotation for the "Boys of Summer" Dodgers and was one of baseball's dominant forces from 1949 to 1956.

After one season with the Negro League Newark Eagles, Newcombe signed with the Dodgers, arriving in Brooklyn in 1949. He immediately helped the Dodgers to a pennant. He shut out the Reds 3–0 in his May 22 debut and finished 17–8, 3.17, with a league-leading five shutouts. In the heat of the pennant race, which the Dodgers won by a single game over the Cardinals, Newcombe pitched 32 consecutive scoreless innings. He was named Rookie of the Year by both *TSN* and the BBWAA.

Newk was a strong 19–11 in his sophomore season, but on the last day of the season suffered the first of many late-season failures that would plague his otherwise outstanding career. Brooklyn needed a

win to force a playoff with the Phillies when Newcombe served up a tenth-inning three-run homer to Dick Sisler to lose 4–1. Newk rebounded to go 20–9 in 1951, fanning a NL-high 164, and shut out the Phillies on the second-to-last day of the season to help force a three-game playoff with the Giants. He started Game Three, and appeared headed for a victory, the WS, and redemption from the previous year with a 4–2 lead in the bottom of the ninth. He left the game with two runners on base, and Bobby Thompson won the pennant for the Giants with a three-run home run.

After two years in the military, Brooklyn's number 36 suffered a disappointing 1954 (9–8, 4.55), but returned to form in 1955, going 20–5, 3.20. He peaked the following year, with a sterling 27–7 record, five shutouts, and a 3.06 ERA, and was named NL MVP and recipient of the first-ever Cy Young Award, then given to only one pitcher each year (rather than one from each league).

In addition to his success on the mound, Newk was a threat at the plate, with a powerful right-handed stroke and a lifetime .271 average (9th best ever among pitchers). In 1955 he hit .359 with 7 home runs (a NL record for pitchers), including two two-home-run games. He hit two homers in a game a third time the next year, and found a place as a first baseman in Japan when his ML pitching days were over.

Still, the postseason was a personal nightmare for the usually dominating Newcombe. He pitched well in his first WS outing, fanning 11 and allowing only 4 hits in Game One of the 1949 Series, only to lose 1–0 on Tommy Henrich's ninth-inning homer. In his four other WS starts he allowed 20 earned runs in 14 innings. /(FK)

Dave Newhouse — 1938– . *Writer.*

In 1989, Newhouse completed 25 years as a baseball writer for the Oakland *Tribune*. He is also the author of three football books: *Rose Bowl Football Since 1902, The Jim Plunkett Story*, and *Heismen: After the Glory.* /(NLM)

Hal Newhouser (Prince Hal) — 1921– . LHP 1939–55 **Tigers**, Indians 2993 ip, 207–150, 3.06. 20 wins: 44–46, 48 *2 WS, 21 ip, 2–1, 6.53*
☛ *Most Valuable Player—44–45. Led League—w 44–46, 48. Led League—era 45–46. Led League—k 44–45. All-Star—42–44, 46–48.*

For three years in the mid-1940s, Newhouser was the most dominant pitcher in baseball. He is the only pitcher to win two consecutive MVP awards.

But he never had a winning season before he blossomed during the war years. And that has been an obstacle to his gaining the respect due his prowess, despite the fact that Newhouser won 26 games in 1946, the year the war veterans returned. A congenital heart ailment kept Newhouser out of the service and for a time threatened his baseball career.

Newhouser signed with the Tigers for $400 while a Detroit schoolboy star. Moments later, the story goes, Cleveland Indians superscout Cy Slapnicka arrived to offer $15,000 and a new car, but the deal was done. Newhouser appeared briefly in the majors at age 18 in 1939 and returned for good in 1941. But he recorded only a 25–43 record through 1943, when he led the league in walks. Failure frustrated Newhouser, an intense competitor, and he alienated teammates with his tantrums. But he resolved to control both his behavior and his pitching, and he won a career-high 29 games in 1944. Pinpoint control of his fastball and overhand curve became Newhouser's trademark. "He is smart and tough in any pinch," said the Yankees' Bill Dickey. Newhouser won two complete-game victories, including the seventh-game clincher, in the 1945 World Series against the Cubs. He engaged in many classic matchups with the Indians' Bob Feller, the dominant righthander of the era. The "big one," in Newhouser's words, came on the final day of the 1948 season, when he outpitched Feller on one day's rest to force Cleveland into a playoff with Boston for the AL title. The victory was a league-best 21st for Newhouser, but also marked the beginning of shoulder trouble that would limit his effectiveness after one more 18-victory season in 1949. Newhouser closed his career as Feller's teammate in 1954, when he won seven, saved seven, and appeared in one more World Series. /(KT)

Al Newman — 1960– . 2B-SS-3B 1985– Expos, **Twins** 476 g, .229, 1 hr, 95 rbi. *1 LCS, 1 g, .000. 1 WS, 4 g, .200*

A 5′9″ utility infielder who stole 63 bases in his first minor league season (Memphis, 1982), the switch-hitting Newman was used sparingly in Montreal. He saw more playing time after his 1987 trade to Minnesota. In 1988, he started at third base in 41 of the Twins' last 45 games after Gary Gaetti was injured. /(JCA)

Fred Newman — 1942– . RHP 1962–67 **Angels** 610 ip, 33–39, 3.41

Newman used good control to go 13–10, 2.75 (1964) and 14–16, 2.93 (1965) in his two best seasons. /(JFC)

Hal Newhouser

Jeff Newman — 1948- . C-1B 1976–84 **A's**, Red Sox 735 g, .224, 63 hr, 233 rbi. *1 LCS, 2 g, .000.*
   Manager 1986 **A's** 2–8, .200
☛ *All-Star—79.*

Newman spent six years in the Indians' system but reached the majors with Oakland. He had his best year, by far, in 1979, leading the A's in home runs (22), games (143), and at-bats (516), sharing catching duties with Jim Essian and playing first base and some third. Traded to Boston with Tony Armas in a December 1982 deal for Carney Lansford, Newman played and hit little his final two seasons. He was the A's bullpen coach for 1986 and served as their acting manager for 10 games in June and July after Jackie Moore was fired and before Tony LaRussa was hired. /(JCA)

Bobo Newsom [Louis Norman] (Buck) — 1907–62. RHP 1929–30, 32, 34–48, 52–53 Dodgers, Cubs, Browns, **Senators**, Red Sox, Tigers, A's, Yankees, Giants 3759 ip, 211–222, 3.98. 20 wins: 38–40 *2 WS, 28 ip, 2-2, 2.86*
☛ *Led League—k 42. All-Star—38–40, 44.*

Bobo Newsom, a massive, barrel-chested man, toured the major leagues for 20 years, traveling a path that reached eight clubs, rewinding to Washington five times, Brooklyn three times, and the Athletics twice. Bobo was what he called most of his teammates, because he was rarely around long enough to learn their names. He moved through baseball, talkative, boastful, with a supreme self-confidence he usually backed up with a superlative performance, only to have it negated somehow. Three seasons in a row he won 20 or more games, but four times he led the league in losses. He is one of two pitchers to win over 200 games and lose even more.

   Misfortune plagued Newsom. He once pitched nine no-hit innings only to lose 2–1 on a 10th-inning hit; he was suspended by his own manager for throwing a spitball; he had his kneecap broken by a line drive yet hobbled on to a complete-game victory. He showed great courage in the 1940 World Series. He had a 21–5 record that year and pitched three complete games for the Tigers in the seven-game Series. His father died suddenly after seeing him win the opener. Tearfully, Newsom dedicated his next start to his dad and won that as well. But his fortunes reversed in Game Seven, as he lost to the Reds, 2–1. /(JK)

Dick Newsome [Heber Hampton] — 1909–1965. RHP 1941–43 **Red Sox** 526 ip, 35–33, 4.50

Bobo Newsom

As a rookie in 1941, the rugged Newsome led the Red Sox in wins and innings pitched, going 19–10 despite a 4.13 ERA. He was supported by an all-star offense that hit .283 (17 points above the league average) and included Ted Williams's .406 bat. Newsome won only eight games in each of his two subsequent ML seasons. /(EW)

Skeeter Newsome [Lamar Ashby] — 1910- . SS-2B-3B 1935–39, 41–47 A's, **Red Sox**, Phillies 1128 g, .245, 9 hr, 292 rbi

This fast infielder was a valuable utility man and a pesky batter who had the ability to come off the bench and get on base. /(EW)

Doc Newton [Eustace James] — 1877–1931. LHP 1900–02, 05–09 Reds, Dodgers, **Yankees** 1201 ip, 53–73, 3.22

Newton set the single-season NL record for errors by a pitcher (since 1900) with 17 for Cincinnati and Brooklyn in 1901. He had his best season in 1902 for Brooklyn, when he went 15–14 with a 2.42 ERA. New York manager Clark Griffith claimed that Newton's failure to stay in condition cost the Highlanders the 1906 pennant; Newton was suspended mid-season for dissipation. /(NLM)

Gus Niarhos [Constantine Gregory] — 1920– . C 1946, 48–55 **Yankees**, White Sox, Red Sox, Phillies 315 g, .252, 1 hr, 59 rbi. *1 WS, 1 g, --*

Slender for a catcher, the 6′ 160-lb Niarhos hit .268 for the 1948 Yankees, platooning with Yogi Berra. A backup after 1948, he batted a career-high .324 in 41 games after a 1950 trade to the White Sox. /(MC)

Simon Nicholls — 1882–1911. SS-2B-3B 1903, 06–10 Tigers, **A's**, Indians 314 g, .251, 4 hr, 58 rbi

Nicholls's great speed allowed him to beat out many infield hits. He hit .302 in his rookie 1907 season with the Athletics, fifth in the AL, but dropped to .216 the next year and fielded just .913. He lost the shortstop job to Jack Barry in 1909 and died from typhoid fever and peritonitis in 1911. /(NLM)

Chet Nichols [Chester Raymond, Sr.] — 1897–1982. RHP 1926–28, 30–32 Pirates, Giants, **Phillies** 123 ip, 1–8, 7.19

Father of pitcher Chet Nichols, Jr., Chet Nichols, Sr. refused Connie Mack's offer to sign with the A's for $400 a month, remaining with a Ware, MA semi-pro team that was paying him $500. He developed a spitball, but when he did agree to major league contracts, was unsuccessful. /(JVM)

Chet Nichols [Chester Raymond, Jr.] — 1931– . LHP 1951, 54–56, 60–64 **Braves**, Red Sox, Reds 603 ip, 34–36, 3.64
☛ *Led League—era 51.*

Tutored by his father, NL pitcher Chet Nichols, Sr., the younger Nichols went 11–8 with a league-best 2.88 ERA (156 innings) as a Braves rookie in 1951. Less effective after losing two years to military service, he won nine games in both 1954 and 1955 and was sent down. Arm troubles thwarted his comeback attempts, but he returned as a Red Sox reliever in the 1960s. He later became vice president of the Pawtucket Red Sox (International League). /(JVM)

Kid Nichols [Charles Augustus] — 1869–1953. RHP 1890–1901, 04–06 **Braves**, Cardinals, Phillies 5084 ip, 360–202, 2.94. 20 wins: 1890–99, 1904
    Manager 1904–05 **Cardinals** 94–108, .465
☛ *Led League—w 1896–98. Hall of Fame—1949.*

A star from the moment he made his major league debut at age 20 in 1890, Kid Nichols topped the 25-

Kid Nichols

victory mark in each of his first nine seasons, leading Boston's staff, and sparking his club to five National League championships. A durable overhand pitcher with a smooth delivery, he depended on control and a fastball reportedly equal to that of famed Giant righthander Amos Rusie. He went 27–19 his rookie season (leading the league with seven shutouts), then achieved seven consecutive seasons of 30 or more triumphs -a feat never matched. He recorded a career-high 35 victories in 1892 and paced the league in wins in 1896, '97, and '98. The workhorse threw at least 400 innings a season from 1890 through 1894. In six of the seven years that followed, he registered more than 300 innings.

By 1898, Nichols was earning $2,400, the top salary permitted by the league. Although he never pitched a no-hitter, he came close on several occasions. He threw 48 shutouts and had 11 complete-game, 1–0 victories. One of his most memorable games came in his rookie season, when he faced Rusie and the Giants at the Polo Grounds. The teams battled in a scoreless tie until, with two out in the 13th inning, Mike Tiernan drove a Nichols fastball for a home run.

Following the 1901 season, Nichols bought a part interest in the Western Association's Kansas City team and served as the club's manager for 1902 and 1903 while also recording 48 victories as a pitcher. Returning to the majors, he pitched for and managed the Cardinals in 1904 and part of 1905. He won 21 games in '04, struck out 15 Brooklyn batters in a 17-inning game, and pitched two complete games in one day against the Reds. Released by St. Louis with the club in sixth place, he joined the Phillies for the remainder of the 1905 season. He retired after pitching only 11 innings in 1906.

Nichols subsequently formed a partnership with Joe Tinker, former Cub shortstop, and entered the motion-picture business. Later he coached the Missouri Valley College baseball team. While managing a bowling alley in Missouri, he was recognized as one of Kansas City's finest bowlers, winning the Class A Championship at age 64.

Nichols stands seventh all-time in victories (360) and fourth in complete games (533). With John Clarkson, Charles Radbourne, Tim Keefe, and Cy Young, he was one of the five premier 19th-century pitchers. He had the most remarkable and consistent record of all pitchers in their twenties; nine months and 23 days past his 30th birthday, he became the youngest pitcher to win 300 ML games. That record stands to this day. /(JLE)

Reid Nichols — 1958– . OF 1980–87 **Red Sox**, White Sox, Expos 539 g, .266, 22 hr, 131 rbi

Nichols lasted parts of eight seasons in the ML as a reserve outfielder and righthanded pinch hitter, appearing in 100 games only once. With the Red Sox in 1983 he reached career highs in average (.302), HR (7), and RBI (33). /(SCL)

Rod Nichols — 1964– . RHP 1988- **Indians** 141 ip, 5–13, 4.72

Nichols struggled with his control in a disastrous trial with the Indians in 1988 after starting the season on the DL, but did have three complete games. His solid performance in 1989 while Greg Swindell was on the DL won him a spot in the rotation; Nichols finished 4–6 with a 4.40 ERA. /(SFS)

Bill Nicholson (Swish) — 1914– . OF 1936, 39–53 A's, **Cubs**, Phillies 1677 g, .268, 235 hr, 948 rbi. *1 WS, 7 g, .214, 8 rbi*
☛ *Led League—hr 43, 44. Led League—rbi 43, 44. All-Star—40, 41, 43, 44.*

Whenever Nicholson took one of his tremendous swings, fans would yell, "Swish!" Started by Brooklyn fans, it was a sign of respect, because the big cut often resulted in a home run. Nicholson was struck out his share of times, as sluggers are; he led the league with a modest 83 strikeouts in 1947. The muscular outfielder struggled as Athletics property after signing out of Washington College. Sent to the minors, he was helped by Hall of Famer Kiki Cuyler, his manager at Chattanooga (Southern League) and later a Cub coach. Cuyler instructed him to open his stance, get set for each pitch, and stop lunging at the ball. During 1939, Nicholson's second straight season as a minor league home run champ, he was purchased by the Cubs.

During talent-starved WWII Nicholson's batting feats became legend. He once hit a ball that just missed the Wrigley Field scoreboard; only Roberto Clemente came as close. After hitting four consecutive homers in a July 23, 1944 doubleheader at the Polo Grounds, he was intentionally walked with the bases loaded in the seventh inning, on orders from Giants manager Mel Ott. (Up 12–9 at the time, the Giants won 12–10.) He led the NL with 29 HR and 128 RBI in 1943 and with 33 HR and 122 RBI in 1944, when he scored a league-high 116 runs and lost MVP honors by one vote to Marty Marion.

Although Nicholson helped the Cubs to the 1945 pennant, his failing eyesight resulted in a slip in production. He was aided somewhat when the seats in Wrigley's centerfield were blocked off. Cubs fans were furious when he was traded to the Phillies after the 1948 season for Harry "The Hat" Walker. After he became weak and lost weight, it was disclosed on Labor Day, 1950, that Nicholson was diabetic. He was unable to play in the World Series with his "Whiz Kids" teammates. He hung on until 1953, primarily as a pinch hitter. He retired with eight pinch homers, and as one of the game's toughest men to double up—he hit into double plays only once every 90.7 at-bats./(DB)

Dave Nicholson — 1939– . OF 1960, 62–67 Orioles, **White Sox**, Astros, Braves 538 g, .212, 61 hr, 179 rbi

Signed by the Orioles for a reported $100,000 bonus in 1958, Nicholson hit with power wherever he went, but became the easiest batter in major league history to strike out, fanning once every 2.48 at-bats. He led the Northern League with 35 HR in 1959 and was rushed to Baltimore, where he struck out 55 times in just 113 trips in 1960. Unsuccessful again in 1962, he was sent to the White Sox in a 1963 trade for Luis Aparicio. He hit a team-leading 22 home runs in 1963, but struck out 175 times to set a since-broken ML record. Platooned by the Astros in 1966, Nicholson batted a career-high .246 before being traded to Atlanta and subsequently returning to the minors./(MC)

Fred Nicholson — 1894–1972. OF 1917, 19–22 Tigers, Pirates, **Braves** 303 g, .311, 12 hr, 107 rbi

Over a 10-year period, Nicholson was the property of 11 clubs in eight leagues. In 1920 he hit .360 in part-time duty for the Pirates, with NL highs of 12 pinch hits and 38 pinch at-bats. That winter the Texan was traded with Billy Southworth, Walter Barbare, and $15,000 for Boston's Rabbit Maranville. Nicholson was in the military in 1918./(NLM)

Steve Nicosia — 1955– . C 1978–85 **Pirates**, Giants, Expos, Blue Jays 358 g, .248, 11 hr, 88 rbi. *1 WS, 4 g, .063*

A platoon starter for the 1979 Pittsburgh Pirates, Nicosia's career was done in by poor speed and defensive skills. The righthanded hitter was best on offense, setting a San Francisco record with eight consecutive hits in 1984. He caught Game Seven of the 1979 World Series as a rookie./(ME)

Tom Niedenfuer — 1959– . RHP 1981– **Dodgers**, Orioles, Mariners 588 ip, 36–40, 3.28. *3 LCS, 8 ip, 0–2, 4.50. 1 WS, 5 ip, 0–0, 0.00*

By pitching well at AA San Antonio (Texas League)

during the 1981 major league baseball strike, Niedenfuer earned a promotion to the Dodgers for the second half of the season. He capped a successful rookie season with 5–2/3 scoreless postseason innings. His 94-mph fastball made him the Dodgers' bullpen stopper after Steve Howe's departure. Niedenfuer gave up two notorious homers to Ozzie Smith and Jack Clark in the final two games of the 1985 NLCS, with Clark's home run sending the Cardinals to the World Series./(TG)

Bert Niehoff — 1884–1974. 2B-1B 1913–18 Reds, **Phillies**, Cardinals, Giants 581 g, .240, 12 hr, 207 rbi. *1 WS, 5 g, .063*

Niehoff spent more than 50 years in baseball. He switched from third base to second for 1915 after the Phillies acquired him and led NL second basemen in errors, but his good range (second in the league in assists) and tolerable hitting (.238 with 21 steals and 60 runs) helped Philadelphia to the NL pennant. In 1916 he led the league with 42 doubles, led second basemen in errors and double plays, and finished second in assists again. A broken leg in mid-

Joe Niekro

1918 finished his ML career. He played, then managed in the minors, coached for the Giants, and scouted for the Yankees and Angels, retiring at age 85./(NLM)

Joe Niekro — 1944– . RHP 1967–88 Cubs, Padres, Tigers, Braves, **Astros**, Yankees, Twins 3585 ip, 221–204, 3.59. *1 LCS, 10 ip, 0–0, 0.00. 1 WS, 2 ip, 0–0, 0.00* ☛ *All-Star—79.*

The younger, underrated half of the winningest brother duo in major league history, despite decent early seasons as a starter and reliever, Joe Niekro struggled between the majors and minors before perfecting his knuckleball in the Atlanta system. Purchased by the Astros, Joe soon proved his value. In 1979, Joe and Phil tied for the NL win lead, but Joe was *TSN* NL Pitcher of the Year and runner-up in the Cy Young vote. Joe won the one-game playoff between the Astros and Dodgers in 1980, then pitched a record 10 shutout innings to a no-decision in the third game of the LCS. From 1980 to 1987, Joe, the winningest pitcher in Astros history, had

Phil Niekro

104 wins to Phil's 100. He was 5–4 head-to-head against Phil and homered off him in 1976. He was suspended during the 1987 season when found carrying a nail file in his back uniform pocket. He finally appeared in the 1987 World Series a record 19 years' and 138 days' service (over the course of 21 seasons) after beginning his big league career./(ME)

Phil Niekro (Knucksie) — 1939– . RHP 1965–87 **Braves**, Yankees, Indians, Blue Jays 5403 ip, 318–274, 3.35. *2 LCS, 14 ip, 0–1, 3.86* ☛ *All-Star—69, 75, 78, 82, 84. Gold Glove—78–80, 82–83.*

A longtime symbol of the Atlanta Braves, Phil Niekro holds many major league records, nearly all of which are as a result of his trademark pitch, the knuckleball, which kept him in the majors until he was 48. Niekro's records tend to center on longevity, durability, and unpredictability, as his reliance on the knuckler saved his arm, fooled batters, and caused catchers to consider a new occupation.

A boyhood pal of basketball Hall of Famer John Havilcek, Phil, and his younger brother Joe, came out of the Ohio River valley for 46 major league seasons. Teammates briefly on the Braves and Yankees, they would eventually combine to pass Gaylord and Jim Perry as baseball's winningest brother act in 1987, finishing with 538.

Along with Niekro's longevity, his loyalty to a floundering Atlanta franchise won him the admiration of fans and players. He contributed greatly to charitable groups in Atlanta and won the 1979 Lou Gehrig Award for his exemplary character. There was little indignation in Atlanta when Phil finally signed with the Yankees as a free agent; the consensus was that he deserved an opportunity to pitch for a contending team. Niekro's effectiveness did not falter with age and his undistinguished records reflected the ragged teams behind him more than anything. In his forties Niekro was able to fashion a 17–4 mark with Atlanta in 1982. At age 45, the gray-haired Niekro went 16–8 for the 1984 Yankees.

Niekro's statistics were compiled with little national fanfare. The 300-game winner pitched a total of 1.1 innings in two All-Star games nine years apart and was selected to only three other squads, possibly because All-Star catchers were unfamiliar with his pitch. His two LCS starts, thirteen years apart, produced no wins, and his playing 24 years without a Series appearance represents a major league mark for futility. His most celebrated game came on the final day of the 1985 season at age 46. Relying on everything except his knuckler until the final batter, former teammate Jeff Burroughs, Niekro became the thirteenth pitcher to win 300 games. He seems destined for Cooperstown. The oldest player to regularly play in the majors, Niekro's outstanding character and his ability to master the most difficult pitch will always be recognized. /(PB)

Scott Nielsen — 1958– . RHP 1986– Yankees, **White Sox** 143 ip, 9–11, 5.49

Signed out of Brigham Young by the Mariners, Nielsen recovered from 1985 arm surgery to debut with the 1986 Yankees. He led their weak staff with two shutouts. Shipped to the White Sox in January 1987, he was reacquired with Rich Dotson in November. Nielsen holds the distinction of winning a 17–0 decision over the Cleveland Indians on July 5, 1987. That equaled a White Sox club record for the widest shutout margin against an opponent. On June 9, 1988 he pitched the first nine-inning no-hitter in Columbus (International League) history, defeating Maine 3–0. /(RL)

Bob Nieman — 1927–1985. OF 1951–62 Browns, Tigers, White Sox, **Orioles**, Cardinals, Indians, Giants 1113 g, .295, 125 hr, 544 rbi. *1 WS, 1 g, --*

The only player to homer in his first two major league at-bats, Nieman accomplished that feat for the Browns at Fenway Park on September 14, 1951 against Boston's Mickey McDermott. His next time up, he beat out a bunt. The following year, he became an everyday St. Louis outfielder, reaching career highs of 18 HR and 74 RBI. He later played regularly with the Tigers and Orioles, batting a high of .325 for Baltimore in 1958. He ended his ML career as a pinch hitter for the 1962 pennant-winning Giants, then played a year in Japan. A scout for the Indians, Dodgers, A's, White Sox, and Yankees, he died suddenly while preparing to leave for spring training in March of 1985. /(JK)

Butch Nieman [Elmer LeRoy] — 1918– . OF 1943–45 Braves 332 g, .256, 37 hr, 167 rbi

A rugged lefthanded slugger for the wartime Braves, Nieman led eighth-place Boston with 16 home runs in 1944. Five of his 30 HR in 1944–45 came as a pinch hitter. /(EW)

Randy Niemann — 1955– . LHP 1979–80, 82–87 Astros, Pirates, White Sox, Mets, Twins 200 ip, 7–8, 4.64

Forkballer Niemann pitched 14 years of pro ball, but never spent a full season in the majors. He signed with the Yankees in 1975 and retired in 1988 to become a Mets minor league coach. He threw shutouts for two of his first three ML wins, with Houston in 1979. Elbow surgery in 1981 damaged his chances. He pitched for the 1986 World Champion Mets, but did not appear in postseason play. /(EW)

Tom Nieto — 1960– . C 1984– **Cardinals**, Expos, Twins, Phillies 234 g, .207, 5 hr, 65 rbi

Pitchers like Nieto behind the plate for the way he calls games and his strong arm. The Cardinals hoped he would be Darrell Porter's successor, but Nieto never came within 50 points of his .279 rookie average. His one moment in the spotlight came in Game Four of the 1987 World Series, when he surprised with a two-strike suicide-squeeze bunt that scored the final run of St. Louis' 3–0 win. /(FO)

Juan Nieves — 1965– . LHP 1986–88 **Brewers** 491 ip, 32–25, 4.71

On April 15, 1987 22-year-old Juan Nieves became the first Milwaukee Brewer and the first Puerto Rican-born pitcher to throw a no-hitter, as he blanked the Orioles 7–0 in Baltimore. Centerfielder Robin Yount made a dramatic diving catch for the last out. Many baseball observers had anticipated such a feat by Nieves. A Connecticut prep-school star with a 90-mph fastball, he was scouted by dozens of colleges and every ML club. Since he was born in Puerto Rico he did not need to go through the amateur draft. He was won over by the Brewers for a reported $150,000 signing bonus in 1983. He compiled a 33–9 record in three minor league seasons and struggled to an 11–12 rookie record in 1986, but matured in 1987, going 14–8. A shoulder injury sidelined him for two months of 1988 and all of 1989. /(JCA)

Johnny Niggeling — 1903–1963. RHP 1938–46 Braves, Reds, **Browns**, Senators 1251 ip, 64–69, 3.22

Knuckleballer Niggeling was 35 when he first reached the major leagues, throwing two innings for the Braves in 1938. He won two games as a late-season addition to the pennant-winning 1939 Reds, but did not appear in the World Series. His most successful season was 1942, when he went 15–11 for the Browns. Traded to Washington in 1943, he was one of four knuckleballers on the wartime Senators' staff. Niggeling took his own life in 1963. /(JK)

Harry Niles — 1880–1953. OF-2B-3B 1906–10 **Browns**, Yankees, Red Sox, Indians 608 g, .248, 12 hr, 152 rbi

Niles perpetrated a classic baserunning error during a 1909 Red Sox game in Washington. With lumbering Babe Danzig on first, Niles hit a shot to the outfield and began to race around the bases. Danzig, thinking the ball would be caught, stayed put, while the fleet Niles, head down, steamed past him. The ball was chased down and relayed in, but Niles never slowed, sliding home in a cloud of dust under the tag. Sure that he had hit an inside-the-park home run, he jogged nonchalantly to the bench, but was called out for passing Danzig, who was standing forlornly on second base. Niles was credited with a single. /(JK)

Al Nipper — 1959– . RHP 1983–88 **Red Sox**, Cubs 774 ip, 44–47, 4.46. *1 WS, 6 ip, 0–1, 7.11*

The junkballing Nipper was named the Red Sox' Co-Rookie Pitcher of the Year, with pal Roger Clemens in 1984, when he went 11–6. Plagued by illness and injury, he never had another winning season for Boston. He lost his 1986 World Series start against the Mets, and was pounded in relief in Game Seven. After the 1987 season, he was traded with Calvin Schiraldi (who had lost Games Six and Seven) to the Cubs for reliever Lee Smith. /(EW)

Ron Nischwitz — 1937– . LHP 1961–63, 65 **Tigers**, Indians 115 ip, 5–8, 4.21

A reliever, Nischwitz led the Tigers with 48 appearances in 1962, but was unsuccessful in 1963 after his trade to Cleveland. He later coached at Wright State University in his hometown, Dayton, OH. /(KT)

Michio Nishizawa — 1919–Unk. P-OF-1B 1937–58 **Chunichi Dragons** 1704 g, .286, 212 hr, 939 rbi
☛ Led League—hr 50.

Nishizawa was one of the most popular players Japan ever had, despite playing for the lackluster Chunichi Dragons. He rose to stardom as a pitcher in Japanese baseball's early years, but injured his arm during two years of WWII service. Despite a .196 batting average at that point, he became a position player. Demonstrating exceptional desire and dedication, he won a regular job by lifting his average into the .260 range. In 1949, while batting .309 with 114 RBI, he hit 37 home runs, which would have been a Japanese record had not Tomio Fujimura hit 45 that season. In 1950, Nishizawa topped Fujimura with 46 HR. Age and injuries slowed him some thereafter, but he batted .353 in 1952, and remained a solid-hitting regular and an RBI threat until his retirement. He later managed Chunichi. /(MC)

Al Nixon — 1886–1960. OF 1915–16, 18, 21–23, 26–28 Dodgers, **Braves**, Phillies 422 g, .277, 7 hr, 118 rbi

A reserve outfielder who batted righthanded but threw lefthanded, the 5′ 7–1/2″ Nixon once won a long-distance throwing contest with a 400-foot heave. He later umpired in the Evangeline League. /(NLM)

Donnell Nixon — 1961– . OF 1987– Mariners, **Giants** 200 g, .277, 4 hr, 33 rbi. *1 LCS, 3 g, .000. 1 WS, 2 g, .200*

The exceptionally speedy Nixon is a better hitter than older brother Otis, but the start of his ML career was delayed by injuries and by 1988 he was stuck behind Brett Butler, of similar talents, in San Francisco. /(WOR)

Otis Nixon — 1959– . OF 1983– Yankees, **Indians**, Expos 506 g, .222, 3 hr, 55 rbi

Nixon was Cleveland manager Pat Corrales's "secret weapon." Among the fastest men in baseball, he would pinch run late in close games. At the plate, the switch-hitter could only bunt or slap the ball. When the Indians failed in 1987, Nixon became a luxury and was sent down. He underwent drug rehabilitation later that year. The Expos gave him a chance in 1988, and he stole 46 bases in 271 at-bats while providing far-ranging defense in centerfield. Otis claimed to be faster than his brother, Mariners and Giants outfielder Donnell Nixon. /(JCA)

Russ Nixon — 1935– . C 1957–68 Indians, **Red Sox**, Twins 906 g, .268, 27 hr, 266 rbi.
Manager 1982–83, 88-**Reds**, Braves 206–307, .402

Twin brothers Russ and Roy Nixon were both signed by the Indians, but only Russ made it to the majors. He batted a career-high .301 as the Indians' regular catcher in 1958. In 1960, he was twice traded from Cleveland to Boston; the original March deal was called off when Sammy White refused to report, but a second trade was completed in June. Often felled by injuries, Nixon appeared in nearly a quarter of his ML games as a pinch hitter. A longtime resident of the Cincinnati area, he managed in the Reds' farm system from 1970 to 1975, joined their ML coaching staff in 1976, and replaced John McNamara as ML manager in July of 1982. Dismissed after a last-place 1983 finish, he coached for the Expos and Braves and then was named Braves manager in 1989. /(EW)

Willard Nixon — 1928– . RHP 1950–58 **Red Sox**
1234 ip, 69–72, 4.39

Although sometimes used in relief early in his career, Nixon was a regular member of the Red Sox rotation from 1954 through 1957. He won 12 games in both 1955 and 1957, enjoying particular success against the top American League clubs—especially the Yankees. He beat New York four times in '55, allowing only five runs in the four games. A competent lefthanded hitter, he batted .242 lifetime, and led all AL pitchers with a .293 average in '57. /(EW)

Ray Noble [Rafael Miguel y Magee] — 1919– . C
1951–53 **Giants** 107 g, .218, 9 hr, 40 rbi. *1 WS, 2 g, .000*

A Cuban veteran of the Negro National League, Noble capably backed up catcher Wes Westrum during the Giants' drive toward their "miracle" 1951 pennant. /(MC)

Matt Nokes — 1963– . C 1985– Giants, **Tigers** 370 g,
.265, 60 hr, 186 rbi. *1 LCS, 5 g, .143, 1 hr, 2 rbi*
☛ *All-Star—87.*

Nokes, who had come to the Tigers from the Giants, was asked in 1987 to fill the hole left when slugging catcher Lance Parrish opted for free agency. A lefthanded-hitting rookie who never had more than 14 home runs in a minor league season, Nokes blasted 32, drove in 87 runs, and batted .289 to help spark Detroit to the AL Eastern Division title. He also broke up a Tom Candiotti no-hitter in the eighth inning. His performance gained him selection to the AL All-Star and Silver Slugger teams. Though manager Sparky Anderson liked his work habits, few could deny Nokes's shortcomings as a catcher—his inexperience calling games, his erratic arm, and his often too-slow reactions. Mike Heath caught 75 of the Tigers' games in 1988. AL pitchers got the book on Nokes—throw him breaking stuff—and, without the rabbit ball of 1987, Nokes hit just .251 with 16 HR in 1988. Injuries slowed him in 1989. /(JCA)

Gary Nolan — 1948– . RHP 1967–73, 75–77 **Reds**,
Angels 1675 ip, 110–70, 3.08. *4 LCS, 27 ip, 1–0, 1.35.
4 WS, 33 ip, 1–2, 4.96*
☛ *All-Star—72.*

When Nolan reached the majors as a 19-year-old fireballer in 1967, he went 14–8 with a 2.58 ERA (fourth in the NL) and 206 strikeouts (also fourth) and led the league in strikeouts per nine innings (8.2). He finished a distant second to Tom Seaver (16–13, 2.76, 170 strikeouts) in the NL Rookie of the Year voting, and thereafter his achievements were reduced by frequent injuries.

Arm problems reduced Nolan's playing time in 1968 and 1969, although he didn't go on the DL. He lost a bit off his fastball but was still one of the league's hardest throwers, and he began to improve his control. In 1970 he was 18–7 with a 3.26 ERA as the Reds won the NL pennant, and he pitched nine innings of shutout ball in Game One of the LCS against Pittsburgh, winning after the Reds scored three in the top of the tenth inning. He was hit hard by the Orioles in both his World Series starts and took the loss in the opener.

Nolan dropped off to 12–15 in 1971 despite a 3.16 ERA, but won 13 before the 1972 All-Star break to earn a spot on the NL squad. He was suffering neck and shoulder problems by that point, however, skipped the All-Star Game, and finished the year at 15–5, 1.99. He led the NL in winning percentage and was second to Steve Carlton in ERA. In the LCS, against Pittsburgh once again, he had to leave Game Three with a 2–1 lead after six innings when his arm tightened, and the Reds' bullpen lost the game. In the World Series against Oakland he lost Game One 3–2 and couldn't last five innings in Game Six despite a big lead (the Reds won 8–1).

More arm problems forced him to miss most of 1973 and all of the 1974 campaign, but he made yet another comeback in 1975. He had become the consummate control pitcher, leading the NL in fewest walks per nine innings (1.24) while going 15–9 with a 3.16 ERA. The postseason was another disappointment, as he was hit hard by the Red Sox in the WS.

Nolan's 1976 season was a virtual duplicate of 1975: he went 15–9 again, with a 3.46 ERA, and once again paced the NL in fewest walks per nine innings with an amazing 1.02, just 27 bases on balls in 239 innings. He also won his first WS game, beating the Yankees 7–2 in the finale of a four-game sweep. Arm miseries struck again in 1977, finally ending his career. He finished with a .611 lifetime winning percentage. /(SH)

Joe Nolan — 1951– . C 1972, 75, 77–85 Mets,
Braves, Reds, Orioles 621 g, .263, 27 hr, 178 rbi. *1 LCS,
1 g, .000. 1 WS, 2 g, .000*

One of the few catchers to wear glasses, Nolan rejected a football scholarship to the University of Missouri to sign with the Mets. A second-stringer, in 1981 he batted .309 and caught a career-high 81 games for Cincinnati in place of an injured Johnny Bench. He had four knee operations in nine years. /(EW)

Dickie Noles — 1956- . RHP 1979-88 Phillies, **Cubs**, Rangers, Indians, Tigers, Orioles 859 ip, 36-52, 4.56. *1 LCS, 3 ip, 0-0, 0.00. 1 WS, 5 ip, 0-0, 1.93*

Noles was ineffective both as a starter and in relief for five different teams in his nine ML seasons, and was hurt as much by his problems with alcohol as he was by opposing batters. He pitched well in the WS for the Phillies in 1980, allowing only one run to the Royals in Game Four after starter Larry Christenson was knocked out in the first inning, and in 1982 he won a career-high 10 games for the Cubs. /(SCL)

Eric Nolte — 1964- . LHP 1987- **Padres** 79 ip, 2-6, 4.20

Nolte saw the most action with the 1987 Padres, going 2-6 with a 3.21 ERA as a starter. /(JFC)

Katsuya Nomura — 1934- . C 1954-80 **Nankai Hawks**, Seibu Lions

Nomura was the winner of nine consecutive home run titles in Japan from 1962 through 1971, but his slugging feats were tainted by the small size of his home park, Nankai's Osaka Stadium—280 feet down the lines, 350 feet to centerfield. Consistent and durable, he often caught every game of the season. He recorded career highs of 52 HR and 135 RBI in 1963. In 1966, he convinced pitcher Masanori Murakami to return to Nankai after Murakami's successful 1965 season with the San Francisco Giants; for that, Nomura became a national hero. He served as Nankai's player-manager late in his career, and played 28 years, the longest career of any Japanese player. /(MC)

Jerry Nops — 1875-1937. LHP 1896-1901 Phillies, **Baltimore (NL)**, Dodgers, Baltimore (AL) 988 ip, 71-41, 3.70. 20 wins: 97

Nops was only 22 in 1897, but was one of Baltimore's three 20-game winners (20-6, 2.81.) Five years later he was out of the ML. /(DAS)

Wayne Nordhagen — 1948- . OF-DH-C 1976-83 **White Sox**, Blue Jays, Pirates, Cubs 502 g, .282, 39 hr, 205 rbi

Nordhagen had limited range as an outfielder and saw mostly reserve duty. In 1980, the only year in which he played regularly, he hit 15 home runs for the White Sox. He had a strong arm and caught 25 ML games; he is one of the few players to pitch and catch for the same club in the same year (1979). His 1982 trade from the Blue Jays to the Pirates was canceled after one game when he developed back spasms. With Toronto, he led AL pinch hitters in 1982 with a .423 average (11-for-26). /(EW)

Irv Noren — 1924- . OF-1B 1950-60 Senators, **Yankees**, A's, Cardinals, Cubs, Dodgers 1093 g, .275, 65 hr, 453 rbi. *3 WS, 11 g, .148, 2 rbi*
☛ *All-Star—54.*

A Dodger farmhand in the late 1940s who never made the talent-rich Brooklyn team, Noren played for the Yankees in the 1952, 1953, and 1955 World Series against the Dodgers. A lefthanded contact hitter and an excellent fielder, he was named to the All-Star team in 1954 when hit .319 as the Yankees' left fielder. He hit his career-high 14 home runs as a Senator rookie in 1950, and tied a since-broken AL record for most putouts in a game by an outfielder with 11 (9/25/51). Noren often played in pain from chronic knee problems. He played for the Chicago Gears of the NBA. /(EW)

Fred Norman — 1942- . LHP 1962-64, 66-67, 70-80 A's, Cubs, Dodgers, Cardinals, Padres, **Reds**, Expos 1939 ip, 104-103, 3.64. *3 LCS, 13 ip, 1-0, 6.10. 2 WS, 10 ip, 0-1, 6.10*

The 5'8" 155-lb Norman took a long time to stick, always having to prove a little more to make up for his stature. He pitched in 14 cities in his first 11 pro seasons, and it wasn't until 1972-73 with San Diego that he started two consecutive seasons in the same city. The Padres didn't have many good pitchers, and they stuck with him after acquiring him in June 1971 despite his 3-12 record; his 3.33 ERA for San Diego showed that he wasn't pitching that poorly. He went 9-11, 3.44 in 1972, his first full season in the majors, and six of his wins were shutouts, third in the NL. When Norman started 1973 1-7, Cincinnati, always short of solid pitching, acquired him for almost nothing. He went 12-6 the rest of the way to help the Reds to a second consecutive division championship. He pitched one-run ball for five innings in Game Four of the NLCS as the Reds won in twelve innings.

Norman went on to have five straight winning seasons for the Reds, including a 12-4, 3.73 record in 1975 followed by 12-7, 3.10 in 1976. He got his sole postseason victory in the 1975 LCS, winning Game Two 6-1. In 1978, he set a since-broken ML record by making 31 starts without a complete game. After going 11-13 for the Reds in 1979, he closed out his career as a relief pitcher and spot starter for the Expos. /(SH)

Jim Norris — 1948- . OF-DH-1B 1977-80 **Indians**, Rangers 489 g, .264, 7 hr, 110 rbi

Without great talent, Norris hustled his way into Cleveland's 1977 outfield, leading the club with 26 stolen bases and receiving the Indians' "10th Player Award." His early career was hampered by eight injuries, which cost him 66 weeks in casts. /(ME)

Leo Norris — 1908– . SS-2B 1936–37 **Phillies** 270 g, .262, 20 hr, 112 rbi

A home run hitter for three years in Minneapolis's (American Association) cozy ballpark, Norris started at shortstop as a rookie for the last-place Phillies in 1936 (.265, 11 HR, 76 RBI), but had his career cut short by a beaning. /(NLM)

Mike Norris — 1955– . RHP 1975–83 **A's** 1097 ip, 57–59, 3.91. 20 wins: 80 *1 LCS, 7 ip, 0–1, 3.68* ☛ *All-Star—81. Gold Glove—80–81.*

Norris was a brilliant pitcher for one season, but drug problems sidetracked his career. The San Francisco native shut out the White Sox in his first ML start in 1975. After four faltering years, Norris went 22–9 in 1980 under new manager Billy Martin as the A's finished a surprising second. Norris was probably the best pitcher in the league that year, but lost a close Cy Young vote to Baltimore's Steve Stone. Norris lead the AL in fewest hits per nine innings (6.8), tied for second in wins, and was second in ERA (2.54), complete games (24), and innings (284). He declined somewhat in 1981, but his 12–9, 3.75 performance helped the A's win the first half of the strike-split season. Norris pitched a four-hit shutout in the first game of the division playoff, working out of two bases-loaded jams, as the A's swept the Royals. He took a tough 3–1 loss in the opener of the LCS, allowing all three Yankee runs in the first inning.

Drug use and arm fatigue took their toll in the next two seasons, and Norris was made persona non grata on the major league level. He pitched for the rest of the decade with the independent San Jose Bees, always attempting to be reinstated. /(SFS)

Billy North — 1948– . OF 1971–81 Cubs, **A's**, Dodgers, Giants 1169 g, .261, 20 hr, 230 rbi. *3 LCS, 11 g, .029, 1 rbi. 2 WS, 9 g, .080, 2 rbi*

The speedy North had a four-year run as one of the premier centerfielders in the game. After the A's acquired him in November 1972 for Bob Locker, North posted stolen-base totals of 53, 54, 30, and 75, leading the AL in 1974 and 1976 and finishing second in 1973. He turned an unassisted double play on July 28, 1974 against the White Sox. North also utilized his speed in the field to lead AL outfielders three times in total chances per game, twice in putouts, and once each in assists and double plays.

A good leadoff hitter, he walked often and scored a career-high 98 runs in 1973, when he also had his highest batting average, .285. In 1974, despite a LCS average of .063 and a WS average of .059, North was productive, scoring three runs in each series. Hampered by hand, foot, and ankle injuries in 1977, he was traded to the Dodgers after a slow start in 1978. Granted free agency after another disappointing season, he returned to form with the Giants in 1979, hitting .259 and finishing second in the NL in steals (58) and fourth in walks (96). The 58 steals were a San Francisco record, and North missed the overall franchise mark of 62 because injuries kept him out of 20 games. After a similar season in 1980, he tailed off in 1981. /(JFC)

Lou North — 1891–1974. RHP 1913, 17, 20–24 Tigers, **Cardinals**, Braves 463 ip, 21–16, 4.43

One of the first pitchers to work primarily as a reliever, North led the NL with 7 saves in 1921 and 53 appearances in 1922. /(NLM)

Ron Northey (The Round Man) — 1920–1971. OF 1942–44, 46–50, 52, 55–57 **Phillies**, Cardinals, Reds, Cubs, White Sox, Phillies 1084 g, .276, 108 hr, 513 rbi

Northey was a beefy lefthanded hitter, a slow-moving outfielder with an exceptionally strong arm. Dodger outfielder Carl Furillo claims that he and Northey were the only two players to hit the famous sign on Ebbets Field's right-field wall and win a free suit from Abe Stark. Northey had his best season with the 1944 Phillies, hitting 22 HR with 104 RBI, and leading NL outfielders with 24 assists. Gone from the majors by 1951, he returned to become a top pinch hitter, leading the AL with 15 hits in that role for Chicago in 1956. He had nine career pinch-hit home runs, three of them grand slams—a ML record. Altogether, he hit eight grand slams in his career. His son Scott played OF with the Royals in 1969. /(JL)

Jim Northrup (The Gray Fox) — 1939– . OF-1B 1964–75 **Tigers**, Expos, Orioles 1392 g, .267, 153 hr, 610 rbi. *1 LCS, 5 g, .357, 1 rbi. 1 WS, 7 g, .250, 2 hr, 8 rbi*

Northrup declined offers to play quarterback for the Chicago Bears and New York Titans to sign with the Tigers. A classic streak hitter and one of Detroit's best in the clutch during the 1960s, he played right and center in a talented but crowded outfield that included Al Kaline, Willie Horton, and Mickey Stanley. In their 1968 World Championship season, he led the Tigers with 153 hits and 90 RBI, and broke up three no-hitters in April and May. He hit four grand slams that year. Two came in consecutive at-bats on June 24, and he added another on June 29 for three in one week, a ML record. He hit yet another off the Cardinals' Larry Jaster in Game Six of the World Series. His two-run triple was the crucial blow in Game Seven. On August 28, 1969 against Oakland, he became the first Tiger since Ty Cobb to go six-for-six, finishing the game with a 13th-inning home run over the Tiger Stadium roof. In 1973, he had a second eight-RBI game, against Texas, and hit a career-high .307. Dealt twice in 1974, he retired a year later. /(KT)

Willie Norwood — 1950– . OF-DH 1977–80 **Twins** 294 g, .242, 18 hr, 93 rbi

Norwood stole 25 bases in 1978, his only year as a regular, but committed a Twins-record 14 errors in left field. /(NLM)

Joe Nossek — 1940– . OF 1964–67, 69–70 Twins, **A's**, Cardinals 295 g, .228, 3 hr, 53 rbi. *1 WS, 6 g, .200*

Nossek was a backup outfielder and pinch hitter who hit .218 in 87 games for the 1965 AL champion Twins. Traded to the A's in 1966, he had by far his best year, batting .261 with 27 RBI in 230 at-bats while going 8-for-17 in the pinch. He declined to .205 in 1967 and was used sparingly thereafter. /(SFS)

Don Nottebart — 1936– . RHP 1960–67, 69 Braves, **Astros**, Reds, Yankees, Cubs 928 ip, 36–51, 3.65

Nottebart broke in with the Braves as a competent reliever who could spot-start and was acquired by the fledgling Colt .45s for 1963. He had his best season, going 11–8 with a 3.17 ERA as Houston's third starter, and on May 17 he no-hit the Phillies, walking two and winning 4–1. Nottebart slumped to 6–11, 3.90 in 1964 and then to 4–15, 4.67 in 1965. The Reds picked him up and returned him to the bullpen, and he had two more decent seasons, going 5–4 with 11 saves and a 3.07 ERA in 1966, and 0–3, 1.93, with four saves in 1967. /(JFC)

Lou Novikoff (The Mad Russian) — 1915–1970. OF 1941–44, 46 **Cubs**, Phillies 356 g, .282, 15 hr, 138 rbi

A four-time minor league batting champion and *TSN* Minor League Player of the Year in 1939, Novikoff could hit, but was a butcher in the outfield. He had trouble locating fly balls, and would leap at a line drive and appear to wrestle it to the ground. A wartime Cub fill-in and an entertaining, storytelling

eccentric, he feared touching Wrigley Field's ivy-covered walls. He once stole third with the bases loaded because, he said, "I got such a good jump on the pitcher." Known for a prodigious appetite, he was assisted by his pet Russian wolfhound, which reputedly dined only on caviar. Novikoff, who had played softball as Lou Nova, went back to the game after he retired from baseball. He played until he was fifty-three, and was inducted into the Softball Hall of Fame. /(JK)

Wynn Noyes — 1889–1969. RHP 1913, 17, 19 Braves, **A's**, White Sox 247 ip, 11–15, 3.76

Noyes saw his only significant action in 1917 with the last-place Athletics, going 10–10 with a 2.95 ERA. He was the only staff member with 40 or more innings who didn't have a losing record. He was unable to come back after his 1918 military service. /(WOR)

Gerry Nugent — Unk.–Unk. *Executive.*

A furniture salesman and avid Phillies fan, Nugent married the secretary of Phillies owner William F. Baker in 1925. He was so full of suggestions for the club that Baker hired him to work in the office. Four years later Baker died and left Mrs. Nugent substantial ownership of the club. Nugent became president in 1932 and remained until he sold the team in 1941. He never had a winner, nor any money to work with, and had to sell players each year to finance the next spring training. /(NLM)

Les Nunamaker — 1889–1938. C 1911–22 Red Sox, **Yankees**, Browns, Indians 715 g, .268, 2 hr, 215 rbi. *1 WS, 2 g, .500*

Nunamaker was the Yankees' number-one catcher for three and a half seasons, 1914–17. His best year was 1916, when he hit .296 with career highs of 14 doubles and 25 runs scored. In January 1918 he was traded with Fritz Maisel, Nick Cullop, Urban Shocker, and Joe Gedeon to the Browns for Hall of Famer Eddie Plank, Del Pratt, and $15,000. He spent the rest of his career as a backup. Despite his 6'2" 190-lb frame, the catcher won medals in the 220– and 440-yard dash. /(NLM)

Edwin Nunez — 1963– . RHP 1982– **Mariners**, Mets, Tigers 397 ip, 19–25, 4.15

Nunez was signed by the Mariners as a sixteen-year-old from Puerto Rico. When he first played in the majors in 1982, the eighteen-year-old Nunez became the youngest player to appear for the Mariners. Over the next half-dozen seasons Nunez showed sustained periods of excellence between frequent trips to the disabled list. By the time the Mariners traded him to the Mets midway through the 1988 season, Nunez was third in career saves as a Mariner and fourth in games. /(TF)

Jose Nunez — 1964– . RHP 1987– **Blue Jays** 137 ip, 5–3, 4.40

This Dominican went 5–2 in 1987, mostly in middle relief, on the strength of the Blue Jays' ability that year to come from behind. /(WOR)

Joe Nuxhall — 1928– . LHP 1944, 52–66 **Reds**, A's, Angels 2303 ip, 135–117, 3.90
☛ *All-Star—55–56.*

The youngest player of the 20th century to reach the majors, Nuxhall was an exceptionally promising schoolboy pitcher, signed by the Reds with special permission from his school principal. He was 15 years, 10 months, and 11 days old on June 10, 1944, when manager Bill McKechnie sent him in to pitch the ninth inning of a game hopelessly lost to the Cardinals. He yielded five runs on two hits and five walks, while retiring only two batters. He pitched seven years in the minors to earn a second chance and returned to the Reds in 1952. He won a career-high 17 games in 1955, leading the league with five shutouts, and pitching 3–1/3 scoreless innings in the All-Star Game. He began having arm trouble in 1960, was traded to the A's in 1961, and hooked on with the Angels briefly in 1962. A lifetime .198 batter with 15 home runs, in 1961 he hit .292 and contemplated continuing his career as a pinch hitter/first baseman. But he bounced back as a pitcher, returning to the Reds for the 1962 stretch drive and going 5–0. In 1963, he was 15–8, with a career-low 2.61 ERA. Nuxhall retired just before Opening Day 1967, to make room on the roster for rookie Gary Nolan and become a Reds broadcaster. /(MC)

Rich Nye — 1944– . LHP 1966–70 **Cubs**, Expos, Cardinals 478 ip, 26–31, 3.71

As a rookie in 1967, 6′4″ Rich Nye went 13–10 (3.20) to help the Cubs climb out of the second division for the first time since 1946. He followed with three lackluster seasons and returned to college to study veterinary medicine. /(ARA)

Jerry Nyman — 1942– . LHP 1968–70 **White Sox**, Padres 110 ip, 6–7, 4.58

Nyman showed promise in his first call-up with the White Sox, going 2–1 with a 2.01 ERA in seven starts and one relief outing, but went 4–4, 5.29 in 1969 and was bombed in two starts with the Padres in 1970. /(JFC)

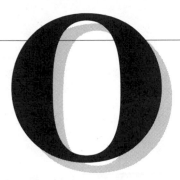

Rebel Oakes [Ennis Telflair] — 1886–1948. OF 1909–15 Reds, **Cardinals**, Pittsburgh (FL) 985 g, .279, 15 hr, 397 rbi.
    Manager 1914–15 **Pittsburgh (FL)** 144–141, .505

A substantial centerfielder who never played fewer than 120 games a season, Rebel had his best years with the Bresnahan-Huggins Cardinals, then jumped to the Federal League at age 27 as the league's youngest manager. /(ADS)

Oakland A's — 1968– . Team. 1811–1690, .517. *AL West Champions 71–75, 81, 88–89 AL Champions 72–74, 88–89 World Champions 72–74*

Charlie Finley moved the A's to Oakland in 1968 hoping to duplicate the Western success stories of the Dodgers, Giants, and Angels. Attendance in Kansas City was bad for the most obvious reason: the A's had finished in last place in three of the previous four seasons.

    The team won in Oakland, but success at the gate was still elusive. Although the farm system was delivering stars each season and the club won five straight division crowns beginning in 1971 (following second-place finishes in 1969 and 1970), home attendance didn't pass one million until 1973. It dropped back to six figures the following season, as the A's won their third consecutive World Series.

    Finley certainly did everything he could to get attention for his team: orange baseballs; a wide variety of multi-colored uniforms, some assigned to specific days of the week; Herb Washington, the pinch-running specialist; a constantly changing procession of managers and fights with managers; encouraging players to grow mustaches; and colorful stars such as Reggie Jackson, Vida Blue, and Rollie Fingers. But competing with the Giants across the bay for customers, the team couldn't draw. In the face of free agency's higher costs and a rosterful of stars who hated Finley and saw their chance to escape, Finley dismantled the team as much as Commissioner Bowie Kuhn would let him, and sold it after manager Billy Martin led the club to a division championship in the strike-distorted 1981 season. Sold to area businessmen, the team was rebuilt in the 1980s to become, by the end of the decade, the powerhouse of the division, featuring sluggers Jose Canseco and Mark McGwire, speedster Rickey Henderson, local hero Dave Stewart, and bullpen ace Dennis Eckersley. /(SH)

Oakland-Alameda County Coliseum Oakland A's 1968– . LF-330, CF-397, RF-330

A simple bowl-shaped stadium with a three-level grandstand and outfield bleachers, the Oakland Coliseum was built in 1965 adjacent to an indoor arena, and in 1968 it became home to the A's, who had moved from Kansas City. A natural grass field with normal dimensions, the Coliseum has vast foul territory along both lines that favors pitchers, as many pop fouls that would land in the seats in any other stadium are caught for outs. The Coliseum's light standards are mounted on tall support poles high above the stadium, rather than on the stadium's rim itself, and the park is much more accessible by freeway than public transportation. It became more popularly known as the Oakland Mausoleum in the late 1970s, when the A's had slipped to last place and the drab, gray stadium was largely devoid of spectators. An April 17, 1979 game against the Mariners attracted 650 fans. /(SCL)

Johnny Oates — 1946– . C 1970, 72–81 Orioles, **Braves**, Phillies, Dodgers, Yankees 593 g, .250, 14 hr, 126 rbi. *1 LCS, 1 g, .000. 2 WS, 2 g, .500*

Oates, a lefthanded batter, was platooned his first four seasons but was a backup from 1976 on. In his best season, he drove in 27 runs; he was kept for his defense. He backed up Steve Yeager with Los Angeles in the 1977–78 World Series. /(PB)

Ken Oberkfell (Obie) — 1956– . 3B-2B 1977- **Cardinals**, Braves, Pirates, Giants 1431 g, .281, 28 hr, 410 rbi. *2 LCS, 6 g, .158, 2 rbi. 2 WS, 11 g, .300, 1 rbi*

A line-drive hitter with little long-ball power, Oberkfell twice batted above .300 and was not prone to slumps. A tough and durable player, he averaged 130 games per season despite knee surgery, a broken thumb, and an elbow injury.

    Signed as a shortstop, Oberkfell came up with the Cardinals as a second baseman. Later he moved to third base to make room for Tommy Herr. His glove proved adequate, as he led the league at both

The 1973 Oakland A's

positions in fielding average. Atlanta acquired him during the 1984 campaign to replace the injured Bob Horner at third. With Horner mended, the Braves opted to continue with the steady Oberkfell, moving Horner to first base. Pittsburgh traded Tommy Gregg to acquire Oberkfell for the 1988 stretch run; the Giants acquired him for 1989 and he led the NL with 18 pinch hits. /(FO)

Buck O'Brien [Thomas Joseph] — 1882–1959. RHP 1911–13 **Red Sox**, White Sox 432 ip, 29–25, 2.63. 20 wins: 12 *1 WS, 9 ip, 0–2, 7.00*

O'Brien went 20–13 for Boston's 1912 World Champions. Sold to the White Sox in 1913, from the Massachusetts native's perspective, they "might just as well have shipped me to Hawaii." He left the major leagues after six more games. /(EC)

Eddie O'Brien — 1930– . SS-OF 1953, 55–58 **Pirates** 231 g, .236, 0 hr, 25 rbi

The embodiment of the pitiful Pirates of 1946 to 1957 was the set of identical twin brothers, Johnny and Eddie O'Brien. Both had been business majors at Seattle University. Branch Rickey signed them each to a $40,000 bonus contract to be Pittsburgh's double-play combination. The pair debuted in 1953, then served in the military in 1954. Eddie's light bat was tried everywhere, including pitcher.

The fun-loving brothers derived great pleasure from confusing managers, and the Topps baseball card company, as to who was who; Topps solved the problem one year by putting both of them on one card. Both became successful out of baseball, Johnny as a King County (Washington) commissioner and then head of security at the Kingdome and Eddie as an energy consultant in Alaska. Eddie was also athletic director at Seattle University (1958–1968) and a coach for the 1969 Seattle Pilots. /(ME)

Jack O'Brien — 1873–1933. OF 1899, 1901, 03 **Washington (NL)**, Senators, Indians, Red Sox 326 g, .259, 9 hr, 133 rbi. *1 WS, 2 g, .000*

A journeyman outfielder at the turn of the century, O'Brien was used twice as a pinch hitter by the Red Sox in the first World Series without a hit. /(BC)

Johnny O'Brien — 1930– . 2B-RHP 1953, 55–59 **Pirates**, Cardinals, Braves 339 g, .250, 4 hr, 59 rbi; 61 ip, 1–3, 5.61

Johnny and Eddie O'Brien, baseball's only twins, came up together with the 1953 Pirates, with Johnny the second baseman of the family double-play combination; they each played in 89 games that season, each spent the following season in the military, and each came back up in 1955. They both tried pitching; Johnny was both the better pitcher (although his record was worse) and hitter (.299 in 1955). He was an All-American basketball player at Seattle University. /(WOR)

Pete O'Brien — 1958- . 1B 1982- **Rangers**, Indians 1101 g, .271, 126 hr, 542 rbi

O'Brien made himself into a reliable hitter with some power and a knack for getting on base. He constantly changes his batting stance during the hot and cold periods he experiences within each season, but his season totals are consistent. From 1984 to 1988 he hit between 16 and 23 home runs. He had a high of 92 RBI in 1985, but has generally been in lineups where he had few RBI opportunities and wasn't driven in by those behind him. O'Brien is one of the best fielders in the league, and he led AL first basemen in assists in 1983 and 1987. When he started three double plays in a game on May 22, 1984, it tied the ML record for first base. He was traded to Cleveland with Oddibe McDowell and Jerry Browne in the blockbuster deal that brought Julio Franco to Texas. /(SH)

Syd O'Brien — 1944- . 3B-SS-2B 1969-72 Red Sox, White Sox, **Angels**, Brewers 378 g, .230, 24 hr, 100 rbi

A poor fielder, O'Brien played on four clubs in his four major league years. He exemplified the ghastly 1970 White Sox, who lost a club-record 106 games, by committing 23 errors at second and third base in just 111 games for a .948 fielding average. /(RL)

Tom O'Brien — 1873-1901. OF-1B 1897-1900 Baltimore (NL), **Pirates**, Giants 427 g, .278, 10 hr, 229 rbi

A Pirate for most of his career, O'Brien became a New York favorite when he was loaned to the Giants in 1899. He later fell ill on a trip to Cuba and died of typhoid and pneumonia. /(ME)

Tommy O'Brien (Obie, Pigskin) — 1918-1978. OF 1943-45, 49-50 **Pirates**, Red Sox, Senators 293 g, .277, 8 hr, 78 rbi

A pinch hitter and little-used outfielder with the wartime Pirates, O'Brien batted .335 in 1945. He hit .359 at Birmingham (Southern Association) in 1948 to earn another major league shot, but again saw limited action. /(ME)

Hiromitsu Ochai — 1953- . **Lotte Orions**, Chunichi Dragons
☛ *Led League—ba 82, 85-86. Led League—hr 82, 85-86. Led League—rbi 82, 85-86.*

Ochai and Leron Lee became one of the top slugging duos in Lotte Orions history. Ochai won Japan's Pacific League triple crown in 1982, hitting .367 with 32 homers and 99 RBI. He collected a second triple crown in 1985, again hitting .367, with 52 HR and a Japanese baseball record 146 RBI—more than one per game. He followed with 50 HR, 116 RBI, and a .364 average for a third triple crown in 1986, but was traded interleague to the Chunichi Dragons for 1987. His $812,500 contract made him the highest-paid Japanese player ever. /(MC)

Danny O'Connell — 1927-1969. 2B-3B-SS 1950, 53-59, 61-62 Pirates, **Braves**, Giants, Senators 1143 g, .260, 39 hr, 320 rbi

Branch Rickey upset Pittsburgh fans when he traded O'Connell, a hustling and intelligent infielder, to the Braves in 1953. O'Connell became Milwaukee's second baseman for three seasons. Though he was considered the weak link in their awesome offense, on June 13, 1956, he tied a major league record with three triples in a game. He played with the Giants from June 1957 until his demotion in 1959, resurfaced with the new Washington Senators for 1961 and '62, then coached them for two seasons. He died in an auto accident in 1969. /(ME)

Jimmy O'Connell — 1901-1976. OF 1923-24 **Giants** 139 g, .270, 8 hr, 57 rbi. *1 WS, 2 g, .000*

Claiming that coach Cozy Dolan and all the Giants were behind it, O'Connell confessed to offering Phillies shortstop Heinie Sand $500 to throw a game in 1924. Sand had turned him down and reported it; the other Giants denied their involvement. Dolan and O'Connell, for whom New York had paid $75,000 two years earlier, were banned from baseball for life. /(NLM)

Jack O'Connor — 1958- . LHP 1981-85, 87 **Twins**, Expos, Orioles 318 ip, 14-17, 4.89

O'Connor's only winning record came in his first season, when he went 3-2, 5.91 in 28 relief appearances for the Twins. He was moved into the rotation in 1982 and went 8-9 with a 4.29 ERA. /(WOR)

Hank O'Day — 1863-1935. RHP-OF 1884-90 Toledo (AA), Pittsburgh (AA), **Washington (NL)**, Giants, New York (PL) 232 g, .190, 1 hr, 43 rbi; 1633 ip, 71-112, 3.79. *Umpire* NL 1893-1927 *10 WS*

One of the most famous umpires, O'Day spent most of his playing career as a pitcher, suffering three 20-loss seasons. His best year was his last, when he had a 23-15 record for New York of the Players' League in 1890. He umpired for 35 years in the NL, only two fewer than Bill Klem. Only Klem worked in more WS than O'Day's ten. Tom Connolly and O'Day were chosen to umpire the first WS in 1903. In a career that spanned five decades, perhaps O'Day's two most memorable incidents occurred in 1908, when he was the senior umpire who called Fred Merkle's blunder, and in 1920, when he was the second-base umpire as Bill Wambsganss executed the only unassisted triple play in WS history./(RTM)

Ken O'Dea — 1913–1985. C 1935–46 Cubs, Giants, **Cardinals**, Braves 832 g, .255, 40 hr, 323 rbi. *5 WS, 10 g, .462, 1 hr, 6 rbi*

O'Dea spent his career as a lefthanded pinch hitter and backup to three star catchers: Gabby Hartnett with the Cubs; Harry Danning with the Giants; and Walker Cooper with the Cardinals. He led the NL with 42 pinch-hit appearances for New York in 1941. In five World Series, he went 6-for-13, including a since-tied record three pinch hits./(JK)

Billy O'Dell (Digger) — 1933– . LHP 1954, 56–67 Orioles, **Giants**, Braves, Pirates 1817 ip, 105–100, 3.29. *1 WS, 12 ip, 0–1, 4.38*

Nicknamed Digger after a comic character from the radio show "The Life of Riley," O'Dell was an eccentric lantern-jawed extrovert. A gentleman farmer from South Carolina, he bragged more about his quail shooting than his pitching, and at times kept opponents from stealing his catcher's sign by throwing what he wished. He went 19–14 for the 1962 NL champion Giants, then lost the World Series opener to the Yankees. He relieved in more than half his ML games and was the Braves' bullpen ace in 1965, when he saved 18 and won a league-high 10 in relief./(JK)

Tiny O'Dell [John Francis] — 1899–Unk. LHP

O'Dell was 6'6" at the age of 17, and the star of the Butterfield, Arkansas town team. On April 1, 1916, O'Dell and a team of local amateurs played an exhibition game against the World Champion Red Sox, who held their spring training in nearby Hot Springs. O'Dell held Boston to four hits and one run, and went 4-for-4, doubling twice off starter Smokey Joe Wood and hitting a game-winning, ninth-inning homer off Babe Ruth. He was offered a contract on the spot, but declined without giving a reason. Less than two weeks later, he was walking along the railroad tracks to a game in a neighboring town

when he was struck by a train, losing his left arm from the elbow down. Shortly after his release from the hospital, he left town and vanished into anonymity./(BS)

Blue Moon Odom [Johnny Lee] — 1945– . RHP 1964–76 **A's**, Indians, Braves, White Sox 1509 ip, 84–85, 3.70. *3 LCS, 22 ip, 2–0, 0.40. 3 WS, 17 ip, 1–1, 2.08* ☛ *All-Star—68, 69.*

A lean, righthanded starter for the A's in both Kansas City and Oakland, the highly-touted Odom made his ML debut only three months after graduating high school in 1964, but did not reach the ML for good until 1966. A's owner Charlie Finley ordered the 19-year-old Odom into the starting rotation at the end of 1964, and he made five starts, pitching one shutout but lasting only eight innings total in the other four, and recording a 10.06 ERA. Odom spent spent most of 1965 and parts of 1966 and 1967 in the minors, but made the AL All-Star team in 1968, finishing 16–10 with a 2.45 ERA. Odom was 15–6, 2.92 as Oakland's third starter in 1969, and made the All-Star team for the second consecutive year, but was shelled for five runs while retiring only one batter in the All-Star Game.

Elbow problems began to hamper Odom at the end of 1969 and throughout 1970, then after an off-season in 1971 he was 15–6 again in 1972, helping Oakland to the first of three consecutive World Championships. He was dazzling in the LCS, shutting out the Tigers on three hits in Game Two and allowing a single unearned run in the deciding Game Five, and in the WS he lost Game Three to the Reds 1–0 and allowed only one run while getting no decision in Game Seven. Odom slumped to 5–12, 4.49 in 1973, and spent most of 1974 in the bullpen before being traded to the Indians with cash for Dick Bosman and Jim Perry in 1975, then was traded to the Braves for Roric Harrison three weeks later. His ERA was 7.22 in 1975, and he spent his final ML season with the White Sox in 1976, winning only two of eight starts. One, however, was against the A's on July 28, when he combined with reliever Francisco Barrios to pitch a no-hitter./(SCL)

John O'Donoghue — 1939– . LHP 1963–71 **A's**, Indians, Orioles, Pilots/Brewers, Expos 750 ip, 39–55, 4.08 ☛ *All-Star—65..*

Despite five mediocre minor league seasons, O'Donoghue became the winningest starter for the cellar-dwelling A's of 1964–65, winning 19 and losing 32, with a league-high 18 losses in '65. He was later effective as a late-inning set-up man and occasional closer for the Seattle Pilots in 1969, saving six and winning two in relief. /(FJO)

Lefty O'Doul [Francis Joseph] — 1897–1969. OF-LHP 1919–20, 22–23, 28–34 Yankees, Red Sox, Giants, Phillies, **Dodgers**, 970 g, .349, 113 hr, 542 rbi; 78 ip, 1–1, 4.87. *1 WS, 1 g, 1.000, 2 rbi*
☛ *Led League—ba 29, 32. All-Star— 33.*

In New York, O'Doul was called The Man in the Green Suit, exploiting an Irish-sounding name of French origin. But he was a hero in his home town of San Francisco, where his fame lives on through Lefty O'Doul's Bar. He spent most of his career in the Pacific Coast League, first as a 12–8 pitcher in 1918. Sore-armed, he saw little action while with the Yankees in 1919, 1920, and 1922, but went 25–9 for San Francisco (PCL) in 1921. He earned his two major league decisions as a Red Sox reliever in 1923. Then his arm went dead. He returned to the

Lefty O'Doul

PCL, where he pitched unsuccessfully in 1924 and began his second career, as an outfielder, to make use of his great natural hitting ability.

With Salt Lake, Hollywood, and San Francisco (PCL) from 1924–27, O'Doul batted between .338 and .392, and hit with power. He was an OF for the Giants in 1928 before being traded to the Phillies, with cash, for the more-established Fred Leach—a lifetime .307 hitter. Playing in 154 games for Philadelphia in 1929, O'Doul had 32 home runs, and set a National League record with 254 hits, batting .398 to win the NL batting crown. He hit .383 in 1930, then was traded to Brooklyn in a five-player deal. His .368 average in 1932 again won him the NL batting title. After spending 1934 with the Giants, he returned, at age 37, to the PCL.

O'Doul managed the San Francisco Seals from 1935–51 (and other PCL teams through 1957), pitching and pinch hitting some, and becoming a renowned teacher of young players. He sent Joe DiMaggio up to the Yankees, claiming the most significant thing he did for his fellow San Franciscan was to change nothing. Making annual visits to Japan in the 1930s as a baseball ambassador of good will, he became an idol of fans there. He took the attack on Pearl Harbor as a personal affront. O'Doul died in San Francisco on December 7, 1969. /(JK)

Fred Odwell (Fritz) — 1872–1948. OF 1904–07 **Reds** 411 g, .258, 10 hr, 168 rbi
☛ *Led League—hr 05.*

Odwell hit only one home run as a Reds rookie in 1904, but his nine the next season led the NL. Teammate Cy Seymour, with eight homers and the league batting and RBI titles, missed the Triple Crown because of Odwell's home run championship. In two more ML seasons, Odwell never homered again. /(BC)

Bryan Oelkers — 1961– . LHP 1983, 86 Twins, **Indians** 103 ip, 3–8, 6.01

Oelkers was the Twins' number-one pick in the June 1982 draft, chosen before Dwight Gooden. Though he threw hard, his fastball had no movement, and he was pounded in a 1983 trial with Minnesota (0–5, 8.65). He lasted one season after his 1986 trade to Cleveland. /(JCA)

Joe Oeschger — 1892–1986. RHP 1914–25 Phillies, Giants, **Braves**, Dodgers 1818 ip, 83–116, 3.81. 20 wins: 21

The Braves' Joe Oeschger battled Brooklyn's Leon Cadore for 26 innings in the longest game in major league history, played to a 1–1 deadlock on May 1, 1920. Oeschger gave up only nine hits, walked four, and set a single-game ML record by pitching 21 consecutive scoreless innings. He was "a little tired" at the end, but said he benefited from the short seventh inning, when he retired the side on three pitches. It was not Oeschger's first marathon performance against Brooklyn; on April 30, 1919, facing Burleigh Grimes, he had pitched the Phillies to a 20-inning, 9–9 tie. Oeschger lost a league-high 18 games for Philadelphia in 1918 and won a career-high 20 with Boston in 1921. He faltered the following year, going 6–21. Before his death in 1986, he was the last survivor of the 22 participants in the 1920 marathon game. /(LRD)

Ron Oester — 1956– . 2B 1978– **Reds** 1212 g, .264, 42 hr, 331 rbi

A slick-fielding shortstop in the minors, Oester couldn't beat out Dave Concepcion there and became the Reds starting second baseman in 1980 instead. The scrappy switch-hitter with occasional power played at least 150 games each year from 1982 to 1986 before breaking his leg in a collision with the Mets' Mookie Wilson in July 1987, then missed the remainder of the 1987 season and the first half of 1988 before regaining his job from Jeff Treadway with a .280 average in 54 games upon his return. In 1985 Oester hit a career-high .295. /(SCL)

Bob O'Farrell — 1896–1988 . C 1915–35 **Cubs**, Cardinals, Giants, Reds 1492 g, .273, 51 hr, 549 rbi. *2 WS, 10 g, .269, 2 rbi.*
 Manager 1927, 34 **Cardinals**, Reds 118–119, .498
☛ *Most Valuable Player—26* .

A National League receiver for 21 years, O'Farrell caught such greats as Grover Alexander, Dizzy Dean, and Carl Hubbell—whose 1929 no-hitter he caught. In 1926 he was named league MVP, batting .293 and catching 146 games for the World Champion Cardinals. He threw out Babe Ruth trying to steal with the Yankees down, 3–2, to end the '26 World Series. In a surprising move, he was chosen to succeed Rogers Hornsby as Cardinal manager for 1927, and lost the pennant by a game and a half to the Pirates. /(JK)

Rowland Office — 1952– . OF 1972, 74–83 **Braves**, Expos, Yankees 899 g, .259, 32 hr, 242 rbi

Sometimes unlikely players get hot. For Office it was in mid-1976 when he hit in 29 consecutive games, batting at a .397 clip. The skinny outfielder also made the greatest defensive play in Atlanta Stadium

history, falling over the seven-foot-high centerfield fence to rob Mike Ivie of a homer in 1975. /(PB)

Curly Ogden [Warren Harvey] — 1901–1964. RHP 1923–26 A's, **Senators** 378 ip, 18–19, 3.79. *1 WS, 0.1 ip, 0–0, 0.00*

The brother of pitcher Jack Ogden, Curly went directly from Swarthmore College to the A's, but developed arm trouble and was sold to Washington in 1924. A righthander, he started Game Seven of the 1924 World Series as a decoy; manager Bucky Harris wanted to get lefthanded hitter Bill Terry, who batted .429 for the Series, out of the Giants lineup. Ogden struck out Fred Lindstrom and walked Frank Frisch, and was then replaced by southpaw George Mogridge. John McGraw lifted Terry for righthanded-hitting Irish Meusel in the sixth inning. Washington won the game in 12 innings. /(NLM)

Jack Ogden — 1897–1977. RHP 1918, 28–29, 31–32 Giants, **Browns**, Reds 529 ip, 25–34, 4.24

Brothers Jack and Curly Ogden came from Swarthmore College to the major leagues. En route, however, Jack got stuck in the International League, becoming the star pitcher of seven successive Baltimore champions (1919–25), and winning 191 games. His years with Baltimore were lucrative, though, due to high salaries and Little World Series shares. /(JK)

Ben Oglivie — 1949– . OF 1971–86 Red Sox, Tigers, **Brewers** 1754 g, .273, 235 hr, 901 rbi. *1 LCS, 4 g, .133, 1 hr, 1 rbi. 1 WS, 7 g, .222, 1 hr, 1 rbi*
☛ *Led League—hr 80. All-Star—80, 82–83.*

Tall and slender with a strong-wristed lefthanded stroke, Oglivie spent 16 ML seasons in the AL's Eastern Division, but didn't blossom as a power hitter until the latter half of his career. He hit three home runs in a game for the Brewers three times, all after turning 30, and he lead the AL with 41 HR in 1980. The native Panamanian was a free-swinger who disdained bases on balls, yet he rarely flailed wildly, striking out 80 times in a season only twice.

 Originally signed by the Red Sox, he could not crack Boston's starting lineup in 1971–73, and was traded to the Tigers for second baseman Dick McAuliffe. Oglivie played more regularly in Detroit, but was still on the bench enough to lead the AL in pinch hits in 1976, and after hitting .262 with 21 HR as the Tigers rightfielder in 1977, he was traded to the Brewers for pitchers Jim Slaton and Rich

Folkers. He hit .303 in his first season in Milwaukee, then belted 29 HR in 1979 before recording career highs across the board in 1980, batting .304 with 41 HR and 118 RBI. His batting average plummeted into the .240s in 1981–82, but he still hit 34 HR in 1982 to help the Brewers to their only WS appearance, and in the WS he homered in a losing effort against the Cardinals in Game Seven.

Oglivie's HR production waned after the 1982 season, and after hitting only five in 103 games in 1986, he left the ML to play in Japan. He returned to the U.S. in 1989, and signed a minor league contract with the Brewers. /(SCL)

Sadaharu Oh — 1940– . 1B 1959–81 **Yomiuri Giants** .301, 868 hr

☛ *Led League—ba 74–75. Led League—hr 62–74. Led League—rbi 74–75.*

Oh's 868 home runs in Japan set an all-time pro baseball record. The son of a Chinese father and a Japanese mother, he had trouble gaining acceptance with Japanese fans after signing for a $60,000 bonus as a pitcher. Switched to first base, he couldn't hit the curveball until he took up samurai swordsmanship as a practice method; he adopted a foot-in-the-air stance similar to Mel Ott's, though he was unaware of Ott's existence. He was noted for taking 30 to 40 minutes of batting practice a day.

In 1965 Oh set the Japanese record of 55 HR in a 140-game season. His record of 54 HR for the revised 130-game schedule was tied by Randy Bass in 1986. He averaged 45 HR a year in winning 13 consecutive HR titles. On the dominating Yomiuri Giants, Oh batted third and Shigeo Nagashima hit clean-up as Japan's equivalent of Babe Ruth and Lou Gehrig. Oh won triple crowns in 1974 and 1975. He broke Hank Aaron's career HR mark in 1978, but Aaron, six years Oh's senior, out-homered him in contests held in 1974 and 1984. Oh became Yomiuri's manager upon retirement. /(MC)

Koichi Ohta — 1951– . RHP 1969–Unk. **Kintetsu Buffalos**

A respectable but undistinguished Japanese starter and reliever, Ohta became a celebrity overnight by pitching brilliantly in the nationally televised high school playoffs. The blue-eyed son of Russian and Japanese parents became a teen idol. Upon turning pro, he led all players in fan voting for the all-star team six years in a row. His first year, he was elected despite a 1–4 record; his second year, he was elected while in the minor leagues. Yet fellow players apparently never held this popularity against him.

When he finally earned selection on merit, he was considered vindicated. /(MC)

Bob Ojeda — 1957– . LHP 1980– **Red Sox**, Mets 1364 ip, 88–73, 3.65. *1 LCS, 14 ip, 1–0, 2.57. 1 WS, 13 ip, 1–0, 2.08*

Ojeda was an occasionally brilliant but inconsistent starter while with the Boston Red Sox; he led the AL with five shutouts in 1984, but finished at 12–12 with a 3.99 ERA. His repertoire of pitches includes the "dead fish," a changeup that acts something like a screwball. But finesse pitchers are on dangerous ground in the confines of Boston's Fenway Park. Traded to the Mets in an eight-player deal after the 1985 season that garnered Boston Cal Schiraldi and Wes Gardner, he sparkled once out from under the shadow of Fenway's Green Monster. He went 18–5 to lead the NL in winning percentage in 1986, and his 2.57 ERA was second in the league. Arguably the Mets' ace that year, Ojeda led the staff in victories as the team won the World Championship. He won Game Two of the LCS 5–1, and although he gave up three runs in five innings in starting Game Six, the Mets went on to win the dramatic contest in 16 innings. In the World Series, he beat his old team at Fenway in Game Three after the Red Sox had taken the first two games from the Mets. It started the Mets' turnaround; they became the first team ever to win the Series after losing the first two games at home. He got a no-decision in the Mets' memorable comeback in Game Six, giving up two runs in six innings.

Ojeda missed most of 1987 after a May elbow operation in which his pinched ulnar nerve was moved and chips were removed. He came back strong in 1988, but pitched with poor support and finished 10–13 despite a 2.88 ERA. He missed the last three weeks of the season after severing his left middle finger while trimming the hedge at his home. The tip of the finger was deliberately reattached crookedly; he lost feeling and strength in it, but the different angle was designed to help him continue to throw his curveball. In 1989 he dispelled fears that his career was over but, inconsistent and lacking his former fine control, went 13–11 with a 3.47 ERA. /(SH)

Daniel Okrent — 1948– . *Writer.*

A graduate of the University of Michigan, Okrent was an editor at several publishing houses before becoming editor of *New England Monthly* in 1983. The inventor of the Rotisserie Baseball League (1980–1983), he was a contributor to *Rotis-*

serie League Baseball (1984), co-editor of *The Ultimate Baseball Book*, a collection of photos, anecdotes and statistics, (1979), and author of *Nine Innings* (1985). /(NLM)

Red Oldham [John Cyrus] — 1893–1961. LHP 1914–15, 20–22, 25–26 **Tigers**, Pirates 854 ip, 39–48, 4.15. *1 WS, 1 ip, 0–0, 0.00*

This wild starter saw his only significant action when he posted losing records for the Tigers in 1920–22. /(SFS)

Rube Oldring — 1884–1961. OF-3B 1905–16, 18 Yankees, **A's** 1237 g, .270, 27 hr, 471 rbi. *3 WS, 15 g, .194, 1 hr, 3 rbi*

Oldring was a reliable outfielder for four Athletics pennant-winners. He batted a career-high .308 in 1910, then broke his leg on the eve of the World Series, giving gifted fielder Amos Strunk the chance to play centerfield. Upon his return in 1911, Oldring moved to left field, and the strengthened A's rolled on to three more pennants in four years. /(JK)

Charley O'Leary — 1882–1941. SS-2B-3B 1904–13, 34 **Tigers**, Cardinals, Browns 954 g, .226, 4 hr, 213 rbi. *3 WS, 11 g, .103*

Popular and witty Charley O'Leary was the regular shortstop for the Tigers from 1904 through 1907 and played on the 1907–09 Detroit pennant winners. In the off-season, he and Tiger prankster Germany Schaefer worked a comic vaudeville act. O'Leary coached for the Yankees from 1920 to 1930, then worked for the Cubs and Browns. He was 51 in 1934 when he asked the Browns for one last chance to improve on his lifetime .226 average. Appearing as a pinch hitter, he singled, raising his average by .00024. /(JK)

Frank Olin — 1860–1951. OF-2B 1884–85 Washington (AA), Washington (UA), **Toledo (AA)**, Detroit (NL) 49 g, .316, 1 hr, 0 rbi (inc.)

Olin financed his engineering education at Cornell by playing ball, including a brief ML career in three different leagues. He went on to become one of America's industrial giants as founder and head of what today is the Olin Corporation. /(FIC)

Tony Oliva [Pedro] — 1940– . OF-DH 1962–76 **Twins** 1676 g, .304, 220 hr, 947 rbi. *2 LCS, 6 g, .440, 2 hr, 3 rbi. 1 WS, 7 g, .192, 1 hr, 2 rbi*
☛ *Rookie of the Year—64. Led League—ba 64–65, 71. All-Star—1964–71. Gold Glove—66.*

The only player in major league history to win batting titles in his first two full seasons, Oliva was one of the most graceful, natural hitters of all time, but had his career cut short by a bad knee. The native Cuban was signed by scout "Papa Joe" Cambria upon the recommendation of Roberto Fernandez, a former outfielder in the Senators' organization. In his first year in the minors, Oliva won the Silver Louisville Slugger award as the top hitter in professional baseball when he hit .410 playing for Wytheville in the Appalachian League.

Following brief .400-hitting trials with the Twins in 1962 and 1963, he earned a permanent spot in their outfield in 1964. That year *Baseball Digest*'s scouting report on rookie prospects underestimated Oliva. It read, "Fair hitter, can make somebody a good utility outfielder." Oliva enjoyed a sensational Rookie of the Year season, leading the AL in batting (.323), hits (217), runs (109), and doubles (43). His 217 hits established an AL rookie mark. He also led the majors with a club-record 374 total bases, 84 extra-base hits, and 71 multi-hit games.

Oliva surprised the Twins with his power as he walloped 32 home runs. He recalled, "They wanted somebody on base for [Harmon]Killebrew and [Bob] Allison. When I started to play I hit home

Tony Oliva

runs too. I think the long ball was contagious on the Twins."

Oliva suffered no sophomore jinx. He once again led the AL in batting (.321) and hits (185) for the pennant-winning Twins. He ultimately would lead the league in hits five times. He was named the AL player of the year in 1965 by *TSN*. In Game Two of the 1965 World Series he helped defeat Sandy Koufax when he doubled off the Dodgers' ace in the sixth inning of the Twins' 5–1 win.

In 1966 Oliva hit .307, second best in the AL. He also captured a Gold Glove award as the league's best defensive right fielder. In 1969, Oliva tied Joe DiMaggio's record of having been named to the All-Star team in each of his first six seasons in the league but missed the game with the chicken pox. He won his third batting title in 1971 (.337) despite a serious knee injury suffered in Oakland while chasing a Joe Rudi fly ball. With the exception of ten games in June, he missed the entire 1972 season because of his ailing right knee, which went under the surgeon's knife seven times during his career.

Because of his knee, Oliva was used mainly as a designated hitter and pinch hitter in his final years. On April 6, 1973 in Oakland, he belted the first home run ever by a DH. It was as a pinch hitter for a DH that Oliva recalled the most amusing story of his career. "Frank Quilici, the manager said, 'Go up and pinch-hit for Greg Kusick, the DH.' After I batted, I stayed on the bench for an inning then went upstairs to take a shower thinking I was out of the game. I forgot that I was the new DH. While I was taking a shower, they came looking for me since it was my turn to bat. I was embarrassed. I was all wet. I never dressed so fast in my life. Rod Carew had walked and the umpire was looking for me. I had to rush. When I got up to the plate they walked me on four pitches."

Oliva's actual name is Pedro, but he used his brother's passport to enter the U.S. to play pro ball in 1961, and he's been known as Tony ever since. /(NLM)

Al Oliver (Scoops) — 1946– . OF-1B-DH 1968–85 **Pirates**, Rangers, Expos, Giants, Phillies, Dodgers, Blue Jays 2368 g, .303, 219 hr, 1326 rbi. *6 LCS, 23 g, .233, 3 hr, 15 rbi. 1 WS, 5 g, .211, 2 rbi*
☛ *Led League—ba 82. Led League—rbi 82. All-Star—72, 75–76, 80–83.*

Al Oliver started slashing line drives as a Pirate rookie in 1969 and continued to do so for 18 seasons. Primarily playing first base (where, on May 23, 1969 he made three errors in the fourth inning),

Al Oliver

the smooth lefthanded hitter batted .285 with 17 home runs to tie for second behind Ted Sizemore in the 1969 NL Rookie of the Year voting. More frequently used in the outfield from 1971 on, he hit .312 in 1972, his first of seven All-Star seasons. He was batting .360 at the 1976 All-Star break, but an inner ear infection sidelined him in the second half, and he finished at .323. It was his first of nine straight .300 seasons. In the years 1970 through 1975, he played on five Pirate division champions, but in December of 1977, Pittsburgh traded him to Texas with Nelson Norman in exchange for Bert Blyleven and John Milner. He is among the Pirates' all-time leaders in doubles (276), home runs (135), RBI (717), and extra-base hits (467).

In 1980, Oliver played in all of Texas's 163 games and reached career highs with 209 hits and 117 RBI. On August 17 in Detroit, he established an AL record with 21 total bases in a doubleheader (four home runs, a double, and a triple). Wearing number 0, he became the Rangers' all-time leading hitter (.319), and reached the club's top ten in every batting category before being sent to Montreal in a March 1982 trade for third baseman Larry Parrish.

Playing first base for the Expos in '82, Oliver batted a career-high .331 to capture the NL batting title. He also led the NL in hits (204) and doubles (43), and tied with Dale Murphy for the RBI lead with 109. He made the *TSN* Silver Slugger team for three straight years, at three different positions (left field in 1980, DH in '81, 1B in '82). He was the first player to amass 200 hits and 100 RBI in a season in both the AL and the NL.

After spending 1984 with the Giants and Phillies and the first half of 1985 with the Dodgers, Oliver wound up in Toronto, for whom he delivered a pair of game-winning hits in the 1985 LCS. He retired among baseball's all-time top 50 in games played (2368), hits (2743), total bases (4083), RBI (1326), and extra-base hits (825). /(ME)

Bob Oliver — 1943- . 1B-OF-3B 1965, 69-75 Pirates, **Royals**, Angels, Orioles, Yankees 847 g, .256, 94 hr, 419 rbi

The versatile Oliver was primarily an outfielder in his 1969 rookie season for the expansion Royals. That May 4 he had six hits in a game. Kansas City's primary first baseman the next year (although he also played 46 games at third base), Oliver had his best season, batting .260 and reaching career highs with 27 HR, 99 RBI, 83 runs, and 24 doubles. In 1971 he returned to his utility role, and he tied the AL mark for double plays by a first baseman in a game with six on May 14. He was dealt to the Angels after the season for pitcher Tom Murphy. Playing first base in 127 games for California, by far his most at a single position in a season, Oliver rebounded to hit 20 HR while batting a personal-best .269. He duplicated his offensive performance in 1973 as a utility man. /(SFS)

Gene Oliver — 1935- . C-1B-OF 1959, 61-69 Cardinals, **Braves**, Phillies, Red Sox, Cubs 786 g, .246, 93 hr, 320 rbi

Oliver had some power, hitting three HR in a game on July 30, 1966. He reached a high of 21 HR in 1965 as the Braves' backup to Joe Torre at catcher and Felipe Alou at first base, a big enough role that he got 392 at-bats in 122 games. His 21 HR on a team with Hank Aaron, Eddie Mathews, Mack Jones, Torre, and Alou enabled the Braves to set a NL mark with six 20-HR men in one season. Oliver was a regular catcher twice, for the Cardinals in 1962 and for the Phillies in 1967 after they traded Bob Uecker to get him. Oliver's career was effectively ended by a 1968 knee injury. /(JFC)

Nate Oliver [Pee Wee] — 1940- . 2B-SS 1963-69 **Dodgers**, Giants, Yankees, Cubs 410 g, .226, 2 hr, 45 rbi. *1 WS, 1 g, --*

Oliver was supposed to make the Dodgers forget former All-Star second baseman Charlie Neal, and push Jim Gilliam closer to retirement. His glove won him the second base job on Opening Day in 1963, and again in 1966, but his bat did not let him keep it. An accomplished singer, he cut a record album, and often performed "The Star Spangled Banner." /(TG)

Tom Oliver (Rebel) — 1903-1988. OF 1930-33 **Red Sox** 514 g, .277, 0 hr, 176 rbi

A graceful centerfielder whose defensive ability sportswriter Fred Lieb likened to that of Tris Speaker and Joe DiMaggio, Oliver thrilled Boston fans with his speed and strong arm. He lacked power but posted acceptable averages, and led the AL with 646 at-bats as a rookie in 1930. /(EW)

Chi Chi Olivo [Frederico Emilio Maldonado] — 1926-1977. RHP 1961, 64-66 **Braves** 141 ip, 7-6, 3.96

Olivo was a Braves relief specialist who first reached the majors at the age of thirty-five. He saw the most action in 1964 (2-1, 5 saves) and 1966 (5-4, 7 saves). The Dominican's brother was Diomedes Olivo. /(WOR)

Diomedes Olivo — 1919-1977. LHP 1960, 62-63 **Pirates**, Cardinals 107 ip, 5-6, 3.10

The brother of Braves pitcher Chi Chi Olivo, Diomedes was a forty-three-year-old major league rookie with Pittsburgh in 1962—possibly the oldest rookie ever, depending on when Satchel Paige was really born. The Dominican reliever baffled hitters that year, going 5-1 (2.77) with seven saves in 62 games, but was ineffective with St. Louis the following season. /(ME)

Luis Olmo — 1919- . OF-3B-2B 1943-45, 49-51 **Dodgers**, Braves 462 g, .281, 29 hr, 272 rbi. *1 WS, 4 g, .273, 1 hr, 2 rbi*

Puerto Rico's Luis Olmo got his chance with Brooklyn during the WWII talent shortage, and proved to be a solid ballplayer, batting .313 with a league-high 13 triples in 1945. Lured to the Mexican League in 1946 by the promise of higher salaries, he was among those suspended by Commissioner Chandler for jumping the major leagues. Reinstated in 1949, he returned to the Dodgers for the stretch drive, and batted .305 to help win the pennant. /(JK)

Fred Olmstead — 1883–1936. RHP 1908–11 **White Sox** 359 ip, 19–20, 2.74

On September 8, 1910, St. Louis's Frank Truesdale scratched an infield single on Olmstead's first pitch. After that, Olmstead no-hit the Browns. This one-hitter was the career highlight both for Olmstead, a swingman with one worthy year (10–12 in 1910), and for Truesdale, a lifetime .220 batter./(DB)

Silk O'Loughlin [Frank] — Unk.–Unk. *Umpire* AL 1902–18 *5 WS*

Legendary O'Loughlin holds the umpires' record for calling the most no-hitters with seven. He often answered arguing batters with the following: "I have never missed one in my life and it's too late to start now. The Pope for religion, O'Loughlin for baseball. Both infallible."/(RTM)

Andy Olsen — 1931– . *Umpire* NL 1968–81

A quiet, likable Brooklynite, Olsen spent six years as a pitcher in the Pirates' chain. He played a role in the "longest" steal in baseball annals. On May 27, 1970, Tommy Agee of the Mets stole home against the Cardinals as a balk was called on pitcher Steve Carlton. According to scoring rules, the balk would nullify the steal. But official scorer Dick Young believed Agee already had the base stolen, balk or not. He consulted with Olsen, who agreed, then credited Agee with the steal. The case went to NL president Chub Feeney for his deliberation. Three weeks after Agee took his lead off third, he officially was safe at home with a steal./(RTM)

Vern Olsen — 1918– . LHP 1939–42, 46 **Cubs** 516 ip, 30–26, 3.40

Olsen was 13–9 as a 22-year-old rookie in 1940, and was in the Cubs' rotation through 1942. But he went off to war, missed the 1943–45 seasons, and pitched in only five major league games after his return./(ARA)

Gregg Olson — 1966– . RHP 1988– **Orioles** 96 ip, 6–3, 1.87
☛ *Rookie of the Year—89.*

Olson received a $200,000 bonus to sign with the Orioles in 1988, when he was the fourth pick in the country. He came up before the end of the season after just 24 innings in the minors. In 1989 he set the ML rookie record with 27 saves and was AL Rookie of the Year./(SFS)

Ivy Olson — 1885–1965. SS-2B-3B 1911–24 Indians, Reds, **Dodgers** 1572 g, .258, 13 hr, 446 rbi. *2 WS, 12 g, .293, 2 rbi*

Olson was the steady-fielding shortstop of the 1916 and 1920 pennant-winning Dodgers, adept at the hidden-ball trick. The cunning leadoff hitter led the NL in at-bats in 1919 and 1921 and in hits in 1919, when he batted a career-high .278. He later managed in the minors and coached for the Dodgers and Giants. He and Casey Stengel, teammates in Brooklyn, went to grade school together in Kansas City. Stengel said Olson, five years his senior, was the school bully. "They let him be the boss. He was the strongest boy in school." He became a tough competitor in pro baseball. Recounted Stengel, "If a man came in with his spikes high, Ivy would say, 'The next time you come in like that, I'll put this ball down your throat.' "/(JK)

Karl Olson (Ole) — 1930– . OF 1951, 53–57 **Red Sox** Senators, Tigers 279 g, .235, 6 hr, 50 rbi

Despite his 6'3″ 205-lb frame, Olson never hit for power and couldn't crack the Red Sox lineup. Like many other Boston rejects, he was traded to Washington, where he played one season, appearing in a career-high 106 games in 1956./(PB)

Ed Olwine — 1958– . LHP 1986–88 **Braves** 90 ip, 0–1, 4.52

Olwine was plagued by wildness, and when not wild was hittable. He had three mediocre seasons as a mop-up reliever with Atlanta./(WOR)

Olympic Stadium (Le Stade Olympique, The Big O) Montreal Expos 1977– . LF-325, CF-404, RF-325

Built for the 1976 summer Olympics, Olympic Stadium and the adjacent 55-story observation tower form baseball's most visually distinctive complex. The stadium itself is a squat, circular disc supported by 38 "ribs," while the futuristic tower, vaguely resembling a concave pyramid, is the world's largest inclined structure. Originally, Olympic Stadium's roof extended only slightly beyond the seating areas, leaving a large hole above the playing field, but baseball's first retractable roof was added for 1988, allowing the Expos to play either outside or indoors, depending on the weather. The roof itself is orange canvas (gray on the outside), and takes 45 minutes to open or close. Inside, Olympic Stadium has artificial turf, symmetrical fences, and 59,266 seats on seven levels./(SCL)

Tom O'Malley — 1960– . 3B 1982– **Giants**, White Sox, Orioles, Rangers, Expos, Mets 384 g, .259, 10 hr, 117 rbi

O'Malley hit .448 in 26 games with Phoenix (Pacific Coast League) to earn a promotion to the Giants in

1982, and was San Francisco's regular third baseman in 1983 before a horrible start in 1984 sent him back to Phoenix. A career .300 hitter in the minors (with over 3,000 at-bats), O'Malley has played for ten different teams in six organizations since 1984, never lasting more than a few months at a time in the ML. /(SCL)

Walter O'Malley — 1903–1979. *Executive.*

Under the ownership of Walter O'Malley, who became the National League's most influential owner, the Los Angeles Dodgers became the most prosperous and most stable franchise in ML baseball. He took control of the team in the midst of its Boys of Summer era in Brooklyn, inheriting a group of regulars who played together for about 10 years. O'Malley installed a new manager, Walter Alston, who served consecutive one-year contracts, through good years and bad, until a retirement in gracious seniority. Alston passed the reins to Tommy Lasorda, a pitcher not quite good enough to crack the Brooklyn-era staff who had served the organization as a coach and minor league manager. First Alston and then Lasorda managed the longest-running intact infield in ML history. And throughout the O'Malley years, which were extended beyond Walter's death by the leadership of his son Peter, the Dodgers have had a continuous broadcast voice, Vin Scully. The Dodgers promote from within, take care of alumni when they need help, and play in a clean, commodious ballpark. They were the first franchise to draw three million fans in a season, and through the end of the 1980s did it more times than every other ML team combined.

People who grew up with the Brooklyn Dodgers see a different Walter O'Malley. In a famous incident, writers Pete Hamill and Jack Newfield wrote their own list of the three worst villains of the 20th century on a piece of paper to settle a discussion they were having over lunch. They each wrote the same three names in the same order: Hitler, Stalin, Walter O'Malley.

O'Malley, born into a wealthy family, graduated from Fordham Law School in 1920. During the Depression he built a practice by representing bankrupt companies. He joined the Dodger management as the lawyer protecting the interests of the Brooklyn Trust Company in 1933. As the McKeever family stock was sold, O'Malley took a personal position as a minority owner and was a substantial shareholder by the time Branch Rickey took control in 1942. Rickey built the Boys of Summer team, in no small part because he also broke the color line, but O'Malley outmaneuvered him for majority control of the team in 1950. Rickey left an enduring on-field legacy, but under O'Malley the sometimes casual Dodger franchise was carefully managed for profit.

The move of the Braves from Boston to Milwaukee for the 1953 season was the first ML franchise shift in 50 years. Suddenly drawing a nearly-unprecedented two million fans each year, the previously moribund Braves were suddenly an economic threat to compete with any NL team, even one as prosperous as the Brooklyn Dodgers. And the franchise shift, and the others that quickly followed (St. Louis Browns to Baltimore, Philadelphia A's to Kansas City), made the previously sacrosanct ML map considerably less binding.

O'Malley saw real limits to the Dodger situation in Brooklyn. Ebbets Field was small, seating under 35,000 (three-million-attendance requires an *average* game attendance of nearly 37,000), without adequate parking, and in a deteriorating neighborhood. O'Malley lobbied local politicians for a new stadium in downtown Brooklyn. In the meantime, he started serious discussions with the city of Los Angeles. When he was able to strike a deal for a valuable parcel of real estate tucked in the hills above downtown called Chavez Ravine, he agreed to build his own stadium and move the team to the West Coast. In the meantime, he brokered the marriage of his rivals, the New York Giants, with the city of San Francisco. In a brilliant business stroke, O'Malley had moved baseball's greatest rivalry from New York to California. The presence of both teams made it easier for the other NL owners to support the move because the then long and novel West Coast flight would cover two road series each time. The Giants' move was officially announced first—they were in a truly weak financial condition where economic motivation was compelling. But O'Malley had orchestrated the move.

The Dodgers played their first four Los Angeles seasons in the Memorial Coliseum, a football stadium that converted to baseball only with considerable difficulty. O'Malley refused to share the Los Angeles Coliseum with the expansion Angels because the city, not O'Malley, would get the money. In 1962 O'Malley's own Dodger Stadium opened, with novel dugout-level seats and vast acres of terraced parking, O'Malley cheerfully rented it to the Angels. The team won frequent championships: a cluster in the 1960s on the backs of a dominating pitching staff, a pair in the late 1970s with ubiquitous home run power. Meanwhile, O'Malley designed the golf courses surrounding the Dodgertown spring training facility at Vero Beach, Florida, and supervised the installation of profitable orange groves on part of the adjoining land.

O'Malley's success and vision put him in a kingmaker position among NL owners. He didn't throw his weight around in public very often, but his influence was nonetheless apparent; Bowie Kuhn was his choice as Commissioner, and O'Malley kept Kuhn in office as long as he lived. His influence also came through the imitation of successful Dodger policies by other teams; the Dodgers' use of a five-man pitching rotation was almost universally adopted.

O'Malley made himself richer time after time; when the Dodgers moved west, he got a great land deal out of it. But the organization benefited greatly, and the institutional memory of the Dodgers has made them one of the most benevolent franchises toward its retired players. /(MS)

Ollie O'Mara — 1891- . SS-3B 1912, 14-16, 18-19 Tigers, **Dodgers** 412 g, .231, 2 hr, 77 rbi. *1 WS, 1 g, .000*

Dodger manager Wilbert Robinson called O'Mara "the most peppery and persistent man on the Brooklyn squad" and considered him superior to Rabbit Maranville at shortstop. Yet he eventually concluded that O'Mara's hands were too small and moved him to third base for 1918. /(TG)

Leo O'Mealia — 1884-1960. *Cartoonist*

A sports cartoonist for the New York *Daily News* from 1943 to 1960, O'Mealia began in Rochester in 1923 and moved to the New York *Journal-American* in 1927. He also drew a syndicated strip called "Wedlocked." Several of his cartoons hang in the Hall of Fame museum. /(NLM)

Alex Oms [Alejandro] (El Caballero) — Unk.–Unk. OF Negro Leagues 1921-46 Cuban Stars East, **Cuban Stars**, New York Cubans, Venezuela statistics not available

Oms, a lefthanded outfielder, starred on black Cuban teams in the United States from 1921 through 1935. A colorful player, he entertained fans by catching fly balls behind his back in one-sided games. He batted approximately .325 during his Negro League career. He also played in Venezuela into the 1940s, and was Venezuela's top defensive outfielder in 1943.

Oms made his greatest impact in his native Cuba,

collecting 537 Cuban Winter League hits in 1531 at-bats for a lifetime .351 average. He won batting crowns in 1924-25 (.393), 1928-29 (.432), and 1929-30 (.380). He led the CWL with 76 hits in 1928-29 and with 44 in 1931-32, when his 14 stolen bases were also the league high. He played on championship teams in Santa Clara, Havana, Almendares, and Cienfuegos. /(MFK)

Randy O'Neal — 1960- . RHP 1984- **Tigers**, Braves, Cardinals, Phillies 394 ip, 16-19, 4.41

O'Neal, a sinkerballer and split-finger pitcher, bounced from the Tigers' starting rotation to bullpen to Triple-A affiliate in 1985-86, never winning manager Sparky Anderson's confidence. He opened the 1987 season with Atlanta, posted a 5.23 ERA in 11 games, and got into a scuffle with manager Chuck Tanner when told he was being sent down. He was traded to St. Louis for Joe Boever the next month. /(JCA)

Buck O'Neil [John Jordan] — 1911- . 1B-MGR Negro Leagues 1938-55 Miami Giants, Shreveport Acme Giants, Memphis Red Sox, Kansas City Monarchs statistics not available
☛ *Led League—ba 46. All-Star—42-43.*

O'Neil became the first black coach hired by a major league team when he was signed by the Cubs in 1962. From 1948 through 1955, he managed some of the finest Kansas City Monarch clubs, leading them to five pennants and two Black World Series. He managed East-West all-star teams in 1951-54. Among his players were more than 20 future major leaguers, including Ernie Banks, Elston Howard, and Hank Thompson. O'Neil had been an excellent clutch hitter and a top first baseman. He led the Negro National League with a .353 batting average in 1946, then hit .333 with two home runs in the BWS. O'Neil was the first officially recognized black coach ever hired by a major league team. /(LL)

Mickey O'Neil [George Michael] — 1900-1964. C 1919-27 **Braves**, Dodgers, Senators, Giants 672 g, .238, 4 hr, 179 rbi

O'Neil was a clever catcher who boasted he had caught more than 2,000 major and minor league games without having broken a finger. He coached for the Indians and Pirates and managed in the minors. /(JK)

Emmett O'Neill (Pinky) — 1918- . RHP 1943-46 **Red Sox**, Cubs, White Sox 356 ip, 15-26, 4.76

O'Neill was a righthander on the 1939 St. Mary's College Pacific College Conference champions, coached by former major leaguer Earl Sheeley. /(NLM)

Mike O'Neill — 1877-1959. LHP-OF 1901-04, 07 **Cardinals**, Reds 137 g, .255, 2 hr, 41 rbi; 664 ip, 34-43, 2.87

Four O'Neill brothers played major league baseball. The two eldest, Mike and Jack, were born in Ireland, and formed a brother battery for the 1902-03 Cardinals. Mike went 18-14 in 1902. He had a strong bat, occasionally played the outfield, and that year made a league-high 12 pinch-hitting appearances with one hit—a grand slam on June 3, the first ever by a pinch hitter. /(JL)

Paul O'Neill — 1963- . OF 1985- **Reds** 354 g, .262, 38 hr, 176 rbi

O'Neill won the Reds' right-field job in 1988, hitting 16 HR with 73 RBI in 485 at-bats. The excellent fastball hitter was third in the NL in RBI in 1989 when he went on the DL at the end of July. His father, Charles W. O'Neill, was a minor league pitcher (1945-48). /(JFC)

Steve O'Neill — 1891-1962. C 1911-25, 27-28 **Indians**, Red Sox, Yankees, Browns 1586 g, .263, 13 hr, 537 rbi. *1 WS, 7 g, .333, 2 rbi.*
Manager 1935-37, 43-48, 50-54 Indians, **Tigers**, Red Sox, Phillies 1039-819, .559. First place: 45 *1 WS, 4-3, .571*

Of the four O'Neill brothers (Jack, Jim, Mike, and Steve) who came out of Pennsylvania's anthracite mines to play major league baseball, Steve was the most successful. A star catcher for Cleveland, he played a total of 17 seasons, and caught more than 100 games nine consecutive seasons (1915-23). He batted .311 or better each year from 1920 through 1922, and was behind the plate for all seven games of the Indians' 1920 World Series victory. A low-key manager who never had a losing season in 14 years, he gained a reputation as a developer of players. At Cleveland's helm from 1935 to 1937, he made a shortstop of Lou Boudreau and helped guide the young Bob Feller toward stardom. He managed the Tigers from 1943 to 1948, winning his one World Championship in 1945, mostly by keeping the previously volatile Hal Newhouser focused on winning ballgames instead of arguing with umpires. /(JK)

Tip O'Neill [James Edward] — 1858-1915. OF-P 1883-92 New York (NL), **St. Louis (AA)**, Chicago (PL), St. Louis (AA), Reds 1054 g, .326, 52 hr, 429 rbi; 289 ip, 16-16, 3.39
☛ *Led League—hr 1887. Led League—ba 1887-88.*

O'Neill was a star slugger in the dead-ball era, a vital member of the St. Louis teams that won four straight American Association pennants, 1885-88. In 1887, the year a base on balls was counted as a hit and charged as an at-bat, O'Neill hit a league-high .435, and was one of 11 players to bat more than .400. Even without that advantage, his performance that year was phenomenal: he led the league in hits, doubles, triples, home runs, runs scored, and slugging average. Because James O'Neill foul-tipped many balls in order to wait out the pitchers, hoping they eventually would walk him and build up his average, he became known as "Tip." He was a hero to Irish-American fans, who frequently named their sons after him. The next year, when bases on balls were not considered hits, his league-leading average was .335. /(JK)

Steve Ontiveros — 1951- . 3B-1B-OF 1973-80 Giants, **Cubs** 732 g, .274, 24 hr, 224 rbi

The switch-hitting Ontiveros spent four years each with the Giants and Cubs but had his only two full seasons with Chicago, batting .299 in 1977 and .285 in 1979. As a third baseman, he had little range and an average throwing arm. In Chicago, he is remembered for doing testimonials for a scalp treatment clinic that specialized in re-sodding balding heads. /(ARA)

Steve Ontiveros — 1961- . RHP 1985- **A's**, Phillies 383 ip, 18-18, 3.80

Ontiveros had 8 saves with a 1.93 ERA as a rookie in 1985 and saved 10 while leading the A's with 46 appearances in 1986. He became a starter in 1987, then was released after injuries limited him to only 10 starts (3-4, 4.61) in 1988. He signed with the Phillies for 1989 but spent most of the season on the DL. /(SCL)

Jose Oquendo — 1963- . SS-2B-OF 1983-84, 86- Mets, **Cardinals** 704 g, .268, 10 hr, 158 rbi. *1 LCS, 5 g, .167, 1 hr, 4 rbi. 1 WS, 7 g, .250, 0 hr, 2 rbi*

Called the Cardinals' "Secret Weapon" for his ability to play any infield or outfield position, Oquendo was the Mets' regular shortstop in 1983. He was a fine fielder, but New York despaired of ever seeing him become an adequate hitter. With the

Cardinals, he became a reliable, switch-hitting .270-.280 singles hitter and batted .385 as a pinch hitter in 1987. In 1988 he lost his "super-sub" status in mid-season when he took over the regular second-base job, but he did pitch in relief once, earning the first decision (a loss) in the majors by a non-pitcher in twenty years. He also caught a game, becoming the first National Leaguer to play all nine positions in a season. /(FJO)

Joe Orengo — 1914– . 3B-1B-2B-SS 1939–41, 43–45 Cardinals, **Giants**, Dodgers, Tigers, White Sox 366 g, .238, 17 hr, 122 rbi

Orengo played regularly for the Cardinals in 1940, was sold to the Giants, and became a handy utility infielder for four major league teams during the WWII player shortage. /(JK)

Red Ormsby (Emmett) — 1895–1962. *Umpire* AL 1923–41 *1 ASU 4 WS*

Ormsby was umpiring in the old Three-I League when a Western League umpire dropped a gun from his pocket as he ran across the diamond to call a play at third. The ump was fired, and Ormsby was promoted to the Western League. A WWI veteran, Ormsby suffered from the effects of a wartime gas attack. According to veteran catcher Birdie Tebbetts, on some days Red would feel light-headed behind the plate. AL catchers knew of his problem, and on such occasions would help him call balls and strikes. /(RTM)

Jesse Orosco — 1957– . LHP 1979, 81– **Mets**, Dodgers, Indians 726 ip, 53–53, 2.66. *2 LCS, 10 ip, 3–0, 4.35. 1 WS, 6 ip, 0–0, 0.00*
☛ *All-Star—83–84.*

Orosco was the hero of the 1986 LCS, setting a playoff record with three wins. His gutsy effort in the series-clinching sixth game featured his strikeout of the Astros' Kevin Bass with the tying and winning runs on base in the bottom of the 16th. In the 13th inning he had given up a game-tying HR to Billy Hatcher. Nearly exhausted in his fourth outing of the series, Orosco lacked his good moving fastball and was having trouble getting out righthanded batters. He did the job with his "backdoor" slider, which started outside to righthanders and broke late to catch the corner of the plate. Orosco also won Games Three and Five with scoreless relief, and until Game Six had given up only one hit in five innings. He saved Games Four and Seven of the WS and was again on the mound as the Mets celebrated the World Championship. He even had an RBI single in the clincher.

Orosco became a Met because Jerry Koosman forced a trade to his home-state Twins in December 1978. Orosco emerged as the Mets' bullpen ace in 1983, saving 13 games with a 1.47 ERA and winning a league-high 13 in relief. He saved a career-high 31 in 1984. Starting in 1985, he shared the stopper role with righthander Roger McDowell. Manager Davey Johnson tended to use sinkerballing, groundout-inducing McDowell more on grass, with flyball pitcher Orosco used heavily in the artificial-turf parks (including the Astrodome), which in the NL tend to be the more spacious stadiums. Throughout the 1985 and '86 seasons Orosco was rumored to have a tender elbow, and after going 3–9 with a 4.44 ERA in 1987, he was traded to the Dodgers in a three-way deal that also included the A's. The clubhouse cutup was involved in a notorious 1988 spring training episode with the intense Kirk Gibson, who reacted strongly and humorlessly when Orosco smeared the sweatband of Gibson's cap with eyeblack. Orosco's nine saves helped Los Angeles to a World Championship, although Orosco compiled a 7.71 ERA against his former teammates in the LCS and was not used in the World Series. After the season he signed a big free-agent contract with the Indians, and spent 1989 as an effective set-up man for Doug Jones. /(SH)

Frank O'Rourke (Blackie) — 1891–1986. 3B-SS-2B 1912, 17–18, 20–22, 24–31 Braves, Dodgers, Senators, Red Sox, Tigers, **Browns** 1131 g, .254, 15 hr, 430 rbi

Blackie O'Rourke, a dark-complected Ontario native, spent more than 70 years in pro baseball. After four major league stops, he became Detroit's everyday second baseman in 1925. When he came down with the measles in 1926, rookie Charlie Gehringer took over and headed for the Hall of Fame. Traded to the Browns after the season, O'Rourke was St. Louis's third baseman through 1930. A minor league coach and manager, he was a scout for the Reds (1941–51) and the Yankees (1952–83). /(JK)

Jim O'Rourke (Orator Jim) — 1852–1919. OF-C-1B-3B-SS 1872–93, 1904 Middletown (NA), Boston (NA), Boston (NL), Providence (NL), Buffalo (NL), **Giants**, New York (PL), Washington (NL) *NA:* 225 g, .317; *ML:* 1774 g, .310, 51 hr, 830 rbi.
Manager 1881–84, 93 **Buffalo (NL)**, Washington (NL) 246–258, .488.
Umpire NL 1895
☛ *Led League—hr 80. Hall of Fame—1945.*

O'Rourke batted .300 or better in 13 of his 22 years in the National Association, National League, and Players' League, and was a member of seven championship clubs—five of them in Boston during the 1870s. He was the first man to gain a hit in National League history (April 22, 1876). From 1881 to 1884 he was player-manager for Buffalo (NL). He managed in the minors, served as president of the Connecticut League and Eastern Association, and returned to the Giants to catch one game on September 22, 1904, at age 52 the oldest man to complete a major league game. Because of his verbosity, players and umpires called him "Orator Jim." One obituary eulogized, "Words of great length and thunderous sound simply flowed out of his mouth." His son, Queenie O'Rourke, was a utility man for the Highlanders (Yankees) in 1908. /(EC)

Dave Orr — 1859–1915. 1B 1883–90 **New York (AA)**, Giants, Brooklyn (AA), Columbus (AA), Brooklyn (PL) 791 g, .342, 37 hr, 269 rbi.
    Manager 1887 **New York (AA)** 28–36, .438
☛ *Led League—hr 1886* .

Orr's 250 pounds and great strength made him one of the best power hitters of the 1880s. An able-fielding first baseman despite his heft, he played most of his eight seasons in the American Association for Jim Mutrie's Metropolitans and never batted below .300. In 1886 he became the first player to top 300 total bases in one season, as he recorded league highs in hits (193), triples (31), and home runs (7). In 1887 he batted .368, and was the second of three unsuccessful Met managers. Orr is one of the few 19th-century players with a lifetime slugging average over .500. In 1890, while with Brooklyn of the Players' League, he hit .373 with 124 RBI in 107 games before suffering a paralyzing, career-ending stroke. /(ADS)

Ernie Orsatti — 1903–1968. OF-1B 1927–35 **Cardinals** 709 g, .306, 10 hr, 237 rbi. *4 WS, 13 g, .273, 2 rbi*

The 5'7" Orsatti was a football player, boxer, and auto racer who hung around Buster Keaton's movie lot before entering baseball. One of six Cardinal regulars to hit more than .300 in 1929, he batted a high of .336 in 1932. /(EW)

John Orsino (Horse) — 1938– . C 1961–67 Giants, **Orioles**, Senators 332 g, .249, 40 hr, 123 rbi. *1 WS, 1 g, .000*

A 6'3" 215-lb highly touted Giant prospect, "Horse" was traded to the Orioles in 1962 and hit 19 home runs as their first-string catcher in 1963.

He did not play regularly after suffering a hand injury in 1964. /(EW)

Joe Orsulak — 1962– . OF 1983–86, 88- **Pirates**, Orioles 546 g, .278, 17 hr, 126 rbi

A starter on some non-contenders, the aggressive, speedy singles-hitter hit .300 in 1985, his first full season. He stole 24 bases that year and in 1986, but was let go after his average dropped to .249. He came back with Baltimore in 1988 and hit a career-high eight HR, then led the resurgent 1989 Orioles with a .285 average. /(ME)

Jorge Orta [born Jorge Orta Nunez] — 1950– . 2B-DH-OF-3B-SS 1972–87 **White Sox**, Indians, Dodgers, Blue Jays, Royals 1755 g, .278, 130 hr, 745 rbi. *2 LCS, 5 g, .067, 1 rbi. 1 WS, 3 g, .333*
☛ *All-Star—75, 80.*

The son of Pedro Orta, known as the Babe Ruth of Cuban baseball, Jorge turned down a basketball scholarship to UCLA to play baseball in the Mexican League. There he batted .391 in 1971 and was purchased by the White Sox. He began 1972 as Chicago's shortstop but was sent down for some seasoning and returned as a second baseman. Uncomfortable with American ways, the soft-spoken young Mexican struggled with English and his fielding before blossoming into a hitting star in 1974. That year he finished second in the AL batting race to Rod Carew (.364 to .316), three times collecting five hits in a game.

Orta batted .304 with a career-high 83 RBI in 1975. In 1976 he was named to Mexico's Baseball Hall of Fame. The White Sox shuttled him around the infield and outfield in an effort to keep his bat in the lineup, but he never developed fielding consistency at any position. He signed as a free agent with Cleveland in December 1979 and batted .291 in 1980, tying a ML record with six hits in a game on June 15. His performance began to decline in 1981, and he spent his final four seasons as a platooned Royals DH. /(RL)

Phil Ortega [Filomeno Coronado] (Kemo) — RHP 1960–69 Dodgers, **Senators**, Angels 952 ip, 46–62, 4.43

Ortega finally stuck in the majors in 1964, going 7–9 with a 4.00 ERA for the Dodgers, and was included in the big Frank Howard—Claude Osteen deal that winter. His best season with the Senators was 1967, 10–10 with a 3.03 ERA. On May 29, 1966 he struck out seven consecutive Red Sox batters. /(SFS)

Al Orth (The Curveless Wonder) — 1872–1948. RHP-OF 1895–09 **Phillies**, Senators, Yankees 3355 ip, 202–184, 3.37; 603 g, .273, 12 hr, 184 rbi. 20 wins: 01, 06
☛ Led League—w 06. Led League—era 1899.

A durable hurler, Orth won 202 games without ever throwing a curve. Instead, The Curveless Wonder changed speeds masterfully on his fastball. For the 1899 Phillies, he led the National League with a 2.49 ERA. His control was among the best; he walked 19 in 145 innings that season, and with the 1902 Senators allowed just 40 walks in 324 innings. He fell to 10–22 in 1903, and in 1904 was traded to the New York Highlanders. There he picked up the spitball from Jack Chesbro, and in 1906 he led the AL with 27 wins, 36 complete games, and 339 innings pitched. In 1907 he lost a league-high 21 games. A fine hitter, he ranks seventh all-time among pitchers with 389 career hits. He sometimes played in the field and was used 78 times as a pinch hitter./(JCA)

Alfredo Ortiz — 1944– . Mexican League Star.

Ortiz is believed to have won over 300 games between the Mexican and Mexican Central leagues, but his 1985 statistics were lost in the Mexico earthquake. After breaking in with Leon, Ortiz won 19 games for Fresnillo in 1962, then pitched 17 years with the Mexico City Reds, where he and Ramon Arano, the only other 300-game winner in Mexico, teamed from 1963 to 1971. Ortiz peaked at 23–9 in 1969. He finished up with Veracruz, following four years with Tabasco and one with Nuevo Laredo./(MC)

Junior Ortiz [Adalberto Colon] — 1959– . C 1982–**Pirates**, Mets 407 g, .257, 5 hr, 104 rbi

Initially buried in Pittsburgh's farm system, Ortiz emerged as a capable reserve with a dependable bat. The bearded Puerto Rican backstop led the Eastern League in batting (.346) in 1980. Traded to the Mets in 1983, he was drafted back to Pittsburgh in 1984./(ME)

Roberto Ortiz — 1915–1971. OF 1941–44, 49–50 **Senators**, A's 213 g, .255, 8 hr, 78 rbi

A 6′4″ reserve outfielder from Cuba, Ortiz jumped to the Mexican League after WWII. Among those suspended, he was reinstated in 1949, and returned to the Senators. His younger brother, Oliverio "Baby" Ortiz, pitched and lost two games for Washington in 1944./(EW)

Bob Osborn [John Bode] — 1903–1960. RHP 1925–27, 29–31 **Cubs**, Pirates 446 ip, 27–17, 4.32

Primarily a reliever but occasionally a starter, Osborn never had a losing season during his short ML term. He was 10–6 for the Cubs in 1930, and led the NL with six relief wins for the Pirates in 1931./(ARA)

Bobo Osborne [Lawrence Sidney] — 1935– . 1B-3B 1957–59, 61–63 **Tigers**, Senators 359 g, .206, 17 hr, 86 rbi

Not as big as his father, pitcher Tiny Osborne, Bobo was a powerfully built lefthanded hitter who spent most of his Detroit tenure as a backup first baseman. With the Senators for 1963 (his last season), he hit 12 home runs in a career-high 125 games./(CC)

Tiny Osborne [Earnest Preston] — 1893–1969. LHP 1922–25 **Cubs**, Dodgers 646 ip, 31–40, 4.72

The 6′4″ 215-lb Tiny was the father of AL first baseman Bobo Osborne. On August 25, 1922, Tiny preserved the Cubs' 26–23 victory over the Phillies, the highest-scoring game in major league history./(ARA)

Hiroshi Oshita — Unk.–Unk. OF 1946–59 **Toei Flyers**

Oshita broke Tetsuharu Kawakami's Japanese single-season record by hitting .382, a mark that stood nearly 15 years. During Oshita's career, his Toei Flyers were among the most successful Japanese teams, regularly drawing two million fans each year. After his retirement, attendance plummeted, and the team was sold, becoming the Nippon Ham Fighters./(MC)

Dan Osinski — 1933– . RHP 1962–67, 69–70 A's, **Angels**, Braves, Red Sox, White Sox, Astros 590 ip, 29–28, 3.34. *1 WS, 1 ip, 6.75*

Though the hard-throwing Osinski would often freeze batters with his icy blue eyes and blazing, inside fastballs, teammates claim he wasn't half as mean as his reputation. Generally a long reliever, he was given a starting shot by the Angels in 1963, and threw a two-hitter and a three-hitter. His 3–1 (2.54) record (despite arm trouble) helped keep the Red Sox in the race for their 1967 "miracle" pennant./(MC)

Claude Osteen (Gomer, Wimpy) — 1939– . LHP 1957, 59–75 Reds, Senators, **Dodgers**, Astros, Cardinals, White Sox 3461 ip, 196–195, 3.30. 20 wins: 69, 72 *2 WS, 21 ip, 1–2, 0.86*
☛ All-Star—67, 70, 73.

Osteen won in double figures each year from 1964 through 1973. Obtained from Washington in a seven-player deal for Frank Howard in December 1964 after winning 15 for the ninth-place Senators, he became the Dodgers' third starter behind Sandy Koufax and Don Drysdale. After Drysdale and Koufax lost Games One and Two of the 1965 World Series, Osteen put Los Angeles on track by shutting out Minnesota in Game Three. Don Sutton's arrival in 1966 gave the Dodgers one of the most dominant rotations ever, with four pitchers who each threw at least 40 lifetime shutouts. Typical of Osteen's hard luck, his 40 shutouts were topped by the 47 thrown against him.

Gomer (so named for his resemblance to TV's Gomer Pyle) helped carry the Dodger staff through the lean years from 1967 to 1973. After losing a league-high 18 games in 1968, the deliberate worker went 20–15 in 1969, despite allowing the most hits in the NL. His best year was 1972, when he went 20–11 (2.64) and finished strong with seven complete-game victories in his last nine starts. He pitched three shutout innings to win the 1970 All-Star Game, and threw two more scoreless innings in the 1973 contest. He became a pitching coach for the Cardinals and Phillies. /(TG)

Fritz Ostermueller [Frederick Raymond] — 1907–1957. LHP 1934–48 **Red Sox**, Browns, Dodgers, Pirates 2067 ip, 114–115, 3.99

Ostermueller began playing pro ball with his hometown club in Quincy, IL. Elbow surgery saved his career early on. As a Red Sox rookie, he walked 12 Senators in a July 30, 1934 game. He three times recorded 13 wins, the last time with Pittsburgh in 1946, and pitched for the Pirates until age forty-one. Considered a good-hitting pitcher, he batted .234 lifetime. /(EW)

Joe Ostrowski (Professor) — 1916– . LHP 1948–52 Browns, **Yankees** 456 ip, 23–25, 4.54. *1 WS, 2 ip, 0–0, 0.00*

Ostrowski was a sinkerballing reliever on three Yankee pennant-winners (1950–52). The bespectacled Professor taught high school mathematics during the off-season. /(JL)

John Ostrowski — 1917– . OF-3B 1943–46, 48–50 **Cubs**, Red Sox, White Sox, Senators 216 g, .234, 14 hr, 74 rbi

A native Chicagoan who spent most of his ML career warming the Cubs' and White Sox' benches, Ostrowski hit a high of .266 with 31 RBI in 49 games for the 1949 White Sox. /(ARA)

Amos Otis (A.O.) — 1947– . OF 1967, 69–84 Mets, **Royals**, Pirates 1996 g, .277, 193 hr, 1007 rbi. *4 LCS, 13 g, .279, 3 rbi. 1 WS, 6 g, .478, 3 hr, 7 rbi* ☛ *All-Star—70–73, 76. Gold Glove—71, 73–74.*

Originally signed by the Red Sox, Otis was drafted by the Mets and went to the Royals with pitcher Bob Johnson in a lopsided December 1969 trade for third baseman Joe Foy. Foy was gone from the majors within 2 years, while Otis starred in centerfield with Kansas City for 14. During his tenure, one of the most popular chants in Royals Stadium was "A-O, A-O." The dapper Otis was criticized at times for a casual demeanor, lack of aggressiveness, and one-handed catches, but he won three Gold Gloves and three times was named Royals Player of the Year. He tied for the American League lead in doubles his first full year, 1970, and led in 1976. In 1971, the speedster stole five bases in a September 7 game and captured the league stolen-base title (52). In 1975 he tied an AL record by stealing seven bases in two consecutive games, April 30 and May 1. He batted .300 twice and hit for power, with a career-high 26 HR in 1973. He starred on four Kansas City division champions. When the Royals won their one AL title, he led all players in the 1980 World Series with 11 hits. He left the Royals in 1983 as their all-time leader in several offensive categories, including runs, hits, and RBI. /(FJO)

Jim O'Toole — 1937– . LHP 1958–67 **Reds**, White Sox 1615 ip, 98–84, 3.57. *1 WS, 2 g, 0–2, 3.00* ☛ *All-Star—63.*

O'Toole was a reliable starter with the Reds in the 1960s, and his 19–9 record in 1961 as their top lefthanded starter was a major contribution to their surprise NL pennant that year; his .679 winning percentage and 3.10 ERA were second in the NL, and he finished third in wins and fourth in strikeouts. He received no support in the World Series. He faced Whitey Ford in both his starts and saw his team shut out each time.

O'Toole followed with seasons of 16–13, 17–14, and 17–7, the last mark in 1964 placing him third in the NL in winning percentage (.708). But he dropped off to 3–10 in 1965, and his career was ended in 1967 by a shoulder injury. His brother, Denny, had brief trials with the White Sox. /(SH)

Marty O'Toole — 1888–1949. RHP 1908, 11–14 Reds, **Pirates**, Giants 599 ip, 27–36, 3.21

A minor league phenom who had an 18-strikeout game in the Western League and a 17-strikeout game in the American Association, O'Toole was purchased by Pittsburgh from St. Paul for a then-exorbitant $22,500. In 1912, the spitballer was 15–17 with NL highs of six shutouts and 159 walks, and lost a pair of games to the Giants' Rube Marquard before sellout crowds. O'Toole's name ultimately became a metaphor for unsuccessful Pirate prospects. /(ME)

Ed Ott — 1951– . C 1974–81 **Pirates**, Angels 567 g, .259, 33 hr, 195 rbi. *1 LCS, 3 g, .231. 1 WS, 3 g, .333, 3 rbi*

Ed Ott was a rough-and-tumble catcher, adept at blocking the plate, and a dependable lefthanded hitter. The converted outfielder was Pittsburgh's starting catcher from 1977 to 1980, and batted a career-high .273 with 51 RBI in the Pirates' 1979 World Championship year. After he spent 1981 with the Angels, his career was ended by a torn rotator cuff. /(ME)

Mel Ott (Master Melvin, Ottie) — 1909–1958. OF-3B 1926–47 **Giants** 2732 g, .304, 511 hr, 1860 rbi. *3 WS, 16 g, .295, 4 hr, 10 rbi.*
   Manager 1942–48 **Giants** 464–530, .467
☛ *Led League—hr 32, 34, 36–38, 42. Led League—rbi 34. All-Star—34–44. Hall of Fame—51.*

Ott was the consummate all-around ballplayer. Pie Traynor said, "I can't name a player who has exerted as strong an influence upon so many games as Mel . . . . and players I talk to express the same thought." Ott's lefthanded power was perfectly suited to the Polo Grounds' inviting right field fence, only 257' from home plate. He was the first National Leaguer to hit 500 home runs, and was the all-time NL HR leader until passed by fellow Giant Willie Mays in 1967. He had a fine eye at the plate, and held the NL record for most walks until 1982, when it was broken by Joe Morgan, then a Giant. He stands eighth among all major league players with 1860 career RBI, and ninth with 1859 runs scored.

   Swinging or walking, Ottie usually left his "cousins" cursing. He referred to his favorite opposing pitchers (the ones he handled so well and so consistently, like Larry French) as his "cousins." The demurely charming native of the New Orleans suburbs was more often on the receiving end of friendly needling. The ribbing began early, as teammates and scribes laughed at his batting stance. By stepping high (the classic "foot in the bucket," about which every batting coach has nightmares), then shifting his weight into the pitch with his bat

swooping low and then nearly upright, Ott constructed a swift, snapping action. Instead of making jokes, mentor John McGraw, the Giant manager, expressed concern to Ott about his swing. Ott replied with a raucous hitting spree which continued long after McGraw's passing. McGraw's only other comment to Ott about his stance was, "Just keep swinging that way, son."

   Ott was sixteen, playing semi-pro ball in cities near his hometown Gretna, Louisiana, when he was befriended by the Patterson Braves team owner, lumberman-millionaire Harry Williams. Stopping off in New York on his way back from Europe in late August 1925, Williams met with John McGraw

Mel Ott

and told him about Ott. That evening, Williams fired off a terse postcard to Ott: "Report to McGraw at the Polo Grounds for a tryout September 1." Ott believed one of his cheerful batterymates was pulling a prank, and quietly continued his catching duties at Patterson. When Williams returned there a few days later, he was shocked to see Ott, bought him a train ticket, and almost had to drag him to the station.

Greatly impressed by the hitting ability of the 5'9" 170-lb teenager, McGraw decided to keep Ott with the team. Casey Stengel, then managing the Giants' Toledo farm team, offered to take "the kid" under his wing for a few years. But McGraw didn't want Ott tampered with. "Ott stays with me!" he growled in reply. For two years, Ott was planted on the bench next to his tutor, who didn't want the youngster sitting with any of the veteran ballplayers. Though McGraw used him mostly as a pinch hitter (he led the NL with 46 pinch at-bats in 1927), Ott learned how to play right field, centerfield, third base, and second base.

Dubbed Master Melvin by New York writers when he became a regular at age nineteen, Ott had career highs of 42 HR and 151 RBI the following year, 1929, when he led the league in walks for the first of six times. He shared the HR crown with Chuck Klein in 1932, Ripper Collins in 1934, and Ducky Medwick in 1937, but had the title to himself in 1936, 1938, and 1942. He was the NL RBI champ in 1934, with 115, and led the league in runs scored in 1938 and 1942. He played for 22 seasons until chronic leg problems forced him to stop. (The ever-insightful McGraw had converted the teenage catcher into an outfielder in order to preserve his legs as long as possible.) Performing in New York his entire career, Broadway became his playground; he enjoyed "most favored ballplayer" status among the likes of Tallulah Bankhead and Toots Shor.

When Giant owner Horace Stoneham and manager Bill Terry decided it was time for Terry to step up to the front office, Ott was their only choice as field leader. Ill prepared, he became player-manager in 1942. The Giants' third-place finish that year was their highest under Ott. If not for his winning personality, his losing management style would have cost him his job long before his departure in 1948. Normally mild-mannered, he suffered the Giants' poor play with outbursts stemming from frustration. He levied numerous player fines and made public criticisms of the team's performance. It is said he acted out of character those first few years, trying to explode his "shy and retiring" image. In 1946 he

became the first manager to be thrown out of both games of a doubleheader.

In 1947 Ott was the target of Dodger manager Leo Durocher's classic quip, "Nice guys finish last." Durocher was actually misquoted; his barb was not so sharp. Directing attention to the Giant dugout, he said, "Do you know a nicer guy than Mel Ott? Or any other Giants? The nice guys over there are in last place!" The Giants finished fourth, but less than a year later, Durocher replaced Ott in mid-season.

Ott worked with his ex-roommate and longtime friend, Carl Hubbell, running the Giants' farm system until the end of his contract in 1950. He managed the Oakland Oaks (Pacific Coast League) in 1951–52, and was a Detroit Tiger broadcaster during the late 1950s. On a November night in 1958, returning home from dinner with his wife, his car was hit head-on by a drunken driver. The efforts of a team of doctors, which included his son-in-law, kept him alive only a few days. He is remembered variously as sincere, disciplined, dedicated, warmhearted, honorable, the embodiment of sportsmanship. /(AA)

Jim Otten — 1951– . RHP 1974–76, 80–81 White Sox, **Cardinals** 118 ip, 1–6, 5.48

A highly regarded college prospect, Otten bounced around the White Sox farm system before surfacing with the Cards in 1980. He lost all five of his ML starts and was used mainly in mop-up relief. /(FJO)

Jimmy Outlaw — 1913– . OF-3B 1937–39, 43–49 Reds, Braves, **Tigers** 650 g, .268, 6 hr, 184 rbi. *1 WS, 7 g, .179, 3 rbi*

A 5'8" contact hitter, Outlaw first arrived as a Reds third baseman in 1937, but saw regular major league action only as a wartime Tiger outfielder. He batted .273 with a career-high 57 RBI for Detroit in 1944. Though he played just 21 games at 3B in 1945, he started all seven World Series games there so that slugger Hank Greenberg, just back from the war, could play left field. /(CC)

Orval Overall — 1881–1947. RHP 1905–10, 13 Reds, **Cubs** 1532 ip, 106–71, 2.24. 20 wins: 07, 09 *4 WS, 51 ip, 3–1, 1.58*
☛ *Led League—k 09.*

Though Overall's career lasted just seven years, it was brilliant, as his 2.24 lifetime ERA, eighth best in major league history, indicates. Traded to the Cubs in July 1906, after a year and a half in Cincinnati, Overall emerged as Chicago's top pitcher in 1907, going 23–8 (1.70) and tying Christy Mathewson for the league lead with eight shutouts. In World Series competition, he beat the Tigers once in 1907 and twice in 1908—including a Series-clinching three-hit shutout in Game Five in which he struck out four men in an inning (the first inning), the only man to do so in WS history. Posting a 1.42 ERA in 1909, he went 20–11, and led the NL with nine shutouts and 205 strikeouts. He had a sore arm in 1910, and in his final WS start was knocked out after allowing the A's three runs in three innings. He retired for two years, then failed to crack the Cubs' excellent staff when he attempted a comeback in 1913. /(ARA)

Stubby Overmire [Frank] — 1919–1977. LHP 1943–52 **Tigers**, Browns, Yankees 1131 ip, 58–67, 3.96. *1 WS, 6 ip, 0–1, 3.00*

The 5'7" 170-lb Stubby went 9–9 with four saves for the 1945 World Champion Tigers. He started and lost Game Three of the '45 Series, 3–0, as Detroit was one-hit by the Cubs' Claude Passeau. Never a flamethrower, Overmire twice won 11 games for Detroit (in 1944 and 1947) before moving on to the Browns after the 1949 season. /(CC)

Bob Owchinko — 1955– . LHP 1976–84, 86 **Padres**, Indians, A's, Pirates, Reds, Expos 889 ip, 37–60, 4.29. *1 LCS, 2 ip, 0–0, 5.40*

The Padres' first-round selection in the June 1976 draft was named NL Rookie Pitcher of the Year by *TSN* in 1977, going 9–12, 4.45 for the fifth-place Padres as the number-two man in their weak rotation. His only winning record (4–3) and only ERA below 3.50 (3.23) came as a reliever (2 saves) after Oakland acquired him from Pittsburgh for Ernie Camacho and cash. /(JFC)

Frank Owen (Yip) — 1879–1942. RHP 1901, 03–09 Tigers, **White Sox** 1368 ip, 82–67, 2.55. 20 wins: 1904–06 *1 WS, 6 ip, 0–0, 3.00*

From 1904 through 1906, Owen was one of the best righthanders in the American League, winning 64 games for the White Sox with pinpoint control and a swift fastball. The fine-fielding Owen induced batters to hit up the middle or to his sharp defense. Yip (a Ypsilanti, MI native) was a fine cold-weather pitcher—an asset in Chicago. After impressing his manager with three victories against the Cubs in a 1903 post-season exhibition series, he earned a rotation spot and went on to help make winners of the "Hitless Wonders." On July 1, 1905, he became the first of only ten AL pitchers ever to win two complete games in one day. He was the first AL pitcher to steal home. He later became a physician. /(DB)

Marv Owen — 1906– . 3B-SS 1931, 33–40 **Tigers**, White Sox, Red Sox 1011 g, .275, 31 hr, 497 rbi. *2 WS, 13 g, .061, 2 rbi*

Owen was the Tigers' anchor at third base for five years in the 1930s. He hit .317 and knocked in 96 runs in 1934, when his four infield mates each topped 100 RBI. During the 1934 World Series, he was involved in a celebrated scrap at third with the Cardinals' Ducky Medwick, who slid into the base unnecessarily hard on a triple when the Cardinals already had the game sewn up. Owen added a career-high 105 RBI in 1936. He managed Portland to the Pacific Coast League pennant in 1945. /(KT)

Mickey Owen [Arnold Malcolm] — 1916– . C 1937–45, 49–51, 54 Cardinals, **Dodgers**, Cubs, Red Sox 1209 g, .255, 14 hr, 378 rbi. *1 WS, 5 g, .167, 2 rbi*
☞ *All-Star—41–44.*

"The condemned jumped out of the chair and electrocuted the warden." That's how one writer described the Yankees' ninth-inning comeback in Game Four of the 1941 World Series, after catcher Mickey Owen let the apparent game-ending third strike on Tommy Henrich get by. Had Owen held onto Hugh Casey's pitch, the Dodgers would have won, 4–3. Instead, the Yankees rallied to win, 7–4, and became World Champions the next day. Rumor had it that Casey had thrown a spitter; Leo Durocher said no, Pee Wee Reese called it "a little wet slider," and Billy Herman thought that Owen might have "nonchalanted" it. Ironically, that season, Owen had set the National League catchers' record of 476 consecutive errorless chances accepted while setting a Dodger season record by fielding .995. A scrapper who batted as high as second in the order, Owen was blackballed after leaving the Dodgers in 1946 to be a player-manager in the Mexican League. He returned in 1949 with the Cubs, coached, scouted, ran a baseball camp, and was still playing in oldtimers' games in his seventies. /(TG)

Spike Owen — 1961– . SS 1983– **Mariners**, Red Sox, Expos 867 g, .240, 25 hr, 253 rbi. *2 LCS, 8 g, .429, 3 rbi. 1 WS, 7 g, .300, 2 rbi*

A steady-fielding switch-hitter with little power from either side of the plate, Owen was named captain of the Mariners at the start of the 1986 season, but was traded to the Red Sox that August 19. In his third game with Boston (8/21/86) he tied a ML record with six runs in a 24–5 rout of Cleveland. He was traded to Montreal for John Dopson before the 1989 season and became the Expos' starting shortstop. /(SCL)

Brick Owens [Clarence] — Unk.-Unk. *Umpire* AL 1916-37 *1 ASU 5 WS*

Owens received his nickname from an object once thrown at him during a game. On June 23, 1917, he made one of baseball's most famous ejections. Babe Ruth, pitching for the Red Sox, walked the Washington leadoff man. The Babe complained so violently about the call (reportedly even striking the umpire) that Owens threw him out of the game and Ernie Shore relieved. The Washington runner was caught stealing and Shore retired the next 26 consecutively to be credited with a perfect game. /(RTM)

Jim Owens (Bear) — 1934- . RHP 1955-56, 58-67 Phillies, Reds, **Astros** 885 ip, 42-68, 4.31

Fond of throwing the inside fastball, Owens was a minor league strikeout and walk leader who discovered control while in the military during 1957 and 1958. He had his best season as a rookie in 1959, going 12-12 for the Phillies. Known as a reveler as a young player, he slumped, was traded, and was demoted before straightening out and becoming a top Houston reliever from 1964 through 1966. After arm trouble ended his career, he served as the Astro's pitching coach from 1967 to 1972. /(MC)

Rick Ownbey — 1957- . RHP 1982-84, 86 Mets, **Cardinals** 147 ip, 3-11, 4.11

A power pitcher, Ownbey hurled back-to-back complete games when called up in September 1981. Traded with Neil Allen to the Cardinals for Keith Hernandez in 1983, Rick was plagued by injuries. /(FO)

Ray Oyler — 1938-1981. SS 1965-70 **Tigers**, Pilots, Angels 542 g, .175, 15 hr, 86 rbi. *1 WS, 4 g, --*

The archetypal "good-field, no-hit" player, Oyler relinquished the Detroit shortstop job to centerfielder Mickey Stanley to strengthen the Tiger offense in the 1968 World Series. Still, Dick McAuliffe called him "the best shortstop I ever played with." Seattle fans, feeling Oyler was the Pilot most needy of support, organized the "Ray Oyler Fan Club" in spring training. Oyler almost ruined it by homering to win the Pilots' first home game. He was supposed to be an underdog. He ended up filling the role perfectly, batting .165 as their regular shortstop. /(KT)

Yukio Ozaki — 1944- . P 1962-Unk. **Toei Flyers**

Ozaki, who went 20-9 as a rookie, and veteran Masayuki Dobashi looked as if they would give the Toei Flyers the best pitching duo in Japan during the 1960s. But they were rarely both healthy at the same time. Ozaki tried to emulate Dobashi's endurance and spent much of his sophomore season on the disabled list. As Dobashi declined due to overwork, Ozaki picked up the slack, working 181 games in 1964-66. At his best, he went 27-12 (1.88) in 1965. However, like Dobashi and other Japanese ironmen, Ozaki burned out early. /(MC)

Danny Ozark (Ozark Ike) — 1923- . Manager 1973-79, 84 **Phillies**, Giants 618-542, .533. *3 LCS, 2-9, 182*

Signed as a first baseman by the Dodgers in 1942, Ozark played and managed in their farm system until 1964. He then coached under Walter Alston until he was named Phillies manager in 1973. He tried an easy-going, kid-glove approach, but by September '73, the players were in rebellion and the press was on his back. "I felt like I was fighting five other clubs and the press," he said. In a closed meeting near the end of the season, he told the players off, accusing them of acting like spoiled brats. He finished third the next year, then second. The Phillies won three Eastern Division titles from 1976 to 1978 but lost the LCS each time. Ozark was known to throw equipment in frustration and to toss reporters out of the clubhouse for dumb questions. Fired September 1, 1979, he returned to the Dodgers as a coach until 1982, then moved to the Giants, where he was interim manager for the last two months of 1984. /(NLM)

John Pacella — 1956- . RHP 1977, 79-80, 82, 84, 86 **Mets**, Yankees, Twins, Orioles, Tigers 191 ip, 4-10, 5.74

The Mets first called up Pacella in 1977, the year he pitched a no-hitter for Jackson (Texas League) against Tulsa in April. The Brooklyn native had no great success for the Mets, but threw with such effort that his cap fell off after nearly every pitch. The Mets traded him with infielder Jose Moreno to the Padres for former Cy Young winner Randy Jones in December 1980. /(SH)

Pacific Coast League — 1903- . League.

The Pacific Coast League has operated continuously since 1903, making it the second-oldest extant minor league. The original six-team membership consisted of San Francisco, Los Angeles, Oakland, Sacramento, Portland, and Seattle. During its early years the PCL battled several outlaw leagues for fan support; by 1909 it had established itself as the predominant Western baseball organization, and remained so until the arrival of NL teams in 1958.

Thriving under strong local ownership, the PCL expanded to eight teams in 1919. A 200-game March-to-October schedule was the PCL norm, producing extraordinary season statistics such as Tony Lazzeri's 60 home runs and 222 RBI for Salt Lake City in 1925.

In the years following WWII, supported by minor league attendance records set in 1946–47 at San Francisco, Oakland, and Los Angeles during close pennant races, a strong movement developed to grant the PCL major league status. Open Classification, just a step below major league level, was obtained in 1952. However, the transfer of the Dodgers and Giants in 1958 robbed the PCL of its largest cities and ended its major league aspirations. /(DBv)

Pat Pacillo — 1963- . RHP 1987-88 **Reds** 50 ip, 4-3, 5.90

A member of the 1984 U.S. Olympic baseball team, Pacillo was the fifth selection overall in the June 1984 draft. He was traded to the Expos in mid-1988. /(JFC)

Tom Paciorek — 1946- . OF-1B 1970-87 Dodgers, Braves, **Mariners**, White Sox, Mets, Rangers 1392 g, .282, 86 hr, 503 rbi. *2 LCS, 7 g, .272, 1 rbi. 1 WS, 3 g, .500* ☛ *All-Star—81.*

At the University of Houston, Paciorek was a defensive back, drafted in the ninth round by the Miami Dolphins, and a NCAA All-American outfielder who set school hitting records. In 1971 at Albuquerque, he was named Minor League Player of the Year, but in the majors he was tagged as a part-time platoon player and was never given a chance to play regularly until he signed as a free agent with Seattle in 1978. Finally blossoming with the Mariners, he hit .326 in 1981 and was named an All-Star. Traded to the White Sox the next season, he twice more topped .300. Paciorek was once picked by a Chicago newspaper as the second-best-looking ML ballplayer, runner-up to Jim Palmer. His brother John owns a 1.000 career BA and is the only one to do it with three hits. His brother Jim also played in the ML. /(NLM)

Gene Packard — 1887-1959. LHP 1912-19 Reds, **Kansas City (FL)**, Cubs, Cardinals, Phillies 1410 ip, 86-67, 3.01. 20 wins: 14-15

Like many other Federal League pitchers, Packard had outstanding records in the two years of the Feds' existence, but could not top the .500 mark in his six other ML seasons. He was the ace of the Feds' Kansas City staff, going 21-13 in 1914 and 20-11 in 1915. He was a respectable hitter who batted as high as .288, in 1917. /(ADS)

Dick Padden (Brains) — 1870-1922. 2B-SS 1896-99, 1901-05 **Pirates**, Washington (NL), Cardinals, Browns 874 g, .258, 11 hr, 334 rbi

A regular infielder for three NL clubs, Padden jumped from the Cardinals to the Browns in 1902 at the height of the war between the NL and the upstart AL. /(ME)

Tom Padden — 1908–1973. C 1932–37, 43 **Pirates**, Phillies, Senators 399 g, .272, 2 hr, 110 rbi

A singles-hitting catcher for six years with the Pirates, Padden was usually platooned with Earl Grace. His .321 was the best BA among NL catchers in 1934. /(ME)

Don Padgett (Red) — 1911–1980. C-OF-1B 1937–41, 46–48 **Cardinals**, Dodgers, Braves, Phillies 699 g, .288, 37 hr, 338 rbi

After a strong rookie season in the 1937 Cardinals outfield (.314, 10 HR, 74 RBI), Padgett slumped the next year and was converted to catcher, a position he never really mastered. In 1941, three days after Pearl Harbor, the Dodgers purchased his contract for $30,000, waited four years while he served in the Navy, and then sold him to the Phillies in June 1946. /(JK)

Ernie Padgett (Red) — 1899–1957. 3B-2B-SS 1923–27 **Braves**, Indians 271 g, .266, 1 hr, 81 rbi

Padgett came up for four games with the Braves in 1923. Playing shortstop that October 6, he made an unassisted triple play; he caught a line drive hit by the Phillies' Walter Holke, stepped on second to double up Cotton Tierney, and tagged Cliff Lee off first base.

Padgett was the Braves' regular third baseman in 1924 and hit .255 with his lone home run, and reached career highs of 25 doubles, 42 runs, and 46 RBI in 502 at-bats. The rest of his career was spent as a utility man. /(NLM)

Andy Pafko (Handy Andy, Pruschka) — 1921– . OF-3B 1943–59 **Cubs**, Dodgers, Braves 1852 g, .285, 213 hr, 976 rbi. *4 WS, 24 g, .222, 0 hr, 5 rbi*
☛ *All-Star—47–50.*

Pafko was an excellent outfielder with a strong arm and power who played on pennant winners in three cities. His 110 RBI helped the Cubs win the 1945 NL pennant, and after WWII he compiled three .300 seasons in Chicago, and also hit 36 HR in 1950. He was often used at third base by Cub manager Charlie Grimm, who gave him his "Handy Andy" nickname. Pafko was extremely popular, so his 1951 trade to the Dodgers was very unwelcome in Chicago. He gave Brooklyn its greatest outfield, with Duke Snider in center and Carl Furillo in right. Pafko's 19 homers and 85 RBI helped a powerful Brooklyn club win a pennant in 1952. Brooklyn traded him to the Braves after the 1952 season, moving Jackie Robinson into the vacated left field

position for a year, and Pafko platooned on Milwaukee's World Champions of 1957 and pennant winners of 1958. /(AA)

Dave Pagan — 1949– . RHP 1973–77 **Yankees**, Orioles, Mariners, Pirates 232 ip, 4–9, 4.97

Pagan was primarily a reliever, but was 0–5 lifetime in that role while going 4–4 in 18 starts. He was dealt to Baltimore from the Yankees along with Rick Dempsey, Scott McGregor, Tippy Martinez, and Rudy May for Ken Holtzman, Doyle Alexander, Grant Jackson, Ellie Hendricks, and pitcher Jimmy Freeman, one of the most unprofitable deals the Yankees ever made. /(JFC)

Jose Pagan — 1935– . SS-3B 1959–73 **Giants**, Pirates 1326 g, .250, 52 hr, 372 rbi. *2 LCS, 2 g, .250. 2 WS, 11 g, .324, 1 hr, 4 rbi*

The flashy Puerto Rican was the Giants' regular shortstop in the early 1960s. He had his best season in 1962, when he played every game, led NL shortstops in fielding, and batted .259 with 77 RBI. The Giants won the pennant, and in the WS loss to the Yankees he hit .368.

Traded to the Pirates for shortstop Dick Schofield in 1965, he began a new career as a utility man and pinch hitter. In 1969 he led all NL pinch hitters with 19 hits, only one short of the league record. In the 1971 WS, he drove in the deciding run in the Pirates' 2–1, seventh game win over the Orioles. /(FS)

Joe Page (Fireman, The Gay Reliever) — 1917–1980. LHP 1944–50, 54 **Yankees**, Pirates 790 ip, 57–49, 3.53. *2 WS, 22 ip, 2–1, 3.27*
☛ *All-Star—44, 47–48.*

The highly visible success of Page, a star reliever for three Yankee World Champions, hastened the widespread use of the relief specialist. Page succeeded Johnny Murphy as the Yankee bullpen ace, and while not as good or as durable as Murphy, he worked more games per season. In 1949 (although the statistic did not officially exist at the time), he set a ML save record of 27 that stood until 1961, and his 14 relief wins in 1947 was the AL record until Luis Arroyo broke that one too in 1961. He led the league twice each in saves, relief wins, and appearances (but three times in relief losses).

Page spent his first three seasons as a struggling starter before Bucky Harris put Page into the bullpen in 1947. Page had just two starts that year and one final start in 1948, and he went 14–8 with 17 saves and a 2.48 ERA (2.15 in relief). Page saved

Game One of the 1947 World Series, lost Game Six, and won the clincher, holding the Dodgers to one hit in five scoreless innings. In 1949 he was even better, saving the record 27 while going 13–8 with a 2.59 ERA. In the World Series, he won Game Three and saved the clincher. He dropped off the next year and failed in a comeback attempt with the Pirates in 1954./(SFS)

Mitchell Page — 1951– . DH-OF 1977–84 **A's**, Pirates 673 g, .266, 72 hr, 259 rbi

Oakland got Page from the farm system of the heavy-hitting Pirates of the 1970s, and for one season the acquisition looked brilliant. Page was named *TSN*'s 1977 AL Rookie of the Year (but lost out to Eddie Murray in the BBWAA award vote by three points) when he broke in with 21 HR, 42 steals, 75 RBI, 85 runs, eight triples, 28 doubles, and a .307 batting average. He also led AL outfielders in errors. He never matched even one of those totals again, and in 1979 was made a DH. /(WOR)

Ted Page (Terrible Ted) — 1903–1986. OF Negro Leagues 1926–37 Brooklyn Royal Giants, Baltimore Black Sox, Homestead Grays, Pittsburgh Crawfords, New York Black Yankees, Newark Eagles, Philadelphia Stars statistics not available

One of the Negro Leagues' most feared baserunners, Terrible Ted was a rugged competitor, a solid hitter, and a skilled bunter and hit-and-run man. He was a valuable member of some of the greatest Negro League teams of all time—the 1931 Homestead Grays and the 1932–34 Pittsburgh Crawfords. The lefthanded-hitting outfielder batted .375 in postseason all-star games against white major leaguers. He was offered a football scholarship to Ohio State, but dropped out of high school to play pro baseball. He batted .316 in recorded Negro League games. In 1934 he injured a knee while sliding and lost much of his great speed. The injury hastened his retirement in 1937./(PG)

Vance Page — 1905–1951. RHP 1938–41 **Cubs** 314 ip, 15–16, 4.03. *1 WS, 1 ip, 0–0, 13.50*

Page was 32 before he set foot on a ML mound. Called up to the Cubs in August 1938, he lost his first start 1–0, but contributed five wins to Chicago's successful pennant drive./(NLM)

Jim Pagliaroni (Pag) — 1937– . C 1955, 60–69 Red Sox, **Pirates**, A's, Pilots 849 g, .252, 90 hr, 326 rbi

Pag signed for a $70,000 bonus with the Red Sox. After two years as Boston's regular catcher, he was sent to the Pirates in 1963 as part of the trade for slugger Dick Stuart. In 1965 he set a Pirate record for homers by a catcher (17) while leading NL catchers in double plays (14) and fielding percentage (.997)./(ME)

Mike Pagliarulo (Pags) — 1960– . 3B 1984– **Yankees**, Padres 753 g, .227, 108 hr, 351 rbi

This lefthanded power hitter became the Yankees' regular third baseman in July 1984. Pagliarulo also became known as a hard-nosed player, literally, missing just one game after being hit in the face by a pitch in May 1986. He homered in his next three games. A consistent mid-season player, he often slumped during September; some blamed over-intense work habits. He went to the Padres in mid-1989 in the Walt Terrell deal./(EG)

Satchel Paige [Leroy Robert] — 1906–1982. RHP Negro Leagues 1926–47, 55 Birmingham Black Barons, Nashville Elite Giants, Chattanooga Black Lookouts, Cleveland Cubs, Pittsburgh Crawfords, Kansas City Monarchs, New York Black Yankees, Satchel Paige's All-Stars, Philadelphia Stars, Baltimore Black Sox statistics not available.*ML: 1948–49, 51–53, 65 Indians,* **Browns**, A's 476 ip, 28–31, 3.29. *1 WS, 0.2 ip, 0–0, 0.00* ☞ *All-Star—34, 36, 41–43; All-Star—52–53. Hall of Fame—1971.*

For more than four decades in the Negro Leagues and the majors, Satchel Paige used his pitching prowess and flashy, outspoken style to fashion a legendary career. He had excellent control, despite a wild, windmill delivery, and several distinctive pitches, each of which bore a descriptive nickname: the "two-hump blooper," a moving changeup; "Little Tom," a medium fastball; "Long Tom," his hard fastball; and the "hesitation pitch," for which he momentarily stopped his delivery halfway through before continuing. The lanky, 6'3" hurler's charismatic reputation made him the Negro Leagues' preeminent gate attraction. His frequent successful outings against such barnstorming major leaguers as Babe Ruth, Rogers Hornsby, and Bob Feller helped boost the credibility of black baseball and lent support to those who called him the greatest pitcher of all time. They also won him a major league career in his forties.

Paige's status as a folk hero had its roots both in his durability and in the confusion about his date of birth. The seventh of 11 children, he was born in Mobile, Alabama, at a time when accurate records were not always kept. A birth certificate bearing

Satchel Paige with the Miami Marlins of the International League

what is now the generally accepted date, 1906, was questioned for years because the family name was misspelled. The uncertainly became part of his persona. As he pitched on, he joked about his age, told fanciful stories about his youth, and titled his autobiography *Maybe I'll Pitch Forever.* After Paige's death, Mobile-born Ted "Double Duty" Radcliffe maintained that Paige was born in 1900: "Satchel was two years older than I was. I know that because we started playing together when he was 17, and I was 15." The truth may never be known.

Paige's nickname had a more certain origin. As a boy, he earned money toting suitcases at the Mobile train depot, where he rigged a pole and some rope to carry three or four bags at once. That ingenious arrangement prompted friends to call him Satchel. He was 12 in 1918 when an episode of shoplifting and truancy sent him to the state Industrial School for Negro Children, where he was able to hone his pitching skills until his 1923 release.

The following summer, Paige won a job with a local semi-pro team. Two years later he advanced to the Chattanooga Black Lookouts of the Negro Southern League. For two decades he pitched whenever the opportunity arose. In the summers he hurled for the Birmingham Black Barons, Nashville Elite Giants, Cleveland Cubs, Pittsburgh Crawfords, and Kansas City Monarchs. Between league games and in the off-season, he barnstormed, often opposing the best ML players. When the money was right, he journeyed to Mexico, Venezuela, and the Dominican Republic. He drew huge crowds everywhere and was able to earn an annual income near $40,000, higher than most major leaguers.

Paige's Negro League record was impressive, especially when he teamed with Josh Gibson on the Crawfords, but it was his exhibition performances that made him a legend. On more than one occasion, he called in his outfielders before an inning and struck out the side. After the 1934 season, he toured with Dizzy Dean and won four of the six games they pitched against each other. The following year, he defeated Dick Bartell's All-Stars, whose centerfielder, Joe DiMaggio, called Paige "the best I've ever faced and the fastest."

When baseball's color line fell, Paige was over 40 and had endured a serious arm injury. Bill Veeck signed him to a Cleveland Indians contract on July 7, 1948, making him the first black pitcher in the American League. He proved to be much more than a drawing card. Manager Lou Boudreau first used him exclusively in relief, but on August 3, Paige started and beat Washington 5–3 before 72,434 fans. He later shut out the White Sox twice, and finished 6–1 (2.48) to help Cleveland to the pennant. He worked in 31 games in 1949 but was released after the season when Veeck sold the Indians, only to be signed by Veeck again for the 1951 St. Louis Browns. He pitched for three more years, in 1952 going 12–10 with ten saves and a league-high eight relief wins.

In 1954 Paige was released again and resumed barnstorming. He played another year for the Monarchs and three for Veeck's International League Miami Marlins. He continued to pitch into the 1960s and finished his career with a farewell, three-inning stint as a starter for Charley Finley's A's on September 25, 1965. He was given a job as an Atlanta Braves coach in 1968–69 to help him gain his pension. In retirement, he embellished his legend through frequent interviews and public appearances. He became known for his rules for longevity, including the classic maxim "Don't look back. Something might be gaining on you." He was elected to the Hall of Fame by the Committee on Negro Baseball Leagues in 1971. /(SG)

Phil Paine (Flip) — 1930–1978. RHP 1951, 54–58 **Braves**, Cardinals 150 ip, 10–1, 3.36

While on leave from the U.S. military in 1953, Paine and Leo Kiley became the first U.S. major leaguers to play in the Japanese leagues. In nine games for the Nishitetsu Lions, Paine was 4–3 with a 1.77 ERA. His only full season in the U.S. was 1956 with the Cardinals, when in 46 relief appearances he was 5–1. /(MC)

Steve Palermo — 1949– . *Umpire* AL 1977–87 *1 ASU 3 LCS 1 WS*

An off-the-field fashion plate, Palermo earned a reputation as one of the top ball-and-strike umpires in the majors. His disdain for the ball-and-strike indicator used by most umpires once resulted in Minnesota's Jose Morales doubling with a count of "four balls and two strikes." /(RTM)

Erv Palica [born Ervin Martin Pavliecivich] — 1928–1982. RHP 1945, 47–51, 53–56 **Dodgers**, Orioles 839 ip, 41–55, 4.22. *1 WS, 2 ip, 0–0, 0.00*

Clem Labine said, "Erv probably had the best stuff of any pitcher that I've ever seen . . ..But [manager] Charley [Dressen]challenged his guts once in the clubhouse in front of everybody . . .and he lost confidence entirely." /(TG)

Rafael Palmeiro — 1964– . OF-1B 1986– **Cubs**, Rangers 414 g, .287, 33 hr, 159 rbi
☛ *All-Star—88.*

A June 1985 first-round draft choice, Palmeiro (pronounced Palm-AIR-oh) showed excellent power in a half-season trial with the Cubs in 1987, hitting 14 HR in 221 at-bats. The Cuban's power dropped off considerably in 1988 (eight HR in 580 at-bats), and though he hit .307 and made the All-Star team, he drove in only 53 runs and had no game-winning RBI, a record. He played errorlessly in the outfield.

Traded to the Rangers that winter and made their regular first baseman to replace the departed Pete O'Brien, Palmeiro was very productive initially in 1989 but slumped badly in mid-season and had trouble at first base. /(WOR)

David Palmer — 1957– . RHP 1978–80, 82, 84– **Expos**, Braves, Phillies, Tigers 1086 ip, 64–59, 3.78

David Palmer was disabled every year from 1980 through 1988. He came to the Expos with a live

fastball and superb control (he set a Florida State League record in 1978 by pitching 37 consecutive innings without issuing a walk) and notched a club-record eight consecutive victories after being placed in Montreal's starting rotation in 1979. He finished the year at 10–2, 2.63, but needed knee surgery after the season. He missed all of 1981 and 1983 after elbow operations, but returned with determination in 1984. In his second start, on April 21, he retired all 15 Cardinals he faced for a five-inning, rain-shortened perfect game. By August he was out again with shoulder stiffness. He signed as a free agent with Atlanta after another stint on the DL in 1985 and recorded career highs of 11 wins and 35 starts in 1986 before his elbow woes returned. /(JCA)

Jim Palmer — 1945– . RHP 1965–67, 69–84 **Orioles** 3948 ip, 268–152, 2.86. 20 wins: 70–73, 75–78 *6 LCS, 60 ip, 4–1, 1.96. 6 WS, 65 ip, 4–2, 3.20*
☛ *Led League—w 75–77. Led League—era 73, 75. Cy Young Award—73, 75, 76. All-Star—70–72, 75, 77, 78.*

High-kicking Jim Palmer spent his entire career with the Baltimore Orioles, becoming the greatest pitcher in their history. Signed in 1963, he replaced the departed Milt Pappas in Baltimore's rotation in 1966, and led the club with 15 wins. That October 6, he became the youngest pitcher (20 years, 11 months) to win a complete-game, World Series shutout, defeating Sandy Koufax and the Dodgers in Game Two. But Palmer was almost finished by arm, shoulder, and back problems; during the next two years, he pitched in the minors for 17 of his 26 games. He was left unprotected in the draft, but there were no takers.

Finally, thanks to surgery, work in the 1968 Instructional League and in winter ball, Palmer regained his form. He was still disabled for 42 days in 1969, but four days after coming off the DL, on August 13, he no-hit Oakland 8–0. He led the American League in winning percentage (.800) by going 16–4. He won the deciding game of the first AL Championship Series, but lost Game Three of the WS to the Mets.

Having overcome the wildness and arm miseries of his early career, Palmer became one of the most dependable and durable pitchers in baseball. His eight 20-win seasons were interrupted in 1974 when he was downed for eight weeks with elbow problems. Only two other AL pitchers had as many 20-win seasons as Palmer: Walter Johnson (12) and Lefty Grove (eight). He won his first ERA title (2.40) in 1973, when he went 22–9, and his second in

Jim Palmer

pitching in six LCS and winning four games.

Meanwhile, Palmer established a much-publicized running feud with manager Earl Weaver. Their love-hate relationship seemed largely theater, and neither man could hide his admiration for the other. Palmer gained more widespread attention in 1980 when, because of his attractive physique and matinee idol looks, he became sports representative and model for Jockey Underwear.

The elder statesman of the Orioles during the 1980s, Palmer added a 16–10 mark in 1980, and a 15–5 record in 1982, good for a league-best .750 winning percentage. Used sparingly in 1983, his last ML win came in relief of Mike Flanagan in the third game of the 1983 WS; he defeated Carlton to become the first pitcher in ML history with WS wins in three different decades. On May 23, 1984, he was released by the Orioles after refusing to go on the voluntarily retired list. He retired as the Orioles' all-time leader in wins, losses, strikeouts, games, innings, and shutouts. He went on to broadcast on both local and national TV. /(ME)

Lowell Palmer (Lulu) — 1947– . RHP 1969–72, 74 **Phillies**, Indians, Cardinals, Padres 317 ip, 5–18, 5.28

Palmer was nicknamed Lulu by his sister. He pitched a 7–0 no-hitter for Tidewater (Carolina League) in 1967. Relieving in 81 of his 106 appearances, he went 2–4 lifetime in relief and 3–14 as a starter. When the Yankees dumped Mike Kekich on the Indians after the Kekich-Fritz Peterson wife-swapping incident, they received Palmer in return (6/12/73). /(SFS)

Pete Palmer — 1938– . *Statistician.*

A Raytheon Corp. radar systems engineer, Palmer was among the first and most innovative users of computers to analyze baseball statistics. He made the cover of *The Sporting News* in 1982 after discovering that Napoleon Lajoie rather than Ty Cobb was the AL batting champion in 1910; Cobb was awarded the title because a Detroit scorekeeper recorded the same two hits twice. Palmer's greatest achievement was the creation of the Linear Weights Player Win Formula, publicized in *The Hidden Game of Baseball* (co-authored with John Thorn, Doubleday 1984). The complex formula assesses the value of each play in creating or preventing runs, taking into consideration park factors and seasonal fluctuations in the level of offense. On average, Palmer found, 10 runs created or prevented have equaled one victory throughout the 20th century. In 1987 a SABR panel voted *The Hidden Game of*

1975 (2.09) when he threw a league-high 10 shutouts and tied for the lead with 23 wins. His 22 victories in 1976 and 20 in 1977 were again league highs. He started more games in 1976–77, and threw more innings in 1976–78 than any other AL pitcher.

Palmer's three Cy Young Awards were matched only by Steve Carlton (four), Tom Seaver (three), and Sandy Koufax (three). His picture-perfect delivery and all-around athleticism helped him to four Gold Gloves (1976–79). His clutch wins included the Orioles' pennant-clinchers in 1966, 1969, 1970, and 1971. He established LCS records for strikeouts (46) and complete games (five), and tied records by

Baseball one of the three most important books on baseball records ever compiled. Palmer and Thorn also collaborated on *Total Baseball* (1989). /(MC)

Emilio Palmero — 1895–1970. LHP 1915–16, 21, 26, 28 Giants, **Browns** Senators, Braves 141 ip, 6–15, 5.17

Brought to the United States by John McGraw in 1914, Palmero became one of the first Cubans to appear in the majors. After going 0–5 with the 1915–16 Giants, he lingered in the minors until 1921, when he appeared in 24 games with the Browns. /(WAB)

Jim Pankovits — 1955– . 2B-OF 1984–88 **Astros** 316 g, .250, 9 hr, 55 rbi. *1 LCS, 2 g, .000*

Pankovits was the Orioles' second-round pick in the 1980 June draft but spent his entire career as a utility man, playing every position but pitcher. /(JFC)

Jim Panther (Pink) — 1945– . RHP 1971–73 A's, **Rangers**, Braves 131 ip, 7–13, 5.22

Oakland traded Panther and Don Stanhouse for the washed-up Denny McLain in 1972. Panther, usually a reliever, lost all four of his lifetime starts that year with the Rangers. After the season he was traded to the Braves for Rico Carty. /(JFC)

Al Papai — 1919– . RHP 1948–50, 55 Cardinals, **Browns**, Red Sox, White Sox 240 ip, 9–14, 5.37

Papai was one of 29 players to pitch for both St. Louis teams. In 1949, one of his two full ML seasons, he appeared in 42 games for the Browns, going 4–11. He once tripped over the chalk line on the way off the field. /(WAB)

Joseph Paparella — 1909– . Umpire AL 1946–65 *4 WS*
☛ *All-Star—4.*

Paparella found himself in a embarrassing position once at Fenway Park. While working behind the plate, he was unaware that first base ump Ed Hurley had called "time" and subsequently allowed Detroit pitcher Paul Foytack to pitch to Frank Malzone and register two strikes. After the mess was cleared up, Paparella had to cancel the two strikes on Malzone, which obviously didn't sit well with Foytack. /(RTM)

Stan Papi — 1951– . 3B-2B-SS 1974, 77–81 Cardinals, Expos, Red Sox, **Tigers** 225 g, .218, 7 hr, 51 rbi

Papi reportedly received a $40,000 bonus when he signed with the Astros in 1969. When the Red Sox dumped the outspoken Bill Lee after their 1978 pennant-race loss to the Yankees, they got Papi from the Expos. /(WOR)

Frank Papish (Pap) — 1917–1965. LHP 1945–50 **White Sox**, Indians, Pirates 581 ip, 26–29, 3.58

The 6'2″ Papish joined the White Sox in 1945 and recorded a 12–12 record in 1947, his only year as a regular starter. After baseball, he joined the sheriff's staff in his native Pueblo, CO. /(JK)

Milt Pappas (Gimpy) — 1939– . RHP 1957–1973 **Orioles**, Reds, Braves, Cubs 3186 ip, 209–164, 3.40. *1 LCS, 2 ip, 0–0, 11.57*
☛ *All-Star—62, 65.*

Maligned as a "five-inning pitcher" and a hypochondriac early in his career, Pappas reached double figures in wins every year but one from 1958 to 1972, but he is best remembered as part of one of the worst trades in Reds history, when he was acquired with journeymen Jack Baldschun and Dick Simpson for Hall of Famer Frank Robinson after the 1965 season. Despite a good fastball and hard slider, the consistent righthander never achieved the stardom many felt he was capable of, yet when he retired he was only one NL victory shy of 100 in each league, and he won 209 ML games without ever winning more than 17 in a single season.

Pappas pitched only three games in the minors before going 10–10 as a 19-year-old rookie for Baltimore in 1958, and was 15–9, 3.27 in 1959, but had already earned a reputation as a brash, impetuous youngster. He would show up the umpires with his griping and posturing on the mound, and once called the press box during a game to complain about an official scorer's decision that had cost him four earned runs. He also had trouble completing his starts, but still averaged nearly 15 wins a season for the Orioles from 1960 to 1964. Pappas tossed seven shutouts (including a one-hitter against the Twins) on the way to a 16–7 record in 1964, and started the All-Star Game for the AL in 1965, then was traded to the Reds in the off-season. In Cincinnati, he went only 12–11, 4.29 in 1966 while Frank Robinson was winning the Triple Crown in Baltimore, and after a 16–13 season in 1967 he was traded to the Braves the following year.

Pappas compounded his reputation problems by frequently squabbling with management as a player representative, but in time he did tone down his on-field antics considerably, and after the Braves sold him to the Cubs in 1970 he enjoyed two of his better ML seasons. He was 17–14 in 1971, but with a career-high 14 complete games and an NL-best five shutouts, and in 1972 he was 17–7 with a 2.77 ERA. On September 2, 1972, he was one out away from a perfect game against the Padres when he walked Larry Stahl, but settled for an 8–0 no-hitter. He retired after going 7–12 in 1973.

Pappas was also dangerous at the plate with 20 career home runs, including two in one game August 27, 1961. /(SCL)

Freddy Parent — 1875–1972. SS-OF 1899, 1901–11 Cardinals, **Red Sox**, White Sox 1327 g, .262, 20 hr, 471 rbi. *1 WS, 8 g, .281, 3 rbi*

When early baseball history was being made, this 5'5" Maine native with a bemused look and pouty smile was often around. In the first WS (1903), he was the winning Boston team's shortstop, and was the last surviving participant. When Yankee Jack Chesbro threw his famous wild pitch on the last day of the 1904 season to blow the pennant, Parent was the batter. His fine defensive plays saved four no-hitters, including Cy Young's perfect game. Parent's solid hitting, running, and fielding made him a popular hero in Boston. Parent denied three pitchers no-hitters when he got his club's only hits. He provided the dramatic conclusion for Frank Smith's no-hitter when, refusing to accept an intentional walk, he reached out to drive in the game's only run in the bottom of the ninth. /(DB)

Ace Parker [Clarence McKay] — 1912– . SS-2B 1937–38 **A's** 94 g, .179, 2 hr, 25 rbi

One of many players to hit a home run in his first ML at-bat, Parker was a triple-threat All-American at Duke. For two seasons he played full-time baseball and full-time football with Brooklyn of the NFL. Finally the wear, conflicting schedules, and his difficulty with curveballs made him concentrate on football. NFL MVP in 1940, he became the league's second-highest-paid player at $12,000 in 1941. In 1972 he was elected to the Pro Football Hall of Fame. /(NLM)

Dan Parker — 1894–1967. *Writer.*

A 6'5" 230-lb hard-hitting columnist who used a cutting sense of humor and could back up every word he wrote, Parker had the truest ear for the spoken word since Ring Lardner. He occasionally spiced his New York *Daily Mirror* column with poetry. He started as a baseball writer in 1924 under sports editor Gene Fowler and wrote a column for 37 years until the *Mirror* folded in 1963. Before his death in 1967, he did a brief stint with the New York *Journal-American.* /(NLM)

Dave Parker (The Cobra) — 1951– . OF-DH 1973- **Pirates**, Reds, A's 2177 g, .293, 307 hr, 1342 rbi. *5 LCS, 16 g, .190, 2 hr, 5 rbi. 3 WS, 14 g, .283, 1 hr, 6 rbi* ☛ *Most Valuable Player—78. Led League—rbi 85. Led League—ba 77–78. All-Star—77, 79–81, 85–86. Gold Glove—77–79.*

The three stages of Dave Parker's career began when he replaced Roberto Clemente as right fielder of the Pirates. As Parker's tall frame filled out, he became an imposing hitter, capable of batting for power and average. His powerful right arm compared with Clemente's and was best shown off during the 1979 All Star-Game, when Parker cut down two runners on the bases. He won three Gold Gloves. In 1978, despite playing with a broken jaw, Parker almost single-handedly led Pittsburgh's second-half charge that fell just short of catching Philadelphia. He became the first Pirate since Clemente to earn the Most Valuable Player award. Knee and weight problems began to rob Parker of his power in 1979 and 1980. His reduced quality was also attributed to drug problems. Owning a million-dollar contract, with millions more in deferred payments, Parker became a villain in Pittsburgh, the object of boos, thrown objects, and threats as the Pirates sank in the NL East. Parker regained his status as a run-producing threat when traded to his hometown, Cincinnati, but had become a defensive liability. He was traded to the Athletics following the 1987 season and contributed to their 1988 and 1989 AL pennants as a DH and team leader. /(ME)

Harry Parker — 1947– . RHP 1970–71, 73–76 Cardinals, **Mets**, Indians 315 ip, 15–21, 3.86. *1 LCS, 1 ip, 0–1, 9.00. 1 WS, 3 ip, 0–1, 0.00*

Parker's best season came as a reliever and spot starter for the Mets in their surprise 1973 NL championship season. He went 8–4 with five saves and a 3.35 ERA, all career bests; he never had another winning season. In Game Four of the LCS, he surrendered a 12th-inning homer to Pete Rose, taking the loss in relief. He also lost Game Three of the World Series in the 11th inning on an unearned run. His brother Jack was an infielder in the Indians' organization. /(SFS)

Wes Parker — 1939- . 1B-OF 1964–72 **Dodgers** 1288 g, .267, 64 hr, 470 rbi. *2 WS, 11 g, .278, 1 hr, 2 rbi* ☛ *Gold Glove–-67–72.*

Graceful Wes Parker was in the lineup for his outstanding glove work at first base, although he felt he was a better centerfielder. In 1965 and 1966 he teamed with Wills, Lefebvre, and Gilliam in the only all-switch-hitting infield. His only 1968 error was controversial, coming on an Astroturf bounce, after which the Los Angeles writers assured him that the Houston scorer had been drinking. His one exceptional year at the plate was 1970, when he hit .319 with 111 RBI and led the NL with 47 doubles. He retired at 32 with a ML career-record .996 fielding average and six straight Gold Gloves, "to enjoy the whole spectrum of life." Parker came out of retirement in 1974 to play in Japan, and he hit .301 with 14 HR for Nankai. He then became a broadcaster and TV actor. /(TG)

Frank Parkinson — 1895–1960. 2B 1921–24 **Phillies** 378 g, .256, 24 hr, 149 rbi

Parkinson was a semi-pro playing for the Pennsylvania Railroad Car Shops team when the Phillies signed him in 1920. In 1922, his only full ML season, he led NL second basemen in assists, errors, and total chances per game while striking out a league-leading 93 times. /(NLM)

Roy Parmelee (Bud) — 1907–1981 RHP 1929–37, 39 **Giants**, Cardinals, Cubs, A's 1120 ip, 59–55, 4.27

A hard thrower, Parmelee never achieved his potential because of a lack of control. Not always a regular starter, he nevertheless led the NL four times in hit batsmen and once in bases on balls. In 1933, his best season, he was 13–8 for the Giants. On July 2 he beat Dizzy Dean of the Cardinals 1–0, striking out 13 and walking none. Two weeks later he lost a 15-inning, 1–0 game to Red Lucas of the Reds. /(LRD)

Mel Parnell — 1922- . LHP 1947–56 **Red Sox** 1752 ip, 123–75, 3.50. 20 wins: 49, 53 ☛ *Led League—w 49. Led League—era 49. All-Star—49, 51.*

Reminiscent of graceful Herb Pennock, Parnell was one of the most stylish and successful Red Sox lefthanders ever, as well as a consummate gentleman. Successful in Fenway Park (70–30) with its looming Green Monster, he handled righthanded hitters with baffling inside sliders. In 1949 he was the AL's leader in wins (25) and ERA (2.77). He

won 18 in each of the next two seasons. After an off-year in 1952, he rebounded with a 21–8 mark in 1953. Parnell struggled with a bad elbow for three more years before retiring, but in his final season, he threw the Red Sox' first no-hitter in 33 years (7/14/56). "I never did reach a state of nervousness," he said afterward, "because I just didn't expect it to happen." /(EC)

Jeff Parrett — 1961- . RHP 1986- **Expos**, Phillies 280 ip, 31–17, 3.28

After several excellent seasons in the Expos' bullpen-by-committee (12–4 in 1988), Parrett was traded to the Phillies in December 1988. By the middle of 1989, he was sharing the role of bullpen stopper with Roger McDowell after ace Steve Bedrosian was traded. /(SFS)

Lance Parrish — 1956- . C 1977–89 **Tigers**, Phillies, Angels 1523 g, .256, 261 hr, 877 rbi. *1 LCS, 3 g, .250, 1 hr, 3 rbi. 1 WS, 5 g, .278, 1 hr, 2 rbi* ☛ *All-Star—80, 82–86. Gold Glove—83–85.*

A onetime bodyguard for singer Tina Turner, Parrish was the Tigers' sturdy catcher for nine years, and made the AL All-Star squad six times. He was converted from third base to catcher in his second year in the minors, and as a rookie in 1978 he platooned with Milt May in Detroit. Playing full-time in 1979, Parrish hit .276 with 19 HR and 65 RBI, but was struggling defensively. He had an outstanding throwing arm but committed 21 passed balls to lead the AL. In 1980 Parrish widened his batting stance and flattened his swing to produce an All-Star year (.286, 24 HR, 82 RBI), and in 1982 he broke Yogi Berra's AL record for HR by a catcher with 32 (Carlton Fisk broke his record the following year). Defensively, Parrish improved enough to win three straight Gold Gloves (1983–85). Back problems plagued him in 1985–86, and in 1987 he signed with the Phillies as a free agent. He never adjusted to the NL, however, and after two subpar seasons he began 1989 as Bob Boone's successor with the Angels. /(SG)

Larry Parrish — 1953- . 3B-OF-DH 1974–88 **Expos**, Rangers, Red Sox 1891 g, .263, 256 hr, 992 rbi. *2 LCS, 9 g, .200, 2 rbi* ☛ *All-Star—79, 87.*

Powerful-looking Larry Parrish produced impressive slugging records at Montreal and Texas. Playing third base, he was a Topps All-Rookie Team member in 1975 and Montreal's Player of the Year in 1979. A consistent run producer when healthy, Parrish left the Expos, in the Al Oliver deal, as the club's all-time leader in games, at-bats, hits, and doubles. Moving to the outfield, Parrish was Rangers Player of the Year in 1984 and 1986, with a severe knee injury in 1985. After the injury, he was primarily a designated hitter, with some action at third base. He was the AL's top DH from 1985 to 1987. In 1987, with a Texas-record 32 homers, Parrish became the 13th player with 30-HR seasons in both the AL and NL. His four three-homer games rank him among a select few with that many. With younger but similarly-talented Pete Incaviglia in Texas, Parrish became expendable and went to Boston in 1988. He left Texas as the club's all-time leading home run hitter. /(ME)

Harold Parrott — 1909-1987. *Writer-Executive*.

A graduate of St. John's, Parrott wrote for the Brooklyn *Eagle* until the Dodgers hired him as their traveling secretary in 1943. Later the ticket manager, he was director of promotion and publicity for the club when it moved to Los Angeles. Parrott went west with them and later worked for Seattle, San Diego, and the Angels. He also wrote magazine articles and was sometimes a *Sporting News* correspondent. In 1976 he wrote a book, *The Lords of Baseball*, about his experiences as a baseball executive. /(NLM)

Mike Parrott — 1954- . RHP 1977-81 Orioles, **Mariners** 494 ip, 19-39, 4.88

The Orioles' top draft pick in 1973, Parrott was acquired by the Mariners in 1978 and set a club record with 14 wins the next year. After winning the Seattle opener in 1979, he lost 16 straight. /(EW)

Bill Parsons — 1948- . RHP 1971-74 **Brewers**, A's 521 ip, 29-36, 3.89

Parsons was the number-two starter for the last-place Brewers, going 13-17, 3.20 in 1971 and 13-13, 3.91 in 1972. He was named *TSN*'s AL Rookie Pitcher of the Year for his 1971 effort, and was runner-up to Chris Chambliss in the BBWAA vote for Rookie of the Year. /(JFC)

Tom Parsons (Long Tom) — 1939- . RHP 1963-65 Pirates, **Mets** 114 ip, 2-13, 4.72

In 1965, with the last-place Mets, the 6'7" 210-lb Parsons went 1-10 for a staff that boasted two 20-game losers. He was gone from the majors at age 25. /(KT)

Roy Partee — 1917- . C 1943-44, 46-48 **Red Sox**, Browns 367 g, .250, 2 hr, 114 rbi. *1 WS, 5 g, .100, 1 rbi*

A fancy catcher with the ability to call a good game behind the plate, Partee returned from the army (in which he took part in the invasion of the Philippines) just in time to share catching duties down the stretch for the 1946 pennant-winning Red Sox. /(EW)

Ben Paschal — 1895-1974. OF 1915, 20, 24-29 Indians, Red Sox, **Yankees** 364 g, .309, 24 hr, 139 rbi. *2 WS, 8 g, .214, 2 rbi*

Paschal, a swift, hard-hitting outfielder, could have been a regular for any team except the one he was on: the Yankees of the late 1920s with Ruth, Combs, and Meusel. He once pinch hit for Ruth. The Babe had homered in the ninth inning and headed for the clubhouse. The Yankees batted around, and Ruth was nowhere to be found, so Paschal pinch hit for him. /(NLM)

Camilo Pascual (Little Potato) — 1934- . RHP 1954-71 **Senators/Twins**, Senators, Reds, Dodgers, Indians 2930 ip, 174-170, 3.63. 20 wins: 62-63 *1 WS, 5 ip, 0-1, 5.40*
☛ *All-Star—59-62, 64.*

Despite a recurring bad arm and years pitching for bad teams, Pascual was one of the dominant AL righthanders for a decade beginning in the late 1950s. Originally recommended to the Senators by his older brother, Carlos "Big Potato" Pascual, who pitched briefly for the team in 1950, Camilo arrived in Washington in 1954 and spent five seasons struggling to a 28-66 with the hapless team. But his stuff was overpowering when he developed a wicked sidearm curve in 1959 to go with his blazing fastball and sharp control, and he posted a 17-10 record for a last-place club. Two years later the Senators moved to Minnesota and built a powerful lineup. Pascual prospered, going 20-11 and 21-9 seasons in 1962 and 1963. He led the AL in strikeouts for three straight seasons, beginning in 1961. In the second '61 All-Star Game he pitched three hitless innings and fanned four. He was 9-3 for the pennant-winning Twins in 1965, as arm miseries reduced him to a spot starter. After a trade sent him to the new Washington franchise, he won 25 games over the 1967-68 seasons. /(MC)

Larry Pashnick — 1956- . RHP 1982-84 **Tigers**, Twins 170 ip, 7-8, 4.17

The 999th player to wear a Tiger uniform, Pashnick divided his time between starting and relieving in

1982. His proclivity for giving up home runs spoiled his ML career. /(EW)

Dode Paskert [George Henry] (Honey Boy) — 1881–1959. OF 1907–21 Reds, **Phillies**, Cubs 1715 g, .268, 42 hr, 577 rbi. *1 WS, 11 g, .175, 2 rbi*

Paskert was more widely admired for his speed and defensive skills in centerfield than for his underrated offensive contributions. In 1917, when he led NL outfielders in fielding average, one sportswriter judged him "better than [Amos] Strunk" going back for long shots, "better than Speaker" going to his left, and able to outdistance Cobb "in any direction." A solid leadoff hitter whose high in runs scored was 102 (1912), he stole 293 bases lifetime, with a high of 51 in 1910, and walked often. The Phillies snared Paskert (and Hans Lobert) from Cincinnati for four nobodies in 1911; the Cubs traded home run champ Cy Williams for him, even up, in late 1917. /(ADS)

Dan Pasqua — 1961– . OF-DH 1985– **Yankees**, White Sox 477 g, .243, 73 hr, 209 rbi

Despite being an outstanding minor league player, the lefthanded-hitting Pasqua never lived up to New York's high expectations and was traded after 1987. Pasqua was the International League 1985 Rookie of the Year and MVP even though he played in just 78 games (.321, 18 HR, 69 RBI) before being called up. He homered in his second major league at-bat. /(EG)

Art Passarella — 1909–1981. *Umpire* AL 1941–42, 45–53 *2 ASU 3 WS*

Passarella was the first ML umpire to be inducted into military service during WWII. He returned in 1945 and worked in the AL for nine more years. Later he became a cast member of the TV show *The Streets of San Francisco*. He made a controversial call in the bottom of the 10th inning of Game Five of the 1952 WS when he called Yankee runner Johnny Sain out at first. The Dodgers won in the 11th inning. A published photo taken with a high-speed camera later showed that Sain had been safe. /(RTM)

Claude Passeau — 1909– . RHP 1935–47 Pirates, Phillies, **Cubs** 2719 ip, 162–150, 3.32. *1 WS, 16 ip, 1–0, 2.70*
☛ *Led League—k 39. All-Star—41–43, 46.*

Passeau was a competitive righthander, not averse to throwing close to batters. After three seasons with

the cellar-dwelling Phillies, he was traded to the Cubs in mid-1939. He was 20–13 for Chicago in 1940 and won 19 in 1942 and 17 for the 1945 pennant winners. In Game Three of the WS, he hurled a one-hit shutout against the Tigers. Unlike most players, Passeau had no qualms about wearing 13 as his uniform number. He once said: "That's my lucky number. My auto tag is 13. The serial on my rifle is 13. The last two digits on my life insurance are 13, and my address is 113 London Street." He also spent 13 years in the majors, and his name is 13 letters long. /(ARA)

Frank Pastore — 1987– . RHP 1979–86 **Reds**, Twins 986 ip, 48–58, 4.29. *1 LCS, 7 ip, 0–0, 2.57*

Pastore went 13–7 (3.26) to lead the 1980 Reds staff in wins; it was to be his only year with more than nine victories and a winning record. He missed most of 1984 after being hit in the right arm with a line drive off the bat of the Dodgers' Steve Sax. After an unrelated elbow operation in 1985, he returned without his good fastball or breaking stuff and was accused by some of throwing a spitter. /(JCA)

Jim Pastorious — 1881–1941. LHP 1906–09 **Dodgers** 727 ip, 31–55, 3.12

With the 1908 Superbas (later the Dodgers), Pastorious, Harry McIntyre, and Kaiser Wilhelm each had at least 20 losses, with Nap Rucker adding 19. Pastorious (4–20) dropped 14 in a row, lost a one-hitter, and was shut out eight times. His only win the following year was a one-hitter. /(TG)

Freddie Patek [Freddie Joe] (The Flea, Moochie) — 1944– . SS 1968–81 Pirates, **Royals**, Angels 1650 g, .242, 41 hr, 490 rbi. *4 LCS, 15 g, .288, 1 hr, 11 rbi*
☛ *All-Star—72, 76, 78.*

The 5'5" 148-lb Patek was the smallest ML player of his time, but he possessed the range and arm to be an outstanding shortstop, three times an All-Star. He was particularly adept at turning double plays. His speed and aggressive baserunning were his primary offensive weapons. He led the AL in triples (11) in 1971 and stolen bases (53) in 1977. For his career he totaled 385 steals. He hit for the cycle at Minnesota on July 9, 1971, in his first year with the Royals. Not usually a power hitter, he hit three home runs in one game for the Angels in Boston (6/20/80). /(EW)

Max Patkin (The Clown Prince of Baseball) — 1920–

Wherever Bill Veeck ran a major league team (Indians, Browns, White Sox), Max Patkin was a baseline coach and a comic attraction. The gangly, double-jointed Patkin barnstormed the minor league circuit with his pantomime, contortionist act. When Al Schacht retired, Patkin took over the billing and role of The Clown Prince of Baseball. Proud of being a bona fide baseball man, capable of doing an actual coaching job, Patkin was a one-time minor league pitcher. /(JK)

Van Patrick — 1916–1974. *Broadcaster.*

For 22 years the voice of the Detroit Lions and Tigers, then sports director for the Mutual Broadcasting System, Patrick was an announcer for 39 years. When he died he owned four radio stations. /(NLM)

Casey Patten [Case Lyman] — 1876–1935. LHP 1901–08 **Senators**, Red Sox 2062 ip, 105–127, 3.36

Patten was the ace of the dismal Senators from 1901 to 1907, averaging 15 wins and almost 300 innings per season. He had three straight 20-loss seasons (1903–05), and in 1904 he lost nine shutouts. /(ADS)

Daryl Patterson — 1943– . RHP 1968–71, 74 **Tigers**, A's, Cardinals, Pirates 231 ip, 11–9, 4.09. *1 WS, 3 ip, 0–0, 0.00*

Patterson had seven saves and a 2.12 ERA in relief for the 1968 World Champion Tigers. A 4.85 ERA in 1970 signaled his decline, but ironically he finished the season 7–1. /(WOR)

Pat Patterson [Andrew] — Unk.–Unk. 3B-2B-SS-OF Negro Leagues 1939–49 Cleveland Red Sox, Homestead Grays, Pittsburgh Crawfords, Kansas City Monarchs, **Philadelphia Stars**, Newark Eagles, Houston Eagles statistics not available

Patterson was an outstanding switch-hitting infielder in the Negro Leagues, Mexico, and the Dominican Republic during a career that produced a batting average of approximately .330. Available data shows him hitting .346 with the Pittsburgh Crawfords in 1935; .349 in the 1937 Dominican League; .340 in the 1940 Mexican League and .321 there in 1946; and .320 with the 1947 Newark Eagles. He hit .313 for Pittsburgh in the 1935 NNL playoffs, and .261 for Newark in their 1946 Black World Series triumph. In four all-star appearances, including starts at third base for the East in 1939 and 1942, he batted .300. He was one of seven Negro Leaguers named in a 1938 New York *Daily News* column by white sportswriter Jimmy Powers

as being capable of helping the New York Giants win the pennant. /(MFK)

Roy Patterson (The St. Croix Boy Wonder) — 1876–1953. RHP 1901–07 **White Sox** 1365 ip, 81–72, 2.75. 20 wins: 01

In 1898 Charles Comiskey's St. Paul Saints, the best team in the Western League, lost an exhibition game in Duluth to the local nine. The Duluth Dukes prevailed that day behind the pitching of Roy Patterson, who was rewarded with a Saints contract the following year. In 1900, when the Saints moved to Chicago to become the White Sox, the Boy Wonder from St. Croix Falls, WI, was the team's best pitcher. When the American League declared itself a major league in 1901, Patterson was on the mound April 24 in the league's first game. Since the day's other games were rained out, Patterson became the AL's first winning pitcher, downing the Cleveland Blues 8–2. He was 20–16 that season, 19–14 the next. After his ML career ended in 1907, Patterson spent a decade with the Minneapolis Millers (American Association). /(RL)

Marty Pattin (Duck, Bulldog) — 1943– . RHP 1968–80 Angels, Pilots/Brewers, Red Sox, **Royals** 2038 ip, 114–109, 3.62. *3 LCS, 7 ip, 0–0, 5.14. 1 WS, 1 ip, 0–0, 0.00*
☛ *All-Star—71.*

A well-traveled and durable journeyman, Pattin was drafted off the Angel roster by Seattle in the 1969 expansion draft. In 1970 the team moved to Milwaukee and Pattin was named an All-Star the next year (14–14, 3.12). A 10-player trade brought him to Boston, where he had his best season (17–13, 3.23). Traded to the Royals in 1974, he split his time over seven seasons in Kansas City between starting and relieving. In 1975 he was AL Pitcher of the Month in June as a starter and in September as a reliever. Sometimes called Bulldog because he was a battler, he was more often called Duck by teammates because of his imitation of the Disney character's voice. Pattin earned his bachelor's and masters degrees at Eastern Illinois and is a member of the NAIA Hall of Fame. /(EW)

Gabe Paul — 1910– . *Executive.*

Gabe Paul's baseball career began at 16 when he was publicity and ticket manager for Rochester (International League) and it ended when he was president of the Cleveland Indians in 1984. Along the way he was general manager of the Reds and the Houston Colt .45s, president and general manager of the Indians for 10 years, and president of the

Yankees before returning to head the Indians in 1978–84. He was responsible for changing the minor league draft system from drawing numbers out of a hat to drafting in reverse order of the finish in the standings. He led the fight to split each major league into two divisions, and pushed through the free agent drafting of players. He supported the designated hitter rule, and put through the rule change that requires fielders to bring their gloves in off the field after each half-inning. /(NLM)

Mike Paul — 1945– . LHP 1968–74 **Indians**, Rangers, Cubs 627 ip, 27–48, 3.92

A journeyman who moved between starting and relieving, Paul's best season was 1972 with Texas, when he was only 8–9 but had a 2.17 ERA. /(ME)

Gene Paulette — 1892–1966. 1B-2B 1911, 16–20 Giants, Browns, **Cardinals**, Phillies 500 g, .269, 2 hr, 165 rbi

Paulette saw little action as the backup first baseman to George Sisler. He was traded to the Cardinals in 1917, and the following year he played every position except catcher. He hit .288 in a career-high 562 at-bats for the Phillies in 1920, but after the season he was banned from baseball by Commissioner Landis for accepting gifts from gamblers. /(NLM)

Don Pavletich — 1938– . C-1B 1957, 59, 62–71 **Reds**, White Sox, Red Sox 536 g, .254, 46 hr, 193 rbi

A solid catcher who could fill in at first base, Pavletich was a career backup. In 1966, his most active season, he hit 12 home runs in 83 games for the Reds. /(EW)

Mike Paxton — 1953– . RHP 1977–80 Red Sox, **Indians** 467 ip, 30–24, 4.70

After breaking in as the Red Sox co-Rookie of the Year (10–5, 3.83) in 1977, Paxton went to Cleveland in the Dennis Eckersley deal. After going 12–11 in 1978, he suddenly lost his effectiveness. /(ME)

Jimmy Payton — Unk.–1955. *Scout.*

Payton scouted for the Cubs from 1940 to 1955, and the former minor league shortstop and manager was instrumental in the signing of eventual Hall of Famer Ernie Banks. /(FVP)

Johnny Peacock — 1910–1981. C 1937–45 **Red Sox**, Phillies, Dodgers 619 g, .262, 1 hr, 194 rbi

A former University of North Carolina quarterback, Peacock was an aggressive catcher with virtually no long-ball power. He shared receiving duties for the Red Sox for a half-dozen years, in part because he batted lefthanded. /(EW)

Dickey Pearce — 1836–1908. SS 1871–77 New York (NA), **Brooklyn (NA)**, St. Louis (NA), St. Louis (NL) *NA:* 257 g, .254; *ML:* 33 g, .198, 0 hr, 14 rbi.
    Manager 1872, 75 New York (NA), **St. Louis (NA)** 73–49, .598

One of baseball's most famous early players, Pearce broke in with the Brooklyn Atlantics in 1856. He and James Creighton were probably the two earliest players to be paid. A brilliant fielder, Pearce is generally given credit for molding the shortstop's play into its present form. A good hitter, and fast, he was legendary for introducing and mastering his "tricky hit," known today as the bunt. For much of his career, the rules permitted it to roll foul and still be a hit.

Pearce played professionally for 22 years, spanning the generation from the game's beginnings to the National League. The *St. Louis Times*, June 30,

Dickey Pearce

1868, applauded Pearce, summarizing his contributions: "Pearce has been noted as a superior shortstop for ten years and to-day has no equal in the base ball field. He bats with great judgment and safety . . ." Following his playing days, he umpired into the mid-1880s. /(DAS)

George Pearce — 1888-1935. LHP 1912-17 **Cubs**, Cardinals 510 ip, 35-27, 3.11

In each of Pearce's six ML seasons, he played for a different manager, five of whom would reach the Hall of Fame: Joe Tinker, Johnny Evers, Frank Chance, Roger Bresnahan, and Miller Huggins. Pearce won 13 games for both the 1913 and 1915 Cubs. /(DB)

Pearson Cup Game 1977- .

An annual mid-season exhibition game played between the Montreal Expos and Toronto Blue Jays for the mythical "Canadian Baseball Championship", the Pearson Cup is named for the late Lester Pearson (1895-1972). A lifelong baseball fan, Pearson was instrumental in bringing the Expos to Montreal. He won the Nobel Peace Prize in 1957 for his role in ending the 1956 Arab-Israeli war, and served as Canadian prime minister, 1963-1968. Proceeds of the Pearson Cup game benefit Canadian amateur baseball programs. /(MC)

Albie Pearson — 1934- . OF 1958-66 Senators, Orioles, **Angels** 988 g, .270, 28 hr, 214 rbi
☛ *Rookie of the Year—58. All-Star—63.*

The smallest player in the ML throughout his career, the 5'5" 140-lb Pearson was AL Rookie of the Year in 1958 when he hit .275 for the Senators. After a couple of poor seasons, he was grabbed by the Angels in the 1961 expansion draft. He learned to use his size to advantage to draw walks, raised his BA, and led the AL with 115 runs scored in 1962. He hit a career-high .304 the next year, but recurring back spasms restricted his play after that and eventually ended his career. After tries at pro golf and disc jockeying, he became a radio evangelist in southern California and Nevada. /(MC)

Ike Pearson [Issac Overton] — 1917-1985. RHP 1939-42, 46, 48 **Phillies**, White Sox 559 ip, 13-50, 4.83

Pearson pitched for the Phillies through four straight last-place finishes. In 1941 he led all NL relievers with a 2.07 ERA in 36 appearances, winning 4, losing 4, and saving 6. But he lost 10 starts to finish 4-14. /(JK)

Monte Pearson — 1909-1978. RHP 1932-41 Indians, **Yankees**, Reds 1429 ip, 100-61, 4.00. *4 WS, 36 ip, 4-0, 1.01*
☛ *Led League—era 33. All-Star—36, 40.*

Pearson was AL ERA leader (2.33) as a rookie with the Indians in 1933. The next year he was 18-13, but after a disappointing 1935 season, he was traded to the Yankees with Steve Sundra for Johnny Allen. He bounced back with his best year, 19-7, and an AL-leading .731 percentage. In 1937 he pitched a no-hitter against his old team, the Indians. Pearson had control problems (in four seasons he walked more than 100) but he often benefited from strong batting support. He also suffered various arm and body ailments and was reluctant to pitch unless he felt in top condition. An outstanding WS pitcher, he won four well-pitched games for the 1936-39 Yankees, including a two-hit shutout of the Reds in 1939. /(LRD)

Hal Peck — 1917- . OF 1943-49 Dodgers, A's, **Indians** 355 g, .279, 15 hr, 112 rbi

After a brief trial with the Dodgers, Peck suffered a hunting accident that cost him part of his foot. The A's acquired him after a .346 season at Milwaukee (American Association). In 1948 he led the AL in pinch hits (8) with the pennant-winning Indians. /(EW)

Roger Peckinpaugh (Peck) — 1891-1977. SS 1910, 12-27 Indians, **Yankees**, Senators, White Sox 2012 g, .259, 48 hr, 739 rbi. *3 WS, 19 g, .250, 1 hr, 4 rbi.*
*Manager 1914, 28-33, 41 Yankees, **Indians** 499-489*
☛ *Most Valuable Player—25.*

Peckinpaugh was the premier AL shortstop in his day. Rangy, full-chested, and broad-shouldered, with big hands and bowed legs, he pursued the ball relentlessly and effectively, if not always gracefully. A steady hitter, he had a 29-game streak in 1919. After nine years with the Yankees, including their first pennant-winning season, he was traded to the Senators. There he paired with young second baseman Bucky Harris in a top combination that produced a record 168 double plays in 1922. Peckinpaugh was a WS hero in 1924, doubling home the winning run in Game Two and saving Game Six with a key fielding play. In 1925 he had a great regular season, hitting .292 and being named AL MVP. But the WS was a disaster. The old pro looked to for reliability made eight errors, several in key spots, as the Senators allowed the Pirates to come back from a 3-1 deficit and lost the Series.

Roger Peckinpaugh

Peckinpaugh had managed the Yankees for 14 games in 1914, and returned to managing with the Indians after retiring as a player. He later served as Cleveland president and general manager. In 17 years as a player, he was thrown out of only one game. /(ADS)

Al Pedrique — 1960– . SS 1987– Mets, **Pirates**, Tigers 174 g, .247, 1 hr, 36 rbi

After ten seasons in the minors, Pedrique was traded to the Pirates in mid-1987 and hit .301 the rest of the way as Pittsburgh's primary shortstop. But the 6′ 155-lb Venezuelan dropped off to .180 in 1988 and was sent down. /(WOR)

Westbrook Pegler — 1894–1969. *Writer.*

Pegler entered sports journalism when he returned from WWI service in the Navy and joined UPI as a baseball reporter. He introduced a tough and rowdy way of reporting, replacing the style of noncritical hero worship which had become hackneyed. He became a daily sports columnist for the Chicago *Tribune* and for several years wrote a weekly column for *The Sporting News.*

Pulitzer Prize-winner Pegler's fame as a mainstream journalist is kept alive by those against whom he fulminated most viciously in his syndicated columns; liberals continue to view him as a glaring example of a reactionary newspaperman. His lost libel suit against Quentin Reynolds is often cited in both journalism and law courses. /(JK)

Heinie Peitz [Henry Clement] — 1870–1943. C-3B-1B-2B 1892–06, 13 Cardinals, **Reds**, Pirates 1234 g, .271, 16 hr, 560 rbi

One of the better catchers around the turn of the century, Peitz was a reliable hitter (career-high .315 in 1902) who often played other positions as well. He usually caught lefthander Ted Breitenstein and the duo became known as the Pretzel Battery because of their German ancestry and a mutual fondness for postgame beer and pretzels at a Cincinnati saloon. Peitz's older brother Joe played a few games in the Cardinal outfield in 1894. /(JK)

Chris Pelekoudas — 1918–1984. *Umpire* NL 1960–75 *3 ASU 2 LCS 2 WS*

A decision by Pelekoudas had a bearing on one of baseball's most famous records. On August 18, 1965 Hank Aaron hit a home run in Sportsman's Park, St. Louis. Except he didn't; Pelekoudas ruled it an illegal hit because Aaron's left foot touched outside the batter's box as he reached out for the pitch. As a result, the record for most homers is 755 instead of 756. Pelekoudas was also the first to eject Gaylord Perry from a game for using an illegal greasy substance on the ball. When the umpire retired, he sent Perry a three-pound jar of Vaseline. /(RTM)

Eddie Pellagrini — 1918– . SS-2B-3B 1946–49, 51–54 Red Sox, **Browns**, Phillies, Reds, Pirates 563 g, .226, 20 hr, 133 rbi

Pellagrini homered in his first ML at-bat, but didn't hit enough to play regularly through the rest of his career. A utility man who visibly hustled, he was a fan favorite. /(EW)

Barney Pelty — 1880–1938. RHP 1903–12 **Browns**, Senators 1918 ip, 92–117, 2.62

One of the first Jewish players in the American League, the Yiddish Curver was a workhorse for the Browns, a member of their starting rotation from 1904 through 1911. His peak year was 1906, when he went 16–11 with a 1.59 ERA (second in the AL). The following season he lost a league-high 21 games. /(WAB)

Alejandro Pena — 1959– . RHP 1981– **Dodgers** 769 ip, 38–38, 2.93. *3 LCS, 9 ip, 1–1, 3.86. 1 WS, 5 ip, 1–0, 0.00*
☛ *Led League—era 84.*

Pena's poise and 95-mph fastball won him the NL ERA title (2.48) in 1984, when he went 12–6 with four shutouts. But the young Dominican was already suffering from a sore shoulder, which required surgery in February of 1985. More than a year of rehabilitation followed, but by late 1987, Pena had established himself as one of the Dodgers' best relievers. /(JCA)

Jose Pena — 1942– . RHP 1969–72 Reds, **Dodgers** 112 ip, 7–4, 4.97

As a starter in Mexico, Pena posted a 246–192 record (1961–66, 1969, 1973–84). But in his four major league trials with the Reds and Dodgers, he was used only in relief. He won as many as 22 games in a Mexican League season (1978). In 1982, at age 40, he went 10–1 for Ciudad Juarez. /(MC)

Orlando Pena — 1933– . RHP 1958–60, 62–67, 70–71, 73–75 Reds, **A's**, Tigers, Indians, Pirates, Orioles, Cardinals, Angels 1203 ip, 56–77, 3.70

Noted for his large assortment of off-speed pitches, Pena was a standout in the minors (146–85). He was used regularly as a major league starter only by the A's, for whom he lost a league-high 20 games in 1963. He teamed in Kansas City's rotation, and later in the St. Louis bullpen, with fellow Cuban Diego Segui. After a poor year in Triple-A ball in 1969, he was signed by the Royals in 1970 as a batting practice pitcher, and was impressive enough that the Pirates signed him that June. His 22–3 (1.25) record in two minor leagues in 1972 earned him three final ML seasons. He later scouted for the Tigers. /(FJO)

Roberto Pena [born Roberto Cesar Zapata y Pena](Baby) — 1937–1982. SS-3B-1B 1965–66, 68–71 Cubs, Phillies, Padres, A's, **Brewers** 587 g, .245, 13 hr, 154 rbi

This Dominican led AL shortstops in fielding in 1970. His best season offensively was 1968, when he hit .260 with 56 runs in 500 at-bats, all career highs, for the Phillies. /(SFS)

Tony Pena — 1957– . C 1980– **Pirates**, Cardinals 1207 g, .274, 82 hr, 472 rbi. *1 LCS, 7 g, .381. 1 WS, 7 g, .409, 4 rbi*
☛ *All-Star—82, 84–86, 89. Gold Glove—83–85.*

This Dominican catcher was a favorite in Pittsburgh with his low, one-leg-out crouch, snap throws, and line-drive hitting. He was a Gold Glove winner in 1983–85. He hit 15 homers in both 1983 and 1984, but his production tailed off in 1985 and 1986. Still, fans were shocked when he was traded to the Cardinals in April of 1987. The players the Pirates received—Andy Van Slyke, Mike LaValliere, and Mike Dunne—became keys in their resurgence, while Pena recovered from an early-season thumb injury to help St. Louis to the World Series. He batted only .214, but began wearing glasses at the end of the season, and led Cardinal regulars with a .381 average in the LCS and a .409 mark in the WS. His brother Ramon became a pitcher and outfielder in the Pirates and Tigers organizations. Tony and Ramon were taught baseball by their mother, an outstanding softball player. /(ME)

Jim Pendleton — 1924– . OF 1953–59, 62 **Braves**, Pirates, Reds, Astros 444 g, .255, 19 hr, 97 rbi

One of the top shortstops in the Negro National League during the late 1940s, Pendleton shaved two years off his age when he signed with the Dodgers. However, with Pee Wee Reese at short for Brooklyn, Jim sat in the minors for four years despite excellent hitting. Traded to the Braves in 1953, he switched to the outfield and hit .299 in a part-time role. Up and down thereafter, he hit .305 in 46 games for the 1957 Pirates, but was back in the minors in 1958. /(MC)

Terry Pendleton — 1960– . 3B 1984– **Cardinals** 806 g, .263, 38 hr, 384 rbi. *2 LCS, 12 g, .209, 5 rbi. 2 WS, 10 g, .300, 4 rbi*
☛ *Gold Glove—87, 89.*

Although groomed for second base for most of his minor league career, Pendleton took over as Cardinal third baseman after a midseason call-up. Like his predecessor, Ken Oberkfell, the switch-hitting

Pendleton was a good contact batter who showed promise of hitting for average but with limited power. He did not have the speed of many of his teammates, but good judgment and good jumps enabled him to steal 24 bases in 1986.

From the beginning, the 5'9" 180-lb Pendleton showed great range, lightning reflexes, and a rifle arm at third. In 1986 he led NL third basemen in chances, putouts, and assists. The following campaign he was awarded his first Gold Glove. /(FO)

Herb Pennock (The Squire of Kennett Square) — 1894–1948. LHP 1912–17, 19–34 A's, Red Sox, **Yankees** 3558 ip, 240–162, 3.61. 20 wins: 24, 26 *5 WS, 5–0, 1.95*
☛ *Hall of Fame—1948.*

Pennock pitched with grace, economy, and style. Nothing he did was overpowering; everything he did was tantalizingly effective. A typical Pennock game

Herb Pennock

had few strikeouts, but even fewer walks—2.3 on average. He was hittable. Over 22 years, he allowed more than a hit an inning, yet those hits somehow produced only 3.61 earned runs a game. He seemed to give up many lazy flies to the outfield. Even-tempered, Pennock never got rattled under pressure. He threw with an effortless, unvarying motion, and it was said that a peek inside his head would reveal the weakness of every batter in the league. He pitched 35 shutouts.

Pennock came from historic Kennett Square, PA, amid comfortable country acres whose owners were horsemen and fox hunters. Pennock himself was an expert rider and a master of hounds. As a profitable hobby, he raised silver foxes for their pelts. Hence, the cumbersome but appropriate nickname: the Squire (or Knight) of Kennett Square.

Originally an unpromising first baseman, Pennock found his true talent on the mound, pitching a no-hitter in 1911, which his catcher, Earle Mack, brought to the attention of his father, Connie Mack. Only 18 when he joined the Athletics, Pennock steadily improved, even earning a brief World Series appearance in the 1914 loss to the Braves. Early in 1915, Mack waived Pennock to the Red Sox.

After two mediocre seasons and a year in the WWI Navy, Pennock hit his stride and, in 1923, became one of the many prizes the Yankees stripped from Boston. The price: three nondescript players and $50,000. In that first year with New York, he led the league in winning percentage (.760), going 19–6, the first of four over-.700 seasons. He then won two games in the 1923 Series triumph over the Giants. He followed with a 21–9 record in 1924, and was a combined 59–25 in 1926–28. He added two more WS victories in 1926, and one in 1927—a jewel in which he retired the first 22 Pirates he faced and ended with a three-hitter.

The Squire retired in 1934 after one year as a Red Sox reliever. He was a Boston coach, 1936–40, then became the supervisor of their farm system. In 1944 Bob Carpenter made him general manager of the Phillies, a post he held until his death in 1948, the year of his induction into the Hall of Fame. /(ADS)

Gene Pentz — 1953– . RHP 1975–78 Tigers, **Astros** 191 ip, 8–9, 3.62

Pentz was a fair reliever, going 3–3 with five saves and a 2.95 ERA in 1976 and 5–2, 3.83 in 1977 for the Astros, but an injury ended his career in May 1978. /(JFC)

Joe Pepitone (Pepi) — 1940– . 1B-OF 1962–73 **Yankees**, Astros, Cubs, Braves 1397 g, .258, 219 hr, 721 rbi. *2 WS, 11 g, .154, 1 hr, 5 rbi* ☛ *All-Star—63–65. Gold Glove—65–66, 69.*

Pepitone joined the Yankees in 1962, playing behind Moose Skowron at first base. Fun-loving and carefree, he spent his $20,000 signing bonus on a fancy car and a motorboat. Pepitone had a powerful swing and an excellent glove, and some of Pepitone's tougher friends thought he should be the regular first baseman ahead of Skowron. They offered to help Joe out by breaking Skowron's legs; Pepitone declined. The Yankee brass believed he could handle the job and before the 1963 season traded Skowron to the Dodgers. Pepitone responded admirably, hitting .271 with 27 HR and 89 RBI. He went on to win three Gold Gloves, but in the 1963 World Series he made an infamous error. With the score tied 1–1 in the seventh inning of Game Four, he lost a routine Clete Boyer throw in the white shirtsleeves of the Los Angeles crowd, and the batter, Jim Gilliam, went all the way to third base and scored the Series-winning run on a sacrifice fly. He redeemed himself somewhat in the 1964 Series against the Cardinals with a Game Six grand slam.

The ever-popular Pepitone remained a fixture throughout the decade, even playing centerfield after bad knees reduced Mickey Mantle's mobility. After the 1969 season he was traded to the Astros for Curt Blefary. Later he played for the Cubs and finished his major league career with the Braves.

Pepitone played baseball in Japan for three years, but the regimented Japanese didn't know what to make of the free-spirited Pepitone, who was unhappy away from home. He jumped the Yakult Sparrows in 1973 while hitting .163, becoming a one-man international incident. In the 1980s he was arrested on gun and drug charges while hanging out with the wrong people and served a small amount of time in prison; he eventually got out on a work-release program, working in the Yankee front office. /(TJG)

Laurin Pepper — 1931– . RHP 1954–57 **Pirates** 109 ip, 2–8, 7.06

A football and baseball star at Mississippi Southern, Pepper was a sixth-round draft pick of the NFL Pittsburgh Steelers in 1954 but chose to sign a $35,000 bonus contract with the Pirates. Forced by the bonus rule of the time to spend two years on the big league roster before he could be farmed out, he saw little action and never fulfilled expectations. /(ME)

Ray Pepper — 1905– . OF 1932–36 Cardinals, **Browns** 339 g, .281, 14 hr, 170 rbi

Pepper held a starting job only in 1934 for the Browns. That year he hit .298, batted in 101 runs, and led AL outfielders by assisting in four double plays. /(NLM)

Oswaldo Peraza — 1962– . RHP 1988 **Orioles** 86 ip, 5–7, 5.55

Peraza was originally a catcher who led his league in fielding in 1982, but hit just .218. Converted to pitching, he had control problems. The Orioles obtained him for Mike Flanagan in a Toronto stretch-run deal in 1987. He missed 1989 with injuries. /(JFC)

Jack Perconte — 1954– . 2B 1980–86 Dodgers, Indians, **Mariners**, White Sox 433 g, .270, 2 hr, 76 rbi

Perconte, a Murray State (Kentucky) University graduate, made three all-star teams in the minors, but did not win a regular spot until 1984 with the Mariners. In 155 games he hit .294 with 29 stolen bases. He had no home run power, but he was good at getting on base. Despite good range in the field, he was criticized as a poor pivot man on double plays. When he slumped the next season, he was sent to the minors one day before he became eligible for free agency. The resulting protests by teammates and fans brought his recall and the resignation of the Seattle GM. /(NLM)

Hub Perdue [Herbert Rodney] (The Gallatin Squash) — 1882–1968. RHP 1911–15 **Braves**, Cardinals 918 ip, 51–64, 3.85

Perdue was 16–13 for the 1913 Braves. After a 2–5 beginning the next year, he was traded to the Cardinals, thus missing Boston's "Miracle" finish in 1914. His odd nickname came from famous sportswriter Grantland Rice as a combination of Perdue's hometown (Gallatin, Tennessee) and the vegetable called Hubbard squash. /(JK)

Marty Perez — 1947– . SS-2B-3B 1969–78 Angels, **Braves**, Giants, Yankees, A's 931 g, .246, 22 hr, 241 rbi

Perez was a member of heavy-hitting Braves teams for five-plus seasons, replacing Sonny Jackson at shortstop in 1971 and moving to second base in 1974. Though he was in the lineup for his glove, he had eight homers and 57 RBI in 1973, and batted as high as .275 in 1975. He was traded from Atlanta to San Francisco to New York to Oakland within 11 months. /(PB)

Melido Perez — 1966– . RHP 1987– Royals, **White Sox** 391 ip, 24–25, 4.47

The younger brother of NL pitcher Pascual Perez, Melido was a top AL rookie in 1988. Signed in 1983 by the Royals, the spidery Dominican impressed the White Sox by winning his ML debut against them on September 4, 1987. That December, Chicago shipped the disappointing, high-salaried Floyd Bannister to the Royals for four young players, with Perez the key. Inserted into the rotation in 1988, Perez, brandishing a split-fingered fastball, became the first White Sox rookie to win in double digits since 1980, going 11–10. /(RL)

Pascual Perez — 1957– . RHP 1980–85, 87– Pirates, **Braves**, Expos 1156 ip, 64–62, 3.48. *1 LCS, 9 ip, 0–1, 5.19*
☛ *All-Star—83.*

No matter what his win-loss record, Perez was always in the spotlight for his antics, intensity, fines, suspensions, and incarcerations. His showmanship pleased fans but could annoy opponents: shooting batters with an imaginary finger-gun, pounding the ball into the ground, and running full speed to the dugout (gold chains and long, curly locks bouncing) after an inning-ending strikeout. He eventually added the "Pascual pitch" (his version of the "eephus") to his repertoire. And he was involved in more than one beanball incident.

The animated, rail-thin Dominican hot dog became a legend in Atlanta on August 19, 1982, the day he was to make his first start for the Braves. He had just passed his driver's test and got lost on his way to the stadium. He circled Atlanta three times on I-285, ran out of gas, and arrived 10 minutes after gametime.

Perez went 15–8 in 1983 but faced drug charges in the Dominican Republic that winter and found himself in jail. By May he was allowed to rejoin the Braves, and he went 14–8. Disabled three times in 1985 with shoulder pain, he went AWOL on the way to Montreal after a July 21 loss in New York and was suspended until August 5. He finished the year 1–13 and was released the following April.

Though he was out of organized ball in 1986, the Expos signed Perez to a minor league contract for 1987. Visa problems kept him from reporting until May. He joined the Expos in August and went 7–0. One of his 12 wins in 1988 was a five-inning, rain-shortened 1–0 no-hitter in Philadelphia on September 24. He also pinch ran 14 times that year. He started slowly in 1989, but by mid-season was back to his 1988 form.

Pascual's brothers Melido, Dario, and Valerio, were all signed as pitchers by Kansas City. Melido pitched for the White Sox in 1989. /(JCA)

Tony Perez — 1942– . 1B-3B 1964–1986 **Reds**, Expos, Red Sox, Phillies 2777 g, .279, 379 hr, 1652 rbi. *6 LCS, 20 g, .234, 3 hr, 13 rbi. 5 WS, 27 g, .242, 3 hr, 11 rbi*
☛ *All-Star—67–70, 74–76.*

One of baseball's greatest run producers, Perez retired as the 14th-best RBI man in ML history. After sharing Cincinnati's first-base job in his first two years, Perez was switched to third base from 1967 to 1972 to get slugger Lee May into the lineup. For ten years (1967–76) Perez was one of the leaders of The Big Red Machine, six times topping 100 RBI. With Perez in the infield, the Reds won four pennants. In 1970, his top season, he hit .317 with 40 homers and 134 RBI. He belted three home runs in the 1975 WS against the Red Sox, two in Game Five, and one in Game Seven when Bill Lee tried to fool him with a soft lob.

He later had several excellent years for Montreal and Boston, and he remained a dangerous pinch hitter for several seasons after his days as a regular ended. He was often compared to first baseman Orlando Cepeda, and Perez's final homer in 1986 tied him with Cepeda at 379 for the most career homers by a Latin player. /(MM)

Broderick Perkins — 1954– . 1B-DH **Padres**, Indians 516 g, .271, 8 hr, 157 rbi

Perkins was a singles hitter who looked promising after he hit .370 in 100 at-bats in 1980, but his norm was about 100 points lower. San Diego got Ed Whitson from Cleveland in exchange for Perkins and Juan Eichelberger in November 1982. /(WOR)

Cy Perkins [Ralph Foster] — 1896–1963. C 1915, 17–31, 34 **A's**, Yankees, Tigers 1171 g, .259, 30 hr, 409 rbi

It took Hall of Fame catcher Mickey Cochrane to take Cy Perkins's job away. After six seasons (1919–24) of smooth glove work as the A's first-string receiver, the light-hitting Perkins lost out to the hard-hitting rookie. What's more, Perkins helped turn Cochrane into a defensive replica of himself, and stayed on as Cochrane's backup through 1930. Perkins became greatly valued as a Yankee, Tiger, and Phillie coach, helping develop pitchers Robin Roberts and Curt Simmons. /(JK)

Tony Perez scoring the winning run in Game Three of the 1972 World Series

Harry Perkowski — 1922– . LHP 1947, 49–55 **Reds,** Cubs 697 ip, 33–40, 4.37

Despite his smooth motion, Perkowski was plagued by wildness, averaging a walk every two innings. He won 12 for the Reds in both 1952 and 1953. /(MC)

Ron Perranoski — 1936– . LHP 1961–73 **Dodgers,** Twins, Tigers, Angels 1175 ip, 79–74, 2.79. *2 LCS, 7 ip, 0–1, 10.29. 3 WS, 7 ip, 0–0, 5.87*

Originally signed by the Cubs, Perranoski went to the Dodger organization in 1960 in a four-player deal that sent Don Zimmer to Chicago. Switched from starting to relieving, he was used exclusively against lefthanders when he first came to the Dodgers but became the stopper in 1962 and led the majors with 70 appearances. The next year he was brilliant (16–3, 1.67), leading the NL in winning percentage and appearances. Using a fastball, curve, and sinker, Perranoski remained the mainstay of the

Los Angeles bullpen through 1967, when he again led the league in appearances. Traded to Minnesota before the 1968 season, Perranoski started slowly in the new league, but benefited from increased work in 1969–70. He led the AL in saves and was *TSN* AL Fireman of the Year both seasons. The Michigan State graduate retired with 179 saves. He served for years as the Dodgers pitching coach under manager Tom Lasorda. /(MM)

George Perring — 1884–1960. 3B-1B-SS-2B 1908–10, 14–15 Indians, **Kansas City (FL)** 513 g, .248, 8 hr, 183 rbi

Perring used a bat that was more than 30 years old, made from a prison scaffold, which he carried in a special case. His father had used it for 20 years. He was the Indians' shortstop for Addie Joss's 1908 perfect game, but saw most action as a Federal League third baseman. /(NLM)

Pol Perritt [William Dayton] — 1892–1947. RHP 1912–21 Cardinals, **Giants**, Tigers 1469 ip, 92–78, 2.89. *1 WS, 8 ip, 0–0, 2.16*

Perritt was a promising young Cardinal pitcher. However, after he signed a Federal League contract in 1915, St. Louis traded him to the Giants. Manager John McGraw talked Perritt into returning to the NL, and he blossomed with the Giants. He won 18 games in both 1916 and 1918, and was 17–7 in the 1917 championship season. /(AAs)

Gaylord Perry — 1938– . RHP 1962–83 **Giants**, Indians, Rangers, Padres, Yankees, Braves, Mariners, Royals 5351 ip, 314–265, 3.10. 20 wins: 66, 70, 72, 74, 78 *1 LCS, 14 ip, 1–1, 6.14*
☛ *Led League—w 70, 72, 78.. Cy Young Award—72, 78. All-Star—66, 70, 72, 74, 79.*

Perry is the only pitcher to win the Cy Young Award in both leagues. Over 22 seasons, he won 314 games by frustrating batters and umpires with his (allegedly) illegal pitches.

Perry signed a $90,000 contract with the Giants and won a regular spot on the ML staff in 1963 after four years in the farm system. Pitching in the shadow of the Giants' great righthander, Juan Marichal, Perry didn't become a recognized star in his own right until 1966. By August of that year he had an incredible 20–2 record, but he slipped in September to finish 21–8. Three good seasons followed. On September 17, 1968, he pitched a no-hitter to beat Bob Gibson and the Cardinals 1–0. In 1970 he led the NL in victories with a 23–13 mark. Perry won 134 games for the Giants before he was traded to Cleveland in 1972.

Perry led the AL in wins in 1972, going 24–16 with a 1.92 ERA for the fifth-place Indians. He was voted the AL Cy Young Award for 1972. He won 19 in 1973 and 21 in 1974 when he was joined by his brother Jim, a longtime AL star, who won 17. Traded to Texas in June 1975, he won 42 for the Rangers in two and a half seasons before he was traded back to the NL. With San Diego in 1978, he went 21–6, led in winning percentage, and again received the NL Cy Young.

Perry was constantly accused of throwing a spitball, a charge he felt gave him an edge against batters. He titled his autobiography *Me and the Spitter*. He fidgeted constantly on the mound, touching his face, glove, uniform, and the bill of his cap before delivering the ball. Umpires nearly undressed him looking for jelly, grease, or Vaseline, and he inspired new rules in 1973 about throwing the

Gaylord Perry

spitter. He remained effective after several teams gave up on him, and won his 300th career game for Seattle in 1982. /(FS)

Gerald Perry — 1960– . 1B-OF 1983- **Braves** 643 g, .270, 37 hr, 246 rbi
☛ *All-Star—88.*

A lefthanded line-drive hitter with outstanding speed for a first baseman, Perry was leading the NL in hitting for most of the summer in 1988 before finishing fifth at .300. He was a part-time player with the Braves in 1984–85, then was returned to Richmond (International League) for most of 1986, where he hit .326. In 1987 Perry finally won the Braves first base job and hit .270 with 42 stolen bases, an Atlanta Braves record and the most by a ML first baseman since Rod Carew's 49 in 1976. Perry has been plagued by recurring shoulder problems since 1988. /(SCL)

Jim Perry — 1936– . RHP 1959–75 Indians, **Twins**, Tigers, A's 3286 ip, 215–174, 3.45. 20 wins: 69–70
2 LCS, 13 ip, 0–1, 7.43. 1 WS, 4 ip, 0–0, 4.50
☛ *Led League—w 60, 70. Cy Young Award—70. All-Star—61, 70–71.*

The less-famous half of the second-winningest brother combination in ML history, Jim Perry won 215 games in 17 seasons, and younger brother Gaylord added 314 to boost the family total to a whopping 529. A tall, trim righthander, Perry overcame several seasons in Twins manager Sam Mele's doghouse, as well as the rap that he was "too nice" to win consistently in the ML, and in 1970 won the AL Cy Young Award with a 24–12 record.

Perry was first signed by the Indians, and in his second season he led the AL in starts (36), wins (18), and shutouts (four) as Cleveland's number-one starter. His ERA jumped to 4.71 in 1961, and after a 12–12 season in 1962 he was traded to the Twins for pitcher Jack Kralick in May 1963. Perry shuttled between the bullpen and starting rotation in his first six seasons with the Twins, usually only starting when injuries or doubleheaders necessitated it, and he pitched well, posting only one ERA above 3.00 from 1965 to 1968. In 1965 Minnesota even placed Perry on waivers, and after he went unclaimed he won seven straight games to help the Twins to the World Series.

Billy Martin became the Twins' manager in 1969, and Perry immediately took over as the number-one starter, going 20–12 with a 2.82 ERA as the Twins won the AL West. The following year, he won the AL Cy Young Award with his 24–12, 3.03 record as the Twins won a second straight division title, but they were swept by the Orioles in the LCS for the second year in a row, with Perry losing Game One. He averaged over 15 wins a year from 1971 to 1974, but was traded to the Tigers in 1973 and to the Indians in 1974 before finishing his career with Cleveland and Oakland in 1975.

At the plate Perry was a switch-hitter, and boasted a respectable .199 career average. /(SCL)

Pat Perry (Atlas) — 1959– . LHP 1985– **Cardinals**, Reds, Cubs 256 ip, 12–10, 3.34

Released by the Astro and Indian organizations due to arm problems, Perry was given a change by the Cardinals. He tallied a 1.85 ERA over two-plus minor league seasons and became a capable short reliever at St. Louis. /(FO)

Scott Perry — 1891–1959. RHP 1915–21 Browns, Cubs, Reds, **A's** 893 ip, 41–68, 3.07

Perry had one big year, for the last-place 1918 Athletics, winning 21 with league highs in innings, starts, complete games, hits, and losses (19). His success reminded the Boston Braves that they had a technical claim to him. The National Commission agreed, but Connie Mack, with Ban Johnson's backing, went to court to retain Perry. The uproar weakened the Commission's authority and fostered the owner hostility that led to Johnson's downfall. Ultimately, the Braves accepted a cash settlement, and Mack kept Perry, who then went 4–17, lost a league-high 25 in 1920, and departed in 1921. /(ADS)

Bill Pertica — 1897–1967. RHP 1918, 21–23 Red Sox, **Cardinals** 331 ip, 22–18, 4.27

The 5'9" Pertica peaked in his rookie season, going 14–10 in 1921 as the Cardinals enjoyed their best season since 1899. Control problems contributed to his sophomore jinx as his ERA shot up from 3.37 to 5.91. /(FJO)

Stan Perzanowski — 1950– . RHP 1971, 74–76, 78 White Sox, **Rangers**, Twins 143 ip, 5–11, 5.11

A cousin of Ron Perranoski, Perzanowski broke in with his hometown White Sox, but was hit hard. His only good season came in 1975 after being traded to the Rangers; he went 3–3 with a 3.00 ERA, his only ERA below 5.00. /(JFC)

Johnny Pesky [born John Michael Paveskovich] — 1919– . SS-3B-2B 1942–54 **Red Sox**, Tigers, Senators 1,270 g, .307, 17 hr, 404 rbi. *1 WS, 7 g, .233.*
    Manager 1963–64, 80 **Red Sox** *147–178, .452*
☛ *All-Star—46.*

A slick fielder, Pesky is best remembered for plays he didn't make, the main one in the seventh game of the 1946 World Series. The Cardinals and the Red Sox were tied 3–3 in St. Louis, with Enos Slaughter on first with two out. Harry Walker blooped a double into centerfield, and Slaughter was running with the pitch. Pesky took the cutoff throw with his back to the plate, checked Walker at first, then saw too late that Slaughter was racing home. Pesky's throw was late, and the Cardinals won the game and the Series. Seven years later in 1952, while Pesky was playing with Detroit, came another memorable nonplay. Virgil Trucks, who had pitched a no-hitter earlier in the season for the Tigers, was mowing down the Yankees. In the third inning, Phil Rizzuto hit a grounder to short that Pesky had trouble getting out of his glove. The scorer originally called the play a hit. But as the game wore on and Trucks looked as if he could get another no-hitter save for Rizzuto's hit, the scorer called the Tiger dugout in the seventh inning. Pesky admitted he had misplayed the ball, the play was scored an error, and Trucks had his second no-hitter.

These famous plays tend to cloud Pesky's otherwise distinguished career. In his rookie season, the lefthanded-hitting Pesky collected 205 hits (a Red Sox rookie record) to lead the league, and finished second in the batting race to teammate Ted Williams with a .331 average. After spending the next three years in the service, he came back in 1946 to lead the Red Sox to their first pennant since 1918 with another league-leading 208 hits, including 11 in a row at one stretch, for a .335 average. On May 8, he set an AL record by scoring six times in one game, later tied by another Red Sox shortstop, Spike Owen. In 1947, after getting married and gaining 30 pounds in the off-season, he had an AL-high 207 hits to lead the league for the third straight year, compiling a .324 average. He also had a 27-game hit streak during the season. In 1948, with the acquisition of Vern Stephens, new manager Joe McCarthy moved Pesky to third, and Pesky hit only .281, but led the majors in double plays. After switching him back to shortstop in 1951, the Red Sox traded him to Detroit during the 1952 season in a nine-player deal, where he played mainly second base. He ended his career with the Senators in 1954. A contact hitter, he struck out just 218 times, never striking out more than 36 times in a season.

After ending his playing career, he managed in the Tiger minor league system from 1956 to 1960 and in the Red Sox' system in 1961 and 1962. He was brought up to manage the big club in 1963, but was fired with two games to go in the 1964 season. He coached with the Pirates in 1965 and 1966, then moved back to Boston and into the broadcast booth from 1969 to 1974. In 1980 he was interim manager at the end of the season after Don Zimmer was fired. /(SEW/EC)

Gary Peters — 1937- . LHP 1959–72 **White Sox**, Red Sox 2081 ip, 124–103, 3.25. 20 wins: 64
☛ *Rookie of the Year—63. Led League—w 64. Led League—era 63, 66. All-Star—64, 67.*

After four brief call-ups with the White Sox, Peters was AL Rookie of the Year in 1963 with a 19–8 mark and league-leading 2.33 ERA. He followed with a 20–8 season in 1964, but arm miseries struck. He rebounded with a second ERA title in 1966 (1.98) and 16 wins in 1967 and again in 1970 after he'd been dealt to the Red Sox.

A good-hitting pitcher (.222 with 19 homers), he was often used as a pinch hitter. On May 26, 1968, manager Eddie Stanky batted him sixth in the order, ahead of Luis Aparicio, Duane Josephson, and Tim Cullen. /(RL)

Ricky Peters — 1955- . OF-DH 1979–81, 83, 86 **Tigers**, A's 307 g, .277, 2 hr, 80 rbi

In his only season as a regular (1980), Peters hit .291 with 2 HR, 79 runs, and 42 RBI as the Tigers' centerfielder, all career highs. /(WOR)

Rusty Peters [Russell Dixon] — 1914- . 2B-SS-3B 1936–38, 40–47 A's, **Indians**, Browns 471 g, .236, 8 hr, 117 rbi

The bespectacled Peters was a poor hitter, but his ability to play any infield position earned him ten years in the ML. His best and busiest campaign was in 1937 with the A's (.260, 43 RBI in 116 games). /(ME)

Cap Peterson [Charles Andrew] — 1942–1980. OF 1962–69 **Giants**, Senators, Indians 536 g, .230, 19 hr, 122 rbi

Signed as a shortstop for a reported $64,000 bonus, Peterson hit well in the Texas League and was used primarily as a pinch hitter for the Giants. He was given a chance to play regularly in the Washington outfield following a 1967 trade, but his .240 BA with only eight home runs put him back on the bench. /(MC)

Fritz Peterson [Fred Ingels] — 1942- . LHP 1966–76 **Yankees**, Indians, Rangers 2218 ip, 133–131, 3.30

As a 1966 Yankee rookie with an average fastball and curve, but with great control and finesse, Peterson went 12–11. By 1970 he had improved to 20–11. Peterson's pitching career plateaued, but he and teammate Mike Kekich made headlines in 1973 when the two traded wives and families. The awkward situation prompted the Yankees to send

Kekich to the Indians. By the time Peterson was exiled to Cleveland with three other pitchers the following year, Kekich was no longer there. /(GDW)

Kent Peterson — 1925- . LHP 1944, 47-53 **Reds**, Phillies 420 ip, 13-38, 4.95

Rushed to the majors by the wartime Reds as an 18-year-old, Peterson retired all three men he faced in the one inning he worked. As a regular starter, he was 6-13 in 1947 and 2-15 in 1948. /(MC)

Geno Petralli [Eugene] — 1959- . C-3B 1982- Blue Jays, **Rangers** 436 g, .287, 20 hr, 120 rbi

Knuckleballer Charlie Hough put Texas catcher Geno Petralli in the record books in 1987. With Hough on the mound on August 22, Petralli committed four passed balls in one inning to tie a major league record. Eight days later, Petralli let six of Hough's evasive deliveries get by him in one game to tie another ML record. Petralli's 35 passed balls that year (32 with Hough) set the ML record for a season. Though he caught Hough in nine more games in 1988 than he had in 1987, Petralli had only 20 passed balls—still enough to lead the majors again. On the positive side, in 1987 Petralli became the first Rangers catcher to hit more than .300 (.302). Originally a switch-hitter, he batted from the left side 92% of the time, and abandoned the right side totally in 1988. /(JCA)

Rico Petrocelli — 1943- . SS-3B 1963, 65-76 **Red Sox** 1553 g, .251, 210 hr, 773 rbi. *1 LCS, 3 g, .167, 1 hr, 2 rbi 2 WS, 14 g, .261, 2 hr, 7 rbi*
☛ *All-Star—67, 69.*

For a decade, Petrocelli was a home-run threat with the Red Sox infield. He was with Boston for their 1967 and 1975 pennants, maturing from a volatile young player to become a steadying influence on his teammates. In Game Six of the 1967 World Series, Petrocelli, Carl Yastrzemski, and Reggie Smith set a WS record by hitting three HR in an inning (the fourth). It was Petrocelli's second shot to clear Fenway's Green Monster that game. His rare combination of power and infield glove work was displayed best in 1969, when he set an AL record for most home runs by a shortstop, with 40, and tied a then-record for fewest errors by a shortstop, with 14.

Petrocelli was moved to third base in 1971 after Boston acquired Luis Aparicio, and led the league in fielding his first year at his new position. But elbow problems in 1974, and a leg injury and beaning in 1975, cost him playing time. He hit just seven HR in '75, but batted .308 in the WS. Inner-ear problems helped to end his career. /(PB)

Dan Petry — 1958- . RHP 1979- **Tigers**, Angels 1830 ip, 113-92, 3.85. *2 LCS, 10 ip, 0-0, 1.74. 1 WS, 8 ip, 0-1, 9.00*
☛ *All-Star—85.*

Petry was a consistent, durable starter for nearly a decade in Detroit, winning at least 10 games in six consecutive seasons and at least 15 in four. He was 19-11 in 1983, leading AL pitchers with 38 starts, and 18-8, 3.24 in 1984 as the number-two starter for the World Champion Tigers. Petry lost Game Two of the WS to the Padres (Detroit's only loss in the Series), and was the starter in the deciding Game Five, but got no decision. In 1985 Petry was 15-13 while pitching over 230 innings for the fourth straight season, but in 1986 he went on the DL for the first time in his ML career, missing over two months after having bone chips removed from his elbow. Petry's ERA ballooned to 5.61 in 1987 and he was traded to California for outfielder Gary Pettis after the season. In 1988 he spent two more months on the DL and won only three games in 22 starts for the Angels. /(SCL)

Gary Pettis — 1958- . OF 1982- **Angels**, Tigers 832 g, .239, 17 hr, 197 rbi. *1 LCS, 7 g, .346, 1 hr, 4 rbi*
☛ *Gold Glove—85-86, 88, 89.*

A breathtaking defensive centerfielder with an anemic bat, Pettis has won three Gold Gloves but hit only .208 and .210 in 1987 and 1988. The slender switch-hitter has sprinter's speed, enabling him to chase fly balls deep into either outfield gap and to steal at least 44 bases in four of his five full ML seasons, but he also strikes out often and rarely hits the ball hard. He won the Angels' centerfield job in 1984, and by 1986 his average was up to a career-high .258 as the Angels won the AL West. Pettis had nine hits in the Angels' seven-game loss to the Red Sox in the 1986 LCS, but in 1987 his average dropped to .208, and when Devon White, a comparable defensive player, emerged from the Angels' farm system, Pettis was traded to Detroit for pitcher Dan Petry. He is the Angels' all-time stolen-base leader with 186. /(SCL)

Jesse Petty (The Silver Fox) — 1894-1971. LHP 1921, 25-30 Indians, **Dodgers**, Pirates, Cubs 1208 ip, 67-78, 3.68

Petty was "tried and found wanting" in a famous mock trial by the Big Four, the central committee of Brooklyn's Daffiness Boys, because he didn't know the meaning of the word "ignominy." In 1926 he led the Dodger staff with 17 wins, while tying for the NL lead with 17 losses. /(TG)

Bruce Petway — 1886–1941. C-OF-MGR Negro Leagues 1906–25 Leland Giants, Brooklyn Royal Giants, Philadelphia Giants, **Chicago American Giants**, Detroit Stars statistics not available

Petway dropped his pursuit of a career in medicine at Nashville's Meharry Medical College in 1906 to play pro baseball. He quickly became known as one of the best black catchers; he proved himself in a series against the Detroit Tigers played in Cuba in 1910 in which he batted .390 and threw Ty Cobb out at second several times. He is reported to have been the first catcher to consistently throw to second base without rising from the squat. A good baserunner, he led the Cuban League with 20 stolen bases in 1912. He played on the dominating Chicago American Giants from 1911 to 1918, then served as a player-manager for Detroit until his retirement. A consistent hitter with little power, he batted .349 in 1923 and .341 in 1924 as his career was winding down. /(BP)

Big Jeff Pfeffer [Francis Xavier] — 1882–1954. RHP-OF 1905–08, 10–11 Cubs, **Braves** 112 g, 695 ip, 31–40, 3.30; .204, 2 hr, 28 rbi

Big Jeff Pfeffer was the older brother of more-successful pitcher Jeff Pfeffer, though neither was really named Jeff. The name was first given to Francis Xavier when he came up in 1905 while James J. Jeffries (Big Jeff) was the heavyweight champ; Pfeffer resembled the prizefighter. He hurled a no-hitter for the Braves against the Reds in 1907. Edward Joseph Pfeffer came along in 1911, Big Jeff's last season, and was called simply Jeff. /(JK)

Fred Pfeffer (Dandelion) — 1860–1932. 2B-SS 1882–97 Troy (NL), **Cubs**, Chicago (PL), Louisville (NL), Giants 1670 g, .255, 95 hr, 1019 rbi

When Pfeffer hit 25 home runs in 1884, a staggering total for the time, three other Chicago teammates topped 20. Lake Front Park had the shortest foul lines ever in ML baseball: 180' in left, 196' in right. Balls hit over the short fences were counted as two-base hits in other seasons, but a ground-rule change in 1884 made them homers. Pfeffer's significant contribution to baseball is that he was the first infielder to cut off a catcher's throw to second base on a double-steal attempt and cut down the runner at the plate. /(JK)

Jeff Pfeffer [Edward] — 1888–1972. RHP 1911, 13–24 Browns, Dodgers, **Cardinals**, Pirates 2407 ip, 158–112, 2.77. 20 wins: 14, 16 *2 WS, 0–1, 2.63*

Jeff was Brooklyn's best pitcher in the years between Nap Rucker and Burleigh Grimes. An impressive figure on the mound (manager Wilbert Robinson always preferred his pitchers to be big fastballers), he was a strong, fast righthander with no qualms about throwing brush-back pitches at hitters who crowded the plate. In 1916 he led the Dodgers to a pennant with 25 wins. He had a loss and a save in the Series.

Pfeffer served a year in the naval reserve in 1918 and returned to help Grimes win the 1920 flag. In 1921, while there still was life in his arm, the Dodgers traded him to the Cardinals for two used-up players, infielder Hal Janvrin and pitcher Ferdie Schupp. Pfeffer won 19 for St. Louis the next season.

Called Ed, he was nicknamed after Big Jeff Pfeffer, his elder brother. /(ADS)

Jack Pfiester [born John Albert Hagenbush] (Jack the Giant Killer) — 1878–1953. LHP 1903–04, 06–11 Pirates, **Cubs** 1058 ip, 71–44, 2.04. 20 wins: 06 *4 WS, 1–3, 3.97* ☛ Led League—era 07.

Pfiester (often and wrongly spelled Pfeister) was a Cub lefthander adroit at holding runners on base. He earned his nickname by compiling a remarkable career record of 15–5 against New York. In two starts against Christy Mathewson in 1908, however, he was first saved from defeat when Fred Merkle failed to touch second base, then was shelled in the first inning of the Cubs' victory in the subsequent playoff game. His 1907 ERA of 1.15 ranks fifth on the all-time single-season list. /(ADS)

Charles Pfirman — 1891–1937. *Umpire* NL 1922–36 *1 ASU 3 WS*

Pfirman was the plate umpire in the 1934 All-Star Game when Carl Hubbell struck out Babe Ruth, Lou Gehrig, Jimmie Foxx, Al Simmons, and Joe Cronin in succession. Earlier, in the 1928 WS, he made a call on Ruth that was more to the Bambino's liking. In the seventh inning of Game Four, Cardinal pitcher Willie Sherdel had apparently struck out Ruth, but Pfirman ruled he had done it with a "quick pitch," legal at the time but illegal in the Series. Given a new life, Ruth connected for his third homer of the game. /(RTM)

Dan Pfister — 1936– . RHP 1961–64 A's 249 ip, 6–19, 4.87

Pfister three-hit Detroit in his first ML start in 1962 but lost 1–0. Plagued by wildness, he went 4–14 that season. /(MC)

Art Phelan (Dugan) — 1887–1964. 3B-2B 1910, 12–15 Reds, **Cubs** 401 g, .236, 8 hr, 131 rbi

Phelan went to the Cubs in a 1912, eight-player deal that sent declining Hall of Fame shortstop Joe Tinker to Cincinnati. A utility man in 1913–14, Phelan left the majors after hitting .219 as the Reds' third baseman in 1915. /(DAS)

William A. Phelon — 1871–1925. *Writer.*

A poet and satirist, Phelon spent 36 years as a baseball writer, beginning with the Chicago *Daily News* at age 18. He worked for the Chicago *Tribune* and New York *Morning Telegraph* before moving to the Cincinnati *Times-Star* in 1910. He was a founding member of the BBWAA, and his magazine articles gave him a national reputation. /(NLM)

Babe Phelps [Ernest Gordon] (Blimp, The Grounded Blimp) — 1908– . C 1931, 33–42 Senators, Cubs, **Dodgers**, Pirates 726 g, .310, 54 hr, 345 rbi
☛ *All-Star—38–40.*

The 6'2" 225-lb lefthanded batter hit .367 in 1936, the record for a catcher qualifying for the batting title. Hypochondria and a refusal to fly (The Grounded Blimp) limited Phelps' career. /(TG)

Ed Phelps — 1879–1942. C 1902–13 **Pirates**, Reds, Cardinals, Dodgers 629 g, .251, 3 hr, 205 rbi. *1 WS, 8 g, .231, 2 rbi*

As a rookie in 1903, Phelps was Pittsburgh's regular catcher in the first modern World Series. Though he was a weak hitter, he was a solid ML catcher for a decade. /(JK)

Ken Phelps — 1954– . DH-1B 1980– Royals, Expos, **Mariners**, Yankees, A's 705 g, .245, 122 hr, 307 rbi. *1 LCS, 1 g, 1.000. 1 WS, 1 g, .000*

Seattle native Phelps had a total of 34 at-bats with the Royals and Expos before being traded to the Mariners in 1983. He was expected to be the regular first baseman for 1984, but he broke a finger in the first week of the season; Alvin Davis was called up and won the job. Phelps was subsequently used primarily as a platooned designated hitter, occasionally subbing for Davis at first base. With an excellent eye and patience at the plate, Phelps was often among league leaders in on-base percentage. His power was well-suited to the Kingdome, giving him one of the AL's best ratios of at-bats to home runs. For a while, he received quite a bit of publicity about being underpublicized. At the time he was traded to the Yankees for Jay Buhner, Phelps was the Mariner franchise leader in HR and slugging percentage. /(TF)

Ray Phelps (Babe) — 1903–1971. RHP 1930–32, 35–36 **Dodgers**, White Sox 602 ip, 33–35, 4.93

When the Dodgers made their 1930 pennant run, they were touting Phelps, from the Alabama coal hills, as the rookie pitcher of the year. Phelps was 14–7 that season, his only successful campaign. /(TG)

Philadelphia Athletics — 1901–1954. Team. *AL Champions 02, 05, 10–11, 13–14, 29–31 World Champions 10–11, 13, 29–30*

The history of the Athletics in Philadelphia is in effect the story of Connie Mack's postplaying career. One of the major figures, with Ban Johnson and Charlie Comiskey, in the founding of the American League, Mack had managed the Milwaukee franchise of the league in 1900, before the AL declared itself a major league. Johnson asked him to lead the new Philadelphia franchise, which would be in head-to-head competition with the NL's Phillies, and Mack was given a quarter-ownership of the Athletics (the name of several former teams in the city). He would eventually become the majority owner of the team (in 1940), and from the start he was the architect of the franchise's growth into a league powerhouse. His 50-year tenure as manager of the club has never been equaled anywhere.

The Athletics lost the services of superstar Nap Lajoie after the Phillies, whose property he had been before jumping to the AL, obtained a court order prohibiting him from playing in Pennsylvania (unless for the Phillies, of course). For the good of the AL, he was transferred to the Cleveland club. But the Athletics nonetheless became league champions the next year (1902), and again in 1905, on the basis of the league's best offense, led by Topsy Hartsel, Lave Cross, and Socks Seybold, and the outstanding pitching of Rube Waddell, by far the best pitcher in the league both seasons. Contending most of the time, the team won back-to-back pennants in 1910–11 and again in 1913–14 with the Hall of Fame talents of Eddie Collins and Home Run Baker (half of the $100,000 Infield), Eddie Plank, Chief Bender, and Herb Pennock, as well as Jack Coombs and Bob Shawkey. In three of those years they also

The 1910 Philadelphia Athletics

won the World Series, but following their upset by the Braves in 1914, Mack broke up the team rather than continue to fight the Federal League for the services of his stars. The Athletics lost an AL-record 117 games in 1916, finished dead last until a seventh-place finish in 1922, and didn't finish above .500 until 1925.

By then, Mack had rebuilt his team, and they finished second that year. After two more second-place finishes behind the Yankees in 1927 and 1928 (Mack liked second-place teams; he said they brought in enough fans to make money, but their stars couldn't ask for high salaries), the new dynasty won three straight pennants and two World Championships, led by four Hall of Famers: sluggers Jimmie Foxx, Al Simmons, and Mickey Cochrane, and pitching ace Lefty Grove. The Depression took its toll, however, and once again Mack had to sell off his stars following the 1932 season. This time the slide to the bottom was more gradual, but last place was the Athletics' nine times in the years 1935–46. It looked like Mack was building a new contender following WWII, but it was not to be. In 1946 the aging gentleman skipper divided his club shares among his three children, and he increasingly relied on right-hand man Jimmie Dykes in the dugout. After the rebuilding plan collapsed into a last-place finish in 1950 following three seasons above .500, Mack's sons forced him into retirement. The club

struggled to near-respectability under Dykes, but after a last-place finish in 1954, with a corresponding slump in attendance, Mack's sons sold out to Arnold Johnson and the franchise, following the example of the Braves, moved west, taking up business in Kansas City. /(WOR)

Philadelphia Phillies (Quakers, Blue Jays) — 1883– . Team. 7456–8576, .465 *NL East Champions 76–78, 80, 83 NL Champions 15, 50, 80, 83 World Champions 80*

In 1883 Alfred Reach, a former player and a sporting-goods manufacturer, united with Colonel John Rogers, a lawyer and politician, to purchase the Worcester Brown Stockings of the National League and move them to Philadelphia. The name the club adopted as a takeoff on their hometown, Phillies, is now the oldest name in the NL.

The team would become known more for its failures than its successes, so its first-season record of 17–81 was appropriate. The team named baseball pioneer Harry Wright manager for 1884, and in 1885 the Phillies finished third with their first winning record, 56–54. They contended in 1887, the year they moved into what would become known as Baker Bowl, and finished second. They remained respectable for the rest of the century, and their outfield in the years 1891–95 contained three Hall of Famers: Billy Hamilton, Sam Thompson, and Ed Delahanty.

The 1915 Philadelphia Phillies

The franchise's troubles began at the dawn of the 20th century. Reach and Rogers had a falling out, and Reach sold his share of the club in 1902. There would be nine more ownership changes before stability returned to Philadelphia. The crosstown Athletics and Connie Mack were unprecedentedly stable, and their emergence with the new American League caused the Phillies grief. Superstar Nap Lajoie jumped to the Athletics in 1901. Although the Phillies were able to obtain a court order that forced his transfer to the AL's Cleveland franchise and prevented him from playing in Pennsylvania, his loss, and Ed Delahanty's death the following season, left the Phillies' offense crippled. One of baseball's biggest disasters struck in 1903, when the Baker Bowl's leftfield bleachers collapsed, killing 12 and injuring 232.

The Phillies contended off and on, winning their first pennant in 1915 on the strength of Grover Cleveland Alexander's first of three straight seasons leading the NL in wins, ERA, and strikeouts, topping 30 victories each year. Gavvy Cravath led the league in HR and RBI. But the Red Sox won the WS in five games, and the Phillies were not to have another chance at the World Championship until 1950. The pitching was usually to blame. After trading away Alexander following the 1917 season, the Phillies topped .500 only once in the next 31 years, and finished last 17 times. During this period, they were tagged the Phutile Phils. The 1930s Phillies, led by slugger Chuck Klein (1932 MVP), became legendarily bad. The owner from 1933 through 1942, Gerry Nugent, was in constant financial need and sold off or traded (in deals that included cash) most of his promising players. In 1943 the NL took the club away from Nugent, but their choice was no better, as new owner William Cox was barred from baseball for betting on the

Phillies. Robert Carpenter, Jr., bought the team before the end of 1943, and he or his son Ruly owned the franchise until 1982. The Carpenters would, by that point, be anachronistic as owners who made their living exclusively from baseball. To stimulate interest in the club, Robert Carpenter conducted a contest to rename the club, and although it was never official, in the years 1944–45 the team was known as the Blue Jays.

Hall of Famer Herb Pennock was named GM in 1943 and spent the last five years of his life building the club that would become known as the Whiz Kids. MVP relief ace Jim Konstanty led the club to the 1950 pennant, leading the NL in appearances and saves. Del Ennis led in RBI, and Richie Ashburn topped NL outfielders in putouts for the second of a ML-record-tying nine seasons. They won the flag from Brooklyn in the last game of the season on a tenth-inning Dick Sisler HR. Ashburn cut down Cal Abrams at the plate in the bottom of the inning. But the Yankees swept the Series, and the Phillies remained without a World Championship. They maintained respectability until 1958, when they began a four-year streak of last-place finishes. Eddie Sawyer, their manager in 1950, came back in 1958 but quit after just one game of the 1960 season, saying, "I'm 49 years old, and I'd love to live to be 50." His replacement was Gene Mauch, who with GM John Quinn rebuilt the team into a contender. The Phillies lost a ML-record 23 straight games in 1961, but by 1962 they were back above .500. In 1964 they lost the pennant on the last day of the season and Mauch was criticized for overusing his three best starters down the stretch. Each appeared in more than 40 games. Jim Bunning, the staff's ace, pitched the NL's first 20th-century perfect game that year, and Richie Allen ran away with the Rookie of the Year award.

After Mauch was fired during the 1968 season, the team dropped below .500 again. They finished last in the NL East for three straight seasons (1971–73) before GM Paul Owens, appointed in 1972, turned things around. The first good signs were the 1972 acquisition of Steve Carlton, who won 27 of the Phillies' 59 victories in 1972 and won the first of a record four Cy Young Awards, and the emergence in 1973 of Mike Schmidt, the greatest third baseman of all time. The Phillies went on to win three straight division titles (1976–78) and finally achieved what had eluded them for so long when they defeated the Royals in six games in the 1980 World Series. No other franchise has waited so long for its first World Championship. Schmidt was the Series MVP.

After the 1981 season the Carpenter family sold the club to a group headed by Bill Giles, who had been with the front office since 1969 and whose father was Warren Giles. The Phillies won another pennant in 1983. /(WOR)

Dave Philley — 1920– . OF-1B 1941, 46–62 **White Sox**, A's, Indians, Orioles, Tigers, Phillies, Giants, Red Sox 1904 g, .270, 84 hr, 729 rbi. *1 WS, 4 g, .125*

Endowed with excellent speed and a fine arm, Philley led AL outfielders in assists three different years. But he is best remembered for his pinch hitting in the late 1950s. In 1958 the switch-hitter had a league-high 18 hits off the Phillies' bench, including eight consecutive pinch hits to end the season. On Opening Day of 1959, he poked a pinch double, establishing a record of nine straight successful pinch-hit appearances. In 1961 Philley collected an AL record of 24 pinch hits with Baltimore. Overall, he hit .299 (93-for-311) off the bench. /(RTM)

Deacon Phillippe [Charles Louis] — 1872–1952. RHP 1899–11 Louisville (NL), **Pirates** 2607 ip, 186–108, 2.59. 20 wins: 99, 01–03, 05 *2 WS, 50 ip, 3–2, 2.88*

One of the greatest control artists of all time, Phillippe averaged just 1.25 walks per nine innings over his career. He broke in with Louisville of the NL in 1899, winning 20 and pitching a no-hitter (5/25/99) to beat the Giants 7–0. When the NL pared to eight teams the next year, Phillippe was one of the players former Louisville owner Barney Dreyfuss took to Pittsburgh when he purchased the Pirates. The tall righthander won 22, 20, and 24 for Pirate pennant winners in 1901–03. After a slump in 1904, he came back to win 22 in 1905. He was the Pittsburgh star in the first World Series (1903) when injuries decimated the Pirate pitching staff. He pitched a six-hitter to defeat Cy Young in Game One of the best-of-nine, a four-hitter to win Game Three, and, following a rain-out, a nine-hitter to win Game Four. After two straight Pirate losses, Phillippe pitched his fourth complete game but lost to Young. Three days later, he threw his record fifth complete game and allowed only three runs on eight hits, but Boston's Bill Dinneen ended the Series with a three-hitter. In 1910, after several years battling a sore arm, he won 13 straight games to go 14–2. /(ME)

Deacon Phillippe

Adolfo Phillips — 1941- . OF 1964-70, 72 Phillies, **Cubs**, Expos, Indians 649 g, .247, 59 hr, 173 rbi

Cub manager Leo Durocher called Phillips "another Willie Mays" when he joined Chicago in 1966. Three years later when he was traded away, Durocher termed him the most disappointing player he'd ever managed. A natural leadoff hitter, the fleet Panamanian refused to bat leadoff. Durocher often batted him eighth, limiting the opportunities to utilize his speed (32 stolen bases in 1966) and power. He hit 16 homers in '66, but drove in only 36 runs. He improved to 17 homers and 70 RBI in 1967, then regressed to 13 and 32. /(MC)

Bill Phillips (Whoa Bill, Silver Bill) — 1868-1941. RHP 1890, 95, 99-1903 Pirates, **Reds** 1289 ip, 71-77, 4.10

Phillips didn't stick in the ML until he was 31, when he was 17-9 for the 1899 Reds. In 1914 he managed the Federal League's first pennant winner at Indianapolis, with Benny Kauff, Bill McKechnie, and Edd Roush as the team's stars. /(JK)

Bubba Phillips [John Melvin] — 1930- . 3B-OF 1955-64 Tigers, White Sox, **Indians** 1062 g, .255, 62 hr, 356 rbi. *1 WS, 3 g, .300*

Phillips began as an outfielder, but didn't hit well enough to play regularly. In 1957 he moved to third base for the White Sox and by hard work made himself into a competent infielder. He had his best season (.264, 18 HR, 72 RBI) in 1961 with Cleveland, leading all AL third basemen in homers. /(ME)

Dave Phillips — 1943- . *Umpire* AL 1970-87 *1 ASU 4 LCS 3 WS*

Phillips was the umpire in charge on July 12, 1979, when Bill Veeck promoted Disco Demolition Night at Comiskey Park, during which fans burned disco records in a huge bonfire on the field between games of a doubleheader. The field became such a mess that Phillips deemed it unplayable and forfeited the game to the Tigers. In 1982, in another highly publicized decision, Phillips ejected Gaylord Perry for throwing an illegal grease ball. Perry was suspended for ten days. A former Missouri Valley Conference basketball referee, Phillips became their supervisor of basketball officials after his umpiring career ended. /(RTM)

Dick Phillips — 1931- . 1B 1962-64, 66 Giants, **Senators** 263 g, .229, 12 hr, 60 rbi

Utility man Phillips was most active for the Washington Senators in 1963 when he hit .237 with 10 HR and 32 RBI in 321 at-bats. /(SFS)

Eddie Phillips — 1901-1968. C 1924, 29, 31-32, 34-35 Braves, Tigers, **Pirates**, Yankees, Senators, Indians 312 g, .237, 14 hr, 126 rbi

This star athlete at Boston College played one season each for six different ML teams, and was several times called up to fill in for a sidelined standout catcher, taking over for Bill Dickey, Luke Sewell, and Frank Pytlak. /(JK)

Jack Phillips (Stretch) — 1921- . 1B 1947-52, 55-57 Yankees, **Pirates**, Tigers 343 g, .283, 9 hr, 101 rbi. *1 WS, 2 g, .000*

A defensive replacement throughout his ML career, the stringbean Clarkson College graduate spelled Johnny Hopp and Ralph Kiner at Pittsburgh and later saw part-time duty at Detroit. /(ME)

Mike Phillips — 1950- . SS-2B-3B 1973-83 Giants, Mets, **Cardinals**, Padres, Expos 712 g, .240, 11 hr, 145 rbi

A poor hitter with little power, Phillips played eleven ML seasons because he was a reliable infield backup. His only period as a regular came in 1975 with the Mets when he replaced injured shortstop Bud Harrelson. In 126 games he hit .251. /(FJO)

Taylor Phillips (Tay, T-Bone) — 1933- . LHP 1956-60, 63 **Braves**, Cubs, Phillies, White Sox 438 ip, 16-22, 4.82

Hard-throwing and wild, Phillips ranks as the fourth-worst-hitting pitcher (minimum 100 at-bats) in ML history, going 6-for-113 (.053). He was 7-10 on the mound for the Cubs in 1958, his most active season. /(DAS)

Tony Phillips — 1959- . 2B-SS-3B 1982- **A's** 835 g, .251, 33 hr, 259 rbi. *2 LCS, 7 g, .200, 1 rbi. 2 WS, 6 g, .238, 1 hr, 3 rbi*

Phillips was a regular at both second base and shortstop for the A's in 1983-84, leading the club in games each year, but then suffered a series of freak injuries that kept him a part-time player. First signed by the Expos, Phillips was traded to the Padres organization for Willie Montanez in 1980, then traded to the A's in 1981. He began the 1983 season as Oakland's starting shortstop, then moved to second when Donnie Hill arrived in mid-season, only to move back the following year when Hill was injured. In 1985 Phillips broke his foot twice before the season started and did not play until August, and in 1987 his wrist was broken by a Mark McGwire line drive in batting practice. In between, he became the first Oakland A's player to hit for the cycle on May 16, 1986 at Baltimore, and on July 6, 1986 he tied the ML record with 12 assists in a nine-inning game at second base. In 1988 Phillips was a utility player for the AL champion A's, playing most often at third base and in the outfield. In 1989 he set a WS record when he played three positions (second base, third base, and left field) in Game Three. /(SCL)

Tom Phoebus — 1942- . RHP 1966-72 **Orioles**, Padres, Cubs 1030 ip, 56-52, 3.33. *1 WS, 2 ip, 1-0, 0.00*

Phoebus was one of the Baby Birds, the group of young pitchers who came out of the Orioles' system in the mid-1960s. He pitched shutouts in his first two ML starts, September 15 and 20, 1966 (only the fourth AL pitcher ever to accomplish this feat) to help the Orioles win a World Championship. He was named *TSN*'s AL Rookie Pitcher of the Year in 1967, going 14-9 with a 3.33 ERA, and in 1968 he pitched a no-hitter against the Red Sox on April 27.

He had his best record in 1969, going 14-7, 3.52. Used less in 1970, he did win Game Two of the World Series in relief. He went to San Diego in the deal that brought Pat Dobson to Baltimore that December, and went 3-11 with the last-place Padres in 1971, while Dobson became one of the Orioles' four 20-game winners. /(JFC)

Wiley Piatt (Iron Man) — 1874-1946. LHP 1898-1903 **Phillies**, A's, White Sox, Braves 1390 ip, 85-78, 3.60. 20 wins: 98-99

Piatt, an Ohio State graduate, earned his Iron Man title in 1903, his final ML year, by pitching two complete games on June 25 for the Braves. He broke in with two impressive seasons with the Phillies, winning 24 games in 1898 and 23 in 1899. /(JK)

Rob Picciolo — 1953- . SS-2B-3B 1977-85 **A's**, Brewers, Angels 730 g, .234, 17 hr, 109 rbi. *1 LCS, 2 g, .200*

Picciolo was Oakland's starting shortstop in 1977 (batting .200 in 148 games) and 1979 (.253 in 115 games) but was platooned or used as a utility man after that. Among his shortcomings was his inability to draw a walk. He drew just 25 in almost 1,700 career plate appearances and none at all in 1983 or 1984. /(JCA)

Ron Piche — 1935- . RHP 1960-63, 65-66 **Braves**, Angels, Cardinals 221 ip, 10-16, 4.19

Piche saved nine games and won three for the 1960 Braves, then bounced between the majors and minors for six years. An apocryphal story holds that he became a pitcher when his first manager asked his position and the French-speaking youngster, thinking he'd been asked his name, answered, "I Piche." /(MC)

Val Picinich — 1896-1942. C 1916-33 A's, **Senators**, Red Sox, Reds, Dodgers, Pirates 1048 g, .258, 27 hr, 298 rbi

A backup catcher for nearly all of his 18 ML seasons, Picinich had an apparent knack for catching no-hit games. As an A's rookie right out of prep school in 1916 he caught Joe Bush's no-hitter. Four years later with the Senators, he handled Walter Johnson's only no-hitter. Traded to the Red Sox in 1923, he arrived in time to catch Howard Ehmke's no-hitter. /(JK)

Charlie Pick — 1888–1954. 2B-3B 1914–16, 18–20 Senators, A's, Cubs, **Braves** 367 g, .261, 3 hr, 86 rbi. *1 WS, 6 g, .389*

The speedy Pick led AL third basemen in errors (42) in 1916 during his lone season with the Athletics. Two years later, after a mid-season callup, he started at second base for the Cubs in the 1918 World Series and hit .389./(BC)

Ollie Pickering — 1870–1952. OF 1896–97, 1901–04, 07–08 Louisville (NL), Cleveland (NL), Cleveland (AL), **A's**, Browns, Senators 885 g, .272, 9 hr, 287 rbi

Pickering was a speedy centerfielder with good range who batted a high of .309 for Cleveland in 1901, their first American League season. He had 194 career stolen bases./(DAS)

Urbane Pickering (Dick) — 1899–1970. 3B 1931–32 **Red Sox** 235 g, .257, 11 hr, 92 rbi

Pickering showed little power and led AL third basemen in errors in 1932, his only season as a regular./(JFC)

Jeff Pico — 1966– . RHP 1988– **Cubs** 203 ip, 9–8, 3.98

Pico split his rookie season between starting and relief, going 6–7 with a 4.15 ERA. He was used almost exclusively out of the bullpen in 1989./(SFS)

Billy Pierce [Walter William] — 1927– . LHP 1945, 48–64 Tigers, **White Sox**, Giants 3306 ip, 211–169, 3.27. 20 wins: 56–57 *2 WS, 19 ip, 1–1, 1.89*
☛ *Led League—w 57. Led League—k 53. Led League—era 55. All-Star—53, 55–59, 61.*

This prep sensation from Detroit was acquired by the White Sox from the Tigers before the 1949 season in a lopsided deal for journeyman catcher Aaron Robinson and $10,000. In the 13 years he wore a Sox uniform, Pierce was a pitching anchor. He threw four one-hitters, and in 1953 he had seven shutouts, pitching 51 consecutive innings without yielding an earned run. His 186 strikeouts that year led the league. But his Sox teammates had trouble scoring runs. Following one particularly dry stretch, after the Sox put across a run, Nellie Fox turned to Pierce and said: "Here's your run. Now go out there and hold it." And most of the time he did. Trouble was, AL managers saved their best for Pierce. In head-to-head competition against Whitey Ford, Pierce won eight and lost six lifetime; against Bob Lemon, he won seven of nine decisions.

In 1955 Pierce's 1.97 ERA led the league, and in 1957 only Pierce and Jim Bunning won 20 games in

Billy Pierce

the AL. Pierce tied for the league lead in complete games each year from 1956 through 1958. A seven-time All-Star, Pierce missed a chance at immortality in a June 27, 1958 game against Washington. He had allowed no baserunners through 8–2/3 innings when backup catcher Ed Fitz Gerald pinch hit. He whacked a Pierce curveball that landed fair down the right-field line, depriving Pierce of a perfect game.

Pierce concluded his career with the Giants, and it was with San Francisco's 1962 NL pennant winners that he earned his WS decisions, including a three-hit 2–0 victory in Game Six./(RL)

Tony Pierce — 1946– . LHP 1967–68 **A's** 130 ip, 4–6, 3.25

Pierce broke into the majors with seven saves and a 3.04 ERA for the A's in their last season in Kansas City. He was unable to match that season in Oakland./(WOR)

Bill Piercy (Wild Bill) — 1896–1951. RHP 1917, 21–24, 26 Yankees, **Red Sox**, Cubs 604 ip, 27–43, 4.29. *1 WS, 1 ip, 0–0, 0.00*

Piercy earned his Wild Bill nickname by averaging nearly three walks for every two strikeouts. In his only year as a regular starter, he went 8–17 for the 1923 Red Sox. /(EC)

Marino Pieretti (Chick) — 1920–1981. RHP 1945–50 **Senators**, White Sox, Indians 674 ip, 30–38, 4.53

The 5′7″ 155-lb Pieretti worked in a slaughterhouse during the off-season, killing cattle with a baseball bat. The native Italian won 14 for the Senators in 1945 as a wartime player. He lasted five more seasons as a spot starter after the regulars returned, hitting a respectable (for a pitcher) .217 lifetime. /(JK)

Jimmy Piersall — 1929– . OF-SS 1950, 52–67 **Red Sox**, Indians, Senators, Mets, Angels 1734 g, .272, 104 hr, 591 rbi
☛ *All-Star—54, 56. Gold Glove—58, 61.*

Piersall broke in as a centerfielder but switched to shortstop at the major league level in 1952 after posting .346 and .339 averages for Boston's minor league affiliate at Birmingham. His season was curtailed by a nervous breakdown, recounted in Piersall's book, *Fear Strikes Out*, which was later made into a movie.

Piersall's comeback with Boston in 1953 was

Jimmy Piersall

marked by a 6-for-6 performance on June 10, 1953 and a new philosophy for dealing with fans who taunted him about his well-publicized illness: "Give 'em their money's worth." His career was characterized by numerous zany stunts, including hiding behind the monuments at Yankee Stadium while with the Indians and running backward around the bases after hitting his 100th career homer as a Met in 1963.

Piersall became the Red Sox' regular centerfielder in 1954, taking over for Dom DiMaggio. Playing the shallowest centerfield in the majors, he won two Gold Gloves. Piersall's best years at the plate included a league-leading 40 doubles, 91 runs, 87 RBI, and .293 average for the 1956 Red Sox; 19 HR and 103 runs for the Red Sox in 1957; 18 HR, 66 RBI, and a .282 average for Cleveland in 1960, with a career-high 18 steals, fifth in the league; and a .322 average, fourth in the league, for the 1961 Indians.

Piersall joined Cleveland in exchange for Vic Wertz and Gary Geiger after the 1958 season, and the Senators gave up three players to get him two years later. Waived to the Mets in 1963, Piersall averaged .194, irked manager Casey Stengel, and was released. He hit .314 for the Angels in 1964 as a part-timer before retiring in 1967. He became an outspoken and controversial broadcaster with the White Sox and was ultimately fired for criticizing their management. /(MC/CR)

Tony Piet [born Anthony Francis Pietruszka] — 1906–1981. 2B-3B 1931–38 **Pirates**, Reds, White Sox, Tigers 744 g, .277, 23 hr, 312 rbi

The slim infielder shortened his surname from Pietruszka to accommodate sportswriters. He batted .323 for the Pirates in 1933 to finish second in the NL. /(JL)

Joe Pignatano — 1929– . C 1957–62 **Dodgers**, A's, Giants, Mets 307 g, .234, 16 hr, 62 rbi. *1 WS, 1 g, --*

Pignatano spent his career as a backup catcher. The Brooklyn native began with the Dodgers in their last season in his home borough, but ultimately lost out to John Roseboro in the competition to succeed Roy Campanella as the Dodgers' catcher. Pignatano saw the most action with the A's in 1961, reaching career highs of .243, four HR, and 22 RBI in 243 at-bats. He became the Senators' bullpen coach under manager Gil Hodges, a former Dodger and Met teammate, and followed him to the Mets in 1968. He got extensive publicity for the tomato garden he planted in the bullpen. Met pitcher Pete Falcone was his cousin. /(SFS)

Al Pilarcik — 1930– . OF 1956–61 A's, **Orioles**, White Sox 668 g, .256, 22 hr, 391 rbi

Originally signed by the Yankees, the smooth-fielding Pilarcik had his best season in 1957 with the Orioles, when he hit .278 with nine homers and finished second in the AL in outfield assists (15). He averaged .261 in 115 pinch-hitting appearances. /(MC)

Duane Pillette (Dee) — 1922– . RHP 1949–56 Yankees, **Browns/Orioles**, Phillies 904 ip, 38–66, 4.40

Duane was the son of Tiger pitcher Herman Pillette. Duane lost to Chicago 2–1 in the last game the Browns played in St. Louis (9/27/53). He moved with the franchise to Baltimore and recorded the Orioles' first win in 1954. He never had a winning season; in 1951 he tied for the AL lead with 14 losses. /(WAB)

Herman Pillette (Old Folks) — 1895–1960. RHP 1917, 22–24 Reds, **Tigers** 564 ip, 34–32, 3.45

Pillette played 29 years of pro ball, pitching until age 49. He went 19–12 as a rookie with the 1922 Tigers, but his 19 losses in 1923 tied for the league high. He left the majors in 1924 after an illness, but went on to set a Pacific Coast League record by pitching in 671 games. His son Duane was a ML pitcher for eight years. /(NLM)

Horacio Pina — 1945– . RHP 1968–74, 78 Indians, **Senators/Rangers**, A's, Cubs, Angels, Phillies 432 ip, 23–23, 3.25. *1 LCS, 2 ip, 0–0, 0.00. 1 WS, 3 ip, 0–0, 0.00*

Pina was a journeyman reliever whose best season came with the last-place 1972 Rangers, for whom he saved a career-high 15 games. Traded to the A's after the season for Mike Epstein, he went 6–3 with eight saves in helping them to a World Championship. He went home to Mexico after being released in 1975, and pitched a 3–0 perfect game in the Mexican League in 1978. /(WOR)

Babe Pinelli — 1895–1984. 3B-SS 1918, 20, 22–27 White Sox, Tigers, **Reds** 774 g, .276, 5 hr, 298 rbi.
Umpire NL 1935–56 4 ASU 6 WS

Pinelli started in baseball as a ML third baseman, twice batting over .300 as a member of the Reds. In 1924 the 5'9"speedster stole 24 bases for Cincinnati. He once caught veterans Sam Rice and Stuffy McGinnis with the "hidden-ball trick" on consecutive days.

Pinelli became one of baseball's best-known and most respected umpires and had a "soft thumb,"

less likely than most to throw players or managers out of games. His final ML game was as the plate umpire for Don Larsen's perfect game in the 1956 WS. He called a third strike against pinch hitter Dale Mitchell for the final out. Pinelli claimed that he did not miss a single regulation game in his 22 years as an NL umpire. /(RTM/JK)

Lou Piniella (Sweet Lou) — 1943– . OF-DH 1964, 68–84 Orioles, Indians, Royals, **Yankees** 1747 g, .291, 102 hr, 766 rbi. *5 LCS, 18 g, .305, 2 hr, 6 rbi. 4 WS, 22 g, .319, 10 rbi.*
*Manager 1986–88, 90 **Yankees**, Reds 224–193, .537*
☛ *Rookie of the Year—69 . All-Star—72.*

Lou Piniella was a fiery ballplayer with a sweet swing. Not always the most graceful on the field, he seemed to consistently make the big play or take the extra base. He was drafted by the Washington Senators, played briefly in 1964 for the Orioles, and came back to the majors to stay in 1968 with Cleveland. Birdie Tebbetts, a former catcher managing Cleveland, planned to make Piniella a catcher. Tebbetts worked with him and all seemed to be going well until in practice Piniella was called on to catch Sam McDowell. Piniella was hit by so many bad pitches, he declared he would be an outfielder or nothing at all.

Pinella was drafted by the expansion Seattle Pilots for 1969 but was traded to the Royals and won AL Rookie of the Year honors. After the 1973 season Pinella was traded to the Yankees for Lindy McDaniel. His consistent play and clutch hitting made him popular with the fans. Since his retirement in 1984 Lou has managed the Yankees as well as acted as hitting coach and scout. Kicked upstairs after the 1987 season, which featured former manager Billy Martin consistently second-guessing Piniella's moves from the Yankee broadcast booth, Piniella's loyalty to the pinstripes led him to finish the 1988 season after Martin was fired for the fifth time. Piniella was named Reds manager in November 1989. /(TJG)

Al Pinkston — 1917– . OF 1951–65 Minor and Mexican Leagues

After years of touring with black teams, Al Pinkston, at age 35 in 1952, became the second triple crown winner in Provincial League history. He went on to win back-to-back RBI titles with Amarillo (Western League) in 1957–58. Then, at 42, he joined the Mexico City Reds, and won Mexican League batting titles his first four seasons, with marks of .369, .397, .374, and .381. When he

Vada Pinson (l.) and Frank Robinson

missed his fifth title, it was with a .368 average. He retired at age 48. In 1975 he became the first American player elected to the Mexican League Hall of Fame. /(MC)

Vada Pinson — 1936- . OF 1958–75 **Reds**, Cardinals, Indians, Angels, Royals 2469 ip, .286, 256 hr, 1170 rbi. *1 WS, 5 g, .091*
☛ *All-Star—59–60. Gold Glove—61.*

Pinson received a $4,000 bonus to sign with the Reds out of McClymonds High School in Oakland. Cincinnati had signed Frank Robinson and Curt Flood out of the same school a couple years earlier. Pinson quickly convinced the Reds he was ready for the majors by assaulting California League and PCL pitching for a .357 average in 1957–58. He could do it all—hit for power and average, steal bases, get to a ball in the deepest reaches of the outfield, and fire a bullet back in.

Called up briefly in 1958, he hit a grand slam in his second game. The next year he led the NL in runs (131) and doubles (47), was fourth in batting (.316), belted 20 home runs, and was only the fourth NL rookie to collect 200 hits. Yet the BBWAA passed him over for Rookie of the Year honors, selecting Willie McCovey instead, who played only 52 games for the Giants.

Pinson proved his sensational start was no fluke. Over his first five full seasons with the Reds he averaged 197 hits, 108 runs scored, 37 doubles, 20 home runs, 88 RBI, 26 stolen bases, and a .310

batting average. In three of those campaigns he also led NL outfielders in putouts. NL president Warren Giles said, "There's no telling how good he can become, maybe the best we've ever seen." For ten years Pinson owned center in Crosley Field. Never on the disabled list, the durable Pinson averaged 154 games and 624 at-bats for a decade. Despite his fantastic production and consistency, he was often overshadowed in Cincinnati by the mighty power production of Frank Robinson and later by Pete Rose and Tony Perez.

Pinson was acquired by the Cardinals after the 1968 season to join fellow speedsters Lou Brock and Curt Flood in the spacious reaches of Busch Stadium, replacing the retiring Roger Maris. A broken leg hampered Pinson, who was dealt to Cleveland at the end of the season. He finished with two seasons each for the Angels and Royals.

After service as hitting instructor in the Mariner farm system, Pinson was hitting coach for the Tigers, 1985–89. /(FO)

George Pipgras — 1899–1986. RHP 1923–24, 27–35 **Yankees**, Red Sox 1488 ip, 102–73, 4.09. 20 wins: 28 *3 WS, 26 ip, 3–0, 2.77.*
Umpire AL 1938–46 1 ASU 1 WS
☛ *Led League—w 28.*

After serving overseas with the army engineers during WWI, Pipgras became one of the Yankees' most successful pitchers. The fastballer led the AL in wins (24), starts (38), innings (301), and hits allowed (314) in 1928, and in shutouts in 1930. The Yankees' pitcher when Ruth supposedly called his home run shot in 1932, Pipgras won all of his WS starts (one each in 1927, 1928, and 1932), but when he was robbed in a railroad station, it was his 1923 World Series watch that was taken. Brother Ed had a brief stint with the Dodgers in 1932.

In 1938 Pipgras became an AL umpire. Once during a Browns-White Sox game, he ejected 17 players. /(NLM/RTM)

Wally Pipp — 1893–1965. 1B 1913, 15–28 Tigers, **Yankees**, Reds 1872 g, .281, 90 hr, 996 rbi. *3 WS, 19 g, .224, 7 rbi*
☛ *Led League—hr 16–17.*

When the Yankees won three straight pennants in 1921–23, Pipp was their solid, sure-handed first baseman. When they again won three in a row in 1926–28, he read about it in the *Cincinnati Enquirer*. In 1925, his eleventh Yankee year, he had asked for a day off because of a headache. A beaning in practice a few days later prolonged his hiatus. By the time he was fit, Lou Gehrig owned his position (for 2,130 consecutive games). Pipp, a good hitter with three .300 seasons and six 90-plus RBI years, was shunted to the Reds and obscurity. /(JK)

Rodger Pippen — 1887-1959. *Writer.*

Perhaps the man most responsible for the return of ML baseball to Baltimore in 1954, Pippen was sports editor of the Baltimore *News-Post* from 1906 to 1958. He wrote a daily column and led the campaign to build Memorial Stadium and woo a ML team for years, despite powerful opposition led by the rival Baltimore *Sun*. In spring training in 1914, Pippen played in the intrasquad game that was Babe Ruth's first professional appearance. /(NLM)

Jake Pitler — 1894-1968. 2B 1917-18 **Pirates** 111 g, .232, 0 hr, 23 rbi

Pitler was the Pirates' second baseman in 1917, then played and managed in the minors for many years. He coached the Brooklyn Dodgers under four managers, and was a loyal lieutenant to all and a friend to a generation of players. He became a scout rather than move to Los Angeles with the Dodgers. /(JK)

Skip Pitlock [Lee Patrick] — 1947- . LHP 1970, 74-75 Giants, **White Sox** 193 ip, 8-8, 4.52

This native Chicagoan was the White Sox' long man in 1974. For a while, Pitlock's herky-jerky motion fooled hitters. He allowed the World Champion 1974 A's just one hit in his 5.1 innings against them, and they demanded his inclusion in a 1975 deal for Chet Lemon, yet he never played another ML game. /(RL)

Pinky Pittenger [Clarke Alonzo] — 1899-1977. SS-3B-2B-OF 1921-23, 25, 27-29 **Red Sox**, Cubs, Reds 373 g, .263, 1 hr, 83 rbi

A graduate of Ohio University, where he was a dental student, Pittenger played several positions. In 1928 he signed a five-year contract with the Reds for $9,000 per year but played the last two years of it in the minors. /(NLM)

Togie Pittinger [Charles Reno] — 1871-1909. RHP 1900-07 **Braves**, Phillies 2040 ip, 116-113, 3.10. 20 wins: 02, 05

A 29-year-old rookie in 1900, Pittinger became a workhorse who topped 335 innings pitched 4 straight seasons. When he and Vic Willis each won 27 in 1902, they set the Braves' post-1900 record for wins in a season, later matched by Dick Rudolph.

Pittinger won 23 for the 1905 Phillies, but in between he lost 23 and 21 for the Braves. /(ADS)

Pittsburgh Pirates [aka Innocents] (Bucs) — 1882- 1882-86 AA, 1887- NL 8061-7431, .520. *NL East Champions 70-72, 74-75, 79 NL Champions 01-03, 09, 25, 27, 60, 71, 79 World Champions 09, 25, 60, 71, 79*

Though professional baseball was first played in Pittsburgh in 1876, the team that evolved into the Pirates, the Pittsburgh Alleghenies, joined the American Association in 1882, and the National League in 1887. Then known as the Innocents, they became the Pirates by "pirating" second baseman Lou Bierbauer from Philadelphia (AA) following the Players' League revolt of 1890.

In 1900 Barney Dreyfuss bought the club and virtually merged it with his Louisville Colonels. Hall of Famers Fred Clarke and Honus Wagner came from the Colonels and formed the nucleus of baseball's winningest team (938-538) in the 20th century's first decade. The Pirates were the best in the NL in 1901 and 1902. In 1903 Dreyfuss and Harry Killilea, owner of the American League Boston Pilgrims (Red Sox), agreed to hold the first World Series, won by Boston 5-3. Pittsburgh made its second WS appearance in 1909 with a club-record 110 wins, and defeated Detroit in seven games. That season also marked the club's move from Exposition Park to brand-new Forbes Field.

The Pirates won pennants in 1925 and 1927, led by Pie Traynor, Max Carey, Kiki Cuyler, brothers Paul and Lloyd Waner, and manager Bill Mc-Kechnie. They took another seven-game Series from Washington in 1925, but dropped four straight to the awesome 1927 Yankees. There was a near-pennant in 1938, spoiled by Gabby Hartnett's "Homer in the Gloamin'" for the Cubs.

When Dreyfuss died in 1932, he was succeeded as club president by son-in-law Bill Benswenger. In 1947 a group led by John Galbreath and featuring Bing Crosby bought the club from the Benswenger family. Despite the presence of Ralph Kiner (1946-53) and GM Branch Rickey (1951-55), the Pirates compiled a 326-597 record from 1950 through 1955. New GM Joe L. Brown and manager Danny Murtaugh turned the club around. Pittsburgh defeated the Yankees in the 1960 WS in dramatic fashion on Bill Mazeroski's seventh-game, ninth-inning homer.

The 1960s were dominated by the brilliance of Roberto Clemente, the magnificence of Mazeroski, and disappointing finishes. The Pirates could never quite muster enough pitching to go with their

The 1925 Pittsburgh Pirates

outstanding offense and defense. Then things began to change. On July 16, 1970, they moved to new Three Rivers Stadium. They became the first team to wear double-knit uniforms. The Lumber Company seemed to have an endless supply of talented young hitters. Joined by Willie Stargell, Manny Sanguillen, and Al Oliver, Clemente led the Pirates to an upset victory over Baltimore in the 1971 WS. When Clemente died in a plane crash on New Year's Eve of 1972, Stargell took over as team leader.

In 1977 new manager Chuck Tanner brought speed to the offensive attack. Stargell led The Family to a seven-game, 1979 WS win against Baltimore. But the Pirates finished last from 1982 to 1984. Dismal attendance forced the sale of the club by the Galbreath family and Warner Communications to a public-private coalition called Pittsburgh Associates. The rebuilding job went to GM Syd Thrift and manager Jim Leyland. /(ME)

Juan Pizarro — 1938- . LHP 1957-74 Braves, **White Sox**, Pirates, Red Sox, Indians, A's, Cubs, Astros 2034 ip, 131-105, 3.43. *1 LCS, 0-0, 0.00. 2 WS, 3 ip, 0-0, 8.10*
☛ *All-Star—63, 65.*

The fireballing Puerto Rican-born Pizarro broke in with the Braves at 19 after going 23-6 for Jacksonville (Sally League) in 1956. He reached his pinnacle during the early 1960s with the White Sox. In 1962 Pizarro threw a pair of two-hitters, and in 1964 he went 19-9 (2.56). He was used mostly in relief from 1966 on, but once outdueled Met ace Tom Seaver

1-0, homering for the Cubs' only run. Pizarro and Dennis Lamp are the only pitchers to throw one-hitters with both the Cubs and the White Sox. /(RTM)

Eddie Plank (Gettysburg Eddie) — 1875-1926. LHP 1901-17 **A's**, St. Louis (FL), Browns 4505 ip, 327-193, 2.34. 20 wins: 02-05, 07, 11-12, 15 *4 WS, 54 ip, 2-5, 1.32*
☛ *Hall of Fame—1946.*

Eddie Plank had never played baseball before entering college. He was signed by the Athletics as an elderly rookie of 25 when he graduated from Gettysburg in the American League's first year, 1901. He became the principal lefthander for the first generation of great Athletics teams. Until Warren Spahn, he was the winningest lefthander in ML history. When he jumped to the Federal League's St. Louis Terriers (as Connie Mack, dismantling his 1914 losers, sought to deal Plank to the Yankees), he had won 285 games for Philadelphia—23% of the team's total victories.

Like many turn-of-the-century pitchers, Plank threw with finesse, mixing a fastball with a sidearm curve (his "cross-fire") that cut the plate at an angle disconcerting to batters. He had superb control (under two walks per nine innings), low ERA (including 1.79 in his final season, 1917), 69 shutouts (fifth all-time), and 412 complete games.

He was a serious, self-contained man, and annoyingly deliberate on the mound. Although the times of some of his World Series games do not seem slow

Eddie Plank

by today's standards — 1:55, 1:46, and 2:33 for a seven-run, 10-inning contest — he evidently irritated players, fans, and sportswriters.

He had a hard-luck Series record. In four of his five losses, the A's were shut out, and in 1910 he was sidelined by a sore arm and did not pitch at all. The arm recovered by the next spring, enabling Plank to post two of his finest seasons: 23–8 in 1911, and 26–6 in 1912, for winning percentages of .742 and .813.

After winning 21 for the St. Louis Terriers in 1915, the Federal League collapsed, and Plank was assigned to the Browns. In 1918 he was packaged with Del Pratt and $15,000 in a trade to the Yankees for Urban Shocker (and four others) but chose to retire rather than report. /(ADS)

Whitey Platt [Mizell George] — 1920–1970. OF 1942–43, 46, 48–49 Cubs, White Sox, **Browns** 333 g, .255, 13 hr, 147 rbi

Platt worked as a bat boy for the Browns one spring in his hometown, West Palm Beach, FL. He spent his two final and most active seasons with the Browns, in 1949 leading the AL with 34 pinch-hitting appearances. /(JK)

Players' League — 1890. League.

The Players' League was the product of the revolt of the Brotherhood of Baseball Players in 1890. Many of the best players chose to join the attempt to form a league without the reserve clause and salary limits, and the quality of play in the new circuit was the equal of the established leagues, the National League and the American Association. Even though the attendance competition was won by the Players' League, only the NL had the financial resources to absorb the losses resulting from the division of the attendance among three, rather than two, leagues. Had the PL been better financed, there is a good chance it would have been successful, but the NL, represented by the wily Al Spalding, used the inexperience and uncertainty of the neophyte owners to wait them out until divisions in the players' ranks led to the collapse of the PL that winter. /(SH)

Bill Pleis — 1937– . LHP 1961–66 **Twins** 281 ip, 21–16, 4.07. *1 WS, 1 ip, 0–0, 0.00*

Pleis defeated Washington 5–4 in relief for the Twins' first victory in Minnesota on April 22, 1961. Used primarily as a short reliever by the 1965 pennant winners, he registered four wins, four saves, and a 2.98 ERA. /(FK)

Dan Plesac (Sac-Man) — 1962– . LHP 1986– **Brewers** 284 ip, 19–19, 2.63
☛ *All-Star—87–89.*

Milwaukee's first pick in the June 1983 draft, the 6'5" Plesac was used exclusively as a starter in the minors but became one of the AL's premier relievers after his arrival in 1986. Using his 95-mph fastball, devastating slider, and remarkable control, he logged a 10–7 (2.97) mark with 14 saves as a rookie. Though he injured his left elbow shagging flies in August 1987, he finished with 23 saves. He was knocked out again in August 1988, this time with tendinitis in his pitching shoulder, but set a Brewers record for saves in a season by a lefthander, with 30. /(JCA)

Herb Plews — 1928– . 2B-3B 1956–59 **Senators**, Red Sox 346 g, .262, 4 hr, 82 rbi

Part of a seven-man trade that included Whitey Herzog in February 1956, reserve infielder Plews tied a since-broken ML record by participating in five double plays at second base September 26, 1958. /(FK)

Bill Plummer — 1947– . C 1968, 70–78 Cubs, **Reds**, Mariners 367 g, .188, 14 hr, 82 rbi

Plummer stuck with the Reds in 1972 after hitting 17 HR at Indianapolis (American Association), and remained in Cincinnati through 1977 backing up Johnny Bench. Plummer hit above .200 in only three seasons. /(SFS)

Eric Plunk — 1963– . RHP 1986– **A's**, Yankees 293 ip, 15–15, 4.51. *1 LCS, 0.1 ip, 0–0, 0.00. 1 WS, 2 ip, 0–0, 0.00*

The big, hard-throwing Plunk started occasionally for the A's in 1986–87 but had terrible control. In 1988 he settled into the bullpen as an effective set-up man for stopper Dennis Eckersley and was 7–2, 3.00 for the AL champion A's with 79 strikeouts in 78 innings. Plunk was one of five players the Yankees traded to Oakland for Rickey Henderson after the 1984 season, and in 1989 he returned to the Yankees with two others as Henderson was dealt back to the A's. New York returned him to the starting rotation. /(SCL)

Ray Poat — 1917– . RHP 1942–44, 47–49 **Indians**, Giants, Pirates 400 ip, 22–30, 4.55

After three lackluster seasons in Cleveland and a couple of years in the minors, Poat was picked up by the Giants. He won 11 games in 1948, and one baseball magazine cracked that other NL GMs had "missed the Poat." He failed to win another ML game. /(FS)

Biff Pocoroba — 1953– . C-3B 1975–84 **Braves** 596 g, .257, 21 hr, 172 rbi. *1 LCS, 1 g, .000*
☛ *All-Star—78.*

Biff (his real name) first attracted attention when he threw out 11 straight runners in 1975 spring training. After a couple of promising seasons, he tore his rotator cuff. The injury ended his days as a full-time catcher and, after a brief trial at third base, made him primarily a pinch hitter. It also forced him to give up switch-hitting and bat exclusively righthanded. /(EW)

Bud Podbielan [Clarence Anthony] — 1924–1982. RHP 1949–55, 57, 59 Dodgers, **Reds**, Indians 641 ip, 24–42, 4.49

One of many young pitchers developed by the Dodgers after WWII, Podbielan finally got a chance to start regularly when he was traded to the Reds. He had little success. One day in June 1953, Reds manager Rogers Hornsby mercilessly left him on the mound into the eighth inning while the powerful Dodgers pounded him for 17 hits, including seven doubles, a triple, and two home runs. /(NLM)

Johnny Podgajny — 1920–1971. RHP 1940–43, 46 **Phillies**, Pirates, Indians 510 ip, 20–37, 4.20

The bespectacled Podgajny started and relieved but found little success for the last-place Phillies of 1941–42. /(EW)

Johnny Podres — 1932– . LHP 1953–55, 57–67, 69 **Dodgers**, Tigers, Padres 2265 ip, 148–116, 3.67. *4 WS, 38 ip, 4–1, 2.11*
☛ *Led League—era 57. All-Star—58, 60, 62.*

The 23-year-old Podres became a Brooklyn legend in 1955 when he pitched the Dodgers to their first-ever World Championship. Only 9–10 during the regular season, he beat the Yankees 8–3 in Game Three and shut them out 2–0 in Game Seven, giving Brooklyn its only title after five consecutive Series losses to their Bronx rivals. After spending 1956 in the Navy, Podres was a consistent winner on strong Dodger staffs from 1957 to 1963. He used a good fastball, a curve, and an outstanding changeup. In 1957 he led the NL in both ERA (2.66) and shutouts (6). In 1961 he won a career-high 18 games and led the NL in winning percentage (.783), and on July 2, 1962, he pitched his finest game, retiring the first 20 Phillies before Ted Savage singled, and striking out eight batters in a row. /(FK)

Jimmy Pofahl — 1917– . SS-2B-3B 1940–42 **Senators** 225 g, .220, 2 hr, 70 rbi

Washington moved Cecil Travis to third base to make room for the cat-quick Pofahl, for whom they'd paid $40,000. But Pofahl had injured his arm in an off-season taxi accident and could barely get the ball to first base. His .234 BA didn't help his case. Travis was back at shortstop in 1941, and Pofahl, after returning to the minors, gave up baseball for wartime defense work. /(JK)

Boots Poffenberger [Cletus Elwood] (The Baron) — 1915– . RHP 1937–39 **Tigers**, Dodgers 267 ip, 16–12, 4.75

The Tigers couldn't control the eccentric Poffenberger, and he was sent to Brooklyn as a form of rehabilitation. He had been 10–5 as a rookie, and both teams' managements hoped he would be intimidated by the even more notorious Dodger cut-ups. It didn't work as planned. After three appearances, Boots left the team. /(JK)

Tom Poholsky — 1929– . RHP 1950–51, 54–57 **Cardinals**, Cubs 754 ip, 31–52, 3.93

Poholsky was named 1950 International League MVP for his 18–6 record and 21 complete games. One of them was a 22-inning marathon in which he did not give up a run after the second inning, leading Rochester to a 3–2 victory over Jersey City. After going 7–13 for the 1951 Cardinals, he spent two years in the army, and returned in 1954 to post three losing seasons. /(FJO)

Dick Pole — 1950– . RHP 1973–78 **Red Sox**, Mariners 531 ip, 25–37, 5.05. *1 WS, 0 ip, 0–0, infinite*

A big righthander with a strong arm and a sinking fastball, Pole saw his career sink after he was hit in the head by a drive off Al Bumbry's bat. /(EW)

Spot Poles [Spotswood] (The Black Ty Cobb) — 1887–1962. OF Negro Leagues 1909–23 Philadelphia Giants, **New York Lincoln Giants**, Brooklyn Royal Giants, Lincoln Stars, Hilldale statistics not available

Many experts on black baseball say that Hall of Famer Cool Papa Bell was the fastest man who ever played in the Negro Leagues, but some who remember the early years say that Spotswood Poles was even faster. The 5'7" 165-lb Poles, a bowlegged, switch-hitting outfielder, played in an era from which most statistics have been lost, but an indication of his great talent was his nickname, The Black Ty Cobb.

Poles broke in as the centerfielder and leadoff hitter for the powerful 1909 Philadelphia Giants. He moved on to the New York Lincoln Giants in 1911, when he batted .440 and stole 41 bases in only 60 games. He hit .398 in 1912, and .487 in 1914. With the Lincoln club in the 10-game 1915 Black World Series, he batted only .205 (9-for-44), but, because of his baserunning ability, scored 11 runs. He averaged .319 in four winters in Cuba. In ten exhibition games against major league opposition, he collected 25 hits in 41 at-bats for an amazing .610 average.

Poles enlisted in the 369th Infantry in 1917 at the age of 30, and earned five battle stars and a Purple Heart fighting in France. He resumed his baseball career after WWI, but became tired of the constant travel and retired in 1923. He died in 1962 and was buried in Arlington National Cemetery. /(JM)

Gus Polidor — 1961– . SS-3B 1985– **Angels**, Brewers 204 g, .213, 2 hr, 34 rbi

This good-fielding Venezuelan utility man's best year was 1987, when he hit .263 in 137 at-bats. After dropping off to .148 in 1988 he was traded to the Brewers for Bill Schroeder. /(WOR)

Howie Pollet — 1921–1974. LHP 1941–43, 46–56 **Cardinals**, Pirates, Cubs, White Sox 2107 ip, 131–116, 3.51. 20 wins: 46, 49 *2 WS, 11 ip, 0–2, 4.68* ☛ *Led League—w 46. Led League—era 43, 46. All-Star—43, 46, 49.*

Pollet came up through the Cardinals' farm system, going 20–3 for Houston (Texas League) in his final minor league season. He was 8–4 after 14 starts in 1943, then departed for WWII, but his 1.75 ERA that year still led the league. Pollett returned in 1946 and picked up where he had left off. He led the NL with 21 wins and a 2.10 ERA, helping the Cardinals to the pennant. In the WS against the Red Sox he got no decision in two starts, but St. Louis won in seven games. Pollett faltered in 1947–48, but rebounded in 1949 with a 20–9 record and a 2.77 ERA, and he led the NL with five shutouts. His effectiveness diminished thereafter, and from 1951 to 1956 he changed teams four times. He pitched mostly in relief in his final two seasons. /(SOM)

Polo Grounds New York Giants 1911–57, New York Yankees 1913–22, New York Mets 1962–63. LF-279, CF-483, RF-258

Most famous for its unusual shape, the Polo Grounds was baseball's most unique stadium. Built by Giants owner John T. Brush to replace the original Polo Grounds, which burned down April 14, 1911, the Polo Grounds stood on Manhattan's East 159th Street, between Coogan's Bluff and the Harlem River. It was New York's first concrete-and-steel stadium, and the first 16,000 seats were ready for spectators by June 28, 1911. The stadium wasn't fully completed until the following season, when it was formally dedicated with 34,000 seats in a double-decked grandstand and bleachers. By 1923 the grandstand had been extended into the outfield in both left and right, leaving bleachers only in dead centerfield, but it was the configuration of the field itself that made the Polo Grounds unique. Often described as ovular or horseshoe shaped, it is more accurately bathtub shaped with a small square added to one end. Round behind home plate, the sides did not run parallel to the foul lines, but rather to a line drawn from home to second, extending straight into the power alleys before curving toward the middle in deep left and right centerfields. The center field wall ran straight across, except for a large cutout square in dead center that was the entrance to the clubhouses. Its back wall was usually 60′ high, 480–500′ from home plate, and no ball ever hit that wall, much less cleared it. The park's straight sides made every batter a home run threat, with the foul lines only 279′ and 258′ in left and right, but the fences merely ran away from the plate, and were approximately 450′ at the left- and right-center field bullpens, which were on the field and in play. The upper deck in left extended 23′ over the field, intercepting many balls that might have been caught, and the outfield was slightly downhill, meaning a manager in the dugout could not see his outfielders' legs. At the base of the wall in center stood a five-foot-high memorial to Eddie Grant, a former ML player killed in action during WWI. Like the bullpens, it was in play, but rarely in the way.

The Polo Grounds hosted several World Series as the Giants battled the Yankees for city supremacy, and was the scene of Willie Mays's sensational over-the-shoulder catch in Game One of the 1954 WS. Babe Ruth was the first batter to hit a home run over the right field roof, and Luke Easter (in a Negro League game), Joe Adcock, Lou Brock, and Hank Aaron were the only batters to reach the centerfield bleachers.

The Polo Grounds was home to the Giants until they moved to San Francisco in 1958, then stood empty until the Mets arrived in 1962. When Shea Stadium was completed two years later, the Polo Grounds was abandoned and demolished. A housing project (the Polo Grounds Towers) and playground (Willie Mays Field) occupy the site today. /(SCL)

Luis Polonia — 1964– . OF 1987– **A's**, Yankees 334 g, .293, 9 hr, 122 rbi

Polonia is a fast singles hitter who stole a career-high 29 bases in 1987 for the A's and scores a lot of runs. He switch-hit all through the minors, even in 1988, but only bats lefthanded in the majors. The Dominican is an erratic fielder, although he covers a lot of ground and has a quick release on his throws. The Yankees acquired him in the Rickey Henderson deal in mid-1989.

Polonia was sentenced to 60 days in prison in October 1989 after pleading no contest to a charge of having sex with a minor while in Milwaukee that August. /(JFC)

Elmer Ponder — 1893–1974. RHP 1917, 1919–21 **Pirates**, Cubs 378 ip, 17–27, 3.21

After he returned from WWI, Ponder won a spot in Pittsburgh's starting rotation. In 1920, his only notable season, he was 11–15 with a 2.62 ERA. /(ME)

Ed Poole — 1874–1919. RHP 1900–04 Pirates, **Reds**, Dodgers 595 ip, 34–34, 3.04

A second-line pitcher with the pennant-winning Pirates in 1901, Poole was purchased by the Reds, who gave him a shot as a regular. He was 12–4 his first season in Cincinnati but quickly faded. /(JK)

Jim Poole (Easy) — 1895–1975. 1B 1925–27 **A's** 283 g, .288, 13 hr, 140 rbi

An active player for 34 seasons, until he was 51 in 1946, Poole spent only three years in the majors. In the minors, he played for 30 teams, often as a player-manager. His last managing job was in 1960. He once hit 50 home runs at Nashville of the Southern Association. /(NLM)

Dave Pope — 1925– . OF 1952, 54–56 **Indians**, Orioles 230 g, .265, 12 hr, 73 rbi. *1 WS, 3 g, .000*

Pope batted .294 as an extra with the 1954 AL Champion Indians. In the 1954 World Series opener, Pope made a futile leap at pinch-hitter Dusty Rhodes's 260-foot 10th-inning game-winner, which barely cleared the Polo Grounds' short right field fence. /(FK)

Paul Popovich — 1940– . 2B-SS-3B 1964, 66–75 **Cubs**, Dodgers, Pirates 682 g, .233, 14 hr, 134 rbi. *1 LCS, 3 g, .600*

A sure-handed utility infielder, Popovich spent most of his career with the Cubs. He played in a career-high 134 games with the 1968 Dodgers, filling in for an injured Jim Lefebvre at second and a fading Zoilo Versalles at short. In the 1974 LCS, he went 3-for-3 as a pinch hitter for Pittsburgh. /(DAS)

Tom Poquette — 1951– . OF 1973, 76–79, 81–82 **Royals**, Red Sox, Rangers 452 g, .268, 10 hr, 136 rbi. *3 LCS, 8 g, .174, 4 rbi*

Coming off two knee operations, Poquette was the Royals' Rookie of the Year in 1976 when he batted .302; he set a club record that June 15 by scoring five runs in a game. The aggressive line-drive hitter was a platooned outfielder on Kansas City's 1976–78 AL West division winners. /(FJO)

Chuck Porter — 1956– . RHP 1981–85 **Brewers** 237 ip, 13–13, 4.15

Porter never spent a full season in the ML, shuttling between Milwaukee and Vancouver (Pacific Coast League) from 1981 to 1985 after being released by the Angels before the 1980 season. Usually a starter, he won seven games for the Brewers in 1983 and six in 1984. /(SCL)

Darrel Porter — 1952– C 1971–87 Brewers, Royals, **Cardinals**, Rangers 1782 g, .247, 188 hr, 826 rbi. *5 LCS, 20 g, .317, 4 rbi. 3 WS, 17 g, .211, 1 hr, 5 rbi* ☛ *All-Star—74, 78–80.*

Porter was a top defensive catcher with a strong arm and was regarded a good handler of pitchers. He hit as many as 20 home runs, and his low batting averages were usually balanced by his bases on balls.

Porter took over regular catching duties at Milwaukee in his first full season, 1973, and hit 16 homers. He was traded to Kansas City in 1977, and replaced the popular Buck Martinez. Two years later, he had a career year, hitting .291 with a league-leading 121 walks. He hit 20 homers and matched Mickey Cochrane as the second catcher to amass over 100 runs, RBI, and walks in a single season.

In 1981 he rejoined former Royals manager Whitey Herzog in St. Louis and publicly stated that he was a recovered alcoholic. Although not as productive offensively with the Cardinals as with the Royals, Porter dominated postseason play in 1982. He hit .556 in the LCS as the Cardinals swept the Braves, and his key hits and perfect defense were central to the Cardinals' World Series victory over the Brewers. /(FO)

Dick Porter (Twitchy) — 1901–1974. OF 1929–34 **Indians**, Red Sox 675 g, .308, 11 hr, 284 rbi

Porter was an outstanding hitter trapped in the minor leagues until he was 28. He hit better than .300 six straight years with Baltimore (International League) before Cleveland was at last able to purchase his contract. In his first four years with the Indians, he continued at a .300 clip, including a career-high .350 in 1930. Twice he scored more than 100 runs. Known as Twitchy because of his batting style, he constantly wiggled, gyrated, and waved his bat. /(NLM)

J.W. Porter (Jay) — 1933– . C-OF-1B 1952, 55–59 Browns, **Tigers**, Indians, Senators, Cardinals 229 g, .228, 8 hr, 62 rbi

A utility man valuable for his catching skills, Porter never had more than 140 at-bats in a season and never hit above .250. His full name was in fact J.W.; the initials stood for nothing else. /(SFS)

Bob Porterfield [Erwin Cooledge] — 1923–1980. RHP 1948–59 Yankees, **Senators**, Red Sox, Pirates, Cubs 1568 ip, 87–97, 3.79. 20 wins: 53 ☛ *Led League—w 53. All-Star—54.*

Porterfield was outstanding in 1953, leading the AL with 22 wins and 9 shutouts for the fifth-place Senators while batting .255 with three home runs, including a May 5 grand slam. In 11 other ML seasons, he never won more than 13 games. /(FK)

Arnie Portocarrero — 1931–1986. RHP 1954–60 **A's**, Orioles 817 ip, 38–57, 4.32

After three losing seasons plagued by wildness, including a 9–18 record in his first season, Portocarrero found his control in 1957 but nonetheless went 4–9 for the seventh-place Athletics. Traded to the Orioles for Buddy Daley, Portocarrero had his best season in 1958, going 15–11 with a 3.25 ERA. /(SFS)

Mark Portugal (Porch) — 1962– . RHP 1985– **Twins**, Astros 347 ip, 18–20, 4.39

Tough to steal against, Portugal's time with the Twins was distinguished only by a 13-strikeout, five-hit 2–1 loss to Texas (9/21/86). Gradually moving into a relief role, he was 7–1 with a 2.75 ERA a set-up and middle reliever for the 1989 Astros. /(WOR)

Bill Posedel (Sailor Bill) — 1906– . RHP 1938–41, 46 Dodgers, **Braves** 679 ip, 41–43, 4.56

Posedel joined the peacetime Navy as a teenager and, after he'd pitched the U.S.S. Saratoga to the Pac Fleet championship, was offered a professional contract. In 1939 he won 15 games for the seventh-place Braves. He returned to the Navy during WWII. Later, he became a ML coach. /(JK)

Cum Posey [Cumberland Willis] — 1891–1946. OF-MGR Negro Leagues 1910–46 **Homestead Grays** statistics not available

Posey joined the Homestead Grays as an outfielder in 1910, but his great success in black baseball came as a result of his managerial and business acumen.

In 1916 he was named the Homestead manager. He fielded consistently talented, uncompromising teams that played high-caliber baseball. He possessed a great baseball mind and was a literate and dictatorial manager.

By the early 1920s, Posey owned the Grays, and he turned the team into a profitable business venture. After taking leadership roles in the organized black baseball leagues, he returned to run the Grays. Homestead continued to be a barnstorming power and eventually became the dominant team in the second Negro National League. Posey remained one of the most powerful men in black baseball until his death. /(JO)

Wally Post (Wallopin' Wally) — 1929–1982. OF 1949, 51–64 **Reds**, Phillies, Twins, Indians 1204 g, .266, 210 hr, 699 rbi. *1 WS, 5 g, .333, 1 hr, 2 rbi*

Post peaked in 1955–56, when he hit 40 and 36 HR respectively for the power-hitting Reds. His numerous tape-measure homers led many to consider him the most powerful slugger in the NL during this period. Following the 1957 season, he was traded to the Phillies for Harvey Haddix, but Post returned to Cincinnati during the 1960 season. His career-high .585 slugging percentage in part-time duty helped the 1961 Reds to the NL pennant. In the World Series, his two-run homer in Game Five went for naught as the Yankees clinched with a 13–5 win.

Post broke into baseball as a pitcher in 1946 and went 17–7 in 1947 for Muncie (Ohio State League), but he was soon switched to the outfield to take advantage of his heavy hitting. He had brief stints with the Reds before finally sticking in 1954. Besides his 40 HR in 1955, he had other career highs with 109 RBI, 116 runs, 33 doubles, and a .309 average, but led the league in strikeouts for the first of three times. Much-used as a pinch hitter from 1958 on, his best effort in that role came in 1962 (9-for-27). /(RTM)

Nels Potter — 1911– . RHP 1936, 38–41, 43–49 Cardinals, A's, Red Sox, **Browns**, Braves 1686 ip, 92–97, 3.99. *2 WS, 15 ip, 0–1, 3.60*

Potter was the only ML pitcher ever suspended for throwing a spitball. He had a habit of wetting his fingers before picking up the resin bag. On July 20, 1944, pitching for the Browns against the Yankees, he was warned by umpire Cal Hubbard, then on the next occasion thrown out of the game. He was suspended for ten days, although he always denied throwing a spitter. The incident probably cost him a

20-win season; he was 19–7 for the pennant-winning Browns. He gave up only one earned run in two World Series starts, but six Browns errors left him with an 0–1 record.

In 1948, while a reliever with the Athletics, he got into a clubhouse argument with Connie Mack and demanded his release. When it was granted, he signed for a bonus with the Braves and went 5–2 to help them win the NL pennant.

Potter relied on the screwball and slider. With the 1938–40 Athletics he compiled a poor 19–38 mark, and in 1941 when an old knee injury failed to respond to surgery, he was sold to the Red Sox. Returned to the minors, in 1943 he was drafted by the Browns. /(NLM)

Shirley Povich — 1905– . *Writer.*

Povich arrived in Washington in 1924 from Bar Harbor, ME, and worked as a copy boy for the *Post* while studying law at Georgetown. He was still a student when he became sports editor. His column, "This Morning," appeared from 1926 to his retirement in 1974, except for time he spent as a war correspondent. Povich was president of the BBWAA in 1975 and a longtime correspondent for *The Sporting News.* In 1975 he received the J.G. Taylor Spink Award from the Hall of Fame. /(NLM)

Boog Powell [John Wesley] — 1941– . 1B-OF 1961–77 **Orioles**, Indians, Dodgers 2042 g, .266, 339 hr, 1187 rbi. *5 LCS, 12 g, .306, 4 hr, 11 rbi. 4 WS, 21 g, .234, 2 hr, 7 rbi*
☛ *Most Valuable Player—70. All-Star—68–71.*

An immense lefthanded slugger, Powell batted cleanup for the Orioles for over a decade and helped them to the WS four times in six years from 1966 to 1971. Standing slightly over 6'4" and weighing at least 230 lb, Powell had bulging biceps and a thick neck, as well as a youthful-looking face topped by a shock of reddish hair. He batted behind Frank Robinson beginning in 1966 to form half of Baltimore's fearsome power combination, and in the field he was an ample target at first base as well as a master at scooping low throws from the dirt.

Powell joined the Orioles after leading the International League in home runs at Rochester in 1961, and spent his first three seasons as a slow-footed left fielder before switching to first base in 1965. Offensively, he was an immediate success, hitting 25 HR in 1963, then leading the AL in slugging percentage (.606) in 1964 while blasting a career-high 39 HR despite missing several weeks because of a broken wrist. He slumped to .248 with 17 HR in 1965, then

Boog Powell

won AL Comeback Player of the Year honors in 1966 (.287, 34 HR, 109 RBI) while being hampered by a broken finger.

Before the 1967 season, Powell lamented, "Once, just once, I'd like to through a whole season without an injury," and he did just that, playing over 150 games each of the next three seasons. In 1968 he hit a career-high .304 with 37 HR and 121 RBI, and in 1970 he was the AL MVP, narrowly missing a .300 average on the last day of the season and hitting 35 more HR with 114 RBI. In the WS, Powell homered in the first two games as the Orioles whipped the Reds. Powell helped Baltimore to a third straight WS the following year, blasting a pair of home runs in Game Two of the ALCS, but he hit only .111 in the WS as Baltimore lost to Pittsburgh in seven games.

The aging slugger was traded to Cleveland with Don Hood for Dave Duncan and a minor leaguer before the 1975 season, and he hit .297 with 27 HR for the Indians that year, but he hit only nine home

runs in 1974 and none as a pinch hitter for the Dodgers in 1975. Powell hit three home runs in a game three times, and is second only to Eddie Murray on the Orioles all-time home run list. /(SCL)

Dennis Powell — 1963– . LHP 1985– **Dodgers**, Mariners 193 ip, 7–16, 4.81

Powell came up to the Dodgers in mid-1985 as a minor league sensation after he had gone 9–0 at Albuquerque (Pacific Coast League). He had surgery for bone chips in his throwing elbow before a trade to Seattle. Control problems prevented him from substantial success in his first five years in the majors. /(TG/TF)

Hosken Powell — 1955– . OF 1978–83 **Twins**, Blue Jays 594 g, .259, 17 hr, 160 rbi

Powell showed early promise for Minnesota, hitting .293 in 1979 and scoring 58 runs with 14 stolen bases in 485 at-bats in 1980. He never demonstrated any power, and his career floundered after two seasons with the Blue Jays. /(JFC)

Jack Powell — 1874–1944. RHP 1897–1912 Cleveland (NL), Cardinals, **Browns**, Yankees 4388 ip, 246–255, 2.97. 20 wins: 98–99, 02, 04

Powell, a contemporary of Cy Young, was built along the same lines, and threw with a free and easy sidearm delivery. He was the workhorse of every staff on which he pitched, but in 16 seasons was never on a pennant winner. He was 24–15 in his second season, for Cleveland (NL), and was part of the wholesale transfer of players from Cleveland to St. Louis in 1899. Powell went 23–21 for the Cardinals that year. He was 22–17 with the Browns in 1902, and lost an AL-high 19 in 1911. He spent a couple of seasons playing in New York, but continued living in St. Louis to run a saloon with his brother-in-law and former batterymate, Jack O'Connor. /(JK)

Jack Powell (Cornelius) — Unk.–1971. *Umpire* NL 1923–24, 33

Powell, who never used an indicator to keep track of balls and strikes, thrived on confrontation. His short stay in the NL was attributed to his frequent run-ins with Giants manager John McGraw. He umpired 22 years in the Pacific Coast League, then served as supervisor of umpires for the National Association in 1953–54. /(RTM)

Jake Powell [Alvin Jacob] — 1908–1948. OF 1930, 34–40, 43–45 **Senators**, Yankees, Phillies 688 g, .271, 22 hr, 327 rbi. *3 WS, 8 g, .435, 1 hr, 5 rbi*

Powell hit his peak with a 10-for-22 showing for the Yankees in the 1936 World Series. Reckless and prejudiced, he broke Tiger first baseman Hank Greenberg's wrist in 1935, continually fought with other players, and was suspended in 1938 because of antiblack slurs during a radio interview. At age 40, he committed suicide in a Washington, D.C. police station while being questioned on a bad-check charge. /(FS)

Ray Powell (Rabbit) — 1888–1962. OF 1913, 17–24 Tigers, **Braves** 875 g, .268, 35 hr, 276 rbi

A fleet centerfielder, Powell's low averages at the end of the dead-ball era jumped when the lively ball was introduced. A free swinger, he twice led the league in strikeouts. Powell was a minor league manager for two decades. /(JK)

Ted Power — 1955– . RHP 1981– Dodgers, **Reds**, Royals, Tigers, Cardinals 876 ip, 57–56, 4.15

A hard-throwing righthander who pitched almost exclusively in relief in his first six ML seasons, Power led the NL with 78 appearances in 1984 and saved 27 games for the Reds in 1985. He was forced into the Reds' starting rotation late in 1986 when Mario Soto and John Denny were injured, and went 6–1 down the stretch to earn a regular spot in the rotation the following year. Power started 34 games in 1987, finishing 10–13, 4.50, then was traded to Kansas City with Kurt Stillwell for Danny Jackson after the season, and was traded again to Detroit in August after going 5–6 for the Royals.

Originally drafted by the Dodgers, Power earned a promotion to the ML with an 18–3 record at Albuquerque (Pacific Coast League) in 1981. /(SCL)

Vic Power — 1931– . 1B-2B-OF-3B 1954–65 **A's**, Indians, Twins, Dodgers, Phillies, Angels 1627 g, .284, 126 hr, 658 rbi

☛ *All-Star—55–56, 59–60. Gold Glove—58–64.*

Power was a stylish, exuberant, showboating first baseman who won seven Gold Gloves. The righthander made all catches one-handed with a wide, sweeping motion. He frequently led AL first basemen in every fielding category. After leading the American Association with a .349 BA in 1953, the black Puerto Rican joined Elston Howard as the first black players on the Yankees' roster, but Power was traded to the Athletics before the season began. A good contact hitter, he batted over .300 three times in his dozen ML seasons. Although not a big basestealer, he stole home twice in one game against Detroit in 1958.

A quick-witted wisecracker, he was once arrested for jaywalking in the South. "I thought the 'Don't Walk' sign was for whites only," he told the judge. "I've seen so many of those signs in this town." /(NLM)

Jimmy Powers — Unk.-Unk. *Writer.*

A graduate of Marquette University, Powers worked in Oklahoma, Milwaukee, and Cleveland before joining the New York *Daily News* in 1928. His column, "The Powerhouse," ran until 1957. He was sports editor of the *News*, 1935–57. His book *Baseball Personalities* was published in 1949. /(NLM)

Mike Powers (Doc) — 1870–1909. C 1898–99, 1901–09 Louisville (NL), Washington (NL), **A's**, Yankees 647 g, .216, 4 hr, 199 rbi. *1 WS, 3 g, .143*

When Powers left Holy Cross to continue his education at Notre Dame, his friend Lou Sockalexis followed him. A great handler of young pitchers, while with the Athletics Powers was Eddie Plank's personal catcher. He died from internal injuries sustained or worsened while chasing a foul ball in Shibe Park's inaugural game, April 12, 1909. /(CAP)

Johnny Pramesa — 1925– . C 1949–52 **Reds**, Cubs 185 g, .268, 13 hr, 59 rbi

A consistent .300 hitter in the minors, the hefty catcher was named to the NL All-Rookie team in 1950 when he hit .307 in 74 games. /(NLM)

Del Pratt [Derrill Burnham] — 1888–1977. 2B-1B 1912–24 **Browns**, Yankees, Red Sox, Tigers 1835 g, .292, 43 hr, 966 rbi

Yankee rookie manager Miller Huggins was strongly criticized in the New York press when he sent Urban Shocker to the Browns in a trade for six-year second baseman Del Pratt in 1918. But Huggins, a former second baseman himself, knew a good second baseman when he saw one, and the hard-nosed, hard-hitting Pratt was the AL's best after Eddie Collins. A former All-American back at Alabama, for three years he plugged a hole in the Yankee infield that eight players had failed to in the previous decade. He was traded to the Red Sox in late 1920.

Pratt averaged 141 games a season, had good range, and led the league five times in total chances

Del Pratt

per game. He hit over .300 each of his last five seasons. Of his nearly 2,000 career hits, a quarter were doubles and triples. With the Browns in 1916, he led the AL with 103 RBI. He argued with his managers and even sued Browns owner Phil Ball for slander when Ball charged his team with easing up on an opponent. Pratt won an out-of-court settlement. /(ADS)

Mike Prendergast (Iron Mike) — 1888–1967. RHP 1914–19 **Chicago (FL)**, Cubs, Phillies 908 ip, 41–53, 2.74

Nicknamed Iron Mike when he was a hard-working pitcher in the Three-I League, Prendergast pitched for the Chicago Whales of the Federal League. He became a Cub when the NL team was purchased by Whales owner William Wrigley, Jr., after the FL folded. /(JK)

Bobby Prescott [George Bertrand] — 1930– . OF 1961 **A's** 10 g, .083, 0 hr, 0 rbi

Prescott left the black outlaw leagues in 1952 to post career minor league numbers of 2,268 games, 398

homers, 1,531 RBI, and a .293 average. He played third base and hit 24 HR for the 1952 Phoenix Giants, outslugging teammates Willie McCovey, Leon Wagner, Felipe Alou, and Willie Kirkland—all of whom were promptly promoted. Prescott, believed older than his listed age, was passed over. He moved on to the Mexican League in 1963, hit 193 HR in six seasons, and won HR titles in 1965–66 and RBI titles in 1966 and 1968. /(MC)

Joe Presko (Little Joe) — 1928– . RHP 1951–54, 57–58 **Cardinals**, Tigers 490 ip, 25–37, 4.61

The 5'9 1/2" 165-lb Presko saw his ERA rise almost one run each of his four seasons with the Cardinals, never winning more than seven games. /(FK)

Jim Presley — 1961– . 3B 1984– **Mariners** 799 g, .250, 115 hr, 418 rbi
☛ *All-Star—86.*

For three years, Presley was an effective power hitter for the Mariners, clubbing 28, 27, and 24 homers before slumping to 14 in 1988. He is second to Alvin Davis in career RBI for Seattle and is only the third player to hit 100 homers for the Mariners. In 1986 Presley was the Mariners' representative in the All-Star Game, and led Seattle with 33 doubles, 27 home runs, 107 RBI, and 172 strikeouts. The franchise leader in career strikeouts and strikeouts in a season, Presley also holds the Mariners' season record for most times grounding into double plays. While not exactly a defensive liability, he did set a major league record in 1982 for the fewest putouts by a third baseman playing in a minimum of 150 games. His career seemingly on the wane, Presley saw reduced playing time in 1989 following the arrival of rookie Edgar Martinez. /(TF)

Tot Pressnell [Forest Charles] — 1906– . RHP 1938–42 **Dodgers**, Cubs 526 ip, 32–30, 3.80

Adequate as a starter with the Dodgers, the stocky knuckleballer had control problems that limited his effectiveness when he was switched to relief. /(FS)

Jim Price — 1941– . C 1967–71 **Tigers** 261 g, .214, 18 hr, 71 rbi. *1 WS, 2 g, .000*

Price's career was spent backing up Bill Freehan in Detroit. In his most active season, Price hit .234 with nine HR while catching 51 games. /(JFC)

Joe Price — 1956– . LHP 1980– **Reds**, Giants, Red Sox 826 ip, 41–44, 3.61. *1 LCS, 6 ip, 1–0, 0.00*

Price worked his way into the Reds' starting rotation in 1983 after three seasons as a reliever, and was the

NL Pitcher of the Month in July with a 5–0, 1.24 record. He finished the season 10–6, 2.88, but slipped to 7–13 the following year before encountering elbow problems in 1985. He tied a NL record by striking out six consecutive Phillies in relief May 8, 1985, but went on the DL in July with a sore elbow and had surgery to remove a calcium deposit in September. Price struggled in 1986, spending two more months on the DL, and in 1987 signed as a free agent with the Giants. After starting the season 6–0 at Phoenix (Pacific Coast League), Price joined the Giants in July, and later won Game Five of the NLCS against the Cardinals with five shutout innings of relief (one hit, six strikeouts) to help San Francisco to a 3–2 series lead. He was 1–6 with four saves in 1988, and in 1989 pitched for the Red Sox./(SCL)

Bob Priddy — 1939– . RHP 1962, 64–71 Pirates, Giants, Senators, White Sox, Angels, **Braves** 536 ip, 24–38, 4.00

Usually a reliever, Priddy made 18 starts for the 1968 White Sox and finished 3–11. He won five and saved eight for the 1970 Braves despite a career-worst 5.42 ERA./(FK)

Gerry Priddy — 1919–1980. 2B-3B 1941–43, 46–53 Yankees, **Senators**, Browns, Tigers 1296 g, .265, 61 hr, 639 rbi. *1 WS, 3 g, .100, 1 rbi*

An outspoken infielder who gained a reputation as a clubhouse lawyer, Priddy teamed with Phil Rizzuto as a keystone combination (1938–40) in the Yankee farm system but couldn't oust Joe Gordon once he reached the majors. After criticizing Yankee manager Joe McCarthy for not playing him, he was traded to the Senators in 1943. A smooth, reliable fielder, he had his best seasons with the bat in 1948–49 with the Browns, when he hit .296 and .290. After leaving baseball he tried professional golf. Later he was convicted of attempting to extort $250,000 from a shipping company by placing a bomb on a ship./(NLM)

Ray Prim (Pop) — 1906– . LHP 1933–35, 43, 45–46 Senators, Phillies, **Cubs** 351 ip, 22–21, 3.56. *1 WS, 0–1, 3.56*

A 3–7 pitcher in his first ML stint from 1933–35, silver-haired Pop Prim resurfaced at age 36 with the 1943 wartime Cubs. In 1945 his 13–8 (2.40) record helped the Cubs win the pennant./(DAS)

Bob Prince (Gunner) — 1916–1985. *Broadcaster.*

A Pirates fan in a broadcasting booth, the zany, unpredictable, and intentionally controversial Prince was Pittsburgh's beloved voice of the Pirates on KDKA radio for over two decades until he was unceremoniously fired in 1975. Nicknamed Gunner when the husband of a woman he was talking to pulled a gun on him in a bar, Prince joined Rosey Rowswell in the Pirates' broadcast booth in 1948 and took over when Rowswell died in 1955.

On the air, Prince was always colorful, yelling "Arriba" when Roberto Clemente came to bat, and, "Spread some chicken on the hill" for Willie Stargell. His signature home run call—"You can kiss it goodbye"—became a broadcasting standard, and close Pirates victories invariably concluded with Prince announcing, "We had 'em all the way!"

Off the air, Prince was also colorful. He once dove into a hotel pool from a third-story window. But he had a serious side as well, cofounding the Allegheny Valley School for retarded children in 1960. When Prince was fired after squabbling with station management over his style, Pittsburgh held a downtown parade in his honor. He returned part-time in 1985, but after being released from the hospital broadcast only three games before falling ill again, and died less than a month later. He was inducted into the Writer's Wing of the Hall of Fame in 1986./(SL)

Lou Proctor — Unk.–Unk.

Proctor was a telegraph operator in Cleveland who inserted his own name into an Indians box score in 1912, walking once as a pinch hitter for the Browns. The fictitious plate appearance was expunged from the records in 1987 when suspicious researchers from the Society for American Baseball Research uncovered the stunt./(SCL)

Mike Proly — 1950– . RHP 1976, 1978–83 Cardinals, **White Sox**, Phillies, Cubs 546 ip, 22–29, 3.23

A Cardinals and Twins farmhand, Proly was signed as a free agent by the White Sox in 1977. Though sidelined by a fractured thumb and elbow injuries in 1978 and 1979, he fared well as a spot starter and reliever. He precipitated two bench-clearing brawls in 1980 when his errant pitches knocked down Baltimore's Doug DeCinces and Milwaukee's Ben Oglivie. As a middle reliever with the 1982 Cubs, he recorded a career-best 2.30 ERA./(RL)

Doc Prothro [James Thompson] — 1893–1971. 3B 1920, 23–26 Senators, **Red Sox**, Reds 180 g, .318, 0 hr, 81 rbi.
Manager 1939–41 **Phillies** 138–320, .301

Doc Prothro practiced dentistry in the off-season. He managed the Phillies to three successive last-place finishes in 1939–41. His son, Tommy Prothro, was a successful college and professional football coach. /(JK)

Hub Pruett (Shucks) — 1900–1982. LHP 1922–24, 27–28, 30, 32 **Browns**, Phillies, Giants, Braves 745 ip, 29–48, 4.63

Celebrated for his dominance of Babe Ruth, he struck out the Babe 10 of the first 13 times he faced him, but had much less success against other hitters. The screwball that baffled Ruth gave Pruett a chronic sore arm. He studied medicine in the off-season and left baseball to set up practice in St. Louis. /(JK)

Tex Pruiett [Charles LeRoy] — 1883–1953. RHP 1907–08 **Red Sox** 232 ip, 4–18, 2.83

Pruiett was a wild fireballer bought by the Red Sox from Dallas (Texas League) after the 1906 season. He won only four games in the majors, but three of them were shutouts. In 1907 Pruiett led AL relievers in appearances (18) and ERA (2.01), but went 2–10 in his starts. He dropped to 1–7 in 1908 despite a 1.99 ERA. /(NLM)

Ron Pruitt (Do-It) — 1951– . OF-C-DH 1975–83 Rangers, **Indians**, White Sox, Giants 341 g, .269, 12 hr, 92 rbi

Michigan State graduate Pruitt was a handy utility man and a decent hitter off the bench. He hit .302 in 56 games for the Indians and White Sox in 1980. /(ME)

Greg Pryor — 1949– . 3B-SS-2B 1976, 78–86 Rangers, **White Sox**, Royals 789 g, .250, 14 hr, 146 rbi. *1 LCS, 1 g, --. 1 WS, 1 g, --*

One of the last Washington Senator draft picks to play in the majors, Pryor signed in 1971 and reached the Rangers for five games in 1976. He was dealt to the Yankees in 1977, but was signed by the White Sox as a free agent after a year in the minors. He was primarily a utility infielder, and his only season as a regular was 1979, when he was at shortstop for 119 games and batted .279. He did not relish the role of supersub, neither with Chicago nor with Kansas City, where he often spelled an injured

George Brett. His father, George Pryor, played for the NFL Baltimore Colts, and his brother Jeff pitched in the Angels organization from 1968 to 1972. /(RL)

Paul Pryor — 1927– . *Umpire* NL 1961–81 *3 ASU 4 LCS 3 WS*

Pryor spent four seasons as a minor league pitcher before he started umpiring. In his 21 years as a NL ump, his most unusual play came in Houston on May 15, 1973. The Braves had runners on first and second with one out in the ninth inning when Dave Johnson grounded to third baseman Doug Rader, who tossed to Tommy Helms at second. Helms relayed to first baseman Lee May for an apparent inning-ending double play. May flipped the ball to Pryor. But the second base umpire ruled that Helms had missed the base and the runner was safe. As soon as he saw that call, Pryor dropped the ball, which was still in play. Before May could pick it up, the Braves' runner who had started on second raced home from third to score. /(RTM)

George Puccinelli (Count) — 1906–1956. OF 1930, 32, 34, 36 Cardinals, Browns, **A's** 187 g, .283, 19 hr, 102 rbi. *1 WS, 1 g, .000*

The good-hitting, poor-fielding Puccinelli was the International League MVP in 1935, when he led in nearly every batting category. The next year, his only full ML season, he batted .278 for the last-place A's. /(NLM)

Kirby Puckett — 1961– . OF 1984– **Twins** 924 g, .323, 96 hr, 506 rbi. *1 LCS, 5 g, .208, 1 hr, 3 rbi. 1 WS, 7 g, .357, 3 rbi*
☛ *Led League—ba 89. All-Star—86–89. Gold Glove—86–88, 89.*

Built like a fireplug, 5'8" 210-lb Kirby Puckett set baseball ablaze upon signing with Minnesota. He was *Baseball America*'s Appalachian League Player of the Year in 1982, California League Rookie of the Year in 1983, and Minnesota's Rookie of the Year in 1984, becoming the ninth player in major league history to debut with four hits in a nine-inning game and leading AL outfielders with 16 assists. The ballhawk went almost one year, until April 22, 1985, before hitting his first big league homer. The following year, Puckett hit 31 homers, becoming the first player ever with 0- and 30-home run seasons (500 or more at-bats) in a career. He was starting centerfielder in the 1986 All-Star Game, received Gold Glove and Silver Slugger honors, and was the Twins' Most Valuable Player. His rise continued in 1987 with a .332 batting average, best for Minnesota since Rod Carew's .333 in 1978, a league-best (tied) 207 hits, an unofficial eight home run-saving catches, and a World Series-high (tied) 10 hits. He hit only eight HR in 1989 but led the AL with a .339 batting average, only the second righthanded batter to do so in 20 years. /(ME)

Terry Puhl — 1956– . OF 1977– **Astros** 1479 g, .280, 62 hr, 424 rbi. *2 LCS, 8 g, .545, 3 rbi* ☛ *All-Star—78.*

An excellent line-drive hitter, the Canadian-born Puhl was signed by the Astros as a free agent in 1973. He hit .301 in 60 games as a rookie in 1977, and in 1978 was the lone Astro All-Star, hitting .289 with 32 stolen bases as Houston's left fielder. He started for the Astros through 1984, averaging over 20 steals a year, rarely striking out, and providing sure-handed defense. A severe hamstring pull in 1985 and an ankle injury in 1986 curtailed his playing time. In 1987 Puhl emerged as the Astros' best lefthanded pinch hitter, and in 1988, playing in 113 games, he hit a career-high .303. Through 1989, Puhl was fourth on the Astros' all-time hits list, third in games, fourth in at-bats, runs, triples, and stolen bases, and fifth in doubles. His .526 batting average in the 1980 LCS remains a record for a five-game series. /(SCL)

Luis Pujols — 1955– . C 1977–85 **Astros**, Royals, Rangers 316 g, .193, 6 hr, 81 rbi. *1 LCS, 4 g, .100*

A weak-hitting catcher, Pujols backed up Alan Ashby in Houston from 1980 to 1983, never batting better than .239. The native of the Dominican Republic hit four of his six career home runs in 1982, and later played four games with the Royals in 1984 and one game with the Rangers in 1985. /(SCL)

Charlie Puleo — 1955– . RHP 1981–84, 86–89 Mets, Reds, **Braves** 633 ip, 29–39, 4.25

The Mets traded Puleo and two minor leaguers to reacquire Tom Seaver after the 1982 season, Puleo's rookie year and the best he ever had (9–9, 4.47). /(SFS)

Frank Pulli — 1935– . *Umpire* NL 1972–87 *1 ASU 4 LCS 2 WS*

One of Pulli's closest calls came in the sixth inning of Game Four of the 1978 WS between the Dodgers and Yankees. New York had Thurman Munson on second and Reggie Jackson on first when Lou Piniella hit a shot to shortstop Bill Russell. Russell dropped the ball, picked it up, stepped on second,

and threw toward first, but his throw hit Jackson. Pulli ruled no interference despite Dodger manager Tom Lasorda's argument that Jackson had intentionally deflected the toss. /(RTM)

Harry Pulliam — 1869–1909. *Executive.*

Pulliam, "an idealist, a dreamer, a lover of solitude and nature," was city editor of the Louisville *Commercial* when Barney Dreyfuss convinced him to become club secretary for the Louisville team he'd purchased in the NL. In 1900 he moved with Dreyfuss to Pittsburgh. His reputation for honesty and his businesslike approach to baseball won him election as NL president in 1903. He helped forge a peace between the AL and NL that resulted in the National Agreement that governed baseball through 1920. Fearless and honest in enforcing league rules, he was strongly criticized by New York's John McGraw over the 1908 Merkle incident and also came into conflict with Charles W. Murphy, the Chicago owner, over a ticket-scalping controversy. Pulliam was of a nervous temperament and proved unable to cope with criticism. In February 1909 he showed signs of mental illness and was given a leave of absence. He returned to work but remained moody and uncommunicative. On July 25, 1909, he committed suicide. /(NLM)

John Purdin — 1942– . RHP 1964–65, 68–69 Dodgers 110 ip, 6–4, 3.92

Purdin won his first two starts in a late 1964 call-up, but was usually a reliever thereafter. /(JFC)

Bob Purkey — 1929– . RHP 1954–66 Pirates, **Reds**, Cardinals 2114 ip, 129–115, 3.79. 20 wins: 62 *1 WS, 11 ip, 0–1, 1.64*

Knuckleballer Purkey was a top starter for the Reds in the late 1950s and early 1960s. Unlike most knuckleball specialists, one of his strengths was excellent control. He was usually hittable but his control helped him avoid big innings. In 1960 he pitched an 11-hit shutout. He lost a heartbreaker in Game Four of the 1961 WS when Roger Maris homered in the ninth inning to give the Yankees a 3–2 win. Twice Purkey won 17 games for the Reds, and in 1962 he led the NL in winning percentage (.821) with a sparkling 23–5 mark. /(BC)

Billy Purtell — 1886–1962. 3B-2B 1908–11, 14 **White Sox**, Red Sox, Tigers 333 g, .230, 2 hr, 104 rbi

Purtell was a journeyman infielder, a regular only in 1910, at third base with the White Sox and Red Sox. He followed his ML career with 12 seasons in the International and Pacific Coast leagues. /(JK)

Pat Putnam — 1953– . 1B-DH 1977–84 **Rangers**, Mariners, Twins 677 g, .255, 63 hr, 255 rbi

Putnam tied for fourth in the 1979 Rookie of the Year voting on the strength of an 18-HR, .277-BA season. His power declined in the following seasons until the Seattle Kingdome became his home park in 1983, and he hit a career-high 19 HR in 469 at-bats. He dropped to just .176 in 1984, though, ending his career. /(WOR)

Ewald Pyle (Lefty) — 1910– . LHP 1939, 42–45 Browns, Senators, **Giants**, Braves 270 ip, 11–21, 5.03

The curveballer's undistinguished career was extended by the WWII player shortages. His Giants career was marred by an off-the-field scuffle for which he was fined a month's pay. /(FS)

Frankie Pytlak — 1908–1977. C 1932–41, 45–46 **Indians**, Red Sox 795 g, .282, 7 hr, 272

Pytlak was a small catcher at 160 pounds and seldom completed a full season in an injury-plagued career. He was a good contact hitter who batted over .300 four times. His greatest thrill, he said, was when he threw out Ty Cobb in an exhibition game. /(ME)

Mel Queen [Melvin Joseph] — 1918–1982. RHP 1942, 44, 46–48, 50–52 Yankees, **Pirates** 557 ip, 27–40, 5.09

A wild fireballer, Queen was among the NL strike-out leaders (with 123) as a Pirate in 1951, his most active season. He was a winner only in 1944, going 6–3 for the Yankees. His son, Melvin Douglas Queen, was a major league outfielder-turned-pitcher. /(ME)

Mel Queen [Melvin Douglas] — 1942– . RHP-OF 1964–72 **Reds**, Angels 269 g, .179, 2 hr, 25 rbi; 390 ip, 20–17, 3.14

Queen failed to hit in three trials as an outfielder, but switched to pitching at the major league level during the 1966 season and went 14–8 in 1967 with a 2.76 ERA and good control. He missed most of 1968 with a sore shoulder and spent most of 1969 coming back in the minors. Traded to California, he was moved to the bullpen and collected nine saves in 1970, and also went 3-for-4 as a pinch hitter that year. He went 2–2 with four saves and a 1.77 ERA in 1971, but faded the next year. His father, also named Mel, pitched for the Yankees and Pirates. /(SFS)

Jim Quick — 1943– . *Umpire NL 1976–87 2 ASU 2 LCS 1 WS*

Quick is one of the few umpires ever to eject a trainer from a game. Rain was falling in the sixth inning of a game between Cincinnati and Atlanta on May 1, 1985. Reds trainer Larry Starr called, "Why don't you stop the game before someone gets hurt?" Quick's reply: "Why don't you take a walk? You're out of here." /(RTM)

Ernie Quigley — Unk.–1960. *Umpire AL, NL 1906, 1913–37 6 WS*

Quigley didn't let being short hinder him in becoming an outstanding umpire for 26 years in the NL. After he retired as an active umpire, he became supervisor of NL umps. In one of his first acts, he had to decide between two candidates for a vacant umpiring slot. One aspirant was a bulky football type who had a good deal of support among Quigley's contemporaries. Instead, Quigley chose the other nominee, a small man like himself. The candidate was Jocko Conlan, who went on to a Hall of Fame career. /(RTM)

Frank Quilici (Guido) — 1939– . 2B-3B 1965, 67–70 **Twins** 405 g, .214, 5 hr, 53 rbi. *1 LCS, 3 g, .000. 1 WS, 7 g, .200, 1 rbi.*
   Manager 1972–75 **Twins** *280–287, .494*

Quilici made the record books when, in the third inning of Game One of the 1965 World Series, the light-hitting utility man singled and doubled off Don Drysdale, tying the WS record for hits in an inning. /(JFC)

Jack Quinn [born John Quinn Picus] — 1883–1946. RHP 1909–15, 18–33 **Yankees**, Braves, Baltimore (FL), White Sox, Red Sox, A's, Dodgers, Reds 3934 ip, 247–217, 3.27. 20 wins: 14 *3 WS, 10 ip, 0–1, 8.44*

Spitballer Quinn pitched for eight teams in three major leagues during four different decades and made his final ML appearance at age 50. One of the major league pitchers allowed to continue using the spitter after the pitch was outlawed in 1920, Quinn was effective as both a starter and reliever. He helped pitch the Yankees to their first pennant in 1921 and aided the A's to two successive flags in 1929–30. His best and worst seasons were in the Federal League: 26 wins in 1914 and 22 losses the following year. On three occasions he won 18, including an 18–7 mark and 2.90 ERA with the 1928 A's at age 45.

Always vague about his birth date, Quinn set records as the oldest player to win a ML game (49), start a WS game (46), finish a WS game (47), and lead in a major pitching category (49) with six saves in 1932. He is also the oldest player to hit a home run (47). He was the teammate of 31 Hall of Famers. /(JL)

Joe Quinn — 1864–1940. 2B 1884–86, 1888–1901 St. Louis (UA), **Cardinals**, Braves, Boston (PL), Baltimore (NL), Cleveland (NL), Reds, Senators 1768 g, .261, 30 hr, 796 rbi.
   Manager 1895, 99 Cardinals, **Cleveland (NL)** *25–131, .160*

Jack Quinn

Quinn was the first Australian-born major leaguer; there wasn't another until Craig Shipley was called up by the Dodgers in 1986. Originally an "Onion," as Union Association players were called, Quinn became a fine second baseman who changed teams 11 times in his 17 ML seasons. He managed Cleveland for most of 1899 after Frank Robison, who owned both clubs, sent the team's best players to the Cardinals. Cleveland finished 20–134 with the lowest winning percentage (.130) in ML history. In the off-season Quinn was a mortician. /(ADS)

Luis Quinones — 1963– . SS-3B-2B 1983, 86– A's, **Giants**, Cubs, Reds 259 g, .225, 13 hr, 68 rbi

Quinones improved a little each year, and saw the most action on the Reds in 1989, filling in at third base for Chris Sabo. He hit a surprising 12 HR in 340 at-bats and batted .244. /(SFS)

Rey Quinones — 1963– . SS 1986–89 Red Sox, **Mariners**, Pirates 451 g, .245, 29 hr, 159 rbi

The Pirates acquired Quinones from the Mariners during the 1989 season with the hope that he would fill the hole at shortstop that had plagued them for years, but released him a few months later. Quinones had an outstanding arm and the ability to make spectacular plays, but showed himself to be an inconsistent player and unstable person. In 1988 he was the subject of controversy when he left the Mariners without consulting the team to attend the funeral of a relative in Puerto Rico. He also demonstrated an unwillingness to play with a series of minor injuries that failed to reveal anything on X-ray examinations. Quinones started his career with the Red Sox and, despite being billed as Boston's shortstop of the future, was traded to the Mariners in 1986 for Spike Owen and soon-to-be playoff hero Dave Henderson. /(TF/CR)

Jamie Quirk — 1954– . C-DH-3B 1975–89 **Royals**, Brewers, Cardinals, White Sox, Indians, Yankees, Orioles 774 g, .237, 37 hr, 193 rbi. *2 LCS, 5 g, .125, 2 rbi*

A shortstop in the minors, Quirk built a long career on his ability to fill in almost anywhere. He started catching in 1979, and he was above average defensively and throwing out would-be basestealers. His career as an effective backup catcher ended with the Yankees in 1989. /(FO)

Dan Quisenberry (Quiz) — 1953– . RHP 1979- **Royals**, Cardinals 1036 ip, 56–45, 2.69. *3 LCS, 12 ip, 1–2, 2.19. 2 WS, 15 ip, 2–2, 4.30*
☛ *All-Star—82–84.*

Groomed from the beginning as a reliever, Quisenberry employed bullseye control and a submarine delivery to keep hitters offstride. His bread-and-butter pitch was a sharp-breaking slider. Only three times in ten years did he issue more than 15 walks in a season despite pitching over 125 innings five times.

In his first full season Quiz won a dozen and saved 33 while appearing in 75 games. He led the American League in saves five times, including a record-setting 45 in 1983 and 44 the following season. Five times *TSN* awarded him AL Fireman of the Year honors. Quisenberry signed a lifetime guaranteed contract with the Royals worth over $30 million.

His bullpen dominance apparently fading, Kansas City released Quisenberry in July 1988, but he was quickly picked up by the Cardinals and his former manager, Whitey Herzog. He continued to have difficulty retiring lefthanded batters, but was a useful role-player in St. Louis' "Bullpen by committee." /(FO)

Dick Radatz (The Monster) — 1937– . RHP 1962–67, 69 **Red Sox**, Indians, Cubs, Tigers, Expos 694 ip, 52–43, 3.13
☞ *All-Star—63–64.*

This 6'6" 230-lb flamethrower was a devastating reliever from the time he joined the Red Sox in 1962 through 1965, saving 100 games in four years and winning 49 more. Radatz had unusually fine control for a one-pitch strikeout artist. As a rookie in 1962, he led the AL with 62 appearances, nine relief wins, and 24 saves to gain Fireman of the Year honors.

Radatz was even better in 1963. He won 10 consecutive decisions on the way to a 15–6 record, a 1.97 ERA, and 25 saves. Yankee manager Ralph Houk called him "the greatest relief pitcher I have ever seen." Houk named him to the 1963 All-Star squad, and Radatz struck out Willie Mays, Dick Groat, Duke Snider, Willie McCovey, and Julian Javier while working the last two innings. Another Fireman of the Year season followed in 1964, when Radatz made 79 appearances and led the league with 29 saves, 16 wins, and nine losses in relief. He recorded a win or a save in 45 of Boston's 72 wins and struck out 181 batters in 157 innings. But he called the 1964 All-Star Game his biggest disappointment; he gave up a three-run homer to Johnny Callison with two out in the ninth to lose 7–4.

Radatz saved 22 in 1965, but by 1966 he was losing movement on his fastball, and he was traded to Cleveland. Unable to convert to finesse pitching, he was out of the majors in 1968. He resurfaced with the 1969 Tigers and finished with the expansion Expos. He never made a start in 381 ML games, and he retired with 122 saves. /(FK)

Old Hoss Radbourn [Charles Gardner] — 1854–1897. RHP 1880–91 Buffalo (NL), **Providence (NL)**, Braves, Boston (PL), Reds 4535 ip, 308–191, 2.67. 20 wins: 81–87, 89–90
☞ *Led League—w 83–84. Led League—era 84. Led League—k 82, 84. Hall of Fame—1939.*

Dubbed Old Hoss for his dependability and endurance, Radbourne was a marvel even in an era when teams commonly used only two starting pitchers.

Already an outstanding pitcher in 1882 when he led the NL in strikeouts and shutouts, in 1883–84 Radbourne won more games for Providence than four entire NL teams. He made 68 starts in 1883, winning a league-high 49 games, including a no-hitter over Cleveland July 25. The next season, Radbourne completed all 73 of his starts, with 60 wins, 441 strikeouts, and a 1.38 ERA in 678.2 innings. He also won 18 consecutive games that year and pitched 11 shutouts. After the season, Providence met New York, champions of the American Association, in a forerunner to the modern World Series. With Radbourne pitching every inning, the Grays swept three games in New York and the series was defaulted before ever reaching Providence.

Radbourne joined Boston in 1886, but was not nearly as dominating as he had been in Providence, often losing as many as he won. In 1890 he led the Players' League in winning percentage for the Boston league champions, but in mid-1891 he dropped out of baseball. Radbourne, who had continued to pitch submarine-style even after the overhand delivery was legalized, was inducted into the Hall of Fame in 1939. /(JK)

Rip Radcliff [Raymond Allen] — 1906–1962. OF-1B 1934–43 **White Sox**, Browns, Tigers 1081 g, .311, 42 hr, 532 rbi
☞ *All-Star—36.*

Radcliff didn't reach the majors until age 28. He reported to the White Sox in 1934, having had a Triple Crown season with Selma (Southeastern League) in 1930. In his second full ML season, 1936, he was voted to the All-Star team on the strength of his hitting. However, he stood out with his glove that game, making a dramatic catch on a deep fly hit by Joe Medwick. The next day, July 8, he went 6-for-7. Radcliff batted .335 that season. After a trade to the Browns, he tied for the AL lead with 200 hits in 1940, finishing at .342, fourth in the league. In his last ML year, 1943, he led the league with 44 appearances as a Tiger pinch hitter. /(JK)

Old Hoss Radbourn

Alex Radcliffe — 1905– . 3B-SS Negro Leagues 1926–45 Chicago Giants, Dayton Marcos, **Chicago American Giants**, New York Cubans, Kansas City Monarchs, Cincinnati Clowns, Indianapolis Clowns, Memphis Red Sox statistics not available
☛ *Led League—hr 44–45(NAL).*

Radcliffe was generally acclaimed the best third baseman in Negro American League history. A 6' 200-lb righthanded hitter, he was a vital cog in the Chicago American Giants' 1932 Negro Southern League pennant (batting .283) and in their disputed 1933 and 1934 NNL claims. From 1933 to 1936 he batted .330. His manager, Dave Malarcher (himself a famed American Giant third baseman), said, "Radcliffe, in my estimation, became one of the truly great third basemen in baseball history; a fast man, a powerful hitter and one who possessed the mind which enabled him to fit into [our system]."

Radcliffe batted .325 during the 1945 NAL season. When he made his 11th and final East-West all-star game appearance in 1946, he had played in more of them than any other player. His 44 at-bats and 15 hits (.341) were East-West game highs, and he scored seven runs and drove in ten. His older brother Ted also starred in the Negro Leagues. /(MFK)

Ted Radcliffe (Double Duty) — 1902– . C-RHP-MGR Negro Leagues 1928–50 Detroit Stars, St. Louis Stars, Homestead Grays, Pittsburgh Crawfords, Columbus Blue Birds, New York Black Yankees, Brooklyn Eagles, Cincinnati Tigers, Memphis Red Sox, Birmingham Black Barons, Chicago American Giants, Louisville Buckeyes statistics not available
☛ *All-Star—37–39, 41, 43–44.*

Radcliffe was a star Negro League pitcher and catcher of the 1930s and 1940s. He was nicknamed Double Duty by Damon Runyon, who saw him in the 1932 Negro League World Series at Yankee Stadium. Radcliffe caught Satchel Paige in a 5–0 victory in the first game of a doubleheader, then pitched a shutout in the nightcap.

The 5'9" 210-lb Radcliffe was a smart, strong-throwing catcher. On the mound he was the master of the emery ball and other pitches of questionable legality. Statistics available for 8 of his 23 seasons show him hitting .273, with a top mark of .316 for the 1929 Detroit Stars. In 6 of the 21 seasons he pitched during the 1930s, he went 33–17 with seven saves. He appeared in six East-West all-star games, three as a pitcher, three as a catcher.

Radcliffe hit .376 (11-for-29) in nine exhibition games against major leaguers. In 1934 he managed a white team that barnstormed through Canada, playing a major league all-star team. Radcliffe's team was 2–1 when Hall of Famer Jimmie Foxx was beaned, and the tour canceled. Ted's brother Alex was a top Negro League third baseman. /(JJM)

Dave Rader — 1948– . C 1971–80 **Giants**, Cardinals, Cubs, Phillies, Red Sox 846 g, .257, 30 hr, 235 rbi

San Francisco's number-one pick in the June 1967 draft, Rader was *TSN* NL Rookie Player of the Year in 1972, when he caught 127 games and batted .259. After five years as the Giants' first-string catcher (1972–76), he spent each of the following four seasons with a different team. He was the Cubs' regular catcher in 1978, though he hit just .203. /(JCA)

Doug Rader (Rojo, Rooster) — 1944- . 3B-1B-DH 1967-77 **Astros**, Padres, Blue Jays 1465 g, .251, 155 hr, 722 rbi.
   Manager 1983-85, 89- **Rangers**, White Sox, Angels 247-272, .476
☛ *Gold Glove—70-74* .

The freckle-faced redhead was a wild, eccentric, clowning character off the field who played and managed aggressively. He won five consecutive Gold Gloves (1970-74) at third base with Houston. Three times he hit more than 20 home runs. Named Ranger manager for 1983, the high-strung and combative Rader guided his club to a third-place finish that year and held the Texas helm until May 1985. He was interim manager of the White Sox for two games in 1986 and led the 1989 Angels into contention. /(JCA)

Ken Raffensberger — 1917- . LHP 1939-41, 43-54 Cardinals, Cubs, Phillies, **Reds** 2151 ip, 119-154, 3.60
☛ *All-Star—44.*

After a shoulder injury slowed his fastball, Raffensberger became a top control pitcher; over one four-year stretch he threw just two wild pitches. Representing the last-place Phillies in the 1944 All-Star Game, he was credited with the victory, but finished the season with a league-high 20 losses. With the Reds, he shared the league lead in shutouts in 1949 and 1952 (his only two winning seasons) and led with 38 starts in '49. But in 1951, no NL pitcher lost more than Raffensberger's 17. He threw four career one-hitters, two against the Cardinals in 1948. /(NLM)

Pat Ragan — 1888-1956. RHP 1909, 11-19, 23 Reds, Cubs, Dodgers, **Braves**, Giants, White Sox, Phillies 1609 ip, 76-104, 2.99

Ragan overcame what a contemporary journalist described as "an inexplicable tendency to become as wild as a Prohibitionist's statistics." On October 5, 1914 Ragan struck out the side on nine pitches, exactly two years after pitching Brooklyn's final game in Washington Park. /(TG)

Tim Raines (Rock) — 1959- . OF-2B 1979- **Expos** 1275 g, .303, 87 hr, 490 rbi. *1 LCS, 5 g, .238, 1 rbi*
☛ *Led League—ba 86. All-Star—81-87.*

This multi-talented outfielder achieved early stardom as American Association batting champion (.354) and *TSN* Minor League Player of the Year in 1980 as a second baseman. Converted to the outfield in 1981, Raines captured the first of four straight stolen base titles and finished a close second in Rookie of the Year voting. The switch-hitter established a record with an 87.4% success rate in over 300 stolen base attempts through his first 1,021 major league games (1979-87). He reached career highs in steals (90) and runs (133) in 1983, leading the NL in both categories. Opting for free agency after his 1986 batting championship season, he found that the baseball owners' collusion on free agents left him without an offer. Raines returned to the Expos in May 1987 with neither spring training nor a warm-up stint in the minors, homered in his first game, and led the NL in runs scored (123) for the second year in spite of the missed time. Replacing the departed Andre Dawson in the lineup instead of hitting in his usual leadoff spot, Raines also hit a career-high 18 HR. Injuries in 1988, including a first-ever trip to the disabled list, hampered Raines. /(ME)

Chuck Rainey — 1954- . RHP 1979-84 **Red Sox**, Cubs, A's 670 ip, 43-35, 4.50

Rainey was a winner in most of his big-league seasons while laboring in hitters' paradises Fenway Park and Wrigley Field. He went 8-5 in his 1979 rookie season with a 3.81 ERA, then improved to 8-3, 4.86 in 1980. Traded to the Cubs for Doug Bird after a 7-5, 5.02 mark in 1982, he posted a 14-13, 4.48 record but missed out on Chicago's division championship when he was traded in July 1984 for player-to-be-named-later Davey Lopes of the A's. /(WOR)

Dave Rajsich — 1951- . LHP 1978-80 Yankees, **Rangers** 115 ip, 3-4, 4.60

The 6'5" forkballer, used mostly in long relief, went from New York to Texas in the 1978 nine-player deal that made Dave Righetti a Yankee. After the end of his major league career, Rajsich played briefly in Japan. His younger brother Gary was a Met outfielder in 1982-83. /(JCA)

Ed Rakow (Rock) — 1936- . RHP 1960-65, 67 Dodgers, **A's**, Tigers, Braves 761 ip, 36-47, 4.33

Rakow tied for the AL lead in losses in 1962 when he went 14-17 (4.25) as the ace of the ninth-place A's. /(SFS)

Bob Ramazzotti — 1917- . 2B-3B-SS 1946, 48-53 Dodgers, **Cubs** 346 g, .230, 4 hr, 53 rbi

Ramazzotti became a Cub in 1949 through one of the many trades Chicago made with the Dodgers during the late 1940s and early 1950s. The utility infielder proved to have limited range, and he hit one home run each year from 1949 through 1952. /(DAS)

Rafael Ramirez (Raffy) — 1958– . SS 1980- **Braves**, Astros 1233 g, .262, 49 hr, 414 rbi. *1 LCS, 3 g, .182, 1 rbi* ☛ *All-Star—84.*

One of a handful of ML players from the town of San Pedro de Macoris in the Dominican Republic, Ramirez was the Braves' speedy, smooth-fielding shortstop from 1981 to 1986, leading NL shortstops in double plays four straight years while hitting quite well for his position. He made the NL All-Star team in 1984 with a .304 average at mid-season, but in 1987 torn knee ligaments limited him to only 56 games and he was traded to Houston after the season. With the Astros in 1988, Ramirez posted his best batting average since 1983 (.276) and drove in a career-high 59 runs. /(SCL)

Domingo Ramos — 1958– . SS-3B-2B 1978, 80, 82- Yankees, Blue Jays, **Mariners**, Indians, Angels, Cubs 409 g, .234, 6 hr, 68 rbi. *1 LCS, 1 g, .000*

Ramos is a utility infielder from the Dominican Republic. After brief appearances with the Yankees and Blue Jays amid an eight-season minor league career, he latched on with the Mariners in 1982, where he filled in at all four infield positions, never appearing in more than 75 games. Primarily a glove man, Ramos hit over .200 just twice, .283 in 1983 and .311 in 1987 (in 103 at-bats). The Mariners released him after the 1987 season. He played for the Cubs in 1989 after signing as a free agent. /(TF)

Pedro Ramos (Pete) — 1935– . RHP 1955–67, 69–70 **Senators/Twins**, Indians, Yankees, Phillies, Pirates, Reds, Senators 2355 ip, 117–160, 4.08 ☛ *All-Star—59.*

Ramos led the AL in losses four straight years, 1958–61, as the Senators finished last in 1958–59 and below .500 all four years. The Cuban also led in starts in '58 and '60, and set a since-broken AL record by surrendering 43 homers. The Washington franchise moved to Minnesota in 1961, and the Twins traded Ramos for Vic Power and Dick Stigman after that season; he went 10–12 on sixth-place Cleveland as the Twins climbed to third.

Switching to relief partway through 1964, he finally played for a winner when the Yankees picked him up on September 5 for their tough pennant drive, surrendering Ralph Terry, Bud Daley, and $75,000. He proved well worth the cost, going 1–0 with a 1.25 ERA and saving eight games down the stretch. He was their bullpen stopper for the next two seasons, with 19 saves in 1965 and 13 in 1966, but the Yankees collapsed, finishing last in '66.

After a stint in the NL, Ramos returned to Washington for his final season, playing for the franchise that had replaced the original Senators in the 1961 expansion.

Ramos was known for more than just his pitching. He hit 15 HR lifetime, tied for 20th among pitchers, and even hit a grand slam off Baltimore's Chuck Estrada on May 30, 1962. He also hit two in one game on July 31, 1963; in the sixth inning, his homer was the second of four straight by the Indians, the first AL team ever to accomplish that feat. He was also used frequently as a pinch runner, around ten times a season when he was with the Senators, and insisted that he was the fastest runner in the majors. He repeatedly challenged Mickey Mantle to a footrace in his attempt to prove his claim but was never granted the match. His switch to relief ended his pinch-running career. /(SH)

Willie Ramsdell (Willie the Knuck) — 1916–1969. RHP 1947–48, 50–52 Dodgers, **Reds**, Cubs 480 ip, 24–39, 3.83

James Willard Ramsdell was originally christened Jess Willard, in honor of the world heavyweight champion. He was a knuckleballer whose trademark good humor was severely tested during a 40-inning stretch in which his Reds teammates failed to provide him with a run. In 1951 he tied for the league lead with 17 losses. /(JL)

Mike Ramsey — 1954– . 2B-SS-3B 1978, 80–85 **Cardinals**, Expos, Dodgers 394 g, .240, 2 hr, 57 rbi. *1 WS, 3 g, .000*

Ramsey was a utility infielder with the Cardinals in the early 1980s. Seeing the most action in 1982 (256 at-bats), the singles hitter contributed to St. Louis's World Championship. /(SFS)

Toad Ramsey [Thomas A.] — 1864–1906. LHP 1885–1890 Louisville AA, St. Louis AA 2100 ip, 114–124, 3.29. 20 wins: 86–87, 90 ☛ *Led League—k 87.*

Ramsey struck out 499 batters in 1886 (to finish second to Matt Kilroy's record 513), the second highest ML total ever. He won 38 games that year and 37 in 1887 when he led the league in strikeouts with 355. /(FIC)

Bob Randall — 1949– . 2B 1976–80 **Twins** 460 g, .257, 1 hr, 91 rbi

A heads-up second baseman, Randall turned double plays adeptly and set a Twins second basemen's fielding average record (.985) in 1977. A contact hitter, he played regularly until the emergence of Rob Wilfong. /(JCA)

Lenny Randle — 1949– . 3B-2B-OF-DH 1971–82
Senators/Rangers, Mets, Yankees, Cubs, Mariners
1138 g, .257, 27 hr, 322 rbi

The acrobatic switch-hitter had played seven positions in five years with Texas when, in spring training of 1977, angry that the second base job was going to rookie Bump Wills, Randle punched out 49-year-old manager Frank Lucchesi. Randle said Lucchesi provoked him by calling him a "punk." The manager needed plastic surgery, and the usually good-natured Randle was suspended, fined, and shipped to New York; he led the Mets in six offensive categories that year. Back in the AL as a free agent, Randle got down on all fours to try to blow a slow roller foul in the Kingdome in 1981./(JCA)

Willie Randolph — 1954– . 2B 1975– Pirates,
Yankees, Dodgers 1869 g, .274, 50 hr, 588 rbi. *5 LCS,
18 g, .258, 1 hr, 6 rbi. 3 WS, 16 g, .158, 3 hr, 4 rbi*
☛ *All-Star—76–77, 80–81, 87, 89.*

Known as a stabilizing influence on a tumultuous team, Randolph's consistency on offense earned the respect of teammates and opponents. After a 30-game stint with the Pirates in 1975, Randolph was one of three players traded to the Yankees for pitcher Doc Medich in the off-season. Randolph immediately became the starting second baseman, and stayed in that role through 13 seasons and 32 shortstops. During Randolph's first six seasons with the Yankees, they won five division championships, four AL pennants, and World Series titles in 1977 and 1978. During 1980, when the Yankees won 103 games, Randolph led the AL in walks with 119, the most by a Yankee since Mickey Mantle's 122 in 1962, and he was second in the league in on-base percentage (.429). He was named to postseason all-star teams in 1977, 1978, and 1980. He had typical Randolph years throughout the 1980s, and he established career highs in 1987 in batting average (.305) and RBI (67). Randolph, however, suffered through an injury-plagued .230 season in 1988 and was not re-signed by New York. Instead, he signed a free-agent contract with the Dodgers. He left the Yankees ranking high on their star-studded all-time lists: second in stolen bases, seventh in at-bats and runs, eighth in games, tenth in hits, and nineteenth in triples./(EG)

Merritt Ranew — 1938– . C 1962–65, 69 Astros,
Cubs, Braves, Angels, Pilots 269 g, .247, 8 hr, 54 hr

One of the Cubs' early-1960s hopes, Ranew had his best year in 1964, when he batted .338, led the National League with 17 pinch hits, and participated in a triple play./(DAS)

William H. Rankin — 1849–1913. *Writer.*

Said to have been the first official scorer, Rankin had a bitter running argument with Henry Chadwick over who deserved the title "Father of Baseball." Rankin claimed he began writing about baseball while Chadwick was still covering cricket, but Chadwick gained the greater recognition. Rankin was with the New York *Clipper* for 30 years, succeeding Al Wright as editor. He left an extensive baseball library, having saved everything of interest from the time he first covered the game./(NLM)

Goldie Rapp [Joseph Aloysius] — 1892–1966. 3B
1921–23 Giants, **Phillies** 276 g, .253, 2 hr, 73 rbi

Rapp led NL third basemen in total chances per game in his rookie 1921 season, split between the Giants and the Phillies; he was dealt, after a .215 start, in the trade that brought Casey Stengel to the Giants. But he was a light hitter in an era that saw the homer become a major offensive weapon./(JFC)

Bill Rariden (Bedford Bill) — 1888–1942. C 1909–20
Braves, Indianapolis/Newark (FL), Giants, Reds 986 g,
.237, 7 hr, 272 rbi. *2 WS, 10 g, .281, 4 rbi*

Named for his hometown of Bedford, Indiana, Rariden was a light-hitting catcher who became a regular in the Federal League and later was involved in one of the most famous plays in World Series history. He helped the Indianapolis Hoosiers to the pennant in 1914, leading FL catchers in putouts and assists. He repeated in those categories in 1915, also leading in total chances per game and errors, and had his best offensive season, batting .270 and setting career highs with 30 doubles, seven triples, and 49 runs. He also showed a good eye, walking 60 times for a .357 on-base percentage.

A standout behind the plate, Rariden was purchased from Newark by John McGraw when the Federal League folded, and caught most of the games in the Giants' 26-game winning streak in 1916. He led NL catchers in putouts and total chances per game in 1916 and helped the Giants to the NL pennant in 1917 with a career-high .271 average. In the World Series, he drove in a run in New York's 3–2 Game Four victory, but in Game Six White Sox runner Eddie Collins eluded him in a rundown, and Rariden then neglected to cover home as Heinie Zimmerman vainly chased Collins across the plate. In February 1919 he was traded to the Reds for Hal Chase and was a backup on their

World Championship team in that, his final, season. /(NLM)

Vic Raschi (The Springfield Rifle) — 1919– . RHP 1946–55 **Yankees**, Cardinals, A's 1819 ip, 132–66, 3.72. 20 wins: 49–51 *6 WS, 60 ip, 5–3, 2.24*
☛ *Led League—k 51.. All-Star—48–50, 52.*

Raschi was already 28 when he broke into the Yankees' starting rotation for good in 1948. He then ran off consecutive records of 19–8, 21–10, 21–8, and 21–10. The Springfield, Massachusetts native had tremendous determination and a blazing fastball. His size (6'1" 205 lbs.) and the menacing scowl on his dark, unshaven face were helpful, too. He never missed an assignment although his knees deteriorated painfully.

With the Yankees, Raschi was a big-game winner. He won the 1948 All-Star Game, driving in the winning run. And he beat Boston on the final day of the 1949 season to break a first-place tie with the Red Sox, then won the WS clincher against Brooklyn, a feat he duplicated against the Giants in 1951. He two-hit the Phillies 1–0 in the 1950 WS, and won twice more against the Dodgers in the 1952 WS. Raschi was a fair hitter (.184 career average). On August 3, 1953 his seven RBI set an AL single-game record for pitchers. In February 1954, he was sold to the Cardinals for $85,000 after contract battles with the Yankees. /(MG)

Dennis Rasmussen — 1959– . LHP 1983– Padres, **Yankees**, Reds 1045 ip, 69–45, 4.07

Despite being the Yankees' top starter in 1986, the 6–7 Rasmussen was traded to Cincinnati for Bill Gullickson in August 1987. The Reds traded him to San Diego in June 1988 after a bad start and he won 10 of his next 11 decisions.

Originally Pirates property, Rasmussen was traded from the Padres to the Yankees in 1984 for Graig Nettles. /(EG)

Eric Rasmussen (Harold) — 1952– . RHP 1975–80, 82–83 **Cardinals**, Padres, Royals 1017 ip, 50–77, 3.85

Rasmussen did not have overpowering stuff and relied on mixing his pitches. He pitched a shutout against the Padres in his first ML start (7/21/75), but never had a winning season. After an 11–17 year in 1977 and a 2–5 start the next year, the Cardinals traded him to the Padres for George Hendrick in late May. He was 12–10 for the remainder of the '78 season. /(FJO)

Morrie Rath [Maurice Charles] — 1886–1945. 2B-3B-SS 1909–10, 12–13, 19–20 A's, Indians, White Sox, **Reds** 563 g, .254, 4 hr, 92 rbi. *1 WS, 8 g, .226, 2 rbi*

When Morrie Rath was hit by Eddie Cicotte's pitch to lead off the 1919 World Series, it was a pre-arranged signal to the gamblers that the Black Sox fix was on. The 5'8" 160-lb Rath had been the White Sox' second baseman in 1912 and led AL second basemen in assists and fielding average. The left-handed batter reached career highs of 104 runs, 95 walks (third in the league, giving him a .380 on-base percentage), a .272 BA, and 30 steals that year, but, amazingly, had only 19 RBI in 157 games (he was Chicago's leadoff batter). His average dropped to .200 the following season, and he lost the second base job.

Rath reappeared with the Reds for their World Championship 1919 season after spending 1918 in the Navy. He led NL second basemen in putouts, assists, double plays, and total chances per game while batting .264 with 64 walks, 77 runs, and a career-high 29 RBI. On August 26, in a 15-inning game, he had 13 assists, the second-highest total ever and the modern (post-1900) NL mark. He hit only .226 in the World Series, but scored five runs in the eight-game Series.

Rath finished his ML career by leading NL second basemen in fielding in 1920, but had only 36 walks to supplement his .267 BA, ending his usefulness as a leadoff batter. /(SH)

Doug Rau — 1948– . LHP 1972–79, 81 **Dodgers**, Angels 1260 ip, 81–60, 3.35. *3 LCS, 7 ip, 0–1, 6.75. 2 WS, 4 ip, 0–1, 6.23*

In his first major league start, in 1972, the poised 23-year-old shut out the Cardinals on three hits. A smart hurler with a wide assortment of pitches, Rau became a consistent winner for the Dodgers, averaging more than 14 victories a season from 1973 to 1978, and was usually a fast starter. In 1976 he was second in ERA (2.57 to John Denny's 2.52) as he won a career-high 16 games. He did not recover well enough from a 1979 rotator-cuff injury to successfully continue his career. /(JCA)

Shane Rawley — 1955– . LHP 1978–88 Mariners, Yankees, **Phillies**, Twins 1871 ip, 111–118, 4.02
☛ *All-Star—86.*

Rawley broke into the ML as a short reliever, earning 36 saves in four seasons with the Mariners despite suffering a broken hand in 1979 and a broken foot before the 1981 season. He was traded to the Yankees in 1982 and became a starter that

July. Rawley preferred starting, because it allowed him more time to warm up, and he became a dependable member of the Yankees' rotation, winning 14 games in 1983. After a 1984 trade sent him to Philadelphia, Rawley had 11 wins by July in 1985 before a fractured shoulder ended his season, and in 1986 he was 17–6 in late August, but lost his last five decisions. After a miserable 1988 (8–16, 4.18), he was traded to Minnesota for Tom Herr. /(SG)

Johnny Rawlings — 1892–1972. 2B-SS 1914–15, 17–26 Reds, Kansas City (FL), **Braves**, Phillies, Giants, Pirates 1080 g, .250, 14 hr, 303 rbi. *1 WS, 8 g, .333, 4 rbi*

Rawlings was a deft fielder and acceptable hitter who kept losing his middle infield jobs to better players. He played second base for the Braves until Buck Herzog arrived and shortstop while Rabbit Maranville was in WWI. He played 2B for the Giants until Frankie Frisch switched back from third, and for the Pirates until Glenn Wright bumped Maranville from short to second. He handled 48 chances flawlessly in his only World Series with the Giants in 1921. /(ADS)

Jim Ray (Sting) — 1944– . RHP 1965–66, 68–74 **Astros**, Tigers 617 ip, 43–30, 3.61

Ray was a winning reliever with a sharp-breaking curveball and a hard, "stinging" fastball. In the 24-inning, 1–0 Astros-Mets marathon of April 15, 1968, Ray pitched seven scoreless innings, striking out 11 while allowing just two hits. /(JCA)

Johnny Ray — 1957– . 2B-OF 1981– **Pirates**, Angels 1248 g, .291, 48 hr, 551 rbi
☛ *Rookie of the Year—82. All-Star—88.*

In 1982 Ray became the first Pirate selected as NL Rookie of the Year, playing 162 games and hitting .281. Though he led NL second basemen in errors, he also led in putouts, assists, and total chances. The disciplined, switch-hitting gap hitter tied for the NL lead with 38 doubles in both 1983 and 1984, and proved one of baseball's toughest batters to strike out. In 1986 he tied a ML second basemen's record for fewest errors (150 or more games), with five. Traded to the Angels late in 1987, he was tried in left field, but moved back to second base when Mark McLemore was injured. /(ME)

Floyd Rayford (Sugarbear) — 1957– . 3B-C 1980, 82–87 **Orioles**, Cardinals 390 g, .224, 38 hr, 117 rbi

A stocky reserve, Rayford was traded from the Orioles to the Cardinals in June 1983, then sold back to the Orioles before the 1984 season. He was outstanding in 1985, hitting .306 (50 points higher than his next-best season batting average) with 18 HR in 105 games, but spent most of 1986–87 at AAA Rochester (International League). /(SCL)

Fred Raymer — 1875–1957. 2B-3B-SS 1901, 04–05 Cubs, **Braves** 371 g, .218, 1 hr, 101 rbi

A light-hitting, speedy infielder, Raymer started a triple play for Chicago in a losing effort on June 14, 1901. He was Boston's regular second baseman in 1904–05. /(DAS)

Bugs Raymond [Arthur Lawrence] — 1882–1912. RHP 1904, 07–11 Tigers, Cardinals, **Giants** 854 ip, 45–57, 2.49

The stereotypical hard-drinking baseball bum, Raymond was considered a better pitcher when lacking in sobriety, and unfortunately his managers took advantage of this; all except John McGraw, who made a serious effort to save the man. Despite Raymond's 2.03 ERA in 1908, the spitballer lost a league-high 25 games for the Cardinals. He was 18–12 for the Giants in 1909, his most effective season. Finally axed in 1911, he died shortly thereafter of a blow to the head in a barroom brawl. /(ARA)

Claude Raymond (Frenchy) — 1937– . RHP 1959, 61–71 White Sox, Braves, **Astros**, Expos 721 ip, 46–53, 3.66

The Milwaukee Braves needed an interpreter to help sign the mild-looking yet tough French-Canadian hurler. Raymond quickly learned English. He logged 83 lifetime saves, 23 in 1970 for the Expos, for whom he became a French-language broadcaster. /(JCA)

Al Reach — 1840–1928. 2B-OF 1871–75 **Philadelphia (NA)** 81 g, .252

Born in London, Reach first attracted attention on Brooklyn baseball diamonds in the 1850s. In 1865, he was brought to Philadelphia for $25 a week "expenses," making him one of the earliest professionals. A second baseman, although by most accounts a lefthanded thrower, he was considered an excellent batter. In 1871, when Philadelphia won the first National Association championship, he hit .348. After retiring as a player, he was one of the founders of the Phillies and served as team president from 1883 to 1902. He later was part owner of the Athletics. A sporting-goods company he founded in the 1870s prospered and eventually made him millions. In 1889 he sold out to A.G. Spalding, although he continued in an executive position. An annual baseball guide that he began in the 1880s was instrumental in developing interest in baseball statistics. /(BC)

Randy Ready — 1960– . 3B-2B-OF Brewers, **Padres**, Phillies 459 g, .268, 33 hr, 163 rbi

The two-time minor league batting champion shuttled between Vancouver (Pacific Coast League) and the Brewers for three seasons, never hitting below .325 at Vancouver, before a 1986 trade brought him to San Diego. With the Padres, Ready excelled in a utility role, filling in whenever necessary in the infield or outfield. His career minor league batting average is .343. /(SCL)

Ronald Reagan — 1911– . *Broadcaster.*

Known as Dutch Reagan in the 1930s, when he did studio re-creations of Cubs games for WHO radio in Des Moines, Iowa, Reagan left baseball broadcasting to pursue a successful movie career. He was president of the United States from 1981 to 1989. /(SCL)

Beans Reardon [John] — 1897–1984. *Umpire* NL 1926–49 *3 ASU 5 WS*

One of baseball's most colorful umpires, Reardon acquired his nickname because he was raised in Boston. He was famous for heavy language and heavy beer drinking. In 1946 Anheuser-Busch awarded him a lucrative franchise in Los Angeles. One day Reardon ejected Frankie Frisch from a game in Pittsburgh and ran into him later that evening in a hotel pub. They had a few beers together, and Frisch told Reardon about his new Packard automobile. Beans asked if he could take it for a spin. Frisch reluctantly agreed. When Reardon got to the hotel garage, he found the Packard out of gas and had the attendant call Frisch to replenish the supply. Reardon remembered, "That day it cost him a $50 fine for the ejection, five rounds of beer, and a tank of gas." Another of Reardon's friends was actress Mae West, and he appeared in many of her movies. Reardon worked many important and historic games. He was behind the plate when Babe Ruth hit his 714th and final home run. /(RTM)

Jeff Reardon (The Terminator) — 1955– . RHP 1979–Mets, **Expos**, Twins 892 ip, 57–62, 3.03. *2 LCS, 6 ip, 1–1, 8.53. 1 WS, 5 ip, 0–0, 0.00*
☛ *All-Star—85–86.*

Jeff Reardon's bullpen exploits lifted both Montreal and Minnesota to unexpected success. A good 1980 season with the Mets prompted Reardon's trade to the Expos for Ellis Valentine. The bearded New Englander was the only hurler with 20 or more saves each season from 1982 to 1988. He led the majors with 41 saves in 1985, but slumped slightly in 1986. At age 31, the University of Massachusetts history major was traded to the Twins. After a shaky start, the hard thrower's relief work earned him Minnesota's Most Valuable Player award and a World Championship ring in 1987; he saved two games and won one in the LCS. During the season, he had more strikeouts than innings. A true stopper, Reardon rarely worked more than one inning in any game. He surpassed 30 saves each year from 1986 to 1988, becoming one of the game's all-time save leaders. /(ME)

Frank Reberger (Crane) — 1944– . RHP 1968–72 Cubs, Padres, **Giants** 389 ip, 14–15, 4.51

The slender 6'5" Idaho rancher was overlooked in the draft but signed on with the Cubs after a Pioneer League tryout. Reberger appeared solely in relief in 67 games for the 1969 Padres but was a spot starter with San Francisco. /(JCA)

Dick Redding (Cannonball) — 1891–1940. RHP-OF-MGR Negro Leagues 1911–38 New York Lincoln Giants, Lincoln Stars, Indianapolis ABC's, Chicago American Giants, Brooklyn Royal Giants, Bacharach Giants statistics not available

The 6'4" 210-lb Redding may have been the hardest-throwing pitcher in black baseball history. Negro Leaguer Jesse Hubbard said Redding had a better fastball than did Satchel Paige or Cum Posey. Frank Forbes, Cannonball's teammate on the 1914 New York Lincoln Giants, said, "Dick Redding was like Walter Johnson. Nothing but speed." Like Johnson, Redding did not develop a curveball until late in his career. He used the hesitation delivery decades before Paige made it famous, balancing on one foot with his back to the hitter before cutting loose his devastating fastball.

In his first season, 1911, Redding reeled off 17 consecutive wins. Through 1914, he teamed with Smokey Joe Williams to give the New York Lincoln Giants one of the all-time-great one-two pitching punches. He went 43–12 in 1912, including a 17-strikeout perfect game against the Eastern League Jersey Skeeters. He struck out 24 in defeating a United States League team. Jumping to the Lincoln Stars in 1915, he won 20 straight, including several games against major league all-star squads. In that year's Black World Series, he went 3–1 with a shutout over the Chicago American Giants, and batted .385.

Redding fought in France in 1918, then returned as player-manager of the Bacharach Giants. In 1920 he led them to the Eastern Colored League championship. He spent 16 years with the Brooklyn Royal Giants, pitching occasionally. Though he never achieved great managerial success, he was well liked by his players. Hall of Famer Buck Leonard said Redding "was a nice fellow, easy going. He never argued, never cursed, never smoked as I recall; I never saw him take a drink." He died in a mental hospital under mysterious circumstances shortly after leaving the Royal Giants./(JJM)

Pete Redfern — 1954– . RHP 1976–82 **Twins** 714 ip, 42–48, 4.54

Redfern went 8–8 with a 3.51 ERA as a rookie in 1976, but was slowed by injury in 1977. He made a comeback in 1979, mostly in the bullpen, going 7–3, and was a solid starter for the next two seasons./(SFS)

Gary Redus — 1956– . OF 1982– **Reds**, Phillies, White Sox, Pirates 794 g, .250, 68 hr, 260 rbi

An erratic hitter with blazing speed, Redus was third in the AL with 52 steals for Chicago in 1987, and twice stole 48 bases with the Reds. He had career highs in HR (17) and RBI (51) as a rookie with the Reds in 1983, but has never hit better than .254. He hit his only two ML grand slams in a span of five days in 1988, and has been a part-time player since his acquisition by the Pirates in August 1988./(SCL)

Howie Reed — 1936–1984. RHP 1958–60, 64–67, 69–71 A's, Dodgers, Angels, Astros, **Expos** 515 ip, 26–29, 3.72. *1 WS, 3 ip, 0–0, 8.10*

The broad-shouldered reliever and swingman played a small role in helping the Dodgers to the 1965 pennant, winning a career-high seven games. Though troubled by a bad arm after 1966, he persevered./(JCA)

Jeff Reed — 1962– . C 1984– Twins, **Expos**, Reds 362 g, .222, 7 hr, 70 rbi

Reed bounced between the ML and minors for four seasons before a July 1988 trade sent him to the Reds, and an injury to Bo Diaz made him a starter in 1989. Normally excellent defensively (he led his league's catchers in assists five times in the minors), Reed tied a 68-year-old record for catchers with three errors in the seventh inning, July 28, 1987./(SCL)

Jerry Reed — 1955– . RHP 1981–83, 85– Phillies, Indians, **Mariners** 427 ip, 18–17, 3.83

Trained as a short reliever in the Phillies organization, Reed found success as a Triple-A starter but did his best work in relief for the last-place 1985 Indians (eight saves) and the 1987 Mariners (seven saves). He pitched the first no-hitter in Western Carolina University history./(ME)

Jody Reed — 1962– . SS 1987– **Red Sox** 264 g, .290, 4 hr, 76 rbi. *1 LCS, 4 g, .273*

Making Reed the everyday shortstop was one of the changes made by new manager Joe Morgan in 1988 that turned the team around, leading to a division title. Reed finished third in AL Rookie of the Year voting, batting .293 and scoring 60 runs in 338 at-bats while providing solid defense./(WOR)

Ron Reed — 1942– . RHP 1966–84 Braves, Cardinals, **Phillies**, White Sox 2476 ip, 146–140, 3.46. *6 LCS, 21 ip, 0–2, 6.53. 2 WS, 5 ip, 0–0, 1.69*
☛ *All-Star—68.*

Reed was a basketball standout at Notre Dame. He was an NBA forward in 1965–67 as the sixth man for Dave DeBusschere's Pistons. He was also playing pro baseball in the summers, and he finally yielded to a two-year contract from the Braves that required him to abandon basketball. In 1969 he went 18–10, helping Atlanta to its first division title, but lost to the Mets in Game Two of the LCS.

Reed was the Braves' winning pitcher on April 8, 1974, the day Hank Aaron hit his record-breaking 715th home run. A 1975 trade sent him to St. Louis, where he went 9–8 before being dealt to the Phillies. Converted to relief by manager Danny Ozark, he teamed with Tug McGraw for eight seasons to give Philadelphia a powerful lefty-righty tandem. He recorded career bests of 17 saves and a 2.23 ERA in 1978 and saved the Phillies' division clincher. He led the majors with 13 relief wins in 1979. He was the loser in Game Two of the 1980 LCS, but he saved Game Two of the World Series against Kansas City. When he left the majors at age

42, he stood 15th on the all-time list for games pitched (751). He recorded 103 career saves. /(CG)

Andy Reese — 1904–1966. OF-3B-2B 1927–30
Giants 331 g, .281, 14 hr, 111 rbi

Reese appeared at every position except catcher and pitcher with the Giants. An arm injury cut short his ML career, but he played nine more seasons with the Memphis Chicks (Southern Association) and was voted the most popular player in the club's history. /(JK)

Jimmie Reese [born James Herman Soloman] — 1905– . 2B 1930–32 **Yankees**, Cardinals 232 g, .278, 8 hr, 70 rbi

Legendary for his precision with the fungo bat, Reese's 70-year pro baseball career began in 1917 as a batboy for Los Angeles (Pacific Coast League). He began playing in 1924, and managed, coached, and scouted. A former roommate of Babe Ruth, he became an Angels coach in 1972. /(EW)

Pee Wee Reese [Harold Henry] (The Little Colonel) — 1918–. SS-3B 1940–42, 47–58 **Dodgers** 2166 g, .269, 126 hr, 885 rbi. *7 WS, 44 g, .272, 2 hr, 16 rbi* ☛ *All-Star—42, 47–54. Hall of Fame—1984.*

Pee Wee Reese got his nickname as a young champion marble shooter; a "pee wee" is a type of marble. A Kentucky native, he earned the monicker The Little Colonel as the star shortstop on the Louisville Colonels (American Association). After his arrival in Brooklyn, he was named captain of the Dodgers, and many called him The Captain. The title was well earned, as he was the leader of Dodger teams that won seven pennants in the 1940s and 1950s. When Jackie Robinson arrived in Brooklyn amid enormous pressures and player resentment, it was Reese who set the example of acceptance, putting his arm around Robinson's shoulder on the field, showing the world he was Robinson's teammate and friend.

After being signed by the Red Sox, the 5'10" 160-lb Reese proved his worth in Louisville. Managing and playing shortstop for Boston at the time was Joe Cronin, who wasn't ready to make room for the talented youngster by moving himself to third base. He was sold to Brooklyn for $75,000, but Reese's rookie 1940 season was marred by a fractured heel. He recovered in 1941 to lead the Dodgers to their first pennant since 1920. From 1941 through 1956, with a three-year absence in the navy during WWII, he averaged 148 games a year.

Pee Wee Reese with the Louisville Colonels of the American Association

A smooth fielder, he became the premier shortstop of his era, an All-Star each year from 1947 to 1954. He was also a great leadoff hitter, leading the NL in walks (104) in 1947, in runs scored (132) in 1949, and in stolen bases (30) in 1952. He was also noted for his clutch hitting and excellent bat control. Reese's highest average was .309 in 1954.

Reese was one of the most popular players on an idolized team. For his birthday in 1955, the Dodgers threw a party at Ebbets Field, showering him with $20,000 worth of gifts, and 35,000 fans lit candles and sang "Happy Birthday" to him as the lights went dark in the fifth inning. When the Dodgers moved to Los Angeles, Reese went along. He played 59 games in 1958 and became a coach. But he soon retired and went to work for the Louisville Slugger bat company. His leadership on the Dodgers' pennant-winning teams gained him election by the Veterans Committee to the Hall of Fame in 1984. /(EW)

Rich Reese — 1941– . 1B-OF 1964–73 **Twins**, Tigers 866 g, .253, 52 hr, 245 rbi. *2 LCS, 5 g, .158, 2 rbi*

Known as a playboy, Reese was a slick-fielding first baseman who hit to all fields with occasional power. He helped bring the Twins their first divisional championship in 1969 with career highs of .322 and 16 homers. His three pinch grand slams with the

Twins tie him with Willie McCovey and Ron Northey for first all-time. /(JCA)

Bobby Reeves (Gunner) — 1904– . 3B-SS-2B 1926–31 Senators, **Red Sox** 502 g, .252, 8 hr, 135 rbi

With Washington on August 7, 1927, the fine-fielding Reeves set an AL record with 13 assists at shortstop in a nine-inning game. In 1928, by far his best offensive season, he was one of six Senators regulars to hit over .300. /(EW)

Bill Regan — 1899–1968. 2B 1926–31 **Red Sox**, Pirates 641 g, .267, 18 hr, 292 rbi

On June 16, 1928 the Red Sox' Regan came to bat twice in the fourth inning and homered both times—equaling his HR output of the previous season. He was more typically a doubles hitter whose speed got him as many as ten triples a year. /(EW)

Phil Regan (The Vulture) — 1937– . RHP 1960–72 Tigers, Dodgers, **Cubs**, White Sox 1372 ip, 96–81, 3.84. *1 WS, 2 ip, 0–0, 0.00*

As a starter for Detroit, 6'3" Phil Regan won a career-high 15 games in 1963 but was optioned to Syracuse (International League) after poor showings in 1964 and 1965. While there, he purportedly added a "greaseball," which was said to "slide" 15–16 inches. Picked up in the off-season by the Dodgers in 1966 and converted to a reliever, The Vulture (so nicknamed by Sandy Koufax for picking up wins in short relief) went 14–1 (1.62, NL-high 21 saves) to garner Comeback Player of the Year and Fireman of the Year honors. Regan and Jim Hickman were shipped to the Cubs in April of 1968, and Regan again was named Fireman of the Year, leading the league with 12 relief wins and 25 saves. On July 7 that season he gained victories in both ends of a doubleheader. /(JCA)

Wally Rehg — 1888–1946. OF 1912–15, 17–19 Pirates, Red Sox, **Braves**, Reds 258 g, .250, 2 hr, 66 rbi

Speedy Wally Rehg was never an everyday out-fielder. He led the AL with 10 pinch hits and 36 pinch at-bats for the 1914 Red Sox, but hit .219 overall that year. He missed most of the following season with a bad knee. Coming back with the Braves in 1917, he hit .270, earning the most playing time in his career and reaching personal highs of 48 runs and 31 RBI. /(NLM)

Rick Reichardt [Frederic Carl] — 1943– . OF 1964–74 **Angels**, Senators, White Sox, A's 997 g, .261, 116 hr, 445 rbi

Wooed by 18 ML teams, Reichardt became the highest-priced bonus baby in baseball history when he signed with California for a reported $200,000 in 1964. A handsome and articulate scholar-athlete (Joe Garagiola: "The first time I saw him I thought he fell off a Wheaties box"), the fleet outfielder looked like he'd live up to expectations when he hit .288 with 16 homers in only 89 games in 1966, before illness forced the removal of a kidney in August. Although he led the Angels with 21 homers and 73 RBIs in 1968, he was an erratic fielder and much more was expected of him than his consistent .250 BAs. /(JCA)

Joe Reichler — 1916–1988. *Writer.*

A graduate of St. John's University, Reichler probably wrote more baseball stories than anybody. With the Associated Press from 1943 to 1966, when he joined the Commissioner's office as director of public relations, he was known for his scoops on the Dodgers' move to Los Angeles, Joe DiMaggio's retirement, and many other stories. A prolific writer of magazine articles, he also edited the Macmillan *Baseball Encyclopedia*. Other books include *It's Good to Be Alive* (with Roy Campanella), *Baseball's Greatest Moments*, and *The Game and the Glory*. He received the J.G. Taylor Spink Award from the Hall of Fame in 1975. /(NLM)

Bill Reidy — 1873–1915. RHP 1896, 99, 1901–04 Giants, Dodgers, **Milwaukee (AL)/Browns** 602 ip, 28–39, 4.17

Reidy was the ace of the last-place Brewers' staff in the AL's inaugural 1901 season, going 16–20 with a 4.21 ERA. The club moved to St. Louis for 1902, and Reidy slipped to 4.45. With Brooklyn in 1904 he attempted to prolong his career by moving to second base (five games) but hit only .156 that year, worse than when he was a full-time pitcher. /(WOR)

Long John Reilly [John Good] — 1858–1937. 1B-OF 1880, 1883–91 Cincinnati (NL), **Cincinnati (AA)** 1142 g, .289, 67 hr, 335 rbi
☛ *Led League—hr 1884, 88. Led League—rbi 1888.*

Reilly was one of the major league American Association's stars, and he played his entire career in his hometown of Cincinnati. A smooth-fielding, 6'3" first baseman, Long John tied for the AA lead with 11 home runs in 1884 and led with 13 HR and 103 RBI in 1888. He also stole 82 bases in 1888 and had 226 career stolen bases. /(DAS)

Art Reinhart — 1899-1946. LHP 1919, 25-28 Cardinals 445 ip, 30-18, 3.60. *1 WS, 0 ip, 0-1, infinite*

Plagued by wildness, Reinhart was constantly getting into and (sometimes) working his way out of jams. Relieving in Game Four of the 1926 World Series, he faced five Yankee batters and gave up four walks and a hit. He was a lifetime .301 batter. /(NLM)

Jerry Reinsdorf — 1936- . *Executive.*

Reinsdorf and his group purchased the White Sox and Comiskey Park from Bill Veeck in 1981. Reinsdorf, also an attorney and CPA, made his fortune in Chicago real estate, heading up the multi-billion-dollar Balcor Corporation. Reserved, and uncomfortable in the spotlight, Reinsdorf also purchased the controlling interest in the NBA Chicago Bulls in 1985. /(RL)

Bobby Reis — 1909-1973. - . RHP-OF-3B 1931-32, 35-38 Dodgers, **Braves** 175 g, .233, 0 hr, 21 rbi; 243 ip, 10-13, 4.27

The versatile Reis played nearly every position during his career. Coming up as a third baseman, the singles hitter failed in two trials before reappearing in 1935 as an outfielder and pitcher. Traded to the Braves after the season, he was used primarily as a relief pitcher in 1936 and went 5-1 in that role. He caught one game in 1938 and filled in around the infield when necessary. /(WOR)

Pete Reiser [Harold Patrick] (Pistol Pete) — 1919-1981. OF-3B 1940-42, 46-52 **Dodgers**, Braves, Pirates, Indians 861 g, .295, 58 hr, 368 rbi. *2 WS, 10 g, .214, 1 hr, 3 rbi*
☛ *Led League—ba 41. All-Star—41, 42, 46.*

In 1941, Pete Reiser, in his first full season with the Dodgers, became the National League's youngest batting champion ever, hitting .343. He tied for the league lead with 39 doubles and led with 17 triples, 117 runs scored, and a .558 slugging percentage. "The feeling about him in 1942 was that he was as great a star as there ever was in the game," said the Braves' Tommy Holmes. Leo Durocher, who managed Willie Mays and played with Babe Ruth, thought that Reiser "just might have been the best ballplayer I ever saw," but that he "had everything but luck."

Reiser played too recklessly to have luck. He was hitting .383 on July 2, 1942, when he smashed into the centerfield wall in St. Louis. It was one of 11 times, according to writer Red Smith, that Reiser had to be carried off the field. He suffered a severe concussion and a shoulder separation and finished the season batting just .310. He still won the NL stolen-base title with 20.

Reiser spent 1943 through 1945 in the military, during which time he first encountered Jackie Robinson at Fort Riley, Kansas. He later became one of Robinson's biggest supporters. Reiser returned to the Dodgers in 1946, and won another stolen-base title. His seven steals of home set a ML record. In 1947, he was hurt so severely after hitting the centerfield wall at Ebbets Field that he was given last rites. Although Reiser's mishaps are credited with prompting the padding of outfield walls and the universal use of warning tracks, the move came too late to preserve what many felt was the greatest talent Brooklyn had ever seen. Reiser played in only 64 games in 1948 and was traded to the Braves. He later coached for the Dodgers, Cubs, and Angels. /(TG)

Doc Reisling [Frank Carl] — 1874-1955. RHP 1904-05, 09-10 Dodgers, **Senators** 312 ip, 15-19, 2.45

A practicing dentist, Reisling didn't reach the majors until he was 30 years old and pitched regularly only in his final season, for the 1910 Senators. His year was interrupted by illness and he finished at 10-10, 2.54. He later managed in the Canadian League. /(NLM)

Ken Reitz — 1951- . 3B 1972-82 **Cardinals**, Giants, Cubs, Pirates 1344 g, .260, 68 hr, 548 rbi
☛ *All-Star—80. Gold Glove—75.*

Reitz was called "The Zamboni Machine" in St. Louis for the way he sucked ground balls off the carpet. In both of his first two seasons, he led NL third basemen in fielding percentage (.974 in 1973 and '74), but captured his Gold Glove in 1975. His nine errors at third in 1977 were the fewest ever in the NL, and he bettered that mark by committing just eight miscues in 1980. A handsome figure with long, dark hair, Reitz was with the Cardinals from 1972 to 1980, except for 1976, which he spent in San Francisco. A consistent yet unspectacular hitter, in 1977 he smashed 17 homers, by far his greatest show of power. /(JCA)

Jerry Remy — 1952- . 2B-DH 1975-84 Angels, **Red Sox** 1154 g, .275, 7 hr, 329 rbi

A clutch lefthanded hitter and an excellent bunter, the consistent second baseman played 147 games for the Angels his first year to win a spot on the 1975 Topps All-Rookie team. California's captain in 1977, Remy was traded to the Red Sox that

December. Boston's only basestealing threat, he hit .313 in 1980 and .307 in 1981 but missed large parts of the 1979 through 1981 and 1984 seasons due to knee problems. /(JCA)

Rick Renick — 1944– . 3B-OF-SS 1968–72 **Twins** 276 g, .221, 20 hr, 71 rbi. *1 LCS, 3 g, .167*

A three-sport star as an Ohio schoolboy, Renick broke in with the Twins by hitting a home run in his first ML at-bat, July 11, 1968. A useful utility man with occasional power over the next two seasons, Renick suffered a knee injury in 1971 that limited him to 27 games. Although he returned in 1972, he could hit only .172. /(CP)

Hal Reniff (Porky) — 1938– . RHP 1961–67 **Yankees**, Mets 471 ip, 21–23, 3.27. *2 WS, 3 ip, 0–0, 0.00*

An effective reliever for the Yankee pennant winners of 1963–64, Reniff saved 18 in 1963 and 9, with six wins, in 1964. /(GDW)

Steve Renko — 1944– . RHP 1969–83 **Expos**, Cubs, White Sox, A's, Red Sox, Angels, Royals 2493 ip, 134–146, 4.00

Renko frequently fell just short of stardom in an erratic, 15-season ML career. He was drafted out of Kansas University by the Mets in 1965 and began in the minors as a first baseman (a position he returned to for two games in 1972) but switched to pitching in 1967. He joined the Expos in 1969. Wild at first, the 6'5" righthander threw 19 wild pitches in 1974 and once tossed 3 in one inning. He won 15 games for Montreal in both 1971 and 1973, but was 1–10 in 1972. After seven and a half seasons with the Expos, he became an oft-traded player, pitching sometimes effectively for six teams in his remaining eight seasons. On October 3, 1972 he struck out seven consecutive Mets. /(CP)

Bill Renna (Big Bill) — 1924– . OF 1953–56, 58–59 Yankees, **A's**, Red Sox 370 g, .261, 28 hr, 119 rbi

One of the first of several Santa Clara University graduates to reach the majors, Renna was traded to the A's as part of a 10-player deal after the 1953 season. He hit 13 homers in '54, but low batting averages sent him to the bench and then the minors. With the Red Sox in 1958, he was primarily a pinch hitter, batting in 18 runs on only 15 hits. /(MC)

Dutch Rennert (Lawrence) — 1934– . *Umpire* NL 1974– *2 ASU 4 LCS 2 WS*

A 1983 *New York Times* poll labeled Rennert the best all-around arbiter in the NL. His style of calling a strike gets everyone's attention. First he pivots, to his right if the batter is righthanded or left if the batter is lefthanded, points his arm (right arm for righthanders and left for lefthanders) toward the dugout, then sweeps his arm behind his back while booming in a voice suitable for warning ships away from rocks: "Striiike Wuuuun!" /(RTM)

Rud Rennie — 1897–1956. *Writer.*

After covering a variety of beats, Rennie began writing sports in 1925 for the New York *Tribune* (later the *Herald-Tribune*). His simple, declarative leads could be masterpieces of understatement. He began his account of Lavagetto's double that spoiled Bill Bevens's no-hitter in the '47 WS: "Harry Lavagetto, a pinch hitter, made a timely hit yesterday." /(NLM)

Andy Replogle — 1953– . RHP 1978–79 **Brewers** 157 ip, 9–5, 4.00

Replogle was the Orioles' number-one draft pick in 1977, but was waived to the Brewers the next year. The Hoosier righthander was 9–5 in 1978 for Milwaukee but slipped back to the minors in '79. /(CP)

Roger Repoz — 1940– . OF-1B 1964–72 Yankees, A's, **Angels** 831 g, .224, 82 hr, 261 rbi

The lefthanded Yankee outfielder was touted as the heir to Mickey Mantle. Instead, he became a platoon player who sank to a .164 average in 103 games for the 1969 Angels. /(JCA)

Rip Repulski [Eldon John] — 1927– . OF 1953–61 **Cardinals**, Phillies, Dodgers, Red Sox 928 g, .269, 106 hr, 416 rbi. *1 WS, 1 g, --*
☛ *All-Star—56.*

Repulski became the Cardinals' regular centerfielder as a rookie in 1953. A streaky power hitter, he played in over 100 games in each of his first five seasons, then faded fast. /(AL)

Xavier Rescigno (Mr. X) — 1913– . RHP 1943–45 **Pirates** 335 ip, 19–22, 4.16

Resigno debuted with the Pirates at the age of 29 in 1943. He lasted three seasons with a decent curveball, leading the NL with eight relief wins in 1944, but was out of work when the regulars returned from WWII. /(FS)

Merv Rettenmund — 1943– . OF-DH 1968–80
Orioles, Reds, Padres, Angels 1023 g, .271, 66 hr, 329 rbi.
6 LCS, 12 g, .160, 2 rbi. 4 WS, 13 g, .200, 2 hr, 6 rbi

Rettenmund played halfback at Ball State and was
drafted by the Dallas Cowboys. He chose baseball
and played in four World Series and six LCS with
three different clubs. He was named *TSN* Minor
League Player of the Year in 1968 when he batted
.331 with 22 HR for Rochester (International
League). He was the AL champion Orioles' leading
hitter in 1970 (.322) and 1971 (.318). In the NL he
became a platoon player and top pinch hitter, and
he went a league-leading 21-for-67 in the pinch for
the 1977 Padres, the eighth most pinch hits ever in a
single season. /(JCA)

Ken Retzer — 1934– . C 1961–64 **Senators** 237 g,
.264, 14 hr, 72 rbi

Signed by the Indians, Retzer spent seven years in
the minors because he was considered a poor hitting
prospect. Sold to the Senators in 1961, he hit .285 in
1962 as the lefthanded-hitting half of a platoon with
Bob Schmidt. He slipped to .242 the next year, then
opened 1964 in a terrible slump before going to the
minors after 17 games. /(MC)

Ed Reulbach (Big Ed) — 1882–1961. RHP 1905–17
Cubs, Dodgers, Newark (FL), Braves 2633 ip, 181–105,
2.28. 20 wins: 08, 15 *4 WS, 33 ip, 2–0, 3.03*

Chicago's Ed Reulbach was the only pitcher to
throw a doubleheader shutout, allowing just eight
hits; the two victories on September 26 were among
nine he collected against Brooklyn in 1908. Chicago
was locked in a tight pennant race with Pittsburgh
and New York, and the Cubs' staff was getting
weary. Reulbach's wins helped his club finish first,
after a one-game playoff.

Reulbach's eyesight was poor, so his catchers used
white-painted gloves. He set a still-standing record
of leading the NL in winning percentage three years
in a row, 1906 through 1908, with records of 19–4,
17–4, and 24–7. Yet his spectacular career was
often overshadowed by his teammate, Three Finger
Brown, and crosstown rival Ed Walsh. Reulbach
took the limelight with the first one-hitter in the
World Series (1906). His 1906 hits-per-inning ratio
of 5.33 per nine innings is the third best in history.
His career ERA of 2.28 has been bettered by only
ten pitchers. Not counting the 1915 season, which
he spent in the Federal League, he allowed only 35
home runs in 2,363 innings. /(CG)

Ed Reulbach

Paul Reuschel — 1947– . RHP 1975–79 **Cubs,**
Indians 392 ip, 16–16, 4.52

Paul relieved for the 1975–78 Cubs while younger
brother Rick was a regular starter. The two combined in a shutout of the Dodgers (8/21/75). In
1977, his busiest season, Paul appeared in 69 games,
going 5–6 with four saves. /(JCA)

Rick Reuschel (Big Daddy) — 1949– . RHP 1972–81,
83–**Cubs,** Yankees, Pirates, Giants 3452 ip, 211–183,
3.36. 20 wins: 77 *2 LCS, 19 ip, 0–2, 5.78. 2 WS, 8 ip,
0–1, 8.21*
☛ *All-Star—77, 87, 89. Gold Glove—85, 87.*

Rick Reuschel's two-part career began as a stellar
starter for the Cubs. The portly Illinois native won
10 or more games each of nine straight seasons

(1972–80), becoming one of the club's all-time leaders in wins, games and strikeouts. Teammate Mike Krukow tagged Reuschel Big Daddy during this period. Rick and Paul became the first brothers to combine on a major league shutout, August 21, 1975.

Reuschel missed the 1982 season with a torn right rotator cuff that threatened to end his career. His renaissance came when he was given a chance by the floundering Pirates. His 1985 season (14–8, 2.27) earned Comeback Player of the Year honors. Possessing outstanding control, Reuschel tied a Pittsburgh record with 13 wins at Three Rivers Stadium in 1985. He also won a Gold Glove, testimony to athletic skills belied by his physique. Traded by the rebuilding Pirates, he helped San Francisco reach post-season play in 1987 and remained a big winner to the end of the decade despite DL time in 1989. /(ME)

Rick Reuschel

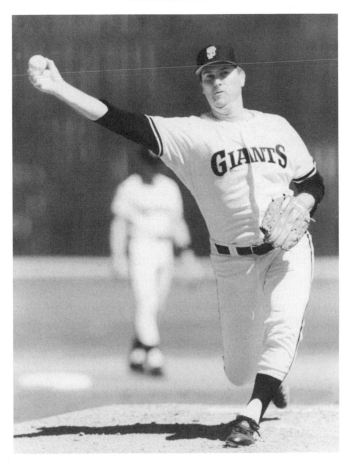

Jerry Reuss (Rolls) — 1949– . LHP 1969-Cardinals, Astros, Pirates, **Dodgers**, Reds, Angels, White Sox, Brewers 3661 ip, 220–191, 3.63. *5 LCS, 33 ip, 0–7, 5.45. 1 WS, 12 ip, 1–1, 3.86*
☛ *All-Star—75, 80.*

TSN named Reuss Comeback Player of the Year in 1980, when he finished second in Cy Young voting and pitched a no-hit, no-run, no-walk game marred only by an error by shortstop Bill Russell. He struck out all three batters he faced in that year's All-Star Game, and his lifetime 1–0, 0.00 in those games made up a little for his lack of playoff success. Reuss outdueled Ron Guidry in the pivotal fifth game of the 1981 World Series, and the Astros failed to score upon him in 19 innings of that year's divisional playoff.

Reuss came up with the Cardinals in 1969 and was a .500 pitcher for three years. He then spent two seasons with Houston; he led NL pitchers in walks in 1973 (117), but later became one of the best control pitchers in the league. Going to Pittsburgh in return for Milt May after the 1973 season, he became the anchor of the Pirates' staff and helped the slugging team to division titles in 1974 and 1975, having his best Pirate season the latter year (18–11, 2.54). Traded straight up for the similarly-talented Rick Rhoden just prior to the start of the 1979 season, he was 7–14, but he rebounded with his Comeback year and from 1980 to 1983 was one of the Dodgers' more consistent winners (18–6, 10–4, 18–11, 12–11). Three straight losing, injury-plagued seasons (1984–86) led to his release after just one game in 1987; picked up by the Reds, he was 0–5 and was released again. A stint with the Angels was slightly more successful (4–5), but at the end of 1987 he was allowed to become a free agent. Signed by the pitching-poor White Sox near the end of spring training in 1988, he again came back, going 13–9 with a 3.44 ERA despite being supported by the worst defense (and offense) in the league. /(TG)

Dave Revering — 1953– . 1B 1978–82 **A's**, Yankees, Blue Jays, Mariners 557 g, .265, 62 hr, 234 rbi. *1 LCS, 2 g, .500*

With Tony Perez and Dan Dreissen to play first base, the Reds traded minor leaguer Revering to the A's along with $1.75 million for Vida Blue in December 1977. After deliberating nearly two months, Commissioner Kuhn voided the deal for exceeding the two-year-old $400,000 limit on cash transactions. In February 1978, Revering was again traded to the A's, this time for Doug Bair. He had three promising years with the A's, hitting .271, .288, and .290, with 50 home runs, before injuries led to deep slumps, frequent trades, and a premature end to his career. /(MC)

Nap Reyes — 1919- . 3B-1B 1943-45, 50 **Giants** 279 g, .284, 13 hr, 110 rbi

Reyes was a Giants wartime regular in 1944-45 who provided occasional power. His Cuban citizenship made him ineligible for U.S. military service. His ML career effectively ended when he jumped to the "outlaw" Mexican League in 1946. /(FS)

Allie Reynolds (Superchief) — 1915- . RHP 1942-54 Indians, **Yankees** 2492 ip, 182-107, 3.30. 20 wins: 52 *6 WS, 77 ip, 7-2, 2.79*
☛ *Led League—era 52. Led League—k 43, 52. All-Star—49-54.*

Reynolds was primarily a hard-throwing starter, but Yankee manager Casey Stengel often used him from the bullpen as well. In six WS relief appearances, Reynolds recorded either a win or a save each outing, including the WS finales in 1950, 1952, and 1953. As a starter, Reynolds beat the Dodgers 1-0 on a two-hitter in the 1949 WS.

Reynolds came to the Yankees in an October 1946 trade that sent Joe Gordon to the Indians, and led the AL in winning percentage in his first season in New York. He won 16 games in 1950 despite bone chips in his pitching elbow. In 1951 Reynolds became the first AL pitcher to hurl two no-hitters in one season, winning 1-0 against Cleveland July 12 and then 8-0 against Boston September 28. In the second game, Reynolds had to get Ted Williams for the final out twice because Yogi Berra dropped his easy foul pop. Reynolds won the Hickock Belt in 1951 as the top professional athlete of the year, and in 1952 he was second in the AL MVP voting, recording 20 wins and six saves, and leading the AL in both ERA (2.06) and shutouts (6). Reynolds's one-quarter Creek Indian ancestry gave rise to his nickname, Superchief. /(MG)

Bob Reynolds (Bullet Bob) — 1947- . RHP 1969, 71-85 Expos, Brewers, Cardinals, **Orioles**, Tigers, Indians 254 ip, 14-16, 3.15. *2 LCS, 7 ip, 0-0, 2.57*

A reliever with a blistering fastball, Reynolds worked for seven different organizations but earned all his ML wins with the Orioles in 1973-74, going 7-5 each year. In '73 he had career bests in ERA (1.95) and saves (9). /(JCA)

Carl Reynolds — 1903-1978. OF 1927-39 **White Sox**, Senators, Browns, Red Sox, Cubs 1222 g, .302, 80 hr, 695 rbi. *1 WS, 4 g, .000*

Reynolds was a hard-hitting outfielder who topped .300 six times in a checkered career. His best season was 1930 with the White Sox, when he finished third in the AL at .359, with 22 homers and 100 RBI. Three of his homers came in consecutive at-bats (5/2/30) at Yankee Stadium. He was slowed by leg injuries the next year. White Sox Manager Donie Bush considered him temperamental and traded him to the Senators. He was traded twice more after the next two seasons and returned to the Senators in 1936. After hitting only .276 as a part-timer, he was sent to the minors. A big year at Minneapolis (.355) won him a promotion to the Cubs before the 1937 season ended. He hit .302, his career average, for the Cub pennant-winners of 1938. /(RL)

Craig Reynolds — 1952- . SS 1975- Pirates, Mariners, **Astros** 1491 g, .256, 42 hr, 377 rbi. *3 LCS, 10 g, .231*
☛ *All-Star—78, 79.*

Reynolds was an AL All-Star in his second full ML season, hitting .292 as the Mariners shortstop in 1978. An off-season trade sent him to Houston in exchange for pitcher Floyd Bannister, and Reynolds started at shortstop for the Astros until Dickie Thon emerged in 1982, and again from 1984 to 1987 after Thon's career was nearly ended by a beaning. In 1981 Reynolds led the NL with 12 triples, including a ML-record 3 in one game on May 16. /(SCL)

Harold Reynolds — 1960- . 2B 1983- **Mariners** 693 g, .266, 6 hr, 150 rbi
☛ *All-Star—87-88. Gold Glove—88, 89.*

The speedy Reynolds is a defensive stalwart with excellent range. In 1987 he led AL second basemen in games started, total chances, putouts, assists, and double plays. The switch-hitter steadily improved his batting average and holds the Mariner record for fewest strikeouts (34) by a batter with at least 530 plate appearances. He stole a club-record 60 bases in 1987, becoming the first Mariner to lead the AL in a major offensive category. He also became the first player ever to lead the league in steals while batting ninth in the order. In 1988, he lost his stolen-base touch, getting caught 29 times while stealing 35. That year Reynolds became the first player to represent the Mariners in the All-Star game more than once. He also won a Gold Glove, despite leading AL second basemen in errors, because he also led in assists and double plays. His brother Don played briefly for San Diego in 1978 and 1979. /(TF)

Ken Reynolds — 1947– . LHP 1970–73, 75–76
Phillies, Brewers, Cardinals, Padres 375 ip, 7–29, 4.46

Reynolds was good Triple-A pitcher who never did well in the majors. In 1972 he lost 12 consecutive games with the Phillies and finished 2–15. Those two wins were his last in the majors. /(JCA)

R.J. Reynolds [Robert James] (Shoes) — 1959– . OF 1983– Dodgers, **Pirates** 691 g, .264, 35 hr, 275 rbi

Reynolds began switch-hitting in his third pro season, and compiled a .307 minor league average. But leg injuries, his trouble with righthanded pitching, and propensity to strike out kept him a fourth outfielder. He was dubbed Shoes by Dodger teammates for his vast assortment of footwear. /(ME)

Tommie Reynolds — 1941– . OF 1963–64, 67, 69–72 **A's**, Mets, Angels, Brewers 513 g, .226, 12 hr, 87 rbi

Reynolds never hit enough to keep a regular outfield job. He hit a career-high .257 in 1969 in his second stint with the A's. /(JFC)

Flint Rhem (Shad) — 1901–1969. RHP 1924–28, 30–36 **Cardinals**, Phillies, Braves 1726 ip, 105–97, 4.20. 20 wins: 26 *4 WS, 10 ip, 0–1, 6.10*
☛ *Led League—w 26.*

Rhem's achievements as the fireballing Cardinals ace (20–7) in their 1926 championship year are obscured by a bizarre episode arising from his weakness for drink. In 1930, with St. Louis and Brooklyn in a stretch-run battle for first place, Rhem vanished. Reappearing two days later, he said he had been kidnapped, evidently by Dodger partisans, sequestered in a hotel room, and forced to drink an incapacitating amount of liquor. Rhem survived the incident, lasted six more years in the NL, and was disappointingly ineffective in World Series appearances. /(ADS)

Billy Rhiel — 1900–1946. 3B-2B-1B-OF 1929–30, 32–33 Dodgers, Braves, **Tigers** 199 g, .266, 7 hr, 68 rbi

In his most active season, this utility man hit .280 with 38 RBI for the 1932 Tigers and went 13-for-27 (.481) as a pinch hitter. /(SFS)

Bob Rhoads (Dusty) — 1879–1967. RHP 1902–09 Cubs, Cardinals, **Indians** 1692 ip, 97–82, 2.61. 20 wins: 06

Rhoads had five consecutive winning seasons for Cleveland (1904–08) including a 22–10 (1.80) campaign in 1906. On September 18, 1908 he no-hit the White Sox. Yet, he said, his fondest pitching memory was of surrendering 23 hits in a game against the Browns that Cleveland won 6–5 on just six hits. /(ME)

Rick Rhoden — 1953– . RHP 1974– Dodgers, **Pirates**, Yankees, Astros 2593 ip, 151–125, 3.60. *2 LCS, 8 ip, 0–0, 1.08. 1 WS, 7 ip, 0–1, 2.57*
☛ *All-Star—76, 86.*

Rhoden overcame childhood osteomyelitis (a bone disease; he wore a brace until he was 12, and had surgery to remove part of his left knee so it would not outgrow his right) and serious shoulder surgery in 1979 to become one of the more dependable pitchers of the 1980s. An All-Star in his rookie 1976 season (12–3) with the Dodgers, he followed with a 16–10 mark. In April 1979, he was traded to Pittsburgh for Jerry Reuss, but was disabled for all but one game. An intelligent, fastball-slider pitcher, from 1982 through 1986 he went 63–63, averaging 236 innings a year. He led the Pirates in wins in 1981 (nine), 1984 (14), and 1986 (15), and the Yankees in 1987 (16). An all-around athlete, he committed only six errors in his first 14 seasons, and won three NL Silver Slugger awards for pitchers in 1984–86, compiling a .239 NL batting average. /(ME)

Dusty Rhodes (James) — 1927– . OF 1952–57, 59 **Giants** 576 g, .253, 54 hr, 207 rbi. *1 WS, 3 g, .667, 2 hr, 7 rbi*

An indifferent outfielder who never was a regular in seven seasons with the Giants, Rhodes was a streaky, lefthanded pull hitter and a home run threat in the Polo Grounds, with its short right-field fence. He twice hit three home runs in a game.

Rhodes became a minor legend in 1954. He cracked 15 homers that year, and batted .333 as a pinch hitter. In the WS, he almost single-handedly led the Giants' sweep of the Indians. His pinch homer off Bob Lemon with two on in the 10th inning won Game One, 5–2. In Game Two, he tied the game with a pinch single off Early Wynn in the fifth and then homered off Wynn in the seventh for the final run in a 3–1 win. And his pinch single in the third inning of Game Three drove in two runs. All told, he was 4-for-6 with two homers and seven RBI. /(FS)

Gordon Rhodes (Dusty) — 1907–1960. RHP 1929–36 Yankees, **Red Sox**, A's 1048 ip, 43–74, 4.85

One of the few Nevada natives to make the majors, Rhodes twice won 12 for the Red Sox. Limited by poor control and a shoulder injury, he was sent to the A's in the trade for Jimmie Foxx before the 1936 season, then went 9–20 to lead the AL in losses. /(DB)

Hal Rhyne — 1899–1971. SS-2B 1926–27, 29–33 Pirates, **Red Sox**, White Sox 655 g, .250, 2 hr, 192 rbi. *1 WS, 1 g, .000*

Rhyne broke in as the Pirates' second baseman, but illness limited his role in the team's 1927 year. The Red Sox' shortstop in 1929–31, Rhyne hit only .203 in 1930, the greatest hitter's year ever, but batted a surprising .273 the next year. /(EW)

Dennis Ribant — 1941– . RHP 1964–69 **Mets**, Pirates, Tigers, White Sox, Cardinals, Reds 519 ip, 24–29, 3.87

By going 11–9 in 1966, Ribant became the first Mets starting pitcher to top the .500 mark. He left the majors as the property of the Royals, for whom he never played, after pitching for five teams in three years. /(KT)

Del Rice — 1922–1983. C 1945–61 **Cardinals**, Braves, Cubs, Orioles, Angels 1309 g, .237, 79 hr, 441 rbi. *2 WS, 5 g, .333.*
   Manager 1972 **Angels** 75–80, .484
☛ *All-Star—53.*

A brainy and gifted defensive catcher, Rice made up for his poor hitting and lack of speed (two stolen bases in 17 years) with his arm, glove, and handling of pitchers. He had some home run power (12 homers in 1947, 11 in 1952), but several batting-stance changes failed to raise his average. Rice was Bob Buhl's "personal catcher" on the Braves in the late 1950s; Buhl regularly beat the Dodgers, Milwaukee's main rivals in several close pennant races. In 1971 he was *TSN* Minor League Manager of the Year when he led Salt Lake City to the Pacific Coast League pennant, but he couldn't get the Angels out of fifth place when given a ML club the next year. /(JK)

Grantland Rice (Dean of American Sports Writers) — 1880–1954. *Writer.*

The best-loved sportswriter ever could capture the drama of an event with a lead paragraph that perfectly set the stage for the story which followed. In his most famous lead, he gave immortality to a quartet of merely above-average football players by dubbing them the Four Horsemen of Notre Dame, a comparison to the Four Horsemen of the Apocalypse. Rice often used self-penned poetry in his columns, a famous example being "Game Called," on the date of Babe Ruth's death ("Game called by darkness—let the curtain fall,/ No more remembered thunder sweeps the field."). The well-known saying "It's not whether you win or lose, it's how you play the game" is derived from his poem "Alumnus Football."

   Rice's long, eventful career was described in the autobiography he finished shortly before his death, *The Tumult and the Shouting.* A well-rounded, polished writer, Grantland Rice is the benchmark those who would write sports are measured against. /(JK)

Hal Rice (Hoot) — 1924– . OF 1948–54 **Cardinals**, Pirates, Cubs 424 g, .260, 19 hr, 162 rbi

Rice earned a reputation as a fine defensive outfielder while in the minors, where he batted as high as .349. He never won a regular job in the majors, appearing in almost a quarter of his games as a pinch hitter. /(EW)

Harry Rice — 1901–1971. OF 1923–31, 33 **Browns**, Tigers, Yankees, Senators, Reds 1023 g, .299, 48 hr, 506 rbi

A versatile defensive player with an outstanding arm, Rice didn't settle in the outfield until his third ML season, when he hit .359 for the Browns. Four other seasons he hit .300 or better, ending with a career mark of .299. /(JK)

Jim Rice — 1953– . OF-DH 1974–89 **Red Sox** 2089 g, .298, 382 hr, 1451 rbi. *2 LCS, 11 g, .159, 2 hr, 7 rbi. 1 WS, 7 g, .333*
☛ *Most Valuable Player—78. Led League—hr 77, 78, 83. Led League—rbi 78, 83. All-Star—77–80, 83–86.*

As a successor to Ted Williams and Carl Yastrzemski in left field for the Boston Red Sox, Jim Rice emerged as the AL's most feared slugger in the late 1970s and early 1980s. The rock-solid 6'2" 200-lb righthander used his quick, compact stroke and immensely strong wrists to send home runs crashing into upper decks or soaring completely over the screen above Fenway Park's Green Monster. Rice was the classic "strong, silent type," and his silence was often perceived as moodiness. But his feats of strength spoke for themselves. He once broke a bat on a checked swing without hitting the ball, and he has reportedly had golf clubs bend in his hands on

Jim Rice

the downswing. Rice always had the ability to hit the ball to all fields, but as he aged he began to concentrate on slapping the ball to the opposite field almost exclusively, keeping his batting average near .300 while still averaging over 20 HR per year. His average declined in the late 1980s, reaching career lows in three consecutive seasons through 1989.

After winning the Eastern League batting title at Bristol in 1973 and the International League Triple Crown (.337, 25 HR, 93 RBI), Rookie of the Year, and MVP awards at Pawtucket in 1974, Rice teamed with Fred Lynn in the Red Sox' outfield in 1975 to form baseball's most powerful rookie tandem. Rice hit .309 with 22 HR and 102 RBI and Lynn was AL Rookie of the Year and MVP as Boston reached the WS. But Rice missed the entire postseason after Tiger pitcher Vern Ruhle broke his left hand with a pitch during the last week of the regular season. Rice came back to hit .282 with 25 HR in 1976, and he led the AL in home runs for the first time in 1977 with 39, while batting .320. In 1978, Rice established himself as the AL's premier

power hitter. He finished third in batting with a .315 average while leading the league in HR (46), RBI (139), hits (213), triples (15), and slugging percentage (.600). His 406 total bases were the highest AL total since Joe DiMaggio's 418 in 1937, and he edged Yankee pitcher Ron Guidry (25–3, 1.74) for the AL MVP award. However, the Yankees beat the Red Sox in a one-game playoff and went on to win the WS.

In 1979, Rice hit .325 with 39 HR and 130 RBI, and became the only player in ML history with three consecutive 35 HR-200 hit seasons. Rice suffered subpar seasons in 1980–82, missing 31 games in 1980 with a fractured wrist and one-third of 1981 due to the players' strike, but he led the AL in HR (39) and RBI (126) a final time in 1983, while batting .305. He drove in at least 100 runs each season from 1983 to 1986, and in 1986 he recorded the second-highest batting average of his career, .324, as the Red Sox won the AL East. Getting his first opportunity in postseason play, Rice struggled against the Angels in the LCS, but his three-run HR clinched Game Seven. He went 9-for-27 against the Mets in the seven-game WS, scoring six runs. In 1987 his batting average fell below .280 for the first time, and he hit only 13 HR. Off-season knee surgery failed to correct the problem in 1988. Rice was forced into the DH role by the emergence of Mike Greenwell and hit only .264 with 15 HR. His frustration came to a head when he engaged in a much-publicized shoving match with 57-year-old manager Joe Morgan after Morgan sent Spike Owen up to pinch hit for him. Boston released Rice after an injury-marred season in 1989.

Rice was never blessed with great speed or agility in left field, but he mastered the intricacies of Fenway Park's left-field wall. He was particularly adept at decoying opposing baserunners, who would often be surprised to slide into outs at second base after ripping line drives high off The Wall. In 1983, Rice recorded a career-high 21 assists. Rice's consistent failing throughout his career was his penchant for grounding into double plays. A slow-footed righthanded batter who usually hit the ball hard, he grounded into a ML-record 36 double plays in 1984, and 35 in 1985.

On the Red Sox' all-time leader lists, he trails only Williams and Yastrzemski in HR, RBI, hits, and total bases. /(SCL)

John Rice — 1920– . *Umpire* AL 1955–73

Rice was a hard man to slip one past. On the night of July 17, 1969, Orioles' catcher Clay Dalrymple came out with his regular catcher's mitt on his left hand and a fielder's glove in his back pocket. Dalrymple figured he might better make a play at the plate by using the more flexible glove. Rice was nonplussed for only a moment, then ordered Dalrymple to return the fielder's glove to the bench, citing the rule that there cannot be extra gloves on the field. /(RTM)

Sam Rice [Edgar]1890–1974. OF 1915–34 **Senators**, Indians 2404 g, .322, 34 hr, 1078 rbi. *3 WS, 15 g, .302, 0 hr, 4 rbi*
☛ *Hall of Fame—1963.*

One of baseball's greatest singles hitters, Rice fell only 13 hits shy of 3,000. In 20 ML seasons, he never hit below .293 and averaged .322. Although he lacked power (21 of his 34 career home runs were hit inside the park), he met every other requirement for stardom. At bat, he usually made contact, averaging only one strikeout in every 34 at-bats. On the bases, he was fast and intelligent, leading the AL with 63 stolen bases in 1920. In the outfield, he was swift and had an excellent arm.

His most famous play was on defense. In Game Three of the 1925 WS, he raced full-tilt after Pirate Earl Smith's drive, leaped and backhanded it. He and the ball disappeared into the stands, but when Rice emerged with the ball in his glove, the umpire called Smith out. Had he really caught the ball? He refused to say but left a sealed letter at the Hall of Fame to be opened after his death. In it, he'd written: "At no time did I lose possession of the ball."

Rice joined the Senators as a pitcher in 1915 but by the next season was moved to right field. A lefthanded hitter, he stood nearly erect in the batter's box, crowding the plate. Although his speed helped him to 497 career two-base hits and the AL lead in triples in 1923, his forte was the slap single. Of his 2,987 career hits, 2,272 went for one base. With a good batting eye he added 709 walks, and he scored 1,515 runs in his career. In 1924, when the Senators won the World Championship, Rice led the AL in hits with 216 and had a 31-game hitting streak. The next year, for Washington's second pennant winner, he amassed 227 hits and batted a career-high .350. He led the AL with 216 hits in 1926. All told, he topped 200 hits seven times.

At age 40 in 1930, he told *Baseball Magazine*, "I can still smack the ball," and proved it by hitting .349 with 207 hits, while scoring a personal-best 121 runs. He was able to contribute a .294 average to the Senators' third and final pennant win as a part-timer

Sam Rice

in 1933. In 1963, Rice was named to the Baseball Hall of Fame. /(ADS)

J.R. Richard [James Rodney] — 1950– . RHP 1971–80 **Astros** 1606 ip, 107–71, 3.15. 20 wins: 76
☛ *Led League—k 78–79. Led League—era 79. All-Star—80.*

Among the most tragic figures in baseball annals is 6'8″ J.R. Richard. With a fastball clocked as high as 100 mph, the Louisianan signed with Houston as their first pick in 1969, passing up 200 basketball scholarship offers. Facing the Giants on September

5, 1971, he fanned 15 batters to tie Karl Spooner's record for most strikeouts in a major league debut. But he pitched mostly in the minors until 1975, and later blamed racism for his failure to advance. Explained teammate Enos Cabell, "He's very sensitive to racial conditions . . . . He's a country boy, a Bible reader. He's not used to pressure or criticism."

Richard was intimidating. With his gigantic stride, he made batters feel as if they were "facing someone who is throwing at them too fast from too close and too great a height," said *Sports Illustrated* in 1978. He mixed in a superb slider and, because he was wild, hitters could not dig in against him. His six wild pitches in a 1979 game tied a modern NL record. Bob Watson claimed, "I've never taken batting practice against him and I never will. I have a family to think of." Richard led the NL in walks three times, but won 20 games in 1976 and 18 each year from 1977 to 1979. The Astros' ace led the NL with 303 strikeouts in 1978 and 313 in 1979, winning the league ERA title (2.71).

In June 1980, Richard began complaining of "a dead arm." The media, fans, and some teammates accused him of loafing (though he hadn't missed a start in five years), gutlessness (the Astros were in a pennant race), jealousy of Nolan Ryan's bigger contract, and even drug abuse. He was 10–4 (1.89) and had started the All-Star Game when, in a July 14 assignment, he appeared dazed and had trouble seeing the catcher's signs, and his movements became awkward. He was put on the disabled list, and though tests revealed a blockage in an artery leading to his right arm, doctors felt there was no danger. Richard resumed workouts, but on July 30, he collapsed. Finding no pulse in his right carotid artery, surgeons removed a clot to restore blood flow to his brain.

The stroke virtually paralyzed Richard's left side, but, in an attempt to restore his chances of pitching again, another operation was performed. With therapy, most of his strength and speech returned, and he tried a comeback the following spring. But his reflexes and coordination were gone, he was unable to make spatial perceptions and could not field his position. He pitched some in the minors, but eventually "traded baseball for a life of God," he explained, and sold cars. Said wife Carolyn, "I've never seen a player dragged through the mud like this . . . . It took death, or nearly death, to get an apology. They should have believed him." /(JCA)

Lee Richard (Bee Bee) — 1948– . SS-2B-3B-OF 1971–72, 74–76 **White Sox**, Cardinals 239 g, .209, 2 hr, 29 rbi

Dick Williams once called this utility player "the fastest man in baseball." Richard scored from first on singles several times, and as a White Sox rookie once scored from second on a sacrifice fly. But in 1971 he led AL shortstops in errors despite playing only 68 games at shortstop. Because he was a strikeout pitcher in high school and college, teammates dubbed him Bee Bee. /(KC)

Gene Richards — 1953– . OF-1B 1977–84 **Padres**, Giants 1026 g, .290, 26 hr, 255 rbi

Before Tony Gwynn came along, Richards's .291 lifetime batting average was the highest in Padres history. He excelled at all three outfield positions and led the majors in outfield assists with 21 in 1980. As a rookie in 1977, he stole 56 bases. In 1980 Richards, Ozzie Smith, and Jerry Mumphrey each stole over 50 bases, becoming the first teammate trio in NL history to do so. /(JCA)

Paul Richards — 1908–1986. C 1932–35, 43–46 Dodgers, Giants, A's, **Tigers** 523 g, .227, 15 hr, 155 rbi. *1 WS, 7 g, .211, 6 rbi.*
    Manager 1951–61, 76 White Sox, **Orioles** 923–901, .506

Paul Richards neither led a team to a pennant as a field manager nor presided over a winner as a general manager. He often got a team ready to win, only to move to another franchise before success was realized. He was considered among baseball's most brilliant and innovative strategists, an astute judge of pitching talent, and a skilled teacher.

After a playing career as a reserve catcher, Richards became a successful minor league manager with the Atlanta Crackers. He credited Bill Terry, for whom he had played briefly in New York, with teaching him the techniques of managing. When WWII brought manpower shortages, Richards resurfaced as a major league catcher with Detroit. He was the Tigers' regular catcher in the 1945 WS. When players came back after WWII, Richards returned to minor league managing. He got his chance to manage in the major leagues in 1951, taking over the White Sox. His "Go-Go" Sox had four winning seasons, but they always finished behind the Yankees and Indians.

His success in Chicago earned him the challenge of converting the perennially dismal Browns into a winner in their new identity as the Baltimore Orioles. He served as both field manager and general manager of the transplanted club. He built the franchise into a winner, developing a pitching staff called The Kiddie Korps, strong-armed throwers backed up by knuckleball reliever Hoyt Wilhelm. Richards invented the oversized catcher's mitts that have been used since to handle knuckleball pitchers. Just as the Orioles moved toward pennant contention, the Texan from Waxahachie went home to the Lone Star State to head up the newly formed Houston Colt .45s.

He brought Houston to a competitive position when another new challenge beckoned. The Braves had gone south, from Milwaukee to Atlanta, and Richards, who had led the old Crackers to glory, was deemed the man to rejuvenate the Braves in their new setting as vice president for baseball operations. The team won a divisional title in 1969. It was as close as Richards came to a pennant, and he left Atlanta and was out of baseball for the first time in 45 years. Not for long, however, as Bill Veeck had taken over the White Sox and hired the sixty-seven-year-old Richards as manager. Richards's White Sox finished last in 1976. /(JK)

Bobby Richardson — 1935– . 2B 1955–66 **Yankees** 1412 g, .266, 34 hr, 390 rbi. *7 WS, 36 g, .305, 1 hr, 15 rbi* ☛ *All-Star—57, 59, 62–66. Gold Glove—61–65.*

Respected as a competitor and as a clean-living, God-fearing gentleman, Richardson played a solid second base on seven Yankee pennant-winners. He had great range and was particularly adept at turning the double play; teamed with shortstop Tony Kubek, he led the AL in double plays four times. He won five consecutive Gold Gloves (1961–65).

Though Richardson hit .301 in 1959, the singles hitter was not usually one of the Yankees' major offensive threats. An exception was his sensational performance in the 1960 World Series, which won him Series MVP honors. He batted .367 with 11 hits, a grand slam, and eight runs scored. He set WS records with 12 total RBI and 6 RBI in Game Three, though he had driven in only 26 runs during the regular season. In 1961, he tied records for a five-game Series with nine hits and 23 at-bats, for a .391 average. He dramatically ended the 1962 Series when he caught Willie McCovey's hard liner with two on and two out in the ninth inning of Game Seven to preserve the Yankees' 1–0 victory over San Francisco.

Manager Casey Stengel platooned Richardson with Jerry Lumpe in 1957 and 1958, and never gave

Bobby Richardson

Richardson more than 469 at-bats a year. He once said of the young second baseman, "He don't smoke, he don't drink, and he still can't hit .250." Ralph Houk, who took over the Yankees in 1961, liked a set lineup. He played Richardson every day and placed him at the top of the order. The combination of leading off for the best offense in the league and rarely walking resulted in Richardson leading the AL in at-bats each year from 1962 through 1964, setting an AL record with 692 in '62. That year his 209 hits were the AL high. He batted .302 and finished second to Mickey Mantle in MVP voting. On June 24, he tied a ML record by coming to bat 11 times in a 22-inning game against Detroit.

His Yankee teammates were a down-and-dirty bunch, but they tried to clean up their act around the religious Richardson. Once Moose Skowron struck out three times in a game and came storming into the dugout, threw his equipment down, and was cursing as he walked down the bench. As he passed Richardson, still cursing, he threw in an "Excuse me, Bobby," and continued with his obscenities, cracking up the whole team. After the collapse of the Yankee dynasty in 1965 Richardson and shortstop Tony Kubek decided between themselves that it would be bad for the team if they both retired at once. Kubek's injuries limited his effectiveness, so he called it quits after the 1965 season, with Richardson staying through 1966. He coached college ball after his playing days. /(FK)

Gordie Richardson — 1939– . LHP 1964–66 Cardinals, **Mets** 118 ip, 6–6, 4.04. *1 WS, 2/3 ip, 0–0, 40.00*

Richardson helped the Cardinals to the pennant (4–2, 2.30) after being called up to their bullpen in mid-1964. Traded to the Mets after the season, he had little success there in a year and a half. /(KT)

Hardy Richardson (Old True Blue) — 1855–1931. 2B-OF-3B 1879–92 **Buffalo (NL)**, Detroit (NL), Braves, Boston (PL), Boston (AA), Washington (NL), Giants 1331 g, .299, 73 hr, 645 rbi (inc.)
☛ *Led League—hr 86. Led League—rbi 90.*

Richardson played every position on the field at one time or another but he was best known as one of the greatest second basemen of the 19th century. He was a member of the "Big Four," a star infield for Buffalo's NL team that also included first baseman Dan Brouthers, shortstop Jack Rowe, and third baseman Deacon White. When Buffalo dropped out of the NL after the 1885 season, the Detroit team paid $7,000, an astonishing sum at the time, for the entire Buffalo roster just to acquire the Big Four. Richardson hit .351 and led the NL in hits (189) and home runs (11) in 1886. The next season the Big Four led Detroit to the NL pennant, with Richardson contributing another 11 home runs, 94 RBI, and a .328 batting average. /(BC)

Mike Richardt — 1958– . 2B 1980, 82–84 **Rangers**, Astros 186 g, .226, 4 hr, 60 rbi

Injuries made Richardt "the pinup boy of the American Medical Association." A top minor league hitter, he suffered a broken jaw from a bad-hop grounder; wrist, neck, shoulder, and knee injuries; a tonsillectomy; and abcessed teeth. He stayed healthy long enough in 1982 to play 119 games and bat .241. /(JCA)

Lance Richbourg — 1897–1975. OF 1921, 24, 27–32 Phillies, Senators, **Braves**, Cubs 698 g, .308, 13 hr, 247 rbi

A University of Florida infielder in 1919 when the Giants trained at Gainesville, Richbourg signed with New York but never played for them. He hit over .300 four consecutive seasons as a Braves regular (1927–30). On May 14, 1927 he set a National League record by playing 18 innings in right field without a fielding chance. He later spent four years managing Nashville (Southern Association). /(NLM)

Pete Richert — 1939– . LHP 1962–74 Dodgers, Senators, **Orioles**, Cardinals, Phillies 1165 ip, 80–73, 3.19. *1 LCS, 1 ip, 0–0, 0.00. 3 WS, 1 ip, 0–0, 0.00* ☛ *All-Star—65–66.*

In his first major league appearance, with the Dodgers on April 12, 1962, Richert fanned the first six men he faced -four in one inning—to tie three ML records. Four years later, he fanned seven batters in a row (4/24/66). Primarily a starter his first six seasons, he came into his own as a relief specialist with Baltimore. Well-suited as a closer, he was calm and aggressive, and had a blistering fastball and sharp slider. He recorded ERAs of 2.60 or less five times; in 1970, when he was 7–2 with 13 saves, his ERA was 1.96. /(JCA)

Lew Richie — 1883–1936. RHP 1906–13 Phillies, Braves, **Cubs** 1359 ip, 74–65, 2.54. *1 WS, 1 ip, 0–0, 0.00*

Lew Richie was more than a good, useful pitcher. He was with the Chicago Cubs when the emerging humorist Ring Lardner traveled with them and filed hilarious stories with *The Sporting News*. Richie was also a gifted pantomimist, readily falling in with Lardner's pranks to pass the time on long train trips. What immortality clings to Richie results from his being the source of many of Lardner's comic inspirations. /(JK)

Arthur Richman — Unk.– . *Writer.*

The brother of Milt Richman, Arthur was a sportswriter with the New York *Mirror* for 21 years. When it folded in 1963, he joined the Mets as director of promotions and public relations. As traveling secretary, he received a half share of the 1986 WS pool. When he was given only a quarter LCS share in 1988, he blasted Mets players for the insult, claiming they came to him "like children with their stupid requests; when they get in jail they call me at 4 A.M. to get them out. Next time they can sit there." He then began working for the Yankees. /(NLM)

Milton Richman — 1922–1986. *Writer.*

Born in the shadow of the then-under-construction Yankee Stadium, Richman was a light-hitting infielder in the Browns' farm system when he quit baseball to go to work for United Press (later UPI) in 1944. He was known for his passion for golf and a willingness to do a series of one-hand pushups at a moment's notice. Credited with many scoops, he enjoyed a reputation for honesty and fairness. In 42 years, he missed only two days from work. Richman received the J.G. Taylor Spink Award from the Hall of Fame in 1980. /(NLM)

Lee Richmond — 1857–1929. LHP-OF 1879–83, 86 Braves, **Worcester (NL)**, Providence (NL), Cincinnati (AA) 251 g, .257, 3 hr, 57 rbi (inc.); 1583 ip, 75–100, 3.06. 20 wins: 80–81

A future doctor and educator, Richmond won 79% of Worcester's victories in the club's three ML seasons (1880–82). On June 12, 1883, four days before graduating from Brown University, he pitched the first ML perfect game, defeating Cleveland 1–0. /(FIC)

Francis C. Richter — 1854–1926. *Writer.*

The editor of the *Reach Guide* from its inception in 1901, Richter died the day after completing the 1926 edition. As a writer and associate of baseball officials, he was influential in the early development of the game. Beginning with the Philadelphia *Day* in 1872, then the *Sunday World* and *Public Ledger*, he was the first to set up a sports department for any newspaper. Richter helped form the original American Association in 1882 and to place the Philadelphia Athletics in it. The next year he helped organize the Phillies in the NL. In 1883, he started *Sporting Life*, a weekly newspaper, which became a great force in baseball. In 1907, he was offered the presidency of the NL, but turned it down. Richter was a WS official for many years and wrote a history of baseball. /(NLM)

Tex Rickart — Unk.–Unk.

The Brooklyn Dodgers' long-time PA announcer began when the public address "system" consisted of a megaphone. He became famous for his malaprops: "A little boy has been found lost." And, to fans who had hung their coats in a way that distracted the hitters, "Will the fans along the outfield railing please remove their clothes." When not in Ebbets Field, he made his living as a film distributor. /(SFS)

Marv Rickert (Twitch) — 1921–1978. OF 1942, 46–50 **Cubs**, Reds, Braves, Pirates, White Sox 402 g, .247, 19 hr, 145 rbi. *1 WS, 5 g, .211, 1 hr, 2 rbi*

On June 23, 1946 back-to-back inside-the-park homers by Rickert and Eddie Waitkus were a ML first, but the Cubs still lost 15–10. The Braves

rescued Rickert from the minors late in 1948 when slugger Jeff Heath broke his ankle, and the much-traveled Rickert homered in Game Four of the WS. /(DAS)

Branch Rickey [Wesley] (The Mahatma) — 1881–1965. C 1905–07, 14 Browns, Yankees 119 g, .239, 3 hr, 39 rbi.
    Manager 1913–15, 19–25 Browns, **Cardinals** 597–664, .473
☛ *Hall of Fame—1967.*

The honorific The Mahatma combined respect for Rickey's baseball sagacity with amusement at his pontifical manner and florid speech, which gave him the air of a con man playing a parson. He could have been either, but essentially he was that traditional American type, the sharp trader. The basis of his success was a nearly infallible eye for baseball talent. Over and over again, he saw the potential in raw youth (George Sisler, Dizzy Dean), brought hidden qualities to light (Billy Cox, Preacher Roe), and calculated precisely the productive time left in a veteran (Dixie Walker, Joe Medwick).

For the discovery and nurture of such talent he elaborated the primitive device of "farming out" into a network of 32 minor league clubs controlling a "chain gang" of some 600 players. Their quality was so high that the parent club, the once-floundering Cardinals, became a National League power, and so numerous that at one time some 65 Cardinal graduates could be found playing in the majors. As the organization grew under Rickey's direction, he sustained it with a handpicked faculty of managers, coaches, and scouts to give the youngsters big-league polish. It was a complete change of purpose and focus for the minor leagues, and it was fought by Commissioner Landis for its effect on the competitiveness and independence of minor league clubs. In 1937 Landis released 91 Cardinal farmhands, who were property of St. Louis in a way that is now the norm, but seemed threatening to organized baseball at the time. But the benefits for major league teams were obvious, and too tempting to ignore; within a decade, Rickey's idea had been universally adopted.

Moving on to the Dodgers, who would become the Cardinals' challengers and successors, he created the spring-training complex at Vero Beach, where players by the hundreds could be instructed, evaluated, and assigned. And he encouraged such innovations as batting cages, pitching machines, batting helmets, and a string outline of the strike zone rigged over home plate for pitchers working on control.

Branch Rickey

Rickey's all-seeing eye enhanced his knack for trades, for he always knew precisely the players he wanted and exactly the players he was prepared to give up. Add to this his psychological ploys and circumlocutory argument, and his trading partners often departed shirtless, but persuaded he had done them a favor. Perhaps the eye also prompted the most significant action of his career: destruction of baseball's persistent discrimination against blacks. For however noble his motives, he was undeniably the first beneficiary of the change. It certainly was a brave move to sign Jackie Robinson, breaking the silently-upheld color barrier that had existed since the 1880s. But by exploiting the Negro Leagues as a new source of talent, Rickey built a dynasty that won the NL pennant seven times from 1947 through 1956.

Rickey was not much of a ballplayer himself, although he came to the Reds in 1904 well-recommended as a catcher. A youthful vow to his mother would not allow him to suit up on Sundays, however, or even carry his gear to the depot if it was a travel day. Manager Joe Kelley, a no-nonsense old Oriole, cut him before he ever caught a game. The Browns and Highlanders (later renamed the Yankees) tried him as a backup catcher until an injured throwing arm ended his playing career. At New York, he was behind the plate on a day Washington stole 13 bases.

By 1913 he had coached at the University of Michigan (where George Sisler was a pitcher), earned a law degree, and taken a front-office job with the Browns. Toward the season's end he replaced George Stovall as field manager. His record was well under .500, and he never got along with Phil Ball, who took over the Browns in the maneuvering that divided the Federal League spoils. In 1919, after brief military service, Rickey became president and field manager of the Cardinals. Soon he began his long and profitable partnership with hardheaded Sam Breadon, the automobile-dealer-turned-baseball-magnate.

The Cardinals were chronic losers, with two third-place finishes as their finest achievements since 1892. The cashbox was empty. The team was wearing used uniforms. Breadon, now president, made a public stock offering to raise capital. Rickey, now vice president, made his first investment in a minor league farm team. Branch also managed for seven seasons, again slightly under .500. After finishes between third place and seventh place, Breadon ousted him as manager in favor of a harder head, Rogers Hornsby, who promptly took the squad Rickey had assembled to the first of many Cardinals pennants and World Championships.

Rickey was now a man of prominence. Yet with success came other qualities less easy to fathom. The jowly lawyer, with his bushy eyebrows, bow ties, and big cigars, was a slick article, an ambiguous personality. As manager he had arranged substitutes for Sunday games, usually Burt Shotten, who had been with him on the Browns and would turn up again in Brooklyn. Cynics used to say there was a vantage point outside Sportsman's Park where Rickey could watch the game through field glasses, technically not on the premises, but happy enough to profit from the doubleheader crowds who were. He neither cursed ("Judas Priest" was his strongest expletive), nor did he drink, and he was a frequent and moralistic speaker at boys' clubs and YMCAs. Yet he played baseball's cozy gentleman's agreements to the limits in waiving players, he diddled his minor league rosters, and double-talked his players into contracts for stingy salaries. In this, of course, he was not unique, just more sanctimonious.

He was equally successful in Brooklyn in the 1940s, crowning his achievement with the skillfully manipulated introduction of Jackie Robinson. He was eventually squeezed out of the picture by Walter O'Malley, but even after moving to Los Angeles, the Dodgers continued to be successfully run according to his principles. In 1950 he undertook to put new life into the Pirates, but the Mahatma's magic was gone. After five doormat finishes, Joe L. Brown stepped in to take his place. However, Rickey did succeed in making the batting helmet standard gear during his time in Pittsburgh.

In 1959 Rickey launched an effort to form a third major league, the Continental League. The majors reacted with alarm. They could not confront the new venture directly without raising antitrust concerns, so they preempted the new league's prime franchises in the expansion of 1961–62, an expansion Rickey had long advocated. He was elected to the Hall of Fame in 1967 by the Veterans Committee. /(ADS)

Frank Rickey — 1888–1953. *Scout.*

The younger brother of Branch Rickey, Frank worked as a sheriff and an FBI agent before joining his brother's scouting staff in 1926. He scouted for the Cardinals for almost 20 years, and briefly for the Giants, Dodgers, and Pirates, signing Enos Slaughter, Preacher Roe, Johnny Mize, and Marty Marion. Unlike most of his contemporaries, he seldom offered signing bonuses. /(FVP)

Harry Riconda — 1897–1958. 3B-2B-SS 1923–24, 26, 28–30 **A's**, Braves, Dodgers, Pirates, Reds 243 g, .247, 4 hr, 70 rbi

While with the Athletics, Riconda made seven putouts in a game at third base, tying the AL record (7/5/24, second game). He broke his leg during the Braves' fourth game of 1926, and was out for the year. He was a semi-pro basketball player during the off-season. /(NLM)

Elmer Riddle — 1914–1984. RHP 1939–45, 47–49 **Reds**, Pirates 1023 ip, 65–52, 3.40. 20 wins: 43 *1 WS, 1 ip, 0–0, 0.00*
☛ *Led League—w 43. Led League—era 41. All-Star—48.*

Sportswriters punned on the righthander's name: when he was good, he was a nearly unsolvable riddle to opposing batters. In 1941, his first full season, he was 19–4 and led the NL in winning percentage (.826) and ERA (2.24). The next year he was a

riddle to his own team, slumping to 7–11. Then in 1943 he bounced back to 21–11, 2.63. He won only four games over the next four seasons. In 1948 he made a comeback with the Pirates (12–10) and was named an All-Star, but he was a dreadful 1–8 when he was released the next season. Riddle, an excellent fielder, played 102 errorless games. His brother John was a NL catcher and his teammate on the Reds for three seasons. /(JK)

Denny Riddleberger — 1945– . LHP 1970–72 **Senators**, Indians 133 ip, 4–4, 2.77

Riddleberger was a reliever in all of his 103 games. Control problems hindered him, and he recorded only one save. /(WOR)

Steve Ridzik — 1929– . RHP 1950, 52–58, 63–66 Phillies, Reds, Giants, Indians, **Senators** 782 ip, 39–38, 3.79

Ridzik pitched 21 years of pro ball. After appearing in eight major league seasons, mostly in relief, he spent more than four in the minors, resurfacing in 1963 with Washington after developing a knuckleball. /(AL)

Lew Riggs — 1910–1975. 3B 1934–42, 46 Cardinals, **Reds**, Dodgers 760 g, .262, 28 hr, 271 rbi. *2 WS, 6 g, .182, 1 rbi*

Tall and slender, Riggs was a good glove man but an unreliable hitter as the Reds' third baseman for four years. He lost his job to Billy Werber in 1939, when Cincinnati won the NL pennant. He became a good pinch hitter, leading the NL (10) with Brooklyn in 1941. /(EM)

Dave Righetti (Rags) — 1958– . LHP 1979, 81– **Yankees** 1083 ip, 73–60, 3.09. *1 LCS, 6 ip, 1–0, 0.00. 1 WS, 2 ip, 0–0, 13.50*
☛ *Rookie of the Year—81. All-Star—86–87.*

The Yankees' all-time save leader, Righetti set the major league single-season mark of 46 in 1986. He began his career as a starter and threw a no-hitter against the Red Sox on a hot day at Yankee Stadium on the Fourth of July, 1983. Acquired from the Rangers as part of the Sparky Lyle trade after the 1978 season, Righetti appeared in three games in 1979. His next trip to the majors, 1981, resulted in the AL Rookie of the Year award, based on his 8–4 record and 2.06 ERA. Righetti was effective during the postseason, winning two games over Milwaukee in divisional play and once over Oakland in the LCS. He went 11–10 in 1982 and 14–8 in 1983, including the no-hitter, the Yankees' first since Don Larsen's perfect game in the 1956 World Series.

Moved to the bullpen to replace Goose Gossage as the Yankees' closer, Righetti saved 31 games in 1984 and 29 in 1985 with 12 wins. Then came record-setting 1986, when he converted on 29 of his final 30 save opportunities, including both ends of a season-ending doubleheader against the Red Sox, to break the record of 45 held by Dan Quisenberry and Bruce Sutter. Righetti finished fourth in voting for the AL Cy Young Award that season. His save totals dropped to 31 in 1987 and 25 in 1988 and 1989, prompting increased speculation that he might be returning to the starting rotation. On the Yankee's all-time lists, he ranks 2nd in games and 12th in strikeouts. /(EG)

Cy Rigler [Charles] — 1882–Unk. *Umpire 1905–22, 24–35 1 ASU 10 WS*

One of baseball's most illustrious umpires, Rigler was a mountain of a man who stood over 6 feet and weighed 240. In 1903 he played right tackle for the original Massillon Tigers professional football team. He later coached football and baseball at the University of Virginia and was athletic advisor to many colleges. He is usually credited with beginning the practice of signaling strikes with the upward movement of his right arm. However, the oft-repeated explanation that he did it for the benefit of deaf player Dummy Hoy is unlikely since Hoy was out of the majors by the time Rigler arrived. A more likely version is that Rigler began using signals while at Evansville, Indiana during his second year as a pro umpire. Then when Rigler came to the majors he found that his signal system had preceded him. Rigler called Sam Rice's controversial "mystery catch" in the 1925 WS, when the Senators' Rice fell backward into the temporary bleachers while pursuing a long drive off the bat of Pirates batter Earl Smith. Rice refused to talk about it but left a letter to be opened after his death. Rice died in 1974; the letter stated he had made the catch as Rigler called it. /(RTM)

Bill Rigney (Specs, The Cricket) — 1918– . *2B-3B-SS 1946–53 **Giants** 654 g, .259, 41 hr, 212 rbi. 1 WS, 4 g, .250, 1 rbi.*
*Manager 1956–72, 76 Giants, **Angels**, Twins, 1239–1321, .484. First place: 70 1 LCS, 0–3, .000*

An 18-year major league manager, Rigney took the reins of the Giants in 1956, succeeding Leo Durocher, for whom he had played from 1948 to 1953. "I learned a lot from Leo Durocher," he said. "I learned about the hit-and-run, about gambling and going against the percentages. You can't play it the same all the time." Rigney was a shrewd, sharp needler who was often ejected by umpires. He managed the Giants in New York and San Francisco until 1960. He then became the expansion Los Angeles Angels' first manager, moved with them to Anaheim, and remained until 1969. His only division title came as manager of the Twins in 1970, but he was swept by Baltimore in the LCS. A light-hitting infielder, he turned a weakness on inside pitches into a strength by altering his stance, and hit 17 HR in 1947. He did not play regularly after 1949. A native of California, Rigney scouted for the Padres and Angels, and became a TV commentator with the Angels and A's. /(NLM)

Johnny Rigney — 1914–1984. *RHP 1937–42, 46–47 **White Sox** 1186 ip, 63–64, 3.59*

A top pitcher with the White Sox before WWII, Rigney pitched the first night game at Comiskey Park in 1939, when he was 15–8. In 1941 he married the daughter of the White Sox' president. After military service (1942–45), he returned with a sore arm and moved into club administration, eventually becoming Chicago's vice president. /(JK)

Topper Rigney [Emory Elmo] — 1897–1972. *SS 1922–27 **Tigers**, Red Sox, Senators 694 g, .288, 13 hr, 314 rbi*

Rigney led AL shortstops in errors in his first season but improved to lead the league in fielding in 1924 and in assists, fielding, and total chances per game in 1926 after he was sold by the Tigers to the Red Sox. He hit .300 his first two seasons but had his best offensive year in 1924, when he drew 102 walks, second in the AL, while batting .289 and driving in 93 runs. Usually batting seventh in the Tigers' lineup, he often had the heart of their star order on base ahead of him, including Ty Cobb, Harry Heilmann, and Heinie Manush. /(JFC)

Jose Rijo — 1965– . *RHP 1984– Yankees, A's, **Reds** 675 ip, 39–44, 3.87*

The Yankees wanted a hard-throwing rookie pitcher to counter the emergence of Dwight Gooden for the rival Mets in 1984, so they rushed the 18-year-old Rijo to the ML after he had been named Florida State League MVP with a 15–5, 1.68 record in 1983. The wild young Dominican proved too raw, and was returned to the minors after winning just two games before being traded to Oakland as part of a five-player package that pried Rickey Henderson from the A's. Rijo struggled for three seasons in Oakland, although he did strike out 16 Mariners April 16, 1986, and in December 1987 was traded to the Reds with Tim Birtsas for Dave Parker. Rijo was still only 22 when the 1988 season began, but it was his fifth year in the ML, and he finally emerged as a consistently overpowering starter, going 13–8, 2.39 for the Reds with 160 strikeouts in 162 innings. /(SCL)

Ernest Riles — 1960– . SS-3B 1985- **Brewers**, Giants 586 g, .270, 29 hr, 207 rbi. *1 LCS, 1 g, .000. 1 WS, 4 g, .000*

A versatile infielder who finished third in the 1985 AL Rookie of the Year voting behind Ozzie Guillen and teammate Teddy Higuera, Riles started at shortstop for the Brewers in 1986, but injured an index finger in a household accident before the 1987 season and spent the first half of the year on rehabilitation in the minors. The former Texas League batting champion (.349 at El Paso in 1983) was traded to the Giants in 1988 for Jeffrey Leonard. /(SCL)

Andy Rincon — 1959– . LHP 1980–82 **Cardinals** 107 ip, 8–5, 3.11

A hard thrower with excellent control, Rincon won his first three ML starts in September 1980 and was 3–1 with a 1.75 ERA to start 1981. Then, on May 9, his career was destroyed by a line drive that broke his pitching arm. /(JCA)

Jimmy Ring — 1895–1965. RHP 1917–28 Reds, **Phillies**, Giants, Cardinals 2389 ip, 118–149, 4.06. *1 WS, 14 ip, 1–1, 0.64*

With the Reds in the 1919 World Series, Ring beat Ed Cicotte 2–0, in a game the crooked "Black Sox" pitcher might have been trying to win. Ring ran up against honest Dickey Kerr in Game Six, losing after allowing one run in five innings of relief. Ring may have had previous experience with game-fixing; in 1918, he allegedly was paid $25 by notorious teammate Hal Chase after losing a game. With the Phillies, Ring led the NL in walks each year from 1922 through 1925, yet won a career-high 18 in 1923. /(JK)

Jesus Rios — Unk.– . Mexican League Star.

The top pitcher in Mexico in the late 1980s, Rios joined the Mexico City Tigers in 1984, just as the Mexican League ball was souped up. He was among

the ERA leaders every season, winning 61 games in his first four years. /(MC)

Billy Ripken — 1964– . 2B 1987- **Orioles** 323 g, .239, 6 hr, 80 rbi

The son of Orioles coach and former manager Cal Ripken, Sr., the brother of Cal, Jr., and the nephew of minor league outfielder Bill Ripken (1947–49), Billy played way above his abilities in his first season, hitting .308 in 58 games for his father. Showing good range afield, he remained Baltimore's regular second baseman in 1988 despite hitting .207 for new manager Frank Robinson. /(JFC)

Cal Ripken, Sr. — 1935– . *Manager* 1985, 87–88 **Orioles** 68–101, .402

Ripken, a long-time Orioles coach, filled in as manager for one game in 1985 and then took over from Earl Weaver after the team's 1986 collapse. Lacking the talent to field a respectable team, he finished last in 1987 and, with tears in his eyes, was forced by ownership to end son Cal Jr.'s consecutive-innings streak, but was able to make son Billy the regular second baseman in the second half of the season. Cal Sr. was fired after the Orioles lost the first six games of the 1988 season. They went on to lose a ML-record 21 before finally registering a victory. Ripken rejoined the club in his old coaching role in 1989. /(SFS)

Cal Ripken, Jr. — 1960– . SS-3B 1981- **Orioles** 1315 g, .277, 204 hr, 744 rbi. *1 LCS, 4 g, .400, 1 rbi. 1 WS, 5 g, .167, 1 rbi*
☛ *Rookie of the Year—82. Most Valuable Player—83. All-Star—83–89.*

From a baseball family, Cal Ripken, Jr. emerged as one of the great players of the 1980s. Baseball's tallest full-time shortstop (6′4″) combined power and defense in a way matched by few of his predecessors. In 1989 he broke Ernie Banks's shortstop record with his eighth straight 20-homer season. The first shortstop to start four straight All-Star games (1983–87), Ripken started slowly as a rookie third baseman in 1982. He was moved to short by manager Earl Weaver on July 1 and finished the campaign as AL Rookie of the Year, hitting .264 with 28 HR and 93 RBI. He also began a streak of consecutive innings played that did not end until September 14, 1987. His consecutive-games streak continued to climb among the all-time leaders, and he reached third behind Everett Scott and Lou Gehrig in 1989.

Ripken defied the sophomore jinx in 1983 by winning Most Valuable Player honors, hitting .318

with 27 HR and 102 RBI, and leading the AL in hits, doubles, and runs scored. He also made the final putout in the 1983 World Series as the Orioles defeated the Phillies. Slow afoot, Ripken hit into a club-record-tying 32 double plays in 1985. Still, great range accounted for an AL-record 583 assists, among 906 total chances, in 1984 when Ripken led the league in putouts and double plays (defensive) as well. He also led the league in assists in 1983, 1986, and 1987; putouts in 1985; and double plays in 1983 and 1985. Disbelievers in his fielding ability, who found it hard to reconcile the images of great-fielding shortstop and heavy hitter, claimed his fielding totals were the product of everyday play, but he also led AL shortstops in total chances per game in 1983 and 1984; his strong arm allowed him to play deep. Ripken led all major league shortstops in home runs, RBI, runs scored, and slugging percentage each year from 1983 to 1986. He was the American League's top All-Star vote getter for the in 1985 and 1986. In 1987 Cal Jr.'s manager was Cal Ripken and his double play partner was younger brother Billy. /(ME)

Allen Ripley — 1952– . RHP 1978–82 Red Sox, **Giants**, Cubs 464 ip, 23–27, 4.51

Ripley was playing semi-pro ball in Rhode Island when he was signed by the Red Sox, for whom his father, Walt, pitched briefly in 1935. He was 9–10 with the 1980 Giants but completed only 2 of 20 starts. He was the winning pitcher in the Cubs' 8,000th victory, a fact reported in *Ripley's Believe It or Not*. /(JCA)

Jimmy Ripple — 1909–1959. 1936–41, 43. OF **Giants**, Dodgers, Reds, Phillies 554, .282, 28 hr, 257 rbi. *3 WS, 17 g, .320, 2 hr, 9 rbi*

An outfielder with a knack for being in the right place at the right time, Ripple played on three pennant-winning teams in his seven ML years. He hit .305 in 95 games for the 1936 Giants as their answer to the rival Yankees' rookie Joe DiMaggio. Ripple improved to .317 the next year. After he was traded to Brooklyn in 1939, Ripple was sent to their Montreal farm club early in the 1940 season. But the Dodgers failed to use the waiver system properly and Judge Landis made Ripple a free agent. He signed with the Reds and hit .307 down the stretch. In the 1940 WS, he hit .333, homering to win Game Two and scoring the winning run in the final game. /(JK)

Swede Risberg [Charles August] — 1894–1975. SS 1917–20 **White Sox** 476 g, .243, 6 hr, 175 rbi. *2 WS, 10 g, .111, 1 rbi*

Risberg helped destroy a team that might have rivaled the great Yankees of the 1920s. Barred for life for throwing the 1919 Series, he also fixed games in his rookie year and in 1920. Rough and rangy, he once knocked out a minor league umpire with one punch after a called third strike. Though he didn't have the incredible range he's sometimes credited with, he had a powerful arm. Risberg's arrival allowed Buck Weaver to move back to third base, his natural position. Risberg despised his double play partner, Eddie Collins, for his talent, character, education, air of superiority, and above all, salary. He preferred the tough Chick Gandil, who enlisted the young shortstop as his first lieutenant in the fix. During the ensuing trial, Joe Jackson requested protection after Risberg threatened to kill him if he dared talk. "The Swede is a hard guy," said Jackson.

Later in the 1920s, in an attempt to discredit players he called "white lilies," Risberg claimed that Detroit had thrown four games in 1917 to help the Sox clinch the flag. Along with other charges, this led to a major investigation of more than 30 players, among them some of the most famous names in the AL. During the hearing, Tiger pitcher Bernie Boland yelled at Risberg, "You're still a pig!"

When only Gandil and Happy Felsch backed up Swede's story, Commissioner Landis dismissed the charges. The case, however, resulted in strong anti-betting edicts, a statute of limitations, and the abolition of the common practice of teams rewarding other teams with "gifts" for defeating pennant rivals. During his exile, Risberg played semi-pro ball, worked on a dairy farm, and ran a tavern which proudly displayed his name. He was the last survivor of the eight Black Sox. /(DB)

Claude Ritchey (Little All Right) — 1873–1951. 2B-SS 1897–1909 Reds, Louisville (NL), **Pirates**, Braves 1672 g, .275, 18 hr, 673 rbi. *1 WS, 8 g, .111, 2 rbi*

Ritchey was a deft, quick fielder and a clever hitter. He led NL second basemen in fielding percentage five times and double plays three times, and teamed with Honus Wagner as the Pirates' double-play combo for four years. He was the Pirates' second baseman in the first World Series, in 1903. /(ADS)

Jay Ritchie — 1936– . RHP 1964–68 Red Sox, **Braves**, Reds 291 ip, 8–13, 3.49

With the 1967 Braves, the 6'4" 175-lb reliever pitched more than the equivalent of a perfect game, retiring 28 batters in a row (five Reds, four Phillies, three Pirates, and 16 Mets) over four consecutive outings. He made a career-high 52 appearances that season. /(KC)

Wally Ritchie — 1965- . LHP 1987–88 **Phillies** 88 ip, 3–2, 3.57

Ritchie saw the most action in his first season, compiling a 3–2, 3.75 record in 49 relief appearances. /(SFS)

Lawrence Ritter — 1922- . *Writer.*

Holder of a Ph.D. from the University of Wisconsin, Ritter is a finance professor at NYU. His book, *The Glory of Their Times: The Story of Early Days of Baseball Told by the Men Who Played It* (1966), is the first and best collection of interviews with former players. He also wrote *The Image of Their Greatness* (with Donald Honig), an *Illustrated History of Baseball from 1900* (1979), *100 Greatest Baseball Players of All Time*, with Honig (1981), and *The Story of Baseball* (1983). /(NLM)

Lou Ritter (Old Dog) — 1875–1952. C 1902–08 **Dodgers** 462 g, .219, 1 hr, 120 rbi

Ritter was a 5'9" 150-lb catcher who had 55 stolen bases in his career. Despite his lifetime .219 batting average, for several years he was Brooklyn's "hitting catcher," as he alternated with Bill Bergen, who had the lowest BA (among players with at least 2,500 at-bats) in major league history—.170. /(TG)

Bombo Rivera [Jesus Torres] — 1952- . OF 1975–76, 78–80, 82 Expos, **Twins**, Royals 335 g, .265, 10 hr, 83 rbi

A righthanded platoon outfielder, happy-go-lucky Bombo was the darling of Minnesota fans in 1978, when a song was written about him. Teammates sometimes attributed the strong-armed outfielder's popularity to his nickname, but he earned the fans' appreciation by hitting .281 in 1979. He had more at-bats (541) in his two years (1985–86) in Japan; playing for Kintetsu, he hit .240 with 37 HR and 86 RBI. /(JCA)

Jim Rivera [Manuel Joseph] (Jungle Jim) — 1922- . OF-1B 1952–61 Browns, **White Sox**, A's 1171 g, .256, 83 hr, 422 rbi. *1 WS, 5 g, .000*

This young Puerto Rican outfielder from the Bronx captured the imagination of White Sox fans with his daring basepath antics and belly-slides. In 1955 he swiped a league-high 25 bases. In Game Five of the 1959 WS, Rivera's catch with his back to the infield of Charley Neal's long drive preserved a 1–0 Sox

victory in front of over 90,000 screaming Dodger fans. And Jungle Jim was a character. To former First Lady Bess Truman, in attendance at an A's game, Rivera said: "I'm sure sorry my homer beat your team, but it was a helluva wallop, eh, Bess?" To President Kennedy, on Opening Day 1961, when Rivera asked for an autograph: "What's this? This is just a scribble! I can hardly make it out! You'll have to do better than this, John." /(RL)

Luis Rivera — 1964- . SS 1986- **Expos**, Red Sox 289 g, .230, 9 hr, 73 rbi

When the Expos became dissatisfied with Hubie Brooks's defense at shortstop, they called on this slick-fielding Puerto Rican. But Rivera hit just .205, and spent most of 1987 in the minors. After hitting .224 in 123 games in 1988, he was traded to Boston with John Dopson for Spike Owen and a minor leaguer. Used as a backup infielder, he hit better in 1989 than he had ever hit at any level. /(WOR)

Riverfront Stadium Cincinnati Reds 1970- . LF-330, CF-404, RF-330

Riverfront Stadium, on the bank of the Ohio River and visible from neighboring Kentucky, is another circular, multi-purpose stadium with artificial turf and symmetrical outfield fences. Opened in 1970, the 52,392-seat stadium has already hosted four World Series, and was the first baseball stadium with the now-standard "cut out" infield (dirt only in sliding areas around the bases), as well as the first to post metric distances on the outfield fences. Despite its small foul territory and hard playing surface it does not favor batters over pitchers. The stadium itself sits atop a large underground parking garage, meaning most fans enter the stadium from below, and home plate was imported from Cincinnati's now defunct Crosley Field. An April 17, 1976 game was delayed when a large swarm of bees descended on the field. /(SCL)

Mickey Rivers [John Milton] (Mick the Quick, Gozzlehead) — 1948- . OF-DH 1970–84 Angels, **Yankees**, Rangers 1467 g, .295, 61 hr, 499 rbi. *3 LCS, 14 g, .386, 2 rbi. 3 WS, 15 g, .238, 2 rbi* ☛ *All-Star—76.*

An often-quoted, off-the-wall character, Rivers had a language all his own. He called people "Gozzlehead" and "Warplehead" (words he said heard in the ghetto) and presided over kangaroo courts with a unique wisdom. Some of his more memorable quotes included his goals for the 1983 season, "I'd like to hit .300, score 100 runs and stay injury-prone," and his philosophy of life, "Ain't no sense worrying about things you got no control over, 'cause if you got no control over them ain't no sense in worrying. And ain't no sense worrying about things you got control over, 'cause if you got control over them, ain't no sense worrying." When Reggie Jackson claimed he had an IQ of 160, Rivers said, "Out of what, 1,000?" His slouching walk made teammate Sandy Alomar call him the "Almighty Tired Man." But Rivers was an intimidating, left-handed-hitting leadoff man, a line-drive hitter who led the AL in triples with the Angels in 1974 and 1975 and stole a league-high 70 bases in 1975. He made up for many mistakes and a weak arm with his speed in centerfield. Traded to the Yankees in December 1975, he was New York's sparkplug for three straight pennant-winners (1976–78). Yet he often sulked when criticized, lost confidence in his basestealing, and spent money unwisely, often at the racetrack. Owner George Steinbrenner traded him to Texas in 1979, saying, "We had to get him out of the New York environment. He's just a sweet, sweet kid." Rivers excelled in Texas, hitting .333 in 1980. Plagued with knee and ankle injuries, he retired after 1984. /(JCA)

Eppa Rixey [Eppa Jephtha] — 1891–1963. LHP 1912–17, 19–33 Phillies, **Reds** 4494 ip, 266–251, 3.15. 20 wins: 16, 22–23, 25 *1 WS, 6 ip, 0–1, 4.05*
☛ *Led League—w 22. Hall of Fame—1963.*

Rixey was a man of contrasts. Playing his entire 21-year career in the National League, he was its winningest lefthander prior to Warren Spahn, and also its outstanding loser, ranking seventh all-time among all pitchers.

Contemporary accounts describe him as a Virginia gentleman of easy charm and boyish humor. In teammates' memories, he was a fierce competitor, crafty on the mound, but hot-tempered after a loss and destructive to clubhouse furniture.

Despite his height (6'5") and pretzel windup, he was a fielder of agility and precision. His 1,196 assists are tenth on the lifetime list; in 1917 he handled 108 chances without an error.

He starred in basketball as well as baseball while earning a degree in chemistry at the University of Virginia, and he was encouraged to become a professional by Cy Rigler, a NL umpire who coached the University of Virginia Cavaliers. Signed by the Phillies in 1912 on Rigler's recommendation, Rixey became one of the few major leaguers to never play a minor league game.

Eppa Rixey

He was 10–10 (2.50) in 1912, but after four seasons had an under-.500 record. He finally blossomed under the patient and expert handling of Pat Moran, the former catcher who managed the Phillies to a pennant in 1915, their only one between 1883 and 1950. Rixey had a good but not overpowering fastball, a swift curve, and a change of pace he used when he got behind in the count. He had only a brief losing appearance in the 1915 World Series, as Moran preferred to use righthanders against the Red Sox' lefthanded power.

Eppa also acquired a middle name: Jephtha. It was invented by a sportswriter inspired by the resonance it had when spoken between "Eppa" and "Rixey." In time, the pitcher accepted it as his own.

In 1916 Rixey went 22–10 (1.85), but despite a

2.27 ERA the following year, lost a league-high 21. He missed the 1918 season, serving overseas with an army chemical-warfare division. In 1920 he finished 11–22, again leading the NL in losses.

In 1921 Manager Moran, now at Cincinnati, gave up outfielder Greasy Neale (better known in his later years as a football coach) and pitcher Jimmy Ring to get Rixey again. Eppa had eight fine years with the Reds, three with 20 or more wins, including 1922 when he led the league with 25. He was a member of two second-place Reds teams, but never another pennant-winner. In 1932, at age 42, he pitched a string of 27 scoreless innings. A year later, he retired to run his insurance agency. He was elected to the Hall of Fame by the Veterans Committee in 1963, the year of his death. /(ADS)

Johnny Rizzo — 1912–1977. OF 1938–42 **Pirates**, Reds, Phillies, Dodgers 557 g, .270, 61 hr, 289 rbi

Rizzo's 23 home runs, 111 RBI, and .301 as a rookie in 1938 helped the Pirates to a strong second-place finish. He slumped badly the next year (.261, 6 HR, 55 RBI) and the Pirates plunged to sixth. He rebounded with the Phillies in 1940, smashing 24 homers. /(EGM)

Phil Rizzuto (Scooter) — 1917– . SS 1941–42, 46–56 **Yankees** 1661 g, .273, 38 hr, 562 rbi. *9 WS, 52 g, .246, 2 hr, 8 rbi*
☛ *Most Valuable Player—50. All-Star—42, 50–53.*

Phil Rizzuto was in the right place at the right time. The New York native was with the powerhouse Yankees in the period of their greatest domination, and as a result is among the all-time leaders in many World Series statistics: 52 games (6th), 183 at-bats and 45 hits (7th), 21 runs (10th), 30 walks (4th), and 10 steals (3rd). One of the best shortstops in the AL in his time, he led three times each in double plays and total chances per game, twice each in fielding and putouts, and once in assists.

Rizzuto was a fair hitter for a shortstop and a superb bunter. He moved Frankie Crosetti aside in 1941 and 1942, but spent 1943–45 in the military. On an all-star service team, coach Bill Dickey played Pee Wee Reese at shortstop and Rizzuto at third base. The peak of Rizzuto's career came in back-to-back standout seasons in 1949 and 1950. Though he had previously been the Yankees' number-seven or number-eight batter, his hot 1949 moved him to the leadoff spot, and he produced 110 runs while batting .275 and walking 72 times. He finished second in the MVP voting (behind Ted Williams, who missed his third Triple Crown by a fraction of a point). Rizzuto's 1950 season earned

Phil Rizzuto

him the MVP award by over a hundred points: he had career highs with a .324 batting average (sixth in the AL), 125 runs (tied for second), 91 walks, 36 doubles (third), and a .439 slugging average, the only time he topped .400.

Rizzuto continued at the top of the lineup (first or second in the order) until he slumped badly in 1954, hitting just .195. Thereafter he was a backup used mostly for his defense. He moved into the Yankee broadcast booth immediately following his last season and has remained ever since, known for advocating the bunt in most situations and for his expressions "holy cow" (whenever something astonishes him, which is frequently) and "that huckleberry" (an unserious putdown). He is the inventor of the scoring symbol "WW," for "wasn't watching." The Yankees retired his number 10 in 1985. /(SH)

Mel Roach — 1933- . 2B-OF-3B 1953-54, 57-62 Braves, Cubs, Phillies 227 g, .238, 7 hr, 43 rbi

Signed out of the University of Virginia for a substantial bonus, Roach gathered splinters on the Braves' bench for two years before going to the minors for seasoning. Recalled in May 1957 when Red Schoendienst was hurt, he hit .309 until he tore up his knee in August. Two years later he managed .300 in 48 games as a utility man. /(MC)

Mike Roarke — 1930- . C 1961-64 **Tigers** 194 g, .230, 6 hr, 44 rbi

A fine handler of pitchers, Roarke didn't make the majors until he was 30. He spent four seasons backing up Bill Freehan for the Tigers. /(CC)

Bert Roberge — 1954- . RHP 1979-80, 82, 84-86 **Astros**, White Sox, Expos 219 ip, 12-12, 3.99

Exclusively a relief pitcher, Roberge won 12 games and saved 10 in brief stints with three different ML teams. On December 7, 1984 the 6'4" righthander was traded with Vance Law to the Expos for Bob James and Bryan Little. /(SCL)

Skippy Roberge [Joseph Albert Armand] — 1917- . 3B-2B 1941-42, 46 **Braves** 177 g, .220, 3 hr, 47 rbi

This utility man hit a career-high .231 in 1946 after coming back from military service in 1943-45. /(WOR)

Robert F. Kennedy Stadium Washington Senators 1962-1971. LF-335, CF-410, RF-335

Originally called D.C. Stadium, RFK was home to the expansion Senators until they departed for Texas as the Rangers. It is a modern stadium (circular, double-decked, and symmetrical) with over 45,000 seats, and several of the centerfield seats were painted different colors to denote the landing spots of Frank Howard's more prodigious home runs. On September 30, 1971 the last ML game played there was forfeited to the Yankees with the Senators leading 7-5 and two outs in the ninth inning when angry fans stormed the field to protest the home club's impending move. It is now the home of the National Football League's Washington Redskins. /(SCL)

Bip Roberts [Leon Joseph III] — 1963- . 2B-3B 1986, 88- **Padres** 223 g, .282, 4 hr, 37 rbi

Roberts was handed the Padres' second base and leadoff jobs by new manager Larry Bowa in 1986, but hit a disappointing .253 with no extra-base power, rarely walked, stole 14 bases but was caught 12 times, spent time on the DL, and was only average afield. He resurfaced in 1989, mostly playing third base, and hit .301 (.391 on-base average) with 81 runs scored in only 329 at-bats. /(JFC)

Curt Roberts — 1929-1969. 2B 1954-56 **Pirates** 171 g, .223, 1 hr, 40 rbi

Roberts was the Pirates' first black player. He had been a shortstop with the Negro League Kansas City Monarchs before playing three years at Denver (Western League), where manager Andy Cohen made him a defensive star at second base. /(NLM)

Dave Roberts [David Arthur] — 1944- . LHP 1969-81 Padres, **Astros**, Tigers, Cubs, Giants, Pirates, Mariners, Mets 2098 ip, 103-125, 3.78. *1 WS, 0 ip, 0-0, 0.00*

Roberts changed organizations 11 times in his pro baseball career. "The way I look at it," he said, "either I'm a bum or everybody wants me." Approached by 14 teams after graduating from high school, he was a Phillies, A's, and Pirates farmhand before being taken by San Diego in the 1968 expansion draft. He went 14-17 (2.10) for the last-place 1971 Padres. With Houston in 1973, he recorded a career-best 17-11 record, setting a club record with six shutouts. After a 16-17 season with the 1976 Tigers, he had surgery to correct an arthritic knee. From 1977 through 1981, he worked for six teams, never winning more than six games. /(KC)

Leon Roberts — 1951- . OF 1974-84 Tigers, Astros, **Mariners**, Rangers, Blue Jays, Royals 901 g, .267, 78 hr, 328 rbi

Roberts signed with Detroit out of the University of Michigan. He was voted the Mariners' MVP in 1978 (.301, 22 HR, 92 RBI), and his first hit for Seattle was a grand slam (4/9/78). /(NLM)

Robin Roberts — 1926– . RHP 1948–66 **Phillies**, Orioles, Astros, Cubs 4688 ip, 286–245, 3.41. 20 wins: 50–55 *1 WS, 11 ip, 0–1, 1.64*
☛ *Led League—w 52–55. Led League—k 53–54. All-Star—50–56. Hall of Fame—1976.*

A hard-nosed competitor, Roberts ranks as the winningest righthander in Phillies history. A baseball and basketball star at Michigan State, Roberts was disappointed when assigned to Wilmington of the Inter-State League his first pro season, 1948. He wasn't there long; the Phillies recalled him in June when he ran up a 9–1 record. In his first full season, Roberts won 15 games. In 1950, he helped pitch the Phillies to their first pennant in 35 years, going

Robin Roberts

20–11. When he won his 20th on the final day of the season at Brooklyn, in a pennant-deciding, 10-inning game, he became the Phillies' first 20-game-winner since Grover Alexander in 1917.

Roberts won 20 games six straight years, from 1950 to 1955, with league highs in wins for four straight, starting in 1952, when he went 28–7. Six times he led the NL in games started, and five times in complete games and innings pitched. He once pitched 28 straight complete games in an era when relief pitchers were regularly employed. He was able to get the outs he needed with men in scoring position, and he helped himself as a fielder and at the plate.

His Achilles' heel was the home run ball, but in his prime he rarely gave one up with men on base. He allowed 46 in 1956, then a major league record. Primarily a power pitcher until late in his career, Roberts had a smooth, flowing motion and threw strikes consistently. Though he pitched over 300 innings in six straight seasons, he never walked more than 77 batters.

All those innings may have taken their toll with shoulder problems that began in 1956. He went 19–18 that season, breaking his 20-win streak. No longer able to muster overpowering speed, he had his worst and most frustrating year in 1957. Though the Phillies were contenders for the first half, Roberts struggled, finishing with only 10 wins, and losing a league-high 22 games.

After going 1–10 in 1961, Roberts was sold to the Yankees, but was released in April 1962, without pitching an inning. But he had made the mental adjustments to become a finesse pitcher. He signed with Baltimore and had a winning record there for three years. Released in mid-1965, he signed with Houston, then moved to the Cubs in 1966, winning his final ML game that September. Roberts was not ready to hang it up at age 40, and joined the Phillies' Eastern League Reading farm club with hopes of returning to the majors.

In his prime, pitching was easy for Roberts, who used to say, "Too many people try to make it more complicated than it really is." He was active in the players' union during his ML time, and served as head coach of the University of South Florida in Tampa and roving minor league instructor for the Phillies. He was made a member of the Hall of Fame by the BBWAA in 1976. /(AL)

Andre Robertson — 1957– . SS-2B-3B 1981–85 **Yankees** 254 g. .251. 5 hr, 54 rbi. *1 LCS, 1 g, .000. 1 WS, 1 g, --*

After two seasons of limited action, Robertson became the Yankees' shortstop in 1983, but a serious car accident ended his season in August. He returned for stints in 1984–85, but a 1985 knee injury prevented him from regaining his starting spot. /(EG)

Bob Robertson — 1946– . 1B 1967–79 **Pirates**, Mariners, Blue Jays 829 g, .242, 115 hr, 368 rbi. *5 LCS, 14 g, .321, 4 hr, 7 rbi. 1 WS, 7 g, .240, 2 hr, 5 rbi*

The stocky, red-haired slugger, a three-time minor league home run champ, was touted in Pittsburgh as another Ralph Kiner. He missed all of 1968 due to a kidney obstruction. An excellent fielder, he set a ML record for first basemen with eight assists in one game (6/21/71). His best offensive year was 1970 (.287, 27 HR, 82 RBI). He nearly matched those figures in 1971, when he was a postseason wrecking crew. He hit three homers (a record) and drove in five runs (also a record) in Game Two of the LCS against the Giants, homered again in Game Three, and homered twice in the WS. He slumped in the next two years, and was only a part-time player after surgery on both knees in 1974. /(JCA)

Charlie Robertson — 1897–1984. RHP 1919, 22–28 **White Sox**, Browns, Braves 1005 ip, 49–80, 4.44

In his third ML start for the White Sox, Robertson was perfect. On April 30, 1922, at Detroit, he beat the Tigers 2–0 with the sixth perfect game in ML history. A diving foul-line catch by left fielder Johnny Mostil preserved the win. His subsequent career was a disappointment: he nursed a sore arm through six more seasons, never winning more than he lost. /(JK)

Dave Robertson — 1889–1970. OF 1912, 14–17, 19–22 **Giants**, Cubs, Pirates 801 g, .287, 47 hr, 364 rbi. *1 WS, 6 g, .500, 1 rbi*
☛ *Led League—hr 16–17.*

Although this quiet, lefthanded slugger did not clear the fences in the 1917 WS, his .500 average set the record for a six-game Series, a mark unmatched for 36 years. His 12 HR in both 1916 and '17 were enough to tie him for the NL lead. /(JL)

Gene Robertson — 1899–1981. 3B-SS 1919, 1922–26, 28–30 **Browns**, Yankees, Braves 656 g, .280, 20 hr, 249 rbi. *1 WS, 3 g, .125, 2 rbi*

A 5'7" football player signed by the baseball Browns out of St. Louis University, Robertson topped all ML third basemen in 1924 with a .315 batting average. /(NLM)

Jerry Robertson — 1943– . RHP 1969–70 **Expos**, Tigers 49 g, 194 ip, 5–16, 3.93

As a reliever in the Cardinal organization from 1965 to 1967, Robertson posted no ERA higher than 1.98. Chosen to be an original 1969 Expo, he went 5–16. /(JCA)

Rich Robertson — 1944– . RHP 1966–71 **Giants** 302 ip, 13–14, 4.94

Powerful Rich Robertson, who grew up in the San Francisco Bay area, was drafted by the Giants and went 18–9 in the Pacific Coast League in 1968. Battling control problems, he turned in a ML career-best 8–9 performance in 1970. /(JCA)

Sherry Robertson — 1919–1970. OF-2B-3B 1940–41, 43, 46–52 **Senators**, A's 597 g, .230, 18 hr, 151 rbi

Signed out of the University of Maryland by his uncle, Senators owner Clark Griffith, Robertson opened 1943 as Washington's third baseman despite uniformly terrible minor league stats. He hit .217 in 59 games before being drafted into the service. In seven postwar seasons, all but the last with the Senators, he appeared in over 100 games only in 1949, when he hit .251 with 11 homers. From 1953 on, he worked in the Senators' front office, serving as farm director from 1958 to 1970. /(MC)

Billy Jo Robidoux — 1964– . 1B-DH 1985– **Brewers**, White Sox 146 g, .212, 4 hr, 39 rbi

Robidoux (pronounced ROE-ba-doe) won the Brewers' first base job in 1986 from the aging Cecil Cooper on the basis of an outstanding 1985 minor league season. Robidoux slumped badly, lost his power, and was on the DL twice, finishing with a .227 batting average. /(SFS)

Aaron Robinson — 1915–1966. C 1943, 45–51 **Yankees**, White Sox, Tigers, Red Sox 610 g, .260, 61 hr, 272 rbi. *1 WS, 3 g, .200, 1 rbi*

Robinson had a small role in three ML success stories. A solid catcher with fair home run power, he lost his job with the World Champion 1947 Yankees to Yogi Berra and was traded to the White Sox for lefthanded pitcher Eddie Lopat. After one season in Chicago, he was traded to Detroit for another lefthanded pitcher who became a star, Billy Pierce. /(JK)

Bill Robinson — 1943– . OF-1B-3B 1966–69, 72–83 Braves, Yankees, Phillies, **Pirates** 1472 g, .258, 166 hr, 641 rbi. *2 LCS, 5 g, .000. 1 WS, 7 g, .263, 2 rbi*

Robinson was unfortunate in being ballyhooed as "the next Mickey Mantle" after the Yankees traded the popular Clete Boyer to Atlanta to obtain him. He struggled for three years with the Yankees, toiled in the Phillies system, and almost quit before finally maturing and hitting 25 homers in 1973. With Pittsburgh, Robinson never had a position, as manager Chuck Tanner used his "super-regular" in the outfield, at first base, and at third base. In 1977, he reached career highs of .304, 26 HR, and 104 RBI. He hit 24 HR in 1979 when Pittsburgh became World Champions and collected another World Series ring as batting coach for the 1986 Mets./(JCA)

Brooks Robinson (Brooksie) — 1937– . 3B 1955–1977 **Orioles** 2896 g, .267, 268 hr, 1357 rbi. *5 LCS, 18 g, .348, 2 hrs, 7 rbi. 4 WS, 21 g, .263, 3 hr, 14 rbi* ☛ *Most Valuable Player—64. Led League—rbi 64. All-Star—60-75. Gold Glove—60-75. Hall of Fame—1983.*

Setting the standard by which all who followed him are judged, Robinson played third base with style, class, and an uncanny ability to turn in spectacular plays with startling regularity for 23 seasons. In 16 of those seasons, he was the Gold Glove award winner. For 15 straight seasons, he was the American League's starting All-Star third baseman. He led AL third basemen in assists 8 times and in fielding 11 times. He holds almost every lifetime record for third baseman by a wide margin: most games (2,870), best fielding percentage (.971), most putouts (2,697), most assists (6,205), most chances (9,165), and most double plays (618). After he almost singlehandedly won the 1970 World Series for the Orioles, Reds manager Sparky Anderson quipped: "I'm beginning to see Brooks in my sleep. If I dropped this paper plate, he'd pick it up on one hop and throw me out at first." Robinson is also one of the kindest, gentlest, and most generous ballplayers ever to make a diving stop.

Robinson didn't play high school ball, and was playing second base in a church league when he was discovered. He worked in slowly as a replacement for Hall of Famer George Kell, who was finishing his career at third base for the Orioles. The Oriole dynasty that developed in the 1960s was built on pitching and defense, but Brooks was head and shoulders above all his smooth-fielding teammates. Wearing his trademark short-billed batting helmet,

Brooks Robinson

he was a fair hitter with some power, winning the 1964 MVP award on the strength of his only .300 season (.317), with 28 HR and 118 RBI. He was named MVP of the 1966 All-Star Game after getting three hits and scoring the AL's lone run in a 2–1 loss.

But it was his glove that regularly won games. In the 1966 World Series, his presence at third discouraged the heavily favored Dodgers from employing their bunting game. The Orioles won four straight close games. In the 1970 Series, the Reds nicknamed him "Hoover," expanding upon the "human vacuum cleaner" tag he had been known by. After Robinson won the Series MVP award with a .429 average, two home runs, and a slew of dazzling defensive plays, Reds catcher Johnny Bench noted that "if he wanted a car that badly, we'd have given him one." On one unbelievable play, Brooks fully extended to backhand a sharp grounder by Lee May behind third and a full body length into foul territory, whirled off-balance, and threw a perfect one-hopper off the Riverfront Stadium Astroturf to Boog Powell at first for the out. He won Game One with a seventh-inning solo homer, and homered again in Game Four.

Robinson also holds the dubious distinction of playing on the most All-Star losers, 15 in all, including both 1960 games. Toward the end of his career, his finances were in rough shape. Some naive business deals had gone sour, and he was heavily in debt. The Orioles kept him on, without asking, for two seasons more than Robinson would have realistically played. The balding and slightly paunchy veteran never complained about his problems, and ultimately solved them with the help of a new career as a popular Orioles broadcaster. A classy legend in his own time, Robinson's Hall of Fame induction in 1983 drew one of the largest Cooperstown crowds ever. /(SEW)

Craig Robinson — 1948– . SS-2B 1972–77 Phillies, **Braves**, Giants 293 g, .219, 6 hr, 42 rbi

A good glove man who led Pacific Coast League shortstops in total chances and double plays in 1971–72, Robinson was handed a regular job with the 1974 Braves but simply didn't hit enough. His .230 batting average and lack of power (four doubles, six triples, no home runs) relegated him to a reserve role for his remaining ML seasons. /(CP)

Don Robinson — 1957– . RHP 1978– **Pirates**, Giants 1619 ip, 92–86, 3.62. *3 LCS, 7 ip, 2–1, 4.05. 2 WS, 7 ip, 1–1, 9.45*

The hard-throwing, 6'4" 225-lb Robinson bounced back from elbow surgery to win *TSN* NL Rookie Pitcher of the Year honors in 1978, when he went 14–6 for Pittsburgh. But he underwent shoulder operations in 1979 and 1981 before winning a club-high 15 games in 1982. His shoulder again kept him out for most of 1983. He returned in 1984 as a relief pitcher. His acquisition by the Giants in mid-1987 helped them win the NL West title; he tied teammate Scott Garrelts with a league-high 11 relief wins, going 5–1 with seven saves down the stretch. He won the pennant-clincher on September 28, homering to break a 4–4 tie with San Diego.

An exceptional fielder and hitter with home run power, he played right field in the 1983 Instructional League when he wasn't on the mound. His lifetime average of .254 is the highest among active pitchers, and he has been used as a pinch hitter. /(ME)

Eddie Robinson — 1920– . 1B 1942, 46–57 Indians, Senators, **White Sox**, A's, Yankees, Tigers, Orioles 1314 g, .268, 172 hr, 723 rbi. *2 WS, 10 g, .348, 0 hr, 2 rbi* ☛ *All-Star—49, 51, 52, 53..*

Robinson contributed 16 home runs and 83 RBI to Cleveland's pennant drive ine 1948 and batted .300 in the WS. Traded to the Senators after the season, he was dealt again early in 1950 to the White Sox, where he had his best seasons. In 1951 he hit 29 homers, the club record until 1970, and drove in 117 runs. The next year he hit 22 homers with 104 RBI. Although he was the only legitimate power hitter for the Go-Go White Sox, GM Frank Lane nevertheless traded him before the 1953 season to the A's for two-time batting champion Ferris Fain, another singles hitter. Robinson had one more top year, hitting 22 homers and batting in over 100 runs for the third straight season. He moved on to the Yankees in 1954, and became their premier pinch hitter, leading the AL with 15 hits in 49 at-bats. /(RL)

Floyd Robinson — 1936– . OF 1960–68 **White Sox**, Reds, A's, Red Sox 1012 g, .283, 67 hr, 426 rbi

In the 1960s, the White Sox had several exciting young players who peaked early, then faded inexplicably. Robinson, a chunky ex-Marine, was the prime example. After hitting .310 as a rookie in '61, he raised that to .312 the next year, with 109 RBI and a league-leading 45 doubles. On July 22, he went 6-for-6 against Boston. That winter, Chicago sportswriters named him the city's top athlete. He slumped in 1963 and was a salary holdout in '64. Although he hit .301 that year, his power stats fell off badly. When Eddie Stanky took over as manager, Robinson was put in his doghouse as a complainer. He was traded to Cincinnati in 1967, and was out of the majors within two years. /(RL)

Frank Robinson — 1935– . OF-1B 1956–76 **Reds**, Orioles, Dodgers, Angels, Indians 2808 g, .294, 586 hr, 1812 rbi. *3 LCS, 9 g, .206, 2 hr, 5 rbi. 5 WS, 26 g, .250, 8 hr, 14 rbi.*
    *Manager 1975–77, 81–84, 88-Indians, **Giants**, Orioles 591–642, .479*
☛ *Rookie of the Year—56. Most Valuable Player—61, 66. Led League—ba 66. Led League—hr 66. Led League—rbi 66. All-Star—56–57, 59, 61–62, 65–66, 69–71, 74. Gold Glove—58. Hall of Fame—1982.*

Robinson came out of nowhere in 1956 to win the Reds' left-field job. Crowding the plate, challenging pitchers, and sliding hard, he tied Wally Berger's

A few days later, he slid hard into Braves third baseman Eddie Mathews, precipitating one of the most memorable brawls in baseball history and the first between black and white stars. Booed intensely, Robinson responded with a grand slam against the Braves and took off on a batting tear climaxed by three homers against the Phillies on August 22. He finished with 36 HR, 125 RBI, a .311 batting average, and 106 runs. Despite more arm pain, Robinson won his first of three straight NL slugging titles with .595 in 1960. The angry young civil-rights advocate began carrying a gun in self-defense in response to numerous death threats. He was eventually arrested for brandishing it at a short-order cook who had refused to serve him.

In 1961 Robinson led the Reds to their first pennant since 1940 with his first MVP season, hitting .323 with 37 HR, 124 RBI, and 117 runs. His .611 slugging percentage led the NL, and he stole 22 bases in 25 attempts to lead in stolen base percentage. He was especially torrid in the stretch run. So dangerous was Robinson after being brushed back that Phillies manager Gene Mauch began fining any of his pitchers who worked Robinson inside. Robinson's third straight slugging title came in 1962 (.624), when he also led the league with 51 doubles and 134 runs. He hit .342 with 39 HR and 136 RBI, and missed leading in total bases and batting average when, respectively, Willie Mays of the Giants and Tommie Davis of the Dodgers surpassed him during the three-game playoff after Los Angeles and San Francisco were tied at the end of the regular schedule.

Playing through injuries in 1963, Robinson saw his offensive output plummet. He broke his slump by choking up two inches on the bat, chopping at the ball. His speed garnered him a career-high 26 steals. Returning to form in 1964, Robinson hit .306 with 29 HR and 96 RBI, and followed with a .296 average, 33 HR, and 113 RBI in 1965. But Reds GM Bill DeWitt traded Robinson to the Orioles with outfield prospect Dick Simpson for pitchers Milt Pappas and Jack Baldschun. The deal was immediately the most unpopular in Reds history, and attendance, offense, and morale all dropped sharply until Johnny Bench assumed the leadership and cleanup roles three years later. DeWitt, who defended the deal by calling Robinson "an old thirty," eventually lost his job. In 1966 Robinson led the Orioles to the first pennant and a World Series upset sweep of the Dodgers. The first Triple Crown winner since Mickey Mantle in 1956, Robinson led the AL with 49 HR, 122 RBI, a .317 batting

Frank Robinson

rookie record of 38 homers, made the NL All-Star team, led the league with 122 runs scored, and was hit by pitches a rookie-record 20 times. The Reds as a team hit a NL-record 221 homers that season, improving 16 games in the standings to finish just two games out of first place. For the next ten seasons, Robinson was their undisputed leader. Batting .322 as a sophomore, Robinson was one of eight Reds elected to the NL All-Star starting lineup in 1957, and was the only outfielder who wasn't removed by Commissioner Ford Frick after the details of a ballot-stuffing campaign by Cincinnati management was exposed.

Recurring arm trouble caused Robinson to slump to .269 in 1958, as he experimented at first and third bases while winning a Gold Glove in left field. Shifted to first base full-time in 1959, Robinson sat on the bench during the first of that year's two All-Star Games. Seething, he came back with three straight hits, including a homer, in the second game.

average, a .637 slugging percentage, and 122 runs. He capped his season with two home runs off Don Drysdale in the World Series. When he was voted MVP, he became the first man to win the award in both the NL and AL. He appeared to be headed toward a second straight Triple Crown in 1967 until he was hurt late in the season. Carl Yastrzemski won the Triple Crown instead, while Robinson finished second in batting (.311) and slugging (.576), third in RBI (94), and fourth in HR (40) while playing only 129 games. Injuries continued to hamper him in 1968, but he rebounded in 1969, leading the Orioles to the AL pennant while hitting .318 with 32 HR, 100 RBI, and 111 runs.

On June 26, 1970 Robinson hit grand slams in consecutive innings. He finished the year with 25 HR, 78 RBI, and a .306 batting average, his last .300 average. After 28 HR, 99 RBI, and a .281 BA in 1971, Robinson was sent to the Dodgers in a six-man deal. He hit only .251 for Los Angeles, with 19 homers in 103 games, before moving on to the Angels in a seven-man trade the next winter. Robinson rebounded to .266 with 30 HR and 97 RBI. By this time Robinson was managing in winter ball, making no secret of his ambition to become the first black manager in the major leagues. When the Indians, well out of contention, acquired him on waivers late in 1974, rumors of a managerial change soon surfaced.

After the season, in which Robinson hit 22 homers, the Indians appointed him playing manager for 1975. Cleveland's ace pitcher Gaylord Perry, a South Carolina native, promptly questioned Robinson's ability to manage. Gaylord's brother Jim was also the Indians' second-best pitcher. Robinson settled the issue in characteristic style, homering to give Gaylord the Opening Day victory. Shortly afterward, he traded both Perrys. Easing himself out of the lineup, Robinson led the Indians to their first winning record (81–78, fourth place) since 1968 and only their third .500-plus season since 1959 in 1976, but he was fired when they started slowly in 1977. He coached for the Angels the balance of 1977, coached for the Orioles and managed at Rochester through 1980, and then managed the Giants from 1981 through August 1985, contending in 1981 and 1982 and finishing only two games out in 1982 despite having only a few talented players.

In 1986 Robinson returned to the Orioles as a coach. Early in 1988 he was installed as manager after Cal Ripken, Sr. had lost the first six games. The streak extended to a record 21 losses from the start of the season before the Orioles finally won. Robinson turned the club around in 1989, guiding the Orioles to first place at the All-Star break and second place at the end of the season; Baltimore wasn't eliminated until the final series of the season, against Toronto. When the Orioles faced the Blue Jays, managed by Cito Gaston, on June 27, 1989, it was the first ML game in history to feature a pair of black managers. /(MC)

Hank Robinson [Born John Henry Roberson](Rube) — 1889–1965. LHP 1911–15, 18 **Pirates**, Cardinals, Yankees 701 ip, 41–37, 2.53

Robinson was Pittsburgh's ace lefthander in 1912 and 1913, going 12–7 and 14–9. But his best work came in the Southern Association, where the Arkansas native had four 20-win seasons with Little Rock from 1916 to 1922. /(ME)

Humberto Robinson — 1930– . RHP 1955–56, 58–60 Braves, Indians, **Phillies** 213 ip, 8–13, 3.25

Although he was 110–58 as a starter in the minors, Robinson was used almost exclusively in relief in the ML. The slender Panamanian started only seven of his 102 ML appearances. He won two and saved another in 19 relief chances for the 1958 Braves' pennant-winners but, though eligible, was not used in the WS. /(MC)

Jackie Robinson — 1919–1972. 2B-3B-1B-OF 1947–56 **Dodgers** 1382 g, .311, 137 hr, 734 rbi. *6 WS, 38 g, .234, 2 hr, 12 rbi*
☛ *Rookie of the Year—47. Most Valuable Player—49. Led League—ba 49. All-Star—49–54. Hall of Fame—1962.*

The most historically significant baseball player ever, Jackie Robinson was the first black man to play in the majors in the 20th century, to win the MVP award, and to be elected to the Hall of Fame; was also the first Rookie of the Year and the first baseball player, black or white, on an American postage stamp. Babe Ruth changed baseball; Jackie Robinson changed America.

In the 1987 survey "Player's Choice," Robinson was called the greatest of his era at second base, where he set a club record for fielding average and teamed with Pee Wee Reese as one of the game's great double-play combinations, and was also named fifth best at third. Yet the 28-year-old rookie broke in at first base, because veteran Ed Stanky was at second.

Robinson's 37 steals in 1949 not only led the majors (he'd led the NL with 29 his rookie season), it was the highest in the NL in 19 years. He stole home 19 times in his career, the most since WWI, and in 1955 (at age 36) became one of only 12 to steal home in the World Series. In 1954 he was the first National Leaguer to steal his way around the

Jackie Robinson stealing home, catcher Johnny Pramesa (Cubs), umpire Art Guglielmo; on-deck batter Preacher Roe

bases in 26 years. Bobby Bragan called him "the best I ever saw at getting called safe after being caught in a rundown situation."

Among the first group of black players in the 1949 All-Star Game, Robinson hit .333 in the six in which he played. But the statistical records of the player Dodger general manager Branch Rickey considered the "most competitive" man he'd known since Ty Cobb only hint at his achievements. Reese called Robinson's integration of baseball "the most tremendous thing I've ever seen in sports."

Since 19th-century star Cap Anson refused to appear with black pitcher Harry Stovey, blacks had been informally barred from the majors. Near the end of WWII, Rickey assigned scouts to recruit for what he told them would be a Dodgers-owned Negro League team. He was really looking for the right ballplayer to break the color line. Clyde Sukeforth found Robinson playing shortstop for the Negro League Kansas City Monarchs.

In a meeting which has been portrayed and

described many times since, Rickey confronted Robinson with the wide range of abuse he knew Robinson would face. Robinson finally blew up, asking Rickey, "Do you want a player afraid to fight back?" Rickey replied that he wanted someone "with the guts not to fight back." Robinson promised a passive response and kept his word, not an easy task for a man who had faced an army court martial for refusing to move to the back of a bus.

Called the "Jim Thorpe of his race" for his multi-sport skills, Robinson was the first four-letter man at UCLA. When he averaged over 11 yards per rush as a football halfback as a junior, *Sports Weekly* called him "the greatest ball carrier on the gridiron today." One coach called Robinson "the best basketball player in the U.S." when he led the Pacific Coast Conference in scoring as a junior and senior. Yet he was not named to the first, second, or third all-conference teams. His brother Mack Robinson was the 1936 Olympic long-jump runner-up behind Jesse Owens, and Jackie won the 1940 NCAA long-jump title. He undoubtedly would have gone to the 1940 Olympics had the war not canceled them. He reached the semi-finals of the national Negro tennis tournament, won swimming championships at UCLA, and played professional football with the Honolulu Bears.

Robinson spent the 1946 season with Montreal, based on Rickey's reasonable belief that the racial confrontations would be less severe in Canada. The first black in the International League in 57 years, he led in batting and runs scored, and led the Royals to a pennant by 19–1/2 games and victory in the Little World Series. When jubilant fans chased him for three blocks after the last game, a black journalist wrote, "It was probably the only day in history that a black man ran from a white mob with love instead of lynching on its mind." Fans later erected a statue of him near the ballpark.

Entry into the majors in 1947 was much tougher. Dodgers manager Leo Durocher had to squelch plans for a players' petition against Robinson in a midnight spring-training meeting. Robinson was often forced to accept road accommodations separate from the rest of the team. The famous Dodgertown complex later erected was in part a response to the problems that Robinson and other blacks faced with spring-training racism. After the start of the season, the St. Louis Cardinals were rumored to be planning a strike in protest of Robinson. Phillies manager Ben Chapman baited him so cruelly that Robinson later said it "brought me nearer to cracking up than I had ever been." The Chapman episode galvanized Robinson's support group. Rickey said it "made Jackie a real member of the Dodgers." Public reaction against Chapman was so harsh that Phillies management asked Robinson to pose for a photo with him to clear Chapman's reputation.

Baseball's "Great Experiment" electrified America. Probably the only rookie given a day in his honor, Robinson trailed only Bing Crosby in a year-end national popularity poll. Virtually the entire black population of America became Dodger fans. He later starred in the movie *The Jackie Robinson Story*. He wrote several autobiographical works, had a weekly newspaper column and radio show, and after his death was the subject of a Broadway musical, "The First".

Robinson's agreement with Rickey only required silence for one full season. When he started to speak out, he became a major public figure. In 1949 he was summoned before the House Un-American Activities Committee to rebut Paul Robeson's con-

tention that American blacks would not fight against the Soviet Union because of racism at home. Ironically, Robeson had once addressed Commissioner Landis and the team owners on the need for integration in the majors. Robinson later felt apologetic about his being used against Robeson, and said, "I would reject such an invitation if offered now." Robinson later told a "Youth Wants to Know" audience that "the Yankee management is prejudiced." When Dodger owner Walter O'Malley announced Robinson's sale to the Giants, Jackie had already decided to retire, but not from public life. A supporter of Martin Luther King and the NAACP, he surprised even his wife, Rachel, by endorsing Richard Nixon for president in 1960 (a move later regretted) because he felt Kennedy had not made it "his business to know colored people."

In 1962 Robinson and Bob Feller were the first elected to the Hall of Fame in their first year of eligibility since Lou Gehrig in 1939.

Robinson's number 42 was retired at Dodger Stadium in 1972 a few months before 2,000 people packed Riverside Church to hear his eulogy delivered by the young Reverend Jesse Jackson. Tens of thousands lined the streets of Harlem and Bedford-Stuyvesant to watch the passage of his mile-long cortege. Joe Black spoke for all future black ballplayers. "When I look at my house . . . I say 'Thank God for Jackie Robinson.'" In 1987, during the 40th anniversary of Robinson's rookie season, major league baseball celebrated by naming the Rookie of the Year award for him. /(TG)

Jeff Robinson [Jeffrey Daniel] — 1960– . RHP 1984– **Giants**, Pirates 678 ip, 39–45, 3.80

San Francisco dealt this promising fastball/forkball reliever for veteran Rick Reuschel during the 1987 stretch drive. Robinson combined with stopper Jim Gott to give the Pirates an outstanding bullpen in 1988, but when Gott was injured on Opening Day 1989, Robinson failed to hold the stopper job by himself and was switched to starting before the end of the season. /(ME)

Jeff Robinson [Jeffrey Mark] — 1961– . RHP 1987– **Tigers** 377 ip, 26–17, 4.15. *1 LCS, 0.1 ip, 0–0, 0.00*

After an unspectacular rookie season, Robinson was 13–6, 2.98 for the Tigers by August 24, 1988 but spent the rest of the year on the DL. The 6'6" righthander shut out the Yankees 8–0 on August 7, 1987, retiring the last 24 batters in a row. /(SCL)

Neil Robinson — Unk.–Unk. OF-SS Negro Leagues 1936–50 Cincinnati Tigers, Homestead Grays, **Memphis Red Sox** statistics not available
☛ *All-Star—38–41, 43–45, 48.*

From 1938 to 1948 Robinson played in eight East-West Negro League all-star games, compiling a batting average of .476 with two home runs and an .810 slugging percentage—figures exceeded only by Hall of Famer Buck Leonard. He batted .376 in his rookie 1936 season with the Cincinnati Tigers. Yet most of his career was spent with the Memphis Red Sox, for whom he batted as high as .333 in 1948. He led the league in RBI in 1944. He was a capable fielder with an erratic arm. /(BP)

Ron Robinson — 1962– . RHP 1984– **Reds** 581 ip, 33–27, 3.60

Robinson was the Reds first round draft pick in the 1980 free-agent draft, and he reached the ML for good in 1985, winning seven games while splitting his time between the starting rotation and the bullpen. He was a reliever exclusively in 1986, making 70 appearances, but by 1988 had returned to the starting rotation, and on May 2, he was within one strike of a perfect game when Expos pinch hitter Wallace Johnson singled. Tim Raines then homered, and Robinson needed relief help. He missed half of 1989 with an elbow injury. /(SCL)

Wilbert Robinson (Uncle Robby) — 1863–1934. C 1886–1902 Philadelphia (AA), Brooklyn-Baltimore (AA), **Baltimore (NL)**, Cardinals, Baltimore (AL) 1374 g, .273, 18 hr, 622 rbi.
   Manager 1902, 1914–31 Baltimore (AL), **Dodgers** 1397–1395, .500. First place: 16, 20 *2 WS, 3–9, .250*
☛ *Hall of Fame—1945.*

The jovial Robinson came from New England and played baseball for a living as soon as he could sign on in the New England League. He became the catcher of the storied Baltimore Orioles, where he joined forces, under manager Ned Hanlon, with Willie Keeler, Hughie Jennings, and John McGraw, the scrappy third baseman who was the dominant force of the team. Robinson was the cornerstone of the team, its catcher, directing the play of the others. He was one of Baltimore's better hitters, once making seven hits in a game, and he was durable enough to catch a rare triple header in 1896 and a double header the next day.

Robinson became John McGraw's partner, off the field and on; the pair owned a billiards parlor in Baltimore. When McGraw took over the New York Giants, Robinson came along to run the pitching

Wilbert Robinson

staff. The men remained close friends until a sudden, bitter parting of the ways. Why they split is not known. Robinson became the Dodgers' manager in 1914 and left a larger than life imprint on the team, which was called the Robins during much of his 18-year managerial tenure. Yet, Uncle Robbie won more than a place in the hearts of players and fans. He won ball games, and twice won pennants (1916 and 1920) with teams not given a pre-season chance. He remained through 1931, running his club far differently than the despotic McGraw ran the Giants. The Dodgers were known for their easy-going ways. Because Robinson gave his roster of cast-offs and characters freedom, the team was a constant source of oddities and anecdotes. He had a gift for cadging winning performances from discarded pitchers, preferring hard throwers over curveball pitchers. Dazzy Vance, a fireballer who only achieved stardom after age thirty, was Robinson's ace during the 1920s after Robinson gave him more rest between starts than was the norm in those days. Robinson asked his pitchers to hold the other team in check until his own hitters could win the game. He looked to Babe Herman, Jake Daubert, Zach Wheat, Casey Stengel, Jack Fournier and other batters to get a key hit. This simple approach kept the team in contention for many years and made them always entertaining.

Robinson is perhaps best known for a spring training incident. He vowed to outdo Gabby Street's stunt of catching a ball dropped from the Washington Monument. He would catch a ball dropped from an airplane. The stunt was set up, but someone (many say it was Casey Stengel) substituted a grapefruit, which exploded on impact. With his eyes shut and his chest wringing wet, Robinson believed himself covered with his own blood until he heard his team laughing. /(JK)

Mickey Rocco — 1916– . 1B 1943–46 Indians 440 g, .258, 30 hr, 186 rbi

Cleveland's smooth-fielding first baseman led the AL with 653 at-bats in 1944. In a doubleheader sweep of the Yankees before a New York crowd of 72,000 in 1945, he hit two HR, two doubles, and two singles. /(NLM)

Andre Rodgers — 1934– . SS-1B-3B 1957–67 Giants, **Cubs**, Pirates 854 g, .249, 45 hr, 245 rbi

A talented Bahamian cricket player, Rodgers paid his own way to a Giants tryout in Florida in 1954. He had to learn the rules of baseball, and not to jump away from curveballs. A graceful 6'3", Rodgers adjusted. He became the Cubs' shortstop in 1962 as Ernie Banks moved to first. /(JCA)

Buck Rodgers [Robert Leroy] — 1938– . C 1961–69 **Angels** 932 g, .232, 31 hr, 288 rbi.
  Manager 1980–82, 85–Brewers, **Expos** 539–495, .521

Rodgers caught 155 games in 1962, breaking Mickey Cochrane's rookie record of 133, and finished second to Tom Tresh in AL Rookie of the Year voting. A switch-hitting starter for six years until beset by injuries in 1968, he was always considered a good handler of pitchers. Rodgers coached for the Twins and Giants, managed in the minors, and, while a Brewer coach, replaced the ailing George Bamberger as manager in 1980. He led Milwaukee to a second-half title in strike-torn 1981, but lost to the Yankees in a playoff and was fired in June of 1982. He became the Expos' manager in 1985 and was named NL Manager of the Year when Montreal finished third (91–71) in 1987. /(JCA)

Aurelio Rodriguez (Leo) — 1947– . 3B-SS-2B, 1967–83 Angels, **Tigers**, Padres, Yankees, White Sox, Orioles 2017 g, .237, 124 hr, 648 rbi. *4 LCS, 10 g, .091. 1 WS, 4 g, .417*
☛ *Gold Glove—76.*

In 1970, playing for California and Washington, Rodriguez had career highs of 19 HR and 83 RBI. He proved not to be that good a hitter, but he was a nimble third baseman with a powerful arm. He was a Tiger regular for almost a decade after Detroit obtained him in the 1970 deal that sent Denny McLain to the Senators. He led AL third basemen in fielding percentage in 1976 and 1978, winning a Gold Glove in 1976. /(JCA)

Ed Rodriguez — 1952– . RHP 1973–79 **Brewers**, Royals 734 ip, 42–36, 3.89

A consistent and versatile reliever and spot starter for six years in Milwaukee, the Puerto Rican went 7–0 (3.49) with seven saves in 1975, his top season. He recorded 32 lifetime ML saves. /(JCA)

Ellie Rodriguez — 1946– . C 1968–76 Yankees, Royals, **Brewers**, Angels, Dodgers 775 g, .245, 16 hr, 203 rbi
☛ *All-Star—69, 72.*

Born in Puerto Rico, Rodriguez grew up in the Bronx idolizing Yogi Berra but played just nine games with the Yankees. He was an agile catcher with a strong arm. With the Angels in 1974 he tied an AL record with 19 putouts in a nine-inning game and set another with 21 in an extra-inning game as Nolan Ryan struck out 19 each time. On June 1, 1975 he caught Ryan's fourth no-hitter. /(JCA)

Francisco Rodriguez — 1943– . SS 1964–84 Mexican League Star.

The elder brother of major leaguer Aurelio Rodriguez, Francisco spent 20 years as an everyday shortstop in the Mexican League. He established himself over eight seasons with Aguila and ten with Aguascaliente, compiling a lifetime batting average of .273. /(MC)

Rick Rodriguez — 1960– . RHP 1986– **A's**, Indians 74 ip, 3–4, 5.62

Rodriguez was the second-round June 1981 draft pick of his hometown A's. His progress was slowed by injuries; he was on the DL five times in 1982–84. Control problems have diminished his effectiveness. /(WOR)

Roberto Rodriguez — 1943– . RHP 1967, 70 A's, Padres, **Cubs** 112 ip, 4–3, 4.82

Signed as a catcher, after seeing his A's teammates pitch in his first minor league camp, the Venezuelan decided he could do better. He was converted to pitching at his request. A strikeout artist, Rodriguez had impressive spring trainings, but little luck in the majors. /(JCA)

Preacher Roe [Elwin Charles] — 1915– . LHP 1938, 44–54 Cardinals, Pirates, **Dodgers** 1914 ip, 127–84, 3.43. 20 wins: 51 *3 WS, 28 ip, 2–1, 2.54*
☛ *Led League—k 45. All-Star—49–52.*

Roe was *TSN* Pitcher of the Year in 1951 when he went 22–3 with Brooklyn for an .880 winning percentage—a record for NL pitchers with more than 20 wins. From 1951 through 1953, he went 44–8 for the Dodgers. The hillbilly raconteur said, "I got three pitches: my change; my change off my change; and my change off my change off my change." But after he retired, he sent the baseball world into a tizzy by admitting to having a fourth pitch in a 1955 *Sports Illustrated* article, "The Outlawed Spitball Was My Money Pitch."

Roe was the NL's strikeout leader in 1945, when he went 14–13 (2.87) for Pittsburgh. He suffered a fractured skull in a fight in '45 while coaching a basketball game and dropped to 3–8 and 4–15 before being traded to Brooklyn in December of 1947. In 1949, his record was 15–6; his .714 winning percentage was the league's best. He shut out the Yankees 1–0 for the Dodgers' only win in the '49 World Series. In the 1952 Series, he hurled a complete-game, 5–3 win over New York in Game Three. In his final WS showdown with the Yankees, Game Two in 1953, he gave up a tie-breaking, eighth-inning homer to Mickey Mantle to lose, 4–2. /(TG)

Ed Roebuck — 1931– . RHP 1955–58, 60–66 **Dodgers**, Senators, Phillies 791 ip, 52–31, 3.35. *2 WS, 6 ip, 0–0, 1.42*

A solid complement to Clem Labine in the Dodger bullpen, Roebuck missed all of 1959 with a shoulder injury, but returned to win eight and save eight in 1960, and he won ten with nine saves in 1962. On September 4, 1957, he struck out twice in the eighth inning. /(FK)

Gary Roenicke — 1954– . OF 1976, 78–88 Expos, **Orioles**, Yankees, Braves 1063 g, .247, 121 hr, 410 rbi. *2 LCS, 5 g, .444, 1 hr, 5 rbi. 2 WS, 9 g, .087*

Roenicke was the righthanded-hitting half of manager Earl Weaver's outstanding left field platoon in Baltimore from 1979 to 1985, alternating with John Lowenstein and often pinch hitting on days he didn't start. In 1982 Roenicke and Lowenstein combined for 45 HR and 140 RBI, and in '83 the duo hit 34 HR with 124 RBI, as the Orioles beat the Phillies in the WS. Roenicke was always content with his role as a semi-regular, and usually responded when called upon, topping 20 HR in a season twice (despite never reaching 400 at-bats) and providing solid defensive play in the outfield. In the 1983 LCS, he scored three times and hit a two-run HR as the Orioles beat Chicago 4–0 in Game Two. By 1986, however, the long-haired veteran role-player had been traded to the Yankees, and in 1987 he signed with the Braves, who released him outright in July 1988. His brother Ron was also a ML outfielder. /(SCL)

Wally Roettger — 1902–1951. OF 1927–34 Cardinals, Giants, **Reds**, Pirates 599 g, .285, 19 hr, 245 rbi. *1 WS, 3 g, .244*

Roettger hit .341 in part-time duty with the 1928 Cardinals, but only a soft .283 when handed a regular job for the Giants two years later. His older brother Oscar played briefly in the ML. /(FS)

Bullet Joe Rogan [Wilbur] — 1889–1967. RHP-OF-1B-3B-SS-MGR Negro Leagues 1920–30 Fred Palace's Colts, Kansas City Giants, **Kansas City Monarchs**, Los Angeles White Sox 494 g, .339, 47 hr; 1164 ip, 111–43 (inc.)

One of the Negro Leagues' most versatile players, Rogan attained mastery both on the pitcher's mound and at the plate. His career .721 winning percentage (111–43) is the highest recorded in Negro League history. In 11 seasons with the Kansas City Monarchs, he compiled a .339 batting average, 10th among all Negro Leaguers.

Rogan used a no-windup delivery and possessed a devastating fastball and an array of curveballs. He also threw a forkball, a palmball, and a legal spitter. Chet Brewer, another Monarch pitching great who played with Satchel Paige and Rogan, insisted that "Rogan should have been put in the Hall of Fame before Satchel. Rogan could throw a curveball faster than most pitchers could throw a fastball." Paige once said Rogan "was the onliest pitcher I ever saw,

I ever heard of . . . pitching and hitting in the clean-up place. He could throw as hard as Smokey Joe Williams." Hall of Famer Judy Johnson said, "Satchel Paige was fast, but Rogan was smart." Rogan was also regarded as the Negro Leagues' finest-fielding pitcher.

Rogan began as a catcher, but eventually played every position. He was a great low-ball and curveball hitter. He had thin but powerful legs and tremendously strong wrists, and would attack the ball with a smooth swing and a heavy bat. He helped the Kansas City, KS Giants to 54 consecutive wins in 1909 against semi-pro and local competition. In 1911 he began his pitching career with the 25th Infantry Wreckers army team. After nine years of army ball, he was discovered at age 30 by Casey Stengel, and referred to Monarchs owner J.L. Wilkinson.

As a Monarch in 1922, Rogan hit 13 home runs in 47 league games. He led the league with 16 victories and batted .411 in 1924. He then starred in the first Black World Series, against Hilldale. In the 10-game series, he went 2–1 (2.57) in four games, and played the outfield the other six, hitting .325. The following year he notched a league-high 14 wins to lead the Monarchs to another BWS. But a freak knee injury forced him to watch from the sidelines as his club lost the championship to Hilldale.

In 25 games against white major leaguers, Rogan batted .329. At the age of 48, he participated in his last such exhibition; playing left field against the Bob Feller All-Stars, he went 3-for-4 and stole a base. Dizzy Dean said, "Old Rogan was a showboat boy, a Pepper Martin-type ballplayer. He was one of those cute guys, never wanted to give you a good ball to hit." /(LL)

Billy Rogell — 1904– . SS-3B-2B 1925, 27–28, 30–40 Red Sox, **Tigers**, Cubs 1481 g, .267, 42 hr, 609 rbi. *2 WS, 13 g, .283, 5 rbi*

The keystone combo of Rogell and Charlie Gehringer was a key factor in the Tigers' 1934 and 1935 pennants. Switch-hitter Rogell had four RBI in Game Four of the 1934 WS as the Tigers won 10–4. He led AL shortstops in fielding for three years, 1935–37, and in assists for two, 1934–35. He injured his shoulder playing handball after the 1938 season; in 1939, his arm went dead. After the season, he was swapped to the Cubs for Dick Bartell, a trade accurately characterized as "one worn-out shortstop for another." /(NLM)

Steve Rogers — 1949– . RHP 1973–85 **Expos** 2839 ip, 158–152, 3.17. *1 LCS, 10 ip, 1–1, 1.80* ☛ *Led League—era 82. All-Star—74, 78–79, 82–83.*

The winningest pitcher in Expos history, Rogers cracked double figures in wins in 10 of his first 11 ML seasons and was an NL All-Star five times before arm problems ended his career. He was touted as the Expos guaranteed first 20-game winner after going 10–5 with a 1.54 ERA as a rookie in the second half of 1973, but became the club's first 20-game loser instead, finishing a disappointing 15–22 with a 4.46 ERA in his first full ML season. He was still named to the NL's mid-season All-Star team that year after only one full year in the ML, and although he never did win 20 games, for the next nine seasons the unimposing righthander posted only one ERA above 3.29.

Rogers led the NL in losses a second time in 1976, finishing 7–17 for a team that lost 107 games, then had winning records every year until 1984 as the Expos rose to prominence in the NL East. As the staff ace, he led the NL with five shutouts in 1979 and was 16–11 in 1980, then reached the playoffs for the only time in his career after winning 12 games in the strike-shortened 1981 season. In the special divisional playoff series, Rogers held the Phillies to one run in Game One and shut them out in the deciding Game Five to send the Expos to the LCS. There, Rogers beat the Dodgers 4–1 in Game Three, but lost Game Five in relief 2–1 when he surrendered a two-out ninth-inning home run to Rick Monday.

Rogers rebounded in 1982 to lead the NL in ERA (2.40) while winning a career-high 19 games, and was 17–12 in 1983, only to see his career crippled by arm woes the following year. Rogers was only 6–15 in 1984, and logged a 5.68 ERA in eight appearances in 1985 before retiring. /(SCL)

Tom Rogers (Shotgun) — 1895–1936. RHP 1917–19, 21 **Browns**, A's, Yankees 414 ip, 15–30, 3.95. *1 WS, 1 ip, 0–0, 6.75*

Rogers had most of his success in the Southern Association, where he played a role in two unforgettable occurrences in 1916. On June 11, he pitched a perfect game for Nashville against Chattanooga. Eleven days later, he hit former major league infielder John Dodge in the face with a pitch, and Dodge died the next day. /(JK)

Clint Rogge — 1889–1969. RHP 1915, 21 **Pittsburgh (FL)**, Reds 290 ip, 18–14, 2.73

In his first college game, Rogge struck out four batters in one inning, as his catcher couldn't hold his sharp curve and live fastball. All but six of his ML games were pitched in the 1915 Federal League. His 17–12, 2.55 record helped the Pittsburgh Rebels move from next-to-last in 1914 to third in 1915, just a half-game out of first. /(NLM)

Garry Roggenburk — 1940– . LHP 1963, 65–66, 68–69 **Twins**, Red Sox, Pilots 126 ip, 6–9, 3.64

Plagued by elbow problems throughout his career, the 6'6" sidearmer was 2–4 (2.16) in 1963, his only full ML season. He later was the GM of Boston's Winter Haven farm club and became a Red Sox minor league pitching coach in 1983. /(JCA)

Saul Rogovin — 1922– . RHP 1949–53, 55–57 Tigers, **White Sox**, Orioles, Phillies 883 ip, 48–48, 4.06
☛ *Led League—era 51.*

The sleepy-eyed Rogovin got a late start as a ML pitcher. He began as a third baseman and then was bothered by a sore arm. Traded to the White Sox early in 1951, he went 12–8 and led the AL in ERA after manager Paul Richards made a few corrections in his delivery to get him to throw straight overhand. Rogovin, who was reported to sometimes fall asleep on the bench, compiled a 14–9 record the next season. On September 14, 1952 he pitched perhaps his best game, striking out 14 Red Sox in 16 innings before he was relieved. /(RL)

George Rohe — 1875–1957. 3B-2BSS 1901, 05–07 Baltimore (AL), **White Sox** 267 g, .227, 3 hr, 92 rbi. *1 WS, 6 g, .333, 4 rbi*

Rohe was an unheralded utility infielder until he became the underdog White Sox' hero in the 1906 World Series. When shortstop George Davis was injured on the eve of the Series, Rohe was pressed into service at third base, with Lee Tannehill moving to short. Rohe had seven hits in the Series. In Game One, he tripled and scored in a 2–1 White Sox victory, and in Game Three, his bases-loaded triple drove in all three Sox runs as Ed Walsh shut out the Cubs. After the game, owner Charles Comiskey proclaimed, "Whatever George Rohe may do from now on, he's signed for life with me!" Rohe played regularly in 1907, hit .213, and was released at the end of the season. /(RL)

Billy Rohr — 1945– . LHP 1967–68 **Red Sox**, Indians 61 ip, 3–3, 5.64

Starting against Hall of Famer Whitey Ford, Rohr made his ML debut with the Red Sox on Opening Day at Yankee Stadium, April 14, 1967, and was one strike away from a no-hitter when Elston Howard drilled a clean single to right-centerfield. The slender, 21-year-old lefthander retired the next batter for a shutout, then beat the Yankees again in his next start, 6–1, but would win only one more game in the ML after that. /(SCL)

Cookie Rojas [Octavio Rivas] — 1939– . 2B-OF-3B 1962–77 Reds, Phillies, Cardinals, **Royals** 1822 g, .263, 54 hr, 593 rbi. *2 LCS, 5 g, .308, 1 rbi.*
Manager 1988 **Angels** 75–82, .478
☛ *All-Star—65, 71–74.*

The studious-looking, Cuban-born Rojas was selected in 1969 as the Phillies' greatest second baseman ever. The popular five-time All-Star played all 10 positions during his career, pitching one scoreless inning in 1967, and DHing in the AL. He played 70 games in the outfield for the famed 1964 great-collapse Phillies. In 1968 he led NL second basemen with a .987 fielding percentage, and in 1973 he helped set a Royal record 192 double plays. In his most productive year at the plate, the slightly-built Rojas drove in 69 runs and scored 78 in 1973. He replaced Angels manager Gene Mauch in spring training of 1988 when Mauch resigned due to ill health, but Rojas was fired in September. /(JCA)

Minnie Rojas — 1938– . RHP 1966–68 **Angels** 261 ip, 23–16, 3.00

The AL's 1967 Fireman of the Year, the Cuban-born Rojas was 12–9 with a league-leading 27 saves. He was felled by a sore arm the next season, and his career ended tragically in 1970 when he was paralyzed (and his two young daughters killed) in a car accident. /(JCA)

Stan Rojek — 1919– . SS 1942, 46–52 Dodgers, **Pirates**, Cardinals, Browns 522 g, .266, 4 hr, 122 rbi

Rojek came up in 1942 but then lost the next three seasons to military service. Stuck behind Pee Wee Reese in Brooklyn, he was sold to Pittsburgh for 1948 and was their everyday shortstop for two years, leading the league in at-bats and NL shortstops in assists in 1948 and reaching career highs in BA (.290), steals (24, third in the league), HR (4), RBI (51), runs (85), and doubles (27). He dropped to .244 in 1949 and was never again a regular. /(JFC)

Jim Roland — 1942- . LHP 1962-64, 65-72 **Twins**, A's, Yankees, Rangers 449 ip, 19-17, 3.22

As a wild, flamethrowing 19-year-old, this Minnesota bonus baby threw a shutout in his first major league start. Mostly a long reliever, he was 5-1 (2.19) for Oakland in 1969, his most successful season. /(JCA)

Red Rolfe [Robert Abial] — 1908-1969. 3B-SS 1931, 34-42 **Yankees** 1175 g, .289, 69 hr, 497 rbi. *6 WS, 28 g, .284, 6 rbi.*
   Manager 1949-52 **Tigers** 278-256, .521
☛ *All-Star—37-40.*

Rolfe was a capable leadoff man and reliable third baseman for some of the best Yankee teams. During his seven years as a regular, they won six pennants and five World Championships. Although he suffered from painful stomach ulcers, he hit .300 or better four times, with a career-high .329 in 1939 when he led the AL in hits (213), doubles (46), and runs scored (139). He scored at least 100 runs every year he was a regular. Twice he led AL third basemen in fielding. A Dartmouth graduate, he served as Yale baseball coach after leaving the Yankees. From 1949 to mid-1952 he managed the Tigers, bringing them in second in 1950. /(JK)

Rich Rollins — 1938- . 3B 1961-70 **Twins**, Pilots/Brewers, Indians 1002 g, .269, 77 hr, 399 rbi. *1 WS, 3 g, .000*
☛ *All-Star—62.*

The stocky redhead broke in with a strong rookie season in 1962 (.298, 16 HR, 96 RBI), receiving the most All-Star votes of any AL player and starting both All-Star Games that year. He worked hard to become an adequate third baseman and helped the Twins contend in the 1960s. After hitting .307 in 1963, his average declined for a ML-record seven consecutive years. /(JCA)

Ron Romanick — 1960- . RHP 1984-86 **Angels** 531 ip, 31-29, 4.24

Romanick was drafted by the Blue Jays in 1979 and the Padres in 1980 but did not sign, then was selected by the Angels in 1981. He won 12 games as a rookie starter in 1984 and was 14-9 in 1985, but a 5.50 ERA in 18 starts in 1986 ended his ML career. /(SCL)

Johnny Romano (Honey) — 1934- . C 1958-67 White Sox, **Indians**, Cardinals 905 g, .255, 129 hr, 417 rbi. *1 WS, 2 g, .000*
☛ *All-Star—61-62.*

A slugging, 5'11" catcher, Romano tended to be overweight, so he was buried in the White Sox system, where he set a Three-I League record with 38 homers at Waterloo in 1955. He went 8-for-13 as a pinch hitter in 1959, when he and Earl Battey backed up Sherm Lollar on Chicago's AL championship team. He became the Indians' regular catcher in 1960 and was an All-Star in 1961 and 1962, when he hit 21 and 25 HR. He fractured a hand in 1963, and it bothered him for several years. Romano was reacquired by the White Sox in 1965 in a three-team deal that also brought them Tommy John and Tommie Agee. /(JCA)

Ed Romero — 1957- . SS-2B-3B 1977, 80- **Brewers**, Red Sox 698 g, .248, 8 hr, 151 rbi. *2 LCS, 2 g, .000. 1 WS, 3 g, .000*

Romero was a handyman who could play any infield position, but never hit well enough to play regularly. The native Puerto Rican hit .317 in 145 at-bats with the Brewers in 1983, but never hit over .280 in any other major or minor league season. /(SCL)

Kevin Romine — 1961- . OF 1985- **Red Sox** 217 g, .255, 2 hr, 34 rbi. *1 LCS, 2 g, --*

Romine did not make an error in his first three major league trials (68 games). The backup outfielder filled in while the injured Dwight Evans DHed in the first half of 1989, and Romine hit better than ever before. /(JFC)

Ed Rommel — 1897-1970. RHP 1920-32 **A's** 2556 ip, 171-119, 3.54. 20 wins: 22, 25 *2 WS, 2 ip, 1-0, 9.00.*
   Umpire AL 1938-59 6 ASU 2 WS
☛ *Led League—w 22, 25.*

The father of the modern knuckleball, Rommel used it to win 19 games as a starter and another 8 in relief for the 1922 Athletics to lead the AL with 27 wins. He led the league in victories again in 1925 with a 21-10 mark for the A's. He led the AL in relief wins in three different seasons. When the Athletics scored 10 runs in the seventh inning of Game Four of the 1929 WS to overcome an 8-0 Cubs lead, Rommel got the win in relief. In his final season on July 10, 1932, the Athletics defeated the Indians 18-17 in an 18-inning marathon. Rommel pitched 17 innings of relief and earned the win despite giving up 29 hits, 8 walks, and 14 runs. He served 22 years as an AL umpire. One of his more unusual calls came in a 1957 game. Boston had Dick Gernert on third with one out and Gene Mauch at bat. Mauch grounded to the first baseman who stepped on first and threw home. Mauch threw up his hands and deflected the ball. Rommel declared both Mauch and Gernert out for Mauch's interference. /(RTM)

Enrique Romo — 1947– . RHP 1977–82 Mariners, **Pirates** 603 ip, 44–33, 3.45. *1 LCS, 1/3 ip, 0–0, 0.00. 1 WS, 5 ip, 0–0, 3.86*

The bearded, fierce-looking reliever pitched 11 outstanding seasons in Mexico before signing with Seattle. Using a large repertoire of pitches, including a sharp-breaking screwball, he notched 52 career saves. /(JCA)

Vincente Romo — 1943– . RHP 1968–74, 82 Dodgers, Indians, Red Sox, White Sox, **Padres** 645 ip, 32–33, 3.36

After leading Cleveland relievers with 12 saves (1.63) as a 1968 rookie, Romo was traded to Boston the next year and finished that season with 11 saves. In 1973 he became the Padres' first Mexican-born player in 1973. He returned to Mexico, where he pitched for eight years before reappearing in the majors with the Dodgers in 1982. He went 1–2 with a save, giving him career totals of 33 losses and 52 saves, exactly the same as his brother Enrique. /(JCA)

John Romonosky — 1929– . RHP 1953, 58–59 Cardinals, **Senators** 101 ip, 3–4, 5.15

Romonosky had control problems and had a 2–4, 6.51 record in his most active season, 1958, with the pitching-poor Senators. /(WOR)

Phil Roof — 1941– . C 1961, 1964–77 Braves, Angels, Indians, A's, Brewers, **Twins**, White Sox, Blue Jays 857 g, .215, 43 hr, 210 rbi

A journeyman catcher, Roof was highly respected for his defensive abilities and handling of young pitchers, but was weak at the plate. His .302 mark for 63 games in 1975 was a full 67 points higher than his previous best. The bowlegged Kentuckian played a career-high 127 games for the 1966 A's. Five Roof brothers played pro ball; brother Gene was an outfielder with the Cardinals and Expos for parts of 1981–83. Phil became a Mariner coach in 1983. /(JCA)

Jim Rooker — 1941– . LHP 1968–80 Tigers, Royals, **Pirates** 1811 ip, 103–109, 3.46. *2 LCS, 11 ip, 0–1, 4.91. 1 WS, 8 ip, 0–0, 1.04*

Known for his willingness to speak his mind during his playing days, Rooker later became a Pirates radio and TV broadcaster. The red-haired left-hander was acquired by Pittsburgh in 1973 from

Kansas City, where he was the first Royal to hit two home runs in a game. He twice won 15 for the Pirates and had three other seasons with double-digit wins. In 1979, he was near the end, with only four victories in 19 appearances. But, in the WS, with the Pirates trailing Baltimore three games to one, he held the Orioles to three hits and one run in five innings of Game Five. Bert Blyleven relieved and held the Orioles scoreless the rest of the way and the Pirates rallied to win. They won the next two games and the Series. /(EW)

Rookie of the Year Award — 1947– .

The Rookie of the Year Award has a chaotic history. Arising from a Chicago BBWAA chapter award begun in 1940, it went national in 1947, officially named the J. Louis Comiskey Memorial Award after the former White Sox executive who was the son of Hall of Famer Charles Comiskey. The first winner was Jackie Robinson; during the fortieth-anniversary celebration of his career in 1987, the award was renamed the Jackie Robinson Award. It has been presented to the top rookie in each league since 1949, after being given to only one player in both 1947 and 1948.

It took ten years before "rookie" was officially defined, and the definition would change twice; in 1989 it stands as a player who has not, in previous seasons, had 130 at-bats, 50 innings pitched, or 45 days on a major league roster. The voting structure has also changed several times; it currently consists of two writers for each team voting for three players each with votes weighted 5–3–1. /(SFS)

Roosevelt Stadium Brooklyn Dodgers 1956–1957. LF-330, CF-411, RF-330

The Dodgers played 15 games at Roosevelt Stadium, located in Jersey City, New Jersey, to dramatize their need for a new ballpark if they were to remain in Brooklyn. A WPA project completed in 1937, it housed the Giants' International League club, and more Giants fans than Dodger fans turned out for the Dodgers "home" games. On August 15, 1956 Willie Mays hit the only home run ever hit completely out of the stadium, to give the Giants a 1–0 win. /(SCL)

Charlie Root (Chinski) — 1899–1970. RHP 1923, 26–41 Browns, **Cubs** 3198 ip, 201–160, 3.58. 20 wins: 27 *4 WS, 22 ip, 0–3, 6.75* ☛ *Led League—w 27.*

A durable, top-flight pitcher for the Cubs for 16 seasons, Root had at least 10 wins in ten different seasons, with a top mark of 26–15 in 1927. In 1969 he was named the all-time Cubs righthander. Yet he was dogged during his later years by the tale that Babe Ruth "called his shot" when he homered off Root in the 1932 WS. The leathery, tobacco-squirting Root denied the claim, stating he'd have decked Ruth with a fastball had the Babe really gestured that he'd hit the next pitch out of the park. "He was just saying he had one strike left," Root insisted. /(JK)

Buddy Rosar [Warren Vincent] — 1914–1979. C
1939–51 **Yankees**, Indians, **A's**, Red Sox 988 g, .261,
18 hr, 367 rbi. *2 WS, 2 g, 1.000*
☛ *All-Star—42–43, 46–48.*

Rosar was a fine defensive catcher who played behind the Yankees' Bill Dickey for four years. Although he appeared in two World Series for the Yankees, he batted only once, producing a pinch-hit single in 1942. Traded to Cleveland after the 1942 season, he became an All-Star. In 1946 with the A's, he set the record for errorless games by a catcher, fielding 1.000 in 117 games. The next year he extended his perfect play to 147 games, second only to Yogi Berra's 148-game streak. /(JK)

Pete Rose (Charlie Hustle) — 1941– . 2B-OF-3B-1B
1963–86 **Reds**, Phillies, Expos 3,562 g, .303, 160 hr,
1,314 rbi. *7 LCS, 28 g, .381, 3 hr, 11 rbi. 6 WS, 34, .269,
2 hr, 9 rbi.*
   *Manager 1984–89 **Reds** 426–388, .523*
☛ *Rookie of the Year—63. Led League—ba 68–69, 73.
All-Star—65, 67–71, 73–82, 85. Gold Glove—69–70.*

Pete Rose is the career leader in hits (4,256), singles (3,215), at-bats (14,053) and games played (3,562). He is second all-time in doubles, fourth in runs, and collected at least 100 hits in his first 23 seasons, a record. He had more than 200 hits in a season 10 times, also a record, led the league in hits in seven seasons, and is the most prolific switch-hitter in history. He is the only player to play 500 games at five different positions and was named the Player of the Decade for the 1970s by *TSN*. He revived the head-first slide and popularized running to first base on a walk after seeing Enos Slaughter do it. Because of his seemingly boundless enthusiasm, he was nicknamed "Charlie Hustle" by Whitey Ford. Rose once said that he'd "walk through hell in a gasoline suit to keep playing baseball." He has also been endlessly compared to Ty Cobb, including allegations of betting on his own team, an accusation Cobb faced in the final years of his career. Rose's statistical standing in major league history is ensured, but his reputation and eventual election to the

Pete Rose

Hall of Fame is in serious doubt following his lifetime suspension by Commissioner Giamatti in 1989.

   Born and raised in Cincinnati, the brash, crewcut rookie broke into the Reds' starting lineup in 1963 and was named Rookie of the Year. In the top of the ninth in a scoreless game in the new Astrodome on April 23, 1964, Rose reached first on an error and scored on another error to make Houston rookie Ken Johnson the only pitcher to lose a complete game no-hitter. But Rose slumped late in 1964, was benched, and finished with just a .269 average. He came back in 1965 to lead the league in hits (209) and at-bats (670), and hit .312, the first of 15 consecutive .300 seasons. He hit a career-high 16 homers in 1966, then moved from second base to the right field the following year. In 1968, he started the season with a 22-game hit streak, missed three weeks, including the All-Star game, with a broken thumb, then had a 19-game hit streak late in the season. He had to finish the season 6-for-9 to beat out Matty Alou and win the first of two close NL batting-title races. In 1969, Rose and Roberto Clemente were tied for the batting title going into the final game. Rose bunted for a base hit in his last at-bat of the season to beat out Clemente. Rose's hustle won the All-Star Game in 1970 for the NL, and may have spoiled the career of Oakland catcher Ray Fosse, Rose's dinner companion the night before the game in Cincinnati. In the 12th inning, Rose led off with a single and went to second on a single by the Dodgers' Bill Grabarkewitz. The Cubs' Jim Hickman then singled sharply to center. Amos Otis' throw beat Rose to the plate, but Rose barreled over Fosse, separating the catcher's shoulder, to score the winning run. Rose sparked the The Big Red Machine to a sweep of the LCS against Pittsburgh that year. He drove in a run to snap a scoreless tie in the 10th inning in the first game, then singled during the eighth inning rally that produced the winning run in the third game.

In 1972, Rose, now in left field, again led the league in hits and at-bats, hit .450 in the LCS against Pittsbugh, but managed only a .214 average in the seven-game loss to Oakland in the World Series. Rose enjoyed his best-ever season in 1973. He won his third and final batting title with a .338 average, collected a career-high 230 hits and was named the NL MVP. The Reds, however, lost the LCS to the upstart Mets, despite Rose's eighth-inning homer to tie Game One and his 12th-inning homer to win Game Four. The Mets were spurred on by Rose's fight with diminutive Met shortstop Bud Harrelson in Game Three, which prompted a bench-clearing brawl. Rose slumped badly in 1974, hitting only .284, although he did lead the league in runs scored with 110. In 1975, Rose was moved to third base to make room for rookie outfielder Ken Griffey, and led the Reds to the first of two straight World Series victories. Rose was named the 1975 World Series MVP on the strength of 10 hits and a .370 average. The Reds swept the Yankees in the 1976 Series, despite only a .188 average for Rose. In 1978, Rose mounted the last serious threat to Joe DiMaggio's 56-game hit streak. Rose hit safely in 44 straight games, the most by a NL player in the 20th century. On May 5, he became the youngest player ever to reach 3,000 hits. After the season, Rose became a free agent and, after a fierce bidding war, signed with the Phillies. Installed at first base, his fifth position in the majors, he hit .331. The next season, despite only a .282 regular-season average,

he helped the Phillies win their first-ever World Championship. With one out in the ninth inning of the sixth and final game of the World Series, the Phillies were leading 4–1 with Tug McGraw on the mound, but the bases were full of Royals. Frank White's foul pop bounced out of catcher Bob Boone's glove, but Rose grabbed it in the air to prevent a possible tragedy.

In the strike-shortened 1981 season, Rose led the league in hits and had his last .300 season, batting .325. Now 40 years old, it was clear his career was winding down, but the question of whether he could catch Cobb and the all-time hit record of 4,192 kept his name in the news. The night after the strike ended on August 10, he passed Musial as the NL all-time hit leader. He hit just .271 in 1982, but collected 172 more hits. In 1983, the last year of his contract with the Phillies, he hit just .245. Rose, Joe Morgan, and Tony Perez, aging remnants of the Big Red Machine teams, helped the Phillies to the World Series, losing to the Orioles in five games. It was clear that the Phillies were moving toward youth, and the question was, who would want a forty-two-year-old player? The Expos, needing some help at the gate, signed him, and on April 13, a day before his forty-third birthday, he collected his 4,000th hit. But he wasn't hitting consistently, and was benched in July. On August 16, he was traded back to his hometown Reds, was named player-manager, and responded by batting .365 the rest of the season. In 1985 the city named a street near the ballpark after him as the Cobb hoopla built. On September 11 in Cincinnati, batting lefthanded, he hit a line single to left off the Padres' Eric Show for hit number 4,193 to pass Cobb. In order to reach Cobb, Rose collected more than 1,000 hits after the age of 38. He guided the Reds to a second-place finish in the NL West that year, and again in 1986, his last year as an active player. Cincinnati finished second again in 1987, and for the fourth time in a row in 1988. During the 1988 season, Rose got into a shoving match with umpire Dave Pallone, and was suspended for 30 days. Early in 1989, his job in jeopardy because of consistent second-place finishes, Rose was accused of being in massive debt to gamblers and of betting on his own team. He resorted to months of legal stratagems, challenging the Commissioner's authority, until finally agreeing on August 24 to a deal in which he dropped his suit against baseball and accepted the lifetime suspension. In return, there were no official findings announced. By that time, testimony and documents from a federal case involving one of his bookmakers had revealed everything anyway, but Rose obdurately denied that he had done anything deserving censure. /(SEW)

Johnny Roseboro — 1933- . C 1957-70 **Dodgers**, Twins, Senators 1585 g, .249, 104 hr, 548 rbi. *1 LCS, 2g, .200. 4 WS, 21 g, .157, 1 hr, 7 rbi*
☛ *All-Star—58, 61-62, 69. Gold Glove—61, 66.*

When Juan Marichal hit Roseboro over the head with a bat in August 1965, Roseboro went down in history as the center of one of baseball's biggest brawls. Marichal claimed that Roseboro had ticked his ear with the ball (Marichal was at bat) while throwing it back to the pitcher

Roseboro caught two of Sandy Koufax's no-hitters and ranks in the top 25 all-time in games caught. Not including his first and last seasons, the durable receiver caught more than 100 games every year but 1960. Helped by Los Angeles's high-strikeout pitching staff, he set ML records for putouts in 1959 and 1961. Roseboro led NL catchers six times in total chances per game (five straight seasons, 1958–62), four times in putouts, and twice in double plays, and also led AL catchers in double plays in 1969 as he contributed to the Twins' divisional title. Adequate with the bat, the left-handed batter hit as high as .287 in 1964 and hit as many as 18 HR in 1961, although he was never in double figures in HR after the Dodgers moved to Dodger Stadium. He won Game One of the 1963 World Series with a three-run homer off Whitey Ford and won Game Three of the 1965 WS with a two-run single off Camilio Pascual. Early in his career he had good speed for a catcher, stealing as many as 12 bases (in 15 attempts) in 1962 and averaging more than six triples a year in his first six full seasons (1958–63). /(SFS)

Dave Rosello — 1950- . 2B-SS-3B 1972-77, 79-81 **Cubs**, Indians 422 g, .236, 10 hr, 76 rbi

Born in Puerto Rico, Rosello was the American Association's all-star shortstop three times, but in the majors was limited to utility work, backing up Don Kessinger and Glenn Beckert. He saw his most action with the Cubs in 1976, when he appeared in 91 games. /(JCA)

Al Rosen (Flip) — 1924- . 3B-1B 1947-56 Indians 1044 g, .285, 192 hr, 717 rbi. *2 WS, 4 g, .231*
☛ *Most Valuable Player—53. Led League—hr 50, 53. Led League—rbi 52, 53. All-Star—52-55.*

Flip got his nickname as a quick-wristed softball pitcher on Miami's sandlots. A tough guy and amateur boxer, Rosen had his nose broken eleven times. Determined, exuberant, and prematurely gray, Rosen came up in 1947, but his glove work was so bad that he posed no immediate threat to slick-fielding Indian third baseman Ken Keltner. But in 1950, his first full season, he led the AL with 37 homers (a league record for rookies at the time), and he honed his fielding skills sufficiently to lead the AL in assists. In 1953, with his shirt sleeves cut to show his bulging biceps, Rosen led the AL in homers (43) and RBI (145), but lost the batting title to Mickey Vernon on the last day of the season. He was the unanimous choice for AL MVP.

In the 1954 All-Star Game, played in Cleveland, Rosen cracked two consecutive home runs. Nagging injuries—including whiplash suffered in an auto accident—and booing from Cleveland fans caused Rosen to quit at age 32 to sell stocks and bonds. He reentered baseball 20 years later as president of the Yankees, then the Astros, and then president and general manager of the Giants. His maneuvering brought San Francisco from last place in 1985 to the NL West title in 1987. /(JCA)

Goody Rosen [Goodwin George] — 1912- . OF 1937-39, 44-46 **Dodgers**, Giants 551 g, .291, 22 hr, 197 rbi

As the Dodgers' right fielder in 1938, Rosen led NL outfielders in fielding and assists. The lefthanded Canadian batted .325 (third in the league) and scored 126 runs (second) in 1945 in a .300-hitting outfield with Luis Olmo and Dixie Walker. Sold to the Giants, in mid-1946 he crashed into a fence and sustained a career-ending clavicle injury. He was inducted into the Canadian Baseball Hall of Fame. /(JJM)

Larry Rosenthal — 1912- . OF 1936-41, 44-45 **White Sox**, Indians, Yankees, A's 579 g, .263, 22 hr, 189 rbi

The injury-plagued Rosenthal became a favorite in Chicago for some timely hitting when he first arrived. In 1937 his nine pinch hits were an AL high. /(EW)

Buck Ross [Lee Ravon] — 1915-1978. RHP 1936-45 **A's**, White Sox 1365 ip, 56-95, 4.94

Always battling control problems, Ross had a good fastball and excellent changeup. Ross's only winning season came with the 1943 White Sox, when he went 11-7. /(EW)

Chet Ross — 1917- . OF 1939-44 **Braves** 413 g, .241, 34 hr, 170 rbi

Ross's first full season (1940) was his only as a regular. He led the NL with 127 strikeouts, but batted .281 with 17 HR. A Braves extra after that, he was rated as a fine outfielder, but hit poorly. /(EW)

Don Ross — 1914- . 3B-OF-SS 1938, 40, 42-46 **Tigers**, Dodgers, Indians 498 g, .262, 12 hr, 162 rbi

Ross was a utility man and valuable pinch hitter, except for 1945 when, acquired from Detroit by the Indians, he was their regular third baseman. /(EW)

Gary Ross — 1947- . RHP 1968-77 Cubs, **Padres**, Angels 712 ip, 25-47, 3.93

Ross was a long reliever in his seven NL seasons, averaging one save a year. He had a 2.45 ERA in 60 appearances for the 1972 Padres. Made a starter by California in 1976, he recorded a 3.00 ERA but finished 8-16, thanks to the Angels' .235 batting average. /(JCA)

Claude Rossman — 1881-1928. 1B-OF 1904, 06-09 Indians, **Tigers**, Browns 511 g, .283, 3 hr, 238 rbi. *2 WS, 10 g, .308, 5 rbi*

Rossman was the first baseman for Tiger pennant-winners in 1907 and 1908, adept at laying down a bunt so that Ty Cobb could streak from first to third. However, a peculiar emotional quirk shortened his career: he couldn't throw the ball when he became excited. Runners would lead off first to draw a throw from the pitcher, then run to second when Rossman froze. /(JK)

Braggo Roth [Robert Frank] (The Globetrotter) — 1892-1936. OF-3B 1914-21 White Sox, **Indians**, A's, Red Sox, Senators, Yankees 811 g, .284, 30 hr, 422 rbi
☛ *Led League—hr 15.*

Often traded, Roth played with six different AL teams in eight seasons and earned an alternative nickname: The Globetrotter. Braggo had little cause for immodesty, other than that his seven home runs won the 1915 AL title; no AL batter ever led with fewer. His older brother Frank was a ML catcher for six seasons. /(JK)

Philip Roth — 1933- . *Writer.*

The noted American novelist grew up in Newark as a fan of the Bears' outstanding Triple-A teams of the 1930s. In 1973, he wrote *The Great American Novel*, a satire about a team of 50-year-olds trotted out of retirement during WWII who lose their stadium and play all their games on the road. /(NLM)

Jack Rothrock — 1905-1980. OF-SS-2B 1925-32, 34-37 **Red Sox**, White Sox, Cardinals, Phillies 1014 g, .276, 28 hr, 327 rbi. *1 WS, 7 g, .233, 6 rbi*

A sometimes brilliant all-around player with little power but good speed, with the Red Sox in 1928 Rothrock performed at all nine positions. He led the victorious Cardinals with six RBI in the 1934 WS. /(EW)

Rotisserie League Baseball — 1980- .

Rotisserie leagues are games where a group of players each "draft" a team drawn from major league rosters before the season starts and then trade, sign, call up, and cut the players just like general managers in the major leagues. Points are awarded to Rotisserie League teams based on their players' current ML statistics. The concept in its current form was begun in January 1980 by a small group of New York City authors, editors, and other professionals, at a Manhattan restaurant called La Rotisserie Francaise (thus the name Rotisserie League). Among the original owners who have since spread the Rotisserie gospel are Dan Okrent and Glen Waggoner.

The players' performance in various statistical categories is added up for each team and ranked at the end of the season to determine standings. Variations on the original idea have resulted in similarly structured leagues referred to as "fantasy baseball" and "statistical baseball" to differentiate them from the stricter rules and more traditional statistical categories of the original. The game grew in popularity throughout the 1980s, bringing prosperity to companies designed to bring together owners and calculate standings. The growth even had an influence on *USA Today*'s weekly major league statistical summary. /(JFC)

Edd Roush — 1893-1988. OF 1913-29, 31 White Sox, Indianapolis (FL), Newark (FL), Giants, **Reds** 1967 g, .323, 68 hr, 981 rbi. *1 WS, 8 g, .214, 7 rbi*
☛ *Led League—ba 17, 19.*

Roush was the National League's most feared hitter in the dead-ball era, batting more than .300 11 straight years, and capturing the batting title in 1917 and 1919. He was also the highest-paid outfielder of his day. Contemporaries called him hardworking, classy, game, and stubborn. As a baserunner, he thought nothing of going out of his way to spike an

Edd Roush

infielder. He hated spring training, was always in shape, and frequently held out—once for a whole year (1930).

Born lefthanded, Roush learned to throw with his right arm when lefthanded gloves were scarce. He broke in as a shortstop with Evansville (Kitty League) in 1912. A shoulder injury weakened his right arm, and he went back to throwing lefthanded, moving to the outfield. After a brief stint with the White Sox in 1913, making $100 a month, he jumped to the Federal League and earned $2,000 for the season with Indianapolis. In 1915 Newark (FL) paid him $4,000. Then the league folded. The better players were put into a pool and sold, the Giants buying Roush for $10,000. After batting .188 through 39 games in 1916, he was traded to the Reds with Christy Mathewson and Bill McKechnie for Buck Herzog and Wade Killefer.

Roush quickly became the NL's premier centerfielder, relying as much on brains as speed. He studied his team's pitchers and opposing hitters, and knew where to move for every pitch. In the thick of the 1919 pennant race, Reds left fielder Sherry Magee was sidelined for a few weeks, with no backup outfielder to replace him. Roush suggested that manager Pat Moran put strong-hitting pitcher Rube Bressler in left. "Greasy Neale (the rightfielder) and I can carry the load," Roush said, "and I'll move Bressler and tell him where to play." At the end of two weeks Bressler told him, "There's nothing to this outfielding. We're right in front of every line drive. What I can't understand is why we have to move around so much."

Though he beat out Rogers Hornsby for the NL batting crown by hitting .341 in 1917 and .321 in 1919, it was in 1921 that Roush reached his career high of .352. He batted .351 in 1923, topping the league with 41 doubles, and in 1924 led with 21 triples. He had 27-game hitting streaks in both 1920 and 1924. In ten full seasons with Cincinnati, the lowest he batted was .323, in 1926. The following February, he was sent to the Giants for George Kelly, and was given a three-year contract at $22,500 a year.

Roush developed an iconoclastic view of Giants manager John McGraw. "McGraw expected every player to be perfectionist. He had his men so scared they couldn't follow his many orders." In 1928 Roush tore stomach muscles diving for a line drive, and in 1929 his legs began to go. As a result, the Giants cut him to $15,000 in 1930, and added this clause: if the 1928 abdominal injury returned, there would be a further cut in salary. He refused to sign the contract, and sat out the year. The next spring, he was sold back to the Reds, with whom he played his last season.

Throughout his career, Roush used the heaviest bats in the game, weighing from 46 to 48 ounces. The bats were not long, but had incredibly thick handles, giving them the appearance of being all barrel. With them he could hit to all fields, bunt, drag, and hit-and-run. He is reputed to have slapped seven hits in one season on pitchouts, including a triple./(NLM)

Jack Rowan — 1887–1966. RHP 1906, 08–14 Tigers, **Reds**, Phillies, Reds 671 ip, 31–40, 3.07

Rowan was in Cincinnati's rotation for two seasons; in 1910, he went 14–13 with four shutouts and a

2.93 ERA in his only winning season. He was traded to the Phillies in February 1911 and was reacquired by the Reds that August. /(NLM)

Jack Rowe — 1857–1911. SS-C-OF 1879–90 **Buffalo (NL)**, Detroit (NL), Pirates, Buffalo (PL) 1044 g, .286, 28 hr, 645 rbi.
Manager 1890 **Buffalo (PL)** 36–96, .273

The Detroit Wolverines purchased the entire Buffalo club for $7,000 in August 1885 to acquire Rowe, Dan Brouthers, Hardy Richardson, and Deacon White, known as the Big Four. The deal brought the previously weak franchise a pennant in 1887 and Rowe scored a career-high 135 runs. Primarily a catcher for his first six seasons (he led NL catchers in fielding in 1884), Rowe began playing shortstop regularly in 1885. He hardly ever struck out (177 times in 12 seasons and 4,386 at-bats), and went the entire 1882 season without fanning once, playing in 75 of his team's 84 games.

Rowe and White bought the International League's Buffalo franchise after the 1888 season, planning to co-manage the team and play, but Detroit sold them to Pittsburgh, whose owner threatened to have them blacklisted if they played on their new team. Rowe and White held out well into the 1889 season, but capitulated on the advice of Brotherhood of Ballplayers leader Monte Ward, who filled them in on the upcoming players' revolt. They jumped to the Players' League in 1890, becoming part-owners of the Buffalo franchise. Rowe managed; the club finished in last place, but he led the league's shortstops in fielding. Managing the Buffalo franchise in the Eastern League later on, he was the basis of manager Delaney in Zane Grey's story "The Redheaded Outfield," inspired when Grey's brother R.C. played under Rowe in 1897 in a real redheaded outfield. /(JFC)

Schoolboy Rowe [Lynwood] — 1910–1961. RHP 1933–43, 46–49 **Tigers**, Dodgers, Phillies 2219 ip, 158–101, 3.87. *3 WS, 46 ip, 2–5, 3.91*

"How'm I doin', Edna?" asked Rowe of his wife during a 1934 radio interview. He was ribbed unmercifully for the ingenuous question, but Edna and everyone else had to admit he was doing very well. Schoolboy, a name he picked up as a teenaged sandlotter, was one of the top AL righthanders of the Depression years. In his career year, the rugged, broad-shouldered Arkansan compiled a 24–8 mark to lead the Tigers to the '34 pennant. Sixteen of his wins were consecutive to tie the AL record. He followed with two 19-win seasons before chronic arm trouble forced him temporarily back to the minors. He bounced back to lead the AL in winning percentage in 1940 with a 16–3 record, as the Tigers won another pennant.

Waived to the NL in 1942, Rowe pitched briefly for the Dodgers before embarking on a productive five-year stint with the Phillies. A career .263 hitter, he was often used as a pinch hitter, and led the NL in pinch hits and appearances in 1943, going 15-for-49. /(JL)

Bama Rowell [Carvel William] — 1916– . 2B-OF 1939–41, 46–48 **Braves**, Phillies 574 g, .275, 19 hr, 217 rbi

Rowell, an Alabaman, hit .305 as a rookie for the 1940 Braves. He made three errors at second base in one inning in 1941, a year in which he led ML second basemen with 40 miscues. /(JK)

Pants Rowland [Clarence] — 1879–1969.
Manager 1915–18 **White Sox** 339–247, .578. *1 WS, 4–2, .667.*
Umpire AL 1923–27

Rowland had a varied baseball career. Beginning as a reserve catcher in the minors, he became a manager and team owner in the minors before becoming White Sox manager in 1915. Although he won the AL pennant and WS in 1917, he was let go after the 1918 season. He later served as an AL umpire for five seasons and president of the Pacific Coast League, and became executive vice-president of the Cubs in 1954. /(NLM)

Rosey Rowswell [Albert Kennedy] — Unk.–1955.
Broadcaster.

One of the first broadcasters to enthusiastically and unabashedly cheer on the air, Rowswell was a long-time Pirates fanatic who was given their broadcasting job in 1936 and remained the club's radio voice until his death in 1955. Always called Rosey, he was physically frail—barely 110 lb—but his creativity and untempered exuberance brightened the broadcasts of even the most dismal Pirates teams. Away from the microphone he authored four books of poetry and aphorisms, but in the booth his energies were focused on his beloved "Buccos." A Pirates extra-base hit was a "doozie marooney," a strikeout was a "dipsy-doodle," and the bases were never "loaded," they were "FOB" (full of Bucs). His most famous trademark, however, was his outrageous home run call, "Raise the window, Aunt Minnie!" followed by his partner dropping a tray filled with nuts and bolts onto the floor, simulating the sound of broken glass. /(SCL)

Royals Stadium Kansas City Royals 1973– . LF-330, CF-410, RF-330

A rare modern stadium that retains much of the charm and beauty of classic ballparks, Royals Stadium was built exclusively for baseball in 1973 and has excellent sight lines, with all 40,762 seats facing home plate. Like most modern parks, it has symmetrical fences and artificial turf, but it also includes numerous features that distinguish it from the typically uniform multi-purpose facilities. Royals Stadium has a very small foul territory, and the seating area barely extends beyond the foul poles, leaving room behind the outfield fences for 322 feet of colorfully lighted waterfalls and fountains. Behind the water display stand two grassy inclines onto which longer home runs fall, and in dead center stands a 12-story scoreboard in the shape of the Royals' home plate and crown logo. Royals Stadium is part of Kansas City's Harry S. Truman sports complex, and is adjacent to Arrowhead Stadium, home of the NFL's Kansas City Chiefs. /(SCL)

Jerry Royster — 1952– . 3B-2B-SS-OF 1973–88 Dodgers, **Braves**, Padres, White Sox, Yankees 1428, .249, 40 hr, 352 rbi. *1 LCS, 3 g, .182*

In 1975 Royster was named Pacific Coast League Player of the Year with a .333 batting average, 91 runs scored, and 33 stolen bases, but he never hit nearly as well in the majors. He saw his most action in 1979, playing 80 games at third base and 77 at second base for the Braves, and hit .273 with career highs of 103 runs, 51 RBI, 25 doubles, and 35 stolen bases. He spent most of his career as a useful utility man. /(CP)

Dave Rozema — 1956– . RHP 1977–86 **Tigers**, Rangers 1106 ip, 60–53, 3.47

After leading the Southern Association with a 1.57 ERA at Montgomery in 1976, Rozema was *TSN* AL Rookie Pitcher of the Year with the Tigers in 1977, going 15–7 with a 3.10 ERA. The 15 wins would be a career high for the slender finesse pitcher, as he found himself working mostly in long relief by 1980. Rozema missed most of 1982 after tearing cartilage and ligaments in his left knee in a fight with the Twins' John Castino, and he didn't pitch in the 1984 postseason for the Tigers. /(SCL)

Dave Rucker — 1957– . LHP 1981–88 Tigers, **Cardinals**, Phillies, Pirates 320 ip, 16–20, 3.94

The sidearmer depended on a moving fastball but often had trouble with location with runners on base. Rucker posted a 2.21 ERA over two seasons and 84 appearances for the Cardinals. /(FO)

Johnny Rucker (The Crabapple Comet) — 1917–1985. OF 1940–41, 43–46 **Giants** 705 g, .272, 21 hr, 214 rbi

Johnny, like his uncle, Dodger pitcher Nap Rucker, came from Crabapple, Georgia. A graceful left-handed hitter, as a rookie Johnny was *Life*'s cover boy for an issue reporting on spring-training prospects. He led the NL in at-bats in 1941. /(JK)

Nap Rucker — 1884–1970. LHP 1907–16 **Dodgers** 2375 ip, 134–134, 2.42. 20 wins: 11 *1 WS, 2 ip, 0–0, 0.00*

In the years prior to WWI, the Brooklyn Dodgers fielded teams in which little civic pride could be taken. However, when the redheaded Nap Rucker took the mound the fans could be sure of a chance to cheer, particularly when he faced the rival New York Giants. He spent barely ten seasons in the big leagues, all with the Dodgers, and failed to provide Hall of Fame statistics, but there were many who insisted he was the best of his time. In Brooklyn, if nowhere else, his memory is revered by those who know of his heroic efforts for a futile ball club. /(JK)

Joe Rudi — 1946– . OF-1B 1967–82 **A's**, Angels, Red Sox 1547 g, .264, 179 hr, 810 rbi. *5 LCS, 19 g, .214, 1 hr, 6 rbi. 3 WS, 19 g, .300, 2 hr, 9 rbi* ☛ *All-Star—72, 74–75. Gold Glove—74–76.*

Rudi was an underrated superstar for the mighty A's of the early 1970s, overshadowed on his own team with better stats and more dynamic personalities. Oakland won three consecutive World Series (1972–74) with a lineup that featured Reggie Jackson, Sal Bando, and pitchers Catfish Hunter, Vida Blue, and Rollie Fingers. But nobody was more important to the A's overall success than Rudi. He was an excellent defensive player, a smart hitter, and a good baserunner. His arm was strong and accurate, and he was outstanding in the clutch. In Game Two of the 1972 WS against Cincinnati, Rudi homered, then saved the 2–1 win with a spectacular ninth-inning catch. And in Game Seven against the Dodgers in 1974, his seventh-inning homer broke a 2–2 tie, and Oakland held on to win 3–2.

Rudi broke into the ML with the Kansas City Athletics in 1967, but never hit better than .189 while playing infrequently in his first three seasons. He came into his own in 1970, hitting .309 in 350 at-bats, and for the next six seasons he would be a mainstay in the Oakland lineup, often playing first base or DH. He led the AL in hits and triples in 1972, and in doubles in 1974.

When owner Charlie Finley began to break up the A's in the mid-1970s, he tried to sell Rudi and Fingers to the Red Sox, but Commissioner Bowie Kuhn voided the deal. Rudi then signed with the Angels as a free agent after the 1976 season, but was hampered by injuries for most of his four seasons with California. He finally made it to Boston in 1981, arriving in the trade for Fred Lynn, but he hit only .180 in limited playing time and closed out his career with Oakland again in 1982. /(SCL)

Dick Rudolph (Baldy) — 1887-1949. RHP 1910-11, 13-20, 22-23, 27 Giants, **Braves** 2049 ip, 122-108, 2.66. 20 wins: 14, 15 *1 WS, 18 ip, 2-0, 0.50*
☛ *Led League—w 14.*

With Bill James and Lefty Tyler, spitballer Dick Rudolph rotated in a trio that pitched the 1914 Braves from last place on July 4 to the pennant. Rudolph paced the staff with 27 wins (tying him for the NL lead with Grover Alexander) and added two more in the World Series as the Braves swept the Athletics in four games. Rudolph was one of those allowed to continue using the spitter after 1919, though he was never successful again. After baseball, Rudolph became a mortician. /(JK)

Don Rudolph — 1931-1968. LHP 1957-59, 62-64 White Sox, Reds, Indians, **Senators** 450 ip, 18-32, 4.00

After several ML failures, Rudolph led the Pacific Coast League with an 18-9 record and won another chance at age 31. He was 8-10 (3.62) for the 1962 Senators, but fell to 7-19 (4.55) the following year. /(MC)

Ken Rudolph — 1946- . C 1969-77 **Cubs**, Giants, Cardinals, Orioles 328 g, .213, 6 hr, 64 rbi

Rudolph was a career second-string catcher who didn't stick in the majors until his fourth trial with the Cubs. He backed up Randy Hundley in Chicago and Ted Simmons in St. Louis, in between which he batted a career-high .259 with the 1974 Giants. /(ARA)

Joe Rue — 1897-1984. *Umpire* AL 1938-47 *1 ASU 1 WS*

Perhaps the high point of Rue's ten-year AL career came on July 13, 1943, at Shibe Park, Philadelphia when he was one of the umpires who worked the first night All-Star Game, a contest broadcast via shortwave radio to American servicemen throughout the world. /(RTM)

Muddy Ruel [Herold Dominic] — 1896-1963. C 1915, 17-34 Browns, Yankees, Red Sox, **Senators**, Tigers, White Sox 1461 g, .275, 4 hr, 532 rbi. *2 WS, 14 g, .200, 1 rbi.*
Manager 1947 **Browns** 59-95, .383

Muddy Ruel picked up his nickname as a boy, improvising a messy game using a mud ball. He became one of baseball's most diversified participants, ranging from star catcher to assistant to Commissioner Happy Chandler. He had a law degree from Washington University, and was admitted to practice before the U.S. Supreme Court.

Small but durable, the 5'9" 150-lb Ruel caught over 1,400 games and was a steady clutch hitter. Ruel platooned with Truck Hannah in New York, became an everyday catcher with the Red Sox in 1921, and was Washington's first-stringer from 1923 to 1928. Batting over .300 three times, his high was .316 in 1923. Ruel led AL catchers in putouts, assists, double plays, and fielding three times each.

In the 1924 World Series, he helped Walter Johnson to his first Series victory; in the twelfth inning of the final game, Ruel hit a foul pop, which Giants' catcher Hank Gowdy, stumbling over his mask, dropped. Given a second chance, Ruel doubled, and scored the winning run.

Ruel was the Tigers GM before joining Chandler's staff, and field manager of the 1947 Browns after leaving it. Ruel's most painful baseball memory came as a young Yankee catcher in 1920. He watched in horror as Ray Chapman froze while Carl Mays's submarine pitch hurtled toward his head. The thud of the ball and the struggle of the doomed player to regain his feet haunted Ruel. He said Mays was blameless, and believed Chapman lost sight of the pitch. /(JK)

Dutch Ruether [Walter Henry] — 1893-1970. LHP 1917-27 Cubs, Reds, **Dodgers**, Senators, Yankees 2123 ip, 137-95, 3.50. 20 wins: 22 *2 WS, 18 ip, 1-1, 3.93*

Though Ruether had a reputation as a trouble-maker, in 1919 his .760 winning percentage (19-6) for the Reds was the NL's best. The lefthander beat the Black Sox in Game One of the 1919 WS. One of the better-hitting pitchers in the game (.258, 7 HR, 111 RBI), Ruether ranks fifth all-time in pinch hits by a pitcher (34).

He went 13-6 as the fourth starter on the great 1927 Yankee club. He should have learned a lesson from Wally Pipp's experience with Lou Gehrig. One day Ruether was too ill to pitch, and lost his job to George Pipgras. /(EW)

Bruce Ruffin — 1963– . LHP 1986- **Phillies** 621 ip, 32–38, 3.94

Ruffin teamed with Roger Clemens, Greg Swindell, and Calvin Schiraldi to help the University of Texas win the 1983 NCAA baseball championship. He had a splendid rookie season in 1986, going 9–4, 2.46 after a mid-season promotion from AA Reading. Control problems (80 walks in 144.1 innings in 1988) have hindered him since. /(SG)

Red Ruffing [Charles Herbert] — 1904–1986. RHP 1924–42, 45–47 Red Sox, **Yankees** 4344 ip, 273–225, 3.80. 20 wins: 36–39 *7 WS, 85 ip, 7–2, 2.63*
☛ *Led League—w 38. Led League—k 32. All-Star—38–42. Hall of Fame—1967.*

Ruffing's career was made by a change of scenery. He joined the Red Sox at age 19, and from 1924 through May 1930, toiled for consistently last-place Boston clubs, compiling an unimpressive 39–96 record. The righthander led the AL in losses in both 1928 (25) and 1929 (22), as his team was always last in batting and averaged a meager 35 HR annually.

Yankee manager Miller Huggins was interested in him, seeing his strength, foreseeing durability and effectiveness, and knowing that Yankee power could give Ruffing the support he deserved. In 1930, Boston ownership, badly in need of money, sold Ruffing to New York for backup outfielder Cedric Durst and $50,000.

Ruffing went 15–5 for the Yankees that first year, though his ERA remained high. In the 15 seasons that followed, the Yankees won seven pennants and six World Series, averaging .276 with 146 homers a year. Ruffing contributed a 231–124 record and had four straight 20-win seasons, coinciding with four Yankee championships, from 1936–39. He threw 42 of his 48 career shutouts for New York. In 1938 his 21 wins topped the AL, as did his .750 (21–7) winning percentage and four shutouts.

In World Series competition, he was 7–2, tying him for second place in wins behind Whitey Ford.

Ruffing was also one of the best-hitting pitchers of all time, with lifetime marks of .269 (10th among pitchers with 500 at-bats), 36 HR (3rd), 273 RBI, and 58 hits in 228 pinch-hitting appearances. He batted over .300 eight times, his .364 (40-for-110) in 1930 standing as the second-best single-season average for a pitcher (Walter Johnson hit .433 in 1925).

The determined Ruffing accomplished what he did despite having lost four toes on his left foot in a mine accident as a youngster. The injury cut down on his speed, and the pain, he said, never ceased.

Red Ruffing

He spent three years in the army in WWII, but lasted for only three injury-plagued seasons upon his return. After retiring at age 43, he managed in the minors, scouted, and in 1962 became the Mets' first pitching coach. He was admitted to the Hall of Fame in 1967 by the BBWAA in his last year of eligibility. /(EC)

Vern Ruhle — 1951– . RHP 1974–86 Tigers, **Astros**, Indians, Angels 1411 ip, 67–88, 3.73. *2 LCS, 8 ip, 0–0, 4.70*

Ruhle had by far his best season as the Astros' number-four starter in 1980, when the team won its first division title. He went 12–4 with a 2.38 ERA and was the center of a controversial play in his Game Four LCS start. With two runners on in the fourth inning, Ruhle fielded a soft liner off the bat of Garry Maddox and threw to first base for the double play. However, Philadelphia players raced out of the dugout to argue that Ruhle had trapped the ball. During the argument, first baseman Art Howe stepped on second base and claimed a triple play.

After 20 minutes, it was ruled a catch, but the triple play, "completed" after time had been called, was disallowed. Ruhle had a no-decision as the Astros lost in the tenth inning.

Houston won the second half of the strike-split 1981 season, and in Game Four of the divisional playoff Ruhle matched Dodger ace Fernando Valenzuela with a four-hitter but lost 2–1. /(WOR)

Chico Ruiz [Hiraldo Sablon] — 1938–72. 2B-3B-SS 1964–71 **Reds**, Angels 565 g, .240, 2 hr, 69 rbi

One of the few utility men to appear on the cover of a national magazine, Ruiz had his career cut short when he was killed in an automobile crash at the age of 33. This "Cuban swifty" pulled a gun on Alex Johnson in the California Angels' clubhouse in 1971. /(KC)

Ed Rumill — Unk.–Unk. *Writer.*

Rumill was a baseball writer and columnist for *The Christian Science Monitor* for 40 years until he retired in 1972. /(NLM)

Ed Runge — 1918– . *Umpire* AL 1954–70 *4 ASU 3 WS*

An AL umpire for 17 years, Runge won the Cardinals' Tim McCarver's respect in the 1967 WS: "Most umps won't publicly reveal their [strike zones]. But . . . [he] was fair-minded enough to tip me on how he preferred to see them. When I came to bat, Ed said to me, 'I don't know if you know my strike zone; it's a wide plate.' I stored away the knowledge not only for batting purposes, but to guide my own pitchers." Runge threw out the ceremonial first ball to begin Game Two of the 1984 WS, a game in which his son Paul, a NL ump, worked third base. /(RTM)

Paul Runge — 1958– . 3B-2B-SS 1981–88 **Braves** 183 g, .232, 4 hr, 26 rbi

This utility man spent only two whole seasons in the majors, 1985 and 1988. He never had more than 90 at-bats and was used mainly for defense. /(SFS)

Pete Runnels [born James Edward Runnells] — 1928– . 1B-2B-SS 1951–64 **Senators**, Red Sox, Astros 1799 g, .291, 49 hr, 630 rbi.
      Manager 1966 **Red Sox** 8–8, .500
☛ *Led League—ba 60, 62 . All-Star—59–60, 62.*

Runnels, with his line-drive swing, was the American League batting champion with Boston in 1960 (.320) and '62 (.326). A true sportsman and gentleman, he once said, "I enjoyed (Ted) Williams's

1958 catching me (for the batting crown) on the final day more than the later titles of 1960 and 1962 because of the great competition. Wasn't he capable!" Quite capable himself, and versatile, Runnels was first a Washington shortstop, but ultimately played 644 games at first base, 642 at second base, and 463 at shortstop. A graceful fielder, he led the AL in fielding at second base in 1960 and at first base in 1961. He was consistent at the plate in the years 1958–62, hitting over .300 each year, varying only 12 points. In 1966 Runnels managed the Red Sox for 16 games. /(EC)

Damon Runyon — 1884–1946. *Writer.*

Best known for the movies and plays based on his short stories about Broadway characters and sporting types, Runyon began his newspaper career in Denver in 1901. After a brief stop in San Francisco, he joined the New York *American*, covering the Giants from 1911 to 1920. A fun-loving man with a sense of humor, he seldom smiled or laughed openly. He considered himself an observer, not a judge, and never indulged in bitter or destructive reporting. An immaculate dresser who sported a porkpie hat, he was at one time a heavy drinker, but gave it up and stuck to coffee most of the time when he socialized with other writers. In 1920 he left the baseball beat to write a syndicated column and short stories. One collection, *Take It Easy*, was published in 1939. He also published a volume of poetry. For a while he owned a string of racehorses and a stable of fighters. An operation for throat cancer in 1944 left him speechless, but he continued writing his syndicated column until his death. Connie Mack called him "a master of characters and plots such as we see every day in our grandstands." /(NLM)

Jake Ruppert (Colonel) — 1867–1939. *Executive.*

A colonel in the seventh regiment of the National Guard, Ruppert was a member of the New York social register and a lifelong bachelor. He went to work in the family brewery at 19 and was elected to four terms in Congress beginning in 1898. He became president of the brewery in 1915. At the suggestion of John McGraw, Ruppert and Tillinghast Huston, an engineer who had made a fortune in Cuba, bought the Yankees in 1914 for $450,000. When Ruppert hired Miller Huggins as manager in 1917 against Huston's wishes (Huston was in Europe), a rift developed between the partners.

The hiring of Huggins, the acquisition of Babe Ruth in 1919, and the selection of Ed Barrow as general manager in 1920 were the most important moves in turning the Yankees into a powerhouse. Ruppert let Huggins and Barrow handle the day-to-day affairs of the club, although he designed the Yankees' famous pinstripe uniform (in hopes it would make the bulky Ruth look slimmer). Yankee Stadium was opened in 1923 at a cost of $2.5 million. Shortly thereafter, Ruppert bought out Huston for $1.2 million.

With the Yankees dominating the AL in the late 1930s, Ruppert answered proposals that the team should be broken up: "I found out a long time ago there is no charity in baseball. Every club owner must make his own fight for existence. I went into baseball purely for the fun of it. I had no idea I would spend so much money . . . the only return I ever sought was to make ends meet." /(NLM)

Bob Rush — 1925– . RHP 1948–60 **Cubs**, Braves, White Sox 2410 ip, 127–152, 3.65. *1 WS, 0–1, 3.00* ☛ *All-Star—52.*

Rush, who delivered with a long, high-kicked windup, was a talented pitcher with the second-division Cubs for his first ten seasons. The 1952 team was the only .500 Cub team on which he played. He went 17–13 (2.70) in '52, including a seven-game win streak with three shutouts, and was the winning hurler in that year's All-Star Game. There were four other seasons in which he won 13 games, though his 20 losses in 1950 led the NL. Traded to the Braves in 1958, Rush helped them to the pennant with a 10–6 record. /(ARA)

Amos Rusie (The Hoosier Thunderbolt) — RHP 1889–95, 97–98, 1901 Indianapolis (NL), **Giants**, Reds 3770 ip, 243–160, 3.07. 20 wins: 90–95, 97–98 ☛ *Led League—w 94. Led League—era 94, 97. Led League—k 90–91, 93–95. Hall of Fame—1977.*

They called the big farmer from Indiana "The Hoosier Cannonball," and he personified sheer power pitching in the 1890s. Amos Rusie was the principal reason the pitcher's mound was moved back from 50′ to the present 60′6″ in 1893.

Rusie had a crackling curveball and a change of pace, hit well, and played outfield on an occasional day off from the mound. He came to the New York Giants, after a season with his hometown Indianapolis team, to fill a gap created by the defection of several Giants to the Players' League. When the rebellion of the star players ended after a single season, Rusie was well established. In their absence he had led the league with 36 wins and in winning percentage and strikeouts.

In 1895 one of the most oppressive men to own a

Amos Rusie with the Giants

big league team, Andrew Freedman, bought the Giants and began to feud with Rusie. Fined that year for missing curfews when he insisted he wasn't out of his room, Rusie demanded his money be restored as part of his 1896 contract. Freedman refused and Rusie stayed home, missing the entire season. He sued the Giants for $5,000 in lost salary and damages and challenged the reserve clause. Freedman refused to knuckle under, but the other owners feared the legal challenge and raised the sum Rusie demanded. He was happy to have had an idle summer and make several thousand dollars more than he would have had he pitched.

When Rusie reported in 1897, Freedman refused to let him suit up and forbade manager Bill Joyce to use him. But when the team lost a string of games and the fans rebelled, Freedman allowed Rusie back in the lineup, and he went 28–10. The next season, with the league's basestealing champion, Bill Lange, on first, Rusie picked him off with a sudden throw.

He tore muscles in his shoulder and had to rest for five weeks. He returned, apparently restored. However, when he tried to pitch in 1898, he found he couldn't and retired. To clear Christy Mathewson, then a prospect, from a claim by the Cincinnati Reds, the Giants swapped the still-contracted Rusie for Matty. Rusie tried a comeback but failed; Mathewson went on to win 373 games.

John McGraw brought Rusie back to the Polo Grounds in the 1920s to work eight years as superintendent of the ballpark. /(JK)

Allan Russell — 1893–1972. RHP 1915–25 **Yankees**, Red Sox, Senators 1393 ip, 71–77, 3.52. *1 WS, 3 ip, 0–0, 3.00*

A spitballer legally allowed to use the pitch after its banning, Russell was primarily a reliever. He led the AL with five saves for the Yankees and Red Sox in 1919 and with nine for the Senators in 1923. His brother, Lefty Russell, pitched in 13 games for the A's (1910–12). /(EW)

Bill Russell — 1948– . SS-OF-2B 1969–86 **Dodgers** 2181 g, .263, 46 hr, 627 rbi. *5 LCS, 21 g, .337, 8 rbi. 4 WS, 23 g, .263, 8 rbi*
☛ *All-Star—73.*

A prep basketball star, Russell was signed to a baseball contract out of a Kansas high school too small to field a baseball team. He played in the outfield his first two years with the Dodgers, and manager Walt Alston considered him an even better outfielder than Willie Davis. But Alston needed a shortstop to replace Maury Wills in 1972, and Russell was chosen. After a rough start, leading NL shortstops in errors in 1972, he was named to the 1973 All-Star team. He teamed with Steve Garvey, Davey Lopes, and Ron Cey for over eight years, baseball's longest-lasting infield. Only Zack Wheat had more games and seasons as a Dodger than Russell. A finger injury made his throws erratic in later days, and he retired after 1986 to become a Dodger coach. /(TG)

Jack Russell — 1905– . RHP 1926–40 **Red Sox**, Indians, Senators, Tigers, Cubs, Cardinals 2050 ip, 85–141, 4.47. *2 WS, 12 ip, 0–1, 0.75*
☛ *All-Star—34.*

Russell was a loser as a starting pitcher, compiling a 41–91 record with the Red Sox from 1926 through 1932. Made a reliever when he joined Washington in 1933, he responded by leading the AL with 13 saves and 11 relief wins. In the final game of the 1933 World Series, he pitched 4–2/3 scoreless

innings before Mel Ott homered off him in the tenth to win it for the Giants. Russell's 54 appearances and seven relief victories were league highs in 1934, as he became the first reliever named to the AL All-Star squad. After retiring, he settled in Clearwater, Florida, and became City Commissioner. He helped put through the construction of a new spring training stadium, named after him, for the Phillies. /(NLM)

Jeff Russell — 1961– . RHP 1983– Reds, **Rangers** 753 ip, 39–48, 4.02
☛ *All-Star—88–89.*

Acquired from the Reds in the Buddy Bell deal, Russell pitched almost exclusively in relief for the Rangers in 1986–87, but made the starting rotation in May 1988 and after an 8–2, 3.16 first half was the only Ranger selected to the AL All-Star team. He pitched one scoreless inning in the All-Star Game, but slumped in the second half of the season and finished 10–9. Russell debuted in the ML as a starter for the Reds (his hometown club), and in 1985 led the NL with 18 losses. /(SCL)

Jim Russell — 1918–1987. OF 1942–51 **Pirates**, Braves, Dodgers 1034 g, .267, 67 hr, 428 rbi

A fine-fielding, regular Pirate outfielder from 1943 to 1947, Russell hit a career-high .312 in 1944. In a 1945 game, he had a home run disallowed when a baserunning teammate called time to tie a shoelace, and the pitcher, not hearing, delivered. /(EW)

John Russell — 1961– . C-OF 1984– **Phillies**, Braves 333 g, .223, 31 hr, 115 rbi

Russell made the Phillies in 1984 as a 23-year-old outfielder with impressive power (27 HR at Portland the year before), but never got his batting average high enough to stay in the lineup. He began catching in 1986 and hit .241 with 13 HR and 60 RBI, but the arrival of Lance Parrish in 1987 curtailed his playing time. /(SG)

Reb Russell [Ewell Albert] — 1889–1973. LHP-OF 1913–19, 22–23 **White Sox**, Pirates 417 g, .268, 21 hr, 172 rbi; 1291 ip, 81–59, 2.34. 20 wins: 13 *1 WS, 0 ip, 0–0, infinite*

As a rookie sensation with the White Sox in 1913, Russell was 22–16 (1.91). Although he never matched those figures, he was 18–11 in 1916 and led the AL in winning percentage (.750) with a 15–5 mark for the World Champion Sox of 1917. Released with a dead arm early in 1919, he returned to the ML as an outfielder with Pittsburgh in 1922, hitting .368 with 12 home runs and 75 RBI in only 60 games. /(RL)

Rip Russell [Glen David] — 1915–1976. 1B-3B 1939–42, 46–47 **Cubs**, Red Sox 425 g, .245, 29 hr, 192 rbi. *1 WS, 2 g, 1.000*

As the Cubs' rookie first baseman in 1939, Russell batted .273 with 79 RBI. Injuries marred his next two seasons, but in 1942 he led the NL with 31 pinch-hitting appearances. In 1946–47 he was a part-time third baseman for the Red Sox. /(ARA)

Marius Russo (Lefty) — 1914– . LHP 1939–43, 46 **Yankees** 680 ip, 45–34, 3.13. *2 WS, 18 ip, 2–0, 0.50*

Russo twice won 14 for the Yankees, but was particularly effective in the World Series. In Game Three of 1941, he matched elderly Dodger Freddie Fitzsimmons through seven scoreless innings. In the eighth, Russo's line drive hit Fitzsimmons in the knee, causing him to limp off the diamond, and the Yankees scored two runs to win 2–1. In 1943 Russo held the Cardinals to one unearned run in Game Four, then doubled and scored the winning run. /(JK)

Babe Ruth [George Herman] — 1895–1948. OF-LHP 1914–35 Red Sox, **Yankees**, Braves 2503 g, .342, 714 hr, 2204 rbi; 1221 ip, 94–46, 2.28. 20 wins: 16–17 *10 WS, 41 g, .326, 15 hr, 33 rbi; 2, 31 ip, 3–0, 0.87*
☛ *Led League—ba 24. Led League—hr 18–21, 23–24, 26–31. Led League—rbi 19–21, 23, 26, 28. Led League—era 16. All-Star—33–34. Hall of Fame—1936.*

Widely considered to be the best player of all time, Ruth was the prototype of the modern superstar. He was the first player to hit 30, 40, 50, and 60 home runs in a season, and his slugging style forever changed the way baseball was played.

Although it was his unprecedented hitting that would make him a charter member of the Hall of Fame, the barrel-chested, spindle-legged Ruth began his career as a pitcher with the minor league Baltimore Orioles (International League) before being sold to the Red Sox. With Boston, he became one of the game's best pitchers, posting 29 consecutive scoreless innings in World Series play, a record that stood for 42 years. He led the AL with a 1.75 ERA and nine shutouts in 1916, going 23–12 for the World Champion Red Sox, and won a career-high 24 in 1917. However, the Red Sox could not ignore the abilities of a hitter who would establish a career-record .304 batting average as a pitcher. In 1917, his .325 batting average (in 123 at-bats) trailed only superstars Cobb, Sisler, and Speaker. He began

playing some outfield in 1918 and led the AL in home runs in 1918 and 1919, with a ML-record 29 in 1919. Aside from five more appearances (winning four) scattered over the next 14 seasons, his pitching career was over.

To bankroll his Broadway ventures, Boston owner Harry Frazee sold Ruth to the Yankees prior to the 1920 season for $100,000, twice the highest price previously paid for a player. (Frazee also got a $300,000 loan.) Ruth responded by shattering his home run record with 54, and went on to break his own record twice more with 59 in 1921 and 60 in 1927. The sale initiated the enduring rivalry between the two teams and shifted the balance of American League power from Boston to New York. Whereas the Red Sox had won six pennants and five World Series in the American League's first nineteen seasons, the Yankees, who had never won a pennant, would rule in the 1920s and 1930s and win fourteen flags before the Red Sox would clinch another.

As an everyday player, Ruth rewrote the record books. The league home run leader a record 12 times, he lost another title by four in 1922 when he missed the first six weeks of the season under suspension by Commissioner Landis for participating in a prohibited barnstorming tour. From 1926 through 1931 he averaged better than 50 home runs a year. Over the course of his career, he homered once every 11.76 plate appearances, well ahead of runner-up Ralph Kiner's one home run per 14.11 appearances. Ruth led the league in RBI six times, runs scored eight times, and walks 11 times. His 170 walks in 1923 and his career total of 2056 are still records. No one has matched his slugging average of .847 in 1920, nor his career record of .690, to which Ted Williams's .634 average is a distant runner-up. Among his other hitting records are his 457 total bases in 1921 and his combined total of 375 hits and walks in 1923. Using his pitcher's arm as an outfielder, he twice recorded more than 20 assists in a season.

Ruth appeared in ten World Series. He holds the dubious distinction of being the only player to be caught stealing to end a World Series. Representing the tying run, he was nabbed trying for second by Cardinals' catcher Bob O'Farrell in the ninth inning of Game Seven of the 1926 WS. That year, he was the first to homer four times in a Series. He batted .625 in the 1928 Series. Whether Ruth actually called his shot when he homered off the Cubs' Charlie Root in his last Series in 1932 is still debated, but the incident typified the enormity of

Babe Ruth

the Ruth legend. He returned to Chicago in 1933 for the inaugural All-Star Game and hit the first homer in All-Star history.

Sportswriter Bill Broeg said that "to try to capture Babe Ruth with cold statistics would be like trying to keep up with him on a night out." On and off the field, Ruth's gargantuan appetites, charisma, and ego kept the media scurrying in the wake of his latest generosities and indiscretions. The same Ruth who would happily spend hours of free time with needy children was ejected for swinging at an umpire who called ball four on the first batter the young pitcher faced in a June 23, 1917 game. Red Sox teammate Ernie Shore relieved Ruth, the runner Ruth had walked was caught attempting to steal, and Shore retired the next 26 batters to earn credit for a perfect game. As for Ruth's legendary carousing, roommate Ping Brodie quipped, "I don't room with him. I room with his suitcase."

Ruth's abilities and personality made him a tremendous drawing card throughout the league and made him the highest-paid player of his era. When informed that the $80,000 dollar salary he received in 1930 was $5,000 more that that of President Hoover, Ruth was reported to have said, "I had a better year than he did." Sportswriter Red Smith always claimed the story had to be apocryphal, because "Ruth was too uninformed about politics." Just as his hitting redefined the game, his salary breakthrough affected others to the point that former teammate Waite Hoyt said, "Every big league player and his wife should teach their children to pray: 'God bless Mommy, God bless Daddy, and God bless Babe Ruth.'"

When the Yankees released him to sign with the Braves in 1935, Ruth's skills had diminished, but he did manage to hit his last three homers in a single game at Pittsburgh. His final homer may not have actually traveled the 600 feet some claimed, but it was considered to have been the longest ever hit in Forbes Field. In 1938, he coached for the Dodgers, but he was never offered the manager's job he hoped for.

Ruth's last public appearance came at the time of the premier of the movie about his life, "The Babe Ruth Story." Three weeks later, he was dead of throat cancer and lay in state in Yankee Stadium, widely known as "The House That Ruth Built." At his funeral, pallbearer and former teammate Joe Dugan, noting the heat of the August day, said, "I'd give a hundred dollars for a beer." Waite Hoyt replied in the spirit of Ruth, "So would the Babe." /(TG/CR)

Dick Ruthven — 1951- . RHP 1973–86 **Phillies**, Braves, Cubs 2109 ip, 123–127, 4.14. *2 LCS, 14 ip, 1–1, 3.29. 1 WS, 9 ip, 0–0, 3.00*
☛ *All-Star—76, 81.*

Ruthven had little success as a temperamental young starter with the Phillies in 1973–75, and led the NL with 17 losses for the Braves in 1976. A dispute with Braves owner Ted Turner sent him back to Philadelphia in mid-1978 and he was 13–5, 2.98 with the Phillies that year to help them win the NL East. He was 6–0 in 1979 before an injury curtailed his effectiveness. Ruthven rebounded in 1980 to go 17–10 as Philadelphia reached the WS, and he won the deciding game of the NLCS in relief, pitching the final two innings of a 10-inning, 8–7 win over Houston. After a 6–1 start earned him a spot on the 1981 NL All-Star team, his ERA ballooned to 5.14 and he finished the season 12–7. He was traded to the Cubs in 1983 and was 10–17 in his final three seasons with Chicago. /(SG)

Blondy Ryan [John Collins] — 1906–1959. SS-3B White Sox, **Giants**, Phillies, Yankees 386 g, .239, 8 hr, 133 rbi. *2 WS, 6 g, .263, 1 rbi*

The lanky Ryan gained immortality with a telegram he sent as a brash rookie to dour Bill Terry, manager of the Giants. Notified to report to the team to play shortstop in place of Travis Jackson, whose broken knee from 1932 would not hold up the next season, Ryan wired: "We can't lose now. Am en route!" He was right. The Giants went on to the pennant and won the World Series with Blondy Ryan hollering loudly on every play. His energy and enthusiasm failed to be matched by his bat and he lapsed into a utility role. /(JK)

Connie Ryan [Cornelius] — 1920- . 2B-3B 1942–44, 46–54 Giants, **Braves**, Reds, Phillies, White Sox 1184 g, .248, 56 hr, 381 rbi. *1 WS, 2 g, .000.*
Manager 1975, 77 **Braves**, Rangers 10–22, .313
☛ *All-Star—44.*

A fancy-fielding, all-around infielder, Ryan was a regular at second base for about half his 12-year career. Remembered as a good team player, he became a coach, briefly taking over as manager of both the Braves and Rangers. /(EW)

Jack Ryan — 1869–1952. C-1B 1889–91, 94–96, 98–99, 1901–03, 12–13 Louisville (AA), Braves, Dodgers, Baltimore (NL), **Cardinals**, Senators 616 g, .217, 4 hr, 154 rbi (inc)

Ryan was a good-field, no-hit catcher in the 1890s and early 1900s. He later became a successful minor league manager, highly respected for his ability to develop young players. /(BC)

Jack Ryan — 1878–1958. *Scout.*

A former minor league umpire, Ryan scouted for a variety of ML clubs for almost 40 years, 20 of which were spent with the Cardinals. He began scouting for the Browns in 1917, but in 1926 switched to the crosstown Cardinals, where he remained until 1945. From 1946 to 1955, Ryan evaluated talent for the Dodgers, Cubs, and Pirates. /(FVP)

Jimmy Ryan — 1863–1923. OF-SS-LHP 1885–1900, 02–03 **Cubs**, Chi (PL), Senators 2012 g, .309, 118 hr, 1093 rbi; 117 ip, 6–1, 3.62

One of the game's early power hitters, Ryan led the NL in HR (16), hits, and doubles for Chicago in 1888. A lefty thrower, he also pitched some, that season leading the league with three relief wins. He was a leader in the movement that established the Players' League in 1890, and was a member of the

Jimmy Ryan

Chicago entry, switching back to the NL in 1891. Ryan was a jolly, free-speaking joker whose openness disturbed some of his teammates. When another convivial player, Tom Burns, replaced Cap Anson as Chicago's manager in 1898, he named Ryan captain. The team rebelled, insisting the honor be given to Bill Lange, and staged a sit-down strike before the season's opener in Louisville. Burns capitulated and lost control of the team. /(JK)

Mike Ryan — 1941– . C 1964–74 Red Sox, **Phillies**, Pirates 636 g, .193, 28 hr, 161 rbi. *1 WS, 1 g, .000*

Though he failed to hit as high as .200 in seven of his 11 ML seasons, Ryan was kept for his outstanding defensive skills. He only twice caught over 100 games, once each for the Red Sox and Phillies. After managing and instructing in the minors, he became a Phillies coach in 1980. /(AL)

Nolan Ryan [Lynn Nolan] (The Express) — 1947– . RHP 1966, 68– Mets, Angels, **Astros**, Rangers 4786 ip, 289–263, 3.15. 20 wins: 73–74 *4 LCS, 41 ip, 1–1, 3.70. 1 WS, 2 ip, 0–0, 0.00*
☛ *Led League—era 81, 87. Led League—k 72–74, 76–79, 87–89. All-Star—72–73, 75, 77, 79, 81, 85, 89.*

Baseball's all-time strikeout leader and the author of a ML-record five no-hitters, Nolan Ryan is in many ways the most remarkable pitcher ever to play the game. He was often maligned as a ".500 pitcher" despite his high strikeout totals, and he walked over 4.5 batters per nine innings each year until 1980, his 14th ML season. But only a physical wonder could still overwhelm hitters with a 95-mph fastball and attain the unbelievable milestone of 5,000 strikeouts at the age of 42.

Growing up in little Alvin, Texas, Ryan was a high schooler with an awesome fastball but almost no control. The Mets selected him in the eighth round of the 1965 free-agent draft. In 1966, he blazed his way to 272 strikeouts, 127 walks, and 17 wins (all Carolina League highs) at Greenville, frightening batters and catchers alike with his velocity. He missed most of 1967 in military service, and in 1968 the raw righthander was rushed to the Mets.

Despite a chronic blister problem (he tried several remedies, including soaking his fingers in pickle brine) and a month on the DL, Ryan struck out 133 batters in 134 innings as a rookie starter for the Mets in 1968. In 1969 the pitching-rich club used him as both a starter and in relief. Ryan won the deciding game of the LCS with seven innings of relief, and saved Game Three of the WS as the Miracle Mets

Nolan Ryan

Detroit batters in the process. In his next start, he was six outs from back-to-back no-hitters when Mark Belanger spoiled the bid. Ryan entered the final week of the season in striking distance of Sandy Koufax's all-time single-season strikeout record of 382, and in his last start he fanned 16 Twins in 10 innings to eclipse the record by one. He struck out Rich Reese for the record 383rd strikeout. In 39 starts that year, Ryan struck out 10 or more batters 23 times, yet he finished second to Jim Palmer for the Cy Young Award.

Already Ryan was the first pitcher with back-to-back 300-strikeout seasons, and he made it three in a row in 1974. He also threw his third no-hitter in his last start of the season, September 28, against the Twins. On August 20 that year, a sophisticated timing device clocked a Ryan fastball at 100.9 mph, putting him in the Guinness Book of World Records. An off-year in 1975 was highlighted by a fourth no-hitter (Ryan fooled Bobby Grich with a changeup to end it), and on August 23, 1975, Ryan underwent elbow surgery. He came back throwing as hard as ever, with 327 strikeouts in 1976, and was *TSN* AL Pitcher of the Year in 1977, finishing 19–16, 2.77, with 341 strikeouts. Injuries hindered him again in 1978, but he was selected for his first All-Star Game start in 1979, before becoming a free agent at the end of the season.

Grabbing the chance to return to his native Texas, Ryan signed a three-year contract with the Houston Astros, and became baseball's first $1-million-per-year player. Ryan's performance fell off in his first season back in the NL, although he struck out Cesar Geronimo for his 3,000th career strikeout on July 4. He returned to form in the strike-shortened 1981 season. He led the NL with a 1.69 ERA and pitched his fifth no-hitter September 26 against the Dodgers. Although he was no longer an annual cinch to lead his league in strikeouts, Ryan still fanned nearly a batter an inning. When he struck out Montreal's Brad Mills on April 27, 1983, he broke Walter Johnson's all-time strikeout record. On July 11, 1985, the Mets' Danny Heep became his 4,000th strikeout victim.

The 1984 and 1985 seasons were filled with injuries and frustrations for Ryan, but 1986 marked a remarkable return to dominance for him, with 194 strikeouts in 178 innings, his best ratio since 1978. In the 1986 LCS, his two-hit, 12-strikeout effort in Game Five against the Mets earned no decision. In 1987 the forty-year-old Ryan continued to defy the calendar with 270 strikeouts in 212 innings and his second ERA title while becoming the only pitcher

beat the mighty Orioles in five games. After opening the 1970 season with a one-hitter, Ryan struggled, and he grew unhappy with the big-city atmosphere of New York. In 1971 he requested a trade and the Mets obliged, sending him to the Angels with three other players to obtain Jim Fregosi, a deal that has been called the worst in Mets history.

In California, Ryan enjoyed the tutelage of pitching coach Tom Morgan and veteran catcher Jeff Torborg, and the Ryan Express arrived. Pitching with a more compact motion in 1972, Ryan became the first righthander since Bob Feller to fan 300 batters in a season and won 19 games with a 2.28 ERA. In 1973 Ryan was even more overpowering, and became the fifth pitcher to toss two no-hitters in one season. He no-hit the Royals on May 15, and on July 15 he repeated against the Tigers, fanning 17 with 2,000 strikeouts in each league. Unfortunately, the Astros' dismal offense left him with an 8–16 record that cost him the Cy Young Award. Ryan added yet another strikeout title with 228 in 1988, and in the off-season he signed with the Texas Rangers. In 1989 the forty-two-year-old struck out an AL-leading 301 batters, by far the most ever for a man his age, and had several near-no-hitters. He announced that he would play another year to reach 300 wins. /(ME)

Rosy Ryan [Wilfred Patrick Dolan] — 1898–1980. RHP 1919–26, 28, 33 **Giants**, Braves, Yankees, Dodgers 881 ip, 52–47, 4.14 *3 WS, 17 ip, 3–0, 1.59*
☛ *Led League—era 22.*

A star reliever and occasional starter in the early 1920s, Ryan was the long man out of the Giants' bullpen, teaming with closer Claude Jonnard. In 1923, Ryan and Jonnard each appeared in 45 games, the league high. While Jonnard led the NL in saves in 1922 and 1923, Ryan led in relief wins (seven and nine). Ryan's 3.01 ERA in '22 led the league. He holds the record for most WS relief wins (three), with one in each Series, 1922–24. In 1924, he became only the second pitcher to hit a WS home run. When the ban on spitballs was declared in 1920, Ryan, who had debuted briefly in 1919, was not on the protected list and was forced to develop a curveball. /(ARA)

Mike Ryba [Dominic Joseph] — 1903–1971. RHP 1935–38, 41–46 Cardinals, **Red Sox** 784 ip, 52–34, 3.66. *1 WS, 0.2 ip, 0–0, 13.50*

A fair reliever whose only losing season came when he went 0–1 in his last year, Ryba had his best season with the 1944 Red Sox (12–7, 3.33). One of the most versatile players ever, he was referred to as The One-Man Team. At various times (but not in the majors) he caught and played the infield and outfield. He also managed, coached and scouted. /(EW)

Jack Ryder [Frederick B.] — 1871–1936. *Writer.*

Along with Sid Mercer, Ryder was one of the most active in creating the BBWAA. After two years with the *Ohio State Journal* in Columbus, he moved to the Cincinnati *Enquirer*, where he spent more than 30 years as baseball editor. /(NLM)

Gary Ryerson — 1948– . LHP 1972–73 **Brewers** 125 ip, 3–9, 4.39

A childhood case of polio afterward forced Ryerson to wear a leg brace, yet he was signed by the Giants at age 19. His control and good curveball prompted Brewers manager Del Crandall's optimism when he said of Ryerson, "He's got talent that grows on you." /(KC)

Byrum Saam — 1914– . *Broadcaster.*

As the voice of Philadelphia baseball for over 40 years, Saam broadcast for more losing teams than any other announcer and called games for 11 teams that lost 100 or more games, 19 last-place clubs, and not one pennant winner. The former Texas Christian University basketball player joined the Athletics in 1938 and broadcast both the Phillies and A's home games from 1939 to 1949. In 1950 both clubs decided to allow live road broadcasts, rather than studio re-creations, and Saam was forced to choose. He chose the A's, and the Phillies won the pennant. He moved back to the Phillies when the A's left for Kansas City after 1954, and remained there until his retirement in 1975. Saam was a straightforward announcer with a knack for malaprops. He once recapped a lengthy rundown late at night for the benefit of "all you guys scoring in bed." /(SCL)

Bret Saberhagen (Sabes) — 1964– . RHP 1984-
Royals 1329 ip, 92–61, 3.23. 20 wins: 85 *2 LCS, 15 ip, 0–0, 4.11. 1 WS, 18 ip, 2–0, 0.50*
☛ *Led League—w 89. Led League—era 89. Cy Young Award—85, 89. All-Star—87. Gold Glove—89.*

Saberhagen was not selected until the 19th round in the 1982 draft but quickly proved to be a fine acquisition for Kansas City. After logging an 18–7 record in his first year of minor league play, Saberhagen earned a berth in the Royals' rotation at the tender age of twenty, and demonstrated control and poise beyond his years.

In 1985 Saberhagen dodged the sophomore jinx by becoming the youngest pitcher ever to capture the Cy Young Award. He ran away with WS MVP honors by limiting the Cardinals to twelve baserunners and one run over 18 innings, and became a father during the Series.

Saberhagen has sharp control (1.8 walks per nine innings over his first five seasons) and a 93-mph fastball, but had trouble putting it all together for a full season, often having an outstanding first half and then faltering. But in 1989 he again excelled, leading the AL in wins (23–6) and ERA (2.16, lowest in the AL since 1978) and winning the AL Cy Young Award. /(FO)

Sabermetrics

Bill James, the person most closely associated with quantitative techniques for assessing baseball performance, defines sabermetrics as "the search for objective knowledge about baseball." This objective search for knowledge usually takes the form of hypothesis-testing research, in contrast to traditional baseball wisdom that goes with "the book" without checking actual data. The term is based on the acronym for the Society for American Baseball Research (which includes many baseball analysts who are not interested in quantitative techniques). The yearly *Bill James Baseball Abstract* did a great deal to popularize sabermetrics in the 1980s, as did *The Hidden Game of Baseball* by John Thorn and Pete Palmer, considered the classic survey of quantitative methods in baseball. Another breakthrough in the development of sabermetrics has been Project Scoresheet, which is a network of scorers who record every pitch and play of each major league game in formats that facilitate computerized analysis. /(TF)

Chris Sabo (Spuds) — 1962– . 3B 1988- **Reds** 219 g, .267, 17 hr, 73 rbi
☛ *Rookie of the Year—88. All-Star—88.*

Sabo came out of nowhere to win the Reds' third base job when Buddy Bell began the 1988 season on the DL. He went on to capture NL Rookie of the Year honors and pinch run in the All-Star Game in his home park, stealing a base. He finished third in the NL in doubles (40) and tied for fourth in steals (46). But after hitting .312 before the All-Star break, he tailed off in the second half to finish at .271, and rarely walked. He endeared himself to the fans and manager Pete Rose with his hustling style and received his nickname, Spuds, for always wearing protective goggles that made him look like a bull terrier. He led NL third basemen in fielding and double plays. On April 7, 1988 he tied the ML record with 11 assists at third base in a nine-inning game.

Sabo started more slowly in 1989, and went on the DL in June with a hyperextended left knee. /(WOR)

Ray Sadecki — 1940- . LHP 1960-77 **Cardinals**, Giants, Mets, Braves, Royals, Brewers 2498 ip, 135-131, 3.79. 20 wins: 64 *2 WS, 11 ip, 1-0, 5.73*

A bonus baby, Sadecki went 9-9 as a 19-year-old, earning 1960 Cardinal Rookie of the Year honors. He led the World Champion 1964 Cardinals' staff with a 20-11 record. He beat the Yankees in the Series opener, but was knocked out in the first inning of Game Four. After dropping to 6-15 in 1965, he was traded to the Giants for Orlando Cepeda on May 8, 1966. In 1968, despite posting a 2.91 ERA, his 18 losses tied him for the league lead. After dropping to five wins in 1969 for the Giants, he was traded to the Mets, who used him as the swingman (reliever and fifth starter in a four-man rotation) on their staff. He relieved in four games of the 1973 WS, recording a save. /(FJO)

Mike Sadek — 1946- . C 1973, 75-81 **Giants** 383 g, .226, 5 hr, 74 rbi

Sadek's entire career was spent as the Giants' second- or third-string catcher. He had a good arm, but his highest batting average was .252 in 1980, when he had his most at-bats (151) and RBI (16). /(SFS)

Bob Sadowski [Robert F.] — 1938- . RHP 1963-66 **Braves**, Red Sox 440 ip, 20-27, 3.87

Bob Sadowski was the youngest of three Pittsburgh-born brothers to play in the major leagues; Ted pitched for the Senators and Twins in 1960-62, and Eddie caught for the Red Sox, Angels, and Braves in 1960-63 and 1966. Bob came through the Cardinal organization but debuted with the Braves after a 1963 trade that sent Lew Burdette to St. Louis. He tied a ML record on April 20, 1964 when he was struck out five times in a nine-inning game. On April 15, 1965, he pitched the Braves' final home opener in Milwaukee, defeating Pittsburgh 5-1. /(GB)

Tom Saffell — 1921- . OF 1949-51, 55 **Pirates**, A's 271 g, .238, 6 hr, 40 rbi

Saffell spent most of his career in the American Association and Pacific Coast League, but was an extra outfielder and pinch hitter in four seasons with Pittsburgh. While managing Reno (California League) in 1964, he was suspended for 30 days and fined $250 when he refused to field his team as a protest against poor umpiring. /(NLM)

Vic Saier — 1891-1967. 1B 1911-17, 19 **Cubs**, Pirates 864 g, .263, 55 hr, 395 rbi

Saier replaced Frank Chance at first base when "The Peerless Leader" began to phase himself out of the Cubs' lineup. In 1913, he batted .288 with a league-leading 21 triples and drove in a career-high 92 runs. His career was essentially ended by a 1917 back injury; he made an unsuccessful comeback attempt with the Pirates in 1919. /(ARA)

Johnny Sain — 1917- . RHP 1942, 46-55 **Braves**, Yankees, A's 2125 ip, 139-116, 3.49. 20 wins: 46-48, 50 *4 WS, 30 ip, 2-2, 2.64*
☛ *Led League—w 48. All-Star—47-48, 53.*

"Spahn and Sain and pray for rain," was the Braves' motto for the 1948 stretch drive, as they pushed toward their first pennant since 1914. That season Spahn was actually not much more effective than the Braves' third and fourth starters, Bill Voiselle and Vern Bickford. Sain, however, led the NL with 24 wins, 39 starts, 28 complete games, and 314 innings.

A rookie in 1942, he spent 1943-45 in the military, but lost no time establishing himself upon his return. He won 20 each year from 1946 to 1948, slumped in 1949, but came back with a 20-13 mark in 1950. Although Sain could strike men out when the occasion demanded, the 6'2" Arkansan had pinpoint control and a let-'em-hit-it philosophy. In three of his 20-win seasons, he led the league in hits allowed. Sent to the Yankees in August 1951 for Lew Burdette and $50,000, he contributed 11-6 and 14-7 marks to the 1952 and '53 Yankee pennants, then led the AL with 22 saves in 1954.

An excellent-hitting pitcher (.245), Sain averaged .346 in 1947 and .353 in 1954, and led the NL with 16 sacrifice hits in 1948. He became an instructor and ML pitching coach with the A's, Yankees, Twins, Tigers, Angels, White Sox, and Braves. He became known for developing 20-game-winners in tight, four-man rotations. Whitey Ford, Jim Kaat, Earl Wilson, Denny McLain, Clyde Wright, Stan Bahnsen, and Wilbur Wood all had their biggest seasons under Sain's supervision. Loved by his pitchers, often hated by his jealous managers, he coached five ML teams that won pennants. Jim Bouton has called Sain "the greatest pitching coach who ever lived."

Lenn Sakata — 1954- . 2B-SS 1977-87 Brewers, **Orioles**, A's, Yankees 565 g, .230, 25 hr, 109 rbi. *1 WS, 1 g, .000*

One of the many bit players on manager Earl

Weaver's 1983 World Champion Orioles, Sakata was a reserve infielder his entire ML career, seeing his most action in 1982 when he hit .259 in 136 games for Baltimore. The diminutive Honolulu native could have refused a demotion to Rochester (International League) in 1985 as a veteran with over five years of ML service. Instead, he accepted, hit only .214 there, and was not offered a contract for 1986 by the Orioles. In 1986–87 he played briefly with the A's and Yankees. /(SCL)

Mark Salas — 1961– . C 1984– Cardinals, **Twins**, Yankees, White Sox, Indians 402 g, .258, 28 hr, 112 rbi

The much-traveled Salas enjoyed career highs in virtually every offensive catagory in his first full ML season (1985) when he hit .300 with 9 HR and 41 RBI as the Twins number-one catcher, but hasn't hit above .250 since. He was traded to the Yankees for Joe Niekro in June 1987, then dealt to the White Sox with Dan Pasqua for Rich Dotson and Scott Nielsen in November. /(SCL)

Angel Salazar [Argenis] — 1961– . SS 1983–84, 86–88 Expos, **Royals**, Cubs 383 g, .212, 2 hr, 59 rbi

Angel followed a series of shortstop candidates to Kansas City. Despite a weak bat and back problems, Salazar's capable defense enabled him to hold the Royals' regular shortstop job two seasons. /(FO)

Luis Salazar — 1956– . 3B-OF-SS 1980– **Padres**, White Sox, Tigers, Cubs 986 g, .267, 63 hr, 345 rbi. *2 LCS, 7 g, .333, 1 hr, 2 rbi. 1 WS, 4 g, .333*

An extremely versatile reserve who has played every position but catcher in 10 ML seasons, Salazar has been a Padre three different times, having been traded once to the White Sox before returning as a free agent, then signing with the Tigers before being traded back to San Diego. The Venezuela native was the Padres third baseman in 1982–83, hitting 22 HR and stealing 56 bases over two seasons, and in 1988 played 130 games for Detroit (mostly in the outfield), hitting .270 with 12 HR and 62 RBI. /(SCL)

Al Salerno — 1931– . *Umpire* AL 1961–68 *1 ASU*

The union efforts of NL umpires were ahead of their counterparts in the AL during the 1960s. At the annual meeting of the NL umpires' association on September 13, 1968, Salerno and Bill Valentine attended in hopes of joining the group. Three days later, both Salerno and Valentine received calls from AL president Joe Cronin, who informed them that their contracts would not be renewed for the following season because of incompetence. /(RTM)

Bill Salkeld — 1917–1967. C 1945–50 **Pirates**, Braves, Cubs 356 g, .273, 31 hr, 132 rbi. *1 WS, 5 g, .222, 1 hr, 1 rbi*

A knee injury in 1938 nearly ended Salkeld's career, but he broke into the ML with 15 home runs and a .311 BA for the Pirates in 1945, his best year. His homer in Game Five of the 1948 WS tied the score at 5–5 and helped the Braves to one of their two victories. /(NLM)

Slim Sallee [Harry Franklin] — 1885–1950. LHP 1908–21 **Cardinals**, Giants, Reds 2819 ip, 173–143, 2.56. 20 wins: 19 *2 WS, 29 ip, 1–3, 3.14*

In his first eight and one half major league seasons, Sallee toiled for Cardinal teams that only once finished in the first division (1914). Yet the lean, 6'3" Slim won consistently and, after his rookie

Slim Sallee with the Giants

season, never recorded an ERA higher than 2.97 for St. Louis. He won 18 games in both 1913 and 1914, and his six saves in both 1912 and 1914 were league highs. Sold to the Giants in July 1916, Sallee helped pitch New York to the 1917 NL pennant by going 18–7 with a league-high four saves. After he was picked up on waivers in March 1919, his 21–7 record led the 1919 World Champion Reds' staff. Gifted with fantastic control at his best, the junkballer walked only 20 batters in 227.2 innings that season and is the only 20-game winner for a championship team not to top 20 walks. He posted a complete-game victory and a loss in the World Series against the Chicago Black Sox. He returned to the Giants in September 1920 (on waivers again) and, in 1921, for the third time in his career, played for a pennant-winner the season after changing teams. Sallee was known to quit the field when practice sessions grew tiresome, repairing to a nearby bar; his drinking led teams to give up on him despite his obvious talent. /(JL)

Chico Salmon [Rutherford Eduardo] — 1940– . 2B-SS-1B-OF-3B 1964–72 **Indians**, Orioles 658 g, .249, 31 hr, 149 rbi. *1 LCS, 1 g, .000. 2 WS, 3 g, 1.000*

Salmon was the utility man for the 1964–68 Indians and the 1969–71 pennant-winning Orioles. In between, he was drafted by the expansion Pilots and traded to Baltimore. For five straight seasons, the Panamanian played every infield position and the outfield. In his only World Series at-bat, in Game Two of the 1970 classic, Salmon's fifth-inning pinch-hit single started the Orioles' game-winning five-run rally. /(ME)

H.G. Salsinger (Harry, Sol) — 1887–1958. *Writer.*

Salsinger started with the Cincinnati *Post* in 1907, and two years later began 49 years as sports editor of the Detroit *News*. Likely to smoke half a cigar and chew on the other half while watching an athletic contest, Salsinger was called the best sportswriter in the country by Westbrook Pegler. In 1968, he posthumously received the J.G. Taylor Spink Award. /(NLM)

Jack Saltzgaver [Otto Hamlin] — 1905–1978. 3B-2B 1932, 34–37, 45 **Yankees**, Pirates 278 g, .260, 10 hr, 82 rbi

The Yankees paid St. Paul $45,000 for Saltzgaver late in the 1931 season, taking him away from the Cubs, who rated him better than Billy Herman, but Saltzgaver was never able to win more than a utility job in New York. /(NLM).

Jack Salveson — 1914–1974. RHP 1933–35, 43, 45 Giants, Pirates, White Sox, **Indians** 272 ip, 9–9, 3.99

The last rookie signed by John McGraw, the fast-working control artist failed to impress then and in a later wartime stint with the Indians, but he won 204 games in 16 years in the Pacific Coast League. In a bit part in the movie *Pride of the Yankees* he was to "bean" star Gary Cooper, actually using a cotton ball. It took him seven tries. "It just wouldn't go straight!" he said. /(NLM)

Manny Salvo (Gyp) — 1913– . RHP 1939–43 Giants, **Braves** , Phillies 721 ip, 33–50, 3.69

Salvo, who was polite, neat, and conservatively dressed, was facetiously called "Gyp"—short for gypsy. Though he was only 10–9 for the seventh-place 1940 Braves, he shared the league lead with five shutouts. /(JK)

Joe Sambito — 1952– . LHP 1976–82, 84–87 **Astros**, Mets, Red Sox 628 ip, 37–38, 3.04. *2 LCS, 4 ip, 0–1, 4.15. 1 WS, 0.1 ip, 0–0, 27.00*
☛ *All-Star—79.*

One of the NL's best relievers with the Astros from 1978 to 1981, Sambito saw his career ruined in 1982 by an injury to his pitching elbow. The hard-throwing lefthander had been a starter in the minors, and led the Southern League in strikeouts at Columbus in 1975 before being promoted to Houston as a reliever the following season. In 1978, he led the Astros in saves for the first of four consecutive seasons, and in 1979 he notched a career-high 22 saves with a 1.78 ERA. Sambito was off to a fast start in 1982, surrendering one earned run and collecting four saves in his first nine appearances, but was forced onto the DL with what was first diagnosed as tendinitis. When the pain in his elbow lingered, it was discovered that bone chips had damaged the ligaments, and Sambito missed the rest of 1982 and all of 1983 recuperating from surgery. Comeback attempts with the Astros and Mets failed in 1984–85, but Sambito made the Red Sox staff in the spring of 1986 and helped Boston to the WS that fall, then retired after posting a 6.93 ERA in 1987. /(SCL)

Billy Sample — 1955– . OF 1978–86 **Rangers**, Yankees, Braves 826 g, .272, 46 hr, 230 rbi

The 5'9" Sample began his pro career as a second baseman but was quickly converted to the outfield, and in 1978 he hit .352 and scored 141 runs at Tucson (Pacific Coast League) to earn a job with the

Rangers the following year. Sample hit .292 as a rookie in 1979 and was the Rangers regular left fielder until 1985, when he was traded to the Yankees for Toby Harrah. He spent less than a year in New York before another trade sent him to Atlanta for his final ML season, where he hit .285 as a reserve outfielder and righthanded pinch hitter. He now works as an announcer on Braves radio and television broadcasts. /(SCL)

Juan Samuel (Sammy) — 1960– . 2B-OF 1983-
Phillies, Mets 938 g, .260, 103 hr, 441 rbi. *1 LCS, 1 g, --.*
1 WS, 3 g, .000
☛ *All-Star—84, 87.*

A speedy runner with great power but unsure hands for a second baseman, Samuel set a rookie stolen-base record of 72 in 1984 (broken by Vince Coleman the following year.) He had a NL-record 701 at-bats in 1984 and hit .272 with 15 HR and 69 RBI as the Phillies' leadoff hitter to win *TSN* NL Rookie Player of the Year honors. He also struck out 168 times to lead the NL, rarely walked, and committed 33 errors, weaknesses that plagued his career. The Phillies moved the strikeout-prone Samuel (at least 141 in each of his six ML seasons through 1988) from the leadoff spot and in 1988 switched him to the outfield, where his speed partially compensated for bad fly-ball judgment. Samuel's best offensive season was 1987, when he hit .272 with 28 HR, 100 RBI, 113 runs, 35 stolen bases, and a NL-high 15 triples. He became the only player in ML history to post double figures in doubles, triples, home runs, and stolen bases in each of his first four ML seasons. In 1988 he missed the feat by one triple. Samuel was traded to the Mets for Len Dykstra and Roger McDowell in mid-1989 and became New York's leadoff hitter and centerfielder. /(SG)

San Diego Chicken

The first of the wave of costumed team mascots that inundated baseball in the late 1970s, the Chicken was the brainchild of Ted Giannopolis. After cutting his ties with the Padres to pursue a nationwide audience, he had to use the name The Famous Chicken. /(WOR)

San Diego Padres (Pods) — 1969– . Team.
1481-1857, .444. *NL West Champions 84 NL Champions 84*

The Padres were the dream come true of San Diego sportswriter Jack Murphy, who sought to bring major league baseball to the city. Murphy, the brother of Mets announcer Bob Murphy, cam-

paigned for years and even pushed the city to build a new stadium before a team had been offered. Thus, in 1969, the Padres were the only one of the four expansion teams to open in a new park. After Murphy's death, San Diego Stadium was renamed Jack Murphy Stadium in his memory.

Like most expansion teams, the Padres were weak in their early years, but their period of weakness lasted longer than most. The team finished in last place their first six seasons; in four of them, they lost 100 or more games. This made it difficult to attract fans, and owner C. Arnholt Smith had arranged to sell the team to a buyer who would move it to Washington, D.C. The move was so expected that not only had the club packed everything to ship, the Topps baseball card company had printed the Padres' cards for the 1974 season without giving the team name; in its place was Washington. But McDonald's founder Ray Kroc stepped in at the final hour to purchase the team and keep it in San Diego.

Dave Winfield had come up in 1973, and Kroc built around him, spending money freely. Home attendance improved as Kroc brought his controversial style to the team. He once commandeered the ballpark's public-address system to apologize to the fans for a particularly poor on-field performance. With the turnaround of Randy Jones, who won 20 games, the club climbed to fourth place in 1975. Jones won the Cy Young Award in 1976. Each year new talent was added (relief ace Rollie Fingers in 1977, Gaylord Perry in 1978), and the franchise had its first winning record in 1978. Although they lapsed back into last in 1979, they were a relatively close 19-1/2 games out.

Trader Jack McKeon became head of baseball operations in 1980 and rebuilt the team. San Diego won the Western Division title in 1984 on the strength of acquisitions Steve Garvey, Graig Nettles, and Goose Gossage and homegrown talents Carmelo Martinez and Kevin McReynolds. They upset the Cubs in the LCS in a championship dedicated to Ray Kroc, who had died that January. His wife, Joan, took over the team and became known for her antipathy toward ballplayers with drug problems in their past. She almost sold the Padres to Mariners owner George Argyros in 1987 before deciding that his parsimonious fiscal policies would hurt the franchise. /(JFC)

San Francisco Giants — 1958- . Team.
2632–2462, .517. *NL West Champions 71, 87, 89 NL Champions 62, 89*

The Giants moved from New York to San Francisco after the 1957 season, with Horace Stoneham continuing as club president and controlling stockholder. Their home in 1958–59 was Seals Stadium; they played their first game at Candlestick Park on April 12, 1960. Led by centerfielder Willie Mays, first baseman Willie McCovey, and pitcher Juan Marichal, the Giants had several powerful clubs in the 1960s, and won a pennant under manager Alvin Dark in 1962. Charlie Fox piloted them to a division title in 1971. In January of 1976, Stoneham negotiated to sell the team to Labatt's Breweries of Toronto, but a court order prevented the club's transfer to Canada. Native San Franciscan Bob Lurie stepped in, and with Arizona cattleman Bud Herseth, purchased the Giants and kept them in San Francisco. Lurie bought out Herseth in 1978. In 1987, under the astute presidency of Al Rosen, the Giants, managed by Roger Craig, won their second NL West title. They made it to the World Series in 1989, aided by the strong bats of Will Clark and Kevin Mitchell. The Series was interrupted for ten days when an earthquake measuring 7.1 on the Richter scale struck just before Game Three was to begin at Candlestick Park. Oddly, the 1962 World Series was also delayed in San Francisco, for three days, due to rain. /(FS)

Irving Sanborn (Sy) — Unk.–Unk. *Writer.*

One of the top baseball writers of the 1920s, Sanborn retired in 1930 after 40 years with the Chicago *Tribune.* The Dartmouth graduate contributed many articles to magazines and guides and was one of the founders of the BBWAA. /(NLM)

Celerino Sanchez — 1944- . 3B 1972–73 **Yankees** 105 g, .242, 1 hr, 31 rbi

One of Mexico's greatest infielders, Sanchez batted .448 for Campeche (Mexican Southeast League) in 1966, leading professional baseball. With the parent Mexico City Tigers, he batted .345 in 1970 and .368 in 1971, and was acquired by the Yankees. The flashy third baseman did not hit well in New York and returned to Mexico in 1974, remaining a regular through 1979. /(MC)

Luis Sanchez — 1953- . RHP 1981–85 **Angels** 370 ip, 28–21, 3.75. *1 LCS, 3 ip, 0–1, 6.75*

After six years in the minors, two years in Mexico, and two years out of organized baseball altogether, Sanchez made his ML debut with the Angels in 1981. The skinny Venezuelan won 10 games in relief for California in 1983 and saved 11 in 1984. /(SCL)

Orlando Sanchez — 1956- . C 1981–84 **Cardinals**, Royals, Orioles 73 g, .218, 0 hr, 12 rbi

Sanchez began ripping the ball for Puebla of the Mexican League in 1985, but his record was lost in the earthquake that devastated Mexico City just after the close of the season. He rebounded to bat .402 with 24 HR and 113 RBI in 1986 and .415 with 25 HR and 115 RBI in 1987. He was first player at any level to post back-to-back .400 seasons since the early 1950s, helped considerably by the lively ball used in Mexico after 1984. /(MC)

Heinie Sand [John Henry] — 1897–1958. SS-3B 1923–28 **Phillies** 848 g, .258, 18 hr, 251 rbi

Sand was a slick fielder and fair hitter in six seasons as the regular Phillies shortstop. In September 1924, the Giants needed to win only one game in a series against the seventh-place Phillies to secure the NL pennant. Sand was approached by Giants outfielder Jimmy O'Connell, who said the New York players would make it worth $500 if Sand didn't "bear down too hard." Sand reported the bribe offer, and O'Connell and Giant coach Cozy Dolan, the instigator, were suspended for life. /(JK)

Ryne Sandberg (Ryno) — 1959- . 2B-3B 1981- Phillies, **Cubs** 1234 g, .285, 139 hr, 549 rbi. *2 LCS, 10 g, .385, 1 hr, 6 rbi*
☛ *Most Valuable Player—84. All-Star—84–89. Gold Glove—83–88, 89.*

A "can't miss" prospect, Ryne Sandberg more than equaled his billing. A shortstop in the minors, he was a throw-in in the deal that brought proven veteran Ivan DeJesus from the Cubs. Moved to third in 1982, Sandberg set a Cubs record for steals at the position (32) and a club rookie record for runs scored (103). He was named Chicago Rookie of the Year and a member of the Topps Major League All-Rookie Team. At second base in 1983, Ryne won a Gold Glove in his first full season at that spot. His 1984 MVP campaign featured more stellar fielding and a starting spot in the All-Star Game. He was one triple and one homer from being the first major leaguer ever with 200 hits and 20 doubles, triples, homers and steals in one season. He became the third 25-homer, 50-steal player in major league history in 1985 and established the NL record for fewest errors (5) and highest fielding percentage (.9938) at second base in 1986. At the end of 1989 he broke Manny Trillo's second base record of 89 consecutive errorless games, with manager Don Zimmer playing him for only one inning each in the last three games of the season. /(ME)

Ken Sanders (Daffy) — 1941– . RHP 1964, 66, 68, 70–76 A's, Red Sox, **Brewers**, Twins, Indians, Angels, Mets, Royals 656 ip, 29–45, 2.98

Ken Sanders may be best remembered for the number of teams for whom he pitched, the Mets in the National League and eight different American League clubs, including two named the Athletics (Kansas City and Oakland) and two in Kansas City (the A's and the Royals). His best years were in Milwaukee with the Brewers. In 1971 he appeared in 83 games, compiled 31 saves and 1.92 ERA, and set an American League record by finishing 77 games. His 12 losses that season (against 7 wins) are the third-most relief losses in a season.

Sanders also led the league in relief losses in 1966 with the Red Sox when he was 6–10, and again in 1972 with Milwaukee, when he was 2–9. He had only one start in his 408 major league games. /(GB)

Ray Sanders — 1916–1983. 1B 1942–46, 48–49 **Cardinals**, Braves 630 g, .274, 42 hr, 329 rbi. *4 WS, 14 g, .275, 2 hr, 3 rbi*

A Missouri native, Sanders was impressive as a Cardinal farmhand, allowing St. Louis to trade Johnny Mize to the Giants in 1941. Sanders played first base for Cardinal pennant winners in 1942, 1943, and 1944; he reached career highs of 12 HR, 102 RBI, and a .295 batting average in 1944 while leading NL first basemen in fielding. Sold to the Braves in 1946 so Stan Musial could play first base, Sanders suffered an arm injury that August, after which he played in only 15 ML games. /(JK)

Scott Sanderson — 1956– . RHP 1978– **Expos**, Cubs 1620 ip, 98–89, 3.55. *2 LCS, 7 ip, 0–0, 4.05*

A lanky NL starter for over a decade, Sanderson was pitching for the Expos in only his second professional season, and in 1980 was 16–11 with a 3.11 ERA. He was traded to the Padres for Gary Lucas on December 7, 1983, and the Padres dealt him to the Cubs the same day, for Carmelo Martinez, Craig Lefferts and Fritz Connally. Sanderson has struggled in Chicago, often battling injuries and never winning more than nine games in a season. /(SCL)

Fred Sanford — 1919– . RHP 1943, 46–51 **Browns**, Yankees, Senators 744 ip, 37–55, 4.45

Sanford lost an AL-high 21 games for the Browns in 1948, but the Yankees thought enough of him to send three players and $100,000 to St. Louis for him

and another player. Never more than a second-line starter in New York, he was dubbed the $100,000 Lemon by the New York press. He won only 12 games in a little over two seasons with the Yankees, before he was traded away to the Senators. /(NLM)

Jack Sanford — 1929– . RHP 1956–67 Phillies, **Giants**, Angels, A's 2049 ip, 137–101, 3.69. 20 wins: 62 *1 WS, 23 ip, 1–2, 1.93*
☛ *Rookie of the Year—57. Led League—k 57. All-Star—57.*

After seven years in the minors and a stint in the military, 28-year-old Jack Sanford compiled a 19–8 record for the fifth-place 1957 Phillies, striking out a league-high 188 batters and winning NL Rookie of the Year honors. He fanned 13 Cubs in one game, tying what was then a club record.

After falling to 10–13 in 1958, Sanford was dealt to San Francisco. When Sandy Koufax fanned 18 Giants on August 31, 1959, Sanford was his final strikeout victim. Though Sanford had just 12 victories in 1960, he led the NL with six shutouts. In 1962, he won 16 consecutive games, his 24–7 record sparking the Giants to the pennant. He had tough luck in the World Series after shutting out the Yankees on three hits in Game Two. He struck out 10 in a 5–3 Game Five loss, and lost 1–0 to Ralph Terry in the final contest.

Sanford pitched more than 200 innings each of his first five seasons with San Francisco, and topped the NL with 42 starts in 1963. He suffered a shoulder injury in 1964 that limited him to 18 games. Moved to the bullpen by the Angels, he recorded a league-high 12 wins in relief in 1966. /(GB)

Manny Sanguillen — 1944– . C-OF-DH-1B 1967, 69–80 **Pirates**, A's 1448 g, .296, 65 hr, 585 rbi. *5 LCS, 19 g, .239, 1 hr, 3 rbi. 2 WS, 10 g, .375, 0 hr, 1 rbi*
☛ *All-Star—71–72, 75.*

Speedy for a catcher, free-swinging Manny Sanguillen had great hitting ability, a strong arm, and a cat-like quality behind the plate. The ever-smiling Panamanian twice finished third in the NL batting race: in his second full season (1970), when he batted .325, and again in 1975, when he hit a career-high .328. The bad-ball-hitting Sanguillen was a good contact hitter, but rarely walked. Overshadowed by Johnny Bench, he edged out the Cincinnati catcher on *TSN*'s NL All-Star Team in 1971 -the only time between 1967 and 1975 that Bench was not selected. He was durable, catching more than 100 games in seven of his first eight full seasons with the Pirates. The exception was 1973, the season after his close friend, Roberto Clemente, was killed in an airplane crash; Sanguillen was chosen to replace Clemente in right field. The move did not work and Sanguillen returned to catching. After playing for five division-champion Pirate clubs, Sanguillen was sent with $100,000 to Oakland for Chuck Tanner in a rare player-for-manager trade on November 5, 1976. Pittsburgh reacquired the popular Sanguillen in April 1978. His pinch single with two out in the ninth in Game Two of the 1979 World Series gave the Pirates a 3–2 victory./(ME)

Rafael Santana — 1958– . SS-2B 1983–88 Cardinals, **Mets**, Yankees 661 g, .246, 12 hr, 153 rbi. *1 LCS, 6 g, .176. 1 WS, 7 g, .250, 2 rbi*

Santana was a light hitter valued by the defensively erratic 1986 World Champion Mets for his consistency at shortstop. Always a slow starter offensively, he hit a career-low .218 that season, not getting his average above .200 until the end of August, but was nonetheless in the lineup almost every day. He did have an important RBI in the Mets' game-winning rally in the seventh inning of Game Seven of the World Series.

Not a wide-ranging fielder, he used his strong arm to compensate for his lack of speed, although he also gained notoriety for his "rainbow" throws that always just beat the runner. He only gunned the ball when necessary. After joining the Yankees for 1988, he played most of the season with an arm injury. Advised by the team doctor that a winter's rest would cure his ills, it was discovered during spring training that surgery was in fact necessary. He missed all of 1989, with any continuation of his career in doubt./(SH)

Benito Santiago — 1965– . C 1986– **Padres** 431 g, .264, 47 hr, 193 rbi
☛ *Rookie of the Year—87. All-Star—89. Gold Glove—88, 89.*

Able to zip the ball on a line to any base from his knees, Santiago has the deadliest throwing arm among active ML catchers, but he has struggled offensively after a sensational rookie season, and his all-around defensive play remains sloppy. He was a unanimous choice as NL Rookie of the Year in 1987, when he hit .300 with 18 HR, 79 RBI, and 21 stolen bases, threw out 33% of the opposition's basestealers, and set a ML rookie record with a 34-game hitting streak (finally broken by Orel Hershiser). The streak was also a club record, and a ML record for catchers. Santiago's throwing improved in 1988, as he began to show off his lightning-quick from-the-knees throw more regularly. He threw out 45% of the basestealers who dared run against him, and picked off nine runners—seven at second base.

His hitting, however, slumped badly (.248, 10 HR, 46 RBI), and although he won a Gold Glove, he still led NL catchers in errors for the second consecutive season with 12./(SCL)

Jose Santiago — 1940– . RHP 1963–70 A's, **Red Sox** 556 ip, 34–29, 3.74. *1 WS, 10 ip, 0–2, 5.59*

Santiago contributed as a reliever and spot starter to the Red Sox's "Impossible Dream" of 1967, going 5–0 in September, including two successive victories over second-place Detroit. He finished at 12–4, with five saves. He then became the only pitcher in World Series history to lose a game in which he homered, as the Cardinals defeated the Red Sox, 2–1, in the 1967 opener. Elbow problems in 1968 ended Santiago's career./(EW)

Ron Santo — 1940– . 3B 1960–74 **Cubs**, White Sox 2243 g, .277, 342 hr, 1331 rbi
☛ *All-Star—63–66, 68–69, 71–73. Gold Glove—64–68.*

Santo made his ML debut on June 26, 1960, and remained the Cubs' third baseman for nearly 14 years. Emotional and sometimes hot-tempered, he played with a visible desire to win. His best overall season was 1964, when he hit .313, with 30 homers,

Ron Santo

114 RBI, and a league-leading 13 triples. He followed with three more seasons of 30 or more home runs and twice more topped 100 RBI. He led the NL in walks four times. In 1966 Santo enjoyed a 28-game hitting streak, and in 1967 he set a record (since broken) with 393 assists at third base.

A fine defensive third baseman, he won five Gold Gloves. He topped NL third basemen in putouts seven times, assists seven times, and double plays four times.

When the Cubs made their ill-fated run for the pennant in 1969, Santo became one of the team's cheerleaders by clicking his heels after every victory at Wrigley Field. Although some writers called it "bush," the victory dance was a hit with Cubs fans, until the team stopped winning. By the end of the year there was no more heel clicking. /(ARA)

Louis Santop [born Louis Santop Loftin](Top) — 1890–1942. C-OF-MGR Negro Leagues 1909–1926 Fort Worth Wonders, Oklahoma Monarchs, Philadelphia Giants, New York Lincoln Giants, Chicago American Giants, Lincoln Stars, Brooklyn Royal Giants, Hilldale statistics not available

This 6'4" 240-lb lefthanded-hitting catcher was one of black baseball's earliest superstars, a slugger who slammed tape-measure homers during the deadball era. A consummate showman who sometimes called home runs before he hit them, Santop was paid the astounding sum of $500 a month by Hilldale in the early 1920s. He reached his prime with the New York Lincoln Giants and Lincoln Stars from 1911 through 1916, catching pitching greats Smokey Joe Williams and Dick Redding. He is credited with batting as high as .470 against all levels of competition in '11. After serving in the WWI Navy, he spent 1918 through 1926 with Hilldale. In 1924, the only year for which complete records are available, Santop hit .389. When Hilldale won its third straight pennant in 1925, he reportedly batted .415. In 14 exhibition games against white major leaguers, he hit .296. /(JJM)

Al Santorini — 1948– . RHP 1968–73 Braves, **Padres**, Cardinals 494 ip, 17–38, 4.28

Santorini's first ML season was marred by arm problems, and he was on Atlanta's disabled list from July on. The Padres took him in the 1968 expansion draft, but after he recorded 8–14 and 1–8 marks in 1969 and 1970, he was traded to the Cardinals. /(GB)

Nelson Santovenia — 1961– . C 1987– **Expos** 191 g, .243, 13 hr, 72 rbi

Santovenia won the Expos' catching job in 1988 and hit .235 with eight HR and 41 RBI in 309 at-bats. The Cuban improved his average in 1989 while sharing the job with Mike Fitzgerald. /(JFC)

Manny Sarmiento [born Manuel Eduardo Sarmiento Aponte] — 1956– . RHP 1976–80, 82–83 **Reds**, Mariners, Pirates 514 ip, 26–22, 3.48. *1 LCS, 1 ip, 0–0, 18.00*

Sarmiento was a fine fielder with a lively split-finger fastball and a singing voice good enough to once sing the National Anthem before a game. As a 20-year-old rookie in 1976, the slender Venezuelan helped the Reds to a World Championship with five relief wins. /(EW)

Bill Sarni — 1927–1983. C 1951–52, 54–56 **Cardinals**, Giants 390 g, .263, 22 hr, 151 rbi

Sarni played for the Los Angeles Angels (Pacific Coast League) as a 15-year-old in 1943, but didn't make it to the ML to stay until 1954. He led NL catchers in fielding as a rookie, while hitting .300. During spring training of 1957, he suffered a heart attack that ended his playing career. /(EW)

Mackey Sasser (Hacker) — 1962– . C 1987– Giants, Pirates, **Mets** 146 g, .280, 2 hr, 41 rbi. *1 LCS, 4 g, .200*

Sasser saw the most playing time in 1989, when both Gary Carter and Barry Lyons went on the DL. The contact hitter's lack of power and low on-base average prevented him from winning the job, and observers blamed his game-calling during Carter and Lyons's absence for the problems of the Mets' pitching staff. /(SFS)

Tom Satriano (Satch) — 1940– . C-3B-1B-2B 1961–70 Dodgers, **Angels**, Red Sox 674 g, .225, 21 hr, 157 rbi

After many years as a versatile reserve, playing all infield positions, Satriano became the Angels' regular catcher in 1968 and had career-best totals in home runs (8) and RBI (44). In 1961, while at USC, he set a record in the College World Series with 10 hits in five games. /(EW)

Kevin Saucier (Hot Sauce) — 1956– . LHP 1978–82 Phillies, Tigers 203 ip, 15–11, 3.32. *1 LCS, 0.2 ip, 0–0, 0.00. 1 WS, 0.2, 0–0, 0.00*

This reliever had his best season with the 1980 World Champion Phillies, when he posted a 7–3 record in middle relief. Traded to Texas for Sparky Lyle after the season, he was sent on to Detroit three months later. He saved a career-high thirteen games in 1981. /(AL)

Hank Sauer — 1917- . OF 1941-42, 45, 48-59 Reds, **Cubs**, Cardinals, Giants 1399 g, .266, 288 hr, 876 rbi
☛ *Most Valuable Player—52. Led League—hr 52. Led League—rbi 52. All-Star—50, 52.*

Sauer was a slow-footed slugger who didn't reach the majors to stay until 1948, when he was 31 years old. That season he hit 35 homers and drove in 97 runs for the Reds, but when he started poorly the next year, he was swapped to the Cubs. He found a happy home in Wrigley Field. In his first full month in Chicago he smacked 11 homers.

In 1952, when he led the NL in RBI and tied Ralph Kiner for the home run championship with 37, Sauer was the NL MVP. After a broken finger slowed him in 1953, he bounced back with 41 homers in 1954.

Sauer was the first player to twice hit three home runs in a game off the same pitcher. The Phillies' Curt Simmons was the victim. On August 28, 1950, just before Simmons went into the service, Sauer slugged three off him at Wrigley to lead a 7-5 win. Two years later, on June 11, 1952, again at Wrigley Field, Sauer hit three solo homers to beat Simmons, 3-0. Sauer finished up with the Giants, slugging 26 HR in their last season at the Polo Grounds before becoming a part-time player when they moved to San Francisco in 1958.

Sauer's brother Ed played for the Cubs, Cardinals, and Braves between 1943 and 1949. /(AA)

Bob Savage — 1921- . RHP 1942, 46-49 **A's**, Browns 423 ip, 16-27, 4.32

Savage worked eight games for the A's in 1942 before entering the military. Wounded in the war, he wrote back to Connie Mack that he "wanted that shrapnel dug out of the shoulder," because he wanted to pitch. He returned in 1946, and went 3-15. /(GB)

Ted Savage — 1937- . OF 1962-63, 65-71 **Phillies**, Pirates, Cardinals, Cubs, Dodgers, Reds, Brewers, Royals 642 g, .233, 34 hr, 163 rbi

His speed and power made eight big league teams give this 6'1" 185-lb righthanded hitter a chance. Only in his rookie year with the Phillies in 1962 was he a regular, because he never became a consistent hitter. His best season came with the 1970 Brewers, when he had career highs of 12 HR, 50 RBI, and a .279 average in 274 at-bats. /(AL)

Bob Saverine (Rabbit) — 1941- . 2B-OF-SS-3B 1959, 62-64, 66-67 Orioles, **Senators** 379 g, .239, 6 hr, 47 rbi

For the Orioles, switch-hitting, speedy Bob Saverine was mainly a pinch runner. Purchased from the Baltimore organization by the Senators in 1965, he spent two years as a utility player, then returned to the minors as a player, coach, and manager. /(MC)

Eiji Sawamura — 1915-1945. P 1935-41 **Yomiuri Giants**

Japan's Sawamura Award, the equivalent of the Cy Young Award, is presented in memory of Eiji Sawamura, the first Japanese native to achieve pitching glory. As a 19-year-old amateur in 1934, Sawamura held a visiting American all-star team scoreless until Lou Gehrig's ninth-inning homer made him a 1-0 loser. In that game, Sawamura fanned Charley Gehringer, Babe Ruth, Jimmie Foxx, and Gehrig in succession. Joining the Yomiuri Giants, Sawamura became their first 30-game winner, going 33-10 in 1937. After the attack on Pearl Harbor, he enlisted in the Imperial Army and was killed in the battle for the Ryukyu Islands shortly before WWII ended. /(MC)

Carl Sawatski (Swats) — 1927- . C 1948, 50, 53-54, 57-63 Cubs, Braves, Phillies, **Cardinals** 633 g, .242, 58 hr, 213 rbi. *1 WS, 2 g, .000*

Carl's nickname, Swats, was a play on his surname rather than an indication of his long-ball prowess, although he belted 132 homers in his final four minor league seasons. A career ML reserve, he enjoyed his best season with the Cardinals in 1961, when he hit .299 with 10 HRs and 10 pinch hits. He was the Cardinal catcher on September 23, 1962 when Maury Wills stole his 97th base of the season, breaking Ty Cobb's modern mark.

Sawatski became president of the Texas League in 1976, following eight years as GM of that league's Arkansas franchise. /(ARA)

Eddie Sawyer — 1910- . *Manager* 1948-52, 58-60 **Phillies** 390-425, .479. First place: 1950 *1 WS, 0-4, .000*

An injury suffered in the minors ended Eddie Sawyer's hopes for a major league playing career. In 1939 he led the Canadian-American League in doubles (53), RBI (103), and batting average (.369). He began managing that year, and succeeded interim manager Dusty Cooke at the Phillies' helm in July 1948, following Ben Chapman's dismissal. In 1950 he led Philadelphia's Whiz Kids to the pennant, though it was almost blown. With nine days to go in the season, the Phillies had a seven-game lead, but lost eight of their last ten. They didn't clinch until the final day of the season, when they defeated the Dodgers in 10 innings at Ebbets Field. They then were swept in the World Series by the Yankees. Sawyer was fired in 1952, but was rehired in 1958. After finishing last in both '58 and 1959, Sawyer quit after losing the first game of the 1960 season. /(AL)

Rick Sawyer — 1948– . RHP 1974–77 Yankees, White Sox, **Padres** 207 ip, 12–9, 4.40

First signed by Cleveland in 1968, Sawyer went to the Yankees in a 1974 three-team deal, and had brief trials with New York. He made his first major league start with San Diego in 1976, throwing a shutout. /(KC)

Steve Sax — 1960– . 2B 1981– **Dodgers**, Yankees 1249 g, .287, 35 hr, 396 rbi. *4 LCS, 18 g, .273, 4 rbi. 2 WS, 7 g, .286*
☛ *Rookie of the Year—82. All-Star—82–83, 86, 89.*

The Dodgers broke up baseball's longest-running infield by trading second baseman Davey Lopes following their 1981 World Championship in order to give Sax a chance. Sax responded by winning the NL Rookie of the Year Award in 1982, the fourth consecutive season the honor was earned by a Dodger; he hit .282, set a Dodger rookie record with 49 stolen bases, and led the club with 638 at-bats, 88 runs, and 180 hits.

An enthusiastic player, Sax once broke coach Joey Amalfitano's finger with a high five while rounding third base on a game-winning homer. In 1983, he mysteriously became unable to make throws to first on easy plays, prompting a clubhouse exchange between manager Tom Lasorda and third baseman Pedro Guerrero: "Pedro, what do you think about when the ball is hit?" Answered Guerrero, "First I think, 'I hope they don't hit it to me.' Then I think 'I hope they don't hit it to Sax.'"

A 25-game hitting streak in September 1986 brought Sax within two points of a batting title; he finished at .332, as Tim Raines batted .334.

Sax became a free agent after the Dodgers' 1988 World Championship and signed with the Yankees. Steve and older brother Dave, a catcher, played on the same minor league team for four straight seasons, and Dave had brief stays with the Dodgers in 1982 and 1983. /(TG)

George Scales (Tubby) — 1900–1976. 2B-3B-OF-SS-MGR Negro Leagues 1920–48 St. Louis Giants, New York Lincoln Giants, Homestead Grays, New York Black Yankees, Baltimore Elite Giants, Philadelphia Stars, Newark Stars, St. Louis Stars 239 g, .311, 29 hr (inc.)
☛ *All-Star—43.*

Hall of Famer Buck Leonard said that Negro Leaguer George Scales was the greatest curveball hitter he ever saw. Scales was a clutch, contact hitter and a quality infielder who compensated for his lack of speed with intelligence and alert play. He batted fifth for the great 1931 Homestead Grays, the team that won 136 games while losing 17; its members included Josh Gibson, Oscar Charleston, Ted Page, and Vic Harris. Scales has been credited with teaching Junior Gilliam (who went on to star for the Dodgers) to switch-hit during their years with the Baltimore Elite Giants. /(LL)

Doc Scanlan [William Dennis] — 1881–1949. RHP 1903–07, 09–11 Pirates, **Dodgers** 1252 ip, 66–71, 3.00

Scanlon was 18–13 for the 1906 Dodgers despite leading the NL in bases on balls (127). Following his ML career, he practiced medicine in Brooklyn. His younger brother Frank pitched in six games for the 1906 Phillies. /(JK)

Randy Scarbery — 1952– . RHP 1979–80 **White Sox** 130 ip, 3–10, 4.50

Scarbery was Houston's first pick in the June, 1970 draft, but turned down an $86,000 bonus and enrolled at USC. He signed with Oakland as their top choice three years later, but reached the majors with the 1979 White Sox, and led their staff with 45 appearances. /(KC)

Ray Scarborough — 1917–1982. RHP 1942–43, 46–53 **Senators**, White Sox, Red Sox, Yankees, Tigers 1429 ip, 80–85, 4.13. *1 WS, 1 ip, 0–0, 9.00*

The Senators considered Scarborough a hot prospect before WWII. After spending 1944 and 1945 in the military, the Wake Forest graduate developed into a reliable, curveballing starter. He had his greatest success in 1948–49, going 15–8 (2.82) and 13–11 (4.60). Purchased by the Yankees from Boston in August of 1952, he went 5–1 during New York's successful pennant drive. /(GB)

Mac Scarce — 1949– . LHP 1972–75, 78 **Phillies**, Mets, Twins 209 ip, 6–19, 3.70

Scarce made all 159 of his major league appearances in relief. In 1973 he led the Phillies' staff with a 2.42

ERA and 12 saves, though he compiled a 1–8 record. /(JCA)

Russ Scarritt — 1903– . OF 1929–32 **Red Sox**, Phillies 285 g, .285, 3 hr, 120 rbi

Scarritt batted .294 as Boston's starting left fielder in 1929, setting a still-standing Red Sox rookie record with 17 triples. Though he batted as high as .377 in the minors, he lasted just two seasons as a ML regular. /(EW)

Les Scarsella — 1913–1958. 1B 1935–37, 39–40 **Reds**, Braves 262 g, .284, 6 hr, 109 rbi

Scarsella was the Reds' regular first baseman as a rookie in 1936, batting .313. The lefthanded hitter led the NL with nine pinch hits in 1937. In need of pitching, the Reds traded Scarsella to Boston for Milkman Jim Turner in December 1939. /(GB)

Paul Schaal — 1943– . 3B 1964–74 Angels, **Royals**, Angels 1128 g, .244, 57 hr, 323 rbi

Schaal was the third baseman on the 1965 Topps Rookie All-Star Team, playing 155 games for the Angels. In Boston on June 13, 1968, he was struck behind the ear by a Jose Santiago pitch, and played only two more games that season. He was taken by the Royals in the 1968 expansion draft, but almost retired because he lost his equilibrium looking up to track high pops. He returned to form in 1971, playing in all of Kansas City's 161 games, and reached base 255 times (103 walks), second best in the AL. /(KC)

Al Schacht (The Clown Prince of Baseball) — 1892–1984. RHP 1919–21 **Senators** 197 ip, 14–10, 4.48

A sore arm limited Schacht to a short ML career, but he was on hand for 25 World Series and 18 All-Star Games in his role as "The Clown Prince of Baseball." After retiring as a player, he was a coach for fifteen years and developed his comic act. At first he teamed with Nick Altrock, a Senators coach and resident clown, reviving many of the routines Altrock had pioneered with Germany Schaefer, his first partner. Eventually, Schacht put on his clown costume, a battered top hat and tattered frock coat, and took to the road. He made his fortune touring America's ballparks with an act that was part pantomime and part anecdotes, always booked for a season's finale wherever the World Series was played. During WWII he toured with the USO, traveling to Europe, Africa, and the Pacific. After his barnstorming days ended, he opened a successful New York restaurant that became a popular meeting place for sports celebrities. /(JK)

Germany Schaefer [Herman A.] — 1877–1919. 2B-1B-3B-SS-OF 1901–02, 05–16, 18 Cubs, **Tigers**, Senators, Newark (FL), Yankees, Indians 1143 g, .257, 9 hr, 308 rbi

One of the zaniest characters in baseball history, Schaefer is most famous for causing a rule change with one of his antics. Actually he had a practical reason for stealing first base. Playing Cleveland, the Tigers had the speed Davy Jones on third base and Schaefer on first in the ninth inning and tried a delayed double steal, but the catcher, Nig Clarke, didn't throw. Schaefer ran back to first base on the next pitch, then shouted across to Jones that he was going to second base again. The catcher, rattled, threw down to second and Jones scored the winning run. That tactic was then outlawed.

Schaefer was a powerless hitter and rarely hit for a good average, but his versatility afield kept him in the majors for 13 seasons (not counting his last two years, when he played in only one game each). In his first two years with the Tigers, 1905–06, he was their regular second baseman, leading the AL in putouts in 1905 and in total chances per game in 1906. He had only one more season in which he played 100 games at a single position. His best season offensively was probably 1908, when he reached career highs with 96 runs (third in the AL), 40 steals (third), and 20 doubles as the Tigers won their second of three consecutive AL pennants (1907–09). Traded to the Senators in mid-1909, he had one more significant season, hitting a career-high .334 in 125 games in 1911, but thereafter spent most of his time on the coaching lines, teamed with fellow clown Nick Altrock. An earlier vaudeville act with Tiger teammate Charley O'Leary was the inspiration for the MGM musical "Take Me Out to the Ball Game," starring Gene Kelly and Frank Sinatra. Schaefer's friend John McGraw made him a Giant scout in 1919, and while on a scouting trip to Canada that year, Schaefer died of a massive heart attack. /(WOR)

Jimmie Schaffer — 1936– . C 1961–68 **Cardinals**, Cubs, White Sox, Mets, Phillies, Reds 314 g, .223, 11 hr, 56 rbi

Schaffer, never a regular, had his best year in 1963, when he hit .239 with career highs of seven HR and 19 RBI. He suffered a broken hand in 1964, hit .205, and never topped .200 after that. /(JFC)

Joe Schaffernoth — 1937– . RHP 1959–61 **Cubs**, Indians 118 ip, 3–8, 4.58

Despite the high hopes of the Cubs, 6'4" Joe Schaffernoth won just three ML games, and saved three others. He recorded a 2.78 ERA in 1960, coming out of the bullpen 33 times. /(DAS)

Ray Schalk (Cracker) — 1892–1970. C 1912–29 **White Sox**, Giants 1760 g, .253, 12 hr, 594 rbi. *2 WS, 14 g, .286, 2 rbi.*
    Manager 1927–28 **White Sox** 102–125, .449
☛ *Hall of Fame—1955.*

Hall of Famer Ray Schalk was one of the premier catchers of his day. He caught a ML-record four no-hitters in his career, including two in May 1914 and Charlie Robertson's perfect game April 30, 1922.

Ray Schalk

He handled perennially strong pitching staffs, including the 1920 White Sox rotation that boasted four 20-game winners. The 5'9"165-lb workhorse caught 100 or more games in 12 seasons (1913–23, '25) and led AL catchers eight times in fielding, eight times in putouts (eight straight years, 1913–20), four times in double plays, and twice in assists. His .989 fielding average in 1922 tied the AL record at the time. He set ML catching records for career games and putouts, and still holds the ML career record for double plays and the AL career mark for assists. An important innovator, he is credited with being the first catcher to back up plays at first and third base. A powerless, merely adequate batter, he set a record for catchers by stealing 30 bases in 1916. He hit for the cycle on June 27, 1922. His best batting came in the 1919 World Series, when he hit .304 as eight of his teammates threw the Series to gamblers; he could tell what was happening, and almost came to blows with pitcher Lefty Williams. /(JFC)

Roy Schalk — 1908– . 2B 1932, 44–45 **Yankees**, **White Sox** 282 g, .233, 2 hr, 109 rbi

A classic WWII player, Schalk returned to the majors at age 35, 12 years after a three-game 1932 tryout with the Yankees. He was the White Sox' second baseman in 1944 and 1945, finishing among the league leaders in four fielding categories. He led AL second basemen with 65 RBI in '45. /(GB)

Art Schallock — 1924– . LHP 1951–55 **Yankees**, Orioles 170 ip, 6–7, 4.02. *1 WS, 2 ip, 0–0, 4.50*

Schallock was a reliever and spot starter with the Yankees at the peak of their dominance, and went 3–1 as a starter in his rookie 1951 season. /(WOR)

Wally Schang — 1889–1965. C-OF-3B 1913–31 **A's**, Red Sox, Yankees, Browns, Tigers 1840 g, .284, 59 hr, 710 rbi. *6 WS, 32 g, .287, 1 hr, 8 rbi*

One of baseball's best catchers throughout most of his 18-year ML career, Schang played for top teams and caught most of the leading AL pitchers of his time, including Hall of Famers Herb Pennock, Eddie Plank, Chief Bender, Babe Ruth, Waite Hoyt, and Lefty Grove. A strong hitter (six seasons over .300) and good baserunner (one of the few catchers to steal more than 100 bases), his defensive work was also outstanding, although he holds the AL career record for most errors by a catcher, 218. When not catching, managers sometimes played him in the outfield or at third base to keep his bat in the lineup.
    Schang broke in as a rookie with Connie Mack's

champions of 1913–14. He was traded to the Red Sox in 1918 and helped them to a World Championship. He was the Yankees' regular catcher when they won their first three pennants in 1921–23. He was a reserve for the 1930 Athletics, his seventh pennant-winning team. He is the only player to be on three different World Championship clubs. On May 12, 1915, catching for the Athletics, he threw out six Browns runners attempting to steal; on the same date in 1920 he had eight assists for the Red Sox in a game against the Indians. Both feats are AL records. His older brother Bobby caught briefly in the NL before WWI. /(JK)

Charley Schanz — 1919– . RHP 1944–47, 50 **Phillies**, Red Sox 627 ip, 28–43, 4.34

As a rookie, Schanz was the Phillies' best pitcher in 1944, with a 13–16 mark. He never again won more than six games in the majors. His 22 victories with Seattle (Pacific Coast League) in 1949 earned him a final shot with the Red Sox. /(AL)

Art Scharein (Scoop) — 1905–1969. 3B-SS 1932–34 **Browns** 205 g, .244, 0 hr, 70 rbi

Scharein had more range than any other third baseman in his time. Although he never played enough games to qualify for percentage titles, he led AL third basemen in double plays in 1933 (in 95 games). He hit .304 in his rookie 1932 season but dropped exactly 100 points the next year. The arrival of heavy-hitting Harlond Clift effectively ended his career. His brother was Phillies' shortstop George Scharein. /(WOR)

George Scharein (Tom) — 1914–1981. SS-2B 1937–40 **Phillies** 388 g, .240, 2 hr, 119 rbi

Scharein was a regular only in his rookie 1937 season, when he led NL shortstops in putouts and double plays and hit .241 with a career-high 57 RBI in 146 games. His younger brother was Art "Scoop" Scharein. /(SFS)

Dan Schatzeder — 1954– . LHP 1977– **Expos**, Tigers, Giants, Phillies, Twins, Indians, Astros 1241 ip, 68–65, 3.80. *1 LCS, 4 ip, 0–0, 0.00. 1 WS, 4 ip, 1–0, 6.23*

A lefthander who can start or relieve, Schatzeder has pitched for seven different clubs, but was often more effective with his bat, hitting .249 with 5 HR. In 1986 his five pinch hits were the most by a ML pitcher since Don Newcombe in 1959. Schatzeder debuted with the Expos in 1977 after less than two full seasons in the minors, and in 1979 his 2.83 ERA was best among NL lefthanders. He was traded

to Detroit for Ron Le Flore and won a career-high 11 games for the Tigers in 1980, but was only an occasional starter after 1981. Overall, Schatzeder was traded four times, sold once, and released twice before signing with the Astros for the 1989 season. He made his only postseason appearances with the 1987 Twins, and won Game Six of the '87 WS in relief. /(SCL)

Rube Schauer [Alexander John, born Dimitri Ivanovich Dimitrihoff] — 1891–1957. RHP 1913–17 **Giants**, A's 400 ip, 10–29, 3.35

One of only five native Russians in ML history, Schauer was pitching with a semi-pro team in Garrison, ND, when the Giants bought him for $10,000. He was much talked about when he went 28–6 for Superior (Northern League, Class C) and was brought up to New York. Yet he was unable to win in the majors, and he saw the most action in his last season, 1917, going 7–16 for the Athletics. /(NLM)

Bob Scheffing — 1913–1985. C 1941–42, 46–51 **Cubs**, Reds, Cardinals 517 g, .263, 20 hr, 187 rbi. *Manager* 1957–59, 61–63 **Cubs**, Tigers 418–427, .495

A solid defensive catcher, Scheffing hit .300 in 102 games with the 1948 Cubs. He managed the 1961 Tigers to 101 wins but finished second to the Yankees, who won 109. He was the Mets' GM from 1970 to 1975. /(ARA)

Carl Scheib — 1927– . RHP 1943–45, 47–54 **A's**, Cardinals 1072 ip, 45–65, 4.88

Signed by the Athletics out of high school, hard-throwing Carl Scheib became the youngest player to appear in an American League game (16 years, eight months, five days) when he made his pro debut in the second game of a September 6, 1943 doubleheader. He pitched in 25 games with Philadelphia before being called to military duty in 1945. He returned in 1947, went 14–8 in 1948, but dropped to 3–10 with a league-high nine relief losses in 1950. For a pitcher, he was an outstanding hitter (.250, 5 HR). /(AL)

Richie Scheinblum — 1942– . OF-DH 1965, 67–69, 71–74 **Indians**, Senators, Royals, Reds, Angels, Cardinals 462 g, .263, 13 hr, 127 rbi
☛ *All-Star—72.*

The switch-hitting Scheinblum frustrated his managers by being a slow starter. "Never in my career have I batted over .200 the first month of the season," he once said. A perennial prospect with Cleveland, he batted just .186 in 1969, was sold to

Washington, and was soon back in the minor leagues. After he led the American Association with a .388 batting average and 108 RBI in 1971, he was purchased by the Royals, for whom he hit .300 as an everyday right fielder in 1972. That November, Kansas City sent him to Cincinnati in the trade for Hal McRae. He batted .222 for Cincinnati in the first 29 games in 1973, was traded to California, and batted .328 the rest of the way—.371 after the All-Star break, and .419 in September. /(KC)

Hank Schenz — 1919– . 2B-3B 1946–51 **Cubs**, Pirates, Giants 207 g, .247, 2 hr, 24 rbi. *1 WS, 1 g, --*

A peppery hustler, Schenz had good minor league records that earned him yearly ML trials, but he never won more than a utility role in parts of six seasons. /(EW)

Fred Scherman — 1944– . LHP 1969–76 **Tigers**, Astros, Expos 536 ip, 33–26, 3.66. *1 LCS, 1 ip, 0–0, 0.00*

A mainstay of the Tiger bullpen in the early 1970s, Scherman relieved 170 times in three years. In 1971 he set a club record with 69 appearances, earning 20 saves and an AL-high 10 relief wins. In 1973 Tiger manager Billy Martin ordered him to throw a spitball in retaliation for Gaylord Perry's alleged use of the illegal pitch. The resulting uproar led to Martin's dismissal. /(CC)

Bill Scherrer — 1958– . LHP 1982–88 **Reds**, Tigers, Orioles, Phillies 311 ip, 8–10, 4.08. *1 WS, 3 ip, 0–0, 3.00*

Scherrer's best season was 1983 when he appeared in 73 games for the Reds, saving 10, with a 2.74 ERA. His ERA has not dipped below 4.18 since, and in 1987–88 he was released three times by three different minor league clubs. /(SCL)

Chuck Schilling — 1937– . 2B 1961–65 **Red Sox** 541 g, .239, 23 hr, 146 rbi

As a rookie in 1961, Schilling batted a career-high .259 and committed only eight errors in 854 chances (a .991 fielding percentage), then an AL record for fewest errors by a second baseman (150 games). When traded to Minnesota in 1966, he announced his retirement. /(EW)

Calvin Schiraldi — 1962– . RHP 1984– Mets, Red Sox, **Cubs** 445 ip, 29–30, 4.17. *1 LCS, 6 ip, 0–1, 1.50. 1 WS, 4 ip, 0–2, 13.50*

The 6'5" Schiraldi emerged as the Red Sox' bullpen ace in the latter half of 1986, saving nine games and fanning 55 batters in 51 innings, but he self-destructed in the postseason, losing Game Four of

the ALCS and Games Six and Seven of the WS. Traded to the Cubs with Al Nipper for Lee Smith, he was an ineffective starter in 1988 and was returned to the bullpen in 1989. In 1983, he was a teammate of Roger Clemens, Greg Swindell, and Bruce Ruffin for the University of Texas NCAA baseball champions. /(SCL)

Admiral Schlei [George Henry] — 1878–1958. C 1904–11 **Reds**, Giants 636 g, .237, 6 hr, 209 rbi

Schlei, whose name sounded the same as that of a bluff, popular, and controversial Spanish-American War admiral, was a pretty good defensive catcher who went to the Giants in the three-way trade that sent Roger Bresnahan to St. Louis. /(ADS)

Ray Schmandt — 1896–1969. 1B-2B 1915, 18–22 Browns, **Dodgers** 317 g, .269, 3 hr, 122 rbi. *1 WS, 1 g, .000*

As a tall, thin first baseman at St. Louis University, Schmandt caught Browns' manager Branch Rickey's eye and was signed upon graduation. After going 0-for-4, he went to the minors but returned in 1918 to put in five years with the Dodgers. /(JK)

Gus Schmelz — 1850–1925. Manager 1884, 86–91, 94–97 Columbus (AA), Cardinals, Cincinnati (AA), Cleveland (NL), **Washington (NL)** 623–703, .470

He never won a pennant, but Schmelz was a highly respected manager. He believed the most important factor in success was the players' confidence, in themselves, one another, and the manager. He had a big, thick beard and supposedly gave signals by pointing with it. An opponent of the Brotherhood League, he advocated banning for life all who played in it. Schmelz gave John Heydler his start in baseball. When an assigned umpire failed to appear for a game, Schmelz called Heydler out of the stands to substitute. Heydler went on to become a regular umpire and eventually rose to NL president. /(NLM)

Bob Schmidt — 1933– . C 1958–63, 65 **Giants**, Reds, Senators, Yankees 454 g, .243, 39 hr, 150 rbi
☛ *All-Star—58.*

In 1958 rookie Schmidt won the Giants' catching job and a spot on the NL All-Star team with an early-season batting tear. He finished with 14 HR, led NL catchers in double plays, and set a since-broken record with 22 putouts in one game. After 1958, Schmidt was platooned. /(MC)

Boss Schmidt [Charles] — 1880–1932. C 1906–11
Tigers 477 g, .243, 3 hr, 124 rbi. *3 WS, 14 g, .159, 5 rbi*

A brawler who boxed an exhibition with heavyweight champ Jack Johnson, Schmidt became the
leader of three Tiger pennant winners (1907–09) by
whipping Ty Cobb in several fights. He made the
last out in consecutive World Series in 1907–08, the
only player ever to do so. Walter Schmidt was his
younger brother. /(JK)

Butch Schmidt [Charles John] — 1886–1952. 1B-LHP
1909, 13–15 Yankees, **Braves** 297 g, .272, 4 hr, 145 rbi;
5 ip, 0–0, 7.20. *1 WS, 4 g, .294, 2 rbi*

Schmidt pitched one game for the Highlanders (later
the Yankees) in 1909, then reappeared with the
Braves. He was the everyday first baseman on the
1914 Miracle Braves and led NL first basemen in
double plays while batting .285 with a career-high
71 RBI. /(WOR)

Dave Schmidt — 1957– . RHP 1981– **Rangers**, White
Sox, Orioles 847 ip, 51–51, 3.76

The only pitcher on the Orioles with a winning
record in both 1987 and 1988, Schmidt was almost
exclusively a reliever with the Rangers and White
Sox before pitching his way into Baltimore's starting
rotation in 1987. He was leading the AL in ERA on
June 24 (2.24), but a bone spur in his pitching elbow
sidelined him after August 22 and required surgery,
and he spent most of 1988 back in the bullpen.
Schmidt has excellent control, walking only 2.4
batters per nine innings in his ML career. /(SCL)

Freddy Schmidt — 1916– . RHP 1944, 46–47
Cardinals, Phillies, Cubs 225 ip, 13–11, 3.75. *1 WS, 3 ip,
0–0, 0.000*

Schmidt had a blazing fastball and a fine change of
pace. After going 7–3 with the 1944 Cardinals, he
went into military service and did not regain his
form upon his return. /(EW)

Henry Schmidt — 1873–1926. RHP 1903 **Dodgers**
301 ip, 21–13, 3.83. 20 wins: 03

Schmidt was 29 years old when Brooklyn manager
Ned Hanlon discovered him pitching in the Pacific
Coast League. In his only ML season, he went 21–13
for Brooklyn in 1903. The Texan returned his 1904
contract unsigned, with a note that simply said, "I
do not like living in the East and will not report."
Adamant in his refusal to continue in the majors, he
returned to the West Coast, where the lifestyle better
suited him. /(JK)

Mike Schmidt — 1949– . 3B 1972–89 **Phillies**
2404 g, .267, 548 hr, 1595 rbi. *5 LCS, 20 g, .241, 1 hr,
7 rbi. 2 WS, 11 g, .220, 2 hr, 7 rbi*
☛ *Most Valuable Player—80–81, 86. Led League—hr
74–76, 80, 81, 83, 84, 86. Led League—rbi 80, 81, 84,
86. All-Star—74, 76–77, 79–84, 86–87, 89. Gold
Glove—76–84, 86.*

By the time he retired early in the 1989 season,
Schmidt had established himself as the best all-
around third baseman of all time. He was the NL's
premier power hitter in the 1970s and 1980s, failing
to hit 30 HR only three times in 16 ML seasons
through 1988. He won the home run crown eight
times, led the NL in slugging five times and RBI
four, and is seventh on the all-time HR list. He led
the league in walks four times and strikeouts four
times, and owns the fourth-highest strikeout total in
ML history. He also won 11 Gold Gloves.

Strikeouts were particularly troublesome to
Schmidt early in his career. He averaged 150 over
his first four seasons and was nicknamed "A-choo!"
by teammate Willie Montanez. But once he learned
to be more selective at the plate, Schmidt became
the consummate all-around ballplayer, hitting for
both power and a high on-base average, stealing
15–20 bases per year, and providing stellar defense
at third base.

The Phillies drafted Schmidt from Ohio University in the second round of the 1971 draft, and he
spent two seasons in the minors before being called
up in September 1972. He hit only .196 in his first
full season but showed promising power with 18
HR. A season of winter ball in Puerto Rico and
following advice from manager Danny Ozark and
coach Bobby Wine helped him come into his own in
1974. He doubled his HR total to lead the NL and
raised his average almost 100 points. Hitting third
ahead of Greg Luzinski, Schmidt still drew 106
walks. He also hit one of the longest singles in ML
history that year, crushing a Claude Osteen fastball
off a speaker dangling from the roof of the Astrodome, 329 feet from the plate and 117 feet in the air.

Playing with a sprained left shoulder, Schmidt
struck out a career-high 180 times in 1975, but still
led the NL in home runs and stole 29 bases, also a
career high. On July 17, 1976 Schmidt hit four HR
in one game at Wrigley Field, as the Phillies rallied
from a 13–2 deficit to beat the Cubs 18–16 in 10
innings. He hit his first homer that day off Rick
Reuschel, and the fourth off Rick's brother, Paul.

Schmidt was uncomfortable with his new role as

Mike Schmidt

team captain in 1978 and suffered an off-year. Pete Rose's arrival in 1979 gave the club an additional spiritual leader, and Schmidt enjoyed a resurgence. He began to hit the ball to all fields, rather than trying to pull each pitch over the left-field fence, and recorded the highest HR totals of his career, 45 in 1979 and 48 in 1980. He was the runaway choice for MVP in 1980 and took WS MVP honors as well, with a .381 average and 2 HR in the Phillies' six-game victory. His double keyed a four-run eighth-inning rally in Game Two that led to a 6–4 win, he homered in a losing cause in Game Three, homered again in Game Five and scored the tying run in the ninth inning, and drove in a pair of runs in the Phillies' final 4–1 win. The 1981 players' strike did not slow him down, as he hit .316 with 31 HR to win his second straight MVP award.

Schmidt cracked the 40-HR and 100-RBI barriers again in 1983 but suffered a miserable post-season, with only one single in 20 at-bats in a WS loss to the Orioles. That winter he became baseball's highest-paid player, signing for $2.1 million per year, and his next four seasons were typically productive. The Phillies shifted Schmidt to first base in 1985 to allow Rick Schu to play third, but the experiment didn't last the season, and in 1986 he won his third MVP award, despite the Phillies finishing a distant second to the Mets, over 20 games out. Schmidt led the NL in homers (37) and RBI (119) for the final time that year, and batted .290. In 1987, he hit .293 with 35 HR and 115 RBI. Schmidt suffered the first serious injury of his career in 1988, a rotator cuff problem requiring surgery that forced him to miss the final one-third of the season. He returned to hit six homers early in 1989, but when his average dipped to .203 in May he retired. Fans elected him to the starting lineup of the NL All-Star team despite his retirement, but he did not play. /(SG)

Walter Schmidt — 1887–1973. C 1916–25 **Pirates**, Cardinals 769 g, .257, 3 hr, 234 rbi

The younger brother of Boss Schmidt, who caught for Detroit from 1906 through 1911, Walter was a light-hitting, platooned Pirate catcher for nine seasons. He had to buy his release from San Francisco (Pacific Coast League) to sign with Pittsburgh. /(ME)

Willard Schmidt — 1928– . RHP 1952–53, 55–59 **Cardinals**, Reds 586 ip, 31–29, 3.93

Schmidt was up with the Cardinals for brief trials in 1952–53, stuck in 1955, and went 10–3 (5–0 as a starter) at his best in 1957. That winter he was sent to Cincinnati in a deal for Curt Flood. Schmidt (4/26/59) and Frank Thomas are the only two ML players to have been hit by a pitch twice in the same inning. /(GB)

Crazy Schmit [Frederic M.] (Germany) — 1866–1940. LHP 1890, 92–93, 99, 1901 Pirates, Baltimore (NL), Giants, **Cleveland (NL)**, Baltimore (AL) 361 ip, 7–36, 5.45

Schmit was dubbed "Crazy" by teammates who regarded the drinker as the most eccentric player of his time. He was only allowed one complete season with a single team, the 20–134 1899 Cleveland Spiders, for whom he went 2–17. /(JK)

Johnny Schmitz (Bear Tracks) — 1920– . LHP 1941–42, 46–56 **Cubs**, Dodgers, Yankees, Reds, Senators, Red Sox, Orioles 1812 ip, 93–114, 3.55
☛ *Led League—k 46. All-Star—46, 48.*

Bear Tracks (inspired by his shuffle to the mound) was an underrated lefty who spent most of his career with weak teams. After returning to the Cubs from the service in 1946, he led the NL in strikeouts and was named to the All-Star team. He led the league in losses (18) the next year but reversed his record to 18–13 (2.64) in 1948, despite the Cubs' last-place finish. Again he made the All-Star team. A noted Dodger-killer (he won 18 lifetime against Brooklyn), he was traded to the Dodgers in 1951 as part of the deal that also put Andy Pafko in a Brooklyn uniform. A variety of arm and shoulder ailments confined him to spot duty after that, with his high point an 11–8 season for the sixth-place 1954 Senators./(ARA)

Dan Schneider — 1942– . LHP 1963–64, 66–67, 69 Braves, **Astros** 166 ip, 2–5, 4.72

Signed out of the University of Arizona for a reported $100,000 bonus in 1962, Schneider was a sinkerballer. In his busiest year he made 54 relief appearances for the 1967 Astros./(MC)

Pete Schneider — 1895–1957. RHP 1914–19 **Reds**, Yankees 1283 ip, 58–86, 2.62. 20 wins: 17

Schneider lost a league-high 19 games for the 1915 Reds, but in 1917 went 20–19 (1.98). He struggled with his control, leading the NL in walks in both 1917 and '18, and was sent back to the minors after a brief fling with the 1919 Yankees. A good-hitting pitcher (.221), he gradually converted to the outfield. With Vernon in the Pacific Coast League on May 11, 1923, he belted Salt Lake City pitching for five home runs and a double, knocking in 14 runs. He continued playing in the minors until 1926./(LRD)

Red Schoendienst [Albert Fred] — 1923– . 2B-OF-SS-3B 1945–63 **Cardinals**, Giants, Braves 2216 g, .289, 84 hr, 773 rbi. *3 WS, 19 g, .269, 3 rbi.*
   Manager 1965–76, 80 **Cardinals** 1028–944, .521. First place: 67–68 *2 WS, 7–7, .500*
☛ *All-Star—46, 48–55, 57.*

Although he suffered a severe eye injury in the Civilian Conservation Corps, Schoendienst signed a minor league contract with the Cardinals for $75 a month in 1942. At Rochester the following season, he was named International League MVP. After spending most of 1944 in the army, he was discharged early in 1945 because of eye problems and an injured shoulder, yet he made the Cardinals as a starting left fielder a few months later. He finished the season with a NL-high 26 stolen bases.

When Lou Klein jumped to the Mexican League in 1946, Schoendienst moved to second base, and led NL second basemen in fielding average for the first of seven seasons. With sure hands and quick reflexes, he handled 320 consecutive chances without an error in 1950. He set a NL record in 1956 with a .9934 fielding average at 2B, eclipsed 30 years later by Ryne Sandberg.

Schoendienst was one of the best switch-hitters of his day. He led the league in at-bats in 1947 and again in '50, when he also led in doubles. In the 1950 All-Star Game, he hit a dramatic 14th-inning home run to win it for the NL. He batted .342 to finish second behind Carl Furillo in the 1953 NL batting race.

Schoendienst was sent to the Giants as part of a multi-player deal on June 14, 1956. A year and a day later, he was traded to the Braves, and led the NL with 200 hits. A key component of Milwaukee's consecutive pennant-winners, he played 106 games in 1958 despite bruised ribs, a broken finger, and pleurisy. Tuberculosis cost him part of a lung in 1959, causing him to miss all but five games of the season. His struggle to come back drew national attention. He returned to the Cardinals in 1961, and in 1962 led the league with 22 pinch hits in 72 attempts. He was a .303 career pinch hitter.

A Cardinal coach under Johnny Keane, Schoendienst succeeded him in 1965, beginning the longest managerial tenure in club history. Under his direction, St. Louis won pennants in 1967 and 1968, and defeated the Tigers in the '68 World Series. Friendly and popular, he had an easy-going managerial style. Fired in 1976 after 12 years at the helm, he spent two years coaching for the A's before returning in that capacity to the Cardinals in 1979. He again served as Cardinal manager for six weeks in 1980 as Whitey Herzog temporarily left the dugout to become general manager./(FJO)

Dick Schofield [John Richard] (Ducky) — 1935– . SS-2B-3B 1953–71 Cardinals, **Pirates**, Giants, Yankees, Dodgers, Red Sox, Brewers 1321 g, .227, 21 hr, 211 rbi. *2 WS, 5 g, .333*

Schofield started as an 18-year-old and played 19 seasons in the majors, mostly as a utility infielder. In 1963–64 as Pittsburgh's regular shortstop, he had back-to-back .246 BA's, nearly 20 points above his career average. Although a notoriously weak hitter, he was used as a pinch-hitter more than 300 times. His son, also named Dick, came up with the Angels in 1983./(FJO)

Red Schoendienst (l.), Billy Queen

Dick Schofield — 1962- . SS 1983- **Angels** 827 g, .231, 47 hr, 229 rbi. *1 LCS, 7 g, .300, 1 hr, 2 rbi*

Schofield led the Midwest League in hitting (.360 at Danville) in 1982 and hit .284 with 94 RBI with Edmonton (Pacific Coast League) the following year before earning the Angels starting shortstop job in 1984. He is extremely quick, and has surprising power for a 5'10" shortstop, but has never hit better than .251 in the ML. On August 29, 1986, his grand slam on an 0–2 pitch with two out in the ninth gave the Angels a 13–12 win over Detroit, after they had trailed 12–5 entering the inning. His father, Dick, was also a longtime ML shortstop. /(SCL)

Mike Schooler — 1962- . RHP 1988- **Mariners** 125 ip, 6–15, 3.08

Schooler became Seattle's bullpen ace in the second half of 1988, saving 15 games and striking out better than a batter an inning. He surpassed that performance in 1989, his first full season, improving his control by half and finishing in the league leaders in saves. /(WOR)

Gene Schott — 1913– . RHP 1935–39 **Reds**, Phillies 587 ip, 28–41, 3.72

The fireballer was 11–11 for the 1936 Reds, with a 3.80 ERA. The next season he brought his ERA down to 2.97, but his record slipped to 4–13 as last-place Cincinnati made the second-most errors in the league while scoring the second fewest runs. /(NLM)

Ossee Schreckengost — 1875–1914. C-1B 1897–99, 1901–08 Lousville (NL), Cleveland (NL), Cardinals, Red Sox, Indians, **A's**, White Sox 893 g, .271, 9 hr, 338 rbi. *1 WS, 3 g, .222*

Highly rated by Connie Mack as a defensive catcher and handler of pitchers, Schreckengost and Hall of Famer Rube Waddell formed a devastating battery for the early Athletics. Off the field, the two were cohorts in mischief; Mack later called the catcher "the Harpo Marx of his time." When they roomed together on road trips, Schreckengost had written into Waddell's contract that he was not to eat crackers in bed. Schreckengost disdained shin guards (invented near the end of his career), and used a one-handed catching style over fifty years before it became an accepted technique. /(JK)

Pop Schriver [William Frederick] — 1866–1932. C-1B 1886, 1888–95, 1897–1901 Brooklyn (AA), Phillies, **Cubs**, Giants, Reds, Pirates, Cardinals 800 g, .264, 16 hr, 374 rbi

Chicago's Cap Anson insisted his star catcher, Pop Schriver, could catch a ball dropped 500 feet from the top of the Washington Monument. On August 25, 1894, he did. Clark Griffith, then a Chicago pitcher, flipped the ball from the top of the obelisk. The apprehensive Schriver let it drop, but after deciding the stunt was not dangerous, caught the next ball Griffith sent down. Washington catcher Gabby Street duplicated the feat in 1908. /(JK)

Bill Schroeder — 1958– . C-1B 1983– **Brewers**, Angels 358 g, .241, 57 hr, 143 rbi

Schroeder enjoyed career-highs in BA (.332), HR (14), and RBI (42) while sharing the Brewers catching duties with B.J. Surhoff in 1987, but slumped badly to .156 in 41 games in 1988 and was traded to the Angels in December. In 1980–82 Schroeder led three different minor leagues in strikeouts. /(SCL)

Al Schroll (Bull) — 1933– . RHP 1958–61 **Red Sox**, Phillies, Cubs, Twins 118 ip, 6–9, 5.34

Schroll won one game for the Red Sox in 1959 and was traded to the Cubs that winter for an over-the-hill Bobby Thomson, who played just 43 more games. Schroll pitched two games for Chicago, then went 4–4 for the 1961 Twins. /(GB)

Ken Schrom — 1954– . RHP 1980, 82–87 Blue Jays, **Twins**, Indians 900 ip, 51–51, 4.81
☛ *All-Star—86.*

Schrom earned a spot on the 1986 AL All-Star team with a 10–2 start for the Indians, then won only 10 more ML games in his career, concluding with a dreadful 6–13, 6.50 record in 1987. In 1983, Schrom was the Twins Pitcher of the Year, winning a career-high 15 games. /(SCL)

Rick Schu — 1962– . 3B 1984– **Phillies**, Orioles, Tigers 501 g, .247, 35 hr, 118 rbi

Schu appeared to be the successor to Mike Schmidt at third base for the Phillies when he hit .301 with 14 triples at AAA Portland in 1984, and Schmidt was moved to first base to make room in the lineup in 1985. The experiment was abandoned when Schu drove in only 24 runs in 416 at-bats, and he has been a reserve player ever since. /(SG)

Heinie Schuble [Henry George] 1906– . SS-3B 1927, 29, 32–36 Cardinals, **Tigers** 331 g, .251, 11 hr, 116 rbi

A utility man who spent parts of seven seasons warming ML benches, Schuble filled in for 101 games with the Tigers in 1932 and hit .271. /(JK)

Ron Schueler — 1948– . RHP 1972–79 Braves, **Phillies**, Twins, White Sox 914 ip, 40–48, 4.08

As an Atlanta farmhand, the 6'4" Schueler threw a no-hitter for Shreveport (Texas League) on September 7, 1970. He went 11–16 in his busiest season as a starter, with the 1974 Phillies, then spent most of his career in long relief. He was on the White Sox staff in June 1979 when pitching coach Freddie Martin died; just 31 years old, Schueler retired as a player and took Martin's place. He joined Oakland's coaching staff for 1983. /(AL)

Wes Schulmerich — 1901–1985. OF 1931–34 **Braves**, Phillies, Reds 429 g, .289, 27 hr, 192 rbi

Schulmerich was a powerful, 5'11" 210-lb right-hander who starred as a fullback at Oregon State. He once batted .380 for Los Angeles of the Pacific Coast League. He hit .318 for the Braves and Phillies in 1933, but was soon back in the PCL. /(JK)

Fred Schulte (Fritz) — 1901–1983. OF 1927–37 **Browns**, Senators, Pirates 1178 g, .292, 47 hr, 593 rbi. *1 WS, 5 g, .333, 1 hr, 4 rbi*

The mild-mannered Schulte was a reliable performer, a top centerfielder, and a consistent hitter. A Browns regular from 1928 through 1932, he was traded to the Senators and led AL outfielders in putouts as Washington won the 1933 pennant. In the World Series, which the Giants won in five games, Schulte led Washington hitters with a .333 average and four RBI. He later managed in the minors and scouted for four organizations from 1947 to 1964. /(JK)

Wildfire Schulte [Frank M.] — 1882-1949. OF 1904-18 **Cubs**, Pirates, Phillies, Senators 1806 g, .270, 93 hr, 823 rbi. *4 WS, 21 g, .309, 9 rbi*
☛ *Most Valuable Player—11. Led League—hr 10-11. Led League—rbi 11.*

A valuable member of the pennant-winning Cubs of 1906–08 and 1910, Schulte was probably the only ML player with a nickname taken from his pet horse. In 1911 he led the NL in RBI (121) and homers (21) and hit .300 with 30 doubles, 21 triples, and 23 stolen bases. He is one of only two men in history (the other was Willie Mays in 1957) to collect more than 20 doubles, triples, homers, and stolen bases in a single season. He also hit four grand slams that year, the ML record until Ernie Banks's five in 1955. For his efforts, he was awarded a new Chalmers automobile as the NL's MVP. /(ARA)

Barney Schultz [George] — 1926- . RHP 1955, 59, 61-65 Cardinals, Tigers, **Cubs** 346 ip, 20-20, 3.63. *1 WS, 4 ip, 0-1, 18.00*

This knuckleball reliever set a since-broken ML record in 1962 by making relief appearances in nine consecutive games for the Cubs, climaxed by a pair of wins in a doubleheader against the Phillies. He had 14 saves and a 1.64 ERA on the 1964 NL-champion Cardinals, but he lost Game Three of the WS when Mickey Mantle homered off his first pitch after Schultz relieved in the bottom of the ninth. /(ARA)

Bob Schultz — 1923-1979. LHP 1951-53, 55 **Cubs**, Pirates, Tigers 183 ip, 9-13, 5.16

Plagued by wildness (125 walks in 183 innings), Schultz's only effective ML season came with the 1952 Cubs, when he was 6-3, with 4 wins in relief. /(ARA)

Buddy Schultz [Charles Budd] — 1950- . LHP 1975-79 Cubs, **Cardinals** 240 ip, 15-9, 3.68

Schultz was a useful middle reliever for the Cardinals (6-1 in 1977, 6 saves in 1978) until tendinitis sidelined him in 1979. /(ARA)

Howie Schultz (Steeple, Stretch) — 1922- . 1B 1943-48 **Dodgers**, Phillies, Reds 470 g, .241, 24 hr, 208 rbi

The 6'6" Schultz played pro basketball for six seasons in the NBL and NBA, including two with the champion Minneapolis Lakers. He was a fan favorite at Ebbets Field until the Dodgers sold him to the Phillies for $50,000 in 1947. /(NLM)

Joe Schultz, Sr. (Germany) — 1893-1941. OF-3B-2B 1912-13, 15-16, 19-25 Braves, Dodgers, Cubs, Pirates, **Cardinals**, Phillies, Reds 703 g, .285, 15 hr, 249 rbi

Schultz was a righthanded hitter who was devastated by righthanded pitching and played parts of 11 ML seasons without having a regular job. He managed in the minors and coached for the Cardinals and Pirates. As a Pittsburgh scout, he signed his own son, Joe Schultz, Jr. /(JK)

Joe Schultz, Jr. (Dode) — 1918- . C 1939-41, 43-48 Pirates, **Browns** 240 g, .259, 1 hr, 46 rbi.
*Manager 1969, 73 **Pilots**, Tigers 78-112, .411*

At the age of thirteen, Schultz pinch hit in a regular league game with Houston (Texas League). He was the batboy; his father, Joe Sr., was the manager. After a career as a back-up catcher, Schultz became a coach and a minor-league manager. In his only full season as a major league manager, he led the expansion Seattle Pilots with a down-to-earth style affectionately chronicled in Jim Bouton's *Ball Four*. /(WOR)

Al Schulz (Lefty, Heinie) — 1889-1931. LHP 1912-16 Yankees, **Buffalo (FL)**, Reds 933 ip, 48-61, 3.32. 20 wins: 15

Schulz, who was epileptic, complained he couldn't win with the weak-hitting Yankees and jumped to the Federal League. He went 21-14 in 1915 (tied for fifth in the FL in wins) despite leading the FL with 149 walks. /(NLM)

Don Schulze — 1962- . RHP 1983-87, 89- Cubs, **Indians**, Mets, Yankees, Padres 339 ip, 15-25, 5.47

The temperamental Schulze had trouble transferring minor league success to the majors. Arm trouble also hindered the 6'4" 230-lb fastballer. He led the International League in winning percentage (11-1, .917) in 1987. /(ME)

Garry Schumacher — 1901-1978. *Writer.*

Schumacher's Brooklyn accent sounded like the parodies popularized by radio comedians in the 1930s and 1940s. He broke in with the New York *Globe* in 1920, then moved to the Brooklyn *Standard-Union*, where he covered the Giants. In 1946

Hal Schumacher

he started a 25-year stint as public-relations director for the Giants in both New York and San Francisco./(NLM)

Hal Schumacher (Prince Hal) — 1910– . RHP 1931–42, 46 **Giants** 2481 ip, 158–120, 3.36. 20 wins: 34 *3 WS, 33 ip, 2–2, 4.13*

Prince Hal helped King Carl Hubbell pitch the Giants to pennants in 1933, 1936, and 1937. In 1934 he won a career-high 23, losing 10. He threw a "heavy" ball that hit the catcher's mitt like a cannonball, and he had an effective overhand curve. A 1935 shoulder injury diminished his fastball, and he developed a palmball, but never again got more than the 13 wins he notched each year from 1937 through 1940. He almost died on the mound on a hot day in St. Louis. After pitching the sixth inning, he collapsed, with no discernible heartbeat. He was packed in ice and revived./(NLM)

Ferdie Schupp — 1891–1971. LHP 1913–22 **Giants**, Cardinals, Dodgers, White Sox 1054 ip, 61–39, 3.32. 20 wins: 17 *1 WS, 10 ip, 1–0, 1.74*

In one season with Decatur in the Three-I League, Schupp pitched 356 innings in 51 games. He reputedly had so much "stuff" that some teammates were afraid to catch him. He became the regular closer for rebuilding Giants teams. In his one season as a full-time starter for the Giants, he was 21–7 for the 1917 NL champions, leading the league in winning percentage. He was knocked out in the second inning of Game Two of the World Series, but came back to shut out the White Sox in Game Four. Schupp lost his effectiveness after serving in WWI./(AAs)

Don Schwall — 1936– . RHP 1961–67 Red Sox, **Pirates, Braves** 743 ip, 49–48, 3.72
☛ *Rookie of the Year—61. All-Star—61.*

Schwall, a 6'6" All-Big Eight basketball star at the University of Oklahoma, was signed by the Red Sox and won 1961 AL Rookie of the Year honors by going 15–7 (3.22). He pitched three innings in the second 1961 All-Star Game. A disappointment in 1962 (9–15), Schwall was sent to Pittsburgh in a November trade for slugger Dick Stuart. He went 6–12 in 1963, and was made a reliever, recording a career-best 2.92 ERA while winning nine games for the 1965 Pirates./(EW)

Pius Schwert — 1892–1941. C 1914–15 **Yankees** 11 g, .217, 0 hr, 6 rbi

Schwert had 23 at-bats for the Yankees in 1914–15, then returned to the minors, where he played until 1922. He became a U.S. Congressman from Buffalo, NY long after his playing days had ended, and was in his second term when he died of a heart attack at a Washington, DC dinner party in 1941./(SCL)

Mike Scioscia — 1958– . C 1980– **Dodgers** 1070 g, .261, 45 hr, 316 rbi. *3 LCS, 18 g, .264, 2 hr, 4 rbi. 2 WS, 7 g, .222, 1 rbi*
☛ *All-Star—89.*

Dodger Vice President Al Campanis called Scioscia the best plate-blocking catcher he had seen in 46 years of baseball. In July 1985, the fearless Scioscia was knocked unconscious in a collision with the Cardinals' Jack Clark, but held on to the ball. With a good eye at the plate, he finished second in the National League in on-base percentage in 1985, batting .296. He missed most of 1983 after tearing his rotator cuff throwing out Padres speedster Alan Wiggins. Scioscia hit a game-tying, ninth-inning homer off Dwight Gooden in Game Four of the 1988 LCS as the Dodgers won in the 12th./(TG)

Daryl Sconiers — 1958– . 1B-DH 1981–85 **Angels** 234 g, .265, 15 hr, 84 rbi

Considered a promising, pure hitter, Sconiers was the Angels' Rookie of the Year in 1983, DHing and backing up Rod Carew. Sconiers missed most of 1984 with a herniated disc, and shortly thereafter was in drug rehabilitation. /(EW)

Herb Score — 1933– . LHP 1955–62 **Indians**, White Sox 858 ip, 55–46, 3.36. 20 wins: 56
☛ *Rookie of the Year—55. Led League—k 55–56. All-Star—55–56.*

With a catapulting delivery that left him in an awkward fielding position, Score simply overpowered American League hitters for the first two years of his career. In that short time, he joined Whitey Ford and Billy Pierce as the league's dominant lefthanded pitchers. One can only speculate about the kind of career he might have put together had his fortunes not been irreversibly altered on May 7, 1957.

As AL champions in 1954, the Indians used a starting rotation comprised exclusively of righthanders, three of whom, Bob Feller, Bob Lemon, and Early Wynn, would become Hall of Famers. Because the three were also in their mid-thirties, Score's debut in 1955 was propitiously timed. He was the first and best of a young crop of Cleveland pitchers that included Gary Bell, Mudcat Grant, and Jim Perry, and he was expected to lead the new staff in replacing the old.

Score astonished. He won 16 games, fanned a league-leading, rookie-record 245 batters, and was named AL Rookie of the Year. His 1956 seaon was more than an encore. He upped his strikeouts to 263 while taming some of the wildness he had shown in his rookie season. He posted 20 wins, pitched a league-leading five shutouts, and held opposition batters to a minuscule .186 average. Teammate Hal Newhouser, who was at the end of a career that saw him lead the AL in victories four times and in ERA and strikeouts twice, said he would trade his past for Score's future in a minute.

On May 7, 1957 at Cleveland's Municipal Stadium, Gil McDougald hit a line drive that struck Score in the eye and ended his season. Questions were raised in the aftermath of the bloody scene as to whether Score would ever see properly again. He made a partial comeback in 1958, and pitched a full season in 1959. Perhaps it was the layoff or fear or loss of vision; whatever the reason, he was no longer unhittable, despite retaining a fine ratio of strikeouts to innings pitched.

As the Indians' young staff of the late 1950s came into its own, Score became expendable. He was traded to the White Sox for Barry Latman after the 1959 season. He pitched for Chicago in 1960 and for fragments of 1961 and 1962 before retiring. In 1988, Score celebrated his 25th anniversary as a play-by-play announcer for the Indians. /(ME/CR)

Ed Scott — 1874–1933. RHP 1900–01 **Reds**, Indians 447 ip, 24–27, 3.98

Although his record was only 17–21 as a rookie with the seventh-place Reds in 1900, Scott was a workhorse, pitching 323 innings with 32 complete games. The next year he was lured to Cleveland of the new American League by more money but did not pitch well. /(BC)

Everett Scott (Deacon) — 1892–1960. SS 1914–26 **Red Sox**, Yankees, Senators, White Sox, Reds 1654 g, .249, 20 hr, 549 rbi. *5 WS, 27 g, .156, 5 rbi*

Scott led American League shortstops in fielding average for eight straight seasons (1916–23) and played 1,307 consecutive games, a streak record that Lou Gehrig would eventually demolish but that no

Everett Scott

other player ever matched. He took over in Boston in 1914, as the Tris Speaker-Joe Wood era was ending, and went to the Yankees eight years later as Roger Peckinpaugh's replacement. His iron-man effort was ended in May 1925 by lame knees that reduced his efectiveness. /(ADS)

George Scott (Boomer) — 1944- .1B-3B 1966-79 **Red Sox**, Brewers, Royals, Yankees 2034 g, .268, 271 hr, 1051 rbi. *1 WS, 7 g, .231*
☛ *Led League—hr 75. Led League—rbi 75. All-Star—66, 75, 77. Gold Glove—67-68, 71-76.*

Likable and colorful George Scott, with his well-spaced gold teeth and sometimes bulging waistline, was a fan favorite in Boston. A flashy fielder, he collected eight Gold Gloves, a record for first basemen. He was the Eastern League triple crown winner and MVP in 1965, then tied a rookie record by playing 162 games with the Red Sox in 1966. He was the AL's starting first baseman in the 1966 All-Star Game, only the second rookie first baseman to start an All-Star Game (Walt Dropo was the first). Though he struck out an AL-high 152 times, he also hit 27 home runs and was nicknamed Boomer for his booming shots. He batted .303 as a key member of the "Impossible Dream" pennant club of 1967. But in 1968 his offense took a tumble; he hit just .171, establishing a ML record for the lowest batting average for a first baseman playing 100 games.

Scott regained his stroke while playing mostly third base in 1969-70. He was traded to Milwaukee in a 10-player deal after the 1971 season. In 1975 he tied Reggie Jackson for the AL lead with 36 HR, driving in an AL-high 109 runs. Sent back to Boston in a trade for Cecil Cooper before the 1977 season, he had his final power year, hitting 33 HR. He went on to play and manage in the Mexican League. /(EW)

Jack Scott — 1892-1959. LHP 1916-17, 19-29 Pirates, Braves, Reds, **Giants**, Phillies 1814 ip, 103-109, 3.85. *2 WS, 12 ip, 1-1, 3.00*

Scott led the NL in appearances and had a 15-13 mark for Cincinnati in 1921, but when he tore a shoulder muscle in April 1922, the Reds released him. He signed with the Giants and went 8-2, then added a four-hit shutout of the Yankees in the World Series. His best season followed in 1924 when he went 16-7 for the Giants' fourth straight NL pennant winner. He lost 21 games in a season twice, in 1920 with the Reds and in 1927 with Phillies. Batting righthanded he had a career average of .275, topped by .341 in 1921. /(NLM)

Jim Scott (Death Valley Jim) — 1888-1957. RHP 1909-17 **White Sox** 1872 ip, 107-113, 2.32. 20 wins: 13, 15

At the start of his rookie year, Scott was hailed in the Chicago press as "an Ed Walsh, Mordecai Brown and Cy Young combined." Scott relied on a spitter and a fadeaway (screwball). In 1913 the 235-lb Scott won 20 games while leading the AL with 38 starts and 20 losses. He finally found consistency in 1915, with a 24-11, 2.03 record that included a 7-0 mark against the weak Athletics. One of his wins over Philadelphia was a 5-0 gem played on August 29 in just 68 minutes. The streaky Scott threw two career one-hitters, and a no-hitter against Washington on May 14, 1914, which he lost in the 10th inning. Finished in 1917, he became a minor league umpire after serving in France during WWI. Published reports in the 1920s say that he formed a religious cult outside of Los Angeles. /(RL)

Mickey Scott [Ralph Robert] — 1947- . LHP 1972-73, 75-77 Orioles, Expos, **Angels** 172 ip, 8-7, 3.71

Scott was born in Germany, where his father was serving in the military. Upon finally getting into a game after a long burial in Baltimore's bullpen, he inquired, "Which way to the mound?" The reliever found his way there a career-high 50 times for the Angels in 1975, going 4-2. /(KC)

Mike Scott — 1955- . RHP 1979- Mets, **Astros** 1855 ip, 115-93, 3.47. 20 wins: 89 *1 LCS, 18 ip, 2-0, 0.50*
☛ *Led League—w 89. Led League—era 86. Led League—k 86. Cy Young Award—86. All-Star—86-87, 89.*

After compiling a nondescript 14-27 record with the New York Mets, Mike Scott went to Houston for Danny Heep and became a star. Scott learned to throw the split-finger fastball from Roger Craig, then led the Astros past Craig's Giants and Cincinnati to win the 1986 NL Western Division pennant. Scott won the pennant clincher by pitching a no-hitter against the Giants. He became the second right-hander in NL history and 11th pitcher overall to reach 300 strikeouts (306) and won the Cy Young Award. He was the Most Valuable Player of the Championship Series with a part of complete-game victories, including a LCS-record 14 strikeouts in the first game, the first 1-0 decision in NLCS history. In 1987 Scott and Nolan Ryan became the first teammates since Sandy Koufax and Don Drysdale to finish first and second in the NL strikeout race. His won-loss record suffered in 1987, possibly due to increasing complaints that Scott was scuffing the baseball. When Craig had taught him the split-finger, he had warned Scott that accusations would result; Craig was among the first to charge Scott with chicanery. /(ME)

Pete Scott — 1898–1953. OF 1926–28 **Cubs**, Pirates 208 g, .202, 8 hr, 88 rbi

A solid hitter, Scott was trying to break into a 1928 Pirate outfield that already had the Waner brothers. While chasing a deep fly at Forbes Field, he crashed into the wall and suffered a concussion that ended his major league career. /(JK)

Rodney Scott — 1953– . 2B-SS-3B-DH 1975–82 Royals, **Expos**, A's, Cubs, Yankees 690 g, .236, 3 hr, 150 rbi. *1 LCS, 5 g, .167*

Scott was a speedy, surehanded infielder who had 205 career stolen bases. Montreal manager Dick Williams called him the most valuable .224 hitter in baseball in 1980 when Scott stole 63 bases and combined with Ron LeFlore to steal 160—then a ML record for teammate stolen bases duos. Scott also tied for the NL lead with 13 triples in 1980. Kansas City teammate John Mayberry called Scott "Cool Breeze" because "he didn't let things get to him." When Williams's replacement in Montreal, Jim Fanning, released Scott, Rodney's friend Bill Lee walked off the team in protest. /(KC)

Tony Scott — 1951– . OF 1973–75, 77–84 Expos, **Cardinals**, Astros 991 g, .249, 17 hr, 253 rbi

Speedy and reliable, Scott led NL outfielders in fielding in 1980, committing only one error. Of the four seasons in which the weak hitter played in over 100 games, his best all-around season was 1979 with the Cardinals, when he hit .259 with 69 runs scored and 68 RBI. /(EW)

Vin Scully — 1927– . *Broadcaster.*

Proudly boasting "I never say 'we.' Never, ever," Scully is the stylistic antithesis of outspoken home-team rooters Harry Caray and Bob Prince, and perhaps the most highly praised announcer in ML history. The consummate professional, he is as knowledgeable as he is lyrical, weaving accurate play-by-play with understated color in a calm resonant voice that is a joy to hear. After playing centerfield for Fordham in the late 1940s, Scully joined Red Barber in the Brooklyn Dodgers' booth in 1950 and by 1954, at the age of 26, had become their top announcer. He called Brooklyn's only

World Championship the following season, but it would be in Los Angeles where he would earn his greatest renown. Scully's voice captivated Southern California, where millions of fans, starved for ML baseball, followed the Dodgers on radio from the freeways and beaches. He was helped to his vast audience by the Dodgers' reluctance to televise games. By 1976, it was Scully, and not a Dodgers player, who was named the club's Most Memorable Personality in a fan poll. He joined CBS as a reporter in 1975, adding national football, tennis, and golf broadcasts to his local Dodgers duties, and in 1983 returned to national baseball broadcasts as NBC's number-one play-by-play man. /(SL)

Rod Scurry — 1956– . LHP 1980–86, 88 **Pirates**, Yankees, Mariners 461 ip, 19–32, 3.24

Scurry had one of the best curveballs of his day, but the ace reliever's career fell apart due to his cocaine habit. His best season was 1982, when he had 14 saves and a 1.74 ERA while going 4–5 for the Pirates.

Scurry pitched a seven-inning minor league no-hitter, beating Richmond 2–0 on July 25, 1977 while with Columbus (International League). His cousin, Joe Rose, was a tight end for the Miami Dolphins. /(SFS)

Seals Stadium San Francisco Giants 1958–59. LF-361, CF-400, RF-350

The longtime home of the Pacific Coast League's San Francisco Seals, cozy Seals Stadium, with no warning track and a 30-foot-high centerfield wall, was the downtown home of the Giants until Candlestick Park opened in 1960. /(SCL)

Ray Searage — 1955– . LHP 1981, 84–87, 89 Mets, Brewers, **White Sox**, Dodgers 256 ip, 10–13, 3.59

First signed by the Cardinals, the Mets got Searage in a 1979 straight-up trade for Jody Davis. Searage drifted through six organizations and didn't spend a full season in the majors until 1987. As a situational lefthanded reliever, he led the White Sox with 58 appearances that year. He threw hitters off with a herky-jerky delivery that included a tucking of his head. In 1984 he recorded a 0.70 ERA in 21 games and finished with 28 consecutive scoreless innings to equal a Brewers record. /(RL)

Ziggy Sears [John] — Unk.–1956. *Umpire* NL 1934–45 *1 ASU 2 WS*

Thousands of youngsters were admitted free to the Polo Grounds on September 26, 1942, for making a scrap-metal contribution to the war effort. In the bottom of the eighth inning of the second game between the Braves and Giants, the kids overran the field. When order could not be restored, Sears forfeited the game to the Braves although the Giants were winning 5–2. As a result, Hall of Famer Warren Spahn's 1942 record shows no wins, no losses, but a complete game. Sears's son Ken caught for the Yankees and Browns in the 1940s. /(RTM)

Tom Seaton — 1887–1940. RHP 1912–17 **Phillies**, Brooklyn (FL), Newark (FL), Cubs 1340 ip, 94–64, 3.14. 20 wins: 13–14
☛ *Led League—w 13.*

When knuckleballer Seaton jumped to the Federal League in 1914, he was the most coveted of the defectors, having led the NL with 27 wins for the Phillies in '13. He won 25 for the Brooklyn Feds in 1914, but thereafter his fortunes declined. In 1920, as baseball purged itself after the "Black Sox" scandal, the Pacific Coast League barred three players as "known gamblers" and San Francisco released Seaton. When he tried to move to the Southern Association his contract was not approved. He sued and won in Federal Court but left baseball before an appeal was reviewed. /(JK)

Tom Seats — 1911– . LHP 1940, 45 Tigers, **Dodgers** 177 ip, 12–9, 4.47

After a trial with the Tigers in 1940, Seats spent most of the war years as a shipyard worker, pitching for San Francisco of the Pacific Coast League. In 1945 he was 10–7 for the Dodgers. /(EW)

Seattle Kingdome Seattle Mariners 1977– . LF-316, CF-405, RF-316

The Kingdome was completed in March 1976, and in 1977 became the AL's first indoor stadium as the home of the expansion Mariners. The Kingdome is a standard circular, domed structure. Its roof is 250' above the field at its highest point, but several speakers, which are in play, dangle considerably lower and have been hit numerous times by both fair and foul balls. On April 11, 1985, Dave Kingman lost a certain home run when the ball struck a speaker and was caught for an out. Unlike in the Astrodome, the ball carries extremely well here, and in 1982 the right-field fence was raised to 23', currently the second highest in the ML. The field, of course, is artificial turf, and the outfield fences are symmetrical. The Kingdome has a baseball capacity of 58,850, and is also home to the NFL's Seattle Seahawks. /(SCL)

Seattle Mariners — 1977– . Team. 860–1190, .420

After years of futility, the 1989 Mariners showed signs of developing a good young team. Playing in the Kingdome, the American League's first domed stadium, the Mariners were born of controversy. When Seattle's original franchise, the Pilots, moved in 1970 to Milwaukee and became the Brewers, the city of Seattle threatened the American League with litigation and was awarded an expansion franchise in 1977. Owned by a group that included entertainer Danny Kaye, the Mariners made Kansas City outfielder Ruppert Jones their first pick in the league expansion draft and played their first game under manager Darrell Johnson on April 6, 1977, losing 7–0 to the California Angels.

For several years, the Mariners seemed to develop faster than the American League's other 1977 expansion team, the Blue Jays. However, the fortunes of the two franchises soon reversed. The Mariners' nosedive began on January 14, 1981, when California tycoon George Argyros purchased the franchise from the original owners. Argyros was quick to hire and fire managers and general managers and insisted that the Mariners pay their players the lowest average salaries in the major leagues. Demoralized and disgruntled players demanded trades, and Argyros, with an eye focused more on maintaining a low payroll than assessing playing talent, accommodated them in a series of disastrous transactions. Through the end of the 1980s, the Mariners failed to have a single winning season.

Of note in Mariner history are the following: Willie Horton's 300th home run (June 9, 1979); Gaylord Perry's 300th win (May 6, 1982); the delightful 1982 season (managed by Rene Lachemann and starring relief ace Bill Caudill); Alvin Davis's 1984 season, in which he set a club record with 116 RBI en route to winning the American League Rookie of the Year Award; AL strikeout crowns by Floyd Bannister (in 1982) and Mark Langston (in 1984, 1986, and 1987); and Harold Reynolds's franchise-record 60 stolen bases, which led the AL in 1987. Of dubious distinction is the Mariners' identity as victims of Roger Clemens's ML-record 20 strikeouts in a nine-inning game on April 29, 1986. /(TF)

Tom Seaver (Tom Terrific, The Franchise) — 1944- .
RHP, 1967-86 **Mets**, Reds, White Sox, Red Sox 4783 ip,
311-205, 2.86. 20 wins: 69, 71-72, 75, 77 *3 LCS, 32 ip,
2-1, 2.84. 2 WS, 30 ip, 1-2, 2.70*
☛ *Rookie of the Year—67. Led League—w 69, 75, 81.
Cy Young Award—69, 73, 75. All-Star—67-73, 75-77,
81.*

An intelligent, hard-working perfectionist and the quintessential professional, Seaver was the first true star for the Mets and led them to their miracle World Championship in 1969. In his 10 years in New York from 1967 to 1977, he won 25% of the Mets' games. The 17th 300-game winner in major league history, Seaver set a major league record by striking out 200 or more hitters in 10 seasons, nine in a row from 1968 to 1976.

Seaver came to the Mets via a strange lottery: In 1966, the Braves offered him $40,000, but the NCAA and baseball commissioner William Eckert voided the offer and made Seaver, still at USC, available to any team willing to match the Braves' offer. The Phillies, Indians, and Mets were willing and, in a drawing held in the commissioner's office, the Mets were picked out of a hat. Seaver was an immediate star, picked to the All-Star team in his first season when he won 16 games for a Met team that won just 61 games, and captured Rookie of the Year honors. In 1969 he won his first of three Cy Young awards with a 25–7 record and a 2.21 ERA and led the NL in wins and winning percentage. On July 9, Seaver lost a perfect game when rookie Jimmy Qualls of the Cubs singled with one out in the ninth. The game was more important, however, since the Mets won 4–0, and began to make their move on the Cubs on their way to the World Championship. In Game One of the LCS against the Braves, Seaver was pinch hit for in the eighth inning, down 5–4, and emerged the winner over Phil Niekro as the Mets rallied for five runs. Seaver had less luck in Game One of the World Series, as he surrendered a homer to the Orioles' first batter, Don Buford, and lost 4–1. He came back to win a 2–1 ten-inning thriller in Game Four, helped by Ron Swoboda's game-saving catch in the ninth inning.

Seaver picked up where he left off the next season. On April 22, 1970, he struck out 19 Padres, including a record 10 in a row to end the game, to tie the then-ML record for a nine-inning game, set by Steve Carlton. Although he didn't duplicate his 20-win season, he led the league in strikeouts (283) and ERA (2.81). Seaver himself felt that 1971 was his best season; he compiled a 20–10 record and led

the league for the second year in a row in with a 1.76 ERA and 289 strikeouts. Overshadowed by Steve Carlton in 1972, in 1973 Seaver became the first non-20-game winner to win the Cy Young Award when he led the NL in ERA (2.08) and strikeouts (251) and tied for the lead in complete games (18) while leading the Mets to another improbable pennant. In Game One of the LCS, Seaver drove in the Mets' only run and almost made it stand for the victory, walking none and striking out 13, but he gave up solo homers to Pete Rose and Johnny Bench in the eighth and ninth innings to take the loss. The Mets' chronically weak offense often let him down during his career, but never so glaringly. He did come back in Game Five to win the clincher 7–2, giving up only one earned run. He took a no-decision in the Mets' 11-inning 3–2 loss in Game Three of the World Series, striking out 12 in eight innings. He pitched another strong game in the sixth contest, surrendering two runs in seven innings, but once again lost a tough one 3–1.

A sore hip caused Seaver's worst season in 1974 with an 11–11 record and his first ERA over 3.00 (3.20). He bounced back in 1975 with his last great season for the Mets, going 22–9 and leading the league in strikeouts, wins, and winning percentage to capture another Cy Young trophy. In September, Seaver put together a seven-game winning streak, including another near no-hitter against the Cubs, broken up by Joe Wallis. By 1976, Seaver was having trouble with Met general manager M. Donald Grant over Seaver's salary and how the team was being run, and the two traded private and public taunts. On April 17, 1977, Seaver pitched his third one-hitter against the Cubs, a single in the fifth by Steve Ontiveros keeping him from the elusive no-hitter. Two months later, on June 15, the bomb dropped. Seaver was unceremoniously dealt to Cincinnati for four players, Pat Zachary, Doug Flynn, Steve Henderson, and Dan Norman, a trade that ripped out the hearts of New York fans. Seaver completed his last 20-win season with the Reds, finishing with a combined 21–6 mark and leading the NL with seven shutouts. Almost exactly a year from the trade, on June 16, 1978, Seaver finally got his no-hitter, blanking the Cardinals 4–0. Seaver had four winning years with the Reds, including 1979, when he went 16–6 and led the NL in winning percentage and shutouts (5). He took another tough no-decision in the LCS when he left Game One after eight innings tied 2–2 with the Pirates' John Candelaria; Pittsburgh won in the 11th inning. In the strike-shortened 1981 season, Seaver

Tom Seaver

went 14–2 and led the majors in victories but lost a controversial Cy Young vote to rookie sensation Fernando Valenzuela.

After Seaver slumped to 5–13 in 1982, the Reds completed the circle by trading The Franchise back to the Mets for three players. Although compiling only a 9–14 record (due mostly to the Mets' usual poor offense; his ERA was a better-than-average 3.55), fans were outraged when he was claimed by the White Sox after he was mysteriously left unpro-

tected in the free agent compensation pool. He won 15 games for the White Sox in 1984, and 16 in 1985 when he set several career standards. On August 4 in Yankee Stadium, he won his 300th game, a 4–1 complete game on a six-hitter. On October 4, he moved past Walter Johnson into third place on the all-time strikeout list. After getting off to a slow start the following season, he was dealt to Boston (closer to his Greenwich, CT home), where he finished his career. An ankle injury prevented him from appearing against the Mets in the World Series, and the Red Sox released him following the season. Seaver tried to latch on with the Mets in 1987, but called it quits when he wasn't satisfied with his performance while getting into shape. After sitting out the 1988 season, Seaver was named to replace newly named National League president Bill White in the Yankee broadcast booth, and replaced Joe Garagiola for NBC Saturday telecasts with Vin Scully. /(SEW)

Dick Seay — 1906- . 2B-SS Negro Leagues 1925-47 Pennsylvania Red Caps of New York, Newark Stars, Brooklyn Royal Giants, Baltimore Black Sox, Philadelphia Stars, Pittsburgh Crawfords, **Newark Eagles**, New York Black Yankees statistics not available
☛ *All-Star—35, 40-41.*

Seay was a 5′8″ 150-lb hustling infielder who performed for more than 20 years in the Negro Leagues. He was a light hitter but a good bunter and hit-and-run man. His splendid throwing arm and sparkling defense gained him recognition as one of black baseball's premier fielders. Besides league play, he performed in Puerto Rico and toured in 1927–28 with Chappie Johnson's Stars, a black barnstorming team operating out of Montreal. He was the second baseman for the 1934 Negro National Association champion Philadelphia Stars, and for three East all-star squads. While available data indicates his lifetime batting average was in the low .200 range, he hit .340 in 15 exhibitions against white major leaguers. /(MFK)

Bob Sebra — 1961- . RHP 1985- Rangers, **Expos**, Phillies 356 ip, 14-27, 4.61

Sebra was one of two players the Expos acquired for Pete Incaviglia in 1985 when the first-round draft choice refused to sign a contract, and he led the Expos with 156 strikeouts in 1987, including 14 against the Cubs July 1. Sebra, who relies on a sharp curveball, began the 1988 season at Indianapolis (American Association), and was traded to the Phillies in September. Oddly, his NL debut is officially listed as July 13, 1986, even though he was not promoted from the minors until July 24, because his first appearance was in the completion of a suspended game. /(SCL)

Jimmy Sebring — 1882-1909. OF 1902-05, 09 **Pirates**, Reds, Dodgers, Senators 363 g, .261, 6 hr, 168 rbi. *1 WS, 8 g, .367, 1 hr, 5 rbi*

Sebring's 11 hits led all participants in the first World Series (Pirates and Red Sox, 1903). He left the Reds in August 1905 to play for a team outside

organized baseball in his hometown of Williamsport, PA; his wife was too ill to be left alone for long periods of time. Most players who jumped to "outlaw" leagues were blacklisted by organized baseball, but the National Commission, headed by Reds owner Garry Herrmann, did not take disciplinary action against Sebring. He led Williamsport, of the outlaw Tri-State League, to a championship. When he returned to the majors in 1909, he had lost his form. /(ME)

Frank Secory — 1912- . OF 1940, 42, 44-46 Tigers, Reds, **Cubs** 93 g, .228, 7 hr, 36 rbi. *1 WS, 5 g, .400.*
Umpire NL 1952-70 *6 ASU 3 WS*

Secory's brief ML playing career was highlighted by a 2-for-5 pinch-hitting performance for the Cubs in the 1945 WS. His 12th-inning single in Game Six helped spark the game-winning rally for Chicago.

Secory was working a Cardinals' game when he called Mike Shannon out at the plate. To "prove" that Shannon had been safe, manager Red Schoendienst demonstrated by sliding into the plate himself. An unamused Secory sent Schoendienst to the showers. /(RTM)

Bob Seeds (Suitcase Bob) — 1907- . OF-1B 1930-34, 36, 38-40 Indians, White Sox, Red Sox, Yankees, **Giants** 615 g, .277, 28 hr, 233 rbi. *1 WS, --*

Nicknamed "Suitcase Bob" for his travels from team to team, Seeds eventually bought a Class-D franchise in Texas, put his wife in charge, and went off to play in higher classifications. In his first 59 games in Newark (International League) in 1938, he hit 28 HR, equaling his entire major league output. Playing at Buffalo on May 6, he singled in his first at-bat, and then hit home runs in four consecutive innings (fourth-seventh). His 12 RBI in the game set an International League record. The next day, also against Buffalo, he hit three more HR, a single, walked, and struck out, for two-day totals of 9-for-10, seven HR, and 17 RBI. /(JK)

Chuck Seelbach [Charles Frederick III] — 1948- . RHP 1971-74 **Tigers** 131 ip, 10-8, 3.37. *1 LCS, 1 ip, 0-0, 18.00*

A one-year wonder, Seelbach won 9 and saved 14 as a rookie in 1972. He saved the Tigers' pennant-clincher against Boston but was unsuccessful in two LCS appearances. A shoulder injury the next year ended his effectiveness. /(CC)

Pat Seerey — 1923–1986. OF 1943–49 **Indians**, White Sox 561 g, .224, 86 hr, 261 rbi

Seerey, just 5'10" but 200 lbs, hit the ball a long way, but he also led AL batters in strikeouts in all four of his seasons as a regular (1944–46 and 1948). Cleveland manager Lou Boudreau exercised great patience with the young slugger in 1946, when Seerey hit a career-high 26 HR, but benched him in 1947. On June 2, 1948, the White Sox sent Bob Kennedy to Cleveland in a much-criticized trade for Seerey and pitcher Al Gettel. That July 18, Seerey became the fifth ML player to hit four homers in a game, blasting two mammoth shots off Philadelphia's Carl Scheib, and one each off Bob Savage and Lou Brissie in an 11-inning, 12–11 Chicago victory. His 16 total bases in the game tied an AL record. But he struck out 102 times in just 363 at-bats that season, and was released early in 1949. Kennedy's career lasted nine more years. /(RL)

Charles Segar — 1903–Unk. *Writer-Executive* .

Born in England, Segar was the youngest member of the BBWAA when he went to spring training with the Dodgers at age 17 for the Brooklyn *Citizen*. In 1926, he moved to the New York *Mirror*. When General Eckert was elected Commissioner of Baseball, Segar was appointed to the Commissioner's office. He was secretary-treasurer of baseball at his retirement in 1971. /(NLM)

Diego Segui (Pablo) — 1937– . RHP 1962–77 **A's**, Senators, Pilots, Cardinals, Red Sox, Mariners 1808 ip, 92–111, 3.81 *1 LCS, 4 ip, 0–1, 5.79 1 WS, 1 ip, 0–0, 0.00* ☛ *Led League—era 70.*

Segui broke in as a regular starter for the A's in 1962, achieving modest success with a mediocre team. He led the AL in losses in 1964 with an 8–17 mark. In 1969, he was the primary reliever for Seattle in the Pilots' only season, saving 12 and winning eight in relief. Returned to the A's the next season, he was used as a reliever and spot starter and led the AL with a 2.56 ERA in 162 innings. The Cardinals acquired him in 1972, and the following year he saved a career-high 17 games. Segui is the only man to play for both the Seattle Pilots and the Seattle Mariners. /(BC)

Socks Seibold [Harry] — 1896–1965. RHP 1915–17, 19, 29–33 A's, **Braves** 1063 ip, 48–86, 4.43

After ten games as a 19-year-old infielder with the A's in 1915, Seibold was converted to the mound in the minors, and he returned as a pitcher the next year. Eventually, he went back to the minors with a sore arm. Twice during the 1920s he retired, once for four years. Rejuvenated in 1929, he became a regular starter for the Braves, a chronic second-division club. His best season was 1930, when he was 15–16. /(JK)

Kevin Seitzer — 1962– . 3B-1B 1986- **Royals** 498 g, .304, 26 hr, 202 rbi ☛ *All-Star—87.*

Seitzer batted .318 over four minor league seasons and facilitated the Royals' move of George Brett to first base. Seitzer would have been a certain Rookie of the Year in most seasons, but in 1987 Mark McGwire hit 49 home runs and Seitzer settled for second. He led the AL in hits, and was only the 13th rookie in history to collect 200. Seitzer had good speed, and although not known for power in the minors, he muscled up for 15 home runs and 83 RBI his first full season. A good batting eye enabled him to draw numerous walks, keeping his on-base percentage near .400. With Kurt Stillwell joining Seitzer in 1988, the Royals had a young, exciting, and productive left side of the infield. His finest game came August 1, 1987, when he clobbered Red Sox pitching for six hits and seven RBI. /(FO)

Kip Selbach [Albert Karl] — 1872–1956. OF 1894–1906 **Washington (NL)**, Reds, Giants, Baltimore (AL), Senators, Red Sox 1614 g, .293, 44 hr, 779 rbi

Short but sturdy (5'7", 190 lbs), Selbach was a regular outfielder with speed and a good eye at the plate. He stole 334 bases and, with Washington in 1895, led the NL in triples. He secured Boston's 1904 pennant (their second in a row) when, in the next-to-last game of the season in New York, he raced in from left field to make a knee-high catch of Kid Elberfeld's hard liner, ending the game. /(EC)

Frank Selee — 1859–1909. *Manager* 1890–1905 **Braves**, Cubs 1299–872, .598. First place: 91–93, 97–98.

A balding little man with a modest demeanor and a formidable mustache that gave his face a melancholy cast, Frank Selee compiled the fourth-best managerial percentage, .598, in baseball history. His Boston teams won five pennants. In a sixteen-year career he never finished lower than fifth. Twelve of his players are in the Hall of Fame. A good case can be made for five or six others, and for Selee himself.

His teams were expert at such maneuvers as the hit-and-run, the 3–6–3 double play, and defensive shifts and signals. Yet his most remarkable talent was recognizing not only a player's potential, but the proper position for him to play. In his three-plus years remaking the Cubs, losers since 1886, he converted, among others, catcher Frank Chance to first base, shortstop Johnny Evers to second base, and third baseman Joe Tinker to shortstop.

In 1905, desperately ill with tuberculosis, he surrendered the team to Chance. Chicago won pennants in four of the next five years. Of thirteen key players on the Selee squad Chance inherited, eight still were regulars in 1910. /(ADS)

George Selkirk (Twinkletoes) — 1908–1987. OF 1934–42 **Yankees** 846 g, .290, 108 hr, 576 rbi. *6 WS, 21 g, .265, 2 hr, 10 rbi*
☛ *All-Star—36, 39.*

Canadian George Selkirk played eight years in the minors before being called upon to replace Babe Ruth as the Yankees' right fielder in 1935, taking Ruth's number 3. While he could not come close to Ruth's home run output (he hit 21 at his best in 1939), he batted better than .300 in five of his first six seasons. He was a valuable part of Joe McCarthy's dynasty, playing for six Yankee pennant winners and five world champions from 1936 through 1942. In 1936 he was one-third of an all-.300 outfield with Joe DiMaggio and Jake Powell. A patient hitter, four times he drew two walks in an inning, and he walked 103 times in 1939. Selkirk hit five home runs in four consecutive games in 1939, and drove in more than 100 runs in 1936 and 1939.

Selkirk was given the nickname Twinkletoes by his teammates at Newark (International League) because he ran with his weight on the balls of his feet. He served in the WWII Navy, managed in the minors, and was a minor league coordinator for the A's and Orioles. In 1962 he became the Senators' GM, and later added the title of vice-president. He returned to the Yankees as a scout in 1970. /(GB)

Jeff Sellers — 1964– . RHP 1985–88 **Red Sox** 330 ip, 13–22, 4.97

Sellers is a young, erratic power pitcher with a Marine-style crew cut. In the spring of 1988, Roger Clemens said Sellers had the best stuff on the Red Sox' staff, but Sellers went 1–7 that year before injuring his shoulder. An off-season trade to the Reds returned him to the minors. /(SCL)

Dave Sells — 1946– . RHP 1972–75 **Angels**, Dodgers 138 ip, 11–7, 3.90

Sells never started a game in the majors and had his best season in 1972 for the Angels (7–2, 10 saves) as their stopper. /(JFC)

Dick Selma (Mortimer Snerd) — 1943– . RHP 1965–74 Mets, Padres, Cubs, **Phillies**, Angels, Brewers 840 ip, 42–54, 3.62

In his second major league start, Selma defeated the Braves 1–0, with a then Mets record 13 strikeouts. In 1969, he won the expansion Padres' first game, but was traded to the Cubs a few weeks later and gained attention by regularly leading cheers for Wrigley Field's bleacher bums. He was 7–1 for the Cubs in '69 until their September skid; he finished at 10–8. In Durocher's doghouse as a result, he was traded with Oscar Gamble for Johnny Callison. In his last effective season, Selma recorded 22 saves in 73 appearances for the 1970 Phillies. When the schedule brought him back to Wrigley Field, the fans showered him with coins. /(KT)

Carroll Sembera — 1941– . RHP 1965–67 **Astros**, Expos 140 ip, 3–11, 4.69

Sembera was a reliever with control problems who never had a winning season. In his most active year, he went 2–6 with three saves for the Astros in 1967. /(WOR)

Andy Seminick — 1920– . C 1943–57 **Phillies**, Reds 1304 g, .243, 164 hr, 556 rbi. *1 WS, 4 g, .182*
☛ *All-Star—49.*

Seminick was the Phillies' first-string catcher from 1946 through 1951 and again in 1955, after a stint with the Reds. On June 2, 1949, the Phillies tagged Cincinnati pitching for a ML record-tying five home runs in one inning (the eighth); Seminick became the ninth major leaguer to homer twice in an inning. In all, he hit three HR in that game.

On August 11–12, 1950, during a series with the Giants, second baseman Eddie Stanky waved his arms whenever Seminick was at the plate. After the first day, the umpires ordered Stanky to stop, but when Seminick slid hard into third baseman Hank Thompson, Stanky declared an end to the truce on Seminick's next at-bat, and umpire Lon Warneke ejected Stanky. When Seminick banged into replacement Bill Rigney at second base a few innings later, the biggest rhubarb of the year took place. Both Seminick and Rigney were fined $25 by league president Ford Frick, and at a hearing August 14 Frick ruled that arm-waving gestures such as those Stanky employed would thenceforth be illegal.

Seminick played hurt during much of his career. An ankle injury incurred on September 27, 1950, bothered him during the World Series against the Yankees; x-rays later disclosed a bone separation.

He also suffered with arm problems for several years. When, on a night given in his honor, Seminick received a wristwatch, one sportswriter quipped, "Now all they have to do is give him an arm to put it on." Seminick was later a Phillies coach (1957–58, 67–69), minor league manager, and scout. /(RTM)

Ray Semproch [Roman Anthony] (Baby) — 1931– . RHP 1958–61 **Phillies**, Tigers, Angels 344 ip, 19–21, 4.42

At mid-season in 1958, Semproch, a 27-year-old rookie, led all NL pitchers in wins with 11. But he faltered in the second half and finished 13–11 with the last-place Phillies. Bothered by asthma, he struggled through the remaining three seasons of his career. /(RTM)

Bill Serena — 1924– . 3B-2B 1949–54 **Cubs** 408 g, .251, 48 hr, 198 rbi

The stocky Serena hit 17 home runs for the Cubs in 1950, his first full season. A broken wrist sidelined him most of the next year, and when he returned in 1952, he'd lost his third base position to Randy Jackson. /(NLM)

Gary Serum — 1956– . LHP 1977–79 **Twins** 271 ip, 10–12, 4.71

Unlike most modern major leaguers, Serum was never drafted, but was signed after attending a Twins tryout camp. As a 21-year-old in 1978, he went 9–9 for Minnesota. Teammate Roy Smalley nicknamed Serum "Truth." /(KC)

Hank Severeid — 1891–1968. C 1911–13, 1915–26 Reds, **Browns**, Senators, Yankees 1390 g, .289, 17 hr, 539 rbi. *2 WS, 8 g, .280, 1 rbi*

Severeid, a strong second-generation Norwegian who swung a hefty 48-ounce bat, was called the most durable catcher in baseball. He caught a record 2,357 games (1,225 in the majors). With the Browns he appeared in over 100 games every year from 1916 through 1924 except for 1918, when he was in the military. In his last two ML seasons, he played on pennant winners, as a backup for the 1925 Senators and the '26 Yankees. After leaving the majors, he batted over .300 for five seasons in the Pacific Coast League. In the Texas League in 1937, he caught his last games at age 46 in both games of a season-ending doubleheader. /(JK)

Al Severinsen — 1944– . RHP 1969, 71–72 Orioles, **Padres** 111 ip, 3–7, 3.08

The 6'3" 220-lb reliever spent a decade in the minors, where he was known as a workhorse. He worked 59 games for the Padres in 1971, recording eight of his nine career saves. /(KC)

Joe Sewell — 1898– . SS-3B 1920–33 **Indians**, Yankees 1902 g, .312, 49 hr, 1051 rbi. *2 WS, 11 g, .237, 3 rbi*
☛ Hall of Fame—1977.

When it came to making contact, no one matched Joe Sewell. Few rookies have faced a tougher assignment than Sewell did in 1920. While Sewell was playing his first professional season in New Orleans, Cleveland hero Ray Chapman was killed by a Carl Mays pitch in August. When Chapman's replacement, Harry Lunte, was hurt on Labor Day,

Joe Sewell

the kid from Alabama was thrust into the American League pennant race with less than 100 professional games played. Little Joe (5′7″) proved equal to the task, batting .329 in and helping Cleveland to its first pennant. From September 13, 1922 to April 30, 1930, he played 1,103 straight games, a major league record at the time. No one threatens to break his record of just 114 strikeouts in 7,132 games. Using a 40-ounce bat called "Black Betsy," Sewell had three full seasons (1925, 1929 and 1933), in which he struck out just four times.

He was, however, far more than just a contact hitter. Sewell led the Indians in RBI three times and hit below .299 just once in Cleveland. He led AL shortstops in putouts four straight years (1924–27), in assists four times, and twice in fielding percentage. Moved to third base in 1929, Joe led the league in assists again. Released after the 1930 season, Sewell filled a trouble spot at third for the Yankees for three seasons before retiring and spent two more years with the Yankees as a coach. He later scouted for the Indians and coached at the University of Alabama, leading the school to a Southeastern Conference title in 1968. /(ME)

Luke Sewell [James Luther] — 1901–1987. C 1921–39, 42 **Indians**, Senators, White Sox, Browns 1630 g, .259, 20 hr, 696 rbi. *1 WS, 5 g, .176, 1 rbi.*
   Manager 1941–46, 49–52 **Browns**, Reds 606–644, .485. First place: 44 *1 WS, 2–4, .333*
☛ All-Star—37.

After an apprenticeship under Cleveland great Steve O'Neill and two years platooning with Glenn Myatt, Sewell was the Indians' catcher from 1926 through 1932. He caught for the Senators and White Sox before returning to the Indians as a player-coach in 1939. He set a since-broken AL record by leading league catchers in assists four years (1926–28 and 1936), and holds the AL record of 20 seasons as an active catcher.

Sewell became manager of the Browns on June 5, 1941, and in 1944 guided them to an 89–65 record and the only pennant in the club's history. Though the Browns lost the World Series to the Cardinals in six games, Sewell was named *TSN* Major League Manager of the Year. Fired in 1946, he managed the Reds for three games in 1949 and from 1950 to 1952, never finishing higher than sixth. Luke's brother, Hall of Famer Joe Sewell, played 14 years in the majors, while a third brother, Tommy, had one at bat with the Cubs in 1927. /(ME)

Rip Sewell [Truett Banks] — 1907– . RHP 1932, 38–49 Tigers, **Pirates** 2119 ip, 143–97, 3.48. 20 wins: 43–44
☛ Led League—w 43. All-Star—43–44, 46.

Sewell was one of the National League's dominant pitchers during WWII, compiling a 70–45 record for the Pirates from 1942 through 1945. Part of his foot had been shot off in a 1940 hunting accident, keeping him out of the war. The injury led to the development of his famous blooper pitch, or "eephus," as it was dubbed by teammate Maurice Van Robays. Ted Williams hit an eephus pitch for his second home run in the 1946 All-Star Game.

Sewell worked seven years in the minors and had a five-game 1932 tryout with Detroit before reaching the Pirates in 1938. He lost a league-high 17 games in 1941, but won 21 in both 1943 and 1944. His 21 wins and 25 complete games in '43 led the league, as he was named NL Pitcher of the Year by the BBWAA. From '40 through '45, he averaged 237 innings per year. He set league records for pitchers with 12 chances accepted in a game and 11 assists in a game in 1941, when he also equaled a ML record with three assists in one inning.

Sewell was an outspoken critic of the burgeoning players' union being organized after WWII by Robert Murphy, with efforts concentrated in Pittsburgh. He led Pirate players against the union, and was reported as saying that he was "glad the owners had finally told these ungrateful players where to get off. First they wanted the hamburg, then filet mignon, eventually the cow and the entire pasture." /(GB)

Socks Seybold [Ralph Orlando] — 1870–1921. OF 1899, 1901–08 Reds, **A's** 996 g, .294, 51 hr, 556 rbi. *1 WS, 5 g, .125*
☛ Led League—hr 02.

Seybold's 16 HR in the second year of the American League set a record that lasted until Babe Ruth shattered it with 29 in 1919. When Connie Mack formed the Philadelphia Athletics for the American League's first season (1901), he brought Seybold with him from the Western Association. Mack later described him as "the steadiest and most serviceable of players." Seybold had a 27-game hitting streak in 1901, when fellow Athletic Nap Lajoie had a 28-game streak. He hit .300 three times, topped 90 RBI three times, and was consistently among the AL leaders in HR, sometimes showing well in RBI (second in 1907 and fourth in 1902). He also led the league in doubles in 1903 with 45. Not an especially good fielder, he nonetheless had two unassisted double plays from the outfield in 1907. An injury in 1908 ended his major league career. /(JK)

Cy Seymour

Cy Seymour [James Bentley] — 1872–1919. OF-LHP 1896–10, 13 **Giants**, Baltimore AL, Reds, Braves 1531 g, .303, 52 hr, 799 rbi; 1047 ip, 63–54, 3.70. 20 wins: 97–98

☛ *Led League—ba 05. Led League—rbi 05. Led League—k 97–98.*

As a hard-throwing lefthander for the Giants in the late 1890s, he won 20 and 25 games. His nickname was an allusion to Cy Young. Seymour led the NL in strikeouts in both 1897 and '98. But he was wild, leading the league in walks for three straight years, with a high of 213 in 1898. A strong lefthanded hitter, he'd occasionally played the outfield when not pitching, and by 1901 he was a regular. In 1905 with the Reds he led the NL in batting (.377), RBI (121), hits (219), doubles (40), and triples (21). Traded to the Giants the next year, he played regularly for McGraw's pennant contenders. He played an unusually shallow centerfield, and in the 1908 playoff a routine Cub fly ball sailed over his head for the winning runs and a Chicago pennant. /(JK)

Harold Seymour — 1910– . *Writer.*

On his way to becoming a history professor, Seymour earned his PhD at Cornell with a dissertation on the history of baseball. Out of that grew the first volume of a planned three-volume history of baseball, *Baseball: The Early Years.* The second volume, *The Golden Age,* covered the 1903–1930 era. Dr. Seymour was a batboy with the Dodgers in the 1920s and managed amateur and semi-pro teams in Brooklyn. /(NLM)

Mickey Shader [George C.] — 1891–1953. *Scout.*

Shader was a former pitcher and minor league business manager who scouted from 1938 to 1953 for the Reds and Giants. His top discoveries included Ace Adams and Vince DiMaggio. /(FVP)

Orator Shaffer [George] — 1852–Unk. OF 1874–75, 77–86, 90 Hartfords (NA), New York (NA), Philadelphias (NA), Louisville (NL), Indianapolis, (NL), Cubs, **Cleveland (NL)**, Buffalo (NL), St. Louis (UA), Cardinals, Philadelphia (AA) *NA:* 28 g, .225; *ML:* 842 g, .283, 10 hr, 179 rbi (inc)

Shaffer was an outstanding fielder, baserunner, and, as his nickname indicates, talker. He was an erratic hitter. He hit .214 in 1882. In 1884 he finished second in the Union Association batting chase with .360 and a league-leading 40 doubles. The next year he dropped to .195. His brother Taylor Shaffer, 18 years younger, was a second baseman for the 1890 Philadelphia American Association team. /(BC)

Art Shamsky — 1941– . OF-1B 1965–72 Reds, **Mets**, Cubs, A's 665 g, .253, 68 hr, 233 rbi. *1 LCS, 3 g, .538, 1 rbi. 1 WS, 3 g, .000*

Shamsky tied a major league record by homering in four consecutive at-bats for the Reds on August 12 and 14 of 1966. He finished the year with 21 HR in only 96 games. He became a favorite of Jewish fans in New York after his 1967 trade to the Mets and his .300 performance as a fourth outfielder and left-handed pinch hitter for the beloved 1969 World Champions. His seven hits led all batters in the 1969 LCS. Nagging back problems hastened Shamsky's departure from the game in 1972. /(JCA)

Howard Shanks (Hank) — 1890–1941. OF-3B-SS-2B-1B 1912–25 **Senators**, Red Sox, Yankees 1664 g, .253, 25 hr, 619 rbi

Shanks's BA usually hovered around .250 with little power, but his defensive versatility kept him in the ML for 14 seasons; he had a strong arm and could play any infield or outfield position well. In 1921, after nine years of constantly switching positions for the Senators, he played the entire season at third base. He hit an uncharacteristic .302 and led the AL in triples (19)./(JK)

Mike Shannon (Moonman) — 1939- . 3B-OF 1962-70 **Cardinals** 879 g, .255, 68 hr, 367 rbi. *3 WS, 21 g, .235, 3 hr, 8 rbi*

A St. Louis native, Shannon became the Cardinals' regular right fielder in their 1964 World Championship season. He hit a game-tying two-run homer off Whitey Ford in the 1964 Series opener, which St. Louis won 9–5. To make room for newly acquired right fielder Roger Maris in 1967, Shannon was moved to third base (a position he quickly learned), and the Cardinals won two straight pennants and the 1967 WS. His HR off Boston's Gary Bell was the key blow in Game Three of the 1967 Series. A solo homer in Game Seven of the 1968 Series was the Cardinals' only run off Mickey Lolich as the Tigers clinched. A kidney disorder forced Shannon to retire prematurely and he became a Cardinal broadcaster in 1972./(FJO)

Mike Shannon — 1951- . *Writer.*

Shannon is the publisher and editor of *Spitball*, a quarterly literary magazine devoted to baseball. Founded in 1981, its focus is on original poetry, but short stories, literary interviews, and book reviews are also featured. Shannon also wrote *Diamond Classics* (1989), essays on the 100 best baseball books./(SH)

Paul Shannon — 1876-1939. *Writer.*

Shannon was a college correspondent for the Boston *Globe* while attending Harvard. When the *Globe*'s sports editor died, Shannon was named to replace him and held that position for 32 years. A frequent contributor to magazines, he was a charter member of the BBWAA and ultimately carried card No. 2, indicating he was second in seniority among all members. He was president of the BBWAA at his death./(NLM)

Red Shannon [Maurice Joseph] — 1895-1970. 2B-SS-3B 1915, 1917-21, 26 Braves, **A's**, Red Sox, Senators, Cubs 310 g, .259, 0 hr, 91 rbi

Red went straight from Seton Hall College to the Braves in 1915 with Joe, his identical twin. Joe's

ML career consisted of five games with Boston, but Red returned to the majors two seasons later and spent several years as a utility infielder./(JK)

Spike Shannon [William Porter] — 1878-1940. OF 1904-08 **Cardinals**, Giants, Pirates 694 g, .259, 3 hr, 183 rbi.
Umpire FL 1914-15

A speedy, sure-handed outfielder, Shannon was aquired by the Giants from the Cardinals in mid-1906 to become John McGraw's leadoff hitter. He led the NL in runs scored (104) in 1907, despite hitting only .265; his 82 walks compensated for his weak bat. When his batting average dropped to .224 the next year, he was sold to Pittsburgh./(JK)

Bobby Shantz — 1925- . LHP 1949-64 **A's**, Yankees, Pirates, Astros, Cardinals, Cubs, Phillies 1936 ip, 119-99, 3.38. 20 wins: 52 *2 WS, 13 ip, 0-1, 4.15* ☛ *Most Valuable Player—52. Led League—w 52. Led League—era 57. All-Star—51-52, 57. Gold Glove—57-64.*

The 5'6" 139-lb Shantz broke in spectacularly, winning a 13-inning game in relief, pitching nine hitless innings along the way while giving up one run and two hits overall. He was handicapped by manager Connie Mack, a former catcher who wouldn't let Shantz use his knuckleball and was predisposed against small pitchers. When Mack finally retired after the 1950 season, Jimmy Dykes took over the club and gave the little lefthander more rest between starts; Shantz blossomed. Finally allowed to use his knuckler, and with a curveball that Ted Williams called the best in the AL, Shantz learned to change speeds and went 18–10 for the 70–84 Athletics.

Shantz reached the peak of his career in 1952, going 24–7 for a fifth-place team to win the MVP award in a landslide. He led the AL in wins, winning percentage, and fewest walks per game (2.03), and finished third with a 2.48 ERA and 152 strikeouts, tied for third with five shutouts, second with 27 complete games, fourth with 255 innings, and fifth in fewest hits per game (7.39).

Plagued by injuries for most of the next four seasons, Shantz went to the Yankees in a 12-player deal before the 1957 season and made a great comeback that year, leading the AL with a 2.45 ERA while going 11–5. After that, he was used more frequently in relief, and contributed 11 saves to the 1960 pennant winners before being traded to the Pirates, who had defeated New York in the World Series; Shantz saved Game Two for the Yankees. He bounced around the NL after that, effective until his last year.

Shantz won Gold Gloves in the first four years of the award (1957–60). His brother Billy was a catcher for the A's in 1954–55 and in one game for the 1960 Yankees. /(WOR)

Bill Sharman — 1926– . OF
Minor League Star.

Sharman was an All-America basketball star at Southern California and played 11 years in the NBA, sharing the Boston Celtics' backcourt with Bob Cousy. He averaged 17.8 points for his career. In 1975 he was elected to the National Basketball Hall of Fame. The Dodgers signed him as an outfielder in 1950. He hit .292 for St. Paul (American Association) in 1952 and .294 for the same club in 1955. Brought up by Brooklyn in September 1955, he became the only man to be thrown out of a ML game without ever playing in one, when one day the whole bench was ejected by the umpire. When the Dodgers did not offer him a ML contract, he quit baseball to concentrate on basketball. /(MC)

Bill Sharp — 1950– . OF 1973–76 White Sox, **Brewers** 398 g, .255, 9 hr, 95 rbi

Sharp was a good defensive outfielder but could not hit for power. The Ohio State graduate saw spot duty with the White Sox, was a Brewers regular in 1975, and put together a 14-game hitting streak in 1976. /(GB)

Bill Sharsig — 1855–1902. *Executive.*
Manager 1884–91 **Philadelphia (AA)** 344–306 .529

At age 25, Sharsig organized the original Philadelphia Athletics, a semi-pro team playing in Oakdale Park, where he held the lease. When the American Association was formed two years later, he joined. The club was profitable, but not very successful on the field. Sharsig hired a new manager every year for four years, beginning in 1884, but none was satisfactory. Each season he took over as manager and finished the season. In 1888 he became the full-time manager. The club jumped to third in the standings but began to lose money. Sharsig turned down several offers to sell the team at a profit. However, the Brotherhood War almost bankrupted him and he was forced to sell in 1891.

An able handler of men and a kind but firm disciplinarian, Sharsig was one of the most popular men in the game. He managed minor league teams in Pennsylvania until he became business manager for the new AL Athletics in 1901. /(NLM)

Shag Shaughnessy [Frank] — 1883–1969. OF 1905, 08 Senators, **A's** 9 g, .281, 0 hr, 1 rbi

Shaughnessy invented a playoff system that bears his name in 1933 to improve minor league attendance by giving teams that were out of the pennant race a postseason opportunity. Captain of the 1904 Notre Dame football team, he later coached at McGill, Clemson, and William and Mary. After a brief ML trial as an outfielder, he became a successful minor league manager and executive, rising to the position of president of the International League in 1938 and holding that office for 24 years. /(NLM)

Joe Shaute (Lefty) — 1899–1970. LHP 1922–34 **Indians**, Dodgers, Reds 1818 ip, 99–109, 4.15

Shaute claimed to have struck out Babe Ruth more than 30 times, including his ML debut when Ruth was the first man he faced. But in 1927, when Ruth hit 60 home runs, three came off Shaute. In 1924 he won 20 games but lost an AL-leading 17. /(JK)

Al Shaw [Albert Simpson] — 1881–1974. OF 1907–09, 14–15 **Cardinals**, Brooklyn (FL), Kansas City (FL) 473 g, .281, 14 hr, 170 rbi

In two full seasons with the Cardinals, Shaw showed speed and some promise as a hitter, but he was too awkward and unreliable in the outfield to play every day. He reappeared in the Federal League, hitting .324 in 1914. /(BC)

Bob Shaw — 1933– . RHP 1957–67 Tigers, **White Sox**, A's, Braves, Giants, Mets, Cubs 1778 ip, 108–98, 3.52. *1 WS, 14 ip, 1–1, 2.57*
☛ *All-Star—62.*

Shaw was sometimes a flake but often a very good pitcher. He wrote an instructional manual called *Pitching* and in his good years was a fine exemplar. In 1959 he was a mainstay of the pennant-winning White Sox, going 18–6 (2.69) and leading the AL in winning percentage (.750). He won 15 games for the Braves in 1962 and 16 for the Giants in 1965. At other times he was not only far less effective, he could be a thorn in the side of management. When Bill Veeck's White Sox wouldn't give him the raise he felt he deserved for 1960, he reportedly stood atop a catwalk outside Comiskey Park and shouted down to fans, "We're not going to win! Why are you people here?" /(RL)

Don Shaw — 1944– . LHP 1967–69, 71–72 Mets, Expos, **Cardinals**, A's 188 ip, 13–14, 4.02

As a Met rookie in 1967, Shaw got the save in Tom Seaver's first career victory (4/20 versus the Cubs). Drafted by the expansion Expos, he won Montreal's inaugural game, relieving in an 11–10 victory at New York on April 8, 1969. /(KT)

Dupee Shaw [Frederick Lander] — 1859–1938. LHP-OF 1883–88 Detroit (NL), Boston (UA), Providence (NL), **Washington (NL)** 1762 ip, 83–121, 3.10

In the midst of a discouraging 1884 season with Detroit (9–18), Shaw abandoned the National League for Boston of the Union Association, where he went 21–15 and struck out a then-ML record 8.81 batters per nine innings. His 451 strikeouts rank fourth on the all-time single-season list. /(FIC)

Jim Shaw (Grunting Jim) — 1893–1962. RHP 1913–21 **Senators** 1600 ip, 83–98, 3.07

Shaw so exerted himself when he pitched that his grunting could be heard in the stands. He led the league in walks in 1914 and 1917. In 1919 he recorded league highs in appearances and innings pitched, but a hip injury ended his ML career in 1921. /(JK)

Bob Shawkey (Sailor Bob, Bob the Gob) — 1890–1980. RHP 1913–27 A's, **Yankees** 2937 ip, 196–150, 3.09. 20 wins: 16, 19–20, 22 *5 WS, 42 ip, 1–3, 4.75.*
  Manager 1930 **Yankees** 86–68, .558
☛ *Led League—era 20.*

For eight years Bob Shawkey was about as good a pitcher as the Yankees had. He was another Connie Mack giveaway, a fine 16–8 sophomore season going for naught after the Braves' 4–0 sweep of the World Series. In mid-1915 he was sold to New York for $18,000. Next year he was the team's workhorse, winning 24 games and achieving a 2.21 ERA in 53 appearances. He had one more win than Boston's phenomenal young Babe Ruth, one less than league-leading Walter Johnson. Seven of his victories (and four losses) were in relief. As was often the case in those days, the staff strong man could be called on to mop up, if he was not pitching his own complete games. Shawkey was credited with eight saves, tops in both leagues.

Most of 1918 was spent in the Navy as a yeoman petty officer aboard the battleship *Arkansas*, whence came his nautical nicknames. The Yankees he returned to were Miller Huggins's team, shortly to

Bob Shawkey

begin its habitual winning ways. Shawkey contributed 20 victories each in 1919, 1920, and 1922, helped along by 10- and 11-game winning streaks the first two of those seasons. He struck out 15 Athletics in 1919, which was a Yankee record for 59 years, and among his 37 career shutouts were seven 1–0 games, also a Yankee mark.

In 1923 he pitched the first game played at Yankee Stadium, beating the Red Sox 3–1; appropriately, Ruth walloped the first Stadium homer, but Shawkey got the second.

The tall, slender Shawkey was a slow, deliberate worker on the mound. He was a gentle, unassuming fellow, yet with all the self-confidence essential to pitching. He constantly studied the great hitters of his era to analyze their success against him and vary his pitches accordingly. He showed Red Ruffing how to get less arm and more body into his motion, even as Chief Bender helped him as a rookie with the Athletics. His only touch of color was a red-sleeved undershirt; he was always a bit overshadowed by the Yanks' array of topnotch pitchers: Mays, Hoyt, Bush, Shocker, Pennock.

His last active season was 1927. He was a coach in 1929 when Huggins died, and Shawkey guided the team to a third-place finish as manager in 1930.

Supplanted by Joe McCarthy in 1931, he began a long career of minor league managing, coaching in the Pittsburgh and Detroit farm systems, and instructing pitchers for several clubs. He was baseball coach at Dartmouth College in the 1950s, and, as an old man, threw out the first ball at refurbished Yankee Stadium in 1976. /(ADS)

Shea Stadium New York Mets 1964– , New York Yankees 1974–75. LF-338, CF-410, RF-338

A triple-decked stadium in Flushing, Queens, Shea Stadium is named for attorney William Shea, who was instrumental in bringing a NL expansion franchise to New York in 1962. It is circular, but unenclosed in the outfield, and features natural grass, symmetrical fences, and the ML's largest scoreboard behind the right-centerfield fence. Left field is home to a small picnic area, while in center a large red apple rises out of a top hat after each Mets home run. Early- and late-season games are plagued by bitter winds from nearby Flushing Bay, while jets from LaGuardia Airport regularly pass overhead with a deafening roar. Shea's ample foul territory favors pitchers, and almost all of its 55,601 seats are in foul territory. The exterior was painted bright blue for the 1987 season. Shea is unusually convenient to both local highways and public transportation, sharing a New York City subway station with the U.S. Tennis Center. Now home only to the Mets, it housed the Yankees while Yankee Stadium was being renovated, as well as the NFL's Jets and Giants. /(SCL)

Merv Shea — 1900–1953. C 1927–29, 33–39, 44 Tigers, Red Sox, Browns, **White Sox**, Dodgers, Phillies 439 g, .220, 5 hr, 115 rbi

Despite a weak bat, Shea parlayed good defense and deft handling of pitchers into eleven ML seasons, ten as a backup. In 1933, in a classic one-sided trade, the Browns sent star catcher Rick Ferrell and pitcher

Shea Stadium

Lloyd Brown to the Red Sox in exchange for Shea and cash. Shea hit .242, the only year in which he played in more than half his team's games. /(RL)

Spec Shea [born Frank Joseph O'Shea] (The Naugatuck Nugget) — 1920- . RHP 1947-49, 51-55 **Yankees**, Senators 944 ip, 56-46, 3.80. *1 WS, 15 ip, 2-0, 2.35*
☛ *All-Star—47.*

Shea would have been AL Rookie of the Year in 1947 if the BBWAA had given separate awards in the NL and AL; Jackie Robinson won in a landslide, but Shea led the AL candidates in votes. Throwing a moving fastball, a change, and a slider, he went 14-5 with a 3.07 ERA that season, led the AL in fewest hits per nine innings (6.4), won the All-Star Game, and helped the Yankees to the World Championship after a pennant drought of three years. His rookie record was achieved despite missing seven weeks in the middle of the year with a pulled neck muscle. He also won Games One and Five of the World Series. In Game Five, Shea threw a four-hitter while getting two hits himself, including an RBI double off Hugh Casey, and won 2-1. Shea came back on two days' rest for the final game and pitched without a decision as the Yankees won. Shea had made the Yankees by a fluke. After missing half of 1942 and all of 1943-46 in the military, he pitched for a local team in Waterbury, Connecticut in an exhibition against the Yankees and beat them 1-0, earning a trip to spring training with them in 1947.

The neck injury in 1947 ultimately caught up with him. He spent the next three seasons pitching in pain and ineffectively, because the doctors and the Yankees misdiagnosed him as having arm trouble, and he spent time in the minors trying to work it out. Finally, he went to a local chiropractor while at home over the winter in 1951; the problem was cured in just 15 minutes, and the chiropractor gave him a list of doctors in each AL city in case it cropped up again. After the season he was traded to the Senators with Jackie Jensen and two others for Irv Noren and Tom Upton, and had two more good seasons for .500 clubs, going 11-7 (1952) and 12-7 (1953).

Shea was called Spec because of his freckles, and was nicknamed the The Naugatuck Nugget by Yankees' broadcaster Mel Allen. /(SFS)

Dave Shean — 1878-1963. 2B-SS 1906, 08-12, 17-19 A's, Phillies, **Braves**, Cubs, Reds, Red Sox 630 g, .228, 6 hr, 166 rbi. *1 WS, 6 g, .211*

Shean and Eddie Collins broke in together with the 1906 Athletics. Shean was a flashy fielder but, because of his weak bat, was a regular in only three seasons. With the Braves in 1910 and the Reds in 1917, he led NL second basemen in putouts, assists, double plays, and chances per game. /(JK)

Jimmy Sheckard — 1878-1947. OF 1897-1913 Dodgers, Baltimore (NL), Baltimore (AL), Cubs, Cardinals, Reds 2121 g, .275, 56 hr, 813 rbi. *4 WS, 21 g, .182, 5 rbi*
☛ *Led League—hr 03.*

Sheckard was one of a handful of Pennsylvania Dutch to play in the majors. Though chiefly remembered for his years with the Cubs, for whom he played in four World Series, Sheckard had his best years with Brooklyn. He batted .353 while leading the league with 19 triples and a .536 slugging percentage for the 1901 Brooklyn Superbas; his 11 HR and 104 RBI were career highs. In 1903 his nine HR were enough to capture the NL title, and he tied for the league lead with 67 stolen bases. (With Baltimore in 1899, he had led the NL with 77 stolen bases.) With the Cubs, he embarrassed himself in the 1906 World Series; boasting that he would bat .400 against White Sox pitching, he instead went 0-for-21 as the Sox upset the Cubs in six games. In 1911 he set a Cub record for most walks (147), leading the NL for the first of two straight seasons. He also scored an NL-high 121 runs that year. /(ARA)

Leonard Shecter — 1926-1974. *Writer.*

A forceful reporter and columnist who never avoided confrontation, Shecter left the New York *Post* in 1968 to write *The Jocks*, an iconoclastic view of sports in America. He co-authored *Ball Four* with Jim Bouton, which sold over 200,000 hardcover copies. He also wrote *Once Upon the Polo Grounds*, about Casey Stengel and the early Mets, and *On the Pad*, written with William Phillips, the bribed policeman whose testimony before the Knapp Commission helped uncover corruption in the New York City police department. /(NLM)

Tom Sheehan — 1894-1982. RHP 1915-16, 21, 24-26 **A's**, Yankees, Reds, Pirates 607 ip, 17-39, 4.00. *Manager* 1960 **Giants** 46-50, .479

Sheehan suffered through an ignominious 1-16 season with the 1916 Athletics, a team that won only 36 games while losing 117. Things were worse for Sheehan's roommate, Jack Nabors, who was 1-20 that year. A coach and minor league manager, Sheehan became a superscout for the Giants in 1948. He managed San Francisco for part of the

1960 season, at 66 the oldest man to be named manager. He then returned to scouting until 1976. /(JK)

Tommy Sheehan — 1877–1959. 3B 1906–08 Pirates, Dodgers 316 g, .236, 1 hr, 88 rbi

An adept bunter, Sheehan hit .214 as Brooklyn's everyday third baseman in 1908, the final season of his brief career. He managed Colon to the Panama Canal Zone League pennant in 1930–31, and died in Panama City at age 81. /(ME)

Earl Sheely (Whitey) — 1893–1952. 1B 1921–27, 29, 31 White Sox, Pirates, Braves 1234 g, .300, 48 hr, 747 rbi

Sheely was a big, slow first baseman with a knack for driving in runs, twice topping 100. He also hit over .300 four times in nine seasons. Although he was criticized for slow play in the field, he was sure-handed and led AL first basemen in fielding in 1926 and NL first basemen in 1929. His son, Hollis, played briefly for the White Sox in the early 1950s. /(RL)

Larry Sheets — 1959– . OF-DH 1984- Orioles 606 g, .268, 84 hr, 286 rbi

In the minors Larry Sheets was a mystery—an outstanding lefthanded slugging prospect who apparently had no great desire to play baseball professionally. He was drafted by the Orioles in 1977 but did not attend spring training until 1983, both because of college commitments and his personal indecision about his future. He still led the Appalachian League in home runs with 14 in only 37 games for Bluefield in 1980, but then chose not to play organized ball at all in 1981. He returned midway through the 1982 season, and in 1983 he tied Glenn Davis for the Southern League HR title with 25 for Charlotte. By 1985 the enigmatic Sheets had reached the ML, where he made the Topps and *Baseball Digest* All-Rookie teams with a .262 average and 17 HR as Baltimore's designated hitter. In 1987 Sheets was outstanding, hitting .316 with 31 HR, including five two-home-run games and one blast onto the roof of Chicago's Comiskey Park, but he fell apart in 1988, hitting just .230 with 10 HR. /(SCL)

Gary Sheffield — 1968– . SS 1988- Brewers 119 g, .246, 9 hr, 44 rbi

Sheffield, Dwight Gooden's nephew, was the pre-season favorite in 1989 for AL Rookie of the Year but was sent down in mid-season for "indifferent fielding." He was batting .248 with four HR at the

time and had been the Brewers' regular shortstop. Before the season, he had removed the gold inlays from his teeth to project a better image to young fans. /(JFC)

John Shelby — 1958– . OF 1981- Orioles, Dodgers 880 g, .243, 63 hr, 283 rbi. *2 LCS, 10 g, .182, 3 rbi. 2 WS, 10 g, .296, 2 rbi*

Shelby showed surprising offensive prowess when obtained by Los Angeles from Baltimore in May 1987, hitting .271 with 21 HR in 120 games for the Dodgers. Always a good outfielder, Shelby had been a free swinger with little power, and he reverted to form the following year. A high-percentage base stealer, he led his minor leagues' outfielders in assists three times, and in 1983 once threw out three baserunners in a game. His shoestring catch of the last out of Game Four of the 1988 NLCS saved the Dodgers' 12-inning victory. /(TG)

Rollie Sheldon [Roland Frank] — 1936– . RHP 1961–62, 64–66 Yankees, A's, Red Sox 725 ip, 38–36, 4.08. *1 WS, 3 ip, 0–0, 0.00*

Benefiting from American League expansion and the Yankees' need for pitching, Sheldon jumped to the majors in 1961 after going 15–1 in Class-D ball his first pro season. He achieved an 11–5 mark as a rookie, but never again matched that success. /(GDW)

Frank Shellenback — 1898–1969. RHP 1918–19 White Sox 217 ip, 10–15, 3.06

A spitball pitcher, Shellenback was at Vernon in the Pacific Coast League when the pitch was outlawed for pitchers coming up to the majors. Still allowed to throw his spitter in the minors, he compiled a 295–178 record in 20 PCL seasons. He later served as pitching coach for several ML clubs, most notably the Giants. /(DB)

Jim Shellenback — 1943– . LHP 1966–67, 69–74, 77 Pirates, Senators/Rangers, Twins 455 ip, 16–30, 3.80

Shellenback suffered severe injuries, including a broken leg, in an auto wreck on October 1, 1967—five days after defeating the Dodgers 2–1 in 11 innings in his first major league start. That turned out to be his last victory for Pittsburgh. At his best, he won six games with the 1970 Senators. He became a longtime minor league coach for the Twins. His uncle Frank Shellenback pitched for the White Sox. /(KT)

Bob Shepard — Unk.- *Announcer.*

The PA announcer at Yankee Stadium since 1951, Shepard became ubiquitous to the point that all other stadium announcers are judged against his authoritative, resonant tones and straightforward style. /(SFS)

Jack Shepard — 1932- . C 1953-56 Pirates 278 g, .260, 12 hr, 75 rbi

Shepard earned three degrees at Stanford and was elected to the university's Hall of Fame. He was a member of *TSN*'s All-Rookie Team and was the Pirates' Rookie of the Year in 1954, when he batted .304. After struggling in 1955-56, he turned to a career in business. /(ME)

Bill Sherdel (Wee Willie) — 1896-1968. LHP 1918-32 **Cardinals**, Braves 2708 ip, 165-146, 3.72. 20 wins: 28 *2 WS, 30 ip, 0-4, 3.26*

Sherdel, a happy craftsman who often whistled or sang on the mound, couldn't overpower batters but relied on guile. His quick pitch of Babe Ruth in the 1928 WS caused an uproar, somewhat tempered when Ruth homered a few moments later. Wee Willie (actually 5'10" and 160-lb) was a key Cardinals pitcher for over a dozen seasons, working as both a starter and reliever. He won 21 for the 1928 pennant winners, twice won 17, and led the NL in winning percentage (.714) in 1925 with a 15-6 mark. As a reliever, he led the NL in saves three times. He once entered a game with the bases loaded and no outs. His first pitch was turned into a triple play. /(JK)

Roy Sherid — 1907-1982. RHP 1929-31 **Yankees** 418 ip, 23-24, 4.65

Pitching for the Yankees against the A's in 1930, Sherid was ordered by manager Bob Shawkey to walk Al Simmons with the bases loaded to keep Simmons from overtaking Lou Gehrig in the batting race. A's first baseman Jimmie Foxx followed with a grand slam. /(NLM)

John Sheridan — Unk.-Unk. *Umpire* 1890 PL, 92-93, 96-97 NL, 01-14 AL

On May 31, 1901, Detroit was down 5-4 to Baltimore in the bottom of the ninth when Ducky Holmes hit a shot to centerfield and circled the bases for an inside-the-park home run, sliding into home plate in a close play. Baltimore catcher Wilbert Robinson objected strenuously and was tossed out of the game. Robinson's teammates carried on the shouting and Mike Donlin heaved a bat at Sheridan. When Baltimore refused to take the field for the tenth inning, Sheridan forfeited the game to Detroit, the first AL forfeit. /(RTM)

Pat Sheridan — 1957- . OF 1981, 83- **Royals**, Tigers, Giants 814 g, .255, 47 hr, 250 rbi. *4 LCS, 20 g, .163, 3 hr, 5 rbi. 2 WS, 6 g, .200, 1 rbi*

The Royals hoped Sheridan, a .300 hitter in the minors, would be their regular right fielder for the 1980s. Given the opportunity, he was unable to put a lock on the job due to his inability to hit lefthanders consistently, and to injuries. Released by the Royals, he won an everyday job in Detroit but remained just a so-so hitter.

Each of his three home runs in LCS play came in dramatic situations in winning causes. In 1985 his ninth-inning pinch homer tied Game Two; in Game Seven his long solo shot in the fourth inning for the second run of the game proved important in the Royals' series-clinching 6-2 victory. And with the Tigers in 1987, his two-run, eighth-inning HR won Game Three. /(FO)

Harold Sherman — 1898-Unk. *Writer.*

From 1926 to 1933 Sherman churned out an average of five books a year, including adventure and sports books for boys such as *Hit by Pitcher*, *Bases Full*, and *Safe* in 1928, *Batter Up* in 1930, and *Double Play and Other Baseball Stories* in 1932. He also wrote two plays, a screenplay, and many nonfiction books on ESP and other subjects. /(NLM)

Larry Sherry — 1935- . RHP 1958-68 **Dodgers**, Tigers, Astros, Angels 799 ip, 53-44, 3.67. *1 WS, 13 ip, 2-0, 0.71*

A 24-year-old rookie reliever called up by the Los Angeles Dodgers in the midst of the 1959 pennant race, Sherry went 7-2, won the first game of a best-of-three playoff with the Braves, and became the hero of the World Series. Relieving in all four Dodger victories, he recorded saves in Games Two and Three, and wins in Games Four and Six. In 12-2/3 innings of work, he allowed just one run and eight hits. For the first time in Series history, no member of either club's staff pitched a complete game.

A power pitcher who threw a slider at several speeds, Sherry led the NL with 13 relief wins in 1960. He recorded 82 career saves, with a high of 20 for Detroit in 1966. He later returned to the Dodger organization as a minor league coach. Sherry was born with two club feet, but his problem was corrected by surgery when he was six. His brother, reserve catcher Norm Sherry, was a Dodger team-mate from 1959 to 1962. /(RTM)

Bill Shettsline — 1863–1933. *Manager 1898–02*
Phillies 367–303, .548

Shettsline was in baseball for 44 years, beginning as a ticket seller for the Philadelphia team in the Union Association in 1884. He became assistant secretary of the Phillies, and managed the team five years, finishing second in 1901. In 1902 he also managed a Phillies pro football team. He became the team's business manager and then served as president from 1905 to 1915. He went back to being business manager from 1915 to 1927, when he joined the A's one year before retiring. /(NLM)

Shibe Park Philadelphia A's 1909–54, Philadelphia Phillies 1938–70. LF-334, CF-410, RF-329

Named for Athletics stockholder Ben Shibe, Shibe Park opened April 12, 1909 as baseball's first concrete-and-steel ballpark, and on May 16, 1939 it hosted the AL's first night game. Double-decked in 1925, Shibe's left and right field walls met at a virtual right angle in deep centerfield, originally 515' from home plate and not shortened to below 440 until 1969. The park was renamed Connie Mack Stadium to honor the retired A's manager in 1953, but two years later the A's had moved to Kansas City, leaving the Phillies as sole occupants. In 1956 a plexiglass shield was installed to protect fans seated behind home plate, replacing the standard wire screen, and a large scoreboard from Yankee Stadium was added to the right field wall, which was simultaneously reduced from 50' to 36'. Richie Allen hit the only ball ever to clear that scoreboard. Shibe Park's bright red seats were filled for the last time October 1, 1970, and the stadium was torn down in June 1976. /(SCL)

Steve Shields — 1958– . RHP 1985– Braves, Royals, Mariners, **Yankees**, Twins 219 ip, 8–8, 5.26

Shields spent seven seasons in the Red Sox minor league system and two more with the Richmond Braves (International League) before finally reaching the ML with Atlanta in 1985. He was traded to the Royals for Daryl Motley September 1986 and then to Seattle as part of a package for Danny Tartabull three months later, before signing with the Yankees as a free agent before the 1988 season. In 1987 he spent a month on the DL after Kirby Puckett hit him in the face with a line drive. /(SCL)

Art Shires (Art the Great) — 1907–1967. 1B 1928–30, 32 **White Sox**, Senators, Braves 290 g, .291, 11 hr, 119 rbi

Shires broke into the majors on August 20, 1928 with three singles and a triple off Red Ruffing. Cocky and brash, he embodied the Jazz Age twenties. Appointed team captain in 1929, Shires became involved in fist fights with manager Lena Blackburne on two occasions that season, once after refusing to discard a red felt hat which he wore to the plate during batting practice, and once when discovered drinking bootleg whiskey in his Philadelphia hotel room. During that first winter of the Depression, Shires arranged a number of professional boxing matches for himself, and he won all but his contest against George Trafton, center for the Chicago Bears. His challenge of crosstown rival Hack Wilson and fears that Shires might become involved with gamblers led Commissioner Landis to intervene in Shires's boxing career, and Shires retired from the ring. After demanding a $25,000 contract for the 1930 season, Shires was traded to Washington on June 16 and was out of baseball by 1932. /(CR)

Bob Shirley — 1954– . LHP 1977–87 **Padres**, Cardinals, Reds, Yankees, Royals 1432 ip, 67–94, 3.82

Shirley was very impressive as a 22-year-old rookie in 1977, striking out 11 Reds in his first ML start on April 10, and retiring the first 25 Astros he faced on April 23 before settling for a 4–2 win. By season's end he had led the Padres in wins (12), innings (214), and strikeouts (146), but those totals would all be career highs, as he spent the next ten seasons spot-starting and in the bullpen. He was traded to the Cardinals with Rollie Fingers and Gene Tenace for seven players in December 1981, then traded to the Reds the following year before signing with the Yankees as a free agent in 1983. In New York, he posted a career-best 2.64 ERA as a lefthanded set-up man in 1985. His high school catcher was Seattle Seahawks wide receiver Steve Largent. /(SCL)

Tex Shirley [Alvis Newman] — 1918– . RHP 1941–42, 44–46 A's, **Browns** 446 ip, 19–30, 4.25. *1 WS, 3 ip, 0–0, 0.00*

Shirley's only winning season was 1944, when the Browns won their only pennant; he was 5–4 in spot starts and long relief. /(NLM)

Urban Shocker — 1890–1928. RHP 1916–28
Yankees, **Browns** 2675 ip, 187–117, 3.17. 20 wins: 20–23
1 WS, 8 ip, 0–1, 5.87
☛ *Led League—w 21. Led League—k 22.*

Shocker is a dim figure, an unappreciated, almost-forgotten great pitcher. In a 13-year career, he never had a losing season and compiled a .617 winning percentage. He was well-enough known in his time, yet he labored in relative obscurity. His best years were spent with the Sisler-era Browns, a so-so team that had the bad luck to be good when the Yankees were fantastic. His final years were spent as a Yankee, but as perhaps the least flamboyant of that vivid ensemble. And he died at the untimely age of 38, much too early to have become a legend.

Shocker came late to the big leagues and did not even become a pitcher until 1913, his first professional season. Originally a catcher, he demonstrated such speed and accuracy in his throws that he was switched to the mound. He acquired a spitter, which he threw infrequently and as a breaking slow ball, and a variety of curves. His delivery was aided by a permanent crook in the end joint of his ring finger, suffered when he speared a ball while still a catcher. He always said the crooked finger improved his grip and thus the effectiveness of his pitches.

Two fine seasons with Ottawa, of the Canada League, brought him to the Yankees in 1916 for $750. In one of Miller Huggins's rare misjudgments, however, he was traded to the Browns in 1918, with Les Nunamaker, Fritz Maisel, Nick Cullop, and Joe Gedeon, for Del Pratt, Eddie Plank, and $15,000.

Thereafter, Shocker hit his stride, stringing together four 20-win seasons and proving a particular nemesis of the Yankees. In 1924 the Yanks stole him back for Joe Bush, Milt Gaston, and Joe Giard. Shocker had his only .500 season in 1925, the year of the great Yankee slump, but pitched marvelously well in 1926 and 1927.

After the 1927 season he voluntarily retired (he did pitch three innings in 1928). He had a successful radio shop in St. Louis, but evidently was too ill to run it. His death was attributed to an overstrained "athlete's heart."

Shocker was an intense, unsmiling fellow, a studious pitcher widely admired for an artful delivery and a profound knowledge of hitters. He allowed almost exactly a hit per inning, yet, as his ERA shows, not many runs. He was stingy with walks, averaging one every four innings. A serious professional, he was known as an excellent fielder and capable hitter, perhaps too serious to have a nickname. /(ADS)

Urban Shocker

Milt Shoffner [Milburn James] — 1905–1978. LHP 1929–31, 37–40 Indians, **Braves**, Reds 577 ip, 25–26, 4.59

In his ML debut with the Indians in 1929 Shoffner relieved against the Yankees and struck out Babe Ruth. But he was known as a hard-luck pitcher throughout his career, plagued by a sore arm and odd happenings. In the minors an irate fan fractured his skull with a bat, and a week after he was married, his league folded. In 1939 with the Braves, the lefty pitched the last eight innings of a scoreless tie, and later 16 scoreless innings to no decision. /(NLM)

Toots Shor [Bernard] — 1904–1977.

The famous bartender whose saloon in New York was a popular watering hole for both players and sportswriters became an oft-quoted observer of the social and sports scenes. He was a special favorite of Casey Stengel. /(SFS)

Ernie Shore — 1891–1980. RHP 1912, 14–17, 19–20 Giants, **Red Sox**, Yankees 987 ip, 65–42, 2.45. *2 WS, 34 ip, 3–1, 1.82*

Shore's baseball career was intertwined with Babe Ruth's. They went to the Red Sox together from Baltimore. When starter Ruth was ejected from a June 23, 1917 game for protesting a walk to the first batter he faced, Shore relieved, and, after the runner was caught stealing, pitched a perfect game. The two later were roommates with the Yankees. Shore was a winner in his four years with the Red Sox, including a 19–8 (1.64) 1915 mark, but was ineffective after spending 1918 in WWI military service. /(ADS)

Bill Shores — 1904–1984. RHP 1928–31, 33–36 **A's**, Giants, White Sox 395 ip, 26–15, 4.17. *1 WS, 1 ip, 0–0, 13.50*

A powerful pitcher who used overhand, sidearm, and underhand deliveries, Shores was a reliever and spot starter for the 1929–31 championship A's. He peaked with a 12–4 record in 1930. /(NLM)

Bill Short — 1937– . LHP 1960, 62, 66–69 **Yankees**, Orioles, Red Sox, Pirates, Mets, Reds 131 ip, 5–11, 4.73

Touted by the Yankees as the next Whitey Ford, Short threw a variety of junk pitches. Pitching for the 1966 World Champion Orioles, he beat Minnesota 2–0, for his only ML shutout, but was sold to Boston later that season. /(GDW)

Chris Short (Style) — 1937– . LHP 1959–73 **Phillies**, Brewers 2325 ip, 135–132, 3.43. *20 wins: 66*

Known as Style because of his meager wardrobe as a rookie, 6'4" Chris Short was slow to develop, but emerged in the mid-1960s as a mainstay of the Phillies' pitching staff. He won 17 or more games four times between 1964 and 1968; in 1966 he became the first Phillies southpaw to win 20 since Eppa Rixey won 22 in 1916. Facing the Mets on October 2, 1965, he tied what was then the post-1901 NL record for most strikeouts in a game, fanning 18 in 15 innings; the game was called after 18 frames without a run being scored. Back trouble curtailed Short's career. /(AL)

Chick Shorten [Charles] — 1892–1965. OF 1915–17, 19–22, 24 Red Sox, **Tigers**, Browns, Reds 527 g, .275, 3 hr, 134 rbi. *1 WS, 2 g, .571, 2 rbi*

Shorten spent eight seasons as a reserve in the ML, leading the AL in pinch hits (9) in 1921. He extended his baseball career to more than 50 years as a longtime scout for Cleveland. /(JK)

Burt Shotton [Barney] — 1884–1962. OF 1909, 1911–23 **Browns**, Senators, Cardinals 1388 g, .270, 9 hr, 290 rbi.
    Manager 1928–34, 47–50 **Phillies**, Reds, Dodgers 697–763, .477. First place: 47, 49 *2 WS, 4–8, .333*

A dependable outfielder and leadoff batter who, with the Browns, led the American League in walks in 1913 and in walks and at-bats in 1916, Shotton gained greater attention as a manager. He was a close friend of Branch Rickey, whom he replaced as a "Sunday manager" because Rickey would not appear at the ballpark on the Sabbath. He served as patient skipper of the Phillies from 1928 to 1933, never finishing higher than fourth, and piloted the Reds for one game in 1934. In 1947 Rickey's Brooklyn manager, Leo Durocher, was suspended for the season by Commissioner Happy Chandler. Rickey was bringing Jackie Robinson to Brooklyn to break the major league color line and, in need of an experienced and steady hand, persuaded Shotton to come out of retirement.

Shotton, who managed from the bench wearing street clothes, was not the tactical genius that Durocher was, but with the talent he managed, his calm, steady approach guided the Dodgers into a '47 World Series loaded with drama. The Yankees' Bill Bevens was one out away from pitching a no-hitter in Game Four when Cookie Lavagetto hit a pinch double, driving in the winning runs. Though Al Gionfriddo's catch of Joe DiMaggio's drive saved Brooklyn in Game Six, the Yankees won the Series the following day.

Durocher retook the Dodger helm in 1948, and Shotton went back into retirement, only to return when Durocher stunned Brooklyn fans by leaving to join the rival Giants midway through the season. Shotton's club won another pennant in 1949, and again lost to the Yankees in the WS. In 1950 the Dodgers were defeated by Philadelphia's Whiz Kids on the last day of the season, missing a chance to tie for the pennant. Before the season, Walter O'Malley had gained control of the Dodgers, and Rickey had departed. O'Malley fired Shotton, who retired for good. /(JK)

Clyde Shoun (Hardrock) — 1912–1968. LHP 1935–44, 46–49 Cubs, **Cardinals**, Reds, Braves, White Sox 1287 ip, 73–59, 3.91

Shoun went 7–7 in his first full year with the Cubs before going to the Cardinals in a headline-generating trade for Dizzy Dean the following April. He led the National League in appearances in 1939 and 1940; his nine saves in '39 tied him for the league lead. Sold to Cincinnati in 1942, he went 14–5 in 1943, topping the NL with 13 wins out of the bullpen. Shoun made a career-high 21 starts in 1944. On May 15, he faced Boston's Jim Tobin, who had thrown a no-hitter 18 days earlier. Shoun matched the feat, and missed a perfect game only by walking Tobin in the third inning. /(GB)

Eric Show — 1956– . RHP 1981– Padres 1497 ip, 94–79, 3.43. *1 LCS, 5 ip, 0–1, 13.50. 1 WS, 3 ip, 0–1, 10.13*

San Diego workhorse Eric Show might best be remembered as the pitcher who surrendered Pete Rose's record-setting 4,192nd hit. He also ranks as the Padres' winningest righthander and among the all-time club leaders in ERA, innings pitched, strikeouts, complete games, and shutouts. He led the Padres in innings pitched each season from 1983 to 1987 except 1986. In the midst of his best season, Show was removed from an August 1986 game against the Mets after retiring the first seven batters. He was found to have flexor tendinitis in the right elbow and missed the rest of the season. An intelligent, all-around athlete, Show was San Diego's leading winner in 1983 and 1984.

He gained notoriety as one of several Padres pitchers who were members of the John Birch Society. His behavior following Rose's record-setter was also remarked upon; during the long presentation of the ball to Rose, the ovation, etc., Show sat on the mound, disgruntled (perhaps rightly so) at the lengthy interruption of the contest. /(ME)

George Shuba (Shotgun) — 1924– . OF 1948–50, 52–55 **Dodgers** 355 g, .259, 24 hr, 125 rbi. *3 WS, 7 g, .333, 1 hr, 2 rbi*

A utility outfielder and lefthanded pinch hitter during the Dodgers' Boys of Summer era, Shuba delivered a pinch-hit homer in the 1953 World Series opener, which the Yankees won 9–5. Knee surgery reduced his effectiveness after that season. /(EGM)

Frank Shugart [born Frank Harry Shugarts] — 1866–1944. SS-OF 1890–95, 97, 1901 Chicago (PL), **Pirates**, St. Louis [Perfectos] (NL), Louisville (NL), Phillies, White Sox 745 g, .267, 21 hr, 384 rbi

Shugart was, for short stints, the starting shortstop for Pittsburgh, Louisville, and Chicago, and the centerfielder for St. Louis. He hit three homers for St. Louis on May 10, 1894, and three triples for Louisville on June 30, 1895. /(ME)

Sicks Stadium Seattle Pilots 1969. LF-305, CF-402, RF-320

Opened in 1938, 25,420-seat Sicks Stadium was named for Emil Sick, owner of the Pacific Coast League's Seattle Rainiers. Home to the Pilots in their only season of existence, the park's bleacher section was still being expanded on Opening Day, delaying the start of the game. Sicks offered an excellent view of nearby Mt. Rainier. /(SCL)

Norm Siebern — 1933– . 1B-OF 1956, 58–68 Yankees, **A's**, Orioles, Angels, Giants, Red Sox 1408 g, .272, 132 hr, 636 rbi. *3 WS, 7 g, .167, 1 rbi*
☛ *All-Star—62–64. Gold Glove—58.*

Though Siebern won a Gold Glove as an outfielder in 1958, his defensive miscues made him the goat of the Yankees' 3–0 Game Four loss to the Braves in the 1958 World Series. Playing in left, Yankee Stadium's difficult sun field, Siebern lost track of two fly balls in the sixth and seventh innings, setting up all three of Milwaukee's runs. After being *TSN*'s 1957 Minor League Player of the Year and hitting .300 as a rookie, Siebern went to Kansas City in the 1959 deal that brought Roger Maris to New York. The three-time All-Star first baseman reached career highs of 25 HR, 114 runs, 117 RBI, 110 walks, and a .308 batting average for the 1962 A's. /(RTM)

Dick Siebert — 1912–1978. 1B 1932, 36–45 Dodgers, Cardinals, **A's** 1035 g, .282, 32 hr, 482 rbi
☛ *All-Star—43.*

A flashy fielder, Siebert led the AL in assists in 1945. He later became baseball coach at the University of Minnesota for 31 years, and won the College World Series in 1956 and 1960–64. He was named Coach of the Year twice, and in 1978 he won the Lefty Gomez award for his contribution to college baseball. His son, Paul, pitched in the 1970s. /(NLM)

Paul Siebert — 1953– . LHP 1974–78 Astros, **Mets** 129 ip, 3–8, 3.78

Siebert was a reliever with poor control. When the Mets dumped Dave Kingman in the "Midnight

Massacre" (they traded Tom Seaver the same night because both wanted more money) on June 15, 1977, they got Siebert and Bobby Valentine in return. Siebert's father Dick had an 11-year ML career./(JFC)

Sonny Siebert [Wilfred Charles] — 1937- . RHP 1964-75 **Indians**, Red Sox, Rangers, Cardinals, Padres, A's 2153 ip, 140-114, 3.21
☛ *All-Star—66, 71.*

Drafted by both the Indians and the NBA St. Louis Hawks, Siebert was an outfielder his first two pro seasons before taking the mound in 1960. A late bloomer, he developed control and a devastating curveball, and blossomed with 16-8 records in both 1965 and 1966. His .667 winning percentage in '66 led the AL. He no-hit the Senators that June 10, and threw two scoreless innings in the All-Star Game.

After two injury-marred seasons, Siebert went to the Red Sox in a controversial but beneficial 1969 trade for Ken Harrelson. He led Boston's starters in winning percentage in 1970 and 1971, going 15-8 and 16-10. He dropped to 12-12 in 1972 after he injured an ankle climbing rocks at the seashore. Pitching for St. Louis on September 11, 1974, he beat the Mets in the second-longest game, by innings (25), in NL history. Siebert hit six of his 12 career home runs in 1971, including two in one game./(ME)

Dwight Siebler — 1937- . RHP 1963-67 **Twins** 117 ip, 4-3, 3.45

Siebler relieved in 40 of his 48 ML games. In his first start, on August 29, 1963, he defeated the Senators, 10-1, on a three-hitter; the Twins' offense supported him by walloping eight home runs to tie a ML record./(RTM)

Ruben Sierra — 1965- . OF 1986- **Rangers** 589 g, .273, 98 hr, 374 rbi
☛ *Led League—rbi 89. All-Star—89.*

Sierra debuted with the Rangers at the age of 20 in 1986, and in 1987 the right fielder became the youngest player to hit 30 HR in a season since Tony Conigliaro in 1965. A compact, powerful switch-hitter who hits equally well from either side of the plate, Sierra also drove in 109 runs in 1987 and set a Rangers record with 69 extra-base hits. In 1988, he became only the third player in club history to be named team MVP two consecutive years, batting .254 with 23 HR and 91 RBI. In his All-Star 1989 season, he led the AL with 119 RBI and broke his own team record with 78 extra-base hits while hitting .306 with 29 HR and 101 runs scored./(SCL)

Ed Siever — 1877-1920. LHP 1901-04, 06-08 **Tigers**, Browns 1507 ip, 83-83, 2.60. *1 WS, 4 ip, 0-1, 4.50*
☛ *Led League—era 02.*

Pitching for the seventh-place 1902 Tigers, Siever led the AL with a 1.91 ERA but went 8-11. He had broken into the majors the year before, going 18-15 with 30 complete games in 33 starts. Sold to the Browns after the 1902 season, he went 13-14 and 10-15 with them before being let go. Reappearing with the Tigers in 1906, he helped them to their first pennant in 1907 with an 18-11, 2.16 record, but lost Game Three of the World Series 5-1./(WOR)

Roy Sievers (Squirrel) — 1926- . 1B-OF-3B 1949-65 Browns, **Senators**, White Sox, Phillies, Senators 1887 g, .267, 318 hr, 1147 rbi
☛ *Rookie of the Year—49. Led League—hr 57. Led League—rbi 57. All-Star—56-57, 59.*

A St. Louis native signed by the Browns, Sievers was the American League Rookie of the Year in 1949, batting .306 with 16 home runs and 75 RBI. He hit just .238 the following season, then was hindered by a shoulder separation suffered while making a diving catch in 1951; after reporting early for spring training in 1952, he dislocated his right arm during infield practice. The Browns traded him to the Senators for Gil Coan in February 1954. In Washington, Sievers became a favorite of Richard Nixon (then vice president), driving in 100 or more runs and playing at least 144 games each year from 1954 through 1958. In 1957, though his club came in last, Sievers led the AL with 42 home runs and became the first Senator to win the RBI crown (114) since Goose Goslin in 1924. He tied an AL record in July and August of 1957 by homering in six consecutive contests—a mark since eclipsed by Don Mattingly. He remained productive through 1963 with the Phillies; that year, he matched Jimmie Foxx as the only players to pinch hit grand slams in both the AL and NL. In mid-1964 he was sold to the expansion Senators. He acquired his nickname as a high school basketball player, from hanging around the "cage" all the time./(RTM)

Charlie Silvera (Swede) — 1924- . C 1948-57 **Yankees**, Cubs 227 g, .282, 0 hr, 52 rbi. *1 WS, 1 g, .000*

Playing behind Yogi Berra and Elston Howard, Silvera spent most of his nine Yankee years warming up pitchers in the bullpen. Eligible for seven WS, he played in only one game./(JK)

Al Sima — 1921- . LHP 1950-51, 53-54 **Senators**, White Sox, A's 309 ip, 11-21, 4.61

Sima, a curveballer, apprenticed with seven teams over nine seasons in the minors. He finally broke in as a spot starter with the 1950 Senators and won his major league career-high four games. /(GEB)

Al Simmons (Bucketfoot Al, The Duke of Milwaukee) — 1902–1956. OF 1924–41, 43–44 **Phillies**, White Sox, Tigers, Senators, Braves, Reds, A's 2215 g, .334, 307 hr, 1827 rbi. *4 WS, 19 g, .329, 6 hr, 17 rbi* ☛ *Led League—ba 30–31. Led League—rbi 29. All-Star—33–35. Hall of Fame—1953.*

Connie Mack kept only one picture of a former player in his office, and it was of the swaggering, hard-hitting Al Simmons. Once, when asked who could provide the most value to a team, Mack reflected on half a century of managing and sighed, "If I could only have nine players named Simmons."

Late in his career Simmons announced his goal of attaining 3,000 base hits. He played beyond when he should have retired but still came up 73 short. Looking back, he grieved about the times he had begged off playing to nurse a hangover or left a one-sided game early for a quick shower and a night's pleasures. Proud of his Polish ancestry, Simmons, as a grizzled coach, imparted his realization to another player from a Polish family. "Never relax on any time at bat; never miss a game you can play," he advised a young Stan Musial.

On the field Simmons was a warrior, intent on damaging the enemy and demolishing pitchers with his bat, stifling rallies with his glove, and upsetting infielders with take-out slides. Despite playing most of his career before night games became customary, Simmons never seemed to tan. In fact, his most evident physical characteristic was his pale complexion. His face would grow whiter as he concentrated on a tense situation.

In the most exciting rally in WS history, Philadelphia came from behind the Cubs, who led 8–0 in the seventh inning of Game Four of the 1929 World Series. It was Simmons who led off the inning with a home run. By the time Simmons batted again in the inning the Athletics trailed only by one run. He singled to keep the WS-record 10-run inning alive.

Once Simmons burst a blood vessel in his knee in the first game of a doubleheader. The team doctor didn't want to leave and thus miss the second game, so he advised keeping Simmons available on the bench for possible pinch hitting. Eventually, with the A's trailing 7–4, they filled the bases and summoned Simmons, who limped to the plate. He avoided having to run by hitting a grand slam.

Al Simmons

Simmons was described as a hitter who put his foot "in the bucket," striding with a natural step toward third base. Although that is generally considered a technical flaw, Connie Mack would not let anyone tell the righthanded slugger to change his style. The long-armed Simmons, using a longer bat than most players, could still hit with power to any field. With long uniform sleeves dangling below the elbows, he was a player of singular skills who could be spotted on the ball field by his unique style and appearance. Simmons's greatest years were with Connie Mack's Athletics, where, as an emerging great, he teamed one season with two other outfielders then in the twilight of their careers, Ty Cobb and Tris Speaker. /(JK)

Curt Simmons — 1929– . LHP 1947–50, 52–67 **Phillies**, Cardinals, Cubs, Angels 3348 ip, 193–183, 3.54. *1 WS, 14 ip, 0–1, 2.51* ☛ *All-Star—52–53, 57.*

A native of Egypt, PA, Simmons received one of the largest bonuses paid to a teenager during his day when he signed with the Phillies for $65,000 in 1947. Promoted to the majors at the end of that season, he did not master his control until 1950, when he became a key member of the NL champion Whiz Kids. He went 17–8 that season despite missing more than a month for National Guard training. Because his unit was activated, he missed the World Series. He returned in 1952 to go 14–8 with a league-high six shutouts. In 1953 he missed a month after slicing off part of his left big toe in a lawn mower accident. Released by the Phillies in 1960 after suffering arm trouble the previous season, Simmons signed with the Cardinals and made a successful adjustment from hard thrower to breaking-ball pitcher. In his last winning season, he recorded a career-high 18 victories for the 1964 World Champion Cardinals. He allowed the Yankees one run in eight innings of WS Game Three, but was not involved in the decision; in the sixth inning of Game Six, he gave up home runs to Roger Maris and Mickey Mantle on consecutive pitches, and lost. /(AL)

Ted Simmons (Simba) — 1949– . C-DH-1B 1968–88 **Cardinals**, Brewers, Braves 2456 g, .285, 248 hr, 1389 rbi. *1 LCS, 5 g, .167, 1 rbi. 1 WS, 7 g, .174, 2 hr, 3 rbi* ☛ *All-Star—72–74, 77–79, 81, 83.*

Tagged Simba for his long locks, he often played hurt and always played hard. Only average defensively, Simmons wreaked havoc on pitchers. Seven times he batted above .300, six times reached 20 HR, and eight times exceeded 90 RBI. He switch-hit home runs in a game three times and established the NL career record for home runs by a switch-hitter (182). Although not a threat to steal, Simmons had enough speed to amass 477 doubles.

Simmons had just turned 19 when he played his first games for the Cardinals. He was groomed to succeed the extremely popular and talented Tim McCarver. After annihilating minor league pitching with power and average for three seasons, Simmons became the regular St. Louis catcher for eleven years. He went to the Brewers for 1981 after feuding with manager Whitey Herzog. Simmons helped the Brewers win the second-half AL East title in the strike-split season and hit a crucial two-run homer in Game Three of the division playoff as the Brewers staved off elimination. The following year Milwaukee went all the way to the World Series. As usual, Simmons hit for a poor average in the postseason, but he hit home runs in the first two games of the WS against his old team. His greatest clutch performance may have come in 1983, when he drove in

Ted Simmons

108 runs with only 13 HR. He closed out his career in 1986–88 as a member of the Braves' utility men's self-dubbed Bomb Squad, playing first base, catcher, and third base, and serving as a valuable pinch hitter. In October 1988, Simmons was named director of player development for St. Louis by GM Dal Maxvill, a former teammate. /(FO)

Mike Simon — 1883–1963. C 1909–15 **Pirates**, St. Louis (FL), Brooklyn (FL) 378 g, .225, 1 hr, 90 rbi

Simon backed up catcher George Gibson for Pittsburgh in 1911–13, seeing most action when Gibson was hurt in 1913. He then caught two seasons in the Federal League, bringing down his career batting average. /(ME)

Dick Simpson — 1943– . OF 1962, 64–69 Angels, **Reds**, Cardinals, Astros, Yankees, Pilots 288 g, .207, 15 hr, 56 rbi

A light-hitting, 6′4″ outfielder, Simpson's greatest asset was his speed. For many years, pitcher Pedro

Ramos claimed to be the fastest runner in baseball. At Cleveland on the last day of the 1962 season, Simpson won a 75-yard dash, handily defeating the other contestants, headed by Ramos. /(RTM)

Harry Simpson (Suitcase) — 1925–1979. OF-1B 1951–53, 55–59 Indians, **A's**, Yankees, White Sox, Pirates 888 g, .266, 73 hr, 381 rbi. *1 WS, 5 g, .083, 1 rbi*

One of the early black players in the American League, Simpson earned the nickname Suitcase by playing for 17 teams in 11 years. Casey Stengel once called him the best defensive right fielder in the AL. A minor league HR and RBI champion, his best major league year was 1956, when he batted .293 with 21 HR and 105 RBI for the A's. His 11 triples in 1956 and nine in 1957 tied him for the league lead. /(RTM)

Joe Simpson — 1951– . OF-1B 1975–83 Dodgers, **Mariners**, Royals 607 g, .242, 9 hr, 124 rbi

A clean-cut All-American out of the University of Oklahoma, Simpson was called up to the Dodgers every September from 1975 through 1978, then spent four years as a generally unproductive Seattle outfielder. On August 17, 1979, he became the first Mariner to have five hits in a game. He was hired as a Mariners broadcaster in 1987. /(JCA)

Wayne Simpson — 1948– . RHP 1970–73, 75, 77 **Reds**, Royals, Phillies, Angels 636 ip, 36–31, 4.37
☛ *All-Star—70.*

In his first season, Simpson started the year by winning 13 of his first 14 decisions (the loss came when a dropped pop fly let in two unearned runs), including a one-hitter, a two-hitter, and a three-hitter, and was selected for the All-Star team. But shoulder problems limited him to just two appearances after July; he finished 14–3, 3.08. The injury hampered him for the rest of his career; in his only other good season, 1972, he went 8–5 with a 4.14 ERA. /(SH)

Duke Sims [Duane B] — 1941– . C-1B-OF 1964–74 **Indians**, Dodgers, Tigers, Yankees, Rangers 843 g, .239, 100 hr, 310 rbi. *1 LCS, 4 g, .214*

The lefty-hitting catcher had good home run power, belting 18 in 1969 and 23 in 1970 as a platoon player with Cleveland. In 1971 the Indians dealt him to the Dodgers, who sold him to Detroit in August of the next year. Normally a low-average hitter, Sims's .316 down the stretch helped the Tigers to the 1972 division title. /(CC)

Bill Singer (The Singer Throwing Machine) — 1944– . RHP 1964–77 **Dodgers**, Angels, Rangers, Twins, Blue Jays 2174 ip, 118–127, 3.39. 20 wins: 69, 73
☛ *All-Star—69, 73.*

Singer's injury-plagued career included two standout seasons of 20–12 (1969) and 20–14 (1973). Teamed with Nolan Ryan on the 1973 Angels' staff, the two combined for more strikeouts than any other duo ever. Ryan's record 383 and Singer's 241 (third in the AL) added up to 624, 32 more than the next-highest total for teammates. The other highlight of Singer's career came when he threw a no-hitter against the Phillies on July 20, 1970. /(SFS)

Elmer Singleton (Smoky) — 1918– . RHP 1945–48, 50, 57–59 Braves, **Pirates**, Senators, Cubs 327 ip, 11–17, 4.83

After parts of five ML seasons as an undistinguished reliever, Singleton became a standout in the Pacific Coast League, earning another shot at the majors at the age of 39. He posted a 2.72 ERA for the Cubs in 1959, his final ML year. /(EW)

Ken Singleton — 1947– . OF-DH 1970–84 Mets, Expos, **Orioles** 2082 g, .282, 246 hr, 1065 rbi. *2 LCS, 8 g, .321, 3 rbi. 2 WS, 9 g, .345, 3 rbi*
☛ *All-Star—77, 79, 81.*

Singleton was a consistent power hitter who topped 20 HR in five seasons, with a high of 35 in Baltimore's 1979 AL championship year. He was in double figures in homers in all but three of his 15 seasons and hit .300 four times.

The native New Yorker started his career with the Mets, but was not given a chance to play regularly and was traded to the Expos in April 1972 with Mike Jorgenson and Tim Foli in exchange for Rusty Staub. In his first season with Montreal, Singleton had troublesome rashes that were finally traced to an allergic reaction to the Expos' wool uniforms; the club had to order double-knit uniforms especially for him. He had perhaps his best year, considering the circumstances, in 1973. Playing on a losing team with only one other significant power hitter, Singleton hit 23 HR with 103 RBI (fifth in the NL), 100 runs, 123 walks (one behind the league leader), and a .302 BA. After dropping off in 1974, he was traded to the Orioles with Mike Torrez for Dave McNally and two throw-ins.

With the Orioles, Singleton became a star. When he hit .328 in 1977 (third in the AL), it set the club record, as did his .438 on-base percentage (second in the AL). He also holds Oriole season marks with 118 walks in 1975 and 35 switch-hit HR in 1979. In major league history, only Singleton, Mantle, and Howard Johnson have switch-hit 35 or more HR in a season. Singleton also ranks high in most Baltimore career offensive categories, including fourth in hits, HR, RBI, and total bases. Twice with Baltimore he had 100 RBI and three times he topped 100 walks. His production dropped off after 1982, when he had muscle deterioration in his right forearm. Until then, he had had a strong throwing arm (he led the NL in assists with 20 in 1973), but that and his decreasing speed, never good even when he was young, forced him into a DH role. That confined his 1983 WS action to two pinch-hit appearances, but in one of them, in Game Four, he walked with the bases loaded to force in the tying run in the Orioles' 5–4 victory. He had an excellent postseason in 1979, hitting .375 with two RBI and four runs in the four-game LCS and .357 with two RBI in the Orioles' WS loss. /(JFC)

Fred Sington — 1910– . OF 1934–39 **Senators**, Dodgers 181 g, .271, 7 hr, 85 rbi

A member of the College Football Hall of Fame, the 220-lb Sington turned down pro football and wrestling offers to play baseball. Originally a pitcher, he became an outfielder noted for his speed and strong arm. Although he hit well in the minors, he never played a full ML season. /(NLM)

Doug Sisk — 1957– . RHP 1982–88 **Mets**, Orioles 507 ip, 20–19, 3.22. *1 LCS, 1 ip, 0–0, 0.00. 1 WS, 0.2 ip, 0–0, 0.00*

Doug Sisk and Jesse Orosco were an effective relief duo for the Mets in 1983 and 1984, with Sisk saving 11 games in 1983 and a career-high 15 in 1984. The excellent movement on his pitches caused some of his frequent control problems. An excellent ground-ball pitcher, he rarely allowed home runs, especially to righthanded batters, and he went all of the Mets' 1986 World Championship season without giving up a single homer. Recurring periods of ineffectiveness starting in 1985 reduced him to a set-up and then a mop-up role. His wildness caused him problems, and his strength as a ground-ball pitcher was negated by the New York infield, which was fairly immobile except for first baseman Keith Hernandez. Limited effectiveness after going to Baltimore for 1988 ended his career. /(SH)

Tommy Sisk — 1942– . RHP 1962–70 **Pirates**, Padres, White Sox 928 ip, 40–49, 3.92

A highly sought California pitching prospect, Sisk led the Pirates in appearance (57) as a rookie in 1963 and in complete games in 1967. His return west via the 1968 expansion draft resulted in one terrible season at San Diego for the fastball-, curve-, and sinker-throwing righthander. /(ME)

Dave Sisler — 1931– . RHP 1956–62 **Red Sox**, Tigers, Senators, Reds 656 ip, 38–44, 4.33

The youngest son of Hall of Famer George Sisler and brother of major leaguer Dick Sisler, Dave was a 6'4", bespectacled Princeton graduate. Upon returning from the military in 1956, he started and relieved for Boston, but worked exclusively out of the bullpen after his 1959 trade to Detroit. In 1960 he recorded a career-best 2.48 ERA with seven wins and six saves. /(EW)

Dick Sisler — 1920– . 1B-OF 1946–53 Cardinals, **Phillies**, Reds 799 g, .276, 55 hr, 360 rbi. *2 WS, 6 g, .053, 1 rbi.*
    Manager 1964–65 **Reds** 121–94, .563
☛ *All-Star—50.*

Son of Hall of Famer George Sisler and brother of pitcher Dave Sisler, Dick returned from three years of military duty to debut with the 1946 World Champion Cardinals. Dealt to the Phillies in 1948, he was moved from first base to left field in 1950, and hit a dramatic tenth-inning, game-winning home run at Ebbets Field on the final day of the season to clinch the pennant. In 1953 he returned to the minors, where he played and managed until made a Reds coach in 1961. He succeeded an ailing Fred Hutchinson as Cincinnati manager in late 1964 and piloted the club to an 89–73 mark in 1965. He went on to coach for the Cardinals, Padres, Mets, and Yankees. /(AL)

George Sisler (Gorgeous George) — 1893–1973. 1B-LHP 1915–22, 24–30 **Browns**, Senators, Braves 2055 g, .340, 100 hr, 1175 rbi; 111 ip, 5–6, 2.35.
    Manager 1924–26 **Browns** 218–241, .475
☛ *Most Valuable Player—22. Led League—ba 20, 22. Hall of Fame—1939.*

Sisler was the greatest St. Louis Brown of them all and one of the half-dozen finest first basemen in baseball history. Like Babe Ruth, he came to the majors as a lefthanded pitcher. Like Ruth, his hitting was too phenomenal to be restricted to a pitcher's schedule. He arrived in St. Louis in 1915,

George Sisler

the same year as Rogers Hornsby, and for 11 seasons they were rivals in excellence.

Branch Rickey was his mentor: Coach at Michigan in George's undergraduate days as an outstanding college pitcher, wily counselor in the maneuvering that eventually led him to the Browns, and manager of the team when he got there.

Other major league clubs were interested in him; Barney Dreyfuss was certain that the Pirates owned him and, under baseball law, perhaps he did. In 1911 underage and without parental consent, George signed a professional contract. He received no money and played no games, but while he pursued his education the contract was sold to Pittsburgh. After four years of anguish, argument and indecision, the National Commission ruled the contract invalid and made Sisler a free agent. He graduated with a mechanical engineering degree, considered a fistful of offers, including one from Pittsburgh, and decided for manager Rickey and the Browns. His was the first of several player-allocation cases that eventually moved irate club owners like Dreyfuss to unseat the Commission and replace it with Judge Landis.

Sisler had promise as a pitcher. His ERA was impressive, and among his five wins were two complete-game victories over Walter Johnson. Still, it was unthinkable not to have his bat in the lineup every day, and his glove at first base, a chronic Brown weak spot where seven players had been tried in the previous six years. In the field Sisler was fast, adroit, and graceful, a combination that gave elegance to his execution of plays. He led the AL seven times in assists and his career total of 1,528 heads the all-time list. In double plays he topped the league three times, starting 13 deft 3–6–3 double plays in 1920. On one occasion against Washington, with Joe Judge on third, George anticipated a squeeze bunt by Roger Peckinpaugh. Darting in with the pitch, he fielded the ball before the right-handed Peck was fairly started down the line, brush-tagged him, and flipped to Hank Severeid to nip Judge at the plate. Two outs on a squeeze are not usual, but that was George.

Sisler's career batting average is tied with Lou Gehrig's for fifteenth lifetime, although he never had Lou's power or his size. An inch or two under six feet and a trim 170 pounds, Sisler swung a 42-ounce bat, often choking up, and had six seasons with more than 200 hits. His 257 in 1920 is the best single-season mark ever. As a run producer, he was good, if not overwhelming. On the lifetime list his 1,175 RBI are one ahead of Vern Stephens; he is tied with Jake Daubert for triples and Sherry Magee for doubles.

His 1920 season was as mighty a performance as any player has ever produced. Playing every inning of 154 games, he hit .407. Among his 399 total bases were 49 doubles, 18 triples and 19 home runs. He went hitless in only 23 games and climaxed the season with prodigious averages of .442 and .448 in August and September. He drove in 122 runs, his high mark, and stole 42 bases. In 1922, when the Browns missed the pennant by one game, he hit safely in 41 consecutive games and achieved a .420 average.

In 1923 severe sinusitis infected his optic nerves and for a time he saw double. He missed the entire season. Dutch Schliebner, acquired from Brooklyn, spent his one major league season as Sisler's replacement. He hit .275 as the Browns slumped to fifth. Sisler returned in 1924 with a $25,000 contract as player-manager. He hit .305 in 151 games and moved the Browns to third. In 1925 he was on track with 224 hits and a .345 average. In fact, he only had one sub-.300 season in seven after the illness. They were seasons most players would have been proud of, but he was not really himself. His eyes never regained their former acuity.

In the winter of 1927 the Browns made a good trade, sending Harry Rice, Elam Vangilder, and Chick Galloway to Detroit for Heinie Manush and Sisler's successor at first, Lu Blue. Washington bought Sisler for $25,000, then moved him along to the Braves, where he was reunited with Hornsby. The St. Louis prodigies put on a good show, Rogers leading the league with .387, George contributing a handsome .340. In 1929, at age thirty-six, he batted .326 average with 205 hits.

After 1930 he drifted into the minors, ran a Sisler printing company in St. Louis, then a Sisler sporting-goods firm. Rickey recalled him to baseball in the 1940s as a scout and special hitting instructor at Brooklyn and Pittsburgh.

Sisler's sons were baseball men. George Jr. was president of the International League. Dick and Dave both had major league careers. /(ADS)

Sibby Sisti [Sebastian Daniel] — 1920- . 2B-3B-SS-OF 1939–42, 46–54 **Braves** 1016 g, .244, 27 hr, 260 rbi. *1 WS, 2 g, .000*

Sisti was a Braves regular at third and second base from 1940 to 1942 before being called to military service. In 1946, he sharpened his skills with Indianapolis of the American Association, batting .343 to win *TSN* Minor League Player of the Year honors. Returning to the majors, he became one of the top utility men of his day; in the Braves' 1948 pennant-winning season, he spelled both Alvin Dark and Eddie Stanky in the middle infield. Sisti had a small acting role as a coach in the movie *The Natural.* /(RTM)

Pete Sivess — 1913- . RHP 1936–38 Phillies 201 ip, 7–11, 5.46

The 6'3″ Sivess had great confidence, but not the ability to match. Farmed out in 1937 after a 3–4 rookie season starting and relieving, he went 15–5 for Baltimore (International League), but won only four more games with Philadelphia. /(AL)

Ted Sizemore — 1946- . 2B-SS 1969–80 Dodgers, **Cardinals**, Phillies, Cubs, Red Sox 1411 g, .262, 23 hr, 430 rbi. *2 LCS, 8 g, .308, 1 rbi*
☛ *Rookie of the Year—69.*

Sizemore was the 1969 NL Rookie of the Year, batting .271 in 159 games for the Dodgers and tying a ML season record with three bases-loaded triples. Originally a catcher, he was the Opening Day shortstop in 1969 but moved to second base when Los Angeles reacquired Maury Wills. He was sent to St. Louis in a trade for Richie Allen following the 1970 season. Lou Brock credited Sizemore with helping him break Wills's ML stolen-base record in 1974. "You have to have the right man batting behind you," said Brock. "I do. Ted Sizemore. He has to be unselfish, because hitting behind me isn't going to do any good for his batting average. He's going to be distracted by me instead of giving his complete concentration to the pitcher." Sizemore's batting average did drop, to .250 from .282 the previous year. After a year back with the Dodgers, Sizemore was the second baseman for the Phillies' 1977 and 1978 division championships. /(RTM)

Dave Skaggs — 1951- . C 1977–80 **Orioles**, Angels 205 g, .241, 3 hr, 49 rbi. *1 LCS, 1 g, .000. 1 WS, 1 g, .333*

Until back problems ended his career, Skaggs was a good-fielding reserve catcher, popular with his mates for his humor. Oddly, his first two (of only three) ML home runs came on the last days of two different seasons, both off Rick Wise. /(EW)

Bob Skinner — 1931- . OF-1B 1954, 56–66 **Pirates**, Reds, Cardinals 1381 g, .277, 103 hr, 531 rbi. *2 WS, 6 g, .375, 2 rbi.*
Manager 1968–69, 77 **Phillies**, Padres 93–123, .431
☛ *All-Star—58, 60.*

A three-time .300 hitter with Pittsburgh, Skinner batted a career-high .321 and was the National League's All-Star left fielder in 1958. As a rookie in 1954, he set a ML first base record with eight assists in a game. In 1956 he led the NL with 54 pinch-hitting appearances. During a torrid three-game stretch against Cincinnati in 1959, he hit five homers, including a grand slam and a three-run shot on May 31. He went 2-for-3 as a Cardinal pinch hitter in the 1964 World Series, then led the NL with 15 pinch hits in 1965. His last 45 at-bats came off the bench, in 1966. Skinner became manager of San Diego, at that time the Phillies' Triple-A affiliate, and by June 1968 he had replaced Gene Mauch at the helm of the parent club. He lasted until the following August. A coach for Pittsburgh, San Diego, and California, he served one game as the Padres' interim manager in 1977. He returned to the Pirates in 1979, working for manager Chuck Tanner, and moved with him to the Braves, 1986–88. Bob's son, Joel Skinner, became a catcher with the White Sox and Yankees. /(RTM)

Joel Skinner — 1961– . C 1983– White Sox, **Yankees**, Indians 416 g, .221, 14 hr, 96 rbi

Known primarily for his defense, Skinner never caught for the White Sox on an everyday basis. He did most of the Yankees' catching after his July 1986 acquisition, but as a reserve in 1987, hit just .137 and spent two months in the minors. The Yankees traded him to the Indians at the start of 1989 for Mel Hall. /(EG)

Lou Skizas (The Nervous Greek) — 1932– . OF-3B 1956–59 Yankees, **A's**, Tigers, White Sox 239 g, .270, 30 hr, 86 rbi

In the batter's box, The Nervous Greek would, at times, put his right hand in his back pocket and swing the bat with his left until the pitcher delivered. Considered a colorful, carousing goofball, Skizas was described by Mickey Mantle as a "hippie from the streets and alleys of Chicago who had a girl under his arm before and after every game." /(RTM)

Craig Skok — 1947– . LHP 1973, 76, 78–79 Red Sox, Rangers, **Braves** 150 ip, 4–7, 4.86

The Florida State grad lacked an outstanding fastball, but good control and an excellent curve earned him 87 relief appearances with the Braves in 1978–79. /(EW)

Bill Skowron (Moose) — 1930– . 1B 1954–67 **Yankees**, Dodgers, Senators, White Sox, Angels 1658 g, .282, 211 hr, 888 rbi. *8 WS, 39 g, .293, 8 hr, 29 rbi*
☛ *All-Star—57–61, 65.*

As a joke, Skowron's grandfather called him Mussolini, but his family shortened the nickname to Moose. A kicker for Purdue, he signed to play baseball in 1951, and joined the Yankees in 1954. A powerful opposite-field hitter, he topped the .300 mark five times with New York and was *TSN* all-star first baseman in 1960. He once lamented, "I hit over .300 three straight years for the Yankees and they wouldn't give me a raise."

Making up for the disappointment of making the final out of the 1957 WS when Milwaukee won, he became a hero of the 1958 World Series versus the Braves. He drove in what proved to be the winning run in Game Six, and hit a three-run homer in the eighth inning of the final game to give New York a 6–2 victory as they came back from a 3-games-to-1 deficit. When Skowron homered in the 14th inning on April 22, 1959, the Yankees and Senators set the AL record for the longest game to end 1–0 on a home run. After playing in his seventh WS with New York in 1962, Skowron was traded to the Dodgers, for whom he hit just .203 while platooned in 1963. But, facing his former team in the 1963 WS, he went 5-for-13, including a HR, as the Dodgers swept the Yankees. /(RTM)

SkyDome Toronto Blue Jays 1989– . LF-328, CF-400, RF-328

Featuring a retractable roof, the SkyDome opened in June 1989. The multi-purpose stadium is a pitcher's park, with deep power alleys (375') and lots of foul territory. The Blue Jays were 12–0 with the roof closed in 1989. The stadium has five decks, one of which contains luxury boxes that have to be bought for every event scheduled. The park's popularity enabled the Blue Jays to set an AL attendance record in 1989. The SkyDome features baseball's largest scoreboard, 150' wide and 35' high, and includes a restaurant and a miniature golf course. Jose Canseco hit a memorable 480' home run into the uppermost deck in Game Three of the 1989 LCS. /(JFC)

Gordon Slade (Oskie) — 1904–1974. SS-2B-3B 1930–35 Dodgers, Cardinals, **Reds** 437 g, .257, 8 hr, 123 rbi

After four years as a part-timer, Slade was purchased by the Reds for the 1934 season and reached career highs by playing 138 games at shortstop and second base and batting .285. /(EGM)

Jimmy Slagle (Rabbit, Shorty, The Human Mosquito) — 1873–1956. OF 1899–1908 Washington (NL), Phillies, Braves, **Cubs** 1298 g, .268, 2 hr, 344 rbi. *1 WS, 5 g, .273, 4 rbi*

Nicknamed Rabbit because of his speed, Shorty and Human Mosquito because of his height (5'7"), Slagle was a regular NL outfielder for a decade. His best year was 1902, his first with Chicago, when he batted .315 with 40 stolen bases. A singles hitter with good sense on the bases, his speed and defensive skills kept him in the lineup when his hitting tailed off. In the 1907 World Series against the Tigers, he set a record with six stolen bases, which stood until Lou Brock stole seven 60 years later. /(ARA)

Cy Slapnicka (Slap) — 1886–1979. RHP 1911, 18 Cubs, **Pirates** 73 ip, 1–6, 4.30

Slapnicka pitched in the minors for 18 seasons, but won only one game in two brief trips to the ML. He discovered Bob Feller and Herb Score for the Indians, and scouted for Cleveland from 1923 to 1941 (he also served as club vice president, 1935–41) and 1947 to 1960. In between, he worked briefly for the Browns and Cubs. When Commissioner Landis considered declaring Feller a free agent in 1937, Slapnicka suffered a heart attack. /(FVP)

Jim Slaton — 1950– . RHP 1971–86 **Brewers**, Tigers, Angels 2683 ip, 151–158, 4.03. *1 LCS, 5 ip, 0–0, 1.93. 1 WS, 3 ip, 1–0, 0.00*
☛ *All-Star—77.*

Drafted by the Seattle Pilots in 1969, Jim Slaton rose to the top of Brewers pitching records in two stints with Milwaukee. He was the all-time club leader in games, starts, wins, innings, strikeouts, and shutouts. Ironically, his best campaign came in his only year away from Milwaukee between 1971 and 1983. Traded to Detroit for Ben Oglivie, the dependable Slaton had a career-high 17 wins in 1978, then went back to Milwaukee as a free agent. Following his winningest season with the Brewers (15–9 in 1979), he suffered a slight rotator cuff tear in 1980. His complete comeback climaxed with a club-high 14 wins, all in relief, in 1983. Slaton was used as a starter and reliever with the Angels. /(ME)

Don Slaught (Sluggo) — 1958– . C 1982– Royals, **Rangers**, Yankees 756 g, .269, 50 hr, 256 rbi. *1 LCS, 3 g, .364*

Slaught set a UCLA record by batting .428 and he hit as high as .333 at the AA level in the minors. He singled in his first two big league at-bats, and after assuming regular status in 1983 he batted .312 and did a good job handling a young Royals pitching staff. He was traded to Texas for the 1985 season.

Slaught continued to hit well until he suffered a broken nose and cheekbone when hit by a pitch in 1986, and he was traded to the Yankees the following year. He provided New York with dependable catching and a reliable bat. /(FO)

Enos Slaughter (Country) — 1916– . OF 1938–42, 46–59 **Cardinals**, Yankees, A's, Braves 2380 g, .300, 169 hr, 1304 rbi. *5 WS, 27 g, .291, 3 hr, 8 rbi*
☛ *Led League—rbi 46. All-Star—41–42, 46–53. Hall of Fame—85.*

Slaughter was a lefthanded batter who hit .300 or better ten times, a superb outfielder with a deadly accurate throwing arm, and the quintessential hustler. While playing for the Columbus, Georgia, Redbirds (Sally League) in 1936, Slaughter was rebuked for not hustling by manager Eddie Dyer, and he vowed never again to walk while on a ball field.

Slaughter had an unusually swift rise through the vast Cardinal farm system. When he arrived in St. Louis in 1938, he was making $400 a month, but when he learned the Cubs had offered $100,000 for him, he persuaded the Cardinals to give him a $200 raise. He led the NL with 52 doubles in 1939 and with 188 hits in 1942, and led in triples in 1942 and 1949. He captured the league RBI title with 130 in

Enos Slaughter

1946. He had extra-base power to all fields, and his level swing made him a fine contact hitter and a good man in the clutch; he spoiled three no-hitters. In 1947 he knocked in ten runs in a doubleheader.

Slaughter was the leader of and top hitter (.318) on the 1942 World Championship Cardinals. In the deciding game of the 1946 Series, he made his electrifying mad dash home from first on Harry Walker's hit, scoring the winning run as Boston shortstop Johnny Pesky hesitated making the relay throw.

Slaughter, who was a North Carolina tobacco farmer, and fellow Southerner Terry Moore tried to persuade their Cardinal teammates to go on strike in May 1947 to protest Jackie Robinson's admittance to the National League. Though his strike plans were thwarted, Slaughter expressed his attitude that August. Robinson was playing first base for the Dodgers when Slaughter hit an infield ground ball and was thrown out by several steps. With Robinson stretched out to make the catch, Slaughter spiked him in the leg.

Slaughter split the 1955 season between New York and Kansas City, leading the AL with 16 pinch hits. He was with the Yankees for their 1956, 1957, and '58 pennants. He had 48 pinch at-bats in each of his last two seasons, leading the AL in 1958. In 1985 he was elected to the Hall of Fame by the Veterans Committee. /(EW)

Bill Slayback — 1948- . RHP 1972-74 **Tigers** 139 ip, 6-9, 3.82

In his 1972 debut, Slayback hurled seven no-hit innings against the Yankees until John Callison singled. He later achieved fame for his recording of a song about Hank Aaron's home run chase, "Move Over, Babe." /(CC)

Lou Sleater — 1926- . LHP 1950-52, 55-58 Browns, Senators, A's, Braves, **Tigers**, Orioles 301 ip, 12-18, 4.70

Mostly a reliever, Sleater battled control problems, walking more batters (172) than he struck out (152). Pitching for the Senators against Boston in 1952, he halted Walt Dropo's ML-record streak of hitting safely in 12 consecutive at-bats. /(RTM)

Bill Slocum, Jr. — 1912-1974. *Writer.*

When Slocum started his career with the New York *American* in 1935, his father was the sports editor, and they both covered New York teams. In the 1940s, Bill Jr. was with the *World-Telegram and Sun* and was a war correspondent for CBS News and CBS Director of Sports. In later years, he was a columnist for the Philadelphia *News*, New York *Mirror*, and New York *Journal-American*, covered the Vietnam War for the Hearst News Agency, and was a travel and drama editor until he retired in 1972. /(NLM)

Roy Smalley, Sr. — 1926- . SS 1948-58 **Cubs**, Braves, Phillies 872 g, .227, 61 hr, 305 rbi

The father of major league infielder Roy Smalley, the elder Smalley was an error-prone, strong-armed shortstop. He was a Cub regular from 1948 through 1950, leading the league's shortstops in errors each year, but he also led NL shortstops in total chances per game in 1949 and 1950, and in putouts, assists, and double plays in 1950. He hit 21 home runs in 1950 while striking out a league-leading 114 times. He married teammate Gene Mauch's sister. /(DAS)

Roy Smalley, Jr. — 1952- . SS-DH-3B 1975-87 Rangers, **Twins**, Yankees, White Sox 1653 g, .257, 163 hr, 694 rbi. *1 WS, 4 g, .500* ☛ *All-Star—79.*

Drafted by the Expos, Red Sox, and Cardinals, but opting to attend the University of Southern California, Roy Smalley turned pro with Texas as the nation's number-one draft choice in January 1974. Soon acquired by Minnesota in a six-player-plus-cash deal, the Californian began a five-year stint playing for his uncle, manager Gene Mauch, a former teammate of his father, Roy Sr. A switch-hitting, wide-ranging shortstop with power, Roy Jr. led pro baseball in homers at his position in 1978 (19) and 1979 (24). He was the Twins' MVP the former year and a starter in the All-Star Game the latter. His success diminished after suffering with spondylolysis, a condition in his lower back, in 1981, though he continued to be a dependable hitter and versatile performer. He spent two-plus unhappy years (1982-84) with the Yankees, being moved among all four infield positions. He was used primarily as a designated hitter upon returning to Minnesota in 1985. Smalley set a Twins record for career sacrifice bunts and is among the club all-time leaders in homers, hits, and RBI. /(ME)

John Smiley — 1965- . LHP 1986- **Pirates** 497 ip, 31-24, 3.46

After two years in the Pirates' bullpen, Smiley became a starter in 1988 and went 13-11 with a 3.25 ERA. In 1989 he established himself as the Pirates' number-two starter. /(SFS)

Al Smith — 1907-1977. LHP 1934-45 Giants, Phillies, **Indians** 1662 ip, 99-101, 3.72. *2 WS, 3 ip, 0-0, 10.80* ☛ *All-Star—43.*

Smith was most famous as one of the two Cleveland pitchers (with Jim Bagby, Jr.) who stopped Joe DiMaggio's 56-game hitting streak in 1940. Earlier, he'd been a steady winner with the Giants' pennant winners of 1936 and 1937. A sore arm in 1939 sent him back to the minors, where he developed his pitching finesse. Given a chance with the Indians in 1940, he responded with a 15-7 season. In 1943 he had his top season (17-7) and made the AL All-Star team. /(EW)

Al Smith (Fuzzy) — 1928- . OF-3B 1953-64 Indians, **White Sox**, Orioles, Red Sox 1517 g, .272, 164 hr, 676 rbi. *2 WS, 10 g, .235, 1 hr, 3 rbi* ☛ *All-Star—55, 60.*

A multitalented player, Smith took over as regular left fielder for the pennant-winning 1954 Indians and in 1955 led the AL in runs scored and batted .306. He was traded to the White Sox in 1958 for Minnie Minoso in a deal that was very unpopular with Chicago fans. To counteract some of the Comiskey Park boo birds, owner Bill Veeck held an Al Smith Night on August 26, 1959. Any fan named Smith, Smythe, Schmidt or Smithe was admitted free and given a button that said, "I'm a Smith and I'm for Al." On his big night, Smith hit into two double plays and dropped a fly ball that led to Boston's winning run. The 1959 White Sox were Smith's second pennant winner, and he finally won some of the fans over by hitting .315 in 1960 and slugging 28 homers in 1961. /(RL)

Billy Smith — 1953- . 2B-SS 1975-79, 81 Angels, **Orioles**, Giants 370 g, .230, 17 hr, 111 rbi. *1 LCS, 1 g, .000. 1 WS, 4 g, .286*

The erratic but wide-ranging Smith platooned with Rich Dauer at second base for the Orioles in 1977-79, but was released when Dauer's hitting improved. Frank Robinson brought Smith to the Giants for the 1981 stretch drive. /(MC)

Bob Smith — 1898-1987. RHP 1923-37 **Braves**, Cubs, Reds 2238 ip, 106-139, 3.95. *1 WS, 1 ip, 0-0, 9.00*

Smith spent two seasons as a good-fielding but light-hitting shortstop for the Braves before switching to the mound in 1925. By 1926 he was a regular starter for the second-division Braves. He had five straight losing seasons but won at least ten games each year. On May 17, 1927, he pitched a complete-game, 22-inning 4-3 loss to the Cubs for the fifth-longest pitching effort in ML history. Traded to the Cubs in 1931, he had his best season, 15-12. In 1933 he returned to the Braves, where he remained through 1937, pitching mostly in relief. /(EW)

Bob Smith — 1931- . LHP 1955, 57-59 Red Sox, Cardinals, **Pirates**, Tigers 167 ip, 4-9, 4.05

Smith's career was as undistinguished as his name. Although he had two complete-game wins with the Pirates in 1957, most of his three-plus ML seasons were spent pitching middle relief. /(EW)

Bobby Gene Smith — 1934- . OF 1957-62, 65 **Cardinals**, Phillies, Mets, Cubs, Angels 476 g, .243, 13 hr, 96 rbi

Smith homered in his first major league game, with the Cardinals in 1957. Never a regular, he was described by ex-teammate Bill White as "the ultimate six o'clock hitter," meaning he would homer in batting practice, but rarely in a game. /(RTM)

Bryn Smith — 1955- . RHP 1981- **Expos** 1400 ip, 81-71, 3.28

A durable, consistent, control specialist, Smith has won 10 or more games for the Expos every year since 1984, peaking with an 18-5, 2.91 mark in 1985. He was ignored by all 24 ML clubs in the 1974 free agent draft, but signed with the Orioles, and a 1977 trade brought him to the Expos' farm system. He debuted in the ML at the age of 26, after almost seven full seasons in the minors, and on September 21, 1981, he earned his first win by retiring one batter in a 1-0, 17-inning Expos victory. He joined the Expos' starting rotation late in 1983, and has been a starter exclusively ever since. Smith has averaged only 2.2 walks per nine innings in his career. /(SCL)

Charley Smith — 1937- . 3B-SS 1960-69 Dodgers, Phillies, White Sox, **Mets**, Cardinals, Yankees, Cubs 771 g, .239, 69 hr, 281 rbi

A steady third baseman, Charley Smith led the 1964 Mets with 20 HR. He was sent with Al Jackson to the Cardinals after the 1965 season for 1964 MVP Ken Boyer, and the following winter was traded to the Yankees for an aging Roger Maris. When he pinch hit for the Cubs in two 1969 games, Smith became the first player to appear with both New York and both Chicago teams (the only other is Dick Tidrow). /(RTM)

Charlie Smith — 1880–1929. RHP 1902, 06–14 Indians, **Senators**, Red Sox, Cubs 1350 ip, 66–87, 2.81

In his first start, with the Indians in 1902, Cleveland native Charlie Smith beat A's Hall of Famer Rube Waddell, but he soon dropped to the minors. He resurfaced in 1906 to go 31–61 in four years with dreadful Senators teams, but had greater success with the Red Sox (11–6 in 1910) and Cubs (league-high six relief wins in 1912). His brother was National and Federal League infielder Fred V. Smith. /(JK)

Chino Smith [Charles] — 1903–1932. OF-2B Negro Leagues 1924–30 Philadelphia Giants, Brooklyn Royal Giants, **New York Lincoln Giants** 214 g, .406, 41 hr (inc.)
☛ *Led League—ba 29–30 (NAL). Led League—hr 29 (NAL).*

Smith was a powerful, 5′6″ lefthanded line-drive hitter who rarely struck out. Satchel Paige called him one of the two greatest hitters in Negro League history, and available statistics seem to support Paige's assessment. From 1925 through 1930, Smith batted .406 in Negro League competition, .335 in the Cuban Winter League, and, reportedly, .405 in exhibitions against major leaguers. He batted third for the powerful New York Lincoln Giants of the late 1920s. In 1929 he collected 118 hits in 67 games, leading the Negro American League with a .463 average, 24 HR, and 28 doubles. His .429 mark in 1930 was again the league high. Smith's career ended tragically before his 30th birthday; playing in Cuba the following winter, he died from what was probably yellow fever. /(JM)

Dave Smith — 1955– . RHP 1980– **Astros** 702 ip, 47–41, 2.54. *2 LCS, 4 ip, 1–1, 6.23*
☛ *All-Star—86.*

Dave Smith outlasted relievers like Joe Sambito and Frank DiPino to become Houston's bullpen ace and the Astros' all-time saves and games-pitched leader. In his only major league start (1982), Smith committed three balks. He became Houston's closer in 1985, with 27 saves in 31 opportunities. In 1986 Smith set a Houston record with 33 saves and was a member of the All-Star team. After allowing a home run to Darryl Strawberry of the Mets on July 19, 1986, Smith did not allow another until Len Dykstra's game-winning blow in the ninth inning of the third game of the LCS. In the decisive sixth game, won by New York in 16 innings, Smith surrendered two walks and a game-tying sacrifice fly in the ninth. (Smith has consistently had trouble with the Mets.) The following season, he did not allow any home runs. /(ME)

Earl Smith — 1891–1943. OF-3B 1916–22 Cubs, **Browns**, Senators 495 g, .272, 9 hr, 186 rbi

An undistinguished reserve for parts of seven ML seasons, Smith was sent to Minneapolis of the American Association in 1922. He became one of the great minor league hitters, active until he was 44. Playing mostly in the American Association, he consistently hit over .300. His minor league highs were a .353 BA, 64 doubles (which led the league), 25 stolen bases, and 139 runs in 1924, and 31 HR and 156 RBI in 1925. /(JK)

Earl Smith (Oil) — 1897–1963. C 1919–30 Giants, **Pirates**, Cardinals 860 g, .303, 46 hr, 355 rbi. *5 WS, 17 g, .239*

A pugnacious, strong-willed catcher for five NL pennant winners, Smith received his nickname from columnist Westbrook Pegler's Brooklynese pronunciation of his first name. With the champion Giants of 1921–22, he ignored manager John McGraw's signals and defied bed checks. Traded to the Pirates, he hit .313 for the 1925 World Champions and a career-high .346 the next season. He missed a month with the 1927 NL champions when he was suspended for smashing the jaw of Braves manager Dave Bancroft in an unprovoked attack. Sold to the Cardinals the next year, he helped them to the 1928 NL pennant. /(JK)

Eddie Smith — 1913– . LHP 1936–43, 46–47 A's, **White Sox**, Red Sox 1595 ip, 73–113, 3.82

One of those pitchers fated to spend their careers with floundering teams, the portly Smith was the losing pitcher in Bob Feller's 1–0 Opening Day no-hitter against the White Sox in 1940. Smith had his only winning ML season that year, going 14–9 for Chicago. In 1942, when he led the AL with 20 losses, his defeats included a 2–0, two 2–1, and three 1–0 games. /(RL)

Elmer Smith — 1868–1945. OF-LHP 1886–89, 1892–1901 Cincinnati (AA), **Pirates**, Reds, Giants, Braves 1239 g, .311, 37 hr, 637 rbi [inc.]; 1219 ip, 74–59, 3.35. 20 wins: 87, 88
☛ *Led League—era 87.*

As a pitcher, Smith won 33 games for Cincinnati and led the American Association in ERA (2.94) in 1887. A lame arm sent him to the minors, but he returned as a Pittsburgh outfielder in 1892 and played ten more years in the majors. He hit over .300 five times, with a career-high .362 in 1896. /(JK)

Elmer Smith — 1892–1984. OF 1914–17, 19–23, 25 **Indians**, Senators, Red Sox, Yankees 1012 g, .276, 70 hr, 540 rbi. *2 WS, 7 g, .267, 1 hr, 6 rbi*

Smith had his best year with the 1920 World Champion Indians, hitting .316, with 12 home runs and 103 RBI. In that year's World Series, his homer off Hall of Famer Burleigh Grimes of Brooklyn in the first inning of Game Five was the first grand slam in Series history. /(JK)

Frank Smith [born Frank Elmer Schmidt] (Piano Mover) — 1879–1952. RHP 1904–1915 **White Sox**, Red Sox, Reds, Baltimore (FL), Brooklyn (FL) 2273 ip, 138–111, 2.59. 20 wins: 07, 09
☛ *Led League—k 09.*

Occasionally great, he pitched two no-hitters and twice won 20 for the early White Sox. But Smith was also a malcontent, and in 1908 he jumped the team to take up his off-season profession of piano moving. White Sox owner Charles Comiskey angrily accused him of habitual drunkenness, but Smith returned to Chicago and had his best season in 1909: 25–17, with a 1.80 ERA and an AL-high 177 strikeouts. /(RL)

Frank Smith [Frank Thomas] — 1928– . RHP 1950–56 **Reds**, Cardinals 496 ip, 35–33, 3.81

Smith, who was not afraid to knock down hitters, was a workhorse Reds reliever, appearing in 50 or more games each year from 1951 to 1954. Though his nine relief losses in 1952 and eight in '54 were league highs, his 20 saves in '54 put him second in the NL. /(RTM)

Fred Smith — 1886–1961. 3B-SS 1913–15, 17 Braves, **Buffalo (FL)**, Brooklyn (FL), Cardinals 438 g, .226, 8 hr, 158 rbi

As a utility infielder with the Braves in 1913, Smith was paid $1,500. He jumped at the chance to join the Federal League for higher pay in 1914 and missed the Braves' "Miracle" pennant drive and World Series win. /(BC)

George Smith (Columbia George) — 1892–1965. RHP 1916–23 Giants, Reds, Dodgers, **Phillies** 1143 ip, 39–81, 3.89

Smith, a Columbia graduate, had little ML success, losing over two-thirds of his decisions. His only full-season winning mark came in 1918 when he was 8–7 while pitching for three different NL teams. In 1921 with the Phillies he led the NL in losses (20) while winning only four. After retiring from base-ball, he was head of a high school math department. /(JK)

George Smith — 1901–1981. RHP 1926–30 **Tigers**, Red Sox 331 ip, 10–8, 5.33

A reliever in all but 7 of his 132 career appearances at a time when that was an uncommon specialization, Smith's best season came in 1927 (4–1, 3.91). /(SFS)

George Smith — 1938–1987 . 2B-SS 1963–66 Tigers, **Red Sox** 217 g, .205, 9 hr, 57 rbi

Smith signed with Detroit after two seasons with the Negro League Indianapolis Clowns. His only season as a ML regular was 1966, when he batted .213 as the Red Sox' second baseman. Smith's career ended when he tore cartilage in his knee in spring training of 1967. /(EW)

Germany Smith — 1863–1927. SS 1884–98 Altoona (UA), Cleveland (NL), Brooklyn (AA), Dodgers, **Reds**, St. Louis [Perfectos] (NL) 1710 g, .243, 45 hr, 618 rbi

A reliable shortstop in the days when a fielding average below .900 could lead the league, Smith was noted for his far-ranging play. His .886 fielding average did, in fact, lead the American Association in 1887. When the AA folded in 1890, he moved from its Brooklyn team to the National League's new Brooklyn franchise. In 1891 John Montgomery Ward took over as manager and shortstop, and Smith was off to Cincinnati. There he led NL shortstops in assists each year from 1891 to 1894. /(JK)

Hal Smith — 1902– . RHP 1932–35 **Pirates** 210 ip, 12–11, 3.77

After a far-flung minor league career, Smith reached the ML with Pittsburgh late in 1932 at age 30, and in his first start he shut out the Cubs. After going 8–7 with a 2.86 ERA the next season, he faded and slipped back to the minors. /(EW)

Hal Smith [Harold Wayne] — 1930– . C-3B 1955–64 Orioles, **A's**, Pirates, Colt .45s, Reds 879 g, .267, 58 hr, 323 rbi. *1 WS, 3 g, .375, 1 hr, 3 rbi*

An excellent defensive catcher, Smith played in a career-high 135 games as a Baltimore rookie in 1955, and in 1957 batted .303 as Kansas City's first-string receiver. Originally Yankee property, he returned to haunt New York in the final game of the 1960 World Series when he delivered an eighth-inning, three-run, pinch-hit homer to give Pittsburgh a 9–7 lead in the game they ultimately won on Bill Mazeroski's ninth-inning HR. /(RTM)

Hal Smith [Harold Raymond] (Cura) — 1931- . C
1956–61, 65 **Cardinals**, Pirates 570 g, .258, 23 hr, 172 rbi
☛ *All-Star—57, 59.*

Smith was an All-Star catcher in 1957 and again in
1959, when he hit 13 home runs for St. Louis.
Disabled in June of 1961 after experiencing heart
problems, Smith was made a Cardinal coach, then
managed in the minors. He played four games with
Pittsburgh in 1965, coached for the Pirates, Reds,
and Brewers, and became a longtime Cardinals
scout. /(RTM)

Harry Smith — 1874–1933. C 1901–10 A's, **Pirates**,
Braves 343 g, .213, 2 hr, 89 rbi. *1 WS, 1 g, .000.*
    Manager 1909 **Braves** 22–53, .293

Born in England, Harry Smith learned baseball as a
boy in Ohio. Though one of Connie Mack's early
discoveries, he played most of his career in the
National League, where he was a fun-loving, light-
hitting backup catcher. Called Peck's Bad Boy of
Baseball, he entertained fans and teammates with
practical jokes (some aimed at umpires) even after
becoming a minor league manager. He piloted the
Braves for half of 1909. /(JK)

Heinie Smith — 1871–1939. 2B 1897–99, 1901–03
Louisville (NL), Pirates, **Giants**, Tigers 311 g, .238, 3 hr,
91 rbi.
    Manager 1902 **Giants**, 5–27, .156

During his one season as a regular, 1902, Smith took
over as Giants manager during the season and lasted
32 games, winning five of them, before being
replaced by John McGraw. He later had success as
an International League manager. /(JK)

Hilton Smith — 1912–1983. RHP-OF 1932–48
Monroe Monarchs, **Kansas City Monarchs** statistics not
available
☛ *All-Star—37–42.*

Smith was an outstanding pitcher for the Kansas
City Monarchs. He had an excellent curveball and
used a variety of pitches intelligently. Smith threw a
no-hitter against the Chicago American Giants in
1937 and didn't lose a game in 1938, according to
teammate Buck O'Neil. Statistics are available only
for the latter, and poorer, portion of his career; he
had a sore arm in 1943, but published Negro
American League figures give him a 23–13 mark for
1944 through 1948. He went 6–1 in exhibitions
against white major leaguers and 10–5 over two

Cuban Winter League stints. He was the top pitcher
(8–5) for the 1946–47 Venezuelan Winter League
champion Vargas club. On March 1, 1947 in
Caracas, Vargas defeated the New York Yankees
4–3; Smith started, allowing no runs and just one
hit in five innings.

Smith won two NAL playoff games in relief,
against the Chicago American Giants in 1937 and
the St. Louis Stars in 1939. His two Black World
Series wins came as a starter, the first in Kansas
City's 1942 sweep of the Homestead Grays, the
second in the 1946 Series loss to the Newark Eagles.
He appeared in every East-West all-star game played
from 1937 through 1942, starting twice for the West
and going 1–2. A fine hitter, he was used off the
bench and in the outfield. Published figures give him
a .326 NAL average from 1944 through 1948, with
a high of .431 late in 1946. /(MFK)

Jack Smith [born Jan Smadt] — 1895–1972. OF
1915–29 **Cardinals**, Braves 1406 g, .287, 40 hr, 382 rbi

A swift outfielder with a good arm, Smith stole 228
bases in his 15 ML seasons. He had four straight
.300 seasons with the Cardinals (1920–23), with a
career high of .332. In 1917 he made five straight
hits as a pinch hitter, and in 1928 he led the NL
with nine pinch hits for the Braves. /(NLM)

Jimmy Smith — 1895–1974. SS-2B-3B 1914–19,
21–22 Chicago (FL), Baltimore (FL), Pirates, Giants,
Braves, Reds, Phillies 370 g, .219, 12 hr, 101 rbi. *1 WS,
1 g, .000*

One of the few major leaguers whose careers began
in the Federal League, Smith debuted as a 19-year-
old shortstop with the 1914 Chicago entry. He was a
first-stringer only in 1915. When the Feds folded, he
went on to appear in six seasons with five National
League teams. /(AL)

Ken Smith — 1902–Unk. *Writer.*

A longtime secretary-treasurer of the BBWAA,
Smith began covering the game for the New York
Graphic in 1925. Two years later he switched to the
Mirror and covered the Giants for 30 years until the
team moved to San Francisco. He was director of
the Hall of Fame from 1963 to 1975, when he
became public relations director. Smith was posthumously awarded the J.G. Taylor Spink Award in
1983. /(NLM)

Lee Smith — 1957– . RHP 1980– **Cubs**, Red Sox 836 ip, 50–57, 2.96. *2 LCS, 5 ip, 0–2, 8.44*
☛ *All-Star—83, 87.*

The intimidating, 6'6" 245-lb Lee Smith recorded at least 29 saves each year from 1983 to 1988 with a menacing glare and a 95-mph fastball. He led the NL with 29 saves for the Cubs in 1983, then strung together four straight seasons above 30, joining Dan Quisenberry and Jeff Reardon as the only pitchers to accomplish that feat. He won the 1987 All-Star Game for the NL with three shutout innings, but amid rumors that his bulk was beginning to affect his knees, he was traded to the Red Sox for Calvin Schiraldi and Al Nipper in the off-season. In his Fenway Park debut he blew a lead and surrendered a game-winning home run, but he recovered to post 29 saves, 96 strikeouts in 83.2 innings, and his best ERA (2.80) since 1983 as Boston won the AL East. He is the Cubs' all-time saves leader. /(SCL)

Lonnie Smith (Skates) — 1955– . OF 1978– Phillies, **Cardinals**, Royals, Braves 1134 g, .290, 68 hr, 385 rbi. *3 LCS, 13 g, .295, 2 rbi. 3 WS, 20 g, .311, 6 rbi*
☛ *All-Star—82.*

A first-pitch hitter, good with the hit-and-run, and a fine bunter, Smith was named *TSN* 1980 Rookie of the Year when he batted .339. His one liability proved to be erratic defensive play; he earned his nickname Skates for his tendency to slip while pursuing balls in the outfield, and he twice led NL outfielders in errors.

Smith was a catalyst for the 1982 World Champion Cardinals when he led them in hits, doubles, triples, batting average, runs, and stolen bases. He also tied a NL record by stealing five bases in a game. He experienced drug problems in 1983; he fought through them, but wasn't the same player. Traded to Kansas City for outfielder John Morris in May 1985, Smith faced his old teammates in the World Series that fall and contributed a .333 average, four RBI, five runs, and two stolen bases to the Royals' victory.

Released after a disappointing 1987 season, Smith signed with Atlanta's Richmond (International League) farm club and worked his way back to the majors in 1988. He exhibited newfound power in 1989 as Atlanta's left fielder and had his best season ever (.315, 21 HR, 79 RBI, .415 on-base average). /(FO)

Mayo Smith — 1915–1977. OF 1945 **A's** 73 g, .212, 0 hr, 11 rbi.
Manager 1955–59, 67–70 Phillies, Reds, **Tigers** 662–611, .520. *1 WS, 4–3, .571*

A minor league outfielder for more than 20 years, Smith spent half of the 1945 season with the A's. He managed in the Yankees' farm system before becoming the Phillies' manager in 1955. Smith was once kicked out of a game in the tunnel going to the dugout before the teams took the field; he asked umpire Frank Dascoli if they were going to play that day's game according to the rules.

A scout with the Yankees through most of the 1960s, he was hired as manager of the Tigers in 1967 and took them to a pennant in 1968. In the 1968 World Series, Smith made a bold move by moving outfielder Mickey Stanley to shortstop and benching the weak-hitting Ray Oyler to keep all his potent outfield bats (Al Kaline, Jim Northrup, and Willie Horton) in the lineup. The move worked as the Tigers beat the Cardinals in seven games. /(NLM)

Ozzie Smith (The Wizard of Oz) — 1954– . SS 1978– Padres, **Cardinals** 1783 g, .256, 18 hr, 550 rbi. *3 LCS, 16 g, .351, 1 hr, 7 rbi. 3 WS, 21 g, .173, 3 rbi*
☛ *All-Star—81–89. Gold Glove—80–89.*

Ozzie Smith was simply the best shortstop of the 1980s and probably the best ever. After a mere 69 games of minor league play, he took over at shortstop for the Padres and immediately displayed his unparalleled glove wizardry. He came to the Cardinals in 1982 for fellow shortstop Garry Templeton.

To watch The Wizard of Oz (or The Wizard of Ah!'s, as some put it) is to see a combination of baseball, ballet, and gymnastics. He repeatedly dives, bounces to his feet, and fires to first in one fluid motion. He prefers to throw on the run rather than planting his feet, even on routine plays. St. Louis manager Whitey Herzog has argued that at his peak Smith saved 75 runs per year with his glove. His nine consecutive Gold Gloves and numerous fielding records attest to his prowess and great reflexes. His barehanded snag, while diving headlong, of a bad-bounce grounder hit by Bob Horner is perhaps the most frequently-shown feat in fielding highlight films. He set major league shortstop records for assists in a season (621) and most years with 500 or more assists and tied ML shortstop marks for most years leading a league in assists (7), most years leading in chances accepted (7), and most double plays in an extra-inning game (6, in 19 innings). He also tied NL shortstop standards for most consecutive years leading in assists (4), for most years leading in fielding average in 100 or

Ozzie Smith

more games (6), and for the highest fielding average in 150 or more games (.987, in 1987). He also led NL shortstops in putouts twice and in double plays twice, and tied for the double play lead an additional two times. And in 1982, he set the World Series record for most putouts by a shortstop in a seven-game Series (22).

With the Cardinals, Smith developed into a fine hitter, reaching .303 in 1987. He rarely strikes out, yet draws a high number of walks for a singles hitter. In 1987 he became the highest-paid player in baseball, drawing around $2.3 million annually for three years. /(FO)

Paul Smith — 1931– . 1B-OF 1953, 57–58 **Pirates**, Cubs 223 g, .270, 7 hr, 56 rbi

Smith batted .280 as a Pirate rookie in 1953, but suffered a concussion the following spring and wound up in Havana (International League). After serving in the military, he rejoined Pittsburgh in 1957, mostly as a lefthanded pinch hitter. /(RTM)

Pete Smith — 1966– . RHP 1987– **Braves** 369 ip, 13–31, 4.20

Smith was rushed to the majors and went 7–15 in 1988, his first full ML season. He declined even further in 1989 and had control problems. /(WOR)

Red Smith [James Carlisle] — 1890–1966. 3B-OF 1911–19 Dodgers, **Braves** 1117 g, .278, 27 hr, 514 rbi

Smith was sold by the Dodgers to the Braves in August of 1914, shortly after Boston began its "Miracle" climb from last to first place. Consistently among the best third basemen in the league, that season he led his position peers in putouts, assists, double plays, and total chances per game. His .314 batting average in 60 games was the team high, but he missed the World Series when he broke his leg in a hesitant slide in the last game of the regular season. /(JK)

Red Smith (Walter) — 1906–1982. *Writer.*

His 1976 Pulitzer Prize cited Red Smith for his literary quality, vitality, and freshness of viewpoint. His criticism was always professional, never personal. He wrote with a light, wry touch even when taking aim at favorite targets like Bowie Kuhn and George Steinbrenner. Born in Green Bay, Wisconsin, Smith graduated from Notre Dame in 1927 and went to work for the Milwaukee *Sentinel* at $25 a week as a general assignment reporter. The next year, with the St. Louis *Star*, his first sports assignment was a night football game, which he wrote from the viewpoint of an indignant glowworm on the field.

He formed close friendships with Grantland Rice and Fred Lieb while spending ten years with the Philadelphia *Record*. In 1945 he moved to the New York *Herald-Tribune*. By 1954 he was the most widely syndicated sports columnist, eventually appearing in 500 newspapers, including *Women's Wear Daily*. When the *Tribune* folded in 1966, he continued the column and, in 1971, he joined *The New York Times*.

"Sports is the real world," he wrote. "People we're writing about, they're suffering, living and dying, loving and trying to make their way through life just as bricklayers and politicians are." He wrote an 11-word sentence that immortalized him for all sportswriters: "Baseball is a dull game only for those with dull minds." Collections of his columns were published as *Strawberries in the Wintertime* and *Out of the Red*. /(NLM)

Reggie Smith — 1945– . OF-1B 1966–82 **Red Sox**, Cardinals, Dodgers, Giants 1987 g, .287, 314 hr, 1092 rbi. *3 LCS, 9 g, .212, 3 rbi. 4 WS, 21 g, .247, 6 hr, 13 rbi* ☛ *All-Star—69, 72, 74–75, 77–78. Gold Glove—68.*

An ambidextrous, all-state high school football and baseball player from California, Smith had a tryout with Houston at Dodger Stadium his senior year, but signed with Minnesota as a shortstop in 1963. Left unprotected by the Twins after his first pro season, the strong-armed switch-hitter was drafted

Reggie Smith

by the Red Sox, who made him an outfielder. As a rookie, he helped Boston to the 1967 pennant and homered twice in the World Series. A fixture from 1967 through 1973 in potent Fenway outfields, first in center, later in right, he batted .300 three times and won a Gold Glove in 1968 when he led AL outfielders in putouts. In 1968 and 1971, he topped the league in doubles.

Traded to St. Louis with Ken Tatum for Rick Wise and Bernie Carbo in October 1973, Smith had two All-Star seasons for the Cardinals in 1974 and 1975. He hit three HR in a May 22, 1976 game before moving on to the Dodgers in June. On the way to the 1977 NL pennant, Smith, Steve Garvey, Dusty Baker, and Ron Cey became the first four teammates in baseball history to each hit 30 or more HR; Smith hit a career-high 32. He was a major factor in the Dodgers' 1978 league title, hitting a club-high 29 HR, and adding three HR in the WS loss to New York.

Shoulder, neck, knee, and ankle injuries plagued Smith in his final four ML seasons. He batted .284 as a Giants first baseman in 1982 before signing to play in Japan. He retired second to Mickey Mantle in HR by a switch-hitter; as the only switch-hitter with 100 HR in each the AL and NL; and as the only player to homer from both sides of the plate in a game twice in each league. Only Smith and Frank Robinson appeared in WS and All-Star Games for both leagues. /(EW)

Roy Smith — 1961– . RHP 1984– Indians, **Twins** 385 ip, 20–17, 4.30

Strictly a starter in the minors, Smith saw little action in brief big league trials. A fastballer and California League Pitcher of the Year in 1980, he tended to deliver home run balls in his initial major league trials. /(ME)

Sherry Smith [Sherrod Malone] — 1891–1949. LHP 1911–12, 15–17, 19–27 Pirates, **Dodgers**, Indians 2052 ip, 114–118, 3.32. *2 WS, 30 ip, 1–2, 0.89*

Steady, if unspectacular, in 14 ML seasons, Smith was described by one news story as "strong as a horse and tireless as a Missouri Mule." An excellent fielder, he went through both the 1923 and 1926 seasons without committing an error. Smith pitched three strong WS games, but lost two of them. In 1916 he lost a 14-inning duel to Babe Ruth of the Red Sox, 2–1. In 1920 he won a Game Three three-hitter, 2–1, but lost a 1–0 heartbreaker in Game Six. /(NLM)

Vinnie Smith — 1916– . C 1941, 46 **Pirates** 16 g, .259, 0 hr, 5 rbi.
  Umpire NL 1957–65 *2 ASU 1 WS*

Smith's ML playing career was brief and interrupted by military duty. After managing Richmond in the Piedmont League for two years, he turned to umpiring. Smith was behind the plate on May 26, 1959, when Harvey Haddix pitched 12 perfect innings before losing his masterpiece to Milwaukee in the 13th. Smith worked both All-Star Games in 1960, one of only six umpires ever to do so. /(RTM)

Willie Smith (Wonderful Willie) — 1939– . OF-1B-LHP 1963–71 Tigers, **Angels**, Indians, Cubs, Reds 691 g, .248, 46 hr, 211 rbi; 61 ip, 2–4, 3.10

An amateur boxer, Wonderful Willie earned his nickname while with Syracuse (International League) in 1963 when he batted .380 and was 14–2 on the mound. He debuted as a pitcher with Detroit that season. After going 9-for-15 as an Angels pinch hitter in 1964, he won a job in their outfield. That June 4 in Cleveland, he pinch hit, played the OF, and relieved in the eighth inning. He is the only black player in ML history to appear in at least 20 games as a pitcher and 20 as a fielder. /(RTM)

Zane Smith — 1960– . LHP 1984– **Braves**, Expos 901 ip, 39–59, 3.93

Smith was the lefthanded starter on *TSN*'s 1987 NL all-star team, going 15–10, 4.09 for the Braves while leading the NL in games started with 36. He struggled with elbow and shoulder problems the following year, and was 5–10 in late August when elbow surgery ended his season. /(SCL)

Mike Smithson — 1955– . RHP 1982– Rangers, **Twins**, Red Sox 1356 ip, 76–86, 4.58. *1 LCS, 2 ip, 0–0, 0.00*

A gangly 6'8″ sinkerballer, Smithson led the AL in games started in 1984 and 1985, winning 15 games each year for the Twins, but was released after a 4–7, 5.94 season in 1987. He then signed with the Red Sox as a free agent (he had spent his first six pro seasons in Boston's minor league chain), and was 9–6 as an occasional starter for the 1988 AL East champs. /(SCL)

John Smoltz — 1967– . RHP 1988– **Braves** 272 ip, 14–18, 3.54
☛ *All-Star—89.*

The Braves' front office was heavily criticized in 1987 after trading Doyle Alexander to the Tigers for Smoltz. Alexander went 9–0 for Detroit and was a major factor in their division title, while Smoltz was coming off a 4–10, 5.68 record with Detroit's Glen Falls (Eastern League) farm club. Smoltz was rushed to the majors in 1988 and went 2–7 while learning to pitch at the major league level, but in 1989 he was called "the new Tom Seaver" and was the ace of the Braves' staff. He was in the NL leaders in ERA, wins, and strikeouts. /(JFC)

Homer Smoot — 1878–1928. OF 1902–06 **Cardinals**, Reds 680 g, .290, 15 hr, 269 rbi

Smoot was a fleet centerfielder and—until his eyesight began to fail—a .300 hitter. In an age when ballplayers did not wear glasses, Smoot dropped to the minors, playing and managing. A son, Roger, was a Cardinals farmhand. /(JK)

Nate Snell — 1952– . RHP 1984–87 **Orioles**, Tigers 219 ip, 7–6, 3.29

Snell didn't reach the ML until he was 32 years old. He served as a slender righthanded set-up man in the Orioles' bullpen in 1985–86, winning five games and saving five over two seasons, and in 1987 he was 1–2 for the Tigers. /(SCL)

Duke Snider [Edwin Donald] (The Silver Fox, The Duke of Flatbush) — 1926– . OF 1947–64 **Dodgers**, Mets, Giants 2143 g, .295, 407 hr, 1333 rbi. *6 WS, 36 g, .286, 11 hr, 26 rbi*
☛ *Led League—hr 56. Led League—rbi 55. All-Star—50–56. Hall of Fame—1980.*

Along with Willie Mays of the Giants and Mickey Mantle of the Yankees, the Dodgers' Snider was one of a trio of Hall of Fame centerfielders about whom fans debated one of the most frequently asked baseball questions of the 1950s: "Who's the best centerfielder in New York?"

Snider debuted in Brooklyn with Jackie Robinson in 1947, but it wasn't until 1949, after Branch Rickey hired George Sisler to help Snider "establish an acquaintance with the strike zone," that Snider showed the form that would make him the leading home run hitter of the 1950s, with 326. In the four years (1954–1957) that Mays, Mantle, and Snider starred simultaneously in New York in full-time capacities, it was Snider who led the three in homers and RBI. His power stroke was well suited to the bandbox structure of Ebbets Field, and the drives he hit that didn't leave the ballpark regularly pounded the stadium's high right-field wall for extra bases. From 1947 to 1961, Snider teamed with Gil Hodges to hit 745 homers, the third-highest total for a duo in National League history, and the fourth-highest total in the majors.

In 1955 *TSN* named Snider Major League Player of the Year in recognition of the completeness of his game. At one time or another, Snider finished among the top three in the National League in batting average, slugging average, hits, runs, RBI,

Duke Snider

doubles, triples, home runs, total bases, and stolen bases. He was also speedy and graceful as an outfielder. Stan Musial named Snider, Carl Furillo, and Andy Pafko "the best-throwing outfield I ever saw." He also named Snider, Mays, and Aaron his all-time NL outfield.

Although Snider did not hit lefthanders well, he was protected from facing them often by the Dodgers' lineup, which was heavily weighted with right-handed hitters Reese, Robinson, Hodges, Campanella, and Furillo. With those five Boys of Summer, Snider participated in five World Series from 1949 to 1956. He made his sixth and final Series appearance in 1959, en route to posting National League World Series home run and RBI records of 11 and 26. He hit four homers in each of the 1952 and 1955 Series, and is the only man to accomplish that feat twice.

Snider was not the darling of the press during his career. Over 50 newspaper articles castigated him following the publication of a 1956 *Collier's* article in which he told Roger Kahn that he wouldn't be playing baseball if it weren't for the money. Nevertheless, he was a favorite of Brooklyn fans, who rued his departure and that of the Dodgers to Los Angeles in 1958. From 1958 through 1961, the Dodgers played their home games in the Los Angeles Coliseum, a football stadium converted to house the Dodgers. A vast right field compensated for a short left-field line and combined with injuries to end Snider's days as a dominant home run hitter. Snider was named team captain in 1962, his last season as a Dodger. He collected the first hit in Dodger Stadium, which opened that year.

The Mets acquired Snider for sentimental reasons in 1963, and he finished his career, ironically, with the Giants in 1964. After he retired, the Dodgers retired his uniform number 4, ending the use of the number by New York's original teams; Lou Gehrig and Mel Ott had already had their uniforms retired by the Yankees and Giants. Snider scouted for the Dodgers and Padres and managed in the minor leagues before becoming an announcer for the Montreal Expos. He was elected to the Hall of Fame in 1980.

Snider is the subject of *The Occurrences of Duke Snider*, one of the strangest books ever written about a baseball player. This small, surrealistic cartoon book by Lee Dejasu features a fantasy Duke Snider who meets up with characters as diverse as Bill "Bojangles" Robinson and Pallas Athene. Snider's own autobiography became a best-seller in 1988. /(TG/CR)

Fred Snodgrass (Snow) — 1887–1974. OF-1B 1909–16 **Giants**, Braves 946 g, .275, 11 hr, 351 rbi. *3 WS, 16 g, .182, 3 rbi*

The feisty, quick-tempered Snodgrass was a regular on three consecutive Giant pennant winners (1911–13). In the 1912 World Series, the centerfielder made the "$30,000 muff," dropping a routine fly ball in the tenth inning of the deciding game and helping the Red Sox to a 3–2 victory. Apparently, only John McGraw remembered the spectacular catch Snodgrass made on the very next play. McGraw gave Snodgrass a generous raise the next season. /(AAs)

Cory Snyder — 1962– . OF-SS 1986- **Indians** 534 g, .247, 101 hr, 285 rbi

Snyder was an instant hit in Cleveland with his power, strong throwing arm, and matinee-idol looks framed by long, shaggy blond hair. He has never hit fewer than 20 HR in a season, with a high of 33 in 1987, and has hit as high as .272 twice. However, he soon revealed several flaws, striking out frequently while rarely walking. In a 1989 game, Pete O'Brien was intentionally walked three times in favor of pitching to Snyder. Later that season, while hitting .229, Snyder went on the DL with a bad back.

A member of the 1984 U.S. Olympic baseball team, Snyder was the fourth pick overall in the June 1984 draft. A third baseman and shortstop in the minors, his poor fielding necessitated a move to right field, where he led AL outfielders in assists in 1988. His 24 HR and 69 RBI in 416 at-bats in 1986 earned him fourth place in AL Rookie of the Year voting. His father, Jim Snyder, was a minor league infielder in 1961–62 in the Braves' system. /(SFS)

Frank Snyder (Pancho) — 1893–1962. C-1B 1912–27 Cardinals, **Giants** 1392 g, .265, 47 hr, 525 rbi. *4 WS, 17 g, .273, 2 hr, 5 rbi*

The durable Snyder, a big, hard-hitting Texan, established himself as one of the NL's better catchers with St. Louis. Acquired by the Giants in 1919 for lefthander Ferdie Schupp, he had his best seasons in New York. He hit .320 in 1921, .346 in 1922, and .302 in 1924. With Snyder doing the bulk of the catching, the Giants won four straight pennants from 1921–24. Snyder led NL catchers in fielding three times. /(JK)

Jerry Snyder — 1929– . SS-2B 1952–58 **Senators** 266 g, .230, 3 hr, 47 rbi

A utility infielder who never appeared in more than 64 games in a season, Snyder participated in five double plays at second base on July 18, 1955, to tie a then-ML record. He missed most of the 1956 season after his wrist was broken by a Virgil Trucks pitch. /(RTM)

Russ Snyder — 1934– . OF 1959–70 A's, **Orioles**, White Sox, Indians, Brewers 1365 g, .271, 42 hr, 319 rbi. *1 WS, 3 g, .167, 1 rbi*

Snyder was a gum-cracking rookie in 1959, when he hit .313 in 73 games for the A's. A Baltimore outfielder from 1961 through 1967, he twice batted higher than .300, reaching .306 for the 1966 World Champions. On April 29, 1962, he hit safely as a pinch hitter twice in one inning. He once scored from second base on a sacrifice fly off the bat of Brooks Robinson. /(RTM)

Hank Soar — 1914– . *Umpire* AL 1950–71 *4 ASU 5 WS*

A Little All-American in football at Providence College, he quit school to play semi-pro baseball, then played pro football for ten years, nine with the New York Giants. In the 1938 NFL title game, he scored the winning touchdown on a 23-yard pass from Ed Danowski, as the Giants defeated Green Bay before a then-record championship game crowd of 48,120 at the Polo Grounds. One year after he left football, Soar coached the Providence Steam Roller (Basketball Association of America) to a woeful 2–17 record in 1947.

In the army during WWII, Soar caught Connie Mack's eye when he umpired an exhibition game, and Mack alerted AL officials. Soar umpired in the New England League in 1947–48 and the American Association in 1949 before spending 22 seasons as one of the AL's top arbiters. /(JMM)

Society for American Baseball Research — 1971– .

The Society for American Baseball Research (SABR) was organized on August 10, 1971, when 16 researchers interested in baseball history and statistical analysis met in the library of the Hall of Fame in Cooperstown. By the end of the 1980s, the society had grown to more than 6,000 members while maintaining its original stated objectives: to foster the study of baseball as a significant social and athletic institution; to establish an accurate historical account of baseball through the years; to facilitate the dissemination of research information; to stimulate the best interests of baseball as our national pastime; to cooperate in safeguarding proprietary interests of individual research efforts of members of the society. SABR meets in regional groups and in an annual national convention. Its publications include *The Baseball Research Journal*, *The National Pastime*, and a variety of monographs. /(NLM)

Lou Sockalexis (Chief) — 1871-1913. OF 1897-99 **Cleveland (NL)** 94 g, .313, 3 hr, 55 rbi

Sockalexis, a Penobscot Indian from Maine, was educated and played baseball at Holy Cross and Notre Dame, from which he was expelled for creating a drunken disturbance. He was quickly signed by the Cleveland National League club in 1897, and was an instant success, having no trouble with major league pitching, playing sensationally in right field, and displaying a powerful throwing arm. He is credited as being the first American Indian to play in the major leagues. At first fans would often let out derisive war whoops when he came to bat, but they quickly took to him because of his skill and proud demeanor.

In July Sockalexis sustained a leg injury, which contemporary accounts reported followed a "tryst with a pale-faced maiden" as well as "dalliance with grape." He began stumbling around and making bad plays in right, but continued to hit, going 9-for-18 in his next five games. From July 25 until September 12, he played only once. In his last game he committed two errors. He finished the season batting .338, but made only brief appearances in 1898-99, and left the game in 1903. He drifted throughout New England, a laborer and a transient, and died of alcoholism in 1913. So strong had been his influence that when a Cleveland newspaper ran a contest to rename the AL Naps, Indians was the winner. /(CG)

Eric Soderholm — 1948- . 3B 1971-75, 77-80 **Twins**, White Sox, Rangers, Yankees 894 g, .264, 102 hr, 383 rbi. *1 LCS, 2 g, .167*

The Twins' number-one draft pick in 1968, Soderholm homered in his second ML at-bat in 1971 but struggled for three seasons until he became a steady hitter and fielder for Minnesota. He missed the entire 1976 season when his torn-up left knee required two operations. In 1977, after signing with the White Sox as a free agent, he was AL Comeback Player of the Year, hitting .280 with career highs of 25 home runs and 67 RBI. /(EW)

Rick Sofield — 1956- . OF 1979-81 **Twins** 207 g, .243, 9 hr, 66 rbi

A good baserunner who seldom hit into double plays, Sofield hit .301 in 35 games with the Twins in 1979 but only .247 the next year, when he was given a chance to play regularly. /(EW)

Tony Solaita [Tolia] — 1947- . 1B 1968, 74-79 Yankees, Royals, **Angels**, Expos, Blue Jays 525 g, .255, 50 hr, 203 rbi

The native Samoan was regarded as one of the strongest men in the ML. He occasionally hit with tremendous power, including a three-homer game (9/7/74), but not often enough to be more than a part-time ML player and DH. When he was first called up, in 1968, he had just hit 49 HR with a .302 BA for High Point-Thomasville of the Class-A Carolina League, but had also made 20 errors at first base. In four seasons of Japanese baseball (1980-83) he hit 155 homers. /(EW)

Claudio Solano — 1926- . OF-SS 1945, 53-58, 61, 66-67 Minor and Mexican Leagues

Solano managed to get a trial with San Diego (Pacific Coast League) as a teenaged shortstop during the player shortage in 1945, but otherwise spent his early career in the then-outlaw Mexican League. After the Arizona-Texas League absorbed some of the Mexican League franchises in 1953, Solano hit 199 homers with 799 RBI in five years. He hit as many as 45 HR in 1956, and batted as high as .402 in 1957. /(MC)

Julio Solano — 1960- . RHP 1983-88 **Astros**, Mariners 174 ip, 6-8, 4.55

A career reliever, Solano never spent a full season in the ML, usually shuttling Houston and Tucson (Pacific Coast League). He pitched a career-high 50.1 innings for the Astros in 1984, posting a 1.95 ERA with 33 strikeouts. /(SCL)

Eddie Solomon (Buddy) — 1951-1986. RHP 1973-82 Dodgers, Cubs, Cardinals, **Braves**, Pirates, White Sox 719 ip, 36-42, 3.99. *1 LCS, 2 ip, 0-0, 0.00*

The high-spirited, well-traveled Solomon was talented but erratic. His best seasons were with Pittsburgh in 1980-81 when he was 7-3 and 8-6 as both a starter and reliever. /(EW)

Mose Solomon [Morris H.] (The Rabbi of Swat) — 1900-1966. OF 1923 **Giants** 2 g, .375, 0 hr, 1 rbi

Nicknamed The Rabbi of Swat when he hit 49 home runs in the Southwestern League in 1923,

Solomon was purchased by the Giants, who hoped for a "Jewish Babe Ruth" as a drawing card. He had three hits in two games, but his fielding deficiencies sent him back to the minors. /(NLM)

Moose Solters [Julius Joseph, born Julius Joseph Soltesz] — 1906-1975. OF 1934-41, 43 Red Sox, **Browns**, Indians, White Sox 938 g, .289, 83 hr, 599 rbi

A big, heavy-hitting outfielder, Solters had three consecutive 100-RBI seasons (1935-37). He hit three home runs in one game (7/7/35) with the Browns and a career-high 20 homers in 1937 after being traded to Cleveland. He was sometimes called Lemons because of his craving for citrus fruit. /(EW)

Charles W. Somers — 1869-1934. *Executive.*

One of the three key men, with Ban Johnson and Charles Comiskey, involved in the launching of the American League, Somers owned the Cleveland club and put up the money to start the Boston and Philadelphia clubs. He built one of the first concrete grandstands at Cleveland's League Park in 1909. He never had a winner at Cleveland, the closest finish being a half-game back of Detroit in 1908. /(NLM)

Don Songer — 1899-1962. LHP 1924-27 **Pirates**, Giants 202 ip, 10-14, 3.38

Songer was a 7-8 spot starter and reliever for the 1926 Pirates, but missed pitching for a pennant winner when he was sold to the Giants the following May. /(NLM)

Lary Sorensen — 1955- . RHP 1977-85, 87-88 **Brewers**, Cardinals, Indians, A's, Cubs, Expos, Giants 1736 ip, 93-103, 4.15
☛ *All-Star—78.*

Sorensen's good sinker helped him to go 18-12 in 1978, his first full season with the Brewers, and throw three shutout innings in the All-Star Game. Preparing himself for life after baseball, he worked at a Milwaukee radio and TV station during the off-seasons. He pitched for four teams in five years, finishing after going 3-7 for the 1985 Cubs. His parents named him Lary with one *r* because they liked four-letter names; they named his siblings Gary, Lynn, and Gail. /(KC)

Vic Sorrell — 1901-1972. RHP 1928-37 **Tigers** 1673 ip, 92-101, 4.43

A steady pitcher with the Tigers for ten years, Sorrell won 16 games in 1930 and had four other seasons of 11 or more wins. By the time Detroit won pennants

in 1934 and 1935, he was only a spot starter, and he did not play in either WS. /(JK)

Elias Sosa [born Elias Sosa Martinez] — 1950- . RHP 1972-83 Giants, Cardinals, Braves, Dodgers, A's, **Expos**, Tigers, Padres 919 ip, 59-51, 3.32. *2 LCS, 3 ip, 0-1, 9.00. 1 WS, 2 ip, 0-0, 11.57*

As a rookie reliever for the Giants in 1973, Sosa went 10-4 with 18 saves (tied for fifth in the NL) in 71 appearances (third in the NL). He dropped to 9-6, seven saves in 1974, when Randy Moffitt took over as the Giants' stopper, and Sosa was traded after the season. He pitched poorly for three teams in the next two years before rebounding with the NL champion Dodgers in 1977, going 2-2 with a 1.97 ERA. He lost the LCS opener and was also hit hard in the World Series. Waived to the Pirates in January 1978, he was then traded to the A's on April 4 and went 8-2 with 14 saves.

The Expos picked up Sosa for 1979, and he rewarded them with an 8-7, 1.95, 18-save season. He went 9-6, 3.06 with nine saves in 1980, and declined thereafter. /(WOR)

Denny Sothern — 1904-1977. OF 1926, 28-31 **Phillies**, Pirates, Dodgers 357 g, .280, 19 hr, 115 rbi

Sothern utilized his speed on the basepaths and in centerfield. A regular with the 1928 Phillies, he had 17 stolen bases and led NL outfielders in assists and double plays. Used part-time in 1929, he batted a career-high .306. /(AL)

Allen Sothoron (Dixie) — 1893-1939. RHP 1914-15, 17-22, 24-26 **Browns**, Red Sox, Indians, Cardinals 1582 ip, 91-100, 3.31. 20 wins: 19
Manager 1933 Browns 1-3, .250

Sothoron shared the AL lead with 19 losses for the Browns in 1917, but went 20-13 two years later. A spitballer who was among those permitted to continue to use the outlawed pitch after 1919, he was a clever baseball man and respected teacher. Called Dixie because of his usually misspelled and mispronounced name, Sothoron managed in the minors and coached for both St. Louis teams, briefly taking over as Browns manager in 1933. /(JK)

Mario Soto — 1956- . RHP 1977-88 **Reds** 1730 ip, 100-92, 3.47. *1 LCS, 2 ip, 0-0, 0.00*
☛ *All-Star—82-84.*

The hard-throwing Soto started making his mark as the Reds' outstanding pitcher in 1980, working short relief, long relief, and starting. From 1981 to 1985, Soto had more strikeouts than any major league pitcher, including a club-record 274 in 1982. He received the Buck Canel Award as the outstanding Latin-American in the majors in 1983 and started that year's All-Star Game. He led the NL in complete games in 1983 and 1984, was Cincinnati's MVP in 1982 and 1983, tied a club record by starting on Opening Day five straight years (1982–86), and set a club record with four Opening Day wins in Cincinnati. Soto developed severe shoulder trouble in 1986. He worked hard to make Cincinnati's 1988 squad and even started the Reds' home opener, but he was ineffective and was released before the All-Star break. Soto ended his Cincinnati career second on the club's all-time strikeout list. A comeback attempt with the Dodgers later that season failed amidst more injuries. /(ME)

Steve Souchock (Bud) — 1919– . OF-1B 1946, 48–49, 51–55 Yankees, White Sox, **Tigers** 473 g, .255, 50 hr, 186 rbi

Decorated for his heroics in the Battle of the Bulge, Souchock was MVP of the Eastern League in 1942. A backup with occasional power in the ML, he hit .302 with 11 home runs in 89 games for the Tigers in 1953. A broken wrist in 1954 ended his effectiveness. /(JK)

South End Grounds Boston Braves 1876–1914. LF-250, CF-440, RF-255

This was originally one of baseball's more majestic double-decked ballparks, but on May 15, 1894 a fire broke out in the bleachers during a Boston-Baltimore game and quickly engulfed the park before spreading to the surrounding neighborhood and destroying 177 buildings. The South End Grounds were rebuilt on a smaller scale, due to insufficient funds from the insurance settlement, and the Braves played their 1914 WS games at larger Fenway Park before moving into Braves Field the following season. /(SCL)

South Side Park Chicago White Sox 1901–1910.

Now a housing project four blocks from Comiskey Park, South Side Park was used by Negro League clubs until it burned down Christmas Day, 1940. /(SCL)

Billy Southworth — 1893–1969. OF 1913, 15, 18–27, 29 Indians, Pirates, **Braves**, Giants, Cardinals 1192 g, .297, 52 hr, 561 rbi. *2 WS, 12 g, .333, 1 hr, 4 rbi.*
  Manager 1929, 40–51 **Cardinals**, Braves 1815–1064, .593. First place: 42–44, 48 *4 WS, 11–11, .500*

A boyish Nebraskan, Southworth entered professional baseball against his father's wishes and spent four decades in the game as a player and manager. As a lefthanded-hitting outfielder, he displayed consistency at the plate, speed on the bases, and sure-handedness afield. He tied for the NL lead with 14 triples for Pittsburgh in 1919 and had his best all-around season with the Giants and World Champion Cardinals in 1926, batting .320 with 16 HR and 99 RBI. His three-run homer in Game Two of the '26 Series secured the victory for Grover Cleveland Alexander.

Southworth managed Rochester to the 1928 International League pennant and was promoted to the Cardinals the following year. Attempts to force his methods on former teammates led to dissension, and he was dismissed in July. Returning to Rochester, he won three successive pennants from 1929 to 1931, but because of bitterness and personal difficulties, he continued to incur the disfavor of the Cardinals organization. He coached the Giants in 1933, but was soon out of baseball.

Offered another chance by the Cardinals in 1935, Southworth worked his way back to the majors. Taking over in July of 1940 with St. Louis in sixth place, he guided the club to third. Under his direction, the Cardinals finished second in 1941 and then captured three successive NL pennants (1942–44) and two World Championships. He was a strict taskmaster, but displayed great skill with young players. A $50,000 offer lured him to the Braves in 1946, and two years later he led them to their first pennant since 1914.

In 13 years as a ML manager, Southworth only once finished in the second division. *TSN* named him Manager of the Year in 1941 and 1942. His .593 won-lost percentage places him sixth among ML pilots. /(JL)

Bob Spade — 1877–1924. RHP 1907–10 **Reds**, Browns 426 ip, 25–24, 2.96

Spade shone briefly for Cincinnati, going 17–12 in 1908, but trouble with management curtailed his career. When he died penniless, fans raised funds to pay for his burial. /(JK)

Warren Spahn — 1921– . LHP 1942, 46–65 **Braves**, Mets, Giants 5244 ip, 363–245, 3.09. 20 wins: 47, 49–51, 53, 54, 56–61, 63 *3 WS, 56 ip, 4–3, 3.05*
☛ *Led League—w 49, 50, 53, 57–61. Led League—era 47, 53, 61. Led League—k 49–52. Cy Young Award—57. All-Star—47, 49–54, 56–59, 61–63. Hall of Fame—1973.*

The winningest lefthanded pitcher of all time, and possibly the best as well, Warren Spahn was a complete player who helped himself at bat and in the field. He was the mainstay of the Braves' pitching staff for two decades. Spahn won 20 games a ML record-tying 13 times, pitched two no-hitters, and led the NL in strikeouts four consecutive years. He had a deceptive pickoff move to first base, and teammate Johnny Sain called him "one of the smartest men ever to play the game."

Spahn's career was delayed by WWII, and he did not earn his first ML win until 1946 at the age of 25. He had been with the Braves in the spring of 1942, but was reportedly sent down to the minors by manager Casey Stengel because he refused to brush back Pee Wee Reese in an exhibition game. He went 17–13 with a 1.96 ERA at Hartford that year, and pitched four games without a decision for the Braves at the end of the season.

In 1946, Spahn relied mostly on a fastball and curve, and had a modest 8–5 record, but in 1947 he was 21–10 and led the NL in ERA (2.33). Spahn's emergence coincided with the Braves' resurgence—a third-place finish in 1947 and a NL pennant in 1948—and in 1948 he was immortalized in baseball lore by the jingle "Spahn and Sain and pray for rain," a reference to the Braves' lack of pitching depth. Oddly enough, 1948 was actually Spahn's worst season until 1964. He was only 15–12 with a relatively high 3.71 ERA. He managed to win key assignments, including a 14-inning 2–1 win over the Dodgers that put the Braves in first place for good, and his 5–2/3 innings of one-hit relief won Game Five of the WS, which the Braves lost to Cleveland in six games.

From 1949 to 1963, Spahn was clearly baseball's most successful lefthander. He won 20 games 12 times in 15 seasons, led the NL in wins eight times, and never had an ERA above 3.50. He won consistently pitching for Braves clubs that ranged from seventh place to World Champions. He was aided by the addition of two new pitches: a wicked screwball that became more important as his fastball lost its pop, and a slider that gave him four quality pitches.

He won 21 games in both 1949 and 1950, and 22 in 1951, but fell off to 14–19 (with a still-excellent 2.98 ERA) in 1952 as the Braves finished 32 games out in their last year in Boston. A June 15 loss to the Cubs that year typified Spahn's frustration. He fanned 18 batters in 15 innings and hit a solo home run, but lost, 2–1. Spahn turned down a contract that would have paid him 10 cents a head based on

Warren Spahn

home attendance in 1953, and the decision proved costly when the Braves moved to Milwaukee and attendance skyrocketed. Spahn led the NL in ERA in 1953, and failed to win 20 games only once between 1953 and 1961, as he began to master changing speeds and location to keep hitters off balance. Braves pitching coach Whitlow Wyatt said, "He makes my job easy. Every pitch he throws has an idea behind it."

In 1957, at the age of 36, Spahn led the Braves to the pennant with a 21–11, 2.69 record, and began a

string of five consecutive seasons leading the NL in
wins. In the WS, he won Game Four in relief as the
Braves beat the Yankees in seven games. He also
won the Cy Young Award. Spahn improved to
22–11 in 1958, and won two more games in the WS
rematch with the Yankees, in which New York
prevailed. The Braves lost a playoff against the
Dodgers in 1959, and would never again reach the
WS during Spahn's tenure, but several personal
milestones remained.

On September 16, 1960, Spahn pitched the first
no-hitter of his career against the Phillies, and the
4–0 win was his 20th of the season. The following
year he no-hit the Giants 1–0 on April 28, five days
after his 40th birthday. Then, on August 11, he beat
the Cubs in a packed Milwaukee County Stadium
for his 300th victory. Despite slumping to 18–14 in
1962, Spahn still led the NL in complete games and
had a 3.04 ERA, and in 1963, at the age of 42, he
tied his career-best record with a 23–7 mark. It was
his last hurrah. Spahn had been overtaken by Sandy
Koufax as the NL's premier lefthander, and his
ERA ballooned to 5.29 in 1964 when he spent
much of the summer in the bullpen. A further
indignity occurred in the off-season, when he was
sold to the fledgling New York Mets. He started
4–12 for the Mets in 1965 and was released in July,
then added three more wins for the Giants before
being released again.

Spahn did not leave gracefully, grumbling, "I
didn't quit; baseball retired me," and he pitched
briefly in Mexico and in the minors until 1967
before finally giving up for good. He was elected to
the Hall of Fame in 1973, his first year of eligibility.
He holds the NL record for career home runs by a
pitcher with 35. /(PB)

Albert Spalding — 1850–1915. RHP-1B-OF-2B
1871–78 **Boston (NA)**, Cubs *NA*: 273 g, 207–56, .320 ba;
ML: 540 ip, 48–13, 1.78; 127 g, .287, 0 hr, 79 rbi. 20
wins: 1871–78
   Manager 1876–77 **Cubs** 78–47, .624. First place: 76
☛ *Led League—w 76. Hall of Fame—1939.*

Spalding's Hall of Fame plaque acclaimed him as
the "organizational genius of baseball's pioneer
days" and as a star pitcher. As a teenager in the
1860s, Spalding played for the Forest City team in
his hometown of Rockford, IL, where he gained a
reputation for his straight-armed, underhand
fastball and for his hitting. He went to work for the
National Association Boston Red Stockings in 1871,
and soon was hailed as the "champion pitcher of the
world." Through 1875, he compiled a 207–56

Albert Spalding

record to become baseball's first 200-game winner.
Boston won four consecutive NA pennants from
1872–75, with Spalding leading the league in victories each year; in 1874 he pitched all of Boston's
games, and in 1875 he went 57–5. He also played in
the field, batting .320 in the NA.

Spalding and several other players were then lured
from Boston to become the heart of the National
League Chicago White Stockings (later known as the
Cubs). On Opening Day, April 25, 1876, Spalding

pitched the NL's initial shutout (the first of his eight that year), and had three hits in Chicago's 4–0 win over Louisville. He lost the league's first 1–0 game to St. Louis that May 5, but also received some lusty support, winning one game 23–3. He finished the season with a league-leading 46 wins, losing 12, and managed his team to the pennant.

The arm strain of years as a workhorse pitcher soon took its toll. Spalding played mostly at first base in 1877, pitching only four games. He retired at age 28 to devote himself to his sporting-goods business. In February 1876, the Chicago *Tribune* had announced Spalding's opening of a "large emporium in Chicago where he will sell all kinds of baseball goods and turn his place into the headquarters for the Western Ball Clubs." His company, eventually named A.G. Spalding & Brothers, emerged as the era's dominant sporting-goods firm. Spalding proved a skilled businessman, capitalizing on his fame as a ballplayer. His motto, "Everything is possible to him who dares," guided his company's growth. With a fierce drive to succeed, he became a captain of industry and created a tight monopoly.

From 1882 to 1891, Spalding served as president of the Chicago team. He sought to improve baseball's image around ballparks by reducing rowdiness and eliminating the influence of gamblers. Chicago, meanwhile, emerged as the decade's powerhouse, winning five pennants.

A skillful diplomat and first-rate organizer, Spalding promoted baseball's interests nationally and internationally, and simultaneously further his own sporting-goods enterprises. In 1874 he arranged a tour of England and Ireland for two baseball teams, and in 1888–89 led the first world baseball tour. His Chicago team and a squad of all-stars performed at such stops as Hawaii, Australia, Egypt, Italy, and England. A pyramid served as a backstop for one of the games. Spalding was inducted into the Hall of Fame by the Committee on Baseball Veterans in 1939, the year the Hall opened. /(DS)

Al Spangler — 1933– . OF 1959–71 Braves, **Astros**, Angels, Cubs 912 g, .262, 21 hr, 175 rbi

The speedy, slap-hitting Spangler was drafted from the Braves by the expansion Colt .45s (later the Astros), and led the .45s in hitting their first two seasons (.285 in 1962, .281 in 1963). He might have become the prototypical Astrodome player but was waived to the Angels in mid-1965, the year the Dome opened. After a stint in the minors, he joined the Cubs, and throughout Leo Durocher's tenure as Chicago manager, Spangler played sparingly,

coached, and was reportedly resented by teammates for being too close to the boss. /(MC)

Tully Sparks [Thomas Frank] — 1874–1937. RHP 1897, 99, 1901–10 **Phillies**, Pirates, Milwaukee (AL), Giants 2336 ip, 121–138, 2.79. 20 wins: 07

A Pittsburgh rookie in 1899 when relief pitching was a rarely practiced art, Sparks topped the National League in relief innings pitched and relief ERA. He settled into the Phillies' rotation in 1903 for a stretch of satisfactory seasons, highlighted by a 22–8 mark in 1907. /(JK)

Joe Sparma — 1942–1986. RHP 1964–70 **Tigers**, Expos 864 ip, 52–52, 3.95. *1 WS, 1/3 ip, 0–0, 54.00*

Sparma was a star quarterback at Ohio State, but quit after three years because of differences with coach Woody Hayes. He signed for a bonus with the Tigers in 1963, and had mixed success, often battling control problems. After going 2–7 in 1966, he rebounded for a 16–9 mark in 1967. He lost his spot in the rotation after a run-in with manager Mayo Smith late in 1968, but, called on to start in an emergency on September 17, he defeated the Yankees to clinch the pennant. /(JK)

Harry L. Sparrow — 1875–1920. *Executive.*

Sparrow, business manager of the Yankees from 1915 until his death five years later, was one of the most popular men in baseball. His cheerful disposition concealed a long history of failing health. A close friend of John McGraw, he traveled with the Giants and managed their 1914 trip to Europe with the White Sox. When Ruppert and Huston bought the Yankees, Sparrow was put in charge of the business side of the operation at McGraw's suggestion. /(NLM)

Bob Speake (Spook) — 1930– . OF-1B 1955, 57–59 **Cubs**, Giants 305 g, .223, 31 hr, 104 rbi

Speake is remembered for a hot start and little else. After hitting 10 homers by June of his rookie year, he managed only 21 the rest of his career. The Cubs traded him to the Giants for a fading Bobby Thomson in 1958. /(NLM)

Tris Speaker (The Gray Eagle, Spoke) — 1888–1958.
OF 1907–28 Red Sox, **Indians**, Senators, A's 2789 g,
.344, 117 hr, 1881 rbi. *3 WS, 20 g, .306, 3 rbi.*
　　Manager 1919–26 **Indians** 616–520, .542. First place:
20 *1 WS, 5–2, .714*
☛ *Most Valuable Player—12 . Led League—ba 16. Led
League—hr 12. Led League—rbi 23. Hall of Fame—1937.*

The seventh player elected to the Hall of Fame, Tris
Speaker's plaque there is inscribed "greatest
centerfielder of his day." From the start of his 22-
year career, he maintained confidence in his eventual success despite some early setbacks. Bought in
1907 by the Red Sox for $750 from Houston of the
Texas League, he did not hit, and the next spring,
without a Boston contract, he was left behind at
Little Rock as payment for the use of the training
camp. His quick Southern League success convinced
the Red Sox to recall him, as previously agreed, for
$500.

He was anxious to improve his fielding and later
recalled, "When I was a rookie, Cy Young used to
hit me flies to sharpen my abilities to judge in
advance the direction and distance of an outfield-hit
ball." Blessed with great speed and a powerful
batting swing, he also worked to make himself a
better batter and baserunner. Speaker played a
shallow centerfield to catch potential hits.

He did not take kindly to personal criticism. In
1910 he sustained an early-season batting slump and
manager Patsy Donovan politely suggested he temporarily yield his third batting spot. "Like hell I
will!" replied Speaker, who finished the season at
.340 as Boston's best batter.

From 1910 to 1915, Speaker was the leader of
Boston's legendary outfield which included Duffy
Lewis and Harry Hooper, and made 161 of their
record 455 assists. In Lewis's words, "Speaker was
the king of the outfield . . .It was always 'Take it,' or
'I got it.' In all the years we never bumped each
other."

In his first several years he enjoyed fringe benefits.
His 1912 Chalmers AL award (predecessor of the
MVP) brought him a $1,950 automobile, and a
Boston jeweler donated a sterling-silver bat valued at
$500 for his accomplishments. Speaker received $50
each time he hit the Bull Durham sign, first at
Huntington Avenue, later at Fenway Park. He
advertised Boston Garters, had a two-dollar straw
hat named in his honor, and received free manufac-
turers' mackinaws and heavy sweaters. Hassan ciga-
rettes created the most popular tobacco trading
cards of Speaker, with four depicting his progress
around the bases.

Tris Speaker

Relations within the Boston team were so cordial
that Larry Gardner described the club as a "big
happy family," enjoying group outings at Revere
Beach when the team was at home. The same was
not true between the players and the owner. President Joe Lannin infuriated Speaker after the 1915
Series victory by proposing a salary cut to under
$10,000 because of his falling batting average; from
1912's .383 to .365, then to .338, and in 1915 to a
mere .322. Angry, the resolute Speaker would not
sign and the obdurate Lannin traded him to Cleveland. For the next eleven years he averaged .354 and
in 1920 he piloted the Indians to their first World
Series title while batting .388 and cracking 50
doubles.

He was player-manager for the Indians for part of
1919 and the following seven full seasons. In 1926 a
gambling scandal broke concerning a questionable

game between Detroit and Cleveland in 1919. Speaker and Ty Cobb were alleged to have participated, and AL president Ban Johnson secured their "resignations" as managers to protect baseball's image. Speaker ended his career with single seasons with the Senators and Athletics.

Although Speaker played only seven full seasons with Boston, he is second on the club all-time in both triples (106) and stolen bases (266), and is third behind Wade Boggs and Ted Williams in batting (.337). He is the all-time ML leader in doubles (793), leading the AL eight times. Speaker is also the all-time ML leader in outfield assists (448) and double plays (139), as well as the AL leader in outfield putouts (6,706). He is fifth in hits, seventh in triples and fewest strikeouts, eighth in runs, ninth in extra-base hits, and tenth in total bases. /(EC)

Chris Speier — 1950- . SS-3B-2B 1971- **Giants,** Expos, Cardinals, Twins, Cubs 2260 g, .246, 112 hr, 720 rbi. *3 LCS, 12 g, .229, 1 hr, 1 rbi*
☛ *All-Star—72-74.*

Speier's steady glove, bat, and all-around smart play have kept him in the ML for 19 seasons, where he evolved from a twenty-one-year-old rookie into an All-Star shortstop in one season, and later settled into a role as a much-traveled and respected reserve infielder. Speier debuted with the Giants in 1971, starting at shortstop for the NL West champions after only one season in the minors, and in 1972 Speier hit .269 with 15 HR and 71 RBI. He made the All-Star team three straight years, showing surprising power at the plate, and in 1975 he led NL shortstops with a .982 fielding percentage. His average slipped to .226 in 1976, and in 1977 he was traded to Montreal for shortstop Tim Foli. Speier was the Expos' starting shortstop through 1982, when he hit .257 in 156 games, but his range at shortstop was shrinking, and he began to experiment at third base as well. Speier was traded to the Cardinals for Mike Ramsey in July 1984 and sold to the Twins in August, before signing with the Cubs as a free agent. After two seasons in Chicago, he returned to his native San Francisco in 1987, where his teammates voted him the club's annual Willie Mac award for inspirational play. Filling in primarily at second and third base, his 11 HR in 1987 was his best output since 1973, and in May he hit two grand slams in a span of five days. Speier has hit for the cycle twice, and still shares the Expos record with eight RBI in one game against Philadelphia, September 22, 1982. /(SCL)

Stan Spence — 1915-1983. OF 1940-44, 46-49 Red Sox, **Senators,** Browns 1112 g, .282, 95 hr, 575 rbi.
☛ *All-Star—42, 44, 46-47.*

Spence was a superlative outfielder with fine range and throwing ability, and a lefthanded hitter with some power. He batted a career-high .323 and led the AL with 15 triples for Washington in 1942, his first year as a regular. In 1944 he drove in 100 runs, but spent 1945 in the military. Holding his own with returning veterans, he hit 50 doubles in 1946, and in 1947 became an AL All-Star for the fourth time. /(JK)

Daryl Spencer (Big Dee) — 1929- . SS-2B-3B 1952-53, 56-63 **Giants,** Cardinals, Dodgers, Reds 1098 g, .244, 105 hr, 428 rbi

Spencer hit a career-high 20 HR in his rookie 1953 season, although he batted only .208. He was used flexibly at shortstop, third base, and second base in manager Leo Durocher's complex lineup manipulation. After missing 1954-55 in the military, Spencer returned to his everyday utility role in 1956, then won the shortstop job in 1957. After leading the league's shortstops in errors in 1957 and 1958, he was moved to second base in 1959. Meanwhile, his hitting improved, although he sacrificed some power for average. In 1958, the Giants' first year in San Francisco, he hit .256 with 73 walks, 17 HR, and career highs of 71 runs and 74 RBI. After the 1959 season, he was traded to the Cardinals with Leon Wagner for Don Blasingame and then joined the Dodgers in mid-1961, resuming his supersub role. After his retirement he became one of the earlier exports to Japanese baseball (1964-68, 71-72), and introduced hard sliding to that country; he was reportedly the first baserunner to break up a double play there. He pursued HR titles in 1964 and 1965, but was walked almost every time he batted down the stretch both years. He totaled 152 HR in Japan, topping 30 three times, and hit .275. /(SFS)

George Spencer — 1926- . RHP 1950-55, 58, 60 **Giants,** Tigers 251 ip, 16-10, 4.05. *1 WS, 3 ip, 0-0, 18.90*

Spencer went 10-4 with six saves in his rookie 1951 season to help the Giants to the NL pennant. He declined to 3-5, 5.55 in 1952 and was used only sporadically thereafter. /(JFC)

Glenn Spencer — 1905-1958. RHP 1928, 30-33 **Pirates,** Giants 534 ip, 23-31, 4.53

Spencer split his time between starting and relieving for the Pirates, leading the NL in relief losses (5) in

1930. In 1933 he was traded to the Giants as part of a three-team deal that brought Hall of Famer Fred Lindstrom to Pittsburgh. /(NLM)

Jim Spencer — 1946– . 1B-DH 1968–82 **Angels**, Rangers, White Sox, Yankees, A's 1553 g, .250, 146 hr, 599 rbi. *2 LCS, 3 g, .000. 1 WS, 4 g, .167* ☛ *All-Star—73. Gold Glove—70, 77.*

Defensive stalwart Spencer won two Gold Gloves and might have been entitled to be named in several other years. He lacked the bat consistency that could have ranked him among the top first basemen, but he had good home run power, twice slugging 18 in a season and getting 23 in only 295 at-bats for the Yankees in 1979. Two years earlier with the White Sox, on May 14 and again on July 2, he drove home eight runs with two homers in a single game.

Spencer moved eastward through most of his career, starting in California, moving to Texas, then on to Illinois and New York, before a final return to California. His time with the Yankees was a home-coming of sorts: He'd first caught the attention of scouts by slugging a home run as a high schooler in the annual Hearst sandlot game held at Yankee Stadium.

Jim's grandfather, Ben Spencer, played eight games for the 1913 Senators. /(RL)

Roy Spencer — 1900–1973. C 1925–27, 29–34, 36–38 Pirates, **Senators**, Indians, Giants, Dodgers 636 g, .247, 3 hr, 203 rbi. *1 WS, 1 g, .000*

After parts of three seasons with the Pirates, Spencer became a free agent when Judge Landis ruled Pittsburgh had unfairly restricted his ML chances. He signed with the Senators and was their regular catcher from 1930 to 1932, hitting .275 in 1931, his busiest season. /(JK)

Tubby Spencer [Edward Russell] — 1884–1945. C 1905–09, 11, 16–18 **Browns**, Red Sox, Phillies, Tigers 449 g, .225, 2 hr, 132 rbi

A backup catcher, Spencer was an admitted alcoholic. He dropped out of baseball in 1910 and, after a few games with the Phillies in 1911, disappeared again. He rode the rails, a hobo, until the Tigers gave him a chance in 1916. He responded by batting .370 in 19 games, and lasted through 1918. /(JK)

Ed Spiezio — 1941– . 3B-OF 1964–72 **Cardinals**, Padres, White Sox 554 g, .238, 39 hr, 174 rbi. *2 WS, 2 g, .500*

Hustling but erratic, Spiezio was Ken Boyer's heir apparent at third base for the Cardinals until injuries wrecked his 1965 season. A backup for St. Louis's 1967 and 1968 pennant-winners, he played on a platoon basis with the Padres, hitting .285 with 12 HR in 1970. /(MC)

Charlie Spikes — 1951– . OF 1972–80 Yankees, **Indians**, Tigers, Braves 670 g, .246, 65 hr, 256 rbi

Laid-back Charlie Spikes went to the Indians in the deal that sent Graig Nettles to the Yankees. Spikes led Cleveland with 23 HR as a rookie in 1973, and with 22 in 1974, but fanned over 100 times each season. Frank Robinson made him a special project upon becoming Cleveland manager in 1975, but Spikes skidded under Robinson's often caustic criticism, winding up in the minors before closing his career as a productive pinch hitter for Atlanta. /(MC)

Dan Spillner — 1951– . RHP 1974–85 Padres, **Indians**, White Sox 1493 ip, 75–89, 4.21

Spillner, who relied mostly on a fastball, was prone to giving up home runs. After suffering through three losing seasons as a Padre starter, he was part of the major leagues' busiest bullpen in 1977: He and Dave Tomlin each had 76 appearances; Rollie Fingers, 78. A Cleveland starter in 1980, Spillner was 16–11 despite a 5.29 ERA. He had one fine year as an Indians reliever, going 12–10 (2.49) with 21 saves in 1982. /(MC)

Harry Spilman — 1954– . 1B 1978–88 Reds, **Astros**, Tigers, Giants 563 g, .237, 18 hr, 117 rbi. *2 LCS, 5 g, .250, 1 hr, 1 rbi*

A lefthanded pinch hitter and occasional first baseman for most of his career, Spilman lasted 11 ML seasons with little power and less speed. On April 30, 1987, Spilman stole the only base of his ML career, and was promptly removed for a pinch runner by Giants manager Roger Craig, and in 1988 he hit his lone ML triple. In 1977 he was the Eastern League MVP with a .373 batting average for Three Rivers. /(SCL)

Alfred H. Spink — Unk.–Unk. *Writer.*

Although Spink is best known as the founder-editor of *The Sporting News* in 1886, his connection with baseball began much earlier. He had been sports editor of the Missouri *Chronicle* and St. Louis *Chronicle* and founder-editor of the St. Louis *World*, a sporting and theatrical newspaper. He helped create the American Association as a rival major league to the NL in 1882. He was one of the organizers of the St. Louis Browns and brought

Chris von der Ahe in as owner. He also formed the Sportsman's Park Club. /(NLM)

J.G. Taylor Spink — 1888–1962. *Writer.*

Spink was honored by the Hall of Fame in 1962 with an award subsequently named for him. The J.G. Taylor Spink Award recognizes journalists who have made outstanding contributions to baseball. Taylor Spink was born two years after *The Sporting News* was founded by his uncle, whom he succeeded as editor in 1914. Under his direction the paper grew from one undergoing financial difficulties to become "the Bible of Baseball," with a small core of permanent staff and 250 correspondents. Spink worked at it seven days a week. He would call anybody at any time of the day or night to get a story. He took the paper's guardianship of the game seriously, furnishing officials with leads to players involved in gambling and helping to uncover the 1919 Black Sox scandal. He was on a permanent campaign to improve baseball and keep it honest. He supported expansion, started annual awards for rookies, pitchers, and relievers, and carried on the MVP awards when the major leagues dropped them, until the BBWAA picked it up.

Spink was known for his ambiguities, outbursts of temper, profanity, and changeability. He was dynamic, argumentative, gruff, sentimental, sensitive, and generous. His signature was an illegible flourish of ink. Dan Daniel, a longtime correspondent and columnist for *TSN*, once said Spink had fired him 16 times. He supported Ban Johnson and disliked Judge Landis, who looked with disfavor on the paper's policy of charging minor leagues to carry their box scores. His son, C.C. Johnson Spink, succeeded him as publisher until the paper was sold in 1977. /(NLM)

William MacDonald Spink — 1840–1884. *Writer.*

For 20 years sports editor of the St. Louis *Globe-Democrat*, Spink was the first baseball writer and booster of the game in the West. A reporter for the Cincinnati *Gazette* in the 1860s, he may have been the first to call the local team the Reds in 1869; he was known to have tagged the St. Louis club the Browns and the Chicago club the White Stockings. He was the first official scorer for the St. Louis NL club, and later he dubbed their grounds Sportsman's Park. /(NLM)

Scipio Spinks — 1947– . RHP 1969–73 Astros, **Cardinals** 201 ip, 7–11, 3.70

Hard-throwing but extremely wild, Spinks seemed to have gotten it together in 1972, when, after joining the Cardinals, he went 5–5 (2.67) in 16 starts. The next spring he couldn't find the plate. /(MC)

Paul Splittorff — 1946– . LHP 1970–84 **Royals** 2555 ip, 166–143, 3.81. 20 wins: 73 *4 LCS, 37 ip, 2–0, 2.68. 1 WS, 2 ip, 0–0, 5.40*

Splittorff was the first player originally signed by the Royals to make it to the majors, and in 1973 he became their first 20-game winner. A thinking control pitcher with a fine sinkerball, he led the AL with a .727 winning percentage by going 16–6 in 1977 (despite a 1–4 start), helping the Royals to their second of three consecutive division titles. He threw two one-hitters, including one on August 3, 1975, in which he set down the last 26 Oakland batters. Beleaguered by back problems, after 17 years in the Royals' organization, he retired as the club's all-time leader in games and innings pitched, starts, wins, and losses. /(FJO)

Watson Spoelstra — Unk.–Unk. *Writer.*

Spoelstra was president of the BBWAA in 1968. He retired in 1973, after 30 years with the Detroit *News* and as a correspondent for *The Sporting News*, to join evangelist Bill Glass in a public relations capacity which included coordinating Sunday chapel services for major league teams. /(NLM)

Al Spohrer — 1902–1972. C 1928–35 Giants, **Braves** 754 g, .259, 6 hr, 199 rbi

Spohrer was a rugged catcher who never ducked a fight. When colorful and egocentric teammate Art Shires took up boxing between seasons, a promoter matched the two. Commissioner Landis warned them that he would ban them from baseball for making fighting a second career. On the field, Spohrer was a competent catcher who showed fair "doubles power" in 1929 and 1930. He hit a career-high .317 in '30 but declined thereafter. /(JK)

Karl Spooner — 1931–1984. LHP 1954–55 **Dodgers** 117 ip, 10–6, 3.09. *1 WS, 3 ip, 0–1, 13.50*

Spooner joined the Dodgers at the end of the 1954 season and wowed the baseball world by pitching back-to-back shutouts against the Giants and Pirates, striking out 27 in the two games. He had deceptively long arms, a blazing fastball with movement, and great confidence. But he injured his arm the following spring training, went 8–6, and lasted just one-third of an inning in his World Series start—his final major league appearance. /(JK)

Sportsman's Park St. Louis Browns 1902–53, St. Louis Cardinals 1920–66. LF-351, CF-422, RF-310

Home to the National Association's Brown Stockings as early as 1875, Sportsman's Park added a second deck in 1909 and seating was extended to the foul poles in 1925, while the outfield bleachers were constructed in 1926. When the Browns moved to Baltimore they sold the park to August Busch, who promptly renamed it Busch Stadium, and a large Anheuser-Busch logo was mounted atop the left-field scoreboard, with the eagle flapping its wings after each Cardinal home run. A grass field with straight outfield fences extending from the corners to deep center, Sportsman's Park was the scene of midget Eddie Gaedel's sole ML appearance, and, when Bill Veeck owned the Browns, home to the Veeck family in an apartment beneath the grandstand. /(SCL)

Ed Sprague — 1945– . RHP 1968–69, 71–76 **A's**, Reds, Cardinals, Brewers 408 ip, 17–23, 3.84

Sprague didn't play baseball in school, but scouts discovered him in the army in Germany. The hard-throwing, 6'4" pitcher was signed by St. Louis and debuted with the A's as a reliever in 1968, his third pro season. He had compiled a career-best 7–2 record with Milwaukee in 1974, when, on July 19, he twisted knee ligaments on Comiskey Park's short-lived Astroturf infield and missed the rest of the season. Sprague became the owner of the Stockton franchise and his wife the owner of Lodi in the California League. Their son, Stanford third baseman Ed Sprague, was the Blue Jays' first pick in the June 1988 draft. /(TO)

Jack Spring — 1933– . LHP 1955, 57–58, 61–65 Phillies, Red Sox, Senators, **Angels**, Cubs, Cardinals, Indians 186 ip, 12–5, 4.26

After brief trials with three major league clubs, Spring joined the expansion 1961 Angels. He appeared in a staff-high 57 games in 1962, going 4–2 with six saves as the Angels finished a surprising third. /(RTM)

Marty Springstead — 1937– . *Umpire* AL 1965–85 *3 ASU 5 LCS 3 WS*

The popular Springstead is the AL supervisor of umpires. Many AL umps had run-ins with Earl Weaver, but Springstead had a disagreement that

resulted in a forfeit. On September 15, 1977, Weaver's Orioles trailed 4–0 after 4-1/2 innings at Toronto. Weaver pulled his team off the field to protest a tarpaulin in the bullpen that he claimed posed a hazard to his fielders. When the Orioles didn't return within five minutes of a warning, Springstead awarded the game to the Blue Jays. /(RTM)

Charlie Sproull — 1919–1980. RHP 1945 **Phillies** 130 ip, 4–10, 5.94

Hampered by wildness, Sproull improved his control enough in the American Association to go 16–7 (2.40) in 1944 and earn a spot with the 1945 Phillies for his one major league season. He walked 80 and struck out 47. /(AL)

Freddy Spurgeon — 1901–1970. 2B-3B 1924–27 **Indians** 316 g, .285, 1 hr, 100 rbi

A bright infield prospect, Spurgeon became the Indians' regular second baseman in 1926, hitting .295. A fractured arm the next season cut short his career. /(JK)

Mike Squires (Spanky) — 1952– . 1B-3B 1975, 77–85 **White Sox** 777 g, .260, 6 hr, 141 rbi. *1 LCS, 4 g, .000*
☛ *Gold Glove—81.*

When the White Sox clinched their first Western Division title in 1983, they chose Squires, an 11-year veteran of the organization, to hoist the pennant flag. Squires was a Gold Glove first baseman in 1981. From 1982 through 1984, Tony LaRussa regularly used him as a late-inning defensive replacement; Squires had only 153 at-bats in 143 games in 1983, while leading AL first basemen in fielding average. A gifted glove man at virtually any position, on May 4, 1980, Squires became the first lefthanded catcher to appear in a ML game since the Cubs' Dale Long in 1958. He caught again three days later, without an error. At Kansas City on August 23, 1983, he gained attention by becoming the first lefthanded third baseman in at least 50 years. In 1984 he made 13 appearances at third base, including one start. He also played the outfield, and when he pitched he retired the only man he faced, the Tigers' Tom Brookens. /(RL)

Randy St. Claire — 1960– . RHP 1984– **Expos**, Reds, Twins 206 ip, 12–6, 3.98

Primarily a middle-reliever, St. Claire has yet to spend a full season in the ML. He saved seven games for the Expos in 1987, and in 1988 was traded to the Reds with Jeff Reed and Herm Winningham for

The 1944 St. Louis Browns

Tracy Jones and Pat Pacillo. His father, Ebba, was a ML catcher in the early 1950s. /(SCL)

St. Louis Browns — 1902–1953. 3414–4465, .433. *AL Champions 44*

The old expression about the St. Louis Browns was, "First in shoes, first in booze, and last in the American League." In their 52-year history, the Browns finished in the cellar 14 times, and seventh 12 times. They made only a dozen appearances in the first division. Once, in 1944, they treated their fans to a pennant.

After the 1901 season, the Milwaukee Brewers, charter members of the American League, moved to St. Louis and became the Browns—a name that recalled the glorious history of Chris von der Ahe's Brown Stockings. In their first St. Louis season, the Browns finished second. After years of prosperity at the gate, in 1916 owner Robert Hedges sold the team to Philip Ball, who had owned the St. Louis Terriers of the defunct Federal League. Ball's tenure, lasting until 1933, was one of failure.

Ball's first major blunder was allowing Branch Rickey, the resident genius in the Browns' front office, to jump to the Cardinals because of a conflict of egos. In 1920 Sam Breadon, who had just purchased the Cardinals, beseeched Ball to allow his team to cohabit the Browns' home, Sportsman's Park. Breadon put the money from the sale of the Cardinals' Robison Field into the minor league system, which eventually produced a host of star players that brought the Cardinals far more drawing power than the Browns.

The 1922 Browns excited their owner by almost beating the Yankees to a pennant. The club was boasting the best players in franchise history, including future Hall of Famer George Sisler, and an outfield trio—Ken Williams, Baby Doll Jacobson, and Jack Tobin—that batted .300 or better in 1919–23 and in 1925. Ball confidently predicted that there would be a World Series in Sportsman's Park by 1926. In anticipation, he increased the capacity of his ballpark from 18,000 to 30,000. There was a World Series in Sportsman's Park in 1926—with the Cardinals upsetting the Yankees. St. Louis had been considered a "Browns' town" until then.

The Browns drew only 80,922 fans for the entire 1936 season—the first year of Donald Barnes' ownership. The downward spiral reached its nadir in 1939; from 1937 to 1939, the Browns compiled a 144–316 record. The franchise was developing a hard-luck aura; in 1941 Barnes tried to move his team to Los Angeles. The league meeting for approval was held in Chicago one day after the attack on Pearl Harbor. Understandably, Barnes was denied.

With the arrival of manager Luke Sewell in 1941, the Browns began a rebuilding program that culminated in their only World Series appearance, in 1944. It took two home runs by outfielder Chet Laabs against the Yankees on the final day of the season to clinch the pennant. After leading the Cardinals two games to one in the Trolley Series, the Browns lost the final three contests, and the World Championship. Due primarily to WWII, the 1940s have been described as a time when "even the Browns" won a pennant, demeaning their only legitimate success. One-armed Pete Gray was employed in their 1945 outfield, further enhancing their negative legacy.

The owners that followed the 1944 pennant, Richard Muckerman (1945–49), and Bill and Charlie DeWitt, were caught in a spiral of rising inflation and sagging expectation. The Browns had to sell off players to pay their bills; when attendance dropped as a result, they were forced to sell more talent.

In 1951 Bill Veeck bought the noncontending Browns with the expressed purpose of driving the Cardinals out of town. Cardinals owner Fred Saight had income tax troubles that resulted in a prison term, but August Busch restored order by purchasing the team. To draw fans, Veeck gave them "fun 'n' games," including midget Eddie Gaedel. The stunts so angered the other owners that Veeck was forced to sell the club to Baltimore interests in 1953, putting an end to the St. Louis Browns. /(WAB)

St. Louis Cardinals [aka Browns, Perfectos] — 1881– . Team. 1882–91 AA, 1892– NL
7568–7410, .505. *American Association Champions 85–88 NL East Champions 82, 85, 87 NL Champions 26, 28, 30–31, 34, 42–44, 46, 64, 67–68, 82, 85, 87 26 WS, 31, 34, 42, 44, 46, 64, 67, 82*

St. Louis had the Red Stockings and Brown Stockings in the NL when it opened in 1876, but did not have a permanent franchise there until Chris von der Ahe brought his Browns in after the American Association disbanded in 1891. The Browns had dominated the AA for much of its existence; some say that he deliberately broke up the team after 1888 for the good of the league. The club did not do well in the NL at first. Renamed Cardinals in 1899 for the color of the trim on their uniforms, it was not until Branch Rickey became president of the team in 1916 that it began moving toward the great success that has characterized the franchise. He invented the farm system as we know it today, which, combined with his great nose for talent, produced a steady flow of good ballplayers. It finally paid off in 1926, under manager Rogers Hornsby, as St. Louis won its first NL pennant and World Championship. They won again in 1928, and the Gas House Gang grabbed

The 1930 St. Louis Cardinals

three more pennants in the early 1930s. The Cardinals, featuring a young slugger named Stan Musial, dominated the 1940s, winning four pennants and three World Championships.

The Redbirds found new vigor in the 1960s as Bob Gibson's heroics on the mound and Lou Brock's daring on the bases led them to three pennants and two World Championships. Red Schoendienst was at the helm more than a dozen seasons, a record for Cardinal managers. Whitey Herzog restructured the team around speed and pitching, guiding them to three pennants and a World Championship in the 1980s. Through the end of the 1980s the Cardinals had won 14 pennants and more World Championships, nine, than any NL team. /(FO)

Eddie Stack — 1887–1958. RHP 1910–14 Phillies, **Dodgers**, Cubs 491 ip, 26–24, 3.52

Signed by the Phillies from a Chicago city league team, in 1910 Stack shut out the Cubs in his first ML start and won his next three, all complete games. Then, on a trip to Boston, he got ptomaine poisoning from a lobster and never again pitched as well. /(AL)

Marv Staehle — 1942– . 2B 1964–67, 69–71 **White Sox**, Expos, Braves 185 g, .207, 1 hr, 33 rbi

Staehle's only significant playing time came with the year-old 1970 Expos, for whom he hit .218 with no power in 104 games. /(WOR)

Bill Stafford — 1939– . RHP 1960–67 **Yankees**, A's 786 ip, 43–40, 3.52. *3 WS, 4 g, 1–0, 2.08*

Swaybacked Bill Stafford had an erect strut that exuded confidence. In 1961 the poised, determined 22-year-old went 14–9 for the Yankees, with a 2.68 ERA that was second best in the league. He was 14–9 again in 1962, and was shutting out the Giants in the eighth inning of World Series Game Three when he was nailed in the shin by a Felipe Alou line drive. He courageously continued, allowed two runs in the ninth, but limped off with a 3–2, four-hit victory. In his first start of 1963, on a particularly cold night, he injured his arm, and struggled through the remainder of his career. /(GDW)

Chick Stahl [Charles Sylvester] — 1873–1907. OF 1897–1906 Braves, **Red Sox** 1304 g, .307, 37 hr, 623 rbi. *1 WS, 8 g, .303, 3 rbi.*
    Manager 1906 **Red Sox** 5–13, .278

Chick Stahl

Unrelated to contemporary Jake Stahl, who is often misidentified as his brother, Chick was a fine hitter. He batted .358 as a rookie for the Braves in 1897 and topped .300 five of his first six seasons. He had six hits in one game on May 31, 1899. As the Red Sox' centerfielder he hit three triples in the first World Series, in 1903, and led the AL with 19 triples in 1904. In 1906 he became the Red Sox' player-manager when his best friend, Jimmy Collins, decided to concentrate solely on playing, but Stahl committed suicide the following spring, confiding to Collins that he couldn't stand the strain of managing. /(JK)

Jake Stahl [Garland] — 1879–1922. 1B-OF 1903–06, 08–13 **Red Sox**, Senators, Yankees 981 g, .260, 31 hr, 437 rbi. *1 WS, 8 g, .281, 2 rbi.*
    Manager 1905–06, 12–13 **Senators**, Red Sox 263–270, .493. First place: 12 *1 WS, 4–3, .571*
    ☛ *Led League—hr 10.*

College-educated and independently wealthy, Stahl played baseball for the love of the game. A good fielder, he was generally an indifferent hitter, although he led the AL in home runs (10) in 1910. He managed the Senators to two seventh-place finishes in 1905 and 1906. On his second try at managing, his Red Sox won the 1912 World Championship, but he was dismissed from a dissension-torn team halfway through the next season. Some sources erroneously list him as being the brother of Chick Stahl. /(JK)

Larry Stahl — 1941- . OF 1964-73 A's, Mets, **Padres**, Reds 730 g, .232, 36 hr, 163 rbi. *1 LCS, 4 g, .500*

Stahl saw the most action in 1966, hitting .250 with five HR and 34 RBI in 312 at-bats as an outfielder and pinch hitter for the A's. He was selected by the Padres in the expansion draft and led the NL in pinch at-bats in 1969, going 6-for-44. After two more years as a semi-regular, he was bought by the Reds and went 11-for-45 as a pinch hitter in their 1973 NL West championship season, and hit .500 in the LCS in his last ML play. /(SFS)

Tuck Stainback [George Tucker] — 1910- . OF 1934-46 **Cubs**, Cardinals, Phillies, Dodgers, Tigers, Yankees, A's 817 g, .259, 17 hr, 204 rbi. *2 WS, 7 g, .176*

Stainback was a good-natured journeyman outfielder whose ejection from the Cub bench for riding umpire George Moriarty during the 1935 Chicago-Detroit World Series led to the entire dugout being cleared. In 1938 Stainback went from the Cubs to the Cardinals with Curt Davis, Clyde Shoun, and $185,000 for Dizzy Dean. /(NLM)

Gerry Staley — 1920- . RHP 1947-61 **Cardinals**, Reds, Yankees, White Sox, A's, Tigers 1981 ip, 134-111, 3.70 *1 WS, 8 ip, 0-1, 2.16*
☛ *All-Star—52-53, 60.*

Staley was a sinker and knuckleball pitcher who won 19, 17, and 18 games for the Cardinals from 1951 to 1953. When he slipped to 7-13 in 1954, he was dealt to the Reds, then on to the Yankees, but he continued to be ineffective as a starter. When he arrived with the White Sox in 1956, his old manager, Marty Marion, converted him to relief and opened a second career for him. He and fellow reliever Turk Lown helped lead the Sox to the 1959 pennant. On September 22, he made one pitch, a game-ending double play with the bases loaded, to nail down the flag. In 1960 he led the AL with 13 wins in relief. /(RL)

Tracy Stallard — 1937- . RHP 1960-66 Red Sox, **Mets**, Cardinals 765 ip, 30-57, 4.17

Stallard was a Red Sox rookie when he took the mound in Yankee Stadium on the last day of the 1961 season. In the fourth inning, he allowed the only run of the game—Roger Maris's record-breaking 61st home run. Said the 6'5" Stallard, "I have nothing to be ashamed of. He hit 60 others, didn't he?" With the Mets in 1964, Stallard suffered one of his NL-high 20 losses in the longest game in ML history, a 7-hour 23-minute marathon against San Francisco on May 31; another loss came when Philadelphia's Jim Bunning pitched his perfect game on June 21. /(RTM)

Virgil Stallcup (Red) — 1922- . SS 1947-53 **Reds**, Cardinals 587 g, .241, 22 hr, 214 rbi

Stallcup was the Reds' regular shortstop from 1948 through 1951, and led NL shortstops in fielding in 1951. Traded to the Cardinals, who had Solly Hemus at shortstop, in early 1952, Stallcup was soon out of the majors. In 1949 he had only nine bases on balls in 575 at-bats. /(SFS)

George Stallings (The Miracle Man) — 1867-1929. C 1890, 97-98 **Dodgers**, Phillies 7 g, .100.
Manager 1897-98, 01, 09-10, 13-20 Phillies, Tigers, Yankees, **Braves** 880-900, .494. *1 WS, 4-0, 1.000*

Stallings managed one of the most memorable pennant-winning teams of all time. His 1914 Miracle Braves were last on the Fourth of July before charging to the pennant, then swept the favored A's in the World Series. Stallings signed his first contract as a player with Harry Wright and the Phillies in 1887 but played in only seven ML games. He was the Tigers' first manager, but Stallings first attracted attention as a manager in 1910 when he brought the Yankees (then called Highlanders) to second place. He described his 1914 Braves team as "one .300 hitter, the worst outfield that ever flirted with sudden death, three pitchers, and a good working combination around second base." A wealthy Georgia plantation owner, he was suave in the parlor but profane and sadistic on the bench. He had a sharp, sarcastic tongue and used it freely on his players. But, with his 1914 Braves 11-1/2 games back in last place, he began using a softer psychology, telling his players they couldn't lose. They roared to the pennant, the only one Stallings ever won.

Stallings was extremely superstitious; scraps of paper or peanut shells around the dugout drove him to distraction. He hated bases on balls. An apocry-

George Stallings

phal story says that on his deathbed, he was asked what had caused his bad heart. Supposedly, he groaned, "Oh, those bases on balls!" and turned to the wall. /(NLM)

Oscar Stanage — 1883–1964. C 1906, 09–20, 25 Reds, **Tigers** 1094 g, .234, 8 hr, 321 rbi. *1 WS, 2 g, .200, 2 rbi*

Stanage joined the Tigers in 1909 and eventually replaced Boss Schmidt as the regular catcher. An excellent defensive player, he was a light hitter, but the Tigers, with Cobb, Crawford, and Veach, felt they could carry his poor bat. /(JK)

Burt L. Standish — 1866–1945. *Writer.*

Standish was the pen name for Gilbert Patten, who created Frank Merriwell for *Tip Top Weekly,* a Street & Smith pulp magazine, in 1896. Merriwell was the star pitcher for Yale, the terror of every Harvard team and the inventor of the "double shoot," which curved twice on the way to the plate.

He always triumphed and was as honest as he was manly, in 245 dime novels. Frank's exploits reached 500 million printed copies.

Patten received $50 for every 20,000-word weekly segment; he kept it up for 17 years. The series was so popular the publishers hired an understudy to take over if anything happened to Patten; the understudy was Upton Sinclair. Patten eventually earned up to $150 per story, but he never owned the copyright and died broke in 1945. /(NLM)

Lee Stange (Stinger) — 1936– . RHP 1961–70 Twins, Indians, **Red Sox**, White Sox 1216 ip, 62–61, 3.56. *1 WS, 2 ip, 0–0, 0.00*

Stange had hard luck with the 1967 pennant-winning Red Sox, going 8–10 despite a 2.77 ERA. He was slated to start the playoff game had Boston and Detroit ended the season in a tie, but instead he relieved in the World Series. Working out of the bullpen in 1968, he saved a staff-high 12 games. Stange's best season was 1963, when he went 12–5 for Minnesota. With Cleveland on September 2, 1964, he struck out four Senators in an inning. He later became a pitching coach for the Twins, A's, and Red Sox. /(PB)

Don Stanhouse (Stan the Man Unusual) — 1951– . RHP 1972–80, 82 Rangers, Expos, **Orioles**, Dodgers 760 ip, 38–54, 3.84. *1 LCS, 3 ip, 1–1, 6.00. 2 WS ip, 0–1, 13.50*
☛ *All-Star—79.*

Moved to the bullpen by the Expos in 1977 after a lifetime record of 13–33 as a spot starter, Stanhouse went 6–2 with 10 saves. In December the Orioles traded Rudy May and Bryn Smith to acquire Stanhouse, Gary Roenicke, and Joe Kerrigan. Used solely in relief by Baltimore, Stanhouse went 6–9 with 24 saves (third in the league) and a 2.89 ERA. He followed with a 7–3 record, 21 saves (tied for third in the AL), and a 2.84 ERA in the Orioles' 1979 AL pennant season. He beat the Angels in Game One of the LCS with a tenth-inning appearance, but just barely hung on in Game Two as the Orioles and Mike Flanagan won 9–8, and took the loss in Game Three on an unearned run (retiring none of the three batters he faced). He also lost Game One of the World Series, and was hit hard in two other appearances. He then signed an expensive free agent contract with Los Angeles after the season, but flopped, posting ERAs above 5.00 in his final two seasons. /(JFC)

Eddie Stanky (The Brat, Mugsy) — 1916- . 2B-SS
1943-53 Cubs, **Dodgers**, Braves, Giants, Cardinals
1259 g, .268, 29 hr, 364 rbi. *3 WS, 19 g, .213, 4 rbi.*
   Manager 1952-55, 66-68, 77 **Cardinals**, White Sox,
Rangers 467-435, .518
☛ *All-Star—47, 50.*

Hustling, hard-boiled Eddie Stanky debuted in 1943
as the Cubs' second baseman and scored 92 runs.
Traded to Brooklyn, Stanky prompted manager Leo
Durocher to make his famous (and imprecisely
remembered) "nice guys finish last" remark: "Look
at Mel Ott over there [in the Giant's dugout]. He's a
nice guy, and he finishes second. Now look at The
Brat (Stanky). He can't hit, can't run, can't field.
He's no nice guy, but all the little SOB can do is
win." The Dodgers played Jackie Robinson at first
base as a rookie to keep Stanky at second base.
   Stanky led the NL in runs scored with 128 in
1945, when he drew a then-record 148 walks. He led
the NL in walks three times. Swapped to the Braves
for 1948, Stanky hit .320 in a year shortened by
injuries. The Giants gave up Sid Gordon, Willard
Marshall, and two others to get Stanky and double
plays partner Alvin Dark for 1950. Stanky hit .300
that year, then contributed 115 runs and a career-
high 14 HR to the Giants' miracle pennant in 1951.
He started the ninth-inning rally that culminated in
Bobby Thomson's pennant-winning home run.
   Sent to the Cardinals that winter, Stanky was
named player-manager and eased himself out of the
lineup. He lasted until May 1955, as the Cardinals
skidded from contention. He managed the White
Sox to fourth-place finishes in 1966 and 1967 before
being fired midway through 1968. When he later
became a college coach, Stanky surprised observers
with his patience toward young players, adopting a
"no-cut, everyone plays" philosophy. He returned
to manage the Rangers in 1977 but quit after one
game, disgusted by the attitudes of modern-day
players. /(MC)

Bob Stanley (Bigfoot, The Steamer) — 1954- . RHP
1977-89 **Red Sox** 1708 ip, 115-97, 3.64. *2 LCS, 7 ip,
0-0, 5.40. 1 WS, 6 ip, 0-0, 0.00*
☛ *All-Star—79, 83.*

A heavyset sinkerballer, Stanley led the ML in relief
innings each year from 1981 to 1983, setting an AL
record with 168.1 relief innings in 1982. He is the
Red Sox' single-season (33 in 1983) and career (128
through 1988) saves leader. In the infamous tenth
inning of Game Six of the 1986 WS, Stanley's two-
out wild pitch to Mookie Wilson allowed the Mets

to tie the score. In 1987, working primarily as a
starter for the first time since 1979, he was 4-15
with a 5.01 ERA. /(SCL)

Fred Stanley (Chicken) — 1947- . SS-2B 1969-82
Pilots/Brewers, Indians, Padres, **Yankees**, A's 816 g, .216,
10 hr, 120 rbi. *4 LCS, 11 g, .304 1 rbi. 3 WS, 8 g, .182,
1 rbi*

Signed by the Astros and drafted by the Pilots,
Stanley was never an everyday regular but outlasted
virtually every other shortstop of his generation by
providing slick late-inning defense. His best average
was .261 in 46 games, 1977. /(MC)

Mickey Stanley [Mitchell Jack] — 1942- . OF
1964-78 **Tigers** 1516 g, .248, 117 hr, 500 rbi. *1 LCS, 4 g,
.333. 1 WS, 7 g, .214*
☛ *Gold Glove—68-70, 73.*

An outstanding outfielder but an ordinary hitter,
Stanley was the subject of Tiger manager Mayo
Smith's daring experiment in the 1968 WS. To get
Al Kaline's bat into the Detroit lineup, Smith took
Stanley out of centerfield and started him at shortstop in all seven games. Although Stanley committed two errors, the Tigers won the Series. As a
centerfielder, Stanley won four Gold Gloves, had a
1.000 fielding average in both 1968 and 1970, and
tied an AL record for putouts in a game with 11 (7/
13/73). When he retired after 1978, he held the
Tiger record for highest career fielding average
among outfielders (.991). /(CC)

Mike Stanley — 1963- . C-1B-3B 1986- **Rangers**
254 g, .253, 11 hr, 76 rbi

Stanley showed promise in his rookie 1987 season,
batting .273 with six HR in 216 at-bats, but
declined thereafter. /(WOR)

Leroy Stanton (Lee) — 1946- . OF-DH 1970-78
Mets, **Angels**, Mariners 829 g, .244, 77 hr, 358 rbi

First signed by the Mets, Stanton was acquired by
the Angels in the 1971 deal that also brought them
Nolan Ryan. He hit three home runs in a July 10,
1973 game at Baltimore to tie an Angel record. He
led California with 14 HR and 82 RBI in 1975, and
was the 1977 expansion Mariners' MVP, hitting a
club-high 27 HR. /(NLM)

Mike Stanton — 1952- . 1975, 80-85 Astros,
Indians, **Mariners**, White Sox 384 ip, 13-22, 4.59

Four clubs drafted Stanton before he signed with
Houston in 1973. An excitable reliever with a
sinking, 90-mph fastball and a hard slider, he

worked 50 or more games four times with the Indians and Mariners, and compiled 30 saves. He threw from the stretch even with no runners on. /(JCA)

Dave Stapleton — 1954– . 1B-2B-SS 1980–86 **Red Sox** 582 g, .271, 41 hr, 224, rbi. *1 LCS, 4 g, .667. 1 WS, 3 g, .000*

With an unusually erect righthanded batting stance in which he rested his bat lazily on his shoulder, Stapleton hit .321 as the Red Sox' rookie second baseman in 1980. His batting average declined each season thereafter, bottoming out at .128 in 1986, when he was a late-inning defensive replacement for the hobbling Bill Buckner at first base. /(SCL)

Victor Starfin — Unk.–Unk. P 1936–55 **Yomiuri Giants**

Starfin's White Russian parents fled to the Japanese island of Hokkaido following the Russian Revolution. When the first Japanese professional league was organized in 1936, young Starfin was promptly recruited. At 6′4″ 230-lb, he was the biggest player in Japan for many years, and reputedly threw the hardest. With Eiji Sawamura, and later Takehiko Bessho, Starfin gave the Yomiuri Giants the best one-two pitching combinations in Japanese baseball for nearly 20 years. /(MC)

Willie Stargell [Wilver Dornell] (Pops) — 1940– . OF-1B 1962–82 **Pirates** 2360 g, .282, 475 hr, 1540 rbi. *6 LCS, 22 g, .253, 4 hr, 12 rbi. 2 WS, 14 g, .315, 3 hr, 8 rbi* ☛ *Most Valuable Player—79. Led League—hr 71, 73. Led League—rbi 73. All-Star—64–66, 71–73, 78. Hall of Fame—1988.*

As a young slugger, as a superstar, and as a veteran captain, Willie always brought class, and often victory, to the Pittsburgh Pirates. A menacing figure at the plate, Stargell would slowly twirl his bat round and round as he prepared for the pitch, almost like winding a powerful spring. Among his "collect-call" homers were four into the upper deck at Three Rivers Stadium, seven over the right field roof in Forbes Field, two completely out of Dodger Stadium (the only two ever to leave that park), and a shot estimated at 535′ into the 500 level at Montreal's Olympic Stadium.

On July 22, 1964 Stargell hit for the cycle. That year, the burly, lefthanded slugger began a string of 13 consecutive 20-homer seasons, and also made his first of seven All-Star Game appearances. In 1970 he tied a ML record with five extra-base hits in one game. He opened 1971 on a tear, setting an April

Willie Stargell

record with 11 HRs, and inspiring Pirate broadcaster Bob Prince to coin the phrase "spread chicken on the hill" (in reference to Willie's chain of chicken restaurants) each time he blasted a homer. He spread chicken 48 times in 1971 and had 125 RBI, both career highs (as were his 154 strikeouts), to help the Pirates to a pennant. In the WS dominated by Roberto Clemente, he hit a disappointing .132.

When Clemente died, Stargell became the Pirates' leader, but his spectacular 1973 season (.299, 44 HR, 119 RBI) went largely unrecognized because the team slumped. Knee problems forced his move to first base in 1974, and a series of injuries ended his string of 20-HR seasons in 1977. However, he earned *TSN*'s Comeback Player of the Year award in 1978 (.295, 28 HR, 97 RBI).

Although he'd had seasons with higher totals, 1979 was his most noteworthy year: As captain of The Family, he drove the team to a pennant with his bat (.281, 32 HR, 82 RBI) and leadership, awarding Stargell Stars to deserving teammates. In the WS win, he set records with 25 total bases and seven extra-base hits (three HR, four doubles). He was NL co-MVP, LCS and WS MVP, *TSN* Man of the Year, and *Sports Illustrated* co-Man of the Year (with Steeler Super Bowl quarterback Terry Bradshaw). After three injury-plagued seasons, he retired as Pirate career leader in HR, RBI, and eight other categories. Since his retirement, Stargell has been a coach with the Pirates and the Braves. He was selected for the Hall of Fame by the BBWAA in his first year of eligibility. /(ME)

Abe Stark — 1894–1972.

Stark was the Brooklyn borough president, but it was through his clothing store that he gained his measure of immortality. On Ebbets Field's right-field fence was an ad that said, "Hit sign. Win suit." But it was near the ground, and the batter had to hit it on the fly, so Stark was in no danger of losing much money on his proposition. /(SH)

Dolly Stark (Albert) — Unk.–1968. *Umpire* 1928–35, 37–39, 42 NL *1 ASU 2 WS*

Stark, a native New Yorker, was popular in the city. During the 1935 season he was given a "day" at the Polo Grounds and presented with an automobile before the scheduled game between the Giants and Cubs, an event virtually unheard of for umpires. During the game, Stark called a strike on Giants star Mel Ott to even the count at 2–2. Ott turned to Dolly, which ignited the boobirds in the stands. When Ott was called out looking on the next pitch, he said something to Stark on his way to the bench, and the home crowd showered the umpire with abuse on his "day." Stark later explained: "Mel knew they were both strikes. The first time he said, 'Dolly, I'd give ten bucks to have that one back.' The second time he said, 'How can I take two beautiful pitches like that in a row?' " /(RTM)

Dick Starr — 1906–1963. RHP 1947–51 Yankees, **Browns**, Senators 345 ip, 12–24, 5.25

One of many Yankee prospects exiled to the Browns in exchange for the occasional competent St. Louis player, Starr was traded with two others and $100,000 in the 1949 deal that put Fred Sanford and Roy Partee in Yankee uniforms. Illness handicapped Starr, and Sanford, a flop in New York, was sent on to the Senators. In 1951 Starr was traded to Washington even up for Sanford. /(NLM)

Ray Starr (Iron Man) — 1906–1963. RHP 1932–33, 41–45 Cardinals, Giants, Braves, **Reds**, Pirates, Cubs 699 ip, 37–35, 3.53

Starr earned the nickname Iron Man by pitching both ends of more than 40 minor league doubleheaders during his 20-year career. Each season he followed the unusual practice of pitching fastballs and curves for two hours on the first day of spring training. As a wartime pitcher with the Reds, he won 15 games in 1942. /(JK)

Joe Start (Old Reliable) — 1842–1927. 1B 1876–86 Giants, Hartford (NL), Cubs, **Providence (NL)**, Washington (NL) 798 g, .300, 7 hr, 220 rbi (357, N/C)

One of the foremost stars of baseball's early years, Start first gained prominence with Brooklyn's Atlantics (1861–70), whom he helped go undefeated in 1864 and 1865 to win the national championship. He played five years with the New York Mutuals of the old National Association and was in his thirties when the National League was formed in 1876. After leading the NL in hits (100) in 1878 with Chicago, he joined the Providence Grays, helping them to a pennant in 1879 and captaining the 1884 pennant winners. Start is credited as the first first baseman to play his position away from the bag (although some say it was Charlie Comiskey), an advantage underscored by the fact that his chances per game and putouts per game exceeded those of other first basemen of his time. /(FIC)

Jigger Statz [Arnold John] — 1897–1988. OF 1919–20, 22–28 Giants, Red Sox, **Cubs**, Dodgers 683 g, .285, 17 hr, 215 rbi

An excellent outfielder and good basestealer, the 150-lb Statz had little power. His best ML year was 1923 with the Cubs, when he hit .319, with 110 runs scored, 209 hits, and 29 stolen bases. He arrived in the majors in 1919 directly from Holy Cross College but ended up playing 18 years with Los Angeles of the Pacific Coast League, a minor league record. For many years he held the record (since broken by Henry Aaron and Pete Rose) for most games played in organized baseball with 3,473. /(LRD)

Rusty Staub [Daniel Joseph] (Le Grand Orange) — 1944– . OF-DH-1B 1963–85 Astros, Expos, **Mets**, Tigers, Rangers 2951 g, .279, 292 hr, 1466 rbi. *1 LCS, 4 g, .200, 3 hr, 5 rbi. 1 WS, 7 g, .423, 1 hr, 2 rbi* ☛ *All-Star—67–71, 76.*

Rusty Staub never resembled an athlete so much as a 205-lb Sherlock Holmes who'd taken an intense

Rusty Staub

interest in the game of baseball. Staub began with modest natural skills and honed them to precision through perpetual practice. Baseball was equal parts discipline and sport to Staub, whose broad, curious world view attracted him to the study of history and gourmet cookery. "He leads the league in idiosyncrasies," said one Staub observer. "He makes a science of getting ready to play to the point where it almost becomes an obsession to him." For years, Staub operated Rusty's restaurant on the Upper East Side of Manhattan. He'd often embarrass teammates who joined him for dinner on the road by sending his meal back two or three times until the chef got it right.

Staub retired with 2,716 hits and an unmatched reputation as a batter. "He is a pure hitter," said Duke Snider. Staub said, "I discovered at a very early age that nothing was going to come easy for me, that I'd have to work for my success." Despite a lack of speed, Staub led his league four times in outfield assists. When he was placed at DH by the Tigers, he knocked in a career-high 121 runs in 1978. The Mets made him a pinch hitter in his final few years, and he tied records in 1983 for consecu-

tive pinch hits (8) and RBI (25), and had a record 81 pinch at-bats (he hit .296).

Staub signed with the Houston Colt .45s (later the Astros) for $100,000 in 1961 and played in 150 games as a 19-year-old rookie. He and Ty Cobb are the only players to homer before age 20 and after age 40, and Staub is the only player to appear in 500 games for four teams and collect 500 hits for four teams. His short, lefthanded stroke produced line drives and a .333 average for the Astros in 1967, with a league-leading 44 doubles. Always popular, Staub became a national hero (and was nicknamed Le Grand Orange for his red hair in French-speaking Quebec) in Canada as a star for the expansion Expos. He hit 30 homers for Montreal in 1970. A broken hand, his first major injury, sidelined him with the Mets in 1972, but he played a dramatic role in the postseason in 1973. Staub hurt his shoulder against the Reds in Game Four of the playoffs when he caught Dan Driessen's 11th-inning drive and smashed into the right-field wall at Shea Stadium. He took cortisone shots and threw underhand in the World Series against the A's. Though unable to pull the ball, he socked an opposite field homer off Oakland's Ken Holtzman to win Game Four. /(KT)

John Steadman — 1927 – . *Writer.*

Beginning in 1945, Steadman spent nine years with the Baltimore *News-Post* and *Sunday American*, and three years as assistant GM and PR director of the Baltimore Colts before becoming sports editor of the *News-American* until the paper's death in 1985. He then became a columnist for the Baltimore *Evening Sun.* /(NLM)

Turkey Stearnes [Norman] — 1901–1979. OF Negro Leagues 1921–42 Montgomery Grey Sox, **Detroit Stars**, New York Lincoln Giants, Kansas City Monarchs, Chicago American Giants, Philadelphia Giants, Detroit Black Sox 789 g, .350, 172 hr, (inc.)
☛ *All-Star—33–35, 37.*

Negro League great Cool Papa Bell once said, "If they don't put Turkey Stearnes in the Hall of Fame, they shouldn't put anybody in." Satchel Paige called Stearnes "one of the greatest hitters we ever had. He was as good as anybody ever played ball." Stearnes was the complete player, a lefthanded batter who, said Paige, "hit with his right foot in the bucket and twisted his right heel and pointed his big toe up." Research confirms that he had a .350 career batting average, a .664 slugging average, and 172 home runs in 750 games. In the short Negro League seasons, he hit as many as 24 HR in 310 at-bats, and led the league seven times.

Stearnes joined the Negro National League Detroit Stars in 1923, and, batting third, hit .353 and tied for the league lead with 17 HR. He won the NNL HR title four of the next five seasons, and was among the leaders in doubles, triples, and batting and slugging averages throughout the 1920s. With a change of ownership in Detroit in 1930, he joined the great New York Lincoln Giants, playing his customary centerfield and batting fourth. He was hitting .323 with a league-high four HR when he was lured back to Detroit by a team that needed his leadership and box office appeal. During the second half, he hit .353 and led Detroit to a playoff with St. Louis for the pennant. In the seven-game series, he hit .481 with three HR and 11 RBI. One shot in St. Louis off ace Ted Trent went well over 500 feet. But Stearnes's heroic efforts could not prevent a St. Louis victory.

Stearnes jumped to the Kansas City Monarchs when Detroit failed to pay his salary late in the Depression year of 1931. He again led the league in HR with eight, and hit .350. With the collapse of the NNL, he joined the Chicago American Giants in the newly formed East-West League. Manager Dave Malarcher batted Stearnes leadoff to take full advantage of his talents. He hit five HR—enough to lead the league—and helped Chicago to the championship. When the American Giants folded after 1935, he joined the Philadelphia Stars, hitting .350 with nine HR in 100 at-bats. He returned to Detroit for a season when the Stars rejoined the league in 1937, and played again for Chicago and Kansas City.

Stearnes was voted to the West squad for the East-West all-star game in four of its first five years. He was the top vote-getter among outfielders in 1933. /(DC)

John Stearns (Dude) — 1951- . C-1B-3B 1974-84 Phillies, **Mets** 810 g, .260, 46 HR, 312 RBI
☛ All-Star—77, 79-80, 82.

Stearns was drafted out of the University of Colorado by the NFL Buffalo Bills, but signed with the Phillies as their first pick in 1973 (number two overall). Traded to the Mets in 1974, by late 1976 he was their first-string catcher. He was an adept bunter and line-drive hitter, and in 1978 stole 25 bases -a league record for catchers. But his all-out "football attitude" play led to injuries that began limiting his action. He broke a finger on a foul tip in 1980, and, after representing the Mets at his fourth All-Star Game, was disabled with elbow tendinitis in

August of 1982. He played just 12 games his final two seasons. His older brother, Bill, was a catcher in the Yankee organization. /(KT)

Bill Steele (Big Bill) — 1885-1949. RHP 1910-14 **Cardinals**, Dodgers 676 ip, 37-43, 4.02

Steele survived when Cardinals manager Roger Bresnahan dropped five pitchers following a 63-90 finish in 1910. He worked 287 innings and led the NL in losses with an 18-19 record in 1911. The following year he was hit hard, 245 hits in 194 innings. He went to the bullpen, then to the Dodgers, and finally to the minors. /(FJO)

Bob Steele — 1894-1962. LHP 1916-19 **Cardinals**, Pirates, Giants 488 ip, 16-38, 3.05

Steele went 5-15 with the weak-hitting, poor-fielding Cardinals his rookie year. In 1917 with the basement-dwelling Pirates, he hit for a higher average than three everyday players. /(FO)

Elmer Steele — 1884-1966. RHP 1907-11 **Red Sox**, Pirates, Dodgers 418 ip, 18-24, 2.41

Steele compiled a 244-5 semi-pro record as a young phenom in New York's Hudson Valley. He failed with the Red Sox but posted a 9-9 record for the 1911 Pirates before suffering a career-ending arm injury. /(JK)

Bill Steen — 1887-1979. RHP 1912-15 **Indians**, Tigers 597 ip, 28-32, 3.05

Steen, Cleveland's number-four starter in 1912, was troubled by a broken wrist in 1913 and 1914. He won 30 games at Portland (Pacific Coast League) in 1911 and posted a 1.55 ERA at San Francisco (PCL) in 1915. /(ME)

Gus Steiger — 1897-1988. *Writer.*

Steiger covered the Dodgers for the Brooklyn *Times*, the New York *Morning World*, the New York *Journal-American*, and for more than 30 years the New York *Daily Mirror* until that paper folded in 1963. He was a president of the New York chapter of the BBWAA. /(NLM)

Bill Stein — 1947- . 3B-2B-1B-OF 1972-85 Cardinals, White Sox, **Mariners**, Rangers 959 g, .267, 44 hr, 311 rbi

Stein's first ML hit was a home run off the Phillies' Ken Reynolds. He was a regular in only one of his 14 ML seasons, as the Mariners' third baseman in 1977, their first season. He hit .259 with 13 homers and 67 RBI. A back injury hampered him the next season, and he returned to his utility role. In 1981 with the Rangers, he set an AL record with seven straight pinch hits and led the league with nine. /(NLM)

Randy Stein — 1953– . RHP 1978–79, 81–82 **Brewers**, Mariners, Cubs 133 ip, 5–6, 5.75

Stein was a reliever with exceptionally bad control: 5.5 walks per nine innings lifetime. /(WOR)

Terry Steinbach — 1962– . C 1986– A's 362 g, .275, 34 hr, 153 rbi. *2 LCS, 6 g, .211, 1 hr, 5 rbi. 2 WS, 7 g, .364, 1 hr, 7 rbi*
☛ *All-Star—88–89.*

Steinbach's election to the 1988 AL All-Star squad as starting catcher was ridiculed (he was hitting only .216 at the All-Star break and was platooning with Ron Hassey as the A's catcher), but he silenced his critics with a home run in his first at-bat and a sacrifice fly that just missed being a grand slam in his second at-bat to win All-Star Game MVP honors.

Steinbach homered in his first ML at-bat. As a rookie in 1987, he hit .284 with 16 HR, and he finished the 1988 season at .265. In the 1989 LCS, he hit only .200 but had a homer and five RBI as the A's defeated the Blue Jays in five games. He led the A's with seven RBI, and another home run, in their sweep of the Giants. /(SCL)

George Steinbrenner — 1930– . *Executive.*

George Steinbrenner made himself synonymous with owner meddling, involving himself with the day-to-day fortunes of his ballclub to an extent unmatched by any owner since Connie Mack, who was his own manager. Only Charlie Finley can approach Steinbrenner in this, but not even Finley equaled Steinbrenner's record of 17 managerial changes in his first 17 seasons. Finley rehired Alvin Dark as manager just once; Steinbrenner gave Billy Martin five separate terms. Graig Nettles commented, "Every year is like being traded—a new manager and a whole new team."

The son of a Great Lakes shipping family, Steinbrenner made his money as chairman of the American Shipbuilding Company, a Cleveland-based firm. In his youth he was an assistant football coach at Northwestern and Purdue universities (Jim Spencer said of his employer, "George Steinbrenner knows nothing about baseball. He doesn't understand that this is a major league team, not Purdue") and assembled national champions in the National Industrial and American Basketball leagues. In 1973 he put together the group that bought the Yankees from CBS, promising at the time, "I won't be active in the day-to-day operations of the club at all." But one-time associate John McMullen, who later owned the Astros, said, "Nothing is more limited than being a limited partner of George's."

The advent of free agency proved a boon to Steinbrenner although he said of it early on, "I am dead set against free agency. It can ruin baseball." After Catfish Hunter was released from his A's contract in 1974, the Yankees paid him the unheard-of salary of $2.85 million for four years. He signed Reggie Jackson after the team won the AL pennant in 1976, and the move was largely responsible for back-to-back World Championships in 1977–78. However, in that period Steinbrenner had solid baseball minds such as Al Rosen and Gabe Paul in the front office making trades like the one that brought Graig Nettles and Chris Chambliss from Cleveland, and also refusing to trade Ron Guidry. Steinbrenner's initial success purchasing free agents led to a tendency to overstock the team with superstars to the point where there wasn't room in the lineup for them all. His preference for name

George Steinbrenner

players came from the conviction that "you measure the value of a ballplayer by how many fannies he puts in the seats." The departure of general managers nearly matched the turnover of managers and apparently was accompanied by a corresponding lack of GM control over major decisions. A series of disastrous acquisitions in the early 1980s (Ed Whitson, John Mayberry, Doyle Alexander, Mike Armstrong) was made worse by a steady stream of departing stars escaping from what had been dubbed The Bronx Zoo. From 1979 through the end of the next decade, the Yankees won only one more pennant, in the strike-split 1981 season; the 1980s were the first decade since the 1910s in which the Yankees did not win a World Championship. /(SH)

Mel Steiner — 1920- . *Umpire* 1961-72 NL *2 ASU 1 LCS 2 WS*

On June 14, 1965, the Reds' Jim Maloney no-hit the Mets for 10 innings before Johnny Lewis hit an 11th-inning homer. Two months later, on August 19, Maloney no-hit the Cubs for 10 innings. The umpire behind the plate for both overtime no-hitters was Steiner. He also worked the plate for Sandy Koufax's no-hitter against the Mets on June 30, 1962. /(RTM)

Harry Steinfeldt — 1877-1914. 3B-SS 1898-1911 **Reds**, Cubs, Braves 1648 g, .268, 27 hr, 762 rbi. *3 WS, 21 g, .260, 8 rbi*

The only member of the Tinker-to-Evers-to-Chance infield left out of Franklin P. Adams's poem, Steinfeldt was a reliable third baseman with an unusually powerful arm. He originally hoped for a theatrical career but did so well in a baseball game put on by his touring troupe that he switched to the diamond. After eight years with the Reds, he was traded to the Cubs in 1906 and responded with his best season, leading the NL in hits (176) and RBI (83) and batting .327. /(JK)

Dick Stello — 1934-1987. *Umpire* 1968-87 NL *2 ASU 5 LCS 2 WS*

Onetime nightclub comedian Stello first got interested in umpiring when he attended the George Barr umpiring clinic in Tokyo while he was in the Air Force. Ten years later, in 1963, he became a professional umpire in the Georgia-Florida League. He rose rapidly, reaching the NL in 1968. He was the second base umpire on September 10, 1974, when the Cardinals' Lou Brock broke Maury Wills's single-season basestealing record by swiping number 105 against the Phillies. /(RTM)

Casey Stengel [Charles Dillon] (The Old Professor) — 1889-1975. OF 1912-25 **Dodgers**, Pirates, Phillies, Giants, Braves 1277 g, .284, 60 hr, 535 rbi. *3 WS, 12 g, .393, 2 hr, 4 rbi.*
 Manager 1934-36, 38-43, 49-60, 62-65 Dodgers, Braves, **Yankees**, Mets 1926-1867, .508. First place: 49-53, 55-58, 60 *10 WS, 37-26, .587*
☛ *Hall of Fame—1966.*

The Casey Stengel legend is well-known among baseball enthusiasts. A prime contender for the title of greatest manager ever, his greatest fame came from managing the Yankees to ten pennants and seven World Championships between 1949 and 1960. His quotes, delivered in a personal language dubbed "Stengelese," are famous for their practicality, their humor, and their longwindedness.

The Stengel story begins in late 1912 when the rookie, renamed for his hometown of Kansas City, went 4-for-4 in his first game ever to set a since-broken record. In 1913 he became the Dodgers' regular centerfielder; in 1914 the team moved him over to right field. When Wilbert Robinson took over the team as their manager in 1915, Stengel's education began. Stengel, through long practice, made himself an expert at the tricky caroms off the oddly angled concrete wall in Ebbets Field. He would later astonish the young Mickey Mantle by taking him out there to teach Mantle how to play the caroms before the 1952 World Series; Mantle couldn't conceive of Stengel as having been a player 35 years earlier.

Stengel played fairly regularly for Brooklyn, sometimes being platooned, until 1917. He was a line-drive hitter, a hard swinger who, unlike most players of the era, held the bat down at the end instead of choking up. In 1916 he got his first taste of postseason play and hit .364 in the World Series for Brooklyn. On January 9, 1918 he was traded along with infielder George Cutshaw to the Pittsburgh Pirates for infielder Chuck Ward, pitcher Burleigh Grimes, and pitcher Al Mamaux. He sat on the bench for Pittsburgh in 1918 and 1919. It was during 1919 that one of Stengel's most famous antics took place. During the course of a rough Sunday afternoon in Brooklyn against his old teammates, Stengel had received a small bird from one of the Dodger pitchers in the bullpen and when he came up to bat, Stengel tipped his hat to the jeering crowd; out flew the bird, to the delight of the fans. This along with other antics caused Stengel to be traded to the Philadelphia Phillies in August for

Casey Stengel with the Giants

would go on to teach him most about managing. He became a backup outfielder for the Giants and was on three pennant winners from 1921 to 1923. He sat on the bench in the 1921 WS but did well in 1922 in a limited role. In 1923 he hit two game-winning home runs. In Game One his inside-the-park homer with two out in the ninth inning gained added drama from his seemingly torturous course around the bases; sportswriters assumed it was due to age, but in fact one of his shoes was falling apart, making him limp.

On November 12, 1923 the Giants shuffled him along with Dave Bancroft and Bill Cunningham to the Boston Braves for Bill Southworth and Joe Oeschger. He was the regular right fielder for the cellar-dwelling Braves in 1924, but by 1925 his playing days in the majors were over. In 1926 he was hired to manage the Toledo Mud Hens of the minor leagues, but he lost that job in 1931 when the team went bankrupt and into receivership. In December 1931 he was hired as a coach for the Brooklyn Dodgers and on February 23, 1923 he took over as the Dodger manager from the fired Max Carey. His greatest thrill of that first year was beating the Giants in the final series of the season and thus gaining revenge for a comment Giants manager Bill Terry had made earlier in the year ("Is Brooklyn still in the league?"). Casey struggled with the Dodgers for three years, with a sixth-place finish in 1934, a fifth-place finish in 1935, and a seventh-place finish in 1936. Years later, he mused, "Brooklyn, that borough of churches and bad ball clubs, many of which I had."

Stengel was fired by Brooklyn at the end of the 1936 season and in 1938 was named manager of the Boston Braves, then called the Bees. He managed the team for six years from 1938 through 1943, never finishing higher than fifth place (in his first year there). He was let go in spring 1944 and went back to managing in the minor leagues. He took over the Milwaukee Brewers (American Association) in 1944 and led them to a first-place finish. Quitting there in 1945, he took over Kansas City of the American Association and led them to a seventh-place finish before he was pushed out of that job. Taking over Oakland (Pacific Coast League), whose GM was George Weiss, in 1946, Stengel led the Oaks to a second-place finish, a fourth-place finish (1947), and a first-place berth (1948).

In 1949 the New York Yankees, whose GM was old friend Weiss, called on Casey to take over the managerial reins from Bucky Harris. At a press conference, Casey summed up his naivete with the

outfielder Possum Whitted. He played right field until, on July 1, 1921, he was traded to the New York Giants along with infielder Johnny Rawlings and pitcher Red Causey for outfielder Goldie Rapp, outfielder Lee King, and outfielder Lance Richbourg. He was ecstatic that he would be playing under the skilled hands of John McGraw, who comment, "This is a big job, fellows, and I barely have had time to study it. In fact, I scarcely know where I am at." The baseball establishment, judging him by his previous failures with bad ballclubs, dismissed Stengel as a clown, but he shocked them with a World Championship; the Yankees had finished third the year before. Stengel went on to make it five consecutive World Championships, a record not only for World Championships, but even for pennants, breaking McGraw's consecutive-pennants record set from 1921 to 1924, with Stengel on that team for the first three years. Stengel began to use an extensive platooning strategy that was soon emulated elsewhere, although never with the same complexity. He took the idea from the way Robinson and then McGraw had platooned Stengel himself years before.

Stengel had inherited a team already considered a powerhouse that included the immortal Joe DiMaggio. Within three years he had remade it into a completely different type of ballclub. Rather than featuring superstars at most every position, Stengel built his team around just three: Mickey Mantle, Yogi Berra, and Whitey Ford. Mantle in particular was a special project of Stengel's; the manager wanted his protege's fame to exceed that of any other player and reflect credit on Stengel himself. The rest of the team consisted of role-players, many of whom would have preferred to be regulars; Stengel had them compete against each other for playing time, which drove them to perform at their highest level whenever they were in the game. Some players found it hard to take; Hank Bauer and Gene Woodling in particular chafed under their restricted playing time. Stengel once said, "The secret of managing is to keep the five guys who hate you away from the five who are undecided." But some of his players worshiped him, in particular Billy Martin. Stengel treated the scrappy second baseman like a son, and later, when in Oakland for Stengel's funeral, Martin slept in Stengel's bed overnight.

It has been said of Stengel that he never established a pitching rotation in his 12 seasons with the Yankees. He was protective of Ford to the point that Whitey didn't get enough starts to win 20 games until 1961, when new manager Ralph Houk gave him the 39 starts that were normal for a staff ace; only in 1955 had Ford's starts exceeded 30. The Big Four of Stengel's best staff, Ford, Vic Raschi, Allie Reynolds, and Ed Lopat, were all used in relief.

The Yankees finished in second place in 1954 despite their most wins under Stengel (103); Al Lopez's Indians set the AL wins record that season

with 111. Lopez was a catcher for Stengel in 1934 at Brooklyn. In 1955 the Yankees were back on top and continued winning AL pennants in 1956, 1957 and 1958. In 1958 he was involved in perhaps his most famous off-field incident. On July 9 he was called in front of the Senate Subcommittee on Antitrust and Monopoly to testify on why baseball should be exempt from antitrust regulation. He gave an hour's worth of classic Stengelese to the baffled and amused politicians. After Stengel left the stand, Mantle was asked to testify. "My views are about the same as Casey's," he replied with a straight face.

The Yankees finished third in 1959 to the White Sox, managed, like the 1954 Indians, by Al Lopez. In 1960 New York finished on top again, only to lose the World Series to the Pittsburgh Pirates and Bill Mazeroski. The Yankees fired Stengel a few days later for being too old. "I'll never make the mistake of being seventy again," Casey quipped. His friend Weiss was also fired. In the 12 years that Stengel had managed the Yankees, he set records, including the most years as a championship manager in the American League (10); the most consecutive first-place finishes (5); the most World Series games managed (63); and the most World Series wins (37). He won seven World Championships: 1949–53, 1956, and 1958.

However, the Stengel story was not over. In 1962 he was named manager of the newly founded New York Mets, and George Weiss was named GM. Stengel said, "It's great to be back in the Polar Grounds again with the New York Knickerbockers." The 1962 Mets went on to become one of the worst teams in baseball history, finishing with a 40–120 record. Some 1962-vintage quotes: "Can't anybody here play this game?" "Look at him. He can't hit, he can't run and he can't throw. That's why they gave him to us." The Mets became quite popular despite, or perhaps because of, their ineptness, and Stengel skillfully distracted the press with his endless string of witticisms. Comedian George Gobel said of Stengel, "If he turned pro, he'd put us all out of business."

Stengel managed until mid-1965, when a broken hip forced him to retire a week before his 75th birthday. He spent his retirement working in a bank in Glendale, California with a sign on his desk that read, "Stengelese Spoken Here." He died on September 29, 1975. His career was summed up perfectly by The Old Professor himself: "There comes a time in every man's life and I've had plenty of them."/(AJA)

Dave Stenhouse — 1933- . RHP 1962-64 **Senators** 372 ip, 16-28, 4.14
☞ *All-Star—62.*

Stenhouse was a 28-year-old rookie sensation for Washington in 1962. With a 10-4 mark at mid-season, he was selected the AL's starting pitcher in the year's second All-Star Game, and allowed one earned run in two innings. But he went 1-8 in the second half to finish 11-12. Over his two remaining seasons, he compiled a 5-16 record. A University of Rhode Island graduate, he became Brown University's baseball coach. His son Mike was an outfielder with the Expos, Twins, and Red Sox, while another son, Dave, was signed as a catcher by the Blue Jays. /(RTM)

Rennie Stennett — 1951- . 2B-SS 1971-81 **Pirates,** Giants 1237 g, .274, 41 hr, 432 rbi. *4 LCS, 13 g, .196, 1 rbi. 1 WS, 1 g, 1.000*

On September 16, 1975, Stennett became the only player in the 20th century to collect seven hits in a nine-inning game, going 7-for-7 in a 22-0 rout of the Cubs. Stennett was good enough to beat out Dave Cash and Willie Randolph for the Pirates' second base job. The strong-armed Panamanian was used frequently at shortstop and in the outfield in 1972 and 1973 before Pittsburgh traded Cash to make room at second base. Stennett responded by leading NL second basemen in both putouts and total chances per game (and did it again in 1976) while batting .291 with 84 runs. He just missed Ken Hubbs's record of 418 consecutive errorless chances, falling short by eight.

The contact hitter had his best season in 1977, finishing second to teammate Dave Parker in the batting race with a .336 mark while stealing 28 bases, both personal highs. He never hit above .250 thereafter, however, and was pushed out of the 2B job by Phil Garner. Stennett was signed by the Giants to a big free agent contract after the 1979 season, but was replaced by Joe Morgan in 1981. /(WOR)

Bryan Stephens — 1920- . RHP 1947-48 Indians, **Browns** 214 ip, 8-16, 5.16

Stephens was one of the Detroit farmhands declared free agents by Commissioner Landis after the 1940 season, when Landis was cracking down on minor league rule violations. He lost the ring finger on his nonpitching hand during WWII military service. /(NLM)

Gene Stephens — 1933- . OF 1952-53, 55-64 **Red Sox**, Orioles, A's, White Sox 964 g, .240, 37 hr, 207 rbi

On June 18, 1953, Stephens had three hits in one inning against the Tigers, but he spent his most promising ML years as a late-inning substitute for Ted Williams and was often called Williams's "caddy." From 1955 through 1959, he averaged nearly 120 games per season but only 1.67 at-bats per game. Even after being traded to the Orioles in 1960 (Williams's final season), he never became a ML regular. /(JK)

Jim Stephens (Little Nemo) — 1883-1965. C 1907-12 **Browns** 427 g, .227, 3 hr, 97 rbi

In his most active season (96 games caught), Stephens led his AL peers in assists, double plays, total chances per game, and fielding average. His weak bat made him a backup for most of his career. /(SFS)

Vern Stephens (Junior, Buster) — 1920-1965. SS-3B 1941-55 **Browns**, Red Sox, White Sox, Orioles 1720 g, .286, 247 hr, 1174 rbi. *1 WS, 6 g, .227*
☞ *Led League—hr 45. Led League—rbi 44, 49-50. All-Star—43-44, 46, 48-51.*

Stephens was the best homer-hitting shortstop until the appearance of Ernie Banks. His glove was reliable, but his bat made him a seven-time All-Star. Hitting behind Ted Williams for five years with the Red Sox, he formed half of the best one-two punch in the AL.

Vern signed with the Browns for a $500 bonus at age 17. By the time he was 21, he was the regular St. Louis shortstop. In 1944, when the Browns won their only pennant, he led the AL in RBI and finished third in the MVP voting behind Tiger pitcher Hal Newhouser. In 1945 Stephens led the AL in homers with 24. The next year, he narrowly missed a suspension from organized baseball. He signed a five-year, $175,000 contract to play in the outlaw Mexican League of the Pasqual brothers. He had been in Mexico only a few days when his father, a minor league umpire, and Browns scout Jack Fournier drove down and brought him back. Fearing the Pasquals might try to stop him, he exchanged clothes with his father and walked across the International Bridge. Those players who stayed behind in Mexico were suspended by Commissioner Chandler, and only a few were eventually able to pick up their careers at their presuspension level.

After the 1947 season, he and pitcher Jack Kramer were traded to the Red Sox for six players and $310,000. His first three seasons in Boston were the best of his career. He smashed 29, 39, and 30 home runs and drove in 137, 159, and 144 runs, the last two marks leading the AL.

Limited in range as a shortstop, he made up for it with good hands and a strong arm. He led AL shortstops in assists three times and double plays once. In 1948 he tied a ML record for double plays by a shortstop with five in one game. From 1952 on, he played mostly third base, and, hampered by injuries, his hitting declined. /(NLM)

Earl Stephenson — 1947– . LHP 1971–72, 77–78 Cubs, **Brewers**, Orioles 113 ip, 4–5, 3.59

Stephenson's best season was 1972, when he went 3–5 with a 3.26 ERA for the Brewers as a starter and reliever. He never saw much other action. /(SFS)

Jerry Stephenson — 1943– . LHP 1963, 65–70 **Red Sox**, Pilots, Dodgers 238 ip, 8–19, 5.69. *1 WS, 2 ip, 0–0, 9.00*

The son of former ML catcher Joe Stephenson, Jerry played parts of seven ML seasons, but only in 1968 (2–8) did he pitch in more than 15 games. /(NLM)

Joe Stephenson — 1921– . C 1943–44, 47 Giants, Cubs, **White Sox** 29 g, .179, 0 hr, 4 rbi

As a Red Sox scout since 1950, Stephenson has been instrumental in unearthing talent for Boston's productive farm system. He has signed or discovered numerous ML players, including Fred Lynn, Bill Lee, Rick Burleson, Dwight Evans, and his own son, Jerry Stephenson. /(FVP)

Johnny Stephenson — 1941– . C-3B Mets, Cubs, Giants, **Angels** 451 g, .216, 12 hr, 93 rbi

Stephenson struck out as a Mets pinch hitter for the last out of Jim Bunning's Father's Day 1964 perfect game. Stephenson was a backup catcher for most of his career, seeing the most action in 1972 with the Angels and batting .219 with 25 RBI in 279 at-bats. /(JFC)

Riggs Stephenson (Old Hoss) — 1898–1985. OF-2B-3B 1921–34 Indians, **Cubs** 1310 g, .336, 63 hr, 773 rbi. *2 WS, 9 g, .378, 7 rbi*

Stephenson batted .319 or better in 12 of his 14 major league seasons, but was poor defensively. Signed as a second baseman, he had a weak arm that kept him from playing regularly in his five years with Cleveland (1921–25). Converted to the outfield during a stint in the minors, he still had to depend on his potent bat to keep him in the Cubs' lineup. His throwing difficulties were the result of a shoulder

injury sustained while playing football at the University of Alabama. It hindered him on pivot throws at second base, and, during one season in the Cubs outfield, he had only one assist. In 1927, his first full season with Chicago, he led the NL with 46 doubles. In the Cubs' 1929 pennant-winning year, he combined with Hall of Famers Hack Wilson and Kiki Cuyler in the only outfield in NL history in which each member had more than 100 RBI. (Stephenson 110, Wilson 159, Cuyler 102). Arm and leg injuries forced him to leave the Cubs in 1934, but he played and managed in the minors through 1939. /(JK)

Chuck Stevens [Charles Augustus] — 1918– . 1B 1941, 46, 48 **Browns** 211 g, .251, 4 hr, 55 rbi

A good fielder who lacked home run power, Stevens spent 23 years in organized baseball but only three seasons in the ML. As the Browns' regular first baseman in 1946, he hit a soft .248. After his retirement as a player, he served for many years as secretary-treasurer of the Association of Professional Ball Players of America. /(DB)

Ed Stevens (Big Ed) — 1925– . 1B 1945–50 Dodgers, **Pirates** 375 g, .252, 28 hr, 193 rbi

Stevens played well in 55 games as a Dodger rookie in 1945, and was platooned in 1946. But when Jackie Robinson debuted in 1947 at first base, Stevens was sent down. Purchased by the Pirates, he led NL first basemen in fielding in 1948, but poor offense cut short his career. /(ME)

Harry M. Stevens — 1856–1934. Concessionaire.

This London-born caterer to crowds at racetracks, ball parks, and arenas began by selling scorecards in Ohio. He moved to New York and won the right to sell scorecards at the Polo Grounds, which led to handling all concessions. When the grandstand burned in 1911, he advanced the money to John T. Brush to rebuild it. His company eventually operated concessions from New York to Mexico. /(NLM)

John Stevens — 1912–1981. *Umpire* AL 1958–71 *6 ASU 4 WS*

After 14 years as an AL umpire, Stevens worked as a roving supervisor of league umpires until his death. He also worked as a NBA official. During the 1950 season, Stevens thumbed the Yankees' Johnny Lindell out of a game in a "delayed call." It seems Johnny made some unkind remarks from the bench, and Stevens booted him, but did not notice that Lindell remained on the bench. For his part, Lindell did not realize he'd been banished from a game he wasn't playing in, and was surprised a few days later when he received word from the AL office of his $25 fine./(RTM)

Bill Stewart — 1895-1964. *Umpire* NL 1933-54
4 ASU 4 WS

Two incidents stand out in Stewart's umpiring career. He was the plate umpire at Brooklyn the night Johnny Vander Meer of Cincinnati pitched his second consecutive no-hitter on June 15, 1938. And as the second base umpire in the first game of the 1948 WS, Stewart made a controversial safe call on the Braves' Phil Masi when Bob Feller and Lou Boudreau tried a pickoff play; Masi later scored the only run of the game.

In addition to his work as a baseball umpire, Stewart served nine years as a referee in the NHL. During the 1937-38 hockey season, he coached the Chicago Black Hawks to a Stanley Cup championship. He also coached the hockey team at M.I.T. for seven years./(RTM)

Bob Stewart (Stewsie) — 1915- . *Umpire* AL 1959-70
2 ASU 2 WS

Stewart umpired 12-1/2 years, mostly in the American Association, before making it to the majors. He hated the inside chest protector and advocated a return to the balloon protector long and often around the league./(RTM)

Bud Stewart [Edward Perry] — 1916- . OF 1941-42, 48-54 Pirates, Yankees, **Senators**, White Sox 773 g, .268, 32 hr, 260 rbi

Stewart led the NL in pinch hits (10) as a Pirate rookie, but he slumped the next season and blamed Pirate manager Frankie Frisch's constant carping. After three years in the military and time in the minors, he returned to the ML at 31 in 1948 with the Yankees, who traded him to the Senators after six games. After three years in Washington, he was traded to the White Sox, where he led the AL in pinch hits (9) in 1951./(NLM)

Bunky Stewart [Veston Goff] — 1931- . LHP 1952-56 **Senators** 187 ip, 5-11, 6.01

After parts of four seasons as the tenth man on the staff of the pitching-poor Senators, Stewart threw 105 innings in 1956. He won only four in relief and never returned to the ML./(NLM)

Dave Stewart (Smoke) — 1957- . RHP 1978, 81-Dodgers, Rangers, Phillies, **A's** 1561 ip, 101-74, 3.68. 20 wins: 87-89 *2 LCS, 29 ip, 3-0, 2.15. 3 WS, 32 ip, 2-1, 2.25*

☛ *Led League—w 87. All-Star—89.*

Overcoming physical and personal problems, Dave Stewart became a star in his native Oakland. Originally signed as a catcher by the Dodgers, the hard-throwing Smoke pitched well, in limited use, with Los Angeles, but struggled with Texas and Philadelphia. He earned some respect by successfully fending off a karate kick by Indians manager Pat Corrales, then flattening him, during a brawl on July 1, 1986. Encouraged that year by A's coach Dave Duncan to add a forkball to his fastball and slider, Stewart became a Cy Young Award candidate in 1987. He led the club in wins, strikeouts, innings pitched, complete games, and starts, becoming the second Oakland A's pitcher (with Vida Blue) to notch a 200-strikeout season. Preferring to pitch in hot weather, Stewart keyed the A's successful pennant effort in 1988 with his second straight 20-win season and became a respected team leader in the Oakland community. On September 22, 1989 Stewart's 100th career victory made him the only pitcher of the 1980s with three consecutive 20-win seasons. He won two games in both the LCS and the World Series that year, the only man ever to do so, and was the WS MVP./(ME)

Jimmy Stewart (Little Stew) — 1939- . OF-2B-SS-3B 1963-73 **Cubs**, Reds, Astros 777 g, .237, 8 hr, 112 rbi. *1 LCS, 2 g, .000. 1 WS, 1 g, .000*

Stewart was a pesky switch-hitter whose aggressiveness was as big an asset as his speed. After Ken Hubbs's death in 1964, Stewart was his replacement at second base but played just 61 games there, serving as a handyman the remainder of his career./(JCA)

Lefty Stewart [Walter Cleveland] — 1900-1974. LHP 1921, 27-35 Tigers, **Browns**, Senators, Indians 1712 ip, 100-98, 4.19. 20 wins: 30 *1 WS, 2 ip, 0-1, 9.00*

Stewart nearly died in 1927 when his appendix burst while he was on a winter hunting trip. Although he recovered, he was told his career was over. Browns manager Dan Howley, for whom he'd pitched in the minors, gave Stewart a chance with St. Louis. In 1930 he was 20-12 for the fifth-place Browns, with five wins over the second-place Senators. Washington acquired Stewart in a 1933 trade that also brought Goose Goslin back to the capital. When the Senators won the 1933 pennant, Stewart, 15–6 on the season, started but lost the opening game of the WS. /(NLM)

Sammy Stewart — 1954– . RHP 1978–87 **Orioles**, Red Sox, Indians 957 ip, 59–48, 3.59. *1 LCS, 4 ip, 0–0, 0.00. 2 WS, 8 ip, 0–0, 0.00*

Stewart fanned seven consecutive Indians in his ML debut September 1, 1978, and was an effective middle reliever for the Orioles for seven seasons, posting a career-high 13 saves in 1984. He was traded to the Red Sox for Jackie Gutierrez in December 1985. /(SCL)

Dave Stieb (Sir David) — 1957– . RHP 1979– **Blue Jays** 2458 ip, 148–117, 3.37. *2 LCS, 32 ip, 1–3, 4.26*
☛ *Led League—era 85. All-Star—80–81, 83–85, 88.*

Originally signed as an outfielder, Stieb made rapid progress through the Blue Jays' system as a pitcher. He finished second on the team in wins (8) in 1979 despite breaking in midway through the season. With an 11–10 record in 1981, Stieb became the first starting pitcher for the expansion Blue Jays with a winning record, and in 1982 he was named *TSN* AL Pitcher of the Year, with a 17–14 record and a 3.25 ERA. He has also been a very good fielder. Stieb was among league leaders in innings pitched, complete games, and ERA consistently while the Jays were making the transition from an expansion team to a contender. He was outspoken in his frustration about his teammates' capabilities, often asking to be traded. He glowered at teammates who made errors and at umpires whose calls he disliked.

Despite his talent, Stieb has never had an impressive won-lost record (although no Blue Jay pitcher has won more games), and he has shown a tendency to self-destruct late in close games as well as to lose his concentration after temper tantrums. On August 24, 1985, he had a no-hitter through eight innings, then surrendered consecutive home runs to slap-hitters Rudy Law and Bryan Little in the ninth.

Stieb had a team-record streak of 26 scoreless innings in 1985 and led the AL with a 2.48 ERA, the fifth consecutive season he was Blue Jay team leader in ERA. Stieb also led the Blue Jays in innings pitched every season from 1981 through 1985, and led the AL in 1984.

Perhaps chastened by his 7–12 record and 4.74 ERA in 1986, Stieb announced he had become a born-again Christian early in the 1987 season. He regained his form in 1988, posting a 3.04 ERA while going 16–8. Stieb pitched a one-hitter against the Brewers in May, allowing only a single to B.J. Surhoff, and in his last two starts of the season he was one strike away from a no-hitter, only to settle for one-hitters each time. Julio Franco spoiled the first bid with a bad-bounce grounder past the second baseman, and Jim Traber ruined the second with a clean single to right. In his second start of 1989, Stieb one-hit the Yankees, giving him three one-hitters in four starts. /(TF)

Dick Stigman — 1936– . LHP 1960–66 Indians, **Twins**, Red Sox 922 ip, 46–54, 4.03
☛ *All-Star—60.*

The aloof Stigman was an All-Star as a hard-throwing, 6'3" rookie with Cleveland in 1960, though he finished the season 5–11. He won a career-high 15 games for Minnesota in 1963. /(JCA)

Rollie Stiles — 1906– . RHP 1930–31, 33 **Browns** 298 ip, 9–14, 5.91

Stiles had three trials with the Browns but was returned to the minors each time after winning three games. His best ERA was 5.01. /(NLM)

Kurt Stillwell — 1965– . SS-2B 1986– Reds, **Royals** 493 g, .252, 21 hr, 166 rbi

Ron Stillwell had a brief stint with the Senators, but his son was destined for a longer big league stay. Kurt progressed through the Reds' system with another promising shortstop, Barry Larkin, both vying to succeed Dave Concepcion. Although Stillwell performed well, the Reds traded him to the Royals, who were desperate for an everyday shortstop, in return for Danny Jackson. Stillwell responded in 1988 with his best year offensively while holding his errors to 13. /(FO)

Bob Stinson [Gorrell Robert] — 1945– . C 1969–80 Dodgers, Cardinals, Astros, Expos, Royals, **Mariners** 652 g, .250, 33 hr, 180 rbi. *1 LCS, 2 g, .000*

Nicknamed Scrap Iron because he played with pain, Stinson had been a reserve for eight ML years when, in 1977, he became the Mariners' first Opening Day catcher. The switch-hitter set an AL record the next year by reaching first six times on catcher's interference. /(JCA)

Snuffy Stirnweiss [George Henry] — 1918–1958. 2B-3B 1943–52 **Yankees**, Browns, Indians 1028 g, .268, 29 hr, 281 rbi. *3 WS, 9 g, .250, 3 rbi*
☛ *Led League—ba 45.*

Stirnweiss, a star college football halfback at North Carolina, was the outstanding AL second baseman during WWII when gastric ulcers and hay fever kept him out of the service. He led the league in hits, doubles, and runs in both 1944 and 1945. On the morning of the last day of the 1945 season, Chicago's Tony Cuccinello led the AL with a .308 BA; Stirnweiss was at .306. The White Sox were rained out. Stirnweiss had two hits and was given a third when the New York official scorer reversed an error ruling, to win the batting title at .3085 to Cuccinello's .3077. Stirnweiss's legs gave out when he was 30 and he retired at 33./(NLM)

Jack Stivetts (Happy Jack) — 1868–1930. RHP 1889–99 St. Louis (AA), **Braves**, Cleveland (NL) 2886 ip, 207–131, 3.74. 20 wins: 90–92, 94, 96
☛ *Led League—era 89. Led League—k 91.*

Stivetts was a star pitcher and power hitter before the turn of the century. He played more than 200 games at field positions in addition to a heavy mound load, and had a career average of .297 with 35 homers. Three times he hit two homers in a game.

Among the many players of his time to hail from the Pennsylvania anthracite coal fields, he joined the St. Louis Browns of the American Association in 1889, and led the league in ERA in his first year. In 1891 he went 33–22 and led in both strikeouts and walks. When the AA dissolved, he joined Boston of the NL, and combined with Hall of Famer Kid Nichols to give them the league's best one-two pitching punch. Nichols was a control artist, while Stivetts was a power pitcher. Jack won 35 games for Boston in 1892, including a no-hitter. They took the team to pennants in 1892 and 1893. In the latter year, Stivetts fell off to 19 wins, as he had trouble adjusting to the new pitching distance of 60'6". In 1894 he bounced back with 28 wins./(JK)

Chuck Stobbs — 1929– . LHP 1947–61 Red Sox, White Sox, **Senators/Twins**, Cardinals 1920 ip, 107–130, 4.29

On April 7, 1953, Stobbs threw the pitch that Mickey Mantle hit out of Griffith Stadium for his famous 565-foot home run. A regular winner with Boston, he registered a career-high 15 wins for the Senators in 1956. In 1957 Stobbs dropped his first 11 decisions; he changed his uniform number to 13, and on June 21, fans came to Griffith Stadium with rabbits' feet and other lucky charms to help him end the jinx. It worked for that one day, but before the season ended, Stobbs had become Washington's first 20-game loser since 1916, when Walter Johnson went 25–20./(JCA)

Milt Stock — 1893–1977. 3B-2B-SS 1913–26 Giants, Phillies, **Cardinals**, Dodgers 1628 g, .289, 22 hr, 696 rbi. *1 WS, 5 g, .118*

Stock became a regular with the 1916 Phillies, taking over third base from a slumping Bobby Byrne. Just 5'8", he had little power, but ran well and rarely struck out. In 1919 he was traded to the Cardinals and became their sixth regular third basemen since 1913. He solidified a good infield, and ran off four straight .300 seasons. In 1920 he led the NL with 639 at-bats.

On the last day of the 1950 season, the Dodgers, one game out of first, blew a chance for the pennant when Brooklyn's Cal Abrams was thrown out at the plate by Phillies outfielder Richie Ashburn in the ninth inning of a tie game. Stock was the third base coach who waved Abrams home. He was fired several days later and never again coached in the majors./(FJO)

Wes Stock — 1934– . RHP 1959–67 **Orioles**, A's 517 ip, 27–13, 3.60

Although his career save total was not outstanding (22), Stock compiled excellent win-loss marks in relief with the Orioles. He was 5–0 in 1961 and went 100 games from July 1962 to July 1964 without a defeat, including 7–0 in 1963. He later became a successful pitching coach. /(FK)

J. Roy Stockton — Unk.–Unk. *Writer.*

Stockton quit Washington University (St. Louis) to cover the 1917 Jack Johnson-Jess Willard boxing match for the St. Louis *Post-Dispatch* and remained with that paper until he retired in 1958, serving as sports editor from 1946. Respected for his integrity, he was president of the BBWAA in 1931. Stockton wrote many profiles for *The Saturday Evening Post*; his book, *The Gashouse Gang and a Couple of Other Guys*, was published in 1945. In 1921 he was part of the first remote radio coverage of a golf tournament, the U.S. Amateur in St. Louis, and he broadcast an evening sports program on radio for 15 years. After his retirement, he became president of the Florida State League. He received the J.G. Taylor Spink Award from the Hall of Fame in 1972./(NLM)

Bob Stoddard — 1957– . RHP 1981–87 **Mariners**, Tigers, Padres, Royals 434 ip, 18–27, 4.03

Stoddard was a failed starting pitcher who was unsuccessfully converted to relief by the Mariners. He had short tours of duty with three teams in his last three seasons./(WOR)

Tim Stoddard — 1953- . RHP 1975, 78-88 White Sox, **Orioles**, Cubs, Padres, Yankees, Indians 729 ip, 41-35, 3.95. *1 LCS, 2 ip, 0-0, 4.50. 1 WS, 5 ip, 1-0, 5.40*

The 6'7" Stoddard started at forward for North Carolina State's 1974 NCAA basketball champions. He was originally signed by the White Sox in 1975, but was released after two minor league seasons. Stoddard reached the ML for good in 1979, posting a 1.71 ERA in 29 appearances for the AL champion Orioles. He had an RBI single in the World Series against the Pirates, the first player ever to drive in a WS run in his very first ML at-bat. In 1980 he led the Orioles with 26 saves. Stoddard shared the Orioles closer role with lefthander Tippy Martinez from 1981 to 1983, but in 1983 his ERA was 6.09, and he was traded twice before the 1984 season, first to Oakland and then to the Cubs. Stoddard won 10 games and saved 7 in his one season with the Cubs, then signed with the Padres in 1985, and was traded to the Yankees for Ed Whitson in July 1986. In New York, Stoddard was mostly a set-up man for Dave Righetti, and was released in August 1988 with a 6.38 ERA. Stoddard never started a game in 12 ML seasons. /(SCL)

Dean Stone [Darragh Dean] — 1930- . LHP 1953-57, 59, 62-63 **Senators**, Red Sox, Cardinals, Astros, White Sox, Orioles 686 ip, 29-39, 4.47

 All-Star—54.

Stone, a 6'4" 205-lb pitcher, won a career-high 12 games for Washington in 1954, his rookie season. He was the winning pitcher in that year's All-Star Game, though he did not officially face a single batter. He came in with two outs in the eighth, the AL down 9-8, and Red Schoendienst on third. Schoendienst tried to steal home, and Stone nailed him at the plate. When the AL scored three runs in the next half-inning, Stone was the winning pitcher. /(JCA)

George Stone — 1877-1945. OF 1903, 05-10 Red Sox, **Browns** 848 g, .301, 23 hr, 268 rbi

Stone led the AL in hits (187) in 1905 and the next year edged Nap Lajoie for the batting title with .358. After that, he declined and, not a brilliant fielder, dropped out of the majors. He later owned the Lincoln, NB, team and became a minor league president. /(JK)

George Stone — 1946- . LHP **Braves**, Mets 1020 ip, 60-57, 3.89. *2 LCS, 8 ip, 0-0, 2.35. 1 WS, 3 ip, 0-0, 0.00*

Stone was a journeyman starter for the Braves who was acquired by the Mets in November 1972, after his worst season (6-11, 5.51), along with Felix Millan in exchange for Gary Gentry and Dan Frisella. The trade was vital to the Mets' surprise 1973 NL pennant. Stone was 12-3 with a 2.80 ERA in that season, his best, and won eight straight decisions at the end of the year as the Mets vaulted from last to first. He made up for an incident the previous season, when his pitch broke Rusty Staub's hand, depriving the contending Mets of their best hitter for the balance of the season. In Game Three of the 1973 LCS, Stone pitched six innings of shutout ball, but then surrendered a solo homer to Tony Perez, tying the game, which was won by the Reds in the 12th inning. He was never effective again, posting ERAs above 5.00 the next two seasons before he was released. /(SFS)

Jeff Stone — 1960- . OF 1983-89 **Phillies**, Orioles, Red Sox 362 g, .277, 11 hr, 71 rbi

A swift outfielder who showed great promise, Stone never developed as the Phillies hoped. Recalled from Portland in late 1984, he hit .362 and stole 27 bases in 51 games with the Phillies, but succeeding seasons featured more strikeouts than stolen bases, and long stints at the Triple-A level. He was traded to Baltimore in 1988, but spent most of the season with the Rochester Red Wings. /(SG)

John Stone (Rocky) — 1905-1955. OF 1928-38 **Tigers**, Senators 1198 g, .310, 77 hr, 707 rbi

Stone hit .300 seven times and was so highly thought of that the Senators traded Hall of Famer Goose Goslin straight-up for him in December 1933. He was one season removed from his career year, 1932, when he hit .297 with personal highs of 17 HR, 35 doubles, 108 RBI, and 106 runs, not particularly remarkable totals at the time. Goslin went on to help the Tigers to a pennant in 1934 while the Senators, who had won in 1933, dropped to seventh place. The only time the lefthanded-hitting Stone approached the level of his 1932 statistics again was in 1936, when he hit .341 with 15 HR, 90 RBI, and 95 runs. An illness in 1938 ended his major league career.

In his first season as a regular, 1930, Stone had a 34-game hitting streak, which at the time tied him with George Sisler for the fourth-longest streak in AL history. On May 30, 1933, he hit two HR and four doubles in a doubleheader; he was the first player to have six extra-base hits in a doubleheader without extra innings (five others have since matched him). /(JFC)

Ron Stone — 1942- . OF 1966, 69–72 A's, **Phillies** 388 g, .241, 6 hr, 89 rbi

Stone was a fourth outfielder and a less-than-successful pinch hitter in four seasons with the Phillies (1969–72). He hit a career-high .262 in 1970, with 39 RBI in 321 at-bats. /(SFS)

Steve Stone — 1947- . RHP 1971–81 Giants, **White Sox**, Cubs, Orioles 1789 ip, 107–93, 3.96, 20 wins: 80 *1 WS, 2 ip, 0–0, 9.00*
☛ *Led League—w 80. Cy Young Award—80. All-Star—80.*

Baseball's "galloping gourmet," a restaurateur, published poet, chess player, and table-tennis whiz, Stone was Thurman Munson's batterymate at Kent State and a mediocre pitcher who never won more than 15 games until his tenth ML season, when he went 25–7 for Baltimore to capture the 1980 AL Cy Young Award. He pitched three perfect innings in the All-Star Game that year, and led the AL in victories and winning percentage (.781). A flame-thrower with the Giants, Stone had arm trouble and became a control pitcher. He joined Baltimore as a free agent in 1979, found a "metaphysical" approach to the game, switched his uniform to Koufax's 32, and helped the Orioles to a pennant. He became a Cub broadcaster in 1983. /(JCA)

Bill Stoneman (Stoney) — 1944- . RHP 1967–74 Cubs, **Expos**, Angels 1237 ip, 54–85, 4.08
☛ *All-Star—72.*

Stoneman was selected by the Expos in the expansion draft and quickly established himself as their ace starter. He tossed a 7–0 no-hitter at Philadelphia on April 17, 1969 in his fifth major league start. He finished the year 11–19, 4.39, the only pitcher on the staff with more than seven wins, but led the NL in walks. He also established a record as the easiest pitcher to strike out, fanning 55 times in 73 at-bats that year, 75 percent of the time; he hit just .086 for his career. Stoneman dropped to 7–15 in 1970, but had his best season in 1971, going 17–16 (his only winning record) with a 3.14 ERA, tying for the NL lead in starts, and leading again in walks.

Stoneman threw his second no-hitter on October 2, 1972, a 7–0 victory over the Mets in which he walked eight; it was the first major league no-hitter pitched outside the United States. He was 12–14 with a 2.98 ERA that year, but declined thereafter. When he was sold to the Angels at the start of 1974, he was the Expos' team leader in wins (51), shutouts (15), and strikeouts (851); he still holds the team record for strikeouts in a season (251 in 1971). He

went on to work his way up through the Expos' front office and became general manager in 1987. /(SH)

Lil Stoner [Ulysses Simpson Grant] — 1899–1966. RHP 1922–31 **Tigers**, Pirates, Phillies 1004 ip, 50–58, 4.76

Stoner won 27 games in the Texas League in 1923, including a no-hitter, an 18-strikeout game, and a 13-inning shutout. He won his ML career-high 11 games in 1924, and pitched unspectacularly for Detroit through 1929. /(JK)

Mel Stottlemyre — 1941- . RHP 1964–74 **Yankees** 2662 ip, 164–139, 2.97. 20 wins: 65, 68, 69 *1 WS, 20 ip, 1–1, 3.15*
☛ *All-Star—65, 66, 68–70.*

Called up from Richmond in midsummer 1964 for the pennant race, the sinkerballer went 9–3 to help the Yankees win their fifth consecutive AL pennant. In the World Series against the Cardinals, he won Game Two with a complete-game 8–3 victory and pitched well in Game Five, surrendering two runs in seven innings for a no-decision. But, coming back on two days' rest (ace Whitey Ford had arm trouble), Stottlemyre lost the final game when he surrendered three runs in the fourth inning.

Even as the Yankee dynasty collapsed around him in 1965, Stottlemyre went 20–9, leading the AL in innings and complete games. He led the league with 20 losses in 1966, and tied for the lead with 18 losses in 1972, his only losing seasons before his final campaign. Through the Yankees' fallow period he remained the classy, reliable staff ace and had two more 20-win seasons (1968–69), serving as one of the team's few ties to a more successful era. He pitched at least 250 innings in each of his nine full seasons. A torn rotator cuff forced his retirement in 1974, just before the Yankees began a new era.

Stottlemyre is currently the Mets' pitching coach, and supervised the conversion of Dwight Gooden from a pure power pitcher to a wilier and hopefully more durable style. His son Todd pitches for the Blue Jays, and Mel Jr. played in the Mets' farm system. /(TJG)

Todd Stottlemyre — 1965- . RHP 1988- **Blue Jays** 226 ip, 11–15, 4.67. *1 LCS, 5 ip, 0–1, 7.20*

The son of Mel Stottlemyre, Sr., Todd has had control problems but won a spot in the Blue Jays' rotation in mid-1989 (7–7, 3.88). /(JFC)

Allyn Stout (Fish Hook) — 1904–1974. RHP 1931–35, 43 **Cardinals**, Reds, Giants, Braves. 457 ip, 20–20, 4.54

After seven years in the Cardinals farm system, Stout contributed a 6–0 record to the 1931 St. Louis pennant drive. In 1935 he left the ML with one more loss than win on his career, but a short wartime stint with the Braves eight years later gave him a single relief win to even his record. /(JK)

George Stovall (Firebrand) — 1878–1951. 1B-2B-3B 1904–15 **Indians**, Browns, Kansas City (FL) 1412 g, .265, 15 hr, 564 rbi.
   Manager 1911–15 Indians, Browns, **Kansas City (FL)** 313–376, .454

Hot-tempered George Stovall played more games at first base for the Indians than anyone but Hal Trosky. His fine scoop of third baseman Bill Bradley's low throw saved, and ended, Addie Joss's perfect game in 1908. The Cleveland captain engineered a one-day "strike" in 1911 so the team could attend Joss's funeral in Toledo. Popular with the players, Stovall became Cleveland manager 17 games into the 1911 season, but was sold in January to the Browns, managing them from June 1912 until late in 1913. Stovall was the first star to join the Federal League, and convinced others to follow. He later was president of the Association of Professional Ball Players of America. His brother, pitcher Jesse Stovall, compiled an 8–14 record with the Indians and Tigers in 1903 and 1904. /(ME)

Jesse Stovall (Scout) — 1875–1955. RHP 1903–04 Indians, **Tigers** 204 ip, 8–14, 3.76

The older brother of George Stovall, Jesse started promisingly when he went 5–1 with a 2.05 ERA for the Indians in 1903, but fell off to 3–13, 4.42 after the Tigers acquired him for 1904. /(WOR)

George Stovey — Unk.–Unk. LHP-OF Negro Leagues 1886–96 Jersey City (EL), Newark (IL), Worcester (New England League), Trenton (Mid-Atlantic League), York (Pennsylvania League), Ansonia (Connecticut League), Cuban Giants, New York Gothams, Cuban X-Giants statistics not available

Stovey is considered to have been the first great black pitcher, a 19th-century pioneer. He played for several white clubs before complete segregation in the late 1880s. In 1886 he was the top pitcher for Jersey City (International League), holding opposing hitters to a .167 batting average. He moved to Newark in 1887 and went 34–14, setting a still-standing IL record for wins. He also played the outfield, and hit .255. He was scheduled to pitch an exhibition game against the National League Chicago White Stockings on July 19, but Chicago's Cap Anson refused to take the field. Stovey, feigning illness, withdrew from the game. Apparently, John Ward of the New York NL club tried to buy Stovey in 1887, but Anson again protested so strenuously that the deal died. The color line was drawn in the International League that winter and Newark released Stovey. He went on to play mostly for black teams, and none of his records survive. /(JJM)

Harry Stovey [born Harry Duffield Stowe] — 1856–1937. OF-1B 1880–93 Worcester (NL), **Philadelphia (AA)**, Boston (PL), Braves, Baltimore (NL), Dodgers 1488 g, .301, 120 hr, 518 rbi (907 N/C)
☛ *Led League—ba 84. Led League—hr 80, 83–86, 89. Led League—rbi 89.*

Stovey combined slugging power with great running speed and a strong arm. He was the first to wear sliding pads and among the first to slide feet first. A home run hitter in the dead-ball era, he led his

Harry Stovey

league in homers six times, with a personal high of 19 in 1889. He led in hits twice, doubles once, triples three times, runs four times, batting (.404 in 1884) and stolen bases (97 in 1890) once each. Gentlemanly and articulate in an age when few ballplayers were, he played as Stovey rather than Stowe (his real name) so that his mother would not see his name in box scores. /(JK)

Mike Strahler (Skinny) — 1947- . RHP 1970-73 **Dodgers**, Tigers 159 ip, 6-8, 3.57

Strahler started as a reliever with the Dodgers. Sometimes used as a starter with Detroit in 1973, he had his best season, 4-5 with a 4.39 ERA. His lack of control was his downfall; lifetime, he walked 79 in 159 innings. /(JFC)

Joe Strain — 1954- . 2B-3B 1979-81 **Giants**, Cubs 169 g, .250, 1 hr, 29 rbi

A solid .300 hitter and basestealer in the minor leagues, Strain batted .286 and committed just two errors in 77 games with San Francisco in 1980. Traded to Chicago, he left the majors after hitting .189 in 25 games. /(JCA)

Les Straker — 1959- . RHP 1987-88 **Twins** 237 ip, 10-15, 4.22. *1 LCS, 3 ip, 0-0, 16.88. 1 WS, 9 ip, 0-0, 4.00*

Straker spent 10 full seasons in the minors, including seven in the Reds' organization, before making the Twins as their number-three starter in 1987. He went 8-10, 4.37 that year, and became the first Venezuelan ever to pitch in the WS when he started Games Three and Six. He spent most of 1988 on the DL. /(SCL)

Paul Strand — 1893-1974. OF-LHP 1913-15, 24 **Braves**, A's 115 g, .201, 0 hr, 18 rbi; 95 ip, 7-3, 2.37

As a 20-year-old pitcher, Strand won six games for the Braves in their 1914 "Miracle" pennant drive. He then suffered arm trouble, and became a minor league outfielder. With Salt Lake City (Pacific Coast League) in 1923-24, he hit 71 homers, batting .394 and .384. Philadelphia's Connie Mack bought him for a reported $100,000. When Strand batted .228 in 167 at-bats without a HR, Mack sold him to the minors for virtually nothing. /(NLM)

Sammy Strang [born Samuel Strang Nicklin] (The Dixie Thrush) — 1876-1932. 3B-2B-OF-SS 1896, 1900-08 Louisville (NL), Cubs, **Giants**, White Sox, Dodgers 903 g, .269, 16 hr, 253 rbi. *1 WS, 1 g, .000*

Strang spent several ML seasons as a regular, but in 1905 he was the Giant's main utility man. That season he led the NL with eight pinch hits, and legend says that it was his penchant for "coming through in the pinch" that gave rise to the term "pinch hitter." /(JK)

Alan Strange (Inky) — 1909- . SS 1934-35, 40-42 **Browns**, Senators 314 g, .223, 1 hr, 89 rbi

As the Phillies' bat boy, Strange saved a bat broken by Rogers Hornsby as a memento. In 1934 as manager of the Browns, Hornsby installed Strange as his shortstop. Strange was called Inky because he worked as a printer in the off-season. /(NLM)

Edward Stratemeyer (aka Lester Chadwick) — 1862-1930. *Writer.*

Stratemeyer wrote articles, short stories, and books under many pen names, and in 1906 formed a syndicate that produced 700 books that sold in the millions, including the popular Tom Swift, Hardy Boys, Nancy Drew, and Bobbsey Twins series. Under the name of Lester Chadwick he wrote the Baseball Joe series from 1912 to 1928. /(NLM)

Monty Stratton (Gander) — 1912-1982. RHP 1934-38 **White Sox** 487 ip, 36-23, 3.71 ☛ *All-Star—37.*

Relying primarily on a trick pitch called the "Gander," Stratton posted 15-5 and 15-9 marks for the White Sox in 1937-38 before his major league career was tragically ended at age 26. While he was hunting rabbits near Greenville, Texas in November 1938, his pistol accidentally discharged, sending a bullet into his right knee, severing the femoral artery. The leg was amputated the next day. In 1939 White Sox management sponsored a charity game in Comiskey Park between the Cubs and the White Sox, the proceeds of which (about $28,000) went to Stratton. In a touching, courageous display, Stratton took the mound to demonstrate that he could still pitch, though he was unable to transfer his weight effectively to the artificial leg. After coaching for the White Sox, he was given a minor league contract; in 1946 he posted an 18-8 record in the East Texas League. Stratton's story was made into a fictionalized Hollywood movie starring Jimmy Stewart and June Allyson which was a 1949 box office smash. /(RL)

Darryl Strawberry (The Straw Man) — 1962- . OF
1983- **Mets** 957 g, .260, 215 hr, 625 rbi. *2 LCS, 13 g,
.269, 3 hr, 11 rbi. 1 WS, 7 g, .208, 1 hr, 1 rbi*
☛ *Rookie of the Year—83. Led League—hr 88. All-
Star—84-88.*

Strawberry has never hit fewer than 26 HR in a
season, and he led the NL with 39 in 1988, the year
the ball was supposedly deadened. In 1987, when he
stole a career-high 36 bases and hit 39 HR, he and
Howard Johnson became the first 30–30 teammates
in baseball history. Only once has Strawberry
slugged less than .500, and he led the NL with a .545
slugging average in 1988. He had 100 runs and 100
RBI in both 1987 and 1988. Since his first full
season in 1984 after winning the Rookie of the Year
award in 1983, he has been one of the most popular
players in the country with the All-Star voters,
earning a starting spot every season except 1989,
when he was injured during much of the voting. The
number-one pick in the nation in the June 1980
draft, after his seventh year in the majors his career
was a close match to that of certain Hall of Famer
Reggie Jackson.

Strawberry's home runs are often hit to
centerfield or the other way. The lefthander's big
looping swing, starting with the head of the bat
cocked towards the pitcher, is sometimes slightly
behind the pitch even when he crushes the ball. He
prefers low or outside pitches that he can extend his
arms for. The streaky hitter has never struck out
fewer than 96 times in a season, and that was 1985,
when he played in only 111 games. He draws a lot of
walks and is a fairly patient hitter who learned to
wait for his pitch, but he is poor at protecting the
plate with two strikes and often strikes out looking.
Strawberry has had at least one month each season
when he slumped horribly. When the Mets were
battling the Cubs for the division title in 1984, he
went all of August without a home run. But his hot
streaks have carried the Mets for months at a time,
and his tape-measure home runs earned him the
cleanup spot in the batting order. The Mets for years
have had an apple rise out of a top hat beyond deep
centerfield after home team homers. One of Strawberry's shots went into the hat, jamming the apple.
In a crucial October series against the first-place
Cardinals in 1985, Strawberry hit a tremendous
blast off Ken Dayley that hit the big St. Louis
scoreboard and supposedly broke its clock. He
struck out 12 times, a NLCS record, in 22 at-bats in
the 1986 LCS, but had a three-run homer in the

Mets' 6–5 Game Three triumph. He also had a
game-tying solo shot off Nolan Ryan in New York's
2–1, ten-inning victory in Game Five. His double
leading off the 16th inning of Game Six started the
Mets' pennant-winning rally. He got his only RBI of
the World Series on a long home run in the Mets'
Game Seven victory.

After running around the bases on that WS
homer, he had to be quickly convinced at the plate
by on-deck batter Ray Knight to shake manager
Davey Johnson's hand. In the midst of the Mets'
stirring victory the night before, he was sulking in
the clubhouse after Johnson took him out in a
double switch during a pitching change. Throughout
his young career Strawberry made statements in the
press that he was, or that he wanted to be, a team
leader. But, as a youngster, he has often acted
immaturely, creating several embarrassing run-ins
with Johnson and some of the older team leaders.
After one of his interviews in 1988, he was the
subject of derogatory replies in the press from
teammates, and in 1989 he punched team co-
captain Keith Hernandez during the team photo
shoot over a Hernandez quote. Strawberry often
stated an intention to leave the Mets for his
hometown Dodgers, and he and former high school
teammate Eric Davis frequently expressed their
desire to play on the same team. Thrown at even by
AL pitchers during exhibition games, he has charged
the mound to start brawls, including several during
the regular season. In 1989 he and Juan Samuel
were intercepted by Shea Stadium security as they
headed toward a postgame confrontation with three
Reds pitchers. His personal life has also been
marked by turmoil.

In the field, Strawberry has had concentration
lapses that led to the criticism that he was not a
hustling player. He tore ligaments in his right thumb
in 1985 while making a diving catch and he missed
seven weeks. He was considered overly cautious in
the outfield for some time thereafter. He has a strong
but erratic throwing arm. He never positions himself
according to the hitter or the situation; over the
course of a season, he wears out a small area in right
field that is critically referred to as the "Strawberry
Patch" by broadcaster Tim McCarver. However,
Strawberry's long strides make his play seem effortless; his attitude has led critics to identify as loafing
that which in a more proven team player might be
called graceful instead. He performs under the close
scrutiny of the New York press corps, magnifying

everything he does. As the 1980s end, Strawberry's curse has been that he is measured by his seemingly unlimited potential rather than by his quite tangible accomplishments. /(SH)

Gabby Street [Charles Evard] (Old Sarge) — 1882–1951. C 1904–5, 08–12, 31 Reds, Braves, **Senators**, Yankees, Cardinals 503 g, .208, 2 hr, 105 rbi.
  Manager 1929–33, 38 **Cardinals**, Browns 368–339, .521. First place: 30–31 *2 WS, 6–7, .462*

Street became famous for catching a baseball dropped from the top of the Washington Monument on a windy day in 1908. He missed 14 before he caught one. In 1894 catcher Pops Schriver had done it on the first try. Gabby, a loquacious Southerner, picked up the nickname Old Sarge during service in WWI. Often referred to as "Walter Johnson's catcher," he was actually with the Washington immortal only four years (1908–11). He brought the Cardinals a pennant as their rookie manager in 1930, and repeated in 1931, defeating the A's in the World Series. Unable to deal with the brash behavior of young Dizzy Dean, Street was replaced in 1933 by Frank Frisch. He managed the Browns to seventh place in 1938, and became a Cardinal broadcaster. /(JK)

Sam Streeter — 1900– . LHP Negro Leagues 1920–35 Montgomery Grey Sox, Atlanta Black Crackers, Chicago American Giants, Bacharach Giants, New York Lincoln Giants, Birmingham Black Barons, Homestead Grays, Cleveland Cubs, Pittsburgh Crawfords statistics not available
☛ *All-Star—33.*

Spitballing Sam Streeter pitched in the Negro Leagues for 15 years and was the starting pitcher in the 1933 East-West all-star game. In the Negro Southern League's first season, 1920, he helped the Montgomery Grey Sox to the pennant. He pitched a perfect game in a 3–0 win over Atlanta and threw 20 consecutive strikes in a game against the Chicago Black Sox, a barnstorming team. In 1924 and 1927 he led the Birmingham Black Barons in innings pitched, strikeouts, and wins. He led the Negro National League in games and innings pitched in 1930. /(BP)

George Strickland (Bo, Clown) — 1926– . SS-2B-3B, 1950–57, 59–60 Pirates, **Indians** 971 g, .224, 36 hr, 284 rbi. *1 WS, 3 g, .000.*
  Manager 1966 **Indians** 15–24, .385

The shortstop for the last championship Indian team in 1954, Strickland was unimpressive with the

Pirates, but Cleveland obtained him in 1952 to replace shortstop Ray Boone, who had ailing knees. Although always a weak hitter, Strickland became a smooth fielder with an accurate arm and led AL shortstops in double plays in 1953 and fielding in 1955. He shares the ML shortstop record with five double plays in a game (9/27/52). A Cleveland regular for four seasons, in 1959 he played more games at third base than at shortstop. He coached for the Twins and Indians and managed Cleveland for parts of 1964 and 1966. /(JCA)

Elmer Stricklett — 1876–1964. RHP 1904–07 White Sox, **Dodgers** 765 ip, 35–51, 2.85

Stricklett is often credited with introducing the spitball to the major leagues, though it was his disciples, Jack Chesbro and Ed Walsh, who became Hall of Famers with it. He was a sore-armed minor leaguer in 1904 when he learned the pitch from its accidental discoverer, George Hildebrand. Stricklett approved the banning of the spitball years later, believing it was too dangerous and hard to control. /(JK)

Nick Strincevich (Jumbo) — 1915– . RHP 1940–42, 44–48 Braves, **Pirates**, Phillies 890 ip, 46–49, 4.05

Acquired from Boston in 1941 for 35-year-old Lloyd Waner, Strincevich won 40 games for Pittsburgh from 1944 through 1946. The sidearming curveballer had a club-high 16 wins in 1945. He completed an unassisted double play in 1940. /(ME)

Lou Stringer — 1917– . 2B 1941–42, 46, 48–50 **Cubs**, Red Sox 409 g, .242, 19 hr, 122 rbi

Tabbed as Billy Herman's replacement in the Cubs' infield, Stringer led NL second basemen in assists in 1941 and errors in 1942. His weak bat sent him back to the minors. In September 1948 an injury to Bobby Doerr gave him a fill-in shot with the Red Sox, and he hung on two more years. /(NLM)

Joe Stripp (Jersey Joe) — 1903– . 3B-1B-OF 1928–38 Reds, **Dodgers**, Cardinals, Braves 1146 g, .294, 24 hr, 464 rbi

A hustling, hard-hitting third baseman/first baseman, Stripp batted .300 six times as a regular. After he hit a career-high .324 in 1931, the Reds sent him in a three-for-three swap to the Dodgers. He was an annual holdout, always trying to negotiate a better contract. While still playing, he opened Jersey Joe Stripp's Baseball School in Orlando, FL, a development school for Depression-era boys who wanted to make a living playing baseball. /(JK)

John Strohmayer — 1946– . RHP 1970–74 **Expos**, Mets 312 ip, 11–9, 4.47

Drafted by Montreal out of the A's organization, Strohmayer made the jump from Double-A to the Expos in 1970 and went 3–1. Though primarily a reliever, he started 14 games in 1971 and was 7–5. /(JCA)

Brent Strom — 1948– . LHP 1972–73, 75–77 Mets, Indians, **Padres** 501 ip, 22–39, 3.95

Strom pitched the University of Southern California to two NCAA championships before signing with the Mets in 1970. He was beginning to blossom in 1976, going 12–16 for San Diego, when an elbow injury effectively ended his career. /(ME)

Ken Strong — 1906–1979. *Minor League* OF 1929–31

An outstanding Yankees prospect, Strong led the New York-Penn league with 41 home runs (including four in one game) for Hazelton in 1930 and hit .340 for Toronto (International League) in 1931, but a shoulder injury ended his baseball career before he ever reached the ML. Instead, he turned to professional football and became a Hall of Fame halfback and kicker for the New York Giants. /(JK)

Ted Strong — Unk.–Unk. OF-SS-MGR Negro Leagues 1937–48 Indianapolis ABC's, Indianapolis Clowns, Kansas City Monarchs, Indianapolis Athletics statistics not available
☛ *All-Star—37–39, 41–42.*

An outstanding all-around athlete, Strong played baseball in the Negro Leagues and basketball for the Harlem Globetrotters. He appeared in five East-West all-star games at three different positions—first base, outfield, and shortstop. The switch-hitter helped the Kansas City Monarchs to four consecutive pennants (1939–42). After Jackie Robinson broke the color line, Strong played several seasons in the Texas League. On the basketball court, his unusually large hands made it easy for him to palm the ball and, consequently, play "pitcher" in the Globetrotters' baseball routines. /(BP)

Ed Stroud (The Creeper) — 1939– . OF 1966–71 White Sox, **Senators** 529 g, .237, 14 hr, 100 rbi

The Creeper was a three-time minor league stolen-base leader. Stroud played in more than 100 games each year from 1967 through 1970, his finest ML season, when he batted .266, scored 69 runs, and stole 29 bases for Washington. /(JCA)

Sailor Stroud (Ralph) — 1885–1970. RHP 1910, 1915–16 Tigers, **Giants** 361 ip, 17–20, 2.94

Stroud had a good curve and changeup in his arsenal, but he was erratic. He gained a temporary spot as a starter for the Giants in 1915 when he beat the Phillies by outdueling Grover Alexander. /(BC)

Amos Strunk — 1889–1979. OF-1B 1908–24 **A's**, Red Sox, White Sox 1507 g, .283, 15 hr, 528 rbi. *5 WS, 18 g, .200, 2 rbi*

Serious and dependable, highly regarded for his defensive skills, Strunk topped AL outfielders in fielding average five times. He was a solid lefthanded hitter who rarely struck out. A native Philadelphian, he played in four World Series with the A's before Ed Barrow obtained him from Connie Mack to bolster the 1918 Red Sox defense. With Strunk in centerfield, Boston won the 1918 WS. Mack reacquired him in June 1919. With the White Sox in 1923, Strunk led the AL with 12 pinch hits in 39 attempts. /(EC)

Dick Stuart (Dr. Strangeglove, The Ancient Mariner) — 1932– . 1B 1958–66, 69 **Pirates**, Red Sox, Phillies, Mets, Dodgers, Angels 1112 g, .264, 228 hr, 743 rbi. *2 WS, 8 g, .136*
☛ *Led League—rbi 63. All-Star—61.*

Unfortunately for the slugging Dick Stuart, he played before the advent of the designated hitter. Known as Dr. Strangeglove, and The Ancient Mariner ("he stoppeth one in three"), he was perennially the league's worst-fielding first baseman. After the immodest, lead-footed 6'4" strongman hit 66 homers at Lincoln (Western League) in 1956, he plastered "66" on his belongings and included the number in his autograph. From 1959 through 1961, he hit 85 homers for Pittsburgh, including three in one game June 30, 1960.

Colorful and controversial, he sold plenty of tickets for Boston in 1963, where they cheered the Comeback Player of the Year's 42 HR and league-high 118 RBI and booed his 29 errors. Stuart was outraged when Boston traded him to Philadelphia for little-known pitcher Dennis Bennett in November 1964. In 1965, for the first time in eight years, Stuart managed not to lead or tie for the league lead in errors at first base. By 1967 he was playing for Taiyo in Japan. Unhappy there, he recrossed the Pacific and played briefly with California in 1969. /(JCA)

Johnny Stuart (Stud) — 1901–1970. RHP 1922–25 **Cardinals** 357 ip, 20–18, 4.76

Stuart, a .228 hitter, sometimes helped himself more with his bat than his arm. He was often behind in the count, resulting in walks or grooved pitches. Although he twice won nine games for the Cardinals, his best ERA was 4.27. /(FJO)

Marlin Stuart — 1918- . LHP 1949-54 Tigers, **Browns/Orioles**, Yankees 485 ip, 23-17, 4.65

The screwballer was 30 years old before he pitched in the majors, and he bounced up and down for several seasons, throwing a perfect game for Toledo of the American Association in 1951. In 1953 he led the Browns' staff in wins with an 8-2 record, which until the 1987 Cleveland Indians, was the lowest win leadership mark for a pitching staff. /(NLM)

Franklin Stubbs — 1960- . 1B-OF 1984- **Dodgers** 542 g, .227, 59 hr, 178 rbi. *1 LCS, 4 g, .250. 1 WS, 5 g, .294, 2 rbi*

Stubbs led the Dodgers with 23 homers in 1986, but hit no better than .233 in his first five ML seasons. A husky lefthanded hitter, he has held the Dodgers' first base and left field jobs several times, but has never been able to keep either one. /(TG)

John Stuper — 1957- . RHP 1982-85 **Cardinals**, Reds 495 ip, 32-28, 3.96. *1 LCS, 6 ip, 0-0, 3.00. 1 WS, 13 ip, 1-0, 3.46*

With the 1982 Cardinals, Stuper became the 14th rookie to start two games of a World Series. He threw all nine innings of a 13-1 victory over Milwaukee in Game Six, which took over five hours, due to two rain delays. /(FJO)

Tom Sturdivant — 1930- . RHP 1955-64 **Yankees**, A's, Red Sox, Senators, Pirates, Tigers, Mets 1137 ip, 59-51, 3.74. *3 WS, 18 ip, 1-0, 4.34*

Using a fastball, slider, and knuckleball, Sturdivant won 16 games for the Yankees in both 1956 and 1957. In the 1956 WS, won by New York, he six-hit the Dodgers in Game Four to pull the Yankees even at two games each. After a sore arm in 1958, he worked as a journeyman with several clubs. On May 31, 1964, his final ML season, he was one of four Met relievers who held the Giants scoreless through 19-2/3 innings before New York finally lost in the 23rd. /(GDW)

Bobby Sturgeon — 1919- . SS-2B 1940-42, 46-48 **Cubs**, Braves 420 g, .257, 1 hr, 80 rbi

Sturgeon was the Cubs' shortstop as a rookie in 1941, but a severe leg injury and a three-year military stint followed. He returned to find himself a backup. While playing shortstop against the Dodgers in 1947, he passed up a double play opportunity to throw the relay at rookie Jackie Robinson, striking him in the chest with the throw. About six weeks later, Robinson reached base and ran on the first pitch. Not sliding, Robinson threw a block at Sturgeon and knocked him halfway into left field. Sturgeon suffered two broken ribs. In Sturgeon's final season he spelled Eddie Stanky at second base for the 1948 pennant-winning Braves. /(DB)

Ken Suarez (Piggy) — 1943- . C 1966-69, 71-73 A's, Indians, **Rangers** 295 g, .227, 5 hr, 60 rbi

Suarez caught for the 1964 U.S. amateur all-star team that toured the Orient. His first pro hit was a grand slam for Lewiston (Northwest League) in 1965. He was an backup every year except 1973, when he played 93 games with Texas. /(ME)

Miguel Suarez — 1952- . OF 1969-87 Mexican Leagues

Lefthanded-hitting Miguel Suarez batted .393 for Tampico (Mexican Center League) in 1970 to lead all of professional baseball. In his first 16 seasons (half of them spent with the Mexico City Reds), he dipped below .300 just once. /(MC)

Jim Suchecki — 1927- . RHP 1950-52 Red Sox, **Browns**, Pirates 104 ip, 0-6, 5.36

With time out for military service, Suchecki spent seven years in the minors. He had six starts for the Browns in 1951, lost five, and never got another. /(NLM)

Bill Sudakis (Suds) — 1946- . 3B-C-1B-DH 1968-75 **Dodgers**, Mets, Rangers, Yankees, Angels, Indians 530 g, .234, 59 hr, 214 rbi

The switch-hitting Sudakis homered for Los Angeles in his first major league game. The Dodgers' third baseman in 1969, he was made a catcher and had won the everyday job in 1970 when he broke a finger. He became a versatile utilityman. More than one-third of Sudakis's hits were for extra bases. /(JCA)

Pete Suder (Pecky) — 1916- . 2B-3B-SS 1941-43, 46-55 **A's** 1421 g, .249, 49 hr, 541 rbi

A versatile infielder, Suder was best known as the pivot man on the Athletics' Joost-Suder-Fain double play combination of the late 1940s. They helped set a team record of 217 double plays in 1949. Normally a weak hitter, he hit 10 homers and had 75 RBI that year. /(NLM)

Willie Sudhoff (Wee Willie) — 1874–1917. RHP 1897–1906 **Cardinals**, Cleveland (NL), Browns, Senators 2086 ip, 103–136, 3.56. 20 wins: 03

Wee Willie, just 5'7", created a stir when he jumped the Cardinals for the Browns in 1902, becoming one of the first to play for both St. Louis franchises. He was at his best in 1903, going 21–15 with a 2.27 ERA./(WAB)

Ed Sudol — 1920– . *Umpire* NL 1957–76 *2 ASU 3 LCS 2 WS*

Sudol, a former beer-truck driver, enjoyed a distinguished 20-year career in the NL, where, with a little help from the Mets, he became known as The Extra-Inning Umpire. On May 21, 1964, he called the pitches in the 23-inning contest between the Giants and Mets that lasted a NL record seven hours and 23 minutes. On September 11, 1974, he was behind the plate when the Cards and Mets went 25 innings. And early in 1976, the Mets and Cards logged 17 innings with Sudol as plate umpire./(RTM)

Joe Sugden — 1870–1959. C-1B 1893–99, 1901–05, 12 Pirates, Cardinals, Cleveland (NL), White Sox, **Browns**, Tigers 831 g, .255, 3 hr, 283 rbi

The catching platoon of switch-hitting Joe Sugden and Bill Merritt replaced Connie Mack in Pittsburgh in 1895. Sugden was Mack's designated pinch runner when Mack had an injury that hindered his running, an arrangement which was then legal. He platooned with Mike Kahoe in 1902 as the AL Browns' initial catching combo. A longtime scout, he served the Cardinals from 1928 until his death./(ME)

George Suggs — 1883–1949. RHP 1908–15 Tigers, **Reds**, Baltimore (FL) 1652 ip, 101–88, 3.11. 20 wins: 14

In four seasons with the mediocre Reds, righthander Suggs pitched 74 complete games, winning 61. In 1914, as ace of the Baltimore Feds, he won 25 games, including six shutouts, and had 26 complete games. He was always stingy with walks, averaging about 1.5 per game, and had 24 decisions and 14 saves in relief./(ADS)

Tadoshi Sugiura — 1935– . P 1958–69 **Nankai Hawks** 180–90, 2.40

The bespectacled Sugiura looked too frail to be an athlete, but proved talented and durable, going 27–12 in 1958 as a Japanese rookie. His .905 winning percentage (38–4) in 1959 is the highest in

the history of baseball, Japanese or American, for a pitcher with more than 30 decisions. He followed in 1960 with a 31–11 mark, but slumped because of overwork in 1962 and 1963. He was 8–1 in 1965 when he suffered the arm blowout that eventually ended his career. He retired that fall after losing two games in the Japan Series, but was persuaded to come back, becoming an effective spot reliever./(MC)

Gus Suhr — 1906– . 1B 1930–40 **Pirates**, Phillies 1435 g, .279, 84 hr, 818 rbi

Suhr arrived in Pittsburgh after batting .381 with 51 homers and 177 RBI in 202 Pacific Coast League games in 1929. A slick-fielding, lefthanded-hitting first baseman, he had a 107-RBI rookie season, then was benched due to poor hitting. On September 11, 1931, he began what was then a NL-record streak of 822 games played, which ended June 4, 1937, when he attended his mother's funeral. He topped 100 RBI in three NL seasons, in 1936 finishing third in the league with 118./(ME)

Clyde Sukeforth (Sukey) — 1901– . C 1926–35 **Reds**, Dodgers 486 g, .264, 2 hr, 96 rbi. *Manager* 1947 **Dodgers** 2–0, 1.000

Sukeforth was a backup catcher in the NL for 10 seasons, playing more than 100 games only in 1931. He served as a Dodger coach for many years and, for two days in 1947 after Leo Durocher's suspension, was interim manager./(NLM)

Billy Sullivan [William Joseph, Sr.] — 1875–1965. C 1899–1912, 14, 16 Braves, **White Sox**, Tigers 1146 g, .212, 21 hr, 378 rbi. *1 WS, 6 g, .000.* *Manager* 1909 **White Sox** 78–74, .513

Sullivan earned a reputation as a terrible hitter and a superior catcher. His .212 lifetime batting average makes him the second worst hitter of all time (to Bill Bergen) among those with 3,000 at-bats. But from 1901 through 1911, with Sullivan calling the pitches, the White Sox won two pennants, came within two games of two others, and never finished lower than fourth. The two years he was injured, Chicago finished more than 30 games back. The sinewy Sullivan excelled in all aspects of catching—calling the game, blocking the plate, catching foul pops, and throwing out runners. Ty Cobb called him the best catcher "ever to wear shoe leather."

When Johnny Kling, star catcher of the crosstown Cubs, boasted that he was going to be the first man to catch 1,000 games, a check of the records revealed that Sullivan had already done it. In 1909

Sullivan managed the White Sox and obtained a patent on the first chest protector that featured a wind pad for compressed air. Although he was one of the early White Sox promised "lifetime employment" by Charles Comiskey, the vow was broken with his 1914 release. When his son, Billy Jr., caught in the 1940 World Series for Detroit, the two became the first father-son team to have played in the WS.

Official records indicate the 1906 Hitless Wonders hit only six home runs. Historian Rich Lindberg discovered the Sox had actually hit seven—the missing homer belonging to Sullivan. /(DB)

Billy Sullivan [William Joseph, Jr.] — 1910- . C-1B-3B-OF 1931-33, 35-42, 47 **White Sox**, Reds, Indians, Browns, Tigers, Dodgers, Pirates 962 g, .289, 29 hr, 388 rbi. *1 WS, 5 g, .154*

The son of famous early White Sox catcher Billy Sullivan, Billy Jr. attended Notre Dame with the young Ed Walsh, son of the star White Sox pitcher. It was rumored that Chicago owner Charles Comiskey paid their tuition in hopes they would duplicate the playing ability and drawing appeal of their fathers. Billy Jr. had played mostly third and first, but as a publicity stunt, he and Walsh appeared as a battery once, late in 1932. Sullivan began catching regularly only after joining Cleveland in 1936, and never caught more than 99 games a season. He turned out to be a much better hitter than his father; his .351 average in 1936 was seventh in the league. A top lefthanded pinch hitter, he was extremely difficult to strike out, fanning only 119 times in 2,840 at-bats. /(CG)

Charlie Sullivan — 1903-1935. RHP 1928-31 **Tigers** 205 ip, 4-9, 5.66

An ineffective reliever, Sullivan claimed he learned to pitch as a boy by throwing rocks at squirrels, and developed a curve so he could hit the ones hiding behind trees. He was killed at 32 when the car in which he was riding was struck by a train. /(JK)

Frank Sullivan — 1930- . RHP 1953-63 **Red Sox**, Phillies, Twins 1732 ip, 97-100, 3.60
☛ *Led League—w 55. All-Star—55, 56.*

Sullivan was a Red Sox workhorse in the mid-1950s. He went 18-13 in 1955, tying for the league lead in wins, and leading in starts (35) and innings pitched (260). That summer, he served up Stan Musial's 12th-inning, All-Star Game-winning home run. Sullivan was the tallest pitcher in the AL

(6'6-1/2") when he was traded to Philadelphia for the NL's taller pitcher, 6'8" Gene Conley, in December of 1960. His 3-16 record in 1961 for the 47-107 Phillies dropped his lifetime record below .500. /(PB)

Haywood Sullivan — 1930- . C 1955, 57, 59-63 Red Sox, **A's** 312 g, .226, 13 hr, 87 rbi.
Manager 1965 A's 54-82, .397

Sullivan signed as a catcher for $50,000 with the Red Sox in 1952. He never hit for the Red Sox but played regularly for the A's in 1961-62, and managed them to a last-place finish in 1965. He later became the Red Sox' general manager and was part of the group that bought the team when Tom Yawkey died, becoming president of the franchise. His son Marc caught for the Red Sox in the 1980s. /(NLM)

Joe Sullivan — 1910-1985. LHP 1935-36, 39-41 Tigers, **Braves**, Pirates 588 ip, 30-37, 4.01

A spot starter and reliever, Sullivan was 6-6 as a rookie for the 1935 pennant-winning Tigers. He left baseball during WWII for a defense job in the Puget Sound naval shipyard. /(JK)

John Sullivan — 1920- . SS 1942-44, 47-49 **Senators**, Browns 605 g, .230, 1 hr, 162 rbi

A weak-hitting wartime regular shortstop, Sullivan turned down a University of Wisconsin football scholarship to play pro baseball. In a 1947 game he fielded a grounder behind second and "centered" the ball between his legs to the waiting second baseman, Eddie Lyons. The ball went over Lyons's head and a run scored. /(NM)

Homer Summa — 1898-1966. OF 1920, 22-30 Pirates, **Indians**, A's 840 g, .302, 18 hr, 361 rbi. *1 WS, 1 g, .000*

A two-time minor league batting champion, Summa hit .328 in his first full major league season, 1923, and remained an Indians regular through 1928. On May 31, 1927, he lined into an unassisted triple play turned by Detroit first baseman Johnny Neun. Sold to the A's before the 1929 season, he appeared as a pinch hitter in the 1929 World Series. Dropped to the Pacific Coast League in 1930, he played there until 1933. /(JK)

Bill Summers — 1895–1966. *Umpire* AL 1933–59 *7 ASU 8 WS*

A boxing enthusiast, Summers developed into one of the best umpires in the AL and shares the record with Al Barlick of working seven All-Star Games, six behind the plate. One of his most controversial calls came in a game between the Indians and the Red Sox in 1949. Boston's Johnny Pesky hit a double with the bases loaded that was turned into a triple because Summers ruled that Cleveland outfielder Dale Mitchell threw his glove at the ball. The rule was later changed to state that a thrown glove must touch the ball to be a violation./(RTM)

Champ Summers [John Junior II] — 1946– . OF-DH 1974–84 A's, Cubs, Reds, **Tigers**, Giants, Padres 698 g, .255, 54 hr, 218 rbi. *1 LCS, 2 g, .000. 1 WS, 1 g, .000*

The solidly built Vietnam veteran bounced between the minors and majors, mostly as a pinch hitter, until Sparky Anderson brought him to Detroit as a DH. Thriving on righthanded pitching, Summers hit .313 with 20 homers in 1979 and .297 with 17 homers the following year./(CC)

Ed Summers (Kickapoo Chief) — 1884–1953. RHP 1908–12 **Tigers** 999 ip, 68–45, 2.42. 20 wins: 08 *2 WS, 22 ip, 0–4, 5.73*

Summers went 24–12 as a rookie with the pennant-winning Tigers in 1908. That September 25, he hurled two complete-game victories over the A's. He had 19 wins in 1909, but his best-pitched game was not one of them; on July 16, he hurled 18 innings to a scoreless tie against Washington, allowing seven hits and one walk. He lost all four of his World Series assignments in 1908–09. He was a notoriously poor hitter, and both of his ML home runs came in a September 17, 1910 game against the Athletics. Rheumatism hampered his pitching, and he faded to the minors in 1912./(LRD)

Billy Sunday (The Evangelist) — 1862–1935. OF 1883–90 Cubs, **Pittsburgh (NL)**, Phillies 499 g, .248, 12 hr, 170 rbi

At the height of his career, the fleet-footed Sunday (who had just stolen 84 bases in 1890) quit baseball to enter Christian work. From beginnings as a YMCA secretary, he rose to fame as a fiery evangelist, spearheading the Prohibitionist movement and attempting to outlaw Sunday baseball. He often would "slide" onto the stage as if sliding into a base./(FIC)

Jim Sundberg — 1951– . C 1974–89 **Rangers**, Brewers, Royals, Cubs 1962 g, .248, 95 hr, 624 rbi. *1 LCS, 7 g, .167, 1 hr, 6 rbi. 1 WS, 7 g, .250, 1 rbi* ☛ *All-Star—74, 78, 84. Gold Glove—76–81.*

Sundberg became the Rangers' regular catcher after a single season of AA ball, batting .298 and demonstrating great defensive skills. For a decade he averaged 140 games per season behind the plate. In his second big league season, he tied the AL record for games caught with 155. Seven times he led AL receivers in fielding average, and he led in putouts and assists six times each. He was also deadly at gunning down would-be basestealers, nailing as many as 50% in a season. Sundberg was the only catcher to be awarded six Gold Gloves, and on his retirement in 1989 was in third place for career games caught.

Billy Sunday

Offensively, Sundberg tried to pull everything early in his career but eventually developed into a productive .270 hitter for a number of years. /(FO)

Steve Sundra (Smokey) — 1910–1952. RHP 1936, 38–44, 46 **Yankees**, Senators, Browns 859 ip, 56–41, 4.17. *1 WS, 3 ip, 0–0, 0.00*

When the Yankees traded Johnny Allen to Cleveland for Monte Pearson in December 1935, they received Sundra as a throw-in. He won his last four starts in 1938, then ran off 11 straight wins (three in relief) for the 1939 pennant winners before losing his final start of the season. With the Browns in 1943, he recorded a career-high 15 victories. /(JK)

Tom Sunkel (Lefty, Long Tom) — 1912– . LHP 1937, 39, 41–44 **Cardinals**, Giants, Dodgers 230 ip, 9–15, 4.34

Sunkel's left eye was damaged by a popgun shot when he was a child. He developed a nonoperable cataract in 1941, lost all sight in the eye, and compensated by pitching and batting with his head cocked to the side. /(JK)

B.J. Surhoff — 1964– . C-3B 1987- **Brewers** 380 g, .262, 17 hr, 161 rbi

A member of the 1984 U.S. Olympic Team and *TSN* College Player of the Year at North Carolina in 1985, Surhoff was the first player chosen overall in the 1985 free agent draft, and hit .299 as a rookie in 1987. Surhoff played more regularly in 1988, often at third base when not catching, and although his average dipped to .245 he still stole 21 bases. His father, Dick, played briefly in the National Basketball Association. /(SCL)

Max Surkont [Matthew Constantine] — 1922–1986. RHP 1949–57 White Sox, **Braves**, Pirates, Cardinals, Giants 1194 ip, 61–76, 4.38

Surkont was signed at age 15 by the Cardinals (his "bonus" was a hotel meal of beans and frankfurters), but it took him 12 seasons to reach the majors. A regular starter with the Braves in the early 1950s, he had his only winning record for a complete ML season in 1953, when he was 11–5. On the night of May 25, 1953, the burly fastballer set a ML record (since broken) by striking out eight Cincinnati batters in a row, the last one after a 35-minute rain delay. /(JM)

George Susce — 1931– . RHP 1955–59 **Red Sox**, Tigers 410 ip, 22–17, 4.42

The son of George "Good Kid" Susce, a marginal catcher and longtime ML coach, the younger Susce

went 9–7 as a Red Sox rookie, including a one-hitter against the A's, for whom his father was then a coach. Used mostly in relief in subsequent years, he won six games out of the bullpen in 1957. /(PB)

Rick Sutcliffe — 1956– . RHP 1976, 78- Dodgers, Indians, **Cubs** 2109 ip, 133–103, 3.813. 20 wins: 84
2 LCS, 19 ip, 1–1, 3.72
☛ *Led League—w 87. Led League—era 82. Cy Young Award—84. All-Star—83, 87, 89.*

Change of scenery always seemed to help Rick Sutcliffe. The 6'7" 215-lb native of Independence, Missouri followed in a long line of star Dodger rookies, but by 1980 he was exiled to the Los Angeles bullpen. Rescued by Cleveland, he led the AL in ERA in 1982. By 1984, unhappy playing with a noncontender, Sutcliffe was ready to become a free agent when he was dealt to the Cubs. After 4–5 start in Cleveland, he went 16–1 for Chicago to earn a unanimous vote as NL Cy Young Award winner, the first winner ever to split a season between the AL and NL. He won Chicago's pennant-clinching game and Game One of the 1984 LCS, but lost the decisive fifth game. Injuries and control problems hampered Sutcliffe following his great 1984 campaign. He rebounded in 1987 to lead the NL in wins (18–10) and, healthy again, was the club's workhorse starter that year and the next two seasons. /(ME)

Darrell Sutherland — 1941– . RHP 1964–66, 68 **Mets**, Indians 122 ip, 5–4, 4.78

The older brother of Gary Sutherland, Darrell was used mostly in relief by the early Mets. He was 5–0 lifetime in relief but was 0–4 in his six starts. /(WOR)

Gary Sutherland — 1944– . 2B-SS 1966–78 Phillies, **Expos**, Astros, Tigers, Brewers, Padres, Cardinals 1031 g, .243, 24 hr, 239 rbi

The brother of pitcher Darrell Sutherland, Gary was a spray-hitting utility man for Philadelphia when he was selected by Montreal in the 1968 expansion draft. He was the Expos' second baseman for much of their first two seasons, but was sent down in 1972 and sold to Houston. A regular again with Detroit, he led the Tigers with 157 hits in 1974. Sutherland was a backup guard on three UCLA national champion basketball teams. /(CC)

Bruce Sutter — 1953– . RHP 1976–86, 88 **Cubs**, Cardinals, Braves 1040 ip, 68–71, 2.84. *1 LCS, 4 ip, 1–0, 0.00. 1 WS, 7 ip, 1–0, 4.70*
☛ *Cy Young Award—79. All-Star—78–81.*

Arm surgery in 1973 nearly ended Sutter's career, but, with the help of Cub pitching coach Mike Roarke, he developed a split-finger fastball. The pitch, which dropped like a rock as it reached the plate, made him an instant success in the Cubs' bullpen. He saved 31 games while recording a microscopic 1.35 ERA in his sophomore season. In 1979 his 37 saves earned him the NL Cy Young Award.

He continued his dominance from the bullpen with the Cardinals, peaking with 45 saves in 1984.

Bruce Sutter

The Cardinals even hired Roarke to monitor Sutter's pitching mechanics. Sutter won two games and saved two in All-Star Game competition. He holds the NL record for career saves and was voted NL Fireman of the Year four times by *TSN*.

Sutter signed a six-year, eight-digit contract with the Braves in December 1984. Shoulder problems caused him to miss most of 1986 and all 1987, but he returned in 1988 to again be Atlanta's closer. He lifted his career saves to an even 300, despite a mid-season bout with Bell's palsy, which forced him onto the DL. More shoulder problems again threatened his career. /(FJO)

Jack Sutthoff (Sunny Jack) — 1873–1942. RHP 1898–99, 1901, 03–05 Washington NL, Cardinals, **Reds**, Phillies 648 ip, 32–37, 3.65

Although the Cincinnati native was a respectable 16–10 for the 1903 Reds, Sutthoff is often confused with a contemporary (and better pitcher), Wee Willie Sudhoff. In 1899 they were teammates on the Cardinals. /(JK)

Mule Suttles [George] — 1901–1968. 1B-OF-UMP Negro Leagues 1918–48 Birmingham Black Barons, St. Louis Stars, Baltimore Black Sox, Washington Pilots, Detroit Wolves, Chicago American Giants, Newark Eagles, New York Black Yankees, Bacharach Giants 673 g, .328, 131 hr (inc.)
☛ *All-Star—33–35, 37, 39.*

Suttles began playing Negro League baseball at age 17 and lasted until 42. He would say, regarding his longevity, "Don't worry about the Mule going blind, just load the wagon and give me the lines." During his five years with the St. Louis Stars (1926–30), he led the league in homers twice and in doubles, triples, and batting average once. Though noted primarily as a power hitter, he could also hit for average; in five East-West all-star games he batted .412 with an .883 slugging average (two HR, six RBI). His initial HR was the first ever hit in the all-star game, and his second won an 11-inning battle in 1935. His average in 26 documented games against white major leaguers was .374, with five HR. /(BP)

Don Sutton — 1945– . RHP 1966–88 **Dodgers**, Astros, Brewers, A's, Angels 5280 ip, 324–256, 3.26. 20 wins: 76 *5 LCS, 49 ip, 4–1, 2.02. 5 WS, 51 ip, 2–3, 5.26*
☛ *Led League—era 80. All-Star—72–73, 75, 77.*

The pitching matchup between Sutton and Phil Niekro on June 28, 1986 was the first between 300-game winners since Tim Keefe and Pud Galvin opposed one another in 1892. It put into perspective an era that began in the 1960s. A new breed emerged, pitchers who would go on to win over 300 games by staying consistently effective into their forties. Although he lacked the overpowering stuff possessed by others of this group—Perry, Carlton and Seaver—and never earned the Cy Young awards they did, Sutton, a fanatic about conditioning, never spent a day on the disabled list in 22 seasons. He combined longevity with excellence, even brilliance, to put together an impressive career.

Sutton was chosen *TSN* Rookie Pitcher of the Year in 1966, when his 209 strikeouts were the most by a NL rookie since Grover Cleveland Alexander's 227 in 1911. He was the fourth starter behind Sandy Koufax, Don Drysdale, and Claude Osteen. That foursome proved to be the only rotation in which each member would amass 40 or more career shutouts. As the years passed, Sutton became the ace of the Dodger staff. Without having the dominant individual seasons that his predecessors had, he still became the Dodgers' career leader in wins, losses, games pitched, games started, strikeouts, innings pitched, hits allowed, shutouts, and Opening-Day starts (seven).

Sutton's all-time statistics reflect his consistency and longevity. En route to defeating every major league team, he earned a spot among the career leaders in losses (sixth), games started (second), strikeouts (fourth), innings pitched (sixth), and shutouts (eighth) at the time he retired. He never pitched a no-hitter, but he did pitch five one-hitters and nine two-hitters. He became the first pitcher to win 300 games while only once winning 20 in a season. He made his way past the 3,000-strikeout mark by racking up a record 21 consecutive 100-plus strikeout seasons (recording 99 in his final season), with a high of 217 in 1969.

Seven times Sutton was a starter on the NL staff with the best ERA, and he was a frequent member of pennant-bound teams. Sutton earned a reputation as a money player. He allowed no earned runs in eight All-Star innings, including his start and win in the 1977 game of which he was named MVP. He pitched the Dodgers' first-ever LCS game in 1974, shutting out the Pirates, and beat them in the fourth and final game as well. He was acquired by the Brewers toward the end of their 1982 pennant drive, and beat Jim Palmer and the Orioles in the division clincher on the last day of the season. In 1986, at age 41, he won 15 for the Western Division champion Angels. In total, he competed in five League Championship Series and four World Series with three different teams.

Don Sutton

Sutton's repertoire featured the curveball, although he was often accused, especially toward the end of his career, of throwing illegal pitches. In 1978 he was ejected from a game for defacing the ball. When he threatened a lawsuit against the league, he was let off with a warning. He once claimed that when he met Gaylord Perry, "he gave me a jar of Vaseline. I thanked him and gave him a piece of sandpaper."

A polished speaker, Sutton served as a postseason announcer during his baseball career. Following his retirement, he became a full-time Braves TV announcer./(TG/CR)

Ezra Sutton — 1850–1907. 3B-SS 1871–88 Cleveland (NA), Philadelphia Athletics (NA), Athletics (NL), **Boston (NL)** *NA*: 231 g, .327. *ML*: 1031 g, .288, 21 hr, 457 rbi

Uncle Ezra, as admiring Boston fans called him, was a power hitter in the bare-handed days. He once hit three consecutive triples in a single game and had respectable numbers for slugging average and total bases. Originally a cross-handed batter (from the righthander's side of the plate), he adopted the normal grip to enhance his effectiveness against pitchers' ever-increasing speed.

Essentially a third baseman, he played all infield positions as needed, had a strong throwing arm and unflinching courage facing "fair-foul" hits down the line. Except for a league-leading .908 in 1884, however, his fielding percentages were usually in the .800s. While with the Athletics he made the first error in the first National League game ever played.

A solid contributor to Boston's 1877, 1878, and 1883 champions, he came to a sad end, dying crippled and impoverished. /(ADS)

Larry Sutton — 1858-1944. *Scout.*

Sutton became one of baseball's first full-time scouts when he joined the Dodgers in 1909. For many years as a semi-pro manager and umpire, he had recommended talent to ML clubs. He quickly discovered Zack Wheat for the Dodgers, and then spent single seasons with the Tigers, Phillies, and Reds before returning to the Dodgers from 1920 to 1936. He sent more than 100 players on their way to the ML. /(FVP)

Dale Sveum — 1963- . SS-3B 1986-88 **Brewers** 373 g, .47, 41 hr, 181 rbi

An aggressive hitter with good power for a shortstop but a tendency to strike out, Sveum (pronounced "Swaim") hit 25 HR while batting ninth for the Brewers in 1987, including three in one game against California July 17. He made the Topps All-Rookie Team as a third baseman in 1986, despite leading the AL in errors at the position in only 65 games there, and was made a full-time shortstop in 1987. In 1988 Sveum led AL shortstops in errors as well. A broken leg caused him to miss all of 1989. /(SCL)

Harry Swacina (Swats) — 1881-1944. 1B 1907-08, 14-15 Pirates, **Baltimore (FL)** 322 g, .256, 1 hr, 151 rbi

The brash Swacina was a defensive whiz whose one-handed catches at first base made fans overlook his .216 batting average. In 1908 he wrote an abrasive letter to Pirate owner Barney Dreyfuss; banished as a result, he did not appear in the majors again until the formation of the outlaw Federal League in 1914. /(JK)

Craig Swan — 1950- . RHP 1973-84 **Mets**, Angels 1235 ip, 59-72, 3.75
☛ *Led League—era 78.*

Swan won the 1978 NL ERA title (2.43) despite missing a month with gastroenteritis, recording just nine victories for the Mets. After winning a career-

high 14 in 1979, he signed a five-year contract—at the time the most lucrative in Met history. A rotator cuff tear in 1980 took away his fastball, and an arm injury in 1983 curtailed his career. /(KT)

Evar Swanson — 1902-1973. OF 1929-30, 32-34 Reds, **White Sox** 515 g, .303, 7 hr, 170 rbi

A three-sport star at Lombard College in Illinois, Swanson played three years in the NFL (1925-27) as an end for the Chicago Cardinals before turning exclusively to baseball. He was one of the fastest men in baseball during a period of heavy hitting. He stole 33 bases and scored 100 runs in his rookie year for the 1929 Reds. In a contest held between games of a doubleheader (9/15/29), he circled the bases in 13.3 seconds, a record that still stands. /(LRD)

Ed Swartwood — 1859-1924. OF-1B 1881-87, 90, 92 Buffalo (NL), Pittsburgh (AA), **Brooklyn (AA)**, Toledo (AA), Pirates 724 g, .299, 15 hr, 4 rbi (inc.)
☛ *Led League—ba 1883.*

In 1882 and 1883, Swartwood ranked among American Association leaders in nearly every offensive category, including league-leading marks of 86 runs and 162 total bases in 1882 and a .356 BA in 1883. He also led the AA in walks in 1886, with 70. He hit .327 with 106 runs and 53 stolen bases for Toledo in 1890. /(FIC)

Bill Sweeney [William J.] — 1858-1908. P 1882, 84 Philadelphia AA, **Baltimore UA** 708 ip, 49-31, 2.67. 20 wins: 84
☛ *Led League—w 84.*

The leading pitcher for the Union Association in its single year of existence, Sweeney's 40 wins represented 69% of his Baltimore team's total. /(FIC)

Bill Sweeney [William John] — 1886-1948. 2B-3B-SS 1907-14 Cubs, **Braves** 1039 g, .272, 11 hr, 389 rbi

After switching to the heaviest bat in the league in midcareer, Sweeney hit in 31 consecutive games in 1911, and in 1912 his .344 average was third in the NL. A regular infielder at three different positions for the Braves from 1908 to 1913, he was traded back to the Cubs for Johnny Evers before the Braves' 1914 World Championship season. /(JK)

Bill Sweeney [William Joseph] — 1904-1957. 1B 1928, 30-31 Tigers, **Red Sox** 308 g, .286, 5 hr, 107 rbi

Sweeney led AL first basemen in fielding percentage and total chances for the Red Sox in 1931, and recorded 21 putouts in one game June 24, but his

.295 average with one home run wasn't enough to keep his job. He was replaced the next year by Dale Alexander, who hit .367 to lead the AL. /(JK)

Charlie Sweeney — 1863–1902. RHP-OF-1B 1882–87 Providence (NL), St. Louis (UA), **St. Louis (NL)**, Cleveland (AA) 233 g, .251, 2 hr, 65 rbi (inc.); 1031 ip, 64–52, 2.87. 20 wins: 84

In 1884 Sweeney won 41 games, helping pitch two major league clubs to pennants. After winning 17 for Providence (NL), he was expelled from the league for leaving the field in the middle of a game, and promptly signed with St. Louis in the rival Union Association, where he won 24. With Providence on June 7, he struck out 19 Boston batters to set a ML record for a nine-inning game that, though tied four times, was not broken until Roger Clemens struck out 20 in 1986. In 1894 Sweeney killed a man in a San Francisco saloon. Sentenced to prison, he died there eight years later. /(FIC)

Jeff Sweeney [Edward Francis] — 1888–1847. C 1908–15, 19 **Yankees**, Pirates 644 g, .232, 3 hr, 151 rbi

In 1914 Sweeney stole 19 bases—the most ever by a Yankee catcher. He did the bulk of New York's catching from 1910 through 1914. He reportedly played a role in star first baseman Hal Chase's fall from grace in 1913. Sweeney didn't like the way Chase was mocking manager Frank Chance for the team's amusement. He told Chance, and Chase was suddenly dealt to the White Sox. /(MG)

Rick Sweet — 1952– . C 1978, 82–83 Padres, Mets, **Mariners** 272 g, .234, 6 hr, 57 rbi

A switch-hitting, platooned catcher, Sweet homered in his first Kingdome at-bat after joining Seattle in 1982. He remained with the Mariners after his playing days as a bullpen coach, advance scout, and minor league manager. /(NLM)

Les Sweetland (Sugar) — 1901–1974. LHP 1927–31 **Phillies**, Cubs 741 ip, 33–58, 6.10

Called up by the Phillies in mid-1927, Sweetland defeated Boston 5–4 in his ML debut, but lost 25 of his next 29 decisions over two seasons. In 1929, when he managed a 13–11 record despite a 5.11 ERA, one of his wins was an 11-hit shutout at Pittsburgh. /(AL)

Steve Swetonic — 1903–1974. RHP 1929–33, 35 **Pirates** 595 ip, 37–36, 3.81

Swetonic was a solid contributor to second-place Pittsburgh clubs in 1932 and 1933, going 11–6 and

12–12. In '32, he tied for the NL lead with four shutouts, though his activity was limited by a sore arm, which curtailed his career. /(ME)

Bill Swift [William Vincent] — 1908–1969. RHP 1932–41, 43 **Pirates**, Braves, Dodgers, White Sox 1638 ip, 95–82, 3.58

A sidearming fastball pitcher, Swift was successful his first five seasons with the Pirates, winning 70 games in the years 1932–36. Used mostly in relief his final six years, he won only 25 more. As a late-season Dodger pickup in 1941, he chipped in three victories and a save to help Brooklyn beat St. Louis for the NL pennant. /(JK)

Bill Swift [William Charles] — 1961– . RHP 1985–86, 88– **Mariners** 541 ip, 23–34, 4.78

Swift pitched on the 1984 U.S. Olympic team and was second choice overall in that year's free agent draft. The Mariners rushed him to the majors after only two months in the minors (the shortest stay in the minors in the history of the franchise). Swift was not ready and had a five-game losing streak on the way to a 6–10 record with a 4.77 ERA. In 1986, shuttling between Calgary and Seattle, Swift had a 2–9 record with a 5.46 ERA. He then spent 1987 on the DL due to bone spurs in his elbow. Swift has had moments of brilliance, including a 1–0 win over the Yankees and Tommy John in 1986 in which he went 7–2/3 innings without allowing a base hit. /(TF)

Bob Swift — 1915–1966. C 1940–53 Browns, A's, **Tigers** 1001 g, .231, 14 hr, 238 rbi. *1 WS, 3 g, .250. Manager 1965–66* **Tigers** 56–43, .566

A 14-year AL catcher, Swift was a smart handler of pitchers. But, behind the plate for the Tigers on August 18, 1951, he couldn't crouch low enough to frame a strike zone when the Browns sent midget Eddie Gaedel to bat. A skilled instructor, he was a winning minor league manager, a major league coach, and an interim manager for the Tigers in 1965 and 1966, filling in for the ailing Chuck Dressen. /(JK)

Greg Swindell (Zeke, Flounder) — 1965– . LHP 1986– **Indians** 590 ip, 39–30, 3.69
☛ *All-Star—89.*

Swindell was the youngest member of the 1984 U.S. Olympic Team. Possessing impeccable control and a 90-mph fastball, he was the Indians' number-one pick in the June 1986 draft and was brought to Cleveland August 21 after just three Class-A starts. His debut was inauspicious; he was removed in the fourth inning of a 24–5 loss to Boston. At 6'3" and indisputably chubby, he acquired a nickname he hated, Flounder, after the glutton from *Animal House*. But the front office stopped worrying about the cocky youngster's weight. He struck out 15 Royals in a May 10, 1987 game. Like Roger Clemens, he came from the University of Texas, where he would pitch a complete game one day and relieve the next. Resembling Clemens physically, and wearing Clemens's number 21, Swindell suffered the same medical fate as the Boston hurler; he was felled by arm trouble (elbow ligament damage) before completing a full ML season. He was disabled from July 2 on. He rested, slimmed down, and on the following May 30 became the first ML pitcher to reach ten victories in 1988. He did not win again for almost two months, but finished 18–14 with a 3.20 ERA. /(JCA)

Steve Swisher — 1951– . C 1974–82 **Cubs**, Cardinals, Padres 509 g, .216, 20 hr, 124 rbi
☛ *All-Star—76.*

The White Sox made Swisher their number-one draft choice in June of 1973, but sent him to the Cubs in the deal for Ron Santo that December. Though Swisher proved to be a disappointment, in 1976 he was the sole Cub named to the NL All-Star team; a special project of coach Lew Fonseca, he hit well in the first half, and was batting .394 against the Reds, whose manager, Sparky Anderson, chose the squad. Swisher finished the season at .236. Cleveland made him a minor league manager in 1986. /(DB)

Ron Swoboda (Rocky) — 1944– . OF 1965–73 **Mets**, Expos, Yankees 928 g, .242, 73 hr, 344 rbi. *1 WS, 4 g, .400, 1 rbi*

As a 20-year-old Met rookie in 1965, Swoboda hit a career-high 19 home runs. Though his subsequent career performance was a relative disappointment, he was a key member of the 1969 "Miracle Mets." He collected half of his 52 RBI in the last five weeks of the season, and hit two home runs to beat Steve Carlton 4–3 the night Carlton struck out 19 (September 15). In Game Four of the World Series, Swoboda's daring ninth-inning diving catch of Brooks Robinson's line drive in right-center field saved the day for New York. A vivacious character with an engaging sense of humor, Swoboda became a sportscaster after his career ended. /(CR)

Tom Swope — 1888–1969. *Writer.*

After brief stints with the Dayton *Herald* in 1908 and Cleveland *Press* in 1914, Swope was named sports editor and baseball writer of the Cincinnati *Post* in 1915 and stayed for 41 years. After one season as statistician on the Reds' TV broadcasts, he rejoined the *Post* to work on the night sports desk. President of the BBWAA in 1941, he was named in 1949 to a five-man committee to revise the scoring rules and did most of the writing. He had a large collection of baseball equipment, books, and writings, dating back to 1916. /(NLM)

Bob Sykes — 1954– . LHP 1977–81 Tigers, **Cardinals** 456 ip, 23–26, 4.65

A part-time starter and long reliever for five ML years, he was traded to the Yankees by the Cardinals even-up for future MVP Willie McGee after the 1981 season. /(CC)

Pat Tabler — 1958– . 1B-OF-DH-3B-2B 1981– Cubs, **Indians**, Royals 979 g, .287, 44 hr, 446 rbi
☛ *All-Star—87.*

Tried at first base, second base, third base, and in the outfield by the Yankee organization, the Cubs, and the Indians, Tabler eventually became Cleveland's first baseman. He was best suited for the DH role he inherited from Andre Thornton in 1987. A remarkably clutch, line-drive hitter, he gained attention for his amazing success in bases-loaded situations: 29-for-55 (.527) through 1987. He batted .326 in 1986, but frustrated the homer-happy Indians with his lack of power. In mid-1988 he was traded to Kansas City for pitcher Bud Black. /(ME)

Jim Tabor (Rawhide) — 1913–1953. 3B 1938–44, 46–47 **Red Sox**, Phillies 1005 g, .270, 104 hr, 598 rbi

The rough hewn Tabor had 95 RBI as a Red Sox rookie in 1939 but was overshadowed that year by another Red Sox freshman, Ted Williams. In a 1940 game against the Browns, Williams, Jimmie Foxx, and Joe Cronin hit consecutive homers, Bobby Doerr tripled, and then Tabor hit the fourth homer in five batters. His 21 homers in 1940 and 101 RBI in 1941 were career highs. /(JK)

Koichi Tabuchi — 1946– . C-1B 1968–Unk. **Hanshin Tigers**, Seibu Lions

Some consider the powerful 6'3" 210-lb Tabuchi the greatest Japanese catcher. After two years of challenging Sadaharu Oh for the home run crown, Tabuchi finally won it with 43 in 1975. Traded by Hanshin to Seibu, he switched to first base to prolong his career, and continued to hit between 20 and 30 HR a year into the mid-1980s. /(MC)

William Howard Taft — 1857–1930.

Taft became the first U.S. president to throw a ceremonial "first pitch" when he opened the 1910 season at Washington's League Park on April 14. An overflow crowd estimated at 15,000 attended the spectacle, and the Senators' Walter Johnson responded by pitching a one-hitter, beating the Athletics and Eddie Plank 3–0. Johnson might have recorded the first Opening Day no-hitter if not for the excess fans who spilled out of the grandstand and surrounded the outfield. In the seventh inning, Frank Baker lofted a fly ball to right field, but Washington's Doc Gessler collided with a youngster while giving chase and the ball fell for a double. Taft stayed for the entire game and enjoyed himself so much that the presidential "first pitch" became an annual event in Washington.

Taft was President from 1909 to 1913 and later became Chief Justice of the Supreme Court. /(SCL)

Doug Taitt (Poco) — 1902–1970. OF 1928–29, 31–32 **Red Sox**, White Sox, Phillies 258 g, .263, 4 hr, 95 rbi

A longtime minor leaguer, Taitt played regularly in the majors only with the 1928 Red Sox. He was a sparring partner for his brother-in-law, light-heavyweight boxer Jimmy Byrne. He died of Lou Gehrig's disease. /(NLM)

Take Me Out to the Ballgame — 1908.

One of the best-known songs in America, "Take Me Out to the Ballgame" was written by vaudeville's Jack Norworth in 1908. The music is by Albert von Tilzer, whose York Music Company published it. The song became a sensation when it was included with a set of picture slides in nickelodeons across the country. The verse has been largely forgotten, but the chorus is still sung at most ballparks in the country during the seventh-inning stretch. The complete song goes: Katie Casey was baseball mad, Had the fever and had it bad; Just to root for her hometown crew, Ev'ry sou, Katie blew. On a Saturday, her young beau Called to see if she'd like to go To see a show, but Miss Kate said, "No, I'll tell you what you can do. Take me out to the ball game, Take me out with the crowd. Buy me some peanuts and cracker jack, I don't care if I never get back. Let me root, root, root for the home team, If they don't win it's a shame. For it's one, two, three strikes you're out At the old ball game!" /(SCL)

Fred Talbot (Bubby) — 1941- . RHP 1963-70 White Sox, A's, **Yankees**, Pilots 854 ip, 38-56, 4.12

A journeyman who received little offensive support from his teams, Talbot's career-best ERA (3.36) came in 1968 with the Yankees, when he lost nine of ten decisions. /(GDW)

Vito Tamulis — 1911-1974. LHP 1934-35, 38-41 Yankees, Browns, **Dodgers**, Phillies 692 ip, 40-28, 3.97

Tamulis shut out the Athletics in his first ML start, September 25, 1934. The fun-loving junkballer couldn't stick with the staid Yankees despite a 10-5 rookie 1935 season. He landed in Brooklyn, where fans loved his encounters with Cardinals slugger Johnny Mize. Tamulis would come halfway to the plate, telling Mize he would strike him out with his rainbow change. Mize would often take futile swings at the floater. /(JK)

Frank Tanana — 1953- . LHP 1973- **Angels**, Red Sox, Rangers, Tigers 3404 ip, 198-188, 3.49. *2 LCS, 10 ip, 0-1, 4.35*
☛ *Led League—era 77. Led League—k 75. All-Star—76-78.*

Frank Tanana made the transition from a classic flamethrower with California to a crafty, curveballing veteran with Texas and Detroit. The Detroit native was *TSN* AL Rookie Pitcher of the Year in 1974, notched the first of three straight 200-strikeout seasons in 1975, and led the AL in ERA and shutouts in 1977. By age 25, however, his arm was thrown out, and a sore shoulder sidelined him for much of 1979. Tanana was second to Nolan Ryan among California's all-time leaders in wins, starts, complete games, strikeouts, innings and shutouts when he was traded to Boston, where he spent one forgettable season. Learning to compensate for his lost fastball, he was Texas Pitcher of the Year in 1984. Traded to the Tigers in June 1985, Tanana became a mainstay of the Detroit staff. His victory on the final day of the 1987 season against Toronto put Detroit in the playoffs. /(ME)

Jesse Tannehill — 1874-1956. LHP-OF 1894, 97-1909, 11 Reds, **Pirates**, Yankees, Red Sox, Senators 2770 ip, 197-116, 2.77; 505 g, .256, 5 hr, 141 rbi. 20 wins: 1898-1900, 02, 04-05
☛ *Led League—era 01.*

Jesse Tannehill was an outstanding turn-of-the-century pitcher and a switch-hitting outfielder who compiled a better batting average than his brother Lee, a ten-year White Sox infielder. He won 20 or more games six times; his 20-6 record for the Pirates in 1900 gave him the league's best winning percentage (.769). His 2.18 ERA in 1901 led the NL. In 1902 he again went 20-6 (1.95).

In 1903 Tannehill jumped to the Highlanders (later the Yankees) of the fledgling American League after a salary dispute with tight-fisted Pirates owner Barney Dreyfuss. He was with the Red Sox on August 17, 1904 when he no-hit the White Sox; brother Lee helped by going 0-for-3. Used in the outfield 87 times and as a pinch hitter 57 times, with his career winding down he actually played more games in the outfield for the 1909 Senators than he pitched (nine to three). /(DB)

Jesse Tannehill

Lee Tannehill — 1880–1938. 3B-SS 1903–12 **White Sox** 1089, .220, 3 hr, 346 rbi. *1 WS, 3 g, .111*

In 1905, Tannehill's bat slipped out of his hands and broke teammate Gus Dundon's jaw. That was one of the few things Lee hit all year. A season earlier, his 0-for-3 helped his older brother Jesse pitch a no-hitter. Appropriately, the tall and angular third baseman was a regular for a team called "The Hitless Wonders." In fact, four different managers kept him in the lineup for nearly a decade because he was the Brooks Robinson of his day in the field. He's the only shortstop to execute two unassisted double plays in one game. Ironically, this weak batsman hit the first home run in Comiskey Park, a windblown fly that bounced through a picket gate for a ground-rule grand slam. The year after he hit a career-high .254, he was released. /(DB)

Chuck Tanner — 1929– . OF 1955–62 **Braves**, Cubs, Indians, Angels 396 g, .261, 21 hr, 105 rbi.
Manager 1970–88 White Sox, A's, **Pirates**, Braves 1352–1381, .495. First place: 79 *1 LCS, 3-0, 1.000 1 WS, 4-3, .571*

Tanner debuted with the Milwaukee Braves on April 12, 1955, and became the third pinch hitter ever to homer on the first major league pitch he saw, tagging the Reds' Gerry Staley. But his only solid season as a player was 1957, with the Braves and Cubs, when he batted .279 with 48 RBI. In 1958, his 53 pinch-hitting appearances led the NL.

At the end of his eighth season as a minor league manager, Tanner took over the helm of the White Sox. He became known for his enthusiasm and eternal optimism. He brought Chicago in second in 1972 to win *TSN* ML Manager of the Year honors, but was fired after a fifth-place finish in 1975. He spent a year piloting Oakland before Charley Finley traded him to Pittsburgh for Manny Sanguillen and $100,000. Tanner's 1979 Pirates won the NL pennant, and defeated Baltimore in the World Series after falling behind three games to one.

Fired by Pittsburgh after finishing in the cellar in 1984–85, Tanner was hired by the Braves' Ted Turner, whom Tanner had defeated when Turner managed Atlanta for one game, on May 11, 1977. But Tanner's positive outlook could not prevent his third straight last-place finish in 1986, nor his dismissal after the Braves had gone 12–27 in 1988. He had come into 1988 with 17 consecutive full seasons as a manager—tops among active ML skippers. His son Bruce pitched ten games for the 1985 White Sox and was later traded to Oakland.

Another son, Mark, pitched in the Cub, White Sox, and Rangers organizations. /(RTM)

Danny Tartabull — 1962– . OF 1984– Mariners, **Royals** 603 g, .283, 106 hr, 375 rbi

A shortstop in the minors, Tartabull made it to the majors on a potent bat that shattered Pacific Coast League pitching in 1985 with 43 homers and 109 RBI. Moved to the outfield in the Kingdome, Tartabull hit 25 HR in his first full term with the Mariners. A trade sent him to Kansas City, where his father, Jose, had spent his best seasons with the Athletics. Placed in the clean-up spot, Tartabull hit 34 home runs in 1987, the second-highest total in Royals history. He averaged 100 RBI in his first three full seasons. /(FO)

Jose Tartabull — 1938– . OF 1962–70 **A's**, Red Sox 749 g, .261, 2 hr, 107 rbi. *1 WS, 7 g, .154*

Cuban-born Jose Tartabull was one of the fastest men in the American League. He got down the line from home to first in 3.4 seconds. A singles hitter, he batted a high of .312 with the 1965 A's, but never played regularly. He played in all seven games of the 1967 World Series, leading off and playing right field for the Red Sox in three of them. His son Danny hit as many home runs in his first ten games with the Mariners as Jose hit in his career (two). /(KC)

Willie Tasby — 1933– . OF 1958–63 **Orioles**, Red Sox, Senators, Indians 583 g, .250, 46 hr, 174 rbi

Tasby was the Orioles' regular centerfielder as a rookie in 1959. He once played in the Baltimore outfield with no shoes, afraid that lightning would be attracted to his metal cleats. He was drafted from Boston by the expansion 1961 Senators, for whom he hit 17 home runs. /(FK)

Terry Tata — 1940– . *Umpire* NL 1973–87 *1 ASU 4 LCS 2 WS*

Tata, the stepson of former NL umpire Augie Guglielmo, was involved in an unusual incident in 1987, a season of many protests about "scuffed" baseballs. On July 6, Cub manager Gene Michael became so upset with Giants pitcher Mike Krukow that he flung six allegedly scuffed balls in front of Tata, who was behind the plate. Instead of getting Krukow in trouble, Michael got himself sent to the showers by Tata. /(RTM)

Bennie Tate — 1901–1973. C 1924–32, 34 **Senators**, White Sox, Red Sox, Cubs 566 g, .279, 4 hr, 173 rbi. *1 WS, 3 g, --*

A backup catcher for Washington most of his career, Tate was behind the plate when Babe Ruth hit Tom Zachary's offering for his 60th home run in 1927. He pinch hit three times for the Senators in their victorious 1924 World Series, walking each time. /(NLM)

Ken Tatum — 1944- . RHP 1969-74 **Angels**, Red Sox, White Sox 283 ip, 16-12, 2.92

As an Angels rookie in 1969, Tatum went 7-2 with 22 saves and a minuscule 1.36 ERA. He followed with 17 saves in 62 appearances in 1970 before going to Boston in a six-player deal for Tony Conigliaro. Generally ineffective thereafter, he was soon done in by arm trouble. He hit four home runs in just 44 career at-bats. /(PB)

Jackie Tavener — 1897-1969. SS 1921, 25-29 **Tigers**, Indians 632 g, .255, 13 hr, 243 rbi

Tavener was an adequate hitter and a fielding whiz with a strong arm whose career was hurt by his size—5'5", 138 lb. Detroit manager Ty Cobb dismissed him at a glance in 1921, and Tavener did not become the Tigers' shortstop until 1925. He remained a regular for four seasons. /(JK)

Frank Taveras — 1950- . SS 1971-72, 74-82 **Pirates**, Mets, Expos 1150 g, .255, 2, 214. *2 LCS, 5 g, .111*

The volatile Taveras broke Max Carey's Pirate record by stealing an NL-leading 70 bases in 1977. His 206 steals rank sixth in Pirate history, but he had no home run power and was extremely erratic in the field. His 1979 trade to the Mets for steady Tim Foli was a key move in bringing that year's pennant to Pittsburgh. /(ME)

Ben Taylor — 1888-Unk. 1B-MGR Negro Leagues 1913-40 Chicago American Giants, Indianapolis ABC's, St. Louis Giants, Bacharach Giants, Washington Potomacs, Harrisburg Giants, Baltimore Black Sox, Baltimore Stars, Brooklyn Eagles, Washington Black Senators, New York Cubans 288 g, .354, 11 hr (inc.)

Ben Taylor, the youngest of four baseball brothers that included famed manager C.I. Taylor, Candy Jim Taylor, and Steel Arm Johnny Taylor, was the premier Negro League first baseman during the first quarter of the 20th century. He began his career with the St. Louis Giants in either 1911 or 1913, and peaked with the Indianapolis ABC's of 1915-22, managed by his brother, C.I. He went 11-for-18 in the 1916 Black World Series, stealing three bases in

five games. He batted .421 in 1921, with league highs of 106 hits and 19 doubles. He followed with a .362 mark. At the age of 41 he hit .310 in 12 games for the Bacharach Giants. He probably continued to play into the 1930s, but no records survive. He has been credited with a career .333 batting average.

Taylor was not only a great lefthanded hitter, but also a smooth defensive first baseman who made difficult plays look easy. An excellent teacher, he was instrumental in the development of Hall of Fame first baseman Buck Leonard. /(JJM)

C.I. Taylor [Charles Isam] — 1875-1922. MGR Negro Leagues 1904-22 Birmingham Giants, West Baden Sprudels, Indianapolis ABC's statistics not available

The eldest of four baseball brothers, C.I. Taylor was regarded by many players and peers as the finest manager in black baseball history. He was patient and dignified, a strict disciplinarian and a good teacher, scrupulously fair and honest with his players. After ten years managing the Birmingham Giants, he moved with the club to West Baden, IN in 1914. As the Sprudels, the club challenged Rube Foster's American Giants for the Chicago area's supremacy. With the backing of the American Brewing Company, the team settled in Indianapolis in 1915 as the ABC's.

Taylor's teams were perennial powers. At the time of his death, the ABC's were financially sound and one of the top three black teams in the Midwest. Taylor was also instrumental in the founding of the Negro National League and the National Association of Colored Professional Baseball Clubs. /(JO)

Candy Jim Taylor [James A.] — 1884-1948. 3B-2B-MGR Negro Leagues 1904-48 Birmingham Giants, St. Paul Gophers, St. Louis Giants, Indianapolis ABC's, Dayton Marcos, Cleveland Tate Stars, St. Louis Stars, Cleveland Elite Giants, Washington Elite Giants, Chicago American Giants, Homestead Grays, Baltimore Elite Giants, Leland Giants statistics not available

Candy Jim Taylor spent a lifetime in black baseball, sometimes accompanied by brothers Ben, Johnny, and C.I. He peaked as a player in 1916 as a key member of C.I.'s Black World Champion Indianapolis ABC's. Playing third base and hitting third in the order, he batted .478 in a key five-game series with the New York Lincoln Stars, and .360 in seven of ten BWS contests. He had also been instrumental in the successes of the 1909 Black Western champion St. Paul Gophers and the 1913 Chicago American Giants. He gained a reputation as a master strategist, managing three Negro National League teams to pennants—the 1928 St. Louis Stars, and the 1943 and 1944 Homestead Grays. The Grays won the BWS both years. /(MFK)

Carl Taylor — 1944- . C-OF-1B 1968-73 **Pirates**, Cardinals, Royals 411 g, .266, 10 hr, 115 rbi

Signed for a reported $50,000 bonus in 1962, Taylor had 17 pinch hits and hit .348 in 104 games in 1969, but he was weak defensively and never found a position. Boog Powell is his half-brother. /(ME)

Chuck Taylor — 1942- . RHP 1969-76 Cardinals, Mets, Brewers, **Expos** 607 ip, 28-20, 3.07

After eight minor league seasons with some success as a starter, Taylor fashioned a major league career in the bullpen. He was a control pitcher who made batters hit the ball. With the Expos in 1974, he had career bests of 61 games, 11 saves, and a 2.17 ERA. /(FJO)

Danny Taylor — 1900-1972. OF 1926, 29-36 Senators, Cubs, **Dodgers** 674 g, .297, 44 hr, 305 rbi

Taylor was a solidly built 5'10" 190-lb journeyman outfielder who didn't see regular action until he joined Brooklyn in 1932. He batted .319 that season, and never hit less than .290 in five seasons as a popular Dodger. /(JK)

Dummy Taylor [Luther Haden] — 1875-1958. RHP 1900-08 **Giants**, Indians 1916 ip, 115-106, 2.75. 20 wins: 04

Taylor was a deaf-mute. He was a favorite of the Giants' John McGraw, perhaps because he could not talk back. McGraw learned the rudiments of signing so he could communicate with Taylor from the bench. They were sharing opinions of Tim Hurst's umpiring one day without knowing the arbiter had a deaf relative and was also proficient in signing. Hurst ejected them both.

Taylor went 18-27 for New York in 1901, leading the NL in losses, games, starts, and hits allowed. He started the 1902 season with Cleveland but returned to the Giants, and went 21-15 for them in 1904. He compiled a 51-30 record from 1905 to 1908. He later joined the staff of the Illinois School for the Deaf. /(JK)

Harry Taylor — 1919- . RHP 1946-48, 50-52 **Dodgers**, Red Sox 358 ip, 19-21, 4.10. *1 WS, 0 ip, 0-0, 0.00*

Taylor came up as one of several postwar Dodger pitchers who found brief success. He went 10-5 as a

rookie in 1947 and started Game Four of the World Series. But a sore arm forced his removal after he faced just four batters. In that game, the Yankees' Bill Bevens took a no-hitter into the ninth inning. /(JK)

Hawk Taylor [Robert Dale] — 1939- . C-OF-1B 1957-58, 61-67, 69-70 Braves, **Mets**, Angels, Royals 394 g, .218, 16 hr, 82 rbi

Signed by the Braves for a $100,000 bonus as an 18-year-old in 1957, Taylor never lived up to his billing as a power hitter. Milwaukee gave up on him in 1963, selling him to the Mets. He appeared in more than half his ML games as a pinch hitter; in 1969 he led the AL with 49 pinch at-bats for the Royals. /(CR)

Jack Taylor [John W.] — 1874-1938. RHP 1898-07 **Cubs**, Cardinals 2617 ip, 151-139, 2.66. 20 wins: 02-04, 06

☛ *Led League—era 02.*

Taylor achieved one of the most remarkable pitching records of the 20th century: For five years, from June 20, 1901 to August 9, 1906, he was never once relieved in a game. During the span he started and completed 187 games, including one 19-inning and one 18-inning affair, and finished 15 in relief of others. On one occasion he pitched both ends of a doubleheader. /(LRD)

Ron Taylor — 1937- . RHP 1962-72 Indians, Cardinals, Astros, **Mets**, Padres 800 ip, 45-43, 3.93. *1 LCS, 3 ip, 1-0, 0.00. 2 WS, 7 ip, 0-0, 0.00*

Taylor saved 73 games in his career, almost all as bullpen ace for the Cardinals and Mets. In his first start, for the Indians in 1962, he lost a 12-inning duel, 4-0, on a grand slam by Boston's Carroll Hardy. Traded to St. Louis, he recorded a NL-high eight relief wins for the 1964 World Champions. When the Mets took the championship in 1969, Taylor won nine games and, for the second of three straight seasons, saved 13. In six career postseason appearances, he did not allow a run and had three saves. The Toronto native graduated from medical school five years after he finished pitching and became the Blue Jays' team physician. /(KT)

Sammy Taylor — 1933- . C 1958-63 **Cubs**, Mets, Reds, Indians 473 g, .245, 33 hr, 147 rbi

Taylor reached career highs of 109 games, 13 home runs, and a .269 average for the 1959 Cubs. That June 30, he was involved in a bizarre situation when two balls were put into play at one time. With a 3-1 count on Stan Musial, umpire Vic Delmore called ball four, but Taylor argued that the pitch had been fouled. He stood at the plate, arguing, as the ball rolled to the backstop. Musial took off for second as the dispute continued, and third baseman Alvin Dark ran to retrieve the ball, which had been tossed by the bat boy to field announcer Pat Peiper, who let it drop so that Dark could field it. Meanwhile, umpire Delmore had routinely handed a new ball to Taylor. Pitcher Bob Anderson threw the ball to second at the same time that Dark's throw of the first ball reached shortstop Ernie Banks. As Anderson's high throw went into the outfield, Musial thought he would continue to third, but Banks tagged him out with the initial ball. The umpires erroneously ruled Musial out despite the bat boy's having touched the ball. /(RTM)

Tony Taylor — 1935- . 2B-3B 1958-76 Cubs, **Phillies**, Tigers 2195 g, .261, 75 hr, 598 rbi. *1 LCS, 4 g, .133*
☛ *All-Star—60.*

The versatile Cuban infielder started as a third baseman in the Giants organization, but was drafted by the Cubs and played two years as their regular second baseman. In 1960 he was traded to the Phillies along with Cal Neeman for Don Cardwell and Ed Bouchee. The deal proved one of the best in Phillies history; the popular Taylor played 15 seasons in Philadelphia. After a half-dozen years at 2B, he became a valuable utility man and pinch hitter. Dealt to the Tigers in 1972, he helped them to a division title that year before returning to the Phillies in 1974 for his final three ML seasons. During his career, Taylor collected 2,007 hits, scored 1,005 runs, and stole 234 bases. His six steals of home for the Phillies is tied for second place on their all-time list. /(AL)

Zack Taylor [James Wren] — 1898-1974. C 1920-35 **Dodgers**, Braves, Giants, Cubs, Yankees 918 g, .261, 9 hr, 311 rbi. *1 WS, 5 g, .176, 3 rbi.*
Manager 1946, 48-51 **Browns** 235-410, .364

Taylor spent 50 years in organized baseball, and though 16 of them came as a major league catcher, he played regularly only from 1923 to 1929. He coached, managed, and scouted until 1970. He was at the Browns' helm for four-plus seasons, never winning more than 59 games, and was the man who sent pinch hitter Eddie Gaedel to the plate on August 18, 1951, the day the midget had his one famous at-bat. One of Veeck's more regular promotions was to allow fans to vote on managerial moves.

The fans' decisions were tallied up and relayed to Taylor. /(JK)

Bud Teachout [Arthur John] — 1904-1985. LHP 1930-32 **Cubs**, Cardinals 215 ip, 12-6, 4.51

Teachout had a fine rookie year, going 11-4 as a starter and reliever for the 1930 Cubs. He had no success in 1931 and was traded to the Cardinals with one Hall of Famer, Hack Wilson, for another, Burleigh Grimes. /(DAS)

Birdie Tebbetts [George Robert] — 1912- . C 1936-42, 46-52 **Tigers**, Red Sox, Indians 1162 g, .270, 38 hr, 469 rbi. *1 WS, 4 g, .000.*
Manager 1954-58, 61-66 **Reds**, Braves, Indians 781-744, .512
☛ *All-Star—41-42, 48-49.*

A high-voiced, talkative backstop, Birdie's nickname was acquired while at Providence College. A consistent hitter, he made exactly 1,000 hits in a 14-year career interrupted by three years of military service. He managed for 11 ML seasons. /(JK)

Patsy Tebeau [Oliver Wendell] — 1864-1918. 1B-3B-2B-SS 1887, 1889-1900 Chicago (NL), **Cleveland (NL)**, Cleveland (PL), Cardinals 1167 g, .280, 27 hr, 735 rbi.
Manager 1890-1900 Cleveland (PL), **Cleveland (NL)**, Cardinals 732-575, .560

Tebeau, who managed the teams he played for in all but two of his major league seasons, was an impetuous and flamboyant team leader, high-spirited and friendly. He positioned himself all over the infield, and had his best years as a player from 1893 through 1895, batting better than .300 each season. In 1899, when Cy Young and other stars were shifted from Cleveland (NL) to St. Louis (NL), Tebeau, a St. Louis native, continued to manage them. In the midst of only his second losing season, his career ended in 1900 with his team in seventh place. His brother, George "White Wings" Tebeau, played in the American Association before joining Patsy in Cleveland in 1894-95. /(JK)

Kent Tekulve (Teke) — 1947- . RHP 1974-89 **Pirates**, Phillies, Reds 1436 ip, 94-90, 2.85. *2 LCS, 4 ip, 0-0, 4.15. 1 WS, 9 ip, 0-1, 2.89*
☛ *All-Star—80.*

Tekulve is the all-time major league leader in relief appearances with 1,050. He went 10-1 as a set-up man for Goose Gossage in 1977, and took over as the Pirates' closer after Gossage signed with the Yankees that November. He established himself as one of baseball's most successful relievers, ranking among the all-time leaders in games, saves, and relief wins. With his sidearm delivery, the bespectacled, 6'4", rail-thin Tekulve proved baffling to both lefthanders and righthanders. In 1978, he set a Pirates record with 31 saves, which he matched the following year. He led the NL in appearances in both 1978 and 1979, setting a club record with 94 in 1979. That fall, he recorded a World Series-record three saves, striking out 10 Orioles in 9.1 innings.

Tekulve led the NL in appearances (85) and relief wins (12) in 1982. He was the Pirates' all-time leader in saves (158) and was second to Roy Face in games (722) when he was traded to Philadelphia in 1985. On September 16, 1986 he broke Face's NL record of 846 games pitched. Back in the set-up role, in 1987 he became the first NL pitcher to have three 90-appearance seasons and, at age 40, the oldest pitcher to lead the NL in appearances. He broke Sparky Lyle's ML record for career games pitched without a start (finishing the season at 943), and helped closer Steve Bedrosian win the Cy Young Award. Let go after 1988, he signed with the Reds and broke Hoyt Wilhelm's record for relief appearances. Midway through the season, with the Reds sinking in the standings, he retired rather than hang on just for the sake of topping Wilhelm's record for total appearances. /(ME)

Tom Tellman — 1954- . RHP 1979-80, 83-85 Padres, **Brewers**, A's 227 ip, 18-7, 3.05

Tellman was an effective middle reliever for the Brewers in 1983-84, winning 15 games and saving 12 over two seasons with an ERA below three each year. As a minor league starter, he led the Pacific Coast League in shutouts at Hawaii in 1980. /(SCL)

Temple Cup — 1894-1897.

William Temple, the president of the Pittsburgh Pirates, proposed in 1893 that a postseason series be played between the National League's first- and second-place teams. In the 1880s, there had been postseason play between the winners of the NL and the American Association, but in 1892 the NL absorbed the AA (becoming a 12-team circuit) and played a split season. That plan was roundly criticized, and was dropped after just one year; in 1893 the Pirates had finished second to the Boston Beaneaters, and Temple felt they had missed a series that was due them. The Temple Cup series was patterned after the earlier Dauvray Cup; permanent possession of the Cup, which cost $800, would go to the first team to win it three times. Lack of

enthusiasm on the part of the players doomed the series; their apathy spread to the fans, who stayed away in droves in later years. The series was dropped after 1897, with no team taking the Cup, although the Orioles were close with two winning series; had they taken it seriously in their first two efforts, they would most likely have captured it. Instead, the league returned it to Mr. Temple; it is now in the Hall of Fame. /(SH)

Johnny Temple — 1928- . 2B 1952-64 **Reds**, Indians, Orioles, Astros 1420 g, .284, 22 hr, 395 rbi
☛ *All-Star—56-57, 59, 61.*

Temple was the popular second baseman for the Reds during the 1950s, a four-time NL All-Star. He hit .300 three times and tied for the NL lead in walks in 1957 with 94. He led NL second basemen three times in putouts and once each in assists and double plays. /(JK)

Garry Templeton (Jump Steady) — 1956- . SS 1976-Cardinals, **Padres** 1823 g, .275, 58 hr, 643 rbi. *1 LCS, 5 g, .333, 2 rbi. 1 WS, 5 g, .316*
☛ *All-Star—77, 79, 85.*

During his years with the Cardinals, Garry Templeton seemed ready to join the ranks of baseball's great shortstops. But away from Busch Stadium's Astroturf as a San Diego Padre, his statistics declined. Selected by St. Louis in the first round of the June 1974 draft, Templeton became the youngest shortstop in modern history (since 1900) to reach the 200-hit plateau (1977) and finished second in the NL batting race. In 1979 he became the first switch-hitter ever with 100 hits from each side of the plate in one season. He also achieved a NL first with his third straight triples championship. In May 1981, Templeton asked to be traded, preferably to San Diego. That August, he made a series of obscene gestures at fans who booed him for not running out a ground ball. Templeton was suspended, fined, and he agreed to psychiatric examination. On February 11, 1982 the erratic Templeton was traded to the Padres for defensive wizard Ozzie Smith. Though he set a San Diego record for shortstops with 64 RBI in 1982, earned a Silver Slugger Award in 1984, and was San Diego's Most Valuable Player in 1985 when he tied for the NL lead in intentional walks (from the eighth spot in the batting order), Templeton did not approach his St. Louis achievements. He was hampered by knee and back problems, and by consistently swinging at first pitches and bad pitches. /(ME)

Gene Tenace [born Fiore Gino Tennaci] — 1946- . C-1B 1969-83 **A's**, Padres, Cardinals, Pirates 1555 g, .241, 201 hr, 674 rbi. *5 LCS, 18 g, .088, 2 rbi. 4 WS, 24 g, .228, 4 hr, 12 rbi*
☛ *All-Star—75.*

Tenace was an underappreciated talent whose magnificent performance in the 1972 World Series displayed to the world his valuable but rarely spotlighted abilities, abilities which modern-day sabermetric analysis has made more apparent.

Tenace warmed up for his MVP WS effort by driving in the LCS-clinching run in Oakland's 2–1 victory in Game Five against the Tigers; it was his only hit of the series. In Game One of the WS Tenace became the first player ever to hit home runs in his first two Series at-bats, and in the process drove in all the A's runs in their 3–2 victory over the Reds. In fact, it was the first time in his career that he hit two homers in a game. In Game Four, the A's were losing 2–1, with their only run to that point coming on Tenace's solo HR. A ninth-inning one-out rally consisting of four singles, with Tenace's the second and the rest coming from pinch hitters, won the game against Cincinnati's ace reliever, Clay Carroll. Tenace also had a three-run homer in Oakland's Game Five loss, and was the hero of Game Seven, driving in two runs in the A's 3–2 clinching victory. He hit .348 overall, and his four home runs tied what was then the WS record. Tenace had been a second-string catcher for most of the regular season, hitting .225 with five HR in 82 games. The only hint of his ability in the clutch came from his 7-for-17 performance as a pinch hitter.

Tenace's power could not be ignored. He reached 20 HR in five of his seven seasons as a regular, with a high of 29 in 1975. But throughout his career, his low batting averages were focused on. Missed was the fact that, after becoming an everyday player in 1973, he didn't have an on-base average below .370 until his final year; his OBA was above .400 five times and over .390 (about 60 points above the league average) an additional three times. Six times he drew more than 100 bases on balls, and he led his league twice.

Tenace's 1972 World Series performance earned him an everyday job the next season. Not blessed with a strong-enough arm to be a good catcher, he was moved to first base. His versatility was always a strong point; he was even briefly used at second base in the '72 LCS. He had four solid seasons as an Oakland regular, and was appreciated enough that he played 158 games in 1974 despite a .211 batting average. But like most of the A's stars, he escaped via the free-agent route, signing with the Padres after the 1976 season. He actually had some of his best seasons from then on, but San Diego owner Ray Kroc had little understanding of the fine points of baseball and saw only that he had made a millionaire of a man who hit .233 and .223 in his first two seasons with the Padres. Tenace was traded following the 1980 season, going to St. Louis in the 11-player deal that sent Rollie Fingers (briefly) to the Cardinals and brought Terry Kennedy to San Diego. Tenace spent his last three seasons as a utility man. He got into one final World Series in 1982 with the Cardinals, but he never hit another WS home run after 1972. /(SH)

John Tener — 1863-1946. RHP 1885, 88-90 Baltimore (AA), **Cubs**, Pittsburgh (PL) 506 ip, 25-31, 4.30

The first ex-player to become a president of a major league, Tener was born in Ireland, and pitched for Cap Anson's Chicago White Stockings. He went with the club on its 1888–89 tour around the world and, an accountant, was made treasurer for the trip by the players. When they returned to discover the owners had imposed salary restrictions, Tener became secretary of the Brotherhood of Professional Players and jumped to Pittsburgh in the new Players' League. The league folded in 1890. Tener entered banking and politics, and was elected to Congress in 1908. He was governor of Pennsylvania for a four-year term and was asked to become president of the National League. He accepted in 1914 and remained until 1918, when he resigned over a dispute with the American League over the contract of a player, Scott Perry. /(JK)

Fred Tenney — 1859-1952. 1B-OF-C 1894-1909, 11 **Braves**, Giants 1994 g, .295, 22 hr, 688 rbi. *Manager* 1905-07, 11 **Braves** 202-402, .334

Tenney went from Brown University to the Boston Beaneaters (later renamed the Braves) when there were few collegians in the hard-bitten world of 19th-century baseball. Dad Clarke, a rough-and-tumble opposing pitcher, taunted the young Tenney about the courage of players from colleges. Tenney responded by spitting tobacco juice on Clarke's feet. He broke in as a lefthanded catcher, already a vanishing breed, and starting in 1897 was Boston's first baseman for over a decade. He topped the .300 mark seven times in his first ten seasons, and never again. In four years as Boston's player-manager, he twice finished seventh, and twice last. In 1908, his first of two seasons with the Giants, he led the NL with 101 runs scored. He became a regular correspondent for *The New York Times*, offering annual preseason assessments and covering the World Series. /(JK)

Fred Tenney

Frank Tepedino — 1947– . 1B-OF 1967, 69–75 Yankees, Brewers, **Braves** 265 g, .241, 6 hr, 58 rbi

Many thought Tepedino, a top Yankee prospect, had one of the sweetest swings in baseball, but most reports said "good hit, no field." He played only 52 games in five trials with New York, who dealt him to Atlanta in 1973. Tepedino's response to the trade: "I'll never understand why I didn't get a shot with the Yankees. I have a career average of .270, but they said I couldn't hit."/(KC)

Jerry Terrell — 1946– . 3B-SS-2B-DH-1B-OF 1973–80 **Twins**, Royals 657 g, .253, 4 hr, 125 rbi

Terrell built his career on versatility, speed, and a good glove. Known for his team-first attitude, he played every position except catcher in the ML. Terrell's best season was 1975 when he batted .286 in 108 games for the Twins. /(FO)

Walt Terrell — 1958– . RHP 1982– Mets, **Tigers**, Padres, Yankees 1473 ip, 84–89, 4.01. *1 LCS, 6 ip, 0–0, 9.00*

Terrell is a consistent, durable starter, pitching over 200 innings each year since 1984 and winning 15 or more games three times. Originally in the Rangers system, he was traded to the Mets with Ron Darling for Lee Mazzilli in 1982, and was International League pitcher of the year at Tidewater in 1983, going 10–1, 3.12. After an 11–12, 3.52 season with the Mets in 1984, he was traded to the Tigers for Howard Johnson. Terrell won 54 games in four seasons in Detroit, including a career-high 17 in 1987, and was 32–7 at Tiger Stadium. His record slipped to 7–16 in 1988, largely due to poor offensive support from his teammates, and he was traded to San Diego for Chris Brown and Keith Moreland before the 1989 season. On August 6, 1983, Terrell hit two home runs off Ferguson Jenkins./(SCL)

Adonis Terry [William H.] — 1864–1915. RHP-OF 1884–97 **Brooklyn (AA)**, Brooklyn (NL), Baltimore (NL), Pittsburgh (NL), Chicago (NL) 3523 ip, 197–195, 3.72; 668 g, .249, 15 hr, 162 rbi. 20 wins: 1884, 89, 90, 95

Handsome Adonis Terry brought more women to the ballpark than free admission on Ladies' Day. He was usually a pitcher, a four-time 20-game winner who no-hit St. Louis in 1886 and Louisville in 1888 while pitching for Brooklyn (AA). He played other positions, including 216 games in the outfield, in one-third of his ML games. Regarded as a potent hitter, he often batted in other than the ninth spot, even when he was the pitcher. /(JK)

Bill Terry (Memphis Bill) — 1896–1989. 1B 1923–36 **Giants** 1721 g, .341, 154 hr, 1078 rbi. *3 WS, 16 g, .295, 2 hr, 7 rbi*
　　　Manager 1932–41 **Giants**, 823–661, .555 First place: 33, 36–37. *3 WS, 7–9, .438*
☛ Led League—ba 30. All-Star—33–35. *Hall of Fame—1954.*

Terry's .401 batting average in 1930 makes him the last NL player to hit over .400. Though there were unusually high batting averages that year (the entire NL averaged .303), 30 other future Hall of Fame members playing regularly in both leagues in 1930 did not hit .400. Terry was a great hitter who had three other seasons over .350 and averaged .341 for his 14-season career. When he wanted to, he could pull the ball into the stands; in 1932, he slugged 28

Bill Terry

before from an ailing John McGraw. After rebuilding the club, he won pennants in 1936 and 1937.

But despite his accomplishments with a bat and glove, and as a manager, he was never a favorite with the New York writers. He was blunt and unwilling to cater to them. Most of all, they resented his insistence on keeping his private life private. Among other gripes they had was his refusal to hand out his private telephone number; he spent 16–18 hours available at the Polo Grounds and that was enough, as far as he was concerned.

Early in 1934, when he was asked about the perennially tail-end Dodgers, he responded jokingly, "Is Brooklyn still in the league?" His offhand remark was widely considered a contemptuous put-down. When the Dodgers won the last two meetings of the season to knock the Giants out of the pennant, some New York writers insisted Terry's "arrogance" had cost his team the title.

The baseball writers elected Terry to the Hall of Fame in 1954, 18 years after he retired as a player. Terry showed no bitterness that his election was so long delayed and became a regular participant in the annual induction ceremonies for many years. /(JK)

Ralph Terry — 1936– . RHP 1956–67 **Yankees**, A's, Indians, Mets 1849 ip, 107–99, 3.62. *5 WS, 46 ip, 2–4, 2.93*
☛ *All-Star—62.*

Terry could have been remembered only as the man who gave up Bill Mazeroski's legendary Series-winning homer in 1960, but he redeemed himself with an All-Star season in 1962 that was capped by an outstanding World Series.

Terry came up with the Yankees in 1956, but was traded to Kansas City in June 1957 in the eight-player deal that exiled Billy Martin and brought Ryne Duren to New York. He went 4–11 the rest of the season for the seventh-place Athletics, but was reacquired by the Yankees in May 1959 after going 11–13 in 1958, impressive considering the lack of offensive and defensive support the A's offered. He went 10–8 in 1960 as the Yankees' fourth starter. He started and lost Game Four of the World Series to the Pirates, 3–2. After warming up five times while Bobby Shantz, who had a sore arm, pitched five valiant innings in relief, Terry finally relieved in the eighth inning of Game Seven with the Pirates in the midst of a go-ahead rally. He got the last out with no further damage, and the Yankees came back in the top of the ninth inning to tie the game at 9–9. But Terry surrendered a home run to Bill Mazeroski, the Pirates' first batter, on a 1–0 pitch: it might

homers. But more typically, he hit doubles and triples into the deep power alleys of the Polo Grounds.

Defensively, he was the best of his day. In the ten seasons he played regularly, he led NL first basemen in fielding average twice, double plays three times, putouts and assists five times each, and total chances per game nine times. Terry was 26 before he came to the ML and then had to move future Hall of Famer George Kelly off first to play regularly for the Giants. Most of his record was achieved from the age of 30 on, and, during his last five seasons, he also served as the Giants' manager.

Terry's Giants won the 1933 pennant and WS with a tattered team he'd taken over the season be the most famous homer in World Series history. It was Terry's second loss of the Series, and deprived manager Casey Stengel of one last World Championship.

Terry emerged as New York's second-best pitcher in 1961 with an excellent 16–3 mark and a 3.15 ERA. He lost Game Two of the World Series 6–2, the Reds' only victory, but only two of the Reds' four runs off him were earned. Terry was hit hard in Game Five and departed after allowing three runs in 2.1 innings, but the Yankees had already scored six runs by that point and won 13–5.

In 1962 Terry had the best season of his career and finally achieved World Series redemption. He went 23–12 with a 3.19 ERA and led the AL in wins, starts (39), and innings (298.2). He lost Game Two of the WS 2–0 as the Yankees managed only three hits, but finally garnered his first WS win in Game Five, a complete-game 5–3 victory. A three-day rain delay before Game Six allowed him to come back for Game Seven. Pitching a superb four-hit shutout, he won 1–0 after getting Willie McCovey to line right at second baseman Bobby Richardson with two out and two on.

Terry went 17–15 in 1963 with a 3.22 ERA and led the AL with 37 starts and 18 complete games. He also showed the best control of his career, walking just 39 batters in 268 innings. He was only needed in relief in that year's World Series as the Yankees were swept by the Dodgers. Dropping to 7–11 in 1964, he was moved to the bullpen and then traded to Cleveland during the September pennant drive with Buddy Daley and $75,000 for Pedro Ramos, whose relief brilliance down the stretch was crucial to the Yankees' pennant. Terry rebounded to 11–6, 3.59 in 1965 but was out of the majors within two years. He went on to become a golf pro./(WOR)

Scott Terry — 1959– . RHP 1986– Reds, **Cardinals** 347 ip, 18–18, 3.73

Terry was shelled regularly out of the Reds' bullpen his rookie season. He found poise and success in the Cardinal pen, and when inserted into the St. Louis rotation in August 1988, he reeled off seven straight victories. An outfielder in the minors, he achieved an unusual distinction in 1989: his two home runs to centerfield, both traveling more than 400 feet, were the longest hit at Busch Stadium that season./(FO)

Yank Terry [Lancelot Yank] — 1911–1979. RHP 1940, 42–45 **Red Sox** 457 ip, 20–28, 4.09

Terry won his major league debut in 1940, but was sent to the Pacific Coast League for seasoning and in 1941 was the runaway PCL MVP, going 26–8. As a wartime Red Sox hurler he won seven games in 1943./(CG)

Zeb Terry [Zebulon Alexander] — 1891– . SS-2B 1916–22 White Sox, Braves, Pirates, **Cubs** 640 g, .260, 2 hr, 216 rbi

Terry played at a weight less than 130 lb, but batted .275 or better in three of his four seasons as a regular with the Pirates and Cubs./(JK)

Wayne Terwilliger (Twig) — 1925– . 2B 1949–51, 53–56, 59–60 Cubs, Dodgers, **Senators**, Giants, A's 666 g, .240, 22 hr, 162 rbi

A star shortstop at Western Michigan University, Twig collected eight consecutive hits for the Cubs in 1949. The next year, he was included in the deal that sent Andy Pafko to Brooklyn. The ex-Marine later spent two seasons as the Senators' second baseman./(RTM)

Jeff Tesreau — 1889–1946. RHP 1912–18 **Giants** 1679 ip, 119–72, 2.43. 20 wins: 13–14 *3 WS, 32 ip, 1–3, 3.62*
☛ *Led League—era 12.*

Tesreau was a sturdy 6'2" 218-lb hurler who topped the NL in starts in 1913–14. He threw a spitball with the speed of a top fastball. As a rookie in 1912, he led the league with a 1.96 ERA and went 17–7 for the Giants and no-hit the Phillies on September 6. He was John McGraw's choice, over Christy Mathewson and Rube Marquard, to pitch the World Series opener against Boston's 34-game winner, Smoky Joe Wood. Wood won it 4–3, and defeated Tesreau again, 3–1, in Game Four. Tesreau won their matchup in Game Seven of a Series that went eight games.

Tesreau went 22–13 for the '13 pennant winners and 26–10 with a league-high eight shutouts in '14. He proved he could win with a loser in 1915 when he went 19–16 (2.29) for the last-place Giants. He retired with 27 career shutouts. Tesreau later became a successful and popular coach at Dartmouth./(JK)

Mickey Tettleton — 1960– . C 1984– **A's**, Orioles 486 g, .240, 59 hr, 183 rbi
☛ *All-Star—89.*

Tettleton was released before the 1988 season after

four years as an undistinguished part-time catcher for the A's, but signed with Baltimore and hit .261 with 11 HR while platooning with Terry Kennedy. The switch-hitter blossomed as Baltimore's everyday catcher in 1989, reaching a career high in home runs. His wife attributed his newfound prowess to eating Fruit Loops cereal.

With Oakland, Tettleton often fell victim to unusual injuries, missing almost half of 1985 with a pinched nerve in his back and part of 1986 with an infected foot. /(SCL)

Tim Teufel (Tuff) — 1958– . 2B 1983– Twins, **Mets** 679 g, .264, 51 hr, 255 rbi. *2 LCS, 3 g, .111. 1 WS, 3 g, .444, 1 hr, 1 rbi*

Teufel spent two seasons as the Twins' everyday second baseman. Considered deficient defensively, he led AL second basemen in assists in 1984 but established an AL record for fewest double plays by a second baseman in 150 or more games (81). Teufel was traded to the Mets, who needed a righthanded-hitting platoon partner for Wally Backman. He hit only .247 in the Mets' 1986 World Championship season, but lined 20 doubles in 279 at-bats. He hit a career-high .308 in 1987 with 14 HR, 29 doubles, and 55 walks in 299 at-bats. Handed the job on an everyday basis in 1988, he

struggled early and then went on the DL. He hit a career-low .238 but had 20 doubles for the fifth straight season. The highly touted Gregg Jefferies was given the second base job in 1989 and Teufel was reduced to a useful utility role. /(SH)

Bob Tewksbury — 1960– . RHP 1986– **Yankees**, Cubs, Cardinals 215 ip, 11–13, 4.19

An often-injured starter, Tewksbury was 9–5, 3.31 as a rookie in 1986, the only season since 1982 in which he did not spend time on the DL. He led the Florida State League in wins, ERA, and shutouts at Fort Lauderdale in 1982, but after only 29 starts for the Yankees was one of three players traded to the Cubs for Steve Trout. Tewksbury never won a game for Chicago. /(SCL)

Texas Rangers — 1972– . Team. 1334–1511, 469

Futility and instability defined the Texas Rangers in the 1970s and 1980s. Owner Rob Short transferred the second incarnation of the Washington Senators to Arlington, Texas in 1972. The old tradition continued, though, as Texas lost 205 games in two years. The first brought Ted Williams's managerial career to an end. Brad Corbett, who made his money in plastic pipes, acquired the Rangers in May 1974. Manager Billy Martin led the team to second

The 1979 Texas Rangers

place that season, but had burned out by mid-1975. In 1977, Corbett employed four different managers (counting Eddie Stanky, who quit after one day, and interim Connie Ryan). The fourth, Billy Hunter, guided the club to a Ranger-record 94 victories. But cash-poor Corbett all but dismantled the team, and let young pitchers Dave Righetti and Jim Clancy escape as well. Mediocrity was the order under Eddie Chiles, who bought the Rangers in February 1980 and allowed GM Eddie Robinson to deal two more young pitchers, Walt Terrell and Ron Darling, for Lee Mazzilli. In 1985 Bobby Valentine (the team's 13th manager in 15 seasons), innovative pitching coach Tom House, and the president-GM combo of Mike Stone and Tom Grieve began a patient building plan. A devotion to scouting in Latin America introduced young stars such as Ruben Sierra. Chiles, fading in the oil bust, sold out to a group led by George W. Bush, son of the president, in March 1989. Bush began negotiations for a new stadium as neighboring Dallas opened a campaign to usurp the team just as Arlington had from the nation's capital in 1972. /(KT)

Ernest L. Thayer — Unk.–Unk. *Writer.*

Despite other claimants, Thayer is recognized as the author of "Casey at the Bat." The poem first appeared in the San Francisco *Examiner* on June 3, 1888, subtitled "A Ballad of the Republic." Thayer had been writing a humor column for the *Examiner*, which was published by his Harvard classmate, William Randolph Hearst. But at the time the poem was published, Thayer had quit journalism and was in Worcester, Massachusetts to help run the family textile factory.

The actor DeWolf Hopper began reciting the poem to audience approval in 1892. When it first appeared in a volume of poetry in 1902, it was attributed to another writer. /(NLM)

The Sporting News — 1886– .

The first edition of *The Sporting News* was published by Alfred H. Spink and his brother, Charles, on March 17, 1886, in St. Louis. A total of 4,986 issues of the weekly appeared with the Spink name at the top. The eight-page paper sold for five cents, or $2.50 per year, and featured news of baseball, cycling, hunting, boxing, and the stage. Charles C. Spink was in South Dakota trying his hand at homesteading when his brother offered him $50 a week to handle the business end of the publication. The Spinks later published the first baseball guide, as well as record books, *The Sporting News Dealer*,

and many baseball books. The paper stayed in the family until it was sold in 1977 to the Times-Mirror Company for $18 million.

In the early 20th century, it had evolved into a baseball-only paper. After WWII, it began to cover other sports. In 1962 C.C. Johnson Spink removed the traditional eagle with a streamer in his beak reading "Baseball" from the masthead, despite strong objections from longtime readers. Keeping the record straight and siding with whatever it felt was in the best interests of the game were two hallmarks of the paper. In 1981 they discovered an error in a 1910 box score that would have made Nap Lajoie that year's batting champion instead of Ty Cobb. A committee appointed by the Commissioner's office voted unanimously that the records should not be changed. *The Sporting News* answered, "They said we were trying to rewrite history. But if history is wrong it should be righted." /(NLM)

Ron Theobald [The Little General] — 1944– . 2B
1971–72 Brewers 251 g, .248, 2 hr, 42 rbi

Theobald was an All-American at Arizona State. Signed by the Cubs, he played in the Twins and Senators organizations before being traded to the Brewers. Milwaukee's second baseman for two seasons, in 1971 the scrappy, 5'8" Theobald hit .276 (second on the club) and led the AL with 19 sacrifice hits. In 1972 he and Rick Auerbach formed a punchless double play combination with three HR and 49 RBI between them, although Theobald made just six errors in his 113 games at second base. /(PB)

Tommy Thevenow — 1903–1957. SS-2B-3B
1924–38 Cardinals, Phillies, Pirates, Cubs, Braves 1229 g, .247, 2 hr, 456 rbi. *2 WS, 8 g, .417, 1 hr, 4 rbi*

In 1926, Thevenow starred for the Cardinals' first World Champions, led NL shortstops in putouts and assists, and hit his only two regular-season home runs. He was credited with another home run in the WS when Babe Ruth dropped his Game Two fly ball. The next spring, Thevenow held out, and, when he returned, suffered a fractured ankle in June. The injury cost him his speed and left him with a limp. In later seasons, he broke his jaw, a finger, and, in a 1931 auto accident, a leg. All told, he played 100 or more games in only 6 of his 14 ML seasons. /(ME)

Jake Thielman (John) — 1879–1928. RHP 1905–08
Cardinals, Indians, Red Sox 475 ip, 30–28, 3.16

As a rookie in 1905, Thielman led the sixth-place Cardinals in wins with 15, but he was returned to the minors the next season. He had a winning record with Cleveland two years later, completing all of his 18 starts. His younger brother Henry lost 12 straight for the 1902 Reds. /(BC)

Jake Thies [Vernon Arthur] — 1926– . RHP 1954–55 **Pirates** 134 ip, 3–10, 3.90

One of many luckless young pitchers used by the hapless Pirates in the early 1950s, Thies's finest moment came when he defeated the Reds' Herm Wehmeier after Wehmeier had beaten Pittsburgh 11 straight times. /(ME)

Bobby Thigpen — 1963– . RHP 1986– **White Sox** 294 ip, 16–19, 3.06

After his emergence as Chicago's bullpen ace in 1987 following the injury problems of Bob James, Thigpen carried on an odd salary battle with the White Sox front office in the off-season. He stated his case in awkward doggerel verse, with the team responding in like fashion; the exchange was even reprinted in *The Wall Street Journal*. He proved his worth more convincingly in 1988 with 34 saves. /(SH)

Andres Thomas — 1963– . SS 1985– **Braves** 493 g, .237, 37 hr, 198 rbi

Finally taking over the Braves' shortstop job on an everyday basis in 1988 after injuries in 1987 delayed the move, Thomas had a career year, hitting .252 with 13 HR and 68 RBI, although he walked only 14 times while striking out 95 times. The Dominican also led NL shortstops in double plays, but tied for the lead in errors. /(SFS)

Bud Thomas [Luther Baxter] — 1910– . RHP 1932–33, 37–41 Senators, **A's**, Tigers 526 ip, 25–34, 4.96

Thomas lost regularly as a starter for Connie Mack's tailenders in 1937 and '38. In 1939 he arrived in Detroit on waivers and won seven straight in relief. /(JK)

Clint Thomas (Hawk) — 1896–Unk. OF-2B Negro Leagues 1920–37 Brooklyn Royal Giants, Columbus Buckeyes, Detroit Stars, **Hilldale**, Bacharach Giants, New York Lincoln Giants, New York Cubans, Newark Eagles, New York Black Yankees, Philadelphia Stars statistics not available

Thomas entered Negro League baseball as a second baseman before being moved to the outfield by Detroit Stars manager Bruce Petway in 1922. He quickly gained the nickname Hawk as a sharp-eyed hitter and a far-ranging centerfielder. He consistently hit for power, and he ran the bases with skill

and speed. In 1923 he began a six-year stay with the Hilldale club, and was a key player in their 1923–25 Eastern Colored League championships.

In 1929 Thomas hit .322 as a Bacharach Giant, then starred for the 1930 New York Lincoln Giants. He joined the New York Black Yankees in 1931, spending much of the remainder of his career with them. He ruined the 1932 unveiling of Greenlee Field by scoring the only run and making a spectacular, game-saving catch in the Black Yankees' defeat of Satchel Paige and the hometown Pittsburgh Crawfords. Thomas's performance prompted Crawfords outfielder Ted Page to remark, "Clint could chase that ball into another world."

Compiled figures indicate that Thomas's lifetime average was in the .326 range. He played six years in the Cuban Winter League, batting .310. In four exhibitions against white major leaguers, he hit .417 (5-for-12). /(MFK)

Derrel Thomas — 1951– . 2B-OF-SS-3B 1971–85 Astros, Padres, Giants, **Dodgers**, Expos, Angels, Phillies 1597 g, .249, 43 hr, 370 rbi. *2 LCS, 6 g, .500. 1 WS, 5 g, .000*

A jack-of-all-trades, Thomas played every position but pitcher in the majors. The speedster and admitted hot dog was considered one of the NL's better defensive outfielders. He played regularly in the Padres' and Giants' infields his first five seasons. Signed as a free agent by the Dodgers in November 1978, the Los Angeles native was thrilled to wear the uniform number 30 of his boyhood idol, Maury Wills. /(TG)

Fay Thomas (Scow) — 1904– . RHP 1927, 31–32, 35 Giants, Indians, Dodgers, **Browns** 229 ip, 9–20, 4.95

An early practitioner of the forkball, the former USC tackle's success with his new pitch in the Pacific Coast League won him a chance with the Browns in 1935. His 7–15 record sent him back to the West Coast. /(DB)

Frank Thomas — 1929– . OF-3B-1B 1951–66 **Pirates**, Reds, Cubs, Braves, Mets, Phillies, Astros 1766 g, .266, 286 hr, 962 rbi
☛ *All-Star—54–55, 58.*

A strapping, 6'3" 200-lb slugger, Thomas hit 30 home runs in 1953, his first full ML season with his hometown Pirates, and was considered the successor of Ralph Kiner, who was traded to the Cubs that June. Thomas followed with 11 straight years with double-figure home runs, his best campaign coming in 1958 when he finished second in the NL to Ernie

Banks with 35 HR and 109 RBI. That August 16, he hit three HR in a game. A dead-pull hitter who crowded the plate, he smashed more than his share of foul "home runs." He was always willing to bet all comers he could catch their hardest throw barehanded, and he never lost. He was an All-Star outfielder in 1954–55 and was the NL's starting third baseman in the 1958 All-Star Game.

Thomas changed teams eight times between 1959 and 1966. In 1962 he led the expansion Mets with 34 HR and 94 RBI, hitting two homers in each of three consecutive games on the first three days in August. The closest he came to playing for a pennant winner was 1964; that August the Mets traded him to the Phillies, who appeared headed for a championship. But Thomas broke his right thumb in early September, and was ineffective upon his return. The Phillies, meanwhile, made their famous fade into second place. On July 3, 1965 he got into a fight with slugger Richie Allen. Despite hitting a pinch homer in the game, he was immediately placed on waivers. /(AL)

George Thomas — 1937– . OF 1957–58, 61–71 **Tigers**, Angels, Red Sox, Twins 680 g, .255, 46 hr, 202 rbi. *1 WS, 2 g, .000*

A natural wit and self-deprecating bench-jockey, Thomas came up with the Tigers, for whom he played a career-high 105 games in 1964, and went to Boston in a 1965 trade for pitcher Bill Monbouquette. When he didn't pan out as the Red Sox centerfielder, he became their willing handyman, even catching a few games. Although he played sparingly, the Red Sox liked his bat off the bench and his clowning, energetic attitude, and eventually made him a player-coach. /(JCA)

Gorman Thomas (Stormin' Gorman) — 1950– . OF-DH 1973–76, 78–86 **Brewers**, Indians, Mariners 1435 g, .225, 268 hr, 782 rbi. *1 LCS, 5 g, .067, 1 hr, 3 rbi. 1 WS, 7 g, .115, 3 rbi*
☛ *Led League—hr 79, 82. All-Star—81.*

A big, lumberjack-like slugger, Thomas was a premier outfielder until undergoing rotator-cuff surgery in 1984. He was the first player ever picked by the Seattle Pilots in the June 1969 draft. A two-time minor league home run champion, Thomas's frequent strikeouts and low batting average kept him from a steady major league job until 1978. The strikeouts continued (478 from 1978 to 1980), but his homers increased. Defensively, Thomas had fine range and never feared the fences. A controversial trade, disastrous for Milwaukee, sent Thomas to Cleveland in 1983. At Seattle, Thomas made a brilliant comeback in 1985 but became relegated to DH and first base duty. /(ME)

Ira Thomas — 1881–1958. C 1906–15 Yankees, Tigers, **A's** 481 g, .242, 3 hr, 155 rbi. *3 WS, 10 g, .214, 3 rbi*

A cumbersome, 6'2" 200-lb catcher, Thomas was one of Connie Mack's favorites and was a member of four Athletics championship teams. Only in 1911 did Thomas catch as many as 100 games. /(JK)

Lee Thomas [James Leroy] — 1936– . OF-1B 1961–68 Yankees, **Angels**, Red Sox, Braves, Cubs, Astros 1027 g, .255, 106 hr, 428 rbi
☛ *All-Star—62.*

From September 1 to 10 as an Angels rookie in 1961, Thomas went 23-for-39 (.590). On September 5 in a doubleheader at Kansas City, he had nine hits and 19 total bases, with three homers and eight RBI, tying the ML record for hits in a twin bill. He hit 50 homers in his first two seasons and played in both 1962 All-Star Games. /(RTM)

Myles Thomas — 1897–1963. RHP 1926–30 **Yankees**, Senators 435 ip, 23–22, 4.64. *1 WS, 3 ip, 0–0, 3.00*

Yankee manager Miller Huggins included Thomas in his 1927 plans, until New York's aging frontline pitchers, Urban Shocker and Bob Shawkey, began to come through. Thomas had seven wins by mid-July, but found himself working less and less. In June 1929 the Penn State graduate whom Babe Ruth called "Duck Eye" was waived to Washington. /(MG)

Pinch Thomas [Chester David] — 1888–1953. C 1912–21 **Red Sox**, Indians 476 g, .237, 2 hr, 102 rbi. *3 WS, 6 g, .167*

Thomas had three seasons as the primary catcher of the Red Sox, helping them to pennants in 1915–16. He averaged 22 RBI a year as a regular, just over 200 at-bats a season. He led AL catchers in fielding in 1917. After the season, he went to the Athletics with two others and cash in the deal that brought Joe Bush, Wally Schang, and Amos Strunk to the Red Sox; Thomas was sold to the Indians and played on another pennant winner in 1920. From 1913 to 1918 he hit .417 as a pinch hitter (13-for-31), but he failed to get a hit in 16 subsequent pinch at-bats. /(WOR)

Roy Thomas — 1874–1959. OF 1899–1911 **Phillies**, Pirates, Braves 1471 g, .290, 7 hr, 299 rbi

Thomas was the NL walk king at the turn of the

century. His ability to foul off pitches endlessly in pursuit of a free pass led to the rule that fouls were strikes, but that change didn't prevent him from leading the NL in walks in seven of his first nine seasons. He was a fast singles hitter (his highest slugging average was .365) who batted as high as .327 and hit .300 five times. His on-base average topped .400 each of his first seven seasons, and he led the NL in 1902 (.412) and 1903 (.450). Before the Phillies' best players jumped to the AL, the leadoff hitter scored 100 runs his first three years, but after 1901 he topped 100 only once more (118 in 1905). He scored 1,011 runs in his career, but drove in only 299; when he led the league with 132 runs in 1900, he had 33 RBI.

Thomas's speed enabled him to steal 244 bases in his career, with a high of 42 his first season. He also ranged widely in centerfield and led the NL three times in putouts, twice in total chances per game, and once each in fielding and assists. His .986 fielding average in 1906 tied the NL record of the time. At his retirement, he held career fielding records for centerfielders in putouts (NL) and fielding average (ML). /(JK)

Roy Thomas — 1953– . RHP 1977–80, 83–85, 87 Astros, Cardinals, **Mariners** 419 ip, 20–11, 3.83

Thomas was the Phillies' first pick in the June 1971 draft. With Reading (Eastern League) on August 20, 1974, he threw a seven-inning no-hitter. A 6'5" sinker-slider pitcher with an awkward, wild delivery, he moved through seven organizations. In 1983 he appeared in a career-high 43 games for the Mariners and put together 20 straight scoreless innings in relief. Hit with tendinitis in 1984, he was healthy enough to go 7–0 in 1985, but spent 1986 on the disabled list. He was released by Seattle, for a second time, in 1987. /(NLM)

Stan Thomas — 1949– . RHP 1974–77 **Rangers**, Indians, Mariners, Yankees 266 ip, 11–14, 3.69

Thomas pitched with authority out of the Cleveland bullpen in 1976, recording a 2.26 ERA. But after undergoing knee surgery, he was only 3–6 with a 6.12 ERA for the Mariners and Yankees in 1977, and left the ML. /(JCA)

Tommy Thomas [Alphonse] — 1899– . RHP 1926–37 **White Sox**, Senators, Phillies, Browns, Red Sox 2173 ip, 117–128, 4.12. *1 WS, 1 ip, 0–0, 0.00*

Thomas recorded a 32–12 mark for the 1925 International League Baltimore Orioles and attracted the attention of White Sox owner Charles

Comiskey. Thomas was a workhorse for Chicago from 1926 through 1929, leading the AL in starts and innings pitched in 1927, and in complete games in 1929 (24, for the third straight year). He put together three winning seasons, but was known as a hard-luck pitcher who was never able to win the close ones. By 1930 he was an overworked pitcher who generally couldn't go past the fifth inning.

On July 24, 1927 Thomas surrendered a mammoth home run to Babe Ruth. It was the first ball to reach Comiskey Park's spacious upper deck, which had been installed the previous winter. On August 16, Ruth blasted a Thomas offering over the roof; earlier in the day, Chicago architects had declared that such a feat was not possible at the redesigned ballpark. /(RL)

Valmy Thomas — 1928– . C 1957–61 **Giants**, Phillies, Orioles, Indians 252 g, .230, 12 hr, 60 rbi

Thomas was a quick, 5'9" 165-lb catcher who had his best season (six HR, 31 RBI) in 1957 as a Giants rookie. In one of the worst trades in Phillies history, the Puerto Rican-born Thomas was obtained with Ruben Gomez after the 1958 season for pitcher Jack Sanford, who in 1962 won 24 games for the Giants. /(AL)

William Thomas — 1905–Unk. *Minor League* Star.

Thomas, a righthander, became the all-time minor league leader in games pitched (1,015), wins (383), losses (346), runs allowed (3,092) and hits allowed (6,709). Pitching from 1926 through 1952, he appeared at every level from Class-D to Triple-A. A curveballer with excellent control, his inability to throw hard deprived him of any major league trials. His 35–7 mark at Houma (Evangeline League) was the best in organized baseball in 1946. He was suspended from 1947 through 1949 for alleged gambling connections, a charge he refuted. /(GWH)

Gary Thomasson — 1951– . OF-1B 1972–80 **Giants**, A's, Yankees, Dodgers 901 g, .249, 61 hr, 294 rbi. *1 LCS, 3 g, .000. 1 WS, 3 g, .250*

The freckle-faced lefthander was a Topps Rookie All-Star in 1973, as he hit .285 for the Giants. The ball Thomasson hit for a homer on Opening Day at Dodger Stadium in 1977 went into the Hall of Fame as the first ML home run with a Rawlings baseball. A solid fourth outfielder and backup first baseman, he set career highs in every offensive category in '77, hitting 17 homers in 145 games. The next spring he was one of the seven players sent with cash from San Francisco to Oakland for Vida Blue. In 1981–82, playing in Japan, he hit .249 with 20 HR in 477 at-bats for Yomiuri. /(JCA)

Danny Thompson — 1947–1976. SS-3B-2B 1970–76 **Twins**, Rangers 694 g, .248, 15 hr, 194 rbi. *1 LCS, 3 g, .125*

The agile, sure-handed, and well-liked infielder played mostly second base when he came up in 1970 but became Minnesota's regular shortstop in 1972. A contact hitter with alley power, Thompson led all regular ML shortstops that year with a .276 BA. Diagnosed as having leukemia before the 1973 season, he courageously played four more seasons, hitting .270 in 1975. He appeared in 98 games in 1976 and died that winter. /(JCA)

Denman Thompson — 1893–Unk. *Writer.*

A bat boy for the Senators in the early days of the AL, Thompson was city editor of the Washington *Herald* at 18, and became sports editor in 1917. He moved to the same position on the Washington *Star* in 1933. That same year he was president of the BBWAA. /(NLM)

Fresco Thompson (Tommy) — 1902–1968. 2B 1925–32, 34 Pirates, Giants, **Phillies**, Dodgers, Giants 669 g, .298, 13 hr, 249 rbi

Quick-witted Fresco Thompson became a successful executive after playing his best years for the futile 1927–30 Phillies. He was set to be the Giants' second baseman in '27 when New York obtained Rogers Hornsby and sent Thompson to Philadelphia. He batted .303 in 1927, and .324, with 115 runs scored, in 1929. A willing after-dinner speaker, he became an assistant farm director for the Dodgers, moved up the executive ladder, and survived the front-office purge that followed Branch Rickey's departure in 1951. Shortly before his death, he was named the Dodgers' executive vice president and general manager. /(JK)

Hank Thompson [Henry Curtis] — 1925–1969. 3B-OF-2B 1947, 49–56 Browns, **Giants** 933 g, .267, 129 hr, 482 rbi. *2 WS, 9 g, .240, 2 rbi*

Thompson was the first black player for both the Browns and the Giants, and when he batted against the Dodgers' Don Newcombe in 1949, it was the first time in ML history a black batter faced a black pitcher. The lefthanded hitter enjoyed his best season in 1953, when he hit .302 with 24 HR. On June 3, 1954 he hit three homers in one game. In the WS that year against the Indians, he hit .364 and drew a four-game Series record of seven walks. /(RTM)

Jason Thompson — 1954– . 1B 1976–86 Tigers, Angels, **Pirates**, Expos 1418 g, .261, 208 hr, 782 rbi ☛ *All-Star—77, 78, 82.*

Jason Thompson was consistently among the league leaders in walks and on-base percentage, and he became one of the few players with 30-homer seasons in both the AL and NL (31 with the 1977 Tigers, 31 with the 1982 Pirates). He also led each league in total chances at first base (1977 and 1984), though he was never considered exceptional on defense.

Thompson joined Detroit after just 79 minor league games. The powerful lefthander was well suited to Tiger Stadium, and he belted two home runs over its right-field roof in 1977. After hitting 98 HR in four-plus seasons, he was sent to the Angels in May of 1980. He batted .317 for California and was traded to Pittsburgh in a deal that was to have then sent him to the Yankees. But Commissioner Bowie Kuhn nullified the Yankee purchase because the money involved exceeded the cash-purchase limits he was trying to impose. In 1982 Thompson became the third Pirate ever to draw 100 walks and drive in 100 runs in a season. Plagued by injuries in 1984–85, he frustrated Pirate management with his unaggressive hitting and was traded to Montreal in 1986. /(ME)

Junior Thompson [Eugene Earl] — 1917– . RHP 1939–42, 46–47 **Reds**, Giants 687 ip, 47–35, 3.26. *2 WS, 8 ip, 0–2, 14.63*

As a rookie, Thompson was 13–5 with a league-leading eight relief wins for the pennant-winning 1939 Reds. He lost his two World Series starts, one in 1939 and one in 1940. After his return from military duty, he recorded a 1.29 ERA in 39 appearances for the 1946 Giants. /(NLM)

Mike Thompson — 1949– . RHP 1971, 73–75 Senators, **Cardinals**, Braves 165 ip, 1–15, 4.84

Thompson got his only major league victory in his first and most active season, going 1–6 with a 4.84 ERA (1971). /(SFS)

Milt Thompson — 1959– . OF 1984–89 Braves, **Phillies**, Cardinals 621 g, .289, 21 hr, 177 rbi

A speedy spray hitter and decent outfielder who strikes out more often than he walks, Thompson hit .302 as a rookie with Atlanta in 1985 and led the NL in pinch hitting (.433). He was traded to Philadelphia with Steve Bedrosian and in 1987 hit .302 again with 46 stolen bases in his first full ML season as a starter. Dealt to the Cardinals for Curt Ford before the 1989 season, he saw considerable action due to the injuries and decline of Willie McGee. /(SG)

Robby Thompson — 1962– . 2B 1986– **Giants** 567 g, .259, 37 hr, 189 rbi. *2 LCS, 12 g, .184, 3 hr, 5 rbi. 1 WS, 4 g, .091, 2 rbi*

Thompson jumped from Double-A to the Giants in 1986, and finished second to Todd Worrell in the NL Rookie of the Year voting after hitting .271 as San Francisco's starting second baseman. In the field, Thompson is reliable if unspectacular, with a knack for turning double plays, but at the plate he often overswings, striking out over 100 times a year without much power (he hit a career-high 10 HR in 1987). On June 27, 1986 he set a ML record by being caught stealing four times in one game. /(SCL)

S.C. Thompson [Sherley Clark] — 1898–1967. *Writer.*

Thompson was a baseball historian and co-author with Hy Turkin of the first *Official Encyclopedia of Baseball* in 1951. /(NLM)

Sam Thompson (Big Sam) — 1860–1922. OF 1885–98, 1906 Detroit (NL), **Phillies**, Tigers 1410 g, .331, 128 hr, 1299 rbi
☛ *Led League—ba 1887. Led League—hr 1889, 1895. Led League—rbi 1887, 1895. Hall of Fame—1974.*

The 6'2″ 207-lb Thompson was a 24-year-old carpenter when he began playing pro ball in 1884. He was acquired by the Detroit National League club the following year, hit more than .300 for the first of nine seasons and, sporting a powerful throwing arm, won the right field job. He was to become one of the best at his position for the next decade, a consistent long-ball threat in the dead-ball era.

In 1887 Thompson led the NL with 545 at-bats, 203 hits, 23 triples, 166 RBI (the highest RBI total in the 19th century), a .372 batting average, and a .571 slugging percentage. That May 7 he hit two bases-loaded triples. He lost most of the 1888 season to an injury. He moved to the Phillies in 1889 and made a successful comeback, leading the league with 20 HR. His power slipped in 1890, but his 172 hits and 41 doubles were league highs.

After leading the NL in 1893 with 222 hits and 37 doubles, in 1894 Thompson was a member of the only .400-hitting outfield in ML history. He batted .404, left fielder Ed Delahanty hit .400, fourth outfielder Tuck Turner hit .416, and centerfielder Billy Hamilton hit .399. Thompson's .670 slugging percentage was the third best of the

Sam Thompson

century. On August 17 he hit for the cycle in a 6-for-7 game against Louisville.

Thompson's final great season was 1895, when his 18 HR, 165 RBI, and .654 slugging percentage were NL highs. He batted .392. On June 29 and July 1, he tied a ML record for most consecutive doubles in two games, with six. He missed all but three games of the 1897 season with an ailing back, which forced his retirement in 1898. He had the second-best lifetime slugging percentage (.504) and third-highest RBI total (1,296) of any 19th-century player, and his 128 career HR total was the record until Babe Ruth broke it. In 1906, at age forty-six, Thompson attempted a brief comeback with the Detroit Tigers. He was elected to the Hall of Fame by the Committee on Baseball Veterans in 1974. /(AJA)

Scot Thompson — 1955– . OF-1B 1978–85 **Cubs**, Giants, Expos 626 g, .262, 5 hr, 110 rbi

Thompson was the Cubs' first pick in the June 1974 draft and batted .417 in his 19-game 1978 Chicago debut. He proved a consistent but punchless left-handed hitter, batting .289 with just 29 RBI as a rookie in 1979. On July 5, 1980 he was knocked unconscious when he collided with Pirate shortstop Tim Foli, and he finished the season at .212. The

Cubs released him in 1983. He led the NL with 62 pinch at-bats for San Francisco and Montreal in 1985. /(DAS)

Tim Thompson [Charles LeMoine] — 1924– . C 1954, 56–58 Dodgers, **A's**, Tigers 187 g, .238, 8 hr, 47 rbi

Like Clint Courtney, Thompson wore glasses while catching. His best year was 1956, when he hit .272 with Kansas City. /(RTM)

Tommy Thompson [Rupert Lockhart] — 1910–1971. OF-1B 1933–36, 38–39 **Braves**, White Sox, Browns 397 g, .266, 9 hr, 119 rbi

Thompson played alongside Babe Ruth in the Braves' outfield in Ruth's last game (1935). He was platooned in his three-plus years with Boston, played seven years in Triple-A, and became a minor league manager. /(NLM)

Bobby Thomson (The Staten Island Scot) — 1923– . OF-3B 1946–60 **Giants**, Braves, Cubs, Red Sox, Orioles 1779 g, .270, 264 hr, 1026 rbi. *1 WS, 6 g, .238, 2 rbi* ☛ *All-Star—48–49, 52.*

Thomson hit what is perhaps the most famous home run in baseball history. His dramatic "shot heard 'round the world" on October 3, 1951, a three-run, ninth-inning homer off Brooklyn pitcher Ralph Branca, capped the Giants' historic comeback to win the NL pennant. Thomson also hit a sixth-inning homer off Branca in the opening game of the playoffs, which erased a 1–0 Dodger lead.

Born in Glasgow, Scotland, the Staten Island Scot hit 24 or more homers six times in his seven full seasons with the Giants. A key to the 1951 pennant was Thomson's switch to third base, allowing Willie Mays to take over centerfield. Following the 1953 season, Thomson was sent to the Milwaukee Braves in a trade that brought future 20-game winner Johnny Antonelli to the Giants. Thomson broke his ankle in spring training with the Braves in 1954, and that injury kept Hank Aaron from being sent to the minors. Later that year, when Thomson was in the lineup, Aaron pinch ran for him and broke his ankle.

A nice, likable guy, known as a good low-ball hitter, Thomson had a comeback season for the Cubs in 1958, when he hit 21 homers and collected 82 RBI while batting .283. In 1969, Thomson was named to the Giants' all-time outfield along with Mel Ott and Willie Mays. /(RTM)

Bobby Thomson

Dickie Thon — 1958– . SS-2B 1979– Angels, **Astros**, Padres, Phillies 912 g, .270, 49 hr, 273 rbi. *2 LCS, 7 g, .250, 1 hr, 1 rbi* ☛ *All-Star—83.*

Dickie Thon's career was changed with one pitch from Mike Torrez. Before being beaned by Torrez on April 8, 1984, Thon was the NL's premier offensive, and some said defensive, shortstop. Afterward Thon suffered from poor vision and frequently spent time on the disabled list. Though his fielding returned to major league status, Thon's power and baserunning elan were diminished until 1989, when he recalled his past excellence with 15 HR, 60 RBI, and a .271 batting average in 435 at-bats.

A righthanded pull hitter, Thon played briefly for California before being traded to the Astros for Ken Forsch. He became Houston's starting shortstop in 1982 and led the NL with 10 triples. He led all NL shortstops with 20 homers and 533 assists in 1983 and led the league with 18 game-winning RBI, driving in 79 overall. /(ME)

Hank Thormahlen [Herbert Ehler] (Lefty) — 1896–1955. LHP 1917–21, 25 **Yankees**, Red Sox, Dodgers 565 ip, 30–30, 3.33

Thormahlen pitched for the Yankees in the years before they began winning pennants. One day in 1918 he took a no-hitter into the ninth inning of a scoreless game. He got two outs, then gave up two singles and a walk. When the next batter's easy fly was dropped by Ping Bodie, Thormahlen lost 1–0. /(JK)

Paul Thormodsgard (Thor) — 1953– . RHP 1977–79 **Twins** 285 ip, 12–21, 4.74

Thormodsgard was highly thought of in the Reds' system before he had arm problems and was released. He sat out the 1975 season, but in 1977 jumped from A-ball to start 37 games for the Twins (11–15). A 1978 groin injury ended his career. /(KC)

John Thorn — 1947– . *Writer.*

Thorn founded and edited *The National Pastime: A Review of Baseball History*, an annual publication of the Society for American Baseball Research. He is a highly-respected photo researcher and the author of several books, including *The Hidden Game of Baseball* and *Total Baseball* with Pete Palmer. /(NLM)

Andre Thornton — 1949– . DH-1B 1973–79, 81–87 Cubs, Expos, **Indians** 1565 g, .254, 253 hr, 895 rbi ☛ *All-Star—82, 84.*

A quiet slugger, Thornton was Cleveland's most identifiable player during the late 1970s and 1980s. His poise, courage, and overall attitude won the respect of fans, teammates, and opponents. If not for injuries, he would have become Cleveland's all-time home run leader. He hit 214 homers for the Indians, 14 fewer than Hal Trosky, despite missing all of the 1980 season, much of 1981, and parts of 1985 and 1986. He led the club in homers seven times, including four straight seasons, set a club record

(righthanded) by walking 109 times in 1982, and became only the second Indian with 100 walks and 100 RBI in the same season (with Al Rosen). A devout Christian, Thornton was a respectable first baseman until injury relegated him to full-time designated hitting. He was first baseman on the *Baseball Digest* 1974 All-Rookie team. One of the great trades in Cleveland history brought Thornton in exchange for pitcher Jackie Brown. /(ME)

Jim Thorpe — 1887–1953. OF 1913–15, 17–19 Giants, Reds, Braves 289 g, .252, 7 hr, 82 rbi. *1 WS, 1 g, --*

When Thorpe won both the pentathlon and the decathlon at the 1912 Olympics, King Gustav of Sweden, the host country, said, "Sir, you are the greatest athlete in the world." Sadly, Thorpe had to return his Olympic medals when it was discovered he'd played professional baseball in a low minor league for about $60 a month in 1909. Signed by the Giants, Thorpe had an undistinguished six-season ML career. Manager John McGraw claimed Thorpe couldn't hit a curveball, but he actually disliked Thorpe's easygoing personality. In 1919 Thorpe hit .327 in limited play with the Braves. Thorpe was twice All-America at Carlisle Indian School, and his later professional football career earned him enshrinement in the Pro Football Hall of Fame. In 1950 he was voted the greatest athlete of the half-century. He appeared as a bit player in several movies, the best-known being the famous Cagney vehicle *White Heat*. /(JK)

Three Rivers Stadium Pittsburgh Pirates 1970– . LF-335, CF-400, RF-335

Where the Allegheny and Monongahela Rivers meet to form the mighty Ohio stands a generic, circular park planned in the 1960s, with the usual problem of distance between the fans and the action. That, its difficult-to-reach location, and the interminable traffic jams it engenders are partially to blame for the Pirates' woeful attendance. However, visibility for the hitters is outstanding, and a substandard artificial surface increases errors and reduces double plays. Only four batters have ever hit upper-deck home runs: Willie Stargell (four times), Bob Robertson, Greg Luzinski, and Bobby Bonilla. It was the site of the first night WS game, on October 13, 1971. /(JP)

Syd Thrift — 1929– . *Scout-Executive.*

Thrift was a part-time scout for the Yankees and Pirates while working as a high-school teacher from 1953 to 1956, and became the Pirates' scouting supervisor in 1957. He left the Pirates after the 1967 season to join the Royals, first as scouting director and later as director of the Royals Baseball Academy, which produced 14 ML players. After two years with the A's, he entered the real-estate business, and in 1981 he spotted Bobby Bonilla while conducting a baseball clinic and recommended him to the Pirates.

He returned to the Pirates as senior vice-president and GM in 1985 with the club in last place and devastated by a drug scandal. By 1988 the club had returned to respectability and finished second to the Mets with a nucleus of excellent young players. Thrift was fired after the season in a dispute with club ownership. He spent most of 1989 as the Yankees' GM until fired by owner George Steinbrenner. During his scouting days, he was instrumental in signing Don Money, Al Oliver, Woody Fryman, and Bob Robertson. /(FVP)

Faye Throneberry — 1931- . OF 1952, 55-61 Red Sox, **Senators**, Angels 521 g, .236, 29 hr, 137 rbi

Marvelous Marv's older brother lacked his popular sibling's home run power and color. Faye was an average reserve outfielder for eight seasons, appearing in more than 100 games only with the '59 Senators. /(RTM)

Marv Throneberry (Marvelous Marv) — 1933- . 1B-OF 1955, 58-63 Yankees, **A's**, Orioles, Mets 480 g, .237, 53 hr, 170 rbi. *1 WS, 1 g, .000*

Marv Throneberry became one of the most celebrated .237 hitters in baseball history. A highly touted young Yankee with a Mickey Mantle look-alike batting stance, he had the power to be a home run hitter. But he struck out in almost one-half of his at-bats and was a part-timer with the Yankees. He played in obscurity with the A's and Orioles before being acquired by the 1962 Mets. He soon became the living symbol of Met futility (in fact, his initials spelled M-E-T) with his untimely hitting, inept fielding, and atrocious baserunning. Against the Cubs on June 17, he hit a triple but was called out for not touching first base. When manager Casey Stengel went out to argue, the umpire told him that Throneberry had missed second as well. Facetiously dubbed Marvelous Marv, the good-natured first baseman capitalized on his comic ineptitude and became a media and fan favorite. But when he disagreed with Met management over his 1963 salary, he was quickly and unconditionally released. He resurfaced 20 years later as a deadpan comic in popular beer commercials. His brother, Faye, was an AL outfielder. /(GDW)

James Thurber — 1894-1961. *Writer.*

For most of his career Thurber wrote short, whimsical pieces and drew cartoons for *The New Yorker*. Perhaps his least typical story, first published in *The Saturday Evening Post* in 1941, was "You Could Look It Up," about a struggling baseball team that hires a midget to pinch hit. Bill Veeck later acknowledged this tale as the idea behind his Eddie Gaedel stunt, and the title became a baseball catch phrase often repeated by Casey Stengel. /(FDS)

Bob Thurman (El Murcaro) — 1917- . OF 1955-59 **Reds** 334 g, .246, 35 hr, 106 rbi

Thurman's entry into the major leagues was delayed by baseball's color line. He played for the Homestead Grays from 1946 to 1948 and the Kansas City Monarchs in 1949 before being signed by the Yankees. His teammates nicknamed him "El Murcaro" (The Owl). He made the majors as an extra outfielder for the slugging Cincinnati Reds, and made half his ML appearances as a pinch hitter. In 1957 he hit four pinch homers. /(RTM)

Mark Thurmond — 1956- . LHP 1983- **Padres**, Tigers, Orioles 781 ip, 38-43, 3.71. *2 LCS, 4 ip, 0-1, 9.00. 1 WS, 5 ip, 0-1, 10.13*

Thurmond was the lefthanded starter on *TSN*'s 1984 NL All-Star Team, going 14-8, 2.97 for the Padres, but has been used mostly in relief since 1986. In the 1984 WS against the Tigers, Thurmond lost Game One 3-2, and retired only one batter after starting Game Five, surrendering three runs. He was traded to the Tigers for Dave LaPoint in July 1986, and to the Orioles for Ray Knight before the 1988 season. /(SCL)

Sloppy Thurston [Hollis John] — 1899-1973. RHP 1923-27, 30-33 Browns, **White Sox**, Senators, Dodgers 1535 ip, 89-86, 4.26. 20 wins: 24

Sloppy Thurston's nickname was a misnomer. He inherited it from his father, a charitable restaurant owner who would dish out free soup to the poor. But the curveballing pitcher was a meticulous and dandy Jazz Age dresser. In the 12th inning of an August 22, 1923, game against the Athletics, he struck out the side on nine pitches. He had his best season for the last-place 1924 White Sox. He reeled off ten straight victories before the Yankees beat him on July 29, and ended the season at 20-14 with league highs of 28 complete games and 330 hits allowed. He was mediocre from then on.

After Thurston's 6-8 performance in 1926, manager Eddie Collins declared his arm was dead and traded him to the Senators. Thurston was pitching for the Dodgers on August 13, 1932 when he allowed six HR in the first game of a doubleheader, tying the post-1900 ML record. He was one of the best-hitting pitchers of all time, with a .270 lifetime average and four .300 seasons. He became a long-time scout and signed Ralph Kiner to a Pirate contract./(RL)

Luis Tiant, Sr. (Sir Skinny, Lefty) — 1906– . LHP Negro Leagues 1930–47 Cuban Stars, New York Cubans statistics not available
☛ *All-Star—35, 47.*

A Negro League standout, Tiant was a master of changing speeds, a junkball-screwball pitcher with a herky-jerky motion and a superior pickoff move. He was also a fierce competitor; according to one of his beanball victims, the Philadelphia Stars' Ted Page, "he gave no mercy to any batter." In October of 1935, Tiant's New York Cubans defeated the Babe Ruth All-Stars 6–1 and 15–3. Tiant pitched both games and held Ruth to one scratch single. At age 41, still pitching for the Cubans, he fashioned a 10–0 record with eight complete games and three shutouts. In 1975, Cuban leader Fidel Castro allowed Tiant to go see his son, Luis, Jr., pitch for the Boston Red Sox in the World Series./(LL)

Luis Tiant, Jr. [born Luis Clemente Tiant Vega](Looie) — 1940– . RHP 1964–82 Indians, Twins, **Red Sox**, Yankees, Pirates, Angels 3486 ip, 229–172, 3.30. 20 wins: 68, 73–74, 76 *2 LCS, 10 ip, 1–0, 0.93 1 WS, 25 ip, 2–0, 3.60*
☛ *Led League—era 68, 72. All-Star—68, 74, 76.*

Tiant didn't join the Red Sox until mid-career, but he became one of the most popular players in club history. A balding, overweight starter whose age was often estimated as several years higher than its "official" listing, Tiant spoke with a thick Cuban accent and would smoke cigars anywhere, including the clubhouse whirlpool and shower. He was a renowned locker-room prankster, but was serious on the mound, winning 20 games three times for Boston. He baffled hitters with a rocking, twisting windup and an assortment of release points that ranged from over-the-top to nearly underhand. Or as announcer Curt Gowdy noted, "He comes from everywhere except between his legs."

Tiant's father, Luis Tiant, Sr., was one of Cuba's greatest pitchers; former All-Star Bobby Avila signed the younger Luis to his first contract, for the

Luis Tiant, Jr.

1959 Mexican League season. He set a Pacific Coast League record with a .938 winning percentage (15–1) in 1964 before joining the Indians in mid-season, and broke in with a four-hit shutout against the Yankees in his first ML start. He went 10–4 with a 2.83 ERA as a rookie in 1964, and in 1966 he pitched four consecutive shutouts. Tiant really broke through in 1968 after he altered his delivery so that he turned away from the plate during his motion, in effect creating a hesitation pitch. He led the AL with a 1.60 ERA, 9 shutouts, and 5.3 hits per nine innings while striking out more than a batter an inning, and finished 21–9. That July 3 he struck out 19 Twins in a ten-inning game, setting an AL record for games of that length. In his previous start he'd fanned 13 Red Sox, giving him a ML-record 32 strikeouts in consecutive starts.

The Indians were overly protective of their newly hot property and ordered Tiant to skip his usual winter ball. The strategy backfired when he led the AL with 20 losses (while winning 9) and 129 walks in 1969. After the season Cleveland traded him with Stan Williams to the Twins for Graig Nettles, former Cy Young winner Dean Chance, Bob Miller, and Ted Uhlaender. Tiant started the 1970 season with six straight wins, but suffered a hairline fracture in his shoulder, missed June and July, and wasn't the same when he came back. Minnesota released him at the end of spring training in 1971, and he signed with the Braves' minor league Richmond club. He was cut a month later and joined Boston's Louisville farm team. He made it back to the majors late that year, but went only 1–7.

Tiant was the Comeback Player of the Year in 1972 for a contending Red Sox team. He captured his second ERA title with a 1.91 mark and was 15–6. He followed his 20–13 mark in 1973 by going 22–13 in 1974, with an AL-leading seven shutouts. After helping the Red Sox to the AL pennant in 1975 with an 18–14 mark (4.02 ERA), he got real national attention for the first time during postseason play. He beat the three-time World Champion A's in the ALCS opener with a three-hitter, giving up only one unearned run, and followed with a five-hit shutout of the Reds to open the World Series. He also won Game Four, 5–4. Tiant got a hit in each game after batting once all season, and his adventuresome trips from base to base (he scored each time) while bundled in a warm-up jacket provided comic relief in an otherwise tense series. His accent ("Ees great to be weeth a weiner") and his eccentric cigar puffing made him an immediate media favorite. He was rocked in Game Six, but left long before Carlton Fisk's 12th-inning homer ended what has been called the greatest game ever played.

Tiant won 20 for the last time in 1976 (21–12), but he was no longer the overpowering pitcher he once had been. For several years he had increasingly relied on deception, with masterful changes of speed to go with his wide variety of pitching motions. He pitched less, but he kept winning, going 12–8 and 13–8 in his last two years with the Red Sox. He signed with the Yankees as a free agent before the 1979 season and went 13–8, but was ineffective thereafter. /(SH)

Jay Tibbs — 1962– . RHP 1984– **Reds**, Expos, Orioles 805 ip, 36–47, 4.13

An erratic starter who won a career-high ten games for the Reds in 1985, Tibbs has been traded three times since being drafted by the Mets in 1980. He began the 1987 season as the Expos' number-two starter, but was demoted to Indianapolis (American Association). In 1988 he was 4–15, 5.39 for the last-place Orioles. When they jumped to second place in 1989, he contributed a 5–0, 2.82 record. /(SCL)

Dick Tidrow (Dirt) — 1947– . RHP 1972–84 Indians, Yankees, **Cubs**, White Sox, Mets 1747 ip, 100–94, 3.68. *4 LCS, 23 ip, 1–0, 3.91. 3 WS, 11 ip, 0–0, 4.22*

Tidrow broke in with the Indians as a starting pitcher and won 14 games twice with poor clubs. He was *TSN*'s AL Rookie Pitcher of the Year in 1972 when he was the number-two man behind Cy Young Award-winner Gaylord Perry in the rotation. The Yankees acquired him in the big 1974 deal that also brought them Chris Chambliss. In 1975 they moved Tidrow to the bullpen and he was 6–3 with five saves and a 3.13 ERA. He became a valuable set-up man for Sparky Lyle, contributing ten saves and a 4–5 mark to the Yankees' 1976 pennant. Tidrow won the LCS clincher when Chambliss hit his famous ninth-inning homer into the Yankee Stadium bleachers to beat the Royals.

Tidrow had his best season when he went 11–4 with five saves in 1977 for the World Champion Yankees, with a 5–0 record in seven starts. Moved into the regular rotation in 1978, he didn't sustain the previous year's success, finishing 7–11 as the Yankees won their third straight AL title and their second straight World Championship. Traded to the Cubs early in the 1979 season, he became the workhorse of their bullpen as Bruce Sutter's set-up man, leading the NL in appearances in 1980 with 84. His odd nickname reflected his basic, simple approach to the game. Tidrow and Charlie Smith are the only players to play for the New York Mets and Yankees, and the Chicago Cubs and White Sox. /(JFC)

Bobby Tiefenauer — 1929– . RHP 1952, 55, 60–65, 67–68 Cardinals, Indians, Astros, **Braves**, Yankees, Cubs 316 ip, 9–25, 3.84

Tiefenauer spent 21 years in pro baseball. The knuckleballer was 32 years old when he got his first secure ML job as a middle reliever in 43 games with the expansion 1962 Colt .45s. He was the ace reliever (13 saves) for the 1964 Milwaukee Braves. /(RTM)

Mike Tiernan (Silent Mike) — 1867-1918. OF
1887-99 **Giants** 1476 g, .311, 108 hr, 851 rbi
☛ *Led League—hr 1891.*

Tiernan patrolled the Giants outfield for 13 seasons
at a time when players generally flitted from team to
team. The low-keyed, lefthanded slugger spent the
last half of his career tolerating Giants owner
Andrew Freedman, an early baseball tyrant. Tiernan
broke in as a left fielder in 1887, batted .287, and
even pitched five games in relief. On May 16 he tied
a major league record with five outfield errors in a
game; on June 15 he tied the NL mark of six runs
scored in a game.

Tiernan starred in right field on the 1888-89
New York pennant-winners, leading the league with
147 runs and 96 walks in '89. In 1891 he won the
NL home run crown with 17. He topped the .300
mark seven times, with a high of .369 in 1896. In
1899 he was let go after batting .255 as a part-
timer. /(AJA)

Cotton Tierney [James Arthur] — 1894-1953. 2B-3B
1920-25 **Pirates**, Phillies, Braves, Dodgers 630 g, .296,
31 hr, 331 rbi

Better at bat than in the field, the witty Tierney
played second base for the fun-loving Pirates of
1922 and sang in the team quartet. Despite a .345
BA that year, he was traded to the Phillies early in
1923, and when his hitting fell off his ML career was
over. /(ME)

Les Tietje (Toots) — 1911- . RHP 1933-38 **White Sox**,
Browns 513 ip, 22-41, 5.11

As a White Sox starter and reliever in 1934-35,
Tietje went 5-14 and 9-15. Plagued with arthritis,
at one point he went on the voluntarily retired list,
but he returned as a winning minor league
pitcher. /(NLM)

Tiger Stadium Detroit Tigers 1912- . LF-340, CF-440,
RF-325

A large square with rounded corners, Tiger Stadium
is one of baseball's two second-oldest stadiums,
having opened April 20, 1912, the same day as
Boston's Fenway Park. Built on the same site as
Bennett Park by Tiger president Frank Navin, the
park was called Navin Field until 1938 and Briggs
Stadium (for new owner Walter Briggs) until 1961
before receiving its present name. It was originally a
single-decked grandstand, and the second deck was
added in the infield for the 1924 season and today
extends all the way around the park, giving Tiger
Stadium the only double-decked bleachers in the

ML. In addition, the right field roof hangs approximately 10' over the warning track, catching home
runs that might have been outs, and necessitating a
small string of floodlights to light the otherwise dark
warning track at night. Tiger Stadium was the last
AL park to install lights, in 1948.

In the outfield, Tiger Stadium has unusual field-
level seats, behind the screens that serve as the
outfield fences. These fences do not curve at all, but
extend in straight lines from the corners to near
centerfield, where they cut directly across. Center is
440' from home plate, the deepest in any ML park
today, but the power alleys are relatively close (365'
in left, 375' in right, but closer because of the
overhang), making Tiger stadium a favorable home
run ballpark. On October 9, 1934 it was the scene of
one of baseball's uglier incidents when, in the sixth
inning of Game Seven of the WS, with the Tigers
trailing St. Louis 9-0, Tiger fans pelted the
Cardinals' Joe Medwick with so much garbage and
debris he was forced to leave the field for his own
safety. And on July 13, 1971 Reggie Jackson hit the
stadium's most famous home run, a mammoth shot
off a light tower atop the right-field roof during the
All-Star Game. /(SCL)

Bob Tillman — 1937- . C 1962-70 **Red Sox**,
Yankees, Braves 775 g, .232, 79 hr, 282 rbi. *1 LCS, 1 g, --*

The well-liked catcher hit with power, though he
admitted in a radio interview as a rookie that he
"couldn't hit a curveball with an oar." In 1964 he
had career highs of 17 homers, 61 RBI, and a .278
BA, but he slumped to .215 the next year. In Boston
the quiet Tillman caught no-hitters by Earl Wilson
and Dave Morehead. On July 30, 1969, with
Atlanta, he hit three home runs against the
Expos. /(JCA)

Thad Tillotson — 1940- . RHP 1967-68 **Yankees**
108 ip, 4-9, 4.06

After winning his first three decisions in 1967,
Tillotson tied Bill Hogg's 1908 Yankee record for
consecutive losses by dropping nine straight. A relief
win in his only 1968 decision saved him from setting
a new mark. /(RTM)

Tom Timmerman — 1940- . RHP 1969-74 **Tigers**,
Indians 547 ip, 35-35, 3.78

The bespectacled Timmerman spent 9-1/2 years in
the Tiger farm system before becoming the Detroit
sportswriters' "Tiger of the Year" in 1970, when he
set club records for appearances (61) and saves (27).

After relieving in 1969–71, he started 25 games in 1972 and posted a 2.89 ERA. /(JCA)

Ben Tincup — 1890–1980. RHP 1914–16, 18, 28 **Phillies**, Cubs 211 ip, 7–11, 3.10

Erroneously called the "Millionaire Indian" because he owned 500 oil-less acres in Oklahoma, Tincup, a full-blooded Cherokee, numbered three shutouts among his seven 1914 Phillie wins, taking two by 1–0. He never won another ML game. In 1928, after ten years in the minors, he made two appearances with the Cubs. /(AL)

Joe Tinker — 1880–1948. SS 1902–16 **Cubs**, Reds, Chicago (FL), Cubs 1805 g, .263, 31 hr, 782 rbi. *4 WS, 21 g, .235, 1 hr, 7 rbi.*
    Manager 1913–16 Reds, **Chicago (FL)**, Cubs 304–308, .497. First place: 15
☛ *Hall of Fame—1946.*

Tinker was immortalized in Franklin P. Adams's verse, "Baseball's Sad Lexicon," better-known, although incorrectly so, as "Tinker to Evers to Chance." An intelligent, smooth-fielding, mediocre-hitting shortstop, Tinker and second baseman Johnny Evers, first baseman Frank Chance, and third baseman Harry Steinfeldt formed one of the better defensive infields of the day. But the celebrated Chicago trio did not actually turn that many double plays. During that era, none did, compared to today. Yet under Chance's often brilliant guidance, what the trio did was to bring fielding into focus. They devised new defensive strategies to defeat the bunt, the hit-and-run, and the stolen base (the key run-producing techniques of the dead-ball era) and implemented the first known version of the rotation play. They brought Chicago to four World Series, in 1906–08 and 1910. All three went on to manage the Cubs.

Tinker had an aggressive, spirited playing attitude, but otherwise was quite an innocuous character. Yet one day in 1905, he argued with Evers over a cab fare, which led to a fistfight on the field. The contentious Evers would not speak to Tinker for decades, and gave him an unrepeatable nickname. Unbeknownst to one another, both were invited to help broadcast the 1938 Cubs World Series, 33 years after their falling-out. When they saw each other, after a moment's strained silence, they hugged and cried for some time.

Tinker first came up in 1902, and remained Chicago's everyday shortstop for 11 years. Always the elegant fielder, he led NL shortstops four times in fielding percentage, three times in total chances,

Joe Tinker

twice each in putouts and assists, and once in double plays (he also led Federal League shortstops in total chances in 1914). He had superior speed, and stole an average of 28 bases a season for Chicago. On July 28, 1910, he tied a major league record by stealing home twice in one game. Though he was a respectable hitter, few pitchers feared his bat. Yet Christy Mathewson had trouble with him. Tinker registered a lifetime mark against the Giants great of almost 100 points better than his career batting average.

Tinker concentrated on his salary as few players had before. In 1909, earning a reported $1,500, he demanded a $1,000 raise. He sat out the early part of the season before settling for a $200 increase. After the 1912 season, the Cubs traded him to Cincinnati, where he became a shortstop-manager. Throughout the year, Tinker argued with owner Gary Hermann over money. Hermann, tired of the talk, sold Tinker to the Dodgers after the season. In the most outrageous player demand to that time, Tinker refused to play for either team unless "commissioned" with $10,000 of his $25,000 sale price. Federal League agents, always on the lookout for discontented stars, quickly signed Tinker as a player-manager with the Chicago Whales. Tinker brought them in second in 1914, and first in 1915. In 1916, he managed the Cubs, but finished fifth.

Tinker went on to become president and manager of Columbus (American Association), and bought controlling interest in the Orlando Gulls (Florida State League) in 1921. He briefly managed in the International League, and scouted for the Cubs. During the 1920s, he made and lost a fortune in Florida real estate; a stadium named after him was built on one property and was used by the Reds in spring training for decades. On his 68th birthday, he died from complications of diabetes. Along with Evers and Chance, he was elected to the Hall of Fame by the Committee on Baseball Veterans in 1946. /(AA)

Bud Tinning [Lyle Forrest] — 1906–1961. RHP 1932–35 **Cubs**, Cardinals 406 ip, 22–15, 3.19. *1 WS, 2 ip, 0–0, 0.00*

Tinning was a crafty pitcher who started about one-third of his games. Perhaps his finest effort came in relief, when he threw 12–2/3 shutout innings in an August 17, 1932 Chicago win. /(DAS)

Eric Tipton (Dukie, Blue Devil) — 1915– . OF 1939–45 A's, **Reds** 501 g, .270, 22 hr, 151 rbi

Tipton, an All-American footballer at Duke and a Rose Bowl star, skipped a pro-football career to sign with Connie Mack's Athletics in 1939. During WWII he had his only ML success, hitting .288 and .301 as a regular outfielder with the Reds. /(JK)

Joe Tipton — 1923– . C 1948–54 Indians, White Sox, A's, Senators 417 g, .236, 29 hr, 125 rbi. *1 WS, 1 g, .000*

After leading the Eastern League with a .375 BA in 1947, the WWII Navy veteran jumped to the ML as backup catcher for the Indians' 1948 World Champions, hitting .289. Traded or sold four times in the next six seasons (in 1950, from the White Sox to the A's for Nellie Fox), he showed home run power but remained a substitute. /(RTM)

John Titus (Silent John) — 1876–1943. OF 1903–13 **Phillies**, Braves 1402 g, .282, 38 hr, 561 rbi

Titus was a steady player for nine years with the Phillies, then hit a career-high .309 when traded to the Braves. Among his eccentricities were chewing toothpicks while batting and sporting a handlebar mustache long after they'd gone out of fashion. /(JL)

Dave Tobik — 1953– . RHP 1978–85 **Tigers**, Rangers, Mariners 396 ip, 14–23, 3.70

Tobik was an inconsistent, forkballing reliever who also made use of a palmball. Aurelio Lopez's arm problems in 1982 thrust Tobik, who had been a long man, into the role of Detroit's bullpen ace. He worked in a career-high 51 games and led the club with nine saves. The Rangers acquired him in 1983 to be their closer, and again he saved nine games. /(CC)

Jack Tobin [John Thomas] — 1892–1969. OF 1914–16, 18–27 St. Louis (FL), **Browns**, Senators, Red Sox 1619 g, .309, 64 hr, 581 rbi

Tobin was a St. Louis native who began his major league career with his hometown entry in the Federal League. In 1915 he led the league with 625 at-bats and 184 hits. He joined the Browns in 1916 after the Feds folded. A 5'8" 142-lb lefthanded batter, he excelled at dragging a bunt for a base hit. He could also hit away with authority, powering as many as 13 HR and averaging 32 doubles and 12 triples a year from 1920 through 1924. He hit two grand slams off Walter Johnson.

Tobin had four straight 200-hit seasons and batted well over .300 each year from 1919 though '23. His career-high .352 came in 1921, when he led the AL with 671 at-bats. He was the leadoff man for the potent 1922 Browns, who finished one game behind the pennant-winning Yankees. In 1922–23, he joined Ken Williams and Baby Doll Jacobson in a .300-hitting outfield. He coached for the Browns from 1944 through 1948 and then scouted for them. /(JK)

Jim Tobin (Abba Dabba) — 1912–1969. RHP 1937–45 Pirates, **Braves**, Tigers 1900 ip, 105–112, 3.44. *1 WS, 3 ip, 0–0, 6.00*
☛ *All-Star—44..*

A man of extremes, Tobin led the NL in innings pitched (287.2) and losses (21) in 1942. He also startled the baseball world by hitting three home runs in one game on May 13 that year. A more than respectable hitter, he cracked 17 homers in his nine ML seasons.

As a starter for the hapless Braves in the 1940s, he could never get his record over .500 but he twice led the NL in complete games. He pitched a no-hitter on April 27, 1944 against the Dodgers, and added a five-inning no-hitter in June. (As the second game of a double-header, the game was scheduled for only five innings.) Tobin was sold to the Tigers late in the 1945 season, reaching the pennant-bound team in time to contribute four victories. /(JK)

Al Todd — 1902–1985. C 1932–41, 43 Phillies, **Pirates**, Dodgers, Cubs 863 g, .276, 35 hr, 366 rbi

The burly Todd arrived in the ML with an intimidating reputation, having punched out Dizzy Dean in the Texas League for an alleged knockdown pitch. A solid journeyman catcher, his best year was 1937 with the Pirates when he hit .307 with 86 RBI and caught 128 games without allowing a single passed ball, a record that still stands. /(JK)

Jackson Todd — 1951– . RHP 1977, 79–81 Mets, **Blue Jays** 287 ip. 10–16, 4.22

Perhaps the high point of Todd's career came in the minors in 1975, when he came back from successful surgery for cancer to post a 3.17 ERA for Jackson (Texas League). He did not pitch as well in cities that didn't share his name, especially those that had major league hitters. His ML career year was 1980, when he was 5–2 with a 4.02 ERA. He set a Blue Jay record on September 30 that year when he allowed four HR to the Tigers. /(TF)

Jim Todd — 1947– . RHP 1974–79 Cubs, **A's**, Mariners 512 ip, 25–23, 4.22. *1 LCS, 1 ip, 0–0, 9.00*

Rollie Fingers, Todd's teammate in Oakland in 1975–76, once said he could not have been regarded as the best reliever in baseball without Todd as his set-up man. Ralph Houk accused Todd of throwing greaseballs; Todd called them "super sinkers." In '75, his top season, he went 8–3 (2.29) with 12 saves in 58 appearances. /(KC)

Phil Todt — 1901–1973. 1B 1924–31 **Red Sox**, A's 957 g, .258, 57 hr, 453 rbi. *1 WS, 1 g, --*

Likable and consistent, Todt was the Red Sox' first baseman while they finished last in the AL for six straight seasons. He led the league's first basemen in fielding (.997) in 1928, but he was handicapped as a lefthanded hitter by Fenway Park's deep centerfield and right-field fences. /(EC)

Bobby Tolan — 1945– . OF-1B 1965–70, 72–77, 79 Cardinals, **Reds**, Padres, Phillies, Pirates 1282 g, .265, 86 hr, 497 rbi. *3 LCS, 11 g, .286, 1 hr, 6 rbi. 4 WS, 16 g, .229, 1 hr, 7 rbi*

After four seasons as a backup in St. Louis, Tolan got his chance as an everyday outfielder when he and Wayne Granger were traded to Cincinnati for Vada Pinson on October 11, 1968. Using a distinctive batting style, with his bat held high above his head and perpendicular to the ground, Tolan had brilliant seasons in 1969 and 1970. Batting second behind Pete Rose, he had career highs of 21 HR and 93 RBI in 1969. He batted .316 and led the NL with 57 stolen bases in 1970. In Game Two of the 1970 LCS, he homered and scored all three Cincinnati runs in their 3–1 victory over Pittsburgh.

Tolan ruptured his Achilles tendon playing basketball in January 1971 and missed the entire season. He came back in 1972 to bat .283 and steal 42 bases, capturing *TSN* Comeback Player of the Year honors. But he feuded with Cincinnati management, was suspended during a dismal 1973 season, and was traded to San Diego in November. A 1974 knee injury eliminated his speed, and he played sparingly after joining the Phillies in 1976, mostly at first base. He spent 1978 in Japan. Later he served as a major league coach and a minor league manager. /(ME)

Fred Toliver — 1961– . RHP 1984– Reds, **Phillies**, Twins, Padres 249 ip, 8–13, 4.81

Toliver never spent a full season in the majors. He saw the most action in 1988, when he made the Twins' rotation and went 7–6 with a 4.24 ERA in his only winning season. /(SFS)

Wayne Tolleson — 1955– . SS-2B-3B 1981- **Rangers**, White Sox, Yankees 789 g, .244, 9 hr, 129 rbi

Tolleson broke into the ML as a fleet, slap-hitting infielder, starting at second base for the Rangers in 1983–84, then moving to shortstop in 1985, when he hit a career-high .313. He stole 33 bases in his first full season, and at least 17 each year until 1987, but has never hit for power, with only 76 extra-base hits in 2,108 ML at-bats through 1988. Tolleson was traded to the White Sox before the 1986 season, but played only 81 games in Chicago before being shipped to the Yankees with Ron Kittle and Joel Skinner for Ron Hassey. In college, Tolleson was an All-American wide receiver at Western Carolina, leading the nation in pass receptions his senior year. /(SCL)

Dick Tomanek (Bones) — 1931– . LHP 1953–54, 57–59 **Indians**, A's 231 ip, 10–10, 4.95

Tomanek's first ML appearance for the Indians was a complete-game win over Detroit, but he struggled from then on. Cleveland included him in the deal that sent Roger Maris to Kansas City. /(ME)

Dave Tomlin — 1949– . LHP 1972–80, 82–83, 85–86 Reds, **Padres**, Expos, Pirates 511 ip, 25–12, 3.82. *2 LCS, 5 ip, 0–0, 5.79*

Used primarily against lefthanded hitters, Tomlin averaged 60 appearances a year in relief for the 1974–77 Padres. He was traded to Texas with $125,000 for Gaylord Perry in January of 1978, but in March was sold to the Reds, who had first signed him in 1967. He went 9–1 in '78, despite a 5.81 ERA. He spent most of the 1980s in the minors, and in 1982 he led the American Association in appearances. /(ME)

Fred Toney — 1888–1953. RHP 1911–13, 15–23 Cubs, **Reds**, Giants, Cardinals 2206 ip, 137–102, 2.69. 20 wins: 17, 20 *1 WS, 3 ip, 0–0, 23.63*

Toney was a 6'6" 245-lb workhorse who, pitching 340 innings, went 24–16 for the Reds in 1917. That May 2, in one of baseball's all-time classic pitching duels, Toney threw ten innings of no-hit, shutout ball to defeat the Cubs' Hippo Vaughn, who did not give up a hit or a run until the tenth inning. Toney again displayed his skill and stamina on July 1, 1917, when he pitched both ends of a doubleheader, defeating the Pirates 4–1 and 5–1. He had hurled a 17-inning no-hitter as a 21-year-old in the Blue Grass league in 1909, striking out 19 and walking one.

Toney went 15–6 in 1915 with a 1.58 ERA—second in the league to Grover Cleveland Alexander. He had dropped to 6–10 in 1918 when he was sold in mid-season to the Giants, for whom he went 21–11 in 1920. He followed with an 18–11 mark for the 1921 World Champions, but didn't make it through the third inning in either of his World Series starts. He faded to 5–6 in 1922, refused to report when the Giants traded him to the Braves that July, and was waived to the Cardinals in October. /(JK)

Specs Toporcer [George] — 1899– . SS-2B-3B 1921–28 **Cardinals** 546 g, .279, 9 hr, 151 rbi. *1 WS, 1 g, --*

Branch Rickey once told this story about Specs Toporcer: "A 19-year-old boy who weighed 142 pounds and never had played a game of pro ball came off the field at Orange, New Jersey. I watched this kid and saw him take off his glasses and, with his hands outstretched, grope his way along the wall to the showers. My captain turned to me and said, 'For God's sake, who sent him up?' " Toporcer, who never played baseball in high school, college, or the minors, is remembered as the first infielder to wear glasses in the majors. Primarily a Cardinal utility

man, in 1922 he played in a career-high 116 games and batted .324. After leaving the majors, he was the International League's MVP with Rochester in 1929 and 1930.

In 1944 Torporcer wrote a book, *Baseball, from Backyards to the Big Leagues*, still considered one of the best manuals of instruction for coaches and youngsters. Despite five operations, he lost his eyesight while managing Buffalo (International League) in 1951. He also served as farm director for the Red Sox. His life story was featured in a network TV show in which he played the lead. /(NLM)

Topps — 1938– .

Topps Chewing Gum, Inc. manufactures Bazooka gum, Garbage Pail Kids, and many more such products; it is the largest manufacturer of bubble gum and related products in the world. But Topps is known by many not for its gum so much as for what comes with it: baseball cards. It has dominated the baseball-card industry almost since it issued its first set.

Topps's ancestry is the American Leaf Tobacco Company, founded in 1890 by Morris Shorin. Diversification seemed necessary during the Depression, and in 1938 the company began selling gum under the Topps name. They began enclosing baseball cards with gum in 1951, and by 1956 the Brooklyn-based company had beaten its well-entrenched competitor, Bowman, and bought them out. For the next twenty-five years, Topps monopolized the baseball-card market; Fleer issued a few sets of old-timers in the early 1960s, and later produced World Series-history sets, but Topps had locked up the basic concept of the baseball-card set that consisted of most of the active players in the major leagues. Finally Fleer won a court case; it was decided that Topps's monopoly included only the right to sell baseball cards with gum, so other companies sprang up in the 1980s. But Topps remains the top dog in the field, regularly producing a myriad of sets for other companies (department stores, food products, even dog food) and in other countries (Canada, England). /(SH)

Jeff Torborg — 1941– . C 1964–73 **Dodgers**, Angels 574 g, .214, 8 hr, 101 rbi.
Manager 1977–79, 89 **Indians**, White Sox 226–293, .435

Torborg reportedly received the Dodgers' first $100,000 bonus in 1963 when he was signed out of Rutgers, where his .537 batting average in his senior year set an NCAA record which still stands. Though he stayed with Los Angeles from 1964 through

1970, he was always a backup catcher, behind Johnny Roseboro and Tom Haller. He caught Sandy Koufax's perfect game (9/9/65), Bill Singer's no-hitter (7/20/70), and the fifth of Don Drysdale's six consecutive 1968 shutouts. With the Angels in 1973, he caught Nolan Ryan's May 15 no-hitter. He replaced Frank Robinson as Indians manager in June 1977, and lasted through July 1979. A month later he became a Yankee coach. /(TG)

Earl Torgeson [The Earl of Snohomish] — 1924– . 1B 1947–61 **Braves**, Phillies, Tigers, White Sox, Yankees 1668 g, .265, 149 hr, 740 rbi. *2 WS, 8 g, .368, 1 rbi*

A graceful, lefthanded first baseman, Torgeson was an immediate hit with the Braves as a rookie in 1947, batting .281 with 16 homers. In the 1948 World Series, he led all hitters with a .389 batting average (7-for-18). He hurt his left shoulder trying to break up a double play in mid-May 1949 and was sidelined for the remainder of the season. Although the injury hampered him throughout his career, he returned in 1950 to lead the NL with 120 runs scored and in 1951 had career highs of 24 HR and 92 RBI. After he dropped to .230 in 1952, he was sent to the Phillies in a four-team trade, and never had another big season. He appeared with the White Sox in the 1959 WS, was released in 1961, and signed with the Yankees as a player-coach for the final month of the season, and his career. Like Hall of Famer Earl Averill, Torgeson was a native of Snohomish, WA, and inherited Averill's nickname, The Earl of Snohomish. /(AL)

Toronto Blue Jays — 1977– . Team. 983–1064, .480. *AL East Champions 85, 89*

Created in the 1976 American League expansion draft, the Blue Jays won their inaugural game amid snow flurries on April 7, 1977, as Doug Ault hit two home runs. The Jays finished last in each of their first five seasons while building a strong franchise with young talent. Future stars like George Bell (1987 AL MVP) and Willie Upshaw were acquired through the major league draft and Tom Henke (1987 AL saves leader) was acquired in the free-agent compensation pool. Jesse Barfield (1986 AL home run champ), Dave Stieb (1985 AL ERA leader), Tony Fernandez (Gold Glove shortstop 1986–87), and Jimmy Key (1987 AL ERA leader) came up quickly through the farm system. The Blue Jays played their home games in Exhibition Stadium—a converted football field—until June 19, 1989, when they moved into the extravagant and ultra-modern SkyDome. The appointment of Cito Gaston as manager spurred the team to the 1989 division title. /(TF)

Frank Torre — 1931– . 1B 1956–63 **Braves**, Phillies 714 g, .273, 13 hr, 179 rbi. *2 WS, 14 g, .222, 2 hr, 4 rbi*

Torre was known for his fielding, leading NL first basemen in fielding in 1957 and 1958, but on September 2, 1957 he tied a NL mark by scoring six runs in one game, and then hit two homers in the WS to help the Braves to victory over the Yankees. His younger brother Joe became a NL All-Star. /(RTM)

Joe Torre (The Godfather) — 1940– . C-1B-3B 1960–77 **Braves**, Cardinals, Mets 2209 g, .297, 252 hr, 1185 rbi.
  Manager 1977–84 **Mets**, Braves 543–649, .456. First place: 82 *1 LCS, 0–3, .000*
☛ *Most Valuable Player—71. Led League—rbi 71. Led League—ba 71. All-Star—63–67, 70–73. Gold Glove—65.*

An All-Star catcher in the 1960s, in 1971 Torre moved to third base and won the NL MVP award, leading the league with a .363 batting average and 137 RBI.

Torre came up at the end of 1960 and hit a pinch single off Harvey Haddix in his first at-bat. It was the last season that his older brother Frank was on the Braves. Joe was a semi-regular the next two seasons and finished second (behind Billy Williams) in 1961 NL Rookie of the Year voting. Becoming an everyday player in 1963 by playing both catcher and first base, he hit .293 with 14 HR and made the All-Star team that year and the next four seasons. He upped his performance in 1964 (.321, 20 HR, 109 RBI), finishing fifth in MVP voting and leading NL catchers in fielding. In 1965 he hit 27 HR and won the catcher's Gold Glove. His two-run HR in the 1965 All-Star Game was vital in the NL's 6–5 victory. When the Braves moved to Atlanta for 1966, he hit a career-high 36 HR while batting .315 with 101 RBI. He was set back by a broken cheekbone in 1968.

The Braves traded Torre to the Cardinals straight-up for former MVP Orlando Cepeda, whom Torre replaced at first base. He reached 100 RBI each of the next three seasons. He replaced Tim McCarver behind the plate after McCarver was dealt to the Phillies for 1970, but moved to third base in mid-season when Mike Shannon was sidelined by a career-ending illness (Ted Simmons took over the catching job). His .325 average and 21 HR in '70 were topped the next season by his MVP performance. In 1971 he led the NL in total bases (352) and hits (230) in addition to batting and RBI, and hit 24 HR. At third base, he led in putouts, although he tied for the lead in errors. He hit in the .280s the

Joe Torre

next three seasons, but saw his power drop. He also spent more time back at first base, leading NL first basemen with 144 double plays, after the emergence of 1973 fielding leader Ken Reitz. On June 27, 1973 he hit for the cycle.

Following the 1974 season, the Mets traded Ray Sadecki and minor leaguer Tommy Moore for Torre in an attempt to solve their persistent third-base problem. The Brooklyn-born Torre was quite popular in New York, but he was a major disappointment. Never fast, he had slowed down considerably. He hit into 22 double plays in 1974, showed reduced range at third base, and hit only .247; he was no longer an everyday player. He rebounded to .306 in 1975, but with only five HR and 31 RBI. He remained popular, however, and on May 31, 1977 he replaced Joe Frazier as the Mets manager. He retired as a player 18 days later.

Torre was not an especially good manager. He played strictly by the book, bunting more often than most. The Mets had finished in third place the year before, but under Torre from 1977 through 1981 their best finish was fourth place in the second half of the strike-shortened 1981 season. Moving to Atlanta the following season, he rode their 13–0

start to the division title (89–73). The Braves finished second the following two seasons, although their record in 1984, 80–82, led to his dismissal. He went on to become a popular Angels broadcaster. /(RTM/SH)

Pablo Torrealba — 1948– . LHP 1975–79 **Braves**, A's, White Sox 240 ip, 6–13, 3.26

The injury-plagued Venezuelan never succeeded as either a starter or reliever, and gave up as many or more hits as innings in every season but 1979 (only six innings). /(WOR)

Felix Torres — 1932– . 3B 1962–64 **Angels** 365 g, .254, 27 hr, 153 rbi

As a 30-year-old rookie third baseman with the Angels in 1962, Torres hit .259 with 11 homers. During one stretch in 1963, he went 12 consecutive games without making a putout at third base. In the same season, he tied a ML record by starting four double plays in one game from his position. /(RTM)

Gil Torres — 1915–1983. SS-3B-RHP 1940, 44–46 **Senators** 346 g, .252, 0 hr, 119 rbi; 10 ip, 0–0, 5.59

Torres made two appearances as a knuckleball pitcher in 1940 with the Senators, who, having plenty of knuckleballers, converted the Cuban to infielding. He resurfaced in 1944 as Washington's third baseman, and in 1945 was their shortstop. He wore his pants legs long to hide two of the skinniest legs in the majors. His father, Ricardo, was a Senators catcher for 22 games in 1920–22. /(NLM)

Hector Torres — 1945– . SS-2B 1968–73, 75–77 **Astros**, Cubs, Expos, Padres, Blue Jays 622 g, .216, 18 hr, 115 rbi

A regular only in his first season, Torres had his best year with the Padres in 1975 (.259, five HR in 352 at-bats). The Mexican glove man was sent to Cleveland with Johnny Grubb and Fred Kendall in exchange for All-Star George Hendrick in December 1976; the Indians then traded Torres straight-up for the Blue Jays' John Lowenstein. His father, Epitacio Torres, was a minor league manager. /(JFC)

Rusty Torres [Rosendo, Jr.] — 1948– . OF 1971–74, 76–80 Yankees, **Indians**, Angels, White Sox, Royals 654 g, .212, 35 hr, 126 rbi

A defensive specialist with modest home run power, switch-hitting Torres's only season with more than 300 at-bats came in 1973 with the Indians. He hit .205 with seven homers. /(ME)

Mike Torrez— 1946- . RHP 1967-84 Cardinals, Expos, Orioles, A's, Yankees, **Red Sox**, Mets 3042 ip, 185-160, 3.97. 20 wins: 75 *1 LCS, 11 ip, 0-1, 4.09. 1 WS, 18 ip, 2-0, 2.50*

Torrez won more than 15 games six seasons in a row (1974-79) for five different teams. The 6'5" Kansan first achieved consistency with the Expos in 1972, winning 16 games. In 1975 with Baltimore, he went 20-9 with a league-leading .690 winning percentage. He was sent to Oakland in the 1976 seven-player trade that brought Reggie Jackson to the Orioles. Torrez won 16 that year (including three straight shutouts) and 17 in 1977 for the A's and Yankees. He helped New York to a pennant with seven straight wins in July and August. He threw two complete-game victories in the '77 World Series against the Dodgers and was the beneficiary of Jackson's three home runs in the sixth and final game.

Torrez signed as a free agent with the Red Sox after the 1977 season, and in 1978 became Boston's Ralph Branca. In the tension-filled playoff game between the Yankees and Red Sox on October 2, he allowed Bucky Dent's short and dramatic game-winning three-run homer.

Torrez was traded to the Mets in 1983 and lost a league-high 17 games. Typically wild, he led his league in walks for the third time in his career. On April 8, 1984, in his final season, he threw a pitch that struck Houston all-star shortstop Dickie Thon above the eye. /(PB)

Christobel Torriente — 1895-1948. OF-LHP Negro Leagues 1914-32 Cuban Stars, **Chicago American Giants**, Kansas City Monarchs, Detroit Stars, Gilkerson's Union Giants, Atlanta Black Crackers, Cleveland Cubs 533 g, .329, 41 hr (inc.)
☛ *Led League—ba 19.*

Torriente, a slugging Negro League superstar, was one of the three greatest Cuban players (with Jose Mendez and Martin Dihigo) to have been kept out of the American major leagues because of race. He had a light complexion and, according to teammate Jelly Gardner, the New York Giants' John McGraw would have signed him to a major league contract had it not been for Torriente's kinky hair. C.I. Taylor, longtime manager and Negro League executive, said, "If I should see Torriente walking up the other side of the street, I would say, 'there walks a ballclub.'"

Torriente was a powerful, 5'9" lefthanded pull-hitter, and a notorious bad-ball hitter. He began his career in the United States in 1914 with the touring Cuban Stars. An outstanding outfielder with great

range and a strong arm, when he joined the Chicago American Giants in 1919, Hall of Famer Oscar Charleston moved from centerfield to left field. Torriente led the American Giants to consecutive Negro National League championships in 1920-22. He batted .396 in 1920, and until 1925 never dipped below .332. When he dropped to .241 in 1925, he was traded to the Kansas City Monarchs, with whom he bounced back to hit .339 in 1926. From 1919 through 1928, he compiled a 16-5 record as a pitcher. He was absent from league play in 1929-31, but returned for a single game in 1932.

In the 12 documented years that Torriente played in the Cuban League, he hit .352. He led the league in doubles twice, in hits and in stolen bases three times, in triples and in HR four times. Though he captured only one batting title (1919), he topped his league-leading mark of .360 in three other seasons, with a high of .402 in 1916. Against major leaguers in exhibition play, he hit .281 (27-for-96) with three HR. He reportedly died of tuberculosis in Cuba in 1948. /(JJM)

Paul Toth — 1935- . RHP 1962-64 Cardinals, **Cubs** 192 ip, 9-12, 3.80

Toth was a finesse pitcher who was traded from the Cardinals to the Cubs in 1962 and went 5-9 in 1963. He was reacquired by St. Louis in the June 15, 1964 trade that brought Lou Brock to the Cardinals. /(DAS)

Cesar Tovar (Pepito) — 1940- . OF-3B-2B-DH-SS 1965-76 **Twins**, Phillies, Rangers, A's, Yankees 1488 g, .278, 46 hr, 435 rbi. *3 LCS, 8 g, .250, 1 rbi*

Hustling Cesar Tovar divided his 1967 season with the Twins among the outfield, third base, second, and short, playing in an AL-record 164 games and leading the league with 649 at-bats. The 5'9" Venezuelan dramatized his versatility in a September 22, 1968 game when he played all nine positions against the A's. He pitched one scoreless inning in which he struck out Reggie Jackson; the first batter he faced was Bert Campaneris, the only other man to perform in nine positions in a game. In 1969 Tovar stole a career-high 45 bases; on May 18, he and teammate Rod Carew each stole home in the second inning against a Detroit battery of Mickey Lolich and Bill Freehan.

Tovar improved his batting average every year from 1965 through 1971. Finally set in the Minnesota outfield, in 1970 he led the AL with 36 doubles and 13 triples. When he batted .311 in 1971, his 204 hits were the league high. He hit for the cycle on

September 19, 1972. Tovar is the all-time AL leader in breaking up no-hit bids, collecting the only hit in five one-hitters; his victims included Mike Cuellar, Dave McNally, and Catfish Hunter. /(RTM)

Jack Townsend (Happy) — 1879–1963. RHP 1901–06 Phillies, **Senators**, Indians 1138 ip, 35–82, 3.59

Townsend was a hard thrower with control problems who, in 1904, was one of three pitchers to lose 20 games for the 38–113 Senators. His 26 losses is still the AL record. No stranger to defeat, he preceded the '04 season with a 2–11 mark and followed by going 7–16. /(JK)

Jim Traber — 1961– . 1B-DH 1984, 86, 88 **Orioles** 264 g, .227, 27 hr, 117 rbi

Traber's best season came in 1986, when he hit .255 with 13 HR in 212 at-bats. Never a regular, he declined after that. /(WOR)

Dick Tracewski — 1935– . SS-2B-3B 1962–69 **Dodgers**, Tigers 614 g, .213, 8 hr, 91 rbi. *3 WS, 12 g, .133*

A "good-field, no-hit" utility man, Tracewski trained as a shortstop in the Dodgers' system but provided insurance at three infield positions on three World Champions. He filled in brilliantly at second base in the 1963 and 1965 World Series. He started all four games of the Dodgers' 1963 sweep of the Yankees; his fifth-inning, diving stop for a force play in a scoreless tie was the defensive key to the Dodgers' 2–1 Game Four victory. He served in the same capacity with the Tigers as he had in Los Angeles, and appeared in two games of the 1968 Series. /(JL)

Alan Trammell — 1958– . SS 1977– **Tigers** 1689 g, .286, 138 hr, 721 rbi. *2 LCS, 8 g, .258, 1 hr, 5 rbi. 1 WS, 5 g, .450, 2 hr, 6 rbi*
☛ *All-Star—80, 84–85, 87–88. Gold Glove—80–81, 83–84.*

Trammell and Lou Whitaker formed a keystone combination that surpassed all others in consecutive years together, yet Alan emerged as the acknowledged leader of the Tigers. After a Most Valuable Player year (1977) in the Southern League, the righthander graduated to the Tigers. Slight of build, Trammell proved a complete offensive and defensive player. He led the AL in sacrifice hits in 1981 and 1983. After an off-season in 1982, he was AL Comeback Player of the Year in 1983 at age 25. His 30 steals in 1983 were the most for a Detroit shortstop since 1917 and his .319 batting average was best among all AL righthanders. The Tigers reeled off 11 straight winning seasons with Trammell

at shortstop. He was voted smartest and best defensive infielder by AL managers in 1984, drove in all of Detroit's runs in Game Four of the World Series, tied a five-game Series record with nine hits, and was named Series MVP.

A persistent elbow injury, first suffered in 1983, threatened Trammell's stardom. After a subpar 1985, a more muscular Trammell helped Detroit have an all-20 home run infield in 1986. Surprisingly, Sparky Anderson moved Trammell to the cleanup spot in Detroit's 1987 offense. The once-scrawny infielder rose to the occasion with a career season, hitting .343 with 28 HR, 105 RBI, 205 hits, and 109 runs. He narrowly missed the league MVP award. Part of an era of shortstops that includes Ozzie Smith, Cal Ripken, Jr. and Robin Yount, Trammell has held his own in all-around ability. He is among Detroit's all-time leaders in doubles, runs scored, hits, and stolen bases. /(ME)

Bill Travers (Stork) — 1952– . LHP 1974–81, 83 **Brewers**, Angels 1121 ip, 65–71, 4.10
☛ *All-Star—76.*

Travers was a solid starter for the Brewers before they had achieved respectability, and gradually improved along with the team. The 6′4″ 187-lb starter was selected for the All-Star Game in 1976 (he did not play), finishing the year at 15–16 with a 2.81 ERA, despite being set back by Legionnaire's disease (a dangerous form of the flu) in mid-season. He had a 1.91 ERA at the All-Star break, but went 5–10 in the second half. Travers dropped to 4–12 in 1977 and missed five weeks with a sore arm. He went 14–8 in 1979 as Milwaukee contended and followed with a 12–6 year. After signing with the Angels as a free agent for 1981, he lost his effectiveness. /(SFS)

Cecil Travis — 1913– . SS-3B 1933–41, 45–47 **Senators** 1328 g, .314, 27 hr, 657 rbi
☛ *All-Star—38, 40–41.*

The modest Travis was a steady fielder and outstanding hitter for the Senators before WWII. He broke in with five hits in his first ML game (May 16, 1933). Early in his career, the lefthanded batter slapped most of his hits to left field. Later he learned to pull the ball and cracked 19 triples in 1941. In that season, his last before entering the service, he led the AL in hits with 218, had 101 RBI, and batted .359, his eighth time over .300 in nine years. Just before the war, he was named the top ML shortstop by *TSN*, but when he returned from military service in 1945, his skills had eroded. After two poor seasons he retired. /(JK)

Pie Traynor [Harold Joseph] — 1899–1972. 3B-SS 1920–35, 37 **Pirates** 1941 g, .320, 58 hr, 1273 rbi. *2 WS, 11 g, .293, 1 hr, 4 rbi.*
    Manager 1934–39 **Pirates** 457–406, .530
☛ *All-Star—33, 34. Hall of Fame—48.*

Barney Dreyfuss ushered in the second glory era of the Pittsburgh Pirates when he purchased Pie Traynor from Portsmouth (Virginia League) in 1920. The classy, intelligent Massachusetts native had been ignored by both Boston clubs. He came up as a shortstop but was moved to third base by Pittsburgh manager Bill McKechnie in 1922—the first of 12 straight seasons in which he played 130 or more games.

Pie Traynor

Traynor topped the .300 mark ten times, and from 1925 through 1930 batted .342. Yet, playing on teams that featured the Waner brothers, he led the Pirates in hitting just once, with a .356 mark in 1929. When he hit .366 in 1930, teammate Paul Waner hit .368. Traynor usually made contact, striking out only 278 times in his career. He fanned only seven times in 540 at-bats in 1930.

At third base Traynor had a great arm and was outstanding on bunts and slow choppers. Teamed with defensive whiz Glenn Wright at shortstop, and in a lineup with hitting stars Max Carey and Kiki Cuyler, in 1925 Traynor helped Pittsburgh to its first pennant since 1909. He hit .346 in their seven-game World Series victory over Washington, and homered off Walter Johnson in the opener. He handled 24 chances without an error.

Traynor hit .342 in 1927, led NL third basemen in double plays for the fourth straight year, and had three hits on October 1 when Pittsburgh clinched another pennant. In Game Three of the WS, he broke up Herb Pennock's perfect game with an eighth-inning single, but the Pirates were swept by the Yankees.

Playing in spacious Forbes Field, Traynor hit few home runs, but consistently reached double figures in doubles and triples. He tied teammate Carey for the NL lead with 19 three-base hits in 1923. He remains among the Pirates' all-time leaders in every offensive category but home runs.

While posting a record-tying seventh season as the NL putout leader at third base despite a sore throwing arm, Traynor replaced George Gibson as Pirate manager in June 1934. He played occasionally in 1935 and 1937, finishing with a NL record 2,288 putouts at 3B. He managed for six seasons, leaving in 1939 with what was then the second-most wins in Pirate history (457). He came close to a pennant in 1938, but Chicago's Gabby Hartnett's "Homer in the Gloamin'" snatched it away. Traynor scouted for the Pirates until his death.

Widely regarded for years as baseball's greatest third baseman, Traynor was elected to the Hall of Fame in 1948, and was honored as a member of the all-time team selected in 1969 for baseball's centennial. He was one of Pittsburgh's most popular players, eagerly adopted by the community though he never lost his New England accent. The Giants' John McGraw, himself a third baseman, called Traynor the greatest team player in the game. Though there are several stories about his nickname, it seems to have come from Traynor's childhood taste for pies. /(ME)

Jeff Treadway — 1963– . 2B 1987– **Reds, Braves** 260 g, .274, 12 hr, 67 rbi

Treadway hit .333 at the end of 1987, when he replaced Ron Oester at second base after Oester suffered a career-threatening injury. Treadway dropped off to .252 in 1988, and near the end of the year Oester won his job back. Treadway took over the Braves' 2B job in 1989 after the team decided to move the erratic-fielding Ron Gant. /(JFC)

Tom Trebelhorn — 1948– . *Manager* 1986– **Brewers** 265–230, .535

Trebelhorn, a schoolteacher in the off-season, took over the Brewers at the end of 1986 after George Bamberger retired. The former strong-armed minor league catcher led the team to third-place finishes in his first two full seasons, exhibiting a patient style well suited to the streaky team. The club began the 1987 season with 13 straight wins, tying the ML record for fast starts, but lost 12 straight two weeks later. /(SFS)

Ted Trent — 1905–1944. RHP Negro Leagues 1927–39 St. Louis Stars, Detroit Wolves, Homestead Grays, Cole's American Giants, Chicago American Giants, Washington Pilots statistics not available
☛ *All-Star—34–37.*

Teammate Ted Radcliffe called Negro Leaguer Ted Trent "one of the best curveball pitchers that ever lived." Trent was the righthanded ace of the St. Louis Stars teams that won three pennants in the late 1920s, and of the Chicago American Giants in the 1930s. His best recorded season was 1928, when he led the St. Louis staff in virtually every pitching category and topped the league with a 17–4 mark. Available information gives him a 64–33 career record. He pitched in four consecutive East-West all-star games from 1934 to 1937, starting the '34 and '37 contests for the West./(PG)

Mike Tresh — 1914–1966. C 1938–49 **White Sox,** Indians 1027 g, .249, 2 hr, 297 rbi

Highly skilled defensively, Tresh was durable enough to catch all 150 White Sox games in 1945. He had caught 115 or more games each year from 1939 through 1941, batting a high of .281 in 1940. His son Tom, who unlike his father was a power hitter, was an infielder-outfielder with the Yankees and Tigers./(JK)

Tom Tresh — 1937– . OF-SS 1961–69 **Yankees,** Tigers 1192 g, .245, 153 hr, 530 rbi. *3 WS, 18 g, .277, 4 hr, 13 rbi*
☛ *Rookie of the Year—62. All-Star—62–63. Gold Glove—65.*

Tresh, the son of former ML catcher Mike Tresh, was AL Rookie of the Year in 1962 when he hit .286, with 20 home runs and 93 RBI, as a switch-hitting Yankee shortstop when Tony Kubek was in military service. Moved to left field in 1963 when Kubek returned, he continued to hit homers, three times topping 25, but his batting average declined steadily. On September 1, 1963 he became only the eighth player to homer from each side of the plate in a single game. He accomplished that feat twice more in his career, including a June 6, 1965 doubleheader when he hit four home runs, three in the nightcap. A damaged knee in 1967 hastened the end of his career./(RTM)

Alex Trevino — 1957– . C 1978– **Mets,** Reds, Braves, Giants, Dodgers, Astros 881 g, .250, 22 hr, 231 rbi

A journeyman catcher who has played for half of the NL clubs in his 12 ML seasons, Trevino was discovered by the Mets while playing in the Mexican Central League. He hit a career-high .271 in 1979, his first full ML season, while splitting time behind the plate and at third base, and he has filled in around the infield throughout his career. He was one of three players the Mets sent to Cincinnati in exchange for George Foster in 1982 and was the Reds' regular catcher that year, hitting .251 in 120 games. He lacked power, however, and was sold to the Braves, then traded in rapid succession to the Giants and Dodgers, who released him before the 1988 season. Trevino then signed as a free agent with Tucson (Pacific Coast League) and was promoted to the Astros after only 15 games./(SCL)

Gus Triandos — 1930– . C 1953–65 Yankees, **Orioles,** Tigers, Phillies, Astros 1206 g, .244, 167 hr, 608 rbi
☛ *All-Star—57–59.*

Big, powerful, strong-armed, and slow-footed, Triandos came to the Orioles as part of a 17-player trade in 1954 and was their regular catcher for seven seasons. He hit over 20 home runs three times, tying the AL record for catchers with 30 in 1958.

With the Phillies on June 21, 1964 Triandos caught Jim Bunning's perfect game, the first in the NL in 84 years. Oddly, he owns the ML record with 1,206 consecutive games without being caught stealing; he stole only one base./(AL)

Bob Trice — 1928- . RHP 1953–55 **A's** 152 ip, 9–9, 5.80

The first black player with the A's, Trice came to the ML after winning 21 games at Ottawa in the International League in 1953. He was 7–8 in '54 but with a 5.60 ERA. /(RTM)

Manny Trillo (Indio) — 1950- . 2B-3B-1B 1973–87 A's, **Cubs**, Phillies, Indians, Expos, Giants, Reds 1780 g, .263, 61 hr, 571 rbi. *2 LCS, 6 g, .381, 4 rbi. 1 WS, 6 g, .217, 2 rbi*
☛ *All-Star—77, 81–83. Gold Glove—79, 81–82.*

First signed out of Venezuela by Philadelphia, Trillo debuted with Oakland and was the Cubs' second baseman for four years before returning to the Phillies in a 1979 trade. He batted a career-high .292 for the 1980 World Champion Phillies and was named MVP of the LCS when he hit .381 with four RBI against Houston. Winning his third Gold Glove in 1982, he set since-broken major league second base records for consecutive errorless games in a season (89) and consecutive errorless chances accepted (479). He also set a since-broken league records for fielding percentage (.9937) at second base. Sent to Cleveland in a deal for Von Hayes that December, in 1983 he became the first player to be chosen to the starting All-Star squad in successive years in different leagues. Six weeks after the 1983 All-Star Game, the Indians sold Trillo to Montreal. By 1986, he was back with the Cubs as a utility man. /(DAS)

Ken Trinkle — 1919–1976. RHP 1943, 46–49 **Giants**, Phillies 435 ip, 21–29, 3.74

Trinkle routinely walked more batters than he struck out. Nevertheless, after returning from WWII military duty, he led the NL with 48 appearances in 1946 and 62 in 1947 for the Giants. His ten saves in 1947 tied him for second in the league. /(FS)

Coaker Triplett — 1911- . OF 1938, 41–45 Cubs, Cardinals, **Phillies** 470 g, .256, 27 hr, 173 rbi

A high-scoring halfback and baseball team captain at Appalachian State College in Boone, North Carolina, Triplett led the International League in batting in 1948. /(NLM)

Rich Troedson — 1950- . LHP 1973–74 **Padres** 171 ip, 8–10, 4.73

Troedson went 7–9 with a 4.25 ERA in his only full major league season in 1973 (5–9 in 18 starts). /(JFC)

Hal Trosky [born Harold Arthur Troyavesky] — 1912- . 1B 1933–41, 44, 46 **Indians**, White Sox 1347 g, .302, 228 hr, 1012 rbi
☛ *Led League—rbi 36.*

The 1940 Cleveland Indians were heavily favored to win the American League pennant. But the players despised their manager, Oscar Vitt, who made a practice of openly berating them. Led by first baseman Hal Trosky, the "Crybaby" Indians petitioned owner Alva Bradley for Vitt's removal. Vitt lasted out the year, but Trosky and others were roundly criticized. This incident tarnished Trosky's reputation late in a superb career as one of the league's top sluggers and as Cleveland's all-time first baseman.

Trosky batted .330 as a rookie in 1934, exhibiting his lefthanded power with 35 homers, 45 doubles, and 142 RBI—second in the AL to Lou Gehrig. In 1936 he put together a 28-game hitting streak, led the league with an Indians-record 162 RBI, and reached career highs of .343 and 42 HR. He drove in 100 or more runs six straight years. He twice hit three HR in a game, and his 216 HR put him second, behind Earl Averill, on the Indians all-time list.

After the 1941 season, Trosky announced a premature retirement, due to migraine headaches. He returned to his Iowa farm, but during 1943 he made known his wish to play again. He was sold to the White Sox after being declared 4F by the military. He hit just 10 HR in 1944, sat out a season, played in 1946, and then became a White Sox scout. His son, Hal Jr., made two appearances as a White Sox pitcher in 1958. /(RL)

Bill Trotter — 1908–1984. RHP 1937–42, 44 **Browns**, Senators, Cardinals 483 ip, 22–34, 5.40

Trotter's career began and ended in the Cardinal organization, but he spent most of his career with the less successful crosstown Browns, mostly in middle relief. He only once had an ERA under 5.34 (3.77 in 1940). /(JK)

Quincy Trouppe — 1912- . C-OF-MGR Negro Leagues 1930–49 St. Louis Stars, Detroit Wolves, Homestead Grays, Kansas City Monarchs, Chicago American Giants, Indianapolis ABC's, Cleveland Buckeyes, New York Cubans statistics not available; *ML:* C 1952 **Indians** 6 g, .100, 0 hr, 0 rbi
☛ *All-Star—38, 45–48.*

Trouppe was an all-star Negro League catcher who also performed in the Mexican League, Canadian Provincial League, and for the crack semi-pro Bismarck, ND club. He played 14 winters in Latin America and barnstormed with black all-star teams playing white major leaguers. In the twilight of his career, he appeared in 6 games for the 1952 Cleveland Indians and 84 games for their Triple-A farm club. A lifetime .300 hitter, he batted as high as .352 for Chicago in the 1948 Negro American League. He started for the West in five all-star games, four as a catcher in 1945–48. He managed the Cleveland Buckeyes to NAL titles in 1945 and 1947. He was also a nationally recognized amateur boxer who won a major heavyweight tournament title in 1936. His autobiography, *20 Years Too Soon*, was published in 1977. /(MFK)

Dizzy Trout [Paul Howard] — 1915–1972. RHP 1939–52, 57 **Tigers**, Red Sox, Orioles 2725 ip, 170–161, 3.23. 20 wins: 43–44 *2 WS, 15 ip, 1–2, 1.71*
☛ *Led League—w 43. Led League—era 44. All-Star—44, 47.*

The colorful, fun-loving Trout led the AL in wins in 1943 for Detroit, but his best season was 1944, when he won 27 and led the league in ERA (2.12).

Dizzy Trout

He also topped the AL in shutouts (7) and hit five of his 20 career home runs while batting .271. That season, he and lefty Hal Newhouser, who won 29, came closer to teammates winning 30 each than any pair since 1904.

In 1945 Trout was the Tigers' workhorse in the pennant drive, pitching six games and winning four over a nine-game late-season stretch. In Game Four of the 1945 WS, Trout beat the Cubs 4–1 on a five-hitter. He remained a Tiger mainstay into the 1950s. Five years after Dizzy "retired," he signed with the Orioles and pitched twice after an impressive showing in an Old-Timers Game. Dizzy is the father of pitcher Steve Trout. /(RTM)

Steve Trout (Rainbow) — 1957– . LHP 1978– White Sox, **Cubs**, Yankees, Mariners 1502 ip, 88–92, 4.18. *1 LCS, 9 ip, 1–0, 2.00*

Trout was dubbed Rainbow by his high school teammates. Recommended to the White Sox by his father, former pitching great Dizzy Trout, Steve was made Chicago's first pick in the 1976 June draft. Joining their rotation late in 1978, the erratic, 6'4″ lefthander was soon considered the team flake. He was 37–40 with the White Sox when the Cubs, desperate for lefthanded pitching, acquired him in January 1983. He went 13–7 in 1984 and won his LCS start against San Diego. After he garnered a large salary, the sinkerballer began experiencing elbow problems in 1985. When he showed signs he was back in 1987, he was dealt to the Yankees, but he was miserably wild and was sent packing to Seattle. /(RL)

Bob Trowbridge — 1930–1980. RHP 1956–60 **Braves**, A's 330 ip, 13–13, 3.95. *1 WS, 1 ip, 0–0, 45.00*

Known as one of the top bowlers in the ML during his time, Trowbridge had only modest success as a pitcher. Splitting his time between occasional starts and long relief, he was 7–5 during the Braves' championship 1957 season. The Yankees slugged him for five runs in his only WS inning. /(RTM)

Virgil Trucks (Fire) — 1919– . RHP 1941–43, 45–58 **Tigers**, Browns, White Sox, A's, Yankees 2682 ip, 177–135, 3.39. 20 wins: 53 *1 WS, 13 ip, 1–0, 3.38*
☛ *Led League—k 49. All-Star—49, 54.*

While with the Tigers in 1952, this burly Southerner tossed a pair of no-hitters against the Senators and the Yankees, joining such luminaries as Johnny Vander Meer, Allie Reynolds, and Nolan Ryan as the only pitchers to accomplish this feat in a single season. Trucks also had four no-hitters in the minors and a near-miss with the White Sox in 1954. The control pitcher returned from military service in 1945 and appeared in the World Series against the Cubs, winning 4–1. He had appeared in only one game during the regular season. After a decade in Detroit, Trucks arrived in Chicago via St. Louis in 1954. Frank Lane sent Lou Kretlow and $95,000 to Bill Veeck for Trucks and Bob Elliot. Trucks recorded eight straight victories en route to his first and only twenty-victory season. Fading after 1955, he returned to the Tigers in 1956. He wound up his career with the Yankees as a spot starter and relief man in their pennant year of 1958. /(RL)

Mike Trujillo — 1960– . RHP 1985– Red Sox, **Mariners**, Tigers 235 ip, 12–12, 5.02

Trujillo made it to the majors as a middle reliever and spot starter for Boston in 1985. Late in 1986, Trujillo went to Seattle in a waiver deal connected to the trade that sent Dave Henderson and Spike Owen to the Red Sox for Rey Quinones. On September 20, 1986, in his second start as a Mariner, Trujillo threw a one-hitter (the second in franchise history) against the Royals. Trujillo started the 1987 season in the Mariners' rotation but was bounced to the bullpen and then to Calgary (Pacific Coast League). Recalled in 1987, he was plagued by home runs, allowing 12 in 66 innings. /(TF)

John Tsitouris — 1936– . RHP 1957–60, 62–68 Tigers, A's, **Reds** 663 ip, 34–38, 4.13

Although Tsitouris pitched in 11 different ML seasons, he was a regular starter only in 1963–65 with the Reds. In 1963 he used an excellent curveball (and an occasional spitball, some said) to go 12–8, which included three shutouts. /(RTM)

Thurman Tucker (Joe E.) — 1917– . OF 1942–44, 46–51 **White Sox**, Indians 701 g, .255, 9 hr, 179 rbi. *1 WS, 3 g, .333*
☛ *All-Star—44.*

The Chicago press corps concluded that Tucker, a bespectacled White Sox outfielder, was a dead ringer for comedian Joe E. Brown. Fans began calling him Joe E. Tucker. He led the league in hitting for the first part of 1944, with his average hovering near .400 through June. He was the AL's leadoff hitter in the All-Star Game but shortly after, mired in a 0-for-32 slump, was benched. He finished at .287. One of the league's fastest runners, he raced basestealing champ George Case in a wartime Comiskey Park promotion, losing a 75-yard dash by three paces. He was traded to the Indians in time to play part-time for the 1948 World Champions. /(RL)

Tommy Tucker (Foghorn, Noisy Tom) — 1863–1935. 1B 1887–99 Baltimore (AA), **Braves**, Washington (NL), Dodgers, Cardinals, Cleveland (NL) 1687 g, .290, 42 hr, 848 rbi
☛ *Led League—ba 89.*

A flashy first baseman who would make one-handed scoops with his small glove in an era when using two hands was normal, Tucker led the American Association in batting with .372 for Baltimore in his third season. Nicknamed for his loudmouthed style as a base coach, he was once assaulted by Philadelphia fans after leading Boston's stalling tactics in hope of a rainout. He tied the ML record with four doubles in a game on July 22, 1893 and went 6-for-6 on July 15, 1897. /(JK)

John Tudor — 1954– . LHP 1979– **Red Sox**, Pirates, Cardinals, Dodgers 1651 ip, 105–68, 3.18. 20 wins: 85 *3 LCS, 33 ip, 2–2, 3.00. 3 WS, 30 ip, 3–2, 3.86*

Tudor reached the heights and the depths in his greatest season, 1985. He started the year 1–7 after coming from the Pirates with Brian Harper in return for George Hendrick and a minor leaguer. Completely turning his season around, he won 20 of his last 21 decisions, which compensated for Joaquin Andujar's poor pitching in the stretch as the Cardinals won the title. Tudor finished 21–8 with a 1.93 ERA and led the NL with ten shutouts. Possessing pinpoint control, he finished second to Dwight Gooden in Cy Young voting and in ERA, wins (tied for second), complete games (tied for second), and innings pitched. He lost Game One of the LCS 4–1 but came back to win Game Four 12–2. In the World Series, he pitched masterfully at first, winning Game One 3–1 and throwing a five-hit shutout to win Game Four 3–0. But he was knocked out in the third inning of Game Seven, allowing the Twins five runs. He punched a fan (the rotating kind) in the clubhouse, severely cutting his hand, and was even surlier than usual to members of the press.

Tudor honed his talents as a lefthander in the shadow of Fenway Park's Green Monster. After a 1–2 record in his first call-up, he went 8–5 with a 3.03 ERA in 1980 and didn't have a losing record in the 1980s. After two straight 13-win seasons, he went to the Pirates in return for Mike Easler for the 1984 season and went 12–11 for the first team ever to lead the league in ERA but finish last in the standings.

After his fine 1985 season he was plagued by injuries. He continued his fine performance in 1986 (13–7, 2.92) but missed the last three weeks of the

John Tudor

season and had his fewest complete games (3) since 1981. He missed over three months in 1987 after Mets catcher Barry Lyons fell into the St. Louis dugout and broke Tudor's leg; Tudor finished 10–2 but had a 3.84 ERA. He lost Game Two 5–0 to the Giants and tied a NLCS record by allowing 10 hits. Combining with Todd Worrell and Ken Dayley, he won Game Six 1–0. Tudor then won Game Three of the World Series 3–1, but was knocked out in the fifth inning of Game Six, allowing four hits and four runs without retiring a batter. He started 1988 on the DL and was traded to the Dodgers in mid-August for Pedro Guerrero. The Mets hit him hard in his no-decision in Game Four of the LCS, and he had to take himself out of Game Three of the World Series in the second inning with an elbow injury. The same injury limited him to just 8.1 innings in three games in 1989 and left his future in jeopardy./(SFS)

Joe Tumelty — 1905– . *Writer.*

Tumelty began in 1923 with the Philadelphia *Public Ledger* and later wrote for the *Sun* and *Inquirer.* He was one of the first to do a daily sports show on radio, featuring interviews with stars of baseball and other sports, beginning in 1929 on station WFI./(NLM)

Lee Tunnell — 1960– . RHP 1982–85, 87, 89- **Pirates**, Cardinals, Twins 483 ip, 22–28, 4.23. *1 WS, 4 ip, 0–0, 2.08*

Tunnell had an outstanding rookie season (1983) in Pittsburgh (11–6, 3.65). He relied on brains and a

variety of pitches. He was exiled to the bullpen in 1984./(ME)

George Turbeville — 1914–1983. RHP 1935–37 **A's** 185 ip, 2–12, 6.14

Turbeville came from Turbeville, SC, a town established by his ancestors. Though ambidextrous, he pitched righthanded. His failure was linked to his wildness—he walked 157 batters and struck out only 47. In his second ML start, he shut out Cleveland for 14–2/3 innings (walking 13) before being tagged for a two-run homer by Earl Averill./(NLM)

Bob Turley (Bullet Bob) — 1930– . RHP 1951, 53–63 Browns/Orioles, **Yankees**, Angels, Red Sox 1713 ip, 101–85, 3.64. *5 WS, 53 ip, 4–3, 3.19*
☛ *Led League—w 58. Led League—k 54. Cy Young Award—58.*

Turley used a no-windup delivery, turning to the simplified motion to improve his control. He led the AL in bases on balls in 1954, 1955, and 1958. Bullet Bob threw in the 93-mph range and was the league's strikeout king with the 1954 Orioles, fanning 10 or more 17 times. He went to the Yankees as part of an 18-player deal that winter and compiled a 17–13 record in 1955.

Turley pitched in five Yankee World Series. In 1956 he shut out the Dodgers through nine innings of Game Six, only to lose 1–0 when Jackie Robinson singled in the winning run in the tenth inning on a fly misjudged by Enos Slaughter. In 1958 Turley won the Cy Young Award, leading the AL with a 21 wins, a .750 winning percentage, and 19 complete games. Though he was pounded by Milwaukee in the first inning of WS Game Two, he shut them out in Game Five and won the Series finale with six-plus relief innings in Game Seven.

Turley lost his fastball in 1959 and turned to a curveball. Bone chips were found in his elbow, requiring surgery. He never again won more than nine games. A master at picking up opposing hurlers' pitches, he helped his Yankee teammates, particularly Mickey Mantle, by whistling to let them know what was coming./(GDW)

Jerry Turner [John Webber] — 1954– . OF-DH 1974–83 **Padres**, White Sox, Tigers 733 g, .257, 45 hr, 238 rbi

Turner had an extraordinary season as a pinch hitter in 1978, leading the NL with 20 pinch hits; coming in 49 pinch at-bats, good for a .408 average. His overall .280 average earned him the Padres' right-field job for 1979, his only season as a regular. He hit .248 with nine HR and career highs of 61 RBI and 55 runs in 448 at-bats but fielded a startlingly poor .958. /(WOR)

Jim Turner (Milkman Jim) — 1903– . RHP 1937–45 **Braves**, Reds, Yankees 1132 ip, 69–60, 3.22. 20 wins: 37
2 WS, 7 ip, 0–1, 6.43
☛ *Led League—era 37.*

In 1937, 33-year-old rookie Jim Turner and 30-year-old rookie Lou Fette each won 20 games for the fifth-place Boston Bees (Braves). Turner's 2.38 ERA and 24 complete games led the NL. At one point he threw 31 consecutive scoreless innings; he and Fette tied for the league lead with five shutouts. Relying on control and a low curveball, he remained in Boston's rotation through 1939, then went 14–7 for the 1940 World Champion Reds. He relieved for the Yankees until he was forty-two, saving a league-high ten games in his final season, 1945. "He knows all there is to know about pitching," said skipper Joe McCarthy. After managing in the minors for three years, he served as a pitching coach for the Yankees (1949–59, 1966–73) and Reds (1961–65). He was credited with developing Vic Raschi into a winner and convincing Ed Lopat that his inability to win in the spring was 100% mental. In all, he spent over a half century in a pro baseball uniform. Milkman Jim worked for his family's dairy in the winters. /(NLM)

Ted Turner (Captain Outrageous, The Mouth of the South) — 1938– . *Executive.*
Manager 1977 **Braves** 0–1, .000

Ted Turner's career in baseball, marked with controversy but little on-field success, began with his 1976 purchase of the Braves, which kept the team in Atlanta. His creation of the first superstation, TBS, distributed Braves games to cable systems nationwide and propelled the Braves to a self-proclaimed position as America's Team.

Turner attended (but did not graduate from) Brown University. While still in his twenties, he became an advertising and communications mogul in Georgia. He also purchased the NBA Atlanta Hawks and was a four-time Yachtsman of the Year. In 1977 he skippered *Courageous* to the America's Cup.

Turner's aggressive pursuit of Gary Matthews following the 1976 season led to his one-year suspension from baseball for tampering. A risk taker and showman, he put on a uniform in 1977 (during a short period when his suspension was lifted while it was appealed) and managed the Braves for one game, the last contest in a 17-game losing streak. Coach Vern Benson made the strategic moves that

night. Turner was then ordered out of the dugout by NL president Chub Feeney. Turner has been a free spender with free agents, but his major purchases, Andy Messersmith and Bruce Sutter, had arm problems and proved to be busts. /(PB)

Terry Turner (Cotton) — 1881–1960. SS-3B-2B 1901, 04–19 Pirates, **Indians**, A's 1685 g, .253, 8 hr, 528 rbi

Turner played in a Cleveland-record 1,617 games in 15 seasons, splitting most of his time between shortstop and third base. Generally a subpar hitter, he nevertheless hit .308 in 1912 and three times broke up no-hitters. Because normal slides hurt his ankles, he pioneered the use of the headfirst slide. /(ME)

Tuck Turner [George A.] — 1873–1945. OF 1893–98 **Phillies**, Cardinals 377 g, .320, 7 hr, 213 rbi

Utility outfielder Turner played in just over 60% of the Phillies' games in 1894 but drove in 82 runs and scored 91. His .416 batting average that year, though second behind Hugh Duffy's ML-record .438, ranks tenth all-time. /(FIC)

Bill Tuttle — 1929– . OF-3B 1952, 1954–63 **Tigers**, A's, Twins 1270 g, .259, 67 hr, 443 rbi

Signed by Detroit out of Bradley University, where he also played football, Tuttle excelled on defense, twice leading AL outfielders in putouts and in assists. His best offensive year was 1959, when he hit

Terry Turner

.300 for Kansas City. On May 28 of that year, he had four hits, including a home run, against Cleveland. He wore number 13 throughout his career. /(RTM)

Wayne Twitchell — 1948– . RHP 1970–79 Brewers, **Phillies**, Expos, Mets, Mariners 1063 ip, 48–65, 3.98 ☛ *All-Star—73.*

Twitchell's best season by far came in 1973, when he went 13–9 for the last-place Phillies; his 2.50 ERA was the second best in the NL, and he was third in fewest hits per nine innings (6.93) and tied for third in shutouts (5). He pitched a scoreless inning in the All-Star Game. Except for 1976, when he went 3–1, 1.75, mostly in relief, 1973 was his only winning season and his only ERA below 4.00. He suffered a knee injury playing basketball in November 1973 and was out until the end of May 1974. /(SFS)

Wells Twombly — 1936–1977. *Writer.*

Twombly was on his way to becoming the most honored sportswriter in America when he died at forty-one. A 1957 graduate of the University of Connecticut, he had worked for the Willimantic (Connecticut) *Chronicle*, Houston *Chronicle*, Detroit *Free Press*, and a couple of Southern California newspapers before he settled at the San Francisco *Examiner*, where he turned out six columns a week. Anthologies of *Best Sports Stories* include works by Twombly from 16 of his 20 active years. In 1974 *Esquire* named him one of the six best sportswriters for his rich, flamboyant prose. He treasured a fan letter he received from author James Michener. The last of his four books, *200 Years of Sport in America*, was published in 1977. /(NLM)

Lefty Tyler [George Albert] — 1889–1953. LHP 1910–21 **Braves**, Cubs 2230 ip, 127–119, 2.95. *2 WS, 33 ip, 1–1, 1.91*

Tyler was a solid starter for the Braves, but when they finished in last in 1912, he went 12–22 and led the NL in losses. As the Braves improved under manager George Stallings, so did Tyler; he went 16–17 in 1913 but finished first in the NL in complete games (28) and had a 2.79 ERA. He was the number-three starter on the 1914 "Miracle Braves" and was 16–14 with a 2.69 ERA and two saves. His best year for the Braves was 1916, when his six shutouts tied him for second in the league and he was 17–10.

Tyler's finest season came with the 1918 NL champion Cubs. He was 19–9 and tied for first in shutouts (8), second in wins, and fourth in winning percentage; his 2.00 ERA was second in the league, and he finished fourth in complete games and strikeouts. He was almost the hero of the World Series against Detroit. He won Game Two 3–1 on a six-hitter, and had a two-run single. He took a tough no-decision in Game Four, giving up two runs on three hits in seven innings. And in the deciding Game Six, he lost 2–1 on two unearned runs. For the Series, his .200 average (1-for-5) ranked sixth on the club.

Tyler won a 2–1, 21-inning game from the Phillies on July 17, 1918, scattering 13 hits and just one walk while going the distance, tied for fourth all-time in the NL for innings pitched in one game. He had ten complete- game 1–0 victories in his career.

A sore arm sidelined him in 1919, but the extraction of several teeth enabled him to last another full season. He also umpired in the minors for 12 years. A good enough hitter that he played 11 games at first base in 1917 and was sometimes used as a pinch hitter (9-for-39 lifetime in that role), he hit just .217 for his career but batted above .260 twice and had three HR in 1916. His brother, Fred Tyler, caught six games for the Braves in 1914. /(NLM)

Edwin L. Tyson (Ty) — 1888–1968. *Broadcaster.*

Tyson began his radio career in 1922 and broadcast the first play-by-play account of a Tigers game from Navin Field in 1927. He had no booth, so he sat with the fans, with a plank across the arms of his seat to hold the microphone. Tyson's first WS broadcast was in 1936. He covered the Tigers until 1940, missing only one game, the 1933 opener. His style was deliberate and sure, with dry humor. He was replaced by former Tigers star Harry Heilmann, because the sponsor preferred a more famous name. In 1966 Tigers voice Ernie Harwell invited Tyson to work one more game, against the Yankees. /(NLM)

Mike Tyson (Rocky) — 1950– . 2B-SS 1972–81 **Cardinals**, Cubs 1017 g, .241, 27 hr, 269 rbi

The fiercely competitive Tyson made it to the majors on his glove work. He was selected Cardinal Rookie of the Year in 1973, playing 128 games at shortstop. He moved to second base in 1976 to make room for Don Kessinger and was hitting .305 in July when he broke his finger making a tag and then refractured it while getting dressed. On May 8, 1977 against Houston, he started a triple play. Tyson lost the second base job to Ken Oberkfell in 1979 and was traded to the Cubs. /(FJO)

Peter Ueberroth — 1937– . *Executive.*

Ueberroth was Commissioner of Baseball from after the 1984 season until before the 1989 season. The millionaire California travel agent became a public figure for his leadership organizing the 1984 Olympics, which turned a $215-million-dollar profit by exploiting corporate sponsorships and media contracts. As Commissioner of Baseball, he successfully increased owners' revenues through his television contract negotiations and marketing schemes that encouraged big-dollar promotional support from large corporations. The blot on Ueberroth's tenure was the owners' proven collusion against free agency by players. This highly visible restraint of trade left the owners with substantial contingent liabilities which survived Ueberroth's departure. Until final damages are awarded, the profit picture for his reign is incomplete.

Commissioner Ueberroth came down heavily on players who used cocaine, largely on the grounds that they were being poor role models. Several big names, including Dwight Gooden and Lonnie Smith, served drug-related suspensions while Ueberroth was in office. In 1989, Ueberroth turned over the Commissioner's reins to former NL president A. Bartlett Giamatti. /(TF/MS)

Bob Uecker — 1935– . C 1962–67 **Braves**, Cardinals, Phillies 297 g, .200, 14 hr, 74 rbi

Baseball's resident jokester batted over .300 three times in the minors but swung a weak stick in the majors. He survived on good defensive ability and a rifle arm. Playing for Louisville in 1961 in the American Association, he led all catchers in fielding.

Some memorable moments in the big leagues included September 1, 1964 when his ninth-inning homer for the Cardinals beat the Braves 5–4 and kept St. Louis in the pennant race. Playing for the Braves on June 21, 1967, he collected five RBI, including a grand slam, as the Braves beat the Giants 9–2. But when asked to list his greatest achievements as a player, the funnyman answered, "Getting out of a rundown, and driving home the winning run by walking with the bases loaded."

Besides his frequent beer commercial appearances and his role on the TV sitcom *Mr. Belvedere,* Uecker has been a long-time Brewers broadcaster and played himself in that role in the movie *Major League* (1989). /(RTM)

Ted Uhlaender — 1940– . OF 1965–72 **Twins**, Indians, Reds 898 g, .263, 36 hr, 285 rbi. *2 LCS, 4 g, .250. 1 WS, 4 g, .250*

Speed and defense kept Ted Uhlaender in Minnesota's starting lineup as centerfielder from 1966 to 1969. The lefthanded batter led the Pacific Coast League in hitting (.340) in 1965. He led all major league outfielders with a .996 fielding average in 1967, one of his five big league seasons with fewer than three errors. His batting improved, although he was overshadowed by Harmon Killebrew, Tony Oliva, and other hitting stars on the Twins. Traded on December 12, 1969, Uhlaender had two solid seasons in Cleveland. He led the Indians in batting in 1971 (.288), despite announcing his retirement for a time during the season. Traded to the Reds for Milt Wilcox, Uhlaender hit poorly in limited play. /(ME)

George Uhle (The Bull) — 1898–1985. RHP 1919–34, 36 **Indians**, Tigers, Giants, Yankees 3120 ip, 200–166, 3.99; 723 g, .288, 9 hr, 187 rbi. 20 wins: 22–23, 26 *1 WS, 3 ip, 0–0, 0.00*
☛ *Led League—w 23, 26.*

Three times Uhle led the American League in games started, twice in complete games including a 20-inning shut out in 1919, and twice in innings pitched, earning him the approving nickname The Bull. He led the league in victories twice, the second time in 1926, when he also had the best winning percentage. He paid the penalty, a sore arm, the next year and was less effective after that time.

Uhle was an innovator with the slider and named it when describing the motion of the pitch. A lifetime Cleveland resident, he holds the record for most base hits made in a season by a pitcher, 52 in 1923. He batted .361 that year and had a lifetime average of .288 in 723 games. His goal was to win 200 games, but he lacked two victories when the

George Uhle

Tigers cut him loose at the end of 1933. Despite an aching arm, when the Yankees signed him, he managed two more victories. /(JK)

Jerry Ujdur — 1957– . RHP 1980–84 **Tigers**, Indians 261 ip, 12–16, 4.79

Ujdur's only decent season came with the Tigers in 1982, when the starter was 10–10 with a 3.69 ERA (his only ERA below 6.43). /(WOR)

Dutch Ulrich [Frank W.] — 1899–1929. RHP 1925–27 **Phillies** 406 ip, 19–27, 3.48

Ulrich went 8–13 and 8–11 for last-place Phillies teams (1926–27); he had a 3.17 ERA in 1927, tied for sixth in the NL. Illness in 1928 ended his career. /(JFC)

Jim Umbarger — 1953– . LHP 1975–78 **Rangers**, A's 483 ip, 25–33, 4.14

Umbarger's only winning season came for the Rangers in his rookie 1975 season, when he was 8–7 with a 4.12 ERA, starting and relieving. In the rotation the next year, he improved his ERA to 3.15 but was 10–12. Traded to the A's with Rodney Scott and cash in 1977, he was bought back by the Rangers before the end of the season. /(WOR)

Frank Umont — 1918– . *Umpire 1954–73 AL 4 ASU 1 LCS 4 WS*

Although he never played college football, the 220-pound Umont was a tackle with the NFL's New York Giants from 1943 to 1945. He ejected Baltimore's Earl Weaver before a 1969 game for smoking in the dugout. The next day, Weaver came out carrying his lineup card with a white cylinder dangling from his lips. As he handed the card to Umont, Earl casually ate the candy cigarette. Late in his career, Umont had the courage to wear glasses on the field even though it made him a target for bench jockeys. /(RTM)

Tommy Umphlett — 1930– . OF 1953–55 Red Sox, **Senators** 361 g, .246, 6 hr, 111 rbi

Umphlett replaced Dom DiMaggio in centerfield and responded with a career-high .283 his rookie year. Following the season he was traded to Washington in a deal that sent Jackie Jensen to Boston. /(RTM)

Pat Underwood — 1957– . LHP 1979–80, 82–83 **Tigers** 344 ip, 13–18, 4.42

Underwood's first major league start came against older brother Tom, then with Toronto. Pat won 1–0 with eight-and-a-third innings pitched. He reeled off five straight wins at the start of his ML career and finished the year 6–4. It was his only winning season. His wide assortment of pitches had led Detroit to make him the number-two pick in the nation in the June 1976 draft. His father, John Underwood, was a minor league pitcher. /(SH)

Tom Underwood — 1953- . LHP 1974-84 **Phillies,** Cardinals, Blue Jays, Yankees, A's, Orioles 1586 ip, 86-87, 3.89. *3 LCS, 5 ip, 0-0, 3.86*

Plagued by terrible inconsistency, Underwood never fulfilled the promise of his first season. The hard thrower was the lefthander on the Topps All-Rookie Team in 1975 after a career-high 14 wins. Extremely effective at Veterans Stadium (23-5) and against St. Louis (5-0), Tom was switched from starting to relief in 1977, then was traded to the Cards where he moved back to starting. He and Victor Cruz went to Toronto for Pete Vuckovich on December 6, 1977. Underwood led the Blue Jays in strikeouts in 1978 and 1979 and was the club's top pitcher the latter season. At age twenty-six, he seemed ready to blossom during a fine season with the Yankees (13-9, 3.66). A poor start in 1981 brought a trade to Oakland. Used mostly in relief, he led the A's in games pitched in 1982 and 1983. In 1979, Tom started, and lost, a game to his brother Pat of the Tigers. /(ME)

Bob Unglaub — 1881-1916. 1B-3B-2B 1904-05, 07-10 Yankees, Red Sox, **Senators** 595 g, .258, 5 hr, 216 rbi.
    Manager 1907 **Red Sox** 8-20, .286

When Unglaub was traded from the Yankees to the Red Sox for Patsy Dougherty during the 1904 season, the one-sided swap was perceived by many as part of an AL plot to create stiffer competition for the NL Giants in New York. Unglaub finally became a regular in the year he was the playing manager of the Red Sox for 29 games and hit .254 with career highs of 13 triples, 62 RBI, and 49 RBI. /(SFS)

Union Association — 1884. League.

The outlaw Union Association was formed in September 1883, hoping to capitalize on player dissatisfaction with organized baseball's reserve rule, which effectively limited a player's pay by binding him to his club. But the UA lured few top players away from the National League and American Association—and attracted too few fans to their games to succeed financially. The St. Louis club, owned by UA president Henry V. Lucas, ran away with the pennant in 1884. But that winter Lucas precipitated the association's demise by transferring his club to the National League. Reduced to only two clubs by January 1885, the UA disbanded. /(FIC)

Del Unser — 1944- . OF-1B 1968-82 **Senators,** Indians, Phillies, Mets, Expos 1799 g, .258, 87 hr, 481 rbi. *1 LCS, 5 g, .400, 1 rbi. 1 WS, 3 g, .500, 2 rbi*

Unser was *TSN*'s AL Rookie of the Year in 1968, despite hitting just .230 with 66 runs and 30 RBI as Washington's everyday centerfielder, because he established himself as second only to Paul Blair defensively. He led AL outfielders in assists, double plays, and total chances per game and finished just two back in putouts. In 1969 he improved his average to .286 and led the league with eight triples (setting a ML record for fewest to lead the league). Traded to the Indians for 1972 and then to the Phillies for 1973, he improved his hitting in the NL, showing a bit more power; he had his best season in 1974, batting .264 with career highs of 61 RBI and 72 runs in 454 at-bats. After that season he was traded to the Mets with Mac Scarce and John Stearns for Tug McGraw and two utility outfielders, and he reached a new personal best by batting .294. He slumped the next season and was never again an everyday player.

He began pinch hitting in 1977 with the Expos, and although he was not successful at first (7-for-58 in 1977-78), he improved on returning to the Phillies in 1979, batting .304 in the pinch and tying a ML record with homers in three straight pinch at-bats (June 30, July 5, 10). He pinch hit .316 in the Phillies' 1980 World Championship season. In the decisive Game Five of the LCS, he went 2-for-2 after coming in as a pinch hitter and then staying in the game, and he drove in a run and scored two, including the game winner in the tenth inning as the Phillies beat the Astros 8-7 to take the series. In Game Two of the World Series, he hit a pinch double off Royals relief ace Dan Quisenberry in the Phillies' eighth-inning come-from-behind rally. In Game Five, another pinch double off Quisenberry in the ninth inning tied the game; Unser moved to third on a sacrifice fly and scored the game winner on an infield single.

Del's father Al caught for the Tigers and Reds during WWII. /(SFS)

Cecil Upshaw — 1942- . RHP 1966-69, 71-75 **Braves,** Astros, Indians, Yankees, White Sox 563 ip, 34-36, 3.13. *1 LCS, 6 ip, 0-0, 2.84*

This 6'6" 205-lb reliever used a difficult sidearm delivery to help Atlanta to the 1969 division title with 27 saves. He appeared in every game of the LCS. Upshaw's career was sidetracked the following spring when he nearly severed a finger on his pitching hand while showing teammates how to dunk a basketball. He missed the entire season and never became the bullpen stopper he had been prior to his accident. /(PB)

Willie Upshaw — 1957– . 1B-OF 1978, 80–88 **Blue Jays**, Indians 1264 g, .262, 123 hr, 528 rbi. *1 LCS, 7 g, .231, 1 rbi*

Upshaw was drafted by the Blue Jays from the Yankee organization in 1977. After a couple of seasons in the minors and as a part-time first baseman and outfielder, Upshaw took over as the regular Blue Jay first baseman from John Mayberry, who had been the franchise's premier power hitter. In 1982 (his first season as regular first baseman), Upshaw set a team record for extra-base hits. He broke the record the following year, hitting .306 with 27 HR, 99 runs scored, and a team-record 104 RBI. He had at least one RBI in a team-record eight straight games in September 1983.

Although he remained a good defensive first baseman, Upshaw's offensive production declined over the next several seasons. The Blue Jays were deterred from getting rid of him by his penchant for hitting well in spring training and the early season, and because Upshaw was highly respected and popular. But the emergence of Fred McGriff led to Upshaw's 1988 trade to the Indians, where he was disappointing as their full-time first baseman. After the season, he went to Japan to finish his career. Upshaw's cousins Gene and Marvin played in the National Football League, with Gene becoming the director of the NFL Players' Association. /(TF)

Tom Upton (Muscles) — 1926– . SS 1950–52 **Browns**, Senators 181 g, .225, 2 hr, 42 rbi

In 1950 Upton enjoyed the best season of his short career, batting .237 with two homers as the Browns' regular shortstop. Having done graduate work at USC, Upton was called the Bard of the Senators for his ability to quote Elizabethan writers. /(WAB)

Jack Urban — 1928– . RHP 1957–59 **A's**, Cardinals 272 ip, 15–15, 4.83

Urban fell victim to the sophomore jinx after a fine freshman campaign with the Athletics, when he went 7–4 with a 3.35 ERA. In 1954 he pitched a no-hitter for Birmingham in the Southern League. /(RTM)

Bill Urbanski — 1903–1973. SS-3B 1931–37 **Braves** 763 g, .260, 19 hr, 207 rbi

Urbanski was a sure-handed but unspectacular shortstop who held his own for five seasons in the Braves' infield at a time when the team was mired in the second division. He batted over .300 for four seasons in the International League. /(JK)

Jose Uribe [aka Jose Gonzalez] — 1952– . SS 1984–Cardinals, **Giants** 699 g, .241, 15 hr, 167 rbi. *2 LCS, 12 g, .256, 3 rbi. 1 WS, 3 g, .200*

The slick-fielding Dominican shortstop was stuck behind Ozzie Smith in the Cardinal system when he decided to change his name, saying that there were too many other Gonzalezes. Traded to the Giants for 1985 in the Jack Clark deal, he immediately became their regular shortstop. He hit a career-high .291 in 1987 after spending the winter practicing hitting by having his brother pitch peanuts to him. However, a nagging hamstring problem put him on the DL three times before the All-Star break. /(SFS)

John Urrea (Chief) — 1955– . RHP 1977–81 **Cardinals**, Padres 364 ip, 17–18, 3.73

In 1977, Urrea jumped from Double-A to the Cardinals as a reliever and won his first five starts when moved into the rotation. He split each of the three following seasons between St. Louis and Springfield (American Association). /(FJO)

Bob Usher — 1925– . OF 1946–47, 50–52, 57 **Reds**, Cubs, Indians, Senators 428 g, .235, 18 hr, 102 rbi

A star on San Diego's 1941 American Legion National Championship team, Bob went pro in 1942. His best season in the majors came in 1950, when he hit .259 for the Reds. /(RTM)

Mike Vail — 1951- . OF 1975–84 Mets, Indians, **Cubs**, Reds, Giants, Expos, Dodgers 665 g, .279, 34 hr, 219 rbi

The International League Player of the Year in 1975, Vail was called up by the Mets that August and hit in 23 straight games to tie what was then both a club record and a modern NL rookie record. He dislocated his foot playing basketball the following February, missed half of the season, and was sold to Cleveland in 1978. He was an effective pinch hitter and fourth outfielder for the 1978–80 Cubs. /(JCA)

Sandy Valdespino [Hilario Borroto] — 1939- . OF 1965–71 **Twins**, Braves, Astros, Pilots/Brewers, Royals 382 g, .230, 7 hr, 67 rbi. *1 WS, 5 g, .273*

Valdespino saw the most action in his rookie year, the Twins' pennant season of 1965, batting .261 with career highs of 38 runs, 22 RBI, and 245 at-bats. He doubled and scored a run in Minnesota's six-run rally in Game One of the World Series as the Twins sent Don Drysdale to the showers in the third inning. /(JFC)

Jose Valdivielso — 1934- . SS 1955–56, 59–61 **Senators/Twins** 401 g, .219, 9 hr, 85 rbi

This fancy-fielding Cuban shortstop had great range but was a light hitter who, despite playing as many as 115 games a season, never got more than 294 at-bats. His father was a Boston University football player in the 1930s. /(RTM)

Bobby Valentine — 1950- . SS-OF-2B-3B 1969, 71–79 **Dodgers**, Angels, Padres, Mets, Mariners 639 g, .260, 12 hr, 157 rbi.
   Manager 1985– **Rangers** 368–408, .474

Bobby Valentine's reckless abandon led to serious injuries that dimmed his playing career. A versatile performer, the fifth player chosen in the June 1968 draft was Pacific Coast League Player of the Year in 1970, leading the league in batting (.340), total bases, and many other categories. After two seasons as a jack-of-all-trades with the Dodgers, he, Billy Grabarkewitz, Frank Robinson, Bill Singer, and Mike Strahler were traded to the Angels for Andy Messersmith and Ken McMullen on November 28, 1972. Playing centerfield on May 17, 1973, Valentine suffered a broken right leg after crashing into the wall at Anaheim Stadium chasing a Dick Green homer. Leaping for the ball, he caught his spikes in the wall as he descended and suffered a serious spiral fracture. The accident left his leg misshapen and ruined his big league career. He later served as a coach with the Mets and became manager of the Rangers May 16, 1985. Valentine, who wore number 13, turned down hundreds of football scholarship to play baseball. /(ME)

Corky Valentine [Harold Lewis] — 1929- . RHP 1954–55 **Reds** 221 ip, 14–12, 4.81

A wild fastball pitcher, Valentine was a bulldog on the mound. As a rookie in 1954, he tied for the Reds' club lead with 12 wins. /(RTM)

Ellis Valentine — 1954- . OF 1975–83, 85 **Expos**, Mets, Angels, Rangers 894 g, .278, 123 hr, 474 rbi
☛ *All-Star—77. Gold Glove—78.*

Valentine was one of a trio of young Expos outfielders (with Andre Dawson and Warren Cromartie) for whom stardom was predicted in the late 1970s. Only Dawson met those expectations. Valentine had two straight 25-HR, 76-RBI seasons (1977–78; .293, .289) as Montreal's everyday right fielder and hit two inside-the-park homers in Olympic Stadium in 1977. In 1978 he led NL outfielders with 24 assists, winning a Gold Glove; in 1979 he had 21 HR and a career-high 82 RBI. But on May 30, 1980 he was hit in the face with a pitch by Roy Thomas of the Cardinals and was out 40 days with a fractured cheekbone. Larry Parrish had injured his wrist earlier that month, and the two injuries probably cost the Expos the pennant. Valentine could have been on his way to his best season: He finished with a .315 average, 67 RBI, and 13 HR in just 86 games.

In 1981 Valentine hit just .208 and was traded to the Mets at the end of May for Jeff Reardon and Dan Norman. He hit .280 in 1982, but his power was gone. He hit only 8 HR in 1982 and 13 for the Angels in 1983. /(WOR)

Fred Valentine (Squeaky) — 1935– . OF 1959, 63–68 Orioles, **Senators** 533 g, .247, 36 hr, 138 rbi

The switch-hitter was named Carolina League Player of the Year in 1958 when he led the league in hitting (.319). A regular in only two ML seasons, he had 16 homers for the 1966 Senators, leading the club with 29 doubles and 140 hits. /(RTM)

Vito Valentinetti — 1928– . RHP 1954, 56–59 White Sox, **Cubs**, Indians, Tigers, Senators 257 ip, 13–14, 4.73

Valentinetti recorded four of his six 1956 Cub victories against Philadelphia—all in relief. With the Senators in a 1958 game, he two-hit the Red Sox and had two of his club's three hits, but lost 2–0. /(RTM)

Fernando Valenzuela — 1960– . LHP 1980- **Dodgers** 2145 ip, 128–103, 3.19. 20 wins: 86 *3 LCS, 37 ip, 3–1, 1.93. 1 WS, 9 ip, 1–0, 4.00* ☛ *Rookie of the Year—81. Led League—w 86. Led League—k 81. Cy Young Award—81. All-Star—81–86. Gold Glove—86.*

En route to being named *TSN* Player of the Year in 1981, Valenzuela, the Mexican star long sought by the Dodgers, ushered in Fernandomania and turned Dodger Stadium into a Mexican fiesta on the nights he pitched. No one had ever broken in quite like Valenzuela. He won his first ten major league decisions and was the first rookie to win the Cy Young Award, and his eight shutouts (including five in his first seven starts) tied the rookie record in a season a third shorter than usual due to the players' strike.

The secret of this phenomenal success was "Fernando's Fadeaway," a screwball widely regarded as the best since Hubbell's. But he was not intentionally emulating Hubbell or even Christy Mathewson, the master before Hubbell. The youngest of twelve children from a Mexican farm family, Valenzuela, who spoke through an interpreter his rookie year, had never heard of either of these Hall of Famers. He learned the screwball from former Dodger Bob Castillo and had even learned to throw it at two different speeds.

As it turned out, he would evoke further comparisons to Hubbell in 1986 when he tied his record five straight strikeouts in the All-Star Game. All-Star success was not new to him—he had compiled a 0.00 ERA and 9 strikeouts in 7.2 All-Star innings, including 1981, when he became one of a select few rookie pitchers to be an All-Star starter.

Although his rookie success continued all the way to the World Series, when he won his start against

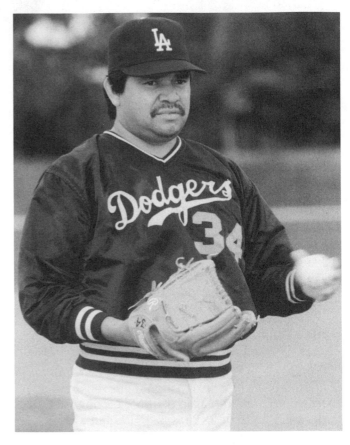

Fernando Valenzuela

Dave Righetti in a matchup of rookies, it would not always be so easy. In April 1986, he became the first to win Pitcher of the Month honors despite a losing record when he went 2–3 with a 0.21 ERA en route to setting a new major league record of 44.1 consecutive innings without an earned run at the start of a season.

His Ruthian physique was deceptive, as he was a good all-around athlete. He won a Silver Bat in 1983 and a Gold Glove in 1986, pinch hit on occasion, and even played outfield during a 21-inning game.

In 1983 Valenzuela became the first player awarded $1 million in arbitration. /(TG)

Dave Valle — 1960– . C 1984– **Mariners** 348 g, .243, 35 hr, 160 rbi

Valle had an apprenticeship of almost seven full seasons in the minors before being promoted to the Mariners. For the next couple seasons he shuttled between Seattle, the minors, and the DL before emerging as the Mariners' regular catcher. /(TF)

Elmer Valo — 1921- . OF 1940–43, 46–61 **A's**, Phillies, Dodgers, Indians, Yankees, Senators/Twins 1806 g, .282, 58 hr, 601 rbi

A native Czechoslovakian, the hustling Valo was noted for his fearless manner in challenging fences. He first played regularly for the A's in 1942 but spent 1944 and 1945 in the military, returning to bat .306 in 1946. A lefthanded line-drive hitter, he hit .300 or better five times in his 20 ML seasons, with a high of .364 playing part-time in 1955. In the latter part of his career he became an outstanding pinch hitter; in 1960, with the Yankees and Senators, he set ML pinch-hitting records for games, walks, and most times reaching first base. He also set a record with 91 career walks as a pinch hitter. After his release, he served as a major league scout and coach through 1982. /(AL)

Russ Van Atta (Sheriff) — 1906–1986. LHP 1933–39 Yankees, **Browns** 712 ip, 33–41, 5.60

In his ML debut with the Yankees on April 25, 1933, Van Atta shut out the Senators 16–0 and went 4-for-4 at the plate. But after cutting his pitching hand the next winter, he was used mostly in relief. Sold to the Browns in May 1935, he led the AL with 58 appearances and six relief wins, and with 52 appearances (despite a 6.60 ERA) the following year. /(LRD)

Chris Van Cuyk — 1927- . LHP 1950–52 **Dodgers** 160 ip, 7–11, 5.16

The 6'6" younger brother of Johnny Van Cuyk, who relieved in seven games for Brooklyn in 1947–49, Chris won five games as a starter for the Dodgers in 1952. He had a reputation for knocking down batters. /(RTM)

George Van Haltren — 1866–1945. OF-LHP-SS 1887–1903 Chicago (NL), Brooklyn (PL), Baltimore (AA), Baltimore (NL), Pirates, **Giants** 1984 g, .316, 69 hr, 1014 rbi; 689 ip, 40–31, 4.05.
    Manager 1891–92 Baltimore (AA), **Baltimore (NL)** 5–16, .238

After Van Haltren walked 16 batters in a game (tying a still-standing major league record) as a Chicago rookie in 1887, manager Cap Anson began to use the lithe, swift youngster in the outfield at times. Van Haltren threw a six-inning no-hitter against Pittsburgh on June 21, 1888, but didn't pitch at all in 1889, and hit .300 for the first of 12 seasons. He jumped to the Players' League in 1890 and went 15–10 for Brooklyn, while batting .335.

George Van Haltren

He played for and briefly managed two Baltimore clubs, and in 1894 he joined the New York Giants.

Van Haltren became a star attraction at the Polo Grounds for a team that had fallen considerably since winning championships in 1888 and 1889. He was a centerfielder and lefthanded leadoff hitter who played with the kind of elan New Yorkers appreciated. His graceful, far-ranging, strong-armed outfield play set a high standard. In 1896 he batted a career-high .351 and tied for the NL lead with 21 triples. His 45 stolen bases in 1900 tied him for the league lead; he had 583 steals lifetime. A broken ankle curtailed Van Haltren's ML career, but he played in the Pacific Coast League from 1904 to 1909. /(JK)

Charles E. Van Loan — 1876–1919. *Writer.*

Grantland Rice called Van Loan "sports' greatest fiction writer." A newspaperman from 1903 to 1910, he then wrote short stories for numerous magazines. Many were later published in four collections: *The Lucky Seventh, Inside the Ropes, Fore,* and *Score by Innings.* /(NLM)

Maurice Van Robays (Bomber) — 1914–1965. OF 1939–43, 46 **Pirates** 529 g, .267, 20 hr, 303 rbi

Because of health problems, Van Robays missed two seasons as a Tiger farmhand and lost the chance to play in his hometown, with the Detroit ballpark's friendly fences. Instead, he played for the Pirates, his power wasted in spacious Forbes Field. /(JK)

Andy Van Slyke — 1960– . OF-1B-3B 1983-
Cardinals, Pirates 962 g, .267, 96 hr, 439 rbi. *1 LCS, 5 g,
.091, 1 rbi. 1 WS, 6 g, .091*
☛ *All-Star—88. Gold Glove—88, 89.*

The popular, clean-cut Van Slyke was chosen by St.
Louis, the sixth overall selection, in the June 1979
draft. He was Cardinals Rookie of the Year in 1983,
playing first base, third base, and all three outfield
positions. The high-percentage basestealer earned a
full-time outfield spot in 1985 and was the top
power man for St. Louis in 1986, hitting .270 with
13 HR and 61 RBI. Traded to Pittsburgh in the
Tony Pena deal, Van Slyke blossomed as
centerfielder for the Pirates. He became the third 20
homer-20 steal Pirate in club history, tied for the
league lead in OF double plays, and was voted most
popular Pirate by the fans and MVP by local
media. /(ME)

Dazzy Vance [Clarence Arthur] — 1891–1961. RHP
1915, 18, 22–35 Pirates, Yankees, **Dodgers**, Cardinals,
Reds 2967 ip, 197–140, 3.24. *1 WS, 1 ip, 0–0, 0.00*
☛ *Most Valuable Player—24. Led League—w 24–25.
Led League—k 22–28. Led League—era 24, 28, 30. Hall
of Fame—55.*

The late-blooming Vance was the dominant strikeout pitcher of the 1920s, leading the National
League a record seven consecutive times (1922–28).
His nickname was fitting; a charter member of the
carousing "Daffiness Boys," he led his Dodger
teammates virtually everywhere but to a pennant.
Vance was one of the three Dodger runners to wind
up on third base at the same time when Babe
Herman "tripled" into a double play (it was actually
scored a double). Vance, starting from second base,
ran much more cautiously than the runners behind
him expected, returning to third base after rounding
the bag.

A 6'2" 200-lb fireballer, Vance burned out his
arm pitching ten years in the minors. He would
break in impressively with one club after another,
only to have his arm tire by mid-season. His great
starts earned him one game with the Pirates in 1915,
and trials with the Yankees in 1915 and 1918. He
pitched poorly each time and was returned to the
minors. An arm operation, and a manager in New
Orleans who allowed him to start on four days' rest
instead of three, proved the cure. Vance went 21–11
in the Southern League in 1921 and was bought by
the Dodgers at the insistence of scout Larry Sutton.
Owner Charlie Ebbets actually wanted Vance's New

Orleans batterymate, defensive catcher Hank De-
Berry, and had to take Vance as part of a package.

Vance, starting every fifth day, won the first of his
seven strikeout titles as a 31-year-old rookie in
1922. He often led by wide margins; in 1924, he
fanned nearly twice as many as his nearest competitor. His style was unique and fearsome. He would
rear back—the ball tiny in his huge, red-flecked
hand—kick his leg high, waggle his foot, and catapult the ball toward the intimidated hitter. After
living and dying by the fastball for a decade in the
minors, he added an outstanding curveball. In a
flamboyant touch of distracting showmanship, he
wore a red undershirt with the sleeves sliced into
twirling ribbons, making his delivery even more
disconcerting. The tatters were subsequently
outlawed.

In 1924, Vance topped the league with a 2.16
ERA and career highs of 28 wins, 262 strikeouts,
and 30 complete games. He had only six losses. The
Dodgers fell one win short of the first-place Giants,
the closest Vance ever came to a pennant in
Brooklyn. He was named NL MVP over Rogers
Hornsby, who batted .424.

Vance led the league in wins a second time in
1925, with 22. That September 13, he no-hit
Philadelphia 10–1, walking one and striking out
nine. The Dodgers committed three errors. He won
22 again in 1928 with a league-best 2.09 ERA, and
he earned a final ERA title in 1930 (2.61). After
going 12–11 at age forty-one, he was traded to the
Cardinals in 1933, where Dazzy joined Dizzy and
Daffy Dean. Though sold to the Reds in 1934,
Vance was waived back to St. Louis in time to earn
a World Series ring. He finished up with Brooklyn as
a reliever in 1935.

During his career, Vance tied for the NL lead in
shutouts four times, compiling a total of 30. He
struck out 2,045 batters and walked only 840. He
was elected to the Hall of Fame in 1955 by the
BBWAA. /(JK)

Sandy Vance [Gene Covington] (Dazzy) — 1947– .
RHP 1970–71 **Dodgers** 141 ip, 9–8, 3.83

Vance had a 7–7 (3.13) rookie 1970 season, but
because of control problems and pitcher Al Downing's comeback, the Dodgers sent him to the minors
for good in 1971. /(TG)

Ed Vande Berg — 1958– . LHP 1982–88 **Mariners**,
Dodgers, Indians, Rangers 519 ip, 25–28, 3.92

Vande Berg made an AL-leading and rookie record
78 appearances for the Mariners in 1982, going 9–4

Dazzy Vance (r.) and Babe Herman

and winning *TSN* AL Rookie Pitcher of the Year honors. Generally used only to get out a lefthanded hitter or two, he continued in relief except for an unsuccessful 17-game stint as a Seattle starter in 1984. He was traded to the Dodgers but released after one season. He signed with Cleveland in 1987 but, incredibly, did not record a decision or save until his 51st appearance, a September 23 victory. /(NLM)

Hy Vandenberg — 1907– . RHP 1935, 37–40, 44–45 Red Sox, Giants, **Cubs** 291 ip, 14–10, 4.32. *1 WS, 6 ip, 0–0, 0.00*

Vandenberg had only brief ML stays until the wartime Cubs found use for him. He started and relieved, going 6–3, during their 1945 championship year, and pitched in three World Series games. /(DAS)

Johnny Vander Meer (The Dutch Master, Double No-Hit) — 1914– . LHP 1937–43, 46–51 **Reds**, Cubs, Indians 2105 ip, 119–121, 3.44. *1 WS, 3 ip, 0–0, 0.00*
☛ *Led League—k 41–43. All-Star—38–39, 42–43.*

Vander Meer is the only pitcher in major league history to have thrown back-to-back no-hitters. The Cincinnati hurler no-hit the Boston Bees 3–0 on June 11, 1938 and followed by no-hitting the Dodgers 6–0 on June 15. The latter contest was the first night game ever played at Brooklyn's Ebbets Field. In his next start, Vander Meer did not allow a hit until Boston's Deb Garms singled in the fourth inning, ending Vander Meer's string of hitless innings at a National League record 21.

Vander Meer recalled the last out of the second no-hitter: "The Dodgers had the bases loaded with two outs. The batter was Leo Durocher, who had a count of one ball and two strikes. On the next pitch I hit the outside of the plate with a fastball for a strike and umpire Bill Stewart called it a ball. On the next pitch Durocher popped out to centerfield for the final out . . .When the game ended Stewart was the first to congratulate me. Stewart said, 'If Leo got a hit, I was to blame as I missed the pitch and the batter should have been struck out on the previous pitch.'"

Vander Meer was the *TSN* Minor League Player of the Year in 1936, when he went 19–6 at Durham and set a Piedmont League record with 295 strikeouts. He copped *TSN* Major League Player of the Year honors in 1938 on the strength of his extraordinary pitching feat. He threw hard and had a good sinker, and he led the NL in strikeouts three consecutive years (1941–43). Yet he often struggled

Johnny Vander Meer

with his control, topping NL pitchers in bases on balls in 1943 and 1948. He won in double figures six times, recording a career-high 18 victories in 1942. In 1943 he tied Carl Hubbell's record by fanning six batters in an All-Star Game, working 2–2/3 innings. Naval duty in 1944–45 and arm trouble shortened Vander Meer's career. /(RTM)

Elam Vangilder — 1896–1977. RHP 1919–29 **Browns**, Tigers 1716 ip, 99–102, 4.29

Vangilder was with the Browns from 1919 through 1927, establishing a club record for games pitched (323). He was 19–13 at his best in 1922 and led the majors with 11 relief wins in 1925. He halted two of minor league baseball's greatest hitting streaks: Joe Wilhoit's 69-game streak, while pitching for Tulsa (Western League) on August 20, 1919; and Reading's Joe Quellich's string of 15 consecutive hits, while on the mound for Montreal (International League) on August 12, 1929. /(LRD)

Ed Vargo — Unk. – . *Umpire* NL 1960–83 *4 ASU 4 LCS 4 WS*

Vargo, the only ML umpire to call no-hitters in three consecutive seasons, was behind the plate for two of Sandy Koufax's no- hitters, including his 1965 perfect game against the Cubs. Vargo was also plate umpire when Hank Aaron tied Babe Ruth's home run record at 714, and he worked the last games played at both the Polo Grounds and Forbes Field. Vargo took a Fourth of July home run away from Tim McCarver in 1976, when the Phillies catcher passed runner Garry Maddox. /(RTM)

Arky Vaughan [Joseph Floyd] — 1912–1952. SS-3B-OF 1932–43, 47–48 **Pirates**, Dodgers 1817 g, .318, 96 hr, 926 rbi. *1 WS, 3 g, .500*
☛ *Led League—ba 35. All-Star—34–42. Hall of Fame—1985.*

Vaughan was a perennial All-Star named to the National League team nine successive years. In 1941 he hit two All-Star home runs. His best years were spent in Pittsburgh, where his mentor, Honus Wagner, roomed with Vaughan while a Pirate coach. Vaughan's 1935 marks, a .385 batting average and .607 slugging average, remain team records. In addition to those league-leading numbers, his performance that year included 19 HR, 99 RBI, 108 runs, and only 18 strikeouts in 499 at-bats plus a league-high 97 walks. Unsurprisingly, he also led in on-base average (.491); from 1934 to 1936 he led in both walks and on-base average. His 1935 season earned him third place in the MVP voting, and he won *TSN* NL Player of the Year honors, at the time as prestigious as the more recently-introduced MVP award.

Vaughan led NL shortstops in errors in his first two seasons (46 each year) but exhibited good range. He settled down to become one of the league's better-fielding shortstops and led in putouts in 1936. By 1938 he may have been the best; from 1938 through 1940 he led three times in assists, twice in putouts, and once each in total chances per game, double plays, and errors.

Playing in spacious Forbes Field, Vaughan was in double figures in triples in all but one of his first nine seasons, and he led the league three times; he reached the 40-double plateau twice. He led in runs three times and topped 100 runs five times. First-place Brooklyn traded four players after the 1941 season to acquire Vaughan. After an off-year (.277, 82 runs) in 1942 while playing third base, he rebounded in 1943 to lead the NL with a career-high 20 stolen bases (at the age of thirty-one) and

Arky Vaughan

with 112 runs. He also had the best of his many excellent strikeout ratios, fanning just 13 times in 610 at-bats plus 60 walks, and hit .305.

Named for his home state of Arkansas, Arky Vaughan was a quiet, gentlemanly ballplayer whose demeanor was only twice disturbed; once by Dick Bartell and then by Leo Durocher. After Bartell had been hit in the head by a throw on a double-play attempt by Vaughan, he was quoted in the press as seeking revenge when the two teams played again. He backed down when a steely-eyed Vaughan walked up to him before the game and proposed they settle their differences under the stands.

Durocher pushed the reserved Vaughan too far. An argument between the Dodger manager and Bobo Newsome raged through the Dodger clubhouse. Finally, Vaughan presented his rolled-up uniform to his manager with a suggestion he dispose of it in an impossible manner. Vaughan stalked out and the rest of the team was ready to follow. Relations were strained the rest of the 1943 season and, in 1944, Vaughan stayed on his California ranch, refusing to give as the reason his obvious loathing for Durocher or his wish to support the war effort by farming.

He remained away from baseball until 1947, the year of Durocher's suspension. Then, after three years of idleness, he hit .325 as a part-time outfielder, third baseman, and pinch hitter (10-for-26). Vaughan drowned in 1952, just forty years old, when a boat from which he was fishing capsized. The Veterans Committee selected him for the Hall of Fame in 1985./(JK)

Irving Vaughan (Mark) — 1888–Unk. *Writer.*

After ten years with newspapers in Milwaukee and Chicago, Vaughan joined the Chicago *Tribune* in 1919 and remained on the sports desk for more than 30 years./(NLM)

Hippo Vaughn [James Leslie] — 1888–1966. LHP 1908, 10–21 Yankees, Senators, **Cubs** 2730 ip, 178–136, 2.49. 20 wins: 14–15, 17–19 *1 WS, 27 ip, 1–2, 1.00*
☛ *Led League—w 18. Led League—era 18. Led League—k 18–19.*

Named Hippo for his running gait, not his 6'2", 215-lb frame, Vaughn won 20 or more games in a season five times and once totaled 19 in a career that just missed being brilliant. A workhorse, he twice pitched the most NL innings, twice started the most games, and twice led in strikeouts. In the 1918 World Series against the Red Sox, he pitched three complete games but lost the opener when Babe Ruth beat him 1–0; two days later Carl Mays topped him 2–1; with only two days off, he finally won on a 3–0 shutout. His ERA for the Series was 1.00.

Vaughn pitched two minor league no-hitters, and on May 2, 1917 he held the Reds hitless for nine innings. However, Cincinnati's Fred Toney no-hit Vaughn's Cubs over the same span. In the tenth inning, Toney kept Chicago hitless, but in the bottom of the inning Hippo gave up a clean single to Larry Kopf; then Hal Chase's fly was dropped for an error, moving Kopf to third. When Jim Thorpe hit a slow roller, Vaughn threw to the catcher, but Kopf scored the winning run./(JK)

Hippo Vaughn

Bobby Veach — 1888–1945. OF 1912–25 **Tigers**, Red Sox, Yankees, Senators 1822 g, .310, 64 hr, 1166 rbi. *1 WS, 2 g, .000, 1 rbi*
☛ *Led League—rbi 15, 17–18.*

Veach was the Tigers' lefthanded-hitting left fielder for more than 11 years and batted .306 or better in 8 of them. He drove in at least 100 runs six times, tied teammate Sam Crawford for the AL lead with 112 RBI in 1915, and led with 103 RBI in 1917 and 78 in the war-shortened 1918 season. Yet Veach was overshadowed by Hall of Fame teammates Crawford, Ty Cobb, and, later, Harry Heilmann. In 1919 he topped the league in hits, doubles, and triples but finished second to Cobb in the AL batting race, hitting .355 to Cobb's .384.

With the Yankees in 1925, Veach once pinch hit for Babe Ruth. He went to the pennant-winning Senators that August, and in the closing weeks of the season he broke up Ted Lyons's bid for a no-hitter with a two-out ninth-inning single. After ending his ML career with his only World Series appearance, he played for Toledo (American Association) in 1926–29. At the age of forty he hit .382 to capture the 1928 AA batting crown. /(JK)

Coot Veal [Orville Inman] — 1932– . SS 1958–63 **Tigers**, Senators, Pirates 247 g, .231, 1 hr, 51 rbi

A basketball player at Auburn, Veal was named to the *TSN* Rookie All-Star team for batting .256 with the Tigers in 1958, though he was not called up until July 30. He was a backup the rest of his career. /(RTM)

Bob Veale — 1935– . LHP 1962–74 **Pirates**, Red Sox 1926 ip, 120–95, 3.08. *1 WS, 1 ip, 0–0, 13.50* ☛ *All-Star—65–66.*

One of the hardest throwers in the majors in an era dominated by fireballers, Veale led the NL in strikeouts in 1964 and finished second in 1965 and third in 1966. He struck out 16 Phillies in a 9-inning game (6/1/1965) and 16 Reds in 12 innings (9/30/1964). His lifetime ratio of 7.96 strikeouts per nine innings ranks fifth all-time (1,500-plus innings). But he also led four times in bases on balls, tying the modern record, and walked 90 or more every year he was in the rotation (1964–70). He won 67 games in his first four full seasons (1964–67), with seven shutouts in 1965. But three losing seasons followed and he was moved to the bullpen in 1971. He went 6–0 as Pittsburgh won the 1971 World Championship, but he posted a 7.04 ERA. Sold to Boston in September 1972, he was the number two man out of their bullpen in 1973, saving 11 games in his last good season. /(SFS)

Bill Veeck — 1914–87. *Executive.*

Perhaps best remembered for sending midget Eddie Gaedel to bat in a game against the Tigers at St. Louis in 1952, Veeck was baseball's most imaginative promoter. He grew up in a ballpark and was never happier than when he was roaming the grandstand and bleachers, mingling with fans. An admitted publicity hound and an imaginative innovator who frequently upset other club owners with his proposals and stunts, he was also a sound baseball man who created winners in Cleveland and Chicago.

His father, William Veeck, Sr., was a baseball writer when William Wrigley installed him as president of the Cubs. By the time he was eleven, Bill Jr. was selling soda in the stands, mailing out tickets, and helping the grounds keepers. When his father

Bill Veeck

died in 1933 Veeck quit Kenyon College and went to work full-time for the Cubs. He became treasurer, but at twenty-seven he quit and bought the near-bankrupt Milwaukee team in the American Association. With $11 in his pocket he arrived in Milwaukee in 1941; four years later he sold the club for a $275,000 profit after setting minor league attendance records and winning three pennants. He gave away live pigs, beer, cases of food; he put on fireworks displays, staged weddings at home plate, played morning games for wartime swing shift workers. But he considered such stunts as extras, not lures, and usually produced them unannounced.

In 1943 he had the backing to buy the Phillies and planned to sign several Negro League players, but he felt the risk was too great and backed out, a move he later said he regretted. Wounds suffered fighting in the South Pacific with the Marines in

WWII forced him to undergo several operations on his leg and eventual amputation. But it didn't slow him down.

In 1946 he put together a syndicate and bought the Cleveland Indians. In 1947 they doubled attendance to 1.5 million; a year later they drew an AL-record 2,620,627 while winning the pennant. He signed Larry Doby, the first black player in the league, and Satchel Paige. After selling the Indians for a large profit, he took over the moribund Browns, then in debt to the league for $300,000, a number about equal to a season's attendance. In 1952 attendance "soared" to 518,000; Veeck said he lost close to $200,000. Despite the opposition of his three partners, Veeck planned to move the team to Baltimore in 1953. August Busch had bought the Cardinals, who were paying $35,000-a-year rent to the Browns for the use of Sportsman's Park. The deal was to sell the park to the Cardinals and raise money by selling shares to the public in Baltimore. Believing he had seven votes lined up, he put it to the league on March 16, 1953. He lost 5 to 3; only former partner Hank Greenberg and Frank Lane of the White Sox supported him. Reasons given for the turndown were too many debts, not enough money, and too little time before the season was to open. He had failed to confer with the president of the International League over the Baltimore territory and had not contacted Washington and Philadelphia officials personally. Veeck said, "I am the victim of duplicity by a lot of lying so-and-sos. Every reason they give for voting me down is either silly or malicious, and I prefer to think they were malicious." Most of the press agreed with him. He was forced to sell out. A year later the club was moved to Baltimore.

Out of baseball, he tried to buy Ringling Brothers circus, researched the Pacific coast for major league possiblities for Phil Wrigley, publicized a passenger ship in Cleveland, worked for ABC sports and NBC game of the week, tried to buy the Tigers in 1957, and went after an NBA franchise for Cleveland. He was back in the game in 1959, heading a group that bought the White Sox. They won their first pennant in 40 years and drew a club-record 1,423,000. In 1960 Veeck unveiled the exploding scoreboard and drew 1,644,460 for a club record that still stands. On advice of his doctors he sold the club and retired to his Maryland farm. But after operating Suffolk racetrack, writing book reviews for newspapers and his own story, *Veeck as in Wreck*, he was back in Chicago in 1975 with Greenberg, paying $7 million

for the White Sox. Five years later they sold the franchise for $20 million.

A heavy smoker and light beer drinker, Veeck gave up both in 1980 and underwent two operations for lung cancer in 1984. His tieless attire was due to a skin condition which made tight collars unbearable. /(NLM)

William Veeck — Unk.–Unk. *Writer-Executive.*

As baseball writer for the Chicago *American*, Veeck was often critical of the management of the Cubs. Club owner William Wrigley, Jr., told him if he thought he could do better he could take over the club. Veeck did just that, and a year later he was named club president. He was not a patient owner and had seven managers in 13 years. When he began to spend Wrigley's money, he produced pennant winners in 1929 and 1932. His last move was the purchase of Chuck Klein from the Phillies. Veeck's son was executive Bill Veeck. /(NLM)

Otto Velez [born Otoniel Velez Franceschi] (Swato) — 1950– . OF-DH-1B 1973–83 Yankees, **Blue Jays**, Indians 637 g, .251, 78 hr, 272 rbi. *1 LCS, 1 g, .000. 1 WS, 3 g, .000*

Otto the Swato was a power-hitting outfielder and DH for the expansion Blue Jays. In April 1977 (the Jays' first month as a franchise), Velez won AL Player of the Month honors with a .442 batting average and .865 slugging average (figures that remain monthly team records). On May 4, 1980 against Cleveland, Velez had the Blue Jays' first three-homer game on the way to tying an AL record with four HR in a doubleheader. /(TF)

Max Venable — 1957– . OF 1979–87 **Giants**, Expos, Reds 532 g, .230, 11 hr, 82 rbi

A reserve outfielder and lefthanded pinch-hit specialist, Venable never had more than 228 at-bats in nine ML seasons. The Giants traded him with Andy McGaffigan to the Expos for Al Oliver before the 1984 season, and in 1985 Venable hit a career-high .289 for the Reds, .371 as a pinch hitter. /(SCL)

Tony Venzon — 1915–1971. *Umpire* NL 1957–71 *3 ASU 3 WS*

Venzon was behind the plate for four no-hitters in his 15 seasons as a NL umpire. He had the unusual experience of working no-hitters on successive days on April 30 and May 1, 1969 when first Jim

Maloney of the Reds and then Don Wilson of the Astros hurled hitless games. /(RTM)

Emil Verban (Dutch, The Antelope) — 1915– . 2B 1944–50 Cardinals, **Phillies**, Cubs, Braves 853 g, .272, 1 hr, 241 rbi. *1 WS, 6 g, .412, 2 rbi*

As a 29-year-old rookie, Verban batted .412 for the Cardinals in the 1944 World Series and went 3-for-3 in the sixth and final game, driving in the winning run to beat the Browns. During the Series he requested a better seat for his pregnant wife, who was put behind a post, but was denied it by the club owner. When the series ended, Verban told the owner, "Now you can sit behind the post, you meathead."

Because of his speed, Verban acquired the nickname The Antelope in the minors. He led the NL in fielding in 1945 and in fewest strikeouts (eight) while with the Phillies in 1947. A latter-day nationwide group of Cub fans calls itself the Emil Verban Society. /(RTM)

Joe Verbanic — 1943– . RHP 1966–68, 70 Phillies, **Yankees** 207 ip, 12–11, 3.26

The Yankees obtained the wiry, 6′ 155-lb Verbanic from Philadelphia for Pedro Ramos in December 1966 and made him their swingman. He handled the role well, going 4–3 in 1967 and 6–7 in 1968 before his career was derailed by a sore arm. /(MG)

Johnny Vergez — 1906– . 3B 1931–36 **Giants**, Phillies, Cardinals 672 g, .255, 52 hr, 292 rbi

When Vergez joined the Giants, he moved aging Hall of Famer Freddie Lindstrom off third base and into the outfield. He was having his best season for the 1933 pennant-bound Giants when felled by appendicitis; he missed the World Series. The following year he batted just .200. /(JK)

John Verhoeven — 1953– . RHP 1976–77, 80–81 Angels, White Sox, **Twins** 204 ip, 3–8, 3.75

Verhoeven never had a winning season; his three victories (against four losses) came as a middle reliever for the Twins in 1980, when he saw the most action (44 games). /(SFS)

Mickey Vernon [James Barton] — 1918– . 1B 1939–43, 46–60 **Senators**, Indians, Red Sox, Braves, Pirates 2409 g, .286, 172 hr, 1311 rbi.
    Manager 1961–63 **Senators** 135–227, .373
☛ *Led League—ba 46, 53. All-Star—46, 48, 53, 55–56* .

One of baseball's most popular players in the 1940s and 1950s, Vernon had a quiet type of charisma. A four-decade player, the consistent, hardy Vernon set the major league record for most games played at first base (2,237).

Vernon led AL first basemen in fielding percentage four times (twice leading the majors) but in three different seasons led ML first basemen in errors. He set the AL mark for most lifetime assists (1,444); his 155 assists in 1949 set the AL first basemen's record. In one 1943 game, he made two unassisted double plays. He was *TSN*'s ML All-Star first baseman in 1953.

The soft-spoken, lefthanded slugger led the AL in batting with the Senators in 1946 (.353), and again in 1953 (.337) at the age of thirty-five. He clinched the 1953 title on the last day of the season in a game against the Athletics. Late in the contest, Vernon hit a line drive that was caught by outfielder Elmer Valo, bringing his average down to .337. Word arrived from Cleveland that Al Rosen, who was vying for the triple crown, was through for the day. If Vernon didn't bat again, he would best Rosen by a

Mickey Vernon after his 2,000th hit

margin of .0011. He would have come up again had not teammate Mickey Grasso, who had doubled, been picked off second base, or had not Kite Thomas been thrown out at second when he "leisurely" tried to stretch a single into a double. Some felt Vernon's teammates were protecting his title.

Vernon collected 2,495 lifetime hits, an average of more than one per game. He led the AL in doubles in 1946, 1953, and 1954, and drove in 80 or more runs 11 times, with a high of 115 in 1953.

Vernon was President Eisenhower's favorite player. On Opening Day 1954, with Eisenhower in attendance, Vernon hit a two-run, tenth-inning homer off the Yankees' Allie Reynolds to win the game for Washington. In Eisenhower's excitement, he started to leave his seat and go on to the field, but was stopped by Secret Service men, who brought the Senators' hero to the President's box.

Vernon managed the Senators from 1961 through 40 games in 1963. Under his leadership, they finished in a tie for last in 1961, and last in 1962. /(RTM)

Zoilo Versalles (Zorro) — 1939– . SS-3B-2B 1959–69, 71 **Senators/Twins**, Dodgers, Indians, Senators, Braves 1400 g, .242, 95 hr, 471 rbi. *1 WS, 7 g, .286, 1 hr, 4 rbi*
☛ *Most Valuable Player—65. All-Star—63, 65. Gold Glove—63, 65.*

The native Cuban was the AL MVP in 1965 when he was the catalyst of the pennant-winning Twins' offense, leading the league with 45 doubles, 12 triples, 126 runs scored, and 666 at-bats. He also stole a career-high 27 bases but struck out 122 times, tops in the league. In the 1965 World Series, his three-run homer was the key hit in Minnesota's 8–2 opening-game win over the Dodgers.

The flashy shortstop won a Gold Glove in 1963. On four occasions during his career, he got his team's only hit in a game. In 1967 Carl Yastrzemski missed receiving unanimous support for the AL MVP Award because one writer cast a vote for Versalles. Versalles was plagued by back problems late in his career and played in the Mexican League in 1970 before one final ML stint with the Braves. /(RTM)

Tom Veryzer — 1953– . SS-2B-3B 1973–84 Tigers, **Indians**, Mets, Cubs 996 g, .241, 14 hr, 231 rbi. *1 LCS, 3 g, .000*

Veryzer became the Tigers' shortstop in 1975, when he was named to the Topps' Rookie All-Star team, and remained through 1977. Supplanted by Alan

Trammell, he was traded to the Indians for Charlie Spikes. In four seasons as a starter for Cleveland, he twice batted .271. Despite an adequate bat and a good glove, he never put solid seasons back to back, partly due to injuries. /(ME)

Veterans Stadium (The Vet) **Philadelphia Phillies** 1971– . LF-330, CF-408, RF-330

Part of a stadium complex that includes the Spectrum and JFK Stadium, the Vet is a typical multi-purpose modern facility, housing both the Phillies and the NFL's Eagles. The stadium is circular, with symmetrical outfield fences and artificial turf, and its 62,382 seats currently make it the NL's largest stadium. It has unusually good visibility for batters, due in part to a black canopy between the outfield fences and the seats. It was opened in 1971, and its fences were quickly raised from 6' to 12' because the lively turf produced an inordinate number of ground-rule doubles. Each section beneath the upper deck contains a small television monitor, allowing fans there to see what is on the otherwise-concealed scoreboard screen. Greg Luzinski is the only batter to hit the replica Liberty Bell that hangs from the third seating level in deep centerfield. /(SCL)

Rube Vickers [Harry Porter] — 1878–1958. RHP 1902–03, 07–09 Reds, Dodgers, **A's** 441 ip, 22–27, 3.04

Canadian-born Rube Vickers recorded 18 of his 22 major league wins for the 1908 Athletics, including a league-high six relief wins. In a doubleheader against the Senators on October 5, 1907 he pitched 12 innings of brilliant relief to win the first game, then hurled a five-inning perfect game in the nightcap. They were his only two ML wins of the season. /(LRD)

Joe Vila — Unk.–Unk. *Writer.*

A graduate of Harvard, Vila was sports editor of the New York *Morning Sun*. A sturdy, individualistic Bostonian, he was a strong AL rooter, but also one of the first journalists to print rumors of the 1919 Black Sox scandal. Known for his enterprise, he reportedly once picked the pocket of the Boston NL owner to get a document for a scoop. /(NLM)

Fay Vincent — 1938– . *Executive.*

Vincent, the deputy commissioner under his friend Bart Giamatti, replaced Giamatti as Commissioner in September 1989 after Giamatti's death. Vincent was previously a securities lawyer who ran Columbia Picture Industries for nearly ten years. /(SH)

Frank Viola (Sweet Music) — 1960- . LHP 1982-
Twins, Mets 1858 ip, 117–98, 3.84. 20 wins: 88 *1 LCS,
12 ip, 1–0, 5.25. 1 WS, 19 ip, 2–1, 3.72*
☛ *Led League—w 88. Cy Young Award—88.*

Viola won the Cy Young Award with a 24–7 record
in 1988, leading the AL in wins and winning
percentage and finishing third in ERA (2.64) and
strikeouts (193). The curly-haired changeup artist
had already established himself as one of the AL's
finest pitchers and the ace of the Minnesota staff,
leading the Twins to the 1987 World Championship
with a 17–10, 2.90 record. In postseason play that
year, he won Game Four of the LCS after a no-
decision in the Twins' Game One victory. He was
the World Series MVP, winning Game One 10–1,
losing Game Four 7–2, and coming back on three
days' rest to triumph in Game Seven 4–2.

Viola came up to the Twins in 1982. After two
losing seasons, he followed with two 18-win years
and a 16–13 record in 1986, when he led the league
in starts. Following his Cy Young season in 1988 he
got into a contract battle with Twins management
that would have gone unremarked upon in most
cities but divided the Twins. He recovered from a
bad start in 1989, turning it around after finally
signing a new contract, but suffered from lack of
support even after his pitching improved. Local hero
Kent Hrbek attacked Viola in the press, and the
notoriously religious Gary Gaetti vented his spleen
regarding Viola's contract later on. Viola was traded
to the Mets for Rick Aguilera, David West, and
three prospects after New York learned that Dwight
Gooden might not pitch again that year; Viola's
arrival gave the Mets a higher-paid starting staff than
the entire White Sox roster. Viola became the
teammate of Ron Darling, whom he had bested in a
famous NCAA playoff game between Yale and St.
John's. Darling no-hit St. John's for 11 innings, but
Viola won 1–0 in the 12th. /(SH)

Jim Viox — 1890–1969. 2B-3B 1912–16 **Pirates**
506 g, .273, 7 hr, 191 rbi

Viox was the Pirates' starting second baseman from
1913, when he batted a career-high .317, until 1916,
when Pittsburgh made wholesale changes. He managed championship clubs at Portsmouth (Virginia
League) in 1920 and 1921. /(ME)

Bill Virdon — 1931- . OF 1955–65, 68 Cardinals,
Pirates 1583 g, .267, 91 hr, 502 rbi. *1 WS, 7 g, .241, 5 rbi.*
   Manager 1972–84 Pirates, Yankees, **Astros**, Expos
995–921, .519 First place: 72, 80–81 *2 LCS, 4–6, .400*
☛ *Rookie of the Year—55. Gold Glove—62.*

Virdon was a graceful centerfielder for a dozen
major league seasons and a manager who stressed
defense and fundamentals for 13 more. The slender,
bespectacled, lefthanded hitter was first signed by
the Yankees. But it was as a Cardinal that he was
named 1955 NL Rookie of the Year, hitting .281
with career highs of 17 home runs and 68 RBI. With
the Pirates in 1962, he won a Gold Glove.

When Virdon got off to a slow start in 1956, St.
Louis GM Frank "Trader" Lane sent him to the
Pirates on May 17 for Bobby Del Greco and Dick
Littlefield. Virdon rebounded to bat a career-high
.319 that season and remained a fixture in center for
the Pirates through 1965. In the 1960 World Series,
Virdon had a key role in three of the Pirates' four
victories. He made two crucial, dazzling catches on
balls hit by Yogi Berra in the opener and Bob Cerv
in Game Four, and he hit the grounder in Game
Seven that struck Yankee shortstop Tony Kubek in
the throat and sparked Pittsburgh's comeback
victory.

Virdon coached in Pittsburgh under Danny
Murtaugh before replacing the popular manager in
1972. He led the Pirates to a division championship
that year but lost to Cincinnati in the final inning of
LCS Game Five. He lost his job late in 1973 after
run-ins with players Dock Ellis and Richie Hebner.
George Steinbrenner's second choice for Yankee
manager in 1974 (Dick Williams was unable to take
the job), Virdon brought the club in second, winning
TSN Manager of the Year honors. Nevertheless, he
was replaced by Billy Martin on August 1, 1975.
Two weeks later, Houston hired him.

In six full seasons with the Astros, Virdon only
once finished lower than third. He guided the club to
postseason play in 1980, when he again was named
TSN Manager of the Year. Again he came within an
inning of the World Series, losing the LCS to
Cincinnati in the tenth inning of Game Five. In
strike-shortened 1981, Houston won the first half of
the split schedule but lost to Los Angeles in the
divisional playoff. When he was fired in August
1982, he was the Houston franchise's winningest
manager (544–522). Virdon was not out of a job for
long. He was hired by Montreal that October and
lasted through late in 1984. /(ME)

Ozzie Virgil [Osvaldo Jose Pichardo] — 1933- . 3B-C-
OF 1956–58, 60–62, 65–66, 69 Giants, **Tigers**, A's,
Orioles, Pirates 324 g, .231, 14 hr, 73 rbi

Father of major league catcher Ozzie Virgil, the
elder Virgil was the first Dominican to play in the
majors. He was also the first dark-skinned player on

the Tigers; he joined them in 1958 and went 5-for-5 in his first game with Detroit. Though used sparingly, he played every position but pitcher during his ML tenure. He began coaching for the Giants in 1969, became Dick Williams's third base coach in Montreal in 1977, and went with him to the Padres and Mariners. /(RTM)

Ozzie Virgil [Osvaldo Jose Lopez] — 1956– . C 1980–89 **Phillies**, Braves, Blue Jays 736 g, .244, 98 hr, 307 rbi. *1 LCS, 1 g, .000. 1 WS, 3 g, .500, 1 rbi*
☛ *All-Star—85, 87.*

The son of Ozzie Virgil, the younger Virgil backed up Bo Diaz for the Phillies in 1982–83 and won the starting job outright in 1984, hitting a career-high .261 wth 18 HR. When the Phillies opted for younger catchers Darren Daulton and John Russell in 1986, Virgil was traded to Atlanta with Pete Smith for Steve Bedrosian and Milt Thompson. In 1987 he belted 27 HR in cozy Atlanta-Fulton County Stadium, and when he was an All-Star that year, his father was an All-Star coach. Virgil declined precipitously and by mid-1988 was sharing the catching job with Bruce Benedict. /(SG)

Ossie Vitt [Oscar Joseph] — 1890–1963. 3B-2B-OF 1912–21 **Tigers**, Red Sox 1062 g, .238, 4 hr, 294 rbi. *Manager* 1938–40 **Indians** 262–198, .578

Detroit's regular third baseman from 1915 through 1917, Vitt was a marginal ballplayer who never batted higher than .254. But he was a smart, scrappy baseball man who became a minor league manager and earned a reputation for leading aggressive teams to pennants. He was hired by the Indians to instill new life into the team in 1938 and finished third in 1938 and 1939, but his tactics were resisted by the Cleveland players. They petitioned for his removal in 1940, becoming known as The Crybabies, and lost the pennant they had been expected to win, finishing a game behind the first-place Tigers. Vitt was replaced by Roger Peckinpaugh for 1941. /(JK)

David Voight — 1926– . *Writer.*

A graduate of Albright College with a Ph.D. from Syracuse, Voight has been a sociology and anthropology professor at Albright since 1964 and is a past president of SABR. His books include *American Baseball from Gentlemen's Sport to Commissioner System* (1966), *American Baseball from Commissioner to Continental Expansion* (1970), *A Little League Journal* (1974), and *America Through Baseball* (1976). /(NLM)

Bill Voiselle (Big Bill, Ninety-Six) — 1919– . RHP 1942–50 **Giants**, Braves, Cubs 1373 ip, 74–84, 3.83. 20 wins: 44 *1 WS, 11 ip, 0–1, 2.53*
☛ *Led League—k 44.*

Big Bill was 6′4″, lived in Ninety-Six, South Carolina, and wore 96, the highest number ever in the major leagues. In his only winning season, as a rookie with the 1944 Giants, he went 21–16, leading the NL with 41 starts, 312-2/3 innings pitched, and 161 strikeouts. He went 13–13 for the Braves in 1948 and lost the last game of the World Series to the Indians. /(NLM)

Clyde Vollmer (Big 'Un) — 1921– . OF 1942, 46–54 Reds, **Senators**, Red Sox 685 g, .251, 69 hr, 339 rbi

Vollmer debuted with the Reds on May 31, 1942 and homered on the first major league pitch he saw, only the third player to do so. Yet he did not get much playing time in the majors until 1949, with the Senators. In 1951, he had a torrid July for the Red Sox, connecting for 13 HR and driving in 30 runs. He homered three times that July 26, and in the 16th inning on July 28 hit the latest-inning grand slam in ML history. /(RTM)

Vic Voltaggio (Vic) — 1941– . *Umpire* AL 1977– *1 ASU 2 LCS*

Voltaggio was the plate umpire on the night of April 29, 1986 when Boston's Roger Clemens set a ML mark by striking out 20 Seattle Mariners. Voltaggio called eight third strikes on the Mariners. The ex-Marine, who served 18 months in Vietnam, is a distant relative of famous songwriter Stephen Foster. /(RTM)

Chris von der Ahe (Der Poss Bresident) — 1851–1913. *Manager* 1892, 95–97 **Cardinals** 59–110, .349

Von der Ahe was the most colorful team owner of the 19th century. In 1882 he helped found the American Association and became owner of the St. Louis Browns. Born in Germany, he knew little about baseball but he owned a saloon near the ballpark and thought the games would provide thirsty crowds. When he hired Charles Comiskey as Browns manager in 1883, the team began to rise in the standings, winning pennants from 1885 to 1888. Although his heavy accent made him the butt of jokes, von der Ahe reportedly cleared $75,000 a year during this period. After each home game he would ceremonially take the receipts to the bank in a wheelbarrow, flanked by armed guards. Supposedly, the word "fan" evolved from von der Ahe's reference to baseball enthusiasts as "fanatics," and he is sometimes credited with introducing the hot dog to ballparks.

The Players' League War destroyed the AA, and von der Ahe moved his team into the 12-team NL, but without Comiskey and most of his stars. He managed the team himself in 1892, finishing 11th. Von der Ahe was known for his promotions and publicity gimmicks. He spent $6,500 to make his ballpark suitable for both ball games and horse races and the games became little more than a sideshow in the 1890s. A number of personal and financial reverses forced him to sell the team in 1898. By 1908, he had become a charity case, and the St. Louis Cardinals played a benefit for him. /(NLM)

Dave Von Ohlen — 1958- . LHP 1983-87 **Cardinals**, Indians, A's 168 ip, 7-7, 3.33

This sinkerballer found some success as a set-up man for Bruce Sutter with the 1983-84 Cardinals. Torn forearm muscles and a twisted knee thwarted a good opportunity with Cleveland. /(FO)

Joe Vosmik — 1910-1962. OF 1930-41, 44 **Indians**, Browns, Red Sox, Dodgers, Senators 1414 g, .307, 65 hr, 874 rbi
☛ All-Star—35.

Vosmik caught the eye of the wife of Indians' general manager Billy Evans at a tryout in Cleveland. Needing to sign one more local boy, Evans asked his wife's opinion. She chose "the good-looking blond boy." Vosmik spent two seasons in the minors, batting .381 and .397, then hit .320 for Cleveland in 1931. He topped the .300 mark in six of his ten seasons as a regular. In 1935 he led the AL in hits (216), doubles (47), and triples (20) and batted .348 to finish one percentage point behind Buddy Myer in the AL batting race. He was traded to the Browns in 1947 and in 1948 had a league-high 201 hits for the Red Sox. /(JK)

Bill Voss — 1943- . OF 1965-72 White Sox, **Angels**, Brewers, A's, Cardinals 475 g, .227, 19 hr, 127 rbi

Voss's first full ML season came after he was acquired by the Angels for 1969; he hit a career-high .261 with 2 HR and 40 RBI in 349 at-bats and was never again a regular. /(JFC)

Pete Vuckovich — 1952- . RHP 1975-83, 85-86 White Sox, Blue Jays, Cardinals, **Brewers** 1455 ip, 93-69, 3.66. *1 LCS, 14 ip, 0-1, 4.40. 1 WS, 14 ip, 0-1, 4.50*
☛ Cy Young Award—82.

Vuckovich was selected by the Blue Jays in the expansion draft and, although mostly used in relief, threw the first shutout in Blue Jay history, a 2-0 victory over Jim Palmer and the Orioles. Traded to the Cardinals for 1978, he started more often and finished third in the NL in ERA with a 2.55 mark while going 12-12. Used almost exclusively in the rotation thereafter, his ERA went up but he posted 15-10 and 12-9 records before being traded to Milwaukee in December 1980 with Rollie Fingers and Ted Simmons for Sixto Lezcano, David Green, Dave LaPoint, and Lary Sorensen. The deal made the Brewers instant contenders and soon led to their first pennant.

Pitching for an offensive powerhouse helped Vuckovich go 14-4 in the 1981 strike season, tying for the AL lead in wins and finishing first in winning percentage despite a mediocre 3.54 ERA. Milwaukee won the second-half title in the split season, and Vuckovich won Game Four of the divisional playoff against the Yankees 2-1.

When the Brewers finally won the pennant in 1982, Vuckovich won the Cy Young Award. He was 18-6, tying for the AL lead in winning percentage and finishing in a three-way tie for second in wins. His 3.34 ERA and 1.03-to-1 strikeout-to-walk ratio were the worst ever at the time for a Cy Young winner, but there were no strong candidates for the award (the wins leader, Lamarr Hoyt, went 19-15 with a 3.53 ERA). The Brewers' unofficial motto that year was "winning ugly," referring to high-scoring games that weren't "pretty." Many players, including Vuckovich, went unshaven on game days to play up the idea, and Vuckovich's record certainly reflected the strong offensive support "Harvey's Wallbangers" provided him. He lost Game Two of the LCS to the Angels 4-2, but did keep Milwaukee in the game in their clinching victory, leaving in the seventh inning down 3-2. In the World Series, the Cardinals beat him 6-2 in Game Three, and he got a no-decision in the final loss.

Vuckovich had been battling shoulder pain for two seasons; in spring training 1983, it was discovered that he'd torn his rotator cuff. He skipped surgery in favor of an exercise rehabilitation program and spent most of the summer doing color commentary on Brewers cable TV broadcasts. He attempted an unsuccessful comeback for three games in September and then missed all of 1984. Subsequent and prolonged comeback attempts all failed. In the 1989 movie *Major League*, Vuckovich played a minor role as the Yankees' slugging first baseman. /(SH)

George Vukovich — 1956– . OF 1980–85 Phillies, Indians 628 g, .268, 27 hr, 203 rbi. *1 LCS, 4 g, .000*

Vukovich was an adequate lefthanded hitter and a strong-armed outfielder. In strike-shortened 1981, his home run off the Expos' Jeff Reardon won Game Four of the NL Eastern Division playoff for Phila-delphia. The Phillies sent him to Cleveland as part of a five-for-one trade for Von Hayes in December 1982. Platooning, he led the Indians with a .304 batting average in 1984, but after hitting .244 in 1985, he was sold to Japan's Seibu Lions. /(ME)

John Vukovich — 1947– . 3B-SS 1970–71, 73–77, 79–81 **Phillies**, Brewers, Reds 277 g, .161, 6 hr, 44 rbi

In Vukovich's ten seasons in the majors, he hit above .200 only twice. The wide-ranging third baseman stayed in the majors by becoming a utility man who played all four infield positions. /(WOR)

Rube Waddell [George Edward] — 1876–1914. LHP
1897, 99–1910 Louisville (NL), Pirates, Cubs, **A's**, Browns
2961 ip, 191–145, 2.16. 20 wins: 02–05
☛ *Led League—w 05. Led League—k 1900, 02–07. Led
League—era 1900, 05. Hall of Fame—1946.*

The colorful, eccentric, and talented Waddell was
"one of the best lefthanders I ever saw," according
to Connie Mack, for whom Waddell had his best
seasons. His great fastball was compared to that of
Walter Johnson, and he threw a sharp-breaking
curve. He collected 50 career shutouts. His strikeout-to-walk ratio was almost 3-to-1.

Waddell grew up on the farmlands around Bradford, PA. "He often missed school," said his sister,
"but I could always find him playing ball, fishing or
following a fire engine." He pitched for a college
team for one year, and for town teams at $25 a
game, before signing his first contract with Louisville
(NL) in 1897. He was playing for Pittsburgh when,
unhappy with the stern discipline of manager Fred
Clarke, he jumped the club. Clarke, preferring not to
have to deal with the flaky hurler, let him go.

Connie Mack "borrowed" Waddell from the
Pirates' Barney Dreyfuss for his Milwaukee team in
the newly christened American League, which was
still a minor league in 1900. On August 19, Milwaukee played a doubleheader against the White Sox.
Waddell went all the way in the 17-inning opener,
winning it 3–2 on his own triple. The two managers
agreed the second game would be five innings.
Mack, knowing Waddell was an avid fisherman,
asked him, " . . .how would you like to go fishing at
Pewaukee for three days instead of going with us to
Kansas City? All you have to do is pitch the second
game." Waddell threw a five-inning shutout.

Waddell joined Mack's Philadelphia Athletics in
1902 and went 24–7, leading the AL in strikeouts
for the first of six straight seasons. In 1904 he struck
out 349—an AL record that stood for over 70 years
until surpassed by Nolan Ryan. (He had been
credited with 343 until after Bob Feller fanned 348
in 1946; further digging later increased Waddell's
total to 349.) In 1905 he led the league with 26 wins,
8 relief wins, 46 appearances, 287 strikeouts, and a
1.48 ERA.

It was rumored that gamblers paid Waddell to
fake an arm injury and sit out the 1905 World Series
against the Giants. "That's ridiculous," maintained
Mack. "Money meant nothing to him." In truth,
Waddell had fallen on his left arm while horsing
around with teammate Andy Coakley. It stiffened
up overnight, and he didn't pitch again that season.
Though he pitched four more ML seasons, he never
again threw with the same snap.

It is believed Waddell never made more than
$2,800 a year, and he spent money as fast as he got
it. For a time the A's paid him in dollar bills, hoping
to make his money last longer. He was forever
borrowing or conning extra money out of Mack.

Waddell enjoyed waving his teammates off the
field and then striking out the side. He actually did
so only in exhibition games, since the rules prohibit
playing with fewer than nine men on the field in
regulation play. But, in a league game in Detroit,
Waddell had his outfielders come in close and sit
down on the grass. He struck out the side. Once the
stunt almost backfired. Pitching an exhibition in
Memphis, he took the field alone with his catcher,
Doc Powers, for the last three innings. With two out
in the ninth, Powers dropped a third strike, allowing
the batter to reach first. The next two hitters patted
flies that fell behind the mound. Waddell ran
himself ragged but finally fanned the last man.

Waddell wrestled alligators in Florida, hung
around in firehouses, married two women who then
left him, and tended bar when he wasn't the saloon's
best customer. He held up the start of games he was
scheduled to pitch while he played marbles with
children outside the park. There was a provision in
Waddell's contract barring him from eating Animal
Crackers in bed. In those days, two players had to
share a double bed on the road, and Ossie Schreckengost was Waddell's catcher and roommate.
"Schreck wouldn't sign unless he saw that clause in
Waddell's contract," said Mack, "so I wrote it in
there, and the Rube stuck to it."

Though Waddell was always a fan favorite, his
erratic behavior and declining effectiveness strained
the tolerance of his teammates. Some threatened not
to report in the spring of 1908 unless Mack got rid of

Rube Waddell

him. Waddell was shipped to the Browns. That July 29, he tied what was then the AL single-game strikeout record by fanning 16 of his former A's teammates.

By 1910 Waddell was back in the minors. He won 20 games for Joe Cantillon's Minneapolis (American Association) club in 1911. In the spring of 1912, he was staying at Cantillon's house in Hickman, Kentucky, when a nearby river flooded. Standing in icy water, Waddell helped pile sandbags on the embankments. The incident affected his health; though he went 12-6 that year, he collapsed while with Virginia (Northern League) in 1913 and landed in a sanatorium in San Antonio, Texas. He died there in 1914 on April Fool's Day.

For several years there was no monument on

Waddell's grave. The president of the San Antonio ballclub told Connie Mack and John McGraw, whose Giants trained there. They raised enough money to put up a six-foot granite marker. Waddell was elected to the Hall of Fame by the Committee on Baseball Veterans in 1946. /(NLM)

Tom Waddell — 1958- . RHP 1984-85, 87 **Indians** 215 ip, 15-11, 4.30

The Scottish-born Waddell was trained as a relief specialist in the Braves organization. He set an Indians rookie record with 58 relief appearances in 1984, going 7-4 with six saves. He could not successfully continue his ML career after a September 1985 elbow operation. /(ME)

Ben Wade — 1922- . RHP 1948, 52-55 Cubs, **Dodgers**, Cardinals, Pirates 371 ip, 19-17, 4.34. *1 WS, 2 ip, 0-0, 15.43*

The younger brother of Jake Wade, Ben went 11-9 for the 1952 pennant-winning Dodgers. Used solely in relief by Brooklyn in 1953, he completed every inning he started during the season but pitched poorly in the World Series. /(RTM)

Jake Wade (Whistlin' Jake) — 1912- . LHP 1936-39, 42-44, 46 **Tigers**, Red Sox, Browns, White Sox, Yankees, Senators 668 ip, 27-40, 5.00

Wade was plagued by poor control, walking 440 batters in 668 ML innings. After his release by the Tigers in 1939, he bounced around the AL, never winning more than five games in any one season. His younger brother Ben pitched in the NL in the 1950s. /(FS)

Charlie Wagner (Broadway) — 1912- . RHP 1938-42, 46 **Red Sox** 528 ip, 32-23, 3.91

Dapper and debonair Broadway Charlie went 12-8 for Boston in 1941 and 14-11 in 1942 before spending 1943 through 1945 in the military. Though he pitched for the Norfolk Naval Training Station (17-5 in '43), his ML career was a casualty of the war, although he appeared in eight final games in 1946. He served in the Red Sox front office and as a scout. /(JK)

Gary Wagner — 1940- . RHP 1965-70 **Phillies**, Red Sox 267 ip, 15-19, 3.71

Wagner was the ace of the Phillies' weak bullpen in his rookie 1965 season, going 7-7 with seven saves and a 3.00 ERA. His only other significant years were 1968 (4-4, 8 saves) for the Phillies and 1970 (3-1, 7 saves) for the Red Sox. /(SFS)

Hal Wagner — 1915–1979. C 1937–44, 46–49 **A's**, Red Sox, Tigers, Phillies 672 g, .248, 15 hr, 228 rbi. *1 WS, 5 g, .000*

Wagner was one of many young players who tried out for the Athletics and were advised by Connie Mack to go to Duke University. He quit after his junior year and signed with the A's but did not catch regularly until 1942. For a time during WWII, he worked in a factory and played only on weekends when the A's were within traveling distance. /(NLM)

Heinie Wagner [Charles F.] — 1881–1943. SS-2B 1902, 06–13, 15–16, 18 Giants, **Red Sox** 983 g, .250, 10 hr, 343 rbi. *1 WS, 8 g, .167.*
   Manager 1930 **Red Sox** 52–102, .338

Wagner was a wide-ranging shortstop who used his exceptionally big feet to block baserunners. He had career highs of .274, 68 RBI, and 75 runs scored for the World Champion 1912 Red Sox. He was a Red Sox coach from 1921 until 1930, when he replaced Bill Carrigan as manager. Carrigan had brought the Red Sox in last the three previous seasons, and Wagner fared no better. /(JK)

Honus Wagner [Johannes Peter] (The Flying Dutchman) — 1874–1955. SS-OF-1B-3B 1897–1917 Louisville (NL), **Pirates** 2786 g, .329, 101 hr, 1732 rbi. *2 WS, 15 g, .275, 9 rbi.*
   Manager 1917 **Pirates** 1–4, .200
☛ *Led League—ba 1900, 03–04, 06–09, 11. Led League—rbi 01–02, 07–08. Hall of Fame—1936.*

For 56 years, Wagner was a fixture in Pittsburgh, as a player for 17 years and as a coach for 39 more. In that time, Wagner was the first player to have his signature on a Louisville Slugger (1905), had his face put on an early baseball card that is now worth more than $100,000 (1909), served as a sergeant at arms for the Pennsylvania state legislature (1929), became one of the first five players elected to the Hall of Fame (1936), and, seven months before he died, saw a statue of himself erected outside Forbes Field. When he died, Branch Rickey declared that Wagner was the greatest player he had ever seen.

One reason for Rickey's pronouncement was the bowlegged, barrel-chested, long-limbed Wagner's skill at shortstop, where he was often likened to an octopus. When he fielded grounders, his huge hands also collected large scoops of infield dirt, which accompanied his throws to first like the tail of a comet. It was said that Wagner threw out runners lying on his back. In one instance, he was caught with his glove hand in his back pocket reaching for a

Honus Wagner

tobacco chaw, so he fielded a sharp grounder in his bare throwing hand and calmly threw the runner out, literally, with one hand behind his back. On another occasion, he used his bulk to keep a runner from stealing second after a wild throw from the catcher. Wagner timed his leap so that he landed on the unsuspecting incoming runner short of the base. By the time the players untangled themselves, the centerfielder had thrown the ball back to Wagner, who tagged the embarrassed runner out.

Ed Barrow discovered the ungainly Dutchman while scouting Wagner's older brother, Al, near the Pennsylvania coal mines where they both worked. Legend says that Barrow spied the 18-year-old Hans flinging rocks across the wide expanse of the Monongahela River and signed him on the spot. Wagner started in Steubenville, Ohio, then joined the NL Louisville club for three years. After the 1899 season, the National League shrunk from twelve to eight teams, and the Louisville franchise was discontinued. In 1900 former Louisville owner Barney Dreyfus bought the Pittsburgh franchise, and brought Wagner back to Pennsylvania for good.

From then on, the good-natured and modest Wagner dominated the league. He led the league in hitting eight times, in steals five times, and in slugging average six times. He hit over .300 17 times and would eventually play every position except catcher. He is also high on the all-time stolen-base, triples, and hits lists. After winning the batting title in 1909, he was pitted against the Tigers and Ty Cobb, the AL batting champ, in the 1909 World Series. In Game Two, Cobb notified the "krauthead" of his intention to steal second on the next pitch. Wagner's message-laden tag in Cobb's mouth resulted in three stitches and Cobb's lasting respect. In Game Three, Wagner drove in three runs and stole three bases. The Pirates won the Series in seven games with Wagner batting .333 and stealing six bases, including home.

Wagner simply loved to play, and reputedly didn't much care about getting paid for it. Ban Johnson tried to lure him to the American League, and Clark Griffith of Washington supposedly offered Wagner a huge sum. But Wagner was loyal and liked Pittsburgh, despite failing ever to earn more than $10,000 a year. Cobb and Nap Lajoie offered him $1,000 a week for a barnstorming tour, but he turned it down. And supposedly, Wagner didn't want his picture on the now-famous baseball card because the sponsor was a tobacco company, and he didn't want to seem to condone smoking, although he chewed tobacco. The story goes that he sent the tobacco company the money it would have earned from the card, which had already been printed.

Wagner was made manager in his final year, 1917, when he was forty-three, but decided he didn't like managing after only five games and one victory. He played semi-pro ball around Pittsburgh for another seven years. He was named a Pirate coach in 1933 and served until 1951, giving batting tips to future Hall of Famers Pie Traynor, Kiki Cuyler, Arky Vaughn, Ralph Kiner, and the Waner brothers. /(SEW)

Leon Wagner (Daddy Wags) — 1934— . OF 1958–69 Giants, Cardinals, Angels, **Indians**, White Sox 1352 g, .272, 211 hr, 669 rbi
☛ All-Star—62–63.

This colorful outfielder hit .317 with 13 home runs in 74 games as a Giants rookie to earn a spot on the *TSN* 1958 Rookie All-Star team. A powerful, left-handed pull hitter, he finished third in the 1962 AL home run race when he hit 37 for the Angels. That summer he played in both All-Star games; in the second contest he went 3-for-4, including a two-run HR off Art Mahaffey in the AL's 9–4 win. As Cleveland's left fielder from 1964 through 1967, he hit 97 HR. A respected pinch hitter, he led the AL with 46 appearances off the bench in 1968, splitting the season between the Indians and White Sox.

Wagner was a professional actor for several years and had a role in *Bingo Long's Traveling All Stars*, a movie about a black barnstorming team. Always well-dressed, he owned a clothing store whose slogan was "Buy Your Rags at Daddy Wags." /(RTM)

Mark Wagner (Peanut) — 1954— . SS-2B 1976–84 **Tigers**, Rangers, A's 414 g, .243, 3 hr, 71 rbi

Wagner hit in his first seven major league games but was otherwise an undistinguished backup to Alan Trammell and Lou Whitaker. Wagner's grandfather Joe Scott was invited by Ty Cobb to Tigers spring training for a tryout, but he reported late and missed his chance. /(SH)

Kermit Wahl — 1922— . 3B-SS-2B 1944–45, 47, 50–51 **Reds**, A's, Browns 231 g. .226, 3 hr, 50 rbi

A graduate of the University of Indiana, Wahl spent his ML days as a utility infielder. His most productive year was 1950, when he hit .257 in 89 games for the Philadelphia Athletics. /(RTM)

Eddie Waitkus — 1919–1972. 1B 1941, 46–55 Cubs, **Phillies**, Orioles 1140 g, .285, 24 hr, 373 rbi. *1 WS, 4 g, .267*
☛ All-Star—48.

Waitkus was a top defensive first baseman and a lefthanded line-drive hitter. After his All-Star 1948 season, he was traded by the Cubs to the Phillies. He was hitting more than .300 in mid-June 1949 when, in a bizarre incident in a Chicago hotel, he was shot in the chest and almost killed by a young woman he did not know—the real-life inspiration for Bernard Malamud's *The Natural*. Waitkus worked hard to come back in 1950 and, as the Phillies' leadoff hitter, helped them to win the NL pennant; he batted .284 and scored 102 runs, playing in 154 games. After being sold to the Orioles during spring training of 1954, he returned to Philadelphia in late 1955 and retired that fall. /(AL)

Rick Waits — 1952- . LHP 1973, 75-85 Rangers, Indians, Brewers 1426 ip, 79-92, 4.25

Waits, a curveball specialist, matched Bob Feller by becoming the second Indian to win back-to-back openers (1979 and 1980). His complete-game victory over the Yankees on the last day of the 1978 season forced the Yankees-Red Sox playoff. In 1979 he led the Indians with a career-high 16 wins. After going 2-13 in 1982, pitching with tendinitis in his right knee, he was traded to Milwaukee. /(ME)

Bozo Wakabayishi — Unk.-Unk. P 1936-53 Japan

An American born of Japanese parents, Wakabayishi attended college in Japan and was among the players recruited when the first Japanese professional league formed in 1936. His American catcher, Bucky Harris (who won the 1937 HR title with only six), was expelled from Japan for his nationality after the 1939 season, but Wakabayishi remained to win 240 games. /(MC)

Dick Wakefield — 1921-1985. OF 1941, 43-44, 46-50, 52 **Tigers**, Yankees, Giants 638 g, .293, 56 hr, 315 rbi

The 6'4", lefthanded-hitting Wakefield was paid a then-record $52,000 bonus to sign with the Tigers off the University of Michigan campus in 1941. He lived up to expectations—but only for a season and a half. As a rookie in 1943 he led the AL with 200 hits, 38 doubles, and 633 at bats; his .316 average was second only to Luke Appling's .328. When the season ended, he entered the Navy as an aviation cadet, but the program was soon discontinued, and he returned in mid-1944 to bat .355 in 78 games.

After naval duties forced Wakefield to miss the 1945 season, he came back to the Tigers in 1946 with his skills diminished, and with what some felt was a lackadaisical attitude. He missed part of the season with a broken arm. He was traded to the Yankees in December 1949 but balked at a cut in pay and was sent down and later released. He tried comebacks with the Indians and Giants, playing three games with New York in 1952 when Monte Irvin was permanently injured and Willie Mays was in the army. His father, Howard Wakefield, was a catcher with the Indians and Senators in 1905-07. /(CTA)

Rube Walberg [George Elvin] — 1896-1978. LHP 1923-37 Giants, **A's**, Red Sox 2644 ip, 155-141, 4.17. 20 wins: 31 *3 WS, 14 ip, 1-1, 1.93*

Walberg was a consistent, durable pitcher who spent over a decade with the Athletics. Yet he fell short of greatness, partly because he was wild, often walking more batters than he struck out. In his one 20-win season, 1931, he led the league with 291 innings pitched but worked just three innings in relief in the World Series. He started only one of the 18 WS games the A's played in 1929-31, losing it 5-0 to the Cardinals in 1930. He was a reliever and spot starter with the Red Sox from 1934 through 1937 and pitched his last game at age forty-one. /(NLM)

Bob Walk — 1956- . RHP 1980- Phillies, Braves, **Pirates** 1099 ip, 66-54, 3.93. *1 LCS, 1 ip, 0-0, 9.00. 1 WS, 7 ip, 1-0, 7.71*
☛ *All-Star—88.*

Journeyman Walk found his niche as elder statesman on a young Pittsburgh pitching staff. The fierce competitor's rookie season at Philadelphia (1980) included 11 wins, plus 1 as the starter in Game One of the World Series. Traded to the Braves, he bounced between Atlanta and Richmond (International League). Released in March 1984, he signed a Triple-A contract for Pittsburgh, led the Pacific Coast League in ERA in 1984, and earned a promotion, only to hurt his right elbow and miss the season's final two months. The native Californian led the Pacific Coast League in ERA and wins in 1985 and earned a trip back to the majors. /(ME)

Bill Walker — 1903-1966. LHP 1927-36 **Giants**, Cardinals 1490 ip, 98-77, 3.59. *1 WS, 6 ip, 0-2, 7.11*
☛ *Led League—era 29, 31.*

Walker was a stylish hurler who in 1929, his second full season, went 14-7 for the Giants with a league-leading 3.09 ERA. He led in ERA again in 1931 (2.26), going 17-9 with a league-high six shutouts. A native of East St. Louis, he was traded to the Cardinals in October 1932. He missed two months of the championship 1934 season but chipped in 12 wins. Pitching in relief in the 1934 World Series, he was the loser in Games Two and Four as the Cardinals defeated Detroit in seven. /(JK)

Curt Walker (Honey) — 1896-1955. OF 1919-30 Yankees, Giants, Phillies, **Reds** 1359 g, .304, 64 hr, 688 rbi

The lefthanded-hitting Walker batted better than .300 in six of his ten full major league seasons. In

1922 he reached a career-high .337, leading the Phillies in six offensive categories. He was speedy enough to stretch doubles into triples, hitting 117 lifetime and 2 in one inning with the Reds on July 22, 1926. He was called Honey because he hailed from Beeville, Texas, and became known as Judge Walker after being elected Justice of the Peace. /(JK)

Dixie Walker [Ewart Gladstone] — 1887–1965. RHP 1909–12 **Senators** 481 ip, 25–31, 3.52

A starter for the Senators, the elder Dixie Walker went 11–11 in 1910 and 8–13 in 1911 before arm problems caused his demotion to the minors. There he played the outfield, as did his brother Ernie and sons Harry and Dixie (Fred) did in the majors. /(JK)

Dixie Walker [Fred] (The People's Cherce) — 1910–1982. OF 1931, 33–49 Yankees, White Sox, Tigers, **Dodgers**, Pirates 1905 g, .306, 105 hr, 1023 rbi. *12 WS g, .222, 1 hr, 4 rbi*
☛ *Led League—ba 44. Led League—rbi 45. All-Star—43, 44, 46, 47.*

Walker spent all or parts of eight seasons in the American League before becoming The People's Cherce in Brooklyn. The lefthanded hitter was purchased by the Yankees off the Greenville (South Atlantic League) roster for a then-record $25,000 in 1930. Though he was highly regarded, he remained in their rich farm system until 1933. He suffered a severe setback when he tore some shoulder muscles, and in 1936 he was waived to the White Sox. He batted .302 and tied for the AL lead with 16 triples in 1937, yet was traded to Detroit. He continued to hit more than .300 but showed little power, and his shoulder problems persisted. After tearing up his knee in 1939, he was placed on waivers and was snatched up by Brooklyn GM Larry MacPhail.

Walker led the 1940 Dodgers in batting (.308) and doubles (37). The likable, 6'1" blond quickly became a favorite of the Brooklyn fans, especially for his heroics against the hated Giants; he batted .436 against New York in 1940. Nevertheless, manager Leo Durocher opened the 1941 campaign with the newly acquired Paul Waner in Walker's outfield spot. Brooklyn fans were outraged. The 38-year-old Waner had won the job in spring training but faded fast and was traded. Walker became part of an all-.300-hitting outfield (with Pete Reiser and Joe Medwick) that led Brooklyn to the 1941 NL pennant. For the next six years, he was a fixture in Brooklyn's right field. He led the NL with a .357

Dixie Walker as a coach

batting average in 1944 and won the 1945 RBI title with 124.

When Jackie Robinson broke the color line with Brooklyn in 1947, Walker, a native of Georgia, initially resisted the idea. But he was soon defending Robinson and giving him pointers. Following that pennant-winning season, in what turned out to be one of the best trades in Brooklyn history, Walker was sent to the Pirates in a six-player deal for pitcher Preacher Roe and third baseman Billy Cox. In 1948 Walker topped the .300 mark for the tenth time in 12 seasons, helping the Pirates to improve by 21 games, from last place to fourth. However, at age thirty-eight in 1949, he played in just 88 contests, led the NL with 13 pinch hits, and left the majors.

Walker managed in the minors for most of the 1950s, coached for the Cardinals, and coached and scouted for the Braves and the Los Angeles Dodgers. Dixie's brother, Harry Walker, was the 1947 NL batting champ. Their father, Ewart "Dixie" Walker, pitched for the 1909–12 Senators, and their uncle, Ernie Walker, played for the 1913–15 Browns. /(ME)

Duane Walker — 1957– . OF 1982–85, 88 **Reds**, Rangers, Cardinals 392 g, .229, 24 hr, 99 rbi

Walker hit .292 with 10 HR for the Reds in 1984, but he was a treacherous fielder and was traded to Texas with Jeff Russell for Buddy Bell in 1985. He was released by the Rangers after 1985 and again by Tucson (Pacific Coast League) in 1986 before signing with the Cardinals' Louisville (American Association) club, where he spent most of 1987–88. /(SCL)

Fleet Walker [Moses Fleetwood] — 1856–1924. C 1884 **Toledo (AA)** 42 g, .263, 0 hr

For sixty years, Fleet Walker was the answer to two trivia questions: who was the first black player in the majors, and who was the last? When the Toledo club, Northwestern League champion in 1883, was admitted to the American Association in 1884, it brought Walker, their regular catcher, into the league. He was a fair singles hitter whose .263 average that year was 23 points above the league average, a fine bare-handed catcher with a strong arm, and a fast and daring baserunner. He was popular with the fans, but not necessarily with his teammates. Toledo's ace pitcher, Tony Mullane, later said that Walker "was the best catcher I ever worked with, but I disliked a Negro and whenever I had to pitch to him I used to pitch anything I wanted without looking at his signals." As much as the quote indicates the problems Walker had to face, its first part is a tribute to his talent as a catcher: The team's other catcher (playing fewer games there than Walker) was star Deacon McGuire, who went on to catch 1,611 games in a 26-year major league career.

Walker, whose brother Welday played five games in the outfield for Toledo that year, was well received by fans in all the league cities, including Baltimore and Washington, except for two southern ones. He was hissed in Louisville, Kentucky, and a pseudonymous letter from Richmond, Virginia (which joined the league after the Washington franchise fell apart in mid-season), promised Toledo manager Charlie Morton that there would be a mob awaiting Walker if he played in a series scheduled there in October. However, Walker had his only major league season interrupted by a July injury (reported variously as a broken collarbone or a broken rib), played sparingly thereafter, and was released in September. Toledo folded following the season, and Walker played the next two seasons in weaker minor leagues. He joined Newark (International League) in 1887, forming, with star George Stovey, the first black battery in organized baseball.

That July 14, Chicago manager Cap Anson prevented the two stars from playing against his team in an exhibition and led league directors to ban blacks, although this was officially reversed. Newark folded after the season, and Walker spent the next two seasons in the International League with Syracuse, helping them to the championship in 1889, his last season.

Off the field, Walker was well educated, handsome, and gentlemanly. He attended Oberlin College for three years and the University of Michigan for one, despite the fact that Oberlin did not even have a baseball team until his final year there. He took classes ranging from Greek, Latin, German, and French, to civil engineering, zoology, astronomy, and chemistry, but never graduated. In 1908 his book *Our Home Colony* advocated black emigration to Africa as the best response to increasing racial intolerance. He also published a newspaper, *The Equator*. He was later tried and acquitted of second-degree murder charges when he was attacked by a convicted burglar and killed him with a knife in self-defense. /(SH)

Gee Walker [Gerald Holmes] — 1908–1981. OF 1931–45 **Tigers**, White Sox, Senators, Indians, Reds 1783 g, .294, 124 hr, 997 rbi. *1 WS, 6 g, .286, 1 rbi*

Gee and elder brother Hub came to the Tigers as rookie outfielders in 1931. While Hub did not stick, Gee—a fiery competitor and a clown -stayed and became a favorite in Detroit. He batted .300 or better in five of his first seven seasons. Though he stole as many as 30 bases a season, he could be a bungler on the basepaths, inattentive and overzealous. He once tried to steal a base while the batter was being given an intentional walk, and in another game he was caught off base twice in the same inning. During the 1934 World Series, he was picked off first while arguing with the Cardinal bench.

Walker reached career highs with 18 HR, 113 RBI, and a .335 average in 1937. Yet Tiger management, unappreciative of Walker's antics, traded him to the White Sox after the season. He continued to hit well for several years but was traded four more times. /(JK)

Greg Walker — 1959– . 1B-DH 1982– **White Sox** 839 g, .262, 113 hr, 442 rbi. *1 LCS, 2 g, .333*

When the Phillies left the 6'3", lefthanded-hitting Walker unprotected in the 1979 major league draft, the White Sox quickly claimed him. Winning Chicago's first base job in 1984, Walker batted .294. He played an AL-high 163 games in 1985, but his 1986 campaign was marred by wrist and hand injuries and seizures cut into his 1988 season. His 27 homers in 1987 were the most by a White Sox first baseman since Dick Allen's 32 in 1974. Commented Walker's former manager, Tony LaRussa, "Everybody sees his swing and knows it's great. But his toughness . . . that's something you don't appreciate until you're around him."/(RL)

Harry Walker (The Hat) — 1918– . OF 1940–43, 46–51, 55 **Cardinals**, Phillies, Cubs, Reds 807 g, .296, 10 hr, 214 rbi. *3 WS, 13 g, .278, 6 rbi.*
   Manager 1955, 65–72 Cardinals, Pirates, **Astros** 630–604, .511
☛ *Led League—ba 47. All-Star—47.*

The son of major league pitcher Ewart "Dixie" Walker and brother of 1944 NL batting champ Fred "Dixie" Walker, Harry is the only player to win a NL batting title playing for two teams in the same season (and the Walker brothers are the only major league siblings to each win a batting average crown). Harry was hitting .200 through May 3, 1947 when the Cardinals traded him to the Phillies. He pounded the ball for a .371 average the rest of the way to finish at .363. It was to be his only outstanding season.

   It was Walker who, in Game Seven of the 1946 WS, drove in Enos Slaughter from first base with the winning run to defeat the Red Sox. He was called Harry the Hat because, at the plate, he would adjust his cap after every pitch. As a result of his tugging, he went through 20 caps a season. He became a manager, taking over the Cardinals from Eddie Stanky for most of 1955 and pinch hitting nine times. He managed Pittsburgh from 1965 through mid-1967 (twice bringing them in third) and Houston from 1968 through late 1972. He continued in baseball as a batting coach./(JK)

Hub Walker [Harvey Willos] — 1906–1982. OF 1931, 35–37, 45 Tigers, **Reds** 297 g, .263, 5 hr, 60 rbi. *1 WS, 2 g, .500*

The brother of major leaguer Gee Walker, Hub was a lefthanded-hitting backup outfielder. He joined the Tigers late in 1945 after a seven-year absence from the majors which included military service from 1942 to 1944. Though Walker was technically ineligible for the World Series, Commissioner Happy Chandler waived the rules. Walker hit a pinch double in two WS at-bats as the Tigers became World Champions./(NLM)

Jerry Walker — 1939– . RHP 1957–64 **Orioles**, A's, Indians 747 ip, 37–44, 4.36
☛ *All-Star—59.*

Walker debuted with the Orioles in 1957 as an 18-year-old bonus baby. In 1959 he went 11–10, won a 16-inning shutout over Chicago, and became the youngest pitcher to start or win an All-Star game. His .368 batting average in 1960 was tops among ML pitchers. With the Indians in 1963 he saved Early Wynn's 300th career victory. He was a manager and scout in the Yankee organization and a ML coach with the Yankees and Astros./(RTM)

Luke Walker — 1943– . LHP 1965–66, 68–74 **Pirates**, Tigers 826 ip, 45–47, 3.64. *2 LCS, 8 ip, 0–1, 3.38. 1 WS, 0.2 ip, 0–0, 40.50*

Walker's best season came in 1970, when he went 15–6, mostly as a starter (3–1, three saves in relief); his 3.04 ERA, .714 winning percentage, and 7.1 hits per nine innings all ranked third in the NL. He took a tough loss in Game Two of the LCS, giving up just one earned run to the Reds in seven innings. He fell off in 1971, going 10–8 with a 3.54 ERA for the World Champion Pirates but almost had a no-hitter against the Dodgers; he gave up a ninth-inning HR to Joe Ferguson. In the World Series, he had a disastrous start in Game Four (the first night game in Series history), retiring only two batters and giving up three runs, but the Pirates won 4–3. In 1972 Walker was bothered by a stiff back and finished 4–6 with a 3.40 ERA in limited use. He declined further in 1973 (7–12) and was sold to the Tigers for his last season.

   Walker was a notoriously bad batter who went without a hit in 1969 (32 at-bats) and was 0-for-39 in 1972 before finally getting a hit, and a rousing ovation, in July. His lifetime average of .059 is the eighth worst of all time for a pitcher (100-plus at-bats)./(SH)

Roy Walker (Dixie) — 1893–1962. RHP 1912, 15, 17–18, 21–22 Indians, Cubs, **Cardinals** 387 ip, 17–27, 3.98

Walker was unrelated to either of the better-known Dixie Walkers. He had only one full ML season in six tries over 11 years. In 1921, he was 11–12 for the Cardinals./(BC)

Rube Walker [Albert Bluford] — 1926– . C 1948–58 Cubs, **Dodgers** 608 g, .227, 35 hr, 192 rbi. *1 WS, 2 g, .000*

Walker was with the Dodgers for their 1951 NL playoff with the Giants, having been traded by the

Cubs that June. Dodger catcher Roy Campanella had injured his thigh, and despite his assertions he could play, manager Charley Dressen had Walker replace him for the second playoff game. Walker caught Clem Labine's shutout and hit a two-run homer. He also caught the final game and was behind the plate when pitcher Ralph Branca served up Bobby Thomson's famed "Shot Heard 'Round the World."

The soft-spoken Walker managed in the minors and became a low-key, patient pitching coach. After stints with the Dodgers and Senators, he coached Met pitchers for 14 years, beginning in 1968. When Joe Torre was fired as New York's manager in 1981, Walker accompanied him to Atlanta. /(NLM)

Tilly Walker [Clarence William] — 1887-1959. OF 1911-23 Senators, Browns, Red Sox, **A's** 1418 g, .281, 118 hr, 679 rbi. *1 WS, 3 g, .273, 1 rbi*
☛ *Led League—hr 18.*

Walker was a powerful hitter and a strong-armed outfielder—one of the dead-ball era's best. He led the AL in assists four times. Playing for the Athletics in 1918, he hit 11 HR to share the league lead with Babe Ruth. He continued as one of the game's leading home run hitters through 1922, when he hit a career-high 37. But in 1923 Athletics manager Connie Mack, stating that long-ball hitting was a fad, announced that he would stress speed and defense in the upcoming season. The Shibe Park fences were moved out, cutting home runs by 63%, and Walker was benched. He then spent six years in the minors. He was an umpire in the Appalachian League in 1938-39 and a manager in 1940. /(LRD)

Tom Walker [Robert Thomas] — 1881-1944. RHP 1902, 04-05 A's, **Reds** 370 ip, 24-16, 2.70

Walker went 15-8 as a rookie for the 1904 Reds but soon became involved in confusion over his contract, which he asked the National Commission to untangle. After 1905 he never again pitched in the majors—some believe because he had the temerity to make the appeal. /(JK)

Tom Walker — 1948- . RHP 1972-77 **Expos**, Tigers, Cardinals, Angels 414 ip, 18-23, 3.87

The highlight of Walker's career came in the minors: a 15-inning 1-0 no-hit victory, the longest ever in pro ball, for Dallas-Fort Worth (Texas League) against Albuquerque on August 4, 1971. His only winning season in the majors came when he went 7-5 with four saves for the Expos in 1973. /(SH)

Jim Walkup [James Elton] — 1909- . RHP 1934-39 **Browns**, Tigers 462 ip, 16-38, 6.74

During a 1938 game, Walkup argued so heatedly when Browns manager Gabby Street came to the mound to take him out that he was fined $100 and suspended for seven days. His record at the time was 0-9. A cousin, James Huey Walkup, pitched for the Tigers in 1927. /(NLM)

Murray Wall (Tex) — 1926-1971. RHP 1950, 57-59 Braves, **Red Sox**, Senators 193 ip, 13-14, 4.20

Wall had his busiest season in 1958, winning eight games and saving ten for the Red Sox. Sent to Washington in a June 11, 1959 trade for Dick Hyde, Wall was returned to Boston after one game because Hyde had a sore arm and was unable to pitch. /(RTM)

Bobby Wallace [Roderick John] (Rhody) — 1873-1960. SS-3B-RHP-2B-OF 1894-1918 Cleveland (NL), Cardinals, **Browns** 2386 g, .267, 35 hr, 1121 rbi; 402 ip, 24-22, 3.89.
 Manager 1911-12, 37 **Browns**, Reds 62-154, .287.
 Umpire AL 1915-16
☛ *Hall of Fame—1953.*

Wallace's association with baseball spanned more than 60 years. He came to the major leagues as a pitcher with the Cleveland Spiders in 1894. Though he won ten games and hurled two shutouts in 1896, he moved to third base in 1897. With the Cardinals in 1899, he shifted to shortstop, remaining a regular at that position for 14 years.

Though known primarily for his fielding skills, Wallace batted better than .300 in 1897, 1899, and 1901 and finished second in the NL with a career-high 12 home runs in 1899. In 1897 and 1899 he drove in more than 100 runs. He became a highly coveted player. In 1902, the Browns lured him away from the Cardinals with a five-year, no-trade contract worth more than $32,000—a fortune at the time. That June 10, he set a still-standing AL record with 17 chances accepted at shortstop in a nine-inning game. He often led the league in one fielding category or another and stands ninth among shortstops in career chances, putouts, and assists. Though his hitting dropped off in the AL, he continued to show good speed, collecting 153 career triples and stealing 201 bases.

As his career wound down, Wallace's time on the diamond was curtailed by a broken hand in 1912 and serious burns in 1914, and was interrupted by a stint as an AL umpire from June 1915 until August

Bobby Wallace with the Browns

1916. He finished his ML playing days with the Cardinals in 1918 at age forty-four. He managed in the minors, coached briefly for Cincinnati, and scouted for them for 33 years until his death. He compiled the worst record in history for a manager with 200 or more ML games—62–154—with the Browns in 1911–12 and the Reds in September 1937. He was elected to the Hall of Fame by the Veterans Committee in 1953. /(FJO)

Mike Wallace — 1951– . LHP 1973–77 Phillies, Yankees, **Cardinals**, Rangers 181 ip, 11–3, 3.94

Wallace showed promise in 1974, when he went 7–0 for the Phillies and the Yankees, but he was never effective again. He pitched a seven-inning no-hitter for Reading (Eastern League) in 1971. /(JFC)

Tim Wallach — 1957– . 3B 1980– **Expos** 1305 g, .263, 161 hr, 675 rbi. *1 LCS, 1 g, .000*
☛ *All-Star—84–85, 87, 89. Gold Glove—85, 88.*

Wallach became Montreal's third baseman when Larry Parrish was traded to Texas. Wallach tied for the most RBI by a third baseman in 1982 and set Expos' sophomore records in homers (28) and RBI

(97). He led NL third basemen in putouts three straight years (1983–85) and assists, total chances, and double plays in 1984 and 1985. The Gold Glove fielder had a career batting season in 1987. Taking over the cleanup spot from injured Hubie Brooks, Wallach set a club record with 123 RBI and led the NL with 42 doubles. He is among Montreal's all-time leaders in homers, doubles, and RBI. /(ME)

Jack Wallaesa — 1919–1986. SS-OF 1940, 42, 46–48 A's, **White Sox** 219 g, .205, 15 hr, 61 rbi

At 6′3″, Wallaesa was one of the tallest shortstops ever. He led the International League with 45 home runs in 1941 but then lost almost four years to WWII. Despite batting lessons from Babe Ruth and Lefty O'Doul, only once in five ML trials did he hit more than .200. /(NLM)

Denny Walling — 1954– . 3B-OF-1B 1975– A's, **Astros**, Cardinals 1166 g, .276, 48 hr, 359 rbi. *2 LCS, 8 g, .143, 4 rbi*

A career platoon player, Walling reached Houston's all-time lists in games played, batting average, and slugging average despite never batting as many 400 times in a season. He also became Houston's all-time leader in pinch hits. A consensus All-American and Atlantic Coast Conference Player of the Year at Clemson, Walling went directly from college to Oakland in 1975. He was traded to Houston for Willie Crawford and cash in 1977, having played just nine games with the A's. A versatile, lefthanded hitter and righthanded thrower, Walling was initially used primarily at first base and in the outfield, but began playing most at third base in 1984, platooning with Phil Garner. Walling led the Astros (350 or more at-bats) with a .312 batting average and set career highs in almost every offensive category. His home run was the winning blow in Mike Scott's 1986 pennant-clinching no-hitter. A tough batter to strike out, Walling was one of a handful of NL players to spend ten straight years with one club from 1978 to 1987. /(ME)

Joe Wallis — 1952– . OF 1975–79 **Cubs**, A's 329 g, .244, 16 hr, 68 rbi

Shortly after his major league debut, the switch-hitting Wallis broke up a Tom Seaver no-hit bid with a two-out, two-strike, ninth-inning single (9/24/75). A fine defensive centerfielder, he missed most of 1977 with a shoulder injury and was traded by the Cubs to Oakland in 1978. /(DAS)

Douglas Wallop — Unk.- . *Writer.*

Wallop was the author of ten novels and *Baseball: An Informal History.* But his most famous book is *The Year the Yankees Lost the Pennant* (1954), a humorous update of the Faust legend in which the devil apparently helps the Washington Senators in the AL race. At the last moment, of course, the devil turns out to be a secret Yankee fan who has set up the Senators for a heartbreaking near-miss, and the hero must choose between saving his soul or winning the pennant for Washington. The book was turned into the long-running Broadway musical and movie, *Damn Yankees.* /(NLM)

Lee Walls (Captain Midnight) — 1933- . OF-3B-1B
1952, 56–64 Pirates, **Cubs**, Reds, Phillies, Dodgers 902 g, .262, 66 hr, 284 rbi

Traded from Pittsburgh to Chicago in 1957 after his first full season, Walls struggled at times but hit for the cycle on July 2. In 1958 he hit .304 with 24 HR and 72 RBI, his best season, and hit three HR in a game on August 24. After a disappointing season in 1959, he shuffled from team to team. Walls was a batboy for the Pacific Coast League Padres in the mid-1940s. Cubs fans nicknamed him Captain Midnight because of his oversized, wire-rimmed glasses. /(DB)

Christy Walsh — 1871–1955. *Writer.*

Walsh was a pioneer of sports licensing. His most frequent device was getting sports stars to put their names on ghostwritten articles in newspapers and magazines. Many a WS game was "analyzed" by a star who was nowhere near the scene of action. A 1911 graduate of St. Vincent's College in Los Angeles, Walsh first worked for the Los Angeles *Express.* In 1921, he started his own syndicate, creating a major industry for stars like Ruth, Gehrig, Rockne, and others. Walsh was sports director for the 1939–40 New York World's Fair. /(NLM)

Ed Walsh [Edward Augustine] (Big Ed) — 1881–1959.
RHP 1904–17 **White Sox**, Braves 2964 ip, 195–126, 1.82. 20 wins: 07, 08, 11, 12 *1 WS, 15 ip, 2–0, 1.80.*
  Umpire AL 1922
☛ *Led League—w 08. Led League—k 08, 11. Led League—era 07, 10. Hall of Fame—1946.*

No American League pitcher ever worked as many innings as Big Ed Walsh did in 1908. The 6'1" spitballer maintained that his main pitch was easy on his arm, allowing him to hurl 464 innings on his way to a 40-win season. No major league pitcher has won as many games since.

Ed Walsh with the Braves

Before playing pro baseball, Walsh worked in a Plains, Pennsylvania, coal mine, driving a mule team. He played two minor league seasons before being drafted from Newark (Eastern League) by Chicago's Charles Comiskey, who acted on a tip from the Red Sox. Walsh joined the White Sox in 1904. Manager Fielder Jones had him room with Elmer Stricklett, who was instructed to teach Walsh the intricacies of the spitter. With the new pitch added to his repertoire, Walsh shut out Washington on two hits that May 19.

It took time for Walsh to master the spitter; he won just six games in 1904, and eight in 1905. But in 1906, he went 17–13 (1.88) for the World Champion Hitless Wonders, leading the league with ten shutouts. In the World Series, he blanked the Cubs on two hits while striking out 12 in Game Three and was the winner in Game Five.

Walsh led the AL with a 1.60 ERA in 1907, going 24–18. In his great, 1908 season, the Iron Man pitched virtually every other day, appearing 17 times in relief and working a total of 66 games. He went 40–15, winning 45.5% of the White Sox' 88 games—the highest percentage of an AL team's wins in history. For the second straight year, he led the league in games, starts, complete games, innings pitched, and saves. He also led in hits allowed and strikeouts. On October 2, during the last days of a pressure-packed, three-way pennant race, he gave up only four Cleveland hits, only to lose 1–0 to Addie Joss and his perfect game.

Walsh's arm began to suffer from overwork. He threw only half as many innings in 1909 as he had in 1908. Yet he retained his effectiveness, shutting out his opponents in 8 of his 15 wins and recording a 1.41 ERA. He rebounded to again lead the AL in appearances in 1910–12, and in innings pitched in 1911–12. His 1.27 ERA in 1910 was the league's and his best. On August 27, 1911, he threw his only nine-inning no-hitter, defeating Boston 5–0. (On May 26, 1907 he had no-hit the Highlanders in a five-inning game.)

After winning 27 games in both 1911 and 1912, Walsh pitched less than 100 innings in 1913. By 1916 his arm was dead. He asked Comiskey for a year off but was released. He made a comeback attempt with the Braves in 1917 but was let go after 18 innings. He managed and pitched some in the Eastern League in 1920 and spent 1922 as an American League umpire. Umpiring was clearly not his forte; he returned to the White Sox as a coach for much of the remainder of the decade. He was coaching when his son, Ed Walsh, also a pitcher, broke in with Chicago. Walsh was elected to the Hall of Fame by the Committee on Baseball Veterans in 1946. /(RL)

Ed Walsh [Edward Arthur] — 1905–1937. RHP 1928–30, 32 **White Sox** 331 ip, 11–24, 5.57

As a publicity stunt, on September 11, 1932 Chicago's Charles Comiskey advertised the battery of Ed Walsh and Billy Sullivan, sons of the star battery of the 1906 World Champion White Sox. The younger Walsh was the victim of rheumatic fever, which robbed him of the strength to capitalize on his inherited talent. However, while pitching for Oakland (Pacific Coast League) on July 26, 1933, he was strong enough to hang an 0–5 collar on Joe DiMaggio, snapping his 61-game hitting streak. /(CG)

Jimmy Walsh — 1885–1962. OF 1912–17 **A's**, Yankees, Red Sox 536 g, .231, 6 hr, 150 rbi. *2 WS, 4 g, .222, 1 rbi*

Born in Ireland, fleet-footed Jimmy Walsh once teamed with Eddie Collins to work two double-squeeze plays in one game. As Collins placed bunts beyond pitcher Walter Johnson, Walsh came in from second on the heels of the A's runner from third. /(JK)

Jimmy Walsh [Michael Timothy] (Runt) — 1886–1947. 3B-2B-OF 1910–15 **Phillies**, Baltimore (FL), St. Louis (FL) 502 g, .285, 25 hr, 212 rbi

Walsh was just a utility man until the Baltimore Terrapins of the Federal League made him their regular third baseman in 1914. He hit .308 with 10 HR (tied for seventh in the FL) and 65 RBI in 428 at-bats. He followed it up with a .294 average and nine HR (fifth in the league) in 1915 but wasn't picked up by any team after the FL fell apart. /(WOR)

Junior Walsh [James Gerald] — 1919– . RHP 1946, 48–51 Pirates 193 ip, 4–10, 5.88

Walsh's busiest year was his last, 1951, when he pitched 73 innings, mostly in relief, and recorded a 6.87 ERA. In each year from 1948 through 1951, he won exactly one game for the Pirates. /(RTM)

Gene Walter — 1960– . LHP 1985–88 **Padres**, Mets, Mariners 183 ip, 4–7, 3.74

Walter appeared in 57 games as a middle-reliever for the Padres in 1986, then was part of the eight-player trade that sent Kevin McReynolds to the Mets before the 1987 season. The Mets traded Walter to the Mariners for Edwin Nunez in mid-1988, and he had a 5.13 ERA in 16 games with Seattle before being demoted to Calgary (Pacific Coast League). /(SCL)

Bucky Walters [William Henry] — 1909– . RHP-3B 1931–48, 50 Braves, Red Sox, Phillies, **Reds** 3105 ip, 198–160, 3.30; 715 g, .243, 23 hr, 234 rbi. 20 wins: 39–40, 44 *2 WS, 29 ip, 2–2, 2.79.*
Manager 1948–49 **Reds** 81–123, .397
☛ *Most Valuable Player—39. Led League—w 39–40, 44. Led League—k 39. Led League—era 39–40. All-Star—37, 39–42, 44.*

Walters broke into pro baseball as a pitcher/third baseman in 1929 but played only the infield from 1930 through 1933. He failed in trials with the Braves in 1931–32 but batted .376 in the Pacific Coast League in 1933 to earn a shot as a third baseman with the Red Sox in 1933. It wasn't until he was sold to the Phillies in 1934 that Walters

Bucky Walters with the Braves

reverted to pitching at the suggestion of manager Jimmie Wilson, a veteran catcher.

The Phillies of the 1930s were losing ballclubs, and in 1936 Walters was the National League's biggest loser, going 11–21. He led the league with 34 starts in 1937, winning 14, and was traded to the Reds in 1938. The sidearming flamethrower, who relied almost exclusively on a sinking fastball, then helped Cincinnati to two straight pennants, going 27–11 in 1939 and 22–10 in 1940. In each season he led the NL in wins, ERA, complete games, and innings pitched. In 1939 he tied Claude Passeau for the league lead with 137 strikeouts. For his performance in 1939, he was named the NL's Most Valua-ble Player, the second of three straight Reds to win the award.

When the Yankees swept Cincinnati in four games in the 1939 World Series, Walters started and lost Game Two and was the loser in relief of the final game, the victim of four Cincinnati errors. In the 1940 WS, he twice defeated the Tigers, throwing a three-hitter in Game Two and a five-hit shutout in Game Six.

Walters had one more superb season in 1944, winning a league-high 23 games while losing only 8, and compiling a career-best 2.40 ERA.

Walters replaced John Neun as Cincinnati's manager during the 1948 season and was relieved by Luke Sewell late in 1949 with the team in seventh place. He coached for the Braves and Giants through 1957. /(JCA)

Ken Walters — 1933– . OF 1960–61, 63 **Phillies**, Reds 259 g, .231, 11 hr, 58 rbi

At Jamestown in 1953, Walters hit .320 and drove in 128 runs. Playing for the Phillies on May 16, 1960, he became the 14th outfielder in ML history to record two assists in one inning. /(RTM)

Roxy Walters [Alfred John] — 1892–1956. C 1915–25 Yankees, **Red Sox**, **Indians** 498 g, .222, 0 hr, 115 rbi

Walters hit below .200 four times and spent most of his career as a strong-armed backup catcher. In the only season he caught more than 65 games, he led AL catchers in total chances per game on the strength of his 94 assists in just 85 games. As a pitcher/outfielder he topped the 1928 Utah-Idaho League with a 15–3 record and fell three points short of the batting title, hitting .382. /(NLM)

Danny Walton (Mickey) — 1947– . OF-DH-1B 1968–71, 73, 75–77, 80 Astros, **Pilots/Brewers**, Yankees, Twins, Dodgers, Rangers 297 g, .223, 28 hr, 107 rbi

Walton was *TSN* Minor League Player of the Year in 1969 when he hit .332 and led the American Association with 25 HR and 119 RBI; that August 31 the Astros traded him with Sandy Valdespino to the Seattle Pilots for Tommy Davis. In the first half of 1970 Walton was among the AL leaders in HR and RBI, but he was slowed down by a knee operation in the latter part of the season. He finished with a .257 batting average, 17 HR, and 66 RBI in 397 at-bats, but struck out 126 times. He was never again a regular. He tried Japanese baseball in 1978, but hit .215 for Taiyo. /(JFC)

Jerome Walton — 1965- . OF 1989- **Cubs** 116 g, .293, 5 hr, 46 rbi. *1 LCS, 5 g, .364, 2 rbi*
☛ *Rookie of the Year—89.*

Walton and fellow rookie outfielder Dwight Smith were vital components in the Cubs' surprising 1989 division title. Using an unusually wide open stance and pivoting at the pitch, he resembles Brian Downing at the plate, but is a line-drive hitting speedster with relatively little power. He won the NL Rookie of the Year award despite spending the middle of the season on the DL./(SFS)

Bill Wambsganss (Wamby) — 1894–1985. 2B-SS-3B 1914–26 **Indians**, Red Sox, A's 1492 g, .259, 7 hr, 519 rbi. *1 WS, 7 g, .154, 1 rbi*

Wamby was the Indians' regular second baseman for much of 1915 through 1923. The slick-fielding infielder gained fame by making the only post-

Bill Wambsganss

Lloyd Waner

season unassisted triple play in Game Five of the 1920 World Series. In the fifth inning, Wambsganss stabbed a line drive off the bat of Brooklyn pitcher Clarence Mitchell, stepped on second to double up Pete Kilduff, and tagged Otto Miller, the runner from first, who thought the ball had gone through for a hit./(JK)

Lloyd Waner (Little Poison) — 1906–1982. OF 1927–42, 44–45 **Pirates**, Braves, Reds, Phillies, Dodgers 1992 g, .316, 28 hr, 598 rbi. *1 WS, 4 g, .400*
☛ *All-Star—38. Hall of Fame—1967.*

The younger half of one of baseball's most famous brother combinations, Lloyd Waner joined the Pirates in 1927 and settled in centerfield, next to brother Paul in right. Paul was known as Big Poison and Lloyd as Little Poison. While Paul captured most of the headlines by winning the 1927 National League batting crown (.380), Lloyd finished third (.355). He set a ML rookie record with 223 hits—198 of them singles, setting the modern ML record. His 133 runs scored led the league. The Waners led Pittsburgh to the 1927 NL pennant;

Lloyd had six hits in 15 at-bats in his first and only World Series, which the Yankees took in four games.

The 5′9″ 150-lb Waner was a lefthanded line-drive hitter. He collected more than 200 hits in each of his first three seasons and led the NL in at-bats in 1928 and 1929 and in triples in 1929. Coming off a .353 season, he missed most of 1930 due to appendicitis but returned with a vengeance in 1931, leading the NL with 214 hits and 681 at-bats (.314). He batted .309 or better in 10 of his 13 seasons as a Pirate regular.

Waner was also an accomplished centerfielder. His arm was not outstanding, but he led the league in putouts four times, using his excellent speed to cover the spacious Forbes Field outfield.

Waner retired after playing 101 games for the Phillies in 1942, but in 1944 he had a change of heart and returned to the Dodgers, to whom he had been traded during spring training of 1943. Released by the Dodgers on June 14, 1944, he signed with the Pirates the next day and remained with them, mostly as a little-used pinch hitter, through 1945. He scouted for Pittsburgh until 1949 and for the Orioles in 1955. The Committee on Baseball Veterans elected him to the Hall of Fame in 1967. /(AL)

Paul Waner (Big Poison) — 1903–1965. OF 1926–45 **Pirates**, Dodgers, Braves, Yankees 2549 g, .333, 112 hr, 1309 rbi. *1 WS, 4 g, .333, 3 rbi*
☛ *Most Valuable Player—27. Led League—ba 27, 34, 36. Led League—rbi 27. All-Star—33–35, 37.*

Paul Waner

Always a threat to break up a ball game but never a party, Waner had the sharpest bloodshot eyes in baseball. He hit doubles and triples during games and drank them after. Nonetheless, he amassed 3,152 hits with good power. One year he announced he was on the wagon, but when his batting average hovered around .250, his manager personally shepherded him to his nearest watering hole. Within a few weeks, he was back over .300.

Waner's merchant father wanted him to be a teacher, but he dropped out of college to join San Francisco (Pacific Coast League), where he compiled batting averages of .369, .356, and .401. In 1926 the Pirates purchased his contract in a $100,000 deal ($40,000 for Waner, $60,000 for second baseman Hal Rhyne). Paul broke into the NL with a .336 batting average and led in triples (22). The next year, he was joined by his brother Lloyd in the Pirate outfield. Together they paced Pittsburgh to the 1927 pennant. Right fielder Paul led the NL in hitting (.380), base hits (237), triples (17), and RBI (131) and was named NL MVP; centerfielder Lloyd hit

.355 and led the league in runs scored (133). Between them, the Waners totaled 460 hits.

They starred for the Pirates throughout the 1930s, continuing their yearly assault on pitchers. Paul led the league in hitting again in 1934 (.362) and 1936 (.373). One day a frustrated Brooklyn fan complained: "Them Waners! It's always the little poison on thoid and the big poison on foist!" From then on Paul and Lloyd were Big Poison and Little Poison. Both were speedy outfielders, and Paul possessed perhaps the strongest arm seen in a Pittsburgh outfield until Roberto Clemente arrived.

After the Pirates released him, Paul played into WWII with the Braves and Dodgers, pursuing 3,000 hits. In 1942 the Braves visited Forbes Field with Waner at 2,999. The shortstop knocked down a drive but Paul beat it out. It might have been a hit, but Paul quickly and openly signaled he didn't want a tainted 3,000th. The scorer obliged by charging the shortstop with an error. On June 19, 1942 he lined the ball off Forbes's right-field wall to become the sixth player ever to reach 3,000 hits.

Waner found steady employment as a hitting coach after his retirement as a player, but his distaste for discipline made him an inappropriate candidate for managing. /(JK)

Paul Wanninger (Pee Wee) — 1902–1981. SS 1925, 27 **Yankees**, Red Sox, Reds 163 g, .234, 1 hr, 31 rbi

Pee Wee was jumped from Class C ball to the staggering, seventh-place Yankees of 1925 as a replacement for fading Everett Scott. His best was none too good, but he is noteworthy as the player for whom Lou Gehrig pinch hit in the first of his 2,130 consecutive games played. /(ADS)

Aaron Ward — 1896–1961. 2B-3B-SS 1917–28 **Yankees**, White Sox, Indians 1059 g, .268, 50 hr, 446 rbi. *3 WS, 19 g, .286, 3 hr, 9 rbi*

Ward was a dependable fielder and a solid hitter for the Yankee pennant winners of 1921, 1922, and 1923. When the next string of pennants began, in 1926, he lost the second base job to Tony Lazzeri and was traded to the White Sox in 1927. /(JK)

Arch Ward — 1901–1956. *Writer.*

As sports editor of the Chicago *Tribune*, Ward was asked to come up with a sports event in connection with the 1933 World's Fair. He knew that July 6 was an open date for both MLs and suggested an all-star game. AL president Will Harridge supported the idea, but some owners openly opposed it. The *Tribune* guaranteed expenses, with any profits to go to the Professional Ball Players of America, a charitable organization. It was expected to be a one-time event but has become an annual institution.

The following year Ward created the College All-Star Game, in which graduated college stars from the previous season opposed the reigning NFL championship team.

A graduate of Notre Dame, Ward was that school's first sports publicity director, in 1920. He was sports editor of the Rockford *Star*, 1921–25, when he joined the *Tribune*, where he served as sports editor and columnist for 25 years. His column was called "In the Wake of the News." Ward's books include *The New Chicago White Sox, Frank Leahy and the Fighting Irish*, and *The Green Bay Packers*. /(NLM)

Chuck Ward — 1894–1969. SS-3B 1917–22 Pirates, **Dodgers** 236 g, .228, 0 hr, 72 rbi

Ward had the impossible task of replacing Hall of Famer Honus Wagner as Pirate shortstop when Wagner stepped down in 1917. In 1918 he left hostile Pittsburgh fans behind to serve in WWI France. There he read in the Paris edition of *The New York Herald Tribune* that he had been traded to the Dodgers, for whom he became a utility infielder upon his return. /(JK)

Duane Ward — 1964– . RHP 1986– Braves, **Blue Jays** 256 ip, 14–15, 4.01. *1 LCS, 4 ip, 0–0, 7.36*

Ward shared stopper duties with Tom Henke in the Blue Jays bullpen in 1988 and 1989, and picked up wins as a middle reliever (9–3 in 1988). A wild, hard thrower, he was the Braves' first-round pick in the June 1982 draft and was traded for Doyle Alexander in July 1986. /(SFS)

Gary Ward — 1953– . OF 1979– **Twins**, Rangers, Yankees, Tigers 1179 g, .277, 121 hr, 551 rbi
☛ *All-Star—83, 85.*

Eight seasons in the Minnesota farm system paid off for Gary Ward when he was named AL Rookie of the Year by *Baseball Digest* in 1981 and followed as Twins Player of the Year and Most Improved Player in 1982. In 1983 he led all outfielders with 24 assists, the most for an AL outfielder since 1944. He started slowly with Texas in 1984 but came on to set a club record with seven triples and a personal high with 97 runs scored. He led the Rangers in batting in 1985 and 1986, then signed with the Yankees as a free agent. A good clutch hitter and best when hitting to all fields, Ward had a great first half in 1987 but slumped badly upon trying to pull everything. /(ME)

John Montgomery Ward (Monte) — 1860–1925. SS-2B-P-OF 1878–94 Providence (NL), **Giants**, Brooklyn (PL), Dodgers 1825 g, .278, 26 hr, 867 rbi; 2461 ip, 161–101, 2.10.
Manager 1884, 90–94 Giants, Brooklyn (PL), **Dodgers** 394–307, .562
☛ *Led League—w 79. Led League—era 78.*

Monte Ward is remembered for his integrity, but he was also a talented player. As a pitcher for Providence, he won 47 games in 1879 and 40 the next year, including the second perfect game in NL history.

When his arm gave out he switched to shortstop and helped the New York Giants win pennants in

John Montgomery Ward with the Giants

1888–89. He was a top basestealer and solid hitter. When he wasn't winning games with his skills on the field, he was planning the strategy as team captain and manager. His instinct for administration and his magnetic personality made him a natural leader.

At the time, the reserve rule, binding a player to a team by self-renewing contracts, was the main source of friction between the owners and players. Ward, assisted by Ned Hanlon, organized the Brotherhood of National League Players and they succeeded in negotiating a compromise with the league: The reserve clause could not be used to bind a player while his salary was being cut. It worked for a year.

Then, while Ward and most of the Brotherhood leaders were on a world tour in 1888, playing as all-stars against the Chicago team in exhibition games arranged by A.G. Spalding, the National League owners met. They adopted a classification system grading the players and established a fixed scale of salaries. The most a player could make, regardless of ability or the team's success, was $2,500 a season.

When Ward and the others learned the league had discarded its agreement with the Brotherhood, they were given no opportunity to appeal. Denied a meeting until the 1889 season was over, Ward and others lined up financial backing for a new league, to be called the Players' League, which the ballplayers would control.

The new league lasted one season, 1890. Ward managed and played for the Brooklyn entry and other teams went into head-on competition with the established franchises. The competition created a financial disaster for both leagues.

The more stable National League won out and Ward joined the new Brooklyn team of the reorganized National League. That team won the pennant in its first season. The next year Ward organized an early all-star game, raising nearly $3,000 for the widow of teammate Hub Collins.

Monte Ward joined Jim Mutrie to fashion the New York team into a strong entry in 1893 and again in 1894, when they defeated Baltimore to win the Temple Cup for the postseason championship. After that season, Ward left baseball to enter a profitable law career.

His concern for ballplayers and loathing for imperious management continued. When the very unpopular Andrew Freedman, who then owned the Giants, discharged Fred Pfeffer, a veteran player, as "a played out old stiff," Ward took the case to court and won Pfeffer his salary. The Giants' owner paid the court costs, appealed the case, and lost again. When Freedman's next legal tangle was a libel suit against the New York *Sun*, the newspaper retained Ward, and Freedman withdrew his suit. As a lawyer, Ward was described as "shrewd, quick-witted and humorous; smiling and sarcastic."

Ward returned to baseball twice. He was president of the Boston Braves in 1911, and when the Federal League arose to challenge the major leagues in 1914, he joined their cause. He became business manager for the Brooklyn Tip Tops, the team backed by the Ward brothers and their baking company. Ward, unrelated to his new associates, became a spokesman for the league. Disappointed with the objectives of the owners and feeling the players were merely pawns in an attempt to force the granting of franchises in the established leagues, he later withdrew.

Ward's legal practice in New York City flourished and he almost became the president of the National League, lacking one vote for confirmation. Too many old enemies still remained among the owners. /(JK)

Pete Ward — 1939- . 3B-OF-1B 1962–70 Orioles, **White Sox**, Yankees 973 g, .254, 98 hr, 427 rbi

Dean Chance once called the dumpy, rumpled Ward the league's toughest clutch hitter. In the 1960s, he was as close as the White Sox came to having a consistent power threat in spacious Comiskey Park. The son of NHL star Jimmy Ward, he was acquired as a throw-in (at the insistence of White Sox coach Charlie Metro, Ward's first minor league manager) in the blockbuster deal that brought Ron Hansen, Dave Nicholson, and Hoyt Wilhelm from the Orioles in return for Luis Aparicio and Al Smith. Placed at third base to replace Smith, he showed good range but led AL third basemen with 38 errors, most of them attributable to his strong but scattershot throwing. But White Sox pitchers didn't complain; he beat Detroit with a seventh-inning HR on Opening Day, the start of an 18-game hitting streak. For the season Ward hit .295, fifth in the AL, with 22 HR, 84 RBI, and 80 runs, and he finished second in the AL in total bases (289), hits (177), and doubles (34). *TSN* named him AL Rookie of the Year.

Lefthanded-hitting Ward used a strange batting stance, crouching with his rear foot pointed straight at the plate and his front foot pointed at the pitcher, and he had a big uppercut. Ward himself observed, "I got a real silly stance. Fundamentally I got a bad swing." He had career highs of 23 HR (including three grand slams) and 94 RBI in 1964 and cut his errors in half (19), but in 1965 he was bothered by recurring muscle spasms in his neck (the result of a minor auto accident in the off-season). He dropped off to 10 HR, 57 RBI, and a .247 average. A back injury in 1966 cut even deeper into both his playing time and his production (84 games, .219, 3 HR) and

forced a move into the outfield. He rebounded somewhat in 1967 with 18 HR and 62 RBI in 467 at-bats, playing outfield, first base, and third, but he hit only .233 and struck out a career-high 109 times.

The White Sox lineup was getting weak in the late 1960s (Ward's 18 HR in 1967 led the team, with Tommie Agee at 14 and Tom McCraw at 11 the only others in double figures), and Ward saw fewer good pitches; he walked 61 times in 1967 and 76 times in 1968, his last decent season (15 HR, .216). By 1969 he was a utility man, but he did pinch hit .370 (17-for-46). He finished his career in limited duty with the Yankees in 1970. /(SH)

Preston Ward — 1927- . 1B-OF-3B 1948, 50, 53–59 Dodgers, Cubs, **Pirates**, Indians, A's 744 g, .253, 50 hr, 262 rbi

When Ward homered in the last game of the 1953 season, it was the 1,197th home run hit in the big leagues that year, then a ML record. The ball and the bat used by Ward were sent to the Hall of Fame.

The 6'4" lefthanded batter, who strongly resembled actor Gregory Peck, led the Western League in 1947 in runs, triples, and RBI. /(RTM)

Robert B. Ward — Unk.–1915. *Executive.*

With Harry Sinclair, Ward was one of the main backers of the Federal League. As owner of the Brooklyn franchise, he poured more than a million dollars into the cause. He offered to share any team profits with his players, but there was never anything to share. A month after Ward died, the league also succumbed. /(NLM)

Curt Wardle — 1960- . LHP 1984–85 **Twins**, Indians 119 ip, 8–9, 6.13

After a brilliant season (6–1, 0.69, 17 saves) in Double-A ball, Wardle struggled in one year of extensive big league play (1985). Rushed to the majors, the slow worker was part of the deal that sent Bert Blyleven back to Minnesota. Wardle moved from reliever to starter with Cleveland. /(ME)

Frank Warfield — 1895–1932. 2B-SS-3B-MGR Negro Leagues 1916–32 St. Louis Giants, Indianapolis ABC's, Kansas City Monarchs, Detroit Stars, **Hilldale**, Baltimore Black Sox, Washington Pilots statistics not available

Warfield was a versatile and intelligent leader as a player and manager. Known primarily for his fielding and baserunning excellence, he also had several good years at the plate. In 1922 he batted .342 for the Detroit Stars, and in four winters in Cuba he hit

.304. He played on the Hilldale teams that won the 1923 through 1925 Eastern Colored League pennants. He became player-manager of the Baltimore Black Sox in 1929 and led them to the Negro American League championship. He and teammates Oliver Marcelle, Dick Lundy, and Jud Wilson became known as the million-dollar infield because their collective talents would have been worth a million dollars to the major leagues had they been white. Warfield was player-manager of the Washington Pilots when he died of a heart attack in 1932./(ETW)

Jack Warhop (Crab, Chief) — 1884–1960. RHP 1908–15 Yankees 1424 ip, 69–93, 3.09

Called "Chief" because his surname sounded like "war hoop" and "Crab" for his disposition, Warhop still holds the Yankee season record for hit batsmen (26). Perhaps most famous for giving up Babe Ruth's first home run (in 1915), he is also one of the few pitchers ever to steal home twice./(JK)

Lon Warneke (The Arkansas Humming Bird) — 1909–1976. RHP 1930–43, 45 **Cubs**, Cardinals 2783 ip, 193–121, 3.18. 20 wins: 32, 34–35 *2 WS, 27 ip, 2–1, 2.63.*
　　Umpire 1949–55 NL
☛ *Led League—w 32. Led League—era 32. All-Star—33–34, 36, 39, 41.*

Warneke won an even 100 games in his first tour with the Cubs, starring for pennant winners in 1932 and 1935. He was traded to the Cards in 1937, where his singing and guitar picking gained him a place in the Mudcat Band, a clubhouse hillbilly combo. He no-hit the Reds on August 30, 1941. The next year, the Cubs paid $75,000 to get him back but soon lost him to military service. After WWII he worked his way back to the NL as an umpire./(JK)

Jack Warner [John Joseph] — 1872–1943. C 1895–1908 Boston (NL), Louisville (NL), **Giants**, Red Sox, Cardinals, Tigers, Senators 1073 g, .249, 6 hr, 303 rbi

Except for 1902, which he spent in Boston, Warner caught for the Giants from late 1896 until replaced in 1905 by Hall of Famer Roger Bresnahan. With his last team, the Senators, he helped develop and was the batterymate of the young Walter Johnson./(JK)

Jack Warner [John Ralph] — 1903–1986. 3B-2B-SS 1925–31, 33 **Tigers**, Dodgers, Phillies 478 g, .250, 1 hr, 120 rbi

Warner spent 60 years in organized baseball. In the major leagues, he was Detroit's third baseman in 1926–27 and a utility infielder thereafter. He coached for the Cubs' Los Angeles farm club for 12 seasons and was a West Coast scout until retiring in 1982. In 1926 he won a $25 bet from Ty Cobb by beating him in a footrace./(JK)

Bennie Warren — 1912– . C 1939–42, 46–47 **Phillies**, Giants 377 g, .219, 33 hr, 104 rbi

Warren was playing his first full season with Philadelphia in 1940 when he was hit in the jaw by a Rip Sewell pitch, losing several teeth and suffering a concussion. After three years in the military, he finished with the Giants as backup catcher to Ernie Lombardi and Walker Cooper./(NLM)

Mike Warren — 1961– . RHP 1983–85 **A's** 205 ip, 9–13, 5.06

The 22-year-old Warren was concluding a mediocre rookie season with the A's in 1983 when, in his last start of the year, he pitched a no-hitter, baffling the White Sox 3–0 on September 29. His success ended there, however, as he won only four more ML games. In 1982, he had led the California League with 19 wins./(SCL)

Rabbit Warstler [Harold Burton] — 1903–1964. SS-2B 1930–40 Red Sox, A's, **Braves**, Cubs 1206 g, .229, 11 hr, 332 rbi

Connie Mack once called the light-hitting Warstler "the best defensive infielder in the American League." Babe Ruth complained that Warstler played so deep and had such a strong arm that he stole hits from him./(JK)

Dan Warthen — 1952– . LHP 1975–78 **Expos**, Phillies, Astros 308 ip, 12–21, 4.30

Warthen's only winning record came in his first season, when he was 8–6 with a 3.11 ERA and three saves as a starter and reliever. He fell off to 2–10, 5.30 in 1976 and was used sparingly thereafter./(WOR)

Carl Warwick — 1937– . OF 1961–66 Dodgers, Cardinals, **Colt .45s**, Orioles, Cubs 530 g, .248, 31 hr, 149 rbi. *1 WS, 5 g, .750, 1 rbi*

Warwick tied a World Series pinch-hitting record with the Cardinals in 1964, collecting three hits in four at-bats off the bench. His pinch single drove in the go-ahead run in St. Louis's 9–5 opening game win over the Yankees. /(RTM)

Jimmy Wasdell — 1914–1983. OF-1B 1937–47 Senators, Dodgers, Pirates, **Phillies**, Indians 888 g, .273, 29 hr, 341 rbi. *1 WS, 3 g, .200, 2 rbi*

From 1937 through 1941, Wasdell was a valued backup—a good outfielder, a smooth first baseman, and a dependable lefthanded pinch hitter. Brooklyn dealt him in a December 12, 1941 package for Arky Vaughan, and he served as Pittsburgh's starting left fielder in 1942. He played regularly with the Pirates and Phillies through the end of WWII. /(JK)

Ray Washburn — 1938– . RHP 1961–70 **Cardinals**, Reds 1209 ip, 72-64, 3.54. *3 WS, 11 ip, 1–1, 8.18*

Washburn was a $50,000 bonus baby who was 12–9 in his rookie 1962 season. He was off to a better year in 1963 when he suffered a shoulder muscle tear, and it took several years to regain his effectiveness. His 10–7, 3.53 and 14–8, 2.26 marks helped the Cardinals to pennants in 1967–68. Washburn pitched a no-hitter against San Francisco on September 18, 1968; the Giants hit only two balls out of the infield. He won Game Three of the 1968 World Series, but was hit hard in Game Six. Washburn was knocked out of the box in the third inning without retiring a batter as the Tigers scored a record-tying ten runs that inning. /(SFS)

Washington Senators (aka Nationals, Nats) — 1901–1960. Team. 4223-4865, .465. *AL Champions 24–25, 33. World Champions 24.*

The old saw about the original Senators, "first in war, first in peace, and last in the American League," was true almost from the first, but has been greatly overinflated. When the American League declared itself a major league in 1901, it was considered important to make a good showing on the East Coast, so players from the 1900 Kansas City franchise were used to form a team in Washington, which had been a National League town until the league pared down to eight teams following the financially troubled 1899 season. The Senators finished last four times in their first nine seasons and didn't rise above sixth place until second-place finishes in 1912 and 1913. The major catalysts in the improvement were the ascendance to greatness of Walter Johnson, who emerged in 1910 as the AL's best pitcher, and the hiring of Clark Griffith as manager in 1912. Griffith acquired first baseman Chick Gandil and pioneered in the use of relief pitchers and in signing Caribbean talent. But the team's new respectability faded a bit over the next decade.

The 1924 hiring of the team's regular second baseman, the 27-year-old Bucky Harris, as player-manager brought instant results with a surprise World Championship in his first season at the helm. The foundation had been laid by Griffith, who had bought the team in 1920. Besides Harris and Johnson, the club featured offensive stars Roger Peckinpaugh (the 1924 MVP) and Hall of Famers Goose Goslin and Sam Rice. Star pitchers included Tom Zachary and Firpo Marberry, considered by most to be the first relief ace. The club repeated as AL champions in 1925 with the acquisition of Hall of Fame pitcher Stan Coveleski.

Washington finished lower than fourth place only once in the next seven years, and then had the city's best season in 1933, capturing the AL title with a team-record 99–53 mark under the leadership of shortstop Joe Cronin. But the club dropped to seventh place in 1934, the team's worst showing since 1916, and Cronin (Griffith's son-in-law) was sold to the Red Sox after the season. The Senators had only four more winning seasons over the next 26 years. The greater incompetence of the Browns and the Athletics generally kept them out of last place, but when the Browns won the pennant in 1944, the Senators finished last. They had finished second the year before, and they finished second in 1945, due to the confusion of the war years, but the hardships of the Depression and the war years cut into attendance and left Griffith, never financially secure, on shaky fiscal ground.

On Clark Griffith's death in October 1955, the club passed to his son, Calvin. The club had finished last that season, the first of four last-place finishes in the space of six years. Clark had pondered the signing of Josh Gibson and other stars of the Negro Leagues to bolster attendance in the 1930s and 1940s, but had ultimately decided not to challenge the unwritten color line; Calvin felt that the team's attendance problem stemmed from Washington's increasingly largely black population, who were less well-off and who tended not to support the Senators, although they had often packed Griffith Stadium for Negro League games. He began lobbying to be allowed to move the franchise to Minneapolis. At first the other owners refused to consider it; the nation's lawmakers were protective of their city's ballclub and often spoke threateningly of reconsidering baseball's anti-trust exemption should the Senators be taken from them. But the decision to expand gave the AL and Griffith a new option, and the AL expanded a year earlier than the NL to allow the Senators to become the Minnesota Twins in 1961, replacing them in the capital with the expansion Senators. /(SH)

Washington Senators — 1961–1971. Team. 740–1032, .418

When Calvin Griffith moved the original Senators to Minnesota, they were replaced by this expansion franchise. It was considered important to keep a team in the nation's capital to placate Congress and thus stave off any reconsideration of baseball's exemption from anti-trust laws. The new club continued the losing tradition of the original team, losing 100 games each of their first four seasons. The Senators had only one winning season, a fourth-place, 86–76 finish under rookie manager Ted Williams. Their only star through most of the club's existence was Frank Howard, who led the AL in homers in 1968 and 1970. In 1972 new owner Bob Short moved the club to Texas. /(SFS)

Claudell Washington — 1954– . OF 1974– A's, Rangers, White Sox, Mets, **Braves**, Yankees, Angels 1867 g, .279, 163 hr, 815 rbi. *3 LCS, 10 g, .281, 1 rbi. 1 WS, 5 g, .571*
☛ *All-Star—75, 84.*

Called up to the majors at age nineteen, Washington played all three outfield positions in the 1974 World Series and was named to Topps' all-rookie team in his third pro season. The Los Angeles native improved in 1975 (.308, 77 RBI, 40 stolen bases) but his batting average and stolen bases were career highs. He played for four teams in five seasons, hitting three home runs in a game in each league, before signing with Atlanta as a free agent for a surprisingly large contract in 1981. He achieved career highs in games, runs, and RBI in 1982 and spurred Atlanta to the playoffs as NL Player of the Month for September. Used exclusively as an outfielder or designated hitter, Washington did not achieve the promise of his youthful talent.

After having his best season in years as a platooned outfielder with the 1988 Yankees, Washington was allowed to sign with the Angels as a free agent. He had developed into a hustling player with a good attitude, perhaps a bit too late. His 1989 season was marred by injury. /(ME)

Herb Washington — 1951– . PR 1974–75 **A's** 104 g, --, 0 hr, 0 rbi

Washington held world indoor track records in both the 50- and 60-yard dashes (5.0 and 5.8 seconds), but hadn't played baseball since his junior year in high school when A's owner Charlie Finley signed him as the club's designated pinch runner two weeks

before the 1974 season. He appeared in 104 games in 1974–75, never batting, and he stole 30 bases, but was not nearly as good a base stealer as his speed would suggest. In the 1974 WS, Washington ran for Joe Rudi in the ninth inning of Game Two after Rudi's single had cut Oakland's deficit to 3–2, and was promptly picked off by Dodgers pitcher Mike Marshall. /(SCL)

Ron Washington — 1952– . SS-2B-3B 1977, 81– Dodgers, **Twins**, Orioles, Indians, Astros 564 g, .261, 20 hr, 146 rbi

Washington was in his 11th professional season when he finally reached the ML for good in 1981, having played for nine different minor league clubs, one team in Mexico, and 10 games with the Dodgers in 1977. He was a utility infielder for the Twins until his release before the 1987 season, then played briefly with the Orioles and Indians. In 1984, he hit a career-high .294. /(SCL)

U.L. Washington — 1953– . SS-2B 1977–87 **Royals**, Expos, Pirates 907 g, .251, 27 hr, 255 rbi. *2 LCS, 5 g, .333, 1 rbi. 1 WS, 6 g, .273, 2 rbi*

Washington's trademark was a toothpick in his mouth whether batting, running, or diving for a ball. The switch-hitting and speedy Washington almost made Royals fans forget his long-time predecessor at shortstop, Freddie Patek. He displayed tremendous range and a strong, accurate arm to provide, with Frank White, a solid middle infield for the Royals through the early 1980s. /(FO)

Gary Waslewski (Was) — 1941– . RHP 1967–72 **Red Sox**, Cardinals, Expos, Yankees, A's 411 ip, 11–26, 3.44. *1 WS, 8 ip, 0–0, 2.16*

Waslewski's moment of glory came in Game Six of the 1967 World Series, when he gave Boston five-plus solid innings (getting a no-decision because of the bullpen) as they went on to beat the Cardinals 8–4. The rookie went 2–2 after being called up that year; it was the only non-losing record of his career. /(SFS)

John Wathan (Duke) — 1949– . C-1B-OF 1976–85 **Royals** 860 g, .262, 21 hr, 261 rbi. *5 LCS, 10 g, .000. 2 WS, 5 g, .250, 1 rbi*
Manager 1987– Royals 197–162, .549

Duke became known for his John Wayne imitations. His surprisingly good speed and ability to adequately play first base and the outfield kept the catcher in the majors for a decade. From 1977 to 1979, he played 92 consecutive errorless games at first base, a Royals record. Despite missing six weeks with a broken ankle, in 1982 he set a ML record for catchers by stealing 36 bases. He was good at working with young pitchers, but was below average at throwing out basestealers. He had managed less than one season in the minors, and was in his 17th year with the Royals organization, when he was named to succeed Billy Gardner as Kansas City manager on August 27, 1987./(FJO)

George Watkins — 1902–1970. OF 1930–36 **Cardinals**, Giants, Phillies, Dodgers 904 g, .288, 73 hr, 420 rbi. *2 WS, 9 g, .231, 2 hr, 3 rbi*

Watkins was 28 years old when he reached the Cardinals, having spent many of his prime years in the well-stocked St. Louis farm system. He batted .373 with 17 home runs as a rookie in 1930, and helped the Cardinals to pennants in 1930 and 1931; his Game Seven, two-run homer proved the difference in their 1931 World Series defeat of the Athletics. His batting average dropped off after his .312 season in 1932./(JK)

Bob Watson (Bull) — 1946– . 1B-OF-DH 1966–84 **Astros**, Red Sox, Yankees, Braves 1832 g, .295, 184 hr, 989 rbi. *2 LCS, 6 g, .375, 1 rbi. 1 WS, 6 g, .318, 2 hr, 7 rbi* ☛ *All-Star—73, 75.*

Watson was a consistent hitter and a dependable team player who, though signed as a catcher, caught only 10 major league games. He played mostly the outfield for Houston until 1975, when he took over at first base for Lee May, who had been traded. He batted a career-high .324 that year and topped the .300 mark in six of his 11 seasons as a regular. In 1976, he scored the one millionth run in ML baseball history. He drove in more than 100 runs in both 1976 and 1977, and was the Astros' all-time leader in hits and RBI when traded to Boston in June 1979.

Helped by the DH rule, Watson had a late-career renaissance in the American League. On September 15, 1979, he became the first ML player to hit for the cycle in both leagues (he did so in the NL in 1977). He signed as a free agent with the Yankees for 1980 and excelled in postseason play. In 1981 he tied a record by homering in his first World Series plate appearance; the three-run shot boosted the Yankees to a 5–3 Game One victory over the Dodgers./(JK)

Doc Watson (Charles) — 1885–1949. RHP 1913–15 Cubs, Chicago (FL), **St. Louis (FL)** 372 ip, 20–25, 2.70

Watson pitched one game for the Cubs in 1913, a complete-game win in which he allowed only one run despite giving up eight hits and six walks. He was easily persuaded to walk away from his $314.50 per month NL salary to sign on with the Federal League in 1914./(BC)

Milt Watson (Mule) — 1890–1962. RHP 1916–19 **Cardinals**, Phillies 424 ip, 21–30, 3.57

The Phillies traded their regular second baseman, Bert Niehoff, and $500 for Watson after he went 10–13 for the Cardinals in 1917. Neither player produced for his new club./(BC)

Mule Watson [John Reeves] — 1896–1949. RHP 1918–24 A's, **Braves**, Pirates, Giants 940 ip, 50–53, 4.04. *2 WS, 3 ip, 0–0, 10.13*

Watson was the Giants' starting pitcher in Game One of the 1923 World Series, the first WS game played at Yankee Stadium. He had complete-game victories in both ends of a doubleheader against the Phillies on August 13, 1921; the second game was a two-hit, no-walk, 8–0 shutout. He performed this iron-man feat in his best season, 14–13 with a 3.85 ERA for the Braves. He was traded to the Giants in June 1923 and went 8–5 the rest of the way as they won the NL flag. He went 9–7 in 1924 as they repeated. In the 1923 WS, he left after giving up three runs in two innings, getting a no-decision; the next year he saved Game Three against the Senators./(NLM)

Eddie Watt — 1942– . RHP 1966–75 **Orioles**, Phillies, White Sox 660 ip, 38–36, 2.91. *3 LCS, 4 ip, 0–0, 0.00. 3 WS, 6 ip, 0–3, 4.26*

Watt spent most of his career as a valuable member of the Orioles' bullpen-by-committee after going 2–5 in 13 starts (the only starts of his ML career) in his rookie 1966 season. That year he was 7–2 with four saves in relief as the Orioles won the franchise's first World Championship. His best effort came in 1969, when he was 5–2 with a career-high 16 saves (tied for fourth in the league). Baltimore won the AL pennant, but Watt lost the fifth and final game of the World Series to the Mets. He also lost Game Four of the 1970 WS. He saved Game One of the 1971 LCS, then lost Game Four of the 1971 WS, the first night game in Series history. Watt never had a bad season in his eight years with the Orioles, and was in double figures in saves for four straight years (1968–71), finishing with 80 for his career.

Watt pitched no-hitters on April 24 and May 6, 1965 for Elmira (Eastern League)./(SFS)

Cliff Watwood [Lefty] — 1905–1980. OF-1B 1929–33, 39 **White Sox**, Red Sox, Phillies 469 g, .283, 5 hr, 148 rbi

In spring training of 1930, John McGraw called Watwood "one of the most natural batters I ever saw." Watwood hit .302 in each of his first two seasons with Chicago, but fielding deficiencies cut short his time in the majors./(NLM)

Jim Waugh — 1933– . RHP 1952–53 **Pirates** 143 ip, 5–11, 6.43

Rushed to the majors in 1952 at age 18, 6'3" Jim Waugh's first victory was a complete game against the Cubs. He lost his other six decisions that year, recorded a 6.48 ERA the next, and left the majors./(ME)

William Weart — 1872–1917. *Writer.*

A baseball writer in Philadelphia for 26 years, Weart was with the *Times* from 1891 to 1909 and the *Evening Telegraph* from 1909 to 1917. He became the Philadelphia correspondent for *The Sporting News*. One of the organizers of the BBWAA, he was its first secretary and held that post until his death./(NLM)

Roy Weatherly (Stormy) — 1915– . OF 1936–43, 46, 50 **Indians**, Yankees, Giants 811 g, .286, 43 hr, 290 rbi. *1 WS, 1 g, .000*

In his 1936 major league debut with Cleveland, Weatherly, a 5'6" 170-lb lefthanded hitter, had a pair of triples and a single. A platooned outfielder for much of his time with the Indians, he was traded to the Yankees in December 1942, but spent all of 1944 and 1945 in the military. He had a reputation among umpires as a complainer./(JK)

Buck Weaver [George Daniel] — 1890–1956. SS-3B 1912–20 **White Sox** 1254 g, .272, 21 hr, 421 rbi. *2 WS, 14 g, .327, 1 rbi*

Slick-fielding Weaver was at his best in the 1919 World Series, cracking 11 base hits. Unfortunately, seven of his teammates were deliberately at their worst; they'd been bribed to throw the games and Buck knew all about it. He hit a career-high .333 the next year, but when the truth about the fix came out, he was lumped with the other Black Sox and banned from baseball for life, his "never-snitch" ethics at odds with Judge Landis's jurisprudence. Chicago fans repeatedly petitioned for Weaver's reinstatement, but he was never pardoned for his failure to warn baseball that his teammates had sold their honor./(JK)

Buck Weaver

Earl Weaver — 1930– . *Manager* 1968–82, 85–86 **Orioles** 1480–1060, .583. First place: 69–71, 73–74, 79 *6 LCS, 15–7, .583. 4 WS, 11–13, .458*

Weaver managed the Orioles for 17 years, including 15 in a row, using the philosophy of "if you play for one run, that's all you get." Throughout his career, Weaver managed for the three-run homer and solid pitching to hold that lead, and liked to use extensive data on past performance to help make decisions, philosophies adopted by his second baseman and current Met manager Davey Johnson. Weaver also liked to bait umpires, and was thrown out of almost 100 games and suspended at least four times. In 1985, he was ejected from both ends of a doubleheader. Weaver, a second baseman, never played in the major leagues, toiling in the Cardinal and Pirate organizations from 1948 through 1957 when he became a manager in the Orioles system. He managed in the minors until 1967 when he was brought in to manage the big club midway through the 1968 season. The next season, he led the Orioles to 109 victories and their first pennant since moving from St. Louis 14 years previous. But his heavily favored team, featuring such future Hall of Famers as Jim Palmer, Brooks Robinson, and Frank Robinson, ran into the Miracle Mets in the World Series. The Orioles won 108 games in 1970, and won the Series over the Reds, thanks largely to Brooks Robinson's glove work at third. In 1971, Weaver and the Orioles won their third straight pennant, but lost to Pittsburgh in seven games in the World Series. Many critics blamed Weaver for the loss, since he had refused to bench injured first baseman Boog Powell, who hit only .111 in the Series. Powell had fractured his wrist in August, aggravated the injury when he was struck on the wrist by a pitch, and was visibly in pain at each at-bat in the Series. The Orioles traded Frank Robinson to the Dodgers after the 1971 season, which signaled the end of the Oriole dynasty. Weaver managed his club to two more divisional championships in 1973 and 1974, mainly on the strength of a superb pitching staff, but lost to the A's in both league championship series. He often had trouble communicating with his players, and was constantly at odds with Palmer. Weaver won his last pennant in 1979 when the Orioles won 102 games, but again was victimized by Pittsburgh in the Series in seven games. He retired in 1982, but came back to manage midway through the 1985 season. In 1986, Weaver suffered his first-ever losing season, winning just 73 games, and retired for good. Weaver won 100 games five times, and is eighth all-time in winning percentage. /(SEW)

Floyd Weaver — 1941- . RHP 1962, 65, 70–71 **Indians**, White Sox, Brewers 155 ip, 4–5, 5.21

Weaver won his first major league start—his one game with the Indians in 1962—then spent most of his career mired in the pitching-rich Cleveland system. Though a starter in the minors, he relieved in 80 of his 85 ML games. /(ME)

Earl Weaver

Jim Weaver (Big Jim) — 1903–1983. RHP 1928, 31, 34–39 Senators, Yankees, Browns, Cubs, **Pirates**, Reds 893 ip, 57–36, 3.88

Big Jim was 6'6" and threw hard, but when he needed another pitch, he became one of the first to throw a forkball. He had extremely large hands, but the use of the pitch left his right hand deformed. Though he never had a losing season, he was cut loose three times by teams about to win a pennant. He went 14–8 for Pittsburgh in both 1935 and 1936. /(JK)

Monte Weaver [Prof] — 1906– . RHP 1931–39 **Senators**, Red Sox 1052 ip, 71–50, 4.36. 20 wins: 32 *1 WS, 10 ip, 0–1, 1.74*

Prof Weaver earned a master's degree in mathematics and taught at Virginia's Emory and Henry College. He had a phenomenal rookie season for the 1932 Senators, going 22–10. Then, impressed by vegetarian theories, he went on a health food diet, became underweight, and lost the zip off his fastball. He struggled to a 10–5 record in 1933, helping the

Senators to their last pennant. In the World Series, he battled the Giants' Carl Hubbell into the 11th inning of Game Four, only to lose 2–1. He dropped to the minors in 1935 before taking the advice of the Senators' trainer, Mike Martin, and dropping the vegetarian diet. Back on beefsteak, he returned to the Senators and had marginal success before retiring in 1939 to devote himself full-time to academia. /(JK)

Earl Webb — 1898–1965. OF-1B 1925, 27–28, 30–33 Giants, Cubs, **Red Sox**, Tigers, White Sox 649 g, .306, 56 hr, 333 rbi

In 1931 the lefthanded-hitting Earl Webb hit a major-league record 67 doubles. He never hit half as many in a season again and was a slow runner, but the record was not necessarily attributable to the dimensions of his home park; the Green Monster, Fenway Park's notorious left-field wall, was not erected until 1934. /(JK)

Hank Webb — 1950– . RHP 1972–77 **Mets**, Dodgers 169 ip, 7–9, 4.31

Webb had only one season of more than 20 IP in the majors, going 7–6, 4.07 for the Mets in 1975. He pitched a seven-inning, 1–0 no-hit victory for Tidewater (International League) against Rochester on June 7, 1974 (second game of a doubleheader). /(JFC)

Skeeter Webb [James Laverne] — 1909–1986. SS-2B 1932, 38–48 Cardinals, Indians, **White Sox**, Tigers, A's 699 g, .219, 3 hr, 166 rbi. *1 WS, 7 g, .185, 1 rbi*

Skeeter was a 5'9" 150-lb, light-hitting infielder who, thanks to his fine glove, WWII, and, perhaps, his father-in-law, managed to play in 12 major league seasons. He saw much action with the White Sox during the WWII player shortage. Traded to Detroit after the 1944 season, he married manager Steve O'Neill's daughter, and was the shortstop for the 1945 World Champion Tigers. /(JK)

Les Webber — 1915–1987. RHP 1942–46, 48 **Dodgers**, Indians 432 ip, 23–19, 4.19

Webber, a 4-F with a heart murmur, was a successful wartime reliever with Brooklyn. Hampered early by arm and rib injuries, abdominal problems, and an appendectomy, he reached the majors at age 27 and led the NL with ten saves in 1943. /(JK)

Mitch Webster — 1959– . OF 1983– Blue Jays, **Expos**, Cubs 671 g, .273, 43 hr, 204 rbi. *1 LCS, 3 g, .333*

A switch-hitting outfielder with good speed and surprising power, Webster was acquired by the Expos when starting centerfielder Herm Winningham was injured in June 1985, and he started for the rest of the season, hitting .274 and setting an Expos record with home runs in four consecutive games. In 1986 Webster hit .290 and led the NL with 13 triples while stealing 36 bases as Montreal's centerfielder, and in 1987 he stole 33 more bases and hit a career-high 15 HR. He was traded to the Cubs for Dave Martinez in July 1988. /(SCL)

Ramon Webster (Monchi) — 1942– . 1B 1967–71 **A's**, Padres 380 g, .244, 17 hr, 98 rbi

Webster hit .256 with 11 HR and 51 RBI in 360 at-bats in his rookie 1967 season. The Panamanian dropped off to .214 in 1968, spending the middle of the year in the minors, and was mostly an unsuccessful pinch hitter thereafter. /(WOR)

Will Wedge — 1889–1951. *Writer.*

A graduate of the Case School of Engineering, Wedge was a baseball writer for the New York *Globe* and later the *Sun.* He covered every WS from 1923 to 1949. Wedge later became librarian for the Hall of Fame. /(NLM)

Mike Wegener — 1946– . RHP 1969–70 **Expos** 270 ip, 8–20, 4.74

Wegener went 5–14 with a 4.40 ERA as the expansion Expos' number-three starter in 1969. /(SFS)

Bill Wegman — 1962– . RHP 1985– **Brewers** 691 ip, 34–42, 4.62

Wegman led the California League in both wins (16) and ERA (1.30) at Stockton in 1982, earning Brewers Minor League Player of the Year honors, and by 1986 was in Milwaukee's starting rotation. The 6'6" righthander was 12–11 in 1987 and 13–13 in 1988. /(SCL)

Herm Wehmeier — 1927–1973. RHP 1945, 47–58 **Reds**, Phillies, Cardinals, Tigers 1803 ip, 92–108, 4.80

"Wehmeier was one of the finest natural athletes we ever had in Cincinnati," said Reds GM Gabe Paul. The three-sport star turned down many college football scholarships to sign with the Reds in 1945. He was extremely wild, leading the league in walks in 1949, 1950, and 1952, and was booed bitterly by the fans, even when he won. After five successive losing seasons, he was sold to Philadelphia in 1954, then traded to St. Louis. He won a career-high 12 games for the Cardinals in 1956. He scouted for the Reds from 1959 through 1961.

Later he worked for a trucking firm, and he collapsed and died while testifying in an embezzlement trial. /(NLM)

Dave Wehrmeister — 1952- . RHP 1976-78, 81, 84-85 **Padres**, Yankees, Phillies, White Sox 158 ip, 4-9, 5.65

Wehrmeister made 30 relief appearances for the Padres in 1977, compiling a 6.04 ERA in 70 innings. He was traded to the Yankees for Jay Johnstone in June 1979, but didn't pitch for New York until 1981. In 1985, Wehrmeister logged his only two ML saves for the White Sox. /(SCL)

Dick Weik (Legs) — 1927- . RHP 1948-50, 53-54 **Senators**, Indians, Tigers 214 ip, 6-22, 5.90

The 6'3" Weik had a blazing fastball but was wild. In 1949, he went 3-12 as a Senators rookie and walked 13 White Sox in one game. He was traded to Cleveland in 1950 for two-time batting champion Mickey Vernon—a deal for which Indians GM Hank Greenberg was widely criticized. Weik pitched in 11 games for Cleveland, spent the next two years in the military, and never won again. /(NLM)

Bob Weiland (Lefty) — 1905- . LHP 1928-35, 37-40 White Sox, Red Sox, Indians, Browns, **Cardinals** 1388 ip, 62-94, 4.24

Weiland, a 6'4" fireballer, shut out the A's in his major league debut with his hometown White Sox on September 30, 1928. Hall of Fame teammate Red Faber made him his protege. In the next seven years, playing with second-division AL teams, Weiland never approximated his premier effort; he compiled a 20-57 record. It wasn't until he joined the Cardinals in 1937, at age 31, that he became a steady starter. He won 15 games in '37 and 16 in 1938. His younger brother Ed relieved in ten games for the White Sox in 1940 and 1942. /(JK)

Carl Weilman [born Carl Woolworth Weilenmann](Zeke) — 1889-1924. LHP 1912-17, 19-20 **Browns** 1521 ip, 85-95, 2.67

Weilman was one of the tallest pitchers of his time, standing 6'5-1/2". After tying for the league lead with 20 losses for the last-place 1913 Browns, he won 18 games in both 1914 and 1915. Yet his career was plagued with illness and injury, and he died only four years after his last ML season. /(JK)

Jake Weimer (Tornado Jake) — 1873-1928. LHP 1903-09 **Cubs**, Reds, Giants 1472 ip, 98-70, 2.23. 20 wins: 03, 04, 06

Weimer went 21-9 (2.30) as a rookie with the 1903 Cubs and 20-14 (1.91) the following year. But Chicago, pitching-rich and desperate to find a third baseman to round out their Tinker-to-Evers-to-Chance infield, sacrificed the hurler in a 1906 trade to Cincinnati for Harry Steinfeldt. After losing Weimer, the Cubs won a ML-record 116 games in '06 and ran off three straight pennants. Weimer won 20 his first year with the Reds, then faded. /(JK)

Lefty Weinert [Philip Walter] — 1901-1973. LHP 1919-24, 27-28, 31 **Phillies**, Cubs, Yankees 437 ip, 18-33, 4.59

Weinert was a wild, hard thrower. In a 1923 game, the Phillies hurler plunked Casey Stengel in the second inning and whizzed a fastball by his ear in the fourth. The enraged Stengel threw his bat at Weinert, attacked him, and had to be escorted off the field by Philadelphia police. Weinert finished the season at 4-17. /(NLM)

Phil Weintraub — 1907- . OF-1B 1933-35, 37-38, 44-45 **Giants**, Reds, Phillies 444 g, .295, 32 hr, 207 rbi

A reserve outfielder and platooned first baseman, Weintraub was a heavy hitter in the minors. In 1934, he was helped to the first .400 season in Southern Association history by Nashville manager Chuck Dressen's ability to tip him off to pitches. As a Giant on April 30, 1944, he drove in 11 runs, one short of the ML record. He had the last hit in Philadelphia's Baker Bowl. /(NLM)

Al Weis — 1938- . 2B-SS-3B-OF 1962-71 **White Sox**, Mets 800 g, .219, 7 hr, 115 rbi. *1 LCS, 3 g, .000. 1 WS, 5 g, .455, 1 hr, 3 rbi*

Weis was the most improbable of heroes in the 1969 Miracle Mets' World Series. The Long Islander's ninth-inning single won Game Two and his seventh-inning homer tied Game Five, making the final Met victory possible. One motivation behind New York's acquisition of the light-hitting utility infielder from Chicago in 1967 was that, at age 29, he couldn't be called for Vietnam-era military duty. Weis, who gave up switch-hitting in 1969, had hit just six career homers prior to the WS smash. /(JCA)

Bob Weisler — 1930- . LHP 1951, 54-58 Yankees, **Senators** 241 ip, 7-19, 5.74

Weisler saw most of his action in 1956, his first year with Washington. Starting 21 games and relieving 16 times for the ninth-place Senators that season, he was 3-12 (all his decisions came as a starter) with a 6.44 ERA. /(FK)

George Weiss (Lonesome George) — 1894–1972.
Executive.
☛ *Hall of Fame—1971.*

By the yardsticks of pennants won and money made, George Weiss was an extremely successful baseball executive. His 29 seasons with the New York Yankees (1932–60) brought 19 pennants, 15 World Championships, and handsome profits. A czar-like general manager, Lonesome George was a shy, colorless, and humorless penny-pincher who clung to his wife and an inner circle of old friends.

Weiss became the baseball entrepreneur of New Haven, CT while attending Yale. His semi-pro team outdrew the local Eastern League club, as Weiss gave the fans what they wanted—big-name stars and Sunday baseball. Ty Cobb demanded $350 for his first game; Weiss gave him $800, and Cobb returned to New Haven frequently. Finally, in 1919, the out-promoted Eastern League club sold out to Weiss.

Upon joining the Yankees in 1932, Weiss built a farm system which at one point boasted more than 20 teams. At Newark (International League), such standouts as Joe Gordon and Charlie Keller were developed. Weiss sold off surplus talent, those players not quite up to Yankee standards. When he was farm director, his bosses were Ed Barrow (who had hired Weiss), and later Larry McPhail. There was a coolness in Weiss's relationship with the territorial Barrow, though the two were much alike. MacPhail, who bought the Yankees in 1945 with Dan Topping and Del Webb, alternately snubbed and abused Weiss. MacPhail brought a turbulence to the Yankees that Topping and Webb eradicated by buying him out in 1947. Weiss was then named GM with absolute authority. As a baseball man rather than a MacPhail-type showman, Weiss ran the club, like Barrow, along conservative lines. When the Yankees finished third in 1948, Weiss fired manager Bucky Harris and hired Casey Stengel. Many felt that Weiss had blundered, that he had hired a clown to manage the Yankees. But Weiss knew the real Stengel, who would reward his faith with 10 pennants in 12 seasons.

Weiss surrounded himself with exceptional people, including a brigade of crack scouts. In 1934, when his scouts told him an injured minor leaguer named Joe DiMaggio would recover and be a star, Weiss convinced owner Jacob Ruppert that the Yankees had to have him. In 1959, he pried Roger Maris from the Kansas City Athletics, offering a package (which included Hank Bauer and Don

George Weiss

Larsen) that the second-division club could not refuse. Dealing with old friend Arnold Johnson, the A's owner, and former employee Parke Carroll, the A's GM, Weiss consistently strengthened the Yankees. "It must be great," said Indians GM Hank Greenberg, "to have your own farm system in the same league."

Weiss was iron-fisted at contract time. He liked to say of his agentless players, "The boys have to be hungry for that World Series money." But Weiss expected his low-salaried players to be well-behaved gentlemen. Billy Martin didn't fit into the GM's idea of the Yankee image, and as soon as he had an excuse (the infamous fight at the Copacabana club), Weiss traded him.

Weiss was named *TSN* Major League Executive of the Year in 1950, 1951, and 1952 (when the Yankees won three of five consecutive World Championships) and again in 1960. He and Stengel were forced to retire after the Yankees lost to the Pirates in the 1960 World Series, with Topping and Webb citing their desire for a more youthful front office. Weiss moped around before coming out of exile in 1961 as president of the expansion New York Mets. His wife had said of his period of forced inactivity, "I married George for better or worse, but not for lunch." Weiss's choice for manager was Stengel. When Weiss retired in 1966—voluntarily—he left the Mets in better shape than were the last-place Yankees; keys to the 1969 World Champion Mets, such as Tom Seaver and Jerry Koosman, were in the farm system. As he bowed out of baseball, Weiss took a jab at the Yankees: "This time I go out with the right kind of taste in my mouth," he said. Weiss was elected to the Hall of Fame by the Committee on Baseball Veterans in 1971. /(MG)

Walt Weiss — 1963- . SS 1987- **A's** 247 g, .252, 6 hr, 61 rbi. *2 LCS, 8 g, .250, 2 rbi. 2 WS, 9 g, .097, 1 hr, 1 rbi* ☛ *Rookie of the Year—88.*

Alfredo Griffin was traded after Weiss had shown he could handle the A's shortstop job. Weiss went on to win the Rookie of the Year award in 1988, the third straight Oakland player to do so, as the A's won the AL pennant. Known primarily for his steady fielding, he made a costly error in Game Four of the World Series, letting in a run in the third inning when Mike Davis's liner went off his glove in a game the A's lost 4–3 to the Dodgers. After hitting .250 in 1988, his average plummeted in 1989. /(WOR)

Johnny Welaj — 1914- . RHP 1939-41, 43 **Senators**, A's 293 g, .250, 4 hr, 74 rbi

Welaj excelled as a baserunner, getting a bigger jump and sliding more elusively than speedier teammate George Case, the AL's top base stealer. /(NLM)

Bob Welch — 1956- . RHP 1978- **Dodgers**, A's 2274 ip, 149-103, 3.18. *6 LCS, 17 ip, 2-2, 6.23. 3 WS, 9 ip, 0-1, 5.79* ☛ *All-Star—80.*

Bob Welch became known in a hurry when he threw nothing but fastballs to strike out Reggie Jackson in the ninth inning to save a 4–3 Dodger win in Game Two of the 1978 series (he also lost Game Four in the tenth inning).

Unfortunately, the next time he achieved national fame was when he had to receive alcoholism treatment. He wrote of his experiences in *Five O'Clock Comes Early: A Young Man's Battle With Alcoholism*, and has since been active in anti-alcoholism efforts. A mainstay on one of baseball's top staffs

with the Dodgers, Welch once played left and right field in a 21-inning game.

Traded to the A's after the 1987 season in a three-way deal that also involved the Mets, Welch helped the A's to the AL pennant with a 17–9 record. He pitched well in Game Three of the WS, allowing one run in five innings, but did not get a decision. /(TG)

Frank Welch — (Bugger) 1897-1957. OF 1919-27 **A's**, Red Sox 738 g, .274, 41 hr, 295 rbi

After his playing days, Welch managed in the minor leagues for a few years. His brother Connie won 24 games in the minors before an arm injury ended his career. /(NLM)

Johnny Welch — 1906-1940. RHP 1926-28, 31-36 Cubs, **Red Sox**, Pirates 648 ip, 35-41, 4.66

Welch was a spindly 19-year-old when the Cubs brought him up to throw batting practice. Put on the roster, he pitched five innings in two full years before being sent down to get game experience. He matured with the Red Sox, going 13–15 at his best in 1934. /(JK)

Mickey Welch (Smiling Mickey) — 1859-1941. RHP-OF 1880-92 Troy (NL), **Giants** 4802 ip, 311-207, 2.71; 606 g, .224, 13 hr, 96 rbi. 20 wins: 80-81, 83-89 ☛ *Hall of Fame—1973.*

The major leagues' third 300-game winner, 5'8" Mickey Welch learned the fundamentals of baseball on the post-Civil War Brooklyn sandlots. Though he did not throw with great velocity, he had an effective curveball, a change of pace, and a version of the screwball. During his 13 major league seasons, he posted 20 or more wins nine times—seven in succession.

After two minor league seasons with Auburn and Holyoke (National Association), Welch joined the National League's Troy Haymakers in 1880, going 34–30 and throwing 574 innings. Diminutive but durable, he pitched two complete-game victories over Buffalo in one day (July 4, 1881), and completed his first 105 major league starts. The Troy franchise moved to New York in 1883, and Welch hurled the first game at the original Polo Grounds. He played 38 games in the outfield that season. In 1884 he completed 62 of 65 starts, winning 39, and had a career-high 345 strikeouts. He established a still-standing ML record that August 28 by striking out the first nine batters he faced.

Mickey Welch

Welch won 17 consecutive games in 1885, threw seven shutouts, and teamed with Tim Keefe (the major leagues' second 300-game winner) to win 76 games. Welch won 44 of them while losing only 11, leading the NL with an .800 winning percentage. Keefe's 1.58 ERA was the league's best; Welch's 1.66 was second. In 1886 Welch went 33–22, yet led NL pitchers in bases on balls for the third consecutive season.

Welch and Keefe accounted for 61 of the team's 84 victories in 1888 as they pitched the Giants to their first pennant. In a postseason series against the St. Louis Browns of the American Association, the Giants won six of ten games, with Welch splitting his two decisions. The Giants repeated as league champions in 1889 as Welch went 27–12. After winning just six games in 1891, he was sent to the Giants' Troy farm club, and he retired after posting a 17–14 record.

Welch remains among baseball's leaders in complete games and innings pitched. He recorded 40 career shutouts, winning 10 by a 1–0 score. He had 492 career base hits—92 of them doubles—and did not bat lower than .200 in his first eight seasons. He was elected to the Hall of Fame by the Committee on Baseball Veterans in 1973. /(JLE)

Harry Weldon — Unk.–1902. *Writer.*

A pioneer among baseball writers and editors, Weldon trained many of the early 19th-century sportswriters while sports editor of the Cincinnati *Enquirer*. /(NLM)

Brad Wellman — 1959– . 2B-SS 1982– **Giants,** Dodgers, Royals 441 g, .231, 6 hr, 77 rbi

Originally signed by the Royals, Wellman was one of four players sent to the Giants in exchange for Vida Blue in 1982, and was a backup infielder with the Giants for three seasons. He spent most of 1986–87 in the minors, then signed with the Royals again as a free agent, and in 1988 hit a career-high .271 for Kansas City. /(SCL)

David Wells — 1963– . LHP 1987– **Blue Jays** 180 ip, 14–12, 3.45. *1 LCS, 1 ip, 0–0, 0.00*

Wells established himself as the Blue Jays' number-three man out of the bullpen in 1988 and '89, showing good control while averaging nearly a strikeout per inning. /(JFC)

Ed Wells — 1900–1986. LHP 1923–27, 29–34 Tigers, **Yankees,** Browns 1232 ip, 68–69, 4.65

Wells was a superb pitcher in the minors; sent down to the Southern Association several times, he would work his way back to the majors. Though never a consistent winner, he recorded a 12–10 record with a league-high four shutouts for Detroit in 1926. He went 12–3 for the 1930 World Champion Yankees, despite a 5.20 ERA, and was not used in the Series. /(JK)

Willie Wells (The Devil, El Diablo) — 1905– . SS-3B-MGR Negro Leagues 1924–50 St. Louis Stars, Detroit Wolves, Homestead Grays, Kansas City Monarchs, Chicago American Giants, Newark Eagles, Baltimore Elite Giants, New York Black Yankees, Indianapolis Clowns, Memphis Red Sox statistics not available

Wells was the best Negro League shortstop during the 1930s and early 1940s. He had great range and sure hands, and he compensated for a weak arm with knowledgeable positioning and a quick, accurate release. Former teammate Monte Irvin said

Wells "always came up with the big play. The opposition would say, 'Don't hit it to shortstop because the Devil is playing out there.'" While playing in Mexico, Wells became affectionately known as El Diablo.

Early in his career, Wells made himself a good, aggressive, clutch hitter. As a St. Louis Star, he won batting titles with a .368 mark in 1929 and a .404 mark in 1930. He helped the Stars to championships in 1928, 1930, and 1931. When the franchise broke up, he played with Detroit, Homestead, and Kansas City before sparking the Chicago American Giants to the 1933 championship. That year, he played in the first East-West all-star game. He went on to appear in eight such contests, batting .281.

Wells's stellar defensive play earned him a spot in the Newark Eagles' "million-dollar infield" in the late 1930s; he batted .386 in 1937. He spent seven winters in Cuba, and hit .328 for the pennant-winning Almendares club to be named league MVP in 1939–40. He recorded a lifetime .364 mark in Negro League competition, and hit .410 against major leaguers in exhibitions. His keen baseball mind and experience made him an excellent teacher and a highly respected player-manager. He continued to top the .300 mark as a batter through the 1940s, and managed into the 1950s.

In his prime, Wells's hot bat and aggressive play made him a frequent beanball target, and he was a pioneer in his use of a batting helmet. But he never backed off, fighting back with his bat and his spikes. "He could run and he'd move you out if you got in his way," said Hall of Famer Judy Johnson. Wells acknowledged that he was filled with a Ty Cobb type of intensity and competitiveness. /(JR)

Chris Welsh — 1955– . LHP 1981–83, 85–86 **Padres**, Expos, Rangers, Reds 538 ip, 22–31, 4.45

Welsh never had a winning record in the majors; his best year came in 1982, when he went 8–8 with a 4.91 ERA for the Padres. He might have developed better as a hitter. His ML average was .208, and he hit .262 in '82. /(JFC)

Jimmy Welsh — 1902–1970. OF 1925–30 **Braves**, Giants 715 g, .290, 35 hr, 288 rbi

The Braves gave up $50,000 in cash and players for Welsh after he hit .350 for Seattle (Pacific Coast League). As Boston's right fielder, Welsh led NL outfielders in assists in 1925 and 1926. He went to the Giants in a 1928 trade for Rogers Hornsby but was returned to Boston in 1929. /(NLM)

Dick Welteroth — 1927– . RHP 1948–50 **Senators** 167 ip, 4–6, 6.48

A teenager signed by the Senators before he was eligible to be drafted into the armed forces, Welteroth didn't reach the ML until 1948, and he had a 7.36 ERA out of the bullpen in 1949, his most active season. /(JK)

Tony Welzer [Anton Frank] — 1899–1971. RHP 1926–27 **Red Sox** 323 ip, 10–14, 4.60

The German-born Welzer was a mediocre starter/reliever who had records of 4–3 (1926) and 6–11 (1927) for the Red Sox. /(WOR)

Harry Wendlestedt — 1938– . *Umpire* NL 1966–88 *3 ASU 6 LCS 3 WS*

Marine Corps veteran Wendlestedt attended the University of Maryland, where he played baseball and basketball. He played a crucial role in Don Drysdale's streak of 58 consecutive scoreless innings for the Dodgers in 1968. In a game at Dodger Stadium, the Giants had the bases loaded with none out in the ninth and catcher Dick Dietz hitting. Drysdale's 2-and-2 pitch hit Dietz, but Wendlestedt ruled that he had made no effort to get out of the way and called the pitch "ball three." Dietz eventually flied out, and Drysdale kept his streak by finishing his fifth straight shutout. /(RTM)

Butch Wensloff [Charles William] — 1915– . RHP 1943, 47–48 **Yankees**, Indians 277 ip, 16–13, 2.60. *1 WS, 2 ip, 0–0, 0.00*

A 21-game winner for Kansas City (American Association) in 1942, Wensloff slipped into the Yankees' 1943 rotation and went 13–11. Then three years of war-plant employment and Army service intervened. He returned in 1947, but his arm was dead; even so, he won twice in a 19-game Yankee winning streak. /(MG)

Bill Werber — 1908– . 3B-SS-OF 1930, 33–42 Yankees, **Red Sox**, A's, Reds, Giants 1295 g, .271, 78 hr, 539 rbi. *2 WS, 11 g, .326, 4 rbi*

Werber, the first All-American basketball player at Duke University, signed with the Yankees after his senior year. Scout Paul Krichell said he had "the best baseball legs I ever saw, including Cobb." Werber won the AL basestealing title with the Red Sox in 1934 and 1935 and tied for it while with the A's in 1937. He once reached second base on a walk while Detroit catcher Ray Hayworth was talking to the umpire. He was the first player to hit four consecutive doubles in one AL game (7/17/35) and on May 13, 1940 became the only man to do so in both leagues.

When Werber held out for $1,500 more than Connie Mack was willing to pay, the A's traded him to Cincinnati in 1939. The Reds gave him the raise, but he turned it back to the club at the end of the season. A fiery competitor, he formed the "Jungle Club" for hustling players, spurring the previously lethargic Reds to pennants in 1939 and 1940. He was the first player to bat in a televised game, leading off for the Reds against Brooklyn, August 26, 1939. /(NLM)

Perry Werden [Percival Wherritt] (Moose) — 1865–1934. 1B-RHP 1884, 88, 90–93, 97 St. Louis (UA), Washington (NL), Toledo (AA), Baltimore (AA), **Cardinals (NL)**, Louisville (NL) 693 g, .282, 26 hr, 367 rbi; 141 ip, 12–1, 1.97

Werden had a sensational rookie mark (12–1) as a pitcher in the Union Association's one year as a major league, 1884, before an arm injury moved him to first base. He twice led his league in triples—with Toledo (American Association) in 1890 and St. Louis (NL) in 1893; when he sought a raise, he was sold to Minneapolis (Western League). There he took advantage of a small park to clout 42 HR and bat .417 in 1894, and hit 45 HR with a .428 average in 1895. No other pro player hit more than 29 HR before 1921. In his minor league career, Werden won five home run titles in all, while compiling a .341 lifetime average and hitting 168 homers. /(MC)

Bill Werle (Bugs) — 1920– . LHP 1949–54 **Pirates**, Cardinals, Red Sox 665 ip, 29–39, 4.69

Werle displayed outstanding control and durability as the NL's top rookie lefthander in 1949 (12–13) after going 25–2 at the University of California. Arm trouble forced his move to relief during the 1950 season and ruined his control. He set a since-surpassed Pirate record with 59 appearances in 1951. /(ME)

Don Wert — 1938– . 3B-SS-2B 1963–71 **Tigers**, Senators 1110 g, .242, 77 hr, 366 rbi. *1 WS, 6 g, .118, 2 rbi* ☛ *All-Star—68.*

A fine glove man, Wert led American League third basemen in fielding in 1965. Playing in all of the Tigers' 162 games that year, he led them with 159 hits. He then followed with his best offensive season

(.268, 70 RBI). Though he batted just .200 in 1968, his ninth-inning, game-winning single on September 17 clinched the pennant for the Tigers. On October 9, 1970, he was shipped to the Senators with Denny McLain in an eight-player deal. /(CC)

Johnny Wertz — 1898– . RHP 1926–29 **Braves** 378 ip, 15–21, 4.29

A sidearmer who sometimes threw fastballs underhand, Wertz went 11–9 as a rookie for the seventh-place 1926 Braves. He slipped to 4–10 in 1927 and soon lost his job. /(JK)

Vic Wertz — 1925–1983. OF-1B 1947–63 **Tigers**, Browns/Orioles, Indians, Red Sox, Twins 1862 g, .277, 266 hr, 1178 rbi. *1 WS, 4 g, .500, 1 hr, 3 rbi* ☛ *All-Star—49, 51, 52, 57.*

Though Wertz had a successful 17-year major league career, it is for one long out with Cleveland that he is best remembered: Wertz hit the drive in the 1954 World Series opener that Willie Mays, racing to the deepest part of the Polo Grounds, caught over his shoulder.

A powerful lefthanded hitter, Wertz drove in 133 runs for Detroit in 1949 and 123 in 1950. He once smashed seven home runs over a five-game span. Capable at two positions, he moved from the outfield to first base when he joined the Indians in 1954. Though he missed part of the 1955 season when stricken with a non-paralytic form of polio, he bounced back in 1956, hit four doubles to tie a ML record in a September 26 game, and finished the season with a career-high 32 HR. A 1958 leg injury caused him to miss most of the season, and by 1961 he was back with Detroit. He led the AL with 17 pinch hits in 1962. /(JK)

West Side Grounds Chicago Cubs 1893–1915 Cleveland (NL) 1898. LF-340, CF-560, RF-340

A small balcony of boxes above the infield grandstand made the West Side Grounds Chicago's first double-decked stadium. An August 5, 1894 game with Cincinnati was suspended due to a fire in the wooden stands. The Cleveland Spiders played their home games here in 1898 after their ballpark burned down. /(SCL)

Joe West (Cowboy Joe) — 1952– . *Umpire* NL 1976, 78– *1 ASU 2 LCS*

West has cut several records with his Texas Cookin' Band. West said, "I don't want to quit umpiring, which has probably helped my music. If I were just a new singer, nobody'd listen. But 'Joe West, NL Umpire,' that gets their attention." He also appeared in the movie *The Naked Gun* as an umpire.

West attended Elon College on a football scholarship and as a quarterback established several school records. /(RTM)

Max West — 1916– . OF 1938–42, 46, 48 **Braves**, Reds, Pirates 826 g, .254, 77 hr, 380 rbi

West was a lefthanded hitter with power and a good outfielder with a superb arm. In the 1940 All-Star Game, he hit a first-inning, three-run homer to give the NL a 3–0 lead. The next inning, he collapsed after leaping for a line drive at the right-field wall; though assisted from the field, he was not seriously hurt. His career was shortened by three years of service in WWII. On April 25, 1948, he walked five times in a game for Pittsburgh. /(JK)

Sammy West — 1904–1985. OF 1927–42 **Senators**, Browns, White Sox 1753 g, .299, 75 hr, 838 rbi
☛ *All-Star—33, 34, 37.*

West was a far-ranging defensive outfielder who set a since-broken American League record with a .996 fielding percentage in 1928. A lefthanded thrower and batter, he joined the Senators in 1927 and was tutored on defense by veteran teammate Tris Speaker. He became Washington's centerfielder in 1928 and remained until his December 1932 trade to the Browns. He batted .300 or better in eight of his twelve seasons as a regular and was named to the first two AL All-Star teams. He had a string of eight consecutive hits in 1933, including a 6-for-6 game on April 13. His lifetime average dropped below .300 in his final season, 1942, when he played 49 games with the White Sox. /(JK)

Wally Westlake — 1920– . OF 1947–56 **Pirates**, Cardinals, Reds, Indians, Orioles, Phillies 958 g, .272, 127 hr, 539 rbi. *1 WS, 2 g, .143*
☛ *All-Star—51.*

Westlake arrived in Pittsburgh in 1947 with power, speed, and a strong arm. In four years as a starting outfielder, he consistently batted .280, and twice hit for the cycle. He had 23 HR and 104 RBI in 1949, and 24 HR and 95 RBI in 1950. He was second to Ralph Kiner in talent and popularity in Pittsburgh when he was traded to St. Louis in 1951 in a seven-player deal. He moved frequently after he left Pittsburgh, never getting established as he had been with the Pirates. He hit .330 in 82 games for the

Indians in 1953. Brother Jim, ten years Wally's junior, had one at-bat with the 1955 Phillies. /(ME)

Wes Westrum — 1922– . C 1947–57 **Giants** 919 g, .217, 96 hr, 315 rbi. *2 WS, 10 g, .250, 3 rbi.*
   Manager 1965–67, 74–75 **Mets**, Giants 260–366, .415
☛ *All-Star—52, 53.*

Westrum set an International League record in 1949 by hitting five grand slams, though he played in only 51 games. In 1950, his first year as a Giants regular, he hit 23 HR, set a still-standing NL record for catchers with a .999 fielding average, and led the league in assists and double plays. He caught every game for the Giants in the 1951 and 1954 World Series. After coaching for San Francisco from 1958 through 1963, he was involved in the only trade of coaches in ML history, going to the Mets for Cookie Lavagetto. When Mets manager Casey Stengel broke his hip during the 1965 season, Westrum replaced him and remained at the helm through 1967. He managed the Giants in 1974 and 1975, finishing third in '75. /(NLM)

Lee Weyer — 1936–1988. *Umpire* NL 1961, 1963–88
4 ASU 5 LCS 4 WS

In a 1987 *Sports Illustrated* poll of NL catchers, Weyer was rated the best at calling balls and strikes. The 6'6" umpire was behind the plate on September 11, 1985, in Cincinnati's Riverfront Stadium when Pete Rose singled off San Diego's Eric Show to break Ty Cobb's career hit record. Weyer, who had done national television commercials for Miller Beer and Coca Cola, was diagnosed in 1980 as having Guillan-Barre syndrome, a potentially life-threatening disorder that affects muscle control and can cause blindness. He rebounded and also returned from a bout with diabetes in 1982. He died during the season in 1988. /(RTM)

Gus Weyhing (Cannonball Gus) — 1866–1955. RHP 1887–96, 1898–1901 **Philadelphia (AA)**, Brooklyn (PL), Phillies, Pirates, Louisville (NL), Washington (NL), Cardinals, Dodgers, Indians, Reds 4324 ip, 264–236, 3.89. 20 wins: 1887–93

Weyhing was one of 19th-century baseball's outstanding pitchers, having his best years before the mound was moved from 50' away from home plate to 60'6" in 1893. He won 30 or more games in four seasons, more than 20 in three others; he was also a seven-time 20-game loser. In 1888, he pitched a no-hitter for Philadelphia against Kansas City (American Association). Weyhing holds the career record for hit batsmen, 286. His younger brother John pitched briefly in the AA in 1888–89. /(AL)

Zach Wheat (Buck) — 1888–1972. OF 1909–27
Dodgers, A's 2410 g, .317, 132 hr, 1261 rbi. *2 WS, 12 g, .283, 3 rbi*
☛ *Led League—ba 18. Hall of Fame—1959.*

From 1909, when he reported to Washington Park after almost three days on a train from Louisiana, until 1926, when his legs gave out at Ebbets Field, Zach Wheat was a fixture in left field for Brooklyn. He was the club's stellar performer, a quiet team leader who was never thrown out of a game in a 19-year career. He batted over .300 13 times, and remains the Dodgers' all-time leader in games played, at-bats, hits, doubles, triples, and total bases.

Wheat was a graceful, lefthanded, line-drive hitter who could handle the curveball so well that Giants manager John McGraw forbade his pitchers to throw him any. Wheat topped the .320 mark only once during the dead-ball era—in 1918, when he had a 26-game hitting streak and won the batting title with a .335 average. He was 32 when the ball was made livelier, and his production soared. He batted .320 or better each year from 1920 through 1925, with .375 marks in both 1923 (when he played just 98 games after a long holdout) and 1924, and a .359 mark in '25. He had averaged about five home runs a year through 1919; from '20 through '25, he averaged more than 12 a season.

Wheat generally batted clean-up and was rarely expected to bunt. One afternoon he found himself in a sacrifice situation, awaiting the obvious sign from manager Wilbert Robinson, who was coaching third. Because Uncle Robby had forgotten the bunt sign, he went through an improvised set of gestures. Realizing they did not convey the message, Robinson simply pantomimed a bunt. Team captain Wheat decided he hadn't received the bunt sign and lined the next pitch out of the ballpark. As Wheat rounded third, the jubilant Robinson slapped him on the back, though he could have slapped him with a fine.

Wheat's last home run for Brooklyn signaled the end of his great Dodger career. He had injured his heel and, with only a few games to play in the 1926 season, was resting his aching legs. Sent in to pinch hit, he pulled a pitch to right field and raced down the line. As the ball cleared the wall, he got a charley horse. As he hobbled on, his other leg failed him, and he lurched into second base. He sat down on the bag as time was called. Robinson and the umpires consulted. Finally, Wheat got his to feet. With the

Zack Wheat

crowd wincing with him on every step, he virtually crept over to third. It took him an estimated five minutes to finally score.

Released by the Dodgers on New Year's Day, 1927, Wheat signed with the Athletics. He batted

.324 his final season, pinch hitting and playing 62 games in the outfield for a Philadelphia team that had ten .300 hitters, including Ty Cobb (.357) and Al Simmons (.392). He finished his career in the American Association in 1928. After retiring to his native Missouri, he was nearly killed in an automobile crash, and was hospitalized for five months. The all-time leader in games played in left field, he was named to the Hall of Fame by the Committee on Baseball Veterans in 1959. His brother, McKinley "Mack" Wheat, caught for the Dodgers for parts of 1915 through 1919, and for the Phillies in 1920–21. /(JK)

John N. Wheeler — Unk.–1973. *Writer.*

One of the original members of the BBWAA, Wheeler was a writer with the New York *Herald* from its founding in 1907. He was a ghostwriter for Ty Cobb, Christy Mathewson, and Eddie Collins, as well as many famous military and political figures. At his death, he was chairman of the board for North American Newspaper Alliances. /(NLM)

Pete Whisenant — 1929– . OF 1952, 55–61 Braves, Cardinals, Cubs, **Reds**, Indians, Senators/Twins 475 g, .224, 37 hr, 134 rbi

Reserve outfielder Whisenant never batted higher than .239 or had more than 11 home runs in a season. Yet, in 1957, he hit five pinch homers for Cincinnati—three off the Cardinals' Vinegar Bend Mizell. /(FK)

Lou Whitaker (Sweet Lou) — 1957– . 2B 1977- **Tigers** 1695 g, .276, 149 hr, 721 rbi. *2 LCS, 8 g, .161, 1 hr, 1 rbi. 1 WS, 5 g, .278*
☛ *Rookie of the Year—78. All-Star—83–87, 89. Gold Glove—83–85.*

With Alan Trammell, Lou Whitaker formed a keystone combination of longevity unsurpassed in baseball history. Yet, Whitaker was in sharp contrast to Trammell. Whitaker's seemingly effortless play left him open to criticism. Expectations for the Brooklyn, New York native were sparked when he was 1976 Most Valuable Player in the Florida State League as a third baseman. He moved to second at Montgomery (Southern League) in 1977 and began his partnership with Trammell. Less than a year senior to the shortstop, Whitaker had the flashier debut in 1978, winning Rookie of the Year honors. He did not immediately improve and was a disappointment until the middle of 1982. A strong finish gave him his best season to that point. Lou was Tiger of the Year in 1983, Detroit's first lefthanded hitter with 200 hits since 1943, and a contender for the batting title. Like Trammell, Whitaker's power improved with maturity. He set a record for Detroit second basemen with 21 home runs in 1985 and was part of the all-20-homer infield in 1986. In spring training of 1985, Sparky Anderson briefly moved him to third base in favor of rookie Chris Pittaro. The experiment came to a quick end. Whitaker was Anderson's leadoff batter until being moved to the number-two slot in 1988. From his rookie season through 1988, he never played on a losing team. But his best season was wasted on the last-place 1989 team.

After a decade with the Tigers, Lou Whitaker is drawing comparisons to Detroit's Hall of Fame second baseman, Charlie Gehringer. Whitaker is among Detroit's all-time leaders in doubles, runs scored, and hits. /(ME)

Lou Whitaker

Steve Whitaker — 1943- . OF 1966–70 **Yankees**, Pilots, Giants 266 g, .230, 24 hr, 85 rbi

The Yankees hoped the lefthanded-hitting Whitaker would hit for power in Yankee Stadium. He played regularly only for the ninth-place 1967 team and hit .243 with 11 HR and 50 RBI. He led AL outfielders in double plays that season. Picked by the Royals in the expansion draft, he was traded with pitcher John Gelnar to the Seattle Pilots just before the start of the season in return for Lou Piniella, who went on to win Rookie of the Year. /(JFC)

Bill White — 1934- . 1B-OF 1956, 58–69 Giants, **Cardinals**, Phillies 1673 g, .286, 202 hr, 870 rbi. *1 WS, 7 g, .111, 2 rbi*
☛ *All-Star—59–61, 63, 64. Gold Glove—60–66.*

White homered for the Giants in his first major league at-bat (5/7/56). Though he topped the 20-HR mark eight times, he was more of a line-drive hitter than a slugger. With the Cardinals in 1961 he tied Ty Cobb's ML record with 14 hits in consecutive doubleheaders July 17 and 18. He topped 100 RBI four times. He was also a stylish, lefthanded first baseman who won seven consecutive Gold Gloves. He retired as a player after the 1969 season and in 1971 began a long career as a Yankee broadcaster. In 1988 he became the major leagues' first black league head when he replaced Bart Giamatti as NL president. /(AL)

Chaney White — Unk.–1965. OF Negro Leagues 1921–36 Hilldale, **Bacharach Giants**, Washington Potomacs, Quaker Giants, Homestead Grays, Darby Daisies, Philadelphia Stars, New York Cubans, Baltimore Black Sox .328 (inc.)

A threat both at the plate and on the bases, White earned high praise from his fellow Negro League players. Catcher Larry Brown said White "was built like King Kong, but he could run like Jesse Owens

Bill White

. . .cut my shinguards off once." Hall of Famer Judy Johnson called him the best one-run getter in baseball because of his speedy, daring baserunning. He was a .328 hitter in the Negro Leagues, and was considered a good outfielder with excellent range but a weak arm. He played with the 1926 and 1927 Eastern Colored League champion Bacharach Giants, and stole five bases in six attempts in the 1926 Black World Series./(PB)

Charles D. White — 1859–1937. *Writer.*

The first compiler of authentic and accurate records of baseball action each year, White started the *Little Red Book*, which was designed by his employer, A.G. Spalding & Bros., and issued through the American Sports Publishing Company. When Spalding discontinued its publication in 1932, White returned and continued to publish *Charles White's Little Red Book*./(NLM)

Deacon White [James Laurie] — 1847–1939. 3B-C-RHP 1871–90 Forest Citys (NA), **Boston (NA)**, Cubs, Reds, Buffalo (NL), Detroit (NL), Alleghenys (NL), Buffalo (PL) *NA*: 259 g, .347. *ML*: 1299 g, .303, 18 hr, 602 rbi; 17 ip, 0–0, 7.20.
    Manager 1879 **Reds** 8–8, .500
☛ *Led League—ba 77. Led League—rbi 76–77.*

The Deacon is a truly historic baseball figure. He began the game early enough to have played, and lost, against the Cincinnati Red Stockings of 1869. He played three championship seasons with Harry Wright's Boston Red Stockings of the National Association. He was with Cap Anson's White Stockings for the first championship of the National League. And, as an ardent supporter of players' rights, he ended his 22-year career as playing owner of Buffalo's Brotherhood team.

His long face, walrus mustache, and sober mien made him look out of place on the ball field in that rough-and-tumble era, but precisely like the abstemious, nonsmoking, Bible-toting, church-going deacon he was.

Nonetheless, he was the best barehanded catcher of his time, and when he joined Buffalo in 1881, with the great Jack Rowe behind the plate, he became the best third baseman, too. He threw righthanded and batted left.

With the Association Bostons he was, with Al Spalding, Ross Barnes, and Cal McVey, one of baseball's first Big Four. They defected to Chicago in 1876, but White returned to Boston for his fifth straight pennant in 1877, plus a league-leading average of .387.

Deacon White

For the next three years Deacon and his brother Will, a righthanded, 222-game winner, were a battery for Cal McVey at Cincinnati. Deacon Jim also had an eight-win, eight-loss stint as manager before handing the job back to McVey. In 1881 he and Will went to Buffalo where, with Dan Brouthers, Hardy Richardson, and Rowe, Jim made up a second Big Four. The owners sold the franchise to Detroit interests in 1886. The lads found Ned Hanlon, Sam Thompson, and Charley Bennett already there, and a Wolverine pennant was won in 1887. In postseason play they thrashed Chris von der Ahe's Browns in a 15-game "World Series" that traveled through ten cities.

White and Jack Rowe bought back into Buffalo in 1889, although Pittsburgh had rights to their services. After a bitter legal fight they were forced to play for the Alleghenys, a situation that gave impetus to formation of the Players' League. When the Brotherhood collapsed, Deacon, then 42, retired, honored and respected by all who knew him./(ADS)

Devon White — 1962– . OF 1985– **Angels** 486 g, .254, 48 hr, 197 rbi. *1 LCS, 3 g, .500*
☛ *All-Star—89. Gold Glove—88, 89.*

An excellent defensive outfielder with blazing speed, White didn't hit higher than .257 in his first three pro seasons, but hit .291 with 14 HR and 60 RBI at Edmonton (Pacific Coast League) in 1986, with a league-leading 42 stolen bases, to win the Angels' right-field job. Debuting in the "lively ball" season of 1987, White smacked 24 HR and stole 32 bases while hitting .263, earning a spot on the Topps All-Rookie Team. In 1988 White moved over to centerfield when Gary Pettis was traded to Detroit, and won a Gold Glove for his often breathtaking defensive play. White stole second base, third base, and home consecutively in a September 1989 game. /(SCL)

Doc White [Guy Harris] — 1879–1969. LHP 1901–13 Phillies, **White Sox** 3050 ip, 190–157, 2.38. 20 wins: 07 *1 WS, 15 ip, 1–1, 1.80*
☛ *Led League—w 07. Led League—era 06.*

Doc White, a graduate in dental surgery from Georgetown, was the mainstay of the Hitless Wonder White Sox pitching staffs. He first signed with

Doc White

the Phillies, tied for the league lead with 20 losses in 1902, and jumped to Chicago. In September 1904 he threw five consecutive shutouts; the string was stopped when he hurled both ends of a doubleheader. During his career he pitched 24 1–0 games, winning 13 of them. The most notable was an 11-inning win over Washington's Walter Johnson; five days later the two battled to a 1–1 tie in 17 innings.

White was an exceptional control pitcher. He set an early American League record by going 65 consecutive innings without issuing a walk. In 1906, when he led the AL with a 1.52 ERA and went 18–6 for the World Champions, he walked only 38 in 219 innings. When he won a league-high 27 the following year, he walked only 38 in 291 innings.

White was also a violinist, balladeer, and songwriter; in 1910, he combined with Ring Lardner on "A Little Puff of Smoke, Goodnight," a bestseller in sheet music. He was a college coach, and, after owning a Texas League franchise for a time, became a traveling evangelist. /(JK/RL)

Ernie White — 1916–1974. LHP 1940–43, 46–48 **Cardinals**, Braves 489 ip, 30–21, 2.78. *2 WS, 9 ip, 1–0, 0.00*

White had an outstanding rookie year for St. Louis in 1941, going 17–7 (2.40). In 1942 he became the first pitcher since 1926 to shut out the Yankees in a World Series, winning the pivotal third game. His career was shortened by arm problems and three years of military service. /(JK)

Frank White — 1950– . 2B 1973– **Royals** 2088 g, .257, 141 hr, 787 rbi. *6 LCS, 26 g, .241, 1 hr, 10 rbi. 2 WS, 13 g, .170, 1 hr, 6 rbi*
☛ *All-Star—78–79, 81–82, 86. Gold Glove—77–82, 86–87.*

White was signed by the Royals from a tryout camp and was one of the few successful products of the baseball school the club operated in the early 1970s. By 1989, White and George Brett had been Royals for 17 seasons, longer than anyone else in the franchise's history. In 1977 White played 62 consecutive games without an error. He collected eight Gold Gloves and is the only second baseman in AL history to win six straight. Three times he led the league in fielding percentage and in 1988 he made only four errors in 150 games.

White also was productive with the bat and on the basepaths. Generally a singles hitter whose speed converted a fair number to doubles, he muscled up late in his career to belt 22 home runs in back-to-back seasons. In 1986 *TSN* awarded him a Silver Bat. /(FO)

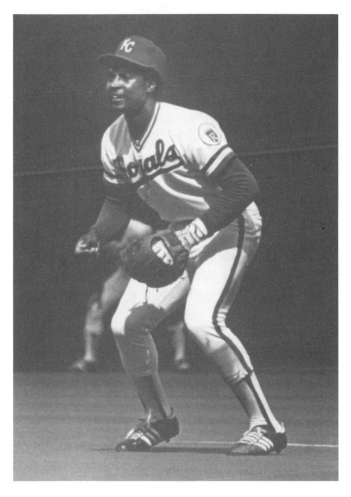

Frank White

Hal White — 1919- . RHP 1941-43, 46-54 **Tigers**, Browns, Cardinals 920 ip, 46-54, 3.78

White went 12-12 with a 2.91 ERA for the Tigers in his rookie 1942 season, but dropped off to 7-12, 3.39 in 1943 and then spent two years in the military. When he came back, he was mostly used in relief with little success. He is one of the players to play for both the Cardinals and Browns. /(SFS)

Jerry White — 1952- . OF 1974-83, 86 **Expos**, Cubs, Cardinals 646 g, .253, 21 hr, 109 rbi. *1 LCS, 5 g, .313, 1 hr, 3 rbi*

White spent most of his career as a fourth outfielder and pinch hitter on the Expos. He saw the most action in 1976, when he hit .245 with career highs of 32 runs and 15 steals. His moment of glory came in the 1981 LCS, when he won Game Three with a seventh-inning three-run homer off the Dodgers' Jerry Reuss after he had hit just .218 in the regular

season. White spent 1984 and '85 in Japan with the Seibu Lions and hit .251 with 37 HR and 113 RBI in 707 at-bats over two seasons. /(JFC)

Jo-Jo White [Joyner Clifford] — 1919- . OF 1932-38, 43-44 **Tigers**, A's, Reds 877 g, .256, 8 hr, 229 rbi. *2 WS, 12 g, .190, 1 rbi.*
   Manager 1960 **Indians** 1-0, 1.000

White was a Texas League basestealing champ with a top-notch throwing arm who couldn't find a regular spot in a crowded Tiger outfield. His ten pinch hits in 1933 were the AL high. Though he left the majors after 1938, he got a second chance with the WWII A's.

He was coaching for Cleveland in mid-1960 when manager Joe Gordon was swapped for Giant manager Jimmy Dykes; White took over while the stunned pair changed teams, winning his one game. His son Mike played 100 games in Houston's infield and outfield in 1963-65. /(JK)

Kirby White (Redbuck Buck) — 1884-1943. RHP 1909-11 Braves, **Pirates** 331 ip, 17-25, 3.24

Unhappy with their aging pitching staff, the Pirates acquired 26-year-old Kirby White from Boston in 1910. He went 11-11, but was deemed expendable the next season. /(ME)

Roy White — 1943- . OF-DH 1965-79 **Yankees** 1881 g, .271, 160 hr, 758 rbi. *3 LCS, 14 g, .316, 1 hr, 4 rbi. 3 WS, 12 g, .244, 1 hr, 4 rbi*
☛ *All-Star—69-70.*

White was the quiet leader of the Yankees in a period when their lackluster, sometimes abysmal play was an embarrassing contrast to the franchise's long winning history. His consistently solid performance was finally rewarded in the mid-1970s when the club regained its winning touch; in that period he provided a dignity beyond many of the team's more obviously talented stars.

White hit home runs from both sides of the plate in the same game five times and also switch-hit triples in a game on September 8, 1970, which nobody has ever done more than once in a season. He had speed, too, and stole 233 bases in his career. He was in double figures in steals every season except for his first and last years, and he stole a career-high 31 bases in 1976 at the age of 32. His fielding was just as steady as his other talents, and in 1975 he fielded 1.000, the first Yankee ever to play an errorless season. League-leading performances offensively came in 1972 (99 walks), 1973 (639 at-bats), and 1976 (104 runs). In 1971 he set the AL record for sacrifice flies in a season with 17.

White came up briefly in 1965, the year of the Yankees' collapse, and stuck in 1966, when they dropped to last place. He achieved everyday status in 1968 and hit .267 with 17 HR, 20 steals, 89 runs, and 73 walks. Military service interrupted his 1969 season, when he made the All-Star team, but he had a career year in 1970 with personal highs of 22 HR, 109 runs, 94 RBI, and a .296 batting average. He continued to provide the Yankees with consistent everyday play at the plate and in left field until an injury in 1978 slowed him. He helped the Yankees to their first pennant since 1964 in 1976, and to back-to-back World Championships in 1977–78. In the 1976 LCS he tied the ML mark for walks in a five-game series (5), and his six doubles tied the ALCS lifetime record. His best postseason came in 1978 despite just having come off the DL; he hit .313 in the LCS, with a game-winning sixth-inning HR in the clincher, and hit .333 with a HR and four RBI in the World Series. He later played in Japan, but returned to the U.S. to coach for the Yankees. /(SFS)

Sammy White — 1928– . C 1951–59, 61–62 **Red Sox**, Braves, Phillies 1043 g, .262, 66 hr, 421 rbi
☛ *All-Star—53.*

White was Boston's first-string catcher from 1952 through 1959. On June 18, 1953, he became the only 20th-century player to score three runs in one inning, as the Red Sox scored 17 in the seventh against the Tigers. His best season with the bat was 1954, when he hit .282 with 14 HR and 75 RBI. But it was for his defensive skills and pitch-calling ability that he was prized. "He steals more strikes from umpires than anyone else," acknowledged Casey Stengel. "I'm not being critical. I'm just bowing to his skill."

White's bowling alley was the scene of a grisly mass murder in the 1970s. /(PB)

Sol White — 1868–1955. 2B-3B-OF-1B-MGR Negro Leagues 1887–1912, 1924–26 Pittsburgh Keystones, Washington Capital Citys, Wheeling (Ohio State League), New York Gothams, York Monarchs (EIL), Cuban Giants, Genuine Cuban Giants, Fort Wayne (WIL), Page Fence Giants, Cuban X-Giants, Columbia Giants, **Philadelphia Giants**, New York Lincoln Giants, Quaker Giants, Cleveland Browns, Newark Stars, Ansonia (Connecticut League) statistics not available

White was a black baseball pioneer who played for several white minor league teams in the 1880s, when blacks were allowed in organized baseball. In 1887 he hit .381 for the Ohio State League's Wheeling, WV, team, playing third base, but was cut when the color line was drawn the next year. In the integrated Eastern Interstate League, he played second base and hit .358 for the 1891 York Monarchs. The last integrated team he appeared with was Fort Wayne, IN (Western Inter-State League). He went on to play for numerous black teams.

With H. Walter Schlichter, in 1902 White founded and captained the Philadelphia Giants, a top black team of the early 1900s. They claimed the Black World Championship in 1905–07. White managed the New York Lincoln Giants in 1911, the Boston Giants in 1912, and the Negro National League Cleveland Browns in 1924. His 1907 book, *Sol White's Official Base Ball Guide*, is the only surviving record of the early years of black baseball. /(JJM)

Will White (Whoop-La) — 1854–1911. RHP 1877–86 Braves, Reds, Detroit (NL), **Cincinnati (AA)** 3542 ip, 229–166, 2.28. 20 wins: 78–79, 82–83
☛ *Led League—w 82–83. Led League—era 83.*

White, in the words of baseball historian Lee Allen, was "one of the game's greats who never received his due." He was the first ML player to wear glasses on the field. Will's brother Deacon was already a star player when Will arrived in the ML in 1877. For a few games they formed a brother battery in Boston, but all except two of Will's 229 career victories came in a Cincinnati uniform. In 1878, he won 30 games for the NL Reds and followed with 43 the next year. In both seasons his ERA was under 2.00. When it rose to 2.14 in 1880, he led the NL in losses with 42. In eight of the losses the weak-hitting Reds were shut out. He returned with Cincinnati's American Association team in 1882 and posted consecutive seasons of 40, 43, 34, and 18 wins. Upon his retirement, he became a successful businessman in Buffalo, New York. /(BC)

Burgess Whitehead (Whitey) — 1910– . 2B-3B-SS 1933–37, 39–41, 46 Cardinals, **Giants**, Pirates 924 g, .266, 17 hr, 245 rbi. *3 WS, 12 g, .135, 2 rbi*

Whitehead was a 160-lb utility infielder for the Cardinals who was often in poor health. The Giants' Bill Terry was criticized when he gave up players and cash for him in December 1935, but Whitehead played in every game for New York in their pennant-winning 1936 and 1937 seasons. He led NL second basemen in total chances per game in 1936, and in putouts, fielding percentage, and double plays in 1937. He missed the 1938 season due to illness, and later spent four years in the WWII Navy. /(NLM)

John Whitehead (Silent John) — 1909–1964. RHP 1935–40, 42 **White Sox**, Browns 944 ip, 49–54, 4.60

A quiet Texan, Silent John broke in with eight straight victories for the White Sox in 1935 but finished at 13–13 in both of his first two seasons. He remained a dependable starter until he was traded to the Browns in 1939. /(JK)

Earl Whitehill — 1899–1954. LHP 1923–39 **Tigers**, Senators, Indians, Cubs 541 g, 3565 ip, 218–185, 4.36. 20 wins: 33 *1 WS, 1 g, 9 ip, 1–0, 0.00*

The handsome, temperamental Whitehill, called The Earl for his flashy wardrobe and temperamental air, was a bear-down lefthander who told off teammates, umpires, and Ty Cobb if he thought they impeded his progress toward victory. Teammates were scorched for less than 100% effort, umpires for bad calls, and Manager Cobb for coming in from centerfield to demand curve balls when Earl wanted to throw the fast one.

A willing worker, he achieved 11 winning seasons despite allowing 3,917 hits lifetime, 1,431 walks (12th all-time), and a league-leading 22 home runs in 1931. His lifetime ERA of 4.36 is higher than any other 200-game winner.

Traded to Washington for pitchers Firpo Marberry and Carl Fischer, he won a career-high 22 games in 1933. He went to the Indians in a three-way trade in 1936. After several seasons as a coach for the Indians, Phillies, and Buffalo (International League), he became a sales representative for the A.G. Spalding sporting-goods firm. /(ADS)

Len Whitehouse — 1957– . LHP 1981, 83–85 Rangers, **Twins** 115 ip, 9–4, 4.68

In his only winning season, Whitehouse went 7–1 with two saves in 60 appearances for the 1983 Twins. /(WOR)

George Whiteman — 1882–1947. OF 1907, 13, 18 **Red Sox**, Yankees 85 g, .272, 1 hr, 31 rbi

Whiteman was 35 when called up by the Red Sox in 1918, and he filled in for Babe Ruth in the outfield whenever Ruth pitched. He was the defensive hero of the 1918 World Series, making a somersaulting catch in the eighth inning of the final game. /(EC)

Fred Whitfield (Wingy) — 1938– . 1B 1962–70 Cardinals, **Indians**, Reds, Expos 817 g, .253, 108 hr, 356 rbi

"Wingy" was a dangerous lefthanded hitter who hit 93 home runs for Cleveland from 1963 to 1967. The underrated first baseman won his nickname for the way he threw. In 1965, he hit 26 HR and drove in 90 runs while batting .293. Though his average withered to .241 in 1966, he hit 27 HR; when it waned to .218 in 1967, Cleveland traded him to Cincinnati, where he pinch-hit and played first base. /(JCA)

Terry Whitfield — 1953– . OF 1974–80 84–86 Yankees, **Giants**, Dodgers 730 g, .281, 33 hr, 179 rbi

After three seasons bouncing between the Yankees and Syracuse (International League), Whitfield was traded to San Francisco, where he played fairly regularly in the outfield from 1977 to 1980, batting between .285 and .296 each year. In 1981 he departed for Japan, and smacked 85 HR in three seasons with the Seibu Lions before returning in 1984 to log three more seasons as a reserve for the Dodgers. /(SCL)

Dick Whitman — 1920– . OF 1946–51 **Dodgers**, Phillies 285 g, .259, 2 hr, 67 rbi. *2 WS, 4 g, .000*

Whitman saw the most action in 1946 for the Dodgers, hitting .260 with 31 RBI and 39 runs. He led the NL in pinch hits in 1950, going 12-for-39 and helping the Phillies to the pennant. /(WOR)

Jim Whitney (Grasshopper Jim) — 1857–1891. RHP 1881–90 **Braves**, Kansas City (NL), Washington (NL), Indianapolis (NL), Philadelphia (AA) 3496 ip, 192–207, 2.97. 20 wins: 81–84, 87
☛ *Led League—w 81.*

A Boston sportswriter described the tall, slender Whitney: "He has a head about the size of a wart, with a forehead slanting at an angle of 45 degrees." "Grasshopper Jim" joined Boston in 1881 and led the NL in both wins (31) and losses (33) as a rookie. In 1883, he was 37–21 as Boston won the pennant. A strong hitter, he often batted cleanup and was usually stationed in centerfield when he was not on the mound. His pitching slump in the next three seasons was blamed by some on the rule change that allowed overhand pitching. After a 24–21 comeback with Washington in 1887, his skills eroded rapidly. He pitched his last game in 1890 and died the following spring of tuberculosis. /(BC)

Pinky Whitney [Arthur Carter] — 1905– . 3B-2B 1928–39 **Phillies**, Braves 1539 g, .295, 93 hr, 927 rbi
☛ All-Star—36.

Obtained by the Phillies in a minor league draft, Whitney was an immediate success, batting .301 as a rookie regular in 1928. He had 200 hits and hit .327 for the 1929 Phillies—the only team in NL history to have four batters reach 200 hits—and .342 in 1930. In four of his first five years, he drove in more than 100 runs. An accomplished defensive player, he led NL third baseman in fielding three times. After batting just .264 in 1933, he was traded to the Braves, but went back to the Phillies in 1936. In 1937, his final season as a regular, he hit .341. /(AL)

Ed Whitson — 1955– . RHP 1977– Pirates, Giants, Indians, **Padres**, Yankees 1933 ip, 108–108, 3.88. *1 LCS, 8 ip, 1–0, 1.13. 1 WS, 0.2 ip, 0–0, 40.50*
☛ All-Star—80.

Ed Whitson's career is best defined by the series of transactions involving him. A promising prospect for Pittsburgh, Whitson was a key to the deal that sent Bill Madlock to the Pirates and brought them a World Championship. After the 1981 season, he went to Cleveland for veteran second baseman Duane Kuiper. He spent a frustrating year in the Indians' bullpen before moving to San Diego for Juan Eichelberger and Broderick Perkins. After an injury-riddled 1983, Whitson attained his best season in 1984, going 14–8 with a 3.24 ERA. He was the first pitcher to win a postseason game for San Diego, the crucial third game of the Championship Series against the Cubs. He made a disastrous mistake by signing with the Yankees as a free agent for 1985. The high-priced pitcher was virtually booed out of town after failing to live up to his price tag. Traded back to San Diego, he was the Padres' top winner in 1987 (10–13) and 1989 (16–11). /(ME)

Ernie Whitt — 1952– . C 1976–78, 80– Red Sox, **Blue Jays** 1266 g, .253, 132 hr, 521 rbi. *2 LCS, 12 g, .162, 1 hr, 5 rbi*
☛ All-Star—85.

Ernie Whitt is the most popular player in the history of the Blue Jays. His personal development from a marginal prospect into an All-Star catcher has paralleled the Blue Jays' development from a hapless expansion team into a pennant contender.

A good defensive catcher and handler of pitchers, Whitt was platooned through most of his career. He became a pull hitter with power, and hit three of the Blue Jays' major league record ten home runs against Baltimore September 14, 1987. His injury while trying to break up a double play in the final week of the 1987 season was an important factor in the AL East pennant race. Playing without Whitt, a Michigan native who had played some of his best ball at Tiger Stadium, Toronto lost the pennant to Detroit on the final weekend of the season.

Whitt was selected by the Blue Jays in the 1976 expansion draft, and of all the players involved in various expansion drafts, only Jim Fregosi played more games with the team that selected him. /(TF)

Possum Whitted [George Bostic] — 1890–1962. OF-3B-1B-2B-SS 1912–22 Cardinals, Braves, **Phillies**, Pirates, Dodgers 1021 g, .270, 23 hr, 451 rbi. *2 WS, 9 g, .138, 3 rbi*

The 5'8″ Whitted acquired the nickname Possum growing up in Durham, NC. A utility man for the Cardinals, he was traded to the "Miracle" Braves in mid-1914 and collected a World Series check. Then sold to the Phillies, he played the outfield in all five of their 1915 WS games with the Braves. He batted a consistent .281 as a Phillies regular from 1915 to 1917 and was traded to Pittsburgh for Casey Stengel in 1919. /(JK)

Whiz Kids

The Whiz Kids were the group of baby-faced youngsters who came up to the Phillies at the end of the 1940s and won a surprise NL pennant in 1950. The best of them included Robin Roberts, Curt Simmons, Richie Ashburn, and Eddie Waitkus. /(SFS)

Harrison Wickel — Unk.–1989. *Scout.*

Wickel hit .300 in the minors eight times and won three pennants in nine seasons as a minor league manager before spending almost four decades as a scout, mostly for the Cardinals and Cubs. He helped sign John Denny, Al Hrabosky, and Bill Caudill, but his best decision may have been as manager of Williamson in 1939, when he used pitcher Stan Musial as an outfielder and pinch hitter. /(FVP)

Bob Wicker — 1878–1955. RHP-OF 1902–06 Cardinals, **Cubs**, Reds 1037 ip, 63–57, 2.73; 172 g, .205, 0 hr, 27 rbi. 20 wins: 03

With the 1903–05 Cubs, Wicker compiled a 49–25 record and played 26 games in the outfield. At New

York on June 11, 1904, he pitched nine innings of no-hit ball, gave up a hit in the 10th, and won 1–0 in 12 innings. /(DAS)

Dave Wickersham (Wick) — 1935– . RHP 1960–69 A's, **Tigers**, Pirates, Royals 1123 ip, 68–57, 3.66

Scouted by Branch Rickey and George Sisler, Wickersham was signed by the Pirates in 1955 but was acquired by Kansas City in the 1959 minor league draft. Slowed by a back injury in 1961, he went 11–4 in 1962 and 12–15 in 1963 and was a major figure in the deal that brought Rocky Colavito to the A's. He responded with his best season for Detroit in 1964, going 19–12 and missing a 20-win season only because of his first ejection from a ballgame; he tied for third in the AL in wins and had a 3.44 ERA. /(SH)

Al Wickland — 1888–1980. OF 1913–15, 18–19 Reds, **Chicago (FL)**, Pittsburgh (FL), Braves, Yankees 444 g, .270, 12 hr, 144 rbi

Wickland saw the most action with the 1914 Chicago Whales of the Federal League, when he hit .262 and had career highs of 157 games, 81 walks (which led the league), 68 RBI, 74 runs, 6 HR, and 31 doubles. In 1915 he was sold to the Pittsburgh Rebels during the season while reaching career highs in batting (.291) and stolen bases (26).

Wickland was earning $230 a month as a Reds rookie when he jumped to the Whales. /(NLM)

Frank Wickware — 1888– . RHP Negro Leagues 1910–25 Leland Giants, St. Louis Giants, Philadelphia Giants, Mohawk Giants, Lincoln Stars, Chicago American Giants, Brooklyn Royal Giants, Detroit Stars, Norfolk Stars, New York Lincoln Giants statistics not available

Wickware was a hard-throwing Negro League pitcher who broke in with the 1910 Leland Giants, a team reported to have had an incredible 123–6 record. In 1912, he went 10–4 to lead the Cuban Winter League in wins, pitching for a team that won only 14 games. In exhibition games in 1913 and 1914, he had three celebrated pitching duels with Hall of Famer Walter Johnson, winning two of the battles. He went 2–2 for the Chicago American Giants in the 1915 Black World Series, completing three of four starts and allowing eight runs in 30 innings. /(JJM)

Al Widmar — 1925– . RHP 1947–48, 50–52 Red Sox, **Browns**, White Sox 388 ip, 13–30, 5.21

Widmar pitched pro ball for 17 years. Solely a reliever for the 1948 Browns, he spent 1949 winning

22 games in the International League and returned to St. Louis as a starter, going 11–24 in 1950–51. He became a minor league manager, and a pitching coach for several ML clubs. /(FK)

Whitey Wietelmann [William Frederick] — 1919– . SS-2B 1939–47 **Braves**, Pirates 580 g, .232, 7 hr, 122 rbi

Though Wietelmann appeared in nine consecutive major league seasons, he was a regular only with the Braves during WWII, playing mostly shortstop. In 1943 he had 534 at-bats but went homerless. He batted righthanded in 1939–40, and 1942; lefthanded in 1943 and 1945; and switch-hit in 1941, 1944, and 1946–47. He later became a minor league pitcher-manager. /(FK)

Alan Wiggins — 1958– . 2B-OF-DH 1981–87 **Padres**, Orioles 631 g, .259, 5 hr, 118 rbi. *1 LCS, 5 g, .316, 1 rbi. 1 WS, 5 g, .364, 1 rbi*

The promising career of Alan Wiggins fizzled amid drug and personality problems. A first-round draft choice of the California Angels in 1977, Wiggins was released, signed by the Dodgers, then drafted away by San Diego in 1980. Playing the outfield and first base in 1983, he set a Padres record with 66 stolen bases. Moving to second base, the switch hitter was the spark plug of the 1984 San Diego Padres with 70 steals and 106 runs scored; his 75 walks compensated for his .258 batting average. Drug involvement ended his San Diego career, but Baltimore hoped the Los Angeles native would solve its lead-off problems. Wiggins did not, and also fell into disfavor with manager Earl Weaver. /(ME)

Bill Wight (Lefty) — 1922– . LHP 1946–53, 55–58 Yankees, **White Sox**, Red Sox, Tigers, Indians, Orioles, Reds, Cardinals 1563 ip, 77–99, 3.95

Wight, an unproven youngster in 1948, was halfway from California to the Yankees' spring training camp in Florida when he heard he had been traded to the White Sox. Chicago trained in Pasadena, CA; Wight had to turn his car around and head west. He became manager Ted Lyons's number-one starter but went 9–20 for the last-place club, walking a league-high 135 batters. He rebounded for his best season in 1949, going 15–13. In 1950, he went 0-for-61 at bat, an AL record for futility. Traded to Boston after the season, he pitched for six teams in the next seven years, never again winning more than nine. /(RL)

Del Wilber (Babe) — 1919– . C 1946–49 51–54 Cardinals, Phillies, **Red Sox** 299 g, .242, 19 hr, 115 rbi

Wilber was a perennial backup catcher and pinch hitter who hit three of his eight 1951 homers in an August 27 game against the Reds. Throughout his career he decorated baseballs for winning pitchers, drawing the line score, highlights, and a humorous cartoon on each memento. /(PB)

Milt Wilcox — 1950– . RHP 1970–75, 77–86 Reds, Indians, Cubs, **Tigers**, Mariners 2015 ip, 119–113, 4.08. *2 LCS, 11 ip, 2–0, 0.00. 2 WS, 8 ip, 1–1, 3.38*

Milt Wilcox knew the exhilaration of World Series victory and the frustration of missing immortality by one pitch. As a freckle-faced 20-year-old, he won the deciding game of the 1970 NLCS. He did not develop as expected at Cleveland, got little chance with the Cubs, and was in the minors when purchased by the Tigers in 1976. Becoming a skilled pitcher, rather than just a thrower, he went on to win 97 games for Detroit, 17 in 1984, despite recurring shoulder problems. Shoulder surgery in 1985 proved a blow from which he could not recover. On April 15, 1983 Wilcox was one out from a perfect game when pinch-hitter Jerry Hairiston singled to end the bid. /(ME)

Rob Wilfong — 1953– . 2B 1977–87 **Twins**, Angels, Giants 959 g, .248, 39 hr, 261 rbi. *2 LCS, 6 g, .286, 2 rbi*

A hustling, sure-handed second baseman, Wilfong started for the Twins from 1979 to 1981, and in 1980 set an AL record for his position with a .995 fielding percentage. He was traded to the Angels with Doug Corbett for Tom Brunansky in May 1982, and remained with the Angels through 1986, usually sharing second base duties with Bobby Grich. An adept bunter and contact hitter, Wilfong's .313 batting average, 9 HR, and 59 RBI in his first season as a regular (1979) all remained career highs. /(SCL)

Hoyt Wilhelm (Snacks) — 1923– . RHP 1952–72 Giants, Cardinals, Indians, Orioles, **White Sox**, Angels, Braves, Cubs, Dodgers 2254 ip, 143–122, 2.52. *1 WS, 2 ip, 0–0, 0.00*
☛ *Led League—era 52, 59. Hall of Fame—1985.*

Knuckleballing master reliever Hoyt Wilhelm appeared in more games (1,070) than any pitcher in major league history, with a late-starting ML career that still spanned 21 years. He established records

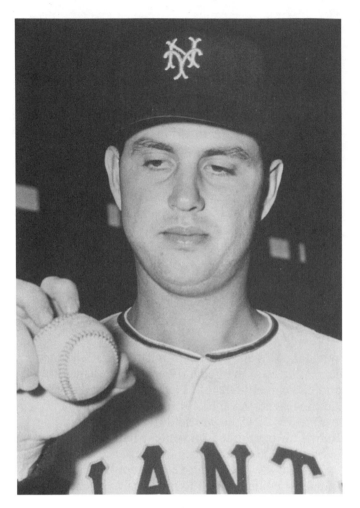

Hoyt Wilhelm

for relief wins (123), games pitched in relief (1,018), games finished by a pitcher (651), and innings pitched in relief (1,870). His 227 saves place him among the all-time leaders. Fittingly, he was the first relief pitcher elected to the Hall of Fame, and the first pitcher inducted with fewer than 150 career wins.

Wilhelm was a high school pitcher in North Carolina when he read an article about knuckleballer Emil "Dutch" Leonard and began experimenting with the pitch. After a year in the minors, his progress was interrupted by WWII, in which he won the Purple Heart for heroic duty during the Battle of the Bulge. He then spent two seasons in the North Carolina State League, winning 21 and 20. Drafted by the Giants in 1948, he remained in their farm system for four years. He was 28 when New York decided to try him in their bullpen in 1952.

Wilhelm hit the only home run of his lengthy career in his first ML at-bat on April 23, 1952 (and his only triple in his second at-bat). That season, he set a then-record with a NL-high 71 appearances, all in relief, and recorded league bests with a 2.43 ERA, an .833 winning percentage (15–3), and 15 relief wins. He led the league in appearances again in 1953 (68), and in 1954 won a league-high 12 in relief, with only 4 losses.

Wilhelm struggled in 1955–56; in 1955 he did not record a save. He was traded to St. Louis and sold to Cleveland in 1957. In 1958, after 363 consecutive relief appearances, he was given six starts by Indians manager Bobby Bragan before being waived to Baltimore in August. In his ninth ML start, on September 20, 1958, pitching through a drizzle on a day with little wind, he no-hit the Yankees on national television. Don Larsen allowed just one hit through six innings, but Wilhelm's batterymate Gus Triandos homered off reliever Bobby Shantz to give Baltimore the 1–0 victory. It was Wilhelm's only win for the Orioles that year.

Kept in the starting rotation in 1959, Wilhelm won his first nine games, finished at 15–11, and won the AL ERA title (2.19). He did not record a relief win or save. His knuckler was largely responsible as Orioles catchers set a modern record with 49 passed balls (28 by Triandos, 21 by Joe Ginsberg). The following year, manager Paul Richards introduced the oversized catcher's mitt that became standard equipment for catching the knuckler. With the emergence of the Orioles' good young pitchers (the "Baby Birds") in 1960, Wilhelm, age thirty-seven, was returned to the bullpen.

After four full seasons in Baltimore, Wilhelm was sent to the White Sox in the January 14, 1963 deal that brought Luis Aparicio to the Orioles. From 1964 to 1968, he rattled off five consecutive seasons with ERA below 2.00, including 1.31 in 1967. He got his career-high 27 saves in 1964. Always one of baseball's most frequently used pitchers, he worked in 361 games in six seasons with Chicago. He set a ML record for pitchers in 1968 when he worked in his 319th straight game without an error. With the knuckleball putting little strain on his arm, he appeared in a career-high 72 games in 1968 at the age of forty-five.

The White Sox lost Wilhelm to the Royals in the 1968 expansion draft, but he was traded to California that same winter. He was reunited with Paul Richards, by then a vice-president of the Braves, when Atlanta purchased the reliever on September 8, 1969. In eight games, Wilhelm went 2–0 with two saves to help Atlanta capture the NL West title. In 1970 he led the Braves in games pitched and

saves before his late-season trade to the Cubs. He pitched briefly for the Braves and Dodgers before retiring in 1972. He was voted into the Hall of Fame by the BBWAA in 1985. /(ME)

Kaiser Wilhelm [Irvin Key] — 1874–1936. RHP 1903–05, 08–10, 14–15, 21 Pirates, Braves, **Dodgers**, Baltimore (FL), Phillies 1432 ip, 58–108, 3.44
   Manager 1921–22 **Phillies** 77–128, .376.
   Umpire NL 1904–05

Wilhelm gained the moniker Kaiser well before the name became hated in WWI. He debuted with the 1903 pennant-winning Pirates, was not used in the World Series, then went 14–22 and 4–23 with Boston. He also lost 22 for Brooklyn in 1908. Given another chance by the outlaw Federal League in 1914, he was 13–17 for Baltimore before his arm went dead. He stayed in baseball as an umpire and a coach for the Cubs and Phillies, and managed two abysmal Philadelphia clubs in 1921–22. /(JK)

Curtis Wilkerson — 1961– . SS-2B 1983-**Rangers**, Cubs 687 g, .254, 4 hr, 116 rbi. *1 LCS, 3 g, .500*

The switch-hitting Wilkerson was the American Association's all-star shortstop in 1983 (.312 at Oklahoma City) and started at short for the Rangers in 1984–85, but has been a utility infielder since. After hitting a career-high .293 in 1988, he was part of the eight-player trade that sent Mitch Williams to the Cubs for Rafael Palmeiro and Jamie Moyer. /(SCL)

Bill Wilkinson — 1964– . LHP 1985, 87–88 **Mariners** 113 ip, 5–8, 4.13

Wilkinson's career has been slowed by constant injuries (he was disabled once a year, 1985–88). He was best in 1987, saving 10 games with a 3.66 ERA. /(SFS)

J.L. Wilkinson [James Leslie] (Wilkie) — 1874–1964. *Executive*, Negro Leagues

Wilkinson was the founder of the Kansas City Monarchs, one of the strongest and most stable franchises in Negro League history. The Monarchs began as the All-Nations Club, a multi-racial team that included blacks, Asians, Hawaiians, Hispanics, native Americans, whites, and a woman second baseman. Wilkinson signed Jackie Robinson to his first professional contract. Highly respected by his players and fellow owners, he was an innovator and the only white owner in the Negro National League when it was organized in 1920. In 1930, his Monarchs became the first pro team to use a portable lighting system for night baseball. The club won a dozen league championships between 1923 and 1950 and made four Black World Series appearances. /(LL)

Roy Wilkinson — 1893–1956. RHP 1918–22 Indians, **White Sox** 381 ip, 12–31, 4.66. *1 WS, 7 ip, 0–0, 3.68*

Wilkinson sat on the bench as his talented but corrupt 1919 Black Sox teammates drove to the pennant. He begged manager Kid Gleason for a chance in September, and blanked last-place Philadelphia in his first ML start, his only career shutout. He pitched in two games of the infamous World Series. When he was summoned to testify against his teammates after the 1920 season, he abided by a code of silence. The Black Sox banned, Wilkinson was counted on to be Chicago's number-two starter. Knowing this, he held out for much of spring training in 1921. He then lost his first nine decisions and finished at 4–20. /(RL)

Ted Wilks (Cork) — 1915– . RHP 1944–53 **Cardinals**, Pirates, Indians 913 ip, 59–30, 3.26. *2 WS, 7 ip, 0–1, 4.91*

When the Cardinals' pitching staff was depleted by the WWII draft in 1944, 28-year-old Ted Wilks was called up. The rookie compiled a sparkling 17–4 record for a league-leading .810 winning percentage. From 1946 to 1950, Wilks went 30–9 as the righthanded complement to southpaw Al Brazle in the St. Louis bullpen. He was undefeated in 1946–47. In 1949, his 59 appearances, 10 relief wins, and nine saves were NL highs. Splitting the 1951 season between the Cardinals and Pirates, Wilks again led the NL in games pitched (65) and saves (13). He was not overpowering, but his excellent control made him effective. /(FJO)

Bob Will (Butch) — 1931– . OF 1957–58, 60–63 **Cubs** 410 g, .247, 9 hr, 87 rbi

An Illinois native, Will had one season as an everyday Cubs outfielder, batting .255 in 1960. Fairly slow, with little power, he led the NL with 52 pinch-hitting appearances in 1961. /(DAS)

Jerry Willard — 1960– . C 1984–87 **Indians**, A's 273 g, .252, 21 hr, 99 rbi

One of five players obtained from Philadelphia for Von Hayes in 1982, Willard caught regularly for Cleveland in 1984–85, batting .270 in 1985. Deficient defensively and poor at calling a game, he was released on April 1, 1986. Signed by Oakland, he platooned that season with Mickey Tettleton. /(ME)

Ed Willett — 1884–1934. RHP 1906–15 **Tigers**, St. Louis (FL) 1696 ip, 102–99, 3.22. 20 wins: 09 *1 WS, 8 ip, 0–0, 0.00*

Willett was among the most powerful men on the mound, but was careless about keeping in shape. After two inauspicious trials, Willett was having his first good season in 1908 when he suffered an ankle injury; he finished 15–8, 2.28 nonetheless, helping the Tigers to their second of three straight AL flags. The following season (1909) was his best, as he went 21–10 with a 2.34 ERA and finished third in the league in wins and fifth in winning percentage (.677). He was effective in limited bullpen use in Detroit's losing WS effort.

Willett won 59 games over the next four seasons for the Tigers, then jumped to the Federal League in 1914 and was one of the few players to see his effectiveness diminish in the new league. He was 4–16 for the last-place St. Louis Terriers and didn't finish the 1915 season, his last. He was the second AL pitcher to hit two HR in a game (6/30/12). /(NLM)

Carl Willey [Carlton Francis] — 1931– . RHP 1958–65 **Braves**, Mets 876 ip, 38–58, 3.76. *1 WS, 1 ip, 0–0, 0.00*

Called up by the Braves in late June 1958, Willey blanked the Giants in his first major league game and finished 9–7 with a league-leading four shutouts. He was named *TSN*'s Rookie Pitcher of the Year. Expected to form a potent trio with Warren Spahn and Lew Burdette, he proved a disappointment, incapable of turning in a complete game. Despite his .099 lifetime batting average, one of his 22 hits was a 1963 grand slam for the Mets. /(JK)

Nick Willhite — 1941– . LHP 1963–67 **Dodgers**, Senators, Angels, Mets 182 ip, 6–12, 4.55

Willhite bounced from team to team in a series of minor deals, never compiling a winning record. He shut out the Cubs for Los Angeles in his first major league appearance, June 16, 1963. He saw the most action in 1965, spent with the Senators and Dodgers, going 2–2 with a 5.59 ERA as a starter and reliever. /(WOR)

Al Williams [born Alberto Williams DeSouza] — 1954– . RHP 1980–84 **Twins** 643 ip, 35–38, 4.24

The Nicaraguan was signed by the Pirates in 1975, but couldn't get a visa to pitch in 1977 and '78, when he was fighting in the Nicaraguan civil war. Williams's best record came in his rookie 1980 season, when he went 6–2 with a 3.51 ERA in 18 games. The streaky pitcher had elbow trouble in 1982 (9–7, 4.22) and '83 (11–14, 4.14). /(SH)

Billy Williams — 1930– . *Umpire NL 1963–87 3 ASU 5 LCS 3 WS*

Williams was a strong union man. He once said in reference to the seven minor league umpires who worked ML games during the 1979 umpires' strike, "Nobody tells me who I have to eat, sleep, or drink with, but when the blue suit goes on, it's a different story." Known for moving a game along, he once called the rare automatic ball on Astros pitcher Larry Dierker for failing to deliver a pitch within 20 seconds with no one on base. In his 25th and final year as a NL umpire, Billy had his leg broken in a play at home plate. /(RTM)

Billy Williams — 1938– . OF-DH-1B 1959–76 **Cubs**, A's 2488 g, .290, 426 hr, 1475 rbi. *1 LCS, 3 g, .000* ☛ *Rookie of the Year—61. Led League—ba 72. All-Star—62, 64–65, 68, 72–73. Hall of Fame—1987.*

Sweet-swinging Billy Williams quietly carved out a Hall of Fame career. Often overshadowed by flashier players during his heyday, he was a dependable star for 14 full seasons as a Cub. From September 22, 1963 to September 2, 1970, he established a National League record of 1,117 consecutive games played that stood until Steve Garvey broke it in 1983. He also set NL marks for games played by an outfielder in one season (164 in 1965) and consecutive years with 600 or more at-bats (nine, from 1962 to '70, broken by Pete Rose). He tied major league records with five homers in two consecutive games (September 8 and 10, 1968), and four consecutive doubles in a game (April 9, 1969).

The Alabama native, inspired by the feats of Hank Aaron, signed with the Cubs in 1956. A lefthanded hitter, he batted better than .300 at every minor league level and had brief trials in Chicago in 1959 and 1960. Hall of Famer Rogers Hornsby worked with him at Houston (American Association) in '60 as a roving instructor, and told the Cubs front office that Williams belonged in the majors. Hornsby proved correct. Williams batted .278 with 25 HR and 86 RBI in 1961 to win the NL Rookie of the Year Award, but received little publicity in light of Mickey Mantle's and Roger Maris's accomplishments that year. That was the first of 13 straight seasons in which Williams delivered at least 20 HR and 84 RBI.

Two of Williams's greatest games came in 1968; he hit for the cycle on July 17, and hit three homers on September 10. But he was stuck on a losing club, and overshadowed by the jovial Ernie Banks and the

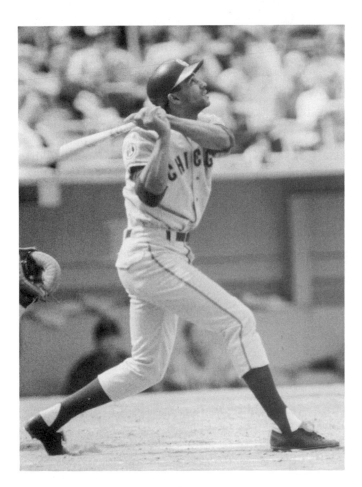

Billy Williams

outspoken Ron Santo. The arrival of Leo Durocher, another flamboyant figure, brought winning back to the Cubs, with Williams leading the way. June 29, 1969 was designated Billy Williams Day at Wrigley Field; the man of honor broke Stan Musial's NL record of 896 consecutive games played, and went 5-for-9 as the Cubs took two from the Cardinals. Chicago seemed pennant-bound that year, but fell before the late-season charge of the "Amazing" Mets. While many of the Cubs slumped, Williams hit .304 in September.

Williams had his most productive season in 1970, leading the NL in hits and in runs scored, and finished second to Johnny Bench in HR (42) and RBI (129). In 1972, he hit .333 to win the NL batting crown. That July 11, he went 8-for-8 in a doubleheader. He finished second to Bench in the RBI race and in NL MVP voting, but was named *TSN* ML Player of the Year.

Williams never played in a World Series. His best chance came after he was traded to Oakland for

Darold Knowles, Bob Locker, and Manny Trillo after the 1974 season. Williams was, by then, perfect for the DH role, and helped the A's to a fifth straight divisional title. But the Red Sox kept Williams and the A's from the WS with a sweep in the LCS.

Williams retired after batting .211 in 1976 and returned to the Cubs as a coach and batting instructor. He served Oakland in the same capacity in 1983–85, then went back to the Cubs. On his sixth try, he was elected to the Hall of Fame in 1987. The following year, he moved into Chicago's front office. /(ME)

Buff Williams [Alva Mitchell] — 1882–1933. C-1B 1911–16, 18 Red Sox, **Senators**, Indians 493 g, .265, 2 hr, 145 rbi

Williams was just 16 years old when he broke in with Keokuk (Iowa State League). The utility man saw better than a quarter of his appearances as a pinch hitter but hit only .175 in that role lifetime. He spent all his time on the Senators (1912–16) backing up defensive specialist John "Bull" Henry. /(NLM)

Charlie Williams — 1947– . RHP 1971–78 Mets, **Giants** 572 ip, 23–22, 3.98

Native New Yorker Williams pitched for the Mets in 1971, before moving across the country in the deal that brought Willie Mays from the Giants. Strong-armed but with unreliable control, he was used mainly in long relief. Although he saved only four games in 235 relief appearances, he had 16 wins out of the bullpen. /(FS)

Cy Williams [Fred] — 1887–1974. OF 1912–30 Cubs, **Phillies** 2002 g, .292, 251 hr, 1005 rbi
☛ Led League—hr 16, 20, 23, 27.

From 1915 through 1927, Williams was one of the National League's most prolific sluggers, winning or sharing four home run titles and finishing among the league's top three in homers 11 times.

An architecture student at Notre Dame, Williams became a fine collegiate sprinter and hurdler and played football with Knute Rockne. Yet it was as a strong-hitting centerfielder that he gained the attention of the Cubs, who brought him directly to the majors after his graduation.

Williams tied New York's Dave Robertson for the NL lead with 12 HR in 1916. Nevertheless, in one of the worst deals in Cubs history, he was traded (after a less productive 1917 season) to Philadelphia for 36-year-old Dode Paskert. Williams starred for the Phillies. His dead-pull, lefthanded stroke was

ideally suited to Baker Bowl. It was for Cy that the first "Williams shift" was created; managers would load up the right side with fielders, knowing it was unlikely he would hit the ball to left.

Williams's 15 homers in 1920 won him his second crown. In 1923 he hit 41, 19 more than the NL runner-up, to tie Babe Ruth for the ML lead. He shared his last title with Chicago's Hack Wilson, hitting 30 in 1927. He hit 12 inside-the-park homers and seven grand slams, and his 11 pinch homers were a record until 1960. From 1918 through his last season, he raised his career batting average every year. He topped the .300 mark six times, with a high of .345 in 1926.

In each of his first 14 seasons, Williams played for a different manager, including Tinker, Evers, and Chance. After his retirement, he became a prominent architect in Eagle River, Wisconsin. /(CG)

Davey Williams — 1927–1955. 2B 1949, 51–55 **Giants** 517 g, .252, 32 hr, 163 rbi. *2 WS, 6 g, .000, 1 rbi* ☛ *All-Star—53.*

Williams was a smooth-fielding second baseman. A NL All-Star in 1953, he was a mainstay for the World Champion Giants of 1954, leading NL second sackers with a .982 fielding average. Chronic back trouble forced his early retirement after one more season. /(BC)

Dib Williams [Edwin Dibrell] — 1910– . 2B-SS-3B 1930–35 **A's**, Red Sox 475 g, .267, 29 hr, 201 rbi. *1 WS, 7 g, .320, 1 rbi*

Williams joined the A's in 1930 and played for two straight pennant winners. A utility infielder, he sat as veteran Joe Boley played shortstop and batted .095 in the 1930 World Series. For the 1931 Series, Connie Mack replaced Boley with the strong-armed Williams; Williams responded by batting .320. /(JK)

Dick Williams — 1928– . OF-3B-1B 1951–1964 Dodgers, **Orioles**, Indians, A's, Red Sox 1023 g, .260, 70 hr, 331 rbi. *1 WS, 3 g, .500.*
Manager 1967–69, 71–88, Red Sox, A's, Angels, **Expos**, Padres, Mariners 1548–1418, .522. First place: 67, 71–73, 84 *4 LCS, 9–9, .500 4 WS, 12–14, .462*

The emotional Williams is the only manager to win pennants with three different teams (the Red Sox, A's, and Padres), as well as win titles in all four divisions. But despite his teams's successes, he always alienated management and players alike with his driving, hard-bitten, "my way or the highway" attitude. He managed six different teams in a career

Dick Williams

that stretched over 21 years and often included clashes with similarly single-minded owners.

A versatile performer in his playing days, Williams played three positions over a 13-year career with five teams, starting in Brooklyn, including three separate short tours with the Orioles, and ending in Boston. In 1967 he took over a Red Sox team that had finished ninth the year before and guided them through a successful four-team pennant race, before losing the World Series to the Cardinals in seven games. Red Sox owner Tom Yawkey grew impatient when Williams didn't repeat the feat in the following two years, and Williams's relationship with his players, especially Carl Yastrzemski, started to deteriorate. Yawkey took Yaz's side, and Williams was fired following a third-place finish in 1969.

After Williams spent a year coaching with the expansion Expos, Charlie Finley hired him to manage the A's, a team with burgeoning stars on the verge of maturity. Williams, Finley's 11th manager in as many years, guided the A's to the division title in 1971, then to their first pennant in 41 years in 1972. Williams was often accused of over-managing, and it almost cost the 1972 Series. The A's were up two games to one, and winning the fourth game 1–0 in the eighth inning. With two on, Williams replaced starter Ken Holtzman with Vida Blue to a chorus of boos. Blue promptly allowed the two runners to score. Williams was exonerated when A's scored two in the top of the ninth on four straight singles, three by pinch hitters, to win the game. They went on to win the first of three straight championships.

The 1973 Series was famous for the Mike Andrews incident. In the second game, defensive replacement Andrews committed two errors in the 12th inning to allow the Mets to win the game and tie the Series at one game each. Finley ordered Andrews to write a "confession" of his errors and claim an injury, and then tried to drop him from the roster, bypassing Williams. Incensed, Williams swore he would quit at the end of the Series, which he did, after the A's won a dramatic seventh game.

George Steinbrenner tried to hire Williams for the Yankees in 1974, but Williams was still under contract to Finley. Finley didn't want Williams to work for Steinbrenner, and prevailed on AL president Joe Cronin to nix the deal for tampering. Although Williams was out of work, he was still entitled to manage the AL All-Star team. Earl Weaver, assigned the task by Cronin, stepped aside to let Williams manage the squad. Right after the All-Star break, Williams replaced Bobby Winkles as manager of the Angels. After finishing no higher than fourth in three seasons, Williams moved back to Montreal, this time to manage. In 1981, Dodger Rick Monday's LCS homer prevented Williams from getting the Expos into their first World Series. In 1982, Williams went back to California as the manager of the Padres. He took the Padres to their only World Series in 1984, where they were overwhelmed by the much stronger Tigers. Williams spent the last three years of his career managing for tight-fisted George Argyros in Seattle, but decided early in the 1988 season that he had had enough of both cheap management and mediocre players, and retired. /(SEW)

Earl Williams — 1948- . C-1B-3B-DH 1970–77
Braves, Orioles, Expos, A's 889 g, .247, 138 hr, 457 rbi.
2 LCS, 7 g, .208, 1 hr, 4 rbi
☛ *Rookie of the Year—71. All-Star—71.*

Williams was an All-Star catcher who didn't want to catch. His 1971 season won him the NL Rookie of the Year award; he reached career highs with a .260 batting average, 33 HR, and 87 RBI while catching and playing first base and third base. He was nearly as good in 1972 (28 HR, 87 RBI, .258), but his constant complaining about playing behind the plate led Atlanta to trade him to Baltimore for 1973 with a throw-in in return for Davey Johnson, Pat Dobson, Johnny Oates, and Roric Harrison. He continued to hit for power, but his average declined and his complaining continued.

Williams is the only Brave besides Hank Aaron to hit a ball into the upper deck at Atlanta—Fulton County Stadium. /(AB)

Frank Williams — 1958- . RHP 1984- **Giants**, Reds, Tigers 472 ip, 24–14, 3.00

Williams led his minor leagues in hit batsmen four consecutive years (1979–82) before being dispatched to the bullpen, and he finally made the Giants as a reliever in 1984. After splitting 1985–86 between San Francisco and Phoenix (Pacific Coast League), he was traded to the Reds and spent two years in their bullpen before being released after the 1988 season. Williams pitched a complete game shutout in his lone ML start. /(SCL)

Gus Williams (Gloomy Gus) — 1888–1964. OF
1911–15 **Browns** 408 g, .263, 12 hr, 143 rbi

Williams struck out 120 times in 1914, only the second year that the AL counted that statistic. It stood as the major league record until 1938 and as the AL record until 1953. Williams's best season was 1913, when he hit .273, stole 31 bases, scored 72 runs, and tied for fourth in the AL with 16 triples. That April 24, he tied the AL record when he hit three triples in a nine-inning game. /(SFS)

Jimmy Williams (Buttons, Home Run) — 1876–1965.
2B-3B 1899–1909 Pirates, **Baltimore (AL)/Yankees**, Browns 1456 g, .275, 49 hr, 794 rbi

Williams was dubbed "Home Run" when he hit a career-high nine homers as a rookie in 1899. He led the NL with 27 triples that season, and led the AL with 21 in both 1901 and 1902. Though he broke in at third base, he was a steady, far-ranging second baseman most of his career. /(JK)

Jimy Williams — 1943- . SS-2B 1966–67
Cardinals 14 g, .231, 0 hr, 1 rbi.
Manager 1986–89 **Blue Jays** 281–241, .538

Williams was Pacific Coast League Manager of the Year in 1976 and 1979, but proved unable to control his major league players. A confrontation with 1987 MVP George Bell during spring training, resulting from Williams's plan to make Bell a DH, undercut his authority. The team was a perennial contender but never rose higher than a second-place finish in 1987, when they faltered at the end of the season and lost the title to the Tigers in two crucial late-season series. Williams was fired in mid-1989 and replaced with batting coach Cito Gaston. /(SFS)

Joe Williams — 1891–1972. *Writer.*

A syndicated columnist for the New York *World-Telegram and Sun* and its predecessor papers for 34 years, Williams arrived in New York in 1927, having worked for the Memphis *Commercial*, Cleveland *News*, NEA, and Cleveland *Press* along the way. /(NLM)

Ken Williams [Kenneth Roy] — 1890–1959. OF
1915–16, 18–29 Reds, **Browns**, Red Sox 1397 g, .319, 196 hr, 913 rbi
☛ *Led League—hr 22. Led League—rbi 22.*

"Brownie Stalwart of the 20s" said his obituary in the *St. Louis Post-Dispatch*. For those with long memories, Ken Williams was one of the cherished, lamented, never-quite-made-it team that finished a game behind the Yankee pennant-winners of 1922. He and the Browns had their best year together. A well-built six-footer who batted left and threw right, Williams led the league in home runs (39) and RBI (155) that year, hit .337 and stole 37 bases. This made him the first player ever to hit 30 home runs, steal 30 bases and hit .300. In one game he swatted three homers, in another, two in one inning; in between he had six in as many consecutive games. He had a pleasant, gap-toothed smile and was popular with teammates and fans.

Born and raised in Grants Pass, OR, Ken was the small-town boy who made it to the big leagues. He was the only ballplayer among six brothers whose mother had been a logging-camp cook and later operated an all-night restaurant serving the train crews when Grants Pass was a junction point on the railroad.

It took him a while to make it. After a two-year trial with Cincinnati, he was returned to the high minors, spent most of 1918 in the military, and began to see action with the Browns in 1919. The following year the club put together its finest outfield, with Ken in left, Baby Doll Jacobson in center, and Johnny Tobin in right. Williams's numbers were always respectable, if not outstanding. In 1925, although he missed some games after being skulled by a pitch, he led the league with a slugging percentage of .613.

The Browns sold him to Boston, where he put in two more .300 years. Portland (PCL) had him for two more, and at 41 he retired to Grants Pass. /(ADS)

Ken Williams — 1964– . OF-3B 1986- **White Sox**, Tigers 204 g, .232, 20 hr, 79 rbi

Williams played football with John Elway at Stanford, but chose to sign with the White Sox in 1982 after his freshman year. Speedy and powerful, he became Chicago's centerfielder in mid-1987, batting .281 with 11 HR, 50 RBI, and 21 stolen bases in 391 at-bats. The front office moved him to third base for 1988. He hurt his ankle in spring training and played with pain until a stress fracture was discovered in late May. He had committed 14 errors, and his confidence had suffered. He hit just .159 that year and was demoted for awhile. Just before the start of the 1989 season he was traded to Detroit for Eric King, but continued to struggle at the plate. /(RL)

Lefty Williams [Claude Preston] — 1893–1959. LHP 1913-14, 16-20 Tigers, **White Sox** 1186 ip, 82-48, 3.13. 20 wins: 19-20 *1 WS, 17 ip, 0-3, 6.75*

Williams had fine seasons for the White Sox in 1916 and 1917, but he worked in a shipyard during WWI and pitched only occasionally in 1918. The moody, inarticulate Williams roomed with hitting star Shoeless Joe Jackson. Williams was at his peak, having gone 22-14 in 1920, when he became one of eight Black Sox banned from baseball for throwing the 1919 World Series, in which Williams went 0-3 (6.61). His poor WS performance was particularly incongruous, as he had gone 23-11 during the season, with a league-leading 40 starts. /(NLM)

Matt Williams — 1965– . SS-3B 1987- **Giants** 220 g, .198, 34 hr, 90 rbi. *1 LCS, 5 g, .300, 2 hr, 9 rbi. 1 WS, 4 g, .125, 1 hr, 1 rbi*

Williams showed good power in his 1987 and 1988 call-ups, hitting eight HR each time, but hit for low average. After being sent down in 1989, he

reemerged and finished with 18 HR and 50 RBI in only 292 at-bats, although he hit only .202 and struck out 72 times. /(JFC)

Mitch Williams — 1964– . LHP 1986– **Rangers**, Cubs 356 ip, 22-23, 3.49. *1 LCS, 1 ip, 0-0, 0.00*

Cubs fans would sing the rock song "Wild Thing" when Mitch Williams emerged from the Chicago bullpen in 1989, in reference to his explosive but uncontrollable fastball. Williams reached a career high in saves with 36 for the Cubs in 1989, but his control problems make him dangerous both to hitters and to his own teams (220 walks in 275 career innings through 1988), and his lunging follow-through leaves him in horrible defensive position after each pitch. Williams set a ML rookie record with 80 appearances for the Rangers in 1986, and he pitched 85 times in 1987, but saved only 14 games over the two seasons. In 1988 the flame-thrower improved his control somewhat (only 6.2 walks per nine innings) and saved 18 games for the Rangers. An eight-player off-season trade made him a Cub. /(SCL)

Pop Williams [Walter Merrill] — 1874-1959. RHP 1898, 1902-03 Washington (NL), **Cubs**, Phillies, Braves 377 ip, 16-25, 3.20

Williams was a much-traveled pitcher who had one strong year, 1902 with the Cubs, when he started 31 games and had a 12-16 record. His career batting average was .217. /()

Rick Williams — 1952– . RHP 1978-79 **Astros** 156 ip, 5-9, 3.58

The Astros picked up Williams for their organization after he was released by the Mets in 1971. He went 4-7 with a 3.27 ERA for the parent club in 1979, his last major league season. /(JFC)

Smokey Joe Williams (Cyclone, Strikeout) — 1886-1946. RHP-MGR Negro Leagues 1905-32 San Antonio Broncos, Austin, Leland Giants, Chicago Giants, New York Lincoln Giants, Chicago American Giants, Bacharach Giants, Brooklyn Royal Giants, Homestead Grays, Detroit Wolves statistics not available

The greatest black pitcher of the opening decades of the 20th century, Smokey Joe Williams was a 6'5" 205-lb fireballer with exceptional control, a soft-spoken man of Negro and American Indian ancestry. He first played in his native Texas with the San

Antonio Broncos. Rube Foster signed him for the Chicago Leland Giants in 1910. He played for the New York Lincoln Giants from 1912 through 1923, and while no complete statistics exist, those were probably his peak years. His best season seems to have been 1914, when he was 12–2 in league play and 41–3 overall. His best-documented season was 1930, when, at age 44, he was 7–1 in league play.

Williams's strikeout feats were legendary. In 1924 he struck out 24 batters in a 12-inning game against the Bushwicks, a powerful semi-pro team. In 1930 he struck out 27 while one-hitting the Kansas City Monarchs over 12 innings. The game was played at night, and Williams was probably aided by the low wattage of the Monarchs' portable lights. Nevertheless, it was an incredible feat for a 44-year-old.

In exhibition games against major leaguers, Williams compiled a 22–7–1 record with 12 shutouts. Two of the losses came when he was 45 years old; two others were in 1–0 games. In 1912 he shut out the National League champion New York Giants 6–0. In 1915 he struck out 10 while hurling a 1–0 three-hit shutout over Hall of Famer Grover Cleveland Alexander and the Phillies. In a 1917 exhibition, he no-hit the Giants and struck out 20, but lost 1–0 on an error. Though no box score has been found to confirm this game, it is firmly rooted in oral history. Legend has it that it was after this game that Giants Hall of Famer Ross Youngs tagged Williams with the name "Smokey Joe." Ty Cobb, never a friend to the black player, said Williams would have been a "sure 30-game winner" if he had played in the majors. Williams threw approximately 40 no-hitters, some against semi-pro competition, recording his last gem in 1928 at forty-two. /(JJM)

Stan Williams (Big Daddy) — 1936– . RHP 1958–65, 67–72 **Dodgers**, Yankees, Indians, Twins, Cardinals, Red Sox 1764 ip, 109–94, 3.48. *1 LCS, 6 ip, 0–0, 0.00. 2 WS, 5 ip, 0–0, 0.00*
☛ *All-Star—60.*

Williams was a hulking 6'4" 225-lb righthander with blistering speed and teammate Don Drysdale's pitching personality. He loved to throw inside to batters and was widely, and appropriately, feared on the mound. But he never gained the control necessary to become a big winner.

Williams won the second game of the 1959 tie-breaking playoff with the Braves to give the Dodgers the first playoff victory in their history. They had lost in 1946 and 1951. He went to the second All-Star Game in 1960 (striking out two in two innings),

a year in which he became a regular member of the Dodger rotation and finished 14–10 with a 3.00 ERA. He struck out 205 to finish second in the league behind teammate Sandy Koufax. He was a winner for the next two years, but his streak of wildness in a relief role cost the Dodgers the '62 pennant in the playoff with the Giants and Williams was traded to the Yankees for Bill Skowron. He helped New York to another AL flag in 1963, going 9–8 with a 3.20 ERA, but he had an off-year in 1964. The Yankees sold Williams to the Indians and he was converted exclusively to relief. In December 1969 he was sent to the Twins with Luis Tiant for Graig Nettles and Dean Chance, and he contributed a 10–1, 15-save, 1.99-ERA record to the Twins' second straight divisional title in 1970. He tied for the AL lead in relief wins in what proved to be his last good season. He later became a coach with the Yankees, serving as their "eye in the sky" by positioning the outfielders from the press box. /(WOR)

Ted Williams (The Kid, The Splendid Splinter, The Thumper, Teddy Ballgame) — 1918– . OF 1939–42, 46–60 **Red Sox** 2292 g, .344, 521 hr, 1839 rbi. *1 WS, 7G, .200, 1 rbi.*
Manager 1969–72 **Senators/Rangers** 273–364, .429
☛ *Most Valuable Player—46, 49 . Led League—ba 41–42, 47–48, 57–58. Led League—hr 41–42, 47, 49. Led League—rbi 39, 42, 47, 49. All-Star—40–42, 46–51, 54–60. Hall of Fame—1966.*

Outspoken, immensely talented, patriotic, iconoclastic, demanding, larger than life: all apply to Ted Williams, for two decades baseball's best hitter and one of the best who ever lived. No one loved hitting more than Williams, who called hitting a pitched baseball "the hardest single feat in sports," and no other ballplayer spent more time at his craft. Williams lost nearly five years of his career to military service in World War II and Korea but managed to hit 521 homers and average .344 for his career, only once hitting below .316.

Signed at seventeen by his hometown San Diego Padres, he produced adequate numbers in the tough Pacific Coast League and then tore up the American Association at Minneapolis. Williams at age nineteen was the brash kid who irritated sportswriters and drove his early managers wild. His cocky manner and disinterest in playing the outfield in spring training of 1938 led to Williams being ragged by veteran Bosox outfielders. Farmed out to the minors, the frustrated youngster blurted, "Tell them I'm going to make more money in this game than all three of them put together"—an accurate prediction.

He arrived in the majors for good in 1939, breaking in with a double off Red Ruffing in Yankee Stadium. Williams completed the season with a .327 average, 31 homers, and a league-leading 145 RBI, the first rookie to be RBI leader. Quickly nicknamed The Splendid Splinter, he commanded attention as a natural hitter. He combined his undeniable talent with an inexhaustible eagerness for hard work where hitting was concerned. His early roommates were sometimes awakened by the pajama-clad Thumper practicing his swing in front of the hotel-room mirror.

In 1941 Williams had one of the greatest individual seasons for any ballplayer in history. At age twenty-three he hit .406, the last ballplayer to reach that magic figure, won his first home run crown, and won the All-Star Game with the most dramatic hit of his career, a ninth-inning two-out homer off Claude Passeau in Briggs Stadium. Williams was hot all season, and his goal of reaching .400 seemed assured when he was at .413 in mid-September, but by the morning of the final day of the season his average had "slumped" to .39955. Given the opportunity by manager Joe Cronin to sit out the doubleheader and save his average, which would have rounded off to .400, Williams characteristically played both games and went 6-for-8.

Williams never got along with the baseball press, particularly Boston beat reporters, whom he dubbed Knights of the Keyboard. Always something of a loner, distrustful of many of the trappings of stardom, he lived alone in a Boston hotel and sought out the company of cab drivers, bellhops, and clubhouse boys. His relationship with the press became adversarial early in his career, but it reached its flash point in 1942, when his request for military deferment attracted disapproval in the press. Williams was the sole support of his mother, a Salvation Army worker, and the notoriety attached to an unhappy family situation hardened his animosity, which lasted throughout his career.

Following the 1942 season, which produced his first Triple Crown (.356, 36 HR, 137 RBI), Williams enlisted in naval aviation and served as a flight instructor. He missed three full seasons (age 24–26). In 1946 there was a return to normalcy, both for America and for baseball. Williams rejoined an already potent Red Sox attack and commenced a five-year period that produced one pennant, one playoff loss and two last-weekend losses to the Yankees. During this stretch Williams accumulated two batting titles, two home run crowns, three RBI

Ted Williams

championships, and his second Triple Crown in 1947.

In 1946, he led the Boston juggernaut to a huge lead (at one point 16 games ahead) and belted two All-Star-Game home runs at Fenway Park, the second a blast off of Rip Sewell's "eephus" lob. He finished the season at .342 with 38 HR and 123 RBI, and was named AL MVP. After winning the AL pennant, the Red Sox played an exhibition against an AL all-star team to stay sharp during the Dodgers-Cardinals NL playoff. Williams was hit on the elbow by a pitch from Mickey Haefner and, playing in pain, hit only .200 with one RBI in the Series as Boston lost in seven games to St. Louis.

Williams's Series output was hobbled not only by an injury but by the Cardinals' application of the "Williams shift," stacking the defense on the right side of the diamond, thereby daring Williams to pull the ball. First employed by Indians manager Lou Boudreau during the middle of the '46 season after Williams had clubbed three homers in the first game of a doubleheader, it challenged Williams by placing as many as six fielders in his hitting zone.

Although Williams occasionally went to left field—he clinched the 1946 pennant with an inside-the-park home run to left against Cleveland—more often than not he responded by driving the ball to right field. The shift became an almost standard defensive alignment against Williams in the AL, and it undoubtedly whittled his lifetime average.

His 1947 Triple Crown performance produced another slap from the sportswriters, who elected Joe DiMaggio MVP by a single vote. DiMaggio had also been named MVP in 1941 when Williams hit .406, and when Williams won the Triple Crown in 1942, New York second baseman Joe Gordon was MVP. Williams won all six of his batting titles in back-to-back pairs, and in 1948 he batted .369 as the Red Sox fell to the Indians and Gene Bearden in the AL's first playoff. The following year produced a second MVP Award, 43 HR, a career-high 159 RBI, and an amazing 162 walks for the second time in three seasons. Williams possessed exceptional eyesight (he was allegedly able to read the label of a spinning record), and had the patience to wait for his pitch. His thorough knowledge of the strike zone produced a nearly 3-to-1 ratio of walks to strikeouts, an unheard-of statistic for a power hitter. He fanned 64 times as a rookie, and never more than 54 in any other season.

Williams had gotten off to an unusually hot start in 1950 as the Red Sox battled the Yankees for the American League lead. But the All-Star Game, which had provided Williams with his share of thrills, now robbed him of another great year. He fractured his elbow crashing into the Comiskey Park wall while catching a Ralph Kiner fly ball in the first inning, but remained in the game. He wound up missing more than sixty games because of the injury,

but still managed 28 homers and 97 RBI in only 89 games. The injury jeopardized his career at age 32. Williams returned in 1951 to hit .318, but the Red Sox slid to fifth and would not challenge the Yankees again.

Williams was called up to active duty in the Korean War after six games in 1952 (with a .400 average); his service in two wars was unique for a star ballplayer. Typically, Williams left with a bang, homering off of Dizzy Trout in his final at-bat on Ted Williams Day at Fenway Park. Unlike many wartime ballplayers, who continued to play baseball for service teams while in uniform, Williams was a pilot and flew combat missions over Korea. Hit by small-arms fire during one run, Williams crash-landed his crippled jet and escaped from the flaming wreckage. Shortly thereafter he contracted pneumonia and was sent stateside after thirty-nine missions.

At age 35, a veteran of two wars, Williams appeared finished; but he homered off Mike Garcia in his first Fenway appearance in 1953 and proceeded to hit .407 for his 37-game season. Included in his feat were 13 home runs and a .901 slugging average—an incredible pace for a veteran whose spring training had been spent inside a fighter plane.

The 1950s included well-chronicled instances of the Williams temper: spitting at the pressbox during a home run trot (he was fined $5,000 by owner Tom Yawkey, although the fine was never paid), flipping his bat into the stands after a strikeout and hitting an elderly woman on the head (she turned out to be Joe Cronin's housekeeper), and a multitude of tirades at the press. Opinionated, and not one to suffer fools gladly, he was his own man and cut a solitary path through the decade. Yet his concern for charitable causes was legendary in Boston and his efforts on behalf of the Jimmy Fund, a New England organization combating children's cancer, were numerous, often unpublicized, and made from the heart. A complex man, Williams was refreshingly human.

Williams continued to play through the 1950s, although his body protested the daily demands. He broke his collarbone diving for a ball in spring training in 1954, missed much of the 1955 campaign with an assortment of injuries, and spent an increasing amount of time fighting nagging aches and pains. There were triumphs, too. Williams's longevity had propelled him to remarkable lifetime power totals and he maintained his high average, hitting no lower than .345 his first four seasons back from Korea. He missed two more batting titles in 1954–55 due to the eligibility rules of the day, which counted at-bats, not plate appearances. In

1954, Williams hit .345 in only 386 at-bats, but was also walked 136 times. Bobby Avila won the title with a .341 average.

His 1957 campaign was arguably the greatest season ever by a veteran player. He hit .388 at age 39, had 38 homers (only 87 RBI), and missed hitting .400 by five leg hits that a younger player might have had. In the second half of the season he batted .453. Williams's charge to reach .400, sixteen years after first attaining that elusive figure, captured the nation's attention, and his popularity reached an all-time high. He finished second to Mickey Mantle in the MVP balloting.

Although his average "slumped" sixty points the following season, he still won the batting crown, rallying to overtake teammate Pete Runnels during the last weekend of 1958.

Bothered by a stiff neck and other pains, Williams had his worst season in 1959. He hit .254 with only 10 homers, and appeared finished to many. He was even advised to quit by Tom Yawkey. "That burned my ass," he recounted in his autobiography *My Turn at Bat.* Clearly Williams felt that he should not conclude his career with a .254 swan song. Instead, he finished strong in 1960, batting .316, with 29 homers. His final at-bat produced his 521st homer.

Retired from the game, Williams became a full-time fisherman. He was easily elected to the Hall of Fame in 1966, his first year of eligibility. Then Williams surprised nearly everyone in baseball when in 1969 he became manager of the Washington Senators. Ignoring critics who said he wouldn't have the patience to deal with ordinary ballplayers, Williams brought his first team in at 86–76, a 21-game improvement over the previous year. For this feat he was voted Manager of the Year. It was his high-water mark and Williams resigned in 1972 when his team, now in Texas, had slumped to 54–100.

A generation after retirement Ted Williams is still regarded as the epitome of hitting. "I want people to say 'There goes Ted Williams, the greatest hitter who ever lived' " he wrote in *My Turn at Bat.*/(PB)

Walt Williams (No-Neck) — 1943– . OF 1964, 67–75 Astros, **White Sox**, Indians, Yankees 842 g, .270, 33 hr, 173 rbi

The 5'6" 185-lb Williams was fast early in his career. But by the time he became a regular in 1969 with the powerless White Sox, he was no longer stealing bases. Although he hit a career-high .304 that year, he hit only three HR and didn't walk much. He hit eight HR twice (1971, 1973), and

fielded flawlessly in 1971. Traded to the Indians after 1972 for infielder Eddie Leon, after one season he was sent on to the Yankees in a three-way deal that brought Jim Perry to Cleveland./(SFS)

Woody Williams [Woodrow Wilson] — 1912– . 2B-SS 1938, 43–45 Dodgers, **Reds** 338 g, .250, 1 hr, 79 rbi

Unable to crack the Dodgers lineup as a shortstop in 1938 (Leo Durocher played there), Woodrow Wilson Williams resurfaced as the Reds starting second baseman in 1943–44. He led the NL in at-bats in 1944, and also led NL second basemen in fielding (.971)./(FS)

Mark Williamson — 1959– . RHP 1987- **Orioles** 350 ip, 23–22, 3.99

Williamson led the Pacific Coast League with 16 saves for Las Vegas in 1986, then was traded to the Orioles by the Padres with Terry Kennedy for Storm Davis. He made 61 appearances for Baltimore as a rookie in 1987 (an Orioles rookie record), and was in the starting rotation briefly in 1988, but was returned to the minors with a 5–8, 4.90 record./(SCL)

Ned Williamson [Edward Nagle] — 1857–1894. 3B-SS-C-RHP 1878–90 Indianapolis (NL), **Cubs**, Chicago (PL) 1201 g, .255, 63 hr, 523 rbi; 35 ip, 1–1, 3.34
☛ *Led League—hr 1884.*

Cap Anson called Williamson "the greatest all-around ballplayer the country ever saw." Williamson led National League third basemen or shortstops in assists seven times, double plays six times, fielding average four times, and putouts twice. Though an unremarkable hitter, he used the short rightfield fence in Chicago's Lake Front Park to set a major league record for doubles, with 49 in 1883, when balls hit over that fence counted for only two bases. In 1884, when the ground rules were changed, he set a ML home run record with an unprecedented 27, nearly doubling the record of 14 set the previous year. The record stood until Babe Ruth hit 29 in 1919./(FIC)

Carl Willis — 1960– . RHP 1984–88 Tigers, **Reds**, White Sox 103 ip, 2–6, 5.90

Willis's lowest ERA was 4.47, for the 1986 Reds. The reliever was both wild and hittable./(SFS)

Mike Willis — 1950– . LHP 1977–81 **Blue Jays** 296 ip, 7–21, 4.60

Willis was the Blue Jays' best lefthanded reliever their first two seasons, saving 12 games in 1977–78.

His only ML complete game came in '78, an 8–1 victory over the Yankees' Ron Guidry, who was 22–2 at the time. /(TF)

Ron Willis — 1943–1977. RHP 1966–70 **Cardinals**, Astros, Padres 238 ip, 11–12, 3.32. *2 WS, 5 ip, 0–0, 11.81*

Signed as an outfielder, Willis was the most-used reliever on the 1967 and 1968 Cardinal pennant winners. In 1967 he saved a career-high 10 games. He later served as GM at Memphis (Southern League). Willis died at age 34 in an auto accident. /(FJO)

Vic Willis — 1876–1947. RHP 1898–1910 **Boston (NL)**, Pirates, Cardinals 3996 ip, 247–206, 2.63. 20 wins: 88–89, 01–02, 06–09 *1 WS, 11 ip, 0–1, 4.76*
☛ *Led League—k 02.*

Willis won 24 games for Boston as a rookie in 1898 and became the anchor of the club's pitching staff for eight years. On August 7, 1899, he won a 7–1 no-hitter against Washington. With a splendid curveball, the durable Willis hurled more than 300 innings eight times; in 1902, he threw a league-high 410 innings and set a modern NL record with 45 complete games. He completed 388 of his 471 career starts.

In 1903, both the American and National Leagues laid claim to Willis's contract, but his services were finally retained by NL Boston. He lost a league-high 25 games in 1904, and in 1905 he set a modern ML record with 29 losses for the first team in history to have four 20-game losers. He regained his winning ways with Pittsburgh, with four consecutive 20-win seasons and a combined 89–46 record with strong clubs from 1906 through 1909. He threw 50 career shutouts, but was on the losing end of 37 others. /(FJO)

Claude Willoughby (Weeping Willie, Flunky) — 1898–1973. RHP 1925–31 **Phillies**, Pirates 841 ip, 38–58, 5.84

In Willoughby's best season, 1929, he was 15–14 with a 4.99 ERA. He compounded the problems of pitching in tiny Baker Bowl with his poor control, walking a league-leading 108 batters (in 243 innings). After falling off to 4–17, 7.59 in 1930, he was traded with Tommy Thevenow for Dick Bartell. /(JFC)

Bump Wills [Elliott Taylor] — 1952– . 2B 1977–82 **Rangers**, Cubs 831 g, .266, 36 hr, 302 rbi

Bump Wills didn't have the success of his father Maury, but he was a fine-fielding second baseman

Vic Willis with the Braves

who hit enough to be useful. He also stole 196 bases in his career at a 75% success rate, slightly better than his father's ratio, and reached a career high of 52 in 1978. Bump led the AL twice each in putouts, assists, and total chances per game. He was consistent offensively, and scored a career-high 102 runs in 1980. /(WOR)

Frank Wills — 1958– . RHP 1981, 83– Royals, Mariners, **Indians**, Blue Jays 332 ip, 16–21, 5.01

Wills was a first-round pick out of Tulane University in the 1980 June draft. He was called up but did not play at the end of the 1981 season. Before the 1985 season he was traded to the Mets and then sent along to the Mariners, where he had a career-high five wins (and 11 losses). /(TF)

Maury Wills (Mousey) — 1932– . SS-3B 1959–72
Dodgers, Pirates, Expos 1942 g, .281, 20 hr, 458 rbi.
4 WS, 21 g, .244, 4 rbi.
  Manager 1980–81 **Mariners** 26–56, .317
☛ *Most Valuable Player—62. All-Star—61–63, 65–66.
Gold Glove—61–62 .*

Wills stole his way into the record books in 1962
and in the process reminded a stagnating baseball
establishment that there could be more to offense
than waiting for your 250-lb slugger to knock one
out of the park.

Maury Wills was an undistinguished minor league
shortstop: scrawny, a poor fielder, and an erratic
hitter. He began his pro career in 1951 and probably
played every position during his time in the minor
leagues; he pitched twice and also caught. The
Dodgers loaned him to the Tigers, and he was given
back. Even the Topps baseball card company
wouldn't sign him to a contract, on the advice of
their scout and the Dodgers' scouts. But Wills
became the first player Topps passed on to make the
majors (and since then, they sign everybody, just to
play it safe). He came up to the Dodgers midway
through the 1959 season and hit .260, but he had
only seven RBI in 83 games. In his first full season in
the majors, 1960, he led NL shortstops with 40
errors. But he also hit a surprising .295 and led the
NL with 50 stolen bases. It was the highest total in
the NL since Max Carey stole 51 in 1923 (although
Luis Aparicio had been stealing bases in the AL for
several years prior to Wills's appearance). In 1961
Wills was not pinch-hit for as often as he had been
in 1960, and he scored 104 runs and drew more
walks while again leading in stolen bases (35). He
also won the first of his two Gold Gloves despite not
leading the NL in any fielding category.

Wills's 1962 season found him at the apex of his
base-stealing ability. His new major league record of
104 stolen bases shattered Ty Cobb's old mark of 96
not only in the final total, but in execution: Wills
was caught stealing only 13 times in 1962, but Cobb
was caught 38 times in 1915. Also, Cobb set his
record in 156 games, and Wills broke it by one in
the same span. In 1962, Wills also led the NL with
10 triples and reached career highs with 130 runs,
48 RBI, six HR, and 208 hits. His 695 at-bats
missed the ML record by one. He won another Gold
Glove. And he beat out Willie Mays by seven points
to win the NL MVP award.

Wills led the NL the next three years in stolen
bases, but his success ratio fell. His six straight
seasons leading the NL in steals set the NL record,

*Maury Wills with his NL record 81st
stolen base*

and he tied the NL record for most years leading in
singles, four (1963–67). He never again scored 100
runs, and he never drew enough walks to really be a
great leadoff hitter, although he hit a career-high
.302 in 1963 and 1966. But he did lead NL
shortstops in assists and total chances per game in
1965. In the 1965 World Series he tied the WS
record with four hits (two singles and two doubles) in
Game Five. In the same game, he tied the record for
double plays started by a shortstop with three.

Traded to the Pirates after 1966 for Bob Bailey
and Gene Michael, Wills played third base in
Pittsburgh due to the presence of Gene Alley at
shortstop. The Pirates didn't protect Wills after
1968, and the Expos selected him in the expansion
draft. After a .222 start, he was traded back to the
Dodgers with Manny Mota for Ron Fairly and Paul
Popovich and regained his stroke. Nearing his 40th

birthday in 1972, he was finally succeeded as Dodger shortstop by Bill Russell.

Wills was named Mariners manager near the end of the 1980 season and promised to teach the team how to steal a pennant. He was fired in 1981 after a 6–18 start, having had serious discipline difficulties. /(JFC)

Ted Wills — 1934– . LHP 1959–62, 65 **Red Sox**, Reds, White Sox 186 ip, 8–11, 5.51

Wills had slightly more success as a relief pitcher than as a starter over the course of his career, compiling a 6–4 record with five saves and a 5.17 ERA in relief. /(SFS)

Art Wilson (Dutch) — 1885–1960. C 1908–21 **Giants**, Chicago (FL), Pirates, Cubs, Braves, Indians 812 g, .261, 24 hr, 226 rbi. *3 WS, 6 g, .200*

A good defensive player, the hard-working Wilson was a reliable reserve catcher for Giant pennant-winners in 1911–13 but did not play regularly until he jumped to the Federal League. In two seasons with the Chicago Whales, he hit .291 and .305. He returned to the NL with the Cubs in 1916 and was Hippo Vaughn's catcher when Vaughn and Fred Toney matched no-hitters through nine innings (5/2/17), a game won by Toney in the tenth when Wilson couldn't handle Vaughn's throw home on a fielder's choice. /(BC)

Artie Wilson — 1920– . SS-1B-2B-3B 1944–57 Negro Leagues; 1951 **Giants** 19 g, .182, 1 rbi

Wilson was the top Negro League shortstop of the 1940s. An ideal leadoff man, he batted lefthanded and slapped the ball to the opposite field. He hit .376 over four seasons (1944–45, 47–48) in the Negro American League and captured the 1948 batting title with a .402 mark. He then won the 1949 Pacific Coast League batting crown (.348) and stolen base title. Opposing managers eventually adopted a special defensive shift to counter his batting style. He was also a superior defensive player, a master at the double play who started at shortstop in four East-West all-star games. The Yankees were awarded rights to him in 1950 after a dispute with the Indians, but Wilson had only 22 major league at-bats, with the 1951 Giants. /(MFK)

Bill Wilson — 1928– . OF 1950, 53–55 White Sox, **A's** 224 g, .222, 32 hr, 77 rbi

Wilson was signed for a reported $75,000 by the White Sox but spent all of 1951 and 1952 in the military. Traded to the A's in June 1954 after a slow start, he was their regular centerfielder and finished the year with 17 HR in 358 at-bats, but struck out too much (64) and hit only .232. /(JFC)

Bill Wilson — 1942– . RHP 1969–73 **Phillies** 258 ip, 9–15, 4.23

Wilson, who spent his whole major league career in relief, had his best season in 1971, when he went 4–6 with seven saves and a 3.05 ERA. /(WOR)

Don Wilson — 1945–1975. RHP 1966–74 **Astros** 1748 ip, 104–92, 3.15

Author of two no-hitters and an 18-strikeout game, Don Wilson had not reached his potential when he died, a suicide, of carbon monoxide poisoning in the garage of his home on January 5, 1975. Wilson was unfairly labeled a troublemaker after run-ins with Astro managers Harry Walker and Leo Durocher. As a rookie, the hard thrower pitched a no-hitter against the Braves on June 18, 1967. He pitched two masterpieces against the Reds: on July 14, 1968, he struck out 18 Cincinnati batters in nine innings, and he no-hit them on May 1, 1969. On September 4, 1974, he pitched eight no-hit innings against the Reds. With Houston trailing 2–1, manager Preston Gomez pulled Wilson for a pinch hitter in a controversial move that prevented a possible third no-hitter. /(ME)

Earl Wilson (Moose) — 1934– . RHP 1959–60, 62–70 **Red Sox**, Tigers, Padres 2052 ip, 121–109, 3.69. 20 wins: 67 *1 WS, 4 ip, 0–1, 6.23*
☛ *Led League—w 67.*

The first black player signed by the Red Sox, Earl Wilson might have been the first to integrate the Boston club had his career not been delayed by military service in 1956–57. Pumpsie Green beat him to Boston in 1959.

Originally a catcher, Wilson threw hard, and switched to pitching in 1953, his first pro season. He reached the majors late in 1959, but did not stick until 1962. That June 26, he no-hit the Angels at Fenway Park. In 1963, he walked a league-high 105 batters and tied an American League record with 21 wild pitches. Though his control improved, he was traded to Detroit on June 14, 1966, in the midst of his fourth straight mediocre season. Just 5–5 when traded, Wilson caught fire with the Tigers, going 13–6 the rest of the way. He earned a spot on *TSN*'s AL All-Star team that year, and again in 1967, when he tied Jim Lonborg for the league lead with 22 wins. A power pitcher averaging better than six strikeouts per nine innings, he was also one of baseball's greatest power-hitting pitchers. He hit 35 home runs in just 740 at-bats, including two in one game August 16, 1965, and seven in a season twice, a feat surpassed only by Wes Ferrell. /(ME)

Glenn Wilson — 1958– . OF 1982– Tigers, **Phillies**, Mariners, Pirates, Astros 1073 g, .267, 88 hr, 466 rbi
☛ *All-Star—85.*

Wilson earned a reputation with a strong, deadly accurate throwing arm, leading NL outfielders in assists in 1985 and 1986 with 18 and 20, respectively. He was a first-round draft choice (eighth overall) of the Tigers in the June 1980 free-agent draft and hit a career-high .292 as a rookie for Detroit in 1982. After a dismal 1984 with the Phillies, Wilson began wearing glasses in 1985 and drove in 102 runs, earning a spot on the All-Star team. His production fell off in 1987, and he was

traded to the Mariners, who shipped him to the Pirates after a disappointing half-season in Seattle. He reestablished himself as a regular in 1989 and was traded to the Astros in mid-season for Billy Hatcher. /(SG)

Hack Wilson [Lewis Robert] — 1900–1948. OF 1923–34 Giants, **Cubs**, Dodgers, Phillies 1348 g, .307, 244 hr, 1062 rbi. *2 WS, 12 g, .319, 3 rbi*
☛ *Led League—hr 26–28, 30. Led League—rbi 29–30. Hall of Fame—1979.*

Hack was, first of all, a physical phenomenon. There were 195 pounds of him on a 5'6" frame: the height of Phil Rizzuto, only 40–45 pounds heavier. As a young man it was all muscle: a barrel-chested upper body, blacksmith arms, and bulging thighs and calves on the short, short legs that tapered to tiny feet. He wore an 18 collar and size 6 shoe. And until the liquor overmastered him, he could hit a ton. Two records, both set in 1930, are still his: 56 home

Hack Wilson

runs in a season, the most for a National Leaguer, and 190 runs batted in, a major league mark no one has approached in 50 years.

His nickname derived either from George Hackenschmidt, an old-time wrestler, or from a resemblance to Hack Miller, another sawed-off heavyweight who preceded him in Chicago.

The Cubs got Wilson on a fluke. Originally a Giant, he performed creditably in 1924, but slumped to .239 the following year and was sent down to Toledo (American Association), then a Giant farm. In the postseason draft the Cubs acquired him for a measly $5,000 over a strenuous Giant protest that Commissioner Landis denied. Thereafter, batting cleanup in the Cubs' awesome array of hitters, he was one of the National League's top power hitters. At the plate he was a sight to see, squat, stumpy, and menacing, with an earnest, clenched-jaw look on the square face. He loved the high fastball and brought the bat around from the right side to meet it with little grace and mighty effort. Like many big swingers, he often led the league in strikeouts, but unlike today's hitters, never exceeded 94 strikeouts in any season. Along the way he had 25- and 27-game hitting streaks, hit for the cycle, and in his best year (1930) had a slugging average of .723.

For all his top-heavy physique, he was a capable centerfielder. Kiki Cuyler may have helped some in right field, but with Riggs Stephenson in left field Hack was on his own. In 1927 he led the league's outfielders with 400 putouts. Although remembered for two crucial hits lost in the sun during the Athletics' memorable 10-run Series rally in 1929, he otherwise fielded without error and led all Series hitters with a .471 average.

His problem was alcohol and the lack of discipline it encouraged. Joe McCarthy knew how to handle him and keep him functioning. Other managers, notably Rogers Hornsby, did not. Following his tremendous 1930, Hack slumped alarmingly, hitting a pussycat .261 with 13 home runs and 61 RBI. Over the winter he was traded to the Cardinals for Burleigh Grimes, and from there to Brooklyn for $45,000 and a minor-league pitcher. He checked his slide briefly, but by 1934 his career had ended. /(ADS)

Highball Wilson [Howard Paul] — 1878-1934. RHP 1899, 02-04 Cleveland (NL), A's, **Senators** 371 ip, 14-27, 3.29

Wilson went 7-5 for the AL pennant-winning Athletics in 1902, but for last-place Washington the next year he struggled to a 7-18 mark. /(BC)

Jack Wilson (Black Jack) — 1912- . RHP 1934-42 A's, **Red Sox**, Senators, Tigers 1132 ip, 68-72, 4.59

Wilson was a weak-hitting third baseman for two years in the minors before taking the mound. In his initial Red Sox outing, in 1935, he relieved Wes Ferrell and hit an 11th-inning homer for his first major league hit and first victory. He went 16-10 at his best in 1937 and 15-15 in 1938, starting and relieving, and saved 20 games in seven years with Boston. /(JK)

Jim Wilson — 1922-1986. RHP 1945-46, 48-49, 51-58 Red Sox, Browns/Orioles, A's, **Braves**, White Sox 1539 ip, 86-89, 4.01
☛ All-Star—54-56.

Wilson's career was almost ended as a rookie when a Hank Greenberg line drive fractured his skull and left him unconscious. He recovered to become a capable starter for a handful of teams, winning in double figures four times but leading the AL with 18 losses for Baltimore in 1955. With the Braves on June 12, 1954 he pitched a no-hitter, defeating Robin Roberts and the Phillies 2-0. /(JK)

Jimmie Wilson (Ace) — 1900-1947. C 1923-40 **Phillies**, Cardinals, Reds 1525 g, .284, 32 hr, 621 rbi. 4 WS, 20 g, .242, 5 rbi.
    Manager 1934-38, 41-44 **Phillies**, Cubs 493-735, .401
☛ All-Star—33, 35.

Wilson was one of the National League's top catchers of the 1920s and 1930s. After catching more than 100 games for the first time in 1927, the native Philadelphian was traded to the Cardinals and helped them to pennants in 1928, 1930, and 1931. A respected handler of pitchers, with St. Louis he led NL catchers in putouts three times, double plays three times, and assists twice. He hit for average with little power, but had 20 or more doubles in five different seasons.

After the 1933 season, Wilson was dealt back to the Phillies to become their playing manager. In five years, he never finished higher than seventh. Given a job coaching for the Reds in 1939, he got an opportunity to play in 1940 when injuries and Willard Hershberger's suicide decimated the Cincinnati catching corps. At 40, after playing in only 16 regular season games, he caught six of seven World Series games against the Tigers, batted .353, and stole the only base of the Series. Replacing the popular Gabby Hartnett in 1941, he managed the Cubs for just over three seasons, all in the second division. The Cubs won their opening game in 1944, then lost 9 straight and Wilson resigned. He joined the Reds again as a coach a few days later, retiring after the 1946 season. /(AL)

Jud Wilson (Boojum) — 1899–1963. 3B-1B-MGR Negro Leagues 1922–45 Baltimore Black Sox, Homestead Grays, Pittsburgh Crawfords, Philadelphia Stars statistics not available
☛ *All-Star—1933–35.*

Wilson was an intense, no-holds-barred dynamo on Negro League baseball fields, intimidating opposing pitchers and umpires with his potent bat and powerful fists. He was built like a wrestler, and his fights with umpires and players were as legendary as his will to win. His nickname, Boojum, derived from the sound of his line drives slamming off the fences.

Playing for the Baltimore Black Sox, Wilson was the Eastern Colored League's batting champ (.408) in 1927. In 1929 he led the league in stolen bases, helping Baltimore win the pennant as a member of their "million-dollar infield." He led the league in doubles in 1930 while batting .372. He played winter ball in Cuba from 1925 to 1929, twice leading the league in average by hitting more than .400.

Wilson was briefly a Homestead Gray before he and most of his teammates jumped to the Pittsburgh Crawfords in 1932. In 1933 he joined the Philadelphia Stars. Webster McDonald, the team's pitcher-manager, appointed him team captain in order to constructively channel Wilson's competitive spirit. While this tactic was somewhat successful (Wilson hit a league-high .412 in leading the club to the 1934 pennant), it did not prevent the pugnacious slugger from punching an umpire in the 1934 playoffs.

The Homestead Grays had won three straight pennants when Wilson joined them in 1940. When he retired at age 46 after the 1945 season, the Grays had won nine consecutive pennants, a pro sports record. Wilson topped the .339 mark three times and played in three Black World Series for Homestead.

Wilson played in the East-West all-star games from 1933 to 1935, batting .455. He holds the third highest average in Negro League history, and ranks 10th in lifetime home runs. He hit .356 in 26 games against white major leaguers. /(ETW)

Mookie Wilson [William Hayward] — 1956– . OF 1980– **Mets**, Blue Jays 1170 g, .277, 62 hr, 359 rbi. *3 LCS, 15 g, .172, 4 rbi. 1 WS, 7 g, .269*

Mookie Wilson will forever be remembered for one World Series at-bat lasting ten pitches. With the Red Sox one strike away from clinching the 1986 WS in the bottom of the tenth inning of Game Six, Wilson fouled off pitch after pitch with last-second swings. With a 2–2 count, he fouled off two pitches. Then, reliever Bob Stanley threw one in the dirt at Wilson's feet, and the long-time Met favorite skipped rope to avoid being hit. The wild pitch allowed Kevin Mitchell to score, tying the game, and moved Ray Knight to second base. Wilson fouled off two more pitches and then hit a slow grounder to first baseman Bill Buckner, playing well behind the bag. The speedy Wilson would have been safe anyway, but Buckner let the ball go between his legs, allowing Knight to score the winning run. With drama quite different from a game-winning home run, the accumulated excitement of the slowly building rally capped by the tension of Wilson's at-bat made the game one of the most exciting in Series history.

For most of his career, Wilson was a hustling fan favorite whose at-bats were greeted at home with cries of Moooooo-kie. However, he had serious flaws as a leadoff man. He struck out more than 100 times in two of his three seasons as an everyday player, and when he led the NL with 638 at-bats in 1983, he drew only 18 walks, giving him a career-low .300 on-base average. Not until 1985 did he have an on-base average above .330, which is roughly the NL average, including pitchers, in a normal year. With the arrival of the more patient Lennie Dykstra in 1985, Wilson had to walk more to keep even a platoon job, and to his credit he did get his OBA as high as .360 (1987). He was a good basestealer, with highs of 58 in 1982 and 54 in 1983. And although he had wild swings between hot and cold during the season, from year to year he was a model of consistency. He hit .276 three years in a row (1983–85) and, after hitting .248 in his first call-up, hit between .271 and .299 from 1981 through 1988.

Wilson's speed helped him outrun mistakes in the outfield and compensated for a weak arm; he led NL outfielders with six double plays in 1984. Arm surgery in 1985 weakened his arm even further and gave Dykstra the playing time that reduced the streaky, switch-hitting Wilson to a platoon player. His career was threatened by a freak eye injury suffered in spring training in 1986, when he was hit in the glasses by a Rafael Santana throw during an infielders' rundown drill. When he came back after five weeks on the DL, he had trouble judging fly balls, especially during day games, that has persisted for the rest of his career.

As the senior member of the team in the second half of the 1980s, Wilson was an important clubhouse influence. His hustle, even when the Mets had been notorious non-contenders, set an example for younger players. He grumbled about his reduced playing time, but continued to be an unselfish team leader until he was traded to Toronto in the second half of 1989. He sparked the Blue Jays to the 1989 division title and fittingly scored the run that clinched first place./(SH)

Owen Wilson (Chief) — 1883–1954. OF 1908–16 **Pirates**, Cardinals 1280 g, .269, 59 hr, 571 rbi. *1 WS, 7 g, .154, 1 rbi*

Wilson is best known for hitting 36 triples for the Pirates in 1912. This was easily the highest figure in organized baseball history. A lefthanded line drive hitter, he hit 24 of the triples in spacious Forbes Field in Pittsburgh. He also hit 31 of his 59 career home runs inside the park. The tall and taciturn Texan was a good outfielder with a strong throwing arm. With the Cardinals in 1914 he led the NL in assists and fielding percentage. He was the only National Leaguer to play the full schedule of games in 1912 and 1913, and would have been in 1914 as well but sat out the last two games to prepare for the St. Louis city series. He batted only .154 in seven Series games against the Tigers in 1909./(LRD)

Red Wilson [Robert James] — 1929– . C 1951–60 White Sox, **Tigers**, Indians 601 g, .258, 24 hr, 189 rbi

Wilson, a former University of Wisconsin football star, was never an everyday catcher, but he caught at least 59 games each year from 1953 through 1960. With the Tigers he was the primary catcher of "The Yankee Killer" Frank Lary; Lary was 16–3 (with two no-decisions) against New York with Wilson behind the plate. In addition, Wilson batted .354 in those 21 contests—96 points above his career average./(FK)

Trevor Wilson — 1966– . LHP 1988- **Giants** 61 ip, 2–5, 4.26

The Giants' staff's injury woes gave Wilson chances in 1988 and '89./(WOR)

Willie Wilson — 1955– . OF 1976- **Royals** 1672 g, .289, 38 hr, 467 rbi. *4 LCS, 16 g, .271, 1 hr, 6 rbi. 2 WS, 13 g, .268, 3 rbi*
☛ *Led League—ba 82. All-Star—82–83. Gold Glove—80.*

Wilson was a first-round draft choice for Kansas City in 1974 after he turned down a football

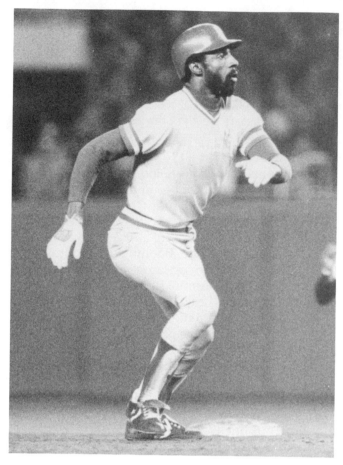

Willie Wilson

scholarship to the University of Maryland. His great speed made him an acceptable leadoff hitter, although he hardly ever walked, and an exciting outfielder in spacious Royals Stadium.

Once Wilson started playing every day, he hit .300 for four successive seasons, and he had stolen more than 30 bases in eleven consecutive seasons through 1988. In 1980 Wilson became the second player to collect 100 hits from each side of the plate in a season. He was Royals Player of the Year in 1981. Five times he led the AL in triples. He played 148 straight errorless games in 1987 (325 chances).

Wilson's twelve strikeouts in the 1980 World Series set a record, but he exonerated himself by batting .367 in the 1987 "I-70 Series" against the Cardinals.

In October 1983 Wilson was one of four Royals to plead guilty to charges of attempting to possess cocaine and served a brief prison sentence./(FO)

Hal Wiltse [Whitey] — 1903–1983. LHP 1926–28, 31 **Red Sox**, Browns, Phillies 500 ip, 20–40, 4.87

Wiltse was a 5′9″ blond who once tried to change a run of bad luck by dyeing his hair red. He compiled an 18–33 record with the Red Sox in 1926–27, but calcium deposits caused him arm problems and curtailed his use for the Phillies. /(JK)

Hooks Wiltse [George LeRoy] — 1880–1959. LHP 1904–15 **Giants**, Brooklyn (FL) 2112 ip, 139–90, 2.47. 20 wins: 08, 09 *2 WS, 3 ip, 0–0, 18.90*

Though overshadowed on the Giants staff by Christy Mathewson, Wiltse won in double figures for New York in each of his first eight seasons and was with them for five pennants. He had a sensational rookie year in 1904, winning his first 13 starts and finishing 13–3. On May 15, 1906, he struck out seven consecutive Cincinnati batters in two innings. He pitched 29 career shutouts.

Wiltse's nickname did not come from his curveball but from the way he would reach out with

Hooks Wiltse

his long right arm to snare line drives and high bounders coming back through the box. Frank Bowerman, his catcher with the Giants, would shout, "That's hooking them, George," and the name Hooks stuck. Wiltse's brother Lewis pitched with four ML teams in 1901–03.

In the first game of a July 4, 1908 doubleheader, Wiltse pitched a 10-inning, 1–0 no-hitter against Philadelphia. He almost had a 30-out perfect game. With two out in the ninth, umpire Cy Rigler failed to give Wiltse a third strike, which he later admitted could have been called. The next pitch hit the batter. Wiltse got the next man, and was perfect in the tenth after his team scored a run.

Wiltse pitched in relief in two 1911 World Series games, but appeared in the 1913 WS only at first base. Regular first baseman Fred Merkle was hurt, and his replacement, Fred Snodgrass, injured his leg sliding in the second game. Wiltse, a great fielder who loved to work out at first base, was sent in, and made several sensational plays to save Christy Mathewson's shutout of Philadelphia. /(JK)

Snake Wiltse [Lewis DeWitt] — 1871–1928. LHP 1901–03 Pirates, **A's**, Baltimore (AL)/Yankees 537 ip, 30–31, 4.59

Snake Wiltse never achieved the success of his younger brother Hooks, who twice won 20 for the Giants. Snake won 13 games for the 1901 A's in the AL's first year but was sold to Baltimore's AL team in July 1902. For the season he gave up a league-leading 397 hits in 302 innings. /(BC)

Bobby Wine (Wine-O) — 1938– . SS-3B 1960, 62–72 **Phillies**, Expos 1164 g, .215, 30 hr, 268 rbi.
Manager 1985 **Braves** 16–25, .390

Known for his strong arm, Wine rarely played enough, or enough full games, to accumulate high statistical totals; he was bothered by a bad back and missed most of the 1966 and '68 seasons because of it (he had surgery for a ruptured spinal disc in 1968). However, he won a Gold Glove in 1963, led the NL in fielding in 1967, and, playing for the Expos in 1970, he set a ML shortstop record with 137 double plays (it was his only season with more than 420 at-bats; he had 501). His best batting average came in his rookie 1962 season, when he hit .244; his .215 lifetime average is the fourth-worst all-time (2,500 or more at-bats).

After retiring, Wine was a coach for the Phillies (1972–83) and scouted for the Braves (1984, '86). While a coach with Atlanta in 1985, he was named interim manager. His son Robbie, a catcher for the Astros, was a first-round draft pick in 1983. /(SFS)

Ralph Winegarner — 1909– . RHP-3B 1930, 32, 34–36, 49 **Indians**, Browns 194 ip, 8–6, 5.33; 136 g, .276, 5 hr, 28 rbi

Winegarner had a long minor league career as a pitcher, infielder, and outfielder, and several trials with the Indians. He relieved in nine games in 1949 while a coach for the Browns after a 13-year absence from the majors. /(ME)

Dave Winfield (Winny) — 1951– . OF 1973–88 **Padres**, Yankees 2269 g, .287, 357 hr, 1438 rbi. *1 LCS, 3 g, .154, 2 rbi. 1 WS, 6 g, .045, 1 rbi*
☛ *Led League—rbi 79. All-Star—77–88. Gold Glove—79–80, 82–85, 87.*

Before back surgery sidelined him for the 1989 season, Winfield was one of baseball's most dominant and durable outfielders. During eight seasons with the Padres and eight seasons with the Yankees, he hit for average and power, played outstanding defense in left field and right field, and was the prototypical hustling professional.

Winfield was a star pitcher and basketball player at the University of Minnesota. He batted over .400 and compiled a 13–1 pitching record for the Golden Gophers, and he was named MVP of the 1973 College World Series. Winfield was drafted by four teams in three sports after his senior year. A fifth-round selection of the NBA's Atlanta Hawks, a sixth-round draftee of the ABA's Utah Stars, and a seventeenth-round choice of the NFL's Minnesota Vikings despite not having played college football, Winfield signed with the Padres, who made him the fourth overall selection in the June 1973 draft. He joined the Padres immediately, bypassing the minors altogether.

By 1977, his fourth full season, Winfield established himself as an All-Star, posting 25 home runs, 92 RBI, 104 runs, 169 hits, and 29 doubles. In 1979, Winfield dominated NL pitching, hitting .308 for the second consecutive year, while pounding 34 homers and driving in a league-leading 118 runs. It was that kind of performance that led Yankee owner George Steinbrenner and Ted Turner, owner of the Atlanta Braves, to court Winfield as a free agent after the 1980 season. Winfield chose New York and signed a landmark 10-year contract. Soon after he signed, conflict arose between Winfield and Steinbrenner when the Yankee owner realized he had incorrectly interpreted the contract's first cost-of-living escalator and that the deal would probably

Dave Winfield

cost him $23 million rather than the $16 million he had expected. For the next decade, the relationship between the two men was uneasy, and controversy arose about Steinbrenner's alleged delinquency in making contractually required payments to the Winfield Foundation, a charitable organization for children.

The press expected controversy on the field as well. Although he was denied much of the media recognition that was his due when with San Diego, there was no question that Winfield was the certifiable star of the Padres. Joining the Yankees, Winfield found himself on a team famous for controversy and big player egos, Reggie Jackson's among them. However, Winfield made the adjustment seamlessly, and he hit .294 in 1981 to help the Yankees defeat Milwaukee in divisional play and Oakland in the LCS, before going 1-for-22 in the six-game World Series loss to the Dodgers.

The Yankees did not made it back to postseason competition in the 1980s, but Winfield had tremendous individual success. He drove in over 100 runs from 1982 through 1986 to become the first Yankee since Joe DiMaggio to do so in five consecutive seasons. He came up three shy of 100 with 97 in 1987, but collected 107 RBI in 1988. He hit 24 or more homers in each of his seven full seasons with New York except for 1984, when he consciously shortened his stroke in an attempt to win the batting crown. He hit a personal-best .340 that year but lost the title to teammate Don Mattingly on the season's final day. He won Silver Bat awards from 1981 through 1984.

Winfield's defensive play was superb and featured his innovative way of digging his cleats into the padding to climb the outfield wall and snatch home runs from the seats. He garnered six AL Gold Gloves to go with his NL Gold Glove. His outfield arm, already respected as arguably the best in baseball, was accorded further notoriety when Winfield accidentally fatally beaned a seagull between innings of a 1983 game in Toronto.

Winfield appeared in 12 consecutive All-Star Games, and he holds All-Star records for most doubles (seven) and most consecutive games with at least one hit (seven). Prior to the back surgery that forced him out of the Yankee lineup in 1989 and led to speculation about his chances of making a comeback in 1990 at age thirty-eight, he showed no signs of slowing, hitting .322 with 25 homers and 107 RBI in 1988. At the start of 1989, Winfield was the active leader in RBI (1,438), and his 1,107 RBI from 1979 to 1988 were more than any other major leaguer. He finished the 1980s tied for seventh with Roger Maris on the Yankees' all-time list for homers. /(EG/CR)

Jim Winford (Cowboy) — 1909–1970. RHP 1932, 34–38 **Cardinals**, Dodgers 276 ip, 14–18, 4.56

When Paul Dean's arm gave out in 1936, Winford, with only 32 major league innings under his belt, stepped into the Cardinal rotation to win 11 games, second on the staff to Dizzy Dean's 24. /(FJO)

Ernie Wingard (Jim) — 1900–1977. LHP 1924–27 **Browns** 696 ip, 29–43, 4.55

Wingard went 13–12 in his first season and his 3.51 ERA was the best on the Browns' staff. He never had another winning season, and he fell to 2–13 in his last year. He was a fair hitter, slugging .462 and batting .288 in 1925. He played three games in the outfield in his career and twice hit three homers in a season. /(SH)

Ted Wingfield — 1899–1975. RHP 1923–27 Senators, **Red Sox** 553 ip, 24–44, 4.18

Wingfield fought in WWI and was hospitalized after exposure to mustard gas. Originally a shortstop, he fielded so poorly that he eventually became a pitcher. He batted .234 in the majors, but never came close to a winning season on the mound. /(NLM)

Al Wingo [Absalom Holbrook] (Red) — OF 1919, 24–28 A's, **Tigers** 493 g, .308, 9 hr, 191 rbi

When Wingo hit .370 in 1925, he had the lowest batting average in the Detroit outfield. Harry Heilmann led the league at .393 and player/manager Ty Cobb hit .378. It was the only time that every member of an outfield has hit .370 or better. It was by far Wingo's career high, as were his 104 runs, 68 RBI, 14 steals, and five HR. It was a time of high averages, and when he fell off to .282 in 1926, he lost his regular status to Fatty Fothergill, who hit .367. Wingo's brother was Ivy Wingo. /(NLM)

Ivy Wingo — 1890–1941. C 1911–26, 29 Cardinals, **Reds** 1326 ip, .260, 25 hr, 455 rbi. *1 WS, 3 g, .571, 1 rbi. Manager 1916 **Reds** 1–1, .500*

Wingo was a durable catcher who retired in 1929 with a National League record for games caught (1,231). He topped the mark set by George Gibson, but was eventually passed by Al Lopez, who had played three games when Wingo retired. Wingo caught 90 or more games in 8 of his 17 major league seasons. He was behind the plate for Cincinnati in three games of the 1919 Black Sox World Series, and later coached for the Reds. Wingo holds the post-1900 ML career catchers records for errors (234) and most years leading the league in errors (7), and ranks seventh in assists (1,487). His younger brother Al was an outfielder with the Athletics and Tigers. /(JK)

Jim Winn — 1959– . RHP 1983–88 **Pirates**, White Sox, Twins 308 ip, 12–17, 4.67

Hard-throwing Jim Winn was plagued by gopher balls as a pro. Converted from starter to reliever in Pittsburgh's 1983 spring camp, Winn modeled himself after relief star Goose Gossage. He was Chicago's closing reliever the second half of 1987. /(ME)

Herm Winningham — 1961- . OF 1984- Mets, **Expos**, Reds 581 g, .240, 14 hr, 112 rbi

A speedy outfielder who has struggled at the plate in the ML, Winningham was one of four players traded from the Mets to the Expos for Gary Carter in December 1984, and was starting in centerfield for the Expos in 1985 until his June knee injury gave Mitch Webster a chance to play. He stole a career-high 29 bases in 131 games for Montreal in 1987, then was traded to the Reds in 1988, where he has remained a reserve. Aside from a .407 average in 14 games with the Mets in 1984, Winningham has hit better than .237 only once in the ML. /(SCL)

George Winter (Sassafras) — 1878–1951. RHP 1901–08 **Red Sox**, Tigers 1656 ip, 83–101, 2.87. *1 WS, 1 ip, 0–0, 0.00*

A Gettysburg College teammate of Eddie Plank, Winter was not signed by the Athletics because Connie Mack believed he was too small to pitch in the ML at 133 pounds. Winter joined the Red Sox instead, put on 20 pounds, and won 16 games for for them in 1901, the AL's first year, and another 16 in 1905. He was 9–8 for the 1903 champions but did not appear in the WS, as Boston used only its three 20-game winners Cy Young, Bill Dineen, and Long Tom Hughes, in the eight games. Instead, Winter served as a ticket taker. A Red Sox official had scalped all the reserved-seat tickets in the grandstand, affecting the players' share of the receipts. The players decided to print and sell their own tickets to the games in Boston. Winter and Jake Stahl supervised. In 1908 he was sold to the Tigers. He pitched one inning of the 1908 WS, his last ML appearance. /(BC)

Jesse Winters (T-Bone) — 1893–1986. RHP 1919–23 Giants, **Phillies** 405 ip, 13–24, 5.04

After two seasons of largely ineffectual relief for the Giants, Winters was packaged with Butch Henline, Curt Walker, and $30,000 in the trade that brought Irish Meusel to New York. Given a chance to start, he went 5–10 with a 3.63 ERA and was soon back in relief. He was mayor of Abilene, Texas in the 1950s. /(NLM)

Nip Winters [Jesse] — 1899–1971. LHP Negro Leagues 1919–33 Norfolk Stars, Bacharach Giants, Norfolk Giants, **Hilldale**, Philadelphia Stars, Harrisburg Giants, New York Lincoln Giants, Darby Daisies, Washington Pilots, Newark Dodgers statistics not available

Winters was one of the Negro Leagues' best left-handed pitchers. The ace curveballer starred in the first modern Black World Series in 1924 as a member of the Hilldale club. Backed by Hall of Famers Judy Johnson and Pop Lloyd and stalwarts Frank Warfield and Biz Mackey, Winters went 3–1 (1.16) versus the Kansas City Monarchs. He led the Eastern Colored League with marks of 26–4 in 1924, 21–10 in 1925, and 18–6 in 1926. In barnstorming games against Babe Ruth's All Stars, Winters split two decisions with Lefty Grove. /(PG)

Rick Wise — 1945- . RHP 1964, 66–82 **Phillies**, Cardinals, Red Sox, Indians, Padres 3127 ip, 188–181, 3.69. *1 LCS, 7 ip, 1–0, 2.45. 1 WS, 5 ip, 1–0, 8.44* ☛ *All-Star—73.*

A star high-school athlete in Portland, Oregon, Wise signed a bonus contract with Philadelphia in 1963 and had to be kept on their 1964 major league roster; he went 5–3 as an 18-year-old for Gene Mauch's "Great Collapse" Phillies. The hard thrower was sent to the minors to learn how to pitch in 1965, returned in 1966, and had mixed success for several years. In 1971 he went 17–14 and no-hit Cincinnati on June 23, becoming the only pitcher in ML history to hit two home runs in a no-hitter. He was one of the best-hitting pitchers in the National League, with a .195 career average and 15 home runs—6 in 1971 alone. In the spring of 1972, he was sent to the Cardinals in a controversial trade for Steve Carlton.

Wise won 16 games for St. Louis in both 1972 and 1973 and was the winning pitcher in the '73 All-Star Game before going to the Red Sox in a deal for Reggie Smith. After overcoming arm trouble, he won a staff-high 19 games for the 1975 AL champion Red Sox. He was the winning pitcher, in relief, in the sixth game of the World Series, won by Carlton Fisk's dramatic home run.

With last-place Cleveland in 1978, Wise lost a league-high 19 games. He signed as a free agent with San Diego after the 1979 season and won ten games in two seasons before the Padres released him in April 1982. Wise's brother, Tom, was a infielder in the Astros organization from 1970 through 1974. /(AL)

Mickey Witek [Nicholas Joseph] — 1915- . 2B-SS-3B 1940–43, 46–47, 49 **Giants**, Yankees 580 g, .277, 22 hr, 196 rbi

Originally signed by the Yankees, Witek debuted with the Giants after being named 1939 International League MVP. In 1943, he hit a league-high

172 singles while batting .314, and led NL second basemen in putouts, assists, and errors. /(JL)

Bobby Witt — 1964– . RHP 1986– **Rangers** 669 ip, 39–42, 4.85

A wild righthanded starter, Witt pitched for the 1984 U.S. Olympic Team and was the third player chosen in the nation in the 1985 free-agent draft, then made his ML debut with Texas in 1986 after pitching only 35 innings in the minors. In his first two seasons the raw flamethrower led the AL in both strikeouts per nine innings (9.93 and 10.07) and walks (143 and 140), and as a rookie uncorked a league-high 22 wild pitches. He was 19–19 over the two seasons, but his ERA was above 5.00, and he completed only one of his 56 starts. In 1988 Witt started horribly, and was 0–5, 7.68 when he was demoted to Oklahoma City (American Association) on May 10. When he returned on July 7, however, he was a different pitcher, completing his first nine starts and 13 overall, walking "only" 66 batters in 138 innings, and posting a 2.93 ERA. He has tied Rangers records for most strikeouts in a game with 14 (7/6/86), and most walks in a game with nine (4/24/87). /(SCL)

George Witt (Red) — 1933– . RHP 1957–62 **Pirates**, Dodgers, Astros 229 ip, 11–16, 4.32. *1 WS, 3 ip, 0–0, 0.00*

Witt justified his billing as a rising star by going 9–2 (1.61) as a Pirate rookie in 1957. The redhead won just two more games after trying to pitch with a sore elbow in 1959. /(ME)

Mike Witt — 1960– . RHP 1981– **Angels** 1945 ip, 109–104, 3.76. *2 LCS, 21 ip, 1–0, 3.05*
☛ *All-Star—86–87.*

The 6'7" California native entered his prime years in position to become one of baseball's great pitchers. Behind him was the 13th perfect game in major league history, a 1–0 win September 30, 1984 in Texas; and selection to the 1986 and 1987 All-Star squads. Using a great curveball and a good fastball, and changing speeds well, Witt climbed among the California leaders in wins, games pitched, starts, complete games, strikeouts, innings pitched, and shutouts, leading the club in each of those categories (except shutouts) each year from 1984 to 1987. He joined Dean Chance (1962–65) as the only pitcher to lead the Angels in wins four straight seasons and was the Angel MVP in 1986. But he lost his overpowering stuff in the middle of 1987 and declined thereafter, still good but not great. /(ME)

Whitey Witt [Lawton Walter][born Ladislaw Waldemar Wittkowski] — 1895– . OF-SS-2B 1916–17, 19–26 **A's**, Yankees, Dodgers 1139 g, .287, 18 hr, 302 rbi. *2 WS, 11 g, .233, 4 rbi*

Witt was a punch hitter and good bunter who reputedly got about 40 infield hits a year and often walked. Tired of playing for last-place A's teams, he badgered Connie Mack into trading him to New York. There he became a favorite party-mate of Babe Ruth. On the day that the Yankees beat the Browns to win the 1922 pennant, Witt was hit on the head with a bottle and knocked unconscious. To avoid further inciting the St. Louis fans, American League president Ban Johnson announced that Witt had stepped on the bottle, causing it to leap up and strike him in the head. /(NLM)

Johnnie Wittig (Hans) — 1914– . RHP 1938–39, 41, 43, 49 **Giants**, Red Sox 307 ip, 10–25, 4.89

A journeyman righthander with poor control, Wittig had his best season in 1943 when, despite a 5–15 record for the last-place Giants, he allowed only 77 hits in 164 innings. /(FS)

John Wockenfuss — 1949– . C-1B-DH-OF 1974–85 **Tigers**, Phillies 795 g, .262, 86 hr, 310 rbi

Wockenfuss spent eight seasons in the minors before making the ML for good in 1975, then lasted 12 ML seasons as a backup catcher and a solid but slow-footed righthanded-hitting reserve. 1980 was the only year in which he played more than 100 games, and he hit .274 for the Tigers that year with career highs in HR (16) and RBI (65). Wockenfuss played for Detroit for ten years, then was traded with Glenn Wilson to the Phillies for Willie Hernandez and Dave Bergman in March 1984, as the Tigers embarked on a World Championship season. /(SCL)

Jim Wohlford (Wolfie) — 1951– . OF 1972–86 **Royals**, Brewers, Giants, Expos 1220 g, .260, 21 hr, 305 rbi. *1 LCS, 5 g, .182*

Wohlfor was a Topps junior college All-American in 1970. Two years later he was American Association rookie of the year while playing second base for Omaha. A line-drive hitter, Wohlford displayed good speed in the outfield and on the basepaths for the Royals. After departing Kansas City, he spent a decade as an extra outfielder and pinch hitter, reaching the .300 plateau in 1984. /(FO)

Chicken Wolf [William Van Winkle] — 1862–1903. OF-SS-1B-C 1882–92 **Louisville (AA)**, St. Louis (NL) 1198 g, .290, 17 hr, 206 rbi.
Manager 1889 **Louisville (AA)**, 15–51, .227
☛ *Led League—ba 1890* .

Wolf, who played right field for Louisville throughout the American Association's ten years as a major league, is considered to have been one of the AA's best outfielders. Normally a solid but unspectacular hitter, he erupted in 1890 to lead the AA (which had been weakened by defections to the upstart Players' League) with a .363 batting average, 197 hits, and 260 total bases. /(FIC)

Bill Wolfe [Wilbert Otto] (Barney) — 1876–1953. RHP 1903–06 Yankees, **Senators** 511 ip, 20–38, 2.96

Wolfe's best season was 1905, when he went 8–14 with a respectable 2.57 ERA for the seventh-place Senators. He never had a winning season. /(JFC)

Edgar F. Wolfe — Unk.–Unk. *Writer-Cartoonist* .

Working under the name of "Jim Nasium," Wolfe was a nationally known baseball writer and cartoonist for the Philadelphia *Inquirer* from 1907 to 1922. He got to know the players by working out with them in spring training and morning practices during the season. He was a scout for the Phillies for two seasons and wrote many articles for *The Sporting News* in the 1920s and 1930s, analyzing the game and the players. His articles were often accompanied by his own cartoons. /(NLM)

Bob Wolff — Unk.– . *Broadcaster.*

Wolff was the radio and TV voice of the wretched Washington Senators from 1947 to 1960 and followed the club to Minnesota for one season in 1961. He left the following season for a spot on NBC's national baseball broadcasts. A New York City native and Phi Beta Kappa graduate of Duke, Wolff returned home in 1966 for a long stint at Madison Square Garden, calling everything from hockey to horse shows, but no baseball. On October 8, 1956, he called the final innings of Don Larsen's WS perfect game. /(SCL)

Roger Wolff — 1911– . RHP 1941–47 A's, **Senators**, Indians, Pirates 1025 ip, 52–69, 3.41. 20 wins: 45

Wolff was a knuckleball pitcher used both as a starter and in relief. The Senators cornered the knuckleballer market during WWII, carrying four; they traded Bobo Newsom for Wolff after the 1943

season. In 1945 Wolff won 20 for Washington while Newsom lost 20 for the A's. /(JK)

Mellie Wolfgang — 1890–1947. RHP 1914–18 **White Sox** 326 ip, 15–14, 2.18

The 150-pound Wolfgang was rejected by three ML teams as too small despite three 20-win seasons in the minors. He hooked on with the White Sox in 1914 and won nine games, using mainly a spitball and curve. His greatest thrill came when he beat Walter Johnson 2–1 (8/29/14) while making a record-tying 11 assists. Two days later he beat Johnson again in a relief appearance. When illness limited his play in 1917–18, he became the White Sox' batting-practice pitcher. /(BC)

Harry Wolter — 1884–1970. OF-1B-LHP 1907, 09–13, 17 Reds, Pirates, Cardinals, Red Sox, **Highlanders/Yankees**, Cubs 587 g, .270, 12 hr, 167 rbi; 78 ip, 5–6, 4.04

Wolter won 5 of 11 decisions as a pitcher before becoming a full-time outfielder in 1910. He twice led the Pacific Coast League in batting. A native Californian, he coached at Stanford University for 26 years. /(JK)

Harry Wolverton — 1873–1937. 3B 1898–05, 12 Cubs, **Phillies**, Senators, Braves, Yankees 782 g, .278, 7 hr, 352 rbi.
Manager 1912 **Yankees** 50–102, .329

Wolverton was a solidly-built third baseman who batted more than .300 for the Phillies in 1901 and 1903. He rapped out three triples in a July 13, 1900 game. While managing the Highlanders (later called the Yankees) to a last-place finish in 1912, he frequently used himself as a pinch hitter. /(JK)

Dooley Womack [Horace Guy] — 1939– . RHP 1966–70 **Yankees**, Astros, Pilots, A's 302 ip, 19–18, 2.95

Womack was considered a non-prospect until he won a spot in the depleted bullpen of the last-place 1966 Yankees. In 1967 he was New York's relief ace, saving 18 games and tying a club record for most appearances in a season with 65. A torn rotator cuff ended his career in 1970. /(GDW)

Bob Wood — 1865–1943. C 1898–1902, 04–05 Reds, **Indians**, Tigers 382 g, .281, 2 hr, 168 rbi

Wood backed up catcher Heinie Peitz in Cincinnati in 1898–1900 before jumping to the new American League in 1901. He then batted more than .290 in both his seasons with Cleveland. /(ME)

Jake Wood — 1937– . 2B-1B-OF 1961–67 **Tigers**, Reds 608 g, .250, 35 hr, 168 rbi

Wood came to the majors in 1961 after hitting .300 in all four of his minor league seasons, and he seemed to show great promise his rookie year. Among the fastest men in the AL at that time, he led the league in triples (14) and finished third in steals (30), batting .258 with 96 runs, 11 HR, and 69 RBI. However, he set a major league record with 141 strikeouts, and led AL second basemen in errors, looking especially bad on the double play. He led in errors again in 1962, and injuries cut into both his playing time and his batting (.226). A finger injury in 1963 limited him to 85 games, although he hit .273; thereafter he was a utility man. Used with some initial success as a pinch hitter (7-for-29 in 1964, 9-for-25 in 1965), he lost that knack as well and soon faded from the majors. /(SH)

Joe Wood [born Howard Ellsworth Wood] (Smoky Joe) — 1889–1985. OF-RHP 1908–15, 17–22 Red Sox, **Indians** 695 g, .283, 24 hr, 325 rbi; 1434 ip, 116–57, 2.03. 20 wins: 11, 12 *2 WS, 8 g, .235, 1 rbi; 22 ip, 3–1, 3.68* ☛ *Led League—w 12. Led League—era 15.*

Few pitchers have ever had a season like the one 22-year-old Smoky Joe Wood had in 1912. Coming off a 23–17 performance for the Red Sox in 1911, including a July 29 no-hitter against St. Louis, Wood won 34 games while losing only 5. He led the league with 35 complete games and ten shutouts and also batted .290. In the World Series, he defeated the Giants with complete games in the first and fourth contests, lost Game Seven, but came back in relief to beat Christy Mathewson in the eighth and final game (Game Two was a tie).

Wood had one of the best fastballs in baseball history, comparable to that of his contemporary Walter Johnson. In 1912 Johnson said, "Can I throw harder than Joe Wood? Listen, my friend, there's no man alive can throw harder than Smoky Joe Wood." The two had 27 matchups, with Wood winning 11. At the time of one duel in 1912, Wood had won 13 straight games and was closing in on Johnson's record of 16 straight, set earlier that season. Before an overflow crowd at Fenway Park, Wood won 1–0. He went on to record two more consecutive victories to tie Johnson's record, but lost his bid to break it.

In the spring of 1913, Wood slipped on wet grass while fielding a ground ball and broke his thumb. He resumed pitching after the cast came off several weeks later, but wasn't the same. He could still

Joe Wood

throw, but was pitching with pain, and had lost some velocity. In 1915 he led the league with a .750 winning percentage (15–5) and a 1.49 ERA. But the pain had become unbearable, and, at the age of 26, Wood had to give up baseball.

In 1917, intent on resuming his career, Wood persuaded the Cleveland Indians to give him another chance. He worked in five games that year, but in 1918 he abandoned pitching and was tried in the outfield and at second base. He batted .296 in 119 games. One afternoon at the Polo Grounds, he hit a home run to tie a game in the 7th inning and hit another to win it in the 19th.

Though a part-timer the next three seasons, Wood played the outfield in four games of the 1920 WS. In 1921, he batted .366. After appearing in 140 games and hitting .297 in 1922, he accepted the head coaching job at Yale University, where he stayed until 1942. His son Joe pitched in three games for the 1944 Red Sox. Wood remained a vigorous and entertaining follower of baseball until his death at age 95. /(JK)

Ken Wood — 1924- . OF 1948-53 **Browns**, Red Sox, Senators 342 g, .224, 34 hr, 143 rbi

Wood was a regular only with the Browns in 1950 and 1951. He had highs of 62 RBI, 42 runs, and 369 at-bats in 1950 and 15 HR and a .237 BA in 1951. In 1950 he was just 4-for-32 as a pinch hitter, and he went 6-for-63 lifetime in that role. /(JFC)

Wilbur Wood — 1941- . LHP 1961-65, 67-78 Red Sox, Pirates, **White Sox** 2684 ip, 164-156, 3.24. 20 wins: 71-74
☛ Led League—w 72, 73. All-Star—71-74.

Overweight Wilbur Wood was one of the busiest and most effective lefthanders of the 1970s. Signed out of a Massachussetts high school by the Red Sox in 1960, he struggled in the Boston and Pittsburgh farm systems, throwing a fastball and a curve that flattened out when it reached the plate. He had learned the knuckleball from his father, and had occasionally used it in high school, but it wasn't until 1967, his first year with the White Sox, that he made it his bread-and-butter pitch. Chicago teammate and knuckleball master Hoyt Wilhelm advised Wood to forget everything else and go with the knuckler.

Wood quickly established himself as a top reliever, throwing the knuckleball with exceptional control and leading the AL in appearances in 1968-70. He helped himself with a deceptive and effective pickoff move. He was named Fireman of the Year in '68, winning 12 in relief, saving 16, and setting an AL record by pitching in 88 games.

In 1971 Chicago manager Chuck Tanner and pitching coach Johnny Sain moved Wood into the starting rotation. Wood was so successful that he was soon pitching regularly on two days' rest. He became the first White Sox pitcher to record 20 or more victories in four consecutive seasons. In 1972 he was named *TSN* AL Pitcher of the Year, tying for the league lead with 24 wins. He also set the ML season record for most strikeouts by a pitcher as a batter (65). For the second straight year in 1973, he led the AL in innings pitched, again recording a

league-high 24 victories. Each year from 1972 through 1975, he started more games than any AL pitcher. In 1973, he even started both ends of a doubleheader, but was hit hard by the Yankees.

Wood dropped to 16-20 in 1975, leading the league in losses. His ERA, which had increased each year since his 1.91 in 1971, ballooned to 4.11. He was pitching well early in 1976 when a line drive hit by Detroit's Ron LeFlore shattered his kneecap. He sat out the rest of the season, but came back to pitch two more. /(RL)

Larry Woodall — 1894-1963. C 1920-29 **Tigers** 548 g, .268, 1 hr, 160 rbi

Woodall was a smart, solid backup catcher for almost a decade with the Tigers. He joined the Red Sox as a coach under manager Joe Cronin in 1942 and became the director of publicity when Cronin became Boston's GM. He continued with the Red Sox as a scout and director of tryout camps. /(JK)

Hal Woodeshick — 1932- . LHP 1956, 58-67 Tigers, Indians, Senators, **Astros**, Cardinals 847 ip, 44-62, 3.56. *1 WS, 1 ip, 0-0, 0.00*
☛ All-Star—63.

Woodeshick spent most of his career as a relief pitcher and had his best seasons in that role. After going 5-16 for the expansion Colt .45s (later the Astros) in 1962, mostly as a starter, he was used exclusively out of the bullpen and had his three best years. He had a 1.97 ERA in 1963 and a league-leading 23 saves in 1964. St. Louis acquired him in June 1965 with Chuck Taylor in exchange for Mike Cuellar and Ron Taylor, but Woodeshick was behind Joe Hoerner and Nellie Briles in the Cardinals bullpen and saw less crucial action thereafter. In Game Six of the 1967 World Series, he was the eighth Cardinals pitcher in the game, tying a record. /(WOR)

Gene Woodling (Old Faithful) — 1922- . OF 1943, 46-47, 49-62 Indians, Pirates, **Yankees**, Orioles, Senators, Mets 1796 g, .284, 147 hr, 830 rbi. *5 WS, 26 g, .318, 3 hr, 6 rbi*
☛ All-Star—59.

After two years in the Navy and several unsuccessful stints in the majors, Woodling, a four-time minor league batting champion, stuck with the Yankees in 1949 and played a large role in the club's record five consecutive World Championships (1949-53).

Yankee manager Casey Stengel usually platooned the lefthanded-hitting Woodling with Hank Bauer in left field, but he sometimes played both in the outfield, getting each about 400 at-bats a season. Woodling was not a typical platooned player. He was, in Stengel's opinion, the best defensive left fielder Casey managed in New York. He could run and throw, and was a clutch hitter; Old Faithful was particularly effective against the Indians and Dodgers—the Yankees' main rivals at the time. He topped the .300 mark in 1952 and 1953, and hit a solo HR in each World Series from 1951 through 1953.

Following the 1954 season, Woodling was traded to Baltimore as part of a record 17-player deal. He moved on to Cleveland, with whom he reached career highs of 19 HR, 78 RBI, and a .321 average in 1957. A few months before his 40th birthday, his contract was purchased from Washington by the lowly 1962 Mets, managed by Stengel. "He gave me hell all those years about wanting to play," said Stengel. "Now he can play all he wants."/(MG)

Harvey T. Woodruff — 1875–1937. *Writer.*

Woodruff was sports editor of the Chicago *Times-Herald* and *The Record* before joining the *Tribune* where he wrote the column "In the Wake of the News" before the more-famous Arch Ward. /(NLM)

Al Woods — 1953– . OF-DH 1977–82, 86 **Blue Jays,** Twins 618 g, .271, 35 hr, 196 rbi

In the expansion Blue Jays' first ballgame (4/7/77), Woods became the 11th player to hit a pinch homer in his first ML at-bat. In 1980 he batted .300 and had six hits in six straight at-bats on July 20–21. His sub-standard defensive skills and apparent lack of interest in improving them limited his career. /(TF)

Gary Woods — 1954– . OF 1976–78, 80–85 A's, Blue Jays, Astros, **Cubs** 525 g, .243, 13 hr, 110 rbi. *2 LCS, 5 g, .222, 1 rbi*

Woods was the 1977 Blue Jays' Opening Day centerfielder, and had the franchise's first stolen base. A fine outfielder with an accurate arm, he spent most of his career with the Cubs as a defensive replacement and useful pinch hitter against lefthanders. /(DB)

Jim Woods (Possum) — 1917–1988. *Broadcaster.*

An excellent number-two announcer in the ML, Woods teamed with Mel Allen and Bob Prince before joining Ned Martin in an extremely popular Red Sox radio duo in the 1970s. Nicknamed Possum, Woods had replaced Dutch Reagan on University of Iowa football broadcasts and Ernie Harwell on Atlanta Crackers baseball broadcasts before joining

the Yankees, but was suddenly fired in late 1956 to make room for Phil Rizzuto. Woods had a phenomenal memory, and could, among other things, name every Kentucky Derby winner. /(SCL/NLM)

Parnell Woods — 1912–1977. 3B-MGR Negro Leagues 1933–49 Birmingham Black Barons, **Cleveland Bears,** Jacksonville Red Caps, Cincinnati Buckeyes, Louisville Buckeyes statistics not available
☛ *All-Star—39–42.*

Woods was a star Negro League third baseman who appeared in the 1939–42 East-West all-star games. He batted .335 as a key member of the 1945 Black World Champion Cleveland Buckeyes. He played a number of winters in Venezuela, winning the 1947 batting title with a .354 mark and leading the league with 28 runs, 13 doubles, and three triples. He had a reputation as a fighting leader, a strong hitter, and a good fielder. He closed out his career in 1949, batting .275 in 40 games with Oakland of the Pacific Coast League. For 27 years he was business manager for the Harlem Globetrotters basketball team. /(MFK)

Pinky Woods [George Rowland] — 1915–1982. RHP 1943–45 **Red Sox** 379 ip, 13–21, 3.97

The 6'5" Woods was a fireballer when he first joined the Red Sox, but his velocity was sharply reduced after he lost a big toe in a spiking incident. He became a sidearm pitcher and had success in the minors. /(DB)

Ron Woods — 1943– . OF 1969–74 Tigers, Yankees, **Expos** 582 g, .233, 26 hr, 130 rbi

Woods spent most of his career as a platoon outfielder and a frequently used but poor pinch hitter. After hitting a career-high 10 HR in 221 at-bats for Montreal in 1972, he saw his most action in 1973 but hit .230. Speedy and sure-handed, he started his ML career with 182 consecutive errorless chances. /(SH)

Walt Woods — 1875–1951. RHP-2B-OF 1898–1900 **Chicago (NL),** Louisville (NL), Pirates 404 ip, 18–26, 3.34; 91 g, .164, 1 hr, 22 rbi

A good-fielding pitcher who also played the infield and outfield, Woods walked twice as many as he struck out. /(DAS)

Dick Woodson — 1945- . RHP 1969-70, 72-74 **Twins**, Yankees 590 ip, 34-32, 3.46. *2 LCS, 3 ip, 0-0, 10.13*

In his first two seasons, Woodson was on division-winning Twins teams, going 7-5 in 1969 as a starter and reliever. Returning as a full-time starter in 1972, he went 14-14 and 10-8. /(WOR)

Rob Woodward — 1962- . RHP 1985-88 **Red Sox** 100 ip, 4-4, 5.04

Woodward was called up repeatedly by Boston but failed to impress. /(JFC)

Woody Woodward [William Frederick] — 1942- . SS-2B-3B 1963-71 **Braves**, Reds 880 g, .236, 1 hr, 148 rbi. *1 LCS, 3 g, .100. 1 WS, 4 g, .200*

Woodward signed with the Braves for a $50,000 bonus in 1963 and made it to the majors to stay before the end of the year, mostly on the strength of his glove. When in 1970 he hit his only homer, off Ron Reed of the Braves (his former team), Reds teammate Wayne Granger said, "We've figured it out. It will take him 4,189 years to catch Babe Ruth."

He was a utility man in the beginning, playing all four infield positions in 1964 while batting .209, but by 1964 he was the Braves' regular second baseman, batting .264. In 1965 he led NL second basemen in fielding average. Woodward was acquired by the Reds in a big 1968 trade that included Clay Carroll, Tony Cloninger, and Milt Pappas, and was expected to be their regular shortstop. Instead, he lost the job twice to rookies, first to Darrel Chaney and then to Dave Concepcion.

In 1980, after two years as the Reds' minor league field coordinator, Woodward was named their assistant general manager. From there, he went on to become the Yankees' general manager in 1984. Actress Joanne Woodward is his first cousin. /(SFS)

Chuck Workman — 1915-1953. OF-3B 1938, 41, 43-46 Indians, **Braves**, Pirates 526 g, .242, 50 hr, 230 rbi

Lefthanded-batting Chuck Workman led two minor leagues in home runs as a Cleveland farmhand in 1940 (Three-I League) and 1942 (Southern Association). He saw regular major league action only with the Braves during WWII; as their third baseman in 1945, he hit 25 HR. He floundered in spacious Forbes Field after his 1946 trade to Pittsburgh and was bothered by ulcers. Falling back to the minors, he set Southern Association records with 52 HR and 182 RBI for Nashville in 1948 and led the American

Association with 41 HR for Minneapolis in 1949. /(ME)

Ralph Works (Judge) — 1888-1941. RHP 1909-13 **Tigers**, Reds 499 ip, 24-24, 3.79. *1 WS, 2 ip, 0-0, 9.00*

Works was called Judge by teammates for his scholarly countenance. At his best, he was 11-5 for the 1911 Tigers. He died with his wife in an apparent double suicide. /(JK)

World Series — 1903- .

There was ample precedent for postseason play in the unofficial contests arranged by the winners of the NL and the American Association from 1882 to 1891. The first World Series, in 1903, was a best-of-nine affair arranged by the winners of the NL and the AL and won by the AL's Boston Pilgrims in a 5-3 upset over the Pittsburgh Pirates. The feud between AL president Ban Johnson and the 1904 NL-champion Giants' manager John McGraw precluded a World Series that year, but the popularity of the 1903 Series led the National Commission to establish an official World Series starting in 1905, with the length of the contest set at seven games. The Giants won 4-1 that year, with all the games being shutouts; Christy Mathewson permitted only 14 hits and one base on balls in his three shutouts. The 1906 Series matched the White Sox and the Cubs in the first World Series between teams from the same city. The White Sox, known as the Hitless Wonders for having the lowest team batting average in the AL that year, upset the mighty Cubs team that had set a still-standing major league record by winning 116 games (while losing only 36).

The unlikely star emerging in the World Series to lead his team to victory became a recurring scenario. The first example came in 1909, when the Pirates' Babe Adams, a rookie pitcher who was 12-3 during the year and not considered the team's ace, was given the starting assignment in the Series opener. He went on to win three games as Pittsburgh won 4-3 despite only two batters (Honus Wagner and Tommy Leach) batting above .250. In the 1911 WS the Athletics' Frank Baker, already established as a fine player, won his nickname Home Run by hitting a game-winning homer off the Giants' Rube Marquard in Game Two and a game-tying home run off Christy Mathewson the next day.

Another Series motif is the "goat," the player whose lapse costs his team the World Championship. Fred Snodgrass wore the horns for the Giants in 1912 after dropping a routine fly ball in the tenth inning of the final game. In 1914 the Braves upset the Athletics in four games, contributing to Philadelphia owner Connie Mack's decision to break up his dynasty. Babe Ruth began his record scoreless innings streak pitching the Red Sox to victory in Game Two of the 1916 WS; after surrendering a first-inning home run, he blanked Brooklyn for 13 innings to win 2–1. He extended the streak to 29-2/3 innings in 1918. That year the Red Sox won their fifth World Championship; over the next 70 years, they failed to win another despite four chances.

The 1917 Series was memorable for Giants third baseman Heinie Zimmerman's futile chase to home plate of Eddie Collins as the White Sox took the lead in the Series clincher; neither catcher Lew McCarty nor pitcher Rube Benton covered home. The White Sox became known as the Black Sox two years later when eight conspirators on the 1919 team threw the Series after gamblers induced them to "lay down." When the fix became public knowledge the next year, it led to the appointment of Commissioner Landis, who became a fixture at World Series games thereafter and ruled on several controversies on the spot. The 1919 Series had returned to the best-of-nine format to take advantage of the renewed popularity of baseball following World War I, which had cut into the 1918 schedule. The 1920 Series, played under close scrutiny due to the previous year's events, featured several Fall Classic firsts in Game Five. The Indians' Elmer Smith hit the first WS grand slam in the first inning, Cleveland's Jim Bagby became the first pitcher to hit a WS home run in the fourth inning, and the only unassisted triple play in Series history was turned by Indians second baseman Bill Wambsganss in the fifth.

The first New York Subway Series took place in 1921, with the Giants defeating the Yankees and holding Babe Ruth to one home run in the last best-of-nine Series. Brothers Bob and Irish Meusel played on the opposing teams. The Giants repeated with a sweep of the Yankees in 1922, notable for Ruth hitting only .118 and for Game Two being called "on account of darkness," while tied 3–3 in the 10th inning, despite the sun still shining. Instantly it was rumored that it had been done to force an additional game (and additional profits). An irate Judge Landis ordered the gate receipts to be donated to charity. Babe Ruth became the first to hit three home runs in a Series in 1923 as the Yankees finally overcame the Giants. Casey Stengel hit two game-winning homers for the Giants, the first coming in Game One with two out in the ninth inning. An inside-the-park shot, it was immortalized by reporter Damon Runyon. The Giants lost again in 1924 as Walter Johnson (in relief) and the Senators won Game Seven in twelve innings as Earl Mc-

Neely's grounder to third base hit a pebble and hopped over Fred Lindstrom's head. The Senators and Johnson were the losers in 1925 when Game Seven was played in extremely dark and muddy conditions under a continuous rain. The Pirates were the first team to win a seven-game Series after going down 3–1 in games.

The Yankees returned to the Fall Classic in 1926, but were defeated by the Cardinals in their first appearance. Ruth was thrown out stealing by Bob O'Farrell for the last out of the Series in the game made famous by Grover Cleveland Alexander's relief appearance. He came in in the seventh inning, after having won his second complete game of the Series the day before, and struck out Tony Lazzeri with two out and the bases loaded. The first consecutive sweeps in WS history came in 1927–28 as the Yankees devastated the Pirates and the Cardinals. In 1928 Lou Gehrig became the first man to hit four home runs in one Series, and in Game Four Ruth set a record with three homers. With Gehrig and Cedric Durst also homering, the Yankees set a record for HR by a team in a single Series game.

The Athletics represented the AL the next three years. Howard Ehmke was the surprise starter in the opener in 1929 and set a Series record with 13 strikeouts, and in Game Four the A's scored 10 runs in the seventh inning to overcome the Cubs' 8–0 lead. Philadelphia was finally bested in 1931 as the Cardinals' Pepper Martin hit .500 and stole five bases. The Yankees swept again in 1932, setting a record with 12 consecutive WS wins. Ruth's "called shot" off the Cubs' Charlie Root in Game Three was the highlight in a contest featuring six home runs, two each by Ruth and Gehrig and two by the Cubs, for a new WS game mark. Ruth's 15 career WS HR stood as the record until Mickey Mantle broke it three decades later.

Landis ruled on another controversy in 1934 when he removed the Cardinals' Joe Medwick from Game Seven rather than forfeit the game after Detroit fans showered the left fielder with debris following his hard slide into third baseman Marv Owen. The Cardinals won 11–0. The tremendous offensive output of the era was best typified by the Yankees' 18–4 victory in Game Two of the 1936 WS, won 4–2 over the Giants in a renewal of their subway rivalry. The two teams met again in 1937, with the Yankees again victorious. Yankee sweeps in 1938 (the Cubs) and 1939 (the Reds) gave manager Joe McCarthy a record four consecutive World Championships. The final game of the '39 Series became famous for "Schnozz's snooze" when Reds catcher Ernie Lombardi lay stunned, unable to tag Joe DiMaggio, after a collision with Charlie Keller.

The Reds came back in 1940 to defeat the Tigers.

The first Yankees-Dodgers Series came in 1941 and was won by New York 4–1. Brooklyn won Game Two and was leading Game Three 1–0 when Yankee pitcher Marius Russo's line drive off the knee of Dodger pitcher Fred Fitzsimmons forced him out of the game in the seventh inning; the Yankees scored two runs off reliever Hugh Casey. In Game Four Casey was again on the mound with the Dodgers leading 4–3 in the ninth with two out. He struck out Tommy Henrich, but the ball got past catcher Mickey Owen, starting a four-run Yankee rally. The Cardinals' defeat of the Yankees in 1942 was New York's first WS defeat since 1926. St. Louis fell to the Yankees in 1943.

The exigencies of wartime baseball led to the Browns' first pennant in 1944. The quality of play in the World Series, won by the Cardinals, was still fair, featuring a Game Five pitchers' duel between Mort Cooper (12 strikeouts) and the Browns' Denny Galehouse (10 strikeouts). But the 1945 Series was considered a travesty; reporters predicted that neither team could win. In fact, the Tigers prevailed in seven games in what proved to be the Cubs' last World Series appearance. The return to peacetime ball in 1946 began the Red Sox' string of seven-game Series defeats when Enos Slaughter scored from first base in the eighth inning on Harry Walker's double as Boston shortstop Johnny Pesky hesitated with the relay. Leon Culberson had bobbled the ball in centerfield, where he was subbing for the injured Dom DiMaggio. Red Sox star Ted Williams hit .200 for the Series, and the Cardinals' Stan Musial hit .222. There was more drama in 1947 as Brooklyn and New York met again. Game Four saw the Dodgers tie the Series when Cookie Lavaghetto broke up Bill Bevens's no-hitter with two out in the ninth inning. The Series was once again knotted in Game Six when reserve outfielder Al Gionfriddo's running catch of Joe DiMaggio's 415′ blast against the left-field fence with two runners on in the sixth inning preserved the victory for the Dodgers and provoked a rare display of emotion by DiMaggio, who kicked the ground when the catch was made. The Yankees prevailed in Game Seven when Joe Page pitched five innings of one-hit relief. Lost in the excitement was Yogi Berra's pinch-homer in Game Three, the first in Series history. The Indians defeated the Braves in 1948, with Larry Doby's HR in Game Four being the first by a black player. Game One included one of the most controversial umpire's calls in Series history. Bill Stewart's safe call on Bob Feller's attempted pickoff at second base of Phil Masi

allowed Masi to score the only run of the game two batters later as Johnny Sain pitched a shutout.

Casey Stengel was named manager of the Yankees in 1949 and started a record streak of five World Championships by defeating the Dodgers 4–1. Phillies ace reliever Jim Konstanty was the surprise starter in the 1950 opener but lost 1–0, and the Yankees went on to a sweep. The Yankees' skein was threatened in 1952 when the Dodgers took a 3–2 lead in the Series (Joe Black becoming the first black pitcher to win a WS game), but New York won the last two games, at Ebbets Field. Billy Martin saved the last win with a catch at his knees of a routine pop-up that neither the first baseman or the pitcher, who were closer, got under; the bases were loaded. Gil Hodges finished the Series 0-for-21, the most famous WS slump in history. In 1953 Carl Erskine struck out a Series-record 14 batters in Game Three, but the Yankees were unstoppable in winning their fifth World Series in five years. But the Indians won the AL pennant in 1954 and were then swept by the Giants on the strength of Dusty Rhodes' pinch-hit heroics.

The Dodgers finally beat the Yankees in 1955 for the NL's first back-to-back Series triumphs since 1933–34. Johnny Podres was the pitching hero for his Game Seven shutout, saved by Sandy Amoros's long run to catch Berra's fly in the left-field corner. The Yankees returned to form in 1956, with Don Larsen pitching a perfect game in Game Five, but they were no longer invincible. They lost to the Braves in 1957 as Lew Burdette won three complete games (two were shutouts), although they turned the tables on the Braves in 1958. The 1959 contest saw the Dodgers beat the White Sox in six games, with Chuck Essegian hitting two pinch-homers. In Stengal's last year at the Yankee helm, the Bronx Bombers outscored the Pirates 55–27 but lost on Bill Mazeroski's dramatic home run in the bottom of the ninth in Game Seven. Under Ralph Houk the Yankees handily defeated the Reds in 1961 and squeaked past the Giants in seven games in 1962. The latter Series featured Chuck Hiller's grand slam in Game Four, the NL's first, and was ended by Willie McCovey's lineout to Yankees second baseman Bobby Richardson with two on and two out in the ninth inning of Game Seven. The Dodgers stunned the Yankees with a four-game sweep in 1963, holding New York to four runs overall. Sandy Koufax struck out a record 15 batters in the opener. The Yankees appeared in their last World Series for the next 12 years in 1964 and lost to the Cardinals, led by Bob Gibson. The Dodgers' pitching gave them another WS victory in 1965, over the Twins, but they received a dose of their own medicine in 1966 when the Orioles swept them, with shutouts in the last three games. Bob Gibson won three games in 1967 to lead the Cardinals over the Red Sox in seven games and appeared set to be the hero in 1968 as well. He struck out a still-standing record 17 Tigers in the opener and won Game Four, but Mickey Lolich won his third game, on two days' rest, to defeat Gibson in Game Seven.

The Miracle Mets of 1969 stunned the favored Orioles in five games. Outfield defense saved two games for New York, with Tommie Agee making two spectacular catches in Game Three (and hitting a leadoff homer) and unlikely hero Ron Swoboda making a foolhardy—but successful—diving, sliding catch in the ninth inning of Game Four to hold the Orioles to a tie. The Orioles used 10 home runs and the spectacular defense of third baseman Brooks Robinson to triumph over the Reds in 1970. Roberto Clemente starred in 1971, which featured the first Series night game in Game Four. Clemente hit .414 and extended his Series hitting streak to 14 games as the Pirates defeated Baltimore in seven games. The surprise hero in 1972 was the A's Gene Tenace, who became the first player to homer in his first two WS at-bats. He had two more HR in the Series and also figured in two game-winning rallies as Oakland beat the Reds in seven games. The A's made it three straight World Championships in 1973 and 1974. The 1973 contest, against the Mets, included the longest WS game by time (4:13) in Game Two, won by New York 10–7.

The Red Sox lost in seven games again in 1975, but to listen to their fans, you'd think they had won. Luis Tiant pitched a five-hitter and ran wild on the basepaths in Game One, and came back with a 163-pitch victory in game Four. And in the famous sixth game, a seesaw contest that saw Bernie Carbo hit a record-tying second pinch-homer for the Series, Carlton Fisk's 12th-inning HR, just barely fair, won the thrilling game for the Red Sox to tie the Series. But the Reds won Game Seven in the ninth inning on a Joe Morgan two-out single. The Reds went on to sweep the Yankees in 1976, a Series that featured the two catchers, Johnny Bench and Thurman Munson, hitting .533 and .529 respectively. The Yankees returned in 1977 and won in six games over the Dodgers when Reggie Jackson earned his "Mr. October" nickname by homering in three consecutive at-bats (each time on the first pitch he saw) in the clincher. New York repeated over the Dodgers in 1978, the last time anybody repeated as World Champions. Graig Nettles was the fielding star with a Brooks Robinson-like display of prowess

at third base in Game Three; his four gems enabled Ron Guidry to hold the Dodgers to one run despite allowing eight hits and seven walks. Bucky Dent hit .417 and was the unlikely Series MVP. The Pirates overcame a 3–1 deficit to beat the Orioles in 1979 despite playing the last two games away.

The Phillies won their first World Championship, ending the sport's longest-such drought, by overcoming the Royals in 1980. Kansas City leadoff hitter Willie Wilson was the goat, batting only .154. In 1981 high-priced free agent Dave Winfield went 1-for-22 and was publically humiliated by Yankee owner George Steinbrenner as the Dodgers won in six games. Mike Schmidt suffered a similar slump in 1983 when Baltimore pitched around him, going 1-for-20 as the Orioles won 4–1. Sparky Anderson became the first manager to win World Championships in both leagues in 1984 as the Tigers blasted the Padres in five games. In 1985 umpire Don Denkinger's safe call, clearly wrong, on Jorge Orta's single in Game Six started Kansas City's comeback. When they defeated St. Louis 11–0 in the finale, they became the first team to come back from a 3–1 deficit after losing the first two games at home. The Series hero was Bret Saberhagen, who surrendered only one run in his two complete games and became a father during one of them.

The Mets triumphed in 1986 as the Red Sox lost yet another seven-game Series. Bill Buckner was the goat in Game Six after the Mets' spectacular comeback in the tenth inning was climaxed by a Mookie Wilson grounder going through Buckner's legs. Wilson most likely would have been safe even if Buckner had fielded the ball, but the winning run wouldn't have scored from second base. To get to that point, the Mets had strung together three two-out singles and a Bob Stanley wild pitch. The Twins, with the worst record of any World Champion during the regular season (85–77), won all four home games during the Series, the first time that had happened. Dan Gladden hit a grand slam in Game One. In 1988 Orel Hershiser shut down the powerhouse A's in his two starts and was the hitting star of Game Two, going 3-for-3. Kirk Gibson, barely able to run, pinch-hit a stunning home run off Oakland relief ace Dennis Eckersley with two out and one on in the ninth inning to win. The A's managed only a lone win in Game Three, but came back in 1989 to sweep the Giants in the first Bay Area Series despite a ten day interruption after an earthquake measuring 7.1 on the Richter scale struck shortly before the start of Game Three at Candlestick. /(SFS)

Todd Worrell — 1959– . RHP 1985– **Cardinals** 362 ip, 28–30, 2.64. *2 LCS, 11 ip, 1–0, 1.69. 2 WS, 12 ip, 0–1, 2.31*
☛ *Rookie of the Year—86. All-Star—88.*

A college All-American and the Cardinals' first-round draft choice, the fireballing Worrell struggled as a starter in the minors. During the 1985 season he was moved to the bullpen, and an overnight transformation occurred. Called up to St. Louis, he won three in relief, saved five, and tied a World Series record by fanning six straight Royals in Game Five.

Worrell consistently threw in the 93–95 mph range utilizing a fastball and very hard slider. In 1986 he was a near-unanimous choice for NL Rookie of the Year as he set a league record for saves (36) by a rookie. In 1988 Worrell became the only pitcher in history to record 30 saves in each of his first three full seasons and the only Cardinal to have three 30-save seasons. On occasion the 6'5″ righthander would move to right field in a pitching platoon arrangement. /(FO)

Rich Wortham — 1953– . LHP 1978–80, 83 **White Sox**, A's 355 ip, 21–23, 4.89

Wortham showed promise in a 1978 trial (3–2, 3.05 in eight starts), but went 14–14 with a 4.90 ERA in 1979. He was used largely in relief in 1980 and then was traded by the White Sox to Montreal for Tony Bernazard. /(JFC)

Al Worthington (Red) — 1929– . RHP 1953–54, 56–60, 63–69 **Giants**, Red Sox, White Sox, Reds, Twins 1247 ip, 75–82, 3.39. *1 LCS, 1 ip, 0–0, 6.75. 1 WS, 4 ip, 0–0, 0.00*

Worthington pitched shutouts in his first two ML starts, 6–0 wins over the Pirates and Dodgers July 6 and 11, 1953, but was only a mediocre pitcher in six seasons with the Giants. He became a reliever exclusively in 1960 and with the Twins he blossomed into one of the AL's best, saving 21 games in 1965 and a league-high 18 in 1968. /(FS)

Red Worthington [Robert Lee] (Bob) — 1906–1963. OF 1931–34 **Braves**, Cardinals 292 g, .287, 12 hr, 111 rbi

Worthington led NL outfielders in fielding in his rookie 1931 season while hitting .291 as the Braves' regular left fielder. He was having a great season in 1932 before he broke his ankle. In 105 games that year he had career highs of .303, eight HR, 61 RBI, and 62 runs. He was never the same after the injury. /(WOR)

J. Edward Wray — 1874–1961. *Writer.*

Wray joined the St. Louis *Post-Dispatch* in 1900 and, except for four years with the *Globe-Democrat*, remained there until he retired in 1946 after 38 years as sports editor. He continued writing "Wray's Column" until 1955. He also worked for the St. Louis *Racing Form*, where he was co-inventor of the past-performance chart that became the backbone of handicapping. When reformers shut down racing in Missouri, the Chicago *Racing Form* bought his copyrighted system. Wray covered the Browns, but after they lost a close pennant race in 1922, he became convinced he was a jinx. He was an unsuccessful candidate to succeed Ban Johnson as AL president in 1927. /(NLM)

Bill Wright [Burnis] (Wild Bill) — Unk.–Unk. OF Negro Leagues 1932–45 Nashville Elite Giants, Columbus Elite Giants, Washington Elite Giants, Baltimore Elite Giants, Philadelphia Stars statistics not available
☛ *All-Star—35–39, 42, 45.*

Wright was a 6'4″ 220-lb outfielder, a fast runner who often batted cleanup. Though statistics for his career are fragmentary, he is credited with a league-leading .488 batting average in 1939, and probably had a career Negro League mark of over .350. He hit .318 in seven East-West all-star games, and .371 in 27 exhibition games against major leaguers. He also played several seasons in Mexico, where he led the league in hitting (.390) in 1941 and won the Triple Crown in 1943 (.366, 13 HR, 70 RBI). After 1945 he played exclusively in Mexico, making it his permanent home. /(JJM)

Clarence Wright — 1878–1930. RHP 1901–04 Dodgers, **Indians**, Browns 324 ip, 14–26, 4.50

Wright pitched back-to-back no-hitters for Dayton (Western Association) in 1901. In 1902 he rejoined Cleveland manager Bill Armour, who had Wright at Dayton. But the Cleveland native went 7–11 with a 3.95 ERA and declined further thereafter. /(ME)

Clyde Wright (Skeeter) — 1941– . LHP 1966–75 **Angels**, Brewers, Rangers 1729 ip, 100–111, 3.50. 20 wins: 70
☛ *All-Star—70.*

Wright threw a four-hitter in his major league debut. In 1968 he pitched 25 consecutive innings without allowing a walk, and combined with Ricky Clark to no-hit the Orioles on August 20. But after a disappointing 1–8 season in 1969, the Angels gave up on Wright, waiving him. He went unclaimed. Teammate Jim Fregosi convinced the drawling, boyish-faced pitcher to accompany him to winter ball, where Wright experimented with a screwball/change and regained his confidence. He returned to the Angels in 1970 and had won 11 of his first 16 decisions when, on July 3, he pitched a no-hitter against Oakland at Anaheim Stadium. He was the loser in the All-Star Game, which was played 11 days later, but went on to a 22–12 record and was named AL Comeback Player of the Year. His ERAs were under 3.00 from 1970 through 1972, when he went 18–11. He was dubbed Skeeter by Freddie Frederico because, the trainer said, "You can't call a major leaguer Clyde." /(JCA)

Ed Wright — 1919– . RHP 1945–48, 52 **Braves**, A's 398 ip, 25–16, 4.00

Ten wins at mid-season for Indianapolis (American Association), including a no-hitter, earned Wright a spot in the Braves' rotation in the second half of 1945. He was 12–9, 3.52 in 1946, but faded rapidly. /(JK)

George Wright — 1847–1937. SS-2B 1871–82 **Boston (NA)**, Braves, Providence (NL) *NA*: 262 g, .353; *ML*: 329 g, .256, 2 hr, 123 rbi.
   Manager 1879 Providence (NL) 59–25, .702 First place: 1879
☛ *Hall of Fame—37.*

George Wright was baseball's first franchise player. His older brother Harry was asked to form the first pro team, the 1869 Cincinnati Red Stockings, and the first player Harry recruited was George, a shortstop. The Wrights transferred operations to Boston when the National Association was formed, and won four of five pennants. George was the team's sparkplug, Harry the manager. They joined the National League in its first season, 1876, and won pennants in 1877 and 1878, with George leading the league in at-bats. George managed Providence to a pennant in 1879, with Harry's Boston club finishing second.

   George gave up baseball almost entirely to establish a sporting-goods business. Since Albert Spalding and A.J. Reach already had strong footholds in baseball, Wright looked to other sports for development. He was helped in this goal when his son, Beals, became an early tennis star. When the Hall of Fame opened in 1939, Wright was one of its first inductees. /(JK)

George Wright of the Red Stockings

George Wright — 1958– . OF 1982–86 **Rangers**, Expos 627 g, .245, 42 hr, 208 rbi

The lefthanded-hitting Wright was the Rangers centerfielder from 1982 to 1984, and in 1983 he played in all 162 games, hitting .276 with 18 HR and 82 RBI. His average dropped rapidly to .190 by 1985, and in 1986 he was sold to Montreal, where he hit .188 in 56 games. /(SCL)

Glenn Wright (Buckshot) — 1901–1984. SS 1924–33, 35 **Pirates**, Dodgers, White Sox 1119 g, .294, 93 hr, 723 rbi. *2 WS, 11 g, .175, 1 hr, 5 rbi*

Wright was an outstanding shortstop who led the NL in assists and double plays his first two seasons. He also led the NL with 616 at-bats as a Pirate rookie in 1924. In 1925 he made an unassisted triple play on a line drive hit by the Cardinals' Jim Bottomley. He batted more than .300 in three of five seasons with Pittsburgh and played in the 1925 and 1927 World Series. Though he reached career highs of 22 HR, 126 RBI, and a .321 batting average with

Brooklyn in 1930, the strong, accurate arm that had earned him the nickname Buckshot was gone, ruined in a 1929 handball accident. His playing career quickly declined, but he remained in baseball as a minor league manager and scout. /(JK)

Harry Wright [William Henry] — 1835–1895. OF-RHP 1871–77 **Boston (NA)**, Boston (NL) *NA*: 179 g, .263; 4–1; *ML*: 2 g, .000.
    Manager 1871–93 Boston (NA), Braves, Providence (NL), **Phillies** *NA*: 225–60, .789; *ML*: 1000–825, .548. First place: 1872–75, 77–78
☛ *Hall of Fame—53.*

Wright was born in England and came to America when his father, a famous cricket player, was hired by the fashionable St. George Cricket Club in New York. Harry and brothers George and Sam scandalized their father by taking up the new American game of baseball. Harry became baseball's most innovative proponent and most influential force, shaping a Hall of Fame career as a pioneer and manager.

Wright joined the Knickerbockers, a club of young New York City sportsmen that included Alexander Cartwright, who had laid out the first diamond and constructed the game's first rules. He played wherever he could and became the recognized leader of others who took up the game. When Cincinnati's city fathers decided after the Civil War that a winning ballclub would put their town on the map, they hired Wright and gave him free rein to recruit the first openly paid baseball team. The result was the undefeated 1869 Red Stockings, whose 56-game nationwide tour helped spread the popularity of baseball.

Wright and Albert Spalding led a tour to England in 1874 to demonstrate the game. The British were indifferent to baseball, but were mildly impressed when the Americans, few of whom had ever seen cricket, took some tips from Wright and won a few matches.

Wright managed the National Association Boston Red Stockings in 1871–75, winning the pennant the last four years. He started an 18-year career in the National League when the circuit formed in 1876, taking the helm of the Boston Red Caps, winning titles his second and third years but never again. His brother George, who became a Hall of Famer, was an infielder on Harry's NA club and his NL Boston and Providence teams. An early student of statistics, Harry kept his own detailed box scores and studied them so avidly that he lost his sight for a year in 1890 and had to temporarily relinquish the reins of

Harry Wright

the Phillies. He is credited with introducing the practice of one fielder backing up another. He was elected to the Hall of Fame by the Committee on Baseball Veterans in 1953. /(JK)

Jim Wright [James Clifton] — 1950– . RHP 1978–79 Red Sox 139 ip, 9–4, 3.82

After nine years in the Red Sox farm system, Wright went 8–4 for Boston in 1978, throwing three shutouts. He recorded only one subsequent ML decision, as he was disabled much of 1979. James Leon Wright, four inches taller at 6′5″ and unrelated, pitched for the Royals in 1981–82. /(JCA)

Ken Wright — 1946– . RHP 1970–74 **Royals**, Yankees 236 ip, 11–15, 4.54

The hard-throwing Wright had trouble controlling his fastball and his weight. Lifetime, he struck out 181 and walked 180. He was dealt with Lou Piniella to the Yankees for Lindy McDaniel in 1973. /(JCA)

Rasty Wright [Wayne Bromley] — 1895–1948. RHP 1917–19, 22–23 **Browns** 451 ip, 24–19, 4.05

Wright went 8–2 with a 2.51 ERA in his second season but dropped off to 0–5 the next year. Resurfacing in 1922, he went 9–7 with five saves and a 2.92 ERA as the Browns challenged for the AL pennant. /(SFS)

Taffy Wright [Taft Shedron] — 1911–1981. OF 1938–42, 46–49 Senators, **White Sox**, A's 1029 g, .311, 38 hr, 553 rbi

Wide-shouldered Taffy Wright was a lefthanded hitting machine with adequate fielding skills. He was switched from pitcher to outfield in the minors and, as a Senators rookie in 1938, led the AL with 13 pinch hits and 39 attempts. He had a career .328 average when called to military duty in 1942. After three-plus seasons, he returned having lost some sharpness, and though he batted .324 in 1947, he dropped to .235 in 1949, his final season. /(JK)

Tom Wright — 1923– . OF 1948–56 Red Sox, Browns, **White Sox**, Senators 341 g, .255, 6 hr, 99 rbi

Wright was a backup outfielder with little power who was used as a lefthanded pinch hitter in nearly half his ML games. Splitting 1952 between the Browns and White Sox, he had a league-high 10 pinch hits. /(PB)

Russ Wrightstone — 1893–1969. 3B-1B-OF-SS-2B **Phillies**, Giants 909 g, .297, 60 hr, 425 rbi

During the 1920s, the Phillies needed only to look to the versatile, hard-hitting Wrightstone to plug any gap on the field. He batted .300 five times, and was often used as a lefthanded pinch hitter. /(JK)

Wrigley Field Chicago (FL) 1914–15, Chicago Cubs 1916– . LF-355, CF-400, RF-353

More than 40 years after Detroit's Tiger Stadium became the second-to-last ML ballpark to install lights, Chicago's Wrigley Field followed suit, and the all-day-game era officially came to an end on August 9, 1988, when the Cubs beat the Mets 6–4 in Wrigley Field's first night game. The inaugural night contest had been scheduled for the previous evening, but the Phillies-Cubs game was rained out in the fourth inning.

While baseball purists and neighborhood residents fought fiercely against the lights, often turning to the courts for help, the local statutes now allow the Cubs 18 night games per season until 2002. And despite the presence of light standards on the roof, Wrigley Field remains one of baseball's most old-fashioned parks, rivaled only by Fenway Park in simplistic charm and beauty. It has the smallest capacity in the NL, 38,143, with an ordinary double-decked grandstand that runs along each foul line and very small bleacher sections in the outfield. The outfield walls are still made of red brick, and are covered with thick green ivy, into which balls often disappear for ground-rule doubles. The large centerfield scoreboard is still manually operated, and it carries the complete line scores of all NL games each day.

Wrigley was built as Weeghman Field in 1914 by Charles Weeghman, owner of the Federal League's Chicago Whales, and when he assumed control of the Cubs in 1916, he immediately moved the club there. By 1927, the park had assumed its current name in honor of new owner William Wrigley, and a second deck had been added, doubling the capacity to near 40,000. Since then, it has been modernized periodically, but has changed little in appearance or scope.

Aside from its lack of lights, Wrigley Field's most distinctive feature has been its winds. Usually strong, when they are blowing out, the tiny park is a pitcher's nightmare (the Cubs once beat the Phillies here, 23–22), but when they are blowing in, home runs are virtually non-existent. The foul lines are surprisingly deep (353′-355′), but the fences do not curve away from the plate as is the norm. Rather, the power alleys are only 10′-15′ deeper, and home runs frequently leave the park completely, landing on either Waveland or Sheffield Avenue behind the tiny bleachers. There is little foul territory, and the field, of course, is natural grass.

Wrigley Field has not hosted many World Series games, but on October 1, 1932, Babe Ruth allegedly

Chicago's Wrigley Field

"called his shot" here in Game Three. And on May 2, 1917 Fred Toney and Hippo Vaughn pitched baseball's only double no-hitter, with Toney winning 1–0 in the 10th inning. Interestingly, the debate over the necessity of lights in Wrigley was almost rendered moot in the winter of 1941, when the Cubs had lights in the ballpark ready to be installed. But when the Japanese attacked Pearl Harbor, the lights were donated to the war effort, and Wrigley Field remained a daylight ballpark for 47 more years. /(SCL)

Wrigley Field Los Angeles Angels 1961. LF-340, CF-412, RF-339

Named for Cubs owner William Wrigley when the Pacific Coast League Angels were a Cubs farm club, Wrigley Field was home to the expansion Angels in their first ML season. A ML-record 248 HR were hit there in its lone season, thanks to 345-foot power alleys. /(SCL)

Philip K. Wrigley — 1894–1977. Owner.

Known as P.K. to his close associates, Wrigley succeeded his father as president of the Cubs (and of the chewing gum company) in 1932 and continued until his death. He was generous to his players and former players with advice and financial help. His favorite was Charlie Grimm, whom he kept on the payroll all his life. Although honest and accessible to print reporters, he gave no radio or TV interviews and insisted on maintaining his privacy. With meticulous integrity, he would dock his salary as president of the gum company for time spent with the Cubs. He could be innovative, as witness his "rotating coaches" experiment with the Cubs' manager job. But he was also responsible for keeping Wrigley Field free of lights. /(NLM)

John Wyatt — 1935– . RHP 1961–69 **A's**, Red Sox, Yankees, Tigers 687 ip, 42–44, 3.47. *1 WS, 4 ip, 1–0, 4.91*
☛ *All-Star—64.*

Wyatt saved 70 games in four years as the ace of the woeful A's bullpen (1962–65). In 1964, his All-Star year, he led the AL with 81 appearances, then a ML record. Traded to the Red Sox in mid-1966, he had another fine year as Boston's stopper in 1967, playing an important part in their "Impossible Dream" pennant with a 10–7, 20-save season. In Game Six of the World Series he let the Cardinals tie the score, but when the Red Sox rallied for four runs in the bottom of the seventh he became the fourth black pitcher to get a WS victory. /(SFS)

Whit Wyatt [John Whitlow] — 1907– . RHP 1929–37, 39–45 Tigers, White Sox, Indians, **Dodgers**, Phillies 1762 ip, 106–95, 3.78. 20 wins: 41 *1 WS, 18 ip, 1–1, 2.50*
☛ *Led League—w 41. All-Star—39–42.*

As a high-school phenom in Georgia, Wyatt struck out 23 Oglethorpe University batters in a game. Signed by the Tigers, he had 16 straight victories for Evansville (Three-I League) in 1929. Then, for eight frustrating seasons, Wyatt was expected to become a top American League pitcher but was sidetracked year after year by injuries. From 1929 through 1937, he compiled a 26–43 AL record. In 1931 his 1.53 ERA tied Dizzy Dean for the Texas League crown. After an MVP season in the American Association in 1938, he was purchased by the Dodgers and became a four-time All-Star.

Wyatt went 15–14 for Brooklyn in 1940, tying for the NL lead with five shutouts. In 1941 he and teammate Kirby Higbe each won 22 games, tops in the majors, to lead the Dodgers to the pennant. Wyatt's seven shutouts were also the ML high. He threw two complete games in the World Series, beating the Yankees 3–2 in the second game, but losing 3–1 in the Series finale. Over the next two seasons Wyatt was 33–12, but he faded in 1944.

Wyatt was unafraid to knock a batter down, earning the reputation as a headhunter. Joe DiMaggio called him "the meanest guy I ever saw." When Wyatt became a ML pitching coach (Phillies, Braves), his pupils said he encouraged them to throw at hitters as well. /(JK)

John Wyckoff — 1892–1961. RHP 1913–18 **A's**, Red Sox 574 ip, 23–24, 3.55. *1 WS, 4 ip, 0–0, 2.45*

As a hard-throwing youngster, Wyckoff went 11–7 for the 1914 pennant-winning Athletics. With nearly all of their stars sold, traded, or lost to the Federal League, Philadelphia finished last in 1915. Wyckoff outpitched Boston's Babe Ruth that Memorial Day, winning 2–1 and striking Ruth out twice. He emerged as the team's ace, winning 10 games, but led the league with 22 losses and 165 walks. A sore arm ended his career. /(JL)

Butch Wynegar — 1956– . C 1976–88 **Twins**, Yankees, Angels 1401 g, .255, 65 hr, 506 rbi
☛ *All-Star—76–77.*

An outstanding defensive catcher, Wynegar was *TSN* AL Rookie of the Year in 1976 and represented the Twins at the All-Star Game his first two seasons, becoming the youngest player (to that point) to appear in the mid-summer game in 1976. A slow-footed switch-hitter, he had initial success after being traded to the Yankees, batting .295 for them in 1982–83 and catching Dave Righetti's 1983 no-hitter. He became a full-time starter in 1984. After an injury-riddled 1985, Wynegar succumbed to the high-pressure atmosphere and suffered from physical and mental fatigue in 1986. Various foot problems in 1987 caused more trouble.

Wynegar won the Appalachian League batting title (.346) in his first pro season (1974). /(ME)

Early Wynn (Gus) — 1920– . RHP 1939, 41–44, 46–63 Senators, **Indians**, White Sox 4564 ip, 300–244, 3.54; 796 g, .214, 17 hr, 173 rbi 20 wins: 51–52, 54, 56, 59 *2 WS, 20 ip, 1–2, 4.95*
☛ *Led League—w 54, 59. Led League—k 57–58. Led League—era 50. Cy Young Award—59. All-Star—55–60. Hall of Fame—1972.*

The vanishing breed of scowling, intimidating pitchers is best typified by Hall of Famer and 300-game-winner Early Wynn. He walked into a Senators tryout camp and signed a pro contract at age 17. After three starts in 1939, he made the majors to stay in 1941. Armed with a blazing fastball and little else, Wynn gave scant evidence of his future in his 191 appearances with Washington. Seasons of 18 and 17 wins were offset by a league-high 17 losses in 1944 and 19 defeats, with a 5.82 ERA, in 1948.

Indians owner Bill Veeck obtained Wynn on December 14, 1948 with Mickey Vernon for Joe Haynes, Ed Klieman, and Eddie Robinson, one of the best deals in Indians' history. Wynn came under

Early Wynn

the tutelage of Cleveland pitching coach Mel Harder, who taught the portly righthander a curve, knuckleball, slider, and changeup. Wynn threw all his pitches with an easy, effortless motion. After a year of adjustment in 1949, he led the AL with a 3.20 ERA in 1950. He had the first of his 20-win seasons in 1951. With Bob Lemon, Mike Garcia, and, first, aging Bob Feller and then Herb Score, Wynn was in one of baseball's all-time great pitching rotations. In 1952 he won 23 games, Lemon and Garcia won 22 each, and the three were named Cleveland's Men of the Year. They made the Indians a close second to the Yankees in 1952 and 1953. In 1954 Wynn and Lemon tied for the AL

lead with 23 wins and the Indians won a league-record 111 games before suffering a stunning World Series sweep to the Giants. Wynn allowed an RBI single and a home run to Series star Dusty Rhodes in losing Game Two.

Though he led the AL in strikeouts, Wynn suffered his first losing season with Cleveland in 1957 (14–17). That December, he and Al Smith went to the White Sox for Minnie Minoso and Fred Hatfield. In 1958, Wynn became the first ML pitcher to lead his league in strikeouts in consecutive years with different teams, but still posted a 14–16 record. But at the age of 39 in 1959 he led the White Sox to the AL pennant, leading the AL in wins

(22–10), starts, and innings. He won Game One of the WS over the Dodgers 11–0, but was hit hard in his two other starts and lost Game Seven.

In the 1950s, Wynn was 188–119 with more strikeouts, 1,544, than any other pitcher. He led the league with four shutouts in 1960 and pitched well in his illness-curtailed 1961 season (8–2), but struggled to a 7–15 record in 1962 as his 300th win proved elusive. He was released that November and was cut during spring training in 1963, needing just one more victory for the landmark plateau. Signed by Cleveland, Wynn reached the milestone on July 13, 1963, going five innings to defeat the Athletics. He spent most of the year in the bullpen and retired after the season. He pitched more seasons (23) than any pitcher to that time, despite battling gout from 1951 on. Wynn believed in running and kept his legs in great shape. He also walked a record 1,775 batters.

Wynn's distinct personality led him to call the pitching mound his "office." He worked with a grim, fierce appearance, and might be best remembered for saying he would knock down his grandmother if she dug in against him. Feared on the field, Wynn was an easygoing, fun-loving practical joker off the field. A dangerous batter who is among the all-time pitchers' leaders in hits, he was used as a pinch hitter 90 times during his career and hit .270 or better five times. /(ME)

Jimmy Wynn (The Toy Cannon) — 1942– . OF
1963–77 **Astros** , Dodgers, Braves, Yankees, Brewers
1920 g, .250, 291 hr, 964 rbi. *1 LCS, 4 g, .200, 2 rbi.*
1 WS, 5 g, .188, 1 hr, 2 rbi
☛ *All-Star—67, 74–75.*

Wynn, the Astros' first slugging star, played most of his career in a big ballpark with a poor supporting cast. The speedy, 5′9″ outfielder had an explosive bat—hence the nickname, the Toy Cannon. When he left Houston after 11 seasons, he held club records in virtually every offensive category, including hits (1,291), home runs (223), and RBI (719).

The Cincinnati native first signed with the Reds, but was drafted from them by the expansion Houston club in 1962. In 1965, Wynn's first full season, he led the Astros with a .275 batting average, 22 home runs, and 73 RBI. He also stole a career-high 43 bases. Two years later he broke club records with 37 HR and 107 RBI, but he struck out a league-high 137 times. Seeing fewer good pitches to hit in 1969, he tied the NL record with 148 walks, but still hit 33 HR.

Wynn's career, and life, nearly ended when he was stabbed in the abdomen during a quarrel with

his wife in December 1970. He recovered physically, but slumped dramatically in 1971, hitting just seven homers. He rebounded in 1972 (.273, 24 HR, 90 RBI), but another poor year in 1973 paved the way for his trade to the Dodgers for pitcher Claude Osteen. Wynn gave Los Angeles a desperately needed righthanded power hitter, and replaced the recently traded Willie Davis in centerfield.

Wynn carried the pennant-winning Dodgers for the first part of 1974, hit three HR in a game for the second time in his career, set a Los Angeles record with 32 HR, and was named *TSN* NL Comeback Player of the Year. Nursing a sore elbow, he spent one more season with the Dodgers before being sent to Atlanta in a six-player deal for Dusty Baker. He led the NL in walks a second time in 1976, but batted just .207, and split a final, dreadful, 1977 campaign between the Yankees and Brewers. /(ME)

Jimmy Wynn

Billy Wynne — 1943– . RHP 1967–71 Mets, **White Sox**, Angels 187 ip, 8–11, 4.32

The 6'3" Mets prospect never had a decision for New York, and in 1967 he went to Chicago in the six-player deal that brought Tommie Agee and Al Weis—two heroes of the 1969 World Series—to the Mets. Wynne went 7–7 for the White Sox in 1969./(JCA)

Marvell Wynne — 1959– . OF 1983– Pirates, **Padres**, Cubs 848 g, .250, 36 hr, 225 rbi. *1 LCS, 4 g, .167*

Wynne's skills were similar to those of his centerfield predecessor in Pittsburgh, Omar Moreno. The far-ranging ballhawk was usually a light hitter who, unlike Moreno, was a poor basestealing threat. Above-average defense and flashes of offense kept Wynne in the majors. He surprised with 11 HR in 1988 for the Padres./(ME)

Johnny Wyrostek — 1919–1986. OF 1942–43, 46–54 Pirates, Phillies, **Reds** 1221 g, .271, 58 hr, 481 rbi ☛ *All-Star—50–51.*

Signed out of high school by the Cardinals in 1937, the lefthanded-hitting Wyrostek first became a regular with the 1946 Phillies after a stint in the army. Traded to Cincinnati, he had a career-high 17 home runs in 1948 and batted .311 in 1951—his second straight year as an All-Star right fielder. He hit 20 or more doubles each year from 1946 through 1951./(AL)

Hank Wyse (Hooks) — 1918– . RHP 1942–47, 50–51 **Cubs**, A's, Senators 1258 ip, 79–70, 3.52. 20 wins: 45 *1 WS, 8 ip, 0–1, 7.04*

Wyse was a sinkerballing control pitcher. He suffered a spine injury that not only made him 4-F during the war, but also sometimes forced him to wear a corset while pitching. Nonetheless, he started an average of 32 games a year from 1943 through 1946. His 22–10 record in 1945 helped Chicago to the pennant, and included an April 27 no-hit bid lost in the eighth inning when Pittsburgh's Bill Salkeld singled with one out. In the 1945 World Series, touched for a three-run homer by the Tigers' Hank Greenberg, Wyse lost Game Two; he pitched in relief in Games Six and Seven./(DAS)

Koji Yamamoto — 1947– . OF 1968– **Hiroshima Carp**

Combining power with speed, Yamamoto was a key member of Hiroshima's 1979 and 1981 Japanese pennant winners, contributing 42 homers with 113 RBI in 1979, and 43 homers with 103 RBI in 1981./(MC)

Bill Yancey — 1904–1971. SS Negro Leagues 1923–36 **New York Lincoln Giants**, Hilldale, New York Black Yankees, Brooklyn Eagles, New York Cubans, Philadelphia Giants, Philadelphia Tigers, Darby Daisies statistics not available

Yancey was a shortstop for 14 Negro League seasons. He was a good fielder and baserunner, a smart player who managed in Latin America and helped develop baseball in Panama in the 1930s. He later scouted for the New York Yankees. In 1932 he became a guard with The Renaissance Five basketball team, which was inducted as a unit into the National Basketball Hall of Fame in 1963./(BP)

Yankee Stadium (The House That Ruth Built) New York Yankees 1923–73, 76– . LF-312, CF-410, RF-310

Asked to leave the Polo Grounds when his Yankees began outdrawing the Giants in 1920, owner Jacob Ruppert seized the opportunity to build what would become the most famous stadium in all of baseball, a triple-decked wonder called Yankee Stadium. Erected on the site of a Bronx lumberyard just across the Harlem River from the Polo Grounds, Yankee Stadium was quickly dubbed The House That Ruth Built to honor the Yankee whose home runs were revolutionizing the game (and filling Ruppert's coffers), and on April 18, 1923 Ruth's three-run home run led the Yankees to a 4–1 win over the Red Sox in the stadium's first game. The grandstand was extended around the foul poles by 1928, with wooden bleachers surrounding the rest of the outfield, and the top of the stadium was ringed with a distinctive white fence facade.

Like the stadium, the playing field itself was quite remarkable. The left- and right-field corners were only 281′ and 295′ in 1923, but left sloped out dramatically to 460′ while center was a near-impossible 490′ away. Deep left and center fields became known as Death Valley as many a right-handed slugger watched towering fly balls die there. Eventually, stone monuments to Ruth, Lou Gehrig, and Miller Huggins were erected in deep left center, and they were in play, although rarely reached by batted balls. Lights were added in 1946, and the stadium remained virtually unchanged until 1973, when it was closed completely for two years of renovations and modernization.

The stadium was reopened in 1976 with major structural improvements. Bulky support poles for the upper decks had been eliminated, along with the corresponding obstructed-view seats, and escalators improved access to the upper decks. The left- and center-field fences had been drawn in considerably, but were still a hefty 430′ and 417′ respectively. The monuments were relocated to Monument Park behind the left-field fence, open to fans before and after games, and numerous plaques have been added to the original trio of Yankee greats. The field remains natural grass, but recently under the direction of George Steinbrenner the left- and center-field fences have been brought even closer, reducing Death Valley to a relatively timid 399'. Yankee Stadium's still-spacious outfield favors pitchers, although it has little foul territory and a close right-field corner that is extremely inviting to lefthanded sluggers.

Naturally, Yankee Stadium has been the scene of many of baseball's greatest moments. Babe Ruth belted his 60th home run here in 1927, and Roger Maris broke the single-season record with his 61st in 1961. It has hosted far more World Series than any other park, and in WS play Don Larsen pitched his perfect game October 8, 1956, and on October 18, 1977 Reggie Jackson hit three home runs on three consecutive pitches to win the Series in Game Six. Despite the presence of sluggers like Ruth, Gehrig, Mantle, and Jackson, no ML batter has ever hit a fair ball completely out of the stadium, although legend says Negro Leaguer Josh Gibson pulled a home run over the left-field roof in 1934./(SCL)

Yankee Stadium

Carl Yastrzemski (Yaz, Captain Carl) — 1939– . OF-1B-DH 1961–83 **Red Sox** 3308 g, .285, 452 hr, 1844 rbi. *1 LCS, 3 g, .455, 1 hr, 2 rbi. 2 WS, 14 g, .352, 3 hr, 9 rbi* ☛ *Most Valuable Player—67. Led League—ba 63, 67–68. Led League—hr 67. Led League—rbi 67. All-Star—63, 65–79, 82–83. Gold Glove—63, 65, 67–69, 71. Hall of Fame—1989.*

Signed as a shortstop off the Notre Dame campus in February 1959, Yastrzemski replaced Ted Williams in left field for the Boston Red Sox in 1961 and followed him into the Hall of Fame in 1989. When he retired after 23 years, Yastrzemski ranked first in career games (3,308), third in at-bats (11,988) and walks (1,845), sixth in total bases (5,539), seventh in hits (3,419) and doubles (646), and ninth in RBI (1,844). He's the only American League player with both 3000 hits and 400 homers.

Although he won three batting titles, played in 18 All-Star games, and was acknowledged as the finest defensive left fielder of his time, Yastrzemski will be primarily remembered by Red Sox rooters for his 1967 season, the year of The Impossible Dream. Starved for a pennant for 21 seasons, Fenway partisans had no reason to think that 1967 would be any different from the miserable ninth-place finish of 1966. But, going into the final week, four teams were still in the race and three teams would finish within a game of one another. Yastrzemski almost single-handedly carried the club during the last month. In the final 12 games, he had 23 hits in 44 at-bats (.523), with five home runs, 14 runs and 16 RBI. The Red Sox needed to win the last two games with the Twins to avoid a three-way tie with them and Detroit. Yastrzemski went 7-for-8 with five RBI, including a three-run homer in the first game. He also snuffed out a Twin rally by throwing out Bob Allison at second base on what looked like a sure double.

Yastrzemski hit .400 with three homers in the World Series. He won the Triple Crown by hitting .326 with 44 HR and 121 RBI and also led the AL in hits (189), runs (112), total bases (360), and slugging average (.622). He missed a unanimous vote for the MVP award because one sportswriter thought that Cesar Tovar (.267, 6 HR, 47 RBI) of the Twins was more valuable.

Yastrzemski's .301 batting average in 1968, "The Year of the Pitcher," is the lowest ever to lead a league, but some sabermetric analysts consider it the equivalent of Bill Terry's .401 in 1930 if the contexts are considered. Yastrzemski constantly tinkered with his batting stance, but remained consistent. Outside of the brilliance of 1967 and his three batting crowns, it was his consistency as much

as anything that earned him Hall of Fame honors, but he was also a clutch hitter. Besides his 1967 feats, he hit .455 in the 1975 LCS and .310 in that year's World Series, and he hit a home run off the nearly-unbeatable Ron Guidry in the 1978 playoff game. He went 4-for-4 with two walks in the 1970 All-Star Game.

In addition, Yastrzemski was a great fielder with a strong arm who made himself expert in playing the tricky caroms off the Green Monster, Fenway Park's left field wall. In the 1975 LCS, he returned to left field after playing first base for three-quarters of the season and shone defensively. In 12 years as a left fielder, Yastrzemski won seven Gold Gloves and led in assists seven times. On July 21, 1982 he played centerfield and went 2-for-3 with a run and an RBI. Nearing 43 years, he may have been the oldest major leaguer to play center. /(CG)

Tom Yawkey [born Thomas Austin] — 1903–1976. *Executive.*
☛ *Hall of Fame—1980.*

Yawkey spent 44 years as the sole owner of the Boston Red Sox, often spending lavishly in pursuit of a winner. Yawkey was born Thomas Austin; his grandfather had a lumber and iron empire worth millions and was negotiating to purchase the Detroit Tigers when he died. Tom's uncle completed the deal, and when Tom's father died, the uncle adopted the boy, who took the Yawkey name. Tom inherited a sizable estate when the elder Yawkey died. Armed with a degree from the Sheffield Scientific School at Yale, he actively headed up the family business empire. In 1933, at the age of 30, he paid Bob Quinn $1.5 million for the Red Sox, and found himself with a perennial second-division club and a decaying Fenway Park.

Yawkey quickly hired an astute baseball man in Eddie Collins, and spent another $1.5 million to refurbish Fenway Park. With Collins supplying the know-how and Yawkey the money, the Red Sox brought future Hall of Famers Rick Ferrell, Joe Cronin, Lefty Grove, Jimmie Foxx, Bobby Doerr, and Ted Williams to Boston. Yawkey never lost his willingness to open his coffers for proven players or to pay his players handsomely even before it was normal to do so. Only three times did his beloved Red Sox reward him with the AL pennant—in 1946, 1967, and 1975. And they never won a World Series.

Yawkey took great pride in becoming a pillar in the baseball world. Yet he was not active in social circles, and was more at ease in his baseball togs, working out on the Fenway diamond. Respected for

Carl Yastrzemski

the sound baseball advice he gave to other owners, Yawkey was named to the Hall of Fame by the Committee on Baseball Veterans in 1980, four years after his death. He left the Red Sox to be operated by his widow, Jean Yawkey. /(EW)

Emil Yde — 1900–1968. LHP 1924–27, 29 **Pirates**, Tigers 705 ip, 49–25, 4.02. *2 WS, 2 ip, 0–1, 11.57*

Submariner Emil Yde was a sensational Pirate rookie in 1924, going 16–3 to lead the NL with an .842 winning percentage. His 17–9 record helped Pittsburgh win the 1925 pennant. He was defeated by Washington's Walter Johnson in Game Four of the World Series, removed after allowing back-to-back homers in the third inning—an event that seemed to signal his decline. He won only eight games the following season and was back in the minors by 1927. Yde was a good switch-hitter (.233); used 34 times as a pinch hitter, he even pinch hit in the 1927 WS. /(JK)

Joe Yeager [George Y.] (Little Joe) — 1873–1940. 3B-RHP-SS-2B 1898–1903, 05–08 Dodgers, **Tigers**, Yankees, Browns 574 g, .252, 4 hr, 201 rbi; 705 ip, 33–49, 3.74

Starting out as a pitcher, Yeager went 12–22 for Brooklyn in his first season and was used sparingly the next two years as a pitcher and a shortstop. He then jumped to the new American League. Detroit initially used him as a pitcher; he went 12–11, 2.61 in 1901, but dropped to 6–12, 4.82 in 1902. The Tigers made him their regular third baseman in 1903; he hit .256 and fielded adequately, ending his pitching career. Reappearing with the Highlanders (later the Yankees) in 1905, he played 90 games at 3B and 21 at SS, batting .267, and he was a utility man in 1906, hitting a career-high .301. He played in the most games of his career with the 1907 Browns, chiefly at third, but was hampered by a hand injury and hit just .239. Illness ended his career the following season. He is credited by some with originating the squeeze play. /(NLM)

Steve Yeager (Boomer) — 1948– . C 1972–86 **Dodgers**, Mariners 1269 g, .228, 102 hr, 410 rbi. *6 LCS, 15 g, .178, 1 hr, 4 rbi. 4 WS, 21 g, .298, 4 hr, 10 rbi*

Longtime Dodger Steve Yeager was well-respected behind the plate, and Lou Brock called him "the best-throwing catcher in the game." He was an intelligent game-caller and a team leader on six Dodger division winners. He shared the three-way MVP award in the 1981 World Series, largely due to

his home run off the Yankees' Ron Guidry that won Game Five.

In an extra-inning game on August 8, 1972, Yeager tied a NL record for catchers with 22 putouts and set another with 24 chances accepted. In 1974 the Dodgers won their first 24 games in which Yeager started behind the plate. He never batted more than .256 as a regular, but he reached double figures in home runs six times.

Yeager introduced the neck protector, the flap attached to the catcher's mask, first donning it after a freak 1976 accident; he was hit with the jagged end of a broken bat while in the on-deck circle, and had nine splinters removed from his neck. The nephew of legendary pilot Chuck Yeager, Steve became accustomed to notoriety. He gained attention by posing for a *Playgirl* centerfold. The best man at his wedding was Los Angeles mayor Tom Bradley. /(TG)

Stan Yerkes — 1874–1940. P 1901–03 Baltimore (AL), **Cardinals** 319 ip, 14–23, 3.66

By the simple expedient of averaging one and a quarter hits per inning, Yerkes led the NL in losses with his 11–20 in 1902. His 3.66 ERA was nearly a run over the league average. /(BC)

Steve Yerkes — 1888–1971. 2B-SS 1909, 11–16 **Red Sox**, Pittsburgh (FL), Cubs 711 g, .268, 6 hr, 254 rbi. *1 WS, 8 g, .250, 4 rbi*

The 1912 WS was the high point of Yerkes's career. He drove in the winning run for the Red Sox in Game One with a two-run seventh-inning single, and he scored the Series-winning run in the tenth inning of Game Eight (Game Two had been a 6–6 tie). In that final game, Yerkes drew a walk off Giants ace Christy Mathewson two batters after outfielder Fred Snodgrass's famous error, and later scored on Larry Gardner's sacrifice fly. That season, his first as Boston's regular second baseman (he'd been their shortstop in 1911), he hit .252 with a career-high 73 runs. After three solid seasons with Boston he jumped to the Federal League in mid-1914 (while earning $3,500 a year with the Red Sox) to make $6,500. He hit a career-high .288 for the 1915 Pittsburgh Rebels. He later managed in the minors and coached Yale's freshman team. /(NLM)

Rich Yett — 1962– . RHP 1985– Twins, **Indians** 410 ip, 22–24, 4.98

First signed by Minnesota in 1980, Yett was sent to Cleveland in a 1985 trade for Bert Blyleven. On September 22, 1986, two weeks after learning a forkball, he used it to shut out the first-place Angels on four hits. /(JCA)

Earl Yingling (Chink) — 1888–1962. LHP-OF 1911–14, 18 Indians, **Dodgers**, Reds, Senators 568 ip, 24–34, 3.22; 139 g, .267, 1 hr, 23 rbi

Yingling never had a winning season as a pitcher, but he added to his value by being able to pinch hit. A .267 batter, he earned a 13-game tryout in Cincinnati's outfield in 1914. /(JK)

Wally Yonamine — 1925– . OF 1951–62 **Tokyo Yomiuri Giants**, Chunichi Dragons 1219 g, .311, 82 hr, 480 rbi
☛ *Led League—ba 54, 56, 57.*

Yonamine is considered the greatest leadoff man in Japanese baseball history. Born in Honolulu of Japanese parents, he was the fifth foreigner, but only the third American (and the first after WWII) to play in Japan. Yonamine starred at halfback for the San Francisco '49ers in 1950, but was injured and turned to baseball the following spring. The Yomiuri Giants had asked San Francisco Seals manager Lefty O'Doul to recommend any star Japanese-American players to them. When Yonamine's average reached .360 for Salt Lake City of the Class C Western League, Yonamine joined the Giants in May 1951, hitting .354 and leading them to the Japan Series despite fan abuse reminiscent of Jackie Robinson's debut with the Brooklyn Dodgers. He introduced the Japanese to hard sliding, running out bunts and infield grounders, and diving for fly balls. Hitting over .300 his first seven years, Yonamine beat out teammate Tetsuharu "The God of Batting" Kawakami for three batting championships. A Japanese nationalist, Kawakami didn't forgive or forget, and released Yonamine upon becoming Giants manager in 1961. At that time, Yonamine's career average was the best in Japanese baseball despite three consecutive off-seasons. Determined to show up Kawakami, Yonamine signed with the Chunichi Dragons, and homered to beat the Giants in their first encounter. It was his last home run, however, and when he finally retired, Yonamine's average had dropped two points below Kawakami's. Yonamine remained in Japan as a coach and scout. /(MC)

Tetsuya Yoneda — Unk.–Unk. P 1956–76 **Hankyu Braves** 342–Unk. *9 JWS*

Second only to Masaichi Kaneda in Japanese career wins, Yoneda pitched his entire career outside the Tokyo media spotlight and was, in contrast with Kaneda, a model of comportment. He received little recognition for outstanding longevity and consistency. /(MC)

Jim York — 1947– . RHP 1970–76 Royals, **Astros**, Yankees 174 g, 284 ip, 16–17, 3.79

The sidearming sinkerballer pitched for UCLA in the 1969 College World Series, and then signed with the Royals. In 1971 he relieved in 53 games, winning five, with a 2.90 ERA. Sent to Houston in a December 1971 deal for John Mayberry, York spent part of each successive year through 1976 in Triple-A. /(JCA)

Rudy York — 1913–1970. 1B-C 1934, 37–48 **Tigers**, Red Sox, White Sox, A's 1603 g, .275, 277 hr, 1152 rbi. *3 WS, 21 g, .221, 3 hr, 10 rbi.*
    Manager 1959 **Red Sox** 0–1, .000
☛ *Led League—hr 43. Led League—rbi 43.*

Always threatening at the plate, the 6'1" 210-lb York overcame defensive troubles and jibes at his ancestry (he was half American Indian) to become a productive ML first baseman. As MVP of the Texas League in 1935 and the American Association in 1936, York was trapped behind the Tigers' first baseman Hank Greenberg, who was AL MVP himself in '35. As a rookie in 1937, York put together one of the greatest months in baseball history, breaking Babe Ruth's record for home runs in one month with 18 in August, while driving in 49 runs, another ML one-month record. He finished at .307 with 35 HR and 103 RBI in only 375 at-bats while splitting time between catcher and third base. When Mickey Cochrane suffered a career-ending skull fracture, York became Detroit's everyday catcher, but by 1940 Tiger management realized York belonged at first base. They paid Greenberg a bonus to move to left field, and he hit 41 home runs that year. York added 33, and the Tigers won the pennant.

Greenberg left for WWII in 1941, leaving York to supply the Tigers' power, but he slipped to 27 and 21 HR in 1941–42, although he hit three in one game on September 1, 1941. York rebounded in 1943 to lead the AL in both HR and RBI, but fell below 20 the next two years. When the Tigers switched Greenberg back to 1B at the end of his career, York was traded to the Red Sox. He hit only 17 HR for Boston in 1946, but added two in the WS, including a game-winner in the tenth inning of Game One.

York was never a defensive whiz, leading AL first basemen in errors three times and prompting one sportswriter to quip, "Rudy York is part Indian and part first baseman." He was, however, extremely dangerous with the bases loaded, belting 12 career grand slams, including two in one game July 27, 1946, a game in which he drove in ten runs. /(JK)

Yoshio Yosheda — 1933- . SS 1953-69 **Hanshin Tigers** .268, 70 hr, 400 rbi

Japan's "Mr. Shortstop," the 5'3" Yosheda was a source of national pride during the 1950s and 1960s when shortstops in Japan tended to be minor league American imports. Usually batting leadoff or second, Yosheda hit his peak with a .318 mark in 1964, when he matched his career high of eight homers. /(MC)

Eddie Yost (The Walking Man) — 1926- . 3B 1944, 46-62 **Senators**, Tigers, Angels 2109 g, .254, 139 hr, 683 rbi.
    Manager 1963 **Senators** 0-1, .000
☛ *All-Star-52*.

Yost earned distinction through his ability to draw bases on balls, but was also a dependable hitter and a record-setting third baseman. He never played in the minors, going right from the Brooklyn sandlots and New York University to the Washington Senators, but lost time in 1944–46 to military service. His keen eye earned him eight seasons with 100 or more walks; he led the American League six times. He led the AL with 36 doubles in 1951, and scored an AL-high 115 runs for the Tigers in 1959.

Yost led third basemen in putouts a major league record eight times. When he retired in 1962, he had played a major league record 2,008 games at 3B, and held AL records for putouts, assists, and chances at 3B. He played 838 straight games from July 6, 1949 until sidelined by tonsillitis in 1955. No player with fewer than 200 HR has matched Yost's 1,614 career walks. His 28 home runs leading off the game in his career set a since-surpassed ML record. Yost became a third base coach for the Senators, Mets, and Red Sox. /(ME)

Ned Yost — 1955- . C 1980-85 **Brewers**, Rangers, Expos 219 g, .212, 16 hr, 64 rbi. *1 WS, 1 g, --*

Yost hit .309 at Vancouver (Pacific Coast League) in 1980 to earn a promotion to the Brewers, but was never more than a backup catcher in the ML. After four seasons with Milwaukee he was one of two players traded to Texas for Jim Sundberg, and he played a career-high 80 games with the Rangers in 1984, hitting .182. /(SCL)

Floyd Youmans — 1964- . RHP 1985- **Expos**, Phillies 539 ip, 30-34, 3.74

An extremely talented hard-throwing starter, Youmans's problems with drugs have hampered what should have been an outstanding career. He was a high-school teammate of Dwight Gooden for two years in Tampa, FL and was the Mets second-round selection (behind Gooden) in the 1982 draft, before becoming one of four players traded to the Expos for Gary Carter in December 1984. Youmans joined the Expos' starting rotation at the age of 22 in 1986, and had several brilliant outings en route to a 13–12, 3.53 record. He pitched a one-hitter against the Phillies June 8, threw three two-hitters, and struck out 15 Phillies on September 27. He also led the NL in walks with 118. In 1987 he again showed flashes of brilliance, pitching a one-hitter against the Astros July 8 on his way to NL Pitcher of the Month honors (4–1, 1.13), but was on the DL three times, and after the season checked into a drug rehabilitation program. Youmans returned to pitch in 1988, only to check back into rehabilitation for most of July and August, and in December 1988 the Expos traded their troubled young pitcher to the Phillies with Jeff Parrett for Kevin Gross. /(SCL)

Babe Young [Norman Robert] — 1915-1983. 1B-OF 1936, 39-42, 46-48 **Giants**, Reds, Cardinals 728 g, .273, 79 hr, 415 rbi

Young graduated from Fordham University in the Bronx in 1936 and was working out at Yankee Stadium when he broke his hand. He received a call at the ballpark from the Giants, inviting him to travel with them. They farmed him out in 1937 and, after his MVP 1939 season in the Southern Association, made him their first baseman. Though he drove in more than 100 runs in both 1940 and 1941, Young did not meet New York's expectations. In 1943 he joined the Coast Guard. He returned in 1946, led the NL with 32 pinch-hitting appearances, and moved on to the Reds and Cardinals. After being invited by the Yankees to spring training in 1949, he injured his leg and left baseball. /(JK)

Bobby Young — 1925-1985. 2B 1948, 51-56, 58 Cardinals, **Browns/Orioles**, Indians, Phillies 687 g, .249, 15 hr, 137 rbi

Young was a smooth second baseman who rose through the Cardinal farm system and was bought in 1951 by the Browns, for whom he batted a career-high .260 as a rookie. When the franchise shifted to

Baltimore in 1954, Young, a Maryland native, was the first player signed to a contract. /(JK)

Curt Young — 1960- . LHP 1983- A's 832 ip, 51–42, 4.20. *2 LCS, 2 ip, 0–0, 0.00. 1 WS, 1 ip, 0–0, 0.00*

Young started 17 games for the A's in 1984 after his recall from Tacoma (Pacific Coast League) in June, then was hampered by tendinitis most of 1985, but joined Oakland's starting rotation for good in 1986, finishing 13–9, 3.45, and tossing a one-hitter against the Royals on the final day of the season. He pitched a second one-hitter June 9, 1987 against the White Sox on his way to another 13-win season, and in 1988 he was 11–8 as the fourth starter for the AL champion A's. He did not start a game in the postseason, but was unscored upon in two relief appearances. /(SCL)

Cy Young [Denton True] — 1867–1955. RHP 1890–1911 Cleveland (NL), Cardinals, **Red Sox**, Indians, Braves 7356 ip, 511–313, 2.63. 20 wins: 91–04, 07–08 *1 WS, 34 ip, 2–1, 1.59*
☛ *Led League—w 95, 01–03. Led League—era 92, 01. Hall of Fame—1937.*

The man who won 511 major league games has his glory reprised annually when the Cy Young Awards are given to the season's best pitchers. He takes two bows retrospectively, one in each league, as he divided both the number of seasons he pitched and the staggering number of games he won almost evenly between the National and American leagues.

Young had already established a pitching record in the NL that might have earned him a place in the Hall of Fame when, in 1901, he joined the new American League and started phase two of his fabulous career. He led the league in victories its first three seasons. He also pitched in the first World Series, in 1903, and won two games for the victorious Red Sox.

Young's career spanned more than just 22 seasons; he bridged the time from when the pitcher's box was 50′ from home plate until the introduction of the present distance, 60′ 6″, with the ball thrown from a mound, was introduced. He pitched against superstars such as Cap Anson, who was an established player when the National League was formed in 1876, and against Eddie Collins, who played in 1930. Young was born just after the Civil War and was still alert and in good physical condition at the time of the Korean War.

Cy Young had his nickname given him in wonderment by a young catcher who warmed him up when he tried out for the Canton, Ohio minor league team. He was judged to be "as fast as a cyclone." Reporters shortened it to "Cy" and Denton True Young had a lifelong nickname.

Among Young's 511 major league victories were three no-hitters. One of them, on May 5, 1904 against the Athletics, was a perfect game in which he outdueled Rube Waddell. Young was so intent on defeating the great lefthander that he didn't realize he had pitched a perfect game until he was congratulated for doing so.

Most noteworthy about Cy Young is the durability that permitted him to amass 511 victories. It also produced 316 losses, another all-time record. He credited his off-season farm work, chopping wood and doing heavy chores, with keeping him in shape to play until he was 44 years old. Then, portly, but without a twinge of pain in his arm, he was unable to field his position and was bunted into retirement.

Occasionally Cy Young is seen in photos taken in his retirement years wearing a uniform that says "Old Timers" on its shirt front. This was a souvenir from a special game played in Cleveland in 1921 to

Cy Young

celebrate the city's 75th anniversary. It brought back the stars of the past to play a team of sandlot stars and, of course, Cy Young was named to start the game. With players like Nap Lajoie, Elmer Flick, and Jesse Burkett behind him, and Chief Zimmer, who had been his barehanded batterymate when he broke in back in 1890, old Cy Young fanned a pair in his two innings as his team of veterans won the game.

It is fitting that baseball honors its most prolific winner, whose career winning percentage was .620, by giving his name to the annual Cy Young Awards. His name invokes the tradition and sense of history some of the recipients of the award seem to lack. When Denny McLain became the latest pitcher to win 30 games, in 1968, he had to ask about the man for whom his Cy Young Award was named. He was told, "You've done it once; Cy Young topped 30 victories five times."/(JK)

Del Young [Delmer Edward] — 1912–1979. SS-2B 1937–40 **Phillies** 309 g, .224, 3 hr, 76 rbi

Del Young was a good-fielding, weak-hitting middle infielder with the futile Philadelphia Phillies in the pre-WWII period. The compactly-built Cleveland, Ohio native's father, Delmer John Young, played 94 games in the majors, mostly with Buffalo of the Federal League./(FS)

Dick Young — 1918–1987. *Writer.*

Young received the J.G. Taylor Spink Award from the Hall of Fame in 1979. For over 30 years he covered baseball with a breezy style that antagonized many in the game and attracted millions of readers to his column, "Young Ideas." He began as a messenger boy with the New York *Daily News* and, in his 45 years there, rose to sports editor. In 1982 he moved to the New York *Post.*

Young railed against drug abuse, coming down hard on users among athletes. When Dwight Gooden came back from treatment in 1987, Young advised fans to stand up and boo him. He criticized the Commissioner's office for its lenient drug policy, and founded a Memorial Fund for the Phoenix House Foundation Drug Education and Prevention Program. Nobody was immune from criticism; while covering the Dodgers, Young was barred from the clubhouse by two managers./(NLM)

Gerald Young — 1964– . OF 1987– **Astros** 366 g, .260, 1 hr, 90 rbi

Switch-hitting Gerald Young challenged Vince Coleman for the NL stolen-base title in 1988 with 65 steals, but tied for the league lead with 27

unsuccessful steal attempts. The powerless Honduran hit only .233 in 1989 and was caught stealing a NL-leading 25 times in his 59 attempts./(SFS)

Irv Young (Young Cy, Cy the Second) — 1877–1935. LHP 1905–08, 10–11 **Braves**, Pirates, White Sox 1384 ip, 63–94, 3.11

Young won 20 games for the Braves in 1905 and set post-1900 rookie records that still stand for innings (378) and complete games (41). Boston's NL fans called him Young Cy while Old Cy was still pitching brilliantly for the Red Sox. But Irv Young also lost 21 games in his first year and ended comparisons with his crosstown namesake by losing 25 and 23 in his next two years./(BC)

Kip Young — 1954– . RHP 1978–79 Tigers 149 ip, 8–9, 3.85

Control pitcher Young went 6–7 (2.81) his rookie year, winning his first four starts, and 2–2 (6.34) his final season./(JCA)

Matt Young — 1958– . LHP 1983– **Mariners**, Dodgers, A's 693 ip, 42–56, 4.36

Young's career started auspiciously with the 1983 Mariners. His 11–15 record made him the staff ace of the last-place team, and his 3.27 ERA set the team mark for lowest ERA by a starter. The anticipation inherent in starting was too much for him, and after leading the AL with 19 losses in 1985 he was converted to relief. He led the Seattle staff with 13 saves in 1986 but was traded to the Dodgers for Dennis Powell that winter. He was unimpressive in the NL, and after a trade to Oakland for 1988 developed injury problems that caused him to miss the whole season./(TF)

Mike Young — 1960– . OF-DH 1982– **Orioles**, Phillies, Brewers, Indians 635 g, .247, 72 hr, 236 rbi

A strikeout-prone switch-hitter, Young was red hot in August 1985, hitting 11 HR with an Orioles one-month record 32 RBI on his way to his best professional season, .273 with 28 HR and 81 RBI. Young cooled considerably in 1986, hitting just nine home runs, and after hitting .240 in 1987 he was traded to Philadelphia in 1988, where he struggled for half a season as an outfielder-pinch hitter. On May 28, 1987 he became only the fifth player in ML history to hit two extra-inning home runs in the same game, homering in the 10th to tie the score, and again in the 12th to beat the Angels./(SCL)

Pep Young [Lemuel Floyd] — 1907–1962. 2B-SS-3B 1933–41, 45 **Pirates**, Reds, Cardinals 730 g, .262, 32 hr, 347 rbi

In his Forbes Field debut, Young went 4-for-4 against Carl Hubbell. A timely hitter, he drove in 82 runs in 1935, his first full year. He was the Pirates' regular second baseman for four seasons. /(JK)

Ralph Young — 1889–1965. 2B-SS 1913, 15–22 Yankees, **Tigers**, A's 1022 g, .247, 4 hr, 254 rbi

The 5′5″ Young was one of the smallest American Leaguers ever. The switch-hitter's ability to draw walks helped compensate for his lifetime .247 batting average. He failed in a seven-game trial with the 1913 Yankees, but was the Tigers' first-string second baseman from 1915 through 1921. In his best year, 1920, he scored 84 times while batting .291. Young led AL second basemen in errors in 1915 and 1918 and in assists in 1917. He later coached at Temple and St. Joseph's in his native Philadelphia. /(NLM)

Joel Youngblood — 1951– . OF-3B-2B 1976– Reds, Cardinals, Mets, Expos, **Giants** 1408 g, .265, 80 hr, 422 rbi
☛ *All-Star—81.*

Youngblood started in right field for the Mets in 1979 and in center in 1980, but has been a reserve for most of his 14 ML seasons, and has blossomed into a fine righthanded pinch hitter since 1986. Originally drafted by the Reds in 1970, Youngblood didn't reach the ML until 1976, and was traded twice in 1977, first to the Cardinals, then to the Mets, where he emerged as a good-hitting outfielder and was the club's sole All-Star in 1981. In 1982, Youngblood became the first ML player ever to collect hits for two different teams on the same day, when he singled for the Mets against the Cubs in the afternoon, was traded to the Expos after the game, and flew to Philadelphia in time to hit a pinch single off the Phillies' Steve Carlton that night. Youngblood signed as a free agent with San Francisco after the 1982 season, and the Giants desperately tried to get his bat into their everyday lineup by playing him at second base in 1983 and at third in 1984. Although Youngblood did hit a career-high 17 HR in 1983, the experiment failed defensively, as he led NL third basemen with 36 errors the following year. He returned to reserve duty in 1985, and from 1986 to 1988 rapped 16, 13, and 15 pinch hits. The veteran missed his only chance at postseason play in 1987 when he broke his wrist chasing a foul fly on September 19. /(SCL)

Ross Youngs [Royce Middlebrook] (Pep) — 1897–1927. OF 1917–26 **Giants** 1211 g, .322, 42 hr, 592 rbi. *4 WS, 26 g, .286, 1 hr, 9 rbi*
☛ *Hall of Fame—72.*

On the wall behind the desk of John McGraw's Polo Grounds office hung portraits of pitcher Christy Mathewson and Ross Youngs, whom McGraw called his "greatest outfielder." Youngs had a brief but outstanding career; in eight full seasons with the Giants, the lefthanded hitter was consistently among the league leaders in several offensive categories. He topped the league with 31 doubles in 1919. His .351 average in 1920 put him second in the NL behind Rogers Hornsby; his .356 in 1924 placed him third.

In 1921, the 5′8″ 162-lb Texan became the first player in World Series history to connect for two hits in an inning, collecting a double and a triple in the eight-run seventh inning of Game Three. The right fielder on New York's four straight pennant winners (1921–24), his superb throwing arm and track-star speed helped to obscure his overenthusiastic defensive style. He recorded league-high totals in outfield assists and errors in both 1920 and 1922.

Ross Youngs

In the wake of the Black Sox scandal, claims were made by baseball insiders that Youngs had taken bribes from New York gamblers. Teammate Jimmy O'Connell, who was banned from baseball, alleged that Youngs knew about an attempt to fix a 1924 game. Highly regarded in the baseball world, Youngs made a quick, calm, and direct denial of the charges, and was acquitted.

Youngs had the first sub-.300 performance of his career in 1925. The following spring, he was diagnosed as suffering from Bright's disease, a terminal kidney ailment. The Giants hired a full-time nurse to travel with him, and Youngs valiantly managed a .306 average in 95 games. Bedridden in 1927, he died after watching the Giants slip to third place. He had some support for the Hall of Fame in 1938, but wasn't inducted until the Committee on Baseball Veterans recognized him in 1972. /(ASNEN)

Robin Yount — 1955– . SS-OF 1974- **Brewers** 2291 g, .292, 208 hr, 1124 rbi. *1 LCS, 5 g, .250. 1 WS, 7 g, .414, 1 hr, 6 rbi*
☛ *Most Valuable Player—82, 89. All-Star—80, 82–83. Gold Glove—82.*

A youthful beginning and sustained performance, despite injuries, put Robin Yount in position to join baseball's all-time greats in several statistical categories. Yount was just eighteen years old when he earned Milwaukee's rookie of the year award in 1974. By 1986 he was the seventh-youngest player in major league history to reach the 2,000 hit mark. Yount reached both the 1,000- and 2,000-hit plateaus in games against the Indians. One of the youngest everyday starters ever, Yount overcame a spring ankle injury to post his first outstanding offensive season in 1978. In 1980 he led the majors with 49 doubles and 82 extra-base hits and became the first shortstop in 15 years with more than 300 total bases. Extensive weight training in 1979 and 1980 accounted for Yount's increased power. He peaked in 1982, leading Milwaukee to the World Series with a Most Valuable Player season: .331, 29 HR, and 114 RBI, all career highs. He led the league in hits, tied for the lead in doubles, and led shortstops with 489 assists. Yount was the top vote-getter for the 1983 All-Star Game.

Robin Yount

Shoulder surgery after the 1984 season ended Yount's career at shortstop. Though he adapted well to the outfield, Yount's power was significantly reduced. But just when his best years seemed gone, he posted big years in '87, '88, and '89, winning his second AL MVP award in the last year. His mark secure in Brewers history as club leader in virtually every offensive category, Yount appeared most likely among active players to become baseball's next 3,000-hit man. /(ME)

Eddie Yuhas — 1924–1986. RHP 1952–53 **Cardinals** 100 ip, 12–2, 2.87

Yuhas went 12–2 with six saves and a 2.72 ERA in his first season, but a sore arm ended his career the next year. /(JFC)

Chris Zachary — 1944– . RHP 1963–67, 69, 71–73 Astros, Royals, Cardinals, Tigers, Pirates 321 ip, 10–29, 4.57. *1 LCS, 0 ip, 0–0, infinite*

Zachary never had a winning season, but in his one good year, 1972, he helped the Tigers to a division championship with a 1.42 ERA in 25 games, all but one in relief. /(JFC)

Tom Zachary — 1896–1969. LHP 1918–36 A's, Senators, Browns, Yankees, Braves, Dodgers, Phillies 3134 ip, 186–191, 3.72. *3 WS, 28 ip, 3–0, 2.86*

Zachary, a solid starter for almost two decades, was the pitcher who gave up Babe Ruth's 60th home run of 1927. He broke in by winning two games for the A's in 1918, playing under the assumed name of Zach Walton to protect his college eligibility. The son of a minister, he went overseas with a Quaker Red Cross unit during WWI. He resumed his career with the Washington Senators, compiling an 85–82 record for them from 1920 through 1925, winning a high of 18 in 1921.

Zachary helped Washington to the pennant with a 15–9 record in 1924. While ace Walter Johnson lost his two World Series starts to the Giants, Zachary won Games Two and Six. Traded to the Browns in 1926, he was back with Washington in 1927 when he allowed Ruth's 60th HR on September 30. (Walter Johnson pinch hit for Zachary in the ninth inning that day in what proved to be his last ML appearance.) He was waived to the Yankees in August 1928 and, as a surprise starter in Game Three of the WS, defeated the Cardinals 7–3. In 1929 he became the only major league pitcher to win as many as 12 games in a season without a defeat. /(JK)

Pat Zachry — 1952– . RHP 1976–85 Reds, Mets, Dodgers, Phillies 1178 ip, 69–67, 3.52. *2 LCS, 9 ip, 1–0, 3.00. 1 WS, 6 ip, 1–0, 2.70*
☛ *Rookie of the Year—76.*

The 6'5" 180-lb Zachry got off to a fast start, sharing NL Rookie of the Year honors with Butch Metzger in 1976 when he went 14–7 (2.74) for the World Champion Reds. One of four players traded for

Tom Seaver in 1978, Zachry pitched respectably for the Mets in five-plus seasons as an injury-prone starter. He led the NL with 14 losses in strike-shortened 1981. Usually bearded, Zachry pitched mostly in relief for Los Angeles and Philadelphia. /(JCA)

Geoff Zahn — 1945– . LHP 1973–85 Dodgers, Cubs, Twins, Angels 1849 ip, 111–109, 3.74. *1 LCS, 4 ip, 0–1, 7.36*

Zahn was a minor contributor to the Dodgers' 1974 NL pennant, going 3–5 with a 2.03 ERA in spot starts and relief. Traded to the Cubs in May 1975 with pitcher Eddie Solomon for Burt Hooton, he spent most of the rest of the year on the DL and was released by Chicago after a disappointing 1976, during which he had bone fragments removed from his elbow. Picked up by the Twins, he used a hard slider to become one of their more reliable starters, winning 12–14 games each of four straight years (1977–80) for mediocre teams. He joined California as a free agent for the 1981 season and had his best season in 1982. He was 18–8 with a 3.73 ERA and finished sixth in the Cy Young Award voting as the Angels won the AL West. Zahn was hit hard by the Brewers in his Game Three start in the LCS and took the loss. In 1983 he lost a month to an inflamed shoulder, stopping his six-year string of victories in double figures (he finished 9–11). He rebounded to go 13–10, 3.12 in 1984, but arm miseries cropped up again in 1985 and ended his career. /(WOR)

Paul Zahniser — 1896–1964. RHP 1923–26, 29 Senators, Red Sox 619 ip, 25–47, 4.66

Zahniser was a consistent 20-game winner in the Southern Association and once won 15 straight. He pitched respectably until he joined the Red Sox; in 1926, he went 6–18, tying for the AL lead in losses. /(NLM)

Oscar Zamora — 1944– . RHP 1974–76, 78 Cubs, Astros 225 ip, 13–14, 4.52

Zamora was the Cubs' main righthanded reliever in 1974–75, saving ten each season despite fighting a back injury. He threw strikes, but, as one writer put it, "When the pitch is so fat, that the ball hits the bat, that's Zamora." Bruce Sutter's 1976 arrival made the Cuban reliever expendable. Zamora pitched a seven-inning perfect game for Denver (American Association) on September 2, 1972. /(DB)

Dom Zanni — 1932– . RHP 1958–59, 61–64, 65–66 Giants, **White Sox**, Reds 183 ip, 9–6, 3.79

Technically, Zanni never pitched a complete game in the majors, but he did pitch all nine innings of a victory. On June 22, 1962 he relieved injured Joel Horlen for the White Sox with two on and none out. He continued the rest of the way, scattering seven hits in a 5–1 win. Moreover, in the seventh inning, he was knocked unconscious in a collision while covering first base. After clearing his head, he went back to the mound and finished the game. /(BC)

Al Zarilla (Zeke) — 1919– . OF 1943–44, 46–53 **Browns**, Red Sox, White Sox 1120 g, .276, 61 hr, 456 rbi. *1 WS, 4 g, .100, 1 rbi*
☛ *All-Star—48.*

Zarilla was on the Browns' only pennant winner, hitting .299 in 100 games and scoring and driving in a run as the Browns won Game Three of the World Series 6–2. After returning from 1945 military service, the right fielder won more playing time each year and made the All-Star team in 1948, when he reached career highs with a .329 batting average (fourth in the AL), 12 HR, 39 doubles, and 11 steals. The Red Sox traded Stan Spence and cash to get him in May 1949, and he had another fine season in 1950, finishing fifth in batting (.325), behind Dom DiMaggio and ahead of Ted Williams in the Red Sox' all-.300 outfield. Zarilla had career highs in slugging (.493), runs (92), and walks (76). That June 8, he tied the major league record for doubles in a game (4). He was traded to the White Sox and he declined thereafter, returning to the Browns and Red Sox before his career finished. /(WOR)

Norm Zauchin [Norbert Henry] — 1929– . 1B 1951, 55–59 **Red Sox**, Senators 346 g, .233, 50 hr, 159 rbi

The 6'5" 220-lb Zauchin, Boston's hope as a right-handed, power-hitting first baseman, hit 27 HR with 93 RBI as a rookie in 1955. He also struck out an AL-high 105 times. He had three homers and drove in ten runs against Washington that May 27. Failing to hit after 1955, he was traded to the Senators in 1958. /(PB)

Rollie Zeider (Bunions) — 1883–1967. 2B-3B-SS-1B 1910–18 **White Sox**, Yankees, Chicago (FL), Cubs 936 g, .240, 5 hr, 253 rbi. *1 WS, 2 g, .000*

This likable utility man held the AL rookie stolen-base record (49) for 76 years until John Cangelosi, another White Sox player, broke it in 1986. Once called Hook because of his beak-like nose, Zeider became Bunions when he contracted bloodpoisoning after a Ty Cobb spiking sliced into his bunion. When he was traded along with another run-of-the-mill player to the Yankees for defensive star Hal Chase, the *New York Globe*'s Mark Roth wrote in disgust: "[Manager Frank] Chance traded Chase for a bunion and an onion." Zeider and Dutch Zwilling are the only two men in the twentieth century to play in three different major leagues in the same city. /(DB)

Bill Zepp — 1946– . RHP 1969–71 **Twins**, Tigers 188 ip, 10–5, 3.63. *1 LCS, 1 ip, 0–0, 6.75*

In the only good season of his short major league career, Zepp was 9–4 with a 3.22 ERA and two saves as a starter and reliever to help the Twins to their second straight division title in 1970. /(JFC)

Gus Zernial (Ozark Ike) — 1923– . OF-1B 1949–59 White Sox, **A's**, Tigers 1234 g, .265, 237 hr, 776 rbi
☛ *Led League—hr 51. Led League—rbi 51. All-Star—53.*

The 6'3" 210-lb, free-swinging Zernial trailed only Mickey Mantle, Yogi Berra, and Larry Doby in American League home runs in the 1950s. Despite tying what was then a White Sox record with 29 home runs in 1950, he was sent to the Athletics in a blockbuster, three-way deal that brought Minnie Minoso to Chicago on April 30, 1951. Zernial went on to lead the league with 33 HR, 129 RBI, and 17 outfield assists that year, while leading AL hitters in strikeouts a second straight time. In 1953, he stroked 42 HR, one less than league leader Al Rosen.

Zernial twice broke his collarbone chasing fly balls. Finishing with Detroit, he led the AL with 15 pinch hits in 1958. When Fred Haney broadcast Zernial's games with the Pacific Coast League Hollywood Stars, he nicknamed the brawny, blond Texan Ozark Ike after the popular comic strip character. /(ME)

George Zettlein (The Charmer) — 1844–1905. RHP 1871–76 **Chicago (NA)**, Troy (NA), Brooklyn (NA), Philadelphia (NA), Phillies *NA*: 217 g, 125–90; *NL*: 234 ip, 4–20, 3.88. 20 wins: 73, 74, 75

After naval service in the Civil War, Zettlein returned to Brooklyn, where he starred for the Atlantics, one of the top teams of the day. He was the winning pitcher in 1870 when the Atlantics ended the Cincinnati Red Stockings' undefeated streak. With the formation of the National Association, he joined the Chicago team that seemed certain of the first pennant until its ballpark burned down during the Chicago Fire. Zettlein won 125 NA games in five years but slumped to 4–20 in 1876, his only NL year. /(BC)

Benny Zientara — 1920–1985. 2B-3B 1941, 46–48 **Reds** 278 g, .254, 2 hr, 49 rbi

Zientara had a "cup of coffee" with the Reds and then spent four years in the military. He hit .289 as a backup in 1946 and won the second-base job in 1947, reaching career highs of 60 runs and 24 RBI while batting .258 (418 at-bats). His career ended after he dropped to .187 in 1948. /(WOR)

Chief Zimmer [Charles Louis] — 1860–1949. C 1884, 1886–1903 Detroit (NL), New York (AA), Cleveland (AA), **Cleveland (NL)**, Louisville (NL), Pirates, Phillies 1280 g, .269, 26 hr, 620 rbi.
Manager 1903 **Phillies** 49–86, .363

Zimmer was with Cleveland (American Association) in 1887 when he became the first catcher to play directly behind the batter on every play; previously, catchers would move farther back of the plate with runners on base. The new style soon caught on. For a decade beginning in 1889, Zimmer caught for the National League Cleveland Spiders, becoming the finest defensive catcher of his day; he repeatedly led the NL in putouts, assists, and double plays. In 1895 he batted a career-high .340. He was dealt to Louisville in mid-1899, and in January of 1900 was part of the package of players that Barney Dreyfuss lifted from Louisville to bolster the Pittsburgh Pirates when the NL went from 12 teams to 8. Waived in 1903, he was picked up by the Phillies as player-manager. He hit .220 and brought the Phillies in seventh. /(AJA)

Don Zimmer (Zim, Popeye) — 1931– . 3B-2B-SS-C 1954–65 **Dodgers**, Cubs, Mets, Reds, Senators 1095 g, .235, 91 hr, 352 rbi. *2 WS, 5 g, .200, 2 rbi.*
Manager 1972–73, 76–82, 88– Padres, **Red Sox**, Rangers, Cubs 790–754, .512. First place: 89 *1 LCS, 1–4, .200*
☛ *All-Star—61.*

Zimmer was leading the American Association with 23 HR and 63 RBI on July 7, 1953 when he was hit in the head by a Jim Kirk pitch. He was unconscious for almost two weeks, lost his speech for six, and dropped 44 lbs. Inserted in his head were four "buttons . . .like tapered corkscrews in a bottle," he explained. He returned in 1954 and was Brooklyn's second baseman in the 1955 World Series. He was doing well in 1956 when a pitch from the Reds' Hal Jeffcoat fractured his cheekbone and ended his season.

Built like a fireplug and nicknamed Popeye for his strength, the scrappy Zimmer came back again and was the Dodgers' starting shortstop in 1958, reaching career highs of 17 HR and 60 RBI. He lost the job to Maury Wills with a woeful 1959 season, spent his two busiest years with the 1960–61 Cubs, and was an original New York Met. He finished his playing career in Japan.

Zimmer managed in the minors and coached for the Expos and Padres before spending 1972 and 1973 as San Diego's manager. He was a Boston coach when named manager in mid-1976. In 1978, his Red Sox won 99 games, but lost the AL East title in a one-game playoff with the Yankees. He piloted the Rangers in 1981–82, coached for the Yankees, Cubs, and Giants, and was named Cubs manager by his high-school buddy, GM Jim Frey, for 1988. He won the division title, and AP Manager of the Year in 1989 with unorthodox strategic moves (he likes the squeeze bunt with the bases loaded) and with lots of rookies and journeymen in his lineups. /(ME)

Heinie Zimmerman [Henry] — 1887–1969. 3B-2B-SS-1B 1907–19 **Cubs**, Giants 1456 g, .295, 58 hr, 800 rbi. *3 WS, 12 g, .163, 2 rbi*
☛ *Led League—ba 12. Led League—hr 12. Led League—rbi 12, 16, 17.*

A utility man until 1911, Zimmerman peaked in 1912, his first season as the Cubs' everyday third baseman, when he led the NL with 14 home runs, 103 RBI, 41 doubles, and a .372 batting average. The native New Yorker was traded to the Giants in 1916, and he helped them to the 1917 pennant by capturing his third RBI title. But he was made a goat in the 1917 World Series against the White Sox. In the fourth inning of the sixth and final game, he made a throwing error. Then, in a botched rundown, he pursued Eddie Collins down the third base line; Collins scored as nobody covered home plate. New York lost 4–2.

Zimmerman and teammate Hal Chase were abruptly suspended by the pennant-contending Giants toward the end of the 1919 season. The two had allegedly tried to entice teammates into fixing games. Both were banned from baseball./(JK)

Jerry Zimmerman — 1934- . C 1961-68 Reds, **Twins** 483 g, .204, 3 hr, 72 rbi. *2 WS, 4 g, .000*

The clever clubhouse prankster backed up the often-injured Earl Battey most of his career. Weak at the plate but superb behind it, Zimmerman handled pitchers extremely well; he was Montreal's bullpen coach from 1969 to 1975./(JCA)

Guy Zinn — 1887-1949. OF 1911-15 Yankees, Braves, **Baltimore (FL)** 314 g, .269, 15 hr, 139 rbi

When Zinn hit six home runs for the 1912 Yankees (then called the Highlanders), he tied the then-existing club record. He was sold to the Braves that December and, after a salary dispute, jumped to the Federal League. In 1914 he broke his leg, an injury that eventually ended his career./(BC)

Jimmy Zinn — 1895- . RHP 1919-22, 29 A's, **Pirates**, Indians 299 ip, 13-16, 4.30

Zinn spent little time in the majors, but in a 22-year minor league career he was 295-198 with five 20-win seasons. He was also a switch-hitting outfielder, and batted .301 in the minors, playing mostly for Kansas City (American Association) and San Francisco (Pacific Coast League)./(ME)

Richie Zisk — 1949- . OF-DH 1971-83 **Pirates**, White Sox, Rangers, Mariners 1453 g, .287, 207 hr, 792 rbi. *2 LCS, 6 g, .400*
☛ *All-Star—77-78.*

A three-time minor league home run champ, Zisk replaced Roberto Clemente as Pittsburgh's right fielder in 1973. He moved to left field to accommodate stronger-armed Dave Parker in 1975. From 1973 to 1976, Zisk averaged .299 with 17 HR a season, but felt unappreciated among the Parkers and Stargells, saying he was "buried alive in Pittsburgh." Manager Danny Murtaugh thought Zisk was a lazy dreamer. Zisk welcomed his trade to the White Sox for Goose Gossage and Terry Forster after the 1976 season and reached career highs of 30 HR and 101 RBI in 1977. He then signed a lucrative ten-year contract with Texas as a free agent. After three Ranger seasons, Zisk was traded to Seattle and hit .311 as a DH in 1981, setting a Mariner record with homers in five straight games, and earning AL

Comeback Player of the Year honors. After multiple knee operations and a wrist injury, he retired after 1983./(JCA)

Billy Zitzmann — 1897-1985. OF 1919, 25-29 Pirates, **Reds** 406 g, .267, 3 hr, 89 rbi

Zitzmann was a journeyman minor leaguer and a platooned Reds outfielder. He played in 104 games in 1925, but a broken foot kept him out for much of 1926. He left baseball after breaking his ankle sliding in a 1932 International League game./(JK)

Sam Zoldak (Sad Sam) — 1918-1966. LHP 1944-52 **Browns**, Indians, A's 929 ip, 43-53, 3.54

Zoldak helped the 1944 Browns and the 1948 Indians to pennants. He was especially valuable to the '48 Indians, going 9-6 with a 2.81 ERA as their fifth starter and reliever after a mid-season trade./(SFS)

Bill Zuber (Goober) — 1913-1982. RHP 1936, 38-47 Indians, Senators, **Yankees**, Red Sox 786 ip, 43-42, 4.28. *1 WS, 2 ip, 0-0, 4.50*

Zuber was a sidearming sinkerballer whose 4-F status made him available to the WWII Senators and Yankees. As a reliever and spot starter, he won a career-high nine games for Washington in 1942. He is the only Amish player in ML history./(JK)

George Zuverink — 1924- . RHP 1951-52, 54-59 Indians, Reds, Tigers, **Orioles** 642 ip, 32-36, 3.54

Zuverink was 9-13 for the Tigers in 1954, his only year as a starter. Sold to Baltimore and returned to the bullpen, he led the AL in appearances twice and saved an AL-high 16 games in 1956./(JK)

Dutch Zwilling [Edward Harrison] — 1888-1978. OF 1910, 14-16 White Sox, **Chicago (FL)**, Cubs 366 g, .284, 29 hr, 202 rbi
☛ *Led League—hr 14. Led League—rbi 15.*

Zwilling, just 5'6", was the star centerfielder of the Federal League Chicago Whales. He tied for the league lead with 15 HR in 1914, led with 94 RBI in 1915, and topped league outfielders in putouts both seasons. When the Feds folded, he served as a lefthanded pinch hitter for the Cubs. He and Rollie Zeider were the only players to play for all three Chicago clubs./(DAS)

CONTRIBUTORS

We are grateful for the efforts all our contributors, those who researched hundreds of biographies and those who provided us with just one article. Occasionally their work was used nearly word for word; more often the requirements of *The Ballplayers* necessitated considerable rewriting. However their efforts were utilized, they were indispensable to us. The initials at the end of each entry identify the main researcher or researchers of that article. In the following section, those initials appear after the contributor's personal sketch. Contributors are identified by more than one set of initials, and in a few instances authors share the same set of initials.

Michael B. Ackerman is an entertainment lawyer working in New York City and a published music critic. (MA)

Art Ahrens has co-authored four books about the Cubs and has written dozens of freelance articles on both the Cubs and other subjects of baseball history. He has been a Cub fan since age seven and has been doing original research since he was fifteen. (ARA, AA)

Al Arthurs lives in Hamilton, Ontario and publishes an annual book about the Ontario Replay League. This proud possessor of a magnificent handlebar mustache is researching the baseball events of 1894. (AJA)

Alan Asnen is a writer, SABR member, former editor, and reporter, and has had numerous biographical sketches published in the *Biographical Dictionary of American Sport*. (ASNEN, AAs, ASN, AA)

Alice B. Belgray is a children's book editor. She has had many articles published, mostly in the field of music (she holds a Ph.D. in musicology). Her love of baseball extends back to the days of the Brooklyn Dodgers. (AB)

Phil Bergen is the librarian at The Bostonian Society, the historical society for the city. He has compiled two indexes of SABR publications and has contributed to the *Hall of Shame* series. (PB)

Richard E. Beverage is the author of *Hollywood Stars* and *The Angels: Los Angeles in the Pacific Coast League*. (DBv, DBev, DB)

Rev. Gerald E. Bierne has been a Catholic priest since 1962 and is now the pastor of St. Rita's Church in Warwick, Rhode Island. He is the author of *The New England Sports Trivia Book* and of the article "The Team with the Most Members in the Hall of Fame" (*Baseball History Magazine*). He and several SABR cohorts run an annual charity Baseball Quiz Bowl in the New England area. (GEB, GB)

Dennis Bingham is currently editor of the Chicago Police Department's Publications Section and a freelance cartoonist, writer, and caricaturist. He served as associate editor of SABR's publication *Baseball in Chicago*. An umpire for semi-pro, youth, and high school leagues in the Chicago area, his particular passions are the study of rules and the White Sox. He served as a historical adviser for the movie *Eight Men Out* and had a bit part therein as umpire Billy Evans. (DB, DBing)

Todd Bolton is a ranger in Maryland whose interests are ballparks and Negro Leaguer Judy Johnson. (TB)

William A. Borst is known in St. Louis as the "Baseball Professor" for his course at Webster University. A SABR member, he does a weekly radio show on WGNU and is the author of several books and articles on baseball, including *Last in the American League* and *The Brooklyn Dodgers: A Fan's Memoir*. As first president and founder of the St. Louis Browns' Fan Club, he edited *The Brown Stocking*. (WAB, WB)

Jesus Francisco Cabrera (JFC)

Clarke Carmody is a co-author of *Baseball's Milestone Season*, a day-by-day account of the record-breaking 1985 year. A former sports anchor and reporter for WLUC-TV in Marquette, Michigan, he is currently employed by Public Interest Communications in Pittsburgh. (CC)

Bob Carroll is a freelance writer and illustrator. The longtime SABR member is also the founder and executive director of the Professional Football Researchers Association and the author of *The Hidden Game of Football* (with Pete Palmer and John Thorn), several other books, and many articles. (BC)

Jim Charlton (JC)

Jane Charnin-Aker began covering major league baseball for New York radio while she was still an English major at Brown University. Over the next nine years, as a broadcaster, writer, minor league media liaison, statistician, and fan she saw professional baseball played in 70 ballparks in North America and the Caribbean. Her baseball poetry has been published in *Spitball*. She dedicates her work on this project to the memory of her mother, Sylvia Bushell Charnin. (JCA)

Dick Clark is the chairman of SABR's Negro Leagues Committee. (DC)

Ellery Clark has authored three books on the Red Sox and has contributed articles to *Baseball Magazine*, *Biographical Dictionary of American Sports: Baseball*, and the Boston Red Sox yearbook. The SABR member received a SABR Salute award in 1984. A retired line-officer Navy captain, U.S. Naval Academy professor of naval history, and Naval Academy A.A. coach of plebe and J.V. cross-country and track, he has also authored many articles on naval history and naval studies. (EC)

Merritt Clifton is a veteran Vermont town team pitcher and makes his living as a freelance writer on environmental subjects and baseball. He is also the editor and publisher, since 1973, of the *Samisdat* literary magazine and chapbook series. The oft-published author's baseball books include *Relative Baseball*, *Relative Baseball II*, and *Japanese Baseball Makes the Big Leagues*. (MC)

Ken Cohen (KC)

L. Robert "Bob" Davids, the founder and first president of SABR, has edited the SABR publications *Baseball Research Journal*, *This Date in Baseball History*, *Great Hitting Pitchers*, and *Minor League Stars* volumes I and II. He also edited *Insider's Baseball* (1983) and contributed articles to *The Sporting News* from 1951 to 1964. He currently publishes the newsletter *Baseball Briefs*. Mr. Davids served in the USAF in 1944-46 and was a U.S. government official from 1951 to 1981. (LRD)

John Devaney (JD)

Morris A. Eckhouse, Executive Director of Cleveland Sports Legends Foundation, has continually focused on the preservation of sports history. An avid collector of sports memorabilia, he worked in the Pittsburgh Pirates publicity department in 1979 and 1980 and began his writing career by co-authoring *This Date in Pittsburgh Pirates History*, and he has also written day-by-day histories of the Cleveland Indians and Cleveland Browns, among other published works. He founded M&M Publications in 1985. (ME, MM, MN)

John L. Evers, a former member of the U.S. Marine Corps, served as a teacher, coach, and administrator for 35 years. He is a member of SABR, PFRA, and CFRA and has contributed to *Detroit Tiger Trivia* and the *Biographical Dictionary of American Sports*. (JLE, JE)

Tony Formo is a leftover Hippie Idealist who has been trying to develop public domain libraries of electronic baseball data through the SABR Computerization Committee. He is also running a guerrilla theater campaign for Commissioner of Baseball. As a draft dodger from Seattle he has been happy to have been a franchise-long Blue Jay fan rather than suffering the Mariners. He has been published by *The Great American Stat Book*, *Left Field*, *Blue Jay Chatter*, and *Replay Magazine*. (TF)

Cappy Gagnon joined SABR in 1977, has served on the Board of Directors since 1983, and was SABR president in 1984-86. He has had articles in *Baseball Digest* and *Baseball Research Journal* and is an authority on the 65 Notre Dame men who played in the major leagues. He is the Director of Special Programs for the Los Angeles County Sheriff's Department. (CG, CAP)

Mark Gallagher, born in 1953, was already a diehard Yankee fan when he entered kindergarten in New Jersey. A writer and SABR member, he still roots for the Yankees from his Rockville, Maryland home and plays softball every summer. Besides articles in SABR publications and in the Yankees' Program and 1987 Yearbook, he has written *The Yankee Encyclopedia*, *Day by Day in New York Yankees History*, *50 Years of Yankee All-Stars*, and *Explosion! Mickey Mantle's Legendary Home Runs*. (MG)

Tom Gallagher is a member of SABR and the Southeastern New England Brooklyn Dodgers Fan Club. He is the director of the New England Equity Institute, a policy center which studies economic issues from the point of view of poor and working people. He is a former three-term member of the Massachusetts House of Representatives. (TG)

Ed Gefen is a sports copy editor for *The Times Herald-Record* of Middletown, NY. He graduated from the University of Pennsylvania in 1988 with a degree in economics. He was sports editor of his college paper in 1986, when *The Daily Pennsylvanian* was selected the top collegiate daily paper in the nation. (EG)

Steven Gietschier is Director of Historical Records for *The Sporting News* and wrote our Roy Campanella and Satchel Paige articles. (SG)

Phil Grabar is a SABR member who is interested in the Negro Leagues. (PG)

Steven Greenfield, a lifetime Phillies fan, wrote and edited sports articles in the *Collier's* and *Merit Students* encyclopedias while working for Macmillan Publishing. He is currently an editor at the Twentieth Century Fund, a nonprofit policy-oriented foundation in New York City (where he avidly roots against the Mets). (SG)

Thomas Griesel is a professional photographer and a baseball fan. (TJG)

George W. Hilton is Professor of Economics at UCLA. He has written mainly on rail transportation, but has published several articles on baseball history and is working on an edition of the baseball stories of Ring Lardner. His published articles include "The Cable Car in America" and "The Transportation Act of 1958." (GWH)

Stephen Holtje is a freelance editor, a published poet, and a classical composer whose works have been performed in New York City recitals. (SH)

Fred Ivor-Campbell is a baseball researcher and writer, specializing in the early history of the game. He is a member of SABR, the North American Society for Sport History, and the Rhode Island Historical Society. He has contributed articles to many SABR publications and to the *Biographical Dictionary of American Sports: Baseball, Harvard Magazine*, and *Sports Collectors Digest*. (FIC)

Tom Jozwik, a former director of SABR, has contributed to several SABR publications, has written sports articles for many newspapers, and has reported on the Milwaukee Brewers as a stringer for the Associated Press. He works full-time as an insurance inspector. (TJ)

Jack Kavanagh is spending his retirement as a sports historian and writer and has contributed to SABR publications and *Baseball History*. (JK)

Francis H. Kinlaw, a member of SABR, is a property tax administrator in Guilford County, North Carolina. He frequently reviews sports books for the Greensboro *News and Record*, and several of his articles on contemporary issues of public administration and political science have also been published. (FK)

Merl F. Kleinknecht has been a SABR member since 1971. A past chairman of SABR's Negro Leagues Committee, he remains a committee member. He has had three articles published in SABR's *Baseball Research Journal* and wrote 13 sketches for the *Biographical Dictionary of American Sports*. He has been an employee of the U.S. Postal Service since 1962. (MFK)

Jim Langford is the author of *The Game Is Never Over*, about the Cubs. (JL)

Joseph Lawler lives in Kingston, Rhode Island, and is a frequent contributor to various publications. His article "Perfection in June" appears in *The Fireside Book of Baseball, 4th Edition*. (JL, LAW)

Larry Lester's main interest is Negro League baseball. The SABR member is a systems analyst. (LL)

Allen Lewis was a sportswriter for the Philadelphia *Evening Ledger* briefly before entering the service in mid-1941 as a private. Discharged as captain (Army Air Force) in 1945, in 1946 he became a sportswriter for the Philadelphia *Inquirer* and remained until his retirement in 1979. He was honored with the J.G. Taylor Spink Award in 1981. Lewis was the Phillies correspondent for *The Sporting News* for 16 years and authored or co-authored three books on the Phillies. (AL)

Richard C. Lindberg is a member of SABR and has authored four books, including *Who's on Third? The Chicago White Sox Story*, the *White Sox Encyclopedia*, and *Chicago Ragtime: Another Look at Chicago, 1880-*1920. He has written for the Chicago *Tribune Magazine* and *Chicago History* and is currently working on a history of the Chicago Police Department. He also serves as a historical consultant to the White Sox. (RL)

Shepard C. Long, a recent Columbia graduate and former sports editor of the *Columbia Daily Spectator*, is a lifelong Red Sox fan. He contributed to *The Baseball Fan's Guide to Spring Training* and is Assistant to the Managing Attorney at the New York law firm of Donovan Leisure Newton & Irvine. (SCL, SL)

Norman L. Macht has been an assistant to broadcasters Ernie Harwell and Jim Woods, a statistician for Howe News Bureau, a general manager of minor league clubs in the Braves and Orioles organizations, and is now a freelance writer on sports history and finance. He is chairman of the SABR Oral History Committee. Besides his numerous articles on baseball and other sports in *The Sporting News*, *Baseball Digest*, *Sports Heritage*, *The Main Event*, and several newspapers, he is the co-author, with Dick Bartell, of *"Rowdy Richard," a Firsthand Account of the National League Baseball Wars of the 1930s and the Men Who Fought Them* (1987). (NLM, NM)

Edward G. Maher works in Human Services for the Commonwealth of Massachusetts and is a self-described Brooklyn Dodger fanatic. (EGM, EM)

Jerry Malloy is interested in Negro Leagues history. His articles on baseball's color line have been published in *The National Pastime*. (JMa)

Rich Marazzi has authored four baseball books: *The Rules and Lore of Baseball* (1980), *The Stein and Day Baseball Date Book* (1981), *Aaron to Zuverink: A Nostalgic Look at the Players of the Fifties* (1982), and *Aaron to Zipfel* (1985). He is a columnist for *Yankees Magazine*, *The Baseball Bulletin*, *Referee Magazine*, and *Sports Collectors Digest*. From 1983 to 1986 he was a research consultant for ESPN's *Inside Baseball*. A high school History and Economics teacher at O'Brien Tech in Ansonia, Connecticut, he is also the school's athletic director and has umpired baseball for 23 years. (RTM, RM)

John Miller (JM, JMM)

Jim Murphy, a retired newspaperman (chiefly in Pawtucket, Rhode Island) has authored numerous articles and two books, *The Gabby Hartnett Story: From a Mill Town to Cooperstown* and *Napoleon "Larry" Lajoie: Modern Baseball's First Superstar* (the latter constituting the 1987 issue of SABR's *The National Pastime*. (JM, JMM, JMu)

Raymond Murphy, a SABR member since 1985, has

written for the *NewPaper*, the Warwick *Beacon*, Pawtucket *Evening Times*, and the Providence *Journal*, and since 1987 has been a sportswriter for the Kent County *Daily Times* in West Warwick, Rhode Island. (RVM, RM, RMu)

Sean O'Malley (SOM)

Francis J. "Frank" Olmstead is a theology teacher and cross country coach at De Smet Jesuit H.S. in St. Louis, Missouri. A SABR member since 1978, he contributed a dozen articles to the *Biographical Dictionary of American Sports: Baseball*. (FJO, FO)

Jim Olson is a physical education specialist whose interests as a SABR member include socio-cultural aspects of baseball and Negro Leaguers. (JO)

Tom Osowski is Season Ticket Sales Director of the Brewers. (TO)

Joseph M. Overfield is the author of *100 Seasons of Buffalo Baseball* and has contributed to SABR publications, *Total Baseball*, *Baseball Digest*, *The Sporting News*, and other magazines. (JO)

John Pastier is an architecture critic and an expert on ballparks. (JP)

Claudia Perry (CP)

Frank V. Phelps has been the chairman of SABR's Bibliographical Committee since its inception and has also served SABR as its treasurer and then on its Board of Directors. His articles have been featured in SABR publications, and he is researching a history of tennis. (FVP)

Bill Plott is a SABR member whose specialty is the ballplayers and baseball history of Alabama. (BP)

Christopher D. Renino is an English teacher in the Scarsdale, New York, public school system. (CR)

James A. Riley is the author of *Dandy, Day, and the Devil* and an expert on the Negro Leagues. His articles have been featured in SABR publications. (JR)

Warner Oliver Rockford (WOR)

Frederic D. Schwarz is an assistant editor at *American Heritage*. (FDS)

Mike Shatzkin (MS)

Duane A. Smith, Professor of History at Fort Lewis College, Durango, Colorado, has published many books about mining and Colorado and articles about baseball and urban history. (DAS, DS)

Fred Stein, a retired Federal Civil Service official, is an environmental and dairy industry consultant. A SABR member since 1975, he has written *Under Coogan's Bluff: A Fan's Recollection of the New York Giants*

Under Terry and Ott and *Giants Diary: A Century of Giants Baseball in New York and San Francisco*. He has also authored several articles on baseball which have appeared in *Giants Yearbook* and *The National Pastime*. (FS, FSt)

Sheldon Fairchild Stewart (SFS)

A.D. Suehsdorf, the former editorial director of The Ridge Press, has authored *The Great American Baseball Scrapbook* and a number of articles in SABR publications and *Baseball History*. He also contributed to the *Biographical Dictionary of American Sports: Baseball*. (ADS)

Richard "Dixie" Tourangeau is a parks ranger. The SABR member is the author of the "Play Ball!" baseball calendars. (RT)

Ken Turetzky has published features and essays, many about sports, in various newspapers and magazines. Although he seized opportunities to meet and interview several heroes of his youth, he remained speechless in the presence of Al Kaline. (KT)

David Quentin Voigt is the author of the scholarly and respected history *American Baseball*, in three volumes. He is a baseball historian and professor at Albright College (Pennsylvania) and a past president of SABR. (DQV, DV)

Ed Walton is Director of Administrative Services at the University of Bridgeport (Connecticut), a baseball historian, and a lifelong baseball fan. The SABR member is a frequent contributor to the Boston media guide and programs, the newsletter "Major League Monthly," and *Diehard* (where his column "Ed Walton's Nostalgia Notebook" is a feature). He often appears on radio and TV talking about baseball. His research resulted in the only change ever sanctioned in a major batting category when he discovered Tris Speaker had hit ten home runs in 1912, tying him with Frank "Home Run" Baker for the AL leadership. Walton's books include *Red Sox Triumphs and Tragedies* and *The Rookies*. (EW)

Edith Williams, a SABR member, is a special education teacher and a specialist in the history of the Baltimore Black Sox. (ETW)

George D. Wolf is the ultimate authority on Yankee uniform number history. He published his first book, *Yankees by the Number*, in 1986. He is a New York commercial banker by profession. (GW, GDW)

Stewart Wolpin is a former sportswriter with the Newark *Star-Ledger* and is currently a freelance writer. He is the author of *The Rules of Neighborhood Poker According to Hoyle*. (SEW)

PHOTO CREDITS

We have made every effort to ascertain the ownership of all copyrighted photographs reproduced herein and to secure permission from copyright holders. In the event of any inadvertent omission of credit, we will be pleased to make the necessary corrections in future printings.

Hank Aaron: National Baseball Library. Babe Adams: National Baseball Library. Jack Aker: New York Yankees. Grover Cleveland Alexander: Mark Rucker. Dick Allen: National Baseball Library. Walter Alston: Mark Rucker & John Thorn. Red Ames: National Baseball Library. Sparky Anderson: Bettmann Archive. Cap Anson: National Baseball Library. Luis Aparicio: Bettmann Archive. Luke Appling: National Baseball Library. Richie Ashburn: Wide World. Earl Averill, Sr.: National Baseball Library.

Dusty Baker: National Baseball Library. Frank Baker: National Baseball Library. Dave Bancroft: National Baseball Library. Sal Bando: National Baseball Library. Ernie Banks: Wide World. Red Barber: National Baseball Library. Al Barlick: Mark Rucker & John Thorn. Ed Barrow: National Baseball Library. Dick Bartell: Wide World. Don Baylor: National Baseball Library. Jake Beckley: National Baseball Library. Buddy Bell: National Baseball Library. Cool Papa Bell: National Baseball Library. Johnny Bench: National Baseball Library. Chief Bender: Dennis Goldstein. Wally Berger: National Baseball Library. Yogi Berra: National Baseball Library. Max Bishop: National Baseball Library. Vida Blue: Wide World. Bert Blyleven: National Baseball Library. Wade Boggs: Tom Griesel. Bobby Bonds: National Baseball Library. Bob Boone: National Baseball Library. The 1914 Boston Braves: National Baseball Library. The 1908 Boston Red Sox: National Baseball Library. Jim Bottomley: National Baseball Library. Lou Boudreau: Carl Seid. Larry Bowa: National Baseball Library. Ken Boyer: Mark Rucker & John Thorn. Bill Bradley: National Baseball Library. Harry Brecheen: National Baseball Library. Roger Bresnahan: National Baseball Library. George Brett: National Baseball Library. Tommy Bridges: National Baseball Library. Briggs Stadium: Mark Rucker & John Thorn. Lou Brock: Bettmann Archive. The 1955 Brooklyn Dodgers: National Baseball Library. Dan Brouthers: National Baseball Library. Three Finger Brown: National Baseball Library. Bill Buckner: National Baseball Library. Charlie Buffington: National Baseball Library. Morgan Bulkeley: National Baseball Library. Jim Bunning: Mark Rucker & John Thorn. Lew Burdette: National Baseball Library. Jesse Burkett: National Baseball Library. George Burns: Western Reserve Historical Society. George J. Burns: National Baseball Library.. Busch Stadium: Mark Rucker & John Thorn. Donie Bush: National Baseball Library. Joe Bush: National Baseball Library.

The 1986 California Angels: National Baseball Library. Roy Campanella: National Baseball Library. Bert Campaneris: National Baseball Library. Rod Carew: Wide World. Max Carey: National Baseball Library. Steve Carlton: National Baseball Library. Chico Carrasquel: National Baseball Library. Bill Carrigan: National Baseball Library. Gary Carter: National Baseball Library. Alexander Cartwright: National Baseball Library. Norm Cash: Bettmann Archive. Cesar Cedeno: National Baseball Library. Orlando Cepeda: National Baseball Library. Ron Cey: National Baseball Library. Henry Chadwick: National Baseball Library. Chris Chambliss: National Baseball Library. Frank Chance: National Baseball Library. Ben Chapman: Western Reserve Historical Society. Ray Chapman: National Baseball Library. Oscar Charleston: National Baseball Library. Hal Chase: National Baseball Library. Jack Chesbro: National Baseball Library. The 1938 Chicago Cubs: National Baseball Library. The 1917 Chicago White Sox: National Baseball Library. Eddie Cicotte: National Baseball Library. The 1972 Cincinnati Reds: National Baseball Library. Fred Clarke: National Baseball Library. John Clarkson: National Baseball Library. Roberto Clemente: National Baseball Library. The 1954 Cleveland Indians: National Baseball Library. Ty Cobb: Western Reserve Historical Society. Mickey Cochrane: Mark Rucker & John Thorn. Rocky Colavito: Mark Rucker. Eddie Collins: National Baseball Library. Jimmy Collins: National Baseball Library. Shano Collins: National Baseball Library. Earle Combs: National Baseball Library. Charlie Comiskey: National Baseball Library. Comiskey Park: National Baseball Library. Dave Concepcion: Bettmann Archive. Jocko Conlan: National Baseball Library. Roger Connor: National Baseball Library. Cecil Cooper: National Baseball Library. Walker Cooper: National Baseball Library. Wilbur Cooper: Mark Rucker & John Thorn. Tommy Corcoran: National Baseball Library. Stan Coveleskie: National Baseball Library. Doc Cramer: National Baseball Library. Gavvy Cravath: National Baseball Library. Sam Crawford: National Baseball Library. Joe Cronin: National Baseball Library. Frankie Crosetti: National Baseball Library. Lave Cross: National Baseball Library. Jose Cruz: National Baseball Library. Candy Cummings: Mark Rucker. Kiki Cuyler: National Baseball Library.

Bill Dahlen: National Baseball Library. Alvin Dark: TV Sports Mailbag. Jake Daubert: National Baseball Library. George Davis: National Baseball Library. Harry Davis: National Baseball Library. Tommy Davis: National Baseball Library. Willie Davis: National Baseball Library. Andre Dawson:

National Baseball Library. Dizzy Dean: National Baseball Library. Ed Delahanty: National Baseball Library. Paul Derringer: Mark Rucker & John Thorn. The 1935 Detroit Tigers: Mark Rucker & John Thorn. Art Devlin: National Baseball Library. Bill Dickey: National Baseball Library. Martin Dihigo: National Baseball Library. Dom DiMaggio: Mark Rucker & John Thorn. Joe DiMaggio: Wide World. Larry Doby: National Baseball Library. Bobby Doerr: Mark Rucker & John Thorn. Patsy Donovan: National Baseball Library. Wild Bill Donovan: National Baseball Library. Larry Doyle: National Baseball Library. Don Drysdale: Wide World. Hugh Duffy: National Baseball Library. Leo Durocher, umpire Art Gore: Wide World. Jimmy Dykes: National Baseball Library.

Luke Easter: National Baseball Library. Ebbetts Field: Mark Rucker & John Thorn. Howard Ehmke: National Baseball Library. Billy Evans: National Baseball Library. Darrell Evans: National Baseball Library. Dwight Evans: National Baseball Library. Johnny Evers: National Baseball Library. Buck Ewing: National Baseball Library.

Red Faber: National Baseball Library. Roy Face: National Baseball Library. Ferris Fain: Wide World. Ron Fairly: National Baseball Library. Bob Feller: Wide World. Fenway Park: Mark Rucker & John Thorn. Rick Ferrell: National Baseball Library. Wes Ferrell: Western Reserve Historical Society. Rollie Fingers: National Baseball Library. Carlton Fisk: Wide World. Fred Fitzsimmons: National Baseball Library. Art Fletcher: National Baseball Library. Elmer Flick: Western Reserve Historical Society. Curt Flood: National Baseball Library. Forbes Field: National Baseball Library. Whitey Ford: National Baseball Library. George Foster: National Baseball Library. Rube Foster: Wide World. Jack Fournier: National Baseball Library. Nellie Fox: Mark Rucker & John Thorn. Jimmie Foxx: Western Reserve Historical Society. Bill Freehan: National Baseball Library. Buck Freeman: National Baseball Library. Larry French: Mark Rucker & John Thorn. Ford Frick: Mark Rucker & John Thorn. Frankie Frisch: Mark Rucker & John Thorn. Carl Furillo: National Baseball Library.

Pud Galvin: National Baseball Library. Joe Garagiola: Mark Rucker & John Thorn. Danny Gardella: National Baseball Library. Steve Garvey: Bob Bartosz. Lou Gehrig: Western Reserve Historical Society. Charlie Gehringer: Western Reserve Historical Society. Bob Gibson: Bettmann Archive. Josh Gibson: Wide World. Warren Giles: National Baseball Library. Jim Gilliam: National Baseball Library. Jack Glasscock: National Baseball Library. Kid Gleason: National Baseball Library. Lefty Gomez: Bettmann Archive. George Gore: National Baseball Library. Goose Goslin: National Baseball Library. Goose Gossage: Mark Rucker & John Thorn. Hank Greenberg: Bettmann Archive. Bobby Grich: National Baseball Library. Griffith Stadium: Mark Rucker & John Thorn. Clark Griffith: National Baseball Library. Burleigh Grimes: TV Sports Mailbag. Charlie Grimm: National Baseball Library. Dick Groat: TV Sports Mailbag. Heinie Groh: National Baseball Library. Lefty Grove: Mark Rucker & John Thorn.

Stan Hack: TV Sports Mailbag. Chick Hafey: National Baseball Library. Jesse Haines: National Baseball Library. Billy Hamilton: National Baseball Library. Ned Hanlon: National Baseball Library. Mel Harder: Mark Rucker & John Thorn. Will Harridge: National Baseball Library. Bucky Harris: National Baseball Library. Gabby Hartnett: National Baseball Library. Jim Hegan: Wide World. Harry Heilmann: National Baseball Library. Rickey Henderson: National Baseball Library. Babe Herman: National Baseball Library. Billy Herman: Bettmann Archive. Keith Hernandez: National Baseball Library. Whitey Herzog: National Baseball Library. Gil Hodges: National Baseball Library. Harry Hooper: National Baseball Library. Rogers Hornsby: National Baseball Library. The 1980 Houston Astros: National Baseball Library. Elston Howard: TV Sports Mailbag. Frank Howard: Bettmann Archive. Dummy Hoy: National Baseball Library. Waite Hoyt: National Baseball Library. Cal Hubbard: National Baseball Library. Carl Hubbell: Mark Rucker & John Thorn. Miller Huggins: National Baseball Library. William Hulbert: National Baseball Library. Catfish Hunter: National Baseball Library. Fred Hutchinson: Bettmann Archive.

Monte Irvin: National Baseball Library.

Shoeless Joe Jackson: National Baseball Library. Reggie Jackson: National Baseball Library. Travis Jackson: National Baseball Library. Ferguson Jenkins: National Baseball Library. Hughie Jennings: Western Reserve Historical Society. Tommy John: TV Sports Mailbag. Ban Johnson: National Baseball Library. Indian Bob Johnson: Mark Rucker & John Thorn. Davey Johnson: National Baseball Library. Judy Johnson: National Baseball Library. Walter Johnson: National Baseball Library. Fielder Jones: National Baseball Library. Addie Joss: National Baseball Library.

Jim Kaat: National Baseball Library. Al Kaline: Mark Rucker & John

1229

Thorn. The 1977 Kansas City Royals: National Baseball Library. Tim Keefe: National Baseball Library. Willie Keeler: National Baseball Library. George Kell: National Baseball Library. Joe Kelley: National Baseball Library. George Kelly: Mark Rucker & John Thorn. King Kelly: National Baseball Library. Harmon Killebrew: National Baseball Library. Ralph Kiner: National Baseball Library. Silver King: Ken Felder. Chuck Klein: Mark Rucker & John Thorn. Bill Klem: National Baseball Library. Johnny Kling: National Baseball Library. Ted Kluszewski: National Baseball Library. Ed Konetchy: National Baseball Library. Jim Konstanty: National Baseball Library. Jerry Koosman: National Baseball Library. Sandy Koufax: Mark Rucker & John Thorn. Harvey Kuenn: National Baseball Library. Bowie Kuhn: Bettmann Archive.

Nap Lajoie: Western Reserve Historical Society. Judge Landis: National Baseball Library. Bill Lange: Mark Rucker. Don Larsen: National Baseball Library. Tom Lasorda: TV Sports Mailbag. Vern Law: National Baseball Library. Tony Lazerri: National Baseball Library. Tommy Leach: Carnegie Library of Pittsburgh. Bob Lemon: Mark Rucker & John Thorn Buck Leonard: National Baseball Library. Freddie Lindstrom: National Baseball Library. Pop Lloyd: National Baseball Library. Hans Lobert: National Baseball Library. Mickey Lolich: Mark Rucker & John Thorn. Sherm Lollar: Mark Rucker & John Thorn. Ernie Lombardi: National Baseball Library. Herman Long: National Baseball Library. Davey Lopes: National Baseball Library. Al Lopez: National Baseball Library. The 1966 Los Angeles Dodgers: National Baseball Library. Bobby Lowe: National Baseball Library. Fred Luderus: National Baseball Library. Dolf Luque: National Baseball Library. Sparky Lyle: National Baseball Library. Fred Lynn: National Baseball Library. Ted Lyons: National Baseball Library.

Connie Mack: Western Reserve Historical Society. Larry MacPhail: Mark Rucker & John Thorn. Bill Madlock: National Baseball Library. Lee Magee: National Baseball Library. Sal Maglie: Wide World. Gus Mancuso: Mark Rucker & John Thorn. Mickey Mantle: National Baseball Library. Heinie Manush: National Baseball Library. Rabbit Maranville: National Baseball Library. Firpo Marberry: National Baseball Library. Juan Marichal: National Baseball Library. Marty Marion: Mark Rucker & John Thorn. Roger Maris: Wide World. Rube Marquard: Mark Rucker. Mike Marshall: Bettmann Archive. Billy Martin: National Baseball Library. Pepper Martin: National Baseball Library. Eddie Mathews: National Baseball Library. Christy Mathewson: National Baseball Library. Gary Matthews: National Baseball Library. Don Mattingly: National Baseball Library. Gene Mauch: National Baseball Library. Lee May: National Baseball Library. Carl Mays: National Baseball Library. Willie Mays: San Diego Historical Society. Bill Mazeroski: National Baseball Library. Joe McCarthy: Western Reserve Historical Society. Tommy McCarthy: National Baseball Library. Tim McCarver: National Baseball Library. Willie McCovey: Bob Bartosz. Gil McDougald: National Baseball Library. Sam McDowell: National Baseball Library. Joe McGinnity: National Baseball Library. John McGraw: National Baseball Library. Tug McGraw: National Baseball Library. Deacon McGuire: National Baseball Library. Stuffy McInnis: National Baseball Library. Ed McKean: National Baseball Library. Bill McKechnie: Bettmann Archive. Denny McLain: National Baseball Library. Roy McMillan: National Baseball Library. Dave McNally: National Baseball Library. Hal McRae: National Baseball Library. Joe Medwick: Bettmann Archive. Sam Mele: Wide World. Fred Merkle: National Baseball Library. Bob Meusel: National Baseball Library. Irish Meusel: National Baseball Library. Clyde Milan: National Baseball Library. The 1969 Minnesota Twins: National Baseball Library. Minnie Minoso: National Baseball Library. Johnny Mize: Mark Rucker & John Thorn. Joe Morgan: Wide World. Jack Morris: National Baseball Library. Wally Moses: National Baseball Library. Tony Mullane: Mark Rucker. Van Lingle Mungo: Bettmann Archive. Thurman Munson: Bettmann Archive. Bobby Murcer: National Baseball Library. Dale Murphy: National Baseball Library. Johnny Murphy: National Baseball Library. Eddie Murray: National Baseball Library. Stan Musial: Bettmann Archive.

Art Nehf: National Baseball Library. Graig Nettles: Bettmann Archive. The 1922 New York Giants: National Baseball Library. The 1986 New York Mets: National Baseball Library. The 1927 New York Yankees: National Baseball Library. Don Newcombe: Mark Rucker & John Thorn. Hal Newhouser: Wide World. Bobo Newsom: National Baseball Library. Kid Nichols: National Baseball Library. Joe Niekro: National Baseball Library. Phil Niekro: National Baseball Library.

The 1973 Oakland A's: National Baseball Library. Lefty O'Doul: National Baseball Library. Tony Oliva: National Baseball Library. Al Oliver: National Baseball Library. Mel Ott: National Baseball Library.

Satchel Paige: National Baseball Library. Jim Palmer: Bettmann Archive. Dickey Pearce: National Baseball Library. Roger Peckinpaugh: Mark Rucker & John Thorn. Herb Pennock: National Baseball Library. Tony Perez: Wide World. Gaylord Perry: National Baseball Library. The 1910 Philadelphia Athletics: National Baseball Library. The 1915 Philadelphia Phillies: National

Baseball Library. Deacon Phillippe: National Baseball Library. Billy Pierce: National Baseball Library. Jimmy Piersall: National Baseball Library. Vada Pinson: Bettmann Archive. The 1925 Pittsburgh Pirates: National Baseball Library. Eddie Plank: National Baseball Library. Boog Powell: National Baseball Library. Del Pratt: National Baseball Library.

Jack Quinn: National Baseball Library.

Old Hoss Radbourn: National Baseball Library. Pee Wee Reese: National Baseball Library. Ed Reulbach: National Baseball Library. Rick Reuschel: TV Sports Mailbag. Jim Rice: TV Sports Mailbag. Sam Rice: Mark Rucker & John Thorn. Bobby Richardson: TV Sports Mailbag. Branch Rickey: Bettmann Archive. Eppa Rixey: National Baseball Library. Phil Rizzuto: TV Sports Mailbag. Robin Roberts: Wide World. Brooks Robinson: Charles Segar. Frank Robinson: National Baseball Library. Jackie Robinson: Bettmann Archive. Wilbert Robinson: National Baseball Library. Pete Rose: Bettmann Archive. Edd Roush: National Baseball Library. Red Ruffing: Western Reserve Historical Society. Amos Rusie: National Baseball Library. Babe Ruth: National Baseball Library. Jimmy Ryan: Mark Rucker. Nolan Ryan: National Baseball Library.

Slim Sallee: National Baseball Library. Ron Santo: National Baseball Library. Ray Schalk: National Baseball Library. Mike Schmidt: Mark Rucker & John Thorn. Red Schoendienst: Wide World. Hal Schumacher: National Baseball Library. Everett Scott: National Baseball Library. Tom Seaver: Bettmann Archive. Joe Sewell: National Baseball Library. Cy Seymour: National Baseball Library. Bob Shawkey: National Baseball Library. Shea Stadium: National Baseball Library. Urban Shocker: National Baseball Library. Al Simmons: Mark Rucker & John Thorn. Ted Simmons: National Baseball Library. George Sisler: National Baseball Library. Enos Slaughter: National Baseball Library. Ozzie Smith: National Baseball Library. Reggie Smith: National Baseball Library. Duke Snider: National Baseball Library. Warren Spahn: National Baseball Library. Al Spalding: National Baseball Library. Tris Speaker: National Baseball Library. The 1944 St. Louis Browns: National Baseball Library. The 1930 St. Louis Cardinals: National Baseball Library. Chick Stahl: National Baseball Library. George Stallings: National Baseball Library. Willie Stargell: Bettmann Archive. Rusty Staub: National Baseball Library. George Steinbrenner: National Baseball Library. Casey Stengel: National Baseball Library. Harry Stovey: National Baseball Library. Billy Sunday: National Baseball Library. Bruce Sutter: TV Sports Mailbag. Don Sutton: National Baseball Library.

Jesse Tannehill: National Baseball Library. Fred Tenney: National Baseball Library. Bill Terry: National Baseball Library. The 1979 Texas Rangers: National Baseball Library. Sam Thompson: John Thorn. Bobby Thomson: TV Sports Mailbag. Luis Tiant, Jr.: National Baseball Library. Joe Tinker: National Baseball Library. Joe Torre: National Baseball Library. Pie Traynor: National Baseball Library. Dizzy Trout: National Baseball Library. John Tudor: National Baseball Library. Terry Turner: National Baseball Library.

George Uhle: National Baseball Library.

Fernando Valenzuela: TV Sports Mailbag. Dazzy Vance: National Baseball Library. Johnny Vander Meer: National Baseball Library. George Van Haltren: National Baseball Library. Arky Vaughan: National Baseball Library. Hippo Vaughn: National Baseball Library. Bill Veeck: Mark Rucker & John Thorn. Mickey Vernon: Bettmann Archive.

Rube Waddell: National Baseball Library. Honus Wagner: National Baseball Library. Dixie Walker: National Baseball Library. Bobby Wallace: National Baseball Library. Ed Walsh: National Baseball Library. Bucky Walters: National Baseball Library. Bill Wambsganss: National Baseball Library. Lloyd Waner: National Baseball Library. Paul Waner: National Baseball Library. John Montgomery Ward: National Baseball Library. The 1924 Washington Senators: National Baseball Library. Buck Weaver: National Baseball Library. Earl Weaver: National Baseball Library. George Weiss: Mark Rucker & John Thorn. Mickey Welch: National Baseball Library. Zack Wheat: National Baseball Library. Lou Whitaker: National Baseball Library. Bill White: National Baseball Library. Deacon White: National Baseball Library. Doc White: National Baseball Library. Frank White: National Baseball Library. Hoyt Wilhelm: National Baseball Library. Billy Williams: TV Sports Mailbag. Dick Williams: National Baseball Library. Ted Williams: National Baseball Library. Vic Willis: National Baseball Library. Maury Wills: Bettmann Archive. Hack Wilson: National Baseball Library. Willie Wilson: TV Sports Mailbag. Hooks Wiltse: National Baseball Library. Dave Winfield: National Baseball Library. Joe Wood: National Baseball Library. George Wright: Mark Rucker. Harry Wright: National Baseball Library. Wrigley Field (Chicago): Mark Rucker & John Thorn. Early Wynn: Wide World. Jimmy Wynn: National Baseball Library.

Yankee Stadium: National Baseball Library. Carl Yastrzemski: National Baseball Library. Cy Young: Western Reserve Historical Society. Ross Youngs: National Baseball Library. Robin Yount: National Baseball Library.